INTERNATIONAL LAW REPORTS

CONSOLIDATED INDEXES

VOLUMES 1—35 AND 36—125

Volumes published under the title:

ANNUAL DIGEST AND REPORTS OF PUBLIC INTERNATIONAL LAW CASES

Vols. 1 *and* 2	Edited by Sir John Fischer Williams, KC, and H. Lauterpacht, LLD
Vols. 3 *and* 4	Edited by Arnold D. McNair, CBE, LLD, and H. Lauterpacht, LLD
Vols. 5—16	Edited by H. Lauterpacht, QC, LLD, FBA

References in these volumes may be cited in the form 1 *AD* 567.

Volumes published under the title:

INTERNATIONAL LAW REPORTS

Vols. 17—23 Edited by Sir Hersch Lauterpacht, QC, LLD, FBA

Vol. 24 Edited by Sir Hersch Lauterpacht, QC, LLD, FBA, and E. Lauterpacht

Vols. 25—68 *and* Consolidated Tables and Index to Vols. 1—35 *and* 36—45
Edited by E. Lauterpacht, QC

Vols. 69—125 *and* Consolidated Index to Vols. 1—80; Consolidated Tables of Cases and Treaties to Vols. 1—80; Consolidated Tables of Cases and Treaties and Consolidated Index to Vols. 81—100; Consolidated Indexes to Vols. 1—35 and 36—125; Consolidated Tables of Cases to Vols. 1—125 *and* Consolidated Table of Treaties to Vols. 1—125
Edited by Sir Elihu Lauterpacht, CBE, QC, and Professor C. J. Greenwood, CMG, QC

References in these volumes may be cited in the form 17 *ILR* 567.

Lauterpacht Research Centre for International Law
University of Cambridge

INTERNATIONAL LAW REPORTS

Edited by

SIR ELIHU LAUTERPACHT, CBE QC
Honorary Professor of International Law, University of Cambridge
Bencher of Gray's Inn

C. J. GREENWOOD, CMG QC
Professor of International Law, London School of Economics and Political Science
Bencher of Middle Temple

A. G. OPPENHEIMER
Associate Editor: Civil Law Jurisdictions
Fellow of the Lauterpacht Research Centre for International Law, University of Cambridge

KAREN LEE
Assistant Editor
Fellow of the Lauterpacht Research Centre for International Law, University of Cambridge
Fellow of Girton College, University of Cambridge

CONSOLIDATED INDEXES
VOLUMES 1—35 AND 36—125

Prepared by

M. E. MacGLASHAN, CMG
Fellow of the Lauterpacht Research Centre for International Law, University of Cambridge

GROTIUS PUBLICATIONS
CAMBRIDGE
UNIVERSITY PRESS

PUBLISHED BY THE PRESS SYNDICATE OF THE UNIVERSITY OF CAMBRIDGE
The Pitt Building, Trumpington Street, Cambridge, United Kingdom

CAMBRIDGE UNIVERSITY PRESS
The Edinburgh Building, Cambridge CB2 2RU, UK
40 West 20th Street, New York, NY 10011–4211, USA
477 Williamstown Road, Port Melbourne, VIC 3207, Australia
Ruiz de Alarcón 13, 28014 Madrid, Spain
Dock House, The Waterfront, Cape Town 8001, South Africa

http://www.cambridge.org

First published 2004

Printed in the United Kingdom at the University Press, Cambridge

Typeface Adobe Garamond 9/9.5 pt. *System* LaTeX 2ε [TB]

A catalogue record for this book is available from the British Library

ISBN 0 521 80777 8

CONTENTS

	Page
Preface	vii
Introduction	ix
Consolidated Index to *ILR* volumes 1—35	1
Consolidated Index to *ILR* volumes 36—125	275

PREFACE

This is the fifth consolidation of the indexes and tables of the *International Law Reports*, the previous consolidations appearing in 1969 (volumes 1-35), 1973 (volumes 36-45), 1991 (volumes 36-80 for the index, volumes 1-80 for the tables) and 1996 (volumes 81-100). The present consolidation has been yet more ambitious, covering as it does the indexes from volumes 36 to 125 and the tables from volumes 1 to 125. The intention in due course is to have a consolidated index which covers also volumes 1-35, but the considerable difference in presentation of material together with changes of terminology and indexing style means that this will be a matter of reindexing rather than consolidation, and will take time. For the convenience of readers, the existing index to volumes 1-35 is reproduced at p. 1.

As far as the tables are concerned, the principal tasks have been to ensure accuracy and consistency of presentation, and to make the material as accessible as possible. The *Annual Digest* volumes were revisited and previous table of cases entries amended to conform so far as possible to later practice. Case names in the alphabetical table, while remaining faithful to the official version, also appear under their popular name or names with double-posting in preference to cross-referencing. And steps have been taken to reduce the variety of style in referring to countries and government bodies, all in the hope of making the tables easier to consult and more transparent. The same principles underlie the work that has been done on the table of treaties and the index to the table of treaties.

The consolidated index was originally intended to be just that – a consolidation or rather a consolidation of consolidations. But it quickly became clear that this would not be enough. The difficulty remains as described in the Introduction to the 1991 consolidation (reprinted at page ix), to coax disparate material into a harmonious whole. This is a problem with the simplest of indexes but it is magnified many times with an index such as the consolidated index to the *International Law Reports*, an index which seeks to handle material going back over eighty years, and which crosses jurisdictions and languages. Indexers now have at their disposal excellent computer programs which improve accuracy and comprehensiveness, but the downside to this is that they also highlight inaccuracy, gaps and inconsistency and leave the indexer no choice but to try to do something about it. So it proved with this

consolidation. Computer tools showed up exciting linkages but also forced the realization that in some cases differences of approach over the years meant there was no alternative but to fundamentally reorganize or even reindex. The resulting index will be familiar to users of previous versions but there will be some surprises, for example in the handling of material relating to State immunity. This is and will remain work in progress, the challenge always being to handle diversity and change within a frame that is secure but itself open to change in such a way, as William Wordsworth put it in *The Prelude*, as to produce a 'marble index of a mind for ever voyaging through strange seas of thought'. Thomas Macaulay's 'index-maker in ragged fustian cloth' carries a heavy responsibility!

These volumes have been four years in the making. The task could not have been accomplished, in the first instance, without the contribution of my predecessors, whose work remains much in evidence. For these particular volumes I have had very considerable assistance from Mrs Diane Ilott and Ms Karen Lee. Ms Finola O'Sullivan (CUP) was the first to urge that the task be undertaken and has shown much patience, for which I am grateful, when it turned out much more time-consuming than she or I could have dreamed. And finally a real debt is owed to the Editors of the *International Law Reports* for the support and enthusiasm they have always shown for those indispensable tools, the indexes and tables.

M. E. MacGLASHAN

Lauterpacht Research Centre for International Law
University of Cambridge

August 2003

INTRODUCTION

(Reprinted from the Consolidated Index to volumes 36-80)

> Every other author may aspire to praise; the lexicographer can only hope to escape reproach . . .
>
> When I took the first survey of my undertaking, I found our speech copious without order, and energetic without rules. Wherever I turned my view, there was perplexity to be disentangled, and confusion to be regulated; choice was to be made out of boundless variety without any established selection; adulterations were to be detected, without a settled test of purity, and modes of expression to be rejected or received, without the suffrages of any writers of classical reputation or acknowledged authority.
>
> Samuel Johnson: *Dictionary of the English Language*

Not a bad description of the task as it seemed to this indexer on taking up the consolidation of the indexes to volumes 36-80 of the *International Law Reports* in August 1988. The consolidation had already been some time in the making. The original idea had been to harness the powers of modern technology for a task which was thought at that stage to be little more than the sorting and consolidation of existing material. A sophisticated computer program was devised and the relevant data fed in with great care. But different indexing styles over the years, the changing nature of the subject matter and the idiosyncrasies of individual indexers (quite apart from the many trivial variations of no consequence to the reader but seized on by the computer as an excuse to scatter related entries far and wide) meant that the material was simply not homogeneous enough for this approach. The only result was an amorphous mess beyond the control of man or machine.

This left essentially two alternatives: to undertake a complete reindexing of the 45 volumes in question; or to adopt the old-fashioned method of cumulation. The former, which might have been the preferred method, was ruled out for reasons of time and cost; but, in fact, the cumulative method had its own attractions, including the fact that a contemporary indexer might have been inclined to work exclusively on the basis of modern concepts thus losing the historical element inescapable in a cumulative index. The present index is, therefore, essentially a consolidation of the existing indexes to volumes 36-80 of the *International Law Reports*. There has been much reordering of material, checking of entries which for one reason or another suggested possible error in the original index, and a good deal of additional material

included. But the temptation to engage in any reindexing was almost without exception resisted. While the consolidated index is thus probably better than the sum of its parts it still reflects much of the variation of quality, balance, style and density apparent in the original volumes. Nor has there been any systematic check on the accuracy of the original entries, a herculean task which would not have brought commensurate benefits. The frequent checks incidental to the process of cumulation suggested that, on the whole, important error was not escaping notice.

The decision to adopt a cumulative approach having been made, the question was whether to begin at the beginning with the earliest volumes (the normal way) or at the end, with the latest. In fact, the end seemed clearly to make more sense, since then the frame of the index would be similar to that used in current indexes and, therefore, more coherent for both indexer and user, as well as a better base for future consolidation. It also fitted in with the fact that the consolidation and the indexing of individual volumes were now in the hands of the same person. It proved extremely helpful, particularly in the early stages, to be creating new indexes and consolidating old ones simultaneously.

The making of almost any index is likely to offer intellectual challenge, a challenge all the greater in the case of a work such as the *International Law Reports* because of the range of issues, variety of sources and amount of translated material, compounded, in the case of this consolidation, by the thirty-year time-span. There is a long way to go before all the problems of serial indexing are brought under control but it is hoped that, at least as far as indexing of materials relating to international law is concerned, this consolidation makes some contribution.

The indexer in this case has had the unusual privilege of working for a publisher who sets particular store by the index and has always given the fullest acknowledgment to the indexer. The pressures of time were particularly great in the case of the present exercise, but otherwise the only requirement laid upon the indexer was to make the best possible index to the work in question. There was no constraint of space (though one has tried not to be pointlessly lavish with it) and never any call to cut back on an index entry unless this was in the interests of the index itself.

As is often the case, the indexer was a novice when the work began and had to derive the principles of indexing in general and the rules to be applied in particular to the *International Law Reports* from the material presented to her. Fortunately several of her predecessors' indexes were excellent and provided most useful models, especially in

demonstrating the value of a very detailed index with multiple entries of the same point (the aspect of preparing an index which continues to present the most difficulty, but is vital if the index is to serve its user fully). However, as pointed out above, the consolidation presented peculiar problems. Solutions could only be developed gradually, and proved far from stable. What seemed the sensible answer at one point in the exercise often seemed quite wrong a few volumes later, and that meant reworking several sections of the index several times over. Inevitably, there remain unevennesses and inconsistencies to be put right as they reveal themselves.

The present indexer's concept of an index is that it should stand in its own right; almost, as it were, offer 'a good read'. The index ought to present the substance of the work in such a way as not only to reflect what has been written, but also to shed new light on the subject-matter and reveal different relationships and perspectives. As a friend who recently indexed her own Ph.D. thesis put it, 'I thought I knew my thesis inside out, but indexing it has identified all sorts of new ideas I did not know were there.' It would be disappointing (and not the best use of the index) if the user simply looked up his word, and was not tempted, as so often with a dictionary, first to explore the surrounding and related material, and then to browse more generally.

Finding one's way

Good read or not, the first function of any index must be to lead the user quickly and confidently to what he is seeking, or give him the assurance that what he is looking for is not there. There are various techniques to help achieve this end. It is, for example, in the present indexer's view, important to establish a pattern so that a regular user will soon move instinctively to the right place. It is, for example, now the normal practice in individual *ILR* indexes, as has been done in this volume for non-English speaking jurisdictions, to gather references to legislation under the sub-heading 'law of'. Most countries will have such a sub-heading even if the entries below it are few. Signatories to treaties appear in alphabetical order (e.g. France–UK, not UK–France). The various issues of privileges and immunities, when dealt with in the context of individual countries, have been treated in identical fashion, not simply ordered according to the language of a particular case. Main entries use full titles, not acronyms (important to know for the alphabetical order), but, to avoid disproportion, familiar acronyms are used in sub-headings. An enormous number of decisions of this order have been taken which it is hoped will quickly become apparent to the user.

Every effort has been made to make it clear to the user where in the index he is at any given moment, not as easy as it may sound in an index where entries even under sub-headings often run to several pages; and to show at a glance the hierarchical structure. To this end the entries have been kept as uncluttered as possible. Prepositions have been eschewed unless essential to the sense, and commas within headings (or, to put it another way, headings with several elements or needing inversion) have been avoided whenever possible. This has been the easier to achieve because of the practice of making a key word a heading on its own, and its qualifers sub-headings, a practice which has also helpfully served sometimes to bring together related ideas which would otherwise have been distributed according to alphabetical accident and lost. To aid clarity further, for the first time in *ILR* practice, the index is presented as a single column on the page, a practice likely to be followed in future single-volume indexes. Problems of overrunning headings and confusion with subsidiary headings, awkward hyphenation and misleading spacing have more or less disappeared; and it has become possible to give much fuller continuation headings. It has also eased the task of proof-reading: a surprising number of errors which escaped when the proofs were still in the traditional two-column format leapt to the eye when the change was made. The single column approach is also less greedy of space than expected; not more perhaps than an extra 35%, a price the publishers deemed well worth paying for the great improvement in the usability of an essential research tool.

Dealing with synonyms and related concepts

It is often said that an author is his own best indexer. Sometimes this may be so, but not infrequently the author's index is little more than a glorified table of contents, cast entirely on the lines of the book, and using principally the terms and concepts familiar to the author, rather than ones to which the reader is accustomed. One has to turn to the book in order to use the index, which is not quite the way it should be. The advice usually given to the new indexer is to use the most common expression, easier said than done since half-a-dozen people may well offer as many different suggestions as to where they would first look for a particular item. Certainly, in the 45 indexes that have been consolidated here there has been a great variety of different entries to reflect the identical idea (sometimes the choice of the indexer but often simply reflecting the terminology of the text). One of the objectives of this consolidation has been to iron out variation in nomenclature. So far as possible, entries relating to the same subject matter have been grouped together under

a single heading. Consolidating diverse entries in this way has been a source of much satisfaction as, volume by volume, a pattern has built up; what may have started as, say, minor subject entries under different headings in three or four volumes spread over 20 years and scarcely worth a researcher's time on an individual basis, by slight re-presentation have suddenly shown themselves to belong together and so to offer the enticement of a substantial and varied body of jurisprudence well worth exploration. It has been both encouraging and reassuring to find this continuity both of substance—so many of today's legal issues turn out also to be the legal issues of yesterday—and of appreciation, through the indexer's eyes, of what those issues are. It was the consolidation process on the basis described which has brought this most tellingly home.

Of course, a passion for form and tidiness must not be taken too far. Some ideas may be close but not identical, or the identity insufficiently certain (perhaps because the precise meaning of the original text is unclear) to justify amalgamation. There have been many examples of this in the present index particularly because of slight variations of usage between English-speaking jurisdictions, because of changing usage over time, and because of the problems of translation. It is not for the indexer to take decisions of substance which may in fact be matter for long debate. 'Applicable law', 'governing law' and 'proper law' seem to be used interchangeably, but there seemed just enough of a possibility that they were used as discrete concepts to justify, at least for the time being, retaining all three. 'Competence' and 'jurisdiction', 'interim measures' and 'provisional measures', examples of the penetration into English usage of the anglicized French term, require that a choice be made. 'Jurisdiction' has probably a secure future, but 'interim measures' may succumb if the International Court of Justice becomes consistent in its use of 'provisional measures'. What about 'sovereign immunity', the normal term at the beginning of the period covered by the index and still used in the United States, but otherwise largely superseded by what is now the more appropriate 'State immunity'? After much reflection, it was decided to place all the entries under 'State sovereignty'. The few instances of genuine immunity of sovereigns appear as 'Heads of State, immunity'. The decision might have been different had the consolidation reached back to volume 1 (1919-22). And what about 'ambassadors', 'envoys' and the like? Did they deserve their own entries or should they be subsumed in entries picking up the language of the Vienna Convention on Diplomatic Relations, which is beginning to become the received language of the courts? Eventually, the latter course was chosen.

Translation problems

The problems of dealing with translated material are even greater, particularly where the translator is not a legal specialist or where the concepts under discussion do not have an English equivalent. It may need a leap of the indexer's imagination (if the translator has failed in his task) to seek exactly where, in an English index, to lodge the particular item. The problem is at its most glaring in dealing with legislation. 'Penal' and 'criminal' are clearly interchangeable—and alphabetically a long way apart. The 'Law on the Organization of the Judiciary' may also be the 'Constitution of the Courts Act', the 'Courts Act' or the 'Judicial Organization Act', to name but some of the options. Often, the only way of determining whether items are one and the same is by reference to their title or abbreviation in the original language, but in many cases this vital information is missing, either omitted altogether, or the proffered abbreviation derived from the English translation. It is *ILR* policy, wherever possible, to retain in the translation the original language abbreviation and this is then incorporated in the index; and to achieve as much identity of translation, where appropriate, as possible. But this is still a counsel of unattainable perfection. In the meantime, the new system of bringing all legislation together under 'law of', of pushing 'Act' or 'Law' to the end, and giving an indication, wherever possible, of the substance of a Law known only by its number, has helped to eradicate some of the previous dispersion, and has reduced the field of search to a manageable few inches of sub-heading rather than to what may be pages of a whole country entry.

Cross references

> I find . . . the order in some respects not so good, that a man may think a place is missing, when it is only put in another place.
> Samuel Pepys on Newman's *Concordance* (*Diary*, 8 June 1663)

By and large, things in an index are not in the wrong place. It is simply that they may not be where a particular user expects to find them. Some of the reasons why this should be so have been outlined above. The problem can largely be resolved by generous cross-referencing. The hard pruning of the original *ILR* indexes to give the consolidation coherent shape has meant that many of the old headings are no longer used. However, a high proportion of them are retained, with a cross reference to where material once listed under them may now be found. And other new headings have been introduced in the same way. The present indexer's rule is quite simple: if it is likely that anyone will seek an item in the 'wrong' place, add that 'wrong place' with

a cross reference. (The range of new headings is always being further extended on much this principle, in that a colleague's suggestion, casual or serious, that a particular issue warrants study alerts this indexer to the need to look out for material which might be indexed under that head. Sometimes this can only work in respect of future indexes, but the opportunity has been taken in this consolidation, whenever possible, to group existing material additionally under the newly conceived heading.)

Organizational problems

Some sections of the index have remained resistant to satisfactory ordering, largely because of the intractability of the material. Two of the most troublesome have been 'jurisdiction' and 'maritime delimitation'. An 'alien' is also a 'national abroad'. Is it helpful to talk of a 'foreign ship'? How does one cope with the problem when the material sometimes encourages an entry under 'Jurisdiction, criminal', but on other occasions, for what is, in fact, an identical point, calls out for inclusion, for example, under 'Jurisdiction, territorial'? How does one deal with the fact that 'jurisdiction' has several quite different meanings? The problems under 'Jurisdiction' are endless, and are unlikely to sort themselves out until the courts and the textbooks have worked out a more ordered presentation of the issues. In the meantime, it has seemed acceptable, because it is so familiar, to retain the confusion of the source material. On the whole, jurisdictional issues have been entered exactly as they appear in the cases being indexed, with only minimal tidying-up, but with full cross-referencing.

The maritime delimitation problem is of a different kind. Most of the material so far generated on this subject is related to continental shelf delimitation. Some indexers have therefore chosen to enter it principally under 'Continental shelf delimitation'. Others have opted for 'Maritime delimitation'. The choice has probably been made instinctively, the material probably sometimes seeming to deal more with general principles of maritime delimitation, with reference to specific jurisdictions; and sometimes to be more tied to the particular jurisdiction in question, with occasional more general references. On a volume-by-volume basis this presents no problem, but when it comes to the point of consolidation, a uniform decision has to be made. As the work on this consolidation proceeded, sometimes 'Continental shelf delimitation' had the upper hand, sometimes 'Maritime delimitation'. In the end the latter won. But the decision is not entirely satisfactory, and this is one area of the consolidation that is likely to be reconsidered as new cases come to hand.

Implicit headings

When indexing a monograph, one can assume the subject matter of the book as a main heading, and for most purposes start one or two levels lower. This has also occasionally been the case with individual *ILR* indexes, where a volume has been largely devoted to a single case or to a limited range of issues. Some of the entries over the years now appear decidedly esoteric, and only make sense if one happens to know that the volume under reference was a 'single-item' volume (as for instance with the *South West Africa* cases). A few such references it has seemed best to delete, but the more usual course has been to provide the missing main heading, unnecessary in the monograph but crucial in a larger work covering many subjects.

Another trap—all too easy to fall into—is to forget that, detached from their context, it may not be obvious to which countries entries refer. There have been several examples over the years of particular pieces of legislation appearing as main headings, or, likewise, legal concepts, peculiar, perhaps, to the International Court of Justice, the European Court of Human Rights, the United Kingdom or the United States, the reader being expected to supply the missing information. A real effort has been made in this consolidation not to build in assumptions (and, in particular, not to assume that the user is a British lawyer), but to make it all comprehensible regardless of the user's background and regardless of whether the individual volumes are available for clarification.

Added value

It came as a surprise how much time had to be spent, whether in respect of a single volume or the consolidation, on research. Dictionaries in several languages, a good atlas, *The Stateman's Yearbook*, United Nations documents, texts and table of treaties were all matter for frequent consultation, to resolve ambiguity or to supply essential information quite absent from the original text. It may well be that it is only the indexer, forced to allocate information very precisely, who is really confronted with these problems. Legislation once again presents special difficulties as do resolutions, for example, of the United Nations, sometimes referred to simply by number, sometimes by description. But most difficult of all has been the treatment of countries which have changed their name, status, boundaries, form of government, sometimes several times. Where the only differences are in name and form of government, the practice adopted has been to use the most recent version with cross references from earlier ones. If the change has been more substantial, entries are made under all the variants according to which was in operation at the relevant time. Useful items of information (such as dates of

treaties) are incorporated into the index. Apparent gaps mean only that the information—sometimes exceedingly elusive—could not be tracked down in the time available, a deficiency which will be gradually put right.

Techniques

Fellow indexers may be interested in the techniques used to produce this index. The process had almost no computer, as opposed to word processing, assistance. The whole text was keyed in by the indexer, eschewing all machine codes in favour of ones developed in conjunction with the printers so that they could print, with relatively little modification, direct from disk. This method of preparing material for the printers, tested in a variety of contexts over the last couple of years, presented negligible problems and has the great advantage that it can be used with any word processing package capable of producing an ASCII file.

The work was carried out entirely on-screen, and apart from the occasional print-out of selected sections at the behest of colleagues anxious to have access to the consolidation, appeared in hard copy only at the galley proof stage. Much of the initial keying-in (as well indeed as the subsequent multiple checking) was extremely tedious, and there were patches where it would have been better undertaken by a competent copy-typist; but these were surprisingly few and there was no question of delegation since it was at this initial stage that much of the error in the original indexes (not necessarily apparent to the non-legal eye) was corrected, and the bulk of the reorganization carried out. The task was bearable because of the high level of intellectual input; it was rarely possible to switch off mentally—and when one did, one paid the penalty of carrying over from the original mis-ordered page numbers, alphabetical curiosities, scattering of entries and the like, some of which may still lurk in the final product. For the purpose of such operations as spell checks and 'search and replace' it proved necessary to break the index up into some 50 sections, but, because of the Word window option making it possible to have several sections of the index on screen simultaneously, this was not usually too much of a disadvantage. It did become a serious irritation when it came to final preparation of the disks for the printers or for transfer to the Cambridge University mainframe. Because of the number of files, the latter exercise could take the better part of a day and so was not to be undertaken lightly; but it was indispensable if one was to take advantage of facilities such as the Muscat Library program which was of great help in the final stages in checking punctuation, matching brackets (crucial in the context of codes for the printer), verifying alphabetical order of main headings, making global changes and the like—operations well beyond the capacity of a personal computer

for a task of this size. But this combination of personal computer and mainframe was not a panacea. A spellcheck could correct error, but would not produce the consequential alphabetical reordering, so that entries which were once in the 'right' place became wrong. Neither system offered any real help with cross references which may have started life quite properly but which, with modification to the index, needed deletion or amendment. A slip of the finger when keying-in could cause, all unbeknown, the insertion of material in a place which made no sense at all, to lie in wait for the mystified proof-reader months later. Quirks of the two systems, separately and in interaction, threw up all sorts of other diverting problems which will be all too familiar to anyone who has tried these methods. But whatever the shortcomings, use of the computer made it possible to complete within eighteen months (from when this system was adopted) a task for which (at least to someone who has never used them) 5 x 3-inch cards and shoe boxes seem inadequate.

Current indexes are being prepared using the Macrex indexing program. As with any new program, it is taking time to coax it to perform in the way the indexer wishes, and there are some minor respects in which it may prove more sensible to adjust the *ILR* system to Macrex, rather than Macrex to the *ILR*. But experience already suggests that Macrex will go a long way towards taking the tedium and error out of indexing while leaving the fun and challenge.

The future

It is clear from what has been said that the present index falls even further short of perfection than one would normally hope for, but financial considerations and the pressing need for a consolidated index to such a large and important body of material as the *International Law Reports* decreed that it be published sooner rather than later. It was all the easier to opt for imperfection knowing that the system of continuous consolidation now in operation means that revised and updated consolidations (possibly also incorporating the indexes to volumes 1-35) can be produced whenever it seems appropriate. It is in actual use of the index, both to seek out material and as a basis for subsequent indexes, that its shortcomings and errors best show themselves. In identifying these, the assistance of users, addressed to the Editors at this Research Centre, will be most warmly welcomed.

M. E. MacGLASHAN

May 1990

CONSOLIDATED INDEX

VOLUMES 1—35 INCLUSIVE

For references to particular articles of treaties, see the Consolidated Tables of Cases and Treaties.

A

Aach River, **4,** 128
Aachen, Boundary Treaty of (1816), **6,** 355; **8,** 162–163; **12,** 59–60
Aaland Islands Demilitarization Agreement (1921), **22,** 681
Abbeville–Paris, Treaty of (1259)
  See Paris, Treaty of (1259)
Absorption of States
  German Länder (1934), **8,** 349; **22,** 141–146; **26,** 91–92; **28,** 47, 96
  non-recognition of, **10,** 70–97; **13,** 19–20: *see also under* Annexation
  Serbia and Yugoslavia, **21,** 71
Abu Dhabi (Sheikh of), Concession Agreement with Petroleum Development (Trucial Coast) Ltd. (1939), **18,** 144–151, 158–160
Abuse of the Optional Clause, **24,** 848
Abuse of process of the Court, **20,** 556
Abuse of right (*abus de droit*), **1,** 237–238, 476–477; **3,** 107–108, 294; **4,** 128–133, 235–236; **5,** 16, 17, 86–87, 204; **8,** 28, 315–318; **15,** 337, 346; **16,** 157, 159, 167; **18,** 104, 108, 110, 111; **19,** 433, 530, 532; **21,** 326, 329; **22,** 321, 366, 370, 372–373, 687, 777; **23,** 562, 570; **24,** 129, 140, 141, 806–808, 821, 836, 848, 864; **27,** 512, 547; **30,** 445;
  see also Discretions *and* Good Faith
Abuse of right of petition to the European Commission of Human Rights, **24,** 355, 388, 389, 390–391; **25,** 229–230; **30,** 346, 348
Abyssinia: *see* Ethiopia
Accession to treaties. *See under* Treaties
Acquiescence, **1,** 88; **18,** 99–102, 154; **20,** 110–111; **22,** 765; **27,** 80; **30,** 480; **33,** 81–82; *see also* Estoppel, Preclusion
  absence of protest, **18,** 100–102, 154; **33,** 76, 80–81, 91, 92, 96, 110, 114, 135–136
  adoption of map of frontier region, **33,** 61, 66, 70–71
  estoppel and, **33,** 91, 137
  evidential value, **33,** 137, 145
  failure to assert rights, **20,** 110–111
  failure to reserve rights, **33,** 81–82
  foreign jurisdiction, **4,** 518–519
  unilateral act, consequences, **33,** 145
"*Acquerront*", meaning, **4,** 73–74
Acquired rights, respect for, **2,** 57, 71–78, 78–79, 163, 271; **3,** 82, 83–84, 87–88; **4,** 89–90, 92–93, 93–94, 292, 507; **6,** 67–68, 69, 70–71, 107; **7,** 95–99, 102–104, 317, 320, 486–487; **8,** 26–29, 136–137, 137–140; **9,** 152; **13,** 200–201; **17,** 54–55; **18,** 108; **20,** 507–508; **21,** 339, 376–377, 382; **22,** 677, 817; **23,** 96, 454, 456–457, 529–532, 533, 548–550, 554–555; **24,** 701–702, 754, 759–760; **27,** 205, 213; **29,** 257; **32,** 517–518, 532, 537–540. *See also under* Cession of territory
  concessionary contracts, under, **27,** 144, 168, 205; **35,** 183–184
  international officials and, **13,** 199–202; **20,** 506–509; **21,** 376; **24,** 753–756; **29,** 257; **32,** 517–518, 532, 537–540
  meaning, **6,** 66–71; **8,** 136–140; **9,** 54
  ordre public and, **25,** 277
  retroactive affect of legislation, **4,** 192; **9,** 152
  right of transport as, **27,** 134, 206
Acquisition of territory: *see* Cession of territory *and* Territorial sovereignty, acquisition of
Acquisitive prescription: *see* Prescription
Act of Algeciras (1906), **9,** 52–54, 56, 59, 507
  consular jurisdiction, adoption of system of, **19,** 290
  interpretation, **19,** 290
Act of sovereignty: *see* Act of State
Act of State, **1,** 21–22, 60; **2,** 11–13, 424; **3,** 41; **4,** 27–28; **6,** 32–35, 270; **7,** 506; **13,** 315, 321; **14,** 37–39, 289; **24,** 75; **27,** 31, 33, 54, 58; **31,** 12, 14–18; **34,** 125, 127
  see also Act of State, foreign, recognition of
  acquisition of property in war, **26,** 690
  acquisition of territory as, **22,** 132, 139; **27,** 31, 33; **31,** 12
  act of administration distinguished, **11,** 146
  affecting nationals, **35,** 15
  appropriation of enemy property and, **26,** 690

Act of State—*continued*
cession, treaty, Britain and King of Lagos, **26,** 109–111
comity and, **35,** 47
conflict of laws and, **35,** 48–49
conquest as, **1,** 60
constitutional aspects (U.S.A.), **35,** 35–37
crimes by former dictator, extradition request, **33,** 353–356
doctrine, and international law, **30,** 28–31; **34,** 12–16; **35,** 13, 25, 33–35, 37–43, 45–48
doctrine, basis of, **33,** 355
doctrine, U.S.A., **32,** 10–11; **35,** 2–50 *passim*
English law principle, **2,** 11–13, 424–425; **26,** 110
French practice, **5,** 28, 31; **7,** 56–57, 489–490, 505–506
injury inflicted by, **22,** 136
invalidity under foreign law, **35,** 12
jurisdictional immunity and: *see* Foreign States, exemption from jurisdiction, —public acts
meanings, **31,** 14–15, 18
nature of, **31,** 16
merger creating new State, **26,** 81–85
merger with existing State, **26,** 88–89
Mixed Courts of Egypt, jurisdiction of, and, **2,** 172–173; **3,** 21; **4,** 27–28; **11,** 224–226
plea of, **2,** 11–13, 424–425
—in relation to aliens, **1,** 231–234, **2,** 11–13
—war crimes, **13,** 221–222; **14,** 289; **15,** 682; **16,** 408, 523–524
power of courts to enquire into, **9,** 118; **7,** 506; **21,** 52–53: *see also* Act of State, foreign, recognition of
private law transactions, **2,** 13–15
protectorate, and, **5,** 17
" public act ", jurisdictional immunity, **35,** 112, 119, 124n.
public policy exception, **35,** 12–13
requisition as, **6,** 446
State succession and, **1,** 60; **10,** 99–102; **14,** 37–39; **21,** 52–53; **23,** 103–105; **24,** 75; **26,** 79–87; **31,** 14–18
State's own subjects and, **22,** 131–138
treaty, judicial review of, **14,** 39
treaty making and legislation, **27,** 261–262, 271, 273–274, 275, 279
U.S. law, immunity of government officials, **9,** 19
Act of State, foreign, recognition of, **4,** 34, 173–174; **7,** 19–28; **8,** 31–39; **11,** 13; **26,** 30, 39; **30,** 28–31; **32,** 10–11; **33,** 16–36
see also Foreign law, recognition of
contrary to international law, **33,** 30–36; **35,** 2, 6–50

Act of State, foreign, recognition of—*continued*
exchange control legislation, **33,** 28–30
Acta jure gestionis and *acta jure imperii*: *see under* Consuls; Diplomatic envoys; Foreign States
Acte de gouvernement, **12,** 183
armistice as, **12,** 413–414
theory of, **7,** 56–57, 489–490, 506
Actio personalis moritur cum persona, **5,** 174–177
" Acts committed " (Versailles Treaty), **2,** 216; **3,** 380–381; **4,** 466–467, 544, 569–571; **5,** 504, 509, 518
" Acts in excess of its powers ", **4,** 559
Ad hoc judges, **8,** 488–489
Adjective law, substantive law, distinguished, **6,** 304–305
Administration for International Assistance, **23,** 510, 511
Administration, State succession and: *see under* State succession
" Administrative control ", meaning, boundary disputes, **7,** 118–119
Administrative discretions: *see under* Discretions
Administrative law: *see under* International organization
Administrative rulings, expulsion cases: *see under* Expulsion of aliens
Administrators of firms, occupied territories, **11,** 108–110
Admiralty actions, foreign public ships, **1,** 137–144, 146–150, 156; **2,** 117–119, 120–121, 137–138, 141–144; **3,** 186–189; **5,** 112–113; **9,** 177–178, 250–263, 272–277, 279–282, 284–289; **10,** 199–204, 217–230, 240–247; **11,** 153–161; **12,** 105–112, 143–149; **13,** 82–85; **14,** 83; **16,** 142–143; **17,** 167–170; **32,** 127–136
Admiralty Court, British jurisdiction, disputes between foreigners, **8,** 208–209
disputes relating to foreign territory, **13,** 97–107
Admiralty jurisdiction, **35,** 120
U.S.A., **11,** 125, 152; **33,** 42
Admission of aliens: *see* Aliens, admission of
Admission of liability, **1,** 374; **3,** 416–417
Admissions, in diplomatic negotiations, **4,** 489; **6,** 101–102, 104
Adrianople, Vilayet, responsibility for obligations of, **4,** 206
Adverse possession of land, **9,** 115: *see also* Prescription
Advisory Opinions: *see under* International Court of Justice, *and* Permanent Court of International Justice

Advowson, continuation of, State succession and, **8,** 145
Aegean Sea, status of Greek islands, **23,** 666, 669
Aerial bombardment: *see also* Air warfare
 analogy with land bombardment, **4,** 570–572; **5,** 516–517
 applicability of Hague Regulations, **5,** 516–517; **32,** 630–631
 legality, **15,** 660–661
 rules relating to, **32,** 629–633
Aerial navigation: *see* Air space; Air transport agreements; Aircraft; Aviation
Affidavits, **4,** 404–405
 admissibility of, **4,** 483–485; **5,** 452–454; **6,** 199
Africa, provisions of Berlin Conference (1885), **4,** 110–111
After-discovered evidence
 arbitral awards and, **8,** 485–487
Agency: *see also under* Belligerent occupation
 contract of, belligerent occupation, effect, **23,** 787, 789
 creation by treaty, **26,** 364
 effect of war on, **12,** 327; **15,** 447–450; **27,** 645–648
Agents of States, jurisdictional immunity: *see* Foreign States, immunities of
Aggravating circumstances in crimes, extradition and, **8,** 380–381
Aggression, German attack on Poland (1939), **30,** 505
Aggression, war of, **15,** 415–417, 621, 636–638; **18,** 592–595
 belligerent occupation and, **16,** 455
 laws of war in, **16,** 529
 legality of, **16,** 345–347
 responsibility for, **16,** 348–349; *see also under* War crimes
Agrarian reform, Italy, **26,** 48
Agreements, inter-governmental, legislative consent, **1,** 313–315: *see also under* Treaties
Agrément, **16,** 282–283
Agriculture—
 International Institute of, **10,** 363
 —juridical nature, **5,** 413–415
 regulation of conditions of: *see* International Labour Organization
Air space: *see also* Aviation
 jurisdiction over, **17,** 191–196; **33,** 202–204
 sovereignty over, **5,** 82; **6,** 112; **7,** 114–115; **8,** 159–160; **9,** 119, 124; **11,** 85–91; **12,** 55–59; **17,** 118–123; **19,** 148; **22,** 157–167; **27,** 58–61; **30,** 73
 violation of foreign, **30,** 69–75
Air transport agreements, provisions *re* nationality of carriers, **31,** 416–424
Air Transport, International, Warsaw Convention (1929), **8,** 453, 459, 463; **9,** 445; **12,** 59, 271-273; **19,** 467–469; **20,** 41–46, 156–163, 418–424; **22,** 157–167; **24,** 267, 271, 554–557, 581–583, 630, 632, 645–647, 664–665; **28,** 99, 106
 "*dol*", meaning, **34,** 201–210
 Hague Protocol (1955), **34,** 208; **35,** 246
 "international transportation", **20,** 420–421; **22,** 160–167
 interpretation of, **35,** 239–252
 limitation of carrier's liability, **28,** 99–106
 limitation period for actions under, **28,** 99–106
 ticket, delivery of, **35,** 244–252
 venue provisions, **34,** 210–213; **35,** 239–243, 247–248
Air warfare, applicable rules, **4,** 570–572; **5,** 516–517; **32,** 630–631: *see also* Aerial bombardment
 nuclear weapons, legality of, **32,** 626–642
Aircraft—
 airships, status of, **5,** 82
 crash over high seas, applicable law, **26,** 242n.
 definition, **11,** 85–89
 nationality, **7,** 114–115
 forced landing, jurisdiction over passengers, **23,** 151–153
 foreign, innocent passage, French law (1920), **9,** 125
 jurisdiction, crime committed in, **14,** 88; **17,** 191–196; **33,** 202–204
 law of the flag, application, **28,** 115–138
 part of territory of national State, **27,** 115–116; **28,** 122–124
 seaplanes, **6,** 112
Airships, status of, **5,** 82
Aix la Chapelle, Protocol of (1818), **9,** 427
Alabama claims, indirect damages, **2,** 195–198
Alabama, seaward boundary, claim to six leagues, **31,** 151, 182, 187, 195, 204
Alaska, cession to U.S.A. (1867), **22,** 562–565
 Yakutat Bay, closing line, **35,** 84–88
Albania—
 Banking Convention, Italian Financial Group (1925), **20,** 446–449, 451; **21,** 414
 Declaration of Principal Allied Powers Concerning (1921), **22,** 681
 Extradition Treaty with Greece, **5,** 282

Albania—*continued*
Germany, Protocol, Gold Looted from Rome (1944), **20,** 451
Italian occupation of (1939), **20,** 450–451
Italy, Economic, Monetary and Customs Convention (1939), **20,** 450, 462, 468–469, 477–479
monetary gold, claims to, **20,** 442–443, 454–455; **21,** 399–400, 405–406
Nationalization Law (1945), **21,** 400, 405, 406, 408, 410, 411
Alfonso, King of Spain, confiscation of property of, **8,** 198–200
Algeciras, Act of (1906), **5,** 117; **9,** 52–54, 56, 59, 507; **19,** 255–263 *passim,* 272–290 *passim,* 294–302 *passim,* 343
Algerian hostilities—
whether covered by Geneva Refugees Convention, **32,** 230–232
Algerian Liberation Movement, activities in, political crimes, whether, **34,** 143–147
Algerian nationalists—
refugees under Geneva Convention, whether, **32,** 230–232
Alien enemy: *see* Enemy alien
Alien Land Law of California, application against Japanese, **11,** 233
Alien Property Custodian: *see also* Custodian of Enemy Property
recognition of acts abroad, **11,** 106–107
sale of land by, **11,** 250–251
Alien seamen—
declaration of naturalization, diplomatic protection, **3,** 269–270
desertion from ship, **9,** 170; **28,** 360
detention of, **11,** 114–115
jurisdiction over claims by: *see* Jurisdiction, ports, in
Alienage, recognition of—
recognition of foreign nationality, distinguished, **5,** 225
Aliens: *see also* Corporations, foreign; Enemy aliens; Refugees; State responsibility
1, 231–259; **2,** 262–273; **3,** 286–299; **4,** 328–340; **5,** 254–268; **6,** 268–292; **7,** 299–334; **8,** 315–347; **9,** 364–394; **10,** 291–326; **11,** 187–198; **12,** 202–236; **13,** 138–151; **14,** 125-137; **15,** 269-292; **16,** 231–265; **17,** 229–260; **19,** 339–360; **20,** 264–363; **21,** 190–231; **22,** 458–512; **23,** 374–403; **24,** 476–492; **26,** 466–512; **27,** 247–250; **28,** 293–318; **30,** 374–376; **31,** 327–355; **32,** 195–275; **33,** 245–293; **34,** 121–132; **35,** 205–216

Aliens—*continued*
abroad, jurisdiction over, **4,** 198–199; **6,** 135–136; **7,** 145–150; **8,** 182–184; **11,** 111–112; **12,** 68–73; **13,** 54–56, 58, 69–75, 95–96; **14,** 72–73, 127–128; **16,** 86–94; **19,** 229–254; **20,** 197–210; **21,** 89–94; **22,** 200–208; **23,** 150–151; **24,** 156–160; **26,** 160; **27,** 341–346; **32,** 112–117; **34,** 51–80; **35,** 97–109
access to courts, **1,** 243; **5,** 260–263; **6,** 276; **7,** 303–309; **8,** 325–326; **11,** 230, 235; **12,** 202–208; **16,** 253–256; **17,** 241–242; **23,** 314, 323–333; **24,** 481; **34,** 101–102, 104
—unlawful entrants, **8,** 325–326
acquired rights: *see* Acquired rights *and* Aliens, expropriation of property of
acquisition of land, **1,** 242; **2,** 265–266; **4,** 329–330; **6,** 279–280; **8,** 319–322; **9,** 379; **13,** 138–142; **16,** 247–253, 257–258; **28,** 37; **31,** 1–3
—foreign companies, **1,** 245–246
Act of State, plea of, **1,** 231–234; **2,** 11–13
admission of, **1,** 231; **3,** 286–287; **4,** 328–329; **5,** 254; **6,** 268–271; **7,** 299–302; **8,** 315–317; **10,** 291–295; **14,** 71–72, 125–127; **15,** 269–279; **16,** 231–238; **17,** 229–234; **18,** 282–286; **20,** 264–286; **22,** 458–460; **26,** 466–474; **28,** 252–253; **31,** 327–329; **33,** 245–252
—clandestine entry, **20,** 285–286
—conditional, **22,** 460
—detention pending leave to land, **26,** 466–474
—duty of, **21,** 210
—English law, **26,** 466–474
—illegal entry, **23,** 374–375; **31,** 327–329
—illegitimate children, **20,** 284–285; **22,** 458—459
—implied leave to land, **33,** 251
—landing to change planes only, **26,** 467–473
—leave to land, **33,** 245–252
—notice of refusal of leave to land, **33,** 249–250
—parole, on, **26,** 476–479
—permission improperly given, **22,** 490–497
—readmission, right of, **6,** 268–271
—right of State to control, **26,** 479–480
—status pending determination of admissibility, **26,** 476, 533

Aliens—*continued*
admission of—*continued*
—visitor requesting permanent admission, **27**, 247–248
allegiance of, **1**, 231–233; **9**, 374; **14**, 128; **15**, 281–285; **17**, 242; **18**, 265–276; **19**, 554; **22**, 468–470, 471–472; **22**, 468–470
arrest of, **6**, 206–207
asylum, right of: *see* Asylum
bankruptcy jurisdiction over, **16**, 86–94
civil action between, jurisdiction, **34**, 49–50
civil jurisdiction over, **3**, 291; **16**, 86–94; **21**, 89–92; **33**, 173–181, 253–254
civil rights, **12**, 202–208
co-belligerency and, **19**, 638–640
companies formed by: *see also* Corporations
—equality of treatment, **7**, 307–309
—establishment rights, **3**, 291
—requirement of registration, **5**, 261–262
—restrictions upon, **1**, 245–246
compensation for war damage, right to, **9**, 374
confiscation of property: *see* Confiscation, foreign property
constitution, right to invoke, **3**, 290
control of, public policy and, **21**, 281–283; **22**, 478–471
court martial jurisdiction, **12**, 12–15
criminal jurisdiction over, **1**, 107–109; **2**, 109; **3**, 148–150; **4**, 153–159, 519; **6**, 151–152; **11**, 111–112; **12**, 68–73; **13**, 54–56, 58, 69–75, 95–96; **14**, 72–73, 127–128, 196–201; **16**, 86–99, 432; **17**, 136–140; **18**, 206–210; **19**, 163; **21**, 92–94; **22**, 203–209; **23**, 147–149, 150–151; **24**, 156–164
—acts committed abroad, **1**, 107–109; **3**, 148–150, 158–160; **4**, 153–159; **11**, 111–112; **12**, 68–73; **13**, 54–56, 58, 69–75, 95–96; **14**, 72–73, 127–128; **22**, 203–209; **23**, 147–149, 150–151; **28**, 341–346
—crime committed in national waters, **15**, 108–110; **32**, 117–119
—Occupant, nationals of, **15**, 550
—occupation forces, **14**, 196–201
currency laws and, **9**, 382
damage to property: *see under* State responsibility
deceased, jurisdiction over estate of, **7**, 162
declaration of receiving State creating obligation, **22**, 479
denial of justice: *q.v.*
deportation of, **27**, 14–15, 245–250; **34**, 21–26: *see also* Expulsion of aliens

Aliens—*continued*
deportation of—*continued*
—Canadian law, **6**, 291–292
—English law, **33**, 257–259, 261–293 *passim*
—invasion of home State, effect, **10**, 316–326
—judicial review, **32**, 198
—national State, to, **33**, 291
—non-recognition of governments, effect, **1**, 258–259; **4**, 340
—onus of proof of citizenship, **27**, 14, 245–247
—procedure, interim injunction, **27**, 14–15
—revocation of deportation order, **27**, 249–250
—subject to, position of, **27**, 249–250
deportation proceedings, effect, **16**, 253–256
detention of, **7**, 477–478; **15**, 278; **18**, 294–298, 310–314; **26**, 473–474
—excessive, **20**, 264–276, 343–350
—*incommunicación*, **5**, 256
—permanent, **9**, 378
disabilities of, **11**, 194
discrimination against, **1**, 240–241, 244–247; **2**, 418–419; **5**, 264, 395; **11**, 1–5, 192–193; **12**, 230
—application of labour laws, **28**, 115, 121
—arms, possession of, **2**, 268
—criminal proceedings, in, **7**, 311–312
—Czech measures against German property, **26**, 41, 47, 51
—discretionary matters, **2**, 267–268
—*ex gratia* payments, **2**, 267–270
—fishing rights, **1**, 237; **2**, 269; **14**, 129–130
—guardianship, **2**, 269–270
—Indonesian measures against Dutch property, **26**, 38–39; **28**, 17–19, 21, 25, 34, 36–37; **30**, 28–33, 375–376
—legislation, **9**, 333, 371: *see also* non-discrimination, plea of, *infra*
—prohibition of, **7**, 312–323
—prohibition of, exception for criminal proceedings, **7**, 311–312
—property, measures affecting, **26**, 39; **30**, 28–33, 375–376
—religion, on ground of, **4**, 55–56
—Soviet law, **32**, 213
divorce proceedings by, **24**, 488–489
domicile, acquisition of, **17**, 241–242
domicile, loss of, **9**, 384
due process of law, **4**, 151–152; **20**, 296–300, 304, 330–333, 340–342, 343–350; **24**, 479
enemy aliens: *see* Enemy alien
entrant, **20**, 276–281, 281–284, 343

Aliens—*continued*
equality of treatment, **1,** 241; **6,** 9–10, 276, 277–278, 280–284, 347–348; **8,** 317–318, 327–336; **11,** 192–193; **13,** 144–145; **17,** 242–249; **19,** 283–287; **24,** 796; **31,** 329–330, 344–345.
See also discrimination against, *supra, and* National treatment clause
—employers' liability and, **9,** 377
—free access to courts, **6,** 276, **8,** 331–333
—freedom of trade, **7,** 314–316
—workmen's compensation, **6,** 347–348; **7,** 468, 469, 470; **18,** 506–507; **22,** 580–583; **26,** 482–487
exclusion of, **18,** 297–299; **20,** 264–276, 286; **33,** 272
—judicial review, **32,** 195–198
expropriation of property of, **1,** 238–239; **2,** 163, 270–272; **3,** 81–83, 133–136, 207, 231–232; **4,** 147–151, 338–339; **5,** 254–265; **6,** 51–52; **7,** 27–28, 255–257, 323-325; **8,** 336–337; **9,** 150, 380–382; **14,** 187–189; **15,** 24–27; **20,** 305–330; **22,** 32–33, 40–41, 483–485; **30,** 133, 214; **32,** 233–237.
See also Confiscatory legislation; Expropriation; Nationalization measures, *and under* Concession agreements
—discriminatory, **35,** 4, 7, 9, 11, 19–23
—interference with property, **2,** 170–171
—Netherlands enterprises in Indonesia, **33,** 32–33
—Peace Treaty, under, **32,** 233–237
—revocation of concessions, **28,** 16–39
expulsion of: *see* Expulsion of aliens
extradition of: *see* Extradition
false imprisonment, action for, **26,** 473–474
freedom of commerce, **9,** 379
freedom of movement, right of, **23,** 383–385; **31,** 330, 331, 332–341
freedom of residence, **19,** 339–340, 345
guardian, alien acting as, **1,** 239; **2,** 269–270
health laws, submission to, **7,** 310–311; **9,** 367
illegal entry—
effect, access to courts, **8,** 325–326
effect, national treatment clause, **31,** 344–345
immigrants, detention of, **15,** 278–279
immigration laws, violation of, **9,** 378
inheritance, right of, **19,** 393–394, 398–399; **20,** 292–296, 386–389; **21,** 203–208; **22,** 475–478; **24,** 482; **26,** 487–489, 585–587, 692,

Aliens—*continued*
inheritance, right of—*continued*
694–699; **28,** 300–309; **32,** 74–76, 203–223; **35,** 205–216, 235–236, 239
insurance policies, payment of, **24,** 476
land, right to bequeath, **12,** 222–224
—right to inherit, **5,** 257–260; **12,** 224–229; **26,** 585–587
—right to own, **2,** 265–266; **4,** 329–330; **6,** 279–280; **8,** 319–322; **9,** 379; **13,** 138–142; **16,** 247–253, 257–258; **19,** 312–316; **31,** 1–3; **35,** 209–210
—security of tenure, **26,** 599–602
language, own, use of, **2,** 262–263; **5,** 264; **6,** 283
legal aid, right to, **23,** 381–382
local law, subject to, **6,** 271–272; **9,** 366–368; **15,** 279–280; **17,** 234–239; **18,** 286–287; **20,** 290–292; **26,** 234–236
—exemption under treaty, **33,** 383–384
—production of documents held abroad, **32,** 100–102; **33,** 158–163; **34,** 43–46
mandated territory, in, **12,** 12–15
meaning, **19,** 327
measure affecting " aliens as such ", **33,** 165, 169
military service, **10,** 116–123; **11,** 187–192; **12,** 208–221; **16,** 244–247; **17,** 234–237; **19,** 342–344; **20,** 286–290; **21,** 199–203; **22,** 460–466, 474; **28,** 293–296; **32,** 189–192
national treatment clause: *q.v.*
non-discrimination, meaning of obligation, **6,** 284
non-discrimination, plea of, **1,** 244–247, 448; **3,** 133–136, 207, 227–232, 297; **4,** 333–339; **6,** 9–10, 276, 277–278, 280–284; **7,** 311–323; **22,** 480, 580–583; **31,** 344–345
non-resident,
—application of statutes, **34,** 78
—capacity to sue, **32,** 195–198
—inheritance, right of, **19,** 393–394, 398–399; **20,** 292–296, 386–389; **21,** 203–208; **22,** 475–478; **24,** 482; **26,** 487–489; **28,** 300–309; **32,** 74–76, 203–223; **34,** 121–126; **35,** 205–216, 235–236, 239
—jurisdiction over, **4,** 198–199; **7,** 145–150; **12,** 68–73; **13,** 54–56, 58, 95–96; **14,** 72–73
See also criminal jurisdiction, *supra*
—right to sue, **5,** 261; **33,** 173–181
—taxation of, **6,** 135–136
—U.S. Constitution, application, **26,** 2–3

Aliens—*continued*
obligations of, **16**, 238–239. *See also* allegiance *and* military service, *supra*
passports, **9**, 383–384
—proof of nationality, **9**, 339
" permitted to reside ", meaning, **22**, 479
petition of right by, **9**, 372; **12**, 202–208
police measures, application to, **6**, 181
poor persons' procedure, **11**, 242–243
position of, **1**, 231–235; **3**, 287–291; **5**, 257–263; **6**, 271–287; **7**, 303–424; **8**, 317–336; **10**, 295–304; **11**, 187–195; **12**, 202–221; **13**, 138–145; **14**, 127–131; **15**, 279–285; **16**, 238–265; **17**, 234–239; 247–248; **18**, 286–287, 292–300; **20**, 286–336; **21**, 199–212; **22**, 460–475; **23**, 377–381, 382–385; 386–391; **24**, 483–489; **26**, 480–502; **27**, 247–248; **28**, 293–309; **30**, 374–375; **31**, 329–345; **32**, 195–237; **33**, 253–255; **34**, 121–127; **35**, 205–216
—attorneys, as, **9**, 376; **15**, 281–285
—enemy aliens, assimilation to, **17**, 237–239
—habeas corpus, **33**, 275
—Federal State, in, **10**, 295–304
—mandated territories, in, **15**, 281–285
—most favoured-nation clause: *q.v.*
—profession, exercise of, **20**, 302–304; **22**, 468–472
—undertaking not to harm existing foreign businesses, **31**, 341–344
privileged, **18**, 300; **21**, 222–225, 284–286, 303
prohibited immigrants, **18**, 294–308
prohibition of employment of, **26**, 311
property of
—acquisition, **1**, 242; **2**, 265–266; **4**, 329–330; **6**, 279–280; **8**, 319–322; **9**, 379; **13**, 138–142; **16**, 247–253, 257–258
—business tenancy, **23**, 392
—enforcement of rights, **18**, 292–293
—expropriation: *see* expropriation of property, *supra*
—interference with, **2**, 170–171
—landlord, right of eviction, **16**, 311
—nationalization: *q.v.*
—respect for, **23**, 701–706: *see also* vested rights, respect for, *infra*.
—right to inherit, **19**, 393–394, 398–399; **20**, 292–296, 386–389; **21**, 203–208; **22**, 475–478; **24**, 482; **26**, 585–587, 692, 694–699; **28**, 300–309; **32**, 74–76, 203–223; **34**, 121–126; **35**, 205-216, 235, 236, 239
—tenant, rights as, **18**, 291–292

Aliens—*continued*
property of—*continued*
—war damage legislation, rights under, **7**, 310, 323–325
protection of
—acquired by provisional entry, **9**, 365
—former imperial country, by, **17**, 199–202
—wartime, **4**, 282–283
See also Diplomatic protection
reciprocal treatment, **4**, 453–454; **7**, 307–309; **8**, 328–329, 335–336; **9**, 376–377; **12**, 420–426; **13**, 144–145; **16**, 259–260; **19**, 393–398; **31**, 329; **32**, 198–200, 210–223
—in absence of treaty, **9**, 376
See also Reciprocity
re-entry of former resident, **9**, 364
registration of, **10**, 295–304; **19**, 317–318; **22**, 479, 501–505; **30**, 353–354, 360
requisitioning of property, **21**, 211, 278
" residence " of aliens, meaning, **1**, 234; **22**, 504
residence—
—permanent, **23**, 453–454
—permit obtained on untruthful statements, **28**, 297–298
—requirement of, **16**, 263
—right of, **22**, 479; **23**, 377–379, 383–385, 386–388
residence permits, **19**, 478–487; **22**, 501–503, 505–507; **28**, 297–298
resident distinguished from entrant, **20**, 281–284
retaliation in treatment of, **3**, 287–288
right to leave State, **20**, 296–300; **26**, 481
—fulfilment of local obligations, **26**, 482
right to question legislation, **18**, 286–287
right to sue, **5**, 261; **9**, 277, 372; **16**, 253–256; **18**, 289–290; **19**, 344, 562–563; **23**, 379–381, 382–383; **24**, 932.
See also access to courts, *supra*
rights acquired abroad, jurisdiction, **20**, 197–210
security for costs, exemption from requirement of, **1**, 243; **5**, 263; **13**, 185, 187, 232
security for costs, liability for, **18**, 52–53; **21**, 210–211, 358, 303–304
standing to sue, nationalized company, **34**, 126–127
sterilization of, **8**, 322–323
subjection to local law, **6**, 271–272; **9**, 366–368; **15**, 279–280; **17**, 234–239; **18**, 286–287; **20**, 290–292

Aliens—*continued*
subjection to local law—*continued*
—régime of capitulations, and, **26**, 234–236
suit *in forma pauperis*, **12**, 113–115
supervision of, **22**, 478–479
taxation of, **4**, 151–152, 332–333, 335–337; **6**, 19–20, 135–136, 280–281; **8**, 336–337; **9**, 380; **11**, 1–2. *See also* Aliens, non-resident, taxation of
—enforceability in home State, **2**, 263–264
—estates of, **12**, 230, 273–276
—exemption, **1**, 333–334; **5**, 255; **15**, 3–4; **18**, 280–281; **20**, 263–264; **21**, 8, 280–281; **25**, 320
—income earned outside State, **27**, 103–107
—non-discrimination, relevance, **26**, 312–313
—war taxation, **4**, 333
temporary resident, subject to health laws, **9**, 367
trade, right to, **11**, 195; **18**, 291; **19**, 339–340, 341–342, 344; **20**, 301–302; **23**, 376–377; **26**, 490–492, 494–496
treason by, **13**, 69–75, 138; **14**, 127–129; **15**, 78–90; **16**, 239–244
treaties, rights under, **3**, 344–345, 383–384; **5**, 154–155, 394; **9**, 371, 379; **13**, 183–184; **14**, 160–162, 164; **22**, 580–583; **23**, 311, 313–314, 317, 323–333; **26**, 490–492, 494–496.
See also Foreign armed forces
treatment of, **1**, 237–247; **3**, 294–297; **5**, 255–256, 263–265; **6**, 269–270, 276–284; **9**, 368–379; **12**, 222–231; **13**, 144–145; **15**, 286–290; **17**, 239–249; **18**, 288–292; **19**, 339–345; **20**, 290–330; **21**, 203–211; **22**, 475–479; **23**, 376–377, 381–385, 392–393; **24**, 476–483; **26**, 482–502; **27**, 141, 248; **28**, 297–309; **31**, 329–344; **32**, 195–233; **33**, 253–255; **34**, 121–127; **35**, 205–216
—capitulations, under, **19**, 342–344
—claims against State, right to bring, **32**, 198–202
—denial of justice: *q.v.*
—detention after refusal to admit, **33**, 246–252
—detention pending deportation, **33**, 258
—equality of: *see* equality of treatment, *supra*
—exemption from taxation: *see* taxation of, exemption, *supra*
—federal States, in, **10**, 295–303; **12**, 224–229

Aliens—*continued*
treatment of—*continued*
—France, law of: *see under* France
—" international standard ", **3**, 214, 227–228, 295
See also International standards
—" legislative reciprocity ", **26**, 493–494
—limitation of movement, **31**, 330–331, 332–341
—maltreatment in prison, **3**, 227–228, 295; **4**, 250
—national treatment: *see* National treatment clause; *and* discrimination *and* non-discrimination, *supra*
—nationals of former colonial power, **28**, 36
—ownership of property, frontier zone, **9**, 379
—reciprocity, **4**, 453–454; **7**, 307–309; **8**, 328–329, 335–336; **9**, 376–377; **12**, 420–426; **31**, 329; **32**, 198–200, 210–223
See also Reciprocity
—war, effect of: *see* Enemy aliens *and* War, outbreak of, effects
—withdrawal of privilege, need for notice, **1**, 237–238
unlawful entry or stay, **8**, 325, 340; **31**, 344–345
vested rights, respect for, **6**, 270; **7**, 317; **11**, 226
See also Acquired rights; Aliens, expropriation, *supra*, *and* Nationalization
violation of duty to, by officials, **21**, 208–209
visa, effect of issue, **34**, 167–168, 170
witness, duty to appear as, **6**, 271–272
workmen's compensation, **6**, 347–348; **7**, 468, 469, 470; **11**, 194; **18**, 506–507; **22**, 580–583; **26**, 482–487; **31**, 344–345
Alimony—
suits against consuls, **4**, 378–379
—against international officials, **32**, 334
Allegiance—
aliens, of, **1**, 231–233; **12**, 202–208; **13**, 69–75, 138; **14**, 127–129; **15**, 78–107, 281–285; **34**, 101, 104, 105
basis of jurisdiction, as, **15**, 78–107; **30**, 107, 108, 109–110
change of, in war, **15**, 83–90, 97; **26**, 430
disciplinary jurisdiction, compared, **26**, 220
domicile and, **16**, 242; **34**, 101, 104
dual nationality and, **18**, 265–276
issue of habeas corpus and, **28**, 49, 61
naturalization and, **15**, 91–104

Allegiance—*continued*
oath to foreign State, expatriation, **8**, 297–299; **10**, 276–278; **16**, 197–198; **22**, 437–442; **25**, 147; **26**, 460–463; **31**, 326
passport and, **15**, 91–104
protectio trahit subjectionem et subjectio protectionem, **15**, 84, 88, 92
treason and, **15**, 78–104; **19**, 554
Alliance
attack on ally, legal effect, **26**, 635
enemy State with, whether involving ally in war, **12**, 285–286
Allied Control Commission: *see under* Italy
Allied Control Council: *see under* Germany
Allied forces, jurisdiction over, **10**, 111–129; **13**, 85–92; *see also* Foreign armed forces
Allied Military Government: *see under* Italy
" Allied national ", meaning, **12**, 210
resident abroad, compulsory military service by, **12**, 208–218
Ally of enemy, status of, **9**, 575
Alsace Lorraine—
binding force of judgments of courts, **7**, 105
liquidation of Germany property, **4**, 408
nationality of natives of, **7**, 273; **12**, 185–188
occupation of, **6**, 447–448
—by French army, **7**, 511–512
railways, **2**, 57–58; **4**, 83–84
reunion with France, **1**, 448–449
Treaty of Versailles, **1**, 92; **7**, 105, 273
Ambassador: *see also* Diplomatic envoys
conclusiveness of certificate of, **16**, 129–137
Ambassadors, Conference of, **2**, 381–383, 386–387
Amboina, Amboinese. *See* South Moluccas, Republic of
Ambulance service, foreign, loss of nationality and, **8**, 301
American Civil War, questions of succession, **3**, 211
American States—
arbitral awards, right to contest, regional custom as to, **30**, 481–483, 490
American Treaty of Pacific Settlement (1948), United States' reservation, **27**, 546–547
Amnesty—
grant of, denial of justice and, **4**, 212–213
peace treaties, under, limits of, **2**, 435; **4**, 553–554
Amnesty—*continued*
right of occupant to grant, **12**, 454–455
Amnesty law, effect on extradition, **7**, 352–353; **8**, 372–375
8, 372–375
Amsterdam, collective fine by occupation authorities, **11**, 294–295
Anarchism, advocacy of, ground for expulsion, **1**, 251–253
Ancón, Treaty of (1883), **2**, 241; **6**, 110
Andorra, legal status, **7**, 56–57
Angary, right of, **1**, 414–418; **2**, 420–427; **3**, 456–458; **10**, 639; **13**, 238–239; **23**, 706–754
compensation—
—counterclaim for expenditure, **23**, 749–750
—currency of payment, **23**, 752–754
—*damnum emergens*, **23**, 740–744
—interest, **1**, 191; **23**, 750–751
—*lucrum cessans*, **23**, 745–749
—measure of, **1**, 188–189; **23**, 732–754
—use, for, **23**, 744–745
history, **23**, 714–717
nature of, **23**, 717–720
necessity, **23**, 723–726
neutral ships, Institute of Internanational Law, Resolutions on (1898 and 1906), **23**, 715
neutrals, exercise by, **23**, 709, 713–714, 717, 728–732
requisition and, **23**, 726–728
requisitioned vessels, jurisdictional immunity, **1**, 152–153
sovereignty and, **23**, 720–722
Anglo-Italian Conciliation Commission jurisdiction, competence to determine, **22**, 867–875
Anglo-Japanese Property Commission
applicable law, **28**, 310
general principles of law on patents in industrial countries, **29**, 312
settlement by parties, decision giving effect to, **29**, 318–320
Ankole Agreement, 1901: *see under* Uganda
Annam, French protectorate, **11**, 43, 46–47
Annexation: *see also* Absorption of States; Territorial sovereignty, change of
Austria, **9**, 19, 87–90, 407; **10**, 103–106, 530–534; **12**, 23–29, 187–194; **15**, 51, 214–216; **16**, 61–62, 63–64, 66–67, 347, 348, 361; **17**, 203, 302; **18**, 47–49, 245; **19**, 144, 335–336; **20**, 89–91, 93, 250–251; **21**, 82, 262–264; **22**, 58–59, 89, 100–101, 146, 430–432, 530, 620–621; **23**, 123–124

Annexation—*continued*
Austria—*continued*
—nationality and, **18,** 244–246, 248–249; **21,** 175–177; **22,** 430–432; **23,** 364–369; **32,** 153
Bessarabia, **2,** 224–227; **5,** 61–62; **6,** 60–61
continuation of laws, **9,** 103; **10,** 104–106
continuation of treaties, **5,** 69
Cyprus, **1,** 199, 201–202
Czechoslovakia, **9,** 84; **10,** 78–79
Estonia, **10,** 70–78, 86–97; **12,** 29–39
See also under U.S.S.R.
Ethiopia, **9,** 94, 172
Eugen, Malmédy and Moresnet (1940), **15,** 60–61, 528, 536
Hague Regulations and, **15,** 672
Hawaii, **10,** 279–281
Latvia, **12,** 39–43. *See also under* U.S.S.R.
laws of war, applicability in annexed territory, **15,** 655
Lithuania, **10,** 80–86. *See also under* U.S.S.R.
Luxembourg, **11,** 226–227
meaning, **7,** 98
nationality, effect on, **1,** 199–202; **2,** 240–241; **3,** 265–268; **7,** 112; **9,** 339–340; **10,** 281–284; **11,** 83–85; **12,** 188–195; **13,** 115–120; **14,** 46, 112, 114, **15,** 48–50, 206–207, 214–216; **16,** 184–188; **17,** 203; **18,** 49–50, 244–246, 258–262; **19,** 319–326; **20,** 250; **21,** 175–177; **22,** 430–432; **23,** 34; **24,** 434, 439–440; **32,** 153
non-recognition of, **10,** 70–97; **12,** 27, 29, 39–44, 47; **15,** 47; **18,** 63, 79–80, 288–289; **19,** 69–71; **20,** 193–195; **22,** 97–100; **23,** 706; **26,** 76; **28,** 95–97, 386, 388–389; **32,** 73–76; **33,** 43–46
non-retroactivity, **6,** 71–72
occupation, distinguished, **14,** 49
occupied territory, of, **10,** 581–583; **12,** 43–47; **13,** 220–221, 358, 386–387, 388; **14,** 45–49
private rights, effect on, **3,** 83–84; **6,** 71–72, 85; **7,** 77–99; **13,** 35–36; **23,** 110–111; **24,** 74–76
recognition of, **9,** 87, 93; **12,** 23–47; **14,** 112; **15,** 45–50
requisites, **13,** 188–192
South African Republic, **2,** 67–68
Trieste, **1,** 455
Anschluss: see under Austria
Anti-trust laws: *see also* Restrictive practices, *and* Shipping conferences
extraterritorial effect, **19,** 158–163; **22,** 168–184; **23,** 130–133; **24,** 673–675
national treatment clause, and, **24,** 673–677
Antioquia, Government of, **1,** 285
Antwerp, German occupation of, **1,** 420; **3,** 473–474
"*Appartenant*", meaning, **2,** 421
"Appeal", meaning, **4,** 464
Appeal against arbitral awards, **4,** 462–465, 491–492; **8,** 480–487; **24,** 774–781
Appearance, waiver of immunity by, **10,** 199–204
Arabs, whether "white persons", U.S. law, **12,** 197
Aramco, oil concession by Saudi Arabia (1933), **27,** 117–122
applicable law: *see under* Concessions, applicable law
"exclusive right" of exploitation, meaning, **27,** 175–179
Arbitration Agreement with Saudi Arabia (1955), **27,** 229–233
fundamental law of parties, as, **27,** 168
international character, **27,** 166
legal nature, **27,** 203–204: *see also under* Concessions
Offshore Agreement, 1948 . . . **27,** 120–122, 143, 181–183, 195
protests against Agreement between Saudi Arabia and Onassis, **27,** 129–130
right to "deal with" oil, **27,** 184–185, 187, 223
right to "export" oil, **27,** 185–186
royalty provisions, **27,** 123
transport of oil abroad, **27,** 123–126, 140–143, 176–184, 186–190, 194–195, 198–202, 209, 228–229
"Aranha Plan" (1934), **10,** 186
Arbitral Awards, Foreign, Geneva Convention (1927), **7,** 419–420; **27,** 36; **28,** 526–538; **31,** 20–22; **34,** 29–36
Arbitration Clauses, Geneva Protocol (1923), **7,** 419–420; **8,** 434–435; **15,** 4–5; **23,** 634, 638, 639; **27,** 36; **28,** 532; **31,** 20–22; **34,** 29–36
Arbitral Commission on Property, Rights and Interests in Germany: *see under* Germany, Federal Republic
Arbitral tribunals. *See also* Arbitration, international; Arbitrators; Mixed arbitral tribunals, *and* names of various tribunals
applicable law, *non liquet* provision, **29,** 295, 297
collège arbitral, sitting as, **22,** 500, 507, 840–843
competence, **2,** 183, 371–379; **3,** 402–407; **4,** 470–477; **5,** 429–448; **6,** 421–423; **7,** 252–254, 255–257, 484–487; **10,** 421–422; **20,** 547–566; **23,** 342–344, 594–595; **25,** 517–544; **29,** 289–304

Arbitral tribunals—*continued*
competence—*continued*
—arbitration clause in private agreement, whether restricted by, **3,** 402–403
—basis of, **6,** 417–420
—claim not presented to respondent Government, **30,** 448–450
—constitutional limitations, **8,** 478–479
—determination of competence, **2,** 183; **4,** 470–471; **5,** 440–442; **7,** 484–487; **10,** 421–422; **25,** 530–533
—extension by subsequent legislation, **6,** 425–426
—*forum prorogatum,* **25,** 530
—municipal law, question of, **7,** 92–94
—nationality acquired *in fraudem legis,* right to examine, **3,** 403–404
—ouster of, **20,** 565–566
—*perpetuatio fori,* **25,** 55
—review of municipal decisions, **29,** 289–291
—special procedures, effect, **23,** 544
compromis, competence to interpret, **30,** 466, 485
conciliation commissions, distinguished, **22,** 820, 867, 872
constitution of, **35,** 161–162, 164, 166–168
equity, application of. *See* Equity
ex aequo et bono decisions. *See Ex aequo et bono*
historical survey by, **23,** 663
individuals, position before: *see under* Individual in international law
jurisdiction: *see* competence, *supra*
law applied by, **1,** 369–371; **2,** 164, 367–368; **3,** 397–400; **4,** 466–469; **5,** 423, 453; **6,** 374; **7,** 477–483; **8,** 479; **20,** 534–547; **22,** 820–839, 871; **23,** 632–658; **25,** 501, 503, 506, 529, 551–552 n., 554; **28,** 544–549; **30,** 485, 486; **35,** 164, 168–176. *See also* Equity *and Ex aequo et bono*
—consent of parties as to, **23,** 634, 636–637, 639
legislative functions, **7,** 121–127. *See also Ex aequo et bono*
mixed: *see* Mixed arbitral tribunals
one treaty, set up by, conflicting decisions, **25,** 53–54
procedure, **1,** 371; **2,** 368–370; **3,** 403; **4,** 469–470; **5,** 426–428; **6,** 420–421; **18,** 470; **20,** 444, 565–566; **22,** 840; **23,** 676–681; **25,** 206, 544–547; **27,** 137–139; **28,** 563–566; **29,** 297–303, 304–307,

Arbitral tribunals—*continued*
procedure—*continued*
318–319: *see also under* Arbitration, international
—competence to determine, **18,** 470; **25,** 206
quasi-arbitral bodies, **2,** 383–384
regrouping of claims by, **23,** 661–663
termination of jurisdiction, **6,** 344–345
Arbitration, civil—
award, foreign, execution of, **7,** 419–420; **8,** 434–435; **27,** 35–44; **28,** 526–528; **31,** 20–22; **34,** 27–36
Geneva Convention on Execution of Foreign Arbitral Awards (1927), **7,** 419–420; **27,** 36; **28,** 526–538; **31,** 20–22; **34,** 29–36
Geneva Protocol (1923) on Arbitration Clauses, **7,** 419–420; **8,** 434–435; **15,** 4–5; **23,** 634, 638, 639; **28,** 532; **31,** 20–22; **34,** 29–36
submission to, waiver of immunity, **2,** 124–128, 139; **35,** 110–121
treaty creating obligation to arbitrate, **31,** 401–405
validity of German bonds, disputes concerning, **31,** 401–405
Arbitration, foreign company and Government, between, **18,** 144; **20,** 534; **23,** 633–658, 670–671; **24,** 761–767; **27,** 116–232; **35,** 136, 140–142, 161–165, 166–168
—administrative contracts, **23,** 640–642; **35,** 183
—*amiables compositeurs,* **24,** 761; **35,** 175
—applicable law, **23,** 636–638; **27,** 153–172; **35,** 164, 168–176
—award, devaluation of currency, effect, **24,** 762–766
—award, interest on, **24,** 766; **35,** 190
—*clausula rebus sic stantibus,* application, **23,** 635
—costs, **35,** 190
—damages, **24,** 761, 766; **35,** 181–190
—declaratory award, **27,** 144–146
—default, judgment in, **35,** 170
—documents, custody of, **27,** 137; **35,** 191
—functions of tribunal, **27,** 146–147, 148
—interest on award, **24,** 766; **35,** 190
—interpretation of *compromis,* **27,** 146–153
—jurisdiction to deal with questions of sovereignty, **27,** 149–153
—parties, severance of plaintiffs, **23,** 634
—parties, notification of award to, **35,** 190–191
—procedure, **23,** 634, 638–640

Arbitration, international, **1,** 367–381; **2,** 359–387; **3,** 419–423; **5,** 423–459; **6,** 417–427; **7,** 477–490; **15,** 339–341; **22,** 820–843
admission of liability, **3,** 416–417; **4,** 489
agreement, **6,** 417–420; **20,** 547–565; **23,** 659–660; **24,** 761–767; **27,** 130
—challenge of awards, provision for, **30,** 481–482
—earlier case, for, relevance, **23,** 83–85, 87
—execution of, partial impossibility, **6,** 365–366
—interpretation, **6,** 190–191, 275, 431; **7,** 85–87; **23,** 670–671, 672, 676, 681
—material error in, **6,** 206–207
—negotiations preceding conclusion, **7,** 116–117
—reparation, provisions as to, **4,** 502–503
—restrictive interpretation, **22,** 840–843
—superiority over municipal law, **7,** 481–482
amendment of claim, **3,** 402; **6,** 420–421; **23,** 316
appeal, admissibility, time-limits, **29,** 292–304
applicable law, **1,** 369–371; **2,** 164, 367–368; **3,** 397-400; **4,** 466–469; **5,** 423, 453; **6,** 374; **7,** 477-483; **8,** 479; **20,** 534–547; **22,** 820–839, 871; **23,** 632–658; **25,** 501, 503, 506, 529, 551–552 n., 554; **28,** 544–549; **30,** 485, 486
See also Equity
—Arbitral Commission on Property, Rights and Interests in Germany, **28,** 544–549
—municipal case-law, **25,** 554
—" principles of equity ", **4,** 467–469
—" principles of international law, justice and equity ", **1,** 369; **2,** 415; **3,** 233, 235–237, 397–400; **4,** 466–467, 467–469; **7,** 477–480
—" principles of justice and equity ", **5,** 452–455
—" principles of justice, equity and good conscience ", **20,** 534–545
—" principles of justice, equity and good faith ", **2,** 368; **3,** 231–232
—" principles of law and equity ", **1,** 369–371, 377–378; **6,** 188–190
—" treaty rights and the principles of international law and equity ", **1,** 377; **2,** 419
arbitrability, concept of, **2,** 359–366
arbitration clause in private agreements, effect, **3,** 402–403
award, **7,** 488–490; **16,** 339–341; **21,** 316; **23,** 682
See also damages, *infra*

Arbitration, international—*continued*
award—*continued*
—after-discovered evidence, **8,** 481, 485–487
—appeal against, **4,** 462–465, 491–492; **8,** 480–487. *See also* revision *infra*
—appeal and revision *de novo*, **24,** 774–781; **34,** 482–488
—apportionment among claimants, **2,** 184
—binding force, **2,** 381–386; **21,** 323–325, 329; **23,** 85–86; **30,** 457–492 *passim*
—currency of payment, **23,** 673–675
—declaratory, **1,** 375
—devaluation of currency, effect, **23,** 302; **24,** 762–766
—effectiveness, **1,** 88
—enforcement, European Convention on Human Rights and, **30,** 306, 309
—*ex aequo et bono*: *q.v.*
—execution, time of, **23,** 673
—finality, **2,** 383–385; **3,** 420–421; **10,** 424–430
—finality, analogous tribunals, **3,** 420–421
—incomplete form, **3,** 419
—interest on, **22,** 409–416; **23,** 675–676. *See also* Equity *and* *Ex gratia* payments
—interpretation of, **5,** 456–457; **22,** 843
—legal nature, **5,** 157, 457
—municipal courts, disregard by, **5,** 5
—municipal courts, effect on decisions of, **4,** 493–494; **23,** 351
—municipal courts, review by, **10,** 424–430
—*non liquet*, admissibility of, **4,** 492–493: *see also* Equity, *non liquet* and
—nullity: *see* award, nullity, *infra*
—partial execution, **1,** 87–89
—payment, method of, **23,** 673–675
—quasi-arbitral decisions, **2,** 381-386, 386–387; **23,** 632–633
—rate of exchange, **4,** 205, 479; **23,** 101
—recommendations as act of grace, **1,** 376–377
—*res judicata*, **1,** 373–374; **3,** 421–423; **4,** 490; **5,** 182–183, 428, 448, 457; **6,** 425–427; **8,** 487–488; **9,** 324, 326, 522–526; **16,** 339–341
—revision of, **1,** 379–381; **2,** 386–387; **4,** 462–465, 491–492; **5,** 458–459; **9,** 324–333; **30,** 490
—revision, essential error, **9,** 331; **30,** 470, 475–476, 488–489
—scope, **20,** 567
—signature, dissenting members, **2,** 385–386

Arbitration, international—*continued*
award—*continued*
—signature, refusal, **1,** 377–378
—*ultra petita,* **2,** 214–215; **3,** 258, 419–420; **30,** 86, 87
—umpire, participation in deliberations, **6,** 427
—validity, **30,** 457–492 *passim: see also* award, nullity, *infra*
—validity, consent of Parties, **30,** 478
award, nullity, **21,** 316, 323–325, 329; **30,** 457–392 *passim*
—contradictions and obscurities, **30,** 476, 490
—delay in raising objections, **30,** 480–481, 490–492
—effects, **30,** 479–481
—essential error, **9,** 331; **30,** 470, 475–476, 488–489
—excess of jurisdiction, **30,** 470, 474–475, 489
—extrinsic defects, **30,** 484–485
—failure to object, effect, **30,** 470, 473–474, 478–479, 480, 490–492
—good faith of objecting State, **30,** 477
—Hague Conferences, 1899, 1907 . . . **30,** 481, 490
—inadequacy of reasons, **30,** 470, 476, 489
—intrinsic defects, **30,** 485–490, 492
—regularity, intrinsic and extrinsic, **30,** 477
boundary disputes: *q.v.*
claim, delay in presenting, **23,** 306, 313, 314–317
—petition for amicable settlement, distinguished, **25,** 519
—previously dismissed by Great Powers, **23,** 632–633
compromis: see agreement, *supra*
compulsory, **20,** 559
—Hague Conference, 1907 . . . **30,** 481
concept of, **4,** 461–462; **8,** 272; **22,** 820
consent to arbitrate, revocation, **6,** 417–420
Convention on Relations, Germany and Western Powers, **28,** 6
costs, **2,** 379–380; **3,** 408–410; **9,** 21, 322
—by whom determinable, **3,** 409
—exclusion of award of, **23,** 680–681
—security for, **3,** 408, 413; **6,** 40–43, 276, 349
—shared, common interest in dispute, **3,** 409–410
—to whom chargeable, **3,** 408
damages: *see also* Equity, compensation and
—calculation of, **23,** 342, 348
—token, **23,** 297: *see also* award, *supra*

Arbitration, international—*continued*
declaratory judgments, **1,** 375
delay in presenting claim, **23,** 306, 313, 314–317
denial of justice, allegation of, **23,** 309, 312, 314, 324–327, 334–340
disputed awards, boundary cases, **30,** 482–483
dominus litis, powers of, **23,** 671
Draft Convention on Arbitral Procedure, International Law Commission (1953)—
—abstention from voting, **28,** 565
—disqualification of arbitrator, **28,** 560, 563, 568
earlier arbitration on related matter, **23,** 667–668
earlier conciliation award on related matter, **23,** 301
" essential error ", meaning, **9,** 331–332; **30,** 475–476
estoppel, **3,** 417–419; **25,** 499; **30,** 457–492 *passim*
evidence, **2,** 380–381; **3,** 414–416; **4,** 479–489; **5,** 450–456; **6,** 423–426; **7,** 118–121, 127–128, 135; **24,** 778–781; **25,** 555; **27,** 62, 72–77, 87, 90, 95, 97; **28,** 523, 577–578; **29,** 448, 463–468; **30,** 451–456
—Acts of Notoriety, **30,** 449
—admissibility, discretion of tribunal, **29,** 448, 463–468
—burden of proof, **3,** 414–416; **4,** 479–489; **6,** 207–208; **7,** 231–241; **22,** 825; **23,** 306, 318, 334–336, 677–680; **30,** 452–454, 455–456
—defendant, in possession of, **23,** 677–678
—documentary, **27,** 72–76, 79–80, 82, 87–89, 94, 95
—documents submitted after hearing, **25,** 73
—evaluation by tribunal, **30,** 476
—experts, **1,** 371; **3,** 413–414; **4,** 273, 522–523; **5,** 390; **23,** 673
—facts relating to another case, **25,** 555–556
—fraudulent, **8,** 485–487
—maps, **4,** 487–488; **7,** 122–123, 125–126; **27,** 75, 77, 90, 95; **33,** 43–149 *passim*
—municipal principles, applicability, **4,** 237
—newly-discovered, re-hearing, **6,** 425; **8,** 485–487
—oral, corroboration, **26,** 624–625
—paucity of, **23,** 677–678, 679–680
—presumptions, **30,** 454–456
—privileged documents, **23,** 332–334
—self-serving declaration, **30,** 448, 449, 451, 453
—subpoena of witnesses, **6,** 425–426
—sufficiency, **30,** 448–450, 461–456

Arbitration, international—*continued*
evidence—*continued*
—valuation, expert evidence of, **35**, 159–161, 188–189
ex aequo et bono decisions: *see Ex aequo et bono*
exhaustion of local remedies: *q.v.*
fraudulent evidence, **8**, 485–487
function of, **1**, 367
—*de lege ferenda*, **9**, 332
good faith, principle of, **23**, 342, 345–346; **25**, 505, 551–552 n. *See also* Good faith
Hague Convention for Pacific Settlement (1907), **1**, 85, 870, 378; **2**, 361, 367; **4**, 479–481
historical survey by tribunal, **23**, 663
inquiry, refusal to order, **23**, 679–680
interest, claim for, **22**, 409–416; **23**, 675–676. *See also* Equity, interest; *Ex gratia* payments
interim measures of protection, **25**, 517–522, 538–540, 555–556
—inherent power to order, **25**, 522–523
interlocutory orders, **3**, 410–413; **4**, 479
international character, one party not a State, **23**, 670–671
International Court of Justice and, **20**, 547–565
interpretation of incidental agreements, **20**, 458–462
—decision on claim distinguished, **25**, 47
intervention, right of, **4**, 478; **5**, 449
judicial native, **35**, 168–169
laches, doctrine of, **3**, 246
League of Nations, Council, arbitral functions, **3**, 387–390
—P.C.I.J. and, **4**, 497
lis, distinct nature of, **23**, 86–87
municipal courts and, **4**, 493–494; **5**, 5; **10**, 424–430; **23**, 351
—review of decisions of, **4**, 462–465
municipal law in, **22**, 824–825
nationality of claims: *q.v.*
non liquet, admissibility of, **4**, 492–493
"past disputes", reservation of, **2**, 392–393
pleadings, new arguments, **25**, 521
—reply and rejoinder, **25**, 521
—subject-matter, incorporation by reference, **25**, 549
prescription, plea of, **23**, 306, 313, 314–316, 671–672. *See also* Prescription
presumptions, bad faith, **24**, 126: *see also* Good faith
private persons, rights of, **10**, 424–430

Arbitration, international—*continued*
procedure, **1**, 371; **4**, 469–470; **5**, 426–428; **6**, 420–421; **20**, 444, 565–566; **22**, 840; **23**, 676–681; **25**, 206, 544–547; **27**, 137–139; **28**, 563—566; **29**, 297–303, 304–307; 318–319; **34**, 474–482
—admissibility, **34**, 475–478
—amendment of claim, **3**, 402; **6**, 420–421; **23**, 316
—competence to determine, **18**, 470; **25**, 206
—compromise by parties, award incorporating, **29**, 304–307, 318–319
—default of appearance, **20**, 444; **35**, 164, 168–169, 170
—intervention, **25**, 544–545, 546–547: *see also* intervention, right of, *supra*
—late claims, **23**, 678–679. *See also* laches, *supra*
—time-limits, **34**, 479–482
—time-limits, general principles, **29**, 297–300
—time-limits, principles of justice and equity, **29**, 300–303. *See also* Laches *and* Prescription, extinctive
—translation of proceedings, **27**, 137–139
proceedings involving private rights, nature of, **9**, 324
recommendations as act of grace, **1**, 376–377. *See also* Equity, compensation; *Ex gratia* payments
recourse to—
—American States, nineteenth century, **30**, 481, 482
—Europe, nineteenth century, **30**, 481, 482
recovery of debts, **24**, 791
regrouping of claims, **23**, 661–663
re-hearing, admissibility of, **6**, 421, 425; **8**, 481, 485–487
res judicata, **1**, 373–374; **3**, 421–423; **4**, 490; **5**, 428, 448, 457; **8**, 487–488; **9**, 324–326; 522–526. *See also Res judicata*
Saudi Arabia and Aramco, between, Rules of Procedure, **27**, 135–137
set-off, **4**, 478–479
stare decisis, **1**, 376
submission to arbitration, validity, **6**, 420: *see also* Error
supervisory rights of State of forum, **27**, 155; **35**, 169
treaty: *see* agreement, *supra*
unanimity, rule of, **2**, 368–370
Arbitrators: *see also* Arbitral tribunals
abstention from voting, **28**, 564–566
amiables compositeurs, **24**, 761
appointment of, **3**, 401; **5**, 424–426; **20**, 443–444; **28**, 554–556; **35**, 161–162, 163, 164, 166–168

Arbitrators—*continued*
appointment of—*continued*
—Council of League of Nations, by, **5,** 58
—revocability of, **3,** 401
—third party, by, in default, **17,** 318–322; **23,** 594; **24,** 767–770
challenge of, **28,** 549–571
competence, **20,** 455–458. *See also* Arbitral tribunals, competence
death of arbitrator, procedure on, **27,** 136–137
designation of, requirements, **30,** 465–468, 478, 484
disqualification of, **28,** 549–571
—municipal rules, **28,** 554–555
duty to apply law *ex officio*, **23,** 652
equity, power to apply, **2,** 419; **25,** 501, 503, 506, 529, 551–552 n.; **30,** 485–486. *See also* Equity
evidence, competence to appraise, **30,** 476
function, **5,** 57–59
national judges, role and function, **28,** 555–557
refusal to act, **24,** 767–770
unanimity requirement, **2,** 368–370
withdrawal of, **28,** 558–559
Ardeatine Caves massacre (1940), **15,** 471–482
Argentina—
Belgium, Extradition Treaty (1886), **21,** 283–289
Bolivia, frontier with, **1,** 106
Code of Civil Procedure (consul, evidence by), **9,** 442
Constitution, jurisdiction in matters of diplomatic immunities, **2,** 299–300; **5,** 301–302
Constitution (1853)—
—Art. 14 (fundamental rights), **9,** 364; **23,** 396
—Art. 17 (expropriation), **9,** 381
—Art. 20 (rights of aliens), **9,** 381
—Art. 31 (treaties supreme law), **9,** 473; **26,** 567–568
—Art. 101 (jurisdiction, diplomats and consuls), **1,** 308; **5,** 302; **9,** 428, 434; **22,** 538; **23,** 50
Constitution (1949)—
—Art. 26 (fundamental rights), **23,** 396–397
—Art. 96 (jurisdiction, diplomats and consuls), **19,** 382; **22,** 538–539, 556; **23,** 430, 438
—equality, principle of, **22,** 473
Consular Regulations (1947), **23,** 449
—copyright law, **30,** 395–398
Criminal Procedure Code—
—extradition, **6,** 294; **28,** 11–12
—jurisdiction, diplomatic personnel, **9,** 434; **23,** 430
Argentina—*continued*
diplomatic immunities, Law concerning, **22,** 538–540, 556; **23,** 430, 449–451
enemy property legislation, **30,** 494–496
expulsion of aliens, Law of 1902 . . . **9,** 392; **18,** 315
extradition, law concerning, **5,** 285–289; **22,** 525–527; **28,** 12
Falkland Islands, claim to, **8,** 180
frontier with Bolivia, **1,** 106
Germany, Consular Treaty (1857), **1,** 303
Great Britain, Consular Treaty (1825), **1,** 303
immigration into, **6,** 270–271; **7,** 302; **19,** 471–473
income tax law, **22,** 473
Inheritance Taxes, Laws of 1923 and 1932 . . . **9,** 380
Internal War, Law declaring State of, **22,** 474
Italy, Consular Convention (1885), **1,** 303
—Extradition Treaty (1886), **5,** 286–287; **6,** 313; **19,** 376; **23,** 412–414
—Immigration Agreements with (1947 and 1948), **19,** 471–473
—Workmen's Compensation Convention (1920), **10,** 411
jurisdiction, diplomats and consuls, **1,** 308; **2,** 299–300; **5,** 237, 302; **9,** 428, 443; **19,** 382; **22,** 538–539, 556; **23,** 430, 438, 450
Low Countries, Treaty with (1893), **18,** 334
nationality laws, **1,** 214–215
naturalization laws, **1,** 210–211
Penal Code, acts against foreign States, **9,** 11
Spain, Extradition Treaty (1881), **9,** 408; **16,** 276
Spain, Treaty on Workmen's Compensation (1922), **2,** 317
trade marks, Decree of 1915 . . . **9,** 10
treaty as supreme law, **9,** 473; **26,** 567–568
U.S.A., Consular Treaty (1853), **9,** 487
—Extradition Treaty (1896), **23,** 404
U.S. military mission in, immunity, **30,** 392–393
Arica, occupation of, law applicable during, **6,** 110–111
" Arising out of recent revolutions ", **4,** 475–478
Arkansas, admission to American Union, **1,** 96
Armed forces—
acts of, State responsibility for, **3,** 223–224; **11,** 177–178
employment outside national territory, **26,** 216–217

Armed forces abroad, criminal jurisdiction, **33**, 190–210
Armed forces, foreign: *see* Foreign armed forces
Armed merchantmen, status, **14**, 84–90
Armenian Refugees, Geneva Conference (1928), **7**, 406–408
Armenian Republic, extinction of, **2**, 18–19
Armistice: *see also* War, capitulations
acts committed in war, damage after armistice, **3**, 469–470
belligerent occupation, effect on, **15**, 552–553, 559; **16**, 478
cessation of hostilities and signature of, **1**, 439
contraband, carriage of, during, **1**, 435
definition, **12**, 466
effect of, **7**, 508; **13**, 193–194, 309–311, 403, 404, 406; **15**, 505; **16**, 415; **19**, 600; **22**, 931; **31**, 512–514
—internal legislation, on, **1**, 437–438, 440
interned civilians, position under, **11**, 266
legal nature, **12**, 412–414; **18**, 318; **22**, 931
military observers, authority of, **18**, 469
object of, **22**, 931
observance of, **14**, 213–215
occupation under, **4**, 549–551
pre-armistice agreements, **3**, 471
prize, capture after, **12**, 460–462, 466–471, 504, 539–542; **16**, 414
prize during, **20**, 617, 675–677
prize jurisdiction, effect on, **12**, 414–415
rights from participation in, **3**, 348
surrender and, **18**, 549, 706–707, 711
termination of war, **1**, 441, 443; **14**, 226, 320; **24**, 929–932, 932–938
" time of war ", whether ended by, **22**, 896–898
treaties, effect on, **16**, 381–382
" twenty-four hours' rule ", effect on, **14**, 320
Armistice agreements—
Franco-German Convention (1940), **11**, 231–232, 266, 271, 281–282, 283–284
interpretation, **11**, 231–232
Israel–Egypt (1949), **28**, 652–653; **31**, 512–514
Italy and United Nations (1943), **14**, 249, 320
November, 1918..**1**, 435–441, 443, 444, 448–449; **2**, 71; **4**, 416–417, 549–550; **11**, 232, 269–270
—Alsace-Lorraine, position under, **6**, 447
Armistice demarcation line, Egypt–Israel, proof of location, **32**, 80–82
Arms—
indiscriminate use of, **4**, 223–224, 233–234
possession of, discrimination against aliens, **2**, 268
prohibition of import of, **8**, 49
Arms, national: *see* National arms
Arrangements, intergovernmental, binding force, **7**, 406–409
Arrest—
illegal, jurisdiction, effect on, **7**, 188–192, 250–251, 337–338
public ships, **1**, 154–156
without extradition, **10**, 327–328
Ashburton Treaty, 1842: *see* Webster–Ashburton Treaty
Asylum—
alien within State, U.S.A., **26**, 475
Caracas Convention (1954), **24**, 518–523
" common crimes " and, **17**, 287–288; **32**, 292–294
customary international law, **17**, 284–286
discretion of deporting State, **28**, 315–318; **31**, 346–349; **33**, 270
extradition and, **2**, 251–252; **7**, 361–362; **17**, 281–284; **20**, 370–371, 373; **22**, 520–525; **24**, 518–524; **28**, 349–350; **31**, 365; **32**, 292–294
Germany, Federal Republic—
—Basic Law, Art. 16 . . . **26**, 498; **28**, 349–350
—Decree on Asylum (1953), **26**, 499
—political offenders, whether limited to, **28**, 350
Havana Convention (1928), **17**, 281, 283–295, 341; **18**, 350–354, 356, 357
Italy, Constitution, Art. 10 . . . **26**, 500
legation buildings in, **17**, 280–295; **18**, 349–357
Montevideo Convention (1933), **17**, 284
—(1939), **16**, 1, 2
natural justice and, **17**, 288–294
neutral, **9**, 583; **10**, 639–643; **12**, 538; **23**, 610–613
non-intervention, **17**, 292
political, claim of, **7**, 188–191, 361–363; **11**, 101–104; **13**, 148–149; **14**, 136–137; **17**, 282; **18**, 282–286, 309, 336–345; **20**, 286, 330–333, 370–371; **22**, 474, 520–525
—U.S. law, **24**, 153–154
safe-conduct, duty to grant, **17**, 286–287
ship equated to territory, **24**, 153
urgent cases, **17**, 288–294
Assurance: *see* Insurance

Assam, Agricultural Income Tax Act, **22**, 65–66
Athens, Treaty of (1926), **20**, 328, 330
Athos, Mount—
cession of, **23**, 664
exterritoriality of monasteries, **3**, 315–316
nationality of monks, **21**, 195–196
Atlantic Charter, **14**, 96
Attachés, diplomatic immunities of, **12**, 241–243. *See also under* Diplomatic envoys
Attachment—
foreign public ships, **32**, 127–136
foreign State property, **10**, 230–239
funds belonging to foreign State, **32**, 137–140
property abroad, **6**, 140, 145–146
ship chartered to Government, **12**, 113–115
Attorney, admission of alien as, **9**, 376
Attorney, power of—
certified by unrecognized government, **35**, 51–57, 62–65
given by resident in enemy-occupied territory, **12**, 349–352
Attorney's lien, property interest, whether, **26**, 298–300
Audi alteram partem, **2**, 396–397; **17**, 338; **21**, 406, 408; **23**, 540–541; **33**, 292
Aufbringungsgesetz, **4**, 332
Auflassung, **1**, 242; **2**, 71–76
Australia—
acquisition of property, Commonwealth power, **32**, 575–577
Air Navigation Act, 1920 . . . **7**, 54–56; **9**, 119
Air Navigation Regulations, **30**, 399–402
appellate jurisdiction, **7**, 51–52
"Australian national", meaning, **8**, 66–69
Charter of the United Nations Act, 1945 . . . **20**, 597–598
Citizen Military Forces, service of aliens in, **12**, 209–215, 219–221
Commonwealth of Australia Act, 1900 . . . **8**, 80
Communist Party Dissolution Act, 1950 . . . **20**, 592, 594, 596
Constitution, **23**, 479–481
Constitution, compared with Canadian, **8**, 58–59
Controller of Enemy Property, functions, **32**, 560–562, 573
Defence Act, 1903–1939 . . . **12**, 218, 220
Defence (Citizen Military Forces) Act, 1943 . . . **12**, 214
defence of Commonwealth, legislative power, **32**, 574–577, 579
Australia—*continued*
Defence Preparations Act, 1951 . . **20**, 594–596
External Affairs, certificate of Secretary, **11**, 15–16; **12**, 44; **15**, 139–140; **20**, 597–598
extraterritorial effect of legislation, **30**, 113, 114
foreign relations, conduct of, **8**, 48–54
Germany, termination of state of war with, **24**, 898; **32**, 571, 572
High Commissioner Act, 1909 . . . **11**, 214–216
High Commissioner, official reports, privilege, **11**, 213–217
immigration into, **7**, 299–301
Judiciary Act, **23**, 478–483
Mandatory, as, **8**, 98–109; **15**, 147–173
National Security Act, 1939–1943, **12**, 290 *et seq.*
Nationality Act, 1920–1946 . . . **19**, 327
naturalization in, **1**, 203–204
—effect in U.K., **5**, 235
New Guinea Act, 1920–1935 . . . **19**, 328
New Guinea, legislation for, **7**, 46–50
New Guinea Mandate, **15**, 147–173
overseas territories, application of legislation to, **30**, 114
Papua and New Guinea Act, 1949–1957 . . . **32**, 38–43
Parliamentary Papers Act, 1908, **11**, 214
Sea Carriage of Goods Act, relevance of treaty, **33**, 397–399
States of, jurisdictional immunity, **2**, 130–131
Trading with the Enemy Act, 1914–1916 . . . **4**, 439
Trading with the Enemy Acts, 1939–1952 . . . **20**, 625–627; **23**, 477; **24**, 898; **32**, 570–581
termination of state of war with Germany (1952), **24**, 898; **32**, 571, 572
Trust Territories, administration of, **32**, 38–43
U.K., Reciprocal Agreement on Social Security (1958), **30**, 420–423
U.S. forces in, **12**, 133–141, 173–175
War-Time Refugees Act, 1949, **19**, 327
Wills, Probate and Administration Act, 1898–1954 . . . **27**, 612
Austria: *see also* Austrian Empire; Austrian Republic; Austro-Hungarian Monarchy
Aliens Police Law, **28**, 310
Allied occupation of, **15**, 173–175; **17**, 411–414, 424–426; **18**, 630–635; 694–700; **19**, 622–628; **20**, 433–434, 649–650, 663–664; **22**, 996–998

Austria—*continued*
Allied occupation of—*continued*
—Allied Control Agreement (1946), **19**, 623–625
Amnesty Law, 1955 ... **22**, 996–998
Anschluss with Germany (1938), **9**, 19, 87–90, 407; **10**, 103–106, 530–534; **12**, 23–29; **15**, 51, 214–216; **16**, 61–62, 63–64, 66–67; **17**, 203, 302; **18**, 47–49; **19**, 144, 335–336; **20**, 89–91, 93, 250–251; **21**, 82, 262–264; **22**, 58–59, 89, 100–101, 146, 430–432, 530, 620–621; **23**, 123–124
—Inter-Allied Declaration concerning (1943), **18**, 245
—nationality and, **12**, 187–194; **18**, 244–246, 248–249; **21**, 175–177; **22**, 430–432; **23**, 364–369; **32**, 153
—prior treaties, effect of, on, **22**, 530
—State succession and, **10**, 103–106
Civil Aviation Law, **24**, 640
compulsory administration of businesses, **11**, 21
Constitution (Federal), **19**, 460, 461; **20**, 433; **21**, 102, 212–213; **23**, 383, 411, 469; **24**, 640
—international law provision, **32**, 5–6
Criminal Code, s. 25 (expulsion of convicted aliens), **28**, 310–311
Criminal Code, s. 40 (proceedings against aliens for offence committed abroad), **28**, 341–346
Czechoslovakia, Commercial Treaty (1922), **5**, 103
European Convention on Human Rights, reservation, **28**, 264, 424–429; **30**, 274, 275, 302, 315
foreign exchange law, **22**, 725–727
France, Treaty on Judicial Assistance (1925), **21**, 262–264; **22**, 58, 100–101
French army in, **16**, 144–145
Geneva Protocol (1922), loan to, **6**, 26–31
German invasion of, **16**, 347, 349, 361
See also Anschluss, supra
German racial legislation, application, **11**, 172–173
German discriminatory measures, responsibility for, **26**, 610, 612
Germany—
—Agreements concerning Frontier Traffic (1955), **25**, 47, 48–49
—Double Taxation Agreement (1922), **23**, 123–124
—Treaty for Settlement of Claims (1957), **32**, 33–37, 152–153
Hague Regulations, applicability after *Anschluss*, **15**, 671–672
Hungary, Commercial and Transport Convention (1907), **4**, 41; **5**, 58–59

Austria—*continued*
independence of, proposed customs union with Germany and, **6**, 26–31
Italy, Extradition Treaty (1922), **2**, 319
Jewish property, expropriation of, **9**, 19, 87
Jurisdiction, Law concerning, **5**, 320
nationality, **1**, 213; **15**, 217–218; **17**, 203; **20**, 250–251; **21**, 175–177; **22**, 430–432
Nationality Law, 1945...**21**, 176–177, 194–195; **22**, 430–432; **24**, 433
Nationality Law, 1949...**19**, 335–336; **24**, 445, 446
Nationality Law (Transitional), 1945, **20**, 250; **23**, 365–367, 367–369
Nationalization Law, **21**, 212–213
Netherlands, Agreement for Return of Austrian Assets (1951), **24**, 40, 433
Netherlands, Double Taxation Agreement, **22**, 530–531
Occupation Damage, Law concerning, 1958...**28**, 424–427, 428–429
ordre public, foreign confiscatory legislation and, **28**, 14, 16, 30–31
Penal Code, counterfeiting currency, **1**, 317
re-establishment of, **22**, 58–59. *See also* State Treaty, *infra*
Roumania, Convention (1924), debts and credits, **5**, 118–120, 216
Russia, Treaty with (1815), boundaries, **21**, 87
Russian occupation of, **19**, 623–625, 626–628; **21**, 212; **23**, 797–798
Second World War, position in, **17**, 165; **21**, 262–264
separation from Germany (1945), **15**, 217–218; **17**, 34–35, 312; **20**, 93, 250–251; **22**, 430–432; **23**, 364–369
State Treaty (1955), **23**, 469–471, 798; **24**, 45, 639–641; **28**, 424–429, 646
—German assets, seizure of, **26**, 40, 41, 77
—U.N. nationals, tax exemptions, **26**, 609–612
—waiver of claims against Germany, **32**, 152–153, 154–161
status (1945), **16**, 186; **22**, 89, 398, 400–401
Switzerland, Extradition Treaty (1896), **24**, 497
Tax Act, **22**, 531
U.K., Commercial Treaty (1924), **5**, 263
U.K., termination of war with (1946), **18**, 245
U.S.A., Agreement on Occupation Costs (1947), **20**, 431–432

Austria—*continued*
U.S.A., Claims Settlement Agreement (1947), **18**, 9; **19**, 459–461; **20**, 433–434; **22**, 402
Unlawful Competition, Law Against, **24**, 45
Yugoslavia, Commercial and Railway Convention, **5**, 364
Austria–Hungary
Switzerland, Extradition Treaty —Czechoslovakia, application to, **20**, 364
U.S.A., termination of war with, **6**, 437–438
Austrian Empire—
Austrian Republic, identity with, **4**, 37–38
dissolution of, **1**, 20, 28, 132, 457
extradition treaties, application to Czechoslovakia, **1**, 259–260
Germany, Commercial Treaty (1891), **1**, 68–69
Hungary, union with, **4**, 40–41
Poland, succession to rights of, **5**, 55
property of, succession to, **1**, 58, 130–131
protected subjects in Egypt, **1**, 202
State succession treaties, **1**, 72–73
Treasury Loans, **4**, 74–75
U.S.A., Treaty of Commerce and Navigation (1848), **1**, 387–388
Austrian Republic—
Austrian Empire, continuity, **2**, 64–65; **3**, 34–35; **4**, 37–38; **5**, 24–25
—law of, maintenance in force, **5**, 24–25
—liability for obligations of, **1**, 66–68; **4**, 79–82, 443–445
—officials, liability to take over, **1**, 74
beginning of existence, **1**, 13, 20, 21; **4**, 25; **5**, 16
Constitution (1929), **18**, 695
Austro-Hungarian debt, apportionment of, **4**, 82
Austro-Hungarian Monarchy—
dissolution of, **1**, 453; **4**, 79–82
Montenegro, occupation of, **4**, 556–557
State succession and, **1**, 130–131; **17**, 77–78, 87–88
status of, **4**, 79–82
" Autonomous ports ", system of (France), **12**, 123
Autonomous States, international position, **8**, 189, 193, 200–203
Auxiliary forces, responsibility for acts of, **4**, 233–234
Auxiliary vessels, **5**, 510–514
Aviation: *see also* Aircraft; Air space; Air Transport, International
aerial navigation—
—" aerodrome " in Navigation Regulations, **30**, 399–402
Aviation—*continued*
aerial navigation—*continued*
—International Convention for Regulation of (1919), **6**, 45; **7**, 114–115; **8**, 54–59, 159; **9**, 119, 124; **17**, 162, 307; **30**, 73, 399–402
Aerial Navigation, Sanitary Convention for (1933), **18**, 382
air law, international, **19**, 467–469; **21**, 287; **22**, 157–167
air transport agreements, provisions *re* nationality of carriers, **31**, 416–424
death of passenger during flight, **20**, 417–424
overflying, right of, **31**, 113
seaplanes, **6**, 112
status of airships, **5**, 82
Aviation, Civil, Chicago Convention (1944), **19**, 86, 110, 372; **20**, 154; **24**, 9–10, 54–55, 597; **33**, 410–414
Avulsion, **1**, 84, 96; **2**, 98; **7**, 133–135; **8**, 31–32; **11**, 94–100
Awards: *see under* Arbitration, civil *and* Arbitration, international
" Ayant droit ", meaning, **4**, 291–292, 418

B

Baden—
Germany, Treaty (1920), railways, **5**, 330–332
international personality, end of, **22**, 141
Switzerland, Treaty (1856), inheritance, **22**, 141–146
utilization of flow of Danube by, **4**, 128–133
Bahrain, jurisdiction of British Crown, **30**, 94–100
Bail—
aliens, restriction of movement of, **31**, 332–341
deportation proceedings, **10**, 309–313
extradition proceedings, **5**, 290–291; **6**, 317–318
Bailee, action for loss or damage, **34**, 186
Balkan Wars, territorial changes after, **23**, 663–668
Bancos, sovereignty over, **11**, 94–100
Banks, documents of foreign branch, order to produce, **28**, 138–142; **31**, 219–226
Banks, licence to operate in foreign State, continued subjection to national law, **28**, 141
Banks, nationalization of—
creditors, effect on, **26**, 288
deposits, whether " taken ", **30**, 120–122, 134–135, 189–190
" drafts ", effect on, **26**, 304–306
pensions, effect on, **26**, 287

Bank accounts—
blocking of, **26**, 301; **30**, 208
situs of, **25**, 358–360
Bank for International Settlements, debts to, place of payment, **25**, 74
Bank deposits—
confiscation of, **26**, 297; **30**, 128–130, 134–135, 148, 189
prohibition on transfer, **26**, 292–295
Bankruptcy—
debtor out of jurisdiction, **15**, 75–77; **16**, 86–88
foreign, effect of, **6**, 148–149; **30**, 24–25
Baptismal certificate, proof of nationality, **5**, 224–225
" Barbarossa " Order, **15**, 388, 389, 392
Barcelona Convention and Statute on Freedom of Transit (1921), **5**, 341; **6**, 404–406; **9**, 121
Barratry, **26**, 72–73; **32**, 132
Base line—
delimitation of bays, **3**, 122–123; **6**, 123–125; **7**, 136; **8**, 169–170, 173–177; **9**, 130–140, 300–304; **18**, 94, 111, 117–118
new international law and: *see* New International Law
territorial waters, **3**, 122–123; **4**, 133–134; **6**, 123–126; **7**, 136–137; **8**, 169–170; **9**, 130–140, 300–304; **18**, 86–144 *passim*
Bases, foreign military, jurisdiction in, **23**, 201–202, 241–244, 245–250
Basle, German railway establishment, **4**, 136–138
Basque Government, **8**, 189–190, 200–201
Battle Monuments Commission, jurisdictional immunities of members, **8**, 227–228
Bavaria—
Germany, Treaty (1920), railways, **5**, 330–332
nationality, **1**, 38–39
occupation of, applicable law, **4**, 119–120
U.S.A., Treaty, inheritance tax, **5**, 403–404
Bayonne, Treaties of (1856, 1862, 1866), **24**, 101–142 *passim*
Bays, **3**, 126–128; **4**, 134–136; **6**, 123–126, 128–129; **8**, 178–179; **18**, 94, 111, 117–118, 164
base line, **3**, 122–123; **6**, 123–125; **7**, 136; **8**, 169–170, 173–177; **9**, 133–140, 300–304; **18**, 94, 111, 117–118
Cancale, **4**, 136
Chesapeake, **4**, 136; **9**, 137
closing line, **35**, 84–88
Conception, **4**, 136

Bays—*continued*
Delaware, **4**, 136; **9**, 136
fishing rights in, **6**, 123–126, 128–129
Monterey Bay, California, **4**, 135–136; **8**, 169–170
"national waters", concept of, **4**, 135
Penobscot, **9**, 128–133
public domain, as, **8**, 173–178
Santa Monica, **9**, 133–140, 300–304
sovereignty over, **3**, 126–128; **4**, 134–135; **9**, 128–132
territoriality of, **8**, 169–170, 173–177
thalweg, **11**, 91–93
Treaty concerning the Delimitation of (1901), **6**, 126
Walvis Bay, **7**, 53–56
Beamtenabkommen, Danzig and Poland (1921), **4**, 288–289; **7**, 184, 415–417
Bearer bonds, seizure as enemy property, **18**, 513–515
Bearer shares, " property, rights and interests ", **2**, 344
Bechuanaland, protectorate of, **8**, 106
—habeas corpus, from England, **28**, 56–58, 64–66
Behring Sea Arbitration Award, **1**, 177–178
Belgium—
Aliens Advisory Commission, **31**, 354
Aliens Control, Law of 1952...**28**, 210
aliens—
—arrest of, Law of 1874...**5**, 290
—domicile, establishment of, **31**, 331, 352–353
—expulsion, procedure, **31**, 352–355
—military service, **11**, 10–12
—registration, **9**, 339
Allied armies in, **13**, 85–86
areas of frontier land, disputed sovereignty with Netherlands, **27**, 62–98 *passim*
Bulgaria, Conciliation Treaty (1931), **9**, 512
China, denunciation of Treaty of 1865...**4**, 513–515
Civil Code, quasi-contract, **5**, 500
coal production, costs, **25**, 427–428
commercial leases, Law of 1926...**9**, 456
competence of courts, Law of 1876, **6**, 165
—*Cour de Cassation*, Law of 1832, **25**, 181
Congo, Treaty of Cession with (1907), **7**, 29–30, 172–173, 409–410; **22**, 226–227; **23**, 191–192
enemy property, sequestration of, **1**, 405; **28**, 430, 434
—disposal of sequestrated, **28**, 432, 434–435
Finland, recognition of, **1**, 153
France—
—Agreement (1947), nationality of married women, **19**, 358

Belgium—*continued*
France—*continued*
—Arbitration Agreement (1936), **8,** 478–479
—" Arrangement " (1945), damage by French troops in Belgium, **22,** 614–616
—Boundary Convention (1886), **7,** 431–432
—Convention on Civil Jurisdiction (1899), **3,** 86; **5,** 380; **7,** 409
—Convention (1945), restitution of illegally seized goods, **20,** 659, 660
—Extradition Treaty (1874), **9,** 400–401; **14,** 139–142; **16,** 275, 278; **18,** 395; **20,** 369; **23,** 410
—Tardieu-Jaspar Agreement (1930), **8,** 479
—Treaty on Conditions of Residence (1927), **4,** 452; **9,** 456; **11,** 10–12, 235–236; **14,** 160–162
German occupation of, **1,** 321–322, 457–467, 481, 489; **4,** 565–566; **12,** 432–433, 448–452
—competence of Belgian courts, **11,** 288
—maintenance of sovereignty, **1,** 445–447
—trading with the enemy, **1,** 420–422
Germany—
—Extradition Treaty (1874), **5,** 272
—reparations from, **4,** 13–14
—Treaty (1912), Workmen's Compensation, **2,** 410
Hague Convention, 1902, Divorce, Law concerning, **5,** 352
Hungary, Extradition Treaty, **5,** 275
Italy, Treaty of Commerce (1882), **4,** 452
jurisdiction, nationals abroad, **5,** 102
landlord and tenant legislation, **4,** 452
legal assistance, Law of 1929, **6,** 277; **9,** 376
Luxembourg, Treaty establishing Economic Union (1921), **28,** 511–513
military law, offence by soldier abroad, **31,** 268–269
nationality, Law of 1909, **1,** 404
—restoration, Law of 1953, **28,** 241
nationals abroad, jurisdiction over, **5,** 102
Netherlands, Boundary Treaty with (1842), **27,** 64, 69, 82, 90
—Boundary Treaty with (1843), **27,** 64–66, 71–72, 76–77, 79–80, 81, 89, 90, 93, 95
—Boundary Treaty with (1843), Descriptive Minute on frontier communes, **27,** 65–67, 72, 74, 76, 79–81, 85–89, 95–97

Belgium—*continued*
Netherlands—*continued*
—Treaty, Civil Procedure (1925), **11,** 221
—Treaty of London (1839) for Separation of Territories, **8,** 166–168; **27,** 64, 71
—Treaty on navigation of Scheldt, **9,** 121
occupation by British forces, 1944, civilian inhabitants, **32,** 588–594
Penal Code, amendment, loss of civil and political rights, **33,** 215, 216–219, 244
Penal Code, Art. 3 (criminal jurisdiction over aliens), **26,** 160
Penal Code, Art. 123 (forfeiture of rights), **25,** 172–174, 176–178, 179–181, 186–189; **33,** 208–210, 214–215
Penal Code, Art. 496 (swindling), **5,** 272
Penal Procedure, crimes committed abroad, **1,** 446
recognition by Great Powers (1831), **5,** 14
refugees, recognition of status of, **31,** 327–329, 331–332
reparations from Germany, **4,** 13–14
requisition of ships abroad, **10,** 141–147, 152–154
requisitions, Law of 1887, **1,** 121
sequestration of enemy property, **1,** 405
Soviet Government, non-recognition of, **2,** 50–51; **5,** 47
—, recognition of, **4,** 69–71
State aids to coal mines, **25,** 423–424
statelessness, **5,** 243
Switzerland, Treaty of Establishment (1887), **11,** 11
taxation, immunity from, **5,** 323–324
—, salaries of international officials, **29,** 56–73
transfers by belligerent occupant, annulment of, **31,** 508–509
treaties, operation of, **11,** 11
U.S.A., Commercial Treaty (1857), **9,** 490
—forces of, in, **1,** 121–122; **21,** 121–122
Belgium-Luxembourg, Economic Union, **31,** 425–426
Belligerency—
automatic, vassal States, of, **3,** 435
co-belligerency, **15,** 106–107; **18,** 426, 473; **19,** 638–640
meaning, **1,** 385
non-recognition of, **4,** 533–534; **9,** 79; **31,** 29
recognition of, **3,** 65–68
—effect on other belligerents, **3,** 435
vassal States, automatic, **3,** 435

Belligerent—
acts of, in regard to neutral property in occupied territory, **1,** 124–129
co-belligerent, enemy character of national, **23,** 756
de facto, **1,** 386
neutral property in occupied territory, acts in regard to, **1,** 124–129
subjects of, intercourse between, **4,** 538–539. *See also* Enemy alien; Trading with the enemy
unlawful acts by, obligation to compensate individuals, **32,** 635–636
unlawful, status of, **24,** 988
Belligerent forces, **1,** 386; **2,** 405–410; **3,** 435–437; **12,** 303–304; **13,** 228–231; **14,** 168–170; **15,** 423–437; **16,** 378–380, 514–515; **21,** 431–432. *See also* Guerillas; Partisans
internment in neutral State, **10,** 639–643
militia, **15,** 641
volunteer corps, **15,** 641
Belligerent occupation, **1,** 445–483; **2,** 439–451; **3,** 472–482; **4,** 556–562; **5,** 485–486, 495–502; **6,** 174, 206, 447–450; **7,** 509–513; **8,** 503–505; **9,** 571; **10,** 581–594; **11,** 270–299; **12,** 420–459; **13,** 334–400; **14,** 228–311; **15,** 519–687; **16,** 418–445; **17,** 404–440; **20,** 634–667; **23,** 750–850; **24,** 941–990; **26,** 691–735; **27,** 649–652; **28,** 643–652; **30,** 538–540; **31,** 508–509; **32,** 588–601
See also Hague Regulations
abandoned private property, **11,** 298
abrogation of laws of occupant, **15,** 560–561
acts of occupant, liability of occupied State, for, **8,** 612–614
administrative acts under orders of occupant, **12,** 452–454; **15,** 551–557
administrative control, transfer of, **18,** 591
administrative functions of occupant, **3,** 475–477; **11,** 283, 284–285, 288–295; **20,** 646–647; **21,** 484–488; **22,** 998–1006; **23,** 699, 795–801; **24,** 945–951, 954–960
—delegation of, **21,** 487–488
—municipal functions, distinction, **18,** 630–631
—notarial acts, formal requirements, **26,** 716–717, 722–723
—occupant's police, disciplinary jurisdiction over, **26,** 210–221
administrative measures of occupant, **12,** 64–68; **16,** 468, 471–479, 504–506; **19,** 607–608, 614–620
—compliance with, **21,** 485–487
administrators of firms, **11,** 108–110

Belligerent occupation—*continued*
agency contract, effect on, **23,** 787–789
agency of occupant, jurisdiction over, **23,** 783–787
agency of occupant, status of, **23,** 783–787
agency, parties in occupied countries, **24,** 947
aggressive war and, **15,** 636–638; **16,** 455; **18,** 592–595; **23,** 822, 845
amendment of penal law, **11,** 294
amnesty law of occupied State, **22,** 996–998
amnesty, occupant's right to grant, **12,** 454–455
annexation of occupied territory, **10,** 581–583; **11,** 226–227; **13,** 220–221, 358, 386–388; **14,** 45–49, 287; **18,** 608–609
—illegal, **24,** 960–962, 966–970; **26,** 723
applicable law, **2,** 440–441; **4,** 556–558; **16,** 462–464, 466–467; **17,** 407–411, 415–418; **18,** 444–445
armistice, effect of, **3,** 9–10; **15,** 552–553, 559; **16,** 478
army of liberation, authority of commander, **15,** 535
army of occupation—
—civil jurisdiction over, **32,** 162–163
—crimes against member, **15,** 682–684; **18,** 625–629; **26,** 731
—crime by member of, **2,** 442–443; **15,** 533–535; **18,** 234–235, 532–533; **20,** 634–635
—criminal law, existing, application to, **2,** 442–443; **18,** 532–533
—enlistment in, **15,** 682–684
—fiscal immunity, **12,** 443–444
—jurisdiction over, **14,** 196–201
—local law, application to, **20,** 634–635
—national law, **18,** 234–235
—offences against, **15,** 682–684; **18,** 625–629; **26,** 731
—status of, **15,** 104–105
—status of members, **2,** 439–440; **18,** 571–573
army of occupied State, matériel of, **15,** 604
art treasures, restitution of, **15,** 619
assimilation to national territory, **3,** 441–442
bank, liquidation by occupant, **23,** 689, 692–696; **24,** 946
banking, regulation of, **23,** 694
booty, **15,** 610–611; **16,** 500–504; **18,** 683–684, 696–697, 701
—sale of, to inhabitant, **19,** 625–626
capitulatory régime, territory under, **1,** 452–453
certificate of executive as to, **15,** 7–9

Belligerent occupation—*continued*
civil administration, establishment of, **14,** 241; **16,** 490: *see also* administrative functions of occupant, *supra*
civil law, effect on, **24,** 972: *see also* local law, *infra*
civilian inhabitants: *see* inhabitants, *infra*
commander-in-chief, authority, **18,** 573–574
commencement, **15,** 550
company incorporated in occupied territory, enemy character, **33,** 444–450
concessions in occupied territory, **23,** 780–783, 801–809, 810–850
—duty of occupant, **23,** 801–805
—nature of concessionary receipts, **23,** 806–809
—seizure of installations, **23,** 810–850
confiscation of private property, **12,** 445–447; **16,** 457; **24,** 42–45
conservation, property of nationals of co-belligerents, **15,** 696
constitution adopted under, **20,** 645–646
consummation of, **15,** 7–9
contract for sale of immovable property, **24,** 962–966
contracts on behalf of occupant, **16,** 455–456, 458–459; **17,** 414–415
contracts, private, and, **15,** 525–526, 537–548, 611–612
contracts with occupant, **15,** 567–572; **20,** 464–467; **24,** 983–985
control of company, effect on patent rights, **27,** 649–652
courts of occupied State, **12,** 447–450; **13,** 334–342
—competence, **19,** 183–185, 622–623
—competence to pass on validity of occupant's legislation, **12,** 447
courts set up by occupant, **12,** 433–437; **13,** 342–349; **15,** 539–540, 586–589; **19,** 609–611; **30,** 506, 509
—common crimes, for, **28,** 643–645
—decisions of, **4,** 558–560; **5,** 497–498; **6,** 448–449; **14,** 235–239, 242–245; **20,** 653–654
—in whose name judgments delivered, **14,** 260–261
—nature of, **18,** 608–609
—power of occupant to set up, **19,** 609–611
—previous conviction by, **21,** 479–484
—recognition of judgments, **23,** 795–797
—sentence of, **21,** 478–479
—status of, **16,** 467, 480–481; **19,** 608–609; **20,** 649–650; **21,** 479–484; **22,** 996–998; **23,** 789–791

Belligerent occupation—*continued*
courts set up by occupant—*contd.*
—validity of judgments, **18,** 629–630, 638–640
—whether foreign or municipal, **18,** 614–620
courts-martial set up by occupant, **16,** 463–464
crime by national of occupant, **16,** 439–455; **18,** 571
crime within territory formerly occupied, extradition request by lawful Government, **28,** 326–327, 329–330
crimes within army of occupation, **18,** 532–533; **28,** 646–647
criminal jurisdiction, effect on, **18,** 318–324; **28,** 330
criminal law, effect on, **18,** 318–324; **26,** 731
currency, issue by occupant, **15,** 576–583; **18,** 576, 584, 585–590, 592–593, 599–604, 641–677; **19,** 619–620; **22,** 994–996; **23,** 800; **26,** 719–721
currency reform, **21,** 476–477
currency regulation by occupant, **18,** 636–637; **23,** 694, 696–698
damage to private property, **19,** 622–623
debts, payment to occupant authorities, **18,** 642–677; **23,** 799–800
decrees of occupant, validity, **11,** 286–295
delegation of powers to authorities of occupied State, **11,** 271–272; **18,** 620–621
devastation of territory, **15,** 632, 647–649; **16,** 484–486, 521–523
diplomatic protection of inhabitants, **28,** 648–652
divorce by occupation court, validity, **20,** 648–650
economic assets, spoliation of, **15,** 624; **16,** 487–491
employee of occupant, judgment against, **19,** 211–212
enemy character and, **18,** 521–528, 575–585; **33,** 444–450
enemy property, appropriation of, **20,** 462, 465–470
Enemy Property Custodian, effect of payment to, **23,** 799–800
enemy property, sequestration of, **15,** 602–604; **18,** 681
enemy territory and, **18,** 575–585
espionage under, **15,** 573–575
evidence of effectiveness of, **12,** 349–352
expenditure by occupant, recovery of, **23,** 782–783
extradition and, **18,** 318–324; **19,** 379–381; **28,** 329–330
fact, state of, **30,** 505

Belligerent occupation—*continued*
fiscal system, modification of, **19,** 616–619
forced sale under, **18,** 635
foreign courts, competence as to acts done under, **20,** 655–662
friendly allied territory, occupation of, **32,** 588–594
functions of occupant, **12,** 444–459; **13,** 360–371; **15,** 551–593; **16,** 469: *see also* administrative, judicial and legislative functions
government-in-exile, legislation by, **15,** 530–533; **16,** 428–432; **18,** 558–570; **21,** 475
government of occupied territory, act done at direction of occupant, **24,** 954–959
government set up by occupant, **15,** 561–563
—powers of, **11,** 275–278; **29,** 45
guerilla warfare under, **16,** 514–516
habeas corpus, application to military tribunals of occupant, **16,** 422–428
Hague Convention on Civil Procedure (1905) and, **11,** 222
Hague Regulations and, **16,** 490; **23,** 820–822, 833; **17,** 408, 420–422; **22,** 992–994, 998–999; **26,** 723
hostages, taking and killing of, **15,** 393, 641–644, 663, 687; **16,** 391, 401–407, 518–520, 547–548, 551–552; **17,** 392–393
immovable property, contract for sale of, **24,** 962–966
—right of occupant to, **23,** 809–810
independence, conferment by occupant on occupied territory, **23,** 787–789
inhabitants—
—arson of houses of, **17,** 393, 431–435
—authority of occupant over, **32,** 588–594
—collective fine, **11,** 294–295
—confiscation of external assets, **32,** 565–570
—conscription of, **13,** 385–387; **15,** 399, 402, 405, 408–411; **16,** 357–358
—deportation of, **13,** 213–214; **14,** 302; **15,** 399, 402, 405, 408–410, 412–414, 620–626, 632–653, 668, 678, 681; **16,** 509–510, 521–523, 526, 531, 550, 552–553, 557; **17,** 393–397; **30,** 500. *See also under* War crimes
—duties of, **13,** 350–354, 384, 396; **15,** 434–436; **16,** 409, 536–537
—duty of obedience, **15,** 435; **20,** 665; **24,** 925
—duty of occupant to, **15,** 572; **16,** 435; **18,** 597–598
—employment of, **13,** 350–354, 394–395; **15,** 625–626, 668, 679

Belligerent occupation—*continued*
inhabitants—*continued*
—employment of—*continued*
— —prohibited, work on, **15,** 633; **16,** 509, 520–521
—enslavement of, **14,** 291–292, 302; **15,** 620, 625–626, 668, 679
—execution of, **14,** 306; **15,** 412–414, 632, 645–646, 654–655, 656, 662–665, 680–684, 685–687; **16,** 279–280, 396–398, 508, 509–525, 553–556; **17,** 399, 431–438; **30,** 500
—fair trial, denial of, **17,** 438–439
—forced labour, **15,** 393–394, 408–408–410, 620, 625–626, 632, 678
—ill-treatment of, **16,** 397, 507–508, 509–525; **17,** 397–399, 434–438
—personal injury to, **19,** 620, 632–634
—religious persecution, **16,** 356–357, 557
—religious worship, interference with, **30,** 538–539
—reprisals against, **15,** 644–646, 687; **16,** 391, 459–461, 484–486, 518–520, 531, 538–542, 545–552, 557
—resistance by, **16,** 450–461, 462–464, 508
See also Resistance movements
—torture of, **17,** 388
—trading with, **23,** 754–756
—treatment of, **13,** 273, 383–400; **14,** 278–311; **15,** 620–686; **16,** 505–557; **18,** 701; **19,** 632–634; **20,** 666–667; **24,** 986–990
— —" protective custody ", **18,** 701–702
—use of, against resistance, **18,** 677, 702–703
Inter-Allied Declaration against Acts of Dispossession Committed in Territories under Enemy Occupation or Control (1943), **15,** 594–595; **16,** 261, 263–265; **18,** 660, 661, 663, 675
invasion, compared to, **13,** 365–366; **15,** 638–641
irregular forces, acts against occupant, **15,** 638–641; **16,** 514–516; **24,** 986–990
Japan, Supreme Commander Allied Powers, powers of, **20,** 635–643
joint occupation, **22,** 982–987
judges, appointment of, **22,** 795–797; **26,** 714–716
judges, criminal liability, **17,** 398, 439–450
judgment against employee of occupant, **19,** 211–212
judicial functions of occupant, **1,** 457–475; **2,** 444–445; **3,** 473–475; **4,** 556–558, 560–561; **5,** 495–498; **6,** 447–448; **11,** 279–283; **16,** 459–467, 470–471, 480–481, 553–556;

Belligerent occupation—*continued*
judicial functions of occupant—*continued*
18, 614–621, 629–630, 635; **19**, 602–607, 608, 613; **20**, 648–650, 653–654; **21**, 478–479; **22**, 996–998; **23**, 789–791; **24**, 943–945
—finality of judgment for war crime, **26**, 707–711
—illegal war and, **24**, 941–943
jurisdiction of local courts, suspension of, **26**, 705–707
jurisdiction over nationals of occupant, **15**, 550
law applicable, **16**, 462–464, 466–467; **17**, 407–411, 415–418
laws and customs of war, **23**, 821–822, 833
lease of property to occupant, **15**, 550, 583–585
legislation by government-in-exile, **15**, 530–533; **16**, 428–432; **21**, 475
legislation, lawful sovereign, by, **12**, 420–432; **15**, 548–549, 550
legislation by occupant, **12**, 437–443, 445, 450–452; **15**, 551–575; **16**, 431, 455–459, 471–479; **17**, 415–423; **18**, 592, 605–607, 609–612, 633–634, 636, 641–677, 689–690; **19**, 600–601, 611–613; **20**, 650–652, 654–655; **21**, 475, 476–477; **22**, 101–102, 994–996, 1007
—abrogation of, **15**, 560–561
—application by local court, **20**, 650–657
—currency, as to, **18**, 636–637
—extension of application by analogy, **28**, 400–401, 404
—extraterritorial operation, **20**, 658
—international law, contrary to, **20**, 28–31; **28**, 371, 373, 387, 394
—liberation, effect, **16**, 478–479
—marriage, as to, **20**, 654–655
—nature of, **20**, 651–652
—penal law, amendment of, **11**, 294; **26**, 705–707
—ratification by legitimate government, **14**, 250–260
—recognition of, **14**, 243, 262–263; **20**, 57–62; **21**, 23–25, 488
—validity, **11**, 286–295; **20**, 635–643
—validity after occupation, **14**, 238–239, 250–260
legislative functions of occupant, **1**, 457–475; **2**, 444–445; **3**, 473–475; **4**, 556–558, 560–561; **5**, 495–498; **6**, 447–448; **11**, 283, 284–285, 288–295; **14**, 228–233, 234, 242–266; **15**, 551–575; **16**, 431, 455–459, 471–479; **17**, 415–423; **18**, 592, 605–607, 609–612, 633–634, 636, 641–677, 689–690; **19**, 600–601, 611–613; **20**, 635–643, 650–655; **21**, 475–477, 488; **22**, 101–102,

Belligerent occupation—*continued*
legislative functions of occupant—*continued*
994–996, 1007; **23**, 791–795; **24**, 960–977
—acts exceeding, legal effect, **14**, 246–248, 258, 261
See also legislation by occupant, validity
—applicability of international law to, **28**, 387
—conformity with international law, **28**, 371, 373, 394
legislative powers of occupant
—currency legislation, **18**, 636–637; **26**, 719–721
—limitation of, **11**, 277; **28**, 400–401, 404
legitimate government, acts of, **13**, 349, 357–358; **14**, 239–240
levée en masse, **16**, 380, 515, 516
liberation, effect, **18**, 590–591
liquidation of bank by occupant, **23**, 689, 692–696; **24**, 946
local courts, jurisdiction of, **11**, 270–271
local law, effect on, **19**, 602–607; **20**, 643–645
—criminal law, **11**, 294; **26**, 705–707
—laws of personal status, **26**, 704
—Nazi Laws on inheritance, **26**, 694
local law, respect for, **4**, 560–561; **5**, 496–497; **6**, 448; **11**, 294; **13**, 336–338, 341–342, 346–348, 363, 366–368; **15**, 526–529; **16**, 432; **18**, 677; **22**, 102, 998–1001; **30**, 505
marriage by occupation authorities, **15**, 527, 589–592; **16**, 470–471
meaning, **18**, 595–596
military commander, responsibility for war crimes, **15**, 386–388, 652–653. *See also under* War crimes
military courts of occupant, **11**, 270–271; **26**, 707
—decisions, *res judicata*, **11**, 279–282
—status, **16**, 422–428, 439–451
military governor, powers of, **16**, 440–441, 464–466
mortgages, measures by occupant regarding, **22**, 1008
municipality created by occupant, **21**, 484–485
national courts of occupant, jurisdiction, **16**, 147–150; **17**, 409–411; **19**, 602–607
nationality and, **15**, 527; **19**, 327–329, 329–336
nationals of occupant, jurisdiction over, **15**, 550
nature and effects, **1**, 445–457; **3**, 472–473; **11**, 270–279, 283–284; **12**, 420–444, 456–457; **13**, 334–358; **14**, 228–245; **15**, 519–550;

Belligerent occupation—*continued*
nature and effects—*continued*
16, 418–455; **17,** 404–415; **18,** 235, 549–570, 585–591; **19,** 600–601; **20,** 634–646; **21,** 475; **22,** 987–994; **23,** 780–789; **26,** 691–707; **27,** 649–652; **28,** 326, 329–330; **29,** 44–45; **30,** 496, 505–506; **32,** 339, 341
neutral alien, arrest of, **5,** 509
non-enemy territory—
—Hague Regulations, applicability, **26,** 731
—requisition, **26,** 730–731
notaries of occupant, validity of acts, **24,** 971–976
obedience to occupant, **20,** 665; **24,** 925
occupant, authorities of, status of, **2,** 443–444; **5,** 495–496
occupant, powers of: *see* administrative, judicial, legislative functions of occupant, *supra*
occupation forces: *see* army of occupation, *supra*
occupation government, status of, **15,** 561–563; **23,** 695
occupied State—
—act of Government of, **22,** 982–987
—compensation for requisitioned property, **18,** 399–400; **19,** 626–628, 630–631
—liability for acts of occupant, **18,** 612–614; **21,** 475
—liability for contracts of occupant, **20,** 646–647
—sovereignty of, **15,** 105, 323; **16,** 441–442; **18,** 549–558; **22,** 994
occupied territory—
—applicable law, **3,** 477–478; **18,** 444–445
—definition, **11,** 278
—devastation of, **16,** 484–486, 521–523
—foreign State, whether, **16,** 418–421; **17,** 404–407, 413; **18,** 549–558
officials, appointment by occupant, **11,** 284–285; **19,** 614–615
officials, authority of, **15,** 529; **18,** 680; **19,** 600–601
oil installations, seizure of, **23,** 810–849
orders of occupant, continuation after occupation, **23,** 797–798
personal injury to inhabitants, **19,** 620, 632–634
plunder, **2,** 174; **15,** 399, 404, 408, 619, 620, 622–625, 632, 653, 657, 668, 672–677; **16,** 358–361, 482
police measures, enforcement of, **18,** 677
postal charges, **23,** 591–596

Belligerent occupation—*continued*
pre-occupation debts, settlement of, **24,** 945–951
prisoners of war under, **17,** 399–400
private contracts and, **15,** 525–526, 537–548, 611–612
private law, effect on, **12,** 452; **15,** 566–567, 587
private property—
—compensation for use of, **22,** 402–403
—confiscation of, **16,** 457; **18,** 558–570, 571; **20,** 665; **24,** 966–970; **26,** 728–729
—damage to, **19,** 622–623
—forced sale, **21,** 484–485
—liquidation, **24,** 31
—requisition of, **20,** 664, 665; **23,** 810–850; **24,** 979
—requisitioned, recovery of, **20,** 656–657, 659–660, 663–664
—requisitioned, title to, **24,** 979–982
—respect for, **4,** 564–567; **5,** 498–502; **6,** 449–450; **11,** 296–299; **12,** 457–459; **13,** 371–383; **14,** 266–277; **15,** 536–537, 551–552, 604–611; **16,** 471–475, 481–497; **17,** 424–430; **18,** 511–512, 646–660, 677, 678–686, 701; **19,** 621–632; **20,** 655–663; **21,** 488; **22,** 1007–1008; **23,** 801–850; **24,** 978–985; **29,** 474
—retention of seized, **24,** 954–959
—sale of, **4,** 561–562
—seizure of, **23,** 806–809; **30,** 150; **31,** 508–509
—sequestration, **24,** 966–970
—sequestration, *specificatio* and, **23,** 827–830, 839
—transfer of, **20,** 662–663
—treatment of, **20,** 663–664; **21,** 475
—unlawfully seized, **20,** 655–662
public enemy property, concessionary receipts, **23,** 806–809
—*res nullius,* as, **23,** 814–817, 819–820, 827, 833–836, 838–839, 841, 843
public officials, appointment of, **11,** 284–285; **19,** 614–615
public order, legislation for, **18,** 689–690
—safeguarding, **15,** 563–565
public property, rights of occupant to, **14,** 271–272, 277; **15,** 594–601; **18,** 686–689, 690–692
—consular official, of, **26,** 725–727
—sale of, **22,** 1001–1006
—seizure of, **11,** 296; **13,** 356–357; **15,** 553–557; **22,** 991–994; **26,** 724–725, 729, 732–734
purchases by army, applicable law, **4,** 28–29
railways run by occupant, **16,** 475–578

Belligerent occupation—*continued*
recognition of acts of occupant, **3,** 27–29; **11,** 20–21, 23, 28–30, 33
reprisals against civilian population, **15,** 644–646, 687; **16,** 391, 459–461, 484–486, 518–520, 531, 538–542, 545–552, 557; **17,** 392–393, 431–432, 435–438
reprisals by occupant, **24,** 986–990
requisition by civil authorities, **16,** 433–434
requisition by occupant, **1,** 475–483; **2,** 446–450; **3,** 478–482; **4,** 562–563, 565–566; **5,** 503–508; **12,** 448, 450, 453; **13,** 350–354, 356–357; **15,** 551–552, 594–620, 626, 674, 684–685; **16,** 456, 471–475, 479–480, 481, 486–491, 493–499, 504–507; **17,** 412–415, 419–423, 424–430; **23,** 810–850; **28,** 636; **30,** 150
—bailment and, **18,** 693–694
—compensation for, **15,** 614–619; **22,** 1008–1009
—construction contract for military installation, **32,** 595–601
—land, of, **18,** 612–613, 697–698
—services, of, **13,** 350–354; **18,** 679–680
—subsequent sale, **18,** 699–700
—transfer to third party, **18,** 694–697
—validity, **16,** 493–497; **18,** 682–684; **22,** 1007–1008
requisitioned ship, maritime lien on, **17,** 167
resistance movement and, **15,** 413–414; **16,** 459–461, 462–464, 508; **21,** 431–432
resistance of civilian population, **16,** 459–461, 462–464, 508; **17,** 431; **26,** 653–654
responsibility of military commander for war crimes, **15,** 386–388, 652–653. *See also under* War crimes
revenue laws, effect on, **24,** 976–977
rights of occupant, **23,** 693–695
—exercise of rights of territorial State, **23,** 780–781
rival government in occupied State, **29,** 45
safeguarding public order, **15,** 563–565
seized property, retention by government of occupied State, **22,** 982–987
seizure of property, later annulment of, **31,** 508–509
sequestration by occupant—
—bank assets, **18,** 642–667
—enemy property, **15,** 602–604; **16,** 491–492; **18,** 681
services for occupant, **17,** 439–440
sovereignty and, **11,** 275–277, 279–282; **15,** 520–523, 613–614; **16,**

Belligerent occupation—*continued*
sovereignty and—*continued*
455, 476, 498; **18,** 558–560; **22,** 994; **24,** 944; **26,** 702–703; **29,** 44; **30,** 505
—acquisition *pendente bello*, **26,** 702–703
sovereignty, effect on, **15,** 105, 323; **16,** 441–442; **18,** 549–558; **22,** 233, 994; **28,** 651
spoliation of economic assets, **15,** 624; **16,** 487–491; **18,** 684–686; **21,** 488
State responsibility and, **22,** 982–987
State-owned railways and, **15,** 557–560
stationing of troops, distinguished, **12,** 150–152, 154–164
status, laws of, effect on, **26,** 704
supplies and services for occupant, **30,** 177, 180
surrender, after, **18,** 475
taxation on orders of occupant, **12,** 452–453
termination of, **20,** 635–643; **22,** 987–991
Germany, in, **23,** 769–772. *See also under* Germany
termination of war, and **22,** 944
tort, liability of occupant for, **20,** 666–667; **32,** 161–165
trading with inhabitants, **23,** 754–756
trading with the enemy laws and, **15,** 530–531, 540–548; **16,** 429–431; **18,** 578–581, 703; **23,** 693–694
treason during, **12,** 444–445
treaties, effect on, **18,** 574–575
treaty between occupied State and occupant, **19,** 413–415
ultra vires measures, **26,** 703–704
voting under, nationality, effect on, **17,** 413
war crimes against inhabitants: *see* inhabitants, *supra*. *See also* War crimes
war crimes legislation and, **16,** 400–402
war material, seizure, **23,** 810–849 *passim*; **24,** 978–979
wills, form of during, **3,** 477–478
Belligerent rights—
armistice and, **20,** 617. *See also* Armistice
surrender and, **18,** 549
termination of war and, **18,** 711–712
" Belonging to ", meaning, **2,** 421
Benares, Maharajah of, whether independent sovereign, **10,** 43–47
Benelux, agreements restricting agricultural imports, **31,** 425–426
Berlin—
Allied Commanders, control by Governments, **28,** 5–6

Berlin—*continued*
Allied control authority in, **21,** 116–121
Allied Kommandatura Law No. 7 (jurisdiction of German courts), **28,** 400
Allied Kommandatura, Restitution Ordinance, **32,** 151–153
application of West German legislation to, **29,** 336
Conference (1945), Protocol, German assets in Japan, **26,** 574
Constitution (1950), **18,** 198; **32,** 152
Declaration of Assumption of Supreme Authority over Germany (1945), **16,** 423, 442; **23,** 770; **24,** 940
division of, **20,** 77–78
General Act (1885), **4,** 110–111; **6,** 107–108; **7,** 29, 312–321, 409; **22,** 226; **23,** 191
status of (1955), **22,** 988–989
Supreme Restitution Court, jurisdiction, **28,** 369 n
Treaty of (1878), **5,** 216, 220–221; **23,** 663
— (1921) (Peace Treaty with U.S.A.), **2,** 198–199, 210–211, 367, 405; **4,** 413, 543; **14,** 173, 175–176; **19,** 583; **22,** 416
whether part of " Federal territory ", **34,** 270, 272, 274–275
Bermuda, leases of territory to U.S.A., **22,** 154–156
Berne Conventions, Rail Transport, **1,** 71; **4,** 40–41; **6,** 35, 418–420; **7,** 58, 411–412, 420–422; **8,** 468; **11,** 230; **15,** 439
Berne Copyright Conventions, **5,** 226; **7,** 403; **8,** 9–10; **15,** 439–441; **23,** 263
Austria and, **18,** 47–48
Bessarabia—
annexation by Roumania (1918), **2,** 224–227; **5,** 61–62; **6,** 60–61
secession of, effect on nationality, **2,** 224–227
" *Biens et propriétés* ", **4,** 73–74, 76, 429, 446
" *Biens meubles* ", **6,** 381–382
Bigamy, national abroad, by, **31,** 272
Bills of Exchange and Negotiable Instruments, Convention (Geneva, 1930), **22,** 820, 836
Bills of lading—
enemy character of goods and, **12,** 391–392, 395, 559–562
to order, **12,** 560–562
Bills of Lading, Brussels Convention (1924), **11,** 223
Bills of Lading, Hague Rules, **21,** 297–300
Birds Protection Treaty (1902), **11,** 222
Birth on high seas, nationality, **4,** 295–296
Black Army, German Society of, **5,** 293–294
Black Sea Company, Italian, **1,** 26–27
Blaine-Pauncefote Treaty (1889), **6,** 298–302, 315
Blockade—
British and French, First World War, **16,** 571
bunker control, **10,** 267–272
establishment, insurgents, by, **4,** 531–533; **9,** 79–83
meaning, **9,** 80–81
prize courts, necessity for, **9,** 83
Bogotá, Charter of OAS, **18,** 63, 441–443
Bogotá, Conference of American States (1948), **17,** 46
Bogotá, Pact of (1948), **24,** 814; **25,** 48
U.S. reservation, **27,** 546–547
Bohemia,
Czechoslovak sovereignty, **1,** 17–20
territory of, **1,** 11–14
Bohemia and Moravia
German protectorate over, **11,** 24–25, 243; **16,** 14–15; **22,** 76, 152–153
German racial legislation, extension to, **11,** 173
nationality in, **11,** 179–180
Bolivia—
Argentina, frontier with, **1,** 106
Chile, Treaty of Peace and Friendship (1904), **9,** 103
Great Britain, Commercial Treaty (1911), **20,** 554, 555; **23,** 313, 320–322
Venezuela, Extradition Treaty (1883), **22,** 518
Bolivarian Treaty on Extradition (1911), **17,** 281, 282, 285; **19,** 378, 379; **22,** 518; **23,** 414–415
Bombardment: *see* Aerial bombardment
Bonds, government, **29,** 4–20, 431–437: *see also* State loans
agreement between government and certain bondholders, application, **29,** 433, 436
award for repudiation, date for conversion into claimant's currency, **26,** 272–274
award for repudiation, guaranteed exchange rate, relevance, **26,** 273–274
compensation, loss of option to be paid in foreign currency, **29,** 431–437
currency of payment, **29,** 7–8
de facto repudiation, **26,** 261
default on, State responsibility, **20,** 213–214
—acceleration clause, effect of, **26,** 258–262
former Government, of, repudiation, **30,** 151, 158–159, 160–161

Bonds, government—*continued*
interruption of service in war, **29**, 4–20
issue of, effect on original debt, **24**, 763
law governing obligations under, **9**, 23
national ownership, proof of, **26**, 341–342; **30**, 172–173
non-negotiable, valuation, **30**, 177–178
revalorization, **29**, 5, 8–11, 19
situs of, **32**, 108–109
Bonn Conventions, 1952/1954: *see under* Germany, Federal Republic
Booty, **12**, 458–459; **15**, 610–611; **16**, 493–496, 500–504, 506–507; **18**, 683–684, 696–697, 701; **19**, 625–626; **20**, 465, 634; **21**, 472, 473–475; **22**, 980–982; **26**, 689–691, 732; **32**, 585–588
individual right to, **2**, 438–439
larceny of, **16**, 500–503
private property as, **11**, 299
prize distinguished, **11**, 300–302, 303–304
taken after termination of hostilities, **23**, 775–776
Borneo, occupation by Japan (1942), **15**, 8–9
Boundaries, land, **1**, 95; **4**, 120–121; **5**, 83, 113–116; **7**, 115–128; **8**, 160–163; **12**, 59–60; **30**, 76–90
arbitral award on, supplementary evidence, **30**, 79, 85
arbitration, fixing by, **1**, 371–372; **30**, 475, 487–488
—cession, distinguished, **6**, 113–116
—existence of State and, **5**, 11–15
armistice demarcation line, **32**, 80–82
boundary commissions, functions, **1**, 89; **27**, 72, 76, 80, 95; **30**, 86, 89, 457–458
boundary commissions, legal nature, **1**, 84–89
conciliation commission as boundary commission, **20**, 577
delimitation of, **27**, 69, 72–73; **30**, 76–89; **33**, 56–60, 61, 118–130 *passim*
delimitation of, importance for establishment of new State, **5**, 14–15
determination of, enclosed areas, **27**, 62–98 *passim*
disputed, acts of recognition of, **30**, 84; **33**, 48 *et seq.*
disputed arbitral awards, **30**, 482–483
disputed territory jointly administered, **3**, 120–121
disputes, compensation, discretion as to, **30**, 475
estoppel: *q.v.*
frontier districts—
—jurisdiction, **5**, 104; **8**, 162–163
—port regulations, **21**, 86–87

Boundaries, land—*continued*
frontier districts—*continued*
—taxation, **12**, 59–60
future determinations of, **3**, 105–106
object of certainty and finality, **33**, 72–73, 87–88, 90, 114
peace treaty, adjustment of frontiers under, **20**, 63–77
preclusion: *see* Estoppel *and* Preclusion
prescription, effect of, **3**, 105–106 113–114
See also Prescription
provisional, **8**, 160–163
rectification of, claim for, **33**, 64, 67, 72, 88
rectification of, effect on private rights, **17**, 81–82
rectification of, legislation on, **19**, 133–135, 148
Treaties of Aachen and Cleve (1811) between Holland and Germany, **12**, 59–60
treaties on, interpretation, **3**, 376–377; **11**, 94–99
watershed line, **33**, 48–148 *passim*
Boundaries, water, **1**, 96–98; **2**, 96–99; **4**, 121–122; **5**, 83–88; **6**, 129, 157–159; **7**, 128–135; **8**, 164–165; **10**, 109–110
Beaufort Convention, S. Carolina and Georgia (1787), **1**, 97
historic title, **35**, 68–83
islands, **7**, 133–135
regulation of, **34**, 180–182
rivers, as, **9**, 113
condominium over, **6**, 50
river mouth, **30**, 476, 490
river *thalweg*, **14**, 56; **30**, 476–490
sea, nature of, **31**, 157
Boundary Commission (Mexico and U.S.A.), **11**, 96–98
Boundary disputes: *see under* Boundaries, land. *See also under* Disputes
Boxer Rebellion, war, whether, **26**, 628
Bratislava, part of Czechoslovakia, **1**, 15–17
Brazil—
aliens, admission of, **5**, 254
—exercise of professions, **1**, 246–247
—expulsion of, **1**, 254–256; **5**, 266; **9**, 390–393
—Revised Constitution (1926) under, **5**, 266
—naturalization of, **5**, 236
attachment of ships, **9**, 167
code of Judicial Organization, **22**, 556
Colombia, Extradition Treaty (1938), **26**, 526
extradition, law of, **5**, 280–281, 288; **6**, 312; **22**, 527–528
—mandated territory, national of, **5**, 32

Brazil—*continued*
" grand naturalization ", **5,** 235–237; **6,** 254–255
Italy, Extradition Treaty (1931), **18,** 339
nationality, constitutional provisions, **1,** 215; **6,** 254; **7,** 281–282
naturalization of aliens, **2,** 247; **5,** 236; **6,** 254–255; **26,** 377–378
Penal Code, territorial scope, **1,** 158, 308
States of, jurisdictional immunity, **4,** 39–40
tacit naturalization, **2,** 267; **6,** 254–255
U.S.A., Treaty concerning inheritance, **5,** 403
U.S.A., Treaty of Commerce (1828), **23,** 716
U.S.A., Commercial Agreement (1935), **20,** 1
U.S.A., forces in, **13,** 86–90
war with Germany, termination, **1,** 444
Bremen—
status of, **18,** 500–501
U.S.A., Treaty (1827), **18,** 500–501, 504
Brest, Bay of, **6,** 123–126, 128–129; **8,** 173–177
Brest Litowsk, Peace Treaty of (1918), **1,** 242, 434; **2,** 434; **5,** 14
abrogation, **3,** 262
Brétigny, Treaty of (1360): *see* Calais, Treaty of
Bretton Woods Agreements (1944): *see* International Monetary Fund, Articles of Agreement
Bretton Woods Conference (1944), Final Act, **20,** 464–466
Brioni, Agreement (1942), **18,** 3; **24,** 622
Bristol Channel, **3,** 126–128; **9,** 136–137
Britain: *see* England; Great Britain; *and* United Kingdom
British Commonwealth: *see* Commonwealth
British Nationality and Status of Aliens Act, 1914...**1,** 212; **4,** 43
British North America Act, 1867...**6,** 45–46, 159; **8,** 41, 59, 74; **12,** 125; **14,** 22–28; **18,** 286; **19,** 58–59; **26,** 173, 176
" British possession ", meaning, **23,** 292
Broadcasting—
from outside territorial waters, **31,** 274–275
law prohibiting, acquired rights, **9,** 52–55
Brünn, Treaty of (1920), **1,** 214, 223
Brussels Anti-Slavery Conference (1890), **4,** 311
Brussels Conference, Copyright (1948), **18,** 48
Brussels Conferences on Maritime Law (1905, 1909 and 1910), **22,** 636
Brussels Conventions on—
Bills of Lading (1924), **9,** 489; **11,** 223
Collisions at Sea (1910), **6,** 385–386; **9,** 299–300; **11,** 230; **20,** 429–430; **22,** 635–637; **24,** 588–590
Immunity of State-owned Vessels (1926), and Protocol (1934), **9,** 286, 291; **10,** 243–247; **11,** 139–142; **12,** 112–113; **15,** 146; **22,** 4
Limitation of Shipowners' Liability (1924), **16,** 9–10
Maritime Assistance and Salvage (1910), **3,** 3; **5,** 128; **6,** 10; **9,** 300; **12,** 123; **22,** 277
Brussels Court of War Damages, **4,** 558–565
Brussels Draft Declaration concerning Laws and Customs of War (1874), **15,** 600, 641; **16,** 534–535; **19,** 612
Brussels Treaty (1948), accession of Germany and Italy, **23,** 770–771
Bucharest—
bombardment of, **5,** 516
Peace Treaty of (1913), **4,** 425; **5,** 121; **23,** 663–665, 668
Budapest, Peace Treaty of (1921), **4,** 81–82, 543
Buenos Aires, federal district, **1,** 97–98
Buganda Agreement, 1955: *see under* Uganda
Bulgaria—
Belgium, Conciliation Treaty (1931), **9,** 512
Declaration of acceptance of obligations of U.N. Charter (1948), **27,** 585, 598, 607, 608
ex-Tsar of, property in England, **1,** 406–407
foreign exchange laws, **28,** 303–305
France, Mixed Arbitral Tribunal, rules of procedure, **5,** 458
Germany, Extradition Treaty (1911), **7,** 351–352
Greece—
—Extradition Treaty (1929), **7,** 335
—Financial Agreement (1927), **6,** 432; **22,** 681
—Peace Treaty (1913), **23,** 663–665, 668
—Treaty of Alliance (1912), **4,** 425
I.C.J., acceptance of Statute of, nature and effect, **27,** 585
nationalization of banks, **24,** 301–302
occupation of Greece by, **15,** 566–567; **16,** 466–467
P.C.I.J., acceptance of jurisdiction of, **27,** 558, 560–561, 568, 572, 573, 574, 576, 598, 603
Peace Treaty with (1947), **17,** 319–322, 331–339; **27,** 573
Sweden, Commercial Treaty (1942), **21,** 265–272

Bulgaria—*continued*
Turkey, Peace Treaty of Constantinople (1913), **7,** 91–99
vassal State (1904), **8,** 93–94
Bunker control in war, U.S. practice, **10,** 267–272
Burden of proof: *see under* Arbitration, evidence, *and* Evidence
Burma—
Defence of Burma Act (1940), **23,** 754–755, 787–788
Extradition Act, **28,** 313–314
Foreigners Act, s. 3 (right to expel), **28,** 312–314
Immigration (Emergency Provisions) Act, 1947...**28,** 311–313
immunity of foreign States, law on, **31,** 259–266
international law and municipal law, **31,** 262–263
Japanese conferment of independence, **23,** 787–789
" local naturalization ", **22,** 433–436
nationality requirements, **28,** 312
occupation by Japan, **15,** 537–548, 576–583; **18,** 575–585, 641–642; **19,** 619–620; **23,** 754–756
Present War Termination (Definition) Act, 1946...**26,** 682
U.K., agreement on independence, commercial relations, **31,** 341–344
Business name, improper use of, **30,** 43, 52
Bustamante Code of Private International Law (1928), **6,** 12–13; **7,** 444–445; **13,** 88–89, 158; **14,** 86, 138; **17,** 264, 266, 270; **18,** 316, 382; **19,** 378, 383–384; **22,** 283, 519, 528, 540–541; **23,** 414, 417, 425–426, 428; **24,** 492–493, 500, 501
extradition, **5,** 277, 281 n; **7,** 336
municipal law and, **30,** 390–391
Byrnes-Blum Agreement, France-U.S.A. (1946), **19,** 454, 455

C

Cables, submarine, **8,** 173–174
Convention for Protection of (1884), **2,** 417
customs laws and, **9,** 126
destruction of, **2,** 415–419
Cairo Declaration (1943), **17,** 178; **22,** 983
Calais (or Brétigny), Treaty of (1360), **20,** 98, 118, 119, 121, 131, 132, 133, 137, 138
California—
aliens, holding of land by, Law of 1913...**1,** 239
Constitution, provisions on aliens, **2,** 315
California—*continued*
Japanese nationals, rights in, **4,** 447–448
Monterey Bay, **4,** 135–136; **8,** 169–170
Penal Code (jurisdiction), **11,** 200
seaward boundaries, **33,** 149–152
" State Waters ", sea surrounding islands, **1,** 101
Calvo clause, **1,** 236; **2,** 177–179; **3,** 261–262; **5,** 163, 186, 208–211; **6,** 199–201, 273
conditions of admissibility, **6,** 222–224
equity and: *see* Equity
international law, compatibility with, **3,** 292–294
law of nature and, **3,** 5
Cambodia, French protectorate, **11,** 44–45
Cambrai, Treaty of (1820), **7,** 431
Cameroon—
German Protectorate, liabilities of, **2,** 88
mandated territory, **22,** 88–89; **28,** 80–81
—fiscal status, **11,** 52–53
nationality of inhabitants on establishment of State of, **28,** 80–81
public land régime in, **6,** 48–49
Cameroons, British—
plebiscite in, **35,** 358–359, 360, 364, 367–369, 380, 453, 463–464
Trusteeship Agreement, **35,** 353, 355, 356, 357, 403–404, 425, 427, 445–448, 459, 460–461, 468, 476–477
—termination, **35,** 357, 359–360, 368, 369–370, 380, 382–383, 386–387, 428–429, 464, 469–470, 480–482
Canada—
aliens, deportation of, **6,** 291–292; **32,** 247–255
Bill of Rights, relevance to expulsion of aliens, **32,** 274–275
British North America Act, 1867, **6,** 45–46; **8,** 41, 59, 74; **12,** 125; **14,** 22–28; **18,** 286; **19,** 58–59; **26,** 173, 176; **27,** 239–240
Canadian Forces Act, 1954...**23,** 254
" Canadian waters ", **9,** 128
Citizenship Act, 1946...**18,** 293
comity, export of liquor to U.S., **5,** 6–7
Constitution, compared with Australian, **8,** 58–59
Criminal Code, definition of theft, **1,** 275
Criminal Code, jurisdiction over aliens, **5,** 91
Crown Liability Act, 1952–53...**23,** 252–254
Custodian of Enemy Property, **12,** 264–266

Canada—*continued*
Customs Act, 1927...**7**, 207–212; **9**, 128; **22**, 591
—Amendment Act, 1936...**9**, 128
Customs and Fisheries Protection Act, 1927...**6**, 154–159
Defence Regulations (1939), **9**, 543, 544–545
Denmark, Extradition Treaty (1873), **1**, 275
deportation procedure, appeal, **32**, 260–275
Dutch forces in, **10**, 116–119
Exchequer Court Act, 1927...**23**, 251–254
Excise Tax Act, **22**, 591
expulsion of British subjects, **9**, 383–384; **32**, 247–249
Extradition Act, 1927...**9**, 406
Extradition Act, 1952...**21**, 235; **23**, 405–409; **27**, 251–252
Fisheries Act, 1952...**23**, 154, 156–159
foreign armed forces, jurisdiction over, **12**, 124–133
Gold Clauses Act, 1937...**11**, 26, 28
Habeas Corpus Act (Ontario, 1927), **22**, 493
habeas corpus, issue of writ from England (1861), **28**, 53–54, 75
hovering laws, **9**, 127–128
Immigration Acts, 1927 and 1952, **9**, 383; **20**, 284; **22**, 458–459, 491–497, 511; **23**, 401–403; **24**, 466–467, 469–472
—deportation, aliens, **6**, 291–292; **32**, 252–255
—deportation, British subjects, **32**, 247–249
—deportation, crime involving "moral turpitude", **32**, 249–251
immigration into, as privilege, **27**, 247–248
Income Tax Acts, **22**, 604; **23**, 462
Indian Acts, 1927 and 1952..**22**, 604; **23**, 460–461, 467; **27**, 239–245
Indian tribes, position of, **27**, 1–13, 239–245
—nationality, **27**, 239–245
—rights in land, **27**, 2–13, 239–245
—treaties with British Crown, **27**, 4, 6, 12
International Labour Conventions, enforcement of, **3**, 393–394
international law and municipal law, **10**, 338–339, 347–350
international status, **8**, 41–48, 71–78; **20**, 40–41
legislative powers of Dominion Parliament, **8**, 41; **9**, 28
Limitation of Hours of Work Act, 1935, legislative competence, **8**, 41
Minimum Wages Act, 1935, legislative competence, **8**, 41
N.A.T.O. pilots in, **23**, 251–254

Canada—*continued*
naturalization, residence requirement, **28**, 275
New Brunswick Rates and Taxes Act, **23**, 224, 225, 227; **24**, 242, 247; **26**, 173, 178
Newfoundland, Terms of Union (1949), **22**, 272
Ontario Lakes and Rivers Improvement Act, **6**, 8; **22**, 593
Petition of Right Act, 1860 . . . **9**, 372–373
Privy Council, appeals to, **8**, 71–80; **9**, 28
Racial Discrimination Act, 1944, **12**, 179, 182; **15**, 304
Secretary of State for External Affairs, certificate of, **15**, 176–204
Shipping Act, 1934 . . . **9**, 127; **15**, 188, 191
Trade Mark Act, 1952 . . . **23**, 145
trading with the enemy legislation, **9**, 549–552; **12**, 322–327; **15**, 439–441
treaties, concluded by Britain, adhesion, **1**, 348
treaties, Head of State form, **32**, 277, 283–285
treaty-making power, **6**, 44–46
Unfair Competition Act, 1932...**22**, 594
U.S.A.—
—Air Base Agreement (1941), **21**, 114
—Ashburton Treaty, 1842; *see* Webster-Ashburton Treaty, *infra*
—boundary, Niagara river, **4**, 121–122
—Boundary Waters Treaty (1909), **7**, 8; **9**, 316; **24**, 564; **28**, 464–467; **34**, 180–182
—Double Taxation Convention, (1942), **23**, 490–492
— —"permanent establishment", **33**, 400–407
—Extradition Treaties (1842, 1889), 1900, 1905, 1950), **5**, 284; **6**, 298–301, 315; **9**, 406–7; **21**, 235
—forces in, **12**, 124–133; **21**, 114–116
—Joint Commission, Report (1931), **6**, 132
—Trade between, Acts for Regulation of (1796, 1801), **22**, 595–596
—Treaty concerning Uses of Waters of Niagara (1950), **24**, 557–571 *passim*
—Webster-Ashburton Treaty, 1842, **5**, 87–88; **6**, 8–10, 298–301, 393; **7**, 3–8; **20**, 40, 41; **22**, 593; **24**, 568–569
Visiting Forces (North Atlantic Treaty) Act, 1951...**21**, 115; **22**, 272; **23**, 253–254

Canada—*continued*
War-Measures Act, 1927...**15**, 439–441
Weekly Rest in Industrial Undertakings Act, 1935, legislative competence, **8**, 41
Canals, international, **2**, 99–102; **3**, 128–129; **7**, 137–139; **17**, 133–135
See also Panama Canal *and* Suez Canal
tolls, fixing of, **24**, 146–152
war, in, **2**, 99–102; **4**, 27–28; **17**, 445–447
Cancale Bay, **4**, 136
Canon law, Italy, relation to ordinary law, **26**, 186–187
Cape of Good Hope, Colony, naturalization in, **4**, 42–43
Capitulations, military, **15**, 500–505; **16**, 530, 538
legal title to property, effect on, **22**, 930–931; **23**, 766–768
resistance movements and, **15**, 502
surrender of property in, effect of, **23**, 766–768
Capitulations, régime of, **1**, 161–163; **2**, 151; **3**, 191–200; **4**, 189–193; **5**, 69, 134; **6**, 180–182; **7**, 199–200, 395–396; **8**, 255, 262; **19**, 255–302; **20**, 195–197; **21**, 136–140
abolition, in Egypt—
—Montreux Convention (1937), **8**, 256; **9**, 466, 471–472; **11**, 226; **12**, 156; **18**, 429–430; **20**, 195–197
—Treaty of Lausanne (1923), **3**, 192–193; **4**, 192–193
abolition, in Morocco, **11**, 223–224; **19**, 276
abolition, in Syria, **3**, 268–289
abolition, in Turkey, **5**, 136
aliens, submission to local law, **26**, 234–236
consular courts, **4**, 191–192
criminal jurisdiction, **4**, 189–190
criminal law, territoriality, **3**, 194–199
custom and usage, **19**, 275–276, 292–294
Egypt, in, **1**, 40, 42, 161–162; **3**, 20–22, 30–31, 191–193, 194–195, 196–198; **4**, 44–46, 64; **5**, 131–137; **6**, 180–182; **7**, 200–201; **8**, 255–262, **25**, 207
—abolition of: *see* abolition, *supra*
—Russian nationals, position of, **3**, 30–31; **4**, 64
enemy occupation and, **1**, 452
Ethiopia, in, **7**, 199–200
extradition request from State under, **2**, 274–275
immovable property, **3**, 198–199
mandated territories, under, **3**, 48–49
—abolition, **3**, 268–269
—status of nationals, **3**, 191–192
Capitulations, régime of—*continued*
martial law, right to proclaim, **1**, 42
Morocco, in, **2**, 151–152; **19**, 255–302, 342–344; **21**, 136–140
—renunciation of French protectorate, **19**, 263–264, 266, 267, 269–271, 273, 280–281
national territory, assimilation to, **4**, 189–190
nationals, status of, **3**, 193–199
nature of, **4**, 189–190; **26**, 235
protected persons, status under, **3**, 196–197
Syria, in, **3**, 195; **4**, 192–193; **7**, 395–396
Turkey, in, **1**, 452–453; **3**, 194, 267–268
—denunciation by, **4**, 192–193
war, effect of outbreak of, **4**, 534–535
Capture, naval, right of, **2**, 452–454; **3**, 483–484; **13**, 401–406
See also Blockade; Prize: Sea warfare
restrictions on, **13**, 402, 403, 405
unfinished ship, **20**, 674
Caracas, Convention on Territorial Asylum (1954), **24**, 518–523
Cardinals, immunities of, **8**, 235–236, 405
Carinthia, occupation by Yugoslavia, **1**, 467
Carriage by air, international: *see also* Carriage of goods by air
meaning, **20**, 43–46
Warsaw Convention (1929), **8**, 453, 459; **9**, 445; **12**, 271–273; **17**, 162; **19**, 467–469; **20**, 41–46, 156–163, 418–424; **21**, 286–291; **22**, 157–167; **23**, 493–497; **24**, 267, 271, 554–572, 581–583, 630, 632, 645–647, 664–665; **27**, 257–259; **28**, 99–106
—Hague Protocol (1955), **35**, 246
—interpretation of, **35**, 239–252
—ticket, delivery of, **35**, 244–252
—venue provisions, **35**, 239–243, 247–248
Carriage of goods between protecting and protected States, **11**, 43–44
Carriage of goods by air, international meaning, **20**, 156–163
See also Carriage by air, international
Carriage of goods by railway: *see* Rail transport
Catalonia, Government of, **8**, 191–193
confiscatory decrees, **9**, 24–25
nationalization of industries by, **9**, 151
Causa proxima non remota inspicitur, **1**, 188; **2**, 175, 198–199, 199–202, 203–207, 207, 208; **3**, 248, 249–251, 254–255, 469–470; **4**, 230–233, 266–267, 274–275, 276;

Causa proxima non remota inspicitur—continued
5, 150–152, 181–182, 201, 202–203; **6,** 229–231; **8,** 274–276; **9,** 318–324
See also Damages, remoteness of
Cautio judicatum solvi. See Security for costs
Ceara (Brazil), State of, international position, **4,** 39–40
Cemetery, State-owned, administration abroad, **7,** 177–178
Central American Tribunal, disqualification of member, **28,** 559
Central Office for International Transport, as arbitrator, **6,** 417–420
CERN (European Nuclear Research Centre), officials, immunity from jurisdiction, **32,** 334
Cessante ratione legis cessat et ipsa lex, **17,** 106; **28,** 382
Cession of territory, **1,** 84–89; **5,** 55–56, 77; **6,** 108–109; **7,** 172–173; **15,** 62–63; **21,** 81; **22,** 133; **23,** 123; **24,** 75; **25,** 7–8, 10; **27,** 31; **31,** 77–78, 87–88, 108, 115, 125; **32,** 84
See also under particular States and treaties, *and* State succession
acquired rights, effect on, **3,** 81–83; **6,** 66–71; **8,** 135–140
Institute of International Law, Resolution (1952), **20,** 68
See also Acquired rights, *and* private rights, effect on, *infra*
Act of State, as, **26,** 109–111; **27,** 31
boundaries, fixing of, distinguished, **6,** 115–116
collective naturalization, **11,** 49–50
compensation for destruction of property, **20,** 628, 633
conditional, **3,** 105–109
Congo, to Belgium (1907), **7,** 29–30, 173, 409–410; **22,** 226–227; **23,** 191–192
consent of population (French law), **26,** 114
continuity of laws, **6,** 82–83; **8,** 143–144; **11,** 49–50, 78–82; **24,** 83–85
criminal law, effect on, **16,** 81–85
disguised, **8,** 153–157
disposition of assets, right of, **5,** 55, 77
formal delivery of possession, **1,** 84–89
Germany to France, Treaty of Versailles, **1,** 337, 349–350, 367–369
jurisdiction, effect on, **4,** 117; **16,** 64; **22,** 197–200
jurisdiction, transfer of, distinguished, **26,** 116
law applicable after, **6,** 82–83, 108–109

Cession of territory—*continued*
less than full sovereignty, **31,** 77–78, 87–88, 109, 115, 125
maintenance of order, transitional period, **20,** 145–148
meaning, **2,** 341; **22,** 133; **24,** 602–630
nationality, effect on, **1,** 91–94, 202, 243; **2,** 227–239, 241–242; **3,** 108–109, 115–116, 264–265; **4,** 293–294, 304–307, 308–309; **6,** 267; **11,** 49–50, 83–85, 179–180; **12,** 185–188; **14,** 113–114; **15,** 27; **16,** 210; **18,** 249–251, 257–258, 400–401; **20,** 145–158; **21,** 177–178
—persons not resident in ceded territory, **2,** 239
—provisional effect, **2,** 241
nemo plus juris transferre potest quam ipse habet, application of, **4,** 113–114
pending actions, effect on, **1,** 89–91; **2,** 61
prescription, law as to, effect on, **4,** 116–117
private rights, effect on, **2,** 71–77, 78–79; **3,** 81–83; **4,** 88–90; **6,** 66–71, 72–73, 83–85; **7,** 433–434; **8,** 31–32, 125–126; **9,** 102–103; **10,** 98–102; **13,** 41–42; **15,** 52–58; **17,** 81–82; **19,** 133–135; **23,** 102–103; **26,** 82–83, 86; **27,** 35: *see also* Acquired rights
—immoveables, **26,** 83–87
property rights preserved by treaty, right of reverter, **26,** 553–555
protection, exercise of right of, **6,** 109
ratification, effect of, **3,** 336
renunciation, contrasted, **3,** 34–35; **6,** 100, 108
State-owned property, **25,** 7–8
succession to obligations, **23,** 107
Ceylon—
citizenship, **19,** 61–68; **26,** 367–374
Indian and Pakistan Residents (Citizenship) Act, 1949...**26,** 367–374
Chaco. *See* Gran Chaco
Chandernagore, cession to India, **21,** 256–257; **22,** 197–200; **23,** 107
"Change in conditions", effect on treaties, **6,** 362–368
See also Rebus sic stantibus, doctrine of
Change of government, effect on extradition request, **1,** 276
Channel Islands—
autonomy of, proclamation (1226), **20,** 139
islets, status of, **20,** 94–145
Chapultepec, Conference (1945), Problems of War and Peace, **22,** 914–915

Chargé d'affaires—
immunities of, **1,** 298 n; **9,** 427
—*ad interim,* **24,** 528
Charles V, Edict on Sea-fisheries (1567), **11,** 176
Charter of the United Nations (1945), **15,** 335 *et seq.*; **21,** 332, 337, 339, 340, 342, 375; **23,** 67 *et seq.*; **26,** 2–3, 619–620
[For references to particular Articles see the TABLE OF TREATIES]
action outside, **34,** 326
agreements under Art. 43...**34,** 295–296, 354, 360, 368, 373, 381, 389–390, 391,
amendment of, **34,** 315, 341, 388
application to all Members, **27,** 589–591
basis of validity, **27,** 586
discretions under: *see* Discretions
effectiveness, **16,** 326–328
enforcement action, **34,** 294, 352, 356, 387
entry into force, **27,** 568, 571
General Assembly, competence of, **22,** 658, 660
Germany, Federal Republic, acceptance by, **23,** 771
human rights provisions, **12,** 179; **13,** 141–142; **14,** 96–100; **15,** 302–308; **16,** 250–251, 253; **19,** 312–317; **20,** 2, 244–245; **31,** 29–30, 48; **32,** 369–370
—and domestic jurisdiction, **14,** 100
—insurgency, relevance to, **31,** 29–30, 48
immigration laws and, **28,** 463
international society and, **21,** 326
interpretation of, **17,** 330; **19,** 494; **32,** 367–368
—applicable principles, **34,** 286–287, 310–312
—practice of the U.N., **34,** 294, 312–319, 322, 342
—preparatory work, **34,** 328, 353, 379
judicial settlement, provisions on, **35,** 471–472
municipal law and, **20,** 244–246
non-Member States, effect on, **34,** 390
Preamble, **19,** 313, 314, 529; **21,** 326
representatives, immunities of, **34,** 155–159
self-executing provisions, **19,** 312–317, 473; **32,** 369–370
treaties and, **32,** 57
validity, basis of, **27,** 586
war crimes and, **17,** 388
Charterers, jurisdiction, disputes with foreign shipmasters, **4,** 162
Charterparty—
State as charterer, arbitration clause, **24,** 205-206
Charterparty—*continued*
war clause—
—Anglo-French action in Egypt (1956), **26,** 638–651
—China and Japan, hostilities, 1937, **9,** 528–536
—commercial interpretation, **26,** 647, 651
—" government ", unrecognized, **23,** 71–78
Chemical warfare, **5,** 517
Chesapeake Bay, **4,** 136; **9,** 137
Chicago Convention on International Civil Aviation: *see under* Aviation
Children: *see* Minors *and* Nationality
Chile—
Bolivia, Treaty, Peace and Friendship (1904), **9,** 103
Constitution (diplomatic immunities), **2,** 308
Constitution (expropriation), **23,** 740
diplomatic immunities, law as to, **6,** 329–330
extradition from Argentina, **5,** 289
France, Commercial Treaty (1846), **23,** 729–730
France, Extradition Treaty (1860), **2,** 276–277
Maritime Zone, Declaration, 1952.. **22,** 278, 280
Peru, Extradition Treaty (1932), **7,** 335–336
—Treaty of Ancon (1883), **2,** 241; **3,** 357–358; **6,** 110
—Treaty of Santiago (1929), **6,** 110
Trade Mark Convention (1923), **5,** 336–337
treaties and municipal law, **30,** 390–391
U.S.A., Arbitration Convention (1858), **22,** 414
" Chile order ", **1,** 410
China—
" Agreed Announcement " with U.S.A., return of nationals (1955), **20,** 299–300; **35,** 237
Belgium, dispute with (denunciation of 1865 Treaty), **4,** 513–515
Chinese in U.S.A., admission to schools, **4,** 331
civil war in (1945–1948), **22,** 92–94
consular jurisdiction, **10,** 265–266
deportation to, from U.S.A., **34,** 21–26
extraterritorial rights, termination of, **12,** 252; **28,** 195
Foreign Exchange Control Regulations, **16,** 27–36
France, Commercial Treaty (1928), **11,** 229–230
France, Treaty with (1844), **1,** 335; **2,** 326; **12,** 280
—Treaty with (1858), **1,** 335; **2,** 326; **6,** 34, **12,** 280

China—*continued*
France, Treaty on Sino-Indo-Chinese Relations (1946), **16,** 260; **28,** 269–271
Great Britain, Convention with (1898), for lease of Kowloon, **27,** 49–58
Japan, dispute with (1931), **22,** 673
Japan, Treaty of Commerce and Navigation (1896), **2,** 152
leases in, **3,** 118–119
Manchuria and, **22,** 90–97
Nationalist Government, establishment of, **17,** 174
—recognition of, **5,** 52–53; **17,** 177–178, 196; **23,** 72
—status of, **19,** 89, 91
Nine-Power Treaty (1922), **28,** 196
relinquishment of extraterritorial rights by U.K. and U.S.A. (1943), **28,** 195
People's Republic, proclamation of, **17,** 174
—recognition of, **17,** 171, 177–178, 196; **19,** 89
Tientsin, British concession in, **2,** 152–153; **9,** 116
treaties with, effect of revolutionary war, **35,** 235–239
U.S.A., agreement on return of civilians, **20,** 299–300; **35,** 237
—Economic Aid Agreement (1948), **24,** 814; **27,** 547
—Immigration Treaty (1880), **1,** 321; **11,** 10; **23,** 453; **24,** 578
—Treaty of Commerce (1903), **28,** 196
—Treaty of Friendship, Commerce and Navigation (1946), **22,** 90–97; **35,** 236–239
U.S.S.R., Treaty of Friendship and Alliance (1945), **22,** 92
Citizenship: *see also* Nationality
acquisition of, **5,** 219; **6,** 252–254; **26,** 367–375
Ceylon, law of, **19,** 61–68; **26,** 367–374
Italy, law of, **5,** 219; **6,** 252–254
meaning, **8,** 281–282; **12,** 186, 189, 190, 192, 194
nationality, differences, **5,** 238
Citizenship rights, deprivation of, **11,** 183–184
Civil law, application to international relations, **1,** 64
international treaty on (1889), **6,** 110
Civil Procedure, Hague Convention on (1905), **1,** 69–73, 122–124, 244, 300–301, 352; **2,** 84, 323; **4,** 37–38, 59–60; **5,** 30, 47; **6,** 40–43, 90, 349; **7,** 305–306, 308; **8,** 40, 334, 423, 427; **9,** 73, 376; **11,** 67, 222, 226–227; **12,** 277–278; **13,** 185, 187, 232; **14,** 177; **16,** 314–318; **17,** 308–310, 357–359; **18,** 20–22,
Civil Procedure, Hague Convention on —*continued*
434, 574–575; **19,** 29–34; **21,** 211, 303; **22,** 900; **24,** 52–53, 483, 485; **26,** 577; **28,** 494–496
"Civil rights", meaning, minorities treaties, **2,** 290
Civil war: *see also* Spanish Civil War
acts done in course of, extradition for, **2,** 286
—jurisdiction of foreign courts, **5,** 51–52
laws of war, application, **5,** 487
levée en masse, **16,** 367–368, 370, 380
nature of, **16,** 362–372; **19,** 550–556
neutrals, duties of, **22,** 1015–1016
"Civilian population", meaning, **3,** 435–437
Civilian war claimants, rights of, **6,** 237–239
Claims commissions: *see also* U.S.A. Foreign Claims Settlement Commission
evidence, oral, corroboration, **26,** 624–625
international law, application of, **26,** 270
judicial review of award of, **22,** 405–407; **26,** 348–351
valuation of property by, **26,** 315–316
Claims, governmental incorporating private, **34,** 228–229
Claims, international, **1,** 184–186; **2,** 117–192, 361–363; **3,** 234–235; **4,** 248–253; **5,** 174–194; **6,** 216–224; **7,** 261–266; **8,** 271; **9,** 308–324; **16,** 176–181; **20,** 223–228; **21,** 146–165; **22,** 332–417, 843–864, 953–980; **23,** 301–302, 342, 344–345, 675–676; **24,** 301–302, 303–315, 316–318; **25,** 91–167, 185–186; **26,** 316–361; **27,** 559; **28,** 195–200, 470; **29,** 21–54, 421–429; **30,** 171–219; **32,** 148–151, 152–161, 163–164, 638, 641
actio personalis moritur cum persona, **5,** 174–177
admissibility, **6,** 273–275
—arbitrability, distinguished, **2,** 359–366
—merits, distinguished from, **5,** 191–193
assessment of, **22,** 332–336
—compulsory mortgage, allowance for, **22,** 333–334
—inheritance tax, deduction for, **22,** 332–333
assignment of, **16,** 176–181; **21,** 161–162; **26,** 346–347; **30,** 158, 159–160
—conditional, **26,** 324–325, 350
—non-national, by, **26,** 345–346; **30,** 156
—non-national, to, **26,** 323–325

Claims, international—*continued*
award: *see* Damages *and* Interest
bank as agent, loss of drafts, **30,** 184, 185
basis of, **6,** 377–379: *see also* State responsibility
beneficial ownership of property, **21,** 154–156
burden of proof, **21,** 154–155; **22,** 846–866, 972, 978; **30,** 126, 138, 157, 218
—circumstances of loss, as to, **22,** 349, 953–959, 966–972
Calvo clause, effect of: *see* Calvo clause
claims of owner and of State from which property taken, **22,** 953–955, 966–967, 970–972
collateral relatives, on behalf of, **7,** 264–265
compensation, measure of, **4,** 258–260
See also Damages; Equity; *Ex gratia* payments
contract claims, U.S. practice, **26,** 268
counterclaim, admissibility, **3,** 172–173
creditor claims, **21,** 291–293; **26,** 307–308; **30,** 122–128, 128–133, 134–135, 140–143, 153–156, 181, 183, 189, 197
damages: *q.v.*
date when claim arose, **7,** 255–257; **30,** 213, 215; **32,** 154, 155
death of owner at time of destruction, **22,** 338–340
delay in bringing, **25,** 185–186
See also prescription, *infra and* Laches
evidence, **5,** 182; **22,** 843–864
—admissibility, **22,** 349
—*bona fides*, of, **1,** 187; **2,** 189–190
See also Good faith
—burden of proof, **21,** 154–155; **22,** 349, 846–866, 953–959, 966–972, 978; **30,** 126, 138 157, 218
—condition of property, as to, **22,** 338–340
—loss or damage, of, **22,** 864–867, 978
—national ownership of bonds, **30,** 172–173
—ownership of property destroyed, **22,** 858–864
exclusion, compensation from another source, **21,** 149–152
exclusion, possible proceedings in respondent State, **22,** 394, 396–397
exhaustion of local remedies: *q.v.*
expenses of evacuating personnel, **30,** 184, 185–186
fugitives from justice, espousal of claims of, **4,** 248–250
funds set aside to meet, **9,** 336–338

Claims, international—*continued*
"gold tariff" as basis of, **23,** 342, 344–345
guaranteed by another State, effect, **22,** 398–404
immoral character of injured person, **4,** 250–251
indirect shareholder claims, **30,** 181, 183, 198–200, 207–208
—Italian Peace Treaty, **30,** 511–514
—"stockholders' pool", **30,** 171–172
individuals, of, international character of, **1,** 184–188; **2,** 362–364; **4,** 258–260; **5,** 491
—renunciation in favour of government, **5,** 184–186
individuals, of: *see* State control over, *infra*
inheritance and, **7,** 244; **21,** 156–159, 161; **22,** 338–340
See also Nationality of claims
insurer, by, nationality rule, **26,** 316–319
interest: *q.v.*
inter-governmental settlement, effect, **30,** 184, 186
international character, **1,** 184–188; **2,** 362–364, 400–401; **4,** 258–260; **5,** 209
See also nature of, *infra*
investigation by State, **22,** 853–856
joint claims, **2,** 184–185
legal expenses, **30,** 151–153, 184, 185
life interest, valuation of, **26,** 296
local remedies: *see* Exhaustion of local remedies
lump-sum settlement, right of individual to share in, **22,** 405–407, 418; **26,** 347–351
maritime lien, based on, **21,** 148
nationality of: *see* Nationality of claims
nationals, of, against own State, **5,** 183–184
nature of, **6,** 242–246; **21,** 146–148
nominee, property owned by, **26,** 279–280
non bis in idem, **21,** 149
"owner", meaning, **22,** 341–343
peace treaties, under: *see* Peace treaties, claims under
personal tort claims, **30,** 539 n.
pledge of, nationality rule and, **30,** 208–212
prescription, **3,** 246; **4,** 263–265; **5,** 196, 450–452; **23,** 306, 313, 314–316, 671–672
prior war damage claim, **22,** 858–864
property owned by nominee, **26,** 279–280
property seized by hostile third State, **22,** 972–978
real property in interest, **4,** 253

Claims, international—*continued*
reasonable time, brought within, **25,** 185–186
remainderman's interest, valuation of, **26,** 315–316
renunciation of, **6,** 379; **7,** 261–263
See also waiver, *infra*
res judicata: *q.v.*
right of espousal, **2,** 361–363; **4,** 248–253
rights void in municipal law, based on, **2,** 183
set-off, **21,** 152-153
shareholders, by, **6,** 273–275; **21,** 150–155; **26,** 342; **30,** 171–172
State and individual, claims distinguished, **4,** 258–260
State control over private claims, **2,** 180, 191–192, 361–363; **3,** 243–245; **4,** 258–262; **5,** 193–194; **6,** 222–224; **28,** 195–200; **22,** 398–407, 418; **32,** 151–165, 638
—claims against national State, **28,** 195–200
—compensation, individual's right to share in, **9,** 336–338; **18,** 9–10; **22,** 405–407, 418; **26,** 347–351; **30,** 205, 206, 216, 217
State from whose territory private property taken, claim by, **22,** 953–955, 966–967, 970–972
stock held by nominee, **21,** 154–155
subrogation to non-national insurers, **27,** 559
treaty, under, concurrent claims, **22,** 959, 964
trustee, by, nationality of beneficiaries, **26,** 322–323, 464
undisclosed principal as claimant, **4,** 253–254; **5,** 177
valuation of property: *see* Valuation
waiver, **20,** 223–226; **28,** 470; **32,** 148–151, 152–161, 641
—extension to municipal law claims, **32,** 163–164
Clausula rebus stantibus: *see Rebus sic stantibus,* doctrine of
Clearing agreements, **21,** 265–272; **30,** 404–420
Clearing offices (1919 Peace Treaties), **1,** 392; **7,** 505
Cleve, Boundary Treaty of (1816), **12,** 59–60
Coal and Steel Community: *see* European Coal and Steel Community
"Coast", meaning, **4,** 120–121; **23,** 127
Co-belligerency, **15,** 106–107; **18,** 426, 473; **19,** 638–640
Co-belligerent, enemy character of national of, **23,** 756
Coblenz Agreement (1925) (occupation of Ruhr), **4,** 404–405
Cochin, Agreement with British Crown (1899), **26,** 116–117
Cochin China, French, legal status of, **11,** 45
Codification: *see also* International Law Commission
Committee of League of Nations, **18,** 379
—Report on Territorial Waters (1927), **18,** 116, 380
Hague Conference (1930), *see* Hague Codification Conference
Collateral relatives, international claim on behalf of, **7,** 264–265
Collective fine, imposition by occupant, **11,** 294–295
Collective naturalization, conquest, after, **5,** 235–237; **6,** 254–255; **10,** 279–281
Collège arbitral, conciliation commission sitting as, **22,** 317–329, 500–501, 886
Collisions at sea—
Brussels Convention on (1910), **6,** 385–386; **9,** 299–300; **11,** 230; **22,** 635–637; **24,** 588–590
high seas, on—
—jurisdiction over, **4,** 158–159; **7,** 139
—law applicable to, **4,** 158–159
territorial waters, in—
—jurisdiction over, **4,** 198; **7,** 137–139; **9,** 298–299; **10,** 166–168
—law applicable to, **1,** 100; **7,** 480–481; **9,** 298–299
vessel on loan to foreign State, jurisdiction, **12,** 175–177
Collisions, Rhine on, jurisdiction over, **11,** 227–228
Venice Lagoon, in, **8,** 173
Collusive evidence, **8,** 486
Colombia—
Bolivarian Treaty on Extradition (1911), **19,** 378, 379; **22,** 518; **23,** 414–415
boundary with Peru, **5,** 388
Brazil, Extradition Treaty (1938), **26,** 526
Constitution, agreements with Holy See and, **2,** 318–319
—Art. 11 (rights of aliens), **9,** 386
discrimination against aliens, **12,** 230
Ecuador, Extradition Treaty (1911), **14,** 143
extradition, law as to, **28,** 323–325
foreign judgments, enforcement of, **26,** 57–58
Holy See, Concordat (1887), **2,** 318
immigration, Law of 1927..**9,** 385
Peru, Boundary Treaty with (1922), **5,** 388
Peru, Protocol of Friendship (1934), **18,** 349

Colombia—*continued*
Spain, Extradition Treaty (1892), **28,** 324–325
U.S.A., Treaty of Peace, Amity, Navigation and Commerce (1846), **5,** 403
Venezuela, Arbitration Agreement (1916), **1,** 371–372
Venezuela, Extradition Treaty (1911), **23,** 416–417
Colombo Agreement, Allied Powers and Siam (1945), **22,** 1002, 1004
Colonial preference, most-favoured-nation clause and, **25,** 319
Colonies—
application of treaties to, **7,** 409–411
dominion, distinguished, **28,** 55
former German, status of, **6,** 64
jurisdictional immunity, **7,** 173
mandated territories, assimilation to, **11,** 52–53
mandated territories, distinguished, **7,** 45; **23,** 37
national territory, whether part of, **2,** 93
nationality of subjects, **8,** 283–284
protectorates, distinguished, **11,** 44–45
Coloured races, treatment of (U.S.A.), **4,** 331, 355–356
Coloured schools, assignment of aliens to, **4,** 331, 355–356
Combatants, unlawful, **23,** 759–762
Comity, international, **1,** 25; **3,** 302; **4,** 19–21; **5,** 6–8; **6,** 291; **7,** 65–66, 69, 70–74, 208; **9,** 7, 13, 88, 164n, 185–186, 196, 279, 290, 305, 416; **10,** 13, 19, 217, 579; **12,** 253; **13,** 65; **18,** 8–9, 14–16, 182; **19,** 306; **20,** 313–314; **21,** 37; **24,** 15–27, 226; **26,** 163, 174; **27,** 19, 21; **28,** 276; **30,** 8, 23; **33,** 4–5, 8, 10–11, 12, 13, 42, 314, 366
Act of State and, **35,** 47, 52
comity of courts, **30,** 111
consular immunity, official records, **31,** 396
diplomatic immunity and, **35,** 224–225
diplomatic privilege and, **10,** 368
extradition, principle of specialty, **31,** 365
extraterritorial effect of legislation, and, **2,** 412; **7,** 156, 161; **8,** 35; **10,** 16, 53, 140; **15,** 18; **18,** 175; **26,** 386; **30,** 115
foreign Acts of State, recognition of, **35,** 47, 52
foreign corporations, recognition of, **26,** 12, 28
foreign ships, access to ports, **31,** 140
general maritime law, **34,** 71
jurisdiction and, **19,** 158–163; **26,** 163
Comity, international—*continued*
locus standi of foreign States, **34,** 126
reciprocity and, **10,** 97; **18,** 14–16; 31, 223; **35,** 28
recognized States and Governments, limitation of application to, **2,** 40–42
sovereign immunity, **26,** 163; **31,** 248, 396
suits by foreign governments, **35,** 26
"Commando" Order, 1942...**15,** 388–389
Commerce, treaties of: *see* Commercial treaties
Commercial activities of States, jurisdictional immunity: *see under* Foreign States
Commercial attaché, immunities, **11,** 204–205
Commercial Bureau, American Republics, **18,** 441–442
Commercial domicile, **18,** 729
Commercial treaties:
[For particular treaties *see under* respective States parties]
breach by legislation, **25,** 261
"commerce and navigation", meaning of, as including "administration of justice", **23,** 306, 313, 319–322
corporations, right to sue and be sued, **23,** 483–486
equality clause, **25,** 317, 320–321
interpretation of, **1,** 350–351; **4,** 450–451; **5,** 363–364, 401–404; **23,** 306, 313, 319–322
most-favoured-nation clause: *q.v.*
national treatment clause: *q.v.*
reciprocity, **8,** 472–474; **26,** 595, 597
"Commissar" Order, 1941..**15,** 388–389
Commissario del Rè, functions, prize proceedings, **12,** 516–521
Commission of enquiry, functions, fact-finding, **35,** 485–501
Commissioner of Controlled German Revenues, **3,** 208–209
Commissions rogatoires, **6,** 90: *see also* Letters rogatory
Common interest, **24,** 129
Common Market: *see* European Economic Community
Commonwealth, **1,** 39; **7,** 30; **9,** 28–32; **15,** 37–38, 137; **17,** 37–41; **20,** 40–47
British subjects, who are, **19,** 62–68, 318
Canada, appeals to Privy Council, **8,** 71–79
citizenship, nature of, **24,** 56: *see also* nationality in, *infra*
Dominion status, **9,** 28–31
Dominions, independence of, **19,** 35–61; **30,** 113, 114

Commonwealth—*continued*
Dominions, independence of—*continued*
—legislative powers, **6**, 160; **14**, 22–28; **30**, 113, 114
—mandatories, as, **4**, 53–54; **7**, 35–36; **8**, 98–109, 110–113
—naturalization in, **1**, 203–204; **4**, 42–43
—treaty-making power, **6**, 44–46; **8**, 58–66; **26**, 107: *see also* Federal States
Eire, position of, **8**, 81–87
expulsion of subjects of other Commonwealth countries, **32**, 247–249
extradition in, **19**, 362–365; **21**, 46–47
fugitive offenders, **19**, 68, 362–365; **21**, 46–47; **33**, 297–312
—political offences, **32**, 299–306
—refusal to surrender, protest, **33**, 312
High Commissioner of Australia in London, reports, whether privileged, **11**, 213–217
Imperial and Dominion legislatures, relation between, **13**, 23–29
Imperial Conference (1926), **19**, 38, 41
—(1930), **19**, 39, 41
Imperial naturalization, **4**, 42–43
independent members, **18**, 50
India, position of, **8**, 91–92
Irish Free State, appeals to Privy Council, **8**, 81–88
—position of, **10**, 27–38
nationality in, **4**, 41–43; **8**, 66–69; **9**, 32; **19**, 38; **22**, 61–64; **24**, 56, 429–430
Protected States, **18**, 54–55
Protectorates, relation of Crown to territory and inhabitants, **3**, 40–41; **28**, 48–78
South Africa, Union of, status, **1**, 22
Statute of Westminster, 1931...**8**, 56, 57, 71, 84; **9**, 30; **10**, 28; **14**, 24–25, 27; **17**, 244; **19**, 37–49, 49–60; **20**, 40, 41; **23**, 466; **30**, 113, 114
treaties and, **20**, 40–41
visiting forces, **19**, 68
Communis opinio doctorum, source of international law, as, **17**, 163. *See also* International law, sources of
Communist Party, membership as reason for deportation, **8**, 338–339
Comoro Island, French protectorate over, **11**, 47
Companies: *see* Corporations
Comparative law, interpretation of treaties, use in, **25**, 77, 81
Compensation—
confiscation of property, for, **1**, 56–57
Compensation—*continued*
destruction of property, for, **20**, 628, 633
"effective", **30**, 133, 139–140, 179
injuries on board ship, for, **11**, 115–122, 126
equity and: *see* Equity
ex aequo et bono: *see* Equity; *Ex aequo et bono*
ex gratia: *see Ex gratia* payments
"fair": *see* Equity
interest, whether included, **30**, 220–225; *see also* Equity; *Ex gratia* payments
"just", **26**, 357
"just and adequate", **30**, 220–225
lump-sum settlement—
—individual's right under, **22**, 405–407, 418; **26**, 347–351
—interest on awards, **30**, 220–225
market value, **30**, 178–179, 192
prize proceedings, **12**, 525, 530–531, 565–567, 569–573
prompt, adequate and effective, **30**, 178–179
war damage, for, assessment of, **24**, 879
whether due to individual or to State, **4**, 258–260
Competence to determine jurisdiction. *See* Arbitration; International Court of Justice; Permanent Court of International Justice
Competition, restrictions on, E.E.C. Treaty provisions, **28**, 506–511; **31**, 427–428; **33**, 414–416
Complicity, doctrine of, State responsibility, **3**, 218–219
Composite States, **3**, 38; **9**, 28
Compromis: *see* Arbitration, international
Compulsory administration of private enterprises, expropriation, whether, **11**, 21
Compulsory old age insurance, Human Rights Convention and, **33**, 233–238
Conception Bay, **4**, 136
Concession—
British at Tientsin, **9**, 116
Italian at Tientsin, **3**, 198–199
Concession agreements: *see also* Contract, government and foreign company, between
acquired rights and, **27**, 144, 168, 205; **35**, 183–184
administrative contracts, **23**, 640–642
applicable law, **18**, 149–150; **20**, 312; **27**, 144, 168, 205; **35**, 171–176
—choice of law principles, **27**, 165–166
—custom and practice of industry, **27**, 169–170, 171–172, 188

Concession agreements—*continued*
applicable law—*continued*
—general principles of law recognized by civilized nations, **27,** 143, 162, 169
—law of State party, **27,** 167
—public international law, **27,** 172
breach, consequences of, **35,** 181–185
—damages for, **35,** 185–190
breaches of, by government, **3,** 292; **6,** 274. *See also* cancellation *and* nationalization in breach of, *infra*
cancellation of, **6,** 274–275. *See also* nationalization in breach of, *infra*
clausula rebus sic stantibus, effect of, **7,** 430; **23,** 652–658
compensation for cancelled rights, **28,** 18, 34–36; **30,** 178–179
constitutional provisions, disregard of, **2,** 177
de facto government by, responsibility for, **2,** 176–177
English law as to, **27,** 161
"exclusive" and "absolute" rights, distinction, **27,** 175
exemption of concessionaire from regulatory powers of grantor, **27,** 140–141, 159, 214, 216–219
estoppel and, **5,** 180
French law as to, **27,** 160–161, 215–216
good faith in performance, **35,** 172, 181, 183, 185
interference with, **35,** 136–192
interpretation of, **18,** 161–164; **27,** 172–174
—in favour of obligor, **27,** 197
—intention of parties, **27,** 172–173, 189, 198
—restrictions on rights in general clause, **27,** 180
—restrictive interpretation, **27,** 140, 142, 190–195
—subsequent conduct of parties, **27,** 197–202
—teleological, **27,** 189–190
—*venire contra factum proprium*, **27,** 196; **28,** 38
irrevocable rights, grant of, **27,** 168
later contract conflicting with rights under earlier, **27,** 117–229 *passim*, esp. 209–226
modification of, **7,** 424–431
Moslem law, **28,** 163–165
nationalization in breach of, **20,** 305–326; **22,** 19–45; **28,** 16–39; **30,** 178–179
nature of, **2,** 342; **20,** 308; **27,** 143, 157–165
—oil concessions, **27,** 157
occupied territory, in, **23,** 780–783, 801–809, 810–849
—duty of occupant as to, **23,** 801–805

Concession agreements—*continued*
occupied territory, in—*continued*
—nature of receipts, **23,** 806–809
—seizure of installations, **23,** 810–850
oil, ownership of, **20,** 308, 312, 315; **22,** 25–33, 43–45; **27,** 158, 170–171
oil, valuation of, **35,** 160–161
pacta sunt servanda and, **35,** 181, 186
position of buyers and "off-takers", liability to regulatory powers of grantor, **27,** 219–223
public service and exploitation, distinction, **27,** 141, 157, 160–161, 192
purchase under treaty, right of concessionaire to indemnity, **28,** 269–271
scope of concession area, continental shelf, **18,** 144–164
State legislative enactment, whether, **27,** 164, 203–204
State responsibility and: *see under* State responsibility
State succession and: *see under* State succession
tobacco, in Indonesia, nature of concessionaire's rights, **28,** 19, 21, 25
transfer of territory, subrogation on, **23,** 668
treatment of aliens during war, **5,** 264
treaty, whether, **19,** 525–526, 532, 542; **20,** 308–309
validation by subsequent conduct, **5,** 179–182
war, effect on, **5,** 482; **23,** 647–652
Conciliation, **18,** 437, 439; **22,** 843–886 *passim*; **23,** 499–508; **24,** 879–882; **25,** 313–325; **29,** 5–7, 11, 15–16, 437. *See also* names of particular Conciliation Commissions
exhaustion of local remedies rule and, **27,** 503, 554
League of Nations Council, by, **3,** 389–390
settlement of government loan dispute, **29,** 5–7
settlement of municipal loan dispute, **29,** 11, 16
Conciliation Commissions—
affidavits, use of, before, **22,** 843–858; **24,** 880–882
arbitral tribunals,—
—acting as, **18,** 437
—distinguished from, **22,** 820, 867, 872
atti di notorieta, use of before, **22,** 843–858, 858–864
Austrian State Treaty (1955), under, jurisdiction, **26,** 611
collège arbitral, as, **22,** 317–329, 500, 501
—powers of, **22,** 886

Conciliation Commissions—*continued*
decisions of—
—binding force, **18,** 437
—other tribunals, reference to, **22,** 885, 886
—previous decisions as precedents, **22,** 629–630, 633; **23,** 500, 503, 506–508; **25,** 321
—retroactive effect, **20,** 76–77
—substituted for agreement prescribed by treaty, **20,** 70–71, 430
dispute, determination of existence of, **22,** 864–867
equitable principles, observance of, **20,** 75
evidence before, **22,** 843–864; **24,** 880–882
—admissibility, **22,** 886
—affidavits, **22,** 843–858; **24,** 880–882
—*ex parte,* **22,** 313, 315–316, 875; **24,** 879; **25,** 142
—false, **22,** 857–858
—signed statement, **22,** 847–848
—sufficiency of, **22,** 843–864, 886; **24,** 880–882
—title, of, **24,** 880
ex aequo et bono award, *see Ex aequo et bono*
individual claims before, **18,** 437, 439
interest, claim of, **22,** 346–348, 409–417, 886. *See also* Interest
Italian–Swiss Permanent, procedure, **25,** 314–315
jurisdiction, power to determine, **22,** 867–870
municipal courts, concurrent jurisdiction, **18,** 436, 439; **22,** 876–882, 882–885
—contrary decision of, **22,** 886
—ouster of, **18,** 394–395
—supremacy over prior judgment of, **18,** 404–405, 439
Peace Treaty, under—
—jurisdiction of, **22,** 867–875
—*lex fori,* **25,** 107
powers and functions, **20,** 577; **22,** 846–848; **25,** 96–99
procedure—
—amendment of petition, **22,** 346–348
—amendment of typographical error, **24,** 879–880
—legal and factual elements, separation, **25,** 314–315
—power to determine, **22,** 874
—presentation of claims, **18,** 427–429
—rules of, **22,** 847–848, 850, 885
provisional conclusions, **25,** 314–315
settlement, proposed, **25,** 322–325
States as sole parties before, **18,** 437, 439; **22,** 883
Conclusiveness of certificate of ambassador, **1,** 31; **14,** 75–76; **16,** 129–137
Conclusiveness of statements of Executive, **1,** 22, 31, 57–58; **2,** 42–43, 48, 124–129, 301, 325; **4,** 362–363; **6,** 103–105, 305; **7,** 64–65, 74, 421–423, 432; **10,** 20–22, 178–181, 193–196, 202–204, 206–207, 224–226; **11,** 15–16, 157–158, 205; **12,** 3–4, 277–278; **13,** 312–321; **14,** 75–76, 155; **17,** 84–89; **18,** 23; **19,** 7–11, 72–85; **22,** 251–252; **23,** 6, 121; **24,** 203, 226–227; **26,** 105; **28,** 11–13, 50, 68, 165–168, 358, 388–389, **32,** 81–82. *See also* Recognition of governments; Recognition of States
acquisition of title, **9,** 14–15
act of foreign consul, whether in course of duty, **31,** 397–399
boundary, location of, **32,** 81–82
communications with occupied State, **18,** 492
consuls, status of, **11,** 211–212; **20,** 391–393
continuance of foreign State, **28,** 389
diplomatic envoys—
—functions of, **20,** 378, 381
—immunities of, **19,** 390–391; **20,** 378, 381; **22,** 12, 549; **35,** 220
—status of, **2,** 48, 49, 301; **4,** 362–364; **18,** 58–59; **19,** 390–391; **20,** 378, 381; **21,** 120; **23,** 437–445
enemy alien, status of, as to, **15,** 259–260
enemy occupation of territory, **15,** 7, 444
extent of jurisdiction and territory, as to, **16,** 12–14; **27,** 54–55; **28,** 50, 68; **30,** 94–100
foreign government, status of, **9,** 36–38
foreign jurisdiction of Crown, **27,** 54–55; **28,** 50, 68; **30,** 94–100
foreign sovereign, status of, **19,** 186–187, 188, 212–219
foreign State, immunity of, **10,** 178–181, 193–196, 202–204, 206–207, 217–221, 224–226; **20,** 173–176, 177; **22,** 220–224; **24,** 202–203; **28,** 165–168; **31,** 348; **32,** 133–135, 136, 137, 138–140; **33,** 185–189
—agent of, **11,** 76–78; **12,** 80–89; **24,** 226–227
—ships, **9,** 278; **10,** 217–221; **11,** 148; **12,** 108–111, 144–149
—status of, **15,** 138–140; **18,** 211–214
form of certificate, **19,** 72–85
international organization, status of, **21,** 16, 279–280
neutrality of foreign State, **22,** 1012–1014; **26,** 399
non-recognition of annexation, **12,** 39–44; **18,** 63

Conclusiveness of statements of Executive—*continued*
non-recognition of foreign nationalization decrees, **12,** 32–39; **15,** 46–47; **18,** 63
reciprocal grant of diplomatic immunity, **22,** 12, 546, 549
reciprocity in extradition, **28,** 11–12
recognition of annexation, **12,** 26–28
recognition of foreign government, **9,** 78; **15,** 47, 139–140, 176–204; **16,** 46–60; **17,** 117–178; **19,** 72–85; **22,** 99; **23,** 71–78; **26,** 72–75
recognition of foreign States, **1,** 43–44
representative to U.N., immunity of, **24,** 203
right to diplomatic privileges, **34,** 161, 163
sovereignty over foreign territory, **15,** 29–31
succession of States, treaties, **17,** 84–87
supplementation by other evidence, **22,** 12, 99
territory, status of, **15,** 520–521, 525; **26,** 104
title to property, **9,** 14–15
treaties, existence of, **21,** 278
treaties, interpretation of, as to, **1,** 332–333, 348–349; **5,** 347; **6,** 300; **20,** 437–438; **21,** 278–285; **22,** 606–607, 623–626, 649; **24,** 600–601: *see also* Treaties, interpretation of, exchange of notes, by reference to
war, state of, **1,** 8, 529–533; **12,** 286, 417; **15,** 506; **17,** 345–349; **20,** 156, 597–598; **21,** 263; **22,** 100
Conclusiveness of statements of Sovereign-in-exile, **12,** 420–424
Concordats: *see also* Holy See
Colombia and Holy See (1887), **2,** 318
Germany and Holy See, **7,** 399–400; **17,** 116–117; **24,** 592–594
interpretation, **5,** 335
municipal law, relation to, **2,** 318–319
Poland and Holy See (1925), **7,** 14–15, 400–401
treaties, assimilation to, **7,** 399–401
Condominium—
Andorra, **7,** 56–57
boundary rivers, over, **6,** 50–51
Danzig, **7,** 59, 61–62
Lake Constance, **2,** 102–103; **7,** 140–141
Memel Territory, **7,** 63
New Hebrides, **9,** 50; **11,** 55
Rhineland, **7,** 58
Saar Territory, **7,** 59–61, 62
Sudan, **4,** 57
Confiscation: *see also* Acquired rights; Confiscatory legislation; Expropriation; Nationalization

Confiscation—*continued*
annulment of claims against previous government, **26,** 276–277
Argentina, Constitution, **9,** 380–382
Austria, property of Jews, **9,** 19, 87–88
compensation, question of, **1,** 56–57, 238–239; **24,** 8–9
compensation, title to, property owned by nominee, **26,** 279–280
concession agreements: *see* Concession agreements, nationalization in breach of
consuls, property of, in time of war, **26,** 725–727
Cuban measures, **35,** 4, 8–10, 16, 20
currency, of, **30,** 144–147
debts, effect on, **11,** 20, 21, 25
enemy property, **1,** 409–410; **15,** 13–17, 24–27; **20,** 602–609; **24,** 893–896; **26,** 656; **33,** 447, 448–449
—international law, compatibility with, **17,** 164; **22,** 914–915; **24,** 895
—neutral States, effect in, **17,** 164–166
expropriation, distinguished, **4,** 150; **26,** 41, 46
foreign State, property of, **21,** 101–103
Germany, National-Socialist measures, **9,** 19–21, 71, 84–87; **12,** 4–7; **16,** 14–15
inheritance, right to, abolition of, **11,** 110–111
inheritance taxes, **9,** 380–382
Jewish property, Italian war measures, **29,** 30–31, 50, 53
liquidation, distinguished, **4,** 150; **18,** 653–654; **23,** 693
moment of "loss", **26,** 30, 33–38
nationalization, when confiscatory, **28,** 14–15, 25, 34–36
—title of confiscating State, **28,** 20, 47
nationals' property, applicability of international law, **30,** 265, 266
national's property, of, review by foreign court, **32,** 10–12
requisitioning: *q.v.*
sequestration by belligerent occupant, distinguished, **18,** 642–659
Confiscatory legislation—
assets in the United States, liquidation of Dutch, **9,** 150; **10,** 10–23; **15,** 17–18
compulsory administration, **15,** 23–24
confiscation before law operative, **24,** 658
conservatory decrees, distinguished, **10,** 14–15
corporations, dissolution of: *q.v.*
currency legislation, as, **22,** 485–489

Confiscatory legislation—*continued*
discrimination in, **3,** 231–232; **11,** 24; **12,** 230; **16,** 25–27
enforcement abroad, **7,** 158–160; **8,** 198–200; **9,** 151; **15,** 24–27; **18,** 175, 558–570; **21,** 265–272; **22,** 18; **26,** 20, 25
—recognition, distinguished, **12,** 6–7
extraterritorial effect, **7,** 153–155, 157; **8,** 184–187, 189–207; **9,** 19–20, 24–25, 141–153, 181–183, 228–233; **10,** 10–23, 131–154; **11,** 108–111; **15,** 17–18, 23–24, 195–198, 200; **16,** 19–25, 84–85; **17,** 28–31, 163–166; **18,** 24–29, 37–38, 174–183, 197–205, 563; **19,** 11–15, 302–308; **20,** 31–39; **21,** 21–23, 30–39; **22,** 13–16; **23,** 7–15, 19–25; **24,** 29, 32–38, 41, 43–48, 438; **26,** 25, 40–48, 706; **28,** 14–16, 24, 26–31, 40, 45; **32,** 9–10, 12–17, 19–22, 26–29, 31. *See also* recognition, *infra*
jurisdictional immunity and, **7,** 155–158, 184–186; **8,** 195; **9,** 177–180, 226–228, 243–245; **17,** 69–70; **21,** 265, 267, 269–270; **22,** 18; **26,** 229
levy on profits under currency reform, **28,** 544–548
Mexico, **1,** 249–250; **9,** 25, 90; **11,** 16–19; **20,** 326
recognition of, **1,** 56–57; **2,** 15–16; **3,** 25–26; **5,** 22–23; **6,** 22–28; **7,** 22–28, 56–67, 71; **8,** 34–39; **9,** 19–21, 24–25, 87–88, 142–151; **11,** 24–25; **12,** 4–7; **15,** 13–18, 23–27; **16,** 14–15, 25–27; **19,** 11–15; **20,** 34–39, 305–328; **22,** 17–45, 480–490; **23,** 7–15, 21–26; **24,** 28–38, 42–45, 228–229, 435–439; **26,** 29–38, 40–55; **28,** 14, 27–31, 40–42, 45, 47; **30,** 5, 10, 17, 28–54; **32,** 9–10, 12–17, 19–22, 20–29, 31; **34,** 12–21
—Austrian law, **1,** 56–57; **18,** 201–205; **20,** 38–39; **24,** 41; **26,** 40–41; **28,** 14–16
—Belgian law, **9,** 25
—Canadian law, **15,** 176–204
—enforcement, distinguished, **12,** 6–7
—English law, **20,** 316–328; **22,** 480–490; **30,** 5, 10, 17
—French law, **3,** 25–26; **9,** 24–25; **11,** 24–25; **16,** 14–15; **21,** 21–23; **22,** 13–14; **23,** 19–21; **24,** 228–229
—German law, **5,** 22–23; **15,** 24–27; **19,** 12–15; **22,** 17–19; **24,** 28–38; **28,** 16–39; **32,** 12–37
—Italian law, **2,** 15–16; **22,** 19–45; **28,** 39–47;
—Japanese law, **20,** 305–316
—Netherlands law, **9,** 25; **30,** 28–32
—Norwegian law, **30,** 33–54

Confiscatory legislation—*continued*
recognition of—*continued*
—Swedish law, **18,** 37–38; **21,** 30–35, 265–272
—Swiss law, **15,** 23–24; **16,** 84–85; **20,** 34–38; **23,** 24–25
—U.S. law, **7,** 22–28, 65–67, 70–75; **8,** 34–39; **9,** 19–21, 87–88, 142–150; **10,** 48–68; **12,** 4–7; **14,** 11–15; **15,** 13–17, 20–23; **19,** 11–12; **20,** 24–26; **23,** 10–15; **26,** 29–38; **32,** 8–12
recognition of governments, effect, **1,** 56–57; **3,** 24–26; **7,** 65–67, 73–75; **10,** 18–23, 60–66, 138–140; **11,** 65–66; **17,** 65–72; **18,** 61–64, 565–566, 569–570
recognition of States, effect, **9,** 88; **18,** 61–64; **23,** 706–708
ships, **8,** 189–191, 195–198, 200–204; **9,** 152–153, 176–183; **10,** 131–147, 152–154; **15,** 176–204; **23,** 700–708
Soviet Russia, liquidation of companies, **7,** 151–153; **8,** 184–187, 191–193, 204–205, 207; **9,** 141–150; **19,** 302–311; **22,** 13–16
—shipping enterprises, **9,** 243
Spanish Civil War, **8,** 189–193, 195–204; **9,** 24–25, 150–153, 225–233
town and country planning, for, **24,** 8
Congo, legal status of,
—Belgium, Treaty of Cession with (1907) and, **7,** 29–30, 173, 409–410; **22,** 226–227; **23,** 191–192
Congo, U.N. Operation in, **34,** 367–370
authorization by S.C., **34,** 304
enforcement action, whether, **34,** 295, 305, 372–373
financing, **34,** 306–307, 374–378, 389
G.A., support of, **34,** 305, 370
ultra vires character, **34,** 368
" Connected offence ", extradition proceedings in, **7,** 364
Conquest—
acquisition of territory by, **6,** 99–100; **12,** 54; **15,** 60–61, 63; **19,** 144; **31,** 89
collective naturalization after, **5,** 235–237; **6,** 254–255; **10,** 279–281
de facto recognition of, **8,** 119–123; **9,** 84–93
de jure recognition of, **8,** 119–123; **9,** 84–93
grant of territory after, **22,** 127–130
nature of, **6,** 99–100; **22,** 133
private rights, effect on, **16,** 62–63
See also under Act of State; Annexation; State succession
renunciation of rights of, **6,** 99–100; **16,** 62–63
State succession and, **31,** 89
Conseil d'État—
acte de gouvernement and, **5,** 30–31

Conseil d'État—*continued*
mandated territories, jurisdiction in regard to, **5,** 31n
protectorates, jurisdiction in regard to, **5,** 28–29
" Consequence of war ", meaning, **2,** 200–201
Conservatoir derden-arrest, **1,** 22, 130
Conservatory measures, **2,** 375–376
confiscation, distinguished, **10,** 14–15
Consideration, equivalence of, as element in treaty interpretation, **6,** 28
Conspiracy, crime in international law, **15,** 373
Conspiracy, territoriality of criminal law, **7,** 192–193, 197–199
Constance, Lake, **2,** 102; **4,** 128; **7,** 140–141
Constantinople—
Convention of, on Suez Canal (1888), **2,** 101; **17,** 441, 444–447; **24,** 993; **28,** 180–181, 653; **31,** 509–518
Inter-Allied police at, **1,** 277
occupation by British forces, **4,** 34–35
Peace Treaty of (Bulgaria/Turkey, 1913), **7,** 91–99
Peace Treaty of (Serbia/Turkey, 1914), **6,** 389, 391; **7,** 98
Constitutions of States—
concessions granted in disregard of, **2,** 177
international law, relation to, **4,** 9–13; **7,** 9–10; **22,** 914
interpretation of, by P.C.I.J., **8,** 490–491
treaty-making power, limitations on: *see* Treaty-making power
Consular agent: *see also* Consuls
immunity, extent of, **7,** 391
Turkey, position in, **4,** 373–374
Consular archives, immunity of, **1,** 305; **6,** 337; **10,** 389–391; **17,** 141
Consular Convention (U.K. and U.S.A. 1951), effect, **22,** 553–555
Consular courts—
competence, **7,** 199; **22,** 263–264
Danish, in Egypt, **8,** 261–262
Dutch, in Egypt, **1,** 161–162
Greek, in Egypt, **20,** 195–197
Greek, in Ethiopia, **7,** 199–200
Italian, in Tientsin, **3,** 198–199
purporting to act under authority of extinct government, **4,** 191–192
Russian—
—in Constantinople, **4,** 191–192
—in Egypt, **2,** 51–52
United States—
—for China, **10,** 265–266
—in Egypt, **10,** 263–265
Consular functions: *see* Consuls, functions of
Consular jurisdiction, **1,** 161–162; **2,** 150–153; **3,** 30–31, 191–199; **4,** 189–193; **5,** 131–133; **6,** 34; **7,** 199–200; **8,** 232–233, 258–262; **10,** 263–266; **19,** 255–302; **20,** 195–197; **21,** 136–140. *See also* Capitulations
Act of Algeciras (1906), provisions as to, **19,** 274–275, 288, 290, 302
custom and usage, based on, **19,** 275–276, 278, 292–294
extension by agreement, **26,** 247
local law, application of, **19,** 277–278
Morocco–U.S.A., Treaty of 1836, under, **19,** 264
most-favoured-nation clause and, **7,** 199; **19,** 261, 263, 265–266
principle underlying, **19,** 267
right of, derived by third Party to treaty, **19,** 288
ships, disputes in, over, **3,** 327–328; **8,** 208–212, 470–471; **11,** 113–114, 115–116, 120, 122; **15,** 110–114; **16,** 100–102; **34,** 75–76
—local courts and, **8,** 210–212; **9,** 163
—residuary jurisdiction of littoral State, **11,** 120–122
Consular premises—
asylum, **10,** 389–390; **20,** 400–405
execution in, **20,** 401–405
extraterritoriality, **1,** 304–305; **2,** 150–151; **8,** 233; **12,** 68–73; **20,** 181–182
immunities, **1,** 305–306; **2,** 307–308; **6,** 332, 338; **15,** 319–320; **17,** 153–155; **20,** 400–405; **22,** 556–559
—taxation, from, **21,** 432–443
legation buildings, distinguished, **7,** 391
marriages celebrated in, **12,** 252–253
offence committed on, **12,** 68–73
status of, **24,** 532
" Consular Secretary ", position of, **4,** 362–363
Consular treaties—
interpretation, **4,** 384–387, 449
most-favoured-nation clause, **32,** 335, 337
Consulate: *see* Consular premises
Consulate-General, Chancellor of, immunities, **11,** 211–212
Consulate-General, status of, **22,** 399–400; **24,** 532–533
Consuls, **1,** 298–310; **2,** 303–308; **3,** 327–329; **4,** 373–390; **5,** 318–325; **6,** 335–338; **7,** 388–396; **9,** 440–443; **10,** 377–393; **20,** 385–405; **21,** 250–255; **22,** 551–559; **23,** 433–451; **24,** 532–535; **26,** 547–551; **28,** 362; **30,** 161–165; **31,** 395–399; **32,** 335–337
acta jure gestionis and *acta jure imperii: see* immunities, acts of a private law character, *and* immunities official acts, *infra*

Consuls—*continued*
acting for several States, **10,** 389–391
administration of estates by, **1,** 302–303; **4,** 449; **9,** 486; **13,** 174–175; **21,** 203–209; **26,** 76, 547; **30,** 161–165; **31,** 395; **32,** 335–337
affidavits, taking of, **21,** 250–253
agent of sending government, whether, **35,** 232–234
appointment of, **7,** 393; **10,** 377–379; **12,** 243–244; **20,** 391–397
arrested national, right to communicate with, **3,** 294–295
authority to represent State, civil proceedings, **32,** 125
cautio judicatum solvi and, **24,** 532
certificates of, evidential value—
—nationality, in matters of, **5,** 223, 226; **6,** 182, 247–249, 250; **8,** 284, 288
—notary public, certificate of, compared with, **6,** 424–425
—succession, in matters of, **3,** 30–31
—validity of marriage, as to, **16,** 182–184
—will, as to, **18,** 359
commissioner of court of sending State, as, **20,** 262
competence, to claim jurisdictional immunity of vessels, **1,** 146
—to request extradition, **8,** 368–370
confiscation of property of, in war, **26,** 725–727
contracts in official capacity, **4,** 381
criminal investigations by, **7,** 388–389
department of foreign State, as, **20,** 399–402
diplomatic envoys, acting as, **5,** 324–325; **6,** 327–328; **19,** 400–412; **20,** 389–390
diplomatic envoys, distinguished, **1,** 307; **5,** 319–320, 322; **7,** 392; **24,** 533
diplomatic post, appointment to, **23,** 436–445
Egypt, position in, **2,** 304–305; **7,** 393–394; **10,** 263–264
employee at consulate, administrative measures against, **4,** 381–382
—taxation, **4,** 382–383
enemy, sequestration of property of, **1,** 307
exequatur—
—absence of issue, **12,** 243–244; **15,** 126–127; **20,** 385
—appointment and, **34,** 9, 173–174
—defined, **34,** 9
—denial, **23,** 446–448
—nature, **10,** 377–379
—proof, **15,** 126; **22,** 551–552
—revocation, **1,** 298–299
extraterritoriality of, **8,** 232–233

Consuls—*continued*
false statement to, to obtain visa, **32,** 112–117
fees, contingent, for legal services, **30,** 161–165
functions of, **1,** 300–304; **2,** 303–304; **3,** 327; **5,** 318–321; **6,** 177–179, 335; **7,** 177–178, 388–389; **8,** 419; **9,** 485–489; **10,** 380–386; **12,** 245–261; **13,** 171–175; **15,** 311–312, 314–317; **18,** 358–359; **19,** 393–400; **20,** 304, 386–390; **22,** 551–552; **26,** 76, 529, 547–548; **31,** 397–399; **32,** 335–337
—deserting sailors, **11,** 14; **26,** 529; **28,** 360; **31,** 405–408
—diplomatic character, combined with, **5,** 324–325; **6,** 327–328; **19,** 400–412; **20,** 389–390
—receipt of estate for incompetent national, **32,** 335–337
—register of co-nationals, **30,** 353–354
garnishee, as, **10,** 383–391
honorary, **23,** 448–450
immunities, **1,** 304–310; **2,** 305–308; **3,** 328–329; **4,** 378–390; **5,** 321–325; **6,** 332, 336–338; **7,** 390–396; **8,** 397–405; **10,** 386–393; **11,** 205, 207–212; **12,** 261–263; **15,** 317–320; **16,** 289, 300–306; **17,** 141–142; **18,** 359–360; **20,** 391–405; **21,** 254–255; **22,** 553–559; **23,** 436–451; **24,** 527, 528, 532–535; **26,** 548–551; **31,** 395–399
—acts of private law character, **1,** 307–308; **5,** 321–322; **6,** 338; **7,** 390; **8,** 403; **12,** 262; **15,** 318–319; **16,** 303; **17,** 141; **23,** 450–451
—archives, **31,** 395–397
—arrest, from, **4,** 387–388
—Chancellor of Consulate-General, **11,** 211–212
—civil jurisdiction, from, **2,** 307; **3,** 328–329; **4,** 381–382, 383–387, 389–390; **5,** 321–322, 324; **6,** 332, 336–337, 338; **7,** 393–394, 395–396; **8,** 397–403; **10,** 386–389; **11,** 211–212; **15,** 318–319; **16,** 301–306; **18,** 359–360; **19,** 400–412; **20,** 391–405; **21,** 254–255; **23,** 436–446, 448–451; **24,** 527–528, 532–535; **33,** 373–374
—criminal jurisdiction, from, **1,** 307–308; **4,** 387–388, 389–390; **5,** 322, 324–325; **7,** 391–392, 394; **11,** 205; **12,** 262–263; **15,** 318; **23,** 446–448
—divorce and alimony proceedings, **4,** 378–380; **5,** 322; **11,** 211–212
—domestic servants, **24,** 529–531
—evidence, from giving, **19,** 400–412
—execution, from, **17,** 140–143; **24,** 533–534

Consuls—*continued*
immunities—*continued*
—families, **7,** 393–394; **24,** 529
—*franchise de l'hôtel,* **20,** 404
—government property in hands of, **9,** 440–441
—in absence of treaty, **31,** 395–397
—most-favoured-nation clause and, **8,** 397–398
—municipal law, based on, **33,** 371–372
—nationals of receiving State, **11,** 207–211
—official acts, **6,** 336–338; **9,** 443; **16,** 301, 302, 303; **22,** 555–556; **23,** 445–446; **26,** 549–550; **31,** 397–399
—official and private acts, distinction, **6,** 338; **7,** 394–395; **8,** 402–403; **9,** 442–443; **17,** 141
—"personal immunity", **4,** 383–384
—personal liabilities, **5,** 321–322
—property administered by, **9,** 440–441
—property taxation, **21,** 432–443
—rent, action for, **26,** 190–192
—service of process, from, **12,** 261–262
—submission to jurisdiction, **21,** 254–255
—subpoena, **12,** 261–262; **22,** 553–555
—"suggestion" of immunity, **11,** 147–148
—taxation, from, **2,** 305–307; **4,** 382–385; **5,** 322–324, 325; **11,** 207–211; **21,** 432–443
—traffic laws **22,** 555–556; **26,** 534–536, 549–550
—waiver, **1,** 306; **17,** 142; **21,** 255; **26,** 548–549
—war, in, **21,** 432–443
—wife, **7,** 393–394
informe of, evidential value of, **2,** 303
jurisdiction, rights of: *see* Consular jurisdiction
legacy, right to receive, **20,** 386–389
mandated territory, in, **7,** 395–396
Mandatory Power, of, **21,** 250–254
minor nationals, representation of interests, **8,** 418–419
"missi", distinguished from others, **7,** 393; **8,** 400–401
most-favoured-nation clause and, **7,** 199; **8,** 397–398; **19,** 261, 263, 265–266
nationality, **4,** 373
nature of rights exercised by, **4,** 376–377
"non missi", **7,** 393; **8,** 400–401
notarial acts, performance of, **10,** 383–385
notification to foreign ministry, need for, **23,** 446–448

Consuls—*continued*
oath, administration by, **21,** 251
occupied territory, right in, **12,** 254–260, 424–427
powers, government not in control of territory, effect on, **19,** 69–71
privileges—
—coat of arms, **22,** 557–559
—flagpole, **22,** 557–559
—waiver of, **1,** 306
prize proceedings, right in, **12,** 516–521
process, acceptance of service on behalf of Government, **23,** 433–435
professional and non-professional, distinction, **5,** 320; **7,** 393
protected persons, as, **4,** 373–374
protection of, **4,** 374–376; **5,** 318–319
recognition by executive department, need for, **11,** 211–212; **20,** 381, 391–393
recognition of, and annexation, **12,** 46, 48, 191
representation of national, right of, **6,** 335; **8,** 419; **10,** 380–383, 391–392; **12,** 245–251, 253–260, 424–427; **13,** 174–175; **15,** 314–317; **19,** 395–398; **22,** 551–552; **26,** 76, 547; **30,** 161–165; **32,** 335–337; **35,** 51–52, 55–57
—whether independent of treaty, **26,** 547; **32,** 335–337
representatives of their States, how far, **1,** 301–302
responsibility for acts of, **6,** 207
revocation of consular status, **34,** 174
rights, basis of, **22,** 552
seizure of property of, in war, **26,** 725–727
service of summons upon, **32,** 125–126
service of writ by, **18,** 358–359
special protection of, **4,** 374–376; **5,** 318–319
State succession and, **19,** 132–133
statement of Executive as to, **20,** 391–392
suspension of mission, **10,** 380–383
termination of mission, **1,** 298–299; **4,** 388–389; **10,** 380
will, certification of, by, **18,** 359
writ, service by, **18,** 358–359
Contiguity, principle of, **4,** 111–112
Contiguous zone, **1,** 111–113; **2,** 114–115; **3,** 151–169; **4,** 196–197; **5,** 137–141; **6,** 157–159; **7,** 163–164; **8,** 212–218; **9,** 127–128; **13,** 57; **15,** 123; **28,** 170–175; **31,** 157
Continental shelf, **17,** 126–133; **18,** 144–164; **23,** 128–129
air accident above, jurisdiction, **32,** 119–122
doctrine of, **18,** 152–158

Continental shelf—*continued*
federal State, jurisdiction and control, U.S.A., **31**, 141–205 *passim*
high seas covering, **22**, 278–282
jurisdiction and control, **22**, 209; **31**, 144, 158; **32**, 119–122
limit of, **18**, 154–155
natural resources, federal State, claim by, **31**, 141
part of State territory, **18**, 161–164; **30**, 531
proclamations, **18**, 152–154; **20**, 535–537
State territory, as part of, **18**, 161–164; **30**, 531
subsoil, **18**, 156–157, 161–164
Continuity of laws, on State succession: *see under* State succession
Continuity of States, **1**, 30–35; **2**, 16–17; **3**, 33–38; **4**, 37–38; **5**, 24–25; **6**, 40–43, 56, 140–141; **8**, 40; **9**, 27, 89; **10**, 25–27; **16**, 36–37; **17**, 34–35; **18**, 40–49; **21**, 42–45, 55–63, 66–75; **22**, 58–59; **24**, 52–53; **30**, 54–67
German *Reich* and Federal Republic, **32**, 157
Germany after 1945...**22**, 943–944
occupation, despite, **12**, 451–457
revolution, effect, **27**, 22–29
Continuous voyage, doctrine of, **12**, 372–373, 562–564, 572; **13**, 416; **16**, 591; **18**, 724: *see also* Contraband; Enemy destination
Contra bonos mores, agreement void as, **15**, 627
Contra proferentum, interpretation of treaties, in, **6**, 380; **18**, 150, 429
—interpretation of concessions, in, **27**, 196; **28**, 38
Contraband, **1**, 491; **9**, 566; **16**, 577, 578, 601; **17**, 440–449; **18**, 724; **24**, 992–994. *See also* Prize
absolute, **9**, 585; **11**, 305–306; **12**, 286–288, 564–573
burden of proof, **16**, 583, 586
capture *in delicto*, **12**, 542
carriage during armistice, **1**, 435–436
—international law, whether prohibited by, **2**, 455
cheques, **12**, 473, **16**, 594–595
condemnation for carriage of, **10**, 636–637; **12**, 539–542; **16**, 592, 599
—in absence of claim by owners, **9**, 587
—quantitative test, **12**, 572, 573
conditional, **9**, 586; **11**, 306; **12**, 365–373, 543–554, 570–573
continuous voyage, doctrine of: *q.v.*
currency notes, **16**, 583–587, 594–595
enemy destination, **11**, 306–307; **12**, 286–288, 365–373, 543–564, 570–572, 573; **13**, 414–421, 425–432; **18**, 724

Contraband—*continued*
—presumption of, **12**, 287–288, 563 564, 569–570
fodder, **16**, 598–599
food, **16**, 570, 577, 591–594, 595–59
hostile destination: *see* enem destination, *supra*
infection, doctrine of, **16**, 587
knowledge of owner, **16**, 592–593, 59
nature of, **12**, 480, 491–492, 501–50
negotiable instruments, **16**, 594–59
" one year " rule, **9**, 587–591
relief parcels of clothing, **16**, 589–59
seizure *in transitu*, **16**, 597–598
ship at sea on outbreak of hostilities **16**, 597
ship in port for stress of weather, **16** 560, 598–599
" six months " rule, **9**, 565, 578, 587–591
stoppage *in transitu*, **11**, 306
trans-shipment of cargo, **16**, 587–58
U.K. Proclamation, 1939...**9**, 566 585; **19**, 635
women's clothing, **16**, 590–591
" Contracting party ", meaning, **22**, 570–571
" Contracting Powers ", meaning, **4**, 43
Contracts: *see also* Bonds, government; Concession agreements *and* State loans
alien and national of State taking discriminatory measures, between, **30**, 375–376
aliens, with, effect of currency laws on, **6**, 286–287
default on, Johnson Act, 1934 (U.S.A.), **8**, 270
enforceability—
—I.M.F. Articles of Agreement, **16**, 29, 34–35; **22**, 715–732; **23**, 581–584; **28**, 539–543; **30**, 423–425; **32**, 371–376
express—
—Anglo-American law, **25**, 85
—French law, **25**, 84–85
—German law, **25**, 84–85
—Swiss law, **25**, 84–85
foreign legislation, effect on, **7**, 65–75; **9**, 22–25; **12**, 4–7; **16**, 21–22, 23–25; **19**, 11–12, 16–18; **20**, 34–38; **22**, 480–490; **26**, 6, 9–29; **30**, 4–24, 25–28
" Friedensschluss ", meaning of, **5**, 492
frustration, State responsibility, **30**, 141–143
government and foreign company, between: *see also* Concession agreements
—administrative contracts, **23**, 640–642
—*clausula rebus sic stantibus*, **23**, 652–658

Contracts—*continued*
government and foreign company, between—*continued*
—*force majeure* and, **23,** 649–652, 657
—interdependent contracts, **23,** 642–647
—loan agreements, **23,** 642–646
—proper law of, **18,** 149–150
—public interest, affecting, **8,** 26–29
—supply agreements, **23,** 642–646
—war, suspension during, **23,** 647–652
government and individual, between,
—interpretation, **18,** 545–546: *see also under* Concession agreements
—U.S. law, **32,** 129
illegality, public policy, **4,** 19–21; **6,** 31–32
Peace Treaty with Italy, 1947, invalidation by, **18,** 403–406
pre-war debts, interest on, **3,** 443
proper law, **18,** 149–150; **26,** 56–57; **30,** 6, 20
quasi-contracts, **2,** 165–166; **5,** 500
requisitions, assimilation to contracts, **5,** 503
revolutionary government, with, liability of successor government, **3,** 232–234; **30,** 168–171
State loans: *q.v.*
State succession, in regard to: *see under* State succession
treaties, relation to prior private agreements, **9,** 122
U.S.A., Neutrality Act, 1939, violation of, **9,** 38, 42–43
validity—
—connected with hostile expedition, **6,** 31–32
—object hostile to successor State, **5,** 52–54
war, effect of outbreak on, **1,** 390–400; **2,** 410–413; **3,** 440–445; **4,** 538–540; **5,** 480–483; **7,** 501; **10,** 437–442; **11,** 243–247; **12,** 308–327; **14,** 177–180; **15,** 441–443, 512–513; **16,** 171–175; **18,** 521–528; **19,** 557, 559–570; **21,** 443–460, 464–471; **22,** 480–481, 488–489, 901–908; **23,** 787–789; **27,** 629–637; **31,** 490–495
—Anglo-American and Continental doctrines, **1,** 391
—executed and executory contracts, **1,** 369–399; **3,** 444–445; **11,** 246–247; **12,** 322–327; **27,** 629–630
—frustration, **1,** 395; **12,** 509–510
— —*force majeure* clause, **27,** 631–632, 635; **29,** 352–354
—liquidated debt, **12,** 308–322
—partnerships, **1,** 399, 400; **3,** 441–443; **11,** 246; **15,** 443–447
—passing of property, **12,** 367

Contracts—*continued*
war, effect of outbreak on—*continued*
—supervening illegality, **27,** 631–637
Contractual obligations of governments, responsibility for, **3,** 703–704; **4,** 203, 205–208. *See also under* State responsibility
Contractual rights—
property, whether, **26,** 307
seizure by occupant, **31,** 503–509
Control, theory of: *see* Corporations, nationality of
Control of revenue, international, **3,** 208–209
Conventions, international: *see* Treaties
" Converted merchantman ", meaning, **3,** 221–222; **5,** 511–512; **13,** 404; **14,** 88–89
Convoy, vessels under, status of, **2,** 408; **4,** 568
Co-operative society, dissolution, confiscation of assets, **32,** 19–26
Copyright—
enemy aliens and, **15,** 439–441; **18,** 530
enemy property as, **18,** 24–36
international infringement, **18,** 47–49
protection of, **7,** 401–403
Copyright Convention (Berne, 1908, 1952), **5,** 226; **7,** 403; **8,** 9–10; **15,** 439–441; **18,** 47–48; **23,** 263; **30,** 395–398
Corfu Channel incident (1945), **20,** 459–460
Corporations—
acquisition of territorial title by, **4,** 108–110
agreements with foreign governments and States: *see* Concession agreements *and* Contracts, government and foreign company, between
amalgamation by statute, recognition abroad, **26,** 12
branches, separate personality, **31,** 220
compulsory administration of, **16,** 14–15
confiscation of shares, effect, **32,** 12–19, 26–33
—domicile, situs of, **32,** 24–26
—representation in foreign proceedings, **32,** 23–24, 27
—" severed company " theory, **32,** 12–17, 19, 22–23, 25, 30, 33, 35–36
diplomatic protection, corporation of foreign nationality, **2,** 190
— national ownership of capital, **30,** 167
disposition of assets, law governing, **33,** 31
dissolution of: *see under* Corporations, foreign

Corporations—*continued*
domicile, **12,** 505; **32,** 24–26
enemy: *see also* enemy character, *infra*
—discrimination against, **21,** 141–146
—*locus standi,* **9,** 538 n., 559–561; **15,** 109, 452–454
—property of, to whom " belonging ", **18,** 185–188
—right to sue after hostilities, **20,** 622–627
—shareholders, non-enemy, protection of interests of, **11,** 258; **18,** 516–520, 529; **24,** 907–910, 911–916
enemy character, **1,** 229–230, 424–426; **3,** 463–467; **9,** 557–561; **10,** 535–558; **11,** 258–260; **12,** 365–383; **13,** 244–246; **15,** 452–454, 466–467; **16,** 389–390; **17,** 402; **18,** 530, 642, 650; **19,** 592–596; **20,** 615–617; **21,** 464–471; **22,** 923–924; **24,** 907–910, 911–915; **33,** 444–450
enemy stockholder's interest in non-enemy corporation, **3,** 447–448
foreign: *see* Corporations, foreign
friendly, in enemy-occupied territory, **12,** 332–333
liquidation of—
—belligerent occupant, by, **18,** 642–645
—foreign: *see under* Corporations, foreign
local undertakings, **7,** 161–162
nationality of, **1,** 227–230, 245–246; 394; **2,** 259–262; **3,** 282–286, 463–467; **4,** 323–328, 332; **5,** 248–253, 384–385; **6,** 265–268, 280; **7,** 298; **8,** 193, 314–315; **9,** 363; **12,** 387–388; **16,** 229–230; **17,** 228; **18,** 280–281; **19,** 338–339; **20,** 263–264; **24,** 276; **35,** 15: *see also* enemy character of
—air transport agreement, **31,** 416–244
—control test, **1,** 227, 230, 245, 394, 424–426; **2,** 260–261; **3,** 282, 463–464; **4,** 323–325; **5,** 248–253, 384–385; **8,** 314–315; **16,** 229–230; **17,** 228; **26,** 224, 229, 238–239
—control test, distinguished from *siège social* test, **1,** 228 n
—" establishment " test, **5,** 250–251
—incorporation, test of, **6,** 265, 266; **7,** 298
—Italian Peace Treaty, **30,** 511–514
—seat, determined by, **17,** 228; **18,** 280–281; **19,** 338–339
—*siège social,* **1,** 227–228, 345; **2,** 261; **3,** 282–286, 466, 467; **4,** 332; **5,** 248–250, 252, 385; **6,** 266, 268; **7,** 298; **8,** 314–315; **20,** 263–264
nationalization, effect on, **3,** 57–59; **4,** 66–68, 71–72, 141–144; **7,** 65–

Corporations—*continued*
nationalization, effect on—*continued*
75, 82, 152–153; **9,** 141–148; **11** 21–23, 107–108; **16,** 19–20; **17** 65–72; **18,** 201–203; **19,** 302–311 **21,** 38–39; **22,** 13–14; **23,** 7–10 19–21, 24–26; **24,** 40–48; **26,** 45 129–131; **28,** 15, 177–185; **30,** 171–172; **32,** 8–10, 12–19, 23–33, 35–36; **33,** 32–33
—assets of subsidiaries, **33,** 32–33
—capacity to sue abroad, **32,** 8–10
—claims based on stockholders' pool, **30,** 171–172
nationalized, receiver for local assets, **32,** 184, 189
neutral, carrying on business in enemy territory, **3,** 448–449
neutral character, **1,** 229–230
non-resident, standing to sue, **33,** 253–254
personality, law of place of incorporation, **26,** 6, 10, 12, 15, 24–25, 28
position abroad, **3,** 291; **5,** 261–262
property of, assimilation to private property, **6,** 449–450
public, partition of territory and, **6,** 77–82
residence for tax purpose, **27,** 103–107
shareholders, rights in time of war, **22,** 909–911
siège social, need for, **32,** 25
statutory amalgamation, recognition abroad, **26,** 12
substance and form, distinction, **3,** 399–400
taxation, residence, basis of, **27,** 103–107. *See also* Corporations, foreign, taxation
unincorporated associations, alien membership, **5,** 252–253
winding-up: *see* Corporations, foreign, liquidation of
Corporations, foreign—
acts of, jurisdiction of forum, **22,** 168–182
arbitration between concessionaire and State: *see* Arbitration foreign company and Government, between
controlled by foreign State, jurisdiction over, **1,** 133–134; **5,** 110–112; **9,** 198–207, 213–217; **19,** 197–203; **23,** 160–173
dissolution of, **3,** 136–145; **4,** 66–67, 144–146; **6,** 140–143; **7,** 70–75, 82, 151–158; **8,** 184–187, 193–194, 207; **9,** 141–148; **11,** 107–108; **16,** 20; **19,** 302–311; **20,** 34–36; **21,** 38–39; **22,** 13–14; **23,** 19–21; **24,** 40–48; **26,** 45; **30,** 20, 23: *see also* Corporations, nationalization of

Corporations, foreign—*continued*
dissolution of—*continued*
—law of domicile governing, **26,** 15, 360
establishment rights, **3,** 291; **5,** 261–262
foreign-owned, test of, **33,** 157
jurisdiction over, **7,** 161–162; **8,** 181–182; **22,** 168–182
jurisdiction over, State-controlled, **1,** 133–134; **5,** 110–112
liquidation by State of incorporation, effect, **3,** 145; **4,** 143; **7,** 65–70, 80–81; **8,** 204–205; **18,** 199–200
liquidation of property of, **4,** 145; **8,** 184–187, 193–194, 205; **9,** 141, 147; **11,** 107–108; **19,** 302–311; **22,** 13–14; **26,** 130
liquidation of property abroad, jurisdiction, **18,** 189–194
merger of, **30,** 20, 23
powers outside State of incorporation, **27,** 19–22
recognition of, comity, **6,** 278–279; **26,** 28
right to sue, **3,** 291; **5,** 261–262; **8,** 460–464
shareholders, as, claims by, **6,** 273–275
shareholder in, claim by, **21,** 152–153; **26,** 342; **30,** 171–172
taxation, **18,** 280–281; **20,** 263–264; **21,** 280–281
—discriminatory, **22,** 473
Corpus delicti, **5,** 165
Corrupt gift to foreign official, prohibition of, **11,** 32–33
Costa Rica—
Constitution (1871), (expropriation provisions), **23,** 702, 704–706
Constitution (1871), Art. 5 (nationality), **9,** 388
Economic Blockade Law, 1942...**23,** 701–706
Expulsions, Law of, 1894...**9,** 387
Penal Code, crimes committed abroad, **7,** 196–197
—foreigners, jurisdiction over, **4,** 160
U.S.A., Consular Convention (1852), **11,** 208–211
Costs—
arbitration proceedings, of, **2,** 379–380; **3,** 408–410, 413; **9,** 322
—award to Heads of State, **8,** 23
—security for, **3,** 408, 413; **6,** 40–43, 276, 349
Court of Justice of European Coal and Steel Community, in: *see under* European Coal and Steel Community
European Communities Court, in: *see under* European Communities Court
Costs—*continued*
prize proceedings, **10,** 624–626, 632–635; **12,** 485, 510
proceedings by aliens, security for, **2,** 84; **5,** 335; **7,** 406–408, 423, 473; **8,** 333–334; **11,** 183–184; **19,** 556
—Hague Convention on Civil Procedure (1905), **1,** 69 n, 72, 244; **2,** 323; **6,** 40–43, 349; **7,** 308; **8,** 334; **9,** 73–74; **11,** 66–67, 226–227; **12,** 277–278
—most-favoured-nation clauses, **1,** 351–352; **5,** 363–364, 404–405; **6,** 276; **8,** 472–475; **11,** 234–235
—national treatment clauses, **5,** 263; **6,** 276; **7,** 305–309
—Treaty of Versailles (1919), Art. 277, effect, **1,** 243
—war, effect, **18,** 289–290
Council of Europe—
Committee of Ministers, Cyprus, decision relating to, **25,** 171
Counterclaims: *see also* Cross-suit *and* Set-off
diplomatic envoys, immunity from, **7,** 380–381; **10,** 373–374
governments, immunity from, **2,** 119–120
States, immunity from, **1,** 129–130, 132–133, 134–135; **2,** 117–119, 119–120 n; **3,** 101, 172–173; **5,** 113–114, 125–127; **7,** 164–166; **11,** 136–138; **12,** 92–96; **14,** 73–75; **18,** 219–221; **19,** 192–196; **20,** 176–178; **22,** 210–219
Counterfeiting, gold coins, **24,** 48–51
Counterfeiting currency—
foreign State, of, **32,** 344–348; **35,** 65–66
former country, of, **24,** 5–7
Counterfeiting Currency, Convention on Suppression of (1929), **18,** 382
Countervailing duties, m-f-n clause and, **34,** 217–219
Country, defined, **26,** 694–698
Court fees, foreign, action for recovery, **6,** 145
Court of Justice of European Coal and Steel Community: *see under* European Coal and Steel Community
Court of Justice of European Communities: *see* European Communities Court
Courts martial—
aliens, jurisdiction over, **12,** 219–221
deserter irregularly apprehended, **12,** 165–168
—irregularly enlisted, **12,** 219–221
foreign, recognition of judgments, **1,** 29
mandated territory, in, **12,** 12–15
spies, jurisdiction to try, **1,** 431

Courts, municipal—
aliens, access to, **1**, 2[illegible] **5**, 260–263; **6**, 276; **7**, 303–3[illegible] **8**, 325–326; **11**, 230–235; **12**, 202–208; **16**, 253–256; **17**, 241–242; **23**, 314, 323–333; **24**, 481: *see also* Aliens
arbitral awards, enforcement of, **7**, 489–490; **18**, 3–5
cession, effect on jurisdiction, **4**, 117; **16**, 64; **22**, 197–200
change of sovereignty, effect on judgments, **4**, 95–96
competence—
—interpretation of treaties, **2**, 326–328
—matters of immunity, **9**, 174–175, 256–257; **12**, 111–112, 143–149; **21**, 95–101
—political matters, in, **6**, 349–350
decisions of—
—governments, whether binding on, **1**, 171–172, 331–332
—international law, as source of, **4**, 6–7; **18**, 665: *see also* International law, sources of
—international law, contrary to, **5**, 157
extraterritorial effect of acts of, **11**, 104–106
fees, claim for, by foreign State, **6**, 145
findings, conclusiveness of, **1**, 176–177
foreign, recognition of judgments of, **1**, 28–29; **6**, 144–145; **7**, 21–22; **19**, 19–23; **24**, 40
international law, application of: *see under* International law, municipal law and
judgments contrary to international law, **5**, 157
jurisdiction, immunities from: *q.v.*
language used in, **6**, 283
mixed: *see under* Egypt *and* Shanghai
mixed arbitral tribunals: *q.v.*
occupied territory, in: *see under* Belligerent occupation
ouster of jurisdiction by international commission, **9**, 123
treaties, interpretation of: *see under* Treaties, interpretation of
Covenant of League of Nations: *see* League of Nations
Crest of watershed, doctrine of occupation, **4**, 120–121
Crete—
autonomy of, relation to Turkey, **4**, 320; **8**, 154–155
Greece as successor to, **23**, 81–93
State of, **23**, 88, 90, 92, 669
Crews of public ships ashore, responsibility for acts of, **3**, 221–222
Crime in foreign embassy, **34**, 148–150
Crime in violation of " law of nations ", **32**, 3–4. *See also* Humanity, crimes against; War crimes
Crimean War, capture of enemy merchant ships, **2**, 452
Ionian Islands, rights during, **3**, 39
Crimen majestatis, **8**, 89
Crimes against humanity: *see* Humanity, crimes against
Crimes, political: *see* Political crimes
Crimes, war: *see* War crimes
Criminal investigations by consuls, **7**, 388–389
Criminal jurisdiction: *see* Jurisdiction, criminal
Criminal law—
State succession and, **8**, 146–150; **15**, 72–75; **16**, 68–72
territoriality of, **7**, 192–193, 197–199; **26**, 215–216, 219
—armed forces in leased base abroad, **31**, 121–128
—capitulations and, **3**, 194–199; **4**, 189–190
Croatia, independent State of, **21**, 55–63
Cross-suit, **3**, 175, 321; **4**, 163–164, 368. *See also* Counterclaim
consular courts, competence of, **7**, 199
implied submission to, **4**, 163–164
Crown: *see under* United Kingdom
Cuba—
aliens, position of, **6**, 277–278; **7**, 311–312
breach of diplomatic relations with U.S.A., standing to sue in U.S. courts, **32**, 70–72
civil procedure, attachment, alien debtors, **5**, 397–398
Constitution, Art. 12 (retroactive effect of laws), **5**, 337
expropriation measures, **34**, 12–16
fisheries (Decree–Law 704 of 1936), **9**, 346
Government, standing to sue in U.S. courts, **33**, 36–43
lease of Guantanamo Bay to U.S.A., **31**, 125
mail, fraud by, **5**, 278
nationality, **1**, 93
nationalization measures, **32**, 8–12
—banks, **35**, 60
—U.S. property, **35**, 3–5, 8–10, 16, 20
naturalized citizens in, **12**, 197
U.S.A.—
—Arbitration Agreement (1927), **5**, 265
—Convention for Prevention of Smuggling of Liquors (1926), **6**, 127
—Extradition Treaties (1904 and 1926), **5**, 282; **28**, 352–353
—Reciprocal Trade Agreement (1934), **22**, 584; **24**, 670–672

Cuba—*continued*
U.S.A.—*continued*
—Reciprocity and Commercial Treaty with (1902), **2**, 345; **5**, 354; **22**, 583–589; **24**, 670–672
Universal Postal Convention, party to, **1**, 314–315
workmen's compensation in, **1**, 93; **20**, 205
Cujus est solum, ejus est usque ad coelum et ad inferos, **23**, 814. *See also* Air space
Cumulative damages, **4**, 272–273
Currency—
changes, payment and, **6**, 72–73
confiscation of, **30**, 144–147
conversion of values, rate of exchange, **30**, 181–183
depreciation of, **22**, 762–767, 829
—bonds, revalorization, **29**, 5, 8–11, 19
—currency of payment, alternative, **29**, 13
—international officials and, **22**, 762–767
devaluation of, effect on lighthouse dues tariffs, **23**, 342, 347–348
devaluation of, State responsibility, **20**, 211–213; **21**, 150; **26**, 275–276, 278, 284–286, 290, 293, 302; **30**, 146–147
—mortgages, effect on, **26**, 278
discrimination against aliens, State responsibility, **26**, 285
domestic jurisdiction, matter of, **26**, 285
exchange control: *q.v.*
functions, medium of payment and measure of debt, **22**, 830–832
international control of, **22**, 713–737
jurisdiction to regulate, **22**, 732–737
money of account, **22**, 828, 830, 833–834, 835–839
money of contract, **22**, 826–829, 839
occupied territory, in, **22**, 994–996; **26**, 719–721. *See also under* Belligerent occupation
payment between postal administrations, **8**, 418–419
prohibition of transfer, whether a taking, **26**, 293, 295, 302, 305–306
State succession and, **6**, 72–73; **7**, 104–105
transfer to non-resident alien, U.S. law, **26**, 487–489
Treasury bills, equivalent of, **26**, 286–287; **30**, 147
Currency laws—
Canadian Gold Clauses Act, private loans and, **11**, 28
contracts with aliens, effect on, **6**, 286–287
Currency laws—*continued*
enforcement in foreign States, **10**, 6–9; **11**, 29; **15**, 18–20; **16**, 27–36; **24**, 49–51; **26**, 56–57. *See also* Exchange control measures
German, 1923 ... **4**, 338–339
Polish, 1924 ... **4**, 397–398
Yugoslav, **20**, 211–213
U.S. Congress, gold clause resolution, State loans and, **8**, 13–22
—private loans and, **8**, 203; **11**, 26–27
Currency notes, contraband, as, **16**, 583–587, 594–595
" Curzon Line ", **1**, 36
Custodian, appointment of, occupied territory, **11**, 33; **18**, 583–585
Custodian of enemy property: *see also* Trading with Enemy laws *under* particular States
functions, **29**, 386
State responsibility for acts of, **29**, 383–388
transfer to, effect, **30**, 412
Custodian of Enemy Property (Australia), powers, **32**, 560–562
(Belgium), **15**, 460
(Canada), **12**, 264–266; **21**, 460–464
(Ceylon), **12**, 341
(Germany), discriminatory treatment and, **25**, 341–349
(Italy), sale of goods by, State responsibility and, **22**, 307–311
(Japan), powers of, **29**, 383–389
—State responsibility for acts of, **29**, 383–389
(Kenya), effect of vesting orders, **27**, 618–627
— — vesting order, severability of, **27**, 626–627
(Palestine), **12**, 349–352
(Scotland), **1**, 398
(South Africa), **1**, 225, 399; **3**, 453–454
Custodian of Enemy Property (United Kingdom), **1**, 397, 399, 400, 406–409; **12**, 63
disposal of property under treaty, **17**, 1–6
" enemy ", meaning, **23**, 691
functions, **23**, 689, 691–692, 700–701
payment to as discharge of debt, **21**, 445–447
powers, **19**, 572–578; **20**, 602–609
Public Trustee as, **3**, 181–182
status, **23**, 689, 691–692
vesting of property in, effect of, **21**, 460–464; **28**, 605–607; **30**, 412
—after hostilities ended, **33**, 445–446, 448–449
Custodian of Enemy Property (U.S.A.) **3**, 447–450; **9**, 546–547; **11**, 106–107, 250–251; **12**, 329–333, 342–349, 363–364, 424–427; **15**, 261; **17**, 359–367, 372; **18**, 513, 514; **20**, 610–615; **22**, 920; **31**, 498–501

Custom or usage—
as a source of international law, **2,** 368; **4,** 115
termination of régime based on, **21,** 140
Customary international law, **2,** 99–102; **4,** 6–8; **7,** 218–221; **15,** 635–636; **17,** 284–286; **18,** 100–102, 107, 123–131, 134–136, 139, 143; **23,** 210–212; **24,** 130; **26,** 169–170; **29,** 476; **31,** 25, 36, 37, 56, 82, 116, 118: *see also* Hague Regulations, declaratory nature, *and* International law, sources
acquiescence as evidence of, **18,** 100–102, 107, 123–131, 134–136, 139, 143
asylum and, **17,** 284–286
consensus required, **4,** 111; **22,** 372
custom, regime based on, termination of, **21,** 140
extraterritoriality of foreign armed forces, **6,** 174
factors regulating, **17,** 284–285
local custom, **31,** 36, 52, 61, 62, 65, 67–68, 82, 90, 96, 97, 105–106, 108, 115
municipal law and: *see under* International law, municipal law and
opinio juris, **17,** 284–285; **28,** 172; **31,** 25, 67, 85
practice and, **31,** 25, 37, 52–53, 56, 67, 68, 70, 80–81, 89, 91, 93–94, 96, 105, 106, 108
proof of, **17,** 284–285
regional, **17,** 284–286; **30,** 481–483, 490
treaty provisions, relation to, **8,** 450; **19,** 275–283; **21,** 140
war crimes and, **15,** 635–636
Customs authorities, responsibility for negligence of, **4,** 228–229
Customs Co-operation Council, officials, tax exemption, **31,** 393–394
Customs duties—
advance payment, State succession and, **4,** 86–87
assessment, equality of treatment and, **19,** 283–287, 297–302
consumption tax, distinguished, **19,** 282
exemption for diplomats, **32,** 307–308
fiscal duties, distinguished, **19,** 282
unwarranted collection of, **9,** 1–4
Customs Formalities, Convention on Simplification of (1923), **18,** 382
Customs frontier—
importation of goods by sea, when effected, **27,** 98–102
meaning, **31,** 243
Customs frontier between two parts of same State, **27,** 59–60
Customs houses, **2,** 103; **4,** 228–229
Customs laws—
foreign ships, innocent passage and, **31,** 132–137
operation of, **7,** 209–212
submarine cables, **9,** 126
Customs, regulation of—
act of State, whether, **11,** 224–226
transit distinguished from export, **11,** 34–35
treaty rights and, **11,** 229–230
Customs territory, State territory, distinguished, **1,** 83; **3,** 110–111
Customs unions—
Benelux, **28,** 511–513
German, Trade Agreement with France (1862), **6,** 282
Germany and Austria, **6,** 26–31
Monaco and France, **11,** 34–35
Saar Territory and France, **7,** 30; **8,** 70
most-favoured-nation clause and, **25,** 319
tax on imports, compatibility with treaty of union, **28,** 511–513
" Cut-banks ", **2,** 96–98
Cyprus—
annexation by Great Britain, **1,** 199, 201, 202
decision of Committee of Ministers, Council of Europe, relating to, **25,** 171
emergency laws, European Human Rights Convention and, **25,** 169–170
establishment of Republic, **33,** 301
nationality, **1,** 199–202
protectorate status, **5,** 25–27
Zürich and London Agreements (1959), **25,** 31–32
Czechoslovakia: *see also* Bohemia and Moravia
agrarian reform, **4,** 147–151
Austria, Commercial Treaty (1922), **5,** 103
—treaty, salaries of officials (1923), **9,** 465
beginning of existence of, **1,** 11–20, 45; **2,** 10–11; **3,** 13–16; **4,** 26, 148–149; **5,** 15–16; **6,** 20; **7,** 19
Civil Procedure Code (diplomatic immunity), **9,** 429
confiscation of German property in, **20,** 31–34; **24,** 436–438
Constitution, Art. 64 (powers of President), **9,** 465
co-operative societies, dissolution, extraterritorial effect, **32,** 19–26
Denationalization Decree, 1945...**20,** 33
France, Compensation Agreement (1950), **28,** 438–439

Czechoslovakia—*continued*
France—*continued*
—Extradition Treaty (1928), **18**, 340
German conquest of, **9**, 84; **10**, 78–79; **11**, 24–25; **12**, 43–47; **13**, 206, 220–221; **16**, 347, 361; **19**, 319–322
German rule in, **9**, 84–87; **10**, 78–79
Germany, Nationality Treaty (1938), **18**, 250, 251, 257; **20**, 32; **24**, 431–433, 437, 537
language used by aliens in, **2**, 262–263; **6**, 283
military courts abroad, jurisdiction, **10**, 123–128
Monetary Reform Decree, 1945...**22**, 424
nationality, **7**, 289–290; **11**, 179; **18**, 250–251, 257; **22**, 426; **24**, 540
—continuity of, German origin, **26**, 42; **32**, 166–168
nationalization claims, lump sum settlement, **22**, 424–427; **26**, 47; **28**, 438–439; **33**, 186, 187
nationalization measures—
—banks, **20**, 34–36; **23**, 7–9
—mines, **28**, 14–16
—Presidential Decree (1945), **22**, 17–19; **23**, 24–26; **24**, 46–48; **26**, 40, 44, 47; **30**, 33–35, 49; **32**, 31, 32
Netherlands, Agreement (1946) *re* Bretton Woods Agreement, **22**, 713–715
Poland, Treaty (legal and financial) (1925), **4**, 397
recognition of, by U.S.A., **11**, 57–59
status after 1938...**17**, 357–359
successor of Austrian Empire, whether, **1**, 259–260; **4**, 86–87; **5**, 63–64; **9**, 102
—former officials, **1**, 73–74; **9**, 465
—pecuniary obligations, **1**, 62
—taxes, **4**, 78–79
—treaties, **1**, 68, 71
Sudeten Germans and, **18**, 249–251, 257–258
Sudetenland, cession of, **18**, 249–251, 257–258; **20**, 32–33
Switzerland, Commercial Agreement (1953), **24**, 47
—Compensation Agreement (1949), **22**, 424–427
—Judicial Assistance, Agreement on (1926), **22**, 426
taxes, State succession, **4**, 78–79
territory occupied by Hungary, status of, **26**, 700–701
territories under plebiscite, status of, **3**, 109–111
treaties, operation of, **7**, 15
U.K., Compensation Agreement (1949), **26**, 47

D

Damages: *see also* Arbitration; Claims; Equity
absence of actual damage, **3**, 205; **5**, 158, 199
absence of proof of pecuniary loss, **11**, 177–178
angary, in case of, **1**, 189–190
awards, apportionment of, **2**, 184
basis of, **2**, 202–203; **6**, 444–445; **7**, 264–265; **21**, 162–164
bona fides of claims to, **1**, 187
breach of concession, for, **35**, 185–190
breach of contract, for, **5**, 202–203
burden of proof, **5**, 151–152; **8**, 450
causa proxima non remota inspicitur, **1**, 188: *see also* indirect *and* remoteness, *infra*
causation, **5**, 446. *See also causa proxima, supra and* indirect *and* remoteness, *infra*
collateral relatives, claim by, **2**, 202–203; **3**, 247
computation of, **1**, 188–189; **2**, 202–203; **3**, 248; **5**, 166–168, 197–198, 202–203; **6**, 207; **22**, 311; **23**, 342, 348; **27**, 531 n., 553
—basis of, **6**, 225–226; **21**, 162–164
—evidence, lack of, **5**, 197–198
—*ex aequo et bono*, **29**, 234, 241. *See also* Equity *and Ex aequo et bono*
—" generally accepted principles of calculating ", **20**, 492
—set-off, compensation from other sources, **30**, 143
contingent, **4**, 273–274, 276
cost of investigation, for, **9**, 321–324; **30**, 137
cumulative, of independent undertakings, **4**, 272
currency, **6**, 226–227
damnum emergens, **5**, 181–182, 203; **35**, 186, 187–190
—*lucrum cessans* and, **5**, 181–182. *See also* loss of profits, *infra*
date for conversion into claimant's currency, **26**, 272–274, 297
death, claims based on, **2**, 202–203; **3**, 239–240
—life insurance company, by, **2**, 203–206
direct, **2**, 193, 199–202; **3**, 255; **4**, 230, 267–268; **5**, 201. *See also* remoteness, *infra*
exaggerated claims, **1**, 187
exclusive remedy, whether, for illegal taking of alien property, **28**, 22, 26–30
exemplary, **2**, 209–211; **3**, 256. *See also* punitive, *infra*
illegal detention, for, **1**, 188–189
indeterminate, **4**, 273–274

Damages—*continued*
indirect, **1,** 187–188; **2,** 175, 193–198, 199–202, 207–208; **3,** 248–255; **4,** 231–232, 268–272, 274–275; **5,** 201–203; **6,** 228–231; **9,** 321–324; **21,** 164–165; **25,** 347; **30,** 137. *See also* remoteness, *infra*
interest as element of, **2,** 213–214; **3,** 257; **5,** 200–202; **20,** 241; **22,** 409–417; **23,** 675–676; **30,** 220–225. *See also* Interest
interest, " usual rate ", **35,** 190
loss of catch, for, **3,** 249
loss of profits, for, **2,** 207; **3,** 248; **4,** 268–273; **5,** 181–182, 203; **21,** 164–165; **22,** 315–317; **23,** 301–302. *See also lucrum cessans, supra*
—prospective profits, **3,** 253–254; **4,** 273–274
loss of use of money, for, **21,** 165
measure of, **2,** 171; **5,** 151, 158, 198, 203; **6,** 225–231, 445; **7,** 249; **8,** 274–276; **16,** 181; **20,** 238–239, 628–634; **21,** 146; **22,** 301–307, 312–317, 408, 858–864, 958–959; **26,** 352–361; **29,** 375–379
—angary, in case of, **1,** 189–190
—betterment, allowance for, **22,** 306–307, 409
—burden of proof, **4,** 267; **5,** 151–152
—calculation of: *see* computation of, *supra*
—currency, question of, **6,** 226–227
—deduction for property recovered, **22,** 408
—equity: *q.v.*
—*ex aequo et bono*: *q.v.*
—inflation, allowance for, **22,** 345–346
—irregular imprisonment, **7,** 478
—jointly-owned property, **22,** 408
—valuation of property: *see* Valuation
mental suffering, for, **2,** 193–194; **6,** 227
nature of, **4,** 266–267
neutral prizes, destruction of, **5,** 490–491
neutral vessel, detention of, **10,** 604–605
non-material injury, **29,** 234, 237, 239, 241, 269
nuisance, for, **9,** 315, 318–321
pillage, for, **5,** 150–152
prize, in: *see* Prize, indemnities and damages
prospective, **3,** 248–249; **4,** 276
punitive, **2,** 209–211; **3,** 256; **5,** 202; **7,** 264–265
rate of exchange, **5,** 199–200
remoteness, **1,** 158; **2,** 195–202, 203–207; **3,** 249–251. *See also causa proxima non remota inspicitur and* direct *and* indirect, *supra*

Damages—*continued*
requisitions, for, **5,** 150–152, 494; **6,** 441, 445–446
solatium, distinguished from compensatory damages, **4,** 266–267
special, **4,** 267–268
speculative, **3,** 249. *See also* loss of profits, *supra*
State sovereignty, injury to, **7,** 206; **9,** 320–321
treaty, violation of, **9,** 1–4
Danube—
agreement between Austria and Roumania (1955), **32,** 5–6
Definitive Statute (1921), **4,** 441–443; **9,** 121
—*Protocole interprétatif,* **4,** 430–431
Donauversinkung, **4,** 128–133
European Commission of, **4,** 126–128, 430–431, 441–442; **10,** 362
—Roumania, Convention on Privileges and Immunities (1938), **22,** 537, 547–548
fishing, regulation of, **9,** 121–122
freedom of navigation, **4,** 125–127; **9,** 121
Galatz–Braila, sectors of, **4,** 126–128
London, Treaty of (1883), **4,** 429–430, 441–442
utilization of flow of, **4,** 128–132
Danube-Save-Adriatic Railway Co., **18,** 1–3
Danzig, Free City of—
appeals from courts, pending at cession by Germany, **2,** 61
Code of Civil Procedure (alien status), **6,** 257
condominium over, **7,** 59, 61–62
Constitution, **18,** 261
—guarantee by League, **6,** 47
German annexation of, **15,** 206–207; **18,** 258–262; **21,** 485–487; **24,** 434
High Commissioner, functions, **3,** 49; **7,** 61–62
International Labour Organization, membership, **5,** 411–413
jurisdiction of courts, actions begun before German courts, **1,** 89–91; **2,** 61
League of Nations, guarantee of Constitution, **6,** 47
Poland—
—Agreement on Double Taxation (1924), **4,** 411
—conduct of foreign relations by, **5,** 411
—Treaty of Paris with (1920), **5,** 410; **6,** 130, 209–213, 383–384; **7,** 61–62, 270
Polish nationals in, treatment of, **6,** 209–213
Polish officials, status of, **6,** 130–131
railways, cession to Poland, **4,** 287–289

Danzig, Free City of—*continued*
railways, Polish Administration, **3,** 170–171, 340–342; **7,** 182–184
ships registered in, **2,** 454
special status of, **1,** 411–412, 414; **5,** 410–413; **6,** 211–212; **7,** 59; **15,** 206–207
—(1945), **24,** 77
State succession and, **5,** 66–68
Dawes Plan (German reparations), interpretation of, **3,** 208–209; **5,** 33
London Conference of 1924...**3,** 349–350; **9,** 155
Treaty of Versailles, relation to, **3,** 406–407
Dawes-Simon Extradition Treaty, 1931 (U.S.A./Great Britain), **6,** 301; **9,** 410–411; **18,** 339
De facto belligerents, **1,** 386
De facto governments—
decrees of *de jure* government in territory controlled by, **9,** 77
jurisdictional immunities, **9,** 60–65, 67, 171, 250, 273
ratification of treaty by, **30,** 396
recognition of, **1,** 50, 51; **2,** 36–37; **3,** 60–64; **8,** 119–123; **9,** 60-67, 85, 94–101; **10,** 64–65; **12,** 43–47; **15,** 176–204; **17,** 180, 183–186; **18,** 595; **19,** 87–93, 100, 104; **21,** 57, 60–62; **22,** 97–100; **28,** 93–95; **31,** 31
—insurgents, as, **9,** 10–67, 75–78, 227–228
—retroactive effect, **1,** 49–51; **9,** 101; **10,** 65; **15,** 176–185; **22,** 97–100
remedy against, in muncipal courts, **6,** 53–54
representatives of, position after extinction of government, **3,** 62–64
responsibility for acts of, **1,** 182–184; **2,** 176–177; **3,** 232–234, 234–235; **4,** 215–216, 240–241, 244–245, 278–279; **5,** 174; **6,** 213–214; **20,** 220; **21,** 55–63; **22,** 645–646, 648–649; **24,** 306–307, 310–312, 653–654, 659–661
status of, **2,** 36–37. *See also* Governments, conflicting claims
validity of acts of, **9,** 84–87
De facto possession, requirement for requisition, **11,** 160
De facto recognition of conquest, **8,** 119–123; **9,** 84–93
De facto subjects, **1,** 202; **2,** 242–243; **3,** 268–269; **4,** 309–312. *See also* Protected persons
De in rem verso, **4,** 83
De jure governments—
capacity to sue, **6,** 54–55
conflicting claims of *de jure* and *de facto*, **9,** 12, 75, 93–94, 227, 275–279
decrees of, territory controlled by *de facto* government, **9,** 77
De jure governments—*continued*
recognition of, **1,** 50; **3,** 59; **5,** 46; **6,** 55; **7,** 67–69, 78–80; **8,** 119–123; **9,** 66–67, 71–72, 75–78, 94–100; **10,** 65; **12,** 43–47; **15,** 176–204; **17,** 179–180, 183–186; **18,** 595; **19,** 75, 78–79, 100–105, 111–115; **22,** 98–99
—insurgents, as, **9,** 73–74
—relevance, **4,** 203–204
—retroactive effect, **5,** 46; **7,** 67–69, 73; **8,** 34–35; **9,** 101, 188; **10,** 59; **12,** 17–22; **13,** 30; **16,** 49–60; **17,** 66–67, 69, 185–186; **19,** 72–115
De jure recognition of conquest, **8,** 119–123
"*De plein droit*", meaning, **4,** 407
Death duties, extraterritorial enforcement, **6,** 149–150
Death of Missing Persons, Convention on, Declaration of, (1950), **18,** 381; **20,** 425–429
Debellatio, **13,** 189; **15,** 216; **16,** 36–37, 266–268, 435, 441; **19,** 320–324
applied to German-occupied Poland, **30,** 505
—not applied to German-occupied U.S.S.R., **30,** 508
"Débouter", meaning, **4,** 498–499
Debts: *see also* Public debt *and* State loans
currency of payment, **6,** 286–287
due outside jurisdiction, attachment, **4,** 146–147
international control of revenue, **3,** 208–209
international, set-off, **6,** 234
local, State succession and, **7,** 87–88
place of payment—
—American law, **25,** 60, 82
—English law, **25,** 60, 82–83
—French law, **25,** 61, 81
—German law, **25,** 59–60, 80, 81
prescription period, debt to enemy national, **2,** 25–26
public, State succession and, **3,** 78–79; **4,** 443–445; **5,** 64–66; **6,** 62–65; **8,** 128–136; **11,** 78; **23,** 667; **24,** 69–73
situs of, **7,** 153–155; **16,** 18–19, 21–24; **32,** 30–31, 33–37, 108, 568; **33,** 18
State responsibility for: *see under* State responsibility
war, effect on, **29,** 8. *See also* Contracts, war, effect of outbreak of
Decedents' estates, in war time, **12,** 224, 225, 246, 423–424
"Declarant" aliens, **11,** 189–190, 192
Declaration of Cairo (1943), **17,** 178; **22,** 983
Declaration of Death of Missing Persons, Convention on (1950), **18,** 381; **20,** 425–429

Declaration of Human Rights: *see* Universal Declaration of Human Rights
Declaration of intention to become naturalized, diplomatic protection and, **3,** 269–271
Declaration of London (1909), Hague Conventions and, **3,** 486
Declaration of Paris (1856), **1,** 491; **9,** 566; **11,** 303; **16,** 570, 588; **19,** 480; **20,** 673; **31,** 520
Declaration of war: *see* War, declaration of
Declarations, exchange of, distinguished from treaties, **3,** 333–334
Declaratory judgments, **1,** 375; **3,** 429–430; **4,** 506–511; **27,** 145–146, 484; **31,** 74–75, 76: *see also under* International Court of Justice
" De-enemization ", 1946 Agreement on Reparations, **17,** 376–377; **18,** 516
Defamation—
  Heads of foreign States, **9,** 8–9, 11–12
  High Commissioner for Australia, official reports of, **11,** 213–217
  interned belligerents, **9,** 583
  member of armed forces of friendly State, **12,** 133–134
  public officials, **11,** 44–45
Defence of superior orders: *see under* War crimes
Defended and undefended cities, distinction, **32,** 631–632
Defensively armed merchantmen, status of, **2,** 407–408
Delaware Bay, **4,** 136; **9,** 136
Délits mixtes, **3,** 308–311
Delivery, formal, of territory, **1,** 84–89
Demilitarization, self-defence, whether right retained, **32,** 43–64
Demurrage, claim for, **2,** 193; **11,** 304–305
Denationalization: *see under* Nationality
Denial of justice, **1,** 331; **2,** 68, 162–163, 166–168; **3,** 206, 213–219, 223–225; **4,** 208–222, 229–234, 236–238, 248–250; **5,** 153–163, 165, 171, 186, 210; **6,** 188–204; **7,** 231–249; **8,** 271–278; **9,** 308–314, 507, 509; **23,** 309, 312, 314, 324–327, 334–340; **24,** 296; **25,** 47; **26,** 261, 285–286; **30,** 129, 143, 183, 197, 329
  absence of impartiality, **6,** 197
  amnesty, grant of, **4,** 212–213
  burden of proof, **6,** 203–204
  currency matters, **26,** 285–286
  delay, undue, **4,** 218–219; **6,** 201–202
  error by municipal court, **25,** 47
  executive action or inaction, **6,** 199–201, 203–209
  exhaustion of local remedies: *q.v.*

Denial of justice—*continued*
  failure to afford remedies, **26,** 261
  failure to apprehend, **4,** 215–216
  —to bring to trial, **4,** 217–218
  faulty judicial procedure, **6,** 195–196
  improper conduct of prosecution, **7,** 244–246
  inadequate punishment, **4,** 213–215; **7,** 246–249
  municipal law as, **24,** 792, 799
  non-execution of sentence, **4,** 208–210
  reduction of sentence, **4,** 208–210, 213–215
  release of accused on bond, **4,** 217–218
Deniken Government of Russia, claim against, **6,** 53–54
Denizens, **10,** 529–534; **12,** 184–188, 360–362
Denmark—
  Administration of Justice Act, **28,** 214, 215–217, 230–231, 233
  Austro-Hungarian subjects, protection of, **4,** 282–283
  Canada, Extradition Treaty (1873), **1,** 275
  Constitution (1953) (expropriation of property), **24,** 381
  France, Treaty (1645) (angary), **23,** 729
  France, Treaty of Commerce (1910), **4,** 453
  German occupation of, **15,** 452; **16,** 507–508; **17,** 434–438
  Germany, Non-Aggression Pact (1939), **15,** 421
  Germany, Treaty concerning Schleswig (1922), **2,** 83
  Iran, Treaty of Friendship, Establishment and Commerce (1934), **19,** 514–517, 533, 534
  Maritime Law, 1937...**20,** 207
  Norway and Sweden, Convention on Execution of Judgments (1948), **20,** 290
  Penal Code, broadcasting from outside territorial waters, **31,** 274–275
  Prussia, Treaty of Commerce and Navigation (1818), **23,** 715
  Special Court of Revision (criminal), **28,** 215–217, 218–219, 230–231, 233
  Sweden, Treaty, fisheries (1899), **6,** 123
  Sweden–Norway, Commercial Treaty (1826), **6,** 103
  U.K., agreements with, *re Red Crusader* incidents, **35,** 485, 501
  U.K., Fisheries Convention (1901), **9,** 126 n.
  U.K., Treaties of Peace and Commerce (1660 and 1670), **20,** 554; **23,** 313, 321–322; **24,** 296
  U.S.A., Consular Treaty (1826), **4,** 449; **5,** 376; **7,** 390

Denmark—*continued*
U.S.A., Mutual Defense Agreement (1950), **22**, 550–551
U.S.A., Neutrality Act, executive order concerning Denmark, **9**, 6
Denunciation of treaties: *see* Treaties, denunciation of
Dependent States, **9**, 35–43; **10**, 38–48; **23**, 29–35. *See also* Dependent territories *and* Protectorates
capacity to acquire territory, **26**, 104–107
legislative powers of Suzerain, **11**, 47–48
Dependent territories, **17**, 42–47; **22**, 76; **24**, 54–55. *See also* Colonies; Dependent States *and* Protectorates
Deportation of aliens: *see* Expulsion of aliens
Deprivation, meaning, Germany, Settlement Convention (1952/54), **25**, 350, 354
Deprivation of property, unlawful, distinguished from expropriation, **4**, 271–272
Deserters—
irregularly enlisted, **12**, 219–221
irregularly handed over, **12**, 165–168
Deserters, from ships, return of, **9**, 170; **11**, 14; **26**, 529; **28**, 360; **31**, 405–408
Destruction of enemy merchant ships in port, **4**, 569–570; **6**, 438–440
Destruction of neutral ships, **5**, 490, 515, 518
Destruction of property in ceded territory, compensation for, **20**, 628, 633: *see also under* Belligerent occupation, private property
Destruction of submarine cables, **2**, 415–419
Detention: *see also* Enemy aliens, internment of, *and* European Convention on Human Rights
alien seamen, **11** 114–115
irregular, responsibility for, **7**, 477–478
neutral vessels: *see under* Neutral vessels
prolonged, State responsibility, **4**, 226–227, 236–238; **5**, 159, 163–164
Détournement de pouvoir, international organizations, in: *see under* European Coal and Steel Community; European Economic Community; *and* International organization
Devaluation: *see* Currency, devaluation of
Devastation, general, of occupied territory, **15**, 632, 647–649; **16**, 484–486, 521–523
Dictionaries, use of, interpretation of treaties, **4**, 446–447; **6**, 375–376; **20**, 473–474
Dies a quo, Dies ad quem: *see under* Interest
Dignity of States, **8**, 23–25; **9**, 8–12; **10**, 9; **11**, 13; **12**, 3; **18**, 22–23; **21**, 10–11; **22**, 238; **24**, 700
Diligentia quam in suis, **2**, 161
Diplomatic correspondence, interpretation, **19**, 276
Diplomatic envoys—
acta jura gestionis: *see* immunities of, acts of a private law character, *infra agrément*, **16**, 282–283
ambassadors, assistance to, by municipal courts, **18**, 57–60
—recognition of, **18**, 58–59
—whether "authority" of foreign State, **9**, 584
—exchange of, as recognition, **20**, 52–57
appointment of, **7**, 377–378; **16**, 281–285
—consul, to post of, **23**, 436–445
—retroactive effect, **7**, 380–381
asylum, grant of, by, **17**, 280–295
channel of communication with, **16**, 285–286
chargé d'affaires, immunities of, **1**, 298n.; **9**, 427
—*ad interim*, **24**, 528
commercial attaché, proof of status, **11**, 204–205
commercial matters, whether representing State in, **3**, 60–61
consular and diplomatic functions, combination, **5**, 324–325; **6**, 327–328; **19**, 400–412; **20**, 389–390
consuls, distinguished, **1**, 307; **5**, 319–320, 322; **7**, 392; **24**, 533
deserters, authority to apprehend, **28**, 360
Diplomatic List, **16**, 288; **19**, 388–389
domicile of, **1**, 291–292; **15**, 309–311
extraterritoriality, fiction of, **1**, 118–119, 290–292, 305; **3**, 179; **5**, 301, 305; **6**, 327–328; **7**, 385–386; **8**, 232–233; **9**, 107, 436–437; **10**, 339–342; **12**, 241–242; **15**, 309–311; **21**, 249–250; **22**, 242; **26**, 544–546; **28**, 370, 372–374
freedom from intimidation, **9**, 414
functions, **7**, 379; **12**, 240; **15**, 309–311; **19**, 204; **23**, 210–212
—conclusiveness of statement of Executive as to, **20**, 378, 381
Habana Convention on (1928), **9**, 425–427; **12**, 241–242; **22**, 536–537, 540–541, 547; **23**, 423–425, 426
heir, as, liability for, death duty, **22**, 530–531

Diplomatic envoys—*continued*
immunities of, **1**, 285–292; **2**, 299–302; **3**, 319–327; **4**, 361–373; **5**, 299–306, 308–309; **6**, 327–331, 338; **7**, 379–386; **8**, 393–394; **9**, 414, 417–431; **10**, 337–377; **13**, 159–171; **14**, 148–157; **15**, 309–314; **16**, 286–287; **18**, 347–348; **19**, 382–393; **20**, 378–380; **21**, 124, 248–249; **22**, 531–551; **23**, 422–432; **24**, 525–527; **26**, 534–536; **27**, 254–255; **28**, 362–365; **31**, 265–266, 389–392
—absence of claim by sending State, **14**, 149
—absence of recognition of new governmental authority, **11**, 68–74
—absence of specific municipal law, **9**, 427
—absolute, **28**, 371
—acts of a private law character, **4**, 364–366; **7**, 383–384; **9**, 423; **10**, 369–374; **16**, 291–292; **21**, 249; **22**, 533–538, 540–541, 543–544, 545–549; **23**, 425–428; **28**, 371, 413, 416–417
—appointment after jurisdiction acquired by court, **23**, 436–445
—arrest, from, **14**, 151–152
—basis of, **33**, 365, 366
—chargé d'affaires, **1**, 298n.; **9**, 427; **24**, 528
—chauffeur, **3**, 304–305; **9**, 434; **23**, 430; **26**, 543–544
—civil jurisdiction, **7**, 380–381; **9**, 417, 420, 429; **14**, 152–153; **19**, 205; **24**, 525–527
—commercial attaché, **28**, 366
—" Commercial Department " of embassy, **28**, 357–359
—consent of receiving State, **32**, 328
—continuation of prior proceedings, **33**, 361–368
—counterclaims, **7**, 380–381; **10**, 373–374
—criminal jurisdiction, **9**, 430–431; **20**, 378; **23**, 429; **26**, 537–538; **28**, 361; **31**, 389–392; **32**, 307–308; **33**, 368–371
—cross suit, **3**, 320, 321; **4**, 368–369
—documents taken from embassy, **14**, 148–150
—domestic proceedings, **28**, 364
—" domestics ", **16**, 290–291
—domestic servants, **9**, 432–434, 435
—family, of, **1**, 287–288; **5**, 303–304; **16**, 289–291; **18**, 348; **19**, 385–387; **22**, 549–550; **26**, 539–542
—fines, liability to, **4**, 367–368
—foreign States, immunities of, compared, **24**, 224–225
—*franchise de l'hôtel*: *see* Diplomatic premises

Diplomatic envoys—*continued*
immunities of—*continued*
—High Commissioner, quasi-diplomatic character, **11**, 213–217
—history, **22**, 534–537, 545–548
—immovable property: *see* Diplomatic premises
—in transit through third State, **35**, 217–218
—limits of, **11**, 203–204; **16**, 286–287
—method of claiming, **15**, 312–313
—military missions, **21**, 118–119
—national employees, social security laws, **26**, 544–545
—nature of, **1**, 118; **9**, 107, 421–423, 434; **20**, 392–393, 395–397; **22**, 530, 540 n.
—naval mission, national employees, **28**, 413–417
—notification of appointment, requirement of, **16**, 282–285; **27**, 254–255
—official residence: *see* Diplomatic premises
—personal servant, **19**, 387–392
—press counsellors, **16**, 286
—proof of status, **28**, 362–365; **30**, 393. *See also* Conclusiveness of statements of Executive
—rationale of, **14**, 153; **22**, 536
—reciprocal grant, **22**, 12, 544–549
—reciprocity, relevance of, **22**, 544, 548–549
—resignation, after, **16**, 286
—retinue, **1**, 288; **9**, 434; **23**, 430–431; **26**, 543–544. *See also* staff, *infra*
—self-defence, right of, and, **13**, 164–166; **14**, 150
—special agreement, under, **22**, 550–551
—special envoys, **1**, 294–298; **5**, 309–313; **6**, 332–335; **7**, 419
—staff, **1**, 298n.; **4**, 362–363; **7**, 380–381; **9**, 428–429; **10**, 365–369; **12**, 241–243; **16**, 286; **20**, 378; **22**, 538–543; **23**, 422–428; **26**, 535–536; **28**, 361, 413–417; **31**, 265–266; **33**, 361–368. *See also* retinue, *supra*
—staff, subordinate members, **2**, 302; **4**, 364–365; **5**, 302–304; **7**, 384–385; **9**, 417; **10**, 375–376; **11**, 204–205; **16**, 288–289; **19**, 400–412; **20**, 379–380; **22**, 543–549; **23**, 429–431; **26**, 537–539; **28**, 366; **33**, 368–371; **35**, 219–222
—staff, subordinate members, private activities, **22**, 543–549
—staff, subordinate members, waiver, **26**, 537–538
—State immunity, compared, **22**, 535; **24**, 224–225

Diplomatic envoys—*continued*
immunities of—*continued*
—statement of Executive as to, **19,** 390–391; **20,** 378, 381; **22,** 12, 549
—subpoena, exemption from, **22,** 531–533
—suit begun before defendant entitled to immunity, **33,** 361–368
—taxation, from, **2,** 301; **4,** 367–368; **5,** 400; **10,** 196–198, 337–352, 355–364; **22,** 543–549
—third States, in, **2,** 300–301; **14,** 150–154; **28,** 367–386; **31,** 389–392; **32,** 325
—traffic laws, **26,** 534–536. *See also* criminal jurisdiction, *supra*
—waiver, **3,** 320–321, 324; **4,** 361, 368–369; **5,** 299–300; **7,** 380–383; **9,** 18, 435; **10,** 199–204, 365–374; **15,** 312–314; **16,** 287; **19,** 382–385; **21,** 248–249; **22,** 531–533; **23,** 422–425, 430–431 n.; **24,** 525–527; **28,** 359; **33,** 363, 369–370
—waiver, subordinate staff, **26,** 537–538
—waiver, withdrawal of, **22,** 538–539
—war crimes and, **15,** 372–373; **16,** 361; **17,** 279, 434–438
—witness, immunity from prosecution for perjury, **28,** 361
—wives, **5,** 303–304; **16,** 289–291; **18,** 348; **22,** 549–550; **26,** 542–543
insurer of envoy, position of, **5,** 299–300; **9,** 422
mediation by, **7,** 230–231
nationality of children, **22,** 381
nationals of receiving State, **9,** 435; **10,** 356–364
obligations incurred before commencement of mission, **1,** 286
persona grata/non grata, **16,** 282–283
privileges of: *see* immunities, *supra*
protection of, **4,** 359–361; **9,** 414–416
protection of interests of nationals, prize proceedings, **12,** 516–521
residence of: *see* Diplomatic premises
sancta corpora legatorum, **9,** 424
special envoys, **1,** 294–298; **5,** 309–313; **6,** 332–335; **7,** 419–420
staff—
—certification of status of, **22,** 539–540
—immunities: *see under* immunities, *supra*
State merged with another State, of, **20,** 180–182
status, certificate of own government, **35,** 218
status, overthrow of sending government, **2,** 48–49
status, proof of, conclusiveness of statement of Executive, **2,** 48, 49, 301; **4,** 362–364; **18,** 58–59; **19,** 390–391; **20,** 378, 381; **21,** 120; **23,** 437–445

Diplomatic envoys—*continued*
status, proof of, conclusiveness of statement of Executive—*continued*
supplying information on private law matters, liability, **22,** 530–531
termination of mission, effect, **1,** 292–293; **3,** 319, 322–323; **5,** 309; **6,** 40–42; **7,** 379–380; **9,** 18–19, 422–423, 432–434; **10,** 364–365
testimony by, **9,** 18–19
Diplomatic immunities—
diplomatic envoys, of: *see under* Diplomatic envoys
European Commission of Human Rights, members of, in, Cyprus, **25,** 170 n.
foreign military mission, member of, **30,** 392–393
governmental Commission temporarily in foreign State, **34,** 175–179
immunity of U.N. officials, compared, **32,** 308–333
international officials, of: *see under* International officials, *and under particular organizations*
scope of, **35,** 231–232
Supreme Restitution Court, Germany, judges of, **25,** 204
trade delegations, of: *see under* Trade delegations of U.S.S.R.
Diplomatic negotiations, admissions in course of, **6,** 101–102
Diplomatic passport, effect of issue, **34,** 151–152
Diplomatic premises—
asylum in, **18,** 349–357
closing of, whether implying recognition of annexation, **12,** 191
extraterritoriality, **1,** 118–119, 290–291, 305; **3,** 179; **5,** 301, 305–308; **7,** 385–386; **9,** 107, 436–439; **10,** 339–342; **15,** 311; **20,** 181; **21,** 249–250; **22,** 242; **26,** 168, 173, 544–546; **28,** 379
immunity from jurisdiction of, **1,** 289–292; **3,** 179; **4,** 370–373; **5,** 305–308; **7,** 385–386; **9,** 436; **11,** 203–204; **15,** 311; **16,** 291–292; **19,** 392–393; **21,** 249–250, 435–436; **22,** 240–242; **23,** 431–432; **28,** 369–431
—crime committed in, **26,** 546
—distance from capital, relevance, **28,** 410
—*franchise de l'hôtel,* **20,** 404
—" functional necessity ", **28,** 380–382, 388, 396
—intention to use for diplomatic purposes in future, **28,** 405–406, 411–412
—*ne impediatur legatio,* **28,** 379, 384, 399, 409

Diplomatic premises—*continued*
immunity from jurisdiction of—*continued*
—number of, relevance, **28,** 390
—suspension of use, **28,** 383
—termination of use, **28,** 369–413, *passim*
inviolability, **34,** 148–150
waiver, **34,** 150
—in contract of sale, **28,** 374–375
marriage on, applicable law, **27,** 253–254
taxation of, **6,** 331; **10,** 337–352. *See also* Rates
title to, **9,** 72; **11,** 68–74
Diplomatic privileges: *see under* Diplomatic envoys *and* Diplomatic immunities
Diplomatic protection, **1,** 235–236; **3,** 292–294; **9,** 380; **16,** 235
See also Nationals, protection of
Bancroft Treaties of U.S.A., **25,** 128–129, 132
contractual claims, U.S. practice, **26,** 268
corporations, national ownership of capital, **30,** 167
discretionary nature, **25,** 121–122; **34,** 117
dual national, of, **1,** 216; **5,** 189–190; **22,** 452–457; **25,** 149–150; **30,** 369 n.
inhabitants of occupied territory, duties of occupant, **28,** 648–652
Institute of International Law, discussion by (1931), **22,** 452–453
nationality of claims and, **6,** 188–199; **22,** 349–363, 421, 432, 452–454, 455; **25,** 148–150
nationality, status of, distinguished, **3,** 269–271; **5,** 188–189; **22,** 360, 363, 365, 375–377, 380–381, 387
naturalized persons, **3,** 269–270; **22,** 357–361, 368–375, 380–381; **35,** 202
nature of, **6,** 242–246; **32,** 638, 640
protégés, **28,** 650
right to, **12,** 183; **22,** 419–421
—loss of, by residence abroad, **25,** 121
State's title to exercise of, **22,** 356–361, 365, 368, 371–377, 380–381, 387, 452
termination of, effect on citizenship, **5,** 188
waiver of right, Japanese Peace Treaty, **32,** 233, 234–235, 237
Diplomatic relations—
absence of, request for judicial assistance and, **28,** 88–92
legation buildings and property, title to, **9,** 72; **11,** 68–74
Diplomatic relations—*continued*
official communications, " treatment ", meaning, **22,** 705–710
rupture of, **12,** 285, 337–340
—access to courts by government organ, **35,** 25, 26–28, 57–61
—sovereign immunity, effect on, **32,** 70–72
—standing to sue, effect on, **32,** 70–72; **33,** 36–43
—treaties, effect on, **6,** 41–42; **12,** 278–279
" *Directement* ", meaning, **4,** 472–473
Discovery, proof of: *see under* Territory, acquisition of
Discretions—
administrative discretions of international organizations *re* their employees—
—abuse (or misuse) of power (or authority), **18,** 451; **20,** 503–505; 509–512; **21,** 357, 359, 395, 397; **23,** 558; **24,** 751, 755
—improper motivation, **20,** 521; **24,** 728, 737, 746–747. *See also détournement de pouvoir under* European Coal and Steel Community; European Economic Community; International organization
—of Director-General of F.A.O., **21,** 395–398
— —of I.L.O., **21,** 348, 357–359; **24,** 750–755, 755–756
— —of UNESCO, **21,** 355; **22,** 778–782, 802–808; **23,** 549, 560–561, 571
— —of W.H.O., **18,** 469
—of High Authority of E.C.S.C., **23,** 627–628
—of Secretary-General of U.N., **18,** 451–453; **19,** 492–494, 496–497, 499–500; **21,** 361, 370–371, 377–378, 386; **22,** 790–792, 817–819; **23,** 619–620, 623–625; **24,** 728, 737, 746–747
of I.M.C.O. Assembly, discretion to elect Members of Maritime Safety Committee, **30,** 431–443, 444–445, 446–447
—limited by its constitution, **30,** 433–434, 438, 438–439, 443
— —by purpose of Convention, **30,** 439, 443
— —by principle of abuse of right, **30,** 445
— —by rules of international law, **30,** 446–467
of international organizations, limited by reason and good faith, **15,** 336, 339, 344, 345, 346

Discretions—*continued*
—by terms of constitution, **15**, 336–337, 342, 345, 346; **23**, 67–68
of political organs of international organizations, **15**, 335, 336–337, 339–340, 341–342, 343, 344; **21**, 319–320, 330–331, 337–340, 342–343, 347; **23**, 67–68
of Security Council, admission of new members, **15**, 335, 336–337, 339–340, 341–342, 343, 344
of U.N. General Assembly to approve budget, **21**, 319–320, 330–331, 337–340, 342–343, 347
—limited by obligations already incurred, **21**, 320
—limited by *res judicata*, **21**, 320
of U.N. General Assembly to modify its procedure, **23**, 67–68
of states—
—limited by requirement of good faith: *see* Abuse of right *and* Good faith
—*re* administration of Mandates and Trusteeship Agreements, **24**, 686–687
—*re* residence of aliens, **7**, 327
—*re* right of passage to enclaves, **31**, 26, 36, 37, 55, 75, 82
—to appraise validity of reservations to multilateral treaties, **18**, 373–374, 385, 386, 387
—to make reservation to acceptance of compulsory jurisdction of I.C.J., **24**, 806–809, 821, 835–836; **27**, 488–490, 508–512, 522–527, 534–555
— —judicial control of, **24**, 821, 835–836; **27**, 511–512, 526, 547–549
Discrimination: *see also under* Aliens—
belligerent occupant, by, **21**, 144–145
burden of proof, **22**, 741
constitutional provisions, **7**, 311–312
contract between alien and national of legislating State, **30**, 375–376
Cuba, naturalized citizens in, **12**, 197
currency matters, State responsibility, **26**, 285
Czech measures against German property, **26**, 41, 47, 51
enemy property, against, **21**, 140–146; **22**, 365; **25**, 342–344, 346, 354, 359
enemy property, treatment of, Germany, Settlement Convention (1952/54), **25**, 342–344, 346, 354, 359; **29**, 333–334, 339, 341, 355–361, 493, 495–499
European Coal and Steel Community Treaty, **22**, 739–740, 741–744, 748; **23**, 601–604; **24**, 698–699; **25**,
Discrimination—*continued*
European Coal and Steel Community Treaty—*continued*
388–392, 402, 406, 410, 418, 426–427, 437–440, 451–452, 459, 460, 466–468; **29**, 142–147, 203–204, 208, 385–386
—*détournement de pouvoir* and, **25**, 449–451, 479–480, 482
—publication, distinguished, **22**, 741
expropriation and, **3**, 231–232; **8**, 336–337; **26**, 41, 47–48; **30**, 30; **33**, 30–33
fiscal legislation, **26**, 56–57
free access to courts, **23**, 314
Indonesian measures against Dutch property, **26**, 39; **33**, 30–33
mandated territories, in, **8**, 110–113
naturalized citizens, against, **12**, 197; **16**, 195 n.
neutral property, treatment of, Germany, Settlement Convention (1952/54), **25**, 516
prisoners of war, treatment of, Germany, Settlement Convention (1952/54), **25**, 351, 352–356
racial: *see* Racial discrimination
State responsibility and: *see under* State responsibility
trade, defined, **26**, 604–605
" Discrimination of an unfair nature " (railway convention), **5**, 419
Disputed territory, *de facto* jurisdiction over, **1**, 105–106; **8**, 157–158
Disputes, international, **1**, 367–381; **2**, 359–402; **3**, 397–432; **4**, 461–527; **5**, 423–472; **6**, 417–433; **7**, 477–498; **8**, 478–491; **9**, 502–527; **10**, 424–430; **11**, 237; **15**, 349–355; **16**, 399–341; **17**, 331–342; **18**, 470–472; **19**, 501–549; **20**, 534–577; **21**, 399–415; **22**, 820–892; **23**, 632–683; **24**, 761–882; **25**, 495–558; **26**, 624–625; **27**, 472–611; **28**, 544–594; **29**, 289–328; **30**, 448–493; **31**, 489; **32**, 549–551; **33**, 418–443; **34**, 474–489; **35**, 352–501. *See also* Arbitration, international; Permanent Court of Arbitration; Permanent Court of International Justice; International Court of Justice.
admission to United Nations, effect, **35**, 379, 435, 436–437, 465
classification of, **4**, 503–504
Commission of enquiry, fact-finding, **35**, 485–501
development of international law as to, **19**, 529
" difference of opinion ", meaning, **3**, 426–427; **4**, 503–504

Disputes, international—*continued*
existence of—
—condition precedent to jurisdiction, **3,** 426–428; **4,** 506–510; **17,** 336–337
—negotiation and, **2,** 398–402; **3,** 426–427; **4,** 508; **24,** 848–849, 864–865; **25,** 51
facts and situations causing, distinguished, **27,** 486, 514; **31,** 73, 102–103
limitation *ratione temporis,* **35,** 379, 435–437, 465
meaning, **2,** 400; **3,** 427; **4,** 506–510; **17,** 341–342; **24,** 840; **27,** 506, 513; **31,** 42; **35,** 363, 377, 378–379, 381, 409, 422–424, 439–445, 461–463
mediation, **30,** 461
moment when dispute arises, **27,** 484–487, 495–503, 505–508, 513; **30,** 448–450; **31,** 40, 41–44, 58, 71–74, 102
negotiation, proposals made in, evidentiary value, **27,** 91
negotiation, requirement of, **35,** 381, 429–435, 449–450, 463, 469
subject of, distinguished from particular claims, **27,** 493–494, 514, 521
technicalities, role of, **25,** 262, 264–265
territorial: *see* Territorial disputes
Distress, entry into port of ship in, **5,** 129–131; **6,** 154–156; **7,** 208; **9,** 165; **11,** 127–130
Divorce—
Chancellor of Consulate General, **11,** 211–212
consuls, suits against, **4,** 378–380; **5,** 322; **11,** 211–212
Hague Convention on Conflicts of Divorce Laws (1902), **5,** 244–245, 352; **19,** 559
nationality, effect on, **32,** 170–173, 176–177
Russian Orthodox Church, granted by, validity, **4,** 69–71
Soviet decrees, **6,** 144–145
Dodecanese Islands—
occupation of, **15,** 322–323
status of, **19,** 135–137; **20,** 628
" Dol ": *see* Air Transport, International, Warsaw Convention
Domestic claims tribunals—
international law, application of, **26,** 270
judicial review, law of U.S.A., **22,** 405–407; **24,** 316–318; **26,** 347–352. *See also* U.S.A., Foreign Claims Settlement Commission
Domestic jurisdiction, matters of, **2,** 349–354, 362–363; **14,** 100; **24,** 787, 799, 806, 807–808, 830–831, 849–850, 859–860, 866–869; **27,** 488–489, 526, 549, 554; **31,** 33, 34, 39, 40–41, 85: *see also* Art. 2 (7) of U.N. Charter in the Table of Treaties
action by anti-aircraft forces in national airspace, **27,** 559
currency, **26,** 285
seizure of enemy property, **27,** 488–489, 526, 549, 554
U.N. intervention in, **34,** 319, 388–389
Domicile—
allegiance and, **17,** 242
commercial, **18,** 729
diplomatic envoys, **1,** 291–292; **15,** 309–311
enemy character of goods, as test of, **1,** 426–427
establishment, contrasted, **3,** 376
establishment of, illegal entry, effect, **26,** 497–498, 505
nationality, effect on, **3,** 264–265
naturalization and, **17,** 241–242
Dominican Republic—
aliens, right to legal aid, **23,** 381–382
Extradition Treaty with U.S.A. (1909), **34,** 139
nationality law, married women, **32,** 192–194
Dominion, territorial, power and, **28,** 55, 58, 71
Dominions, British; Dominion status: *see under* Commonwealth
Donauversinkung, **4,** 128–133
Dorpat, Treaty of, Finland/Russia (1920), **2,** 395
Double criminality (double jeopardy)
extradition, in: *see under* Extradition
foreign armed forces, and, **22,** 267–270
status of forces agreements, **34,** 192–198
Double nationality: *see* Nationality, dual
Double taxation—
exempt income considered for rate-fixing, **29,** 66–67
non-resident alien's property, **6,** 135–136
situs of intangibles, **6,** 135–136
succession of federal State, effect on treaty, **5,** 350
tax levied by " foreign country " not a State, **6,** 19–20
Double taxation treaties, **33,** 1–14, 400–407
" dividend stripping ", and, **33,** 1–14
effect on nationals of Party, **23,** 489–493

Double taxation treaties—*continued*
  " income ", whether includes capital gains, **27**, 291–293
  income tax, exemption provision, **35**, 278–282
  interpretation, **34**, 187–191, 199–201
  interpretation, purposes of conventions, **35**, 281
  interpretation, same in courts of both Parties, **33**, 407 n.
  Italian–Swiss Establishment Convention (1868), **25**, 313–325
  later inconsistent statute, **33**, 1–14
  Luxembourg/Prussia treaty on, **5**, 350
  most-favoured-nation clauses in, **25**, 318–319
  " permanent establishment therein ", **33**, 400–407; **34**, 200
  Poland/Danzig Agreement (1924), **4**, 411
  taxation of foreign aircraft, **32**, 90–91, 95–100
  U.K./U.S.A. Convention (1945), **24**, 632–637
Dresden, Treaty of (navigation on Scheldt) (1922), **9**, 121
Drugs and narcotics, importation into Egypt, **11**, 169–170
Dual nationality: *see under* Nationality
" Due process of law "—
  aliens, right to, **3**, 287; **11**, 192–194; **20**, 330–333; **21**, 213–218
  meaning, **11**, 81
Dumbarton Oaks, Conference of (1944), U.N. voting system, **22**, 679
Dumping, defined, **26**, 604
Duress—
  in conclusion of treaty: *see under* Treaties
  property removed by, in war, burden of proof, **20**, 488–490
Dutch East India Company, acquisition of territorial sovereignty by, **4**, 103, 108–110
  transfer of sovereignty to Republic of United States of Indonesia, effect on nationality, **17**, 109–110; **19**, 318–319
Duties, customs: *see* Customs duties

E

Easement of necessity, **31**, 70, 81
East Germany: *see* Germany, East
East India Company, as successor to Sikh Kingdom, **24**, 76
East Indies, acquisition of territorial sovereignty over, **4**, 109
Eastern Galicia, status in 1939...**26**, 703
Economic and Financial Control, Systems of, Inter-American Conference (Washington, 1942), **22**, 916; **23**, 703
Economic and Social Council: *see under* United Nations
Economic Conference of Allied Governments (1916), **1**, 401
Economic Statistics, Convention on (1926), **18**, 382
Ecuador—
  Bolivarian Treaty on Extradition (1911), party to, **17**, 281, 282, 285; **19**, 378, 379; **22**, 518; **23**, 414–415
  Colombia, Extradition Treaty (1911), **14**, 143
  Constitution, **22**, 916
  enemy property decrees (1942, 1944 and 1945), **22**, 916
  jurisdiction, litigation of diplomats, **5**, 303
  Maritime Zone Declaration (1952), **22**, 278, 280, 282
" Effective nationality ": *see under* Nationality
Effectiveness, principle of: *see under* Treaties, interpretation
Egypt: *see also* United Arab Republic—
  aliens in, rights of, **6**, 181
  armistice demarcation line with Israel, proof of location, **32**, 80–82
  Bill of Indemnity, 1923, acts by British military authorities, **4**, 45–46, 547
  British forces in, **6**, 174; **7**, 187–188; **13**, 90–92; **14**, 78–79; **16**, 145–146
  capitulations, régime of, **1**, 40, 42, 161–162; **3**, 20–22, 30–31, 191–193, 194–195, 196–198; **4**, 44–46; **5**, 131–137; **6**, 180–182; **7**, 200–201; **8**, 255–262; **25**, 207
  —abolition, **3**, 192–193; **4**, 192–193; **8**, 256; **9**, 466, 471–472; **11**, 226; **12**, 156; **18**, 429–430; **20**, 195–197
  —Russian nationals, position of, **3**, 30–31; **4**, 64
  Constitution (treaties, Parliamentary consent), **9**, 468
  consular courts in—
  —Danish, **8**, 261–262
  —Dutch, **1**, 161–162
  —Greek, **20**, 195–197
  —Russian, **2**, 51–52
  —United States, **10**, 263–265
  consuls in, privileged position of, **2** 304–305; **7**, 393–394; **10**, 263–265
  Customs Administration, decrees of whether acts of State, **11**, 224–226
  Customs Statute, recognition by foreign States, **6**, 369
  Danish consular courts in, **8**, 261-262
  Dutch consular courts in, **1**, 161–162

Egypt—*continued*
exchange control laws, **33,** 16–17
foreign officials (Law of 1923), **5,** 134
France—
—Foreign Legion in, **12,** 154–162
—Military Mission in, **12,** 164
—protectorate over Tunis, recognition of, **4,** 46
—sailors in, jurisdiction over, **12,** 115–119
French Property Commission, immunity of members, **34,** 175–179
Germany, Agreement on consular jurisdiction (1925), **5,** 132
Greece—
—Air Force, in, **11,** 170–171
—Army, in, **12,** 150–152, 152–154
—consular courts in, **20,** 195–197
—sailors in, jurisdiction over, **11,** 165–169, 169–170; **12,** 120–123
independence, **1,** 204–205
Iran, Treaty of Friendship (1928), **6,** 343–344
Israel—
—General Armistice Agreement (1949), **28,** 652–653; **31,** 512–514; **32,** 80–82
—hostilities with (1948), **17,** 345–349, 440–447
—relations with, 1951–1956 ... **31,** 512–515
Japan, Customs Agreement (1930), **11,** 224–226
Khedive, claims against United Kingdom, **4,** 434n.
Lausanne, Treaty of (1923) and, **3,** 53, 192–193; **4,** 48–49, 192–193
Law of June 14, 1958, Compensation Agreement with Suez Canal Company, **28,** 181, 183, 184
" local subject ", meaning, **1,** 205
mandate over Syria and Lebanon, recognition of, **4,** 48–49
Mixed Courts of—
—jurisdiction of, **1,** 40, 161–162; **3,** 21–22; **4,** 48–49, 57, 64, 335–336; **5,** 135–137, 486; **6,** 180–181, 182, 193–195; **7,** 187–188, 200; **8,** 255–261; **9,** 466–468, 471, 478–480; **11,** 146
—jurisdiction, acts of State and, **2,** 172–173; **3,** 21; **4,** 27–28; **11,** 224–226
—jurisdiction, crew-member of Greek warship on shore mission, **11,** 165–166
—jurisdiction, foreign armed forces, **11,** 165–171
—jurisdiction, ships in harbour, **9,** 167
—responsibility for, **25,** 207
—Rules concerning Judicial Organization, **5,** 135; **11,** 166

Egypt—*continued*
Montreux Convention (1937), regarding abolition of capitulations, **8,** 256; **9,** 466, 471–472; **11,** 226; **12,** 156; **18,** 429–430; **20,** 195–197
national tribunals, Organic Law for, **5,** 135
nationality of Ottoman subjects, **1,** 40–41
nationalization of Suez Canal Company (1956), **28,** 177, 180–181
Russian consular courts in, **2,** 51–52
Russian nationals, position under capitulatory régime, **3,** 30–31; **4,** 64
Sanitary and Quarantine Council, **1,** 364; **6,** 414
siege, proclamation of state of, **1,** 42
Soviet Government, non-recognition of, **2,** 51–53; **4,** 64–65, 173–174; **5,** 48–49
Suez Canal, defence of, **17,** 445–447
—prohibition of passage of munitions, **4,** 27–28
Suez Canal Company, contract with Viceroy (1866), **5,** 137
—nationalization of (1956), **28,** 177, 180–181
telegraphic service in, **6,** 413
traffic in dangerous drugs, **11,** 169–170
Turkish suzerainty over, abolition, effect on loans of Suzerain, **3,** 20–22
United Kingdom—
—Convention *re* Sudan (1899), **4,** 57
—military occupation by, **5,** 485–486; **7,** 187–188
—protectorate, **1,** 40–42; **2,** 21–26
— — recognition of, **1,** 42, 162
— — termination of, **31,** 516
—Treaty of Alliance (1936), **9,** 478–479; **11,** 168; **14,** 79; **16,** 145–146; **17,** 445, 447
United States consular courts in, **10,** 263–265
Eire: *see also* Ireland, Republic of
Aliens Act (1935), **18,** 342–343
citizens, liability to national service in U.K., **10,** 27–37
Commonwealth, position in, **8,** 81–87; **10,** 27–37
Constitution (1937), Art. 29 (3), (international law), **12,** 97–98; **18,** 336, 337
Constitution Act, 1922...**10,** 30
Customs Act, 1945...**24,** 95–96
establishment of, Agreement with U.K. (1921), **2,** 368; **3,** 98; **8,** 82; **19,** 46
Estonia, non-recognition of annexation of, **10,** 91–97
Great Britain, whether part of, **10,** 37–38
Offences against the State Acts (1939 and 1940), **24,** 420–425

Eire—*continued*
recognition as independent State, **10,** 36
status, **10,** 27–38; **19,** 46
succession to property of revolutionary Government, **3,** 98–102
U.K., Irish Free State Agreement (1921), **2,** 368; **3,** 98; **8,** 82; **19,** 46
Ejus est interpretare legem cujus condere, **2,** 384
Ejusdem generis, rule of, **1,** 358; **3,** 381–382; **25,** 340: *see also* Treaties, interpretation
Elbe, navigation, Treaties of Dresden (1922) and Prague (1923), **9,** 121
" Elementary considerations of humanity ", **4,** 235–236; **16,** 158
Embargo—
anticipatory, in time of peace, **10,** 512–513
meaning, **6,** 375
occupying authorities, by, **12,** 463–466
use of ships, on, **21,** 12–16
Emergency legislation, most-favoured-nation clause and, **11,** 235–236
Eminent domain, **1,** 418: *see also* Expropriation; Nationalization
Enclaves, territorial, right of passage for access, **31,** 23–121, *passim*
armed police, **31,** 53–56, 61, 63, 64–65, 90, 92, 93, 96, 97, 98, 108, 110–111, 115, 119
arms and ammunition, **31,** 53, 55–56, 61, 65–67, 90, 92, 93, 96, 97, 98, 100–101, 108, 115, 119
civil officials, **31,** 93, 101
content of right, **31,** 67, 104, 108
continuance of administration by one State, relevance, **31,** 61
correlative obligation to permit exercise of right, **31,** 99, 106, 107
de facto government in enclaves, effect on right, **31,** 84
discretion of territorial State, **31,** 26, 36, 37, 55, 75, 82
domestic jurisdiction of territorial State, **31,** 85
exercise of right, control of, **31,** 67, 69, 75, 79, 92, 93, 97–98, 101–102, 105, 108, 111, 114
—effective and regular, **31,** 80
formal authorization, need for, **31,** 62–63, 65, 66–67, 82, 89, 94–96, 106, 111–112, 113, 114
immunity of passengers, **31,** 45, 49, 75, 105, 117
incident of tenure, as, **31,** 78, 81, 98, 109
indivisibility of, **31,** 92
municipal law, **31,** 70, 116
nature of right, **31,** 85, 107, 108, 114
Enclaves, territorial, right of passage for access—*continued*
private persons and armed forces, distinction between, **31,** 52–56, 58, 61, 92–93, 107, 108, 115
reciprocity, **31,** 61, 63, 65, 93, 106, 110, 114
refusal of passage, circumstances justifying, **31,** 57–58
restrictions upon, **31,** 100, 102, 106, 119–121
suspension of, **31,** 83
troops, **31,** 53–56, 58, 61, 63–65, 82, 83, 85, 90, 92, 93, 94–96, 97, 98, 108, 110–111, 115, 119
Enemies, unarmed, killing of, **2,** 436–437
Enemy: *see also* Trading with the enemy; War, effect of outbreak of
Enemy, ally of, status, **9,** 575n.
" Enemy ", definition—
—Belgian law, **15,** 465–466; **22,** 922
—English law, **10,** 530; **19,** 574–575
—United States law, **17,** 372–376; **19,** 581; **26,** 663–664
Enemy aliens—
administration of estate of deceased, **9,** 33–35, 548–549
change of sovereignty and, **18,** 244–246
copyright and, **15,** 439–441; **18,** 24–36, 530
corporations: *see* Corporations, enemy
declaration of war, **5,** 483–484
detention of—
—U.S. law, **12,** 185–194
—writ of habeas corpus, **10,** 317, 450–454; **13,** 314–315, 317–321, 320; **15,** 211–214; **16,** 425
expulsion, **13,** 233–234, 316; **14,** 18–19, 450–451; **15,** 227, 240–242, 450–452, 508–512
extraterritorial courts, in, **1,** 402, 403
finding as to status of, **15,** 259–260
inherit, right to, **5,** 258–260; **11,** 238–242, 251–255; **12,** 222–226; **18,** 499–508; **26,** 675–680
interned—
—right to recover property after war, **31,** 503–508
—subsequent naturalization, **31,** 503–508
internment, **12,** 185–195, 199–202; **14,** 18–19; **15,** 455; **26,** 652, 653–655
—effect on contracts, **31,** 494–495
—judicial review of, **31,** 503–508
—right to effective defence, **10,** 447–450
persona standi in judicio—
—defendant, as, **9,** 536–546; **10,** 446–450, 481, 490–499; **12,** 329–332, 340–341; **14,** 182–184

Enemy aliens—*continued*
persona standi in judicio—*continued*
—habeas corpus, right to, **10,** 317, 450–454; **13,** 314–315, 317, 320; **15,** 211–214; **16,** 425
—right to sue, **3,** 446–447, 454; **6,** 437–438; **9,** 32–35, 559–561; **10,** 442–446, 455–480, 481–490, 535–558; **11,** 245–249; **12,** 113–115, 328–329, 332–336, 339–340; **13,** 234–237, 317; **14,** 179, 181–182, 184–187; **15,** 108–109, 452–454; **16,** 385–388; **18,** 509–512; **19,** 578–579, 588–590; **20,** 622–627; **22,** 909–911; **24,** 932–938; **26,** 668–674
persons assimilated to, **17,** 237–239
pre-war contract with, **31,** 490–495
principal, capacity to ratify agent's acts, **27,** 645–648
prisoners of war, whether, **9,** 539; **10,** 450–454, 529–530
property of: *see* Enemy property
refugees, as, **16,** 260–261
restitution, right to, **16,** 263–265
right to inherit property, **5,** 258–260; **11,** 238–242, 251–255; **12,** 222–226; **18,** 499–508; **26,** 675–680
right to sue: *see persona standi in judicio, supra*
security for costs and, **18,** 289–290
service of writ of summons on, **9,** 537; **10,** 446–447
status of, **4,** 548; **11,** 260–264: *see also* Enemy character
—finding of Executive as to, conclusiveness, **15,** 259–260
—recognition of new State, effect, **11,** 56–61, 247–249
statutes of limitation and, **2,** 413–414; **22,** 909–911
Trading with the Enemy Act, position under (Canada), **9,** 552
treatment of, **13,** 137, 142–143, 233–238; **18,** 291–292
war, outbreak of, effect—
—personal status, **1,** 401–406; **2,** 413–414; **3,** 445–447; **5,** 483–484; **6,** 437–438; **9,** 536–546; **10,** 442–499; **11,** 58–61, 247–250; **12,** 328–341; **13,** 233–237; **14,** 179, 181–187; **15,** 450–456; **16,** 385–388; **17,** 237–239; **18,** 509–512; **22,** 909–911; **24,** 932–936; **26,** 652
—property, **1,** 406–410; **3,** 447–456; **4,** 541; **5,** 484–486; **7,** 501–505; **8,** 492–502; **9,** 546–553; **10,** 500–508; **11,** 250–256; **12,** 342–353; **13,** 237–238; **14,** 187–192; **15,** 24–27, 456–460; **17,** 359–367; **18,** 513–516; **19,** 571, 580–587; **20,** 600–602; **21,** 141–146; **22,** 911–917; **23,** 687–706; **24,** 893–896;

Enemy aliens—*continued*
war, outbreak of, effect—*continued*
—property—*continued*
26, 653–662; **27,** 488; **28,** 605–611; **29,** 329–354; **30,** 33–38, 39, 41, 49; **31,** 495–503: *see also* Trading with the enemy
Enemy character—
belligerent occupation and, **18,** 521–528, 575–585
cargo, of, **17,** 440–448; **31,** 520
corporations, of, **1,** 229–230, 424–426; **3,** 463–467; **9,** 557–561; **10,** 535–538; **11,** 258–260; **12,** 365–383; **13,** 244–246; **15,** 452–454, 466–467; **16,** 389–390; **17,** 402; **18,** 530, 642, 650; **19,** 592–596; **20,** 615–617; **21,** 464–471; **22,** 923–924; **24,** 907–910, 911–915; **33,** 444–450
determination of, **17,** 402–404
goods, of, **1,** 426–427; **4,** 547–548; **9,** 565–570; **10,** 558–564; **12,** 358, 365–373, 386–396, 460–461, 524, 554–557, 559–562, 570–572; **16,** 572; **18,** 531; **20,** 622; **22,** 1008–1011; **24,** 923–924
—control test, **18,** 531
—currency captured from enemy, **28,** 636–638
—domicile test, **1,** 426–427
—transfer of goods at sea, **13,** 428
individuals, of, **1,** 404–405, 422–423; **2,** 427–428; **3,** 461–463; **4,** 546–547; **5,** 483–484; **8,** 502–503; **10,** 529–534; **12,** 360–365; **13,** 240–243, 284–285; **15,** 441–447, 461–466; **16,** 580; **17,** 368–377; **18,** 521–530; **19,** 578–591; **22,** 918–922; **24,** 903–906; **31,** 503–508; **32,** 557–560; **33,** 450; **34,** 494–496
—acquisition, unneutral service, **3,** 461
—" de-enemization ", **17,** 376–377
—dual nationals, **14,** 124, 192
—hostilities, cessation of, effect, **26,** 678
—loss of, effect, **18,** 24–36
—nationality and, **15,** 466; **18,** 244–246; **19,** 587–591
—presumption, **12,** 390
—refugees, **11,** 255–256
—residence and, **1,** 387; **2,** 427–428; **3,** 445–446; **4,** 548; **10,** 529–530; **15,** 461–466; **17,** 372–376; **18,** 521–525, 575–585; **19,** 574–576, 578–591; **22,** 918–921; **24,** 905–906; **26,** 663–666; **28,** 633–635
—stateless persons, **1,** 404–405; **22,** 921–922
—war, state of, and, **23,** 758–759
—war, termination of, effect, **11,** 269
partnerships, **15,** 466

Enemy character—*continued*
ships, of, **9,** 561; **11,** 260–265; **12,** 383–386; **13,** 401–406; **16,** 389–390; **17,** 378–385; **18,** 725–730; **24,** 916–923; **32,** 602, 604, 606, 607, 612, 617–618, 623
—flag, conclusiveness of, **11,** 264–265; **16,** 389–390; **17,** 378–385; **24,** 919–921
—nationality and ownership, distinction, **32,** 610–611, 618
territory occupied by enemy, **13,** 240–246; **14,** 181–182
trademarks, **20,** 600–602
Enemy corporations: *see* Corporations, enemy, *and* Enemy character, corporations
Enemy destination, **11,** 306–307; **12,** 286–288, 365–373, 543–564, 570–572, 573; **13,** 414–421, 425–432; **18,** 724
presumption of, **12,** 287–288, 563–564, 569–570
Enemy government, right to sue, **10,** 454–455; **18,** 493–498
Enemy merchant ships: *see* Enemy character, ships, *and under* Merchant ships
" Enemy national ", meaning, **11,** 259–260; **19,** 586–587; **22,** 918–919
—*locus standi in judicio,* **19,** 587–591
Enemy property: *see also* Custodian of enemy property; Trading with the enemy—
administrator of, fraud or negligence, State responsibility, **21,** 141–146; **22,** 312–317
appropriation of, **2,** 438–439; **20,** 462–471; **22,** 911–912, 980–982: *see also* Booty
—act of State doctrine and, **26,** 690
—domestic jurisdiction, matter of, **27,** 488
—prize decision, whether required, **26,** 690–691
bearer bonds, seizure of, **18,** 513–515
capture of, unfinished ships, **20,** 674
compensation for destruction, **7,** 323–324
compensation for sequestration and sale, **22,** 307–311
confiscation, **1,** 409–410; **15,** 13–17, 24–27; **20,** 602–609; **24,** 893–896; **33,** 447, 448–449
—international law, compatibility with, **17,** 164; **22,** 914–915; **24,** 895
—nationality, reasons of, **26,** 653–655
—neutral States, effect in, **17,** 163–166
—renunciation of power of, **8,** 499
Enemy property—*continued*
confiscation—*continued*
—vesting in Custodian after hostilities ended, **33,** 445–446, 448–449
control of, **22,** 967–972; **29,** 331–340
—Italian law, **29,** 26–29, 47–50
—termination of war, effect of, **22,** 932–935, 935–939; **26,** 672–673, 680
—United States law, **12,** 225–229
conversion of building to air-raid shelter, **22,** 304–305
copyright, **15,** 439–441; **18,** 24–36, 530
corporations, of, **18,** 529. *See also* Corporations, enemy
custodian of: *see* Custodian of Enemy Property
discriminatory treatment, **21,** 141–146; **22,** 305
—Germany, Settlement Convention (1952/54), **25,** 342–344, 346, 354, 359; **29,** 333–334, 339, 341, 345
enemy stockholder's interest in non-enemy corporation, **3,** 447–448
estate of deceased non-enemy, **27,** 615–616, 622–624
expropriation, **22,** 911–912, 913–915
German legislation on (Second World War), **25,** 336–337, 338–340, 341–342, 347
goodwill, whether within Trading with the Enemy legislation, **27,** 639–645
governmental property, **21,** 432–436, 439–442
heirs, rights of, to, **22,** 912–913
lienholder, sale by, with consent of Custodian, **29,** 349–354
liquidation, **23,** 687–701
meaning, **18,** 184–188
naturalization of owner, **18,** 254–255
nature of vesting in Custodian, **28,** 605–607
neutral corporation carrying on business in enemy territory, **3,** 448–449
ownership of appropriating State, nature of, **8,** 499; **18,** 515–516; **22,** 911–912
patent rights, **3,** 450–451
Protecting Power and, **12,** 348–349
relevance of foreign law in determining, **27,** 639–640
restoration, **3,** 450–451; **15,** 261–262; **22,** 916–917; **25,** 341–349, 357–360; **29,** 361–362
retaliatory legislation, proportionality, **29,** 346–347
retention, **22,** 982–987
sale, **11,** 250–251
—compensation for, **22,** 917
seizure of, **30,** 1–3, 41, 44, 48

Enemy property—*continued*
seizure of—*continued*
—belligerent forces, by, **22,** 953–959, 966–972
—beneficial ownership, effect on, **32,** 581
—consistency with prior treaty, **28,** 367–469
—U.S. practice, **8,** 492–502; **18,** 513–515
sequestration, **4,** 541; **7,** 501–505; **8,** 501–502; **11,** 255–256, 258–260; **14,** 16–17; **15,** 602–604; **22,** 317–329, 915–917; **24,** 893
—compensation for, **22,** 306–307, 307–311; **29,** 383–389
—expropriation distinguished, **22,** 912
—nationality, change of, effect of, **15,** 460
—occupied territory, in, **16,** 491–492
—State responsibility, **21,** 141–146; **22,** 301–307, 312–317, 317–329
—trademarks, **26,** 657–662
state of war and, **19,** 555n.
statutes of limitations and: *see* Statutes of limitations, war, effect of
testamentary dispositions in favour of neutral subjects, **3,** 453–456
trademarks, cancellation of, **23,** 701–706
trademarks, confiscation of, **20,** 602–609; **26,** 656
—confiscation of undertaking, whether included in, **17,** 163–164
trademarks, sequestration of, **26,** 657–662
transfer in anticipation of war, **14,** 190–192
trust under will taking effect during war, **3,** 449–450
undivided estate including non-enemy property, **26,** 657
unfinished hulls in shipyard, whether prize, **20,** 667–674
unlawfully vested in Government, right to recover, **28,** 629–633
war, outbreak of, effect, **1,** 406–410; **3,** 447–456; **4,** 541; **5,** 484–487; **7,** 501–505; **8,** 492–502; **9,** 546–553; **10,** 500–508; **11,** 250–256; **12,** 342–352; **14,** 187–192; **15,** 456–460; **17,** 359–367; **18,** 513–516; **19,** 571, 580–587; **20,** 600–602; **21,** 141–146; **22,** 911–917; **23,** 687–706; **24,** 893–896; **26,** 653–662
war, termination of, effect, **22,** 932–935, 935–939; **26,** 672–673, 680
Enemy State—
action commenced by, before outbreak of war, **9,** 93
jurisdictional immunity, **10,** 576–581
right to sue, **12,** 337–340
Enemy status: *see* Enemy character
Enemy stockholder, interest of, in non-enemy corporations, **3,** 447–448
Enemy subjects: *see* Enemy aliens
"Enemy territory"—
meaning, **17,** 369–371; **19,** 555
occupation of: *see* Belligerent occupation
recognition of States and, **11,** 58–61
Enforcement of treaties: *see under* Treaties
England: *see also* Great Britain *and* United Kingdom—
France—
—Commercial Treaties (1606 and 1655), **20,** 99, 132
—Treaty of Calais (1360), **20,** 98, 118, 119, 121, 132, 133, 137, 138
—Treaty of Lambeth (1217), **20,** 98, 128, 129, 131, 132
—Treaty of Étaples (1492), **20,** 132
—Treaty of Paris (1259), **20,** 95, 98, 116, 118, 120, 129–135, *passim*
—Treaty of Picquigny-Amiens (1475), **20,** 128, 132
—Treaty of Troyes (1420), **20,** 99, 116, 120, 132, 133
—Truce of London (1471), **20,** 99, 132, 133
Netherlands, Treaty of Commerce (1654), **23,** 729
Offences at Sea Act, 1536...**24,** 165
Spain, Treaty of Peace and Commerce (1661), **23,** 313, 321, 322
Spain and France, Boundary Treaty (1763), territory in North America, **7,** 131
Sweden, Treaties of Peace and Commerce (1654 and 1661), **20,** 554; **23,** 313, 321, 322
Enlistment for military service against foreign State, **1,** 180–182; **8,** 278
Enlistment for military service, loss of nationality through: *see under* Nationality, loss of
"*Enrichissement sans cause*": *see* Unjust enrichment
Envoys, special: *see* Consuls; Diplomatic envoys; Trade delegations
Epirus, occupation by Greece, **3,** 481–482
"Equal protection" clause of Fourteenth Amendment (U.S. Constitution), **1,** 240 n.; **2,** 265–266, 314; **11,** 192, 196; **19,** 312; **20,** 346; **24,** 478
"Equality in fact and in law", minorities treaties, **2,** 290–291; **8,** 386–391
Equality of opportunity, mandated territories, **8,** 110–113

Equality of parties, **1**, 371; **23**, 523–524, 541, 542, 544, 545
Equality of States, **1**, 24, 332, 371, 418; **2**, 211; **3**, 42; **9**, 8–12; **15**, 26; **17**, 283; **21**, 344; **22**, 445, 448, 454, 455; **24**, 124, 125–126, 845–847, 853. *See also* Independence of States
Equality of treatment of aliens: *see under* Aliens
Equity: *see also Ex aequo et bono*, **1**, 239, 336–337, 349–350, 367–369, 369–371, 373–374, 377; **2**, 38, 158, 170–171, 190, 192, 267, 359–367, 367–368, 379, 419; **3**, 108, 231–232, 246, 357–359, 397–400, 414–415, 419; **4**, 111–112, 131, 275, 466, 467–469; **5**, 59, 64–65, 149, 168, 181, 198–199, 201, 209–210, 439, 450–451, 459–461, 470; **6**, 71, 189–193, 207, 208–209, 214–215, 231–232, 233; **7**, 121–127, 262, 477–479; **8**, 271, 450–451; **9**, 317, 581–583; **14**, 324; **20**, 68–69, 72, 75–76, 541–542, 544, 545, 547, 555–556; **21**, 146, 395, 397, 398; **22**, 104, 347–348, 413–417, 782, 838, 871, 872; **23**, 298, 301, 321–322, 537, 569, 571, 626–627; **24**, 296; **25**, 501, 503, 506, 529, 551–552n.; **30**, 485, 486
acquired rights and, **6**, 71; **20**, 68–69, 72, 75–76
Administrative Tribunal of the I.L.O. and recourse to principles of, **21**, 395; **22**, 782–783; **23**, 537. *See also* Discretions, administrative
Anglo-Italian Conciliation Commission and, **22**, 872
apportionment as a principle of, **20**, 75, 541–547
arbitrability and, **2**, 359–367
arbitration, application of in—
—" *amiables compositeurs* ", **24**, 761, 765, 766, 767, 836
—Germany, Arbitral Commission on Property, Rights and Interests, **25**, 501, 503, 506, 529, 551–552n.
—" justice, equity, and good faith ", **2**, 368; **3**, 231–232
—" principles of international law and equity ", **1**, 377; **3**, 246; **3**, 397–400
—" principles of international law, justice and equity ", **1**, 369; **2**, 415; **3**, 231, 235–237, 397–400; **4**, 466–467, 467–469; **7**, 477–480
—" the legitimate needs of the parties concerned ", **1**, 336, 349, 367–369
—" the principles of justice and equity ", **5**, 452–455
—" the principles of justice, equity and good conscience ", **20**, 541, 545

Equity—*continued*
arbitration, application of in—*continued*
—" the principles of law and equity ", **1**, 369–371, 377–378; **6**, 188–190
—" treaty rights and principles of international law and equity ", **1**, 377; **2**, 419
award taking into account " the equities of a claim ", **1**, 373–374
Calvo Clause and, **5**, 209–210
compensation and, **2**, 419; **4**, 275; **5**, 168, 199; **6**, 207; **7**, 478–479; **8**, 271; **9**, 581–583; **22**, 838; **23**, 298, 301, 626–627
compensation *ex aequo et bono*, **5**, 201–202; **7**, 262–263; **21**, 146; **22**, 782–783; **23**, 537
conflicting interests of States, **2**, 158; **4**, 131
contiguity in territorial claims and, **4**, 111–112
diplomatic protection of corporations of foreign nationality, **2**, 190
discrimination against aliens and, **3**, 231
equitable estoppel, **2**, 381; **3**, 419; **5**, 198–199, 470
expenses of arbitration, **2**, 379
" fair compensation ", **2**, 170–171
force majeure and, **5**, 470
inadimplendi non est adimplendum, **8**, 450
inapplicability of principles of, to " decisions based on law ", **22**, 104
interest, award of, and, **6**, 231–232; **22**, 347–348, 413–417
international responsibility and, **5**, 149; **6**, 208–209, 214–215, 233; **9**, 317
interpretation of treaties and, **22**, 871–872
" justice and equity ", undertaking in treaties, that courts should administer, **20**, 555–556; **23**, 321–322; **24**, 296
laches, **3**, 246
maxims of, **8**, 450–451
meaning, **1**, 370–371, 376–377; **3**, 397–400; **4**, 400
" natural justice and equity ", **20**, 544
natural justice, real interests of claimant, **5**, 181
non liquet and, **4**, 466–467
obligation of claimant State to account for award made to national, **2**, 192
P.C.I.J. Statute, Article 38, and, **8**, 450–451
power of arbitrator to apply, **30**, 485, 486

Equity—*continued*
procedure and evidence, **3**, 414–415; **5**, 451
refuelling, 24 hours rule and, **14**, 324
Treaty of Versailles, **5**, 338–439
unjust enrichment as a principle of, **5**, 65; **9**, 581–583; **23**, 323; **24**, 296
Equity of redemption, **4**, 555; **6**, 241–242
Equity tribunal, factors considered by, **6**, 215
Erie, Lake, **4**, 122
Eritrea, occupation of, **12**, 64–68
—renunciation by Italy, **17**, 101–106
—status of (1947), **16**, 74–75
Erosion, doctrine of, **11**, 100
Error, plea of—
in boundary disputes, **33**, 71, 74, 87–89
in *compromis*, **6**, 206–207, 417–420
in decisions of arbitral tribunals, **9**, 328–332; **30**, 470, 475–476, 488–489
in decisions of Mixed Claims Commission, **8**, 484–485
in relation to acceptance of the jurisdiction of the I.C.J., **33**, 429
preclusion and, **33**, 64, 71, 87–89
Errors in judgment, responsibility for, **1**, 171–172, 172–173, 175, 177–179; **2**, 10–11; **3**, 220–221; **26**, 221, 222
Escape, right of prisoners of war to, **12**, 397–402, 407–410; **13**, 291–293; **17**, 400n.
Espionage, **5**, 5. *See also* Spies
U.N. official charged with, **32**, 308–333
violation of air space for, **30**, 69–75
war crime, as, **15**, 574–575; **16**, 271–272, 405–407; **23**, 759–762
" Essential error " in arbitration proceedings, **9**, 331–332; **30**, 470, 475–476, 488–489
Establishment, contrasted with domicile, **3**, 376
Establishment of new States, **1**, 11–21, 45; **2**, 9–11; **5**, 11–16; **23**, 101–105; **27**, 35–44
Esthonia—
German occupation of, **15**, 525–526
Government of, recognition by Great Britain, **1**, 43–46
nationalization decrees, **12**, 61–62
U.S.A., Treaty of Friendship, Commerce and Consular Rights (1925), **12**, 259–260
U.S.S.R.—
—annexation by, **10**, 70–78, 86–97; **12**, 29–39; **15**, 47, 176–204, 314; **19**, 69–71; **23**, 706
—Treaty with (1920), **9**, 308
Estoppel, **1**, 172, 332, 373–374; **2**, 38; **3**, 220–221, 246, 417–418, 418–419; **4**, 469–470, 471–472, 473, 489, 506; **5**, 180, 198–199, 217, 450–451, 469–470; **6**, 102–104; **7**, 230; **21**, 334; **24**, 837; **25**, 151, 153, 154–156; **30**, 480, 490–491; **33**, 75, 76, 82–83, 91–93. *See also* Acquiescence; Preclusion
acquiescence and, **33**, 91, 137
admissions by government representatives, **4**, 489
based on equitable considerations, **2**, 38, 176
based on public policy, **2**, 38
by conduct, **33**, 79
by decisions of municipal courts, **1**, 172, 332, 373–374
by legislation, **4**, 469–470; **5**, 198–199
by military regulations, **3**, 220–221
conditions for operation of, **33**, 92, 136–137
inconsistency between claim and prior acts, **33**, 82–84, 89
nationality, relating to, **25**, 151, 160
—passport, use of, **25**, 151, 153
non-recognition of government as, **2**, 38–39; **3**, 417–418
nullity of arbitral award, in relation to, **30**, 480, 490–491
treaty interpretation, **25**, 154–155, 156
Étaples, Treaty of (1492), **20**, 132
Ethiopia—
British occupation of, **19**, 609–611
capitulations in, **7**, 199–200
continuation of laws, **8**, 146–150
France, Commercial Treaty (1908), **7**, 199–200
Greece, Commercial Treaty (1922), **7**, 199–200
Italian conquest of, **8**, 119–123; **9**, 93, 94–101, 172
Italy as successor to, **19**, 100
Italy, Treaty of Amity (1928), **8**, 268
recognition of Italian *de facto* government, **8**, 119–123; **9**, 94–101, 172
—withdrawal of recognition of Italian conquest, **9**, 93
United Kingdom, Extradition Agreement (1944), **18**, 282, 283, 285
Eupen, transfer to Belgium (1920), **21**, 177–178
Eupen, Malmédy and Moresnet, annexation of (1940), **15**, 60–61, 528, 536
Euratom, officials, compensation for dismissal, claim for, **32**, 541–544
Europe, Council of: *see* Council of Europe
European Atomic Energy Community: *see* Euratom
European Central Inland Transport Organization, Agreement establishing (1945), **20**, 481, 487

European Coal and Steel Community, **21,** 309–310; **22,** 737–756, 886–892; **23,** 597–605, 627–631; **24,** 693–715; **25,** 369–494; **27,** 301–417; **28,** 496–508; **29,** 56–73, 77–224, 243–288; **32,** 382–439, 544–548, 549–551
administrative acts—
—acquired rights, whether, **29,** 257
—illegality, consequences of, **29,** 263
—presumption of validity, **29,** 263
—revocation of, **29,** 257–259
—severability, **29,** 255, 263–264
Belgium, limit on coal imports, **32,** 400
Caisse for Subsidies on Imported Scrap, **25,** 370, 380, 454; **29,** 168–169, 189–190, 193, 196, 197–199; **32,** 406, 438
coal prices, fixing of maximum, **27,** 334–335
Commission of Presidents, functions and powers, **29,** 251, 256, 259–263
Common Assembly—
—decisions, requirements of, **29,** 256, 259
—*détournement de pouvoir*, **29,** 244, 247
—*faute de service*, **29,** 255–256, 267–269
compensation system for Belgian coal, **25,** 423–424, 428–429, 437–440
competition, fundamental principle of, **22,** 738; **29,** 208; **32,** 429–430. *See also* monopoly, *infra*
competition, interference with, **22,** 602–603; **25,** 463, 482; **27,** 415–417
competition, prohibition of restriction of, **24,** 693–699; **32,** 422, 431–432
Consultative Committee, need to consult, **22,** 746, 749–750; **25,** 429, 458 n.
constitutional laws of member States, alleged violation by High Authority, **27,** 328, 343
Council, consultation, need for, **25,** 390, 399, 429, 446, 458 n.
Court: *see also* European Communities Court—
—access to, distributors, by, **27,** 323, 325, 342
—appeals to: *see* Court, appeals to, *infra*
—capacity of parties, **27,** 327, 329–330
—competence, **23,** 597, 605; **28,** 499: *see also* Court, appeals to, *infra*
—control over officials, **23,** 627–628
—costs, **25,** 403, 411, 413, 416, 440, 453, 456–457, 470, 474, 477–478,

European Coal and Steel Community—*continued*
Court—*continued*
—costs—*continued*
483, 489–490, 492–493; **27,** 354–355, 356, 375, 392; **29,** 85, 249–250, 267, 269
—examination of questions *ex officio*, **22,** 746, 749; **25,** 401; **27,** 413
—function concerning Treaty, **25,** 399
—further evidence, power to call, **25,** 422
—intervention, conditions for, **27,** 386
—joinder of actions, **25,** 414, 485, 488
—judgment, extent of grounds of, **22,** 749
—judgment, interpretation of, **22,** 886–892
—judgment, interpretation, " difficulty ", **22,** 890
—municipal law and, **27,** 343
—pleadings, grounds of appeal modified in reply, **27,** 303
—pleadings, new heads of action, **25,** 447–449
—pleadings, request, contents of, **25,** 441–443, 447–449; **27,** 416
—powers, **23,** 597–605
—provisional measures, grounds for granting, **27,** 322–326
—provisional measures, time for application for, **27,** 322–324
—re-opening of proceedings, **25,** 422
—Statute of, Protocol on (1951), **22,** 888–892; **29,** 67, 89, 165, 178, 283, 321–323
—withdrawal of party, **25,** 489
Court, appeals to—
—challenging several decisions, **25,** 409
—*en pleine juridiction*, **24,** 714, 715; **25,** 373; **27,** 302 n., 399, 403 n.
—enterprise or association, by, **25,** 372, 421, 461, 473, 476, 481, 485–486, 487, 490–492; **27,** 323, 325
—grounds of: *see* High Authority, competence, lack of, *and ibid. détournement de pouvoir*, *and* European Coal and Steel Community Treaty, violation of, *and ibid.* violation of substantial procedural requirement, *infra*
—parties, *locus standi*, **25,** 473, 476, 481, 485–486, 487, 490–492; **27,** 323, 325, 329–330
—time-limit, **25,** 372–373, 378 n.; **27,** 361, 364, 366, 378–379, 380, 383, 385–387
détournement de pouvoir, *see under* Common Assembly, *supra*; High Authority, *infra*; *and* European Coal and Steel Community Treaty

European Coal and Steel Community—*continued*
discrimination: *see under* European Coal and Steel Community Treaty
Experts on Transport, Commission of, **29,** 200, 202–203
fault, responsibility for, **29,** 184, 187–188
faute de service, responsibility for, **27,** 393–398; **29,** 267–269; **32,** 383–384, 386, 405, 406–407, 408–412, 413, 416, 417–418, 419, 434, 437–439
general principles of law, relevance to legality of acts, **32,** 390
German shift bonus scheme, whether State subsidy, **29,** 85–102
High Authority—
—action against wrongful act of enterprises, **25,** 430
—admission of liability by statements in Assembly, **27,** 394–395, 397–398
—amendment of general decisions, **27,** 385, 387
—annulment of decisions of, **22,** 739, 740, 747, 748, 749; **25,** 372, 378, 389, 401, 402, 407, 409, 412, 455–456; **27,** 329, 333; **29,** 87, 102, 129, 140, 150, 155, 162, 166–167, 194, 197; **32,** 385, 398
—appeal to, by associations, **25,** 415–416
—binding nature of decisions of, **28,** 500, 502
—compensation to Belgian mines, determination of, **25,** 443–444
—competence, **27,** 412–413, 415. *See also* powers, *infra*
— —alteration of subsidy system, **27,** 353–354
— —lack of, **25,** 425, 427–432; **27,** 412–413, 415; **29,** 105, 109–110, 155, 156–160, 167, 192, 194–196, 200, 201–202, 212. *See also* E.C.S.C. Treaty, *excès de pouvoir*, appeal alleging
— —to declare State in breach of Treaty, **29,** 155, 159, 164, 167
— —to impose financial obligations, **29,** 192, 193–195
— —trade regulations, **27,** 339–340, 343, 350
— —Transitional Convention, under, **29,** 200–202, 222
— —transport charges, **29,** 113–114, 117, 145–147, 150–158, 161–162, 163–167, 199–209, 219–223
—decisions, annulment of, **22,** 739, 740, 747, 748, 749; **25,** 372, 378, 389, 401, 402, 407, 409, 412, 455–456; **27,** 329, 333; **29,** 87, 102, 129, 140, 150, 155, 162, 166–167, 194, 197; **32,** 385, 398

European Coal and Steel Community—*continued*
High Authority—*continued*
—decisions, challenge by member States, **29,** 122
— —date from which effective, **29,** 121–122, 201–202
— —disguised, **29,** 83–84
— —effect on governments, **29,** 119–124
— —executory force, **25,** 371–372, 380, 455, 457–458, 461–462; **29,** 193–195
— —general or individual, **25,** 417–422, 485–488; **27,** 330–331, 385, 387; **32,** 389
— —" internal measures ", **29,** 179, 181
— —preamble, whether binding, **29,** 176, 180–181
— —reasons, need for, **23,** 599; **25,** 374–375, 412–413, 456; **29,** 106, 127, 129, 130–135, 155, 171, 176–177, 182, 212, 216
— —requirements of, **29,** 83–84
— —time-limit for challenge, **25,** 449, 458, 460, 461–462; **29,** 124
— —time-limit for compliance, **29,** 124
— —whether letter constitutes, **25,** 417–422, 485–488; **27,** 301–303, 352–356, 361, 363, 365, 367, 372, 373, 375–376, 379, 381, 392, 404, 407–408; **29,** 171–172, 184–186; **32,** 383, 384, 385
— —whether silence constitutes, **27,** 361, 363, 366
—delegation of powers, **25,** 372, 375–378, 456; **32,** 411, 438
—*détournement de pouvoir*, **21,** 309–310; **22,** 737–740, 748–751, 754–756, 887; **23,** 604; **25,** 372, 373, 378 n., 380, 383, 385, 387, 388–390, 402, 406–410, 411–413, 417, 420–421, 426, 431–435, 440, 445–447, 449–452, 468, 471, 473, 475, 477, 479, 481, 485–486, 488, 491; **27,** 328, 330, 340, 343, 353, 354, 361, 373–374, 376, 383, 385, 388–390, 391; **29,** 102, 107, 118, 127, 135, 136, 174, 193, 212, 218, 220, 223; **32,** 384, 389, 390
— —action more restrictive than necessary, **25,** 480, 482, 486, 488–489
— —action under wrong Article of Treaty, **25,** 451–452, 459, 461, 468
— —aims of Authority in Memoranda, **25,** 450, 459–460, 461, 468–469
— —avoidance of administrative difficulties, **25,** 451–452, 461, 468–469

European Coal and Steel Community—*continued*
High Authority—*continued*
—*détournement de pouvoir—continued*
— —avoidance of guarantees in Treaty, **25,** 449–450, 468, 473, 477, 481, 488, 492
— —change of purpose, **25,** 447, 450, 459–460
— —decision imposing special charge, **23,** 600–601; **25,** 479, 480, 481–482
— —detriment to working conditions, **25,** 472, 474, 480, 483
— —discrimination, **25,** 449–451, 479–480, 482; **27,** 388
— —fundamental aims, non-compliance with, **25,** 382–387, 471, 473, 477, 481, 488, 492
— —inexact motives, **22,** 752
— —major reason improper, **22,** 748, 749
— —obscure decision, **27,** 354
— —penal taxation, **27,** 389–390
— —proof of, **22,** 740–741, 748, 755; **25,** 421, 446, 450, 468–469
— —unjustified and justified motives, **22,** 748; **25,** 432
— —violation of Treaty, distinguished, **25,** 445–446, 448, 480, 486, 489
—discretionary power, **25,** 377, 431
—discrimination by: *see under* European Coal and Steel Community Treaty, violation of
—disguised individual decision, **25,** 420
—estoppel by decision of, **27,** 376
—foresight, lack of, **25,** 434–435, 447, 450–451
—fraud, repayment of subsidy obtained by, **29,** 189–197
—general decision as series of individual decisions, **25,** 485, 488
—general decision, irregularity, effect, **25,** 374, 378, 456, 462
—general decisions, quasi-legislative, **25,** 421
—general objectives, duty to comply with, **29,** 206–207
—Governments of Members, relation to, **25,** 435–436
—guarantee of proper working of subsidy system, liability under, **27,** 394, 396
—implied decision, **25,** 414
—implied decision from inaction, **29,** 184, 186–188
—implied powers, **29,** 157
—inaction of, appeal against, **27,** 303–304, 378, 380–381; **29,** 86–88; **32,** 387, 413–414, 433–436

European Coal and Steel Community—*continued*
High Authority—*continued*
—individual decision, annulment, **25,** 374, 378, 455
—information, collection of, **22,** 748; **29,** 209–219
—injury to third parties, duty to limit, **25,** 463, 465
—inspection, powers of, **29,** 209–218
—law applied by, **27,** 343
—legislative power, **29,** 157, 160
—levy on scrap consumption, **25,** 370–371, 379, 382–383, 386; **27,** 352–398, *passim,* 403–417; **29,** 168–174; **32,** 382–399, 405–412, 433
—loans to enterprises, **29,** 77
—mixed enterprises, jurisdiction over, **29,** 210, 212, 217
—opinions, nature of, **29,** 84
— —requirement of reasons for, **29,** 80–82
— —time-limits, **29,** 82–83
—penalising particular enterprise, **25,** 472, 474
—powers, **21,** 309–310; **22,** 738–740, 750, 752; **25,** 384, 389, 392–399. *See also* competence, *supra*
— —delegation of, **25,** 372, 375–378, 456; **32,** 411, 438
— —finding of fundamental disturbance in economy, **32,** 400–405
— —imposition of fines, **24,** 711–715; **27,** 398–402; **28,** 503
— —prices and price-lists, **22,** 738–740, 749, 750–755, 890–892; **24,** 711–714; **25,** 403 n., 424, 425–435; **27,** 334–335
— —proposal to extend, **27,** 304–310, 312, 315–320
—price deviations and discrimination, decision on, **22,** 741; **25,** 390, 392, 397, 404 n., 406, 410
—prices and price-lists, powers regarding, **22,** 738–740, 749, 750–755, 890–892; **24,** 711–714; **25,** 403 n., 424, 425–435; **27,** 334–335
—publication of price-lists by, **22,** 742, 744–746, 746–747, 749; **25,** 388, 392, 399, 404 n., 406, 410
—recommendations, validity, **34,** 403, 405–406
—recommendatory powers, **29,** 95–96, 159
—refusal to reply to letter, whether, decision, **32,** 545–546
—safeguard, duty to take measures of, **25,** 462
—sale prices of coal, decision on, **25,** 424, 425–435
—sales at listed prices, decisions on, **25,** 403 n.

European Coal and Steel Community—*continued*
High Authority—*continued*
—subsidy for imported scrap, **25,** 369–370, 372, 375, 377–378, 445, 453, 463; **27,** 368–372, 417; **29,** 189–197; **32,** 382, 383, 405–406, 407, 411, 433, 438
—supply of scrap, decision on, **25,** 369–371, 374–378
—suspension of application of decisions, grounds for, **27,** 322–326
—tax on scrap consumption, **25,** 370–371, 379, 382–383, 386; **27,** 352–398, *passim,* 403–417; **29,** 168–174; **32,** 382–399, 405–412, 433
—transport enterprises, control of, **34,** 405
—wrongful act of enterprises, action against, **25,** 430
illegality of administrative acts, consequences, **29,** 263–265
legal personality, **29,** 260
levy on coal and steel, **29,** 183–188
levy on scrap consumption, **25,** 370–371, 379, 382–383, 386; **27,** 352–398, *passim,* 403–417; **29,** 168–174; **32,** 382–399, 405–412, 433
—exemptions, legality, **32,** 392–397
—exemptions, withdrawal of, **32,** 391, 397–398
—" own resources ", **27,** 352–357, 360–362, 373, 376, 378, 391
—" period of reference ", **25,** 379, 386; **29,** 168
—" purchased scrap ", **32,** 396–397
—scrap from group of companies, **27,** 368–372; **32,** 392–393
—" special " charge, **27,** 417
Luxembourg, removal of import duties on coal, **23,** 598–605
main purposes, **22,** 737–738, 747; **25,** 382–387, 392–393; **29,** 206–207
monopoly, effect of, **22,** 751–752
non-discrimination in sales, offences connected with, **27,** 401
Office Commun of Consumers of Scrap, **25,** 370, 380; **27,** 353, 357 360–361, 363; **32,** 406
officials—
—appeal against inaction of High Authority, **32,** 544–546
—control by Court of Justice, **23,** 627–628
—damages for non-material injury, **29,** 269
—grading, **29,** 252, 254–257, 260, 262, 270–272
—immunity from taxation, **29,** 56–73
—pension contributions, transferability, **29,** 285–286
—position prior to Statute of Service, **29,** 233, 246–249

European Coal and Steel Community—*continued*
officials—*continued*
—resignation, right of, **29,** 276, 281
—resignation, sums due on, **29,** 278–279, 283–286
—resignation, suspension, during, **29,** 274–282
—Statute of Service, admission to, **29,** 251, 255, 264–266
—Statute of Service, withdrawal of admission to, **29,** 255, 264, 268
—sums due on resignation, interest on, **29,** 286
—suspension of employment, resignation during, **29,** 274–282
—transfer to EEC post, **29,** 274–286
—travel allowance, **32,** 354–358
—unilateral termination of contract, **29,** 276, 281
price lists, publication of, **25,** 388–405
—alignment, **22,** 887, 891–892; **25,** 397, 401
—decisions of High Authority as to, **27,** 402–403
—offences connected with, **27,** 400–401
—private law effects, **25,** 395
—reasons for, **27,** 402
privileges and immunities, **22,** 4; **29,** 56–73
prohibited practices, unfair prices, **22,** 738–748
Ruhr coal sales agencies, authorization by High Authority, **27,** 336–338
Statute of Service, adoption and entry into force (1955), **29,** 245, 248, 251, 265
subsidy for imported steel scrap, **32,** 382, 383, 405–406, 407, 433
—delegation of powers by High Authority, **25,** 372, 375–378, 456; **32,** 411, 438
—indirect grant, **25,** 467–468
—ship-breaking scrap, **27,** 393; **32,** 433
—uniform tax, legality of, **25,** 451–452, 459, 460, 466–468
transitional provisions: *see* E.C.S.C., Convention containing Transitional Provisions
transport, partial integration, **29,** 112–113, 147
transport tariffs—
—special rates, **29,** 103–118, 137–151, 199–209, 219–223
—zonal frontiers of Germany, relevance, **29,** 116–117, 223
unjust enrichment, subsidy on scrap, **29,** 196, 197

European Coal and Steel Community, Convention containing Transitional Provisions (1951), contracts of officials, **29,** 233, 246, 254
period of validity, **29,** 105, 107, 111
purpose of, **22,** 740, 744, 747, 749, 886–892; **27,** 346; **29,** 115
time-limits, **29,** 222
European Coal and Steel Community, Protocol on Privileges and Immunities (1951), **22,** 4; **29,** 56–73
European Coal and Steel Community, Treaty establishing (1951), **21,** 309; **22,** 737–756; **23,** 597–605, 627–631; **24,** 693–699, 703–708, 711–715; **25,** 369–494; **27,** 301–417; **28,** 496–508; **29,** 59, 61, 63, 65, 68–69, 72, 77–224, 244–246, 254, 260–262, 267–268; **32,** 382–439, 545
action " in the common interest ", **25,** 459, 460, 465, 492; **27,** 415
agreements for joint selling, conformity with Treaty, **27,** 336, 339–340, 343–344
—relevance of evasion in making agreements, **27,** 341, 348
amendment of, **27,** 304–320; **32,** 422–432
—grant of new power to High Authority, **32,** 428–429, 430–431
breach by enterprise, fines, **27,** 398–402; **28,** 503
breach by member State, **27,** 301–304; **29,** 155, 159–162, 167
—declaration of, appeal against, **29,** 122–123
" common interest ", meaning, **25,** 492
concentration of industry without sanction, effect on legality of dismissal of employee, **28,** 496–497
consumers, equal access to sources of production, **27,** 413–414
continuity of employment, duty to ensure, **29,** 200
date of entry into force of Art. 65, **27,** 340–341, 344–348, 350
détournement de pouvoir, **21,** 309–310; **22,** 737–740, 748–751, 754–756, 887; **23,** 604; **25,** 372, 373, 378 n., 380, 383, 385, 387, 388–390, 402, 406–410, 411–413, 417, 420–421, 426, 431–435, 440, 445–447, 449–452, 468, 471, 473, 475, 477, 479, 481, 485–486, 488, 491; **27,** 328, 330, 340, 343, 353, 354, 361, 373–374, 376, 383, 385, 388–390, 391; **29,** 102, 107, 118, 127, 135, 136, 171, 174, 177, 179, 183, 193, 212, 218, 220, 223; **32,** 384, 389, 390; **34,** 406. *See also under* High Authority, *supra*
directly binding nature, **28,** 502

European Coal and Steel Community, Treaty establishing (1951)—*continued*
discrimination—
—Belgian coal subsidy, **25,** 418, 426–427, 437–440
—deviation from price lists, **25,** 388–392, 406, 410
—meaning, **27,** 353, 363, 369–371, 412–415; **28,** 505; **29,** 106, 109, 112–114, 128, 138–139, 142–147, 203–204
—prohibition of, **25,** 385–386; **28,** 497–508
—third parties, against, by decision of Authority, **27,** 327
—uniform tax to steel subsidy fund, **25,** 451–452, 459, 460, 466–468
—violation of substantial procedural requirement, distinction, **27,** 332
duration, distinction between definite and transitional provisions, **27,** 309
" enterprise ", meaning, **32,** 385, 392, 394, 413–415
excès de pouvoir, appeal alleging, **32,** 383, 386, 435, 436. *See also* High Authority, competence, lack of, *supra*
excès de pouvoir, regarding officials' contracts, **29,** 276
faute de service, **29,** 267–269; **32,** 383–384, 386, 405, 406–407, 408–412, 413, 416, 417–418, 419, 434, 437–439
function of Court concerning, **25,** 399
fundamental economic disturbances, **29,** 206, 207, 219, 221; **32,** 400–405
imports, free circulation of, **32,** 414, 418–419, 420–421
interpretation, **23,** 597–605
—general principles of law of Member States, **25,** 385
—grammatical meaning, **27,** 410
—implied powers, **25,** 430–431
—intention of authors, **27,** 411
—provisions referred to in several places, **23,** 600
—reference to Transitional Convention, by, **29,** 96
—strict, **29,** 160
—Treaty read as a whole, **23,** 600; **25,** 382
joint buying and selling agreements, authorization of, **32,** 422–432
levy on coal production, assessment and collection of, **25,** 419, 424, 438
lowest possible prices, establishment of, **29,** 200, 208
main purposes, **22,** 737–738, 747; **25,** 382–387, 392–393; **29,** 206–207
members' obligations, classic international law and, **29,** 159–160
misconstruction of, **27,** 353

European Coal and Steel Community, Treaty establishing (1951)—*continued*
monopoly agreements, prohibition of, **29,** 130
municipal courts, interpretation of Community law, **28,** 500
municipal law, conflict with, **29,** 128, 130
normal conditions of competition, obligation to ensure, **27,** 415–417
obvious ignoring of provisions, **22,** 753–754
price lists, publication of, **34,** 408
restrictive practices, scope of prohibition of, **32,** 431–432
scope of, " enterprise engaged in production . . . of steel ", **27,** 404–407, 409–412
self-executing provisions, **29,** 155, 156, 167
Special Council of Ministers for amendment of, **27,** 306, 310, 313, 316; **32,** 425, 426, 432
State subsidies—
—meaning, **29,** 90–91
—prohibition, **29,** 85–102, 141, 143, 204, 208
transport rates, discrimination, **34,** 402–410
transport tariffs, publication of, **29,** 151–158, 161–162, 163–167
violation of, **22,** 739, 741–746, 747–748, 751–754; **23,** 599–604; **24,** 696–699, 713–714; **25,** 388, 390–402, 410, 437–440, 458–459, 462–468, 489; **27,** 301–302, 315, 319–320, 327, 340, 343, 353, 374, 383, 385, 387–390, 392, 406, 408–417; **29,** 86, 90, 102, 105, 109, 111–117, 126, 127–128, 135–136, 139, 141, 144–148, 149–150, 170, 171, 173–174, 200, 203–208, 210, 214–217, 219, 222–223; **32,** 392–397
—*détournement de pouvoir,* distinguished, **25,** 445–446, 448, 480, 486, 489
—discrimination, **22,** 739–740, 741–744, 748; **23,** 601–604; **24,** 698–699
— —Belgian coal subsidy, **25,** 418, 426–427, 437–440
— —deviation from price lists, **25,** 388–392, 406, 410
— —uniform tax for steel subsidy, **25,** 451–452, 459, 460, 466–468
—interference with competition, **24,** 696–698; **25,** 462–465, 467, 482
—price discrimination, non-comparable transaction, **25,** 391
—sanctions imposed by Authority, **24,** 713–714

European Coal and Steel Community, Treaty establishing (1951)—*continued*
violation of substantial procedural requirement, **22,** 746, 749; **23,** 599, 604; **24,** 694–695; **25,** 372, 374–375, 401, 455–456; **27,** 328–329, 331–333; **29,** 106, 117–118, 126, 129, 130–135, 200, 202–203, 212, 217–218, 220, 223
—failure to consult Expert Commission, **29,** 200, 202–203
—failure to give reasons for decision, **27,** 328, 331–333, 354, 373, 384; **29,** 106, 117–118, 126, 130, 193, 212, 217–218, 220, 223, 226, 233–234
—failure to obtain Council's agreement, **27,** 354
—State to submit observations on breach, **29,** 155, 161–162
European Commission of Human Rights: *see under* Human rights
European Commission of the Danube: *see under* Danube
European Communities Court: *see also* European Coal and Steel Community, Court—
advisory jurisdiction, **32,** 422, 425, 426
annulment, appeal for, nature of, **32,** 417
appeal against inaction of High Authority, **29,** 86–88, 102, 138, 141, 149
appeal *en pleine juridiction,* **29,** 119, 122, 159
appeals, time-limits, reason for, **29,** 123–124
compensation, action for, **32,** 415–417, 419–421, 434, 437, 439
competence: *see* jurisdiction, *infra*
costs, **29,** 73, 102, 118, 124, 150, 162, 188, 198, 209, 218, 223, 267, 269, 274, 282, 286, 323; **34,** 401, 410, 415, 473
—agreement of parties as to, **29,** 182
—apportionment of, **29,** 136–137, 148–149, 151, 182, 235, 242, 250; **32,** 399, 405
—" thrown away ", **32,** 549–551
—unnecessary, **29,** 182
—vexatious, reimbursement of, **29,** 174, 250
damages, assessment *ex aequo et bono,* **29,** 234, 241
expert examination, use of, **29,** 139, 141, 142, 148–149
finding that State in breach of treaty, **32,** 378
hearing *en pleine juridiction,* **34,** 406
High Authority, remittal of matter to, **29,** 89

European Communities Court—*continued*
interpretation of judgment, **29**, 198–199
intervenors, objections to admissibility raised by, **32**, 387
intervention, conditions of, **29**, 89–90, 165–166
joinder of cases, **29**, 129, 279
judgments—
—declaratory effect, **29**, 60–61
—interpretation, **29**, 198–199
—rectification, **29**, 198–199
—revision, grounds for, **29**, 320–323
jurisdiction—
—appeal against opinion of High Authority, **29**, 83–84
—Commission's acts, review of legality, **29**, 229–231
—Common Assembly, annulment of decisions of, **29**, 244–246
—laws of member States, *re*, **29**, 59, 60–61
—motives for decisions, *re*, **29**, 130, 171, 174
—power of High Authority *re* economic disturbance, over, **32**, 400, 402–405
—to order High Authority to take decisions, **29**, 89
language of procedure, translation of documents, **29**, 320–333
limitation periods, officials, actions by, **29**, 271, 273, 276, 280
limitation periods, Rules of Court, **29**, 271, 273, 276, 280
municipal laws, reference to, **29**, 258–259
national courts, relation to, **29**, 64
officials of Parliamentary Assembly, appeals by, **34**, 467–468
officials, right to appeal to, **29**, 61–63
pleadings, grounds relied on, **32**, 435–436
production of documents, **32**, 395
rectification of judgment, **29**, 198–199
request, subsequent increase in sums claimed, **29**, 278, 283
res judicata, **32**, 546–547
revision of judgment, grounds for, **29**, 320–323
Rules of Court, date from which effective, **29**, 271, 276, 280
suspension of execution of Commission's decision, **29**, 227–229
suspension of execution of High Authority's decision, **29**, 107–109, 154, 177–179, 191–192, 212–213
suspensive effect of appeal to, **29**, 121–122
visits to *locus*, **32**, 395

European Convention for Protection of Human Rights and Fundamental Freedoms: *see under* Human rights
European Convention on Establishment, deportation of aliens, provision for hearing, **33**, 264 n., 277 n., 284 n.
expulsion of aliens after long residence, **32**, 256
European Economic Community—
Commission—
—*détournement de pouvoir*, **29**, 237, 239–241
—*faute de service*, **29**, 226, 233, 239
—legal personality, **29**, 231
common market, transitional period, **26**, 607–608
competition, regulation of, **26**, 606–608; **28**, 508–511; **31**, 427–428; **33**, 414–416
Council, Regulations, nature of, **34**, 412, 413–414
détournement de pouvoir: *see under* Commission, *supra*
fruit and vegetables, common market in, **34**, 410–415
officials—
—contracts of employment, public law nature, **29**, 226, 229–231, 239
—damages for non-material injury, **29**, 234, 237, 239, 241
—dismissal, compensation for, **32**, 541–544
—dismissal, length of notice, **29**, 234–235, 242
—dismissal, requirement of reasons for, **29**, 233, 241
—grading, **29**, 239
—position prior to Statute of Service, **29**, 231–232, 238
—right of appeal to Court, **29**, 230, 238
—security of employment, **29**, 226, 231–233, 239
European Economic Community, Treaty establishing (1957)—
Arts. 85 and 86...**26**, 606–608; **28**, 508–511; **33**, 414–416
breach by Member State, **32**, 377, 379
customs duties, reductions in, **34**, 397–401
détournement de pouvoir, **29**, 237–241
direct application to individual contracts, **31**, 427–428
discrimination, **28**, 23
economic union, establishing, **31**, 425–426
faute de service, **29**, 226, 233, 239
imports, prohibition of, public policy reasons, **32**, 381
imports, prohibition of restrictions on, **32**, 376–382

European Economic Community, Treaty establishing (1957)—*continued*
market-dominating position, abuse of, **31,** 427–428
natural or legal person, challenge of Regulations, **34,** 411–414
prior agreements of Members, **34,** 401
regional economic policy, **29,** 205
Regulations and Decisions, distinction, **34,** 413–414
restrictive practices, prohibition of, **26,** 606–608; **28,** 508–511; **33,** 414–416
self-executing, whether, **26,** 607–608
transitional period, protective measures, **32,** 377, 380–381
European Economic Co-operation, Convention and Protocol for (1948), **21,** 279–280
European Nuclear Research Centre (CERN), officials, immunity from jurisdiction, **32,** 334
European Parliamentary Assembly, officials, contracts of, **34,** 466–473
European States, arbitral awards, right to contest, regional custom as to, **30,** 481–483
Euthanasia, crime against humanity, as, **15,** 654–655
Evidence—
affidavits, importance of, **4,** 483–485; **5,** 452–454; **6,** 198–199; **12,** 8–9
arbitration, international, in: *see under* Arbitration, international
burden of proof, **1,** 217–218, 221; **3,** 243, 414–416; **4,** 479–489; **5,** 151–152, 456; **6,** 207–208; **7,** 231–241; **22,** 825, 972; **23,** 306, 318, 334–336, 677–680; **25,** 28–30, 274; **27,** 96
—abuse of rights and, **3,** 107–108
—counter-proof, **4,** 483
—discrimination, as to, **22,** 741
—duress, as to, **20,** 458–490
—enemy character of corporations, **9,** 559–561
—enemy character of goods, **12,** 390–391; **22,** 1008–1011
—enemy character of ship, **12,** 384–386; **16,** 389–390; **17,** 378–385; **18,** 725–730
—enemy destination, **12,** 543–564; **13,** 414–419, 425–429, 431, 432; **17,** 443; **18,** 724
—enemy nationality, **1,** 423; **2,** 428; **18,** 246
—expatriation and, **4,** 313–314; **26,** 453–454, 456, 458–459, 460 n.
—international claims, in, **21,** 154–155; **22,** 349, 846–866, 953–959, 966–972, 978

Evidence—*continued*
burden of proof—*continued*
—measure of damages and, **4,** 267; **5,** 151–152
—nationality and, **1,** 217–218, 221–222; **4,** 303; **22,** 428–429
—nationality of claims and, **2,** 380–381; **3,** 243; **4,** 485
—naturalization, as to, **1,** 205
—sovereign immunity, **16,** 129–137
—sovereignty, claims to, **20,** 97
circumstantial, **16,** 157
conciliation commissions, before: *see under* Conciliation commissions
consular certificate, value of, **3,** 30–31; **5,** 223, 233; **6,** 182, 247–249, 250, 424–425; **8,** 284–285; **16,** 182–184; **18,** 359
consular *informe*, value of, **2,** 303
consuls, right to collect, **1,** 300–301
détournement de pouvoir, of, **29,** 223
enemy character of goods, as to, **9,** 565–566; **12,** 391–392, 395, 396
experts, use of: *see under* Experts
extradition proceedings, in: *see under* Extradition
foreign armed forces—
—official duties, certificate of agency, **24,** 249; **26,** 203
fraudulent, arbitral proceedings, **8,** 485–487
hearsay, **6,** 316
international claims, in support of, **22,** 338–340, 858–867, 978
International Court of Justice, before, **16,** 157; **20,** 97–115, 577; **25,** 274, 306–307; **27,** 96
jurisdiction, order to produce documents held abroad, **19,** 197; **22,** 184–197; **26,** 123–129; **28,** 138–142; **31,** 210, 214–219, 220–226; **32,** 100–102; **33,** 158–163
lack of, in calculation of damages, **5,** 197–198
maps, **4,** 487–488; **7,** 122–123, 125, 126; **27,** 75, 77, 90, 95. *See also* Maps
—material error, effect, **33,** 43–148, *passim*
municipal principles, application by international tribunals, **4,** 237
nationality, of: *see* Nationality, proof of
newly-discovered, petition for rehearing, **6,** 425; **8,** 485–487
oral, in arbitration, corroboration, **26,** 624–625
Permanent Court of International Justice, before, **3,** 107–108; **4,** 518–519
—experts, **4,** 522–523
public ownership of vessel, **11,** 147–149

Ex gratia payments, State responsibility and, **4,** 376–377; **6,** 214–215; **11,** 177–178
Ex injuria jus non oritur, **4,** 281–282; **19,** 97
Exceptio est strictissimae applicationis, **19,** 481
"Exceptional war measures", meaning, **1,** 244; **5,** 440, 508
Exchange control—
agreement, application limited by, **33,** 28–30
aliens, right to inherit and, **28,** 303
bonds, currency of payment, **29,** 435
compensation payments, subject to, **29,** 397
critical date, **22,** 824, 835–839
discrimination concerning imports, **19,** 261
extraterritorial effect, **16,** 27–36; **26,** 39; **30,** 25–28; **33,** 32, 35
I.M.F. Articles, provisions on, **15,** 20; **22,** 713–732; **23,** 581–584; **28,** 539–543; **30,** 26–28, 423–425; **33,** 35
private international law aspects, **22,** 715–717, 721–722
—choice of law rule, **26,** 233
rates, as matter of international law, **22,** 732–734
recognition of, **15,** 18–20; **22,** 713–732; **23,** 581–584; **28,** 539–543; **30,** 26–28, 423–425; **33,** 32, 35
Exchange of declarations, distinguished from treaty, **3,** 333–334. *See also* Exchange of notes
Exchange of Greek and Turkish populations, **4,** 470–471, 524–525; **19,** 21, 22
Exchange of notes: *see also* Treaties, form—
binding force, **6,** 249–250, 394; **14,** 139–140, 142; **23,** 468
executive agreement, whether, **20,** 413–414
interpretation of treaties by reference to, **5,** 362–363, 405; **6,** 394–395; **7,** 404–406; **8,** 327–328, 424–426; **10,** 407–409; **11,** 231, 234–235; **18,** 401–402; **19,** 476–477; **21,** 280–281; **22,** 622–623; **23,** 468
nature of, **8,** 424–426; **9,** 69; **20,** 369–370, 413
subsequent to treaty, **10,** 407–410
Exchange of telegrams, as form of diplomatic convention, **7,** 79–80 n.
Exchange, rate of—
appropriate date for conversion, **30,** 181–183
arbitral awards, in, **4,** 205, 479
matter of international law, **22,** 732–734
Execution, immunity from, States and State property: *see under* Foreign States
Execution of foreign arbitral awards, **7,** 419–420; **27,** 36; **28,** 526–538; **31,** 20–22
Execution of foreign judgments, **4,** 183–184; **11,** 221; **26,** 57–58
Executive action: *see under* State responsibility
Executive agreements, **1,** 313–315
law of the United States, **8,** 37–38; **20,** 412–417; **22,** 402–404; **26,** 557–560; **28,** 420–423
Executive, conclusiveness of acts and statements of: *see* Conclusiveness of statements of executive
Executive decrees, validity abroad, **11,** 17
Executive, sphere of, boundaries, determination, **31,** 131
Executive, war measures, judicial review of, **30,** 495
Exemplary damages: *see under* Damages
Exequatur, application to colonial judgments, **7,** 409–410: *see also under* Consuls
Exhaustion of local remedies, **1,** 374; **2,** 69, 166–167, 401; **3,** 215, 293; **4,** 265, 471–473; **5,** 211, 429–430, 430–432; **6,** 193, 422; **7,** 92–93, 94–95, 231–241, 478–482; **8,** 271–274; **9,** 58, 311–315; **16,** 281–282; **23,** 306, 314, 334–340, 672; **24,** 274–281, 283–295, 299, 327, 336, 340, 345, 359–360, 361–362, 407, 412–413, 419, 794, 796–799, 837–839; **25,** 30, 38, 42–49, 71, 170, 181–182, 201–202, 210–211, 221–223, 232, 527–529; **26,** 261; **27,** 490–495, 503–504, 525, 528, 529–533, 553–556; **28,** 204–208, 226, 227, 229–231, 233, 247, 251–252, 426, 431, 433, 628–629; **29,** 61, 62–64; **30,** 227, 228, 229, 242, 243, 270–271, 291, 302, 308–309, 311–312, 315, 321, 340, 346: *see also under* Human Rights, European Commission, applications, admissibility
action pending, **24,** 419; **27,** 491, 504, 525, 530–531
adverse decision already given, **9,** 311–312
appeal instituted by wrong person, **24,** 280–281
appeal pending, **24,** 376
appellate rights, exhaustion of, **7,** 238–239; **23,** 314, 338–339; **24,** 274, 277–278, 279, 285–287, 289–291; **24,** 293, 327, 345, 359–360, 361, 407; **25,** 181, 201–202, 494–495

Exhaustion of local remedies—*continued*
allegations of fact and submissions of law presumed valid, **7,** 233–234, 237–238; **23,** 335
—when exhausted, **7,** 240–241
—when unnecessary, **7,** 239; **24,** 275, 293
application of the rule, **24,** 294, 838–839; **25,** 42–49, 170, 224; **27,** 491–493, 493–494, 503–504, 528, 532, 553–554
applied by municipal courts, **16,** 281–282
as a precondition of the right to exercise diplomatic protection, **2,** 401; **9,** 58, 311; **25,** 381; **27,** 490–492, 504
as a rule of substantive law, **9,** 314–315
burden of proof, **23,** 334–335; **25,** 30
Calvo Clause, and, **3,** 292–293; **5,** 210–211
conciliation and, **27,** 503, 554
competence of arbitral tribunals to enquire into, **6,** 193
diplomatic protection and, **27,** 504
direct breach of international law, **7,** 94, 235, 240–241; **27,** 492, 527–529, 532, 556
discovery of documents, **24,** 291–299
European Communities Court, **29,** 61, 62–64
exclusion of the rule, express, **1,** 374; **3,** 215; **4,** 265, 472–473; **5,** 211, 429–430; **6,** 422; **7,** 478–479
—by treaty, **25,** 40, 42, 71
—G.B.–Mexico, Claims Commission, **5,** 211; **6,** 422
—implied, by *compromis,* **20,** 672
—Hungarian–Yugoslav Mixed Arbitral Tribunal, **4,** 473
—Turko–Italian Mixed Arbitral Tribunal, **5,** 429–430
—U.S.A.–Mexico, General Claims Commission, **3,** 215; **5,** 210–211
—U.S.A.–Panama Claims Commission, **7,** 477–479
—Upper Silesia Arbitral Tribunal, **4,** 472–473
extension of rule, **25,** 47–49
extraordinary remedies, **28,** 229–231
failure to seek remedies claimed in international proceedings, **23,** 314, 339–340
failure to assert rights asserted in international proceedings, **24,** 288
failure to sue, **2,** 166–167; **5,** 210–211, 430–432; **23,** 306, 314, 339–340; **24,** 281, 283, 336, 340, 413; **25,** 221
function of the rule, **7,** 235, 239–240; **24,** 837–838; **27,** 503–504, 528, 531–532

Exhaustion of local remedies—*continued*
grounds for non-exhaustion of, **24,** 282–283
lack of financial resources, **24,** 278
limits of the rule, **7,** 235–237; **25,** 42–49; **27,** 503, 530
meaning of the rule, **23,** 334; **24,** 291–292, 293–294
National Claims Commission, **6,** 422
national statutes of limitation, and, **4,** 265
necessary even if contingent and theoretical, **24,** 197–198
no jurisdiction in local courts, **9,** 311–312
non-legal remedy, **25,** 224
no preclusion, **4,** 471–472; **27,** 799
officials, personal action against, **25,** 29
parties' agreement to suspend proceedings, **25,** 527–529
procedural facilities, exhaustion of, **23,** 335–336; **24,** 292–293, 294–295
remedy as of grace, **25,** 29, 181
restricted by terms of treaty, **7,** 92–94
requisition, compensation claims, **28,** 628, 629
settlement, offer of, **25,** 49–50
time limits, need to observe, **25,** 232
undue delay in procedure, **24,** 275, 276
unnecessary when—
—highest court has already given a decision, **9,** 312
—legal remedies inadequate, **7,** 239–240; **8,** 271–274; **24,** 797; **25,** 30, 221, 223; **26,** 261; **28,** 252
—measures taken by the government, **7,** 94–95; **24,** 839; **27,** 491
—no claim based on an infringement of rights is made, **25,** 47
—" no justice to exhaust ", **2,** 69
—no remedy provided, **5,** 429–430
—remedies obviously ineffective or inadequate, **23,** 334–338; **24,** 797; **25,** 30, 181
— —burden of proof, **24,** 797; **25,** 30, 202, 223
—uniform line of decisions in the highest courts, **7,** 239; **8,** 272–274; **24,** 275, 298
—useless, **7,** 951; **24,** 293, 838–839; **25,** 202
witnesses, calling of, **23,** 306, 314, 337–338; **24,** 291–299
Exiled governments: *see* Governments in exile
Exiled Sovereigns: *see* Sovereigns in exile
Expatriation: *see also* Nationality, change of sovereignty, *and* Nationality, loss of—
absence of naturalized citizen, **16,** 194–195

Expatriation—*continued*
acquisition of another nationality, **24**, 445–447; **26**, 364–366, 376–379. *See also* naturalization abroad, *infra*
application for foreign passport, **7**, 283; **26**, 364–366
automatic operation, **26**, 439
avoidance of military service, **34**, 108–121
burden of proof, **4**, 313–314; **22**, 428–429; **26**, 453–454, 456, 458–459, 460 n.
defined, **9**, 354; **14**, 116–117; **25**, 120; **26**, 418, 423, 436–437, 447
dual nationals, **7**, 283–287; **9**, 352, 354–355; **14**, 104, 115–118, 124–125; **15**, 228–230, 262–264; **16**, 195–196, 227–229; **17**, 226–228; **18**, 251–254, 265–270; **26**, 451–463
denaturalization, distinguished, **26**, 447 n.
desertion, by, **26**, 426–448
failure to return, **17**, 215–216
insanity as bar, **8**, 297–298
involuntary, **15**, 230–236; **16**, 204–208; **17**, 215–217; **20**, 255–260; **22**, 437–442
Italian law, **15**, 234–235
leaving country " forever ", **30**, 352–366
marriage, as result of, **5**, 240–242; **8**, 295–296, 302–303; **9**, 347–350; **15**, 248–249
—duress, effect of, **15**, 249
—to enemy in war, **1**, 211–213
minors, expatriation of parents, **7**, 284–287; **14**, 119–120; **25**, 134, 139
monk of Mount Athos, **21**, 195–196
naturalization abroad, by, **1**, 214; **12**, 15–17; **15**, 236–237; **16**, 199–203; **20**, 251–254; **25**, 123, 128; **26**, 246; **28**, 275
—in wartime, **9**, 350; **14**, 104; **26**, 402–404
naturalization by statute later revoked, **15**, 237–248
oath of allegiance to foreign State, **8**, 297–299; **10**, 276–278; **16**, 197–198; **22**, 437–442; **25**, 147; **26**, 460–463; **31**, 323–326
passport, application for, **7**, 283
—Nansen, issue of, **7**, 287–289
Polish law, **25**, 353
presumption of, **3**, 271–276; **4**, 254–256
—burden of proof, **4**, 313–314; **26**, 453–454, 456, 458–459, 460 n.
release, distinguished from option, **7**, 289
residence abroad, **2**, 225–226; **3**, 271–275; **15**, 234–235; **16**, 199, 203–204; **25**, 115–116, 120–121; **26**, 449–450; **30**, 370

Expatriation—*continued*
residence abroad—*continued*
—naturalized citizen, **16**, 194–195
—prolonged, **4**, 313–314; **8**, 299–301; **18**, 251–254
residence in State of birth, **35**, 197–205
right of, **11**, 6–9; **18**, 267; **26**, 406, 417, 456
service in foreign army, **5**, 217, 239–240; **8**, 298–299, 301–302; **10**, 276–278; **11**, 182–183; **14**, 115–118, 124–125; **15**, 209–211, 228–230; **16**, 195–198, 220; **17**, 216–217; **20**, 255–260; **21**, 185–191; **22**, 437–443; **26**, 451–460; **28**, 287–290; **35**, 193–196
service of foreign State, **19**, 334–336
—political subdivision, **30**, 350–352
surrender to foreign Power, **5**, 242–243
Swiss law, **13**, 129–130
transfer of residence as condition, **16**, 215–219
U.S.A., law of, **26**, 407–448
use of foreign passport, **16**, 219
voluntary, **8**, 295, 297–299; **10**, 276–278; **14**, 115–118; **15**, 236–237; **16**, 194–195; **17**, 226–228 **18**, 267–270; **24**, 445–446; **26**, 408–409, 414, 417–421, 424–426, 427, 430, 452–455, 456; **28**, 287–290
voting in foreign election, **17**, 210–212, 226–228; **19**, 329–334; **21**, 185–191; **22**, 437–443; **26**, 404–426; **28**, 287–290
voting in occupied State, **16**, 418–421; **17**, 205–210
war, effect of, **9**, 350; **14**, 104; **26**, 402–404
Expert witnesses—
Commission of enquiry, **35**, 487
valuation, oil concession, **35**, 160–161
Experts—
appointment by international courts, **3**, 248, 413–414; **4**, 273, 522–523; **5**, 390; **9**, 332; **22**, 313, 315–316, 329, 875
European Communities Court, use by, **29**, 139, 141, 142, 148–149
foreign law, on, **26**, 13
functions of, **1**, 371–372; **3**, 413–414; **22**, 315–316, 875
Experts' Plan of April 9, 1924: *see* Dawes Plan
Expressio unius est exclusio alterius, **2**, 340; **5**, 356–357; **6**, 66–68, 191n, 405–406; **7**, 102–104; **9**, 396, 483; **18**, 150–151, 423–426; **20**, 481; **25**, 373, 376–377. *See also* Treaties, interpretation
Expropriation: *see also* Acquired rights; Confiscatory legislation; Nationalization measures; " Taking " of property

Expropriation—*continued*
aliens, property of, **1**, 238–239; **2**, 163, 270–272; **3**, 81–83, 133–136, 207, 231–232; **4**, 147–151, 338–339; **5**, 264–265; **7**, 27–28, 255–257, 323–325; **8**, 336–337; **9**, 150, 380–382; **14**, 187–189; **15**, 24–27; **20**, 305–330; **22**, 32–33, 40–41, 483–485; **24**, 8, 35–38; **28**, 16–39, 544–548; **30**, 28–33, 133, 214, 375–376; **32**, 233–237
—contractual rights, **35**, 29: *see also* concessions, *infra*
—interference with property and, **2**, 170–171
—international law as to, **35**, 38
Catalonia, Government of, validity of decrees, **8**, 191–193; **9**, 24–25, 151
compensation and **1**, 238–239; **2**, 163; **3**, 133–136, 207; **9**, 150–152; **15**, 24–27; **20**, 310–311, 321–323, 324–328; **24**, 8–9. *See also* Confiscatory legislation; Equity
compulsory administration, distinguished, **11**, 21
concessions, and, **7**, 424–431; **20**, 305–328; **22**, 19–45; **28**, 16, 25, 38; **30**, 178–179
confiscation, distinguished, **4**, 150; **26**, 41, 46; **30**, 214, 260
constitutionality, **11**, 16–19
Costa Rica, provisions of Constitution, **23**, 702, 704–706
defence purposes, for, **30**, 133
discrimination, effect, **3**, 231–232; **8**, 336–337; **26**, 41, 47–48
Dutch assets in U.S.A., nationalization by Netherlands, **9**, 150 n.
enemy property: *see* Enemy property, appropriation of
extraterritorial effect, **8**, 191–193; **9**, 150–152, 180–183, 228–233; **26**, 54; **30**, 39, 41, 44, 46, 48, 51
irregularity of proceedings, **5**, 264–265
land, for town planning, **24**, 8–9
legacies, **9**, 70
legality in international law, **4**, 159, 151
liquidation, distinguished, **4**, 150
Mexico, foreign oil installations, **9**, 25, 90; **11**, 16–19
nature of, **7**, 441; **20**, 310–311
option to pay contribution, **24**, 542–546
recognition of, by foreign States, **23**, 706
recognition of, in foreign courts, **4**, 66–68; **7**, 27–28; **9**, 150–152, 180–182; **15**, 24–27; **20**, 305–328; **21**, 38–39; **22**, 14–16; **23**, 10–15, 24–26; **24**, 35–48; **26**, 38–50; **28**, 16–47; **30**, 33–54; **32**, 10–12

Expropriation—*continued*
recognition of, in foreign courts—*continued*
—requirement of possession, **9**, 180, 182
ships, of, **9**, 181–183, 217–219, 224, 228–233
—after writ *in rem*, **9**, 218
—foreign waters, in, **9**, 224
Spain, Bank of, **9**, 12
—industrial enterprises, **9**, 151
—ships, **2**, 177
Spain (Government of Catalonia) decrees of, **8**, 191–193; **9**, 13
Spanish law (1879), right of reverter, **26**, 553–554
title to property, **20**, 320–323
treaty protection, effect, **20**, 328–330
unlawful deprivation, distinguished, **4**, 271–272
Expulsion of aliens, **1**, 251–259; **2**, 273; **3**, 286, 297–299; **4**, 340; **5**, 266–268; **6**, 205–206, 287–292; **7**, 325–334; **8**, 338–347; **9**, 378, 382–393; **10**, 304–326; **11**, 195–199; **12**, 231–236; **13**, 232; **15**, 276–277, 291–292; **16**, 253–256; **17**, 249–260; **18**, 300–315; **19**, 345–360; **20**, 330–363; **21**, 213–231; **22**, 490–512; **23**, 386–388, 393–404; **24**, 490–491; **26**, 503–512; **27**, 249–250; **28**, 93–95, 275, 310–318; **31**, 340–341, 346–355; **32**, 237–275; **33**, 255–296; **34**, 128–132
"accepting" State, effect of non-recognition of Government, **23**, 397–400; **28**, 93–95
administrative reviews of, **8**, 342–345; **20**, 357–363; **33**, 255–293. *See also* discretion of executive, *infra*
aliens brought into State involuntarily, **14**, 133–137
asylum—
—denial of, **20**, 330–333
—discretion, matter of, **28**, 315–318
—U.S. law of, **24**, 153–154
Brazilian law, **1**, 254–257; **5**, 266–268; **9**, 390–391
British subject from Canada, **9**, 383–384; **32**, 247–249
cancellation of residence permit, **20**, 340–342
Commonwealth countries, citizens of, **32**, 247–249
competence of courts, **9**, 391; **10**, 309
competent authority for, **19**, 360; **21**, 224–225
Costa Rican law, **9**, 387
country to which deported, **26**, 509–512; **31**, 349–352; **32**, 237–240
detention pending removal, **17**, 258

Expulsion of aliens—*continued*
discretion of executive, judicial review of, **8,** 342–345; **9,** 309; **17,** 249–252, 256–259; **18,** 314; **19,** 359–360; **20,** 335–340, 350–357; **28,** 314; **33,** 255–293
discretionary character, **11,** 198–199; **18,** 308–309, 314; **28,** 314; **33,** 265–266
due process, right to, **3,** 287; **20,** 330–333, 343–349; **21,** 213–218
enemy aliens, **13,** 233–234, 316; **14,** 18–19, 450–451; **15,** 227, 240–242, 450–452, 508–512
" entry " for purpose of, **6,** 289–290; **20,** 276–281
exclusion, distinction (U.S. law), **26,** 476–477, 512 n.; **28,** 95
extradition and, **22,** 497–500; **33,** 255–293
—distinguished, **7,** 332–333
extraterritorial restraint, right of, **14,** 70–71, 131–133
fair hearing, right to, **3,** 287; **8,** 344; **17,** 259–260; **20,** 343–349; **21,** 219–222; **23,** 401–403
force majeure, plea of, **7,** 331–332
France, law of: *see* France, aliens, expulsion of
general principles of international law, **32,** 256
grounds for, **18,** 301–302; **20,** 333–340; **21,** 222–224
—anarchism, advocacy of, **1,** 251–253
—Communist Party membership, **8,** 338–339; **20,** 330–333; **21,** 213–218; **28,** 275; **32,** 240–243
—crimes, **7,** 328; **15,** 291; **20,** 276–277, 280, 333 n.; **21,** 219–222; **23,** 386–388; **24,** 503–509; **28,** 310–311; **32,** 249–251
—danger to public order, **5,** 266–267; **20,** 335–336; **31,** 352–353, 354–355
—identical with grounds of criminal charge, **10,** 304–307
—notice of, **17,** 257–258; **21,** 219–222, 229–231; **31,** 353–355
—perjury, **11,** 111–112
—political activities, for, **1,** 252, 253; **20,** 336–337; **32,** 240–243
—political offences, **9,** 386–388
—security reasons, **32,** 262–263, 266–267
Havana Convention, 1928, provision on, **32,** 258
human rights and, **23,** 393–395; **28,** 209–210, 246, 251, 253; **32,** 255–260
impossibility, invasion of national State, **10,** 316–326
long residence, **9,** 389–391; **12,** 235–236; **15,** 291; **23,** 395–397; **32,** 255–257

Expulsion of aliens—*continued*
Mexican laws, **1,** 253–254; **12,** 236; **15,** 291
nationality, proof of, and, **10,** 273–274
native-born expatriates, **26,** 416
natural justice, denial of, **22,** 510–511
natural justice, requirement of, **17,** 259–260; **32,** 266
—fair hearing, right to, **3,** 287; **8,** 344; **20,** 401–404; **21,** 219–222; **23,** 401–404
nullification of order, **20,** 343
option of country to which deported, **3,** 298–299; **7,** 332–333; **18,** 310–313, 315; **31,** 340–341; **33,** 266–267, 274, 288
penal act, whether, **26,** 434
permission to enter improperly given, **22,** 490–497
persecution, likelihood of, **19,** 352–358; **20,** 330–333; **26,** 503–511; **28,** 315–318; **31,** 346–349; **32,** 243–246
previous proceedings under extradition legislation, **28,** 313–314
" physical persecution ", **34,** 128–131
privileged aliens, **19,** 350–351
procedure, **1,** 257–259; **7,** 330–334; **8,** 342–347; **10,** 309–315; **13,** 151; **14,** 70–71; **18,** 310–315; **20,** 343–363; **21,** 219–222; **22,** 500–512; **23,** 397–400, 401–403; **26,** 509–512; **27,** 249–250; **28,** 93–95; **31,** 349–355; **32,** 260–275; **33,** 297
—appeal, need for reasons, **32,** 260–275
—bail, grant of, **10,** 309–313
—irregularity in, **17,** 252–256, 259–260
—territory controlled by unrecognized government, **1,** 258–259; **3,** 297–298; **4,** 340; **21,** 225–229; **23,** 397–400; **26,** 478 n.; **28,** 93–95
—unfairness of proceedings, **11,** 195–196
—U.S. regulations, **1,** 257–258; **3,** 298–299; **17,** 252–256; **20,** 350–357; **26,** 510
—whether reasons to be given, **31,** 353–355
prohibited immigrants, **18,** 294–299; **21,** 229–231
reception of expelled nationals, **10,** 316–326
" *refoulement* ", **18,** 301
refugees, **11,** 197–198; **26,** 498, 504, 507–509; **28,** 297–300, 310–311
renvoi (Belgian law), **20,** 333–335; **21,** 222–225
residence permit, cancellation of, **20,** 340–342
resident alien, of, **20,** 343–350

Expulsion of aliens—*continued*
revocation of expulsion order, **22**, 501, 508–510; **27**, 249–250
right of expulsion, **1**, 251–257; **7**, 325–330; **8**, 338–342; **10**, 304–309; **13**, 146–150, 233–234; **14**, 131–137; **18**, 282–286; **19**, 345–350; **20**, 330–343; **21**, 213–219, 225–231; **22**, 490–500; **23**, 393–397; **31**, 346–349
—alien mother of national child born during visit, **32**, 252–255
—independent of statute, **28**, 311–313
—renunciation of, **19**, 478–487
—restrictions on, **5**, 266–267; **7**, 325–327; **9**, 384–389
—treaty limitations, **1**, 251–252; **7**, 326, 327; **21**, 218–219; **23**, 393–395; **28**, 209–210, 246, 251, 253; **32**, 255–260
self-defence, as, **1**, 254–255
South Africa, law of, **17**, 258–260; **18**, 303–308; **20**, 340–342
State responsibility for, **6**, 206
stateless persons, **5**, 268; **6**, 287–289
status pending expulsion, **26**, 475–479
statutes of limitation and, **6**, 287–290
United States policy *re* China, **26**, 478 n
validity, **11**, 197
Expulsion of nationals, **13**, 23–28
Exterritoriality, fiction of: *see* Extraterritoriality
Extinction of States, **1**, 35–38, 130–132; **2**, 18–19; **4**, 166–167; **8**, 349; **14**, 18–19, 176; **15**, 292–293; **16**, 267–268; **17**, 357–359; **18**, 17–20, 49–50, 288–289; **19**, 29, 33; **21**, 59; **22**, 141–146, 943–944; **23**, 123–124; **24**, 78. *See also* Absorption of States; Merger of States
Extinctive prescription, **3**, 246; **4**, 263–265; **5**, 194–197, 450–452; **23**, 306, 313, 314–316, 671–672. *See also under* Extradition, *and* Acquiescence; Estoppel; Preclusion; Prescription
European Communities Court, before, **29**, 271, 273, 276, 280
Extradition, **1**, 259–281; **2**, 274–286; **3**, 299–311; **4**, 341–351; **5**, 269–295; **6**, 293–321; **7**, 334–374; **8**, 347–386; **9**, 394–413; **10**, 327–336; **12**, 237–239; **14**, 137–147; **15**, 292–302; **16**, 266–280; **17**, 260–278; **18**, 315–346; **19**, 361–381; **20**, 363–373; **21**, 232–247; **22**, 512–529; **23**, 404–421; **24**, 492–524; **26**, 513–533; **27**, 251–252; **28**, 319–356; **30**, 376–391; **31**, 356–385; **32**, 275–306; **33**, 297–360; **34**, 132–147. *See also* Extradition treaties
absence of accused, in, **17**, 275

Extradition—*continued*
absence of extradition proceedings, **1**, 262
absence of treaty, in, **2**, 274–275, 279 n.; **3**, 301–302; **5**, 276–278, 289–290; **6**, 293, 294; **14**, 137–138, 142, 143; **17**, 13, 83–84, 265–266, 277; **18**, 315–317, 333, 334, 336–348; **19**, 361; **20**, 363–364, 366–367; **21**, 66–75, 239; **28**, 322–324; **30**, 386–388; **31**, 368; **32**, 290–291
—" assurance of reciprocity ", **5**, 280, 285–286, 288–290; **7**, 351–352; **17**, 263–265; **19**, 361; **28**, 11–12
" accused " or " convicted " person, distinction, **30**, 376–384
aggravating circumstances in crime, **8**, 380–381
amnesty law, effect, **7**, 352–353; **18**, 330–331
—after extradition treaty, **9**, 402
arrest, illegal, **11**, 101–104
arrest without extradition, **10**, 327–328
asylum, right of, and, **2**, 281–282; **7**, 361–362; **17**, 281–284; **20**, 370–371, 373; **22**, 520–525; **32**, 292–294
bail, release on, **5**, 290–291; **6**, 317–318
belligerent occupation and, **7**, 367–369; **18**, 318–324; **19**, 379–381; **22**, 987–991; **28**, 327, 329–330
Bolivarian Agreement on (1911), **6**, 311 n.; **10**, 329; **12**, 238–239; **13**, 155–156; **14**, 143; **17**, 281, 282, 285; **19**, 378, 379; **22**, 518; **23**, 414–416
British Commonwealth, in, **19**, 362–365; **21**, 46–47; **33**, 297–312
Canadian Extradition Act, 1927...**9**, 406
—Extradition Act, 1952...**21**, 235; **23**, 405–409; **27**, 251–252
capital offences, **34**, 145–146
capital punishment, undertaking not to impose, **23**, 412–414
causation, place of, and place of effect, **11**, 199–200
change of government, requesting State, **1**, 276
change of law after treaty, **23**, 412–414
change of sovereignty, requesting State, **9**, 407–408
civil war, acts committed in course of, **2**, 286
collaboration with the enemy, for, **16**, 275–276
" common crimes ", meaning, **9**, 402
—political crimes and, **22**, 520–525, 528–529
Commonwealth countries, between, **19**, 362–365; **21**, 46–47; **33**, 297–312

Extradition—*continued*
competence of requesting authority, **19**, 379–381
concurrent jurisdiction, **11**, 199–200
conditions of, **1**, 270–277; **2**, 277–279; **3**, 305–307; **5**, 282–290; **6**, 294, 298–314; **7**, 335–357; **8**, 361–384; **9**, 395–408; **11**, 199–201; **12**, 237–238; **13**, 151–157; **14**, 139–142; **15**, 295–296, 297; **16**, 266–277; **17**, 260–275; **18**, 318–334; **19**, 362–378; **20**, 363–369; **21**, 232–240; **22**, 514–519; **23**, 405–417; **24**, 493–506; **26**, 513–524; **28**, 322–340; **30**, 376–388; **31**, 356–374; **32**, 275–294
—Executive, question for, **31**, 369
" connected offence ", **7**, 364
convicted criminals, surrender of, **9**, 411
conviction as basis for request, **18**, 325–330
conviction *in absentia*, **5**, 287; **8**, 382–384; **31**, 356, 358, 362–364, 368, 372
crime committed after escape from prison, **23**, 410–411
crime committed during occupation, **7**, 367–369; **18**, 318–324; **28**, 327, 329–330
crime committed in extraditing State, **21**, 234–236
crime committed in third State, **2**, 274–275
crime committed prior to treaty, **9**, 410–411
crime not in treaty, **14**, 139–141; **16**, 275–276; **17**, 11–17; **21**, 234–236
crime on requesting State's ship—
—territorial waters of requested State, in, **24**, 497–499
—territorial waters of third State, in, **3**, 305–306
—undetermined position, in, **26**, 513–518
definition, **15**, 292–293
délits mixtes, **3**, 308–311
depositions, sufficiency of, **21**, 236–238
discretion, exercise of, **22**, 514–517
double criminality, **5**, 277–278; **6**, 298–302, 310–311; **7**, 337–338, 340, 344–351; **8**, 365–367, 372–376, 381; **9**, 399, 402, 405; **11**, 201; **14**, 138, 140; **16**, 275–276; **18**, 325–330; **20**, 365–366; **21**, 234–236; **23**, 414–417; **24**, 502–506; **26**, 518–525; **28**, 324–326; **30**, 385–386, 387; **32**, 275–285, 288–291
double jeopardy, **2**, 280–281
dual nationality, **3**, 303
escaped criminals, **9**, 412–413

Extradition—*continued*
evidence—
—accused, by, **6**, 316–317
—admissibility, **28**, 339
—authentication of documents, **28**, 328–329
—burden of proof, **28**, 355–356; **30**, 389, 390
—law of requested State, application, **27**, 251–252
—new affidavits, **2**, 280–281
—new, on appeal, **33**, 334–336, 339, 346–349
—obtained by subpoena and deposition, **31**, 374–383
—preliminary examination of, **23**, 414–417
—prima facie case, requirement of, **9**, 405–407
—proof of nature of crime, **21**, 238–239
—request for, **17**, 267–275
—sufficiency of, **3**, 307; **5**, 282–283; **6**, 301–302, 310–311, 315–316, 318–319; **8**, 363–365; **9**, 408–411; **17**, 267–275; **24**, 502, 519; **27**, 251–252; **28**, 330–335, 338–340
—time-limit for filing, **28**, 326–328
expulsion, distinguished, **33**, 264–293, *passim*
expulsion order, prior, and, **22**, 497–500
extraditable crimes, **1**, 263–267, 272–273; **3**, 301–302; **4**, 342–343; **5**, 277–280; **6**, 293, 298–302, 305–306; **7**, 337–338, 340–344; **9**, 394; **14**, 139–142; **17**, 266–267; **20**, 364–369; **26**, 518–524; **28**, 324–326; **30**, 381, 387; **34**, 136
—proof of criminality, **6**, 310–311, 315–316, 318–319
failure to hand over accused, **2**, 280–282
finality of order, **9**, 411
fiscal offences, for, **20**, 363–364, 367–369
former jeopardy, plea of, **31**, 371–372
France, law of, **6**, 308–309; **9**, 400–401; **14**, 140; **18**, 324, 344; **19**, 365–366; **20**, 369–370; **22**, 514–515, 517, 519–520
fraud, for, **6**, 308–309
" fugitive from justice ", meaning, **6**, 137–138, 303; **7**, 343, 355
Fugitive Offenders Act (U.K.), political offences, **32**, 299–306
general principles of international law and, **18**, 315–317, 336–345
hearing, presence of accused, **23**, 419–420
homicide, for, **2**, 283–284; **3**, 303–309; **5**, 289; **18**, 318–324
identity of accused, **2**, 279 n.; **5**, 287–288; **16**, 273–274; **23**, 417–418

Extradition—*continued*
identity of punishment, **13,** 155–157
illegal arrest, **11,** 101–104
impartiality of courts of requesting State, relevance, **2,** 283–284
incest, for, **5,** 288
Indian Extradition Act (1903), **17,** 11–17
insanity, effect, **5,** 288–289
Institute of International Law, Draft Convention (1880), **18,** 341
International Penal Law—
—Montevideo, Treaty (1889), **7,** 354–355, 356, 357; **12,** 237–238, 239; **17,** 285; **26,** 525
—Montevideo, Treaty (1933), **22,** 528–529; **24,** 499–501
—Montevideo Treaty (1940), **18,** 333
interruption of proceedings, **2,** 277–279
inter-State, in U.S.A., **15,** 293–295
irregular rendition, **2,** 281–282
irregularity, effect of, **23,** 405–409
judicial review, **19,** 365
jurisdiction of court, **2,** 281–282
kidnapping, for, **5,** 283–284; **7,** 337–338
legislative prohibition, effect, **22,** 512–513
locality of offence, **11,** 199–200
locus delicti commissi, French practice, **6,** 308–309
mandated territories, from, **9,** 50
—to, **2,** 275–276; **5,** 32; **8,** 382–384
merger, theory of, **7,** 340–344
military offence, **7,** 357
Montevideo Treaty (1889), **7,** 354–355, 356, 357; **12,** 237–238, 239; **17,** 285; **26,** 525
Montevideo Treaty (1933), **22,** 528–529; **24,** 499–501
Montevideo Treaty (1940), **18,** 333
nationality and, **18,** 324; **22,** 430–432
nationals, of, **1,** 265, 269; **3,** 302–304; **5,** 280–282; **6,** 295–297, 305–308; **8,** 352–361; **9,** 394; **10,** 329–331; **12,** 237; **17,** 189–191; **18,** 324, 333; **21,** 232–234; **22,** 512–513; **23,** 404; **24,** 492–493; **28,** 319–322
—execution of foreign sentence in lieu of, **6,** 297
—ignorance of nationality, **28,** 319–322
—indirect extradition, **28,** 319–322
—loss of nationality, effect, **20,** 250–251; **22,** 430–432
—prohibition of, extension to members of same race, **5,** 281–282
—prohibition of, principle of, **6,** 307–308; **7,** 335–336; **32,** 142
—re-extradition, **6,** 295–297
—transit facilities by national State, **28,** 319–322
nature of, **28,** 342; **31,** 375, 378

Extradition—*continued*
new request, amendment of former request, **5,** 291
non-extraditable offences, **20,** 371–373; **21,** 125–126; **23,** 410–411
—merger, theory of, **7,** 340–344
objects connected with offence, **1,** 279–280
occupied territory, inhabitant of, **7,** 367–369
occupied territory, to, **22,** 987–991
offence committed before treaty concluded, **31,** 361
offence on ship, jurisdiction of flag State, **3,** 305–306; **24,** 497–499; **26,** 513–518
offence within "territory" of requesting State, **26,** 513–518
"passive extradition", **30,** 390–391
penalty, discrepancy as to, **24,** 499
penalty, nature of, relevance, **14,** 144. *See also* capital punishment, *supra*
Polish law, **30,** 507 n., 510
political offences, **2,** 283–284; **3,** 308–311; **4,** 347–351; **5,** 270–272, 292–295; **6,** 305; **7,** 360–372; **9,** 402, 410; **10,** 331; **14,** 139–142, 145–147; **15,** 297–302; **16,** 4–8, 276; **17,** 276–278; **18,** 325–330, 336–346; **19,** 366–376, 379–381; **20,** 369–371; **21,** 240–247; **22,** 520–529; **24,** 501, 510–517, 518–524; **28,** 326–327, 335–337, 341–356; **30,** 388; **31,** 359, 365–366, 370, 372–373; **32,** 294–306; **33,** 271, 319–352, 353–360; **34,** 139–147
—assurance sought, **30,** 388
—Caracas Convention, Territorial Asylum (1954), **24,** 518–523
—civil war, acts committed in course of, **2,** 286
—common crime and, **9,** 402; **22,** 520–525, 528–529; **32,** 294–298, 304
—Commonwealth, within, **33,** 300, 303–304, 309, 310–312
—crimes by dictator, whether acts of State, **33,** 353–356
—expulsion of aliens, distinguished, **7,** 332–333; **22,** 497–500
—homicide in course of elections, **2,** 283–284
—murder, **4,** 347–351; **5,** 270–272
—request for non-political offence also, **33,** 356
—trading with the enemy, **1,** 265–266
—treason, **15,** 297–300; **22,** 527–528
prescription and, **2,** 279 n.; **5,** 286; **6,** 294, 306–307, 313–314; **7,** 354–355; **8,** 350, 382–383; **9,** 395–398; **16,** 276; **19,** 378; **22,** 514–517; **26,** 525–526; **30,** 389–390; **31,** 369–372

Extradition—*continued*
prima facie case, requirement of, **9,** 405–407
prior expulsion and, **18,** 325–330
probable treatment by requesting State, relevance, **31,** 364–365, 369
procedure, **1,** 277–281; **2,** 280–283; **4,** 343–345; **5,** 285–287, 290–291; **6,** 315–321; **7,** 358–359; **8,** 384–385; **9,** 408–412; **10,** 335–336; **11,** 201–202; **12,** 238–239; **13,** 157–158; **14,** 143–144; **15,** 296–297; **16,** 277–278; **17,** 276; **18,** 335; **19,** 379–381; **22,** 519–520; **23,** 417–421; **24,** 506, 507–510; **26,** 525–528; **27,** 251–252; **28,** 340; **30,** 388–391; **31,** 374–385; **32,** 317–318
—advantages for requesting State, **31,** 382
—appeal, **23,** 421
—conviction *in absentia*, **5,** 287; **8,** 382–384; **31,** 356, 358, 362–364, 368, 372
—formal request, need for, **23,** 405–409
—fresh evidence on appeal, **33,** 334–336, 339, 346–349
—innocence, plea in bar, **30,** 389
—language of proceedings, **31,** 373
—*locus standi* of requesting Government, **26,** 515
—nature of, **5,** 285–287; **6,** 295–297, 317; **15,** 292–293
—passive extradition, **33,** 318
—proof, prima facie case, **31,** 376
—request by telegraph, **30,** 391
—State succession, effect, **18,** 332–333
—time-limit for filing evidence, **28,** 326–328
—treaty requirements, **26,** 525, 526–528; **31,** 385
—waiver, **1,** 280–281; **9,** 401; **23,** 405–409
—warrant, matters to be specified in, **31,** 384–385
—warrant, need for, **33,** 317–318
—witnesses requested by accused, **31,** 366–367
prosecution, relation to extradition: *see* specialty, principle of, *infra*
protection of accused, **9,** 403
provisional detention, request for, **30,** 390–391
reciprocity, principle of, **5,** 280, 285–286, 288–290; **7,** 351–352, 355, 356; **14,** 140; **17,** 263–265; **19,** 361; **20,** 364–365; **28,** 11–12
re-extradition, **6,** 295–297; **7,** 338–340; **8,** 361–362
refusal of extradition, right of, **1,** 268; **5,** 291
rendition, irregular, effect, **2,** 281–282

Extradition—*continued*
rendition within same State, **22,** 512–513
request for—
—absence of, **9,** 413
—amendment of, **1,** 263–264; **5,** 291; **6,** 310
—capitulations, from State under régime of, **2,** 274–275
—conviction as basis of, **18,** 325–330
—formal, need for, **23,** 405–409
—meaning, **1,** 277
—new, **5,** 291
—particulars in, **26,** 518–522
—repeated, **16,** 277; **22,** 517–519
—two States, from, **1,** 278–279; **2,** 274–275
requesting authority, competence of, **19,** 379–381; **30,** 388–390
requesting State—
—change of government in, **1,** 276
—change of sovereignty in, **9,** 407–408
retroactive application of penal law, **14,** 146–147
ship, offence on, jurisdiction of flag State, **3,** 305–306; **24,** 497–499; **26,** 513–518
specialty, principle of, **1,** 260, 272–275; **2,** 283; **4,** 345–346; **5,** 269–278; **6,** 305–306, 310, 319–321; **7,** 334, 351–352; **8,** 350–351, 375–380; **9,** 399–401, 402–405; **16,** 266–272, 275–276; **18,** 331; **19,** 376–378; **20,** 364–365; **21,** 234–236; **23,** 409, 410–411; **24,** 496–497; **30,** 239, 241; **31,** 365; **32,** 286–288, 297; **33,** 313–317; **34,** 132–134, 135, 137–139
—basis of, **33,** 314
—punishment, scope of, **33,** 314–317
stateless persons, **20,** 367–369
statutes of limitation and: *see* prescription, *supra*
subsequent law as " new fact ", **22,** 519–520
substance of charge, competence of requested State to review, **14,** 144
" sufficient cause ", **9,** 408–410
supervision by courts, **14,** 140
surrender, distinguished from voluntary return, **6,** 319–321
temporary, **21,** 232–234
territorial competence of courts of requesting State, **7,** 353
territoriality of offence, **3,** 305–306; **6,** 302–303, 312; **11,** 199–200; **15,** 215–216; **19,** 371–374; **22,** 517; **24,** 497–499; **26,** 513–518
third State, crime committed in, **2,** 274–275
third States, rendition to, **20,** 369
time-barred offences: *see* prescription, *supra*

Extradition—*continued*
transport of accused, **7**, 372–373
treaty and law, conflict between, **30**, 390–391. *See also* Extradition treaties
treaty, dependent upon, **31**, 368. *See also* absence of treaty, in, *supra*
two States, request from, **1**, 278–279; **2**, 274–275
unexpired portion of sentence, for, **23**, 410–411
war crimes, for, **15**, 301–302; **16**, 266–274; **18**, 331; **24**, 516–517; **30**, 506–508, 510
warrant by description, **23**, 417–418
Extradition treaties. *See also under* various States—
absence of, effect: *see* Extradition, absence of treaty, in
change of government, effect of, **10**, 328–329
change of law after treaty, **23**, 412–414
change of status of colony, **20**, 40–41
crimes committed prior to, **9**, 410–411
effect of war on, **28**, 602–604; **31**, 361
individual, rights of, under, **16**, 275
interpretation, **2**, 276–277; **8**, 347–349, 355–359, 365–371; **23**, 418–419
—liberal, **31**, 375
mandated territories, application to, **4**, 47–48
municipal law, relation to, **1**, 260–261; **5**, 273–274; **14**, 140; **17**, 12–20
offence not included in, **14**, 139–141; **16**, 275–276; **17**, 11–17; **21**, 234–236
retroactive operation, **28**, 604
State succession and, **8**, 349; **14**, 42–44; **17**, 15–20, 82–91; **20**, 364
territorial scope, *de facto* authority, **33**, 320, 322–326, 332–333, 340, 345–346, 351
Extraterritorial application of court orders, production of documents, **19**, 197; **22**, 184–197; **26**, 123–129; **28**, 138–142; **31**, 210, 214–219, 220–226; **32**, 100–102; **33**, 158–163
Extraterritorial courts, during war, *persona standi in judicio*, **1**, 402–403
Extraterritorial effect of acts of courts, **11**, 104–106. *See also* Letters rogatory
Extraterritorial effect of deportation order, **14**, 70–71, 131–133
Extraterritorial effect of legislation, **3**, 136–148; **4**, 141–153; **6**, 140–151, 179–180; **7**, 49, 151–162, 212; **8**, 184–207; **9**, 141–156; **10**, 10–23, 131–154; **11**, 107–111; **12**, 8–11;
Extraterritorial effect of legislation—*continued*
13, 12–18, 26, 59–66, 94–95, 135, 137, 142; **14**, 93–94, 122–123; **18**, 195–206; **23**, 130–149; **26**, 129–131, 158, 213; **27**, 108–109; **28**, 14–16, 24, 26–31, 40, 45, 115–138; **30**, 112–115; **31**, 126, 206–219; **32**, 9–10, 12–17, 19–22, 26–29, 31, 140–147; **33**, 191, 196, 199–200
alien seamen on foreign ships, **33**, 155–158
anti-trust legislation, **19**, 158–163; **22**, 168–184; **23**, 130–133; **24**, 673–675: *see also* Restrictive practices, *and* Shipping Conferences
armed forces in leased base abroad, **31**, 121–128
colonial statutes, **33**, 170, 171
comity and, **2**, 412; **7**, 156, 161; **8**, 35; **10**, 16, 53, 140; **15**, 18; **18**, 175; **26**, 386
confiscatory legislation: *see under* Confiscatory legislation
criminal, **13**, 54, 55–56; **14**, 93–95; **15**, 78–90; **26**, 158; **31**, 121–128: *see also* penal decrees *and* traffic laws, *infra*
defence legislation, **13**, 94–95
exchange control measures, **11**, 29; **16**, 27–36; **26**, 39; **33**, 32, 35
government in exile, decree of, **9**, 150; **10**, 10–23; **15**, 17–18
labour legislation, flights outside territory of owner's national State, **28**, 115–138
law of Belgium, **8**, 207
—France, **8**, 193–197
—Germany, **8**, 205–207
—Italy, **8**, 198–200
—Soviet Union, **8**, 184–187
—Spain, **8**, 189–193, 195–197
—U.S.A., **8**, 187–189
nationality laws, **13**, 135–137, 142; **14**, 122–123; **16**, 16
nationalization decrees: *see under* Nationalization
penal decrees, **9**, 180–181; **13**, 12–17: *see also* criminal, *supra*
powers of foreign bank in State of forum, **27**, 19–22
presumption against, **26**, 213, 514; **30**, 113; **31**, 126, 207, 208
recognition, effect of, **10**, 10–23, 131–140, 149; **12**, 9
requisitioning decrees, **8**, 195–197, 200–204; **9**, 289–293; **10**, 131–147
ships, concerning, **9**, 229; **30**, 112–115
taxation laws, **5**, 101–102; **13**, 59–64
trading with the enemy, **9**, 552–553
traffic laws, **32**, 140–147; **33**, 191, 196, 199–200

Extraterritorial jurisdiction, **1**, 161–163; **4**, 189–193; **7**, 160–161, 199–201; **9**, 471–472; **10**, 111–129, 263–266; **13**, 93–96; **14**, 91–95; **16**, 81–84; **20**, 3–4; **22**, 263–265: *see also* Capitulations, régime of; Consular jurisdiction; High seas, jurisdiction over
bankruptcy, **15**, 75–77
high seas, on: *see under* High seas
international public order, **9**, 292
Kuwait, British Court in, **26**, 245–254
law of the Netherlands, **8**, 200–205
marriage, solemnization of, **13**, 93–94
police power measures, states of U.S.A., **31**, 185
territorial waters, outside, **9**, 300. *See also* Contiguous zone
treason, **15**, 78–90
treaty, in virtue of, **5**, 103; **16**, 82
Extraterritorial rights in China, termination of, **12**, 252
Extraterritoriality—
consuls, **8**, 232–233
—premises, **1**, 304–305; **2**, 150–151; **12**, 68–73; **20**, 181–182
diplomatic envoys, **1**, 291; **6**, 327–328; **8**, 232–233; **10**, 341; **12**, 241–242; **15**, 309–311
easements, and, **9**, 457–458
foreign armed forces, **2**, 144–145; **6**, 174; **8**, 248–249; **11**, 171 n.; **12**, 162–163 n.; **13**, 88; **14**, 214; **16**, 95, 145; **22**, 263–264
Holy See, buildings, **9**, 108, 109, 436–439
I.L.O. officials, **5**, 314–318
legation buildings, **1**, 118–119, 290–291, 305; **3**, 179; **5**, 301, 305–308; **7**, 385–386; **9**, 107, 436–439; **10**, 339–342; **15**, 311; **21**, 249–250; **22**, 242; **26**, 168, 173, 544–546; **34**, 149
ships, **9**, 470; **10**, 252–258; **27**, 45–49

F

F.o.b. sales, nature of, **27**, 220–221
Faculties of law, opinions rendered by, **4**, 33
Fair compensation: *see* Damages; Equity
Fair hearing, expulsion procedure, in, **3**, 287; **8**, 344; **17**, 259–260; **20**, 343–349; **21**, 219–222; **23**, 401–403. *See also Audi alteram partem*
Falke, The, affair of, **6**, 31–32
Falkland Islands, Argentine claim, **8**, 180
False imprisonment, alien detained by immigration authorities, **26**, 473–474
Far Eastern Commission, functions and jurisdiction, **16**, 147–149; **22**, 985–986
Federal Republic of Germany: *see* Germany, Federal Republic
Federal States—
aliens, treatment of, **10**, 295–303; **12**, 224–229
Australia, international status, **8**, 54–70
Canada, international status, **8**, 41–48
foreign relations, **1**, 116 n.; **8**, 34–39, 48–69; **10**, 58–59; **12**, 22–23; **26**, 412; **34**, 125
fulfilment of international obligations, **10**, 348–349
International Labour Conventions, **8**, 41–48
jurisdiction, federal courts, of, **6**, 151–152; **12**, 226–229
legislative powers, distribution of, **33**, 166
member States—
—disputes between, applicable law, **4**, 130; **6**, 120
—immunity from jurisdiction, **6**, 162–163; **7**, 166–169; **10**, 178–191; **11**, 143
—international status, **4**, 39–40, 130; **8**, 41–48
—legislative competence, **12**, 224–229
—public policy, **8**, 34–39; **10**, 58–59; **12**, 22–23
—territorial waters, **8**, 171–173
recognition by Federal Government, effect, **10**, 48–70; **13**, 22–23
responsibility for acts of member States, **3**, 203–204; **4**, 203; **5**, 145–149
treaties–
—operation and enforcement, **5**, 330–332; **8**, 41–48, 58–66; **10**, 394–397, 398–403; **15**, 4–5; **24**, 592–594; **25**, 124
—superiority over state law, **14**, 163–165
—ratification, **8**, 41–48, 54–58
treaty-making power, **8**, 41–69, 410–412, 412–414
—administrative agreements, **5**, 331
Fees, court, recovery of foreign, **6**, 145
Ferdinand, ex-Tsar of Bulgaria, property in England, **1**, 406–407
Fez, Treaty of (France/Morocco) (1912), **5**, 117; **7**, 172; **8**, 93, 94; **19**, 255, 259, 260, 263, 269, 296
Fiat executio decree, **11**, 221
Fideikommiss, establishment by Frederick William I of Prussia, **4**, 31–33
Fiji Islands, acquisition of land from chiefs, **2**, 78–79

Finland—
  Constitution (liability for military service), **28**, 289
  German occupation of, **15**, 647
  independence of (1917), **23**, 354, 356
  recognition by Belgium, **1**, 153
  Russia, Peace Treaty, Dorpat (1920), **2**, 394–397
  ships, detention by U.S.A., **10**, 267–272
  U.S.S.R., peace with, **15**, 647
Finland, Gulf of, international maritime routes, **8**, 407–409
Fiord of Varanger, **7**, 136
Fiords, limits of territorial waters, **7**, 136
Firearms: *see* Arms
First World War, termination of: *see* War, termination of
Fiscal legislation—
  German-occupied countries, in, non-recognition of, **26**, 56–57
Fiscus, foreign State as, **3**, 180
Fishery limits, exclusive zone, enforcement of prohibition on fishing, **35**, 485–501
Fishery protection vessels, use of force by, **35**, 498–499, 500
Fisheries: *see also* Fishing rights—
  Charles V, Edict of, 1547...**11**, 176
  conservation, Cuba–U.S.A., Treaty (1958), **32**, 342–344
  Convention for Regulation of (Denmark/United Kingdom) (1901), **6**, 126 n.
  North Sea Fisheries Convention (1882), **6**, 125; **8**, 266; **18**, 101, 116, 117, 127, 128
  pearl, **20**, 167–169
  Zuiderzee, **11**, 175–176
Fisheries zone: *see* Maritime belt
Fishing rights—
  Anglo-American Commission on, **6**, 347
  Anglo-French Convention (1839), **18**, 117, 118; **20**, 95, 96, 101, 102, 103, 120, 121, 123, 127, 141, 142
  —(1867), **20**, 104
  —(1951), **20**, 145
  discrimination against aliens, **1**, 237; **2**, 269; **14**, 129–130
  enclosed parts of high seas, in, **11**, 175–176
  high seas, **18**, 156
  illegal fishing, jurisdiction in regard to, **6**, 157
  territorial waters, in, **1**, 176–177; **6**, 123–126, 154–156; **15**, 71; **18**, 86–144 *passim*; **20**, 166–169; **23**, 127, 154–159
  withdrawal of privileges, **1**, 237–238
Fiume, status of, **6**, 439; **9**, 430–431
Flag, foreign—
  consul, right to fly, **22**, 557–559
  display of, recognition, effect of, **7**, 76–77
Flag, ships, flown by—
  dependent territory, of, **23**, 34
  enemy character, how for determining, **11**, 264–265; **24**, 919–921
  jurisdiction, determining, **22**, 282–286
  non-enemy, **24**, 919–921
Flags of convenience, **26**, 222–227, 227–231, 236–239; **30**, 429–430; **31**, 235–236
  ships, application of penal laws, **35**, 97–101
Florida—
  breadth of maritime belt, **8**, 171–172; **31**, 151, 194, 205
  seaward boundary—
  —admission to United States, upon, **31**, 143, 151
  —claim to three leagues, **31**, 151, 194, 205
Flying boat, whether " ship or vessel ", **12**, 55–59
Food and Agriculture Organization—
  Director-General, powers relating to Staff Rules, **27**, 456
  Personnel Manual of Technical Assistance Board, **21**, 392, 396
  Staff Manual, conformity with Staff Regulations, **27**, 454–457
  Staff Regulations, **21**, 358, 390–397, *passim*
Forced Labour, Convention for Abolition of (1957)—
  complaint of non-compliance, **35**, 285–351 *passim*
  forced labour, meaning, **35**, 327, 347–348
  grievance procedures, **35**, 329, 331, 345–347
  labour inspection service, **35**, 341–343
Force majeure, **1**, 169, 418; **2**, 159–160; **4**, 206; **5**, 470; **6**, 413; **7**, 331–332; **10**, 530; **13**, 201; **18**, 422, 428; **22**, 328; **23**, 354 n., 640, 649–652, 657; **27**, 631–637; **29**, 301. *See also* Duress
  contract between government and foreign company, **23**, 649–652, 657
  contract between State trading corporation and alien, **27**, 631–637
  delay in appeal, **29**, 301
  expulsion proceedings, in, **7**, 331–332
  International Telegraphic Convention (1875), under, **6**, 413
  residence under, enemy character, **10**, 530
  State responsibility and, **1**, 169, 418; **23**, 354 n.
  Treaty of Versailles, Art. 131..**1**, 169

Foreign Affairs, Minister for: *see* Foreign Minister
Foreign air carriers, ownership and control provisions of bilateral agreements, **31**, 416–424
Foreign Arbitral Awards, Convention on Execution of (1927), **7**, 419–420; **27**, 36; **28**, 526–538; **31**, 20–22
Foreign armed forces—
attack by, in time of peace, **22**, 208–209
Australia, in—
—French, **16**, 144–145
—United States, **12**, 133–141, 173–175
Austria, in, French army, **16**, 144–145
Belgium, in—
—Allied armies, **13**, 85–86; **32**, 588–594
—United States, **1**, 121–122; **21**, 121–122
Brazil, in, United States base, **13**, 86–90
Canada, in—
—Dutch, **10**, 116–117
—N.A.T.O. pilots, **23**, 251–254
—United States, **12**, 124–133, **21**; 114–116
damage during military operations, liability for, **23**, 205–208, 214–216
double jeopardy rule, **22**, 267–270; **34**, 192–198
Egypt, in—
– British, **6**, 174; **7**, 187–188; **13**, 90–92; **14**, 78–79, 90; **16**, 145–146
—French Foreign Legion, **12**, 154–162
—French Military Mission, **12**, 164
—French sailors, **12**, 115–119
—Greek Air Force, **11**, 170–171
—Greek Army, **12**, 150–152, 152–154
—Greek sailors, **11**, 165–169, 169–170; **12**, 120–123
employees, action between, **26**, 200–203
employees, crimes committed by, **23**, 245–250
exemption from jurisdiction of host State, **1**, 121; **2**, 143–145; **4**, 180–181; **5**, 486; **6**, 174; **7**, 187–188; **8**, 248–249; **10**, 111–129; **11**, 161–171; **12**, 115–123, 124–143, 150–164; **13**, 86–92; **14**, 78–79, 90; **15**, 147–173; **16**, 144–146; **19**, 220–226; **20**, 182–188; **21**, 111–125; **22**, 263–264; **23**, 239–269; **24**, 595; **26**, 200–203; **31**, 35–36, 85, 405–408. *See also* jurisdiction over, *infra*
—refusal by host State to recognize, **11**, 170–171
—stationing, relevance of, **12**, 150–152, 154–164

Foreign armed forces—*continued*
exterritoriality of, **2**, 144–145; **8**, 248–249; **11**, 171; **12**, 162–163; **13**, 88; **14**, 214; **16**, 95, 145; **22**, 263–264. *See also* jurisdiction over, *infra*
France, in—
—United States, **1**, 333; **20**, 182–184, 186–188; **23**, 255–259; **24**, 251–253; **26**, 196–200
Germany, Federal Republic, in—
—Belgian, **24**, 594–595
—Bonn/Paris Conventions (1952/54), **24**, 595; **26**, 200–203
—British, **26**, 200–203
Greece, in—
—British army, **12**, 163
—United States naval mission, **21**, 122–125
Iceland, in—
—United States defence force, **23**, 260–264
internal discipline, **11**, 161–165; **12**, 124–141
interned members, status of, **9**, 583–584
Italy, in—
—United States, **23**, 201–202; **24**, 253–255
—Yugoslav forces, **15**, 106–107
Japan, in—
—British sailors, **19**, 221–226
—United States, **23**, 239–240
—United States, Administrative Agreement (1952), **22**, 257–266; **23**, 265–268, 455–459; **24**, 227; **26**, 203–208
—United Stâtes, of, Administrative Agreement, Protocol (1953), **23**, 264–265; **24**, 248–250
jurisdiction over: *see also* exterritoriality, *supra, and* North Atlantic Treaty, Status of Forces Agreement
—civil, **1**, 121–122; **6**, 174; **7**, 187–188; **12**, 133–141, 164; **14**, 78–79; 90; **16**, 144–145; **19**, 220–221; **20**, 184–186; **21**, 111–113, 114–116, 116–121, 121–122; **23**, 260–264; **26**, 200–203; **28**, 161, 414
—concurrent and primary, **10**, 128–129; **11**, 161–165; **22**, 264–266, 266–270; **23**, 241–244, 245–250, 255–259, 264–265; **24**, 248–255; **26**, 196–200, 205–208
—criminal, **1**, 333; **8**, 248–249; **11**, 161–171; **12**, 115–123, 124–143, 150–163, 165–168; **13**, 86–87, 87–90, 90–92; **15**, 106–107, 147–173; **19**, 221–226; **21**, 182–184; **22**, 154–156, 208–209; **23**, 239–241, 241–244, 245–250, 264–265, 455–459; **24**, 595; **26**, 196–200; **33**, 190–193

Foreign armed forces—*continued*
jurisdiction over—*continued*
—criminal—*continued*
— —U.N. Command in Korea, **32,** 367–368
—insurance company, position of, **14,** 90
—official duties, act in course of, **1,** 121–122; **7,** 187–188; **12,** 152–154; **14,** 79; **20,** 184–186, 187; **26,** 200–203
—certificate, **11,** 166; **12,** 153; **24,** 249; **26,** 203
—unofficial acts, **11,** 165–169, 170; **12,** 151; **19,** 220–221; **21,** 122–125; **23,** 264–265; **26,** 196–200, 202
—waiver by host State, **22,** 257–266; **23,** 255–259; **24,** 251–253, 253–255; **26,** 196–200
—waiver by sending State, **16,** 144–145; **20,** 187; **23,** 265–268; **24,** 249, 250; **26,** 206
— —implied, **12,** 153–154
leased territory, in, **22,** 154–156
Libya, in, United States, **23,** 241–244
N.A.T.O. Status of Forces Agreement (1951), jurisdiction under: *see* North Atlantic Treaty, Status of Forces Agreement
occupied territory, in: *see* Belligerent occupation
offences against, jurisdiction over, **12,** 152–154; **13,** 85–86
officers' club, employee, offence by, **23,** 265–268
Palestine, in, Polish Army, **12,** 165–168
Panama Canal Zone, in, United States, **4,** 180–181
performing rights, liability in respect of, **23,** 260–264
protected States, in, looting by, **2,** 174
protection of base areas, U.S. forces in Japan, **32,** 43, 45, 48
responsibility for acts of, **7,** 258–259; **12,** 173–175; **23,** 205–208, 214–216, 251–255
Saar territory, in, Italian, **8,** 248–249
sailors on shore mission, criminal jurisdiction over, **11,** 165–169, 169–170; **12,** 115–123, 141–143, 153
service in, expatriation by: *see under* Expatriation
South Africa, in, Dutch, **10,** 119–123
taxation, immunity from, **16,** 145–146
torts, liability for, **12,** 173–175; **23,** 251–255
—libel, **22,** 270–275

Foreign armed forces—*continued*
United Kingdom, in,
—Allied Forces Act (1940), **10,** 111–113, 123, 128; **11,** 162–165; **12,** 126, 138, 165; **15,** 160, 164; **18,** 182
—Belgian, **2,** 144–145
—Canadian Army, **19,** 220–221; **20,** 184–186
—Czech Army, **10,** 123–128; **11,** 161–165
—Dutch, **10,** 111–116
—Polish Army, **10,** 128–129
—United States, of, **21,** 111–113
—U.S.A. (Visiting Forces) Act, (1942), **12,** 125, 139; **15,** 160, 164
—Visiting Forces Act (1952), **19,** 221; **21,** 113 n.
—Visiting Forces (British Commonwealth) Act (1933), **12,** 126, 138, 167; **19,** 220; **20,** 184–186; **21,** 111–113
visiting forces in British Commonwealth, **19,** 68; **20,** 184–186
" Foreign country ", meaning—
taxation purposes, **6,** 19–20
U.S. Federal Tort Claims Act (1938), **24,** 89–93
Foreign courts—
enforcement of criminal sentences, **15,** 72–75
execution of orders of, **19,** 158–163
Foreign decisions *in pari materia,* **4,** 414
" Foreign Government ", definition, **24,** 6
Foreign governments—
acts done within own territory, **21,** 16–21
inducing breach of contract with, **21,** 16–21
recognition of: *see* Recognition, Governments, of
recognition of acts of: *see* Recognition, acts of foreign States and Governments, of
status of, conclusiveness of statement of executive: *see* Conclusiveness of statement of executive
Foreign judgments—
enforcement of, **4,** 183–184; **11,** 221; **26,** 57–58; **30,** 105–111
recognition of, **1,** 28–30; **6,** 144–145; **7,** 21–22; **19,** 19–23; **24,** 40
Foreign jurisdiction of British Crown, Bahrain, **30,** 94–100
Foreign law: *see also* Confiscatory legislation; Penal legislation; *and* Revenue laws
enforcement of, **21,** 23–24; **24,** 15–27, 38–39; **35,** 29, 43
evidence of—
—burden of proof, **28,** 46
—consular *informe,* **2,** 303
—expert, **26,** 13

Foreign law—*continued*
extraterritorial effect: *see* Extraterritorial effect of legislation
recognition of, **1**, 47–51; **3**, 25–27, 29–30, 32–33; **5**, 22–23; **7**, 22–27, 65–75, 80–82; **8**, 34–39; **9**, 84–87; **10**, 48–70; **11**, 16–24, 26–29; **12**, 8–11, 22–23; **13**, 12–17; **15**, 17–18; **16**, 14–16, 19–20; **17**, 32–33; **18**, 38–39; **19**, 16–19; **20**, 26–31, 34–36; **21**, 25–29; **22**, 97–100, 101–102; **23**, 24–26; **24**, 38–39, 40–41, 48–51; **26**, 6–29, 56–57, 702–704; **27**, 19–22; **28**, 184–185; **29**, 31–32, 45–46, 52; **30**, 4–24; **33**, 16–36: *see also* Recognition, acts of foreign States; Confiscatory legislation; Exchange control; Revenue laws
—law providing for lapse of claims against prior Government, **33**, 26–27
—powers of foreign bank, **27**, 19–22
violation of, production of documents, **34**, 44–45
Foreign military missions, jurisdiction over, **12**, 164; **21**, 116–121. *See also* Foreign armed forces
Foreign Minister—
international authority of statements of, **6**, 103–105
interpretation of treaty by, **7**, 404–405
right to represent State, **7**, 63–65
Foreign Office certificate: *see* Conclusiveness of statements of executive
Foreign public ships: *see under* Ships
Foreign relations, conduct of, judicial review, **34**, 8, 10–11
Foreign sovereigns: *see under* Foreign States *and* Heads of State, foreign
Foreign States—
action brought by, **4**, 170–171; **9**, 89; **13**, 9–12; **21**, 265–272; **33**, 36–43
acts of—
—jurisdictional immunities and: *see* immunity from jurisdiction, private law acts, public law acts, *infra*
—recognition of: *see under* Recognition
agencies of: *see under* immunity from jurisdiction, *infra*
ambassador, competence to represent in proceedings, **23**, 210–212
charterers, as, arbitration clause in charterparty, jurisdictional immunity, **24**, 205–206
cross suit, implied submission to, **4**, 163–164

Foreign States—*continued*
embassy, as representing, **23**, 431–432; **24**, 221–222
enforcement of judgment obtained in, **4**, 183–184; **11**, 221; **26**, 57–58; **30**, 105–111
execution of awards against—
—immunity from, **4**, 174–176; **5**, 109–110, 162; **7**, 179–182; **8**, 229–232; **9**, 236, 240–242; **11**, 141, 144, 145; **12**, 104, 112–113; **18**, 3–9; **19**, 211–212; **23**, 198–200; **28**, 156–158; **35**, 126–128: *see also* Foreign States, property, immunity from execution, *infra*
—submission to, **1**, 114–116; **26**, 195
fiscus, as, **3**, 180
High Commissioner, agent or organ of, **24**, 175–195
immunities—
—diplomatic envoys, immunities of, compared, **24**, 224–225
—execution, from, **5**, 109–110, 162; **7**, 179–182; **8**, 229–232; **11**, 144; **12**, 104, 112–113; **18**, 3–9; **19**, 211–212; **23**, 198–200; **28**, 156–158
—taxation, from: *see* taxation, exemption from, *infra*
—waiver: *see* immunity from jurisdiction, *infra*
immunity from jurisdiction, **1**, 22–23, 91, 114–135; **3**, 169–184; **4**, 28–31, 163–179; **5**, 109–129; **6**, 160–173; **7**, 147–150, 164–187; **8**, 218–221, 223–248, 399; **9**, 171–250; **10**, 178–239, 576–581; **11**, 136–146; **12**, 75–104; **13**, 76–82; **14**, 73–83; **15**, 125–136, 138–145; **16**, 103–142; **17**, 140–152, 155–166, 173–183; **18**, 3–9, 210–232; **19**, 163–212; **20**, 91–92, 173–182, 398–400; **21**, 11–12, 17, 95–105; **22**, 210–253; **23**, 160–238, 433–435; **24**, 2–4, 175–228; **26**, 161–195; **31**, 247–266, 395–396; **32**, 122–140, 638; **34**, 81–88; **35**, 110–129
—*acta jure gestionis*: *see* private law acts, *infra*
—*acta jure imperii*: *see* public law acts, *infra*
—actions *in personam*, **35**, 119–120
—actions *in rem*, **3**, 138; **16**, 125, 127; **18**, 221–223; **20**, 398–399; **21**, 95–101; **26**, 174
—agencies, **1**, 120–124, 134; **3**, 182–183; **5**, 110–112, 125–127; **7**, 182–184; **8**, 227–228, 234–235; **9**, 198–207, 213–217, 243–249; **10**, 191–196, 229, 576–581; **11**, 205–207; **12**, 75–89, 97–102; **14**, 78–83; **15**, 132; **16**, 129–137;

Foreign States—*continued*
immunity from jurisdiction—*contd.*
—agencies—*continued*
18, 225–228; **19,** 197–201; **20,** 173–176; **21,** 11–12, 119; **22,** 227–230; **23,** 160–173, 210–212, 265–268, 431–432; **24,** 218–219, 221–222, 226–228; **26,** 180–181; **34,** 12–16; *see also* government departments, *infra, and* Trade delegations
—agent, State bound by acts of, **2,** 116–117
—agents, conclusiveness of statements of executive as to, **11,** 76–78; **12,** 80–89; **24,** 226–227
—arbitration in forum State, party to, **27,** 155–156
—assertion of, **19,** 197–201
—bankruptcy proceedings, **22,** 242–244
—banks, **19,** 202–203; **22,** 227–230; **26,** 180–181
—basis of claim to, **8,** 246; **17,** 179; **19,** 200–201; **31,** 249–250
—conclusiveness of statement of executive, **9,** 179; **10,** 178–181, 193–196, 202–204, 206–207, 217–221, 224–226; **12,** 80–89; **20,** 173–176, 177, 202–203; **24,** 226–227; **28,** 165–168; **31,** 248; **32,** 133–135, 136, 137, 138–140; **33,** 185–189
—corporations controlled by, **1,** 133–134; **5,** 110–112; **9,** 193, 198–207, 213–217, 233; **19,** 197–203, **23,** 160–173; **31,** 215–217
—counterclaims, **1,** 129–130, 132–133, 134–135; **2,** 117–119, 119–120n.; **3,** 101, 172–173; **5,** 113–114, 125–127; **7,** 164–166; **11,** 136–138; **12,** 92–96; **14,** 73–75; **18,** 219–221; **19,** 192–196; **20,** 176–178; **22,** 210–219; **26,** 180; **28,** 150–153; **31,** 247–248, 252–256; **32,** 131: *see also* set-off, *infra*
—cross-suit, **3,** 175; **4,** 163–164
—cultural institution, **24,** 218–219
—damage by foreign forces during military operations, **23,** 205–208, 214–216
—diplomatic immunities, compared, **22,** 534–535; **24,** 224–225
—evidence required, **24,** 195
—examination of, action brought by, **16,** 137–138
—extinct government, **2,** 134–135
—federal States, members of, **2,** 130–131, 162–163; **7,** 166–169; **10,** 178–191; **11,** 143
—French practice, **7,** 174–175; **9,** 240n.; **11,** 30–32

Foreign States—*continued*
immunity from jurisdiction—*contd.*
—garnishee order against legation, **32,** 122–124
—government departments, **3,** 180; **8,** 227–228; **12,** 87–89; **14,** 78–83; **16,** 129–137; **20,** 399; **23,** 160–173, 201–202. *See also* agencies, *supra*
—guarantor, as, **24,** 204–205
—heads of State: *see under* Heads of State
—history of privilege, **22,** 535
—Holy See, **8,** 235–236, 405; **24,** 214–215, 215–217; **26,** 183–190
—immigration office, **9,** 249
—indirect impleading, **1,** 116–118; **7,** 169–170; **9,** 207–213; **12,** 100–101; **17,** 143–152, 177; **18,** 219–221; **20,** 398–399; **21,** 95–101
—interest in subject-matter of action, **6,** 173; **9,** 207–213; **10,** 185–191; **12,** 89–92; **15,** 127–131; **21,** 95–101
—legatee, as, **10,** 196–198; **16,** 138–140
—loan issued in country of forum, **22,** 226–227; **23,** 191–192
—maritime lien, action based on, **26,** 175
—military authorities, **18,** 228–232
—mode of claiming, **2,** 120–122; **9,** 177; **10,** 204–207; **19,** 197–201; **33,** 40–41
—non-recognition, relevance, **10,** 91–97
—officers' club of foreign air force, **23,** 265–268
—officials, **3,** 182–183; **9,** 19; **15,** 125–127; **18,** 232–234
—order in breach of, nullity, **26,** 195–196
—political subdivision, **9,** 234, 242; **15,** 138–145
—principle of, **26,** 168–169
—private law acts, **1,** 118–119, 122–124; **3,** 169–172, 173–179, 184–191; **4,** 28–31, 166, 172, 177–178; **5,** 18–19, 114–115, 121–125; **6,** 169; **7,** 175–177; **8,** 26–31, 225, 237; **9,** 198–207, 245–246; **10,** 230–232, 235–238; **11,** 145–146; **12,** 103–104; **14,** 77–78; **16,** 140–142; **17,** 155–166; **18,** 3–9; 210–219, 225–228; **20,** 178–180; **21,** 101–103; **22,** 224–227, 240–242; **24,** 205–206; **26,** 190–192; **31,** 247–257; **33,** 189–190
—private law and public law acts, distinction, **1,** 22–23, 119, 122–124; **3,** 18–23; **4,** 28–31; **6,** 36–37, 167–173; **7,** 19–22, 171, 177–179, 184–186; **8,** 26–31, 231,

Foreign States—*continued*
immunity from jurisdiction—*contd.*
—private law and public law acts, distinction—*continued*
235, 238, 399; **11,** 140–142, 155–166; **12,** 103–104; **15,** 133–136, 141–145; **16,** 140, 141–142; **17,** 142–143, 155–166; **18,** 225–228; **19,** 203–210; **21,** 119; **22,** 224–225, 237–239, 240–242, 756–757; **23,** 195–201, 203–205, 206–208; **24,** 200, 207–217, 219–220; **26,** 180–182, 191–192; **28,** 153–155, 160; **31,** 250; **35,** 113, 115, 117, 119
—protected States, **2,** 174; **5,** 116–118; **7,** 171–172; **8,** 226
—public law acts, **1,** 22–23, 129–130; **2,** 172–173; **3,** 21; **4,** 27–28; 164–165, 173–174; **6,** 164–169; **9,** 152, 190; **11,** 224–226; **22,** 224–225, 534–535; **23,** 191–192, 206–208, 209–210; **24,** 3–4, 200, 211–213, 218–219; **31,** 250; **34,** 83
—public law and private law acts, distinction: *see* private law and public law acts, *supra*
—public ships: *see* Public ships
—purchaser of goods for armed forces, **22,** 224–225
—real party in interest, **21,** 103–104
—reciprocity, **3,** 23; **8,** 239–240, 246; **26,** 178–180
—recognition of government, relevance, **32,** 138
—renunciation of, **2,** 176–177: *see also* waiver, *infra*
—restrictive theory, **31,** 215–216; **35,** 113–118, 124–125 n.
—rupture of diplomatic relations, effect, **32,** 70–72
—service of process, **31,** 257–259; **35,** 121
—set-off, **7,** 164–166; **8,** 218–221; **11,** 136–138; **12,** 92–96; **13,** 29–32; **18,** 219–221; **30,** 176–178. *See also* counterclaims, *supra*
—State enterprise as plaintiff, **31,** 247–256
—State-owned shipping lines, **31,** 215–217
—State trading corporations, **23,** 160–173; **31,** 247–256
—submission: *see* submission to jurisdiction, *infra*
—suit by national employees on military base, **28,** 158–164
—summons, nullity of, **7,** 186–187
—Tate letter (U.S.A.), **32,** 133; **33,** 185
—trade delegations: *see* Trade delegations

Foreign States—*continued*
immunity from jurisdiction—*contd.*
—trustee of private property, **13,** 78–79
—unenforceability of judgment, relevance, **31,** 255
—waiver, **1,** 134–135, 145, 150–154; **2,** 139; **3,** 176–177; **4,** 168–169; **5,** 112–113; **7,** 184–186; **9,** 190, 205, 219–224, 233–234; **10,** 199–204, 228–229; **18,** 214–216, 218–219, 223–224; **19,** 182–195; **20,** 173–176; **21,** 121; **22,** 233–234, 248–253; **23,** 160–173, 192–195, 210–214; **26,** 191, 195; **31,** 250, 251–252; **32,** 10–12, 124–126, 128–131, 135, 136; **34,** 81, 82, 84, 89, 90; **35,** 122–129
See also submission to jurisdiction, *infra*
—waiver by treaty, **26,** 164; **28,** 159–164
—waiver, defence entered by predecessor non-sovereign body, **18,** 223–224
—waiver, evidence of, **23,** 267–268
—waiver, implied, **3,** 177; **6,** 160–161; **7,** 148–150; **8,** 228; **9,** 190–193, 236–239; **12,** 92–96; **19,** 182–195; **21,** 121; **23,** 212–214; **24,** 201–202. *See also* submission to jurisdiction, *infra*
—war, effect of, **10,** 576–581
meaning of, **24,** 92
ownership of land by, **25,** 10
private acts, jurisdictional immunities: *see under* immunity from jurisdiction, *supra*
property, immunity from attachment, **6,** 164–169; **9,** 198–207; **10,** 178–191, 208–217, 230–239; **15,** 131–133; **22,** 220–224; **26,** 161–164, 181–182; **28,** 165–168
—immunity from execution, **8,** 246; **9,** 236, 239–243; **11,** 141, 144, 145; **12,** 104, 112–113; **32,** 130, 137–140; **33,** 181–183, 184–190. *See also* execution of awards against, *supra*
—immunity from jurisdiction, **3,** 172–179; **6,** 173; **7,** 151–158; **9,** 38, 207–213, 239–240; **10,** 185–191, 230–239; **12,** 89–92; **15,** 127–131; **17,** 173–188; **19,** 163–182, 191–192; **20,** 174, 180–182; **21,** 95–101; **22,** 220–224, 230–234, 248–253, 256; **23,** 217–238; **24,** 231–247; **26,** 162–164; **27,** 111–113; **32,** 137–140; **33,** 181–190. *See also under* Public ships
——bailee, deposited with, **16,** 103–128; **19,** 163–182

Foreign States—*continued*
property, immunity from jurisdiction—*continued*
—chose in action, **24**, 178–182
—conclusiveness of claim to, **2**, 123–124
—*de facto* possession, **23**, 234–238
—immovable property, **4**, 164–165, 174–176, 178–179; **5**, 306–307; **18**, 221–223; **19**, 191–192; **20**, 180–182; **21**, 119; **22**, 230–233; **24**, 221–222, 231–247: *see also* Diplomatic premises
—leasehold, on trust for, **26**, 167, 171
—nationalized banks, **33**, 185, 188
—penal confiscation, **21**, 101–103
—possession or control, **9**, 171–176, 219–233; **10**, 178–191, 208–217, 221–224, 226–230, 230–239; **16**, 103–128; **17**, 173–188; **19**, 163–182; **20**, 398; **22**, 252; **23**, 173–191, 234–238; **24**, 178–182, 247
—tax liens on, **35**, 129–130
—time to raise claim, **33**, 182
—trust created by, **27**, 111–114
—waiver, **33**, 182
property, title to, **11**, 68–74
propriety of acts of, **21**, 105
protection of interests of, **11**, 32–33
public law, recognition and enforcement, **11**, 32–33; **21**, 25–29
recognition of: *see* Recognition, States, of
recognition of acts of: *see under* Recognition
right to sue, **4**, 170–171; **9**, 89; **13**, 9–12; **21**, 265–272; **33**, 36–43, **35**, 26–28
status of, conclusiveness of statements of executive, **15**, 138–140; **18**, 211–214
statutes of limitation, application to, **9**, 184–190; **12**, 17–22; **15**, 130–131
submission to arbitration, **24**, 205–206
submission to execution, **1**, 114–116; **26**, 195
submission to jurisdiction, **7**, 148–150; **8**, 177; **10**, 228–229, 232–234; **11**, 136–138; **14**, 79–83; **22**, 248–253; **23**, 160–173, 210–214; **26**, 195; **32**, 125
—charterparty, arbitration clause, **24**, 205–206
—commercial contract, **18**, 210–219
—cross-suit, **4**, 163–164
—evidence of, **23**, 267–268
—express refusal of, **4**, 163–164; **7**, 169–170
—failure to appear, through, **10**, 232–234
—implied, **1**, 114–116; **4**, 163–164, 170–171

Foreign States—*continued*
summons against, nullity of, **7**, 186–187
taxation, exemption from, **9**, 234–235; **10**, 38–47, 196–198; **17**, 153–155; **23**, 217–233; **24**, 231–247; **26**, 165–178
—return of tax paid on immune property, **26**, 171–172, 176–177
—tax liens, **35**, 129–130
—war and, **21**, 432–443
waiver of immunity: *see under* immunity from jurisdiction, *supra*
Foreign territory, occupation of: *see* Belligerent occupation *and* Occupation of foreign territory
Foreigners: *see* Aliens
Formosa—
status of, **17**, 171, 174, 178; **23**, 71–78
whether "country" within U.S. deportation law, **31**, 349–352
Forum prorogatum, **15**, 352–354; **19**, 520–521, 530–531, 549; **24**, 812
France: *see also* Free French forces; Free French National Committee
aircraft, foreign, passage of, **9**, 125
aliens, expulsion of, **11**, 197–199
—competence of courts, **11**, 199 n.
—Decree-Law (1938), police control, **11**, 198–199
aliens, treatment of—
—Decree-Law (1939), reduction of rents, **11**, 186, 235–236
—Decree-Law (1938), traders' permits, **22**, 606; **26**, 490–492, 494–496
—employment permits (Law of 1926), **9**, 377
—"legislative reciprocity", **26**, 493–494
aliens, war damage reparation and, **6**, 285; **22**, 468
Alsace Lorraine—
—occupation of, **7**, 511–512
—railways in, responsibility for obligations, **2**, 57–58
—reunion of, **1**, 448–449
Andorra, administrative jurisdiction in, **7**, 56–57
Austria, Treaty on Judicial Assistance (1925), **21**, 262–264; **22**, 58, 100–101
Belgium—
—Agreement *re* nationality of married women (1947), **19**, 358
—Arbitration Agreement (1936), **8**, 478–479
—"Arrangement" *re* damage by French troops in Belgium (1945), **22**, 614–616
—Boundary Convention (1886), **7**, 431–432

France—*continued*
Belgium—*continued*
—Convention on Civil Jurisdiction (1899), **3,** 86; **5,** 380; **7,** 409
—Convention on restitution of illegally seized goods (1945), **20,** 659, 660
—Extradition Treaty (1874), **9,** 400–401; **14,** 139–142; **16,** 275, 278; **18,** 395; **20,** 369; **23,** 410
—Tardieu–Jaspar Agreement (1930), **8,** 479
—Treaty *re* Conditions of Residence (1927), **4,** 452; **9,** 456; **11,** 10–12, 235–236; **14,** 160–162
Bulgaria, mixed arbitral tribunal, rules of procedure, **5,** 458
Cameroons and, **22,** 88–89
cession of Italian territory to, **20,** 63–77
cession of Louisiana to U.S.A., **31,** 160, 180, 182
cession of territory to India, consent of population, **26,** 114
Chile—
—Commercial Treaty (1846), **23,** 729–730
—Extradition Treaty (1860), **2,** 276–277
China—
—Commercial Treaty (1928), **11,** 229–230
—Treaty of Commerce (1946), **16,** 260
—Treaty of Friendship and Commerce (1844), **1,** 335; **2,** 326; **12,** 280
—Treaty of Friendship and Commerce (1858), **1,** 335; **2,** 326; **6,** 34; **12,** 280
—Treaty on Sino-Indo-chinese Relations (1946), **28,** 269–271
Civil Code, Art. 8 (nationality provisions), **9,** 361; **11,** 83
—Art. 11 (rights of aliens), **5,** 405; **11,** 235
—Art. 16 (security for costs), **11,** 235
—Art. 214 (position of spouses), **11,** 197
—Art. 1166 (action against debtor's debtor), **1,** 117
—Art. 1179 (retroactive effect of fulfilled conditions), **11,** 181 n.
—Art. 1626 (breach of warranty of title), **1,** 120
—Art. 1733 (tenant's liability), **3,** 173–174
—Art. 1875 (dissolution of company by extinction of object), **28,** 177, 179, 181, 184
—Art. 2279 (restitution of lost property), **11,** 299

France—*continued*
Clearing Office, status of, **7,** 505
Coastal Trade and Fisheries Decree (1862), **23,** 127
Code of Civil Procedure, Arts. 385 and 389 (disqualification of judge), **28,** 566
Code of Criminal Procedure, Art. 7, **1,** 108
—Art. 8...**11,** 271
—Arts. 476, 635 and 637 (contumacy), **9,** 397–398
Code of Military Justice Arts. 63 and 64...**1,** 235
—Art. 192...**22,** 929
—Arts. 235 and 236...**11,** 45 and 46
—Art. 269...**1,** 235
Code of Nationality, Art. 12 (acquisition of nationality by annexation), **28,** 441
—Art. 95 (loss of nationality), **28,** 440–441
Comoro Island, protectorate over, **11,** 47
Conseil de Prud'hommes, competence, **5,** 312
Constitution (1946), **15,** 4, 324–325; **18,** 52, 394, 395; 435, **19,** 1, 340, 342, 475; **20,** 439, 591; **21,** 2, 278, 279, 283; **22,** 60–61, 604–605
—Art. 27 (treaties of cession), **26,** 114
—Art. 31 (treaty making power), **23,** 771
Constitutional Law (1875), **5,** 334
consular immunities, practice, **6,** 332
courts, competence of—
—administrative acts, **11,** 51–52
—expulsion of aliens, **11,** 199 n.
—immunity of States: *see* immunity of States, *infra*
—interpretation of treaties, **1,** 332–335; **2,** 326–328; **5,** 358–363; **6,** 370–371; **7,** 506; **9,** 469; **11,** 46–47, 54, 77–78, 229–232; **12,** 280; **14,** 169; **15,** 688; **17,** 316; **20,** 438–440
—Mixed Tribunal of New Hebrides, **11,** 55
—State loans, **11,** 30–32
criminal law: *see also* Penal Code, *infra*
—application in Morocco, **11,** 45–46
—conviction *par contumace*, **9,** 397–398; **30,** 382–383, 384
—*jugement itératif défaut*, **30,** 377, 379, 380, 383, 384
—*jugement par défaut*, **30,** 377, 379 380, 383, 384
Czechoslovakia—
—Compensation Agreement (1950), **28,** 438–439
—Extradition Treaty (1928), **18,** 340

France—*continued*
Denmark—
—Commercial Convention (1910), **4**, 453
—Treaty of Commerce and Navigation (1645), **23**, 729
employers' liability, Law of 1898..**9**, 377
Egypt, Property Commission in, immunity of members, **34**, 175–179
England: *see also* U.K., *infra*
—Commercial Treaties (1605, 1655), **20**, 99, 132
—Treaty of Calais (1360), **20**, 98 118, 119, 121, 132, 133, 137, 138
—Treaty of Étaples (1492), **20**, 132
—Treaty of Lambeth (1217), **20**, 98, 128, 129, 131, 132
—Treaty of Paris (1259), **20**, 95, 98, 116, 118, 120, 129–135 *passim*
—Treaty of Picquigny–Amiens (1475), **20**, 128, 132
—Treaty of Troyes (1420), **20**, 99, 116, 120, 132, 133
—Truce of London (1471), **20**, 99, 132
Ethiopia, Commercial Treaty (1908), **7**, 199–200
extradition law, **6**, 308–309; **9**, 400–401; **14**, 140; **18**, 324, 344; **19**, 365–366; **20**, 369–370; **22**, 514–515, 517, 519–520
Foreign Exchange Control Regulations, **22**, 730 n.
foreign flag, legality of display, **7**, 76–77
Foreign Minister, statement of, conclusiveness of, **5**, 362–363, 405; **6**, 394; **7**, 404–405; **11**, 231, 234–235; **17**, 316; **18**, 401–402; **19**, 476–477; **21**, 16, 263, 278–285; **22**, 622–623. *See also* treaties—interpretation of, competence of courts, *infra*
French Union, Morocco and, **22**, 60–61
German Customs Union, Trade Agreement (1862), **6**, 282
Germany—
—Agreement *re* civil procedure (1927), **16**, 384
—Armistice (1940), **11**, 231–232; **12**, 412–414; **20**, 489
—Commercial Agreement (1927), **7**, 423
—Commercial Treaty (1937), **9**, 477
—mixed arbitral tribunal, rules of procedure, **5**, 428, 457
—occupation by (1940), **11**, 231–232, 266, 270–271, 281–284; **12**, 427–430, 443–444, 452–454, 457–459; **13**, 377–378, 385—387; **15**, 288, 551–552, 596–597, 619, 684–686;

France—*continued*
Germany—*continued*
—occupation by (1940)—*continued*
16, 359; **18**, 678; **20**, 430–431, 655–662; **22**, 1007–1008; **27**, 650–652
—succession to rights in Alsace, **4**, 85–86
—Trade Agreement (1862), **6**, 282
—Treaty, Commerce and Consular (1927), **7**, 423
—Treaty of Frankfort (1871), **1**, 390; **2**, 255; **14**, 113; **15**, 209–211; **18**, 400–401
—Treaty *re* French protectorate over Morocco (1911), **9**, 507; **19**, 259
—Treaty *re* liquidation of German property in France (1929), **11**, 47
Germany, Federal Republic—
—Agreement concerning the Saar (1954), **22**, 630–632
—extradition between, **22**, 520–525
—Treaty, Settlement of the Saar Question (1956), **24**, 411–412
Gex district, sovereignty over: *see under* Gex, Free Zone of
Gold Looted by Germany, Arbitration Agreement with U.K. and U.S.A. (1951), **20**, 441–463 *passim*, 467, 470, 475
Greece—
—Consular Convention (1876), **12**, 261
—Convention, Commerce and Consular (1926), **4**, 453
—Extradition Treaty (1906), **23**, 418–419
immunity of consuls, practice of courts, **6**, 332
immunity of States—
—procedure of recognition of, **7**, 174–175
—summary of practice, **9**, 240 n.; **11**, 30–32
India—
—Treaty of Cession (1951), **21**, 256–257; **22**, 198, 200; **23**, 107
—Treaty of Cession (1956), **26**, 114
Inter-Allied Supreme Command, Agreement with (1944), **18**, 400
International Monetary Fund, membership, **22**, 729
Israel, extradition between, **21**, 236–238
Italy—
—Agreements *re* Peace Treaty (1951 and 1952), **20**, 71, 74; **22**, 319–320, 324, 325, 327, 841, 842
—Armistice (1940), **11**, 266; **20**, 489
—cession of Nice and Savoy by, **5**, 395

France—*continued*
Italy—*continued*
—Commercial Treaty (1946), most-favoured-nation clause, **26,** 490–492
—claims under Art. 79 of Peace Treaty, **19,** 478; **22,** 501
—Convention, Enforcement of Judgments (1930), **9,** 120; **16,** 382; **18,** 290 n.; **19,** 556; **24,** 890–892
—Convention *re* nationality (1896), **18,** 508
—Convention *re* river Roja (1914), **9,** 120
—Emigration Agreement (1946), **22,** 604–605
— —(1947), **20,** 300–301
—Establishment Agreements (1946 and 1948), **23,** 468
—Establishment Treaty (1862), **7,** 391–392
—Establishment Treaty (1930), **12,** 304, 305 n., 307; **14,** 161 n.; **15,** 327, 437; **16,** 381; **20,** 599; **23,** 468
—Extradition Treaty (1870), **7,** 334, 372; **18,** 324, 327, 328; **22,** 514–515
—occupation of (1796), **15,** 619
—Social Security Convention (1948), **24,** 509
Japan—
—declaration of war on, **32,** 621, 622
—Protocol, Joint Defence of Indo-China (1941), **32,** 603–604, 620
landlord and tenant legislation, **5,** 251, 307, 333–334, 361, 405; **7,** 391, 405; **15,** 327, 437; **16,** 381–382; **18,** 434–435; **20,** 300–301, 406–407; **20,** 1–3, 300–301, 599–600; **22,** 604–605; **23,** 468
Latvia, Commercial Treaty (1937), **18,** 288, 289
Louisiana, extent of territory claimed, **31,** 180
mandated territories, public land régime, **6,** 48–49
Mexico, Claims Convention (1924), **5,** 147, 149, 174, 192–193, 392, 424
Monaco, Customs Union, **11,** 34–35
Morocco—
—protectorate over: *see under* Morocco
—Treaty of Fez (1912), **5,** 117; **7,** 172; **8,** 93, 94; **19,** 255, 259, 260, 263, 269, 296
—Treaties with (1631 and 1682), **19,** 265
— —(1836), **19,** 288
— —(1892), **19,** 285
" National Solidarity Tax ", Law (1945), **21,** 280–281
nationality law, **1,** 38–39; **9,** 361; **11,** 197; **15,** 249; **17,** 225; **18,** 51, 247, 507, 508; **20,** 246–248; **22,** 60

France—*continued*
Netherlands, Commercial Treaty (1935), **21,** 166, **24,** 584–588
neutral status (1943), **22,** 1012–1014
Norway–Sweden—
—Arbitration Convention (1904), **24,** 787
—Treaty of Commerce and Navigation (1881), **11,** 229
officials seconded to mandated territories, status, **11,** 51–52
passage of foreign aircraft, Law of 1920...**9,** 125
patent law, **5,** 359
Penal Code (Art. 78), **1,** 108
—(Art. 177), **11,** 32–33
Poland—
—attitude to restoration of, **1,** 37
—Consular Convention (1925), **6,** 332
—Convention, Commerce (1937), **15,** 1–2; **16,** 312
—Convention *re* private property, (1922), **5,** 387–391
—Extradition Treaty (1925), **7,** 372–373
—Intergovernmental Agreement (exchange of ambassador's residence), **11,** 203
procedure, civil appeals, **28,** 301. *See also* Code of Civil Procedure; Code of Criminal Procedure, *supra*
protection of trade and industry legislation, **21,** 281, 283–285
protectorates, financial régime, **6,** 47–48
refugees, Intergovernmental Arrangement (1928), **11,** 198
reparation for war damage, **5,** 253; **6,** 285; **22,** 468
Roumania, Treaty of Establishment (1930), **21,** 284–285; **28,** 492–493
Saar—
—Convention with (1948), **17,** 36–37; **18,** 431, 432
—submission to French customs régime, **7,** 30
Sardinia, Treaty with (1760), **5,** 69; **18,** 290
—(1860), **15,** 58
Savoy and Nice, annexation (1860), **15,** 58
Seizure of Enemy Goods, Decree (1939), **24,** 923–924
Social Assurance Law, 1930...**11,** 43
Spain—
—Additional Act (Bayonne, 1866) *re* boundary, **24,** 101–142 *passim*
—Arbitration Agreement (1956), **24,** 111
—Arbitration Treaty (1929), **24,** 101
—Bayonne, Treaties of (1856, 1862, 1866), **24,** 101–142 *passim*

France—*continued*
Spain—*continued*
—cession and retrocession of Louisiana, **31**, 181
—Consular Convention (1862), **1**, 333–334; **2**, 305–306; **5**, 323, 361; **6**, 370; **7**, 405–406; **15**, 3–4, 326 n.; **17**, 240, 316; **18**, 280, 360, 435 n.; **19**, 1, 339–342, 474–476; **20**, 264 n., 437–438; **21**, 277–278, 282–284; **22**, 478–479, 606–607, 624–625; **24**, 110, 600–601; **25**, 320; **26**, 490–492, 494–496
—Convention *re* Rights in Spanish Zone of Morocco (1912), **19**, 268, 269, 296
—Declarations on Morocco (1914), **19**, 268, 269, 270, 271, 280, 293–297
—Extradition Treaty (1877), **20**, 370 n.
—Final Act, Delimitation of Frontier of Pyrenees (1868), **24**, 105
—Nationalist Government, Agreement with (1939), **11**, 144
—Treaty, railways (1882), **9**, 488–489
—Treaty, Work and Assistance (1932), **7**, 470
Spain and United Kingdom, Boundary Treaty (1763), **7**, 131
Suez Canal Company, Law of 1957, **28**, 181–182, 184
Switzerland—
—Convention, Judicial Competence (1869), **1**, 122; **5**, 364, 404; **6**, 350; **8**, 421; **18**, 393; **19**, 338; **21**, 211, **27**, 259–260
—Establishment Treaty (1882), **5**, 360, 361, 362 n.; **6**, 394; **8**, 327, 424–425; **16**, 259 n.; **17**, 315; **21**, 284; **23**, 376–377; **25**, 319
—Extradition Treaty (1869), **19**, 365; **22**, 516; **24**, 497; **34**, 144, 145, 147
—Special Arbitral Agreement (1924), **5**, 459–463
Syria, mandate over, **4**, 95–96; **5**, 32; **8**, 110
—evolution of French protectorate over Syrians, **4**, 256–257
taxation, Law of 1914...**5**, 323
tenure of agricultural land, law of 1945...**23**, 468
territorial waters, **9**, 123–126
trading with the enemy legislation, 1939...**9**, 557; **11**, 258–260; **15**, 466
treaties, interpretation of, competence of courts, **1**, 332–335; **2**, 326–328; **5**, 358–363; **6**, 370–371; **7**, 506; **9**, 469; **11**, 46–47, 54, 77–78, 229–232; **12**, 280; **14**, 169; **15**, 688; **17**, 316; **20**, 438–440

France—*continued*
Tunisia—
—Beylical Decrees concerning aliens, **5**, 28; **22**, 501–503, 507–508
—Convention with (1883), **5**, 28
—Convention with (1955), **24**, 767–770
—jurisdiction of French courts, **5**, 28
—jurisdiction of French courts, termination of, **26**, 562–563
—protectorate, **4**, 44, 46; **5**, 28; **8**, 97–98; **17**, 42; **18**, 51–52; **20**, 47–48
—protectorate, treaty establishing (1881), **20**, 47–48; **28**, 79
—Treaty on Independence (1957), **26**, 99, 562–563
United Kingdom: *see also* England, *supra*
—Arbitration Treaty (1903), **20**, 143
—Commercial Treaty (1882), **5**, 360, 404–405; **8**, 426 n.; **12**, 278–279; **14**, 166; **18**, 435; **26**, 200–201
—Commercial Treaty (1882), interpretative Exchange of Notes, **5**, 362–363, 405; **6**, 394; **7**, 404–405; **11**, 231, 234–235; **18**, 401–402; **19**, 476–477; **21**, 280–281; **22**, 622–623
—de Gaulle, Government of, recognition (1944), **17**, 269
—Extradition Treaty (1876), **5**, 269; **6**, 302–303; 319–321; **8**, 91–92; **9**, 399 n.; **21**, 236–237; **30**, 379, 382
—Fisheries Convention (1839), **18**, 117, 118; **20**, 95, 96, 101, 102, 103, 120, 121, 123, 127, 141, 142
—Fisheries Convention (1867), **20**, 104
— —(1951), **20**, 145
—Protocol, New Hebrides (1914), **9**, 51
—Reciprocal Agreement on Social Security (1948), **27**, 284
—Special Agreement (1950), submission of dispute to I.C.J., **20**, 94–96, 97, 103, 145
—Submarine Telegraph Convention (1859), **20**, 104
—Tariff Agreement (1933), **9**, 458
—Treaty abrogating capitulations in Morocco (1937), **11**, 223–224; **19**, 274, 276, 281, 288, 289–302 *passim*
U.K. and Spain, Boundary Treaty (1763), **7**, 131
U.K. and U.S.A., Arbitration Agreement (1951), gold looted by Germany, **20**, 441–463 *passim*, 467, 470, 475
U.S.A.—
—Agreement, jurisdiction over U.S. forces (1918), **1**, 333

France—*continued*
U.S.A.—*continued*
—"Byrnes-Blum" Agreement (1946) **19**, 454, 455
—Consular Convention (1853), **2**, 315; **5**, 251–252, 362; **11**, 211–212; **15**, 324; **16**, 259
—Economic Cooperation Agreement (1948), **19**, 255
—Extradition Treaty (1909), **7**, 339–340; **9**, 396
—forces of, in, **1**, 333; **20**, 182–184, 186–188; **23**, 255–259; **24**, 251–253; **26**, 196–200
—Lend-Lease Agreement (1941), **22**, 980
U.S.S.R.—
—Commercial Agreement (1934), **7**, 19–20, 171; **9**, 238, 246; **11**, 145
—Commercial Agreement (1945), **20**, 439
—recognition of Soviet Government, **4**, 66–69; **5**, 43–44, 46
Vichy Government—
—confiscatory legislation, **10**, 147–151
—legislation, validity, **32**, 621
Vietnam—
—Convention on Nationality (1955), **28**, 436–437
—Joint Declaration (1954), **22**, 225
—recognition of independence (1948), **22**, 224
war damage legislation, **5**, 253; **6**, 285; **22**, 468
Washington Accord on German Property in Switzerland (1946), **27**, 477–478, 492, 497, 499, 501, 503, 507, 528, 556
workmen's compensation, reciprocity, **6**, 347–348; **7**, 468, 469, 470; **18**, 506–507
Yugoslavia, Special Agreement submitting dispute to P.C.I.J. (1928), **5**, 466, 470
Franchise de l'hôtel, **20**, 400–405
Franco, General, Government of, **10**, 25–27. *See also* Spanish Civil War
de jure recognition of, **11**, 144
title to legation property in Norway, **11**, 68–74
Franco-German Mixed Arbitral Tribunal, Rules of Procedure, **5**, 457
Franco-Italian Conciliation Commission, *Collège arbitral*, as, **22**, 317, 501, 841
competence, Exchange of Notes, **22**, 840–843
competence, municipal law and Treaty, **22**, 876–882
jurisdiction, municipal proceedings and, **18**, 404, 471; **22**, 508
"*Francs effectifs*", meaning, **5**, 418
Francs tireurs, **15**, 639; **16**, 380, 500, 500, 510, 516. *See also* Guerillas
Frankfort, Treaty of (1871), **1**, 390; **2**, 255; **14**, 113; **15**, 209—211; **18**, 400–401
Fraud—
claims, **1**, 187; **5**, 131
concept in international law, **25**, 102, 109
extradition for, **6**, 308–309
fraudulent evidence, arbitral proceedings, **8**, 485–487
nationality, acquisition of, **6**, 191; **22**, 365, 366–367, 370, 373, 374, 377, 384
—release from, **3**, 403–404
naturalization, effect on, **7**, 274, 280, 281; **8**, 290; **10**, 285; **16**, 222–224
—law of U.S.A., **16**, 222–224
non-recognition, **2**, 38
Frederick William I of Prussia, establishment of *Fideikommis*, **4**, 32
"Free and open", waterways, **5**, 87–88; **6**, 8–10; **7**, 5
Free French forces, status in 1942, **28**, 282
recognition by U.S.A. as co-belligerents, **28**, 284
Free French National Committee, recognition by Austria, **11**, 15
Free Zones: *see* Gex; Savoy
Freedom of navigation, **7**, 12–13, 317–318. *See also* Danube; Elbe; Rhine
"free and open", meaning, **5**, 87–88; **6**, 8–10; **7**, 5
Freedom of trade, treatment of aliens and, **7**, 314–316
Freedom of Transit, Barcelona Convention (1921), **5**, 341; **6**, 404–406; **9**, 121
Freedom of transit, legal principle, **31**, 81
"Freezing" regulations, **10**, 16. *See also* Trading with the enemy
Freight, claims for, **10**, 626–631, 636–637; **12**, 528–529, 531
compensation in lieu, **13**, 421–425
French Morocco: *see* Morocco, French protectorate
Frenchpet, acquisition by India, 1935.. **26**, 104–105
"*Friedenschluss*", meaning, **5**, 492
Friendly relations with foreign States, disturbance of, **1**, 127–128. *See also* Comity, international
Frontier: *see* Boundaries, land
Frontier estates, taxation of, **12**, 59–60
Frontier land, disputed sovereignty over, **27**, 62–98 *passim*
Frontier traffic—
Austria/Germany, Agreements (1955), **25**, 47, 48–49

Frontier traffic—*continued*
most-favoured-nation clause and, **25**, 318–319
Frontier zone, ownership of land in, **9**, 379
Frustration, contracts, **1**, 395. *See also* Contracts, war, effect of outbreak on; *Force majeure*
Fugitive from justice, irregular seizure, **7**, 190–191, 337–338
" Fugitive ", meaning, **6**, 137–138, 303; **7**, 343, 355
" Fundamental rights of man ", **1**, 198
Funds set aside to meet international claims, **9**, 336–337

G

Gambia, deportation of aliens, **24**, 491
" Gaps " in international law, **2**, 417
Garnishee, consul acting as, **10**, 383–391
Garnishee order—
against foreign legation, **32**, 122–124
against funds of foreign State, **32**, 137–140
attachment of property abroad, **6**, 145–146
Gas and oil concessions, valuation of reserves, **30**, 176–177
Gaza Strip—
administration of, **26**, 221 n.
armistice line, location of, **32**, 80–82
Israel Police Force in, position of, **26**, 211–212, 217
jurisdiction over offences in, **26**, 210–221
military government of, **26**, 217
General Agreement on Tariffs and Trade (1947), **18**, 380; **22**, 565–572; **23**, 487; **24**, 670–672, 677–682; **26**, 558, 560–561; **31**, 410–416; **33**, 375–379, 390–396
customs duties, amendment (1956), **34**, 398, 400, 401
" escape clause ", **31**, 412, 414
general interest, **1**, 343; **4**, 493; **19**, 528
interpretation of, *travaux préparatoires*, **28**, 479–490
national treatment provisions, California " Buy American " Act, **33**, 390–396
reservation, duty on fabrics, U.S.A., **33**, 375–379
General participation clause, Hague Convention (1907), **1**, 411–413, 428; **13**, 212; **15**, 365, **18**, 678–679
General principles of law, **25**, 269, 278, 385, 529, 545; **31**, 25–26, 36, 70, 82, 85, 86, 116, 118. *See also* Good faith
abuse of right: *q.v.*
acquired rights, respect for: *q.v.*

General principles of law—*continued*
actio personalis moritur cum persona
admission of indirect evidence, **16**, 157
application to concessions, **35**, 173–175, 184
audi alteram partem: q.v.: see also Fair hearing
burden of proof: *see* Evidence
causa proxima non remota inspectatur: q.v.: see also Damages, remoteness of
cessante ratione legis cessat et ipsa lex
clausula rebus sic stantibus: see Rebus sic stantibus and Contracts, frustration of
common sense, principles of, **24**, 805
compensation, *q.v.: see also* Equity
contra proferentem: see Concession agreements, interpretation *and* Treaties, interpretation
détournement de pouvoir, see under European Coal and Steel Community; European Economic Community; International organization
easement of necessity: *q.v.*
effectiveness, principle of: *see under* Treaties, interpretation
ejusdem generis rule: *see* Treaties, interpretation
enrichissement sans cause: see Unjust enrichment
equality of parties: *q.v.*
equity: *q.v.*
error: *q.v.*
estoppel: *q.v.*
ex dolo malo jus non oritur: q.v.
ex injuria jus non oritur: q.v.
exceptio est strictissima applicationis- q.v.: see also Treaties, interpretation
expressio unius est exclusio alterius: q.v.
force majeure: q.v.
forum prorogation: q.v.
fraud: *q.v.*
generalia specialibus non derogant: q.v.: see also Treaties, interpretation of
good faith, *q.v.*
human rights, *q.v.*
interest: *q.v.*
interest rei publicae ut sit finis litum: q.v.
international standards: *q.v.*
judgment by default, **16**, 342
juridical conscience of the nations, *see* " New International Law "
ordre public as, **25**, 268, 278
principles or presumptions: *see* Evidence
quasi-contractual obligations, **2**, 166
res inter alios acta: see Treaties, interpretation

General principles of law—*continued*
res judicata: q.v.
restitutio in integrem: q.v.: and see Damages
rules of interpretation, **22,** 825
system of pecuniary penalties as practised by civilized States, **24,** 385–386
ubi jus ibi remedium, **2,** 194; **13,** 202
ultra petita: q.v.
ultra vires: q.v.
unjust enrichment, *q.v.*
respect for the personal liberty of individuals, **5,** 164
right to life, **32,** 564
teleological interpretation, **32,** 56: *see also* Treaties, interpretation of
use of another's property, **29,** 469
general principles of private international law, **5,** 468; **25,** 256–259, 259–260, 265–274, 275–280, 287–293, 297–298, 301–302, 305, 311–312
" General rules of international law "—
State succession, **6,** 78–79, 81, 84
taxation of aliens, **6,** 281
Generalia specialibus non derogant, **27,** 168, 204. *See also under* Treaties, interpretation of
Geneva Conference, Legal Status of Russian and Armenian Refugees (1928), **5,** 248, 333–335, 362; **7,** 406–408
Geneva Conference of Experts (1947), **16,** 535
Geneva Convention, Bills of Exchange and Negotiable Instruments (1930), **22,** 830, 836
Geneva Convention, Execution of Foreign Arbitral Awards (1927), **7,** 419–720; **27,** 36; **28,** 526–538; **31,** 20–22; **34,** 27–36
Geneva Convention on High Seas (1958), nationality of ships, **30,** 443–446; **34,** 59–60
Geneva Convention, Road Traffic (1949), breach, individual liability, effect on, **32,** 382–384
Geneva Convention, Upper Silesia (1922), **4,** 92–93, 472–473, 497, 501, 506; **5,** 346; **6,** 66–71, 83–84, 322; **7,** 102–104, 283–284, 325–327, 411, 433–434; **8,** 136–138. *See also* Upper Silesia
Geneva Conventions, 1929...**15,** 360, 383–384, 471
declaratory nature, **19,** 596–598; **15,** 383–384
municipal law and, **18,** 12–13
Prisoners of War, **11,** 266; **12,** 397–407, 411; **13,** 212, 217–218, 223, 263, 274–276, 278–279, 280–281; **14,** 168–169, 202–203, 206, 208, 210, 211, 302, 307–308, 310;

Geneva Conventions, 1929—*continued*
Prisoners of War—*continued*
15, 364, 368, 370, 395, 401, 404, 455, 477, 499, 626–627, 679; **16,** 349, 351, 352, 353, 354, 403, 408–414, 426–427; **16,** 510, 517, 528–529, 533–536, 539; **17,** 400; **18,** 12–13, 275, 544, 607; **19,** 597; **22,** 925–926, 929; **24,** 927–928; **29,** 495–499
Geneva Convention, Prisoners of War, 1949...**18,** 12–13; **22,** 925, 927–929; **23,** 762–764; **24,** 927–928
Geneva Convention, Sick and Wounded (1906), **3,** 463; **4,** 458
—(1929), **7,** 507–508; **13,** 274, 277, 333; **14,** 212; **16,** 349; **17,** 391–392; **19,** 598
Geneva Conventions, Refugees (1922), **8,** 313
—(1933), **8,** 305, 306, 308–310; **9,** 392; **11,** 186, 187; **14,** 130–131; **15,** 286–287, 326; **21,** 2, 284–285, 304; **22,** 467; **16,** 260–263, 311
—(1936), **9,** 392
—(1938), **13,** 142; **14,** 121–123; **16,** 224, 260–263; **22,** 467
—(1951), **21,** 2, 258, 284–285, 304; **22,** 467–468; **23,** 378–379, 382–391; **24,** 418, 484–489
Intergovernmental Arrangement (1928), **11,** 187, 197–198; **15,** 288–290
Geneva Protocol (1922), loan to Austria, **6,** 26–31
—(1924), Economic Rehabilitation of Austria, **22,** 681
Geneva Protocol on Arbitration Clauses (1923), **7,** 419; **8,** 434; **15,** 4; **19,** 557; **23,** 634; **28,** 532; **31,** 20; **34,** 29
Genocide Convention (1948), **15,** 653, 656
—history, **18,** 370, 375, 383–384
—object, **18,** 368–371
—reservations to, **18,** 364–392
German assets in Japan, disposal of, **26,** 573
German Credit Agreement (1939), **25,** 67–68
German Customs Union, Trade Agreement with France (1862), **6,** 282
German East Africa, succession to private law liabilities, **1,** 61–62; **2,** 59–60
German External Debts, Agreement on (1953), **22,** 611–614; **23,** 772–775; **24,** 207; **25,** 33–89, 326–335
Annex VII, " original written arrangements ", **25,** 332–334
Arbitral Tribunal, jurisdiction, **25,** 38–39, 42–57, 70–72
debt of " specific foreign character ", **35,** 253–261, 268, 271–272

German External Debts, Agreement on (1953)—*continued*
express agreement for payment abroad, **25**, 37, 40, 51, 52, 57, 67–70, 73, 76, 84–88, 334
gold clause, **25**, 64–66, 72–73, 74–76
interpretation, **25**, 57–66; **32**, 158
London Conference, **25**, 63–64, 75–76
Mixed Commission, competence, **35**, 261–278
—costs, **25**, 334–335
non-discrimination among creditors, **25**, 63
obligations of Reich, effect on, **30**, 307
Peace Treaty with Hungary and, **32**, 160–161
specific foreign character, debt with, **25**, 34–38, 52, 65, 72, 74–77, 83–84, 86, 89, 326, 329–334
" German national ", meaning, **1**, 212, 224–225, 423
German South West Africa—
occupation by British forces, **1**, 484–485
reprisals against Portuguese, **4**, 526–527
status of German protectorate, **8**, 131–132
succession to liabilities of, **5**, 60: *see also* South West Africa, mandate over
Germanic Federation, Constitutive Act, 1815...**5**, 348
Germany: *see also* Germany, Democratic Republic; Germany, Federal Republic; *and* Berlin
Advisory Commission for Europe, Protocol on Zones of Occupation (1945), **22**, 988
aggressive war by, **16**, 539–540
Albania, Protocol (1944) regarding gold looted from Rome, **20**, 451
Aliens Police Ordinance, 1938...**26**, 504
Allied and Associated Powers, Rhineland Agreement (1919), **3**, 9–10; **4**, 118–119; **5**, 77–78
Allied Control Council, **15**, 257–259
—Proclamation No. 2, **17**, 309
—Law No. 3 (1945) (trading licences), **24**, 320
—Law No. 5 (1946) (German external assets), **24**, 33; **26**, 52, 54; **32**, 566–570
—Law No. 10 (1945), (trial of war criminals), **14**, 279, 281–282, 283–286, 292–293; **15**, 377, 379, 380, 386, 395, 396, 407, 408, 410, 411, 412, 418, 634, 635, 655, 657, 664, 671, 672, 673, 675, 679; **16**, 269, 347–349, 350, 361; **24**, 514
Allied Control Council laws, effect in Italy, **28**, 45

Germany—*continued*
Allied Governments, Agreement (1924), Experts' Plan, **5**, 33
Allied High Commission, status, **32**, 595, 597
Allied High Commission Law No. 8 (Industrial, Property of Foreign Nations and Nationals), **25**, 496–497, 498, 504, 531; **28**, 584–586; **29**, 344–345
—Art. 2 (impairment due to war measures), **25**, 336–337, 338–340
—Art. 3 (performance of acts omitted because of war), **25**, 335, 337, 339
—Art. 5 (extension of patents), **25**, 335, 338, 496, 504–505, 552
—Art. 7 (protection of acquired rights), **25**, 496, 497
—Art. 10 (national treatment, rights of aliens), **25**, 508
—Art. 14 (" foreign nationals " and " state of war "), **25**, 336–337, 338–339
—Settlement Convention (1952/54), effect, **25**, 498
Allied High Commission Law No. 13, " allied armed forces ", **26**, 708
Allied High Commission Law No. 41 (extension of Law No. 8 to persons treated as enemy), **25**, 336
Allied High Commission Law No. 63 (German property abroad), **24**, 33
Allied occupation of, **16**, 18–25, 358–359, 383, 422–423, 441–442; **17**, 407–411, 415–418; **18**, 234–235, 571–574, 614–621; **19**, 330–331, 602–607, 608–609, 621–622, 632–634; **20**, 79, 651, 656–657, 666, 669; **21**, 476–477; **22**, 987–991; **23**, 789–790; **32**, 596–597
—Hague Regulations, **16**, 435–436, 438; **17**, 408
—recovery of loot, **20**, 656–657, 659–660
—restitution proceedings, **29**, 298, 476–478; **34**, 255–258
annexation of Alsace-Lorraine, **18**, 608–609
annexation of Austria, **9**, 19, 87–89, 407; **10**, 103–106, 530–534; **12**, 23–29, **15**, 214–216; **16**, 61–62, 63–64, 66–67, 347, 361; **17**, 203; **18**, 47–49; **19**, 144, 335–336; **20**, 89–91, 93, 250–251; **21**, 82, 262–264; **22**, 58–59, 89, 100–101, 146, 430–432, 530, 620–621; **23**, 123–124
—Inter-Allied Declaration concerning (Moscow, 1943), **18**, 245
—nationality and, **18**, 244–246, 248–249; **21**, 175–177; **22**, 430–432; **23**, 364–367; **24**, 433
—prior treaties, effect on, **22**, 530

Germany—*continued*
annexation of Austria—*continued*
—recognition by U.S. of, **12**, 47
—recognition of, **15**, 50
—State succession and, **10**, 103–106
annexation of Belgium, nationality and, **24**, 439–440
annexation of Czechoslovakia, **9**, 84; **10**, 78–79; **11**, 24–25; **12**, 43–47; **16**, 347, 361; **19**, 319–322
—nationality and, **24**, 436, 537–540
—Reunion of Sudeten-German Districts with German Reich, Law concerning (1938), **24**, 437, 537–540
annexation of Luxembourg, effect on treaties, **11**, 226–227
Argentina—
Consular Treaty (1857), **1**, 303
—extradition from, **5**, 288
assets abroad, Agreements concerning, **24**, 44, 543–545, 546, 895
Australia, termination of state of war with (1952), **24**, 898
Austria—
—Double Taxation Agreement (1922), **23**, 123–124
—proposed customs union, **6**, 26–31
—separation from (1945), **15**, 217–218; **20**, 668, 675–677; **22**, 430–432
Austria-Hungary, Commercial Treaty (1891), **1**, 68–69
Austrian claims against, waiver in State Treaty, **32**, 152–153, 154–161
Baden—
—absorption of (1934), **22**, 141
—Treaty with (railways) (1920), **5**, 330–332
bankruptcy law, **6**, 149
Bavaria, Treaty with (railways) (1920), **5**, 330–332
"Bavarian" nationality, assimilation, **1**, 39
Belgium—
—Extradition Treaty (1874), **5**, 272
—Protocol of Surrender (1940), **23**, 766–767
—Treaty, Workmen's Compensation (1912), **2**, 410
bombardment of Salonika, **4**, 570–571
bonds, validity after Second World War, **31**, 401–405
Bulgaria, Extradition Treaty (1911), **7**, 351–352
capitulatory rights in Egypt, **4**, 534–535
cessions to France, Treaty of Versailles, **1**, 337, 349–350, 367–369
cessions to Poland, Treaty of Versailles, nationality, effect on, **32**, 339–341
Civil Code, Art. 162 (good faith), **25**, 505

Germany—*continued*
Civil Code, Introductory Law—
—Art. 30 (application of foreign law), **5**, 23
—Art. 88 (acquisition of land by alien), **1**, 242
—Arts. 812 and 818 (unjust enrichment), **5**, 3, 501
Civil Procedure, Code of, **1**, 351; **3**, 412; **9**, 459
Coal Tax Law, 1923..**3**, 9–10
colonial loans, **6**, 62–63
colonies, former, status of, **3**, 93; **6**, 64
compulsory administration of private enterprises, **11**, 20–21
confiscatory legislation, **9**, 19–21, 71, 27; **11**, 20, 24–25; **12**, 4–7; **15**, 464; **16**, 14–15, 19–26
Constitution (1871), **22**, 142
Consitution (1919), **22**, 142
—Art. 2...**1**, 99, 290
—Art. 4...**1**, 151; **4**, 11–13, 130, 332–333; **7**, 11; **15**, 420
—Art. 45...**1**, 314; **19**, 462
—Art. 78...**1**, 116
—Art. 82...**1**, 99
—Art. 131...**21**, 209
—Art. 178...**15**, 243
—treaties and, **7**, 11–12; **15**, 243. *See also* Germany, Federal Republic Constitution
Consular Jurisdiction Act, **5**, 131
continuity after 1945...**19**, 24–34; **32**, 157. *See also* Continuity of States
Criminal Code—
—Arts. 3 and 4 (territorial scope), **9**, 295
—Art. 42 (recidivists), **9**, 378
currency, Law of 1924...**9**, 153–155
—Law of 1936...**9**, 156
Czechoslovakia, conquest of, **9**, 84; **10**, 78–79; **11**, 24–25; **12**, 43–47; **16**, 347, 361; **19**, 319–322
—nationality and, **24**, 436, 537–540
Czechoslovakia, rule in, **9**, 26, 84, 86; **10**, 78–79
Czechoslovakia, Treaty with (1938), **18**, 250, 251, 257; **20**, 32; **24**, 431–433, 437, 537
Danzig and Poland, Convention, Freedom of Transit (1921), **5**, 349
Danzig, annexation of, **15**, 207; **18**, 64, 258–262; **24**, 434
—invasion of, **21**, 485–487
Declaration, Defeat and Assumption of Supreme Authority (1945), **14**, 12; **16**, 267–268; **18**, 573, 706–707; 712, 714; **24**, 940; **32**, 596
Decrees against Jewish property, 1941, 1942...**26**, 31, 37. *See also* racial legislation, *infra*
de-nazification law, **20**, 651–652

Germany—*continued*
Denmark—
—Non-Aggression Pact (1939), **15**, 421
—occupation of, **15**, 452; **16**, 507–508; **17**, 434–438
—Treaty, Commerce and Navigation (1818), **23**, 715
—Treaty (1922) concerning Schleswig, **2**, 83
diplomatic immunities, law as to, **6**, 327–328
Egypt—
—Agreement (1925), consular jurisdiction, **5**, 132
—German-born official in, position at outbreak of war, **4**, 546–547
enemy property, legislation, **25**, 338, 341, 347–348
Expulsion Act, 1934...**9**, 378
extradition law, **5**, 273–274; **6**, 295–297, 304–306; **18**, 248, 330, 340; **22**, 521–523; **24**, 494
Federal Insurance Law, territorial extent, **5**, 306
financial regulations, **9**, 22–23, 71
foreign relations, conduct of, **1**, 39
France—
—Agreement (1927), civil procedure, **16**, 384
—Armistice (1940), **11**, 231–232, 266; **12**, 412–414; **20**, 489
—Commercial Agreement (1927), **7**, 423
—Commercial Treaty (1937), **9**, 477
—Mixed Arbitral Tribunal, rules of procedure, **5**, 428, 457
—occupation of: *see under* occupation *infra*
—succession to rights of, Alsace-Lorraine, **4**, 85–86
—Trade Agreement (1862), **6**, 282
—Treaty of Frankfort (1871), **1**, 390; **2**, 255; **14**, 113; **15**, 209–211; **18**, 400–401
—Treaty with (1911), French protectorate over Morocco, **9**, 507; **19**, 259
—Treaty (1929) (German property in France), **11**, 47
German minorities, protection of, **3**, 312–313
gold, looting from Rome (1943), **20**, 441, 451, 465, 468, 469–470, 476, 479
Greece, Extradition Treaty, **22**, 521–524
Hamburg, contracts of, responsibility for, **4**, 203
hereditary diseases, prevention of, Law of 1933...**9**, 367
Hesse, Treaty (1920) (railways), **5**, 330–332
Holy See, Concordat (1933), **7**, 399–400; **17**, 116–117; **24**, 592–594

Germany—*continued*
Income Tax Act, application to alien, **5**, 75
Italy—
—Agreement, *re* nationality (1939), **15**, 234–236
—Consular Convention, **2**, 274–275
—Convention, Patents and Trade Marks (1892), **5**, 479–480
—Extradition Treaty, **2**, 274–275; **5**, 271, 273, 276; **7**, 360–367
—Extradition Treaty (1942), **21**, 232
Joint Export–Import Agency, immunity from jurisdiction, **23**, 784, 785–786
judicial assistance, law on, **22**, 513
jurisdictional acts in Switzerland, **10**, 6–9
Kamerun Protectorate, liability for obligations of, **2**, 88–89
Länder, treaties concluded by, **22**, 141–146
lapse of claims against, **33**, 27
Latvia, Commercial Treaty (1926), **7**, 305–306
law of, Treaty of Versailles and, **5**, 5
Lithuania, Treaty, Reincorporation of Memel (1939), **11**, 75
Luxembourg Agreement, Officials (1872), **6**, 131
Manual of Military Law, **15**, 659–660, 666–667
marriages, performance abroad, Law of 1870...**5**, 131–133
Mecklenberg–Schwerin, Treaty with (railways) (1920), **5**, 330–332
Memel, succession to Lithuanian rights in, **11**, 74–76
Mexico, Claims Convention (1925), **6**, 215
Military Government Law No. 52 (blocking and control of property), **24**, 33
Military Government Law No. 63 (Conversion Law), **25**, 63
Military Government Ordinance No. 1 (criminal law), **16**, 449–451, 452; **17**, 416
Military Government Ordinance No. 165 (administrative courts), **22**, 609
Military Government Proclamation (1944), **16**, 436–437
Military Government restitution legislation, **28**, 2–4, 6
Military Penal Code, defence of superior orders, **2**, 429–430; **16**, 532, 544, 546
Moratorium Law (1933), **22**, 480–481, 488
Morocco, Treaty with (1890), **19**, 259, 298–299
Nacht und Nebel Order (1941), **15**, 388, 389

Germany—*continued*
" national ", meaning, **6**, 280
nationality laws, **1**, 225–226; **4**, 546
—(1870), **21**, 192–193
—(1913), **21**, 44, 176; **22**, 364, 381; **27**, 237–238
—(1938), **21**, 175, 197
—(1941), **21**, 197
—(1942), **22**, 381
Nazi officials, validity of acts of, **15**, 20–23; **20**, 24–26
Netherlands—
—Boundary Treaties of Aachen and Cleve, (1816), **12**, 59–60
—Extradition Treaties (1896, 1897), **16**, 267
—Treaty of Arbitration and Conciliation (1926), **15**, 417
North German Confederation, nationality laws, **1**, 217
Norway—
—capitulation of, **15**, 503–505
—Extradition Treaty (1878), **24**, 498
occupation of, after 1944: *see* Germany, Allied occupation of, *supra*
occupation of Belgium, **4**, 565–566; **12**, 432–433, 448–452; **13**, 358; **16**, 360; **17**, 388–390; **18**, 683–684; **19**, 631–632; **20**, 26–31, 648, 662–663; **13**, 366; **15**, 104–105, 517–519, 526–529, 536–537, 560–561, 608–609, 626
occupation of Bohemia-Moravia, **16**, 14–15; **22**, 152–153
occupation of Czechoslovakia, **12**, 43–47
occupation of Denmark, **15**, 452; **16**, 507–508; **17**, 434–438
occupation of Estonia, **15**, 525–526
occupation of Finland, **15**, 647
occupation of France, **11**, 231–232, 266, 270–271, 281–284; **12**, 427–430, 443–444, 452–454, 457–459; **13**, 377–378, 385–387; **15**, 288, 551–552, 596–597, 608, 619, 684–686; **16**, 359; **18**, 678; **20**, 430–431, 655–662; **22**, 1007–1008
occupation of Greece, **12**, 431–443, 454–455; **14**, 242–245; **15**, 561–567; **11**, 629–630; **15**, 638
occupation of Italy, **13**, 354–358, 365, 382; **15**, 553–557, 604–608, 610–612, 614–619; **17**, 353, 419–420; **19**, 611–613, 616–619; **22**, 991–994, 998–1001
occupation of Lithuania, **22**, 98–100, 101–102
occupation of Luxembourg, **15**, 537; **16**, 479–480
occupation of the Netherlands, **11**, 271–272, 288–291; **12**, 420–424; **13**, 17–18, 350–354, 366–368, 395–398; **15**, 17, 241, 250–260, 412–414,

Germany—*continued*
occupation of the Netherlands—*continued*
434–435, 442, 500–503, 530–536, 567–572, 599–602, 685–686; **16**, 16–18, 428–432, 455–464, 468, 529–531, 537, 540, 554–555; **17**, 392–397, 399–400, 414–415; **18**, 473, 536–538, 558–570, 609–614, 679–682, 701–702; **19**, 600–601; **20**, 82, 646–647, 665–666; **21**, 431–432, 486–487
occupation of Norway, **9**, 5; **12**, 286–289, 444–447; **13**, 391–394; **11**, 285; **17**, 438–440; **18**, 635, 684–686
occupation of Poland, **4**, 561–562; **12**, 424–427; **13**, 387–391; **15**, 594–595, 680–682; **24**, 80; **30**, 496–511
occupation of Trieste, **16**, 471–475
occupation of U.S.S.R., **4**, 28; **16**, 360–361; **30**, 508
occupation of Yugoslavia, **15**, 638
Occupation Statute, 1949...**32**, 597–598
occupied territories, Law on (1943), **22**, 152–153
occupied territory (Rhineland), legislative sovereignty, **5**, 77–78
Oldenburg, Treaty with (railways) (1920), **5**, 330–332
Penal Code, ss. 263 and 264 (fraud), **5**, 34, 272
Poland—
—Arbitration Treaty (1925), **24**, 814
—Convention, Freedom of Transit (1921), **5**, 393
—Convention, frontier traffic (1924), **6**, 387
—Non-Aggression Pact (1938), **15**, 419
—Paris Agreement (*re* peace treaty) (1920), **1**, 313–314
—Revolution Convention (1929), **6**, 351
—Upper Silesia, Convention concerning (1922), **5**, 346; **6**, 66–71, 83–84, 322; **7**, 102–104, 283–284, 325–327, 411, 433–434
—Vienna Convention, Option and Nationality (1924), **4**, 15–16; **6**, 260–263
Polish subjects, treatment of, **1**, 91–93
poor persons' procedure, stateless persons, **6**, 263–264
Prize Code and Regulations, **11**, 257; **12**, 287–288
protection of German blood and honour, Law of 1935...**9**, 294–295; **11**, 23, 172–173
Prussia—
—incorporation of, **17**, 16–17

Germany—*continued*
Prussia—*continued*
—obligations, succession to, **4,** 84
—rights, succession to, **6,** 74–76
—Treaty with (railways) (1920), **5,** 330–332
Public Authorities Law (1909), **21,** 208–209
R.S.F.S.R.—
—Treaty of Brest-Litovsk (1918), **28,** 37
—Treaty of Rapallo (1922), **1,** 28; **5,** 22–23; **28,** 37
racial legislation, **11,** 23–24, 109–110, 172–173, 183–184, 283; **12,** 8–11; **15,** 469, 652, 656, 661, 663, 667, 682; **16,** 14–15, 27, 224–225, 471–475, 529, 554, 556; **26,** 31, 37, 90, 93
Reconstruction of the Reich, Law concerning (1934), **22,** 141–146
Reich Citizenship Law (1941), **22,** 392
Reich, collapse of, **18,** 40, 45
Reich Post Act, 1871...**6,** 179–180
requisitions of Roumanian property, **4,** 261
responsibility, Art. 231, Treaty of Versailles, **1,** 169
Restitution Law (U.S. Zone, 1947), **25,** 190–193
Roumania—
—Agreement, waiver of claims (1928), **6,** 344–345
—outbreak of war with (1916), **5,** 482
Russia, Treaty with (1894), **1,** 242: *see also* R.S.F.S.R. *supra, and* U.S.S.R., *infra*
Saar Territory and, **18,** 42–44
Saxony, Treaty with (railways) (1920), **5,** 330–332
Seizure of Property of Enemies of the People, Law of 1933...**26,** 90, 93. *See also* racial legislation, *supra*
separation from Austria (1945), **15,** 217–218; **20,** 668, 675–677; **22,** 430–432
South Africa, Agreement, German nationals in S.W. Africa (1923), **15,** 246–247
Soviet occupation of, **23,** 795–797; **24,** 43
Soviet Zone, status of, **21,** 42–45
Spain—
—Extradition Treaty (1878), **18,** 341
—Treaty of Commerce (1868), **23,** 716
Spanish Nationalist Government, *de jure* recognition of, **9,** 73–74
State railways, non-immunity of, **9,** 193
stay of execution, Law of 1934...**9,** 459

Germany—*continued*
sterilization of aliens, Law as to, **8,** 322–323, 341
superior orders, military law, **15,** 495–496, 659–660, 666–667
surrender of (1945), **14,** 215; **15,** 292–293; **16,** 267, 423, 435–439; **17,** 124, 355, 401; **18,** 549, 706–707; **19,** 330–331; **21,** 436, 473–475, 476–477; **22,** 943; **28,** 85
—Potsdam Declaration, **14,** 12; **16,** 267–268; **18,** 573, 706–707, 712, 714; **24,** 940; **32,** 596
—status, after, **16,** 441–442; **18,** 43; **24,** 78
—treaties, effect on, **17,** 308–310
surrender of war criminals, Allied Control Council Law, **30,** 507
Switzerland—
—Arbitration Treaty (1921), **24,** 814
—Clearing Conventions, **9,** 461
—Convention, Recognition of Judgments (1929), **9,** 459
—Extradition Treaty (1874), **1,** 268, 280; **5,** 274; **7,** 352, 353, 369–371; **19,** 34, 380; **24,** 493–495; **34,** 132–134
—Gold Mortgage Agreement (1920), **5,** 378–380; **6,** 386–387
—jurisdictional acts in, **10,** 6–9
territory of—
—Saar Territory, **1,** 42, 83; **7,** 59–61
—territorial waters, **1,** 98–99
Trading with the Enemy Act, 1940, **18,** 650
transfer on death, law concerning, **22,** 141
treaties—
—publication of, **1,** 322–323
—ratification of, **25,** 201, 208
Treatment of Enemy Property Ordinance, 1940..**25,** 336–337, 338–349, 341–342, 347
Turkey, Extradition Treaty (1930), **18,** 339
Turnover Tax Act (*Umsatzsteuergesetz*), **5,** 75
Unemployment Exchanges and Insurance Act, 1927...**5,** 305
U.K.—
—Commercial Treaty (1924), **6,** 280
— —(1925), **7,** 11–12
—London Agreement, release of property (1929), **6,** 240–241
—Reparations Agreement (1929), **6,** 241
United States High Commission, Law No. 21 (Court of Restitution Appeals), **24,** 402
U.S.A.—
—Claims Conventions (1921 and 1922), **22,** 416
—Commercial Treaty (1871), **5,** 475

Germany—*continued*
U.S.A.—*continued*
—Commercial Treaty (1923), **5,** 477; **9,** 71; **14,** 171–176; **18,** 504; **21,** 433, 437, 441, 443; **28,** 467–469
—declaration of war by (1941), **21,** 434
—Extradition Treaty, **7,** 358
—Mixed Claims Convention (1922), **2,** 188, 211; **5,** 185–186; **22,** 851
—Peace Treaty (1921), **2,** 211; **5,** 476–477; **11,** 238, 264; **14,** 173, 175–176; **18,** 503, 505
—termination of war with, **34,** 498
—Treaty of Friendship, Commerce, Consular Rights (1925), **9,** 2, 486, 491; **15,** 460
—Treaty with North German Confederation, *re* naturalization (1868), **1,** 208
U.S.S.R.—
—Conciliation Treaty (1929), **5,** 310
—Convention (1925), *re* Brussels Convention of 1910...**5,** 128
—Economic Agreement (1925), **5,** 310, 311; **6,** 333–334; **7,** 175–177, 419–420
—Frontier Agreement (1941), **15,** 49, 50
—Pact with (1939), **15,** 680; **16,** 347
—Repatriation Convention (1941), **20,** 62
Upper Silesia and, **18,** 49, 67–69. *See also* Upper Silesia
Valorization Law, **4,** 163, 338
Versailles, Treaty of, alleged German violation, **5,** 5
war legislation, enemy-owned patents, **29,** 342–343, 346–348
Wills, Law on Making of (1938), **24,** 970–971
Workmen's Councils, Law on, **6,** 148
Württemberg, Treaty with (railways) (1920), **5,** 330–332
Yugoslavia, Commercial Treaty, **6,** 276
Germany, Democratic Republic—
capacity of agency of, to sue in U.S. courts, **32,** 65–70
Conventions on Protection of Industrial Property and, **28,** 43, 44, 82–88
nationalization decrees, **22,** 14–16; **28,** 39, 42
non-recognition by German Federal Republic, **28,** 82–88
status of, **32,** 69
Germany, Federal Republic—
Aliens Police Ordinance, **28,** 298
Amnesty Law (1954), **21,** 480, 482–484
Arbitral Commission on Property, Rights and Interests—
—access to, **25,** 527–529

Germany, Federal Republic—*continued*
Arbitral Commission on Property, Rights and Interests—*continued*
—admissibility of claims, **34,** 231, 475–478
—applicable law, **25,** 498; **28,** 554–555; **29,** 295, 297, 476
—award, appeal and revision, 482–488
—award, enforceability, 483–484
—challenge of member for prejudice, **28,** 549–571
—Charter, **28,** 569–570; **29,** 465
—competence, absence of provision in Convention, **29,** 293–295, 297
— —appeal from Patent Office, **28,** 585–586
— —case pending in German court, **25,** 524–527
— —claim against enterprise in East Germany, **28,** 572, 578
— —compensation claim against German postal and transport authorities, **28,** 576–578
— —compensation for war damage, **28,** 576, 578
— —damage from conversion of German currency, **29,** 335, 337
— —disputes under Equalization of Burdens Law, 1952...**28,** 581–583
— —limitation of, **25,** 536–538
— —nationality of claimants, **25,** 513–514, 534–535
— —patent royalties, **25,** 499–500
— —procedural questions, **29,** 293–295
— —wage claims, forced labour, **28,** 572, 573, 578
—costs, **25,** 502, 538–540
—declaratory judgment, **25,** 344, 348
—equity, application of, **25,** 501, 503 506, 529, 551–552 n.
—establishment of, **25,** 509–512; **34,** 487
—function in relation to German authorities, **29,** 446
—German courts, relation to, **25,** 498–499, 524–527, 553–554
—ignorance of establishment of, effect, **25,** 509–510, 512
—interim measures of protection, **25,** 522–523, 538–540, 555–556
—intervention, **25,** 544–545, 546–547; **28,** 587–589
—judgments, enforceability, **25,** 501–502
—jurisdiction, Berlin, **34,** 273, 275
— —extension of, **25,** 348, 541–543
— —property situate in Austria, **29,** 344–345
—legal aid, **25,** 513–514

Germany, Federal Republic—*continued*
Arbitral Commission on Property, Rights and Interests—*continued*
—municipal case-law, application of, **25,** 554
—Patent Appeal Board and, **25,** 551
—precise claim, need for, **25,** 515–516
—preliminary objections, effect of upholding one, **28,** 579–580
—procedure, abstention from voting, **28,** 564–566
— —equality of parties, **28,** 567
— —hearing witnesses, **29,** 359; **34,** 232
— —judge challenged for disqualification, **28,** 563–564
— —written statement by challenged member, **28,** 566
—recourse by national of non-signatory State, **25,** 513–514
—recourse by non-national of United Nations, **25,** 534–535, 540–543
—relief against individual, **25,** 536–537
—residence of claimant, **34,** 480–481
—review of municipal decisions, **29,** 289–291
—Settlement Convention and general international law, application of, **29,** 476
—successive applications to, **25,** 344
—time-limits for appeal, **25,** 508–512, 515–516, 525, 528, 530–533, 548–551, 553–554; **28,** 579, 589–591; **34,** 479–482
—time-limits, power to extend, **25,** 548–551; **29,** 292–304
Asylum, Ordinance on, 1953...**28,** 350
Austria—
—Agreements, Frontier Traffic (1955), **25,** 47, 48–49
—Treaty for Settlement of Claims (1957), **32,** 33–37, 152–153
Berlin, whether part of, **34,** 270, 272, 274–275
Brussels Treaty, Protocol of Accession (1954), **23,** 770
Civil Code, Introductory Law, Art. 30 (*ordre public* clause), **28,** 19, 20, 22–23, 24–25, 30, 32–33
Code of Civil Procedure, Art. 17 (jurisdiction—domicile of defendant company), **28,** 20
—Art. 24 (venue for actions concerning real property), **28,** 370, 372, 374, 377, 388, 393, 395, 400
—Art. 42 (disqualification of judge for prejudice), **28,** 554–555
Compensation of Victims of Nazi Persecution, Law of 1953...**24,** 277, 417–418; **32,** 150, 154, 157

Germany, Federal Republic—*continued*
Constitution (Basic Law) (1949), **18,** 41, 44–45, 46, 68, 575, 621; **19,** 25, 26, 33, 413–415, 461–463; **20,** 250, 370–371, 407–409, 652; **21,** 43, 44, 175–176, 208–209, 210, 232; **22,** 430, 512–513, 521–522, 560–561, 608, 609, 610, 631; **23,** 367, 378, 379, 380, 393–395; **24,** 320, 350, 412, 413, 434, 541, 543, 545, 546; **28,** 2, 6–8
—Art. 3 (equality), **24,** 545; **28,** 256
—Art. 16 (extradition and asylum), **20,** 250, 370–371; **21,** 43–44, 232; **22,** 430, 512–513, 521–522; **23,** 367; **28,** 319–322, 347–351
—Art. 25 (international law), **18,** 575; **20,** 371; **21,** 175–176; **22,** 608, 610; **23,** 379; **28,** 22, 31, 321, 372, 387, 393, 545
—Art. 59 (treaties), **19,** 413–415, 461–463; **20,** 408; **22,** 560–561
Constitutional Court, appellate jurisdiction, **25,** 202, 231
Constitutional Court, Law concerning, **24,** 288, 403; **25,** 231
continuity with Reich, **30,** 54–67
Convention on Relations with Western Powers (1952/54), **22,** 990; **28,** 3, 6
currency reform laws, " nationals of the United Nations ", **18,** 55–56
Equalization of Burdens Law, 1952, jurisdiction of Arbitral Commission on Property, etc., **28,** 581–583; **30,** 294, 295–296
—levy on profits under currency reform, application to aliens, **28,** 544–548
Extradition Law, **28,** 320, 348, 349
Federal Compensation Law, 1956, **28,** 521
—s. 43 (compensation for loss of liberty), **28,** 648–651
—s. 160 (rights of stateless persons and refugees), **28,** 649
Finance Convention with Western Powers (1952/54), **26,** 201–203
foreign armed forces in, **24,** 594–595; **26,** 200–203; **33,** 191–193
France—
—Executive Agreement, *re* Saar, (1954), **22,** 630–632
—extradition between, **22,** 520–525
—Treaty with, Saar Question (1956), **24,** 411–412
General Consequences of the War, Decree, 1957...**33,** 26–27
Hardship Compensation Law, **30,** 247, 249

Germany, Federal Republic—*continued*
Homeless Aliens, Law on, 1951...**23**, 378, 383–385, 386–388; **26**, 503–505, 507–509; **28**, 298–299
Industrial Property Conventions, statement on re-application of, **28**, 85; **30**, 57, 58, 64
industrial property rights, restoration after war, **29**, 344
International Monetary Fund, membership, **22**, 730
international status, **30**, 60, 64
Israel, Agreement concerning Reparation (1952), **28**, 88
—waiver of claims, **32**, 148–151
Judicature Act, Art. 18 (diplomatic immunity), **28**, 370, 377, 393, 398
—Art. 20 (jurisdiction over real property), **28**, 370, 372, 373, 374, 377, 388, 393–394, 395, 400
Länder, succession to obligations of former *Länder*, **20**, 79–81; **26**, 89–97
legislation, paid holidays for women, **28**, 255, 258–259
Naturalization, Collective, Law for Unification of (1955), **24**, 541
non-recognition of German Democratic Republic, **28**, 82–88
North Atlantic Treaty, Protocol of Accession (1954), **23**, 770
Petersburg Agreement (1949), *re* occupation régime, **19**, 413–415
Prisoners of War, Laws on Status of (1950 and 1956), **24**, 927
procedure, civil appeals, **29**, 301
Property Law (1950), **24**, 771–773
Public Officials, Law concerning, **24**, 702
Public Procedure, Law concerning, **24**, 289
ratification of treaties, **25**, 201, 208
Reich, successor of, **16**, 36–37; **18**, 40–42, 44–47, 68; **22**, 146, 151; **24**, 593; **26**, 578; **30**, 307, 309
Reichsmark, conversion to Deutsche Mark, **32**, 24
Restitution Appeals, Court of (U.S. Zone), **25**, 194, 198, 200, 203, 210
Restitution Court of Appeal (British Zone), procedure, **25**, 206
Restitution Law (1953), **19**, 25; **24**, 346; **26**, 95–96, 146, 153; **28**, 2–8; **32**, 151
—" affected property ", **26**, 153
—" default " of Reich, whether starting war amounts to, **28**, 191, 193
—international law and, **28**, 384, 387, 389, 399, 404
—liability under, whether tortious, **26**, 95–96

Germany, Federal Republic—*continued*
Restitution Law (1953)—*continued*
—nature of proceedings, **28**, 372
—place of deprivation, relevance of, **26**, 153
—possible claim under Italian Peace Treaty, effect, **32**, 350–351
—principles for assessment of compensation, **28**, 191, 194
—promulgation in Berlin, **28**, 5
Restitution Law (1957), **28**, 519, 521, 523
Restitution Office, competence, **25**, 537–538
Restrictions of Competition, Law against, 1957. . .**28**, 508, 510–511
Rights and Obligations of Foreign Forces, Convention (1952/54), **24**, 595; **26**, 201; **31**, 269
Settlement Convention (1952/1954), **22**, 941, 989, 990; **23**, 21–23, 770–775, 785, 789–791; **24**, 31, 33–35, 36, 576, 895; **26**, 708–711; **28**, 2–7, 470, 515–524, 545–548, 581; **29**, 329–348, 363–369, 442–499; **30**, 246, 327–328; **32**, 17, 109–110, 159
—Allied High Commission Law No. 8, effect on, **25**, 498
—Berlin, application to, **29**, 334, 336, 346
—compensation in lieu of restitution, conditions for, **29**, 289–291
—" deprivation " (Chap. Ten), **25**, 350, 354
—discriminatory treatment, **29**, 333–334, 339, 341, 355–361, 493, 495–499; **34**, 267–269, 272–273
—discriminatory treatment, prisoners of war, **28**, 515–518
—enactments of Occupation Authorities and, **34**, 485–487
—exemption of U.N. nationals from exceptional levies, **28**, 545–548, 581
—external assets, provisions on seizure of, **32**, 109–110
—external assets, waiver, **30**, 246
—external restitution provisions, **29**, 363
—governmental claim incorporating private claim, **34**, 228–229
—"impairment" of property, **29**, 368
—maintenance of certain Allied Laws, **30**, 246
—nature of, **29**, 468
—non-review of decisions of occupation courts, **30**, 327–328
—occupation, powers of, whether based on, **32**, 159
—Peace Treaty with Italy and, **29**, 451, 453, 464
—property removed from occupied territory, **29**, 363–369

Germany, Federal Republic—*continued*
Settlement Convention (1952/1954)—*continued*
—reparation or compensation claims, exclusion of, **29**, 362–363, 367–368, 452–453, 458, 471, 475–476, 484, 493–494
—reparation claims, postponement of, **34**, 233, 240, 247, 265
—reparation provisions, **23**, 774–775
—restitution and compensation provisions, **29**, 329–340, 363–369; **34**, 219–261 *passim*
—restitution and reparation, distinction, **29**, 452, 474–476
—restitution, compensation in lieu, **29**, 442–492; **34**, 235–260
— —concept of property to be restituted, **29**, 450–455
— —expendable and non-expendable property, **29**, 472–473
— —" identification in Germany ", **28**, 518–524; **29**, 481–483; **34**, 235, 237–249, 251–253
— —identification of property, **29**, 442, 445, 448, 455–459, 476–492
— —nationality of claimant, **28**, 522
— —reference to existing procedure for, **29**, 477–479, 485, 487–488
— —shares, of, **25**, 345–346
— —ship declared prize, **34**, 261–267
—restitution claims, burden of proof, **28**, 518–524
— —made after Convention in force, **29**, 479–481, 485–486
—restitution legislation, provisions as to, **28**, 2–7
—restoration claims, **34**, 272
—restoration provisions, **29**, 341–342, 343–348
— —territorial scope, **29**, 344–346, 359, 361–362
—seizure of German external assets, **32**, 17
—*situs* of property restored, **25**, 358–360
—*travaux préparatoires*, **29**, 459–470, 472, 474; **34**, 232, 241–248
—waiver of claims, **28**, 470
sovereignty of, Bonn/Paris Conventions, **25**, 198–200, 204, 209; **32**, 159
Supreme Restitution Court, **25**, 194, 201
—Charter of, **25**, 200–201, 203—204
—international character, **25**, 203–204, 206, 207, 210
—Presidential Council, **25**, 205
—responsibility for acts of, **25**, 198–201, 204–210
—Rules of Procedure, **25**, 200, 205, 209
—status of, whether agency of U.S. Government, **28**, 592–594

Germany, Federal Republic—*continued*
Sweden, Agreement (1956), German property, **25**, 48
Switzerland, Agreements (1952 and 1953), German assets in Switzerland, **22**, 638–642; **26**, 543–545, 546; **32**, 18
taxation, appeal procedure, **29**, 295, 301–302
Termination of Occupation Régime, Protocol (1954), **22**, 990; **23**, 785, 789; **24**, 576, 595, 895
treaties, ratification of, **25**, 201, 208
U.K., Debt Agreement (1953), **24**, 207
U.S.A.—
—Agreement, Settlement for Surplus Property (1953), **24**, 952
—Commercial Treaty with (1954), national treatment clause, **34**, 214–217
—Treaty of Friendship, Commerce and Navigation (1955), **22**, 939; **24**, 8–9; **28**, 470
—Validation of German Dollar Bonds, Agreements (1953), **24**, 774, 777, 779
Validation of German Foreign Currency Bonds, Law for (1952), **24**, 774–780
Gex, Free Zone of, **5**, 16–17, 339, 398, 459–465; **6**, 362–367, 430, 431; **7**, 483; **8**, 178–179
Ghana—
complaint of non-compliance by Portugal with Forced Labour Convention, **35**, 285–351 *passim*
Deportation Act, 1957...**27**, 13–18
Deportation (Othman Lardan and Amadu Baba) Act, 1957...**27**, 15–17
Ghana (Constitution) Order in Council, 1957...**27**, 16–17
Ghandi Agreement (1945): *see* Colombo Agreement
Ghent, Treaty of (1814), boundary provisions, **4**, 122; **14**, 2–3
Glasscock Island, boundary dispute, **7**, 133–135
Gold clause: *see also under* German External Debts, Agreement on (1953)
gold-yen, reference to, **29**, 4–11
government loans and, **5**, 466–471; **8**, 13–22; **24**, 782, 798; **29**, 4–11
—legislation affecting, **9**, 156; **11**, 26–28, 30–32
Gold dollars, payment in, **9**, 24
Gold, monetary: *see also* Tripartite Commission for the Restitution of Monetary Gold
Agreement on restitution of: *see* Reparations Agreement (1946)

Gold, monetary—*continued*
looted, **20,** 444–445, 451, 466–467, 479
meaning, **20,** 466, 469, 476
right to restitution of, **20,** 471–472, 479; **21,** 399–401
Gold, prohibition of export, **11,** 34–35
Gold tariff, as basis of claim, **23,** 342, 344–345
Gold transactions, International Monetary Fund and, **22,** 734–737
Golfe de Juan, **8,** 177–178
Good faith, **2,** 38, 176–177; **3,** 108, 214, 215–217, 358–359; **5,** 156, 168, 171, 265, 428; **15,** 336, 339, 344–346; **18,** 407; **20,** 75; **21,** 325, 343, 347; **22,** 675, 686–687, 790–791, 825; **23,** 45, 53–54, 60, 342, 345–346, 549, 557, 635, 641–642; **24,** 119, 126, 129, 141, 706, 765, 806–809, 811, 836; **25,** 284, 287, 505, 551–552n.; **27,** 96, 598; **30,** 478; **31,** 26, 68, 75, 118; **33,** 77, 88–89, 93, 96, 146
basis of equitable estoppel, **2,** 38, 176; **30,** 498; **33,** 88, 88–89, 93, 96, 146
element in the principle of *uti possidetis*, **27,** 66
impossibility of adjudicating between States on basis of, **24,** 836
administrative decisions, in, **22,** 790–791; **23,** 549, 557
awards of Conciliation Commissions, in, **20,** 75
carrying out arbitral awards, in, **21,** 325; **30,** 478
determinations by States that matters are within their domestic jurisdiction, in, **24,** 806–809, 811, 836
exercise of discretions, in, **15,** 344–346; **21,** 347; **22,** 377, 384; **31,** 26, 68, 75, 118
exercise of sovereignty, in, **31,** 26, 68, 75
interpretation of administrative contracts, in, **23,** 635, 641–642
—concessionary contract, **23,** 345–346, 635, 641–642
—contracts generally, **25,** 505–506
—international agreements, **18,** 407; **22,** 825; **23,** 54, 60; **25,** 284, 287; **27,** 598
nationalization, in, **22,** 377, 384
negotiations, in, **3,** 358–359; **20,** 75; **24,** 119, 126, 129, 141
supervision of Mandates, in, **23,** 45, 53
use of powers by ceding state before transfer of sovereignty, in, **3,** 108
lack of, not to be presumed, **3,** 108, 358–359; **24,** 126, 706
Good faith—*continued*
lack of, as an element in denial of justice, **3,** 214, 217; **5,** 156, 168, 171; **21,** 343
—in expropriation, **5,** 265
nemo judex in re sua as a principle of, **22,** 676
of U.N. General Assembly in refusing to give effect to awards of Administrative Tribunals, **21,** 347
of U.N. Members in interpretation of Article 4 (admission), **15,** 336, 339, 344–346
of States administering Mandate or Trust Territories in considering Assembly recommendations, **22,** 686–687
Goods, enemy character of: *see under* Enemy character
Goodwill—
loss upon nationalization, **30,** 147, 182
vested right, whether, **7,** 317
whether " property " within Trading with the Enemy legislation, **27,** 639–645
Government agencies and departments, jurisdictional immunity: *see* Foreign States, immunity from jurisdiction, agencies
Government loans, applicable law, **5,** 468–469; **8,** 13–22
Governments: *see also De facto* governments; *De jure* governments
acts of foreign, recognition of: *see under* Recognition
change, effects of, **1,** 276; **2,** 34–36, 53; **9,** 408
—judicial notice, **11,** 63–64
de facto and *de jure*: *see De facto, De jure* governments
enemy, right to sue, **10,** 454–455
extinct—
—consular courts established by, **4,** 191–192
—jurisdictional immunity, **2,** 134–135
—Omsk All Russian Government, **1,** 32; **2,** 134–135
immunity from jurisdiction: *see* Foreign States, immunity from jurisdiction
insults by individuals to, **9,** 333
non-recognition, effect on individual's right to sue, **6,** 51–52
recognition of: *see* Recognition of governments
States, distinguished from, **10,** 25–27
statutes of limitation, application to, **9,** 185
succession of, **2,** 18–19, 54–87; **3,** 24–25, 96–102; **4,** 58–59; **5,** 72, 113–114; **6,** 54, 86–88; **7,** 78–79; **19,** 89–90

Governments—*continued*
succession of—*continued*
—functional succession, **26**, 91, 92–93
—liabilities, **26**, 193–194, 276–277
—part of territory only, **26**, 94
—treaties, India, **31**, 20–22, 60
—upon termination of rebellion, **3**, 98–102
trustees for individuals, as, **6**, 240–242
unrecognized—
—acts of, **11**, 64–66
—capacity to sue, **6**, 57; **7**, 75–76; **19**, 192–195; **26**, 70–71
—construction of charterparty, **23**, 71–78
—relations with, **23**, 397–400
—repudiation of treaty by, **5**, 47; **22**, 90–97
—status before municipal courts, **2**, 39–44; **5**, 42–45; **23**, 71–78
—territory controlled by, **11**, 68–73; **21**, 225–229
—validity of acts, **7**, 22–27
Governments in exile, **4**, 166–167; **12**, 420–424
delegation of powers of government, **11**, 271–272
legislation of, **10**, 10–23, 111–123, 131–132, 174–175; **12**, 420–424, 431–433, 444–445; **15**, 17–18, 530–535, 561, 567–471; **16**, 46–60, 428–432; **18**, 558–570; **20**, 26–31; **21**, 475
—occupied territory, effect in, **15**, 530–533
locus standi in judicio, **22**, 230–233
recognition of, **4**, 167; **19**, 72–85; **21**, 25–29
recognition of acts of, **12**, 378–382
rights of, **28**, 651
title to property, **12**, 346–348
"*Gracieusement*", meaning, **4**, 467
Gran Chaco dispute, **1**, 106
prohibition of import of arms during, **8**, 49
Grants in perpetuity, **1**, 94–95; **5**, 80–81; **6**, 111; **7**, 113–114; **31**, 121–128
Great Britain: *see also* England; United Kingdom
France and Spain, Boundary Treaty (1873), **7**, 131
meaning of, **27**, 116
Morocco—
—Treaties with (1721, 1750, 1751, 1760, 1801), **19**, 265
—Treaty with (1783), **2**, 19–20
Greco-Bulgarian Mixed Emigration Commission, status of members, **7**, 387–388
Greece—
Aegean Islands, status of, **23**, 666, 669
Greece—*continued*
Albania, Extradition Treaty, **5**, 282
amalgamation of banks, **26**, 7–8, 15–16, 19, 21–22; **30**, 4–23
Argentina, extradition from, **5**, 288
British army in, **12**, 163
Bulgaria—
—Convention on Emigration (1920), **5**, 4
—dispute with (1925), **22**, 674
—Extradition Treaty (1929), **7**, 335
—Financial Agreement (1927), **6**, 432; **22**, 681
—Peace Treaty (1913), **23**, 663–665
—Treaty of Alliance (1912), **4**, 425
Constitution, **20**, 329; **21**, 195, 196
Crete as successor to, **23**, 81–93
criminal procedure, **22**, 520
Decree blocking Italian-owned shares in Greek companies, **28**, 153
Decree on obligations of amalgamated banks, **26**, 19, 22–23, 26, 28; **30**, 4–23
—penal nature, **26**, 20–21
Egypt—
—Air Force in, **11**, 170–171
—consular courts in, **20**, 195–197
—Treaty, *re* nationality (1918), **1**, 41
Ethiopia—
—Commercial Conventions (1922, 1923), **7**, 199–200
European Court of Human Rights, acceptance of jurisdiction, **25**, 171
France—
—Commercial Convention (1926), **4**, 453
—Consular Convention (1876), **12**, 261
—Extradition Treaty (1906), **23**, 418–419
German legislation in, **12**, 437–443, 454–455
German military courts in, **12**, 433–437
Germany, Extradition Treaty, **22**, 521–524
Government in exile, legislation, **12**, 431–433
Italy—
—Commercial Convention (1926), **19**, 435, 447
—Consular Convention (1880), **7**, 388–389
—Economic Collaboration Agreement (1949), **22**, 241
landing of French troops at Piraeus, **1**, 385
liability for torts of Samos officials, **2**, 70
marriage according to Greek Orthodox Church, **4**, 37–38
military forces abroad, **11**, 165–169, 170–171

Greece—*continued*
Ministry of Foreign Affairs, certificate of, **2**, 301; **12**, 386
Mitylene Island, occupation of, **11**, 277–278
moratorium laws affecting bonds, **26**, 7, 13–15
Mount Athos monasteries, exterritoriality, **3**, 315–316
nationality, law of, **20**, 261–263
neutrality, First World War, **4**, 569, 571
occupation of, First World War, **4**, 570–572
—Second World War, **10**, 164; **11**, 275–278; **12**, 431–443, 454–455; **15**, 561–567, 638; **16**, 466–467; **18**, 629–630
Poland, Trade Convention (1925), **6**, 352–353
Provisional Government of Salonica, Decree of 1916...**5**, 497
Samos and, **23**, 84–85
suits against Government, **34**, 87
Switzerland, Convention, Establishment and Judicial Protection (1927), **21**, 305–307
territorial changes after—
—Balkan Wars, **23**, 663–666, 667–668
—First World War, **23**, 666–669
Turkey—
—successor to, **23**, 79–80, 81–93, 94–99, 99–101
—Treaty of Athens (1913), **1**, 389; **23**, 87
U.K.—
—Conventions on war claims (1925), **5**, 352–354
—Convention, Reciprocal Exemption from Income Tax (1936), **21**, 305–306
—Disposal of Diverted Cargoes, Agreement (1942), **22**, 820–839 *passim*
—Treaties of Commerce (1886 and 1926), **19**, 416–454 *passim*; **20**, 548–565; **23**, 309; **24**, 293–299 *passim*
U.S.A.—
—Accord on military facilities (1953), **21**, 123
—Aid Agreements (1944, 1947), **21**, 122–123
—Consular Convention (1902), **1**, 346–347; **9**, 159; **10**, 158n.; **15**, 110; **16**, 101, 309–310
—Extradition Treaty (1931), **7**, 344–346, 351; **31**, 370–372
—Treaty of Friendship, Commerce and Navigation (1951), **24**, 481; **33**, 408–409; **34**, 85, 88; **35**, 208–215

Greece—*continued*
United States, naval mission to, **21**, 122–125
U.S.S.R., Commercial Treaty (1929), **6**, 334
Guadeloupe Hidalgo, Treaty of (1848), **6**, 113; **11**, 95; **13**, 178–181; **21**, 218–219
Guam—
status of, **32**, 84–85
territorial waters as naval defence area, **32**, 83–86
Guarantee of sovereignty, violation, guarantor State, effect on, **26**, 635
Guardianship—
discrimination against aliens and, **2**, 269
Dutch law, **25**, 263–274, 266, 308, 309–310, 312
English law, **25**, 267
German law, **25**, 263, 264
nature of, **25**, 253, 263–264
tutelle d'autorité, **25**, 263
tutelle de famille, **25**, 263
Guardianship, Hague Convention (1902), *ordre public*, implied exception, **25**, 246, 248, 253, 256, 267, 288, 293–294, 312
purpose of, **25**, 252–254, 260, 264, 285, 302, 307–308
war, effect on, **17**, 357
Guatemala—
Aliens Act (1936), **22**, 354
Constitution, Art. 30 (extradition), **5**, 294
Honduras, Arbitration Treaty (1930), **7**, 115–127
Liquidation of Matters Arising out of the War, Law on (1949), **22**, 386, 387
Penal Code, provisions as to extradition of nationals, **6**, 297
U.S.A.—
—Commercial Convention (1936), **22**, 617–618
—Protocol of Arbitration (1929), **5**, 179
Guerilla forces—
Geneva Convention, 1929, and, **15**, 638–641; **16**, 355
levée en masse, **16**, 514–516
occupied territory, in, **15**, 638–641; **16**, 514–516; **24**, 986–988
Guerilla warfare, **15**, 638–641, 661–662; **16**, 354–356, 380, 510, 516; **17**, 352–353
Guerillas, right to trial, **15**, 392–393
Gulfs: *see also* Bays
Golfe de Juan, **8**, 177–178
Gulf of Finland, **8**, 407–409
Gulf of Mexico, **6**, 128–129

H

Habana Conventions of 1928—
Asylum, **17**, 281, 283, 290–294, 341; **18**, 350–354, 356, 357
Diplomatic Officers, Rights and Duties, **9**, 425–427; **12**, 241–242; **22**, 536–537, 540–541, 547; **23**, 423–425, 426
Maritime Neutrality, **14**, 89
Private International Law (The Bustamante Code: *q.v.*)
Habeas corpus, writ of—
aliens under deportation order, **12**, 231–232, 235–236
Allied Forces, and, **12**, 165–168
determination of nationality, **10**, 275–276
enemy alien, alleged, **12**, 185–188
enemy aliens, availability to, **10**, 450–454; **12**, 199–201, 360–362; **13**, 317–321
foreign country, detention in, **12**, 64–68
history of, **28**, 63
issue by English High Court into protectorate, **28**, 48–78 *passim*
mandated territories, availability in, **12**, 12
means of judicial review of administrative order, **32**, 196–197
nature of writ, **28**, 52, 60, 72, 76–77
political refugees, **12**, 231
" Habitual residence ", meaning, **9**, 339
—nationality, in relation to, **2**, 230–237, 256, 295
Hague Codification Conference (1930), **8**, 410; **9**, 124; **18**, 91, 92, 116, 133; **20**, 563; **22**, 386
—Bases of Discussion, nationality of claims, **6**, 222
—Final Act, **7**, 488; **8**, 266
Hague Conference (1899), **15**, 622, 641; **16**, 486, 534, 539
Hague Conference (1907), deliberations of, **5**, 517; **19**, 431
Hague Convention, Adaptation to Maritime War of Geneva Convention, 1864..**2**, 429–430; **4**, 458; **13**, 274, 277; **30**, 516
Hague Convention, Bombardment by Naval Forces (1907), **15**, 687–688; **32**, 630
Hague Convention, Civil Procedure (1905), **1**, 69–73, 122–124, 244, 300–301, 352; **2**, 84, 323; **4**, 37–38, 59–60; **5**, 30, 47; **6**, 40–43, 90, 349; **7**, 305–306, 308; **8**, 40, 334, 423, 437; **9**, 73, 376; **11**, 67, 222, 226–227; **12**, 277–278; **13**, 185, 187, 232; **14**, 177; **16**, 314–315; **17**, 308–310, 357–359; **18**, 20–22, 434, 574–575; **19**, 29–34; **21**, 211,
Hague Convention—Civil Procedure (1905)—*continued*
303; **22**, 900; **24**, 52–53, 483, 485; **26**, 577; **28**, 494–496
annexed State, continued application in, **11**, 227
national treatment regarding civil imprisonment, **28**, 494–496
poor persons' procedure, **11**, 242–243
Hague Convention, Commencement of Hostilities (1907), **12**, 300–302; **15**, 359, 417; **18**. 599; **20**, 591; **26**, 641 n., 645
Hague Convention, Conflict of Divorce Laws (1902), **5**, 244–245, 352; **19**, 559
Hague Convention, Conflict of Marriage Laws (1902), **5**, 132; **11**, 23; **16**, 380–381; **20**, 654
Hague Convention, Conflict of Nationality Laws (1930), **6**, 192; **15**, 248, 268–269; **20**, 56; **22**, 360, 371, 376, 381, 382, 384, 449–450, 454, 456; **24**, 301; **25**, 149; **30**, 369n.; **32**, 167
Hague Convention, Conversion of Merchant Ships into Warships (1907), **3**, 221–222; **5**, 511; **13**, 404; **14**, 89
Hague Convention, Guardianship, 1902
ordre public, implied exception, **25**, 246, 248, 253, 256, 267, 288, 293–294, 312
purpose of, **25**, 252–254, 260, 264, 285, 302, 307–308
war, effect on, **17**, 357
Hague Convention, Industrial Property, Protection of (1925), **7**, 435–437; **8**, 24; **13**, 1–2
Hague Convention, International Prize Court (1907), **1**, 488
Hague Convention, International Sales of Moveable Property (draft, 1955), **25**, 86
Hague Conventions, Laws and Customs of War (1899, 1907), **2**, 429; **5**, 498–500; **7**, 509, 511–513; **8**, 503–505; **10**, 573; **11**, 274; **13**, 212, 297, 382; **14**, 233, 244–265, 279–281; **15**, 429, 474, 535–536, 553–555, 558, 559, 560, 606–607, 614, 616, 622–623, 635; **16**, 17, 65, 464, 465, 469, 473, 476, 542; **17**, 351; **18**, 690, 691; **19**, 137, 140, 612, 616, 617; **20**, 658, 661, 673, 674; **22**, 991; **23**, 718, 765; **24**, 967, 970, 979, 988; **30**, 503, 504–505, 510; **32**, 591, 628: *see also* Hague Regulations
aerial bombardment and, **5**, 4; **32**, 630
Allied occupation of Germany, application to, **14**, 233, 279–281

Hague Conventions, Laws and Customs of War (1899, 1907)—*continued*
belligerent occupation and, **17**, 408, 420–422, 423. *See also* Belligerent occupation
binding force, **1**, 428; **3**, 468
changed conditions of warfare, **13**, 297
civil wars, application by analogy, **5**, 148
communal penalties, prohibition of, **30**, 506
conditions of entry into force, **24**, 891
customary law, evidence of, **3**, 486
declaratory nature, **13**, 212, 382; **14**, 244, 265; **15**, 606–607, 614, 616, 622–623, 635; **16**, 466
general participation clause, **1**, 428; **13**, 212; **15**, 365; **18**, 678–679
individuals, binding on, **30**, 505, 510
interpretation by municipal courts, **1**, 462, 464, 465
jus cogens, character of, **30**, 503
municipal courts, application by, **30**, 503
occupation of friendly allied territory, application to, **32**, 591
sovereignty of occupied State, preservation of, **30**, 505
Hague Convention, Limitation on Use of Force for Recovery of Contract Debts (1907), **24**, 787, 791, 792, 793, 796
Hague Convention, Neutral Powers and Persons in Land Warfare (1907), **2**, 223, 455; **3**, 461; **12**, 288; **16**, 355; **22**, 931, 1015–1016; **23**, 612, 715, 718, 720
Hague Convention, North Sea, Police and Fisheries (1882), **6**, 125; **8**, 266; **18**, 101, 116, 117, 127, 128
Hague Convention, Pacific Settlement of Disputes, **1**, 85, 370; **2**, 361, 367; **4**, 479–481; **18**, 599; **19**, 440; **20**, 572; **22**, 824, 874; **23**, 671; **24**, 796, 833; **25**, 314n.; **27**, 543
applicability to States not ratifying it, **1**, 3
revision of award made under, **9**, 326
rules of evidence, **4**, 479–481
Hague Convention, Restrictions on Capture, Maritime Warfare (1907), **1**, 430; **12**, 471, 482–483, 488; **13**, 402, 405
coastal fishing vessels assisting enemy, **28**, 661–662
Hague Convention, Rights and Duties of Neutrals, Maritime War (1907), **5**, 510; **12**, 538; **16**, 588
declaratory content, **3**, 486; **14**, 321
Hague Convention, Status of Enemy Merchant Ships (1907), **1**, 410–414; **2**, 452; **3**, 483–484; **5**, 511; **6**, 439–441; **7**, 506, 509–510; **10**, 509–514; **11**, 257, 264–265; **12**, 357–359, 489, 504, 512; **16**, 578; **24**, 921–922; **32**, 612, 622–623, 624
British denunciation, effect, **11**, 257, 265
denunciations, **16**, 559
Hague Regulations, Land Warfare (1899), **16**, 535; **19**, 616
Mertens Clause, **15**, 622
municipal law and, **18**, 13–14, 621–625
Hague Regulations, Land Warfare (1907), **2**, 429; **4**, 570–571; **6**, 448, 449–450; **9**, 375; **11**, 272, 289; **12**, 434, 436–443, 447, 448, 453, 454, 458–459; **15**, 61, 360, 365, 368, 383–384, 393–394, 398, 401, 406, 412, 420, 429, 430, 435, 470, 471, 493–494, 502, 527, 536, 600, 615, 622, 634, 637, 641; **16**, 535; **18**, 532, 567, 602, 626, 661, 692, 701; **19**, 140; **23**, 831, 833, 840; **26**, 718–719, 723, 731; **29**, 44; **30**, 503: *see also* references to Articles of the Regulations in Table of Treaties
aerial warfare, applicability to, **5**, 516–517
Allied occupation of Germany and, **16**, 435–436, 438
annexed territory, applicability to, **15**, 671–672
belligerent occupation and, **17**, 408, 420–422
bombardment, provisions as to, **4**, 571; **32**, 630
customary international law and, **19**, 633; **26**, 732
declaratory nature, **16**, 390–391; **18**, 691; **19**, 633
illegal annexation, application to, **26**, 723
legal basis of, **22**, 992
military authority over occupied territory, **16**, 490
military necessity and, **16**, 511–513
modern interpretation of, **23**, 826
municipal law and, **18**, 13–14, 621–625
" *munitions de guerre* ", meaning, **23**, 822–827, 832, 846–847
non-enemy territory, application to, **26**, 731
poisonous weapons, **32**, 634
requisitions, provisions as to, **4**, 486–487; **17**, 423; **29**, 451
reprisals against civilian inhabitants, **30**, 503
respect for family and private life, **28**, 650
respect for local law, **28**, 644–645; **30**, 505
salaries of public officials, **29**, 497

Hague Regulations, Land Warfare (1907)—*continued*
total warfare and, **15,** 677–678; **16,** 358, 489, 510
U.S.S.R. and, **16,** 510–511; **23,** 795–796
"*valeurs exigibles*", Institute of International Law resolution, **15,** 600
Hague Rules, Carriage by Sea (1921), **21,** 297–300; **33,** 397–399
Haiti, naturalization in (Decree-Law of 1939), **11,** 32
Hamburg—
free port, **1,** 100
State of, distinguished from German State, **4,** 203
U.S.A., Treaty, Friendship and Commerce (1827), **5,** 475, 477
Hartford, Treaty of (1786), New York and Massachusetts, **7,** 128
Havana Charter (1947), dumping, definition of, **26,** 604
Hawaii—
annexation by U.S.A., **10,** 279–281
channels between islands, historic title, **35,** 68–83
"grand naturalization" in, **10,** 279–281
land, title to, **13,** 35–36; **35,** 74
status of, **24,** 5
territorial waters, jurisdiction, **35,** 71–74, 82–83
Hay-Pauncefote Treaty (1901): *see under* Panama Canal
Hay-Varilla Treaty (1903): *see under* Panama Canal
Heads of State—
action by, nature of, **4,** 35–36; **9,** 98
acts of, judicial review, **9,** 16–17, 21, 25–26, 123
co-existence of *de facto* and *de jure*, **9,** 62
defamation of, **9,** 8–9, 11–12
dual nationality of, **3,** 461
dignity, protection of, **8,** 23–25; **11,** 13; **12,** 3; **18,** 23; **21,** 10–11
—ex-King, status of, **24,** 228–229
jurisdictional immunities, **1,** 136–137; **2,** 124–128, 139; **7,** 164–166, 167–168; **11,** 136–171; **12,** 337–340; **19,** 182–192, 212–219; **20,** 91–92, 398–400; **22,** 244–248, 253–256; **24,** 228–231; **26,** 195–196; **27,** 109–111
—cessation of, **22,** 253–256
—*de facto* Sovereign, **9,** 171
—order in breach of, nullity, **26,** 195–196
—partner in firm, as, **27,** 109–111
—trustees, **24,** 229–230
—waiver, **9,** 190, 205
private property of, distinguished from trust property, **4,** 31–33
Heads of State—*continued*
railway owned by, immunity of, **9,** 233
status of—
—conclusiveness of statements of executive, **19,** 186–187, 188, 212–219
—ex-king, **24,** 228–229
taxation, immunity from, **22,** 73–75
Health, International Convention (1892), **1,** 363, 364. *See also* World Health Organization
Hearsay, evidential value, **6,** 316
Heimatrecht, **1,** 15–18, 221; **4,** 25
Helsingfors, Liquor Treaty (1925), **8,** 407–409
Hesse, Treaty with Germany (railways) (1920), **5,** 330–332
"High Contracting Parties", meaning, **9,** 446–453
High Seas: *see also* Hot pursuit; Hovering laws
birth on, question of nationality, **4,** 295–296
broadcasting outside territorial waters, **31,** 274–275
channel more than one league from mainland, status of, **33,** 148–154
collisions on: *see under* Collisions at sea
concept of, **11,** 174–175; **20,** 197; **35,** 69–70
contiguous zone, **1,** 111–113; **2,** 114–115; **3,** 151–169; **4,** 196–197; **5,** 137–141; **6,** 157–159; **7,** 163–164; **8,** 212–218; **9,** 127–128; **13,** 57; **15,** 123; **28,** 170–175; **31,** 157
covering continental shelf, national jurisdiction over, **22,** 277–282; **23,** 128–129
customs laws, enforcement of, **31,** 201–202
enclosed parts, whether inland waters, **11,** 175–176
extent of, **11,** 175–176
fishing rights: *q.v.*
freedom of the seas, **31,** 130 n., 237
—Geneva Convention (1958), **31,** 237, 239; **35,** 70 n.
—nuclear tests, **26,** 2–3
jurisdiction on, **1,** 163; **2,** 112; **4,** 186–189, 193–197; **6,** 183–184; **7,** 201–224; **8,** 262–263; **9,** 298–300; **10,** 252–263; **13,** 57, 97–107; **14,** 69–72, 93–95; **15,** 115–125, 204; **16,** 150–154; **17,** 191–198; **22,** 276–286, 295–299; **23,** 284–295; **24,** 267–271; **26,** 236–244; **27,** 45–49; **28,** 122–124; **30,** 112–115; **31,** 274–275. *See also* Jurisdiction, law of the flag
—continental shelf, covering, **22,** 278–282
—crime begun on, **23,** 147–149

High Seas—*continued*
jurisdiction on—*continued*
—crime committed on, **24**, 161–166
—injuries to seamen on, **11**, 115–116; **26**, 236–239
—salvage by warships, **22**, 277–278
—smuggling by aliens in contiguous zone, **28**, 170–175
marriage contracted on, **1**, 163–164
piracy: *see* Piracy
smuggling in contiguous zone, **28**, 170–175
High Seas, Geneva Convention (1958), nationality of ships, **30**, 443, 446; **34**, 59–60
High treason: *see* Treason
Hindus in Madagascar, taxation of, **11**, 77–78
Hindus, naturalization in U.S.A., **2**, 244
" His Majesty's dominions ", meaning, **27**, 45–47
Historic waters, concept of, **35**, 79–80
Holland: *see* Netherlands
Holy See: *see also* Vatican City
cardinals, exemption from jurisdiction, **8**, 235–236, 405
Colombia, Concordat (1887), **2**, 318
concordats, relation to municipal law, **2**, 318
diplomatic representative accredited to, **9**, 111
exemption from jurisdiction, **8**, 235–236, 405; **24**, 214–215, 215–217; **26**, 183–190
extraterritoriality of buildings, **9**, 108, 109, 436–439
Germany, Concordat (1933), **7**, 399–400; **17**, 116–117; **24**, 592–594
Italy, Concordat (1929), **6**, 90; **26**, 183–189
—Lateran Treaty (1929), **5**, 304; **9**, 103, 105, 109, 111, 425, 435–436, 438; **10**, 106–108, 355–364; **19**, 142–143; **22**, 536; **23**, 115; **24**, 214, 216; **26**, 183–188
Poland, Concordat (1925), **7**, 14–15, 400–401
position of, **4**, 97–99; **8**, 151–152; **19**, 142–143; **23**, 114–115; **24**, 85
private law contracts, **9**, 108
Homicide, ground for extradition, as, **5**, 283, 289
Honduras—
Guatemala, Arbitration Treaty (1930), **7**, 115–127
Nicaragua, Extradition Treaty with, **1**, 269
U.S.A., Treaty of Friendship, Commerce and Consular Rights (1927), **7**, 454–455; **11**, 119; **22**, 283; **34**, 53, 54, 60
Honduras-Nicaragua, Arbitral Award of 1906, litigation concerning, **30**, 457–492. *See also* Boundaries
Hong Kong—
Companies Ordinance, **23**, 235
Importation and Exportation Ordinance, **23**, 236
Japanese occupation of, **15**, 443–447; **18**, 521–529, 636–637
naturalization in, **5**, 234–235
whether " country " within U.S. Immigration Act, **32**, 237–240
Horses, objects of booty, **32**, 585–588
Hospital ships, **2**, 429; **30**, 515–532
Hostages—
killing of, **13**, 216; **15**, 393, 412–414, 471–482, 641–644, 662–663, 687; **16**, 391, 401, 407, 518–520, 547–548, 551–552
right to take, **15**, 641–644; **17**, 392
Hostile destination: *see* Enemy destination
Hostile expedition, **1**, 180–182
nullity of contract connected with, **6**, 31–32
Hostilities—
general, participation in, **12**, 285–286
" imperfect war ", **26**, 627, 630
termination of, **18**, 545–546; **26**, 678
Hot pursuit, **1**, 164; **4**, 194–196; **5**, 137–141; **6**, 157; **7**, 203–206; **8**, 263–267, 410; **9**, 128; **10**, 177
Hovering laws, **1**, 111–114; **2**, 114; **3**, 151–169; **4**, 196–197; **5**, 137–138, 140; **6**, 157–160; **7**, 163–164, 207–212; **8**, 212–218; **9**, 128, 171, 300
Huerta insurrection (1923), responsibility for acts of, **3**, 211, 212, 232–234
Human rights—
adequate standard of living and housing, **24**, 325
adequate time for defence, **28**, 259, 260–261
Charter of the United Nations, provisions of: *see under* Charter of the United Nations
child, right to custody of, **24**, 331
Communist Party of Germany and, **24**, 349–351
Court of, proposed, **19**, 531
decision within reasonable time, **25**, 195
deportation and, **21**, 168
discrimination between sexes, **28**, 253–257
entry into country, right of, **24**, 331–332
European Commission, Convention and Court: *see* separate entries *infra*
expulsion and separation from family, **28**, 209–210
fair hearing, **28**, 216, 223–226, 227, 237, 244, 247, 248, 250, 261; **30**, 273–274, 275–280, 282, 301–302, 303–306, 314, 315, 316–321, 332, 333, 338

Human rights—*continued*
family life, right to respect for, **23,** 393–395; **24,** 366, 372–374; **28,** 244, 251; **30,** 268–272, 289, 290–291, 292
fines, whether violation of, **24,** 385
freedom of expression, **24,** 370; **25,** 174, 187–188; **33,** 211, 213–214, 223, 225, 227
freedom of movement and residence, **23,** 393–395, 617, 625
freedom of religion, **33,** 233–244, 380–382
hearing within reasonable time, **24,** 367
home in foreign country, right to establish, **24,** 338
imprisonment without charge or trial, **25,** 217–230
information of nature of charge, **28,** 216, 220–223, 227, 235–236
justice, right to proper administration of, **24,** 377, 387, 389, 407
law of war and, **15,** 433
legal aid, **24,** 364, 368, 371, 374–375; **30,** 249–253, 310, 311, 312, 324–325, 331, 332–333, 347
liberty, deprivation of, **24,** 348–349, 364
liberty, right to, **21,** 168; **24,** 372; **33,** 211–212
mandated territory, freedom of conscience in, **18,** 237–243
municipal law and, **20,** 244–246
nationality, right to, **24,** 347
non-discrimination, principle of, **24,** 321, 324, 326, 339; **30,** 245, 247, 248, 267, 294, 296–297, 336
non-retroactivity of penal laws, **24,** 378–379; **25,** 174, 176; **30,** 230, 232–234, 237; **33,** 211, 213
Peace Treaties, 1947, provisions of, **17,** 331–339
pension, right to, **24,** 322
petition, right of, **24,** 355–356, 388, 390–391
presumption of innocence, **28,** 216, 218, 226, 233
preventive detention, **25,** 212–216; **28,** 203
property, right to acquire, **19,** 345
public hearing, **25,** 195
public service, right of entry into, **24,** 324, 340, 392
publicity of judgments, **22,** 608–611
reasonable suspicion of commission of offence, **28,** 215, 218
religious freedom, **28,** 245
remedy for violation of, **22,** 611
residence in own country, **25,** 174–175
restrictions for public order and safety, **33,** 240, 241, 242, 243–244
third parties, rights of, **24,** 396–401
time of war, in, **17,** 203

Human rights—*continued*
trade, right to carry on, **24,** 320–321, 326
treaty and conflicting municipal law, **24,** 661–662
trial within reasonable time, **28,** 216, 218–220, 234–235
United Nations and: *see under* Charter of the United Nations, *and* Universal Declaration of Human Rights
Human Rights, Universal Declaration of: *q.v.*
Human Rights, European Commission of—
abuse of right of petition, **24,** 355, 388, 391; **25,** 229–230; **30,** 346, 348
appeal to, questions of fact, **24,** 286
application, right of, hindrance, **28,** 239–240, 268; **30,** 287, 289, 290, 292–293, 341, 343, 344–346, 347–348
applications, admissibility—
—errors by municipal court, **28,** 435
—exhaustion of local remedies, **24,** 273–291, 327, 336, 340–341, 345, 419; **25,** 28–31, 170, 180–182, 201–202, 216, 219–224, 232; **28,** 204–208, 226, 227, 233, 247, 251–252, 426, 431, 433; **30,** 227, 228, 229, 242, 243, 270–271, 291, 302, 308–309, 311–312, 315, 321, 340, 346
—judicial function of Commission, **25,** 168 n.
—*ratione personae,* **24,** 395–401, 401–416, 417–418; **28,** 256; **30,** 226–229
—*ratione temporis,* **24,** 276, 283, 290, 322, 324, 332, 338, 356, 370, 385–387, 407, 419, 546–548, 572–577; **25,** 177–180; **28,** 216–218, 226–233, 235, 240–242, 266, 435; **30,** 241, 327, 329, 339
—time limit, six months, **24,** 407; **25,** 182–186; **28,** 216–218, 226, 227–232; **30,** 244, 291–292
—violation of Convention, requirement, **24,** 322, 324, 325, 326–327, 332, 339, 341, 345–346, 348, 353, 358–359, 363–379 *passim,* 395; **25,** 215; **28,** 240, 242, 265, 268, 435; **30,** 226, 228–229, 242, 243, 280, 282, 285, 305, 320
" applications substantially the same ", **24,** 391–395; **28,** 245, 267, 433; **30,** 249–252
applications, suspending effect, **25,** 215
applications, withdrawal of, **25,** 31–32; **33,** 221, 224, 231, 232
competence—
—alleged errors of fact or law, **24,** 334, 353, 354, 359, 362; **28,** 263–265, 435; **30,** 242, 245, 267, 280, 282, 285, 324, 331, 332

Human Rights, European Commission of—*continued*
competence—*continued*
—compatibility of law with Convention, **25,** 180; **30,** 226, 228–229
—derogation, grounds for, **25,** 170
—jurisdiction, duty to determine *ex officio*, **28,** 234
—provisional measures, **25,** 215
—tribunal outside scope of Convention, **30,** 235
enquiry, request for, **30,** 343
function, **24,** 286; **28,** 435; **30,** 242, 267, 285, 305, 324; **31,** 285
inter-State applications, admissibility, **25,** 169–170
members, diplomatic immunity, **25,** 170 n.
preliminary objections, joinder to merits, **25,** 226, 227
Report to Committee of Ministers, **33,** 213, 229
—communication to applicant, **31,** 279, 281–282, 284, 286–288
Rules of Procedure, **24,** 390, 397, 410, 411
—compatibility with Convention, **31,** 279, 280, 284, 285–286
Sub-Commission to ascertain facts, **31,** 277
Human Rights, European Convention (1950), **18,** 342, 381; **21,** 168, 210; **22,** 10, 523, 608–611; **23,** 379, 393–395; **24,** 321–425 *passim*, 575; **25,** 28–32, 168–233 *passim*; **28,** 201–268 *passim*; **30,** 226–350 *passim*; **31,** 276–315 *passim*
accused to be informed of charge, **31,** 373
appellate proceedings, application to, **30,** 278
arbitral tribunal, enforcement of award of, **30,** 306, 309
Austrian reservation, public hearing, **28,** 264; **30,** 274, 275, 302, 315
—concerning State Treaty, **28,** 424–429
authoritative texts, **28,** 207
Bonn/Paris Conventions (1952/54), compatibility with, **25,** 196, 209
case-file, right to consult, **30,** 273, 283–286, 314, 321
charge not offence in applicant's State, **30,** 232–233, 237
charge not offence under national/international law, **30,** 273, 280
" civil security measure " (Art. 10), **25,** 176–177
continuing violation, **25,** 179–180, 182, 184
defence, opportunity to prepare, **30,** 273, 275, 280–283, 285–286
defence, violation of rights of, **30,** 240, 244
Human Rights, European Convention—*continued*
derogation from, adequacy of notice, **31,** 310–312
derogation from, public emergency, **25,** 227; **31,** 277, 293, 305–312, 313–315
earlier treaties, relation to, **30,** 328
effective remedy before national authorities, **30,** 245, 248, 312, 329; **33,** 380–382
entry of conviction in police record, **30,** 230, 234–237
expulsion of aliens, **23,** 393–395
fair hearing, right to, **28,** 216, 223–226, 227, 237, 244, 247, 248, 250, 261; **30,** 273–274, 275–280, 282, 301–302, 303–306, 314, 315, 316–321, 332, 333, 338
family life, respect for, **23,** 393–395; **24,** 366, 372–374; **28,** 244, 251; **30,** 268–272, 289, 290–291, 292
" final decision " (Art. 26), **25,** 182–184, 211; **28,** 226, 228–232
fines not prohibited, **24,** 385
First Protocol, deprivation of property, **24,** 542–543, 546; **30,** 253–268
—right to education, **28,** 268
forced labour, prohibition, **30,** 341, 342, 345, 347, 348–350
freedom of conscience, **30,** 336
freedom of expression, **30,** 334–337
" friendly settlement ", **33,** 231
ignorance of, relevance, **25,** 182–183, 185
illegitimate child, custody and education, **30,** 268–272
impartial tribunal, right to hearing by, **30,** 297–300, 332, 338
interpretation, plain and natural meaning, **31,** 303
—teleological, **31,** 303
—*travaux préparatoires*, **30,** 252, 266, 279, 305; **31,** 300–302; **33,** 242
judgment pronounced in public, **30,** 323
legal aid, **24,** 364, 368, 371, 374–375; **30,** 249–253, 310, 311, 312, 324–325, 331, 332–333, 347
mitigation of damage, effect of failure, **25,** 229
no exercise of rights to destroy others' rights, **24,** 350–351; **31,** 296–297, 314, 315
non bis in idem, **30,** 249–252
non-discrimination, principle of, **24,** 321, 324, 326, 339; **30,** 245, 247, 248, 267, 294, 296–297, 336
non-retroactivity of penal laws, **24,** 378–379; **25,** 174, 176; **30,** 230, 232–234, 237; **33,** 211, 213
personal security, right to, **30,** 295; **31,** 297–304

Human Rights, European Convention —*continued*
preventive detention, **31**, 305
prisoner's correspondence, censorship, **30**, 287, 289, 291, 323–325, 339–340
private property, right of, **28**, 609, *See also* First Protocol, deprivation of property, *supra*
prompt trial, right to, **30**, 287, 290, 291
proper administration of justice, **30**, 230–237, 292, 323, 332
prosecution after amnesty in another State, **28**, 143–144
public emergency, derogation for, **25**, 227; **31**, 277, 293, 305–312, 313–315
public hearing, right to, **30**, 231, 233, 237–238, 273, 274, 301, 302, 303, 314, 315–316
ratification, need for, **24**, 403, 415–416, 418, 548, 572–577
retroactive creation of offence, **31**, 304
right to life, general principle of law, **32**, 564
signature, need for, **24**, 406, 417–419
sovereign right to control admission of aliens, effect on, **28**, 251
travaux préparatoires, **30**, 252, 266–279, 305; **31**, 300–302; **33**, 242
" victim of a violation " (Art. 25), **24**, 395–401; **28**, 256
vote, right to, **30**, 289–290
witnesses, right to secure attendance, **30**, 314, 315, 321–322, 336, 337–338

Human Rights, European Court of—
amendment of law during proceedings, **33**, 215, 216, 219–223
applicant, position before, **31**, 280, 284–285, 286, 287–289
applicant's observations, presentation to, **31**, 280, 282, 284–285, 288–289, 291–292
competence, *re* Commission's Rules of Procedure, **31**, 285
duty in relation to Convention, **31**, 285–286; **33**, 226, 231
functions, **31**, 306–312; **33**, 205–232
individual, communication from, **33**, 225
interpretation of Convention by, **31**, 285
judge national of respondent State, **33**, 206
nature of proceedings, **31**, 286–287; **33**, 232
opinion on compatibility of legislation, **33**, 228, 230
pleadings, **31**, 279, 282–284, 290–291, 293–294
reference under Arts. 44 and 48...**24**, 425

Human Rights, European Court of— *continued*
request for removal of case from list, **33**, 207, 222, 223, 224–228, 230
submission of case by Commission, **31**, 278, 280

Humanity, crimes against, **13**, 204, 206, 213–214; **14**, 100–102, 272–274, 283–285, 292, 297–298, 302–303; **15**, 491–492, 493–494, 498, 653–655, 656, 663–665; **16**, 356–358, 395–400, 542, 552–553; **17**, 203, 392; **18**, 538–544; **30**, 504, 509
crimes against property, whether, **15**, 671
euthanasia, **15**, 654–655

Hungarian Optants dispute (1925), **22**, 674

Hungary—
Allied subjects, treatment of, **4**, 336
Austria, Convention of Commerce and Transport (1907), **4**, 41
Austro-Hungarian Monarchy, liability for debts of, **4**, 79–82, 443–445
Belgium, Extradition Treaty, **5**, 275
confiscation of assets in, **23**, 10–15
Czechoslovakia, succession to obligations, **9**, 102
foreign exchange regulations, **26**, 489
Hague Convention on Civil Procedure, party to, **1**, 72–73
Italy, Cultural Agreement (1935), **23**, 203–204; **24**, 218
National Government-in-Exile, capacity to sue, **26**, 70–71
Nationalization Decree (1948), **21**, 38–39
nationalization of banks, **26**, 293
occupation of, **1**, 450–452; **2**, 443
—armistice, during, **4**, 566–567
Peace Treaty with (1947), **17**, 319–322, 331–339; **18**, 3, 172–174, 183; **26**, 344
—Hungarian external assets, **32**, 587
—restoration clauses, nationality of claims rule, **30**, 202, 210
—retention of property in satisfaction of claims, **28**, 630
—waiver of claims against Germany, **32**, 160–161
Roumania—
—Claims Convention (1923), **5**, 386
—succession to obligations of, **5**, 61
Russia, termination of war with, **2**, 434
Soviet Government, non-recognition of, **1**, 56–57
Soviet marriages, recognition of, **4**, 36–37
Switzerland, Commercial Agreement (1950), **23**, 197

Hungary—*continued*
U.S.S.R., Agreement on claims to German external assets, **32,** 569
U.S.A., Treaty of Friendship, Commerce and Consular Rights (1925), **20,** 386–389
Hyderabad, India and, **24,** 175
Hydraulic Power, Convention on Development of (1923), **24,** 130

I

Iceland—
taxation of large properties, European Convention of Human Rights and, **30,** 253–268
United States Defence Force in, **23,** 260–264
Ihlen declaration, **6,** 103–105
Illegitimate child, nationality of, Dutch law, **11,** 184–185
Immigrants, prohibited, onus of proof, **18,** 303–308
Immigration—
acquisition of nationality by, **32,** 168–169
administrative orders, judicial review, **32,** 195–198
Argentine law, **6,** 270–271
Australian law, **7,** 299–303
Canadian law, **6,** 291–292; **9,** 383; **20,** 284; **22,** 458–459, 491–497, 511; **23,** 401–403; **24,** 466–467, 469–472; **32,** 247, 249, 252–255, 260–275
Colombian law, **9,** 385
U.S.A., laws of, **1,** 198, 257–258; **4,** 536–537; **6,** 289–290; **15,** 218–220, 265–268, 269–276. *See also* U.S.A., Immigration and Nationality Act
Immobilia obnoxia sunt territorieis, **4,** 148, 175
Immovable property, jurisdictional immunity in respect of, **3,** 325; **4,** 147–149, 164–165, 174–176, 178–179, **10,** 337–352. *See also* Diplomatic premises; *and* Foreign States, property
Immunity from jurisdiction. *See* Diplomatic privileges and immunities; Foreign States, immunity from jurisdiction; Jurisdiction, immunities from
Imperial Russian Government, succession of Soviet Government to, **3,** 172–173; **5,** 72; **26,** 268–269, 267–277; **30,** 117, 151, 158–159, 160–161, 166–168
Implied recognition of governments, **8,** 114–115; **12,** 43–46; **31,** 31
Incest, as extradition crime, **5,** 288
Inchoate title to territory, **4,** 3–5
Inclusio unius est exclusio alterius: see Expressio unius est exclusio alterius
Income tax, **6,** 19–20: *see also* Double taxation; Taxation
business on national ship in foreign waters, **8,** 254–255
consuls, exemption, **11,** 207–211
Income tax conventions (various), **24,** 637
Incommunicacion, Mexican law, **4,** 236–237; **5,** 256
Inconsistency between States' claims and prior acts, **33,** 82–84, 89
Independence of States. *See also* Equality *and* Sovereignty
claims based on prior wrongs, **35,** 436–437
concept of, **6,** 29
foreign intervention, **2,** 158–159
jurisdiction of international tribunals, **2,** 396–397
jurisdictional immunities, **7,** 174–175; *see also* Foreign States, immunity from jurisdiction
reservations of national honour and independence, **24,** 813
respect for, **5,** 8; **6,** 26–32
restrictions not to be presumed, **2,** 102, 329–330; **4,** 155; **5,** 16–17; **31,** 86
significance of, acquisition of territory, **26,** 104–107; **31,** 89
territorial sovereignty and, **4,** 104
India—
aliens, freedom of movement, **31,** 340
Anglo-Tibetan Trade Regulations, 1914..**21,** 272–275
Arbitration (Protocol and Convention) Act, 1937...**27,** 36–38, 40; **34,** 28–31
Bombay Public Trust Act, 1950...**27,** 111–114
Carriage by Air Act, 1947...**20,** 43
Central Provinces States (Administration) Order 1947...**27,** 30
Chandernagore, cession of, **22,** 197–200
citizenship, **20,** 52–57
Citizenship Act (1955), **24,** 56–57, 430; **26,** 372
citizenship provision in Constitution (Arts. 5 and 7), **26,** 364–366
Citizenship Rules (acquisition of foreign nationality), **27,** 246–247
Citizenship Rules, (obtaining foreign passport), **27,** 234–236
civil servants, on independence (1947), **22,** 147–151
Code of Civil Procedure, s. 86 (jurisdictional immunity), **9,** 234; **27,** 110–111
Constitution (1947), **18,** 18–19, 209; **26,** 364–366

India—*continued*
Constitution (1950), **21,** 46, 94, 257; **22,** 67, 68–69, 70, 128, 129, 131, 132, 137, 138, 140, 255, 498–499; **23,** 103; **24,** 56–57, 230, 426–430, 440–441
—Art. 19 (freedom of movement), **27,** 234–235, 245–246
continuity of law after partition, **23,** 112–113; **26,** 100–102; **31,** 22
Defence Order (1947), **24,** 62–63
Dominion of, 1947–1950, sovereign State, **26,** 107
East India Company, successor to Sikh Kingdom, **24,** 76
Essential Supplies Act (1946), **21,** 275
Extradition Act, **20,** 371, 372; **22,** 498–500
Foreign Exchange Regulation Act, **31,** 132–133, 242, 244–246
Foreign States Order (1950), **24,** 429
Foreigners Act (1946), **22,** 498–499; **23,** 374; **24,** 56–57; **27,** 245–247; **31,** 332, 334–335, 337–338
—expulsion provisions, **31,** 340–341
Foreigners Order, 1948...**31,** 332, 334–335, 337–339
France Treaties of Cession (1951, 1956), **21,** 256–257; **22,** 198, 200; **23,** 107; **26,** 114
Fugitive Offenders Act, 1881 (U.K.), application, **19,** 362–365
Hyderabad and, **24,** 175
Income Tax Act, **23,** 112–113
Independence Act, 1947 (U.K.), **17,** 39–41, 96; **18,** 18, 208; **19,** 118, 120, 124, 212, 216, 217; **20,** 6, 43, 54; **21,** 273; **22,** 148–151; **26,** 101, 106; **27,** 43; **34,** 29, 31
independence, effect of, **17,** 37–41, 101
—territorial sovereignty, **31,** 89
—treaties, **31,** 20–22, 60
Indian Extradition Act, 1903...**18,** 209
Indian Independence (International Arrangements) Order, 1947...**27,** 38–40, 41; **31,** 21; **34,** 31, 32–35
Indian Independence (Rights, Property and Liabilities) Order, 1947...**24,** 62–63, 64–68; **19,** 117, 119–126
Instrument of Accession (1947), **18,** 17–20; **20,** 5
Kolhapur State (Application of Laws) Order, 1949...**27,** 32–33
Merger Agreements and Letters of Guarantee (1948), **22,** 69–70, 71, 138–140, 254–257
Naturalization Act, 1852...**22,** 433–434
Orissa Estates Abolition Act, 1952, **24,** 425–426

India—*continued*
Pakistan and, separate States, **17,** 101; **19,** 117–131; **21,** 11–12; **24,** 56
Pakistan as successor State, **15,** 72–75; **19,** 117–131; **21,** 273
partition of, **18,** 207; **19,** 117–131, 212–219; **20,** 3–6, 43–46, 91–92, 145–148; **24,** 62–64, 65–67
Portuguese enclaves, access to, **31,** 23–121 *passim*
Prevention of Corruption Act, 1947, **24,** 83, 85
Preventive Detention Act, 1950...**21,** 272
Punjab, status of, **20,** 91–92
Sea Customs Act, 1878...**24,** 15; **31,** 132, 133, 241, 243, 244–246, 336
States' Merger (Governor's Province) Order, 1949...**27,** 34
status prior to independence, **20,** 41–46, 53
succession to former States of, **23,** 101–105, 109–110; **26,** 81–89, 193–194; **27,** 30–35; **31,** 17–18
territorial waters, breadth, **31,** 244
Union Government, Dominion Government, successor to, **19,** 117–126; **26,** 194
Union of—
—Hyderabad, successor to, **26,** 193–194
—merger of Princely States with, **22,** 138; **23,** 101–105, 109–110; **26,** 81–89; **27,** 30–35; **31,** 17–18
—uncollected tax vested in Dominion, right to, **26,** 100–102
West Bengal, Preventive Detention Act, 1950...**22,** 497–498
Indian Rulers—
classification of, **22,** 67–70
descendants, status of, **22,** 127–130
immunity from jurisdiction, **22,** 67–72, 76, 244–248, 253–256
immunity from taxation, **22,** 64–67, 73–75
status of, **22,** 130, 131–138
succession to obligations of, **10,** 98–102; **23,** 109–110
wives, immunity from taxation, **22,** 73–75
Indian States—
accession to Union, **21,** 51–54, 64–66; **22,** 131
British India, relation to, **7,** 150
cession of territory by, **10,** 98–102
international position of, **10,** 38–48; **17,** 11–17, 95–101; **18,** 17–20, 69–72, 332–333; **19,** 212–219
merger in Union, **22,** 138; **23,** 101–105, 109–110; **26,** 81–89; **27,** 30–35; **31,** 17–18
termination of British protection, **31,** 16–17

Indian tribes in Canada, position of, **27,** 1–13, 239–245
actions against, **27,** 2
nationality, **27,** 239–245
rights in land, **27,** 2–13, 239–245
status in international law, **3,** 237, 238, 246
treaties with British Crown, **27,** 4, 6, 12
Indian tribes in U.S.A.—
treaties with U.S.A., **10,** 1–4, 405–407
Indirect shareholders' claim: *see under* Claims, international
Individual in international law. *See also* Aliens; Expatriation; Extradition; Human rights; Nationality; Naturalization; Statelessness
acquisition of rights, unilateral declaration by State, **22,** 418
claims, settlement of, right to share in proceeds, **18,** 9–10; **22,** 405–407, 418; **26,** 347–351; **30,** 205, 206, 216, 217
claims, State control over, **2,** 180, 191–192, 361–363; **3,** 243–245; **4,** 258–262; **5,** 193–194; **6,** 222–224; **22,** 398–407, 418; **28,** 195–200; **32,** 151–165, 638
de facto subjects, **1,** 202; **4,** 309–312
diplomatic protection, right to, **6,** 242–246; **12,** 183; **22,** 419–421; **25,** 121–122. *See also* Diplomatic protection
enemy character: *q.v.*
international tribunals, before, **1,** 197; **3,** 263; **4,** 291–292; **9,** 58, 338; **13,** 207; **18,** 244, 439; **23,** 669–671; **25,** 523; **32,** 637
minorities treaties, **1,** 17; **2,** 73–74, 221–222, 230–237, 250–251, 287–296; **3,** 311–316; **4,** 352–356; **6,** 37, 260, 322, 359–360; **7,** 497; **8,** 386–392. *See also* Minorities
minorities, treatment apart from treaties, **4,** 355–356
position of, **2,** 219; **3,** 261–262; **4,** 288–290; **5,** 207–213; **6,** 237–247; **7,** 269–272; **8,** 280–281; **9,** 336–413; **12,** 178–183, 215; **14,** 96–102; **15,** 205–206, 419–421; **16,** 118, 348–349, 356–357; **17,** 199–203; **21,** 166–167; **22,** 209, 418, 505–506, 591–597, 611–614, 973–975; **23,** 242–243, 360–363, 459–467, 489–492; **26,** 362–364; **32,** 636. *See also* Human rights *and* Treaties, rights of individuals under
protected persons, *q.v.*
responsibility for violation of rights, **13,** 221; **14,** 197–198, 289–290; **15,** 362, 366–369, 373–374, 376, 379–383, 384–392, 395–397, 419–421; **16,** 344, 348–349; **22,** 208–209. *See also* War crimes
Individual in International Law—*continued*
settlement of claims, right to share: *see under* Claims, international, State control of
treaties, effect on and rights under: *see under* Treaties
violation of territorial sovereignty of foreign State by, **22,** 208–209
war, effect on: *see* Enemy aliens; Enemy character; Trading with the enemy
Indo-China, French protectorates in, **11,** 43, 44–47
Indonesia: *see also* South Moluccas, Republic of
control of foreign estates, legality, **30,** 28–33; **33,** 32–33
Dutch East Indies and, **21,** 63–64
exchange control laws, **30,** 25–28, 32–33, 423–425; **33,** 31–36
measures affecting Dutch property, **26,** 38–39; **28,** 17–19, 21, 25, 34, 36–37; **30,** 28–33, 375–376; **33,** 32–33
nationality of citizens of, **17,** 109–110; **19,** 318–319
Netherlands—
Agreement on Transitional Measures (1949), **20,** 80–89; **24,** 71–72
—Convention on Transfer of Sovereignty (1949), **19,** 132, 318, 337; **24,** 71
—Financial and Economic Agreement (1949), **24,** 71–72; **28,** 17, 37
—Linggadjati Agreement (1947), **17,** 147–149, 151; **19,** 5
—Round Table Conference Agreements (1949), **17,** 109–110, 199–202; **19,** 5, 337; **21,** 77–79; **24,** 88
—succession to, continuity of laws, **17,** 82–91; **19,** 138–139; **20,** 82–89
— —contractual obligations, **24,** 60
— —private rights, effect on, **20,** 81–82; **21,** 63–64; **24,** 73–74
preliminary Constitution, 1950, Art. 95 (non-reviewability of legislation), **28,** 22, 31
Republic of United States of, **17,** 144–152; **19,** 116–117, 132–133, 138–141; **20,** 80–89
—former colony of Indonesia and, **18,** 223–224
South Moluccas, secession of, **17,** 199–202; **19,** 4–6
transitional period pre-independence, **15,** 70
Union Statute as treaty, **18,** 433–434
Industrial Property, Protection of—
Paris Convention (1883), **7,** 435–437; **20,** 602; **22,** 18; **24,** 46, 47–48, 438, 596; **28,** 44, 82, 87

Industrial Property, Protection of—*continued*
Madrid Convention (1891), **22,** 17–18; **26,** 614–616; **28,** 43–44
Washington Convention (1911), **5,** 262; **4,** 413
Hague Convention (1925), **7,** 435–437; **8,** 24; **13,** 1–2; **21,** 260; **26,** 53, 613; **27,** 649; **30,** 42, 43, 45, 52
London Convention (1934), **21,** 258–262; **23,** 134–142; **24,** 46, 47–48, 438, 596; **28,** 82–88, 472–473; **30,** 45, 52, 54–67
registration by infringer of trade mark in foreign State, **23,** 276–284
unfair competition, effect in municipal law, **28,** 471–473
" Industry ", meaning of, **1,** 330–331
Industrial property, international protection of, **34,** 276–278
Infection, doctrine of, **16,** 587
Informe, Colombia, meaning, **2,** 4
Inheritance—
abolition of right of, **11,** 110–111
aliens, right of, **19,** 393–394, 398–399; **20,** 292–296, 386–389; **21,** 203–208; **22,** 475–478; **24,** 482; **26,** 487–489, 585–587, 692, 694–699; **28,** 300–309; **32,** 74–76, 203–223
enemy alien, right to, **5,** 258–260; **11,** 238–242, 251–255; **12,** 222–226; **18,** 499–508; **26,** 675–680
Injunctions, **3,** 411–413
foreign court, preliminary to action before, **11,** 139
restraining non-resident alien from bringing suit, **33,** 173–181
Innocent passage, meaning, **9,** 165; **10,** 177
—right of, **21,** 110; **31,** 132–137
Insanity, plea of, extradition proceedings, **5,** 288
Institute of International Law—
diplomatic protection, discussion of (1931), **22,** 452–453
effect of territorial change on acquired rights, Resolution (1952), **20,** 68
exhaustion of local remedies, Resolution (1956), **25,** 49
extradition, draft convention (1880), **18,** 341
immunities of foreign States, Resolution (1954), **23,** 200
ships and crews in foreign ports, Resolution on, **11,** 167–168
Insults—
governments, to, **9,** 333
heads of State, **8,** 25
States, to, Mexican law, **9,** 334
Insurance companies—
claims against, jurisdictional immunity of assured, **14,** 90
Insurance companies—*continued*
claims by, special nature of, **6,** 216–219
dissolution by Soviet Government, **3,** 57–59
Insurance contracts—
" act of war ", meaning, **26,** 626–638
annulment, State responsibility, **30,** 151–153
effect of war on, **4,** 540
marine, flying boat, whether ship or vessel, **12,** 55–59
neutral property clause, **1,** 230
term " war " in, **10,** 432–435
war risks, exclusion of, **12,** 282–384, 289–300; **32,** 552–556
Insurance policies, territorial limits clause, **34,** 37–41
Insurers—
international claim based on assured's death, **2,** 203–207
relevance of nationality of, protection of nationals, **27,** 558
subrogation to international claim, **26,** 316–319; **27,** 559
Insurgency—
neutrality, application to, **31,** 29, 48
third States, rights of, **31,** 29, 38, 48
U.N. Charter, human rights provisions, **31,** 29–30, 48
Insurgents—
acts of, **5,** 172
blockade by, **9,** 80
closing of ports occupied by, **4,** 531–533
decrees of, territorial scope, **29,** 31–32, 44–47, 52
—principle of effectiveness, **29,** 45–46, 52
recognition of, **5,** 51–52; **7,** 118–119; **9,** 75–78
—*de facto* government as, **9,** 10–67, 75–78, 227–228
—*de jure* government, as, **9,** 73
responsibility for acts of, **4,** 239–245; **5,** 172–173; **7,** 259–261; **9,** 333–334
Insurrection, damage to foreign property in suppression of, **3,** 225
Integrity, territorial, respect for, **5,** 8
Intellectual Co-operation, International Institute of, **18,** 458–465; **22,** 762–767
Agreement with UNESCO (1946), **20,** 533
Staff Regulations, **22,** 766–767
Inter-Allied Accounting Rules for German Property (1947), **20,** 601
Inter-Allied Control Agreement on German Property (1946), **19,** 623, 624

Inter-Allied Declaration against Acts of Dispossession Committed in Territories under Enemy Occupation and Control (1943), **15,** 594–595; **16,** 261, 263–265; **18,** 660, 661, 663, 675; **20,** 27, 28, 29, 31, 406–407, 464, 465–466, 482, 484, 487, 490, 656–661, 663–664; **21,** 59; **23,** 758–759, 771, 827, 848; **24,** 39; **28,** 493; **30,** 2, 504
Inter-Allied Declaration on Restoration of Independence of Austria (1943), **21,** 263; **22,** 100–101, 399–401
Inter-Allied Declaration on Transactions in Gold by Neutrals with Axis Powers (1944), **20,** 464, 465–466
Inter-Allied Railway Committee, authority of decisions of, **6,** 32–33
Inter-Allied Rhineland High Commission, binding force of decrees, **5,** 36; **6,** 35; **7,** 58
legal status, **3,** 50
legislative function, **5,** 77–78
powers, **3,** 9–10
Inter-Allied Supreme Command, France, Agreement with (1944), **18,** 400
Inter-American Conferences—
Maintenance of Peace (Buenos Aires, 1936, Lima, 1938), **23,** 702–703
Systems of Economic and Financial Controls (Washington, 1942), **22,** 916; **23,** 703
Inter-American Economic and Financial Advisory Committee, Resolutions, **23,** 731, 736, 737, 748
Inter-American General Treaty of Arbitration (1929), United States' " understanding ", **27,** 546
Interest—
agreement to compensate *ex gratia*, **6,** 231–232
angary, right of, **1,** 191
award of, **1,** 191–193; **2,** 211–216, 393; **3,** 257–258; **4,** 277–281; **5,** 204; **6,** 231–232, 445–446; **20,** 240–242; **22,** 346–348, 409–417; **23,** 675–676; **30,** 220–225
compound, **1,** 191–192; **2,** 214–215; **4,** 280
conventions authorizing award of, **3,** 257–258
damages, as element of, **2,** 213–214; **3,** 257; **5,** 200; **20,** 241; **22,** 409–417; **23,** 675–676
dies a quo, **1,** 192–193; **2,** 213, 215–216; **4,** 281; **6,** 446; **7,** 101; **26,** 358–359
dies ad quem, **2,** 214–216; **3,** 258
personal tort claims, **30,** 539 n.
rate of, **2,** 213–215, 393; **4,** 280–281; **6,** 446; **20,** 241–242
—interlocutory judgments, **4,** 479
Interest—*continued*
remoteness of damage, **6,** 446
war damage claims, **30,** 220–225
Interest rei publicae ut sit finis litium, **33,** 77
Intergovernmental agreements, **1,** 313–315; **7,** 406–409; **8,** 37–38
Inter-Governmental Maritime Consultative Organization
Assembly, **30,** 427, 429, 431, 440, 441, 443, 444, 445, 446, 447
Convention, entry into force, **30,** 440
Council, **30,** 427, 440
establishment, draft conventions, **30,** 434–438
expenses, apportionment of, **30,** 441
Maritime Safety Committee, composition, **30,** 427–447
Maritime Safety Committee, constitution, interpretation, **30,** 426–447
—functions, **30,** 427, 443
Interim measures of protection: *see under* names of particular tribunals
Interlocutory decisions, whether *res judicata*, **3,** 410–413; **4,** 479
International Bank for Reconstruction and Development—
Charter, **22,** 705–707, 710–711
communications of, " treatment " of, **22,** 705–712
President as conciliator, **29,** 11, 16
International canals: *see* Canals, international
International carriage by air, meaning: *see* Carriage by air
International Civil Aviation Convention (1944), **19,** 86, 110, 372; **20,** 154; **24,** 9–10, 54–55, 597; **33,** 410–414
International Civil Aviation Organization, **24,** 10
Council, powers *re* personnel, **34,** 421–422
International Civil Law, Treaty of Montevideo (1889), **6,** 110
International claims: *see* Claims, international
" International claims ", meaning, **3,** 235–237
International comity: *see* Comity
International control of revenue, **3,** 208–209
International conventions: *see* Treaties
International Court of Justice—
abuse of rights and, **24,** 821, 836. *See also* Abuse of right
acceptance of jurisdiction, **19,** 508–509, 522; **20,** 568, 573–576; **21,** 399–415; **24,** 782–878 *passim*; **27,** 574; **33,** 418–443
—" automatic " reservation, **24,** 800–803; **27,** 509–512, 523–525, 534–535, 537–542, 547–549, 550–552

International Court of Justice—*contd.*
acceptance of jurisdiction—*continued*
—contractual and consensual aspect, **24,** 853–856
—defect, whether nullifying consent, **33,** 433
—domestic jurisdiction reservation, **24,** 782–878 *passim*; **27,** 509–512, 523–525, 534–535, 540–544, 547–549, 551–552, 554–555; **31,** 33, 34, 39, 40–41
—form, **33,** 430–431, 440
—Germany, by, **23,** 771
—notification to Secretary-General, **24,** 845–847
—reciprocity, effect of, **24,** 785–790, 820; **27,** 487
—reservations, compatibility with Statute of Court, **24,** 782–878 *passim*; **27,** 509–512, 523–525, 534–535, 540–544, 547–549, 551–552
—reservations, future, as to, **24,** 842–845
—reservations *ratione temporis,* **19,** 507–514, 521–525, 538–539, 543–544; **24,** 858–852; **27,** 484–487, 495–503, 505–508, 512–522, 558, 560; **31,** 33–34, 35, 39–40, 41–44, 71–72, 103–104
—reservations, reciprocity, as to, **24,** 844, 845–847, 784
—retroactive effect, **31,** 43
—severability of Declarations, **24,** 809–811; **27,** 510–512, 524–525, 533, 535, 540, 551
—Switzerland, by, **27,** 483
—termination of, **24,** 844
—U.S.A., by, **27,** 482, 484, 486, 495, 500, 505, 508–512, 523–524, 533, 536, 540, 543, 547, 554
—withdrawal of certain categories of disputes, **24,** 842
access to, submission of dispute to other tribunals, **30,** 519, 522
admissibility, questions of, **35,** 374, 417, 418, 419–420, 435–436
advisory jurisdiction, **17,** 327; **18,** 366; **22,** 873; **23,** 574, 682–683; **34,** 284–285, 348, 358, 394; **35,** 365–366, 466
—request by G.A., relevance, **34,** 286, 308, 332–333, 344–347, 351, 356, 382–383, 396
advisory opinions, **15,** 337–339, 345–346, 349–355
—appeal from I.L.O. Administrative Tribunal, **23,** 517–537, 540, 543, 551, 572–573, 578–580
—binding force, **23,** 522, 538, 540, 573, 577

International Court of Justice—*contd.*
advisory opinions—*continued*
—competence to request, **18,** 366–367
—duty as to, **23,** 47–48
—General Assembly and, **18,** 470
—judicial function, **30,** 426–427
—domestic jurisdiction and, **17,** 333–334
—nature of, **17,** 335
—non-participation of interested party, **17,** 334–336
—political character of request, **17,** 327–328
—procedure, **34,** 283–284, 382
aliens, equality of treatment and, **24,** 796
appellate tribunal, as, **30,** 474
application, nature of claim and grounds, **35,** 363–364, 376, 468
application, right of, **35,** 364
basis for decision, *jura novit curia,* **27,** 575
burden of proof, **16,** 343; **25,** 274
compensation, measure of, experts' report, **16,** 342–343
conclusions of Parties, whether exclusive, **25,** 266
contentious jurisdiction, **17,** 339–342; **19,** 501–549; **20,** 567–576; **23,** 574–578, 682; **24,** 782–878 *passim;* **27,** 475–608 *passim;* **33,** 418–443
decision on point not before Court, **21,** 408–409
decisions, binding force, on other courts, **21,** 136–137, 415
decisions binding only on parties, **33,** 426
Declaration under Optional Clause of Statute
—interpretation of, **19,** 510–514, 536–540, 542–544; **33,** 431–432
—legal character, **27,** 540, 543, 550
—most-favoured-nation clause and, **19,** 514–517, 537–539
—operation of, **19,** 514–517
—ratification of, **19,** 509–510, 522, 543; **24,** 784
—renewal, **33,** 418–443
—secondary acts, as, **27,** 533–534
—severability, **24,** 809–811; **27,** 510–512, 524–525, 533, 535, 540, 551
—unlimited and fixed term, **27,** 572, 574–575
declaratory judgment, **27,** 484; **31,** 74–75, 76; **35,** 372, 390–392, 445, 451–452, 465–467, 482–484
disqualification of judge, **28,** 558–559
doctrinal function, **25,** 275
establishment of, **27,** 577
evidence—
—circumstantial, **16,** 157
—incomplete facts, **25,** 306–307

International Court of Justice—*contd.*
evidence—*continued*
—procedure as to, **20,** 577
—production, onus on Parties, **25,** 274; **27,** 96
ex-enemy States, temporary exclusion from access to, **27,** 595–596
execution of judgments, **18,** 470
exhaustion of local remedies, **24,** 784, 797; **27,** 490–492, 494, 503–504, 525, 526, 529–533, 539, 553–554, 555–556, 560
—burden of proof as to, **24,** 797–800
expert inquiries, **16,** 341, 342; **33,** 97–98, 116
forum prorogatum, **15,** 349–353; **19,** 520–521, 549; **21,** 405; **27,** 549
functions, **18,** 105–106
interim measures of protection, **19,** 501–507, 521; **24,** 870–878
intervention procedure, **18,** 470
—application to tribunal for individuals, **28,** 588
interpretation of judgments, **17,** 339–342; **35,** 422
Judges, eligibility for re-election, **16,** 335
Judges, privileges and immunities, **32,** 321
judgment—
—boundary dispute, execution of, **30,** 76–89
—by default, **16,** 341–342
—grounds, freedom to select, **25,** 247, 266
—interpretation of, **17,** 339–342
—*res judicata,* **35,** 443, 444–445, 466–467, 484
judicial function—
—advisory opinions, **30,** 426–427
—inherent limitation on, **35,** 365, 369, 373, 375, 392, 417–422, 473–474, 479
—precision required for determination of legal rights, **31,** 49
—difficulties in exercise of legal rights, relevance, **31,** 49
jurisdiction—
—acceptance of: *see* acceptance of jurisdiction, *supra*
—compensation, to assess, **16,** 167–170
—competence to determine, **20,** 567, 571–573; **27,** 534
—compulsory, discussions on establishment of I.C.J., **27,** 578–579
—consensual basis, **27,** 549, 576, 586, 596–597, 600; **31,** 30, 73, 74
—" dispute ", meaning, **35,** 363, 377, 378–379, 381, 409, 420, 422–424, 438, 461–463
—dissolution of P.C.I.J., effect, **27,** 582

International Court of Justice—*contd.*
jurisdiction—*continued*
—divesting after Application, **20,** 573–576; **24,** 843
—incidental, **35,** 419
—" moot " case, **35,** 415–417
—nature of, **35,** 365, 369
—objections to, **15,** 349–355; **19,** 416–454, 507–549; **20,** 567–576; **21,** 399–415; **24,** 782–840, 841–870; **27,** 475–556, 557–608; **33,** 418–443; **35,** 374
—objections to, domestic jurisdiction, **27,** 487–490, 509–512, 526, 536
—objections to, exhaustion of local remedies, **27,** 490–492, 494, 503–504, 525, 526, 529–533, 539, 553–554, 555–556, 560
—objections to, objection to admissibility, distinguished, **27,** 487, 525, 529, 555
—objections to, *ratione temporis,* **27,** 484–487, 495–503, 505–508, 512–522, 558, 560
—objection to, whether abandonment may be presumed, **24,** 789
—preliminary question, **35,** 353, 373, 376, 418–419, 426 n.
—questions settled by arbitration, Pact of Bogotá, **30,** 491
—raising of issue of, **21,** 401–404, 410
—reasonableness, test of, **27,** 600
—third States interested in dispute, **31,** 31, 48
—treaty, based on, **19,** 416–454, 514–520, 525–527, 532–535, 537–540, 544–548; **20,** 547–565
—Treaty of Peace with Japan, **30,** 519, 522
—voluntary submission, **15,** 349–355
Mandates, jurisdiction under, **17,** 55
municipal law, examination of, **25,** 268, 273–274
nature of, **19,** 529
oral proceedings, **23,** 545
parties before, **23,** 541–542, 573, 575
Permanent Court of International Justice and, **17,** 48, 55, 342; **18,** 106; **27,** 577–578, 584, 587; **33,** 418–443
pleadings, Court limited to Parties' submissions, **31,** 76
—relevance of Applicant's submissions, **31,** 44, 76
preliminary objections, **35,** 374
—joinder to merits, **24,** 784, 841–842, 849–852, 860; **27,** 532–533, 549, 555
priority of claims, **21,** 410–415
reparation, failure to claim, **35,** 415–417, 430, 442, 445, 452, 465
right of transit as cause of action, **24,** 850

International Court of Justice—*contd.*
Rules of—
—Art. 32...**21,** 409–410; **27,** 493
—Art. 41...**24,** 873–877
—Arts. 41 and 47...**19,** 429, 501, 508
—Art. 48...**22,** 366, 367, 389
—Art. 61...**19,** 502, 504, 508; **24,** 871–878 *passim*
—Art. 62...**19,** 427, 429, 540; **21,** 403; **24,** 871–878 *passim*
—Art. 66...**18,** 356, 357
—Art. 69...**21,** 404
—Arts. 82 and 83...**23,** 577
seising of, consequences, **35,** 365, 419, 478–479
State not party to proceedings, and, **21,** 399, 401, 404–408
Statute: *see also* the Table of Treaties
—application of, test of reasonableness, **27,** 597–598, 599
—Art. 36 (5), **27,** 558–608 *passim*; **35** 446
—Art. 38, application to concessions, **27,** 143, 162, 169
—Art. 38 (general principles of law), **16,** 280, 554; **18,** 106–107; **20,** 547
—derogation from, **27,** 534–535
—general application of, **27,** 589–594, 596
—inconsistency of "automatic" reservation with, **27,** 542
—interpretation of, **27,** 573–574
—preservation of declarations made under Statute of P.C.I.J., **27,** 561–608 *passim;* **33,** 424–427
—relation to Declarations under Art. 36...**27,** 533–534, 540
subject-matter of dispute undetermined, **24,** 848–849
treaties, duties as to, **19,** 535–536
treaty, finding of abrogation, Contracting Party not represented, **19,** 296
International courts: *see* International tribunals. *See also* names of particular tribunals
International criminal law, general rules as to extradition, **6,** 309
International government, territories under, **9,** 52–58
International Labour Conventions—
application of, **7,** 466–470
Canada, obligations under, **6,** 46
Draft, adoption of, **8,** 42
Employment of Women during the Night (1919), **6,** 410–413
enforcement of, **3,** 393–394; **7,** 466–470
execution of, **6,** 347–348; **9,** 472–474
federal States and, **8,** 41–48
interpretation of, **6,** 348, 410–413
Liability of Shipowners (1939), **16,** 10
International Labour Conventions—*continued*
municipal legislation, need for, **9,** 474–475
obligation to make effective, **35,** 328–329, 331, 347
Reciprocity in regard to Workmen's Compensation (1925), **6,** 347–349
Unemployment Indemnity in case of Loss or Foundering at Sea (1920), **5,** 344
Workmen's Compensation for Accidents (1925), **6,** 347–349; **7,** 468–470
Workmen's Compensation in Agriculture (1921), **9,** 472–474
International Labour Organization—
Commission of Inquiry, non-compliance with Convention, **35,** 285–351 *passim*
—judicial function, **35,** 292, 324
—*prima facie* case, **35,** 325, 326
—procedure, **35,** 293–297, 302–307
—recommendations, **35,** 323, 328, 335, 336, 337, 338, 339, 342, 344, 346–347, 350–351
—reports *re* recommendations, **35,** 349, 350–351
—visits to *locus*, **35,** 296, 307–312, 326, 336, 337, 338, 340
—witnesses, **35,** 295–296, 299–305, 326
competence, **1,** 328–330, 338, 342, 357–361; **3,** 363, 390–393
Conventions, obligation to make effective, **35,** 328–329, 331, 347
Danzig, membership, **5,** 36, 410
membership, **5,** 410–413
objects, **1,** 358–360
officials, contracts and conditions of service: *see under* International officials
officials, immunities, **5,** 314–318
—waiver, **5,** 315–318; **10,** 376
restrictive interpretation of Constitution, **3,** 363
Staff Regulations, **18,** 465–466; **20,** 523–531 *passim;* **21,** 348; **22,** 795; **24,** 749, 751, 754–756, 757–759; **27,** 447, 449–450; **31,** 481–482
—amendment, **24,** 756
workers' delegates, designation of, **1,** 361–363
International Labour Organization, Administrative Tribunal—
appeal against awards of, **23,** 517–537, 551, 572, 578–581
applicable law, **24,** 751
change in title of officials, **24,** 757–760
competence, **18,** 457, 460; **23,** 518–519, 521, 535, 545–547, 565–571; **32,** 478, 513–515, 519–526
—interim injunctions, **32,** 518–519
—*ratione materiae*, **32,** 487–488

International Labour Organization, Administrative Tribunal—*contd.*
competence—*continued*
—*ratione personae*, **32**, 488–489, 529–531
—receivability, to investigate *proprio motu*, **32**, 499, 500
— technical assistance staff, as to, **24**, 750
costs, intervenors, **32**, 540
judgments, *res judicata*, **27**, 295–298
—oral proceedings, need for, **27**, 450
—time limit for appeals to, **27**, 445–446
nature of, **23**, 534, 545–547
provisional measures, **32**, 519
Staff Association, intervention by, **32**, 533, 535–536
Statute and Rules, **20**, 525–529; **21**, 355; **22**, 778, 779, 783, 784, 792; **23**, 518–519, 522–581 *passim*; **24**, 751; **27**, 296–298, 445–446, 471–472; **32**, 475–476, 485, 486, 488, 489, 492, 494–495, 498, 519, 530, 534
International law—
acts of foreign governments contrary to, recognition of, **15**, 24–27; **20**, 309–312, 323–328; **22**, 39–42; **28**, 14, 16, 18–20, 22, 24–39; **30**, 28–33; **32**, 9; **33**, 30–36; **34**, 12–16; **35**, 13, 25, 33–35, 37–43, 45–48. *See also* Act of State doctrine
arbitration, application in, **22**, 820, 824–825. *See also* Arbitration
binding force, **1**, 3; **3**, 3; **4**, 3–5, 178–179; **20**, 312; **22**, 1
cantonal law of Switzerland and, **15**, 4–5
Claims Commissions, application by, **26**, 270
codification, questionnaire, **5**, 423
comity and, **4**, 19–21; **5**, 6–7; **18**, 15–16. *See also* Comity
Constitutions of States and, **4**, 1–13; **7**, 9–10; **22**, 914. *See also* particular States
customary: *see* Customary international law
development of, **7**, 128–133, 218–221; **16**, 345
—State practice, **26**, 169–170
effectiveness, concept of, **2**, 36–37; **4**, 4, 103–107, 108–110, 111–112, 114–115, 492–493; **5**, 13–15, 25–27, 183; **6**, 107–108, 225; **7**, 117–120; **31**, 80. *See also* Treaties, interpretation of
E.C.S.C. Treaty and, **29**, 159–160
enforcement of, **14**, 283
—when contrary to municipal law, **6**, 158–159
evidence of, **12**, 129–132; **34**, 60 n.
International law—*continued*
evolution of: *see* " new international law ", *infra*
evolution of, effect upon acquired rights, **4**, 3–5
—limitation of occupant's rights, **20**, 465
extent of, **1**, 3; **3**, 3; **4**, 5
fraud, concept of, **25**, 102, 109. *See also* Fraud
general conventions, evidence of, **34**, 60 n.
general maritime law, **16**, 10
general principles of, **6**, 67–68; **18**, 12–13, 106–107, 315–317, 336–345; **24**, 4, 132, 210, 283. *See also* General principles of law
—acquiescence, *q.v.*
—arbitral procedure, time-limits, **29**, 297–300. *See also* under Arbitration
—equity, *q.v.*
—expulsion, concerning, **32**, 256
—extradition, concerning, **32**, 287
—general principles of law, application to concessions, **18**, 149; **27**, 143, 162, 169
— obligation not to allow territory to be used for acts contrary to rights of other States, **9**, 317–318; **16**, 158
—right of access to enclosures, **31**, 56, 70, 116
—treaties, interpretation of, *q.v.*
—unity of river basin, principle of, **24**, 125
" general rules of ", **6**, 281
—whether treaties included in, **22**, 608–611
inter-temporal, **4**, 3–5; **20**, 101. *See also* Treaties, interpretation of
jus cogens, **31**, 115
justice as part of, **15**, 633–634
lack of conflict rules, **5**, 468; **27**, 156, 162
means of creating, **4**, 8
members of federal States, application to, **4**, 130
morality and, **35**, 14
municipal decisions as evidence of, **4**, 6–7; **18**, 665
municipal decisions contrary to, **5**, 157
municipal law, relation to, **1**, 4–8, 124–129; **2**, 3–5, 425; **3**, 5–10; **4**, 9–21, 333; **5**, 4–6; **6**, 3–15, 158–159, 443–444; **7**, 3–15, 411–412; **8**, 7–12; **9**, 1–7, 56, 252, 259; **10**, 1–5, 338–339, 347–350; **11**, 1–12, 187–192, 278; **12**, 1–2, 97–101, 124–141, 221, 241; **13**, 1–5, 26–27, 55–56, 164, 178–186, 193, 232–233, 262–267, 279, 315, 337, 341–342, 347–348, 372; **14**, 1–5, 29–32, 39,

International law—*continued*
municipal law, relation to—*continued*
96–97, 100, 151, 156, 158–162, 244, 249, 286–287, 295; **15**, 1–6, 169, 324–325, 327, 328–330, 485–490, 555–557; **16**, 3–11, 262–263, 281–285, 461; **17**, 1–22, 72–81, 393–397, 420; **18**, 3–14, 475–477, 595, 688; **19**, 1–3, 229–254, 337–340, 342–344; **20**, 1–2, 244, 246, 317, 323–324; **21**, 1–9, 256–275; **22**, 5–11, 64–67, 73–75, 253–256, 424–427, 608–611, 884–885, 914, 991; **23**, 1–5, 195–201, 284–295, 710; **24**, 5–15, 423, 425–428, 432, 661, 868; **25**, 98, 108–109, 126–127, 279, 299; **26**, 1–5, 270, 483, 487; **27**, 13–18, 491; **28**, 2–10, 467, 470; **29**, 375, 392; **30**, 1–3; **31**, 1–8, 262; **32**, 1–7; **33**, 1–15; **34**, 1–6; **35**, 6, 14, 24, 45. *See also under* Treaties
—cantonal law, Switzerland, **15**, 4–5
—construction of legislation, **6**, 443–444; **7**, 7; **8**, 11; **16**, 8–9; **34**, 62
—general maritime law, **16**, 9–10
—Germany, Constitution (1919), **4**, 11–13; **6**, 327–328
—Germany, Basic Law (1949), **18**, 575; **20**, 371; **21**, 175–176; **22**, 608, 610; **23**, 379; **28**, 22, 31, 321, 372, 387, 393, 545
—German, Restitution Law, **28**, 384, 387
—Iceland, law of, **30**, 263, 264
—inconsistent legislation, **1**, 7; **4**, 333, 474–475; **6**, 157–159; **12**, 208–218; **18**, 10–11; **24**, 661; **27**, 17–18; **28**, 467, 470; **31**, 246–247
—Ireland (Republic), Constitution, **12**, 97–98
—Japan, Imperial Constitution, **32**, 635
—judgment contrary to, **1**, 124–129
—legislative power, extent of, **27**, 17–18. *See also* Extraterritorial effect of legislation
—Mandates, **14**, 29–32
—Mexico, Constitution (1857), **4**, 9–11
—municipal law as fact, **3**, 5–6; **25**, 121
—nationality questions, **25**, 102, 108–109, 126; **32**, 166–168
—permissive rules of international law, **14**, 196–201
—Philippines Constitution, **13**, 372
—presumption of consistency with international law, **6**, 443–444; **7**, 7; **12**, 221; **13**, 26–27; **30**, 204–206, 216, 217
—Tangier, Statute, **9**, 52–58

International law—*continued*
municipal law, relation to—*continued*
—torts in violation of international law, **32**, 1–4; **34**, 1–6
nature of, **1**, 3; **4**, 3–5; **12**, 217–218; **16**, 345; **17**, 389; **22**, 1; **34**, 3–6
"new international law", **18**, 107–110, 388–392; **19**, 528–532; **21**, 324–331
—application of, to baselines, **18**, 108–110
— —Charter of the U.N., **21**, 326–331
— —compulsory jurisdiction of the I.C.J., **19**, 528–532
— —multilateral conventions, **18**, 389–392
— —powers of General Assembly of the U.N., **21**, 327–331
—characteristics of, **18**, 107–108; **21**, 326
novelty of action in, **2**, 417
offense against, **15**, 486–487; **32**, 3–4. *See also* War crimes
private and public, **19**, 229–254
private law concepts and, **31**, 84; **33**, 430
prize courts and, **16**, 569–572
reason and, **31**, 70
requirements of form, **2**, 313
sources, **1**, 3, 4; **2**, 3, 164, 367–368; **3**, 4–5; **4**, 5–9; **5**, 3–4; **7**, 214; **8**, 1–2, 450–451; **13**, 97–107, 341; **17**, 1; **18**, 1; **19**, 1; **21**, 1; **22**, 1, 536, 560; **23**, 710; **25**, 1, 77–79, 81, 253–254, 269, 278, 529, 545; **28**, 1, 172, 55, 557; **29**, 1, 476
—analogy, **2**, 99, 164; **4**, 105, 280, 466–467; **5**, 175–177; **23**, 55, 628–630
—*communis opinio doctorum*, **2**, 368; **17**, 163
—custom and usage, **2**, 368; **4**, 8, 115; **19**, 275–276, 292–294; **23**, 710–712, 868; **31**, 25, 36, 52, 61, 62, 65–68, 82, 90, 96, 97, 105–106, 108, 115; *see also* Customary international law
—decisions of international tribunals, **18**, 385, 388
—draft codes, Rules of Air Warfare, **32**, 631
—equity, *q.v.*
—foreign decisions *in pari materia*, **4**, 414
—general principles of law, **2**, 368; **5**, 3–4; **6**, 81; **8**, 450–451; **18**, 106–107, 370; **23**, 52, 55–56, 569; **24**, 130, 804, 859, 868; **25**, 269, 278, 529, 545; **28**, 555, 557; **31**, 1, 25–26, 36, 56, 70, 82, 85, 86, 116, 118; **33**, 1, 75–84, 91, 136–137, 145–146; **35**, 173. *See also* General principles of law

International law—*continued*
sources—*continued*
—international standards: *q.v.*
—juridical conscience of peoples, *see* "new international law", *supra*
—law and practice of the U.N., **18,** 385, 390
—municipal decisions, **3,** 18; **4,** 6–7, 105; **9,** 318; **22,** 836
—municipal legislation **3,** 5–6; **4,** 156–157, 280; **22,** 836
—natural law, **3,** 5–4. *See also* Natural law
—principles of private international law, **5,** 128; **25,** 77–78
—State practice, **3,** 5; **10,** 369; **22,** 836; **24,** 855–856. *See also* Customary international law
—treaties, **4,** 6–7; **16,** 1–3; **22,** 560, 836; **29,** 476
—writings of publicists, **3,** 4; **4,** 6–7; **18,** 385
statute of limitation, absence of, **24,** 540
subjects of, **4,** 9; **8,** 2–7, 280–281; **13,** 221–222; **15,** 419; **16,** 321; **17,** 1; **18,** 1–3; **21,** 1; **22,** 1–5; **24,** 1–4; **27,**1–13: *see also* Individuals; Protected States *and* Protectorates
—effect of non-recognition, **28,** 87
—Indian tribes in Canada, **27,** 1–13
tacit reference to, **4,** 426–427
taxation and, **6,** 281
Vereinbarung, creation of by, **4,** 8
"International law and equity", **3,** 397
International Law Commission, draft code on diplomatic intercourse, **28,** 380, 407–409
—on territorial sea (1956), **28,** 172
International Law Commission, Reports on—
Continental Shelf, **18,** 156, 157
High Seas, **18,** 158
Treaties (1953), **24,** 807
International leases: *see* Leases, international
International maritime law, **16,** 9-10; **20,** 197–210
International Military Tribunals: *see under* War crimes
International Monetary Fund—
Articles of Agreement, **16,** 29, 34–35; **22,** 705–707, 713–737; **23,** 581–584, 753; **28,** 539–543; **30,** 26–28, 423–425; **32,** 204, 208, 371–376; **33,** 35
—"exchange contract", meaning, **32,** 372–373
—exchange regulations, private international law aspects, **22,** 715–717, 721–722
—exchange regulations, right of non-resident aliens to inherit, **32,** 204, 208
International Monetary Fund—*continued*
Articles of Agreement—*continued*
—interpretation of, **22,** 706, 710–711, 718–719, 727–730
—gold transactions, **22,** 734–737
—superseded by bilateral agreement, **33,** 35
communications of, "treatment" of, **22,** 705–712
membership, **22,** 720, 721–722, 726, 729, 730
—effect of, **22,** 715–717, 718–719, 721–722
—withdrawal, **22,** 719–720
President as conciliator, **29,** 5
International obligations, lapse, change of circumstances, **31,** 38. *See also under* Treaties
International officials: *see also under* European Coal and Steel Community; European Economic Community; I.L.O. Administrative Tribunal; League of Nations; O.E.E.C. Appeals Board; United Nations, *and* U.N. Administrative Tribunal
acquired rights and, **13,** 199–202; **20,** 506–509; **21,** 376; **24,** 753–756; **29,** 257; **32,** 517–518, 532, 537–540
acquired rights, amendment of Service Code, **34,** 424
—amendment of Staff Regulations, **34,** 462, 465
administrative decisions, withdrawal of, **31,** 472–474, 483–486
advisory administrative bodies, duty to give opinion, **32,** 495
allowances, head of household, **31,** 403–486
appeals by—
—admissibility of evidence, **27,** 465 n., 472 n.
—award of administrative tribunal, from, **23,** 517–537, 551, 572, 578–581
—costs, **27,** 464, 465
—exhaustion of administrative remedies, **32,** 485, 494–495, 535
—form, **32,** 497–498
—intervenors, **27,** 466 n., 471–472
—legal representation, **32,** 458, 462
—time-limits, **22,** 767, 793–797; **27,** 445–446, 458–461; **31,** 452–455, 456–458; **32,** 458, 461, 472, 473, 474–476, 482–483, 486–487, 490, 492, 493–498
appearance before national court, **21,** 349–353, 379
briefing on conditions at duty station, **32,** 469
casual employees, claims by, **32,** 529–531

International officials—*continued*
classification and grading, **27,** 451–453; **29,** 252, 254–257, 260, 262, 270–272; **32,** 440–456, 468, 469, 480–483, 499–503
communication of information by State, **21,** 356–360, 379
communication with authorities outside organization, **32,** 508–512
compensation for wrongful dismissal, tax on, **23,** 625–627
competence, **24,** 723–728
competition for posts, failure to appoint, **32,** 473
conditions of service, contractual or statutory, **34,** 462–463
—municipal law and, **23,** 613–615
—unilateral amendment, **31,** 467–470; **32,** 515–518, 531–540; **34,** 415–427, 446, 461–466
conduct damaging to repute of organization, **21,** 349–355
contracts of service, **18,** 450–469; **21,** 314, 320, 328; **23,** 628–631; **29,** 226, 231, 239; **31,** 429–486 *passim*
—frustration of, **18,** 463–465, 467
—interpretation, **23,** 628–631
—novation of, **34,** 440, 447, 459
—probation period, **18,** 465–466, 468–469; **34,** 467, 469–470
—proper law, **31,** 446–450; **34,** 457–458
—public law nature, **29,** 226, 229–231, 239
—termination, **18,** 450–456, 465–467; **19,** 491–494; **23,** 628–631; **24,** 778–741; **31,** 429–433, 436–439, 450–452, 458–462, 470–472, 474–479. *See also* fixed term appointments *and* termination, *infra*
— —damages, **19,** 492–494; **23,** 268–631; **24,** 728–735, 740–741; **31,** 429–431, 447, 450, 460–462
— —*détournement de pouvoir,* **31,** 474–479
— —*détournement de procédure,* **31,** 432–433, 470–472
— —procedural irregularities, **31,** 450–452
— —procedural requirements, **31,** 474–477
— —reappointment as auxiliary, **31,** 436–437
— —reorganization of departments, **31,** 432–433
—types of, **31,** 437–439
—voidable, **34,** 450, 456
copyright in work done for organization, **32,** 526–528
damage to personal effects, compensation for, **32,** 471
damages for non-material injury, **29,** 234, 237, 239, 241, 269

International officials—*continued*
death benefits, **31,** 472–474
disability pension, **34,** 429
disciplinary proceedings—
—access to documents, **27,** 435–438, 440–444
—due process requirement, **27,** 432–445 *passim*
—equity and justice, requirements of, **27,** 441
—publicity by Organization, effect upon due process, **27,** 438–439
—representation by counsel, **27,** 435, 438, 439–440
disloyalty to State during war, **22,** 784–793
dismissal, **18,** 460–463; **20,** 493–533; **21,** 372–379; **29,** 224–242, 243–250; **32,** 491–493, 509–512, 541–544; **34,** 467–473. *See also* termination, wrongful, *infra*
—Administrative Tribunal, competence, **20,** 523–531
—applicable law, **20,** 523–531
—claim for compensation for, **32,** 541–544
—compensation for, **34,** 472–473
— —tax on, **23,** 625, 627
—damages against home Government, **20,** 531–533
—damages against organization, **20,** 499–501; **29,** 229, 235, 237–238, 241–242
—due process, requirement, **32,** 510–512
—equity, compensation on basis of, **34,** 460, 466
—equity, rules of, **20,** 530
—illegal, **34,** 467–473
—length of notice, **29,** 234–235, 242
—misconduct, **27,** 437; **32,** 491–493, 509–512
—refusal to reply to questions, **21,** 372–379
—requirement of reasons for, **29,** 233, 241
—subversive activities, for, **20,** 493–518
—summary, grounds for, **32,** 508–512
dual nationals, master nationality, **22,** 809–819; **32,** 513–515
equality between officials in same position, **32,** 528
establishment allowance, **34,** 472
European Communities, position prior to Statute of Service, **32,** 541–544
failure to reclassify, compensation for, **32,** 445–446, 455–456
family allowances, **32,** 539–540
fixed term appointment—
—expiry, **27,** 461–471

International officials—*continued*
fixed term appointment—*continued*
—expiry, due process, **27**, 461, 464, 466, 469–471
—non-renewal, **18**, 454–456; **19**, 494–499; **21**, 361–362; **22**, 768–784; **23**, 517–521, 525–534; **24**, 742–747; **32**, 471–474, 476–480, 519–526
—non-renewal, health grounds, **34**, 452–457
—non-renewal, misuse of power, **22**, 777, 778–782; **32**, 472
good faith, requirement of, **32**, 543
immunities, **3**, 325–326; **5**, 314–318; **22**, 537; **32**, 308–334
—espionage, charge of, **32**, 308–333; **34**, 151–153
—taxation, **5**, 314–315; **23**, 616, 621, 625–627; **29**, 56–73; **31**, 393–395
—waiver, **23**, 616–625
indemnity payable to, depreciation of currency, **22**, 762–767
independence of, **22**, 798–809
integrity of, **22**, 784–793
interests of organization, relevance, **22**, 768–784, 798–809
League of Nations, immunities of, **3**, 325–326
—rights against League, **13**, 199–202
—relationship with, **10**, 416–418
—Staff regulations, **6**, 406–409
leave, home and annual, **31**, 452–455
leave, home, determination of place of, **27**, 428–432
leave, maternity, **32**, 483–485
leave, refusal of, **27**, 447–450
locally recruited, criteria, **32**, 489–491
money paid to by mistake, recovery, **31**, 483–486; **32**, 467, 468, 469–470
non-resident allowances, **23**, 609–613; **32**, 515–518
pensions fund, **10**, 416–418; **18**, 456–457, 467–468; **32**, 537–538
—participation in, **34**, 436–450
privileges and immunities: *see* immunities, *supra*
probation, need for reasonable period, **23**, 627–628
probationary appointment, termination, **21**, 356–360; **27**, 418–422, 422–427; **32**, 505–508
probationary period, termination, **27**, 418–422
reassignment of, **22**, 793–797
reclassification of, review by Administrative Tribunal, **27**, 451–453
refusal of appointment, effect of procedural irregularities, **27**, 470
repatriation, payment during voyage, **32**, 503–505

International officials—*continued*
representation by counsel, **22**, 793–797
residence allowance, **31**, 439–446
resignation, claim for compensation, **32**, 541–544
retirement, age of, **21**, 348
salary, delay in payment, **32**, 470
salary *en disponibilité*, **18**, 458–460
salary increases, **31**, 479–482
salary scales, **32**, 499–503
Staff Association officials, freedom of action, **32**, 473
Staff Rules and Regulations, relation between, **31**, 439–444, 467–469
Staff Rules, commentary on, **31**, 452–455, 474–477
—express exclusion of application, **31**, 446–450
—statutory and contractual provisions, **32**, 536
—subsidiary rules not in comformity with, **27**, 454–457
status of, **5**, 314–318; **6**, 33–34, 406–410; **10**, 416–418; **20**, 508; **24**, 715–722
subversive activities, allegations of, **21**, 372–379
—enquiries into, **22**, 768–784, 798–809
summary dismissal, grounds for, **32**, 508–512
taxation, position as to, **5**, 314–315; **23**, 616, 621, 625–627; **29**, 56–73; **31**, 393–395
temporary appointments, termination, **18**, 452–456; **21**, 379–388; **22**, 784–793; **24**, 723–728; **27**, 422–427; **29**, 233; **31**, 434–436
terminal emoluments, **23**, 614–615
termination indemnity, **22**, 762–767; **23**, 628–631
termination of appointment: *see also* contracts of service, termination, *and* fixed term appointments, *supra*
—abolition of post, **21**, 361–372; **32**, 538–539; **34**, 459
—due process, requirement, **18**, 462; **22**, 792; **34**, 430, 433, 434
—grounds for, **27**, 421, 424–427, 456; **32**, 457–466, 505–508
—health grounds, **22**, 793–797; **34**, 428–436
—misconduct, **32**, 505–508
—notice, period of, **34**, 460
—professional incompetence, **20**, 518–522; **21**, 360–361, 365; **23**, 784–793
—reduction of staff, **21**, 388–398
—requirement of reasons for, **19**, 497
—right to hearing, **32**, 506
—unsatisfactory service, **20**, 513–518; **21**, 356–360

International officials—*continued*
termination, wrongful, **18,** 450–451; **19,** 492–498; **20,** 493–506, 510–522; **21,** 356–360, 361–372, 388–398; **22,** 798–809; **23,** 628–631; **24,** 683–684, 688, 715, 728–741; 748–749, 750, 751–753; **27,** 445–446, 454–457, 458–461; **32,** 457–471, 505–508. *See also* contracts of service, dismissal, *and* fixed-term appointments, *supra*
—complaint, **27,** 295–298, 298–300, 418–427, 445–446, 454–461, 461–471
—damages, **24,** 735–741, **27,** 457, 471
—misuse of power, **20,** 503–504, 509, 512, 521; **21,** 360, 393–394, 395; **24,** 751
transfer to another station, refusal to accept, **27,** 454–457
travel allowance, **32,** 354–358, 503-505
U.N. and specialized agencies, harmonization of conditions, **32,** 445, 449–450, 481, 482
undisclosed allegations against, **22,** 784–793
Walters Selection Committee, **20,** 510–512, 519–522
International organization: *see also* names of particular organizations
action against Member State, **17,** 323–326
action by, procedural requirements, **23,** 515–516
adherence to, **21,** 348
administrative tribunals—
—effect of G.A. budgetary resolutions, **32,** 443, 445, 451–452
—judgments, *res judicata,* **27,** 295–298
—judgments of, revision of, **27,** 297–300
constitution, interpretation of, **23,** 597–605; **30,** 426–447; **34,** 311: *see also under* Charter of the United Nations
—practice, relevance, **30,** 440–441
continuity of organizations, **18,** 441–443
détournement de pouvoir, **21,** 309–310; **22,** 739–741, 748–750, 751, 753, 754–756; **23,** 556–564, 604. *See also under* European Coal and Steel Community; European Economic Community
excès de pouvoir, **34,** 337
implied powers, **34,** 352
International Court of Justice and, **23,** 541–542, 573
legal personality—
—N.A.T.O., **22,** 756–762
—United Nations, **16,** 318–331
—U.N.R.R.A., **19,** 490–491
International organization—*continued*
membership, admission, **15,** 333–346; **17,** 326–330
military observers supervising armistice agreements, **18,** 469
nullity of acts, **34,** 337
officials of: *see* International officials
organs, discretionary power, **30,** 431–434, 439, 444, 445, 446
ouster of jurisdiction of municipal courts, **9,** 123
powers of, **22,** 737–756
privileges and immunities, **18,** 444–449; **21,** 279–280; **22,** 4, 276, 709–711, 756–762; **23,** 509–510, 510–515; **26,** 620–621; **32,** 308, 315–323. *See also* International officials, immunities of
—land owned by, **21,** 398
resolutions, interpretation, practice, **31,** 479–482
specialized agencies of the U.N., **18,** 444–446
status of, **18,** 16
—conclusiveness of statement of executive as to, **21,** 16, 279–280
status of members of, **6,** 32–34
succession of, **18,** 441–443; **19,** 490–491
succession, jurisprudence of I.C.J. on, **27,** 587–588
ultra vires acts, **21,** 309–310
ultra vires, concept of, **34,** 297, 321
voidability, concept of, **34,** 336
International Penal Law, Treaty of Montevideo (1889), **7,** 259–260, 354–355, 365, 357
International Postal Conventions: *see* Postal Conventions
International public interest, **1,** 343; **4,** 493; **18,** 387, 389; **19,** 528; **21,** 387
International public policy, **1,** 370; **23,** 61
International Red Cross: *see* Red Cross, International
International Refugee Organization: *see under* Refugees
International standards, **3,** 214, 215–217, 227–228, 294–295; **4,** 132–133, 227, 236–237, 249–250; **5,** 168, 171, 256; **7,** 239, 241–244
International Telecommunications Union, Administrative Council, functions concerning officials, **27,** 451–453
International tribunals: *see also* Arbitration, international, *and* names of particular tribunals
access to, individuals, **1,** 197; **3,** 263; **4,** 291–292; **9,** 58, 338; **13,** 207; **18,** 244, 439; **23,** 669–671; **25,** 523; **32,** 637

International tribunals—*continued*
competence to determine jurisdiction, **27**, 542
concurrent jurisdiction, **9**, 58
decisions *ex aequo et bono*, **22**, 103, 106
dispute, existence of, condition for jurisdiction, **3**, 426–428
equity, application of, **8**, 450–451 n.; **25**, 501, 503, 506, 529, 551–552 n.
—compensation and, **2**, 419
extinctive prescription, application of, **23**, 314–315
form, questions of, attitude to, **25**, 223
laches, doctrine of, applicability, **3**, 246
municipal proceedings pending, **18**, 438–439
presumption of conformity with recognized standards, **25**, 209
procedure, power to determine, **25**, 205, 209; **28**, 562
responsibility of local State, **25**, 206–207
statutes of limitation, applicability, **5**, 196–197
International waterways, freedom of navigation on: *see* Freedom of navigation
Internment—
belligerent forces, in neutral countries, **9**, 583; **10**, 639–643
civilians, of, prisoners of war, whether, **11**, 266
enemy aliens, of, **12**, 185–195, 199–202; **14**, 18–19; **15**, 455; **26**, 652, 653–655
—contracts, effect on, **31**, 494–495
—judicial review of, **31**, 503–508
—right to effective defence, **10**, 447–450
enemy vessel in neutral port, of, **12**, 538
political refugees, **7**, 259–261
Interpretation of treaties: *see under* Treaties
" Inter-temporal " law, **4**, 3–5; **20**, 101
Intervention—
diplomatic, nature of, **6**, 242–246
hostilities, in course of, **5**, 472
international arbitration, in, **4**, 478; **5**, 449
Invasion, meaning, **16**, 347
" Inventory ", compensable property under peace treaty, **29**, 389–391, 438–440
Investment, protection of, **35**, 42
Ionian Islands, Protectorate, **3**, 39; **28**, 67
Iran: *see also* Persia
co-belligerant, as, **19**, 638–640
Iran—*continued*
Concession Agreements with Anglo-Iranian Oil Company (1933 and 1937), **19**, 502, 507–549 *passim;* **20**, 305–316, 317, 321; **22**, 21–45 *passim*
Denmark, Treaty with (1934), **19**, 514–549
Egypt, Treaty with (1928), **6**, 343–344
Great Britain, Treaties with (1857 and 1903), **19**, 515–549 *passim*
nationalization of oil industry, **19**, 501–503, 508–509; **20**, 305–316, 317, 321, 328; **22**, 19–45 *passim*
P.C.I.J. and, **19**, 523
Petroleum Law, 1957...**35**, 136, 137
Switzerland, Treaty with (1934), **19**, 514–549 *passim*
Turkey, Treaty with (1937), **19**, 514–549 *passim*
Iraq, determination of frontier, **3**, 376–377
Ireland, Republic of: *see also* Eire
Bank of Ireland Act, 1929...**27**, 20–21
boundary with Northern Ireland, **24**, 95
Constitution, **24**, 421–424
Double Taxation Agreement with U.K., **33**, 1–14
Government of Ireland Act, 1920..**2**, 369
Offences Against the State Act, 1939, **25**, 216–217
Offences Against the State (Amendment) Act, 1940...**25**, 217, 220, 222–223; **31**, 276, 277, 280, 293, 295, 297, 302, 304, 305, 306, 308–311, 313, 315
status of nationals, **20**, 286–290
U.S.A., Treaty of Friendship, Commerce and Navigation (1950), **28**, 286 n.
—military service provision, **31**, 320
Irish Free State: *see* Eire
Irish Free State Agreement (1921), **2**, 368; **3**, 98; **8**, 82; **19**, 46
Iroquois Tribe of the Six Nations, **4**, 535
Irregular apprehension—
enemy alien, of, prior to belligerency, **14**, 133, 135
jurisdiction in regard to, **7**, 188–192, 250–251, 337–338; **13**, 55–56, 67–69
State responsibility, **7**, 188–192, 250–251
Irregular combatants, insignia, **15**, 424, 639, 661
Irregular forces, status of, **16**, 379–380, 514–516. *See also* Guerillas
Irregular imprisonment, State responsibility, **7**, 477–478

Islands—
acquisition of sovereignty over, **7,** 109–111
boundaries, as, **7,** 133–135
channels between, historic title, **35,** 68–83
contiguity, principle of, in relation to, **4,** 111–112
offshore, claims to, effect on status of intervening waters, **31,** 178–179, 186, 195
territorial waters of, **1,** 100–102; **9,** 127; **33,** 152
uninhabited, **5,** 91–92; **15,** 71
Israel—
Air Navigation Act (1920) (U.K.), **20,** 154
Arab invasion of, **19,** 550–556
Areas of Jurisdiction and Powers Ordinance, 1948...**26,** 211
—(Amendment) Law, 1956...**23,** 295
Armistice Agreements with Arab States (1949), **19,** 555; **28,** 652–653
armistice demarcation line with Egypt, **32,** 80–82
British army, status after end of Mandate, **22,** 123–127
Custodian of Enemy Property, rights of, **17,** 113–115
Defence (Finance) Regulations (1941), **22,** 702
Defence Service Law (1949), **18,** 11; **19,** 344; **24,** 533
demilitarized zones, **18,** 164–170
Egypt—
—hostilities with (1948), **17,** 345–349, 440–447
—non-recognition by, **17,** 345–349, 440–447
—relations with, 1951–1956...**31,** 512–515
Extradition Law (1954), **21,** 238
France, extradition between, **21,** 236–238
General Administrative Law in Palestine, Law Amending (1949), **21,** 458
Germany—
—Agreement (1952), **26,** 362–364; **28,** 88
—waiver of claims, **32,** 148–151
independence of, **15,** 58–59, 573; **16,** 68; **17,** 314, 444
—declaration of, **15,** 7; **16,** 43; **18,** 166; **19,** 554; **20,** 49; **21,** 444
Invalids (Nazi Persecution) Law, **32,** 148–151
Jerusalem, occupation of, **15,** 573–575
Jerusalem, status of, **26,** 68–69; **33,** 320, 322, 324, 333, 340, 345–346, 351
Jordan, armistice with (1949), **22,** 5–9
Israel—*continued*
Law and Administration Ordinance (1948), **17,** 115; **18,** 65, 66, 73, 75, 76; **19,** 230, 233, 588; **20,** 50, 155, 393; **21,** 251–253, 444; **22,** 114–122, 126, 702; **23,** 285–288, 293, 294
Law of Return, 1950...**26,** 376, 379
Lebanon, armistice with (1949), **22,** 698–701
Legal Assistance to Foreign States Law, 1956...**28,** 89
legislation of Palestine Government
—adoption of, **17,** 113–115
—repeal of, **17,** 107–109
Ministry for Foreign Affairs, certificate of, **20,** 7, 389–399
Nationality Law (1951), **18,** 56; **20,** 49–51; **32,** 168–169
nationality of residents, **17,** 110–111
Nazi and Nazi Collaborators (Punishment) Law (1950), **18,** 538–540, 542, 543
occupation of Arab territory, **16,** 464–466
Palestine Mandate and, **21,** 254
recognition of, **16,** 38–39; **17,** 348, 444; **21,** 49, 444, 457–459; **33,** 320, 340, 345, 351
religious and political controversy, political offence for extradition, **33,** 319–352
succession to Palestine—
—obligations of Government, **17,** 72–81, 92–94; **22,** 113–122
—proceedings commenced by Government, **18,** 72–77
—punishment for offences, **19,** 141–142
—rights of Government, **18,** 64–67
Syria, General Armistice Agreement with (1949), **18,** 164, 167, 168
territory of State, **18,** 10–11
Trading with the Enemy Ordinance (1939), **22,** 702
United Arab Republic, state of war between, **31,** 509–520
U.K., Financial Agreement (1950), **18,** 398; **22,** 123–126; **28,** 442–460
war criminals, treatment of, **18,** 538–544
Istanbul: *see* Constantinople
Italian property in Germany, restitution of, **29,** 442–492
Italian-United States Conciliation Commission—
applicable law, **25,** 107
arbitral character, **22,** 850
claim denied by, whether not "provided for" in Peace Treaty, **30,** 532–536
competence, **30,** 449–450
—dispute as pre-condition, **22,** 864–865

Italian-United States Conciliation Commission—*continued*
competence—*continued*
—Italian municipal law, question of, **29,** 375
decisions of other Commissions, authority of, **22,** 950
decisions, rectification of, **24,** 880
evidence, **30,** 448–450, 451–456
—nature and sufficiency, **22,** 843–864; **24,** 880–882
expenses of establishing claims, **29,** 23, 33, 50–51
experts, partial and impartial, **24,** 879
municipal claims settlement, relation to, **30,** 532–536
Rules of Procedure, **22,** 847–848, 850
time limit on work, **30,** 535
witnesses, power to call, **22,** 853
Italy—
administrative jurisdiction, law of, **22,** 998
agrarian reform, **26,** 48
Albania—
—Economic, Monetary and Customs Convention (1939), **20,** 450, 462
—occupation of (1939), **20,** 450–451
Allied Control Commission in, **15,** 288, 552
Allied Military Government, validity of acts, **15,** 602–604
Allied occupation of, **15,** 602–604, 613–614; **16,** 433–434; **17,** 421–423; **18,** 625–629, 686–690; **19,** 613–615
Alto Adige, status of, **16,** 215–219
Amnesty Decree, 1922...**2,** 286
anti-Jewish legislation in, **20,** 217–222; **22,** 389–393, 643–646, 647–648; **24,** 303, 305, 307, 312, 314–315, 654; **29,** 21–22, 30–32, 35, 40, 49–50, 52–53
Argentina—
—Consular Convention (1885), **1,** 303
—Extradition Treaty (1886), **5,** 286–287; **6,** 313; **19,** 376; **23,** 412–414
—Immigration Agreements (1947 and 1948), **19,** 471–473
—Treaty *re* workmen's compensation (1920), **10,** 411
Armistice (1943), **16,** 477, 560, 561, 566; **18,** 716; **19,** 614, 616; **20,** 490; **22,** 444, 445, 455, 643, 644; **24,** 650, 653–654, 655, 658, 659; **29,** 31, 36, 38, 40, 52
Articles of War, 1938...**15,** 424–426, 431; **16,** 477; **18,** 622–624, 626, 627, 628, 688, 690–691; **19,** 617; **29,** 27
Austria—
—Extradition Treaty (1922), **2,** 319
—succession to property of, **4,** 78
Belgium—
—Commercial Treaty (1882), **4,** 452
Italy—*continued*
Belgium—*continued*
—Extradition Treaty (1875), **19,** 366–368
belligerent, definition, Decree-Law (1938), **24,** 987
Brazil, Extradition Treaty (1931), **18,** 339
Brussels Treaty, 1948, accession, **23,** 770
canon law, relation to ordinary law, **26,** 186–187
Capital Levy Decrees (1946, 1947 and 1948), **22,** 876–882. *See also* special capital levy duty, *infra*
cession of territory to France, **20,** 63–77
citizenship, re-acquisition of, **5,** 219; **6,** 252–253
Civil Code, Art. 3 (rights of aliens), **1,** 136
Civil Code (intestate succession) **5,** 235
Civil Procedure, Code of (jurisdiction, aliens), **28,** 153–154, 416–417
Civil Procedure, Code of (jurisdiction, non-resident aliens), **1,** 136
co-belligerent, as, **18,** 426
—occupation of Germany, **26,** 712–713
Commercial Code, (collisions at sea), **9,** 299
Commercial Code (extradition under), **5,** 288
Commissario del Rè, functions, **12,** 516–521
Constitution, **22,** 36, 42, 78, 884, 992, 999; **23,** 203; **24,** 4, 12–13, 210, 212, 217
—Art. 10 (conformity of Italian with international law), **28,** 155, 157–158, 160, 171–172, 174, 609
—Art. 42 (expropriation of private property), **28,** 156–158, 609, 610
—implied incorporation of customary international law, **18,** 622; **28,** 155, 157–158, 160, 171–172, 174, 609
—treaty-making power, **2,** 320
consuls, jurisdiction over, **6,** 336
—law concerning, **1,** 300
Criminal Code in Time of War, **15,** 472, 477, 478, 481, 482
Criminal Procedure, Code of, **1,** 260–261, 277, 294, 305; **4,** 189–190; **5,** 288
customs duties, reduction, E.E.C. Treaty and, **34,** 397–401
Customs Law, 1940 (jurisdiction in contiguous zone), **28,** 170–175
" defending of Italian race ", Decree Law (1938), **24,** 648
Dodecanese and, **19,** 135–137
enemy property legislation, **29,** 26–29, 47–50

Italy—*continued*
Eritrea and, **16**, 73–75; **18**, 389
—renunciation of, **17**, 101–106
Ethiopia—
—conquest, British recognition of, **8**, 119–123; **9**, 93, 94–101, 172
—succession to, **19**, 100
—Treaty of Amity (1928), **8**, 268
execution on foreign State property, Law of 1926...**28**, 156–158
extradition to, **5**, 288, 295
financial administration, law concerning (1923), **22**, 1000
firm or partnership, legal nature, **32**, 558
foreign corporations, position, **6**, 278–279
France—
—Agreements with (1949, 1951, 1952) *re* Peace Treaty, **19**, 478; **20**, 71, 74; **22**, 319–320, 324, 325, 327, 501, 841, 842
—Armistice (1940), **11**, 266; **20**, 489
—cession of Nice and Savoy to, **5**, 398
—Commercial Treaty (1946), most-favoured-nation clause, **26**, 490–492
—Convention *re* nationality (1896), **18**, 508
—Convention *re* river Roja (1914), **9**, 120
—Convention, Mutual Enforcement of Judgments (1930), **9**, 120; **16**, 382; **18**, 290 n.; **19**, 556; **24**, 890–892
—Emigration Agreements (1946, 1947), **20**, 300–301; **22**, 604–605
—Establishment Agreements (1946, 1948), **23**, 468
—Establishment Treaty (1862), **7**, 391–392
—Establishment Treaty (1930), **12**, 304, 305 n., 307; **14**, 161 n.; **15**, 327, 437; **16**, 381; **20**, 599; **23**, 468
—Extradition Treaty (1870), **7**, 334, 372; **18**, 324, 327, 328; **22**, 514–515
—occupation by (1796), **15**, 619
—Social Security Convention (1948), **24**, 599
"General Provisions" (foreign law and public policy), **26**, 185–189
German occupation of (1943), **15**, 553–557, 604–608, 610–612, 614–619; **17**, 419–422, 426–428; **18**, 690–694; **19**, 611–613, 616–619; **22**, 991–994, 998–1001
German trade-marks in, Memorandum of Understanding (1956), **26**, 52, 54–55

Italy—*continued*
Germany—
—Agreement with (Alto Adige) (1939), **15**, 234–236
—convention, patents (1892), **5**, 479–480
—Consular and Extradition Treaties, **2**, 274–275
—declaration of war against (1943), **17**, 353
—Extradition Treaty (1871), **5**, 271, 273–274; **7**, 360–367
—Extradition Treaty (1942), **21**, 232
Greece—
—Agreement for Economic Collaboration (1949), **22**, 241
—Consular Convention (1880), **7**, 388–389
—Commercial Treaty (1926), **19**, 435, 447
Guarantees, Law of 1871...**4**, 97–98; **22**, 536, 548
Holy See—
—Concordat, **6**, 90; **26**, 186–188
—Lateran Treaty (1929), **5**, 304; **9**, 103, 105, 109, 111, 425, 435–436, 438; **10**, 106–108, 355–364; **16**, 82; **19**, 142–143; **23**, 115; **24**, 214, 216; **26**, 183–188
Hungary, Cultural Agreement (1935), **23**, 302–204; **24**, 218
International Institute of Agriculture, Law of 1930...**5**, 415
Italian Social Republic (1944), **15**, 612, 618–619
—acts of, **20**, 217–222; **29**, 30, 36, 37, 40, 42–47, 49–50, 51, 54
jurisdiction, crimes committed in territory under capitulations, **4**, 189–190
Kingdom of, constitution of, by annexation, **5**, 69
landlord and tenant legislation, **20**, 300–301; **23**, 392
League of Nations, application of sanctions against, **8**, 422–423, 476
Libya and, **17**, 106–107; **18**, 77–78
—transfer of sovereignty to, (1955), **22**, 103–113
Libya, State property in—
—administration, transfer of, **25**, 518–522
—Agreement with U.K. (1951), **22**, 104–113; **25**, 15–20
—Peace Treaty, Art. 23, effect, **25**, 4–5, 7–9
—succession to, **25**, 2–26
Lubiana, annexation of, **19**, 322–326
Maritime Code, Art. 2 (territorial waters), **28**, 170–171, 174
Mexico, Mixed Claims Commission, Agreement (1927), **22**, 851
Military Penal Code, **23**, 764–766

Italy—*continued*
Ministry for Foreign Affairs, certificate of, **22,** 549, 547
monetary revaluation decrees (1940, 1948), **22,** 876–882
National Committee of Liberation, **15,** 426, 428
Nationality Law, 1912...**9,** 26, 340; **24,** 302, 459, 460, 462; **30,** 369–370
nationality, married women, **5,** 235
nationality, Sardinian citizens, **9,** 27
North Atlantic Treaty, 1949, ratification of, **23,** 202
obligations of Sardinia, how far bound by, **4,** 91–92
Peace Treaty with (1947), **15,** 62, 63, 106–107, 323; **16,** 273–274, 316–317, 560, 561, 562; **17,** 2, 3–5, 101–106; **18,** 3, 77–78, 290, 319–320, 323, 389, 394–395, 406–428 *passim*, 436–439, 471, 714; **19,** 145–147, 322–326, 366–369, 459, 478–487 *passim*; **21,** 141, 400, 405, 410; **22,** 241, 418, 607–608, 938; **23,** 468, 499–508, 663; **24,** 209–211; **25,** 4–5, 7–9, 314, 316, 319, 360–362, 366; **26,** 54, 686–687; **28,** 602–603, 608, 609; **29,** 21–25, 29–54, 372, 374, 399, 451, 435, 464–465; **30,** 204, 366–374, 448–450, 451–454, 456, 511–514, 533–535; **31,** 3, 359–360; **32,** 335, 336, 350–351: *see also* Anglo-Italian Conciliation Commission; Conciliation commissions; Franco-Italian Conciliation Commission, *and* Italian-United States Conciliation Commission
—Albanian authorities, agreements with, **20,** 450, 479
—" as a result of the war " (Art. 78), **22,** 949–953
—" ceded territories " (Art. 78), **24,** 601–630
—ceded territory, boundaries, **20,** 63–77
—ceded territory, property in, **24,** 602–630
—ceded territory, public property, **20,** 63–77
—cession of Dodecanese, **23,** 663, 669
—claims, death of claimant, **22,** 338–340
—claims, dual nationals, **22,** 443–457; **24,** 301–302, 452–456; **30,** 366–374
—claims, expenses of establishing, **29,** 23, 33, 50–51; **30,** 368, 372, 374
—claims, nationality of, **24,** 301–315
—claims, nationality, material dates, **30,** 368–370
—compensation, exemption from tax, **29,** 369, 371–382

Italy—*continued*
Peace Treaty with (1947)—*continued*
—compensation for war damage, **18,** 414–423; **20,** 218–222; **22,** 340–348; **30,** 511–514
—compensation, two-thirds standard, **20,** 491–492; **22,** 305–306; **29,** 376–382
—contracts, dissolution clause, **18,** 403–406
—Decree Law bringing Treaty into operation (1947), **22,** 884–885
—" disputes ", meaning, **30,** 449–450
—Eritrea and Libya, renunciation of, **16,** 73–75; **17,** 101–107; **18,** 77–78; **19,** 145–148
—Ethiopia, " ceded territory ", whether, **24,** 601–630
—exemption from progressive property tax, **29,** 22, 24, 33–38, 51
—forced sale of property, claim based on, **30,** 532
—French law, effect in, **18,** 394; **22,** 607–608
—frontier adjustments, **20,** 63–77
—German property in Italy, **26,** 54
—indirect corporate claims, **30,** 511–514
—interpretation, *travaux préparatoires*, **18,** 414, 418, 420–422; **24,** 612–613, 620, 623–625
—Italian property abroad, seizure, **19,** 478–487; **22,** 500–510; **26,** 163
—Law of October 29, 1954...**28,** 608–609
—" laws in force in Italy during war " (Art. 78), **24,** 306, 647–663; **29,** 31–32, 36, 37, 42–47
—loss of property in transit, **26,** 686
—" measure taken against property ", **22,** 964–965; **23,** 500–506
—nationality provisions, **19,** 322–326; **22,** 445–448
—Prize Court, revision of decision, **22,** 1008–1011
—prize, effect on, **18,** 714
—requisition, responsibility for, **22,** 959–966; **23,** 499–503, 506–508
—restitution claims, time-limit, **18,** 427–429
—restoration provisions, **18,** 403, 423–426, 435–440; **20,** 482–492; **22,** 305–306, 945–979; **23,** 499–508; **29,** 21–54; **30,** 511–514
—sequestration, responsibility for, **21,** 141–146; **22,** 302–304, 307–329
—Settlement Convention with Germany and, **29,** 451, 453, 464
—special war taxes, exemption from, **18,** 406–413; **22,** 876–885; **25,** 314, 319; **29,** 379
—" successor " (Art. 78), **22,** 340–345

Italy—*continued*
Peace Treaty with (1947)—*contd.*
—" treated as enemy " (Art. 78), **22**, 389–390, 642–646; **24**, 303–315, 654, 658–661; **25**, 153–164; **29**, 22–54; **30**, 451–454
—treaties kept in force, **22**, 607–608; **24**, 890–892
—treaties, revival, **18**, 320; **19**, 556; **23**, 468; **24**, 883–892; **28**, 602; **31**, 3; **32**, 336–337
—Trieste, renunciation of, **18**, 81–84; **19**, 144–145
—" United Nations nationals ", **22**, 445–446, 647; **24**, 308, 313, 647; **26**, 327; **29**, 22–54
—victims of discriminatory measures, **29**, 47–48
—waiver of claims, **19**, 459; **20**, 223–225; **22**, 972–975
—waiver of claim against Germany, **29**, 453
Penal Code (territorial scope), **9**, 297
Penal Military Code of War, **18**, 346
property transferred to Allied Government for reparations, claims for compensation, **28**, 607–611
provinces, recovery of, **1**, 454
Rhodes, occupation of, **1**, 452–453
Sardinia, continuation of, **9**, 27
sequestration measures, **25**, 363–364, 366–367. *See also under* Peace Treaty, *supra*
Serb–Croat–Slovene State, Consular Convention (1924), **7**, 392
Sicily, restoration of control over, **31**, 362
Social Republic of Salò, status of, **20**, 217–222; **24**, 308–310, 651–652, 655, 663, 666; **29**, 42–47
Somaliland and, **22**, 76–80
special capital levy duty (Law of 1947), French nationals, application to, **18**, 406–413
—Swiss nationals, application to, **25**, 313–325
—U.S. nationals, application to, **24**, 647–648
—valuation of property under, **25**, 323–324
succession tax on indemnity under Peace Treaty, **29**, 369, 371–382
Switzerland—
—Conciliation Treaty (1924), **25**, 313–315, 321
—Convention, recognition and enforcement of judgments (1933), **21**, 264–265
—Establishment and Consular Convention (1868), **25**, 313–314, 316–317, 320

Italy—*continued*
Switzerland—*continued*
—Extradition Treaty (1868), **1**, 261, 273–274; **4**, 343–345; **6**, 307–308; **9**, 402; **18**, 345; **19**, 370, 375; **34**, 135, 136, 137
—Fisheries Convention (1912), **9**, 122
Trading with the Enemy Act (1938), **18**, 650
Turkey, Extradition Treaty (1926), **9**, 402
U.K.—
—Extradition Treaty (1873), **9**, 50, 394
—Financial Agreement (1947), **17**, 1, 3
—Libya, Agreement concerning (1951), **22**, 104–113; **25**, 15–20
—Social Insurance Convention (1951), **27**, 288–291
—Treaty of Commerce and Navigation (1863), **25**, 320
U.S.A.—
—Claims Agreement (Lombardo, 1947), **22**, 411, 946; **24**, 304, 655, 656, 658, 659; **25**, 164–166; **26**, 338–339
—Commercial Treaty (1871), **1**, 350–351; **7**, 322; **11**, 5
—Commercial Treaty (1913), **1**, 241; **7**, 322
—Consular Convention (1878), **5**, 403; **6**, 398–400; **9**, 71, 487
—Establishment Treaty, **11**, 194
—Exchange of Notes implementing Peace Treaty (1949), **22**, 411, 864
—Extradition Treaty (1868), **6**, 301–302; **18**, 320; **24**, 883, 885, 888; **28**, 340 n., **31**, 356
— —conviction *in absentia*, **31**, 362–364
— —effect of war on, **31**, 359–361
—Financial and Economic Agreements (1947), **22**, 846, 854, 859, 863; **25**, 164–165
—Friendship, Commerce and Navigation Treaty (1948), **22**, 580–582
— —compatibility of U.S. Ship Mortgage Act, **33**, 385–390
— —m.f.n. clause, **31**, 1–3
—Treaty, workmen's compensation, **1**, 319–320
U.S. bases in, **23**, 201–202
U.S. forces in, **23**, 201–202; **24**, 253–255
U.S. naval base, Agreement on conditions of employment, **28**, 159, 163
—suit by Italian employee against U.S. Government, **28**, 158–164
U.S.S.R.—
—Commercial Agreement (1921), **1**, 26–27; **2**, 15–16

Italy—*continued*
U.S.S.R.—*continued*
—Commercial Treaty (1924), **6**, 55, 170; **7**, 179–182; **9**, 248; **15**, 142, 143
—Commercial Treaties (1924 and 1948), **22**, 235–240
—Government, non-recognition of, **1**, 58, 294–295
—Italian property in, confiscation of, **2**, 16
—Trade Delegation in Italy, **9**, 247–249
Vatican City, jurisdiction, crimes committed in, **23**, 114–115
Venezuela—
—Arbitration Agreement (1920), **5** 154
—Commercial Treaty (1861), **5**, 154
—Extradition Treaty (1930), **22**, 518; **24**, 507, 509–510; **26**, 527
Victor Emmanuel III, estate of, **17**, 1–6
war criminals, surrender of, **16**, 273–274
War Law (1938), **22**, 3, 309, 389, 391–393, 446–447, 642–646, 647–648, 949, 960, 1010; **24**, 312; **25**, 155, 157–158, 160, 162
Yugoslavia, occupation of, **15**, 106; **18**, 621–625

J

Jan Mayen Island, occupation of, **7**, 109–111
Japan: *see also* Anglo–Japanese Property Commission; Netherlands–Japanese Property Commission, *and* United States–Japanese Property Commission
aliens, right to sue State or Government, **32**, 200–201
Allied occupation of (1945), **19**, 225; **20**, 635–643; **21**, 105–108; **22**, 982–987; **24**, 956–959; **32**, 175. *See also* U.S.A., occupation by
Allied Powers Property Compensation Law, 1951—
—bonds, compensation for non-restoration of, **29**, 435–436
—cancellation of contracts, **29**, 438–440
—compensation, exchange control, subject to, **29**, 397
—compensation, exemption from tax, **29**, 394–401
—depreciation, allowance for, **29**, 404–408
—excessive war-time depreciation, **29**, 438–440
—" inventory ", compensable property, **29**, 389–391, 438–440

Japan—*continued*
Allied Powers Property Compensation Law—*continued*
—nationality provisions, **29**, 422, 428
—patents, compensation for cancellation or transfer of, **29**, 309–318
—property acquired after outbreak of war, deduction for, **29**, 391, 393
—quantum of compensation, **29**, 391–394, 401–408, 420–421
—time-limits for claims, **29**, 428–429
—valuation of property, **29**, 401–408, 418, 425–427, 429
—war damage, compensation for, **29**, 318–319
—war damage, items covered, **29**, 351 n.
—war-time special measures, damage due to, **29**, 383–389
anti-Jewish measures in war, whether " caused " by German Government, **28**, 649
armistice (1945), **30**, 516–517
British sailors in, **19**, 221–226
Cairo Declaration (1943), **22**, 983
China—
—Commercial Treaty (1896), **2**, 152
—dispute with (1931), **22**, 673
City of Tokyo Loan of 1911, settlement of dispute, **29**, 11–20
Civil Affairs Manual, **18**, 652
Civil Code, sale, provisions on, **29**, 314–316
Civil Procedure Code (arbitral awards), **28**, 526–529, 531, 532, 535, 537
Commission of Three Countries, **26**, 573, 576
Constitution, **19**, 221, 222, 224; **20**, 306, 311, 312, 636–643; **23**, 265; **26**, 480
—human rights provisions, **32**, 172, 178
—international law provision, **32**, 60
—renunciation of right of war, **32**, 43–64
criminal jurisdiction, suspension, 1945–1951...**26**, 705–707
Egypt, Customs Agreement (1930), **11**, 224–226
Enemy Property Custody Law (1941), **24**, 955
—Imperial Ordinance *re* Enforcement of, **24**, 955
—whether " war-time special measure ", **29**, 383–389
Family Registration Law, revision of, **32**, 178
France, Protocol on Joint Defence of Indo-China (1941), **32**, 603–604, 620
German assets in, disposal of, **26**, 573–577

Japan—*continued*
Government Loan of 1910, settlement by creditors, **29,** 4–11
Hōrei (Law No. 10 of 1898 embodying private international law), **20,** 306, 311, 312, 313, 315, 316
Juvenile Law, **34,** 194
Korea—
—effect of union with, **17,** 15; **32,** 174, 180–181
—renunciation of, Peace Treaty, **32,** 179, 182
Labour Union Law (1954), **22,** 266
Ministry of Foreign Affairs, certificate of, **24,** 226–227
Nationality Law, 1899...**32,** 175, 180, 181
Nationality Law, 1950...**32,** 171, 172, 173, 177, 178, 180
occupation of—
—Borneo, **15,** 8
—British territories in Asia, **23,** 687–701
—Burma, **15,** 537–548, 576–583; **18,** 575–585, 641–642; **19,** 619–620; **23,** 754–756
—Hong Kong, **15,** 443–447; **18,** 521–529, 636–637
—Malaya, **15,** 449, 548–549; **18,** 585–590, 638–640; **19,** 183–185; **20,** 653–654
—Netherlands Indies, **15,** 682–684
—New Guinea, **15,** 155
—Philippines, **18,** 590–607, 642–677, 702–703; **20,** 643–646; **22,** 994–996
—Singapore, **19,** 183–185
patent infringement, law as to, **29,** 314–315, 317
Peace Treaty with (1951), **18,** 494; **19,** 224, 225; **20,** 314, 636, 639–643; **21,** 82–86, 108; **22,** 939; **23,** 211, 698–699; **24,** 89–91
—compensation, completion of process of, **29,** 394–395, 397, 400–401
—compensation, exemption from tax. **29,** 394–401
—compensation unpaid, interest on, **29,** 441
—debts provision, **29,** 8, 14–15
—external assets, seizure, **32,** 578
—" inventory ", compensable property, **29,** 389–391, 438–440
—Korea, renunciation of, effect on nationality, **32,** 170–186
—Kurile Islands, renunciation of, **32,** 582–583
—nationality requirements, **29,** 421–429
—presence of foreign forces, **32,** 51
—" property in Japan of an Allied Power ", **30,** 515–532
—property not restored, measure of compensation, **29,** 431–437

Japan—*continued*
Peace Treaty with (1951)—*continued*
—reparations, diplomatic property, **28,** 404–405
—responsibility for acts of trade association, **29,** 414–417, 420, 427
—restoration, compensation for failure, **29,** 409, 412
—restoration, " disposal " by owner, **29,** 409–412
—Ryukyu Islands, position of, **21,** 82–86, 308; **32,** 583–584
—shareholders' claims, **29,** 389, 438–440
—validity in municipal law, **32,** 162, 164–165
—waiver of claims, **30,** 518, 519, 520, 521, 529; **32,** 161–165, 233–237, 640–642
prisoners of war, treatment of, **15,** 364–372
Prize Court Review Commission, **32,** 601, 621
Property Commissions under Peace Treaty—
—applicable law, **29,** 437
—*ex aequo et bono*, authority to decide, **29,** 437
—jurisdiction, **29,** 304, 308, 398
—procedure, **29,** 389–390, 393
—reference to each other's decisions, **29,** 390–391
—reference to decision of Italian–United States Conciliation Commission, **29,** 398–400
protests, order of U.S. court, production of documents, **33,** 159–160
requisition legislation in war, **29,** 417, 419, 420, 430–431
Ryukyu Islands and, **21,** 82–86, 308; **33,** 583–584
surrender of (1945), **15,** 356, 362, 375; **18,** 494; **20,** 618–621, 635; **21,** 106, 108, 109, 475; **22,** 939, 982, 984; **32,** 49
—status after, **21,** 106–109
termination of war with, by U.S.A., **28,** 595–596; **34,** 498
Thailand—
—invasion of (1941), **22,** 1001–1006
—Treaty of Alliance (1941), **22,** 1001
Trading with the Enemy Act, **18,** 650, 652
treaties—
—judicial review of, **32,** 52, 59
—self-executing, **32,** 61–62
—status in municipal law, **32,** 60
U.K., Commercial Treaty (1911), **23,** 313
U.S.A.—
—attack on (1941), whether " war ", **12,** 283–284, 289–300

Japan—*continued*
U.S.A.—*continued*
—Commercial Treaty (1911), **1,** 320; **4,** 447–448; **11,** 1–5, 194, 195, 233; **15,** 509
—Commercial Treaty (1953), **24,** 673–677; **31,** 210, 217–218
—discrimination against Japanese in, **11,** 1–2, 233
—forces of, in, **22,** 261; **23,** 239–240
—forces of in, Administrative Agreement, *re* (1952), **22,** 257–266; **23,** 265–268, 455–459; **24,** 227; **26,** 203–208; **32,** 53
—forces of in, Administrative Agreement *re*, Protocol to amend (1953), **23,** 264–265; **24,** 248–250
—instruction of Japanese in, **4,** 330–331
—occupation by, **15,** 524–525; **17,** 204, 208. *See also* Allied occupation of, *supra*
—prohibition of trade with, 1941.. **29,** 353
—Security Treaty, constitutionality, **32,** 43–64
—Security Treaty, military action, limitations on, **32,** 57, 63
—Status of Forces Agreement (1960), **34,** 192–198
—termination of war with, **28,** 595–596; **34,** 498
—territory granted to, applicable law, **31,** 121–128
Yoshida Letter (1952), **19,** 223, 224
Jay Treaty (1794), **4,** 535–536; **5,** 480; **9,** 369; **10,** 396–397; **13,** 181–182; **14,** 1–3; **19,** 435, 436; **22,** 10, 591–604; **23,** 460–467; **24,** 564; **26,** 483–486
Jerusalem, status of, **15,** 573; **26,** 68–69; **33,** 320, 322, 324, 333, 340, 346–346, 351
Jewish refugees: *see under* Refugees
Jews—
confiscation of property of, **9,** 19–21, 71, 84–87; **11,** 24–25; **18,** 24–36, 558–570
crimes against the Jewish people, **18,** 538–544
discrimination against, **9,** 383; **11,** 23–24, 172–173, 183–184, 283; **28,** 649
German legislation against, **12,** 4–11, 199–201
—deprivation of nationality, **12,** 191, 194; **15,** 250–252, 255–260, 287–288
German treatment of, **15,** 20–22, 656, 661, 663, 667, 682
immigration into Palestine, **15,** 115–125
Iraq legislation concerning, **21,** 35–36
Jews—*continued*
Italian legislation concerning, **20,** 217–222; **22,** 389–393, 643–646, 647–648; **24,** 303, 305, 307, 312, 314–315, 654; **29,** 21–22, 30–32, 35, 40, 49–50, 52–53
judicial notice of fate of, in Lithuania, **19,** 91
liquidation of businesses, **11,** 109–110
restrictive covenants against, public policy of Canada, **12,** 178–182; **15,** 302–308
Roumania, in, status of, **5,** 213–218
sequestration of property by German occupant, **19,** 631–632
Jodhpur, Treaty of Alliance, United Kingdom (1818), **22,** 128
Joint government, territories under, **9,** 50, 59. *See also* Condominium; International government
Jordan—
Constitution, **22,** 619
Israel, armistice with (1949), **22,** 5–10
Proclamation of General Military Governor of Western Side, jurisdiction, **21,** 458
recognition of, **21,** 49, 444
U.S.A., Economic Assistance Agreements with (1952 and 1954), **22,** 619
Judgments, foreign—
execution of, **4,** 183–184; **11,** 221; **26,** 57–58
extraterritorial operation, **7,** 160–161
recognition of, **1,** 29–30; **26,** 57–60
Judgments, State succession and, **1,** 77–79; **2,** 87; **3,** 92–96; **4,** 95–96; **5,** 71; **7,** 105; **9,** 103; **13,** 19–20, 43; **15,** 58–59; **18,** 69–72, 78; **20,** 89–90, 93
Judicial assistance—
absence of diplomatic relations, effect, **28,** 88–92
letters rogatory, **6,** 90; **9,** 305; **11,** 63, 104–106; **31,** 223
Judicial authorities, pronouncements, how far binding on governments, **1,** 22, 171, 172, 331, 332
Judicial Committee of the Privy Council: *see under* United Kingdom
Judicial function, limits of, **1,** 371; **2,** 396–397; **17,** 322, 335–336, 338; **18,** 352; **21,** 406, 408; **23,** 522–532, 538–541, 541–544, 544–545, 572–581; **33,** 292
" Judicial measures ", meaning, **5,** 507
Juridical persons: *see* Corporations; Partnership
Jurisdiction: *see also* Extraterritorial jurisdiction; Maritime frontier, jurisdiction at
admiralty, **35,** 120

Jurisdiction—*continued*
abduction from foreign country: *see* criminal, irregular apprehension, *infra*
agreement between States, whether necessary, **24,** 127
air space, over, **17,** 191–196; **33,** 202–204
aliens abroad, over, **6,** 135–136; **7,** 145–150; **8,** 182–184; **11,** 111–112, **12,** 68–73; **13,** 54–56, 58, 69–75, 95–96; **14,** 72–73, 127–128; **15,** 91–104; **16,** 86–94; **19,** 229–254; **20,** 199–210; **21,** 89–94; **22,** 200–209; **23,** 150–151; **24,** 156–160; **26,** 160; **28,** 341–346; **32,** 112–117; **33,** 173–181
—act against State interests, **11,** 111–112
—submission, by, **4,** 198–199
aliens, over, **1,** 107–109; **2,** 109; **3,** 148–150; **4,** 153–159, 519; **6,** 151–152; **13,** 69–75; **14,** 72–73; **16,** 86–99; 432, **17,** 136–140; **18,** 206–210; **23,** 147–149, 150–151; **26,** 160–161; **28,** 143–144, 293–296, 341–346; **31,** 132–137; **32,** 112–117. *See also* aliens abroad, over, *supra*
—action against non-resident corporation, **33,** 253–254
—deceased aliens, **7,** 162
allied territory, in, **10,** 116–119; **14,** 214
anti-trust laws, extraterritorial application of, **4,** 182–183; **19,** 158–163; **23,** 130–133; **24,** 673–677
armed forces abroad, **26,** 217; **31,** 268–269; **33,** 190–201
—leased territory, in, **31,** 121–128
aviation conventions: *see* Air Transport, International, Warsaw Convention
belligerent occupation, during: *see under* Belligerent occupation
capitulations: *q.v.*
cession, after, **16,** 64–65
coercion and, **20,** 318–320
collisions at sea: *q.v.*
comity, requirements of, **19,** 158–163
concurrent, **4,** 181–182; **6,** 139, 183–184; **9,** 163
—Status of Forces Agreement (1960), **34,** 192–198
consuls, of: *see* Consular jurisdiction
continental shelf, over: *see under* Continental shelf
continuity of, State succession, **16,** 68–70
corporations, over, **7,** 161–162; **8,** 181–182; **22,** 168–184; **33,** 253–254
—assets of, **18,** 189–194

Jurisdiction—*continued*
corporations, over—*continued*
—controlled by foreign State, **1,** 133–134; **5,** 110–112; **9,** 193, 198–207, 213–217, 233; **19,** 197–203; **23,** 160–173; **31,** 215–217
courts-martial, of, **1,** 431; **12,** 12–15, 165–168, 219–221
criminal—
—aircraft, crime committed in, **17,** 191–196; **33,** 202–204
—aliens, over, **1,** 107–109; **2,** 109; **3,** 148–150, 158–160; **4,** 153–159, 519; **6,** 151–152; **7,** 191–192; **8,** 181–184; **11,** 111–112; **12,** 68–73; **13,** 54–56, 58, 69–75, 95–96; **14,** 72–73, 127–128, 196–201; **16,** 86–99, 432; **17,** 136–140; **18,** 206–210; **19,** 163; **21,** 92–94; **22,** 203–209; **23,** 147–149, 150–151; **24,** 156–164; **26,** 160–161; **28,** 143–144; **31,** 132–137; **32,** 112–117
—cession of territory, effect, **16,** 81–85
—consuls, over, **7,** 392, 394–395
—crew-members of foreign warship, **12,** 115–123
—crime begun within territory, **12,** 169–172
—crime committed abroad, **2,** 109–111; **6,** 137–140, 175–177; **7,** 192–199; **8,** 181–184; **10,** 251–263; **11,** 161–165, 172–173; **15,** 78–90, 173–175; **17,** 136–140, 189–191; **18,** 206–210, 234–235; **19,** 142–143, 226–227; **21,** 125–126; **23,** 270–284; **24,** 264–266, 673–677; **26,** 209–221; **28,** 341–346; **31,** 267–272; **32,** 115–116, 140–147; **33,** 194–201
—crimes committed abroad, concurrent jurisdiction, **4,** 159, 181–182; **6,** 139
—crime committed on national ship on high seas, **24,** 161–167; **26,** 242–244
—crime completed in national territory, **4,** 181–182
—crime within territorial waters, **35,** 73
—"effects" doctrine, **2,** 109–111; **8,** 253; **11,** 111–112; **17,** 138–140; **22,** 207–208
—embassy premises, offence committed on, **26,** 546
—enforcement of sentence of foreign court, **15,** 72–74
—English law as to, **26,** 214–215
—foreign amnesty, **28,** 143–144
—foreign ships in port, **4,** 160; **6,** 175–177; **8,** 210; **9,** 167, 169–170; **14,** 84–90; **15,** 108–109; **16,** 143–144; **20,** 154–155; **31,** 241–247; **32,** 117–119. *See also* ports, in, *infra*

Jurisdiction—*continued*
criminal—*continued*
—frontier districts, in, **5,** 104; **8,** 162–163
—irregular apprehension, **7,** 188–192, 250–251; **10,** 327–328; **11,** 101–104; **13,** 55–56, 67–68; **15,** 115–125, 173; **18,** 232–234; **26,** 528–533
—location of crime, **4,** 153–159, 182–183; **10,** 251; **22,** 150–151; **26,** 209
—*ne bis in idem,* **1,** 470; **28,** 143–144
—occupying force, crimes against, **18,** 625–629
— — crimes by, **28,** 646–647
—protective principle, **3,** 149–150; **6,** 151–152; **11,** 130, 132–134; **15,** 115, 123, 125; **17,** 136; **32,** 112–113, 116
—territorial limits, **2,** 109–111; **7,** 197–198; **12,** 64–68; **14,** 65–68; **15,** 78–90; **20,** 188–193; **22,** 203–208; **26,** 158; **32,** 142, 145; **33,** 164—173: *see also* ports, *infra, and* Territorial waters, jurisdiction in
—territorality principle, **3,** 194–199; **4,** 189–190; **7,** 192–193, 197–199; **24,** 156–160; **26,** 215–216, 219; **30,** 102–103; **32,** 142, 145
—U.N. officials, over, **35,** 222–227
currency offences, **18,** 206
currency regulation, limitation of jurisdiction, **22,** 732–736
demilitarized zones, **18,** 164–170
disciplinary, nature of, **26,** 215, 218–220
domestic jurisdiction, matters of: *q.v.*
duality of jurisdictions, **5,** 390
enforcement of international conventions, **22,** 278–282
extraterritorial: *see* Extraterritorial jurisdiction
federal States, in, **6,** 151–152; **12,** 226–229
foreign, acquiescence and absence of protest, **4,** 518–519
foreign armed forces, over: *see under* Foreign armed forces
foreign courts, of, acts done in civil war, **5,** 51–52
foreign government agency, immunity: *see under* Foreign States
foreign merchant ships, over, in war, **10,** 267–272; **23,** 354–357
foreign military bases, in, **23,** 201–202, 241–244, 245–250
foreign States, submission by, **7,** 148–150; **8,** 177; **10,** 228–229, 232–234; **11,** 136–138; **14,** 79–83; **22,** 248–253; **23,** 160–173, 210–214; **26,** 195; **32,** 125

Jurisdiction—*continued*
foreign States, submission by—*continued*
—charterparty, arbitration clause, **24.** 205–206
—commercial contract, in, **18,** 210–219
—cross-suit, **4,** 163–164
—evidence of, **23,** 267–268
—express refusal of, **4,** 163–164; **7,** 169–170
—failure to appear, through, **10,** 232–234
—implied, **1,** 114–116; **4,** 163–164, 170–171
foreign territory, in, **30,** 94–100
frontier districts, **5,** 104; **8,** 162–163
general nature of, **24,** 176, 194, 196, 197, 199–200
government agency, service of process, **35,** 121
grant of " full and exclusive power and jurisdiction ", **26,** 116–118
high seas, on: *see under* High seas, *and* nationals abroad, over, *infra*
hot pursuit: *q.v.*
hovering laws: *q.v.*
immovable property abroad, over, **4,** 185; **22,** 197–200
immunities from: *see also* Consuls; Diplomatic envoys; Foreign States; Heads of State; Public ships; Trade delegations of U.S.S.R.; Waiver, jurisdictional immunities; Warships
—agent of Occupant of enemy territory, **23,** 783–787
—army of occupation, **14,** 196–201
—basis of claim to, **17,** 179; **19,** 200–201, 206–210
—cardinals, **8,** 235–236, 405
—colonies, **7,** 173: *see also* dependent States, *infra*
—comity and, **9,** 279
—corporations controlled by foreign State, of, **1,** 133–134; **5,** 110–112; **9,** 198–207, 213–217, 233; **19,** 197–203; **23,** 160–173; **31,** 215–217
—*de facto* governments, **9,** 62, 64–65, 67, 171
—*de facto* government, immunity as against *de jure* government, **9,** 250, 273
—dependent States, **9,** 250: *see also* colonies *above*
—diplomatic envoys: *see under* Diplomatic envoys
—diplomatic and State immunity contrasted, **24,** 224–225
—enemy States, **10,** 576–581
—federal States, member States and, **2,** 130–131; **6,** 162–163; **7,** 166–169; **10,** 178–191; **11,** 143

Jurisdiction—*continued*
immunities from—*continued*
—foreign armed forces, of: *see under* Foreign armed forces
—foreign military bases, **23,** 201–202, 266–267
—foreign military missions, **21,** 118–119
—foreign State property: *see under* Foreign States
—foreign States: *see under* Foreign States
—foreign trade delegations: *see under* Trade delegations
—French practice, summary of, **7,** 174–175; **9,** 240; **11,** 30–32
—government property administered by consuls, **9,** 440–441
—High Commissioner, **24,** 177–178
—Holy See, of, **8,** 235–236, 405; **24,** 214–215, 215–217; **26,** 183–190
—immunity from arrest, distinguished, **4,** 387–388
—implied grant of, **11,** 124–140
—Intergovernmental Committee for Refugees, **11,** 205–207
—international organizations, **18,** 444–449; **21,** 279–280; **22,** 4, 276, 709–711, 756–762; **23,** 509–515; **26,** 620–621
—international organizations, land owned by, **21,** 398
—loan issued by foreign State, **22,** 253; **23,** 191–192
—mixed commissions, **7,** 387–388
—mode of claiming, **2,** 120–122; **9,** 177; **10,** 204–207; **19,** 197–201; **33,** 40–41
—nature of immunity, **17,** 187; **22,** 256
—non-governmental association, **10,** 226–230
—North Atlantic Treaty Organization, **22,** 756–762
—protectorates, **2,** 174; **5,** 116–118; **7,** 171–172; **8,** 226
—public ships: *q.v.*
—rulers of vassal States, **22,** 67–72, 76, 256
—ships entering in distress, **5,** 129–131; **6,** 154–156
—United Nations, **26,** 260–621
—United Nations, representatives acredited to, **23,** 436–445; **24,** 203; **34,** 154–172
—United Nations staff, **15,** 346–348; **17,** 295–299; **32,** 308–334; **34,** 151–154
—war, effect of, **10,** 578–581
—warships: *q.v.*
immunity from, as denial of justice, **17,** 160
industrial property, protection of, **23,** 134–147, 149

Jurisdiction—*continued*
labour relations law, application to aliens, **28,** 115–138; **34,** 51–80: *see also* ports, labour disputes, *infra*
law of the flag, **1,** 163; **2,** 114; **4,** 157–158, 186–189; **5,** 75–76; **8,** 262; **9,** 299, 470; **10,** 252–258; **11,** 116; **13,** 54, 57; **14,** 93–95; **15,** 115, 124; **16,** 152, 183–191; **20,** 197, 205–206; **22,** 282–286; **23,** 287–291; **24,** 174, 271–272; **26,** 242–244; **27,** 45–49; **30.** 112–115; **34,** 38, 40, 55, 65, 71, 73–74, 76
leased territory, over, **20,** 148–153; **27,** 49–58; **31,** 121–128
legislation, scope of application: *see* Extraterritorial effect of legislation
locality of cause of action, **7,** 146–147
meaning, **22,** 869
national waters, in, **1,** 109–111; **2,** 111–114; **5,** 129–131; **6,** 153–157, 175–177; **7,** 208; **8,** 208–212; **9,** 164–166; **10,** 110; **14,** 84–90; **15,** 108–115; **24,** 167–171, 172; **28,** 145–149; **30,** 90–93, 103–104; **31,** 227–247; **32,** 117–119: *see also* ports, *infra*
—collision between foreign ships, **9,** 298–299; **10,** 166–168; **11,** 124–127
—crime on foreign ship, **4,** 160; **6,** 175–177; **8,** 210; **9,** 167, 169–170; **15,** 108–109; **16,** 143–144; **20,** 154–155; **31,** 241–247; **32,** 117–119
—involuntary entry, **2,** 111–112; **5,** 129–131; **6,** 154–156; **7,** 207–208; **9,** 164–166; **23,** 151–153
—navigable rivers, **10,** 110
nationals abroad, over, **1,** 158–161; **2,** 145–150, 411–412; **4,** 181–185; **6,** 175–179; **7,** 192–199; **8,** 66–67, 249–255; **13,** 93–95; **14,** 91–92; **16,** 96–99; **19,** 227–254; **20,** 193–195; **21,** 125–135; **24,** 673–677; **26,** 209–221; **28,** 115–138; **30,** 105–111; **31,** 273–274; **32,** 140–147; **33,** 194–201; **34,** 91–97
—act crime and civil wrong, **31,** 268–269
—bigamy, **31,** 272
—cheating, **31,** 270–271
—civil matters, **30,** 105–111
—crime committed while prisoner of war, **23,** 764–766
—criminal, **1,** 158–161; **2,** 145–147; **4,** 181–183, 184–185; **6,** 175–177; **7,** 192–197; **8,** 249–254; **10,** 250; **11,** 172–173; **14,** 91-92; **15,** 173–175; **17,** 189–191; **19,** 226–227; **20,** 188–193; **21,** 125–126; **22,** 560–561; **23,** 114–115, 269–270; **26,** 209–221; **31,** 140–147, 267–272; **33,** 194–201; **35,** 131–135

Jurisdiction—*continued*
nationals abroad, over—*continued*
—high seas, on the, **4**, 186–189; **7**, 212–213; **10**, 252–263; **23**, 284–295; **26**, 242–244; **31**, 274–275
—property, **15**, 176–204
—taxation, **2**, 147–148; **8**, 254–255; **31**, 273–274
nationals, over: *see also* personal, *infra*
—ceded territory, in, **20**, 145–148, 195
—foreign military bases, in, **20**, 193
—foreign ships, on, **20**, 195
—former nationals, war crimes, **14**, 200–201
—passports, **26**, 131–145
—property abroad, **4**, 185; **15**, 176–204; **23**, 270–284
ouster by conciliation commission, **18**, 394–395
passenger on aircraft making forced landing, **23**, 151–153
personal, **1**, 158–161; **4**, 181–189; **6**, 175–180; **7**, 192–199; **9**, 294–298; **14**, 91–92; **17**, 189–191; **18**, 234–235; **19**, 226–254; **20**, 188–195; **21**, 125–135; **23**, 269–284; **24**, 256–266; **26**, 209–234; **28**, 115–138; **30**, 105–111; **31**, 267–274; **32**, 140–147; **33**, 194–201; **34**, 46, 91–97; **35**, 131–135
See also nationals abroad, over *and* nationals, over, *supra*
—exchange control, **26**, 232–234
—foreign employees of national air carrier, application of labour legislation, **28**, 115–138
—nationality alone as basis, **30**, 105–111
—protection of foreign commerce, **12**, 169–172
—reason for, **32**, 142
—waiver of international claims and, **32**, 156
piracy, in respect of: *see* Piracy
ports, in **1**, 109–111; **4**, 160–162; **5**, 129–131; **6**, 153–157, 175–177; **8**, 182–184, 208–212; **9**, 157–171; **10**, 155–176; **11**, 113–124, 127–128; **12**, 73–75; **15**, 110–115; **16**, 100–103, 309–311; **20**, 197–210; **23**, 151–153; **24**, 167–171; **31**, 227–247: *see also* national waters, *supra*
—alien seamen, wages claims, **1**, 109–110; **4**, 161–162; **9**, 157–161; **10**, 155–159, 165–166; **11**, 113–114; **12**, 73–75; **16**, 309–311
—armed merchantmen, **14**, 84–90
—attachment of foreign ship, **9**, 167–169
—consular jurisdiction, **8**, 208–209, 210–212, 470–471; **9**, 157–163, 169–170; **15**, 110–114; **16**, 100–103

Jurisdiction—*continued*
ports, in—*continued*
—crime on foreign ship, **4**, 160, 184–185; **6**, 175–177; **8**, 210; **9**, 167, 169–170; **15**, 108–109; **16**, 143–144; **20**, 154–155; **24**, 173–174; **31**, 241–247; **32**, 117–119
—detention of foreign ships in war, **10**, 267–272; **23**, 354–358
—foreign ships with emigrants, **9**, 166–167
—injury to alien on foreign ship at sea, **10**, 172–174; **11**, 115–116
—" internal economy " doctrine, **31**, 228–229, 231, 239–240
—" internal order " doctrine, **15**, 110–114; **16**, 100–103
—labour disputes on foreign ships, **24**, 167–171; **31**, 227–240
—Mixed Courts of Egypt, **9**, 167
—torts on foreign ship, **6**, 153–154; **8**, 208–209; **10**, 159–161, 169–171; **11**, 116–124; **20**, 197–210; **28**, 145–149
prisoners of war, over, **23**, 764–766
production of documents from abroad, **19**, 197; **22**, 184–197; **26**, 123–129; **28**, 138–142; **31**, 210, 214–219, 220–226; **32**, 100–102; **34**, 43–46
property situate abroad, **18**, 210
protective principle: *see* criminal, *supra*
reciprocity as basis, **24**, 223–226
restriction on exercise of, in treaty, **24**, 127–128
revenue laws, **5**, 101–102
sea bed, over, **20**, 535
ships, foreign territorial waters, in, **1**, 176–177; **6**, 123–126, 154–159, 175–177; **15**, 71; **21**, 126–135. *See also* law of the flag, *supra*
ships on high seas: *see* law of the flag, *supra*
ships, national owned, registered abroad, **26**, 222–226, 227–231, 236–239; **28**, 108–109, 112–113; **31**, 230–240
ships, tort on foreign, **26**, 240–241: *see also under* ports, *supra*
sovereignty, derived from, **34**, 50
State loans, *re*, **5**, 116–118, 468–469; **8**, 13–22
State succession, effect of, **4**, 117; **16**, 64; **18**, 77–78; **22**, 197–200
submission to—
—diplomatic envoys: *see* Diplomatic envoys, immunities, waiver
—foreign States: *see under* Foreign States
territorial, **1**, 105–109; **3**, 133–150; **4**, 141–181; **5**, 95–104; **6**, 135–174; **7**, 145–192; **11**, 107–111;

Jurisdiction—*continued*
territorial—*continued*
12, 61–168; **15,** 72–75; **17,** 136–188; **18,** 171–189, 197–206; **19,** 158–226, 229–254; **20,** 123, 170–188; **21,** 89–125; **22,** 168–209; **23,** 130–268; **24,** 161–166; 255, 867; **26,** 123–131, 145–160; **27,** 103–107; **28,** 108–142; **30,** 94–104; **31,** 206–267; **32,** 90–140; **33,** 155–173; **34,** 43–91; **35,** 89–109
—aliens, over, **34,** 51–80
—civil actions between aliens, **34,** 49–50
—confiscatory legislation: *q.v.*
—control of enemy property, **12,** 63
—effectiveness, principle of, **26,** 147, 155, 157
—effects doctrine, **2,** 109–111; **8,** 253; **11,** 111–112; **17,** 138–140; **22,** 207–208; **31,** 212, 213
—foreign seaman on foreign ship, **34,** 46–49
—foreign seaman, right of action, **35,** 101–103
—issue of habeas corpus from English High Court to protectorate, **28,** 48–78
—judgment confiscating debt situate abroad, **32,** 107–110
—objective principle, **24,** 156–160, 264–265
—over nationals, freedom to travel, **35,** 89–96
—penal laws, **35,** 97–101
—presence of defendant, **26,** 156
—presumption, scope of statutes, **35,** 107
—production of documents situate abroad, **19,** 197; **22,** 184–197; **26,** 123–129; **28,** 138–142; **31,** 210, 214–219, 220–226; **32,** 100–102; **33,** 158–163; **34,** 43–46
—property, taxation, foreign-registered aircraft, **32,** 90–100
—protest by foreign government, **35,** 104, 108–109
—public law rights, **30,** 27, 29
—Restitution Authorities, Germany, former British Zone, **26,** 145–149, 150–158
—service of process, **31,** 258
—tangibles and intangibles, **26,** 151, 154, 156–157
—taxation of aliens, income earned outside State, **27,** 103–107
—universality principle, **24,** 166
territorial waters, in: *see under* Territorial waters
territoriality principle: *see under* criminal, *supra*
territory, distinguished, **26,** 513–518
tort on foreign ship on high seas, **26,** 240–241

Jurisdiction—*continued*
transfer of, cession, distinguished, **26,** 116
treaty, creation by, **23,** 493–497
treaty, restriction in, **24,** 127–128
treaty rights, waiver of, **23,** 255–259
trespass to land abroad, **23,** 27–28
venue and, **33,** 172
warlike operations, **17,** 151–152
warships and crews abroad, resolutions of Institute of International Law (1928), **11,** 167–168; **12,** 118–123, 142
Jurisdiction, international, absence of compulsory, nullity of arbitral awards, **30,** 479
Jury, trial by, law of U.S.A., **11,** 49–50
Jus gentium, **16,** 152
Jus posteriori derogat priori, **25,** 279
Jus postliminii: *see Postliminium*
Jus puniendi, **17,** 189
Jus sanguinis and *jus soli*: *see under* Nationality
Just and unjust wars, **5,** 229

K

Kamerun, Protectorate: *see* Cameroon, Protectorate
Kellogg–Briand Pact: *see* Renunciation of War, General Treaty for
Kentucky, boundary with Indiana, **31,** 192
Kenya—
Indian Succession Act, s. 212, **27,** 622
Trading with the Enemy Ordinance, **27,** 615–628
Kerensky Government: *see* Russia, Provisional Government of 1917
Khedive of Egypt, claims against United Kingdom, **4,** 434
Kidnapping—
extradition for, **5,** 283–284; **7,** 337–338
offender from foreign territory, **11,** 101–104
Kiel Canal—
international servitude, **2,** 329–330
jurisdiction in, **17,** 133–135
"King's Resolution", Norway, **1,** 114
status of, **2,** 99–102, 329; **3,** 128–129
Treaty of Versailles, **3,** 128–129
Kiel, Treaty of (1814), **6,** 95
Kitchener, Lord, Proclamation to Boer forces, **2,** 419
Kommissarische Verwalter, appointment in German-occupied territory, **11,** 20–21, 25, 33
Korea—
hostilities in (1950–1953), **23,** 684–686; **24,** 929–932
—after Armistice (1953), **22,** 896–898

Korea—*continued*
hostilities (1950-1953)—*continued*
—Armistice Agreement, **24**, 929, 931, 932
—whether war, **20**, 578–599; **21**, 416–430; **22**, 893–899; **26**, 626–638
independence, date of, **32**, 179, 182
Japanese Peace Treaty, effect on nationality, **32**, 170–186
merger with Japan, effect of, **17**, 15; **32**, 174, 180–181
North, non-recognition by Japan, **32**, 183
two governments, legal status, **32**, 186
U.N. Command in, criminal jurisdiction, **32**, 367–368
Krassin, M., head of Russian mission in U.K., **1**, 296–297
Kriegsräson geht vor Kriegsmanier, **16**, 543; **17**, 433
Kurile Islands, status of, **32**, 582–583
Kuwait, British Court—
—applicable law, **26**, 248–250
—jurisdiction, **26**, 245–254
Kwajalein Islands: *see* Pacific Islands

L

Labour Conventions: *see* International Labour Conventions
Labour legislation—
aliens, application to, **34**, 51–80
foreign ships in port, **24**, 167–171; **31**, 227–240
ships on high seas, application to, **30**, 112–115
Labrador boundary dispute, **4**, 120–121
Laches, doctrine of, international tribunals, application, **3**, 246. *See also* Prescription, extinctive
Laholm Bay, **6**, 123–124
Lake Geneva, Convention on Control of Navigation, **32**, 348–350
Lakes—
Constance, **2**, 102; **4**, 128; **7**, 140–141
Erie, **4**, 122
Geneva, **32**, 348–350
Lanoux, **24**, 101–142
Ontario, **4**, 122
sovereignty over, **7**, 140–141
status of, **2**, 102–103
Superior, **11**, 92, 124
thalweg in, **11**, 91–93
La Marsa, Treaty of, **5**, 360
Lambeth, Treaty of (1217), **20**, 98, 128, 129, 131, 132
Land reform, taking of property under, **30**, 118–120
Landlocked seas, **20**, 167–169
" Largest ship-owning nations ", **30**, 426–447, *passim*
Lateran Treaties, **8**, 151–152, 236, 254
Treaty of 1929... **9**, 103, 105, 109, 111, 425, 435–436, 438; **10**, 106–108, 355–364; **16**, 82; **19**, 142–143; **22**, 536; **23**, 115; **24**, 214, 216; **26**, 183–188
Latvia—
annexation of, by U.S.S.R., **10**, 73, 80–86, 91–97; **11**, 142–143; **12**, 39–43; **15**, 45–48; **18**, 49–50, 61–64, 251, 288–289; **20**, 180–182; **22**, 103, 230–233; **24**, 483; **28**, 95–97, 386, 388–389
—non-recognition of, **10**, 73, 91–97; **12**, 39–43; **15**, 45–48; **18**, 61–64, 288–289; **22**, 230–233; **28**, 95–97, 386, 388–389; **35**, 62–65
evacuation by Russian authorities, **1**, 456
France, Commercial Treaty (1937), **18**, 288, 289
Germany, Commercial Treaty (1926), **7**, 305–306
Red Cross Association of, **4**, 458
Soviet Republic, nationalization decrees, **10**, 73, 80, 91; **11**, 142–143; **15**, 45–48; **18**, 61–64
U.S.A., Treaty of Friendship, Commerce and Consular Rights (1928), **18**, 63; **28**, 96
U.S.S.R., Treaty with (railways, 1920), **9**, 308
Latvia and Esthonia: *see* Latvia, *supra*
Lausanne, Convention on Exchange of Greek and Turkish Populations (1923), **20**, 329
Treaty of (1923), **2**, 334, 387–389; **11**, 277; **13**, 113–114; **14**, 3–5, 36–40, 110; **16**, 230, 312; **19**, 19, 21, 22, 23, 136, 137; **20**, 628; **22**, 663; **23**, 94, 305, 354, 667, 782
—" allied nationals ", **5**, 25–26
—amnesty, **4**, 553–554
—capitulations, abrogation of, **3**, 192–193; **4**, 192–193
—claims, lodging of, **5**, 429
—concessions, **3**, 204–205; **8**, 153–154; **23**, 79–80, 87, 90, 96, 98, 107, 108, 343–348, 667–668
—currency of debt payments, **6**, 286
—decisions of occupying authorities, **4**, 34, 414 n.
—enemies, definition, **5**, 483–484
—financial clauses, **23**, 95–96
—forced contracts, **5**, 372
—life assurance policies, **6**, 267
—liquidation of property, **4**, 435–436
—loan contracts, **23**, 97
—minorities, **23**, 667
—mixed arbitral tribunals, jurisdiction, **5**, 434, 444

Lausanne, Treaty of (1923)—*contd.*
—nationality provisions, **3**, 48; **4**, 48; **9**, 47; **28**, 291–292
—option of nationality, **4**, 257, 301–302
—Ottoman Public Debt, distribution of, **7**, 473
—pre-war contracts, **4**, 562–563
—ratification, **2**, 312
—recognition of effects by Egypt, **3**, 53, 191–192; **4**, 49, 192–193
—renunciation of claims, **4**, 435–437; **5**, 372; **6**, 345
—restitution of property, **4**, 29–30, 395, 433; **5**, 25–26, 183, 444, 448–449
—restoration of ships, **4**, 439–440
—State succession and, **8**, 123–127
Law: *see* International law; General principles of law; Municipal law
"Law and equity", meaning of, **1**, 369–371
Law, continuity of, change of sovereignty, **4**, 95–96; **8**, 143–151
Law governing contract (bonds), **9**, 23: *see also* Bonds *and* State loans
"Law of nations", crime against, **32**, 1–4
Law of nature: *see* Natural law
Laws of war: *see* Hague Conventions *and* Regulations; War
League of Nations—
Administrative Tribunal, **21**, 322, 344
—jurisdiction, **7**, 461–465; **13**, 200
—law applied by, **6**, 408
—revision of judgments of, **27**, 296–297
admission to, **5**, 412
—effect of recognition of government, **8**, 114–115
Albania, financial reform, **20**, 445–446
Assembly—
—powers, officials' salaries, **6**, 409–410
—powers, contracts concluded by organization, **13**, 199–202
—Resolution of 1922 (French mandate over Cameroons), **11**, 53
—resolutions, legal effect, **22**, 688–689
—Rules of Procedure, **22**, 680, 681
Assembly of 1946...**17**, 51–52, 54, 58
Codification Committee, **18**, 379
—Report on Territorial Waters (1927), **18**, 116, 380
Council—
—arbitral functions, **3**, 387–390
— —concurrent jurisdiction with P.C.I.J., **4**, 497
—arbitrators, appointment of, **5**, 58
—decisions, binding force, **5**, 346; **22**, 688–689

League of Nations—*continued*
Council—*continued*
— —interpretation, **6**, 381–382
—jurisdiction under Art. 15 of Covenant, **2**, 390–391
—Mandates system and, **22**, 664, 667, 670, 672–677
—minorities, function in respect of, **2**, 289–290, 291
—minorities treaties, amendment of, **22**, 681
—report under Art. 11 of Covenant, **5**, 409, 423, 443; **7**, 494
—reservations to treaties, report on, **18**, 372, 379, 380
—residuary powers, U.N. General Assembly and, **23**, 42–43, 45, 50, 67
—resolutions, binding force, **6**, 405
—Rules of Procedure, **22**, 680, 681
—voting, effect of, **22**, 664
— —unanimity rule, **22**, 656, 657, 663, 664, 667, 669, 672, 673–674, 689
Covenant—
—annexation of territory, **14**, 49; **15**, 61
—*bona fides*, principle of, **19**, 209
—interpretation of, **2**, 354; **6**, 28; **7**, 465–466
—mandates provision, and nationality, **15**, 211–213
—mandates provision, legal effect, **17**, 49, 50, 51, 54, 57; **22**, 655, 663, 666; **23**, 40, 68
—requirement of unanimity, **7**, 494
—treaty application, judicial questions, **19**, 431
Danzig, guarantee of Constitution, **6**, 47
delegates, immunities of, **3**, 325–326; **5**, 313
dissolution, effect of, **17**, 51–52
domestic jurisdiction, matters of, **2**, 350–354
—provisional nature of decision, **2**, 351–352
—relative character, **2**, 351
functions, mandated territories, **14**, 66
—succession of U.N. to, **17**, 53–55
Mandates, practice as to, **23**, 41–42, 45, 48–52
officials—
—immunities of, **3**, 325–326; **5**, 314–317, 318; **32**, 321–322
—rights against organization, **13**, 199–202
refugees and, **15**, 290
sanctions against Italy, **8**, 422–423, 476
Secretariat—
—claims against, **7**, 461–465
—conditions of service, **6**, 406–410

League of Nations—*continued*
Secretariat—*continued*—
—diplomatic immunities of staff, **3**, 325–326; **5**, 314–317, 318; **32**, 321–322
—status of officials, **10**, 416–418
Secretary-General, diplomatic immunities, **5**, 314–317, 318; **8**, 395–397
Staff Pensions Fund, **18**, 456–457, 467–468
supervisory responsibilities, U.N. and, **22**, 660, 669–671
Switzerland, Agreement on Privileges and Immunities (1926), **22**, 537, 547, 548
treaties, reservations, practice as to, **18**, 379, 380
U.N. as successor to, **17**, 53–55; **23**, 66–67
winding-up Resolution (1946), **22**, 655
Leases, grant of, during enemy occupation, **8**, 503–504
Leases in perpetuity, **9**, 118
Leases, international, **2**, 95–96; **3**, 118–119; **4**, 180; **5**, 80–82; **7**, 112–113; **9**, 116; **13**, 48–49; **14**, 49–55; **15**, 64–68; **20**, 148–153; **22**, 154–156; **32**, 77–79
Cochin, Agreement with British Crown (1899), **26**, 116–117
foreign military bases, **32**, 77–79
issue of writ of habeas corpus from lessee State, **28**, 59
jurisdiction over, **20**, 148–153
Kowloon, Convention of 1898, China and Great Britain, jurisdiction in walled city, **27**, 49–58
military purposes, grant for, application of law of lessee State, **31**, 121–128
U.S. base in Philippines, whether " foreign country ", **32**, 77–79
Lebanon: *see also* Syria and the Lebanon—
citizenship, **4**, 301–302
Israel, armistice (1949), **22**, 698–701
Mandate, **4**, 48–49, 52–53; **8**, 113
Legal Assistance, Treaty of, continuance in force, **5**, 47
Legal rights, uncertainty, effect of, **31**, 35, 49, 104
Legation buildings: *see* Diplomatic premises
Legislation, confiscatory: *see* Confiscatory legislation
Legislation, extraterritorial effect: *see also* Extraterritorial effect of legislation
fiscal, German-occupied countries, in, non-recognition of, **26**, 56–57
Legislation, extraterritorial effect—*continued*
" gold clauses ", concerning, **9**, 156; **11**, 26–28, 30–32
incompatible with international obligations, responsibility for enactment, **31**, 72
international law, presumption of consistency with, **6**, 443–444; **7**, 7; **12**, 221; **13**, 26–27; **30**, 204–206, 216, 217; **34**, 62
" principles of modern legislation ", taxation of aliens and, **8**, 336–337
Legislatures, debates in, treaty interpretation and, **2**, 336–337
Legitimacy, municipal law doctrine, **2**, 35–37
" Legitimate interest ", meaning, **4**, 478
Legitimatio per subsequens matrimonium, **7**, 272–273
Lend-Lease Agreements: *see under* U.S.A. and other States concerned
Lèse majesté, **8**, 89–90
Letters rogatory, **9**, 305; **31**, 223
execution of, **11**, 63
Hague Convention on Civil Procedure (1905), under, **6**, 90
limitation of proceedings, **11**, 104–106
Levée en masse—
civil war, **16**, 367–368, 370, 380
occupied territory, **16**, 514–516
Lex fori, Conciliation Commission, of, **25**, 107
Lex locus actus, **15**, 24
Lex non cogit ad impossibilia, **15**, 543
Lex posterior derogat legi priori, **6**, 355, 357
Lex rei sitae, **15**, 24; **18**, 393
Lex situs, **18**, 171, 175: *see also* Debts
Lex specialis derogat legi generali, **5**, 400–401, 440; *see also under* Treaties, interpretation
Libel: *see* Defamation
Libel *in rem*, foreign public ships, **1**, 137–144, 146–150, 156; **2**, 117–119, 120–121, 137–138, 141–144; **3**, 186–189; **9**, 177–178, 250–263, 272–277, 279–282, 284–289; **10**, 199–204, 217–230, 240–247; **11**, 153–161; **12**, 105–112, 143–149; **13**, 82–85; **14**, 83; **16**, 142–143; **17**, 167–170; **32**, 127–136
Liberal Professions, Convention on Exercise of (1889), **7**, 442–443
Liberec, district of, Czechoslovakia, **1**, 11–13, 17–19
Liberia—
U.S.A., Consular Convention (1938), **34**, 70, 75–77
U.S.A., Treaty of Friendship, Commerce and Navigation (1938), **26**, 228, 230; **34**, 70, 75

Libya—
Italian State property in—
—administration, transfer of, **25**, 518–522
—Agreement, Italy–U.K. (1951), **22**, 104–113; **25**, 15–20
—Italian Peace Treaty (Art. 23), **25**, 4–5, 7–9
—succession to, **25**, 2–26
Italy and, **17**, 106–107
status of, **18**, 77–78
transfer of power (1955), **22**, 103–113
U.S.A., Base Rights Agreement (1954), **23**, 241–244
Liechtenstein, nationality law (1934), **22**, 350–351, 359, 362, 364, 369, 379–380, 384
Liens: *see* Attorney's lien *and* Maritime liens
Life interest, valuation of, **26**, 296
Lighthouse as military objective, **15**, 687–688
Lighthouses concession, international character, **23**, 342, 346. *See also under* State succession
Lima, Inter-American Conference, Declaration of (1938), **23**, 703
Limitation of actions: *see* Prescription *and* Statutes of limitation
Limited partnership, whether " permanent establishment ", **33**, 400–407
Liquidation, measures of, **4**, 88–90
expropriation and confiscation, distinguished, **4**, 150; **18**, 653–654; **23**, 693
Liquidation of corporations—
belligerent occupant, by, **18**, 642–645; **23**, 687–701
foreign: *see under* Corporations, foreign
Liquor—
importation into Norway, **1**, 113–114
importation, prohibition of, **11**, 130–135
International Convention, Suppression of Contraband Traffic (1925), **8**, 406–410
Liquor traffic, U.S. prohibition treaties, **1**, 111–112; **3**, 151–168; **5**, 138–140; **6**, 3–7, 127; **7**, 163–164, 203–205, 454–455
Literary and Artistic Property, Convention for Protection of (Brussels, 1948), news photographs, **28**, 478–479
South American Convention (1889), **7**, 401–403
Lithuania—
annexation by U.S.S.R., **10**, 80–86; **15**, 48–50; **18**, 79–80; **20**, 57–62; **22**, 97–100, 101–102; **26**, 76; **32**, 73–76; **33**, 43–46
Lithuania—*continued*
annexation by U.S.S.R.—*continued*
—non-recognition of, **10**, 80–86; **20**, 193–195; **22**, 230–232; **26**, 76; **32**, 73–76; **33**, 43–46; **35**, 51–57
foreign consuls in, functions, **6**, 335
German occupation (1941), **20**, 58; **22**, 101–102
Germany, Treaty of Cession (1939), **11**, 75
Jews in, judicial notice of fate of, **19**, 71
Memel, Convention and Statute (1924), **6**, 21–25, 384, 404–406; **22**, 681
Memel Territory, relations with, **6**, 21–25
Poland, termination of war with, **3**, 446–447; **5**, 491–492
Soviet occupation (1940 and 1944), **20**, 58, 59
status of (1947), **22**, 97–100
U.S.S.R., Peace Treaty with (1920), **6**, 150; **7**, 456; **9**, 308
Litispendence, **3**, 425; **4**, 505–506; **5**, 446–448, 499
Litvinov Assignment, 1933: *see under* United States of America
Loans—
colonial, German guarantee, **6**, 62–65
compulsory, State responsibility, **5**, 173–174, 190
government: *see also* Bonds *and* State loans—
—applicable law, **8**, 13–22
—currency of payment, **29**, 7–8
—interruption of service in war, **29**, 4–11
municipal, suspension of payment in war, **29**, 11–20
public—
—assimilation to private law transactions, **6**, 36–37
—private law or administrative contract, **11**, 30–32
Locality of cause of action, **7**, 146–147
Local remedies rule: *see* Exhaustion of local remedies
Locarno, Treaties (1925), **4**, 12; **22**, 681; **24**, 814
jurisdiction of P.C.I.J. under, **4**, 500–501; **24**, 814
Locks, Meuse waterworks, in, **8**, 445–450
Locus delicti commissi, jurisdiction and, **4**, 157–158
French extradition law, **4**, 157–158; **6**, 308–309
Lombardy, cession to France, **1**, 88
London Conference on Reparations (1924), **3**, 349–350; **9**, 155
London, Cyprus Agreement (1959), **25**, 31–32

London, Declaration of (1885), **17,** 445–446
London Naval Agreement (1930), **13,** 218, 219
London Naval Conference, 1909...**17,** 447
London, Naval Declaration of (1909), **4,** 568, 569; **5,** 342, 423, 488–490, 515, 518; **11,** 262, 303; **12,** 288, 552, 558, 565; **16,** 582, 589, 591, 592–593, 595, 596, 597, 601; **19,** 480; **20,** 673; **23,** 715
customary international law, evidence of, **3,** 486
Hague Conventions and, **3,** 486
London, Peace Treaty of (1913), **7,** 99; **8,** 155; **23,** 87, 346, 663, 665, 666
clauses on Crete, **4,** 320
London, Protocol (1924), occupation of Ruhr, **4,** 404–405
London, Treaty of (1883) *re* the Danube, **4,** 429–430, 441–442
London, Truce of (1471), **20,** 99, 132
Loot, replevin of, **15,** 17–18
Looting, **2,** 174–175
gold from Rome by German forces (1943), **20,** 466–467, 470
troops of protecting power, by, **2,** 174
Lorraine, reunion with France, **1,** 448–449: *see also* Alsace-Lorraine
Loss of profits: *see under* Damages
Louisiana—
acts of sovereignty over marginal sea, **31,** 184–185
admission to U.S.A., 1812...**31,** 177, 180, 182
cession and retrocession, France–Spain, **31,** 181
cession to U.S.A. by France, **31,** 160, 180, 182
Mississippi, boundary with, **31,** 179
seaward boundary, claim to three leagues, **31,** 151, 177–185, 195, 204; **32,** 86–89
Lübeck Bay, **1,** 98, 99; **4,** 134–135
claims to, **4,** 8, 115–116
Lucrum cessans: *see* Damages, loss of profits
Luneville, Peace Treaty of (1801), **7,** 131
Luxembourg—
Allied Supreme Command, Agreement (1944), **18,** 361–362
Belgium—
—Double Taxation Agreement (1931), **18,** 11–12; **23,** 27
—Treaty of Economic Union (1921), **17,** 9–11; **18,** 396–397; **28,** 511–513; **31,** 425–426
Constitution, **18,** 13, 362
German occupation of, **15,** 537; **16,** 479–480; **18,** 633–634
Luxembourg—*continued*
Germany—
—Agreement, railways (1872), **6,** 131
—annexation by, **11,** 226–227
—respect for sovereignty of Luxembourg, **5,** 8
import duties on coal, removal, **23,** 598–605
Import Office for Fuel, **25,** 413
International Monetary Fund, membership, **22,** 729
Prussia, Double Taxation Treaty (1909), **5,** 350
treaty-making power, **31,** 425–426

M

Madagascar—
annexation by France, State succession, **11,** 77–78
U.K., Commercial Treaty (1865), **11,** 77–78
Madrid, Convention (1880), right of protection in Morocco, **4,** 311; **15,** 328; **16,** 9; **19,** 263, 266, 267, 272, 273, 275, 279, 280, 291–302, *passim*; **22,** 17–18
Magna Carta, **18,** 156
punishment, limitation of, **26,** 435
right to travel, provision on, **26,** 135
Maratha Empire, Treaties with Portugal—
(1741), **24,** 368; **31,** 54, 95, 96
(1779), **24,** 850, 852, 859; **31,** 36, 40–41, 50, 51, 77, 90, 91, 109, 115, 117
(1785), **24,** 859; **31,** 68, 77, 88, 90, 91, 109
Mails, fraud committed through, **12,** 68–74
location of offence, **31,** 270–271
Main navigable channel, doctrine of: *see Thalweg*
Majestas, meaning, **8,** 89–90; **15,** 79–86
Malaya—
criminal jurisdiction, crime by national abroad, **31,** 272
Federated Malay States, protectorate status, **9,** 33
Japanese occupation of, **15,** 449, 548–549, 583–592; **18,** 585–590, 638–640; **19,** 183–185; **20,** 653–654
state of emergency, in, whether amounting to war, **27,** 612–614
Malines, Great Council, judgments of 1559, Dutch fishing disputes, **11,** 175–176
Malta, Sovereign Order of, **8,** 2–7
competence of Italian courts and, **6,** 88–89
status of, **22,** 1–5; **24,** 1–4
Malum prohibitum and *malum in se*, **4,** 20
Manchuria, status of, **22,** 90–97

Mandated territories—
" A " and " B " mandates, administrative officials, **11,** 51–52
Act of State, French practice, **5,** 17
aliens in, **12,** 12–15; **15,** 281–285
appellate jurisdiction of mandatory, **7,** 50, 51–52
assimilation to colonies, fiscal purposes, **11,** 52–53
British Dominions as mandatories, **4,** 53–54; **7,** 36–56; **8,** 98–109
" C " mandates, **8,** 98–109; **9,** 44
capitulations in, **3,** 48–49
capitulations in, abolition of, **3,** 191–192, 268–269
Cameroons, French mandate: *see* Cameroons
colonies, assimilation to, **11,** 52–53
colonies, distinguished, **7,** 45; **23,** 37
consular officers in, powers, **21,** 251–253
—immunities, **7,** 395–396
courts of, competence, claim for tortious acts of administration, **22,** 88–89
discrimination in, **8,** 110–113
equality of opportunity in, **8,** 110–113
extradition from, **9,** 50
—to, **2,** 275–276; **5,** 32; **8,** 382–383
extradition treaties, application to, **12,** 47–48
former, and Trusteeship Agreements, **22,** 83–86
foreign relations of, **21,** 253
human rights in, **18,** 236–243
interpretation of mandates, **2,** 331–334; **4,** 50–52
jurisdiction of mandatory, **15,** 115–125, 149
Lebanon, French mandate over, **4,** 48–49, 52–53; **7,** 35–36
—status of nationals, **8,** 113: *see also* Syria and Lebanon, *infra*
legislation of mandatory contrary to mandate, **15,** 40–42
legislative powers of Dominion Parliament, **4,** 53–54
legislative powers of mandatory, **7,** 36–41, 44–50, 53–56; **8,** 98–109; **9,** 45; **15,** 38–39, 42–44; **16,** 39–41
nationality in, **3,** 47–48; **8,** 113; **9,** 44–51; **15,** 211–213; **16,** 38–39; **18,** 55–56; **19,** 69, 327–329; **20,** 49–51; **22,** 87–88; **28,** 80–81
neutrality of, **15,** 693–694
New Guinea, Australian mandate over, **7,** 46–52; **8,** 98–109; **15,** 147–153
officials of mandatory, status, **7,** 35–36
open door, **8,** 110–113
Palestine, British mandate over, **8,** 110–113; **11,** 51; **16,** 38, 42–45; **17,** 347–348, 444

Mandated territories—*continued*
Palestine, British mandate over—*continued*
—applicable law, **14,** 33–35, 66
—citizenship, **3,** 47–48; **9,** 43–46; **14,** 32–33; **17,** 111–112
—detention of Palestinian citizen abroad, **12,** 64–68
—discrimination, religious, **4,** 55–56
—immigration provisions, **13,** 53, 54–55; **15,** 115–125; **21,** 12–15
—interpretation of mandate, **2,** 331–334, 387–389, 392, 393, 398, 399; **3,** 46–47; **4,** 50–52
—powers of mandatory, **13,** 52–53
—termination of, **16,** 68; **17,** 313
protectorates and, **5,** 31 n.; **12,** 14
public land régime, **6,** 48–49
recognition of foreign government by mandatory, binding force, **11,** 51
relationship to mandatory, **15,** 38–39
rights and duties of mandatory, **2,** 27; **3,** 44–47, 204–205; **4,** 50–57; **7,** 36–56; **11,** 54; **12,** 12–15; **14,** 29–32; **16,** 41–45; **21,** 250–253; **23,** 38–70, *passim*
South West Africa, South African mandate over, **2,** 27–31; **7,** 53–56; **9,** 45; **15,** 211–213; **16,** 39–41; **17,** 47–60; **22,** 651–689 *passim*
—nationality in, **15,** 237–248
—petitions, admissibility of, **23,** 38–44, 46, 50
—status of, **3,** 42–44; **4,** 47–48; **5,** 30–32; **16,** 39–41; **17,** 47–60; **22,** 651–652, 662, 666; **23,** 38–39, 40, 54, 292–293
— —modification of, **17,** 57–60
—status of German protectorate, **8,** 131–132
—U.N. supervision, **22,** 86
sovereignty over, **2,** 27–31; **6,** 48–49; **7,** 35–36; **8,** 98–109; **12,** 12
State succession in, **8,** 128–136
supervision by U.N. General Assembly, **22,** 655, 683–689
Syria, French mandate over, **4,** 48–49, 52–53; **7,** 35–36; **11,** 54
—administrative acts, whether reviewable, **5,** 30–31
—applicable law, **8,** 110
—capitulations, effect on, **7,** 395–396
—position of mandatory, **4,** 55
taxation in, **11,** 52–53
treaties, application to, **4,** 47–48, 52–53
—authority to make, **4,** 47–48, 52–53
United Nations, position regarding, **22,** 652, 655, 658, 664, 681
Western Samoa, New Zealand mandate over, **7,** 36–45, 46
Mandates—
continuation after dissolution of League, **17,** 51–52

Mandates—*continued*
Council of League and, **22,** 664, 667–670, 672–677
enforceability of provisions, municipal courts, **14,** 29–32
I.C.J., supervision by, **17,** 55
law of territory, as part of, **16,** 41–45
League of Nations practice, hearing of petitioners, **23,** 41–42, 45, 48–53
Mandates Commission, position of, **22,** 675, 687–688; **23,** 68
Mandatory, responsibility for tortious acts of local administration, **22,** 88–89
Mandatory, vote in Council of League, **22,** 663, 670, 674, 677
nature of, **7,** 42–43; **17,** 48–51
obligation to place territory under Trusteeship, **17,** 55–57
petition, right of, **17,** 48, 54–55
petitions, oral hearing, **23,** 41–42, 45, 48–52, 57–58, 63–64
recognition by Mandatory of continuation of obligations, **17,** 52–53
sovereignty under, **17,** 444
succession to concessions granted by Mandatory, **22,** 113–122
—land requisitioned by Mandatory, **22,** 123
supervising authority, rights and duties, **22,** 86
termination of, **15,** 40–42, 58–59; **16,** 68; **21,** 444, 458
transitional period before Trusteeship, **35,** 458
Trusteeship system and, **17,** 48, 51, 55–57; **22,** 83–86
Mannheim, Act of (1868), **4,** 123–124; **5,** 88–90; **6,** 117–119, 355; **7,** 12–13; **8,** 166–169; **11,** 228; **13,** 49–50; **15,** 69; **16,** 78–80; **17,** 123–125, 354–356; **18,** 85; **19,** 149–157, 469–470, 487–488; **20,** 164–165, 409–410; **21,** 3–8, 276–277, 300–303; **24,** 97–100, 172
German denunciation (1936), **20,** 165; **24,** 99
Manus Island, status, **15,** 152–156
Maps—
acquisition of treaty character, **33,** 50, 71–72, 86, 93, 99–103, 108
adoption of, by State, **33,** 61–65, 70, 86–87, 105
evidence from, **4,** 487–488; **7,** 122–123, 125, 126
—material error, effect, **33,** 43–148, *passim*
—probative value, **27,** 75, 77, 90, 95
Mare clausum/mare liberum, **18,** 132
Marianas: *see* Saipan
Maritime Assistance, Brussels Convention (1910), **12,** 123
Maritime assistance, "*résultat utile*", **11,** 230
Maritime belt: *see* Territorial waters
Maritime Committee, international conventions under auspices of, **13,** 103–105
Maritime conventions, interpretation, **30,** 442: *see also* Inter-Governmental Maritime Consultative Organization
Maritime frontier, jurisdiction at, **1,** 111–114; **3,** 151–169; **6,** 157–160; **7,** 163–164, 209–212; **8,** 212–218; **9,** 127–128; **15,** 115–125; **20,** 171–172; **23,** 154–159; **27,** 45–49; **28,** 170–175
Maritime law—
Brussels Conferences (1905, 1909, 1910), **22,** 636
international, **20,** 197–210
judicial notice of, **16,** 9–10
tort on ships, application of *lex loci delicti*, **28,** 146–147
Maritime liens—
Brussels Convention (1926), **9,** 300; **33,** 389
extinction on condemnation of cargo, **12,** 529–530
foreign public ships, **1,** 148–150; **2,** 137–138, 141–144; **3,** 185, 187–189; **17,** 167–168; **26,** 175: *see also* Libel *in rem*, foreign public ships
privately-owned ships under requisition, **2,** 141–144
prize law, **10,** 613–618
requirements for enforcement, **17,** 198
social security contributions, for, **33,** 22
Maritime property, capture on land, **1,** 483–485; **32,** 601, 605, 608, 611, 614, 616–617
Maritime reprisals, conditions of legality of, **1,** 429; **12,** 543–554
Maritime warfare: *see* Sea warfare
Maritime Zone, Declaration by Peru, Chile and Ecuador (1952), **22,** 278–282
Marriage—
certificates, requirement of legalization, **10,** 410
consular premises, on, **12,** 252–253
diplomatic premises, on, applicable law, **27,** 253–254
Hague Convention, Conflicts of Marriage Laws (1902), **5,** 132
high seas, on, **1,** 163, 211–212
nationality of wife, effect on: *see* Married women, nationality of
polygamous, admission of aliens, **18,** 294–298
polygamous, nationality of children, **4,** 296–297
U.S.S.R., in—
—recognition by Hungary, **4,** 36–37
— —by Switzerland, **4,** 62–64

Married women—
alien, expulsion of, **11**, 197
denationalization of husband, effect, **11**, 182–183
nationality of, **1**, 212; **2**, 221–222; **3**, 275–276; **4**, 315–317; **5**, 240–241; **6**, 255–258, 263–264; **8**, 303–304; **11**, 6–9; **12**, 184; **14**, 109, 110, 111, 121; **15**, 268–269; **16**, 182–184, 227–229, 230–231; **18**, 248–249, 276–280; **20**, 246–248; **21**, 194–195; **26**, 418–419, 463–465; **28**, 436–437; **32**, 170–185, *passim*, 192–194
naturalized, denationalization of, **5**, 237–238
right to option of nationality, **1**, 220–221; **28**, 436–437
stateless, poor persons' procedure, **6**, 263–264
Martial law—
consideration by courts, **1**, 21
Egypt, in, **1**, 42
" Material damage to tangible things ", meaning, **3**, 251–254
Mavrommatis concessions, re-adaptation of, **4**, 50–52
Mayence, Act of (1831), **8**, 166–168; **16**, 78; **21**, 6
—(1867), **21**, 7
Measure of damages: *see* Damages
Mecklenberg-Schwerin
—claim to Bay of Lübeck, **4**, 8
Germany, Treaty (railways) (1920), **5**, 330–332
Mediation—
compulsion to submit to, **20**, 559
Council of League of Nations, by, **3**, 389–390
joint, **30**, 461
nature of, **8**, 272
Medium filum, doctrine of, **4**, 121–122
Memel, Convention and Statute (1924), **6**, 21–25, 384, 404–406; **22**, 681
Memel Territory—
autonomy of, **6**, 21–25; **7**, 63
cession to Germany, State succession, **11**, 74–76
Lithuania, relations with, **6**, 21–25
Men-of-war: *see* Warships
Mental suffering, damages for, **2**, 193–194
Merchant ships: *see also* Neutral merchant ships—
armed, submarine warfare, **13**, 219
conversion of, **3**, 221–222; **5**, 511–513; **13**, 404; **14**, 88–89
—reconversion of, **5**, 512
convoy, under, **2**, 408; **4**, 568
criminal jurisdiction over, **22**, 295–299: *see also* Jurisdiction, law of the flag
defensively armed, status, **2**, 407–408
Merchant ships—*continued*
enemy, capture of, **2**, 452–454; **3**, 483–484; **13**, 401–406
—removal from occupied territory, whether equivalent, **34**, 261–263, 265–266
enemy, Hague Convention (1907), Status at Outbreak of Hostilities, **7**, 506; **11**, 264–265
enemy, in port, **1**, 410–414; **2**, 452–454; **3**, 483–484; **4**, 542; **5**, 487, 515, 518; **12**, 353–359: *see also* War, outbreak of
—destruction of, **4**, 569–570; **6**, 438–440
—requisition of, **6**, 440–441
—seizure of, **3**, 483–484
— —sequestration of, **12**, 353–357
exterritoriality of, **9**, 470; **10**, 252–258; **27**, 45–49
flag as determining jurisdiction over: *see* Jurisdiction, law of the flag
foreign port, in, jurisdiction: *see* Jurisdiction, ports, in
foreign territorial waters, in, jurisdiction over, **14**, 84–90; **20**, 171–172. *See also under* Territorial waters
manifest, requirement of production of, **11**, 130–135
men-of-war, distinguished, **6**, 94
mercantile fleet, foreign State as owner of, **2**, 138–139
neutral: *see* Neutral merchant ships
publicly owned, jurisdictional immunity: *see under* Public ships
public user of, **11**, 156–161
requisition of, **11**, 148–149, 153–154, 156–161
seaplanes, assimilation to, **5**, 82
status of, **5**, 510
—effect of salvage, **5**, 512
transport of troops by, **2**, 140
Merger of States—
contractual obligations, effect on, **27**, 30–31; **31**, 10–13
diplomatic envoys after, **20**, 180–182
nationality, effect on, **9**, 341
non-recognition of, **20**, 180–182, 193–194; **22**, 230–233
private rights, effect on, **27**, 32–35
sovereign State within Union, **18**, 69–72
Merger, theory of, extradition proceedings, **7**, 340–344
Methodist Church, position in Italy, **4**, 337
Meuse, River, waterworks on, **8**, 445–450
Mexico—
aliens and naturalization legislation, **18**, 280
boundary with U.S.A., **1**, 105–106; **31**, 171 n., 173, 183, 196–199

Mexico—*continued*
Carranza Government, **1,** 53; **3,** 59
—decrees of, **3,** 59
Civil Code (jurisdiction in contract), **11,** 105
Constitution, **1,** 249; **15,** 329; **18,** 309; **20,** 411–412; **22,** 616–617
—Art. 4 (freedom of commerce), **9,** 365
—Art. 8 (property in frontier districts), **9,** 379
—Art. 27 (frontier zone), **9,** 379
—Art. 30 (acquisition of nationality), **6,** 251
—Art. 33 (aliens), **9,** 365
—land ownership, **1,** 249
detention *incommunicado*, **5,** 256
enemy alien property, Vesting Decree, 1951... **22,** 913–915
Escobar revolution, **5,** 51–52
expropriation of oil installations, **1,** 249–250; **9,** 25, 90; **11,** 16–19; **20,** 326
expulsion of aliens, law as to, **1,** 253–254
Federal Judiciary Law, **23,** 486
France, Claims Convention (1924), **5,** 147, 149, 174, 192–193, 392, 424
Germany, Claims Convention (1925), **6,** 215
government, non-recognition by U.S.A., **2,** 49–50
independence from Spain, **31,** 160
Industrial Property Law, **24,** 596
Italy, Agreement on Mixed Claims Commission (1927), **22,** 851
jurisdictional immunity in U.S.A., **1,** 25–26
Penal Code, **5,** 162; **9,** 334
real property, Law of 1902...**9,** 379
recognition by U.S.A., 1822...**31,** 160
Texas, declaration of independence, 1836...**31,** 158, 160, 165
Texas, invasion of, 1846... **31,** 170
territorial waters, nine mile claim, **31,** 203
—three leagues, **31,** 174
U.K.—
—Claims Commission, rules of procedure, **5,** 221
—Claims Convention (1926), **5,** 166, 452; **6,** 219–220
U.S.A.—
—Boundary Treaties (1848–1905), **5,** 85, 176, 398; **6,** 114–116; **11,** 94–99; **13,** 178–181; **21,** 218–219; **26,** 120–121; **31,** 171 n., 173, 183, 196–199
—Claims Convention (1923), **5,** 176, 453; **6,** 275; **26,** 261
—Extradition Treaty (1899), **6,** 318–319; **24,** 257, 261, 262; **26,** 518, 520, 522

Mexico—*continued*
U.S.A.—*continued*
—Military Service Agreement (1943), **28,** 294
—Treaty concerning Stolen Vehicles (1936), **17,** 20–22; **20,** 411–412; **22,** 616
—Treaty of Guadeloupe Hidalgo (1848), **5,** 85, 176, 398; **6,** 113; **21,** 218–219; **26,** 119–121; **31,** 171, 173–174
—Utilization of Waters of Colorado, etc., Rivers, Treaty (1944), **22,** 573–580; **23,** 360–363; **26,** 556–557
Mexico, Gulf of, submerged land rights, **31,** 142–143, 144
Military attaché, privileges and immunities, smuggling, **32,** 307–308
Military Courts, Allied, jurisdiction of, **11,** 162–165
Military government before surrender, provisional nature, **26,** 698
Military missions, foreign, jurisdiction over, **12,** 164; **21,** 116–121; **30,** 392–393: *see also* Foreign armed forces
Military necessity, Hague Regulations and, **16,** 511–513
Military occupation of foreign territory, British forces in Palestine after termination of mandate, **22,** 127: *see also* Belligerent occupation
Military offence, extradition for, **7,** 357
Military operations, damage, State responsibility, **2,** 161; **4,** 234–236; **30,** 116–117
Military service—
acquisition of citizenship and, **6,** 253–254; **10,** 276–278
aliens, liability for, **10,** 116–123; **11,** 187–192; **12,** 208–221
enlistment in foreign army, effect on nationality, **5,** 217; **10,** 276–278; **11,** 182–183
exemption provision in treaty, **31,** 320
police service, distinguished, **11,** 182–183
Minefields, obligation to notify, **16,** 155–170
Ministère public, functions, **7,** 78–79, 174
Minorities, protection of, **2,** 287–296; **3,** 311–316; **4,** 352–356; **8,** 386–392; **14,** 26
"civil rights", meaning, **2,** 290
Council of League, function, **2,** 289–290
"equality in fact and in law", **2,** 290–291; **8,** 386–391
exterritoriality of monasteries of Mount Athos, **3,** 315–316

Minorities, protection of—*continued*
general conception of minorities, **2**, 292–294
linguistic minorities, **3**, 289–290, 313–314
national minorities, language of aliens, **2**, 262; **3**, 289, 313–314; **5**, 295
parent State, position, **3**, 312–313
religious minorities, **3**, 315–316
treaties, effectiveness, **2**, 294–295
—interpretation, **3**, 311–314; **4**, 352–354
—voting procedure provisions, **22**, 681
treatment apart from treaty, **4**, 355–356
Treaty for (1919, Czechoslovakia), **1**, 17; **3**, 313–314
Treaty for (Poland), **2**, 73–74, 221–222, 230–237, 250–251, 287–296; **6**, 37, 260, 322; **7**, 497
-effect on U.S.S.R., **6**, 359–360
Minors—
nationality of, **2**, 221–222; **3**, 238–239; **4**, 296–297, 319; **5**, 235–237; **7**, 272–273, 284–289, 290–294; **9**, 341, 354–358; **11**, 197; **12**, 195–196; **14**, 108–109, 110; **15**, 221–224; **16**, 227–229; **18**, 278; **20**, 248–249; **23**, 370; **27**, 236–238; **28**, 239
—adoption and, **20**, 248, 261–263
—Brazil, compulsory and collective naturalization, **5**, 235–237
—declaration of option, **4**, 319
—diplomats' children, **22**, 381
—foreign enlistment, **11**, 183
—illegal immigrants, **9**, 389
—illegitimate, **11**, 184–185
—loss of nationality of parent, **7**, 287–289, 290–294
naturalization of parent, effect, **7**, 284–287; **9**, 341, 351; **11**, 7–9; **12**, 195–196; **25**, 134, 136–138, 139–141, 144
polygamous marriage, children of, **4**, 296–297
Mississippi—
admission to the Union, **1**, 96; **31**, 186
cession by Britain to Spain, **31**, 186
cession by France to Britain, **31**, 185
cession by Spain to France, **31**, 186
Louisiana, boundary with, **31**, 179
seaward boundary, claim to six leagues, **31**, 151, 182, 185–187, 195, 204
Mitylene Island, Greek occupation of, **11**, 277–278
Mixed arbitral tribunals. *See also* Arbitral tribunals; Arbitration, international; Versailles, Treaty of, Art. 304
Mixed arbitral tribunals—*continued*
arbitrators, termination of appointment, **3**, 401; **5**, 424–426
awards, binding effect, **24**, 773
awards, execution of, **4**, 174; **30**, 306, 309
—revision of, **5**, 458–459
character of, **4**, 425; **5**, 423
jurisdiction, **2**, 371–378; **3**, 404–407; **4**, 89–90, 151, 476–477, 505–506; **5**, 434–442, 446–448; **6**, 421–423; **8**, 427, 432–433; **24**, 771
—exclusion, in favour of national courts, **5**, 184
—relation to Reparation Commission, **3**, 405–406
—termination of, **6**, 344–345
late applications, admission, **5**, 194–196
law applied by, **6**, 374; **7**, 477–483; **22**, 872–873
League of Nations, report of Council and, **5**, 409, 443
legislative functions, **7**, 121–127
locus standi of individuals, **32**, 637
position of, **5**, 423
review of decisions of national courts, **4**, 303
rules of procedure, **5**, 428, 449, 457
stare decisis, practice of, **1**, 376
termination of jurisdiction, **6**, 344–345
Mixed boundary commissions: *see* Boundary commissions
Mixed commissions, status, **7**, 387–388
Mixed Courts of Egypt, **1**, 40–41, 161–163; **2**, 172–173, 248; **3**, 20–22; **4**, 27–28, 48–49, 57, 335–336; **5**, 135–137, 486; **6**, 180–181, 182, 193–195; **7**, 200; **8**, 255–262; **9**, 298, 466, 471, 478; **11**, 146
jurisdiction—
—Acts of State, **11**, 224–226
—crew member of foreign warship, **11**, 165–166
—foreign armed forces, over, **11**, 165–171
—vessels in harbour, **9**, 167
Rules concerning Judicial Organization, **5**, 135
Mixed interest, theory of, **8**, 255–257
Mobilia sequuntur personam, principle of, **6**, 136; **18**, 174
Moluccas: *see* South Moluccas, Republic of
Monaco, Customs Union with France, **11**, 34–35
Monarch, private property of, distinguished from trust property, **4**, 31–33
Monetary gold looted from Albania, claims to, **20**, 442–443, 454–455; **21**, 399–400, 405–406

Money: *see* Currency; Exchange control; Exchange regulation; International Monetary Fund
Monopoly, governmental, effect outside State, **4**, 141–146
Monroe Doctrine, treaties inconsistent with, **9**, 454
Montenegro—
Hague Convention No. VI and, **1**, 410–411
Kingdom of, end of, **4**, 166–167
occupation by Austria-Hungary, **4**, 356–557
Monterey Bay, California, **4**, 135–136; **8**, 169–170
Montevideo, Convention on Extradition (1933), **22**, 528–529; **24**, 499–501
Montevideo, Convention on Political Asylum (1933), **16**, 1, 2; **17**, 284
Montevideo, Treaties of (1889) on—
Exercise of Liberal Professions, **7**, 442–443
International Civil Law, **5**, 288, 319; **6**, 110; **10**, 410
International Penal Law, **7**, 259–260, 354–355, 356, 357; **12**, 231, 237, 239; **14**, 86–87; **17**, 285; **26**, 525
Law of Procedure, **20**, 429
Protection of Literary and Artistic Property, **7**, 401–403
Montevideo, Treaty of (1940), International Penal Law, **14**, 87 n.; **18**, 333
Montreux, Conference of (1937), **19**, 289
Montreux, Convention of (1937), abolition of capitulations in Egypt, **8**, 256; **9**, 466, 471–472; **11**, 226; **12**, 156; **18**, 429–430; **20**, 195–197
Moratorium law, foreign, recognition of, **22**, 480–489; **30**, 15
Moravia, territories of, **1**, 13–14
Moresnet, status of, **3**, 120–121
Morgan Loan, 1924...**11**, 30
Morocco: *see also* Tangier
aliens, general fiscal immunity, **19**, 294–295
Bank of, at Tangiers, nationality, **9**, 59
capitulatory régime, **19**, 255–302, 342–344; **21**, 136–140
—abolition of, **11**, 223–224; **19**, 276
carriage of goods between Morocco and France, **11**, 43–44
commercial treaties (1631–1892), **19**, 262–263
—Treaty of Fez (1912), **5**, 117; **7**, 172; **8**, 93, 94; **19**, 255, 259, 260, 263, 269, 296
—Treaties with (1631, 1682), **19**, 265
— —(1836), **19**, 288
— —(1892), **19**, 285
Morocco—*continued*
French protectorate, **5**, 116–118; **6**, 350; **7**, 171–172; **8**, 92–93, 94–97; **11**, 42–43
criminal jurisdiction, **8**, 92–93; **11**, 45–46
—establishment of, **19**, 263
—financial régime, **6**, 47–48
—France/Spain, declarations on, **19**, 268, 269, 270, 271, 280, 293–297
—France-Germany, Treaty (1911), **9**, 507; **19**, 259
—immunity of public services, **8**, 226
—internal sovereignty, **7**, 171–172
—jurisdiction in, **7**, 31–35
—nationality of State bank, **9**, 59
—new courts in, **19**, 268, 294
—status of, **17**, 41–42; **19**, 260
—treaty obligations of France, **19**, 263
—treaty-making power, **19**, 269
—whether "foreign territory", French law, **11**, 45–46
French Union and, **22**, 60–61
French Zone: *see* French protectorate, *supra*
Germany, Treaty of Commerce (1890), **19**, 259, 298–299
Government, immunity from jurisdiction, **5**, 116–118
International Zone, **2**, 169–170
Madrid Convention, 1880 (right of protection), **4**, 311; **15**, 328; **16**, 9; **19**, 263, 266, 267, 272, 273, 275, 279, 281, 291–302, *passim*
—(1891), **22**, 17–18
nationality law, **2**, 349–350; **16**, 8–9
Netherlands, renunciation of capitulations, **2**, 151–152
Spain—
—Commercial Treaty (1861), **19**, 259, 262, 265, 272, 280, 281
—Consular Treaty (1861), **19**, 263, 271, 292–302, *passim*; **21**, 139, 146
—Treaties with (1799), **19**, 262
— —(1912), **21**, 139
— —(1914), **19**, 266; **21**, 139
Spanish protectorate, **2**, 20–21, 163–164; **10**, 47
Spanish Zone, **2**, 169–170; **6**, 348; **18**, 51
—France/Spain, Convention (1912), **19**, 268, 269, 296
U.K.—
—Commercial Treaty (1856), **19**, 259, 262, 265, 267, 282; **21**, 139, 140
—Consular Treaty (1856), **19**, 263
—General Treaty (1856), **19**, 265, 266, 272, 274, 280, 281, 289, 290, 292
—Treaties with (1721, 1750, 1751, 1760, 1783, 1801), **2**, 19–20; **19**, 265

Morocco—*continued*
U.K.—*continued*
—Treaties with—*continued*
— —(1937), **19**, 264, 266; **21**, 139, 140
— —(1938), **19**, 298, 301
U.S.A.—
—Treaties with (1787), **19**, 262; **21**, 139
— —(1836), **19**, 255–266, *passim*, 274, 275, 276, 282, 283, 288–302, *passim*, 343; **21**, 139
Mortgagee, effect of nationalization of debtor, **30**, 122–128
Moscow, Agreement of (1945), **15**, 356; **22**, 985
Moscow, Declaration of (1943), **13**, 263; **14**, 198, 292; **16**, 273, 400, 533; **18**, 245; **21**, 263; **22**, 100–101, 399–401
Most-favoured-nation clause, **1**, 347–349, 390; **4**, 339, 451–454; **7**, 404, 450–452; **8**, 472–475; **9**, 2–3, 370, 487; **11**, 10–12, 224–226; **13**, 183–184, 198; **15**, 1–2; **16**, 381; **18**, 288–289, 435; **20**, 599–600; **22**, 479; **23**, 468; **26**, 490–492, 600; **31**, 1–3; **32**, 206, 208; **35**, 212–213
bequest to alien, taxation of, **26**, 592–598
colonial preference and, **25**, 319
consular immunities and, **8**, 397–398
consular jurisdiction and, **7**, 199; **19**, 261, 263, 265–266
customary law limitations on, **25**, 318–319
customs union and, **25**, 319
discrimination, absence of, **21**, 307–308
double taxation conventions, in, **25**, 318–319
emergency legislation and, **11**, 235–236
establishment treaty, in, **28**, 492–493
exceptions for valuable consideration, **33**, 413
failure to exercise right by other Party, effect, **19**, 297
frontier traffic and, **25**, 318–319
incorporation by reference, method of, **19**, 267, 280
interpretation of, **5**, 363–364; **6**, 398–400; **7**, 452–455; **8**, 426 n.; **11**, 234–236; **14**, 166; **17**, 315–316; **23**, 377 n., 468; **33**, 408–409; **34**, 217–219
lease, application to, **26**, 599–601
operation in relation to multilateral convention, **28**, 494–496
private rights based on, **33**, 413–414
reciprocity, requirement of, **1**, 352; **5**, 404–405; **7**, 408, 456; **8**, 472–475; **9**, 457; **21**, 305–307
Most-favoured-nation clause—*continued*
security for costs, exemption from requirement, **1**, 351–352; **5**, 363–364, 404–405; **6**, 276; **8**, 472–475; **11**, 234–235
taxation, exemption from, **19**, 279; **25**, 313–321; **26**, 592–598
U.S.A., unconditional policy, **26**, 594–595
Motor Traffic, Convention of Paris (1926), **6**, 354–355
Mount Athos, cession of, **23**, 664
exterritoriality of monasteries, **3**, 315–316
Mount Athos monks, expatriation of, **21**, 195–196
"Movable things", meaning, **6**, 381–382
Multilateral treaties: *see* Treaties, multilateral
Multiplicity of suits, jurisdiction of international courts and, **3**, 424–425; **4**, 476–477
Munich Agreement (1938), Germany, Italy, France and U.K., **18**, 249, 250, 257; **22**, 101; **24**, 431, 432, 437, 537–539
Municipal courts—
competence in regard to treaties, **7**, 506; **9**, 4, 476
decisions as source of international law, **4**, 6–7
extraterritorial effect of acts of, **11**, 104–106
free access to, **11**, 230, 235. *See also under* Aliens
interpretation of treaties by: *see under* Treaties, interpretation of
Municipal law—
arbitral decisions, relation to, **1**, 3, 7
arbitration agreement, superiority over, **7**, 481–482
arbitration in, **22**, 820, 824–825
armistice agreements, effect, **1**, 437–440
Charter of the United Nations and, **20**, 244–246
extraterritorial operation of: *see* Legislation, extraterritorial effect of
international courts, consideration of, by, **3**, 5–6, 423–424
—treaties referring to, **3**, 378–379; **5**, 4–5, 345–347, 349, 392
International Labour Conventions and, **6**, 347–348; **9**, 474–475
international law and, **1**, 4–8, 124–129; **2**, 3–5, 425; **3**, 5–10; **4**, 9–21, 333; **5**, 4–6; **6**, 3–15, 158–159, 443–444; **7**, 3–15, 411–412; **8**, 7–12; **9**, 1–7, 56, 252, 259; **10**, 1–5, 338–339, 347–350; **11**, 1–12, 187–192, 278; **12**, 1–2, 97–101,

Municipal law—*continued*
international law and—*continued*
124–141, 221, 241; **13,** 1–5, 26–27, 55–56, 164, 178–186, 193, 232–233, 262–267, 279, 315, 337, 341–342, 347–348, 372; **14,** 1–5, 29–32, 36, 96–97, 100, 151, 156, 158–162, 244, 249, 286–287, 295; **15,** 1–6, 169, 324–325, 327, 328–330, 485–490, 555–557; **16,** 3–11, 262–263, 281–285, 461; **17,** 1–22, 72–81, 393–397, 420; **18,** 3–14, 475–477, 595, 688; **19,** 1–3, 229–254, 337–340, 342–344; **20,** 1–2, 244, 246, 317, 323–324; **21,** 1–9, 256–275; **22,** 5–11, 64–67, 73–75, 253–256, 424–427, 608–611, 884–885, 914, 991; **23,** 1–5, 195–201, 284–295, 710; **24,** 5–15, 423, 425–428, 432, 661, 868; **25,** 98, 108–109, 126–127, 279, 299; **26,** 1–5, 270, 483, 487; **27,** 13–18, 491; **28,** 2–10, 467, 470; **29,** 375, 392; **30,** 1–3; **31,** 1–8, 246–247, 262; **32,** 1–7; **33,** 1–15. *See also under* Treaties
—cantonal law, Switzerland, **15,** 4–5
—construction of legislation, **6,** 443–444; **7,** 7; **8,** 11; **16,** 8–9
—general maritime law, **16,** 9–10
—Germany, Basic Law (1949), **18,** 575; **20,** 371; **21,** 175–176; **22,** 608, 610; **23,** 379; **28,** 22, 31, 321, 372, 387, 393, 545
—Germany, Constitution (1919), **4,** 11–13; **6,** 327–328
—Germany, Restitution Law, **28,** 384, 387
—Iceland, law of, **30,** 263, 264
—inconsistent legislation, **1,** 7; **4,** 333, 474–475; **6,** 157–159; **12,** 208–218; **18,** 10–11; **24,** 661; **27,** 17–18; **28,** 467, 470; **31,** 246–247
—Ireland (Republic) Constitution, **12,** 97–98
—Japan, Imperial Constitution, **32,** 635
—judgment contrary to, **1,** 124–129
—legislative power, extent of, **27,** 17–18: *see also* Extraterritorial effect of legislation
—Mandates, **14,** 29–32
—Mexico, Constitution (1857), **4,** 9–11
—municipal law as fact, **3,** 5–6; **25,** 121
—nationality questions, **25,** 102, 108–109, 126; **32,** 166–168
—permissive rules of international law, **14,** 196–201
—Philippines Constitution, **13,** 372
—presumption of consistency with international law, **6,** 443–444; **7,** 7; **12,** 221; **13,** 26–27; **30,** 204–206, 216, 217; **34,** 62

Municipal law—*continued*
international law and—*continued*
—Tangier, Statute, **9,** 52–58
—torts in violation of international law, **32,** 1–4
interpretation by reference to treaties, **7,** 12–14, 447–448, 465–466; **11,** 222
necessity of, treaties: *see* Treaties, Municipal legislation, need for
reference to, by European Communities Court, **29,** 258–259
reference to, in interpretation of treaties, **6,** 381–382, 387; **7,** 445–448; **9,** 389
treaties and: *see* Treaties, municipal law and
Municipalities, property of, assimilation to private property, **6,** 449–450
Munitions: *see* Arms
Munitions de guerre, oil as, **23,** 810, 822–827, 832, 846–847
Munster, Treaty of (1648), **4,** 115; **31,** 113
Murmansk, Provisional Russian Government of, **1,** 50
Muscat Dhows, case of, **4,** 311
Museum, national, whether governmental agency, **10,** 576–581
Mysore State, international position, **10,** 38–43

N

Nacht und Nebel Order (1941), **15,** 388, 389
Nansen International Office for Refugees, **7,** 464–465; **8,** 306, 313
Nansen passport, **7,** 287–288
Napoleon, restoration of Poland and, **1,** 37
Narcotic Drugs, Convention (1931), **12,** 268
National arms, use in trade marks, **9,** 10; **10,** 9
National judges of P.C.I.J., right of appointment, **4,** 494–495; **8,** 488–489
" National ", meaning, **2,** 22–25, 378; **4,** 549; **6,** 280
" *ressortissant* ", distinguished, **4,** 44; **5,** 213–218
"National of the former Austrian Empire ", meaning, **2,** 238–239; **4,** 325–328
" National of the former Kingdom of Hungary ", meaning, **4,** 304–306
National treatment clause, **8,** 327–328; 12, 305 n.; **14,** 161 n.; **15,** 324–326,

National treatment clause—*continued*
327, 437; **16**, 259, 381; **19**, 339–342; **20**, 300–301; **21**, 211, 281–284; **22**, 478–479, 606–607; **23**, 376–377; **24**, 480–481, 600–601; **26**, 594, 598–599
anti-trust laws, alleged violation, **24**, 673–677
discrimination, absence of, **21**, 307–308
illegal entry, effect, **31**, 344–345
interpretation, **34**, 214–217
patents, **32**, 364–365
property, enjoyment of, **2**, 315; **15**, 324; **16**, 259–260
reciprocity, requirement of, **16**, 259–260; **20**, 300–301; **21**, 282, 284 n.; **23**, 377
security for costs, under, **5**, 263; **6**, 276; **7**, 305–309
National waters, conception of, **4**, 135; **8**, 173–178
jurisdiction in, **1**, 109–111; **2**, 111–114; **5**, 129–131; **6**, 153–157, 175–177; **7**, 208; **8**, 208–212; **9**, 164–166; **10**, 110; **14**, 84–90; **15**, 108–115; **24**, 167–171, 172; **28**, 145–149; **30**, 90–93, 103–104; **31**, 227–247; **32**, 117–119. *See also* Ports
—collision between foreign ships, **9**, 298–299; **10**, 166–168; **11**, 124–127
—crime on foreign ship, **4**, 160; **6**, 175–177; **8**, 210; **9**, 167, 169–170; **15**, 108–109; **16**, 143–144; **20**, 154–155; **31**, 241–247; **32**, 117–119
—involuntary entry, **2**, 111–112; **5**, 129–131; **6**, 154–156; **7**, 207–208; **9**, 164–166; **23**, 151–153
navigable rivers, **10**, 110
Nationality: *see also* Citizenship *and* Option of nationality
acquisition of, **1**, 197–198; **4**, 14–15, 295–297; **5**, 218–219; **6**, 251–254, 359–360; **7**, 273; **8**, 281–288; **10**, 279–284; **13**, 110–115; **14**, 108–114; **15**, 208–227, 265; **16**, 184–188; **18**, 51, 244–251; **19**, 319–326; **20**, 246–251; **21**, 175–178; **22**, 430–432; **23**, 364–372; **24**, 431–441; **25**, 112–123, 234–236, 357, 513–514; **26**, 367–379; **27**, 236–239; **28**, 80–81, 312; **30**, 37–38, 41, 44, 47, 50; **31**, 316–319; **32**, 166–169
—adoption, by, **31**, 316–318
—after commission of crime, **21**, 92–94
—birth on foreign ship in territorial waters, **23**, 371–372
—birth on high seas, **4**, 295–296

Nationality—*continued*
acquisition of—*continued*
—Ceylon, law for Indian residents, **26**, 367–374
—change of sovereignty, on: *see* change of sovereignty, effect, *infra*
—compulsory, **18**, 247–248
—date of, after option, **1**, 218–219; **2**, 254
—descent, by: *see jus sanguinis, infra*
—" First Papers ", law of U.S.A., **25**, 235, 359
—immigration, by, **32**, 168–169
—Israel, immigrants to, **26**, 376, 379
—re-acquisition, **4**, 546–547; **6**, 252–253; **7**, 288–289; **9**, 340
—recognition by foreign States, **22**, 356–357
—residents abroad, **27**, 236–238
—" return to territory ", **6**, 192, 259–262
—violation of treaty, in, **24**, 435–439
allegiance, **34**, 101, 104, 105
annexation, effect: *see under* Annexation
apparent nationality, theory of, **25**, 150–153
Austria, *Anschluss* with Germany, **12**, 187–194; **18**, 244–246, 248–249; **21**, 175–177; **22**, 430–432; **23**, 364–369; **32**, 153
basis of jurisdiction, as, **30**, 105–111. *See also under* Jurisdiction
belligerent occupation and, **15**, 527; **19**, 327–329, 329–336
British Commonwealth, in, **4**, 41–43; **8**, 66–69; **9**, 32; **19**, 38; **22**, 61–64; **24**, 56, 429–430
Burma, birth or residence in, **28**, 312
cession of territory, effect: *see* change of sovereignty, *infra*
change of, during legal proceedings, **3**, 403; **6**, 57, 196, 221–222
—during marriage, **13**, 113–114
—enemy property and, **1**, 211–213; **15**, 460
—extent of freedom to change, **5**, 220–221
—treason and, **14**, 103–106; **15**, 78–90; **18**, 265–276
change of government, effect, **2**, 53
change of sovereignty, effect, **1**, 91–94, 199–202, 243; **2**, 224–242; **3**, 108–109, 115–116, 263–268; **4**, 293–294, 304–307, 308–312; **6**, 267; **7**, 112; **9**, 339–340; **10**, 281–284; **16**, 208–215; **18**, 257–262; **19**, 318–326, 329; **20**, 145–158, 250–251; **21**, 175–178; **22**, 428–429, 430–432; **23**, 34, 364–369; **24**, 431–433; **25**, 513–514; **27**, 3; **32**, 170–186, 339–341
children, of: *see* minors, *infra*

Nationality—*continued*
" citizen " and " subject ", meaning, **34**, 99–107
citizenship and, law of U.S.A., **26**, 415 n., 443
citizenship, naturalization, political rights, nationality, differences between, **5**, 238
claims, of: *see* Nationality of claims
colonial subjects, **8**, 283–284
compulsory conferment, **32**, 166–168
consuls, of, **4**, 373–374
corporations, of: *see under* Corporations
Cuba, residents of, **1**, 93
Cyprus, in, **1**, 199–202
Czechoslavakia, in, **15**, 250–251, 257
—continuity, persons of German origin, **26**, 42; **30**, 37–38, 41, 44, 47, 49–51
—decree on loss of (1945), **24**, 540
—law of, 1920...**11**, 179
—law on Acquisition and Loss of (1949), **22**, 426
—re-acquisition of, **7**, 289–290
de facto subjects, **1**, 202; **3**, 268–269
denationalization, **4**, 314–315; **5**, 243; **7**, 290–295; **13**, 23–28, 133–137; **14**, 108–109, 121–123; **15**, 250–261, 287–288; **16**, 222–226; **17**, 212–215, 217–222, 225; **20**, 33, 261; **24**, 447–452; **25**, 359–360; **31**, 323–326
—Canadian nationals of Japanese race, **13**, 23–28
—enemy government, by, **12**, 199; **15**, 250–252
—foreign, judicial review of, **14**, 107–108
—fraud in obtaining naturalization, **16**, 222–224
—penal nature, **16**, 226; **26**, 434, 436–437, 440–441, 446–447
—recognition of, **13**, 133–137; **14**, 107–108; **25**, 359–360
—right of, **18**, 258–259
—repeal of German decrees, **14**, 121–123; **16**, 224–225
—wife, effect on, **11**, 182–183
deportation, for purposes of, **34**, 21–26
deprivation of, **11**, 183–184; **20**, 261; **21**, 197–198; **22**, 921–922; **32**, 194. *See also* Expatriation
diplomatic protection and, **6**, 188–199; **22**, 349–363, 421, 432, 452–454; **25**, 148–150
—distinguished, **3**, 269–271; **5**, 188–189; **22**, 360, 363, 365, 375–377, 380–381, 387
disputed, applicable law, **25**, 107
division of State and, **21**, 43–45
divorce, effect of, **32**, 170–173, 176–177

Nationality—*continued*
domicile, effect on, **3**, 264–265
dominant: *see* effective, *infra*
dual, **1**, 215–218; **2**, 249; **3**, 276–281; **4**, 299–301, 315–317; **5**, 189, 244–245, 447; **7**, 283–287, 295–298; **9**, 351–360; **10**, 290; **14**, 103–106, 115–118, 124–125; **15**, 228–230, 248–249, 261–264; **16**, 195–196, 227–229; **17**, 226–228; **18**, 251–254, 265–278; **19**, 318–319; **20**, 230–232, 261–263; **22**, 443–457, 809–819; **24**, 452–453, 455–457, 457–464, 464–465; **25**, 147–153; **26**, 460–462; **28**, 88; **30**, 366–374
—active nationality principle, **3**, 277–280; **11**, 184–185
—allegiance and, **18**, 265–276
—arbitral decisions, **22**, 450–452
—Bancroft Treaties concluded by U.S.A., effect, **25**, 130
—burden of proof, **1**, 217–218
—claims, international, effect on, **1**, 216; **3**, 277–279; **5**, 189; **6**, 192–193; **22**, 443–457; **25**, 149–150
—diplomatic protection, **1**, 216; **5**, 189–190; **22**, 452–457; **25**, 149–150
—enemy character and, **5**, 258–260; **14**, 124, 192
—expatriation, **7**, 283–287; **9**, 352, 354–355; **14**, 104, 115–118, 124–125; **15**, 228–230, 262–264; **16**, 195–196, 227–229; **17**, 226–228; **18**, 251–254, 265–270; **26**, 451–463
—extradition of persons with, **3**, 303
—heads of State, **3**, 461
—international officials, **32**, 513–515
—juror (German law), **2**, 249
—literature on, **22**, 452–454
—military service, whether voluntary, **26**, 453, 456–458
—naturalization without consent of former country, **11**, 188
—oath of allegiance to one State, **26**, 460–463
—prima facie evidence, **4**, 299–301
—principles of international law, **22**, 449–454
—residence of family, relevance of lack of permanent visa, **30**, 371–373
—rules as to, **22**, 455–456
—treason and, **18**, 265–276
—treaties concerning, **26**, 137
effective, **3**, 279–280; **5**, 244–245; **9**, 358–360; **10**, 290; **18**, 276–277; **22**, 358–359, 362–363, 381–383, 419–421, 443–457; **24**, 452–465; **25**, 147–150; **30**, 366–370
—critical date, **22**, 455; **24**, 658, 659; **30**, 370
—principle of, **6**, 191–192; **22**, 840

Nationality—*continued*
election of, **3,** 242–243
—law of U.S.A., **9,** 358–360; **25,** 94–95, 136–137, 139–142, 145
enemy, acquisition of, **1,** 211–213; **9,** 350; **14,** 104, 200–201; **18,** 263–264
enemy character and, **1,** 422–423; **15,** 466; **18,** 244–246; **19,** 587–591
estoppel, **25,** 151, 160
—passport, use of, **25,** 151, 153
expatriation: *q.v.*
extradition and: *see* Extradition, nationals, of
federal States, in, **1,** 38–39; **4,** 292–293
French law, **1,** 38–39; **9,** 361; **11,** 197; **15,** 249; **17,** 225; **18,** 51, 247, 507, 508; **20,** 246–248; **22,** 60
German and Polish law, **11,** 179–180
German law, person of German ethnic origin, **25,** 513–514
habitual residence, **2,** 228, 230–237; **9,** 340
Hague Convention, Conflict of Nationality Laws (1930), **6,** 192; **15,** 248, 268–269; **20,** 56; **22,** 360, 371, 376, 381, 382, 384, 449–450, 454, 456; **24,** 301; **25,** 149; **30,** 369n.; **32,** 167
heads of State, **3,** 461
illegitimate child, Dutch law, **11,** 184–185
imposition of, **24,** 537
international air law, rights under, **19,** 467–469
international officials, **22,** 809–819
international tribunals, competence to inquire into, **25,** 102–106, 108–110, 112, 122
Italy, Sardinian citizens, **9,** 27
jus sanguinis and *jus soli*, **6,** 56–57, 248–249; **7,** 295–296; **11,** 184–185; **23,** 370–371; **24,** 440–441; **25,** 112–113, 122, 141, 144, 146; **26,** 374–375
kinds of, **8,** 282–283
legislation—
—extraterritorial effect, **13,** 135–137, 142; **14,** 122–123; **16,** 16
—retroactive application, **25,** 116
legitimatio per subsequens matrimonium, **7,** 272–273
loss of, **1,** 211–215, 225–226; **2,** 191; **3,** 273–276; **4,** 313–315; **5,** 242–244; **6,** 256–258, 259–263; **7,** 274, 283–290; **8,** 295–304; **9,** 350–341, 354; **11,** 179–180; **13,** 130–132; **14,** 121, 200–201; **15,** 237–248, 250–261; **16,** 219–222; **17,** 212–215, 217–225; **18,** 254–265, 280; **19,** 144, 322–326; **20,** 261; **21,** 181, 192–195, 197–198; **22,** 428–429, 437–443; **27,** 245–247. *See*

Nationality—*continued*
loss of—*continued*
also change of sovereignty, *and* denationalization, *supra, and* Expatriation
—burden of proof, **18,** 262–264; **21,** 174; **30,** 357
—denationalization: *q.v., supra*
—denaturalization, **17,** 212–215, 217–220, 225; **21,** 181–185
—enemy territory, transfer to, **18,** 264
—foreign ambulance service, **8,** 301
—Italian law, **24,** 302; **30,** 369–370
—married women, **19,** 334–335; **20,** 246–248; **21,** 194–195; **26,** 464–465
—non-residence, for, **21,** 168–174
—procedure, constitutional guarantees, **27,** 245–247
—revocation of naturalization, **7,** 274, 276–281; **16,** 222–224; **17,** 217–222
—wife, effect on, **11,** 182–183
mandated territory, in, **17,** 111–112; **18,** 55–56; **19,** 69, 327–329; **20,** 49–51; **22,** 87–88
mandated territory under capitulatory régime, **3,** 191–192
married women and minors, **1,** 211–212; **2,** 221–222; **3,** 275–276; **4,** 315–317; **5,** 240–241; **6,** 255–258, 263–264; **7,** 284–289, 290–294; **8,** 303–304; **11,** 6–9, 197; **12,** 184, 195–196; **14,** 109, 110, 111, 121; **15,** 221–224, 268–269; **16,** 182–184, 227–229, 230–231; **18,** 248–249, 276–280; **20,** 246–248, 248–249; **21,** 194–195; **23,** 370; **26,** 418–419, 463–465; **27,** 236–238; **28,** 436–437; **32,** 170–185 *passim*, 192–194
—declaration by, **11,** 197
—law of U.S.A., **26,** 418–419, 464–465
—uniform nationality doctrine, **32,** 182
meaning, **8,** 67, 281–282
mediatised princes, **26,** 374–375
merger of States, effect, **9,** 341
military service and, **18,** 246–247; **20,** 255–261
minors, **2,** 221–222; **3,** 238–239; **4,** 296–297, 319; **5,** 235–237; **7,** 272–273, 284–289, 290–294; **9,** 341, 354–358; **11,** 197; **12,** 195–196; **14,** 108–109, 110; **15,** 221–224; **16,** 227–229; **18,** 278; **20,** 248–249; **23,** 370; **27,** 236–238; **28,** 239
—adoption and, **20,** 248, 261–263
—declaration of option, **4,** 319
—diplomat's children, **22,** 381
—foreign enlistment, **11,** 183
—illegal immigrants, **9,** 389

Nationality—*continued*
minors—*continued*
—illegitimate, **11,** 184–185
—loss of nationality of parent, **7,** 287–289, 290–294
—naturalization of parents, **7,** 284–287; **9,** 341, 351; **11,** 7–9; **12,** 195–196; **25,** 134, 136–138, 139–141, 144
—polygamous marriage, children of, **4,** 296–297
" natives " and " denizens ", **12,** 23–28, 184–188
naturalization: *q.v.*
nature of, **22,** 360, 365
option of: *see* Option of nationality
outbreak of war, effect of, **15,** 455; **18,** 265, 507–508
Palestine citizenship, **9,** 43, 49; **12,** 15–17; **18,** 56; **20,** 251–252
partnerships, of, **6,** 218–220
" passive ", **15,** 491–492
passports: *q.v.*
Peace Treaty with Italy and, **19,** 322–326; **22,** 445–448
polygamous marriage, children of, **4,** 296–297
presumption of, **4,** 304
presumption of continuance, **22,** 422–424
proof of, **3,** 274–275; **4,** 297–303, 483–487; **5,** 213–226, 233; **6,** 181, 247–251; **7,** 272–273, 275; **8,** 281–288; **9,** 339; **10,** 273–278; **14,** 103–108; **15,** 207–208; **16,** 182–184; **18,** 244, 262–264; **19,** 21, 317–318; **20,** 52–57, 246; **21,** 168–174, 192–194; **22,** 378–380, 419–422, 422–429; **24,** 429–430; **25,** 99–106, 109, 353; **28,** 431; **29,** 423–424
—administrative statement, **25,** 111
—burden of proof, **1,** 217–218, 221–222; **4,** 303; **22,** 428–429
—certificate from International Refugee Organization, **28,** 274
—certificate of citizenship, **22,** 422–424; **25,** 98–101, 107, 112
—deportation proceedings, in, **10,** 273–274; **27,** 13–16
—error or fraud, **25,** 112
—passports: *q.v.*
protected persons, **3,** 268–269; **4,** 309–312; **17,** 41–42; **27,** 239–245
public character of question, **2,** 219–221; **5,** 220
questions of, reference to municipal law, **25,** 102
race, how far including membership of, **5,** 226
re-acquisition of: *see* acquisition of, *supra*

Nationality—*continued*
recognition by other States, **2,** 219–221, 224–227; **22,** 349, 353–363, 371–377, 384–388; **25,** 148; **27,** 236–238; **32,** 167
redintegration, **11,** 218; **15,** 209–211, 321
regulation of, **2,** 219–221, 292
renunciation of, **5,** 225; **7,** 283–284; **16,** 215–219; **32,** 169
—under duress, **15,** 230–234
reserved domain of States, **25,** 98–99
residence and, **34,** 480–481
right to, **24,** 347
secession, effect on, **2,** 224–227
ships, of: *see under* Ships
" Soviet " and " Russian ", **6,** 56
State succession and, **17,** 109–112; **19,** 318–319. *See also* change of sovereignty, *supra*
statelessness: *q.v.*
treaties, effect of entry into force, **2,** 226–227
—municipal law inconsistent with, **28,** 439–441
—U.S.A., Bancroft Treaties, **25,** 111, 115, 123–138, 140, 143, 145
—Versailles and St. Germain, provisions, **6,** 37–40; **7,** 445–448
treaty as source of, **25,** 126, 143
unity of the family, principle of, **6,** 258; **13,** 113–114; **14,** 110, 111
Universal Declaration of Human Rights, deprivation, **32,** 194
war, effect on, **15,** 455; **18,** 265, 507–508
works of art, nationality distinct from that of author, **5,** 225
Nationality of claims, **1,** 185; **2,** 185–191; **3,** 237–243; **4,** 254–257; **5,** 187–193; **6,** 190, 193, 216–222; **7,** 95, 263; **9,** 334; **16,** 324; **20,** 226–238 ; **21,** 156–160; **22,** 349–397; **24,** 303–308; **25,** 91–167; **26,** 320–346; **29,** 21–54, 421–429; **30,** 198–218
acquisition of nationality after claim arises, **30,** 204–206
assignment by non-national, **26,** 345–346; **30,** 156
basis of rule, **30,** 214
burden of proof, **2,** 380–381; **3,** 243; **4,** 483–487
change of nationality, **29,** 421–429
continuous national ownership, presumption, **30,** 172–173
continuity rule, **5,** 190–191; **20,** 233–236; **21,** 157–159, 160, 161–162; **24,** 316–318; **26,** 320, 328, 334–335, 344; **30,** 119, 201–204, 207–215
death of claimant, **21,** 156–159

Nationality of claims—*continued*
diplomatic protection and, **6,** 188–199; **22,** 349–363, 421, 432, 452–454, 455; **25,** 148
dual (double) nationality, effect of, **1,** 216; **5,** 189; **6,** 191; **20,** 230–232, 263; **22,** 397, 443–447; **24,** 301–302, 452–465; **30,** 366–370
effective (dominant) nationality, **6,** 191–192; **22,** 358–359, 362–363, 381–383, 397, 419–421, 443, 457, 840; **24,** 452–465; **25,** 147–150
effective nationality, critical date, **22,** 455; **24,** 658, 659
indirect shareholder claims, **26,** 342; **30,** 181, 183, 198–200, 207–208, 511–514
insurer, claim by, **26,** 316–319
modification by statute, **26,** 262–266, 330, 334, 336–339; **30,** 204–206, 216, 217
modification by treaty, **26,** 330, 334, 336–339
naturalization of claimant, **21,** 159–160; **22,** 394–397
naturalization of property owner after date of treaty, **22,** 389–393, 397; **24,** 658, 659
Peace Treaty claims, treatment as enemy; *see under* Italy, Peace Treaty with
pledge, **30,** 208–212
stateless owner, **22,** 391–393
succession to claim of non-national, **30,** 215
trustee claims, **26,** 322–323, 464
Nationality of Married Women, U.N. Convention (1957), **32,** 192–194
Nationalization measures: *see also under* Acquired rights; Concession agreements; Expropriation: **1,** 47–50; **2,** 44–47; **3,** 25–26, 55, 57–59, 136, 137, 141–142, 143–145; **4,** 61, 66–68, 71–72, 141–146; **5,** 22–23, 38–42, 49–51, 97–101; **6,** 141–143, 144, 150–151; **7,** 22–27, 65–75, 151–153, 157; **8,** 34–39, 184, 187, 193–194; **9,** 141–150; **10,** 48–68 *passim*; **11,** 21–23; **12,** 29–39; **13** 12–17, 30; **14,** 15; **15,** 176–204; **16,** 18–20; **17,** 32–33, 65–72; **18,** 38–39, 61–64, 201–203, 204–205; **19,** 14–19; **20,** 34–36, 193, 215–217, 305–328, 435–436; **21,** 34–35, 38–39, 148, 152–153, 212–213, 291–297; **22,** 13, 17–45; **23,** 7, 19–21, 24–26; **24,** 40–48, 211–213; **26,** 40–51, 129–131, 287–290, 294–295, 301–302, 306, 309, 313; **28,** 14–39; **30,** 33–54, 120–128, 134–135, 140–143, 171, 177–179, 187, 190; **32,** 8–10, 30–33; **33,** 30–36, 184
acts *jure imperii*, **26,** 182
Nationalization measures—*continued*
administration of enterprises, **11,** 108–110
annulment of pre-nationalization debt, **26,** 303–308
banks, **6,** 140–143, 150–151; **7,** 151–153; **8,** 184, 187; **9,** 207; **11,** 142–143; **17,** 65–72; **18,** 189–190; **19,** 14–15; **20,** 34–36, 215–217; **22,** 13; **24,** 211–213
—depositors' rights, effect on, **26,** 129–131, 293–295, 301–302; **30,** 120–122, 134–135, 189–190
belligerent occupation and prior unexecuted measures of local sovereign, **15,** 176–204
business name, effect on, **30,** 52
compensation, absence of, penal sanction, **30,** 50
compensation, adequacy, **30,** 30–31, 41; **35,** 4, 7, 9–10, 11, 12, 16–19
compensation, duty of, **19,** 18–19; **21,** 212–213; **22,** 19–45
compensation, market value, **30,** 179
corporations, effect on, **3,** 57–59; **4,** 66–68, 71–72, 141–144; **5,** 38–42, 97–101; **6,** 140–143, 150–151; **7,** 65–75, 82, 152–153; **8,** 184, 187, 193–194; **9,** 141–148; **11,** 21–23, 107–108; **14,** 15; **16,** 19–20; **17,** 32–33, 65–72; **18,** 38–39, 201–203; **19,** 302–311; **21,** 38–39; **22,** 13–14; **23,** 7–10, 19–21, 24–26; **24,** 40–48; **26,** 45, 129–131; **28,** 15, 177–185; **30,** 171–172; **32,** 8–10, 12–19, 23–33, 35–36; **33,** 32–33: *see also* Corporations, foreign, dissolution of
creditors' rights, effect on, **26,** 303–308; **30,** 140–143
Cuba, in, **35,** 3–5, 8–10, 16
Czechoslovakia, in, **20,** 34–36; **22,** 17–19; **23,** 7–9, 24–26; **24,** 46–48; **26,** 40, 44, 47; **28,** 14–16; **30,** 33–35, 49; **32,** 19–26, 31, 32
debtor corporation, creditor, effect on, **26,** 298–300, 303–308; **30,** 140–143
—mortgagee, effect on, **30,** 122–128
discriminatory, **30,** 30; **33,** 33; **35,** 4, 7, 9, 11, 19–23. *See also* Discrimination
enforceability in territorial waters of foreign State, **15,** 176–204
extraterritorial effect, **3,** 136–148; **4,** 141–144; **6,** 150–151; **7,** 65–75, 80–82, 151–153, 157–160, 184–186; **8,** 34–39, 191–193; **9,** 141–150, 232–233; **11,** 21–23, 107–111; **12,** 61–62; **13,** 12–17; **15,** 176–204; **16,** 18–20; **17,** 32–33, 155–166; **18,** 38–39, 179; **19,** 16–18; **20,** 34–36; **21,** 30–33, 38–39; **22,**

Nationalization measures—*continued*
extraterritorial effect—*continued*
13–19; **23,** 7–16, 19–25; **24,** 41, 43–48; **26,** 41, 45, 48–49, 50–51, 54; **28,** 14–39; **30,** 39, 41, 44, 46, 48, 51; **32,** 30–33
goodwill, loss of, **30,** 147
international law and, **20,** 313–314
joinder of nationalizing government in action, **23,** 10–12
jurisdictional immunity and, **11,** 142–143, 155–161; **17,** 156–163; **26,** 181–182
land, condemnation, **23,** 27–28
life interest, affecting, **26,** 296
Mexican decrees, **9,** 90–93
nationalized company, action on behalf of, **23,** 19–21. *See also* corporations, effect on, *supra*
nationalizing State as universal successor, **24,** 40
Netherlands enterprises in Indonesia, **28,** 17–19, 21, 25, 34, 36–37; **30,** 30; **33,** 32–33
Netherlands, liquidation of Dutch assets in United States, **9,** 150
partnership, effect on, **26,** 46
pension rights, **26,** 287–288
political motives, relevance, **28,** 38; **30,** 30; **33,** 33
proof of, **23,** 7–10
public purpose requirement, **35,** 6, 8
rent, loss of, **26,** 289–290
right to adjudicate on, **20,** 312–314. *See also* Act of State doctrine
ships, **3,** 137; **11,** 155–161; **12,** 61–62; **13,** 12–17; **15,** 176–204; **23,** 706–708
State as universal successor, **24,** 40
State responsibility for, **20,** 215–217; **21,** 156, 291–297
title, whether acquired by, **20,** 305–328; **21,** 19–42; **23,** 706–708; **28,** 16–39
Nationalized foreign company, *locus standi*, **23,** 19–21; **34,** 126–127
Nationals—
de facto subjects, **1,** 202; **2,** 242–243; **3,** 268–269; **4,** 309–312. *See also* Protected persons
expulsion of, **13,** 23–28
extradition of: *see under* Extradition
ressortissants, distinguished, **4,** 44; **5,** 213–218
right to return, **35,** 132, 134
Nationals abroad, jurisdiction over, **1,** 158–161; **2,** 145–150, 411–412; **4,** 181–185; **6,** 175–179; **7,** 192–199; **8,** 66–67, 249–255; **13,** 93–95; **14,** 91–92; **16,** 96–99; **19,** 227–254; **20,** 193–195; **21,** 125–135; **24,** 673–677; **26,** 209–221; **28,** 115–138; **30,** 105–111; **31,** 273–274; **32,** 140–147; **33,** 194–201: *see also* Jurisdiction, nationals, over
—act crime and civil wrong, **31,** 268–269
—bigamy, **31,** 272
—cheating, **31,** 270–271
—civil matters, **30,** 105–111
—crime committed while prisoner of war, **23,** 764–766
—criminal, **1,** 158–161; **2,** 145–147; **4,** 181–183, 184–185; **6,** 175–177; **7,** 192–197; **8,** 249–254; **10,** 250; **11,** 172–173; **14,** 91–92; **15,** 173–175; **17,** 189–191; **19,** 226–227; **20,** 188–193; **21,** 125–126; **22,** 560–561; **23,** 114–115, 269–270; **26,** 209–221; **31,** 140–147, 267–272; **33,** 194–201
—high seas, on the, **4,** 186–189; **7,** 212–213; **10,** 252–263; **23,** 284–295; **26,** 242–244; **31,** 274–275
—property of, **15,** 176–204
—taxation, **2,** 147–148; **8,** 254–255; **31,** 273–274
"Nationals of the United Nations", German currency reform laws, **18,** 55–56
Nationals, protection of: *see also* Diplomatic protection
corporations, national ownership of capital, **30,** 167
dual nationals, **1,** 216; **5,** 189–190; **22,** 452–457; **25,** 149–150; **30,** 369 n.
—insured damage, relevance of nationality of insurer, **27,** 559
"Native", meaning, **12,** 23–28, 184–188
Native chiefs, treaties with **9,** 444, 462
Natural justice—
expulsion of aliens and, **17,** 259–260; **22,** 510–511
laws contrary to, **12,** 8–11
Natural law—
source of international law, **3,** 4–5
State succession and, **1,** 63
Natural Resources, Exploitation of, G.A. Resolution (1952), **22,** 40–41
Naturalization, **1,** 203–211; **2,** 243–248; **3,** 269–271; **4,** 312–313; **5,** 226–239; **6,** 254–255; **7,** 274–283; **8,** 292–294; **9,** 341–347; **10,** 285–289; **11,** 180–181; **12,** 195–197; **13,** 121–128; **14,** 115; **15,** 218–227; **16,** 188–193; **17,** 204; **20,** 251–254; **21,** 178–181; **22,** 433–436; **23,** 373; **24,** 442–445: *see also* Naturalized citizens
allegiance and, **15,** 91–104
application for, effect of annexation of former State, **12,** 189–194
attachment to State of origin, **16,** 192

Naturalization—*continued*
Australia, in, **8,** 68
British Commonwealth, in, **22,** 433–436
British self-governing dominions, in, **1,** 203–204; **4,** 43; **8,** 68
cancellation of, **1,** 209–210; **6,** 292; **7,** 274, 276–281; **9,** 345–347; **10,** 288–289; **12,** 197–199; **13,** 121–123; **17,** 212–215, 217–222, 225; **25,** 117–118, 121. *See also* revocation of, *infra*
Cape of Good Hope, in, **4,** 42–43
collective, **11,** 180–181
—after cession, **11,** 49–50
—after conquest, **5,** 235–237; **6,** 254–255; **10,** 279–281
compulsory, **20,** 57, 59–61; **21,** 181, 195; **32,** 166–168
conscientious objectors, **5,** 226–232; **7,** 9–10; **13,** 124–128
consent of State of origin, **2,** 243, 247, 304; **5,** 233; **7,** 275; **8,** 293
declaration of intention, effect, **3,** 269–271; **11,** 187–192
diplomatic protection and, **3,** 269–270; **22,** 357–361, 368–375, 380–381
discrimination against naturalized citizens, **9,** 346
disregarded, **26,** 401–402
disqualification—
—claim of exemption from military service, **11,** 187–192; **13,** 124–128; **14,** 115; **15,** 218–220, 224–226; **16,** 191–192; **21,** 178–181; **22,** 460–466; **24,** 442–444; **26,** 397–401; **28,** 277–286; **31,** 318–323; **32,** 189–192
—prior political activities, **32,** 186–189
domicile and, **17,** 241–242
eligibility for, **22,** 1012–1014; **23,** 373, 453–454
enemy character of property resulting from, **18,** 254–255
English law, eighteenth century, **26,** 382
evidential value, **25,** 103
formality, **21,** 181
former citizenship, effect on, **6,** 191–192; **12,** 15–17; **15,** 236–248; **16,** 199; **25,** 123, 128; **26,** 401–404
—in wartime, **9,** 350; **14,** 104
fraud in obtaining, effect of, **7,** 274, 280–281; **8,** 290; **10,** 285; **16,** 222–224; **17,** 217–222
—law of U.S.A., **25,** 114–115, 118
French law, **11,** 180–181; **17,** 225
good morals, as requirement of, **1,** 206–207
" grand naturalization ": *see* collective, after conquest, *supra*
Hong Kong, in, **5,** 234–235

Naturalization—*continued*
limitation of right of, **12,** 197
marriage, by, **15,** 227
military service, by, **10,** 276–278
minors, **5,** 235–237; **7,** 284–287; **9,** 341–357; **11,** 7–9; **12,** 195–196; **15,** 221–224; **20,** 252–254; **25,** 134, 136–138, 139–141, 144
motive, relevance, law of U.S.A., **25,** 114, 117, 119
nationality, citizenship, political rights, naturalization, differences between, **5,** 238
nature of, **22,** 361; **26,** 400
non-retroactivity of, **23,** 373
recognition of, by foreign States, **4,** 312–313; **22,** 349–363, 365, 381
recognition of, by home State, **2,** 243–244
refusal of (Latin-American practice), **10,** 286–288
refusal to fight against State of origin, **15,** 224–226
re-naturalization by *force majeure,* **18,** 254–255
renunciation of, **1,** 208–209; **9,** 345
renunciation of right of, **19,** 638–640
residence, requirement of, **16,** 188–191; **17,** 204; **23,** 35–37
—national service in lieu, **17,** 204–205
retention of former nationality, **7,** 281–282
return to country of origin, effect, **1,** 204–205
revocation of, **13,** 23, 28; **17,** 212–215, 217–222, 225; **21,** 181–184. *See also* cancellation of, *supra*
right to, **15,** 226; **22,** 363
Saar Territory, **11,** 180–181
status of naturalized citizens, **12,** 197; **16,** 194–195
statute, by, **15,** 237–248
—naturalization of royal family, **26,** 380–397
tacit, **2,** 267; **6,** 254–255; **10,** 286
U.S.A.—
—Arabs, **12,** 197
—Constitution and, **7,** 9–10
—Hindus, **2,** 244–246
validity of, **22,** 364, 366, 370–376, 383–384, 388–389
—challenged in courts of another State, **28,** 275–277
—competence, international tribunals, **25,** 106
—competence, Mixed Courts of Egypt, **2,** 247–248; **8,** 292–294
voluntary character, **15,** 236–237; **18,** 254–255
waiver of privileges and immunities as condition of, **23,** 616–625
war, during, **16,** 417–418
war, effect on, **9,** 350

Naturalization—*continued*
women, military service and, **5,** 237–239
—naturalized, denationalization of, **5,** 237–238
Naturalized citizens—
diplomatic protection of, **35,** 202
expatriation of, **35,** 197–205
Nauru, Trusteeship Council and, **22,** 685
" Naval and military works or materials ", meaning, **2,** 405–409
Naval attaché, diplomatic immunity, **12,** 243
Naval capture: *see* Capture, naval *and* Sea warfare
Naval Protocol (1936), **13,** 218, 219
Naval warfare: *see* Sea warfare
Navicerts, system of, **12,** 532–537
Navigation, freedom of, **7,** 12–13, 317–318. *See also* Danube; Elbe; Rhine
" free and open ", meaning, **5,** 87–88; **6,** 8–10; **7,** 5
Navigation, International Rules of U.S. Act to Adapt Regulations for Preventing Collisions (1890), **7,** 480–481
Ne bis in idem, principle of, **1,** 470; **6,** 313–314; **11,** 282
Ne impediatur legato, **24,** 224
Necessity, plea of: *see under* War crimes
Negotiations, diplomatic: *see also* Treaties, preparatory work, consideration of
admissions in course of, **6,** 101–102
dispute, existence of, and, **2,** 398–402; **3,** 426–427; **4,** 508; **24,** 848–849, 864–865; **25,** 51
function of, **2,** 398–402
proposals in, evidentiary value, **27,** 91
Negotiorum gestio, **5,** 502; **12,** 255. *See also* Unjust enrichment
Nemo judex in re sua, **3,** 387–388; **22,** 673, 674, 676
Nemo plus juris transferre potest quam ipse habet, **4,** 113–114
Nepal, status of Indian Ambassador, **23,** 269
Netherlands—
acquisition of territory through Dutch East India Company, **4,** 108–110
Agreement for return of Austrian Assets in Netherlands (1951), **24,** 40, 433
—annexation by Germany, recognition of, **13,** 46–47
—Double Taxation Agreement, **22,** 530–531
Austrian Monarchy and Republic, dispute as to identity of, **4,** 37–38

Netherlands—*continued*
Belgium—
—Boundary Treaties (1842 and 1843), **21,** 87; **24,** 93–95; **27,** 64–66, 69, 71–72, 76–77, 79–80, 81, 89, 90, 93, 95
—Boundary Treaty with (1843), Descriptive Minute on frontier communes, **27,** 65–67, 72, 74, 76, 79–81, 85–89, 95–97
—Treaty of Establishment and Labour (1933), **20,** 338
—Treaty of London (1839), Separation of Territories, **8,** 166–168; **27,** 64, 71
—Treaty on Civil Procedure (1925), **11,** 221
—Treaty, Scheldt Navigation (1925), **9,** 121
—Treaty on Territorial Jurisdiction in Bankruptcy (1925), **24,** 638–639
Birds Protection Act, 1936... **11,** 222
Capitulation of Rijsoord (1940), **15,** 500–503; **16,** 414, 527, 530, 536–537
—status of armed forces after, **17,** 399–400
Cartel Act, 1957...**26,** 606–609; **33,** 416
Civil Code, Art. 2014 (reclamation of movables), **13,** 379–380
conflict of laws, foreign political legislation, **14,** 17
Constitution (1953)—
—Art. 1 (definition of Kingdom), **24,** 69
—Art. 58 (treaty-making power), **21,** 166–167; **24,** 584–585
—Art. 65 (treaties and legislation), **21,** 8; **22,** 635, 637; **24,** 923
Constitution (1956)—
—Art. 65 (self-executing treaties), **22,** 637; **30,** 424–425
—Art. 66 (treaties and legislation), **22,** 637; **24,** 588, 589; **26,** 606–607; **28,** 269; **30,** 1–2; **33,** 234–240, 381–416
—Art. 158 (expropriation), **19,** 17
—Arts. 181–187 (freedom of conscience and religious worship), **33,** 235, 239–244, 380, 381
courts of—
—assistance to enemy during occupation, **11,** 288–291
—review of foreign legislation, **11,** 16–19
Criminal Code—
—Art. 1 (change in law after offence), **11,** 294
—Art. 8 (scope of application), **11,** 291
—Art. 43 (superior orders), **13,** 397
—*nulla poena sine praevia lege poenali*, **15,** 533; **16,** 527, 528, 542–543
Currency Decree (1945), **18,** 206

Netherlands—*continued*
Czechoslovakia—
—Agreement in execution of Bretton Woods Agreement (1946), **22,** 713–715
" Destination Act ", 1951, disposal of enemy property, **24,** 434, 436
Economic Competition Act, 1956, **33,** 414, 416
Enemy Property, Decree on, **13,** 46–47, 349–350; **14,** 124; **18,** 250, 255, 256, 257, 258–259, 515–516; **19,** 571; **20,** 600–601; **22,** 911–912; **23,** 21–24; **24,** 31–32, 61, 434–435, 436, 437, 439, 893–896
forces in Germany, jurisdiction over, **33,** 191–193
Foreign Exchange Control Decree (1945), **22,** 722–725; **24,** 94, 95
France, Commercial Treaty (1935), **21,** 166; **24,** 584–588
freight traffic on inland waterways, **7,** 12–13; **21,** 3
frontier districts, " treaty pastures ", **21,** 86–87
frontier land, disputed sovereignty with Belgium, **27,** 62–98 *passim*
Germany—
—Boundary Treaties of Aachen and Cleve (1816), **12,** 59–60
—Extradition Treaties (1896, 1897), **16,** 267
—frontier, rectification of (1949), **17,** 81–82
—Treaty of Arbitration and Conciliation (1926), **15,** 417
Gold Clauses Law, 1937. . . **11,** 28
Government in exile, decrees of, **10,** 10–23, 111–123; **12,** 420–424; **14,** 239, 250; **15,** 17–18, 530–535, 567–571; **16,** 399, 428–432, 457, 460; **18,** 172–174, 558–570; **20,** 31, 83–85; **21,** 25–29, 431, 487; **24,** 917–923
Great Britain, Commercial Treaty (1654), **23,** 729
guardianship, law concerning, **25,** 263–264, 266, 308, 309–310, 312
I.L.O., designation of workers' delegates, **1,** 361–363
Indonesia, and, **17,** 82–91, 109–110, 144–152; **19,** 132–133, 138–141, 318–319, 337–338; **20,** 80–89; **21,** 48–49, 77–79; **24,** 60
—Agreement on Transitional Measures, **20,** 80, 87, 88; **24,** 71
—continuity of law, **20,** 80–89
—Linggadjati Agreement with (1947), **17,** 147–149, 151; **19,** 5
—Round Table Conference Agreements (1949), **17,** 109–110, 199–202; **18,** 434; **19,** 132, 318–319, 337; **21,** 77–78; **24,** 71–72, 88; **28,** 17, 37; **33,** 28–30

Netherlands—*continued*
Indonesia, and—*continued*
—succession to liabilities, **19,** 116–117; **20,** 80–81
—transfer of sovereignty, **18,** 224; **21,** 63–64
—Union Statute (1949), **18,** 434
Industrial Property Emergency Act (1947), **24,** 438
interrogation of witnesses abroad, **6,** 90
Judicature Act, **19,** 487, 488, 599
Judicial Organization, Law of 1827, **11,** 17–19, 291, 292
legislation, international law and, **1,** 23, 125–129
Mannheim, Act of (1868), German denunciation, effects in Netherlands, **13,** 49–50
military service, nationals resident abroad, **10,** 116–123
nationality, Emergency Decrees (1943 and 1945), **18,** 254, 256, 277, 278
Nationality Law, 1892. . . **11,** 182–183; **15,** 248–249; **16,** 227–229; **18,** 277, 279; **19,** 335; **24,** 473
nationalization of Dutch assets in U.S.A., **9,** 150
" Netherlands Forces of the Interior ", status, **14,** 170
neutrality, duties of, **1,** 489–490
Norway, Treaty of Commerce and Navigation (1912), **21,** 308
occupation by Germany, **11,** 271–272, 288–291; **12,** 420–424; **13,** 17–18, 350–354, 366–368, 395–398; **15,** 17, 412–414, 434–435, 442–443, 500–503, 530–535, 567–572, 599–602, 685–686; **16,** 16–18, 428–432, 455–464, 468, 529, 537, 540, 554–555; **17,** 392–397, 399–400, 414–415; **18,** 473, 536–538, 558–570, 609–614, 679–682, 701–702; **19,** 600–601; **20,** 82, 646–647, 665; **21,** 431–432, 486–487
—competence of Dutch courts, **11,** 288–295
—Decree on Occupation Measures, **14,** 250–255, 256–258; **18,** 609–611, 681; **19,** 601; **21,** 487
—non-recognition by U.S.A., **10,** 587
—property seized by enemy, legislation, **16,** 493–496
—public order, **11,** 33
—Reichskommissar's Ordinance, May, 1940. . . **11,** 291
Old Age Insurance Act, European Convention on Human Rights and, **33,** 233–238, 380–382
P.C.I.J., Agreement with (1928), **22,** 537
poor person's procedure, **11,** 242–243

Netherlands—*continued*
Prize Rules (1940), 917–923
Prussia, Frontier Agreement (1816), **6,** 50–51
recognition, acts of Allied troops in Istanbul, **4,** 34–35
resistance movement, status, **14,** 170
Restoration of Legal Rights, Decree on (1944), **21,** 25–28, 487
Road Traffic Act, territorial extent, **26,** 158
Soviet Government, non-recognition of, **4,** 59–60; **6,** 42; **11,** 66–67
—recognition of, **4,** 71–72
Supervision of Religious Communities Act, 1853...**33,** 233, 236, 239
termination of war with Germany, Decree-Proclamation (1951), **24,** 939
Texel island, mutiny (1945), **13,** 308
Trade Marks Act, **20,** 601
Trading with the Enemy Decree, **14,** 239–240
treaties, operation in Dutch law, **6,** 354–355. *See also* Constitution, Arts. 65 and 66, *supra*
U.K.—
—Extradition Treaty (1898), **16,** 267; **17,** 83, 84, 86, 89
—Property Agreement (1944), **18,** 172, 173
—Social Security Agreement (1954), **27,** 285–287
U.S.A., Claims Convention (1948), **16,** 307–308
U.S.A., Treaty of Friendship, Commerce and Navigation (1956)—
— —alleged breach, **31,** 218–219
— —most-favoured-nation clause, **28,** 495
— —Trading with Enemy Act, action, **33,** 449
Union of Utrecht, 1579, freedom of religion, **33,** 235
war crimes, special decrees concerning, **14,** 196–201; **15,** 491–496; **16,** 398, 399, 482, 527, 528, 529, 533, 542, 554; **17,** 394–397
West New Guinea, Law of 1958 on, **28,** 37
Zuiderzee, fishery rights in, **11,** 175–176
Netherlands Indies—
Accountability Act, **24,** 70
Constitutional Act, **24,** 77
legal personality of Government, **15,** 28–37
Mining Law (1891), **23,** 815–816, 834–844
occupation by Japan, **15,** 682–684
status of, **15,** 138–140
Netherlands–Japanese Property Commission—
competence, **30,** 516–525
Netherlands–Japanese Property Commission—*continued*
competence—*continued*
—jurisdiction, to determine, **30,** 524
—preliminary objection as to, **30,** 524–525
—prorogated jurisdiction, **30,** 523
composition, **30,** 515
finality of decisions, **30,** 521–522
Neuchatel, Arrangement of (1947), Industrial Property Rights affected by the War, **17,** 7
Neuilly, Peace Treaty of (1919), **23,** 666–668
Neutral alien, arrest of, **5,** 509
Neutral asylum, **9,** 583; **10,** 639–643; **12,** 538; **23,** 610–613
Neutral character, corporations, of, **1,** 229–230
Neutral corporation carrying on business in enemy territory, **3,** 448–449
Neutral merchantships—
capture of, for probable cause, **11,** 304–305
—goods with enemy character, **28,** 652–656
—owned or controlled by enemy, **31,** 509–520
chartered to enemy, **12,** 539–452
convoy, under, **4,** 568–569
destruction of, **1,** 485–487; **2,** 420–421; **5,** 487–491, 515, 518
detention, **6,** 442–446; **10,** 598–605; **14,** 318–319
—damages for, **10,** 604–605
—probable cause and, **10,** 601–605
non-enemy flag, sailing under, **24,** 916–923
requisition, **2,** 420–421; **6,** 442–446
rescue and recapture, **1,** 485–487
search in port, **1,** 486, 487; **14,** 311–316
transfer, **11,** 260–264
visit and search, Suez Canal, **31,** 509–520
Neutral nationals—
exemption from military service, claim by, **31,** 318–319
testamentary dispositions in favour of, **3,** 453–456
Neutral Powers and Persons, Hague Convention on Rights and Duties of, 1907: *see under* Hague Conventions of 1907
Neutral property—
angary, **1,** 414–418; **2,** 420–427; **3,** 456–458; **10,** 639; **13,** 238–239; **23,** 708–754; **28,** 611
destruction in course of military operations, **2,** 415–419; **5,** 494
discriminatory treatment, Germany, Settlement Convention (1952/54), **25,** 516
pillage, **30,** 116–117

Neutral property—*continued*
requisition of, **1,** 414–418; **2,** 421–427; **4,** 542–545
—assessment of compensation, **1,** 189–191; **28,** 614 n., 625–628
—waiver of compensation claim, effect, **28,** 611, 617–621
—whether a " taking ", **28,** 621–625
sequestration of, **7,** 501–504; **14,** 187–189, 192–194; **30,** 494–496
Neutral property clause, insurance policy, **1,** 230
Neutral subjects, enemy-controlled corporations and, **18,** 516–520, 529
Neutrality
angary, right of, and, **1,** 414–418; **2,** 420–427; **3,** 456–458; **10,** 639; **23,** 709, 713–714, 717, 728–732
belligerent forces, internment, **10,** 639–643
civil war, duties of neutrals, **22,** 1015–1016
courts, competence of, effect on, **10,** 637–638
determination of neutral status, **22,** 1012–1014
formal acts, absence of, state of war, **26,** 650
Free French forces, position in 1942 . . . **28,** 282, 284
insurgency, application to, **31** 29, 48
mandated territory and, **15,** 693–694
nature and duties of, **9,** 583; **12,** 301–302; **14,** 319–327. *See also* Hague Conventions, 1907
neutrality orders, international law and, **2,** 4
qualified, **19,** 638–640
Palestine, Second World War, **26,** 397–400
prisoner of war in neutral territory, **23,** 610, 612
prohibition of passage of munitions, **4,** 572
right to repel attack, **12,** 289
state of war, notification of, **12,** 300–302
statement of executive as to, **22,** 1012–1014; **26,** 399
transport of goods acquired by act of war, **1,** 489–490
treaty permitting trade with enemy, **1,** 436
unneutral service, **3,** 461; **4,** 572; **5,** 517–518; **9,** 82–83; **12,** 462–466, 532–542; **31,** 517
—acquisition of enemy character, **3,** 461
—carriage of contraband, **12,** 539–542
—condemnation for, **12,** 533–537; **31,** 517
Neutralization of States, **20,** 51–52
Neutrals, reprisals against, **5,** 490, 517
New Guinea, occupation by Australia (1914), **19,** 327
New Guinea, mandated territory, **8,** 98–109
—appellate jurisdiction of mandatory, **7,** 51–52
—legislative powers of mandatory, **7,** 46–50
New Guinea, Trusteeship Agreement, **32,** 38–43
—absence of disputes clause, **35,** 406–407, 411, 412
New Hebrides, condominium, **9,** 50; **11,** 55
—French administrative courts, jurisdiction, **11,** 55
—Mixed Tribunal, French magistrates, **11,** 55
New States, establishment of, **1,** 11–21, 45; **2,** 9–11; **5,** 11–16
" New States ", meaning, **1,** 346
New York—
State of, public policy of, **8,** 39
theatre of war, as, **1,** 432
New Zealand—
aliens, admission as barrister, **22,** 468–472
British Nationality and New Zealand Citizenship Act, 1948 . . . **22,** 87
British Nationality and Status of Aliens (in New Zealand) Act, 1928, **22,** 87
Constitution Act, 1852 . . . **9,** 462; **19,** 53, 54
Crown Redress Act, 1871. . . **12,** 207
Crown Suits Act, 1908...**12,** 202–208
Emergency Forces Act, 1950. . . **22,** 899
Immigration Restriction (Amendment) Act, 1920...**22,** 87–88
Law Practitioners' Act, 1931...**22,** 468–472
Minister of External Affairs, certificate of, **12,** 417
Native Land Act, 1873. . . **22,** 597
Native Purposes Act, 1935. . . **9,** 462–464
petition of right, **12,** 202–208
Social Security Agreement with U.K. (1955), **27,** 48–49
status of, **19,** 49–61
termination of war with Germany, **12,** 415–420
Waitangi, Treaty of (1840), **9,** 462–464
Western Samoa and, **22,** 87–88
Western Samoa, legislation as mandatory for, **4,** 53–54; **7,** 36–45
Wills Act, 1837. . . **22,** 899
Newfoundland—
American Bases Act, 1941. . . **22,** 272
Canada, Terms of Union (1949), **22,** 272

Newfoundland—*continued*
claims on Labrador boundary, **4,** 121
U.S. bases in, **15,** 64–68; **21,** 114–116
Niagara, "Peace Bridge" over, **4,** 121–122
Niagara, Treaty concerning Uses of Waters of, between Canada and U.S.A. (1950), **24,** 557–571 *passim*
Nicaragua—
Honduras, Arbitral Award of 1906, litigation concerning, **30,** 457–492. *See also* Boundaries
Honduras, Extradition Treaty (1907), **1,** 269
U.S.A.—
—Consular Convention (1868), **11,** 208–211
—Extradition Treaty (1923), **12,** 237
Nigeria—
U.K., Treaty, British Crown and King of Lagos (1861), **26,** 109–111
Night Work of Women in Industry, Convention (1906), **6,** 412
Nine-Power Treaty (1922), **13,** 223
No man's land, property rights in, **7,** 109–111
Nominee, property owned by, claim concerning, **26,** 279–280
Non-belligerency, **19,** 638–640
Non bis in idem, principle of, **1,** 470; **6,** 313–314; **11,** 282
Non-combatant—
meaning, **3,** 435–437
respect for life and property of, **5,** 516
Non concedit venire contra factum proprium, **25,** 151, 156. *See also* Estoppel
Non-discrimination, plea of: *see under* Aliens
Non-governmental association, jurisdictional immunity, **10,** 226–230
Non-intervention, **2,** 158–161; **31,** 38
Non liquet, admissibility in international arbitration, **4,** 492–493
"*Non missi*" consuls, **8,** 400
Non-recognition of governments: *see under* Recognition, governments, of
Non-retroactivity of laws, principle of, **14,** 140, 146–147, 268, 285–286, 327
Non ultra petita, **2,** 214–215; **3,** 419–420; **16,** 343
North Atlantic Treaty (1949), **20,** 186–187; **22,** 272, 276, 756, 758–760; **23,** 201
Germany, accession of (1954), **23,** 770
Italy, ratification by, **23,** 202
North Atlantic Treaty Organization (N.A.T.O.)
Canada, Visiting Forces (North Atlantic Treaty) Act, 1951...**21,** 115; **22,** 272; **23,** 253–254
North Atlantic Treaty Organization (N.A.T.O.)—*continued*
jurisdictional immunity, commercial relations, **28,** 414–416
—Headquarters, **22,** 756–762
nature of, **22,** 756–757, 759, 761
officials, exemption from tax on salaries, **29,** 58; **31,** 394
Status of Forces Agreements (1951 and 1952), **22,** 264, 267–270, 758, 760; **23,** 246–247, 255–259; **24,** 249, 251–255, 551; **26,** 196–199; **28,** 159–163, 415–417; **34,** 193
member of a "force", **32,** 359–363
Status of International Military Headquarters Protocol (1952), **22,** 758, 760–762
taxation of officials' salaries, **29,** 58; **31,** 394
North German Confederation, nationality laws, **1,** 217
North Sea Fisheries (Police) Convention (1882), **6,** 125; **8,** 266; **18,** 101, 116, 117, 127, 128
Northern Ireland—
Administration of Estates Act, 1955, **27,** 19–22
Parliament, legislative competence, **33,** 164–169
Northern Rhodesia—
Emergency Powers Regulation, 1956, **28,** 48, 51
native reserves in, **11,** 35–42
status of, statement of Colonial Secretary, **28,** 50, 68, 71, 75
whether "foreign dominion" of British Crown, **5,** 29; **28,** 48–78 *passim*
Northern Russia, Provisional Government, **1,** 43–44; **3,** 62–64
Norway—
capitulation to Germany, **15,** 503–505
Citizenship Acts, 1888, 1924, 1946 and 1950 ... **13,** 73; **18,** 263; **30,** 353, 356–359, 360–365
compulsory public service, European Human Rights Convention and, **30,** 348–350
Constitution (1814), **18,** 635
—Art. 97 (retroactive operation of laws), **13,** 262–266
consuls of, jurisdiction in U.S.A., **10,** 157–158, 160
contracts "against decency", Law of 1687 ... **13,** 394–395
Criminal Code, 1902, Art. 86 (assisting enemy), **13,** 73, 267
Denmark and Sweden, Convention on execution of judgments (1948), **20,** 290
Enemy Property Law, 1946 ... **18,** 263
expatriation, leaving country "forever", **30,** 352–366

Norway—*continued*
Extradition Law (1908), **24,** 497–498
fisheries zone (Decrees of 1935 and 1937), **18,** 86–88, 95–96, 102, 105, 110–111, 113–114, 119–124, 131, 134, 144
Foreign Minister, declaration by, **6,** 103–105
Germany, Extradition Treaty (1878), **24,** 498
Gold Payments Law (1923), **24,** 782, 828, 829, 831, 833, 837, 838
Government in exile, decrees of, **10,** 131–132
importation of liquor, **1,** 113–114
international law as part of law of, **13,** 262–267
Netherlands, Treaty of Commerce and Navigation (1912), **21,** 308
occupation by Germany, **9,** 5; **10,** 158; **13,** 391–394; **14,** 305–307; **17,** 438–440; **18,** 635, 684–686; **23,** 791–795
—competence of Norwegian courts, **11,** 285–288
—interference with courts, **11,** 286–288
Prize Law, **14,** 316–317; **22,** 1011–1012
requisition of ships abroad, **10,** 131–140
Territorial Waters Boundary Commissions (1911 and 1912), **18,** 97, 102, 129, 138, 142
territorial waters—
—delimitation, **18,** 86–105 *passim*, 110, 114, 119–132, 133, 136–144
—extent, **1,** 102, 114; **4,** 133–134; **7,** 136
—illegal fishing, penalties for, **20,** 166–167
U.K., Extradition Treaty (1873), **26,** 513–516
U.S.A.—
—Agreement permitting trade with Germany (1918), **1,** 435
—Arbitration Agreement (1921), **1,** 369–371
—Claims Convention with (1940), **28,** 611, 625, 629
—Naturalization Treaty (1869), **11,** 8
—Neutrality Act, executive order concerning Norway, **9,** 5–6
—Treaty of Amity and Commerce (1932), inheritances, **5,** 394; **9,** 5, 157, 162; **11,** 219
U.S.S.R., Commercial Treaty (1925), **6,** 333
Varanger Fiord, **7,** 136
war crimes, Decree of 1945 ... **13,** 263–267
Whaling Laws (1939 and 1946), **21,** 307–308
Norway–Sweden—
Denmark, Commercial Treaty (1826), **6,** 103
France—
—Arbitration Convention (1904), **24,** 787
—Treaty of Commerce and Navigation (1881), **11,** 229
U.S.A.—
—Treaty of Establishment (1827), **11,** 113–114, 123–124
Notary public, certificate, consular certificate, distinguished, **6,** 424–425
Notification—
—acquisition of territory, and, **4,** 115; **6,** 108
—state of war of, **12,** 300–302
Novelty of action, international law and, **2,** 417
Nuclear weapons, legality of, **32,** 626–642
Nuisance—
State responsibility for, **9,** 315–333
violation of sovereignty by, **9,** 321
Nullity, burden of proof, **22,** 369
acceptance of compulsory jurisdiction of I.C.J., **33,** 422–434, 436–438, 439–443
arbitral awards, **30,** 463, 468–477, 477–478, 478–479, 479–492
awards of U.N. Administrative Tribunal, **21,** 316, 323
dismissal of arbitrator, **5,** 425
illegal act, **5,** 158–159
international law, in, **34,** 343
naturalization, **22,** 388
reservations to acceptance of compulsory jurisdiction of the I.C.J.: *see* Discretions
Nullum crimen sine lege: *see under* War crimes
Nullus commodum capere de sua injuria propria, **4,** 506; **5,** 426; **33,** 76

O

Obscuritas pacti nocet ei qui opertius loqui potuit, **2,** 330
Occupation—
creation of territorial title, **6,** 95–98
requirement of effectiveness, **6,** 107
Occupation forces, costs, Austrian State Treaty, **26,** 609–612
Occupation of enemy territory: *see* Belligerent occupation; War
Occupation of foreign territory—
administration, joint, **7,** 58
armistice agreement, under, **1,** 450
—after armistice, **3,** 173–174; **4,** 549–550
—during armistice, **4,** 566–567

Occupation of foreign territory —*continued*
British Army in Egypt, jurisdictional immunity, **5,** 486; **7,** 187–188
de facto, **7,** 157–158
extradition of inhabitant, **7,** 360–369
peace, in time of, **1,** 94; **3,** 9–10, 27–29, 116–117, 234–235; **4,** 34–35, 118–120; **5,** 77–78; **12,** 43–47; **22,** 127, 152–154
—applicable law, **6,** 110–111
protectorates and, **5,** 25–27
" Occupied territories ", Saar territory distinguished, **5,** 33–34
Occupied territory: *see also under* Belligerent occupation
devastation of, **15,** 632, 647–649; **16,** 484–486, 521–523
enemy character of, **13,** 240–246; **14,** 181–182
extradition to, **22,** 987–991
foreign armed forces in, **5,** 485–486; **6,** 174, 206
—looting by, **2,** 174
inhabitants of, extradition, **7,** 367–369
sequestration of private property, **16,** 491–492
Oder, International Commission of, **5,** 83–84, 339–341
Officials: *see also* International officials, *and under* State responsibility
acts of, private and official capacity, **4,** 213–215
—ratification of, implicit, **1,** 170
—State responsibility for, **1,** 170, 171, 172; **4,** 250–252; **7,** 244–247, 250–254, 481–482; **20,** 221; **22,** 301, 840
contracts made by, **4,** 207–208
foreign, status of, **6,** 130–131
international: *see* International officials
mandated territory in, status of, **7,** 35–36
State succession, rights of, **1,** 73–75; **2,** 85; **3,** 87–91; **4,** 92–95; **5,** 70; **7,** 102–104, 509–510; **8,** 141–142; **17,** 92–94; **21,** 75–79
—pensions, **1,** 66–67
Oil and gas concessions, valuation of reserves, **30,** 176–179
Oil, *munitions de guerre,* whether, **23,** 810, 822–827, 832, 846–847
Oil, nationalization by Iran (1951), **19,** 501–506, 507, 546; **20,** 305–328; **22,** 19–45
Okinawa, status of, **15,** 524–525; **18,** 549–558; **21,** 82–86; **24,** 89; **32,** 584
—U.S. occupation of, **17,** 404–407
Oldenburg, Treaty with Germany (railways) (1920), **5,** 330–332
Omnia rite acta praesumuntur, **25,** 107
Omsk All Russian Government, extinction of, **1,** 32; **2,** 134–135
Ontario, Lake, **4,** 122
Open door, mandated territories, in, **8,** 110–113
Open sea: *see* High Seas
Opinio juris sive necessitatis, **4,** 6–7. *See also* Customary international law
Opium—
prevention of smoking, **1,** 110–111
traffic in, **5,** 416
Opium Convention (1912), **12,** 267–270
Opium and Drugs Convention (1925), **18,** 379
Option of nationality, **1,** 218–223; **2,** 249–258; **4,** 301, 317–320; **5,** 213, 245–247; **6,** 57, 258–263; **7,** 289–290; **10,** 290; **15,** 265; **19,** 337–338
annexed territory, in, **7,** 112
burden of proof, **1,** 221–222
cession, on, **15,** 27
conditions of validity, **1,** 219; **2,** 249–252
constitutive or declaratory, **1,** 218–219; **6,** 259
co-operation of authorities of former State, **2,** 255
date of acquisition of nationality, **1,** 218
death of optant before acceptance by new State, **2,** 257
descendants of optants, effect on, **2,** 253
divorced wife, **4,** 318
exercise before treaty enters into force, **28,** 291–292
expulsion subsequent to, **1,** 219–220
failure to exercise right, **3,** 268
form of application, **2,** 256–257
minors, **4,** 319; **7,** 285–287
persons over 18 years old, **1,** 219
release, distinguished, **7,** 289–290
removal to country of option, **2,** 252
residence, continued, in country of origin, **2,** 255
retroactive effect, **2,** 253; **5,** 245–247
withdrawal of, **2,** 255; **4,** 319
women, **1,** 220
Optional clause (Statutes of I.C.J. and P.C.I.J.): *see under* International Court of Justice *and* Permanent Court of International Justice
Oral declaration, binding force—
judicial proceedings, in course of, **6,** 367
Minister of Foreign Affairs, by, **6,** 103–105
" Ordinarily resident ", meaning, **1,** 199
Ordre public—
application, " removal case ", **25,** 272–273
—retroactive effect, **25,** 277, 294

Ordre public, application—*continued*
—territorial connection, requirement of, **25**, 272, 279
expulsion of aliens, **11**, 198
general principle of law, as, **25**, 268, 278
international, **6**, 31–32; **7**, 185; **9**, 291–292, 459; **16**, 15; **22**, 25, 39; **25**, 278, 288–289
national, **5**, 46; **11**, 29, 221; **21**, 280–281; **24**, 215; **25**, 277–278, 289: *see also* Public policy
public law, distinguished, **25**, 277, 291–292
public policy and, **25**, 268
scope, **25**, 267–269, 311
treaties,
—implied exception to, **25**, 246, 248, 253, 256, 267, 278, 288, 290, 293–294
—reservation, **11**, 221
O.E.C.D., succession to O.E.E.C., **34**, 463
Organization for European Economic Co-operation (O.E.E.C.) Appeals Board—
—competence, discovery of documents, **31**, 486–488
—decisions, *erreur matérielle*, **31**, 462–466
—decisions, nullity, **31**, 462–466
—decisions, rectification of, **31**, 456–458, 462–466
—power of review, limit of, **31**, 429–432
O.E.E.C., Secretary-General, powers of, **31**, 479, 482
ONUC: *see* Congo, U.N. Operation in
Organization of American States—
Charter, **18**, 63
Union of American Republics and, **18**, 441–443
Ottoman Bank, nationality of, **4**, 323–324
Ottoman Empire: *see also* Turkey
law of personal status, **4**, 95
nationality of subjects of, in Egypt, **1**, 40–41
—in Cyprus, **1**, 199–202
Republic of Turkey, whether continuation of, **3**, 36–37, 78–79
Ottoman Laws of Nationality (1861, 1869), **2**, 304, 305
Ottoman Public Debt—
Council of, status, **7**, 473; **23**, 96, 97
transfer of, **23**, 667–668
Overflying, right of, **31**, 113
Outbreak of war, effects: *see under* War

P

Pacific Islands—
Kwajalein, status of, **24**, 58; **26**, 62–68
Pacific Islands—*continued*
Trusteeship Agreement for (1947), **23**, 36; **26**, 2–3, 62–67
Trusteeship Council and, **22**, 685
Pacific Settlement of International Disputes, General Act (1928), **9**, 425; **18**, 381, 383; **24**, 787, 814, 822
Pacific Settlement of Disputes, Hague Convention (1907), **1**, 85, 370, 378; **2**, 361, 367; **4**, 479–481; **23**, 85, 671, 681
applicability to States not ratifying it, **1**, 3
disqualification of arbitrator, **28**, 559
evidence, rules of, **4**, 479–481
res judicata, **9**, 326
Pacta sunt servanda, **24**, 534; **25**, 255, 288, 302; **32**, 5. *See also* Treaties
Pacta tertius nec nocent nec prosunt; see Treaties, third States, effect on
Pactum de contrahendo, **2**, 19–20; **3**, 357–359; **4**, 393; **5**, 339–341; **6**, 405
Pactum in favorem tertii, **4**, 409. *See also under* Treaties
Pakistan—
Adaptation of Existing Laws Order, 1947...**27**, 43, 44
Aircraft Act, 1934...**27**, 61
Citizenship Act, 1951...**19**, 218, 219
Constitution (1956), annulment of, **27**, 23
Constitution (1956), Art. 5, equal protection of the law, **27**, 22–24, 28
creation of, succession to treaties, **34**, 27–36
customs frontier between East and West Pakistan, **27**, 59–60
Frontier Crimes Regulation, **27**, 22–23, 28
Income-Tax Act, 1922...**27**, 103–107
Indian Independence (International Arrangements) Order, 1947...**21**, 273; **27**, 38–40, 41; **34**, 31, 32–35
Laws (Continuance in Force) Order, 1958...**27**, 23–24, 26–29
membership of international organizations, **34**, 33–34
Railways Act, 1890...**27**, 108–109
Sea Customs Act, 1878...**27**, 58–61
separation from India, effect, **17**, 37–41, 101; **21**, 11–12, 92–94, 273; **24**, 62, 64, 65–67; **27**, 35–44; **34**, 27–36
succession to multilateral treaties on partition, **27**, 35–44; **34**, 27–36
status of, **18**, 50, 210–214; **24**, 56–57
status of Ruler of State in, **19**, 68, 216, 219
status of States of, **19**, 212–219
successor State of India, as, **15**, 72–75; **19**, 117–131, 212–219

Palestine: *see also under* Mandated territories
Arab–Jewish hostilities, **19,** 550–556
British consuls in, **21,** 251–253
" British possession ", as, **23,** 292–293
Citizenship Order, 1925...**9,** 43, 49; **12,** 15–17; **20,** 251–252. *See also* nationality of inhabitants, *infra*
concessions granted by Turkey, recognition of, **2,** 57
Custodian of Enemy Property, **12,** 349–352
detention of Palestinian citizens abroad, **12,** 64–68
enforcement of foreign revenue laws, **10,** 24–25
extradition from, **9,** 50
freedom of conscience provision in Mandate, **18,** 237–243
Immigration Ordinance (1933), **9,** 126
Immigration Ordinance (1941), **15,** 116–117, 119–125; **20,** 50–51
Interpretation Ordinance (1945), **22,** 116, 119, 120
Israel, succession to, **17,** 72–81, 92–94; **18,** 64–67, 72–77; **19,** 141–142; **22,** 113–122
jurisdiction, protective on, high seas, **15,** 115–125
legislative power of U.K. Parliament, **12,** 12–15; **15,** 40–44
Mandate over—
—immigration, restriction of, **15,** 116–125; **20,** 50–51; **21,** 12–15
—" public control ", meaning, **2,** 331–334; **4,** 50–52
—termination of, **15,** 40–42, 58–59; **16,** 68; **17,** 110–112, 313; **21,** 444–458; **22,** 114–116, 123–126
—termination of, effect on nationality, **17,** 110–112
nationality, former Turkish subjects, **9,** 46–50
nationality of inhabitants, **18,** 56. *See also* Citizenship Order, 1925, *supra*
neutrality, **15,** 693–694; **26,** 397–400
Order in Council, 1922...**17,** 74; **23,** 288–290, 295; **26,** 213–215
partition (1947–1948), **17,** 347, 444; **31,** 517
Polish Army in, **12,** 165–168
readaptation of Mavrommatis concessions, **4,** 50–51
recognition of foreign government by Mandatory, **11,** 51
State Railways Administration, **11,** 146
State succession in, **8,** 123–127
status, before and after Mandate, **17,** 347–348, 444

Palestine—*continued*
termination of mandate, **15,** 40–42, 58–59; **16,** 68; **17,** 110–112, 313; **21,** 444–458; **22,** 114–116, 123–126
Palmyra Island, sovereignty over, **12,** 49–54
Pan-American Conference, Problems of War and Peace (1945), **22,** 914–215
Pan-American Convention, Status of Naturalized Citizens (1906), **22,** 359, 372
Pan-American Extradition Convention (1933), **18,** 316
Pan-American Union, **18,** 441–443
Organization of American States and, **18,** 441–443
Panama—
Labour Law, **22,** 285
U.K., Special Arbitral Agreement (1932), **7,** 251
U.S.A.—
—Boundary Conventions (1903 and 1914), **1,** 94; **2,** 101; **5,** 82; **7,** 438–441; **9,** 118
—Claims Convention (1926), **7,** 255–257, 477–480
—Treaty *re* Canal Zone (1936), **9,** 118
Panama Canal—
Convention, Panama–U.S.A. (1903), **7,** 439; **9,** 118; **23,** 116–118
Hay–Pauncefote Treaty (1901), **2,** 101; **24,** 147
tolls, **24,** 146–152
U.S. sovereignty, extent of, **31,** 125
Panama Canal Zone, **4,** 180–181; **9,** 118
Civil Code, **1,** 77
extradition to, **6,** 111
flags flying in, **34,** 7–12
jurisdiction in, **1,** 94; **3,** 119; **7,** 138–139
law applicable in, **2,** 113; **7,** 482
maritime belt, breadth, **7,** 139
Penal Code (crimes committed abroad), **5,** 104
—(extradition), **5,** 277
sovereignty within, **34,** 7–12
status of, **2,** 95–96; **7,** 113–114; **23,** 116–123
" territory of the United States ", **34,** 38
—whether foreign territory, **5,** 81
U.S.A., agreements with, **34,** 10
U.S. Act of 1950...**24,** 146–152
U.S. forces in, **4,** 180–181
Panay, incident, **12,** 298–299
Papal States, nationality and citizenship, **3,** 265–266
Par in parem non habet imperium/jurisdictionem, **4,** 364; **6,** 169; **15,** 136, 144; **20,** 401; **24,** 4, 210, 224; **26,** 181; **28,** 160, 162. *See also* Foreign States, immunity from jurisdiction

Paraguay, U.S.A., Reciprocal Trade Agreement (1946), **24,** 678–681
Paris—
Agreement on German Assets (1945), **17,** 166
Declaration of (1856), **1,** 491; **9,** 566; **11,** 303; **16,** 570, 588; **19,** 480; **20,** 673; **28,** 653–654
Pact of (1928): *see* Renunciation of War, General Treaty for
Peace Conference (1947), **18,** 420–422
Peace Treaty of (1815), **5,** 16–17, 461–462; **11,** 83
—(1898) (Spain and U.S.A.), **4,** 3–4, 113–114, 419
Protocol of (1815), **5,** 461, 464
Reparations Agreement (1946), **20,** 31, 431, 440, 441–462 *passim*, 463–468, 469, 616; **23,** 478–483
—restitution of monetary gold, **21,** 399–400, 405
Treaty of (1259), **20,** 95, 98, 116, 118, 120, 129–135 *passim*
Treaty of (1902), Bird Protection, **11,** 222
Treaty of, 1920, (Poland/Danzig), **5,** 410; **6,** 130, 209–213, 383–384; **7,** 61–62, 270
Parliamentary debates, in interpretation of statutes, **2,** 263
—interpretation of treaties, **6,** 51
Parliamentary papers, whether publication privileged, **11,** 213–217
Partisans: *see also* Guerillas; Resistance movements
belligerents, as, **15,** 661–662
criminal jurisdiction of, **15,** 433–434
insignia worn by, **15,** 639, 661
regular forces, relation to, **15,** 424–427
requisitions by, **15,** 428–433
resistance by, whether acts of war, **12,** 303–304
status of, **17,** 350–354
warfare by, **15,** 638–639
Partition of territory—
local debts, effect on, **7,** 87–88
public corporations, effect on, **6,** 77–82
Partnerships—
dissolution of, **20,** 38–39
enemy character, **15,** 466–467
illegal, when, **4,** 19–20
limited, whether "permanent establishment", **33,** 400–407
nationality, **6,** 218–220
nationalization of assets, **30,** 33–54
—effect on existence of firm, **30,** 42, 45, 47–48
war, effect of outbreak on, **1,** 399, 400; **3,** 441–443; **11,** 246; **15,** 443–447; **27,** 629–631
Passing of property in cargo, **12,** 495–501, 564–567
enemy character and, **12,** 390, 392–395
Passing of property *in transitu*, **10,** 558–563
"Passive extradition", **30,** 390–391
"Passive nationality", principle of, **15,** 491–492
Passport—
Andorra, citizens of, **18,** 53
application for, effect on nationality, **7,** 283–284
defective, **9,** 384
denial of, **35,** 89–96, 238
evidential value, **5,** 226; **9,** 339; **16,** 182–184; **21,** 169–170; **26,** 366; **27,** 234–236; **30,** 352, 354–355, 357, 359, 360, 361, 363, 365
false information, tort in violation of international law, **32,** 1–3
foreign, possession of, **27,** 234–236
foreign, use of, **16,** 219
issue of, discretionary act, **26,** 134–135, 139, 143
legal effect of holding, **15,** 91–104; **30,** 352, 354–355, 357, 359–361, 363, 365
Nansen, effect of, on former nationality, **7,** 287–288
nature of, **17,** 23–27; **18,** 53; **19,** 7–10; **20,** 273–377; **21,** 169–170; **26,** 132, 137; **32,** 4
need for, war measures, **26,** 143–144
Palestinian, validity after termination of mandate, **20,** 49–51
re-entry without valid, **35,** 131–135
refusal to issue, **16,** 301
right of expulsion, effect on, **9,** 383
right to, **17,** 203, 206
withholding of, law of United States, **26,** 131–144
"Past disputes", reservation as to, **2,** 392–393
Patents: *see also* Patent Acts, etc., under various States
claims under U.S. War Claims Act, 1928...**4,** 542
Convention for Protection of Industrial Property and, **7,** 435–437; **27,** 649
enemy-owned, suspension of rights during war, **3,** 450–451; **27,** 649–652
French law, **5,** 358–359
German, in U.S.A., **4,** 541–542
German law, **5,** 358–359
German, London Agreement on (1946), **17,** 166
impairment by German war measures, restitution, **25,** 335–340, 496–497, 503
infringement, comparison of various laws, **29,** 312–315

Patents—*continued*
inter-governmental release of, **23,** 16–19
national treatment clause in treaty, **32,** 364–365
ownership of, **25,** 504–505
rights in, effect of war on, **3,** 450–451; **27,** 649–652
royalties, assessment of, **25,** 499–500
war measures affecting, compensation for, **29,** 309–318
war measures, appropriation of royalties, **29,** 341–348
Patiala Union, Covenant of—
Act of State, whether, **26,** 81, 85
Constitution, whether, **26,** 81–82, 86
Payments agreements, **30,** 404–420
Pays de Gex, Free Zone of, **5,** 16–17, 339, 398, 459–465; **6,** 362–367, 430, 431; **7,** 483; **8,** 178
Peace, crimes against, **15,** 620–621; **16,** 345–350. *See also* War crimes
conspiracy to wage aggressive war, **15,** 621
planning war, **15,** 668
responsibility for, **15,** 669–671
Peace treaties: *see also under* various States Parties to
adjustment of frontiers under, **20,** 63–77
" Allied Powers ", meaning, **24,** 668–669
amnesty, **2,** 435; **4,** 553–554
analogous instruments: *see* German External Debts Agreement; Germany, Federal Republic, Arbitral Commission on Property, etc., *and* German Federal Republic, Settlement Convention
" as a result of the war ", meaning, **22,** 330–331, 945–953; **23,** 504
Bulgaria, Hungary and Roumania (1947), interpretation of, disputes provisions, **17,** 331–339
claims—
—indirect corporate, **30,** 511–514
—rights of ownership, **22,** 953–959
compensation—
—concurrent right under several clauses, **22,** 959
—exemption from tax, **29,** 369, 371–382
—loss from measure before war, **22,** 945–953
—loss of requisitioned ship, **22,** 965–966
—loss of seized ship, **22,** 966–972, 972–978
—property lost in war, **22,** 953–959, 966–972, 972–978
—requisition of domestic metal ware, **22,** 959–964
—requisition of premises, **22,** 964
—sequestration of property, **22,** 917
Peace treaties—*continued*
consent of defeated State, necessity for, **19,** 481; **22,** 448; **25,** 317–318
contractual character, **7,** 297; **18,** 419–420; **19,** 480–481; **22,** 445, 448, 650, 871; **25,** 317–318; **29,** 468
date of taking effect, **11,** 268–270
effects of, **4,** 551–555; **21,** 82–86, 108–109; **22,** 317–329, 945
" encumbrances and charges ", meaning, **23,** 503–504
equality, principle of, and, **22,** 448
imposed, interpretation of, **7,** 297
" in the course of prosecution of the war ", meaning, **23,** 698–699
individuals, rights under, **23,** 469–470, 698–699
interpretation of, **11,** 250–251; **18,** 419–420; **19,** 481; **22,** 642–649, 871; **24,** 647–654, 655–665
—by reference to events connected with war, **24,** 666–668
—municipal courts, by, **23,** 699
" laws in force in Italy during the war ", meaning, **24,** 306, 647–663; **29,** 31–32, 36, 37, 42–47
liquidation of enemy property, **28,** 629–633
" measure taken against property ", meaning, **22,** 964–965; **23,** 500–506
municipal legislation, need for, **23,** 698
nationality and, **19,** 322–326; **22,** 12, 445–448; **32,** 170–186
Order based on, interpretation of, **18,** 440
performance of, **20,** 628–634; **22,** 647–649; **26,** 685–688; **29,** 369–500; **30,** 511–537
political nature, **22,** 945
postliminium: q.v.
prize and, **16,** 560–565
renunciation of territorial sovereignty, **32,** 582–585
reparations clauses, **18,** 414–429
—" injury or damage as result of war ", **18,** 414–423
—municipal legislation, satisfaction by, **18,** 435–439
—restitution of requisitioned property, **18,** 423–426, 435–440
—time limit for claims, **18,** 427–429; **20,** 483–484
—claim by owner against own Government, **28,** 607–611
—waiver of claims, **32,** 233–237
requisitioning, nature of, **23,** 500, 505, 507
restitution and reparation, **20,** 481–488, 491–492; **22,** 649–650, 864–867, 945–978; **23,** 499–508; **34,** 219–261 *passim. See also under* Germany, Federal Republic, Settlement Convention

Peace treaties—*continued*
restitution and reparation—*contd.*
—assessment of compensation, **20,** 491–492
—evidence of loss or damage, **22,** 979
—" free of all encumbrances ", **24,** 666
—naturalization of property owner, effect, **22,** 979
retroactive effect, **23,** 665
sequestration, nature of, **22,** 389–393
sequestration and sale, whether war loss, **22,** 389–393
settlement of disputes, provisions for, **17,** 331–339; **23,** 62
sovereignty of defeated State, limitation of, **22,** 945
State succession and, **23,** 106–107
transfer of territory under, **7,** 413, 415, 491–496, 509–510; **23,** 664
" treated as enemy ", meaning, **22,** 389–390, 642–646; **24,** 654, 658–661; **25,** 153–164; **29,** 22–54; **30,** 451–454
treaties kept in force, **22,** 607–608; **24,** 890–892
treaties, revival, **5,** 479–480; **11,** 241–242; **18,** 320; **19,** 556; **23,** 468; **24,** 883–892; **28,** 602; **31,** 3; **32,** 336–337
tribunals set up under: *see* titles of various tribunals and commissions
unequal character, reparations provisions, **32,** 233–234, 235–236
" United Nations nationals ", meaning, **22,** 445–446, 647; **24,** 308, 313, 647; **26,** 327; **29,** 22–54
validity in municipal law, **32,** 162, 164–165
victor, right to seize property of vanquished, **22,** 980
waiver of claims under, **23,** 662, 698; **32,** 164, 233–237
Peaceful Settlement of Disputes, European Convention for (1957), **24,** 814
Pearl Harbour, Japanese attack on, **12,** 283–284, 289–300
Penal legislation—
characterization as, **26,** 431–434
foreign, operation of, **7,** 158–160; **8,** 198–200; **24,** 16–21; **30,** 10. *See also* Recognition, foreign legislation, of
Penobscot Bay, **9,** 128–133
Pension rights—
nationalization, effect on, **26,** 287–288
State succession and, **1,** 66–68; **2,** 58, 65–66; **3,** 79–80; **5,** 66–68; **6,** 83–84; **7,** 433–434; **24,** 69
Perduellio, **8,** 88; **15,** 80–85
Perjury—
deportation for, **11,** 111–112
evidence before foreign military tribunal, **11,** 270–271
Permanent Court of Arbitration, non-accessibility to individuals, **9,** 58
Permanent Court of International Justice
ad hoc Judges, **8,** 488–489
advisory function, **23,** 538–540
Advisory Opinions—
—competence to render, **1,** 381; **2,** 394–397
—duty to render, **8,** 489–491
—non-members of League and, **2,** 394–397
—refusal to give, **23,** 541–545
—request for, **4,** 524; **6,** 432–433
—scope, **5,** 412, 471
appellate jurisdiction, **7,** 493; **8,** 487–488
capitulations and, **19,** 523–524
constitutions of States, interpretation of, **8,** 490–491
contentious jurisdiction: *see* jurisdiction, *infra*
counterclaims, **4,** 499–501, 516–518
declaratory decisions, **4,** 506–511; **27,** 145–146
dissolution of, effects, **27,** 559, 562–563, 568, 571, 577, 581–583, 586–587
evidence, **3,** 107–108; **4,** 518–519
experts, appointment of, **4,** 522–523
function, **5,** 459–461
—agency of pacific settlement, **5,** 461–463
I.C.J. and, **17,** 48, 55, 342; **18,** 106; **27,** 577–578, 584, 589
individuals, non-accessibility, **9,** 58
interim measures of protection, **6,** 428–430; **7,** 497–498
joinder of actions, **6,** 430
Judges—
—*ad hoc,* **8,** 488–489
—disqualification, **28,** 558
—immunities, **10,** 362–363
Judgments—
—basis of, **5,** 460
—binding force, **4,** 149–150, 519–520
—contents, **6,** 431
—declaratory, **4,** 506–511; **27,** 145–146
—effectiveness, **4,** 516–518
—execution of, **2,** 393; **6,** 367
—finality, **5,** 461, 471
—interpretation of, **3,** 430–432; **4,** 506–511
—" judgment by consent ", **5,** 461
—municipal courts, authority before, **18,** 3–9
—*res judicata,* **4,** 506–511; **9,** 325–326, 522–525; **23,** 83, 84–88
—time-limit for compliance, **2,** 394; **6,** 367

Permanent Court of International Justice—*continued*
jurisdiction, **3,** 423–432; **4,** 495–511; **5,** 467–468, 471; **6,** 428–431; **7,** 490–498; **19,** 521–523; **23,** 578–579
—acceptance, forms of, **4,** 499
—acceptance, implied, **4,** 496, 499, 501–505
—acceptance, renewal in relation to I.C.J., **33,** 418–443
—alteration in character of dispute, **9,** 526
—basis of, **3,** 423–424
—concurrent instruments, under, **9,** 511
—concurrent jurisdicton of other tribunals, **4,** 505–506
—continuing situation, **9,** 503, 516
—Council of League and, **2,** 390–391; **4,** 497
—dispute arising after Application, **9,** 519
—dispute arising after ratification of Optional Clause, **9,** 505, 516
—dispute, as condition precedent, **3,** 426–428; **4,** 506–510
—exhaustion of local remedies, **9,** 311–315, 513; **27,** 532
—interpretation of Judgments, **4,** 506–511
—interpretation of treaties, **4,** 503–504
—limitation *ratione temporis,* **9,** 505, 516
—*litispendence,* **3,** 425; **4,** 505–506
—nationality of claims and, **9,** 309, 314
—negotiations as condition of, **2,** 399–400, 401; **9,** 521
—objections to, **2,** 391–392; **3,** 425–426; **9,** 515
—relation to jurisdiction of other bodies, **2,** 387–389
—reparation for damage, **4,** 501–505
—requirement of form, **4,** 497–498
—restricted, presumption of, **4,** 495–497
—special arbitral agreements, **6,** 366; **24,** 817
law applicable, **3,** 429–430; **4,** 466–467; **8,** 450–451
multiplicity of suits, **3,** 424–425
municipal decisions, authority of, **5,** 469
municipal law, interpretation of, **3,** 423–424
negotiate, imposition of obligation to, **9,** 521
non-exhaustion of local remedies, **27,** 532
objections to jurisdiction: *see* jurisdiction, objections to, *supra*

Permanent Court of International Justice—*continued*
Optional Clause: *see* Statute, Art. 36, *infra*
Orders, force of, **5,** 464
organization of, **4,** 494; **5,** 459–465; **6,** 427–428; **9,** 502
pleadings
—Application, form of, **6,** 25
—submissions, change in, **9,** 503
preliminary objections and decisions on merits, **3,** 425–426; **9,** 503
Privileges and Immunities, Agreement with Netherlands (1928), **22,** 537
procedure, **4,** 506–519; **6,** 428–431; **7,** 497–498
—defects of form, **4,** 511–512
—fresh submissions, **4,** 512
—provisional measures, **4,** 315–316
res judicata, **4,** 506–511; **9,** 325–326, 522–525; **23,** 83, 84–88
status of members and officials, **9,** 425
Statute, Art. 36 (Optional Clause), **2,** 361; **5,** 468; **6,** 96; **9,** 309, 503–510
submissions of parties, how far binding on Court, **5,** 464
treaties, interpretation of, **3,** 428
—preparatory work, **6,** 384–385
—previous decisions, **6,** 411
U.S.A., reservation to adherence to Statute, **27,** 546
Perpetuatio fori, principle of, **25,** 55
Perpetuity, grants in, **1,** 94–95
leases in, **9,** 118. *See also* Leases, international
Persia: *see also* Iran
Concession Agreements with Anglo-Persian Oil Co. (1933 and 1937), **19,** 502, 507–549 *passim;* **20,** 305–316, 317, 321
—Gass-Golshoyan Agreement, **20,** 322
Constitution (1907), **22,** 32, 33, 34, 36, 38
Switzerland, Commercial Treaty (1934), **19,** 514–549 *passim*
U.K., Commercial Treaties (1857 and 1903), **19,** 515–549 *passim*
U.S.A., Consular Convention (1856), **6,** 398–400; **11,** 209
Persian Gulf, continental shelf under, **18,** 154
Persona grata/non grata, **16,** 282–283
Persona standi in judicio, **1,** 410–404; **3,** 445–447; **17,** 144, 151; **19,** 210: *see also under* Enemy alien
" Personal immunity ", consular, meaning, **4,** 383–384
Personal jurisdiction: *see under* Jurisdiction

Peru—
Air Transport Agreement with U.S.A., nationality of carrier, **31,** 416–424
Bolivarian Convention (1911), **22,** 518
Chile—
—Extradition Treaty (1932), **7,** 335–336
—Treaty of Ancón (1883), **2,** 241; **3,** 357–358; **6,** 110
—Treaty of Santiago (1929), **6,** 110
Colombia—
—Boundary Treaty (1922), **5,** 338
—Protocol of Friendship (1934), **18,** 349
Maritime Zone Declaration (1952), **22,** 278, 282
territorial waters, claim to 200-mile belt, **31,** 129–131
U.K., Commercial Treaty (1830), **23,** 313
U.S.A.—
—Extradition Treaty, **24,** 263
—Treaty of Commerce and Navigation (1870), **23,** 715
Petersberg Agreement (1949) Federal Republic of Germany and Western High Commissioners, **19,** 413–415
Petition of right, power of alien to bring, **9,** 372–373
Philippines, Commonwealth of—
Constitution, 1935...**9,** 40
—1943...**20,** 644–646
nationality in, **7,** 282; **9,** 38
occupation by Japan, **18,** 592–607, 642–677, 702–703; **20,** 643–646; **22,** 994–996
Penal Code, piracy, **1,** 164
Spanish Penal Code, application of, **1,** 77
State succession of U.S.A. to Spain, **1,** 59, 77
status of, **9,** 35, 38; **16,** 208–215; **20,** 276–281, 343; **23,** 29–35
suppression of insurrection, damage to alien property, **3,** 225–226
taxation in, **11,** 47–48
Treaty of Cession (1898), **24,** 447, 448
whether included in territorial possessions of U.S.A., **5,** 76, 354
Philippines, Republic of—
independence (1946), **18,** 562; **21,** 40; **24,** 448
nationality in, **16,** 208–215
U.S. bases in, **23,** 124–126; **32,** 77–79
U.S.A., Military Bases Agreement (1947), **20,** 148–153
Picquigny-Amiens, Treaty of (1475), **20,** 128, 132
Pillage, **15,** 619, 674–677; **23,** 833
damages for, **5,** 150–152
Piracy *jure gentium,* **1,** 164–165; **7,** 213–224; **11,** 129–130
Piracy *jure gentium—continued*
definitions of, **7,** 215–216, 221–224; **11,** 174–175
high seas, bays, territorial waters, whether, **8,** 169–170
robbery as essential element, **7,** 216–218, 221–224
" Place of business ", meaning, **8,** 181–182. *See also under* Double taxation
Plebiscite, **1,** 43, 179; **2,** 241; **3,** 107–112; **4,** 306–307
conduct of, **3,** 112
occupation of foreign territory pending, law applicable, **6,** 110–111
State succession and, **6,** 83–84
status of territory under, **3,** 107, 108, 110–111
—pending decision, **2,** 93–95, 241
termination of, frustration, **3,** 112
Plebiscite Commission, Upper Silesia, authority, **3,** 109, 110, 112
legal status of agents, **2,** 93–94; **6,** 33
responsibility of Prussia for, **1,** 179–180
Pledge, subject-matter of international claim, **30,** 208–212
Plunder, acts of, responsibility for, **2,** 160
Plunder of occupied territory: *see under* Belligerent occupation
Poland—
alien property in, **1,** 247–248
Austrian railways, liability for obligations of, **2,** 63
cession of Posen to, **2,** 58–59
Congress Poland, territory of, **5,** 12, 14
Constitution (1921), Art. 81 (non-reviewability of statutes), **1,** 7
—Art. 95 (admission of aliens), **1,** 247, 248; **4,** 328–329
—Art. 99 (limitations on land ownership), **1,** 248
Constitution (1952), **21,** 242
continuity of, **1,** 33–38; **5,** 72, 493
Czechoslovakia, Treaty on Legal and Financial Matters (1925), **4,** 397
Danzig—
—Agreement on Double Taxation (1924), **4,** 411
—conduct of foreign relations of, **5,** 411
—nationals in, treatment of, **6,** 209–213
—official in, status of, **6,** 130–131
—railway administration, **3,** 170–171, 340–342; **7,** 182–184
—Treaty of Paris (1920), **5,** 410; **6,** 130, 209–213, 383–384; **7,** 61–62, 270
Danzig and Germany, Convention with (1921), **5,** 349, 393
Economic National Bank, jurisdictional immunity, **9,** 213

Poland—*continued*
establishment of, **1,** 47; **2,** 9–10, 229–230; **5,** 11–15
ex-German Property, Decree of 1946, **24,** 943
foreign exchange regulations, **28,** 308
France—
—Consular Convention (1925), **6,** 332
—Convention, Private Property (1922), **5,** 387–391
—Extradition Treaty (1925), **7,** 372–373
—Intergovernmental Agreement (exchange of ambassador's residence), **11,** 203
—Treaty of Establishment (1937), **15,** 1–2; **16,** 312
General Principles of Civil Law (1946), **24,** 80, 962, 967, 969, 970
German property in, liquidation of, **4,** 258–260, 268–270
German State property, succession to, **2,** 55
Germany—
—Arbitration Treaty (1925), **24,** 814
—Convention with (Danzig) (1921), **5,** 349, 393
— —(1924) *re* frontier traffic, **6,** 387
—Geneva Convention on Upper Silesia (1922), **5,** 346; **6,** 66–71, 83–84, 322; **7,** 283, 325–327, 411, 433–434
—Non-Aggression Pact (1938), **15,** 419
—Paris Agreement (1920), **1,** 313–314
—Revaluation Convention (1929), **6,** 351
—Vienna Convention (1924), **4,** 15–16; **6,** 260–263
Greece, Trade Convention (1925), **6,** 352–353
Hague Convention on Civil Procedure (1905), as party to, **1,** 70–71
Holy See, Concordat (1925), **7,** 14–15, 400–401
independence, effect of recovery of, **6,** 59–60
international law, as part of municipal law, **1,** 7
Land Reform Law, 1920...**1,** 248
Lithuania, dispute with (1928), **22,** 673
—relations with, **3,** 446–447
—termination of status of war with, **5,** 491–492
military jurisdiction in U.K., **10,** 128–129
Minorities Treaty (1919), **5,** 13; **6,** 37–40, 260, 322, 359
Nationality Act, 1920...**11,** 179–180
Nationality Law, 1951...**22,** 429
nationals in Danzig, treatment of, **6,** 209–213
nationals, Second World War, enemy aliens, whether, **26,** 726–727

Poland—*continued*
Notaries Public, Law on, **24,** 956–966, 972
occupation by Germany, **4,** 561–562; **10,** 581–583; **11,** 33; **12,** 424–427; **15,** 594–595, 680–682; **24,** 80; **30,** 496–511
—destruction of as subject of international law, **30,** 505
—local law, failure to respect, **30,** 506
—local law, modifications, **26,** 714–723
—sovereignty, effect on, **28,** 651
occupation by U.S.S.R., **11,** 145
—requisitions, **26,** 730–732
partition, legal effects of, **1,** 33–34; **2,** 81
partition, rights of Powers, **4,** 551–553
partition (1939), **15,** 680
private rights of political origin, **2,** 77, 80–81
recognition of, **1,** 33–34
restoration of, **1,** 35–38
" Recovered Territories ", Decree on Government of (1945), **24,** 77–82
recognition of Government of (1945), **16,** 46–60; **19,** 72–85
Sequestration of Private Property Order (1940), **24,** 963, 964
State succession and, **2,** 54–55; **5,** 52–57, 71
—Austria-Hungary, **2,** 64–65, 83–85
—Austrian rights, **1,** 63–64; **4,** 73–77; **5,** 55
—German State property, **2,** 55
—officials, **4,** 92–95
—Prussian obligations, **1,** 64–65
—Russian rights, **2,** 54–55
Succession, Law of, **24,** 967, 970, 971
Succession Procedure, Law of, **24,** 962
treaties, law on binding force of, **6,** 352–353
U.K., Extradition Treaty (1932), **21,** 240, 242, 244
U.S.A., Treaty of Friendship, Commerce and Consular Rights (1931), **12,** 245, 425; **21,** 204–205; **28,** 307
U.S.S.R., Peace Treaty of Riga (1921), **6,** 353, 360, 450
valorization of claims, Decree of 1924...**5,** 392
War Criminals, Decree of 1944...**24,** 943; **30,** 497
Wills, German Law, introduction of, **24,** 970–971
Police, serving outside national territory, disciplinary jurisdiction, **26,** 210–221
Police measures, application to aliens, **6,** 181
Police service, military service distinguished, **11,** 182–183

Political crimes: *see also* Extradition
bomb outrages, **5,** 292–293
common crimes and, **9,** 402; **22,** 520–525, 528–529; **32,** 294–298, 304
Communism, crime committed to combat, **5,** 293–295
concept of, **4,** 347–351; **7,** 360–367; **33,** 271, 319–352, 353–360
murder, **4,** 347–351; **5,** 270–272
trading with the enemy, **1,** 265–266
treason, **15,** 297–300; **22,** 527–528
"Political question", **10,** 22. *See also* Act of State; Conclusiveness of statement of Executive
Political refugees, internment of, **7,** 259–261
Political rights—
State succession and, **1,** 76, 77
taxation of aliens and, **6,** 280–281
Polygamous marriage, nationality of children, **4,** 296–297
Poor person's facilities—
aliens, **11,** 242–243
stateless persons, **4,** 321–322; **8,** 311–312, 314
Ports: *see also* Blockade
access for foreign merchant ships, **27,** 212; **31,** 137–140
belligerent rights, exercise in, **31,** 518
closure by insurgents, **4,** 531–533
Convention on International Regime of, **31,** 140 n.
crime on foreign ship in, **1,** 158–159; **4,** 160, 184–185; **6,** 175–177; **8,** 210; **9,** 167, 169–170; **15,** 108–109; **16,** 143–144; **20,** 154–155; **24,** 173–174; **31,** 241–247; **32,** 117–119
crimes on national ship in foreign port, **4,** 184–185
entry in distress, **5,** 129–131; **6,** 154–156; **7,** 208; **9,** 164–166; **11,** 127–130; **23,** 151–153
jurisdiction in, **1,** 109–111; **4,** 160–162; **5,** 129–131; **6,** 153–157, 175–177; **8,** 182–184, 208–212; **9,** 157–171; **10,** 155–176; **11,** 113–124, 127–128; **12,** 73–75; **15,** 110–115, 193–194; **16,** 100–103, 309–311; **20,** 197–210; **23,** 151–153, 354–358; **24,** 167–171; **31,** 227–247
—bunker control, **10,** 267–272
—"internal economy" doctrine, **31,** 228–229, 231, 239–240
—Mixed Courts of Egypt, **9,** 167
—personal injury action, **28,** 145–149
Portugal—
Abolition of Forced Labour Convention—
—non-compliance, allegation of, **35,** 285–351 *passim*
—ratification of, **35,** 286, 288, 292, 323, 333
Portugal—*continued*
confiscation of property of aliens, **1,** 238–239
divorce, law of 1910...**5,** 244
enclaves in India, access to, **31,** 23–121 *passim*
Holy See, relation to, **4,** 97–98
Mahrathas, Ruler of, Treaties with (1741), **24,** 868; (1779) **24,** 850, 852, 859; (1785), **24,** 859
nationality, law of, **5,** 244; **10,** 290
Spain, Extradition Treaty (1867), **9,** 403
U.K., Extradition Treaty (1892), **24,** 502–506
Posen, cession to Poland, **2,** 58–59
Possession, as condition for invoking jurisdictional immunity, **10,** 208–217
Possession, forcible, **10,** 211–216
Post, offence of cheating through, location of offence, **31,** 270–271
Postal Conventions—
arbitration under, **23,** 587, 592, 594, 595, 596
Brussels Convention (1952), **23,** 591–593
compensation for loss of registered packet, **23,** 596–597
Convention of 1897...**22,** 414
gratuitous transport of mail, liability for cost of, **23,** 605–609
Madrid Convention (1920), **23,** 585–590
Paris Convention (1947), **23,** 592
reply coupons issued in puppet State, payment for, **23,** 591–596
Rome Convention (1906), **5,** 401, 416, 418; **23,** 585–590
sea transit charges, "contrary arrangements", **23,** 585–590
transit charges from enemy occupied territory, **23,** 591–596
Postal correspondence, exemption from capture as prize, **12,** 473–481
"Postal correspondence", meaning, **1,** 432
Postal Union of the Americas and Spain, Conventions (1932, 1936, 1955), **23,** 606, 608, 609
Postliminium, **2,** 55; **4,** 551–553; **5,** 492; **11,** 58–60; **14,** 250–258; **15,** 584, 592; **18,** 638–640; **20,** 465, 634; **21,** 108–109, 471–473
funds taken by occupant, restoration of, **26,** 718–719; **28,** 636
Potsdam, Agreement and Declaration (1945), **13,** 271; **15,** 356, 362, 363, 374; **17,** 166, 178; **18,** 259, 261; **19,** 624; **21,** 106, 486; **22,** 400, 984; **24,** 44, 77, 955
Potsdam Conference (1945), German assets in Japan, **26,** 574

Practice, customary international law and, **31,** 25, 37, 52–53, 56, 67, 70, 80–81
Prague, Treaty of (1866), **4,** 84
—(1923), **9,** 121
Preamble of treaties, interpretation; *see under* Treaties
Preclusion: *see also* Acquiescence *and* Estoppel
adoption of map of frontier region, **33,** 61, 66, 70, 86–87, 91, 105, 114
common law estoppel and, **33,** 91
elements of, **33,** 146
failure to object to arbitral award, **30,** 470, 473–474, 478–479, 480, 490–492
good faith as basis of, **33,** 146
" Pre-investigation " of national status, (U.S.A.), **1,** 197
Preparatory work: *see under* Treaties
Prescription—
acquisition of territory by, **4,** 103, 115; **9,** 112
boundary disputes and, **3,** 105–106, 113–114
duration of, **4,** 263–264
extinctive (laches), **3,** 246; **4,** 263–265; **5,** 194–197, 450–452; **20,** 483–484; **23,** 306, 313, 314–316, 671–672; **24,** 296; **27,** 80; **30,** 480. *See also* Statutes of limitation
—European Communities Court, before, **29,** 271, 273, 276, 280
extradition proceedings, in, **2,** 279; **5,** 286; **6,** 294, 306–307, 313–314; **7,** 354–355; **8,** 350, 382–383; **9,** 395–398; **16,** 276; **19,** 378; **22,** 514–517; **26,** 525–526; **30,** 389–390; **31,** 369–372
general principle of law, as, **4,** 263–264
periods of, in treaty, **20,** 483–484
war, effect on, **2,** 26, 413–414
Pre-war contracts: *see* Contracts, war, effect of outbreak on
Princeps in alterius territorio privatus, **15,** 144
" Principles of equity ", meaning, **4,** 467–469. *See also* Equity
Principles of international law, justice and equity: *see* Arbitration *and* Equity
Prisoners of war: *see also under* Geneva Conventions
"aiding and relieving the enemy", **24,** 925, 926
civilian internees, distinguished, **11,** 266
communication with enemy, **23,** 762–764
conduct of, responsibility to home State, **2,** 434

Prisoners of war—*continued*
criminal proceedings against, **12,** 403–411; **23,** 764–766
detention after conclusion of peace treaty, **1,** 434
duty of obedience, **22,** 926–928; **23,** 762–764; **24,** 925
employment of, **13,** 285–286
—coalmines, in, **16,** 352–353
—prohibited work, **13,** 218, 296; **14,** 210, 211, 300–302; **15,** 394, 401, 411–412, 679; **16,** 509, 516–518
enemy aliens, whether, **10,** 450–464
enemy character of, **9,** 539; **10,** 529–530
escape, right or duty, **12,** 397–402, 407–410; **13,** 291–293; **17,** 400 n.
escaped, status in neutral territory, **23,** 609–613
escaping, shooting of, **16,** 403
espionage, use for, **16,** 354
execution of, **13,** 281–282, 286–287, 293–296, 297–299, 305–306, 332–333; **14,** 205–207, 307; **16,** 353
exposure to danger, **14,** 211; **15,** 394–395
forced marches, **16,** 351–352
French laws on reinstatement, **12,** 281–282
ill-treatment of, **16,** 351–352, 554
internment, **23,** 609–610, 612
interrogation, **13,** 290–291
irregular volunteers, as, **16,** 356
law governing conduct, **14,** 202–203, 207–208
legal effect of treatment as, **22,** 925
legal position, **1,** 433; **4,** 548–549
offences against, **15,** 477; **16,** 351–354, 403, 404, 509–525; **17,** 399, 431–434
—exposure to danger, **14,** 211; **15,** 394–395
—handing over to civil authorities, **15,** 395
—unlawful employment, **13,** 218, 296; **14,** 210, 211, 300–302; **15,** 394, 401, 411–412, 679; **16,** 509, 516–518
offences by, **16,** 534–536
pay of, **18,** 544
—officers, **25,** 349–353, 355–356; **28,** 517; **29,** 495–499
—rate of exchange, **16,** 408–414
persons liable to capture, **13,** 284–285
punishment of, **14,** 210
reprisals against, **15,** 477
" resident " in enemy territory, whether, **10,** 529–534
responsibility for lives of, **4,** 226–227
right to treatment as, **17,** 399
rights of, **22,** 927–928
service of process on, **9,** 539
status of, **13,** 306–308; **24,** 926–928

Prisoners of war—*continued*
status of—*continued*
—continued membership in national forces, **14,** 207–208
subordination to own officers, **14,** 203–204
treatment of, **2,** 431–433; **13,** 216–218, 290–300; **14,** 205–207, 209–210; **16,** 351–352, 554; **18,** 544; **19,** 596–598
trial of, **13,** 274–276, 278–279, 280–281, 300–305; **16,** 414, 427; **22,** 929
unauthorized communication with, **22,** 926–929
war crimes concerning, **15,** 364–372, 394–395, 404, 411–412, 499, 500, 620, 626–627, 633; **16,** 351–354, 403–404, 414, 509–525, 554; **18,** 533–535; **19,** 596–598
war criminals, as, **18,** 544; **22,** 929
Private international law—
Act of State doctrine, **35,** 48–49
aircraft, crash over high seas, applicable law, **26,** 242 n.
application to jurisdiction of Restitution Authorities, Germany, **26,** 146
arbitrator under concession, **35,** 170
contracts for sale of land, proper law, **25,** 79
Conventions concerning—
—breach by legislation, **25,** 260–261
—interpretation of, **25,** 268–269, 285, 302
—municipal courts, effect on, **25,** 269
—*ordre public*, implied exception, **25,** 253, 256, 257–258, 268–269, 271, 278, 288, 290, 293–294
damage, items recoverable, **35,** 251–252
debt relationships, applicable law, **25,** 39
defined, **26,** 270
expropriation of alien property and, **4,** 147–151
form, *lex loci actus*, **35,** 54
public international law and, **5,** 468; **19,** 229–754
Hague Convention, Guardianship of Infants (1902): *see* Guardianship, Hague Convention (1902)
jurisdiction, principles of, **26,** 148
municipal law character, conventions, effect of, **25,** 275–276
ordre public, concept of, **25,** 256–257, 268, 270, 277, 289–290, 299
place of performance, concept of, **25,** 78
purpose of, **25,** 270
public law, distinguished, **25,** 277
public policy, **35,** 54
tort on ship in foreign territorial waters, applicable law, **26,** 226–227 n.
Private international law, Bustamante Code (1928), **5,** 277, 281; **6,** 12–13; **7,** 336, 444–445; **22,** 283, 519, 528, 540–541; **23,** 425–426, 428; **24,** 492–493, 500, 501
Private law transactions by States, **2,** 13–15
Private property, interference with, recognition of: *see* Act of State *and* Foreign legislation, recognition of
Private property, respect for: *see under* Aliens; War. *See also* Private rights, respect for
Private rights, cession of territory, effect of: *see under* Cession of territory
Private rights, respect for, State succession and, **1,** 68; **2,** 71–83; **3,** 81–84; **4,** 88–91, 551–553; **5,** 68; **6,** 66–73, 83–85; **7,** 91–101, 433–434, 486–487; **8,** 32, 125–126, 136–141; **9,** 102; **10,** 98–102; **11,** 76–77; **13,** 35–42; **14,** 36–40; **15,** 52–58; **16,** 62–63; **17,** 81–82; **19,** 132–137; **20,** 74–75, 81–82; **21,** 51–54, 63–66; **23,** 101–105, 109–111; **24,** 73–76; **26,** 82–83, 86; **31,** 13–19: *see also* Acquired rights
continuance of contractual obligations, **23,** 109–110; **24,** 61
land grants, **5,** 71; **9,** 102; **22,** 127–130; **23,** 109–110; **31,** 13–19
leases, **1,** 63–66; **23,** 109–110
new currency, effect on debts, **24,** 73–74
title to land, **23,** 110–111
Privilege, official reports of commercial representative, **11,** 213–217
Privileges and Immunities of the United Nations, Convention on (1946), **23,** 619
Privileges and Immunities of (U.N.) Specialized Agencies, Convention on, (1947), **22,** 4, 709, 710
Privileges exceeding requirements of international law, withdrawal of, **1,** 237–238
Privy Council, Judicial Committee of: *see under* United Kingdom
Prize: *see also* London, Declaration of (1909); Paris, Declaration of (1856)
ally, former, cargo destined for territory of, **9,** 573
ally of enemy, status of, **9,** 575
applicable law, **1,** 487–488; **3,** 486; **9,** 570; **10,** 606–623; **16,** 569–572
armistice and, **12,** 414–415, 460–462, 466–471, 504, 439–542; **16,** 414; **20,** 617, 675–677
black list, cargo shipped to firm on, **16,** 574–575

Prize—*continued*
booty and, **11,** 300–302, 303–304; **21,** 473–475
burden of proof, **16,** 574–575, 578, 586; **17,** 443–444
capture—
—absence of declaration of war, **12,** 471–472
—after hostilities, sunk outside territorial waters, **30,** 515–532
—armistice, after, **12,** 460–462, 466–471, 504
—enemy port, in, **20,** 669, 672
—in war, in dock, **32,** 601–625
—land forces, by, **12,** 471–472; **32,** 601–625
—meaning of, **18,** 704, 706
—nature of, **20,** 668, 670–672
—neutral flag, effect, **32,** 607, 612, 623, 624
—neutral property, subsequent outbreak of war, **12,** 513–516
—neutral territorial waters, in, **32,** 611
—on land, **11,** 302; **32,** 601–625
—place of, **12,** 460–466, 481, 488, 497, 500, 501, 516
—port, in, **16,** 560–565, 568; **18,** 705–706, 710–713; **32,** 601–625
—Port-Admiral, by, **12,** 511
—procedure, **32,** 604, 606, 611, 618–619
—restrictions on, **12,** 473–489; **16,** 557–560; **31,** 509–520
—termination of hostilities, after, **22,** 1011–1012
—time of, **12,** 460–462, 466–471, 504–505, 510–513
—validity, Japanese Prize Court Review Commission, **32,** 601–625
—validity, need for intent to seize, **15,** 688–692
—validity, presumption of, **12,** 526
—" vessel " capable of capture, **32,** 603, 605, 606, 608, 610, 611, 616–617
—whether transferring property, **11,** 303–304
capturing State, rights of, **12,** 514–515
cargo, enemy ship on, presumption of enemy character, **31,** 520
cargo of wreck, **11,** 301–302
cargo shipped before outbreak of hostilities, **16,** 600–601
claim, need for, **16,** 572
compensation for capture, **9,** 578; **12,** 525, 530–531, 565–567, 569–573
—goods wrongly seized, **22,** 832
—use and delay, for, **9,** 580; **19,** 634–638
condemnation, setting aside, **18,** 727–730

Prize—*continued*
continuous voyage, doctrine of, **17,** 441–442
contraband: *q.v.*
corporations, enemy nationality, ground for condemnation, **12,** 554–557
costs, award of, **10,** 624–626, 632–635; **12,** 485, 510
courts: *see* Prize courts
days of grace, **12,** 489
decree, effect of condemnation of ship, **1,** 107
delay, damages for, **9,** 580; **19,** 634–638
demurrage, claim for, **11,** 304–305
diversion of ship from course, **16,** 581–583
documents, **16,** 573, 576, 587
—order for production of, **22,** 193
domicile, commercial, **18,** 727
domicile, test of, **17,** 447–448
enemy character of goods, **16,** 572; **17,** 440–448
—persons, **16,** 580
enemy destination, **16,** 574–580, 600; **17,** 448–449
enemy goods, proof of nationality of owner, **22,** 1008–1009
enemy property, presumption as to, **12,** 511–512
enemy purchaser, c.i.f. contract, **9,** 567
enemy ship in captured port, **15,** 692
enemy ship in dock, **32,** 601–625
enemy ship in ignorance of war, **16,** 558–559,
entry into belligerent port for stress, **16,** 560, 598–599
evidence, **16,** 573–581
existence of state of war, **17,** 347
extra-judicial release of, **13,** 407–412
fishing vessels, exemption, **12,** 469–471
—assisting enemy, **28,** 661–662
flag, conclusiveness of, **11,** 264–265; **16,** 389–396; **17,** 378–385; **24,** 919–921; **28,** 652–656; **31,** 509–520
freight of condemned goods, claim for, **10,** 626–631; **13,** 421–425
goods for use of enemy, **28,** 656–660
goods shipped before hostilities, **17,** 448–449
governmental authorization, need for, **15,** 691–692
hulls, **20,** 667, 673
indemnities and damages, **9,** 578–583; **10,** 626–637; **12,** 527–532; **13,** 412–413, 432; **14,** 318–319; **16,** 581–583
Japanese Prize Court Review Commission, **32,** 601–625
maritime liens, **10,** 613–618; **12,** 529–530

Prize—*continued*
mortgagees, rights in prize proceedings, **9**, 562, 564
municipal rule altering international law rule, **9**, 575
nationality of libellant, **15**, 689
nature of, **12**, 492–494
navicerts and ships' warrants, **12**, 532–537, 546, 553
Netherlands Prize Rules (1940), **24**, 918–923
neutral flag covers enemy goods, **16**, 570, 588, 602
neutral goods, capture of, **12**, 512; **31**, 509–520
neutral's ignorance of outbreak of war, **12**, 568–570
neutral ship carrying enemy goods, **28**, 662–664; **31**, 509–520
neutral ship carrying produce of enemy State, **16**, 572; **28**, 655
neutral ship chartered to enemy company, **28**, 662–664
passing of property, **12**, 390, 392–395, 495–501, 564–567
peace treaty and, **16**, 560–565
port, capture in, **16**, 560–565, 568; **18**, 705–706, 710–713; **32**, 601–625
postal correspondence, exemption, **12**, 473–481
private property, liability to capture, **11**, 299–302
"probable cause", capture for, **1**, 172; **9**, 579; **10**, 601–605; **11**, 304–305; **12**, 543–548
procedure, **9**, 575–578; **10**, 623–631; **12**, 516–521, 524–526; **13**, 409, 419–420; **14**, 316, 317; **16**, 573–581
—*Commissario del Rè*, functions, **12**, 516–521
proceedings, need for, **21**, 473–475, 489
produce of soil of enemy, **16**, 572; **28**, 655
release from requisition for purpose of seizure, **18**, 725
requisition out of Prize Court, **16**, 569–570
residence, relevance of, **18**, 728–730
revision of judgment, **22**, 1008–1011; **32**, 601–625; **34**, 261, 263–264
right of, Italian practice, **12**, 466–469
—when originating, **12**, 388
sale of goods before judgment, **12**, 527–528
salvage claims and, **10**, 608–613
salvage ships, exemption, **12**, 486–488
search and capture, **19**, 634–638
second seizure, validity, **12**, 462–466, 496–498
seizure, nature of, **20**, 667; **21**, 473

Prize—*continued*
seizure—*continued*
—requirements for, **16**, 562–568; **24**, 992–994
—time for, **20**, 669, 675
—unlawful, **24**, 991–992
setting aside condemnation, **18**, 727–730
ship aground in captured port, **16**, 560–565
"ship", meaning, **12**, 506
ships as booty, **21**, 489
ships scuttled in bay, **16**, 566
ships under neutral flag, enemy controlled, **11**, 264–265; **16**, 389–390; **17**, 378–385; **24**, 919–921; **28**, 652–656; **31**, 509–520
"small craft", exemption, **12**, 482–483, 487–488
subject of, **18**, 713–714, 719; **20**, 667, 673
suspicion, grounds for, **19**, 633
tackle, furniture and apparel, **12**, 505–510
territory under enemy control, **12**, 568–570
third party rights, **12**, 511.
toute prise doit être jugée, **12**, 492
transfers *in transitu*, **11**, 306–307
unfinished hulls, **20**, 667–674
unneutral service: *see under* Neutrality
unsecured creditors, rights in prize proceedings, **9**, 563
validity of capture—
—need for intent to seize, **15**, 688–692
—presumption of, **12**, 526
visit and search, **17**, 440–447
volition, need for, **18**, 713
wrecks, **22**, 1011–1012
yachts, exemption, **12**, 481–486, 488
Zamora, The, rule in, **1**, 429; **9**, 572–573, 576–577
Prize Courts—
British, Commission under Great Seal, **20**, 670
condemnation of cargo, information required, **9**, 575; **10**, 636–637
confiscation of bonds, effect on debt, **32**, 108
contraband: *q.v.*
damages against captor, **10**, 631–635; **13**, 432; **14**, 318–319
effect of decisions in neutral courts, **1**, 487–488; **2**, 452
finality of decisions, **5**, 489, 515
Japanese Prize Court Review Commission, **32**, 601–625
jurisdiction of, **12**, 353–357, 490–516; **13**, 407, 412; **14**, 318; **15**, 689; **18**, 722–725; **20**, 667, 670; **22**, 1008–1011

Prize Courts—*continued*
jurisdiction of—*continued*
—nature and extent of, **3,** 485–486; **9,** 571, 585; **10,** 611–615; **32,** 107–110
jurisdiction of, British, **1,** 491
—" six months " rule, **9,** 565, 578, 585–587
—*Zamora, The,* rule in, **1,** 429; **9,** 572–573, 576–577
law applied by, **1,** 487–488; **3,** 486; **9,** 570; **10,** 606–623; **16,** 569–572
need for, to constitute blockade, **9,** 83
parties to proceedings, **12,** 494–495
procedure, **9,** 575–578; **10,** 623–631; **12,** 516–521, 524–526; **13,** 409, 419–420; **14,** 316, 317; **16,** 573–581
—consuls, rights of, **12,** 516–521
—diplomatic envoys, rights of, **12,** 516–521
—law governing, **22,** 193
proceedings, " exceptional war measures ", **2,** 108
requisitioning, ship in custody of, **9,** 572, 578–579; **10,** 608–610
review of judgment, **22,** 1008–1011; **32,** 601–625; **34,** 261, 263–264
" Probable cause ", capture for: *see under* Prize
Procedural provisions, date of effective operation, **25,** 532–533
Procedure, conciliation commissions, before: *see under* Conciliation commissions
Procedure in Civil Cases: *see under* Hague Conventions
" Prohibition " laws, enforcement of: *see* Liquor traffic, prohibition treaties of U.S.A.
Promulgation of treaties: *see* Treaties, publication of
Proof: *see* Evidence
Property: *see also under* Aliens; Confiscatory legislation; Expropriation; Nationalization; War
governmental, title to, **9,** 14–15
immovables abroad, jurisdiction, **4,** 185–186
respect for, **22,** 480–490. *See also* Confiscatory legislation; Nationalization
seized in violation of international law, restitution, **15,** 467–470
Property, State-owned: *see* Foreign States, property of, *and* State-owned property
" *Propriété commerciale* ", meaning, **4,** 454
Prospective profits, damages for: *see under* Damages
Protected persons, **1,** 202; **2,** 152, 242; **4,** 309–312
Protected persons—*continued*
capitulations, status under régime of, **3,** 196–197
consuls, as, **4,** 373–374
nationality, **3,** 268–269; **4,** 309–312
naturalization of, **4,** 312–313
status in protecting State, **11,** 43
Protected States, **19,** 68–69; **20,** 47–48; **22,** 76
exemption from jurisdiction, **2,** 174; **7,** 171–172; **8,** 226
jurisdiction of British Crown, Bahrain, **30,** 94–100
jurisdiction of local courts, Kuwait, **26,** 245–254
protecting State, troops of, looting by, **2,** 174
Protecting Power—
enemy property and, **12,** 348–349
recognition of, **21,** 436
Protection of Birds, Treaty on (1902), **11,** 222
Protection of minorities: *see* Minorities, protection of
Protection of nationals: *see* Diplomatic protection
Protective jurisdiction, **11,** 130–134
Protectorates, **1,** 40–42; **2,** 19–26; **3,** 38–42; **4,** 44–46; **5,** 25–29; **6,** 47–48; **7,** 31–35; **8,** 92–98; **10,** 47; **17,** 41–42; **18,** 51–55
Act of State and, **5,** 17
Andorra, **7,** 56–57
Annam, French protectorate, **11,** 43, 46–47
assimilation to States, **5,** 28
Bohemia-Moravia, German protectorate, **11,** 24–25, 173, 179–180, 243
British, relation of Crown to territory and inhabitants, **3,** 40–41; **28,** 48–78
Cambodia, French protectorate, **11,** 44–45
carriage of goods between protecting and protected States, **11,** 43–44. *See also* Berne Convention (1890)
colonies, distinguished, **11,** 44–45; **28,** 67, 70, 73
Comoro Island, French protectorate, **11,** 47
conquered territory, distinguished, **28,** 66, 68, 70
Cyprus, British protectorate, **5,** 25–27
Egypt and U.K., relation during First World War, **4,** 44–46
—termination of, **21,** 516
equality of treatment, foreign and national workers, **6,** 347–348
Federated Malay States, **9,** 33
financial régime (French practice), **6,** 47–48
German, status in German law, **2,** 88–89

Protectorates—*continued*
immunity from jurisdiction, **5**, 116–118; **8**, 226
inhabitants and nationals, status, **2**, 22–25; **4**, 44
internal sovereignty, **7**, 171–172
jurisdiction of protecting State, **27**, 279
legislative powers of protecting State, **11**, 35–42
looting by troops of protecting State, **2**, 174
mandated territories and, **12**, 14
modern conception of, **28**, 49
Morocco, French protectorate, **11**, 42–46
—capitulatory régime in, **19**, 255–302 *passim*. *See also under* Capitulations
Morocco, Spanish protectorate, **10**, 47
nationals of protected State, legal status, **4**, 44, 46; **8**, 97–98; **11**, 43; **18**, 51–52
native reserves, **11**, 35–42
nature of, **28**, 66–70, 72
Northern Rhodesia, extent of British jurisdiction, **5**, 29; **11**, 35–42; **28**, 48–78 *passim*
occupying State, establishment of protectorate by, **22**, 152–153
powers of protecting State, **2**, 353
relation to protecting State, **28**, 48–78 *passim*
responsibility of protecting State, **2**, 163–164, 174; **28**, 79
State succession and, **11**, 77–78
treaties concluded by protecting State, application of, **6**, 348, 350; **19**, 269
treaties of protection, interpretation by municipal courts, **11**, 46–47
Tunisia, French protectorate, **4**, 44, 46; **5**, 28; **8**, 97–98; **17**, 42; **18**, 51–52; **20**, 47–48
waters of, rights of capture in, **13**, 402–403, 404
when at war with enemy of protecting State, **9**, 33
"*Protégé*", meaning, **4**, 311–312
Protest: *see under* Territory, acquisition of
Protest, absence of, questions of jurisdiction, **4**, 518–519
Protocols—
not submitted for ratification, **1**, 315
unratified, distinguished from treaties, **1**, 186
Provisional measures: *see under* International Court of Justice *and* Permanent Court of International Justice
Proximate damages, **3**, 249–251
Prussia—
Brandenburger family trust, position of, **4**, 31–33
Danube, utilization of flow, **4**, 128–133
foreign affairs, conduct of, **1**, 116
Germany, Treaty with (railways) (1920), **5**, 330–332
incorporation into Germany, **17**, 16–17
Luxembourg, Double Taxation Treaty (1909), **5**, 350
Netherlands, Frontier Agreement (1816), **6**, 50–51
special position in Third Reich, **26**, 94
Tribunal for Conflicts of Jurisdiction, **1**, 115–116
U.S.A., Treaty of Amity and Commerce (1799), **18**, 503; **23**, 735
—Treaty of Friendship, Commerce and Navigation (1828), **5**, 260, 475–478; **6**, 74–76; **11**, 238–242; **18**, 500, 503, 504, 505
Upper Silesia, responsibility for acts of Inter-Allied Plebiscite Commission, **1**, 179–180
Public debt, State succession and, **3**, 78–79; **4**, 443–445; **5**, 64–66; **6**, 62–65; **8**, 128–136; **11**, 78; **23**, 667; **24**, 69–73
Public interest, **3**, 409–410; **8**, 27–28
Public law—
meaning, **25**, 292
private law, distinguished, **25**, 277
public policy, distinguished, **25**, 277, 291–292, 311
Public law rights, territorial limitation on exercise, **30**, 27, 29
Public loans, assimilation to private transactions, **6**, 36–37
Public order,—
concept of, **1**, 122; **8**, 112 n., 399 n.; **11**, 198, 221; **17**, 446; **21**, 24
See also Ordre public and Public policy
expulsion of aliens as contrary to, **9**, 391–392
naturalization, cancellation of, **12**, 197–198
Public policy: *see also Ordre public and* Public order
confiscatory legislation, **10**, 149, 150–151; **16**, 84; **26**, 24–25, 41, 48; **32**, 9–10
control of aliens, whether a matter of, **21**, 281–284; **22**, 478–479
currency control, German-occupied countries, law of Israel, **26**, 56–57
dependent States and, **9**, 42
discriminatory legislation, **26**, 51
enemy aliens and, **10**, 446; **11**, 251; **14**, 165; **22**, 478–479, 485, 486, 489

Public policy—*continued*
exclusion of jurisdiction by agreement of Parties, **10,** 130
executive agreements and, **20,** 416–417
federal States, in, **8,** 34–39; **10,** 58–59; **12,** 22
foreign armed forces and, **21,** 115
foreign, consideration of, **23,** 27
immunity of States and, **4,** 178; **7,** 185; **8,** 232; **9,** 189, 193–198
contracts of employment and, **16,** 217
international, **9,** 155, 291–292; **20,** 439; **21,** 277–278; **22,** 624–625; **24,** 206; **33,** 77
international comity and, **24,** 16–18 21, 24
international declarations as evidence of, **12,** 178–182
Italian concept of, **26,** 185
ordre public and, **25,** 268
international officials and, E.E.C., **29,** 228
interpretation of diplomatic act, **19,** 475
moratorium legislation, **26,** 14
political policy, distinguished, **18,** 181–182
prohibition of imports, E.E.C. Treaty, **32,** 381
recognition *de jure* and, **3,** 26–27; **4,** 66–67, 68; **5,** 46; **7,** 65–66, 69, 70–74, 81, 82; **8,** 35–39; **10,** 56–60, 63
recognition of foreign acts and decrees, **8,** 193; **9,** 21, 25, 88, 148, 150, 151, 153; **10,** 14, 16, 18–19, 21–22, 53–59, 61–66, 592; **11,** 17, 20, 22–25, 26–30, 66; **12,** 6–7, 22–23; **13,** 136; **15,** 17, 18, 198, 203; **16,** 15, 20, 29, 35–36; **18,** 199; **19,** 12; **20,** 34–38; **21,** 19, 20, 25–29, 31; **22,** 14, 23, 25; **23,** 13, 20, 23; **24,** 38; **26,** 24–25, 45, 48, 57
recognition of foreign law and, **30,** 5, 10, 26, 28, 31–32, 41, 375; **33,** 26–27, 28, 30, 408–409
registration of trade marks and, **8,** 24
revenue laws, foreign, **32,** 372, 374
Soviet nationalization decrees and, **7,** 65–66, 69, 70–74, 81
territorial, principles of, **26,** 45
title to property and, **10,** 216; **18,** 566
treaties and, **22,** 622–623; **25,** 262
treaties, interpretation of, **21,** 280–281; **22,** 622
Public ships—
commerce, engaged in, **1,** 137–138, 140–141, 146, 154, 157–158; **5,** 129; **12,** 112–113
concept of, **12,** 123
crew ashore, responsibility for, **3,** 221–222
Public ships—*continued*
crimes committed on, jurisdiction, **9,** 264
jurisdictional immunities, **1,** 137–158; **2,** 117–119, 120–121, 136–144; **3,** 184–191; **5,** 112, 127–129; **9,** 177, 250–294; **10,** 199–230, 240–250; **11,** 139, 147–161; **12,** 29–30, 105–124, 143–149; **13,** 82–85; **14,** 83–90; **15,** 146, 193–194; **16,** 142–144; **17,** 167–172; **21,** 105–110; **31,** 405–408; **32,** 127–136; **34,** 88–91; **35,** 113, 117, 122–129
—competence of consul to claim, **1,** 146
—conclusiveness of statements of executive, **12,** 108–111, 144–149
—crew members, immunity of, distinguished, **12,** 141–143
—irregular taking of possession, **11,** 155–156
—operated by private company, **12,** 143–149
—possession as determining, **1,** 137–139
—privately-owned ship chartered to government, **12,** 113–115
—privately-owned ships requisitioned, **9,** 250–259
—proof, **11,** 147–152
—requisitioned, **9,** 250–263; **10,** 239–250
—waiver, **1,** 145, 150–154; **2,** 136–144
libel *in rem*, on foreign, **1,** 137–144, 146–150, 156; **2,** 117–119, 120–121, 137–138, 141–144; **3,** 186–189; **9,** 177–178, 250–263, 272–277, 279–282, 284–289; **10,** 199–204, 217–230, 240–247; **11,** 153–161; **12,** 105–112, 143–149; **13,** 82–85; **14,** 83; **16,** 142–143; **17,** 167–170; **32,** 127–136
maritime lien on foreign, **1,** 148–150; **2,** 137–138, 141–144; **3,** 185, 187–189; **17,** 167–168; **26,** 175
non-recognition of government ownership, **1,** 142
requisition of, **9,** 250–263; **10,** 239–250
sale to private persons, position after, **1,** 148–150; **2,** 137–138; **3,** 185
salvage, claims for, **1,** 146–147; **2,** 141–142
warrant of arrest, **1,** 154–156
Public user, merchant ship, of, **11,** 156–161
" Public utility undertaking ", meaning, **2,** 342
Publication of treaties: *see under* Treaties
Publicists, teachings of, evidence of international law, **3,** 4; **4,** 6

Puerto Rico—
law of, **1,** 76
Organic Act of, **9,** 481
rights of citizens after cession to U.S.A., **11,** 49–50
Spanish law, continuance of, **26,** 555
status of, **17,** 42–47
trade mark legislation, **9,** 481
Punitive damages: *see under* Damages
Punjab, status of, **20,** 91–92
Pursuit, right of, on high seas: *see* Hot pursuit
Pyrenees, utilization of flow of waters in, **24,** 101–142

Q

Quarantine Council of Egypt, **1,** 364; **6,** 414
Quarter, refusal of, **15,** 377, 633
Quasi-arbitral bodies, decisions of, **2,** 383–384
Quasi-contractual obligations, **2,** 165–166; **5,** 500
Qui sentit commodum sentire debet et onus, **3,** 210

R

Race—
meaning, **1,** 222–223; **4,** 317–318
membership of, nationality and, **5,** 226
Racial discrimination, **12,** 179; **13,** 141–142; **14,** 96–100; **15,** 302–308; **20,** 244–245
German legislation, **11,** 23–24, 172–173, 183–184, 283; **12,** 4–11, 191, 194, 199–201
—territorial nature, **11,** 109–110
Radio Conventions, Atlantic City (1947), **22,** 710–712
Radio Telegraphic Convention (1912), **7,** 471–472
—(1927), **5,** 416; **6,** 45–46
Railway administration, foreign jurisdictional immunity, **8,** 234–235; **9,** 193, 233
Railway agency operated by foreign government, jurisdictional immunity of, **10,** 191–196
Railway transport, Berne Conventions (1890 and 1933), **7,** 58, 411–412; **12,** 266
Railway Transport, International Convention (1890), **6,** 418–420
Railways—
Inter-Allied Commission, authority of decisions, **6,** 32–33
International Régime of, General Convention (1923), **5,** 419
—war, effect of, **2,** 410
Railways—*continued*
nationalization by Soviet Government (1918), **11,** 21–23
officials, responsibility for acts of, **4,** 229
operation of, whether governmental function, **2,** 50
transfer of, **7,** 424–431, 484–487
Rapallo, Treaty of (1922), **1,** 28; **5,** 22–23
Rastadt, Congress of (1797), **7,** 131
Rates: *see also* Taxation—
diplomatic envoys, exemption, **10,** 346–352
—liability for, **6,** 331; **10,** 337–352
power to assess and power to enforce, **10,** 347–352
Ratification—
municipal law, of, **7,** 85
tacit, of acts of officials, **1,** 170
treaties, of: *see under* Treaties
Re-acquisition of nationality: *see under* Nationality
Real party in interest, **4,** 253
Real unions, States of, **1,** 38–39; **7,** 29–30
Rebellion—
damage to foreign property, **3,** 225–226; **6,** 208–209
termination of, succession of governments, **3,** 98–102
Rebus sic stantibus, doctrine of, **1,** 393–395; **2,** 323–325, 353–354; **3,** 22, 352–354; **4,** 420–423; **5,** 332; **6,** 362–368, 413; **7,** 424–431; **8,** 423; **12,** 279; **22,** 427, 621; **23,** 652–658; **25,** 351; **31,** 88
recognition of governments and, **10,** 58–59
Reciprocity: *see also under* Aliens, treatment of, *and* Commercial treaties
comity, distinguished, **18,** 14–16
defined, **26,** 697
evidence and production of documents, **31,** 223
extradition proceedings, **5,** 280, 285–286, 288–290; **7,** 351–352, 355–356; **14,** 140; **17,** 263–265; **19,** 361; **20,** 364–365; **32,** 290
most-favoured-nation clauses, **1,** 352; **5,** 404–405; **7,** 408, 456; **8,** 472–475; **9,** 457; **21,** 305–307
national treatment clauses, **16,** 259–260
poor persons' procedure, **7,** 322–323, 456
right of passage to enclaves, **31,** 61, 63, 65, 93, 106, 110, 114
workmen's compensation, **6,** 348; **7,** 468, 469, 470; **18,** 506–507
Recognition—
absorption of States, of, **10,** 70–97

Recognition—*continued*
acts of foreign States and governments, of, **1,** 24–26, 28; **2,** 15–16; **3,** 23–33; **4,** 33–37; **5,** 22–23; **6,** 37–40; **7,** 22–28; **8,** 31–39; **9,** 12–26, 63, 90; **10,** 10–25; **11,** 13–34, 155–156; **12,** 4–11; **13,** 12–20; **14,** 8–17, 107; **15,** 10–27; **16,** 14–36; **17,** 28–33; **18,** 24–40, 61–64, 558–570; **19,** 11–23; **20,** 2, 7–39, 305–328; **21,** 16–42; **22,** 13–57; **23,** 7–28, 277–281; **24,** 28–52; **26,** 6–60; **27,** 19–22, 237–238; **28,** 14–47; **30,** 4–54; **32,** 8–37; **33,** 16–36; **35,** 2–50: *see also* foreign legislation, of, *infra, and* Act of State doctrine; Confiscatory legislation; Extraterritorial effect of legislation; Nationalization measures
—confiscatory, **34,** 12–21; **35,** 9–10, 16–19, 45
—contrary to international law, **15,** 24–27; **20,** 309–312, 323–328; **22,** 39–42; **28,** 14, 16, 18–20, 22, 24–39; **30,** 28–33; **33,** 30–36; **35,** 2–50
—non-recognition, public policy, **9,** 193; **35,** 12–13, 46
—review by foreign courts, **9,** 16, 17, 21, 25, 26, 63, 90; **33,** 353–356
annexation, of, **9,** 88; **12,** 23–47, 188–194; **13,** 32–35; **15,** 45–50; **17,** 49–50, 61–64, 79–80; **19,** 144; **20,** 57–62, 309–310, 311–312; **22,** 100–103: *see also* conquest, *infra*
—non-recognition, **26,** 76; **28,** 95–97; **32,** 73–76
—withdrawal of, **9,** 93
belligerency, of, **3,** 65–68; **9,** 79, 85; **17,** 345–349
—non-recognition, effect, **31,** 29
belligerent, opposing, non-recognition as a State, **17,** 345–349
conditional, **1,** 45–47; **10,** 57
conquest and other titles to territory, **8,** 119–123; **9,** 84–93: *see also* annexation, *supra*
de facto control of territory, Jerusalem, **26,** 68–69
federal government, by, **10,** 48–70
foreign judgments, **1,** 28–30; **6,** 144–145; **7,** 21–22; **19,** 19–23; **24,** 40
—occupation court, **23,** 795–797. *See also under* Belligerent occupation
foreign legislation, of, **1,** 47–51; **3,** 25–27, 29–30, 32–33; **5,** 22–23; **7,** 22–27, 65–75, 80–82; **8,** 34–39; **9,** 84–87; **10,** 48–70; **11,** 16–24, 26–29; **12,** 8–11, 22–23; **13,** 12–17; **15,** 17–18; **16,** 14–16, 19–20; **17,** 32–33; **18,** 38–39; **19,** 16–19; **20,** 26–31, 34–36; **21,** 25–29; **22,** 97–100, 101–102; **23,** 24–26; **24,** 38–39, 40–41, 48–51; **26,** 6–29,

Recognition—*continued*
foreign legislation, of—*continued*
56–57, 702–704; **27,** 19–22; **28,** 184–185; **29,** 31–32, 45–46, 52; **30,** 4–24; **33,** 16–36. *See also* Confiscatory legislation; Currency laws; Exchange control measures; Expropriation; Extraterritorial effect of legislation; Nationalization measures; Revenue laws
—claims against prior government, law on lapse of, **33,** 26–27
—powers of foreign bank, **27,** 19–22
—social security laws, **33,** 21–76
foreign property rights, of, **23,** 26–27
governments, of: *see* Recognition of governments
implied, **8,** 43–46, 114–115; **12,** 23–28, 48, 188–194; **15,** 50; **28,** 88–90; **31,** 31
insurgency, of, **5,** 51–52; **8,** 118–119; **9,** 75–78
insurgents as *de facto* government, **9,** 61, 75
—as *de jure* government, **9,** 73
nationality, conferment of, **22,** 349, 353–363, 370–376, 378, 380–381, 384–385
States, of: *see* Recognition of States, *infra*
States, merger of, **20,** 180–182, 193–195; **22,** 230–233
title to territory, of: *see* annexation *and* conquest, *supra*
treaty, by, **22,** 224–225
unrecognized government: *see under* Recognition of governments
Recognition of governments, **1,** 44, 47–58, 141–142; **2,** 34–35; **3,** 54–64; **4,** 59–73; **5,** 36–51; **6,** 51–59; **7,** 63–83; **8,** 34–39, 114–118; **9,** 60–74, 84–85; **10,** 48–70; **11,** 61–74, 138–139; **12,** 17–23; **13,** 29–32; **15,** 45, 176–204; **16,** 46–60; **17,** 61–72, 177–178; **18,** 57–60; **19,** 72–116, 192–195, 202–203, 398–400; **21,** 55–63; **22,** 90–100; **23,** 71–78; **24,** 306, 311; **26,** 70–75; **28,** 93–95; **29,** 31–32, 45–46, 52; **32,** 65–72, 186, 614–615, 621–622; **33,** 36–46; **34,** 21–27; **35,** 51–67
Carranza Government of Mexico, **3,** 59
conclusion of treaty, effect, **10,** 58–59
conditional, **10,** 57
counterfeiting currency and, **35,** 65–66
de facto, **1,** 49–51; **2,** 36–37; **3,** 60–64; **8,** 119–123; **9,** 60–67, 85, 94–101; **10,** 64–65; **12,** 43–47; **15,** 176–204; **17,** 180, 183–186; **18,** 595; **19,** 87–93, 100, 104; **21,** 57, 60–62; **22,** 97–100; **28,** 93–95; **31,** 31

Recognition of governments—*continued*
de facto, retroactive effect of, **1,** 49–51; **9,** 101; **10,** 65; **15,** 176–185; **22,** 97–100
de jure, **1,** 50; **3,** 59; **5,** 46; **6,** 55; **7,** 67–69, 78–80; **8,** 119–123; **9,** 66–67, 71–72, 75–78, 94–100; **10,** 65; **12,** 43–47; **15,** 176–204; **17,** 179–180, 183–186; **18,** 595; **19,** 75, 78–79, 100–105, 111–115; **22,** 98–99
—relevance, **4,** 203–204
—retroactive effect, **1,** 47–50; **5,** 46; **7,** 67–69, 73; **8,** 34–35; **9,** 101, 188; **10,** 59; **12,** 17–22; **13,** 30; **16,** 49–60; **17,** 66–67, 69, 185–186; **19,** 72–115; **28,** 269, 348, 360; **32,** 622; **34,** 20
de jure and *de facto*, conflict of jurisdiction, **8,** 119–123
—conflicting claims, **9,** 94–101
—distinction, **33,** 340, 351
distinguished from recognition of States, **4,** 58–59
effects, **9,** 68–74; **10,** 63–65. *See also* retroactive effect, *supra.*
exchange of telegrams, by, **7,** 79–80
Executive, statement of, *see under* Conclusiveness of statements of Executive
Federal States, foreign legislation and, **10,** 48–70; **12,** 22–23
flag, display, effect on legality of, **7,** 76–77
foreign State immunity and, **32,** 138
implied, **8,** 114–115; **12,** 43–46; **31,** 31
Mandatory, by, effect on mandated territory, **11,** 51
non-recognition, **2,** 51–53; **4,** 59–72, 173–174, 340; **5,** 36–51; **6,** 51–59; **7,** 65–67, 75–76, 80–83; **8,** 115–118; **9,** 74, 184–189, 408; **10,** 68–70; **11,** 22, 62–67; **12,** 29–43; **13,** 19–20; **15,** 176–186; **17,** 61–65; **19,** 194–195, 399; **21,** 225–229; **22,** 90–97; **23,** 71–78, 397–400; **26,** 70–75; **28,** 93–95; **32,** 65–70; **33,** 43–46
—agency as plaintiff, **32,** 65–70
—claims to assets abroad, **17,** 61–65
—consuls of former government, **5,** 49–50
—deportation of aliens, **4,** 340; **34,** 21–26
—effect on power of attorney, **35,** 51–57, 62–65
—estoppel, as, **2,** 38–39; **4,** 417–418
—expulsion of aliens, **1,** 258–259; **4,** 61–62, 340; **21,** 225–229; **23,** 397–400; **28,** 93–95

Recognition of governments—*continued*
non-recognition—*continued*
—extradition, **9,** 408
—government as defendant, **6,** 53–54
—government as plaintiff, **6,** 57–58; **8,** 117–118; **9,** 187; **17,** 61, 63; **19,** 192–195; **26,** 70–71
—nationality, proof of, **6,** 56–57; **8,** 117
—nationalization and confiscation, **3,** 54–59; **4,** 66–68; **5,** 50–51; **7,** 65–74; **10,** 61; **11,** 22; **12,** 29–43; **15,** 176–186
—recognition of State, distinguished, **11,** 141–142
—representation in court of nationals, **33,** 43–46
—significance, **35,** 27
—State-owned ships, immunities of, **1,** 141–142
—State ships, ownership, **26,** 72–75
—statutes of limitation, **10,** 68–70
—transactions within territory, effect abroad, **32,** 69–70
—treaties, effect on, **4,** 59–60; **6,** 40–42; **22,** 90–97; **35,** 235–239
organs of recognition, **1,** 47–51
recognition of States, distinguished, **4,** 58–59
standing to sue, breach of relations, **35,** 25, 26–28, 57–61
treaties, and, **10,** 58–59; **30,** 60, 61
unrecognized government,
—capacity to sue, **6,** 57; **7,** 75–76; **19,** 192-195; **26,** 70–71
—construction of charterparty, **23,** 71–78
—relations with, **23,** 397–400
—repudiation of treaty by, **5,** 47; **22,** 90–97
—status before municipal courts, **2,** 39–44; **5,** 42–45; **23,** 71–78
—territory controlled by, **19,** 399; **21,** 225–229; **22,** 90
—validity of acts and decrees, **1,** 47–51; **3,** 59; **7,** 22–27; **11,** 64–66
—withdrawal of recognition, **9,** 93; **11,** 67; **19,** 72–115
Recognition of States, **1,** 36, 43–47; **3,** 53–54; **4,** 58–59, 173–174; **5,** 11–15; **6,** 55; **11,** 56–61; **13,** 8–9; **17,** 60; **18,** 39–40; **19,** 69–71; **20,** 52–57; **21,** 48–49; **22,** 89
accession to multilateral treaty, **28,** 82–88
boundary of new State and, **11,** 56–58
breach of diplomatic relations, **33,** 39
capacity to sue, effect on, **17,** 145–147
citizenship, **11,** 58–61
conditional, **1,** 58

Recognition of States—*continued*
de facto, exchange of ambassadors, **20,** 52–57
discretion as to, **24,** 2
enemy aliens, status of, **11,** 56–61, 247–249
implied, **3,** 53; **28,** 88–90
need for, **18,** 17–20, 57
non-recognition, effects, **14,** 15–16; **17,** 345–349, 440–447
—effect on jurisdictional immunity, **10,** 91–97
recognition of governments, distinguished, **11,** 141–142
revocability, **1,** 43–45
state of war and, **18,** 244–246
succession to debts, **23,** 595–596
unrecognized States, law of, **21,** 457–459
—subject to international law, whether, **28,** 87
Recommendations—
act of grace, as, **1,** 376–377
treaty obligations, distinguished, **7,** 406–409
Reconversion of merchant ships, **5,** 512
Red Cross, International, **4,** 458
abuse of emblem, **7,** 507–508; **13,** 333; **19,** 598–600
immunities, **3,** 326–327
national branches, position of, **4,** 458
Red Cross surgeon serving in enemy army, **3,** 462–463
Red River, boundary, Oklahoma-Texas, **11,** 100
Redemption, equity of, **4,** 555
Redintegration, French practice, **11,** 218
Re-extradition to third State: *see under* Extradition
" Refoulement ", expulsion and, **18,** 301
Refugees—
Administration for International Assistance, **23,** 510, 511
Convention on Status of (1951), **20,** 371; **21,** 2, 258, 284–285, 304; **22,** 467–468; **24,** 418, 484–485, 486–487, 488–489; **26,** 496–499, 506–507; **28,** 297–299, 310–311, 343, 350; **31,** 327–329; **32,** 223–227
domicile, change of, **26,** 498, 506
enemy aliens, as, **16,** 260–261
enemy character, whether endowed with, **11,** 255–256
expulsion of, **11,** 197–198; **26,** 498, 504, 507; **28,** 297–300, 310–311
—appeal against, **26,** 508–509
—public order, **26,** 507–508
Geneva Convention (1933), **8,** 306–307, 308–310; **9,** 392; **11,** 186, 187; **14,** 121–123, 130–131; **15,** 287, 289, 326; **16,** 260–263, 311; **17,** 239–241; **21,** 2, 304; **22,** 467
Refugees—*continued*
Geneva Convention (1938), **13,** 142; **14,** 121–123, 130–131; **16,** 224–225, 260–263; **22,** 467
Homeless Aliens, German Law on (1951), **23,** 378, 383–385, 386–388; **26,** 503–505, 507–509; **28,** 298–299
identity card and travel document, **32,** 490–491
illegal entry, effect under 1951 Convention, **26,** 506–507; **31,** 327–329
illegal entry, German law, **26,** 496–498,504–507
immigration law, relaxation in favour of refugees, **9,** 383
Intergovernmental Committee, immunity from suit, **11,** 205–207
International Refugee Organization, **15,** 290; **21,** 200–202
—Agreement with Commander-in-Chief, Eucom (1948), **18,** 444–446, 572
—Agreement with Italy (1948), **23,** 510, 513
—Constitution, **18,** 380, 445, 447; **21,** 200–202
—contract of employment with, **23,** 510–515
—legal personality, **18,** 447–449, 572
—privileges and immunities, **18,** 444–446
—U.S.A. and, **21,** 348
Jewish, deportation of, **9,** 383. *See also* Jews
law applicable to, **23,** 388–390, 390–391
Montevideo, Treaty of (1939), **16,** 1, 2
Nansen International Office, **7,** 464–465; **8,** 306, 313
nationality, proof, I.R.O. certificate, **28,** 274
political, habeas corpus and, **12,** 231; **22,** 474
political, internment of, **7,** 259–261
right to return to country of residence, **24,** 486–487
rights under Conventions, **16,** 311; **21,** 1–3, 258, 304
Russian and Armenian, Intergovernmental Arrangement (1922), **8,** 313
— —(1928), **5,** 248, 33–335, 362; **7,** 406–408; **11,** 187, 197–198; **15,** 289–290; **21,** 304
sojourn, right of, **26,** 500–501
status of, **22,** 467–468; **24,** 488–489; **26,** 496–499; **28,** 297–300; **32,** 230–232
—loss of, **26,** 498–499, 506
—recognition of, **26,** 496–499; **31,** 327–329, 331–332; **32,** 227–230
—voluntary return to country, **32,** 223–227
Travel Documents, International Arrangement (1946), **22,** 426

Refugees—*continued*
treatment of, **21,** 211
U.N. High Commissioner, budget, **34,** 381
U.S.A., Refugee Relief Act (1953), **24,** 153–154; **26,** 511–512; **28,** 315–317; **33,** 293–296
Registration—
aliens, of, **10,** 295–304; **19,** 317–318; **22,** 479, 501–505; **30,** 353–354, 360
treaties, of, **4,** 393–394; **7,** 465–466
Re-hearing—
—admissibility in international arbitration, **6,** 421, 425
after-discovered evidence, for, **8,** 481, 485–487
Reichskommissars, appointment in German-occupied territory, **11,** 20–21, 25, 33
Relatives, collateral claim for damages, **3,** 247–248
Remainderman's interest, valuation of, **26,** 315–316
Remaindermen, change of nationality, **10,** 529
Remission of sentence, denial of justice and, **4,** 213–215
Remoteness of damage: *see* Damages, direct, indirect, proximacy
Rentengutsverträge, **2,** 71–76
Renunciation of territory, cession contrasted, **3,** 34–35; **6,** 100, 108
Renunciation of War, General Treaty for (1928), **7,** 9–10; **13,** 208–209, 223; **15,** 359, 361, 362, 364, 372, 373, 382, 405, 417, 419, 420, 421, 488, 637; **16,** 344, 346, 347, 349, 361; **24,** 942, 962–966
just and unjust wars, **5,** 229
U.S. Constitution and, **7,** 9–10
Renvoi, expulsion and, **20,** 333–335; **21,** 222–225
Reparation agreements, Second World War, **34,** 234
Reparations. *See also* Paris, Reparations Agreement (1946)
different kinds of, **3,** 468–469
Germany and Allied Powers, 1924 Agreement, Experts' Plan, **5,** 33
Germany, Inter-Allied Agreement on Payments (1946), **17,** 377; **18,** 516; **29,** 465, 470, 475; **32,** 571, 574, 580
—Settlement Convention with (1952/1954), provisions concerning, **23,** 774–775; **29,** 362–363, 367–368, 452–453, 458, 471, 474–476, 484, 493–494
—Three Power Agreement (1945), **32,** 569
Italian acceptance, **29,** 465
London Conference (1924), **9,** 155
nature of, **29,** 474; **32,** 233–234, 235–236
Reparations—*continued*
New Plan, Hague Agreement (1930), **7,** 413–415, 484–489; **8,** 479
obligation to pay compensation, **20,** 629–630, 632
war damage, for, **6,** 237–239, 285; **7,** 503, 506; **14,** 13–14, 17
Reparations Commission, **4,** 416–417
employees, legal status of, **6,** 33
practice, in apportioning Austro-Hungarian debt, **4,** 82
Reprisals—
civilian inhabitants of occupied territory, against, **13,** 392–394, 396, 397–398; **15,** 471–482, 644–646, 652, 662–663; **16,** 459–461, 484–486, 518–520, 531, 538–542, 547, 548–552; **17,** 392–393, 431–432, 435–438
civilian population, against, **30,** 503
economic, Indonesian measures against Netherlands enterprises, **28,** 38
German Order of 1942 (Commando Order), **13,** 281–282
how far within province of courts, **8,** 437–438
individuals, by, **4,** 174
justification for, **4,** 527; **15,** 652, 662; **16,** 531, 539–540, 547
maritime, British Orders in Council, **1,** 429, 430; **12,** 543–554
nature of, **13,** 258–261
neutrals, against, **5,** 490, 517
pacific, **6,** 406
preliminary request for redress, **4,** 527
prisoners of war and, **15,** 477
proportionality, **4,** 527; **13,** 396, 398; **15,** 642, 645, 663; **16,** 518
treaties, suspension by way of, **1,** 414; **2,** 325
war crimes as, **13,** 258–261, 393–394; **15,** 482, 687
Requisitioning—
abandonment of requisitioned property, **19,** 628–630
aliens' property, **21,** 211, 278
applicable law, **19,** 470–471
cargo not found contraband, compensation, **12,** 525
compensation for, **5,** 150–152, 494; **6,** 441–442, 445–446; **18,** 697–699; **19,** 454–459, 632; **23,** 706–754 *passim*: *see also under* Peace treaties
contract, assimilation to, **5,** 503
contrary to international law, **1,** 475–476; **2,** 446–449
de facto possession, requirement of, **11,** 160
decrees, **1,** 427–428, 475–483; **2,** 446–450; **3,** 478–481; **4,** 565–567; **5,** 503–508; **7,** 511–513; **8,** 184–207, 237–239

Requisitioning—*continued*
decrees—*continued*
—extraterritorial effect, **8,** 195–197, 200–204; **9,** 289–293; **10,** 131–147
—judicial measures, distinguished, **5,** 507–508
—legal nature, **3,** 480–481; **4,** 562–563; **5,** 373, 503–508; **6,** 440–441
disguised, **5,** 505
economic war and, **23,** 501
enemy ships, **10,** 608–610
—in port, **6,** 440–441
enforced, defence to charge of assisting enemy, **16,** 496–497
governmental character, **1,** 24–25
land, of, **18,** 612–613
means of conveyance, **11,** 296–299; **16,** 481, 486
military, judicial review of, **1,** 120–121
—in times of revolution, **4,** 545–546
neutral property, of, **1,** 414–418; **2,** 421–427; **4,** 545
—assessment of compensation, **28,** 614 n., 625
—waiver of compensation claim, effect, **28,** 611, 617–621
occupying Power, by, **12,** 450, 453, 457–459; **16,** 481, 486, 487; **17,** 412–415, 419–423, 424–430
—illegal, **16,** 487–490, 497–499
—payment for, **17,** 424–426, 430
—review by local courts, **16,** 497–499, 504–506
property abroad, **10,** 211–216, 240–247
—not accompanied by actual possession, **10,** 221–224
public property, **2,** 450–451
puppet government for occupant, by, **18,** 629
racial grounds, **19,** 631–632
receipts for, **1,** 481, 482; **4,** 485–487
restoration of property, **18,** 423–426
sale of property, **22,** 991
scope of, whether a "taking", **28,** 621–625
services, of, **16,** 553
ships, of, **6,** 440–441; **9,** 225, 273, 277; **10,** 131–155, 608–610; **11,** 148–149, 153–154; **16,** 494, 496
—angary and, **23,** 726–728, 732–733
—civil war, in, **11,** 155–161
—compensation for, **23,** 706–708
—confiscation, distinguished, **6,** 440–441
—evidence of possession, **9,** 151–153, 281
—extraterritorial effect of legislation, **8,** 189–191, 195–198, 200–204; **9,** 152–153, 176–183, 228–233; **10,** 131–147, 152–153; **15,** 176–204
—foreign waters, in, **1,** 161; **9,** 273, 281
—high seas, on, **1,** 24–25

Requisitioning—*continued*
ships, of—*continued*
—maritime lien on, **17,** 167
—neutral port, in, **22,** 336–338
—privately owned, **2,** 141–142, 408
—prize court, in custody of, **9,** 572, 579
—public ships, **9,** 250
State responsibility for, **5,** 151, 374
temporary occupation, for, **11,** 54
transfer of property, whether conferring title, **1,** 474–479, 482–483; **16,** 493–494, 506–507
use, for, **22,** 946–966
validity of, **16,** 493–497
Res extra commercium, **11,** 303–304
Res inter alios acta: *see under* Treaties
Res judicata, **1,** 172, 373–374; **2,** 381–385, 386–387; **3,** 410–411, 420–423; **4,** 490–491, 506–511, 515; **5,** 182–184, 428, 448, 457, 489; **6,** 421-423, 425, 427, 448; **8,** 487–488; **9,** 324–328, 456, 522–526; **16,** 339, 341, 342; **18,** 353, 357, 437, 439; **21,** 312–314, 316–317, 320, 323–324, 335–337, 340, 406–407; **23,** 81–88, 632–633; **24,** 392, 403
Administrative Tribunal of the United Nations, **21,** 312–314, 316–317, 320, 323–324, 335–337, 340
appointment of arbitrator, **35,** 167–168
arbitral awards, **1,** 373–374; **3,** 421–423; **4,** 490; **5,** 182–183, 428, 448, 457; **6,** 425, 427; **7,** 487–488; **9,** 324, 326, 522–526; **16,** 339–341
awards of Mexican National Claims Commission, **6,** 421–423
Conciliation Commissions, **18,** 437, 439
conditions of application, **3,** 421–423
courts set up by Occupant, decisions of, **6,** 448
decisions of prize courts, **5,** 489
European Commission of Human Rights, **24,** 392
Hague Convention No. I (1907), under, **9,** 326
interlocutory decision and, **3,** 410–411; **4,** 479
International Court of Justice, **16,** 342; **18,** 353, 357; **21,** 312–314, 316–317, 320, 323–324, 335–337, 340, 406–407; **35,** 443, 444–445, 466–467, 484
international tribunals and, **24,** 392
interpretation of statutes by municipal court, **1,** 172
Permanent Court of International Justice, **4,** 506–511, 515–516; **9,** 325–326, 522–525; **23,** 81–88

Res judicata—continued
quasi-arbitral body, **2,** 381–386, 386–387; **23,** 632–633
United States Court of Restitution Appeals, **24,** 403
Res perit domino, **15,** 612
Residence, establishment of illegal entry, effect, **26,** 497–498, 505, 507
" Residence ", meaning, **4,** 445, 548; **19,** 482–484
nationality on change of sovereignty, determining, **1,** 94. *See also* Habitual residence
" Resident ", meaning, **1,** 200, 201; **30,** 420–423
enemy territory, in, **3,** 445–446
Residential ties, criterion for home leave of international official, **27,** 428–432
Residuary sovereignty, **8,** 155–156
Resistance movements, **13,** 228–231, 305, 393; **14,** 169–171; **15,** 412–416; **18,** 474; **21,** 431–432: *see also* Guerillas; Partisans
acts of, whether a war risk, **15,** 435–436; **17,** 349–350
capitulation and, **15,** 502
legality of, **15,** 434
responsibility of State after liberation for acts of, **16,** 378–379
status of, **13,** 228–231, 305, 393; **14,** 169–171; **15,** 412–416; **16,** 508
Respect for private rights: *see under* Acquired rights; Cession of territory; State succession
Respect for territorial sovereignty, **2,** 158–159; **16,** 167
Respondeat superior, **1,** 78
Responsibility of States: *see* State responsibility
" *Ressortissants* ", meaning, **2,** 22–25, 222–224, 260
Jews in Roumania, position of, **5,** 248–249
nationals, distinguished, **4,** 44; **5,** 213–218
stateless person, distinguished, **5,** 215
Restitutio in integrum, principle of, **6,** 67–68; **7,** 99–100; **18,** 425, 428, 436–439; **20,** 484–486; **24,** 603. *See also* Damages
Restitution: *see also under* Peace treaties—
as remedy for expropriation, **35,** 24
compensation or, question of, **7,** 99–100
French Commission of, in Belgium, **1,** 120
Germany, Settlement Convention
—compensation, distinguished, **25,** 536–538; **29,** 329–340, 363–369
—compensation in lieu, **29,** 442–492
Restitution—*continued*
Germany, Settlement Convention—*continued*
—shares, of, **25,** 345–346. *See also under* Germany, Federal Republic, Settlement Convention
nature of proceedings, **28,** 372
rolling stock, of, **20,** 482–483, 486–489
" Restraint of Princes ", **11,** 30
Restrictive interpretation of treaties: *see under* Treaties, interpretation of
Restrictive practices—
E.E.C. Treaty provisions, **31,** 427–428; **33,** 414–416
shipping conferences, jurisdiction to investigate, **31,** 209–219; **32,** 100–102; **33,** 158–163; **35,** 103–109
" *Résultat utile* ", maritime assistance, **11,** 230
Retaliation in treatment of aliens, **3,** 287–288
Retaliation, nationalization as, **35,** 19–21
Retinue of diplomatic envoy: *see under* Diplomatic envoys
Retorsion: *see also* Reprisals
courts, by, for non-compliance with treaty, **9,** 459
meaning, **4,** 525; **6,** 73
treaties and, **9,** 459
Retroactive legislation, extraterritorial effect, **16,** 16; **30,** 18, 21
Revenue, international control of, **3,** 208–209
Revenue laws—
aliens, application to, **6,** 280–281. *See also* Aliens, taxation of
enforcement as between States of U.S.A., **15,** 10–13
foreign, enforcement of, **2,** 148–150, 263–264; **4,** 35–36; **6,** 149–150: **10,** 24; **15,** 18–20; **22,** 46–57; **23,** 27; **24,** 16–17; **28,** 90; **33,** 16–26
—high seas, on, **8,** 254
foreign, non-recognition of, **4,** 20; **17,** 32; **18,** 37–38; **20,** 7–24; **22,** 46–47; **23,** 26–27; **24,** 15–27; **28,** 90; **30,** 10, 24–25; **32,** 372, 374; **33,** 16–26
Revision of arbitral awards: *see* Arbitral awards, revision of
Revolts, successful and unsuccessful, State responsibility, **4,** 243–245
Revolution: *see also* Rebellion; Riots
international entity, effect on, **2,** 34–36; **27,** 22–29
military requisitions during, **4,** 545–546
responsibility for damage suffered in, **4,** 239–245; **7,** 259–261

Revolutionary forces—
contractual obligations, responsibility for, **3,** 232–234
responsibility for acts of, **5,** 173–174
Revolutionary governments, responsibility for acts of, **2,** 34–37, 176–177; **3,** 232–234; **6,** 213–215; **20,** 217–222; **30,** 168–171
Rhine—
Central Commission for Navigation of, competence, **5,** 88–90
collision on, jurisdiction over, **11,** 227–228
crews of foreign ships on, **4,** 124–125
embouchures du Rhin, **8,** 166–168
freedom of navigation on, **7,** 12–13; **16,** 77–80; **17,** 123–125, 354–356; **18,** 84–85; **19,** 149–157, 469–470; **20,** 164–165, 409–410; **21,** 3–8, 88, 276–277, 300–303. *See also* Mannheim, Act of (1868)
internationalization of, **4,** 123–125; **8,** 166–169
Modus vivendi (1936), **15,** 69
Rhine Navigation Convention (1868): *see* Mannheim, Act of
Rhine navigation tribunals, competence, **5,** 88–89; **21,** 300–303
Rhineland—
Agreement of 1919...**3,** 9–10; **4,** 118–119; **5,** 77–78
British courts-martial in, **1,** 469
High Commission—
—binding force of decrees of, **5,** 36; **6,** 35; **7,** 58
—legal status, **3,** 50
—legislative function, **5,** 77–78
—powers, **3,** 9–10
—military occupation of, **1,** 445; **5,** 351
Rhodes, courts of, **1,** 452–453
Riga, Peace Treaty of (1921), **4,** 14–17; **6,** 353, 360, 450
Right to tax, **5,** 255; **6,** 69
Rights: *see* Acquired rights; Human rights; Private rights, respect for; *and under* State succession
of population of Mandated territories, **23,** 46
Rio Negro, territory of, **1,** 98
Riots—
damage to foreign property, responsibility for, **1,** 173–174; **2,** 159–160; **28,** 189, 193
protectorate, in, responsibility of protecting State, **2,** 174–175; **20,** 47–48
Riparian landowners, rights of, **4,** 122
River commissions, international, competence, **5,** 83–84, 88–91
Rivers: *see also* named rivers *and* Thalweg, doctrine of
boundaries, as, **1,** 84, 96–98; **9,** 114; **7,** 128–135
Rivers—*continued*
boundaries, as—*continued*
—accretion, doctrine of, **2,** 98–99; **11,** 100
—erosion, doctrine of, **11,** 100
—joint jurisdiction over, **6,** 50
—Niagara river, **4,** 122
changes in course of, **1,** 97–98
" cut-banks ", **2,** 96–98
diversion of waters, **6,** 119–121
inter-state, utilization of flow of, **6,** 119–121
medium filum, doctrine of, **4,** 121–122
mouth, whether fixed point for boundary, **30,** 476, 490
navigable, Argentine law, **10,** 110
riparian landowners, rights of, **4,** 122
Rivers, international—
construction of works on, **23,** 360–363
freedom of navigation on, **4,** 123–126; **5,** 83–88; **7,** 12–13; **8,** 166–169; **16,** 77–80; **17,** 123–125; **18,** 84–85; **19,** 149–157, 469–470; **20,** 164–165; **21,** 3–8, 88, 276–277, 300–303
jurisdiction on, **6,** 117–119; **17,** 123–125; **21,** 300–303; **24,** 97–100
prevention of pollution, **28,** 464–467
treaty regulating, **22,** 572–580
tributaries, **5,** 83–84
utilization of flow of, **4,** 128–133; **6,** 119–121; **9,** 120; **24,** 101–142 *passim*
Road Signs and Signals, Protocol and Final Act (1949), **18,** 382
Road Traffic, Convention on (1926), **9,** 367; **18,** 235
—(1949), **18,** 382; **24,** 11–12, 591–592
Road traffic convention, breach of effect on individual liability for offences, **33,** 382–384
Roadsteads, part of public domain, **8,** 173–178
Roja River, utilization of flow of, **9,** 120
Rolling stock, restitution of, **20,** 482–483, 486–489
Rome, Treaty of (1957): *see* European Economic Community, Treaty (1957)
Roumania—
agrarian legislation, **4,** 88–90
Allied Powers, Convention with (1920), **5,** 62
Austria, Claims Convention (1924), **5,** 118–120, 216
Austria-Hungary, occupation by, **1,** 477–478
Bessarabia, annexation of, **6,** 60–61
—succession to, **5,** 61, 63
European Danube Commission, Convention on Privileges and Immunities (1938), **22,** 537, 547, 548
France, Treaty of Establishment (1930), **21,** 284–285; **28,** 492–493

Roumania—*continued*
Germany—
—Agreement on actions before Mixed Arbitral Tribunal, (1928), **6**, 344–345
—outbreak of war with (1916), **5**, 482
government bonds, default on, **26**, 259–261
Hungary, Claims Convention (1923), **5**, 386
Jews in, status of, **5**, 213–218
Monopolies Institute, jurisdictional immunity, **9**, 198
nationalization of banks, **26**, 294–295
Peace Treaty with (1947), **17**, 319–322, 333–339
—losses covered by, **26**, 334, 687
—Roumanian assets in Allied States, charge on, **30**, 406–407, 411, 416, 419
—retention of property for claims, **28**, 630
—United Nations national, meaning, **26**, 327
Soviet Government, non-recognition of, **5**, 49–51
succession to obligations of, **5**, 61
Switzerland—
—Arbitration Treaty (1926), **16**, 282
—Commercial Agreement (1951), **23**, 197
U.K., Trade and Payments Agreement (1939), **30**, 404–420
"Royal personage", meaning, **1**, 341; **4**, 33
Ruhr, military occupation of, **2**, 327–328; **4**, 404–405; **5**, 79–80
"Rum-running", **5**, 6–7: *see also* Liquor
Russia, Empire of—
administrative measures, enforceable in Poland, **1**, 75–76
Austria, Treaty with (1815), **21**, 87
Bessarabia, annexation of (1878), **5**, 61–62
—separation of, **2**, 224–227
continuity of, **1**, 31–33
contractual obligations in Bessarabia, succession of Roumania, **5**, 61–63
Deniken Government, claim against, **6**, 53–54
dismemberment, **1**, 70, 71
Germany, Commercial Treaty (1894), **1**, 242
Government of, **1**, 30–31
Omsk All Russian Government, extinction of, **1**, 32; **2**, 134–135
property in England, succession of Soviet Government, **3**, 172–173
Provisional Government of 1917...**1**, 30–33, 43–44
—North Russian Government of 1918...**3**, 62–64
—overthrow, **11**, 63–65

Russia, Empire of—*continued*
Provisional Government of 1917—*continued*
—recognition by Belgium, **4**, 70
representative in U.S.A., 1917...**1**, 52–53; **2**, 48–49
U.S.A., Convention for Cession of Alaska (1867), **22**, 562–565
Russian Orthodox Church, validity of divorces, **4**, 69–71
Russian Red Cross, succession to property of, **4**, 458
Russian refugees—
Intergovernmental Arrangement (1922), **8**, 313
—(1928), **5**, 248, 333–335, 362; **7**, 406–408; **11**, 187, 197–198; **15**, 289–290
Russian Socialist Federal Soviet Republic—
Civil Code, frustration of contract, **27**, 633–636
Germany, Treaty of Brest-Litovsk (1918), **28**, 37
—Treaty of Rapallo (1922), **28**, 37
nationalization of banks (1917), **26**, 130
Russian Trade Delegations: *see* Trade Delegations of U.S.S.R.
Russian Volunteer Fleet (Dobroflotte), **5**, 114–115
claim for compensation for services of, **3**, 210–211
Ryukyu Islands—
nationality of inhabitants, **21**, 178
status of, **21**, 82–86; **24**, 88, 90; **32**, 583–584

S

Saar, Territory of, **1**, 83; **3**, 50–52; **8**, 70
extradition to, **4**, 341
France, Judicial Convention (1948), **17**, 36–37; **18**, 431, 432
Franco-German Agreement on (1954), **22**, 630–632
Franco-German Treaty on (1956), **24**, 411–412
French customs régime, submission to, **7**, 30
Germany, whether part of, **1**, 42, 83; **7**, 59–61, 62
integration into Federal Republic, effect, **24**, 408–413, 413–415; **28**, 501
Italian Military Force in, **8**, 248–249
nationality of inhabitants, **11**, 180–181
"occupied territories", distinguished, **5**, 33–34
status of, **2**, 32–33; **5**, 33–35; **17**, 36–37; **18**, 42–44; **22**, 59, 512–513, 630–632

Saar, Territory of—*continued*
taking over of former Prussian officials, **3,** 90–91
Treaty of Versailles and, **4,** 341–342
Sabotage, legality, **23,** 759–762
Saboteurs, punishment of, **10,** 568–573
Safe-conduct—
return visa, expulsion order and, **7,** 331–332
violation of, **6,** 438–440
Safety of Life at Sea, International Convention (1929), **22,** 460, 589–591
Saigon, whether neutral port in 1941, **32,** 603–604, 619–622
St. Germain, Peace Treaty of (1919), **1,** 454; **2,** 237–239; **4,** 399; **13,** 115–119; **15,** 234; **16,** 82, 216; **17,** 161
acquisition of Austrian nationality and, **1,** 20–21; **4,** 25
Austrian Republic, establishment of, **1,** 20, 21; **4,** 255, 399 n.
Czechoslovak State, establishment of, **4,** 149
nationality provisions, **6,** 37–40
—option, **6,** 258–259
" *ressortissants* ", meaning, **5,** 213–218
Rome Agreements (1923) *re* Danube–Save–Adriatic Railway Company, **18,** 1–3; **22,** 607–608
signature, effect of, **11,** 268
State succession, questions of, **1,** 75
St. James, Declaration of, on War Criminals (1942), **13,** 263; **14,** 198; **16,** 268
St. Peter, Basilica of, **4,** 99
St. Peter's Square, duty to maintain, **10,** 106–108
St. Petersburg International Telegraphic Convention (1875), **5,** 416–417; **6,** 413; **7,** 471–472
Saipan (Marianas), U.S. occupation of, **15,** 519–524
Sales f.o.b., nature of, **27,** 220–221
Salonica—
Allied occupation of, **4,** 571
bombardment by German forces, **4,** 570–571
Salvage—
Brussels Convention on (1910), **6,** 10; **7,** 201–202; **9,** 300; **22,** 277; **34,** 85, 87
—" *résultat utile* " (Art. 2), **11,** 230
—third States, application to, **3,** 3
claims for—
—jurisdictional immunity of foreign public ships, **1,** 146–148; **2,** 141–142
—own crew, salvage by, **16,** 150–153
—prize law, in, **10,** 608–613
goods from land, **11,** 85–91
jurisdiction in, **4,** 198–199; **16,** 151–152
Salvage—*continued*
law governing, **16,** 150–153
maritime liens in respect of, **10,** 616–620
neutral merchantships, **1,** 485–487
ship, exemption from prize, **12,** 487–488
warship, by, jurisdiction as to, **22,** 277–278
Samoa, Western: *see* Western Samoa
Samos—
cession to Greece, **2,** 70; **23,** 84–85
international position of, **3,** 38–39; **8,** 153–155; **23,** 666
Sancta corpora legatorum, **9,** 424
Sanitary Convention for Aerial Navigation (1933), **18,** 382
Sanitary, Maritime and Quarantine Council of Egypt, **1,** 364; **6,** 414
Santa Monica Bay, **9,** 133–140, 300–304
São Paulo, immunities of, **10,** 178–191
Sarawak, Japanese occupation of, **24,** 943–951, 979–985
Sardinia, Kingdom of—
France, Treaty (1760), **5,** 69; **18,** 290
—(1860), **15,** 58
nationals abroad, acquisition of Italian nationality, **9,** 26
succession of Italy to obligations of, **4,** 91–92
Switzerland, Treaty (1816), **5,** 462
Sardinia and Piedmont, Kingdom of, continuation of, **9,** 27
Saudi Arabia—
Agreement with Onassis on transport of oil, 1954...**27,** 126–130, 202–209
—conflict with Aramco Concession, **27,** 209–226
—legal nature, **27,** 202–206
—protests by Aramco, **27,** 129–130
Aramco, oil concession of 1933: *see* Aramco, oil concession by Saudi Arabia, 1933
Arbitration Agreement with Aramco (1955), **27,** 229–233
Continental Shelf Proclamation (1949), **18,** 153, 154
Savoy and Nice, annexation by France (1860), **15,** 58
Savoy, Upper, Free Zone of, **5,** 16–17, 459–465; **6,** 362–367, 430, 431; **7,** 483; **8,** 178
Saxony, Treaty with Germany (1920) (railways), **5,** 330–332
Scheldt, navigation on, Treaty of 1924...**9,** 121
Schleswig—
Northern, cession to Denmark, **2,** 82, 83
plebiscite in, **1,** 93
Scotland, Custodian of Enemy Property in, **1,** 398–399

Scuttling of ships, whether ground for condemnation, **10,** 594–598
Sea bed and subsoil: *see also* Continental shelf
jurisdiction over, **20,** 535
rights of littoral States over, **18,** 151–152, 155
territorial waters and, **9,** 126
Sea fisheries: *see* Fisheries
Sea, law of the, **16,** 9–10. *See also* Geneva Conventions on the Law of the Sea (1958)
Sea warfare, **1,** 483–488; **2,** 452–454; **3,** 482–484; **4,** 568–570; **5,** 510–515; **6,** 438–446; **9,** 571–583; **10,** 594–637; **12,** 460–574; **13,** 400–407; **15,** 687–694; **16,** 557-600; **17,** 440–449; **19,** 634–640; **21,** 489; **23,** 851; **24,** 916–923, 991–994; **28,** 652–664; **31,** 509–520: *see also* Contraband; Prize *and under* the relevant Hague Conventions
belligerents, rights of, **2,** 417
capture of enemy merchant ship, *see* Merchantships, enemy
capture of maritime property on land, **1,** 483–485
conversion of merchantships, **23,** 341–342, 801–805
Declarations of Paris (1856) and London (1909): *see* London, Declaration of; *and* Paris, Declaration of
enemy merchantships: *see* Merchantships, enemy
lighthouses, bombardment of, **15,** 687–688
minefields, obligation to notify, **16,** 155–170
navicerts, system of, **12,** 532–537
—absence of navicert, **12,** 546, 553
neutral merchantships: *q.v.*
requisition, distinguished from confiscation, **6,** 440–441
requisitioned ships, whether " warships properly so-called ", **23,** 341–342, 801–805
saboteurs, **10,** 564–576
safe-conduct, violation of, **6,** 438–440
search in port, legality of, **3,** 484–485
submarine warfare, **13,** 218–220, 246–250
Submarine Warfare, Treaty of Washington (1922), **14,** 198
surrender, **18,** 707–709
unneutral service, **12,** 462–466, 532–542
—condemnation for, **12,** 533–537
visit and search, **10,** 594–605; **14,** 311–316
—resistance to, **10,** 596–598
warships, types of, **23,** 341–342, 801–805
Seamen, alien: *see* Alien seamen
Seamen's Articles of Agreement, Convention (1926), **24,** 643–644
Seaplanes, status of, **5,** 82; **6,** 112
whether a ship, **11,** 85–89; **12,** 55–59
Search—
port, in, legality of, **3,** 484–485
neutral merchantships, of, **1,** 485–487
Secession, nationality, effect on, **2,** 224–227
Second World War, Treaty of Versailles and, **11,** 219. [For Second World War generally, *see* War *and under* particular States]
Secretary-General, League of Nations, immunities of, **8,** 395–397
Secretary-General, United Nations: *see under* United Nations
Securities, regulation of sale of, application to sale by foreign dealer, **31,** 206–209
Security Council of United Nations: *see under* United Nations
Security for costs: *see under* Costs
" Seizure " of ships, meaning, **3,** 485–486: *see also* Prize
Seizure of ships outside national territorial waters, **11,** 130–135, 156–161
Self-defence, **32,** 54–55, 58, 62–64
defence of State interests and, **4,** 12, 174
diplomatic immunities and, **13,** 164–166; **14,** 150
limitation by treaties, **2,** 4, 417
limits of, **13,** 210–211
right of, **24,** 126
retention of right of, renunciation of war in Constitution, **32,** 43–64
Self-determination, **31,** 38
Charter provisions, insurgency, relevance to, **31,** 29–30, 48
legal principle, whether, **31,** 30
Self-executing treaties: *see under* Treaties
" Self-governing ", meaning, **5,** 409, 413
Self-help, entry into foreign waters as, **16,** 165–167
Self-preservation, State's right of: *see also under* Sovereignty
rules of war and, **1,** 427–428; **2,** 428–429
Sequestration, enemy property, of: *see under* Enemy property
" *Sera* ", meaning, **4,** 428
Serb–Croat–Slovene State, Consular Convention with Italy (1924), **7,** 392
Serbia—
Hague Convention No. VI, party to, **1,** 410–411
Switzerland, Extradition Treaty (1897), **19,** 371
Turkey, Peace Treaty of Constantinople (1914), **6,** 389, 391; **7,** 98

Serbia—*continued*
U.S.A.—
—Commercial Convention (1881), **7**, 452–453; **20**, 293–295; **21**, 71, 72
—Consular Convention (1881), **19**, 393, 395; **21**, 71, 72
—Extradition Treaty (1901), **21**, 67–68, 72, 73, 74; **24**, 510, 517
Yugoslavia and, **21**, 66–75
Service commandé, crime committed abroad during, **11**, 165–169
Servitudes, **2**, 103; **4**, 136–138, 420–423; **8**, 178–179; **31**, 86
Kiel Canal and, **2**, 329–330
restrictive interpretation of, **2**, 329–330; **6**, 130–131
specific delimitation, need for, **24**, 867
Set-off: *see also* Counterclaims—
international debts, **6**, 234
jurisdictional immunity of States and, **7**, 164–166; **8**, 218–221; **11**, 136–138; **12**, 92–96; **13**, 29–32; **17**, 66, 72; **18**, 219–221; **20**, 176–178
validity of, **3**, 210–211; **4**, 478–479; **7**, 164–166
severance, **5**, 158; **24**, 708–710, 809–812, 816, 862
—impossibility of, **2**, 177: *see also under* Treaties
Severance, theory of, confiscation of shares, **32**, 12–17
Sevres, Peace Treaty of (1920), **1**, 205; **2**, 334; **23**, 667
Shanghai, French Settlement at, **1**, 334, 335
French consular court at, **2**, 326
termination of International Settlement (1943), **28**, 195, 199
Shareholders—
corporations as, claims by, **6**, 273–275
enemy territory in, service on, **10**, 520–528
foreign corporations, in, claims by, **21**, 152–153; **26**, 342
nature of interest, **18**, 185
non-enemy, in enemy corporation, protection of interests of, **11**, 258; **18**, 516–520, 529
Shares—
cancellation by foreign government, effect, **4**, 141–144
enemy-owned, " blocking " of, effect, **25**, 366
restitution of, Germany, Settlement Convention, **25**, 345–346
situs of, **26**, 154; **32**, 14
" Ship ", definition, **12**, 521–523
Shipmasters, foreign, jurisdiction in disputes with foreign charterers, **4**, 162
Shipowners Liability (Sick and Injured Seamen) Convention (1936), **19**, 464–467
burial expenses, shipment of body home, **28**, 514
Shipping: *see also* Inter-Governmental Maritime Consultative Organization *and* Ships
conferences, jurisdiction to investigate, **31**, 209–219; **32**, 100–102; **33**, 158–163; **35**, 103–109
Hague Rules, interpretation of statute based on, **33**, 397–399
State-owned lines, immunity from jurisdiction, **31**, 215–217
Ships: *see also* Auxiliary ships; Merchant ships; Neutral merchant ships; Prize; Public ships; Sea warfare; Warships
abroad, requisition of, **10**, 131–147, 152–154
arrest of, in innocent passage, **7**, 138–139
asylum on, high seas, on, **24**, 153
attachment of, **9**, 167
belligerent-owned, transfer to neutral flag, **11**, 260–264
chartered to government, immunity of, **9**, 283–284; **12**, 113–115. *See also* Public ships
collisions: *q.v.*
contract for construction, requisition of, **1**, 189–191, 369–371, 377–378, 414–418; **28**, 611–629
contract for construction, transfer of rights to occupant, **31**, 508–509
crimes committed on, **9**, 167–169, 250, 259, 297; **15**, 108–109, 110–115. *See also* Jurisdiction, criminal *and* Ports, jurisdiction in
—extradition for, **24**, 497
—flag State, jurisdiction of, **26**, 514, 517–518
—foreign territorial waters, in, **26**, 226–227, 236–239
deserters from, **9**, 170; **11**, 14
disputes in, jurisdiction over, **11**, 113–124: *see also* Consular jurisdiction
distress, entry in, **5**, 129–131; **6**, 154–156; **7**, 208; **9**, 165; **11**, 127–130
embargo on use of, **21**, 12–16
emigrants, carrying of, **9**, 167
enemy character of, **9**, 561; **11**, 260–265; **12**, 383–386; **13**, 401–406; **16**, 389–390; **17**, 378–385; **18**, 725–730; **24**, 916–923
—flag, conclusiveness of, **11**, 264–265; **16**, 389–390; **17**, 378–385; **24**, 919–921
—State with whom relations severed, **24**, 916–923
enemy, in port, effects of outbreak of war, **1**, 410–414; **2**, 452–454; **4**,

Ships—*continued*
enemy, in port, effects of outbreak of war—*continued*
542; **5,** 487; **6,** 438–441; **7,** 505–506; **10,** 509–514; **12,** 353–359
expropriation of, **9,** 217, 224
exterritoriality, fiction of, **2,** 144
fishing vessels, exemption from seizure as prize, **12,** 469–471; **28,** 661–662
flag flown by—
—dependent territory, of, **23,** 34
—enemy character, conclusiveness as to, **11,** 264–265; **16,** 389–390; **17,** 378–385; **24,** 919–921
—jurisdiction, determining, **5,** 75–76; **22,** 282–286
—nationality, determining, **9,** 299; **31,** 237–240
flag, genuine link, **30,** 446
"flag of convenience", **26,** 222–227, 227–231, 236–239; **34,** 61, 69
—application of law of port, **31,** 230–240
"floating island" theory, **10,** 252–258; **27,** 45–49; **28,** 123: *see also* territorial character, *infra*
flying boats, whether, **12,** 55–59
foreign, application of local labour law, **34,** 51–80
foreign, detention in territorial waters, **10,** 267–272
foreign ports, access to, **31,** 137–140
foreign ports, in—
—application of local law, **26,** 228–229; **31,** 132–137
—jurisdiction over: *see* Ports, jurisdiction in
—status of, Institute of International Law, Resolutions (1928), **23,** 804
foreign territorial waters, in, jurisdiction over, **6,** 123–126, 154–159, 175–177; **20,** 154–155; **21,** 126–135
internal discipline, jurisdiction, **34,** 63–64, 74
internal economy doctrine, **34,** 73–74, 76; **35,** 97
jurisdiction over, on high seas, **4,** 186–187; **17,** 196–198; **26,** 242–244; **27,** 45–49
—flag, determined by, **22,** 282–286; **30,** 112–115
law of the flag, **34,** 38, 40, 55, 65, 71, 73–74, 76; **35,** 102
—criminal jurisdiction, **26,** 514, 517–518
—importance of, **32,** 104–105
—jurisdiction in personal injury action, **28,** 108–114, 149
—origin of doctrine, **31,** 237, 239
—treaty provisions, **31,** 238

Ships—*continued*
maritime lien, ships requisitioned by government, **2,** 141–144; **17,** 167–168
Maritime Liens, Brussels Convention (1926): *see under* Maritime liens
national-owned, registered abroad, applicable law, **26,** 222–226, 227–231, 236–239
national territory, whether part of, **34,** 37–41, 54, 266
nationality of, **9,** 299; **31,** 237–240; **34,** 59–60: *see also* flag flown by, *supra*
—Geneva Convention on High Seas, **30,** 443, 446
nationalization of, **11,** 155–161; **15,** 176–204
neutral: *see* Neutral merchant ships
public purposes, when used for: *see* Public ships
requisitioned—
—jurisdictional immunity, **9,** 250, 279
—status, **2,** 141, 408–410
—whether "warships", **23,** 341–342, 801–805
requisitioning of: *see* Angary *and under* Requisitioning
seizure by foreign State, protection against, U.S. law, **31,** 130
seizure outside national territorial waters, **11,** 130–135, 156–161
seizure under enemy property legislation, **30,** 1–3
seizure, wrongful, **1,** 171–179
ship mortgages and maritime liens, ranking, **33,** 385–390: *see also* Maritime liens
stateless, **9,** 299
State-owned, Brussels Convention on Immunity of (1926), **9,** 286–291
State-owned, immunities: *see under* Public ships
State-owned, statement of executive as to, **12,** 108–111, 144–149
territorial character, **4,** 107, 188–189, 295–296; **5,** 75–76; **6,** 93–94, 175–177, 179, 183, 290, 293; **7,** 212–213; **10,** 252–258, 323–325; **23,** 284–295; **27,** 45–49; **28,** 123
tort on foreign, on high seas, jurisdiction, **26,** 240–241
tort on, in foreign territorial waters, applicable law, **26,** 226–227, 236–239
trading vessels, jurisdictional immunities, **11,** 160, 161
transfer *flagrante bello*, **16,** 390
"wreck", meaning, **7,** 466
Ship's papers—
absence of, enemy character and, **11,** 264–265; **12,** 383–386; **13,** 401–406

Ship's papers—*continued*
hostile destination evidenced from, **12,** 559
spoliation of, **10,** 594–598
Ship's warrants, system of, **12,** 532–537
Siam: *see also* Thailand—
acceptance of jurisdiction of P.C.I.J., **33,** 421, 423
Siege, state of—
establishment in protected State, **11,** 42–43
proclamation in Egypt, **1,** 42
Siège social, **1,** 344–345
test of nationality of corporation, **1,** 227–228; **2,** 259–261; **3,** 282–286; **5,** 248–250, 253
Sikh Kingdom, East India Company as successor to, **24,** 76
Silesia, territories of, **1,** 13–14
Silesia, Upper: *see* Upper Silesia
Singapore—
application of Warsaw Convention, 1929, in, **27,** 257 n.
Japanese occupation of, **15,** 448–449; **19,** 183–185
trading with the enemy legislation, **15,** 447–449
Sitka, Russian church at, **15,** 52–58
Situs, bank account, of, **25,** 358–360
debts, of, **7,** 153–155; **16,** 18–19, 21–24; **32,** 30–31, 33–37, 108, 568; **33,** 18
property in transit, of, **26,** 685–686
shares, of, **26,** 154
trade marks, of, **30,** 42, 45, 48
Slavery Convention (1926), **18,** 378
Slovakia, establishment of Czecho-slovak sovereignty, **1,** 15–17; **4,** 26
" Small craft ", exemption from prize, **12,** 482–483, 487–488
Smuggling, jurisdiction in respect of, **7,** 163–164, 203–204
U.S.A., Prohibition Law, **3,** 151–169: *see also* Liquor traffic
Smyrna, occupation of, **5,** 496
Social security treaties, **27,** 48–49, 283–291; **30,** 420–423
employment legislation, consistency with, **33,** 165, 168
place of residence and of employment, **27,** 285–287
Société en nom collectif, assimilation to partnership, **5,** 252–253
Soldiers, responsibility for acts of, **3,** 220–224, 225, 226; **4,** 233–234, 242–243; **5,** 147–149, 170–173, 392
shooting in accordance with orders, **11,** 177–178
Solicitor's retainer, **10,** 557–558
Somaliland—
status of, **22,** 76
Trusteeship Agreement, **22,** 77–80
Somaliland—*continued*
Trusteeship, powers of Administering State, **22,** 76–80
Sources of international law, **1,** 3, 4; **2,** 3, 164, 367–368; **3,** 4–5; **4,** 5–9; **5,** 3–4; **7,** 214; **8,** 1–2, 450–451; **13,** 97–107, 341; **17,** 1; **18,** 1; **19,** 1; **21,** 1; **22,** 1, 536, 560; **23,** 710; **25,** 1, 77–79, 81, 253–254, 269, 278, 529, 545; **28,** 1, 172, 555, 557; **29,** 1, 476
communis opinio doctorum, **17,** 163
custom and usage, **4,** 8; **19,** 275–276, 292–294; **23,** 710–712, 868; **31,** 25, 36, 52, 61, 62, 65–68, 82, 90, 96, 97, 105–106, 108, 115: *see also* Customary international law
draft codes, Rules of Air Warfare, **32,** 631
foreign decisions *in pari materia,* **4,** 414
general principles of law, **5,** 3–4; **6,** 81; **8,** 450–451; **18,** 106–107; **24,** 130, 859; **25,** 269, 278, 529, 545; **28,** 555, 557; **31,** 1, 25–26, 36, 56, 70, 82, 85, 86, 116, 118
municipal decisions, **4,** 6–7
natural law, **3,** 4–5. *See also* Natural law
principles of private international law, **25,** 77–78
treaties, **4,** 6–7; **16,** 1–3; **22,** 560; **29,** 476
writings of publicists, **3,** 4; **4,** 6–7
South Africa, Cape Colony, Aliens Naturalization Act, 1883...**4,** 42
South Africa, Union of: *see also* South West Africa—
Aliens Act, 1937...**20,** 340–342
Constitution, **19,** 36–49, *passim*
Custodian of Enemy Property, **1,** 225, 399
Dominion status and Statute of Westminster, **19,** 35–49
Dutch forces in, **10,** 119–123
Germany, Agreement (1923) *re* South-West Africa, **15,** 246–247
Immigrants Regulation Act, 1913, **21,** 220, 221, 230
Immigration Acts, 1931 and 1937, **18,** 295–296, 303–308; **21,** 220
Imperial legislation, application of, **9,** 31
King, position of, in, **8,** 88–91
legislation, enforceability in South-West Africa, **16,** 39–40
mandate obligations, recognition of, **17,** 52–53
nationality laws, **17,** 229–232
naturalization in, under former law, **4,** 41–43
recruitment of mine workers, Forced Labour Convention and, **35,** 294, 298, 331–332, 338–339

South Africa, Union of—*continued*
South Africa Act, 1909...**8,** 80
State succession in, **1,** 60
—succession to Imperial legislation, **9,** 32
status (1921), **1,** 22–23
—treason, in regard to, **15,** 78–90
South African Republic—
annexation by U.K., **2,** 67–68
U.K., London Convention (1884), **2,** 69–70
South Moluccas, Republic of—
proclamation of, **17,** 143–152, 199; **19,** 4–6; **21,** 48–49
recognition of, **17,** 60, 143–152
South West Africa—
mandate over, **2,** 27–31; **7,** 53–56; **9,** 45; **15,** 211–213; **16,** 39–41; **17,** 47–60; **22,** 651–689, *passim*; **23,** 38–70. *See also* German South West Africa
G.A. Resolution establishing Committee (1953), **22,** 653–660
legislative powers of Mandatory, **7,** 53–56; **9,** 45
nationality in, **15,** 237–248
petitions, admissibility of, **23,** 38–44, 46, 50
status of, **17,** 47–60; **22,** 651–652, 662, 666; **23,** 38–39, 40, 64
status of former German protectorate, **8,** 131–132
U.N. supervision, **22,** 86
Southern Rhodesia, Extradition Act, **24,** 502
Sovereign, foreign: *see* Foreign States; Heads of State
Sovereign immunity: *see* Foreign States, immunity from jurisdiction
Sovereign-in-exile—
conclusiveness of statements of, **12,** 420–424
legislative competence, **12,** 420–424, 431–433, 444–445: *see also* Governments in exile
Sovereign Order of Malta: *see* Malta, Sovereign Order of
Sovereignty: *see also* Territorial sovereignty—
acquisition of: *see* Territory, acquisition of sovereignty over
acts of, private transactions, distinguished, **1,** 22–23; **3,** 18–23; **5,** 181; **6,** 36–37; **7,** 19–22; **8,** 26–31; **18,** 113. *See also under* Foreign States, jurisdictional immunity of
air, over the, **5,** 82; **6,** 112; **7,** 114–115; **8,** 159–160; **9,** 119, 124; **12,** 55–59; **17,** 118–123; **19,** 148; **20,** 153–163; **22,** 157–167; **27,** 58–61; **28,** 99, 115–138; **30,** 69–75
angary and, **23,** 720–722
beginning of, **7,** 82–83

Sovereignty—*continued*
belligerent occupation and, **11,** 275–277, 279–282; **12,** 420–432, 434, 456–457; **15,** 520–523, 613–614; **16,** 455, 476, 498; **18,** 558–560; **22,** 994; **24,** 944; **26,** 702–703; **29,** 44
change of, effects: *see also* State succession
—concession agreement, on, **23,** 26
—extradition, **9,** 407–408
—judgments, **4,** 95–96
—minorities, protection of, **3,** 312–313
—nationality, on: *see under* Nationality
—operation of local laws, **4,** 95–96; **8,** 143–151; **11,** 79–81
—pending actions, **1,** 89–96; **2,** 61; **18,** 72–77; **26,** 99
—private rights, **1,** 90–91; **3,** 115–116; **11,** 74–77, 94–99; **13,** 35–42; **19,** 133–135; **22,** 134–135; **23,** 110–111
—treaties, **23,** 123–124
control of admission of aliens, effect of European Convention on Human Rights, **28,** 253
disputed, deportation of aliens, **2,** 273
divisible, whether, **6,** 23–24; **20,** 3–4; **28,** 67, 69
domestic jurisdiction and, **21,** 12–16; **22,** 11
eminent domain and, **23,** 721
exceptions to, **20,** 447
foreign relations, in, **17,** 23–27; **19,** 6, 11; **21,** 10–14; **22,** 12
government loans abroad, juridical nature, **11,** 30–32. *See also* State loans
guarantee of, violation, effect on, guarantor State, **26,** 635
imperium and *dominium*, **28,** 376
import and export, right to control, **27,** 211
internal and external aspects, **2,** 28–31; **8,** 13–25; **20,** 4–6
international leases and, **15,** 64–68
jurisdictional acts of foreign States within national territory, **10,** 6–9
jurisdiction and control, distinction, **31,** 124
jurisdiction of arbitral tribunals and, **19,** 432, 536; **23,** 533
legislative power, extent of: *see* Extraterritorial effect of legislation
less than full, cession of, **31,** 77–78, 87–88, 108, 115, 125
limitations on—
—contractual, restrictive interpretation, **8,** 26–30
—new international law and, **18,** 109–110, 112–113, 389; **19,** 528

Sovereignty—*continued*
limitations on—*continued*—
—rights of other States, **18,** 109–110; **24,** 119–120, 127
—rules of international law as, **4,** **11**; **18,** 387; **24,** 849–850, 866–869
—Sovereign Order of Malta, **24,** 2
—State responsibility and, **6,** 197–198
—treaties, in, **5,** 364–365
—treaties, in, restrictive interpretation, **1,** 338; **2,** 329–330; **3,** 362–366; **4,** 427–428; **5,** 16–17, 382; **6,** 374–377; **24,** 127–128
loss of, **6,** 99–100, 108; **13,** 187–192; **16,** 73–77; **17,** 118; **19,** 144–148; **24,** 87–88
mandated territories, in, **2,** 27–31; **6,** 48–49; **7,** 35–36; **8,** 98–109; **17,** 49
nationality, determination of, **28,** 291–292
nature of, **1,** 83–84; **5,** 101–102; **6,** 93–94; **18,** 7–8, 79; **23,** 721–722
negotiation, requirement of, and, **2,** 402
occupied States, of: *see* belligerent occupation, *supra*
peace treaty as limitation on, **22,** 448
ports, right to control, **27,** 211
renunciation of, **32,** 173, 176, 179, 182
reservations with regard to, in arbitration clauses, not to be presumed, **5,** 443
reservations to multilateral treaties and, **18,** 371
residuary, **8,** 155–156; **24,** 90–92
restrictive interpretation of treaties, reason for, **1,** 338; **2,** 329–330; **6,** 374–377
restrictions on not to be presumed, **3,** 364; **4,** 153; **16,** 335–336; **17,** 283; **18,** 109–110; **24,** 127–128
rights less than, **31,** 60
rights of, as subject-matter of arbitration, **27,** 149–153
—enforcement of, **6,** 145, 149–150
—police power, **5,** 85–87; **10,** 423
—taxation, **5,** 255–256
self-preservation, **5,** 17
State trading and, **5,** 18–21, 309–313
States of the United States, **31,** 146, 183
suzerainty, **2,** 69–70; **20,** 117, 133–134
Telecommunications Convention of Madrid (1932) and, **10,** 421–423
territorial limits of, **28,** 60. *See also* Jurisdiction, territorial limits of
transfer of, **24,** 604
—contractual obligations, effect on, **24,** 61
—expressions in treaties, **31,** 50–51

Sovereignty—*continued*
transfer of—*continued*
—occupation, effect of, **6,** 447–448
—ratification of treaty, effect of, **3,** 336
treaties, conclusion of, and, **2,** 329–330; **5,** 364; **22,** 448
treaties, limitation of, as, **2,** 329, 330; **22,** 874, 945
trespass on, issue of writ by foreign court, **28,** 60, 75
U.N., members of, **21,** 344
various meanings, **28,** 62
violation of, **10,** 6–9
—nuisance, by, **9,** 321
without citizens, **24,** 2
without territory, **22,** 1–5; **24,** 2
Soviet Government: *see also* R.S.F.S.R. *and* U.S.S.R.—
capacity to sue, **7,** 75–76, 82–83
non-recognition, effects of, **7,** 80–83
property in England of Imperial Government, succession to, **3,** 172–173
recognition, by France, **7,** 76–80
—by U.S.A., **7,** 63–75; **9,** 68–70, 145, 149, 184. *See also under* U.S.A., Litvinov Assignment
repudiation of claims connected with 1914 War, **26,** 276–277
repudiation of Czarist bonds, **26,** 268–269
Soviet Union: *see* U.S.S.R.
Spa, Armistice Protocol of (1918), **2,** 71; **4,** 402
Spain: *see also* Spanish Civil War—
adoption law, **31,** 316–318
arbitration between Colombia and Venezuela, **1,** 84–89
Argentina, Extradition Treaty (1881), **9,** 408; **16,** 276
—Workmen's Compensation Treaty (1922), **2,** 317
Civil Code, intestate succession, **5,** 235
—separation decrees, jurisdiction, **5,** 351
civil law, application in Puerto Rico, **1,** 76
Civil Procedure, Law of, actions between aliens, **34,** 49–50
Colombia, Extradition Treaty (1892), **28,** 324–325
France—
—Additional Act (Bayonne, 1866) *re* boundary, **24,** 101–142, *passim*
—Agreement of Nationalist Government (1939) *re* property in France, **11,** 144
—Arbitration Treaty (1929), **24,** 101
—Arbitration Agreement (1956), **24,** 111
—cession and retrocession of Louisiana, **31,** 181

Spain—*continued*
France—*continued*
—Consular Convention (1862), **1,** 333–334; **2,** 305–306; **5,** 323, 361; **6,** 370; **7,** 405–406; **15,** 3–4, 326n.; **17,** 240, 316; **18,** 280, 360, 435n.; **19,** 1, 339–342, 474–476; **20,** 264n., 437–438; **21,** 277–278, 282–284; **22,** 478–479, 606–607, 624–625; **24,** 110, 600–601; **25,** 320; **26,** 490–492, 494–496
—Declarations on Morocco (1914), **19,** 268–271, 280, 293–294
—Extradition Treaty (1877), **20,** 370 n.
—Final Act of Delimitation of Pyrenees Frontier (1868), **24,** 105
—Treaties with (Bayonne, 1856, 1862 and 1866) *re* frontier, **24,** 101–142, *passim*
—Treaty concerning railways (1882), **9,** 488–489
—Treaty of Work and Assistance (1932), **7,** 470
—Treaty (1912) *re* Spanish Zone of Morocco, **19,** 268, 269, 296
France and United Kingdom, Boundary Treaty (1763), **7,** 131
Franco, Government of, **10,** 25–27
Germany—
—Extradition Treaty (1878), **18,** 341
—Treaty of Commerce (1868), **23,** 716
Great Britain, Treaty of Peace and Commerce (1667), **23,** 313, 321, 322
government by decree, Law of 1937, **9,** 15
Morocco—
—Commercial Treaty (1861), **19,** 259, 262, 265, 272, 280, 281
—Consular Treaty (1861), **19,** 263, 271, 292–302, *passim*; **21,** 139, 140
—Protectorate over, **2,** 20–21, 163–164; **10,** 47
—Treaties (1799), **19,** 262; (1912), **21,** 139; (1914), **19,** 266; **21,** 139
Penal Code (insults to authorities), **9,** 8–9
—(insults to public officials), **9,** 583
—Philippines, in, continuing validity, **1,** 77
—(piracy), **1,** 164
Portugal, Extradition Treaty (1867), **9,** 403
State succession of U.S.A. in Philippines, **1,** 59
Switzerland, Establishment Convention (1879), **28,** 461–462
U.K., Arbitration Agreement (1923), **2,** 359; **5,** 148
U.K. and France, Boundary Treaty (1763), **7,** 131

Spain—*continued*
U.S.A.—
—Agreement for settlement of Cuban claims (1871), **25,** 100–101
—Boundary Treaty (1795), **7,** 131
— —(1819), **2,** 96
—Peace Treaty of Paris (1898), **1,** 93–94; **5,** 354, 397; **17,** 43; **24,** 447, 448, 569; **26,** 553–555
—Treaty of Friendship and General Relations (1902), **22,** 461–462; **26,** 529–532
Venezuela, Extradition Treaty (1894), **19,** 378; **22,** 517–518
Spanish Civil War—
alien's military service in, effect on nationality, **11,** 182–183
Bank of Spain, claims against Loyalist Government, **9,** 12
blockade, establishment by insurgents, **9,** 79–81
Catalonia Government, confiscatory decrees, **8,** 191–193; **9,** 24
concurrent recognition of *de facto* and *de jure* governments, **9,** 275, 279
consular jurisdiction, disputes between ship's master and crew, **8,** 210–212
decrees of legitimate government, territory controlled by *de facto* government, **9,** 75, 227
enlistment in, French prohibition of, **8,** 278
—ambulance corps, **8,** 301–302
expropriation, industrial enterprises, **9,** 151
—ships, **9,** 176; **11,** 155–161
extradition, effect of change of government, **9,** 408
insurance, war risks clause, **16,** 362–372
jurisdictional immunities of Spanish Government, **8,** 247–248
—waiver of, **8,** 229–232
recognition—
—decrees of Loyalist Government, **9,** 12–16
—Nationalist Government as *de facto* government, **9,** 61
—Nationalist Government as *de jure* government, **9,** 73–74
Republican Government, nationalization of ships (1936), **11,** 155–161
requisitioning of ships, **8,** 189–191, 195–197, 200–204, 237–239; **9,** 151, 225, 273, 277, 280; **11,** 156–161
title to State property, **11,** 68–73
Special envoys, **1,** 294–298; **5,** 309–313, 316–317
" Special protégé ", status of, **4,** 311
Specialized Agencies of the U.N.: *see under* United Nations, *and* names of particular agencies

Specialty, principle of: *see under* Extradition
Speculative damages, **3,** 249
Spies, **1,** 235, 431, 432; **10,** 564–576; **13,** 281, 293, 294–295, 298–299; **15,** 423–424, 434, 435, 483–484, 497, 636, 640; **16,** 271–272, 406; **17,** 434; **30,** 69–75
captured after rejoining armed forces, **15,** 483–484
conditions of trial, **1,** 431, 432; **13,** 281, 293–295, 299
definition, **1,** 235; **15,** 423–424; **16,** 271, 405–406
espionage as lawful means of combat, **15,** 435; **16,** 271–272
occupied territory, in, **15,** 573–575
peacetime and wartime espionage, **16,** 271–272, 405–406
punishment of, **10,** 568–573; **15,** 435, 636, 640; **16,** 406; **17,** 434; **30,** 69–75
trial of, court-martial, **1,** 431
Spoliation of occupied territory: *see under* Belligerent occupation
"*Staatnotstand*", doctrine of, **5,** 271
Stare decisis, **1,** 376
State control over private claims: *see under* Claims, international
State enterprise, foreign, taxation of employees, **32,** 5–6
State loans: *see also* Bonds, government
colony, issued by, State as guarantor, **6,** 62–65
currency of payment, **5,** 468
force majeure, **5,** 470
France, jurisdiction of courts, **11,** 30–32
gold clause, **5,** 469, 470–471; **24,** 782–783, 825, 826–828; **29,** 4–11
interruption of service, **29,** 4–11
law governing, **5,** 468–469; **6,** 36–37
legal nature, **6,** 36–37; **11,** 30–32; **24,** 825
municipal law, matter of, **24,** 790, 830–833
war, effect on, **29,** 4, 8
State of war: *see* War, state of
State-owned foreign company, whether foreign "national", **18,** 20–22
State-owned property—
cession of territory, effect, **25,** 7–8
jurisdictional immunity of, **7,** 151–158; **9,** 239–243; **10,** 230–239
State-owned Ships, Brussels Convention on Immunity of (1926), **9,** 286, 291; **12,** 112–113; **34,** 85–86
State responsibility: *see also* Calvo clause; Claims, international; Concession agreements; Denial of justice; Exhaustion of local remedies; Expropriation; Nationality of claims; Nationalization

State responsibility—*continued*
absolute, **16,** 155–170
acceptance of obligation by debtor State, **22,** 348
administrator of enemy property, neglect or defraud, **21,** 141–146; **22,** 312–317: *see also* sequestrator of enemy property, negligence, *infra*
annulment of valid claims, **30,** 117
armed forces, acts of, **2,** 161, 174–175; **3,** 220–224, 225; **4,** 233–234; **5,** 147–149, 170–173, 392, 494; **7,** 258–259; **11,** 177–178; **30,** 116–117, 538–539
—abroad, **7,** 258–259; **12,** 173–175; **23,** 205–208, 214–216, 251–255
arrest, detention or deportation of aliens, **6,** 206–207
attributability: *see* imputability, *infra*
bank accounts, blocking, **30,** 208
bank deposits, confiscation, **26,** 297
basis, **2,** 158–159; **5,** 150; **6,** 229–231; **22,** 300, 322
belligerent occupation and, **22,** 982–987; **30,** 150, 538–539
bonds: *see also* debts, *infra*
—acceleration clause, effect, **26,** 258–262
—currency in which payable, relevance, **26,** 266–272
—date for conversion into claimant's currency, **26,** 272–274
—default on, **20,** 313–214, 434–437
—issued by former government, repudiation of, **30,** 151, 158–159, 160–161
breach of contract: *see* contracts, *infra*
breach of treaty, **1,** 170; **3,** 204–207; **4,** 205–208; **24,** 273–290
—later inconsistent treaty, **25,** 196–197, 199, 208–210
burden of proof, **6,** 203; **21,** 154–155; **22,** 349, 846–866, 972, 978; **23,** 678–679
business, prohibition on carrying on, **30,** 136–137
calculation of loss, **21,** 150–152, 163
—rate of exchange, **21,** 151–152, 153
Calvo clause: *q.v.*
causal connection, need for, **23,** 352–354
claims: *see* Claims, international
complicity, doctrine of, **3,** 218–219
compulsory liquidation, **30,** 119
concessions, with regard to: *see also* contracts, *infra, and* Concession agreements
—breach of contract, **23,** 83, 89–93, 341–342, 342–349
—eviction of concessionaires, **23,** 352–353

State responsibility—*continued*
concessions, with regard to—*contd.*
—interference with contracts, **23,** 296–298; **35,** 136–192
—later contract conflicting with rights under earlier, **27,** 117–229, *passim,* esp. 209–226
—nationalization, alleged to infringe, **20,** 314
—no derogation from grant, **27,** 212
—occupied territory, in, **23,** 780–783, 801–809, 810–849
—payments on moral grounds to employees, **23,** 298
—redemption of concession, **23,** 299–304
—revocation of contract, **23,** 298, 299–304
—seizure of concession property, **23,** 299–304
—suspension during war, **23,** 647–652
concurrent rights of compensation, **20,** 217–222
conditions of, **3,** 204–206
constitutional provisions and, **6,** 209–213
consuls, obligation to give special protection, **4,** 374–375; **5,** 318–319
contracts, breach of or interference with, **16,** 171–175; **23,** 306–348; **24,** 291–299; **26,** 310; **30,** 161–168, *see also* concessions, *supra*
contracts, frustration of, **30,** 141–143
contractual claims, **3,** 203–204; **4,** 203, 205–208
—U.S. practice, **26,** 268
cost of defending title to land, **23,** 349–352
creditors' rights, annulment of, **26,** 288–289
criminal gangs, acts of, **22,** 330–331
currency, confiscation of, **30,** 144–147
custodian of enemy property, sale of goods by, **22,** 307–311
customs authorities, negligence, **4,** 228–229
date of taking of property, **30,** 118–120, 156, 190, 213, 215
de facto governments, acts and omissions, **1,** 182–184; **2,** 176; **4,** 246–248
de jure governments, acts of, **4,** 203
debtor, nationalization of, **30,** 122–128, 140–143
debts, **3,** 208–211; **20,** 211–214; **21,** 292–293; **23,** 304–306; **29,** 4–20; **30,** 158–161
—annulment of, **30,** 128–133, 140–143, 153–156
—municipal loans, **29,** 15
—set-off, **6,** 234

State responsibility—*continued*
debts—*continued*
—settlement by creditors, effect of earlier unimplemented settlement, **29,** 11, 14–19
—settlement by creditors with consent of government, **29,** 4–11
—war, effect of, **29,** 4–20
—war-time puppet State, of, **23,** 591–596
decisions of municipal courts for, **1,** 171–172; **22,** 328–329; **25,** 210–211
denial of justice: *q.v.*
dependent territory, liability of protecting State, **2,** 163–164, 174; **28,** 79
detention " *incommunicado* ", **4,** 236–237
detention of neutral ships, **6,** 442–446
detention of foreign ships in war, **23,** 354–358
devaluation, **20,** 211–213; **21,** 150; **26,** 275–276, 278, 284–286, 290, 293, 302
—mortgages, effect on, **26,** 278
discrimination, as condition of, **7,** 493–494; **9,** 333; **22,** 303, 305, 626–628
—absence of, relevance, **11,** 177–178
discriminatory measures against aliens, **21,** 144–145; **26,** 311
—currency, with regard to, **26,** 285
—sale in contemplation of, **30,** 118–120
documents of title, confiscation of, **26,** 303–304
domestic jurisdiction, matters of, and, **2,** 362–363
drafts on nationalized banks, non-presentment, **26,** 304–306
error of judgment, **6,** 443
executive action or inaction, **1,** 171–179; **3,** 213–225; **4,** 223–239; **5,** 163–170, 172; **6,** 199–201, 203–209; **7,** 250–254, 481–482; **10,** 267–272; **23,** 349–358; **28,** 79
ex gratia payments and, **4,** 376–377; **6,** 214–215; **11,** 177–178
exhaustion of local remedies: *q.v.*
expropriation of alien property: *see* Expropriation
expulsion of aliens, for, **6,** 206
failure to bring to trial, **4,** 217–218
—prosecute, **2,** 161–162, 169; **4,** 225–226, 234; **5,** 161–162
federal States, responsibility for acts of member States, **3,** 203–204; **4,** 203; **5,** 145–149
fire damage, for, **23,** 352–353
firearms, indiscriminate use of, **4,** 223–224, 233–234
force majeure, plea of, **1,** 169, 418; **23,** 354n.

State responsibility—*continued*
forced sale, **30,** 118–119, 136–138, 179–180, 209, 212–213
foreclosure for unpaid tax, **26,** 282
foreign exchange controls and, **20,** 242–243; **21,** 149–150; **22,** 394–397; **26,** 301–302
fraud of administrator of enemy property, **21,** 141–146; **22,** 312–317: *see also* sequestrator of enemy property, negligence, *infra*
" free access to courts ", meaning, **23,** 306, 314, 319, 322–325, 332–333
hostile expeditions, **1,** 180–182
illegal taxes, **30,** 145, 146–147
imputability—
—bonds issued by municipalities, **26,** 255–256, 274
—bonds issued by private company, guaranteed by government, **26,** 257
—nationalized corporation, unauthorized acts of, **26,** 313–314. *See also* armed forces, acts of, *and* executive action or inaction, *supra*; individuals, acts of, *and* officials, acts of, *infra*
inadequate diplomatic protection, **4,** 225–226; **6,** 242–246
inadequate punishment of offenders, **7,** 246–249
indirect injury, **30,** 126, 127
individuals, acts of, **9,** 333; **22,** 330–331; **28,** 189, 193
insurance claims, confiscation of, **30,** 149. *See also* Claims, international, insurers, by
insurance contracts, annulment of, **30,** 151–153
insurgents and rioters, acts of, **4,** 239–245; **5,** 172–173; **7,** 259–261; **9,** 333–334
interest, liability for: *see* Interest, award of
interference with contracts, **16,** 171–175; **23,** 306–348; **24,** 291–299; **26,** 310; **30,** 161–168. *See also under* Concession agreements
interference with property, **2,** 170–171; **26,** 279–308; **30,** 118–157. *See also* Confiscatory measures; Concession agreements; Expropriation; Nationalization measures
—" effective compensation ", **30,** 133, 139–140
—" just compensation ", **26,** 357
international tribunal, acts of, responsibility of local State, **25,** 206
irregular apprehension, **7,** 250–251
irregular imprisonment, **7,** 477–478
joint, **22,** 982–987
" judicial measures ", meaning, **5,** 506
judicial sale, authorization of, **22,** 330

State responsibility—*continued*
judiciary, acts of, **1,** 171–172; **22,** 328–329; **25,** 210–211
—legal error, **25,** 47
—municipal decision absorbed by international decision, **25,** 211
labour riots, **30,** 145, 146–147
land reform measures, **26,** 280–281; **30,** 118–120
legal services, breach of contract for, **30,** 161–165
legislation, in respect of, **6,** 209–213; **7,** 255–257; **20,** 215–217; **24,** 796; **31,** 72
licence to do business, revocation, **26,** 309–310
limitations of sovereignty and, **6,** 197–198
looting, for, **4,** 174–175
maltreatment in prison, **4,** 236–237, 248–250
mandatory, of, tortious acts of local administration, **22,** 88–89
measure of damages: *see under* Damages
military operations, damage due to, **2,** 161, 168, 174–175; **3,** 225; **5,** 494; **30,** 116–117
Mixed Courts of Egypt, for, **6,** 197–198; **25,** 207
mortgaged property, taking of, **30,** 122–128
mortgages, **22,** 334–336
—cancellation of, **22,** 335
—compulsory, **22,** 333–334, 335, 336
—payment off, after taking, **22,** 336
—unpaid taxes, for, **22,** 335–336
national emergency, plea of, **6,** 444
nationality of claims: *q.v.*
nationalization: *q.v.*
negligence of officials, **22,** 301–307, 312–317, 317–329; **23,** 379–381
nuisance, for, **9,** 315–333
occupying forces, acts of, **30,** 538–539
officials, acts of, **1,** 170, 171, 172; **4,** 250–252; **7,** 244–247, 250–254, 481–482; **20,** 221–222; **22,** 301–330, *passim*, 840–843
officials, negligence of, **22,** 301–307, 312–317, 317–329; **23,** 379–381
pension rights, loss through nationalization, **26,** 287–288
prescription: *q.v.*
prohibition of employment of aliens, **26,** 311
prolonged detention, **4,** 226–227, 237–238; **5,** 159, 163–164
protection of interests of foreign nationals, **4,** 282–283
protectorates, responsibility of protecting Power, **2,** 163–164, 174; **28,** 79
proximate cause, **30,** 126, 127

State responsibility—*continued*
quasi-contractual obligations, **2,** 165–166
rebellion, damage suffered in, **2,** 174–175; **6,** 208
rent, loss of, through nationalization, **26,** 289–290
reparation for culpability, **30,** 222, 223. *See also* Damages
requisitions, for, **1,** 414–418; **5,** 151, 374; **22,** 336
—refusal to pay dues on requisitioned ships, **23,** 341–342: *see also* Requisitioning
restrictions on ownership, **26,** 283, 291–292; **30,** 120–122, 134–135
revocation of concessions, adequacy of compensation, **28,** 18, 34–36: *see also under* Concession agreements
revolution, damage suffered in, **4,** 239–245; **7,** 259–261
revolutionary forces, acts of, **5,** 173–174
revolutionary forces, contractual obligations of, **3,** 232–234
revolutionary government, acts of, **2,** 34–37; **3,** 232–234; **6,** 213–215; **20,** 217–222; **30,** 168–171
riot, damage suffered in, **2,** 172–173
rioters, acts of, **1,** 173–174; **2,** 159–160; **20,** 47–48, 217; **28,** 189, 193
sequestration of enemy property, for, **22,** 840–843
sequestrator of enemy property, negligence, **22,** 301–307, 312–317, 317–329
State from whose territory private property taken, claim by, **22,** 953–959, 966–972
tax liens, foreclosure for, **26,** 282
taxation of alien property, **26,** 312–313; **30,** 265–266, 295–297. *See also* Taxation
Treasury bills, currency, equivalent to, **26,** 286–287
treatment of goods in transit at outbreak of war, **22,** 626–630
unilateral declaration of State as creating, **22,** 505–506
unjust enrichment, **5,** 3, 501; **6,** 228–231; **21,** 150–152; **23,** 781; **24,** 296
use of territory, actions against neighbouring State, **31,** 27–28, 46–47
vicarious responsibility, **12,** 173–177
war, acts of, **5,** 494
war damage, **22,** 301–307
State servitudes: *see* Servitudes
State, subdivision of, continuity of, **9,** 89
State succession—
accrued claims of taxpayers, **4,** 86–87

State succession—*continued*
Act of State and, **23,** 103–105; **24,** 75
administration, in matters of, **4,** 92–95; **6,** 77–82; **21,** 75–79
administrative acts, **2,** 61–63
administrative debts, **5,** 64–67; **6,** 60–61; **26,** 92
advowsons, continuation of, **8,** 145
annexation, on, **5,** 61–63. *See also* conquest, *infra*
annuity under court order, **5,** 61
—under settlement *inter partes*, **21,** 49–51
assets in form of debts, **20,** 77–78
binding force of law of successor State, **7,** 104–105
cession of territory, applicable law: *see* Cession of territory
concessions, as to, **1,** 58–59; **2,** 57; **5,** 57–60; **7,** 84–87, 424–431; **22,** 113–122; **23,** 79–80, 81–93, 94–99, 99–101; **26,** 79–89
—abortive expenditure of predecessor State, **23,** 83, 89
—assignment by predecessor State of share of revenue, **23,** 94–99
—breach by predecessor State, **23,** 83, 89–93
—claim for operating costs, **23,** 99–101
—division of rights and obligations, **23,** 79–80
—subrogation, **23,** 668
—torts, duty to compensate for, **23,** 108
—treaty provision, effect, **23,** 79–80
conquest and, **16,** 62–63; **22,** 127–130; **31,** 89. *See also* annexation, *supra*
consuls, power of attorney of, effect on, **19,** 132–133
continuity of laws, **1,** 76–78; **2,** 86–87; **4,** 95–96; **5,** 71–72; **6,** 82–85; **8,** 143–150; **10,** 104–106; **11,** 49, 78–81; **13,** 43; **19,** 138–142; **20,** 82–89, 91–92; **23,** 112–113; **24,** 78–81, 83–85; **31,** 17
—uncollected tax in former dependent State, **26,** 100–102
contracts: *see also* concessions, *supra, and* leases, *infra*: **1,** 59; **2,** 57; **3,** 70, 72–77; **4,** 82–84, 85–86; **5,** 60, 61–63; **7,** 91, 95–97; **15,** 51; **19,** 117–131; **21,** 51–54; **22,** 113–122; **23,** 109–110; **24,** 60–67; **26,** 192–193; **27,** 30–31; **31,** 10–13
criminal law, **8,** 146–150; **15,** 72–75; **16,** 68–72
critical date under treaty, **23,** 108
currency of successor State, **7,** 104–105
—debts, whether payable in, **6,** 72–73; **24,** 73–74
Danzig, in, **5,** 66–68

State succession—*continued*
date, effective, of, **9,** 101
de facto and *de jure* governments, **17,** 183–186
debts: *see also* administrative debts, *supra, and* local debts *and* public debts, *infra*: **16,** 61–62; **18,** 40–42, 44–45; **19,** 116–117; **24,** 72, 604, 629
—claim for damages, **2,** 57–58, 63–65; **4,** 79–82
—need for recognition of successor State, **23,** 595–596
—new currency, effect, **6,** 72–73; **24,** 73–74
duty, advance payment of, and, **4,** 86–87
extradition, effect on—
—process of, **18,** 332–333
—treaties of, **8,** 349; **14,** 42–44; **17,** 15–20, 82–91; **20,** 364
federal States and unions of States, **4,** 79–82, 84–85; **5,** 350; **6,** 74–76
fiscal funds, to, **20,** 77–78
former mandated territory, Israel and, **15,** 41–44; **17,** 72–81
functional succession, **20,** 79–81
" general rules of international law ", **6,** 78–79, 81, 84
Germany, position after 1945...**19,** 24–34: *see also under* Germany *and* Germany, Federal Republic of
government bonds, **5,** 65–66
governments, in regard to: *see* Governments, succession of
international law rules, **6,** 78–79, 81, 84
international obligations, upon conquest, **31,** 89
Israel, Government of, and U.K. Government, **28,** 445
judges, contracts of service of, **26,** 97–98
judgments of courts of predecessor, **1,** 77–79; **2,** 87; **3,** 92–96; **4,** 95–96; **5,** 71; **7,** 105; **9,** 103; **13,** 19–20, 43; **15,** 58–59; **18,** 69–72, 78; **20,** 89–90, 93
jurisdiction of courts, **16,** 64–65; **18,** 77–78; **20,** 93; **21,** 458
land grants, **5,** 71; **9,** 102; **22,** 127–130; **23,** 109–110; **31,** 13–19
laws and judicial organization, as to, **17,** 95–109
leases by former government, **1,** 63–66; **23,** 109–110
local debts, **6,** 79, 82; **7,** 87–88; **31,** 79
merger—
—contractual obligations, **27,** 30–31; **31,** 10–13
—private rights, **27,** 32–35
military pay, **1,** 62–63; **24,** 72

State succession—*continued*
money paid in error to predecessor State, **3,** 70–71
nationality and. *See* Nationality, change of sovereignty, effect
oath of allegiance and, **16,** 63–64
obligations, to, **17,** 72–81; **18,** 45–47, 67–69; **23,** 107. *See also* debts, *supra*
obligation to pay liquidated sum, **24,** 67–68
officials, **1,** 73–75; **2,** 85–86; **3,** 87–91; **4,** 92–95; **5,** 70; **7,** 102–104, 509–510; **8,** 141–142; **17,** 92–94; **21,** 75–79
partial, **6,** 60–61
partition of territory, **6,** 77–82; **7,** 87–90
peace treaties and, **23,** 106–107
pending litigation, **1,** 89–91; **2,** 57, 60–61; **8,** 72–77; **26,** 99
pension rights, **1,** 66–68; **2,** 58–59, 65–66; **3,** 79–80; **5,** 66–68; **6,** 83–84; **7,** 433–434; **24,** 69
plebiscite and, **6,** 83–84
private rights, respect for, **1,** 68; **2,** 71–83; **3,** 81–84; **4,** 88–91, 551–553; **5,** 68; **6,** 66–73, 83–85; **7,** 91–101, 433–434, 486–487; **8,** 32, 125–126, 136–141; **9,** 102; **10,** 98–102; **11,** 76–77; **13,** 35–42; **14,** 36–40; **15,** 52–58; **16,** 62–63; **17,** 81–82; **19,** 132–137; **20,** 74–75, 81–82; **21,** 51–54, 63–66; **23,** 101–105, 109–111; **24,** 73–76; **26,** 82–83, 86; **31,** 13–19
public debt, **3,** 78–79; **4,** 443–445; **5,** 64–66; **6,** 62–65; **8,** 128–136; **11,** 78; **23,** 667; **24,** 69–73
public law claims, **26,** 77–78
public property and rights, **1,** 130–131; **2,** 54–57; **3,** 68–69; **4,** 73–79; **5,** 52–57, 68; **6,** 59–60, 84–85, 229; **7,** 90; **8,** 123–127; **9,** 94, 102; **11,** 74–76; **18,** 64–67; **20,** 63–78; **22,** 103–113; **23,** 78; **25,** 2–25
railways and, **7,** 424–431, 484–489; **21,** 49–51
rent, arrears of, **1,** 61–62
reparations under peace treaty and, **20,** 631
requisitioned property, **22,** 123–127
restitution obligations of Reich, Federal Republic and, **28,** 7
set-off of claims, **18,** 40–42
tax, collection of, **4,** 78–79
tax exemption, right to, **21,** 51–54; **26,** 79–87
tax legislation, **16,** 66–67, 71
title to land, **23,** 110–111
torts, liability for, **1,** 63–64; **2,** 66–70; **3,** 80–81; **7,** 89–90; **13,** 6–9; **14,** 41; **20,** 79–81; **21,** 55–63; **23,** 92–93, 106–108; **26,** 89–97

State succession—*continued*
trading with the enemy legislation and, **17,** 113–115
treaties and, **1,** 68–73; **2,** 83–84; **3,** 70–77, 84–87; **4,** 84–85, 91–92; **5,** 69, 133–134; **6,** 74–76; **8,** 141, 349; **10,** 103; **14,** 42–44; **17,** 15–20, 82–91; **20,** 82, 364; **21,** 66–75; **22,** 141–146; **23,** 112; **24,** 52, 593; **27,** 35–44; **31,** 20–22, 60; **33,** 420, 421, 422; **34,** 27–36
treaties of protectorate, **11,** 77–78
unincorporated territory, **11,** 78–81
—rights of citizens of, **11,** 49–50
unions of States, **4,** 79–82
State territory: *see* Territory
State tourist agency, jurisdictional immunity, **8,** 227
State trading, sovereignty and, **5,** 18–21, 309–313. *See also* Public ships *and* Trade Delegations of U.S.S.R.
Stateless persons—
assimilation to citizens, **11,** 186
distinguished from "*ressortissants*", **5,** 215
expulsion of, **5,** 268; **6,** 287–289; **8,** 304–311, 313; **9,** 392; **33,** 293–296
extradition of, **20,** 367–369
poor persons' facilities, grant of, **4,** 321–322; **6,** 263–264; **8,** 311–312, 314
unemployment benefit, **4,** 321–322
Statelessness, **1,** 224–226; **2,** 258–259; **3,** 274–275, 282; **4,** 321–323; **5,** 243, 247–248; **6,** 257–258, 263–264; **8,** 304–314; **9,** 361–363; **10,** 290; **14,** 121–123; **15,** 208–209, 237, 255–257, 260, 265–268; **16,** 3–4, 220–222, 225; **21,** 197, 198–199, 303–304; **22,** 391–393, 419–421, 422–424; **24,** 465–472; **26,** 416, 436, 441; **30,** 41; **34,** 111
cause, **24,** 472–473
enemy character and, **1,** 404–405; **22,** 921–922
extradition and, **20,** 367–369
illegitimate children, **24,** 473–475
jurisdiction of court to determine, **28,** 80
married women, **11,** 182–183
ships, **9,** 299
U.N. Convention, naturalized persons expatriated, **35,** 203
States: *see also* Annexation; Continuity of States; Federal States; Foreign States; Merger of States; Recognition of States; Sovereignty; State succession; Territorial sovereignty
agents, acting as, **21,** 11–12
beginning of existence of, **1,** 11–21; **2,** 9–11; **3,** 13–17; **4,** 25–26; **5,** 11–16; **6,** 20; **7,** 19; **15,** 7; **17,** 23; **18,** 17–20; **23,** 101–105, 787–789

States—*continued*
changes in condition of, **6,** 74–76
commercial activities, character of, **3,** 172–179; **6,** 172–173; **7,** 182–183. *See also* Foreign States, immunity from jurisdiction, *and* Public ships
composite, **1,** 38, 39; **4,** 39–43; **15,** 28–38
contractual obligations, binding nature of, **8,** 26–29; **27,** 192
continuity of: *q.v.*
dependent, **15,** 38–44; **17,** 42–47. *See also* Colonies; Mandated territories; Protectorates; Trust territories
dignity of, **8,** 23–25; **9,** 8–12; **10,** 9; **11,** 13; **12,** 3; **18,** 22–23; **21,** 10–11; **22,** 238; **24,** 200
dissolution into two separate States, **9,** 32
economic unions, **17,** 36–37; **18,** 396–397; **28,** 511–513; **31,** 425–426. *See also* unions, *infra, and* Customs unions
enemy—
—action commenced by, before outbreak of war, **9,** 93
—jurisdictional immunity, **10,** 576–581
—right to sue, **12,** 337–340
equality of, **1,** 24, 332; **3,** 42; **9,** 8–12; **15,** 26; **22,** 448; **24,** 125–126
establishment of, **1,** 11–21, 45; **2,** 9–11; **5,** 11–16; **23,** 101–105
extinction of, **1,** 35–38, 130–132; **2,** 18–19; **4,** 166–167; **14,** 18–19, 176; **15,** 292–293; **17,** 357–359; **18,** 17–20, 49–50, 288–289
federal: *q.v.*
heads of: *q.v.*
independence of, jurisdictional immunities and, **6,** 21–32; **7,** 174–175
jurisdictional immunities of: *see* Foreign States, immunity from jurisdiction
neutralization of, **20,** 51–52
notion of, in statute, **6,** 19–20
recognition of: *q.v.*
requirements of Statehood, **32,** 173
right to sue, **4,** 170–171; **9,** 89; **13,** 9–12; **14,** 6–7; **21,** 12
sovereignty and independence, **1,** 21–23; **2,** 11–15; **3,** 17–23; **4,** 27–33; **5,** 16–21; **7,** 19–22; **10,** 6–9; **12,** 3–4; **13,** 20–21; **15,** 7–9; **16,** 12–14; **17,** 23–27; **18,** 20–23; **20,** 3–6; **21,** 10–16. *See also* Sovereignty
succession of: *see* State succession
unions of, **1,** 38–39; **7,** 29–30; **12,** 11; **15,** 28–37; **17,** 36–37; **22,** 60–61; **23,** 92. *See also* economic unions, *supra*

States—*continued*
unrecognized, acts of judicial authorities, **1**, 28–30
vassal, **22**, 64–76
States and governments, distinction, Korea, **32**, 186
States of the U.S.A.—
continental shelf, rights to, vis-à-vis Federal Government, **31**, 141–205, *passim*
seaward boundaries of, **31**, 149–155
sovereign equality, territory and, **31**, 146, 183
Stationing of troops, distinguished from occupation, **12**, 150–152, 154–164
Status, laws of—
belligerent occupation, effect, **26**, 704
meaning of, **26**, 673
Status of forces agreements: *see under* Foreign armed forces
Statutes: *see also* Municipal law—
construction of—
—against extraterritorial effect, **28**, 124–125, 132, 134–135
—consistent with treaty, **24**, 588–590; **31**, 405–408; **33**, 6, 10–11, 12, *see also* Treaties, municipal law and
—English law, **26**, 381–397
—extension to new things, **27**, 60–61
—international law, having regard to, **12**, 209–221; **34**, 62
—no change in law, **34**, 95
—Parliamentary debates and, **2**, 262–263
—presumption of territorial scope, **35**, 107
—treaties, by reference to, **12**, 273–276
criminal, territorial scope, **33**, 164–168, 169–173
Statutes of limitation—
applicability before international tribunals, **5**, 196–197
cession, effect, **4**, 116
change of sovereignty, effect, **4**, 116–117
deportation of aliens and, **6**, 287–290
extradition proceedings, in, **2**, 279; **5**, 286; **6**, 294, 306–307, 313–314; **7**, 354–355; **8**, 350, 382–383; **9**, 395–398
foreign armed forces and—
—official acts, **20**, 184–186
—unofficial acts, **19**, 220–221
foreign States, application to, **9**, 184–190; **12**, 17–22; **15**, 130–131
national, relevance for international claims, **4**, 264–265; **5**, 196–197; **22**, 337
non-recognition of governments, effect, **10**, 68–70
prescription and, **4**, 264–265; **5**, 196–197
Statutes of limitation—*continued*
recognition of governments, retroactive effect, **12**, 19–21
termination of war and, **20**, 618–622
Versailles, Treaty of (Art. 300), **2**, 26, 321
war, effect on, **2**, 413–414; **3**, 451–452; **5**, 484–485; **6**, 437–438; **9**, 502–503; **11**, 247–249, 263–264, 268–270; **18**, 474, 477–492; **19**, 559–570; **22**, 909–911
Sterilization of aliens, German law, **8**, 322–323, 341
Stockholders, enemy, interest in non-enemy corporation, **3**, 447–448
"Stockholders' pool", indirect claims based on, **30**, 171–172
Straits, **16**, 159–165; **33**, 148–154
"Stress of weather", meaning, **6**, 154–156
Subcarpathian Russia, establishment of Czechoslovak State, **4**, 26. *See also under* Czechoslovakia
Subjects abroad, jurisdiction over: *see* Jurisdiction, nationals abroad, over
Subjects of international law, **4**, 9; **8**, 2–7, 280–281; **13**, 221–222, 264, 265, 279; **14**, 268–269; **15**, 419–421; **16**, 318, 321–322, 330, 569–570; **17**, 408; **18**, 1–3; **21**, 3–8; **22**, 1–5; **24**, 1–4; **26**, 1–3, 667–668; **27**, 1–13; **28**, 2–6; **32**, 627, 636–638, 641. *See also* Individual in international law; International organization
Subjects of laws of war, **13**, 250–257, 264, 265; **14**, 205–207
civilians as authors of war crimes, **13**, 250–254
responsibility of military commander for acts of subordinates, **14**, 205–207, 292
Subjugation of territory, **19**, 144
requirements for title by, **26**, 700–701
Submarine, attempted theft of, **11**, 152–153
Submarine cables, **8**, 173–174
destruction of, **2**, 415–419
Submarine warfare—
armed merchant ships, against, **13**, 219
neutral merchant ships under convoy of enemy warships, **4**, 568–569
shipwrecked survivors, duty towards, **13**, 220, 246–247, 248–250
Treaty of Washington (1922), **14**, 198
unrestricted, **13**, 218–220
Subpoena of witnesses—
German law, **6**, 271–272
inadmissibility of, in international arbitration, **6**, 425–426
service abroad, **6**, 177–179

Substantive law, distinguished from adjective law, **6,** 304–305
Subversion, duty of State to prevent incursion into foreign State, **31,** 46
Succession of governments: *see* Governments, succession of
Succession of States: *see* State succession
Sudan—
Egypt, Arrangement *re* Judicial Assistance (1902), **23,** 472–477
status of, **4,** 57
Sudditanza, Italian nationality law, **8,** 283
Sudeten Germans, nationality of, **18,** 250–251, 257–258; **20,** 32–33
Suez Canal—
belligerent rights in, **17,** 135, 445–447; **28,** 653; **31,** 509–520
Constantinople Convention on (1888), **2,** 101; **17,** 441, 444–447; **24,** 993; **31,** 510, 512, 515–516
defence of, Egypt and, **17,** 445–447; **24,** 993; **28,** 653
hostilities, 1956, whether war, **26,** 638–651; **32,** 552–556
passage of munitions in war in which Egypt neutral, **4,** 27–28
Suez Canal Company—
dual status of, **6,** 268
duration of concession, relation to existence of company, **28,** 180
Indemnity Agreement with United Arab Republic (1958), **28,** 181–182, 185–187
—rights of shareholders under, **28,** 176–187
nationalization of—
—Constantinople Convention (1888) and, **28,** 180
—denial of validity by France, **28,** 180–181
—effect on legal personality, **28,** 177–185
renunciation of concession, **28,** 181–182
termination of concession, **28,** 177, 180
Viceroy of Egypt, contract with (1866), **5,** 137
Suez hostilities, whether "war", **26,** 638–651; **32,** 552–556
Sulu Islands, Exchange of Notes (1930), U.K. and U.S.A., **23,** 107
Sumatra, Japanese occupation of, **23,** 810–849
Superficies solo cedit, **4,** 83
Superior, Lake, **11,** 124
Superior orders: *see under* War crimes
Suppression of Counterfeiting Currency, Convention for (1929), **18,** 382
Suretyship, contract of, trading with the enemy, **10,** 514–529
Surrender: *see* Capitulations, military
Surrender, unconditional, effect on state of war, **12,** 415–420
Suzerainty, **2,** 69–70; **20,** 117, 133–134
taxation in dependent State, **11,** 47–48
Sweden—
breadth of maritime belt, **3,** 122–123
Bulgaria, Commercial Treaty (1942), **21,** 265–272
Children, Law for Protection of, 1924...**25,** 243, 247, 248, 252–253, 258–259, 260, 264, 275, 279, 280–281, 286, 295, 297–298, 301, 302, 304, 306, 310–311
Denmark, Convention on Fishing Rights (1899), **6,** 123
Denmark and Norway, Convention on Execution of Judgments (1948), **20,** 290
Distraint, Law of, **24,** 354
Extradition Law (1913), **18,** 340
Germany, Agreement on German property in Sweden (1956), **25,** 48
Great Britain, Treaties of Peace and Commerce (1654 and 1661), **20,** 554; **23,** 313, 321, 322
international payment obligations, Laws concerning (1927 and 1934), **21,** 266, 268, 271
Marriage Law (1904), **22,** 419
nationality law, **9,** 352; **22,** 419–421
Parents' Law, **24,** 336
prosecution of nationals for crimes abroad, **32,** 143
protective upbringing of children, **25,** 249, 252–253, 260
recognition of Estonian nationalization decrees, **12,** 61–62
recognition of Soviet Government, **1,** 54–56
Swedish State Railways, exemption from jurisdiction, **2,** 121–122
traffic law, extraterritorial application, **32,** 140–147
U.S.A.—
—Consular Convention (1910), **6,** 399; **9,** 487; **11,** 120, 123
—Income Tax Convention (1940), **24,** 637
—Naturalization Convention (1869), **9,** 352
—Treaty of Amity and Commerce (1783), **6,** 372–378; **11,** 220
Sweden–Norway—
Denmark, Commercial Treaty (1826), **6,** 103
France—
—Arbitration Convention (1904), **24,** 787
—Treaty of Commerce and Navigation (1881), **11,** 229

Switzerland—
Aliens, Law on Establishment, **20,** 301–302
Austria-Hungary, Extradition Treaty (1896), **20,** 364; **24,** 497
Baden, Consular Treaty (1856), **22,** 141–146
Bank Law, secrecy of records, **26,** 124; **27,** 478
bankruptcy, federal law, **5,** 123
Belgium—
—Extradition Treaty, **20,** 367–368
—Treaty of Establishment (1887), **11,** 11
Cantons of Thurgau and St. Gallen, border between, **4,** 420–423
Congress of Vienna, accession to settlement of, **5,** 461–464
Constitution, **18,** 293; **19,** 31; **21,** 265; **24,** 543, 544
consuls, jurisdiction over, **6,** 337
courts, competence in political matters, **6,** 349–350
Criminal Code (crime committed by national abroad), **31,** 267–268
Criminal Code (transmission of economic secrets), **26,** 124; **27,** 478
Czechoslovakia—
—Commercial Agreement (1953), **24,** 47
—Compensation Agreement (1949), **22,** 424–427
—Judicial Assistance, Agreement on (1926), **22,** 426
Extradition Law of 1892...**5,** 274; **6,** 307–308; **18,** 341, 345; **20,** 364, 369; **22,** 516–517; **24,** 497
Federal Council, arbitration between Colombia and Venezuela, **1,** 84–89
France—
—Arbitral Agreement (1924), **5,** 459–463
—Convention on Judicial Competence (1869), **1,** 122; **5,** 364, 404; **6,** 350; **8,** 421; **18,** 393; **19,** 338; **21,** 211; **27,** 259–260
—Establishment Treaty (1882), **5,** 360, 361, 362n.; **6,** 394; **8,** 327, 424–425; **16,** 259n.; **17,** 315; **21,** 284; **23,** 376–377; **25,** 319
—Extradition Treaty (1869), **19,** 365; **22,** 516; **24,** 497; **34,** 144, 145, 147
German property in, Agreements (1952 and 1953), **22,** 638–642; **24,** 543–545, 546; **32,** 18
—provisional agreement as to blocking of, **27,** 476
—Swiss Compensation Office, functions, **27,** 476
—Washington Agreement (1946), **20,** 616; **27,** 477–478, 492, 497, 499, 501, 503, 528, 556

Switzerland—*continued*
German railway establishment, Basle, competence of German courts, **4,** 136–138
Germany—
—Arbitration Treaty (1921), **24,** 814
—Clearing Conventions, **9,** 461
—Convention, Recognition and Enforcement of Judgments (1929), **9,** 459–460
—Extradition Treaty (1874), **1,** 268, 280; **5,** 274; **7,** 352–353, 369–371; **19,** 34, 380; **24,** 493–495; **34,** 132–134
—Gold Mortgage Agreement (1920), **5,** 378–380; **6,** 386–387
Greece, Convention, Establishment and Judicial Protection (1927), **21,** 305–307
Hungary, Commercial Agreement (1950), **23,** 197
Iran, Establishment Convention (1934), **19,** 514–549, *passim*
Italy—
—Conciliation Treaty (1924), **25,** 313–315, 321
—Convention, Recognition and Enforcement of Judgments (1933), **21,** 264–265
—Establishment and Consular Convention (1868), **25,** 313–314, 316–317, 320
—Extradition Treaty (1868), **1,** 261, 273–274; **4,** 343–345; **6,** 307–308; **9,** 402; **18,** 345; **19,** 370, 375; **34,** 135, 136, 137
—Fisheries Treaty (1912), **9,** 122
—Treaty of Commerce and Establishment (1868), **4,** 345
Judiciary, Organization of, Laws on, **23,** 196; **28,** 563, 566
jurisdictional acts of foreign States in, **10,** 6–9
League of Nations, Agreement on Privileges and Immunities (1926), **22,** 537, 547, 548
League of Nations, diplomatic immunities of representatives, **3,** 325–326
nationality law, **7,** 287–289, 290–294; **9,** 348
Nationality Laws, 1947 and 1952, **21,** 192; **22,** 382, 428; **27,** 237
Nationality Law, 1953...**24,** 473–475
nationality law, marriage to alien, **32,** 192–194
neutralization of, **20,** 51–52
procedure, civil appeals, **29,** 301
property restitution, law of, **15,** 467–470
recognition of Soviet Government, **4,** 62–64
Rhine, navigation of, **15,** 69–70

Switzerland—*continued*
Roumania—
—Arbitration Treaty (1926), **16,** 281–282
—Commercial Agreement (1951), **23,** 197
Sardinia, Treaty, Customs Zones (1816), **5,** 462
Serbia, Extradition Treaty (1897), **19,** 371–372
Spain, Establishment Convention (1879), **28,** 461–462
Swiss Tug Navigation Company, position of, on Rhine, **4,** 124–125
Versailles, Treaty of, and, **3,** 351; **5,** 462–465
U.K.—
—Extradition Treaty (1880), **1,** 270–271
—Treaty of Commerce and Establishment (1855), **6,** 242, 245
United Nations, Agreement concerning properties in Geneva (1946), **21,** 341
U.S.A.—
—Convention on Military Obligations of Dual Nationals (1937), **20,** 256–257
—Double Taxation Convention (1951), **27,** 291–293; **34,** 199–201; **35,** 278–282
—Treaty of Arbitration and Conciliation (1931), **22,** 197; **27,** 480–482, 489, 503
—Treaty of Friendship, Commerce and Extradition (1850), **5,** 402; **7,** 307–309; **16,** 245; **21,** 178; **26,** 133
U.S.S.R., Agreement on Russian trade delegation (1948), **23,** 197
Syria—
capitulations in, **4,** 192–193; **7,** 395–396
Christian subjects in, position of, **4,** 95–96
crimes committed in, law governing, **5,** 32
extradition to, **8,** 382
French mandate over, **4,** 95–96; **5,** 32; **8,** 110
—evolution of protectorate over Syrians, **4,** 256–257
High Commissioner, finality of acts of, **5,** 30–31
—position of, **4,** 55
Israel, General Armistice Agreement with (1949), **18,** 164, 167, 168
military requisition, for temporary occupation, **11,** 54
Syria and Lebanon—
decisions of French High Commissioner, juridical nature, **11,** 51–52
recognition of mandates over, **4,** 48–49
treaties on behalf of, **4,** 52–53

T

Tacit ratification, acts of officials, State responsibility, **1,** 170
Tacit renewal of treaties, **1,** 68–69
Tacna, Province of, provisional cession, **2,** 241
Tacna-Arica—
occupation of, law applicable, **6,** 110–111
plebiscite in, **3,** 112
"Taking" of property—
absorption of property into "farmers' co-operatives", **26,** 281
devaluation of currency, **20,** 211–213; **26,** 275–276, 278, 293, 302; **30,** 146–147
nationalization of debtor companies, **26,** 306–308; **30,** 140–143
prohibition of disposition of property, **26,** 283, 291–292; **30,** 120–122, 134–135
prohibition of enforcement of rights to goods, **26,** 304
prohibition of enjoyment of property, **26,** 291–292
prohibition of transfer of currency, **26,** 293, 295, 302, 305–306
Taganak, Island of: *see* Sulu Islands
Tanganyika—
customary religious laws, jurisdiction as to, **22,** 81–86
Trusteeship Agreement (1946), **22,** 81–86
Trusteeship Council and, **22,** 685
Tangier—
abolition of international régime, **28,** 197
capitulations, aliens, submission to local law, **26,** 234–236
Diplomatic Corps, supervisory functions, power of Sultan over aliens, **19,** 263, 295
International Tribunal, **21,** 136–140
status of, **9,** 7, 52–53, 56, 59; **15,** 328
Tangier Zone, Paris Conventions (1923 and 1945), **19,** 284, 301; **21,** 136, 137, 138
Tardieu-Jaspar Agreement, Belgium and France, German reparation payments (1930), **8,** 479
Tariffs and Trade, General Agreement on (GATT): *see* General Agreement on Tariffs and Trade
Tax liens, on foreign State property, **35,** 129–130
Taxation: *see also* Double Taxation; Foreign revenue laws; Income tax; Rates
aliens, of, **2,** 148, 263–264; **4,** 151–152, 332–333, 335–336; **6,** 19–20, 135–136, 280–281; **8,** 336–337; **9,** 380; **26,** 312–313

Taxation—*continued*
aliens, of—*continued*
—enforceability in home State, **2**, 263–264
—estates of, **12**, 273–276
—exemption from, **1**, 333–334; **5**, 255; **15**, 3–4; **18**, 280–281; **20**, 263–264; **21**, 280–281; **25**, 320
—non-discrimination, relevance, **26**, 312–313
claim to social security contribution, **33**, 21–26
confiscatory, European Convention on Human Rights, Protocol, **30**, 253–268, 295, 296
dependent State, in, **11**, 47–48
diplomatic exemptions, **2**, 301; **4**, 367–368; **5**, 300; **6**, 331; **10**, 196–198, 337–352, 355–364
residence of envoy, **6**, 331; **10**, 337–352
double: *see* Double taxation
exemption of corporations, **18**, 280–281; **20**, 263–264; **21**, 280–281
extraterritorial effect, **5**, 101–102; **13**, 59–64
foreign armed forces, immunity, **16**, 145–146
" foreign country ", tax paid to, credit, **6**, 19–20
foreign-registered aircraft, tax on, **32**, 90–91, 95–100
foreign States, exemption from, **10**, 196–198; **17**, 153–155; **23**, 217–233; **24**, 231–247; **26**, 165–178
—return of tax paid on immune property, **26**, 171–172, 176–177
—war and, **21**, 432–443
foreign States, liability to, **10**, 38–47
frontier estates, of, **12**, 59–60
illegal, State responsibility, **30**, 145, 146–147
import tax, compatibility with customs union, **28**, 511–513
income of alien earned outside State, **27**, 103–107
income tax, exemption of consuls, **11**, 207–211
international officials' salaries, exemption, **31**, 393–395
mandated territories, in, **11**, 52–53
nationals abroad, **2**, 147–148; **31**, 273–274
occupying forces, immunity, **12**, 443–444
occupying power, levied on orders of, **12**, 452–453
" presence in foreign country ", meaning, **31**, 129–131
private rights and, **6**, 69–70
reciprocal exemption and " foreign country ", **23**, 29–35
residence of corporations, **27**, 103–107

Taxation—*continued*
sovereign right to protect revenue laws from abuse, **33**, 11
sovereignty, attribute of, **28**, 582; **30**, 265
State responsibility and, **26**, 312–313; **30**, 265–266, 295–297
State succession and, **1**, 91–93; **4**, 78–79
territorial waters, in, **9**, 123–126
treaty, compatibility with **11**, 77–78
treaty restrictions on right of, **28**, 582
war taxation, aliens and, **4**, 333
Telecommunications Convention, Madrid (1932), **5**, 417; **10**, 419–423
Telecommunications Convention (Atlantic City, 1947) and Regulations (1949), **22**, 710, 711, 712; **28**, 473–476
Telegrams—
exchange of, recognition of government by, **7**, 79–80
international telegraphic service, immunity of private companies, **6**, 413
requirement of secrecy in transmission, **5**, 416–417
Telegraphic Convention of St. Petersburg (1875), **5**, 416–417; **6**, 413; **7**, 471–472
Terra nullius, **7**, 109–111
Territorial asylum: *see* Asylum, territorial
Territorial disputes, **7**, 115–135
absence of conclusive evidence, **7**, 120–121
arbitration, discretion to grant territorial compensation, **30**, 475, 487–488
boundary commission, effect of award of, **11**, 95–99
burden of proof, **33**, 55
critical date, **33**, 55, 84
decisions *ex aequo et bono*, **7**, 121–127
effective possession, **7**, 119–120
evidence, **7**, 119–121
—maps, **4**, 487–488; **7**, 122–123, 125, 126; **27**, 75, 77, 90, 95
—maps, material error, **33**, 43–148 *passim*
Latin America, *uti possidetis* principle, **1**, 84–89; **7**, 115–127; **27**, 86, 96; **30**, 477, 483, 487, 488
restitution of objects, claim for, **33**, 74–75
topographical factors, relevance, **33**, 85, 97
Territorial integrity, respect for, **5**, 8
Territorial sovereignty: *see also* Annexation; Cession of territory; Leases, international; Prescription; Servitudes; Territorial disputes
abuse of, **31**, 120–121
accretion, doctrine of, **2**, 98; **11**, 100

Territorial sovereignty—*continued*
acquisition, **1,** 84–89; **2,** 93–94; **3,** 105; **4,** 108–113; **6,** 95–108; **12,** 49–54; **13,** 44–47; **14,** 45–49; **15,** 60–68; **16,** 73; **17,** 118; **18,** 79–80; **22,** 100–102; **23,** 123, 664–668; **27,** 77–79, 91–93, 95–96. *See also* Annexation; Cession of territory
—acquiescence, **27,** 77, 92–93. *See also* prescription, *infra*
—Act of State, as, **1,** 60; **22,** 132, 139; **24,** 75; **27,** 31, 33; **31,** 12
—changes in international law, effect, **4,** 3–5
—conquest, by, **6,** 99–100; **12,** 54; **15,** 60–61, 63; **19,** 44; **31,** 89. *See also* Annexation
—corporations by, **4,** 103, 108–110
—dependent States, by, **26,** 104–107
—discovery, by, **4,** 103–106, 108–111; **6,** 105–107
—Dutch East India Company, by, **4,** 103, 108–110
—force, by, **12,** 39–43
—independence, upon, **31,** 89, 162, 178
—individuals, by, **12,** 49–54
—no man's land, property rights in, **7,** 109–111
—non-sovereign State, by, **26,** 104–107
—notification, duty of, **4,** 115; **6,** 108
—occupation, by, **6,** 95–97; **7,** 109–111
—*pendente bello*, **26,** 702–703
—prescription, by, **4,** 103, 115; **9,** 112; **31,** 84, 192; **33,** 68. *See also* acquiescence, *supra*
—protest, **20,** 110, 115, 142–143
—remote regions, **33,** 92–93, 111–113
—subjugation, **26,** 700–701
—territorial waters included, **32,** 84
—treaties as evidence of sovereignty, **6,** 100–101
changes of, nationality and, **1,** 91–94, 199–202, 243; **2,** 224–242; **3,** 108–109, 115–116, 263–268; **4,** 293–294, 304–307, 308–312; **6,** 267; **7,** 112; **9,** 339–340; **10,** 281–284; **16,** 208–215; **18,** 257–262; **19,** 318–326, 329; **20,** 145–148, 250–251; **21,** 175–178; **22,** 428–429, 430–432; **23,** 34, 364–369; **24,** 431–433; **25,** 513–514; **27,** 3; **32,** 170–186, 339–341
de facto exercise of, **5,** 11–15
enclaves, right of passage for access, **31,** 23–121 *passim*
—discretion of territorial State, **31,** 26, 36, 37, 55, 59–60
—immunity of passengers, **31,** 45, 49 75, 85

Territorial sovereignty—*continued*
enclaves, right of passage for access —*continued*
—refusal of passage, circumstances justifying, **31,** 57–58
equality of different sovereignties, **31,** 69
Executive, statement of, as to, **15,** 29–31
" His Majesty's dominions ", meaning, **27,** 45–47
imperium distinguished from *dominium*, **28,** 376
landlocked seas and, **20,** 167–169
loss of, **6,** 99–100, 108; **16,** 73–77; **17,** 118; **18,** 81–84. *See also* renunciation of, *infra*
nature of, **1,** 83–84; **2,** 93; **3,** 105; **4,** 103–107; **5,** 75–76; **23,** 116–123; **31,** 98, 104, 107; **34,** 37–41
neighbouring, mutual respect, duty of, **31,** 59, 67, 70, 116–117
ownership of land by foreign State, **25,** 10
recognition of, **9,** 84–93; **31,** 117–118, 162. *See also* States, recognition of
—Executive, function of, **31,** 131
—tacit, **31,** 51, 59, 68–69, 91–92, 98, 117
renunciation of, **3,** 34–35; **6,** 100, 108; **17,** 101–106; **18,** 77–78; **32,** 173, 176, 179, 182; **33,** 79–80, 84. *See also* loss of, *supra*
—cession, contrasted, **3,** 34–35
rivers, inter-state, **24,** 101–142
uti possidetis principle, **1,** 84–89; **7,** 115–127; **27,** 86, 96; **30,** 477, 483, 487, 488
violation of, **10,** 6–9; **21,** 80–81
Territorial waters: *see also* Bays; Ports
baseline, **3,** 122–123; **4,** 133–134; **6,** 123–126; **7,** 136–137; **8,** 169–170; **9,** 130–140, 300–304; **18,** 86–144 *passim*
belligerent rights, exercise in, **31,** 518
breadth, **1,** 98–102; **3,** 122–124; **4,** 133–134; **6,** 123–128; **7,** 136–137, 139; **8,** 169–172; **9,** 127–128; **28,** 172–174; **30,** 528–529; **31,** 129–131; **33,** 151–154
—Alabama, **26,** 118–121
—extension, for certain purposes, **5,** 141; **6,** 3–7, 158–159
—Florida, **8,** 171–172
—nine-mile limit, **8,** 171–172
—Norwegian claims, **1,** 114
—three leagues, Spanish practice, **31,** 155–156
—three leagues, validity, **31,** 167, 201–203
—three mile rule, **31,** 130 n, 203

Territorial waters—*continued*
breadth—*continued*
—two leagues, Spanish claim, **31,** 200–201
broadcasting from outside, prosecution for, **31,** 274–275
channel more than marine league from mainland, **33,** 148–154
claim to offshore islands, effect, **26,** 118–121
collisions in: *see under* Collisions at sea
concept of, **35,** 76–78, 82
—historical origin, **31,** 181
continental shelf and, **17,** 126–133; **18,** 144–164
crimes committed in, **9,** 126, 264, 297; **20,** 171–172; **32,** 117–119
customs territory, as, **1,** 98
definition, need for statute, **9,** 126, 132
entry in distress, effect on jurisdiction, **7,** 208; **9,** 164–166. *See also under* Ports
fishing rights, **1,** 176–177; **6,** 123–126, 154–156; **14,** 61–64; **20,** 166–167; **23,** 127
France, of, **9,** 123–126
Geneva Convention on Territorial Sea (1958), **28,** 171–174; **31,** 134; **35,** 84–86, 88
hovering laws: *q.v.*
" importation ", meaning, **24,** 142–146; **27,** 98–102
India, six miles, **31,** 244
innocent passage, **9,** 164–166; **16,** 160–162; **21,** 110; **31,** 132–137
Institute of International Law, Draft Rules (1928), **18,** 109
jurisdiction in, **3,** 124–126; **5,** 91–92, 141; **6,** 154–157, 175–176, 179–180; **7,** 137–139, 209–212; **9,** 123, 126, 140; **13,** 51–58; **14,** 84–90; **20,** 154–155, 171–172; **23,** 154–159; **31,** 132–137, 241–247; **32,** 83–89, 117–119; **35,** 71. *See also* Jurisdiction, criminal, foreign ships in port
—involuntary entry, effect, **2,** 111–112; **5,** 129–131; **6,** 154–156; **7,** 208; **9,** 164–166; **23,** 151–153
—nature of, **9,** 123–126
—protective, outside territorial waters, **9,** 300; **11,** 130–135. *See also* Hovering laws
—tort on foreign ship, **28,** 108–114. *See also* Jurisdiction, ports, in
legal principles, **18,** 108–110
limits of, chank fisheries, **20,** 167–169
meaning, **23,** 155–159
minefield in, knowledge of littoral State, **16,** 157–158
minesweeping in, by foreign ships, **16,** 165–167

Territorial waters—*continued*
national waters and, **5,** 91–92; **9,** 164
nature of, **1,** 112; **3,** 122; **6,** 121; **18,** 150–152
piracy, jurisdiction in, **1,** 164–165; **8,** 169–170
prohibition of fishing in, **23,** 127
protective jurisdiction outside, **9,** 300; **11,** 130–135. *See also* Hovering laws
State territory, whether part of, **6,** 121–122; **32,** 84
status, **15,** 70–71
subsoil of, ownership, **14,** 56–61; **18,** 151–152, 156–157
—federal States, **31,** 146–151
taxation in, **9,** 123–126
Thailand, law of, **26,** 243
warships, passage of, **16,** 160–162; **31,** 83
Territoriality, principle of, **6,** 93–94, 147–149, 175–177, 179, 183, 290, 293; **32,** 29, 31. *See also* Extra-territorial effect of legislation *and* Jurisdiction, territorial
Territoriality of ships, **4,** 107, 188–189, 295–296; **5,** 75–76; **6,** 93–94, 175–177, 179, 290, 292; **7,** 212–213; **10,** 252–258, 323–325
Territory: *see also* Annexation; Bays; Canals, international; Cession of territory; Islands; Lakes; Leases, international; Plebiscite; Prescription; Rivers; Servitudes; Territorial disputes; Territorial sovereignty; Territorial waters
air space, sovereignty over, **5,** 82–83; **6,** 112; **7,** 114–115; **8,** 159–160; **9,** 119, 124
canals, international: *q.v.*
cession of: *q.v.*
changes of sovereignty, effect of: *see under* Territorial sovereignty *and* State succession
colonies, whether part of national territory, **2,** 93
condominium: *q.v.*
contiguity, principle of, **4,** 111–112
continental shelf: *q.v.*
customs zone and, **1,** 83, 98–99; **2,** 103; **3,** 110–111
damage suffered outside, claim for compensation, **30,** 100–104
delivery of, formal, **1,** 84–89
demilitarized zones, **18,** 164–170
disputed, jurisdiction over, **1,** 105–106; **8,** 157–158
disputes over: *see* Territorial disputes
extension of, **5,** 75–77
extent, statements of Executive as to, **16,** 12–14

Territory—*continued*
grants in perpetuity, **1,** 94–95; **5,** 80–81; **6,** 111; **7,** 113–114. *See also* Leases, international
injurious use of, **6,** 132; **9,** 315–324, 332–333
islands: *q.v.*
lakes: *q.v.*
joint or international government, under, **1,** 83, 179; **2,** 32–33; **3,** 49–52; **4,** 57; **5,** 33–36; **7,** 56–63
jurisdiction distinguished, **26,** 513–518
land boundaries: *see* Boundaries
leases, international: *q.v.*
meaning, in extradition treaties, **33,** 324–325, 332
occupation in peace time, **1,** 94; **3,** 116–117; **4,** 118–120; **5,** 77–80; **6,** 110–111; **7,** 58, 109–111, 187–188, 360–369
occupation in war time: *see* Belligerent occupation
occupied, devastation of, **15,** 632, 647–649; **16,** 484–486, 521–523. *See also* Belligerent occupation
partition of, **6,** 77–82; **7,** 87–90
partition, public corporations and, **6,** 77–82
plebiscite: *q.v.*
prescription: *q.v.*
rivers: *q.v.*
servitudes: *q.v.*
ships, assimilation to, **4,** 107, 188–189, 295–296; **5,** 75–76; **6,** 93–94, 175–177, 179, 183, 290, 293; **7,** 212–213; **10,** 252–258, 323–325; **23,** 284–295; **27,** 45–49; **28,** 123
straits: *q.v.*
water boundaries; *q.v.*
Territory, use of—
actions against neighbouring State, responsibility, **31,** 27–28, 46–47
injurious, **6,** 132; **9,** 315–324, 332–333
Terrorism, Convention for Prevention and Punishment of (1937), **18,** 382–383
Teschen, extension of Polish Nationality Act, 1920, to, **11,** 179–180
Texas—
admission to Union, effect, **17,** 15
annexation by U.S.A., **31,** 159, 161, 162–165, 167–168, 175, 196, 197
Boundary Act, 1836...**31,** 158, 159, 160–161, 165, 166, 168, 169, 170, 171–172, 174, 196, 200
invasion by Mexico, 1846...**31,** 170
independence from Mexico, 1836.. **31,** 158, 160, 165
recognition by U.S.A., 1837...**31,** 159, 162
Texas—*continued*
seaward boundary, claim to three leagues, **31,** 151, 154, 158–176, 188, 189, 194
status of (1836–1845, and after 1845), **17,** 126–131
Thailand—
Allied occupation of, **22,** 1001–1006
Colombo Agreement with Allied Powers (1945), **22,** 1002, 1004
Constitutions (1932 and 1952), **23,** 485
India and U.K., Agreement for Termination of State of War (1946), **22,** 1004
Japan, Treaty of Alliance (1941), **22,** 1001
Japanese invasion (1941), **22,** 1001–1006
Japanese nationals, Act for control of (1945), **22,** 1005
Nationality Act, 1953...**19,** 317
territorial waters, law as to, **26,** 243
Trade Marks Act, 1931...**23,** 483
U.K., Treaties of Commerce and Navigation (1925 and 1937), **23,** 484–486
Thalweg, doctrine of, **1,** 96–97; **7,** 128–135; **8,** 164–165; **9,** 114; **11,** 91–93; **30,** 476, 490
" Theatre of war ", meaning, **1,** 432
Theft, Canadian Criminal Code, **1,** 275
Third parties, effect of treaties on: *see under* Treaties
Third party opposition to judgment (Dutch law), **1,** 126
Three-mile limit: *see* Territorial waters, breadth of
Tibet—
India, Anglo-Tibetan Trade Regulations (1914) and, **21,** 272–275
status of, **21,** 272–273
U.K., Commercial Treaty (1914), **21,** 272–275
Tientsin—
British Concession, **2,** 152–153; **9,** 116
issue of habeas corpus from England, **28,** 59
Italian concession, **3,** 198–199
Tientsin, Treaty of (1858), **1,** 335; **2,** 326; **6,** 34
Tinoco Government, Costa Rica, **2,** 34–39
Tort on foreign ship in territorial waters of forum, jurisdiction, **28,** 108–114
Torts in violation of international law, **32,** 1–4; **34,** 1–6
Torts, liability of successor State: *see under* State succession
Tourist agencies, State, jurisdictional immunities, **8,** 227
" Trade ", meaning, **2,** 315; **10,** 412–415

Trade agreements—
concessions granted under, implementation in municipal law, **31,** 410–416
"escape clauses", **31,** 411, 412, 415
Trade delegations of U.S.S.R.—
character of, **6,** 169–170
Foreign Trade Corporation, whether separate from State, **27,** 633–634, 636
jurisdictional immunities, **1,** 294–298; **3,** 174–175; **5,** 18–19, 114–115, 124; **6,** 169–170, 332–335; **7,** 19–20, 170–171, 175–177, 178–182; **8,** 30–31, 223, 225, 241–245; **9,** 237, 245–249; **10,** 407–410; **11,** 140–142, 145; **12,** 101–102; **13,** 80–82; **15,** 141–145; **22,** 235–240
position of, in—
—England, **1,** 295–298
—France, **3,** 174–175; **4,** 30–31; **5,** 18–21, 114–115, 312; **6,** 57–58; **9,** 237, 246
—Germany, **5,** 309–312; **6,** 333–334; **7,** 419–420
—Greece, **5,** 312; **6,** 334
—Norway, **6,** 333
—Sweden, **13,** 80–82
right to sue, **6,** 54–55, 57–58
status of, **4,** 30–31; **5,** 18–21, 309–313; **6,** 54–55, 57–58, 169–170; **7,** 170–171, 419–420
Trade Mark and Commercial Protection, General Inter-American Convention (1929), **9,** 481
Trade marks—
assignment, pre-war contract with enemy, **31,** 490–495
confiscation as enemy property, **17,** 163; **20,** 602–609; **26,** 656; **31,** 495–503
Convention for International Registration of (Paris, 1883), **22,** 18; **26,** 613–614. *See also* Industrial Property, protection of
—"*telle quelle*" protection, **26,** 53
Convention for International Registration (Madrid, 1891), **24,** 47; **26,** 50–51
—fees, effect of non-payment, **26,** 614–616
—international registration, effect, **26,** 614–616; **28,** 84
—similarity, refusal to register, **26,** 615–616
Convention of Chile (1923), **5,** 336–337
denial of validity, reliance on prior user, **28,** 44, 46
enemy—
—cancellation of, **23,** 701–706
—confiscation of, **20,** 602–609
—sequestration of, **26,** 657–662
enemy character of, **20,** 600–602
Trade marks—*continued*
expropriation of rights to, **23,** 24–26
foreign confiscation and nationalization, effect—
—Austrian law, **26,** 40–43
—French law, **26,** 50–51
—Italian law, **26,** 44–49; **28,** 29–47
—Norwegian law, **30,** 33–54
images of foreign heads of State, **8,** 24; **12,** 3
in gross or appurtenant to business, **28,** 42; **31,** 495–503
infringement abroad, jurisdiction in respect of, **23,** 270–275, 276–284
international protection of, **34,** 276–278
lapse of right by non-exercise, **30,** 53
national arms, use of, **9,** 10; **10,** 9
nationalization of registered owner **22,** 17–19; **23,** 24–26; **30,** 33–54
outbreak of war, effect, **23,** 701–706
registration by infringer, **23,** 28
registration, priority, effect of expropriation, **28,** 40, 42, 45–46
registered abroad, sale by Alien Property Custodian, **11,** 106–107
reparations, as, **20,** 438–439
rights in, ownership of enterprise distinguished, **26,** 43
sequestration of, **26,** 657–662
situs of, **30,** 42, 45, 48
use of, on national ship in foreign port, **5,** 76
validity in Member States of Union, effect of incapacity of State, **28,** 86
validity, law governing, **26,** 53–54
vesting in Custodian under Trading with the Enemy legislation, **27,** 638–641
Washington, Convention on (1929), **9,** 481
Trade names—
presumption of enemy character by reference to, **12,** 382–383
protection of, abroad, **6,** 282–283
Trading with the enemy, **1,** 419–422; **3,** 358–460; **10,** 514–529; **11,** 30, 250–251, 253, 264, 269; **12,** 359; **15,** 460–461; **20,** 602–615; **21,** 460–464; **22,** 184–197; **23,** 754–756; **27,** 646–648; **32,** 557–562; **33,** 444–450; **34,** 490–494: *see also* Custodian of enemy property
action against non-enemy guarantor of debt to enemy, **9,** 555
actions in tort without Custodian, **21,** 460–464
agency of enemy bank, **20,** 610–615
aliens resident in belligerent State, **11,** 243–245
allied country under enemy occupation, **1,** 420–422

Trading with the enemy—*continued*
Australia, Act of, 1939–1952...**24,** 898
Belgium, Art. 115, Penal Code, **15,** 461, 465–466
—Law of 1944, release from Custodian, **15,** 407
belligerent occupation and, **15,** 530–537, 540–548; **16,** 429–431; **18,** 578–581; **23,** 754–756
Canada—
—Orders of 1916...**9,** 549–552
—Regulations of 1939...**15,** 439–441
—War Measures Act, 1927...**15,** 439–441
change of sovereignty, effect, **17,** 368
choses in action, assignments of, **9,** 553
construction of legislation, **27,** 619, 643
contingent interests in remainder, **10,** 529
contract executory at outbreak of war, **12,** 322–327
control of enemy property, **12,** 225–229
copyright and, **18,** 24–36
countries subject to capitulations, **1,** 419
enemy interest in company, **11,** 258–260
" enemy national ", French law, **11,** 259–260
enemy territory, meaning of, **19,** 555, 567
extradition and, **1,** 265–266
extraterritorial effect on legislation, **9,** 156
France, Decree of 1939...**9,** 557; **11,** 258–260; **15,** 466
intercourse for religious purposes, **22,** 917
legislation, nature of, in occupied territory, **23,** 693–694
licences, **3,** 458–460; **20,** 615
liquidated debt, **12,** 308–322
loan contract, pre-war, **22,** 480–481, 488–489, 917
moratorium law, effect, **22,** 480–481, 488
neutral interests, protection of, **22,** 184–197
Palestine, Order of 1939...**17,** 114
payment to Custodian as discharge of debt, **21,** 445–447
permitted transactions, **18,** 496–498
political crime, as, **1,** 265–266
power of attorney given by residents of enemy-occupied territory, **12,** 349–352
prohibition of, **18,** 581–584, 649–652; **22,** 701–705
purpose and scope of, **9,** 550; **13,** 235

Trading with the enemy—*continued*
residence in enemy territory, involuntary, **19,** 572–575, 580–589
right of action of enemy alien, **11,** 58–61
right of action of enemy as shareholder, **22,** 909–911
Russian prohibition of, **2,** 411–412
sale agreement, inchoate, validation of, **18,** 25–36
separation agreement between spouses, **22,** 901–908
sequestration and confiscation distinguished, **9,** 551
shareholders, whether company property " belongs " to, **18,** 184–188
Singapore, Custodian of Property Proclamation, **15,** 447–449
State succession and, **17,** 113–115
suretyship, contract of, **10,** 514–529
termination of war and, **20,** 622–627; **22,** 918, 932–935, 935–939
U.K., **1,** 394, 406–408
—Act of 1939...**9,** 537–538, 546, 554–555; **10,** 514–529; **17,** 3, 369–371; **18,** 25–36, 171–172, 174, 176, 184; **19,** 572–578; **21,** 462, 466, 470, 471; **24,** 899
—Proclamations, 1914, 1915...**1,** 419–412
U.S.A.—
—Act of 1917...**8,** 493; **14,** 172, 174–176, 182, 187–189, 191, 192, 193–194; **15,** 261–262, 441–443
—Act of 1917, amendment of 1941... **14,** 172, 174, 187–189; **15,** 45–48, 453, 456–460, 462–465; **17,** 359–367, 372–376; **21,** 39–42, 433, 438, 439, 440, 442, 443; **24,** 903–906, 907–915, 932–938
—neutral property, seizure of, **14,** 187–189, 192–194
vesting of property in Custodian, **21,** 460–464; **28,** 605–607; **30,** 412; **33,** 445–446, 448–449
vesting of securities outside country, **18,** 513–515
vesting orders, **17,** 368; **18,** 172; **27,** 618–627
voluntary residence in enemy territory, **22,** 918–921
Trans-Jordan, status of, **12,** 15–17
Transit, freedom of, **6,** 403–406; **31,** 81, 112–113
Transport—
European Central Inland Transport Organization, Agreement establishing (1945), **20,** 481, 487
Transport by air: *see* Air Transport, International
Transport, international, Central Office for, as arbitrator, **6,** 417–420

Transport of Goods by Rail, Berne Convention for (1890), **7,** 58, 411–412
—(1933), **12,** 266
Travaux préparatoires: *See under* Treaties, interpretation
Treason, **8,** 89–90; **16,** 239–244. *See also Perduellio*
allegiance and, **15,** 78–104; **19,** 554
—*protectio trahit subjectionem et subjectio protectionem*, **15,** 84, 88, 92
annexation, before, **2,** 240–241
change of nationality and, **15,** 78–90; **18,** 265–276
enemy character and, **15,** 425
enemy occupation, during, **12,** 444–445
extradition for, **15,** 297–300; **17,** 261–263
mandated territories, in, **2,** 27–31
passport held by alien, **15,** 91–104
war treason, **13,** 384–385; **16,** 460
Treasury bills, nature of, **26,** 286–287
Treaties: *see also* Protocols, *and* Commercial treaties; Double taxation treaties; Extradition treaties; Peace treaties, etc.
abrogation—
—adopting statute, effect on, **14,** 158–162
—changed conditions, as result of, **6,** 362–365
—mutual consent, by, **3,** 354–357
—subsequent legislation, by, **1,** 7, 251–252; **11,** 135; **16,** 6–8, 309–311
acceding parties, **34,** 245
accession to, **3,** 334–335
—in advance, **25,** 541
—stipulations for third parties, **5,** 461
adhesion to, **7,** 401–404
adhesion, of Canada, to treaty concluded by Great Britain, **1,** 348
agency created by, **26,** 364
aliens, rights under: *see under* Aliens; *see also* most-favoured-nation clauses *and* national treatment clauses *infra*
amendment, **9,** 55
annexation of Party, effect, **21,** 443
—Austria and Berne Copyright Union, **18,** 47–48
—war between other Party and annexing State, **21,** 262–264; **22,** 100–101
annexed declaration as part of, **19,** 422–425, 430–431, 433, 441–444, 445–447, 449–450, 452–454
application distinguished from interpretation, **5,** 390
application, reasonableness, test of, **27,** 599–600
apportionments under, **20,** 70–75
—bilateral adjustments, nature of, **20,** 71–72
Treaties—*continued*
apportionments under—*continued*
—municipal law and, **20,** 71–72
arbitration clauses in, **19,** 425–426, 433, 440, 448
arbitration treaties: *q.v.*
armistice, effect on, **16,** 381–382
"arrangements" distinguished, **7,** 408–409
authority of signatory, Belgian law, **32,** 591–592
belligerent occupation, effect, **18,** 574–575
—Occupant, treaty with, **19,** 413–415
bilingual: *see* interpretation, bilingual treaties, *infra*
boundary treaty, interpretation of, **11,** 94–99; **27,** 62–98 *passim*
breach of, **6,** 195; **9,** 1–4; **31,** 53, 54, 210, 217–219
—action for, **23,** 360–363
—comity and, **33,** 13
—competence of municipal court, **9,** 1–4
—E.E.C. Treaty, **32,** 377
—later inconsistent treaty, **25,** 208
—legislation, by, **25,** 260–262, 265, 291, 297, 299
—municipal law, effect in, **28,** 500–506
—remedy for, **23,** 61
British (Imperial), application to independent Commonwealth States, **20,** 40–41
British India as Party, devolution to independent India, **20,** 41–46
cause of action arising out of, **19,** 471, 473; **20,** 417–424
change of sovereignty, effect, **23,** 123–124
changed conditions, effect, **6,** 362–368, 413; **12,** 279. *See also Rebus sic stantibus*, doctrine of
civil war, effect, **22,** 90–91, 94–95, 479, 619
clausula rebus sic stantibus: *see Rebus sic stantibus*, doctrine of
clerical error in copying, effect, **27,** 87, 89
colonies, application to, **7,** 409–411
"commerce and navigation", meaning, as including "administration of justice", **23,** 306, 313, 319–322
commercial: *see* Commercial treaties; *see also* most-favoured-nation clauses, *infra*
communication to third parties, **4,** 418–419
compatibility between later and earlier, **19,** 318–319; **20,** 429–430; **23,** 241–244; **30,** 328–329; **31,** 425–426
composite States, with, unification, effect of, **28,** 124–125

Treaties—*continued*
conception of, **19,** 413–415; **20,** 409
concession agreement as, **19,** 525–526, 532, 542; **20,** 308–309
conclusion of: *see also* parliamentary approval, need for, *infra*
—authentic text, **31,** 86
—capacity to conclude, **22,** 448
—constitutional limitations: *see* Treaty-making power
—contracts, comparison with, **26,** 571
—contracting party, meaning, **9,** 446–453; **22,** 565–572
—federal States, in, **8,** 41–69
—lack of parliamentary approval, effect on individual rights, **19,** 459–461
—mandatory power, by, **4,** 47–48, 52–53
—member state of federation, with, **25,** 124
—peace treaties, not freely negotiated, **18,** 419–420; **19,** 481; **22,** 448. *See also* Peace treaties, contractual character
—sovereignty, whether implying abandonment of, **2,** 329–330; **5,** 364; **6,** 100–101
conclusiveness of statements of Executive as to existence of, **21,** 278
concordats: *q.v.*
conflict between—
—earlier and later multilateral, **20,** 429–430
—executive agreement after treaty, **23,** 241–244
—multilateral and later bilateral, **19,** 318–319
continuance by later treaty, **22,** 607–608
continuance during war, **12,** 304–308
continuity of States and, **22,** 58–59
contra bonos mores, **11,** 218–219
contract contrary to, **23,** 470–471, 582–584; **27,** 257–259
"contracting party", meaning, **9,** 446–453; **22,** 570–571
"Contracting Powers", meaning, **4,** 52, 43
courts, competence to pass on validity of, **9,** 471; **31,** 3–7; **32,** 59
—self-executing treaties, **32,** 61–62
courts, interpretation by, **1,** 331–335; **5,** 345–347, 349, 392; **7,** 506; **9,** 118, 461, 469, 476, 478. *See also* Treaties, interpretation of, *infra*
customary international law and, **21,** 140; **22,** 11, 608–611, 824; **28,** 547
—incorporation of provisions of, **23,** 306, 318, 320. *See also* Hague Convention on Laws of Land Warfare (1907)

Treaties—*continued*
customary international law and—*continued*
—source of, as, **4,** 6–7; **16,** 1–3; **22,** 560
declarations, exchange of, distinguished, **3,** 333–334
déclaration interprétative, as part of, **5,** 363–364
definition, **8,** 37
—agreement with foreign port authority, **20,** 407–409
—multilateral declarations, **20,** 406–407
denunciation, **17,** 123–125
—general participation clause, effect, **11,** 257
—recognition by courts of other Party, **22,** 95
—subsequent withdrawal of, **7,** 423
—unilateral, **8,** 441–442; **11,** 219, 224–225, 227–228; **21,** 276–277; **33,** 28–30
—unrecognized government, by, **22,** 94–95
diplomatic relations, breach, effect of, **12,** 278–279
disputes, procedure as to, **17,** 335–339
dual nationality, concerning, **25,** 137
duration, **14,** 48, 159; **30,** 468–470, 478, 484–485. *See also* extinction and termination, *infra*
duress, invalidity for, **18,** 249–251, 363; **22,** 448; **24,** 437, 538. *See also* Peace treaties, contractual character
effects of—
—before entry into force, **2,** 74–75; **28,** 430–436; **32,** 256
—individuals, on: *see* individuals, *infra*
—private rights, **4,** 403–404; **6,** 240–242; **9,** 458
—third States: *see* third States, effects on, *infra*
enforceability in territory of other Party, **9,** 476
enforcement: *see* operation and enforcement, *infra*
entry into force, **4,** 396–415; **22,** 562–565; **30,** 468, 478, 484; **32,** 339–341, 349
—effect before, **2,** 74–75; **28,** 430–436; **32,** 256
—exchange of ratifications, relevance, **4,** 400–401
—future date, at, **24,** 11
—signature, from, **28,** 436–437
—subject to ratification, **23,** 665
equality of parties, **22,** 448, 572
"equality of treatment" clauses, **7,** 305–306
estoppel as a result of, **6,** 102–103

Treaties—*continued*
exception clauses: *see also under* interpretation, *infra*
—good faith, **25,** 274, 294
—" public emergency ", **25,** 227
—reasonableness, **25,** 274, 280, 294
—unilateral determination, **27,** 49–58
exchange of declarations, distinguished from treaty, **3,** 333–334
exchange of notes—
—binding force, **6,** 249–250, 394; **11,** 231, 234–235; **14,** 139–140, 142
—extending prior treaty, **14,** 139–140
—interpretation of treaty by: *see under* interpretation, *infra*
—ratification and publication of, **20,** 369–370, 413
—revalidation of prior treaty by, **24,** 498
—subsequent to treaty, **10,** 407–410
—whether a treaty, **8,** 424–426; **9,** 69; **31,** 86–87
exchange of ratifications: *see* ratification, *infra*
exchange of telegrams, **7,** 78–80
execution of, **6,** 349–350; **8,** 451–452. *See also* need for municipal legislation, *infra*
executive agreements, **1,** 313–315
—law of the United States, **8,** 37–38; **20,** 412–417; **22,** 402–404; **26,** 557–560; **28,** 420–423
Executive, statements of as to existence, **21,** 278
extinction, **11,** 226–227. *See also* duration, *supra, and* termination, *infra*
extradition, of: *see* Extradition treaties
foreign law, as evidence of, **22,** 96
form of, **2,** 311; **5,** 329–335; **6,** 367; **7,** 78–80, 399–401; **11,** 231; **19,** 416–459 *passim*; **20,** 409; **21,** 256; **33,** 140
—" agreements " and, **21,** 167
—conclusions of conference, **22,** 562
—conduct, agreement inferred from, **33,** 143
—executive agreement, **23,** 244; **24,** 549–553; **27,** 492
—informal agreements, **5,** 351
—inter-governmental agreements, **1,** 313–315; **7,** 406–409; **8,** 37–38; **23,** 486
—interpretative exchange of notes, **22,** 562
—inter-State financial agreement, **22,** 824
—ministerial agreement, **22,** 560–561
formalities, effect of absence of, **9,** 56
frontiers, adjustment under, **20,** 63–77

Treaties—*continued*
general—
—majority decisions in conclusion of, effect, **18,** 368–371
—non-signatories, effect on, **3,** 3
—withdrawal from, **22,** 565–572
general conventions, evidence of international law, **34,** 60 n.
general international law and, **34,** 234
general participation clause, **1,** 411–413, 428; **11,** 257
generally recognized rules of international law and, **18,** 12–13, 106–107, 315–317, 336–345
Germany, Reich and States, **5,** 330–332
Harvard Research Draft Convention, **18,** 380
" High Contracting Parties ", meaning, **9,** 446–453
implied exceptions, unilateral determination of, **25,** 269, 273
implied powers, **29,** 157
inconsistency with national declarations of policy, **9,** 455
inconsistent obligations, priority, **19,** 318–319; **20,** 429–430; **23,** 241–244; **30,** 328–329; **31,** 425–426
incorporation into subsequent treaty, **7,** 91–92
individuals—
—absence of legislation, **22,** 418; **28,** 442–460
—application to relations between, **14,** 96–97, 98–100
—benefits or rights under, **3,** 340–342; **4,** 314–315, 403–409, 414; **5,** 154–155, 348–349, 352–353; **6,** 181, 240–242; **7,** 269–271, 413–415; **8,** 193–194, 280–281, 378; **9,** 1, 338; **10,** 427–430; **12,** 179; **13,** 279; **14,** 96–100; **18,** 9–10, 399, 698-699; **19,** 149–154, 459–461, 626–628; **20,** 148–153, 219, 430–434; **21,** 1, 4–8, 278; **22,** 563–565, 575–577, 589–591; **23,** 205–208, 241–244, 317, 360–363, 455–459, 469–471, 698–699, 826; **24,** 10, 320–428 *passim*; **26,** 362–364, 588; **28,** 269–271; **30,** 246–247, 248; **31,** 401–405; **32,** 59, 346, 637; **33,** 10, 12, 382–384, 411
—binding force, **5,** 212–213, 351; **6,** 181; **13,** 209, 221, 279; **20,** 409–410; **21,** 166–167; **24,** 585; **26,** 603; **33,** 380–381, 414–416
—contracts, effect on, **28,** 494–495
—extradition treaty, **14,** 139–140; **16,** 275
—national of third State, **19,** 467–469; **27,** 259–260
—preparatory work and, **18,** 429–430
—regulation of exercise of, **26,** 490–492, 494–496

Treaties—*continued*
individuals—*continued*
—"reliance" on treaty, meaning, **28,** 447–450
—waiver of claims in treaty, **20,** 223–226; **22,** 611–614, 972–978; **28,** 470. *See also under* Italy, Peace Treaty with
intergovernmental agreements, **1,** 313–315; **7,** 406–409; **8,** 37–38; **23,** 486
interpretation of: *see* Treaties, interpretation of
jurisdiction created by, **23,** 493–497; **24,** 549–553
jus cogens, Hague Convention, Laws of War, **30,** 503
kinds of, special: *see* Commercial treaties; Peace treaties, etc.
languages of text, relevance. *See under* Treaties, interpretation of, *infra*
Labour Conventions, obligation to make effective, **35,** 328–329, 331, 347
lapse, **30,** 468–470; **31,** 65
law in execution of, whether binding on other Parties, **9,** 155
law-making, **19,** 479–482; **23,** 55
lend-lease agreement, transfer of war booty, **22,** 980–981
minorities, for protection of: *see under* Minorities, protection of
mistake, effect of, **27,** 67, 72–77, 97
modification, **7,** 420–431, 435–437; **11,** 224–226; **20,** 430
—before ratification, **26,** 571–572
—exchange of letters, by, **2,** 19–20
—municipal law, by, **22,** 604–605, 884–885; **33,** 1–14
—mutual agreement, by, **20,** 70–71
most-favoured-nation clauses, **1,** 347, 350–352, 390; **4,** 451–454; **5,** 363, 400, 403–405; **6,** 398–400; **7,** 450–456; **8,** 472–475; **9,** 2–3, 370, 457, 486, 490–500; **11,** 234–236; **13,** 198; **14,** 160–162, 165–166; **15,** 1–2; **17,** 300, 315; **18,** 433–435; **20,** 294, 480, 553, 554–556, 564; **21,** 139, 305–308; **22,** 604–605; **23,** 468; **24,** 670–672, 673–677, 677–682
—consular jurisdiction and, **19,** 261–275
—nature and scope, **23,** 306, 313, 318–323
multilateral conventions: *see also under* Treaties, interpretation of
accession to, **28,** 87
—application to nationals of non-party, **28,** 494–496
—bilateral treaties *in pari materia* between Parties to, **8,** 406–410

Treaties—*continued*
multilateral conventions—*continued*
—commencement of operation for each Party, **27,** 581
—*communis opinio juris*, as, **22,** 450
—interpretation, **25,** 303
—modification, **25,** 542
—re-application after war, **28,** 85–86
—right to enact exceptions, **26,** 564–567
municipal courts and—
—direct application by, **23,** 483–485
—enforcement by, **4,** 409–410; **9,** 2, 4, 6, 459; **15,** 327; **21,** 265–272, 274
—international court, reference to, **32,** 33–34
—jurisdiction, rights arising from treaties, **21,** 51–54
municipal law and, **1,** 319–324; **2,** 314–322; **3,** 6–9; **4,** 403–415; **5,** 345–347, 349, 392; **6,** 3–15, 24–25, 65, 240–242, 286–287, 345–348, 351–357, 443–444; **7,** 3–15, 401–403, 415–417, 465–466; **8,** 7–12, 418–419; **9,** 4, 57, 459, 482; **13,** 2–4, 178–184; **14,** 1–5, 158–162, 163–165; **15,** 54–55, 324–325, 327, 328–330; **17,** 1–22, 116–117, 300–303, 306–308, 355; **18,** 11–14, 393–395, 398–399; **19,** 1–2, 339–340, 464–467, 470, 474–476, 482; **20,** 1–2, 40–46, 244–246, 294–295, 328–330, 369–370, 406–407, 412–417; **21,** 1–9, 168, 256–275, 284; **22,** 580–583, 608–611, 914–915; **23,** 383, 393–395; **24,** 577–591, 594–595, 596; **25,** 220, 250–251, 265, 291, 293, 297, 299–300, 301; **26,** 483–487, 491–492, 554–558, 606–607, 613, 676, 679–680; **27,** 38, 43, 492; **28,** 322, 324, 439–467, 471–473, 475, 509–511; **29,** 375, 392; **30,** 246–247, 263, 264, 423–425; **31,** 401–409; **32,** 258–259; **34,** 180–183; **35,** 208, 211–212, 236: *see also* parliamentary approval, need for, *infra*
—abrogation by later statute, **6,** 3–7, 12–13; **8,** 7–10; **9,** 5–6; **13,** 181–182; **16,** 6–8
—absence of legislation, **6,** 7–10; **22,** 5–9, 10; **28,** 442–460
—action under, contrary to treaty, **29,** 70–72
—adhesion, effect in, **7,** 401–403
—adopting statute, effect of, **14,** 158–160
—anti-trust legislation, **24,** 673–677
—assimilation of treaties to, **7,** 412–414
—avoiding treaty obligations, **9,** 480
—conflict with, provision for negotiation on, **26,** 491–492

Treaties—*continued*
municipal law and—*continued*
—conflict, reservation as to, **30**, 391
—*consensus gentium* and, **22**, 537
—constitution, conflict with, **17**, 310–311; **21**, 264–265; **22**, 403–404; **32**, 61–62
—constitutional requirements, compliance with, **22**, 560–561, 614–617, 618–619, 620, 630–632; **24**, 549–553, 554
—contract contrary to, **23**, 470–471, 582–584; **27**, 257–259
—effect on earlier statutes, **6**, 353; **13**, 1–2; **23**, 468
—enforcement, in relation to national of non-signatory State, **14**, 206
—exception clause retaining freedom of action, **28**, 473, 475
—executive agreements, U.S. law, **8**, 37–38; **20**, 412–417; **22**, 402–404; **26**, 557–560; **28**, 420–423
—existing law, effect on, **30**, 395–398
—federal States, state laws, **11**, 1–5; **14**, 163–165; **32**, 342, 343–344, 349; **33**, 390–396
—French law, **26**, 199, 492. *See also under* France
—implementation by, **20**, 66–67, 425–429; **24**, 638–639
—inconsistent provisions, **1**, 6–7, 319–321; **2**, 4–5; **3**, 8, 346–347; **4**, 11–15, 409; **5**, 4–5, 16–17; **6**, 3–9, 11–15, 303; **7**, 11–15, 415–417; **8**, 9–11, 418–419; **9**, 467, 476; **10**, 1–5, 155–159, 405–407; **11**, 1–10, 113–114, 219–221; **12**, 238, 266; **13**, 183–184; **14**, 1–3; **15**, 2–3, 324–326; **16**, 4–8; **17**, 7–11; **18**, 393–398, 434–435; **19**, 1–2; **20**, 492; **21**, 128, 130, 375; **22**, 10, 11, 460–466, 480, 580–591, 619–620, 991–994; **23**, 453–454, 468, 472–477; **24**, 12–13, 552, 677–682; **25**, 126–127, 297; **26**, 556–557, 558, 606–607, 613, 676, 679–680; **27**, 257–259; **28**, 439–441, 464–467; **29**, 128, 130, 375; **31**, 1–3, 322, 344–345, 407; **32**, 61, 203–209, 259–260, 364–365; **33**, 1–14, 165, 385–396; **35**, 208, 211–212, 236
—incorporation into, **6**, 10–11; **21**, 265–275; **24**, 8–9, 11; **33**, 4. *See also* municipal legislation, need for, *infra*
—Japan, law of, **32**, 59–60
—legislation giving effect to, interpretation of, **7**, 466; **27**, 261, 270; **31**, 405–408; **32**, 352–353; **33**, 6, 10–11, 397–399
—legislation, interpretation to conform with treaty, **16**, 311–312
—modification by, **22**, 604–605, 884–885
—Netherlands Constitution, **33**, 234, 239
—non-self-executing treaties, **28**, 471–473
—prior contracts, effect on, **9**, 122; **33**, 410–414
—provision for non-replacement of legislation, **28**, 2–8
—right to enact exceptions, **26**, 564–567
—same subject matter, **32**, 350–351
—self-executing treaties: *q.v.*, *infra*
—statute and treaty waiving claims, **32**, 148–151
—subsequent change of, **23**, 412–414; **24**, 579
—supremacy of treaty, **4**, 14–15; **7**, 13; **8**, 419; **9**, 370, 459; **12**, 238, 266; **14**, 163–165; **15**, 2, 3; **17**, 7–8, 9–11; **18**, 393–395, 396–398, 434–435; **19**, 1–2; **22**, 580–585, 617–618; **23**, 304–305; **26**, 567–568; **28**, 322, 324, 461–462
—supersession by municipal law, **9**, 6
—Swiss law, **32**, 346
—taxation, compatibility with customs union treaty, **28**, 509–511
—U.S.A., law of, **26**, 483–487; **32**, 94–95. *See also under* U.S.A.
municipal legislation, effect, **34**, 180–183
municipal legislation, need for, **3**, 6, 7, 9, 10, 339–347; **4**, 403–410; **5**, 345–346; **6**, 65; **7**, 15; **9**, 462, 464, 472, 474, 482; **12**, 267–270; **16**, 307–314; **17**, 19, 89–91, 307–308; **18**, 398; **20**, 431–434; **22**, 417, 572–580; **23**, 455–467, 477–483, 698; **27**, 38, 43; **31**, 401–405, 427–428; **32**, 342–344; **33**, 380–381
municipal legislation overriding, **7**, 450–451; **8**, 7–9; **9**, 493; **20**, 328–330; **22**, 460–463, 583–589, 590–591, 619–620, 991–994; **24**, 12–13, 552; **25**, 126–127; **26**, 554–555
municipal legislation, presumption of conformity with treaty, **24**, 588–590; **31**, 405–408; **33**, 6, 10–12
municipal legislation subject to treaty, **21**, 258–262
national treatment clause, **20**, 300–301, 338–339; **21**, 307–308; **26**, 598–599
—anti-trust laws, and, **24**, 673–677
nationality, concerning, (U.S.A., Bancroft Treaties), **25**, 111, 115, 123–138, 140, 143, 145
native chiefs, with, **9**, 444, 462
—inhabitants, right retained by, **26** 109–111
nature, Inter-Allied Declaration on Enemy Acts of Dispossession, **30**, 2

Treaties—*continued*
non-metropolitan territories, application to, **21,** 211, 275
non-parties, rights of, **35,** 427
non-recognition of governments, effect, **4,** 59–60; **11,** 66–67
obligations under parallel instruments, **20,** 486–488
obligations under, whether determinable by municipal courts, **9,** 4
Occupant, with, **19,** 413–415
operation and enforcement, **1,** 313–315, 319–324; **2,** 314–325; **3,** 339–347; **4,** 15–18; **5,** 342–355; **6,** 6, 259–262, 342–343; **7,** 404–418, 507–508; **8,** 418–440; **9,** 454–476; **10,** 394–412; **11,** 219–226; **12,** 264–278; **13,** 232–233; **14,** 1–5, 158–162; **15,** 324–331; **16,** 307–314; **17,** 304–308, 310–311; **18,** 392–399; **20,** 338–339, 409–410; **21,** 258–276; **22,** 562–572, 572–620; **23,** 452–489; **24,** 549–557; **26,** 553–572; **27,** 257–280; **28,** 483–476; **30,** 395–399; **31,** 401–409; **32,** 338–354; **33,** 380–384
—after signature, before entry into force, **2,** 341; **23,** 470–471
—condition of compliance with local law, **20,** 338
—constitutional limitations, **20,** 410–412
—dependent territory, in, **24,** 54
—federal States, in, **5,** 330–332; **8,** 41–48, 58–66; **10,** 394–397, 398–403; **14,** 163–165; **15,** 4–5; **24,** 592–594; **25,** 124
—limitation of rights conferred by treaty, **10,** 394–403; **11,** 219–221
—modification by acts of sovereignty, **11,** 224–226
—municipal courts, enforcement by, **4,** 409–410; **9,** 2, 4, 6, 459; **15,** 327; **21,** 265–272, 274
—national of non-signatory State, in relation to, **14,** 206
—non-performance by one Party, **3,** 357–359
—non-self-executing agreement, **23,** 455–456
—reasonableness, test of, **27,** 599–600
—retroactive effect, **5,** 336–337; **6,** 344–345; **7,** 20, 405–406, 457; **8,** 420–422, 434; **11,** 223–224
—war, in time of, **11,** 222
ordre public, implied exception, as, **25,** 246, 248, 253, 256, 269, 278, 288, 290, 293–294
—reservation, **11,** 221
outbreak of war, effect on, **1,** 387–390; **2,** 410; **3,** 438–440; **4,** 534–538; **5,** 475–480; **11,** 218, 238, 242–243; **12,** 304–308; **13,** 232–233; **14,** 2, 158, 171–177; **15,** 437–

Treaties—*continued*
outbreak of war, effect on—*continued*
441, 508–512; **16,** 266–267, 380–384; **17,** 354–359; **18,** 499–508; **19,** 474, 556–559; **20,** 599–600; **21,** 262–264, 277, 432–443; **22,** 100, 592, 597–603, 900–901; **23,** 459–467; **25,** 125, 351; **26,** 577–578, 677–678; **28,** 86, 492–493, 602–604; **30,** 45, 58; **31,** 3, 358, 359–361
—Cardozo, Judge, on, **11,** 239–240
—multilateral treaties, **18,** 506–507
—revival by agreement, **26,** 577–578; **32,** 27, 28
—revival by notice from party, **17,** 87–89
—revival by peace treaty, **5,** 479–480; **11,** 241–242; **18,** 320; **19,** 556; **23,** 468; **24,** 883–892; **28,** 602; **31,** 3; **32,** 336–337
pactum de contrahendo, **2,** 19–20; **3,** 357–359; **4,** 393; **5,** 341; **6,** 405; **17,** 56–57; **24,** 128; **25,** 8–9
parallel obligations, assumption of, **21,** 256
parliamentary approval, need for, **19,** 413–416, 459–463; **20,** 407–409; **21,** 167, 256–258, 275; **22,** 11, 604, 614–616
Parties: *see also* " contracting party" *and* " High Contracting Parties ", *supra*
—dependent territories, **31,** 341–344
—territorial change, effect, **30,** 54–67
peace treaties: *q.v.*
performance: *see* operation and enforcement, *supra*
" permanent " treaty, **14,** 48, 159
personal validity, extent, **5,** 216
preamble, interpretation of, **6,** 374–375, 396; **8,** 428–429, 452–453; **19,** 273
preparatory work, consideration of: *see under* Treaties, interpretation of, *infra*
prior acts of international organization, effects, **20,** 486–488
prior inconsistent obligations, **33,** 412
prior private contracts, relation to, **9,** 122; **33,** 410–414
prior usage, incorporating, **19,** 292
private agreement in, **9,** 475
private law, concerning, **18,** 1–3
—legislation in public law sphere, conflict, **25,** 264–265
private international law, treaty concerning—
—interpretation, **25,** 268–269, 285, 302
—municipal courts, effect on, **25,** 269
private rights, affecting, **4,** 403–404; **6,** 240–242; **7,** 413–415; **9,** 458; **10,** 404; **20,** 431–434; **22,** 563–565; **24,** 542; **26,** 588

Treaties—*continued*
private rights, affecting—*continued*
—effect between signature and ratification, **22**, 562–564
—ratification, effect of, **26**, 586
—termination of treaty, **3**, 262
—violation, whether municipal tort, **26**, 603
procedural provisions, date of effective operation, **25**, 532–533
promise by government distinguished, **9**, 444, 454
promulgation of, **3**, 343; **19**, 460–461; **23**, 472–477
promulgation, dependent territory, in, **24**, 56–57
property rights of aliens, concerning, effect on vesting of alien enemy property, **28**, 467–469
protocols not submitted for ratification, **1**, 315
protocols, unratified and, **1**, 186
provisional agreements, **18**, 361–363
public policy and, **22**, 424–427; **25**, 246, 248, 253, 256, 269, 278, 288, 290, 293–294: *see also ordre public, supra*
publication, **1**, 322–323; **5**, 348; **6**, 342–343, 351–353; **19**, 469–470; **20**, 409–410; **24**, 595; **26**, 563, 569–570; **28**, 438–439
punctuation, discrepancies in, **9**, 478–480
ratification, **1**, 316–319; **2**, 312–313; **3**, 335–339; **4**, 395–403; **5**, 339–342; **6**, 342–344; **7**, 411–412; **8**, 418; **16**, 307; **21**, 258; **24**, 13
—annexed documents, **19**, 435
—binding force prior to, **2**, 74–75, 80–81, 313; **3**, 339
—cession of territory, effect on, **3**, 336
—*de facto* government, by, **30**, 396
—effect of, **4**, 396–399; **6**, 347–348
—effect, nationality of claims, **3**, 335–336
—effect prior to, **26**, 562–563, 586; **27**, 79, 91, 97
—exchange of ratifications, **4**, 400–401
—federal States, **8**, 41–48, 54–58
—legislative assent distinguished, **3**, 337–339
—measures between signature and, **4**, 395–396, 402–403
—multilateral convention, **22**, 450, 572
—nature of, **6**, 351
—nature of, German law, **25**, 201, 208
—need for, **11**, 267–270; **15**, 322–323; **18**, 361–363, 392–393, 395; **22**, 563–564; **28**, 436–437
— —agreement subsidiary to earlier treaty, **32**, 53, 64

Treaties—*continued*
ratification—*continued*
—need for—*continued*
— —by " high contracting parties ", **9**, 445
—*ratihabitio*, by, **23**, 665
—reliance on unratified treaty, **1**, 316–318
—retroactive, **23**, 87
—transfer of sovereignty, effect, **3**, 336
—treaty subject to, provisional entry into force, **23**, 87
—unratified but signed, **9**, 471
rebus sic stantibus: see Rebus sic stantibus, doctrine of
reciprocity, notification of, **23**, 471–472
reciprocity, requirement of, **20**, 294, 300–301
recognition of governments and, **10**, 58–59
recognition of States and, **22**, 224–225
redundancy, presumption against, **6**, 390–391; **7**, 257
registration of, **4**, 393–394; **7**, 465–466
renewal of, tacit, **1**, 68–69
repudiation, unrecognized government by, **5**, 47
res inter alios acta, **6**, 346; **19**, 516, 546
reservations, **18**, 364–392; **24**, 557–572
—" compatability ", **18**, 371, 384–388
—consent of other Parties, need for, **18**, 371–373, 384, 392
—effect on other Parties, **18**, 373–374
—extension to later legislation, **28**, 424–429
—history of practice, **18**, 377–380
—implied, public policy, **11**, 221; **25**, 246, 248, 253, 256, 269, 278, 288, 290, 293–294
—interpretation, **24**, 558; **28**, 429
—invalid, effect of, **24**, 563
—limitation on right to make, **27**, 543
—municipal law and, **30**, 391
—objections before ratification, **18**, 374–376
—objections to, **18**, 365–366, 367–368
—practice of L. of N., U.N. and Pan-American Union, **18**, 379–383
—ratifications, included in exchange of, **24**, 558–572
—reliance on, estoppel and, **24**, 565
—rights for individuals, whether creating, **22**, 589–591
respect for, clerical errors and, **27**, 89
retorsion for non-compliance, **9**, 459
retroactive effect, **6**, 344–345; **7**, 20, 405–406, 457; **8**, 420–422, 434; **11**, 223–224; **19**, 421–422, 432, 471–

Treaties—*continued*
retroactive effect—*continued*
473; **22,** 344; **25,** 178–179, 550; **31,** 2
review of, consistency with national policy, **9,** 461
revival of Party, effect, **17,** 312
revived by peace treaty, **5,** 479–480; **11,** 241–242; **18,** 320; **19,** 556; **23,** 468; **24,** 883–892; **28,** 602; **31,** 3; **32,** 336–337
rights acquired under, violation by subsequent legislation, **19,** 260
rule of law, created by, **31,** 86
rupture of diplomatic relations and, **12,** 278–279
self-executing, **4,** 406–410, 413–414; **5,** 349, 355; **6,** 347–349; **12,** 271–273; **16,** 307–314; **19,** 312–317, 464–467, 473; **22,** 580–583, 635; **23,** 137–139; **24,** 13, 577–579, 584–588; **28,** 461–462; **29,** 155, 156, 167; **30,** 2–3; **31,** 427; **32,** 61, 342, 343, 346, 349, 369–370; **33,** 234, 411, 414–416; **35,** 241
severability of provisions, **24,** 809
severance of States, effect, **22,** 530, 620
signature, **9,** 476; **11,** 267–270
—constraint, effect of, **22,** 448. *See also* duress, *supra*
source of international law, as, **4,** 6–7; **16,** 1–3; **22,** 560
sovereignty—
—abandonment of, whether implied, **2,** 329–330; **5,** 364; **6,** 100–101
—as evidence of, **6,** 100–101
—limitation of, restrictive interpretation, **1,** 338; **2,** 329–330; **5,** 382; **6,** 374–377; **22,** 874; **28,** 582, 586
special kinds of: *see* Commercial treaties; Double taxation treaties; Peace treaties; Social security treaties, etc.
State succession and: *see under* State succession
subsequent treaty—
—abrogation by, **22,** 711–712
—supersession by, **22,** 621
suspension and revival of obligations, **27,** 569, 583, 585, 588
suspension by way of reprisals, **1,** 414; **2,** 325
tacit renewal, **1,** 68–69
termination of, **1,** 327–328, 414; **2,** 322–325; **3,** 352–359; **4,** 420–424; **5,** 352, 357–358; **6,** 352–353, 362–369; **7,** 420–431; **8,** 441–444; **12,** 278–279; **13,** 187–192; **14,** 48, 159; **16,** 314–315; **17,** 312–314; **20,** 434; **21,** 276–277; **22,** 424–427, 621; **27,** 569–570, 580; **28,** 95–97, 307. *See also* duration *and* extinction, *supra*

Treaties—*continued*
termination of—*continued*
—annexation of party, **11,** 226–227; **17,** 312; **23,** 123–124; **28,** 95–97
—effect on private rights, **3,** 262
—mutual consent, by, **3,** 354–357; **28,** 37
—non-performance by other Party, **3,** 357–359
—reprisals, as result of, **1,** 414; **2,** 325
—revolutionary war and conquest, **35,** 235–239
—war, by, **11,** 238; **12,** 304
third States, effect on, **1,** 324–326; **2,** 322; **3,** 3, 6–7, 348–352; **4,** 393, 409, 416–419; **5,** 332, 355–357, 464; **6,** 359–361, 363–364; **7,** 269–271, 419–420; **9,** 468; **11,** 223; **14,** 206; **16,** 314; **19,** 474, 516, 546; **20,** 430–434; **26,** 573–577; **32,** 193–194
—national of, benefits under treaty, **19,** 467–469; **25,** 513–514, 541
—nationality treaty, **25,** 125–126
—*res inter alios acta,* **6,** 346; **19,** 516, 546
third Parties, rights of, **19,** 288
time limits in, **18,** 427; **20,** 483–484; **22,** 157–159
transformation, doctrine of, **3,** 9–10; **4,** 404–412; **9,** 466–470
trilingual, **5,** 365–372, 400
U.N. Charter, compatibility with, **32,** 57
unconditional surrender, effect, **17,** 308–310
"unequal", violation of, **6,** 195
unilateral denunciation, **8,** 441–442; **11,** 219, 224–225, 227–228; **21,** 276–277; **33,** 28–30
unratified, effect, **26,** 562–563, 586; **27,** 79, 91, 97
unrecognized Government and, **22,** 90–97
U.S.A., State laws and, **10,** 394–397, 398–403; **14,** 163–165
usage and, **21,** 140
validity, **2,** 311; **7,** 321, 420–422; **12,** 271–273; **22,** 572; **31,** 50
—conditions of, **11,** 218–219
—declarations by Parties, **31,** 77
—different texts, significance, **31,** 50
—duress, effect of, **18,** 249–251, 363; **22,** 448; **24,** 437, 538
voidance of, **5,** 350
waiver of claims in, **20,** 223–226; **22,** 611–614, 972–978; **28,** 470. *See also under* Italy, Peace Treaty with
waiver of rights under, Treaty of Versailles, **5,** 413
war, effect on: *see* outbreak of war, *supra*
war damage, compensation for, **23,** 207–208

Treaties, interpretation of, **1,** 328–353; **2,** 276–277, 326–346; **3,** 359–384; **4,** 384–381, 424–450; **5,** 358–401; **6,** 369–399; **7,** 431–448; **8,** 347–349, 355–359, 365–371, 444–475; **9,** 476–489; **10,** 410; **11,** 84, 85; **13,** 194–198; **14,** 39–40, 164; **15,** 3, 4, 331–332, 338, 339; **16,** 312, 315; **17,** 315–322; **18,** 399–433; **20,** 126–127, 222, 434–481; **21,** 137, 277–304; **23,** 418–419, 489–508, **24,** 599–669; **25,** 53–54, 58–62, 66, 71, 73, 77–86, 129–132, 135–137, 154–157, 163–164, 172, 180, 185, 189, 240–242, 265, 303, 311, 316–320, 382; **26,** 578–591; **27,** 269–270, 281–282, 291–293, 346–347, 561–567, 574–575, 579–584, 589, 594, 598–600; **28,** 104, 207, 228, 429, 472–473, 478–492, 520, 522, 531; **29,** 31–32, 38–43, 48, 74–76, 260, 294–295, 297, 311, 374–378, 445, 447–474, 480–483; **30,** 399–404; **31,** 5–6, 299–303, 410; **32,** 319–323, 345–346, 354–363; **33,** 192–193, 316–317, 397–414; **34,** 183–219; **35,** 239–253
a contrario and *a fortiori*, **24,** 616–617
absurdity, avoidance of, **22,** 633, 874
accompanying circumstances, **19,** 488
" according to its whole tenor ", **23,** 699
agencies of, **2,** 326–328; **5,** 358–364; **6,** 350, 369–371; **7,** 404–406, 431–432; **8,** 464–465; **9,** 476; **11,** 229–232; **12,** 280; **17,** 316–318; **18,** 399–403; **19,** 474–478; **20,** 434–440; **21,** 277–286; **22,** 606–607, 622–626; **23,** 418–419, 489–493, 699; **24,** 599, 600; **25,** 50–57; **26,** 490–492, 494–495; **31,** 5–6, 410; **34,** 177
aliens, provisions relating to, **5,** 395
ambiguity, narrower interpretation, **31,** 87
analogy, by, **22,** 633; **23,** 506
analytical, **20,** 630
arbitrator, functions of, **20,** 458–462
bene indicat qui bene distinguit, **27,** 575
bilateral, agreed interpretation, **6,** 394–395, 404–406; **8,** 424–426; **10,** 407–409; **11,** 231; **15,** 321–322; **19,** 430–431, 435, 441; **23,** 468
bilingual treaties, **1,** 227–228, 339–341; **2,** 21–22, 331–336; **3,** 368–371; **4,** 428–429; **5,** 215, 365–372; **6,** 376, 381–382; **8,** 468; **9,** 288, 475, 478; **18,** 408, 429–430; **21,** 304; **22,** 634–636; **30,** 444; **33,** 237

Treaties, interpretation of—*continued*
boundary commission, minutes of, **27,** 68–72, 97
boundary treaty, **11,** 94–99; **27,** 62–98 *passim*
certainty and practicality, **30,** 441, 446
changed circumstances and, **21,** 300–303
" clear and ordinary meaning ", **24,** 836
" clear and unambiguous clauses ", **22,** 632, 825
clear provisions requiring no interpretation, **2,** 339; **18,** 415; **24,** 121, 641; **25,** 135
comparative law, use of, **25,** 77, 81
conditions, of, **8,** 451–452
conduct of parties: *see* interpretation by reference to subsequent conduct, *infra*
consideration, equivalence of, **6,** 28
consular treaties, **4,** 448–450
contemporaneous interpretation, **6,** 375; **20,** 458, 461; **26,** 485–486; **34,** 311–312
—by one party, **23,** 489–493
contra proferentem rule, **6,** 380; **18,** 150
customary international law as element of, **5,** 392; **8,** 450
déclaration interprétative, **5,** 363–364
deduction *a contrario,* **18,** 405–406
definition clauses, of, **22,** 633
dictionaries, use of, **4,** 446–447; **6,** 375–376; **20,** 473–474
disparate parts of treaty, **20,** 69–70
drafting party, construction against, **2,** 340; **3,** 366–368
effectiveness, principle of, **1,** 336–337; **3,** 360–361; **5,** 390, 399–401; **11,** 221; **17,** 318–322; **19,** 488; **20,** 471, 476; **22,** 632, 825; **24,** 626; **25,** 265; **29,** 460
—*ejusdem generis,* rule of, **1,** 358; **3,** 381–382; **35,** 410
equality of obligations, **8,** 444–446
equivalence of consideration as element of, **6,** 28
estoppel in relation to, **25,** 154–155, 156
exceptio est strictissimae applicationis, **19,** 481
exception clauses, **25,** 157, 185; **28,** 478–479; **29,** 260, 476
exchange of notes, by reference to, **5,** 362–363, 405; **6,** 394–395; **7,** 404–406; **8,** 327–328, 424–426; **10,** 407–409; **11,** 231, 234–235; **18,** 401–402; **19,** 476–477; **21,** 280–281; **22,** 622–623; **23,** 468
executive authorities, by, **1,** 332–333, 348–349; **5,** 347; **6,** 300

Treaties, interpretation of—*continued*
executive authorities, by, conclusiveness of statements, **7,** 404–409; **20,** 437–438; **21,** 278–285; **22,** 606–607, 649. *See also* exchange of notes, *supra*
Executive, matter for, **34,** 177
expressio unius est exclusio alterius, **2,** 340; **5,** 356–357; **6,** 66–68, 191 n., 405–406; **7,** 102–104; **9,** 396, 488; **18,** 150–151, 423–426; **20,** 481; **25,** 373, 376–377
expressum facit cessare tacitum, **20,** 479
extensive, **11,** 235
foreign minister, by, **7,** 404–405
function of, **18,** 415
gaps, apparent, in treaty, **8,** 465; **9,** 489; **20,** 75–76
generalia specialibus non derogant, **18,** 177; **34,** 330
geographical terms, **6,** 101
good faith, **18,** 407–408; **20,** 75, 479, 490; **22,** 638–642, 825; **23,** 345–346; **24,** 139, 626; **29,** 52
governmental declaration of policy and, **9,** 497
grammatical construction, **22,** 633; **23,** 108; **24,** 640; **27,** 292. *See also* literal, *infra*
grammatical meaning, repudiation of, **23,** 108
heading and text, discrepancy, **24,** 641
historical, **3,** 371–375; **19,** 511–512; **27,** 292
I.C.J., function of, **17,** 321, 328; **19,** 535–536
identical terms in other treaties, **5,** 375, 385; **33,** 192–193
" illogical or irrational ", **22,** 633, 978
implied powers, **25,** 430–431
in claris non fit interpretatio, **18,** 415
inclusio unius est exclusio alterius: *see expressio unius, supra*
incorporation in statute, law applicable, **21,** 297–300
Institute of International Law, resolution (1953), **22,** 870
intention of Parties, **18,** 420; **19,** 478–487, 488; **20,** 543–545; **21,** 273; **22,** 325–329, 575–578, 632, 633, 634, 368–642, 825, 831, 838, 872; **25,** 136, 137, 156; **26,** 581–584, 588, 608; **27,** 565–567, 570, 572, 577–579, 583–585, 592–593, 595, 604; **29,** 48, 294, 377, 460, 465, 468; **34,** 183–187, 190, 241, 252; **35,** 213
international law, conformity with, **20,** 481; **22,** 633, 874
international law, provisions in derogation of, **23,** 447; **30,** 368–370

Treaties, interpretation of—*continued*
jurisdictional clauses: *see under* Arbitration agreements; International Court of Justice; Permanent Court of International Justice
knowledge of local conditions, **20,** 73–74
languages of text, comparison of, **18,** 408, 429–430; **20,** 536; **22,** 106–107, 343–344, 629, 632, 633, 647–648, 872; **23,** 472–477; **24,** 641; **25,** 154–156, 163
law applicable, **20,** 544–546
legislation embodying treaties, **9,** 489; **23,** 477–483
legislative bodies, deliberations of, **2,** 336–337; **18,** 411–413, 431–433
legislative, interpretation relied on before, **19,** 512–514, 532
lex generalis and *lex specialis,* **5,** 400–401, 439; **7,** 494–495
liberal, **3,** 344–345; **4,** 447–448; **5,** 377, 400; **6,** 300–301, 393, 399; **7,** 338; **9,** 369, 480, 482, 489; **10,** 412–415; **11,** 233; **12,** 246–249, 275; **14,** 164; **15,** 4; **19,** 393–397, 488; **21,** 272–275, 308; **22,** 633; **23,** 304–305; **24,** 635; **26,** 483; **28,** 465; **33,** 411
" linguistic analysis ", **22,** 634, 961–962
literal, **2,** 345; **3,** 359–360; **7,** 253–254; **9,** 477, 488; **18,** 427–429; **20,** 22, 445–447, 489; **22,** 633, 634, 874, 969, 977–978; **25,** 135; **26,** 588; **27,** 574, 579–580, 594; **29,** 40–42, 52; **30,** 529; **32,** 357; **35,** 240–241. *See also* grammatical construction, *supra*
logical, **5,** 375, 382; **22,** 344, 633
Minister of Foreign Affairs, by (French law), **17,** 316–318; **18,** 400–402; **19,** 474–477; **20,** 437–438; **21,** 278–285; **22,** 478, 606–607, 622–626, 649; **23,** 376–377, 418–419, 623–625; **26,** 492, 495–496
most-favoured-nation clauses, **1,** 347, 350–352, 390; **5,** 363, 400, 403–405; **8,** 472–475; **11,** 234–236; **19,** 489
multilateral, **25,** 303
—conduct of parties, **34,** 314–315
—intention of parties, **34,** 310
—*travaux préparatoires,* resort to, **29,** 460–468; **34,** 242–246, 311
multilingual, **27,** 579–580; **29,** 377, 480; **30,** 444; **31,** 301
municipal courts, by—
—competence of, **1,** 331–335; **2,** 326–328; **5,** 347, 358–363; **6,** 370–371; **7,** 12–14, 412–413, 447–448, 506;

Treaties, interpretation of—*continued*
municipal courts, by—*continued*
—competence of—*continued*
9, 469, 478–480; **11,** 46–47, 54, 77–78, 224–226, 229–232; **12,** 280; **14,** 169; **15,** 688; **20,** 438–440; **23,** 418–419
—conclusiveness of, **1,** 331, 332
—divergent practice, **9,** 476
—views of Executive, **32,** 207
municipal law and, **6,** 381–382, 387; **7,** 445–448; **9,** 389; **10,** 410; **15,** 596; **16,** 4–9, 262; **19,** 487–488; **22,** 157–159, 460–463, 575–577, 632; **25,** 268–269; **26,** 517, 529, 711; **27,** 261, 279, 292; **28,** 104
natural and ordinary meaning, **17,** 322, 328–329; **19,** 535; **22,** 633, 647–648, 950; **25,** 58, 62, 66, 155; **29,** 39–40, 449; **30,** 399–402, 420–423, 433, 530; **31,** 303; **32,** 357; **33,** 94, 139; **35,** 408
necessity for, **18,** 415
"normal meaning of words", **19,** 466; **21,** 343; **34,** 187, 189
numbering of paragraphs, relevance, **7,** 495–496
official language, **26,** 588, 591
parliamentary debates, **2,** 336–337; **18,** 411–413
"patent misconstruction of treaty", meaning, **22,** 649
peace treaties: *see under* Peace treaties
penal clauses, **2,** 339
P.C.I.J., jurisdiction of, **4,** 503–504
"plain meaning", **24,** 565
practical construction by parties, **5,** 378; **8,** 447–449
preamble: *see* Treaties, interpretation by reference to preamble
preparatory work: *see* Treaties, interpretation by reference to preparatory work
presumptions, **22,** 630–632
—extension of terms, against, **9,** 485
—redundancy of terms, against, **6,** 390–391; **7,** 257
prevailing text, **34,** 203
"principles of justice, equity and good conscience", **20,** 541
private international law conventions, **25,** 268–269, 285, 302
private transactions, provisions, affecting, **11,** 229–320
public policy and, **21,** 280–281; **22,** 622
punctuation, discrepancies in, **9,** 478–480
reasonable, **8,** 461–463; **19,** 488; **25,** 68, 431; **27,** 598–600
"reasonable meaning", **18,** 417–418
reductio ad absurdam, **18,** 426; **22,** 633; **23,** 504

Treaties, interpretation of—*continued*
redundancy, presumption against, **6,** 390–391; **7,** 257
restrictive, **2,** 329–330; **3,** 362–366; **4,** 427; **5,** 364, 397; **6,** 118–119, 345, 372–380; **7,** 318; **8,** 467; **9,** 477; **12,** 358–359; **18,** 426; **19,** 478; **20,** 480; **21,** 303–304; **22,** 447, 874; **27,** 574; **28,** 582, 586; **29,** 38–39
—exception clauses, **25,** 157, 185; **28,** 478–479; **29,** 260, 476
—provision going beyond international law, **29,** 159–160
—provisions in derogation of sovereignty, **1,** 338; **2,** 329–330; **5,** 382; **6,** 374–377; **24,** 120; **26,** 597
—provisions derogating from general international law, **1,** 177–178; **22,** 447
rules of, **1,** 344–350; **2,** 329–340, 345; **3,** 376–384; **4,** 426–427, 441–450; **5,** 395–399, 400; **7,** 448–449; **8,** 470–472; **14,** 164; **16,** 316–317; **18,** 403–429; **19,** 478–488; **20,** 449–481; **21,** 286–304; **22,** 626–650; **23,** 493–498; **24,** 602–642; **25,** 240–242; **26,** 579–589; **27,** 281–282; **28,** 478–491; **29,** 74–75; **30,** 399–403; **33,** 397–400
"sense of the words", **18,** 415–416
similar treaties, comparison with, **2,** 339, 367; **30,** 442, 446. *See also* Treaties, interpretation by reference to other treaties
"spirit of the treaty", **18,** 419–426; **22,** 447–449; **23,** 504
state of knowledge of parties, relevance, **27,** 565–567, 590, 606
subject-matter, according to, **25,** 284
subsequent local ordinance, **26,** 111
superfluity of terms used, **19,** 488
surrounding circumstances, **22,** 632, 825; **27,** 594
teleological, **1,** 329–331; **5,** 394; **8,** 447–448, 452–459; **9,** 483; **19,** 272–273, 483; **21,** 286–291; **22,** 632, 825; **23,** 493–497; **24,** 632–637, 640; **25,** 77, 80, 135, 156–157; **28,** 531; **29,** 32, 52, 460, 470, 482; **30,** 399–402, 443, 530; **31,** 303; **32,** 203, 205–206; **33,** 315–317, 412; **34,** 241, 311; **35,** 213, 239–243
texts, authenticated originals, **25,** 156
texts *in pari materiae,* **19,** 488
travaux préparatoires: see Treaties, interpretation by reference to preparatory work
trilingual treaties, **5,** 365–372, 400
ubi lex non distinguit nec nos distinguere debemus, **25,** 135
unforeseen circumstances, **11,** 235–236

Treaties, interpretation of—*continued*
unilateral, **5,** 70, 329, 357; **7,** 404–405, 437
Treaties, interpretation by reference to—
absence of specific mention of relevant criteria, **23,** 600
all interests involved, **24,** 138–139
authoritative writings, **22,** 452–454, 634; **24,** 609
changed conditions, **23,** 846–847
circumstances in which concluded, **22,** 632, 825; **27,** 594
contemporaneous customs, **23,** 321
contemporaneous memorandum of signatory, **22,** 633, 952
context, **6,** 362–363; **16,** 332–334; **18,** 403–405; **23,** 599–600; **24,** 603, 609, 610; **25,** 382; **27,** 96; **30,** 433, 530
decisions of other tribunals, **21,** 304; **22,** 301–307, 629–630, 633, 950; **23,** 86–87; **24,** 610
drafting amendments, **23,** 86
exchange of notes, **6,** 394–395
facts of the case, **22,** 330–331, 633
historical circumstances, **6,** 383–384, 391–392
intention of Parties, **3,** 359–360; **4,** 424–426; **5,** 399; **6,** 117–118, 380; **7,** 297–298; **22,** 160, 444, 445, 634; **23,** 97, 320; **24,** 634; **28,** 465; **33,** 411
international law, principles of, **22,** 449–450, 634
legislative history of implementing law, **20,** 566; **21,** 293–297
letter from consular authority, **26,** 598–599
municipal law, **6,** 381–382, 387; **7,** 445–448; **9,** 104, 389; **19,** 486; **21,** 304; **22,** 632; **23,** 306, 321–322; **24,** 630
negotiations, **3,** 371–375; **4,** 81–82, 438–440; **5,** 400; **6,** 300–301; **9,** 468, 497
object of treaty, **1,** 329–331; **5,** 394; **8,** 447–448, 452–459; **9,** 483; **19,** 272–273, 483; **21,** 286–291; **22,** 632, 825; **23,** 493–497; **24,** 632–637, 640; **25,** 77, 80, 135, 156–157; **28,** 531; **29,** 32, 52, 460, 470; **30,** 399–402, 443, 530; **31,** 303; **32,** 203, 205–206; **33,** 315–317, 412
" only possible meaning ", **24,** 33–34
original text, **21,** 297–300
other articles of treaty, **2,** 22–23, 199; **18,** 418–419; **20,** 479; **22,** 107, 317–329, 632, 634; **23,** 599–600, 602–603; **25,** 382
other treaties, **2,** 339, 367; **4,** 435–436, 443–446, 475–476; **5,** 216, 368, 375, 385–386, 389, 400; **6,** 276, 376; **7,** 98–99, 318; **11,** 208–

Treaties, interpretation by reference to —*continued*
other treaties—*continued*
211; **16,** 335; **19,** 510–511; **20,** 434–436, 458–459; **22,** 632, 633; **29,** 96; **30,** 442, 446
parliamentary debates, **2,** 336–337; **18,** 411–413, 431–433
parliamentary report of signatory, **20,** 434–436
practice and policy of signatory, **20,** 234, 436; **21,** 157–158, 291–293
preamble, **6,** 374–375, 396; **8,** 428–429, 452–453; **19,** 273; **26,** 585–586; **29,** 43
preparatory work, **1,** 342–344; **2,** 97, 266, 334, 336–338, 365–367; **3,** 371–375; **4,** 90, 429–441; **5,** 372–383, 388, 401, 442; **6,** 190–191, 383–389, 391, 408, 412; **7,** 85–87, 406–408, 433–438, 443, 510; **8,** 2, 391, 436–437, 468–469; **9,** 468; **14,** 39–40; **15,** 343; **16,** 316, 336–337; **17,** 322, 328–329; **18,** 409–410, 411, 420–422, 429, 431–433; **19,** 273, 469–470, 488–489; **20,** 480; **21,** 3–8, 291–293, 302, 304; **22,** 106, 107–108, 629, 632, 634–642, 962; **23,** 86, 97, 498, 575–577; **24,** 612–613, 623–624, 643–644, 645–647; **25,** 62–63, 77, 184, 189, 257, 271, 294; **26,** 591; **27,** 97, 269, 291–293, 565–566, 578, 589, 591–593; **28,** 228, 482–490; **29,** 376–448, 459–470, 472, 474; **30,** 252, 266, 279, 305, 434–438; **31,** 300–302; **32,** 320–322, 345–346, 354–358; **33,** 242; **34,** 201–209, 212, 232, 241–248; **35,** 243–251
previous decisions of other tribunals, **21,** 304; **22,** 301–307, 629–630, 633, 950; **23,** 86–87; **24,** 610
previous decisions of same tribunal, **22,** 629
ratio legis, **22,** 634
report of legislative committee, **21,** 291–293
statement of Executive, **23,** 376–377
subsequent conduct of parties, **1,** 328–329, 335, 344; **5,** 401, 418; **16,** 335; **22,** 632; **34,** 199–201, 313–314, 316
subsequent statement of parties, **24,** 638–639; **25,** 76
surrounding circumstances, **35,** 411
title of part of treaty, **20,** 67–68; **22,** 107; **24,** 641
treaty as a whole, **6,** 362–363; **16,** 332–334; **18,** 403–405; **23,** 599–600; **24,** 603, 609, 610; **25,** 382; **27,** 96; **30,** 433, 530; **34,** 341
unpublished protocol, **25,** 543
usage in the subject-matter, **30,** 442, 446

Treaties, interpretative agreements, **5,** 363–364
retroactive effect of, **9,** 457
Treaty-making power: *see also* Treaties, conclusion of
Australia, for, **8,** 56–58
Canada, for, **6,** 44–46
constitutional limitations, on **1,** 4–6; **2,** 20; **5,** 336–339; **7,** 84–85; **8,** 41–48, 48–54, 56–58, 410–418, 479; **13,** 179; **19,** 461–463; **23,** 771
—federal States, **8,** 56–58
—Turkey, **7,** 84–85
Luxembourg, **31,** 425–426
U.S.A., **1,** 4–7; **2,** 315–316; **9,** 488; **11,** 1–10; **12,** 269; **13,** 179; **19,** 455; **22,** 934; **24,** 554, 885; **28,** 420–423
"Treaty merchants", Chinese in U.S.A., **23,** 453–454
Treaty of Versailles: *see* Versailles, Treaty of
Trianon, Treaty of (1920), Rome Agreements under (1923), **18,** 2
Trieste—
annexation by Italy, **1,** 455
German occupation of, **16,** 471–475
Permanent Statute of Free Territory, **18,** 81, 82
status, under Italian Peace Treaty, **15,** 107; **16,** 64–65, 76–77; **18,** 81–84; **19,** 144–145
Tripartite Agreement (1925) (U.S.A., Austria, Hungary), **4,** 262
Tripartite Commission for Restitution of Monetary Gold (1946), **20,** 442–443, 448, 452–463, 467–479
Tripoli, status of, **18,** 77–78; **19,** 145–148
Troops: *see* Armed forces
Troyes, Treaty of (1420), **20,** 99, 116, 120, 132, 133
Trucial States, Continental Shelf Proclamations, 1949...**18,** 146, 154
Trust, taxable entity, as, **34,** 188, 189
Trust, war, taking effect during, **3,** 449–450
Trust Territories—
Administering State, duties of, **22,** 76–86, 684, 686
—customary religious laws, as to, **22,** 81–86
—judicial system, as to, **22,** 76–80
Administering State, jurisdiction of, **15,** 149–150
"administration of the Territory", meaning, **32,** 39–40
"foreign country", whether (law of U.S.A.), **26,** 62–68
immigration into, **24,** 58
joint government with non-trust territory, legality, **32,** 38–43
Trust Territories—*continued*
Pacific Islands, **23,** 35–37; **26,** 2–3, 62–68
status of, **22,** 76; **23,** 35–37; **24,** 58–59
Trusteeship Council recommendations, **22,** 684–685
U.N. General Assembly and, **22,** 684–687, 688
Trustee, claim by, nationality of beneficiaries, relevance, **26,** 322–323, 464
Trusteeship Agreements—
disputes clause, **35,** 353, 356, 361, 370, 371, 376–379, 392–393, 397, 398–402, 405–411, 414, 424–435, 445–446, 448–450, 455, 460, 463, 468–470, 481
drafting, **35,** 406–407, 412–413
Japanese mandated islands (former), **15,** 520–521, 523
judicial protection, **35,** 371–372, 377, 378, 385, 395–396, 455–459, 472–473
parties, **35,** 428
Trusteeship system, **17,** 46
Mandates and, **17,** 48, 51, 55–57; **22,** 83–86
nature of, **26,** 65, 66
objects of, **35,** 400, 459
Tunisia—
France—
—Beylical Decrees concerning aliens, **5,** 28; **22,** 501–503, 507–508
—Convention, Arbitration of Disputes (1955), **24,** 767–770
—Conventions creating protectorate (1881 and 1883), **5,** 28; **20,** 47–48
—courts of, jurisdiction, **5,** 28
—courts of, jurisdiction, termination of, **26,** 562–563
—protectorate over, **4,** 44, 46; **5,** 28; **8,** 97–98; **17,** 42; **18,** 51–52; **20,** 47–48
—Treaty on Independence (1957), **26,** 99, 562–563
status of, before independence, **28,** 79
Turkey: *see also* Ottoman Empire
abolition of suzerainty over Egypt, **1,** 40–42; **4,** 48–49
Bulgaria, Peace Treaty of Constantinople (1913), **7,** 91–99
capitulations, denunciation of, **4,** 192–193
Civil Code, Art. 601 (tenant, liabilities of), **3,** 173–174
Concession Agreement concerning lighthouses (1860), **20,** 628–633
constitutional limitations on treaty-making power, **7,** 84–85
consular agents in, **4,** 373–374
Crete, relation to, **4,** 320; **8,** 154–155
Germany, Extradition Treaty (1930), **18,** 339

Turkey—*continued*
Greece as successor to, **23**, 79–80, 81–93, 94–99, 99–100
Greece, Treaty of Athens (1913), **1**, 389; **23**, 87
Iran, Establishment Convention (1937), **19**, 514
Italy, Extradition Treaty (1926), **9**, 402
Penal Code, 1858 (bankruptcy and swindling), **5**, 32
Purchases Commission in Germany, **1**, 114–115
recognition of French protectorate over Tunis, **4**, 46
recognition of French mandate over Syria and Lebanon, **4**, 48–49
recognition of Treaty of Versailles, **4**, 435–436
Republic, whether continuation of Ottoman Empire, **3**, 36–37, 78–79
responsibility for obligations of Adrianople, **4**, 206
Serbia, Peace Treaty of Constantinople (1914), **6**, 389, 391; **7**, 98
Tariff Act, 1878...**5**, 495
U.K., Treaty concerning Cyprus (1878), **5**, 26–27
U.S.A., diplomatic relations with, **1**, 142

U

Ubi jus ibi remedium, **2**, 194; **13**, 202
Ubi lex non distinguit nec nos distinguere debemus, **25**, 135
Uganda—
Ankole Agreement, 1901, whether a treaty, **27**, 277
—whether part of municipal law, **27**, 275–280
British protectorate, establishment of, **27**, 263
Buganda Agreement, 1955, interpretation of, **27**, 260–274, *passim*; **32**, 352–353
Legislative Council, composition, **27**, 261, 263–267, 272
Ukraine: *see* West Ukraine Republic
Ultimate destination: *see* Enemy destination
Ultimatum, need for: *see* War, declaration or ultimatum, need for
Ultra petita award, **2**, 214–215; **3**, 258, 419–420; **30**, 86, 87
Ultra vires, **1**, 185; **2**, 177; **17**, 333; **21**, 311, 322–323, 325, 329, 331, 343; **23**, 537. *See also under* International organization.
Unanimity—
arbitral procedure, in, **2**, 368–370
League of Nations, Art. 15 of Covenant, **2**, 390–391; **3**, 387–388; **7**, 494
Uncertainty of legal rights, effect, **31**, 35, 49, 104
Undertaking by Minister of Foreign Affairs, binding force, **6**, 103–105
Undisclosed principal, claims by, **4**, 253; **5**, 177
UNEF, creation of, **31**, 514–515
enforcement action, whether, **34**, 295, 300, 361, 372–373
financing, **34**, 301–304, 362–367
functions, **34**, 299–300, 360, 361
Unemployment benefit, admission of stateless persons to, **4**, 321–322
UNESCO—
Administrative Tribunal, Statute, **23**, 517–581, *passim*
Advisory Opinion of I.C.J., request for, **23**, 517–581, *passim*
Agreement with International Institute of Intellectual Co-operation (1946), **20**, 533
budget, **34**, 380–381
Constitution, **21**, 354; **22**, 798–799, 801, 802, 803, 808
Director-General, power of appointment of staff, **27**, 470
Executive Board, eligibility for membership of, **16**, 331–337
officials, dismissal of, **23**, 517–537
Staff Regulations and Rules, **21**, 349, 354; **22**, 777, 779–781, 798–806, 808–809; **23**, 517–581, *passim*
staff, responsibilities of, **21**, 354
UNICEF, **17**, 324–325
officials, Review Board, rescission of decision, **27**, 424–426
Unification of Certain Rules of Law, Conventions for: *see under* subject-matter of Convention
Uniform, misuse of, **16**, 540
Uniform, wearing of, **15**, 424, 639, 661
Union of American Republics, Pan-American Union and, **18**, 441–443
Union of South Africa; *see* South Africa, Union of
Union of Soviet Socialist Republics: *see also* Russia, Empire of *and* Russian Soviet Federal Socialist Republic
abrogation of Russian law, **5**, 49
admission to League of Nations, **5**, 49
aliens and citizens, discriminatory provisions, **32**, 213
annulment of claims against Imperial Russian Government, **30**, 117
Armenian Republic, extinction of, **2**, 18–19
Austria, occupation of, **19**, 623–625, 626–628
bonds of former Russian Governments, repudiation of, **30**, 151, 158–159, 160–161
China, Treaty of Friendship and Alliance (1945), **22**, 92

Union of Soviet Socialist Republics—*continued*
Civil Code, Arts. 18, 322, 364 (relating to corporations), **5,** 20
claims against, set-off, **3,** 210–211
claims connected with War 1914–1918, annulment of, **30,** 166–168
confiscation of private property, **1,** 26–28; **19,** 302–311
—legality, **1,** 49–50; **5,** 43–44; **10,** 14–15. *See also* nationalization decrees, *infra, and* Confiscation; Extraterritorial effect of legislation; Nationalization
Constitution, Arts, 15, 17 (jurisdiction of Republics, rights of secession), **11,** 143
Constitution, legislative organs, **32,** 212
consular courts appointed by Imperial Government, position of, **4,** 91–192
consuls, foreign, special protection of, **4,** 375–376
continuity with former Empire, **3,** 35; **6,** 40–42, 56, 141–142
contracts concluded in private capacity, **4,** 172–174
contracts of revolutionary governments in civil war, responsibility for, **30,** 168–171
contracts, pre-1917, ban on enforcement, **30,** 129–130, 154, 156
Copyright Convention and, **30,** 395
deportation of aliens, **4,** 340
dissolution of corporations, extraterritorial effect, **4,** 144–146; **6,** 141–144. *See also under* Extraterritorial effect of legislation
espionage, offence of, **30,** 69–75
Esthonia, annexation of, **10,** 70–78, 86–97; **12,** 29–39; **15,** 47, 176–204 314; **19,** 69–71; **23,** 706–708; **35,** 62–65
—Peace Treaty, (1920), **9,** 308
federation, formation of, **32,** 215
Finland, Peace Treaty of Dorpat (1920), **2,** 394–397
Foreign Minister, position of, **7,** 63–65
Foreign Trade Corporation, whether entity separate from State, **27,** 633–634, 636
France—
—Commercial Agreement (1934), **7,** 19–20, 171; **9,** 238, 246; **11,** 145
—Commercial Agreement (1945), **20,** 439
—recognition of Soviet Government by, **4,** 66–69; **5,** 43–44, 46
German occupation of, **4,** 28; **16,** 360–361; **30,** 508
Germany—
—Commercial Treaty (1925), **5,** 310; **6,** 333–334; **7,** 175–177, 419–420

Union of Soviet Socialist Republics—*continued*
Germany—*continued*
—Conciliation Treaty (1929), **5,** 310
—Convention (1925) *re* Brussels Convention on Maritime Assistance of 1910...**5,** 128
—Frontier Agreement (1941), **15,** 49, 50
—Pact (1939), partition of Poland, **15,** 680; **16,** 347
—Repatriation Convention (1941), **20,** 62
—Treaty of Rapallo (1922), **1,** 28; **5,** 22–23
Greece, Commercial Treaty (1929), **6,** 334
Hague Regulations and, **16,** 510–511
Hungary—
—Agreement on claims to German external assets, **32,** 569
—termination of war with, **2,** 434
inheritance, abolition of right of, **6,** 148; **11,** 110–111
—from abroad, **34,** 122–123
—general law of, **32,** 219–200
—rights of aliens, **32,** 210–223
insurance, State monopoly, **30,** 151
Italy—
—Commercial Agreement (1921), **1,** 26–27; **2,** 15–16
—Commercial Treaty, (1924), **6,** 55, 170; **7,** 179–182; **9,** 248; **15,** 142, 143; **22,** 235–240
—Commercial Treaty (1948), **22,** 235–240
judicial system, **32,** 212–213
Kunashiri Island, occupation of, **32,** 582–583
Latvia, annexation of, **10,** 73, 80–86, 91–97; **11,** 142–143; **12,** 39–43; **15,** 45–48; **18,** 49–50, 61–64, 251, 288–289; **20,** 180–182; **22,** 103, 230–233; **24,** 483; **28,** 95–97, 386, 388–389; **35,** 62–65
—Peace Treaty (1920), **9,** 308
legacies, expropriation of, **9,** 70
League of Nations, admission to, **8,** 114–115
Lithuania, annexation of, **10,** 80–86; **15,** 48–50; **18,** 79–80; **20,** 57–62, 193–195; **22,** 97–100, 102; **26,** 76; **32,** 73–76; **33,** 43–46; **35,** 52
—Peace Treaty (1920), **6,** 150; **7,** 456; **9,** 308
marriage in, validity of, **4,** 36–37, 62–64
nationalization measures, 1917–1919...**30,** 131–132
—banks, **22,** 13–14; **30,** 120–121, 134–135; **34,** 17, 20
—extraterritorial effect of, **3,** 136–145; **4,** 141–144; **5,** 22–23, 38–41, 49–50, 97–101; **6,** 57, 140–144,

Union of Soviet Socialist Republics—*continued*
nationalization measures—*continued*
—extraterritorial effect of—*continued*
150–151; **7,** 65–75, 80–82, 151–153, 157–160, 184–186, 287–289, 290–295; **9,** 141, 150, 232; **12,** 22–23
—metal industry, **30,** 188
—non-recognition, effect of, **12,** 29–39
—railway companies, **11,** 21–23
—shipping, **4,** 67–68; **5,** 45–46; **9,** 243
non-recognition of Soviet Government by
—Belgium, **2,** 50–51; **5,** 47
—Egypt, **2,** 51–53; **4,** 64–65, 173–174; **5,** 48
—Italy, **1,** 294–295; **5,** 45–46
—Netherlands, **4,** 59–60; **6,** 42
—Roumania, **5,** 49–51
—Sweden, **1,** 54–56
—U.S.A., **1,** 51–53; **2,** 39–49; **4,** 60–61; **4,** 340; **5,** 36–42
non-recognition of Soviet Government, effect of, **11,** 22
—private rights, on, **11,** 64–65
—treaties, on, **11,** 66–67
Norway, Treaty concerning trade delegations (1925), **6,** 333
ownership of property, laws concerning, **32,** 214
Poland—
—establishment of, absence of formal cession, **5,** 11–15
—Peace Treaty of Riga (1921), **6,** 353, 360, 450
recognition of Soviet Government by
—Belgium, **4,** 69–71
—Egypt, **4,** 64–65
—France, **4,** 66–69; **5,** 43–44, 46
—Netherlands, **4,** 71–72
—Switzerland, **4,** 62–64
—U.K., **1,** 49–51; **4,** 72; **5,** 51, 96; **23,** 76
—U.S.A., **4,** 58–59, 60–62; **9,** 68, 142, 145, 149, 184; **10,** 55–59, 68–70; **17,** 66
recognition of treaty concluded by Russian Empire, **24,** 52
refugees, inter-governmental Arrangement (1928), **5,** 248, 333–335, 362; **7,** 406–408; **15,** 289–290
refugees, position under Geneva Convention (1933), **15,** 326: *see also* Refugees
responsibility for acts of Imperial Russian Army, **30,** 116–117
State monopoly of trade, **9,** 236, 245: *see also* Trade delegations of U.S.S.R.
succession to property of former Empire, **3,** 96, 170–173

Union of Soviet Socialist Republics—*continued*
Switzerland, Agreement on Soviet Trade Delegation (1948), **23,** 197
trade delegations of: *q.v.*
U.S.A.—
—Litvinov Assignment (1933), **9,** 148–150; **10,** 49, 52–57, 66–68; **12,** 17–19, 22–23; **17,** 65, 68; **26,** 269, 348, 357, 360; **28,** 422; **32,** 212; **34,** 16–21
—Litvinov Assignment, effect on claims of nationals, **30,** 184, 186
Volunteer Fleet, status of, **3,** 482; **5,** 114–115
Unions of States, **7,** 29–30; **12,** 11; **15,** 28–37; **17,** 66; **19,** 35; **22,** 60–61
succession to obligations, **4,** 79–82
United Arab Republic, Israel, state of war between, **31,** 509–520: *see also* Egypt
United Kingdom: *see also* England; Great Britain—
Act of State, **2,** 11–13, 424
—alien subject to deportation order, **33,** 273
admiralty jurisdiction, damage by ship to foreign soil, **13,** 97–107
Admiralty Offences (Colonial) Act, 1849...**23,** 288–289, 291–293
Air Corporations Act, 1949...**17,** 123
Air Navigation Acts, 1920 and 1936...**11,** 88–90, **12,** 55–59
aliens, admission and expulsion of, **13,** 316
aliens, deportation of, **18,** 282–285, 310–313; **27,** 249: *see also* deportation procedure, *infra*
—acquisition of British nationality after deportation order, **13,** 146–147
aliens legislation, emergency basis of, **33,** 272–273, 275–276
Aliens Order, 1920...**13,** 146–147; **18,** 311–313
Aliens Order, 1953...**26,** 467–474; **33,** 245–252, 255–293, *passim*
—leave to land, **33,** 245–252
—power to deport, **27,** 249
—*ultra vires*, whether, **33,** 261–262, 275–276, 282
Aliens Restriction Acts, 1914 and 1919...**13,** 146; **14,** 185; **18,** 283
Aliens Restriction (Consolidation) Orders, 1916 and 1918...**18,** 283, 310–312
Allied Forces Act, 1940...**10,** 111–113, 123, 128; **11,** 162–165; **12,** 126, 138, 165; **15,** 160, 164; **18,** 182
anti-smuggling legislation, **6,** 159
Arbitration Act, 1950...**23,** 74; **27,** 40–41
Argentina, Consular Treaty (1825), **1,** 303

United Kingdom—*continued*
Army Act, 1881, application to mandated territory, **12,** 12–15
—application to U.S. forces, **21,** 112–113
Army Acts, 1881 and 1955, offences committed abroad, **20,** 188–189, 191; **33,** 194–201
Australia, Reciprocal Agreement on Social Security (1958), **30,** 420–423
Austria—
—Commercial Treaty (1924), **5,** 263
—termination of state of war with (1946), **18,** 245
Bankruptcy Act, 1914, extraterritorial effect, **15,** 75–77
Belgium—
—Agreement on Administration and Jurisdiction in Liberated Territory, **32,** 590
—Agreement on Claims, acts of British occupying forces, **32,** 589–590
—Agreement, Mutual Aid (1944), **23,** 207, 208
—forces of, in, **2,** 144–145
Bolivia, Treaty of Commerce (1911), **20,** 554, 555; **23,** 313, 320–322
British Nationality Act, 1870...**22,** 373
British Nationality Act, 1948...**19,** 62, 65–68, 219; **20,** 287–289; **22,** 61–64, 373; **24,** 445, 446
British Nationality and Status of Aliens Acts, 1914–1943...**4,** 43; **9,** 47; **20,** 54; **22,** 61–63; **27,** 47
British North America Act, 1867: *see under* Canada
" British possession ", meaning, **23,** 292
Burma, agreement on independence *re* commercial relations, **31,** 341–344
Burma Independence Act, 1947...**22,** 433–436
Canadian army in, **19,** 220–221; **20,** 184–186
Carriage by Air Act, 1932...**9,** 446; **20,** 156–163, *passim*
—1934...**20,** 41, 43–44, 45
Carriage of Goods by Sea Act, 1924, **21,** 297–300; **33,** 397–399
cession of territory to, **2,** 78–79; **10,** 98–102
Ceylon Independence Act, 1947...**19,** 64
China, Convention with (1898) for lease of Kowloon, **27,** 49–58
Civil Aviation Acts, 1946, 1949...**17,** 118–123; **24,** 163–166
—crime committed on aircraft, **33,** 202–204
Coinage Act, 1870...**24,** 50–51

United Kingdom—*continued*
Colonial Courts of Admiralty Act, 1890...**23,** 292
Colonial Laws Validity Act, 1865...**8,** 75–76; **14,** 23–24; **19,** 37–49, *passim*, 50, 54, 58, 59, 60; **20,** 41; **22,** 63
Colonial Office, certificate of, **5,** 29; **19,** 186–187, 188
Commissioner for Oaths Act, 1883, functions of consuls under, **21,** 252
Commonwealth of Australia Act, 1900...**8,** 80
Commonwealth Relations Office, certificate of, **18,** 211–214; **19,** 212–219; **22,** 251–252
communication from foreign government, Crown privilege, **33,** 259–260, 265, 266, 272, 288
Companies Acts, 1929, 1948...**8,** 181, 185; **20,** 7, 8, 19, 20, 22; **22,** 288, 292–293, 295
Continental Shelf Proclamations (1948, 1949 and 1950), **18,** 153
Contraband Proclamation, 1939...**9,** 566, 585; **19,** 635
Cornwall Submarine Mines Act, 1858...**9,** 126
Criminal Justice Acts, 1925, 1948...**20,** 273; **21,** 247
Crown—
—conclusiveness of statements of, **5,** 29: *see also* Colonial Office; Commonwealth Relations Office *and* Foreign Office, certificates of
—Free French National Committee, relations with, **11,** 15
—grants of land in Africa, interpretation of, **26,** 112
—prerogative to expel aliens, **33,** 278–279
Crown Proceedings Act, 1947...**18,** 212
Currency and Bank Notes Act, 1928...**24,** 50
Custodian of Enemy Property: *q.v.*
Cyprus, annexation of, **1,** 199, 201, 202
—protectorate over, **5,** 25–27
Czechoslovak military courts in, **10,** 123–128; **11,** 161–165
Czechoslovakia, Compensation Agreement (1949), **26,** 47
Defence (General) Regulations 1939, **12,** 64–68
Defence (Trading with the Enemy) Regulations, 1939...**12,** 341
Defence of the Realm Act, 1914...**2,** 422
denationalization decrees of enemy government, non-recognition of, **12,** 199–201; **15,** 250–252
Denmark, agreements with, *re Red Crusader* incidents, **35,** 485, 501

United Kingdom—*continued*
Denmark—*continued*
—Treaties of Peace and Commerce (1660 and 1670), **20,** 554; **23,** 313, 321–322; **24,** 296
deportation procedure, **33,** 258, 266–267, 272
—alien refused leave to land, **33,** 261, 262–263, 276
—deportation to particular State, **33,** 272, 274
—direction to carrier to remove alien, **33,** 256–257
—power of court to inquire into order, **33,** 266–271, 272, 274, 280, 285
—right to make representations, **33,** 274, 275, 276–277, 283, 292, 293
—selection of ship or aircraft, **33,** 266–267, 274, 279, 288
—use for collateral purpose, validity, **33,** 264–293, *passim*
diplomatic privileges and immunities, law as to, **1,** 297–298; **13,** 159–161
Diplomatic Privileges Act, 1708...**9,** 417–419; **19,** 388; **20,** 393, 395; **23,** 443; **26,** 540–541; **28,** 406; **33,** 364
Diplomatic Immunities (Commonwealth and Republic of Ireland) Act, 1952...**28,** 150; **33,** 361, 362, 365, 368, 369
Distribution of German Enemy Property Act, 1949...**18,** 188; **20,** 603, 605–606, 609; **21,** 462; **27,** 638–639, 640–642, 644
Dutch forces in, **10,** 111–116
Egypt—
—Convention with (Sudan) (1899), **4,** 57
—Convention (1936), immunities of British forces in Egypt, **9,** 478–479; **11,** 168; **14,** 79; **16,** 145–146; **17,** 445, 447
—military occupation of, **5,** 486; **7,** 187–188
—protectorate over, **1,** 40–42, 162; **2,** 21–26
—protectorate, termination of, **31,** 516
Eire—
—citizens, liability to national service, **10,** 27–37
—Irish Free State Agreement (1921), **2,** 368; **3,** 98; **8,** 82; **19,** 46
Emergency Regulations, 1939...**12,** 64–68
enemy alien, interned, status of, **13,** 315–321
Esthonia, incorporation into U.S.S.R., recognition of, **13,** 13
Esthonian Government, recognition of, **1,** 43–46

United Kingdom—*continued*
Ethiopia, Agreement (1944), surrender of deserters, **18,** 282, 283, 285
Exchange Control Act, 1947...**24,** 51
Extradition Act, 1870...**1,** 270–271; **9,** 395; **17,** 14; **18,** 338, 341; **19,** 362, 364; **21,** 237, 240, 242–244, 247; **23,** 409; **24,** 157, 513; **26,** 514, 517
—" accused " or " convicted " person, distinction, **30,** 376–384
—basis and purpose, **33,** 303
—" conviction for contumacy ", **30,** 378, 379, 380, 382–383
—" foreign State ", meaning, **33,** 323
—procedure, fresh evidence on appeal, **33,** 334–336, 339, 346–349
Extradition Acts, 1870–1906...**17,** 82–83, 87, 90–91; **24,** 502–506
extradition, law as to, **5,** 269, 280; **6,** 302–303, 319–321; **33,** 326–352
—Indian Extradition Act, 1903...**18,** 209; **21,** 47
—reference to treaty to construe Act, **30,** 379, 383–384
Fiji Islands, cession to, **2,** 78–79
foreign armed forces in: *see under* Foreign armed forces
Foreign Enlistment Act, 1870...**1,** 180
Foreign Judgments (Reciprocal Enforcement) Act, 1933...**20,** 16; **22,** 290; **33,** 25
Foreign Jurisdiction Act, 1890...**4,** 54; **5,** 29; **7,** 36–40; **8,** 111; **9,** 49, 117; **11,** 40; **15,** 41; **19,** 292; **23,** 292; **26,** 251–252; **27,** 278; **28,** 62, 65
Foreign Office, certificate of, **1,** 49; **4,** 362–363; **9,** 75–78, 529–533; **12,** 43–44; **13,** 312–321; **15,** 7–9, 29–31, 444; **16,** 12–14, 46–60; **17,** 84–89, 177–178; **19,** 72–85; **22,** 99; **23,** 71–78
France—
—Arbitration Treaty (1903), **20,** 143
—Commercial Treaty (1882), **5,** 360, 404–405; **8,** 426 n.; **12,** 278–279; **14,** 166; **18,** 435
— —interpretative Exchange of Notes, **5,** 362–363, 405; **6,** 394; **7,** 404–405; **11,** 231, 234–235; **18,** 401–402; **19,** 476–477; **21,** 280–281; **22,** 322–623
—Extradition Treaty (1876), **5,** 269; **6,** 302–303, 319–321; **8,** 91–92; **9,** 399 n.; **21,** 236–237; **30,** 379, 382
—Fisheries Convention (1839), **18,** 117, 118; **20,** 95, 96, 101, 102, 103, 120, 121, 123, 127, 141, 142; **20,** 104
— —(1951), **20,** 145
—New Hebrides, condominium, **9,** 50–51

United Kingdom—*continued*
France—*continued*
—Social Security Agreement (1948), **27,** 284
—Special Agreement for submission of dispute to I.C.J. (1950), **20,** 94–96, 97, 103, 145
—Submarine Telegraph Convention (1859), **20,** 104
—Tariff Agreement (1933), **9,** 458
—Treaty abrogating capitulations in Morocco (1937), **11,** 223–224; **19,** 274, 276, 281, 288, 289–302, *passim*
France and U.S.A., Arbitration Agreement (1951) *re* gold looted by Germany, **20,** 441–463, *passim,* 467, 470, 475
Fugitive Offenders Act, 1881...**8,** 99–101, 384; **19,** 362–365; **23,** 292; **24,** 156, 157; **33,** 297–298, 300–312
Germany—
—Commercial Treaties (1924, 1925), **6,** 280; **7,** 11–12
—London Agreement (1929) *re* transfer of German-owned property, **6,** 240–241
—Reparations Agreement (1929), **6,** 241
—state of war, whether existing in 1946...**13,** 312–315, 317, 319–320
Gold Looted by Germany, Arbitration Agreement with France and U.S.A. (1941), **20,** 441–463, *passim,* 467, 470, 475
Gold Standard Act, 1925...**24,** 50
Gold Standard (Amendment) Act, 1931...**24,** 51
Government of India Act, 1935...**19,** 124, 212, 216, 217; **22,** 65, 131, 147–148, 150, 247
Government of Ireland Act, 1920...**2,** 369; **24,** 95
Great Britain, meaning, **27,** 116
Greece—
—Convention for Reciprocal Exemption from Income Tax (1936), **21,** 305–306
—Conventions (1925), settlement of war crimes, **5,** 352
—Disposal of Diverted Cargoes Agreement (1942), **22,** 820–839, *passim*
—Treaty of Commerce and Navigation (1886), **19,** 416–454, *passim*; **20,** 548–565; **23,** 309–325, 332–337; **24,** 293–299
—Treaty of Commerce and Navigation (1926), **19,** 416–454, *passim*; **20,** 548–565
Habeas Corpus Act, 1679...**7,** 42
Hague Convention No. VI, denunciation of, **11,** 257, 265

United Kingdom—*continued*
"His Majesty's dominions", meaning, **27,** 45–47
hovering laws, enforcement of, **6,** 157–160
Indemnity Act, 1920...**2,** 423
India and Thailand, Agreement for Termination of State of War (1946), **22,** 1004
India Income Tax Acts, 1922, 1947, **22,** 287
Indian Extradition Act (1903), **17,** 11–17
Indian Independence Act, 1947...**17,** 39–41, 96; **18,** 18, 208; **19,** 118, 120, 124, 212, 216, 217; **20,** 6, 43, 54; **21,** 273; **22,** 148–151; **26,** 101, 106; **27,** 43; **34,** 29, 31
Ireland Act, 1949...**18,** 344
Ireland, Double Taxation Agreement, inconsistent statute, **33,** 1–14
Irish Free State, Agreement (1921), **2,** 368; **3,** 98; **8,** 81–82; **19,** 46
Irish Free State (Consequential Provisions) Act, 1922...**18,** 344
Irish Free State Constitution Act, 1922...**10,** 30
Israel, Financial Agreement (1950), **18,** 398; **22,** 123–126; **28,** 442–460
Italian conquest of Ethiopia, recognition of, **9,** 94
—withdrawal of recognition of, **9,** 93
Italy—
—Accord concerning Libya (1951), **22,** 104–113; **25,** 16–17, 19–22
—Extradition Treaty (1873), **9,** 50, 395
—Financial Agreement (1947), **17,** 1–3
—Social Insurance Convention (1951), **27,** 288–291
—Treaty of Commerce and Navigation (1863), **25,** 320
Japan, Treaty of Commerce (1911), **23,** 313
Jodhpur, Treaty of Alliance (1818), **22,** 128
Judicial Committee—
—Canada, appeals from, **8,** 71–80; **9,** 28–29
—history and functions, **8,** 72–75
—Irish Free State, appeals from, **8,** 81–87
Judicial Committee Acts, 1833, 1844...**8,** 72; **9,** 30
Khedive of Egypt, claims against, **4,** 434
Kowloon City Order in Council, 1899...**27,** 51–53, 56, 57–58
Legal Proceedings against Enemies Act, 1915...**1,** 421
Legitimacy Act, 1926, effect on nationality, **7,** 272–273

United Kingdom—*continued*
Limitation (Enemies and War Prisoners) Act (1945), **17,** 368–371
Madagascar, Treaty (1865), **11,** 77–78
Manual of Military Law, **16,** 465, 518, 532; **18,** 588; **20,** 189, 191; **23,** 832, 847
Maritime Conventions Act, 1911...**17,** 368–371
Merchandise Marks Act, 1887...**27,** 639, 641
Merchant Shipping Acts, 1876, 1894, 1906 and 1924...**5,** 343–344; **8,** 182; **11,** 87, 123; **12,** 56; **21,** 127–135, *passim*; **22,** 553; **24,** 161, 162, 165; **34,** 2, 3
Merchant Shipping (International Labour Conventions) Act, 1925, **5,** 342, 344–345, 413; **7,** 466–467
Mexico—
—Claims Commission, proof of nationality, **5,** 221
—Claims Convention (1926), **5,** 166, 452; **6,** 219–226
Morocco—
—Commercial Treaty (1856), **19,** 259, 262, 265, 267, 282
—Consular Treaty (1856), **19,** 263
—General Treaty (1856), **19,** 265, 266, 272, 274, 280, 281, 289, 290, 292; **21,** 139, 140
—Treaty (1937), **19,** 264; **21,** 139, 140
— —(1938), **19,** 298, 301
National Insurance Acts, 1946...**27,** 45–47, 115, 250, 285, 286, 287–289
National Service Act, 1948...**20,** 286–289
nationality law, **10,** 32–34: *see also* British Nationality Acts, *supra*
Naturalization Act, 1870...**12,** 195–196
Naval Prize Act, 1864...**18,** 720; **20,** 671–672
Netherlands—
—Agreement (1944), *re* certain enemy property, **18,** 172, 173
—Extradition Treaty (1898), **16,** 267; **17,** 83, 84, 86, 89
—Social Security Convention (1954), **27,** 285–287
New Territories Order in Council, 1898...**27,** 50–51, 53, 56
New Zealand, Social Security Agreement (1955), **27,** 48–49
Northern Rhodesia, extent of jurisdiction over, **5,** 29
Northern Russia, Provincial Government, recognition of, **1,** 43–44
Norway—
—Extradition Treaty (1873), **26,** 513, 516
—fisheries dispute, **18,** 86–144, *passim*

United Kingdom—*continued*
oath of allegiance, **22,** 469
Official Secrets Act, 1911...**9,** 31–32
—extraterritorial effect, **33,** 171
Palestine Act, 1948...**22,** 116
Palestine, legislation for, under Mandate: *see under* Palestine
Panama, Special Arbitral Agreement (1932), **7,** 251
passport, nature of, **15,** 95–97, 100
Patents and Designs Acts, **15,** 250–252; **21,** 259–262; **27,** 649–652
Patents, Designs, Copyright and Trade Marks (Emergency) Act, 1939...**18,** 25–26, 29–32
Persia, Treaties (1857 and 1903), **19,** 515–549, *passim*
Peru, Treaty of Commerce (1830), **23,** 313
Petroleum (Production) Act, 1934, **23,** 814
Poland—
—army of in, **10,** 128–129
—Extradition Treaty (1932), **21,** 240, 242, 244
Polish military courts in, **10,** 128–129
political asylum, practice as to, **33,** 270, 281
Portugal, Extradition Treaty (1892), **24,** 502–506
Princess Sophia Naturalization Act, 1705...**26,** 380–381
Prize Court Rules: *see* Prize courts, British, jurisdiction of
recognition of
—Israel (1949), **21,** 444
—Jordan, Hashemite Kingdom (1949), **21,** 444
—Soviet Government, **5,** 51, 96
Reprisals Order in Council, 1940...**12,** 543–554
Republic of Ireland Act, 1948...**18,** 344
requisition of ship, certificate of ambassador, **1,** 24–25
Rhodesia and Nyasaland Federation Act, 1953...**28,** 50
Roumania, Trade and Payments Agreement (1939), **30,** 404–420
Sale of Goods Act, 1893...**9,** 569; **24,** 982
Sea Fisheries Act, 1843...**20,** 104
Secretary of State for India, certificate of, **26,** 104
Slave Trade Acts, 1824 and 1843, **20,** 328
South Africa Acts (1909 and 1936), **8,** 80; **19,** 36–49, *passim*
South African Republic—
—annexation of, **2,** 67–68
—Convention of London (1884), **2,** 69–70
Spain, Arbitration Agreement (1923), **2,** 359; **5,** 148

United Kingdom—*continued*
statelessness, recognition by English courts, **15,** 251
Statute of Westminster, 1931...**8,** 57, 71, 84; **9,** 30; **10,** 28; **14,** 24–25, 27; **19,** 37–49, 49–60; **20,** 40, 41; **23,** 446
statutes of limitation, **19,** 220, 221, 564; **20,** 184–185; **23,** 466
Switzerland—
—Commercial and Establishment Treaty (1855), **6,** 242, 245
—Extradition Treaty (1880), **1,** 270–271
termination of war with Germany, **1,** 442–443
Termination of the Present War (Definition) Act, 1918...**11,** 267; **22,** 941
Termination of State of War with Germany, Proclamation (1951), **22,** 940–942
Territorial Waters Jurisdiction Act, 1878...**9,** 126; **24,** 160
Thailand, Treaties of Commerce and Navigation (1925 and 1937), **23,** 484–486
Tibet, Commercial Treaty (1914), **21,** 272–275
Tientsin, concession in, **2,** 152–153; **9,** 117; **28,** 59
Tinoco Government (Costa Rica), non-recognition of, **2,** 34–35
Trade Marks Act, 1938...**20,** 603–609, *passim*; **27,** 639, 641, 644
Trading with the Enemy Act, 1939... **9,** 537–539, 546, 554–555; **11,** 30; **12,** 63; **18,** 26, 29, 30, 32, 36, 171, 172, 174, 176, 177, 184, 185, 186, 189, 511, 579, 646, 650, 726; **19,** 572–578; **20,** 602–609; **21,** 462, 466, 470, 471; **22,** 901–903, 907–908; **24,** 899; **27,** 621, 623–624, 629–631, 638–645, 646, 648; **30,** 406, 412, 416
Trading with the Enemy (Amendment) Act, 1914...**20,** 605, 608
treason, law as to, **15,** 92–104
Treaties of Peace (Italy, etc.) Act, 1947...**16,** 560–561, 562; **17,** 5
Treaty of Peace Act, 1919...**1,** 211
—Orders under, **1,** 224; **4,** 547–548; **6,** 240–241
Treaty of Peace (Italy) Order, 1948, **17,** 5
Turkey, Treaty of Berlin and additional Convention (1878), **5,** 25–27
U.S.S.R.—
—recognition of Soviet Government, **5,** 51, 96
—Trade Agreement (1921), **1,** 295–296
U.S.A.—
—Arbitration Agreement (1910), **1,** 193; **22,** 414; **27,** 545

United Kingdom—*continued*
—Blaine–Pauncefote Treaty (1889), **6,** 298–301, 315
—Boundary Waters Treaty (1909), **7,** 8; **9,** 316; **24,** 564
—Commercial Treaty (1815), **9,** 368–370; **10,** 396–397
—Consular Convention (1951), **22,** 553–555
—Convention (1899), disposition of real and personal property, **1,** 347; **5,** 401–404; **12,** 274–276; **26,** 483–486
—Double Taxation Agreement (1945), **24,** 632–637; **34,** 188–191
—Exchange of Notes (1930), Sulu Islands, **23,** 107
—Executive Agreement (1942), jurisdiction over U.S. servicemen, **24,** 551
—Extradition Treaty (1842), **6,** 315; **11,** 101–104
— —(1900), **1,** 272–273
— —(1931), **6,** 301; **9,** 409–410; **18,** 339
—Fisheries Convention (1818), **1,** 236–237, 331–332, 335–336; **6,** 154–156; **18,** 118
—Fisheries Treaty (1908), **6,** 347
—forces of, in, **21,** 111–113
—General Treaty of Arbitration (1897), **27,** 544–545
—Hay–Pauncefote Treaty (1902), **24,** 147
—Income Tax Convention (1945), **24,** 632–637; **34,** 188–191
—Jay Treaty (1794), **4,** 535–536; **5,** 480; **9,** 369; **10,** 396–397; **13,** 181–182; **14,** 1–3; **19,** 435, 436; **22,** 10, 591–604; **23,** 460–467; **24,** 564; **26,** 483–486
—Jay Treaty (1794), Act of 1797 implementing, **22,** 596, 597, 598
—Lend-Lease Agreement, **34,** 183–187
—Liquor Treaty (1924), **2,** 115; **6,** 3–7; **7,** 163–164, 203–205, 454–455; **11,** 134–135
—Naturalization Treaty (1815), **9,** 368–370
—Naturalization Treaty (1870), **7,** 284–287; **9,** 342; **11,** 6–9; **28,** 275
—Peace Treaty (1783), **22,** 598; **23,** 464
—Treaty of Ghent (1814), **14,** 2–3; **23,** 460, 465–466
—Treaty of Washington (1871), **1,** 327; **5,** 86 n., 176
—Treaty, migratory birds (1916), **1,** 4
—Webster–Ashburton Treaty (1842), **5,** 87–88; **6,** 8–10, 298–301, 315; **7,** 3–8; **20,** 40, 41; **24,** 568

United Kingdom—*continued*
U.S.A. and France, Arbitration Agreement (1951) *re* gold looted by Germany, **20,** 441–413, *passim,* 467, 470, 475
U.S.A. (Visiting Forces) Act (1942), **12,** 125, 139; **15,** 160, 164
Venezuela, Treaty (1942) *re* Gulf of Paria, **18,** 152
Visiting Forces Act, 1952...**19,** 221; **21,** 113 n.
Visiting Forces (British Commonwealth) Act, 1933...**12,** 126, 138, 167; **19,** 220; **20,** 184–186; **21,** 111–113
War Damage Act, 1941...**9,** 375
Washington Accord on German Property in Switzerland (1946), **27,** 477–478, 492, 497, 499, 501, 503, 507, 528, 556
United Nations: *see also* Charter of the United Nations; Congo, U.N. Operation in, *and* UNEF
accredited representatives, jurisdictional immunity, **35,** 227–232
Administration for International Assistance, **23,** 510, 511
admission, effects of, whether retroactive, **27,** 571
budget, **34,** 288–291, 309, 335, 351, 379–380
Charter of: *see* Charter of the United Nations
competence to bring claims, **16,** 320–321, 322–323, 324–325, 329–330
conventions and, legislative functions, **18,** 389
Economic and Social Council, functions, **18,** 449–450
Educational, Scientific and Cultural Organization: *see* UNESCO
enforcement action, **34,** 294, 352, 356, 387
—economic problems, **34,** 296
" expenses of the Organization ", **34,** 285–396 *passim*
—notion of, **34,** 325–326
—obligation of S. C. members, **34,** 354
—right to refuse payment, **34,** 324, 329, 330–332, 343
files, immunities of, **20,** 382–383
financial obligation of Members, **34,** 327, 391–393
forces, right of passage, Charter provisions, **31,** 82, 113
General Assembly—
—Administrative Tribunal and, **21,** 310–311, 316, 317–318, 328, 330–331, 343–347
—Administrative Tribunal, Resolution amending Statute, **23,** 572
— —Resolution approving Statute (1949), **21,** 331, 334
— —Resolution on access to, **24,** 720

United Nations—*continued*
General Assembly—*continued*
—Advisory Opinion of I.C.J. and, **18,** 470
—approval of budget, **34,** 293, 298
—budgetary powers, **21,** 330, 337–339; **32,** 443–444, 445, 453, 454
—Charter, competence subject to, **22,** 658, 660, 681
—decisions, important questions, **34,** 293, 355
—domestic jurisdiction, intervention in, **34,** 319
—Eritrea, Resolution on (1949), **18,** 389; **25,** 9
—Exploitation of Natural Resources, Resolution (1952), **20,** 309, 313; **22,** 40–41
—functions, **21,** 344
—Genocide, Resolution on (1946), **18,** 370
—I.C.J., Resolution on (1947), **18,** 388
—international force, establishment of, **34,** 299, 360, 362
—League, assumption of functions by U.N. Resolution, **23,** 66
—legislative function, **18,** 389–390
—Libya, Economic and Financial, Resolution, **25,** 2–26, 517–521
—mandated territories, supervision of, **22,** 665, 683–689; **23,** 40, 43, 44–45
—Palestine, partition Resolution, **18,** 164, 166; **31,** 517
—peace and security functions, **34,** 292, 294, 321, 350, 359, 361, 371–372, 386
—powers, **21,** 310–347
—powers, supervision of mandates system, **23,** 38–70
—procedure, **22,** 651 *et seq.*
—recommendations of, **22,** 665, 685
—residuary powers of Council of League, **23,** 42–43, 45, 50, 67
—secondary organs, creation, **34,** 390
—Security Council and, **17,** 329–330
—South-West Africa, Committee on, Resolution concerning, **23,** 63, 69
—statements in Political Committee, **25,** 9
—status of, **21,** 344
—subsidiary organs, establishment of, **21,** 318, 333–334
—termination of Trusteeship Agreements, **35,** 359–360, 368, 382–383, 386–387, 429–430, 442, 464, 470, 480–482
—trust territories and, **22,** 684–687, 688
—trusteeship system, functions, **35,** 386–389, 399–400, 402
—voting procedure, **22,** 86, 651 *et seq.*

United Nations—*continued*
General Assembly—*continued*
—voting procedure—*continued*
— —" important questions ", **22,** 652, 656–657, 665, 667–668, 677–683
— —unanimity rule, **22,** 689
—war criminals, Resolutions on, **24,** 511, 515–516
General Assembly Resolutions, **22,** 103 *et seq.*, 651, 652, 653, 657, 659, 660, 664, 665, 684, 685–686, 686–689
—approving Staff Regulations (1952), **20,** 503, 509, 511, 521
—effect, **22,** 665, 668, 683–684, 688; **24,** 511–517; **35,** 430 n., 464
—finality, **34,** 338
—tribunal set up under, **22,** 103–113
Headquarters Agreement with U.S.A. (1947), **14,** 157; **16,** 294, 296, 298, 299; **17,** 296; **20,** 381, 382; **21,** 340–341; **23,** 438; **24,** 203; **32,** 309, 311, 317, 319, 324, 329, 330; **34,** 152, 154, 158, 160–167, 169; **35,** 222–227, 228, 230
—duties of U.S.A. under, **24,** 688–692
—protection against obstruction, **24,** 689
Human rights and: *see under* Charter of the United Nations
Hungary, Special Committee on, custody of documents, **27,** 433–435, 443–444
—Secretariat representative, duties of, **27,** 443
Korean conflict and, **20,** 579, 591, 597
—status of forces in, **20,** 591
League of Nations, successor to, **17,** 53–55; **23,** 66–67
League of Nations supervisory responsibilities and, **22,** 652, 660
—voting procedure, **22,** 654–655
legal capacity, **26,** 622
legal nature, **16,** 318–331; **17,** 323–326; **23,** 515–516
legal personality, **14,** 156; **19,** 490–491; **26,** 622; **32,** 318–319, 326 n.
locus standi, municipal courts, **17,** 323–326
mandated territory and, **22,** 86, 652, 655, 658, 664, 682; **23,** 38–70
mandatory and permissive functions, **34,** 330–331
member of staff of delegation, notification of appointment to receiving State, **27,** 254–255
membership of, **15,** 333–346; **17,** 326–330
military action by, whether act of war for Members, **26,** 634
name, unauthorized use, **26,** 618–620
observers, immunities of, **20,** 380–381

United Nations—*continued*
offer of amnesty by official, whether binding on Member State, **23,** 762–764
officials: *see also* Staff Regulations and Rules, *infra*; U.N. Administrative Tribunal *and* International officials
—Appeals Board, suspensive effect of appeal to, **27,** 436, 438, 440
—classification of, **27,** 451
—conditions of employment, **23,** 609–627
—contractual rights, **19,** 491–494
—crime committed by, **32,** 308–334; **35,** 222–227
—harmonization of conditions, U.N. and specialized agencies, **32,** 445, 449–450, 481, 482
—home leave, determination of place of, **27,** 428–432
—home leave, purpose of, **27,** 430
—Joint Disciplinary Committee, composition, **27,** 438, 439
—privileges and immunities of, **13,** 168–171; **14,** 154–155; **15,** 346–348; **16,** 293–297; **20,** 382–385; **32,** 308–333; **35,** 222–227
—privileges and immunities of, waiver, **23,** 616–625
—professional category, **32,** 449
—protection of, **16,** 326–328, 330–331
—Joint Disciplinary Committee, objection to composition of, **27,** 438, 439
—Review Board, functions, **27,** 420
—Review Board, legal error by, **27,** 418–422
—travelling expenses to attend Appeals Board, **27,** 424, 427
—Walters Selection Committee, **20,** 510–512, 519–522; **21,** 360
organs, competence of, **34,** 297, 318, 323, 352
organization, essentials of, **21,** 343–344
peace and security, powers of S.C. and G.A., **34,** 292, 321, 350, 353, 370–371
peaceful settlement of disputes by, **22,** 698–700
privileges and immunities, **14,** 155–156; **34,** 151–154
—Convention on (1946), **16,** 322; **21,** 336, 341, 345; **23,** 619; **26,** 620–621; **34,** 165
—delegates, **16,** 298–299; **17,** 295–299; **19,** 382–385, 500; **23,** 436–445, 619; **24,** 203
—jurisdiction, from, **23,** 509–510; **26,** 620–621
—U.S. legislation, **13,** 168, 170; **14,** 156; **17,** 323–326; **18,** 444–445, 447–448; **23,** 509; **32,** 312, 315–317, 318, 319, 323, 330

United Nations—*continued*
recommendations, effect on opposing States, **34,** 344
reparation for injuries suffered in service of, **16,** 318–331, *passim*
representatives to, immunity of, **24,** 203; **34,** 154–172
resolutions, categories of, **34,** 334
—formal legality, **34,** 383–385, 394
—intrinsic legality, **34,** 385, 394
San Fransisco Conference, appeal to, Canadian Indians, **27,** 243–244
Secretariat, **20,** 494; **21,** 317–318, 332, 336
Secretary-General—
—custody of documents, **27,** 443
—financial obligations incurred, **34,** 309
—functions, **34,** 393
—Memorandum on High Seas (1950), **18,** 158
—name, power to approve use of, **26,** 619–620
—powers in relation to officials and staff, **18,** 450–456; **21,** 360–388, *passim*; **27,** 439
—proceedings, authority to institute, **26,** 622–623
—Report on reservations to treaties (1950), **18,** 372, 379–380, 382
Security Council—
—admission of new Members and, **15,** 336–341; **17,** 327–328
—delegation, power of, **34,** 305, 385
—General Assembly and, **17,** 329–330
—peace and security functions, **34,** 292, 295–296, 300, 321, 350, 353, 356, 372, 386
—voting in, **22,** 661
—voting, abstention of Permanent Members, **34,** 383–384
South West Africa and, **22,** 86, 652, 655, 658, 664, 682; **23,** 38–70: *see also* South West Africa
sovereignty, renunciation by Members, **34,** 387
Specialized Agencies, **22,** 705–712; **23,** 517–584
—Convention on Privileges and Immunities (1947), **22,** 4, 700, 710
—occupied territory, legal position in, **18,** 444–446
Staff Regulations and Rules, **18,** 453; **19,** 492, 494; **20,** 494–499, 501–504, 506–510, 510–513, 514–518, 520–522; **21,** 312, 313, 320, 338, 342, 343, 363–364, 366–371, 373–377, 379–386, 388; **22,** 692, 787, 788, 792, 810–819; **23,** 610–613, 614–615, 617–623; **24,** 686, 718, 721, 722, 724–728, 731–737, 746–747; **27,** 418–422, 423–427, 429, 432, 435, 436–437; **32,** 443–447, 449, 450, 452–455, 462, 484

United Nations—*continued*
subject of international law, as, **16,** 321
subsidiary organs, **24,** 718
succession to functions of League, **17,** 53–55; **23,** 66–67
Switzerland, Agreement concerning properties in Geneva (1946), **21,** 341
Trusteeship Council, functions, **35,** 399–400, 401
ultra vires expenditure, **34,** 296–297
voluntary contributions, **34,** 330, 331, 343, 350, 374
voting system—
—abstention, significance, **34,** 375, 383–384
—Dumbarton Oaks Conference (1944), **22,** 679
—San Francisco Conference (1945), **22,** 679
war between Members of, **22,** 698–700
U.N. Administrative Tribunal—
—access to, right of, **24,** 719
—appeal limited to procedure, **27,** 442
—appeals from, **21,** 312, 316, 324
—awards of, **21,** 310, 311, 314, 329, 339
— —deductions from, **22,** 697–698
— —income tax and, **22,** 691–694
—competence, **20,** 507; **24,** 683–688, 715–722; **27,** 440–441
—competence to interpret earlier judgments, **22,** 689–691, 694–698
—costs, **32,** 456
—judgments, revision of, **27,** 297–300
—nature of, **21,** 312, 323, 328, 333, 338, 344
—representation by counsel, **22,** 793–797
—Statute of, **20,** 500–502; **21,** 310–324, *passim*, 328–341, *passim*, 343–347, 375; **22,** 692, 694, 696, 814; **23,** 572–576; **24,** 717, 719, 720, 722, 730, 732, 740; **27,** 299–300, 440; **32,** 461, 462
U.N. Appeals Board, function, **24,** 687
U.N. Children's Emergency Fund, **17,** 324–325
officials, Review Board, rescission of decision, **27,** 424–426
U.N. Command in Korea, criminal jurisdiction, **32,** 367–368
U.N. Declaration concerning Acts of Dispossession, etc. (1943), **15,** 287–288; **17,** 238
U.N. Educational, Scientific and Cultural Organization: *see* UNESCO
U.N. Emergency Force: *see* UNEF
U.N. Korean Reconstruction Agency, **23,** 515

U.N. Monetary and Financial Conference (1944): *see* Bretton Woods Conference
U.N. Relief and Rehabilitation Administration
—legal personality, **16,** 337–338; **19,** 490–491
—United Nations as "liquidator" of, **23,** 509–510
U.N. Relief and Works Agency, **24,** 683–688
—officials, status of, **24,** 715–722
—staff members, definition, **24,** 720
—status of, **24,** 718
U.N. Tribunal for Libya, jurisdiction, **25,** 517, 519–520
U.N. War Crimes Commission, **14,** 199, 293
United States of America—
"Act of State" doctrine, **35,** 2–50 *passim*
Administrative Procedure Act, **24,** 151
admiralty jurisdiction, **11,** 125, 152; **33,** 42
admission of states to the Union, **31,** 154 n.: *and see under* Florida, Louisiana *and* Texas
Agricultural Adjustment Act, **24,** 681
Air Transport Agreement with Peru, nationality of carrier, requirements, **31,** 416–424
Alabama, territorial waters, limits, **26,** 119–121
Alaska, cession to Russia, **15,** 52–53
Alien Enemy Act, **12,** 185, 186, 194; **13,** 120; **15,** 206, 207, 259–260, 262–264, 450–451, 509–512, 516–517
Alien Land Law of California, **11,** 233; **13,** 138–142; **20,** 345
Alien Property Custodian, **3,** 447–450; **9,** 546–547; **12,** 329–333, 346–349, 363–364, 424–427; **15,** 261; **17,** 359–367, 372; **18,** 513, 514
—powers, **12,** 342–346; **20,** 610–615
—recognition of acts abroad, **11,** 106–107
—sale of land by, **11,** 250–251
Alien Registration Act, 1940...**19,** 346, 349; **21,** 216; **24,** 889
aliens—
—acquisition of land by, Federal Acts, **5,** 257
— —California Alien Land Law, **11,** 233; **13,** 138–142; **20,** 245
— —state laws, **4,** 329–330; **31,** 1–3
—Acts relating to, **17,** 212–215
—admission to ordinary schools, **4,** 331
—equal protection of the laws, **11,** 195–196
—expulsion of, **1,** 251–253, 257–259; **13,** 148–150
U.S.A.—*continued*
aliens—*continued*
—expulsion in war time, **13,** 233–234
—internment in war, **1,** 208–209
—non-resident, right to inherit, **19,** 69–71, 393–394, 398–399; **20,** 292–296, 386–389; **21,** 203–208; **22,** 475–478; **24,** 482; **26,** 487–489; **28,** 300–309; **32,** 74–76, 203–223
—political rights, limitation to citizens, **11,** 196
—right to sue U.S., **32,** 198–202
annexation of States, implied recognition of, Austria and Germany (1938), **9,** 85; **12,** 26–28, 188–194
annexation of States, non-recognition of—
—Austria and Germany (1938), **13,** 32–34
—Czechoslovakia and Germany (1938), **10,** 78–79
—Estonia and U.S.S.R. (1940), **10,** 70–78, 86–90; **12,** 29–39; **15,** 47; **19,** 69–71; **23,** 706
—Latvia and U.S.S.R. (1940), **10,** 73; **12,** 39–43; **15,** 45–48; **18,** 61–64; **28,** 95–97
—Lithuania and U.S.S.R. (1940), **10,** 80–86; **20,** 193–195; **26,** 76; **32,** 73–76; **33,** 43–46
Anti-Smuggling Act (1935), **8,** 212–217: *see also* liquor treaties, *infra*
Anti-Trust (Sherman) Act, 1890...**4,** 182–183; **19,** 159, 197; **22,** 168, 182–183; **23,** 130–133, 273, 275; **24,** 673, 675; **31,** 213–214
Arabs, whether "white persons", **12,** 197
Arbitration Act, 1925...**31,** 403; **35,** 111, 120, 121
arbitration treaties of 1904 and 1905, **27,** 545
—practice in regard to, **27,** 544–547
—Taft-Knox Treaties (1913), **27,** 545
army, occupation of Germany, **2,** 440
—in France, jurisdiction over members of, **1,** 333
Argentina—
—Air Force Mission to, immunity, **30,** 329–393
—Consular Treaty (1853), **9,** 487
—Extradition Treaty with, **23,** 404
Arkansas, admission to American Union, **1,** 96
—Alien Land Act (1925), **4,** 329–330
Armistice, 1919, and Treaty of Versailles, rights derived from participation in, **3,** 348
Articles of War, **16,** 442–449; **19,** 603, 604, 606; **20,** 149, 588, 589, 621; **21,** 429; **23,** 779–780; **24,** 925–926; **28,** 595–601
Atomic Energy Act, 1954...**26,** 2–3

U.S.A.—*continued*
Austria—
—Claims Settlement Agreement (1947), **18,** 9; **19,** 459–461; **20,** 433–434; **22,** 398, 402
—"Pay as You Go" Agreement (1947), **20,** 431–432
—Peace Treaty of Vienna (1921), **4,** 81–82, 543
—termination of war with, **6,** 437–438; **11,** 268–269
—Treaty of Commerce and Navigation (1829), **18,** 502
—Treaty of Commerce and Navigation (1848), **1,** 387, 388
Bancroft Treaties, **25,** 128–129, 132
base in Philippines, whether "foreign country", **32,** 77–79
Bases (Agreement) Act, 1952...**22,** 154–156
bases in Newfoundland, whether "foreign country", **15,** 64–68
bases in West Indies, whether U.S. "possessions", **13,** 48–49
Basic Field Manual, **16,** 484–485, 532, 552; **18,** 644
Battle Monuments Commission, jurisdictional immunities, **8,** 227–228
Bavaria, Treaty abolishing Droit d'Aubaine and Taxes on Emigration (1845), **5,** 403
Belgium, Treaty of Commerce and Navigation (1875), **9,** 490
Bermuda, leases of territory in, **22,** 154–156
Brazil—
—Commercial Treaty (1935), **20,** 1
—Treaty of Commerce (1828), **23,** 716
Bremen, Hamburg, Lübeck, Treaty of Commerce (1827), **18,** 500–501, 504, 505
Bretton Woods Agreements Act, 1945...**22,** 707–708, 711, 712, 717, 718, 721
bunker control, practice, blockade, **10,** 267–272
"Buy American" Act, consistency with GATT, **33,** 390–396
Canada—
—Air Bases Agreement (1941), **21,** 114
—Ashburton Treaty, 1842: *see* Webster-Ashburton Treaty
—Boundary Convention, 1842: *see* Webster-Ashburton Treaty
—boundary, Niagara river, **4,** 122
—Boundary Waters Treaty (1909), **7,** 8; **9,** 316; **24,** 564; **28,** 464–467; **34,** 180–182
—Double Taxation Convention (1942), **23,** 490–492; **33,** 400–407

U.S.A.—*continued*
Canada—*continued*
—Extradition Treaties (1842, 1889, 1900, 1905, 1950), **5,** 284; **6,** 298–301, 315; **9,** 406–407; **21,** 235
—Report of Joint Commission with (1931), **6,** 132
—Treaty concerning Uses of Waters of Niagara River (1950), **24,** 557–571 *passim*
—Webster-Ashburton Treaty, 1842, **5,** 87–88; **6,** 8–10, 298–301, 393; **7,** 3–8; **20,** 40, 41; **22,** 593; **24,** 568–569
Carriage of Goods by Sea Act, 1936... **22,** 158; **23,** 116–122
Chile, Arbitration Convention (1858), **22,** 414
China—
—agreement on return of civilians, **35,** 237
—consular jurisdiction in, **10,** 265–266
—deportation of aliens to, **23,** 397–400; **26,** 478 n.
—extraterritorial rights, termination of, **12,** 252; **28,** 195
—Immigration Treaty (1880), **1,** 321; **11,** 10; **23,** 453; **24,** 578
—non-recognition of National Government, **5,** 42–43
—Relinquishment of Extraterritorial Rights, Treaty for (1943), **12,** 252; **28,** 195
—Treaty of Commerce (1903), **28,** 196
—Treaty of Friendship, Commerce and Navigation (1946), **22,** 90–97; **35,** 236–239
—(People's Republic) "Agreed Announcement", 1955, *re* return of nationals, **20,** 299–300
—(Republic of) Economic Aid Agreement (1948), **24,** 814; **27,** 547
Chinese Exclusion Act, **1,** 112; **20,** 353
"citizen" and "subject", meaning, **34,** 99–107
citizenship, meaning, **34,** 495–496. *See also under* Nationality
Civil Aeronautics Act, **28,** 117, 127, 131, 135–136
Civil Affairs Manual, **18,** 603, 644, 647
Civil War (1861–1865), **19,** 551
Collisions at Sea, Act to Adapt Regulations for Preventing, **7,** 480–481
Colombia, Treaty of Peace, Amity, Navigation and Commerce (1846), **5,** 403
coloured races, treatment of, **4,** 355–356

U.S.A.—*continued*
coloured schools, assignment of aliens to, **4,** 331
Communications Act, 1934...**22,** 712
Communist Government of China, recognition as *de facto* Government, **28,** 94
confiscation of enemy property, constitutionality, **33,** 447, 448–449
Connecticut, Compensation Act, **1,** 351
conscientious objectors, naturalization of, **5,** 226–232
Constitution—
—Art. 1 (due process clause), **21,** 20, 216–217; **34,** 110, 113–115
—Art. 1 (foreign relations power), **18,** 271–272; **34,** 124
—Art. 1 (power of Congress to declare war), **20,** 578; **21,** 417; **22,** 897, 932, 933, 937
—Art. 1 (regulation of armed forces), **19,** 604
—Art. 1 (regulation of foreign commerce, and offences against law of nations), **24,** 5, 7; **32,** 90, 94
—Art. 1 (retroactive legislation), **19,** 349
—Art. 2 (pardon power of the President), **23,** 763
—Art. 2 (treaty-making power), **1,** 4–7; **2,** 315–316; **9,** 488; **11,** 1–10; **13,** 179; **19,** 455; **22,** 934; **24,** 554, 885; **28,** 420–423
—Art. 3 (diplomatic envoys), **9,** 431; **34,** 153, 171–172
—Art. 3 (right to jury trial), **24,** 553
—Art. 3 (suits with aliens), **34,** 101–103, 105
—Art. 5 (amendment of Constitution), **24,** 552
—Art. 6 (treaties), **9,** 488; **15,** 54–55; **16,** 308; **19,** 313; **22,** 582; **23,** 244; **24,** 427, 551–552, 554; **24,** 558; **26,** 483; **28,** 465; **31,** 402, 404; **32,** 94–95; **33,** 392, 393
—competence of State and Federal Governments, **11,** 192
—expulsion of alien, membership of Communist Party, **20,** 333 n.
—extent of judicial power, **17,** 297
—foreign relations, exclusive powers of President, **18,** 271–272
—" full faith and credit " clause, **20,** 18
—international law and, **15,** 486–487; **21,** 287; **24,** 5, 7; **32,** 324
—non-resident aliens, application to, **26,** 2–3
—offences against law of nations, **34,** 4
—powers of President, **18,** 271–272; **20,** 415–416
—right to travel, **35,** 132

U.S.A.—*continued*
Constitution—*continued*
—treason, provision as to, **18,** 266, 274
—treaties as supreme law, **9,** 488; **19,** 313; **22,** 582; **23,** 244; **24,** 427, 551–552, 554, 558; **26,** 483; **28,** 465; **32,** 94–95
Constitution, Amendments—
—First, **19,** 349; **20,** 346; **24,** 689; **35,** 91
—Fifth, **1,** 416, 417, 431; **2,** 280; **4,** 330–331; **19,** 352, 353, 357; **20,** 268, 272, 282–284, 297–299, 326, 344–349, 493–499, 501–505, 510, 513, 515, 517; **21,** 373; **22,** 267, 398–399, 403, 576, 932; **23,** 245; **24,** 553, 955; **26,** 425, 442; **34,** 16, 18; **35,** 197–205
— —expatriation laws, **35,** 197–205
— —right to travel, **35,** 90, 95
—Sixth, **1,** 431; **11,** 196; **22,** 205; **23,** 245; **24,** 553
—Seventh, **24,** 554, 555, 556
—Eighth, **26,** 442; **35,** 195
—Tenth, **1,** 5; **24,** 552, 553
—Fourteenth, **1,** 240–241; **2,** 265, 314; **10,** 192, 196; **19,** 312; **20,** 346; **21,** 188; **24,** 478, 689; **25,** 113; **26,** 423, 425
—Eighteenth, **1,** 327; **28,** 122–123
consuls, immunity of, state courts, **33,** 371–372
consuls, foreign—
—jurisdiction in U.S.A., **10,** 156–158, 160
—special protection of, **5,** 318–319
continental shelf claims, **17,** 126–133
Continental Shelf Proclamation, 1945, **18,** 152, 153; **23,** 128–129
continental shelf, rights of States and Federal Government, **31,** 141–205 *passim*
contractual claims of nationals, practice regarding, **26,** 268
Costa Rica, Consular Convention (1852), **11,** 208–211
Criminal Code (enlistment in foreign armed force; conspiracy against United States), **1,** 181, 182
criminal jurisdiction of, **6,** 175–177
Cuba—
—breach of relations, actions in U.S. courts, **32,** 70–72; **33,** 36–43
—Convention for Prevention of Smuggling of Liquors (1926), **6,** 127
—Extradition Treaties (1904 and 1926), **5,** 282; **28,** 352–353
—Reciprocal Trade Agreement (1934), **22,** 584; **24,** 670–672
—Reciprocity and Commercial Treaty (1902), **2,** 345; **5,** 354; **22,** 583–589; **24,** 670–672

U.S.A.—*continued*
Cuba—*continued*
—Special Arbitration Agreement (1927), **5**, 264–265
Cuban sugar quota, reduction of, **35**, 3, 7, 19, 21–22
Czechoslovakia, recognition of, **11**, 57–59
Death on the High Seas Act, **24**, 267–271, 581–583; **26**, 119–121, 242 n.; **32**, 86–89, 119, 121; **33**, 148, 149, 153
Declaratory Judgment Act, **21**, 171
Defense Bases Compensation Act, 1941...**13**, 44
Denmark—
—Mutual Defense Agreement (1950), **22**, 550–551
—Treaty of Commerce and Navigation (1826), **4**, 449; **5**, 376; **7**, 390
diplomatic immunity, law as to, **28**, 367; **32**, 314, 324, 331
—Act of 1790...**9**, 433; **23**, 443
Displaced Persons Act, 1948...21, 229
dollar, gold content, Congressional Resolution (1938), **8**, 13–22; **9**, 24; **11**, 211–212
Dominican Republic, Extradition Treaty (1909), **34**, 139
due process of law—
—meaning, **11**, 81
—right of alien to, **3**, 287; **11**, 192–194; **20**, 330–333, 343–349; **21**, 213–218
Emergency Fleet Corporation, **2**, 136–137
Espionage Act, 1917...**24**, 7
Estonia, Treaty of Friendship, Commerce and Consular Rights (1925), **12**, 259–260
Executive, conclusiveness of statement on jurisdictional immunity, **13**, 76–78
exiled governments—
—attitude to, **10**, 10–23
—Dutch Government, **10**, 20
expatriation: *see under* Nationality
Export Trade Act, **12**, 171–172
extradition law, **6**, 301–302; **13**, 157; **22**, 988–991
—inter-State extradition, **13**, 67–69; **15**, 293–295
extradition procedure, **31**, 377
Fair Labor Standards Act, application to leased base areas abroad, **13**, 48–49
Federal Aviation Act, inter-state transport, **35**, 68
Federal Employers' Liability Act, **20**, 202
Federal Maritime Board, extent of jurisdiction, **35**, 103–109
Federal Power Act, **24**, 559, 565, 566, 570

U.S.A.—*continued*
Federal Tort Claims Act, 1938...**17**, 404–407; **18**, 549, 550, 552, 553, 555, 557; **24**, 89–93; **26**, 62–63, 67; **28**, 132; **32**, 77–79, 689
Federal Trade Commission Act, **12**, 170–171
First War Powers Act, 1941...**28**, 640
Fisheries Proclamation, 1945...**18**, 114, 152, 153
Foreign Agents Registration Act, 1938...**34**, 154
Foreign Assistance Act, *Sabbatino* provision, **35**, 49–50
Foreign Claims Settlement Commission, **34**, 19 n. *See also* International Claims Settlement Act, *infra*
—equity, application of, **30**, 153
—evidence, corroboration, **30**, 199, 200, 203
—inquiries on valuation, **30**, 200 n.
—legal status, **30**, 533–534, 536
—panel opinions, **30**, 131 n.
—relation to claims procedure under Peace Treaties, **30**, 532–536
—shareholder claims, practice as to, **30**, 198–200
foreign relations, conduct of, **8**, 48–54
France—
—Agreement, jurisdiction over U.S. forces (1918), **1**, 333
—Byrnes-Blum Agreement *re* certain war claims (1946), **19**, 454, 455
—Consular Convention (1853), **2**, 315; **5**, 251–252, 362; **11**, 211–212; **15**, 324; **16**, 259
—Economic Co-operation Agreement (1948), **19**, 255
—Extradition Treaty (1909), **7**, 339–340; **9**, 396
—Lend-Lease Agreement (1941), **22**, 980
—and the United Kingdom, Arbitration Agreement (1951), *re* gold looted by Germany, **20**, 441–463 *passim*, 467, 470, 475
GATT, quota reservation, legality, **33**, 375–379
Germany—
—Agreement on Settlement for Surplus Property (1953), **24**, 952
—Agreements on Validation of German Dollar Bonds (1953), **24**, 774, 777, 779
—annexation of Austria, non-recognition of, **9**, 85; **12**, 26–28, 188–194; **13**, 32–34
— —recognition of, **9**, 89
—Claims Conventions (1921 and 1922), **2**, 188; **5**, 185–186; **22**, 416, 851
—Commercial Treaty (1954), national treatment clause, **34**, 214–217
—declaration of war (1941), **21**, 434

U.S.A.—*continued*
Germany—*continued*
—Extradition Treaty with, **7,** 358
—hostilities against, 1941...**10,** 433–434
—Naturalization (Bancroft) Treaty (1868), **1,** 208
—occupation of, requisition, **32,** 595–601
—Peace Treaty (1921), **5,** 476–477; **11,** 238, 264; **14,** 173, 175–176; **18,** 503, 505
—sovereignty over Czechoslovakia, recognition of, **9,** 84
—termination of war with, **1,** 443–444
—Treaty of Friendship, Commerce and Consular Rights (1923), **5,** 477; **9,** 2, 71, 486, 491, 495; **14,** 171–176; **18,** 504; **21,** 433, 437, 441, 443; **28,** 467–469
—Treaty of Friendship, Commerce and Navigation (1955), **22,** 939; **24,** 9–8; **28,** 470
—Treaty *re* inheritance of real property (1925), **15,** 460
gold content of dollar, Congressional Resolution (1938), **8,** 13–22; **9,** 24; **11,** 26–27
Gold looted by Germany, Arbitration Agreement with France and U.K. (1951), **20,** 441–463 *passim*, 467, 470, 475
Great Britain—
—Arbitration Agreement (1910), **1,** 193; **22,** 414; **27,** 545
—Jay Treaty (1794), **4,** 535–536; **5,** 480; **9,** 369; **10,** 396–397; **13,** 181–182; **14,** 1–3; **19,** 435, 436; **22,** 10, 591–604; **23,** 460–467; **24,** 564; **20,** 483–486
Greece—
—Accord on military facilities (1953), **21,** 123
—Aid Agreements (1944 and 1947), **21,** 122–123
—Consular Convention (1902), **1,** 346–347; **9,** 159; **15,** 110; **16,** 309–311
—Extradition Treaty (1931), **7,** 344–346, 351; **31,** 370–372
—Treaty of Friendship, Commerce and Navigation (1951), **24,** 481; **33,** 408–409; **34,** 85, 88; **35,** 208–215
Guam, naval defence area in territorial waters, **32,** 83–86
Guatemala—
—Protocol of Arbitration (1929), **5,** 179
—Treaty of Commerce (1936), **22,** 617–618
habeas corpus, scope of proceedings, **31,** 357–358, 366

U.S.A.—*continued*
Hague Convention on Pacific Settlement of Disputes (1907), " understanding " *re* Art. 53...**27,** 545
Hamburg, Treaty with (1827), **5,** 475–477
Harter Act, Hague Rules, 1921 and, **33,** 398
Hawaii, annexation of, **10,** 279–281
—title to land, effect on, **13,** 35–36; **35,** 74
Hawaiian Organic Act, 1900...**35,** 75
high seas, definition of, **11,** 174–175
Hindus, naturalization of, **2,** 244–246
Honduras, Treaty of Friendship, Commerce and Consular Rights (1927), **7,** 454–455; **11,** 119; **22,** 283; **34,** 53, 54, 60
Hungary—
—Treaty of Friendship, Commerce and Consular Rights (1925), **20,** 386–389
—Treaty of Peace (1921), **4,** 81–82
Iceland, Defence Force in, **23,** 260–264
Immigration Act, 1891...**20,** 352
—1917...**20,** 277–278, 280, 350, 351, 353, 354, 355; **24,** 58–59, 444, 449, 450, 451
—1924...**9,** 382; **11,** 9–10; **20,** 357; **21,** 229; **22,** 465, 599, 602; **23,** 35, 453–454; **24,** 450, 578–580
Immigration and Nationality Act, 1952...**20,** 269, 279, 283, 349, 350, 355, 356, 357–359; **21,** 83, 169, 170, 179–180, 182, 185, 187, 188, 226–229; **22,** 423, 461, 465–466, 589–591; **23,** 35–37, 398–400, 616, 620, 623; **24,** 58–59, 444–445; **26,** 133, 141–142, 404, 415, 421, 423, 425, 427, 428–434, 438–440, 442–444, 451–454, 461n., 475–478, 510–512; **28,** 275, 277, 286–287, 316–318, 463; **31,** 346–352; **32,** 186–192, 237–246
—deportable alien, **35,** 196
—deportation provisions, **34,** 21–22, 24–26, 128–131
—expatriation provisions, **34,** 108–121; **35,** 194, 197, 199, 202
immigration laws, **1,** 257–258; **4,** 536–537; **6,** 289–290; **15,** 218–220, 265–268, 269–276
immigration regulations, " diplomatic visa ", **32,** 312–313
immunity of foreign States—
—" suggestion ", **9,** 212–213; **12,** 77–87, 107–111; **28,** 165–168; **32,** 133–134, 136, 137, 139–140; **33,** 185–189; **34,** 13, 89, 125. *See also* State Department, certificate of, *infra*
—Tate letter, **32,** 133; **33,** 185; **35,** 114–115

U.S.A.—*continued*
import regulations, manifest, requirement of, **11,** 130–135
independence, recognition by Great Britain, **31,** 178
Indian tribes, treaties with, **10,** 1–4
Internal Revenue Code, 1939...**22,** 543, 583–588; **26,** 29, 31–32, 34–37
Internal Security Act, 1950...**19,** 352; **20,** 505; **21,** 214–217, 226; **26,** 132 n., 142–143
International Claims Commission, **34,** 18–20
International Claims Settlement Act, 1940...**20,** 211
—1949...**20,** 233, 237–240, 436, 566; **21,** 55, 157, 164, 165, 292, 296; **22,** 332, 405–407; **24,** 317; **26,** 255–360 *passim*; **28,** 629–633; **30,** 116–225 *passim*; **34,** 16, 17, 18–20, 494–495
international law as law of the land, **32,** 324
International Organizations Immunities Act, 1945...**13,** 168, 170; **14,** 156; **17,** 323–326; **18,** 444–445, 447–448; **23,** 509; **32,** 312, 315–317, 318, 319, 323, 330; **34,** 151, 152–153, 158, 166
—U.N. officials, **35,** 224
internment of aliens in war, **1,** 208–209
Interstate Commerce Act, **28,** 115–116, 119, 126, 130, 137
Ireland, Treaty of Friendship, Commerce and Navigation, **28,** 286 n.; **31,** 320
Italy—
—Claims Agreement (Lombardo, 1947), **22,** 411; **24,** 655, 656, 658, 659; **25,** 164–166
—Commercial Treaty (1871), most-favoured-nation clause, **31,** 1–3
—Commercial Treaty (1913), **1,** 241, 351; **7,** 322
—Consular Convention (1878), **6,** 398–400; **9,** 71, 487
—Exchange of Notes implementing Peace Treaty (1949), **22,** 411, 864
—Executive Agreement (1948) under Peace Treaty, **28,** 603
—Extradition Treaty (1868), **18,** 320; **24,** 883, 885, 888; **28,** 340 n.; **31,** 356, 359–361, 362–364
—Financial and Economic Agreements (1947), **22,** 846, 854, 859, 863
—Treaty of Commerce and Navigation (1871), **1,** 241, 351; **7,** 322; **11,** 5
—Treaty of Establishment, **11,** 194
—Treaty of Friendship, Commerce and Navigation (1948), **22,** 580–582; **33,** 385–390

U.S.A.—*continued*
Italy—*continued*
—Treaty on Workmen's Compensation, **1,** 319–320
—War Claims, Memorandum of Understanding (1947), **22,** 949; **26,** 338–339
Japan—
—Acceptance of Surrender (1945), **21,** 107
—commencement of war with, **12,** 283–284, 289–300; **13,** 224–227
—Commercial Treaty (1953), **31,** 210, 217–218
—forces in, **23,** 239–240
— —Administrative Agreement (1952), **22,** 257–266; **23,** 265–268, 455–459; **24,** 227; **26,** 203–208
— — —Protocol to amend (1953), **23,** 264–265; **24,** 248–250
—jurisdiction in, land granted for military purposes, **31,** 121–128
—occupation of, **15,** 524–525
—Pacific islands, whether "acquired", **13,** 44–46
—prohibition on trade with, 1941, **29,** 353
—relinquishment of extraterritorial rights in (1894), **28,** 197
—Security Treaty (1952), **23,** 246, 247, 264–268, 455–459
— —constitutionality under Japanese Constitution, **32,** 43–64
—Status of Forces Agreement (1960), **34,** 192–198
—Treaty of Commerce and Navigation (1911), **1,** 320; **4,** 447–448; **11,** 1–5, 194, 195, 233; **14,** 158–160; **15,** 509
—Treaty of Friendship, Commerce and Navigation (1953), **24,** 673–677
Johnson Debt Default Act, 1934...**8,** 270
Jones Act: *see* Seamen's Act, *infra*
Jordan, Economic Aid Agreements (1952 and 1954), **22,** 619
judicial review of distribution of lump sum settlement, **22,** 405–407; **24,** 316–318; **26,** 347–352
jurisdiction, nationals abroad, over, **1,** 159–161
Kansas Workmen's Compensation Law, **1,** 319
Labor Management Relations Act (Taft-Hartley), **24,** 168, 169, 171
Labor Union Law, 1954...**24,** 226
Latvia, Treaty of Friendship, **18,** 63
Lease-Lend Act, 1941...**10,** 434; **12,** 175–177
Liberia, Consular Convention (1938), **34,** 70, 75–77
—Treaty of Friendship, Commerce and Navigation (1938), **26,** 228, 230; **34,** 70, 75

U.S.A.—*continued*
Libya, Base Rights Agreement (1954), **23,** 241–244
" Liquor " treaties: *see* " prohibition " treaties, *infra*
Lithuania, Treaty of Friendship, Commerce and Consular Rights (1928), **28,** 96
Louisiana—
—admission of, 1812...**31,** 177, 180, 182
—rights over marginal sea, **17,** 131–133
Maritime Commission, **12,** 342
marriage in Japanese Consulate, New York, validity, **13,** 93–94
marriage of women to aliens, Act of 1907...**5,** 240–242
Merchant Marine Act, 1920...**11,** 150–152
Merchant Seamen's Act, penal clauses, **35,** 97, 99–101
merchant ships, requisition of, 1917, **1,** 415, 418; **5,** 510, 514; **28,** 612, 613 n., 621 n.
Mexico—
—boundary, **1,** 105–106
—Boundary Treaties (1848–1905), **5,** 85, 176, 398; **6,** 114–116; **11,** 94–99; **13,** 178–181; **21,** 218–219; **26,** 120–121; **31,** 171 n., 173, 183, 196–199
—Claims Convention (1923), **5,** 176, 453; **6,** 275; **26,** 261
—Extradition Treaty (1899), **6,** 318–319; **24,** 257, 261, 262; **26,** 518, 520, 522
—Military Service Agreement (1943), **28,** 294
—non-recognition of Mexican Government, **2,** 49–50
—Special Claims Convention (1934), **9,** 336
—Treaty concerning Stolen Vehicles (1936), **17,** 20–22; **20,** 411–412; **22,** 616
—Treaty of Peace, etc. (Guadeloupe Hidalgo) (1848), **5,** 85, 176, 398; **6,** 113; **13,** 178–181; **21,** 218–219; **26,** 120–121; **31,** 171, 173–174
—Utilization of Waters of Colorado, etc. Rivers, Treaty (1944), **22,** 573–580; **23,** 360–363; **26,** 556–557
—Vera Cruz, occupation of, **5,** 480–481
Migratory Bird Treaty Act, 1918...**1,** 4
military commissions, authority after cessation of hostilities, **13,** 269–279
Morocco—
—Treaty of Peace and Friendship (1787), **19,** 262, 264, 275; **21,** 139
—Treaty of Peace and Friendship (1836), **19,** 255–266 *passim,* 274,

U.S.A.—*continued*
Morocco—*continued*
—Treaty of Peace and Friendship (1836)—*continued*
275, 276, 282, 283, 288–302 *passim,* 343; **21,** 139
most-favoured-nation clause, unconditional policy, **26,** 594–595
Mutual Defense Assistance Act, 1949, **21,** 419
nationality, acquisition of, " first papers ", **25,** 235, 239
National Labor Relations Act, application to alien seamen, **34,** 51–80
Nationality Act, 1907...**22,** 437–438; **24,** 459, 460, 461; **26,** 449, 454 n.
—1940, certificate of identity pending proceedings, **21,** 170–171
— —citizenship by birth, **21,** 172–173
— —expatriation provisions, **13,** 129; **18,** 268, 269, 272, 273; **19,** 329, 330, 331, 333; **20,** 255; **21,** 159, 169; **22,** 437–440; **26,** 404, 410–411, 415, 420–421, 423; **26,** 425, 427, 428–434, 438–440, 442–444, 446, 451–454, 459, 460–467; **28,** 287–290; **30,** 350–352; **31,** 324–326; **34,** 108–121. *See also under* Nationality
— —naturalization obtained by fraud, **13,** 121–123
— —oath of allegiance, **24,** 302
— —residence for naturalization, maritime service, **20,** 268, 283, 348; **24,** 451
nationality laws, **6,** 256–257; **14,** 115–116; **15,** 218–224, 226–227, 230–234, 252–254, 261–264; **17,** 204–212, 215–216, 219, 220–225, 226–228; **18,** 265–276; **26,** 331–332, 460–465. *See also* Immigration and Nationality Act, 1952 *and* naturalization laws, *infra*
332, 460–465
—Cable Act, Naturalization and Citizenship of Married Women, 1922...**11,** 5–6; **15,** 261
—Citizenship Act, 1934...**20,** 252–253
—Philippine inhabitants, **9,** 40
nationality treaties (Bancroft), **22,** 359, 385; **25,** 111, 115, 123–138, 140, 143, 145
naturalization laws, **5,** 226; **6,** 122; **7,** 9–10; **9,** 341, 344, 347, 351–360; **11,** 189–190; **25,** 113–123; **31,** 318–323
—" Arabs ", naturalization of, **12,** 197
—naturalization, cancellation of, **13,** 121–123
—refusal to bear arms, **13,** 124–128
naturalization practice, **5,** 232; **25,** 128
naval base in Italy, suit against U.S. Government, **28,** 158–164

U.S.A.—*continued*
Naval Code for Time of War, 1900, **23,** 737
Netherlands—
—decrees affecting Dutch assets in U.S.A., **9,** 150
—Treaty of Friendship, Commerce and Navigation (1956), **28,** 495; **31,** 218–219; **33,** 449
Neutrality Act, 1939...**9,** 6, 39–43; **34,** 61 n.
Newfoundland, Bases Agreement (1941), **22,** 270–272
New York Civil Practice Act, **12,** 256, 259; **15,** 128, 130, 314, 316, 453; **22,** 909–911; **34,** 18
—Decedent Estate Law, **12,** 224, 245, 246
—Domestic Relations Court Act, **12,** 252; **13,** 93
—Real Property Law, **12,** 222–224
—Surrogate's Court Act, **9,** 68–71; **22,** 552; **26,** 487–489; **34,** 121, 122
—Workmen's Compensation Law, **22,** 580–583, 911 n.; **26,** 484, 486
Nicaragua—
—Consular Convention (1868), **11,** 208–211
—Extradition Treaty (1923), **12,** 237
non-recognition of absorption of Baltic States, **35,** 51–57, 62–65
non-resident aliens, right of inheritance, **19,** 69–71, 393–394, 398–399; **20,** 292–296, 386–389; **21,** 203–208; **22,** 475–478; **24,** 482; **26,** 487–489; **28,** 300–309; **32,** 74–76, 203–223; **35,** 205–216, 235–239
non-resident corporations, standing to sue, **33,** 253–254
Norris-La Guardia Act, **31,** 138–139, 233–234
—application to foreign ships, **31,** 227–240; **34,** 56–57, 63, 69
Norway—
—Agreement on trade with Germany (1918), **1,** 435
—Claims Convention (1948), **16,** 307–308; **28,** 611, 625, 629
—Consular Convention (1932), **9,** 5, 157, 162
—Naturalization Treaty (1869), **11,** 8
—Treaty of Amity and Commerce, **5,** 394; **11,** 219
Norway–Sweden, Treaty of Establishment (1827), **11,** 113–114, 123–124
Okinawa, occupation of, **17,** 404–407; **18,** 549–558
Opium Poppy Control Act, 1942...**12,** 267–271
Outer Continental Shelf Lands Act, **32,** 119–122; **33,** 153; **35,** 87

U.S.A.—*continued*
Palmas Island, acquisition of title, **4,** 3–4, 103–106, 108–115
Panama—
—Boundary Convention (1903), **1,** 94, 95; **2,** 101; **7,** 438–441; **9,** 118
—Boundary Convention (1914), **7,** 438–441
—Claims Conventions (1926 and 1936), **7,** 255–257, 477–480; **9,** 118
—Convention *re* Canal (1903), **7,** 439; **9,** 118; **23,** 116–118
Panama Canal Zone and: *see* Panama Canal Zone
Paraguay, Reciprocal Trade Agreement (1946), **24,** 678–681
Passport Act 1856...**26,** 134
Passport Act, 1918...**20,** 265, 266, 268, 296–298; **26,** 134, 139–140
Persia, Consular Convention (1856), **6,** 398–400; **11,** 209
Peru—
—Extradition Treaty, **24,** 263
—Treaty of Commerce (1870), **23,** 715
Philippine Islands—
—legislation for, **11,** 47–48
—liability for Spanish obligations, **1,** 58, 59
—nationality, **9,** 40
—part of U.S. territory, **5,** 76, 354
—Philippine Independence Act, 1934, 36–37, 40; **20,** 278–280; **23,** 31, 34; **24,** 448, 449, 450, 451
—Philippine Rehabilitation Act, 1946...**24,** 976
Philippines, Republic of, Military Bases Agreement (1947), **20,** 148–153; **23,** 125–126
Poland, Treaty of Friendship, Commerce and Consular Rights (1931), **12,** 245, 425; **14,** 163–165; **21,** 204–205; **28,** 307
prize law, **15,** 692
"Prohibition" laws, **1,** 327; **2,** 112–114; **4,** 19–20, 152–153, 181–183, 187, 188, 193–197; **6,** 3–7, 127; **11,** 128–135
—execution of, **3,** 151–169; **5,** 6–7
—extraterritorial effect, **4,** 152–153
"Prohibition" treaties, **1,** 111–112; **2,** 114–115; **3,** 151–163
Prussia—
—Treaty of Amity and Commerce (1799), **18,** 503; **23,** 735
— —(1828), **5,** 260, 475–478; **6,** 74–76; **11,** 238–242; **14,** 173–174; **18,** 500, 503, 504, 505
public policy, compensation for taking, **35,** 12
Public Vessels Act, 1925...**12,** 176; **24,** 481; **34,** 85, 87
Puerto Rico—
—maintenance of Spanish law, **1,** 76
—Organic Act of, 1917... **11,** 49–50

U.S.A.—*continued*
Puerto Rico—*continued*
—residents, service in U.S. forces, **17,** 42–47
Refugee Relief Act, 1953...**24,** 153–154; **26,** 511–512; **28,** 315–317; **33,** 293–296
requisition of merchant ships, 1917, **1,** 415, 418; **5,** 510, 514; **28,** 612, 613 n., 621 n.
Revenue Act, 1921—
—" foreign country ", **6,** 19; **23,** 32, 34
—tax on consular fees, **11,** 208
Revenue Act, 1926—
—estates of aliens, **12,** 274
—imported cigars, **22,** 586–587
Revenue Act, 1932, import tax, treaties and, **9,** 1–3
Revenue Act, 1935—
—estates of aliens, **12,** 274
—income tax, foreign government employees, **11,** 208
revenue laws, enforcement between States, **15,** 10–13
Rules of Land Warfare: *see* Warfare Rules *infra*
Russia, Convention ceeding Alaska (1867), **22,** 562–565
Russian Provisional Government, 1917, recognition of, **1,** 31, 51–53: *See also* Soviet Government, *infra*
Seamen's Act, 1915 (La Follette), **1,** 109; **9,** 159; **20,** 202; **24,** 170–171
—1920 (Jones Act), **11,** 119, 121; **20,** 197, 200, 203, 206, 210; **22,** 262; **24,** 269; **28,** 108–114, 145–148; **32,** 103–107; **33,** 155–158; **34,** 64 n., 71–72, 73 n.
—foreign ships, **34,** 46–49, 55
—territorial scope, **35,** 101–103
Securities Exchange Act, 1933...**9,** 405
—territorial scope, **31,** 206–209
Selective Draft Law, 1917...**11,** 191–192
Selective Service Act, 1948 and 1951, **22,** 466
Selective Training and Service Act, 1940...**19,** 638, 639; **21,** 178, 179; **22,** 460, 463–466, 1013–1014; **24,** 442, 444, 445; **26,** 398; **28,** 277–281, 294–296
Serbia—
—Commercial Treaty (1881), **7,** 452–453; **20,** 293–295; **21,** 71, 72
— —application to Yugoslavia, **35,** 206, 207
—Consular Convention (1881), **19,** 393, 385; **21,** 71, 72
—Extradition Treaty (1902), **21,** 67–68, 72, 73, 74; **24,** 510, 517; **28,** 326–328, 336

U.S.A.—*continued*
Settlement of War Claims Act, 1928, **4,** 479, 542–543; **5,** 510–513; **8,** 492–501; **19,** 583, 584
Ship Mortgage Act, compatibility with treaty provisions, **33,** 385–390
Shipping Act, 1916...**11,** 150
—foreign conferences and, **35,** 103–109
—production of documents, **32,** 100–102; **33,** 158–163
—restrictive practices sections, scope, **31,** 209–219
Shipping Board, **1,** 414–416; **2,** 136–139, 409, 420; **3,** 184–185; **11,** 149–152
—diplomatic status of officials, **4,** 390
—State commercial fleet, immunity of, **1,** 152
Ships of, in enemy ports, **10,** 509–514
sovereign immunity, operation of doctrine, **32,** 133, 639; **33,** 185. *See also under* Foreign States, immunity of
sovereignty, in unincorporated territory, **11,** 78–81
Soviet Government, non-recognition of, **1,** 51–53; **2,** 39–49; **3,** 297–298; **4,** 60–61, 340; **5,** 36–42
—recognition of, **4,** 58–59, 60–62; **9,** 68, 142, 145, 149, 184; **10,** 55–59, 68–70. *See also* U.S.S.R., Litvinov Assignment, *infra*
Spain—
—Boundary Treaty (1795), **7,** 131
—Claims Settlement Agreement (1871), **25,** 100–101
—Peace Treaty (1819), **1,** 93–94; **2,** 96
— —(1898), **4,** 3–4, 103, 113–114, 418–419; **5,** 354, 397–398; **17,** 43; **24,** 447, 448, 569; **26,** 553–555
—Treaty of Friendship and General Relations (1902), **22,** 461–462; **26,** 529–532
State Department, certificate of, **2,** 48; **10,** 20–22, 178–181, 193–196, 202–204, 206–207, 217–221, 224–226; **11,** 149, 204–205; **12,** 26–28, 32–42, 80–89, 108–111, 144–149; **14,** 155; **15,** 44–48, 520–521, 524–525; **18,** 58–59, 63, 492; **19,** 390–391; **20,** 173–176, 177, 380–381; **21,** 120; **22,** 220–224, 1012–1014; **23,** 121, 437–445; **24,** 203; **32,** 133–134, 136. *See also* immunity of foreign States, " suggestion ", *supra*
state succession and private rights, practice as to, **13,** 36–40
states of—
—jurisdictional immunity, suit by foreign State, **7,** 167–168
—territorial waters, **32,** 86–89

U.S.A.—*continued*
Submerged Lands Act...**31,** 141–143, 144–146, 152, 156, 173, 189–192, 195, 200; **35,** 82, 87
—legislative history, **31,** 146–158, 194
Subversive Activities Control Act, 1950...**20,** 345, 348; **35,** 89, 91, 92, 95
Sugar Act, 1937...**22,** 585, 587
Suits of Admiralty Act, 1920...**5,** 112–113; **11,** 152; **17,** 323–325
Supreme Court, jurisdiction, suits against ambassadors, **32,** 329, 330–332
Sweden—
—Consular Convention (1910), **6,** 399; **9,** 487; **11,** 120, 123
—Income Tax Convention (1940), **24,** 637
—Naturalization Convention (1869), **9,** 352
—Treaty of Amity and Commerce (1783), **6,** 372–378; **11,** 220
Switzerland—
—Double Taxation Convention (1951), **27,** 291–293; **34,** 199–201; **35,** 278–282
—Dual Nationals, Military Service, Convention (1937), **20,** 256–257
—Treaty of Arbitration and Conciliation (1931), **22,** 197; **27,** 480–482, 489, 503
—Treaty of Friendship, Commerce and Extradition (1850), **5,** 402; **7,** 307–309; **16,** 244–247; **21,** 178; **26,** 133
Tariff Acts, 1799–1894...**22,** 601–602
Tariff Act, 1897...**22,** 583, 584, 602–603
—1922...**5,** 106, 108, 138–140; **6,** 3–7, 20; **11,** 127, 129, 135; **22,** 586
—1930...**6,** 3–7, 20; **11,** 134; **22,** 565–567, 571–572, 583–588; **24,** 670
—1934...**22,** 584
Tariff Commission, functions and jurisdiction, **31,** 410–411
"Tate letter", **32,** 133; **33,** 185; **35,** 114–115
taxation, nationals abroad, **31,** 273–274
termination of war with Germany (1921), **1,** 443–444; **22,** 937
—Second World War, **22,** 932, 933, 935, 936, 937, 938, 939; **26,** 669–670, 672, 674 n., 678–680
territorial waters, breadth, **31,** 155–158, 167, 171, 178 n., 182
Texas—
—admission to Union, **17,** 15
—annexation of, **31,** 159, 161, 162–163, 167–168, 175
—legislation concerning Chinese, **1,** 321

U.S.A.—*continued*
Texas—*continued*
—rights over marginal sea, **17,** 126–131
theatre of war, New York as, **1,** 432
tort in violation of law of nations, **32,** 1–4; **34,** 1–6
Trade Agreements Act, 1934...**22,** 588, 589; **24,** 670–672; **33,** 376–377
Trade Agreements Extension Act, 1951...**31,** 410–411, 412, 414–416
Trade Mark Act, 1905...**23,** 137
Trade Mark Act, 1946 (Lanham Act), **23,** 135–137, 139–143, 270–275, 276–284
Trading with the Enemy Act, 1917, **5,** 260; **9,** 547; **11,** 59–60, 246, 250–251, 253, 264, 269
—amended, 1941...**12,** 225–229, 328, 333, 334, 336, 339, 343–346, 363–365, 378–382; **13,** 235–237; **14,** 172, 174–176, 182, 187–189, 191, 192, 193–194; **15,** 45–48, 261–262, 442–443, 453, 456–460, 462–465; **17,** 372–376; **18,** 482, 486, 494, 496, 498, 499, 513–514, 516–520, 566, 649, 650, 651, 652; **19,** 566, 567, 568, 578–587, 592, 594, 595; **20,** 386–388, 611, 621; **21,** 40, 433, 438, 439, 440, 442, 443; **22,** 184, 189, 478, 909, 918–921, 932–934, 935–939; **23,** 756–757; **24,** 896–902, 903–906, 907–910, 911–915, 932–938; **26,** 126, 162, 663–664, 670–671, 692; **27,** 475–476, 478, 490, 501, 505, 526, 548, 556; **28,** 300, 467, 469, 633–638, 639; **31,** 495–508; **32,** 557–560; **33,** 444–450; **34,** 490–494
—transactions with China, **35,** 238
treaties—
—Congress, power to implement, **12,** 267–270
—federal statutes and, **13,** 181–182; **31,** 1–3. *See also* treaties, supreme law of the land, *infra*
—state legislation and, **5,** 377; **10,** 394–397, 398–403; **11,** 219–221; **14,** 163–165
—supreme law of the land, as, **9,** 488; **15,** 54–55; **16,** 308; **19,** 313; **22,** 582; **23,** 244; **24,** 427, 551–552, 554, 558; **26,** 483; **28,** 465; **31,** 402, 404; **33,** 392, 393
—treaty-making power, **1,** 4–7; **2,** 315–316; **9,** 488; **11,** 1–10; **12,** 269; **13,** 179; **19,** 455; **22,** 934; **24,** 554, 885; **28,** 420–423
—Universal Postal Conventions, **1,** 314–315
Trusteeship, ex-Japanese mandated islands, **15,** 520–521, 523

U.S.A.—*continued*
Turkey, diplomatic relations with, **1,** 142
Uniform Code of Military Justice, **21,** 423, 426, 427, 428, 429, 430; **22,** 257–258, 265, 266–267, 897, 926–928; **23,** 241, 244, 245, 250, 455, 762; **24,** 549, 551, 924–925, 929
U.S.S.R., Litvinov Assignment (1933), **9,** 148–150; **10,** 49, 42–57, 66–68; **12,** 17–19, 23; **13,** 29–32; **17,** 65, 68; **26,** 269, 348, 357, 360; **28,** 422; **34,** 16–21
—effect on claims of nationals, **30,** 184, 186
—treaty nature, **32,** 212
U.K.—
—Arbitration Agreement (1910), **1,** 193; **22,** 414; **27,** 545
—Blaine-Pauncefote Treaty (1889), **6,** 298–301, 315
—Boundary Waters Treaty (1909), **7,** 8; **9,** 316; **24,** 564
—Commercial Treaty (1815), **9,** 368–370; **10,** 396–397
—Consular Convention (1951), **22,** 553–555
—Convention (1899), disposition of real and personal property, **12,** 274–276; **1,** 347; **5,** 401–404; **26,** 483–486
—Double Taxation Agreement (1945), **24,** 632–637; **34,** 188–191
—Exchange of Notes (1930) Sulu Islands, **23,** 107
—Executive Agreement (1942), jurisdiction over U.S. servicemen, **24,** 551
—Extradition Treaty (1842), **6,** 315; **11,** 101–104
— —(1900), **1,** 272–273
— —(1931), **6,** 301; **9,** 409–410; **18,** 339
—Fisheries Convention (1818), **1,** 236–237, 331–332, 335–336; **6,** 154–156; **9,** 2; **18,** 118
—Fisheries Treaty (1908), **6,** 347
—General Treaty of Arbitration (1897), **27,** 544–545
—Hay–Pauncefote Treaty (1902), **24,** 147
—Income Tax Convention (1945), **24,** 632–637; **34,** 188–191
—Jay Treaty (1794), **4,** 535–536; **5,** 480; **9,** 369; **10,** 396–397; **13,** 181–182; **14,** 1–3; **19,** 435, 436; **22,** 10, 591–604; **23,** 460–467; **24,** 564; **26,** 483–486
—Lend-Lease Agreement (1942), **34,** 183–187
—Liquor Treaty (1924), **2,** 115; **6,** 3–7; **7,** 163–164, 203–205, 454–455; **11,** 134–135

U.S.A.—*continued*
U.K.—*continued*
—Naturalization Treaty (1815), **9,** 368–370
— —(1870), **7,** 284–287; **9,** 342; **11,** 6–9; **28,** 275
—Peace Treaty (1783), **22,** 598; **23,** 464
—Treaty of Ghent (1814), **14,** 2–3; **23,** 460, 465–466
—Treaty of Washington (1871), **1,** 327; **5,** 85 n., 176
—Treaty, migratory birds, (1916), **1,** 4
—Webster–Ashburton Treaty (1842), **5,** 87–88; **6,** 8–10, 298–301, 315; **7,** 3–8; **20,** 40, 41; **22,** 593; **24,** 568
U.K. and France, Arbitration Agreement (1951) *re* gold looted by Germany, **20,** 441–463 *passim*, 467, 470, 475
United Nations Headquarters Agreement (1947), **14,** 157; **16,** 294, 296, 298, 299; **17,** 296; **20,** 381, 382; **21,** 340–341; **23,** 438; **24,** 203, 688–692; **32,** 309, 311, 317, 319, 324, 329, 330; **34,** 152, 154, 158, 160–167, 169; **35,** 222–227, 228, 230
United States Bases (Agreement) Act, 1952...**22,** 154–156
" United States ports ", meaning, **23,** 116–123
Universal Military Training and Service Acts (1948 and 1951), **21,** 179, 200, 202, 203
Uruguay, Trade Agreement (1942), m–f–n clause, **34,** 217–219
Validation of German Bonds, Board for, **31,** 401
Venezuela—
—Claims Commission (1903), **5,** 192
—Extradition Treaty (1922), **31,** 378, 379
—Trade Agreement, **22,** 572 n.
Vera Cruz, occupation of, **5,** 480–481
Versailles, Treaty of, reservations to, **27,** 546
—rights derived from, **3,** 348
Virgin Islands, Organic Act, 1917, **11,** 79
Walsh Act, subpoenas abroad, **34,** 92–96
War Claims Act, 1928...**23,** 17
—1948...**17,** 359–364; **22,** 938; **24,** 937
War Department, certificate of, **9,** 36–38
War Powers Act, 1941...**15,** 512–515; **21,** 438
War-Time Prohibition Act, **11,** 130; **20,** 620

U.S.A.—*continued*
Warfare Rules, **10,** 564–576; **15,** 650; **17,** 417–418; **18,** 318, 485, 591, 596; **19,** 458
Washington Accord, German Property in Switzerland (1946), **27,** 477–478, 492, 497, 499, 501, 503, 507, 528, 556
Workmen's Compensation Law of New York, **22,** 580–583, 911 n.; **26,** 484, 486
Yugoslavia
—Claims Agreement (1948), **20,** 211–217, 226–243, 435–437, 565–566; **21,** 55–63 *passim,* 147, 148; **21,** 149–165, 291–297; **22,** 332, 334, 394–397, 405; **24,** 316, 318
—Convention of Commerce and Navigation, **20,** 243
United States–Japanese Property Commission, settlement by parties, decision in terms of, **29,** 304–307
Universal Copyright Convention (1952): *see* Copyright Convention
Universal Declaration of Human Rights (1948), **16,** 269, 279–280, 546; **18,** 259, 342; **19,** 496; **20,** 371, 377, 503, 507, 511, 514; **22,** 387, 524; **23,** 617–618, 625; **24,** 324, 325, 327, 364, 392, 425–428; **25,** 175
confiscatory taxation, **30,** 259, 262, 263, 264
international officials, " equal pay for equal work ", **32,** 443, 444
right of nationality, **34,** 112 n.
right of private property, **28,** 609
war crimes, **16,** 279–280; **17,** 388, 390
Universal Postal Convention (1897), **22,** 414. *See also* Postal Conventions
Cuba, party to, **1,** 315
U.S.A., party to, **1,** 315
Universal Postal Union, Arrangement of Buenos Aires (1939), **23,** 597
Universal succession, concept of, **26,** 12, 17
corporations, of, **30,** 5–24
foreign obligations, effect on, **25,** 6–18
novation distinguished, **26,** 17
Unjust enrichment—
conditions for claim based on, **29,** 197
European Coal and Steel Community Treaty, under, **29,** 196, 197
principle of, **4,** 82–84; **5,** 3–4, 498–502; **6,** 229; **7,** 414–415; **9,** 581–583; **23,** 314, 323; **24,** 296
Venezuelan criminal law, **30,** 386
Unlawful deprivation of property, expropriation, distinguished, **4,** 271–272
Unlawful entry by aliens, access to courts, **8,** 325–326
Unlawful entry by aliens—*continued*
national treatment clause, **31,** 344–345
Unlawful stay by aliens, **8,** 340
Unneutral service, **3,** 461; **4,** 572; **5,** 518; **9,** 82; **12,** 462–466, 532–542
acquisition of enemy character, **3,** 461
carriage of contraband, **12,** 539–542
condemnation for, **12,** 533–537
Unseaworthiness, doctrine of, **34,** 2–3
Upper Savoy, Free Zone of: *see* Savoy
Upper Silesia—
plebiscite in, **1,** 43, 179; **3,** 107–109, 110, 112
plebiscite in, officials of Commission, **2,** 93–94
rights of minorities, **4,** 352–355
severance from Germany, **18,** 49, 67–69
social insurance funds relating to, **3,** 349–350
Upper Silesia, Convention, Germany–Poland, (1922), **6,** 322; **7,** 102–104, 283–284, 325–327, 411, 433–434; **8,** 136–138
acquired rights and compensation, **6,** 66–71, 83–84
customs houses, **4,** 291–292
Uruguay—
extradition to, Treaty of Montevideo, **5,** 288
extradition treaties, application to mandated territories, **4,** 47–48
Trade Agreement with U.S.A. (1942), m–f–n clause, **34,** 217–219
Usage—
consular jurisdiction based on, **19,** 275–276, 292–294
meaning, **19,** 292
treaties and, **21,** 140
Usufruct, valuation of property subject to, **30,** 173–176
Usury, German Decree on, **1,** 83
Ut res magis valeat quam pereat, **17,** 321. *See also* Treaties, interpretation
Uti possidetis, principle of, **1,** 84–89; **7,** 115–127; **27,** 86, 96; **30,** 474–475, 477, 479, 483, 487, 488
Utica award, 1882...**4,** 122
Utrecht, Treaty of (1713), **15,** 27; **27,** 1–3

V

Valeur d'achat, meaning, **11,** 230
Valeurs exigibles (Art. 53, Hague Regulations), **15,** 494, 599–601
Validity of legal acts, **34,** 336, 343
Valorisation of currency: *see also* Currency
German Law, 1923, application to aliens, **4,** 338–339

Valorisation of currency—*continued*
Polish currency reform, 1924...**4,** 397–398
Valuation of property for compensation, **30,** 138, 143, 148–149, 187–197
accounts receivable, **30,** 194
balance sheet valuations, **30,** 181–183, 188, 190
bonds, non-negotiable, **30,** 177–178
conversion of currency, rate of exchange, **22,** 345–346; **30,** 181–183
engineering method, **30,** 176, 178–179
furniture and fittings, **30,** 149, 192–193
insurance valuations, **30,** 191–192
land and buildings, **29,** 401–408; **30,** 138, 191–192
life interest, **26,** 296
machinery and plant, **30,** 138, 148
market value, **30,** 177–178
oil concessions, **35,** 160–161
oil and gas reserves, **30,** 176, 178–179
remainderman's interest, **30,** 173–176
shares, **30,** 143, 181–183, 199, 203–204
standards of, **7,** 100–101
Varangar Fiord, **7,** 136
Vassal States, **3,** 38–39; **8,** 93–94; **10,** 46–47; **22,** 64–76
immunity of Rulers from jurisdiction, **22,** 67–72, 76
—from taxation, **22,** 64–67, 73–75
Vatican City: *see also* Holy See
concordats: *q.v.*
crimes committed in, **8,** 250–251, 253–254; **9,** 103
diplomatic representative accredited to, **9,** 111
exterritoriality of, **8,** 235–236
—buildings within, **9,** 105, 108, 109, 111, 436–439
Italian jurisdiction, crimes committed in, **9,** 103; **23,** 114–115
position of, **4,** 97–99; **8,** 151–152
private law contracts, **9,** 108
Venezuela—
Belgium, Extradition Treaty (1884), **22,** 518
Bolivia, Extradition Treaty (1883), **22,** 518
Bolivarian Convention (1911), **22,** 518
Colombia—
—Arbitration Agreement (1916), **1,** 371–372
—Extradition Treaty (1911), **23,** 416–417
Constitution, treaties and, **24,** 509
extradition law, **30,** 385, 387
extradition treaties, **19,** 377–378
hostile expedition against, **6,** 31–32
Venezuela—*continued*
Italy—
—Arbitration Agreement (1920), **5,** 154
—Extradition Treaty (1930), **22,** 518; **24,** 507, 509–510; **26,** 527
—Treaty of Commerce (1861), **5,** 154
passive extradition procedure, **33,** 317–318
Penal Code, 1926...**5,** 278–279; **6,** 311; **24,** 509
Spain, Extradition Treaty (1894), **22,** 517, 518; **30,** 385
U.K., Aggreement, Gulf of Paria (1942), **18,** 152
U.S.A.—
—Claims Commission (1903), **5,** 192
—Extradition Treaty (1922), **31,** 378, 379
—Trade Agreement, **22,** 572
unjust enrichment, criminal law, **30,** 386
Venice, cession to France, **1,** 88
inland waters of, **8,** 173
Venue for actions, Warsaw Convention (1929), **34,** 210–213
Vera Cruz, occupation by United States, **4,** 483; **5,** 480–481
Vereinbarung, creation of international law by, **4,** 8
Versailles, Peace Treaty of (1919)—
alteration by later treaties, **4,** 15–16
Belgium, application in, **4,** 13–14
Canada, operation in, **12,** 264–266
cession of territory under, **1,** 337, 349–350, 367–369
Danzig, status under: *see* Danzig
Dawes Plan and, **3,** 406–407
denunciation by Germany, **11,** 227–228; **14,** 45, 48
Egypt, application in, **2,** 25
entry into force, **32,** 339–341
German law, as part of, **2,** 4; **4,** 11–13, 406–409; **5,** 5
German nationals reinstated as French citizens, **28,** 439–441
Kiel Canal, provisions relating to, **17,** 134, 135
Mixed Arbitral Tribunals: *q.v.*
nationality provisions, **6,** 37–40; **13,** 110; **14,** 111, 113–114; **24,** 431
—Alsace-Lorraine, inhabitants of, **7,** 273; **14,** 111, 114; **15,** 209–211, 321–322; **17,** 316; **18,** 400–401
—Eupen and Malmédy residents, **21,** 177–178
—German colonies, inhabitants of, **28,** 80–81
nationals of neutral States, application to, **7,** 501–504
Poland, cession to, **5,** 52–53
Polish State, establishment of, **5,** 11–15
recognition by Turkey, **4,** 435–436

Versailles, Peace Treaty of (1919)—*continued*
renunciation by Germany of overseas possessions, **19**, 328–329
reparation provisions—
—"civilian population", meaning, **3**, 435–437
—*force majeure* and, **1**, 169
reparation works under, **6**, 147–148
restitution provisions, **20**, 465; **29**, 475
revival of former treaties with Germany, **18**, 503–505
Rhine navigation provisions, **15**, 69; **17**, 124, 355; **19**, 150, 469; **20**, 409
Saar Basin, French customs régime, **7**, 30
Saar Basin, status under, **4**, 341–342
Second World War, effect of, **11**, 219
system established by, finality of, **5**, 413
termination of war and, **9**, 550; **11**, 267; **14**, 173
U.S.A., rights under, **3**, 348; **18**, 503, 504–505
United States reservations, **27**, 546
validity, **11**, 218–219
violation by Germany, **4**, 11–13; **5**, 5
war crimes, provisions on, **14**, 198
"Vessel bound to the United States", meaning, **5**, 106–109
Vessels: *see* Ships
Vested rights of aliens, respect for, **6**, 270; **7**, 317; **11**, 226
Vichy Government, France, confiscatory legislation, **10**, 147–151
Victor Emmanuel III of Italy, estate of, **17**, 1–6
Vienna, Congress of (1815), **1**, 33–38; **24**, 893–896
Final Act, **8**, 166–169; **21**, 6; **24**, 893–896
free navigation on rivers, **5**, 86
Regulations of, **9**, 427
Vienna Convention (1924), Germany and Poland, **4**, 15–16; **6**, 260–263
Vienna, Peace Treaty, Austria and U.S.A. (1921), **4**, 81, 543; **11**, 268
Vienna, Peace Treaty (1955) (Austrian State Treaty): *see under* Austria
Vienna, Treaty of (1864), **2**, 255; **4**, 84
Vietnam—
France, Convention on Nationality (1955), **28**, 436–437
—Joint Declaration (1954), **22**, 225
recognition of, **22**, 224
status of, **22**, 224–225
Violacion de domicilio, **1**, 309
Virgin Islands, law applicable after cession to U.S.A., **11**, 79–81
Visa, nature of, **6**, 269–270
Visit and search, **10**, 594–605; **14**, 311–316
resistance, forcible, to, **10**, 596–598
Visiting forces: *see* Foreign armed forces
Voie de fait, case of (French law), **11**, 203
Voluntary expatriation: *see under* Expatriation
Volunteer corps, status of, **17**, 431
Volunteer Fleet, Russian, status of, **3**, 482; **5**, 114–115

W

Wages: *see under* Alien seamen
Waiver—
extradition proceedings, **1**, 280–281; **9**, 401
jurisdictional immunities, of—
—diplomatic envoys, by: *see under* Diplomatic envoys
—foreign armed forces, by: *see under* Foreign armed forces, jurisdiction over
—foreign States, by: *see under* Foreign States, immunity from jurisdiction
—heads of State, **9**, 190, 205
—public ships, in respect of, **1**, 145, 150–154; **2**, 136–144
Walvis Bay, position of, **7**, 53–56
Walwal incident, **8**, 268–269
War: *see also* Armistice; Belligerency; Belligerent occupation; Civil war; Enemy aliens; Enemy character; Enemy property; Hague Conventions *and* Regulations; Peace treaties; Prisoners of war; Prize; Sea warfare; War crimes
acts of, by civilian population, **14**, 170; **15**, 104–105, 640
acts of, responsibility for damage caused by, **2**, 161, 168, 174–175; **3**, 225; **5**, 494; **30**, 116–117
"acts of war", insurance policies, **17**, 349–350; **26**, 632–638
"acts of war", state of war, distinguished, **26**, 633–637
"actual military service", meaning, **22**, 898–900
aerial bombardment, **4**, 570–571; **5**, 516–517
—Hague Conventions, applicability, **5**, 4
—nuclear weapons, **32**, 626–642
—war crime, as, **15**, 660–661
aggressive: *see also* illegal, *infra*
—acquisition of title in, **23**, 820–822, 826
—effect on legality of acts, **15**, 415–416
—effect on validity of occupant's currency, **18**, 592–593
—legality, **13**, 307–211; **15**, 379–380, 412–414; **16**, 345–347

War—*continued*
aggressive—*continued*
—responsibility of arms manufacturers, **15,** 620–621, 668–670
—rules of war, application, **14,** 288–289; **15,** 415–422, 636–638; **16,** 378, 529
—taxation and, **23,** 1–3
ally of enemy, status, **9,** 575
aliens, treatment of, during, **5,** 264, 483; **23,** 758–759
amnesty, **2,** 435; **4,** 553–554
angary, right of: *q.v.*
Anglo-French action in Egypt (1956), whether, **26,** 638–651
appropriation of enemy property: *see under* Enemy property
armistice: *q.v.*
belligerency: *q.v.*
belligerent forces: *q.v.*
blockade: *q.v.*
booty: *q.v.*
canals, international, in time of: *see under* Canals, international
capitulations, effect on civilian population, **15,** 500–505
capitulations, effect on title to property, **22,** 930–931; **23,** 766–767
chemical warfare, **5,** 516–517
civilian population, acts of war by, **14,** 170; **15,** 104–105, 640
combatants, unlawful, **23,** 759–762. *See also* Guerillas; Partisans
commencement of, **4,** 534; **13,** 224–227; **14,** 220, 223, 224, 225–227; **15,** 423; **20,** 599
" consequence of war ", meaning, **2,** 200–201
contraband: *q.v.*
convoy, belligerent escort, under, **2,** 408; **4,** 568–569
declaration of—
—capacity, **15,** 538, 544; **23,** 788–789; **26,** 648
—communication of, **26,** 648–649
—definition, **26,** 644 n.
—form, **26,** 647–650
—Hague Convention (No. III), **12,** 300–302; **15,** 359, 417; **18,** 599; **20,** 591; **26,** 641n., 645
—hostilities in absence of, **10,** 431–437; **19,** 555; **20,** 578–590; **26,** 627–632, 644
—need for, **15,** 417, 606; **19,** 555; **20,** 578, 582, 588, 591, 599; **22,** 896–898; **23,** 684–686
—speech by President Nasser, 1956, **26,** 640–641, 647–650
declared and undeclared, **26,** 630–631
definition and meaning, **9,** 529–533; **10,** 431–437; **13,** 224–227, 229; **15,** 432; **16,** 372; **17,** 343–344; **18,** 473, 723; **20,** 578–599; **21,** 416–430; **22,** 893–900, 933–934; **23,**

War—*continued*
definition and meaning—*continued*
684–686; **26,** 626–638, 644; **27,** 612–614; **28,** 595–601; **32,** 552–556
—in charterparty, **9,** 528–536; **26,** 638–651
devastation of occupied territory, **15,** 632, 647–649; **16,** 484–486, 521–523
economic, requisition and, **23,** 501. *See also* Requisition
emergency powers during, **11,** 270n.
enemies, unarmed, killing of, **2,** 436–437
enemy—
—ally of, status of, **9,** 575n.
—definition, Belgian law, **22,** 922
—definition, English law, **15,** 574–575
enemy aliens: *q.v.*
enemy character: *q.v.*
enemy government, right to sue, **10,** 454–455; **18,** 493–498
enemy property: *q.v.*
enemy State—
—jurisdictional immunity of, **10,** 576–581
—right to sue, **12,** 337–340
enemy territory, meaning, **11,** 263–264
" exceptional war measures ", meaning, **1,** 244; **5,** 440, 508
" *fait de guerre* ", meaning, **22,** 626
force, use of, whether essential, **26,** 632–633, 645
francs tireurs, **15,** 639; **16,** 380, 500, 510, 516. *See also* Guerillas; Partisans
freezing of enemy assets, **34,** 492–494: *see also under* Enemy property
Hague Conventions and Regulations: *q.v.*
hostilities in absence of declaration of war, **10,** 431–437; **19,** 555; **20,** 578–590; **26,** 627–632, 644
hostilities, termination of, **18,** 545–549
—effect on power to vest enemy property, **28,** 639–642
—state of war after, **28,** 596–601, 603
illegal, applicability of laws of war, **14,** 288–289; **15,** 412–422, 636–638; **16,** 378, 529
" imperfect " hostilities, **26,** 627, 630
" in time of war ", **34,** 496–501
indemnities, **1,** 487
" injury or damage as result of ", meaning, **23,** 633
invasion, meaning, **16,** 347; **18,** 594
irregular forces, **15,** 424, 639, 661; **16,** 379–380, 514–516. *See also* Guerillas: Partisans

War—*continued*
just and unjust wars, **5,** 229
land, on, **6,** 447–450; **11,** 270–299; *see also* Hague Conventions, Laws and Customs of War (1899, 1907) *and* Hague Regulations
legality of, **13,** 207–211; **15,** 379–383, 412–414; **16,** 345–347
London, Declaration of (1909), **4,** 568, 569; **5,** 342, 423, 488–490, 515, 518; **11,** 262, 303; **12,** 288, 552, 558, 565; **16,** 582, 589, 591, 592–593, 595, 596, 597, 601; **19,** 480; **20,** 673; **23,** 715
naval: *see* Sea warfare
neutral property: *q.v.*
non-combatants, **3,** 435–437
non-hostile relations between belligerents, **22,** 930–931
occupation of enemy territory: *see* Belligerent occupation
occupation of foreign territory during, **5,** 486
occupation of territory by enemy, conclusiveness of statements of Executive, **15,** 7, 444
outbreak of, effects, **1,** 387–422; **2,** 410–427; **3,** 79, 438–460; **4,** 534–546; **5,** 475–487; **6,** 437–446; **7,** 501–506; **8,** 492–503; **9,** 536–557; **10,** 437–529; **11,** 238–260; **12,** 47, 304–359, 505, 506; **13,** 232–240; **14,** 171–195; **15,** 437–461; **16,** 380–388; **17,** 354–368; **18,** 474–520; **19,** 556–578; **20,** 599–615; **21,** 432–464; **22,** 900–918; **23,** 687–756; **24,** 883–902; **25,** 559; **26,** 651–663; **27,** 614–649; **28,** 602–633; **29,** 329–354; **30,** 412, 494–496; **31,** 490–503; **32,** 557–562; **33,** 444–450: *see also* Angary; Enemy aliens; Enemy character; Enemy property; Trading with the enemy
—agency, **12,** 327; **15,** 447–450; **20,** 645–648
—bank accounts, **23,** 689
—capitulations, **4,** 534–535
—compensation for destruction of neutral property, **2,** 415–419
—concessions, **23,** 647–652
—consular privileges, **1,** 307
—contracts, **1,** 390–399; **2,** 411–413; **3,** 440–445; **4,** 538–540; **5,** 480–483; **7,** 501; **10,** 437–442; **11,** 243–247; **12,** 308–327; **14,** 177–180; **15,** 441–449; **16,** 171–175; **18,** 521, 522, 526–528; **19,** 559–570; **21,** 443–459, 464–471; **22,** 488–489, 698–704, 901–908; **23,** 754–756, 787–789; **27,** 629–637; **31,** 490–495
copyright agreements, **18,** 24–36

War—*continued*
outbreak of, effects—*continued*
—diplomatic and consular premises, **21,** 435–436
—enemy government, **10,** 454–455; **18,** 493–498
—enemy merchant ships in port, **1,** 410–414; **2,** 452–454; **4,** 542; **5,** 487, 510–514; **6,** 438–441; **7,** 505–506; **10,** 509–514; **11,** 257; **12,** 353–359
—enemy State, right to sue, **12,** 337–340
—expatriation, on, **26,** 402–404
—functions of organs of States, **22,** 240, 900
—jurisdictional immunities, on, **10,** 576–581
—nationality, **15,** 455; **18,** 265, 507–508
—neutral persons and property, on, **1,** 414–418; **2,** 415–427; **3,** 456–458; **4,** 542–546; **6,** 442–446; **13,** 338–239; **17,** 368; **18,** 516–520, 529; **23,** 706–708; **28,** 611–629; **30,** 494–496
—partnership, **1,** 399–400; **3,** 441–443; **9,** 536–538; **11,** 245–247; **15,** 443–447; **27,** 629–631
—patents, enemy-owned, **3,** 450–451; **25,** 495–502; **29,** 341–348
—right to sue, enemy government, of, **10,** 454–455; **18,** 493–498
—statutes of limitation, on, **2,** 413–414; **3,** 451–452; **5,** 484–486; **6,** 437–438; **9,** 502–503; **16,** 385–388; **18,** 474, 477–493; **19,** 559–570
—trade marks, **20,** 600–609; **23,** 701–706; **26,** 656, 657–662; **31,** 495–503
—treaties, **1,** 387–390; **2,** 410; **3,** 79, 438–440; **4,** 534–538; **5,** 475–480; **11,** 218, 238–243; **12,** 304–308; **13,** 232; **14,** 2, 171–177; **15,** 298, 437–441, 460, 511; **16,** 267, 380–384; **17,** 354–359; **18,** 499–508; **19,** 474, 556–559; **20,** 599–600; **21,** 262–263, 277, 432–443; **22,** 592, 597–603, 620, 621, 900–901; **23,** 455–467, 489; **24,** 883–892; **26,** 577–578, 677–678; **28,** 85, 86, 493, 602–605; **30,** 45, 48; **31,** 2, 357, 359–361
—Cardozo, Judge, on **11,** 239–240
—trusts, **3,** 449
peace treaties, effects of, on, **4,** 551–555; **5,** 492–493. *See also under* Peace treaties
poisonous weapons, **32,** 634
prisoners of war: *q.v.*
private property, respect for, **1,** 475–483; **4,** 564–567; **5,** 498–502; **9,** 571

War—*continued*
protected States, parties to, **9,** 33
Protecting Power, recognition of, **21,** 436
renunciation of: *see* Renunciation of War, General Treaty for
reprisals: *q.v.*
requisitioning: *q.v.*
resistance movements: *q.v.*
right of, **13,** 203–223, 388; **15,** 356–376, 376–412, 419–421; **16,** 344–362. *See also* Self-defence
safe-conduct, **6,** 438–440; **7,** 331–332
sea, at: *see* Sea warfare
" solemn ", **26,** 627, 630
sovereignty, maintenance of, **1,** 445–448, 450–451
spies, **1,** 235, 431, 432; **10,** 564–576; **13,** 281, 293, 294–295, 298–299; **15,** 423–424, 434, 435, 483–484, 497, 636, 640; **16,** 271–272, 406; **17,** 434
—occupied territory, in, **15,** 573–575
starting of, Second World War, whether " default " by Germany, Restitution Law, **28,** 191, 193
state of—
—after hostilities, **16,** 417–418; **17,** 401–404
—conclusiveness of statements of Executive, **9,** 8, 529–533; **12,** 286; **15,** 506; **17,** 345–349; **20,** 156, 597–598; **21,** 263; **22,** 100
—distinguished from " acts of war ", **26,** 633–637
—enemy property and, **19,** 555 n.
—enemy status and, **23,** 758–759
—Israel and Egypt, **31,** 509–520
—proof of existence of, **19,** 555–556; **20,** 156; **24,** 930
—recognition of State and, **18,** 244–246
state of emergency in Malaya, whether war, **27,** 612–614
statute of limitations during, **2,** 413–414; **3,** 451–452; **5,** 484–485; **6,** 437–438; **9,** 502–503; **16,** 385–388; **18,** 474, 477–493; **19,** 559–570
surrender, belligerent rights and, **18,** 549. *See also* Capitulations, military
termination of, **1,** 442–445; **5,** 491–492; **6,** 438; **9,** 550; **13,** 286, 312–332; **14,** 18–19, 216–227; **15,** 505–519; **16,** 416–418; **17,** 401–404; **18,** 474, 486, 545–549; **19,** 600; **20,** 618–627; **21,** 471; **22,** 701, 932–944; **23,** 768–780; **28,** 595; **32,** 553, 565–570; **33,** 445, 448
—absence of formal peace treaty, **24,** 938–940
—belligerent rights and, **18,** 711–712
—"conclusion of peace", **23,** 772–775

War—*continued*
termination of—*continued*
—criminal statute, **34,** 496–501
—date of, **11,** 264, 267–270; **22,** 939, 940–943; **23,** 768–769
—enemy property, effect on, **22,** 932–939; **26,** 672–673, 680
—enemy status, effect on, **11,** 269–270
—" Friedensschluss ", meaning, **5,** 492
—hostilities, termination of, **18,** 545–549; **23,** 775–776; **24,** 929–932, 938–940; **28,** 596–601, 603, 639–642
—municipal law, for purposes of, **26,** 681–684
—official statement, need for, **26,** 682, 684
—prize, capture of, after, **22,** 1011–1012
—" proclamation of peace ", **23,** 776–778
—reparations and, provisions of Settlement Convention with Germany, **23,** 774–775
—" signature of peace ", **23,** 769–775
—statute of limitations and, **20,** 618–622; **22,** 910
—termination of diplomatic relations between defeated State and other States, **28,** 397, 400, 403
—termination of occupation régime in Germany as, **23,** 679–772
—trading with the enemy and, **20,** 622–627; **22,** 918, 932–935, 935–939
—U.S. Congress Joint Resolution (1951), **26,** 669–670, 672, 674 n., 678–679, 680
—war crimes and, **23,** 779–780
theatre of war, New York as, **1,** 385, 432
" total " character of, **14,** 170, 272; **32,** 632–633
trading with the enemy: *q.v.*
treaties, effect on: *see* outbreak of war, effects of, treaties, *supra*
ubi bellum non est pax est, **20,** 592–593
ultimatum: *see* declaration of war, *supra*
unarmed enemies, killing of, **2,** 436–437
United Nations, war between Member States, **22,** 698–700
unlawful belligerency against State by a national, **23,** 759–762
violation of treaties, in, **13,** 208–209; **15,** 361–363, 364, 398–412, 421–422
" war clause ", in insurance policy, **12,** 283–284, 289–300; **16,** 362–377
—in charterparty, **9,** 528–536; **26,** 647, 651

War—*continued*
war treason, **13,** 384–385; **16,** 460
war zones, **13,** 219
weapons causing unnecessary suffering, **32,** 633–634
wounded, treatment of, **7,** 507–508. *See also* Geneva Conventions, Sick and Wounded
War, Peace and Problems of, Pan-American Conference (1945), **22,** 914–915
" War clause " in insurance policy, **12,** 283–284, 289–300; **16,** 362–377
—in charterparty, **9,** 528–536; **26,** 647, 651
War crimes: *see also* Belligerent occupation, inhabitants, treatment of; Germany, Allied Control Council Law No. 10; Hostages; Humanity, crimes against; *and* Prisoners of war, offences against
Act of State and responsibility for, **13,** 221–222; **14,** 289; **15,** 682; **16,** 408, 523–524
aerial bombardment, as, **15,** 660–661
aliens, conscription of, **16,** 357–358
appeals from tribunals, **15,** 485–490
armistice, breaches of, as, **13,** 309–311; **14,** 213–215
authors of, **13,** 223, 250–258; **15,** 498. *See also* individual responsibility for, *infra*
—Chief-of-Staff, unlawful orders, **16,** 513–514
—civilians as, **13,** 250–254; **15,** 640
—collective guilt, **17,** 387–388
—government officials and military commanders, **15,** 366–369, 376
—head of State, **15,** 373–374
—judges of Occupant, **17,** 438–439
—military commanders, unauthorized, acts, **15,** 385–386
—military commanders, occupied territory, **15,** 386–388
—military commanders, responsibility to prevent commission of, **13,** 272–274; **14,** 205–207, 223, 292
—military commanders, transmission of unlawful orders, **15,** 364–383
—police officers, acts of subordinates, **16,** 398–399
—staff officers, unlawful orders, **15,** 388–392
civilian prisoners, execution of, **16,** 396–398, 459–461
coercion, defence of, **16,** 350–351
collaboration by inhabitants of occupied State, defence of, **16,** 488, 490
compatibility with laws of war, defence of, **17,** 388–390
conscription of aliens, **16,** 357–358
conspiracy, **15,** 373
contradictory orders, defence of, **16,** 398–399

War crimes—*continued*
court martial, right of trial by, **15,** 364, 378–379; **18,** 12–13
criminal organizations, **13,** 203 n.; **16,** 393–394; **17,** 392; **18,** 539
customary international law and, **15,** 635–636
definition, Belgian Law of 1947...**16,** 401
—Charter of International Military Tribunal (1945), **13,** 204
—Israel Law of 1950...**18,** 539–540
denial of medical aid, **17,** 392
destruction of lighthouse, whether, **15,** 687–688
destruction of property during retreat, **15,** 647–649; **16,** 521–522
devastation of occupied territory, **15,** 632, 647–649; **16,** 484–486, 521–523
diplomatic immunity and, **15,** 372–373; **16,** 361; **17,** 279, 434–438
espionage as, **15,** 575; **16,** 271–272, 405–407; **23,** 759–762
execution of collaborators by resistance fighters, **18,** 536–537
extradition and, **15,** 301–302; **16,** 266–274; **18,** 331; **24,** 510–517; **30,** 506–508, 510
force majeure, defence of, **17,** 432–434
Human Rights, Universal Declaration of (1948) and, **16,** 279–280; **17,** 388, 390
humanity, crimes against: *q.v.*
ignorance of criminal nature of acts, **16,** 408, 484–486, 553
ignorance of international law rules, **15,** 661; **16,** 404
individual responsibility for, **13,** 221–222, 264, 265; **15,** 627–628, 659, 678–679; **16,** 350–351, 404–407; **30,** 505. *See also* authors of, *supra*
International Military Tribunal (Nuremberg)—
—Agreement establishing (1945), **13,** 203–205, 212, 222; **14,** 198, 281–282, 292; **30,** 504, 507, 508, 509, 510
—Charter, **13,** 203–205; **14,** 14, 100, 101, 281–282, 291; **15,** 362–363, 377, 420, 488–489, 493, 494, 634, 681, 682; **16,** 268, 280, 348, 350, 393, 395, 528, 531, 533, 536, 543; **17,** 385–388; **18,** 539, 540–542; **24,** 514, 942, 964
—defence of superior orders, **15,** 666
—judgment of, **14,** 14, 101, 303; **17,** 8; **24,** 942, 964; **30,** 504, 505
—judicial safeguards recognized by, **14,** 268
—jurisdiction, **13,** 207, 213; **14,** 272
International Military Tribunal (Far East) appeals from, **15,** 485–490

War crimes—*continued*
International Military Tribunal (Far East)—*continued*
—Charter, **14,** 198
—establishment of jurisdiction, **15,** 356–358, 361–364, 375
—legality of, **15,** 360–361
judgment by court of Occupant, finality, **26,** 707–711
jurisdiction over: *see under* International Military Tribunals, *supra, and* punishment, *infra*
limitation period for prosecution, **17,** 388–390
looting of private property, **16,** 526
medical experiments, **14,** 296–298
military tribunals
—composition **15,** 484–485; **22,** 924–926
—jurisdiction, **15,** 657–659. *See also* International Military Tribunals, *supra*
mitigating circumstances, **16,** 408, 544–545
Moscow Declaration (1943), **30,** 504, 506, 508, 510
municipal courts, jurisdiction, **16,** 402–403, 407, 527–528, 533; **30,** 506–508
murder, **15,** 359, 364–365, 376; **16,** 403
—foreign forced labourers, **32,** 563–565. *See also under* Belligerent occupation
national emergency, defence of, **15,** 628. *See also* necessity, plea of, *infra*
national legislation concerning, **14,** 199, 292–295; **18,** 538–543
nature of, **15,** 636, 683
necessity, plea of, **13,** 246–250, 306; **14,** 269–270; **15,** 397–398, 406, 497, 628–632, 646–647; **16,** 349–350, 488, 511–513, 533, 543; **17,** 390, 432–434; **19,** 596–598
nulla poena sine lege, **30,** 504
nullum crimen sine lege, **13,** 208; **14,** 245–246, 285–286; **15,** 362, 378, 405, 470, 471, 634–636
offence against member of same forces, **18,** 532–533
organizations, criminal, **13,** 203 n., **16,** 393–394; **17,** 392; **18,** 539
para-military organization, **15,** 424
peace, crimes against, **13,** 204–206, 207–211, 223; **15,** 358–359, 364, 376–377, 379–383, 398–399, 406–408, 669; **16,** 345–350
pillage, **15,** 619
plunder of occupied territory, **15,** 399, 404, 408, 619, 620, 622–625, 632, 653, 657, 668, 672–677; **16,** 358–361, 482
Polish legislation, **30,** 497

War crimes—*continued*
P.O.W. Convention, 1929, application to war criminals, **16,** 403, 533–536; **18,** 12–13
prisoners of war, trial of, for, **22,** 929, 930
punishment of, **10,** 564–576; **13,** 262–283, 286–287; **14,** 196–201; **15,** 483–499; **16,** 392–408, 426, 485, 544–545, 553, 556; **17,** 385–390, 392–397; **18,** 532–544; **22,** 924–926, 929
—after cessation of hostilities, **13,** 272
—jurisdiction of municipal courts, **14,** 196–201; **17,** 391, 393–395; **18,** 12–13
—universality, **14,** 282–283
quarter, refusal to give, **15,** 377, 633
reprisals, as, **13,** 258–261, 393–394; **15,** 482, 687
—reprisals, legitimate, defence of, **16,** 547; **32,** 563–565
responsibility for international basis, **30,** 503, 510: *see also* authors of, *supra, and* the various defences, *e.g.*, Act of State
retroactive legislation, **13,** 208; **14,** 245–246, 285–286; **15,** 362, 378, 405, 470, 471, 533, 634–636; **16,** 527, 528, 542–543; **17,** 435–436
St. James, Declaration of, on War Criminals (1942), **13,** 263; **14,** 198; **16,** 268
second trial for (Israel Law of 1950), **18,** 543
self-defence, plea of, **16,** 349–350, 508
self-preservation, plea of, **18,** 536–537
superior orders, defence of, **2,** 429–430, 437–438; **13,** 205, 222, 223, 249, 268, 280–282, 292, 294, 298, 304–305, 306, 386, 388–389, 392–394, 396–397; **14,** 202–205, 269, 303–304, 305–307; **15,** 395–397, 418, 483–499, 628–632, 649–652, 655–656, 665–668, 679–684; **16,** 392–393, 400–403, 487–491, 524–525, 532–533, 543–544, 546, 555–556; **17,** 385–396, 432–434; **18,** 532–538; **32,** 563–565
—prisoners, orders of own officers, **14,** 203–204
termination of hostilities, commission after, **23,** 779–780
territorial responsibility for, **30,** 506–507, 511
torpedoed enemy ships, survivors of, **13,** 246–250
" total war " and, **13,** 211–212; **15,** 406
" *tu quoque* ", defence, as, **16,** 347–348, 358–359
uniforms, misuse of, **16,** 540
Versailles, Treaty of (1919), provisions on, **14,** 198

War crimes—*continued*
volentibus non fit injuria, **16**, 395
War damage—
claims, interest on, **30**, 220–225
enemy property by illegal acts, compensation for, **24**, 604. *See also* reparation or compensation for, *infra*
goods, causal relationship with war, **22**, 626–630
reparation or compensation for, **6**, 237–239, 285; **7**, 310, 323–324; **24**, 879
—French legislation, **6**, 285; **23**, 468
War, laws of—
aggressive war, **14**, 288–289; **15**, 412–415, 419–422, 636–638; **16**, 378, 529
annexed territory, applicability in, **15**, 655
binding force, **1**, 427; **2**, 428–430; **3**, 468; **4**, 548; **5**, 487; **11**, 257; **13**, 246–250; **15**, 467–471; **16**, 390–391; **17**, 385; **18**, 532; **19**, 596; **26**, 667–668
—civil wars, application by analogy, **5**, 487
—combatants, lawful and unlawful, **23**, 759–762
customary international law and, **15**, 635–636
enforcement, **2**, 429–431; **3**, 468–469; **5**, 487–491; **15**, 471–482; **16**, 391–392; **17**, 385–398; **18**, 532–544, 678–679; **22**, 924–926; **23**, 759–762
military manuals, status, **16**, 391
military necessity and, **15**, 480–482
nature and development, **16**, 510, 512
non-combatants and, **15**, 359, 365, 658–661
sources, **15**, 635; **16**, 510, 512
subjects of, **13**, 250–257; **14**, 205–207
violation, **2**, 437; **15**, 360, 376
War pensions, State succession and, **7**, 433–434
War profits, taxation of, **1**, 334
War taxation, aliens and, **4**, 333
War treason, **13**, 384–385; **16**, 460
War zones, **13**, 219
Warfare at sea: *see* Sea warfare
Warsaw Convention on International Carriage by Air (1929): *see under* Air Transport, International *and* Carriage by air, international
Warsaw, Duchy of, **1**, 34
Warships—
attempted theft of, **11**, 152–153
definition, **23**, 341–342, 801–805
deserters from foreign, return of, **31**, 405–408
extraterritoriality, **14**, 86
jurisdictional immunity, **11**, 152–153; **14**, 86–88
Warships—*continued*
jurisdictional immunity—*continued*
—crew, **11**, 165–169; **12**, 115–123, 124–133, 141–143; **19**, 221–226; **31**, 406, 408
merchant ships, distinguished, **6**, 94
publicly-owned merchantships, distinguished, **14**, 88–89
refuelling in neutral port—
—armistice, effect of, **14**, 320
—" twenty-four hours ' rule ", **14**, 319–321, 324
—whether neutral State must supply fuel, **14**, 319–324
right of passage through straits, **16**, 159–165
—through territorial waters, **31**, 83
territoriality of, **6**, 93–94, 293
Washington, Arbitration Agreement (1951), Claims to Gold Looted by Germany, **20**, 441–463 *passim*, 467, 470–475; **21**, 400–412
Washington Accord on German Property in Switzerland (1946), **27**, 477–478, 492, 497, 499, 501, 503, 528, 556
arbitral procedure, **27**, 477, 479, 481–482, 489
Joint Commission under, **27**, 477, 485, 507
Swiss Authority of Review, effect of decision of, **27**, 478, 485, 492, 499, 507, 516, 518–519, 527
Swiss Authority of Review, functions, **27**, 477, 518
Water boundaries, **1**, 96–98; **2**, 96–99; 4, 121; **5**, 83–88; **6**, 129, 157–159; **7**, 128–135; **8**, 164–165; **10**, 109; **11**, 91–100. *See also* Rivers
avulsion, **11**, 94–100
changes in course of, **1**, 97
thalweg, doctrine of, **1**, 96–97; **7**, 128–135; **8**, 164–165; **9**, 114; **11**, 91–93; **30**, 476, 490
Waterways: *see* Canals; Rivers
Webster–Ashburton Treaty, 1842...**5**, 87–88; **6**, 8–10, 298–301, 393; **7**, 3–8; **20**, 40, 41; **22**, 593; **24**, 568–569
Weights and Measures, International Bureau of, **12**, 281–282
Weimar, German Constitution of (1919): *see* Germany, Constitution (1919)
West New Guinea—
Netherlands Law of 1958...**28**, 37
status of, **24**, 87–88
West Ukrainian Republic, **1**, 386; **4**, 94, 533
Western Samoa—
appeals from High Court of, **7**, 50
Mandate over, **4**, 53–54; **7**, 36–45; **22**, 87–88
Trust Territory, as, **22**, 87–88

Western Samoa—*continued*
Trusteeship Council and, **22,** 685
Western Thrace, status of, **23,** 666–668, 669
Westminster, Statute of, 1931: *see under* Commonwealth
Wet (Dutch law), meaning, **11,** 291, 292, 293–294
" White race ", meaning (U.S. naturalization laws), **2,** 244–246
Wills—
alien enemy, by, in favour of neutral subjects, **3,** 453–455
form of, during occupation of enemy territory, **3,** 477–478
Winding-up of corporations: *see* Corporations, foreign, liquidation of
Witness—
alien, duty to appear as, **6,** 271–272
subpoena of, **6,** 177–179, 425–426
Women, married: *see* Married women
Workmen's compensation—
aliens and, **6,** 347–348; **7,** 468, 469, 470; **11,** 194; **18,** 506–507; **22,** 580–583; **26,** 482–487; **31,** 344–345
—I.L.O. Convention (1925), 347; **7,** 468, 469, 470; **18,** 507
change of sovereignty and, **8,** 143–144
consul, claim by, **11,** 56–58
consular jurisdiction to hear claims, **11,** 115–116
Cuba, in, **1,** 93; **20,** 205
enemy alien, claim by, **11,** 248–249
treaties as to, **2,** 317–318, 410
World Health Organization—
Constitution, **18,** 380
Staff Regulations, **18,** 468
World War I and World War II, termination of: *see* War, termination of
World War II, Treaty of Versailles and, **11,** 219
Wounded, treatment of: *see under* Geneva Conventions
Wrangel, General, party of, **4,** 191–192
Wreck—
cargo of, as prize, **11,** 301–302
meaning, **7,** 466
salvaged, condemnation as prize, **12,** 521–523
Writers, opinions of, as source of international law, **3,** 4; **4,** 6–7
Württemberg—
Germany, Treaty with (railways) (1920), **5,** 330–332
utilization of flow of Danube, **4,** 128–133

Y

Yachts, as prize, **11,** 265: **12,** 481–486, 488
Yalta, Agreement of (1945), **16,** 437; **22,** 92, 983–984
Yugoslavia—
aliens, acquisition of land by, **4,** 448
Austria, Convention with (railway tariffs), **5,** 364
bonds, default on, **20,** 213–214
Carinthia, occupation of, **1,** 467
currency, revaluation of, **20,** 211–213
Constitution (1946), adoption of, **21,** 58
Constitution, Art. 14 (mineral wealth, property of State), **18,** 227
Croatia
—continuity and identity, **21,** 55–63
—declaration of independent State of, 1941...**28,** 336
declaration of independence of, **2,** 228
Enemy Property Laws, 1944 to 1946, **21,** 147; **22,** 335
Federal People's Republic, establishment of (1945), **21,** 58, 67
France, Special Agreement submitting Serbian Loans Case to P.C.I.J. (1928), **5,** 466, 470
German occupation of, **10,** 172–174; **12,** 456–457; **15,** 638; **23,** 592, 594
Germany, Commercial Treaty with, **6,** 276
inheritance and gift tax decree, 1947, **22,** 333
Italian occupation of, **18,** 621–625
Italy
—Consular Convention (1924), **7,** 392
—occupation of (1945), **15,** 106
National Bank Act, 1931...**20,** 216
Nationalization Laws, 1946, 1948, **20,** 216, 231–232; **22,** 395; **23,** 19–21
nationalization of banks, **20,** 215–217
—property, **20,** 230–232
new State, whether, **1,** 346; **3,** 33–34
Payments to Foreign Countries, Law Regulating, 1945...**20,** 242
position of, 1941, 1942...**28,** 329–330
recognition of, by U.S.A., **11,** 249
Serbia and, continuity and identity, **21,** 66–75
Settlement of Pre-War Obligations, Law on, 1945...**20,** 211–213; **21,** 147
sovereignty, railway tariffs, **5,** 365
U.S.A.
—Claims Agreement with (1948), **20,** 211–217, 226–243, 235–437, 565–566; **21,** 55–63 *passim*, 147, 148; **21,** 149–165, 291–297; **22,** 332, 334, 394–397, 405
—Commercial Treaty with Serbia, **35,** 206, 207
—Convention of Commerce and Navigation with, **20,** 243
—Extradition Treaty with Serbia (1901), **28,** 326–328, 336

Z

Zamora, The, rule in, **1,** 429; **9,** 572–573, 576–577
Zanzibar—
  Customs Management Decree, **24,** 143–145; **27,** 98–101
  Imports Control Decree, 1954...**24,** 143–145; **27,** 99, 101
  Order-in-Council, provisions as to criminal jurisdiction, **24,** 162–166
Zanzibar—*continued*
  Prevention of Cruelty to Animals Decree, **24,** 161, 164
  status of, **18,** 54–55
Zollauschluss, **1,** 100
Zollausland/Zollinland, **1,** 83
Zuiderzee—
  fishery rights in, **11,** 175–176
  inland waters, whether, **11,** 175–176
Zürich, Agreement on Cyprus (1959), **25,** 31–32

CONSOLIDATED INDEX

VOLUMES 36—125 INCLUSIVE

The index as it now stands is the work of many hands over many years. The nature of the material to be indexed and indexing practice both in general and as applied to this particular index have changed considerably over this period. While every attempt has been made to harmonize style, inevitably some variation of approach remains. Current guidelines are:

1) Only points of international law as discussed by the court or tribunal are indexed. Facts and parties' arguments are indexed only in so far as this is essential for an understanding of the legal argument. The summaries to the cases are not indexed except to the extent that they contain relevant legal material not included in the report of the case itself. Points relating solely to issues of municipal law not relevant in the international law context are not indexed.
2) The same material is not indexed repeatedly, i.e., where a case which has already appeared in the *ILR* is cited at length in a subsequent case, it will not be reindexed, but simply subsumed in the indexing of the later case, with occasionally, where the case is particularly important, its name as a subheading.
3) Treaties are indexed by reference to content. For treaties by article, reference should be made to the Table of Treaties.
4) Material is double-posted as follows:

    a) Entries under a country heading normally appear also as self-standing entries, thus bringing together, for example, all treatment of 'extradition' under that heading. To find treatment of 'extradition' specifically in the Canadian or Italian courts, reference should be made to Canada, extradition or Italy, extradition. Material under a particular country heading unique to that jurisdiction is not double-posted, nor normally is there double-posting where the great bulk of the material is to be found in a single jurisdiction, national or international.
    b) Material is also double-posted where this can offer a different perspective, so entries like 'applicable law', 'burden of proof', 'customary international law' bring together all relevant material, but that material can also be found, desegregated, under such headings as 'State immunity, jurisdiction, burden of proof'. Only

when the number of page references becomes 'substantial' is the decision made to choose just one location.

5) Every effort is made to work to a common structure and terminology across jurisdictions and across time. For example, almost every country has a subheading 'law of' under which is gathered together almost all legislation. 'Constitution' is an exception to this rule, as also are those legislative acts (such as the US Foreign Sovereign Immunities Act) generating such a volume of jurisprudence that they warrant elevation in the hierarchy. There are also occasions when it has seemed helpful, for reasons of alphabetical order, to place legislation next to its subject matter (e.g., under Canada, the legislation relating to Indians in Canada and the 'Indians in Canada' subject heading are co-located.) But while consistency of structure and terminology is important, so is accuracy, and important fine distinctions are not to be ironed out simply for the sake of symmetry.
6) One difficulty in an index such as this which deals with material extending across time, jurisdictions and language is to ensure that where different terms (e.g. translations of titles of statutes) are used to describe the same thing, a common term is found for the index. Equally where the same term is used for different things distinct terms are used in the index (examples being where judicial decisions ten years apart both refer to the 'Constitution', but where the Constitutions in question are significantly different, or where a country's short name hides an important change of status). It may also, for example, be crucial to know which of a number of treaties with an essentially identical title is under discussion. With these issues in mind, every effort is made, where clear distinction is required, to include an 'identifying' tag. Legislation from a non-English speaking jurisdiction will, whenever possible, include the foreign language abbreviation. Dates are provided, whenever possible, for treaties and legislation. Where countries have changed their names or their status, cross-references are given to all the alternative versions.
7) Another major difficulty in an ever-growing consolidated index is to keep control of the inevitable strings of page references. It may be perfectly acceptable in a single volume index to have a simple entry 'State immunity, waiver' generating perhaps four or five references. But over 125 volumes, those four or five references will have become four or five hundred and not of much use to anybody. The only escape is to make the index ever more detailed, the aim being never, in an individual volume, to have a string of more than five page numbers, and so far as possible, never to go beyond a string of twenty in the

consolidated index. But there is a further constraint in that, to help the user, the allowable number of subheadings is kept strictly to three. The most frequent escape route, as with 'treaty interpretation', is to combine a main and a subheading to create a new main heading.

8) The consolidated index to the *ILR* was originally exactly that – a retrospective consolidation of the indexes to the individual volumes. It would be more accurate now to describe it as a cumulative index. The indexes to individual volumes are now prepared within the existing consolidation and then extracted, with cross-references added as appropriate. One consequence of this is that individual indexes may sometimes seem curiously structured or oddly balanced. In a volume dealing solely with *Pinochet* cases, or war crimes trials, it would normally be right to make a number of contextual assumptions. But each individual volume of the *ILR* needs to be seen as part of a whole, a whole which the indexing process seeks to reflect.

abandonment of
aboriginal rights **115,** 462
property **42,** 35
right **46,** 140-1
territorial claim **100,** 309, 310, 312, 313-14, 326
territorial sovereignty **38,** 89, **59,** 171
abduction. *See* forcible abduction/unlawful arrest; hostage-taking
aboriginal rights. *See also* Australia, aboriginals in; Canada, aboriginal Indians in; Canada, aboriginal rights; Canada, aboriginal title; Finland, Sami rights; French Polynesia; Murray Islands; New Zealand, State-owned Enterprises Act (SOEA) (1986); Sweden, Sami; territory, aboriginal title; United States of America (USA), Indian tribes
Convention concerning Indigenous and Tribal Peoples in Independent Countries (1989) (ILO Convention 169), accession, Suriname **116,** 279
Croker Island (Northern Territory), territorial sea, rights in **125,** 327-468
in Liberia **36,** 381-2, 396
Abu Dhabi
Continental Shelf Declaration (1949) **41,** 164
Ruler, competence to act on behalf of United Arab Emirates **111,** 609-10
State immunity **111,** 609
status, constituent territory of United Arab Emirates **111,** 609
Abu Dhabi Formula 66, 554-5, 572-3
Abu Musa
continental shelf **64,** 342
Iran, Islamic Republic and **66,** 177, 330-8
maritime delimitation **64,** 336-8, **66,** 177, 330-8, **91,** 663-77
territorial sea
breadth **64,** 277-9, 341-3
Decree of 10 September 1969 **64,** 278
Decree of 4 May 1970 **64,** 278-9
abuse of discretion. *See* executive discretion
abuse of power 56, 385, **58,** 694-9, **62,** 279, 285, **86,** 334, 343, **88,** 250
belligerent occupation, forced deportation **83,** 184
by international organization **43,** 448-53
by mandatory **37,** 440, 461
definition **88,** 250
delay in producing evidence **85,** 107-8
European Commission **47,** 1-2, 5-7
European Convention on Human Rights (1950) and **56,** 385, **86,** 343
executive **118,** 313-14
forcible abduction, jurisdiction and **111,** 556, 561-3
international officials, renewal of short-term contract **38,** 276-80
judicial review and **111,** 556, 561-3, 568-70
treatment of foreign interests as **46,** 498
abuse of process 91, 11
arbitral award, ground for annulment **92,** 39
arbitration (Law of the Sea Convention (1982)) **119,** 554
choice of law and **91,** 152-3
death row delay **124,** 289
ECHR applications **62,** 37, 59-60, 82, **103,** 637-8
extradition **119,** 251
forcible abduction/unlawful arrest and **95,** 406, **111,** 556, 561-3
general principle of international law **62,** 88-9
ICJ proceedings **62,** 88-9, **97,** 22, **105,** 358, **110,** 237-8, 319
ILOAT proceedings **40,** 311-12, 328, 329-30

improper purpose **118,** 325, 336-7, 591-2
judicial review and **111,** 566
judicial role and **95,** 390-5, 401, 407-8, 412-16
political motivation in bringing application to ECHR **103,** 637-8
stay of proceedings and **118,** 409-10, 414, 418-19
universal jurisdiction and **91,** 152
abuse of rights 62, 171, 352-3
damages, effect on obligation to pay **116,** 240
equity **99,** 585
freedom of assembly/association and **122,** 417-18
good faith and **82,** 614
ICJ proceedings, preliminary objections and **115,** 35
as international tort/wrong **46,** 498
treaty rights **82,** 614
access to courts 57, 210, 212, 218, 219-20, 224-30, 238-40, 242-61, **60,** 172-3, **72,** 362-3, **75,** 505-9, 513, 517, 554-6, 585, **78,** 338-9, 342. *See also* aliens, access to courts; American Convention on Human Rights (1969), judicial protection; European Convention on Human Rights (1950), access to courts; fair hearing; fair trial; habeas corpus; legal aid; prompt hearing; stay of proceedings
aliens. *See* aliens, access to courts; enemy aliens, access to courts
American Declaration of the Rights and Duties of Man (1948) **123,** 171-2, 175-8, 180, 185-8
appeal against town-planning procedures and **68,** 113-14
arbitral award, enforcement and **94,** 213-15
arbitration clause and **118,** 634
civilians detained during armed conflict **123,** 171-2, 175-8, 180, 185-8
effectiveness of procedural means, need for **123,** 152-5
execution of judgments and **123,** 45-7
extent of right **78,** 334, **81,** 127-9, **111,** 158, **118,** 134-7, **123,** 37-8, 39-43, 64-6, 84-6
failure to disclose evidence and **119,** 277
as general principle of law **57,** 217-18
margin of appreciation **123,** 39, 64-6, 84-6
national treatment and **44,** 300, **45,** 365-70, **111,** 537
non-disclosure of evidence and **119,** 277, 307. *See also* evidence, disclosure, obligation; evidence, disclosure as offence under law of foreign State
reasonable cause of action, need for **118,** 345-8, 362-4, 586, 591
recognition, government and **94,** 207-8, **108,** 504
refugees **44,** 143-4, **48,** 171-4, **70,** 356-8, **72,** 586-7, 641-5, **111,** 537, **119,** 365
appeal against refusal of refugee status and **99,** 2-3
Appeals Commission, recourse to **73,** 603-5, **74,** 433-44
reciprocity and **48,** 173
State immunity as procedural bar and **123,** 38, 70-3, 81-2, **125,** 157-9
stateless person **44,** 143-4
unconstitutional dismissal of judge and **123,** 152-5
accounting method, calculation of reasonable return on air user charges **102,** 448-54, 456-80, 535-41
accreditation. *See also* ambassador/head of mission; diplomatic agent; diplomatic mission; diplomatic premises; diplomatic privileges and immunities
in absence of diplomatic relations **85,** 56
diplomatic agent, procedural, whether **88,** 328
diplomatic mission **82,** 286
diplomatic mission, special **121,** 601-2
diplomatic privileges and immunities and **82,** 286 n. 8, **99,** 165

accreditation (*cont.*)
diplomatic relations and **85,** 56, 61
recognition of government and **86,** 6, 18
requirements
agreement/*agrément* by receiving State **99,** 166
full-time diplomatic activity **99,** 165-6, **121,** 602 n. 4
non-immigrant visa **121,** 602 n. 4
residence in capital **99,** 165
accretion 91, 453-4, 458, 464. *See also* alluvion; avulsion; erosion
inland waters **50,** 35, 37-8, 41, 390
artificial **42,** 98
rivers **91,** 196, 453-4, 458, 464
accrued rights. *See* acquired rights
accused person, rights. *See* detainees, rights
acquiescence 38, 249-53, **41,** 129-30, 211, 222, **59,** 210, 232, **67,** 62, 89-90, 96-7, 124-5, 191, 300, **74,** 146, **76,** 121-4, 175-6, 194, 305-11, 499, **77,** 667, **81,** 260-1, **82,** 619, 625-6, 652, **97,** 317, 324-5. *See also* doctrine of acknowledgment; estoppel; preclusion; prescription
absence of challenge. *See* protest, absence *below*
acceptance of principles in different context **80,** 479
authority of State representatives **71,** 132-5
between Paramount Power and Vassal State **50,** 99-100, 104, 246, 398
boundary **50,** 90, 409-15, 464, 495, **71,** 107-9, 130-7, **75,** 118-19, **83,** 19-20, **90,** 202-4, 448, **97,** 317, 324-5, 511
breach of international law **90,** 662-5, 674, 691-2
burden of alertness **80,** 326
challenge. *See* protest *below*
consistency of conduct **71,** 121, 123, **80,** 500
continental shelf delimitation **81,** 260-1
definition **75,** 118-19
equality of parties **83,** 81-2
estoppel and **71,** 131-2, **75,** 119-20
as evidence **50,** 28, 90-1
execution of agreement **82,** 65
failure to speak in UN organs **37,** 335, 345
formal protest **38,** 250
good faith and **75,** 118, **120,** 231
historic bays **91,** 418, 420 n. 6, **97,** 507, 511-12, 652
ICJ judgment **37,** 486
implied consent **38,** 250, 251
international law, substantive rule of **44,** 266
jurisdiction
extraterritorial **91,** 71
universal **91,** 144
knowledge of States **71,** 132, 135
as preliminary question **80,** 480
protest **83,** 83, **97,** 444, **100,** 35-6. *See also* silence *below*
absence **76,** 121, 123, **80,** 500, 556-9, **91,** 612, 620-5, 627, 631, **97,** 473, **100,** 35-6, 75-6, **120,** 232-3
conditions determining necessity for **80,** 325-6
entitlement to rely on other party's actions **113,** 79
factors mitigating failure **114,** 83-5, 102-3, 108, 136
force majeure **114,** 112-13
Rhine Boatmen's Certificate Scheme **101,** 441-2

requirements
consistency of conduct **71,** 134, 136
constancy **83,** 81
intention to be bound **75,** 118, **80,** 479-80
North Sea Continental Shelf **83,** 81
uniformity of practice **83,** 81
reservation of rights **71,** 107-9
silence **38,** 249. *See also* protest *above*
tacit agreement **67,** 63, 77, 89-91, 117-22, 170, 299-300
in treaty context **110,** 366
State succession and **80,** 500
territorial sovereignty and **50,** 4, 90, 95, 99-105, 246, 381, 383, 448, 452, 474, 495-500, **91,** 621-5
title **97,** 321-5, 335-6, 338, 482-3
treaty
amendment **101,** 600
termination **70,** 440
unilateral statements as **80,** 475, 477-8
uti possidetis position **97,** 441
acquired rights **73,** 33-5, 37. *See also* estoppel; United Nations Staff Rules and Regulations, acquired rights, respect for
agreement to extradition **106,** 261
aliens **46,** 407
assignment **89,** 497
civil servant's retirement grant **48,** 12
Evian agreements (1962) **73,** 33-5, 37
expropriation and **48,** 153-4
general principle of international law, whether **62,** 352-3, **89,** 497
importance of concept under traditional international law **46,** 484-5
independence, effect **73,** 33-5
international official. *See also* United Nations Staff Rules and Regulations, acquired rights, respect for
competence to determine nature of right **69,** 397
ILOAT jurisprudence **69,** 328-9
repatriation grant **69,** 310, 318-19, 326-30, 373-4, 508-10, 516-17, 522, 533-47, 552-4, 559-61
maritime claims liability, right to apply for limitation of liability decree **107,** 128-9
nature **69,** 328-9, 440
public purpose and **69,** 329-30
of refugees **72,** 443
retroactivity and **62,** 170-1, **69,** 442, 539-40
State succession
continuing liability of successor government **103,** 121-2, **118,** 438-9
statutory retention **118,** 438
statutory **44,** 12-13, 15-17, 22-5
treaties and **101,** 561
acquisitive prescription. *See* prescription
act of God, events following independence **47,** 102-4. *See also force majeure*
act of government. *See also* act of State
decision of EC Council of Ministers **96,** 222
diminishing scope **96,** 220
employment contract, termination **116,** 655, 674-5
European Community (EC), Council of Ministers, decision **96,** 222
immunity for, whether, European Community (EC) **96,** 220-1

act of government (*cont.*)
judicial review **96,** 218, **117,** 423
unilateral, binding nature **83,** 195-6
act of grace 71, 269, 468
act of State 42, 30-44, 47-51, **43,** 34-5, **47,** 152-3, **51,** 11-24, **54,** 286, **56,** 28, 29, 38-9, 227-8, **57,** 26, 44, 336, **61,** 55, 73-5, 77-8, **63,** 317, 501 n. 5, 595, **77,** 183, 186, 218-20, 230-3, **81,** 511, 515, 595, **82,** 309, **84,** 90, 109, 110, 117-19, **85,** 239, **86,** 47-52, **88,** 95-100, 117-26, 163-5, **91,** 343-4. *See also* act of government; administrative act; expropriation/nationalization, as act of State; foreign law, recognition/enforcement; political question doctrine; prerogative; State immunity; United Kingdom, act of State; United States of America (USA), act of State
act committed abroad **64,** 343-4
immunity in own courts **121,** 202
act of government distinguished **96,** 217 n. 48
acta jure imperii/acta jure gestionis distinguished, relevance **64,** 258, **78,** 93, 616
acts attributable to State, [Draft] Articles on State responsibility (1977/1980/1996/1998/2001) **82,** 190-1
acts of. *See also* applicability *below*
de facto government. *See* governments, de facto
deposed government. *See* former officials of deposed government *below*; Head of State, former
former officials of deposed government **81,** 595
government-controlled entity **69,** 626
Head of State
act in violation of international law **103,** 557, **119,** 106-7
private acts **57,** 31, **88,** 164-5, **99,** 163-5, **119,** 82, **121,** 588
burden of proof **99,** 164
Head of State, former **81,** 619-28, **119,** 106-7
basis **81,** 623
personal gain **81,** 623 n. 12, **119,** 82
officials. *See also* classification as *below*; former officials of deposed government *above*
abroad **86,** 138
foreign officials applying own law **84,** 193-4
Nazi **81,** 511
official act, limited to **81,** 595, **92,** 496
State agency **63,** 208-10, **71,** 225-6
administrative action **66,** 163-7
unrecognized government, legislation **77,** 571
administrative act, third State's competence to examine conformity with international law **78,** 93
applicability. *See also* acts of *above*
administrative agencies **66,** 306-10
boundary dispute. *See* territorial dispute *below*
foreign currency laws, insurance contract payable in forum State **38,** 140, 457
high seas **44,** 365-6, **64,** 264
limitation to sovereign States **57,** 31
pragmatic **79,** 587
private acts **81,** 630-3, **111,** 596-7. *See also* acts of, Head of State *above*
territorial dispute **64,** 280, 292-4, 303, 343-4, 348-51, **66,** 180-5, 334-8
applicable law **42,** 149-51, **84,** 127, 193-4, **88,** 119
basis **43,** 22, **57,** 26, 28, 31, 38-9, 47, 114, **66,** 13, 50-7, 98-100, 106-24, 138-9, 150, 181, 204, 221-3, 226-9, 238-9, 249, 252-3, 276-9, 296-8, 306-7, 315, 322-3, 327, 363, 367-8, 383-4, 390-4, 417-18, 427, 480, 491, **79,** 587-8, 596-7, **81,** 646, **84,** 118-19, **87,** 512, 515-16, **88,** 97. *See also* foreign policy considerations *below*

avoidance of embarrassment **63,** 475, **84,** 194
comity **63,** 187, **66,** 105-8, 160-1, 189, **81,** 633, **84,** 130, 195, **86,** 139, **88,** 65, 97, 99, **92,** 389, 474, **112,** 740-3, **119,** 73-4
equality of States **64,** 260-1
extraterritorial enforcement, difficulty **92,** 474
foreign policy considerations. *See* foreign policy considerations *below*
independence of States **81,** 519, **88,** 66, 99, **92,** 496-7
principles of international law **81,** 519
separation of powers. *See* separation of powers *below*
Bernstein exception. *See* United States of America (USA), Bernstein exception
burden of proof **64,** 264-5, 380-1, **66,** 11, 27-8, 218-20, **81,** 519, 593-4, 597, 637, **101,** 533, **103,** 469
changing significance **79,** 363
choice of law and **84,** 119, **87,** 186, **88,** 119
civil law, absence of doctrine **100,** 372
claim of, limitation and **64,** 266
classification as **81,** 525-6, 595, 622, 654-5, **103,** 508, **111,** 603
acquisition of territory **55,** 59-60, **69,** 41, **71,** 42, 46-7, 53-4, **73,** 119-20, 152, 156-7
justiciability **112,** 481-2, 513, 521, 523, 535-8, 642, 670
administration over native State, resumption **49,** 377
administrative act **66,** 163-7
adoption placement **66,** 163-7
aliens and **54,** 286
antitrust claims **63,** 208-11, 475, **80,** 34, **81,** 517, 519-21, 526
insignificant State involvement **66,** 391-5
assassination **63,** 388-9, **101,** 527-32
breach of contract **63,** 153-4, **64,** 266, **66,** 10-11, 21-31, 77, 182, 220-2, 233-6, 343-5, 583, 592-3, 624-5
commercial activities **63,** 188, 190, 209, 456, 595, **66,** 149-50, 220-2, 226-32, 237-40, 263, 315-16, 343, 384-5, 391, 419-20, 449, **80,** 34, **81,** 518,527, **84,** 119-21, 195 n. 5, **86,** 49, **88,** 74, **94,** 151, **103,** 358, 508, **121,** 496
compensate, failure to **66,** 265-8
concession agreement **81,** 527
extension **66,** 182
grant **66,** 182
revocation **66,** 148-50, 182, 189-91, 292, 343-5, 583, 592-3, 624-5, **69,** 9
confiscation of intangible property **87,** 512. *See also* expropriation/nationalization, as act of State
court judgment **66,** 278-9, 384, **70,** 429-34, **88,** 118
criminal conviction **66,** 153-4
debt **103,** 549
collection of extraterritorial **92,** 478
confiscation **87,** 512
expropriation of right to repayment **92,** 411
repudiation **63,** 153, 190, 275-6, **66,** 76-7, 138-9, 218-26, 233-6
situs **81,** 535, 536-7
declaration of diplomat as *persona non grata* **115,** 443-5
demurrage, refusal to pay **63,** 153-4
deportation. *See* expulsion of alien *below*
drug-trafficking, *Noriega* **119,** 65, 82-3
embargo on shipping **63,** 187-90
exchange controls **84,** 119, 120-1, 126-30
exclusion of alien **92,** 502
execution of arbitral award against foreign State **89,** 359 n. 11

act of State (*cont.*)
executive certificate/statement, status of government **39,** 67, 99, 100-2, 103, 212
expropriation/nationalization. *See* expropriation/nationalization, as act of State
expulsion of alien **45,** 106, **63,** 475, **64,** 426
expulsion of enemy alien **44,** 374
extradition. *See* extradition *below*
foreign legislation **64,** 344-6, **86,** 138
formation of united State **49,** 374
genocide **36,** 48
government decree transferring domicile of corporation **71,** 29, 32-3, **72,** 555-6, 562, **73,** 585, 591
holding/disposal of foreign currency **111,** 592-603
implementation of international obligation **77,** 380
import control **66,** 315-16
international law, under **115,** 613
international organizations and **80,** 34, 164-5
issue of currency **111,** 594-7, 600
legal proceedings **69,** 227
military operation, ally's assistance **80,** 21-2
official act. *See* acts of, officials *above*
patent rights
forfeiture **70,** 429-34
grant **66,** 492-3
price-fixing **80,** 34
public act **64,** 383, **81,** 628. *See also* acts of, officials *above*
publication of documents **86,** 138
purchase of cement for undefined purpose **63,** 152-5
quasi-contractual obligation, repudiation **64,** 266, **66,** 76-7, 137-9, 215-20, 232-6, 240-1
ratification of individual's act **77,** 183-4, 186
recognition of alien property vesting orders **74,** 153-6
sale of airline tickets abroad **121,** 496 n. 10
taking of property on own territory **88,** 73
territorial waters, extension of **63,** 317, **66,** 182
terrorist act **121,** 642
tort, legalization of **87,** 186
torture **119,** 96
treaty
conclusion **70,** 41-2, **81,** 700-1
interpretation **107,** 56
margin of discretion in implementing, relevance **106,** 195, 201-2, 265-8
publication **106,** 238
suspension **106,** 208-11
war crimes **36,** 23, 44-8, 254, 308-12, **44,** 11
superior orders **39,** 438
common law doctrine **119,** 94
conditions for. *See* relevant factors *below*
court's right to raise *proprio motu* **64,** 267
criminal conviction **66,** 153-4
criteria. *See* relevant factors *below*
customary international law **84,** 121 n. 18
customs and tax laws, inquiry into and **92,** 476
as a defence **36,** 23, 44-8, 254, 308-12, **41,** 11, **64,** 380-1
defence on merits, whether **103,** 408

defence, superior orders and **39,** 438
definition **44,** 368-9, 371, 373, 383-4, **49,** 407, 412, **57,** 45, **66,** 9-12, 24, 54, 95, 105, 112-13, 119, 129, 148, 153, 160-1, 181, 209-10, 217, 249, 260, 276, 292, 298, 306, 322, 327, 342, 349, 357, 363, 366, 383, 390, 397, 402, 410, 417, 427, 477-8, 491, **70,** 41-2, **79,** 586, **81,** 518-19, 645, **86,** 139, **119,** 73-4
different types **39,** 282
development of doctrine **79,** 363, **81,** 519
disclosure of documents and **92,** 389-91
discretionary nature **63,** 187, **81,** 519, 528, 653-4, **103,** 516, 548 n. 22
domestic policy considerations
foreign armed forces, prohibition on stationing or transit **106,** 240
high seas, destruction of vessel **106,** 240
public service overseas **106,** 239-40
dominium eminens **41,** 10-12
Dunhill doctrine **86,** 48-9
effects **57,** 46
evidence of
conduct **66,** 218-19, 233-6, 268
government agency minutes **66,** 314-15
official declaration **66,** 191, 260-7, 277
statement by Counsel **66,** 77, 217, 219-20, 236-8, 263
exceptions
Bernstein exception. *See* United States of America (USA), Bernstein exception
corruption **81,** 527-8
executive certificate of non-applicability **92,** 435-6
international law **43,** 12-18
ministerial act of foreign government **81,** 518-19
private act **81,** 630-3, **111,** 596-7
violation of international law **77,** 266, **103,** 474-5
extradition **48,** 187-8, **69,** 224-5, 227, **77,** 395, **79,** 447-51
refusal **106,** 235-43
judicial assistance obligation, relevance **106,** 237, 240-2
separability from foreign policy **106,** 253, 260, 272
withdrawal of agreement **106,** 259-60
separability from foreign policy **106,** 260
extraterritorial effect **61,** 75, 79, **70,** 429-34, **79,** 7, 576-8, 580, 586, **84,** 126-30, **88,** 67, 68. *See also* territorial limitation *below*
assets, *situs* **79,** 587-9, **88,** 67, 73-4
basis **79,** 587
compatibility with law of forum State, need for **81,** 597
enforceability of judgments, need for **79,** 587
nexus with foreign country **79,** 588
territorial sovereignty **79,** 586
transfer of Kuwait Airways assets to Iraq Airways **125,** 665-8
failure to compensate **66,** 265-8
federal State **42,** 30-1, **61,** 74
foreign law, recognition/enforcement **64,** 344, **66,** 189-91, 257-63, 266-7, 306-10, 322-4, 465-6, **88,** 306, **116,** 568-78. *See also* recognition of *below*
foreign policy considerations **57,** 157, **66,** 13, 35-6, 50-8, 95-100, 106-23, 138-9, 161, 181, 221-8, 243, 250-3, 276-7, 284, 296-7, 306-10, 315, 322-3, 335-8, 342, 419-20, 493-7, **81,**520-1, 525, 527-8, 536, 589, 590, 624-5, 626-7, 633, 636 n. 9, **88,** 68, **92,** 390, 435, 474, **101,** 533, 534, **103,** 516, 548, **106,** 195, 196-7,200-3, **116,** 573-8
act within territory of foreign State **121,** 496
counterclaim as set-off and **92,** 437

act of State (*cont.*)
deregistration of Iraqi students following invasion of Kuwait **106,** 199-203
EU Council of Ministers, voting at **106,** 238
expropriation, standard of compensation and **92,** 435-6
extradition. *See* extradition *above*
ICJ, submission of dispute to **106,** 239
maritime exclusion zone, establishment **106,** 239
nuclear equipment, executive decision prohibiting export **106,** 194-7
nuclear tests, resumption **106,** 231-2
port regulation prior to war **106,** 238
protection of nationals **106,** 238
respect for foreign State **81,** 535, 594, 596, 619
sale of weapons by private company to foreign State **106,** 220-1
suspension of technical cooperation with Iraq following invasion of Kuwait **106,** 201-2
treaty. *See* classification as, treaty *above*; treaty exception *below*
general principle of international law **36,** 46, **57,** 26, **86,** 119 n. 13, **100,** 372
governmental compulsion distinguished **81,** 519
IMF and **84,** 125 n. 27
immunity
abrogation **96,** 219-20
general principle of law, whether **96,** 220
immunity from own laws **53,** 167-8, 170-1, 174-7
Iran–US Claims Settlement Declaration **81,** 567
Iran–US Claims Tribunal **84,** 503 n. 12, 653, 666 n. 2
judicial abstention **88,** 121, **103,** 409-10
judicial restraint **64,** 264, 279-80, 292-3, 344-51, **119,** 74, 92, **124,** 563-4, **125,** 645, 650-7
judicial review **115,** 445
constitutional compliance **106,** 209
jurisdiction of courts and **66,** 147-51, 160-2, **70,** 42, **78,** 93, 680-2
jurisprudence
Buttes Gas and Oil Co. v. *Hammer* **64,** 255-6, 257-8, 261-2, **111,** 594, 595-6, 597, 601, 603, **116,** 556, 568-70, 575-8, **119,** 63, 74, 91, 95, **125,** 639-40, 655-7, 683-4, 709-10, 718
Duke of Brunswick v. *King of Hanover* **64,** 255-6, 345-6
First National Bank v. *Banco Nacional de Cuba* **125,** 645-6
International Association of Machinists and Aerospace Workers v. *OPEC* **119,** 73
I° Congreso del Partido **111,** 594, 596-7, 602
Kamachee Boye case **64,** 265, 346
Kirkpatrick v. *Environmental Tectonics* **111,** 601, 602, **119,** 74, 91, 95-6, **125,** 646
Luther v. *Sagor* **64,** 256-7, 263, **116,** 570-1, 587-9
Oetjen v. *Central Leather Co.* **64,** 256, 346-7, **116,** 588, **119,** 92
Princess Paley Olga v. *Weisz* **116,** 570-1, 588
Sabbatino **42,** 31, 35-6, **57,** 29, **64,** 259, 347, **86,** 48, **111,** 597-8, **119,** 73, **125,** 643-5
Underhill v. *Hernandez* **64,** 256-7, 346-7, **111,** 596, **119,** 95
justiciability and **45,** 106, **63,** 98, **80,** 124, 177, 201-2, 205, **81,** 517, 700-1, 721-2, **83,** 259, **87,** 185-6, **88,** 119, **92,** 496, **99,** 163, **103,** 406-10, **111,** 592-603, **116,** 568-78, 594, **119,** 73-4, 90-3, 95-6, **125,** 633-57, 709-10, 718-22
commercial acts **63,** 456, **81,** 722
preferred term **119,** 78
limits **57,** 46, **88,** 126
margin of appreciation **89,** 242

nationality, relevance **125,** 633-7
act involving own nationals **44,** 364-70, 374, 379, 387-9, 391, **57,** 39-40, **64,** 259, **70,** 42
nationalization. *See* expropriation/nationalization, as act of State
nature
different types **39,** 282
flexibility **88,** 164
process of law **71,** 46-7
restrictive doctrine **106,** 195, 200-1, 202-3, 236
participation in law suit and **88,** 118
political asylum and **88,** 22-3, 32-3
political offence and **79,** 511-13
political question doctrine and **81,** 626, 645-6, **87,** 515
property rights based on, State immunity **82,** 25-7
protectorates and **71,** 42, 46-7
public policy and **42,** 29-33, **64,** 266, 139, 144, **119,** 106
recognition of **40,** 7-28, **42,** 26-51, **43,** 12-23, **48,** 5, 30-40, **57,** 39-41, **66,** 10, 269, 401, **75,** 271, 279, 283-4, 290, 292, 295-6, 325, **78,** 599, 615-19. *See also* foreign law, recognition/enforcement *above*
acts *jure imperii* **40,** 7-8
compatibility with international law **40,** 7-9
courts' competence to examine **78,** 93, **116,** 571-2, 589-91, 595
confiscation **42,** 29-33, **43,** 18-23, **78,** 615-19
effect, *situs*, relevance **107,** 211-12
expropriation/nationalization **77,** 450, 548-9, **78,** 679, 680-2
government's right to property **96,** 49
guardianship decrees **42,** 26-9
relevance **98,** 65, **99,** 74 n. 8
seizure of property, Nazi Party in Belgium **42,** 34-8
relevant factors **71,** 46-7, 54
diplomatic relations **77,** 571
formality **66,** 77, 137-9, 148-50, 167, 216-20, 233-4, 260-8, 410
legality of actions **81,** 621, **104,** 163, **121,** 642
level of decision **64,** 381
motivation **57,** 39-40, **64,** 381, 383, **81,** 520-1, 526-7, **92,** 496-7
nature of act **111,** 596, 602
prospect of success of suit **81,** 636-7
public interest/good **64,** 200-1, 206-7, 208, **65,** 281-2, **66,** 278-9, 419, 584-5, **81,** 595, 623-4
recognition, government
compatibility with *lex fori* **77,** 571
effectiveness as criterion **77,** 571
recognition, State **77,** 220, 232-3
sovereign function **66,** 150, 220-6, 231-7, 240-1, 292, 315-16, 343, 384-5, 411, 493
sovereignty **57,** 47
status of parties **84,** 195
repudiation **66,** 385
requirements **42,** 35-6, 44, 46, 50
authorization of action **64,** 381, **81,** 621-2, **88,** 117-18, **104,** 163
military officers **88,** 117
declaration of invalidity of foreign act **88,** 97-100
official act **99,** 163
reciprocity, unrecognized government **77,** 571

act of State (*cont.*)
scope **66,** 114-24, 140-1, 181-2, 189-91, 204-6, 252-3, 291-300, 314-16, 323-4, 349-50, 371-3, 388-95, 397-8, 417-20
separation of powers **63,** 187, 567 n. 38, **77,** 226, 230-3, **79,** 6, 446-51, 499-502, 586, 596-7, **81,** 519, 525, 528, 536, 595, 619-20, 625, 636 n. 9, 645, 654, **84,** 119 n. 14, **86,** 48, **88,** 66, 73, 97, 99, 119-20, 121-3, 125-6, **92,** 389, 496, **98,** 65, 108-9, 162, 165
sovereignty, assumption of **49,** 342, 360, 369, 375-6, 385, 389, 427-33, 473
State immunity, execution/attachment and **89,** 359 n. 11
State immunity, jurisdiction and **63,** 317, **64,** 264, 316-18, **65,** 281-2, **66,** 105-6, 120, 123, 222-3, 237-9, 411-12, 418-19, **77,** 521, **78,** 93, **79,** 6-7, 596-7, 599, 601-2, **80,** 124, 164, 205, 581 n. 28, **81,** 518-19, **84,** 118 n. 12, 119 n. 14, 126, **86,** 49, **88,** 81, **99,** 163, 165, **101,** 532, **103,** 356-8, 548-9, **119,** 73, 240
commercial activities **64,** 316-18
distinction **57,** 39, **63,** 153, 187-9, **64,** 255, 258, 260, **104,** 618, **119,** 223, **121,** 496
in own courts for act of State abroad **121,** 202
State succession, contractual obligations **45,** 19-24
summary judgment and **63,** 456
territorial limitation **43,** 18-23, **64,** 382, **81,** 535, 536, 594-9, **87,** 512-15, 516, 518, **88,** 89 n. 7, 89 n. 17, **98,** 65, 108, **111,** 596, 597, 601, **113,** 529, **119,** 95. *See also* extraterritorial effect *above*
act within own territory **63,** 475-6, **64,** 263-4, 426, **113,** 529, **119,** 95-6, **121,** 496, 642, **125,** 633, 650
cause of action **66,** 357-8
wartime exception **66,** 254-5
treaty exception. *See also* classification as, treaty *above*
treaty or other unambiguous agreement **66,** 121, 268, 345, 479-80, **81,** 625 n. 12, 632 n. 4, **84,** 121-6, **86,** 47-8
unambiguous agreement, need for **86,** 49-52
unjust enrichment **66,** 448, **79,** 597
waiver **64,** 266, 381-2
counterclaim **84,** 179 n. 9
possibility of **64,** 266-7, **84,** 119 n. 14
Act of Union between Scotland and England. *See* Union of England and Scotland, Act of Parliament of Scotland ratifying and approving the Treaty of Union with England 1707/Act of Union with Scotland Act 1706
acte de gouvernement. *See* act of government; act of State
adjacency. *See* maritime delimitation, adjacency
administrative act. *See also* act of government; act of State; judicial review; procedural fairness
judicial review **86,** 411
expropriation permits **68,** 104-27
expulsion of alien **68,** 160-73
property use, restrictions on **68,** 104-27
requirements
arbitrary act **86,** 332
flagrant unlawfulness **86,** 332
wrongful acts against aliens
State responsibility for **46,** 191, 204, 324, 327
exhaustion of remedies **46,** 200, 201
administrative claims 80, 22 n.7
administrative contract
applicable law, administrative law of Contracting State **106,** 704
requirements **106,** 704

unilateral amendment, right to **106,** 631-2, 704
refusal to accept proposed changes **106,** 647, 704-5
requirements
adequate compensation **106,** 631
Aminoil **106,** 631
public interest **106,** 631
administrative documents
interpretation, *travaux préparatoires* **80,** 493-4, 507, 510-13
validity **80,** 495
administrative law 54, 619
applicability
administrative contract **106,** 704
occupied territory **125,** 547
discretionary powers, exercise in furtherance of purpose for which granted **117,** 486-9
general principles of **90,** 577, **125,** 547
administrative practice 58, 261-3, 268, 269, 270-2, 305-6, 312-13, **71,** 300-3
definition **58,** 263, **120,** 122-3
'official tolerance' **120,** 122
evidence of **58,** 263-6, **120,** 49-50, 95-6, 101-4
exhaustion of local remedies and **58,** 263, **71,** 302-3, **120,** 61, 62, 63-5, 101-4, 122-3
State immunity, jurisdiction and **58,** 261-3, 312-14
torture **58,** 263-4, 268-9, **71,** 300-3
administrative tribunals. *See* Asian Development Bank Administrative Tribunal; international administrative tribunals; International Labour Organization Administrative Tribunal; International Labour Organization Administrative Tribunal (ILOAT); International Labour Organization (ILO) Conventions; League of Arab States Administrative Tribunal; NATO Appeals Board; United Nations Administrative Tribunal; United Nations Administrative Tribunal (UNAT); World Bank Administrative Tribunal
admiralty jurisdiction 38, 125-6, **48,** 77-81, **54,** 235-9, **55,** 440-1, **69,** 163, **72,** 2-10, **77,** 66, **78,** 570-2, 685, 689-94, **81,** 541, 664-6, **90,** 293-6
between aliens **98,** 19 n. 6
basis **72,** 3-4
common law and **125,** 394-6
foreign ship, action *in rem* against **64,** 186-93, 234, 552-61, **72,** 2-10
sister ship jurisdiction **64,** 231, **90,** 559
State immunity and **63,** 77-80, 215-27, 252-60, 417-18, 529-34, 546, 605-13, 624-8, 640, **64,** 177, 186-93, 234, 552-61, **72,** 2-10, **81,** 540-2, 664-6, **90,** 558-67, **99,** 85 n. 4, **100,** 538-9
territorial fiction **63,** 353, **125,** 394-6
territorial sea and **90,** 292-6, **125,** 394-6
universality **78,** 570
admissibility. *See* exhaustion of local remedies; *forum [non] conveniens*; jurisdiction; justiciability; political question doctrine *and under individual tribunals*
adoption 66, 165, **92,** 233, **95,** 499-500
aliens and **95,** 487-8, 490-3, 498, 503
of illegitimate child by mother, restrictions **58,** 571-93
Adriatic Sea, delimitation agreement, Italy–Yugoslavia (1968) **41,** 122
advisory opinion. *See* Inter-American Court of Human Rights, advisory opinion; International Court of Justice (ICJ), advisory opinion
aerial bombardment
damages for **80,** 20-4
immunity from suit **80,** 22-3
as war crime **105,** 507-8

affiliation
Brussels Convention on the Establishment of Maternal Affiliation of Natural Children (1962) **58,** 574, 583
discrimination **58,** 581-3
establishment of **58,** 580-4, 617
maternal **58,** 571-3
Afghanistan, League of Nations, admission to **37,** 80
Africa
boundaries in **50,** 407-8, **100,** 50-2. *See also uti possidetis*, Africa
colonization, *terra nullius* **49,** 76
customary international law **84,** 30
customary law **41,** 144, **84,** 30
equity **41,** 144
res nullius **41,** 127, **49,** 76
State immunity, jurisdiction **64,** 647-8
sustainable development principle **116,** 113-14
African Charter on Human and Peoples' Rights (1981)
freedom from discrimination, sexual **87,** 110, **103,** 179
retroactive legislation **91,** 141
African Reinsurance Corporation
Headquarters Agreement **86,** 659-60
waiver of privileges and immunities, whether **86,** 659, 661
personality **86,** 686-9
privileges and immunities **86,** 656-91
common law **86,** 672
employment contract **86,** 656-9, 690
tasks of organization distinguished **86,** 690
Headquarters Agreement **86,** 659-60
waiver **86,** 661-7, 668, 673, 676-90
African States
military forces as agent of foreign government **44,** 363, 376, 383
SW Africa, special interest in **37,** 517
age discrimination 58, 358, **84,** 435, 438-9, 453
agency 46, 33-4, 139, **63,** 158-9, 242-4, **69,** 576, 597-8, 599-600, **77,** 89-94, **80,** 46, 53, 110-21, 176-9. *See also* State agency/State-owned corporation/State entity; Trust Territories
capacity
agent **66,** 321-2
principal **66,** 321-2
imputability of acts
general principle of agency law **107,** 233
of principal **107,** 233
to principal **107,** 233
Agency for International Development. *See* United States of America (USA), Agency for International Development
aggression 49, 81, **76,** 606, 624, 672, 675-81, 724-5. *See also* United Nations General Assembly (UNGA) Resolutions, 3314 (XXIX) (14 December 1974) (Definition of Aggression)
aerial espionage and **47,** 109-12
Namibia, South African occupation of **49,** 79-80
treaty provisions **42,** 398
Vietnam **42,** 437
AGIP. *See* Italy, AGIP, USA
AGIP Spa. *See* Congo, Popular Republic of, AGIP Spa
agricultural leases

aliens **44,** 141
refugees **48,** 166-7, 168
agriculture. *See* European Community (EC), agricultural market; Food and Agriculture Organization (FAO); Uruguay Round, Agreement on Agriculture
aid, human rights and **87,** 668-9
Air Force, agency or instrumentality of a foreign State **63,** 263, 266-7, 278
Air Navigation Safety Organization for Africa and Madagascar. *See also* Eurocontrol (European Organization for the Safety of Air Navigation)
immunity, jurisdiction **74,** 690-3
legal status **74,** 691
staff contract claims **74,** 690-3
staff regulations, as ouster of jurisdiction of ordinary courts **74,** 690-3
air traffic control, Antarctica **82,** 682, **100,** 527. *See also* Air Navigation Safety Organization for Africa and Madagascar; air transport agreements; airspace; Eurocontrol (European Organization for the Safety of Air Navigation)
air transport. *See* air transport agreements; aircraft; airports; carriage by air, international; International Air Transport Association (IATA)
air transport agreements. *See also* air traffic control; airspace; carriage by air, international
'Bermuda type' scheduled flights **45,** 393-427
Canada/Netherlands (1974)
'air services' as 'scheduled services' **96,** 335
'designated airlines' **96,** 335-6
directly binding on individuals, whether **96,** 336
failure to object to proposed tariffs, effect **96,** 336-7
Chicago Convention on International Civil Aviation (1944). *See* Chicago Convention on International Civil Aviation (1944)
France–USA Air Services Agreement **38,** 182-260, **54,** 309, 315-17, 328-35, 337, 341-3, 346-9
interpretation **41,** 426-36, **60,** 445, 447-8, 452, **77,** 407-9. *See also* phrases *below*
Italy–USA Air Transport Services Agreement (1948), scheduled flights, cargo only **45,** 393-427
modification, procedure **38,** 224-6, 234, 243-5, 248
Montreal Agreement (1961), liability **96,** 116, 123
phrases. *See also entries under* UK/US (1977) (Bermuda 2) *below*
'Bermuda type' scheduled flights **45,** 396-427
'categories of users' **102,** 307-8
'change of gauge' **54,** 328-9, 332-5, 337, 342
'five freedoms' **45,** 414-15
'international carriage' **43,** 256-7
'Near East' **38,** 217-18
'omission of stops' **38,** 233-4, 260
'reasonably direct route' **38,** 232
'transshipment' **54,** 344-9
premature termination **82,** 321-8
South Africa–USA (1947) **52,** 424-8, 436-42
special relationship between two parties and **48,** 353-4
suspension of **48,** 354, 394-5
war and 437, **48,** 436
UK/US (1946) (Bermuda Agreement) **38,** 197, 221, 233, 238-9
UK/US (1946-77) (Bermuda Agreements) **74,** 45-56, 66, 73-82, 84
settlement of disputes **74,** 47
US anti-trust laws, applicability **74,** 46-58, 73-82
UK/US (1977) (Bermuda 2)
breach of treaty, State responsibility **102,** 357-9

air transport agreements (*cont.*)
'categories of users' **102,** 307-8
'just and reasonable' user charges **102,** 290-491, 529-41
accurate review, need for **102,** 312
'best efforts' to ensure **102,** 290, 291-5, 301-3, 358, 447, 480-2, 531-2
comparability with user charges elsewhere, relevance **102,** 299-300
criteria exclusively determined by treaty, whether **102,** 297-301, 311-12
domestic costs charged to international user **102,** 307-8
obligation of conduct **102,** 290, 295-7, 298, 386, 480-2, 490
Memorandum of Understanding of 6 April 1983 (MoU)
aid to interpretation **102,** 353
arbitration, whether subject to **102,** 353
as consensual subsequent practice **102,** 353
legal obligations, whether **102,** 353
treaty, whether **102,** 351-3
remedies, declaratory relief **102,** 526-7
'user charges' **102,** 303-5
accounting method **102,** 448-54, 456-80, 535-41
consultations, obligation **102,** 308-10, 513-17
'equitable apportionment' **102,** 305-8, 535
ex ante review, need for **102,** 496
exchange of information, best efforts to encourage for purposes of consultation **102,** 309, 310-11, 517-27
income from commercial enterprises, relevance **102,** 342-9, 456
international comparisons, relevance **102,** 342
'just and reasonable'. *See* 'just and reasonable' user charges *above*
marginal costs as measure **102,** 334-42, 355-7, 383, 396, 430-1
'necessary for an accurate review' **102,** 312
non-discrimination between national and international users **102,** 307-8, 384-92, 426, 492-6
peak charging **102,** 353-5, 385, 387-92, 405-19, 430-8
profit, avoidance of excessive **102,** 340, 347-9, 446-8, 531-41
structure of charges at Heathrow **102,** 312-446
total and constituent elements distinguished **102,** 304-5
Warsaw Convention on International Carriage by Air (1929) and Hague Protocol (1955). *See* Warsaw Convention on International Carriage by Air (1929) and Hague Protocol (1955)
air warfare. *See* aerial bombardment; war, air warfare
aircraft 40, 93, 208-10, **71,** 230. *See also* air transport agreements; carriage by air, international; hijacking of aircraft; jurisdiction, foreign aircraft
'air carrier' **82,** 328
'any aircraft', **90,** 217-18
attempted destruction, extraditable crime, whether **40,** 208-10
China, Civil Aircraft, Flight Regulations **40,** 93
crime committed on **40,** 209
in distress **82,** 675
'interest' for purposes of Security Council Resolutions imposing Yugoslav embargo **117,** 280-5, 299-300
as State territory **71,** 230
aircraft piracy. *See* hijacking of aircraft; Montreal Convention for the Suppression of Unlawful Acts Against the Safety of Civil Aviation (1971); terrorism
airline. *See* carriage by air, international, air companies; State agency/State-owned corporation/State entity, classification, national airline

airports
illegal landing at **40,** 92-3
jurisdiction
aircraft in transit **73,** 702-4
baggage in transit **72,** 673-6, **73,** 663
transit zone **73,** 66, 702-4, **77,** 484, **88,** 261-2
landing fees **78,** 521-6
sanctions for non-payment **78,** 521-6
landing rights **78,** 522-5
operation of **78,** 521-6
airspace 76, 385-7, **90,** 245, 252-3. *See also* air traffic control; air transport agreements; airports; sovereignty, foreign military aircraft, overflight
air corridor above airport **89,** 30-1
boundaries **82,** 682
federal State, legislative power **90,** 253
infringement **76,** 385-8
high-level reconnaissance flights **76,** 385-8
low-level reconnaissance flights **76,** 385-7
sonic boom **76,** 385-7
jurisdiction **40,** 92-3, 346, **54,** 316-17, **77,** 280, 484
above the high seas **90,** 215-16
overflight rights **82,** 675
aircraft in distress **82,** 675
charges **82,** 73
India/Pakistan dispute (1971) **48,** 331, 337, 347, 438
safety of **89,** 30-1
sovereignty over **45,** 414, 422, **47,** 109-12, **54,** 316-17, 346, **71,** 231
as territory **47,** 109-12, **71,** 231
Akaba. *See* Aqaba
Alaska. *See* United States of America (USA), Alaska
Albania
Declaration to Council of League of Nations, treaty character **37,** 68
Italy, union with **40,** 29-32, 35
Alexandria Sanitary Bureau 62, 461-5, 537, 540, 567-8, 579. *See also* World Health Organization Regional Office in Egypt
Algeria
civil war in **44,** 439-41
non-combatants, criminal law and **44,** 447
sabotage in France **44,** 440
Compagnie Nationale Algérienne de Navigation **63,** 252-60, 605-13
continuity of law **47,** 101-2, 103-4, 106, **48,** 61-2
courts, municipal, judgments
effect in France **47,** 124
enforcement abroad **71,** 48-9
Evian Agreements (1962). *See* Evian Agreements (1962)
exchange control regulations **47,** 124, **52,** 11-14
expropriation/nationalization measures 1964 **47,** 119-26, **48,** 82-3, **65,** 84-5, **72,** 219-20, **80,** 433-9
employment contract, locally engaged staff, State agency, State immunity, jurisdiction and **65,** 44-6
France, responsibility of **47,** 325-6
insurance **41,** 375
mining enterprises **41,** 384, 385, 390, 393-4

Algeria (*cont.*)
replacement of company directors **41,** 369, 371, 373
foreign property, State administration of **41,** 266-7, 269, 270-1, 273-9
France. *See* France, Algeria and
government decree, annulment for *ultra vires*, effect **72,** 568
independence. *See also* State succession *below*
acquired rights, effect on **73,** 33-5
nationality of companies and **72,** 567-8
jurisdiction, events prior to independence, French courts **48,** 61-2
law of
Maritime Code **87,** 523
Nationality Code, Moslems **41,** 366, 368
recognition, Algerian National Liberation Front **75,** 81
sequestration of ownerless property **47,** 60-2
Sonatrach, immunity **77,** 525-9
State succession **41,** 21, 23, **48,** 59, 60, **75,** 81, **78,** 108
continuity of law **47,** 101-2, 103-4, 106, **48,** 61-2
continuity of State **75,** 81
contractual obligations **47,** 88-9, 94-6, 104-6, **48,** 58-60
dismemberment of States **47,** 79-83, 104-6, **48,** 59
Evian Agreements and **41,** 21, 23
jurisdiction over State-controlled corporations **47,** 152-5
representation of interests abroad **41,** 20-4
State obligations and **72,** 54-8, 256, **74,** 98-100
assumption **47,** 79-83, 104-6, **48,** 59
wrecks **87,** 523
Algerian National Liberation Front, legal status **75,** 81
Algerian war, visit and search on high seas **47,** 164
Algiers Declaration. *See* Iran–US Claims Settlement Declaration; Iran–US General Declaration
aliens 38, 142-59, 261-4, **39,** 431-2, **40,** 95, 96-7, 99, 200-2, **41,** 395-6, **42,** 48-9, 197-232, **43,** 197-231, **44,** 135-73, **46,** 338, 405, 422-8, 510, 529, **47,** 233-74, 412, 416, **48,** 156-86, **53,** 532, **54,** 259-63, **60,** 250, 252-3, 256, 269, 271-3, 278-80, **70,** 347-53, 365-72, **72,** 571-3, 575-80, **73,** 571-3, 596-656, 674, **74,** 398-401, 448, 571-3, **77,** 434-8, 439, 445, 446-7, **79,** 663. *See also* asylum; deportation; deportation withhold/bar; excludability of alien; exclusion of alien; expulsion of alien; extradition; freedom of establishment; naturalization; refugees
abroad, constitutional protection **80,** 592
access to courts **44,** 300, **45,** 365-70, **46,** 496, **47,** 239-40, **54,** 227-9, **63,** 108, 393-7, 564, 574-5, 577-8, 580-2, **73,**599-602, **74,** 116-17, **77,** 212, **79,** 281, **106,** 292-3, **111,** 537. *See also* enemy aliens, access to courts; United States of America (USA), Alien Tort Claims Statute 1789 (28 USC 1350)
European Court of Human Rights **111,** 170-1
legal person **65,** 224-5
non-resident aliens **61,** 122-3
reciprocity **48,** 173
act of State and **44,** 374, **45,** 106, **54,** 286
admission **44,** 135-40, **61,** 270, 392, 397, 398-406, 424-7, 428-9, 571-3, **79,** 648, 660-1, 663. *See also* entry permit *and* residence permit *below*
discretionary **86,** 130, **90,** 23, 25-6, **95,** 486, 500
judicial review **95,** 487
natural justice **90,** 20, 25
power to refuse **86,** 222, 226, **90,** 25-6
intention to settle **99,** 42

temporary pending determination of status **95,** 486, 500
agricultural leases **44,** 141
allegiance **54,** 268-77, 281-91, 294-5, **55,** 492, 494, **56,** 492, 494
infant **43,** 168
outside jurisdiction **41,** 240, 250, 254-5
appeal rights
defence counsel **72,** 418-29
legal aid **72,** 418-29
notification in native language **72,** 321-2, **74,** 413-16
arbitrary detention **87,** 451-60, **95,** 633
armed forces, voluntary enlistment **47,** 233-4
asylum. *See* asylum
cautio judicatum solvi **73,** 601-2
character **54,** 285
children awaiting adoption
access to record **95,** 487-8, 492-3
constitutional rights **95,** 487
custody **95,** 498
habeas corpus **95,** 490-2
interests of child **95,** 498, 503
common law position **69,** 212
compulsory resettlement **78,** 188
constitutional rights **72,** 265-6, 420-1, 575-9, 594-6, **82,** 315 n. 24, **85,** 276-300, **98,** 403, **124,** 358, 403
illegally resident **85,** 277, 290
non-resident **85,** 276-300
voluntarily resident **85,** 282, 287-8, 290
consular access **77,** 541-2
copyright, respect for property **39,** 431-2
courts, municipal
appeal rights. *See* appeal rights *above*
foreign counsel, right to appoint **47,** 251-62
treatment in, USA **77,** 211-12
damage to, necessity as defence **85,** 470
definition **55,** 490
deportation. *See* deportation
detention
international obligations and **92,** 551-3
pending trial, compensation for **72,** 264-6
EC national **93,** 476-80
employment of **53,** 529, **78,** 85-6
enemy aliens. *See* enemy aliens
entry permit **90,** 22
discretionary **90,** 25-7, 159
judicial review **85,** 212
refugee status, relevance **90,** 27-8, 155, 159, 160, 168, **91,** 176
revocation **68,** 171-3
temporary **90,** 22-3, 140, 146, 147, 155, 159
equalization of burdens, levies and **61,** 164, 166, 173-8
establishment. *See* freedom of establishment
exclusion. *See* exclusion of alien
expropriation/nationalization, levies on gains from currency depreciations **44,** 149-56
extradition. *See* extradition
false identity documents, public order and **86,** 334

aliens (*cont.*)
freedom of association **75,** 59-65
freedom of movement **60,** 252, 253, 268-9, 271, 279
alien husband, refusal of residence permit **103,** 230-4
Universal Declaration of Human Rights (1948) and **60,** 268
harmonization of policy respecting, need for **111,** 267-8
human rights, breach by **89,** 73
illegal entry, claim to refugee status **43,** 212-13
immigration. *See* immigration
'integrated aliens' **111,** 193, 269
intention to settle
burden of proof **99,** 43
public order and **99,** 43
request for residence permit as evidence of **99,** 43
judicial delay **84,** 372-3
judicial review, entry permit **85,** 212
jurisdiction. *See* jurisdiction, aliens
labour law, application to **88,** 688, 689-90
legal practitioners, admission as **55,** 492
legislation, applicability to acts committed abroad **54,** 268-73, 281-3
liberty, judicial protection of **38,** 151
most favoured nation clause. *See* standard of treatment of alien
non-discrimination. *See* standard of treatment of alien
non-national, whether synonymous **115,** 338-41
passport, conditions for issue **73,** 608-12
patriality **61,** 392, 397, 398, 404, 428-9
political rights **62,** 397, **72,** 589-90
definition **72,** 589-90
procedural rights **74,** 413-16
property **77,** 435-9, **81,** 3-24, **82,** 43
compulsory purchase **40,** 96-7
confiscation **42,** 48-9, **47,** 412, 416
copyright **39,** 431-2
discrimination **93,** 477
Draft Convention on the International Responsibility for Injuries to Aliens (1961) **85,** 398-9, 402 n. 1
EC membership and **93,** 476-80
national administration of **40,** 95, 99
real/immovable **48,** 169-71
restrictions on acquisition **77,** 434-8, 439
rights of succession **53,** 532
protection **54,** 273, 286, 290, **84,** 326, **89,** 457, 516, 531, 532-3. *See also* diplomatic protection
abuse of right **46,** 420
duty of, customary international law **82,** 219
international law, under **84,** 326
treaty **84,** 326
reciprocity **85,** 291
refugees. *See* refugees
removal, airlines, obligation **90,** 26
'residence' **54,** 287-8, 290
relevance **46,** 423-5
residence permit **47,** 248, **61,** 424, **72,** 571-80, **74,** 398-401, 405, 448, 571-3

alien husband's right to **103,** 230-4
cancellation **70,** 365-72, **72,** 575-80, **73,** 618-26
'conduct giving rise to serious complaints' **72,** 575, 578-9
expulsion distinguished **72,** 579-80
permit procured by fraud, forgery, false, misleading or concealment of information **117,** 644-5
deportation and **92,** 364-5
discretionary **72,** 577-8, **73,** 620-1, **74,** 398-401, 571-3
EEC Regulation **38,** 261-4
establishment permit distinguished **72,** 579
extension **72,** 571
refusal **73,** 608, 612, **74,** 398, 448
'family members', entitlement **74,** 448, 572-3
grant **72,** 577-8, **73,** 620-1, 674
humanitarian grounds
refugee status distinguished **99,** 5-6, 31-2
relevance **111,** 282
prohibition on
civil or criminal proceeding **77,** 446-7
permissibility **77,** 445
refusal **72,** 571-3, 578, **74,** 400-1, 448
economic considerations **72,** 572
public order and **72,** 571-3
request for as evidence of intention to settle **99,** 43
revocation. *See* cancellation *above*
settlement permit distinguished **111,** 281-2
residence, right of **86,** 336, **92,** 310-12
permanent residence status **90,** 22, **104,** 489-90
residence status **62,** 287-8, 290-2, 294
resident and non-resident distinguished **56,** 16-18
restrictions upon **60,** 250, 271-3
right of abode **61,** 428-9. *See also* residence, right of *above*; freedom of establishment
right of entry. *See* admission *above*
right of inheritance **38,** 142-5, **42,** 1-8, 43, 197-212, **43,** 197-212
right to commercial occupation **44,** 145-7
right to control **108,** 353, 408, **111,** 192, 269
customary international law **111,** 184, 265, 288
limitations on
European Convention on Human Rights (1950) **111,** 184, 291-2
treaty obligations **111,** 184, 265
right to cultivate land **47,** 243-8
right to remain in country **124,** 403
rights and freedoms of citizen, entitlement **115,** 653-4
salaried activity **47,** 245, 248, 249-50
shareholders outside jurisdiction of respondent State **46,** 422
social security
entitlement **94,** 602
motivation, relevance **94,** 602
residence requirement **94,** 602, 607
standard of treatment. *See* standard of treatment of alien
State responsibility and. *See* State responsibility for, aliens
stateless person. *See* stateless person
status as

aliens (*cont.*)
burden of proof **54,** 270, 276-80, 291-7
Salvadoreans in US **95,** 573-4
taxation
family allowances **47,** 135
land **43,** 11
levies on gains from currency depreciations **44,** 149-56
war charges and levies **43,** 3, 6, **44,** 151, 154
trade union rights **72,** 589-91
treaties, rights under **74,** 399-401, 572-3, **78,** 100
visa application
misrepresentation of material fact
assisting the enemy in persecuting civilians **95,** 517-21, 525
invalidity of visa **95,** 520-1, 522
war burdens and **61,** 164, 166, 173-8
women married to, discrimination **62,** 287-97
work permit, EEC Regulations **47,** 249-51
allegiance 39, 248, 277-9, 292-3, 314-16, 323, 388, **54,** 270-1, 275-6, 283-91, **60,** 93
accession to independence and **92,** 633-5
aliens **54,** 268-77, 281-91, 294-5, **55,** 492, 494, **56,** 492, 494
infant **43,** 168
outside jurisdiction **41,** 240, 250, 254-5
American Declaration of Independence, effect **39,** 329-30
British Commonwealth **92,** 634
change of **54,** 277-8
continuance of **42,** 450
differing types **54,** 270-1, 275-6, 283-6
divided **39,** 278, 326, 328, 340
duty of **54,** 264-90
establishment of **54,** 270, 282-91
jurisdiction and **41,** 239, 240, 247, 250, 254-6, **42,** 109-12, **43,** 168, **54,** 268-73, 281-91, **92,** 630-5
allegiance of non-citizens **43,** 166-75
nationality and **52,** 72-3, **53,** 525-6, **54,** 268-77, 284, **92,** 631, **103,** 148
oath to foreign State and **53,** 526
passport and **56,** 492, 494
prisoner of war status and **42,** 441-57, 477-8
residence and **92,** 631-2
Rhodesia
after 1965 **39,** 326-9, 336, 340
before 1965 **39,** 324-6, 340
sovereign authority, evidence of **59,** 61, 73-4, 100, 120
temporary **39,** 305, 313, 316, 318, 329, 330
territoriality and **39,** 328
to de facto sovereign **39,** 245-6, 248, 251-2, 279, 294-5, 300, 303-23, 353-5, 359, **52,** 72-3
to State **39,** 294-300, 323, 326, 333, 336
to usurper **39,** 119
treason and **39,** 309, **54,** 268-73, 281-91
de facto sovereign, to **39,** 309, 359, 388
alliance
Axis, Berlin–Rome (1936) **44,** 335
union of States and **91,** 312

alluvion 74, 122-3. *See also* accretion; avulsion; erosion
alter ego. *See* State agency/State-owned corporation/State entity, *alter ego* theory
ambassador/head of mission. *See also* accreditation; diplomatic agent; diplomatic privileges and immunities; diplomatic relations
agrément, need for **99,** 166, **115,** 616-17
State succession and **115,** 616-17
withdrawal to prevent abuses **115,** 611
ambassador to UN, bilateral ambassador distinguished **99,** 130, 135
appointment
as abandonment of territorial claim **100,** 310, 312, 313-14
act of international courtesy **100,** 311, 325
open to constitutional challenge, whether **100,** 311
as political act **100,** 311, 326
recognition, government **86,** 18, **107,** 258
recognition, State **100,** 310, 313, 326
validity **100,** 326-7
countersignature by minister invalidly appointed **100,** 323-4
failure to publish **100,** 308, 323
assassination **63,** 380-90
duty to control actions of members of mission **121,** 486
evidence of status, executive certificate **118,** 300
executive certificate/statement **74,** 173, 176, 179, 187-8
effect **63,** 130-5, 321, **64,** 594-5, **82,** 8, **94,** 360, 361, **120,** 6
nationality **120,** 6
use of mission funds **63,** 130-5, 321, **64,** 594-5, **74,** 173, 176, 179, 187-8, **82,** 8, **94,** 360, 361, **120,** 6
letter of. *See* executive certificate/statement *above*
powers
conclusion of treaties **99,** 130-1
contract distinguished **99,** 136 n. 1
credentials, relevance **65,** 124
disposal of land on behalf of sending State **65,** 123-4
to bind sending State **99,** 130, 135-6
authorization, need for **99,** 130-1
reasonable reliance on apparent authority **99,** 131, 133, 136-8
residence as diplomatic premises **87,** 236
special envoy as **99,** 116
State immunity, jurisdiction, entitlement **65,** 2, **115,** 613-14, **119,** 208-11
status
agent of sending State **64,** 442-4, **99,** 130-4, 136-8, **104,** 412
diplomatic agent **104,** 413
State agency/State-owned corporation/State entity **115,** 613-14
State organ **65,** 269-70, 307
treaties, authority to sign **44,** 202, 204-5, 215, 216
American Arbitration Association 80, 33
American Civil War
Confederacy, validity of laws **39,** 254-5
doctrine of necessity **39,** 121, 125-33, 137-40, 365-8, 388-90, 394-6, **90,** 487-90
American Convention on Human Rights (1969) 75, 5-30, 34-75. *See also* African Charter on Human and Peoples' Rights (1981); American Declaration of the Rights and Duties of Man; European Convention on Human Rights (1950); Inter-American Commission on Human Rights; Inter-American Court of Human Rights; International Covenant on Civil and Political Rights (ICCPR) (1966)

American Convention on Human Rights (1969) (*cont.*)
access to courts. *See* judicial protection *below*
accession to
Peru **116,** 340 n. 8, 347
Suriname **116,** 261, 296 n. 3, 307
adjudication and advisory machinery **67,** 562, 596-609
American Declaration on the Rights and Duties of Man and **96,** 426-9
applicable law
human rights violations
applicable principles of international law **95,** 315, 319
treaty **95,** 315, 319
arbitrary detention **87,** 457, **116,** 308-11, **118,** 77-9, 90
breach
absence of effective remedy for breach as itself a breach **96,** 411. *See also* effective remedy *below*
before entry into force **123,** 141
by individual **116,** 335-6
jurisdiction **116,** 336
critical date, self-executing and non-self-executing laws distinguished **116,** 333-5
enforcement of offending law, relevance **118,** 89
exhaustion of local remedies and **95,** 257, 272
refusal to accept responsibility for events as established before court **116,** 515
State responsibility for. *See* State responsibility and *below*
victim's guilt, relevance **118,** 77, 84
Commission, procedures before, waiver **67,** 581-3, 585-6
compensation **95,** 300-6
accommodation **95,** 309
admissibility of request, need for inclusion in Commission's report **116,** 380
assignees of victim
basis for indemnification **95,** 319
party to determination **95,** 302-3
Commission involvement **95,** 301, 302-6
costs and expenses. *See* costs and expenses *below*
Court approval, need for **95,** 301, 306
currency of payment **118,** 119-20
rate of exchange **116,** 439, 520, **118,** 119
customary international law **116,** 274-5, 410, 498-9
dependants **116,** 282-3
equitable basis **116,** 287, 428-9, 449-50, 511, 513
exemption from tax, duty or other reduction **118,** 120
heirs **116,** 277-82. *See also* next of kin *below*
applicable law **116,** 277-8
burden of proof **116,** 283
in case of death of beneficiaries **118,** 118-19
human rights violation
European Court of Human Rights **95,** 314
UN Human Rights Committee **95,** 314
interest on **118,** 108, 110
lawyer **116,** 480-1
loss of life plan **116,** 431-3, 442-4
justification for inclusion **116,** 448-50
restitutio in integrum compared **116,** 433, 447
lump sum **95,** 316-17
measure

adequate **123,** 156
in case of inferred finding of responsibility **116,** 317-18
currency fluctuations, relevance **116,** 288
expenses **116,** 289, **118,** 108, 110
incurred in prison **116,** 429
fair **95,** 315-16, **118,** 91, 101
lost benefits **95,** 317
lost earnings **95,** 309, 317, **116,** 276, 287-8, 428, 508-9, **118,** 108, 109-10
lost opportunity **116,** 508
lost pension **95,** 317
medical expenses during incarceration **116,** 428
medical expenses of victim and next of kin in the future **116,** 428-9
next of kin's expenses incurred in obtaining information about victims **116,** 284
next of kin's travel expenses **116,** 428, 509-10
patrimonial loss **116,** 509
'prudent estimate' **116,** 287
psychological treatment **118,** 109, 110
psychological treatment of wife **118,** 109, 110
restitutio in integrum **116,** 275-6, 481
victim and assignee of victim distinguished **95,** 317-18
moral injury **95,** 309, 314, 316, 318, **116,** 276-7, 287, 288, 430-1, 511-13
dependants **116,** 283-4, 430-1, **118,** 110-11
equity **95,** 314
family members **116,** 431, 512-13
members of community **116,** 513-14
victims' tribe **116,** 285-6
next of kin. *See also* heirs *above*
by succession **116,** 500
in own right **116,** 411-12, 500-1, 507-15
payment
in instalments **95,** 319
procedure **116,** 291-2
pension **95,** 308-9
postponement of decision on **116,** 384
punitive damages **95,** 315-16, **116,** 514
requirements, causality **116,** 429
third parties **116,** 282-3
time-limits
for agreeing **95,** 306, 313
payment **95,** 319
complaint under, obligation to avoid adversely affecting situation of plaintiff **116,** 355
compliance, obligation of **118,** 88, 90
costs and expenses **95,** 316, **118,** 91, 120
Court's discretion **118,** 117-18
equitable basis **118,** 116
evidence of, need for **118,** 116, 117
incurred in efforts to secure court decision **116,** 437-8
inter-American system proceedings **118,** 116-18
necessary and reasonable **116,** 437, 438, 519, **118,** 116-18
next of kin **116,** 437-8, 519
payment to heirs in case of death of applicant **118,** 118
proceedings in domestic courts **116,** 438, **118,** 115-16
representatives of victim **116,** 437-8
criminal, rights of **95,** 324

American Convention on Human Rights (1969) (*cont.*)
death penalty provisions **70,** 465-77
death row as inhuman or degrading treatment, conditions of detention **123,** 523-4, 533-4, **124,** 227-9
denunciation **123,** 513-14, 527. *See also* suspension of rights *below*
derogation. *See* suspension of rights *below*
detention
incommunicado **118,** 72, 73-4, 79-81, 85-7, 89
arbitrary nature **118,** 87
cruel, inhumane or degrading treatment, whether **118,** 86-7, 91
family, effect on **118,** 110-11
habeas corpus and **118,** 79-83, 91
requirements **118,** 87
'lawful detention'. *See also* arbitrary detention *above*
accordance with the procedures and terms established by law **118,** 77, 78
necessity **118,** 77, 85
order of competent authority **118,** 77, 78-9
reasonableness **118,** 77
preventive **118,** 77-9, 85, 90
disappearances **95,** 292-4, **116,** 476-7
due process **96,** 412-13
effective remedy
absence as breach of the Convention **96,** 411
ineffectiveness
denial of access to judicial remedy **96,** 412
general conditions in country **96,** 411
lack of independent judiciary **96,** 412
state of emergency **96,** 412, **123,** 155
unjustified delay **96,** 412
suspension **96,** 415
enforcement procedure. *See* Inter-American Commission on Human Rights; Inter-American Court of Human Rights, exhaustion of local remedies
exhaustion of local remedies **67,** 581-3, 585-7, 592-3, **75,** 7-8
State benefit, whether solely for **67,** 581-3, 585-6
waiver **67,** 587-8
expulsion **95,** 322
in accordance with the law **95,** 325
administrative act, need for **95,** 326
as extradition **95,** 325
national **104,** 188
security **95,** 325
unlawful arrest as **95,** 326-7
extraterritorial jurisdiction **123,** 168
acts of State agents abroad **123,** 168
fair trial **79,** 346, 374, **96,** 412
lawyer's right of communication with accused **116,** 379
in military courts **116,** 378-80
right to challenge evidence **116,** 379
unconstitutional removal of judge and **123,** 145-52
family, protection of, disappearances and **116,** 480
freedom of expression **75,** 6-30, 35-58, 67-75, **79,** 343, 349-50
definition **75,** 10-11, 40-8, 55
journalism **75,** 3-30, 33-75

freedom of the press **75,** 13-30, 41-57, 66
nature of profession **75,** 9-12, 14-30, 42, 54-7, 63-5, 68-9
professional associations, compulsory membership **75,** 3-30, 35-6, 41-2, 48-57, 68-9
Talloires, Declaration of **75,** 25-6
other conventions compared **75,** 44-8, 66-75
restrictions
legitimacy **75,** 5-6, 11-30, 41-2, 44, 46, 48-57, 68-9
public interest **75,** 5, 10-11, 15, 17, 41-2, 44-6, 50-2, 54-7, **122,** 591
rights and reputations of others and **79,** 343
right of reply **79,** 348, 349, 351
freedom from discrimination **79,** 299-304, 305-7, 308-10, 313-25
freedom of movement **70,** 236-40, **95,** 322
freedom of the press **75,** 13-30, 41-57, 66
journalists, compulsory licensing and **75,** 16-23, 41-2, 48-57
prior censorship **75,** 23-4, 41, 48-57, 68
guarantees
non bis in idem **116,** 380-3, 386
rights distinguished **96,** 397, 400, 412
suspendable, whether **116,** 376-7
habeas corpus **116,** 478-80
amparo and **96,** 401-2, 413-14, 415
detention incommunicado and **118,** 79-83, 91
procedural impediment to exercise **118,** 81-3
purpose **96,** 402, **118,** 83
right of suspension **96,** 394-404, 413-15, **118,** 80, 81-3, 91. *See also* suspension of rights *below*
independent and impartial tribunal **89,** 81-2, **105,** 372
military tribunal **116,** 387
state of emergency and **96,** 400-1, 403, **123,** 155
unconstitutional dismissal of judges and **123,** 151-2
individuals and **67,** 569-70, 584-5, 592-3, **116,** 333-6. *See also* breach, by individual *above*
inhumane treatment **95,** 292, **116,** 377-8
arbitrary detention **95,** 299, **116,** 475
deprivation of communication **95,** 299-300, **116,** 378
detention incommunicado **118,** 86-7, 91
isolation **95,** 299
manner of arrest **116,** 475-8
interpretation **79,** 310-12, 326-35, 338-77
bilingual **67,** 598-9
by Inter-American Court of Human Rights **67,** 596-609, **79,** 326-35, 338-77, **123,** 549, 552
conflicting **67,** 607-8
context **79,** 292
object and purpose **67,** 566-71, **79,** 292-3, 329, 334
ordinary meaning **67,** 603, 606, **79,** 292, 329, 334, 343
other treaties compared **79,** 351-2, 368
restrictions on **75,** 43-8, **79,** 291, 357
rules **67,** 605
travaux préparatoires **67,** 566-7, 598-9, 606-7, **79,** 348-9, 351, 367-8, 369
unilateral **79,** 371
Vienna Convention on Treaties (1969) **67,** 585, 602, 606, **79,** 291-2, 310, 329, 342, 357

American Convention on Human Rights (1969) (*cont.*)
invocation by individual, as disloyalty **95,** 287
judicial guarantees. *See* fair trial *above*; judicial protection *below*
judicial protection **79,** 346, 368-74, 376, **116,** 376-7, 478-80, **118,** 87-9, 91
effectiveness of procedural means, need for **123,** 152-5
unconstitutional dismissal of judge and **123,** 152-5
legal defence, right to **116,** 477-8, **118,** 85-6
freedom to communicate with counsel **118,** 86
life, right to **95,** 292, **116,** 476-7
death in custody **116,** 314-16, 318-19
obligation to take measures to protect and preserve **116,** 318-19, **120,** 53-5
municipal law and **89,** 81-2, 85-7
conflict **116,** 332-7
Convention ancillary to **95,** 257-8
nationality, right to **79,** 294-9
object and purpose, effective protection of human rights **95,** 243-4
obligations
compliance with recommendations of supervisory organ **116,** 383-4
compliance. *See* compliance *above*
prevention of human rights violations **116,** 435-6
amnesty laws and **118,** 167
simple and prompt recourse to a competent tribunal **116,** 435-6, 479-80
to investigate events **116,** 480
amnesty laws and **116,** 522-6
to refrain from adopting measures incompatible with the object and purpose of treaty **116,** 332, 522-6, **118,** 88-9, 90
personal integrity **95,** 299-300
personal liberty **95,** 292-3, **116,** 471-4. *See also* detention *above*
failure to bring promptly before a competent court **116,** 473-4, **123,** 542
illegal detention **116,** 473-4
right of suspension **96,** 395, **116,** 376-7
phrases
'all persons subject to their jurisdiction' **123,** 101-2, 168
'domestic laws' **72,** 326-35, **79,** 290, 341, 343-5, 346, 347
'injured parties' **116,** 498
next of kin **116,** 411-12, 499-501
'interpretation or application of [the] Convention' **95,** 243
'laws' **116,** 256-7
'parties' **95,** 301
assignees of victim **95,** 302-4
Commission, whether **95,** 302-6
'reasonable time' **118,** 82-4
'recommendations' **116,** 383
presumption of innocence **116,** 379-80, **118,** 85
procedural norms
prejudice to State, need to avoid **95,** 244-5
preservation of procedural rights **95,** 244
prompt hearing **95,** 292, **118,** 80, 82-5, 91
'reasonable time' **118,** 83-5, **123,** 553
date of commencement **118,** 84
relevant factors. *See* relevant factors *below*
relevant factors
complexity of case **118,** 84

conduct of judicial authorities **118,** 84
parties' conduct **118,** 84
relevant period **118,** 84
purposes **67,** 584-5, 601
ratification, reservations, subject to **67,** 564-71
remedies. *See* compensation *above*; reparations *below*
reparations
applicable law
Convention **116,** 498
international law **116,** 410-11, 498
beneficiaries **118,** 105
claimant's failure to appear before Court, relevance **116,** 414-15
commission's power to recommend **123,** 542-3
compensation. *See* compensation *above*
evidence submitted during reparations hearing **116,** 415, **118,** 90
instruments of **116,** 411, 498
acknowledgement of responsibility **116,** 434, **118,** 112
amendment of legislation **116,** 333, 434-5, **118,** 114-15
condemnation of facts **95,** 308
information about fate of victims **116,** 293, 481
investigation **95,** 308, 315, **116,** 481, 517-19, 522-3, **118,** 90, 91, 113
judgment **95,** 315, **116,** 434, 514, **118,** 112
non-implementation of consequences of breach **118,** 113, 119
provision of school and dispensary **116,** 289
public apology **116,** 433-4
punishment of those responsible **118,** 90, 91, 113
reinstatement in previous position **116,** 423-4
release of victim **116,** 384, 422-3, **123,** 542
restoration of violated right **116,** 498
right to take proceedings in International Court **116,** 514-15
obligation to make **116,** 274-5, 410-11, 498-9, **118,** 90, 91, 101, 102-3
purpose, *restitutio in integrum* **116,** 499
requirements, proportionality **116,** 411, 499
reply **89,** 84-7
reservations **67,** 564-71
interpretation **70,** 453, 465, 469-77
restrictions, limitation to those authorized by Convention **79,** 330, **116,** 364
retroactive legislation **91,** 80, 140
rights
amparo. See habeas corpus *above and individual rights*
guarantees distinguished **96,** 397, 400, 412
suspension. *See* suspension of rights *below*
self-executing provisions **116,** 258
State responsibility and
change of government **95,** 299
domestic law, relevance **95,** 299
individual's responsibility distinguished **116,** 336
obligation to prevent **95,** 296-9, 300
violation of rights **95,** 296
suspension of rights. *See also* denunciation *above*
'effective exercise of democracy' of paramount importance **96,** 398, 414, 415
essential judicial remedy requirement **96,** 400-1, 415
exceptional **96,** 398

American Convention on Human Rights (1969) (*cont.*)
full and effective exercise distinguished **96,** 398
habeas corpus **96,** 394-404, 413-15
humane treatment **96,** 395
international obligations and **96,** 398
liberty of person **96,** 395, 414
non-discrimination **96,** 398
non-suspendable rights **96,** 395, 398-9, 402, 409-10, 414-15, **116,** 376, **118,** 80
proportionality **96,** 399, 414
reasonableness **96,** 399
rule of law and **96,** 399-400, 414, 415
suppression of rights distinguished **79,** 329
third parties
effect on **67,** 599-607
jurisdiction of Inter-American Commission on Human Rights. *See* Inter-American Commission on Human Rights, admissibility, complaints against States not party to Convention
torture, evidence of **116,** 311-14
truth and information **116,** 480
American Declaration of the Rights and Duties of Man (1948) 37, 455, **79,** 333
access to courts **123,** 171-2, 175-8, 180, 185-8
applicability
armed conflict **123,** 169-70, 182-8
non-combatant deaths and injuries **123,** 134-5
basis in WWII **123,** 169
derogation, in accordance with the law **123,** 176-7
detention. *See also* access to courts *above*; liberty of person, deprivation *below*
civilians in armed conflict, public security **123,** 171-2, 174-5
civilians during armed conflict **123,** 158-88
humane treatment, right to **123,** 171
evolving law and **96,** 426
extraterritorial application **123,** 101, 115
fundamental human rights, statement of **96,** 426-7
interpretation
context, juridical system in force at time of interpretation **123,** 169-70
Inter-American Court of Justice **96,** 422-4, 426, 428-9
legal effect **96,** 429
liberty of person, deprivation, in accordance with established norms and procedures **123,** 171-2, 176-8, 183-8
obligations
non-ratifying OAS members **123,** 133-5
source of **96,** 428, 429, **123,** 167-8
remedies
investigation and attribution of responsibility **123,** 178-80
repair of consequences **123,** 178-80
review of procedures to ensure future conformity **123,** 178-80, 188
treaty, whether **96,** 422-3, 424-5, **123,** 170 n. 10
Inter-American Committee of Jurisconsults **96,** 425
Inter-American Juridical Committee **96,** 425
Ninth International Conference of American States (1948) **96,** 425
American Law Institute, Draft Law of Treaties **37,** 67
'American States', definition **67,** 603
amicus curiae **63,** 162, 338, **64,** 211, 355, 365, **75,** 34, 50, 678, 688, **78,** 554, **79,** 327, 402-3, 504, **103,** 68, **108,** 146, **110,** 618, 681, **116,** 306, **118,** 301, **121,** 228-9, 330. *See*

also Yugoslavia, International Criminal Tribunal for the Former (ICTY), Rules of Procedure and Evidence, 74 (*amicus curiae*)
Aminoil (American Independent Oil Company). *See* Kuwait, Aminoil concession
amnesty 78, 23-4
effective remedy, whether **78,** 25-6
extradition and **106,** 264
International Criminal Court (ICC), jurisdiction **125,** 488
legality under international law **118,** 167, **119,** 86
competence to determine whether **119,** 92
obligation to investigate human rights violations and **116,** 523-6, **118,** 171-2
UNHRC Sub-Commission on Minorities, Report on the impunity of perpetrators of human rights violations **116,** 525
as *res judicata* **119,** 344
torture, UNHRC General Comment No 20 **121,** 261 n. 172
Amnesty International Charity Limited, effect of relationship with on impartiality requirement 119, 113-35
***amparo* 79,** 370, 375, 377, **94,** 428, 430, **95,** 273, **96,** 401-2, 411, 413-14, 415
AMTRAK. *See* United States of America (USA), AMTRAK
ANAD (Accord de non-aggression et d'assistance en matière de défense), Burkina Faso/Mali dispute and **80,** 456, 464
anarchism. *See* political offence, classification as
ancient title. *See* title, historic
Andorra
citizens of, legal status **52,** 27
France and, legal relationship **44,** 176-9, **52,** 16-26
independence **52,** 14-25
nationals of, in France **52,** 26
status **39,** 412-13, **44,** 176-9, 185, **52,** 16-26, 27
Angola
boundary with South West Africa **37,** 409
Constitution
Art. 1 **118,** 530
Art. 2 **118,** 530, 538
Art. 7 **118,** 530
Art. 10 **118,** 530, 538-9
Art. 44 **118,** 530, 539
Art. 45 **118,** 531
Art. 58 **118,** 531, 539
expropriation/nationalization, limited nature **118,** 537
fair trial, probability of **118,** 535-6
independence, continuity of laws **118,** 534, 538
law of, Portuguese law, applicability **118,** 534, 538-9
legal system, changes following independence, forum selection clause and **118,** 529-39
recognition **118,** 529
non-recognition, effect **94,** 204, 206-9
State agency
right to sue **94,** 204-9
Transportes Aeros de Angola **94,** 207
SWAPO detention camps **85,** 219-35
evidence of detention **85,** 223-8
release of detainees
UN High Commissioner for Refugees **85,** 232-4
UN Special Representative **85,** 232-4
UN Mission on Detainees **85,** 219

annexation 82, 418
aboriginal territory/title in Australia **112,** 432-3, 436, 509, 537-8, 557-602
acquired rights and **118,** 438-9
statutory retention **118,** 438, 439
acquisition of territory and **48,** 63-8
by administering power **77,** 628
as act of State **71,** 53-4
application of foreign law as **48,** 63-8
assumption of supreme power by Allied Powers in Germany, whether **91,** 225
Belgian Congo **48,** 14
belligerent occupation and **49,** 267 n. 58, **77,** 629
Bohemia and Moravia **47,** 33
Bophuthatswana **103,** 19
Bosnia-Herzegovina **95,** 152-3, **122,** 51-3, 57
as breach of Mandate **49,** 99, 111-13, 266
by agreement **95,** 153
Czechoslovakia **47,** 31, 33
East Jerusalem **48,** 63-8, 94, 98
foreign law, application to **48,** 63-8
Germany after WWI, opposition to **37,** 56-8, 65, 196
Germany after WWII, whether **91,** 225
Goa, Daman and Diu (1961) **46,** 484, **118,** 431, 432-3
Hawaiian Kingdom **119,** 584-5, 594, 597
implied use of force **95,** 153
Madagascar **11,** 77-8
mediatized rulers **49,** 344
Murray Islands. *See* Murray Islands
Namibia, by South Africa **49,** 80-1, 110-13, 148-9, 151
New South Wales **86,** 212-13
Penguin Island (Cape Colony) **86,** 191, 196, 198, 204
private law, change of **44,** 367
proclamation as means **49,** 387-8
redistribution distinguished **95,** 153
right of **82,** 418
rights against former sovereign **44,** 366-7, 380
self-determination and **49,** 81
South West Africa **49,** 5, 18, 20, 23, 33
title, effect on **95,** 152
Torres Strait islands **86,** 190-1, 193, 195-6
Transvaal **39,** 101
waste and vacant land **71,** 51-6
Antarctica
air traffic control **82,** 682, **100,** 527
applicable law **100,** 533-5, 540-2
US law **100,** 522-30, 532-44
co-ordination of policies **82,** 672
environmental impact statement, need for **100,** 522-30
Antarctic Treaty, Protocol on Environmental Protection (1991), relevance **100,** 527-8
rights relating to, avoidance of prejudice **82,** 683, 688
status **100,** 532 n. 1
'foreign country', whether **100,** 526, 537-40, 553, **108,** 654-6
'global common' **100,** 522, 526-7, 529-30
no-man's-land **108,** 655-6

part of sovereign territory, whether **108,** 656
US legislative control **100,** 526-7, 529
anti-dumping measures. *See* European Community (EC), anti-dumping measures; General Agreement on Tariffs and Trade (GATT) (1947)
Antigua
Constitution **60,** 136-8, 142, 144, 146
discrimination **60,** 143
European Convention on Human Rights (1950) and **60,** 137
human rights in **60,** 138
corporations and **60,** 137-8, 140-1
freedom of expression **60,** 141-4
freedom of the press **60,** 142-3, 147
Newspaper Regulation Acts 1883/1971 **60,** 141-5
property, protection of **60,** 137, 140, 145
restraints, lawfulness **60,** 142-7
Universal Declaration of Human Rights (1948) **60,** 137
antitrust legislation 73, 303-4, 312, 317, 333, 343-4, 353-4, **74,** 39, 43-59, 64-5, 68-9, 73-87. *See also* competition, restraint of trade; United States of America (USA), antitrust legislation
act of State and **80,** 34
bilateral treaty, compatibility with **74,** 46-58, 73-82
carriage by air
applicability of rules **74,** 43-59, 64-5, 68-9, 73-82
disputes under **78,** 526
landing fees **78,** 525
landing rights **78,** 523-5
contract, applicable law **48,** 111, 113, 117
extraterritorial effect **46,** 340, **48,** 106-44, **56,** 32, **63,** 295, **66,** 279-86, 293, 343, 382-3, 490-7, 500-2, **72,** 79-80, **73,** 321, 337-8, 346-7, 357-8, **74,** 39-40, 48-54, 78-82
foreign State and **63,** 106-20, 189, 201-11, 294-7, 298
parent and subsidiary company **48,** 112-13, 117, 120, 135, 140
public law character **48,** 109, 114, 115
stay of proceedings and **118,** 542-65
apartheid
basis and methods **37,** 462
breach of
League of Nations Covenant **37,** 6, 7, 245, 248, 348, 350, 449, 460, 559, 566
Mandate **37,** 557, **49,** 4, 47, 51-4, 70-9, 113-14, 115, 169, 207, 212
UN Charter **49,** 4, 47, 51-4, 70-9, 113-14, 115, 169, 207, 212
civil service **37,** 467-8
crime against humanity **49,** 69
equality and **37,** 461-71, **49,** 68-75, 115-16
fundamental norm of international law, prohibition **82,** 417
Gleneagles Accord (1977) **85,** 207, 208, 215-16
enforceability
exclusion of alien and **92,** 503-4, 507-9
individual, by **92,** 504-8
human rights and **49,** 4, 6, 47, 68-75, **85,** 209
illegality **37,** 466, 470, 553
ICJ and **37,** 470, 540, 553
industries **37,** 468
international public policy and **91,** 369
job reservation **37,** 468

apartheid (*cont.*)
UN General Assembly, resolutions **37,** 454
UN Human Rights Commission, denunciation by **49,** 74
UNGA Resolutions
32/105M (1977) (Apartheid in Sports) **85,** 210
616A (VIII) **85,** 209
3266 (XXIX) (Commission for Implementation of Racial Discrimination Convention) **85,** 209
US legislation, premature termination of air services agreement and **82,** 321-8
appeal, right of. *See* European Convention on Human Rights (1950), appeal, right of; International Covenant on Civil and Political Rights (1966), appeal, right of; *and under individual tribunals*
applicable law 60, 61-2, **77,** 484, **79,** 411-12. *See also under individual tribunals*
act of foreign official **81,** 626
act of State **42,** 149-51, **84,** 127, 193-4, **88,** 119
ad hoc judge **97,** 152
Administrative Tribunal. *See also individual tribunals*
constituent instrument **96,** 235
general principles of law, 'common law' of international organizations **96,** 235
Antarctica **100,** 533-5, 540-2
applicable principles of international law **38,** 75, **89,** 329, 450, 463, 521, 552, 616-22
gaps in municipal law, in case of **89,** 521, 593-4, **106,** 607, 721-2, 724-6
role of international law **89,** 594
Arbitral Commission on Property, Rights and Interests in Germany **42,** 371-2, 378-9
arbitration **53,** 326-7, 328, 431, 433-6, 454-5, **66,** 534, 559-60, **67,** 331-2, 366, **77,** 656, **80,** 633, **82,** 547-51, **89,** 328, 460-1, 463, 465, 494, 503, **90,** 558
agreement of parties **83,** 44
exclusion of national law **102,** 215
express provision, need for **106,** 606-7
applicable principles of international law **89,** 329, 450, 463, 521, 552, 616-22, **122,** 272-84
applicable rules of international law **119,** 633, 653, **121,** 38, 106, 190
arbitral award **82,** 63
arbitral award, annulment **82,** 63
arbitral award, exequatur proceedings
European Convention on International Commercial Arbitration (1961) **82,** 67-8
New York Convention on the Recognition and Enforcement of Foreign Arbitral Awards (1958) **82,** 68
arbitration agreement **65,** 451
BIT **106,** 429-30, 437, 475-8, **125,** 79
supplemented by relevant international or municipal law **106,** 429-30
choice of law clause. *See* choice of law clause
customary international law **106,** 430
'error of law' and **117,** 578
ex aequo et bono **91,** 682, **99,** 479-81, **100,** 319
failure to apply **89,** 544-5
general principles of law **53,** 327-9
ICSID Arbitration Rules **89,** 328, 520-1, 533
international law **82,** 627, **117,** 560, **119,** 598
investment guarantee arbitration **44,** 85-6, 87
jurisdiction
constituent instrument **106,** 555
distinguished **106,** 476-7

international law **106,** 541-2
municipal law of Contracting State **106,** 540-3, 577
municipal law of place of arbitration **53,** 431-2
municipal law of State party **53,** 431-2, **89,** 329, 450, 461, 463, 521, 531, 533, 552, 613-16, **121,** 197-8
'supplemented if need be by any principles of international law' **106,** 430, 475-8
NAFTA (1992) **119,** 633, 653, **121,** 38, 106
need for reference to specific State **65,** 358-9, 362-3
non-contractual dispute **119,** 582, 586
private international law **53,** 326-7
procedure **53,** 308-11, 326-7, **62,** 148-9, 180
absence of connecting factors, relevance **96,** 264-5
forum **82,** 69-70
ICC Rules **65,** 448
ICJ Rules **83,** 13
municipal procedural law **53,** 309, 326
parties' right to choose **82,** 69-70, **96,** 264-5
PCA Optional Rules **119,** 582-3
procedural rules **53,** 454-5
seat of arbitration **53,** 309-11, 326, **65,** 448
seat of tribunal **96,** 260, 264-5
substance and procedure distinguished **53,** 326-7, **82,** 69-70
UNCITRAL Rules **119,** 571-2, 582-3, 584-6. *See also* UNCITRAL (United Nations Commission on International Trade Law), Rules
recognition and enforcement of award, relevance **65,** 358-9, 362-3
right to choose
parties **89,** 328, **96,** 12
tribunal **122,** 326
strictu juris **100,** 319
substantive aspects **53,** 454-5
where neither party a State **56,** 316-17, **119,** 582-3
arbitration clause. *See* arbitration clause, applicable law
armed conflict
American Declaration of the Rights and Duties of Man (1948), detention of civilians **123,** 169-71, 184-5
international humanitarian law **124,** 98-101
detention of civilians **123,** 169, 184
rules relating to State responsibility **108,** 155-6, **124,** 98
armed forces **47,** 234
assets, *situs* **79,** 587
banking contract **40,** 14
bankruptcy proceedings **107,** 345
banks
foreign branch
currency of payment **107,** 216 n. 5
lex situs **107,** 207, 208-10, 215-16
place of payment **107,** 216 n. 5
bays, Law of the Sea Convention (1982) **97,** 504
belligerent occupation. *See* belligerent occupation, applicable law; belligerents in time of war; occupied territory *below*
belligerents in time of war **91,** 23. *See also* belligerent occupation, applicable law
contemporary legal system of place of trial **91,** 26, 28

applicable law (*cont.*)
boundaries
delimitation, *uti possidetis* **97,** 302, 311-17
federal State **86,** 187, 626, **91,** 460, 585-90
federal Constitution **86,** 187
territorial claims, rules governing **91,** 586-7
burden of proof, avulsion **97,** 463
capacity to sue/be sued **108,** 497
central/State-owned bank
status **87,** 244
structure and responsibilities **96,** 735
change **85,** 61
choice of forum clause and **118,** 528-39
choice of law clause. *See* choice of law clause
civil obligation, jurisdiction **87,** 12-13
civil war
Genocide Convention (1948) **115,** 28
laws and customs of war **99,** 78-9, **104,** 73-4, **105,** 444-50, 506-24
Spanish Civil War **105,** 507
claims against foreign State, Head of State's power to change **94,** 220-1
classification of State activity, international law **86,** 577
collisions at sea **65,** 107, 365-7, **70,** 478-9
collisions in internal waters, international convention **74,** 3-4
colonial law **80,** 560
colonies **72,** 204-8, **123,** 583-4
commercial/trade representation/mission
lex loci contractus **64,** 592-4
status **64,** 590-4
company. *See* corporation *below*
compensation
damage caused by offence committed abroad **91,** 240-2
lex loci delicti **91,** 240-1
private international law and **91,** 241
public international policy and **91,** 241
implementation **95,** 305
international law **116,** 274-5, 410-11
rights of heirs **116,** 277-8
standard **85,** 562, 563
customary international law **84,** 523, 557
treaty **84,** 523, 524, 532-5, 557, **116,** 410
competence of courts to make injunction, place of serving order **86,** 581
competition law, place of implementation **96,** 196
concession agreement **47,** 396, 399-400, 403-4, 494, **62,** 171-3, 176, **66,** 133-4, **77,** 44, 51
Conciliation Commission **62,** 109, 111
conflict **110,** 255-9
conservation and management measures **123,** 271-2, 291-302
consular agent
functions
municipal law of receiving State **101,** 372, 482
municipal law of sending State **101,** 372
continental shelf **81,** 261, 262, 278, 294, 300
Law of the Sea Convention (1982) **81,** 262

continental shelf delimitation. *See* continental shelf delimitation
contract **47,** 102-4, 494, **48,** 111, 113, 117, **66,** 133-4, **75,** 375, **77,** 44, 51, **80,** 657
diplomatic agent, made by **41,** 21, 23
exchange **72,** 545
frustration **72,** 243, 248-9
International Tin Council **80,** 71
interpretation **66,** 343-5, 364-5
lex loci contractus **65,** 70, **71,** 22, 29
made by diplomat **41,** 21, 23
performance **42,** 150
place where account kept **114,** 472
Rome Convention on the Law Applicable to Contractual Obligations **114,** 472
State **41,** 455, **66,** 161, 343-5, 364-5, **72,** 154
corporation **47,** 67, 69, 70-1, **57,** 618, **61,** 50-1, 52-4, 63, **73,** 429, 590-2, **80,** 138, 657
authority to act on its behalf, place of incorporation **114,** 473
dissolution **89,** 572-3
domicile **71,** 21-2, 27-30, **72,** 559, 562-3, 567, **116,** 579
foreign **43,** 74, 75-6, **46,** 193
legal capacity **44,** 57
lex fori **85,** 20, 23
multilateral. *See* multilateral corporation *below*
name **72,** 557-60, 563-5
national law of contracting party **96,** 308-9, 319
nationality in dependent territory **106,** 585
place of execution **83,** 468
place of incorporation **54,** 542, **80,** 101, **81,** 710-11, **83,** 468
relations with members **47,** 67, 69, 70-1
status **77,** 28
lex rei sitae **77,** 450
crime **77,** 484
crimes against humanity. *See* crimes against humanity, applicable law
criminal acts committed abroad
by nationals **86,** 560-1
lex fori **94,** 73
currency, place of circulation **111,** 598-9
custody of children **95,** 498-500
Hague Convention Concerning Powers of Authorities and the Law Applicable in Respect of the Protection of Infants (1971) **95,** 499
Hague Convention Regarding Guardianship of Infants (1902) **95,** 499
nationality **95,** 499-500
difficulty of determining **95,** 499-500
customary international law **83,** 32-3, 87
continental shelf delimitation **81,** 261, 300, **99,** 426, 428, 438, 473-4, 657, 660, 666, 672, 673
fishing zones **99,** 495-6, 558
maritime delimitation **83,** 87, **91,** 656, 658-9, **99,** 438, 473-4, 657, 660, 666, 672
reparation for breach of international law **116,** 498-9
damages **46,** 510
municipal law of Contracting State **106,** 467-8
debt **80,** 427
debtor **86,** 310
law of debtor **86,** 310
defamation **88,** 166

applicable law (*cont.*)
denationalization, State contract **106,** 430
dependent territory status **90,** 454, 455
diplomatic mission, locally engaged staff **82,** 22-3, **86,** 584, **94,** 351-2, **104,** 523, **116,** 532, 631, 638, 653, 674
diplomatic privileges and immunity, Vienna Convention on Diplomatic Relations (1961) **107,** 454-5
disclosure of documents as offence against foreign law, *lex fori* **104,** 554, 558
domicile **73,** 590-2
corporations **71,** 21-2, 27-30, **72,** 559, 562-3, 567, **116,** 579
EC law. *See* European Community law
ECJ **53,** 28-31, 37, 44-5, **93,** 370
economic development agreement **83,** 553-4, 555. *See also* State contract, applicable law
EEC treaties **93,** 104, 426-7
EEC Treaty (Rome) (1957) **93,** 557
implementing legislation **93,** 450
effects doctrine, place of effects **86,** 544-5
employment contract. *See individual employment contract headings*
employment contract, international organizations **96,** 325, **116,** 645
employment contract, locally engaged staff at foreign military base, sending State **94,** 268
employment contract, locally engaged staff, consulate **86,** 584, **101,** 372, **104,** 514, **114,** 511-12
employment contract, locally engaged staff, diplomatic mission
local law **86,** 584, **94,** 351-2, **104,** 523, **116,** 532, 631, 638, 653, 674
municipal law of receiving State **82,** 22-3, **94,** 353, **116,** 532
employment contract (municipal law) **96,** 572-3
employment contract, ship **87,** 97
enforcement of foreign judgment **81,** 570, **101,** 445-7
enterprises of different countries, international law **47,** 28-30
equity
parties' consent, need for **97,** 550, **99,** 568
relevance to **80,** 472
European Commission and non-Member States, relations between **107,** 525-7
European Schools
constituent instrument **108,** 665
international law **108,** 642, 651
European Union (EU), Protocol on Privileges and Immunities of the European Communities (1957) **107,** 527-9
European Union (EU) treaties **107,** 519-27, 532-3
evidence, *lex fori* **104,** 559
exhaustion of local remedies **95,** 255-6, 272
expropriation. *See* expropriation/nationalization, applicable law
expulsion of alien **82,** 214-16
extinction of claims against foreign State, change of applicable law **94,** 220
extradition. *See* extradition, applicable law
factors determining **63,** 447 n. 2
federal State. *See* federal State, applicable law
Fonseca Bay dispute. *See* Fonseca Bay, applicable law
forcible abduction/unlawful arrest, effect on jurisdiction **95,** 426
foreign civil aviation companies operating on territory, bilateral air transport agreement **96,** 334-6

foreign investment contract. *See* economic development agreement *above*; State contract *below*
foreign law **104,** 183
foreign official **81,** 626
foreign State, proceedings involving, international law **116,** 635
Gabčíkovo/Nagymaros Project, general treaties **116,** 223-4
GDR post-unification **100,** 371-5, 380, 388, 390-3
general principles of law **53,** 327-9
government agency, status **90,** 612-14
  international law **90,** 612
  law of chartering State **90,** 612
  lex fori **90,** 612
Greenland **91,** 263-75, 276-8
guarantee **80,** 427
Head of State. *See* Head of State, applicable law; Head of State, former, conduct in office, applicable law
headquarters agreement, interpretation **105,** 21-2
high seas **74,** 213-18, **123,** 439
  collisions **70,** 478-9
  submarine cables **74,** 213-18
human rights. *See* human rights, applicable law
ICAO, dispute settlement **48,** 442
ICSID. *See* ICSID (International Centre for the Settlement of Investment Disputes), arbitral tribunal, applicable law
implementation of Convention on the Transfer of Sentenced Persons (1983) **84,** 728
insurance **38,** 138-41
interest
  choice of law clause **106,** 642-3
  express provision in contract **86,** 310
  general principles **86,** 310
  municipal law of Contracting State **106,** 641, 642
  trade usage **86,** 310
international crimes
  international law **91,** 43, 118-19, **104,** 181-3
  lex fori **104,** 181-4, 191-2
International Criminal Tribunal for the Former Yugoslavia. *See* Yugoslavia, International Criminal Tribunal for the Former (ICTY)
international law **53,** 309, 328, 433-6, **80,** 101, 102, 104, 574, **82,** 673
  contract **83,** 555, 559
  corrective role **106,** 726
  enterprises of different countries, between **47,** 28-30
  expropriation, legality **83,** 527-8
  federal State **91,** 460
  incorporation into municipal law, need for **106,** 607
  international crimes **91,** 43, 118-19
  Klöckner v. *Republic of Cameroon* **106,** 725-6
  PCIJ **37,** 81
  principles and rules **78,** 649
  State contract **62,** 170-3
  statehood, determination of **82,** 398
  as supplement **106,** 726

applicable law (*cont.*)
international organizations. *See* international organizations, applicable law *and individual organizations*
international tribunals, norms of international law or agreed by parties **97,** 584. *See also* Iran–US Claims Tribunal, applicable law; Yugoslavia, International Criminal Tribunal for the Former (ICTY), applicable law
interpretation of jurisdiction **84,** 739, 745-6
interpretation of legislation implementing treaty **88,** 206
intertemporal law **80,** 472-3, **83,** 32, **106,** 136, **114,** 46, 115
changed values, effect on law to be applied **112,** 480-1, 546-7, **116,** 122-4, 129-35
treaty implementation **116,** 124
invading enemy forces **42,** 452, 456-7
investment dispute
municipal law of Contracting State **106,** 722-7
'supplemented if need be by any principles of international law' **106,** 607
Iran–US Claims Tribunal. *See* Iran–US Claims Tribunal, applicable law
judicial assistance **81,** 603, **82,** 55, **117,** 100, **121,** 571
jurisdiction
civil obligation **87,** 12-13
EEZ, national of forum State **101,** 447-8
extradition **87,** 408
international law, determined by **91,** 43
ship
contract of employment **87,** 97
lex loci **87,** 97
universal **91,** 40-4
land, disposition and ownership **44,** 57
law of 'Germany as a whole' **43,** 52, 58-9, 62, 75
legal capacity **73,** 240, 672-3
legislation, interpretation, by international tribunals **40,** 70
lex fori rule **85,** 20, 23, **90,** 612, **91,** 26-7, 241, **104,** 181-4, 554, 558, **122,** 534-5
lex situs **84,** 127
life insurance contract **38,** 138-41
limitation of liability **87,** 558-9
loi d'enracinement **83,** 553
mandated territories, law of Mandatory **37,** 34, 358, **52,** 28-9, **82,** 469-99
maritime delimitation. *See* maritime delimitation, applicable law
marriage formalities, *lex loci celebrationis* **41,** 467, 471-2
marriage, right of **72,** 297-300
matrimonial property **73,** 672-3, **74,** 113-15, 531, 548
military courts. *See* military courts, applicable law
military tribunals. *See* military tribunals, applicable law
mining rights in Portuguese Goa **118,** 431, 436-46
multinational corporation **46,** 230-1, **47,** 28-30, **118,** 509, 526
municipal courts **91,** 240
nationality. *See* nationality, applicable law
nationality of corporation. *See* corporation, nationality, applicable law
native title. *See* native title, applicable law
natural resources, EC law **120,** 625
'new situation' **69,** 581, 594
non-liquet **80,** 308
'norms of international law' **83,** 86, 87
absence of substantive law **83,** 44

nuclear weapons, deployment. *See* nuclear weapons, deployment, applicable law
obligations arising on board ship, law of the flag **77,** 560
occupation of Italy **40,** 430, 433
occupied territory. *See* belligerent occupation, applicable law
participation in conduct of public affairs, national law **96,** 712
personal status **72,** 642, **73,** 672-3, **79,** 400
Pitcairn, English rules of equity and statutes of general application **104,** 511-12, 515
place of injury **98,** 124
place where act committed **91,** 26-7
political offence, classification, requested State **104,** 67
private international law. *See* private international law, as applicable law
Privy Council (UK), appeals jurisdiction **123,** 526, 549
prize proceedings **49,** 473, 476-7
property **85,** 61
  belligerent occupation. *See* belligerent occupation, applicable law
  definition, *lex situs* **106,** 414 n. 5
  lex situs **78,** 599, **106,** 414 n. 5, **108,** 592
    movable **104,** 612
    real/immovable **104,** 612
    transfer of personal property **94,** 171
  mobilia sequuntur personam **42,** 414
  real/immovable **42,** 164, 166-7
  rights **42,** 164, 166-7, **77,** 544, 547, 549
    lex situs **77,** 544, 549, **78,** 599
    of refugee **73,** 672-3
  title **73,** 238, 242, 248-9
protecting State, acquisition of land **71,** 47, 54-6
protectorate, acquisition of land by protecting State **71,** 47, 54-6
provisional measures **93,** 698, 699
public international policy and **91,** 241
recognition, State. *See* recognition, State, applicable law
refugees, law relating to aliens **111,** 536, 537
renvoi. See renvoi
restrictive practices agreement, place of implementation **96,** 196
retroactive nature of legislation **91,** 93-4
Rhodesia after Declaration of Independence **39,** 238-61, 328, 347, 350
Saramacas **116,** 278
secession of part of a State
  international law **115,** 546, 579
  municipal law **115,** 133-46, 580, 590
service of process **80,** 370
  forum State **106,** 280
  law of State where process to be served **106,** 281
  lex fori **96,** 78, 79-80
  municipal law **94,** 364
settlers in newly acquired territory **112,** 485, 486-7
shares, cancellation **72,** 18
ship, employment contract **87,** 97
  lex loci **87,** 97
social security entitlement, usual place of residence **86,** 540, 541
social security obligations, place of employment **86,** 540, **102,** 188
South Georgia and South Sandwich Islands
  procedural matters, law of the Falkland Islands **108,** 633
  substantive matters, law of South Georgia and South Sandwich Islands **108,** 633

applicable law (*cont.*)
South West Africa, South Africa, law of **37,** 358, **52,** 28-9
Special Agreement, prescribed by **97,** 302, 473
State activity, classification **80,** 382
State agency/State-owned corporation. *See* State agency/State-owned corporation/State entity, applicable law
State contract. *See* economic development agreement *above*; State contract, applicable law
choice of law. *See* State contract, choice of law clause
common principles **62,** 168, 172-5, 191, 198-9, 201-9, 217
customary international law **95,** 207
general principles **62,** 172-6, 199, 209-18
municipal law of State party **89,** 461, 463, **95,** 207
conflict with **96,** 265-6
parties' right to choose **62,** 178, 190, 196
private international law **62,** 169
public international law **62,** 170-3, **89,** 463, **96,** 262-6
State, creation
international law **115,** 117-20
municipal law **115,** 121-3
State immunity. *See* State immunity, execution/attachment, procedural aspects, applicable law; State immunity, jurisdiction, procedural aspects, applicable law
State responsibility
customary international law **106,** 441, 443-4, 452-4, 458
damages, place of accident **86,** 550
imputability, forum State **94,** 348
international law **125,** 89-93
municipal law **106,** 454
State organ abroad **86,** 549-50
treaty **106,** 440-53
State succession, international law **91,** 354-5, **92,** 165, 166, 205, **94,** 180
State-sponsored terrorism **121,** 632-3
statehood, determination of, international law **82,** 398
State's right of suit in foreign court, dependence on **106,** 244-5, 246
statutory limitation **79,** 404, 407-11, **81,** 533 n. 2
international law **79,** 404
stay of proceedings, *lex fori* **118,** 551
succession
general principles of law recognized by civilized nations **116,** 279-80
mortis causa **94,** 372
taxation, host State **105,** 45, 48
territorial sea. *See* territorial sea, applicable law
territory, acquisition **112,** 482, 521
tort **74,** 3-4, 213-18
committed by foreign State **84,** 104-5
domicile of victim **101,** 527
federal State, domicile of victim **101,** 527
lex loci delicti commissi **66,** 115, **94,** 365-7, **108,** 498-9, **124,** 432-3, **125,** 679-80, 722-7
domicile of offenders **108,** 499
place of injury **108,** 498-9
nexus **94,** 367
trademarks, protection of **40,** 22, 28
treaty as. *See also* treaties, applicable law; treaty interpretation, applicable law
bilateral **82,** 673

incorporated treaty **93,** 426-7
UN Charter **83,** 336
UN Compensation Commission. *See* United Nations Compensation Commission, applicable law
UN General Assembly resolutions **83,** 342, 426, 439
uti possidetis **83,** 57, **97,** 474, 547, 549-54, 582, 590
territory
attribution **97,** 565, 566-7, 570-1, 582, 590
delimitation **97,** 302, 311-17, 582, 590
visiting forces
bases, traffic on **91,** 276-8
metropolitan **91,** 276-8
war crimes
international law **91,** 47-8, **104,** 299-300
municipal law **91,** 45, 47, 92-3, 94-6, **104,** 299-300
withdrawal of approval of project, effect **106,** 523-4
World Health Organization (WHO), international law **110,** 22
appreciation. *See* margin of appreciation
appropriation. *See* confiscation; expropriation/nationalization; requisition; taking of property
appurtenance 52, 123, 179-80, 184
continental shelf **81,** 257, 268, 295, 325, 406
basis of rights **41,** 58-61, 81
equidistance and **41,** 41, 58
just and equitable share **41,** 52, 59
equidistance and **41,** 41, 58
test **41,** 59-62, 65, 81, 158, 189
Aqaba 80, 328
status, 1925 **80,** 260
Aqaba, Gulf of
status **41,** 124
US statement on (1957) **41,** 124 n. 2
Arab Monetary Fund (AMF). *See also* International Monetary Fund Agreement (IMF) (1944) (Bretton Woods Agreement)
agent or instrumentality of foreign State, whether **107,** 414-15
Agreement **85,** 5, 671
applicable law, independence of municipal laws of Member States **108,** 586-7, 591
capacity to sue and be sued **85,** 5, 28, **107,** 415, 418-28
corporation, whether **85,** 5, 10, 14-28
domicile **85,** 7
Headquarters Agreement (AMF–UAE Protocol) **85,** 26-7, 692
personality **85,** 5, 17-19. *See also* corporation, whether *above*
multiplicity **85,** 12, 28, **108,** 581
nationality and **85,** 7
status **83,** 258, 266, 267-8
applicable law, international law **108,** 586-94
Arab Organization for Industrialization 80, 138-41, 171-2, 596-666
applicable law **80,** 610, 611, 636
constituent instruments **80,** 610-12, 657-8, 660
interpretation **80,** 660
State immunity, waiver, whether **80,** 661
debts, Member States' liability for **80,** 138-42, 171, 612-16, 661
legal personality **80,** 610-16, 657-60

Arab Organization for Industrialization (*cont.*)
competence to determine **80,** 636
public company, compared **80,** 660
Member States
liability for obligations **80,** 138-41, 612-16, 636-7, 640-4
applicable law **80,** 613
power to affect status **80,** 611-12
status **80,** 610-12. *See also* legal personality *above*
administrative seat, relevance **80,** 611
applicable law **80,** 611
constituent instruments, determined by **80,** 610, 657-8, 660
supranational, whether **80,** 139, 610-12
Arabian Gulf
continental shelf **64,** 336-8
territorial sea, delimitation **64,** 336-8
Arabian Oil Company 66, 548, 554
arbitral award 52, 268-77, 281-2, **59,** 528, **68,** 530-3, 652-4, **77,**45-50, **84,** 297. *See also* arbitral award, annulment; arbitral award, appeal; arbitral award, binding force; arbitral award, challenge; arbitral award, correction/rectification; arbitral award, enforcement; arbitral award, enforcement, defences against; arbitral award, finality; arbitral award, interpretation; arbitral award, nullity; arbitral award, *res judicata*; arbitral award, resubmission, request for; arbitral award, review; arbitral award, revision; arbitral tribunal; arbitration; Egypt–Israel Arbitration Tribunal (Taba), award; Iran–US Claims Tribunal, award
addition **95,** 222
administrative decision, whether **91,** 684
on agreed terms **68,** 530-3, 652-4, **72,** 225-6, 233
agreements arising under, interpretation or application **82,** 518
announcement, presence of arbitrator, relevance **92,** 39-41
appeal. *See* arbitral award, appeal
applicable law **82,** 63
clarification
clarification of evidence distinguished **102,** 580
revision distinguished **102,** 576-7
compliance **52,** 227, 268, 281-2, **89,** 328
time-limit **52,** 281-2, **53,** 510-11
confirmation **62,** 220-2
currency of payment **75,** 606, 627, 643-51
damages. *See* damages
date **103,** 568-70
'decision'
decision on preliminary objections to jurisdiction, whether **106,** 593
silence as **92,** 137-8
declaratory **53,** 343
definition
binding pronouncement by third party **91,** 572
New York Convention on the Recognition and Enforcement of Foreign Arbitral Awards (1958) **96,** 9
discontinuity **78,** 582-3
acceptability of **78,** 582-3
effect **54,** 37-8, 343, **95,** 724
enforceability, date of **96,** 332
ex aequo et bono **46,** 472, 506, **91,** 682
'fulfilment'. *See* compliance *above*

incomplete **83,** 48-9, 120
inconsistent **80,** 621
avoidance **80,** 621
interest **69,** 654-6, 659-63, **71,** 610, 625, 675, **72,** 492, 724, **75,** 607, 625-6, 648
rate **69,** 660, 662
international law, as source of **70,** 519
international organization, enforceability **80,** 34, 57, 120, 213
language, authentic **105,** 70
modification, avoidance of **82,** 672. *See also* arbitral award, binding force; arbitral award, correction/rectification; arbitral award, finality
payment **71,** 624, 678, **72,** 226, 492, 724
place of award, place of signature, relevance **117,** 564, 568
precedence, over decisions of ordinary courts **71,** 638-49
precedent, as **71,** 94, 101, 120, 129-30, 139, 187, 192, 201, 205-6, 208, 210, 212, 641-2, 655-6, 658-9, 695-6
preliminary award, jurisdiction **53,** 418-19, 429-30
publication
desirability **89,** 580, 657, 660, **121,** 135
right to refuse **89,** 526-7
qualification as **65,** 359
reconsideration
ICJ practice **95,** 222-3
ICSID practice **95,** 223
inherent power of Tribunal **95,** 222-3
timeliness **95,** 222
US Arbitration Act **95,** 223
reformulation of award **92,** 155
remission (opportunity to cure defect) **125,** 470-5
rendering of **54,** 161-2
scope **47,** 396-405
separability **92,** 143-9, 150
avoidance of prejudice **92,** 144, 146
serial awards, possibility **102,** 575-6
State immunity. *See* State immunity, arbitral award, enforcement
supplemental decision **89,** 658-60, **102,** 577-8. *See also* arbitral award, annulment; arbitral award, correction/rectification
suspension **86,** 494-5
third parties and **44,** 436
treaty, effect on **53,** 17-19
treaty interpretation, difference between government and arbitrators, effect **82,** 66-7, 74-5
US–UK Arbitral Tribunal (Heathrow Airport User Charges), supplementary decisions and clarifications **102,** 564-81
validity **53,** 386. *See also* arbitral award, annulment; arbitral award, nullity
differing interpretations of treaty by government and arbitrators **82,** 66-7, 74-5
arbitral award, annulment 86, 481-92, **114,** 243-311. *See also* arbitral award, supplemental decision; arbitral award, correction/rectification; arbitral award, nullity; arbitral award, review; arbitral award, revision
action for **92,** 30-161
'annulment as a whole' **89,** 555, 556
appeal distinguished **89,** 521-2, 548, 562-3, 570, **92,** 38, 83, 97, 110, 155, **114,** 267, 290, 299-300, **125,** 79-80
applicable law **89,** 519-23

arbitral award, annulment (*cont.*)
ICSID Convention **89,** 520
automaticity where ground established **114,** 309-10
burden of proof **92,** 128
damages, effect on **89,** 547, 548-9
discretion **199,** 679-80
effect **89,** 571-2
Committee of Jurists Report to League of Nations (1930) **89,** 539
error of law **114,** 267-8, 306-7. *See also* arbitral award, appeal, error of law
excess of powers **89,** 519-20, 524, 533, 535, 538, 543-4, **92,** 41-3, 69, 76-7, 102-5, 133-4, 138-40, 150, 155, 158-9, **94,** 225, **114,** 245
infra petita **54,** 511, **92,** 104, 133-4, **125,** 85
failure to consider breach of concession contract as breach of BIT **125,** 86-96
lack of jurisdiction under
arbitration clause **114,** 246, 252-65
ICSID Convention **114,** 246
manifest **114,** 246, 248, 251-2, 265
ultra petita **48,** 420, **54,** 511, **83,** 88, 113, **92,** 155, **110,** 224, **117,** 187-9
exhaustion of local remedies and **89,** 525
failure to state reasons, burden of proof **114,** 289
forum, lack of **92,** 149
grounds
absence of arbitrator from announcement of award **92,** 39-41
abuse of process **92,** 39
additional grounds raised by party not requesting annulment **125,** 81-2
arbitration agreement
absence of **86,** 490
failure fully to observe **92,** 12, 43-51, 53-5, 60-1, 75-81, 89-95, 99-102, 106-7, 109-10, 128-9, 133
flagrant violation **86,** 490
departure from fundamental rules of procedure **89,** 520, 524, 540-1
error of law. *See* error of law *above*
excess of powers. *See* excess of powers *above*
failure to apply appropriate applicable law **114,** 266-7, 268-73
failure to observe due process **114,** 276-7. *See also* serious departure from a fundamental rule of procedure *below*
award outside legal framework established by parties **114,** 277
decision based on arguments not advanced **114,** 276-7
equality of parties **114,** 277
failure to state reasons **89,** 520, 524-5, 526-8, 531-5, 544-5, **114,** 245, 284-91, 307, **125,** 80, 96
contradiction of reasons **114,** 287-9, **125,** 80
correctness of reasons, relevance **125,** 80
failure to deal with every question submitted **114,** 285, 291-304, **119,** 678-9
hypothetical **114,** 289
inadequacy of reasons **92,** 43-4, 50, 70-1, 80, **114,** 285-6, 290-1
invalidity of reasons **92,** 44-9
sufficient and relevant as test **114,** 286-7
unelaborated arguments **114,** 298
failure to substantiate legal basis for award **114,** 270-3, 297, 307-9
fraud on the Tribunal **95,** 222-3
ILC Model Rules on Arbitral Procedure (1929) **92,** 104
inconsistent separate declaration of arbitrator **92,** 12, 39, 56, 57-9, 69-70, 72-5, 106

insufficiency of purpose **92,** 64-5
manifest excess of powers. *See* excess of powers *above*
principles and usages of international commerce **86,** 491
serious departure from a fundamental rule of procedure. *See* serious departure from a fundamental rule of procedure *below*
solution based unjustifiably on equity **114,** 267, 272-3, 304, 307-9
subsequent court decision **89,** 549, 564
waiver **89,** 530-1
guidelines, *in favorem validitatis sententiae* **114,** 264, 273
inherent power of Tribunal **95,** 222-3
jurisdiction **82,** 68-9, 70
country where rendered **82,** 70, 96
nullity distinguished **80,** 633-4
partial **89,** 559-60, 579, **114,** 273-4, **125,** 81-2
refusal of application, decision on objections to jurisdiction **106,** 593
request for **80,** 622-66, **82,** 63, 96, **89,** 661
admissibility **80,** 636
applicable law **80,** 633
competence of court **80,** 635-6
effect **80,** 633, 650
enforcement distinguished **82,** 96
jurisdiction **82,** 63, 96
non-applicant and **80,** 633-4, 647
staying effect **80,** 650
suspension of award **86,** 494-5
time-limits **80,** 633
scope **89,** 555-7
serious departure from a fundamental rule of procedure **114,** 245, 274-84, **125,** 85-6
absence of deliberation **114,** 274-5
due process. *See* failure to observe due process *above*
partiality **114,** 277-83
timely complaint, need for **114,** 276
time-limits **89,** 528-30
withdrawal from docket of municipal court as **82,** 68-9
arbitral award, appeal 52, 282. *See also* arbitral award, challenge
admissibility **42,** 380-7
agreement to exclude **117,** 586-7
error of law **117,** 575-93
in case of conflicting evidence **117,** 583-4
determination and application of foreign law as fact **117,** 578-84, 589-92
error of foreign law, jurisdiction **117,** 585-93
grounds. *See* error of law *above*; arbitral award, annulment, grounds
waiver of right to **86,** 483
arbitral award, binding force 47, 396-405, **62,** 176, 179, **69,** 619-21, 628-31, 634-7, 663, **71,** 638, 645, **75,** 180, **80,** 247, 310, **82,** 70, **86,** 494, **89,** 340, 560, **91,** 572, 684, **95,** 222, **96,** 332. *See also* arbitral award, finality; arbitral award, *res judicata*
arbitrator's absence, effect **69,** 620-1, 629, 635-7, 663
European Economic Area disputes **100,** 212
arbitral award, challenge 84, 297
costs **80,** 662, 663, 665-6
eligibility **80,** 661, 663, 665
grounds **80,** 662

arbitral award, challenge (*cont.*)
arbitrariness **80,** 649-50, 661, 664
breach of right to be heard **80,** 648-9
improper assumption of competence **80,** 639-40
irregular constitution of tribunal **80,** 638-9
arbitral award, correction/rectification 89, 352-4, 523-6, 658-60, **95,** 222, **124,** 58-61
accidental error, limited to **102,** 578-9
clerical, arithmetical or similar error **124,** 60
time-limit **102,** 578
arbitral award, enforcement 52, 268, 281, 283, **53,** 17-19, **62,** 198-200, 220-4, 225-7, 362, 384, **63,** 197-8, **65,** 47-50, 52-4, 79-82, **80,** 167-90, 247, 310, 691-4, **86,** 493-5, **89,**521, **90,** 559, **113,** 445. *See also* arbitral award; arbitration; arbitration agreement; foreign judgments, recognition/enforcement; New York Convention on the Recognition and Enforcement of Foreign Arbitral Awards (1958)
access to courts and **94,** 213-15
applicable law, as determined by municipal law of contracting State **65,** 53
appointment of receiver **77,** 45-50
arrest of sister ship **90,** 559
burden of proof **94,** 221
defences against. *See* arbitral award, enforcement, defences against
dependence on qualification as award **65,** 359
enforcement of judgment compared **80,** 189
equitable execution **77,** 45-9
exequatur proceedings **65,** 48-50, 52-3, 76-7, 79-80, 89-92, 170-1, **77,** 14, **113,** 445
applicable law
European Convention on International Commercial Arbitration (1961) **82,** 67-8
New York Convention on the Recognition and Enforcement of Foreign Arbitral Awards (1958) **82,** 68
simplified procedure (ICSID Convention (1965)) **65,** 90-1
standing **65,** 53
foreign State, against **82,** 92, **94,** 221-31
attachment of assets held on behalf of bank of that State **82,** 92
foreign State, in **82,** 68, 70
Graeco-German Mixed Arbitral Tribunal **47,** 424
international organization, against **80,** 34, 57, 120, 213
jurisdiction, as determined by municipal law of contracting State **65,** 53
mechanism **82,** 518
municipal courts **72,** 61-2, 157-71, **75,** 156-7, 162, 166-73, **77,** 14-15
procedure **103,** 569-70
public order/public policy/*ordre public* and **72,** 61-2, **74,** 567-9
refusal, grounds **63,** 198
State immunity. *See* State immunity, arbitral award, enforcement
State succession and **45,** 33-6
statutory limitation **103,** 564, 568-9
stay of **89,** 661
winding-up as **77,** 38, **80,** 187-90
arbitral award, enforcement, defences against
excess of powers
award based on equity **94,** 224-7
damages unsoundly based **94,** 224-7
lack of jurisdiction **94,** 225
fraud

fair hearing and **94,** 223 n. 23, 227
false testimony **94,** 221-4
material **94,** 222, 223 n. 25
opportunity to challenge arbitration proceedings **94,** 223-4
reluctance to invoke **94,** 222
public policy violation **94,** 227-8
arbitral award, finality 82, 70, **92,** 84-5, 97-102, 128-9, 155-6. *See also* arbitral award, binding force; arbitral award, modification; arbitral award, appeal; arbitral award, *res judicata*
Arbitral Procedure of the Institute of International Law (1873/5) **92,** 85, 132
basis
arbitration agreement **92,** 84-5
authority of tribunal **92,** 84-5
burden of proof **82,** 68, 70
compétence de la compétence and **92,** 82, 84-9
customary international law **92,** 85
Geneva Convention on the Execution of Foreign Arbitral Awards (1927) **82,** 70
Hague Conventions (1899/1907) **92,** 132
ILC Model Rules on Arbitral Procedure (1929) **92,** 104, 125, 132-3
reservation of decision on remedy, relevance **102,** 575
arbitral award, interpretation 54, 143-8, 153, 157-8, 160-77, **95,** 222
aids
circumstances of conclusion **113,** 176
conduct of parties subsequent to original arbitration **38,** 89, 90, **113,** 77-9, 123-5, 165-6, 190-1, 202-5
context **113,** 176
travaux préparatoires **38,** 89-90, **113,** 76, 109-10, 176-7
written pleadings **114,** 271-2
burden of proof **113,** 73
by arbitrator **44,** 420-2
definition of terms by drafter, need for **113,** 140-1
dispute as to **54,** 157-8, 162-3, 164-71
ex tunc effect **113,** 76
guidelines
conformity with international law **113,** 45
customary principles of interpretation **114,** 271
distinct meanings for different expressions **113,** 138-9
distinctions to be limited to those in text **113,** 172-3
effectiveness **113,** 70
general practice of previous tribunal **113,** 72
good faith **113,** 55
intention of Tribunal **38,** 89-90, 93
knowledge at time of award **113,** 56, 76, 83-4, 111-14, 123, 129-30, 177, 185-6
meaning of terms at time of award **113,** 55, 62, 67-8
ordinary meaning **113,** 69, 73, 176
stricter than treaty interpretation **38,** 89-90
translation to produce compatible result **113,** 171-2
unity of texts **113,** 146, 163
judicial role **113,** 45
jurisdiction, limited to that of original tribunal **113,** 128-30
limited scope **113,** 45-6
modification distinguished **54,** 166
requirements

arbitral award, interpretation (*cont.*)
disagreement **113,** 229-30
possibility of resolution by interpretation **113,** 230
specificity **113,** 231
responsibility, Tribunal **38,** 90
revision distinguished **113,** 82, 176, 230-1
ICSID Rules of Procedure **102,** 580
arbitral award, nullity 80, 632, **92,** 129-38. *See also* arbitral award, annulment
absence **46,** 472
absolute nullity **92,** 131
declaration of **52,** 268-77, 281-2, **92,** 131-2, 134-7
grounds **53,** 358-74, 381-4, **71,** 641
non-arbitral subject **80,** 634
public order/public policy/*ordre public* **80,** 634
King of Spain's Award (1960) **92,** 141
need for **91,** 573, 577, **92,** 43-4, 138, 140-1, **114,** 237-8, 240
Cerruti (1897) **92,** 141
general principle of international law **92,** 43
ILC Model Rules on Arbitral Procedure (1929) **92,** 140-1
Portendick (1843) **92,** 141
non-existence **92,** 130-2
legal effect **92,** 131
arbitral award, *res judicata* 89, 556-72, 592, 594, 599, 600, 601-2, 624, 627, **113,** 186, **120,** 5. *See also* arbitral award, binding force; arbitral award, finality
general principle of law **89,** 559, 562
international law, in **89,** 560-2
meaning of terms at time of award **113,** 44, 62, 67-8
operative part of award **113,** 43-4, 62
essential elements in reasoning **113,** 44, 62
reasoning, whether **89,** 559, 560-3, 569-72
arbitral award, resubmission, request for 89, 552-662
jurisdiction **89,** 552-80
excluded matter **89,** 566
express annulment **89,** 558, 569
express confirmation **89,** 563-6
new claim/counterclaim **89,** 574-9
obiter findings **89,** 571
ratione materiae **89,** 575-9
unpresented matters **89,** 566-9
arbitral award, review 86, 483
adjournment to allow action to eliminate grounds for setting aside award **125,** 470-5
time-limit **125,** 475
by municipal courts **56,** 329-30, **86,** 483, **119,** 648-82
applicable law, law of place of review **119,** 656-9
standard of review **119,** 659-61
award based on deception **119,** 675-6
conflict with public policy **119,** 673-5
decision beyond scope of submission to jurisdiction **119,** 659-68, 670
misinterpretation of treaty and **119,** 665-6
error of law **119,** 671
failure to address every question **119,** 676-81
patently unreasonable error **119,** 670-3
pragmatic and functional approach **119,** 660-1
ultra vires award. *See* decision beyond scope of submission to jurisdiction *above*

arbitral award, revision 53, 360-1, 380-4, **92,** 38, 68. *See also* Argentina–Chile Tribunal (1994), revision of Judgment
appeal distinguished
Arbitral Award of the King of Spain of 23 December 1906 **113,** 200-1
Baron de Neuflize Case **113,** 200
compensation, effect on **119,** 681-2
ICSID Rules of Procedure **102,** 580
procedure **53,** 361
variation to detriment of appellant (*reformatio in pejus*) **113,** 226
Arbitral Commission on Property, Rights and Interests in Germany 71, 641
appeals, admissibility **42,** 380-7
applicable law **42,** 371-2, 378-9
German Patent authorities **42,** 351, 380-3
nationals of State not party to UN Charter **42,** 351, 380-3
time-limits **42,** 385-7
competence
diplomatic negotiations, to order **42,** 408
restitution appeals, 'party concerned' **42,** 387-90
equity and **42,** 372-3, 379, 387
arbitral tribunal. *See also* arbitral award; arbitration; arbitration agreement; arbitrator; international tribunal *and individual tribunals*
admissibility, representative claims **72,** 732-4
advisory opinion, binding effect **96,** 716
amendment of claim **75,** 129, 147-8
in light of developments subsequent to original finding **119,** 631-3, 669-70
as amicable compositor **82,** 70
applicable law. *See* applicable law, arbitration
Argentina–Chile Arbitral Tribunal. *See* Argentina–Chile Arbitral Tribunal
award. *See* arbitral award
burden of proof **52,** 267, **89,** 326, 564-5
UNCITRAL Rules **95,** 207, 223
claimant, standing **44,** 434-7
compensation commission distinguished **103,** 358-60
compétence de la compétence **53,** 404-8, **80,** 605, 665, **82,** 611-12, 641, **86,** 482, **89,** 319, **92,** 48, 49, 82-90, 104, 142-3, 195, 197, **96,** 260, 266-8, **113,** 42. *See also* jurisdiction, *compétence de la compétence*
arbitral decisions **96,** 267-8
basis **92,** 84-9
derived from arbitrator's appointment, whether **96,** 260-1
equity, rule of **96,** 268
European Convention on International Commercial Arbitration (1961) **96,** 266-7
finality of award and **92,** 82, 84-9
France/Iran Arbitration Agreement (1977) **96,** 267
general principle of international law **96,** 268
ICSID Convention (1965) **96,** 267
ILC Model Rules on Arbitral Procedure (1929) **92,** 104
Interpretation of the Greco-Turkish Agreement of 1 December 1926 **92,** 142
King of Spain's Award (1960) **92,** 87
Orinoco Steamship Co. case (1916) **92,** 86-7
scope **92,** 84, 86
teachings of publicists **96,** 267
Conference on Yugoslavia (Arbitration Commission) **92,** 162-211
confidentiality of proceedings **69,** 628, 631-2, 658, **119,** 622, **125,** 96-102. *See also* disclosure of documents *below*; arbitral award, publication

arbitral tribunal (*cont.*)
constitution **80,** 604-5, **82,** 609, **105,** 11-12, **106,** 512-13
continuance of **52,** 228
counterclaim **89,** 626-7
for Czechoslovakia debts **42,** 162, 171
declaratory judgments **54,** 318-19
delimitation of maritime boundary **92,** 48, 101-2, 126
descent sur les lieux **52,** 226
disclosure of documents **102,** 233-8
dispute, need for **54,** 157-8, 162, 163-71, 318, 323, **59,** 526-7, **82,** 641
between contracting State and national of another contracting State **89,** 321-4, 385-8
agreement to treat as foreign national **89,** 322-4, 385-8
boundary dispute **41,** 104, **54,** 203-4, **77,** 658, 675-92
commercial, limited to **95,** 203
continuing dispute, need for **95,** 202-3, **119,** 587-8
North Cameroons **119,** 587-8
dispute arising from dissolution of union of States **91,** 306, 307
dispute arising under separate treaties **119,** 536-44, 546-9, 557-65
as single dispute **119,** 550
existence as objective matter to be determined by Tribunal **119,** 546-7
extradition dispute **106,** 247
'in respect of an approved enterprise'
denial of justice **95,** 202
expropriation/nationalization **95,** 202
violation of human rights **95,** 202, 203
legal dispute **53,** 416-18, **84,** 273-4, **119,** 577, 578, 587
arising out of investment **89,** 320, 397-8, 535
tax fraud claim **89,** 576-7
nature of dispute **62,** 179, 216
non-legal dispute **84,** 269, 273-4
'outstanding dispute' **91,** 584
termination of dispute, effect **119,** 545-6
dissenting opinion **82,** 638, **102,** 529, **113,** 81
opportunity for other arbitrators to study, need for **114,** 275, 284
duties, to determine boundary **50,** 22, 29-30, 39
equity **80,** 172
competence **80,** 616
Eritrea/Yemen Arbitration Tribunal. *See* Eritrea/Yemen Arbitration Tribunal (1998); Eritrea/Yemen Arbitration Tribunal (1999)
European Molecular Biology Laboratory/FRG, Rules of Procedure, text **105,** 72-4
evidence
absence of key player **102,** 383
admissibility **102,** 239-40
contemporaneous records **95,** 223-4
disclosure of documents. *See* disclosure of documents *above*
exclusion by agreement **102,** 232, **117,** 575-7
standard of proof **95,** 223-4
exhaustion of local remedies
admissibility, question of **102,** 278
treatment of issue **102,** 231, 269-77
expert evidence. *See* expert
findings of fact, incorporation of findings of another court, admissibility **106,** 562
foreign law

evidence of **117,** 575-7
knowledge of **117,** 575-7
freedom of judgment **83,** 88
function **52,** 228
functus officio **52,** 283-5, **106,** 59
ICJ and, similarity of approach presumed **80,** 141
joinder of merits and jurisdiction. *See* jurisdiction, joinder of merits *below*
joinder of parties
arbitrator, effect on choice of **80,** 618
consorité **80,** 617-18, 619-21, 647-8, 663-4
parties' intentions as determining factor **80,** 617
respondents **80,** 617-18, 620
where no relief sought **95,** 205
jurisdiction **62,** 216, **66,** 534, 559-60, **69,** 569-70, 583-4, **70,** 122-7, 484-9, 491-5, 499-526, **71,** 601-2, 607-8, 614-21, 629-30, 633-49, 651-4, 659-62, 667-9, 690-1, 694-7, **72,** 225, 241, 483-9, 496-8, 502, 719-20, 727-32, **78,** 640, **80,** 604, **82,** 280, **86,** 447-55, **89,** 382-400
admissibility distinguished **89,** 399-400
basis
arbitration agreement **53,** 308, 327, **62,** 179-80, **83,** 23, 44, 88-9, **92,** 45, 46, **95,** 673-4, 675, **102,** 353
consent **92,** 129, **95,** 203
between parties to dispute **119,** 577-8
compétence de la compétence. See compétence de la compétence above
completion of incomplete agreements **66,** 579-81
denial of justice, avoidance **80,** 616
determination **77,** 656
by parties **82,** 75, **113,** 45-6
validity of third-party treaty in case of State succession **83,** 21-2
equitable principles **89,** 522-3
equitable rulings **66,** 581-2
ex aequo et bono **89,** 522
power to decide **46,** 472, 506, **50,** 3, 18
excès de pouvoir, subsequent developments, relevance **113,** 187
exclusion, undertaking not to bring proceedings **102,** 288-9
extra compromissum arbiter nihil facere potest **92,** 84, 133, 142
failure to abide by
Chamizal Arbitration (1911) **80,** 314
Northeastern Boundary of the US Case (1827) **80,** 314
formulation of own rules of procedure **106,** 584
inherent powers of revision **102,** 579-81
interim relief **71,** 635-49
interpretation of party's Constitution **117,** 559
joinder of merits **95,** 190, **125,** 104-5
'justice and equity' **46,** 506, **54,** 144-7, **60,** 130, **62,** 159, 179-80, **72,** 162
Law of the Sea Convention (1982), Commission on the Limits of the Continental Shelf **95,** 674
limitations
incomplete boundary **50,** 388
jurisdiction of previous arbitrator **113,** 60, 114
maximum claim of parties **113,** 45-6
acceptance by previous arbitrator, relevance **113,** 59
nature of **53,** 308, 327, 356, 404-8

arbitral tribunal (*cont.*)
objection to
absence of **92,** 198
time-limits **89,** 535
waiver **89,** 535
re-opening of proceedings **53,** 376, 380-8
recommendations **82,** 578, 580
restrictive interpretation **82,** 280
submissions of parties, relevance **82,** 611-12
territorial limitation, evidence of **113,** 114
third parties, dispute involving rights and obligations **119,** 578, 588-92, 594-7. *See also* International Court of Justice (ICJ), intervention of third State; International Court of Justice (ICJ), intervention of third State, 'interest of a legal nature which may be affected by the decision' as requirement; International Court of Justice (ICJ), third States and
treaty interpretation **53,** 523-7, **82,** 66-7, 74-5, **83,** 44
international public policy and **82,** 66-7, 74
private interests in respect of **82,** 67
ultra petita **83,** 88, 113, **113,** 58, 59, 77, **117,** 144, 187-9
written consent, need for **89,** 320-1
language **52,** 265
League of Nations Council as **91,** 575
maps and documents, inspection **50,** 17
nature
international court distinguished **119,** 410
procedure as determining factor **113,** 42
non licet **80,** 307, 308, 310
meaning **80,** 308
non liquet distinguished **80,** 308
non liquet **80,** 347
non licet distinguished **80,** 308
organ of UN, whether, unregistered treaty and **83,** 42
parties
absence **95,** 673-4
arbitration clause
need to be bound by **95,** 203
owner of capital of protected company **95,** 204
party to, relevance **95,** 204
change **95,** 191, 204
non-prejudice **95,** 204
parties' conduct as evidence of acceptance **95,** 204
timeliness **95,** 204
joinder. *See* joinder of parties *above*
peaceful settlement, simultaneous pursuit of alternative methods of **80,** 242-3
pleadings, amendment **69,** 603, 605-6, 610-13
powers. *See* jurisdiction *above and* task *below*
precedent **83,** 70
decisions of another arbitral tribunal **119,** 639, 667-8
procedure **52,** 107-14, 265-7, 270, **62,** 146-51, 165, 176-7, 179, 216, 221
applicable law. *See* applicable law, arbitration
applicable law, ICJ Rules **83,** 13
Arbitral Procedure Convention (Draft) (1955) **53,** 436

determination of **38,** 23, 75, **53,** 380-1, **62,** 180, 216
arbitral tribunal **119,** 579-80
authority **53,** 309
documents filed after hearing **68,** 645-51
hearings **52,** 116
re-opening **71,** 685
ICSID Rules **102,** 228
irregularities **69,** 621, 624-5
joinder of merits. *See* joinder of merits *above*
nature of **62,** 179-80
objection to, opportunity for **102,** 231-2
oral proceedings
new grounds **96,** 294-5
order determined by lots **82,** 609
post-hearing briefs **102,** 238
practice **92,** 198, **96,** 294-5
preliminary proceedings **114,** 9-11
representative claims, admissibility **72,** 732-4
Rules of Procedure, Tribunal's power to determine **102,** 228
time-limits **68,** 646-51
extension **95,** 190
US–UK Arbitral Tribunal (Heathrow Airport User Charges) Rules **102,** 228-40, 577-81
text **102,** 551
varied nature **91,** 682-3
proceedings **53,** 401-2
applicable law **75,** 165-73
law of seat of tribunal **75,** 165-8
failure to appear **53,** 311-13, 370-2, **62,** 151, 181, 216, 230, **63,** 536-7, 539, **114,** 145, 146
institution of **53,** 302-5, 398-401, 426-30, **54,** 311-14
attempt at friendly settlement, need for **53,** 413-15, **75,** 168-73
stay of **80,** 618
recommendations **105,** 70-1
seat **62,** 223, **86,** 490
change of **77,** 646
connection with forum State, need for, arbitration clause as **65,** 449-50
determination of **62,** 177, 180-1, 216
by consent **62,** 223, **66,** 534, **80,** 36, **122,** 258
forum selection clause, effect **71,** 636, 648, 669
neutral forum **122,** 258-9
standing, individual **121,** 133, 143-4
task **91,** 580-5
boundary determination **91,** 582-3, 653, 654
comprehensive presentation of dispute **92,** 101, 152
compromise **113,** 59
definition of scope of dispute **114,** 26
drawing of boundary on map **92,** 49-50, 54-5, 60-1, 71, 79-81, 104
ex aequo et bono decision **91,** 587
fulfilment of parties' wishes **92,** 103
guidance on future conduct **102,** 496
resolution of dispute **92,** 125, 127

arbitral tribunal (*cont.*)
terms of reference
determined by tribunal **102,** 227
establishment **80,** 605
US–UK Arbitral Tribunal (Heathrow Airport User Charges), text **102,** 546
unicum theory **83,** 70
US–UK Arbitral Tribunal (Heathrow Airport User Charges)
Memorandum of Understanding (MoU) (6 April 1983) **102,** 561
procedure **102,** 228-40
Rules of Procedure **102,** 551
terms of reference, text **102,** 546
Arbitral Tribunal for the Agreement on German External Debts. *See* German External Debts Agreement, Arbitral Tribunal
arbitrary act 56, 413-14, **84,** 326, 414-26, **87,** 195, **89,** 207-8. *See also* arbitrary detention
appeal, possibility of and **84,** 421-2
'arbitrary or discriminatory measures' **84,** 378-83, 423
capriciousness **84,** 420-1
compensation, failure to pay and **84,** 420, 421
definition **84,** 380
as denial of justice **84,** 421-2
excess of power **84,** 382, 415, 419-20
interference under law, conformity with provisions, aims and objectives of International Covenant on Civil and Political Rights (ICCPR) (1966), need for **112,** 340-1, **115,** 342-3
International Criminal Tribunal for the Former Yugoslavia **105,** 432-3
international law concept **89,** 621
international law and municipal law distinguished **84,** 380, 415
judicial review **86,** 332
legal framework and **84,** 382-3, 417
motivation **84,** 418-19
partial arbitrariness **84,** 418
Security Council, arbitrary exercise of powers **105,** 561-7
test
proportionality **100,** 384-5, **115,** 348-9
reasonableness **84,** 420-1, **115,** 342-3
tribunal established by law **105,** 563-7
arbitrary detention 78, 26-7, **81,** 125-6, **87,** 448-60, **101,** 300-5, **111,** 485. *See also* arbitrary act; liberty of person, deprivation
aliens **87,** 451-60, **95,** 633
American Convention on Human Rights (1969) **87,** 457, **116,** 308-11, **118,** 77-9, 90
appeal, right of **71,** 316, 321, 328, 349, 361
customary international law **87,** 455-60, **95,** 633
human rights and **87,** 455-60, **95,** 633, **104,** 185
as inhumane treatment **95,** 299, **116,** 475
International Covenant on Civil and Political Rights (ICCPR) (1966) **59,** 442-3, **68,** 31, 35, 36, 38-9, **69,** 192, **70,** 256, **71,** 312, 316, 319, 321, 325-31, 347-53, 355-6, 361, 363, 365, **78,** 26, 27, **79,** 182-6, 189, 191-2, **94,** 414
as international tort/wrong **77,** 210
jus cogens **104,** 185
nationals **95,** 633-4

preventive detention **101,** 304-5
statutory limitation, retroactive withdrawal **78,** 132-6
unfair trial distinguished **118,** 291
arbitrary laws
breach
League of Nations Covenant **37,** 6
Mandate **37,** 6, 347
equality and **118,** 466-7
arbitration 72, 483, 721-2, **75,** 180-268, **77,** 656, **78,** 640, 655, **80,** 650-1, 662, 665-6, **84,** 271, 272-4. *See also* arbitration agreement
applicable law. *See* applicable law, arbitration
application to tribunal **59,** 521-3
arbitrability **62,** 150, 165, 171, 179-80
Arbitration and Conciliation for the Settlement of International Disputes, Rules of (1962) **53,** 436
arbitrator. *See* arbitrator
award. *See* arbitral award
commercial arbitration, definition **119,** 657-9
compulsory **72,** 156, **84,** 272-4
conciliation and **84,** 271
consent, need for **80,** 36-8, **91,** 573, **119,** 585-6
formal agreement, need for **91,** 573, 576
initiation of arbitration proceedings as **122,** 290-1
legislation as **89,** 391
contract
applicable law and procedure, possibility of divergence **82,** 69-70
termination of and **62,** 177-8, 216
costs. *See* costs
counterclaims **62,** 604, **75,** 607
competence of tribunal **70,** 127
jurisdiction over, whether exclusive **71,** 637-8, 641-9
scope **62,** 600
damages. *See* damages
definition
Hague Convention for the Pacific Settlement of Disputes (1907) **91,** 574-5
ICJ **92,** 197
'suit' **64,** 580-4
duty, reprisals, effect on **54,** 338-9, 341
equity **82,** 82
error in law **53,** 358-74, 377-84, **54,** 174
procedural **53,** 367-73
substantive **53,** 362-7
between Euratom Commission and UK Atomic Energy Authority **44,** 409-22
evidence. *See* evidence
exhaustion of local remedies. *See* exhaustion of local remedies, arbitration and
expert witnesses **62,** 150, 166, 210-11, 213, **66,** 534, 538, 544-5
frustration, avoidance of **80,** 308, 309
functions, interpretation of treaties **59,** 526
good faith **84,** 592
ICSID. *See* ICSID Convention (Convention on Settlement of Investment Disputes between States and Nationals of Other States (1965))
ILC and **82,** 273

arbitration (*cont.*)
interim measures **82,** 81, **89,** 34-5
merits, relevance **89,** 34-5
public presentation of case, prohibition **89,** 402-5
reprisals, effect on **54,** 320, 338-41, 343-4
'international', whether limited to inter-State arbitration **96,** 330-1
International Chamber of Commerce. *See* International Chamber of Commerce (ICC)
international contract. *See* concession agreement; economic development agreement; State contract
international law
as applicable law. *See* applicable law, arbitration
institution established by **53,** 454-5
interpretation, treaties establishing rules **54,** 323
intervention
accessoire ou conservatoire **106,** 584
principal ou agressive **106,** 584
request for to be treated as request for arbitration **106,** 584
investment guarantee programmes **56,** 258-330
Iran–US Claims Tribunal. *See* Iran–US Claims Tribunal
judicial control of **78,** 582-3, **102,** 212-13, 214-15
judicial nature **82,** 273, **92,** 197, 198-9
departure from **80,** 640-1
judicial procedure and **84,** 273-4, 276
law, facts distinguished **54,** 322-3
maritime delimitation **99,** 479-81
ILC Draft Continental Shelf Convention **99,** 480
Model Arbitral Rules (ILC) (1958) **91,** 572-3, 575
binding, whether **91,** 575
as customary international law **91,** 572, 575
municipal courts
jurisdiction
effect on **82,** 288-91
provision for ouster **71,** 637-8, 641-9, **75,** 157-8
power to request stay of proceedings **71,** 639-49
nature of, jurisdictional and contractual **53,** 405-8
negotiations as *préalable* **95,** 200-2
'new situations', law governing **69,** 581, 594
obligation
negotiations as *préalable* **82,** 250-2, 258
UN Headquarters agreement, under **82,** 230-82, 288-91
Pact of Bogotá (1948) **84,** 272-4
parties to decision, need for participation in proceedings **91,** 576
place of arbitration. *See* NAFTA (North American Free Trade Agreement) (1992), Arbitral Tribunal, place of arbitration
place of arbitration, confidentiality/freedom of information and **125,** 104
political settlement distinguished **91,** 571-80, 682-3
procedure. *See* arbitral tribunal, procedure
provisional measures. *See* interim measures *above*
refusal to submit to, denial of justice **53,** 475
reparation. *See* reparation
requirements, injury **54,** 318

res judicata, effect on **54,** 167-71, 211
right to **89,** 334
waiver **89,** 401-2
exhaustion of local remedies and **124,** 15-18, **125,** 7, 34, 72-3
third party agreement **102,** 289
in Romania **74,** 561-2, 567-9
settlement **72,** 225-6, 233
UNCITRAL Rules **68,** 530-4
'without prejudice' **68,** 530-3, 652-4
six-month rule **124,** 24
sovereignty and **62,** 165, 178, **78,** 640, **122,** 280-1
State contract. *See* ICSID Convention (Convention on Settlement of Investment Disputes between States and Nationals of Other States (1965)); State contract
State immunity, jurisdiction and **53,** 308-9, 433-4, **65,** 449, 451-3
submission to
burden of proof **80,** 640-1
State's capacity **41,** 452-5, **48,** 329-30
between suzerain and vassal **50,** 399
treaty interpretation **77,** 657
on basis of *travaux préparatoires* **77,** 657
tribunal. *See* arbitral tribunal
two-stage process, relevance
compensation **121,** 136-8
Eritrea/Yemen (1998 and 1999) **119,** 449-50
United Nations, claim against **44,** 433-7
willingness to submit to, as radical reversal of policy **106,** 557-8, 567
arbitration agreement 54, 311-14, 321, **72,** 155, 162, **74,** 561-2. *See also* arbitral award; arbitral tribunal; arbitration; arbitration clause; *and the Index to the Consolidated Table of Treaties*
applicable law **83,** 44
substantive law unspecified **83,** 44
Argentina–Chile 1971 (Beagle Channel Dispute) **52,** 107-14
Argentina–Chile General Treaty of Arbitration (1902) **52,** 269-70
Canada/France (1989), text **95,** 650-4
choice of law clause. *See* choice of law clause
corporation, dissolution, effect on **89,** 572-3
dual nature **92,** 100
Dubai/Sharjah (1976) **91,** 350
effects of **57,** 329-31
unilateral delimitation of continental shelf **54,** 130, 132
existence of, power to determine **86,** 483
France–UK, Continental Shelf dispute **54,** 12-16
France–US Air Transport Agreement **38,** 186-9
function, prevention of unilateral modification of situation **83,** 111
Guinea-Bissau/Senegal (1985) (maritime delimitation) **83,** 9-12, 20, 21, 44
Guinea/Guinea-Bissau (maritime delimitation) **83,** 38
inadequacy **92,** 61-4, 70
interpretation **92,** 45-9
aids
conduct of parties **89,** 389
legislation **89,** 391
promotion literature **89,** 391

arbitration agreement (*cont.*)
applicable law, general rules of international law governing the interpretation of treaties **92,** 45
guidelines
agreement as whole **89,** 389
aim and spirit of ICSID Convention (1968) **89,** 389
pacta sunt servanda **89,** 384-5
restrictive **86,** 310
text as a whole **86,** 311-12
multilingual **89,** 389
discrepancy between French and English text **92,** 24 n. 1
parties' intention **89,** 384, 389, 394
phrases, 'du droit de chacun' **92,** 24-5
investment dispute **86,** 449-50, 451, 491
legal requirements **75,** 156-7, 166
reformulation **92,** 110
responsibilities of parties **68,** 518, 522
substantive rights, effect on **118,** 637-9
UK/US (1977), text **102,** 542
as waiver of State immunity **47,** 150-1, **63,** 197-8, 357-8, 405-7, 462, 519-20, 526, 537-8, 566, 645, **80,** 644-6
'without prejudice' clause **114,** 34
arbitration clause 54, 322, **62,** 147, 152, 159, 176, 216, 220, 227, 229, **82,** 96, **86,** 451-6. *See also* arbitration agreement
acceptance **86,** 489
burden of proof **86,** 448
clear **86,** 448
provisions of agreement implying **95,** 204-5
State agency, by, attribution to government **86,** 449, 451-5, **95,** 204-5, **96,** 275
applicable law **80,** 609
contract in general distinguished **80,** 609
municipal law where tribunal sits **106,** 529
ratione personae, municipal law where tribunal sits **106,** 529
validity *ratione personae,* municipal law where tribunal sits **106,** 529
assignment **89,** 394-5
binding effect **62,** 178-9, **80,** 608-10, **89,** 340
Anglo-Iranian Oil Co. **96,** 277
arbitral decisions **96,** 277
ICSID Convention (1965) **96,** 275
members of international organization **80,** 610, 612-16, 657, 659-60
non-signatories, on **80,** 609, 636, 646-7, 657
teachings of publicists **96,** 275-6
breach
exhaustion of efforts to reach amicable settlement **95,** 200-2
non-objection to establishment of tribunal as waiver **95,** 202
capacity to conclude **48,** 329-30, **62,** 177
public order/public policy and **41,** 452-5, **48,** 329-30
duties of parties. *See* obligation under *below*
effect **53,** 454-5
Egypt/SPP **106,** 603
European Molecular Biology Laboratory/FRG Headquarters Agreement (1973) **105,** 11
as evidence of

intention to be bound **80,** 659-60
State's intention to act as private person **82,** 65
exclusion of alternative fora **89,** 326
exhaustion of local remedies and **82,** 243, 247-8, 260-1
expropriation/nationalization, effect on **53,** 408-13, **62,** 177-8, 216
failure to include as breach of treaty **80,** 173
foreign investment, applicability to **89,** 392
as forum selection clause **68,** 563-4, 586-7, 591-4, 606-7, 609-10, 613, 628-9, **85,** 379, 417-18
imperfect or incomplete **82,** 272-3
international organization, obligation to include in contract **81,** 683-4
interpretation, in accordance with language and circumstances of conclusion **118,** 632
ITC HQ Agreement requirement **77,** 14
judicial control by host State, exclusion **102,** 212-13, 214-15
jurisdiction, basis for, applicable law distinguished **106,** 476-7
maritime commerce contract **48,** 329-30
nullity **82,** 68-9
legislation of State party **96,** 268-9, 274-8
obligation under **62,** 178, **66,** 593-4
partner, binding on **80,** 609
separability **53,** 408-13, 446, **62,** 178, **95,** 205, **96,** 268-74
arbitral decisions **96,** 269
arbitration conventions **96,** 272
Council of Europe Uniform Law on Arbitration **96,** 272-3
European Convention on International Commercial Arbitration (1961) **96,** 272
France/Iran Arbitration Agreement (1977) **96,** 274
ICC Rules **96,** 273
UNCITRAL **96,** 237
BP v. *Libya* **96,** 271
general principle of international arbitration law **96,** 269
international organizations, arbitration rules **96,** 270, 272
LIAMCO **96,** 270-1
Losinger **96,** 270
national arbitration law **96,** 270, 273-4
teachings of publicists **96,** 269-70, 271-2
Texaco **96,** 270
shareholder's right to invoke on own behalf **106,** 476-7
Sri Lanka/UK Bilateral Investment Treaty (1980) **106,** 422-3, 475-6
State obligation to respect **62,** 178, **65,** 452-3
State's capacity to accept **48,** 329-30, **65,** 452-3
successor in contract and **80,** 609, 657
termination of contract, effect **53,** 408-13, **62,** 177-8, 216
terms **53,** 402-5
transferability **89,** 394-5
as waiver of diplomatic immunity **41,** 452-5, **62,** 220, 223, 225, 228, 234-5, **65,** 52, 383-4, **78,** 84
as waiver of international organization's immunity **102,** 212-13, 214-15
as waiver of State immunity **41,** 452-5, **45,** 84, **47,** 150-1, **62,** 220, 222, 223, 225, 228, 234-5, **65,** 48, 52-3, 89-92, 96, 98, 383-4, 449, 452-3, **77,** 523-4, **80,** 36, 619, 659, **82,** 74, **86,** 449, 450, 461-2
war, effect of **67,** 628-9
writing, need for **80,** 609

arbitrator. *See also* arbitral tribunal; arbitration; Iran–US Claims Tribunal, arbitrator; Law of the Sea Convention (1982): Annex VII (settlement of disputes), arbitral tribunal (Annex VII)
absence **69,** 620-1, 629, 635-7, 663, **78,** 670-5
effect **69,** 620-1, 629, 635-7, 663
from announcement of award **92,** 39-41
appointing authority, powers **62,** 586-90
appointment **62,** 147-8, 176, 179, **66,** 532-3, **68,** 517-20, **80,** 618
by ICC **67,** 614
by ICSID **67,** 323, 352, **72,** 155, 159, **77,** 645-6
by President of the ICJ **53,** 304-5, 400, 427, **62,** 147-8, 163, 165, 176, 179, 229, **66,** 532-3
failure **82,** 63, 272-3, **95,** 188-9
obligation, breach, State immunity and **42,** 173-8
right to nominate **80,** 618, 621, 638-40, 664
challenge **62,** 585-94, **68,** 515-22
State right of **68,** 517-18
UNCITRAL Rules **68,** 516-18
competence
determination of jurisdiction **53,** 404-8
enforcement proceedings **53,** 432
death **52,** 120
designation **53,** 302
refusal to designate **53,** 398-401, 427
designation of appointing authority **95,** 188-9
disqualification **68,** 515-22
manifest lack of ICSID Article 14 qualities **125,** 51-8
'appearance of bias' as **125,** 54-5
burden of proof **125,** 54-7
de minimis rule **125,** 52-3, 55, 57
lawyer–client relationship continuing after dispute has arisen **125,** 54-5
real risk test **125,** 54-5
relationship of independent professional partner with party **125,** 51-8
social contacts **125,** 55
unilateral **68,** 518
dissent, right to **37,** 285
expertise, relevance **117,** 576-7
impartiality **68,** 519-20, 522, **75,** 194-5, 197, 267-8, **91,** 573
independence **65,** 452, **91,** 573, 576
neutrality. *See* impartiality *above*
panel, as part of **92,** 74-5
powers **56,** 329, **75,** 266-8
Presiding Arbitrator, selection by appointed arbitrators **95,** 189
refusal to sign award **68,** 549, **69,** 619, 629-31, 634-5, 638, 658, 661, **71,** 611, 625-7, **72,** 492, 500, **86,** 474
reasons **69,** 634-5, 658-61
resignation **69,** 620, 630-1, 638-41, 662, **78,** 670-3, 674
role, ICC Rules **67,** 614
separate declaration, effect **92,** 12, 39, 56, 57-9, 69-70, 72-5, 106
post facto change of mind distinguished **92,** 59
archives. *See* diplomatic archives, inviolability; international organizations, archives
Argentina
ambassador/head of mission, State immunity, jurisdiction, entitlement **65,** 2

American Convention on Human Rights (1969) and **89,** 84-7
citizenship **56,** 562
commercial/trade representation/mission, State immunity, jurisdiction **65,** 1
Constitution 1853 **55,** 413-17
  Art. 31 **89,** 86
  Art. 33 **89,** 86, 87
  Art. 100 **89,** 89, **113,** 435
  Art. 101 **89,** 89, **113,** 435
  Art. 117 **113,** 436-7
  federal or unitary, whether **55,** 416-17
  partial repeal by Junta (26 March 1976) **123,** 146, 149
consular privileges and immunities
  functional **89,** 89
  State responsibility, relevance **89,** 89
Continental Shelf Declaration (1946) **41,** 118, 120, 125, 158
diplomatic privileges and immunities, death of member of family **89,** 93-4
employment contract, State immunity, jurisdiction **113,** 432-4
extradition by, treaty, in absence of **49,** 211-12
foreign State, proceedings involving, action against, agreement of State, need for **113,** 432
human rights
  Constitution, protection by **89,** 86-7
  right of reply **89,** 84-7
international law, compliance, preservation of international standing **113,** 433
international organizations, privileges and immunities
  basis **89,** 91
  State immunity as measure **113,** 436-7
  waiver **89,** 91-2
    express **89,** 91-2
judicial independence, unconstitutional removal **123,** 146-52
judicial protection, right to judicial enforcement of rights **113,** 431
jurisdiction, *ratione personae* **89,** 89
law of
  Code of Criminal Procedure, s 607 (presentation of forged document) **104,** 37
  Criminal Code, s 119 (rape) **121,** 270 n. 208
  Decree-Law No 1285/58, s 24(1)(2) **113,** 431, 432-3, 435, 437
  Decree-Law No 9015/63 **113,** 432
  Law No 23.054 (American Convention on Human Rights (1969)) **89,** 85
  Law No 48 **113,** 431
  Penal Code, Art. 89 **89,** 92
political question doctrine, removal of judges by de facto government **123,** 149-50
Salta and **55,** 414-17
service of process on foreign State or State agency, refusal to accept **65,** 1
sovereignty, violation, Eichman, abduction **36,** 62-4, 67-71
State immunity, jurisdiction, classification of act, personal injury in forum State **65,** 2
State immunity, jurisdiction, entitlement
  commercial/trade representation/mission **65,** 1
  government department **65,** 1
  provincial government **55,** 413-17
State immunity, jurisdiction, theory/doctrine
  basis, reciprocity **113,** 432, 433
  customary international law, absolute theory **113,** 433
State responsibility for

Argentina (*cont.*)
acts of Tucumán authorities **125,** 26-38
damage caused by closure of consular post **89,** 89
Statute of the Revolution **55,** 414-15
treaties
implementing legislation, need for **89,** 85-7
incorporation **89,** 85-7
Argentina–Chile Arbitral Tribunal (1902) 38, 48-50, **113,** 354-6. *See also* Argentina–Chile Arbitral Tribunal (1966); Argentina–Chile Arbitral Tribunal (1994)
Arbitral Award of 1966 concerning **113,** 36, 167-8
Award
compromise nature **113,** 59-60, 76, 107, 145, 179
constituent instruments **113,** 43, 77, 87, 110, 157, 163-5, 169-72, 180-1
effect **38,** 80-9
interpretation. *See also* Argentina–Chile Arbitral Tribunal (1994)
conduct of parties subsequent to original arbitration, relevance **113,** 77-9, 123-5, 165-6, 190-1, 202-5
knowledge at time of award **113,** 56, 76, 83-4, 111-14, 123, 129-30, 177, 185-6
meaning of terms at time of award **113,** 55, 62, 67-8
responsibility **38,** 91
travaux préparatoires, relevance **38,** 89-90
unity of texts **113,** 146, 163
'interpretation and fulfilment' (1966 Compromiso) **38,** 35, 37, 41, 88, 90-1
as 'interpretation and application' **38,** 91
text relating to area of dispute **113,** 38
validity **38,** 81
jurisdiction
areas in dispute **113,** 153-4
territorial limitation **113,** 114, 118, 119-22, 178
'points and sections' **113,** 101-3
maps, role
Award **38,** 80-9, **113,** 118-19, 146, 166-7, 169-72, 181
Demarcator's map (1903) **113,** 119-20, 154-60, 181-3
evidence of territorial jurisdiction **113,** 114, 118, 119-22, 178
travaux préparatoires **113,** 104-5, 106-10, 115-18, 178-80
Argentina–Chile Arbitral Tribunal (1966) 38, 11-99. *See also* Argentina–Chile Arbitral Tribunal (1902); Argentina–Chile Arbitral Tribunal (1994)
applicable law, principles of international law **38,** 75
compromis (1965), text **38,** 23
Compromiso (1965) **38,** 22
'interpretation and fulfilment of part of 1902 Award' **38,** 35, 37, 41, 88, 90-1
as 'interpretation and application' **38,** 91
expert evidence, field mission **38,** 17, 27-8, 55-8, 96
jurisdiction, determined by Compromiso (1965) **38,** 91
procedure, determination **38,** 23
Question, determination **38,** 75-6
burden of proof and **38,** 76
Argentina–Chile Arbitral Tribunal (1994). *See also* Argentina–Chile Arbitral Tribunal (1902); Argentina–Chile Arbitral Tribunal (1966)
applicable law
1902 Award **113,** 42, 82
equity. *See* equity *below*

international law **113,** 42, 82
any act or instrument of international law binding on parties **113,** 42
equity **113,** 85, 174
expert, use of **113,** 204-5, 216-19, 226-7, 323
interpretation of Judgment, subsidiary request for **113,** 194-6, 229-33
basis, *Tratado de Paz y Amistad* (1984) **113,** 229
disagreement, need for **113,** 229-30
Judgment
binding effect **113,** 201
declaratory of content of 1902 Award, *ex tunc* effect **113,** 76
revision. *See* revision of Judgment *below*
jurisdiction
basis, Special Agreement (1991) **113,** 176
compétence de la compétence **113,** 42
limited to jurisdiction of 1898-1902 arbitrator **113,** 60, 85-6, 128-30, 177
limited to maximum claim of parties as presented during 1898-1902 arbitration **113,** 46-51, 56-60, 85-6, 128-34, 177-80
acceptance by arbitrator, relevance **113,** 59
Memorandum of Understanding (1991), text **113,** 24-5
revision of Judgment **113,** 194-262
appeal distinguished **113,** 200
applicable law, *Tratado de Paz y Amistad* (1984) **113,** 199-201
error of fact **113,** 199-200
adoption of changing geographical feature as basis **113,** 209-10
definition of water-parting **113,** 204-6
failure of party to verify work **113,** 227
failure to distinguish single continuous water-parting **113,** 223-6
interpretation distinguished **113,** 227-8
judgment wholly or in part consequent on **113,** 200, 212-15
resulting from act or document of the proceedings **113,** 200, 226-7
resulting from error of law **113,** 202
resulting from error of reasoning **113,** 202
error of law **113,** 200
grounds
error of fact. *See* error of fact *above*
forgery or alteration of document **113,** 199
scale of map used by Tribunal **113,** 215-23
resolution of 22 February 1995 **113,** 194-5
Rules of Procedure
14.1 **113,** 26
18 **113,** 25
28 **113,** 28, 29
adoption **113,** 25
status
1902 Arbitrator and **113,** 42, 176
appointment **113,** 25
autonomous **113,** 42, 176
judicial body **113,** 42
task
determination of boundary as fixed by 1902 Arbitral Award **113,** 41-2, 81-2, 83, 176
Tribunal's freedom of choice **113,** 191
Argentina–Chile boundary 113, 1-262
1903-64 developments **38,** 64-75

Argentina–Chile boundary (*cont.*)
acquiescence **113,** 125-8, 192
aerial survey **38,** 26-7, 56-7
Beagle Channel arbitration, declaration of nullity **52,** 268, 277, 281-2
Boundary Treaty (1881) **52,** 124-35, 270-7
Chile's claim as presented during 1898-1902 Arbitration **113,** 49-51, 56-60, 87-121, 178-80
principle of natural and effective water-parting **113,** 57-8, 59, 93-9, 103-5, 128, 164-5, 177
choice of river channels **38,** 91-8
continental water-parting (*divortium aquarum*) **38,** 97-8, **113,** 50-77, 111-23, 193-4
1898-1902 Arbitration
Report **113,** 143-5, 149-54
travaux préparatoires **113,** 141-3, 188-90
critical date for determining **113,** 211-15
crossing of rivers, admissibility **113,** 70-2, 153, 169
definition **113,** 62-8
matter of law **113,** 224-6
dividing ranges **113,** 149-54, 192-3
spur **113,** 151
glaciers, relevance **113,** 70-2, 206-12
divortium glaciarum **113,** 226
local water-parting and **113,** 68-74, 135-45, 151-2, 160-2, 174-5, 183-5, 187-94
Mount Fitzroy **113,** 58-9, 122-3
identity with continental water-parting **113,** 136-41, 145-6, 160-2, 174-5, 187-9
separating waters flowing ultimately into same ocean **113,** 70
scientific literature **113,** 141
demarcation
1951-4 (Mixed Boundary Commission) **38,** 69-73
following 1902 Award **38,** 61-3, **113,** 154-60
following 1966 Award **38,** 19, 28-9
following 1994 Arbitral Award **113,** 80
following Tratado de Limites (1881) **113,** 30-2
dispute, obligation to submit to arbitration **52,** 230, **113,** 57-8
disputed area, description **113,** 39-41
estoppel
Chile's acceptance of
Argentine jurisdiction over disputed territory **113,** 60
Argentine maps **113,** 203-4
maps used by Tribunal **38,** 77-9, **113,** 219-23
contradiction between Chile's claims **113,** 130-4
geographical developments **38,** 50-5, 64-5, **113,** 125-6
jurisdiction
exercise by Chile **113,** 124, 192
consistency **113,** 78-9
effectiveness **113,** 78-9
maps, relevance **113,** 78-9, 124
land concessions as evidence of **113,** 78-9, 124-5, 192
maps
1898, prior to **38,** 58-9
1898-1902 arbitration **38,** 59-61, **113,** 108-10
1902 Award **38,** 61
1903 Demarcator's, variations from 1902 Arbitrator's **113,** 155-60

1966 demarcation **38,** 29
accuracy **113,** 106-7
dependence on accompanying documentation **113,** 106-7
error. *See* estoppel *above*
pecked lines, significance **113,** 68-9, 77, 105-6, 112-13, 167-9, 181
relevance **113,** 51-5, 58, 93-112
evidence of exercise of jurisdiction **113,** 79
scale **113,** 215-23
glacial area, relevance **113,** 224-6
Mixed Boundary Commission, organization, operation and results **38,** 67-70, 85-7
natural boundary **113,** 57-8
Report of 1902 Arbitral Tribunal. *See* Argentina–Chile Arbitral Tribunal (1902), Report
thalweg **38,** 97
Tratado de Amistad, Comercio y Navegación (1855) **113,** 30
Tratado de Limites (1881) **38,** 47-8, **113,** 30
Additional Explanatory Protocol (1893) **38,** 48, **113,** 31-2, 111
demarcation agreement (1888) implementing **113,** 30
dispute relating to **113,** 30-1
Treaty submitting disagreements to British Government (1896) **38,** 48, **113,** 32-5
uti possidetis **113,** 30
Argentine Airlines 63, 195-6
Aristotle, justice **37,** 463, **46,** 297
armed attack 76, 361-2, 453-5. *See also* armed activities in the Congo; armed conflict; civil war; crimes against humanity, requirements, armed conflict; force, prohibition on the threat or use of; war; war crimes, requirements, armed conflict
definition **76,** 428, 437, 602-3, 605, 877
assistance to rebels **76,** 510, 665-75, 680-1, 877
customary international law **76,** 437
supply of arms **76,** 453, 488-9, 877
supply of funds **76,** 453
armed bands 42, 481-2
aid to **76,** 387-98
armed combat. *See* war
armed conflict. *See also* armed attack; Bosnia-Herzegovina, armed conflict; civil war; force, prohibition on the threat or use of; Geneva Conventions 1949; internal armed conflict; international armed conflict; war
applicable law
American Declaration of the Rights and Duties of Man (1948) **123,** 169-71, 184-5
International Covenant on Civil and Political Rights (ICCPR) (1966) **110,** 189-90
international humanitarian law **112,** 182-3
detention of civilians **123,** 169, 184
law of armed conflict **110,** 190
rules relating to State responsibility **108,** 155-6, **124,** 98
Bosnia-Herzegovina. *See* Bosnia-Herzegovina, armed conflict
Croatia (Republic of Serbian Krajina) **108,** 49, 62
definition **105,** 486-9
Geneva Conventions (1949) **105,** 486-8
geographical scope **105,** 487-9, **112,** 210, **124,** 162
temporal extent **105,** 486-8
detention of civilians. *See also* Geneva Convention (Protection of Civilian Persons in Time of War) (Convention IV) (1949); prisoners of war
American Declaration of the Rights and Duties of Man (1948), applicability **123,** 158-88

armed conflict (*cont.*)
evidence of **108,** 49-50
human rights, applicability in **105,** 500, 505-6, **123,** 135-6, 182-8
peacetime distinguished **123,** 170
inter-ethnic **122,** 58-60
International Humanitarian Law Applicable in, Final Act of Diplomatic Conference on (1977) **74,** 696
legality of participation in, municipal courts' jurisdiction **42,** 393-401
Malaysia–Indonesia 'confrontation' **42,** 458, 464
new concept **105,** 500
Northern Ireland **79,** 97, 147-50
State practice, international and internal, distinction **105,** 498-9
terrorism. *See* terrorism
torture during. *See* torture, armed conflict and
war distinguished **67,** 615, 620-1, 625
extent of hostilities **67,** 621-2, 625
intentions of parties **67,** 621-3
armed force. *See* armed conflict; armed forces; force, prohibition on threat or use of; war
armed forces. *See also* deserter; Germany, Federal Republic, armed forces; jurisdiction, armed forces; military base; military courts; military service; NATO Status of Forces Agreement (1951); State responsibility for acts and omissions of, armed forces; State responsibility, classification of act, armed forces, acts concerning; visiting forces; war
aliens, voluntary enlistment **47,** 233-4
arrest, use in **82,** 338-43, **88,** 182-4
international waters, in **82,** 338
non-regulatory, proscriptive or compulsory **82,** 342-3
use of military aircraft to transport **82,** 341
civilians and **58,** 101
Commander-in-chief, immunity from suit **80,** 22-3
contract. *See* military equipment *and* provisions, supply of *below*
criminal responsibility **74,** 245-56
superior orders defence. *See* superior orders
deployment
interim injunction, requirements **106,** 352
legislative consent, need for **106,** 323-52
collective security, agreement to treaty establishing **106,** 331-3, 347
declaration of state of defence as **106,** 349, 350
legislature's right of initiative **106,** 350-1
prior **106,** 326, 348, 349, 350
obligation
collective security system **106,** 326-34
Security Council Resolutions relating to Bosnia, participation in NATO/WEU implementing action **106,** 332-3
UN Mandate, Somalia **106,** 326, 331-2
deportation of foreign conscript **86,** 223
desertion
detention
military authorities of foreign country, by **85,** 158, 164
permanent resident of foreign country, of **85,** 158-9, 178
place of desertion, relevance **85,** 156-7, 166-8
prerogative matter, whether **85,** 164-5
treaty obligation, whether **85,** 164-5
visiting forces, limited to, whether **85,** 156-81

extraditable offence **85,** 165
jurisdiction **85,** 156-81
disciplinary proceedings (fair trial requirement) **58,** 53-60, 81, 101-2, 105-6, **73,** 395, 554-64, **78,** 227-53, **96,** 650-60. *See also* military courts
discrimination
between ranks **58,** 87, 90, 101
civilians and **58,** 87, 90, 101
European Convention on Human Rights (1950) and
fair trial **58,** 80-7, **73,** 395, 526, 557-64
freedom of expression **58,** 87-90, **73,** 395-6
freedom from discrimination
civilians and **58,** 87, 90, 101
ranks, between **58,** 77-9, 90, 101
liberty of person, deprivation **58,** 71-7
military discipline **58,** 75, 101, 105
extradition and **87,** 177
freedom of expression **58,** 87-90, **73,** 395-6
homosexuality **112,** 371-412
humanitarian law, offences against
evidence of **88,** 10-13
hearsay **104,** 173 n. 4
jurisdiction. *See* jurisdiction, armed forces abroad; jurisdiction, visiting forces; State immunity, jurisdiction, acts of, armed forces; State immunity, jurisdiction, acts of, armed forces abroad; State immunity, jurisdiction, classification of act, armed forces, acts concerning
law governing **47,** 234
liberty of person, deprivation and **58,** 71-3, 74-7
military discipline **58,** 53-60, 71, 72, 73-4, 87, 90, 101, **73,** 395, 557-64, **78,** 231-3, 243-5, 259-62, 279-85
arrest under **58,** 53-60, 71, 73-4, 94-5
civilian life and **58,** 72, 87, 90, 101
European Convention on Human Rights (1950) and **58,** 75, 101, 105
military service, law relating to
evasion, right to asylum and **88,** 5-36
political objective **88,** 8-9
sovereignty and **88,** 8-9
private property
responsibility for
damage to **54,** 244-6
occupation of **54,** 244-6
public order/public policy/*ordre public* and **58,** 88-9
State agency **101,** 558-61
State responsibility. *See* State responsibility for acts and omissions of, armed forces
transfer of power of command to head of Government **106,** 349
uniform, relevance **88,** 187-8
visiting forces
definition **85,** 162-3, 179
diplomatic protection **100,** 436
international law, relevance **85,** 157-8, 164, 169
uncertainty **85,** 157
Armenian massacres in Turkey, representations **37,** 83
armistice 48, 485, **67,** 628
occupation following **40,** 429-34

armistice (*cont.*)
parties' intention **67,** 628
termination of war distinguished **83,** 165-6
armistice agreement
Hungary **44,** 310
Italy **40,** 468-70
Korea **41,** 19
prerogative and **83,** 160
rights, effect on **80,** 263-4
territory, acquisition under **114,** 46, 58
arms dealing. *See also* war
armed conflict, in case of **91,** 253-4
contract
brokerage agreement **91,** 255
enforceability **91,** 252, 254
legality **91,** 253-5
war, effect **91,** 253-5
foreign relations, refusal to issue export licence and **101,** 423-6
arms trade, Brussels Conference (1890) **47,** 27-8
arrest
acquiescence, relevance **61,** 212-13, 215
definition **111,** 471-3
deserter
consular function, whether **42,** 233-4
from foreign forces outside territory **85,** 156-81
extradition. *See* extradition, arrest; extradition, arrest warrant
on foreign soil **68,** 8-14, 31, 45, **69,** 150-8, **85,** 158, 161, 163-5
burden of proof **68,** 8-9
as fraudulent deprivation of liberty **68,** 10
jurisdiction following **61,** 192, 194-202, 210-11, **68,** 9-14
terrorist suspects **69,** 157-8
illegal. *See* lawfulness, requirements *below*; forcible abduction/unlawful arrest
international law violation **68,** 8-14
jurisdiction and **57,** 318-25, **61,** 192, 194-7, 198, 210-11. *See also* forcible abduction/unlawful arrest, jurisdiction, effect on
unlawful, State practice **68,** 12-13
lawfulness, requirements. *See also* forcible abduction/unlawful arrest
accused to be informed of charges **111,** 480-1
non-disclosure of indictment, relevance **111,** 481-3
accused to be informed of rights **111,** 480-1
arrest warrant, entitlement to copy **111,** 483
authorization **69,** 152-3, 155-6, **77,** 333-5, 359-76
persons in transit **73,** 663, **82,** 359-75
protest, relevance **61,** 212-13, 215
use of armed forces **82,** 338-43, **88,** 182-4
in international waters **82,** 338
non-regulatory, proscriptive or compulsory **82,** 342-3
use of military aircraft to transport **82,** 341
provisional **58,** 74-6
ships. *See* ships, arrest; ships, State-owned, immunity, arrest attachment
torture and **61,** 484
'artisanal fishing' 119, 450-3
FAO Fisheries Infrastructure Development Project Report (1995) **119,** 451

Aruba Trough 83, 101 n. 60
Asia, State immunity, jurisdiction **64,** 647-8
Asian Development Bank. *See also* World Bank Group
Administrative Order
No 2.08 **96,** 248
No 2.10 **96,** 246
fixed-term appointment, decision not to convert, review of **96,** 246
performance appraisal **96,** 235-7
Personnel Handbook for Professional Staff, s 5.1 **96,** 236
Personnel Policy Statement (1990) **96,** 236
termination of employment
reasons, unsatisfactory performance **96,** 237
security of tenure **96,** 248-9
Asian Development Bank Administrative Tribunal
admissibility, delay in adopting Rules of Procedure and **96,** 235, 246-7
applicable law
constituent instrument
Bank **96,** 235
Tribunal **96,** 235
general principles of law
'common law' of international organizations **96,** 235
decisions of international and administrative tribunals **96,** 235, 250
employment contract **96,** 235
Personnel Handbook **96,** 235
Staff Rules and Regulations **96,** 235
World Bank Administrative Tribunal, decisions of **96,** 250
costs and expenses **96,** 251
itemization, need for **96,** 251
legal **96,** 251
secretarial **96,** 251
jurisdiction
compétence de la compétence **96,** 238
judicial review, limitations **96,** 237-8
non-observance of terms of employment contract or terms of appointment **96,** 234
assassination
as act of State **63,** 388-9, **101,** 527-32
of ambassador/head of mission **63,** 380-90
as extraditable offence **86,** 180
of Head of State, attempted **72,** 615-17
as inhuman or degrading treatment **99,** 9-10
as political offence **63,** 388-9, **72,** 615-17, **107,** 572
State immunity, jurisdiction **63,** 388-9, **81,** 63, 378-9, 554, **101,** 527-32
assets
attachment. *See* attachment; State immunity, execution /attachment
corporation, of, shareholders' ownership of **82,** 133-4
debt, attachment in case of, existence of corporeal or incorporeal asset, need for **82,** 72
asylum 48, 149, **62,** 278-9, **69,** 275, **71,** 497-8, 501-2, 533, **72,** 582-5, 624, 643, **73,** 608-12, 615-17, 628-34, **74,** 395-6, 402-3, 410-11, 432, 571, **79,** 612-40, 645-64, **80,** 674-82, **87,** 472, 474 n. 20, 479-80, 488. *See also* deportation withhold/bar; excludability of alien; exclusion of alien; expulsion of alien; extradition, political offence; refugees; refugees, non-refoulement
anti-terrorist conventions, effect **80,** 679-80
burden of proof **79,** 615 n. 3, 620, 623, 628 n. 32, 633, 638, **95,** 538, 572

asylum (*cont.*)
concealment of identity **36,** 75-6, 306
conditions **72,** 583-5, **79,** 508 n. 11, **87,** 475
country of first refuge, relevance **88,** 16
customary international law and **87,** 499, **95,** 566-7
deportation and **73,** 615-16, 628-34
political persecution **73,** 615-16
deportation withhold/bar, compelling reasons of national security and **73,** 615-16, 628-34
deportation withhold/bar distinguished **79,** 616 n. 6, **87,** 475-7, **95,** 549, 558-9, 574, 581, 582 n. 11
determination
executive **79,** 657
judicial review **79,** 657
discretionary **79,** 612, 615, 623, 635, 668, **118,** 600
in case of country in breach of European Convention on Human Rights (1950) **118,** 600-1
duty to offer **83,** 388-9
internal armed conflict, flight from
customary international law **95,** 566-7
Geneva Convention on the Protection of Civilian Persons in Time of War (1949) **95,** 566-7
exclusion of application **72,** 645
extradition, offence committed within asylum State **40,** 212-14
fear of persecution **80,** 677, 680, 682
immunity from later prosecution **32,** 66, **36,** 12, 71-6, 305
imprecise term **87,** 475
international officials **83,** 288, 387-90
motivation for offence **80,** 676
possible impediments
acts contrary to purposes and principles of UN **80,** 681
hijacking of aircraft **80,** 676, 679-80
offence completed in asylum State **80,** 681
terrorist offence **80,** 674-82
prima facie case **88,** 9, 28, 30
standard of proof **88,** 28
procedure **79,** 616, 619-20, 624, 657, **88,** 16-17
refugees outside territory, interception on high seas, undertaking not to prosecute for illegal departure **95,** 581-98
refusal **79,** 280, **80,** 674-82
grounds, need to state **86,** 507
refusal, grounds
acts contrary to purposes and principles of UN **80,** 681
country of refuge, crime in **40,** 206
crime against humanity **80,** 679
crime against peace **80,** 681
crime committed in country of refuge **80,** 681
serious crime outside country of refuge **80,** 680
'serious non-political crime'. *See* refugees, 'serious non-political crime'
terrorist offences **80,** 676, 679-80
reprehensible conduct and **72,** 583
requirements **79,** 633 n. 2, 640 n. 8
right of **45,** 94, 95-6, **48,** 155-6, **53,** 533-6, **83,** 388, **86,** 506-7

illegal entry, subsequent to **86,** 507
late application **86,** 506-7
violation of norms relating to, procedure for determining **86,** 506
withhold of deportation/bar distinguished, likelihood of persecution, standard of proof **79,** 617-20, 623-41
Atlantic Charter (1942) 46, 485
freedom of the high seas **120,** 284-5
legally binding, whether **120,** 284-5
atrocities. *See* crimes against humanity; war crimes
attachment. *See also* jurisdiction, acquisition; State immunity, execution/attachment
blocking/freezing of assets as **63,** 427-9, 505, **81,** 646
deposed Head of State's **81,** 613-56
discretionary nature **63,** 307
grounds
arrest before judgment as alternative **63,** 277
burden of proof **63,** 308-10, 509
risk of removal of property from jurisdiction **63,** 277-8, 348
as interim measure **82,** 72
jurisdiction, as basis for **63,** 11, 63-6, 145-52, 215-27, 334-7, 347-50, 500, **64,** 185-6, 669-72, 675-83, 686, 691, 697-8, 710, 715-16, **65,** 172-3, 239-40, **66,** 9, 15, 170
post-judgment attachment distinguished **63,** 270, 307-8, 348-9, **92,** 402-3
requirements
defendant outwith the jurisdiction **63,** 277, 348
evidence ownership **64,** 680-1
impossibility of service within the jurisdiction **63,** 277, 278-9, 348
prima facie cause of action **64,** 697-8, 711
timely implementation **63,** 253-60, 410-11
audi alteram partem
'Anton Piller' order **89,** 281
general principle of law **38,** 386, 404-5, 414-17, **54,** 401, **120,** 317
ICJ proceedings **57,** 410, 585, **76,** 652, **97,** 60, **106,** 47
immigration proceedings **68,** 171-3, **69,** 212-13, **70,** 369-72, **71,** 454, 480, 490, **87,** 128
international official
appeal proceedings **69,** 356
termination of employment **38,** 386, 404-5, 414-17, **40,** 416, 418, **42,** 303, 315, 317, 319, **47,** 377-82
transfer **43,** 267
natural justice **53,** 370-2, **68,** 162-73, **69,** 213, **70,** 265-6, 369-72, **71,** 454, 480, 490
refusal to recognize jurisdiction and **53,** 61, **97,** 60
UNHRC **70,** 265-6, **79,** 177
Yugoslavia, International Criminal Tribunal for the Former (ICTY), appeal, admissibility **110,** 682-4
Austin, de facto governments **39,** 318
Australia
Aboriginal Land Fund Commission **68,** 184-5, 190-3, 213, 224, 236-7, 260-5
legal status **68,** 190-1, 237, 263-5
aboriginals in. *See also* Murray Islands
class/representative action, admissibility **118,** 332, 365
clearances **120,** 360
compensation
breach of fiduciary and trust obligations **118,** 327, 335
dispossession **118,** 327, 335

Australia (*cont.*)
trespass **118,** 327, 335
unlawful alienation **118,** 327, 335
criminal law, right to own **112,** 659-61
Croker Island (Northern Territory), territorial sea, rights in **125,** 327-468
as dependent domestic nation **118,** 330
discrimination against **68,** 193-5, 240, 242-3, 381, 464
fiduciary duty in respect of **112,** 592-8, 622-7, 634, **118,** 331-4
aboriginal interest in land as basis **118,** 364-5
Canadian and US experience, relevance **118,** 365
failure to define **118,** 332-3, 361-2
ICJ Advisory Opinion, requirement to seek **118,** 355, 366-9
legislation authorizing alienation of lands as breach **118,** 333-4, 335, **120,** 415
liability of Commonwealth for acts preceding its establishment **118,** 365
forcible transfer of children **120,** 358-9
as free and independent people **118,** 330
genocide, treatment amounting to **120,** 358-61
denial of access to land **120,** 360
intent, need for **120,** 360-1
jurisdiction over **73,** 152, 156-7, **86,** 210-14
land trust **112,** 640-57
benefit of aboriginals, for **112,** 647-53
consent, need for **112,** 641
correspondence with incidents of native title, need for **112,** 649
lawfulness **112,** 656
racial discrimination, whether **112,** 641
'special measure' under International Convention on the Elimination of All Forms of Racial Discrimination (1965) **112,** 641, 654-5, 656
legislation relating to. *See* law of, Aboriginal Land Rights (Northern Territory), Queensland, Queensland Coast Islands Declaratory Act 1985, Native Title Act 1993 *and* Western Australia, Land (Titles and Traditional Usage) Act 1993 *below*
protection of society and heritage **68,** 285-6, 362-3, 380-2, 425, 440-1, 464-6, 477, 506
protection of access to spiritual places **125,** 439-40
State's duty **118,** 334, **125,** 431
as a race **68,** 437-9, 465
reservation of land **112,** 509-11, 581-6
social and political organization, existence **112,** 488-90, 538-9
Milirrpum **112,** 488-9, 586-8
sovereignty **118,** 328-30
title to land. *See* native title *below*
Wiradjuri **118,** 323-8
abuse of power, executive **118,** 313-14
abuse of process **91,** 11
choice of law and **91,** 152-3
improper purpose **118,** 325, 336-7
stay of proceedings and **118,** 409-10, 414, 418-19
access to courts, reasonable cause of action, need for **118,** 345-8, 362-4
act of State, choice of law rules and **87,** 186
admiralty jurisdiction **69,** 163
territorial sea and **125,** 394-6
aliens **90,** 23, 25-6. *See also* deportation; extradition; immigrants *and* refugees *below*

admission, natural justice **90,** 20, 25
admission as legal practitioners **55,** 492
definition **55,** 490
entry permit **90,** 22
discretionary power **90,** 25-7, 159
refugee status, relevance **90,** 27-8, 155, 160
expulsion **73,** 628-34
permanent residence status **90,** 22
Integrated Departmental Instructions Manual **104,** 489-90
removal, airlines, obligation **90,** 26
sovereign right to refuse entry **90,** 25-6
allegiance
jurisdiction and **92,** 630-2
nationality and **92,** 631
Queen, owed to **92,** 635
residence and **92,** 631-2
sovereign independence of Australia, effect on **92,** 633-5
ambassador/head of mission
State immunity, jurisdiction **104,** 412
status
agent of sending State **104,** 412
diplomatic agent **104,** 413
State agency/State-owned corporation/State entity **104,** 412
applicable law
acts by belligerents in time of war **91,** 23
contemporary legal system of place of trial **91,** 26, 28
law of place where act committed **91,** 26-7
arbitral tribunal, 'error of law' and **117,** 578
English law, relevance **125,** 429-33
intertemporal law, changed values, effect on law to be applied **112,** 480-1, 546-7
retroactive nature of legislation **91,** 93-4
treaty interpretation, international law **104,** 432, 447
war crimes
international law **91,** 47-8
municipal law **91,** 45, 47, 92-3, 94-6
within State **91,** 23, 27
arbitral award, appeal
agreement to exclude **117,** 586-7
error of law
in case of conflicting evidence **117,** 585-93
determination and application of foreign law as fact **117,** 578-84, 589-92
error of foreign law, jurisdiction **117,** 585-93
arbitral tribunal, applicable law, 'error of law' and **117,** 578
armed forces, immunity **52,** 333-5
Australian Federal Police. *See also* law of, Federal Police Act 1979 *below*
Commissioner, liability for acts of **111,** 662-4
legal personality **111,** 628-9
part of government, whether **111,** 646-53, 670-1
State immunity, entitlement **111,** 646-53, 664-71
bankruptcy, sequestration order, annulment **87,** 172-6
bill of attainder. *See* legislation, bill of attainder *below*
boundaries
acquiescence in **91,** 202-4

Australia (*cont.*)
fixing of
colonial ministers, by **91,** 198-203
definition distinguished **91,** 198-202
Imperial legislation **73,** 195-7, 210-11, 222-3
internal **86,** 185-208. *See also* Queensland, boundaries, establishment *below*; South Australia, internal waters, delimitation *and* historic boundaries *below*
alteration **86,** 187, 200, 202-3
Commonwealth Constitution as applicable law **86,** 187
letters patent, effectiveness **86,** 188-9
low-water mark **90,** 242-4
prerogative power **86,** 190-2, 198, 200
New South Wales–Victoria **91,** 190-204
River Murray as **91,** 190-204
permanent nature **91,** 197
rivers as **91,** 190-204. *See also* rivers *below*
variable nature **91,** 196-7
broadcasting
Australian Content Standard. *See also* New Zealand, Closer Economic Relations Trade Agreement (1983)/Trade in Services Protocol (1989) *below*
compatibility with treaty obligations **115,** 386-415
transmission quota as **115,** 391
programme content **115,** 393-5
burden of proof
native title **118,** 336, **125,** 431-2
war crimes **91,** 11, 68-9, 103-4, 134
child care, diplomatic immunity and **118,** 305
child rights
common law, best interests of child **104,** 485-6
standing, parent **104,** 474-5
UN Convention on the Rights of the Child (1989)
'action concerning children' **104,** 472-3, 475-6, 483-4, 498-9
implementing legislation, need for **104,** 470-1, 480
citizens, British subjects **69,** 161-3
civil rights and obligations, property, use of **68,** 262-3
claim, sampling methodology **109,** 75
Cocos (Keeling) Islands
Act of Self-Determination **118,** 318-20
Government's right to acquire territory **118,** 312-21
comity
injunction and **118,** 415
stay of proceedings **118,** 413-14
common law
constitution, conformity with **125,** 414
fundamental rights **118,** 374
human/fundamental rights and **125,** 441-2
jurisdiction and, local and transitory actions distinguished **125,** 389-94
private international law and **125,** 396-8
source, treaty **104,** 431, 472, 494
statutory law, conformity with **125,** 414
territorial sea, applicability in **125,** 334-42, 365-7, 380-407
common law offence **120,** 372, 399-405
common purpose **124,** 1103 n. 290

Commonwealth
Constitution. *See* Constitution *below*
inherent power **68,** 316-17, 364, 382, 402-3, 446-7, 507-8
international personality **68,** 200-1, 237-8, 252
legislative powers **90,** 80-9
courts and **90,** 88, 91
criteria **90,** 81-2, 84-9
Commonwealth executive, Cabinet as **90,** 48
constituent states. *See also* foreign relations *below and individual States*
Commonwealth legislation
primacy **90,** 137
right to challenge **68,** 186
constitutional balance **90,** 81
Crown lands **68,** 407-13, 471-2
executive functions, Federal interference **68,** 345-7, 407-13, 471-2
extraterritorial legislation **51,** 39, **69,** 58, 113-21, 124-5, **70,** 58-60, 66-8, 89-90, 101
Federal discrimination **68,** 336, 345-7, 411-13, 471-2
fishery regulation **69,** 34, 36-7, 40, 54-5, 58, 110-26
internal waters, delimitation, constituent instruments, by reference to **69,** 35-6, 41, 46-53, 57, 59-63, 68-71, 73
international personality **68,** 238
legislation
federal invalidation of **68,** 482-3, 509
federal legislation, inconsistency **69,** 36, 39-40, 55, 58, 71, 118, **70,** 54-101
federal legislation, interaction **86,** 174-5
functions **68,** 211, 219, 227, 241, 249, 310, 395-6, 410-13
'laws for peace, good order and good government' **70,** 58-60, 67, 90
League seas, application to **69,** 55, 58
offshore waters, application to **69,** 117-20
validity **69,** 115-19
legislative powers **51,** 39-80, 89-217
power to bind federal government **90,** 49-50
rights **51,** 24
sovereignty. *See* sovereignty *below*
status **51,** 216
United Kingdom dominions **69,** 14
territorial sea
entitlement **69,** 39-41, 58, 79, 111, **70,** 58, 66, 89
jurisdiction **70,** 60, 67-8, **90,** 242, **125,** 351-6
transfer of control of territory to federal authorities **90,** 78-9
United Kingdom legislation, applicability **69,** 13-15, 17-23
following Statute of Westminster Adoption Act 1942 **69,** 13, 21
Merchant Shipping Act 1958 **69,** 13-15, 17-23
waste lands. *See* Crown lands *above*
water rights **68,** 326, 357-8, 382, 442-5
Constitution **85,** 161
Chapter II **111,** 650
Chapter III **87,** 182, 184, **91,** 75-96, 138-42, 148, 164-8, **101,** 266-8. *See also* judicial power, usurpation *and* legislation, retroactive *below*
retroactive legislation and **91,** 82-3
interpretation **68,** 195-6, 215-16, 230, 309-10, 334-6, 345-7, 397-8, 410-13, 417-19, 490, **118,** 377
justiciability **87,** 184

Australia (*cont.*)
s 51 **118,** 375, 377, 378-9
reserved State powers and **68,** 370
s 51(vi) **91,** 28
s 51(x) (fisheries power) **68,** 284, 319-26, 351-7, 379-80, 399-401, 434-7, 460-3, 500-4, **69,** 39, 54, 73-4, 79, **70,** 58, **101,** 170, 173-4
non-trading activities and **68,** 325-6, 352-5, 380, 399-400, 435-7, 460-3, 502-4
s 51(xxvi) (racial power) **112,** 702-6, 724
scope **68,** 193-5, 211, 213-15, 242, 244-5, 258-9, 285, 318-19, 364, 380-2, 401-2, 437-41, 463-7, 504-7
s 51(xxvii) **91,** 30
s 51(xxix) (external affairs power) **70,** 95, 99, **90,** 61, 73-4, 79, 80-1, 82-3, 91, 101, 103, 109, 127-9, 132, 137, **91,** 11-14, 28-34, 70-5, 146, 161-2, **101,** 173-4, 452-66, **112,** 724-5. *See also* external affairs power *below*
constitutional limitations **68,** 198, 217, 220, 232-3, 240, 307, 309, 315, 346, 397-8, 448, 491-2
independence of other provisions **68,** 198, 252, 307
scope **68,** 195-212, 215-42, 245-58, 281, 283, 290, 306-16, 334-9, 343-7, 371-8, 385-99, 413-17, 419, 427-34, 447-60, 485-500
s 51(xxxi) (just terms) **70,** 68, **112,** 548, **118,** 314, 317
scope **68,** 350-1, 382, 441-2, 472-81, **118,** 314
s 51(xxxix) **91,** 26, 28, 32, 74, 86-8, 98-101, 106, 109, 138-9, 162-3
s 53 (charge or burden on people) **112,** 721
s 61 **87,** 176, 183, 184, 187, 188, **111,** 650-1
s 62 **111,** 650
s 64 **111,** 650
s 67 **111,** 650
s 71. *See* Chapter III *above*
s 75 **85,** 180, **87,** 185, 187, **118,** 344
s 75(i) (matters arising under a treaty) **101,** 262-5
s 75(ii) (matters affecting consuls and representatives of other countries) **101,** 265
s 75(iii) (Commonwealth as party) **101,** 265-6, **118,** 355
s 75(iv) **92,** 624, 625
s 75(v) **90,** 104
s 76 **118,** 344
s 76(i) **92,** 626
s 76(iv) **92,** 624
s 77 **100,** 483
s 100 **68,** 326, 357-8, 364, 382, 442-5
s 107 (legislative powers of States) **112,** 418-19, 706
s 109 (concurrent legislation, conflict) **68,** 364, 406, 448, 483, **69,** 55, 118, **70,** 61, **112,** 418-19, 433, 667, 694-5, 706-9
s 116 **118,** 379
s 122 **118,** 314, 317, 375-7, 378-9
s 128 **118,** 378
s 517(xxiv) **87,** 163-4
consular access, right to, routine questioning at airport **107,** 81
consular agent
functions, safeguarding interests of minors **107,** 102-4
status as, evidence of, executive certificate **107,** 102
consular immunity, jurisdiction, tort **107,** 102
consular privileges and immunities

honorary consul **107,** 102-4
State immunity and, distinction **104,** 412-13
continental shelf
legislative power, federal **91,** 210
seabed, as part of territory **91,** 209-10
waters above, as part of territory **91,** 209-10
corporation, status, quasi-corporation **77,** 85
costs, frivolous proceedings **118,** 370-1
courts, municipal. *See also* judicial power *below*
Chapter III courts **91,** 14
federal jurisdiction **85,** 180
foreign affairs and **87,** 175. *See also* justiciability, foreign relations *below*
jurisdiction, determined by Constitution **118,** 369-70
standing **86,** 187, 205, **87,** 185
Constitution, interpretation of and **87,** 184, 187-8
hypothetical question **118,** 343-4, 365-6
requirements, infringement of personal rights **118,** 344
Crown rights and obligations, devolution **78,** 438
customary international law
fishing zones, 200-mile limit **101,** 173
genocide **118,** 330-1, 379, **120,** 361
incorporation into municipal law **102,** 201
developing international law and **101,** 403, 405, **108,** 535-6
jus cogens and **120,** 371-3, 391-405
transformation doctrine compared **120,** 362-5, 378-91
Darnley Island, Queensland, whether part of **86,** 185-208
defence power **91,** 14, 15-16, 64-5, 138, 148. *See also* external affairs power *below*
proportionality and **91,** 65
purposive nature **91,** 148
deportation **86,** 216-28, **90,** 2-8
extradition distinguished **86,** 217, 226
military service and **86,** 223
prohibited non-citizen **86,** 216-18, 226-8
deserter
detention
military authorities of foreign country, by **85,** 158, 164
permanent resident, of **85,** 158-9, 178
place of desertion, relevance **85,** 156-7, 166-8
prerogative matter, whether **85,** 164, 165-6, 168-71, 177-8
treaty obligation, whether **85,** 164-5
visiting forces, limited to, whether **85,** 156-81
extraditable offence **85,** 165
diplomatic immunity, jurisdiction
appearance in stay proceedings **104,** 416-17
child custody dispute **118,** 304-5
common law **104,** 414-16
equitable interest **118,** 307-8
immunity, execution as independent issue **118,** 308-9
matrimonial jurisdiction **118,** 302-4
declaration of status as divorced person **118,** 304
procedural bar **118,** 309-10
stay of proceedings **118,** 309-10
diplomatic mission

Australia (*cont.*)
diplomatic premises distinguished **101,** 241
functions/'diplomatic activity', joint control of funds for education institution **104,** 413-17
diplomatic premises
demonstration outside embassy, duty to prevent **101,** 227-35, 242-5, 254, 257
duties of host government
freedom of expression and **101,** 243-54, 256, 257
to protect **101,** 207-8, 227
to refrain from entry **101,** 207
inviolability
customary international law **101,** 207
office and residence distinguished **101,** 226
diplomatic privileges and immunities
commercial activity, purchase of property by diplomat for renting **118,** 305-6
State immunity and, distinction **104,** 412-13, 414-17
waiver, requirements, consent of sending State **118,** 301
discovery and settlement of **73,** 138, 141, 144-9, 151-3, 156-63
domicile, married women **118,** 302
double criminality **87,** 150-1, 152-8, **114,** 388
legality in place of offence, relevance **101,** 178-80
double jeopardy, federal and state laws, interrelationship **91,** 74, 82
eminent domain/*dominium eminens*, just compensation and **118,** 317
environment **90,** 34-58, 118-37. *See also* UNESCO Protection of the World Cultural and Natural Heritage Convention (1972) *below*
definition **90,** 122-3
social and economic aspects **90,** 64, 123-5
equitable remedies, injunction **118,** 408, 410-12
estoppel, agreement not to bring court proceedings **118,** 395, 400, 406-7, 410-11
evidence
taking at request of foreign State **86,** 173-4
conformity with local practice, need for **86,** 173-4
extradition distinguished **86,** 181
transcript of evidence, availability **86,** 174, 181
witnesses, compellability **118,** 351-2
executive abuse **118,** 313-14
executive certificate/statement
conclusiveness **87,** 182-3
State immunity, jurisdiction, **104,** 143 n. 7, **118,** 297
state of war **87,** 183
territory, status of **87,** 183
as to facts **114,** 399-401
diplomatic status **118,** 300
judicial review **87,** 183
neutrality **87,** 183
recognition
governments **87,** 183
States **87,** 183
recognition of diplomatic status **73,** 680-2
responsibility for foreign relations **114,** 399-401
executive discretion **86,** 221-2
effect of improper purpose **86,** 228
executive power **55,** 27-8, **87,** 183

exclusive nature **87,** 183
foreign relations **87,** 183
excess of power **87,** 187
expropriation/nationalization
Commonwealth powers **118,** 315
compensation, need for **112,** 423, 554, 561, 634, 642, 715-16, **118,** 319
contract, breach of **118,** 316-17
executive and legislative powers distinguished **118,** 314-15
freedom of movement and **118,** 321
procedure **118,** 317
public interest, legitimate social objective **118,** 317, 318-21
public purpose **62,** 166, 183-5, 194, **118,** 312-21
requirements, compatibility with law **112,** 423, **118,** 315
expropriation/nationalization, compensation, need for, extinction of native title **112,** 693-4, 715-16
external affairs power **70,** 59, 95, 99, **87,** 163-4, **91,** 11-14, 161-4. *See also* defence power *above*; foreign relations *and* legislation, international obligation or concern *below*
abuse **68,** 204-6, 212, 220, 231-2, 252, 309-10, 414-16
acts having effect abroad **91,** 164
'colourable treaty' doctrine **87,** 163-4
crime committed abroad by non-national **91,** 31-4
customary international law obligation **120,** 362
defence power compared **68,** 205, 221, 247-8, 310-11, 428
domestic effect **91,** 13, 100-1, 115
expansion **68,** 230-1, 253-4, 309-10, 334, 490-1
extraterritoriality **91,** 11-14, 70-5, 104, **104,** 454-6, **120,** 361-2
competence **91,** 96-9
need for, whether **91,** 74
fisheries outside territorial sea **101,** 173-4
foreign relations **91,** 34-65. *See also* legislation, international obligation or concern *below*
limitations on
constitutional **68,** 198-9, 204, 217, 227, 241, 249-52, 309-10, 331-9, 386-7, 395-6, 410-13, 448, 490-2
international law, relevance **91,** 30, **104,** 453-66
nexus, need for **91,** 12, 13-14, 28-32, 75, 97, 98, 113-14, 144, 162
purpose **68,** 491, **91,** 28, 38
responsibility for determining whether, Parliament **91,** 13-14, 31-2
scope **68,** 195-212, 215-42, 245-58, 281, 283, 290, 306-16, 329-39, 371-8, 385-99, 413-17, 419, 427-34, 447-60, 485-500
sovereignty and **91,** 72-3, 97-8, 101
Statute of Westminster Adoption Act 1942, effect **91,** 161-2
treaty obligations, implementation **68,** 196-212, 215-42, 245-58, 307-16, 329-33, 337-9, 372, 386-96, 413-17, 419, 427-30, 449-60, 485-500
international concern, need for **68,** 394, 494-7
validity, competence to determine **91,** 99-100, 113
extraditable offence
definition **87,** 147, 148, **101,** 177-8, 183
desertion **85,** 165
equivalent act or omission **87,** 148
jurisdictional elements **87,** 150, 152
extradition
appeal **87,** 161

Australia (*cont.*)
- composite offence **87,** 150, 157
- continuing criminal enterprise **87,** 145-53, 158, **101,** 181-3
- deportation distinguished **86,** 217, 226
- disguised **86,** 216-17, 219-29
- dissatisfaction of foreign government, right of individual to complain **87,** 189
- double criminality. *See* double criminality *above*
- evidence **87,** 148
  - standard **101,** 184-6, 187-90
- executive power **55,** 35, **87,** 168, 176, 188-9, 191
- extradition country **114,** 388-9
- foreign relations, matter of **87,** 164
- fugitive's guilt, relevance **87,** 167
- judicial review **87,** 146, 161, 168-9
- local criminality **87,** 157
- military duty, breach of and **87,** 177
- motivation of requested State **86,** 224-8
- municipal legislation, undertaking to apply in absence of treaty **87,** 176
- political offence. *See* political offence *below*
- prerogative power **77,** 335
- procedure **87,** 146, 161-2
  - defects **87,** 167-9
  - evidence of alleged crime, need for **86,** 218
  - warrant **86,** 218
- reciprocity **87,** 164-6
- 'rendition' distinguished **101,** 287, 293
- speciality **87,** 177-8, 189-90, **114,** 388
  - offences committed after extradition **87,** 190
  - previous conviction, detention for **101,** 289-90
  - reason for rule **87,** 190
  - treaty rule **101,** 286
- statutory basis **85,** 159-60
  - need for **87,** 163, **114,** 388
- USA, to **87,** 159-66

extradition agreement
- informal understanding or arrangement **101,** 283-4, 286-7, 293
- need for **87,** 146-7, 148, 151, 153

extraterritorial legislation
- Native Title Act 1993 **125,** 380-2
- states **51,** 39, **69,** 37, 55, 58, 110-26, **70,** 58-60, 66-8, 89-90, 101

fair hearing **90,** 55-6
- legal representation **118,** 354-5
- natural justice **90,** 56

federal State, Head of State, immunity, jurisdiction **118,** 294-7

fishing zones
- overlapping
  - Australia–Indonesia Provisional Fisheries Arrangement (1981) **101,** 167-9
  - legislative powers **101,** 172-4

foreign law
- as fact **117,** 575-8, 581-2, 587
- interpretation **117,** 575
- Queensland, English law as **117,** 583

foreign relations. *See also* external affairs power *above*
defence distinguished **90,** 95-6
interstate trade **90,** 96
justiciability **90,** 54
responsibility for **87,** 163-4, **118,** 366-70
treaty implementation. *See* treaties, implementation *below*
Foreign States Immunities Act 1985
s 3(1) ('agent or instrumentality') **104,** 412
s 7(1) (transaction prior to act) **101,** 201, **104,** 412
s 9 (general immunity) **104,** 412
s 11 (commercial exception) **104,** 412
s 22 ('agent or instrumentality') **104,** 412
forum [non] conveniens
commencement of proceedings, relative timing and **118,** 399-400
concurrent jurisdiction and **118,** 394
place of conduct as determining factor **118,** 397-9
stay of proceedings and **118,** 415-18
freedom of expression, constitutional right **101,** 251-2
freedom of movement, expropriation and **118,** 321
freedom of navigation
freedom to fish distinguished **125,** 425
territorial sea, common law **125,** 423-5
fundamental rights, common law **118,** 374
GATT Anti-Dumping Implementation Code (1980). *See also* General Agreement on Tariffs and Trade (GATT) (1947) *below*
obligations of confidentiality
'disclosure pursuant to a narrowly drawn protective order' **107,** 93-8
disclosure to accountant **107,** 97-8
disclosure to company lawyer **107,** 97
disclosure to employee **107,** 96
public interest **107,** 93-8
undertaking of confidentiality, terms **107,** 98-9
General Agreement on Tariffs and Trade (GATT) (1947). *See also* GATT Anti-Dumping Implementation Code (1980) *above*
countervailing duties, right to impose **107,** 107-21
individual **107,** 112-13
subsidy
financial burden borne directly or indirectly by government or public body **107,** 112-20
Uruguay Round **107,** 121
genocide
classification as
failure to list site under World Heritage Convention (1972) **120,** 416
failure to list site on World Heritage List **120,** 416
forcible removal of aboriginal children **118,** 372-9
native title, extinction **120,** 357, 374-5, 405-10
customary international law **118,** 330-1, 379, **120,** 361-5
jurisdiction
civil **120,** 366
universal **120,** 361-2, 376, 391-405
offence under Australian law, whether **120,** 361-6, 373, 405
Genocide Convention (1948)

Australia (*cont.*)
applicability, acts committed prior to coming into force of Convention **118,** 330, 372-9
'genocide'
cultural genocide **118,** 361, 374, **120,** 409
'intent to destroy in whole or in part' **118,** 372-3, 376
municipal law and, incorporation, need for **118,** 330, 373, **120,** 377
as part of municipal law **118,** 360-1, 373, 376, 379
ratification **118,** 360, 372, 376, **120,** 377, 391
Governor-General
role **87,** 190-1
extradition **87,** 191
habeas corpus **85,** 159-60, 165-6
abrogation of right **85,** 160, 161
Head of State, immunity, jurisdiction, waiver
counterclaim as **118,** 297-8
extending to execution, whether **118,** 298
High Court Rules
O 26
r 18 **118,** 345-6
r 18(1) **118,** 344
r 18(2) **118,** 344, 346
r 19 **118,** 346, 355
O 58, r 4(3) **118,** 341-2
human rights
implementation, national discretion **104,** 446
incorporation into municipal law **101,** 246-52, **104,** 440, 486
Human Rights Commission Act 1981 **101,** 246-7
jus cogens **104,** 486
State obligation **104,** 485
waiver **104,** 440
immigrants. *See also* aliens *above*
entry permit
compassionate or humanitarian grounds **85,** 185, 188-9, 195-201
discretionary **85,** 185, 199
failure to make proper application for entry, relevance **85,** 202
illegal **85,** 185, 196-7
status **85,** 185-6
Regularization of Status Program **85,** 185
individual in international law, rights **87,** 184
injunction
comity and **118,** 415
equitable remedy, whether **118,** 408, 410-12
stay of proceedings distinguished **118,** 408-9, 414-15
innocent passage
activities prejudicing 'innocence' **125,** 421
exclusion of limited areas **125,** 421-2
statutory provision **125,** 489-90
International Covenant on Civil and Political Rights (ICCPR) (1966)
appeal, right of **104,** 424, 426-36
application for special leave to appeal, sufficiency **104,** 432-6
customary international law **104,** 432
implementing legislation, need for **101,** 247-50, **104,** 428-30

accession to First Optional Protocol, relevance **104,** 430
scheduling to Act, effect **104,** 430
legislation, as aid to interpretation **104,** 430-1
remedies, discretionary where Covenant not part of municipal law **104,** 436-40
waiver of rights **104,** 445-6
international law **90,** 129, **91,** 134-5
application by national courts **91,** 62-3, 134-5
compliance, public interest considerations **107,** 93-8
direct applicability **85,** 157-8
incorporation into municipal law **90,** 28
legislation, interpretation and **91,** 132-8
municipal law and
compatibility, presumption of **90,** 129, 215
harmonization, desirability **69,** 71-2
visiting forces **85,** 157-8
visiting warship and aircraft **85,** 180-1
judge, disqualification
delay in raising **118,** 349-50
for lack of impartiality, 'reasonable man' test **121,** 334
judicial notice, international events **87,** 182
judicial power **91,** 14-21, 76-7, 138-9. *See also* courts *above*
application of existing law **91,** 15
ascertainment of rights and liabilities under law **91,** 75-6, 77-8
critical date **91,** 77
retroactivity and. *See* legislation, retroactive *below*
judicial process, exercise in accordance with **91,** 153-5
law creation **91,** 15
legislation affecting substantive rights and interference with judicial process distinguished **91,** 16
retrospective law, application of **91,** 15-16, 155-7
usurpation **91,** 14-21, 76, 111, 155-7
judicial review
as appeal **85,** 192-3
entry of property on World Heritage List **90,** 122
executive certificate **87,** 183
extradition **87,** 146, 161, 168-9
grounds
abuse of discretion **117,** 628
denial of natural justice **91,** 186-7
error of law **91,** 187-8, **117,** 597, 600
improper exercise of power **85,** 194-5
insufficiency of evidence **85,** 192-4
international obligation, failure to construe correctly **91,** 188
unreasonableness **85,** 195, **90,** 56-7, 140, 142-4, 152, 158, 164-5, 177-80
limited purview **90,** 145, **117,** 606
powers of reviewing body **117,** 609, 623-5
remission to tribunal **117,** 608, 609, 623-5
prerogative and **90,** 34, 35, 50-5
refugees. *See* refugees, judicial review *below*
judicial role, development of law, indirect incorporation of customary international law/treaty distinguished **104,** 472, **120,** 372, 399-405
jurisdiction
aboriginals, over **86,** 210-14

Australia (*cont.*)
acts committed abroad, requirements
actionability if committed in forum State **118,** 406
unjustifiability by law of place where committed **118,** 406
allegiance, relevance **92,** 630-5
armed forces. *See* visiting forces *below*
child-care cases **92,** 620-35
Infants Custody and Settlement Act 1899 **92,** 623
prerogative jurisdiction **92,** 624-6, 630-2
presence of child within jurisdiction, necessary, whether **92,** 635
conspiracy, to commit crime abroad **101,** 180-1
definition **91,** 117
effective service and **92,** 627-8
extraterritorial
past conduct of persons at the time nationals **91,** 73, 162
past conduct of persons at the time non-nationals **91,** 14
federal/constituent State
maritime claims liability **107,** 133-6
matters affecting the Commonwealth **101,** 265-6
matters affecting foreign representatives **101,** 265
matters arising under a treaty **101,** 262-5
territorial **101,** 266-8
nationality, subsequent acquisition of nationality and **91,** 118
ouster **85,** 73-4
sovereignty and **91,** 39, 117, 119
submission to court **92,** 628-9
territorial
aboriginals, applicability **112,** 659-61
criminal **125,** 334-42
universal **91,** 117-21, **118,** 369-70
basis **91,** 119
critical date **91,** 144
external affairs power and **91,** 14, 39, 50-1
genocide **120,** 361-2, 375-6, 391-405
nexus, relevance **91,** 119
permissive nature **91,** 119
unlawfully brought within jurisdiction **87,** 180-1
circumvention of provisions of extradition treaty **87,** 181
visiting forces **85,** 163-4, 173-4
waiver **85,** 174
waiver
consent to entry of foreign forces **85,** 174
prerogative right **85,** 180
jus cogens/peremptory norm, human rights **104,** 486
justiciability **87,** 181-8. *See also* judicial review *above*
act of State **87,** 185-6
Constitution, interpretation **87,** 184
executive certificate. *See* executive certificate *above*
foreign relations **87,** 182, 185, **90,** 54, **118,** 366-9
treaty-making power **87,** 182, 183, **90,** 54-5
law of evidence and **87,** 182
nuclear weapons, deployment **118,** 346-8

political question. *See* political question doctrine *below*
prerogative act **90,** 34, 50
recognition **104,** 456
treaties. *See* treaties, justiciability *below*
law, function **118,** 352
law of. *See also under individual States*
Aboriginal Land Rights (Northern Territory) Act **90,** 39
Aboriginal Land Rights (Northern Territory) Act 1976 **112,** 643-57
discriminatory nature **112,** 653
furtherance of interests of native people **112,** 647-53
Racial Discrimination Act 1975, compatibility with **112,** 653-6
s 12(1)(a) **112,** 641
Acts Interpretation Act 1901 **87,** 190-1, **91,** 209
s 8(c) **107,** 128
s 13 **86,** 195
s 15 **85,** 157, 168, 175, 181
s 15B(4) ('coastal sea') **125,** 329, 370, 412, 450-1, 459-60
Administrative Appeals Tribunal Act 1975, s 45 **91,** 206, 210
Administrative Decisions (Effect of International Instruments) Act 1995 **104,** 707
Administrative Decisions (Judicial Review) Act 1977 **85,** 184, 188, 192-3, 195, 196, **87,** 146, 160, 161, 168, **90,** 2, 10
s 3 **90,** 23, 24, 154, 160, 161
s 3(1) **87,** 132, 135
s 3(2) **87,** 132
s 5 **90,** 6, 7, 20, 28, 56, 140, 142, 147, 152, 154, 158, 159, 160, 166, 168, 178, 180, **91,** 184, 185-6, 188, **107,** 107
s 5(1) **107,** 83
s 5(1)(e) **117,** 607
s 5(1)(f) **91,** 188, **117,** 597
s 5(1)(h) **91,** 177, **117,** 607
s 5(2)(a) **117,** 607
s 5(2)(b) **117,** 607
s 5(2)(g) **104,** 473, **117,** 607
s 5(3) **91,** 177
s 6 **90,** 24, 142, 146, 152, 154, 158, 159, 160, **91,** 184, 186
s 6(1)(a) **91,** 186
s 6(1)(f) **91,** 188
s 6(2) **91,** 185, 188
s 7 **90,** 160
s 13 **87,** 131-4, 135-6, 140, **90,** 16, 18, **91,** 173
s 16(1)(c) **117,** 598, 608
s 16(2) **91,** 187
s 22AA **117,** 608
s 116 **117,** 624
s 166BC(1) **117,** 608
s 176 **117,** 623
s 177 **117,** 623
Admiralty Act 1988
s 3(1) **100,** 477, **107,** 134-5
s 6 **107,** 127
s 9 **107,** 135
s 10 **107,** 135

Australia (*cont.*)
s 25 **100,** 477, **107,** 124, 133-6
s 25(1) **107,** 133-6
Air Navigation Act 1920 **90,** 253
Anti-Dumping Authority Act 1988 **107,** 107
Arbitration (Foreign Agreements and Awards) Act 1974, s 7 **118,** 633-4
Atomic Energy Act 1953 **90,** 49
Australia Act (UK) 1986 **91,** 12, 97
Australian Citizenship Act 1948 **92,** 624-5
Australian Courts Act 1828, s 11 **92,** 624, 633
Bankruptcy Act 1966 **86,** 210, 214, **87,** 172-3, 174-5, 176, 187, 190, 191, 192
Bankruptcy Rules **87,** 172, 191
Broadcasting Services Act 1992
s 4(1) **115,** 400
s 122(1)(a) **115,** 387
s 122(1)(b) **115,** 389-91, 405-7
ss 122(1)(b) and 160(d), conflict **115,** 389-414
s 128(1) **115,** 401
s 158 **115,** 386, 400
s 159 **115,** 386
s 160 **115,** 386-7, 389-91, 400-1
validity of act in breach of **115,** 412-14
Builders Labourers' Federation (Cancellation of Registration) Act 1986 **91,** 16
Coastal Waters (Northern Territory Powers) Act 1980 **125,** 352, 366-7, 453-4
s 5(a) **125,** 352, 403-4, 453, 459-60
s 6 **125,** 403-4
s 7 **125,** 404
Coastal Waters (Northern Territory Title) Act 1980 **125,** 352, 366-7, 453
purpose **125,** 404
s 4 **125,** 352, 404, 459-60
s 4(1) **125,** 454
s 4(2) **125,** 454
seabed rights, limitation to **125,** 404-5
Coastal Waters (State Powers) Act 1980 **125,** 352
Coastal Waters (State Title) Act 1980 **125,** 352
Commercial Arbitration Act 1990
'error of law' **117,** 578-84
extracts **117,** 573-5
s 38 **117,** 573, 578, 586, 590-3
s 38(1) **117,** 567, 592-3
s 38(2) **117,** 566
s 39 **117,** 573, 586
s 40 **117,** 574, 586-7
s 41 **117,** 576-7, 588-9
Commonwealth Electoral Act **118,** 378 n. 245
Constitution Alteration (Referendums) Act 1977 **118,** 378 nn. 246 and 247
Consular Privileges and Immunities Act 1972-3 **104,** 413
s 5 **107,** 102-4
s 5(1) **107,** 81
Crimes Act 1900 (ACT), s 477(1) **120,** 372
Crimes Act 1914 **87,** 173, 177, **91,** 19-20, 85, 164
s 70 **107,** 99
Crimes Act 1915 **91,** 19-21, 86

Crimes (Foreign Incursions and Recruitment) Act 1978 **91,** 164
Crimes (Internationally Protected Persons) Act 1976, s 8 **101,** 261, 262-5
Crimes (Taxation Offences) Act 1980 **87,** 173, 175, 176, 177, 178-81
Criminal Code, s 1.1 **120,** 372, 399-400
Customs Act 1901 **87,** 148
  amendment (Act 150 of 1995) **107,** 121
  s 269TB **107,** 107-21
Customs Administration Act 1985, s 16(2) **107,** 99
Customs Tariff (Anti-Dumping) Act 1975, s 8(2) **107,** 91
Defence Act 1903 **85,** 157, 160, 165, 174-5, 177, 181
Defence Acts Amendment Act 1981 **85,** 157, 160, 165, 174-5, 177, 181
Defence Forces Regulations **85,** 174
Defence (Visiting Forces) Act 1939 **85,** 157, 158, 160, 178
Defence (Visiting Forces) Act 1963
  Part II **85,** 156, 162, 173
  Part III **85,** 156-7, 160-5, 166-7, 169, 171-8
  s 5 **85,** 162, 179
  s 8 **85,** 157, 163-4, 167, 173-5, 179
  s 9 **85,** 173, 174
  s 13 **85,** 173
  s 16 **85,** 173
  s 17 **85,** 173
  s 18 **85,** 173
  s 19 **85,** 156-9, 160-1, 162, 166-8, 171, 175, 177, 178, 179, 181
  s 21 **85,** 158-9, 169, 173
Defence (Visiting Forces) Regulations **85,** 171
Diplomatic Privileges and Immunities Act 1967-73
  s 6 **104,** 413
  s 7 **101,** 205, 210, 211-13, 214-17, 219, 223, 232-4, **118,** 300-1
  s 14 **118,** 300
  s 15 **101,** 206, 211, 215, 218, 219, 233-4
Diplomatic Privileges and Immunities (Amendment) Regulations 1992, SR 7, validity **101,** 205-59
Director of Public Prosecutions Act 1983 **87,** 188-9
Domicile Act 1982
  s 6 **118,** 302
  s 8(1) **118,** 302
Environment Protection (Impact of Proposals) Act 1974 **90,** 119-20, 122, 123-5
Export Expansion Grants Act 1978
  s 3 **91,** 208
  s 4 **91,** 208
  s 13 **91,** 208
Export Market Development Grants Act 1974 **91,** 206
Extradition Act 1988
  codification of law **114,** 387-8
  compliance with treaty obligations **114,** 388
  s 5 **101,** 177, 181-3, 187, **120,** 391
  s 11(5) **101,** 184
  s 12(1) **114,** 388-9
  s 19(2) **101,** 178-9, 181-3, 187
Extradition (Commonwealth Countries) Act 1966 **101,** 283-93
  s 3 **101,** 286
  s 33 **101,** 286-9, 293

Australia (*cont.*)
Extradition (Foreign States) Act 1966 **86,** 173, 175, 176, 177, 178-81, 218, **87,** 145, 162-3
s 4 **87,** 147, 148, 150, 157
s 10(1) **87,** 146, 176
s 10(4) **87,** 164, 176
s 12 **87,** 147
s 15 **87,** 168
s 16(1) **87,** 160
s 17(6) **87,** 146, 147, 148, 153, 161
s 18 **87,** 161
s 31 **87,** 190
Schedule I **87,** 147
Extradition (Foreign States) Amendment Act 1985 **87,** 145
Extradition (Foreign States) Regulations (Statutory Rules 1962, No 47), *ultra vires,* whether **86,** 174-5
Extradition (United States of America) Regulations **87,** 145, 146
Family Law Act 1975
Regulation 16 **118,** 309-10
s 39 **118,** 310
s 39(3) **118,** 302
s 78 **118,** 307-8
s 79 **118,** 300, 302-4, 305-8
Federal Police Act 1979
s 8 **111,** 648, 650
s 13(1) **111,** 648
s 13(2) **111,** 648
s 17(1) **111,** 648
s 25(1) **111,** 650
Fisheries Act 1952 **101,** 165, 166-7, 168-9
Fisheries Act 1976 **86,** 185
Foreign States Immunities Act 1985. *See* Foreign States Immunities Act 1985 *above*
Forestry Act 1920 (Tasmania) **90,** 68
Freedom of Information Act **111,** 623-4
GATT Anti-Dumping Implementation Code (1980), municipal law, effect in **107,** 93-8
Geneva Conventions Act 1957 **91,** 36
Genocide Act 1949 **118,** 360, 379, **120,** 391
Human Rights Commission Act 1981 **101,** 246-7
Human Rights and Equal Opportunity Commission Act 1986 **101,** 247
s 47(1) **104,** 470-1, 496-8
Income Tax Assessment Act 1936 **87,** 173
Infants Custody and Settlements Act 1899, s 5(1) **92,** 623-4
Insurance Contracts Act 1984 **118,** 390
Interpretation Act 1897
s 17 **92,** 623
s 36(2) **100,** 480
Judiciary Act 1903 **86,** 177, **87,** 181, 185, 187, 188
s 13 **91,** 11
s 14 **91,** 11
s 18 **112,** 602

s 23(2)(b) **118,** 328
s 35 **104,** 436, 445
s 38A **92,** 626
s 39(2) **92,** 624-5
s 39B **90,** 104
s 40A **92,** 626
s 56 **90,** 34, 49
s 68 **91,** 11
s 78B **92,** 621
s 79 **92,** 625
s 80 **92,** 625
Lands Acquisition Act 1955 **90,** 39, **118,** 312-28
s 5(1) **118,** 313
s 6 **118,** 312-13, 317
s 10 **118,** 317-18
s 12 **118,** 318
s 51 **90,** 44
Lemonthyme and Southern Forests (Commission of Inquiry) Act 1987
Commission, appointment of **90,** 61, 75
s 6 **90,** 61
s 7 **90,** 61
s 8 **90,** 61-2
s 16 **90,** 61, 64-5, 87, 91, 99-100, 103-5, 113-14
s 18 **90,** 61, 114
s 19 **90,** 104
validity **90,** 60-115
Limitation of Liability for Maritime Claims Act 1989 **100,** 476-88
entry into force **107,** 133
procedural, whether **107,** 166-70
retroactive effect **107,** 128-30, 137-44
s 2 **100,** 480
s 3 **100,** 478
s 6 **100,** 485, 487, **107,** 124, 127-8, 129, 137-44
s 9 **107,** 138
s 17(1) **107,** 127
s 17(3) **107,** 127
Magistrates Court Act 1930 (ACT)
s 12(1) **120,** 372
s 16(1) **120,** 406
s 19 **120,** 372
s 26 **120,** 372, 405-6
Migration Act 1958. *See* Migration Act 1958 *below*
Mining (Northern Territory) Act 1980 **90,** 40, 49
National Parks and Wildlife Conservation Amendment Act 1987 **90,** 34
s 8B **90,** 37-8, 45, 51, 57
s 9 **90,** 67-8
s 10 **90,** 45
National Securities (Inquiries) Regulations **91,** 8
Native Title Act 1993. *See* Native Title Act 1993 *below*
Navigation Act 1912
Part VIII **100,** 476
s 330 **100,** 476

Australia (*cont.*)
s 333 **100,** 477, **107,** 127-30, 133-4, 139
Navigation Amendment Act 1979
s 65 **100,** 476
s 104(3) **100,** 476
s 503 **100,** 476
New South Wales Act 1855 **86,** 187-8
Northern Territory Acceptance Act 1910 **125,** 366
Northern Territory Representation Act 1922 **118,** 378 n. 245
Northern Territory Representation Act 1968 **118,** 378 n. 245
Northern Territory (Self-Government) Act 1978 **90,** 49, **118,** 378 n. 245
s 6 **90,** 50
s 69 **90,** 38, 39
s 70 **90,** 38, 39, 50
Nuclear Non-Proliferation (Safeguards) Act 1987 **118,** 347
Passports Act 1938 **87,** 179
Patents Act 1952, s 160(2) **107,** 82-9
Petroleum (Australia–Indonesia Zone of Cooperation) (Consequential Provisions) Act 1990, validity **104,** 452-9
Petroleum (Submerged Lands) Act 1967 **125,** 353
Racial Discrimination Act 1975
applicability to State legislature **112,** 418, 456
'person aggrieved' **68,** 192-3, 224-5, 236-7, 259-65
protection of persons of another race, colour or national or ethnic origin **112,** 455, **125,** 430-1
remedies **112,** 419, 420
s 8(1) (special measures) **112,** 517, 641, 722-3
s 9 **112,** 418-19, 423-4
s 9(1) **112,** 418-19, 423-4, 433-4, 454-5, 598-600, 635, 641
s 10 **112,** 119-20, 419-20, 424-7, 434-7, 444-7, 454-6, 600-1, 636, **118,** 327
s 10(1) **112,** 682-4, 693-4
s 10(3) **112,** 641
s 11 **118,** 327
Seas and Submerged Lands Act 1973 (including 1994 amendments) **86,** 186, **90,** 242
innocent passage **125,** 420
object and purpose **125,** 454
s 6 **125,** 329, 450
s 7 **125,** 329, 353, 366-7, 450-1, 454-5
Territorial Sea and Contiguous Zone Convention (1958) and **125,** 353
validity **90,** 242
Seat of Government Acceptance Act 1909, s 6 **120,** 372
Senate (Representation of Territories) Act 1973 **118,** 378 n. 245
Sentencing Act 1989, s 53 **104,** 437
Service and Execution of Process Act 1901 **92,** 620, 628
South Pacific Nuclear Free Zone Treaty Act 1986 **118,** 347
Statute Law (Miscellaneous Amendments) Act (No 2) 1982, s 178 **100,** 476-7
Supreme Court Act 1970
s 23 **92,** 624
s 48(2)(i) **104,** 436, 442-3
s 70A **104,** 435
Supreme Court Rules 1970, Pt 55, r 13(1) **104,** 437
Trade Practices Act 1974 **118,** 397, 398

Trading with the Enemy Acts 1939/57 **38,** 464, 466
Treaty of Peace (Japan) Act 1952 **38,** 463, 466
Weapons of Mass Destruction (Prevention of Proliferation) Act 1955 **118,** 347
World Heritage Properties Conservation Act 1983. *See* World Heritage Properties Conservation Act 1983 *below*
legislation. *See also* law of *above*; legislation, interpretation *below*
bill of attainder **91,** 17-18, 139-40, 166-8
ex post facto law and **91,** 20, 21, 79-81
retroactive **91,** 16, 17, 83-6, 107-9
separation of powers and **91,** 18, 107-9
War Crimes Act 1945/88, whether **91,** 109-10
constitutionality, context of operation, relevance **112,** 695-6
extraterritorial. *See* extraterritorial legislation *and* external affairs power, extraterritoriality *above*
federal and State, interaction **86,** 174-5
foreign relations, law relating to, classification **90,** 81-2, 84-9
implementation by broadcasting authority in conformity with treaty obligations **115,** 407
proportionality to purpose and object **90,** 84, 112-13
retroactive. *See* legislation, retroactive *below*
separability **91,** 14, 73-4
subordinate law-making **90,** 121-2, 136-7
treaties, separation of powers **104,** 428-9, 706
ultra vires **68,** 186
unjust, power to overturn **91,** 140
validity
clarity of intention **112,** 422
conflict with international obligations **115,** 410-12
inaccurate declaration of existing law **112,** 430-1
incorporation of common law **112,** 723-6
invalidity of single clause, effect **112,** 726
judicial process, interference with **112,** 422-3
presumption of **68,** 364-6, 381-2
legislation, interpretation **68,** 261-2, 459
aids
context **86,** 196, **91,** 29, **115,** 393-5, 405, 406
executive intention **85,** 59, 157
legislative history **85,** 157, 172, 175-6, **115,** 392-3
long title **118,** 313
marginal note **86,** 194-5
parliamentary proceedings **86,** 203-4, **125,** 374-9, 416-17
preamble **86,** 194-5, 201
title of statute **85,** 172, 173
ambiguity **86,** 196
characterization of subject-matter **68,** 355-7, 380, 400-1, 435-6, 466-7, 500-4
English law **118,** 303
guidelines
absurdity, avoidance **112,** 722-3
clear intention **118,** 313
clear language **91,** 68
consistency between related legislation **112,** 697 n. 192
every word to be given meaning **115,** 405

Australia (*cont.*)
implied provision **91,** 24
intention of legislature **107,** 134-5, **115,** 398-9
liberal **91,** 11, 29, 70, 72, 146, 161, **118,** 321
object and purpose **86,** 202, 204, **91,** 29, 69-70, **115,** 404-5
ordinary grammatical meaning **115,** 406-7
ordinary and natural meaning **87,** 148, 181, **118,** 314
legislation intended to promote justice and **125,** 371
plain meaning **90,** 69
preservation of validity **90,** 69
Statute as a whole **86,** 202, **115,** 404-5
text to prevail **85,** 157
judicial process, interference with **112,** 422-3
phrases
'a law of the Commonwealth' **112,** 725-6
'a person to do any act' **112,** 418
'acquisition of land for a public purpose' **118,** 312-21
'adjacent islands' **90,** 289-90
'alienated Crown land' **112,** 645
'an entry permit not granted' **90,** 22
'arising under a law' **107,** 134
'arising under a treaty' **101,** 262-5
'Australia' **91,** 209-10
'Australian content' **115,** 389-95, 402
'Australian fishing zones' **91,** 210, **101,** 169-70
'Australian waters' **38,** 131, **52,** 39, 52-6, 59, 62, 68-89, **69,** 38, 78, 125, **101,** 170-4
'between residents of different States' **92,** 624, 625
'coastal sea' **125,** 329, 371-2, 412, 450-1, 459
'conduct' **91,** 186, 188
'conduct for purpose of making a decision' **90,** 24
'Crown land' **112,** 509-11, 519, 579-80, 601, 621, 645
'decision under an enactment' **91,** 185-6
'discharge under any other Act' **104,** 437-9
'eligible goods' **91,** 208-10
'environment' **90,** 122-3
'external affairs' **91,** 70-5, 96-101, 104, 112-38, 146, 161. *See also* external affairs power *above*
'extradition country' **114,** 389, 396-9
'identified property' **68,** 281, 431-4, 457-8, 469-70, **90,** 42, 51, 120-1, 126-8, 136-7, **120,** 412-13
'illegal entrant' **91,** 171, 172
'in the course of' **91,** 132, 135
'knowingly concerned' **91,** 143
'laws, customs and usages of war' **91,** 66-7, 68, 132
'matrimonial cause' **118,** 302, 303-4, 308
'matter' **87,** 182, 185, 187-8, **118,** 343-4, 365, 366, 368-70
'native title'. *See* native title, definition *and* Native Title Act 1993 *below*
'occupation' **91,** 10
'ought not to have been made' **87,** 180
'past act' **112,** 696-9, 722-3
'peace, order and good government' **91,** 75, 99, 146-7, 162
'permitted' **91,** 66

'person aggrieved' **68,** 192-3, 224-5, 236-7, 259-65
'personally present' **87,** 180-1
'persons of a particular race, colour or national or ethnic origin' **112,** 444-5, 683
'proclaimed waters' **101,** 170-1
'prohibited non-citizen' **91,** 171, 172
'protected area' **90,** 62, 74, 79-80
'qualifying area' **90,** 62, 74, 79-80
'relating to the same subject matter claimed under the laws of different States' **92,** 624
'required' **107,** 84-5
'serious crime' **91,** 7, 9, 22-3, 51, 54
'State' [of federation] **90,** 43
'subsidy, bounty, reduction or remission of freight or other financial assistance' **107,** 111-21
'territory' **114,** 398
'the [whole] course' **91,** 193-4, 196-7, 199
'traditional Aboriginal owners' **112,** 645-6
'unalienated Crown land' **112,** 645
'under any enactment' **87,** 133-4, 136, 140, 141, 143, **90,** 140, 146, 147, 168-9
'visiting forces' **85,** 162, 173, 179
'war' **91,** 10, 24, 32
'war crime'. *See* war crimes, definition *below*
'within the limits of their several jurisdictions' **92,** 628-9
presumption against
expropriation without compensation **112,** 440
restriction of liberty **85,** 157, 159, 161, 168
retroactivity **91,** 105, **107,** 141-2, 143, **112,** 442
presumption of conformity with Constitution **118,** 314
presumption of conformity with customary international law **118,** 373-4
presumption of conformity with international law **101,** 288-9, **115,** 395, **118,** 373-4
presumption of conformity with international obligations **104,** 471, **107,** 132-3
clear meaning of legislation and **118,** 374-5
presumption of conformity with treaty **68,** 208, 224, 235-6, 242, 258, 307, 312-16, 338-9, 348-9, 373, 427-34, 452, 457-60, 499-500, **115,** 407-10
presumption of human rights protection **101,** 245-51, **120,** 414
principle of double criminality **87,** 151
responsibility
judicial **114,** 400
municipal courts **117,** 575
separability of provisions **68,** 459
treaty as aid **101,** 210, **104,** 494-5, **107,** 87-8, 89, 115
'drawn into' legislation **101,** 210
treaty language, correspondence with **91,** 134-6, **101,** 188
treaty meaning expressly accorded **101,** 210
unincorporated treaty **104,** 430-2, 471, 482-3, 704, **118,** 376
treaty interpretation distinguished **107,** 87
treaty-implementing legislation **68,** 261-2, **107,** 137-44, **118,** 373
legislation, retroactive **91,** 14-21, 27-8, 32-4, 93-6, 140-4, 151, 164-8
bill of attainder. *See* legislation, bill of attainder *above*
civil law **91,** 77, 165-6
clear intention **107,** 142-3

Australia (*cont.*)
criminal legislation **91,** 16-17, 32-4, 77-96, 104-11
non-national at time of offence **91,** 32-4
critical date, acquired right, relevance **107,** 129
declaratory statute **91,** 16, 88
definition **107,** 137
external affairs power and
critical date **91,** 33-4
'war crime', justification, whether **91,** 34
fairness, minimum standards of and **91,** 89
general principle of international law **91,** 141
general principle of law **91,** 80, 156-7
identification of individual or group, relevance **91,** 80-1, 109-11, 139-40, 168
international crime, critical date **91,** 50
international law as applicable law and **91,** 43-4, 47-8
'present execution' and **91,** 106
presumption against **107,** 141-2, 143, **112,** 442
procedural legislation **107,** 137-44
public interest, protection of **91,** 141-2
purposes of legislation, relevance **107,** 143
retrospective distinguished **91,** 166
separation of powers and **91,** 18, 77-86, 89-91, 107-9
sovereignty and **91,** 105
State immunity legislation **104,** 412
test of acceptability, offensiveness **91,** 142-3
treaty implementation, Brussels Convention on Limitation of Liability for Maritime Claims (1976) **107,** 128-30, 133, 137-45
trial, provision for, relevance **91,** 81, 96, 139, 168
universality of crime and **91,** 143, **120,** 394-5
validation of administrative act distinguished **91,** 16
legislative powers **90,** 61, 65-6, 73-4, 81-6, 91-7, 101-5, 109, 127-8. *See also* Constitution, s 51(xxix) *above*
concurrent, conflicting legislation **112,** 419-20, 706-9, 722-3
constituent State **91,** 13, 210
continental shelf **91,** 210
double jeopardy **91,** 74, 82
federal **91,** 72-3, 101
federal legislature's power to restrict State legislature **112,** 418-19, 424, 548, 706-21
inherent **68,** 316-17, 364, 382, 402-3, 446-7, 507-8
international obligation or concern **91,** 14, 34-65, 115-19. *See also* external affairs power *above*
correspondence of municipal and international law, need for **91,** 48, 50-1, 61-2
critical date **91,** 49, 62
federal law **91,** 29
maritime boundaries **91,** 29
obligation and concern distinguished **91,** 38-9, 116-17
resolution of international body **91,** 14, 115
seeking out and trial of alleged war criminals **91,** 34-51, 116-17
State law **91,** 29
treaty obligations **91,** 29
universal jurisdiction and **91,** 14, 39, 50-1, 118-19, 144
just terms, need for **112,** 548
limitations on, international law, relevance **104,** 452-6

over state Crown lands **68,** 407-13, 471-2
over waste lands **112,** 422, 452-4, 514-15, 577-8
'peace, welfare and good government' **112,** 422
'people of any race for whom it is deemed necessary to make special laws' **112,** 702-5
'special' laws **68,** 193-5, 211, 213-15, 244-5, 258-9, 285, 318-19, 360-3, 380-2, 401-2, 437-41, 504-7
territorial **91,** 13
territorial sea **91,** 210
legitimate expectation
knowledge of, need for **104,** 483
legal rule distinguished **104,** 474
procedural fairness **104,** 473-6, 481
distinction **104,** 481-3, 491-4
notice, need for **104,** 475, 486-7, 491-4
standing **104,** 474-5
treaty, ratification **104,** 473-5, 480-1, 483-4, 487, 494-8, 704-6, **122,** 440, **124,** 289
liberty of person, deprivation, detention during extradition hearings **101,** 191-2
lobsters, livestock, whether **91,** 208-10
margin of appreciation
human rights implementation **104,** 446-7
treaty obligations **107,** 93-8
maritime claims, limitation of liability
Brussels Convention on the Limitation of Liability for Maritime Claims (1976)
entry into force **100,** 480
implementing legislation **107,** 124-46
retroactive effect **100,** 483-8
International Convention Relating to the Limitation of Liability of Owners of Sea-going Ships (1957)
denunciation **100,** 480
denunciation, subsequent validity **100,** 482, 488
incorporation into municipal law **100,** 476-7
married women, domicile **118,** 302
Migration Act 1958 **85,** 158, **86,** 216-29, **104,** 464-5
Regulations
1.8 **117,** 610
173A **104,** 465
s 4(1) **117,** 595
s 5 **90,** 147, **104,** 4
s 6 **85,** 184-9, 196-203, **90,** 4, 11, 18, 20-7, 140-1, 146-7, 151, 152-5, 160, 166, 168-9
s 6(2) **91,** 181, 188, **104,** 467
s 6(6) **104,** 468
s 6A **104,** 468, 469
s 6A(1) **87,** 132-4, 135-40, 141-3
s 6A(1)(c) **91,** 171, 175-6, 177, 187-8
s 6A(1)(e) **91,** 172-3, 174
s 7 **85,** 196
s 7(3) **104,** 465
s 13 **90,** 144
s 14 **117,** 595
s 14(2) **91,** 171, 172
s 16(1)(b) **91,** 170. *See also* s 20(1)(b) *below*

Australia (*cont.*)
s 16(1)(c) **104,** 468-9, 490, 497-8
text **104,** 468, 490
s 18 **90,** 159, 161, **91,** 171
s 20(1)(b) **91,** 172
s 22AA **117,** 595, 597, 612
s 31 **90,** 159, 161
s 36 **90,** 19, 20, 147
s 38 **91,** 171
s 47(1)(d) **91,** 172, 175
s 54B **117,** 595
s 60 **91,** 171
Migration Amendment Act (No 2) **85,** 184-5
Murray Islands. *See* Murray Islands
nationality, allegiance and **92,** 631
nationals
State obligation towards **104,** 485
human rights **104,** 485
native title **73,** 138-63, **86,** 210-14, **112,** 419-20, 468-9
alienation, right of **112,** 505, 618
non-member of indigenous people **112,** 506, 514, 529
surrender to Crown **112,** 506, 514, 529, 547, 643
applicable law **112,** 512, 554, 606
change following acquisition of sovereignty **112,** 563
consistency/coexistence with common law, need for **112,** 505, 525-7, 530, 547, 561-2, **125,** 341-4, 355-6, 362-4, 453
English law, relevance **125,** 429-33
international law **125,** 421, 429-33
rules relating to individual rights, need for **112,** 507-8, 551-2
The Case of Tanistry **112,** 505, 591-2
traditional laws and customs **112,** 504, 505-6, 514, 591, 642, 646-7, **125,** 331-3, 355-62
arbitrary deprivation **112,** 435-7
burden of proof **125,** 431-2
Crown grants and common law rights distinguished **112,** 680-1, 684-6
definition **112,** 637, 680-1, 685-6, 695, **125,** 331-2
disposal subsequent to annexation **112,** 432-3, 436
evidence of **125,** 356-62, 436-40
oral histories **125,** 360-2
extinction **73,** 58-62, 65, 68-72, 76-7, 101-2, 107-8, 111-13, 117-27, 132, 141, 151-3, 162
annexation of territory **112,** 509, 537-8, 557-602
applicable law **112,** 643
burden of proof **118,** 336
clear provision, need for **112,** 468-9, 509-11, 535-8, 548-9, 619-20, 627, 651-3, 670, 671, **118,** 335
community's loss of connection with land **112,** 547, 642
compensation, relevance **112,** 432, 440, 468-9, 548, 549, 554, 589, 622, 627, 642, 693, 715-16
creation of reserves **112,** 511, 581-6
Crown as absolute beneficial owner **112,** 643
as genocide **120,** 357, 374-5, 405-10

government's power of **112,** 519, 539
grant in trust **112,** 516-18, 622
inconsistent interest. *See* inconsistent interest *below*
legislation **112,** 548, 550-1, 567-8, 627, 696-729
Native Title Act 1993 and **125,** 383-5
Racial Discrimination Act 1975 and **118,** 327, 336
remedies **112,** 549, 693-4
remedies, declaration **112,** 548, 554-5, 627, 636
remedies, injunction **112,** 555, 622
traditional and common law rights distinguished **112,** 445-6, 605
wishes of native people, relevance **112,** 532, 547, 617-18, 686-93
inconsistent interest **112,** 512-14, 515-16, 530, 538, 539-40, 547, 642, 647, 650-1, **118,** 324, 335-6, **125,** 396-7
authority to prospect for minerals **112,** 647, 687-91
construction of public buildings **112,** 588-9, 642
freehold **112,** 650, 651
land trust **112,** 647-53
lease for establishment of sardine factory **112,** 515-16, 518-19, 552-3, 588, 620-1, 637
lease to Missionary Society **112,** 515, 518-19, 552, 588, 637
non-exclusive nature of claimed rights **125,** 351, 362-4, 418-26, 436, 466-7
pastoral lease **112,** 638
reservation for public purpose **112,** 588-9, 642, 686-7
measures affecting, consent of aboriginals, need for **112,** 711-14
mining and other rights **73,** 139, 146-50
nature
common law concept **112,** 726
common law rights **73,** 142-3, 153, **112,** 435-6, 446, 539, 552, **118,** 328-30, **125,** 377-8
community interest **112,** 506, 527, 529, 539, 547, 605-6
fiduciary relationship **112,** 443-4, **115,** 461, 512-17, 524, 529, **118,** 331-2
ownership **112,** 518
permissive occupancy **112,** 530-3, 569-70, 571, 592, 634
personal right **112,** 529-30, 590
possession, relevance **112,** 592, 613-16, 627-34, **125,** 332, 433-40
proprietary **112,** 525-6, 611-12, **125,** 333-4, 427-9, 433-40
relevance **112,** 618-19, 642
traditional rights **112,** 435-6, 445-6
universal effectiveness **112,** 518, 519
ownership of lands in New South Wales **118,** 323-8
inadequate identification of relevant lands **118,** 324, 335
private title to, relevance **118,** 324, 335-6
protection
common law **112,** 505-7, 533-4, 549-50, 612-13
common law as supplemented by Native Title Act 1993 **125,** 330, 382. *See also* Native Title Act 1993 *below*
representative action **112,** 507, 647
radical and beneficial native titles distinguished **112,** 492-504, 513, 527-8, 540-2, 552, 557-8, 606-8, 641, 671, **125,** 344-7
Administration of Papua and New Guinea v. *Daera Guba* **112,** 497
Amodu Tijani **112,** 497-8, **125,** 332
applicable law **112,** 493

Australia (*cont.*)
feudal tenure and **112,** 494-9, 542-6, 557, **125,** 398-400
'patrimony of the nation', relevance **112,** 499-500
prerogative right **112,** 500-1, 557, **125,** 398-9
private international law and **125,** 396-8
sovereignty over territorial sea and **125,** 346-7, 396-7
The Case of Tanistry **112,** 496-7
remedies, equitable **112,** 549
survival **112,** 627, 667-8, **125,** 345-6
assumption of **112,** 439-40, 445-7, 540, 551, 570
communal proprietary interests **112,** 508, **125,** 427-9
legislative denial **112,** 424-5, 431-7
territorial sea, rights in **125,** 327-468
absence of land/sea distinction under traditional laws and customs **125,** 409
evidence of exercise **125,** 436-40
exclusive rights, claim to **125,** 355, 357-64, 367, 419-21
public rights of fishing, navigation and innocent passage, relevance **125,** 351, 362-4, 419-26, 436, 466-7
statutory fishing licences and **125,** 425-6
traditional laws and customs as basis **125,** 357-62, 436-7
US jurisprudence **125,** 463-6
Native Title Act 1993
Preamble, as endorsement of *Mabo (No 2)* **125,** 368-9, 441-2
Racial Discrimination Act 1975, interrelationship **112,** 696-7, 722-3
s 6 (applicability to coastal sea and any waters over which Australia asserts sovereign rights) **125,** 322, 329, 331, 451-2
high seas, exclusion **125,** 373
offshore rights **125,** 374-9, 380-1, 412
s 7 **112,** 696-7, 722-3
s 10 (recognition and protection of title) **125,** 369
s 11(1) (extinction of native title) **112,** 637, 696, 710, **125,** 330, 369, 374
s 11(2) **112,** 710-11
s 12 **112,** 723-6
s 20 **112,** 715-16
s 211 **112,** 714-15
s 223 (key concepts) **125,** 330-2, 408-9, 451-2
s 223(1) ('native title'/'native title rights and interests') **112,** 637, 695, **125,** 322, 330, 372
critical date **125,** 383-5
source of title distinguished **125,** 371-3, 374-9, 451, 459-60
s 223(1)(a) (possession under traditional laws and customs) **125,** 330, 331-2, 334, 357-62, 372, 436-7
s 223(1)(b) (connection with/relation to land or waters) **125,** 330, 333-4, 341-2, 436-7
'waters' as addition to *Mabo (No 2)* **125,** 370, 413
s 223(1)(c) (recognition under common law) **125,** 330, 332, 342-4, 364-5, 372-3, 374-407
Mabo (No 2) **125,** 343-4, 380-8, 406-9, 412-18, 436-7, 452-3
s 223(2) (hunting, gathering and fishing rights) **125,** 322, 411
s 224 ('native title holder') **125,** 331
s 225 ('determination of native title') **125,** 331, 452-3
s 225(b)(ii) (exclusion of 'all others') **125,** 436

s 253 ('waters') **125,** 331, 370-1, 411-12
'special measure', whether **112,** 703-4, 722-3
Native Title Act 1993, applicability
airspace **125,** 375-6
extraterritorial **125,** 380-1
sea country **125,** 411-18
Native Title Act 1993, constitutionality **112,** 695-729, **125,** 412
interference with legislative powers of State, whether **112,** 706-21
Native Title Act 1993, interpretation
context, aboriginal rights, legislation relating to **125,** 413
object and purpose **125,** 412, 416-17, 451-2
amelioration of injustice, relevance **125,** 371, 406-7, 410-11
ordinary and natural meaning **125,** 372-3
parliamentary proceedings **125,** 374-9
language of Statute, preference for **125,** 416-17
Statute as a whole **125,** 410-11
Native Title Act 1993, retroactive effect **112,** 696-9
Native Title Amendment Act 1998
applicability to offshore waters **125,** 375-6
support for as genocide **120,** 357, 374-5, 405-10
natural justice
aliens, admission **90,** 20, 25
detriment to individual as essential element **90,** 35, 49-50
fair hearing **90,** 56
judicial review and **91,** 186-7
New South Wales
applicable law
aboriginal traditions and customs, survival **112,** 660-1
consent of aboriginals, need for **112,** 659-61
boundaries, Queensland, formation of and **86,** 185-208
evidence, taking of, abroad **84,** 741
law of
Aboriginal Lands Act 1983 **118,** 327
Companies Code **87,** 190
Crown Lands (Validation of Revocations) Act 1983 **118,** 327
Evidence (Evidence on Commission) Amendment Act 1988 **84,** 741
Poisons Act 1966 **87,** 148
territory, acquisition **86,** 210-14
New Zealand, Closer Economic Relations Trade Agreement (1983)/Trade in Services Protocol (1989)
MFN clause
Australian Content Standard (broadcasting), compatibility with **115,** 386-415
text **115,** 387
Northern Territory
history **125,** 448-50
law of
Aboriginal Land Rights Act **90,** 39
Aboriginals Ordinance 1918, genocide and **118,** 372-9
Mining Act 1980 **90,** 40, 49
Off-shore Waters (Application of Territory Laws) Act 1985 **125,** 352, 354, 380
common law, extension of common law within 3-mile territorial sea **125,** 405, 453-4
native title, effect on **125,** 354

Australia (*cont.*)
nuclear weapons, deployment, justiciability **118,** 346-8
official secrets, disclosure in course of duties **107,** 99
passports, property of government **87,** 179
permanent resident status **85,** 158-9, 160-1, 178
political offence **114,** 388
political question doctrine **87,** 185-6, **118,** 345
separation of powers and **118,** 369
precedent in municipal courts **90,** 92-3
ECJ decision **107,** 118-19
GATT Committee on Subsidies and Countervailing Measures **107,** 133
importance of following **112,** 729-32
municipal courts in other countries **107,** 140-1
prerogative
British practice, relevance **118,** 367
constitutional basis **118,** 367
foreign relations **118,** 367
judicial review and **90,** 34, 35, 50-5
private international law, common law rules **125,** 396-8
procedure
amicus curiae brief **118,** 301
class/representative action for equitable relief **118,** 332
proportionality
defence interests **91,** 64-5
war and peace distinguished **91,** 65
legislation **90,** 84, 112-13
public order/public policy/*ordre public*, treaty obligations **107,** 93-8
public purpose, expropriation/nationalization **62,** 166, 183-5, 194, **118,** 312-21
Queensland
boundaries, establishment **86,** 188-208
Australian Colonies Act 1861 **86,** 188
Letters Patent Act 1872 **86,** 188-9, 192-3
Letters Patent Act 1878 **86,** 189, 192-3, 195, 206
Queensland Coast Islands Act 1879 **86,** 190, 193, 195, 200, 206-7
Commonwealth legislation, right to challenge **68,** 186
Darnley Island, part of, whether **86,** 185-208
law of
Land Act 1962 **68,** 184
Letters Patent 1925 **86,** 192-3
Mineral Resources (Adjacent Submarine Areas) Act 1964 **86,** 186
Petroleum Act 1923-1976 **86,** 186
Petroleum (Submerged Lands) Act 1976 **86,** 186
Queensland Coast Islands Declaratory Act 1985. *See* Queensland Coast Islands Declaratory Act 1985 *below*
legislative powers. *See* legislative powers *above*
proprietary interest in land, Crown's power to grant **112,** 508-9
Queensland Coast Islands Act 1879 **86,** 190, 193, 195, 200, 202, 206-7
Queensland Coast Islands Declaratory Act 1985. *See* Queensland Coast Islands Declaratory Act 1985 *below*
separation of powers **112,** 423
Queensland Coast Islands Declaratory Act 1985
declaratory nature **112,** 419, 443
enabling effect **112,** 441-3

extinction of traditional rights of Murray Islanders **112,** 430-2, 435-7, 439-47
judicial process, interference with **112,** 422-3, 442
Racial Discrimination Act 1975, compatibility with **112,** 417-20, 423-7, 433-7, 444-7, 454-6, 598-601, 634-6
retroactive effect **112,** 442, 552
validity **112,** 417-56
racial discrimination
aboriginals **68,** 193-5, 240, 242-3, 381, 464
constitutional provisions **68,** 193-5, 211, 213-15, 242, 244-5, 258-9, 285, 318-19, 364, 380-2, 401-2, 437-41, 463-7, 504-7
equality before the law
other persons enjoying denied rights, need for **112,** 424-7, 446-7, 455-6, 683-5
'special and concrete measures' **112,** 426-7, 517-18, 641, 654-5, 656
extinction of native title **125,** 433
compensation, failure to pay **112,** 693-4
foreign affairs and **68,** 207-8, 223-4, 247-51, 386-8, 489
International Convention on the Elimination of All Forms of Racial Discrimination (1965), implementation **112,** 424, 445, 456, 654-5
recognition
forceful occupation of territory, responsibility, executive **104,** 456
justiciability **104,** 456
refugees **85,** 184-208
definition **90,** 4-6, 16, 27, 28-31, 155-6, 163, 175
flexible **90,** 28-9
Geneva Convention on the Status of Refugees (1951) and Protocol (1967) **117,** 595, 601-3
International Refugee Organization (IRO) **90,** 175
UN Protocol relating to the Status of Refugees (1967) **90,** 159-60
UNHCR *Handbook on Criteria for Determining Refugee Status* (1979) **90,** 145
expulsion **73,** 628-34, **87,** 122-9
family members, extension of rights of refugee to, member of a family unit **117,** 600, 610
judicial review
assessment of facts **117,** 608, 623
grounds **117,** 617
abuse of discretion **117,** 628
error of law **117,** 597-8, 618-19
failure to exercise jurisdiction **117,** 606
unreasonableness **114,** 579, 581-3, **117,** 619
standard, 'not over zealous' **117,** 615-16, 621
'membership of a particular social group' **124,** 485, 496, 502
'persecution'
birth control policy **117,** 601-2, 609-10, 616
denial of employment **90,** 177
denial of fundamental rights or freedoms **90,** 142
disregard of human dignity **90,** 151, 177
selective harassment **90,** 176
serious punishment, penalty or disadvantage **117,** 601
'persecution or well-founded fear of persecution' **90,** 141, 142-5, 149-50, 161-2, 172-7, **91,** 177
burden of proof **90,** 7
changed circumstances **90,** 151, 156-7, 158-9, 162-4

Australia (*cont.*)
clear probability **90,** 162
Convention reason, need for **117,** 601-2, 616-17
damage to foreign relations resulting from finding of **90,** 149
directed at individual **90,** 30-1, 176
discrimination, need for **90,** 142, 143-4, 151-2, 170, **117,** 618
evidence of **87,** 441, 442, **90,** 8, **117,** 614-16, 622
exile **90,** 143
good reason **90,** 175
likelihood of realization **90,** 143, 149-50, 174, 176
political opinion, for **90,** 142-3
political profile prior to departure, need for **117,** 598-600
racial persecution **90,** 29
real and substantial risk **90,** 143
reasonable possibility **90,** 150, 173
relevant date **90,** 141, 144, 150-1, 156-7, 163-4, 178-9
requirements, discrimination **117,** 616
self-created **91,** 178-9
serious possibility **90,** 172
subjective **90,** 149, 156, 164
threat to life or freedom **90,** 151, 165, 179-80
UNHCR *Handbook on Criteria for Determining Refugee Status* (1979) **90,** 29, 150-1, 156, 165, 172-3
variety of interpretation **90,** 173
violation of human rights **90,** 151
well-founded fear, balance of probabilities test **117,** 600, 603-6, 618-19
well-founded fear, possibility of error in determining **117,** 605-6
well-founded fear, real chance **90,** 143, 150, 157, 158, 174, **117,** 602-7, 613-14, 620, 623
political refugee, distinction, whether **90,** 5
status **91,** 175-9
date arising **90,** 21-2, 27, **91,** 175
determination **85,** 186, 188, 191-5
determination, procedures **87,** 127-9, 132-3, 134, **91,** 171, 172
determination, responsibility **87,** 138-40, 141-2, **90,** 163, 172
entry permit, relevance **90,** 27-8, 155, 160, **91,** 176
error of law, possibility **90,** 20, 24-5, 27-31
recognition, relevance **90,** 163, 172
request, need for **90,** 178
statutory basis **85,** 185, 188
status, refusal
judicial review **85,** 192-203, **90,** 20, 21-31, 140-80, **91,** 175, 176
reasons for, right to **87,** 131-2, 140
sur place **91,** 177-9
Refugees, Geneva Convention on the Status of (1951) and Protocol (1967) **87,** 124, 128-9, 132, 141
justiciability **91,** 175, 187
remedies
breach of treaty, discretionary **104,** 436-40
declaratory relief, requirements **117,** 608
extinction of native title
declaration **112,** 548, 554-5, 627, 636

equitable **112,** 549
injunction **112,** 555, 622
Rhodesian sanctions **52,** 2
rivers
ad medium filum aquae **91,** 195
boundary **91,** 190-204
changes **91,** 194-204
avulsion **91,** 196
common law principles **91,** 195, 196
erosion and accretion **91,** 196
'course' **91,** 193-4, 196-7, 199
divided, both channels as river **91,** 197-8
Rosily Island, territorial sea **69,** 81, 84-5
Rules of Court
Order 49 **87,** 175
preservation of subject matter **87,** 175
seabed and subsoil
ownership
common law **125,** 398-401, 427, 433-6
native title **125,** 427-9, 433-6, 449-50
separation of powers **91,** 75, 77, 138, **112,** 423
bill of attainder and **91,** 18, 107-9
exceptions
contempt of parliament, power to punish **91,** 91
international crimes **91,** 92-3
military tribunals **91,** 91
political question doctrine and **118,** 369
recognition **104,** 457
retroactive legislation and **91,** 18, 77-86, 89-91, 107-9
treaties, validity and **104,** 453-6, 706
US doctrine distinguished **91,** 83-6, **118,** 369
ship, national territory, part of **91,** 98-9
South Australia
constitutive instruments
'bays and gulfs' **69,** 35, 41-2, 47-50, 52-4, 57, 59-63, 68-71
interpretation **69,** 35-6, 41-2, 46-53, 59-63, 68-71
criminal jurisdiction, outside territorial sea **38,** 120-7
extraterritorial legislation **69,** 37, 55, 58
Fisheries Act 1971-75 **69,** 34, 36-7, 40, 54-5, 58
conflict with Commonwealth legislation **69,** 40
off-shore waters, applicability **69,** 36-7, 55, 58
historic boundaries **69,** 41, 46-7, 49-53, 59
internal waters, delimitation
Backstairs Passage **69,** 35, 44-5, 53, 55, 61, 65, 68
constitutive instruments **69,** 35-6, 41, 46-53, 57, 59-63, 68-71, 73
historic evidence **69,** 43, 45, 49-52, 56, 59, 69-70
international law considerations **69,** 36, 41-2, 62-7, 72-4
Investigator Strait **69,** 35-7, 41-4, 53-4, 59-63, 65-73
Kangaroo Island **69,** 35-6, 43-5, 53-4, 59, 62, 65-6, 68-9
St Vincent Gulf **69,** 35-7, 41-54, 59-63, 67, 71-3
Spencer Gulf **69,** 35-7, 41-54, 59-63, 67, 71-3
Kangaroo Island

Australia (*cont.*)
delimitation of internal waters **69,** 35-6, 43-5, 53-4, 59, 62, 65-6, 68-9
as extension of mainland **69,** 44-5, 53, 62, 65-6, 68-9
law of
Fisheries Act 1971-75. *See* Fisheries Act 1971-75 *above*
Justices Act 1921 **86,** 174-5
Northern Territory Surrender Act 1907 **125,** 366
Off-shore Waters (Application of Laws) Act 1976 **69,** 37, 58
sovereignty
duality **91,** 73, 101, **125,** 347-8
extraterritorial legislation and **91,** 72-3, 97-8, 101
retroactive legislation and **91,** 105
territorial sea. *See* territorial sea, sovereignty *below*
State agency/State-owned corporation/State entity, classification, ambassador **104,** 412
State immunity, jurisdiction, applicability, in own courts, native title, protection and **112,** 549
State immunity, jurisdiction, classification of act
appointment of civil servant **101,** 200-1
appointment of national airline pilot **101,** 198-201
joint control of funds for education institution **104,** 413-17
military base, civilian clothing hire service **52,** 332-5
nature or purpose of transaction as determining factor **101,** 195, 199-200
State immunity, jurisdiction, entitlement
agency **52,** 333-5
ambassador/head of mission **104,** 412
Australian Federal Police **111,** 646-53, 664-71
Ruler of State of Malaysian Federation **118,** 294-8
State immunity, jurisdiction, procedural aspects
appearance, need for **104,** 416-17
entitlement to raise, bank holding affected funds **104,** 416-17
evidence of
executive certificate/statement, conclusiveness **104,** 143 n. 7, **118,** 297
standard of proof **104,** 413-14
State immunity, jurisdiction, theory/doctrine
acta jure imperii/*acta jure gestionis* distinguished **101,** 192-201
basis, comity **101,** 195
legislation, retroactive, whether **104,** 412
State practice, statutory provision, limitation as precedent **101,** 196
State immunity, jurisdiction, waiver
amendment of claim, effect **107,** 598-9
withdrawal **107,** 592
stay of proceedings
abuse of process and **118,** 409-10, 414, 418-19
agreement not to sue, relevance **118,** 390-1, 395-6, 410
comity **118,** 413-14
injunction distinguished **118,** 408-9
power to order in courts of another State **118,** 381-420
avoidance of injustice **118,** 394-6
concurrent and sole jurisdiction distinguished **118,** 394
greater suitability of foreign court **118,** 395
oppressive proceedings **118,** 400-1, 407, 409-13, 418-19
prevention of distortion of domestic policy **118,** 395, 396-401

relevant factors **118,** 384-6
treble damages proceedings **118,** 397-8, 400-1, 406, 412-13
Tasmania
Criminal Code
arbitrary nature **112,** 340-4
repeal **112,** 342, 344
s 122 **112,** 340-2, 343-4
s 123 **112,** 340-2, 343-4
Crown lands, Federal legislation **68,** 271-2, 407-13
Gordon River dam project **68,** 271, 273, 404-6, 425-6
Hydro-Electric Commission **68,** 271-3, 319-26, 358-60, 364, 380, 399-401, 404-5, 468, 482-3, 509
as trading corporation **68,** 324-6, 358-60, 380, 399-401, 405, 434-5, 481-2, 540
law of
Criminal Code. *See* Criminal Code *above*
Forestry Act 1920 **90,** 68
Gordon River Hydro-Electric Power Development Act 1982 **68,** 271, 273, 364, 405, 468, 482-3, 509
Hydro-Electric Commission Act 1944 **68,** 273, 319-26, 468
National Parks and Wildlife Act 1970 **68,** 272-3, 404, 468
Western Tasmania Wilderness National Parks **68,** 272-8, 374, 381, 404, 425-6, 440-1, 469-70
aboriginal settlements **68,** 277, 381, 440-1
archaeological sites **68,** 276-7, 404, 440-1, 470
cultural heritage significance **68,** 276-8, 425, 469-70
natural heritage significance **68,** 275-6, 425-6
World Heritage Listing **68,** 275-6, 425-6
World Heritage List, inclusion in **90,** 28, 60-115. *See also* UNESCO Protection of the World Cultural and Natural Heritage Convention (1972) *below*
discriminatory effect **90,** 68-70, 105
territorial sea
applicable law, common law **125,** 334-42, 366-7, 380-407, 455-9
delimitation **69,** 77-88, **73,** 174-8. *See also* South Australia, internal waters, delimitation *above*
baselines **69,** 79-80, 85-8
evolution of law **125,** 347-51
extension to 12 miles **125,** 353, 366-7, 412, 454-5
freedom of navigation **125,** 350-1
common law **125,** 423-5
jurisdiction. *See also* law of, Coastal Waters (Northern Territory Powers) Act 1980, Coastal Waters (Northern Territory Title) Act 1980, Off-shore Waters (Application of Territory Laws) Act 1985 *and* Seas and Submerged Lands Act 1973 *above*
statutory basis **125,** 388-9, 401-3
legislative power **91,** 210
native title and. *See* native title, territorial sea *above*
as part of territory **91,** 209-10
seabed and subsoil, sovereignty over **70,** 58, 66, 69, **90,** 242-3, **125,** 347-51
ownership, whether **125,** 350, 354, 427-9, 433-6, 449-50, 455-63
sovereignty **69,** 36-41, 48, 54-5, 67, 71, 73-4, 77-88, 111-12, 118-19, 123-6, **70,** 58-9, 66, 97-8, 100, **125,** 347-51, 398-401
UK Merchant Shipping Act 1894, applicability **70,** 70-2, 90-1, 98-100
wrecks, title **70,** 54-101

Australia (*cont.*)
Territories
democratic rights **118,** 378-9
right to acquire land **118,** 312-21
territory
acquisition, act of State, justiciability **112,** 481-2, 513, 521, 523, 535-8, 642, 670
terra nullius, rejection of concept **112,** 642
Torres Strait **68,** 194, **86,** 186, 189-90, 202, 204
treaties **52,** 2
breach, remedy, discretionary **104,** 436-40
denunciation, effective date **107,** 133
entry into force **100,** 480
applicability and **100,** 485-7
Federal clauses **68,** 200, 297-9, 303, 315, 342, 379, 395, 424, 455-6, 500
implementation **90,** 61, 73, 86-7, 93, 101, 104, 112, **104,** 429, 496
conformity of domestic legislation **68,** 208, 224, 235-6, 242, 258, 307, 312-16, 338-9, 373, 427-34, 453, 457-60, 499-500
legislative responsibility **104,** 495
means, choice **107,** 87
partial **68,** 460
parties' choice of means **100,** 487
State practice, relevance **101,** 258
states' role **68,** 129, 211, 241, 249, 395-6
treaty obligation, need for **90,** 108-10, 111, 135-6
implementing legislation
applicable law **101,** 210-11, 242
effectiveness **100,** 487
need for **101,** 208-9, 248-9, **104,** 428-30, 470-1, 483, 495-6, 704-6, **118,** 330, **120,** 362-5
ratification, effect **120,** 362
regulations 'necessary or convenient' to give effect to, limitations on **101,** 212-17, 218-25, 232-5, 238-9, 254
scheduling to Act, effect **104,** 430, 496-7
separation of powers **104,** 429
as source of obligation **101,** 262-4
incorporation into municipal law, need for **104,** 443
individual **87,** 126-7
GATT (1947) **107,** 112-13
obligations **101,** 209
individual's right to, challenge validity **107,** 77-80
international law, source of, treaty interpretation distinguished **104,** 471
justiciability, treaties between constituent States **87,** 185
municipal law and **104,** 428-30
interpretation, guide to **90,** 27, **101,** 188
part of, ratification, relevance **104,** 428, **120,** 362
statutory approval, effect **101,** 250
obligations **90,** 51, 65-71, 73, 75
anticipated **90,** 71
margin of appreciation **107,** 93-8
means of fulfilling, choice **90,** 77
operation and enforcement **90,** 61, 73, 93, 96-7, 101, 104, 108-10, 111, 135-6

primacy, conflict **107,** 87
prior consultation with constituent State governments **101,** 249-50
ratification
declaration of acceptance of principles **104,** 466, 474, 483, 495, 706
implicit authorization to State agencies to act in accordance with **104,** 484, 704-6
incorporation as result of **104,** 428, 484
legislation, interpretation **104,** 704
national community **104,** 466, 474, 495
retroactive effect **100,** 483-8, **107,** 145-6
context **107,** 142-3
customary international law and **107,** 143
intention **107,** 142-3
termination, subsequent treaty **107,** 127, 143
treaty-making power. *See also* external affairs power *above*
executive **87,** 126
unincorporated treaty **90,** 28
breach, discretionary remedy for **104,** 436-40
courts' right to apply **104,** 428-32
individual's right to invoke before national courts **104,** 429, 447, 471
Vienna Convention on the Law of Treaties (1969)
customary international law and **100,** 478
entry into force **100,** 478
treaty interpretation
aids
context **101,** 242, **107,** 135-6
judicial and arbitral decisions **91,** 177
subsequent practice **101,** 242
teachings of publicists **91,** 177-8
travaux préparatoires **90,** 174-5
UNHCR *Handbook on Criteria for Determining Refugee Status* (1979) **90,** 145, **91,** 178
applicable law, international law **104,** 432, 447
by municipal courts **90,** 129
error, error of fact or law **101,** 210
guidelines
consistency. *See* uniformity *below*
general international purpose **90,** 162
human rights, protection **101,** 245-6
object and purpose **101,** 242, **104,** 433
ordinary meaning **101,** 242, **104,** 483
uniformity **107,** 119, 130
phrases, 'a real action relating to private immovable property' **101,** 360, **118,** 306-7
UN Charter (1945), implementing legislation, need for **52,** 2-3
UN Security Council resolution, effect **52,** 2-3
UNESCO Protection of the World Cultural and Natural Heritage Convention (1972)
cultural heritage, definition **68,** 275, 298
federal clause **68,** 297-9, 303, 315, 342, 379, 389, 395, 424, 455-6, 496-7, 500
indigenous people's rights under **120,** 415
individual's right to invoke before national courts **120,** 414, 415
obligations **90,** 65-71, 73, 75, 87-8, 128-9, 131, 133, 134, 136
identification of areas for protection **90,** 67, 102, 104, 112, 125-6, 134, **120,** 412-13

Australia (*cont.*)
imprecise **90,** 94
interim protection **90,** 67, 103, 104
property rights, protection of **68,** 299, **90,** 66
proportionality and **90,** 67
statement of political intent as **90,** 66
phrases
'cultural heritage' **90,** 40, 62, 63
'natural heritage' **90,** 40-1, 62, 63
purpose **90,** 110
proportionality and **90,** 97
sovereignty, avoidance of encroachment on **90,** 97, 133
World Heritage List **90,** 35, 43-4, 47-8, 129-30, 133, 136-7
criteria **90,** 40-4, 129-30
discriminatory, whether **90,** 68-70
duty of care **120,** 416
economic factors **90,** 64
effect **90,** 130-1, **120,** 413-14
forestry management, effect on **90,** 68-70, 99-100, 113-14, 123-4
justiciability of listing **120,** 413, 416
mining interests, effect on **90,** 44-53
responsibility for decision **120,** 413
UNGA resolutions, municipal law and **52,** 2
United Kingdom and **69,** 14-15, 21-3, **70,** 100
visiting forces
definition **85,** 162-3, 179
immunity **85,** 157-8, 164, 169
international law, relevance **85,** 157-8, 164, 169
uncertainty **85,** 157
war, with Germany **52,** 506-7, 509-11
war crimes
applicable law
federal and State courts **91,** 47
international law **91,** 47-8
military courts **91,** 47-8
municipal law **91,** 45, 47, 92-3, 94-6
burden of proof **91,** 11, 68-9, 103-4, 134
defences
evidence of additional facts **91,** 69
execution of judicial orders **91,** 26-7
lawfulness under laws, customs and usages of war **91,** 10, 25
lawfulness under laws of place where act committed **91,** 26-7
superior orders. *See* superior orders *below*
definition **91,** 7, 8-10, 21-2, 23-8, 47, 51-63, 66, 67, 68-9, 92, 121, 132-8
commission within Australia **91,** 101, 159-60, 163-4
conformity with international law definition **91,** 51-7, 94
crime against humanity **91,** 57-63
international law, relevance **91,** 51-7, 69, 132-8
enforcement, municipal courts **91,** 47
Hetherington Report **91,** 47, 50
National Security (Inquiries) Regulations. *See* law of, National Security (Inquiries) Regulations *above*
obligation to seek out and prosecute

international obligation, whether **91,** 34-51
matter of international concern, whether **91,** 38-9
superior orders **91,** 10, 26-7, 54-7, 92, 136-8, 150
War Crimes Act 1945/88 **91,** 8-11, 21-8
conformity with international law **91,** 51-7
criminal courts **91,** 8
defences under. *See* war crimes, defences *above*
extraterritorial nature **91,** 14, 114-15
international law and **91,** 25-7
implied importation **91,** 26
military courts **91,** 8
s 3 **91,** 8
s 5(1) **91,** 8-9, 32
s 6 **91,** 9, 51-2
s 7 **91,** 8, 10, 23-5, 31-2, 51, 52, 61-2, 66
s 9 **91,** 14-15, 17-18, 21-3, 50-7, 132-8
s 11 **91,** 10, 160
s 16 **91,** 10, 57, 136-7
s 17 **91,** 10, 25-6, 52-4, 66-9, 103-4, 132, 150
s 20 **91,** 27
separability **91,** 10, 14, 73-4
Western Australia
admiralty jurisdiction **69,** 163
Fisheries Act 1905/1975 **69,** 110-12, 121-6
construction **69,** 113, 121-2
jurisdiction, crimes outside territorial sea **38,** 128-32
Land (Titles and Traditional Usage) Act 1993 **112,** 667-70
retroactive effect **112,** 694-5
s 5 (confirmation of titles) **112,** 681, 694-5
s 7 (extinction of title/entitlement to exercise traditional rights) **112,** 681-94
Maritime Archaeology Act 1973 **70,** 54-101
Mining Act 1978 **112,** 687-90
Museum Act 1959-64 **70,** 54-101
Museum Act 1969 **70,** 54-101
Petroleum Act 1967 **112,** 690-1
phrases
'native title' **112,** 680-1, 685-6, 695
'rights of traditional usage' **112,** 693
'title' **112,** 680-1, 685-6
Racial Discrimination Act 1975
Land (Titles and Traditional Usage) Act 1993, compatibility with **112,** 667, 668-9, 680-95
Native Title Act 1993, compatibility with **112,** 667-70
UK Merchant Shipping Act 1894 **70,** 60-1, 64, 70-2, 75, 90-1, 98, 100
ultra vires, whether **70,** 54, 58-60, 62, 63, 66-8, 75, 89-90, 101
waters **69,** 110, 112, 121, 124-5
wrecks legislation
conflict with Commonwealth legislation **70,** 61, 64, 68-70, 72-5, 91-5, 97-101
salvage awards and **70,** 83-4
World Heritage Properties Conservation Act 1983 **87,** 185, **90,** 42, 61, 74, 119
acquisition of property
compensation provisions **68,** 287-90, 478-81
proclamations as **68,** 326, 349-51, 382, 441-2, 472-81

Australia (*cont.*)
appropriateness of measures **68,** 348-9, 373, 427-34, 457-9
constitutional base **68,** 281-90
Environment Protection (Impact of Proposals) Act 1974 and **90,** 119-20, 122, 123-5
foreign affairs power. *See* validity, foreign relations power *below*
identified property **68,** 281, 431-4, 457-8, 469-70, **120,** 412-13
acquisition by Commonwealth **68,** 326, 349-51, 382, 441-2, 472-81
damage to part **68,** 344-5, 348
Proclamations **68,** 274, 282-3, 383, 433-4, 436-7, 458-9, 469-70
Regulations **68,** 274, 434-5, 437, 469-71, 475-6
s 3 **90,** 119, 120-1, 122, 126-9, 134, 136-7
s 4 **90,** 61
s 6 **90,** 119, 120-1, 123, 125-31, 134-7
validity **68,** 306-16, 398, 431-4, 446-7, 507-9
s 7 **90,** 119, 120-1, 123
validity **68,** 319-26, 351-7, 379-80, 399-401, 434-7, 460-3, 500-4, 509
s 8, validity **68,** 318-19, 360-3, 380-2, 401-2, 437-41, 463-7, 481, 504-8, 509
s 9 **90,** 120-1, 123, 132
separability of provisions **68,** 459
validity **68,** 306-16, 347-51, 398, 431-4, 457-60, 508
s 10, validity **68,** 319-26, 351-7, 370-80, 399-401, 434-7, 460-3, 500-4, 507
s 11, validity **68,** 318-19, 360-3, 380-2, 401-2, 437-41, 463-7, 481, 504-8
s 16 **90,** 61
s 17, constitutional 'just terms' requirement **68,** 287-90, 478-81
s 18 **90,** 61
s 21 **90,** 131
separability of provisions **68,** 315, 459
state functions, interference with **68,** 345-7, 407-13, 471-2
trade or commerce regulation, whether **68,** 444-5
validity
corporations' power **68,** 319-26, 351-7, 364, 379-80, 399-401, 434-7, 460-3, 500-4
facts in dispute **68,** 383
foreign relations power **68,** 306-16, 364, 379, 385-99, 413-17, 419, 427-34, 457-60
inherent national power **68,** 316-17, 364, 382, 402-3, 446-7, 507-8
'special laws' power **68,** 318-19, 360-5, 380-2, 401-2, 437-41, 463-7, 504-7
water rights, interference with **68,** 326, 357-8, 382, 443-5
World Heritage Properties Conservation Regulations **68,** 469-71, 475-6
restricted works **68,** 470-1, 475-6
World Heritage (Western Tasmania Wilderness) Regulations **68,** 272, 274, 278-81
validity **68,** 281, 315-27, 343-7, 379, 383, 388-9, 398, 427-30, 467-9, 508
Austria
airspace, sovereignty over **71,** 231
aliens
expulsion. *See* expulsion of alien *below*
property **77,** 435-9, **81,** 3-24
residence
administrative matter **77,** 446-7
restrictions on **77,** 445
Anschluss
nationality and **45,** 353-7
restoration of State and **45,** 355-6
applicable law **47,** 466-8
corporation **77,** 450
employment contract (municipal law) **96,** 572-3

asylum, right of **48,** 155-6
Austro-Hungarian Bank
  funds repaid by US **71,** 267-9
  liquidators, international law status **71,** 268-9
belligerent occupation
  Allied agreement on **44,** 2-3
  Hungarian property, acts of French authorities **44,** 2-4
citizenship, application for **71,** 442-6
civil proceedings in respect of damage to foreign diplomat abroad, reciprocity, need for **86,** 548
claims, waiver by State **40,** 184-6
compensation, for war damage, treaty or statute, need for **65,** 12-13
compensation claims **77,** 427-32, 449-52, 459-66
Constitution 1929
  Art. 7 **56,** 447
  Art. 133 **56,** 448
Constitution 1963 (*B-VG*) **56,** 479-80
  amendment of Hapsburg Law **77,** 476, 479
  Art. 9 **77,** 445, 464, **86,** 577, 585
  Art. 10 **77,** 446
  Art. 15 **81,** 9-10
  Art. 18 **77,** 446
  Art. 20(2) **81,** 12, 23
  Art. 83(2) **81,** 8
  Art. 94 **96,** 576
  Art. 130 **96,** 576, 581
  Art. 131 **96,** 575
  Art. 133(4) **81,** 13
  Art. 140 **77,** 429, 459
  Art. 144 **77,** 428, 435, 444, 459, **81,** 13, **96,** 575
  equality, principle of **48,** 159-61, 175-8, **77,** 432
  inviolability of property **47,** 414-16, **48,** 159-61, 175, 178
  judicial review **48,** 158
  treaties
    political **40,** 179-80, 229, 231, 233, 239, 242
    treaty-making power **40,** 237
Constitution 1965 (*B-VG*)
  Art. 2 (Sending of Austrian Contingents Abroad for Assistance at the Request of International Organizations) **77,** 472, 474
  Art. 3 **71,** 231
  Art. 9 **71,** 38, 231, 541
  Art. 140 **71,** 549
consular immunity, jurisdiction, State immunity, jurisdiction and **86,** 556
consular privileges and immunities
  functional basis **86,** 554-8
  honorary consul **86,** 554-8
    customary international law **86,** 556
    national of receiving State **86,** 556-7
contract, employment. *See employment contract entries below*
corporation, personality **77,** 450-1
courts, municipal
  application of foreign law **71,** 38-9
  determination of sentence, penalties abroad, relevance **71,** 250-1
  preliminary investigations **41,** 347

Austria (*cont.*)
release pending trial **41,** 316-18, 334, 335, 336-7, 342-3, 345, 349-50, 351, 357-8
right of access, constitutional guarantees **56,** 447-9
criminal procedure **67,** 514-16
Enforcement Regulations **81,** 201
examining judges **41,** 340-1, 347, 356
expert evidence, court and expert witness distinguished **81,** 188-98
necessity, defence of **71,** 230, 254
customary international law **71,** 38, 541, 549-51
municipal law and **71,** 38, 541, 549-51
defamation **88,** 520-4, 529-30
burden of proof **88,** 521, 522-3, 530
defences, justification **88,** 521, 522, 529
office-holder **88,** 521
public prosecution, limitation to **88,** 521, 522
parliamentary immunity and **88,** 522
detention pending trial **56,** 461-72
diplomatic agent, State responsibility for actions of **86,** 547-8
diplomatic immunity, jurisdiction
State immunity and, distinction **65,** 22
waiver, initiation of proceedings **77,** 454-6
diplomatic mission
administrative and technical staff, embassy driver **65,** 22
functions/'diplomatic activity', representation of sending State **86,** 584-5
diplomatic privileges and immunities **38,** 161, **77,** 468-9
entitlement, embassy driver **65,** 22
private servants **71,** 548-51
taxation, exemption **71,** 541, 574-6
drug-trafficking
jurisdiction **71,** 484
jurisdiction, obligation to exercise
extradition, request for, relevance **86,** 551-2
ne bis in idem **86,** 551
Single Convention on Narcotic Drugs (1961), jurisdiction, obligation to exercise **86,** 551-2
duress **47,** 464-6, 468-9, 471
embassy
executive certificate/statement, binding nature **71,** 548-9
legal status **77,** 487
embassy or consular bank account/funds, immunity, execution/attachment **65,** 8-9, **77,** 490-4
account as basis for jurisdiction distinguished **65,** 7
as asset **65,** 7
embassy or consular bank account/funds, immunity, execution/attachment, purpose/use
designation, conclusiveness **65,** 9
evidence of
fact of being in name of embassy or State **65,** 9, **77,** 491
Ministry of Justice declaration **65,** 9, **77,** 491-2
extraterritorial, whether **65,** 9, **77,** 491-2
'for its legation' **65,** 9
employment contract, academic appointment in respondent State, jurisdiction **65,** 5-6
employment contract, locally engaged staff, diplomatic mission **86,** 585-6
applicable law, local law **116,** 532

classification of employment, nature of employment obligations as determining factor **86,** 586
employee's right to institute proceedings against employing State **65,** 22
jurisdiction **65,** 22
national of sending State **86,** 594-5
sending State as contractual party **86,** 585
State immunity, jurisdiction **86,** 584-6
dismissal for national security considerations **116,** 530-3
general principle of international law **65,** 22
national of sending State **86,** 584-5
employment contract (municipal law)
applicable law **96,** 572-3
Civil Code (*ABGB*) **96,** 573
Private Employee Act 1921 **96,** 573
dismissal **96,** 573-8
administrative retirement **96,** 573
disabled person **96,** 574-5, 580-2
Disabled Persons (Employment) Act 1970 **96,** 574-5
Industrial Relations Act 1974 **96,** 573-4
procedure **96,** 575-6
enforcement measures, extraterritorial **65,** 9
European Convention on Human Rights (1950)
in constitutional law **45,** 288
municipal law and **38,** 174-80, **71,** 257
primacy, previous legislation **38,** 176-80
ratification **56,** 479-80
reservations **56,** 479-80
expatriation. *See* law of, Habsburg Law *below*
expropriation/nationalization
property of expellees from Czechoslovakia **51,** 22-4
without compensation **51,** 22-4
expulsion of alien
grounds, Nazi propaganda **51,** 237-8
South Tyrol, residents of **71,** 237-8
extradition **51,** 328-39
own national **86,** 551-2
extraterritoriality, Head of State **65,** 14-15, **103,** 585
Federal Distribution Commission **48,** 157-8, 176
foreign State
liability to suit **77,** 488
procedure **77,** 487-8
fraud **41,** 321, 333
freedom of establishment **77,** 477
freedom of expression
journalist, role **88,** 524
limitations **88,** 556
respect for private life **88,** 521
respect for reputation **88,** 521, 524
freedom of movement **71,** 258
general principles of international law, State immunity, jurisdiction, employment contract **65,** 22
German property
Finance and Compensation Treaty (1961) **44,** 322

Austria (*cont.*)
as war booty **48,** 227-8
Head of State, as State **65,** 14-15
Head of State, immunity, jurisdiction
absolute theory **65,** 14-15
executive certificate/statement **65,** 14
extraterritoriality and **65,** 14-15
submission to the jurisdiction as waiver, revocation/withdrawal **65,** 15
Head of State, immunity, jurisdiction, waiver, insurance contract **65,** 14-15
human rights **51,** 236-7
European Convention on Human Rights (1950) **77,** 438-9
determination of civil rights under **77,** 438-9
Protocol IV, reservation **77,** 481-2
right to hearing **77,** 439
IAEA, Headquarters Agreement **38,** 453-6
individual in international law, rights **77,** 445
injunction against foreign State, failure to comply, action for damages **86,** 578
International Covenant on Civil and Political Rights (1966), pensions law and **118,** 147-51
international law
general principles of international law, as part of municipal law **86,** 585-6
municipal law and, derogatory effect of treaty **77,** 469
as part of municipal law **40,** 2, **77,** 445
primacy **40,** 74
judicial officials, bias **56,** 449
judicial review **96,** 576-8
separation of powers **96,** 575-6
jurisdiction
airspace, territorial **77,** 484-5
criminal
acts committed abroad. *See* criminal acts committed abroad *below*
credit card abuse **86,** 562-3
foreign State's rights, protection of **71,** 230, 255-7
fraud. *See* fraud *below*
hijacking of aircraft **71,** 229-31
nationals abroad **71,** 229-31
terrorist offences **71,** 236-7, 243-7
criminal acts committed abroad **86,** 559-61
applicable law **86,** 560-1
double criminality **86,** 560-1
nationals, by **86,** 559-61
private prosecution, requirement for in place of commission, relevance **86,** 560-1
time-barred in place of commission, relevance **86,** 560-1
'designation of competent court' and **86,** 567, 577-8
drug-trafficking. *See* drug-trafficking *above*
effects doctrine **77,** 484, **86,** 562-4
employment contract, academic appointment in respondent State **65,** 5-6
enforcement, impossibility of as impediment **86,** 566, 567, 568, 573, 574
European Convention on Human Rights (1950), violation of **77,** 438-9
exclusion, permanent representative of defendant State, absence of **86,** 566, 581
extraterritorial, enforcement of injunction against foreign State **86,** 581
fraud **71,** 252-8
place of commission **86,** 562-3

international official **77,** 454-7
nexus
advertising campaign, bank account **65,** 7
property within the jurisdiction **65,** 7, 15, 17-18, 19
ratione loci **86,** 566, 567, 570, 573, 574, 577, 578, 580-2
personal **86,** 551-2, 559-61, 562-3
proceedings in defendant's home State, possibility of
bias **86,** 566
certification, need for **86,** 568-9, 574
unreasonable or impossible **86,** 567, 574, 577, 578, 580-2
proprio motu **77,** 429
protective principle **77,** 484
lex loci delicti commissi, relevance **77,** 484
as riparian State, Lake Constance **75,** 83
Single Convention on Narcotic Drugs (1961) **86,** 551-2
territorial, effects doctrine. *See* effects doctrine *above*
just satisfaction, creditors in bankruptcy, payment of compensation to **56,** 499, 501-4, 506-10
law of
Abolition of the Aristocracy Law (3 April 1919) **77,** 478
Abolition of Extraterritoriality Law 1919 **71,** 549-50
Administrative Court Law 1965 (*VwGG*)
Art. 42 **71,** 282-3, 446, 541, 576, **77,** 482, 487-8
Art. 63 **77,** 482
Administrative Offences Law (1950)
Art. 35 **107,** 11, 13
Art. 36(1) **107,** 11, 13
Administrative Procedure Act 1950 **56,** 448
Art. 7 **81,** 12
Art. 17 **81,** 12
Art. 37 **81,** 12
Art. 39 **81,** 12
Art. 43 **81,** 12
Administrative Procedure Laws, Introductory Law (1950)
Art. VIII **107,** 11, 13
Art. IX(1) **107,** 10, 11, 13, 15
Aliens Police Law **77,** 444
appeal, new material **96,** 443-4
Bankruptcy Act **56,** 458-9
Basic Law (*StGG*) **77,** 477
Art. 5 **81,** 8
Civil Code (*ABGB*) **86,** 576
Arts. 33-7 **86,** 549
Art. 364 **86,** 581
Arts. 859 ff **96,** 573
Art. 1409 **71,** 267, 269
Art. 1431 **71,** 268-9
non-retroactivity of laws principle **71,** 38
Civil Procedure Code (*ZPO*) 1960
Art. 34 **56,** 460
Art. 44 **77,** 474
Art. 50 **77,** 474
Art. 57 **77,** 441, 442
Art. 109 **64,** 11

Austria (*cont.*)
Art. 112 **56,** 458
Art. 119 (service of process) **65,** 5, 8, **77,** 454
Art. 175 **56,** 460, 461
Art. 190 **56,** 461, 464, **96,** 577
Art. 197 **56,** 467
Art. 228 **96,** 577
Art. 411(2) **65,** 11
Art. 502 **77,** 491
Art. 503 **71,** 268
Art. 504 **96,** 577
Art. 507 **96,** 577
Art. 508 **96,** 577
Art. 509 **96,** 577
Art. 510 **86,** 550
Art. 530 **96,** 577
Art. 706 **65,** 22
Art. 725 **65,** 22
Civil Procedure Code (*ZPO*) (Amended) 1983 **86,** 567
Constitution. *See* Constitution *above*
Criminal Code (*StGB*)
Art. 2 **71,** 257
Art. 8 **71,** 243-5, 248, 250, 252-6
Art. 25 **71,** 236
Art. 34 **71,** 244
Art. 36 **71,** 250-1
Art. 37 **71,** 231, 237
Art. 38 **71,** 444
Art. 39 **39,** 237, **71,** 230
Art. 40 **71,** 237
Art. 42 **67,** 510-24
Art. 53 **77,** 484
Art. 55 **56,** 455
Art. 58 **71,** 244-5, 444
Art. 63 **86,** 560, 563
Art. 64 **86,** 552
Art. 65 **86,** 552
Art. 66 **71,** 245, 445
Art. 67 **86,** 560, 563
Art. 72 **86,** 560, 563
Art. 88 **77,** 468
Art. 93 **71,** 230
Art. 111 **88,** 519-20, 525
Art. 111(2) **88,** 524
Art. 111(3) **88,** 529
Art. 112 **88,** 520
Art. 116(2) **88,** 521, 522
Art. 134 **71,** 243-5
Art. 135 **71,** 243-4
Art. 136 **71,** 244
Art. 183 **45,** 239
Art. 184 **45,** 239
Art. 197 **45,** 237, 239, **56,** 450, **71,** 252-7

Art. 199 **45,** 237, **71,** 252-7
Art. 201 (rape) **121,** 270 n. 208
Art. 203 **45,** 239, **56,** 455, 456
Art. 205 **45,** 239, **56,** 450
drug offences **86,** 551
Criminal Procedure Code (*ZPO*) **45,** 237-9, 241, 244, 252, 255, 256, 265, 275, 281-2, 284, 288, 291, 292, 296, **47,** 464-6, 468, 472
Arts. 4 ff **71,** 244
Art. 34 **56,** 456
Art. 61 **77,** 467, 468-9
Art. 109 **45,** 239
Art. 112 **56,** 452, 458
Art. 120 **81,** 191, 193, 194
Art. 125 **81,** 191, 193, 194
Art. 126 **81,** 191, 193, 194
Art. 152(1) **81,** 192
Art. 175(1) **45,** 237-8
Art. 265 **56,** 455, 456
Art. 281 **71,** 237, 248, 250-1, 254, 256-7, **77,** 484
Art. 345 **71,** 244-5
termination of proceedings **67,** 510-24
Currency Protection Laws **77,** 449
Decree of 1 February 1922 (Re-application of the Hague Convention on Civil Procedure) **77,** 442
Disabled Persons Employment Act 1970 **96,** 574-5, 580
Distribution Law (Poland) (*VGP*) **77,** 428-32, 462-3
Distribution Law (Romania) **48,** 157-8, 159-61, 176, 177, **77,** 430
Enforcement Law (*EO*), Art. 355 **86,** 578, 580, 581
Execution of Contracts Law **71,** 269
Execution Law (EO)
Art. 54 **77,** 494
Art. 55 **77,** 494
Art. 78 **77,** 491
Explosives Law (*SprengstoffG*) **71,** 236-7, 243-7
Art. 4 **71,** 236, 243-5
Art. 5 **71,** 286
Art. 6 **71,** 236
Food Act 1975 **81,** 188-94
General Administrative Procedure Code 1950 **96,** 575-6
Art. 38 **96,** 577
Habsburg Law (3 April 1919) **77,** 476-82
Art. 2 **77,** 276-82
expatriation of Habsburgs **77,** 476
persons affected **77,** 476-82
State Treaty 1955, entrenchment under **71,** 540-1, 574-6
Income Tax Law 1967 **71,** 540-1, 574-6
Industrial Relations Act 1974 **96,** 573, 580
Jurisdictional Statute, Introductory Act (EGJN)
Art. 9 **65,** 9, 11-12, 14-15, **71,** 548-9, **77,** 455, 494
disputes relating to treaties or principles of international law **65,** 9 n. 3
jurisdiction in relation to 'extraterritorial' persons **65,** 9 n. 3
Jurisdictional Statute (*JN*)
Art. 19(b) **44,** 232

Austria (*cont.*)
Art. 28 **86,** 566, 567-8, 570, 573-4, 577, 578
Art. 42 **65,** 6, **77,** 494
Art. 81 **86,** 576, 577, 578, 580, 582
Art. 99 (claims concerning property rights against persons not domiciled in Austria) **65,** 5, 7, 17-19, **86,** 566, 567, 572-3
Labour Courts Act **96,** 576
Labour Relations Law (*ArbVG*), Art. 105 **77,** 487-8
Labour and Social Courts Act 1985, Art. 63 **96,** 576-7
Land Sales Law (*GVG*) 1970 **77,** 438-9
Legal Assistance Decree, s 12 **65,** 22
Narcotic Drugs Law (*SuchtgiftG*) 1985 **86,** 551
Art. 6 **71,** 248-50
Art. 12 **77,** 484
Nationality Law 1965, Art. 10 **71,** 442-5
Nuclear Energy Law 1978 **86,** 569
Nuclear Energy Liability Law (*AtomHG*) **86,** 572
Occupation Damages Act **45,** 370
Passport Law 1951 **71,** 255-6
Pension Act 1965, compatibility with International Covenant on Civil and Political Rights (ICCPR) (1966) **118,** 147-51
Private Employment Act 1921, Art. 27 **96,** 573
Private International Law Act (New) (*IPRG*) **86,** 544, 545
Art. 44 **116,** 532
Art. 48 **86,** 549
Protection of Personal Freedom Law 1862 **86,** 557
Art. 35 **107,** 10
Public Liability Law. *See* State Liability Law (*AHG*) *below*
Real Property Transactions Act (Upper Austria) **56,** 445-7, 449-50
Rescission of Contracts Law **71,** 269
Road Traffic Offences Law (*VStG*) **86,** 554-8
Sale of Real Property Law (*GVG*) (Tyrol) 1966 **77,** 434, 437-9
Service Law, Art. 11 **77,** 487
State Liability Law (*AHG*) **77,** 471, 472, **86,** 554
Art. 7 **86,** 548
attribution of liability **77,** 472-4
functional test **77,** 472
Organtheorie **77,** 472, 474
State Treaty Execution Act **48,** 228
Transfer of Nationality Law **71,** 237
Usury Act **45,** 236-41
Water Law (*WRG*) **86,** 544-5
Weapons Law (*WaffenG*) 1967 **71,** 236, 286
legal aid **57,** 199
legislation
scrutiny **47,** 413
territorial application **86,** 548
legislation, interpretation
aids
legislative history **86,** 567
Minutes of Constitutive National Assembly **77,** 480
guidelines

intention of legislature **77,** 481-2
teleological **77,** 481
phrases, 'designation of competent court' **86,** 567, 577-8
presumption of conformity with international obligations **40,** 2-3
presumption of human rights protection, restrictive in case of fundamental rights **77,** 481
treaty as aid **40,** 2
treaty reservation **77,** 481
treaty-implementing legislation **77,** 429-32, 463-5
MFN treatment, Austro-German Commercial Agreement (1920) **77,** 435
nationality
Anschluss, effect **45,** 353-7
extraterritorial legislation, effect **43,** 192-4
necessity **71,** 230, 254
property
aliens' rights **77,** 435-9, **81,** 3-24
jurisdiction **81,** 9-10
Provincial Land Sales Authority **77,** 439
Public Administrator, appointment, constitutionality **47,** 412-17
public interest
Public Administrator, appointment **47,** 412-17
transfer of property **56,** 445
Real Property Transactions Authority **81,** 5-6, 10
fair and public trial and **81,** 18-19
independent and impartial tribunal, whether **81,** 15-18, 20-1
membership **81,** 16-18
procedure **81,** 12-13
tribunal established by law, whether **81,** 15
reprisals **47,** 412-17
restitution laws **40,** 238, 342-3
separation of powers **77,** 446
service of process on foreign State or State agency
garnishee order **65,** 22
method, diplomatic channels **65,** 8
refusal to accept **65,** 5, 8
on grounds of prejudice to sovereignty or security **65,** 11
refusal to provide legal assistance distinguished **65,** 11
South Tyrol **71,** 237-8. *See also* Italy, South Tyrol
standard of treatment of alien, equality **45,** 370, **77,** 465
State agency/State-owned corporation/State entity, classification, national airline, separate legal entity **86,** 573
State immunity, execution/attachment, applicability, garnishee order on earnings of embassy employee **65,** 21-2
State immunity, execution/attachment, bank account. *See* embassy or consular bank account/funds, immunity, execution/attachment *above*
State immunity, execution/attachment, entitlement, national airline, separate legal entity **86,** 573
State immunity, execution/attachment, procedural aspects, executive/ministerial authorization, need for **65,** 9
State immunity, execution/attachment, purpose/use of funds/assets
commercial purpose **86,** 570
cultural institute **86,** 573

Austria (*cont.*)
diplomatic functions **77,** 492-4
State immunity, jurisdiction
European Convention on State Immunity (and Protocol) (Basle) (1972), non-party, application to **86,** 585, **116,** 532-3
executive/ministerial authorization, need for **65,** 9
preliminary issue, whether **65,** 7-8
submission to the jurisdiction as waiver
insurance contract **65,** 14-15
revocation/withdrawal **65,** 15
State immunity, jurisdiction, classification of act **65,** 18
expropriation/nationalization **65,** 18-19
legislative act **65,** 12-13, 18
nature or purpose of transaction as determining factor **86,** 586
private law relationship **65,** 6, 12
private person test **65,** 171
production of nuclear power **86,** 569
treaty obligation to pay compensation **65,** 12-13
State immunity, jurisdiction, entitlement, State agency/State-owned corporation/State entity, nationalized industry **65,** 19
State immunity, jurisdiction, procedural aspects
effective remedy, right to, proceedings in defendant's home State, possibility of, unreasonable or impossible **86,** 567, 574, 577, 578, 580-2
enforceability of judgment, relevance **86,** 568-9, 570
State immunity, jurisdiction, theory/doctrine
general principle of international law **86,** 584
restrictive theory **86,** 585-6
State immunity, jurisdiction, waiver **86,** 584
express contractual term **86,** 584-5
implied, insurance contract **65,** 14-15
motor insurance **65,** 14-15
State responsibility for acts and omissions of
consular agent **86,** 556-7
diplomatic agent **86,** 507-8
failure to monitor and control activity **86,** 569
lawful act **86,** 557
nuclear power station, accident **86,** 569
State organ abroad **86,** 547-50
transboundary nuclear pollution **86,** 565-70
unlawful act **86,** 557
State responsibility, procedural aspects
individual's right to remedy **86,** 569, 572
requirements, execution of Austrian law **86,** 549
State Treaty (1955)
applicability to German nationals resident in Austria **45,** 440-1
compensation for
property taken by foreign States **40,** 175-83
requisitioned property **40,** 234-5
Execution Act **48,** 228
Habsburg Law and **77,** 482
interpretation **48,** 227-8
UN nationals, restoration of rights of **40,** 230-2, 233

Supreme Court Rules of Precedent No 28 (restrictive principle of State immunity) **65,** 6, 12, 18, 22, **86,** 586
transboundary nuclear pollution **86,** 565-70
basis of liability
emissions law **86,** 569
ownership of plant **86,** 569
State responsibility for **86,** 569
treason, against foreign State **71,** 243-7, 443-5
treaties
abrogation **77,** 435-6
Austria–Switzerland Commercial Treaty (1950) **77,** 436
German assets, transfer to Austria **40,** 228-9
implementing legislation
conformity with international law **77,** 446
supremacy of treaty **77,** 431-2
pre-1938 **38,** 135
primacy **38,** 176-80, **77,** 446
subsequent treaty **38,** 176-80
reapplication **77,** 436-8
suspension, Austria-Switzerland Establishment Treaty (1875) **77,** 439-40
validity **77,** 435-8
waiver of individual claims **40,** 184-6, **44,** 316, **45,** 440
treaty interpretation **77,** 464-5
Tyrol
Farms Act 1900 **81,** 10
Real Property Transactions Act 1970/73
Art. 3 **81,** 5
Art. 4(2) **81,** 5-6, 7-8
Art. 13(3) **81,** 5, 10
Art. 15(1) **81,** 10
Art. 16(1) **81,** 10
Sale of Real Property Law (*GVG*) 1966 **77,** 434, 437-9
Upper Austria, Real Property Transactions Act **56,** 445-7, 449-50
war, compensation, treaty or statute, need for **65,** 12-13
Austro-Hungarian monarchy, dissolution **39,** 92
aut dedere aut punire/judicare. *See also* war crimes, obligation to seek out and prosecute
crimes against humanity **119,** 356-7
customary international law **110,** 72
extradition **60,** 296, **87,** 166-7, **94,** 507, 534, **95,** 364, **106,** 237, 263, 267-8
refugees **111,** 523
terrorism conventions **94,** 507-8
forcible abduction/unlawful arrest **95,** 364
Geneva Conventions (1949) **105,** 536
genocide **120,** 361-5
Hostages Convention (1979) **119,** 65
jus cogens/peremptory norm **94,** 552, 565
Montreal Convention for the Suppression of Unlawful Acts Against the Safety of Civil Aviation (1971). *See* Montreal Convention for the Suppression of Unlawful Acts Against the Safety of Civil Aviation (1971), *aut dedere aut punire/judicare*
State practice **119,** 86
terrorism **88,** 296-7, **94,** 487-8, 507-8, 534, 551, 556, 564-5, **107,** 564-5, **110,** 702
Torture Convention (1984) **119,** 70-1, 85, 150, 151, 164

aut dedere aut punire/judicare (*cont.*)
universal jurisdiction and **36,** 302-3
war crimes **36,** 302-3, **88,** 296-7, **105,** 449, 497, 536
aviation. *See* air transport agreements; aircraft; carriage by air, international; International Air Transport Association (IATA)
avulsion
acquisition of territory and **91,** 454, 457-8, 464
boundary, effect on **51,** 28-30, **91,** 196, 454, 457-8, 464, **97,** 462-4
critical date **97,** 462-4
erosion distinguished **97,** 462
estoppel and **97,** 466-7
Goascorán **97,** 462-7
Axis, Berlin–Rome (1936) 44, 335

bad faith. *See also* good faith
belligerent occupation, deportation **83,** 184
costs and **89,** 350, **96,** 331-2
evidence of, need for **46,** 333
foreign courts **46,** 332-4
of friendly government **52,** 366
mala fides **71,** 492, **87,** 287, **88,** 702, **91,** 296
malicious prosecution **123,** 492-5
natural persons, limited to **91,** 296
shareholders
fraude . . . la loi **82,** 144
pursuit of compensation relating to company **82,** 142
State contract, revocation for **89,** 610, 613
State responsibility for **91,** 296, **125,** 29-32, 69-71
Baden, France, boundary treaties with **42,** 60
Badinter Commission (Yugoslavia) 92, 162-211, **96,** 713-42, **100,** 228
advisory opinion
binding effect **96,** 716
'subsidiary means for the determination of the rules of law' **96,** 715
competence
basis
agreement of parties **96,** 715, 716
referral by Co-Chairmen of the International Conference on the Former Yugoslavia **96,** 716
non-legal issues **96,** 731
terms of reference **96,** 716
composition and terms of reference **96,** 737-8
equality of parties **96,** 717
Rules of Procedure **96,** 739-42
Yugoslavia, Federal Republic (FRY) and
advisory opinion, effect **96,** 716
letter relating to **96,** 717-18
non-participation **96,** 717
statement relating to **96,** 714-15
Bahamas
Constitution
Art. 15 (fundamental rights) **124,** 292
Art. 16(1) (right to life) **124,** 287-8, 294
Art. 17(1) (torture/inhuman treatment) **124,** 262-4, 266-9, 273-81, 293-8

Art. 19 **85,** 149, 151
Art. 19(1) (deprivation of liberty) **124,** 262
Art. 19(3) (prompt hearing) **124,** 262, 266
Art. 20(1) (fair trial within reasonable period) **124,** 262, 263-4, 266-7, 276-7
Art. 25 **85,** 148, 149
Art. 28 (appeal) **85,** 146, 148, 149, 150, 151, 152, 153, **124,** 262, 276-7
Art. 104 (appeal) **85,** 148, 149-50, **124,** 372
phrases, 'sentence of a court' **124,** 287
continuity of law **85,** 133-9
death penalty
delay in execution, UNHRC, appeal to **124,** 285
prosecution for non-capital charges while on remand **124,** 269-70, 280-1
death row as inhuman or degrading treatment
conditions of detention **124,** 276-8, 281
delay
as abuse of process **124,** 289
before sentencing **124,** 264-6, 273-81
'reasonable' **124,** 290, 296-7
submission to Inter-American Commission on Human Rights, effect **124,** 265, 270-2, 284-98, 1625-6
length of detention **124,** 268-9, 273-81
'reasonable' **124,** 289-90
extradition **85,** 129-45
inhuman or degrading treatment, death row. *See* death row as inhuman or degrading treatment *above*
law of
Bahamas Extradition Act 1960 **85,** 154
Constitution. *See* Constitution *above*
Court of Appeal Act **85,** 145-6, 148, 150
Criminal Procedure Code Act 1968 **85,** 148, 153-4
Crown Proceedings Act 1963, waiver of immunity in US courts, whether **63,** 352
Customs Management Act 1976 **85,** 133
Dangerous Drugs Act **85,** 133
Existing Laws Amendment Order 1974 **85,** 138
Extradition Act 1870 (UK), extension **85,** 137
legitimate expectation, death penalty, non-implementation while petition to Inter-American Commission on Human Rights in train **124,** 289-90, 294-5, 297-8
treaties, State succession **85,** 143-5
Baie du Figuier, co-ownership **97,** 516, 670-1
Balfour Declaration (1926) 86, 607, **90,** 249
Balfour Draft. *See* Mandate, South West Africa, Balfour Draft
Bandung Conference 1955, self-determination and **46,** 485
Bangladesh
boundary demarcation, powers of executive **70,** 43, 46-50
Constitution
s 2(a) **70,** 50
s 36 **70,** 40
s 42, compensation provisions **66,** 255
s 55(2) **70,** 43
s 102(2) **70,** 40
s 142 **70,** 50
s 143(2) **70,** 43, 48, 50
courts, municipal

Bangladesh (*cont.*)
executive treaty-making powers, enquiry into **70,** 38-50
standing of individuals **70,** 39-41
jurisdiction **66,** 196-7, 253-4
East Pakistan, State succession **63,** 53, **66,** 56, 194-7
executive, powers of
constitutional limits **70,** 43, 46-50
treaty-making **70,** 43, 46-50
municipal law restriction **70,** 48-9
India
boundary demarcation **70,** 43-50
Land Boundary Demarcation Treaty (1974)
as cession of land **70,** 43-50
entry into force **70,** 42-3
ratification **70,** 42-3
Industrial Development Corporation
dissolution, effects of **65,** 446-9
extinction of liabilities of, whether confiscatory **65,** 448-9
whether contrary to international law **65,** 449
law of. *See also* Constitution *above*
Abandoned Property (Control, Management and Disposal) Order 1972 **66,** 248
Bangladesh Industrial Development Corporation (Amendment) Order (Order No 78) 1972 **65,** 447
Bangladesh Industrial Development Corporation (Dissolution) Order (Order No 140) 1972 **65,** 447
Bangladesh Industrial Development Corporation Order (Order No 39) 1972 **65,** 446-7
Banks Nationalization Order **66,** 193-4, 247-55
Civil Procedure Code **66,** 253
Disputed Debts Order 1972 **65,** 447-8
Industrialization Enterprises (Nationalization) Order 1972 **66,** 248
secession, emergence as independent State **52,** 487-9
status **57,** 611
bank. *See also* central/State-owned bank; embassy or consular bank account/funds, immunity, execution/attachment; *and under individual countries*
accounts abroad
immunity. *See* embassy or consular bank account/funds, immunity, execution/attachment; State immunity, execution/attachment, funds held in private foreign bank
jurisdiction over **38,** 112-20
branch. *See also* foreign branch *below*
foreign bank to operate through **107,** 205
legal identity **66,** 194-5, 402-3, 447-8, 469-70
confidentiality **84,** 752-3, **86,** 167
expropriation/nationalization
foreign accounts, effect on **66,** 193-7, 250-5
Vietnam **107,** 206-19
foreign branch
applicable law
currency of payment **107,** 216 n. 5
lex situs **107,** 207, 208-10, 215-16
place of payment **107,** 216 n. 5
deposit, *situs* **107,** 207

funding responsibility **107,** 205
liability for loss. *See* liability for loss *below*
liability for loss
currency of payment, relevance **107,** 218
disclaimer
'any loss . . . resulting from government orders, laws . . . or other cause beyond its control' **107,** 206, 208, 209-10, 216, 218-19
clarity, need for **107,** 210
expropriation/nationalization, *Sokoloff* **107,** 217-18
force majeure **107,** 207-10, 216
general principle of banking law **107,** 208, 217
impossibility of performance **107,** 208
revolution **107,** 207-9
seizure of assets, effect on creditor's rights **81,** 534, 538
banking practice 68, 535-6, 543-4, 546-7, 551-2, 555-6
banking contract, applicable law **40,** 14
Barcelona Traction Company **46,** 182-4, 189, 190-1, 192, 234, 325, 458-9, 493-4, 528-9
customary international practice **75,** 136-7
international credit transfers **117,** 241-2
UNCITRAL Model Law on International Credit Transfers (1992) **117,** 242
bankruptcy. *See also* bankruptcy proceedings; liquidators
company's existence, effect on **46,** 493
diplomatic functions, effect on **94,** 368-9
foreign company **46,** 189, 191-2, 235, 277-80, 459
subsidiaries' property **46,** 192-3
German External Debts Agreement (1953) **44,** 318-19
laws **46,** 183, 189, 192-6, 234-6, 281-4, 439, 458
modern trends **46,** 449 n. 2
power to require person to appear for examination **88,** 312-22
proceedings. *See* bankruptcy proceedings
sequestration order, annulment **87,** 172-6
State immunity, execution/attachment and **94,** 368-9
bankruptcy proceedings. *See also* bankruptcy; liquidators; service of process out of the jurisdiction, insolvency/insolvency-related proceedings; winding-up proceedings
applicable law **107,** 345
creditor, international organization as **107,** 416-18
jurisdiction
aliens **101,** 338-51
Enforcement of Judgments in Civil and Commercial Matters Convention (1968) **101,** 348
'right to payment'
enforceability, relevance **107,** 417-18
judgment in favour **107,** 417-18
State immunity, jurisdiction, winding-up order, preferential treatment **101,** 335-7
Barcelona Traction Company
bankruptcy **46,** 182-4, 189, 190-1, 192, 234, 325, 458-9, 493-4, 528-9
Belgian participation **46,** 310-14, 525-6
diplomatic representations by Canada **46,** 184, 199, 217-19, 253-4, 346-50, 355-6
history **46,** 181-5, 190-7, 214-15
local remedies, pursuit of **46,** 322-4, 458-9. *See also* exhaustion of local remedies
valuation of property of **46,** 331
Bari Institute (IAM). *See* International Centre for Advanced Mediterranean Agronomic Studies (CHEAM), Bari Institute (IAM)

Basel Convention on the Control of Transboundary Movements of Hazardous Wastes and Their Disposal (1989). *See* waste disposal, Basel Convention on the Control of Transboundary Movements of Hazardous Wastes and Their Disposal (1989)
baselines 70, 594, **71,** 114, 156-7, 159, **91,** 655-63. *See also* European Economic Community (EEC) fisheries policy, baselines
basepoints. *See* basepoints
bays **57,** 59, 61-2, **59,** 279-80
choice, parties' **99,** 446
closing-line of bay **97,** 523, 661
coastline, turning point and **81,** 477, 478
coasts. *See* coasts
construction lines **52,** 263
continental shelf **81,** 393
territorial sea, outer edge **91,** 669
Continental Shelf Convention (1958), customary international law distinguished **41,** 190-1
full coastline **91,** 463
importance **83,** 105
instability **100,** 133
islands **59,** 300, **67,** 256-9, 264, 293-8, **81,** 393
low-water mark **73,** 176-8, 193-4, 199-200, 205, 216-17, **91,** 416, 660-1, **94,** 25
customary international law **119,** 458
Law of the Sea Convention (1982) **100,** 149, **119,** 458
Territorial Sea and Contiguous Zone Convention (1958) **81,** 485, **100,** 118, 149
modification **81,** 393
erosion of low-tide elevations **100,** 133
extension of territorial waters distinguished **100,** 146-7
peninsulae and **81,** 393
straight **41,** 50, 82, 87, 149, 151, 152-3, 181, **42,** 90-3, **52,** 262, **59,** 225-7, 275, 280, **69,** 35, 44, 63-8, 72-3, 79-81, **73,** 174-8, 217, **81,** 254, **82,** 673, 682, 687, **83,** 20, 95, **91,** 416, **119,** 459-61
construction lines **52,** 263
equity of **41,** 87, 149, 153
internal waters **42,** 90-3
optional **91,** 416, 431 n. 9, 461 n. 7
territorial sea **69,** 35, 63, 72-3, **81,** 254, **91,** 416, **119,** 459-61
Territorial Sea and Contiguous Zone Convention (1958) **73,** 174-8, 217, **81,** 254
territorial sea **41,** 161, **57,** 76-7, 108-9, **81,** 254, 393
internal waters, seaward edge **91,** 416, **119,** 459
low-water mark **69,** 79-80, 85-8, **90,** 238, **91,** 416
at spring-tide **94,** 366-7
Law of the Sea Convention (1982) **119,** 458
outer limit of as **41,** 190
reefs **119,** 460-1
rivers, effect **59,** 241-2, 281
straight **69,** 35, 63, 72-3, **81,** 254, **91,** 416, **119,** 459-61
Territorial Sea and Contiguous Zone Convention (1958) **41,** 153 n. 1, 163, **59,** 225-7, 275, 280, **69,** 44, 63-8, 72, 79-81, **73,** 174-8, 217
economic interests **41,** 153 n. 1
rivers, effect **59,** 241-2, 281
basepoints
average distance curve method and **83,** 107
choice **81,** 288

courbe de la distance moyenne **83,** 107
distance between **81,** 283
Eddystone Rock **81,** 378, 379
equidistance and **41,** 82
harbour works **91,** 660-3
Hague Codification Conference (1930) **91,** 661
State practice **91,** 662
Territorial Sea and Contiguous Zone Convention (1958) **91,** 662
treaty practice **91,** 662
islands **81,** 280, 282-3, 295
Eritrea–Yemen **119,** 455-6
islets **81,** 280, **119,** 459-61
low-tide elevations **83,** 110-11
Law of the Sea Convention (1982) **82,** 110-11, **100,** 149
lighthouses, need for **83,** 110, 111, **119,** 460
Territorial Sea and Contiguous Zone Convention (1958) **100,** 118, 149
number **81,** 413, 414, 419
proportionality **81,** 280
Basutoland. *See* Lesotho
bays 90, 325-8. *See also* gulfs; *mare clausum*; maritime delimitation
baselines and **57,** 59, 61-2, **59,** 279-80
Chesapeake Bay **97,** 653
closed sea **97,** 507
definition
not high seas **97,** 507
not international waters **97,** 507
closing line **69,** 35-6, 43-6, 53-7, 62-5, 70-3, **71,** 95-7, 163, 181-2
6 miles **91,** 438
10 miles **97,** 651, 652, 658
12 miles **97,** 651-2, 655 n. 1
24 miles **91,** 416, **97,** 659, 660
25 miles **97,** 658
as baseline **97,** 523, 661
cartographic evidence **69,** 70-1
coastal configuration **69,** 65
international law rules **69,** 43, 63-5, 71-3
line of sight test **91,** 430, 437-8
off-shore islands **69,** 35-6, 43-6, 53-4, 62, 64-5
Territorial Sea Convention (1958) and **69,** 44, 63-5, 72-3
visual criteria **69,** 43, 56
co-ownership
administrative boundaries, absence **97,** 514-15
agreement, need for **97,** 513
Baie du Figuier **97,** 516, 670-1
community of interests distinguished **97,** 518-19
continued and peaceful exercise **97,** 515
customary law **97,** 513
division, absence **97,** 515-16
as joint sovereignty **97,** 513-14
State succession and **97,** 514-16
coastal State interests, importance **97,** 507-8
community of interests
as co-ownership **97,** 518-19

bays (*cont.*)
communauté de patrimoines **97,** 519
delimitation, need for **97,** 519-20
Territorial Jurisdiction of the International Commission of the River Oder (1929) **97,** 518
Conception Bay **97,** 653
definition **57,** 67, 73-5, **59,** 273, 277, 296
semi-circle test **59,** 296-7
Delaware Bay **97,** 653
delimitation **71,** 95-7, 149, 152, 163, 180-5
fishing rights, title and **90,** 301-5
Fonseca Bay. *See* Fonseca Bay
Fundy **71,** 95-7, 149, 152, 163, 180-5, **81,** 324, **90,** 315, 325-6
geographical concept **97,** 649
gulfs distinguished **69,** 42, 52, 61
historic **42,** 88, 95-7, **57,** 64-5, **59,** 264-73, **69,** 63, 66, 73, **114,** 35
ancient title distinguished **91,** 429-39. *See also* title, ancient
Anglo-Norwegian Fisheries **97,** 671-3
applicable law
Law of the Sea Convention (1982) **97,** 504
Territorial Sea and Contiguous Zone Convention (1958) **97,** 504
Committee of Experts (1927) **97,** 655
criteria
acquiescence **91,** 418, 420 n. 6, 421, 423-4
continuous and open exercise of authority **91,** 418, 420, 421 n. 10, 432
exclusion from innocent passage **91,** 423, 425-6
Judicial Regime of Historic Waters Including Historic Bays 56 (UN Doc A/CN.4/143) (1962) **91,** 418, 425, 431-2
passage of time **91,** 420
vital interests. *See* vital interests *below*
definition **91,** 417, 432 n. 10
exception to rules governing bays **97,** 652, 662
Fonseca. *See* Fonseca Bay, historic bay
historic internal waters and **91,** 417 n. 2
historic waters distinguished **97,** 630 n. 1, 671-3
inconsistent acts by sovereign **91,** 419, 421, 422, 437 n. 18, 438
innocent passage **97,** 508-9
internal waters **97,** 662-3
justification
immemorial possession/continuous peaceful exercise of sovereignty/acquiescence **97,** 507, 511-12, 652
strategic requirements **97,** 507
Law of the Sea Convention (1982) **97,** 660
legal institution, whether **97,** 649, 654, 660-3, 667
North Atlantic Fisheries **97,** 504, 674
Oppenheim (1st edn) (1905) **97,** 653
special regime, whether **97,** 649-50
submerged lands under, ownership **91,** 411-13
territorial nature, closed sea **97,** 509
as territorial sea **42,** 88, 95-7, **57,** 64-5, **59,** 264-73, **69,** 63, 66, 72-3
Territorial Sea and Contiguous Zone Convention (1958) **91,** 432 n. 10
as internal waters **91,** 417
title **42,** 88, 95-7, **57,** 64-5, **59,** 264-73, **69,** 63, 66, 72-3, **114,** 35

Tunisia/Libya **97,** 504-5
UNCLOS I **97,** 659-60
vital interests
economic interests **91,** 418, 420 n. 7
geographical configuration and **91,** 418-20
security **91,** 418, 419-20
inter fauces terrae **69,** 55-7, 59, **91,** 430, 438
as internal waters **42,** 68-9, 74, 83-4, 86, **43,** 114-25, **69,** 35-6, 42-7, 55-7, 61-7, **90,** 238, **91,** 431
development, Law of the Sea Convention (1982) **97,** 661
multilateral approach **69,** 56
pluri-State **97,** 520-1
single State **97,** 660-3
international **90,** 326, 329
juridical
innocent passage **97,** 509
Territorial Sea and Contiguous Zone Convention (1958) **91,** 416, 431
jurisdiction **51,** 230-2
Law of the Sea Convention (1982), as internal waters **97,** 661
legal concept, whether **97,** 649-50
development **97,** 651-63
ILC (1952) **97,** 658
ILC (1953) **97,** 658
ILC (1955) **97,** 658
ILC (1956) **97,** 659
Institut de droit international (1895) **97,** 652
League of Nations Codification Conference (1930) **97,** 654-8
North Atlantic Fisheries **97,** 652
Oppenheim (1st edn) (1905) **97,** 652
Territorial Sea and Contiguous Zone Convention (1958) **97,** 659
UNCLOS I **97,** 659-60
UNCLOS III **97,** 660
territorial waters regime, exception to **97,** 651-2
measurement **57,** 66-71, 73-5, **59,** 296-7, 303
six-mile limit and **57,** 69
Mississippi Sound **91,** 413-26
Monterey Bay **42,** 94
municipal court decision, third State and **91,** 422
pluri-State
absence of rules **97,** 505, 544
ad hoc nature of, *Fonseca Bay* **97,** 544
applicable law
Law of the Sea Convention (1982) **97,** 504
Territorial Sea and Contiguous Zone Convention (1958) **97,** 504
Law of the Sea Convention (1982) **97,** 504
right of access of coastal States **97,** 510
single-State bay rules, applicability **97,** 509-10
territorial sea/high seas regime **97,** 510
UN Secretariat study (1958) **97,** 509-10
rights **57,** 73
rivers and, baselines, effect on **59,** 281
Santa Barbara Channel **42,** 94-5
ten-mile limit **55,** 293

bays (*cont.*)
Territorial Sea and Contiguous Zone Convention (1958) **97,** 504
criteria **91,** 416
thalweg **91,** 421-2
Thames estuary **43,** 114-25
title
'county waters' doctrine and **91,** 430-3, 437-8
discovery and occupation **91,** 430
exploitation **91,** 434-7
tributary waters, effect **59,** 281
Belgian Congo. *See also* Congo, Republic of; Zaire
Belgian civil servants, status **48,** 8-20, 22, 24
cession to Belgium (Treaty of Cession (1907)) **44,** 72, **48,** 9, 13, 17, 23
Colonial Charter 1908 **48,** 8, 9, 11, 13-17, 19, 20, 21, 22, 23-4, **69,** 25-30
legal effect **45,** 25
status under **45,** 25, 27
Fundamental Act 1960 **48,** 11, 17, 21, 22, 24-5
State succession
debts, liability for **45,** 24-32, **47,** 75-8, **48,** 20-5, **82,** 124
pensions **69,** 29-30, **82,** 124
status
in relation to Belgium **48,** 8-25, **69,** 25-30
separate **44,** 72-3, **45,** 25, 29
under Colonial Charter 1908 **45,** 25, 27
UN operation in, destruction of aircraft, claim for **44,** 433-7
Belgium
act of government, judicial review **96,** 218
act of State
declaration of diplomat as *persona non grata* **115,** 443-5
judicial review **115,** 445
acts of war, compensation for **91,** 257-8
adoption **58,** 571-3
aliens. *See also* deportation *and* extradition *below*
expulsion **47,** 263-4
procedure **43,** 229-31
American Battle Monuments Commission, legal personality **115,** 440
Appeals Council, independent and impartial trial, whether **62,** 341-2
applicable law
compensation for damage caused by offence committed abroad **91,** 240-2
lex loci delicti **91,** 240-1
private international law and **91,** 241
public international policy and **91,** 241
lex fori **91,** 241
military courts **91,** 240
municipal courts **91,** 240
service of process
forum State **106,** 280
law of State where process to be served **106,** 281
State immunity, execution/attachment, Vienna Convention on Diplomatic Relations (1961) **106,** 296-7
arbitration in **44,** 435-7
armed forces, civil claims against **69,** 137-9
arms dealing

armed conflict, in case of **91,** 253-4
contract
brokerage agreement **91,** 255
enforceability **91,** 252, 254
legality **91,** 253-5
war, effect **91,** 253-5
human rights and **91,** 253-4
international public policy and **91,** 253-5
arrest, limitation period **43,** 85, 89
Belgian Congo and. *See* Belgian Congo
Belgian National Railways, State distinguished **47,** 241, 242
Belgian Telegraph and Telephone Administration (RTT) **77,** 419-23
Board for Recidivists, judicial status **67,** 537-8
boundary demarcation **70,** 45-6
burden of proof, war risks **82,** 109
choice of law clause, contract **91,** 253
comity, State immunity, execution/attachment **65,** 171
compensation claims, admissibility **77,** 431
compensation for war-related events
Paris Reparations Agreement (1946), reparations payable by Germany, limitation to **69,** 671
private property, damage or loss **69,** 667-71
Congo operations, Agreement with UN for settlement of claims arising from **45,** 446, 450, 452, 453-4
Conseil d'Etat, international civil servants, supervision of **69,** 207
Constitution 1831 (as amended) **48,** 14
s 11 **69,** 9
s 14 **47,** 200
s 68 **77,** 389, 425
s 97 **71,** 417
s 129 **77,** 393
education and language provisions **45,** 116, 144, 149, 151, 154
freedom of association **57,** 270
judiciary, magistrates, status **56,** 363
Constitution 1988 **91,** 97
interpretation, comparative study of principles **93,** 212
s 17(3) (free education), applicability to European Schools **108,** 644-8
s 25 *bis* **93,** 220-1
s 40 **91,** 253
s 68(2) **93,** 222, 223-4
s 97 **82,** 104, **93,** 224-5
s 107 *ter* (2) (constitutional review of legislation) **108,** 645-6
consular privileges and immunities **77,** 399-402
Consultative Commission for Aliens **69,** 207-9
continental shelf
legislation **41,** 137, 180
Netherlands, note to (1945) **41,** 137
contract
applicable law
connecting factors **91,** 253
nationality of parties **91,** 253
place of conclusion **91,** 253
place of performance **91,** 253

Belgium (*cont.*)
arms sales. *See* arms dealing *above*
definition **89,** 462
enforceability **91,** 252, 254
legality **91,** 253-5
Court of Cassation
functions **47,** 178, 181
independent and impartial tribunal, whether **62,** 341-3
judgments and administrative act distinguished **56,** 363
judicial impartiality **68,** 132-5, 140
crimes against humanity
definition **119,** 353-4
immunity, legislation providing for removal **119,** 360
jurisdiction
aut dedere aut punire/judicare **119,** 356-7
universal **119,** 357, 360
jus cogens/peremptory norm **119,** 355
offence under municipal law, whether **119,** 354-6
as part of municipal law **119,** 355
prosecution, possibility of, municipal legislation **119,** 354-5
retroactivity
absence of precise penalty at time of offence **119,** 355
customary international law, relevance **119,** 354-5
statutory limitation **119,** 354-9
criminal law **60,** 156-60, 170-1
criminal procedure
appeals **47,** 169-88
Procureur général, presence of **47,** 169-88
customary international law
crimes against humanity, retroactivity and **119,** 354-5
as part of municipal law **119,** 355
primacy **45,** 25-6
Vienna Convention on Diplomatic Relations (1961) **82,** 98
Vienna Convention on the Law of Treaties (1969) **82,** 98
debt, assignment **48,** 13
deportation **92,** 359-61
discrimination
EC nationals **92,** 369-70
nationals **92,** 369-70
European Convention on Human Rights (1950) **92,** 366-70
family life, respect for and **92,** 366-9
residence permit, relevance **92,** 364-5
right of **92,** 368
diplomatic channels, service of process **106,** 280-1
diplomatic immunity, execution/attachment **106,** 291-2
diplomatic immunity, jurisdiction
translation, in respect of **82,** 116-18
waiver **82,** 99
insurance contract **69,** 282-3
diplomatic immunity, jurisdiction, waiver, authority of sending State, need for **69,** 283
diplomatic mission, receiving State's duty of protection **82,** 125-7
diplomatic privileges and immunities **82,** 122-4
abuse, receiving State's right to protect against **106,** 291-2, 297

basis, efficient performance of diplomatic functions **106,** 291-2, 296-7
entitlement
family member in transit **82,** 97-9
locally engaged staff **82,** 119-21
receiving State's views, relevance **106,** 292
social security legislation **69,** 277-9, **71,** 542-3
State immunity, execution/attachment distinguished **106,** 291-2
Vienna Convention on Diplomatic Relations (1961), customary international law **82,** 98
diplomatic relations, declaration of diplomat as *persona non grata*, act of State **115,** 443-5
diplomatic representations on behalf of
Belgian shareholders **46,** 184-5, 188, 190, 217, 354-6, 474
foreign company **46,** 188, 190, 355, 377, 474
disciplinary proceedings (fair trial requirement), medical **58,** 74, **62,** 319, 321-2, 325-8, 332-4, 358, **71,** 415-36
discrimination, public service appointments, Political Rights of Women Convention (1953) **47,** 196-7
double criminality **100,** 618
Geneva Convention (Treatment of Prisoners of War) (Convention III) (1949) **119,** 351
drugs offence, powers of customs officials in relation to **82,** 105-6
EC law
binding effect **93,** 219-20
direct effect **93,** 218, 224
migrant workers **82,** 112, 114
primacy **93,** 214-23
regulations, limited to, whether **93,** 217
ECJ, judgment, binding on national courts, whether **93,** 216-17
EEC law in **60,** 159-60
employment contract, international officials. *See* international officials, employment contract *below*
employment contract, locally engaged staff, consulate, State immunity, jurisdiction, language teacher **115,** 434
employment contract, locally engaged staff, diplomatic mission
State immunity, jurisdiction **82,** 103
dismissal **115,** 419, 421-3, 435
European Convention on State Immunity (and Protocol) (Basle) (1972), relevance **115,** 422
national of sending State **113,** 432
nationality of employee, relevance **104,** 517, **114,** 533, **115,** 422
European Convention on Human Rights (1950) **56,** 401-3, **61,** 373-4
European Schools
jurisdiction over, municipal courts **108,** 641-2
status
organ of international organization **108,** 641
'public institution'/'body', effect on status as organ of international organization **108,** 641
tuition fees, admissibility **108,** 646-8
evidence of, ships, ownership **65,** 25
extraditable offence
presumption of **100,** 618-19
treaty, defined by **100,** 419-23, 424, 618
extradition **77,** 395-6

Belgium (*cont.*)
act of State **77,** 395
Benelux Extradition Treaty **77,** 395
conditions in receiving State, relevance **100,** 622
cross-border offence, effects doctrine **100,** 618
double criminality. *See* double criminality *above*
jurisdiction limited by terms of request for **77,** 395
legality of
court's right to enquire into **77,** 395
determined by surrendering State **77,** 395
member of, 'organ or employee' of State, whether **77,** 398
procedure **77,** 395-6
need to take court opinion **43,** 244-5
refugee status, relevance **100,** 619
requirements
prima facie case **100,** 617-18
waiver **77,** 395-6
responsibility for damage caused by **77,** 397-9
Extradition, European Convention on (1957), reservations, 'particularly serious offence' **100,** 621-2
foreign judgment, recognition/enforcement
court's power to amend judgment **106,** 279
exequatur proceedings, need for **106,** 293
foreign law, recognition/enforcement **47,** 33-6, **69,** 4-6, 9
expropriation/nationalization **82,** 132-4
international public policy, where contrary to **91,** 253, 254
freedom of religion **47,** 200
full review **62,** 356
Geneva Convention (Treatment of Prisoners of War) (Convention III) (1949)
double criminality **119,** 351
legality requirement **119,** 351
Genocide Convention (1948), incorporation, need for, where principles already part of law **119,** 355
habitual offenders **67,** 535-9, 541-5, **81,** 54
Head of State, immunity, jurisdiction
international crimes **119,** 349
recognition and **119,** 349
statutory limitation, suspension **119,** 358
human rights violations **62,** 318-28
illegitimate child
adoption by mother **58,** 573-4, 586-7
affiliation **58,** 571-3
family life **58,** 572, 580-1
inheritance **58,** 573
voluntary disposition **58,** 573
insurance legislation **69,** 4-6
foreign State rights **69,** 4-6
international crimes
Head of State, immunity, jurisdiction **119,** 349
legislation, retroactive, procedural provisions distinguished **119,** 350-1
universal jurisdiction **119,** 350
presence of offender, relevance **119,** 350
international criminal law, primacy **119,** 355

international humanitarian law, requirements, nexus with armed conflict **119,** 351-2
international law
  European Community law, whether rule of **77,** 391
  primacy **93,** 209-14, 220-1
    customary international law **45,** 25-6
  recommendations of international bodies **77,** 421-3
    ministerial approval, effect of **77,** 421-3
  treaties. *See* treaties *below*
international officials, employment contract, applicable law **115,** 425
international organizations, immunity, execution/attachment
  exequatur proceedings as preliminary step **115,** 429
  nature of assets as test **115,** 428-9
  waiver, need for **115,** 428, 429
international organizations, immunity, jurisdiction, employment contract **115,** 425
international organizations, personality **115,** 426
international organizations, privileges and immunities, waiver **115,** 425
international public order/public policy/*ordre public*
  applicable law and **91,** 241
  expropriation/nationalization, recognition **81,** 132, 136-7
judicial independence **56,** 405, **81,** 43-5
judicial procedure **68,** 136-8
judicial review
  act of government **96,** 218
  commercial relations **96,** 219
  foreign relations, discretionary powers **96,** 219
  treaties, implementing legislation **108,** 645-6
jurisdiction **86,** 42
  Belgian Congo and **69,** 30
  compensation for damage caused by offence committed abroad **91,** 240-2
  contract between aliens **77,** 413-16
  criminal, offence on train outside territory, whether committed in Belgium **82,** 104-6
  deprivation of identity papers **77,** 387
  NATO forces **82,** 112-14
    Belgium/US Agreement **82,** 114
  nexus
    payment of compensation **115,** 417
    registered office **115,** 416
  UNHCR Representative **77,** 417-19
  universal
    international crimes **119,** 350, **125,** 579-80
    presence of offender, relevance **119,** 350
jus cogens/peremptory norm, crimes against humanity **119,** 355
languages
  human rights and **45,** 114-231
  legislation (1932) **45,** 202-4, 223
  legislation (1963) **45,** 147-9, 167, 170-1, 175-7, 187, 191-4, 199, 203-4, 220, 223
law of
  Aeronautic (Penal) Code 1937 **86,** 43
  Aliens Act 1952 **43,** 230, **69,** 207-9
  Aliens Act 1980 **92,** 364
  Children and Young Persons' Welfare Act 1965 **92,** 363-4
  Civil Code **58,** 571-3
    s 3(1) **91,** 240-2, 244, 246, 247

Belgium (*cont.*)
s 6 **91,** 252
s 1131 **91,** 252, 254
s 1137 **77,** 407
s 1162 **82,** 109
s 1235 **93,** 225
s 1382 **91,** 240
s 1961 **82,** 131, 132
Constitution. *See* Constitution *above*
Continental Shelf Bill 1967 **41,** 137
Coordinated Laws on the *Conseil d'Etat,* s 14 **108,** 640, 641
Coordinated Laws on the Contract of Employment
s 1 **82,** 103, **91,** 244, 246
s 14 **91,** 244
s 15 **91,** 244
Criminal Code 1891, s 56 **67,** 535
Criminal Code
s 2 **119,** 351, 355
s 323 **100,** 618
s 324 **100,** 618
Criminal Investigation Code **82,** 104
Art. 61 *quinquies* **119,** 348
Criminal Procedure Code **73,** 464-8
s 8 **81,** 38
s 9 **81,** 38
s 12 **119,** 350
s 47 **81,** 38
s 54 **81,** 38
s 59 **81,** 38
s 60 **81,** 38
s 61 **81,** 38
ss 61ff **81,** 38
s 62 **81,** 38
s 64 **81,** 38
ss 71-86 **81,** 38
s 87 **81,** 38
s 88 **81,** 38
s 89 **81,** 39
ss 91ff **81,** 38
s 92 **81,** 38
s 127 **81,** 38
s 128 **81,** 39
s 129 **81,** 39
s 130 **81,** 39
s 133 **81,** 39
s 138 **81,** 38
s 279 **81,** 38, 39
s 441 **81,** 26-7
Decree-Law of 19 May 1945, s 38 **91,** 257-8
European Convention on Human Rights (1950) and **56,** 401-3
Judicial Code **73,** 464-8, 470-1
s 3 **119,** 350
s 43(6) **82,** 122

s 79 **81,** 37
s 127 **81,** 39, 44-5
s 148 **81,** 38
s 292 **81,** 37, 39, 40
s 455 **111,** 207
s 570 **106,** 279, 280, 282
s 627(9) **82,** 121
s 635 **82,** 121, **115,** 417
s 648 **81,** 36
s 748 **111,** 207, 208
s 751 **111,** 207, 208
s 828 **81,** 37
s 1413 **107,** 241-2
s 1414 **107,** 241
s 1415 **107,** 241
s 1452 **106,** 297, **113,** 396-7
Nationality Code 1984 **92,** 365
Royal Decree of 30 January 1954 (coordination of the laws on war damage to private property) **69,** 667-71
Royal Decree No 79 of 1967 **62,** 328-34
Royal Decree of 16 March 1968 (control of road traffic) **77,** 389
Royal Decree of 25 September 1968 (control of road traffic) **77,** 389, 392
Royal Decrees, ministerial derogation **77,** 392
Social Protection Act 1964 **67,** 535-9, 541-9
Special Law of 6 January 1969 on the Court of Arbitration, constitutional review of legislation **108,** 645
Vagrancy Act 1891 **56,** 399, 410, 411, 412-13
vagrancy provisions **56,** 362-6
Laws of
1 October 1833 (extradition), s 6 **100,** 619
15 March 1874 (amended by Law of 3 July 1985) (extradition), s 3(2) **100,** 617, 619, 622
11 June 1874 (war risks), s 19 **82,** 108-9
18 October 1908 (government of Belgian Congo) **44,** 73
24 February 1921 (drugs traffic) **82,** 104-6
s 7 **82,** 106
19 July 1930 **77,** 423
15 June 1935 **77,** 414
17 December 1949 (Atlantic City Convention) **77,** 422
28 March 1952 (control of aliens) **77,** 385-7, 418
10 June 1952 (security of employment) **82,** 112
26 June 1953 (Status of Refugees Convention) **77,** 417-19
26 December 1956 (Postal Service) **77,** 424, 425
12 May 1960 (New York Convention on the Status of Stateless Persons (1954)) **77,** 385-6
31 May 1961 (language in legislation) **77,** 425, 426
20 August 1962 (Universal Postage Convention) **77,** 424
11 September 1962 (amended 19 July 1968) (arms sales) **91,** 253, 254
13 February 1963 (taxation of small boats) **77,** 405
2 August 1963 (use of languages) **47,** 333-6
18 January 1964 (frontier controls) **82,** 104
30 April 1964 (control of aliens) **77,** 386
3 July 1967 (industrial accidents in the public sector) **77,** 397-9

Belgium (*cont.*)
21 October 1967 (Benelux Extradition Treaty) **77,** 395
30 March 1968 (Vienna Convention on Diplomatic Relations (1961)) **82,** 97, 102, 122, 123
10 April 1971 (accidents at work), s 84 **91,** 257-8
15 June 1971 (Montreux Convention) **77,** 422
29 July 1971 (Geneva Convention on the High Seas) **77,** 540
12 January 1973 (*Conseil d'Etat*) **77,** 418
16 July 1976 (Belgium/Zaire Cooperation Agreement (1976)) **93,** 225-6
15 December 1980 (aliens) **100,** 619
20 July 1990 (preventative detention)
s 16 **119,** 359
s 34 **119,** 359
16 June 1993 (crimes against international law) **119,** 349-53
retroactive effect **119,** 350-1
s 7(2) **119,** 350
s 8 **119,** 358
30 June 1994 **106,** 290
22 March 1996 (recognition of ICTY and ICTR) **119,** 350, 355
February 1999 (crimes against humanity: universal jurisdiction) **119,** 360
lawyers
defence without payment, obligation to provide **73,** 463-81
professional organization **73,** 465-8, 476-8
legislation, interpretation
in absence of ambiguity **82,** 109
aids
comparative study of principles **93,** 212
context **91,** 258
phrases, 'vagrant' **56,** 376
treaty-implementing legislation, treaty as aid **77,** 407-8
legislation, retroactive, international crimes, procedural provisions distinguished **119,** 350-1
Mandate, declaration of continuance **37,** 152, 220, 320, 325
measure of damages/compensation including valuation of company/property/assets **82,** 123
Medical Association **62,** 319-34, 344
disciplinary proceedings **62,** 319, 321-2, 325-8, 332-4, 358, **71,** 415-36
object of sanctions **71,** 420
medical practitioners, professional conduct, whether **62,** 324-8, 358
military courts, jurisdiction, foreign soldier **119,** 350
Minister of Justice, refugee status, competence to rule on **69,** 208-9
nationality
deportation and **92,** 369-70
right to acquire **92,** 365
nationality of claims. *See* nationality of claims
NATO forces in, jurisdiction **82,** 112-14
NATO Status of Forces Agreement (1951), enforcement **69,** 5-6, 147-9
Netherlands
boundary demarcation **70,** 45-6
secession from **39,** 117-18, 240
novation **47,** 77
ordre des médécins. See Medical Association *above*
piracy **77,** 537-41

police, functions **57,** 269-70, 289-90
political offence
  classification as
    bomb-making **100,** 621
    logistical support outside territory **100,** 619-22
  definition/requirements, political character **100,** 619-20
  incidence test, offence connected with political offence **100,** 619, 620
  place of offence, relevance, outside the jurisdiction **100,** 619-22
  relevant factors
    damage to political institutions **100,** 620-1
    motivation **100,** 620-1
ports, freedom of access to **77,** 413-16
Procureur-Générale, functions **47,** 171-2, 175, 177, 178, 183-6
public order/public policy/*ordre public* **69,** 4-6, 137-9
  foreign legislation, recognition **69,** 9
  jurisdiction and **65,** 28
reciprocal agreements **69,** 669-71
religious broadcasting **47,** 198-203
separation of powers **77,** 395
service of process on foreign State or State agency
  applicable law
    forum State **106,** 280
    law of State where process to be served **106,** 281
  date of
    date of handing to postal authorities **115,** 420
    date of transmission of diplomatic note **115,** 420
  means
    courier **106,** 280-1
    court's power to determine **106,** 280-1
    diplomatic channels **106,** 280-2, **115,** 420
    registered post **115,** 420, 440-1
ships, jurisdiction, foreign ship, foreign crew against foreign owners **65,** 24
ships, state-owned
  commercial activity, effect on immunity **64,** 24
  immunity, arrest/attachment, claims for non-payment of wages **65,** 23-6
  ownership, possession or control as test of status **65,** 25
  safeguarding/conservatory measures **65,** 25-6
    ownership, relevance **65,** 25-6
Spain, Treaty of Conciliation, Judicial Settlement and Arbitration, 1927
  denial of justice **46,** 197-200
  jurisdictional clauses **46,** 23-6, 37, 38, 188, 315, 354-5, 448-51
  PCIJ, effect of dissolution **46,** 38-40, 47-51, 105-6, 145-72
State immunity, execution/attachment
  customary international law, restrictive **106,** 290-1
  development of concept **65,** 170-1
State immunity, execution/attachment, doctrine/theory, absolute theory **65,** 170
State immunity, execution/attachment, procedural aspects
  applicable law **106,** 296-7
  exequatur **65,** 170-1, **106,** 277-82
    applicability to **106,** 277-8
    safeguarding/conservatory measures **65,** 26
State immunity, execution/attachment, purpose of proceedings
  safeguarding/conservatory measures **65,** 27-8

Belgium (*cont.*)
State-owned ships. *See* ships, State-owned *above*
State immunity, execution/attachment, purpose/use of funds/assets
burden of proof **106,** 290-1
court's right to verify **106,** 291, 297
evidence of **106,** 290-1, 292, 297
promotion of image of Head of State **65,** 28
State immunity, execution/attachment, waiver, failure to notify status when signing lease **106,** 295-6
State immunity, jurisdiction, classification of act
establishment of Office for Management of Public Debt (recovery of compensation in respect of expropriation of private property) **115,** 417-18
expropriation **101,** 549-50, **115,** 417
nature or purpose of transaction as determining factor **106,** 277
private person test **115,** 421, 433
purchase of furnaces possibly for nuclear weapons production **106,** 277
State immunity, jurisdiction, procedural aspects
court's right/duty to raise *proprio motu* **115,** 431
preliminary issue, whether **115,** 417
State immunity, jurisdiction, theory/doctrine
customary international law, European Convention on State Immunity (and Protocol) (Basle) (1972) **115,** 422
restrictive theory **65,** 340
State responsibility for, failure to protect diplomatic premises **82,** 125-7
statutory limitation **43,** 243-4
crimes against humanity **119,** 354-9
suspension during period of immunity **119,** 358
territorial sea
Geneva Convention on the Territorial Sea and the Contiguous Zone (1958) **77,** 404-5
internal waters distinguished **77,** 404-5
rights over, rights of central authorities **77,** 405
sovereignty over **77,** 405
territory
internal waters part of **77,** 405
territorial sea, whether **77,** 405
terrorist acts
'accident at work', whether **91,** 257-8
acts of war, whether **91,** 257-8
jurisdiction **86,** 42
trade union **57,** 270, 281-3, 284-7, 289-90
public authorities and **57,** 271-5
transsexualism, law relating to **61,** 367-8, 371-7
treaties
constitutional requirements, compatibility with, need for **108,** 646
direct effect **77,** 423
executive agreements **77,** 390-3
administrative act, as **77,** 389
aliens, effect on **77,** 394
directly applicable **77,** 392-3
form **77,** 389
individuals and **77,** 393, 425, 426
ministerial orders, having force of **77,** 390
municipal law and **77,** 391

individuals **93,** 225-6
European Convention on Human Rights (1950) **93,** 226
Geneva Convention on the Status of Refugees (1951) **93,** 226
interpretation **77,** 407-9
municipal law and **47,** 328-40, **77,** 390-3, 422
ratification law and Statute distinguished **93,** 223-4
parliamentary approval, rules governing **77,** 425
primacy **93,** 8, 29, 207-14, 220-4, 234
conventional treaty **77,** 391
European Community law *qua* treaty *stricto sensu* **77,** 391
previous legislation **93,** 213, 224
subsequent legislation **93,** 213, 221-3
publication, need for **77,** 393, 425, **115,** 426, 439-40
in French and Dutch **77,** 426
in *Moniteur belge* **77,** 426
recommendations of international assemblies distinguished **77,** 422
self-executing **93,** 234
complete and precise provision, need for **93,** 225
individual rights and **93,** 225-6
non-infringement of law, need for **93,** 226
parties' intention **93,** 225-6
subsequent legislation, effect of reference to **77,** 397-8
treaty-making power **93,** 222
prerogative **77,** 389
third parties and **115,** 434
treaty interpretation **82,** 105-6
aids, parliamentary documentation **82,** 98
guidelines, strict **82,** 98
Turkey, Payments Agreement 1948 **45,** 85, 89
UN Agreement settling claims resulting from Congo operations **45,** 446, 450, 451, 453-4
UN High Commissioner for Refugees, representative of
Conseil d'Etat supervision **69,** 207
status **77,** 418-19
vagrancy laws **56,** 354-62, 364, 375, 381, 416
administrative nature **56,** 381
procedure **56,** 381
war damage reparation, claim by foreign-owned company **69,** 667-71
war risks
insurance cover **82,** 107-9
burden of proof **82,** 109
Warsaw Convention, ratification **42,** 260
young people, protection of **92,** 363-4
belief, freedom of. *See* freedom of belief
Belize
Guatemalan claim. *See* Guatemala, Belize, claim to
history
1936 proposals **100,** 318-19
Boundary Convention (Great Britain/Guatemala) (1859) **100,** 317
arbitration proposals **100,** 319
Boundary Convention (Great Britain/Guatemala) (1863) **100,** 317-18
denunciation by Guatemala **100,** 318
non-ratification **100,** 318
Clayton–Bulwer Treaty (Great Britain/USA) **100,** 317

Belize (*cont.*)
Dallas–Clarendon Treaty (Great Britain/USA) **100,** 316-17
English incursions **100,** 314-15
English right of enjoyment **100,** 316
Guatemalan protest against exercise **100,** 316, 321
independence (1981) **100,** 319
effect on relations with Guatemala **100,** 324
independence of Guatemala **100,** 315-16
London Convention (England/Spain) (1786) **100,** 315
Paris Peace Treaty (England/Spain) (1763) **100,** 315
London Convention (England/Spain) (1786) **100,** 315
recognition **100,** 319. *See also* Guatemala, recognition, State, Belize
Spanish colony **100,** 314
UN membership **100,** 319
law of, Registration of Merchant Ships Act 1989 **125,** 298-9, 311
Paris Peace Treaty (England/Spain) (1763) **100,** 315
ships, registration/deregistration provisions **125,** 295-300, 301-2, 307-9, 315-16, 318-20
Versailles Peace Treaty (England/Spain) (1783) **100,** 315
belligerency
de jure or de facto **48,** 469-75
recognition, UN in Namibia **49,** 82
belligerent, recognition. *See* recognition, belligerent
belligerent occupation 47, 472-99, **49,** 267 n. 58, **59,** 600-1, **73,** 11, 15-17, 19, 27, 582-3, 589-90, 592-3, **77,** 628-30, **88,** 706-10, **90,** 402-8. *See also* compensation for war-related events; Germany, occupation (post-WWII); Israel, East Jerusalem; Israel, occupied territory; looted property; recognition, forceful occupation of territory; war
allegiance, effect on **54,** 289
annexation and **49,** 267 n. 58, **77,** 629
applicable law **61,** 63-5, **83,** 138, 146, **90,** 405. *See also* Control Council Law No 10
fundamental principles of administrative law **125,** 547
human rights, derogation **125,** 548-50
international humanitarian law **125,** 546-8
law of occupying power **72,** 444-5, **73,** 16, 19, 582, 589-90, **91,** 44
law of war **83,** 165-6
local law **39,** 259, 260, 364, 397
non-discriminatory application **47,** 472-6
occupation forces **41,** 461-74
after cessation of hostilities **91,** 44-6
immunity from local law **91,** 45, 52, 53
occupation of Italy **40,** 430, 433
occupation law **94,** 54-6, 168-70
parallel systems **48,** 489-91
private property, confiscation **53,** 5-6
armistice, after, public property **40,** 429-34
assignment of place of residence, legality **125,** 539-68. *See also* deportation *below*; displacement of people
deportation distinguished **125,** 549-50
as deterrent **125,** 557, 562, 564, 566
discretionary power of military commander, 518-19
for imperative reasons of security (Geneva Convention IV) **125,** 548-60
proportionality **125,** 555-7
standard of proof **125,** 555

as preventive measure **125,** 554-5
'reasonable' test **125,** 559-60
'within the territory subject to belligerent occupation' **125,** 550, 551-2
Bosnia-Herzegovina
Croatia, by **108,** 160-1, **122,** 64
Serbian forces **112,** 186-7
Brezhnev Doctrine, intervention under, whether **90,** 407
Channel Islands, German occupation, courts, position **39,** 236-8
civilian infiltrators, military courts, trial by **47,** 484-7
contract made at occupying power's direction **40,** 467-71
costs
imprisonment of war criminal **90,** 391
jurisdiction, relevance **90,** 394-5
responsibility for, basis **90,** 394-5
courts. *See also* jurisdiction *and* occupation courts *below*
continuance **39,** 237
effect on **48,** 489-91, **52,** 513-17, 524-9, **61,** 675-8
occupation courts. *See* occupation courts *below*
occupying power's right of audience in **42,** 484-7
Cyprus **62,** 12, 39, 45, 57, 75
damage, compensation for **90,** 406
de facto government **88,** 709-10, **116,** 579-87
debt, discharge by payment to occupying power **36,** 497-503
definition **91,** 10, **108,** 161-2
Geneva Convention (Protection of Civilian Persons in Time of War) (Convention IV) (1949) **108,** 160-1
deportation, prohibition **83,** 125-97
absolute, whether **83,** 126, 191-2
abuse of power **83,** 184
administrative detention as alternative **83,** 185
appeal, right of **83,** 155
arbitrariness **83,** 184
bad faith **83,** 184
customary international law, whether **83,** 155
evacuation distinguished **83,** 142
willing evacuation **83,** 193
Geneva Convention on the Protection of Civilian Persons in Time of War (1949) **83,** 129, 137-8, 140-1, 142, 143, 185-97
individual **83,** 137-8, 188
International Red Cross and **83,** 139-40
justification
compelling reasons of national security **83,** 142, 185, 189
extradition **83,** 143, 145-6, 193
imperative military reasons **83,** 142
public order, threat to **83,** 185
unlawful presence **83,** 143, 147, 193-4
mass **83,** 137, 140-1, 143, 147, 148, 193-4
deportation withhold/bar, security **83,** 142, 185, 189
detention without trial **83,** 191
effect **39,** 259, 260, 364, 397, **61,** 407, 675-8, **72,** 444-5, 554-6, 559-61
effective control, need for **90,** 405, **112,** 186-7
espionage **83,** 191

belligerent occupation (*cont.*)
expropriation/nationalization by occupying/administering power. *See* expropriation/nationalization, by occupying/administering power
extradition treaty, feasibility **83,** 194
freedom of communication **83,** 190-1
International Red Cross, with **83,** 190-1
freedom of movement **83,** 189-90
genocide, obligation to prevent **95,** 162
Hague Conventions (1899/1907). *See* Hague Conventions (1899/1907)
Hague Regulations (1907). *See* Hague Regulations (1907)
hostages, execution of **83,** 139
human rights derogation
applicable law **125,** 548
balance of interests of State and individual **125,** 548, 566-8
judicial acts, divorce decree **38,** 470-1
judicial decisions, effect on **61,** 675-8
jurisdiction **88,** 298-301. *See also* courts *above*
de facto **88,** 298-301
extraterritorial **48,** 478-85
military courts **48,** 478-85
civilian infiltrators **47,** 484-7
occupation forces after cessation of hostilities **91,** 44-6
occupying power's nationals **42,** 146-8
war crimes **48,** 484, **57,** 170-3
legislation, validity **83,** 127
local authorities, agents of occupying power, whether **40,** 468
looting of monetary gold, restitution provisions in Italian Peace Treaty **44,** 448-50, 477-9, 482-3
military government, duration **83,** 164-5
motive, relevance **83,** 147-8, 188
Nuremberg Tribunal and **83,** 141
unlawful discrimination **83,** 184
within and beyond occupied territory, distinction **83,** 137, 189
nationality and **61,** 407
nationals, protection of **90,** 397
necessity and **90,** 485-6
obligation, restoration of public order and safety **109,** 595
occupation courts. *See also* courts *and* jurisdiction *above*
competence, over occupying power's nationals **42,** 146-8
Nuremberg Tribunal as **91,** 60, **119,** 225
right to establish **39,** 236, 365
rules and procedure **52,** 524-9
status as municipal courts **91,** 60
validity of judgments **88,** 709-10
occupied territory
definition **75,** 363-5
espionage in **83,** 191
separated areas with shared culture under single occupying power **125,** 551-2
occupying power. *See* occupying power
presence of foreign forces with consent distinguished **90,** 405-6
private property, respect for **36,** 501, **42,** 488-90. *See also* requisition, private property *below*

Hungarian property in Austria, acts of French authorities **44,** 2-4
public property, sale of **40,** 429-34
reprisals **61,** 666-7
requisition
materials **40,** 67, 69
private property **41,** 480-2, **42,** 488-90. *See also* private property, respect for *above*
right of **88,** 707-9
sequestration **61,** 44, 45
confiscation and temporary sequestration distinguished **88,** 709
sovereignty and **61,** 675-8, **72,** 214, **78,** 161, 186-7, **90,** 404-5
of occupied State **40,** 468, 469, 470, **42,** 37
of occupying power **40,** 468, 469, 470, **61,** 675-8
State responsibility for acts in occupied territory **70,** 697-8
de facto organ or agent **112,** 189-92, 262-76
Nicaragua **112,** 189-92, 262
Genocide Convention (1948) **95,** 162
occupation, during **70,** 697-8, **112,** 188-92
persecution of Jews in Hungary **44,** 302, 330-3
termination **90,** 403-8
by Peace Treaty **77,** 629
reservation of right of intervention and **90,** 407
Soviet Statement on Relations between the Soviet Union and the GDR of 25 March 1954 **90,** 404
violation of rights **90,** 403-4
war crimes **86,** 171, 178-9
jurisdiction **48,** 484, **57,** 170-3, **88,** 298-301
Benelux Economic Union
European Union and **113,** 291-2
as intergovernmental organization **99,** 40-2
visa, issue
on behalf of member country **99,** 41-2
need for publication of regulations, relevance **99,** 41-2
Working Party, role **99,** 42
Bergen Declaration on Sustainable Development (1990). *See* environment, precautionary principle
Berlin 78, 157, 162, 172, 175-6
Allied reservation on **78,** 162, 172
Allies, reserved powers **78,** 175
autobahn to FRG **52,** 287-8
citizens
nationality **57,** 50
common nationality with citizens of FRG **78,** 175
FRG–GDR Basis of Relations Treaty, effect on **78,** 175
Constitution (1950)
s 6 **100,** 398
s 8 **100,** 398
s 9 **100,** 398
s 11 **100,** 398
s 20(1) **100,** 398
Constitutional Court (FRG), jurisdiction **78,** 175
East Berlin

Berlin (*cont.*)
GDR, relationship with **78,** 157
legal status **74,** 114-15
FRG and **78,** 172
FRG–GDR Basis of Relations Treaty and **78,** 157, 159, 172
GDR–Senat, agreements between **78,** 172
respect for FRG Constitution **78,** 172
inheritance in **57,** 49-51
Land Berlin
obligation to respect FRG Constitution **78,** 172, 175-6
status **78,** 175-6
Mantelgesetz **78,** 176
nationality
common with that of citizens of FRG **78,** 175
FRG–GDR Basis of Relations Treaty, effect **78,** 175
Quadripartite Agreement (1972) and **78,** 175
Quadripartite Agreement (1972) **78,** 159, 172
extension of agreements and regulations under **78,** 172
Western Sectors of Berlin, ties **78,** 175
nationality **78,** 175
representation of interests, FRG and **78,** 172
reserved powers **78,** 175
status **42,** 464-70, **52,** 287-8, **78,** 162, 172
autobahn leading to **52,** 287-8
FRG–GDR Basis of Relations Treaty, effect **78,** 159, 172
Land **78,** 162
Three Power reservation **78,** 162
treaties, extension to **78,** 157, 172
Berlin clause **78,** 157
Western Sectors
applicable law
FRG and **57,** 114-16
property in west Berlin **65,** 112-13
FRG, relationship with **57,** 114-16, **59,** 323
ties with **78,** 175
nationality **59,** 323, **78,** 175
ties with FRG and **78,** 175
property belonging to East Berlin resident, inheritance **57,** 49-51
sovereignty in respect of **52,** 287-8, **57,** 115-16
status **52,** 287-8, **57,** 114-16, **60,** 222-4
Supreme Court, exhaustion of local remedies and **57,** 115
Berlin Congress 1885 **49,** 76
Bermuda Agreements. *See* air transport agreements, UK/US
Bhopal gas leak disaster. *See also parens patriae*
Bhopal Gas Leak Disaster (Processing of Claims) Act 1985
Civil Procedure Code 1908 and **118,** 491-2, 496-8, 520-1
liability, effect on **118,** 478-9, 499-500
Preamble **118,** 468, 470
purpose
creation of *locus standi* for Indian Government **118,** 468-9, 474
speedy redress **118,** 519
s 2(a) **118,** 490

s 2(e) **118,** 490
s 3 **118,** 462, 465, 470, 479, 483, 486, 491-2, 512, 514-16, 518
s 3(3) **118,** 514-15
s 4 **118,** 462, 465, 483, 491, 492-3, 496-500, 502, 512, 514-16, 517-18, 520-1
s 5 **118,** 462, 491
s 6 **118,** 463, 501-2
s 7 **118,** 462
s 8 **118,** 462
s 9 **118,** 457, 462-3
s 9(2) **118,** 486-7
s 10 **118,** 463
s 10(b) **118,** 487
s 11 **118,** 463, 465, 496
validity **118,** 455-526
reasonableness **118,** 484-8
Bhopal Gas Leak Disaster Scheme (Registration and Processing of Claims) (1985) **118,** 457
Clauses
3 **118,** 463
4 **118,** 463
5 **118,** 463
5(2) **118,** 463
5(3) **118,** 463
9 **118,** 463
10 **118,** 487
10(3) **118,** 463
11 **118,** 464
11(2) **118,** 464
11(5) **118,** 464
claimants
definition **118,** 461, 490
Government of India as **118,** 490
claimants. *See also* representation of claimants *below*
damages
distribution **118,** 501-2, 524
punitive **118,** 481-3, 511, 518
forum [non] conveniens **118,** 457
Government of India's powers and responsibilities in respect of claims **118,** 462-3. *See also* representation of claimants *below*
exclusive right to represent and act in place of victims **118,** 470-1, 512-17
in accordance with procedure of forum State **118,** 470-1
limitation to proceedings abroad **118,** 474
safeguards **118,** 521-3
statutory basis **118,** 485-6
maintenance of victims **118,** 486-8, 519-20
parens patriae **118,** 471-6, 521-3
standing **118,** 468-9, 474
Indian legislation relating to, validity **118,** 459-526
interim relief **118,** 458
liability for **118,** 478-84
Government of India **118,** 488-90
joint tortfeasors, whether **118,** 489-90, 516-17

Bhopal gas leak disaster (*cont.*)
measure of damages/compensation including valuation of company/property/assets
ability to pay **118,** 500
liability, relevance **118,** 470, 481-2
natural justice
disclosure of details before settlement of claim **118,** 500
fairness of proceedings **118,** 491-8, 523-4
nemo judex in sua propria causa principle **118,** 489, 490-1
third party interests **118,** 468
representation of claimants **118,** 462
bona fide representation **118,** 491
duty to notify victims **118,** 498-501, 520-3
fundamental rights and **118,** 464-76, 484-91
government's competence **118,** 488-94
conflict of interest **118,** 488-90, 516-17
natural justice **118,** 489
right to be heard **118,** 496-501, 517-18, 522-3
settlement of claims
criminal liability, relevance **118,** 467, 469-70, 477-8, 499-500, 511, 523
disclosure of details before finalization **118,** 500
failure to consult victims **118,** 467, 496-501
recommendation for **118,** 459-61, 518-19
third party interests **118,** 468-9, 497
natural justice **118,** 468
Biafra. *See* Nigeria, Biafra
bias. *See* freedom from discrimination
Bijagos Archipelago 83, 109, 110, 111
bill of lading
acceptance as waiver of immunity **63,** 356-8
Brussels Convention, 1924 **36,** 429-32
binding force. *See* precedent in international tribunals; precedent in municipal courts
birching. *See* corporal punishment
BITs (bilateral investment treaties). *See also* ICSID Convention (Convention on Settlement of Investment Disputes between States and Nationals of Other States (1965)); investment; NAFTA (North American Free Trade Agreement) (1992)
applicability, breach of BIT, relevance **125,** 77-8
as applicable law **106,** 429-30, 437, 475-8, **125,** 79
compensation for expropriation/nationalization **121,** 143
compensation for loss during war or civil disturbance not attributable to State **106,** 480-1
compliance with national law, need for **124,** 51-2
customary international law **119,** 663-4, **121,** 143, **122,** 380, 382, **125,** 143-51
description **121,** 143-4
dispute settlement provisions
'dispute relating to investments made under this Agreement' **125,** 45, 83
MFN treatment **124,** 18-26
exclusive remedy rule **125,** 76-8. *See also* exhaustion of local remedies requirement *below*; forum selection clause, exclusive jurisdiction
choice of forum **125,** 76-8
'national'/'domestic' courts **125,** 77
claim based on BIT provision, relevance to **125,** 89-96
exhaustion of local remedies requirement **124,** 13-18, **125,** 7, 34, 72-3
fair and equitable treatment, transparency, need for **124,** 54

'investment' **121,** 139-40
'investor', 'body corporate effectively controlled by nationals . . . or having registered office in territory of Contracting Party' **125,** 74-6
nationality of corporation, NAFTA provisions distinguished **125,** 134
separability of contractual obligations **125,** 33, 71-3, 79, 89-96
standard of treatment
customary international law **119,** 663-4, **122,** 380, 382, **125,** 143-51
fair and equitable **122,** 381-4
MFN **124,** 18-26
minimum standard of treatment **121,** 182-3
procedural fairness **121,** 185
US Model BIT (1984) **121,** 143
Art. I(c) **106,** 477
Art. III(3) **106,** 488
waiver of rights, forum selection clause in concession agreement **125,** 24-5
blasphemy laws
freedom of expression and **87,** 434, 436
freedom of religion and **87,** 433, 436
blockade 78, 584. *See also* economic sanctions; embargo
port access **72,** 462-3, **76,** 53
'restraint of princes' **78,** 584
blocking/freezing of assets. *See also* enemy property, blocking/freezing
as attachment **63,** 427-9, 505, **81,** 646
deposed Head of State **81,** 613-56
as property interest **63,** 427-9
Bogotá Pact. *See* Pact of Bogotá (1948)
Bohemia and Moravia
diplomatic protection of citizens **70,** 695
German annexation **47,** 33
German protectorate, citizenship **70,** 694, 696
residence **70,** 694-5
Bombay
Administration Reports **50,** 250-5, 419, 433, 496-7, 513
Government Resolution of 1914 **50,** 21, 23, 289, 304-16, 416, 417-18, 431, 438-42, 466, 468, 474, 487, 489
Miraj, merger with **49,** 474
bondholders, diplomatic protection of **46,** 184, 345-6, 381
bonds
Danube–Save–Adriatic Railway Company, Agreement guaranteeing bonds **45,** 83-5
issued abroad, bankruptcy jurisdiction based on default on **46,** 115, 118, 459
State succession and **47,** 75-8
booty of war 40, 463-7, **42,** 34-5, **44,** 486-7, **48,** 227-8
Bophuthatswana
annexation **103,** 20
Ciskei compared **82,** 420-3
external constraints, absence **82,** 413
general principles of international law, territorial integrity **103,** 21
history, 1989-94 **103,** 13-19
human rights **82,** 413
independence **82,** 394-6, 397-8. *See also* sovereignty *and* State, whether *below*
loss **103,** 19
judiciary, authority post-1994 **103,** 12

Bophuthatswana (*cont.*)
law of
Act 18, 1977 (Constitution Act) **82,** 394-5
human rights **82,** 413
suspension **103,** 12
Act 32, 1979 (Internal Security Act) **82,** 390
Act 51, 1977 (Criminal Procedure Act) **82,** 392
Administration of Bophuthatswana Decree 1 of 1994 **103,** 12
necessity, unconstitutional acts, legitimization **103,** 22, 26
non-recognition, effect **82,** 420
recognition, government
applicable law, constitutional law **103,** 21-2
legitimacy
Kelsen **103,** 22
necessity **103,** 22, 26
'successful revolution' doctrine **103,** 22-6
premature, *in mediis rebus* **103,** 27
requirements
acquiescence of population **103,** 24-6
democratic regime **103,** 25-6
effective control of territory **103,** 22, 24-6
revolution, regime, legal validity, retroactive **103,** 24
South Africa
agent of, whether **82,** 420, 424
annexation by **103,** 20
foreign government, whether **103,** 19
non-aggression pact, breach **103,** 21
sovereignty **82,** 423, **103,** 19-20, **106,** 154-5. *See also* independence *above and* State, whether *below*
breach, deposition of President **103,** 21, 22
State immunity, jurisdiction, classification of act, sovereignty and **103,** 20
State, whether **103,** 19-20, **106,** 154-5. *See also* independence *and* sovereignty *above*
capacity to enter into relations with other States **82,** 415-17
defined territory **82,** 412-13
government **82,** 413-14
permanent population **82,** 412
territory, annexation **103,** 20
treason **82,** 390-4
UN General Assembly Resolutions, legal effect **82,** 418
border controls. *See also* Germany, inter-zonal trade
forged passports **71,** 252-8
State rights, infringement of **71,** 230, 255-7
borders. *See* boundaries
Bosnia-Herzegovina 92, 173-8
annexation of territory
Croatian ambitions **122,** 51-3, 57
FRY, by **95,** 152-3
redistribution distinguished **95,** 153
armed conflict **105,** 488-9, **106,** 488-9, **108,** 35
co-belligerency **122,** 60-3
critical date **105,** 531
declaration of state of war, relevance **105,** 533
existence **105,** 488-9, **112,** 179-84, 208, **121,** 235, 291-2, **124,** 195-200

intensity **112,** 179
organization of parties **112,** 179
Federal Republic of Yugoslavia (FRY) involvement **105,** 532-3
General Assembly Resolution 2675 (1970) **105,** 512
Geneva Conventions (1949), applicability **105,** 443-4, 490-2, 523-4, **108,** 149, 158-61, **112,** 184-200, **121,** 254-5, **122,** 58-64
international, whether **105,** 443, 490-5, 531-4, **108,** 35-6, 132-3, **112,** 179-83, **115,** 174-5, **122,** 43-57, 114, 225, 245-50, **124,** 96-130
after 19 May 1992 **124,** 96-130, 115 nn. 155 and 156, 195-201
Bosnian Croats as agents of Croatia. *See* Bosnian Croats as agents of Croatia *below*
direct involvement of another State, relevance **108,** 150-4, **122,** 43-57, 245-50, **124,** 96-130
Herceg-Bosna **108,** 149-58, **122,** 53, 54, 56
responsibility for determining **112,** 188
Security Council reference to international humanitarian law as evidence of **124,** 115 n. 155
belligerent occupation
Croatia, by **108,** 160-1, **122,** 64
Serbian forces, by **112,** 186-7
Bosnian Croats as agents of Croatia **108,** 154-8, **122,** 48-57
military intervention by Croatia **108,** 151-4, **122,** 45-8
indirect **122,** 48-57
reasonable grounds for believing **108,** 156, 158
Bosnian Muslims
diplomatic protection **122,** 62-3
as protected persons under the Geneva Convention (IV) **122,** 58-64, 216, 248-9
Bosnian Serbs (Srpska)
Constitution 1991/2
s 80 **108,** 122
s 81 **108,** 122
s 111 **108,** 122
Geneva Conventions (1949), applicability **104,** 156 n. 8, **112,** 188
People's Defence Act 1991 **108,** 122-3
President's powers **108,** 122-3
recognition **104,** 146, 152 n. 2, **105,** 441
nation at war with Bosnia, whether **104,** 156 n. 8, **105,** 493-4, **112,** 180-3
responsibility for acts of **104,** 144-6, **112,** 188-200
Dayton Agreements (1995) and **124,** 129-30
FRY **95,** 80-1, **108,** 137-8, **124,** 114-15, 121-30, 195-201
silence in respect of **95,** 81-2
statement by President of Serbia **95,** 80-1
boundaries
administrative dividing lines **115,** 74-80
conversion into international boundaries **115,** 76-80
Arbitration Commission of the Conference on Yugoslavia **115,** 76-7, 116-17
Dayton Agreements (1995) **115,** 79
demarcation lines **115,** 75
Constitution 1974/1990 **92,** 177
federal unit of SFRY, whether **115,** 130-2
Framework Agreement for the Federation (1994) **115,** 77-9
Genocide Convention (1948)
applicability **115,** 23-7, 67-8
date of **115,** 25

Bosnia-Herzegovina (*cont.*)
succession mechanism **115,** 23-7, 183-203
Head of State
authority to act on behalf of State in international relations **115,** 34-5, 102-15
existence of state of war or emergency, relevance **115,** 108-13
human rights, undertaking to protect **92,** 178
ICJ and
jurisdiction *ratione personae* **95,** 27-9
party to Statute, whether **95,** 27
as international protectorate **115,** 94-6
law of
Citizenship Act 1992 **124,** 132
Criminal Code 1992
applicability of Geneva Conventions (1949) **105,** 522, 591
Art. 48 (multiple conviction) **121,** 301
rape **121,** 270 n. 214
torture **121,** 255
Extradition, Decree with Force of Law **110,** 642
minorities, undertaking to protect **92,** 178
proclamation of sovereignty, legality **115,** 115-16, 132-57
recognition **115,** 96-102
FRY reservation **115,** 200-3
political basis **115,** 98-102
secession, right of **115,** 130-57
Security Council Resolutions. *See* United Nations Security Council Resolutions, 713 (1991), 777 (1992), 808 (1993), 819 (1993), 827 (1993) *and* 859 (1993)
Serbs in, acts of
FRY, responsibility for **95,** 148-9
burden of proof **95,** 149
Special Rapporteur of the Commission on Human Rights
General Assembly Resolution 47/121 **95,** 156
imbalance of weaponry **95,** 156
statehood
Dayton Agreements (1995), dependence on effective implementation of **115,** 89-94
effective government **115,** 80-93
population, absence of consensus between separate groups **115,** 73-4
proclamation of sovereignty. *See* proclamation of sovereignty *above*
Republika Srpska and Herceg-Bosna, relevance **115,** 80-8
territory **115,** 71-3, 74-80
succession, date **96,** 721-2
torture, prohibition **121,** 255
treaties, State succession **115,** 23-5, 46-8, 115-17, 183-203
war crimes in
rape **121,** 266
responsibility **104,** 156 n. 8
Botswana
Constitution (1966)
nature **103,** 198
primacy **103,** 144-5
s 3 **103,** 134, 141-4, 150-6, 170, 173, 179, 181, 184-8
preamble, whether **103,** 137, 140-1, 174-5, 184, 193-5
text **103,** 140

s 5(1)(f) **103,** 164-5, 181-2, 197
s 7 **103,** 182, 198
s 14 **103,** 134, 164-7
s 15 **103,** 148-62, 170, 175, 179, 195-7, 202
text **103,** 149-50
s 15(1) **103,** 150, 152, 154
s 15(2) **103,** 152
s 15(3) **103,** 136, 141-4, 150-6, 195-7
s 15(4) **103,** 154-7, 171-2
s 15(9) **103,** 157-8, 187-8, 197
s 18 **103,** 135, 163-4, 180-3, 184
s 18(1) **103,** 141
s 21 (repealed) **103,** 157-9
s 22 (repealed) **103,** 157-8
s 86 **103,** 144-5
s 89 **103,** 187, 190
Constitution, interpretation
guidelines
broad **103,** 135-6, 137, 140, 173, 188, 190-2
effectiveness **103,** 172
intention of legislature **103,** 199-200
'living tree' **103,** 200-1
objective, evolving **103,** 139, 173
purposive **103,** 201-2
text as a whole **103,** 141-2, 172
special rules **103,** 137-40, 190-1
courts, municipal
standing
actual harm **103,** 165-7
infringement of individual rights **103,** 162-8, 180-3
parent **103,** 164-5, 188-9
popularis actio **103,** 162-3, 181
customary law
establishment **103,** 196
primacy **103,** 145, 174, 188, 196
freedom from discrimination
sexual
African Charter on Human and Peoples' Rights (1981) **103,** 179
right of women to transmit citizenship through descent **103,** 133-7, 141-62, 170-2, 174-80, 183, 185-8, 192-7, 202
UN Declaration on the Elimination of Discrimination against Women (1967) **103,** 178-9
freedom of movement, children, restrictions on, effect on parent **103,** 164-7, 197
human rights
Constitution, under, entrenchment **103,** 155
derogation
constitutional provision **103,** 143, 151-5, 159, 186-8
express provision, need for **103,** 155
exceptions
common law **103,** 163
pre-existing legislation **103,** 157-9
strict interpretation **103,** 150
immigration, procedures, inhuman or degrading treatment **103,** 181-2, 198

Botswana (*cont.*)
inhuman or degrading treatment, immigration procedures **103,** 181-2, 198
law of
Citizenship Act 1984
discriminatory, whether **103,** 133-203
s 4, text **103,** 133
s 5, text **103,** 134
Common Law and Customary Law Act **103,** 196
Habit Forming Drugs Act **88,** 241, 242
Interpretation Act 1984
s 24(1) **103,** 145-6, 159, 162
s 26 **103,** 137-8
s 33 **103,** 153
legislation
preamble, effect **103,** 140-1
validity, declaration of invalidity, vacuum as result **103,** 167-8
legislation, interpretation
aids
dictionary **103,** 191, 193-4
grammar **103,** 191
official report **103,** 145-6
parallel legislation **103,** 179-80
parliamentary proceedings **103,** 146
preamble **103,** 141, 194
ambiguity **103,** 191, 195
guidelines, *expressio unius exclusio alterius* **103,** 136, 151, 152-6, 171-2, 184-8, 194-5
phrases
'man' **103,** 186
'whereas' **103,** 193-4
presumptions, conformity, international obligations **103,** 161-2, 179
treaty as aid
unincorporated treaty **103,** 159, 160-1
unratified **103,** 177
unsigned **103,** 177
nationality
acquisition
descent **103,** 148, 183, 192-3
guardianship **103,** 148
territorial **103,** 148
allegiance and **103,** 148
applicable law
Constitution **103,** 148, 149
customary law **103,** 146-8
international law **103,** 148
citizenship distinguished **103,** 147-8
discrimination, right of women to transmit citizenship through descent **103,** 133-7, 141-62, 170-2, 174-80, 183, 185-8, 192-7, 202
dual, avoidance **103,** 148-9
personal law, definition **103,** 156-7
treaties
compliance, obligation **103,** 175-9

incorporation into municipal law, legislation, interpretation and **103,** 177-8
ratification, legislation, interpretation **103,** 177-8
unincorporated, effect, obligation of passive compliance **103,** 178
boundaries 50, 381-4, **59,** 210, 232. *See also* boundaries, air; boundaries, land; boundaries, maritime; boundary treaties,[i] maritime delimitation; territory; title
acquiescence **50,** 90, 409-15, 464, 495, **75,** 118-20, **91,** 202-4, 448, **97,** 317, 324-5. *See also* prescription *below*
failure to object to definition of territory **100,** 35, 75-6
adjacency, 19th century concept **86,** 187-8
in Africa **50,** 407-8, **100,** 50-2. *See also uti possidetis,* Africa
Angola–SW Africa **37,** 409
OAU Charter **50,** 407-8
agreements. *See* boundary treaties
Alaska **73,** 64, 79-80
alignment **81,** 444-6, 484
alteration. *See* modification *below*
applicable law
federal State **91,** 585-7
federal Constitution **86,** 187
international law **91,** 460
principles of international law relating to territorial sovereignty, validity in respect of nomadic peoples **91,** 587-8
Argentina–Chile. *See* Argentina–Chile boundary
in Australia **69,** 32-75, **73,** 195-7, 210-11, 222-3
Australia–Indonesia **81,** 312
Bosnia-Herzegovina. *See* Bosnia-Herzegovina, boundaries
in Canada
New Brunswick **43,** 105
Vancouver Island **73,** 189-90, 206, 218-19
Canada–USA **71,** 57-216
boundary dispute, Special Agreement and Treaty to submit dispute to binding settlement 1979. *See* International Court of Justice (ICJ), Special Agreement
cession of territory and **70,** 43-50. *See also* territory, acquisition
Chad–Liberia
establishment **100,** 22-32
history **100,** 16-21, 91-2
ICJ definition **100,** 32-3, 36-7
parties' attitude to **100,** 33-6
terra nullius, whether **100,** 36, 52-9
changing geographical circumstances **113,** 179-80
concession agreement, effect **81,** 254, 260-1
coterminous **50,** 276-85, 388, 406, 470, 479-80, 481, 499, 512, 514, **95,** 671, 684, 722-3
criteria
demographic pressure **97,** 312
distribution of natural resources **97,** 313
definition **83,** 36, 59
delimitation distinguished **83,** 60 n. 23, 91
development of concept **83,** 63

[i] Distribution between the four boundary headings represents a compromise between precision and an avoidance of repetition.

boundaries (*cont.*)
frontière **83,** 59-60, **100,** 26
limit **83,** 58, 59
distinguished **77,** 662-4, 670, **81,** 294, 328, **119,** 456
line dividing State competences **83,** 58-9
line or zone **77,** 662-4, 670
delimitation
Beagle Channel dispute, treaty of **82,** 684-9
demarcation distinguished **41,** 178, **77,** 665, **113,** 143, 157, 182-3
land and maritime distinguished **113,** 82, 84
determination. *See also* establishment *below*
agreement. *See also* boundary treaties
adjustment under **71,** 586-7, **78,** 169
demarcation, role of **52,** 167
by
boundary commission **73,** 79-80
courts **42,** 101, **57,** 21, **73,** 188-225
conduct of parties **70,** 42-6
crystallization, process of **50,** 424-6, 467, 470
custom, line established by **50,** 212, 406, 466
executive certificate and **48,** 64, 67
geographical error, in case of **38,** 82-4, 86
international agreements, by **73,** 63-4, 79-80, 188-9, 206, 214, 218-20
international law rules **74,** 123, **75,** 117-21
legislation **42,** 101, **69,** 35-6, 41, 46-53, 57, 59-63, 68-71, 73, **70,** 43, 46-50, 190-5, 205-12, 218-25
occupation, effect **70,** 42-6
rules, order of priority **75,** 117-21
State sovereignty and **41,** 86
unilateral, opposability **41,** 108
unilateral recognition **75,** 118-20
differing sorts **78,** 168-9
diversification of regimes **83,** 63
El Salvador–Honduras. *See* El Salvador–Honduras boundary
equity **97,** 430-1
Frontier Dispute **97,** 430
'reasonable and fair' **97,** 430-1
establishment. *See also* determination *above*
administrative decision **91,** 571-80
arbitral award, whether **91,** 571-6, 681-3
binding effect **91,** 572, 578-9, 583, 585
justification *a posteriori* **91,** 577, 605, 607
British Empire, in **91,** 198-203
consent, need for **91,** 566-71
definition distinguished **91,** 198-202
dependent territory **86,** 191, 199-204
duress and **91,** 568-71
economic coercion **91,** 569-71
nomad peoples and **91,** 562, 635-6, **100,** 91-2
official, by. *See* administrative decision *above*
treaty, by **100,** 22-7, 40, 42, 58, 93
Trucial States **91,** 562-5

estoppel. *See* estoppel
evidence of, maps **50,** 4, 7, 23, 25, 101-2, 105-13, 420, 423, 485, 515, **59,** 169-70, 202-3, 206
federal State **90,** 242-4
  applicable law **91,** 585-90
    federal Constitution **86,** 187
    international law **91,** 460
  confederation, at **90,** 271
  disputes, jurisdiction **91,** 450, 459
  equitable principles **91,** 460
  low-water mark as **90,** 242-4, 272
  modification **86,** 187, 200, 202-3
    applicable law, federal Constitution **86,** 187
  permanent nature **91,** 197
  prerogative power **86,** 190-2, 198, 200
  river **91,** 190-204, 442-66
  seaward **91,** 459
  variable nature **91,** 196-7
finality. *See also* modification; respect for *and* stability *below*
  treaty interpretation and **91,** 453, **100,** 42-8
  treaty of limited duration, relevance **100,** 36, 96, 100
force, change by. *See also* intangibility *and* modification *below*; *uti possidetis*
  effect **92,** 172
    Helsinki Final Act **92,** 172
    UN General Assembly Resolution 2625 (XXV) (Declaration on Principles of International Law concerning Friendly Relations and Cooperation amongst States) **92,** 172
'the frontiers' **100,** 22-3
fundamental change of circumstances **113,** 84. *See also* stability *below*
German. *See* Germany, Federal Republic, boundaries; Germany (Reich), boundaries
historical **50,** 4-5, 6, 20, 474-5, 481, 493, 511
India (Nicobar)–Indonesia (Sumatra) **81,** 312
India, under British rule **50,** 80-105, 325, 412, 416, 466, 501
India–Bangladesh **70,** 43-50
India–Pakistan. *See* India/Pakistan relations
Indian States, acquiescence by Paramount Power **50,** 21, 23
inland waters, effect on status **94,** 243-6
intangibility **83,** 61, 67. *See also* force, change by *above*; modification *and* stability *below*; State succession, boundaries, respect for; *uti possidetis*
  Vienna Convention on Succession of States in Respect of State Property, Archives and Debts (1983) **83,** 61
  Vienna Convention on Succession of States in Respect of Treaties (1978) **83,** 61
Iraq–Kuwait Boundary Commission. *See* Iraq–Kuwait Boundary Commission
in Latin America **50,** 407
legal concept **113,** 209-10
legislation **69,** 35-6, 41, 46-53, 57, 59-63, 68-71, 73
  determining factor **69,** 35-6, 41, 46-53, 57, 59-63, 68-71, 73
  necessity for **70,** 43, 46-50
lex generalis **83,** 65
line **52,** 263
mandated territories. *See* mandated territories, boundaries
maps **50,** 4, 7, 23, 25, 101-2, 105-13, 420, 423, 450, 515, **59,** 169-70, 202-3, 206

boundaries (*cont.*)
error **38,** 60, 76-9, **50,** 106, 111, 167, 477, 485
lines on, value **77,** 664
maritime and land distinguished **83,** 37, 58-60, 63-5, 67, 76
marshland **50,** 391, 464
modification **86,** 605. *See also* federal State, modification *above*
by agreement **78,** 169
internal
British Commonwealth, within **86,** 605
prerogative power **86,** 190-2, 198, 200
multiple delimitation lines **83,** 37, 65
natural **81,** 292, 293-4, 297-8, 299-300, 308, **83,** 101. *See also* watershed *below*; continental shelf delimitation; rift zones; rivers, boundary
Argentina–Chile **113,** 57-8
land and maritime distinguished **81,** 337
rift zone as **81,** 267, 308
Timor Trough **81,** 293, 337
topographical superiority **97,** 423
natural frontiers **75,** 116-17, 120-1
origin **50,** 405-9, 466
Paramount Power's decisions, binding nature **50,** 28
Poland, adjustment by treaty **71,** 586-7
prerogative and **86,** 199-204
prescription. *See also* acquiescence *above*
critical date **75,** 120
recognition **97,** 317
treaty, by **100,** 21-2, 26, 41, 42
rectification **50,** 441-2
Red Sea Islands. *See* Red Sea Islands
respect for. *See* modification, by agreement *above*; stability *below and uti possidetis*
rivers. *See* rivers, boundary
stability **50,** 409-10, 520, **67,** 59, 124, **91,** 197, 578. *See also* fundamental change of circumstances *and* intangibility *above*; *uti possidetis*
changing geographical feature as basis **113,** 208-12
treaty interpretation and **100,** 42-3, 47-8
Vienna Convention on the Law of Treaties (1969) **91,** 578
State sovereignty and, right to determine **41,** 86
State succession and. *See* State succession, boundaries, respect for; *uti possidetis*
straight lines
definition **83,** 46-7
geodesic line **83,** 46, 47
loxodromic line **83,** 46, 47, 48
Surinam–Guyana **48,** 77
territory distinguished **113,** 85
third parties, tripoint **80,** 483
title and **80,** 468-9
uncertainty, effect on States' rights **41,** 62
in USA. *See* United States of America (USA), boundaries
uti possidetis. See uti possidetis
variable nature **91,** 197
varying treaty regimes, possibility **78,** 168-9
watershed line **75,** 116, 120-1, **80,** 337n. 29, **97,** 338, 339
boundaries, air, derived from land and maritime boundaries **82,** 682

boundaries, land 38, 11-90. *See also* boundaries; boundaries, maritime; Egypt–Israel Arbitration Tribunal (Taba); *uti possidetis*
administrative boundary, international boundary, conversion to **80,** 471
apportionment of territory compared **80,** 468
Berubari Union (India–Pakistan) **53,** 182-3
territorial sovereignty **70,** 43-50
burden of proof **80,** 531-2
communes
France–Baden **42,** 59-61
Treaties of Paris (1814-15) **42,** 59-61
continental shelf delimitation and **67,** 57-9, 77-8, 86, 109, 249, 264, 301-3
critical date **80,** 474-5, 519, 535, 557
de facto **80,** 498, 500-4, 532
de jure **80,** 324
delimitation
better title as basis **80,** 284, 287
demarcation and **80,** 319, 321
burden of proof **67,** 321
hydrographic **80,** 544
orographic **80,** 544
line of, nature **80,** 563
methods **80,** 492
transboundary rights, separate issue **80,** 519
demarcation **53,** 191, 198-9, **57,** 58-69, **62,** 126. *See also* Argentina–Chile boundary, demarcation
allocation of territory distinguished **94,** 28, 40, **100,** 49-50
arbitral decision distinguished **113,** 43, 157, 182-3
Belgium–Netherlands **70,** 45-6
boundary markers
challenge to **80,** 306
stability of boundaries and **80,** 306, 335-6
boundary pillars **50,** 22, 23, 151-3, 316-21, 442-3, 468, 475, 490
concrete markers, intervisibility **94,** 26
criteria
ethno-cultural **100,** 58-9
geographical features **100,** 53-4, 58-9
religion **100,** 53-4, 58-9
security **100,** 54
definition **50,** 135
delimitation and **41,** 178, **77,** 665
delimitation and **80,** 319, 321
directional poles **94,** 26-7
evidence of, exchange of letters **94,** 11
geographic co-ordinates **94,** 26-7
general international practice **94,** 27, 28
ICJ expert, appointment **80,** 551-2, 564-5
guidelines **80,** 534
latitude, line of **94,** 18
legal–political operation **71,** 104
lines. *See* boundaries
low-water springs line **94,** 22
maintenance **94,** 27, 28-9, 40
costs **94,** 27

boundaries, land (*cont.*)
navigational access **94,** 24, 25
equitable principles **94,** 25
Law of the Sea Convention (1982) **94,** 25
noticeboard **94,** 11, 18-19
plaques on jetties **94,** 26
procedure, agreement on **50,** 17, 155
settlement distinguished **53,** 199
shortest possible line **94,** 22, 25
thalweg **94,** 17-18
establishment **94,** 21
weighted mean **94,** 22, 25
equitable principles **80,** 472
maritime boundaries compared **80,** 472
erroneous border, validity **80,** 325
evidence of
administrative documents **80,** 491, 492-517, 538-9, 545-50
factual error **80,** 544
agreement **80,** 288, 293, 317-19, 533
books **80,** 340
boundary markers **80,** 287, 288, 289, 290, 293, 323, 333, 334-5
burden of proof **80,** 321, 326
cairn **80,** 342
conduct of colonial authorities **80,** 490-1
diary **80,** 320, 349
diplomatic correspondence **80,** 317
guidebooks **80,** 301
intelligence handbook **80,** 317
international organizations, records **80,** 318
legislation **80,** 484-6, 491
maps **59,** 169-70, **80,** 268, 289, 291, 292, 293, 300-1, 303, 324, 340, 343, 349, 350-1, 486-92, 532, 535-8, 544-50, 562, **100,** 32, 33
absence of satisfactory **80,** 287, 289
discrepancies **80,** 295, 333, 334
disputed **80,** 254, 290, 490
lines on, value **77,** 664
neutrality **80,** 487, 490
reliability **80,** 334, 486-8, 491, 532
scale **80,** 287, 295, 300
value **80,** 334, 343-4, 486-7
margin of error **80,** 521
military presence **80,** 301, 344
minutes of meeting **80,** 520
official papers **80,** 318
official publication **80,** 509
oral tradition **80,** 521, 523-4
parliamentary reply **80,** 317
photographic **80,** 260, 264, 268, 301, 303, 340, 342
caption as interpretative aid **80,** 342-3
presence **80,** 301, 344
Statistical Yearbooks **80,** 301, 318, 341
limited value **80,** 301

topography **80,** 350
travel accounts **80,** 340, 344
treaty **100,** 33, 34
trig points **80,** 288, 289, 290, 303
UN publications **100,** 35
foreign inlets, avoidance **50,** 7, 520
intangibility **80,** 478
as general rule of international law **80,** 471
interzonal border **45,** 37-46
Island of Palmas case **80,** 287
mandated territories **80,** 260-3
maritime delimitation distinguished **80,** 472, 482
Nufenen Pass case **80,** 325-6
occupation **41,** 101
opposability **80,** 482-5
recognition **80,** 283, 332, 351-2
implied **80,** 261
stability **80,** 306, 323-4, 334-5
markers and **80,** 306, 335-6
State succession and. *See* State succession, boundaries, respect for; *uti possidetis*
straight line technique **80,** 526
Temple of Preah Vihear **80,** 297-8, 306, 323-6, 334-5
thalweg **38,** 97, **77,** 672-3, **83,** 18, 119, **94,** 17-18, 21
third parties **80,** 482-5
title and, pre-eminence **80,** 391, 470
track-making works, evidence of intentions **80,** 521, 522
tripoint, agreement of all parties, need for **80,** 483
uncertainty, territorial rights, effect on **41,** 62
boundaries, maritime 51, 27-38, **52,** 227, 262, **74,** 122-3, **75,** 126, **77,** 636-92, **82,** 681-2. *See also* continental shelf delimitation; evidence of, maritime boundaries; maritime delimitation
alluvion **74,** 122-3
applicable law, principles, rules and practices of maritime law **114,** 37
azimuth prolonged and raised to superjacent water column **83,** 16, 21
critical date **91,** 460 n. 6
delimitation distinguished **41,** 62-3
delimitation of internal waters, whether **83,** 68
demarcation
absence of, effect **52,** 224-6
median line **94,** 24-5
basepoints **94,** 25
determination
acquiescence **71,** 107-9, 130-7
perimeter line, whether **77,** 662
reservation of rights **71,** 107-9
dispute settlement, geographical and historical framework **77,** 649-56
equitable principles **91,** 460, 461
Eritrea–Yemen. *See* Eritrea/Yemen boundary
France–UK **39,** 425-6
intention to create, whether **77,** 659-75
lakes and rivers **50,** 391-2
Lake Geneva **41,** 135, 149

boundaries, maritime (*cont.*)
land boundaries and **67,** 57-9, 77-8, 86, 109, 249, 264, 301-3, **71,** 86, 89, 100, 160-1, **74,** 123
lex specialis **83,** 65-6
Libya–Malta **81,** 252-90, 292-307, 308-24, 325-35, 336-54, 361-72, 401-2, 410-19, 726
Libya–Tunisia **67,** 58-9, 77-8, 117-18, **81,** 432-47, 469-78, 479, 481-5
Norway–Denmark **81,** 312
review, right to **83,** 42-3
seaward boundary **51,** 30-8, **91,** 459-61
State succession. *See* State succession, boundaries, respect for; *uti possidetis*
boundary dispute. *See also* Argentina–Chile boundary; Burkina Faso/Mali boundary dispute; Egypt–Israel boundary; India–Pakistan relations, boundary dispute
act of State and **64,** 280, 292-4, 303, 343-4, 348-51, **66,** 180-5, 334-8
arbitral tribunal, role **91,** 580-5
avoidance of prejudicial acts **82,** 682
Burkina Faso–Mali Frontier Dispute **80,** 319, 324, 441-563
Indo-Pakistan Boundaries Disputes Tribunal **53,** 187-8
justiciability in US courts **66,** 180-5, 334-8
maps as evidence. *See* maps
settlement **57,** 110-11
demarcation distinguished **53,** 199
spheres of influence, relevance **100,** 37
territorial dispute distinguished **113,** 129-30
boundary treaties 100, 47-8. *See also Index to the Consolidated Table of Treaties*
as comprehensive settlement **100,** 42-8, 95
Jaworzina **100,** 46-7
Monastery at Saint-Naoum **100,** 47
stability of boundaries, relevance **100,** 47-8
Treaty of Lausanne case **100,** 44-6
division of spheres of interest distinguished **100,** 93-4, 95
France–Baden **42,** 60
France–Portugal (Senegal–Guinea-Bissau) (1886) **83,** 17-18, 35, 38
land
Baden–France **42,** 60
Cambodia–Thailand (1904) **70,** 46
maritime
Denmark–FRG (1965) **41,** 29, 37, 40, 46, 89, 90, 130-1, 169
Denmark–Netherlands (1966) **41,** 41-6, 47-8, 50, 57, 84, 114
Denmark–Norway (1965) **41,** 90, 136, 180, 187
Denmark–UK **41,** 41, 48, 90, 166
Finland–USSR **41,** 160
France–Switzerland (1953) **41,** 149
FRG–Netherlands **41,** 90
FRG–Netherlands (1964) **41,** 29, 40-9, 50, 57, 84, 90, 101, 108, 114, 169
Iceland–Norway (Jan Mayen) (1980) **62,** 111-12, 115
Italy–Yugoslavia (1968) **41,** 122
Morocco–Spain (1967) **41,** 136
Netherlands–UK (1965) **41,** 41, 48, 90, 95
Norway–UK (1965) **41,** 90, 102, 166
third States and **41,** 181
purpose **83,** 36
peace, stability and finality **100,** 62-4

State succession and. *See* treaties, State succession, boundary treaties
Brazil
aliens, expulsion, right of **71,** 492-3
Companhia de Navegacao Lloyd Brasileiro **63,** 330-3
Constitution (1988)
s 119(1) **91,** 294, 296, 299, 302
s 125(II) **116,** 630
s 153 **91,** 308
COTAC, State agency **66,** 312-16
courts, municipal
States, dispute between **91,** 296, 299, 315-16
absence of alternative forum **91,** 298, 299, 301
compétence de la compétence **91,** 299
enforceability of decision, relevance **91,** 314-15
international law as applicable law, relevance **91,** 294, 300, 316
real/immovable property **91,** 294, 299
State succession, relevance **91,** 300-1
diplomatic immunity, jurisdiction, State immunity and, States as parties to dispute **91,** 293, 295-6, 299, 306, 307
extradition **55,** 12, 20, 22-3, 32-3
foreign judgment, enforceability **91,** 314
foreign State, proceedings involving, right to sue and be sued **116,** 630
France, lobster war **47,** 22-4
jurisdiction, immovable property, dispute relating to, applicable law **91,** 310-12
law of
Civil Code, s 89(1) **91,** 299, 308
Civil Code Introductory Law, s 12 **91,** 299, 308
Civil Procedure Code, s 267 **91,** 307
Constitution. *See* Constitution (1988) *above*
Fundamental Law (*Lei Maior*) **91,** 308
Legislative Decree No 102/1964 (Vienna Convention on Diplomatic Relations) **91,** 300
State immunity, jurisdiction
diplomatic immunity distinguished, States as parties to dispute. *See* diplomatic immunity, jurisdiction, State immunity, jurisdiction and *above*
international courtesy and **91,** 302
international goodwill and **91,** 309
State immunity, jurisdiction, applicability, immovable property, dispute relating to **91,** 296, 300-1, 302, 308, 310-12
State immunity, jurisdiction, classification of act
diplomatic premises, lease **91,** 297
responsibility for determining **91,** 297
State immunity, jurisdiction, procedural aspects, applicable law, international law **91,** 295, 311-14
State immunity, jurisdiction, theory/doctrine
absolute theory **91,** 309
international goodwill and **91,** 309
par in parem non habet jurisdictionem **91,** 298
USSR and **91,** 296
acta jure gestionis/*acta jure imperii* distinguished **91,** 297, 310
customary international law **91,** 295
restricted, general acceptance **91,** 296-8
State practice **91,** 297-8

Brazil (*cont.*)
State immunity, jurisdiction, waiver, exclusion by Constitution **116,** 629-30
Bretton Woods Agreement (1944). *See* International Monetary Fund Agreement (IMF) (1944) (Bretton Woods Agreement)
Brezhnev Doctrine, belligerent occupation and **90,** 407
Briand–Kellogg Pact, breach 49, 83 n. 1
Brioni Agreement (1942) 42, 403-5, 407
British Columbia. *See* Canada, British Columbia
British Commonwealth. *See also* United Kingdom
allegiance and **92,** 634
Balfour Declaration (1926) **86,** 607, **90,** 249
boundaries within, alteration **86,** 605. *See also* Australia, boundaries; Canada, boundaries
'Commonwealth citizen', Northern Cypriots **108,** 545-56
commonwealth citizens, control of entry into UK **43,** 130-40
'Commonwealth subject', 'British subject', identity of meaning **92,** 634
continental shelf rights, acquisition, Crown in right of colony **86,** 603-7
Crown
obligations, *lex situs* **78,** 435-7, 467-8
unity and diversity **88,** 272
defence, responsibility for **90,** 463
definition **80,** 14-16
fluidity of concept **80,** 16
Dominion status
external sovereignty **86,** 607-8
international personality **37,** 529
League of Nations Council and **37,** 533
legislative competence **43,** 110-11, **88,** 271
extradition between members of **41,** 397-406, **52,** 357, **77,** 344, **78,** 501-5, **80,** 13, 16-18, **88,** 264-7, 270-6
agreement, need for **88,** 276
'designated' **80,** 13, 14-15
membership, need for **80,** 14, 16
extraterritorial legislation, New Zealand **45,** 4-18, **88,** 271
Gleneagles Accord. *See* apartheid, Gleneagles Accord (1977)
head of, role **92,** 634
ICJ jurisdiction, exclusion **97,** 94
Imperial Conference (1926) **78,** 468
Imperial legislation, colonies, application to **69,** 13, 23, **70,** 60-1, 70-2, 90-1, 98-100
independence, evidence of, independent participation in war **88,** 272
legislative powers within **86,** 604
territorial sea, over **86,** 604
membership
Constitutions, autochthonous, whether **90,** 468-72
Fiji **80,** 11-16
independence **53,** 99-102
lapse **80,** 13
Nauru **97,** 94
obligations **90,** 467
requirements **90,** 467
sovereignty, effect on **90,** 467-8
status **53,** 99-101
termination, date of **80,** 15

mutual assistance, Harare Scheme. *See* judicial assistance, Scheme relating to Mutual Assistance in Criminal Matters within the Commonwealth (1986/1990) ('Harare Scheme')
non-interference in internal affairs **42,** 21
Pakistan, withdrawal from **61,** 270, 274
State succession and **78,** 467-8
Statute of Westminster 1931. *See* United Kingdom, law of, Statute of Westminster
succession **78,** 438-47, 451-2
unity and diversity **78,** 425, 429, 431, 433, 443-5
ties, nature **80,** 16
treaty obligations, responsibility for **86,** 699-700
visiting forces, reciprocity **90,** 461-4
British Guiana
admiralty jurisdiction **48,** 77-81
jurisdiction, territorial limits, ship on Corentyne River **48,** 77-81
law of
Criminal Law (Offences) Ordinance **48,** 78
Federal Supreme Court (Appeals) Ordinance 1958 **48,** 81
Supreme Court Ordinance, admiralty jurisdiction **48,** 77-8
British India. *See also* India, State succession
definition **50,** 69
partition **38,** 3-9
effect on contracts **53,** 117-29
British Indian Ocean Territory (BIOT)
British Indian Ocean Territory Order 1965
as exercise of Crown prerogative **123,** 557-8, 585-6, 590, 591-2
extracts **123,** 558-60
ss 3-5 **123,** 558
s 8 **123,** 558
s 8(3) **123,** 558
s 10 **123,** 558
s 11 **123,** 558, 584-91
s 15(1) **123,** 559, 586
s 16 **123,** 559
s 17 **123,** 559
s 19 **123,** 559
as British settlement **123,** 585-7
as ceded colony **123,** 587
constitution of Chagos Archipelago as **44,** 122, **91,** 336
British Indian Ocean Territory Order 1965 **123,** 557. *See also* British Indian Ocean Territory Order 1965 *above*
Ilois
property rights **123,** 561
public law rights **123,** 561
removal to Mauritius **123,** 557, 560-2
compensation for **91,** 334-40
Immigration Ordinance 1971. *See* Immigration Ordinance 1971 *below*
legitimacy **123,** 556-93
Magna Carta 1215 and **123,** 575-9
motivation **123,** 561-9, 590
responsibility for **91,** 334-40
settled population, whether **123,** 562-4

British Indian Ocean Territory (BIOT) (*cont.*)
size of population **123,** 560
Ilois Trust Fund, entitlement to compensation under **91,** 334-40
Immigration Ordinance 1971
drafting process **123,** 564-9
extracts **123,** 559-60
s 4, validity **123,** 557-93
s 9 **123,** 559-60
judicial organization **123,** 569, 572
jurisdiction, UK courts **123,** 569-75, 591-2
law of, Magna Carta 1215 **123,** 575-9, 586
legislative powers
peace, order and good government **123,** 584, 587-91, 592-3
source **123,** 585-7, 591-2
Mauritius–UK Agreement (1982) **91,** 334-40
individuals, rights under **91,** 337-40
nationality **91,** 336
UK–US Exchange of Notes concerning the Availability of BIOT for Defence Purposes (1966) **123,** 562
British New Guinea. *See also* Papua New Guinea; protectorates
administration, authority to acquire land **71,** 42-4, 51-7
land
acquisition by Crown **71,** 41-7, 51-6
waste and vacant land **71,** 51-6
protectorate, proclamation of **71,** 41, 44-6, 52-4
British Petroleum Company 66, 548
'British possession' 42, 52, **79,** 688, **85,** 136, **88,** 274, **91,** 390-1
British Rail. *See* United Kingdom, British Rail
'British settlement' 123, 586
British subject
allegiance, duty of **44,** 379
'natural-born British subjects' **44,** 374, **79,** 391, 689-94
Western Samoans **79,** 689-94
status **39,** 325
British Virgin Islands
continental shelf, proclamation **86,** 605
fishing zones
regulations, power to enforce **86,** 699-700
rights in, preservation **86,** 699
judicial notice, Fishing Rules, of **86,** 695
law of
Fisheries Ordinance 1979/1982 **86,** 693, 694, 697, 699
Fisheries Rules 1982 **86,** 695
municipal law, publication, effect **86,** 693-4
treaties
form, agreed minute **86,** 694, 697
implementing legislation
absence, effect **86,** 699
need for **86,** 697-9
municipal law, primacy **86,** 693-4, 697-9
broadcasting. *See also* European Convention on Human Rights (1950), freedom of expression; freedom of expression
content standard

MFN clause, compatibility with **115,** 386-415
transmission quota as **115,** 391
jurisdiction, high seas **101,** 412-18
programme content **115,** 393-5
religious, human rights and **47,** 198-203
territorial sea
from outside **61,** 184-5, **74,** 201-3
from within **43,** 80-93
Strasbourg Agreement (1965) **74,** 201-3
Brunei, status as British Protectorate **55,** 490, 493
Bulgaria
citizens, USA, right to inherit from estates in **43,** 200, 203
commercial/trade representation/mission, immunity, jurisdiction **65,** 283
exchange control laws **38,** 145
Greece, Caphandaris–Moloff Accord (1927) **47,** 420, 430
bunkering at sea. *See* exclusive economic zone (EEZ), refuelling of fishing vessel
burden of proof 55, 294, **58,** 263-4, 300-1, **60,** 195, **66,** 195-6, **70,** 507-11, 519-20, 525-6, **75,** 133-8, **76,** 148, 653-4, **78,** 38-9, 79, 650 n. 2, **80,** 491, 508, 532, 585, **82,** 202, **83,** 23, **89,** 326
act of State **64,** 264-5, 380-1, **66,** 11, 27-8, 218-20, **81,** 519, 593-4, 597, 637, **101,** 533, **103,** 469
acta jure gestionis **82,** 33
actori incumbit onus probandi **68,** 554, **120,** 221
administrative practice giving rise to alleged breach **58,** 263-6, **120,** 49-50, 95-6
agency relationship **90,** 611
aliens
detention of, purpose **77,** 339
exemption from costs **77,** 442
intention to settle **99,** 43
status **54,** 270, 276-80, 291-7, **95,** 573-4
arbitral award
annulment proceedings **92,** 128
finality **82,** 68, 70
interpretation **113,** 73
arbitral tribunal **89,** 326, 564-5
arbitration **75,** 133-8
submission to **80,** 640-1
arbitration clause **86,** 448
arbitrator, grounds for disqualification **125,** 54-7
asylum **79,** 615 n. 3, 620, 623, 628 n. 32, 633, 638, **95,** 538, 572
attachment, grounds for **63,** 308-10, 509
availability of alternative forum **84,** 105
avulsion as applicable law **97,** 463
bona fides **70,** 372
boundary **80,** 531-2
delimitation and demarcation, conflict **80,** 321, 326
claimant, general principle of international law **106,** 447
compensation, entitlement of third parties **116,** 283
Constitution, breach **98,** 378-9
constitutional compatibility of legislation **87,** 348
costs incurred **106,** 655-6, 731
crimes against humanity, personal motives **124,** 167, 172-3
criminal case, in **94,** 236-7

burden of proof (*cont.*)
civil jurisdiction distinguished **94,** 236-7
damages **106,** 714
default judgment, entitlement **63,** 382, 389-90
default judgment against foreign State, acceptance of **65,** 87-8
delay, justification **79,** 167
deprivation of
constitutional rights **79,** 142
liberty **79,** 39
diplomatic premises **77,** 119-21
'used for purposes of maintaining a diplomatic or consular mission' **98,** 12
diplomatic privileges and immunities **69,** 281-2
waiver **111,** 623
displaced persons **95,** 508, 512, 522, 528-9
due process **79,** 389, **84,** 143
embassy or consular bank account/funds, use for private purposes **77,** 49-50
enemy character **54,** 573, 579, 581-2, 602-3, 606-7
enforcement of arbitral award **94,** 221
environmental damage **106,** 69-70, 122-7
evaluation **82,** 198
exclusion of alien **95,** 538, **104,** 203-4
exhaustion of local remedies **60,** 163, **61,** 383-4, 352, **84,** 353, **94,** 407, **95,** 257, 271-2, **102,** 287, **120,** 50, 95
existence of civil war, rebellion or insurrection **107,** 507
existence of loan **124,** 54
expropriation/nationalization, compensation **121,** 195
extinction of native title **118,** 336
extradition
cause for **79,** 428
conditions in requesting State **104,** 100-1
delay, justification **79,** 167
fair trial **98,** 548
family life, respect for **92,** 311, **111,** 295-6
fishing in prohibited zone, legitimacy **108,** 635
flag State status **125,** 295-7
government, validity **90,** 519-20
Head of State, public nature of acts **99,** 164
human rights **100,** 630-1
human rights violations **71,** 303, **79,** 224, **95,** 284, 287
illegal fishing **125,** 260-1, 263-4
IMF, disapproval of exchange controls **84,** 124 n. 5
immigration controls **81,** 153
impartial tribunal **81,** 42
implied contract **81,** 724-5
inhuman or degrading treatment **98,** 510
'interest of a legal nature which may be affected by the decision' as requirement for intervention by third State **97,** 27-8, 156, 210, 227-8, 235-49, 257, 259-62, 276
interim measures, requesting party **95,** 62
international law **55,** 313-14
jurisdiction **48,** 457, **107,** 346, **121,** 52-3
acquisition **107,** 188
collusion **63,** 102

extraterritorial **36,** 57
ICJ **37,** 115, 164, **84,** 230-1, **123,** 211
legal question, whether **83,** 343
legality of arrest of ship within EEZ **110,** 761
legislation
challenge to **98,** 397
interpretation **90,** 623
likely persecution **79,** 607-9
location of discharge of oil from ship **94,** 236
ministerial acts, *bona fides* **70,** 372
national security defence **110,** 673
nationality, loss or deprivation of **77,** 386
nationality of claim **46,** 262-3, 376, 442, 456-7
North American Free Trade Agreement Arbitral Tribunal **110,** 560, 561, 577-8
nuclear weapons, deployment, legality **110,** 236, 349
onus probandi actori incumbit **106,** 447
ownership of property **64,** 680-1
'persecution or well-founded fear' **108,** 379-80
person alleging fact **106,** 447
persuasive/evidential burden distinguished **122,** 478-80, 482-3
political offence **79,** 53, 59, 94-5, 116, 117, 132-3, 454, **104,** 91, 93, 94
liability to prosecution for **79,** 94
presumption of innocence and **81,** 198, **122,** 445-9, 476-88, 497-8
prisoners of war, status **99,** 185-6
provisional measures, ICSID **124,** 7
recognition, government **103,** 77
refugee **40,** 207
status **77,** 386
refugees **92,** 705, 718, **104,** 233
'persecution or well-founded fear of persecution' **95,** 564-5
'serious non-political crime' **104,** 663-5
reversal **80,** 487
revolution, legal validity of regime **103,** 77
right to attachment of assets **87,** 240-1, 256
Serbs in Bosnia, acts of **95,** 149
shift **106,** 448
ship
nationality **120,** 176-7
registration **120,** 311
sovereignty, violation **105,** 480
standard **91,** 430, **106,** 448
standards of justice, failure to meet **79,** 82, 85, 164, 166
standing **124,** 27
State agency, independence **79,** 565, 566, **80,** 577, **101,** 547, **103,** 496-500, 510
State assets, purpose **87,** 36
State contract, investment **89,** 489-90, 542
State controlled entity **84,** 605
State immunity, execution/attachment, purpose **98,** 12
State immunity, jurisdiction. *See* State immunity, jurisdiction, procedural aspects, burden of proof
State responsibility **82,** 33, 160, 162, 176-7, 202, 214, 223, 224, **86,** 502, **106,** 447-9
for injury outside jurisdictional period **109,** 134

burden of proof (*cont.*)
taxation, exemption **108,** 548-9
time-limits for arbitral claim **122,** 312, 313
title **91,** 651, 686
treaty reservation
admissibility **107,** 71
validity **103,** 650
treaty interpretation **90,** 376
UN Human Rights Committee (UNHRC) **94,** 442
UN Secretary-General's assertion, truth of **83,** 438
UNCITRAL Rules **95,** 207, 223
visiting forces status **79,** 45
waiver of rights under European Convention on Human Rights (1950) **81,** 42
war crimes **91,** 11, 68-9, 103-4, 134, **104,** 355-6
knowledge that act constituted war crime or crime against humanity **98,** 542, 596-7, **104,** 395
lawful authority **98,** 597
superior orders **98,** 599
war risks **82,** 109
well-founded fear of persecution **90,** 7
where evidence difficult to produce **83,** 477
Yugoslavia, International Criminal Tribunal for the Former (ICTY) **121,** 306, 338
burial grounds, family life, respect for and **118,** 264-78
Burkina Faso/Mali boundary dispute 80, 440-563
Mali/Upper Volta Mixed Technical Commission **80,** 520-1
OAU Mediation Commission **80,** 475-80
alleged acquiescence in conclusions **80,** 477-80
failure to complete work **80,** 477
Legal Sub-Commission **80,** 494
limited powers **80,** 477
Technical Sub-Commission **80,** 494
Burma
emergence as separate State **53,** 150-2
extraterritorial legislation, goods shipped from foreign port **36,** 428-33
Hague Regulations (1907), law of **36,** 498
immigration control laws **36,** 345-50
Japanese occupation, debts, discharge in Japanese currency **36,** 497-503
law of
Carriage of Goods by Sea Act **36,** 428-33
Brussels Convention for the Unification of Rules relating to Certain Bills of Lading (1924) and **36,** 428-33
Defence of Burma Act 1940, control of enemy firms **36,** 500-1
Japanese Currency (Evaluation) Act **36,** 502, 503
treaties, primacy **36,** 428-33
Burundi, law of, Decree-Law 1/007 of 20 November 1989, expulsion of alien **96,** 311
Bynkershoek
cannon-shot rule **51,** 110
expropriation/nationalization **41,** 12
usurper, validity of acts of **39,** 118, 258

Cairo Declaration (1964). *See uti possidetis,* Cairo Declaration (1964)
Calvo Clause 46, 465-8, **66,** 319-20
Cambodia

diplomatic premises in UK, status **83,** 233-43
French courts in, independence and **47,** 92-4
independence, jurisdiction, transfer of **47,** 92-4
Thailand, boundary **70,** 46

Cameroons
applicable law, former Republic of Cameroon, French Civil Code **114,** 208
Cameroons Development Bank (CDB), immunity, jurisdiction **77,** 533
French trusteeship, termination **40,** 36-7, **44,** 36-7

Cameroons and Togo, Mandate, drafting **37,** 62-3

Canada
aboriginal Indians in. *See also* United Kingdom, law of, Royal Proclamation 1763
in Alberta (Cree Indians) **78,** 423-53
Bands **78,** 457, 459, 472, 473
Canada Act 1982 and **78,** 423-53, 457-73
constitutional basis **118,** 364
Constitutional Conferences to determine status **96,** 709-10
right of representation under International Covenant on Civil and Political Rights (ICCPR) (1966) **96,** 710-12
customary law of **78,** 424-5
definition **78,** 480-1
British North America Act **78,** 472
Constitution Act 1982 **78,** 460
fiduciary relationship with Crown **104,** 219, 222, **118,** 364
Gitksan and Wet'suwet'en people
demography **115,** 454, 473
history **115,** 454-5
oral histories **115,** 485-8
social organization **115,** 455-6
territorial boundaries **115,** 461-2, 473
Jay Treaty, rights under **104,** 208-17
jurisdiction over
Canadian courts **73,** 127-35
interjurisdictional immunity **115,** 520-1
jurisdiction over land distinguished **115,** 520
Mikmaq tribe **79,** 262-6
recognition **79,** 263
natural resources, right to dispose of freely **96,** 669-73
recognition
government **79,** 262
State **79,** 262
rights **115,** 452-535. *See also* aboriginal rights *below*
Rupert's land **78,** 437, 449
self-determination, right to **96,** 669-73, 706-7
title. *See* aboriginal title *below*
treaties **78,** 429-31, 449-51, 466-72
Indian hunting rights, preservation **53,** 580-6
requirements **104,** 220-1
State succession and **78,** 436, 467-8
aboriginal rights **78,** 425-53, 473. *See also* aboriginal Indians in *above*; aboriginal title *below*
abandonment, burden of proof **115,** 462
alienation, restrictions on **115,** 463, 476, 498-500
basis

Canada (*cont.*)
occupation or use of specific land **115,** 456-7, 463, 467
operation of law rather than Crown grant **115,** 463
practices, customs and traditions pre-dating contact with Europeans **115,** 469-70, 473-4
Charter of Rights and Freedoms and **78,** 475
common law recognition **115,** 467, 469, 481
constitutionalization. *See* aboriginal title, Constitution Act 1982 *below*
consultation with minority representatives, relevance **115,** 516, 534
critical date
contact with Europeans **115,** 469-70, 473-4, 481
England's assertion of sovereignty **115,** 460, 463
development, possibility of **115,** 469-70
extinction
act inconsistent with continuing right and **115,** 460-1, 466-7, 470
clear and plain intention, need for **115,** 460, 464-5, 469, 475, 522-3
Crown's power of unilateral **115,** 457, 460, 464
fiduciary obligation of Crown. *See* fiduciary obligation of Crown *below*
laws of general application, by **115,** 465-6
possibility of **115,** 463, 511
provincial power over. *See* provincial power over *below*
fiduciary obligation of Crown
to ensure aboriginal activities not unduly impaired **115,** 461, 512-17, 529
to enter into and conduct negotiations in good faith **115,** 524
jurisdiction of British courts **78,** 423-53
land rights **115,** 476
nature
ad hoc **115,** 466
communal pursuit of subsistence activities **115,** 456-7, 463, 472-3
jurisdictional **115,** 459, 464, 468, 472, 473-6
personal **115,** 457
proprietary **115,** 457-8, 463, 467
usufructuary **115,** 457
negotiations relating to **115,** 464, 466, 469, 473, 535
Crown's obligation of good faith **115,** 524
oil or gas benefits **115,** 496-7
priority over competing and inconsistent activities **115,** 457
provincial power over **115,** 465-7, 470, 518-23
'core of Indianness' **115,** 520-1
general legislation affecting **115,** 521-2
legislation relating specifically to Indians **115,** 521
rights not relating to land **115,** 521
rights relating to land **115,** 521
reconciliation of prior aboriginal occupation and Crown sovereignty **115,** 481, 504, 514-15
regulation
legitimate and justifiable Crown interests, need for **115,** 457, 533-4
possibility of **115,** 463
requirements
continuity **115,** 481-2, 494-7
integrality to claimants' culture **115,** 467-8, 470, 497-500
long-standing practice **115,** 456, 463-4, 468, 472
occupation pre-dating England's assertion of sovereignty **115,** 459-60, 463-4, 468

occupation of specific territory **115,** 459-60, 463-4, 468
occupation to the exclusion of other organized societies **115,** 459-60, 468, 474
organized society **115,** 459-60
self-government **115,** 470-1, 474-7, 517
as alternative to jurisdiction **115,** 478-9
territorial limits **115,** 476
evidence of **115,** 488-90
title to land distinguished **115,** 520
trapping, whether aboriginal right **115,** 472
aboriginal title **73,** 58-62, 65-127. *See also* aboriginal Indians in *and* aboriginal rights *above*
aboriginal rights distinguished **115,** 511
affirmation by Constitution Act 1982 **115,** 452, 470
alienation, restrictions on **115,** 492, 528-9
basis
activities **115,** 491-2, 503-4
occupation **115,** 472, 493, 528
possession **115,** 472
relationship between common law and pre-existing aboriginal law **115,** 493
Royal Proclamation, 1763 **115,** 493, 532-3
use **115,** 472
at common law **115,** 492-500
Constitution Act 1982 **115,** 500-3. *See also* Constitution Act 1982, s 35(1) *below*
critical date, assertion of sovereignty **115,** 481-2, 504-8, 531-2
evidence of **115,** 452
occupancy **115,** 498
occupation prior to assertion of sovereignty **115,** 504-8
oral histories **115,** 453, 471, 481-90
extinction **73,** 58-62, 65, 68-72, 76-7, 101-2, 107-8, 111-13, 117-27, 132. *See also* power of province to extinguish *below*
interference with
compensation **115,** 516-17, 535
requirements **115,** 514-16
joint **115,** 509-11
nature
aboriginal rights **115,** 469
communal **115,** 493
ownership and jurisdiction **115,** 472, 478, 527-8
right in land **115,** 452, 491-2, 502-3
right to exclusive use and occupation for variety of purposes not necessarily integral to aboriginal cultures **115,** 494-7, 529
sui generis **115,** 453, 469, 481, 492-500, 528
uncertainty **115,** 478-9
power of province to extinguish **115,** 453, 470-1, 535
requirements
continuity **115,** 508-9, 528, 530, 531-2
defined territory **115,** 530-1
exclusive occupation **115,** 509-11, 524, 531, 532
practices relating to traditional way of life **115,** 530, 532
reserve lands, relevance of legislation relating to **115,** 529-30
Alberta
aboriginal Indians in **78,** 423-53
Public Service Employer Relations Act 1977, validity **90,** 183-4, 189-98

Canada (*cont.*)
aliens, right to remain in country **124,** 403
applicable law
secession of part of State
international law **115,** 546
municipal law **115,** 590
tort, *lex loci delicti commissi* **124,** 432-3
treaty interpretation, international law **101,** 313
war crimes
international law **104,** 299-300
municipal law **104,** 299-300
arbitral award, annulment, discretion **199,** 679-80
arbitral award, review
adjournment to allow action to eliminate grounds for setting aside award **125,** 470-5
time-limit **125,** 475
applicable law, International Commercial Arbitration Act RSBC 1966 and Commercial Arbitration Act RSBC 1996 distinguished **119,** 656-9
standard of review **119,** 659-61
award based on deception **119,** 675-6
conflict with public policy **119,** 673-5
decisions beyond scope of submission to jurisdiction **119,** 659-61, 665-8, 670
error of law **119,** 671
failure to address all questions **119,** 676-81
patently unreasonable error **119,** 670-3
pragmatic and functional approach **119,** 660-1
ultra vires award. *See* decisions beyond scope of submission to jurisdiction *above*
arbitral award, revision, compensation, effect on **119,** 681-2
arbitration, commercial arbitration, definition **119,** 657-9
Bill of Rights **69,** 212, 214-15, 242-7, 264, **71,** 528
fair hearing **42,** 230-2
freedom of religion **43,** 188-91
immigration enquiries **44,** 163-4, 166, 167-8, 170, 172
s 1(a) **69,** 242-3, 264
s 1(b) **69,** 214-15
s 2 **69,** 214-15, 243-7, 264
self-incrimination **42,** 219-26
boundaries. *See* provinces, boundaries *below*
British Columbia **43,** 95, 96, 99, **73,** 63, 80, 188, 190-3, 196, 205-12, 218-25, **90,** 284-92
Newfoundland, modification **86,** 605
provinces
boundaries, modification **86,** 605
confederation, at **90,** 271
low-water mark as **90,** 272
settlement by
Imperial legislation **73,** 190-5, 205-12, 218-25
international agreements **73,** 63-4, 79-80, 188-9, 206, 218-20
USA, dispute **71,** 57-216
British Columbia. *See also* United Kingdom, British Columbia, colony of
aboriginal rights in **115,** 452-535
arbitral award, review, International Commercial Arbitration Act 1966 and Commercial Arbitration Act 1996 distinguished **119,** 656-9

boundaries **43,** 95, 96, 99, **73,** 63, 80, 188, 190-3, 196, 205-12, 218-25, **90,** 284-92
Confederation, entry into **43,** 97, 110
constitutional history **43,** 95-6
continental shelf, rights in **43,** 113-14
Crown lands in **43,** 96-7, 106
Crown Procedure Act 1960 **73,** 128
discovery and settlement, history of **73,** 62-5, 67-72, 78-82, 112-17, 120-6, 188-9, 207-9
International Commercial Arbitration Act RSBC 1966
Commercial Arbitration Act RSBC 1996 distinguished **119,** 656-9
review of award, limitations **119,** 679
s 5 **119,** 659-61
s 34 **119,** 659-61, 673, 679-80
s 34(1) **119,** 659
s 34(2) **119,** 660, 675
s 34(3) **119,** 659
s 34(4) **125,** 471, 472-4
s 36 **119,** 679-80
Land Act **73,** 81
offshore minerals, rights to **43,** 93-114
straits. *See* straits *below*
territorial sea **90,** 274-6
entitlement **90,** 238-42
jurisdiction, title distinguished **90,** 311-12
mineral resources, ownership **90,** 239-40
specific act, need for **90,** 311-12, 329
Vancouver Island
as enclave **90,** 288-90
union, effect **90,** 321-2
British North America Act 1867 **51,** 138, **73,** 59, 61, 70-1, 101, 192, 209, 212, 214, **78,** 435, 439-41, 444, 469, 470
aboriginal Indians, effect on **78,** 428, 435
transfer of obligations in respect of **78,** 435
amendment, competence limited to UK Parliament **78,** 474
entrenchment **78,** 429
s 3 **78,** 448, 472
s 5 **78,** 473
s 7 **78,** 448, 472
s 9 **78,** 428
s 12 **78,** 428
ss 55-7 **78,** 441-2
s 65 **78,** 428
s 91 **78,** 428, 441, 444, 482
s 92 **78,** 428, 440
s 109 **78,** 440
s 132 **78,** 448
s 146 **78,** 450
British North America Act 1871 **42,** 82
federal legislative competence **43,** 95, 110, 112
new provinces, establishment of **43,** 98-9
provincial lands, ownership of **43,** 97-8
supremacy of law of Canada **43,** 1-2
British North America Act 1930

Canada (*cont.*)
aboriginal Indians, effect on **78,** 431
Schedule, s 1 **78,** 473
British North America Act 1940 **78,** 482
British North America Act 1946 **78,** 482
British North America Acts 1867/1946 **86,** 613-14
British North America Acts 1870-1930 **78,** 462
British North America (No. 2) Act 1949 **78,** 474, 482
burden of proof **88,** 292-3
Charter of Rights and Freedoms, breach **98,** 378-9
criminal case, in **94,** 236-7
civil jurisdiction distinguished **94,** 236-7
exclusion of alien **104,** 203-4
fair trial **98,** 548
legislation, challenge to **98,** 397
location of discharge of oil from ship **94,** 236
State immunity, jurisdiction **64,** 11, 21-2, 28-9, 35-6, 75
war crimes **104,** 355-6
knowledge that act constituted war crime or crime against humanity **98,** 542, 596-7
Canada–France Trade Agreement 1933, entry into force **55,** 40-5, 46-9
Canada–France Trade Agreement Act 1933 **55,** 39-40, **69,** 285-6, 292-4
'Canadian citizen' **90,** 222-3, 226
'Canadian waters' **94,** 234-7, 243
Carriage of Goods by Sea, Hague Rules and **60,** 2-9
cause of action, illegality as **90,** 231
Charter of Rights and Freedoms **78,** 434, 475, **79,** 263
aliens, entitlement to protection of **98,** 403, **124,** 358, 403
balancing process. *See* fundamental justice, balance of interest *below*
common law and **124,** 378-9
Criminal Code, ss 7(3.71)-(3.77) and **104,** 323-30
extraterritorial application **98,** 379, 381, 388, 403, 417, 418, 423
foreign State, applicability to **90,** 232
freedom of association. *See* freedom of association *below*
international law and **124,** 363
interpretation **88,** 296
International Covenant on Civil and Political Rights as aid **101,** 300-5
preamble, rule of law, whether **124,** 450
religious discrimination **96,** 663
s 1 (rights and freedoms subject to reasonable limits prescribed by law) **88,** 291-7, **94,** 248, 250
extradition in case of death penalty without assurances **124,** 313-14
proportionality, need for **124,** 382-3
'reasonable limits' **124,** 382-3
s 2 (fundamental freedoms), derogation **124,** 377
s 2(b) (freedom of expression) **124,** 352, 376-8
s 2(d) (freedom of association) **124,** 352, 376-8
s 6(1) (right to enter, remain in and leave Canada) **88,** 291-8, **124,** 304, 305-6, 312-17
s 7 (right to life, liberty and security/fundamental justice) **82,** 430-2, 452, 458, 459-60, 462, **92,** 676, 677, **124,** 306
deportation to country where risk of subjection to torture **124,** 347, 350-1, 353, 358-63, 369, 378-84, 394-5, 402-7, 415-27
economic rights and **124,** 447
evidentiary threshold **124,** 385, 403, 416

extradition involving death sentence, compatibility **98,** 374-83, 418-23, **124,** 304, 306, 318-40
extraterritorial jurisdiction and **98,** 573-4, **104,** 338
failure to provide civil remedy for torture outside the forum and **124,** 446-50
nationality, relevance **123,** 495-6
pre-trial delay **104,** 338
procedural fairness and **124,** 378-83
retrospective jurisdiction over war crimes, compatibility **98,** 574-5, **104,** 198
stay of deportation pending consideration by UNHRC **124,** 395, 396-8, 402-12
vagueness of legislation and **104,** 337-8, 396-9, **124,** 370-5
well-founded fear of persecution and **124,** 403
s 8, discriminatory treatment of foreign vessels **123,** 496-7
s 9 (arbitrary detention or imprisonment) **101,** 300-5
s 11 **82,** 433-5, 456-8, 462, 463
s 11(b) (fair trial) **104,** 338
s 11(d) (fair trial), delay in introducing war crimes legislation **98,** 576, **104,** 338
s 11(g) (war crimes/crimes against humanity) **104,** 198, 330, 335-7, 353-4
s 12 (cruel and unusual punishment)
extradition involving death sentence, compatibility **98,** 374, 382, 386, 396-402, 417-18, **124,** 304, 306, 315-18, 323-4
lesser of penalties to prevail **98,** 576
torture **124,** 360-1
s 15 (discrimination) **104,** 198, 254-5, 263-4, 338-9
arrest of foreign vessels under Coastal Fisheries Protection Regulations **123,** 496-9
corporate rights **123,** 497-8
extraterritorial legislation **98,** 577
nationality, relevance **123,** 498-9
s 15(1) **82,** 430-2, 449-51, 453
s 24(1) **82,** 458, 462
s 32 (applicability) **124,** 446-50
s 32(1)(a) **124,** 306, 316
s 32(1)(b) **124,** 307, 316
s 33 **118,** 176-9
s 433 **94,** 240-1, 246
'shocking to the conscience' test **98,** 377, 379, 382-3, 420-1, **124,** 304, 320-1, 353, 360-3
State-imposed harm, need for **124,** 449
Chicago Convention on International Civil Aviation (1944), as part of municipal law **90,** 215, 216-17
citizenship
acquisition **43,** 187-91
application for **60,** 225, 242
civil aviation
Chicago Convention on International Civil Aviation (1944) **90,** 216-17
fees for telecommunication and radio services **90,** 214-20
Civil Procedure Rules
Rule 17 **87,** 204-5
Rule 21 **87,** 198, 200
claim, sampling methodology **109,** 72
claims settlement agreement
customary international law **90,** 227
dual national, right to benefit **90,** 221-8
Foreign Claims Commission, role **90,** 223

Canada (*cont.*)
implementing legislation, interpretation **90,** 221-8
comity **84,** 694-5
extradition in case of death penalty **124,** 322-3, 341
international courtesy and **64,** 13-17
jurisdiction, territorial **104,** 326
common purpose, foreseeability **124,** 158 n. 288
Conception Bay **43,** 105
confederation, history **115,** 550-5
Constitution
amendment of **78,** 474
UK Parliamentary consent required **78,** 474
constitutional/parliamentary supremacy distinguished **115,** 564-5
cultural and linguistic minorities, pursuit of collective goals **115,** 559-60
entrenchment, reasons for
protection of division of powers **115,** 565
protection of human rights **115,** 565
protection of minority groups **115,** 565, 566
referendum. *See* referendum *below*
'repatriation' **78,** 434, 435
sovereignty of people, expression of **115,** 569
unwritten principles
aid to interpretation **115,** 556-7, 558
democracy **115,** 560-3
effect **115,** 557
federalism **115,** 557-60
protection of minorities **115,** 566-8
written nature **115,** 555-7
Constitution Act 1867 **86,** 615, **90,** 258, **118,** 178
s 9 **87,** 232
s 91(24) **115,** 465, 518-19, 520-2
s 92 **86,** 624-5, **90,** 264
s 101 **115,** 540-2
s 109 **86,** 599, 614, 616, **90,** 259-60
s 132 **86,** 605
Constitution Act 1982 **78,** 423, 433-4, 457-84, **79,** 263, **118,** 178
aboriginal Indians under **78,** 433-4
aboriginal rights **104,** 206
fiduciary role of Crown **104,** 219, 222
Preamble **78,** 458, 474-5
'repatriation', Indians under **78,** 434
rights
limitations on **88,** 292-7
national to remain in Canada **88,** 292-7
s 1 **78,** 466, 475
s 2 **78,** 475
s 3 **78,** 475
s 25 **78,** 460
s 35 **78,** 460, 475
s 35(1) **104,** 208, 210-15, 222, **115,** 452-3, 466, 468, 469, 491-517
self-government, right to **115,** 517
s 37 **78,** 460, 475
ss 38-49 **78,** 475

s 52 **88,** 291
s 52(1) **115,** 564, **124,** 307
s 53 **78,** 475
Schedule, Item 17 **78,** 466
supremacy **88,** 291
Constitution, interpretation
aids, unwritten underlying principles **115,** 556-7
guidelines, text as a whole **115,** 556
continental shelf
rights, division between federal and provincial government **86,** 594-625
territorial sea and, separable, whether **86,** 600
corporations in **56,** 225-7
US law and **60,** 33-5
counterclaims
requirements
'arising out of the subject-matter' **120,** 442-6, 457-9
defensive **120,** 441-2, 457
Court Rules, 419(1) **123,** 486, 488-9
crimes against humanity
basis, common problems of civilized nations **104,** 336
customary international law **104,** 200-2, 337-8
defence
any defence available under international law at the time or at time of proceedings **104,** 331-4, 366
any defence available under *lex fori* at the time or at time of proceedings **104,** 331-4, 366
autrefois convict **104,** 366
legality under laws of place where act committed **104,** 296-7, 310, 334, 366, 377-80
manifest illegality **104,** 379, 381
mistake of fact **104,** 367-8
municipal law provision for similar offences **104,** 297-8
definition
municipal law **104,** 197, 357
ordinary law committed in certain circumstances **104,** 361
double criminality **104,** 198
exclusion of alien **104,** 198
general principle of international law **104,** 296, 336-8
international law, existence in, absence of court/code, relevance **104,** 336
jurisdiction
accused within territory **104,** 354
extraterritorial **104,** 298-9
Geneva Conventions (1949) **104,** 298
obligation **104,** 328, 330
universal **104,** 313
knowledge that act a war crime or crime against humanity, relevance **104,** 312-23, 359-66
requirements
actus reus **104,** 312-14
civilian population, acts against **104,** 313
contravention of international law at time of act **104,** 301, 335
lack of clarity **104,** 328-9
mens rea **104,** 314-23, 359-63

Canada (*cont.*)
persecution of identifiable group of people **104,** 357-8, 359
persecution in name of State practising ideological persecution **104,** 365-6
treaty **104,** 337-8
Criminal Code 1927, s 297 **104,** 202-3
Criminal Code 1970-85-87
s 6(2) (territorial principle) **104,** 294, 352-3
s 7(3.71) (war crimes) **104,** 294, 302, 303-23, 335-9, 354-63, 368-77
compatibility with s 1 of Charter **104,** 404
compatibility with s 7 of Charter **104,** 337-8, 399-402, 403-4
compatibility with s 11(g) of Charter **104,** 399-402
compatibility with s 12 of Charter **104,** 404
compatibility with s 15 of Charter **104,** 403-4
fair trial **104,** 396-9
jurisdictional, whether **104,** 303-8
text **104,** 349-50
s 7(3.72) (war crimes), text **104,** 350
s 7(3.73) (defences) **104,** 323, 331-5
s 7(3.74) (legality at time and place of commission) **104,** 297, 366, 377-82
compatibility with s 7 of Charter **104,** 395-6
permissive **104,** 380
text **104,** 350
s 7(3.76) (war crimes) **104,** 197, 198, 296, 337-9
compatibility with s 7 of Charter **104,** 395-6
text **104,** 350, 357-8
s 15 (legality under laws of place where act committed), text **104,** 351
s 25(1) (peace officer defence) **104,** 333, 350-1, 366-7, 379
text **104,** 350-1, 367
s 423(1) (jurisdiction, murder) **104,** 5
s 423(3) (jurisdiction, conspiracy to murder) **104,** 5
s 423(4) (jurisdiction, conspiracy to murder) **104,** 5
s 442a) (procuring an offence) **104,** 6
s 465(3) (conspiracy) **104,** 305-6
s 477.1 (continental shelf) **104,** 305
s 607(6) (*autrefois convict*) **104,** 366
critical date, State immunity **94,** 262
Crown
capacity to enter into obligations in **78,** 470
devolution of rights and obligations **78,** 439-48, 462-9
Custodian of Enemy Property **54,** 609-13
customary international law
municipal law and **123,** 490, **124,** 437-8
diplomatic privileges and immunities **101,** 310
transformation doctrine compared **120,** 386-7
war crimes/crimes against humanity **104,** 299-300
primacy of legislation **124,** 351
damages, punitive, classification of act as criminal and **124,** 433-4
death penalty. *See also* extradition in case of death penalty *below*
abolition **124,** 300-2, 323-4
inhuman or degrading treatment **98,** 381, 398-402, 407, **124,** 323
international initiatives **124,** 324-6
State responsibility **98,** 402-7, 417, **124,** 316-17
wrongful conviction and **124,** 329-81

death row as inhuman or degrading treatment **98,** 379-80, **124,** 336-8
default judgment against foreign State
State immunity, execution/attachment **64,** 70-6
State immunity, jurisdiction, procedural aspects, non-appearance as admission of allegations **124,** 430-1
democracy
majority rule **115,** 561-3, 592
competing majorities **115,** 562-3, 566
referendum, role **115,** 565
rule of law, need for **115,** 562-3, 572. *See also* rule of law *below*
sovereign will of the people, supremacy **115,** 560, 562
dependent status, legislative competence and **84,** 687-8, 693
deportation. *See also* non-refoulement to country of origin or any other country where risk of subjection to torture *below*
appeal **69,** 296-9, **124,** 346-91, 393-427
stay of deportation pending **124,** 412-13
compelling reasons of national security and
compassionate circumstances **124,** 349-50
terrorist activity **124,** 348-51, 360-3, 367-78
terrorist organization, membership of **124,** 375-8
threat to another State, relevance **124,** 371-2
discretion
refugee status, relevance **124,** 354
risk of subjection to torture and **124,** 347, 353-8, 380
procedural fairness **124,** 378-83
reasons for decision, need for **124,** 350, 382
special relief **69,** 298-9
stay of deportation pending appeal **124,** 412-13
stay pending consideration by international body **124,** 403-5, 407, 417-27
to country where risk of subjection to torture **124,** 346-84
assurances that torture will not be used, need to evaluate **124,** 381-2
International Covenant on Civil and Political Rights (ICCPR) (1966) **124,** 365-6
'minimal risk of harm' finding **124,** 390, 403, 409-10, 416
Refugees, Geneva Convention on the Status of (1951) **124,** 367-8
'shocking to the conscience', whether **124,** 353, 360-3
State responsibility and **124,** 361-3
'substantial grounds' test **124,** 358, 380, 389
Torture Convention (1984) **124,** 366-7
UNHRC General Comment No 20 and **124,** 365-6
Deschênes Commission **104,** 292-3, 299-300, 353-4
criminal law, retroactivity **91,** 49, **104,** 307-8
entrenchment of international law **104,** 198-9
general principles of international law as basis of jurisdiction **104,** 299-300
diplomatic immunity, jurisdiction
State immunity and, distinction **64,** 72
waiver, clear and unequivocal communication, need for **120,** 456-7
diplomatic privileges and immunities, entitlement
termination
customary international law **101,** 309-16
permanent departure **101,** 309-16
Vienna Convention on Diplomatic Relations (1961) **101,** 309, 312-16
diplomatic representations, Canadian companies, on behalf of **46,** 184, 199, 217-19, 253-4, 325, 346-50, 355-6, 434-5, 454-5

Canada (*cont.*)
discrimination
on basis of language **118,** 174-83
existence to be determined by context **121,** 117, 154-5
geographic location **82,** 447-53
Dominion status, legislative competence **43,** 110-11
double criminality **88,** 289, **92,** 723-9, 731, 732-4, **98,** 416
identity of crime and **92,** 731, 732-4
international law, rule of, whether **92,** 725-6
jurisdiction, basis for, judge/jury responsibility to determine whether double criterion met **98,** 536-7
war crimes/crimes against humanity **104,** 198
jurisdiction and **98,** 533, 536-7
offence under *lex fori* at the time **104,** 198, 202-4
embassy or consular bank account/funds, immunity, execution/attachment, purpose/use
funds 'in possession' of State **64,** 75-6
governmental **64,** 75
employment contract. *See also* union certification proceedings *below*
employment contract, locally engaged staff at foreign military bases, State immunity, jurisdiction **94,** 271-91, 303-5
employment contract, locally engaged staff, military/naval base
contract for purchase of goods, whether distinguishable **86,** 637, 638-9
State immunity, jurisdiction **94,** 283
contract for supply of goods, whether distinguishable **94,** 283
national security considerations **94,** 283
evidence
affidavit **69,** 242-7, 263-8
bias
access to foreign materials **82,** 455-6
foreign government **82,** 453-5
evidence of
jus cogens/peremptory norm
multilateral treaties **124,** 364, 365-8
State practice **124,** 364
mens rea
law **104,** 380
superior orders **104,** 376-7
territorial limits of aboriginal rights **115,** 488-90
title
occupancy **115,** 498
oral histories **115,** 453
war crimes
admissibility **104,** 386-9
witnesses, judge's right to summon **104,** 389-93
exclusion of alien
burden of proof **104,** 203-4
criminal record **104,** 257-8
justification
crimes against humanity **104,** 198
war crimes **104,** 198
past behaviour, retroactive legislation **104,** 198
right of **98,** 376-7
exclusive fishing zone (EFZ) **82,** 602-70. *See also* fishing zones *below*

establishment **82,** 605, 628
purpose **82,** 628
foreign vessels, rights in **82,** 602-70
executive certificate/statement **55,** 48-9
expropriation/nationalization, applicable law, municipal law of expropriating State **121,** 177-8
expulsion of alien **73,** 618-26
dependants **54,** 301-2
natural justice **43,** 219-24
procedure **43,** 213-29, **44,** 157-73
representation at enquiry **43,** 225-9
extraditable offence
continuing criminal enterprise **92,** 728, 730-2
unlisted in extradition treaty **92,** 730-1, 733
extradition **71,** 511-29
appeal **88,** 287-9
balance of interests **98,** 421
comity **98,** 416, 420
conditions in receiving State, relevance **98,** 381, 416
customary international law **92,** 686
definition **88,** 289-91
deportation distinguished **98,** 377
discretion **88,** 293, **98,** 422, 423
in case of death penalty **124,** 304-5, 309-11
double criminality. *See* double criminality *above*
evidence, affidavit **69,** 242-7, 263-8
executive responsibility **124,** 309-12
foreign relations and **124,** 311-12
judicial review **98,** 378-9, 388, 418, 419-20, 423, **124,** 311-12, 321-2
death penalty and **124,** 312, 321
nationals
death penalty and **124,** 313, 314-15
European Convention on Human Rights (1950), Protocol 4 **88,** 294, 295
extraterritorial crimes, assumption of jurisdiction in respect of and **88,** 294
International Covenant on Civil and Political Rights (ICCPR) (1966) **88,** 293-4
procedure **98,** 387-8
appeals **69,** 219-20
depositions **69,** 228-37, 251-9, 273-5
duty of magistrate **69,** 236-7
political offence **69,** 251-9, 273-5
reasons, whether necessary **98,** 387-8
representation of accused **69,** 228-37
purpose **88,** 289-90
reciprocity **98,** 416, 422
refusal, safe haven, risk of creating **98,** 377-8, 380, 407-8, 422-3, **124,** 342-3
security of extraditing State **98,** 420
speciality
customary international law **92,** 686
limitation **92,** 689
opportunity to return and **92,** 687-90
perpetual immunity, whether **92,** 687-90
treaty rule **92,** 686
State responsibility for acts following **98,** 374, **124,** 316-17

Canada (*cont.*)
Extradition Act, s 25, Charter of Rights and Freedoms, compatibility **98,** 417-23, 474, 476-8
extradition agreement **88,** 289-90
assurances that death penalty will not be carried out **124,** 340-3
conditions in signatory State, relevance **124,** 323-4
definition **92,** 687
need for **92,** 686, 690, **124,** 310
reciprocity, relevance **88,** 292, 294-5
extradition in case of death penalty **124,** 300-43
arbitrary sentencing **98,** 379
assurances that death penalty will not be carried out, need for **98,** 382-4, 386, 404-6, 407, 410, 417-18, 423, 424-5, 477, 478, **124,** 304-5, 310-11, 312-15, 322-43
comity and **124,** 323-4, 341
failure to seek, whether reasonable and justifiable in a free and democratic society **124,** 1403-5
public policy reasons for not seeking **124,** 339
cruel and unusual treatment, whether **98,** 374, 382, 386, 396-402, 417-18, **124,** 316
discretion **124,** 304-5, 309-11
as exile **124,** 304, 305-6
fundamental justice, breach of, whether **98,** 374-80, 381-3
judicial review **124,** 312, 321-2
Model Treaty on Extradition (1990) **98,** 376
nationals **124,** 313, 314-15
'shocking to the conscience', whether **98,** 377, 379, 382-3, 420-1, **124,** 304, 320-1
extraterritorial legislation, presumption against **84,** 695, **92,** 679, **94,** 235
extraterritoriality, State immunity, jurisdiction **64,** 39-40, **95,** 455
fair trial **98,** 659-60
burden of proof **98,** 548
constitution of court, right of election **82,** 458
defence counsel, propriety of closing statement **98,** 547-8, 628-38
delay **82,** 458-60
introducing war crimes legislation **104,** 338
post-charge **82,** 462-3, **104,** 402-3
pre-charge **82,** 460-2, **104,** 338, 402-3
improper calling of evidence **98,** 545-8, 577-8, 639-58
in introducing war crimes legislation **98,** 576
lack of clarity in charge **98,** 575-6
specific offence **82,** 456-8
as federal State **68,** 200-1, 249-50
sovereign immunity **52,** 324, 327
fisheries
closing line **82,** 605, 639
conservation and management measures. *See also* Coastal Fisheries Protection Acts *and* Regulations *below*
freedom of the seas and **123,** 219-27, 229-30, 269-72, 277-8, 354-6
fishing licences
conditions **82,** 622-3
discretionary power **82,** 622-3, 626, 649-50
fishing zones **71,** 92-110. *See also* exclusive fishing zone (EFZ) *above*
adjacent to coast **92,** 678-82
200 miles, whether **92,** 682

foreign judgment, recognition/enforcement, tax **42,** 114-18
foreign relations, conduct of, executive certificate, effect **55,** 48-9
forum [non] conveniens, State immunity, jurisdiction distinguished **120,** 452-3
freedom of association
  margin of appreciation **94,** 250
  right of workers to act in concert **94,** 249-50
  strike, right to. *See* strike, right to *below*
freedom from discrimination
  direct and intentional discrimination, need for **96,** 664
  religious, hard hat, requirement to wear **96,** 663-4
freedom of speech and, terrorist organization **120,** 375-8
fundamental justice. *See also* Charter of Rights and Freedoms, s 7 (right to life, liberty and security/fundamental justice) *above*
  appeal, frustration **124,** 418-19
  applicable law
    international law **124,** 359
    law of the forum **124,** 359
  balance of interests **98,** 375, 379, 421, **124,** 319-21, 338-40, 358-69, 382-3, 404, 416-17, 418
  procedural fairness **124,** 378-83, 390-1
  right to stay of extradition or deportation pending consideration of case by international body **124,** 403-5, 407, 417-27
  war crimes, retroactive/external jurisdiction and **98,** 572-7
General Agreement on Tariffs and Trade (GATT) (1947) and
  implementing legislation **90,** 334-65
    intended purpose **90,** 338, 357-8
general principles of international law
  codification, impossibility **104,** 335
  crimes against humanity **104,** 296, 321
  source of international law **104,** 335
  war crimes **104,** 296, 321
Germany, Treaty of Peace Order 1920 **54,** 609-13
good faith, treaties, applicability of multilateral treaty before incorporation **124,** 413-14
Great Lakes, status **94,** 242-6
Hague Conventions (1899/1907)
  implementing measures, availability of alternative measures to achieve environmental objectives **121,** 105, 118, 133, 175
  prisoners of war, employment, munitions manufacture **104,** 199
Hazardous Wastes, Basel Convention on Control of Transboundary Movements and Their Disposal (1989)
  implementing measures **121,** 88-94
    compatibility with NAFTA (1992) **121,** 115-90
    discriminatory, whether **121,** 115-17, 133, 174-5
    protectionist nature **121,** 98-105, 118, 133, 159-67
'hovering' Acts **43,** 103, 110-11
human dignity, right to **98,** 398-402
Immigration Act 1952 **42,** 207-32, **43,** 214-28, **44,** 135-9, **54,** 301-2
  inquiry under
    powers of Minister **42,** 208-9, 212-13, 216-18
    procedure **44,** 163-73
  seaman remaining behind **42,** 219
Immigration Act 1970 **73,** 619-26
Immigration Act 1976 **84,** 710, **90,** 344, **92,** 663, 669

Canada (*cont.*)
s 2(1) **87,** 195, **92,** 695-9
s 2(1) (refugee: definition) **104,** 226
s 3(g) **92,** 708
s 42 **92,** 710
s 64 **92,** 710
s 71(1) **87,** 197
Immigration Act 1985
'danger to the security of Canada' **124,** 370-3
s 2(1) (refugee: definition) **104,** 226, 246, 258, 265, **107,** 149
s 19(1) **104,** 256-8
'terrorism' **124,** 373-5
text **124,** 352, 387-8
s 19(1)(e)(iii) **124,** 387
s 19(1)(e)(iv)(C) **124,** 349, 387
s 19(1)(f)(ii) **124,** 349
s 19(1)(f)(ii)(B) **124,** 387-8
s 19(1)(f)(iii)(B) **124,** 349, 387-8
s 19(1)(j) **104,** 197, 198, 203-4
s 40.1 certificate **124,** 348, 349, 375-8, 386-91, 394, 400
s 41.1(2)(b) **124,** 386
s 53(1) **124,** 348
discretion and **124,** 347, 354-5, 380-3
judicial review and **124,** 359-80, 541
reasons for decision under **124,** 350, 382
s 19(1) and **124,** 376-8
torture and **124,** 347-8, 368-84
s 53(1)(b) **124,** 349-50, 351, 387-91, 394
text **124,** 352
Immigration Appeal Board **84,** 710, 713
Immigration Appeal Board Act 1970 **69,** 210-15, 296-301
Geneva Convention on the Status of Refugees (1951), effect of reference to **69,** 300-1
s 15, legal effect **69,** 210-11
s 21, legal effect **69,** 213-15
immigration appeals
procedure **42,** 211-13, 229-32
self-incrimination **42,** 209
Immigration Inquiries Regulations **54,** 301-2
Immigration and Refugee Board, impartial and independent, whether **118,** 247, 248-9
Immigration Regulations **54,** 300-2
Indian Act 1952 **73,** 108-9
Band Councils, authority of **68,** 23-4
definition of Indian **68,** 19-20
patrilineal family relationships **68,** 20
discriminatory, whether **68,** 21, 25-6, 28
International Covenant on Civil and Political Rights (ICCPR) (1966), minority rights, infringement **68,** 26-8
laws of general application, applicability to Indians **53,** 577-8, 580-6
marriage to non-Indian, effect on **68,** 21, 22-5
reserve land, rights of residence **68,** 20, 22-5, 27-8

Indian Act 1985 **104,** 206-7
s 88 **115,** 466, 522-3
Indian affairs legislation 1920 **73,** 70-2
Indian Oil and Gas Act **115,** 496-7
Indian peoples in. *See* aboriginal Indians in *above*
Indian treaties. *See* aboriginal Indians in, treaties *above*
inhuman or degrading treatment
death penalty, method of execution, relevance **98,** 379-80
death row. *See* death row as inhuman or degrading treatment *above*
lesser penalty to prevail **98,** 576
proportionality **98,** 396-7, 399, 408
inland waters
Great Lakes **94,** 243, 245-6
international boundary, effect on status **94,** 243-6
internal waters
areas of sea on landward side of territorial sea baseline **94,** 242-3
'sea' **94,** 242
inland waters distinguished **94,** 243
International Covenant on Civil and Political Rights (ICCPR) (1966)
implementing legislation, need for **101,** 300-4, **124,** 396, 404-5, 413-15
right of application to UN Human Rights Committee and **124,** 417-27
international law. *See also* treaties *below*
judicial obligation to observe norms **94,** 252
law, whether **104,** 329
legislation
in breach of **90,** 208
interpretation in accordance with **94,** 291
matter of law for judge **98,** 557, 571
municipal courts, application by **104,** 397, **115,** 545-6, **124,** 359
binding effect on other States or international courts **115,** 545
municipal law and
conflict **90,** 337-8
customary international law **90,** 198, 199-202
entrenchment **104,** 198-9
part of **104,** 334
primacy **43,** 1-2, **123,** 490-1
sources
judicial and arbitral decisions **104,** 329
teachings of publicists **104,** 320-3
subjects, federal State **104,** 296
treaties. *See* treaties *below*
Jay Treaty, aboriginal peoples, rights under **104,** 208-10
judge, disqualification for lack of impartiality, 'reasonable man' test **121,** 334-5
judicial notice
definition **94,** 234-5
general principles of international law **123,** 492
sources of indisputable accuracy
atlases **94,** 235
dictionaries **94,** 235
encyclopaedias **94,** 235
maps **94,** 235
treaties **123,** 491

Canada (*cont.*)
judicial restraint **115,** 574-5
judicial review
extradition **98,** 378-9, 388, 418, 419-20, **124,** 311-12, 321-2
grounds, unreasonableness **124,** 353-8, 388
procedural fairness **124,** 419
standard of review **124,** 353-8, 388-90. *See also* grounds *above*
treaty, implementation **90,** 227
jurisdiction **84,** 687-700
actual commission of war crime/crime against humanity as condition precedent **98,** 528, 531, 564-5
jury responsibility to determine, whether **98,** 553-6, 561-6
whether to be established pre-trial or pre-judgment **98,** 566-71
comity and **84,** 694-5
conspiracy, to commit crime abroad **104,** 307
continuing offence **84,** 688, 691
contract law analogy **84,** 692
effects doctrine **84,** 690
gravamen of offence **84,** 690, 693-4, 696
criminal
completion of offence **84,** 696
ne bis in idem **84,** 697-8
nexus **84,** 695, 698
territorial. *See* territorial *below*
crown proceedings **73,** 127-35
'deemed to have been committed' within territory **98,** 533-6, 614-20, **104,** 302, 304-10, **123,** 202-3, 225-6
creation of new offence distinguished **98,** 570-1, **104,** 304-6, 307-8, 358-9
provisional 'deeming' **98,** 568-9
retroactivity, avoidance **104,** 399
extraterritorial **82,** 443-7, **84,** 688
fundamental rights, breach, whether **98,** 573-4
offences against ship of forum State **98,** 532
piracy **98,** 532, **104,** 307
power to legislate **82,** 445-6
Indian peoples, jurisdiction over land distinguished **115,** 520
international law, rule of, whether **84,** 688
interprovincial **84,** 690-2
jury role in determining **98,** 553-7, 561-6, 601-2, 619-26, **104,** 303, 308-9, 310-11, 317, 355-6
Charter **104,** 324-30
international and domestic elements, distinguishable, whether **98,** 623-6
international elements **104,** 327-30
legislative and adjudicatory distinguished **98,** 604-10
marine pollution, 'while in Canadian waters' **94,** 232-7
nexus
real and substantial connection **124,** 432-3
suffering following injury overseas **124,** 436
tort and contract distinguished **124,** 433
sovereignty issues **92,** 674-5
standard of proof **104,** 311
territorial **55,** 105, **82,** 443-4, **98,** 531-2, 610-14, **104,** 309-10, 352-3. *See also* nexus *above*

avoidance of infringement on third State **104,** 326
civil **84,** 688, 693
comity **104,** 326, 327-8
criminal **104,** 294
efficacy of prosecution **104,** 326
non-exercise **104,** 326
presumption of territoriality. *See* 'deemed to have been committed' within territory *above*
sovereign integrity **104,** 353
universal **82,** 444
crimes against humanity **104,** 313
piracy **82,** 444-5
terrorist offences **82,** 445
war crimes **104,** 299-300
war crimes, accused within territory **82,** 445
jury trial, right to **88,** 297
jus cogens/peremptory norm
evidence of
multilateral treaties **124,** 364
State practice **124,** 364
torture. *See* torture, *jus cogens below*
justice, fundamental principles of, obligation to give notice of possible prosecution **92,** 677
justiciability
advisory jurisdiction
hypothetical question **115,** 546
legal nature of question **115,** 546-7
imprecise or ambiguous question **115,** 548-9
judicial restraint, need for **115,** 574-5
legal problem, limited to **115,** 575-6
secession **115,** 574-7, 593-4
Labrador
property rights, extinction of unclaimed **92,** 673
sovereignty over **92,** 672-5
law of. *See also individual Provinces*
Aeronautics Act 1970 **90,** 215
s 4 **90,** 217-18
s 5 **90,** 217-19
s 6 **90,** 217
Air Regulations 1978 **90,** 215, 218-19
Appropriation Act No 9 of 1966 **90,** 222, 225
Arctic Waters Pollution Prevention Act 1970 **120,** 596-8
Bill of Rights. *See* Bill of Rights *above*
British North America Acts. *See* British North America Acts *above*
C-48 (Bill) (Energy) 1980 **85,** 468
Canada Evidence Act **42,** 219-26, **43,** 188-91
Canadian Corporation for the 1967 World Exhibition Act 1963 **64,** 27, 33
Charter of Rights and Freedoms. *See* Charter of Rights and Freedoms *above*
Citizenship Act 1967 **60,** 225-6
Citizenship Act 1970 **60,** 242-3, **69,** 196-201
Citizenship Act 1974-75-76 **90,** 222, 226
Citizenship Regulations 1968 **60,** 241, 245-6
residence and **60,** 225-6

Canada (*cont.*)
Coastal Fisheries Protection Act 1953/1970 **82,** 621-2, 640, 648, 649, **92,** 677
Coastal Fisheries Protection Act 1994
political motivation **123,** 391-401, 507-8
reservation to acceptance of compulsory jurisdiction of ICJ and **123,** 217-27, 236, 286-90, 292-3
s 2 ('NAFO Regulatory Area') **123,** 201
s 5.1 (straddling stocks: declaration of need for urgent action) **123,** 201-2
s 5.2 **123,** 202, 223
s 6 (power to make regulations) **123,** 504-5
s 7 (boarding by protection officer) **123,** 202, 223
s 7.1 (search) **123,** 202, 223
s 8.1 (use of force) **123,** 202, 223, 226, 471-6
s 18.1 ('deemed to have been committed in') **123,** 202-3, 225-6
Coastal Fisheries Protection Regulations 1976 **82,** 619, 640, 650-1, 657
Coastal Fisheries Protection Regulations 1976 (as amended on 25 May 1994)
ss 19.3-19.5 (use of force) **123,** 203, 226, 471-6
s 21(2)(a) ('straddling stocks') **123,** 203
s 21(2)(b) ('prescribed vessels') **123,** 203, 443-8
s 21(2)(c) ('prescribed conservation and management measures') **123,** 203
Coastal Fisheries Protection Regulations 1976 (as amended on 3 March 1995) **123,** 207, 223, 341, 351, 505
amendment as agreed with EC **123,** 206-7, 351
retroactive effect **123,** 503-4
s 21(2)(b) (prescribed classes of foreign fishing vessels) **123,** 203, 338, 343-8
s 21(2)(c) ('prescribed conservation and management measures' in respect of straddling stocks) **123,** 203
s 21(2)(d) ('prescribed conservation and management measures' in respect of straddling stocks) **123,** 204
s 21, Table 5 (measures applicable to Spanish and Portuguese vessels) **123,** 223
Commercial Arbitration Act **121,** 198, **122,** 255-6
Constitution Acts. *See* Constitution Act 1867 *and* Constitution Act 1982 *above*
Constitutional Questions Determination Act 1970 **90,** 272
Criminal Code 1927
s 68 **82,** 463-4
s 268 **82,** 430
s 297 **82,** 429, 430, 442-3, 451
s 447 **82,** 429, 442-3
Criminal Code 1970-85-87-94 **55,** 106, 108, 435-6, **71,** 528, **88,** 288
bankruptcy offences **43,** 234-42
s 5(2) **84,** 687, 695
s 6(1.91) **82,** 429-31, 432, 442-3, 447-50
s 6(1.93) **82,** 448
s 6(1.94) **82,** 430, 431, 447, 448-53, 464
s 6(1.96) **82,** 430, 431
s 6(2) (territorial principle) **98,** 531, 610-14
s 7(3.71) (war crimes) **98,** 525-663
s 15 **82,** 448-9
s 17 **82,** 452, 453
s 21(2) **124,** 158 n. 288
s 25 **123,** 203, 225-6
s 74(1) **82,** 444
s 269.1 **124,** 358

s 423(1) **84,** 676
s 423(3) **84,** 676, 700
s 427 **82,** 451
s 429 **82,** 451
s 468 **69,** 229, 233-5, 245
s 475 **71,** 512-13, 520, 522
s 510(5) **82,** 456
s 565(2) **82,** 458
s 577 **82,** 458
s 650(3) **82,** 462
s 786(2) **82,** 442
summonses, service **69,** 93, 96-8
Criminal Law Amendment Act 1977 **71,** 339-45
Crown Lands Act 1930 **90,** 253, 254
Customs Act 1916 **90,** 253
Customs Act 1927-28-36 **90,** 247
Customs Act 1928, 'territorial waters of Canada' **43,** 103, 111
Customs Act 1933 **90,** 253
Customs Act 1985 **104,** 206-7
Customs and Excise Act 1938 **90,** 253, 254
Evidence Act 1970 **71,** 518
Evidence Act 1985, s 39 **121,** 196, 197, **122,** 349-51
Extradition Act 1952 **43,** 218, 234-42
Extradition Act 1970 **60,** 282, 321, 323, **69,** 103, 220-2, 228-39, 241-53, 256-9, 263-75, **71,** 511
habeas corpus and **60,** 322-3
s 10 **71,** 511, 520
s 13 **69,** 235-6, 253, 275, **71,** 512, 521, 528
s 14 **69,** 253
s 15 **69,** 253, 274
s 16 **69,** 236, 242-7, 263-8
s 18 **69,** 248-9, 253, 374-5, **71,** 512, 520-2
s 19 **69,** 253
s 21 **69,** 250, 261, 263, 270, 272-5
s 22 **69,** 274-5
s 30 **69,** 230
s 31 **69,** 228-39
Extradition Act 1985 **88,** 289-91
s 3 **88,** 290, **92,** 734
s 10 **88,** 279
s 11 **88,** 297
s 21 **107,** 149
s 25(1) **124,** 307, 309-11
s 33 **92,** 686-90
s 40 **92,** 689-90
Federal Courts Act 1970 **71,** 511, **84,** 713, **90,** 222
s 28 **69,** 241-3, 247, 259, 296
s 28(1)(c) **92,** 716
Fisheries Act 1970 **82,** 457, 621, 648
Fishing by Foreign Vessels Act 1868 **43,** 103
Fishing Regulations 1978 **82,** 621
Foreign Claims (Czechoslovakia) Settlement Regulations 1973 **90,** 222-8
Foreign Investment Review Act (FIRA) **121,** 121, 175

Canada (*cont.*)
Geneva Conventions Act 1970 **88,** 297
Geneva Conventions Act 1985, s 3(1) (offence under Canadian law) **82,** 447, **98,** 532
Hydro-Québec Act 1977 **92,** 660
Immigration Acts. *See* Immigration Acts *above*
Indian Act 1952. *See* Indian Act 1952 *above*
Indian Act 1985. *See* Indian Act 1985 *above*
Indian Oil and Gas Act. *See* Indian Oil and Gas Act 1985 *above*
Industrial Relations and Disputes Investigation Act **42,** 267-8, 270-1
Inquiries Act 1970 **90,** 223
International Boundary Waters Treaty Act 1970 **73,** 167-8
Interpretation Act 1970 **82,** 442
s 12 **92,** 681
s 33(2) **104,** 265
James Bay Region Development Act RSC 1977 **92,** 659
Judicature Act 1824 **92,** 674
Judicature Act 1970 **90,** 236
Labour Code 1985 **86,** 634-9, 727
s 3 **94,** 291
s 136(1) **94,** 291
safety at work provisions **96,** 662-3
Manganese-based Fuel Additives Act, SC 1997, compatibility with NAFTA **122,** 262-4, 283-6
Manitoba Act 1870, validity **90,** 504-5, 506
NAFTA Implementation Act **121,** 198
Narcotic Control Act 1970 **69,** 220
Narcotic Control Act 1975, s 5 **101,** 270-80
Newfoundland Act (UK) 1949 **86,** 612-16, **90,** 258-9
Oath of Allegiance Act **43,** 188-91, **69,** 195-200
Oil Pollution Prevention Regulations 1971 **94,** 232-7
Order in Council of 25 February 1971 (Gulf of St Lawrence closing line) **82,** 605
Parole Act 1970 **70,** 306-13, **71,** 339
Patent Act 1935 **60,** 390
Shipping Act 1970 **60,** 2, **94,** 232-7
inland waters, definition **94,** 243
Special Import Measures Act 1984
s 2 **90,** 341
s 42 **90,** 333-65
State Immunity Act 1980-81-82-83-85. *See* State Immunity Act 1980-81-82-83-85 *below*
Supreme Court Act 1970 **90,** 272
s 55 **86,** 596
Supreme Court Act 1985, constitutional validity of s 53 **115,** 541-9. *See also* Supreme Court, jurisdiction *below*
Territorial Sea and Fishing Zones Act 1964 **43,** 94, 111, **71,** 110, **73,** 193-4, 199-200, 204, 213, 216, **86,** 598, **90,** 240, 242, 273, 276
customary international law, incorporation **90,** 242
internal waters, definition **94,** 242
s 3 **90,** 274
territorial sea, definition **94,** 242
Territorial Sea and Fishing Zones Act 1970, s 4 **92,** 677-82
Trade Marks Act **55,** 45
Trading with the Enemy Regulations 1939 **56,** 224

Treaties of Peace Act 1919 **90,** 198-9, 205-11, 212-13
Visiting Forces Act 1985 **94,** 267. *See also* visiting forces *below*
War Crimes Act 1946 **88,** 297
Law Reform Commission, *Our Criminal Law* **84,** 697
legislation
challenge to, burden of proof **98,** 397
dependent status, effect **84,** 687-8, 693
discretionary power, general rule of conduct and **82,** 623-4
extraterritorial. *See also* Charter of Rights and Freedoms, extraterritorial application *above*
clear intention **94,** 235
extraterritorial effect **69,** 93-8
legislative competence **86,** 624
retrospective, clear intention **82,** 433-4
validity, vagueness **104,** 397-8
legislation, interpretation **88,** 296
aids
ambiguity, in case of **90,** 340, 342, 359
context **90,** 290, 357, **92,** 680, 696, **104,** 304, 305
decisions of US courts **94,** 251, 271
dictionary **92,** 668, 678-9, 680
legislative history **82,** 434, **104,** 304
parallel legislation **104,** 304
parliamentary proceedings **90,** 338
preamble **92,** 681
textbook **90,** 228
UNHCR *Handbook on Procedures and Criteria for Determining Refugee Status* (1979) **92,** 698, 704
guidelines
conformity with Charter **104,** 295
consistency **90,** 292
intention of legislature **98,** 396
object and purpose **88,** 298
ordinary and natural meaning **101,** 273
penal legislation to be interpreted restrictively **92,** 679
perverse conclusions, avoidance of **90,** 342
plain meaning **90,** 225-6, 227, 228, 357
purpose **92,** 680, 696
singular to include plural **104,** 265
legislative competence. *See* Provinces, legislative powers *below*
phrases
'adjacent' **90,** 318-19
'adjacent to the coast' **92,** 678-82
'agency of foreign State' **104,** 280-2
'any aircraft' **90,** 217-18
'arbitrary detention' **101,** 302, 304-5
'Canadian citizen' **90,** 222-3, 226
'Canadian customs waters' **90,** 247-8
'Canadian waters' **90,** 247-8, **94,** 234-7, 243
'claims' **90,** 222-3
'coast' **94,** 244-5
'commercial activity'. *See* State Immunity Act 1980-81-82-83-85, phrases *below*
'conservation and management measures' **123,** 220-3

Canada (*cont.*)
'cruel and unusual punishment' **101,** 302, 305
'demonstrably justified' **88,** 297-8
'extradition agreement' **92,** 687
'fishing' **82,** 648
'fishing vessel' **82,** 621-2
'foreign State' **104,** 280-2
'import'/'export' **101,** 272-9
'Indians' **115,** 520-1
'inland waters' **94,** 243
'internal waters' **94,** 342-5
'lands reserved for the Indians' **115,** 518-20
'Pacific Ocean' **90,** 286-90, 296, 318
'particular social group'. *See* refugees, 'membership of a particular social group' *below*
'penalty' **101,** 303
'prescribe' **90,** 215, 219
'processing' **82,** 621-2
'relating to' **94,** 274, 275-6, 283-90, 304-5
'seaward from the low-water mark on the coast of the mainland and the several islands of British Columbia' **90,** 272-6, 319
'territorial sea' **94,** 241-2
'territorial waters of Newfoundland' **90,** 248-9, 254
'territory' **90,** 290-2, 317, 321
'treaty' **104,** 211-15
'vessels of a prescribed class' **123,** 224-5, 230, 443-8
presumption of conformity with Constitution **104,** 295
presumption of conformity with international law **90,** 215-16, **104,** 397-8
in case of apparent conflict **124,** 437-8
presumption of conformity with treaty **90,** 335, 339-40, 360, **94,** 291, **101,** 275-6, 303-4
presumption of conformity with treaty, in case of apparent conflict **90,** 342
presumption of territorial limitation **84,** 695, **92,** 679, **94,** 235
presumption of validity
of international obligations **92,** 687, 696, 708, 731, 734
intra vires **90,** 205
refugees, 'Convention refugee' **92,** 667-8, 669, 695-6, 713-14, 717-18
treaty as aid **90,** 225-8, 335, 340, **94,** 251-2
in case of ambiguity **101,** 301-4
travaux préparatoires **90,** 225, 226-7, 228, 343, **104,** 236-7, 258
unincorporated **104,** 264-5, **124,** 363, 437-8
treaty-implementing legislation, treaty as aid **90,** 225-8, **94,** 251-2, **124,** 437
legislation, retroactive **82,** 430-41, **84,** 707-8, **90,** 232-3, 270-92
exclusion of alien for past behaviour **104,** 198
express provision **123,** 503-4
extraterritorial extension of jurisdiction distinguished **82,** 432, 443
fishing regulations **123,** 503-4
retrospective distinguished **82,** 432-3, **98,** 574
war crimes **88,** 297
legislative powers, distribution between province and federal government **115,** 557-9
legitimate expectation
stay of deportation pending consideration by international body **124,** 411-12
treaty, right of individual under ratified but unincorporated treaty **124,** 397-8
malicious prosecution **123,** 492-5, 505-6

Mareva injunction
fiduciary obligation of disclosure **120,** 421-7, 439-40
undertaking in damages and **120,** 421-7, 438-46, 455-7
marine pollution
jurisdiction, 'while in Canadian waters' **94,** 232-7
oil discharge
failure to keep records **94,** 232-7
failure to report **94,** 232
Mikmaq tribe **79,** 262-6
recognition **79,** 264
nationality
acquisition of **60,** 242-5
dual nationality
compensation on claims and **90,** 221-8
dominant nationality **90,** 221, 224-8
nationals, right of entry to country **104,** 266-7
native title, nature, *Attorney-General for Quebec* v. *Attorney-General for Canada* **112,** 531-2
NATO Status of Forces Agreement (1951)
bilateral agreement and **94,** 290-1
ratification, need for **94,** 290
natural justice, extradition procedure and **98,** 388
natural law, knowledge of illegality of act **104,** 321
necessity, criminal law defence **101,** 278-80
Netherlands, wartime decrees, recognition **42,** 409-36
Newfoundland
acquisition of territory and **86,** 605, **90,** 254
airspace, rights over **90,** 252-3
Commission of Government **90,** 255-8
continental shelf, rights
adoption into municipal law **90,** 262
American Bases Act 1941 **90,** 257
Crown in right of a colony **86,** 603-7
Customs Act 1898 **90,** 248
Customs Act 1916 **90,** 248-9
date of acquisition **90,** 262
Hibernia Field, rights in **86,** 596-625
title **86,** 596-625
executive powers
extraterritorial **86,** 605
treaty-making **86,** 608
foreign relations, responsibility for **86,** 608, 611
Labrador. *See* Labrador *above*
law of
Air Navigation Act 1929 **90,** 252, 253
American Bases Act 1941 **94,** 267
Newfoundland Act (UK) 1933 **86,** 610, 612-16, **90,** 255
Newfoundland Act (UK) 1949 **86,** 612-16
self-government **86,** 612
sovereignty
external **86,** 604, 607
internal **86,** 604, 607
status **86,** 603-16, **90,** 248-60

Canada (*cont.*)
1934, before **86,** 607-9
1934-49 **86,** 609-12
1949, after **86,** 612-16
Commission of Government **86,** 609
confederation, effect **90,** 258-60, 275, 277
Terms of Union (Canada, Newfoundland Act 1949) (UK) **86,** 612-16
Terms of Union
Term 2 **90,** 260
Term 3 **90,** 258-9
Term 7 **90,** 258
Term 37 **90,** 259-60, 265
territorial sea, right to **90,** 236-60
recognition by UK, UK–USA Agreement on Lease of Bases (1941) **90,** 257
non-refoulement to country of origin or any other country where risk of subjection to torture **124,** 351. *See also* deportation *above*; refugees *below*
compelling reasons of national security, conviction of serious crime, need for **124,** 371
extradition distinguished **107,** 152-4, 161, 167
Nova Scotia, territorial sea, taxation of property **42,** 62-85
offenders, rights, sentencing changes, retroactive benefit **71,** 339-45
offshore mineral rights **73,** 193-5, 199-200, 215-16
Parliament, power to alter treaty provisions **53,** 576, 582, 584
piracy
jurisdiction **82,** 444-5
tort, whether **123,** 502
political offence
classification as
killing and injuring of innocent bystanders **107,** 165-8
terrorist offence **107,** 160-1, 163-4, 166-7
incidence test, acts incidental to violent uprising **107,** 154-8, 161-2
proportionality and **107,** 164, 167
political question doctrine, clarification of legal framework for democratic decisions **115,** 547
precedent in municipal courts, *stare decisis* doctrine **53,** 583, **64,** 15-20
prerogative, treaty-making power **124,** 413, 419
prisoners of war
compensation for unlawful treatment, Peace Treaty with Japan (1951) **118,** 211-22
disability pension rights **118,** 222
munitions manufacture, employment in
Hague Conventions (1907) **104,** 198
war crime **104,** 199-200
procedural fairness
deportation **124,** 378-83, 390-1, 411-12
fundamental justice and **124,** 378-83, 390-1
judicial review **124,** 419
proportionality
inhuman or degrading treatment **98,** 396-7
political offence **107,** 164, 167
Provinces
confederation, equality of Provinces **90,** 258-9
customary international law and **90,** 198, 200-1

legislative powers
customary international law **90,** 198
international law and, breach **90,** 208, 211
international law and, conflict, subsequent legislation **90,** 210-11
source **90,** 208
treaties **90,** 199
territorial sea, rights **90,** 263-6. *See also* British Columbia *and* Newfoundland *above*
Quebec
Charter of the French Language (Bill No 101) **118,** 174
s 58 **118,** 175-6
Charter of the French Language (Bill No 101), Act to Amend 1983, s 1 **118,** 175
Charter of the French Language (Bill No 178) 1988 **118,** 174-83
s 10 **118,** 176-7
Charter of the French Language (Bill No 178) 1988, Act to amend (Bill No 86 of 22 December 1993) **118,** 180-2
Code of Civil Procedure **118,** 177
legislation relating to the use of French, compatibility with International Covenant on Civil and Political Rights (ICCPR) (1966) **118,** 182-3
'people', whether **115,** 594
Regulations on the language of commerce and business of 22 December 1993 **118,** 180-1
right of self-expression **115,** 587-8
secession, right of **115,** 539-95. *See also* secession, right of Province *below*
Queen, role **87,** 232
referendum
democratic, whether **115,** 565, 572
legal effect **115,** 570, 593
legitimacy, conferring **115,** 571
negotiation, obligation following **115,** 570-4, 593
secession, relevance to **115,** 570-1, 592-3
refugees **84,** 710-13, **92,** 663-70, 693-719. *See also* refugees
burden of proof **92,** 705, 718, **104,** 233
refugee **92,** 705, 718
definition **92,** 667-8, **104,** 226, 246, 258, 265, **107,** 149, **124,** 413
Refugees, Geneva Convention on the Status of (1951) and Protocol (1967) **87,** 195
dual nationality, relevance **104,** 229
economic migrants **104,** 250
entitlement to protection of Charter of Rights and Freedoms **124,** 358, 403
'membership of a particular social group' **92,** 695-9, 708-12, 715-16, 717, **104,** 246-58, **124,** 402, 485, 496, 507
women **104,** 263-4
non-refoulement to country of origin or any other country where risk of subjection to torture. *See* deportation *and* non-refoulement to country of origin or any other country where risk of subjection to torture *above*
'persecution' **92,** 699-702
activities committed or condoned by State **92,** 669-70, 698-702, 712-13, 715
arrest, essential element, whether **87,** 196
probability **84,** 711
reasonable chance **84,** 710, 711
responsibility for determining **87,** 196-7
substantial grounds for thinking **84,** 710, 711-12, **124,** 358
well-founded fear **87,** 194, **92,** 669-70, 698-702, 712-13, 715

Canada (*cont.*)
'persecution or well-founded fear of persecution'
basis, religious belief **92,** 668, 670
military service evasion **104,** 269-77
political opinion **104,** 260-3
race **92,** 668, 670
reasons, need to identify, UNHCR *Handbook on Procedures and Criteria for Determining Refugee Status* (1979) **104,** 260
relevant factors **104,** 246-60
intentions of authorities **104,** 274
State complicity, need for **104,** 228, 231, 236-9, 241-2
subjective test **92,** 697
well-founded fear **104,** 236
protection, State's ability to undertake, relevance **104,** 228-9, 231, 232, 234-6, 239-42
denial of admittance to home territory **104,** 267
First *Ad Hoc* Committee on Statelessness and Related Problems (1950) **104,** 240
inability raising presumption of fear of persecution **104,** 242-6
UNHCR *Handbook on Procedures and Criteria for Determining Refugee Status* (1979) **104,** 240-1, 267
unwillingness distinguished **104,** 239-42
right of residence **92,** 710
'serious non-political crime', degree of criminality, relevance **107,** 167-8
status, appeal against decision respecting **87,** 194-7
unwillingness to avail oneself of protection of national authorities **92,** 669-70, 701-6, 714-19
dual nationality and **92,** 704-6, 714-15, **104,** 230, 232-3, 264-7
protection of national State, primacy **104,** 239, 250
right to live in country, relevance **92,** 704-6, 716-18
Refugees, Geneva Convention on the Status of (1951) and Protocol (1967)
extradition law, compatibility **104,** 258
incorporation into municipal law **69,** 300
remedies
need for **115,** 576
political process as **115,** 576
rule of law
definition **115,** 563-6
constitutionalism distinguished **115,** 564-5
remedy for breach **115,** 590-1
St Lawrence River, International Joint Commission, competence **73,** 167-72
secession, right of Province
amendment to Constitution, need for **115,** 568-9, 574
applicable law
international law **115,** 546, 579
municipal law **115,** 590
complementary rights of federal government and other provinces **115,** 571-3
de facto **115,** 578, 589, 595
international law, under **115,** 579-91
legitimacy
recognition **115,** 576, 593
refusal to negotiate, effect **115,** 576-7
referendum **115,** 570-1, 592-3

unilateral **115,** 568-95
service of process on foreign State or State agency
method, diplomatic channels **120,** 450-1
State immunity, jurisdiction and **94,** 261
acknowledgement of receipt, need for **94,** 261-2
service of process out of the jurisdiction
as exercise of extraterritorial jurisdiction **69,** 93-8
jurisdiction over alleged offence, relevance **69,** 96
statutory authority **120,** 450-2
ships, State-owned, immunity, attachment **42,** 125-34
softwood lumber Export Control Regime, compatibility with NAFTA **122,** 302-42
fair and equitable treatment, whether **122,** 379-402
sovereignty
acquisition **43,** 111
date **90,** 240-1
external **86,** 606-7
State agency/State-owned corporation/State entity
'agent or instrumentality of foreign State' **104,** 280-2
alter ego theory **64,** 64-7
classification
applicable law, *lex fori* **64,** 65-6, **80,** 573 n. 11
bank acting at request of State **104,** 280-2
municipal highways authority **64,** 64-9
Securities and Exchange Commission (SEC) **64,** 48-51
separate legal entity test
nature of functions **64,** 66
right to sue/be sued **64,** 66
structure **64,** 66
State Immunity Act 1980-81-82-83-85 **86,** 627, 634-9, **87,** 66
preamble **120,** 430
as codification **94,** 278-80, **120,** 430-2
personal injury exceptions **104,** 282-3
common law, effect on **95,** 451-6
death and personal injury exception **95,** 456, 464
determination of functionaries entitled to **95,** 457-60
s 4(4) as modification **120,** 442, 458
s 7(2) **84,** 707
critical date **95,** 457, 466
injury caused in forum State, limitation to **124,** 436-41
phrases
'commercial activity' **86,** 628-31, 633-9, **94,** 271-91, 302-3, **124,** 434-5
'foreign State' **120,** 430
property, immunity of, attachment **65,** 230-1
purpose
limitation of immunity **120,** 432
transfer of competence to courts **95,** 455
restrictive theory and **65,** 230-1, **124,** 433
retroactive, whether **84,** 707-8, **90,** 232-3
s 2 (interpretation) **86,** 628-31, **87,** 202, **94,** 261, 271, 275, 302-3
s 3 (immunity entitlement) **86,** 631, **87,** 198, 201, **104,** 280, 282, **120,** 420, **124,** 430, 433
compatibility with Charter of Rights and Freedoms, s 7 **124,** 446-50

Canada (*cont.*)
obligation to provide civil remedy for torture **124,** 436-7, 438-41
s 3(1) (general statement of immunity) **94,** 261, **120,** 430
s 4 (submission and waiver) **87,** 220-1, **124,** 433
s 4(1) **94,** 262, **120,** 427
s 4(2) **94,** 271, 275, **120,** 427
s 4(2)(a) (express waiver) **120,** 432, 440, 446, 455-7
s 4(2)(b) (waiver through initiation of proceedings) **120,** 440, 446
s 4(4) (counterclaim arising out of the subject matter) **120,** 426, 427, 441-6, 457-9
s 5 (commercial activity exception) **86,** 628-31, **87,** 201, 204, **94,** 274, 276, 283-4, **104,** 282-3, **124,** 430, 433, 434-6
s 6 (exceptions) **87,** 201, 204, **95,** 465-7, **104,** 282-3, **120,** 427-8, 436
s 6(a) (death or personal injury exception) **120,** 459-60, **124,** 433
s 6(b) (damage to or loss of property exception) **120,** 460
s 9 (service of document) **94,** 263, **120,** 450-2
s 17 (service of document *ex juris*) **120,** 451-2
s 18 (criminal proceedings) **124,** 433-4
classification of proceedings **124,** 433
as sole source of immunity **124,** 438
UK and US legislation distinguished **120,** 430, 432
State immunity, execution/attachment, applicability
default judgment, right to raise jurisdictional immunity **64,** 73-4
default judgment against foreign State **64,** 70-6
State immunity, execution/attachment, theory/doctrine, State immunity, jurisdiction distinguished **64,** 74
State immunity, jurisdiction **86,** 627-9
State immunity, jurisdiction, applicability
counterclaim arising out of the same subject matter, extension of waiver to **120,** 432-40, 442-6, 457-9
criminal proceedings **124,** 433-4
State immunity, jurisdiction, classification of act
act in territory of forum State
decisions of international tribunals relating to **124,** 444-6
State practice **124,** 443-4
commercial activities **87,** 201
damage to or loss of property **90,** 232
electricity poles, transaction concerning **84,** 702, 707, 708
employment of architect for construction of pavilion at exhibition **64,** 2-20, 22, 25-8, 45-6
film, agency contract for distribution of **64,** 56-8
functional test **64,** 53-5
hydro-electric development **92,** 659-61
law enforcement **124,** 434-5
lease of diplomatic premises **64,** 60-2, 70-6
merchant ship **84,** 708
nature or purpose of transaction as determining factor **86,** 630, **94,** 274, 302-3, **124,** 434-5
participation in international exhibition **64,** 21-2, 28
personal injury in forum State **87,** 201, 203-4, **90,** 232, **124,** 436-41
private acts, limitation to **104,** 283-4
Torture Convention (1984) and **124,** 436-41

transit stop in third country **104,** 283-4
private acts **90,** 231-2
private person test **94,** 273, 274, 275, 290, 303-8
public project **92,** 661
securities legislation, enforcement **64,** 48-51
test **84,** 706
tort
abuse of police power **124,** 435
commercial activity distinguished **124,** 434-5
torture, customary international law **124,** 443
union certification proceedings **94,** 274-91, 304-5
State immunity, jurisdiction, entitlement
constituent State of federation
Attorney-General **95,** 457
division of executive **95,** 457
functionaries. *See* officials *below*
Custodian for Enemy Property **56,** 228
government department **84,** 703
officials **87,** 202, 205
illegal nature of acts, effect **95,** 460-2
official receiver **90,** 230-3
scope of duties **87,** 203, **95,** 459
State agency, of **94,** 263, **95,** 457-60
sovereign status, dependence on **84,** 708
State agency/State-owned corporation/State entity **64,** 48-51, **92,** 659-61, **94,** 263
bank acting at request of State **104,** 280-2
State compared/distinguished **64,** 64-9
State-controlled entity **92,** 660-1
State official **104,** 282
State immunity, jurisdiction, procedural aspects
admissibility, question of **84,** 708
burden of proof **64,** 11, 21-2, 28-9, 35-6, 75
cause of action preceding statutory provision **87,** 202, 204, 205
critical date
assertion of claim of sovereignty **84,** 707
cause of action **94,** 262
issue of writ **84,** 703, 707, 708
default judgment, non-appearance as admission of allegations **124,** 430-1
immunity from jurisdiction and liability distinguished **86,** 629, **120,** 432
need to plead **64,** 73-4, **95,** 464-5
as procedural bar **64,** 32, **87,** 201
State immunity, jurisdiction, theory/doctrine
absolute theory **64,** 736, **87,** 200, **90,** 231, **95,** 452-3, 470
agreement by parties to apply **64,** 64
basis
equality of States **86,** 629
extraterritoriality **64,** 39-40, **95,** 455
independence of State **95,** 452
development of concept **64,** 3-20, 21-2, 29-32, 52-9, 60-2, 642, **84,** 703-6, **86,** 628-9, **94,** 297-301, **95,** 369-70, 452-5, **120,** 428-9
restrictive theory **64,** 48-51, 54, 58, 737, **84,** 706, **86,** 628-31, **87,** 201, **92,** 661, **95,** 452-5, 470

Canada (*cont.*)
equality before the law and **64,** 42
State immunity, execution/attachment distinguished **64,** 74
State practice, diversity **95,** 452, **120,** 430
State immunity, jurisdiction, waiver **87,** 201, 204-5
action to stay proceedings as **87,** 205, **95,** 462-4
challenge to the jurisdiction **64,** 34
express waiver, need for **86,** 628
extension to counterclaim **120,** 432-46
NATO Status of Forces Agreement (1951) **86,** 628, 633
personal defendants, extension to **120,** 446-50, 460-1
submission to foreign labour tribunal **94,** 285-6
undertaking in damages as **120,** 432-40, 455-7
State immunity, taxation, property held by public corporation for public use **43,** 162-5
State practice
customary international law, element of **104,** 329, 335
as evidence of *jus cogens*/peremptory norm **124,** 364
State responsibility for acts and omissions outside its jurisdiction
death penalty **98,** 402-7, 417, **124,** 316-17
deportation to country where risk of subjection to torture **124,** 361-3
following extradition **98,** 374, **124,** 316-17
respect for other States **98,** 417-18
statutory limitation **82,** 442
territorial sea, extension to 12 miles **82,** 605
straits
between British Columbia and Vancouver Island, proprietary rights **90,** 269-330
land covered by, ownership **73,** 191-225
strike, right to
public service, in **90,** 183-213, **94,** 250-9
customary international law **90,** 200-1, 211-12
freedom of association and **90,** 185, 186, 187, 199, 205-8, **94,** 249-58
international law, under **90,** 184-7, 195-9, 205, 207-8, **94,** 251-8. *See also* customary international law *above*
State immunity and **94,** 285-6, 305
superior orders **104,** 332-4, 367, 378
Einsatzgruppen case **104,** 375
history **104,** 369-74
Llandovery Castle **104,** 372-3
mens rea, evidence of **104,** 376
moral choice test **104,** 333, 374-6, 381-2
Nuremberg Charter (1945) **104,** 297
R v. *Smith* **104,** 371
requirements **104,** 333, 373-4, 380-1
Supreme Court
advisory function **115,** 543-4
international law, right to apply **115,** 545-6
jurisdiction
advisory function. *See* advisory function *above*
application of federal laws, whether limited to **115,** 541
important questions of fact or law concerning any matter **115,** 544
interpretation of Constitution Acts **115,** 544

original jurisdiction **115,** 541-2
questions concerning the powers of the legislature or government of a Canadian province **115,** 544
primacy over provincial court of appeal **115,** 542
territorial integrity **79,** 264
territorial sea
boundaries **73,** 193-4, 198-200, 205, 216
breadth **43,** 104
Crown in right of a colony **90,** 265
Customs Act 1928, 'territorial waters of Canada' **43,** 103, 111
definition **94,** 242
jurisdiction **51,** 138
taxation of property **42,** 62-85
rights **90,** 241-2
division between federal and provincial governments **86,** 596-625
succession to UK rights **90,** 240-1
seabed and subsoil
federal/provincial ownership **125,** 460
sovereignty over, Crown in right of the Island of Newfoundland **90,** 260
territory, acquisition, legislation, need for **90,** 240
terrorism, definition/requirements, difficulty of **107,** 576, **124,** 373-5
terrorist organization, freedom of speech and **120,** 375-8
tort, applicable law, *lex loci delicti commissi* **124,** 432-3
torture. *See also* deportation, to country where risk of subjection to torture *above*
as cruel and unusual punishment **124,** 360-1
definition **124,** 358
jus cogens/peremptory norm **124,** 363-6, 441-3
obligation to provide civil remedy against foreign State for acts committed outside the forum State **124,** 441-3
State immunity, jurisdiction, theory/doctrine, customary international law **124,** 443
as violation of right to life, security and liberty **124,** 352
Torture Convention (1984)
definition, action 'by a public official or other person acting in an official capacity' **124,** 438-9
deportation to country where risk of subjection to torture **124,** 366-7
obligations, civil remedy **124,** 436-7, 438-41
trading with the enemy legislation, shares held abroad **42,** 415-19, 435
Trading with the Enemy Regulations 1939 **56,** 224
travaux préparatoires, Geneva Convention on the Status of Refugees (1951) **104,** 237
treaties **60,** 391
breach, justification, municipal law **124,** 414
definition
agreement with aboriginal peoples distinguished **104,** 210-15
Jay Treaty (1794) **104,** 210-15
Expo 67 Rules and Regulations, whether **64,** 33-4
federal Statutes and **43,** 1-2
good faith
applicability of multilateral treaty before incorporation **124,** 413-14
implementation **124,** 413-14
implementing legislation. *See also* legislation, interpretation *above*

Canada (*cont.*)
Agreement on Distant Early Warning System 1955 **42,** 267-71
applicable law **101,** 313-14
evidence of purpose **90,** 334-5, 360
Jay Treaty 1794 **42,** 269-70
language of treaty, use of **90,** 342-4
need for **42,** 268-71, **69,** 296-301, **90,** 209, 338-9, **101,** 208-9, 248-9, 300-1, 312, **104,** 216-18, 219, 232, **123,** 491, **124,** 363, 396-8, 404-5, 410-11, 413-15, 420-3
primacy **90,** 338, 340, 343-5, 358-60
as source of obligation **104,** 215
Supplementary Extradition Convention 1905 **43,** 235, 236, 239
individual
rights **104,** 215-18
State as agent for **104,** 218-19
legislature's role, amendment **53,** 576, 582, 584
as part of municipal law **90,** 198, 199-202, 215, 217, **94,** 252
responsibility for, executive **90,** 210
as source of international law **104,** 335
treaty-making power, prerogative **124,** 413, 419
unincorporated, individual's rights under **124,** 414-15
treaty interpretation
aids
context **92,** 687, **124,** 440
customary international law **101,** 309, 310-15
general principles of international law **92,** 724-5
international manual **104,** 237
judicial and arbitral decisions **104,** 238-9
State practice **92,** 725
teachings of publicists **104,** 237-8
applicable law, international law **101,** 313
by international tribunal **124,** 425-6
guidelines
contract law **92,** 731
general principles of international law **92,** 687
object and purpose **92,** 687
purpose **101,** 314
respect for sovereignty **92,** 688
multilingual
authentic languages **104,** 209-10
Vienna Convention on the Law of Treaties (1969) **104,** 209-10
parties' intention **101,** 314
Truman Proclamation 1945, reaction to **71,** 106, 138-9
USA, boundary dispute, Special Agreement and Treaty to submit dispute to binding settlement 1979. *See* International Court of Justice (ICJ), Special Agreement
Utrecht, Treaty of **78,** 449
Vancouver Island. *See also* United Kingdom, Vancouver Island, colony of
boundaries **73,** 189-90, 206, 218-19, **90,** 236-330
discovery and settlement, history of **73,** 65-7, 69, 104, 124-5, 189, 206
enclave **90,** 288-90
low-water mark **90,** 312-16
straits surrounding. *See* straits *above*
visiting forces

NATO Status of Forces Agreement (1951)
locally engaged civilian employees **94,** 267
State immunity, jurisdiction and **86,** 627-39, **94,** 267-306
war crimes
applicable law
international law **104,** 299-300
municipal law **104,** 299-300, 306, 327
burden of proof **104,** 355-6
knowledge that act a war crime or crime against humanity **104,** 395
customary international law **104,** 200-2, 299, 322, 335-6, 337-8
defence
any defence available under international law at the time or at time of proceedings **104,** 331-4, 366
any defence available under *lex fori* at the time or at time of proceedings **104,** 297-8, 331-4, 366
autrefois convict **104,** 366
lawful authority **98,** 597-600. *See also* superior orders *below*
lawful authority, burden of proof **98,** 597
legality under laws of place where act committed **104,** 296-7, 310, 334, 366, 377-80, 381, 395-6
legality under *lex fori* at time of act **104,** 203, 331
military necessity **104,** 331
mistake of fact **104,** 367-8, 379
peace officer defence. *See* peace officer defence *below*
permissibility under laws of place where act committed **98,** 597
reprisals **104,** 331
superior orders. *See* superior orders *below*
definition, municipal law **104,** 197, 335, 358
Deschênes Commission of Inquiry on War Criminals
Decision concerning Foreign Evidence **82,** 453-4
Report **82,** 434-5
double criminality
forced labour/kidnapping/forcible confinement, equivalence **104,** 202-3
notional transfer of act **104,** 198
offence under *lex fori* at the time **104,** 198, 202-4, 354
evidence
admissibility **104,** 386-9
witnesses, judge's right to summon **104,** 389-93
exclusion of alien **104,** 198
fault, need for **98,** 595. *See also* knowledge that act a war crime or crime against humanity, relevance *below*
general principle of international law **104,** 296, 322, 337-8
international law, existence in
absence of court/code, relevance **104,** 336
Hague Conventions (1907) **104,** 200, 336
Nuremberg Charter (1945) **104,** 200-1
UNGA Resolution 95(1) (Nuremberg Charter) **104,** 201-2, **112,** 204-6
as international offence **104,** 356-7
jurisdiction
accused within territory **104,** 354
basis, breach of general principles of law recognized by the community of nations **104,** 299, 353
customary international law **104,** 353

Canada (*cont.*)
extraterritorial **104,** 298-9, 403-4
obligation **104,** 328, 330
universal **104,** 299-300
knowledge that act a war crime or crime against humanity, relevance **98,** 536, 541, 542-6, 558-61, 594, 627-8, **104,** 312-23, 363-6, 376-7, 380, 395
burden of proof **98,** 542, 558-61, 596-7
peace officer defence **104,** 331, 332, 366-7, 378-9
requirements **104,** 333, 350-1, 367, 380-1
requirements
armed conflict **104,** 311, 312
breach of international law at time of act **104,** 301, 335, 354
breach of laws of armed conflict **104,** 358
lack of clarity **104,** 328-9
retroactivity **98,** 564-5
breach of fundamental rights, whether **98,** 574-5, **104,** 335-7, 399-402
Hague Conventions (1899/1907) **104,** 400-1
Nuremberg Tribunal **104,** 322, 400-2
retrospectivity distinguished **98,** 574
retrospectivity. *See* retroactivity *above*
superior orders **98,** 598-9. *See also* defence, lawful authority *above*
burden of proof **98,** 599
treaty **104,** 337-8
whether
question of fact for jury **98,** 528-9, 552-7, **104,** 303
question of law for judge **98,** 536, 539-41, 570
waste disposal measures. *See also* Hazardous Waste, Basel Convention on Control of Transboundary Movements and Their Disposal (1989) *above*
precautionary principle and **121,** 169-74
Cape Colony, Penguin Island
annexation **86,** 191, 196, 198, 204
capital punishment. *See* death penalty
capitulations system 46, 469
carriage by air, international 52, 424-30, 433-6, **54,** 309, 319, 323, 324, 328-35, 340, 342. *See also* air transport agreements; International Air Transport Association (IATA)
air companies, government, relations with **54,** 336
air transport services **54,** 244-9, 332-5
rights and duties of parties **54,** 347
antitrust rules
applicability **74,** 43-59, 64-5, 68-9, 73-82
disputes under **78,** 526
landing fees **78,** 525
landing rights **78,** 523-5
between South Africa and USA **56,** 26
as 'commercial activity' **63,** 134, 195-6, 292, 344, 449-73, 588-9, 617
designated carrier **52,** 424-6, 427-8, 433, **54,** 309, 319, 323, 324-5
dispute
India–Pakistan (1971) **48,** 331, 337, 347, 453
tariffs **74,** 42-4, 46, 67-70
mail **52,** 424-30, 433-4, 438, 446
racial discrimination and **56,** 27-9
regulation **74,** 45-87

by treaty **74,** 45-56, 66-9, 73-82
tariffs, dispute concerning **74,** 42-4, 46, 67-70
Carriage of Goods by Road, Convention on (CMR) (1956) 74, 577-625. *See also* Road Signs and Signals, Geneva Protocol (1949); Road Traffic Convention (1949)
applicability, Jersey and UK **86,** 152-60
carrier's liability **74,** 620-5
compensation
'charges incurred in respect of carriage' **74,** 578, 580, 585-6, 589-90, 592-6, 598-9, 601-4, 607-13
'current market price' **74,** 577, 583-5, 588-9, 591-2, 597, 604-6, 613
value of goods for calculation of **74,** 577-8, 583-6, 589-90, 592-6, 598-9, 601-4, 607-13
municipal law and, direct application **70,** 435-6
Carriage of Goods by Sea, Hague Rules on 60, 2, 6
interpretation **60,** 3, 6-8
in municipal courts **60,** 4-5, 7
municipal law and **60,** 2-5
purpose **60,** 7-9
Cayman Islands
extradition
habeas corpus **124,** 453-9
time-limit
extension **124,** 453-9
'reasonable' **124,** 453-9
extradition agreement, legislation, effect of agreement on legislation **124,** 453-8
treaties, legislation, effect of treaty on **124,** 453-8
censorship
public morals, protection of **70,** 298-304
television, human rights **40,** 188-90
Central African Republic, French Community, status in **44,** 26-8
Central America, Federal Republic of
Constitution (1824)
s 5 (transfer of Spanish sovereignty) **100,** 320
s 197 (prohibition on formation of new States) **100,** 320
Constitution (1835), territorial provisions **100,** 320-1
central/State-owned bank. *See also* bank; *and under individual States*
classification of act
affidavit in interests of public service **65,** 66-7
commercial act **63,** 88-91, **87,** 18
foreign exchange control **65,** 65-6, 349-53, 422-4
letter of credit **65,** 133-7
sale of certificates of deposit **92,** 416
sale of currency **98,** 59
transfer of shares following reorganization of banking sector **124,** 559-63
classification as **86,** 8-9, 12, 13
private law as applicable law, relevance **65,** 65
separate legal entity test **64,** 118-19, **65,** 55, 65-6, 134, 138, 422-3, **82,** 92, **124,** 559-61
Turkiye Garanti Bankasi AS **65,** 422-4
as department of government/State **64,** 119, 134, 136-9, 146-9, 222
functions **63,** 150, **64,** 116-19, 147-8, **86,** 13, **124,** 552. *See also* classification as *and* classification of act *above*; purpose/use of funds *below*

central/State-owned bank (*cont.*)
mixed private/public **64,** 136, 147
restrictions on private banking activities **64,** 119
sovereign nature **63,** 83-4, **64,** 118-19, **82,** 35
jurisdiction, dispute relating to agreement with foreign commercial bank **96,** 736, 737
liability **86,** 13
private funds **86,** 13-14
as organ of government **64,** 133-4
purpose/use of funds **63,** 599
as attachable interest **87,** 240, 255-6
cash and securities accounts **65,** 135
commercial **89,** 364-5
diplomatic relations **82,** 35
funds held for its own account **63,** 599, **64,** 224-5, **92,** 401-3
future use, relevance **65,** 135, 176-7
ILA Draft Articles on State Immunity (1982) **65,** 245
mixed **63,** 527, **89,** 365
monetary **64,** 119
private, liability for **86,** 13-14
public and private distinguished **47,** 158, 161
right of suit in foreign court **86,** 14
as State agency **63,** 65, 90, 104, 150, 175, 347, 360, 391, 425, 460, 490, 496, 558-61, 575, 587, **64,** 115-19, 133-4, 137-9, 147-9, 222, **65,** 65-6, 134, 350-3, 422-3, **66,** 9-10, 22, 39, 41-2, 48-9, 110, 170, 448-50, 457, 507-12, 516, **72,** 122, 165, 174-8, 184, 186, **82,** 34, 92, **86,** 13, **87,** 241, 250, **92,** 483, **96,** 735-6, **106,** 278-80, **107,** 263, **121,** 491
Bancec **80,** 568-82
State Bank of India **63,** 82-5, 88-91
wholly owned commercial bank **107,** 263
State control **87,** 242-3, 246-8
State immunity, execution/attachment **72,** 187-90
assets of nationalized bank **63,** 1-4
burden of proof **87,** 240-1
central and State-owned bank distinguished **92,** 416
currency reserves **63,** 16-17, **64,** 146, **82,** 35-6
failure to honour government contract **63,** 63-6
funds held for its own account. *See* purpose/use of funds, funds held for its own account *above*
immunity, jurisdiction and **64,** 135
Mareva injunction **64,** 222-5
nature of underlying relationship as determining factor **65,** 423-4
period of exposure between transfer of central bank role and transfer of assets/shares **124,** 553, 554
State immunity, jurisdiction, dependence on **64,** 223
US/UK law distinguished **64,** 224-5, 226
waiver. *See* waiver of immunity from execution/attachment *below*
State immunity, jurisdiction **63,** 137-61, 175, 391-407, 460, 490, 558-61, 575, 587-99, **82,** 12, 34, 92, **84,** 109-10, 194, **87,** 248-50
classification of act. *See* classification of act *above*
State immunity, execution/attachment and **64,** 135
State responsibility **84,** 633-4, 643, **96,** 735-6, **124,** 52-4

acts on behalf of State and private acts distinguished **96,** 736
foreign exchange operations **117,** 240-1
State succession
disintegration and **96,** 735
distribution of assets following succession, applicable law **96,** 736
status **87,** 241, 246, 248-52
applicable law, *lex fori* **64,** 138-9
evidence of, ambassador/head of mission certificate **64,** 137, 146
relevance **65,** 350-4
structure and responsibilities, applicable law **96,** 735
waiver of immunity from execution/attachment **92,** 402-3
compatibility with central bank status **124,** 554
reference to applicable legal system, relevance **124,** 554
in respect of bank having lost central bank status **124,** 554
CERN. *See* European Organization for Nuclear Research (CERN)
certificate of executive. *See* executive certificate/statement
cession, territory. *See* territory, acquisition, cession
cetaceans, protection. *See* Habitats Directive (92/43/EEC), cetaceans and *lophelia pertusa*, protection
Ceylon
legislation, retroactive **91,** 18-19
separation of powers and **91,** 18-19, 89-91, 110-11
CFSP. *See* Common Foreign and Security Policy (CFSP)
Chad, independent status **44,** 42-3
Chagos Archipelago. *See also* British Indian Ocean Territory (BIOT)
history and status **123,** 556-69
British Indian Ocean Territory (BIOT), constitution as **123,** 557
changed circumstances 68, 565, 571, 576, 583-4, 591-3, 594, 603-5, 612-24, 633, 635, 639-42, **69,** 581
contract, accession to independence **47,** 102-4
date of change **68,** 641
channel, definition **52,** 170
Channel Islands 81, 378-9. *See also* Minquiers and Ecréhos; St Pierre and Miquelon
German occupation, courts, position of **39,** 237
relation to UK **54,** 92, 96-7, 99
Channel Tunnel, France–UK agreements relating to
Concession Agreement (Eurotunnel)
arbitration clause **119,** 408-11, **125,** 593
Clause 15.1 **119,** 414
Clause 23.2 **119,** 411, 413, 414-16, **125,** 593-601
Clause 40 **119,** 408
Clause 40.4 **119,** 409
extracts **119,** 402-3
dispute settlement provisions
applicable law
principles of equity [if parties agree] **119,** 409
relevant principles of international law **119,** 409
rules of English or French law as appropriate **119,** 408-9
forum **119,** 409-11
conveniens **119,** 410-11
for determining validity of UK legislation **119,** 409-11, **125,** 591, 592-3
implementation

Channel Tunnel, France–UK agreements relating to (*cont.*)
consultation, need for **119,** 411-16, **125,** 593-601
absence of objection, effect **125,** 595-8, 600-1
joint action (*aggissent d'un commun accord*), need for **119,** 413-16, **125,** 595-8, 599-601
interpretation
agreements as a whole **119,** 411-12
equal authority of English and French texts **125,** 595
subsequent practice **125,** 596-7
unconfirmed statements at JSC meeting **125,** 597
Joint Security Committee (JSC) **119,** 403
advisory status **119,** 412, **125,** 597
Special Arrangements on Security Matters relating to the Channel Fixed Link (1993), extracts **119,** 403-4
Treaty concerning the Construction and Operation by Private Concessionaires of a Channel Fixed Link **119,** 400-16
UK legislation relating to. *See* United Kingdom, Channel Tunnel (Security) Order 1994 (Part III) *and* Channel Tunnel Act 1987
Chapultepec, Act of 76, 691-5
Charter of Economic Rights and Duties of States. *See* United Nations General Assembly (UNGA) Resolutions, 3281 (XXIV) (Charter of Economic Rights and Duties of States)
Charter of the Organization of American States, force, prohibition on the threat or use of **76,** 55, 637
Charter of the United Nations. *See* United Nations Charter (1945)
charterparty
arbitration clause **41,** 452-5, **57,** 149, 151
beneficial ownership, whether **64,** 188-94
variation of terms, guarantor, consent, need for **90,** 559
charts. *See* maps
chemical weapons, deployment
human rights and **106,** 395-7
legality, defensive purposes **106,** 362-3
legislative consent, need for
collective security, agreement to treaty establishing **106,** 396-7
Convention on the Presence of Foreign Forces in the FRG (1954) **106,** 396-7
threat to use force, whether **106,** 398-9
cheque, action for payment in case of unenforceable agreement **41,** 238, **118,** 567-78
Chernobyl nuclear accident
liability for **80,** 384-8
State immunity and **80,** 370-1, 372
Chesapeake Bay 97, 653
Chicago Convention on International Civil Aviation (1944)
aircraft in transit, right of search **73,** 699-701, 702-4
Annex 13 (accident and incident investigation) **120,** 558-63
disclosure of records **120,** 558-9, 577, 583
flight recorders
accident or serious incident **120,** 559-60
incident **120,** 560-1
implementation
freedom in respect of **120,** 561-3, 573-6

implementing legislation, need for **120,** 563
State practice **120,** 561-2
as part of municipal law **120,** 569-72
Annexes
Annex 13. *See* Annex 13 (accident and incident investigation) *above*
effect in municipal law **72,** 675-6, **73,** 700, 704, **120,** 561-3
obligation to implement **120,** 558
as part of the Convention **120,** 564
baggage in transit
damage to, notification, time-limit **74,** 633, 646, 649, 654, 672, 682
partial loss **74,** 633-83
right of search **72,** 673-6, **73,** 663
bilateral agreements concluded under **60,** 439
customary international law **120,** 567-8
description **48,** 417
direct effect **73,** 700, 704
drafting and conclusion **45,** 400, 413
fees for telecommunications and radio services **90,** 216-17
non-discriminatory basis **90,** 217
flight into or transit over territory of non-scheduled aircraft, right **40,** 93
hijacking **48,** 434-5
implementation
ad hoc approach **120,** 565-9
legislation, need for **120,** 568-9
international standards and procedures under **120,** 555-63
binding force of rules **120,** 556-7
procedures for rule-making **120,** 557-8
legislation, interpretation, presumption of conformity with treaty **124,** 472-4
object and purpose **54,** 324-5
as part of municipal law **90,** 215, 216-17, **120,** 563-9, **124,** 471-5
legislation, interpretation in conformity with **124,** 472-4
obligation to exercise powers in conformity with **124,** 472
persons in transit, right of search and arrest **73,** 663
phrases
'accident' **96,** 114 n. 2, 124
'air services' **45,** 394, 409, 414, 422, 424
proceedings under
'action' in respect of illegal action **48,** 344-6, 382, 427-9, 430-2
'complaint' in respect of legally permissible action causing hardship **44,** 427-9, **48,** 343-6, 381-4, 426-30
sovereignty over airspace and **54,** 334, 346, **60,** 435-6, **120,** 567-8
child care. *See also* child rights; European Convention on Human Rights (1950), child care; International Covenant on Civil and Political Rights (ICCPR) (1966), child care; young people, protection of
administration **92,** 278-9
adoption. *See* adoption
affiliation. *See* affiliation
care order **92,** 226
appeal against **92,** 226, 281
implementation **92,** 279-80, 338-9
termination or variation **92,** 226, 280-1
care proceedings **92,** 225
'child' **95,** 486 n. 2

child care (*cont.*)
custody
applicable law **95,** 498-500
grandparent's right **95,** 498-500
developing law
abduction of children by parents, conclusion of conventions **96,** 636
parental access
bilateral agreements **96,** 636
Draft Convention on the Rights of the Child **96,** 636
diplomatic immunity and **118,** 305
ECHR and **92,** 233-56, 281-303, 335-49
jurisdiction **92,** 620-35
local authority decisions relating to, judicial review **92,** 230-2
parental access **92,** 231, 243, 280
prohibition on removal and **92,** 343, 346-7
parental rights **92,** 242-4
place of safety order **92,** 224-5
prohibition on removal **92,** 336-8
supervision order **92,** 225
voluntary care **92,** 224, 227, 274-8, 335-6
parental rights resolution **92,** 227-9
reception into care **92,** 227
wardship **92,** 224, 229-30
child rights
common law, best interests of child **104,** 485-6
family interests distinguished **117,** 639
forceful transfer of children of mixed ancestry **120,** 358-9
illegitimate child. *See* illegitimate child
immigration and **117,** 638-9
International Covenant on Civil and Political Rights (ICCPR) (1966) **101,** 459-65, **117,** 628-34, 638-9
religious education **47,** 205-11
standing, parent **104,** 474-5
UN Convention on the Rights of the Child (1989) **101,** 458-60, **117,** 628-35, 638-9
death penalty and **124,** 327-8
declaration of wrongful removal, discretionary nature **114,** 499-500
implementing legislation, need for **104,** 470-1, 480
parental access **96,** 638-9
phrases
'action concerning children' **104,** 472-3, 483-4
'the best interests of child . . . a primary consideration' **104,** 473, 475-6, 498-9
Chile
American Convention on Human Rights (1969) and **89,** 81-2
Argentina. *See* Argentina–Chile Arbitral Tribunal (1902) *and other Argentina–Chile entries*
Centro Nacional de Intelligencia **63,** 380-90
Compania de Acero de Pacifico, SA **63,** 175-8
'agency or instrumentality' **63,** 175-8
Constitution
Art. 19 **89,** 49, 52-4, 56, 75
Art. 20 **89,** 55, 59, 75-7

Art. 86 **65,** 31
nature **89,** 54
primacy, treaty **89,** 53-5, 69, 70
consular agent, functions, consular protection **89,** 66, 67-8
consular privileges and immunities **89,** 70-1. *See also* consular agent *above*; diplomatic privileges and immunities *below*
basis, comity **89,** 71
functional **89,** 66, 67
media interviews **89,** 67-8
waiver **89,** 71
copper industry **65,** 58-60, **73,** 232-8, 245-6, 248-9
foreign enterprises, nationalization of **73,** 235, 237
compensation, non-payment **73,** 235-7
Law No 16,624 (1967) ('Copper Law') **59,** 412, 428-9
Law No 17,450 (1971) **73,** 235, 244, 249
policy **59,** 410-11, 417, 418-21
diplomatic agent, social security, entitlement **70,** 393-4
diplomatic immunity, execution/attachment **89,** 55
diplomatic immunity, jurisdiction
real property contract **65,** 30-1
State immunity and **65,** 30-1
waiver
participation in related proceedings **89,** 51
Vienna Convention on Diplomatic Relations (1961) **70,** 392-3
diplomatic premises, extraterritoriality **70,** 393-4
diplomatic privileges and immunities. *See also* consular privileges and immunities *above*
constitutional rights, proceedings for enforcement of **89,** 49-59
consular distinguished **89,** 52
counterclaim **89,** 51
entitlement **89,** 50
functional **89,** 52-3
executive certificate/statement, conclusiveness, consular privileges and immunities, entitlement **89,** 72
genocide in **119,** 340-2
Head of State, General Pinochet's status as **119,** 56-7, 94, 100
human rights **89,** 67-8, 69
alien, breach by **89,** 73
diplomatic immunity and **89,** 49-59
remedy for breach, right to **89,** 70
right of privacy **89,** 49, 73-7
internal armed conflict in **119,** 352
international law, as part of municipal law **65,** 30-1
law of
Civil Code **73,** 248-9
s 593 **89,** 79
s 595 **89,** 79
Civil Procedure Code
s 170 **89,** 57
s 182 **89,** 56
Code of Commerce **73,** 240
Customs Code **89,** 81, 82

Chile (*cont.*)
Decree-Law 2191 (1978) (Amnesty) **119,** 72-3, 86
universal jurisdiction and **119,** 344
Law No 666 (1967) (Vienna Convention on Diplomatic Relations (1961)) **65,** 30, **89,** 51
Law No 16,624 (1967) ('Copper Law') **59,** 412, 428-9
Law No 17,450 (1971) **73,** 235, 244, 249
Organization of the Courts Code **89,** 71, 79
s 537 **65,** 31
s 540 **65,** 31
s 541 **65,** 31
Penal Code, s 361(2) (rape) **121,** 270 n. 207
legislation, interpretation, aids, legislative history **89,** 54, 69
nationalization measures **59,** 378-83, 403-5, **65,** 58-60
compensation, whether obligation to pay **65,** 58-60
right of action
arbitrary or illegal act, need for **89,** 58, 59, 73, 74-7
continuing breach, need for **89,** 58, 59, 73, 74-7
standard of proof **89,** 58, 73-4
treaties, primacy **89,** 53-5, 69, 70
State immunity, jurisdiction, applicability, real/immovable property, dispute relating to, annulment of contract **65,** 30-1
State immunity, jurisdiction, procedural aspects, effective remedy, right to and **65,** 31
State immunity, jurisdiction, theory/doctrine
absolute theory **65,** 30-1
basis, equality of States **65,** 30
development of concept, codification **65,** 30
general principle of international law **65,** 30
State-owned corporation
expropriation/nationalization **59,** 378-83
government relations with **59,** 376-9
policy towards **59,** 376-9, 403-4
treaties
Constitution, primacy **89,** 53-4, 55, 69, 70
incorporation into municipal law **89,** 81-2
effect **89,** 82
Vienna Convention on Consular Relations (1961), interpretation, restrictive **89,** 66
Chile–USA International Commission (Letelier and Moffitt)
competence, determination of amount of damages **88,** 733, 739
establishment **88,** 730-2
China, People's Republic of. *See also* China, Republic of
aliens **40,** 200-2
China Ocean Shipping Company **63,** 355-8
Civil Aircraft, Flight Regulations **40,** 93
civil proceedings, foreign trade disputes **63,** 358-9
Constitution 1982, s 31 (special administrative regions) **114,** 394-5
equity **41,** 144
flag
adoption **122,** 578
Law on the National Flag 1990 **122,** 578-80. *See also* law of, Law on the National Flag 1990 *below*

International Amateur Athletic Federation, admission to **74,** 107-8
law of
Counter-Revolution, Regulation for Punishment of **40,** 201
Law on the National Flag 1990 **122,** 578-80
Art. 1 **122,** 578-9
Art. 2 **122,** 579
Art. 3 **122,** 579
Art. 17 **122,** 579
Art. 18 **122,** 579
Art. 19 **122,** 579
supplementary provision to the Criminal Law (1990) **122,** 579-80
Penal Code 1997, s 236 (rape) **121,** 270 n. 207
Punishment of Counter-Revolutionaries Law 1951 **47,** 109-12
leased territory, restoration by France **42,** 8-9
occupation of western provinces (Boxer Rebellion) **46,** 465 n. 8
recognition **55,** 64, **74,** 106-11, **84,** 153
withdrawal **55,** 64
State immunity, jurisdiction, theory/doctrine, absolute theory **84,** 152
sustainable development principle **116,** 114-15
China, Republic of. *See also* China, People's Republic of
Constitution **87,** 506
diplomatic relations, termination **96,** 86
freedom of religion **87,** 506
jurisdiction
nationals, crimes committed abroad **40,** 87-8
US forces in **40,** 86-7
law of
Criminal Law 1935 **43,** 177
Law on Deserting Seamen **43,** 177
National General Mobilization Law **43,** 177
People's Republic of China and **96,** 85-7
recognition, withdrawal **96,** 85-7
recognition, withdrawal
continuation of non-diplomatic relations **96,** 86
treaties, effect on **96,** 86-9
ships, State-owned, immunity, jurisdiction, merchant ships **40,** 84-5
treaties
Friendship and Navigation Treaty (US/Republic of China) (1946), validity **96,** 85-7
recognition, effect **96,** 86-9
choice of forum. *See* forum selection clause
choice of law clause 80, 383, **89,** 329, **96,** 262-6, **106,** 19, **107,** 266-7, **120,** 5
absence
in case of arbitration based on treaty provision **106,** 429
parties' conduct to determine **106,** 429, 476-7
act of State doctrine as **84,** 119, **87,** 186, **88,** 119
agreement between State entities **124,** 567
choice of forum as **107,** 350-1
choice of seat of tribunal as **106,** 529, **120,** 5
concession agreement **62,** 171, **66,** 520, 560-1
conflict with national law **96,** 262-3, 274-9
subsequent legislation and **96,** 265-6

choice of law clause (*cont.*)
contract
insurance **42,** 149-52
strike on board ship in port **87,** 97
waiver of immunity, whether **63,** 40, 198, 405-7, 520, 537
deviation from general conflict of laws rules **96,** 263
'equity and generally recognized principles of law and in particular international law' **96,** 262-6
ICJ Statute, Art. 38 and **96,** 265
failure to include **101,** 518
interest **106,** 642-3
lex fori **108,** 498
lex voluntatis **64,** 594
pacta sunt servanda **96,** 265-6
refinancing agreement **118,** 603
State contract **53,** 441-50, 451-2, 454, **62,** 169, 171-5, 190, 200, **117,** 559-60
applicable law **53,** 443
binding nature **53,** 443-4
as waiver of State immunity **63,** 40, 198, 357-8, 405-7, 520, 537, **87,** 232, 235, 414-15, **94,** 271, **101,** 490-1, **107,** 349-52, **113,** 538, **114,** 511, **120,** 614-16
choice of means. *See* margin of appreciation, choice of means
***Chorzów Factory* principle of reparation for wrong**
EC law and **111,** 94
expropriation/nationalization, compensation and **83,** 473, 565-6, 619-22, **95,** 314, **116,** 276, 410, **118,** 102-3, **120,** 199, **121,** 127-8
general principle of international law **121,** 127-8
restitutio in integrum **83,** 566, **88,** 733, **116,** 89, 276, 506, **121,** 127, 190, 191
church
status
capacity to sue/be sued **108,** 497
applicable law **108,** 497
incorporation, relevance **108,** 496-7
legal personality **47,** 24-5
separate legal entity **108,** 496-7
CITES. *See* Endangered Species of Wild Fauna and Flora, Convention on International Trade (CITES) (1973)
citizenship 60, 225-6, 241-6. *See also* nationality
competence of courts to determine **45,** 340-5
division of India, effect **45,** 335, 359
foreign passport, possession of and **53,** 521, 524
intention to reside permanently, relevance **45,** 330, 332, 333-8
loss of **45,** 348-9, 351, 361
voluntary relinquishment **53,** 525-6
religious belief, lack of and **43,** 187-91
civil aviation. *See also* air transport agreements; aircraft; carriage by air, international; Chicago Convention on Civil Aviation (1944); International Air Transport Association; Montreal Convention for the Suppression of Unlawful Acts Against the Safety of Civil Aviation (1971); Warsaw Convention on International Carriage by Air (1929) and Hague Protocol (1955)
fees for telecommunication and radio services **90,** 214-20
Chicago Convention on Civil Aviation (1944) **90,** 216-17
provisional suspension or variation of certificate **124,** 462-75

grounds for challenge
irrationality/unreasonableness **124,** 470-1
unfairness **124,** 467-70
civil law, State immunity, jurisdiction, theory/doctrine, development of concept **64,** 642-6
civil procedure
natural justice, fairness of proceedings **118,** 491-8
request for ruling on jurisdiction, evidence of existence of action **87,** 17
civil proceedings. *See* fair hearing; fair trial; procedural fairness
civil rights and obligations. *See* American Convention of Human Rights (1969); European Commission of Human Rights; European Convention on Human Rights (1950); European Court of Human Rights; human rights; Inter-American Court of Human Rights; International Covenant on Civil and Political Rights (ICCPR) (1966); United Nations Human Rights Committee (UNHRC)
civil strife 76, 448, 519-21. *See also* civil war
civil war distinguished **74,** 28
State, existence in case of **48,** 6-8
civil war 74, 22-8. *See also* civil strife; force, prohibition on threat or use of; rebellion; revolution; war
applicable law
Genocide Convention (1948) **115,** 28
laws and customs of war **99,** 78-9, **104,** 73-4, **105,** 444-50, 506-24
Spanish Civil War **105,** 507
customary international law **105,** 504-24
definition
civil commotion distinguished **74,** 28
civil strife distinguished **74,** 28
for insurance purposes **74,** 7-8, 22-8
international conflict distinguished **80,** 668-9
revolution distinguished **107,** 507, 516
under international law **74,** 22
extradition and **104,** 73-4
in
Algeria **44,** 439-41
America **39,** 121, 125-33, 137-40, 254-5, 365-8, 388-90, 394-6
Angola, insurance against war risks **82,** 109
Bosnia-Herzegovina. *See* Bosnia-Herzegovina, armed conflict
East Pakistan, insurance against war risks **82,** 108-9
Korea **41,** 19
Lebanon (1975-6) **74,** 14-21, 27-8, 32-5
Mozambique **107,** 507-16
Nicaragua, injuries to US national, right of civil action in US court **99,** 58-79
Spain **80,** 666-73
injuries to alien, right of civil action **99,** 68-9, 78-9
insurance against war risks **44,** 439-41, **74,** 7-8, 22-8, **82,** 108-9
international law, private support for rebel forces, whether contrary to **80,** 590-2
intervention by British Crown, effect under Patent Act **41,** 17
nationality of combatants **44,** 439
necessity and **70,** 22, 30
peaceful exercise of *effectivités*, compatibility with **114,** 69
recognition of **74,** 22
responsibility, individual **105,** 520-4, 537-8

claims 72, 133-40, 143-52, 284-9, **79,** 598. *See also* claims settlement agreements; diplomatic protection, extinction of claims against foreign State; Iran–US Claims Tribunal, claims; nationality of claims; reparations; United Nations Compensation Commission
administrative, judicial review **80,** 22 n. 7
advisory report distinguished **54,** 326
assignment **72,** 84-8, **73,** 378-9, **84,** 163
merger of creditor and debtor, effect **72,** 85-8
capacity to bring, substantive issue **46,** 206, 239, 400, 513-14, 529-30
concept **44,** 309
concurrent **46,** 212, 224, 304-5, 525
counterclaims **46,** 199
creditors' claims **42,** 155-8, 161-3, 186
against State wronging debtor **46,** 209, 424
damages, for. *See* damages
direct injury against State, definition **102,** 278-81
dispute, as element of **37,** 178, 179, 181
exhaustion of local remedies. *See* exhaustion of local remedies
force and **46,** 465
foreign nationals **74,** 281-4, 420-4, **79,** 593
grounds, damage or injury **106,** 57-8
individual's rights under international law **80,** 382
international character **74,** 258, 262, 266
international organization, Member States' failure to fund, Member State's right to claim on behalf of injured national **80,** 172-3
Iran–US. *See* Iran–US Claims Tribunal
Litvinov Assignment **84,** 162-4, 165, 175, 176, 177-8, 180 n. 11, 181
mass processing
practice of international tribunals **109,** 252-3
State practice **109,** 252-4
multiple recovery, measures to prevent **109,** 267-8, 477, 613-14
national against own government **52,** 7, **85,** 262-3, 265, 273
nationality of. *See* nationality of claims
private and governmental distinguished **47,** 420, 437, 438, 445
release from future **106,** 630, 649
representative claims **72,** 732-4
reprisals, effect **54,** 337-41
sampling methodology
European Commission of Human Rights **109,** 69-70
European Court of Human Rights **109,** 70
Iran–US Claims Tribunal **109,** 69
legal principle underlying **109,** 68
Mixed Claims Commissions **109,** 70-1
State practice
Australia **109,** 75
Canada **109,** 72
Finland **109,** 71 n. 14
Sweden **109,** 71 n. 14
UK **109,** 74-5
USA **109,** 72-4
UN Compensation Commission. *See* United Nations Compensation Commission, sampling methodology
service on government, need for **69,** 622-3, 631

shareholders in foreign companies **45,** 111-13
State control over private claims. *See* claims settlement agreements, State control over private claims
State responsibility. *See* State responsibility
State's right, individual's right as measure of **46,** 498, 509-10
waiver by State **40,** 184-6, **44,** 301-23, **45,** 436-45
Austrian State Treaty (1955)
individual claims **40,** 184-6, **44,** 316, **45,** 440
Peace Treaty with Hungary (1947) distinguished **45,** 300
compensation by national State **44,** 301, 312
debtor's cooperation **45,** 438
definition **44,** 315-16
Peace Treaty with Hungary (1947) **44,** 301-23, **45,** 436-45
Peace Treaty with Italy (1947) **40,** 64, 69-73
war claims **56,** 536-47
claims settlement agreements 48, 157, 159, 160-1, **72,** 284-9, **81,** 545, 576, **107,** 59-60. *See also* Bhopal gas leak disaster, settlement; diplomatic protection; Iran–US Claims Settlement Declaration; *and Index to the Consolidated Table of Treaties*
Belgium–France (1953) **69,** 667-71
bilateral character **69,** 669
foreign-owned company claim **69,** 667-71
claims under
dual national, right to benefit **90,** 221-8
nationals **72,** 284-9, **73,** 378-80, **74,** 282-9, **75,** 212-13, 225-6
public law nature **48,** 178
criminal liability, relevance **118,** 467, 469-70, 477-8, 499-500, 511, 523
customary international law **90,** 227
disclosure of details before finalization **118,** 500
distribution of compensation **45,** 111-13, **48,** 160-1, 177, 178, **118,** 501-2, 524
discretion of recipient State **46,** 276
extinction of claimant's rights against foreign State **65,** 50, **72,** 282-9, **84,** 90, **87,** 618, **107,** 59-60. *See also* payments under as property of State *below*
legal remedies of individual, effect on **82,** 65-6, 68-9
payment by government of less than full claims **84,** 163
payment of compensation to claimants
duty **84,** 95, **107,** 59-60, **108,** 612, 619
moral obligation **108,** 619
State responsibility **95,** 617, 623
'taking of property' **72,** 150-2, 291-2
US embassy hostages **72,** 134, 137-40, 143-50
Foreign Claims Commission, role **90,** 223
German External Debts Agreement (1953). *See* German External Debts Agreement (1953)
implementation machinery **107,** 472
implementing legislation, interpretation **90,** 221-8
Indonesia–Netherlands **74,** 284-9
lump sum settlement **62,** 205-6, 210, **67,** 375-6, **72,** 285-7, **73,** 378-9, **74,** 282-9
nationalized assets **67,** 375-6
payments under as property of State **108,** 612-14, 618-20. *See also* extinction of claimant's rights against foreign State *above*
contractual agreement relating to disposal **108,** 620

claims settlement agreements (*cont.*)
Restatement of Foreign Relations Law (Third) **108,** 612
treaty, relevance **108,** 612-14, 618
property taken by third States **48,** 175-7
shareholders, provisions concerning **46,** 214, 341, 451-2, 480, 518
State control over private claims **42,** 186-9, **65,** 50, 278-9, 302-3, **84,** 93
nullification of attachment of foreign assets **72,** 274-82
third party interests **118,** 468-9, 497
claims settlement tribunals. *See also* claims settlement agreements; international tribunals; Iran–US Claims Tribunal
Anglo-Italian Conciliation Commission
expert, use of **40,** 269, 283-8
jurisdiction **40,** 439, 441-2
Arbitral Commission on Property Rights and Interests in Germany. *See* Arbitral Commission on Property Rights and Interests in Germany
Canada–US International Joint Commission **73,** 167-72
Chile–USA International Commission (Letelier and Moffitt). *See* Chile–USA International Commission (Letelier and Moffitt)
Conciliation Commission (Italian Peace Treaty) **77,** 566
French–Mexican Claims Commission **78,** 673
German–Mexican Claims Commission **69,** 613
Iran–US Claims Tribunal. *See* Iran–US Claims Tribunal
Mexico–United Kingdom Claims Commission **69,** 612-13
United States–Mexico General Claims Commission **69,** 612, **71,** 653, 655-7
class/representative action 37, 111, 138, **95,** 574, **112,** 507, 647, **118,** 332, 365, **120,** 576-7
clean hands. *See* equity, clean hands
clearing agreements, purchase contract and **47,** 41-3, 44-5
closed sea. *See* continental shelf delimitation, closed sea
closed shop agreement. *See* European Convention on Human Rights (1950), trade union; trade union; United Kingdom, British Rail
co-belligerency
Croatia and Bosnia-Herzegovina, whether **122,** 60-3
diplomatic relations and **122,** 61, 62-3
evidence of **122,** 61-2
protection under the Geneva Convention (IV) **122,** 60-4
co-imperium 52, 19
coastal configuration 41, 49, 50, 75, 83, 109-10, 111, 151, 153, 156, 161, 178, 180, 194, 227, **71,** 114, 149, 157-8, 160, 201, **81,** 289, 296, 316, 376, 414, 3741.6, **83,** 95, 117
amplification effect **41,** 78
bays, closing line **69,** 65
changes in direction **71,** 86, 89, 95, 147, 151-2, 157-8, 160
coastal irregularities **81,** 393
coastal length **81,** 376, **99,** 488-94
concave coastline **71,** 86, 89, 111, 114, 162
Dahlak Islands as integral part of **119,** 459-60
distorting effect **81,** 276, 380, **99,** 556-8
geographical **81,** 380
islands and **83,** 109
Malta **81,** 282-3, 370-1
territorial sea, relative effect **41,** 47, 66-7

coastal facade, continental shelf delimitation **81,** 366-7, 393-5
coastal front 67, 55-6, 75, 79-82, 85-6, 100, 142, 251, 311
continental shelf delimitation **81,** 315-16
extension. *See* continental shelf, natural prolongation
coastal opening, continental shelf rights and **81,** 273
coastal State
bays
closing line, coastal State practice **97,** 520
evidence of, coastal State practice **97,** 506
interests **97,** 507-8
pluri-State, right of access **97,** 510
continental shelf
duties **81,** 303
rights **81,** 296
delimitation of sea areas, opposability **56,** 164
disputes affecting sovereign rights under UNCLOS (1982) **119,** 552-3, 563
EEZ, duties **81,** 303
exclusive fishing zone (EFZ)
inherent right to manage biological resources **82,** 612, 618, 627, 669
administrative function **82,** 628
conservation required objective **82,** 628, 641-4
exercise in general interest **82,** 628
fisheries
conservation measures **56,** 149-51, 191-2
jurisdiction **56,** 86, 132
exclusive **55,** 280-7
preferential rights **55,** 171-5, 258-63, 265-8, 275, 333, **56,** 159, 164-7, 168-9, 220
regulatory authority
protection of fishery **82,** 658
public authority **82,** 658
relation to **55,** 308-9, 344
sovereign rights over **55,** 223-5, 309
high seas
responsibilities of, private acts **71,** 259-61
rights **56,** 119, 132
private acts **71,** 259-61
jurisdiction, ship **87,** 96-7
licensing of foreign vessels, sovereign right **82,** 631
rights
contiguous zone **56,** 117
powers **71,** 260, **74,** 210-12
continental shelf **41,** 58-61, 62, 125, 126, 128, 173, 189, 191, 220, **55,** 170-5, 218, 345, **56,** 85, 119-20, 131, **57,** 147, **67,** 39, 41, 54, 116-17, 166-77, 183-5, 214-15, **70,** 616-17, 684, 688, **71,** 92, 123, 193
customary international law and **41,** 51, 188, 191, **71,** 260, **74,** 206-12
Continental Shelf Convention (1958)
fisheries **56,** 119, 132
sovereign **56,** 119
economic zone **56,** 192
fisheries **55,** 171-5, 223-5, 258-63, 265-8, 275, 333, **56,** 86, 119, 132, 159, 164-7, 168-9, 220

coastal State (*cont.*)
high seas **56,** 117
maritime **71,** 92, 123, 139, 165, 193
patrimonial sea **56,** 90
territorial sea **56,** 116-17, 119-20
Timor Gap, Portugal **105,** 251-4, 259
coastal waters
'coastal sea' **125,** 329, 370-1, 412, 450-1, 459
as 'territorial sea' **120,** 635, **125,** 329, 412
coastline
artificial structures, effect **42,** 98, **57,** 92-4
curvature **81,** 316, **83,** 117
definition **57,** 92, 108, **91,** 413-14
low-water mark **91,** 414, 431
harbours **57,** 88-9, 92, **59,** 210-11, 218-20, 225-7
length **71,** 86, 89, 98, 149-50, 155, 161-4, 180, **81,** 275, 281, 341-3, 353, 419, **83,** 95, 96, 97, 100, 113, 116, 117, **95,** 661, 707-11. *See also* proportionality, maritime delimitation
'following general direction' **77,** 678-9
general direction **95,** 708-9
islands, coastal **77,** 679
islands, scattered **77,** 679
long **77,** 683
measurement. *See* measurement *below*
short **77,** 683
measurement **81,** 304, 342
subjective nature **81,** 342
US Submerged Lands Act **42,** 87
coasts
adjacency **83,** 117
capacity to generate maritime space **83,** 98, 116
change of direction **81,** 316, 443, 454-5, 477-8, **83,** 117
definition, dictionary **94,** 244-5, **95,** 660-3
determination **81,** 281-3, 285, 292
third-State claims and **81,** 282, 285, **99,** 436
distance between **81,** 284, 288, 289, 331-5, 343, 413, 414, 419
general direction **71,** 85, 89-90, 113-15, 140, 144, 146-7, **81,** 304, 316, 394, **83,** 95, 97, **91,** 657, **95,** 708-9
geographical context **81,** 272
indentations **81,** 316, **83,** 117
irregularities **81,** 316
islands and. *See* islands
maritime areas, relationship to **71,** 85, 88, 139-40, 146-7, 157, 207
maritime jurisdiction, capacity to generate **81,** 315
occlusion **81,** 311
opposite **83,** 117
third State, relevance **81,** 312-13
opposite and adjacent
distinction disappearing **81,** 270
equidistance **81,** 283, 342, 371-2
position **81,** 282
primary and secondary coasts, whether distinguishable **71,** 98, 125, 147, 180

projection **81,** 316
proportionality. *See* proportionality, maritime delimitation
radial projection **81,** 308, 310-13, 350
closed sea, in **81,** 310-13, 345
State practice **81,** 310-13, **95,** 686
relationship **81,** 289, 316, 411-14. *See also* adjacency; opposite *and* opposite and adjacent *above*
relevance **81,** 342
relevant **81,** 292, 306, 349-50, **83,** 95, 96-7, 98-9
Anglo-French Arbitration **95,** 710-11
facing area to be delimited **95,** 710
Jan Mayen **99,** 436
leap-frogging **95,** 710-11
role **81,** 272, 275, 306
salients **83,** 117
seacoast, limitation to **94,** 244-6
shore distinguished **80,** 329
special geographic factor, whether **95,** 704
Coccejus, Grotius, commentary on **39,** 119-21
Cocos (Keeling) Islands. *See* Australia, Cocos (Keeling) Islands
codification. *See* customary international law, codification
coercion 71, 244, 254. *See also* duress; force, prohibition on threat or use of
coexistence
'generally recognized rules of international law serving peaceful coexistence and cooperation between peoples' **100,** 382-9
Vitoria and Grotius on **37,** 30
coffee. *See* International Coffee Agreement (1962); International Coffee Council
cohabitation
duty **58,** 630
family life, respect for **58,** 641, 650, **92,** 311-12, 341, 372-3
right of spouses **61,** 399
collective agreements
discrimination **58,** 35
right to conclude **58,** 31-2, 33
freedom of assembly/association and **58,** 31-2, 33
collective security system 76, 62
collective self-defence, distinction **106,** 329
definition **106,** 328
absence **106,** 328
inchoate state **106,** 340-1, **110,** 258
legal interest of all States **76,** 62-4
legislative consent, need for
approval of constituent treaty as **106,** 331, 341, 346-7
prior **106,** 330
programme of integration, agreement to **106,** 381-7
NATO **106,** 330, 369
preservation of peace between members, limitation to **106,** 328
reciprocity of rights and obligations **106,** 329
sovereignty, surrender **106,** 329-30, 331-2
UN **106,** 329, 331
peacekeeping forces as part of **106,** 331, 346-7
collective self-defence. *See* self-defence

collisions at sea. *See also* wrecks
applicable law
International Regulations (1948) **65,** 107, **70,** 478-9
Netherlands–USSR Agreement on Merchant Shipping (1969) **65,** 365-7
EEZ **89,** 78-80
jurisdiction
Convention for the Unification of Certain Rules relating to Penal Jurisdiction in Matters of Collision or Other Incidents of Navigation (1952) **78,** 119
EEZ **89,** 78-80
national in foreign territorial waters **78,** 118-29
State-owned ships **63,** 14-15, 605-12, **64,** 179, **65,** 101-7, 365-7
collisions in internal waters, applicable law, international convention **74,** 3-4
Colombia
appeal rights **71,** 320-3, 328
Compania National de Navigation (Navenal) **63,** 77-8
Constitution 1886 (as amended)
s 26 **71,** 325
s 58 **71,** 326
s 121 **70,** 244, **71,** 320
s 170 **71,** 326
detainees, rights **71,** 319, 321-3, 325-31
disappearances **118,** 290-1
fair trial **71,** 319, 321-2, 324-31
freedom from discrimination, English-speaking protestants, treatment of **96,** 705-6
habeas corpus **71,** 323, 326, 330
human rights, compensation provision **71,** 323
law of. *See also* Constitution 1886 (as amended) *above*
Administrative Code, s 67 **71,** 323
Amnesty Law No 35 of 1982 **94,** 435
Criminal Procedure Code
s 417 **71,** 323, 325-6
s 426 **71,** 325
s 573 **71,** 328
s 580 **71,** 328
s 584 **71,** 328
Decree No 0070 of 1978 **70,** 268-81
Decree No 1923 of 1978 (Security Statute) **70,** 242-8, **71,** 319-37
constitutionality **71,** 320, 325, 328-9
text **71,** 331-7
Decree No 2260 of 1976 **71,** 322, 328
Military Criminal Justice Code
s 108 **71,** 327
s 125 **71,** 327
s 272 **71,** 327
s 309 **71,** 323
Security Statute. *See* Decree No 1923 of 1978 (Security Statute) *above*
military courts, criminal jurisdiction **70,** 242-8, **71,** 320-1, 323, 325-30
police, powers of **70,** 268-81
political question doctrine, state of exception **123,** 149-50
state of siege **71,** 320-2, 326, 329
individual rights, effect on **71,** 321-2, 324, 329
torture **118,** 291

colonies
applicable law **72,** 204-8, **123,** 583-4
authority in **78,** 491-500
Crown prerogative **43,** 130-40, **44,** 110, 113, 117, 127-8, **123,** 557-8, 585-7, 590, 591-2
decolonization **59,** 97-8, 127, **76,** 684-6. *See also* independence, accession to *below*; Western Sahara, decolonization
General Assembly Resolution 1514 (XV) **46,** 464, 478, 484, 485, 488, **49,** 21, 64, **59,** 46-54, 97-8, 139, 183-4, 186-7, **79,** 263, **80,** 554
methods **59,** 97-9
procedures **59,** 97-8, 127
right of **59,** 46-54, 127, 137-9
self-determination **59,** 48-9, 51-3, 127, 138-9
uti possidetis and **80,** 471
fundamental rights **41,** 139
independence, accession to **52,** 87, **70,** 3-15, **72,** 54-8, 65-75, 256, **73,** 33-5, 45-8, 53-4, **83,** 52 n. 19, **87,** 80-1. *See also* State succession; United Nations General Assembly Resolutions, 1514 (XV) (Declaration on the Granting of Independence to Colonial Countries and Peoples)
acquired rights, effect on **73,** 33-5, 37
act of God **47,** 102-4
Angola **118,** 534
Comoros Islands, unilateral declaration **74,** 92
consultation of population
Comoros **74,** 93-4
East Timor **105,** 276-9
New Caledonia **89,** 19-22
debts, liability for **42,** 8-25, **45,** 24-32, **47,** 75-8, **69,** 25-8
French Indo-China **47,** 97-9
interim jurisdiction **71,** 220-1
internal constitutional matters **42,** 11-26
jurisdiction
ecclesiastical courts in Morocco **45,** 53-6
events prior to independence **42,** 11-26, **48,** 61-2
transfer of **47,** 92-4
Lithuania **115,** 622
nationality of companies, effect on **72,** 567-8
pension rights **69,** 29-30
restoration of sovereignty doctrine **50,** 471
social security functions **71,** 220-1
State obligations, effect on **72,** 54-8, 256, **74,** 98-100. *See also* State succession
status before **41,** 388
treaty obligations **70,** 3-15, **71,** 48-9, **72,** 65-74, **73,** 45-8, 53-4, **74,** 116-17, **87,** 314. *See also* treaties, State succession
jurisdiction, UK courts **123,** 569-75, 591-2
legislative powers **69,** 114-15, **84,** 72-3, **123,** 584-91
agent/delegate status of legislature **123,** 584-5
peace, order and good government **123,** 584, 587-91, 592-3
source **123,** 585-7
within competence and jurisdiction **123,** 585
protection of nationals of **78,** 491-500
restoration of sovereignty doctrine **50,** 471

colonies (*cont.*)
sovereignty **39,** 384, **52,** 50, **59,** 162
colonies held in trust **50,** 471
following unilateral declaration of independence **72,** 33-51
restoration of **50,** 471
territorial competence **69,** 89-90
treaties, extension to **83,** 75-6
unilateral declaration of independence, effect **72,** 33-51, **74,** 92-4, **78,** 491-500
State succession **68,** 3-6
colonization
legality **46,** 483
nature **59,** 186
COMECON
dispute settlement under **116,** 166
effect of disappearance on treaty obligations **116,** 203-4, 209-10
comity 52, 297, **54,** 283, **57,** 134, 137-8, **59,** 469, **60,** 82-3, **61,** 77, 78, 147, **63,** 645, **78,** 452, 607, **88,** 65, 262, 308-10. *See also* customary international law; foreign relations; international law; State practice; usage
access to ports **77,** 182
act of State **63,** 187, **64,** 260, **66,** 105-8, 160-1, 189, **81,** 633, **84,** 130, 195, **86,** 139, **88,** 65, 97, 99, **92,** 389, 474, **112,** 740-3, **119,** 73-4
bankruptcy proceedings, power to require person to appear for examination **88,** 316
choice of law and **100,** 599
consular premises, exemption from taxes **53,** 547
courtesy. *See* international courtesy and *below*
criminal law **55,** 127-8, 130, 135, **57,** 136-7, 138
default judgment, failure to serve correctly **118,** 616
definition **42,** 22, **64,** 260, **107,** 425
customary international law distinguished **70,** 401-4
diplomatic privileges and immunities **121,** 379
inviolability of embassy documents **86,** 141-3
termination **101,** 311-12
disclosure of documents and **64,** 280
effects doctrine **96,** 182, 183, 187, 197
extradition **51,** 272, 274, **55,** 23-4, 35, **59,** 74, **74,** 480, **79,** 494, 546, **85,** 115-16, **87,** 164, **98,** 416, 420, **104,** 10, 115, **119,** 305-6
consultation with requesting State **119,** 308-9
death penalty and **124,** 323-4, 341
extraterritorial legislation **91,** 97, **96,** 133-4, **100,** 586-7, 599, 601
in federal State **98,** 8
forcible abduction/unlawful arrest, judicial enquiry into **95,** 403-4, 408
foreign currency, circulation **111,** 593, 598-9, 602-3
foreign judgments, recognition **66,** 156, **73,** 5
foreign law, breach **104,** 536
foreign law, recognition/enforcement **42,** 22-3, 27, 104, **80,** 35, **88,** 308, 310, **104,** 507, **108,** 592
fugitive offenders, detention **55,** 19-20
guardianship decrees, recognition **42,** 27
Head of State immunity and **103,** 585, **119,** 45, 62, 97, **121,** 572-3, 642
injunction and **118,** 415
international courtesy and **64,** 13-17, 39, 49, **80,** 399

international law enforcement and **84,** 174
pronouncement on legality of act of third State **123,** 605
international organizations
immunity **80,** 34-5
municipal law, subjection to **80,** 93
judicial assistance **57,** 167, **86,** 182
in absence of agreement **90,** 411
service of process and **90,** 459
jurisdiction **73,** 265-6, 300, 324, **84,** 50, 677, 684-6, 694-5, 698-9
aliens, construction in favour of **80,** 29
concurrent **57,** 166
examination of foreign witness abroad **90,** 410
extraterritorial **66,** 172, 282-6, 382-3, 493-7, 501-2
impugnment of foreign constitution **42,** 21, 22-3, 25-6
territorial **104,** 326
justiciability **108,** 576, **111,** 598-9, 602-3, **112,** 740
law of the flag and **57,** 164-5
letters rogatory and **73,** 300, 324
municipal law, international law, consistency with **42,** 457
national interest overriding **83,** 265
nationality and **56,** 561
par in parem non habet jurisdictionem. See equality of States *above*
piercing the corporate veil **103,** 500
reciprocity **111,** 598
recognition
foreign corporation **85,** 6-7, 8
foreign legal body **83,** 265, 271-2
international organization **85,** 12, 19, **107,** 424-6
sanctions for non-observance **70,** 402
service of process on foreign State or State agency **90,** 459
State agency/State-owned corporation/State entity, independence **80,** 576, **107,** 379-80
State immunity, execution/attachment **65,** 56, 76-7, 80, 171, 174
State immunity, jurisdiction **42,** 22-3, **63,** 218, 249, 506, **64,** 13-17, 39, 54, 85, 135, 150, 279, 401, 407, 415-16, 421, 456, 595, 666, **65,** 34, 157, 255, 321, 326, 340, **77,** 265, **79,** 6, 11, 552, **80,** 3-4, 30, 33-4, 576, 591, 791, **84,** 20-1, 117, 130, 150, 169-70, 172, 190, **86,** 651, **88,** 193, **92,** 444, 512, **94,** 291, **95,** 476, **101,** 195, **103,** 617, 620, **104,** 517, 557, 570, 576, 586, 616, 624, **107,** 381, **119,** 45, **121,** 639
State immunity, taxation **65,** 321
stay of proceedings in case of concurrent jurisdiction **106,** 529, **118,** 413-14
substance and form **42,** 23
surrender of fugitive from justice **90,** 677
treaty application and **74,** 117
commercial law
banking usages. *See* banking practice
general principles of **84,** 552
maintenance of enterprise principle **37,** 439
commercial relations. *See* commercial/trade representation/mission; European Community (EC); economic relations; General Agreement on Tariffs and Trade (GATT) (1947); most favoured nation (MFN) treatment; Uruguay Round; World Trade Organization (WTO)

commercial/trade representation/mission
applicable law, *lex loci contractus* **64,** 592-4
diplomatic privileges and immunities **64,** 590-3, **74,** 518-19, **99,** 103-12
recognition of State/government, relevance **65,** 56
State immunity, execution/attachment **65,** 55-6, 179-80, 187, 210-11
State immunity, jurisdiction **64,** 590-3, 651-2, **65,** 1, 55-6, 177, 179-80, 210, 283, 313-15, **99,** 103-12
Romania **65,** 313-15
status
agent of State **64,** 591-2
applicable law **64,** 590-4
diplomatic agent **99,** 106
diplomatic mission **64,** 591
private merchant **64,** 591-3
service of process as evidence of **65,** 56
State organ **64,** 592-3
treaty provision **64,** 590-3
Vietnam, Democratic Republic **65,** 55-6
commodity agreements. *See* International Coffee Agreement (1962); International Tin Council (ITC); Natural Rubber Agreement (1979); *and the Index to the Consolidated Table of Treaties*
Common Foreign and Security Policy (CFSP). *See also* European Union (EU)
common commercial policy and **117,** 516-18, 540-2
decision to offer aid to Macedonia, whether **100,** 241
ECJ jurisdiction **100,** 238
fundamental rights, effect **98,** 217
national measures **100,** 238
in accordance with EC law **117,** 516-18, 541
transfer of prerogative powers, whether **98,** 177-9
Common Fund for Commodities 77, 89
common heritage of mankind 83, 90. *See also* environment; natural resources
res communis [omnium] **41,** 125, 173, 179, **55,** 204-5, **56,** 116-17, 181, **57,** 459, **71,** 259
common law
aboriginal rights/native title **73,** 142-3, 153, **112,** 435-6, 446, 505, 525-7, 530, 539, 547, 552, 561-2, **118,** 328-30, **125,** 341-4, 355-6, 362-4, 377-8
admiralty jurisdiction and **125,** 394-6
application by former dependent territory **86,** 643, 647-8, 650, 677-9
constitution, conformity with **125,** 414
definition **87,** 233-4
development in conformity with international law **112,** 482, 490
Optional Protocol to the International Covenant on Civil and Political Rights (ICCPR) (1966), effect of signature **112,** 491
differing interpretations **43,** 55
equity and **41,** 144
freedom of navigation **125,** 423-5
human/fundamental rights and **118,** 374, **125,** 441-2
European Convention on Human Rights (1950) and **41,** 313-14
international organizations, privileges and immunities **86,** 672
jurisdiction and
local and transitory actions distinguished **125,** 389-94
territorial sea, applicability in **125,** 334-42, 366-7, 380-407, 455-9

martial law **87,** 276
necessity **118,** 490
pre-trial procedure **41,** 284, 313, 344
private international law and **125,** 396-8
reception into African law **87,** 116-18
Roman–Dutch **82,** 484
self-incrimination **104,** 582-3, 607
source, treaty **104,** 431, 472, 494
State immunity, jurisdiction **63,** 644, 645, **64,** 419, **80,** 122, **86,** 643, 647-8, **87,** 234, **94,** 276-8, **104,** 510, 514, 520-2, 524-5, **107,** 354-8, **111,** 606
employment contract, locally engaged staff, diplomatic mission **64,** 357-63
State immunity, jurisdiction, acts of, armed forces **119,** 371, 373, 374-5, 380, 381-2
State immunity, jurisdiction, theory/doctrine **87,** 234, 237-8, **94,** 276-7, **104,** 524-5
restrictive theory **94,** 277-8
statutory law, conformity with **125,** 414
supremacy of **39,** 358
torture **119,** 189
common law offence **79,** 95, 100, **120,** 372, 399-405
common purpose. *See also* conspiracy; Yugoslavia, International Criminal Tribunal for the Former (ICTY), Statute, 7(1) (individual responsibility: direct participation)
Convention for the Suppression of Terrorist Bombing (1997) **124,** 154-5
crimes against humanity **124,** 136-62
International Criminal Court (ICC), Rome Statute (1998) **124,** 155-6
State practice **124,** 139, 156-9
Commonwealth. *See* British Commonwealth
communications. *See also* correspondence; telephone-tapping
International Telecommunications Union (ITU) **77,** 422
sovereign right to regulate **77,** 422
Comoros Islands
independence
consultation of population **74,** 93-4
unilateral declaration **74,** 92
United Nations, admission to **74,** 92-3
Compagnie Nationale Algérienne de Navigation. *See* Algeria, Compagnie Nationale Algérienne de Navigation
Compañia National de Navigation (Navenal). *See* Colombia, Compañia National de Navigation (Navenal)
Compañia Pervana de Vapores, SA. *See* Peru, Compañia Pervana de Vapores, SA
companies. *See* corporation
company law
general principles of **84,** 390-1, 392, 393-5
scope **46,** 295
compensation. *See* American Convention on Human Rights (1969), compensation; compensation for war-related events; costs; damages; expropriation/nationalization, compensation; interest; international officials, compensation; just satisfaction (Art. 50 [41] of the European Convention on Human Rights (1950)); measure of damages/compensation including valuation of company/property/assets; remedies; reparation; United Nations Compensation Commission
compensation for war-related events. *See also* claims settlement agreements; United Nations Compensation Commission
aerial bombardment **80,** 20-4
Bretton Woods Agreement **42,** 410, 431-2

compensation for war-related events (*cont.*)
copyright infringement **40,** 427
customary international law **61,** 166, 170, 173-8
disability pension, for injuries in 'connection with the Second World War' **90,** 403
expropriation/nationalization by occupying/administering power
acts not attributable to compensating State **94,** 61-2
discretionary element **94,** 61-2
equalization of burdens **94,** 61-2
individual entitlement, whether **94,** 62-3
reparations distinguished **61,** 50 n. 21, **94,** 51
expropriation/nationalization/confiscation of enemy property **41,** 11-12, **48,** 467-9, **56,** 332-4
as reparation **74,** 153-4, **94,** 51
German reparations
Dawes Plan **47,** 418-19, 426-7, 437-8, 443, 449, 456, 458
London Agreement on German External Debts (1953), deferment of claims **41,** 481, **61,** 235-6
Paris Agreement (1946) **42,** 432-3, **69,** 670
German enemy assets, disposal of **44,** 487-90
individual claims, limitations on **44,** 315
monetary gold **44,** 449, 452, 459, 461, 462-3, 469-70, 472, 475, 476, 484-5
Protocol, Italy and **44,** 452
Tripartite Commission for the Restitution of Monetary Gold **44,** 448-9, 453, 455, 457, 459, 461, 466-70, 471-2, 483, 484
Paris Reparations Agreement (1946)
individual's rights under **56,** 544-5
national treatment to nationals of other contracting States, recommendation for **69,** 670-1
reparations, rights reserved **44,** 462, 478
reparations payable by Germany, limitation to **69,** 671
post-war expropriation
as **94,** 51
distinguished **61,** 50 n. 21
postponement of settlement (London Agreement on German External Debts (1953)), right of individual to compensation for **41,** 480-2
Settlement Convention (1952/4)
internal restitution (Chapter III) and compensation for Nazi persecution (Chapter IV) distinguished **44,** 317-21
reparations, acceptance of measures taken by allies (Chapter VI) **42,** 435
restoration of foreign rights and interests (Chapter X) **42,** 405-8, 489
State succession and **96,** 728-9
World War I **59,** 504-6
value of ceded colonies **49,** 199
World War II **59,** 506-16, 552-60, 598-601
Italy, Peace Treaty (1947) **45,** 500-2, **77,** 563-6
'arrangement' in lieu of compensation **40,** 106, 107, 109
individuals' rights under **77,** 563-6
monetary gold provisions **44,** 448-85
nationality of claim
continuity **77,** 566
nationality of company **45,** 109-10
'owner' and 'successor' **40,** 450, 461

pillage, claims for **40,** 261, 264, 267, 269, 271, 281-2
'property, rights and interests' **40,** 278-9
mining concession **40,** 261, 262, 266-7, 277-81
restitution provisions **40,** 255, 257, 441, 461, **44,** 448-85
limits of obligation **44,** 480
looted property and monetary gold **44,** 448-50, 477-9, 482-3
monetary gold, good faith transactions **44,** 458
shareholders' claims **40,** 144-6
stateless person **77,** 566
waiver of claims **40,** 64, 69-73
war damage
assessment **40,** 147, 164-8, 262, 283
compensation for **40,** 103-11, 129, 457-8
military operations
destruction of property **41,** 11-12
losses arising out of **48,** 467-9, **106,** 451-2
Nazi persecution **70,** 693, **72,** 448, 457, 472, 647-50, **74,** 281-4, 420-4
occupation, damages caused by **90,** 406
occupied territory, State responsibility **70,** 697-8
'owing to war or other armed conflict, revolution, a state of national emergency, revolt, insurrection or riot' **106,** 441, 451
pillage **40,** 261, 264, 267, 269, 271, 281-2
prisoner of war, compensation for earnings as **61,** 235-6, 237
Geneva Convention (Treatment of Prisoners of War) (Convention III) (1949) **61,** 235, 236
Hague Convention No IV on the Laws and Customs of War on Land (1907) **61,** 234-5
private property, loss or damage **56,** 542, 544-5, **69,** 667-71
reciprocity, need for **69,** 669-71
United Nations nationals, entitlement **77,** 563-6
requisition, Hague Convention concerning the Laws and Customs of War on Land (1899) **77,** 566
requisition of private property **56,** 525-6, **72,** 237-8, **84,** 409
substitution of responsibility in post-war agreement **72,** 237-8
requisition of ships
under international law **56,** 525-6
warship **56,** 525-6
restitution of looted property **44,** 448-85
Bretton Woods Agreement (1944) and **42,** 431-2
State responsibility **40,** 103-11, **94,** 61-2
substitution of responsibility in post-war agreement **72,** 237-8
State succession and **96,** 728-9
US Foreign Claims Settlement Commission. *See* United States of America (USA), Foreign Claims Settlement Commission
victims of persecution **74,** 281-4, 420-4
war damage **41,** 12
France–Monaco Agreement (1954) **47,** 312-27
competition. *See also* antitrust legislation; European Community (EC), anti-dumping measures; European Community (EC), common commercial policy; General Agreement on Tariffs and Trade (GATT) (1947), Anti-Dumping Implementation Code (1980); restrictive practices
applicable law, place of implementation **96,** 196

competition (*cont.*)
concerted practices, EEC **48,** 106, 108, 123, 124, 127-34
exclusive dealing contract, EEC **44,** 393-408
public law character **48,** 109, 114, 115
quantitative restrictions, measures with equivalent effect **48,** 233-6
restraint of trade
agreements **52,** 292, 296
legislation, public law character **48,** 109, 114, 115
restrictive practices, EEC Treaty **44,** 393-408
unfair
freedom of expression and **101,** 81-95
margin of appreciation **81,** 219, 226
participation agreements and **118,** 622-36
voluntary import restrictions, as international agreement **61,** 7-9, 12, 13-15, 17-18, 21, 25
compliance. *See* European Community treaties, compliance; European Court of Human Rights, judgment, compliance; European Court of Justice (ECJ), judgment, compliance; International Court of Justice (ICJ), judgment, compliance; International Court of Justice (ICJ), provisional measures, compliance; treaties, compliance; United Nations Security Council Resolutions, compliance
compromissory clause/*compromis* 77, 642-5. *See also* International Court of Justice (ICJ), consent to jurisdiction, compromissory clause; Mandates, compromissory clause
dispute settlement convention distinguished **84,** 267-8
exhaustion of local remedies and **84,** 348
FCN treaties **84,** 348
interpretation, responsibility of tribunal **38,** 23, 75, **77,** 656
need for **37,** 146, 201
compulsory jurisdiction. *See* European Convention for the Peaceful Settlement of Disputes (1957), compulsory jurisdiction of the ICJ and; European Court of Human Rights, jurisdiction, compulsory; International Court of Justice (ICJ), compulsory jurisdiction, acceptance
Conception Bay 43, 105, **97,** 653
concert of Europe, collective negotiation with **37,** 89
concession agreement 83, 502-638, **86,** 298-9. *See also* cooperation agreement; economic development agreement; joint exploitation agreement; State contract
as act of State **66,** 182, **81,** 527
revocation **66,** 148-50, 182, 189-91, 292, 343-5, 583, 592-3, 624-5, **69,** 9
as *acta jure imperii* **47,** 139-41, 147-9
amendment, consent to **62,** 154, 170. *See also* Libya, law of, Petroleum Law 25 1955
Aminoil concession, 'Abu Dhabi Formula', application to **66,** 555, 572-82, 620-1
applicable law **47,** 396, 399-400, 403-4, 494, **62,** 171-3, 176, **66,** 133-4, **77,** 44, 51
law of State party **53,** 397-8
boundaries, effect **81,** 254, 260-1
breach by government, State immunity, jurisdiction **63,** 166-9, 233-5
cancellation. *See* termination *below*
choice of law clause **66,** 520, 560-1
colonial nature **66,** 587
conclusion
State-owned company
applicable law **47,** 396, 399-400, 403-4
by, *acta jure imperii*, whether **47,** 138-49
construction concession **66,** 343-5, 364-5
continental shelf **81,** 254

continental shelf delimitation and **81,** 260-1
contractual nature **53,** 438-41, **62,** 156, 169-70, **66,** 583, 592-3, 624-5
delimitation, effect on **81,** 260-1
dispute settlement, parties' intention **62,** 179
economic value **62,** 203
evolution of terms
  acquiescence or conduct of parties **66,** 588, 590-1, 626-7
  stabilization clauses, effect on **66,** 590-1, 594, 626-7
  State dominance **66,** 590-1
extension **66,** 182
  war damage compensation and **40,** 103-11
force majeure, war **40,** 267, 272, 283
fundamental breach **62,** 147, 181, 199
grant, as sovereign act **66,** 182, **81,** 527
implementation **62,** 179
impossibility of performance **42,** 8-9
incorporeal property **62,** 189, 196
interpretation **62,** 179
labour, Government's assistance to secure **36,** 415-16, 418, 423-4
minerals **59,** 425
mining, property, whether **40,** 266, 273
modification **62,** 159-60
municipal law requirements **44,** 194
nationalization. *See* confiscation; expropriation/nationalization
nature of **62,** 169, 189
negotiation clauses
  deadlocked negotiations **66,** 592
  nature of duty **66,** 565-6, 578
oil concessions. *See also* Kuwait, Aminoil concession; Libya, oil concessions; Mexico, oil concessions; Red Sea Islands, oil concessions; Venezuela, oil concessions
  administrative contract **66,** 588-91
  Arbitration Agreement **66,** 532-5, 559, 561
  arbitration clause **66,** 593-4
  cancellation **63,** 166-7, 233
  colonial nature **66,** 587
  confiscation **60,** 129
  Deeds of Concession **53,** 314, 319-22, 324, 327, 422-3, 437-8
    amendment **53,** 393-4
  Ethiopia/Eritrea **114,** 110-14, 126, **119,** 443-6
  exploration concessions, continental shelf delimitation and **81,** 254
  gold clause **66,** 547-8, 610
  'good oilfield practice' **66,** 552, 596-9
    nature of obligation **66,** 597-9
  Middle Eastern, general trends **66,** 563-4, 572-3
  sovereignty **114,** 100-14, 126, 131-2, 136, **119,** 443-6
  valuation of assets **66,** 609, 613
posted price **62,** 161
provisional variation agreements
  duress, effect on validity **66,** 569-71, 615-16
    quid pro quo, failure of **66,** 568-9, 616-20
  status **66,** 566-9, 615-20
rent **62,** 158
repudiation. *See* termination, repudiation *below*

concession agreement (*cont.*)
royalties **62,** 158
stabilization clauses **66,** 586-91, 621-7
nationalization and **66,** 589-90, 623-5
permanent sovereignty over natural resources, effect **66,** 587-8
State practice **41,** 136
State succession and **44,** 37-8, **48,** 58-9, **66,** 87
succession **44,** 37-8
taxes **62,** 158
termination **63,** 166-7, 233
by agreement **52,** 5-7
compensation
goodwill **40,** 159, 161, 162
lost profit **40,** 159, 161, 162, **46,** 187
for invalidity **121,** 22-8
purchase of equipment **40,** 168-74
repudiation **56,** 319, **66,** 148-50, 182, 189-91, 292, 343-6, 583, 592-3, 624-5, **69,** 8-10
fundamental breach, whether **44,** 99
jurisdiction of arbitral tribunal **70,** 484-9, 491-5
State responsibility and **44,** 79-100, **70,** 484-9, 491-5
State succession and **48,** 58-9
territorial dispute, effect **66,** 183-4, 337
treaty and **42,** 8-9
validity
grant by occupying power **40,** 111-13
rights of concessionaire in case of invalidity **40,** 111-13
termination for invalidity **40,** 111-13, **121,** 22-8
conciliation 62, 108-36, **80,** 314, **84,** 265, 271, 273, 305. *See also* arbitration; conciliation commissions; diplomatic channels; dispute settlement; good offices; mediation; negotiation
arbitration and **84,** 303
Contadora process **84,** 309
dispute settlement, method of, whether **106,** 571
ICJ and **102,** 32, 46
judicial settlement and **84,** 303
Law of the Sea Convention (1982), exclusion from compulsory procedures and **99,** 481
Peace Treaty, disputes regarding **80,** 240
precondition to resort to ICJ, whether **84,** 243-5
treaty provision **82,** 689-95
conciliation commissions
applicable law **62,** 109, 111, 125
composition **62,** 111
court of law distinguished **62,** 109, 111-12
damages, assessment **40,** 427-8
decisions. *See also* recommendations *below*
binding force **45,** 500-2
equitable principles **62,** 125
expert, use of **40,** 427-8
functions **62,** 111-12, 125
judicial distinguished **41,** 109, 111-12
recommendations leading to equitable solution **62,** 125
nature of **62,** 111

procedure
determined by Commission **62,** 111
pleadings, absence **62,** 113
recommendations. *See also* decisions *above*
effect **62,** 111-12, 125
condominium 52, 19, **97,** 519
lakes **75,** 83
conduct of parties. *See* acquiescence; estoppel; maritime delimitation, conduct of parties; preclusion
confederations. *See* federal State
Conference on Security and Cooperation in Europe (CSCE) 76, 434, **77,** 252, 273
Helsinki Final Act (1975). *See* Helsinki Final Act (1975)
confession, extraction of
inhuman treatment, whether **58,** 267
torture, whether **58,** 267, 298
confidentiality, right of 58, 432-4, **74,** 319-22, 336-9, 356
telephone-tapping and **58,** 461, **74,** 319-22, 336-9, 356
confiscation 53, 4-5, **60,** 129-31, **61,** 173, **72,** 18-27, 467-70, 474-6, 554-6, 559-61, **73,** 235-47, **75,** 275-80, 299-308. *See also* expropriation/nationalization; taking of property
act of State **78,** 616-17
compensation **57,** 30. *See also* measure of damages/compensation including valuation of company/property/assets
illusory **40,** 98, 101, **42,** 48-50
State succession, liability of successor government **47,** 79-83
de facto **78,** 187
debt **66,** 69-72
definition **47,** 412, 416
enemy property. *See* enemy property, confiscation
European Convention on Human Rights (1950) and **46,** 447
exchange rates **38,** 143
extraterritorial effect **40,** 16-17, 20, 27, **42,** 29-33, 50-1, **43,** 18-23, **66,** 44, 69-70, 96-9, 132, 169-72, 196, 215, 250-5, 357-8, 403, 455-6, **69,** 9, **72,** 27, 86-7, 559-61, **73,** 237, 244-7, **78,** 616-17
enemy property **43,** 248
Foreign Sovereign Immunities Act (USA) and **63,** 595
legislation. *See also* extraterritorial effect *above*; foreign law, recognition/enforcement, confiscatory legislation
purpose **72,** 20
nationalization and **60,** 131
Nicaraguan measures **63,** 592-6
oil concession **60,** 129
partnership, effect on **40,** 18, 22
physical taking, whether necessary **66,** 33-4, 210
political motives **42,** 49-50
production levy, whether **74,** 231-2
prohibition under international law **46,** 449
public policy and **72,** 19-26
shareholders, rights of **40,** 16-17
ships contravening EEZ **118,** 448-50
State immunity, jurisdiction **63,** 595, 597, **64,** 179
territorial waters claim **66,** 183-4
conflict. *See* civil strife; civil war; dispute; rebellion; revolution; war
conflict of interest, dispute, element in **37,** 178, 180

conflict of laws. *See* private international law
Congo (Brazzaville).[ii] *See* Congo, Popular Republic of
Congo (Kinshasa). *See* Belgian Congo; Congo, Republic of; Zaire
Congo operations, Agreement with Belgium settling claims resulting from 45, 446, 450, 452, 453-4
Congo, Popular Republic of
AGIP (Brazzaville) Spa
expropriation/nationalization **67,** 329, 335-9
compensation **67,** 329, 335-9
share transfers **67,** 326
State agency debts **67,** 327, 335
State shareholder, obligations **67,** 337
AGIP Spa
Agreement (1974) **67,** 322, 326, 331-44
applicable law **67,** 331-2
arbitration clause **67,** 326
breaches **67,** 332-9
compromissory clause **67,** 326
stabilization guarantee **67,** 326, 335-9
compensation **67,** 340-3
credit guarantees **67,** 326-7, 329-30, 333-4
legal capacity **67,** 339-40
arbitral award, enforcement, in France **82,** 92
Banque Commerciale Congolaise (BCC), State agency, whether **82,** 92
Benvenuti and Bonfant, Srl
Agreement (1973) **67,** 351, 361, 366
arbitration clause **67,** 356
breaches **67,** 367-74
finance guarantees **67,** 361, 369
compensation claims **67,** 364-5
government counterclaims **67,** 365-6, 380-3
civil and commercial law **67,** 332, 336-7, 340, 353, 366
Constitution **67,** 332, 366
private property guarantees **67,** 332, 336-7
nationalization and **67,** 336-7
s 33 **67,** 332, 366-7
s 55 **67,** 332, 336
Enterprise de Distribution Congolaise (EDICO) **67,** 363
dissolution **67,** 373
dissolution, compensation **67,** 377-8
France, Agreement on Judicial Matters (1960) **47,** 85-6
Hydro-Congo **67,** 326-30, 334-5
law of. *See also* Constitution *above*
continuity **44,** 434
Law No 1/74 **67,** 325-6
Law No 71/75 **67,** 336
Ordinance No 5/78 **67,** 330-1, 339-40
Ordinance No 6/75 **67,** 329-31, 335-40
nationalization measures **67,** 325-6, 329, 335-9, 366

[ii] Material relating to the Congo is distributed in accordance with the status/name of the territory at the time in question. For entries related to what was the Belgian Congo/Congo (Kinshasa) see Belgian Congo; Congo, Popular Republic of; Congo, Republic of; Zaire. There are no entries relating to the former French colony (Congo (Brazzaville)/Republic of Congo-Brazzaville).

Permanent Mission to the UN **63,** 122-6
petroleum distribution nationalization **67,** 325-6, 366
PLASCO
directors' meetings **67,** 362-4, 368-9
expropriation/nationalization **67,** 364, 374
formation, minutes relating to **67,** 362
government undertakings **67,** 361-2
operating history **67,** 361-4
protectionist measures **67,** 370-1
SODISCA contract **67,** 362, 381-2
tax status **67,** 370
SIACongo **67,** 362-3, 367, 371-2
State agency/State-owned corporation/State entity **67,** 372
Congo, Republic of. *See also* Belgian Congo; Zaire
administrative act, review by Belgian courts **69,** 30
Basic Law 1960 **69,** 25-30
effect on
contractual liabilities **69,** 27-8
pending actions **69,** 30
pension rights **69,** 29-30
Belgium
relation to **69,** 25-30
succession to bonded debts **47,** 75-8
continuity of law **69,** 29-30
international law, municipal law and, general principles of international law in completion of **67,** 338-9, 366
pensions **69,** 29-30
State succession **47,** 75-8
conquest. *See* territory, acquisition
conscientious objection. *See also* European Convention on Human Rights (1950), conscientious objection; International Covenant on Civil and Political Rights (ICCPR) (1966), conscientious objection
discrimination and **78,** 251-2
military service **71,** 497-9, **73,** 383-5, 675-6, **74,** 302-3, **78,** 14-17, 230-2, 258-9
naturalization, eligibility for **69,** 195-201
'persecution or well-founded fear of persecution' and **71,** 498-9, **95,** 550-6, 558-60, **99,** 13
non-governmental group, refusal to join distinguished **95,** 560
political belief **95,** 555
UNHCR *Handbook on Procedures and Criteria for Determining Refugee Status* (1979) **95,** 551, 555
refugees **40,** 202-4, **95,** 550-6, 558-60, **99,** 13
State practice **95,** 552-3
UN Forces, service with **78,** 14-17
wartime obligations **69,** 197-201
conservation. *See* Australia, law of, National Parks and Wildlife Conservation Act *and* World Heritage Properties Conservation; Australia, Tasmania; environment; fisheries, conservation and management measures; forestry conservation measures; Japan, law of, Law for the Conservation of Aquatic Resources Environment; natural resources, conservation
conservatory measures. *See* provisional measures; ships, state-owned, safeguarding/conservatory measures; State immunity, execution/attachment, purpose of proceedings, safeguarding/conservatory measures
consideration, doctrine of **37,** 67
conspiracy. *See also* common purpose

conspiracy (*cont.*)
criminal procedure **91,** 480-5
definition **84,** 44
extraditable offence **48,** 69-76, **73,** 50-2, **85,** 130-43, **104,** 5-6
jurisdiction. *See* jurisdiction, conspiracy
liability for acts after withdrawal from conspiracy **103,** 218-24
Nuremberg Charter (1945), consideration by Tribunal limited to waging aggressive war **121,** 274 n. 217
torture **119,** 148, 183-4, 188-9, 190-2, 250
constitution (international organization) 37, 497, 540, **48,** 415-16, **80,** 657-8, 660. *See also* constitution (State)
as applicable law **80,** 101, 610, 611, 657, 658, **96,** 235, **110,** 14
applicable law
Vienna Convention on the Law of Treaties (1969) **105,** 22-3, **110,** 87
Vienna Convention on the Law of Treaties between States and International Organizations (1986) **105,** 22-3
breach. *See* international organization, Member States, obligations
classification of activities **105,** 42
enforcement **81,** 717, 724
implementing legislation **80,** 67, 68-71
consistency **80,** 68
international status unchanged by **80,** 70
language compared **80,** 69-71, 89, 92-3, 155-61
interpretation **37,** 497, 540, 547, 549, 553, 575, **62,** 471, 547, 549, 553, 575, **80,** 660, **105,** 24-5, 585-6
aids
debates of organization **110,** 146
object and purpose **105,** 585, **110,** 15, 48, 86, 87-8
previous agreement **105,** 585
subsequent practice **110,** 15, 21-2, 138-9, 143, 146
UN Secretary-General's report **105,** 585
UN statement **105,** 585
guidelines **105,** 585
conformity with text **110,** 144
effectiveness **110,** 88, 143
'fairly in factual context' **80,** 170-1
international law as background **80,** 66
liberal **110,** 48, 86, 87
overall UN system **110,** 19-21
primary objective **80,** 143
reasonable result **110,** 143
text **105,** 585
treaty interpretation rules **105,** 586, **110,** 14-15
responsibility
limitation to matters within competence **110,** 22, 27-8, 67-8
Member States' courts' **77,** 53
justiciability **83,** 249
modification **46,** 168, **49,** 272
personality and **77,** 623, **82,** 112
State practice **80,** 67
status and **105,** 21
treaty as **80,** 66, **110,** 14-15, 85-6
'mixed' **80,** 66
voting system, essential part of **49,** 276

constitution (State). *See also* constitution (international organization); *and under individual countries*
aliens abroad and **80,** 592
annulment, 'efficacy of change' principle **53,** 56-7, 65, 66, 73, 74, 76-81
breach of rights, 'matter relating to tort' **103,** 325
British colonies, nature of constitutions **53,** 88
change of
by revolution **39,** 48-50, 65, 81-90, 157-8, 163, 215-19, 281, 301-2, 334, 345, **53,** 71-2, 77-8
status of courts and **53,** 58, 74-5
constitutional/parliamentary supremacy distinguished **115,** 564-5
conventions **39,** 341-2
development in accordance with changing international standards **118,** 509
entrenched provisions
amendment **98,** 210-11, 212, 219
reasons for
protection of division of powers **115,** 565
protection of human rights **115,** 565
protection of minority groups **115,** 565, 566
referendum and **98,** 220
right to remedy/resist if endangered **98,** 210, 212, 220
interpretation **37,** 446, 554, **57,** 294-5, **68,** 195-6, 215-16, 230, 309-10, 334-6, 345-7, 397-8, 410-13, 417-19, 490, **69,** 35-6, 41-2, 48-9, 59-71, 73, **70,** 107, 112-13, 143, 165-7, 193, 201, 207
aids, unwritten underlying principles **115,** 556-7, 558
guidelines
broad **103,** 116, 135-6, 137, 140, 173, 188, 190-2, 228, **124,** 293-4
effectiveness **103,** 172
human rights as underlying consideration **103,** 84
intention of legislature **103,** 199-200
'living tree' **103,** 200-1
objective, evolving **103,** 139, 173
purposive **103,** 201-2
text as a whole **103,** 141-2, 172, **115,** 556
international law and **69,** 36, 41-2, 62-8, 71-3, **118,** 377, **123,** 549, **124,** 363
international tribunals, jurisprudence **123,** 549
special rules **91,** 351, 363-6, **103,** 137-40, 190-1
judicial review **105,** 544-6
judicial role, under revolutionary regime **39,** 230-2, 337
nature **103,** 198
necessity as justification for departure from **70,** 26-7
primacy **89,** 53-5, 69, 70, **91,** 327, 330, **98,** 260, **103,** 144-5
customary law **103,** 145, 174, 188, 196
property rights, protection of **91,** 320, 321-2, **103,** 118-20, **115,** 624-36
rights
abrogation by executive **123,** 579-84
created after coming into force of jurisdiction **123,** 517-18, 519
supremacy. *See* primacy *above*
treaties. *See* treaties, constitutional compatibility
unwritten principles
aid to interpretation **115,** 556-7
democracy **115,** 560-3
effect **115,** 557
federalism **115,** 557-60

constitution (State) (*cont.*)
protection of minorities **115,** 566-8
written **115,** 555-7
role of courts **39,** 356-8
constitutional petition. *See also* judicial review
admissibility, foreign State, against **106,** 360-1
standing. *See* courts, municipal, standing
constitutional review
acts of EC **98,** 250-1
acts of national public authorities, limited to **98,** 250-1
declaration of constitutional compatibility of treaty
binding effect **98,** 260-1
legal nature **98,** 261
procedure **98,** 259-61
direct and current violation of constitutional right **98,** 213
European Union, amendments **98,** 226
referendums **98,** 190
requirements
judgment dependent on validity of norm **98,** 193
laws, regulations or provisions of general nature **100,** 312
treaties. *See* treaties, constitutional review
consul. *See* consular agent
consular access
arrest of national **77,** 542
customary law and **38,** 171, **123,** 608
legal representation, right to provide if asked **77,** 542, **123,** 607-9
obligation to inform consul if so requested **77,** 542
Guantanamo Bay Naval Base detainees **123,** 603, 605-10
notification of detention
failure **118,** 5
remedy **118,** 6-7, 10, 12, 15, 40-3, 49
State practice **118,** 10
right to routine questioning at airport **107,** 81
Vienna Convention on Consular Relations (1963) **77,** 542, **107,** 81, **118,** 4-21, 40-52, **123,** 608
consular agent. *See also* ambassador/head of mission; consular access; consular immunity, jurisdiction; consular privileges and immunities; consular relations; consulate; diplomatic agent
acts attributable to sending State **86,** 556, **99,** 125
diplomatic agent distinguished. *See* diplomatic privileges and immunities, consular distinguished
exequatur **38,** 170-3, **40,** 224-7
functions **53,** 549-50, **57,** 158, **61,** 596-7, **99,** 123-4
administration of international hospital **101,** 371-5
applicable law for determining
municipal law of receiving State **101,** 372, 482
municipal law of sending State **101,** 372
arrest of naval deserters **42,** 233-4
bilateral agreement **101,** 373, 469-70
exclusive, whether **101,** 373
certification, refusal without reason **70,** 239
commercial relations **114,** 564-5
consular protection **89,** 66, 67-8
deceased nationals, protection of property of **56,** 530

discharge of seamen **41,** 416-20
discretionary, wrongful act **101,** 482-3, 494-5
extraterritorial nature of **77,** 594
immigrants' centre **82,** 45
'in accordance with the laws of the receiving State' **94,** 372, **99,** 124-5
indecent assault 'in exercise of' **68,** 179-80
lease of consular premises **101,** 382
oaths and affidavits **44,** 224
protecting interests of sending State and its nationals **99,** 123-4
'in accordance with the laws of the receiving State' **99,** 124-5
purchase of goods for consulate **101,** 382
representation of national in court **101,** 468-70, 479 n. 3
'address the authorities of receiving State' distinguished **101,** 469-70
'assist in proceedings' distinguished **101,** 469-70
safeguarding interests of nationals
in case of succession *mortis causa* **94,** 371-3
'in accordance with the laws of the receiving State' **94,** 372, **99,** 124-5
minors **107,** 102-4
social, economic and political policy, grounded in **98,** 128-9
'subject to practices and procedures obtaining in receiving State' **101,** 470, 479 n. 3
Vienna Convention on Consular Relations (1963) **86,** 556, **94,** 372, **98,** 128-9, 130, **101,** 372-3, 381, 383, 469-70, 479 n. 3, 481, **107,** 102-4
'within the limits permitted by international law' **101,** 373, 481
wrongful act **101,** 481-2, 493-5
identification, means
consular insignia **86,** 558
consulate papers **86,** 558
identity card **86,** 557-8
identification, need for **86,** 557-8
national of receiving State, consent of receiving State, need for **86,** 556
privileges and immunities. *See* consular immunity, jurisdiction; consular premises, inviolability; consular privileges and immunities; consular relations
protection of, duty **61,** 556-9, 583-4, **86,** 557-8
social security
entitlement **86,** 540, 541
FRG–Turkey Social Security Agreement (1960) **86,** 540-1
State immunity, capacity to plead **42,** 245-6
status as, executive certificate as evidence **107,** 102, **108,** 526
consular archives
inviolability **61,** 555-7, 559-60, **82,** 9-10, **94,** 372
documents belonging to estate of national **94,** 372
consular immunity, execution/attachment
honorary consul/consulate, funds in private bank account **82,** 7-10
permitted **77,** 582
police intervention **77,** 584
Vienna Convention on Consular Relations (1963) **82,** 9-10
consular immunity, jurisdiction **77,** 400-2
civil jurisdiction **56,** 529
functional, interference with functioning of consulate and **101,** 384
mixed courts, of **71,** 581
official acts **56,** 530, **57,** 158-9, **77,** 594, 596, 611-12, **82,** 9-10, **86,** 554-8. *See also* consular agent, functions
car, use of **77,** 611-12

consular immunity, jurisdiction (*cont.*)
'connected with' **77,** 594
difficulty of establishing whether **77,** 612
driving to official function, whether **86,** 554-8
employment contract as **77,** 595-7
State immunity and **86,** 556, **101,** 489-96
capacity to plead **42,** 245-6
distinction **104,** 412-13, **113,** 419, 422
tort **107,** 102
traffic offences **73,** 690, **86,** 554-8
honorary consul **52,** 98-405, **77,** 611-12
consular immunity, jurisdiction, waiver 40, 225, **42,** 244-8, **56,** 531, **89,** 71
consular jurisdiction, purpose **124,** 22-3
consular law
development **61,** 566, 569
nature **61,** 564-6, 568-9
consular official. *See* consular agent
consular premises. *See also* consular agent; consular immunity, jurisdiction; embassy or consular bank account/funds
diplomatic premises distinguished **53,** 549-50, **77,** 582, **107,** 241 n. 5, 242
divorce effected in **55,** 581
extraterritoriality **52,** 306-9, **55,** 385-6, 581-3
FRG–Italy Treaty of Friendship (1957), absence of provision regarding **77,** 583
honorary consulate **77,** 582-4
private residence of honorary consul **82,** 6
immunity, local rates **53,** 545-9
inviolability **55,** 582-3, **61,** 558-60, **107,** 240-2
archives. *See* consular archives
Vienna Convention on Diplomatic Relations (1961) **107,** 240-1
liens on **53,** 548
marriages in **55,** 581, 584, 587
'organ of foreign State or political subdivision thereof' **101,** 482, 489
privileges and immunities **52,** 397, **55,** 582-3
residence used as consulate **77,** 583
archives elsewhere **77,** 583
consular privileges and immunities 44, 190-1, **52,** 401-2, **61,** 559-60, 583-4, **71,** 578-83, **73,** 690, **89,** 70-1. *See also* consular access; consular agent; consular archives; consular immunity, jurisdiction; consular premises; consular relations; consulate; diplomatic premises, inviolability; diplomatic privileges and immunities; evidence of, consular status; international organizations, privileges and immunities; State immunity; *and under individual countries*
basis
comity **89,** 70
sovereign nature of consular activity **101,** 372-3, 375, 384
codification
Convention regarding Consular Agents (Havana) (1928) **99,** 200
ILC **99,** 200-1
Inter-American Commission of Jurists (1927) **99,** 200
Vienna Convention on Consular Relations (1963). *See* Vienna Convention on Consular Relations (1963)
customary international law **77,** 594
debts **57,** 152-3
diplomatic privileges and immunities distinguished **56,** 540

employment contract. *See* employment contract, locally engaged staff, consulate
entitlement
executive certificate, conclusiveness **89,** 72
honorary consul. *See* honorary consul/consulate *below*
national of receiving State **75,** 97-8, **86,** 556-7, **101,** 382-5
ushers **77,** 401
evidence, immunity from obligation to give **86,** 556
fiscal exemption, nationals of receiving State **75,** 97-8
functional **45,** 383, **68,** 179-80, **71,** 579-83, **73,** 690, **77,** 594, **86,** 554-8, **89,** 66, 67, **94,** 371-3, **99,** 123, **107,** 101-4. *See also* consular agent, functions
customary international law **101,** 372, 382, 383
media interviews **89,** 67-8
improper performance, relevance **94,** 372
responsibility for determining whether, court **99,** 123
Vienna Convention on Consular Relations (1963). *See* Vienna Convention on Consular Relations (1963), functional immunity under
honorary consul/consulate **77,** 582-4, **82,** 7-10, **86,** 554-8, **107,** 102-4
customary international law **86,** 556
private residence **82,** 6
traffic offences **52,** 98-405, **77,** 611-12
restrictive. *See* functional *above*
State immunity, jurisdiction and **86,** 556
taxation, exemption **108,** 526
waiver, lease, cancellation clause **45,** 383-4
consular relations. *See also* consular access; consular agent; consular immunity, jurisdiction; consular privileges and immunities; diplomatic relations; Vienna Convention on Consular Relations (1963)
damage done by closure of consular post **89,** 89
diplomatic relations, break, effect on **96,** 303, 304
Vienna Convention on Consular Relations (1963) **96,** 303
expulsion of alien, notification to **82,** 675
treaty basis, precedence of bilateral convention **101,** 373, 480, **123,** 608
consulate
'mission', whether **107,** 240-1
as 'property used for commercial purposes' **65,** 241-2
as 'seat' of State/government **65,** 373
Contadora process **76,** 49-52, 411, 698-9, **84,** 248, 251-62, 306-11
Arías Peace Plan **84,** 258, 259
conciliation, whether **84,** 309
conclusion **84,** 281-2
direct negotiations, whether **84,** 248-9
Esquipulas II Accord **84,** 258, 259, 260, 261, 310
nature **84,** 309
Pact of Bogotá (1948)
'pacific measure' **84,** 309-11
'special procedure' **84,** 254, 281-2
provisional measures and **76,** 49-52, 479
regional arrangement under the UN Charter **76,** 149-52, 505-6
contempt of court **58,** 508-18, 519-20, 522, 523, 525, 540, 544, **78,** 396-402, **79,** 48
freedom of expression and **58,** 523-36, 540-1, 544, 548
contentious jurisdiction. *See* Inter-American Court of Human Rights, contentious jurisdiction; International Court of Justice (ICJ), contentious proceedings

contiguity principle 39, 425-6, **41,** 115, 126-7, 152, 189, **50,** 40, **59,** 60-1
contiguous zone. *See also* continental shelf; exclusive economic zone (EEZ); high seas; Territorial Sea and Contiguous Zone Convention (1958)
claim to, Guinea **120,** 259
coastal State obligations, prevention of acts interfering with other States' rights **71,** 260-1
coastal State rights **56,** 117, **71,** 260, **74,** 210-12
'control' **120,** 272-7
Convention on the Territorial Sea and Contiguous Zone (1958) **120,** 275-6
State practice **120,** 275-6
definition **55,** 205, **56,** 117
continental shelf distinguished **41,** 159
high seas, part of **71,** 261, **74,** 206, 210
as part of EEZ **120,** 274
delimitation
fisheries jurisdiction and **55,** 281, 345, **56,** 117
prolongation of land boundary **83,** 43
hot pursuit **120,** 276
islands **62,** 125
jurisdiction **89,** 79
control distinguished **120,** 273-4
customs protection **91,** 524-6, **120,** 272-7
Territorial Sea and Contiguous Zone Convention (1958) **91,** 515
status **74,** 210-12
continental margin 67, 49-50, 180, 183, 208-14, 280, 283. *See also* continental shelf, 200 miles, beyond
limits of continental shelf and **81,** 260-1
rift zone distinguished **81,** 389
continental shelf 41, 284, 313, 344, 356, **43,** 93-114, **62,** 108-36, **77,** 313-21. *See also* contiguous zone; continental margin; Continental Shelf Convention (1958); continental shelf delimitation; continental slope; exclusive economic zone (EEZ); Law of the Sea Convention (1982), continental shelf; maritime delimitation
200 miles, beyond
Commission on the Limits of the Continental Shelf, role **95,** 674-5, 701, 723
leap-frogging **95,** 723
adjacency **67,** 54
applicable law **81,** 261, 262, 278, 294, 300
Law of the Sea Convention (1982) **81,** 262
Art. 76 **81,** 262
appurtenance **81,** 257, 268, 295, 325, 406
basis of rights **41,** 58-61, 81
equidistance and **41,** 41, 58
just and equitable share **41,** 52, 59
test **41,** 59-62, 65, 81, 158, 189
Arabian Gulf **64,** 336-8
Australia **51,** 171
baseline
territorial sea, outer edge **91,** 669
territorial sea, outer limit **41,** 190-1
breadth, Law of the Sea Convention (1982) **70,** 607, 611
claim to. *See also* proclamation *below*
municipal law, adoption into **90,** 262-4
need for **86,** 65, 603, 621-3, **99,** 466

requirements **67,** 62
space or resources, whether **41,** 51
'coastal seabed economic area' **67,** 210-11
coastal State's duties, Law of the Sea Convention (1982) **81,** 303
coastal State's rights **41,** 58-61, 62, 125, 126, 128, 173, 189, 191, 220, **55,** 170-5, 218, 345, **56,** 85, 119-20, 131, **57,** 147, **67,** 39, 41, 54, 116-17, 166-77, 183-5, 214-15, **70,** 616-17, 684, 688, **71,** 92, 123, 193
customary international law and **41,** 51, 188, 191, **71,** 260, **74,** 206-12
nature of **81,** 296
coasts. *See* coasts
common boundary, Malacca Straits **84,** 81
concept **41,** 115, 167, **67,** 36, 38-9, 41, 54, 67-8, 103-14, 166-77, 250, 281-2
Continental Shelf Convention (1958) **90,** 262
delimitation distinguished **41,** 138
evolution **67,** 38, 85, 104, 168-71, **81,** 267-8, 294-9, 302, 326, 337, 382-8, **86,** 600-2, **90,** 260-6, **99,** 465-8
extension, possibility **41,** 222-3
International Law Commission (1949) **90,** 261
Law of the Sea Convention (1982) **81,** 302
legal **41,** 166, 188, **81,** 272, 287, 296, 297, 302, 326, **99,** 552, **105,** 251
Libya/Malta **95,** 665
origin **41,** 88, 116, 118, 132, 167, 220
physical **41,** 51, 60-1, 81, 82, **81,** 302, 326
spatial **81,** 263-4
submarine **81,** 302-3
concessions, grant of **81,** 254
effect on delimitation **81,** 260-1
customary international law **41,** 31, 36, 58, 67-75, 84-6, 106, 116-30, 132, 158, 168, 169-73, 220, **81,** 261-2, 287, 297, 298, 300-1, 351, **86,** 617-24, **99,** 465-6
coastal State's rights **41,** 51, 188, 191, **71,** 260, **74,** 206-12
Continental Shelf Convention (1958) **99,** 426-7, 502-3
delimitation **41,** 31, 36, 38, 58, 159, 168-75, 190, 209
distance and **41,** 119-25
Law of the Sea Convention (1982) and **99,** 467
negotiate, obligation **41,** 86
definition **56,** 137, **67,** 38, 41, 67, 69, 103-7, 174, 210, 280
change **81,** 368, **83,** 46
Continental Shelf Convention (1958) **41,** 118, 123, **67,** 38-9, 41, 67, 103-5, 174-7, 205, **77,** 313-14, **81,** 383, 388
200-metre isobath, limited to **99,** 473
depth/exploitability **83,** 46
distance principle **67,** 41-2, 107-8, 246, 280
exploitability **67,** 39, 41, 104-5, 109, 172-7, 204-6, **81,** 389
UNCLOS I **99,** 465
whole of seabed **99,** 466
Law of the Sea Convention (1958) **81,** 383, 388
legal **67,** 38-9, 41, 103-11, 281-2
North Sea **99,** 473
outer and inner, distinction, whether **81,** 388, 390
status **67,** 39, 108
UNCLOS III **81,** 383, **99,** 467-8
draft convention **67,** 40-1

continental shelf (*cont.*)
delimitation. *See* continental shelf delimitation; maritime delimitation
discontinuities. *See* rift zones
distance **81,** 287, 327, **83,** 71. *See also* continental shelf delimitation, distance
bathymetry and **81,** 327
exploitability and **81,** 327
legal concept **81,** 326
natural prolongation and **81,** 265, 326-31
title and **81,** 329
East Timor **105,** 244, 251-4, 259
EEZ and **71,** 121, 191, 194, 211, **81,** 264-6, 273, 301, 303, 326, 330, 357-8, 359-61, 388
assimilation **67,** 108-9, 215, 218-19, 224-7, 241-2, 278-82, 290-1, 313
coincidence **95,** 674
delimitation line
pre-existing continental shelf line, relevance **92,** 66
single, whether **92,** 66-7, 79, 146-9, 153, 154-5, 157, 158, 159
differences **81,** 301-2, **99,** 464-8
relevant/special circumstances **99,** 477
identity of regime, whether **71,** 198-202, **81,** 388, **92,** 65-7
Law of the Sea Convention (1982) **71,** 121-2, 201-2, **92,** 65, **99,** 467-8
confusion of concepts **99,** 474-6, 477-8
merger of concepts **67,** 108-9, 240-2, **71,** 121, **81,** 301
parallel concepts **99,** 460, 464, 468, 477-8
priority, responsibility for determining **99,** 482
single boundary. *See* maritime delimitation, single boundary
entitlement. *See also* rights *and* title *below*
distance as basis **81,** 288
influence of EEZ **81,** 264, 265, 357-8, 359-61
inherent **81,** 264, **83,** 49-50, **105,** 251
proportionality as basis **81,** 277
epicontinental shelf and **41,** 120-7, 128
equidistance. *See* equidistance
European Community competence **120,** 626-7
exploitation **71,** 106-9
extension of territorial seas **86,** 602
extent
Continental Shelf Convention (1958) **81,** 327
equidistance/special circumstances **81,** 327
Law of the Sea Convention (1982), natural prolongation/outer edge of the continental margin or distance **81,** 327
measurement, surface of waters **81,** 302-3
natural prolongation. *See* natural prolongation *below*
federal State, legislative powers **91,** 210
fisheries, sedentary **67,** 195-202, 241
fisheries jurisdiction and **55,** 280-1, **56,** 119, 134, 189
adjacent coastal States **55,** 320
general principle of law, whether **41,** 138-47
high seas and **55,** 320
distinguished **41,** 187
encroachment **41,** 116, 128-9
historic rights
conflicting **67,** 65, 116-17, 123

distinguished **67,** 67
interrelation **67,** 67, 116-17, 124-5, 203-4
inherent right to **41,** 51, 58-61, 84-5, 116
International Law Commission (ILC) and **86,** 619-20, **90,** 261
islands **64,** 336, **67,** 293
joint exploitation **67,** 312-17
joint exploitation agreement
France–Spain (1974) **81,** 294
Japan–Korea (1974) **81,** 294
Libya–Malta (1970) **81,** 254
jurisdiction **55,** 207, **57,** 147
landlocked States **81,** 315
law of, development **43,** 112-13
Law of the Sea Convention (1982) and **71,** 188, 192, 202, 210, **72,** 121, **91,** 670
legislative powers **43,** 95
federal **91,** 210
limit, delimitation distinguished **81,** 294, 328
low-water mark **81,** 485
meaning. *See* definition *above*
military use of **41,** 129
mineral resources
right to exploit, Crown in right of the Commonwealth **90,** 242
right to explore **90,** 238
right to legislate **90,** 238
natural law of **41,** 58-67, 84-5
natural prolongation **41,** 51, 60-1, 66, 77, 80-1, 86, 113, 115, 127, 149, 152, 158-9, 167, 173, 174, **56,** 131, **67,** 36-51, 73, 85, 96-7, 102-11, 184-5, 187-8, 209, 215, 241, 281-4, **71,** 85, 88-9, 108, 113, 123, 125, 194, **77,** 685, 686-7, **81,** 267-8, 287, 289, 295, 296, 302-3
200 miles, within **81,** 265, 267, 294, 337, 358, 384-5, 389
adjacency and **41,** 86, 174
areas of overlap and **99,** 532-3
bathymetry **67,** 47-50, **81,** 327
closed sea **41,** 86
concept
changed **81,** 326, **99,** 467, 534-5
geological **62,** 116, 119, 124
legal **81,** 287
morphological **62,** 116, 119, 124
physical **41,** 80-1, **99,** 529-34
continental margin and **81,** 385
convergence and **41,** 86, 88-9
definition **81,** 326, 331
direction **67,** 38, 45, 47-50
distance and **41,** 59-60, **77,** 687, **81,** 265, 267-8, 300-1, 326-31, 360-1, **99,** 534-5
equidistance and **41,** 61, 174
equitable delimitation and **67,** 37, 39-40
equitable principles and **67,** 40
Grisbadarna **41,** 159 n. 2
Jan Mayen Ridge, whether **62,** 116, 119, 124
Law of the Sea Convention (1982) **81,** 329, **99,** 534
non-encroachment and **41,** 61, 89
North Sea **81,** 267-8, 385-6, **99,** 473

continental shelf (*cont.*)
proportionality and **41,** 86, **99,** 529-38
relevant/special circumstance. *See* continental shelf delimitation, natural prolongation
third State, attribution to **41,** 61, 66
title and **81,** 263-7, 329, 330, 336
Law of the Sea Convention (1982) **81,** 329
Tunisia–Libya **81,** 268
natural resources **51,** 227-8, **55,** 323, **56,** 137, **81,** 383
occupation **67,** 168-75, 215, 313
relevance **41,** 51, 168, 191
outer limits **41,** 70, 119-20, 123, 220, 222-3, **67,** 175-7, 185, 204-14, 240-1, **81,** 383, 387-8, 390
criteria **67,** 207-9
legal basis **81,** 383
principles and rules, over-conceptualization **67,** 85, 184
proclamation **41,** 51, 85, 88, 113, 118, 120-1, 128, 131, 134, 136, 164, 167, 191, **81,** 294, **90,** 260-1, 263-4
Abu Dhabi **41,** 164
Argentina **86,** 618
Bahamas (1948) **86,** 602, 605, 619
British Honduras (1950) **86,** 602, 605
British Solomon Islands Protectorate (1970) **86,** 605
British Virgin Islands (1972) **86,** 605
Cayman Islands (1978) **86,** 605
Chile **86,** 618
Costa Rica **86,** 618
Ecuador (1947) **41,** 118, 120
El Salvador (1950) **41,** 118, 120
Falkland Islands (1952) **86,** 602, 605
FRG (1964) **41,** 56, 94, 112, 131, 138, 212-14, 221
Honduras (1950) **41,** 118, 120
Iraq (1958) **41,** 136
Jamaica **86,** 602, 605, 619
Mexico **86,** 618
Mexico (1945) **41,** 113, 118, 158
need for. *See* claim to *above*
Nicaragua **86,** 618
Panama **86,** 618
Peru **86,** 618
Peru (1947) **41,** 118, 120
reservations **41,** 85
St Vincent (1970) **86,** 605
Seychelles (1976) **86,** 605
Sierra Leone (1960) **86,** 605
The Gambia Islands (1963) **86,** 605
Trinidad and Tobago (1942) **86,** 602, 605
Truman Proclamation (1945). *See* Truman Proclamation (1945)
UK practice **90,** 263-4
proximity. *See* adjacency *above*
res communis **41,** 173, 187-8
res nullius **41,** 173
rift zones. *See* rift zones
rights **74,** 206-11, **77,** 320, **81,** 263, 295. *See also* entitlement *above and* title *below*

ab initio **67,** 116-17, 166, 183-5
appurtenance theory and **41,** 58-61, 81
delimitation method as corollary **41,** 61-2
North Sea **41,** 51, 58-61, 62
basis **81,** 263, 279
coastal front **81,** 273, 314-15, 327, **99,** 542-3
coastal opening. *See* coastal opening
coastal States' **41,** 58-61, 62, 125, 126, 128, 173, 189, 191, 220
contiguity **41,** 115, 126-7, 152, 189
continental margin **81,** 327
distance **81,** 263-4, 269-70, 296-7, 327
distance, customary international law **81,** 297
exploitation of resources **41,** 84-5, 187, 220
landmass **81,** 273
natural prolongation **81,** 273
proportionality **81,** 277
sovereignty over land **41,** 58
territorial sovereignty **81,** 273, 296, 315, 339, **99,** 658, 660
of coastal State. *See* coastal State's rights *above*
dependent territories **86,** 603-7
Crown in right of a colony **90,** 265
exclusive **41,** 51, 61, 84-5, 116, 126, 128, 167, 168
exercise, whether necessary **41,** 51
extension of territorial rights **41,** 67, 149
extent **41,** 128
external sovereignty, manifestation of **86,** 602, 608
extraterritorial **86,** 602, **90,** 264
historic. *See* historic rights *above*
inherent **41,** 51, 58-61, 62, 84-5, 125, 168, 174, 187, 220, **81,** 264, 296, **90,** 262-4
Continental Shelf Convention (1958) **81,** 295-6
delimitation regime as corollary **41,** 223
ipso facto and *ab initio*, meaning **90,** 263
ipso jure **86,** 603, 617, 621-4
limited nature **86,** 601-2
military **81,** 274
proprietary, whether **86,** 602, **90,** 262-4
retroactivity **86,** 622-4
sovereign **41,** 88, 126, 128, **81,** 327
legislative, executive and judicial **41,** 220
seabed
distinguished **86,** 601
as part of territory **91,** 209-10
res nullius, whether **86,** 618
single shelf **41,** 79, 82, 187
sovereignty over **51,** 218, **77,** 689
natural resources, exploitation **56,** 137
starting point, outer limit of territorial sea **41,** 87, 189, 190-1, **81,** 441-2, 461, **83,** 113, **90,** 238
Statehood, emanation of **81,** 315
status **78,** 530
superjacent airspace **86,** 601
superjacent waters **86,** 601, 618
status **74,** 206-11

continental shelf (*cont.*)
terra nullius, whether **67,** 168-74
territorial sovereignty, extension of **41,** 60, 87, 126, 127-8, **66,** 337, **86,** 601
territorial waters and **67,** 67-8
distinction, whether **41,** 64, 75, 159
territory, whether part of **51,** 224-36, **78,** 538, **83,** 66
as basis of rights **81,** 295-6, 315, **86,** 608
seabed **91,** 209-10
waters above **91,** 209-10
title. *See also* entitlement *and* rights *above*
basis **81,** 263, 279
adjacency **81,** 338
appurtenance **81,** 338
delimitation, relevance to **81,** 265-6
distance **81,** 263-5, 267, 269-70, 296-7, 329, 338-9
distance, customary international law **81,** 297
natural prolongation **81,** 263-7, 296, 329, 330, 336
delimitation
basis for **81,** 260
distinguished **81,** 257, 260, 262, 267-8, 275, 278-9, 328, 329, **83,** 94, 103, **123,** 357-8
Law of the Sea Convention (1982) **81,** 338, **83,** 103
legal **81,** 330
natural prolongation and **81,** 263, 295, **99,** 532
UNCLOS III **81,** 327
UNCLOS III draft convention, modification of concept **67,** 40-1
unilateral claims **67,** 169-70
United States and **51,** 224-8
unity and continuity **71,** 100-2
waters above, as part of territory **91,** 209-10
Continental Shelf Convention (1958) 41, 29-229 *passim*, **43,** 113, **51,** 44, 47, 114, 140, 174, 226, **81,** 328. *See also* continental shelf; continental shelf delimitation; Law of the Sea Convention (1982)
adjacency **41,** 173-4
'adjacent' and 'equidistant' **41,** 126-7
'adjacent' and 'opposite' States **41,** 57, 84, 90, 108, 224
adjacent States, boundary **41,** 30, 31, 37, 38, 49, 53-7, 69
agreement/equidistance/special circumstances rule **41,** 49, 57
absence of agreement **41,** 57
applicability **41,** 53-8, 84, 104, 108, 155, 169-70, 174-5, 202, 217, 229
non-parties **67,** 185-9, **71,** 130
applicable law
continental shelf delimitation **99,** 424, 425-6, 427-8, 473-4, 499-500, 673
'general International Convention establishing rules expressly recognized by the contesting parties' **99,** 500
single boundary **99,** 425, 496, 568
Art. 6(1)
as customary international law **99,** 426-7, 502-3
ILC Commentary **99,** 507-10
independence of Articles 1 and 2 **99,** 503
modification, whether **99,** 500-4
customary international law **99,** 502-3
judicial interpretation **99,** 501, 504

Law of the Sea Convention (1982), Art. 76 **99,** 502-3
Canadian ratification **71,** 106, 108, 128
accompanying declaration **71,** 106, 108, 128
coastal relationship **81,** 270
coastal States
exclusive rights **41,** 51, 70
fisheries, rights over **56,** 119, 132
sovereign rights over **56,** 119
natural resources, exploitation of **56,** 119
continuing validity
Anglo-French Arbitration **99,** 131
Canada–France Arbitration **99,** 500
Gulf of Maine **99,** 499-500
Jan Mayen **99,** 499-500
Law of the Sea Convention (1982) **99,** 502-3
criteria, failure to specify **99,** 470-1
customary international law and **41,** 57-75, 105-15, 117-26, 132, 135-8, 186, 205, **71,** 118-20, 191
Arts. 1-3 **41,** 69, 112-14, 131
Art. 4 **41,** 69
Art. 5 **41,** 69
Art. 6 **41,** 31, 67-75, 84, 106, 112-14, 131, 168-75, 187, 203, 206-11, 223
codification/reflection of **41,** 57-75, 105-15, 117-26, 132, 135-8, 186, 205, **71,** 118-20, 191, **81,** 377, 378, 379, **99,** 426-7, 502-3, 504, 517, 526-7
development **41,** 205, **62,** 571, **99,** 502-4
divergence from **41,** 190-1
equidistance as required method **99,** 506
definition **41,** 118, 123, **67,** 38-9, 41, 67, 103-5, 174-7, 205, **77,** 313-14, **81,** 383, 388
200-metre isobath **99,** 473
status **67,** 39, 108
delimitation under **67,** 58, 180-3
application of provisions concerning **71,** 148-52
by agreement between States **71,** 118-19
equitable criteria **71,** 119
general application to **71,** 118-20, 128-30, 196, 213-14
methods **71,** 119
non-party States, application to **67,** 36, 185-9
principles, as expression of international law principles **71,** 118-20, 129
entry into force **71,** 106, 118
equidistance **41,** 36, 49, 69-70, 84, 90, 104, **71,** 106, 108, 111, 114, 118-20, 127-30, 150-1, 180, 192, 213-15, **91,** 671-2, **95,** 663-4, **99,** 505, 507-10, 634, 673
obligatory, whether **99,** 512-15, 516, 517, 521
special circumstances **71,** 128
equitable result **99,** 627
extent, equidistance/special circumstances **81,** 280, 373-5
fishing rights **55,** 207, 396-7
freedom of the high seas and **41,** 116-17, 123, 128-9, 168
general maritime law rules in **41,** 69
ILC Draft **67,** 177-80, **81,** 374
special circumstances **99,** 489-90
interpretation **71,** 119
islands **64,** 336
continental shelf entitlement, political status, relevance **95,** 665

Continental Shelf Convention (1958) (*cont.*)
lapsed, whether **71,** 194-202
Law of the Sea Convention (1982), interrelationship **99,** 500
methods
equidistance/special circumstances. *See* maritime delimitation, equidistance/relevant circumstances
negotiated/judicial settlement **81,** 328
permissible extent, relevance **99,** 503
natural prolongation **99,** 534
natural resource
definition **56,** 119
exploitation **56,** 119
fish, whether **56,** 119
operation and enforcement **71,** 118, 127-30, 196
overlap and **41,** 108
phrases
'special circumstances' **99,** 488-93, 515-17
ILC draft **99,** 489-90
UNCLOS I **99,** 490-1
ratification **41,** 54, 112, 186, 206-8, 221
rights
co-existence with rights to use of seabed **86,** 601
coastal State **86,** 601-2
'to explore and exploit' **86,** 601
scope **71,** 118, 130
single boundary **95,** 663-4, 700, **99,** 500
UK and **78,** 530
US ratification **71,** 106, 118
continental shelf delimitation. *See also* continental shelf; Continental Shelf Convention (1958); maritime delimitation
200 miles, beyond **81,** 390
acquiescence **81,** 260-1
adjacency **41,** 86, 174, **67,** 54, **81,** 278
coastal opening, need for **81,** 273
adjacent coasts, proportionality **81,** 342
adjacent States **81,** 262
agreement, need for **81,** 280, 293, 299
applicable law **67,** 30-1, 36-7, 52, 85, **70,** 684, **81,** 261, 263, 278, 294, 300. *See also* principles and rules applicable to *below*
adjacency **81,** 278
Continental Shelf Convention (1958) **81,** 294, **99,** 424, 425-6, 427-8, 473-4, 499-500, 673
customary international law **81,** 261, 300, **99,** 426, 428, 438, 473-4, 657, 660, 666, 672, 673
equitable principles **81,** 263
fishing zone boundary, relevance **99,** 426
Law of the Sea Convention (1982) **81,** 261, 294, **99,** 427, 474
third party claims **67,** 35
apportionment **81,** 305, 390
as attribution **81,** 390
baselines. *See* baselines
basepoints. *See* basepoints
basis **81,** 272

appurtenance **81,** 257
better title **81,** 257
inherent right **81,** 257
law **81,** 294
title **81,** 257, 265, 328-9
closed sea
Caribbean **81,** 310
Mediterranean **81,** 284
North Sea **81,** 310, 312
Persian Gulf **81,** 310-12
radial projection **81,** 310-13, 345
termination of delimitation line, State practice **81,** 310-13
coastal configuration. *See* coastal configuration
coasts. *See* coasts
continental shelf
continuity **81,** 330, 390-1. *See also* rift zones
right to, whether distinguishable **81,** 328
rights, basis **81,** 314
delimitation line. *See also* equidistance, line
criterion for **81,** 442, 444, 453
delimitation zone distinguished **81,** 308
terminal point, in closed sea, State practice **81,** 310-13
turning point **81,** 454, 464-8
distance **81,** 278-9. *See also* continental shelf, distance
convenience **81,** 301
customary international law **81,** 297, 300-1
EEZ, effect **81,** 265, 359-61
equidistance and **81,** 269
Law of the Sea Convention (1982) **81,** 327
distributive justice and **81,** 391-2
equal division **81,** 304, 322, 323, 351, 390
equality of States and **81,** 275, 412, 414
equitable principles. *See* equitable principles
expert, role **81,** 455, 460
geographical context **81,** 283
description **81,** 252-3
interests of third States **81,** 336
islands. *See* islands
islets **81,** 411
law of. *See also* principles and rules applicable to *below*
ad hoc nature **81,** 297
customary international law **81,** 298
treaty basis **81,** 298
treaty and case-law, divergence **81,** 340
Law of the Sea Convention 1982. *See* Law of the Sea Convention (1982), continental shelf
littoral **81,** 412
low-water mark
meaning **81,** 485
relevance **81,** 457
maps, relevance **81,** 252
median line. *See* equidistance
method

continental shelf delimitation (*cont.*)
agreement **92,** 18, **105,** 251
arcs of great circles **81,** 726
bisector of angle **81,** 396-7, 398-9
choice **81,** 351, 378
equidistance. *See* equidistance
Law of the Sea Convention (1982), failure to prescribe **81,** 262-3, 317, 328, 372-3, 380
perpendicular to coast **81,** 443, 444
proportionality **81,** 277
State practice **81,** 277
titles, comparison **81,** 328
two-stage **81,** 278
natural boundaries, role **81,** 297-8
natural prolongation. *See* continental shelf, natural prolongation
North Sea **99,** 471-3
as criterion for delimitation **81,** 277, 336-7
islands **99,** 546-7
objective, determination of legal entitlement **81,** 365
opposability **81,** 401-2
opposite coasts, between **81,** 262
200 miles, within **81,** 287-8
adjustment of equidistance line **81,** 283-4, 410-11
coasts, role **81,** 306
opposition, need for **81,** 308, 312-13
petroleum concessions and **81,** 254, 260-1, 443, 444, 445, 469-74
political **81,** 298
principles and rules applicable to **81,** 254-7, 288-90, 295, 296, 325. *See also* law of *above*
Anglo-French Arbitration **81,** 295
domination of sea by land **81,** 300, 339
equidistance **81,** 351
equitable principles. *See* equitable principles
equitable solution. *See* maritime delimitation, equitable result
non-encroachment **41,** 61, 89, **99,** 432
North Sea **81,** 295
over-conceptualization **81,** 297
paucity **81,** 298
proportionality **81,** 274, 304
Tunisia–Libya **81,** 296
proximity. *See* distance *above*
rules and principles. *See* principles and rules applicable to *above*
single shelf **81,** 389, 390-1. *See also* rift zones
territorial delimitation distinguished **81,** 391
territorial sea. *See* territorial sea, delimitation
third States and **81,** 256-60, 401-2
unilateral **81,** 340
continental slope 41, 120, 125, **71,** 101-2. *See also* continental margin
continental terrace 41, 123
contraband
absolute, manganese ore in transit **44,** 495-8
Pakistan proclamations (1965) **40,** 473
sale of

indemnity due to owner **44,** 498
notice of **44,** 497
contract. *See also* administrative contract; bank, liability for loss; concession agreement; cooperation agreement; economic development agreement; participation agreements; State contract
administrative, special rules **66,** 588-92
agency by estoppel **87,** 639
amendment **53,** 423-4
applicable law **43,** 456-8, **47,** 102-4, 494, **48,** 111, 113, 117, **66,** 133-4, 343-5, 364-5, **75,** 51, 375, **77,** 44, **83,** 555-8, 559. *See also* applicable law, employment contract
choice of law clause. *See* choice of law clause *below*
connecting factors **91,** 253
damages for breach of contract **86,** 470-1
depecage **87,** 636
disputes procedure, possibility of divergence **82,** 69-70
employment. *See* applicable law, employment contract
European Convention on the Law Applicable to Contractual Obligations (1980) **86,** 99, **87,** 97, 99
foreign investment contract
choice of law clause **86,** 457
conflict of law rules **86,** 457
ICSID Convention **86,** 457
principles of international law **86,** 456-7
trade usages **86,** 456
implementation **86,** 259
law of parties **86,** 257
nationality of parties **91,** 253
performance **42,** 150
place of conclusion **91,** 253, **94,** 142
place of performance **65,** 127, **86,** 105, **91,** 253, **94,** 142
principal place of business of party required to effect performance **87,** 99, 100
Uniform Act Governing the International Sale of Goods **87,** 99
Warsaw Convention on International Carriage by Air (1929) and **87,** 372, 385
arms sales. *See* arms dealing
binding force **89,** 339
blockade and **78,** 584
breach **78,** 668, 669, 672-3
act of State, whether **86,** 459-69
breach of duty of full disclosure **114,** 174-9, 208-10, 227-9, 269-71
breach of law as **106,** 612-16
damages for **84,** 453-4, **86,** 471-3, **89,** 339, **114,** 209-10
defective performance, waiver **114,** 225
discrimination **84,** 453
evidence of **86,** 468, 484
exchange controls **83,** 583
expropriation/nationalization **66,** 583, 592-3, 624-5, **83,** 551, **118,** 316-17
as cause of unlawfulness **83,** 561-3
failure of condition precedent **114,** 176
failure to follow acceptance procedures **114,** 184-5, 186-7

contract (*cont.*)
government action leading to, responsibility for **64,** 196-203, 319-20, **106,** 194-7. *See also* frustration, government intervention as *below*; *force majeure*, government intervention as
justification, *exceptio non adimpleti contractus. See exceptio non adimpleti contractus below*
liability if due to acts of third party **83,** 560-1
maritime claim **96,** 377
simultaneous breach of law **106,** 524-5
State immunity as defence **86,** 460, 462
State responsibility **86,** 295-6
termination for **86,** 468, **89,** 480
unlawful conduct **106,** 619-20, 705-15
capacity to conclude, revolutionary movement **103,** 266-7
changed circumstances, independence **47,** 102-4
choice of law clause **53,** 443-5, **66,** 171-2, 319-20, 343-5, 364-5, 520-1, 560-1, **68,** 561-5, 575, 589-91, 596, 600, 609-10, 613-14, 626-9, 636, **69,** 596-7, **83,** 555, **86,** 257, 457, **87,** 635-6, **91,** 253, **107,** 266-7
c.i.f.
laws of sale **43,** 142, 143-4, 145, 146
nature of **43,** 143, 148, 150, 152
civil law **86,** 465, 466
concession. *See* concession agreement; oil, concessions; State contract
customs and usages **84,** 452, **86,** 258-9
default, rights of other party **49,** 203
definition **89,** 461-3
civil law **89,** 461-2
common law **89,** 462-3
disinvestment negotiations distinguished **124,** 55-6
duty of management, obligation of result, whether **114,** 230-2, 293-7
employment. *See* employment contract
with enemy company, validity **48,** 475-8
enforceability **74,** 298-301, **91,** 252, 254
enforcement
by agent **64,** 536-7, 538
involving breach of foreign law **78,** 597-8
equilibrium **66,** 588, 590-1, 626-7
European Convention on the Law Applicable to Contractual Obligations (1980)
applicable law and **87,** 97, 99
customary international law, whether **87,** 97, 99
exceptio non adimpleti contractus **54,** 319-20, **114,** 210-21, 304-7
equitable principle **114,** 212
interdependent agreements **114,** 214-15, 219-21
international law **114,** 212
notice of default, need for **114,** 211, 220, 233-7
partial failure **114,** 212-13
test, failure rendering achievement of parties' intention impossible **114,** 215-16
timing of invocation **114,** 211
as exception to legal regime **83,** 556
exchange. *See* exchange contract
exclusive dealing contract, EEC Treaty and **44,** 393-408
force majeure. See force majeure
formation **84,** 445-6, 448-51

duress **86,** 272-3
offer/acceptance **84,** 448-9, **124,** 56
parties' intention **84,** 449
place of **87,** 13, 16, 18
forum selection clause. *See* forum selection clause
fraudulent misrepresentation **87,** 636-9, 643-5
financial and technical capacity of claimants **106,** 616-19
frustration **78,** 583-9
accession to independence and **47,** 102-4
date of **64,** 252-4, 373-4
diplomatic and consular relations, break and **64,** 370-1
government intervention as **64,** 250-4, 372-9, **86,** 453. *See also* breach, government action leading to, responsibility for *above*
State agency/State-owned corporation, right to rely on **64,** 250-4, 377-9
US Iranian Assets Control Regulations **72,** 241-7
'restraint of princes' **78,** 584
war and **78,** 583-91
gas, for supply of
immunity, jurisdiction **80,** 438
nature **80,** 438
government, change of **62,** 172-3
instrumentum, need for **89,** 463
insurance
choice of law **42,** 149-52
contra proferentem **56,** 330
excepted perils **74,** 7-8, 21-35
interdependent contracts
hierarchy **114,** 261
presumption of compatibility **114,** 254-5, 258, 259, 261
self-executing nature of earlier agreement **114,** 255-7, 259-60
international. *See* concession agreement; economic development agreement; State contract
international law of **86,** 258-9
international organizations, applicable law **80,** 27, 71
interpretation. *See* contract, interpretation
legality **91,** 253-5
liability
agent **84,** 582-3
successor to **84,** 582-4
mistake **87,** 640
modification **86,** 265-8
MFN clause **86,** 267
tacit amendment **86,** 265-7
monetary clause **82,** 63
pacta sunt servanda **56,** 139, 283, **66,** 590, **83,** 561-2, **89,** 495-7
parties
'approved, agreed, ratified' stamp, effect **86,** 451-4, 484-7
non-Signatory State **83,** 556-8
performance
abroad, right to sue on **48,** 171-4
collateral guarantee of continuing legality under law of place of **64,** 376-7
evidence of **78,** 667

contract (*cont.*)
promissory estoppel **84,** 446
property right, as **62,** 221, 224, **89,** 339
public policy considerations **113,** 497
public or private law character **47,** 150-1
renegotiation clause **86,** 294-5
rights
foreign State interference or repudiation **66,** 16, 33-4, 182-4, 343-5, 363-5, 369-73, **67,** 332-9, 368-74
personal and real **37,** 187
risk **106,** 657-8, 732-3
seaman's, forum **42,** 104-7
State contract. *See* State contract
State succession and. *See* State succession, contractual obligations
State's duty to respect **83,** 561
pacta sunt servanda distinguished **83,** 561-2
UNGA Resolution 1803 (XVII) (Permanent Sovereignty over Natural Resources) **83,** 561, 613 n. 12
substitute **63,** 156-7
synallagmatic **89,** 465
termination **78,** 668, 673
breach, for **86,** 468, **89,** 480
change of basis for contract **84,** 440
changed circumstances **86,** 270-1
force majeure. See force majeure
non-performance **86,** 465
rescission **86,** 465
third party obligations **81,** 716-17
tortious interference with, State, immunity, jurisdiction **63,** 169, 229, 231, 243-4, 385, 619-21
unilateral **37,** 67
validity **78,** 665-8
continuing, parties' conduct **86,** 268
contract with enemy company **48,** 475-8
evidence of **121,** 23-8
voidable **86,** 465-7
fraudulent misrepresentation **86,** 466
war
arbitration clause **67,** 628-9
effect **52,** 475, 476-81, 483-5, 489-91, **53,** 609-12, **54,** 523-4, 525-7, **78,** 583-91
Warsaw Convention on International Carriage by Air (1929) and **87,** 372, 385
contract, interpretation
aids
conduct of parties **78,** 667
context **77,** 5
applicable law **107,** 216
applicable law **66,** 343-5, 364-5
bilingual **68,** 580, 583, 599
guidelines
clear language **107,** 216
consistency with applicable law **107,** 208, 218
language of **82,** 103
meaning not necessarily fixed **77,** 5

ordinary 'business' meaning **107,** 507
parties' intention **77,** 18
reconciliation of conflicting clauses **87,** 543-4
sentence as a whole **114,** 257
municipal systems **37,** 185, 192-3
phrases
'carry out' **114,** 257-8
'civil war' **107,** 507
'insurrection' **107,** 507
'jurisdiction' **77,** 4-8
'peace treaty' **40,** 434-5
'rebellion' **107,** 507
responsibility, courts **82,** 103
Contras, US aid to **76,** 387-401. *See also* State responsibility, imputability, United States for acts of *Contras*
Control Council Law No 10 91, 48
as applicable law in occupied Germany **36,** 39-41, **91,** 59-60, **111,** 343-4, 398 n. 12, 400-1, 407
former combatants **122,** 81 n. 405
German courts **111,** 417, 420
military tribunals **105,** 451-2, **111,** 398 n. 12, 400-1
rules of procedure those of domestic military courts **121,** 274-5
complicity/aiding and abetting **121,** 275-82
crimes against humanity
definition **36,** 48-9, **119,** 353, **121,** 266
individual responsibility **112,** 225-36
rape **121,** 266
requirements
armed conflict **112,** 208
discrimination **124,** 178
nexus with war crime **105,** 451-2, 525
torture **121,** 255
customary international law **111,** 398, 417, **124,** 178
international law, correspondence with **36,** 39-41, **91,** 48
mens rea **121,** 287 n. 262
retroactivity **91,** 48
statutory limitation **119,** 357
torture **121,** 254-5
war crimes **36,** 31, 39-41, **121,** 254-5, 266
'control', test of. *See* State agency/State-owned corporation/State entity, control, test
Convention for the Conservation of Southern Bluefin Tuna (1993), Law of the Sea Convention (1982) and **117,** 161-2, 182-4
conventions. *See* treaties
convictions. *See* freedom of conscience
Cook Islands
Constitution, Art. 71 **104,** 536-7, 569, 574-6
foreign law, recognition/enforcement
comity and **104,** 507
morality of law, relevance **104,** 507
Government Auditor
immunity from New Zealand jurisdiction **104,** 576
status **104,** 568-9, 574-6, 611

Cook Islands (*cont.*)
law of
Government Property Corporation Act 1969
s 4(3) **104,** 536
s 8 **104,** 536
International Companies Act 1981-82
extraterritorial effect **104,** 540-1, 555, 588-9, 601
s 219 **104,** 504
s 224 **104,** 504
s 227 **104,** 504-6, 541, 551-3, 588
s 227(3) **104,** 540-1
s 227(8) **104,** 540-1, 555, 588-9
New Zealand law **104,** 503-4
legislation, interpretation, phrases, 'in relation to any person who is a resident of the Cook Islands' **104,** 589
nationality, New Zealand **104,** 577
status **104,** 501 n. 1
associated Statehood **104,** 503
good faith **104,** 576-7, 624
Exchange of Letters between Prime Minister of New Zealand and Premier of Cook Islands 1973/4 **104,** 568-9, 577, 624
sovereign **104,** 503-4, 537, 568-9, 611
tax haven, legitimacy **104,** 534-6, 547-8, 620-1
cooperation agreement. *See also* concession agreement; economic development agreement; European Community treaties, EEC/SFRY Cooperation Agreement (1980); State contract for nuclear energy exploitation **65,** 94-8
copyright. *See also* Uruguay Round, Agreement on Trade-related Aspects of Intellectual Property Rights (TRIPS)
film score **65,** 145
Soviet, extraterritorial effect **39,** 431-2
State immunity, jurisdiction and **65,** 143-5
war-related infringement, compensation **40,** 427-8, **44,** 490-4
coroner, jurisdiction 78, 551-63
place of death, relevance **78,** 551-63
purpose **78,** 563
Corporacion Venezolana de Fomento. *See* Venezuela, Corporacion Venezolana de Fomento
corporal punishment
inhuman or degrading, whether **103,** 93-101
arbitrary **103,** 94, 97, 104
attack on dignity **103,** 94, 97, 103
demeaning to State **103,** 94, 97
impersonal **103,** 94, 97
international consensus **103,** 94-6
irrational **103,** 94, 97
judicial organs of State **103,** 84-92
adult offenders **103,** 94-7
juvenile offenders **103,** 97-100, 103-4
method, relevance **103,** 98-100
motive, relevance **103,** 97-8
schools **103,** 92-3, 100-1, 103-4
authority delegated by parent **103,** 101

corporate interests, diplomatic protection of **46,** 70-1, 94, 226-31, 253-7, 295-7, 302-3, 306, 314, 315, 339-41, 369
corporate personality
fiction theory **46,** 294, 306, 471
Gierke's theory **46,** 343
realist theory **46,** 294, 471
relative theory **46,** 298
corporate veil, lifting of. *See* corporation, piercing the corporate veil
corporation 60, 137-40
applicable law. *See* applicable law, corporation
assets
confiscation **73,** 235-6, 239-40, 245-6
effective control of **56,** 319-20, 326
expropriation/nationalization **78,** 678-9, 680-2
effect on existence **44,** 65-6
of mother corporation **78,** 678-9, 680-2
ownership **78,** 681
equitable **78,** 681
shareholders **40,** 24
sole shareholder **40,** 130-1, 142-5
recovery **56,** 300-5, **73,** 233, 247-9
of State-owned corporation. *See* State-owned agency/State-owned corporation/State entity
capacity **73,** 586-7, 599-600
characteristics **46,** 291-3, 298, 305-6
church as **108,** 496-7
confiscation
assets **73,** 235-6, 239-40, 245-6
plant, legal identity following **71,** 14-36, **72,** 27, 554-6, 559, 561, **73,** 582-3, 585, 589-93
control over **56,** 270
effective control of assets **56,** 319-20, 326
creation of, legal consequences **43,** 36
de facto company **40,** 122, 131, 134, 136-40
debts, liability for
enforceability of award **96,** 17
fraudulent intent **96,** 16-17
piercing the corporate veil **96,** 16-17
definition **103,** 362-3
diplomatic protection. *See* diplomatic protection, corporation
dissolution
applicable law **89,** 572-3
arbitration agreement, effect on **89,** 572-3
domicile **42,** 410, 411, **61,** 51-4, 55, 62, 65-8, 79, **71,** 5-36, **73,** 582-93
change of **71,** 13-36, **72,** 555-6, 559, 562-3, 567-8
commercial **40,** 474
election **73,** 580
government decree transferring **71,** 17-35, **72,** 555-6, 562-3, **73,** 585, 591
head office **65,** 203-4
law governing **71,** 21-2, 27-30, **72,** 559, 562-3, 567, **73,** 574-80
nationality and **85,** 7
place of incorporation **85,** 6

corporation (*cont.*)
place of registration **85,** 6
enemy character. *See* enemy character, corporation; enemy corporation
European Convention on Human Rights (1950) and **60,** 137
expropriation. *See* expropriation/nationalization, of corporation; expropriation/nationalization, of corporation assets
foreign
applicable law **43,** 74, 75-6, **46,** 193
capacity to sue in US courts **63,** 109
claims of local creditors **54,** 546
conduct in host country **59,** 388
confiscation of assets
effect on debt owed to State **66,** 409
extinction of corporation **66,** 95-8, 467-70
succession in interest **66,** 467-8
control of **59,** 420
dissolution by State, ownership of assets abroad **66,** 97-9, **69,** 9-10
injury to, compensation for **56,** 271
Legal Personality of Foreign Corporations, Convention on Recognition of (1956) **47,** 217, 226-8
political activity **59,** 390
private **66,** 277, 294
recognition **85,** 6, 10-11, 13, 14, 20, 23-4
common law principle **85,** 23
registration requirements **46,** 230
right to sue **85,** 10-11
State, distinct from **63,** 149
succession in interest **66,** 467-8
in occupied territory **61,** 50
foreign investment
insurance **59,** 423-4
protection of **59,** 378-9
freedom of expression and **60,** 141
hegemony of **46,** 238, 242, 252
holding companies **46,** 228-31, 442, 454
human rights and **60,** 137-40
injury to, protection of shareholders **46,** 23, 26, 55-6, 64-75, 121-5, 180, 188, 199-200, 205-25, 240-57, 289-315, 342-4, 365-75, 379, 399, 402-4, 405-16, 418-38, 446-53, 470-6, 489, 491-507, 509-30
international companies. *See* multinational corporation
international organizations distinguished **77,** 28
international public undertaking
applicable law
constituent instrument **96,** 308-9
national law of contracting party **96,** 308-9, 319
jurisdiction over
non-resident **63,** 42-5, 50, 117, **73,** 579-80
personal and territorial **46,** 340-1
siège administratif **41,** 393
siège social **41,** 391
legal identity **61,** 60-2, 65
liability of members **81,** 681, 708-9
mixed entities **81,** 679

municipal law, as institution of, international law, recognition by **46,** 207-11, 240
name, applicable law **72,** 557-60, 563-5
nationality **39,** 430-1, **41,** 376, 384-95, **44,** 134-5, **46,** 23, 26, 216, 226, 257, 265, 296-7, 314, 356-7, 369, 378-9, 454, 469, 521-2, **47,** 216-32, **54,** 545, **61,** 416-18, **69,** 603, 605-13, 616-17, 621-2, 632, **71,** 604-8, 614-15, 667-8, 690-1, **72,** 567-8, 727-32, **83,** 514, **84,** 490-2, **86,** 246-7, **89,** 386-8
applicable law
dependent territory, in case of **106,** 585
place of incorporation **89,** 387
social seat **89,** 387
BIT/NAFTA provisions distinguished **125,** 134
change
purported **46,** 192, 279
treaty claim, effect on **125,** 75-6
'charter of convenience' **46,** 344, 356, 357, 379, 522
diplomatic protection and **70,** 509-10
dual **46,** 374
evidence of **46,** 378-94, 439, 456-7, **55,** 486, **84,** 490-2, 597, 651, **85,** 377-8, 428-30, **86,** 246-7, **89,** 323-4, 386-8
administrative and adversary proceedings contrasted **70,** 509
burden of proof **70,** 507-11, 519-20, 525-6
certificate of good standing **70,** 505-6, 520-1
inference from public documents **70,** 501, 504-5, 509-10, 523-5
methods **70,** 502-6, 511-26
ownership of company **45,** 109-10
rebuttal evidence **70,** 501, 519-20, 525-6
municipal law **70,** 508-9, 524-5
nationality of owners **84,** 490
neutral **44,** 497
notionality **73,** 573, 575
place of incorporation **84,** 496, **87,** 100-1, **89,** 484
shareholders' nationality **41,** 385, 393, **69,** 616-17, **70,** 123, 499-526, **71,** 607, 614-15, 668, 690, **72,** 727-32
confidentiality and **70,** 500, 519
continuous ownership **70,** 499, 502, 521-3
'subject of the State' **40,** 474
subsidiary companies **40,** 8, **70,** 505-6, **71,** 607, 667-8, **72,** 726-8
test for determining
administration and seat **45,** 442
control **46,** 473-4, **72,** 567-8, **73,** 572-4, 577, 579
domicile **85,** 7
incorporation into municipal law **85,** 6-7
ownership **45,** 109-10
place of incorporation **73,** 574-5, 579
principal establishment **73,** 574-5, 577, 579
registration **85,** 6-7
seat **72,** 567-8
siège social **72,** 567-8, **73,** 574-5, 579
nationalization. *See* expropriation/nationalization, corporation
nature **60,** 137-9
organization **46,** 516
ownership
assignment **83,** 467-9

corporation (*cont.*)
continuity of **83,** 467-9
control **84,** 496-7, 518-21
evidence of, share certificates **83,** 466
interests sufficient to control **84,** 497, 499
ownership and management, separation **46,** 292, 448-9
partnership **78,** 681
legal personality **47,** 33
personality **78,** 681
applicable law, *lex rei sitae* **77,** 450
recognition in State practice **46,** 432, 472
piercing the corporate veil **46,** 213, 249, 265-6, 291, 294, 331, 343 n. 1, 360, 378, **82,** 143, 144-5, **87,** 241-2, 254-5, **96,** 16-17
comity **103,** 500
debts, liability for **96,** 16-17
enemy property legislation **46,** 213, 357, 518
international organizations **80,** 138, 172, 616
State agency/State-owned corporation/State entity **79,** 595, **80,** 574, 578, **107,** 240
'practically defunct' **46,** 215, 246-9, 308, 367-8, 430, 450, 472, 493-4, 518-19
quasi-corporation **77,** 83-5
receiver, appointment, effect on corporate existence **46,** 215, 368
recognition **61,** 51-2, 53-4, 60, 62-3, 65, 77
State recognition and **100,** 253-4
rights, FCN treaty, under **84,** 389-91
seat
State succession, effect on **52,** 488-91
status as **65,** 203-4
transfer **41,** 369-79, 385, 392
effect **47,** 133
shareholders distinguished **84,** 389-91, **85,** 421-2, 431-6. *See also* shareholders
situs, determination **56,** 226-7
split companies **73,** 237, 239-41
State of incorporation, rights **42,** 415-21, 425
State succession, effect on corporate seat **52,** 488-91
status
applicable law
country of incorporation **77,** 28
lex rei sitae **77,** 450
private international law **77,** 28
quasi-corporation **77,** 85
stockholders agreements **54,** 567
subsidiaries
legal personality **80,** 429
whether acting on behalf of **48,** 112-13, 117, 120, 135, 140
succession **61,** 50, **69,** 576, 578-9, 581, 593-4
contractual obligations, liability for, de facto succession **69,** 581, 592-6, 618
supervision by host State **62,** 188
taxation **42,** 413-14
treaty, creation, by **85,** 9
Universal Declaration of Human Rights and **60,** 137
valuation, balance-sheet **96,** 327-8

correspondence. *See also* communications; European Convention on Human Rights (1950), correspondence, respect for; International Convention on Civil and Political Rights (ICCPR) (1966), correspondence; telecommunications; telephone tapping; Universal Postal Union (UPU)
crime committed by post **56,** 236
definition **70,** 183
European Agreement relating to Persons participating in proceedings of the European Commission and the Court of Human Rights **78,** 383-4, 386
exchange control enforcement and **70,** 154-83
foreign sender, right to compel delivery **56,** 238
Costa Rica
American Convention on Human Rights (1969), self-executing provisions **116,** 258
Constitution 1949 **75,** 16
Art. 10 **75,** 8
Art. 28 **75,** 66
Art. 29 **75,** 5, 20, 66
naturalization, proposed amendments **79,** 285-305
proposed amendments, submission to Inter-American Court of Human Rights **79,** 285-305
Continental Shelf Proclamation 1948 **41,** 118, 120
diplomatic privileges and immunities, scope **71,** 567-9, 571-2
freedom of expression, journalists, compulsory licensing **75,** 4-30, 33-75. *See also* law of, Law 4420 *below*
law of. *See also* Constitution 1949 *above*
Basic Law of Journalism **75,** 8
Law 4420 **75,** 8-9, 12, 14, 34-6, 57-8, 64, 71
text **75,** 9-10, 57-8, 60
nationality, acquisition **71,** 570-2
naturalization **79,** 287-9, 294-305
discrimination
non-native Central Americans **79,** 299, 302-3
sexual **79,** 299, 303-4
requirements **79,** 297-8, 302-4
Pact of San José **75,** 5
costs 40, 162, 164, **44,** 96, **46,** 186, 198, **54,** 469-71, **61,** 345, 348-9, 350-7, 359, **62,** 177, 216, 218, **67,** 344, 359, 383, 385, 393-4, **69,** 660, **70,** 127, **71,** 610, 630-1, 677, **72,** 247, 252, 492, 500, 724, **75,** 134, 608, 626, **77,** 189, 581, 668, 694, **78,** 123, **79,** 694, **80,** 650-1, **81,** 18-19, 56, 102, **82,** 375, 387, 477, 498, **84,** 588-9, 601, 638, 661, 671-2, **86,** 473, **88,** 531-2, 676, 677, **92,** 252-3, 298-300. *See also* American Convention on Human Rights (1969), costs and expenses; Asian Development Bank Administrative Tribunal, costs and expenses; damages; ICSID Convention (Convention on Settlement of Investment Disputes between States and Nationals of Other States (1965)), arbitral tribunal; Iran–US Claims Tribunal, costs
actually and necessarily incurred **92,** 299, **96,** 560
appeal
in criminal case **85,** 144-54
international official **43,** 286
arbitration costs **84,** 588, **95,** 230, **96,** 330, **117,** 564-5, **121,** 49
legal fees distinguished **96,** 330
arbitration proceedings **89,** 350-1, 513, 551, 654-7, **96,** 331-2
ICSID Convention (1965) **96,** 331

costs (*cont.*)
practice **96,** 331
UN Commission for International Commercial Law **96,** 331
in case of inferred finding of responsibility **116,** 318
currency of payment, conversion rate **108,** 429
damages for injuries, relevance **54,** 469-71
definition **105,** 64-5
determination, court or tribunal **81,** 227, **105,** 63-4
discretionary **107,** 63
domestic courts, in **88,** 531, 677, **92,** 371
equitable **81,** 31, 204, **88,** 531-2, **92,** 300, 317, 478, **113,** 485, 498
European Court of Human Rights proceedings. *See* just satisfaction (Art. 50 [41] of the European Convention on Human Rights (1950)), expenses *and* legal costs
European Court of Justice **48,** 143, 225
expenses and fees of arbitrators **95,** 211, 230
ICSID rate **95,** 230
President **95,** 230
expenses of witnesses **95,** 211
expert's **85,** 394, **107,** 46
friendly settlement **81,** 105-6, 236
Hague Convention for the Pacific Settlement of Disputes (1907) **105,** 67
ILO Administrative Tribunal **38,** 402, 434-8
doubt as to jurisdiction **43,** 459-62
Inter-American Court of Human Rights **116,** 294
interest on **108,** 428, 429
interpretation **58,** 469-71, 484-5, 706, **107,** 46
Iran–US Claims Tribunal proceedings. *See* Iran–US Claims Tribunal, costs
League of Arab States Administrative Tribunal **116,** 649
legal **57,** 199, **58,** 112, 412, 538, 717, 720, 722, **67,** 393-4
assessment **89,** 262
domestic courts, in **96,** 560, **101,** 159, **107,** 462, **111,** 251
additional costs caused by delay **96,** 450, 518
ECHR, proceedings before **81,** 31, 57-8, 180, 203, **89,** 183, 190, 206, 262, 308, **101,** 159, **107,** 46, **108,** 428, **111,** 187, 231, 251
legal aid, deduction **81,** 180
time spent **96,** 450
legal advice **96,** 584
legal aid, relevance **81,** 180, **89,** 309
legal expenses **96,** 497
legal representation **96,** 584
municipal courts, before **89,** 206, 262, 308
public policy and **86,** 404
reasonable **96,** 497
legal fees **81,** 31, 57-8, 180, 203, **84,** 588, **92,** 350, 371-2, **95,** 211, 231, **96,** 330-1, 497, 534, **98,** 318-19
direct payment to counsel **95,** 231
municipal courts, before **81,** 29-31, 57, **111,** 231
NATO Appeals Board. *See* NATO Appeals Board, costs
parties'
parties to pay own **105,** 67, 79, **121,** 49, **124,** 58, 61
State party to pay claimant's, two-thirds **106,** 473
practice **105,** 67
presumption of innocence and **72,** 399-404

proceedings for annulment of arbitral award **114,** 310-11
reasonable **92,** 299, **96,** 560
relevant factors
absence of fault on part of unsuccessful party **121,** 49
bad faith **89,** 350, **96,** 331-2, **125,** 163
complexity of issues **125,** 39, 96-7
contributory fault of successful party **121,** 28
enforceability **103,** 5, **121,** 28
failure to abandon case **103,** 124-6
frivolous proceedings **118,** 370-1
jurisdiction, termination **103,** 4-5
novelty/public importance of issues **121,** 28, **125,** 39, 96-7, 163
security for
aliens **47,** 239-40
Hague Conventions on Civil Procedure **48,** 215-16
special rapporteur, proceedings in respect of **121,** 404-5, 413-14, 433, 448, 471
translation **96,** 584, **107,** 46
travel and subsistence **58,** 486, 723, **67,** 393, **88,** 532, **92,** 317, **96,** 534, 584, **98,** 318-19
tribunal
equally divided **105,** 63-7, **124,** 1080
State party to pay 60% **105,** 66, 69, **106,** 473
UN Administrative Tribunal **54,** 419-21, 469-71
unsuccessful case, in **92,** 299-300, **121,** 28
witnesses, unnecessary attendance **67,** 445
Council of Europe
Appeals Board **51,** 445-50
time-limits **38,** 439-43
Committee of Ministers **56,** 396, **58,** 578, 644, **62,** 34, 37, 44, 54, 64, 68-9, 81
Consultative Assembly, Resolution 337 **73,** 383-5
death penalty (Resolution 1044 (1944)) **124,** 326
harmonization of law relating to treatment of aliens, need for **111,** 267-8
lawyers, remuneration **58,** 709
municipal law and **58,** 583
officials, employment **51,** 438-56
organs, Commission of Human Rights **41,** 442, 446, 449
practice of **62,** 72
Privileges and Immunities, General Agreement on **41,** 443, 448
Recommendations, R (84) 15 of 18 September 1984 (reparation for damage caused by unlawful act of public authority) **111,** 77, 88 n. 98, 89
Statute **41,** 442-3, 449
counterclaims. *See also* Iran–US Claims Settlement Declaration, counterclaims; Iran–US Claims Tribunal, counterclaims; State immunity, jurisdiction, applicability, counterclaim arising out of the same subject matter; State immunity, jurisdiction, waiver, counterclaim as
admissibility
Court's discretion **115,** 242-3, 245, 250-3
criminal cases **115,** 248-50
ICJ
Bosnia and Herzegovina v. *Yugoslavia* **115,** 206-53
oral hearings, need for **115,** 227, 236
State immunity cases **115,** 241-2
ILC Draft Articles on Jurisdictional Immunities of States and their Property (1991) **115,** 241-2

counterclaims (*cont.*)
autonomy **115,** 216-17, 222-3
basis
consistency of decision-making **115,** 217-18
procedural economy **115,** 217-18, 235-6
defence on merits distinguished **115,** 217
United States Diplomatic and Consular Staff in Tehran **115,** 217
definition **115,** 246-50
equality of parties **115,** 220, 226
for
defective performance, where counter-claimant should have known better **114,** 225-6
unsatisfactory performance **106,** 647-8
ICJ **84,** 282-3
joinder, automatic, whether **115,** 224-6
jurisdiction **106,** 718
legal nature **115,** 223
requirements
'arising out of the subject-matter' **120,** 442-6
defensive **120,** 441-2, 457
'direct connection with the subject-matter of the claim of the other party' **115,** 218, 224-31, 245
Court's discretion to determine **115,** 218, 224-7
Diversion of Water from the Meuse **115,** 229
facts of the same nature **115,** 218
factual connection **115,** 218, 228
legal connection **115,** 218, 228-31
part of the same factual complex **115,** 218, 230
reasonable time-scale for decision **115,** 220
reciprocity of obligations, relevance **115,** 218-19
security, US and non-US actions compared **63,** 417-18
'within the jurisdiction of the Court' **115,** 245
as recognized by the parties **115,** 218
third party
effect on admissibility **115,** 243, 253
protection, transmission of Order **115,** 220
countermeasures 61, 542-4, 569-70, 589, 593-5. *See also* economic sanctions; intervention in affairs of another State, countermeasures; reprisals
customary international law **116,** 229, 239
diplomatic staff, forcible release
attempt at **61,** 543-4
lawfulness **61,** 569-70, 580-1
economic **60,** 645, 650-1, **61,** 542-3, 589, **63,** 455, 504-9, **72,** 249-51
GATT, compatibility with **60,** 646, 648-9
force. *See* force, prohibition on the use or threat of
Foreign Sovereign Immunities Act (USA) and **63,** 432, 503-4
grounds, breach of treaty or rule of international law **116,** 74, 143, 228-35
hostages, forcible release
attempt at **61,** 543-4
lawfulness of **61,** 569-70, 580-1
ILC [Draft] Articles on State responsibility (1977/1980/1996/1998/2001) **116,** 228, 239
lawfulness **61,** 554, 569-70, 580-1
military **61,** 543, 569-70, 580-1
requirements

absence of alternative **116,** 229-30
direction against offending State **116,** 64-5
intention to force compliance with obligations **116,** 65-6, 143, 231, 233
previous wrongful international act of another State **116,** 64-5, 229, 231
prior request to discontinue or remedy wrongful act **116,** 65
proportionality **116,** 61, 65, 143, 215, 221, 229, 231, 232-5
reversibility **116,** 65-6, 239
responsibility for determining validity **116,** 228
self-defence, whether **61,** 570, 593-5
treaties, effect upon **61,** 553-4, 556-9
US measures against Iran **61,** 542-4, 569-70, 589, 593-5, **63,** 432-3, 455, 499, 504-9
as violation of State immunity **63,** 504-9
countervailing duties. *See* General Agreement on Tariffs and Trade (GATT) (1947), countervailing duties
'country', 'whole of the territory subject under one sovereign to one body of law' **108,** 549
'county waters' doctrine 91, 430-3, 437-8
coup d'état. *See* civil strife; civil war; rebellion; revolution
Court of Arbitration for Sport (Ad Hoc Division: Sydney Olympic Games)
ad hoc Rules
16 **120,** 5
17 **120,** 5
18 **120,** 5
applicable law
applicable general principles of law and the rules of law **120,** 5
applicable regulations **120,** 5
Olympic charter **120,** 5
procedure **120,** 5
basis of jurisdiction **120,** 5
procedure
applicable law
CAS ad hoc Rules **120,** 5
Swiss Private International Law Act of 18 December 1987 **120,** 5
courtesy. *See* international courtesy
courts, municipal. *See also* constitutional review; judicial review; jurisdiction; separation of powers
access to. *See* access to courts; European Convention on Human Rights (1950), access to courts
advisory functions **115,** 543-4
appeal court's right to exercise original jurisdiction **115,** 541-2
application of foreign law **93,** 236, 239
arbitral award, review of **56,** 329-40
assumed reluctance of foreign State to use **83,** 238
authority, basis **39,** 233-4, **53,** 56, 59, 62
belligerent occupation. *See* belligerent occupation
boundary disputes, settlement of **57,** 110-11
capacity to determine status of usurping government **53,** 72, 75, 76-81
competence of foreign **52,** 57-8, 67
Constitution, relationship to **39,** 359-60
customary law
modification **87,** 113-16, 118-19
reception into law and **87,** 113-16, 118-19
definition **67,** 468
duty to keep in step with State practice **77,** 17

courts, municipal (*cont.*)
EC, and. *See* European Community law, national courts, role
ecclesiastical courts in Morocco, jurisdiction after independence **45,** 53-6
ECJ and **93,** 416-18, 424-6, 438
enemy aliens. *See* enemy aliens, access to courts
external trade regulation **93,** 262-3
extradition, role **90,** 415, 685
foreign relations and **87,** 175
general principles of law **53,** 460-1
independence **46,** 328. *See also* State responsibility for acts and omissions of, judicial authorities
international law, application. *See* international law, municipal courts, application by
international law, role **90,** 397-8
international relations and **60,** 40, 45-6
judicial assistance and **57,** 167-8
jurisdiction. *See also* jurisdiction
'civil or commercial matters' **84,** 735-51
court's duty to examine *proprio motu* **36,** 20
domestic legislation as basis **84,** 740
foreign legislation, determination of legality **64,** 219-20, **119,** 92
obtaining of evidence for use abroad **84,** 737, 742
ouster, martial law, by **87,** 260, 261, 263-4
legislation, examination of validity of, standing, plaintiff **70,** 57-8, 64-6, 76-7, 86-8, 97, 101
legislative procedures, role **93,** 231, 232
legislature and **55,** 59, **56,** 17, **84,** 761-2
locus standi. See standing *below*
political protest, forum for **80,** 23
refusal of sanctions **80,** 23-4
requirements, standing, sufficiency of interest **106,** 407
role. *See also* separation of powers
interpretation of law **103,** 265
recognition, government, pre-revolutionary **103,** 72, 77-8
war, determination of state of **87,** 273-5
sovereignty of State under which constituted, power to determine **82,** 398-9
standing **80,** 28, **93,** 485-6
capacity distinguished **107,** 418-19
citizen intervener **122,** 636-8
confiscated business, former owner **66,** 94-8, 254-5, 354
consul **101,** 468-70
EC accession, challenge to **93,** 229, 231, 232
foreign corporation **66,** 93, 97-101
hypothetical question **118,** 343-4, 365-6
international organizations, bankruptcy proceedings **107,** 416-18
legitimate expectation **90,** 451-2
parent **103,** 164-5, 188-9
popularis actio **103,** 162-3, 181
representation of persons protected under the Treaty of Waitangi (1840) **120,** 470, 535
requirements
actual harm **103,** 165-7
infringement of individual rights **93,** 511, 512-13, **103,** 162-8, 180-3, **106,** 325-6, **118,** 344
sufficient interest **90,** 451

undisclosed principal **107,** 266-7
wife in respect of refusal of residence permit to alien husband **103,** 231-2
State immunity, responsibility for determining **84,** 153
State responsibility **93,** 200-1
States, dispute between **91,** 296, 299, 315-16
absence of alternative forum **91,** 298, 299, 301
compétence de la compétence **91,** 299
enforceability of decision, relevance **91,** 314-15
immovable property **91,** 294, 299
international law as applicable law, relevance **91,** 294, 300, 316
State succession, relevance **91,** 300-1
supervisory powers **90,** 666, 686
treaties
operation and enforcement **90,** 657-8
powers **73,** 700-1, 704, **74,** 47, 99-100, 144, 311-13, 703-4, **75,** 5-6, 8, **77,** 31
responsibility **77,** 503, 553
UN Administrative Tribunal **40,** 384
creditor claims 42, 155-8, 161-3, 186
against State wronging debtor **46,** 209, 424
creeks 69, 50
crimes against humanity 36, 239-52, 288, **72,** 607-14, **78,** 125-48, **91,** 67-8, 124-32. *See also* Genocide Convention (1948); international crimes; Rwanda, International Criminal Tribunal for (ICTR); terrorism; war crimes; Yugoslavia, International Criminal Tribunal for the Former (ICTY), Statute, 5 (crimes against humanity)
'act of criminal sovereignty', whether **122,** 79
act of State and **36,** 254, 280, **66,** 50-8
aiding and abetting. *See* war crimes, aiding and abetting
applicable law
Geneva Conventions (1949), First Additional Protocol relating to the Protection of Victims of International Armed Conflicts (1977) **112,** 211-12
Nuremberg Charter (1945) **100,** 333
basis
common problems of civilized nations **104,** 336
desire to include crimes outside reach of traditional war crimes law **112,** 204-5
need to protect civilian population **111,** 382-3
civilian population, acts against as requirement **91,** 126, **104,** 313, **108,** 33-5, 62-3, 64, **111,** 328, **112,** 249. *See also* classification, civilian population, acts against *above*
Barbie **112,** 212-13, **122,** 79
Control Council Law No 10 **122,** 81 n. 405
discrimination **112,** 218-19, 241-7, 249, **122,** 94
evidence of **83,** 551, **122,** 114-23, 166-8
former combatants **108,** 64, 133, **112,** 210-14, **122,** 81
as a group **22,** 88-9, **108,** 33-5, 64, **111,** 328, **112,** 214-15, **122,** 76
ICTR Statute **122,** 76
ILC Draft Code of Crimes Against the Peace and Security of Mankind (1994) **112,** 215-17
nexus between act or omission and **124,** 165-6
Nuremberg Charter (1945) **112,** 212
presence of non-civilians, relevance **122,** 81-3
resistance movements and **122,** 81-3
single act **108,** 64-5
status of victim, relevance **122,** 81
widespread or systematic policy. *See* widespread or systematic policy *below*

crimes against humanity (*cont.*)
classification as
civilian population, acts against **108,** 33-5, 91, 130-2, **112,** 207-23, 249. *See also* civilian population, acts against as requirement *above*
destruction of property **108,** 91
detention **108,** 30, 91
Geneva Conventions (1949) and Protocols **108,** 44-5, **112,** 211-12
unlawful appropriation of property **36,** 240-2, **108,** 30, 36
unlawful transfer **108,** 31
confiscation of property **36,** 240-2
crimes of extermination **91,** 124, 131
cruel treatment **112,** 250-2, 257
beating **112,** 253-4, 260
where person already dead **112,** 255-6
deportation or forcible transfer of civilians **36,** 239, 243-52, **78,** 139, 146, **122,** 88, 179
disappearances **95,** 292
enslavement **36,** 239
extermination **36,** 239
genocide **36,** 41, **78,** 147, **119,** 229, **121,** 357
hijacking **80,** 679
human shields **122,** 83-4
inhuman acts **112,** 88, 93, 97, 102, 103, 107, 255, **122,** 22, 244
beating **112,** 253-4, 260
'calling-out' **112,** 258-9
in case of person already dead **112,** 255-6
sexual assault other than rape **121,** 268
wilful infliction of serious mental or physical injury and great suffering **122,** 89-90
inhuman or degrading treatment **108,** 27-8, 56-7, 62-3
confiscation of property **36,** 240-2
genocide as **108,** 91
motivation of victims, relevance **78,** 140, 146-7
murder **36,** 239, **108,** 25-7, 57-8, 62-3, 224, **112,** 106, 258, 259, **122,** 22, 83, 138-9, 244
mass **108,** 58-9
persecution **91,** 124, 131, **112,** 240-1, **122,** 21, 83-9, 126, 206. *See also* persecution in name of State practising ideological supremacy *below*
crimes against the Jewish people **36,** 30-1, 41-2, **122,** 84-7
cultural **112,** 246
customary international law **122,** 84
definition **112,** 237-46, **122,** 83-9
discrimination as **122,** 86-7, 88-9
ILC **122,** 86
as member of group **122,** 88-9
as member of group of which perpetrator is not a member **122,** 89
mens rea **122,** 88, 90-4
nationals **36,** 239
Nuremberg Tribunal **122,** 84-5
plunder of public or private property **122,** 88, 244
political **36,** 239, **108,** 91, **112,** 246
on political, racial or religious grounds **100,** 352, 364, **122,** 88
racial **36,** 239, **108,** 91, **112,** 246
religious **108,** 30, 91, **112,** 246

serious bodily and mental harm **122,** 84-7
violation of individual's right to enjoyment of fundamental rights **112,** 246, **122,** 84-7
persecution in name of State practising ideological supremacy **100,** 350-1, 363, 364. *See also* persecution *above*; widespread or systematic policy *below*
against opponents of policy **100,** 352
at instigation of officer of that State **100,** 363
of identifiable group of people **104,** 357-8, 359
in name of State **104,** 365-6
Nazi Germany **100,** 355-6
Vichy State **100,** 352-5
responsibility of courts **119,** 352
starvation **36,** 239
torture **108,** 29-30, 37, **119,** 229, **121,** 255-6
sexual assault **108,** 29-30, 37
unlawful detention of civilians **122,** 88
wanton destruction and plunder of property not justified by necessity **122,** 88, 139-40, 173-82, 244
common purpose **124,** 136-62
criminalization of offences, State practice **105,** 520-4
customary international law **104,** 200-2, 337-8, **105,** 451, 500-24, 569-70, 586-7, **112,** 205-6, **119,** 106-7, 353-4
armed conflict, need for **105,** 494, 525-6, **124,** 166
internal conflict **105,** 504-24, **108,** 45-6
unconditional respect for fundamental human rights **108,** 46-7
war crimes, nexus **105,** 525
defence
any defence available under international law at the time or at time of proceedings **104,** 331-4, 366
any defence available under *lex fori* at the time or at time of proceedings **104,** 331-4, 366
autrefois convict **104,** 366
behaviour of other party **108,** 46-7
duress **111,** 313, 314, 333-79
absence of alternative **108,** 187-8
imminent physical danger **108,** 187-8
proportionality, need for **108,** 187
legality under laws of place where act committed **104,** 296-7, 310, 334, 366, 377-80
manifest illegality **104,** 379, 381
mistake of fact **104,** 367-8
municipal law provision for similar offences **104,** 297-8
necessity **36,** 340
nullum crimen nulla poena sine lege, absence of precise penalty at time of offence **108,** 195-6
peace officer **104,** 331, 332, 366-7, 378-9
superior orders. *See* superior orders
definition **75,** 342, 359-60, 362-3, **91,** 121-2. *See also* classification as *above*; requirements *below*
Control Council Law No 10 **36,** 48-9, **119,** 353, **121,** 266
customary international law. *See* customary international law *above*
decisions of municipal courts **119,** 353
French Criminal Code (1994) **119,** 353
ICC, Rome Statute (1998) **119,** 354

crimes against humanity (*cont.*)
ICTR **119,** 217, 353
ICTY **105,** 450-2, **119,** 353
municipal law **36,** 239, **104,** 197, 357
Nuremberg Charter (1945) **36,** 48-9, **78,** 131, **91,** 57-8, 60, 126-7, **100,** 349, 350, 363, **105,** 451, 524-5, **119,** 67, 68, 353, **122,** 74
offence against ordinary law committed in certain circumstances **100,** 349, 350, 351, **104,** 361
serious crimes against civilian population **91,** 124, 131, **119,** 217
development of concept **112,** 204-6
double criminality **104,** 198
offence under *lex fori* at the time **104,** 198, 202-4, 354
evidence of **108,** 65-6
authority of accused **108,** 119-29
exclusion of alien for **104,** 198
general principle of international law **104,** 296, 336-8
general principle of law **37,** 456-9
Geneva Conventions (1949) **105,** 500, 503-15, 586-7
genocide. *See* genocide
Hague Conventions (1899/1907) **105,** 500-4
Head of State immunity, jurisdiction **119,** 45-8, 98-9
immunity, legislation providing for removal **119,** 360. *See also* Head of State, immunity, jurisdiction
individuals, acts against **91,** 126
international crimes, whether
before 1945 **91,** 58-61, 131
Commission on the Responsibility of the Authors of the War and on Enforcement of Penalties (1919) **91,** 125
customary international law **91,** 60, 124-30
international law and
absence of court/code, relevance **104,** 336
as violation of **36,** 295-7
judicial assistance, UNGA Resolution 3074 (1973) **91,** 35, **108,** 207, **119,** 99
jurisdiction **36,** 295-6, **78,** 128-31, 136-41, **79,** 545-6. *See also* International Criminal Court (ICC); Rwanda, International Criminal Tribunal for (ICTR); Yugoslavia, International Criminal Tribunal for the Former (ICTY)
absence of provision **125,** 573
accused within territory **104,** 354
aut dedere aut punire/judicare **119,** 356-7
customary international law **110,** 702
extraterritorial **104,** 298-9, **119,** 227
Geneva Conventions (1949) **104,** 298
over nationals **74,** 706-7, **75,** 341, 362
possibility and obligation distinguished **119,** 356-7
protective principle **36,** 49-50, 52, 57
return of suspects to country where acts carried out **78,** 131
universal **36,** 26-9, 40, 298-304, **91,** 119-21, **104,** 313, **119,** 67, 228-9
creation of international tribunals as evidence against **119,** 364
customary international law **105,** 441, **119,** 67, 357, 363-4, 366-7
extradition as alternative **100,** 670-1
legislation providing for **119,** 360
jus cogens/peremptory norm **37,** 458, **119,** 355
means and methods of warfare, restriction

chemical weapons
EU declaration **105,** 517
State practice **105,** 517-19
Turku Declaration of Minimum Humanitarian Standards (1990) **105,** 516
mens rea
discrimination, intent **122,** 94
intent **78,** 139-40, 146
jurisprudence, *Papon* case **122,** 92, 93
knowledge that act a war crime or crime against humanity **36,** 41, 42, 44, **98,** 536, 541, 542-6, 558-61, 594, 627-8, **104,** 312-23, 359-66, 376-7, 380, 395, **112,** 222-3, 229-30
knowledge of widespread or systematic attack **122,** 90-4, **124,** 163, 167
knowledge that attack part of **122,** 91, 92-3, **124,** 167, 172
persecution **122,** 88, 90-4
personal motives, relevance **112,** 222-3, **122,** 163-73, **124,** 193, 202-4
burden of proof **124,** 167, 172-3
customary international law **124,** 167-73
Finta **124,** 171-2
post-WWII cases **124,** 167-73
military tribunals in occupied Germany, Control Council Law No 10 **36,** 48-9, **91,** 59-60, 127-8, **105,** 451-2, **111,** 398 n. 12, 400-1
ne bis in idem. See previous conviction on basis of same acts *below*
Nuremberg Charter (1945). *See* Nuremberg Charter (1945)
obligation to bring offenders to justice **91,** 36, **104,** 328, 330
UNGA Resolution 2712 (XXV) **91,** 36
offence under municipal law, whether **119,** 354-6
as part of municipal law **119,** 355
penalty. *See also* Yugoslavia, International Criminal Tribunal for the Former (ICTY), penalty
death **108,** 193
Nuremberg Tribunal **108,** 193
severity, general principle of law **108,** 193
State practice **108,** 193-6
underlying crime as measure **108,** 193-4
previous conviction on basis of same acts
acquittal **100,** 348
appeal against **124,** 191-3
contacts with the enemy **100,** 347-9
reclassification **100,** 348-9
war crimes **100,** 332-3
prosecution, possibility of
municipal legislation **100,** 348, **119,** 354-5
Nuremberg Charter (1945) **100,** 348
punishment **74,** 701-4, 707-8, 710-13, **75,** 336-68. *See also* Yugoslavia, International Criminal Tribunal for the Former (ICTY), penalty
death penalty **74,** 707-8
imprisonment
appropriate term **75,** 344-5, 366-7
life **74,** 710-13
obligation **78,** 129
purpose **75,** 344
relevant factors
age and health of accused **75,** 366-7

crimes against humanity (*cont.*)
lapse of time since offence **75,** 340-1, 344, 348, 350-3
ministerial undertaking not to prosecute **75,** 340, 348, 355-6, 362
requirements **100,** 363. *See also* definition *above*
act of serious nature inflicted on a human being **112,** 251-2
actus reus **104,** 312-14
armed conflict **91,** 67, **105,** 452, 486, 488, 494, **108,** 32-3, 35-6, 62-3, **119,** 67
Control Council Law No 10 **112,** 208
customary international law **105,** 494, 525-6, **124,** 166
ICTY **112,** 87, 207-10, **122,** 40-2
international conflict **105,** 452, 525-6, 596, **108,** 63
nexus between act or omission and armed conflict **112,** 208-10, **122,** 40, 41-2, **124,** 162-73, 1247
Nuremberg Charter (1945) **112,** 207-8
as objective/jurisdictional element **124,** 165
Rwanda, International Criminal Tribunal for (ICTR), Statute **112,** 41, 208
as temporal condition **122,** 42
civilian population, acts against. *See* civilian population, acts against as requirement *above*
conformity with international law **108,** 44
contravention of international law at time of act **104,** 301, 335, **108,** 44-8
customary international law **108,** 44, 61
general principles of law recognized by community of nations **104,** 335
discrimination **124,** 173-84
Control Council Law No 10 **124,** 1128
customary international law **124,** 174, 177-80, 181
decisions of municipal courts **124,** 178-9
ILC Draft Code of Offences Against the Peace and Security of Mankind (1996) **124,** 180
Military Tribunal for the Far East **124,** 1128
Nuremberg Charter (1945) **124,** 1128
international law, criminality under **91,** 128-9
lack of clarity **104,** 328-9
mens rea. See mens rea above
participation in common plan of extermination or persecution
'heated' criminal reaction distinguished **100,** 356-7
separate offence, whether **100,** 334-6
planned attack **122,** 127-30, **127,** 142-3
treaty **104,** 337-8
binding on parties **108,** 44
binding on parties at time of offence and not in conflict with peremptory norm **108,** 44, 61
reciprocity, relevance **108,** 45
war crime, nexus **91,** 126-8, 131-2, **105,** 451-2, 525-6, **108,** 33, **112,** 208-10
Control Council Law No 10 **105,** 451-2, 525
customary international law **105,** 525, **112,** 209
ILC Draft Code of Offences against the Peace and Security of Mankind (1949/1976/1989/1996) **105,** 452, 525, **111,** 344, **119,** 148, 163, 226
Nuremberg Tribunal **105,** 451, **112,** 205, **119,** 226
Oppenheim (1992) **105,** 452
res judicata. See previous conviction on basis of same acts *above*
responsibility

entity in de facto control **112,** 220-2
individual **112,** 204, **121,** 256-7, **122,** 95-100, **124,** 121 n. 175. *See also* common purpose *above*
Čelibići **122,** 95
commander's obligation to prevent or punish **108,** 31-2, 120, 128-9, **122,** 94, 95, 100-14, 159-62, 187-8, 226
Control Council Law No 10 **112,** 225-36
direct participation **108,** 59-61, 129-30, **112,** 224-36, 249
judicial institution, relevance **110,** 621
Nuremberg Charter (1945) **82,** 438, **104,** 154, **112,** 205-6, 225-36, **119,** 148, **121,** 256-7
position of authority, relevance **108,** 59-61, 119-30, **121,** 257
retroactivity **36,** 20-40
absence of precise penalty at time of offence **108,** 195-6, **119,** 355
customary international law, relevance **119,** 354-5
nullum crimen sine lege **36,** 281-3, **105,** 452
conditions in which penalty to be served **108,** 206
removal of right to non-retroactivity, statutory limitation **78,** 132-6
sovereignty and **91,** 130-1, **105,** 497
statutory limitation **74,** 701-3, 707-8, **75,** 341, 353-4, 357-8, **78,** 133-6, 145, **100,** 333, 342
customary international law **119,** 358
European Convention on the Non-Applicability of Statutory Limitation to Crimes against Humanity and War Crimes (1974) **91,** 35, **119,** 357-8
France **100,** 333, 342, **119,** 358
Nuremberg Charter (1945) **100,** 333
UN Convention on the Non-Applicability of Statutory Limitations to War Crimes and Crimes against Humanity (1968) **79,** 405, **119,** 357-8
where classified also as war crimes **78,** 136
superior orders. *See* superior orders
systematic policy. *See* widespread or systematic policy *below*
terrorism distinguished **125,** 504
war crimes distinguished **36,** 288, **78,** 136-7, 139, 140, 141-7, **79,** 401 n. 2, 511, **91,** 121-2, **108,** 32-6, 64, **124,** 177
Nuremberg Charter 1945 **124,** 230-1
relative seriousness **111,** 327-31, 381-5, **121,** 354-9
Albrecht **111,** 329
Control Council Law No 10 **111,** 383
customary international law **124,** 233, 256
Einsatzgruppen **111,** 329-30
FRY **111,** 385
ICC (Rome) Statute (1998) **124,** 231, 256
ICTR Statute **124,** 233
ICTY **111,** 327-31, 381-5, **121,** 346-7, 348, 354-9, **122,** 240-2, **124,** 225-6, 229-36, 255-6
ILC Draft Code of Offences Against the Peace and Security of Mankind (1996) **124,** 231-2
Nuremberg Tribunal **111,** 382-3
Prosecutor v. *Tadić* **111,** 330-1
Stalag Luft III **111,** 329
UN Convention on the Non-Applicability of Statutory Limitations to War Crimes and Crimes against Humanity (1968) **111,** 384
US War Crimes Act (1996) **111,** 384

crimes against humanity (*cont.*)
widespread or systematic policy **100,** 356-7, **108,** 33-5, 64-6, 133, **111,** 328, **112,** 207, 215-18, 219-22, 249, **122,** 76, 77-81, 164-6, 188-96, 225-6, **124,** 164-5, 183, 232. *See also* civilian population, acts against as requirement *and* classification as, persecution in name of State practising ideological supremacy *above*
criminal act on large scale or repeated and continuous commission of linked inhumane acts **122,** 78
customary international law **124,** 233
as evidence of commander's responsibility **122,** 152, 204-6
evidence of plan **122,** 78-9, 164-6. *See also* requirements, participation in common plan of extermination or persecution *above*
ILC definition **108,** 17, **112,** 214-17, **122,** 78 n. 380, 79-80
implication of high-level political or military authorities **122,** 78
instigation or direction by government or by any organization or group **122,** 79-80
jurisprudence
Akayesu **122,** 78 n. 381
Menten **122,** 78
political objective and plan or ideology directed against community **122,** 78, 87, **124,** 164-5
substantial public or private resources whether or not military **122,** 78
criminal intent 66, 157
criminal law, international. *See* international criminal law; international tort/wrong
criminal procedure
conspiracy **91,** 480-5
evidence, sufficiency **91,** 480, 486
instruction to the jury **91,** 506-7
recours en référé **86,** 331-3
trial in absentia **86,** 330
public policy and **86,** 327
voire dire **91,** 504-5, 507-8
criminal proceedings. *See* European Convention on Human Rights (1950), fair trial; fair trial; International Covenant on Civil and Political Rights (ICCPR) (1966), fair trial; military courts; *and under individual countries*
critical date 80, 284, 291, 299, 324, 474-5, 519, 535, 557
avulsion **97,** 462-4
Bosnia-Herzegovina, classification of armed conflict **105,** 531
boundary, establishment of **91,** 460 n. 6
cause of action **94,** 173-4, 194-7
State immunity **94,** 262
unreasonable delay **94,** 174-7
deportation, facts as at date of decision **111,** 178
double criminality **74,** 451-2, **88,** 287, **119,** 41, 55, 146-7, 159-60, 175-6, 182, 189-93, 202, 214, 250, **120,** 364-5, 367, 384-5
effective remedy before national authority, developments subsequent to communication **45,** 271, 298-9, 301-2, **56,** 370-1, **115,** 364-5
European Court of Human Rights, jurisdiction **103,** 658
evidence **76,** 373, **79,** 658
expropriation/nationalization **108,** 660
federal State
acts committed after federation **91,** 592-3
Argentine National Commission on Inter-provincial Boundaries **91,** 592-3
foreign judgment, recognition/enforcement, date of judgment **106,** 227

ICJ proceedings **37,** 481, 541, **76,** 257, 260, 338
legislation, interpretation **90,** 406
nationality of claims **77,** 431-2, 465, 466
prescription **75,** 120
State agency/State-owned corporation/State entity, change of status after cause of action or institution of legal proceedings **98,** 143, **107,** 362
State immunity, execution/attachment, purpose/use of funds/assets **65,** 393
State immunity, jurisdiction **94,** 262
assertion of claim of sovereignty **84,** 707
cause of action **94,** 262
issue of writ **84,** 703, 707, 708
treaty exception **107,** 388
title **97,** 589, 591-2
uti possidetis. See uti possidetis, critical date
Croatia 92, 179-81, 210-11. *See also* Bosnia-Herzegovina, Bosnian Croats
armed conflict, Republic of Serbian Krajina **108,** 49, 62
Constitution 1991/2 **92,** 181, 210-11
human rights, undertaking to protect **92,** 181
law of, Criminal Procedure Law 1993, Art. 176 **108,** 76
minorities, undertaking to protect **92,** 181
Serbian Krajina, Constitution, Rule 78(5) **108,** 49-50
succession, date **96,** 721
'Croatian nation' 122, 59-60
Crown Colony. *See* United Kingdom, Crown Colony
'Crown land' 43, 96-7, 106, **68,** 407-13, 471-2, **112,** 509-11, 519, 579-80, 601, 621, 645, **120,** 484
Crown prerogative. *See also* prerogative; United Kingdom, prerogative
colonies **43,** 130-40, **44,** 110, 113, 117, 127-8, **123,** 557-8, 585-7, 590, 591-2
cruise missiles. *See* nuclear weapons, deployment
CSCE. *See* Conference on Security and Cooperation in Europe (CSCE); Helsinki Final Act (1975)
Cuba
Bancec
separate legal entity, whether **80,** 568, 570-2, 574-8, 581-2
State immunity, entitlement **80,** 573-4, 578-81
Banco Central de Cuba (BCC)
assumption of central bank functions **124,** 552
as separate legal entity **124,** 550-1
Banco Nacional de Cuba
establishment and functions **124,** 551-2
State agency/State-owned corporation/State entity **66,** 9-10, 22, 39, 41-2, 48-9, 110, 426, 457
alter ego theory **66,** 110, 114, 426, 448, 457, 516
State immunity **66,** 9
transfer of central bank role to Banco Central de Cuba (BCC) **124,** 552
Banco Para el Commercio Exterior de Cuba, State agency, *alter ego* **66,** 507-12
bank, expropriation/nationalization **42,** 45, 48-9, **81,** 532, **87,** 511
bank accounts, freezing **81,** 532, 534
Chile
diplomatic and consular relations, break **64,** 370-1
measures against **64,** 162-4, 246-50, 320, 321, 325
currency regulations
as confiscation **66,** 12-14, 16, 19-20, 31-2, 41-7

Cuba (*cont.*)
extraterritorial effect **66,** 71-2, 133-5
international law violation **66,** 19-21, 31-2, 41-7
Currency Stabilization Fund
Decision No 346 **66,** 8-12, 25-8, 31-2, 41-2, 45-6
State agency/State-owned corporation/State entity **66,** 10, 28
exchange control laws **38,** 138-40, 457
expropriation/nationalization measures **51,** 11, 22, **63,** 2-3
discriminatory nature **92,** 434, 438-9
Industrial Bank, dissolution **63,** 1-3
International Monetary Fund Agreement, withdrawal from **66,** 134-5
'intervention' of Cuban tobacco companies **42,** 41-2
'interventors', sovereign authority **66,** 18, 233, 235
law of
Commercial Code, company dissolutions **66,** 95
Fundamental Law, compensation provisions **66,** 115
Law 13 of 1948 (Banco Nacional de Cuba (BNC)) **124,** 551
Law 78 of 13 February 1959 **81,** 532, 534, **87,** 510-11
Law 793 of 25 April 1960 **80,** 568
Law 851 of 6 July 1960 **42,** 46-51, **66,** 48-52, 96, 115, 424-5, 428, 430, 445, 454, 457, 459, **87,** 511
Resolution 1 **92,** 438
Resolution 2 **92,** 410
Law 890 of 13 October 1960 **66,** 94-6, 424
Law 891 of 13 October 1960 **42,** 50-1, **66,** 424-5, 439, 453, 457-8, 516, **80,** 568, 579
confiscatory effect **63,** 2
Law 930 of 1961 (Banco Nacional de Cuba (BNC)) **124,** 551
Law 930 of 23 February 1961 **66,** 457-8
Law 989 of 5 December 1961 **120,** 7
Law 1256 of 11 September 1973 (freezing of Chilean assets) **64,** 162-4, 246-50, 320, 321, 325, 372-9
discriminatory nature **64,** 374-6
penal nature **64,** 374-6
retroactive effect **64,** 373
territorial limitation **64,** 325
Law Decree 843 **66,** 407
Law Decree 548 of 20 November 1952 **66,** 25, 27
Law Decree 647 of 14 November 1959 **66,** 407
Law Decree 172 of 28 May 1997 (Banco Central de Cuba (BCC)) **124,** 552
nationality, loss or deprivation of, deprivation of civic rights amounting to **120,** 6-8
nationalization measures **66,** 46, **80,** 568-70, 579-80, 582
banks **42,** 45, 48-9, **81,** 532, **87,** 511
powers of attorney, effect on **43,** 20-1
US property **42,** 49, **87,** 511
Penal Code 1982
Art. 135.1 **120,** 7
Art. 214.1 **120,** 7
travel to, US citizens, restrictions **38,** 100-11, **43,** 126-30
USA
boycott **42,** 42
claims against, legislation concerning **40,** 171

confiscation of US property **42,** 49
nationalization of US property **40,** 171
sanctions against **61,** 658-61
trading with the enemy legislation **42,** 198-205
cultural diversity, need to respect 116, 105-20
cultural exchange agreement. *See also* cultural relations
contract pursuant to, commercial act, whether **63,** 229-30
cultural heritage. *See* cultural property, protection; national heritage; UNESCO Protection of the World Cultural and Natural Heritage Convention (1972)
cultural institute
diplomatic status **82,** 2-5
as State agency **82,** 4, **86,** 635-7
State immunity, execution/attachment **86,** 573
State immunity, jurisdiction **40,** 60-3, **65,** 325-8, **82,** 3-5, **87,** 46, **114,** 538-9
status, executive certificate/statement **82,** 4
treaty basis **82,** 4
cultural property, protection
Convention on the Means of Prohibiting and Preventing the Illicit Import, Export and Transfer of Ownership of Cultural Property (1970)
accessions to **118,** 582
'cultural property' **118,** 582
Dealers Code of Practice
disposal of property innocently acquired **118,** 584
provisions **118,** 583-4
forged export documents, effect **118,** 580-92
UNESCO Declarations **73,** 228-9
war, during
Hague Convention on the Protection of Cultural Property in the Event of Armed Conflict (1954), northern Cyprus **108,** 507-8
nuclear weapons, deployment **110,** 416-17
cultural relations. *See also* cultural exchange agreement
State immunity, jurisdiction **63,** 171-2, 229-32, 589
currency
applicable law, place of circulation **111,** 598-9
ownership, outside country of issue **111,** 600
sovereign right to issue
comity **111,** 593, 598-9, 602-3
holding/disposal in foreign country distinguished **111,** 592-603
manufacture distinguished **111,** 595, 602
currency regulations 46, 182, 185, 189, 190, 233, **77,** 449. *See also* exchange controls
as confiscation **42,** 153-5, **66,** 12-14, 16-17, 19-21, 31-2, 41-7, 72
extraterritorial effect **66,** 71-2, 133-5
international law violation **66,** 19-21, 41-7
public law act, whether **63,** 590-5
custodian of enemy property. *See* enemy property, custodian of
custom. *See also* customary international law; customary law
bilateral **83,** 44
establishment **82,** 371-4
customary international law 53, 544-6, **54,** 132-3, **61,** 173-8, 180-1, 622-4, **62,** 233, 559, **66,** 600-1, 605-7, **76,** 135, 342, 467, 471, 583, 722, **79,** 401-6, **88,** 48, **91,** 671-3. *See also* comity; custom; customary law; international law; intervention, in affairs of another State; *jus cogens*/peremptory norm; State practice; usage; *and under individual countries*

customary international law (*cont.*)
act of State **84,** 121 n. 18
aggression **76,** 680, 724
as aid to interpretation of legislation implementing treaty **119,** 161
airspace over high seas, exercise of sovereignty **90,** 215-16
aliens
duty to protect **82,** 219
right to control **111,** 184, 265, 288
applicable law **83,** 32-3, 87
continental shelf delimitation **99,** 426, 428, 438, 473-4, 657, 660, 666, 672, 673
fishing zones **99,** 495-6, 558
ICTY. *See* Yugoslavia, International Criminal Tribunal for the Former (ICTY), applicable law
'applicable rules and principles of international law' **82,** 548
arbitral award, finality **92,** 85
arbitrary detention **87,** 455-60, **95,** 633
arbitration, Model Arbitral Rules (ILC) (1958) **91,** 572, 575
armed attack, definition **76,** 437
armed forces, stationing on foreign territory **106,** 394
arrest on foreign soil **68,** 10
asylum **87,** 499, **95,** 566-7
international conflict, flight from **95,** 567
jus cogens/peremptory norm, absence **95,** 567
baselines **119,** 458
basis, customs and usages of civilized nations **80,** 590
binding force **74,** 145-6
boundary disputes and **75,** 117-21
China, status of Beijing government **82,** 403-4
civil war **105,** 504-24
responsibility, individual **105,** 520-4, **122,** 71
claims settlement agreements **90,** 227
codification. *See also* customary international law, treaties and other international instruments reflecting; international law, codification
desirability **110,** 226
Hague Conference (1930), State responsibility **46,** 495-6
League of Nations Committee **37,** 67
State immunity and **45,** 65, 69, 76
UNGA Resolution 2625 (XXV) **83,** 74
collective self-defence **76,** 439, 690, 719, 864
comity. *See* comity
conservation and management of resources and **123,** 473
consular privileges and immunities **77,** 594
functional **101,** 372, 382
honorary consul **86,** 556
consular relations **38,** 171, **71,** 580-1, **77,** 401, 594, **101,** 481 n. 5
continental shelf **41,** 31, 36, 58, 67-75, 84-6, 106, 116-30, 132, 158, 168, 169-73, 220, **81,** 261-2, 287, 297, 298, 300-1, 351, **86,** 617-24, **99,** 465-6
coastal State's rights **41,** 51, 188, 191, **71,** 260
Continental Shelf Convention (1958) **99,** 426-7, 502-3
delimitation **41,** 31, 36, 38, 58, 159, 168-75, 190, 209
development of concept **81,** 287, 300
distance **41,** 119-25
basis of rights **81,** 300

basis of title **81,** 297, 300-1
equidistance **41,** 36, 38, 57-77, 84-5, 92, 105-15, 133-8, 169-73, 192, 194
equidistance/special circumstances **41,** 84
equitable principles **41,** 86
Law of the Sea Convention (1982) and **99,** 467
negotiate, obligation **41,** 86
continental shelf delimitation **81,** 261-2, 298, 300-1
distance **81,** 297
equidistance/special circumstances **81,** 375, 401
Control Council Law No 10 **111,** 398, 417, **124,** 178
countermeasures **116,** 229
crimes against humanity **79,** 403-4, **91,** 60, 124-30, **104,** 200-2, 337-8, **105,** 451, 500-24, 569-70, 586-7, **112,** 205-6, **119,** 106-7, 353-4
armed conflict, need for **105,** 494, 525-6, **124,** 166
discrimination as requirement **124,** 177-80
internal conflict **105,** 504-24, **108,** 45-6
mens rea, personal motives, relevance **124,** 167-73
retroactivity and **119,** 354-5
statutory limitation **119,** 358
unconditional respect for fundamental human rights **108,** 46-7
war crimes, nexus **105,** 525, **112,** 209
widespread or systematic policy **124,** 233
damages under **77,** 242
right to **116,** 274, 410
standard **84,** 523, 524-5, 527, 529, 535-43, 653, 654-5
definition **71,** 550
derogation from **41,** 71, 105, 209, **121,** 361
deterrence **110,** 318
development **41,** 138-9, **46,** 207, 221, **49,** 57, 62, **54,** 42-3, **55,** 236-7, 291, **56,** 86, 90, 132, 133-4, 162, 182, 183, **57,** 512-13, 580, **64,** 152-3, 168-70, 714, **69,** 63, **71,** 117, 120-7, 129-31, 141, 184-5, 187-9, 191, **74,** 145-6, **79,** 363, **110,** 82, 235-6, 245-7, **119,** 232-3, **125,** 141-51
by international organizations **55,** 304
changing conditions **110,** 356-61
new rules
interpretation of obligations, effect on **37,** 455
treaty rules, effect on **74,** 145-6, **99,** 503
new situation **71,** 126
new States and **41,** 137 n. 3
new trends **46,** 460-9, **67,** 30-1, 40-2, 101-2, 152-4, 240, 276-8, 290-1, 313
slow pace **119,** 68-9
subsequent practice **110,** 329-40, 363
diplomatic immunity, execution/attachment **111,** 158
diplomatic mission, status **102,** 181-2
diplomatic premises
duty to protect **83,** 237
inviolability **71,** 559-61, **99,** 200, 201, **101,** 207
diplomatic privileges and immunities **71,** 536-9, 541, 543, 550-1, 568-9, 571-2, **73,** 679-88, **78,** 102-4, **80,** 423, **86,** 667, **101,** 378
diplomatic agent's spouse, assimilation **87,** 78
evidence of
State practice **71,** 550, 559
treaty **71,** 537-8

customary international law (*cont.*)
jurisdiction **111,** 158
lease **101,** 379
matters not covered by the Vienna Convention on Diplomatic Relations (1961) **65,** 186-7, **70,** 401-2, **115,** 611, **119,** 59
parking spaces **70,** 400-4
State succession, incorporation of receiving State into forum State, effect **115,** 615-16, 618
third State, in **115,** 610-12
waiver **87,** 216
diplomatic protection **88,** 694
disappearances **95,** 634-5
double criminality **75,** 108-13, **92,** 725-6, **101,** 178-80
identity of crime, whether necessary **101,** 182-3
due process **104,** 92
duress **111,** 336-44
economic zones and **74,** 144-6
EEZ **67,** 108, **81,** 264, 330-1, 388, **82,** 642, **83,** 45, 86
equidistance **81,** 299, 374
equitable principles **81,** 359
refuelling of fishing vessel **120,** 263-5
employment contract, immunity, jurisdiction **101,** 383, **114,** 504-5, **116,** 628-33
enclave, right of access and **92,** 574
military, paramilitary and armed police **92,** 574
enforcement **79,** 402-3
environment **106,** 130, **110,** 82, 154, 454-5
development **110,** 82
environmental impact assessment (EIA), need for, nuclear tests **106,** 12-13, 16, 21, 134
precautionary principle **106,** 134, **117,** 174, 179-80, 186
right to equitable and reasonable share of resources of international watercourse **116,** 225, 243-8
equality of application **110,** 476-8
equidistance **99,** 428, 502-4, 506, 512, 516, 517, 519-22, 526-7
equitable principles **99,** 675-6
undefined in **99,** 678
espionage **94,** 74, 77, 78
estoppel. *See* estoppel
European Community law and **117,** 440-1
European Court of Human Rights and **123,** 48-9
evidence, corroboration, need for **112,** 173
evidence of **38,** 164, **55,** 314, **57,** 580, **65,** 166-7, **76,** 431-2, 434, 438, 448, 866. *See also* customary international law, treaties and other international instruments reflecting
doctrine **71,** 126, 550, 561, 568, 580
European Convention on Human Rights (1950) **87,** 457
executive certificate/statement **70,** 391, **94,** 359
ICRC Report **105,** 529
interested parties' views **83,** 164
International Covenant on Civil and Political Rights (ICCPR) (1966) **87,** 457
judicial decisions **74,** 182-3, 481-2, **75,** 191-4, 199-200, 211, 216, 242-4, 610-12, 617-20, 631, 634, **124,** 167-73
judicial practice **94,** 77, **121,** 361-2
Law of the Sea Convention (1982) **99,** 476

legislation **64,** 311-12, **104,** 700-4
need for **87,** 31
negotiating positions **102,** 22-3
OAS Charter **90,** 666 n. 25
State practice. *See* State practice, customary international law, evidence of statement
by international official **95,** 567
at UN **105,** 512, 530
treaty **65,** 422, 431-2, **70,** 376-7, 391, **76,** 438, 448, 866, **77,** 247-8, **95,** 567, **99,** 476, **121,** 256, **124,** 155
conflicting practices **70,** 376-7
draft **94,** 375-6
draft treaty **94,** 77
multilateral **94,** 77, **124,** 155
ratification or signature, relevance **41,** 118-19, **64,** 312
treaty reservation **104,** 186-7
UN Charter **90,** 666 n. 5
UN Commission of Experts' Report **105,** 529
UN Resolution **77,** 247-8, **105,** 329, 331, 346, 354, **110,** 269-70, 482-3, 507
UNHCR *Handbook on Criteria for Determining Refugee Status* (1979) **90,** 145
unilateral declaration/undertaking **41,** 118-19
writings of jurists **77,** 174-5, 245
exchange control, as sovereign activity **84,** 122 n. 21
exhaustion of local remedies **46,** 315-16, 475, **84,** 348, **96,** 278, **102,** 277, 281
diplomatic protection and **120,** 233, 318
expansion **68,** 220-1
expropriation/nationalization **83,** 541-4
compensation **83,** 473-6, 542-3, 565, **84,** 523, 524-5, 527, 529, 535-43, 653, 654-5, **86,** 300, **95,** 228
discrimination **83,** 550
expulsion of alien **82,** 164-5, 197, 213, 214, 215-16, 219
collective **96,** 312
extradition **72,** 636, **74,** 457, 481-2, **78,** 98, 100
aut dedere aut punire/judicare **94,** 507, 534
customary international law, *aut dedere aut punire/judicare* **94,** 507, 534
motivation of requesting State **104,** 115
narcotics offences **99,** 170
nationals **94,** 502, 522
political offence **59,** 474-6
as sovereign act **94,** 507
speciality **92,** 686, **125,** 535-6
extradition in case of death penalty **78,** 98, 100, **124,** 326
extraterritorial jurisdiction, conflicting jurisdictions **96,** 185
family, protection of **85,** 337-8
fishing zones **99,** 495-6
200-mile limit **99,** 462-3, **101,** 173
force. *See* force, prohibition on the threat or use of, customary international law
forcible abduction/unlawful arrest **90,** 695
jurisdiction, effect on **86,** 529
foreign relations, compliance with **68,** 208-11, 223-4, 231-3, 250-1, 492-3
formation **41,** 31, 72, 85, 114, 157, 169, 170-1, 172-3, 174, 209-10, 211, 219, 221, **46,** 476, **55,** 324-5, **67,** 72, 82, 108, 111, 163, 170, 172, 183-5, **70,** 401-4, **82,** 371-4
instantaneous **81,** 301, **83,** 162
International Committee of the Red Cross, role **105,** 511

customary international law (*cont.*)
legal philosophy, relevance **41,** 172-3
Nuremberg Charter provisions, subsequent adoption as **111,** 342, **112,** 205-6
technological development **41,** 170-1, 209, 219
teleological approach **41,** 171, 172, 174
usage. *See* usage
freedom of the high seas, duties of coastal States **71,** 260-1
freedom of navigation **76,** 639
function **71,** 126
fundamental change of circumstances **117,** 409-10, 425-6, 441
general practice recognized by law, evidence of **80,** 173
general principles of international law and **41,** 157, **61,** 180, **115,** 610
special rule derogating from **46,** 418, 435
treaty provision, effect **41,** 71-2, 171
general principles of law recognized by civilized nations and **121,** 350-3, 361-4
genocide **118,** 330-1, 379, **119,** 106-7, **120,** 361
good faith **65,** 282, 340-3
treaty, avoidance of measures before entry into force which would defeat object and purpose **113,** 322-3, **116,** 215
good neighbourliness principle **110,** 455-6
Head of State
definition **99,** 162
functions **119,** 61, 104-5, 193-6
immunity, execution/attachment **91,** 260
immunity, jurisdiction **99,** 161, 162, **102,** 201, 202, **103,** 585, **119,** 43-8, 62-70, 78-87, 104-5, **125,** 495-509
ratione personae **119,** 219
power to override **95,** 378 n. 34
Head of State, former, immunity, jurisdiction **119,** 43-8, 62-70, 78-87, 99-100, 106-7, 203-4, 208-11
ratione materiae **119,** 219, 236-7
high seas **41,** 69, 117
hostage-taking **119,** 106-7
hot pursuit **77,** 590-1
human rights **77,** 173
ICJ
compliance with judgments **85,** 255, 258
individual and **94,** 575-6
interim measures **94,** 575-6
ILC, role in developing **41,** 84
inhuman or degrading treatment **95,** 635
innocent passage **84,** 84, **125,** 420
instant custom **76,** 865-6
internal waters **91,** 415
international crimes **91,** 121, **119,** 65-70
international humanitarian law **110,** 209-10, 223, 514-15, 533-4
international law
compliance **105,** 24
obligations **105,** 350-3
international organizations, privileges and immunities **86,** 666, **87,** 23, 26, **94,** 329, 338, **105,** 21, **107,** 319 n. 3, 324 n. 10, 423-4, **114,** 551, **116,** 647
interpretation, State practice and convention as basis distinguished **41,** 219
intervention **76,** 639

Islamic law and **62,** 174-5
judicial assistance, duty to comply with request **110,** 645-6
judicial impartiality **121,** 350-3, 362-4
judicial notice **122,** 627-9
jurisdiction
  crimes committed by national forces **77,** 559
  examination of foreign witness abroad **90,** 410
  flag State **91,** 524, **120,** 588, **123,** 356
  nationality **84,** 10-11
  ships. *See* ships, jurisdiction *below*
  universal **81,** 662
    crimes against humanity **105,** 441, **119,** 67, 357, 363-4, 366-7
  visiting forces **86,** 534
jus cogens. See jus cogens/peremptory norm
lacunae. *See* international law, gaps
law of the sea and **74,** 144-6
marine pollution, discharge of radioactive waste **106,** 20
maritime delimitation. *See also* maritime delimitation, customary international law
  as applicable law **91,** 656, **99,** 427, 430
    non-parties to 1958 Conventions **91,** 656, 658-9
  equidistance **41,** 36, 38, 46-7, 57-77, 78-80, 84-5, 92, 105-15, 133-8, 169-73, 192, 194
  freedom of navigation **95,** 677
  as relevant factor **95,** 703 n. 4
  relevant/special circumstances **99,** 430
  single boundary **99,** 568, 657
maritime law **41,** 69
maritime limits **91,** 515
maritime zone, right to establish **108,** 637
Martens Clause. *See* Martens Clause (customary international law: applicability in case of gaps)
mine-laying **76,** 463
minorities, protection **68,** 208-11, 221-2, 236
modification **76,** 443
municipal law and **38,** 163, **43,** 3-11, **45,** 58, 60, **57,** 309-10, **64,** 127-8, 142, 600, 670, 714, **65,** 103-5, 116, 120, 128-30, 134-6, 141, 150, 153-5, 157, 159-64, 166-8, 175-7, 184-92, 195-6, 202, 207, 210, 213-14, 219-22, 226-9, 239, 241-5, 266, 268, 274, 278, 282, 292-4, 302-3, 305, 309, 314, 317, 321-2, 326, 335, 339-43, 418-25, **68,** 10, 208-9, **70,** 400-4, **71,** 536-7, 541, 590-1, **73,** 2-3, 47, 53, 244, 372, 687-8, **74,** 167-8, **79,** 401-3, 410, 411, **82,** 479, **83,** 149, 150-1, 152-4, 238, **90,** 242, **92,** 655, **93,** 361-2, **94,** 76, **101,** 403, **102,** 201, **116,** 627-8, **117,** 424, **119,** 78-9, 87, 227, 355, **120,** 362-5, 397-8, **122,** 505-6, **123,** 490
  in case of treaty codifying customary international law **78,** 8
  change of municipal law as consequence of change in customary law **101,** 403, 405, **108,** 535-6
  criminal offence, direct creation **122,** 506-7
  declaratory of **80,** 124, **120,** 403-4
  developing international law and **101,** 403, 405, **108,** 535-6, **120,** 403-5
  diplomatic privileges and immunities **101,** 310
  direct effect **117,** 426
  due process rules **104,** 92
  independence **46,** 510-11
  indirect **84,** 84, 85

customary international law (*cont.*)
jus cogens/peremptory norm and **120,** 371-3, 391-405
primacy **45,** 25-6, **117,** 423-4
legislation **124,** 351
recognition, State **108,** 535-6
role, determination by municipal law **125,** 499
as source of law in absence of legislative or treaty provision **125,** 495
stare decisis doctrine **53,** 583, **64,** 15-20, 89-90, 212-15, 549-50, 714-15, **84,** 69, 683, **90,** 527
subsequent inconsistent legislation **85,** 258-9, 273
transformation doctrine **120,** 362-5, 378-91, **122,** 506-7
universal recognition/UK consent requirement **122,** 505-6
national security defence **110,** 726-7
nationality of claims **117,** 66
ne bis in idem principle **75,** 106
necessity **116,** 49-50, 191, **120,** 191-2
negotiate, obligation to **41,** 86
neutrality **110,** 210-11
non-intervention under. *See* intervention in affairs of another State
non-refoulement **92,** 655, **124,** 368
inconsistent municipal legislation **92,** 655
norms
foreign relations, as aspect of **68,** 208-11, 223-4, 231-3, 250-1, 492-3
racial discrimination, elimination of **68,** 208-9, 221-2, 236
nuclear weapons, deployment **106,** 362-3, 406
authorization of threat or use **110,** 197, 327, 339-40, 346-7, 525, **122,** 502-6, 650-1
prohibition on threat or use **110,** 203-5, 216, 246-7, 267-8, 327, **122,** 502-6
nullum crimen sine lege **111,** 395, 429, **121,** 360, **122,** 76
relevance in case of **122,** 68
obligation to negotiate in good faith **110,** 223-4, 231
opinio juris. See opinio juris
pacta sunt servanda **65,** 452-3, **117,** 409, 426, 441
peaceful settlement of disputes, duty of States **76,** 479
peremptory norm. *See jus cogens*/peremptory norm
persecution **122,** 84
persistent objector rule **41,** 138, 221-2, 225-6, **65,** 181-2, **103,** 471
change of mind distinguished **41,** 215-16, 222
nuclear tests **106,** 107-10
nuclear weapons
deployment **110,** 264-5, 330, 363, 365, 370, 437
possession **110,** 264-5
port State powers on the high seas **120,** 596
President's authority to override **95,** 378 n. 34
as primary source of international law **119,** 236
principles and rules **71,** 115-27, **110,** 442-3
private action in tort, basis for **99,** 65-7
proportionality **110,** 195
public order/public policy/*ordre public* and **72,** 636
rape in time of war **121,** 266-7
recognition of international entity **83,** 248

regional or local **41,** 125, 132, 137-8, **50,** 213, **76,** 518. *See also* regional international law
European Convention on State Immunity (and Protocol) (1972) **94,** 347
North Sea median line and **41,** 89, 90
purpose to remove previous difficulties, where **82,** 21
requirements. *See also* formation *above*
acquiescence **41,** 211
challenge, absence of **41,** 85, 221
consent **53,** 4, **62,** 189
constant and uniform practice **45,** 396, 419, **46,** 74, **56,** 194-5, **86,** 617, **87,** 31, 66, **91,** 37, 116, 123, 124, **95,** 635, **110,** 203-4, 246-7, 259, **111,** 341, **113,** 433, **115,** 186, 610, **119,** 364, **125,** 499
absence of contrary practice **110,** 247, **125,** 499
frequency **41,** 201
general acceptance **45,** 61, **64,** 598, **65,** 141-2, 181-2, 213-14, **81,** 301, **83,** 151, **86,** 617, **105,** 56, 519, 530, 588, **115,** 186, 610, **116,** 104, 628-32, **120,** 392, **122,** 505-6
'appreciable section of the community' **110,** 228, 483
persistent objector rule. *See* persistent objector rule *above*
States specially affected **110,** 364, 485-6
general principle of law **64,** 598
jus cogens. See jus cogens/peremptory norm
majority principle **55,** 327
passage of time **41,** 31, 72, 114, 157, 169, 170, 172, 209-10, 219
precision of rule **95,** 635
reciprocity **83,** 151
recognition by civilized nations **64,** 598
State practice. *See* State practice
usus **81,** 301
resolution of international conference, effect **83,** 153
sanctions **49,** 287
scope **71,** 126
self-defence, limitations on right **110,** 195, 225-6
self-determination **105,** 266, 270, 335, 346, **108,** 553
obligations, international community **105,** 346, 351
ships
arrest, use of force **120,** 196-7, 274
harbouring in distress
aircraft by analogy **82,** 363-4
immunity, jurisdiction **82,** 362-3
jurisdiction
on high seas **77,** 590
ships in territorial sea **77,** 559-60
registration **93,** 729, 761-2
sources **77,** 245
arbitral awards and diplomatic practice **46,** 473
judicially measurable and manageable standards **99,** 67
treaties. *See* customary international law, treaties and other international instruments reflecting; treaties
sovereign immunity. *See* State immunity, execution/attachment, customary international law; State immunity, jurisdiction, theory/doctrine, customary international law
special diplomatic missions **80,** 399-400

customary international law (*cont.*)
standard of treatment of alien **83,** 533, **106,** 441, 443-6, 452-4, 458, 483, **119,** 663-5, **121,** 55, 183, **122,** 379-80, 682
due diligence **106,** 453, 479-80
fair and equitable **125,** 147-51
minimum international standard **106,** 453, 484-5
most favoured nation clause **106,** 487, 488, 490-1
national treatment **106,** 487
procedural fairness **121,** 187
transparency **119,** 664-6
State contract, applicable law **95,** 207
State immunity. *See* State immunity, execution/attachment, customary international law; State immunity, jurisdiction, theory/doctrine, customary international law
State practice. *See* State practice
State responsibility **82,** 213, 215, 219, 548
for actions of diplomatic agents **87,** 59
crimes against humanity **121,** 257
de facto organ or agent **112,** 188-9
Head of State **119,** 200-1
individual, attribution to **110,** 707, 710, 712, **112,** 224-7, **121,** 257
national security **106,** 497-8
revolution **106,** 491-4
State organ **124,** 105 n. 129
State succession **75,** 125
immovable property on territory of successor State **96,** 731
State terrorism **77,** 236-7
statutory limitation **79,** 404
crimes against humanity **119,** 358
straits, Great Belt (Finland/Sweden) **94,** 460
strike, right to **90,** 200, 211-12
supersession **67,** 108
sustainable development principle **116,** 104
taxation, judicial assistance **104,** 579
territorial sea, territory, whether **90,** 46
Third World States and **46,** 482-4, 504, 505
torture **77,** 176, **103,** 472-5, **119,** 106-7, **121,** 255-6, 318
war crimes distinguished **100,** 471
transit, right of **82,** 369-71
treaties **41,** 31, 113, 114, 135, 217, 219, 220-2, **43,** 3, **57,** 580-1, **82,** 550-1. *See also* customary international law, treaties and other international instruments reflecting
accession to, relevance **110,** 207, 208
bilateral **41,** 86-90
change in customary international law, effect **84,** 524, 535, 536
co-existence of identical rule **99,** 503
denunciation **90,** 374-5
denunciation provisions, relevance **110,** 208
derogation from **110,** 726-7
individual, rights **117,** 425
non-retroactivity and **101,** 390, **105,** 588, **107,** 143
omissions, absence of unambiguous provision **78,** 8
primacy **108,** 539
recourse to **72,** 502

reservations **41,** 205-6, 225, **77,** 606, **84,** 240
admissibility **107,** 69-71
possibility of and **41,** 68-70, 71-2, 105-6, 107, 109, 113
reinstatement of customary international law **78,** 100
tacit dispensation **84,** 348
termination and suspension **116,** 71, 222-3, 224, **117,** 441-2
third party **96,** 725
treaties, State succession **74,** 116, **83,** 54, **107,** 173
treaties of a territorial character **116,** 81
treaty interpretation **68,** 304, 419, **83,** 541, 618-19, **90,** 374-5
aid **101,** 309, 310-15, **106,** 441
multilingual treaties
authentic languages equal authority **94,** 603
non-authentic language **94,** 603
presumption of identity of meaning in all authentic languages **94,** 603
obligation to accept treaty partner's constitutional requirements **78,** 174-5
strict in case of deviation **40,** 117, 127
UNGA Declarations **77,** 176-7
Friendly Relations and Cooperation between States **76,** 674-5
UNGA Resolutions **37,** 367-9, 559, 568, 577, **62,** 189, **82,** 479, **84,** 526, 540, 668 n. 2, **105,** 331, 346, 354, **108,** 45-6, **110,** 204-5, 269-70
defining aggression **76,** 679
Resolution 1803 (XVII) (Permanent Sovereignty over Natural Resources) **83,** 474
unilateral undertakings, legislative consent, need for **106,** 371-2
uti possidetis **97,** 550-2
war crimes **82,** 439-41
aiding and abetting **121,** 273-89, 322-3, **122,** 97-8, 100
common purpose **124,** 139-54
obligation to seek out and prosecute **91,** 36-7
responsibility, commander **122,** 100, 104-9
war, laws and customs **99,** 78
applicability **105,** 528-31
civilian population, protection **104,** 91-2, **108,** 45-8, **110,** 537
grave breaches, internal conflict **105,** 538, **108,** 162-3
limitations on means of waging, unnecessary suffering **110,** 352, 435, 447-9, 524-5
means of waging, limitations on, non-discrimination between combatants and non-combatants **110,** 123, 152, 239
war liabilities and **61,** 166, 170, 173-8
world heritage **68,** 311, 396, **106,** 659
customary international law, treaties and other international instruments reflecting **36,** 34-6, **41,** 67-70, **43,** 38, **46,** 479-80, **55,** 584, **61,** 173-8, 623-4, **67,** 31, 39, 67, 163-5, 183-5, 221-2, **68,** 304, 419, **76,** 135-6, 324-7, 426-31, 432-3, 485-8, 517-18, 528, 541, 636-40, **81,** 294, **83,** 152, **95,** 567. *See also* customary international law, treaties; customary international law, treaty interpretation
Agreement Relating to the Conservation and Management of Straddling Fish Stocks and Highly Migratory Fish Stocks (1995) **117,** 180
American Convention on Human Rights (1969) **116,** 274-5, 410, 498-9
application to **81,** 294
non-parties **65,** 254, **77,** 657, 658, 659, **82,** 629, **83,** 162-3, **91,** 476
non-signatories **77,** 401, 657, 658, 659
BITs (bilateral investment treaties) **106,** 483, **119,** 663-4, **121,** 143, **122,** 380, 382, **125,** 143-51

customary international law, treaties and other international instruments (*cont.*)
Brussels Convention on Immunity of State-owned Ships (1926) **64,** 239-40, 312, **65,** 103-4
Brussels Convention on Limitation of Liability for Maritime Claims (1976) **107,** 142-3
change of status **83,** 163
Chicago Convention on International Civil Aviation (1944) **120,** 567-8
co-existence of identical rule **99,** 503
later custom to prevail **99,** 503
codification of existing law **36,** 34-5, **53,** 546, **59,** 529, **62,** 568, 570, 573, **68,** 304, 419, **70,** 391, **71,** 119-21, 568, 571-2, 580-1, **75,** 97-8, **76,** 486, 487, 864-5
declaratory, whether **65,** 419, 431, **78,** 8-9
development distinguished **41,** 218
effect where areas covered not identical **76,** 428
effect where rules identical **76,** 428, 429-31
codification of principles of international law not yet in force **77,** 659
Continental Shelf Convention (1958) **41,** 57-75, 105-15, 117-26, 132, 135-8, 186, 205, **71,** 118-20, 191, **81,** 377, 378, 379, **99,** 426-7, 502-3
Arts. 1-3 **41,** 69, 112-14, 131
Art. 4 **41,** 69
Art. 5 **41,** 69
Art. 6 **41,** 31, 67-75, 84, 106, 112-14, 131, 168-75, 187, 203, 206-11, 223
codification **41,** 112, 117, 132, 186, 205
development of customary international law and **41,** 205, **62,** 571, **99,** 502-4
Council of Europe/OECD Convention on Mutual Administrative Assistance in Tax Matters (1988) **104,** 579
Declaration of Paris (1856) **83,** 162
divergence from **41,** 190-1
European Convention on Extradition (1975) **78,** 96, 97
European Convention on Human Rights (1950) **87,** 457
exhaustion of local remedies **102,** 278
European Convention on State Immunity (and Protocol) (Basle) (1972) **64,** 362, **65,** 178, 419, 421-2, 431, **77,** 607-8, **78,** 116, **82,** 12-13, 21-2, 25, 40, **87,** 27, 32, **94,** 346, 347, **100,** 470, **101,** 383, **114,** 517, 547, **115,** 422, 431, 432-4, **116,** 660-1, **119,** 378, **123,** 38-9, 89
Geneva Conventions (1949) **76,** 447-8, **91,** 36, **105,** 442-3, 503, 506, 508-10, 586-7, **108,** 46-7, 163, 465-6, **110,** 149-50, 207, 523, 530, **112,** 188-9, 201, **122,** 68, 81
First Additional Protocol relating to the Protection of Victims of International Armed Conflicts (1977) **104,** 91-2, **105,** 536-7, **108,** 46, 163, **110,** 515, 530, **122,** 70, 109-10, **123,** 604, **124,** 99 n. 113
Second Additional Protocol relating to the Protection of Victims of Non-International Armed Conflicts (1977) **104,** 156 n. 8, **105,** 506, 514-15, 536-7, **108,** 46, 163, **124,** 99 n. 113
Geneva Convention (Armed Conflict) (1949), Protocol 1 (1977) **88,** 50, 52-3
Geneva Convention (Prisoners of War) (1929) **104,** 400-1
Geneva Convention (Prisoners of War) (1949) **42,** 449, 472, 475
Geneva Convention (Protection of Civilians in Time of War) (1949) **83,** 126, 138, 149, 154-5, 162, 186, 195, 196, **95,** 567, **125,** 547
Geneva Conventions on the Law of the Sea (1958)
codification **74,** 144-6
High Seas Convention (1958) **41,** 69, 117, **91,** 475-6, 514, 528
Geneva Protocol (Prohibition of Asphyxiating, Poisonous or other Gases and Bacteriological Methods) (1925) **110,** 530

Genocide Convention (1948) **36,** 34-6, **120,** 361
Hague Convention for the Protection of Cultural Property in the Event of Armed Conflict (1954) **105,** 506
Hague Conventions (1899/1907) **36,** 293, 294, **82,** 435, **83,** 162, 163, **104,** 400-1, **105,** 447-50, 500, **110,** 150, 207-8, **122,** 67, **125,** 547
Hague Regulations on the Laws and Customs of War on Land (1907) **53,** 3-5, **83,** 85, 163, 194, **94,** 76, **122,** 69
ILC Draft Articles on Jurisdictional Immunities of States and Their Property (1991) **123,** 90-2
incorporation doctrine and **78,** 8
individuals' rights and **91,** 476
  remedies **91,** 476
Inter-American Treaty of Reciprocal Assistance (1947) **76,** 689-90, 691-5
International Covenant on Civil and Political Rights (ICCPR) (1966) **104,** 432
International Criminal Court (ICC), Rome Statute (1998), continuing development for purposes other than Statute **124,** 156 n. 282
International Criminal Tribunal for the Former Yugoslavia, Statute **112,** 184, 224-7, 247, **124,** 180-1
interpretation, differing rules **76,** 866
Jan Mayen **62,** 114
Law of the Sea Convention (1982) **62,** 114, **77,** 658-9, **81,** 261-2, 264, 287, 300 n. 1, 301, 351, **82,** 629, 642, **83,** 86-7, **92,** 66, **97,** 504, **99,** 452, 467, 476, 495-6, 499, 655, **119,** 458
  as evidence of **99,** 476
  fishing zones **99,** 495-6
  freedom of navigation **95,** 705, **120,** 588
  islands, rocks distinguished **99,** 452
legal effect **57,** 549
Montevideo Convention on the Rights and Duties of States (1933) **108,** 537
Montreal Convention for the Suppression of Unlawful Acts Against the Safety of Civilian Aviation (1971) **94,** 489, 521-2, 555, 565, 592
North American Free Trade Agreement (1992), expropriation/nationalization **122,** 336-7
Privileges and Immunities of the Specialized Agencies Convention (1947) **77,** 573
role **81,** 261-2
Rome Statute (1998) **121,** 283-4
signature, effect **41,** 213
Slave Trade Conventions **83,** 162
as source of customary international law **57,** 580-1
  extent of participation and **41,** 72, 85, 107, 112, 114, 206-9
  norm-creating character **41,** 71, 72, 114
  objection and **41,** 131
  passage of time, relevance **41,** 72, 114
  previous jurisprudence, relevance **82,** 117
  ratification, relevance **41,** 186, 206-7
  revision, possibility of and **41,** 106
Sri Lanka/UK Bilateral Investment Treaty (1980) **106,** 441, 479-83, 486-7
States especially affected by, need for concurrence **41,** 114
Straddling Stocks and Highly Migratory Fish Stocks Agreement (1995) **117,** 180, **123,** 471
subsequent development of rules of international law, effect **41,** 71, 85, **76,** 865
Territorial Sea and Contiguous Zone Convention (1958) **73,** 177-8, 195, 214, **90,** 247, **91,** 514
Torture Convention (1984) **119,** 198, **121,** 263-4, 318, **123,** 41, 42, 100

customary international law, treaties and other international instruments (*cont.*)
UN Charter (1945) **53,** 492-3, **76,** 428, 430-5, 439, 485, 487, 637-8, 863-7, **85,** 241 n. 6, **103,** 476, **117,** 58
Art. 2(4) **110,** 247
non-members **76,** 638
UN Convention on Special Missions (1969) **80,** 403-4, 406, 408, 418-20, **121,** 601-2
UN Declaration on the Protection of All Persons from Being Subjected to Torture **104,** 153, **121,** 263
UNESCO Protection of the World Cultural and Natural Heritage Convention (1972) **106,** 658-9
Universal Declaration of Human Rights (1948) **49,** 66, **87,** 45, **103,** 475
Vienna Convention on Consular Relations (1963) **71,** 580-1, **77,** 401, 594, **101,** 481 n. 5
Vienna Convention on Diplomatic Relations (1961) **65,** 254, **75,** 92, **78,** 4, 8, **82,** 57, 98, **94,** 310, **99,** 200, 201, **119,** 59, **121,** 509
break from **116,** 628-9
preservation of customary international law **65,** 186-7, **101,** 219, 309-10, 314-16, 378, **115,** 611, **119,** 59
Vienna Convention on the Law of Treaties (1969) **56,** 111, **57,** 549, **59,** 579, **68,** 304, 419, **77,** 658, **82,** 612, **83,** 32-3, **84,** 402, 403, **85,** 260, **88,** 627, **92,** 46, 125, 160, **97,** 633-4, 635, 645, **100,** 478, **101,** 211, 390, **105,** 25, 26, 30, 53, **106,** 207, 706, **110,** 576, **115,** 196, **116,** 71, **117,** 407, 409, **121,** 51, **122,** 279, **123,** 388, **124,** 183-4, **125,** 499
as partial codification **117,** 425
termination and suspension of treaties **117,** 428, 437, 443
treaty interpretation **82,** 612, **100,** 478, **121,** 51 n. 2, **124,** 439
Vienna Convention on the Law of Treaties between States and International Organizations (1986) **101,** 390, **105,** 25, 26, 30, 53, **117,** 407-8
Vienna Convention on the Succession of States in respect of Treaties (1978) **77,** 657, **92,** 164, 204, **96,** 377, **115,** 185-92, **116,** 79-80
customary law 84, 84. *See also* custom; customary international law
aboriginal Indians **78,** 424-5
Africa **41,** 144, **84,** 30, **103,** 145, 174, 188, 196
establishment of **103,** 196
evidence of **84,** 84
freedom from discrimination, sexual **87,** 107-20
Saramaca
determination of successors **116,** 279-80
recognition by Suriname **116,** 278
customs duty, charge having equivalent effect **113,** 333-4
customs frontier, Free Zones **40,** 53-5
customs jurisdiction, territorial sea and **90,** 254
customs laws. *See* exclusive economic zone (EEZ), customs laws, right to apply
customs officials
drugs control **82,** 106
drugs offence, powers relating to **82,** 105-6
powers **82,** 105-6, **86,** 164
public nature of activity **86,** 644-5, 656
customs waters 84, 211-14, **90,** 247-8, **91,** 526 n. 28
Cyprus, Republic of. *See also* Cyprus, Turkish Republic of Northern (TRNC); United Nations Committee on Missing Persons (Cyprus) (CMP)
aliens, admission, discretionary **86,** 130
citizenship **108,** 519-20

Constitution 1960 **62,** 6, 50, 68, **73,** 12
alleged violation of **62,** 73, 84-5
Art. 15/1 **88,** 232-8
Art. 25 **86,** 111, 112, 117, 121-5, 129-30
Art. 28 **86,** 111, 112, 117, 121-5, 129-30
Art. 122 **86,** 123
Art. 146 **83,** 218
Art. 169 **83,** 218, 226, **88,** 202-3, 206, 224, 229
Art. 169(3) **86,** 113-14, 118-19, 122
Art. 179 **88,** 205
Art. 188 **83,** 228
Art. 198 (citizenship) **108,** 519-20
criminal charge, details of **41,** 360-5
European Convention on Human Rights (1950) and **47,** 189-93, 194-5
exclusion of citizens **41,** 381, 383
freedom of movement **41,** 381, 383
'Greek community' **41,** 381, 383
necessity, doctrine of and **70,** 26-7
practice, relevance **62,** 73, 85
responsibility for upholding **112,** 739-43
continuity **48,** 6-8
'country', whether **108,** 549
death by careless driving **41,** 361, 364-5
EC intervention in affairs of **100,** 299
EC membership, Commission opinion **100,** 267 nn. 6 and 7
emergency courts legislation, validity **90,** 492-3
European Convention on Human Rights (1950) and **41,** 360, 362, **47,** 189-93, 194-5, **86,** 119, 120
executive powers, establishment **83,** 228-30
fair hearing, proceedings for enforcement of provisional foreign maintenance order **47,** 189-93
foreign maintenance orders, enforcement **47,** 189-93
freedom from discrimination **86,** 115-25, 129-30
government
de facto and de jure **73,** 12, 15, 20
recognition **62,** 25-7, 38-40, 42, 69, 72, 84
Turkey's non-recognition **62,** 68, 72-3, 84
status **62,** 39, 43, 72, 83-4
Governor, Council of Ministers, successor to **83,** 228-9
human rights
alleged breaches **62,** 9-24, 51-3, 59-62, 133
broad interpretation **88,** 236-7
illegitimate child, rights, succession **88,** 220
independence, effect of legislation granting **112,** 736-43
insurgents, law concerning trial **48,** 6-8
international law, subjects, States **88,** 213
jurisdiction **62,** 12-13, 75-6, 83
forgery of currency notes abroad **48,** 69-76
Sovereign Base Areas **41,** 25-8
waters off **88,** 238-9
territorial **88,** 238-9
law of
Aliens and Immigration Law **41,** 380-3

Cyprus, Republic of (*cont.*)
Constitution 1960. *See* Constitution 1960 *above*
Convention on Discrimination (Employment and Profession) (Ratification) Law 1968 (Law 3/68) **86,** 111
Criminal Code **48,** 69-76
s 5(1)(3) **88,** 238
s 5(1)(a) **88,** 238
European Convention on Human Rights (1950) (Ratification) Law (Law 39/62) **86,** 111
Illegitimate Children Law **88,** 217
Inland Telecommunications Service Law **83,** 228
International Covenants (Economic, Social and Political Rights *and* Civil and Political Rights) (Ratification) Law 1969 (Law 14/69) **86,** 111, 113, 117, 118, 122
International Telecommunications Conventions and Relevant Protocols (Ratification) Law 1971 (Law 21/71) **83,** 226
Law No 39/62 (European Convention on Human Rights (1950)) **88,** 202
Law No 45/64 (Territorial Waters) **88,** 238
Law No 50/79 (Convention on the Legal Status of Children Born out of Wedlock (1975)) **88,** 201, 214, 216, 220-30
Municipalities (Amendment) (No 3) Law 1986 (Law 25/86) **86,** 111, 113, 117, 121
Municipalities Law 1985 (Law 111/85) **86,** 111, 113, 116, 117, 121-5
National Guard Laws 1964-68-75 **83,** 218, 219
Statutory Functions (Conferment of Exercise) Law 1962 (Law 23/62) **83,** 229
Succession Law **88,** 220
Telegraphs Law **83,** 228
validity in northern Cyprus, principle of self-determination **108,** 552-3
Wills and Succession Law, Convention on the Legal Status of Children Born out of Wedlock (1975), effect **88,** 217, 220-1, 230
legislation, interpretation
aids, structure of Act **86,** 122
law incorporating treaty **88,** 206
phrases
'law' **88,** 205
'national of Cyprus' **86,** 129-30
legislation, repeal by treaty **88,** 225
legislative discretion **86,** 123
nationality
alien spouse **86,** 129-30
marriage to Cypriot citizen **41,** 380-3
necessity **70,** 26-7, **90,** 492-3
privacy, right of
business diary, private, whether **88,** 237
search of premises **88,** 232-8
business premises **88,** 235-8
waiver of right to warrant **88,** 233
telephone directory **88,** 237
prohibited immigrants **41,** 27
separation of powers **86,** 122-3
Sovereign Base Areas, jurisdiction of Cyprus courts **41,** 25-8
sovereignty over northern Cyprus **108,** 549, 550-1
status **73,** 12, 15-20, 22
telecommunications

competent organ **83,** 228-30
interruption **83,** 227-30
treaties
Constitution and **86,** 113-14
direct effect **83,** 228
entry into force, municipal and international law distinguished **88,** 203
implementing legislation **86,** 111-12, 120
need for **88,** 211-14. *See also* self-executing *below*
incorporation into municipal law **88,** 201-6, 220, 223
individuals and **88,** 206, 226
primacy of treaty **83,** 218, 226, **86,** 112, 113-14, 118-19, 120, 122, **88,** 201-6, 217, 221-2, 225, 226
amendment of treaty **88,** 205-6
basis **88,** 205
reciprocity, need for **86,** 118, 122
repeal of existing law **88,** 225, 228
subsequent legislation **86,** 118, 122, **88,** 204-6
termination, reciprocity, lack of **88,** 210
ratification **88,** 223-4
procedures, determined by States party **88,** 223, 228
reciprocity, need for **88,** 206-16, 222
self-executing **88,** 210-14, 224-5, 226-8, 229
Treaty of Establishment (1960), validity **108,** 552
treaty interpretation, aids, Explanatory Report **88,** 215
Turkish occupation **73,** 11, 15-17, 19, 27
UK agreement for restoring civil peace (1963) **44,** 359, 361, 371
UN peace negotiations **73,** 16
UN peacekeeping force **73,** 15
status **44,** 359-60
Status of Force Agreement **44,** 362, 375
Cyprus, Turkish Federated State. *See also* Cyprus, Republic of; Cyprus, Turkish Republic of Northern (TRNC)
authority, exercise of **62,** 45-7, 57-8, 65-7, 70
Constitution 1975 **73,** 16
effects of non-recognition **73,** 12-13, 20, 22, 24-5, 27
establishment **62,** 25, 65
jurisdiction **62,** 13, 27-9, 32, 45, 54-5, 61, 64, 68
recognition **62,** 38-40, 62, 69, 70, 72-3, 84-5
non-recognition, effect **73,** 12-13, 20, 22, 24-5, 27
Turkey **62,** 76
United Kingdom **73,** 12-27, 30
requisition of property by **73,** 15-17, 19, 27
status **62,** 13, 25, 42-5, 49, 61, 66, 70, 75-6
representative in London **73,** 12-13, 20
Cyprus, Turkish Republic of Northern (TRNC)
Constitution 1985
Art. 67 (citizenship) **108,** 520
Art. 156 **120,** 104-5
Art. 159(1)(b) **108,** 453, 461, 462, 474-5, **120,** 64-5, 117-18
validity for international purposes **108,** 462, 468, 474-5, **120,** 42-3
courts, municipal
'established by law' **120,** 76, 118-19

Cyprus, Turkish Republic of Northern (TRNC) (*cont.*)
exhaustion of local remedies and **120,** 40-6, 76, 111, 122, 136-7, 140
independent and impartial, whether **120,** 73-7, 104-6, 113-14, 116, 120-2, 141-2
legal validity of decisions **120,** 120
settled system **100,** 253
cultural protection, war, during, Hague Convention on the Protection of Cultural Property in the Event of Armed Conflict (1954) **108,** 507-8
displaced Greek Cypriots, discrimination **120,** 67-8
effective remedy before national authority **120,** 66, 94-6, 113, 115, 120-2
elections, right to participate in **120,** 96-7, 115
ethnic cleansing, allegations of **120,** 110-11
expropriation/nationalization. *See also* property, denial of return or access to *below*
church property **108,** 490-509
de facto, loss of control **108,** 474
necessity **108,** 468, 481
staged process **108,** 460, 478
family life, respect for **120,** 61, 88
Greek Cypriots living in northern Cyprus. *See also* missing Greek Cypriots *and* property, denial of return or access to *below*
access to medical care **120,** 71-2, 113, 140-1
correspondence, respect for **120,** 89-90, 115
education, right to **120,** 84-6, 114
European Convention on Human Rights (1950), inhuman or degrading treatment, discrimination amounting to **120,** 91-4, 115, 125
fair trial/hearing by independent and impartial tribunal **120,** 73-7, 113-14, 120-2, 141-2
freedom of association **120,** 80-2, 114
freedom of expression **120,** 78-80, 114
freedom of movement **120,** 72, 88-9, 113
freedom of religion **120,** 77-8, 114, 124-5, 142
home, respect for **120,** 86-91, 114
peaceful enjoyment of possessions **120,** 82-4, 114
protection of property **120,** 84, 114
right to dispose of property **120,** 83-4
private life, respect for **120,** 86-91, 114
security, threat to **120,** 72-3, 113
history **122,** 531-3
homosexuality, alleged persecution on account of **118,** 595-601
identifiable territory **100,** 253
inhuman or degrading treatment, treatment of displaced persons **120,** 68
law of
Abandoned Movable Property Law 1975 **108,** 503-5
Antiquities Ordinance 1975 **108,** 503-5
Civil Wrongs Law **120,** 40
Constitution 1985. *See* Constitution 1985 *above*
Law No 52/1995 **120,** 64-5
Prohibited Military Areas Decree **120,** 105-6, 134-5
missing Greek Cypriots. *See also* United Nations Committee on Missing Persons (Cyprus) (CMP)
failure of Turkish authorities to account to families
family life, respect for and **120,** 59-60
information, right to receive and **120,** 59-60

failure of Turkish authorities to investigate
as inhuman treatment of relatives **120,** 58-9, 112, 131
liberty of person and **120,** 55-7, 112
right to life and **120,** 51-5, 111-12
life, right to, alleged killings **120,** 53, 111, 131
nationality
applicable law, law of the Republic of Cyprus **108,** 550-6
power to confer **108,** 555-6, **122,** 536-41
validity of law of the Republic of Cyprus **108,** 553-5
property, denial of return or access to **108,** 462-3, 467-8, 487-8, **120,** 112-13. *See also* expropriation/nationalization *above*
absence of legislative basis **120,** 62
as administrative practice **120,** 61-2, 64-5
discriminatory nature **120,** 67
family life, respect for and **120,** 60-3, 112
historical and political context giving rise to **108,** 471-83, **120,** 125-35
home, respect for and **120,** 60-3, 112
recognition, government **103,** 636-7
recognition, State **100,** 253, **108,** 462
acceptance of courts as 'established by law', effect **120,** 76
EC refusal **100,** 268
executive certificate/statement, State immunity, for purposes of **108,** 519
Hague Convention on the Protection of Cultural Property in the Event of Armed Conflict (1954), applicability **108,** 508
need to clarify **103,** 660-1
non-recognition, effect
administrative act **122,** 536-8
administrative contacts **108,** 519
expropriation/nationalization **108,** 462, 503-5
nationality, power to confer **108,** 555-6, **122,** 536-41
refugees **122,** 533-45
representatives, diplomatic status **108,** 520-1
taxation, exemption **108,** 525-40
validity of acts **120,** 40-6, 76, 111, 117-24, 135-7, 139
UK municipal law **108,** 512-45
responsibility for acts of **103,** 638, 639-49, 654, **108,** 466, 485, **120,** 36-40, 111, 133-5
lawfulness of military intervention, relevance **108,** 466, 473, 481-2
private individuals **120,** 39-40
Security Council Resolution 541/1983 **100,** 268, **120,** 23-4, 36-7, **122,** 532-3, 542
EC Foreign Ministers' support **100,** 268, **120,** 23
Security Council Resolution 550/1984 **100,** 268, **120,** 23-4, 36-7
self-determination, right to **108,** 470-1
sovereignty in, Cyprus, Republic of **108,** 549, 550-1, **120,** 34-5
State, whether **108,** 467
'unrecognized foreign State' **108,** 540-5
Turkish control over **108,** 466. *See also* responsibility for acts of *above*
Turkish Cypriots living in northern Cyprus
administrative practices amounting to breach of rights, whether **120,** 101-4, 106-8, 116, 122-3
effective remedy before national authority **120,** 109-10, 123
freedom of association **120,** 106-8
freedom of expression **120,** 106

Cyprus, Turkish Republic of Northern (TRNC) (*cont.*)
gypsy community's rights **120,** 103-4, 122-3
independent and impartial tribunal **120,** 104-6, 141-2
peaceful enjoyment of possessions **120,** 108-9
political opponents' rights **120,** 101-3
freedom of association **120,** 106-8
gypsies, alleged breach of rights **120,** 103-4, 122-3, 125
Czech Republic
Charter of Fundamental Rights and Freedoms, Art. 11(2) **118,** 190
International Covenant on Civil and Political Rights (ICCPR) (1966), succession to **118,** 185 n. 2
law of, continued application of law of Czech and Slovak Federal Republic **118,** 238
Czech and Slovak Federal Republic
law of
Act 87/1991 (rehabilitation of citizens leaving country under Communist pressure)
compatibility with International Covenant on Civil and Political Rights (ICCPR) (1966) **118,** 193-5, 237-9, 240
continued application in the Czech Republic **118,** 238
s 3 **118,** 186
s 5(1) **118,** 186
s 5(2) **118,** 186-7
s 5(4) **118,** 187
s 6 **118,** 186
Czechoslovakia. *See also* Czech Republic; Czech and Slovak Republic
annexation of part of by Germany **47,** 31, 33
Munich Agreement (1938), validity **44,** 50, 55
compensation agreements. *See Consolidated Index to Table of Treaties*
concession agreement
invalidity, termination for **40,** 111-13
validity, rights of concessionaire in case of invalidity **40,** 111-13
continuity of State **44,** 57-9
currency conversion measures as 'taking' **42,** 153-5
exchange control, extraterritorial effect **47,** 157-63
expropriation/nationalization **40,** 17-28, 94-7, **42,** 159-61, 162-4, 165-9, 170-2, 180-2, **47,** 31-9, **63,** 70-3
against German property **40,** 115, **44,** 67, **47,** 32, **55,** 23-4
currency conversion measures as 'taking' **42,** 153-5
enemy property **56,** 538
extraterritorial effect **55,** 23-4, **77,** 450
expropriation/nationalization, compensation **79,** 593, 595, 597, 598
adequacy **47,** 34-5
undertaking to pay, dishonoured **79,** 593, 595, 598
expulsion of Sudeten Germans **44,** 53, **51,** 23-4, **78,** 187
extraterritorial legislation, fiscal and exchange control **47,** 157-63
freedom of movement, right to leave one's country **74,** 410-11
International Monetary Fund (IMF) (1944)
whether party to **48,** 229-30
withdrawal from **77,** 450
law of
Criminal Code 1961, Art. 109 (leaving Czechoslovakia without permission) **74,** 410-11, **80,** 682
Decree 100/45 of 1945 (nationalization) **79,** 593

Decree 108/1945 of 25 October 1945 (confiscation without compensation of deposits by persons of German or Hungarian nationality) **77,** 450
Decree 41/1953 of 30 May 1953 1945 (annulment of blocked deposits) **77,** 450
Law invalidating transfers during occupation 1945 **40,** 111, 112
Monetary Reform Law 1953 **42,** 153
Nationalization Decrees 1945-6 **74,** 102
Munich Agreement (1938), validity **44,** 50, 55
municipality
law relating to **44,** 59-61, 63-4, 67
as State organ **44,** 63-4
State succession, effect on **44,** 50-70
nuclear energy exploitation **86,** 576-8, 580-2
acta jure imperii **86,** 577
occupation, concession agreement, validity **40,** 111-13
State responsibility, civil liability for public act **86,** 577
State succession (1918)
municipality, effect on legal identity **44,** 50-70
State succession (1993)
compensation for war-related events **109,** 159, 623, 640 n. 1, 645 n. 2, 648, 661 n. 2, 663 n. 4
Czech Republic **118,** 185 n. 2
Slovak Republic as sole successor in respect of Gabčíkovo/Nagymaros Project **116,** 210-11
unauthorized departure from **80,** 682

damage
exercise of right causing **85,** 459
unusual or special, damage caused by Iraq Law No 57 of 16 September 1990 **117,** 389-92
damages[iii] **54,** 508-9, **56,** 201-4, **61,** 320-1, **62,** 147, 169, 197, 200-2. *See also* American Convention on Human Rights (1969), compensation; claims settlement agreements; compensation; compensation for war-related events; costs; European Community law, compensation for breach or failure to implement; European Convention on Human Rights (1950), damages; expropriation/nationalization, compensation; just satisfaction (Art. 50 [41] of the European Convention on Human Rights (1950)); measure of damages/compensation including valuation of company/property/assets; NATO Status of Forces Agreement (1951), damage caused by visiting forces or member of, compensation; remedies; reparation; *restitutio in integrum*; United Nations Compensation Commission, compensation; war damage
amicable settlement **58,** 538, **62,** 205, 208
applicable law **46,** 510
burden of proof **106,** 714
Chorsów Factory. See Chorzów Factory principle of reparation for wrong
claims for. *See also* diplomatic protection
declaratory judgment in respect of **57,** 464
jurisdiction **56,** 221-2
competence to determine **88,** 733, 739
cumulative **46,** 451, 502-3, 505, 525
determination by

[iii] Since it is impossible to maintain a clear distinction between 'damages' and 'compensation', for the purposes of the index except in certain specific cases (such as expropriation/nationalization) material relating to compensation has been subsumed under 'damages'.

damages (*cont.*)
arbitration **40,** 158-64, **62,** 223, **66,** 533, 602-3, **67,** 340-2, 375-83, **75,** 452-8, 505-7, 515, 549-56, 599-643
conciliation **40,** 427-8
special committee **62,** 223, 229
devaluation of currency, adjustment for **106,** 644-6
Aminoil **106,** 645
basis of calculation, US Consumer Price Index **106,** 646
municipal law **106,** 645-6
direct/indirect distinguished **46,** 412, 426, 470-1
Alabama Claims **117,** 247-8
War Risk Insurance Premium Claims case **117,** 248
discrimination and **61,** 242-4, **75,** 279, 479, 483-4, 494-5, 500-4, 707-9, 716, 719
duty to pay. *See* obligation to pay *below*
entitlement **62,** 181-2
actio personalis moritur cum persona **118,** 525
equity **56,** 429, **81,** 56, **107,** 63, **116,** 161, 249
moral injury **95,** 314
Evian Agreements (1962) **62,** 207
evidence of **78,** 681
ex gratia **88,** 733, **106,** 499-500
exemplary **70,** 233, **103,** 294-5
fault, relevance **54,** 509-10, **56,** 196
financial guarantees dishonoured **67,** 376-7
for
aerial bombardment **80,** 20-4
airport noise and pollution **73,** 448-50
aliens, injuries to **56,** 271, 282
arrest of ship not in accordance with rules of international law, International Law of the Sea Convention (1982) **120,** 198-201, 250-1
assault and battery **70,** 234
breach of contract **62,** 181-2, **67,** 340-3, 376-7, **84,** 453-4, **86,** 471-3, **89,** 339, **114,** 209-10
applicable law **86,** 470
breach of International Covenant on Civil and Political Rights (ICCPR) (1966) **114,** 325, 331
breach of international law **37,** 83, **56,** 196, **77,** 239-41, **82,** 516, 571, 586, **116,** 410-11
Greenpeace vessel, damage to **74,** 259, 267-8, 274
inappropriateness **82,** 574-5
breach of international obligations **56,** 178, 201-2
breach of official duty **108,** 673-4, **111,** 9-11
fault, relevance **108,** 673-4
breach of State responsibility **74,** 253, 258-9, 267, 271, **106,** 452-4, 465-72, 479-83, 487-500, **116,** 249
causal link, need for **96,** 323, **117,** 246-50
customary international law **106,** 479-83
discretionary **106,** 499
loss, need for **106,** 452, 465
breach of treaty **84,** 325-6, 327, **93,** 329, **116,** 212
applicable law, treaty provisions **121,** 126
determination as two-stage process **121,** 136-8
conversion of property **116,** 559-62, **125,** 693-706

damage **56,** 174-6, 196
after establishment of proceedings **45,** 270, 305
proof of **56,** 90, 214
damage caused by crash of foreign military aircraft **91,** 283-8
Belgium–USSR Agreement (1989) **91,** 287-8
procedure for determining **91,** 287-8
damage caused by lawful event **86,** 545
damage caused by unlawful acts **86,** 629
damage caused by visiting forces **91,** 283-8
distribution of responsibility **91,** 283-8
procedure for determining **91,** 287-8
damage to reputation **54,** 511-12, **58,** 716, 719, **67,** 440
defective performance **114,** 229-30
difficulty of access to children **92,** 297-8
dividends, absence of **67,** 341
enforced uneconomic operation of concession **52,** 5-7
expenses **88,** 734
legal fees **88,** 744-5, 748
medical **88,** 736, 744, 745
expropriation. *See* compensation; expropriation/nationalization, compensation
expulsion of alien **82,** 177-8, 197-203
attribution to government, need for **82,** 197
failure by diplomat to pay rent **99,** 204
failure to accord national treatment **121,** 190-4
failure to pay bonds **84,** 139
false imprisonment. *See* unlawful detention *below*
fishing dispute, losses during **47,** 22-4
foreign corporation, injury to **56,** 271
foreign investment factor **66,** 602-3
genocide **107,** 460
human rights violations **51,** 239-44, 247, 248, **56,** 419-23, 424-6, 427, 428-31, 499, 501-4, 507-10, **57,** 190-4, **60,** 161, 200-1, 202, **61,** 320-1, **70,** 266, 279, 286, **71,** 316, 353, 365, 392-4, 409-10, **72,** 309-19, 325-33, 379-86, 404-13, 430-2, **78,** 234, 370-1, **79,** 179, 192, 200, 233, 241, **94,** 410, 415. *See also* just satisfaction (Art. 50 [41] of the European Convention on Human Rights (1950))
creditors in bankruptcy, payment to **56,** 499, 501-4, 506-10
equity **78,** 224
lex generalis **57,** 190-1
lex specialis **57,** 190-1
incidental damage **46,** 21, 198
incorporeal assets **44,** 100-1
injury to feelings (solatium) **121,** 647-50
insufficient parental involvement in decision relating to child care **92,** 253-5
intangible loss **67,** 378-9, 382-3
interference with minority rights **115,** 516-17, 535
interim measures, injury caused by **94,** 467
international officials
breach of contract **84,** 438, 440
inadequate handling of termination of appointment **83,** 687-8
international official's contract
breach **40,** 352-4
delay in settling claim **38,** 319, 369, 376
illegal decision, prejudice caused by **43,** 456

damages (*cont.*)
improper failure to renew **48,** 320
irregular termination **42,** 320-1
moral injury **43,** 395, 399
procedural delay **40,** 384-5, **43,** 411, 421-2
sickness **42,** 299-303
termination **38,** 314-16, 318, 417-20, **43,** 339, 359-61, 426, 434, 488-90, 491-4, 495-9
international tort/wrong **82,** 569-70, **116,** 89-91
length of proceedings **92,** 254-5
loss of earnings **92,** 317, 370-1
loss of employment **71,** 392-4, 438-40
loss of income as result of treaty **44,** 292-4
losses due to sanctions **109,** 584, 593-4
mental anguish **92,** 255
miscarriage of justice **94,** 394-5
monetary reform, losses due to **44,** 102-3
moral injury **43,** 395, 399, **54,** 318-19, 511, **57,** 197-9, **58,** 112, 113, 116, 593, **61,** 348, **72,** 329-33, **82,** 569-70, **88,** 734, 735, 736, 743-4, **95,** 309, 314, 316, 318, **96,** 250, **116,** 276-7, 287, 288, 430-1, 511-13
equity **95,** 314
mitigating factors **88,** 736
nationalization. *See* expropriation/nationalization, compensation
Nazi persecution **70,** 693, **72,** 448, 457, 472, 647-50, **74,** 281-4, 420-4
non-availability of judicial remedy **92,** 254
non-pecuniary damage **81,** 56, **92,** 317, 349-50, 371
pain and suffering **107,** 460, **121,** 646-7
passport, improper withdrawal **103,** 291-5
preclusion of claims **81,** 545
rehousing, loss on **67,** 393-4
sale of contraband **44,** 498
State-sponsored terrorism **94,** 494, 514, 517, 557, 569-70
compensatory **121,** 613-14, 645-50
liability of foreign State **121,** 643-5
liability of officials acting within scope of functions **121,** 644
punitive **121,** 614-18, 643-5, 650-2
suffering of hostages **81,** 545
territorial sovereignty, violation **74,** 258-9, 266, 271
torture **70,** 234, **121,** 615-16
treaties, breach of **61,** 532-3, 567-8
UN operation in Congo, destruction of aircraft **44,** 433-7
unlawful detention **45,** 319, **56,** 409, 425, 432-3, 497-8, **57,** 184-9, 190-2, 197, 198-9, **70,** 233-4, **72,** 291-2, 313-16, **78,** 252-3
usurpation of property in absence of damage **125,** 690-1, 739-40
war damage. *See* compensation for war-related events
wrongful nationalization **62,** 202
foreign State, action against **63,** 201-14, 245-51, 286-98, 320-9, 352-3, 460-6, 468-77, 481-93
'general' **72,** 379-81, **78,** 344-5
Geneva Convention on Prisoners of War (1929) **61,** 234, 236
human rights considerations **88,** 736, 737-8, 742-3
impossibilium nulla est obligatio **56,** 425

injured party **58,** 709
interest. *See* interest
international officials **96,** 250
legitimate expectations of parties **66,** 602-11
lucrum cessans. See measure of damages/compensation including valuation of company/property/assets, *lucrum cessans*
material **61,** 348
mitigation **78,** 673, **84,** 576
  burden of proof **78,** 673
  changed circumstances **106,** 647
  justification of wrongful act **116,** 64, 154
  known risk **106,** 647, 735
  lawfulness of expropriation/nationalization **106,** 647
  obligation **106,** 630, **116,** 60-1
    general principle of international law **109,** 388, 502, 618, **116,** 64
  refusal to accept proposed changes to contract **106,** 647
mutual renunciation of claims to **116,** 90
nationality of victim, relevance **88,** 734, 742-3
nationals, against own State **52,** 5-7
nominal **58,** 112, 113, **67,** 341, **82,** 576
non-pecuniary **58,** 718-20, **67,** 440
obligation to pay **59,** 395-6
  general principle of law **54,** 509-10, **56,** 196
  recognition, effect **62,** 208
  State succession and **74,** 98-100
offset, unjust enrichment **106,** 646-7
partial indemnity **62,** 186
payment
  currency **85,** 550, 608, 610
  exchange rate **85,** 550-1, 591
    date of conversion **85,** 550
    date of damage **96,** 328
  method **56,** 506
pecuniary **58,** 720-2, **67,** 393-4
period covered
  commencement of unlawful act **96,** 323
  continuation of unlawful act **96,** 323-4
persecution, bar to
  burden of proof **77,** 119-21
  waiver **77,** 120-1, 130, 134, 157-8
préjudice moral. See for, intangible loss *above*
provisional award **46,** 188
proximity **88,** 742
psychological **67,** 440-1
punitive **58,** 112, **63,** 38, **77,** 189-91, **78,** 344-5, **88,** 741, **95,** 315-16, **116,** 514
  Civil Liability for Acts of State Sponsored Terrorism Act 1996 (USA) **121,** 614
  classification of act as criminal and **124,** 433-4
  extra-judicial killing **121,** 616-17
  Foreign Sovereign Immunities Act (USA), exclusion of actions for. *See* United States of America (USA), Foreign Sovereign Immunities Act (FSIA) 1976/82, 28 USC 1606 (State liability: private person liability: exclusion of punitive damages)
  genocide **107,** 460

damages (*cont.*)
hazardous activities **118,** 481-3, 511, 518
I'm Alone case **77,** 189
purpose **77,** 190
purpose **121,** 614-16
I'm Alone case **77,** 190
State practice **88,** 741
State-sponsored terrorism **121,** 614-18, 643-5, 650-2
torture **121,** 615-16
treble damages action **118,** 397-8, 400-1, 406, 412-13
by foreign State **63,** 106-20
libel suit **88,** 113-14
quantum. See measure of damages/compensation including valuation of company/property/assets
refugee **61,** 241
reparation. *See* reparation
requirements
damage **105,** 418, **106,** 452, 465
loss **91,** 263, **106,** 452, 465
nexus **116,** 559-62
rescission of decision and **96,** 250
restitutio in integrum, See restitutio in integrum
right to **75,** 322, 485, 510, 711
State's right to claim **77,** 464
satisfaction distinguished **46,** 466
settlement and. *See* amicable settlement *above*
special. *See* punitive *above*
specific performance and **48,** 320, **96,** 250
speculative **62,** 144, 214-15
State succession
inequity following **96,** 731
war damage **96,** 728-9
subrogation **96,** 330
symbolic. *See* nominal *above*
third party entitlement **86,** 348, **116,** 282-3
Lusitania **116,** 282-3
UN Human Rights Committee **95,** 314
UNGA Resolutions **66,** 435-7, 588, 601-2
as unjust enrichment **88,** 702. *See also* unjust enrichment
USA, public policy **66,** 69-70, 117, 132, 196, 215, 254-5, 375, 434
vexatious proceedings, for **91,** 263
damnum emergens*. See* measure of damages/compensation including valuation of company/property/assets, *damnum emergens*
Danube
boundaries **116,** 226
description and history **116,** 27-9
European Commission for
functions **73,** 168, 171-2
immunity of officials **71,** 538
fisheries **116,** 226
Gabčikovo/Nagymaros Project. *See* Gabčikovo/Nagymaros Project
right to equitable and reasonable share of resources **116,** 63, 65, 89, 158-61, 175, 211-12, 221-2, 224-5, 243-8
riparian States' obligations

fisheries **116,** 226
in respect of by-pass canal **116,** 226
uninterrupted and safe navigation **116,** 80-1, 226
Danube–Save–Adriatic Railway Company
Agreement guaranteeing bonds of **45,** 83-5
Agreements on Debentures **42,** 403-4
Dawes Plan (German reparations and liabilities) 47, 418-19, 426-7, 437-8, 443, 449, 456, 458
Dayton Agreements (Bosnia-Herzegovina) (1995)
Bosnian Serbs (Srpska), responsibility for acts of and **124,** 129-30
boundaries **115,** 79
Genocide Convention (1948), accession to and **115,** 200-3
statehood and **115,** 89-94
de facto governments. *See* government, de facto
death penalty 112, 288-91. *See also* death row as inhuman or degrading treatment; European Convention on Human Rights (1950), death penalty; European Convention on Human Rights (1950), Additional Protocol No 6 (death penalty); extradition in case of death penalty; International Covenant on Civil and Political Rights (ICCPR) (1966), death penalty; Yugoslavia, International Criminal Tribunal for the Former (ICTY), penalty, death
abolition **124,** 300-2, 323-4
Council of Europe Resolution 1044 (1994) **124,** 326
extradition and **98,** 502
American Convention on Human Rights provisions **70,** 465-77
appeal to international bodies
constitutional right **123,** 516-21, 525-32, 549-51
measures prescribing time-limits, legality **123,** 513-16, 531-2
proportionality **123,** 516, 531-2
suspension of execution during **123,** 540-9
commutation
breach of constitutional rights and **123,** 524, 544
reinstatement following appeal **123,** 524-5
delay in execution
breach of Constitution, whether **98,** 344-5, 347-56
Inter-American Commission on Human Rights, appeal to **98,** 355-6, **123,** 512-16, **124,** 265, 272, 284-98
UNHRC, appeal to **98,** 355-6, **123,** 512-16, **124,** 285
history **98,** 375-6, 388-96, 445-6, **124,** 324-6
inhuman or degrading treatment **98,** 350-6, 381, 398-402, 407, **124,** 323. *See also* death row as inhuman or degrading treatment
appeals procedure, relevance **98,** 350-5, **123,** 520
fault of complainant, relevance **98,** 350, 353-4
interim measures and **118,** 4-21, 39-55
international initiatives **124,** 324-6
mitigating factors **124,** 327-8
age **124,** 327-8
prosecution for non-capital charges while on remand **124,** 269-70, 280-1
restitutio in integrum and **118,** 17
State practice **98,** 445-6, **124,** 323-8
State responsibility **98,** 402-7, 417, **124,** 316-17
wrongful convictions and **124,** 328-36
death row as inhuman or degrading treatment 98, 307-12, 379-80, 447-8, **100,** 631-56, **114,** 368, 375-7, 381-2, **115,** 297-8, **118,** 257-8, **124,** 336-8
age and mental state **98,** 311-12, **124,** 276-8
conditions of detention **98,** 310-11, **123,** 523-6, 533-6, **124,** 276-8, 281

death row as inhuman or degrading treatment (*cont.*)
delay
as abuse of process **124,** 289
'reasonable' **124,** 290, 296-7
delay before sentencing **124,** 264-6, 273-81
delay before trial **123,** 521-3, 533
delay caused by appeal, relevance **100,** 648-51, **123,** 521-3
three-year delay in hearing appeal **115,** 297-8
length of detention **98,** 310
'reasonable' **124,** 289-90
personality of condemned person, relevance **98,** 311-12, **100,** 653, **124,** 276, 277-8
repeated reading of death warrant **123,** 550-1
time-limits **100,** 656, **124,** 268-9
debt
annulment, 'taking' of property **42,** 155-7, 161-3
applicable law **80,** 427
debtor **86,** 310
assignment **48,** 13
attachment of assets
creditor's rights and **81,** 538
existence of corporeal or incorporeal asset, need for **82,** 72
confiscation **66,** 69-72, 132-3
debt restructuring, multilateral agreement, treaty, whether **108,** 601
dependent territory's liability **69,** 25-8
enforcement. *See also* repayment *below*
domicile of creditor and **82,** 34
expropriation/nationalization **92,** 410-11
as act of State **87,** 512, **92,** 411
effect **41,** 267-71, 273-9, **42,** 155-7, **47,** 60-2, 63, 120-6, **48,** 82-3, **74,** 288-9, **79,** 584-9, **80,** 427
obligation of original debtor to repay **92,** 410-11
international organizations, liability of members **81,** 676-725
'localized' **48,** 21
public corporation
State, liability for **87,** 12, 103-5
State immunity and **87,** 12, 103-5
real property right distinguished **82,** 42
repayment. *See also* enforcement *above*
enforcement jurisdiction **87,** 514
situs, relevance **87,** 514, 517-18
repudiation
as act of State **63,** 153, 190, 275-6, **66,** 76-7, 138-9, 218-26, 233-6
commercial action **87,** 610
rescheduling **88,** 65
satisfaction
expropriation/nationalization, whether **66,** 409
payment **66,** 135-6
service of process out of the jurisdiction and **65,** 413-16
settlement agreements, effect on legal remedies available to individual **82,** 65-6, 68-9
situs **43,** 21-2, **48,** 83, **66,** 69-72, 138-9, 218-26, 233-6, **81,** 535, 536-7, **84,** 126-30, **87,** 511-19, **92,** 410-11
act of State and **81,** 535 n. 5
bank deposit **38,** 113
creditor's presence **87,** 516-17

domicile **82,** 34
enforcement jurisdiction **87,** 514, 517-18
jurisdiction over debtor **107,** 212
multiple **87,** 513, 515, 518
place of payment **88,** 67, 73-4
place where deposit held **107,** 212 n. 5
relevant considerations
currency of loan **92,** 410
location of borrowers **92,** 410
place of loan **92,** 410
power to collect **92,** 475
State immunity and **82,** 41-2, **103,** 544-6
State trading enterprise, liability for each other's **82,** 93
UN Compensation Commission **117,** 239-40
Declaration of Mexico (1945) 79, 334
declaration, unilateral. *See* unilateral declaration/undertaking
declaratory award 57, 457-66, 486, 533, 597-8, **62,** 169, 181, 197, 199, 217
enforcement **62,** 200, 217
specific performance distinguished **53,** 364-5
declaratory relief. *See* remedies, declaratory relief
decolonization. *See* colonies, decolonization
defamation 88, 106-9, 116-61, 520-4, 529-30, 602, 609-11
applicable law **88,** 166
burden of proof **88,** 521, 522-3, 530
by diplomats, of Ministers **44,** 31
defences, justification **88,** 521, 522, 529
government official, of **88,** 126-9
Head of State **88,** 164-5
libel-proof defence **88,** 109-13
office-holder **88,** 521
public prosecution, limitation to **88,** 521, 522
official report privilege **88,** 166-75
applicability to foreign government **88,** 166-75
parliamentary immunity and **88,** 522
special damages, relevance **88,** 113-14
State immunity and **63,** 129-34, 464, 590
default judgment against foreign State. *See also* service of process on foreign State or State agency, default judgment
burden of proof
acceptance of judgment **65,** 87-8
entitlement **63,** 382, 389-90
effective date **118,** 618
foreign relations and **84,** 144, **118,** 615-16, 617-18
non-appearance as admission of allegations **124,** 430-1
'process', whether **118,** 615-17
public interest **84,** 144
setting aside, grounds, breach of State immunity, jurisdiction **84,** 161-85, **118,** 607-8, 615-18
State immunity, execution/attachment **64,** 70-6, **92,** 425-6
waiver and **65,** 160
State immunity, jurisdiction
acceptance of judgment as waiver **65,** 87-8
evidential requirements **65,** 87-8, **107,** 265-6
impossibility of performance **107,** 267

defence, right to. *See* European Convention on Human Rights (1950), defence, right to; fair trial; International Covenant on Civil and Political Rights (ICCPR) (1966), defence
degrading treatment, freedom from. *See* inhuman or degrading treatment
Delaware Bay 97, 653
delict
definition **91,** 344, 347
State responsibility for unlawful acts of predecessor government **91,** 343-57, 359-70
delimitation. *See* boundary treaties, maritime; continental shelf delimitation; maritime delimitation
demarcation. *See* boundaries, land, demarcation
democracy
definition **70,** 180
European Convention on Human Rights (1950) and **122,** 418, 422-3
majority rule **115,** 561-3, 592
competing majorities **115,** 562-3, 566
referendum, role **115,** 565
rule of law, need for **115,** 562-3
supremacy of sovereign will of the people **115,** 560, 562
democratic legitimacy. *See* European Community (EC), transfer of powers to, democratic legitimacy; European Parliament, democratic legitimacy
demurrage, foreign State's refusal to pay 63, 153-4, 495-7, 569-72
denationalization, *See* State contract, 'denationalization'
denial of justice 46, 324-34, 346, 348, 354, 407, 433, 448, **56,** 469, **57,** 218, **58,** 182, **75,** 375, 377-8, **77,** 212, **80,** 616, **84,** 399. *See also* due process; fair hearing; fair trial; liberty of person, deprivation
classification as
arbitrary or discriminatory act **46,** 326, **84,** 421-2, **121,** 24
arbitration, refusal to submit to **53,** 475
bad faith of courts **46,** 332-4, **121,** 24
cumulative series of acts or omissions **46,** 319, 325, 448
defence, denial of right to **46,** 197, 320
delay **46,** 197, 327, **84,** 372-3, **121,** 24
error in application of law **46,** 320, 326, 330-2
international tort/wrong incurring State responsibility **46,** 318
judicial discrimination **46,** 196
jurisdiction, absence of **46,** 32, 346, 528
manifestly unjust application of treaty **84,** 398
misapplication of the law **121,** 24
procedural issues **125,** 155
serious departure from previous jurisprudence/new rule **125,** 153-5
failure to consider retrospective application of new rule **125,** 156
unreasonable departure from principles of justice recognized by the principal legal systems of the world **125,** 151-2
valuation, method **46,** 331
damages, basis for **89,** 619-22, 630
exhaustion of local remedies and **46,** 57, 316-21, **124,** 16-17, **125,** 140. *See also* exhaustion of local remedies
expropriation/nationalization measures and **62,** 168
failure of municipal court to provide remedies **53,** 475
international officials, employment contract **116,** 649
judicial acts, limitation to **89,** 621-2
lato sensu **46,** 192, 318, 320, 324-34, 511, 512
nationals, claims in respect of losses abroad **56,** 544

Denmark
applicable law, visiting forces, bases, traffic on **91,** 276-8
Arbitral Commission on Property, Rights and Interests in Germany, accession to Charter of **42,** 384
Constitution 1953
Art. 20, accession to EC and **93,** 231
Art. 62 **88,** 609, 611
Art. 63 **93,** 232
Art. 77 **88,** 609-10, 611
continental shelf legislation **41,** 208
contract, definition **89,** 462
courts, municipal, legislative procedures, role **93,** 231, 232
diplomatic immunity, jurisdiction, civil jurisdiction **78,** 83-4
doctrine of acknowledgement **81,** 63, 65, 66, 70
drug-trafficking
jurisdiction, personal **86,** 589, 591
sentencing **86,** 592-3
Single Convention on Narcotic Drugs (1961) **86,** 589
EC, accession, constitutionality, standing to challenge **93,** 229, 231, 232
education in
discrimination **58,** 145
primary **58,** 124-6
sex education **58,** 126-34, 143-4
estoppel. *See* doctrine of acknowledgement *above*
Germany, Arbitration Convention (1926) **42,** 386
Greenland. *See also* Greenland
applicable law **91,** 263-75, 276-8
jurisdiction in **91,** 277, 278
International Covenant on Civil and Political Rights (ICCPR) (1966), reservation to Optional Protocol. *See* International Covenant on Civil and Political Rights (ICCPR) (1966), Optional Protocol, reservation
judicial proceedings, time-limits **81,** 63-6, 70-1
judicial review
diplomatic protection **96,** 215
diplomatic relations, establishment **96,** 215
legally protected right, need for **96,** 215
recognition, State **96,** 215
jurisdiction, drug-trafficking, personal **86,** 589, 591
law of
Administration of Justice Act, s 456 **81,** 65
Criminal Code **74,** 463, 465
s 1 **86,** 589
s 7 **86,** 589, 590, 591, 593
s 10 **86,** 590, 593
s 19 **86,** 587, 589, 590, 591, 592
s 21 **86,** 592
s 75 **86,** 592
s 76 **86,** 592
Illegitimacy Act 1937 **81,** 63
Income Tax Law, Greenland **91,** 271
Law 143 of 29 April 1955 **91,** 267, 273
Law 252 of 18 June 1968 (Vienna Convention on Diplomatic Privileges and Immunities) **78,** 82

Denmark (*cont.*)
Law of 29 November 1978 (Greenland Local Government) **91,** 270
Legal Status of Children Act 1960/1982 **81,** 65-6
discriminatory, whether **81,** 67-71
s 5(1) **81,** 64
s 5(2) **81,** 63, 64-5
s 5(3) **81,** 63, 65
Legitimacy Act 1937, s 3 **81,** 63
Media Liability Act 1991 **107,** 40-1
Art. 18 **107,** 36-7
Art. 22 **107,** 37
Narcotic Drugs, Minister of Interior Notice No 209 of 5 April 1976 **86,** 590
Narcotic Drugs Law 1969 **86,** 587
s 1 **86,** 589, 592
s 2 **86,** 589, 591
s 3 **86,** 591
Penal Code
Art. 23 **107,** 33, 36, 39
Art. 266(b) **107,** 32-3, 34-6, 39
Royal Decree of 23 May 1945 (Denmark/US Defence Agreement (1941)) **91,** 266
Royal Decree of 10 May 1955 (Status of Forces Agreement (1951)) **91,** 267, 273
Traffic Law
Faroes **91,** 276-8
Greenland **91,** 276-8
s 53 **91,** 278
s 125 **91,** 278
s 127 **91,** 278
s 143 **91,** 278
paternity, establishment of, sexual discrimination and **81,** 62-71
public order/public policy/*ordre public*, non-application of foreign law inconsistent with international law **53,** 367
separation of powers, legislative procedures, role of courts **93,** 231, 232
dependent States. *See also* colonies; dependent territories
Andorra **39,** 412-13
dependent territories 48, 26-30. *See also* British Commonwealth; colonies; dependent States
boundaries, establishment **86,** 191, 199-204
common law, application by **86,** 643, 647-8, 650, 667-9
continental shelf rights **86,** 603-7
debt, liability for **69,** 25-8
EU competence and **105,** 147-9, 196-7
European Convention on Human Rights (1950), extension to **58,** 355-7
French Community, autonomy of members **44,** 26-8
judiciary, role **39,** 349-50
legislative powers **86,** 193-4
concurrent **86,** 191
extraterritorial **86,** 191, 198-9, 205, 207
revolution in, effect on legal order **39,** 65, 89, 92-3, 165, 219, 878
South African 'homelands', status **75,** 679-98
status **86,** 159-60
treaties
applicability to **75,** 582-3, **86,** 152-60
EC competence, in case of, representation by Member State **99,** 371, 393

extension to **45,** 429-30
express declaration, need for **75,** 582-3
power to conclude **86,** 155-6
UN Charter provisions **105,** 320-2, 326-7
World Trade Organization Agreement (1994) **105,** 84
deportation 47, 267, **61,** 244, 257, 259, **62,** 286, 288, 291-2, **73,** 596, 598, 613-51, **78,** 372-8, **86,** 216-28, 329-30, **90,** 2-8, **92,** 359-61. *See also* European Convention on Human Rights (1950), deportation; expulsion of alien; expulsion of national; refugee, non-refoulement
appeal **79,** 603-9, **88,** 5-36
'conducive to the public good' and **73,** 639, 641, **124,** 515, 532
grounds
failure to examine all the evidence **111,** 167
manifest error **111,** 167, 173, 179
independent advisory panel **108,** 381
'court', whether **124,** 515
guarantee against arbitrariness, whether **108,** 420-2, 427-8
procedure **108,** 367
reasons for determination, need for, closed evidence **124,** 527, 530, 536
restraint, need for **124,** 547-8
review of proportionality **111,** 179
right of **124,** 540-2
scope **79,** 606-7
Special Immigration Appeals Commission (SIAC) (UK). *See* United Kingdom, Special Immigration Appeals Commission (SIAC)
stay of deportation pending **124,** 412-13, 515
asylum. *See* asylum
belligerent occupation and. *See* belligerent occupation, deportation, prohibition
compelling reasons of national security and
action directed/targeted at deporting State, need for **124,** 521-2, 523-5, 532-5, 543, 548-59
balance of interests **108,** 370-5, 377-8, 406, **124,** 517, 526-7
belligerent occupation **83,** 142, 185, 189
compassionate circumstances **108,** 382-4, **124,** 349-50
defence of the realm and **124,** 535
matter of law/fact **124,** 544-5
responsibility for determining **124,** 519-22, 523-8, 535-6, 537-9, 544-6
risk of torture and **124,** 546
terrorist activity **108,** 379, **124,** 348-51, 360-3, 367-78, 520-2, 525
terrorist organization, membership of **124,** 375-8
threat to another State, relevance **124,** 371-2
'conducive to the public good' **71,** 456-7, 460-2, 480-2, 485-7, **73,** 637, 639, 641, **108,** 368-70, 377, 409-11, **124,** 514-15
appeal **73,** 639, 641, **124,** 515, 532
foreign relations considerations **124,** 520, 545-6
mutual exclusivity of 'conducive to the public good' grounds **124,** 520, 525, 534-5, 537, 543, 548-9
as contempt of court **79,** 49
country of designation **54,** 252-7
country of origin **54,** 253-7
criminal law, punishment, whether **103,** 292, **111,** 178
critical date, facts as at date of decision **111,** 178
definition **87,** 214, 221

deportation (*cont.*)
discretion **104,** 84, **111,** 170
refugee status, relevance **124,** 354
risk of subjection to torture and **124,** 347, 353-8, 380
to country of citizenship **104,** 83
discrimination
EC nationals **92,** 369-70
nationals **92,** 369-70
disguised extradition. *See* extradition, disguised
due process violation, whether **104,** 83
European Community and **86,** 333
European Convention on Human Rights (1950) **92,** 366-70
exclusion distinguished **95,** 580
exempt persons **111,** 177-8
extradition distinguished **83,** 145-6, **86,** 217, 226
family life, respect for **73,** 617, **74,** 447-8, **78,** 374, **92,** 366-9, **103,** 233, **111,** 169-70, 258, **115,** 341. *See also* European Convention on Human Rights (1950), deportation, family life, respect for; International Covenant on Civil and Political Rights (ICCPR) (1966), deportation, family life, respect for
unlawful or arbitrary interference **115,** 337, 348-9
fear of persecution **73,** 615-17, 628-30
forcible **86,** 332, 336-7, 343-4
forcible abduction **104,** 64 n. 4
foreign relations and **86,** 332
of former Nazi government members **79,** 380-1
grave breach of Geneva Conventions (1949) **108,** 31, 135
grounds
criminal record **115,** 342-3
threat to public order/public policy/*ordre public* **111,** 167-8, 173, 176-7, 258
inhuman or degrading treatment, whether **115,** 330
judicial review **88,** 259
legislation relating to, retroactive effect **111,** 178
long residence, relevance **111,** 189
military service and **86,** 223
nationality and **45,** 346-52, **92,** 369-70, **103,** 282, 288, 297, **111,** 172, 188-9
non-compliance with order **86,** 343-4
order
indefinite duration **111,** 178
request for revocation, repeated **111,** 178
political nature of decision **88,** 28
procedural fairness **124,** 378-83, 390-1
prohibited non-citizen **86,** 216-18, 226-8
proportionality **74,** 616
protection **87,** 221
punishment **79,** 381
reasons, need for **124,** 350, 382
residence permit, relevance **92,** 364-5
retroactivity of legislation **79,** 381
right of **92,** 368
rights of child under international conventions and **117,** 645-9
stay pending appeal **124,** 412-13, 515
stay pending consideration by international body **124,** 403-5, 407, 417-27
stay pending European Commission proceedings **78,** 372-5

suspension **79,** 380
discretionary, whether **79,** 606
to country where risk of subjection to torture **123,** 595-6, 598, **124,** 346-84
assurances that torture will not be used, need to evaluate **124,** 381-2
International Covenant on Civil and Political Rights (ICCPR) (1966) and **124,** 365-6
'minimal risk of harm' finding **124,** 390, 403, 409-10, 416
Refugees, Geneva Convention on the Status of (1951) **124,** 367-8
'shocking to the conscience', whether **124,** 353, 360-3
State responsibility and **124,** 361-3
'substantial grounds' test **124,** 358, 380, 389
Torture Convention (1984) **124,** 366-7
UNHRC General Comment No 20 and **124,** 365-6
to country where risk of threat to life **79,** 502 n. 8
unlawful, remedies **86,** 347-8
waiver **111,** 178
compulsory residence order **111,** 178
withhold. *See* deportation withhold/bar
deportation withhold/bar 79, 612-20, 623-9, 632-9
asylum distinguished **79,** 616 n. 6, **87,** 475-7, **95,** 549, 558-9, 574, 581, 582 n. 11
burden of proof **95,** 572, 574
conditions **87,** 484
eligibility for asylum **95,** 574
deportation to specific country **95,** 549, 581, 604 n. 8
distinguished **87,** 476-7
extended voluntary departure **95,** 568
mandatory **79,** 616, 625, **95,** 543, 549, 558
persecution as ground for **79,** 380, 381
burden of proof **79,** 607, 608
clear probability **95,** 549, 574
evidence of **79,** 607-9
requirements
absence of security risk to State of refuge **79,** 605
likelihood of **79,** 605, 607-9
persecution by government or by group government unable to control **79,** 605
political beliefs, resulting from **79,** 605
threat to life and freedom **87,** 496
well-founded fear **79,** 502 n. 8, 505 n. 11, 605-9, 613, 616-20, 623-41, 657, 662, **87,** 473, 483-8
requirements, absence of security risk to State of refuge **79,** 605
standard of proof **87,** 499
derelict. *See* wreck, derelict (*res derelicta*)
deserter
arrest
consular function, whether **42,** 233-4
from foreign forces outside territory **85,** 156-81
detention
military authorities of foreign country, by **85,** 158, 164
permanent resident, of **85,** 158-9, 178
place of desertion, relevance **85,** 156-7, 166-8
prerogative matter, whether **85,** 164, 165-6, 168-71, 177-8
treaty obligation, whether **85,** 164-5
visiting forces, limited to, whether **85,** 156-81

deserter (*cont.*)
due process and **44,** 232-8
extraditable offence, whether **85,** 165
prisoner of war status **42,** 448
punishment **42,** 177
return, obligation **42,** 232-8, **85,** 158
deserting seamen, punishment **43,** 177
desuetude. *See* treaties, termination, desuetude
detainees, rights 71, 311-16, 347-53, 356-65. *See also* detention; Guantanamo Bay Naval Base detainees
appeal **70,** 221-34
conditions of detention **78,** 34, 35, 36, 39
correspondence, respect for **57,** 211, 220-3, 230-1, 233-7, **69,** 180-2, **72,** 339-72, **78,** 338, 339-42, 343-4, 346-7, 380-8
censorship **78,** 51, 52, 53
complaints concerning, procedure **72,** 351-4
practice of authorities **72,** 354-8
rules concerning **72,** 342-51
defence, preparation **78,** 34, 39
freedom from
discrimination **58,** 77-9, 285-8
ill-treatment **62,** 241, 244-7, 256-8, 260
racial harassment **69,** 177-8
torture **70,** 221-34, 356, 360-6. *See also* torture
as fundamental rights **70,** 231-2
humane treatment **69,** 177-8, **108,** 84
interrogation techniques **71,** 301-3
judicial review **96,** 659-60
judicial supervision **56,** 379
legal proceedings **56,** 379-80, 382, **57,** 210, 230-1
legal representation **71,** 313, **87,** 578-83
legality of detention, challenge to **58,** 71-9, 289, 699-700, **71,** 353, 356, 365, **72,** 409, **79,** 189, 260
medical attention **69,** 192-3, **70,** 258, 294, **79,** 237, 239, 257
private life, respect for **56,** 384, 398
prompt appearance before a judge **118,** 258
prompt notification of charges **62,** 247, 254, **69,** 192, **70,** 227-32, 255-7, 261, **118,** 258
reasons for arrest/detention **62,** 241, **67,** 471-3, **79,** 185, 186, 192
in language understood by detainee **92,** 542-8
regular review **78,** 208
release on completion of sentence **71,** 312, 314-15, 360-1, 363
conditional upon leaving the country **71,** 356, 363
segregation from convicted persons **69,** 177-80
solitary confinement and **69,** 192, **70,** 221-6, **78,** 51, **96,** 655, 657
status as protected persons under the Geneva Convention, Muslim detainees at Bosnian Serb detention camp **108,** 35, 132
to make representation **92,** 248-51
delay in dealing with **92,** 249-51
trial, right to **56,** 378-9, 401, 410, **67,** 545-9
detention. *See also* American Convention on Human Rights (1969), detention; arrest; detainees, rights; detention; European Convention on Human Rights (1950), detention;

European Convention on Human Rights (1950), liberty of person, deprivation; International Covenant on Civil and Political Rights (ICCPR) (1966), detainees; liberty of person, deprivation; United Nations Compensation Commission, detention/forced hiding; Yugoslavia, International Criminal Tribunal for the Former (ICTY), detention
administrative detention **108,** 439, 443
alien **92,** 551-2
convicted prisoner distinguished **92,** 552-3
International Covenant on Civil and Political Rights (ICCPR) (1966) **92,** 551-2
International Covenant on Economic, Social and Cultural Rights (1966) **92,** 551-2
international obligations to be respected **92,** 551-3
Universal Declaration of Human Rights (1948) **92,** 551
armed forces, members of **58,** 72-4, 94-5, 101-2, 107
belligerent occupation
as alternative to deportation **83,** 185
without trial **83,** 191
by illegal regime **78,** 491-500
civilian prisoners during armed conflict **123,** 158-88
conviction, after **41,** 303-4, 311
delegation of powers **88,** 268
detention on island, *mafiosi* in Italy **61,** 310-18
escape from as
offence connected with political offence **79,** 163, 498
political offence **55,** 572-4, 577, **59,** 61-2, 63-5, 73, 482, **79,** 59
habeas corpus
detention incommunicado and **118,** 79-83, 91
as means to test validity **119,** 393-4
in case of detention by peacekeeping forces **119,** 393-8
habitual offenders **67,** 540-9
without trial **67,** 545-9
house arrest
considerations
age **108,** 77
mental health **108,** 77
physical condition **108,** 77
public order/public policy/*ordre public* **108,** 77-8
risk of criminal behaviour continuing **108,** 78
risk of escape **108,** 78
risk of tampering with evidence or witnesses **108,** 78
special merit **108,** 77
Council of Europe Resolution (65)11 **108,** 77
requirements **108,** 77
State practice **108,** 76-8
incommunicado **62,** 242, 246-8, 253, 255-8, 260-1, **68,** 31, 36, 46, **70,** 256, 258, 260-1, 282, 286, 289-90, 295-6, **71,** 311-13, 347, 355-6, 363, 365, **78,** 34, 35, **79,** 183, 186, 214, 218, 224, 232, 259, 260, **118,** 72, 73-4, 79-81, 85-7, 89
arbitrary nature **118,** 87
cruel, inhumane or degrading treatment, whether **118,** 86-7, 91
family, effect on **118,** 110-11
habeas corpus and **118,** 79-83, 91
requirements **118,** 87

detention (*cont.*)
inhuman or degrading treatment, whether **75,** 366-7
inhuman treatment or torture, whether involving **62,** 241, 244-7, 256-8, 260, **71,** 311-13, 315-16, 347-53, 356-65, **78,** 52, 78-9, 80, **79,** 191-2, 204-5, 207-8, 209, 210, 214, 224, 225, 232, 235-6, 239, 241, 257-60
'lawful detention' **58,** 75-6, 79, 94-5, 273-7, 280-1, 667-73, 674-7, **62,** 241-3, 245, 256-7, 260, **72,** 310-12, 314-16, **78,** 203-12, 243-5, 694-9
accordance with the procedures and terms established by law **118,** 77, 78
'fulfilment of obligations prescribed by law' **73,** 394-5
habeas corpus proceedings **67,** 453-4, 468-71
judicial determination/order of competent authority **58,** 676, 678, 695-9, **67,** 466-71, 545-9, **118,** 77, 78-9
military service **58,** 71-6
necessity **118,** 77, 85
public interest **40,** 187
reasonableness **118,** 77
mentally ill person **58,** 667-73, 675-8, **67,** 465, 470. *See also* person of unsound mind *below*
compulsory detention **67,** 450-2, **70,** 326-8, **81,** 118-20, 121-4
trade union activity respecting **81,** 113-16
emergency measures **67,** 463, 465, 470
judicial review **67,** 466-71
regular **67,** 466-8, 470
lawfulness **67,** 462-71
minimum conditions **67,** 462, 465-6
recall into custody, arrest, whether **67,** 472
review procedures **67,** 466-71
pending expulsion **88,** 250-1, 257-9
pending extradition **45,** 316-28, **79,** 244, 248, 249-50, **101,** 191-2, **108,** 441, **111,** 206-10, 249-50
pending trial **43,** 180-1, **56,** 480-4, 487-8, 489-92, **57,** 194-7, **58,** 688-91, **72,** 309-13. *See also* provisional *below*
legality, right to challenge **72,** 409
sentence, as part of **58,** 75-6, 107, 113
person of unsound mind **78,** 203-12, **81,** 121-6. *See also* mentally ill person *above*
conditions of detention, relevance **81,** 121-6
precautionary (*medidas eliminativas de seguridad*) **78,** 78
preventive **118,** 77-9, 85, 90
procedure **56,** 405
provisional **41,** 281-3, 284, **58,** 70, 73, 107, 275-6. *See also* pending trial *above*
provisional release order, following **71,** 312, 316
purpose
breaking of links with offender **92,** 551
prevention of criminal activity **92,** 551
rights, effect on **58,** 679-81
as slavery **120,** 55, 112
SWAPO detention camps **85,** 219-35
tax, for non-payment **40,** 241-2, 244-6
unlawful
dependence on breach of individual's own right **86,** 531
legal effects **56,** 409
remedy **56,** 416

damages **45,** 319, **56,** 409, 425, 432-3, 497-8, **57,** 184-9, 190-2, 197, 198-9, **70,** 233-4, **72,** 291-2, 313-16, **78,** 252-3
remission of prison sentence **57,** 184-8, 197
vagrants **56,** 405-6
without charge **62,** 241-6
without trial **62,** 256, 260
deterrence 110, 204. *See also* nuclear weapons, deployment; Yugoslavia, International Criminal Tribunal for the Former (ICTY), penalty, purpose, deterrence
credibility **110,** 490
customary international law **110,** 318
degrees of **110,** 489
intent, relevance **110,** 490-1
'mutually assured destruction' **110,** 492
as threat **110,** 475-6, 490
UN Charter **110,** 234, 241, 257-9, 273-9, 335-7, 475-6
détournement de pouvoir. *See* abuse of power
devaluation 59, 534-5, 589
development. *See also* environment; sustainable development principle
Declaration on the Right to Development (1986) **116,** 100
definition **116,** 100
Rio Declaration on Environment and Development (1992). *See* environment, Rio Declaration on Environment and Development (1992)
Diplock courts. *See* Northern Ireland, Diplock courts
diplomacy 61, 525-6, 568-9, **77,** 41, 99, 247
collective **37,** 27, 55, 89, 174-5, 181, 453, 565
international law invoked in support **77,** 247
diplomatic agent. *See also* ambassador/head of mission; consular agent; diplomatic mission; diplomatic premises; diplomatic privileges and immunities; diplomatic relations; Vienna Convention on Diplomatic Relations (1961)
accreditation, procedural, whether **88,** 328
action on behalf of ambassador, validity **106,** 250, 254
agent of State-owned corporation **46,** 33-4, 139
appointment **61,** 500, 502
non-acceptability to receiving State **61,** 500-1
termination **61,** 501, 502
assets, State immunity and **87,** 59-62
breach of law
recall of diplomat **94,** 606
remedies **94,** 605-8
civil proceedings for damage, forum **86,** 547-50
contract made by, applicable law **41,** 21, 23
criminal offence, remedy, declaration as *persona non grata* **115,** 607
employee of company established under economic development agreement, whether **96,** 306
employment of, public act, whether **63,** 344
expulsion
aliens distinguished **96,** 313
persona non grata, relevance **99,** 110
extraterritoriality, maintenance of normal residence in sending State **94,** 600
forcible release of, attempt at **61,** 543-4, 569-70, 580-1
functions. *See* diplomatic mission, functions/'diplomatic activity'
Head of State as **119,** 60-1

diplomatic agent (*cont.*)
hostages, detention as **61,** 561, 563
international official, whether **105,** 48-56
obligations, respect for laws and regulations of receiving State **116,** 633
offence against, violation of international law **36,** 293
permanent residence, claim to **42,** 207-10
Police Liaison Officer **111,** 616, 661
dual status **111,** 635, 636-7
ranking, sending State, responsibility of **99,** 116
recognition, need for **61,** 500, **64,** 695-6, **94,** 614
responsibility for **64,** 696
rescue, lawfulness **61,** 543-4, 569-70, 580-1
seizure **61,** 513, 520, 523-4, 538-40, 555
lawfulness **61,** 562-4
service of process on, procedural requirements **77,** 497, 508-9
social security
entitlement **94,** 598-608
civil war in sending State **94,** 607
diplomatic immunity and **70,** 393-4
legal aid, entitlement **94,** 601
performance of functions, effect on **94,** 604-5
requirement to work **94,** 600
sending State, responsibility of **94,** 600, 605
urgent distress **94,** 605, 606-7
Vienna Convention on Diplomatic Relations (1961), implications **94,** 600, 601, 603-6
obligations **94,** 604
employer **94,** 604
special envoy
definition **99,** 116
as head of Mission **99,** 116
spouse, assimilation to **87,** 77-8
customary international law **87,** 78
State responsibility for actions of **86,** 547-50, **87,** 59, **103,** 310
customary international law **87,** 59
status
civil war in sending State, effect on **94,** 607
determination responsibility of executive **113,** 531-2
receiving State's right to refuse **99,** 106-12
special mission. *See* diplomatic mission, special
taxation in sending State, liability **87,** 77-8
trade representative, whether **99,** 106
ILC **99,** 106 n. 3
training, State's duty, Vienna Convention on Diplomatic Relations (1961) **107,** 222, 223-4
treatment, inhumane, whether **61,** 540
diplomatic archives. *See also* diplomatic premises; international organization, archives; State succession, State property, archives and debts
definition **77,** 117-20
functional test **77,** 118
'official', tautologous **77,** 117-18
Vienna Convention on Diplomatic Relations (1961), omission from **77,** 118
inviolability **77,** 117-20

internal embassy documents **86,** 132-51
comity **86,** 141-3
functions of mission, relating to **86,** 138
voluntary **86,** 145
diplomatic bag, smuggling, use for **48,** 236-7
diplomatic channels
dispute settlement **82,** 518
dissolution of union of States, disputes arising from **91,** 309-10
inter-State **84,** 131, 270, 306
means of inter-State communication **106,** 314
means of pursuing claim **57,** 463
as remedy
forcible abduction/unlawful arrest **95,** 404
State immunity, jurisdiction, in case of **102,** 173, 182, **104,** 580, 622, **113,** 434
service of process on foreign State or State agency **80,** 369, 372, 374, 376, **84,** 138, **104,** 686-9, **106,** 280-1
treaty, notice of suspension **106,** 211-12
treaty implementation and **84,** 20
diplomatic envoy. *See* ambassador/head of mission; diplomatic agent
diplomatic functions. *See* diplomatic mission, functions/'diplomatic activity'
diplomatic immunity, arrest 71, 555, **87,** 214, 217-18
disturbance of internal order **87,** 221
diplomatic immunity, execution/attachment 65, 332-3, 386-7, **72,** 658-60, **89,** 55, **106,** 291-2
honorary consul **82,** 6-10
private funds **82,** 7
diplomatic immunity, jurisdiction 60, 380-2, **64,** 365-7, **65,** 332-3, 386-7, **70,** 395-6, 414-19, **71,** 550-1, **74,** 520-2, **75,** 76-8, **87,** 214
absolute **87,** 235, **91,** 315
administrative jurisdiction **75,** 91-5
alternative forum, desirability **114,** 484-5
child custody dispute **114,** 480-5, **118,** 304-5
civil proceedings, employment contract **113,** 452
commercial activity **60,** 377, 382-3, **64,** 590
purchase of property by diplomat for renting **118,** 305-6
common law **104,** 414-16
construction of embassy **78,** 83-4
counterclaims **77,** 455-6, **78,** 5, **89,** 51
effect of withdrawal of original suit **77,** 456
courts' duty to apply *proprio motu* **78,** 485, 489, **86,** 147
criminal **71,** 537, 567-9, 571, **74,** 518-19, **87,** 214, **119,** 60
civil jurisdiction distinguished **86,** 643
functional immunity and **115,** 606, 607
serious violation of law **115,** 607
customary international law **111,** 158
determination by judge considering merits **82,** 57
divorce proceedings **74,** 520-2, **118,** 304
enforcement of covenant proceedings **64,** 364-7, 385-93
equitable interest **118,** 307-8
eviction **77,** 497
functional. *See* diplomatic mission, functions/'diplomatic activity'
immunity from execution as independent issue **118,** 308-9

diplomatic immunity, jurisdiction (*cont.*)
interference with functioning of mission and **65,** 109, 186-91, 210-11
International Criminal Tribunal for the Former Yugoslavia (ICTY) **110,** 652
international organizations, representatives and missions accredited to **48,** 205-8, **70,** 414-18, **71,** 567-73, **74,** 278-9, **75,** 76-7, **77,** 495-7, **82,** 122-3, **99,** 141-3. *See also* State immunity, jurisdiction, entitlement, international organizations, representatives and missions accredited to
Convention on Privileges and Immunities of the UN (1946) **99,** 142, 199
UN Charter **99,** 142, 198, 199
UN delegates **47,** 275-7
UN Headquarters Agreement **99,** 142, 198
Vienna Convention on Diplomatic Relations (1961) **99,** 142, 198, 199
judicial assistance, request for and **82,** 57
legal liability distinguished **64,** 392-3, **114,** 494
matrimonial jurisdiction **78,** 485, **118,** 302-4
'matrimonial cause' **118,** 302, 303-4, 308
official acts attributable to State **78,** 104
penalty for wrongful occupation **77,** 497
private acts **41,** 444-5, 447, 450, **70,** 389-92, 414-19, **71,** 536-8, **78,** 103
procedural bar **41,** 414-15, **80,** 422-4, **118,** 309-10
real/immovable property held on behalf of the sending State for the purposes of the mission, dispute relating to **40,** 80-1, **45,** 75, **65,** 109, 252-4, 257, **78,** 6 n. 1, **94,** 312-13, **118,** 305-10
annulment of contract **65,** 30-1
embassy bank accounts, evidence of purpose **94,** 360
lease **101,** 378-9
customary international law **101,** 379
notice to quit leasehold property **77,** 497
reasons for exception **94,** 311-12
recovery of rent **78,** 102-4, **82,** 122-3, **89,** 44
Vienna Convention on Diplomatic Relations (1961) and **65,** 109, 254, **74,** 181-2
State immunity and **38,** 163-70, **40,** 80-1, **64,** 391, **65,** 22, 185, 190, **77,** 270-1, **86,** 510-11, **87,** 235-6, 415, 416, **89,** 363, **102,** 182, **103,** 310, **106,** 182, 291-2, 310, **111,** 632-4, **115,** 605-6, **119,** 153, 222. *See also* ambassador/head of mission, State immunity, jurisdiction
diplomatic privileges and immunities as basis of State immunity **64,** 419
distinction **45,** 59, **64,** 72, **65,** 22, 30, 109, 161-2, 254, 307, **82,** 2-5, 102, 116-18, **91,** 293, 295-6, 299, 306, 307, **102,** 172, **103,** 309, **104,** 412-13, 414-17, **107,** 636, 639-40, **111,** 606, **113,** 419, 422, 452, 465-6, 467-8, 471-2, **114,** 495, **115,** 608-10, 613-14, **116,** 633, **119,** 210
failure to make **82,** 116-18
overlap **116,** 628-9
primacy **115,** 613-14
State as party to dispute **91,** 293, 295-6, 299, 306, 307, **102,** 181-3
stay of proceedings **118,** 309-10
tenancy agreement **78,** 6 n. 1
traffic offences **75,** 90-6
diplomatic immunity, jurisdiction, waiver 41, 414-15, **86,** 146-7, 520-1, 522, **87,** 214-22, **88,** 40
agreement to authenticate document as **87,** 218, 219-20

authority of sending State, need for **60,** 378, 382-3, **69,** 283, **77,** 523, **78,** 7, **86,** 147, 151, **87,** 222, **94,** 340-1, **111,** 623, 634, 643, 656-7, 663, **114,** 481-3, **118,** 301, **120,** 448-50
burden of proof **111,** 623
by lawyer on behalf of client **111,** 628, 657
compatibility with claim of inviolability of documents **86,** 146-7, 150-1
conditional **87,** 215
counterclaim as **77,** 454-6, **111,** 639-41, 658-9
customary international law **87,** 216
evidence, giving of as **87,** 222
express **86,** 520, **87,** 215, 220, 221, **111,** 626-8, 642-5, 656-8
clear and unequivocal communication, need for **111,** 645, **120,** 456-7
knowledge and intent, need for **111,** 643, 656
writing **111,** 643
failure by sending State to object to proceedings by employee as **116,** 638
failure to appear as **102,** 182
failure to exercise right of appeal as **102,** 182
general **86,** 520
insurance contract as **69,** 282-3
international conventions relating to children's rights, effect **114,** 483-4
limited **87,** 215
need to know of status **99,** 116-17
as part of defence **86,** 135-6, 147, 148, 151
retrospective **86,** 520, **111,** 645
separate waivers for jurisdiction and execution, need for **111,** 645
submission to the jurisdiction as **111,** 642, 656-7
appearance in stay proceedings **104,** 416-17
initiation of proceedings **77,** 455-6, **82,** 16, **99,** 116-17, **111,** 637-41, 658-9, **120,** 448-50
participation in extradition proceedings **42,** 242-8
participation in related proceedings **89,** 51, **111,** 658
term of lease **99,** 204
undertaking to Court by diplomatic agent as **111,** 623, 641-2, 656-8
Vienna Convention on Diplomatic Relations (1961) **70,** 392-3, **75,** 93, 95-6, **87,** 216
withdrawal **87,** 216-17, 218
diplomatic law
development of **61,** 556, 569
inviolability, principle of **61,** 565-7, 568-9
nature of **61,** 564-6, 568-9, 572-3
diplomatic mission. *See also* ambassador/head of mission; consular premises; diplomatic agent; diplomatic mission, special; diplomatic premises; Vienna Convention on Diplomatic Relations (1961)
accreditation **82,** 286
administrative and technical staff **64,** 357, 361-2, **82,** 20-3, **104,** 641-2, **116,** 640
embassy driver **65,** 22
capital, location in as requirement **99,** 108
State practice **99,** 108
commercial/trade representation/mission, status as **82,** 117
jurisdictional nexus **103,** 568
consulate. *See* consulate, 'mission'
cultural institute, part of, whether **82,** 3

diplomatic mission (*cont.*)
definition, absence from Vienna Convention on Diplomatic Relations (1961) **99,** 106-9
diplomatic activity. *See* functions/'diplomatic activity' *below*
diplomatic dignity, international law concept, whether **101,** 230-1
diplomatic premises distinguished **99,** 107-9, **101,** 241, **107,** 240-1
employment contract. *See* employment contract, locally engaged staff, diplomatic mission
functions/'diplomatic activity' **45,** 59
bomb attack, assistance **115,** 600, 603
campaign to embarrass government friendly to host State **57,** 154-9
clerical staff **82,** 22
commercial work **86,** 70-1
cultural relations **63,** 171-2, 231
economic relations **63,** 172
effect on performance of
bankruptcy petition **94,** 368-9
receipt of social security from receiving State **94,** 604-5
employment of domestic staff **107,** 453-6
executive officers **82,** 22
export promotion **98,** 59-60
joint control of funds for education institution **104,** 413-17
medical care **104,** 681
privileges and **56,** 519-25
promotion of friendly relations **63,** 172, **86,** 71
protection of interests of sending State and its nationals **85,** 56
within the limits permitted by international law **119,** 246-7
protection of national **86,** 71
public relations **63,** 171-2
representation of sending State **86,** 548
participation in hunt, whether **86,** 547-8
sale of land on behalf of sending State, whether **65,** 123-4
State immunity in respect of acts concerning **57,** 156-8, **63,** 51, 57, 171-2, 218, 231, **64,** 233, **65,** 187-8, 210-11
telecommunications staff **82,** 20
telephonists **82,** 22
translation **82,** 116-18
head of mission. *See* ambassador/head of mission
jurisdiction of receiving State, whether subject to **72,** 142
lease
breach, diplomatic channels as remedy **102,** 182
sending State as contracting party **102,** 182
locally engaged staff. *See also* diplomatic privileges and immunities, locally engaged staff; employment contract, locally engaged staff, diplomatic mission
enforcement of rights, forum **82,** 20
local law, subject to **82,** 17
'member of the staff of mission', whether **104,** 637-43, **107,** 639-40
unemployment benefit, entitlement **69,** 277-9
medical office, status **104,** 680-1
'member'
diplomatic status, relevance **107,** 635-7
entitlement to privileges and immunities, relevance **104,** 642
locally engaged staff **104,** 637-43, **107,** 639-40
nationality, relevance **104,** 643, **107,** 639-40

notification of appointment, relevance **104,** 637-8, 642-3, 681
staff of medical office **104,** 680-1, **107,** 635-40
purposes of
ownership of residences **87,** 236
property held for **64,** 367, 388-92, **87,** 233, 236
receiving State's duty of protection **61,** 525, 556-9, **82,** 125-7, **89,** 2-3, **123,** 502-3
choice of means **82,** 126
service of process on **42,** 239-41, **63,** 21-3, 60-2, 124-7, **80,** 369, 372, 374, 376
size, receiving State's right to determine **99,** 112
special. *See* diplomatic mission, special
status **71,** 239
agent of sending State **102,** 181-3
customary international law **102,** 181-2
emanation of sending State **103,** 364-5
executive certificate **104,** 682
independence of sending State **102,** 181-2, 207
organ of sending State **65,** 269-70, **77,** 487

diplomatic mission, special
accreditation to **121,** 601-2
as courtesy **80,** 409-10
customary international law **80,** 404, 419-20
establishment **80,** 398-9, 412-22. *See also* requirements *below*
customary international law **80,** 399-400, 404, 406
date **80,** 400-1
ex post facto **80,** 399, 421
UN Convention on Special Missions (1969) **80,** 408
foreign policy considerations **80,** 398, 399, 402, 409
informal agreement **80,** 407
general rules of international law. *See* customary international law *above*
Head of State's family and **81,** 606
mission en passant **80,** 416, 420, 422
privileges and immunities, **81,** 606
requirements
actual existence of mission **80,** 398
agreement **80,** 398, 401-2, 404
evidence of **80,** 406, 412
formation **80,** 404, 420-1
specific task **80,** 398, 399, 401-2, 404, 405, 408-9
evidence of **80,** 405, 410-11
UN Convention on Special Missions **80,** 397, 403, 418-20
customary international law and **80,** 403-4, 406, 408, 418-20, **121,** 601-2
establishment under **80,** 408

diplomatic premises 60, 385-7. *See also* diplomatic agent; diplomatic archives; diplomatic mission; diplomatic privileges and immunities; diplomatic relations
arrest within, legality, individual without diplomatic status **71,** 554-6, 558-61
birth on **55,** 584
burden of proof **77,** 119-21
commercial transactions in **55,** 584
crime
against **55,** 585
committed within **40,** 56-7, **52,** 306-9
definition **77,** 117-20
'official', tautologous **77,** 117-18

diplomatic premises (*cont.*)
residence of head of mission **87,** 233, 236
residence of member of mission **64,** 365-7, 390-1, **71,** 554-61, **72,** 659-60, **78,** 103, **87,** 236, **98,** 10, **101,** 361
'used for purposes of [maintaining] a diplomatic or consular mission' **64,** 367, 388-92, **87,** 233, 236
burden of proof **98,** 12
Vienna Convention on Diplomatic Relations, absence **77,** 118
diplomatic privileges and immunities distinguished **99,** 108
dispute between States relating to **91,** 292-316
duty of host government
to protect **94,** 306-7, 349-50, **101,** 207-8, 227, **102,** 180
to refrain from entry **101,** 207
duty of host government to prevent any disturbance of the peace of the mission or impairment of its dignity **83,** 234-43, **121,** 535-8
customary international law **121,** 509, 532
demonstration outside embassy **101,** 227-35, 242-5, 254, 257
diplomatic considerations, relevance **101,** 245, 253
foreign relations considerations **121,** 504-5, 506-9
freedom of expression and **60,** 385-6, **101,** 243-54, 256, 257, **121,** 503-63
Harvard Draft Convention on Diplomatic Privileges and Immunities (1932) **101,** 227
House of Commons Foreign Affairs Committee (1984-5) **101,** 228-9, 243-4
legislation implementing, constitutionality **121,** 503-66
'congregation' clause **121,** 503, 521-2, 527-8, 538-41, 547-50, 552, 560-3
'display of placard' clause **121,** 503, 518-20, 527-8, 551-60, 563, 566
measures necessary to meet obligation, executive certificate/statement, conclusiveness **121,** 511-12
pre-Vienna Convention (1961) requirement **121,** 506-9
proportionality **101,** 254-7
protection of local government and political figures distinguished **121,** 513
security interest **121,** 535, 540-3
State practice **101,** 231-2, 243-4
duty of host government to protect
customary international law **83,** 237
motives of accused, relevance **94,** 306-7, 349-50
sale as fulfilment **83,** 237, 240
duty of host government to sell **83,** 236
execution, immunity, private residence of diplomatic families **72,** 659-60
extraterritoriality **55,** 584, **65,** 112-13, **69,** 277-9, **70,** 393-4, **71,** 542-3, 554-5, 557, **72,** 214, **86,** 540-1, **87,** 230-1, **101,** 226, **102,** 179
inviolability distinguished **90,** 591 n. 9, **101,** 226, **116,** 632
rejection of theory **72,** 141-2
territory of sending State, whether part of **72,** 141, **90,** 589-90, 593-4, **94,** 351, 352
handing over of keys to host government by disaffected staff, effect **83,** 240-1
inviolability **38,** 162-70, **40,** 56-7, **55,** 584, **61,** 525-6, 556-9, 562, 563-7, 583-4, **65,** 254, **71,** 554-61, **72,** 141-2, 658-60, **87,** 220-1
absolute theory **71,** 558-61
consular premises. *See* consular premises, inviolability
customary international law **99,** 200, **101,** 207, **121,** 509
18th century **99,** 201
damages, action for and **64,** 393
emergencies, in case of **99,** 199-200

entry with consent of head of mission **113,** 480
eviction **101,** 361, **111,** 158-9
obligation of Receiving State to find alternative accommodation **111,** 158
extraterritoriality distinguished **90,** 591 n. 9, **101,** 226, **116,** 632
forcible eviction **99,** 198-204
functional test **71,** 561, **77,** 118, **99,** 201, **101,** 226
illegal occupation **102,** 179
mission to international organization **99,** 198-9
office and residence distinguished **64,** 390, **101,** 226
residence of member of mission **64,** 365-7, 390-1, **71,** 554-61, **72,** 659-60
eviction order **101,** 361
seizure **61,** 539-41, 555
service of notice and **87,** 230-1
service of writ as breach **102,** 182
jurisdiction **61,** 226. *See also* extraterritoriality *above*
lex loci contractus **92,** 533
lex situs **92,** 533, 536
territorial **55,** 585-6
land register, rectification **38,** 169
maintenance, Estonian mission in UK **85,** 62
marriages in **55,** 581, 584, 587
'mission', whether **107,** 240
misuse **71,** 544, 556, 558-60, **77,** 117-20
ownership, foreign sovereign **87,** 236
part of sending State's territory, whether **55,** 584, **63,** 125, **94,** 351, 352
possession **64,** 390-1
premises of international organization **101,** 228
privileges and immunities **55,** 584
taxation **57,** 336, **98,** 3-12
protection **60,** 385, 387, **61,** 525, 556-9, 562
reciprocity and **60,** 385
receiving State, agreement, need for **88,** 40
recognition as such, executive responsibility **94,** 349
repair of, commercial act, whether **63,** 344, 588
seizure, lawfulness **61,** 560-4
State immunity. *See* State immunity, execution/attachment, diplomatic premises; State immunity, jurisdiction, diplomatic premises
status as **61,** 225
dependence on use as such, Iranian Embassy in London **108,** 563-4
loss of **83,** 236, 239
Vienna Convention on Diplomatic Relations (1961). *See also individual duties*
breach **71,** 554-6, 560-1
defence of necessity **71,** 558-9
remedy **71,** 554, 558
*travaux pr*éparatoires and **71,** 558-9
immunities **55,** 586
inviolability **99,** 199-204
customary international law **99,** 200, 201, **101,** 207, **121,** 509
exceptions excluded **99,** 199-203
ILC Report (1958) **99,** 199, 200
State practice **99,** 202
universal acceptance **99,** 201, 202-3
State immunity, analogy **40,** 81, 83

diplomatic privileges and immunities 40, 222-3, **47,** 275-7, **48,** 191-208, **52,** 306-9, **57,** 331, **61,** 500, 501-2, 555-70, **68,** 176-80, **71,** 535-76, **72,** 654-62, **73,** 679-88, **74,** 518-22, **77,** 468-9. *See also* consular privileges and immunities; diplomatic immunity, execution/attachment; diplomatic immunity, jurisdiction; Head of State, diplomatic privileges and immunities, entitlement; Head of State, immunity, jurisdiction; NATO Status of Forces Agreement(1951); State immunity, execution; State immunity, jurisdiction
abuse **55,** 586, **56,** 520-3, **80,** 421
measures to prevent **115,** 608
break of diplomatic relations **115,** 611
refusal of permission to transit **115,** 611
withdrawal of *agrément* **115,** 611
receiving State's right to protect against **106,** 291-2, 297
remedies **99,** 204
expulsion **115,** 618
applicable law, Vienna Convention on Diplomatic Relations (1961) **107,** 454-5
basis **72,** 656, **75,** 91-2
bilateral treaty **82,** 16
comity **101,** 311, **121,** 379
courtesy **80,** 399-400
efficient performance of functions **106,** 291-2, 296-7, **107,** 455
extraterritoriality **86,** 520
foreign relations considerations **80,** 398, 399, 402, **107,** 456, **115,** 607, **121,** 507
judicial review and **80,** 402
historical **77,** 273
ne impediatur legatio **70,** 400, **71,** 572, **78,** 8, 104
protection of own diplomats abroad **107,** 456, **115,** 607
protection of sending State **115,** 609, 616, 617
reciprocity **86,** 140, **99,** 201-2, 203
sovereignty of sending State **86,** 520
Vienna Convention on Diplomatic Relations, Preamble **77,** 510
Congress of Vienna (1815) **99,** 200
constitutional rights, proceedings for enforcement of **89,** 49-59
consular distinguished **53,** 549-50, **56,** 530, **87,** 415, **89,** 52, **99,** 109
courts
jurisdiction to determine **121,** 380-2, 384-8
responsibility for determining **121,** 379, 396
customary international law **86,** 667, **101,** 378
parking spaces **70,** 400-4
State succession, incorporation of receiving State into forum State, effect **115,** 615-16, 618
customs duty, exemption, goods imported for Embassy use **48,** 191-205
death of member of family **89,** 93-4
EEC Convention on Jurisdiction and the Enforcement of Judgments (1968), *in rem* action in sending State, exclusion **94,** 312
employment contract. *See* employment contract, locally engaged staff, diplomatic mission
European Convention on Human Rights (1950) and **111,** 158-9
evidence, obligation to give **87,** 214, 215-16, 217, 219
cross-examination, liability to **87,** 216
subpoena **87,** 217, 218, 219
functional **56,** 519-25, **64,** 591, **71,** 550, 561, 572, **80,** 398, 412, 419, **82,** 117, 122-3, **86,** 520, **87,** 235-6, **89,** 52-3, **99,** 115, 202, **111,** 636, 660-1, **115,** 603, 605-7, **116,** 666. *See also* diplomatic mission, functions/'diplomatic activity'

act attributable to State **115,** 606
act illegal under sending State law **115,** 606
burden of proof **111,** 636
criminal act **115,** 606, 607
failure to prevent bomb attack **115,** 606
nature of act as determinant **121,** 380
personal immunity distinguished **115,** 606, 609-10, 612-13
funds. *See* embassy or consular bank account/funds
insurance, effect **40,** 222-3
inviolability. *See* diplomatic archives, inviolability; diplomatic premises, inviolability; international organizations, archives, inviolability
parking privileges **70,** 398-404
privileges and immunities distinguished **87,** 415, **119,** 61
procedure for asserting **75,** 92-5
purpose. *See* basis *above*
reciprocity **70,** 396, **72,** 654-6
respect for law of receiving State **70,** 399-400
restricted. *See* functional *above*
right of suit **78,** 5, 7-8, **82,** 16-17, **94,** 601-2
bilateral treaty, under **82,** 16
break in diplomatic relations, effect **94,** 206-8, **96,** 74-5
consent of sending State, need for **65,** 269-70, **78,** 5, 7-8
Vienna Convention on Diplomatic Relations (1961) **82,** 16
private acts, in respect of **78,** 5, 103
Vienna Convention on Diplomatic Relations (1961) **94,** 601-2
search **74,** 518
service of process **42,** 239-41, **77,** 497, 508-9, **87,** 230-1
substituted service **87,** 230-1
social security legislation **69,** 277-9, **70,** 393-4, **71,** 542-3
State succession
incorporation of receiving State into forum State, effect **115,** 602, 614, 615-17
customary international law **115,** 615-16, 618
State practice **115,** 615-16
subordinate staff **41,** 407-16
subsisting action, revival of **41,** 407-16
taxation, exemption **71,** 541, 574-6
executive certificate/statement **108,** 524-5
liability of spouse in sending State **87,** 77-8
tenancy agreement, property right distinguished **101,** 360
treaty exception, trade agreement **64,** 590-4
violation **77,** 274-5
justifiable, whether **61,** 563-7
State immunity and **77,** 270-1
diplomatic privileges and immunities, entitlement 69, 281-2, **89,** 50
accreditation/presentation of credentials/*agrément* and **71,** 537, **82,** 286 n. 8, **99,** 165, **115,** 610, 611, 616-17
administrative and technical staff **71,** 537-8, **77,** 468-9, **82,** 15-17
employment contract, applicability **82,** 20
locally engaged **82,** 20
agrément, dependence on. *See* accreditation/presentation of credentials/*agrément* and *above*
break of diplomatic relations and **47,** 276, **115,** 611

diplomatic privileges and immunities, entitlement (*cont.*)
commercial/trade representation/mission **64,** 590-3, **74,** 518-19, **99,** 103-12
of unrecognized State **65,** 56
Vienna Convention on Diplomatic Relations (1961) **64,** 596
cultural institute **82,** 2-5
diplomatic status granted after commencement of suit **99,** 114-16
diplomatic visa, relevance **80,** 407
Economic Counsellor as agent of State-owned corporation **63,** 242-4
embassy driver **65,** 22, **69,** 281-2
European Community (EC) **102,** 186-7
European Parliament **101,** 213
executive certificate/statement **114,** 481
family members **60,** 378
as employees of embassy **121,** 483-4
'forming part of household' **114,** 481
son **71,** 568
step-child **77,** 456
in transit **82,** 97-9
accompanying diplomat **82,** 99
joining diplomat **82,** 99
travelling to diplomat's home **82,** 99
wife **71,** 545-6, 568, **74,** 278-9, **77,** 496
FAO **101,** 388-9
federal State, constituent State **111,** 608-9
Head of State. *See* Head of State, diplomatic privileges and immunities, entitlement
honorary consul/consulate **82,** 6-10
illegal occupant of diplomatic premises **102,** 179-80
Institute for Religious Works (IOR) **82,** 51-2
insurers of embassy vehicles **69,** 282-3
interpreter **77,** 602
locally engaged staff, non-national of sending State **82,** 19-20, 22
location of office in mission premises, relevance **99,** 109-10
membership of diplomatic mission, need for **99,** 105-11
military adviser, diplomatic status **73,** 679-82
nationals of receiving State **70,** 389-92, **71,** 541, **119,** 60
natural persons, limitation to **82,** 102
Palestine Liberation Organization (PLO) **82,** 286
period of
starting date **60,** 378
termination **61,** 502
permanent resident in receiving State **71,** 568, 571-2, **77,** 469, **119,** 60
personal **80,** 398-9, 422, 424, **86,** 510-11
press attaché **38,** 160-2
private servants **71,** 549-51
receiving State's views, relevance **106,** 292
representative of unrecognized State **73,** 12-13, 20
special envoys **48,** 205-8
special missions **80,** 389-424
customary international law **80,** 397, 419-20, **121,** 601-2
establishment of **80,** 406
informal agreement **80,** 406
functional **80,** 398, 412
special advisor to **121,** 600-2

termination, date **80,** 403
UN Convention on Special Missions (1969) **80,** 403
State **82,** 3, **86,** 510-11, **87,** 2, 59, **98,** 6, **99,** 120
Vienna Convention on Diplomatic Relations (1961) **63,** 179, **86,** 510, 516, **98,** 6
termination **41,** 408, 411-12, 413, 443-5, 446, 449-51, **80,** 422-4
customary international law
comity **101,** 311-12
permanent departure **101,** 309-16, **111,** 636, 660-1
effect **78,** 483-90
Vienna Convention on Diplomatic Relations (1961), 'when he leaves the country or on expiry of a reasonable period in which to do so' **101,** 309, 312-16, **119,** 153
termination of diplomatic status **115,** 600, 605-6, 612-13, **119,** 153
acts performed in respect of functions **115,** 600, 605-6, **119,** 3
protection of State as basis **115,** 609
relevance **99,** 109-10, 119-21, **102,** 183, **114,** 495
third State, in **94,** 340-1, **115,** 602
customary international law **115,** 610-12
effects doctrine **115,** 604-5
general principle of international law **115,** 602
Lateran Treaty (1929) as evidence against **115,** 612
recognition of judgment delivered by courts of receiving State **115,** 612
State practice **115,** 612
termination of mission, relevance **115,** 612-13
third State as successor State, relevance **115,** 602
trade representative. *See* commercial/trade representative *above*
while in transit **80,** 407, **82,** 97-9
diplomatic protection 52, 5-7, **55,** 486, **59,** 396, **60,** 210-11, 215-16, **72,** 219-22, 238, 265-6, 284-9, 484-8, 504-49, 650, 728-32, **74,** 283-6, **87,** 582, **88,** 694, 696. *See also* claims; claims settlement agreements; consular access; nationality of claims
abuse of right of **46,** 189, 420
of aliens, interference in affairs of third State **77,** 463
basis **46,** 121, 228, 290, 301, 339, 369-73, 396-7, 428, 436, 443, 461, 466-7, 474, 489, 509
beneficial interest **46,** 310
belligerent occupation and **90,** 397
of bondholders **46,** 184, 345-6, 381
Bosnian Muslims **122,** 62-3
claims settlement agreements. *See* claims settlement agreements
commercial and economic relations and **46,** 207, 301
corporate interests **46,** 67-9, 70-1, 94, 226-31, 253-7, 295-7, 302-3, 306, 314, 315, 339-41, 369
of corporation **46,** 67-8, 69, 94, 226-7, 295-7, 302-3, 306, 314, 339-40, 344-65, 378, 411, 415, 419, 428-9, 433-4, 437, 454
against country of nationality **84,** 396-7, 400
by more than one State **46,** 344-5
group of companies **46,** 442, 457
holding companies **46,** 228-31, 442, 454
by national State **46,** 67-8, 94, 226-7, 295-7, 302-3, 306, 314, 339-40, 344-65, 378, 411, 415, 419, 428-9, 433-4, 437, 454, 473-4
foreign shareholders **46,** 70-1
foreign shareholders **46,** 70-1
genuine link requirement **46,** 253-7, 303, 315, 357-65, 379, 428, 455-6, 469

diplomatic protection (*cont.*)
holding companies **46,** 228-31, 442, 454
nationality and **70,** 509-10
customary international law **88,** 694
definition **70,** 695
diplomatic relations, need for **74,** 423-4
direct injury to State distinguished **84,** 348-9, **118,** 6, 17
discretionary nature **42,** 408, **45,** 453, 454, **46,** 218, 222, 223, 243, 251, 301-2, 304, 369, 414, 433, 437, 469, 492
disposal of private claim **90,** 588, 589
distribution of compensation, discretion of recipient State **46,** 276
dual nationality **46,** 224, 304-5, 345, 373, **75,** 182-4, 189-94, 202-3, 220-65
effect **72,** 484-91, 497-8, 501-49
effective nationality test **72,** 484-91, 497-8, 501-19, 522-9, 535-49, **75,** 191-4, 203, 206, 220, 229, 235-58, 262, 265
non-responsibility theory **72,** 484-5, 504-49, **75,** 190-1, 195, 206, 220, 234-52, 254, 258, 262-4
duty. *See* State responsibility *below*
espousal of claim **88,** 739
effect **88,** 739
nationality, relevance **88,** 739
European Convention on Human Rights (1950) and **45,** 298-9, 302
as exercise of State's own right **45,** 96-7, **82,** 66, **108,** 611-12
agent or trustee, whether **108,** 612, 613
presumption against **108,** 612
investment claims. *See* international investment and *below*
exhaustion of local remedies and **45,** 298, **46,** 237, 321-2, **88,** 738, **96,** 278-9, **116,** 614-15, **118,** 5-6
arbitration cases, limitation to **96,** 278-9
customary international law **120,** 233, 318
deficient or ineffective local machinery **107,** 472-3
direct injury to State distinguished **102,** 278-9, **120,** 233-4, 318, **123,** 337
margin of appreciation **107,** 469-73, 480
Pact of Bogotá (1948) **46,** 467
expropriation of property **53,** 336-7
foreign judgment, recognition/enforcement and **79,** 570 n. 4, **89,** 6-8
functional protection **46,** 305, 520
of Germans **78,** 171-2, 175, 184-6
territories east of the Oder–Neisse **78,** 184-6
individual's right to compensation **56,** 333-4
international investment and
as exercise of State's own claim **121,** 128, 191
investor's right to bring direct complaint **121,** 133, 143-4
BITs **121,** 143-4
NAFTA-based claim distinguished **125,** 132
teleological approach **46,** 301, 308
international organization, by **40,** 297-8, 301
international tribunal, referral of case to **88,** 738-9
Iran–US Claims Tribunal and **84,** 493, 494
judicial review **90,** 395, 397, 398, **96,** 215, 219-20, **116,** 609-22
legal obligation, whether **52,** 5-7, **100,** 413-14. *See also* State responsibility *below*
international law **94,** 344-5
legislature, role **94,** 345

loss of **70,** 693, 695-6
lump sum settlements **73,** 378-80, **74,** 285-9
Member States' failure to fund international organization, Member State's right to claim on behalf of injured national **80,** 173
of multinational corporation **46,** 442, 457
of national entrapped by foreign State **94,** 345-6
of national other than diplomatic agent under death penalty **118,** 54
of national shareholders in foreign companies **72,** 728-32
non-intervention in the affairs of another State **116,** 614, 615-16, 618, 620-2
of persons without government to pursue **109,** 584
Palestinians **109,** 577-8
stateless person **46,** 362, **109,** 577-8
as preferred method **65,** 278-9
proof of nationality **70,** 509-10, 522-4
passport and **43,** 128, 135, 182-3
property abroad, consular protection **56,** 530
'property, rights and interests' **46,** 212, 299-300, 308
'protected person' status under Geneva Convention IV (1949) and **124,** 131
protecting State status as substantive question **46,** 122-3, 188, 199-200, 239
reciprocity and **46,** 230, **72,** 266
refugee status, effect on **43,** 182-3, 184-6
request for
justiciability **89,** 7-8
seisure of ICJ, request for **89,** 6-8
right to
concurrent **46,** 304-5, 373-4, 453
conditional **46,** 300
individual and State distinguished **46,** 443, 501, **88,** 694, **119,** 450
nature and source of **46,** 341-2, 369-73, 382, 428, 461, 499
scope **69,** 144-5
Vienna Convention on Diplomatic Relations (1961) and **46,** 339
of shareholders in foreign company **45,** 111-13, **46,** 23, 26, 55-6, 64-75, 94-5, 121-5, 180, 188, 199-200, 205-25, 240-57, 289-315, 342-4, 365-75, 379, 399, 402-4, 405-16, 418-38, 446-53, 470-6, 489, 491-507, 509-30
beneficial owners of shares **46,** 73, 309, 389, 392-3
nationality of shareholders, proof of **46,** 363, 378-94, 439, 456-7
nominee holders **46,** 309
preponderance of national holding **46,** 302
State immunity, relevance **88,** 740
State responsibility **44,** 308, **70,** 693-8
failure by State **48,** 4-5
municipal law **94,** 344-5
discretion **94,** 345
scope **70,** 695
of victim of Holocaust **103,** 600 n. 3, 614
of visiting forces **100,** 436
diplomatic protest, judicial notice **90,** 696
diplomatic relations 96, 175. *See also* accreditation
accreditation **85,** 61
in absence of **85,** 56
impossibility **85,** 56
break. *See also* suspension *below*
belligerent, recognition of and **80,** 669

diplomatic relations (*cont.*)
Cambodia, whether **83,** 239-40
China, People's Republic, threat **101,** 425
commercial relations, effect on **64,** 370-1
Chile–Cuba **64,** 370-1
consular relations, effect on **96,** 303, 304
Vienna Convention on Consular Relations (1963) **96,** 303
diplomatic immunity, effect on **47,** 276
disadvantages **82,** 318
discretionary act **96,** 303, 313
economic development agreement, effect on **96,** 306-7, 308-9
parties' conduct and **96,** 308
existing treaties **96,** 303, 304-5
nationals in receiving country, effect on **96,** 306
reduction to Chargé d'Affaires status distinguished **101,** 425
right of suit, effect on **94,** 206-8, **96,** 74-5
service of process and **63,** 414-15
treaties, effect on
in absence of need for diplomatic relations **96,** 303, 304, 308
conclusion of new treaties **96,** 303
existing treaties **96,** 303
United States Diplomatic and Consular Staff in Teheran **96,** 305
war, characteristic of state of **80,** 668
declaration of diplomat as *persona non grata,* act of State **115,** 443-5
establishment
judicial review **96,** 215
political act **100,** 327
responsibility for **82,** 333-4
Estonia **85,** 56, 61
evidence of
diplomatic mission, maintenance of **80,** 9
publication of accredited diplomatic representatives **80,** 9-10
as nexus required for jurisdiction **121,** 640-1
protection under the Geneva Convention (IV) and **122,** 61, 62-3
recognition of belligerent and **80,** 669
recognition of State/government, relevance **49,** 45, 209, **62,** 29, 84, **65,** 56, **80,** 5-6, 669, **84,** 177, **87,** 586-7
distinguished **108,** 538
evidence of **108,** 519
state of war and **67,** 623-4
suspension **79,** 170, 176, **88,** 695. *See also* break *above*
Third World influence **46,** 464-9, 495
Vienna Convention on Diplomatic Relations (1961) and **80,** 5
written guarantee of oral statement **99,** 20-1
diplomatic representations, formal claim distinguished **46,** 256
diplomatic status, evidence of/requirements 48, 148, **60,** 380-2, **61,** 502
certificate of Head of Permanent Delegation **77,** 496
certification by receiving State **121,** 602
diplomatic licence plates **99,** 111
diplomatic list **80,** 9-10, **99,** 111
diplomatic passport **99,** 110, 166, **119,** 78
diplomatic visa **99,** 111, 112 n. 19, 166-7
executive certificate **73,** 680-2, **78,** 484, **99,** 116, **101,** 378, **111,** 616

Ministry of Foreign Affairs' identity card **61,** 502, **77,** 455, 496
special mission, member **80,** 420, **121,** 599-602
disappearances
American Convention on Human Rights (1969), breach of rights **95,** 292-4, **116,** 476-7
breach of rights
family, protection **116,** 480, **120,** 59-60
humane treatment **95,** 292, **118,** 156
of relatives through failure to investigate **120,** 58-9, 112
information **120,** 59-60
liberty of person **95,** 292-3, **116,** 467, **120,** 55-7, 112
life **95,** 292, 634, **116,** 477, **118,** 155-6, **120,** 52-5
prompt hearing **95,** 292
respect for integrity of person **95,** 292
torture **118,** 156
crime against humanity, whether **95,** 292
customary international law **95,** 634-5
clear criteria **104,** 185
precision of rule **95,** 635
presumption of disappearance **95,** 635
universality of practice **95,** 635, **104,** 185
definition
abduction by State official under State approval or authority **104,** 185 n. 30
refusal by State to acknowledge abduction and detention **104,** 185 n. 30
domestic remedy, evidence of ineffectiveness or absence **95,** 258
ECOSOC
Resolution 1979/38 **95,** 291
Subcommission for the Prevention of Discrimination and Protection of Minorities Resolution 5B (XXXII) **95,** 291
European Convention on Human Rights (1950), breach of rights **120,** 52-60
evidence of **95,** 276-83
General Assembly of the Organization of American States **95,** 292
General Assembly Resolution 33/173 **95,** 291
habeas corpus and **116,** 479-80
International Covenant on Civil and Political Rights (ICCPR) (1966), breach **118,** 155-6, 207-8
jus cogens/peremptory norm **104,** 185
legislation typifying **116,** 519
State responsibility **79,** 179, **95,** 296-9, **118,** 207-8, 290-1
systematic manner **95,** 289-91
as torture **118,** 156, 291, **119,** 285-6, 328
UN Commission on Human Rights, Resolution 20 (XXXVI) (Working Group on Enforced or Involuntary Disappearances) **95,** 291
disciplinary proceedings (fair trial requirement)
criminal charge **58,** 74, 81-2, 102, **62,** 321-2, 336, 341, 346-7, 352, 357-9, **78,** 324-8, 351-3
medical **58,** 74, **62,** 319, 321-2, 325-8, 332-4, 358, **71,** 415-36
military **58,** 53-60, 81, 101-2, 105-6, **73,** 395, 554-64, **78,** 227-53, **96,** 650-60
judicial review **96,** 651
nature of proceedings **62,** 320, 326, 336, 346-8, 353, 355-6, 358
prison **78,** 310-12, 323-8
safeguards **71,** 423-9
sanctions **71,** 420
discipline, education, whether ancillary to **67,** 493-4

disclosure of documents
act of State and **92,** 389-91
applicable law **104,** 554, 558
arbitral tribunal **102,** 233-8, **125,** 105, 107-10
CIA involvement, relating to **107,** 441
comity and **64,** 280
'document' **122,** 27
extradition and **104,** 50, 116
extraterritorial **103,** 320, 321
fair trial and **104,** 50, 116
immunity from. *See also* State immunity, jurisdiction *below*
Head of State, former **102,** 199-205
international organizations **43,** 260-4, 269, **77,** 166
international administrative tribunals **43,** 260-4, 269, 326-7, 335, 415, 422
professional privilege **64,** 281-2, 287-90, 297-8
waiver **64,** 290, 306
public interest privilege **64,** 285, 290-2, 298-306
balance of interests **64,** 291, 305
communications between States **64,** 285, 291-4, 297-304
State immunity, jurisdiction **43,** 260-4, 269, 326-7, 335, 415, 422, **64,** 280-5, 287-94, 298-306, **84,** 173, **98,** 108, **99,** 162, **102,** 233-8, **103,** 319-21, **104,** 536-40, 556-8, 606, 611-25, **107,** 251-3, 254
confidentiality of financial information **104,** 556-7
tax haven **104,** 536-40, 556-8, 606, 611-25
waiver of right to **121,** 222
discovery. *See* territory, acquisition
discrimination. *See also* expropriation/nationalization, legality, requirements; freedom from discrimination; war, means of waging, limitations on, non-discrimination between combatants and non-combatants
airport user charges
ex ante review, need for **102,** 496
factors for consideration **102,** 492-6
on basis of language **118,** 174-83
belligerent occupation, deportation **83,** 184
compensation by successor government for expropriation of property under communist regime **115,** 268-76
existence to be determined by context **121,** 117, 154-5
geographic location **82,** 447-53
racial. *See* racial discrimination
disinvestment negotiations 124, 55-6
displaced persons. *See also* displacement of people
burden of proof **95,** 508, 512, 522, 528-9
definition, International Refugee Organization, Constitution (1946) **95,** 508
determination of status **95,** 508-9
displacement of people. *See also* belligerent occupation, assignment of place of residence, legality; displaced persons
as breach of human rights **125,** 547-8
State responsibility **91,** 339-40
dispute. *See also* dispute settlement; European Court of Human Rights, dispute (*contestation*) over right; International Court of Justice (ICJ), 'dispute'
avoidance of prejudicial acts **82,** 672, 674
boundary. *See* boundary dispute
categorization **84,** 300

claim, critical date. *See* critical date *below*
contesting claims **37,** 178, 477
critical date **83,** 17, **97,** 472, 623, **113,** 107, 114, **124,** 33-5
establishment of claim **113,** 107, 114, 130-1, **124,** 34
territorial **38,** 79-80, **50,** 27, 388, 389-91, 463, 470, **59,** 55, **91,** 590-4
crystallization of dispute **91,** 591-2, 593-4
State practice **91,** 594
treatment of aliens, concerning **46,** 339-40, 377
definition **37,** 10, 24, 81, 98, 176, 178-9, 200, 240-1, **57,** 472-3, **59,** 87-9
conduct as element **37,** 178, 179-80
existence of **37,** 10, 52, 81-2, 98-9, 165, 175, 176-83, 477, 485-6, 542, 564, **49,** 14, 165, **57,** 416, 422, **83,** 16-17
critical date. *See* critical date *above*
factual situation **54,** 323
international law, interpretation to minimize **41,** 228
justiciability. *See* justiciability
legal. *See also* ICSID (International Centre for the Settlement of Investment Disputes), arbitral tribunal, jurisdiction, legal dispute arising directly out of investment
definition **84,** 270
minimization **41,** 228
overflying rights **48,** 331, 337, 347, 438
political campaign as **37,** 540-2
treaty, concerning the interpretation or application of **48,** 351-5, 371, 376, 389-95, 410-15, 418-19, 430, 433, 437, 438, 454, 456, **97,** 630, **100,** 219. *See also* Inter-American Court of Human Rights, jurisdiction, 'all matters relating to the interpretation or application of [the] Convention'; International Court of Justice (ICJ), dispute; International Court of Justice (ICJ), jurisdiction, interpretation or application of treaty; International Tribunal for the Law of the Sea (ITLOS), jurisdiction, dispute concerning the interpretation or application of the Law of the Sea Convention (1982)
'relating to interpretation or application of the Mandate' **37,** 357-9, 366
Tripartite Commission on German Debts, competence in respect of disputed claims **47,** 450
unilateral redress short of war **47,** 412-17
within organization **37,** 89, 166, 174-5, 181
dispute settlement 41, 76-7, 104, 150, 200, **57,** 416, 492, 554, **62,** 223, 229, **80,** 314. *See also* arbitration; conciliation; diplomatic channels; European Community treaties, dispute settlement; ICSID (International Centre for the Settlement of Investment Disputes); International Civil Aviation Organization (ICAO), Council; International Court of Justice (ICJ); International Tribunal for the Law of the Sea (ITLOS); Law of the Sea Convention (1982): Part XV (settlement of disputes); mediation; negotiations; Permanent Court of International Justice (PCIJ); Straddling Stocks and Highly Migratory Fish Stocks Agreement (1995); United Nations Security Council
'agreed mode of settlement', municipal court proceedings, whether **82,** 289 n. 18
amicable. *See* peaceful *below*
boundaries. *See* boundary dispute
claim
amendment, party's entitlement **113,** 105-6, 107
contradictions in **113,** 130-1
compromissory clause. *See* compromissory clause/*compromis*
compulsory, Argentina–Chile **52,** 230, **113,** 36
concession contract, parties' intention **62,** 179
'conciliation or arbitration' **106,** 556
choice of method **106,** 556

dispute settlement (*cont.*)
need to distinguish in order to establish ICSID jurisdiction **106,** 556, 569-70, 571-2, 585-6
consultation **84,** 271, **105,** 377
conventions. *See also* European Convention for the Peaceful Settlement of Disputes (1957); General Act for the Pacific Settlement of Disputes; Pact of Bogotá (1948)
Barcelona Convention (1922) **37,** 517
compromissory clause distinguished **84,** 267-8
General Convention of Inter-American Conciliation (1929) **84,** 270
legal disputes, compulsory conciliation **84,** 270
General Treaty of Inter-American Arbitration (1929) **84,** 270, 301
PCIJ compulsory jurisdiction and **84,** 270, 301
League of Nations Protocol for the Pacific Settlement of International Disputes (1924) **84,** 291
critical date. *See* dispute, critical date
definition **55,** 360
discontinuance **61,** 593-5
dissolution of union of States, disputes arising from **91,** 505-7
arbitration **91,** 306, 307
diplomatic channels **91,** 309-10
ICJ **91,** 306
international tribunal **91,** 307
mediation **91,** 306, 307
negotiation **91,** 306, 307
duty to resolve quickly and amicably **118,** 631-2
duty to resort to in sufficient time, protection of third parties **47,** 406-11
European Coal and Steel Community **47,** 406-11
failure to make provision for, under COMECON regime **116,** 166
GATT. *See* General Agreement on Tariffs and Trade (GATT) (1947), GATT Panels; Uruguay Round, Settlement of Disputes, Understanding on Rules and Procedures
Genocide Convention (1948). *See* Genocide Convention (1948)
international investment policy, relevance of changing practice **118,** 637-9
international organization, in respect of **81,** 683
need to make provision **102,** 212-13, 214-15
judicial **55,** 339
methods
diplomacy and judicial means distinguished **117,** 185
failure to make treaty provision **106,** 248, **115,** 662
hierarchy **106,** 527-8, 544, 546-7, 549-52, 561, 574-5
parallel **105,** 377
Convention for the Conservation of the Southern Bluefin Tuna (1993) **119,** 555-6, 559-61
peaceful. *See* peaceful *below*
pacific. *See* peaceful *below*
participation agreements, dispute settlement clause **118,** 625-6, 631-4
Peace Treaty, concerning **80,** 240
peaceful **56,** 184-5, 186, **57,** 561-2, **62,** 205
negotiations **41,** 76-7, 150, 200, **54,** 338-41, **56,** 172, 185, **76,** 155-7, 164, 226-7, 267
obligation **76,** 55, 155-7, 164
PCIJ, effect of dissolution of **57,** 479
preferred method **87,** 353
treaty provision for, exhaustion of treaty processes **46,** 37, 92

procedures **54,** 337-8
regional arrangements **76,** 55, 151, 505-7
settlement out of court **106,** 735
negotiations, contract distinguished **124,** 55-6
third-party judgment **48,** 392
treaty provision **85,** 310, 315
adverse admission, risk **48,** 340
individual's right to invoke **107,** 489
interpretation **48,** 413, 450-1
separability **48,** 332, 339-40, 348, 350-1, 390, 413-14, 419
unilateral suspension of treaty, effect **48,** 339-40, 390, 413-14, 432, 434
UN Secretary-General, reference to **74,** 256-7, 264-6
interpretation of ruling, recourse to arbitration **74,** 261, 270, 273-4, 276
ruling **74,** 271-4
distance. *See* continental shelf, distance; continental shelf delimitation, distance
distress. *See also* necessity
aircraft in
absence of restrictions **82,** 675
right to seek refuge **82,** 581
ships in **82,** 696
right to seek refuge **82,** 581
distributive justice. *See* maritime delimitation, distributive justice
divorce 58, 630, 645-6, **89,** 161-3. *See also* marriage, separation
a mensa et thoro **89,** 161
a vinculo matrimonii **89,** 161
diplomatic immunity and **74,** 520-2, **118,** 304
evidence of **53,** 589-90
foreign divorce, recognition **55,** 580, **89,** 162-3, 176-7
unrecognized State **52,** 54
Hague Convention on Conflicts of Divorce Laws (1902) **40,** 29-30, 33-4
Hague Convention on Recognition of Divorces and Legal Separation (1970) **74,** 532-43, 551-3
'divorce following judicial or other proceedings recognized in that State' **74,** 537-8, 541, 543, 552-3
inadmissibility, right of marriage and **89,** 172-5, 185-8
Ireland **58,** 645-6
jurisdiction, refugees **72,** 641-5, **74,** 533-56
Muslim, recognition of **74,** 531-56
occupied territory **38,** 470-1
Djibouti, law of, Constitutional Law No 1 of 27 June 1977 **89,** 13
doctrine of acknowledgement 81, 63, 65, 66, 70
domestic jurisdiction 46, 487, **69,** 111-12, 118-19, 123-6, **76,** 133, **79,** 296
crimes against humanity and **36,** 295-6
de facto governments. *See* government, de facto, implied mandate doctrine
health of national **85,** 342-3
human rights and **77,** 175, **79,** 363, **105,** 483
international tribunal, primacy **105,** 479-84, 576, 578-9
limitation by assumption of obligation **76,** 717
nature of **77,** 182
Optional Clause, reservation **76,** 133
UN Charter (1945) **105,** 439, 441, 479-84, 576, 578-9
Chapter VII enforcement measures **105,** 439, 441, 481, 576, 578-9
domestic law. *See* municipal law

domestic rebellion. *See* civil strife; civil war; rebellion; revolution
domestic remedies. *See* European Commission of Human Rights, exhaustion of local remedies; European Court of Human Rights, exhaustion of local remedies; International Covenant on Civil and Political Rights, exhaustion of local remedies
domicile
as applicable law, corporation **71,** 21-2, 27-30, 559, 562-3, 567, **116,** 579
corporation. *See* corporation, domicile
definition **86,** 540
jurisdiction, basis of, whether **54,** 225
married women **118,** 302
nationality/citizenship and **45,** 336, **79,** 287, 309
neutral persons' commercial domicile **40,** 478
normal residence **86,** 584
real/immovable property and. **82,** 46
Rhodesia and Nyasaland, immigration law **44,** 10-11, 15
situs of debt **82,** 34
taxation and **72,** 669, **74,** 206, 209
basis for liability **72,** 669, **74,** 206, 209
double taxation conventions **87,** 83
official of European Community (EC) **87,** 82-3
tests of **41,** 246, 251
Dominican Republic
disappearances **118,** 153-6
Dominicana **63,** 468-77
expropriatory actions **48,** 179-86
immigration laws **63,** 473-5
dominions. *See* British Commonwealth, dominion status
double actionability. *See* jurisdiction, tort
double criminality 40, 213, **41,** 397-406, **43,** 234-42, **44,** 181, 182, 184, 199, 275, **49,** 507-9, **55,** 515-17, 518-21, 531-8, 539, 540-2, 548, **60,** 295, 300, 323-5, **69,** 100, 220-2, 247-9, **72,** 610-11, 621-2, **73,** 664, **74,** 451-2, 459-72, 502, **78,** 392, 426-7, 495, 501-5, 510, 542-3, **79,** 390-1, **85,** 79-87, **87,** 150-1, 152-8, **88,** 287, 289, **92,** 723-9, 731, 732-4, **98,** 416, **100,** 618, **114,** 388
attempted and unsuccessful crime distinguished **40,** 208-10
conduct test **90,** 414-15
critical date **74,** 451-2, **88,** 287
commission of offence **119,** 41, 55, 146-7, 159-60, 175-6, 182, 189-93, 202, 214, 250, **120,** 364-5, 367, 384-5
Extradition, European Convention on (1957) **74,** 451
customary international law **87,** 154, **101,** 178-80
definition **55,** 534
determination
on basis of law as set out in request **119,** 259-60
evidence of foreign law **90,** 413-15, **119,** 259-60
extradition court's obligation **104,** 48
magistrate's power **78,** 503
responsibility
District Judge **55,** 516, 521, 527
judge/jury **98,** 536-7
equivalent act or omission **87,** 148, **111,** 507
'deemed to have been committed' within territory **98,** 535-7, 617-20
forced labour/kidnapping/forcible confinement **104,** 202-3

identity of crime, need for **92,** 731, 732-4
customary international law **101,** 182-3
reclassification of offence, possibility of **106,** 250-2, 254-5
relevant and comparable offence **41,** 397-406, **78,** 503-5, **85,** 80-4, **88,** 373-6
'substantially analogous' **104,** 48
general principle of international law **92,** 725-6
general standard of international law **87,** 154-5
Geneva Convention (Treatment of Prisoners of War) (Convention III) (1949) **99,** 170-1, **119,** 351
imposition of extraditing State's views on another **98,** 470
Institut de Droit International, Oxford Resolutions (1880) **87,** 151, 156
international law, rule of, whether **92,** 725-6
judicial assistance and **65,** 408, **82,** 57
jurisdiction, basis for, 'deemed to have been committed within territory', need for **98,** 535-7, 617-20
jurisdiction, relevance **88,** 338-9, **104,** 5-6
legality in place of offence, relevance **101,** 178-80
limitation period for prosecution and **72,** 611, **74,** 452
London Scheme (1966) **87,** 156, 157
murder, degrees of **69,** 247-9
nature of act as determining factor **87,** 155-7
need for **87,** 151, 154, **104,** 20
public policy and **100,** 685
punishment, relevance **100,** 410-11
reason for **87,** 255
retroactivity **79,** 391, **119,** 230, **121,** 40-1
specification of charges **88,** 352-5
subsequent legislation, relevance **85,** 82
theft **85,** 83-4
universal validity of rule **75,** 112-13
war crimes/crimes against humanity **104,** 198
jurisdiction and **98,** 533, 536-7
notional transfer of act **104,** 198. *See also* equivalent act or omission, 'deemed to have been committed within the territory' *above*
offence under *lex fori* at the time **104,** 198, 202-4, 354
forced labour/kidnapping/forcible confinement, equivalence **104,** 202-3
double jeopardy/*non bis in idem* **55,** 128, **61,** 249-50, **62,** 34, 55, 63-4, 69, 80-1, **70,** 242, 245-6, **79,** 203, 205, 207, 271, **86,** 538, **100,** 347, **115,** 365, **116,** 380-3, **124,** 191-3. *See also under individual Conventions*
degrading treatment, whether **61,** 249-50
federal and State laws, interrelationship **91,** 74, 82
fundamental right within the European Community (EC) **93,** 397, 431
general principle of law, whether **124,** 191-3
jurisdiction and **55,** 128
multiple extradition requests **104,** 62 n. 2, 82
political offence **104,** 62 n. 2
State practice **124,** 191-3
double nationality. *See* dual nationality
double taxation. *See also* double taxation agreements *and Index to the Consolidated Table of Treaties*
domicile, EC official **87,** 83
exemption, international officials' salaries **56,** 569-71, 572-3

double taxation agreements 74, 205-11, 285-6. *See also* double taxation
'industrial or commercial profit' **45,** 431-5
interpretation **40,** 292-5, **45,** 427-35
municipal law, effect on **72,** 216-17, 448, 668-70, **74,** 206
OECD Model Convention (1963) **74,** 208
Drago doctrine 46, 465
droits acquis. *See* acquired rights
drug-trafficking
definition **86,** 163
export of drugs **73,** 250-1, **74,** 167-9
extradition for **69,** 220-2, **74,** 450-3, **87,** 145-52, **88,** 241-6
import of drugs **71,** 248-50, **73,** 270
conspiracy **69,** 100, 220-2
jurisdiction **69,** 100-1, **73,** 250-1, 270, 274-5, 284, 699-704, **74,** 167-9, **82,** 104-6, **84,** 210-13
obligation to exercise **99,** 157, **101,** 275-7
extradition, request for, relevance **86,** 551-2
ne bis in idem **86,** 551
personal **86,** 589, 591
protective principle **84,** 214-15
transit-lounge **88,** 261-2
'narcotic', psychotropic, whether **86,** 498-9
possession
assumption of **88,** 242
foreign aircraft in transit within territory **73,** 700-4
foreign ship in territorial sea **73,** 180-3, 274-5, 284
public health legislation, territorial scope **71,** 248-50
search and seizure
foreign vessels on the high seas **91,** 470-86, 488-92, 514-38
national vessels in foreign territorial sea **91,** 495-508
sentencing **86,** 592-3
Single Convention on Narcotic Drugs (1961) **86,** 498, 589
aim **74,** 168-9
drugs to which Convention applies **73,** 183, 285
'import'/'export' **73,** 251, **101,** 275-6
jurisdiction, obligation to exercise **86,** 551-2, **99,** 157
country of apprehension **86,** 551
extradition, request for, relevance **86,** 551-2
ne bis in idem **86,** 551
dual criminality. *See* double criminality
dual nationality 39, 327-8, **40,** 148, **60,** 244-6, **72,** 449, 452, 454-5, 483-549, **73,** 568, **78,** 185. *See also* nationality, effectiveness, need for
avoidance **103,** 148-9
forfeiture **103,** 284-8
claims, effect on **40,** 148, **46,** 224, 304-5, 345, 373, **48,** 159-62, **75,** 180-268. *See also* United Nations Compensation Commission, nationality of claim, Iraqi dual national
effective nationality test. *See* effective *below*
Hague Convention on Nationality Laws (1930) and **72,** 484, **75,** 189-91, 220, 228-34, 252-3, 255-6, 262
non-responsibility theory **72,** 484-5, 504-49, **75,** 183-4, 186, 190-1, 193, 195, 206, 220, 234-52, 254, 258, 262-4
compensation claims and **90,** 221-8

diplomatic protection, effective nationality test **72,** 484-91, 497-8, 501-19, 522-9, 535-49, **75,** 191-4, 203, 206, 220, 229, 235-58, 262, 265
dominant and effective **84,** 614-15, **90,** 221-2, 224-8
diplomatic protection **72,** 484-91, 497-8, 501-19, 522-9, 535-49, **75,** 191-4, 203, 206, 220, 229, 235-58, 262, 265
factors **84,** 614-15
enemy character and **72,** 449, 455, 459
Hague Convention on the Conflict of Nationality Laws (1930) **72,** 484-5, 512, 518-29, 547-8
travaux preparatoires **72,** 438, **75,** 189
international law, rules of **71,** 579-80
military service **56,** 557-64
refugee
relevance **104,** 229, **122,** 534
unwillingness to avail himself of protection of national authorities and **92,** 669-70, 701-6, 714-19
Dubai, as independent State **121,** 588
due process 36, 382, 386, 397, 401, **61,** 194-8, **79,** 389, **84,** 102, 112, **86,** 100, **88,** 38, **90,** 652, 655-7. *See also* arbitral award, annulment, grounds, failure to observe due process; international officials, due process
access to international appellate bodies as right under municipal law **123,** 518-19, 530-1, 551-4
on grounds not provided for under Constitution **123,** 531
advisory committee proceedings **123,** 518, 519-20
applicable law **123,** 527, 530
arrest of ships **125,** 313
burden of proof **79,** 389, **84,** 143
changing content **123,** 519, 530
criminal contempt proceedings **88,** 38
customary international law **104,** 92
deportation and **104,** 83
development of concept **123,** 516-17, 528-9
equity **89,** 537-8
evidence of
official international bodies and **88,** 11, 21-2, 31
role of foreign armed forces **88,** 10-12
expropriation/nationalization **121,** 126-7, 192
fair trial as part of **123,** 517
foreign naval deserters, arrest **42,** 232-8
foreign State's right to **107,** 341-2, **121,** 576, 597-9, 637-9
forum conveniens and **84,** 102-3
general principle of law **89,** 537-8
ICTY **105,** 610-11
municipal law and international provisions distinguished **123,** 517, 530
natural justice **87,** 400, 406
nexus, need for **63,** 398. *See also* jurisdiction, nexus
personal jurisdiction and **63,** 257-8, 612, **98,** 146-7, **121,** 495
recognition of judgments not resulting from **79,** 411
refugees, expulsion **74,** 433, 436-7
right to complete legal processes **123,** 518-19
rule of law and **123,** 516-17
separation of powers and **123,** 516-17
Dumbarton Oaks 76, 587-9

duress. *See also* coercion
boundaries, establishment, **91,** 568-71
economic coercion **91,** 569-71
business compulsion **63,** 157-8, 168
concession agreement **66,** 569-71, 615-16
contract negotiations **86,** 272-3
crimes against humanity
defence **108,** 187-8, **111,** 313, 314, 333-79, 395-431
K and L **111,** 418-20
M et al. **111,** 420
Wülfing and K **111,** 417-18
criteria
acquiescence **111,** 427, 431
inevitability of victim's death **111,** 368-9, 371, 379, 396, 425, 451-5
position of accused in relation to danger **111,** 360, 398
Einsatzgruppen **111,** 398 n. 12
Milch **111,** 398 n. 12
rank **111,** 417, 425-6, 431, 435
soldier **111,** 371-2
Spadini **111,** 398 n. 12
Touvier **111,** 398 n. 12
reasonable behaviour **111,** 360, 370-2, 427-8
voluntary membership of group intent upon action contrary to international humanitarian law **111,** 398, 404 n. 35, 435
customary international law **111,** 336-44, 374, 396, 399-427, 428-9
definition **111,** 358
economic pressure, whether **56,** 526-7, **66,** 569-71, 615-16
force majeure **111,** 347
general principle of law recognized by civilized nations **111,** 344-63, 375, 440-2, 456-8
international official, admission of misconduct **48,** 237-8, 240-1
mens rea, effect on **111,** 349, 362, 442
as mitigating factor **111,** 355-8, 363-74, 376-9, 396, 428, 442
Justice Trial **111,** 383
murder **111,** 399-429, 440-58
Abbott **111,** 364-5, 443, 446, 447
Bernardi and Randazzo **111,** 361, 414-15
British Manual of Military Law (1958) **111,** 408
definition **111,** 396 n. 8
Devji Govindiji **111,** 365
Dudley and Stephens **111,** 405, 444, 446
Goliath **111,** 370, 445-6
Gotts **111,** 442, 449-50
Howe **111,** 361, 362-3, 373, 442, 447-9, 451-2
Lynch **111,** 361, 364, 372-3, 442, 443-51
Tyler and Price **111,** 444-5
US Manual for Courts-Martial (1984/1994) **111,** 409
US Model Penal Code **111,** 450, 451, 455
necessity and **111,** 346-7, 348, 349, 396-7, 411-12, 417, 453
British Manual of Military Law (1958) **111,** 397, 408
nuclear weapons, possession and deployment, whether **122,** 509
opinio juris **66,** 606, **111,** 341-2, 440
penalty, mitigating circumstance **108,** 217, 218
proportionality **111,** 334-5, 359-60, 369-70, 376, 396, 397, 423-4, 425, 430, 435, 441, 444, 458

evidence of, need for **111,** 437-8
moral choice **111,** 362-3, 451-6
requirements
absence of alternative **56,** 526-7, **111,** 376, 397, 421 n. 97, 423, 430, 435
imminent danger both serious and irreparable **111,** 376, 397, 403, 417, 423, 430, 435
moral choice **111,** 376
non-voluntary situation **111,** 397, 423
overwhelming fear **111,** 348, 350
proportionality. *See* proportionality *above*
settlement of employment dispute and **85,** 645
State practice **111,** 341-2
Australia **111,** 351-2, 356 n. 130, 357, 367
Belgium **111,** 347
Canada **111,** 352, 356 n. 130
Chile **111,** 350
China **111,** 354
civil law systems **111,** 346-51, 357-8, 359-60
common law systems **111,** 341, 351-4, 356-8, 360-3, 366-7, 409, 441-58
England **111,** 351, 356-7
Ethiopia **111,** 355, 359
Finland **111,** 349-50
France **111,** 347, 375
Germany, Federal Republic **111,** 348, 360, 375, 416-22
India **111,** 353
Italy **111,** 348-9, 359, 414-16
Japan **111,** 354, 359
Malaysia **111,** 353, 356 n. 130, 357, 367
Mexico **111,** 350-1
Morocco **111,** 354
Netherlands **111,** 347-8
Nicaragua **111,** 350, 359
Nigeria **111,** 353-4, 356 n. 130
Norway **111,** 349, 355-6, 359-60, 375-6
Panama **111,** 350
Poland **111,** 355, 375
Scotland **111,** 449
Somalia **111,** 355
South Africa **111,** 352
Spain **111,** 348
Sweden **111,** 349, 359
United States **111,** 341, 351-2, 357, 359
Model Penal Code **111,** 362 n. 152, 371
Venezuela **111,** 350
Yugoslavia, Socialist Federal Republic **111,** 351, 359, 360
superior orders compared **111,** 333-4, 397
teachings of publicists **111,** 338
treaties, effect on validity of **56,** 107, 139
UN War Crimes Commission review (1949) **111,** 336-7
US Manual for Courts-Martial (1984/1994) **111,** 338, 409
war crimes
defence
Eichmann **111,** 340, 358-60, 411, 455-6
Einsatzgruppen **111,** 337-8, 407-8

duress (*cont.*)
Farben **111,** 376-7, 424
Feurstein **111,** 362, 377-8, 401, 404-5, 426
Flick **111,** 376-7, 424
Hölzer **111,** 337, 341, 377, 405-6, 423, 425
Jepson **111,** 337, 377-8, 401-5, 425
Krupp **111,** 376-7
Llandovery Castle **111,** 339, 410-11
Masetti **111,** 340, 368-9, 371, 416
Müller et al. **111,** 339, 411
Nuremberg Tribunal **111,** 338, 376
Papon **111,** 340, 412
Priebke **111,** 359 n. 145, 412
Retzlaff et al. **111,** 340, 412-13
S and K **111,** 340
Sablić et al. **111,** 340, 413
Srà et al. **111,** 415-16
Stalag Luft III **111,** 337, 341, 362, 402-4
Touvier **111,** 412
Warsaw Ghetto **111,** 340, 421
Wetzling et al. **111,** 421-2, 424-5
Z et al. **111,** 420-1

East African Community, Treaty for East African Cooperation **51,** 414-23
East African Currency Board
immunity, jurisdiction **43,** 154-61
powers and duties **43,** 159-60
East Germany. *See* Germany, Democratic Republic (GDR)
East India Company
British supremacy exercised by **50,** 29, 51, 65-6, 67
immunity, jurisdiction **64,** 573-4
treaties with Indian rulers **50,** 54-6, 59-63, 218, 270, 398-401, 424, 425, 459, 464, 465, 470, 477
Miraj Ruler (1819) **49,** 470
East Punjab, Patiala, Union with **49,** 338, 433-4, 449-50, 453, 459
East Timor
Administering Power
demise of status **105,** 257-9, 277, 319-34
exclusive authority, whether **105,** 244-5, 263-5, 276-7, 329-30, 413
physical control, relevance **105,** 320-1, 418
Portugal as **105,** 237-8, 244-5
right of representation **105,** 322-3, 417
Fretilin, status **87,** 75-6
incorporation by Indonesia **105,** 256, 285, 370-4
recognition
Australia **104,** 451, **105,** 238-9, 341-3, 374, 401-6
conclusion of treaty capable of application to **105,** 245, 374, 402-3
de facto **105,** 238, 341
de jure **105,** 239, 341
delimitation of continental shelf as **105,** 239
obligation to avoid **105,** 244, 403-6
UN **105,** 285
State, whether **87,** 74-6

status **105,** 236-9, 254-9, 285-8, 367-75
ICJ and **105,** 276-9
consultation, people of territory **105,** 276-9
consultation, UN organs **105,** 279
non-self-governing territory **105,** 244, 246-7, 362, 368, 400-1
Portuguese position **105,** 255-6, 288, 332-4, 369-70
UN Resolutions **105,** 236-8, 244-5, 255, 256-8, 285-7, 319-20, 323-32, 369, 371-4
Australian position **105,** 343
unilateral act, effect **105,** 401
Timor Gap
coastal State, Portugal **105,** 251-4, 259
continental shelf title, Australia **105,** 251-4, 344-5
Timor Gap Treaty
conclusion **104,** 452, **105,** 374-5
implementation **104,** 452-9, **105,** 288-90
validity **104,** 452-6, **105,** 353, 363
treaty-making power **105,** 246, 263-5, 319, 344-5, 416-17
UN competence **105,** 326-30
Eastern Mediterranean Regional Health Organization. *See* World Health Organization Regional Office in Egypt
Eastern Slavonia
Croatian security forces, absence **111,** 479
Security Council Resolution 1037 **111,** 478-9
United Nations Transitional Administration for Eastern Slavonia (UNTAES)
establishment **111,** 478
'international authority' **111,** 480
obligations, cooperation with the International Criminal Tribunal for the Former Yugoslavia **111,** 479, 491-2
powers
arrest **111,** 474-5, 477-80
full executive authority **111,** 478
safe conduct, issue of **111,** 492-4
Eastern Treaties. *See* Germany, Federal Republic (FRG), Eastern Treaties for the Normalization of Relations with Poland and the USSR (1970) (Moscow and Warsaw Treaties)
EC. *See* European Community (EC)
economic contract. *See also* concession; economic development agreement; State contract
applicable law, general principles of law **96,** 235
economic cooperation, joint commission **82,** 687
economic development, forced or compulsory labour, use of **36,** 415-16, 418, 419-21, 423-4
economic development agreement 53, 455-7, **56,** 271-2. *See also* concession agreement; cooperation agreement; State contract
applicable law **83,** 553-4, **85,** 555
company established under
applicable law
constituent instrument **96,** 308-9
national law of contracting party **96,** 308-9, 319
'measure capable of infringing rights of shareholders or limiting right of company to achieve objects'
nationalization or similar measures, limited to, whether **96,** 315-16
waiver
right of expulsion **96,** 315
right to sever diplomatic relations **96,** 315-16

economic development agreement (*cont.*)
termination, necessity **96,** 316-20
economic interest 62, 111
Economic and Monetary Union (EMU)
automaticity **98,** 238
Bundestag/Bundesrat resolutions (December 1992) **98,** 207
as community of stability **98,** 235, 238-40
constitutional amendment, need for **98,** 186-7, 189
constitutional compatibility **93,** 347-9
convergence criteria **98,** 236-8
watering-down, protection against **98,** 237-8
democratic deficit **98,** 214-15
European Central Bank, commitment to stability and **98,** 237, 239-40
independence **98,** 240-3
Member States' willingness, dependence on **98,** 236, 238
political union, inevitable, whether **98,** 240-1
reversibility of European Union and **98,** 212
separable, whether **98,** 240
economic pressure 76, 403-4
duress, whether **56,** 526-7, **66,** 569-71, 615-16
economic relations. *See also* European Community (EC); General Agreement on Tariffs and Trade (GATT) (1947); most favoured nation (MFN) treatment; Uruguay Round; World Trade Organization (WTO)
development of, diplomatic activity, whether **63,** 172
international law and **46,** 511, 529-30
links with particular State **46,** 515-16, 518, 520
economic reprisals. *See* blockade; countermeasures, economic reprisals; economic sanctions; embargo
Economic Rights and Duties, Charter of. *See* United Nations General Assembly Resolutions, 3281 (XXIV) (Charter of Economic Rights and Duties of States)
economic sanctions. *See also* countermeasures; European Community (EC), economic sanctions; European Community (EC), unilateral measures by Member State (Art. 224 of EEC Treaty); *and relevant European Council Regulations and United Nations Resolutions*
change of policy and, natural justice **117,** 482
countervailing measures **107,** 119
fairness **117,** 477-9, 499
lawfulness **62,** 161
compatibility with GATT **60,** 646, 648-9
retroactive effect **117,** 475-7, 498
economy, State control of, manifestations **46,** 443, 452, 510
ECOSOC. *See* United Nations Economic and Social Council (ECOSOC)
Ecuador
Constitution 1979
s 22(19)(h) **118,** 79
s 28 **118,** 81
Continental Shelf Proclamation (1947) **41,** 118, 120
detention, incommunicado **118,** 78-80, 114-15
habeas corpus **118,** 81-3
procedural impediment to exercise **118,** 81-3
law of
Criminal Code
need for amendment **118,** 114-15
s 114 *bis* **118,** 87-9, 91, 114-15

Criminal Procedure Code
Law on Narcotic Drugs and Substances and **118,** 88-9
s 177 **118,** 78-9
s 458 **118,** 81
education
discipline, ancillary function, whether **67,** 497-9, 504
discrimination **45,** 156, **58,** 145
equality
Elimination of Discrimination in Education, Paris Convention (1960) **96,** 371
European Convention on Human Rights (1950) **96,** 371
International Covenant on Civil and Political Rights (ICCPR) (1966) **96,** 371
refugees **115,** 537
family, measures affecting and **45,** 163, 167, 173, 190, 224-5, **120,** 86
language of **45,** 162, 165-6, 170, 172, 173, 190, 224, 227, **120,** 84-6, 114
morality, protection of **58,** 147-8
official recognition of studies **45,** 162, 173, 201-17, 225-6, 227
parental convictions, respect for **45,** 142, 147-9, **58,** 141, 142, 147-9, **67,** 495-7, 500-3, **72,** 324, **74,** 295-6
religious instruction and **67,** 495-7, 500-3, **72,** 324, **74,** 295-6
primary **58,** 124-6
as 'public service' **113,** 289-90
religious **47,** 205-11
right to **45,** 114, 118, 119-22, 128, 131, 138-231, **57,** 219, **120,** 84-6, 114
access to occupations **45,** 208, 213
right to free **108,** 644-8
sex education **58,** 126-34, 143-4
South West Africa **37,** 375-6, 381, 383, 590
State regulation **67,** 498, 504
State schools, in **58,** 141
subsidies, withdrawal as punitive measure **45,** 177-9
teaching, freedom of **58,** 141, 143, 147, 149
EEC. *See* European Economic Community (EEC)
effective link 79, 14, 295-6, 303, 588
effective remedy before national authority 72, 373-6, **73,** 246, **74,** 310, 325, 381, 446, **102,** 286-8, **104,** 178. *See also* European Convention on Human Rights (1950), effective remedy before national authority; exhaustion of local remedies
absence of evidence **78,** 241-2
absence of legal aid, relevance **98,** 365, **120,** 104
administrative or disciplinary remedies **46,** 233-4, **118,** 207, 286-7, 290
aggregation of ineffective remedies as **89,** 236-9, 241-2
amnesty **78,** 25-6
amparo **95,** 273
availability **62,** 375, **86,** 345-6, **96,** 597
burden of proof **60,** 163, **96,** 597
cassation **95,** 273
complainant misled **94,** 393
constitutional motion bound to fail **98,** 331-2, 355-6
criminal law provision, need for **81,** 98-9
critical date, developments subsequent to communication **45,** 271, 298-9, 301-2, **56,** 370-1, **115,** 364-5
delays **70,** 272-6
in bringing criminal proceedings **118,** 201
unreasonableness **96,** 679, 702

effective remedy before national authority (*cont.*)
diplomatic privileges and immunities, relevance **111,** 158-9
discretionary act **46,** 233-4, **102,** 286-8
judicial review, possibility of **102,** 286
doubts about effectiveness **115,** 364-5
effectiveness **62,** 361, 376, 383, **86,** 339-41
'escape', prohibition on **74,** 299-301, 410-11
exceptional or extraordinary remedies **46,** 203, 235-7, **60,** 166, **62,** 246-7, 251-3, **70,** 284, 293-4, **94,** 392-3
failure to achieve desired result **95,** 273
finding case time-barred **96,** 519
general principle of international law **98,** 331, 366
habeas corpus **62,** 249, 258, **95,** 273, 276
partiality **95,** 273
persons held clandestinely **95,** 273, 276
powerlessness **95,** 273, 275-6
hearing before court with jurisdiction to determine criminal charge **60,** 165-6
inappropriate remedy **61,** 380-3
ineffectiveness
denial of access to judicial remedy **96,** 412
general conditions in country **96,** 411
lack of independent judiciary **70,** 272-6, **96,** 412
state of emergency **96,** 412
unjustified delay **96,** 412
interim measures, non-availability against Crown, relevance **98,** 317
judicial authority, need for **89,** 238-9, 240-1
judicial review **98,** 316-17
asylum procedures **108,** 357-62, 422, 423-7, 430-2, **124,** 515-16, 531-2, 540-1
just satisfaction proceedings and **86,** 348
justification for failure to provide, political solution, need for **120,** 66
lack of independent judiciary **70,** 272-6, 284-5, **96,** 412
legislative changes falling short **115,** 178-9
legislative measures and **62,** 77
margin of discretion **108,** 358
measures constituting **95,** 315
official act, relevance **123,** 154
partial resolution, remedy offering **60,** 164-6, **61,** 371-2, 378
prerogative of mercy **71,** 339-40
presumptive finding of death based on disappearance **95,** 272-3
reasonable chance of success, need for **56,** 371, **60,** 165, **61,** 372-4, 379-80, 384-6, **111,** 170-1
State Party's change of position before Convention institutions **111,** 205
reasonableness **94,** 398-9
relevance to alleged breach, need for **96,** 597
right to challenge legislation **75,** 432-3, 436-7, 508-9, 513, 516-17, 556-7
shareholders' incapacity to bring legal action and **46,** 497
State immunity as bar to suit and **81,** 136-8, **91,** 301, **114,** 566-7, **119,** 372, 373, 376, 377-8, 383-5, **121,** 203-4, 208
State immunity, jurisdiction and **91,** 301
statutory provision, sufficiency **96,** 596-7
suspension **96,** 415
time-limits and **62,** 79

effects doctrine. *See* jurisdiction, effects doctrine
'efficacy of change' principle 53, 56-7, 65, 66, 73, 74, 76-81
Egypt, Arab Republic
administrative contract
requirements **106,** 704
unilateral amendment, right to **106,** 631-2, 704
Alexandria Sanitary Bureau. *See* Alexandria Sanitary Bureau
Anglo-Egyptian Agreement on Compensation (1971) **60,** 115, 118, 122-4, 127
Arab Organization for Industrialization and **80,** 611-12
'nationalization' **80,** 611
arbitration
government's refusal **86,** 489
willingness to submit to, radical reversal of policy **106,** 557-8, 567
Constitution 1971
Art. 34 (compensation for expropriation) **106,** 627, 728, 729
Art. 35 **86,** 458
consular premises of, part of Egyptian territory **55,** 580, 581
contract
breach, damages for **86,** 471-3
termination, non-performance **86,** 465
damages, devaluation of currency, adjustment for **106,** 645-6
divorce regulations **55,** 580-1
validity in foreign country **55,** 580
expropriation/nationalization **60,** 116, 118-20, 126
compensation, need for
adequacy **106,** 627-8, 630
Civil Code **106,** 728
Constitution **106,** 627, 728
discretion as to amount **106,** 730
Law 215 (1951) (Protection of Monuments and Antiquities) **106,** 627
Law 577 (1954) (compensation for expropriation) **106,** 728, 729-30
power of courts to award **106,** 729-30
contractual rights **106,** 627-9
expulsion of alien **72,** 221-2
health, institutions concerned with **62,** 460-6
independence **80,** 259
interest
compound **106,** 641-3
date of commencement, date of award **106,** 642
principal, not to exceed **106,** 641-2
international law, principles, as part of municipal law **86,** 457-8
investment
applicable law
choice of law, admissibility **106,** 722-7
municipal law of Contracting State **106,** 722-7
dispute settlement **86,** 483
investor
approval by General Authority for Arab Investment, need for **106,** 620-3, 718-20
assignment of interest **106,** 719-20
open-door policy **86,** 446, 449
Israel. *See* Egypt–Israel boundary; Egypt–Israel Peace Treaty (1979)
justiciability, government act **86,** 461

Egypt, Arab Republic (*cont.*)
Law 43 (1974)
Art. 2 (definition of investment) **106,** 678
Art. 3 (Arab and foreign capital) **106,** 678, 680-1
Art. 8 (investment disputes)
consent to arbitration, whether **106,** 524-8, 540-3, 545-88
ICSID Convention, reference to, significance **106,** 552-60
Law 90 (1971) and **106,** 558-9
limited to Law 43 obligations, whether **106,** 525-6, 583, 587, 715-18
self-executing, whether **106,** 526-8, 576
withdrawal of approval of project, effect **106,** 523-4, 530
Art. 26 (information relating to investment) **106,** 719
Art. 27 (approval of investment) **106,** 719
consent to arbitration, whether
Decree 375 (1977) and **106,** 550-1
mandatory, whether **106,** 546-9, 561
as offer to submit to **106,** 570-1, 578, 582, 585, 653
Prime Minister's Decision 91-1975 and **106,** 551-2
separate agreement, need for **106,** 552-6
remedies
hierarchy **106,** 527-8, 544, 546-7, 549-52, 561, 574-5
mutually exclusive, whether **106,** 523
translation
agreed by parties for use in ICSID proceedings **106,** 545-6
variations **106,** 572-6
law of
Civil Code
Art. 1 (sources of law) **106,** 721, 726
Art. 125 **86,** 466
Art. 139 **86,** 267
Art. 147 **86,** 458
Art. 148 **86,** 488
Art. 157 **86,** 465
Art. 158 **86,** 465
Art. 216 (offset) **86,** 473, **106,** 735
Art. 221 **86,** 470, 471
Art. 226 (interest) **86,** 472-3, **106,** 643-4, 716-17
Art. 446 (risk) **106,** 733
Art. 447 (known fault) **106,** 733
Art. 805 (compensation for expropriation) **106,** 728
Art. 985 (usufruct) **106,** 728
Constitution. *See* Constitution 1971 *above*
Decree 50 (1976) (Egyptian General Company for Tourism and Hotels (EGOTH)) **86,** 445
Decree 90 (1978) (Al Giza pyramids region as public property) **106,** 625-6
Decree Law 30 (1979) **80,** 611
Law 30 (AMF) **108,** 576, 594-6
Law 60 **86,** 484
Law 215 (1951) (Protection of Monuments and Antiquities) **106,** 626
s 11 (compensation for expropriation) **106,** 627
Law 577 (1954) (compensation for expropriation) **106,** 728, 729-30
Law 90 (1971) (ICSID Convention) **106,** 557-8
Law 1 (1973) **86,** 445, 448, 484

Law 2 (1973) **86,** 445, 448, 484
Law 115 (1975) (Egyptian General Organization for Tourism and Hotels (EGOTH)) **86,** 438, 444
Law 2 (1978) (cancellation of land transfers) **86,** 439, 449-50, 458, 483, 488
siyadat el kanoun (supremacy of the law) **86,** 457
legislation, interpretation
aids
implementing regulation **106,** 551
legislative history **106,** 557, 576, 577
promotional literature **106,** 560-1, 577-81
guidelines
effectiveness **106,** 574, 587
object and purpose **85,** 450
ordinary grammatical meaning **106,** 547
original language to determine, whether **106,** 547-8, 572-3
phrases
'shall be' **106,** 547-9, 574-6
'*sont réglées*' **106,** 547-9, 574-6
'*tatimmu*' **106,** 547-9, 577
'within the framework of the Convention . . . where it applies' **106,** 552-3, 554-6
occupation by Britain **46,** 465 n. 8
State agency/State-owned corporation/State entity
EGOTH **86,** 487
separate legal entity **86,** 484
State contract, approval, need for **106,** 620-3, 667
Suez Canal Company, compensation agreement regarding **46,** 474
termination of protectorate (1922) **80,** 259-60
WHO Regional Office. *See* World Health Organization Regional Office in Egypt
Egypt–Israel Arbitration Tribunal (Taba) (1979) 80, 224-364. *See also* Egypt–Israel boundary; Egypt–Israel Peace Treaty (1979)
admissibility, 'abandoned' claim **80,** 285-6
award
dispositif **80,** 311-12
final and binding **80,** 247, 310
implementation
'as quickly as possible and in good faith' **80,** 247, 310
Liaison System and **80,** 310
rebuilding of pillars **80,** 310
Chamber to explore settlement possibilities **80,** 242-3
arbitral process, provision for termination of **80,** 242
constitution **80,** 242-3
failure **80,** 243
proceedings **80,** 243
Compromis (1986) **80,** 241-7
Appendix A **80,** 284
Great Britain–Turkey Agreement (1906), effect of express reference to **80,** 324, 346
interpretation
'address' **80,** 285
'final' **80,** 308
'recognized international boundary between Egypt and the former mandated territory of Egypt'. *See* Egypt–Israel boundary, 'recognized international boundary between Egypt and the former mandated territory of Egypt'
dissenting opinion **80,** 312-54

Egypt–Israel Arbitration Tribunal (*cont.*)
duty
to establish better title **80,** 284, 287
to weigh evidence **80,** 284
evidence
absence of **80,** 304
books **80,** 340
boundary markers **80,** 287, 288, 289, 290, 293, 334-5
burden of proof **80,** 321, 326
cairn **80,** 342
description cards **80,** 288-9, 290, 291, 292
diary **80,** 320, 349
diplomatic correspondence **80,** 317
Great Britain–Turkey Agreement (1906) **80,** 288, 293
as determinant of boundary **80,** 317-19, 324, 351
guidebooks **80,** 301
intelligence handbook **80,** 317
international organizations' records **80,** 318
maps **80,** 268, 289, 291, 292, 293, 300-1, 303, 324, 340, 343, 349, 350-1
absence of satisfactory **80,** 287, 289
discrepancies **80,** 295, 333, 334
disputed **80,** 254, 290
reliability **80,** 334
scale **80,** 287, 295, 300
value **80,** 334, 343-4
official papers **80,** 318
parliamentary reply **80,** 317
photographic **80,** 260, 264, 268, 301, 303, 340, 342
caption as interpretative aid **80,** 342-3
pillars **80,** 323, 333
Statistical Yearbooks **80,** 301, 318, 341
topography **80,** 350
travel accounts **80,** 340, 344
trig points **80,** 288, 289, 290, 303
Turkish presence **80,** 301, 344
video film **80,** 243
weighing of **80,** 284
'transferability' **80,** 284
expert evidence **80,** 330 n. 24
frustration of arbitration, contrary to parties' intention **80,** 308, 309
functions **80,** 244, 245-6
determination of proper location of pillars **80,** 352
limitations on **80,** 284-5, 314, 347
determination of location of Parker pillar **80,** 286, 299, 308
Great Britain–Turkey Agreement (1906). *See also* Egypt–Israel boundary, Great Britain–Turkey Agreement (1906)
determining factor, whether **80,** 317-19, 324, 351
express reference to, effect **80,** 324
translation adopted by Tribunal **80,** 253
non licet **80,** 307, 308, 310
non liquet **80,** 307
powers. *See* functions *above*

preliminary issues **80,** 282-6
proceedings **80,** 241-7
tasks. *See* functions *above*
Egypt–Israel boundary. *See also* Egypt–Israel Arbitration Tribunal (Taba)
critical date, date of entry into force of Palestine Mandate **80,** 284
critical period **80,** 284, 291, 324
maps **80,** 291
Parker pillar **80,** 299
demarcation
absence of challenge **80,** 283, 322-3
delimitation and **80,** 319, 321
Great Britain–Turkey Agreement (1906) and **80,** 283, 287
authentic interpretation of **80,** 297
conflict with **80,** 297, 316-26, 332-3, 348-52
Joint Commission (1906), Parker's participation as Egyptian representative **80,** 304-5, 322
pillars, replacement of telegraph poles by, whether part of **80,** 320-1
procedure, report, necessity for **80,** 320
Egypt–Israel Peace Treaty (1979) **80,** 240
Egyptian proposal, deviation from 1906 Agreement, whether **80,** 283
evidence. *See* Egypt–Israel Arbitration Tribunal (Taba), evidence
Granite Knob **80,** 300-3, 336-45, 346, 354
Great Britain–Turkey Agreement (1906) **80,** 252-5, 315-16
demarcation **80,** 255-7, 316
conflict **80,** 297, 316-26, 332-3, 348-52
intervisibility **80,** 255, 288, 300, 302-3, 306-7, 322, 329, 330-2, 335-6, 340, 345, 347
representatives of both sides to be present **80,** 255
evidence of situation on ground during critical period **80,** 284, 288, 295
existing water rights retained **80,** 255
interpretation, *travaux préparatoires* **80,** 346. *See also* phrases *below*
maps **80,** 315, 352
phrases
'approximately' straight line **80,** 288, 353
'eastern ridge' **80,** 302
'on the shore' **80,** 309-10, 329
'point' **80,** 309, 329
'ras' **80,** 339-40
'will' **80,** 330
renewal or increase of demarcation pillars **80,** 255
representatives of both sides to be present **80,** 255
separating line as laid down in map, to be determined by **80,** 255
separative administrative line
international frontier, whether **80,** 261, 314
recognition of **80,** 261
text **80,** 253-4, 362-3
translation, lack of authentic **80,** 253
1987 Egyptian translation **80,** 254, 255, 302
1987 Israeli translation **80,** 254, 255, 302
Turkish soldiers
unarmed **80,** 255
water rights **80,** 255

Egypt–Israel boundary (*cont.*)
Great Britain–Turkey Exchange of Notes (1906) **80,** 250
Israeli proposal, 'legal line' **80,** 283
maps
1915 map, publication (1926) **80,** 261
critical period **80,** 291
discrepancies **80,** 295
as evidence **80,** 254, 268, 287, 289, 291, 292, 293, 295, 300-1, 324, 333-4, 350-1
preparation **80,** 257-9
relative value **80,** 343-4
later one by same surveyor **80,** 351
scale **80,** 287, 295, 300
markers. *See also* pillars *below*
cairn **80,** 342, 350
trig point as **80,** 288, 289
UNEF **80,** 265
accuracy and origin uncertain **80,** 287
pillars. *See also* markers *above*
demarcation, whether part of **80,** 319-20, 323
as evidence **80,** 323, 333, 334-5
evidence of **80,** 291
insufficient **80,** 287
Great Britain–Turkey Agreement (1906), conflict with **80,** 297-8, 318-19
intervisibility **80,** 255, 288, 300, 302-3, 306-7, 322, 329, 330-2, 335-6, 340, 345, 347
location, Tribunal's task to determine **80,** 352
Parker **80,** 267-9, 299-310
accuracy **80,** 305-6, 322
Arbitral Tribunal no competence to decide location **80,** 286
during critical period **80,** 299, 303, 304
evidence of **80,** 268, 303-4, 306, 307
legitimacy **80,** 304-5, 322
renewal, implementation of arbitral award and **80,** 310
1909 **80,** 257
1911 **80,** 257
unilateral erection **80,** 319
'recognized international boundary between Egypt and the former mandated territory of Egypt' **80,** 266, 282, 283, 315
'as it was demarcated, consolidated and commonly understood during the period of the Mandate' **80,** 284
change excluded **80,** 260, 263, 323
critical date **80,** 284
critical period **80,** 284, 293, 324
events subsequent to **80,** 284
evolution during **80,** 284
demarcation, relevance **80,** 283, 293, 326
Great Britain–Turkey Agreement (1906)
as aid **80,** 284, 288, 295
subsequent demarcation, relevance **80,** 283, 293
Great Britain/Egypt
Declarations (1926) **80,** 283, 332, 351-2
demarcation, absence of challenge to **80,** 283
separative administrative line, as **80,** 261, 314

State succession and **80,** 184, 441-563
straightness of line as determining factor **80,** 288-9, 290, 291, 292, 299, 353
survey
1906 **80,** 250-2
1908-14 **80,** 257-9
1917 **80,** 259
1943 **80,** 262
1981 **80,** 266-7
boundary pillars **80,** 261
UNEF **80,** 265
Survey of Egypt **80,** 261, 262
Survey of Israel **80,** 265
thalweg **80,** 302, 339
trig points **80,** 288, 289
watershed **80,** 337 n. 29
Egypt–Israel Peace Treaty (1979)
boundary **80,** 240. *See also* Egypt–Israel Arbitration Tribunal (Taba)
1982 Agreement **80,** 240-5
Multinational Force and Observers (MFO) **80,** 244
demarcation **80,** 266-7
interim measures **80,** 244-5
'recognized international boundary between Egypt and the former mandated territory of Palestine' **80,** 266, 282
conclusion **80,** 266
dispute settlement
arbitration **80,** 240
conciliation **80,** 240
negotiation **80,** 240
US participation in **80,** 266, 282
Joint Commission **80,** 266-7
boundary demarcation **80,** 292
establishment **80,** 282
Liaison System, functions transferred to **80,** 267
Liaison System **80,** 267
implementation of Taba Arbitral Award **80,** 310
military government, effect on **83,** 165-6
Multinational Force and Observers (MFO) **80,** 242
Eire. *See* Ireland, Republic of
El Salvador
Constitution 1983, Art. 84 (definition of territory) **97,** 473, 521
Continental Shelf Proclamation (1950) **41,** 118, 120
exclusive fishing zone (EFZ) **41,** 122
expropriation/nationalization
arbitration, offer of, Caribbean Basin Economic Recovery Act **95,** 623
land reform **95,** 617
US encouragement **95,** 622-3
Fonseca Bay islands, claim to
Central American Court of Justice (1916) **97,** 472-3
Constitution 1983 and **97,** 473, 521
El Tigre
acquiescence in Honduran occupation **97,** 482-3
protest at Honduran occupation **97,** 484-5
historical title **97,** 475-6

El Salvador (*cont.*)
'in accordance with the provisions of international law' **97,** 473
Meanguera/Meanguerita, acts of authority **97,** 488-90
Fonseca Bay maritime spaces, Honduras/Nicaragua Delimitation Agreement (1900), acceptance **97,** 520-1
high seas, claim to sovereignty over 200 miles **41,** 120-2, 123
human rights **87,** 668-9
UNESCO Report **88,** 11 n. 6
ICJ
acceptance of compulsory jurisdiction **97,** 299, 300-1
modification **84,** 242
Meanguera/Meanguerita
absence of claims **97,** 627
acts of authority **97,** 488-90, 622
El Salvador protest, Honduran failure to respond **97,** 488, 490, 495, 624-5
Honduran protest **97,** 491-3
Pact of Bogotá (1948), denunciation **84,** 242, **97,** 299
El Salvador–Honduras land boundary. *See also* Fonseca Bay
acquiescence **97,** 317, 324-5
boundary **97,** 511
protest **97,** 444
uti possidetis position **97,** 441
applicable law. *See* Fonseca Bay, applicable law
armed conflict **97,** 298-9
Convention 1895, *uti possidetis* **97,** 298
Convention for the Adoption of a Mediation Procedure (1976) **97,** 299
Cruz–Letona Convention (1884) **97,** 298, 323
legal effect **97,** 323
El Salvador claims **97,** 278-9, 287-91
General Treaty of Peace (1980) **97,** 299-301, 305-6
Joint Frontier Commission **97,** 299, 301
reservations to ICJ compulsory jurisdiction, effect **97,** 300-1
Honduran claims **97,** 281-3, 284-6
King of Spain's Award **97,** 461-2
maps **97,** 319, 327-9, 336, 341, 358, 368, 373, 391, 393-4, 416, 428, 450, 457
Montaña de Naguaterique negotiations (1969) **97,** 298
OAS Special Commission (1969) **97,** 298-9
rivers as
Goascorán **97,** 298, 459-69
avulsion **97,** 462-7
estoppel **97,** 468-9
mouth **97,** 468-9
Las Cañas **97,** 420-1, 422, 423
Negro-Pichiguel **97,** 425-6
Negro-Quiagar **97,** 394-5, 399
Sumpul **97,** 346-7
Torola **97,** 442-4, 446-7, 456-8
Saco negotiations (1880), Goascorán River **97,** 466-7
Saco negotiations (1884) **97,** 467
Special Agreement. *See* International Court of Justice (ICJ), Special Agreement, El Salvador/Honduras (1986)
Special Demarcation Commission **97,** 301-2
ICJ Chamber and **97,** 301-2, 306-7

survey 1829 **97,** 347-9
tripoint (Guatemala/El Salvador/Honduras) (1935) **97,** 297, 317-18, 324
uti possidetis. See uti possidetis
Zelaya–Castellones Convention **97,** 298, 323
Zelaya–Galindo Convention **97,** 298
El Tigre. *See* Fonseca Bay, El Tigre
embargo 76, 586-7. *See also* blockade
as act of State **63,** 187-90
embassy or consular bank account/funds, immunity, execution/attachment 63, 63-6, 599, **65,** 115-19, 150-9, 164, 175-6, 387-8, **72,** 186, **74,** 173-88, **77,** 490-4, **82,** 34-6, 44, **87,** 60-2, 240, 417, **89,** 362-6, 364 n. 4, 636, **113,** 423-5, **124,** 553-6, 569. *See also* ambassador/head of mission; bank account; central/State-owned bank, State immunity execution/attachment; consular funds, immunity, execution/attachment; diplomatic mission; diplomatic premises; diplomatic privileges and immunities; embassy or consular bank account/funds, immunity, execution/attachment
absolute immunity, whether **113,** 427-9
abuse of **65,** 190
account as basis for jurisdiction distinguished **65,** 7
amount involved, relevance **113,** 428
applicable law **65,** 188-9
as asset **65,** 7
economic position of State, relevance **65,** 153, 157, 158, 191
ILC Draft Articles on Jurisdictional Immunities of States and Their Property (1991) **113,** 423
interference with functioning of mission and **65,** 152-3, **74,** 179
mission to international organization **99,** 141-3
in name of honorary consul **82,** 7-10
personal funds, inviolability of archives compared **82,** 9-10
presumption of immunity **77,** 493-4
requirements
certificate of use **74,** 179, 187-8
consent of State **77,** 494
State practice **113,** 423-4
in United Kingdom **74,** 173-88
Vienna Convention on Diplomatic Relations (1961) **65,** 152
embassy or consular bank account/funds, immunity, execution/attachment, purpose/use
account for use of separate legal entity **65,** 210-11
allocation for sovereign purpose **116,** 528
allocation for specific purpose **102,** 208
certificate as to **74,** 173, 176, 179, 187-8
commercial **74,** 174-9, 184-8, **89,** 363, 364
narrow definition **89,** 365
commercial transaction of private nature **77,** 491, 515
court's right to verify **106,** 291, 297
designation
by honorary consul **82,** 7
conclusiveness **65,** 9, 158, 190, **74,** 179, 187-8
difficulty of distinguishing **77,** 493-4, **116,** 527-9
diplomatic mission, expenses **63,** 236, **65,** 151-9, 185-91
evidence of
certificate of **74,** 173, 176, 179, 187-8
diplomatic note **102,** 206, 207

embassy or consular bank account/funds (*cont.*)
conclusiveness **94,** 360
fact of being in name of embassy or State **65,** 9, **77,** 491
failure to provide **106,** 297
manner of possession **77,** 492
Ministry of Justice declaration **65,** 9, **77,** 491-2
statement by bank holding account **106,** 297
exclusively private **116,** 529
extraterritorial, whether **65,** 9, **77,** 491-2
'for its legation' **65,** 9
funds 'in possession' of State **64,** 75-6
governmental use **64,** 75
mixed **63,** 524-7
mixed use **89,** 365, **116,** 528-9
operating account **77,** 490-4
personal funds **82,** 8-10
public relations **65,** 210
right/duty to enquire into **65,** 9, 153, 157-8, 160-1, 188-9, **77,** 493, **116,** 529
running of State's offices in forum State **65,** 115-19
segregation, need for, whether **89,** 363
separability **82,** 8-10
sovereign **82,** 44
emergency legislation **79,** 478-9. *See also* state of emergency
repeal **47,** 483, 487
repeal of other laws by **47,** 481
emigration
freedom of **74,** 299-301, 410-11, **78,** 70
nationality, effect on **72,** 438-41, 469-70, 489-91, 496-8
prohibition
GDR **74,** 299-300
Jews **36,** 194-8
eminent domain/*dominium eminens* **41,** 10-12, **83,** 554, **84,** 91, 197, **105,** 546, **106,** 626, **118,** 317. *See also* sovereignty
international law and **41,** 11-12
just compensation and **118,** 317
protection of antiquities **106,** 626
Pufendorf **41,** 12
employment contract,[iv] **academic appointment in respondent State**

[iv] Material relating to employment contracts is indexed under the following headings (and, where relevant, in parallel entries under individual countries):
employment contract, academic appointment in respondent State
employment contract, locally engaged staff, commercial/trade representation/mission
employment contract, locally engaged staff, cultural institute
employment contract, locally engaged staff, diplomatic mission
employment contract, locally engaged staff, Holy See, nationality, relevance
employment contract, locally engaged staff, information office/news agency
employment contract, locally engaged staff, military cemetery
employment contract, locally engaged staff, military/naval base
employment contract, locally engaged staff, office of Governor of British colony
employment contract, locally engaged staff, public broadcasting network
employment contract, locally engaged staff, Sovereign Order of Malta
employment contract, locally engaged staff, State agency
employment contract, mercenary in Congolese army

applicable law, relevance **65,** 380
jurisdiction **65,** 5-6
contract concluded in forum State **65,** 379-80
State immunity, jurisdiction **65,** 6-7, **107,** 368-70
in case of employment by foreign ministry **65,** 380
nationality of employee, relevance **65,** 379-80
non-State school **65,** 305-8
State school **65,** 378-80, **87,** 53-6, **94,** 314-15
employment contract, international organizations. *See* international officials, employment contract
employment contract, locally engaged staff, commercial/trade representation/mission
classification of employment
act of appointment, relevance **65,** 313-15
non-official nature **65,** 283
private law nature of relationship **65,** 283, 315, 342
State immunity, jurisdiction **65,** 282, 313-15, **98,** 57-61
nationality of employee, relevance **98,** 60 n. 7
national of sending State **82,** 102-3
employment contract, locally engaged staff, consulate
applicable law **86,** 584
lex fori **104,** 514
classification of employment
administrative and technical **65,** 342
chauffeur **116,** 662
commercial secretary **101,** 376
employee performing tasks essential to proper functioning of consulate **101,** 376
sovereign nature of consular acts **65,** 207-8
sovereign nature of functions of employee as test **114,** 504-6, 517-18
consular immunity, jurisdiction, voluntary retirement of employee, relevance **101,** 384-5
immunity, jurisdiction, waiver. *See* waiver of immunity *below*
national of sending State **86,** 584-5
privileges and immunities of employee distinguished **65,** 373
sending State as contractual party **86,** 585
State immunity, jurisdiction **65,** 206-8, 342-6, 372-4, **114,** 504-7, 510-12
applicable law clause, relevance **114,** 511-12
contract as waiver **114,** 512
customary international law **114,** 504-5
failure to pay medical insurance **94,** 356
financial aspects **114,** 535-6, 558, 566
language teacher **115,** 434
nationality of employee, relevance, national of sending State **98,** 60 n. 7
nature of functions of employee as test **65,** 345-6, **114,** 504-6, 517-18
remedies, law of sending State **104,** 525
State practice **104,** 523-4
waiver, choice of law clause in manual of employment **120,** 614-16

employment contract (municipal law)
employment contract, specialized agency
European Convention on State Immunity (and Protocol) (Basle) (1972), employment contract
international officials, employment contract
Iran–US Claims Tribunal, employment contract
NATO Status of Forces Agreement (1951), State immunity, jurisdiction, employment contract
World Bank Group, employment contract.

employment contract, locally engaged staff, cultural institute
State immunity, jurisdiction
archivist/secretary **65,** 325-8, **114,** 538-9
librarian **82,** 3-5
employment contract, locally engaged staff, diplomatic mission 86, 585-6
applicable law **116,** 631, 638, 674
place of employment **86,** 584, **94,** 351-2
receiving State **82,** 22-3, **94,** 353, **116,** 532, 653
sending State **104,** 523
as civil right under European Convention on Human Rights (1950) **123,** 62, 68-70
classification of employment **82,** 17, 18-20, **116,** 633
caretaker **113,** 493
clerical **94,** 353, **104,** 521-2
driver/interpreter **114,** 533
interpreter/translator **116,** 665-8
managerial role **65,** 329-30
medical staff **104,** 681, **116,** 623-4
nature of employment obligations as determining factor **86,** 586
radio-telegraph operator **82,** 15-23
secretary and technical officer **114,** 531
security guard **113,** 451-2
telephonist **114,** 557-8, **116,** 637-42
diplomatic immunity, jurisdiction **113,** 452
discrimination on grounds of sex **123,** 66-7, 70-1
dismissal for national security considerations **116,** 530-3
employee's right to institute proceedings against employing State **65,** 22, **116,** 638
waiver of plaintiff's diplomatic immunity **116,** 638
jurisdiction **65,** 22, **86,** 515-16, **116,** 638, 640
medical insurance, duty to ensure **94,** 356
sending State as contractual party **86,** 585
State immunity, jurisdiction **64,** 354-63, **86,** 510, 511, 515-16, 584-6, **94,** 353, **104,** 636-40, **107,** 603-4, **113,** 432-4, **114,** 557-8, **116,** 639-42
applicable law clause, relevance **114,** 528
commercial purposes of mission **95,** 473
common law **64,** 357-63
customary international law **64,** 357-63, **113,** 432-3, **116,** 628-33, **123,** 71-2
dismissal **64,** 360-1, **94,** 353-4, **114,** 531, 557-8, **115,** 419, 421-3
European Convention on State Immunity (and Protocol) (Basle) (1972), relevance **116,** 532-3, **123,** 59-60
non-party **115,** 422, **116,** 532-3, 632, 658-61
financial aspects **114,** 530-1, 533, **116,** 655, 675
general principle of international law **65,** 22
industrial tribunal as court **104,** 641
inviolability of premises, relevance **116,** 632
nationality of employee, relevance **77,** 607, **82,** 15-23, **94,** 353, **98,** 60 n. 7, **104,** 517, **114,** 533, **115,** 422, **116,** 641
national of sending State **86,** 509-11, 584-5, **87,** 43-7, **104,** 682, **113,** 432, **116,** 663
place of performance, relevance **82,** 16
presumption of **120,** 616
sending State as contractual party **86,** 585
Sengupta **104,** 521-2, 681
sovereign nature of functions of employee as test **82,** 17-23, 102-3, **87,** 43, 45, 46-7, **94,** 281-3, **116,** 658, 666, 670-1, **123,** 69-70

permanent clerical duties and **87,** 46-7
State practice **104,** 523-4, **123,** 65
status as member of mission, relevance **104,** 637-8
termination
acte de gouvernement **116,** 655, 674-5
enquiry into reasons for **116,** 654-5
Vienna Convention on Diplomatic Relations (1961), relevance **116,** 628-9, 632
waiver **116,** 633, 636
employment contract, locally engaged staff, Holy See, nationality, relevance **65,** 335
employment contract, locally engaged staff, information office/news agency
private law nature of relationship **65,** 284
State immunity, jurisdiction
challenge to grading **114,** 524
financial aspects **114,** 522-4
public service responsibilities, relevance **65,** 284-7, **113,** 458-9, 492
employment contract, locally engaged staff, military cemetery, State immunity, jurisdiction, dismissal, refusal of work permit as ground for **115,** 435
employment contract, locally engaged staff, military/naval base
State immunity, jurisdiction **94,** 283
contract for supply of goods, whether distinguishable **86,** 637, 638-9, **94,** 283
international agreement as context **94,** 281
labour relations distinguished **94,** 274, 289, 304-5
collective bargaining **94,** 284-6
labour tribunal, submission to **94,** 285-6
right to strike **94,** 285-6
national security considerations **94,** 283, **116,** 530-3
State immunity, jurisdiction, procedural aspects, applicable law, sending State **94,** 268
employment contract, locally engaged staff, office of Governor of British colony
State immunity, jurisdiction **104,** 513-14, 519-24
national of receiving State **104,** 520
State immunity, jurisdiction, procedural aspects
applicable law **104,** 509-25
receiving State **104,** 520
employment contract, locally engaged staff, public broadcasting network, State immunity, jurisdiction, forum selection clause as waiver **87,** 40-1
employment contract, locally engaged staff, Sovereign Order of Malta
State immunity, jurisdiction **65,** 309-12
in relation to administrative staff **65,** 312
employment contract, locally engaged staff, State agency
expropriation/nationalization, State immunity, jurisdiction and **65,** 44-6
nationalization of employing company following independence **64,** 44-6
State immunity, jurisdiction
arbitration clause as waiver of right **113,** 497
research assistant **113,** 496-7
employment contract, mercenary in Congolese army, State immunity, jurisdiction **64,** 668-72
employment contract (municipal law)
applicable law **96,** 572-3
dismissal, fair hearing and **96,** 573-8
employment contract, specialized agency, State immunity, jurisdiction, functional **77,** 577
employment practice, employee entitlements on termination of employment **109,** 382-8

Ems Estuary Treaty (1960) 43, 252
EMU. *See* Economic and Monetary Union (EMU)
enclaves
Bangladesh/India Agreement providing for the Exchange of Enclaves (1974)
1982 Exchange of Letters as integral part **92,** 564
cession of territory, whether **92,** 535, 560-1, 564, 568, 569, 572-3
constitutional amendment, need for, whether **92,** 575-6
jurisdiction under **92,** 564-5, 574-5
notification in Official Gazette, need for, whether **92,** 575-7
maritime jurisdiction, territory of third State **83,** 90-1
right of access **92,** 571-2
customary international law **92,** 574
military, paramilitary and armed police **92,** 574
UN Headquarters **82,** 285
Vancouver Island **90,** 288-90
Endangered Species of Wild Fauna and Flora, Convention on International Trade (CITES) (1973)
danger of extinction **90,** 578
domestic pets **90,** 576
illegal activity **90,** 578
legality of importation **90,** 578
phrases
'exports' and 're-exports', distinction **90,** 424
'unworked or simply prepared' **90,** 419-22, 425-6
enemy. *See also* enemy aliens; enemy character; enemy corporation; enemy organization; enemy property
definition **53,** 615, **54,** 579, 581, 602-3, **94,** 172-3
trading with **41,** 457-9, **54,** 579, 581, 602-3
benefit to the enemy **52,** 477, 483-5
contract with enemy company **48,** 475-8
control of enemy property **74,** 153-5
enemy aliens 53, 609-12, 616-27, **60,** 211
access to courts **71,** 710, **83,** 162
as defendant **53,** 609-10, 618-22, 624-7
right to sue **53,** 610, 618-22, 624-7
appeals, right of **53,** 621, 626
civil rights **53,** 617-22, 624-7
definition **53,** 617-18, 619-22, 624-7, **54,** 285, **71,** 710
internment, right to sue, effect on **53,** 620
nationality
loss or deprivation of **72,** 449-77
non-recognition by belligerent State **72,** 449, 453, 457, 459-60, 465, 467-70, 474-6
pre-war contract with **53,** 625
property. *See* enemy property
right to sue. *See* access to courts *above*
seizure of assets **54,** 588
enemy character. *See also* enemy corporation; enemy taint
burden of proof **54,** 573, 579, 581-2, 602-3, 606-7
corporation **40,** 479, **52,** 489-91
attempt to disguise **54,** 558-63, 566-9, 576-9, 587-95, 596-602
cloaking operations **54,** 558-63, 566-9, 576-9, 587-95, 596-602
control test **74,** 155

enemy nationals as employees **54,** 575
evidence of, ships **40,** 474
goods **40,** 472-80
ships, proof **40,** 474
enemy corporation. *See also* enemy character, corporation
contract with, validity **48,** 475-8
control of stock **54,** 556-7
enemy shareholder's rights **38,** 460-9
German law (World War II) **54,** 558-63, 595-602
German policy (World War II) **54,** 558-63, 578-9, 587-95, 596-602
enemy organization, membership as offence **36,** 20, 31-2, 252-3, 276, 289
enemy property 61, 671-3
booty, currency captured as **40,** 464-7
cargoes, produce of soil **40,** 472-80
cession by administrator **73,** 582, 588
compensation for acts relating to. *See* compensation for war-related events
confiscation **41,** 459-61, **42,** 198-205, **43,** 248, **44,** 486-94, **74,** 153-6
extraterritorial effect **44,** 490, 493
German patents by allies **48,** 468-9
Peace Treaty with Japan (1951) **44,** 490-4
recognition **74,** 153-6
restrictions on **92,** 478
third States, effect in **74,** 153-6
custodian of
cession by **73,** 582, 588
powers, Canada **54,** 609-13
vesting in
Pakistan **53,** 616
USA **54,** 572
destruction, military necessity **56,** 542
discriminatory treatment of **42,** 401-8
in enemy territory **56,** 543
expropriation/nationalization, after cessation of hostilities **56,** 538
freezing/blocking
in case of country technically not at war **42,** 198-205
government's constitutional powers **42,** 198-205
vesting distinguished **54,** 543-5
legislation
extraterritorial effect **43,** 248
piercing the corporate veil **46,** 213, 357, 518
ownership **56,** 541
patents, sequestration of **41,** 459-61
repayment of funds **71,** 267-9
requisition **41,** 480-2
seizure **54,** 588, 590, **56,** 538, 541, **59,** 599-600
mistake, liability for interest **54,** 582-4
protective custody **54,** 572
recovery **54,** 519, 585, 602-3
sequestration **41,** 459-61, **42,** 198-205
treasure trove, whether **61,** 671, **62,** 672-3
enemy taint 54, 579-80, 605-7. *See also* enemy character
individuals **54,** 606
enemy territory, definition **53,** 615

enforcement measures. *See* arbitral award, enforcement; European Convention on Human Rights (1950), enforcement; foreign judgment, recognition/enforcement; foreign law, recognition/enforcement; foreign maintenance orders, enforcement; New York Convention on the Recognition and Enforcement of Foreign Arbitral Awards (1958); State immunity, arbitral award, enforcement
England. *See* United Kingdom
***Entente Cordiale* 82,** 604
entry permit. *See* aliens, entry permit
environment. *See also* Australia, Tasmania, Western Tasmania Wilderness National Parks; Bhopal gas leak disaster; conservation; development; Endangered Species of Wild Fauna and Flora, Convention on International Trade (CITES) (1973); Greenpeace; hazardous activities; marine pollution; NAAEC (North American Agreement on Environmental Co-operation) (1993); natural resources; nuclear energy exploitation; nuclear weapons, deployment; UNESCO Protection of the World Cultural and Natural Heritage Convention (1972); United Nations Compensation Commission, Category 'F' claims; waste disposal
breach of obligations, standard of proof, prima facie case **106,** 20
burden of proof **110,** 452-3
customary international law **106,** 130, **110,** 82, 154, 454-5
damage, burden of proof **106,** 69-70, 122-7
definition **90,** 122-3
development of law **106,** 127-31, **110,** 79-82, **116,** 87, 186-8
cultural diversity and **116,** 105-20
customary international law **110,** 82
ICJ
Chamber for Environmental Matters **106,** 130
jurisprudence **106,** 130
treaties and **106,** 129, **110,** 80, 82, **116,** 76-7
fundamental change of circumstance, whether **116,** 74
provision for **116,** 76-7, 86-7, 122-4, 132, 133, 187-8
economic imperatives and **116,** 72-3
environmental impact assessment (EIA), need for **106,** 66-7, 133, **116,** 168
activity on high seas **100,** 497, 501-3
activity within foreign jurisdiction **100,** 497-501
alternatives, need to consider **100,** 503-5
Antarctica **100,** 522-30
Antarctic Treaty, Protocol on Environmental Protection (1991), relevance **100,** 527-8
CERN **82,** 88-9
continuous nature **116,** 120-2, 242
European Community directives 85/337/EEC and 97/11/EEC **120,** 629-30
Gabčkovo/Nagymaros Project **116,** 120-2, 242
implied term in treaties having an impact on the environment **116,** 121
national security **106,** 21
nuclear tests **106,** 125-7
customary international law **106,** 12-13, 16, 21, 134
ILC (Draft Articles on International Liability for Injurious Consequences Arising out of Acts Not Prohibited by International Law (1994)) **106,** 127
standard of assessment, contemporaneous norms **116,** 122-4
State responsibility for effects **124,** 50-2
supplementary statement, need for **100,** 505
Trail Smelter Arbitration **116,** 121
treaty provision **106,** 12, 16, 21

as essential interest of State **116,** 50
free trade and. *See* international trade interface *below*
freedom of navigation, right of environmental protection group to interfere **101,** 433-6
Gabčíkovo/Nagymaros Project. *See* Gabčíkovo/Nagymaros Project
global commons **106,** 67
human rights, effect on **110,** 441, **116,** 123-4
intergenerational rights **106,** 63-4, **110,** 405-6
  Stockholm Declaration on the Human Environment (1972) **106,** 63-4
interim measures and **117,** 146
international trade interface
  balance
    GATT (1947/1994) **121,** 142
    NAFTA (1992) **121,** 105-10, 116, 131, 133-4
  impact of free trade agreements on governments' power to regulate in interest of public values **121,** 142, 144-6, 178-80
  protectionism and **121,** 145-6
maritime delimitation **71,** 85, 89
  ecological aspects **71,** 86, 89, 100, 102-5, 113-14, 143, 146, 153-4
noise **73,** 448-50
nuclear tests. *See* nuclear tests
nuclear weapons, deployment. *See* nuclear weapons, deployment
obligations
  action to preserve and enhance the environment **11,** 80-1
  avoidance of harm to others **106,** 68-9, 100-1, **110,** 80-1, 455-6
    Rio Declaration on Environment and Development (1992) **106,** 69
    Stockholm Convention on the Human Environment (1972) **106,** 69
  erga omnes **110,** 81-2, **116,** 126-7, 169
  Geneva Protocol (Prohibition of Asphyxiating, Poisonous or other Gases and Bacteriological Methods) (1925) **110,** 154
  intergenerational rights. *See* intergenerational rights *above*
  in time of war **110,** 124-6, 154-7, 191-3
  to respect obligations **106,** 28
overland cables, installation by international agreement, public utility, whether **72,** 13-14
'polluter pays' principle **110,** 453
pollution
  of air **57,** 533-5, **73,** 448-50
  inhuman or degrading treatment, whether **111,** 229
precautionary principle **106,** 12, 20-1, 64-6, 134, **110,** 452-3, **116,** 161, **117,** 186-7
  Bergen Declaration on Sustainable Development (1990) **106,** 64-5
  customary international law **106,** 134, **117,** 174, 179-80, 186
  Law of the Sea Convention (1982) **117,** 172-7
  Maastricht Treaty (1992) **106,** 65
  NAFTA (1992) **121,** 169-71
  Rio Declaration on Environment and Development (1992) **106,** 66, **117,** 173-4, **121,** 169
protection of **57,** 448-9, **82,** 672
  principle of international law **116,** 100
  State's right to act unilaterally outside territory **120,** 596-9
public interest, international considerations and **72,** 14
rehabilitation of Nauru worked-out phosphate lands. *See also* Nauru
  liability of former Trusteeship Administering Authority **97,** 71-92
    delay in claiming **97,** 20-2, 90-2

environment (*cont.*)
environmental norms as basis **97,** 49
termination of Trusteeship, effect **97,** 17-20
Trusteeship Agreement as basis **97,** 49
waiver of claims **97,** 13-17, 78, 89
right to equitable and reasonable share of resources of international watercourse **116,** 63, 65, 89, 158-61, 175, 202, 211-12, 221-2, 224-5, 243-8
Lake Lanoux **116,** 244-7
Rio Declaration on Environment and Development (1992) **106,** 129-30
avoidance of harm to others **106,** 69
precautionary principle **106,** 66, **117,** 173-4, **121,** 169
radioactive waste **106,** 68
right to development **116,** 100
in time of war **110,** 126, 155, 192
self-defence **110,** 467, 528
social and economic aspects **90,** 64, 123-5
Stockholm Declaration on the Human Environment (1972) **106,** 128-9
avoidance of harm to others **106,** 69
intergenerational rights **106,** 63-4
sustainable development principle **116,** 101
sustainable development. *See* sustainable development principle
treaties
Convention on Biodiversity (1992), European Community (EC) and **120,** 69
Convention on the Conservation of Antarctic Marine Living Resources **108,** 636
Convention on the Modification of the Environment (1977)
'environmental modification technique' **110,** 155
in time of war **110,** 155
Convention for the Protection of Birds (1950), municipal law, conflict with **47,** 336-40
epicontinental platform 41, 120, 122, 125, 127, 128, 134
equality 41, 93, **46,** 478, **79,** 314-15, **91,** 329-32. *See also* equality of parties; equality of States; freedom from discrimination; International Covenant on Civil and Political Rights (ICCPR) (1966), equality; International Covenant on Economic, Social and Cultural Rights (1966), equality
apartheid and **37,** 461-71
arbitrariness and **118,** 466-7
before the law **37,** 450-71, **71,** 307, **79,** 315
juridical equality distinguished **79,** 315
education
Elimination of Discrimination in Education, Paris Convention (1960) **96,** 371
European Convention on Human Rights (1950) **96,** 371
International Covenant on Civil and Political Rights (ICCPR) (1966) **96,** 371
identity of treatment distinguished **91,** 330-2
International Covenant on Civil and Political Rights (ICCPR) (1966) **91,** 329-31
job-reservation **37,** 469
legitimate inequalities **79,** 301
proportionality **79,** 301, 303, 306, 316-17, 319-20, 322
reasonableness **79,** 306, 316, 317, 319, 320, 322, 324
in Namibia, motives for **49,** 6, 46-7, 207
of nations. *See* States, equality
natural law and **37,** 464, **49,** 67
racial, apartheid **49,** 46-7, 68-75, 207
sexual **79,** 303-4
transitional rules **96,** 371-2
of UN Members **44,** 375, 377

equality of arms 105, 542-3, **124,** 80-90. *See also* equality of parties; European Convention on Human Rights (1950), equality of arms; European Court of Human Rights, equality of arms; fair trial, balancing interests of defence and prosecution; International Covenant on Civil and Political Rights (ICCPR) (1966), equality of arms; Yugoslavia, International Criminal Tribunal for the Former (ICTY), equality of arms
applicability to conditions outside court's control **124,** 86-90
as essential element of fair trial **124,** 85-6
failure to provide copy of relevant report **96,** 619
international and domestic proceedings distinguished **124,** 87-8
release pending trial **45,** 277, 295, 296, 308, 315
time to prepare defence and **124,** 86
equality of parties 46, 133, **54,** 435-6, 485-7, **57,** 381-2, **69,** 349-51, 356-8, 367, 386-8, 391-4, 462, 471, **76,** 60-1, 488, 658-9, 662, **81,** 351, **85,** 427, **89,** 540-1, 542, 550-1. *See also* equality of arms
arbitral tribunal
tribunal's verification of nationality **120,** 342
withhold of documents and **122,** 351, 403
Badinter Commission (Yugoslavia) **96,** 717
equal time to question witness **122,** 38
estoppel and **89,** 398-401
good faith and **89,** 401
prejudice, need for **89,** 400-1
respondent disadvantaged, whether **89,** 580
function **89,** 475
ICSID Convention (1965) **106,** 568
Inter-American Court of Human Rights **95,** 266
interim measures and **94,** 476, **95,** 94, 97
International Court of Justice (ICJ) **95,** 55
determination of 'subject of dispute' **123,** 391
interim measures **95,** 94, 97
International Criminal Tribunal for the Former Yugoslavia **105,** 542-3, **122,** 38
judge *ad hoc*, entitlement to choose **106,** 16, **117,** 37
multilateral treaties **47,** 439, 440, 445, 460
municipal courts
relevance of decision **89,** 459, 503, 624-5
res judicata principle **89,** 459, 503, 624-5
proceedings, failure to appear **89,** 324-7, 350
proper claimant **89,** 572-4
proper respondent **89,** 395-8
State contract and **62,** 171
time-limits **89,** 573-4
Yugoslavia, imbalance of arms **95,** 156
equality of States. *See* States, equality
equality of treatment
enforcement of decisions of international tribunals **108,** 206-8
Mandates System **37,** 460, 518-19
equalization of burdens. *See also* aliens, equalization of burdens, levies and
individual's right to demand, FRG–Poland Border Treaty (1990) **108,** 661-2
'social State' and **108,** 661-2
Equatorial Guinea
diplomatic relations, suspension **88,** 695
independence **88,** 693
nationalization measures **88,** 695
special administrative status **88,** 693

equidistance 41, 29-229, 313, **67,** 42, 71-2, 80-1, 98-101, 125-8, 141-4, 178-83, 185-90, 230, 239, 250, 253-60, 285-91, 313, **77,** 679-83, **83,** 15, **91,** 460-1, 463, 653, 663
in absence of adjacency or opposition **81,** 309
in absence of agreement **41,** 57, 106, 177, 202
acceptance for general application
bilateral agreement between parties in dispute **99,** 416-20
bilateral agreement with third party **99,** 679-80
Continental Shelf Convention (1958), signature **99,** 420
diplomatic correspondence **99,** 423-4
fisheries legislation **99,** 422-3
parties' conduct **99,** 420-4
parties' domestic practice **99,** 681
adjacency and **41,** 115, 126-7, 189-90, 193
adjacent States, between **41,** 46, 61, 106, 108, 134, 224
advantages. *See* merits *below*
agreement, in absence of **41,** 57, 106, 177, 202, **91,** 656
appurtenance theory and **41,** 41, 58
automaticity **81,** 256, 392
coastal configuration, amplification effect **41,** 78
coastal projection and **95,** 668
contiguity and **41,** 115
Continental Shelf Convention (1958) **41,** 36, 49, 69-70, 90, 104-15, 176-8, 190, **71,** 106, 108, 111, 114, 118-20, 127-30, 150-1, 180, 192, 213-15, **81,** 270, 280, **91,** 671-2, **95,** 663-4, **99,** 505, 507-10, 634, 673
obligatory, whether **99,** 512-15, 516, 517, 521
relevant/special circumstances **71,** 128
continental shelf delimitation **67,** 72, **81,** 270, 274-5, 293, 298, 339-40, 359
customary international law and **41,** 36, 38, 57-77, 84-5, 92, 105-15, 133-8, 169-73, 192, 194, **81,** 298, 303, 378, **91,** 671-3, **99,** 428, 502-4, 506, 512, 516, 517, 519-22, 526-7
converging equidistance lines **41,** 46-7, 79-80
simplified equidistance line **41,** 78-9
definition **41,** 36-7, 38, 39, 46, 49, 224
as departure point. *See* line, as departure point *below*
development of concept **41,** 62-5, 203-4
disadvantages **77,** 681-2, 684
distortion resulting from **81,** 276
equal division, relevance **99,** 546, 547-50
equitable factor
Gulf of Maine **99,** 633
parity **99,** 633-4
Anglo-French Arbitration **99,** 633-4
Guinea–Guinea-Bissau **99,** 634
priority **99,** 631, 633
North Sea **99,** 633
equitable principles and **81,** 317
equitable result, need for **81,** 391, **119,** 464
equitable, whether **41,** 36, 38, 39, 46-7, 53, 64, 65, 68-80, 106, 146, 147-9, 151-2, 153-5, 177, 178, 179-82, 183-4, 193-5, 197, 216, 227, **81,** 270, 279, 338, 350, 351, 361, 377-8, 379, 392, **95,** 698, **99,** 434, 589-90
adjacent coasts **81,** 380
basepoints, choice **81,** 280
fishing zones **99,** 558

opposite coasts **81,** 279, 338, 380
usual result **99,** 435
proportionality as test **81,** 276
first step **81,** 269
fishing zones **99,** 430, 558
general principle of law **41,** 31, 85, 138, 141, 184, 204
Gulf of Maine **81,** 411
ILC and **41,** 63, 105-6, 146
internal waters **41,** 75
as *jus cogens*/peremptory norm **41,** 175
lateral line **41,** 46, 66, 105, **71,** 118, 151-2, 158-9, **83,** 94, **91,** 663-77
Law of the Sea Convention (1982) **81,** 280, 293, 303, **83,** 15, **99,** 633, 674
territorial sea **97,** 674-5
legal norm **41,** 76, 175-6
legal requirement, whether **41,** 52-75, 83, 92, 105, 111, 112, 114, 132, 168-75, 189-92, 202
line
adjustment. *See* correction *below*
correction **81,** 283, 284, 306, 314-15, 318, 320, 323, 332, 341-5, 352-3, 411, 419, **99,** 429-30, 432, 445, 447-9. *See also* transposition *below*
consistent, whether necessary **99,** 447
cut-off effect, avoidance **81,** 416-18
proportionality **81,** 280, 339, 367-71, 416-18, **99,** 483, 484
State practice **81,** 339
territorial sea delimitation compared **81,** 332
third State claims and **81,** 369-70
as departure point **81,** 269-70, 278, 279-81, 338, 351-2, 358, 374, **99,** 427-9, 430-2, 673-4
as final line **81,** 338
lateral. *See* lateral line *above*
provisional. *See* as departure point *above*
simplified **81,** 378, **91,** 655-6
transposition **81,** 284-5, 325, 332, 353, 371, 399, 412-13, 414-16, **99,** 554-5. *See also* correction *above*
logical necessity **41,** 58-61, 63, 65, 173-5, 189, 217
median line **41,** 41, 46, 61, 65, 66, 74, 89, 90-1, 133-5, 170, 224, **52,** 185, 282, **62,** 125, 126, **67,** 80-1, **71,** 118, 151-2, 158, 161. *See also* equidistance
baseline. *See* baselines
as coastal line **119,** 458
definition
Law of the Sea Convention (1982) **119,** 458
legal writings **119,** 458
Eritrea/Yemen **114,** 114, 131-2, **119,** 443-6, 453-65
inland sea or lake **50,** 35-41, 209
internal waters **41,** 135
islands, sovereignty over and **50,** 35-41, 178, 180-2, 189, 194-5, 208-13, **114,** 114, 131-2, **119,** 443-6, 453-65
lateral line distinguished **41,** 46
natural law concept **50,** 38, 209
North Sea **41,** 41, 89
as regional customary law **41,** 89
obligatory, whether **77,** 681, 682
opposite States, between **41,** 46, 66, 75, 190, **119,** 445

equidistance (*cont.*)
merits **77,** 681
certainty **41,** 157, 175, **81,** 378, 392
convenience **41,** 53, 64, 157, 175, 184, 204, 228, **81,** 378, 392
practicality **71,** 124, 127
as method **41,** 49, 50, 52-3, 104, 105, 106, 109, 113, 156-7, 165 n. 1, 174
equity, requirement of **41,** 80-1
obligatory, whether **41,** 52-75, 83, 92, 105, 111, 112, 114, 132, 168-75, 189-92, 202, **71,** 119, 124, 129-30, 148, 180, 192, 214-15
substantive rule, whether **41,** 49, 53
modified **41,** 78-9
natural law and **41,** 58-62, 84
non-encroachment and **41,** 61
obligatory, whether **41,** 52-75, 83, 92, 105, 111, 112, 114, 132, 168-75, 189-92, 202, **81,** 269, 270, 279, 288, 296, 297, 339-40, 351, 358, 378, 392, 411
Anglo-French Arbitration **99,** 513-14
Canada–France Arbitration **99,** 514-15
Continental Shelf Convention (1958) **99,** 512-15, 516, 517, 521
customary international law **99,** 512, 516
Gulf of Maine **99,** 514
Libya–Malta **99,** 514
North Sea cases **99,** 513
opposite coasts, between **41,** 46, 66, 134, 190, 224, **81,** 288, 351-2, 378-9, 410-11
adjacent coasts, distinction, whether **81,** 270, 283, 293
Jan Mayen **99,** 428-9
North Sea **81,** 410-11
primacy **81,** 269
resultant proportionality **81,** 366
primacy **81,** 269, 288, 293, 358, **99,** 674
opposite coasts, between **81,** 269
proportionality and **41,** 46, 50, 82, 147, 180, 195. *See also* proportionality, maritime delimitation
relationship between coasts **71,** 151-2, 160, 214
rejection **95,** 684, 699, 707
disproportion of coastal lengths **95,** 707, 715
relevant/special circumstances and **41,** 36, 37, 106, 109-10, 140, 143, 146, 148-52, 153, 156, 158, 177, 192-3, 201, 209, 213-16, 223-4, 226-8, **71,** 85, 88, 106, 108, 111, 113-14, 118-19, 124, 129-30, 132-9, 140, 143, 148-52, 156, 158, 192-3, 201, 209, 213-16, **91,** 675, **99,** 430, 634-5, 673-5
appropriateness **71,** 151-2, 214
conduct of parties **71,** 132-9, 148
EEZ, application to **71,** 193
Eritrea/Yemen boundary **119,** 464
fundamental norm, as expression of **71,** 130
lateral equidistance line **71,** 118, 151-2, 158-9
obligatory, whether **71,** 119, 124, 129-30, 148, 180, 192, 214-15
rule of law, whether **91,** 460, **99,** 504-6, 525
security considerations **81,** 274
sovereign equality of States and **81,** 274
State practice **41,** 73-4, 105, 169-71, 190, 208, 223, 227, **62,** 125, **71,** 159, 214, **81,** 270, 274-5, 280, 293, 298, 339-40, 359
as starting point **71,** 159, 214
technical **81,** 293, **99,** 504-6

geometric method **99,** 505
territorial sea **41,** 46, 47, 66-7, 75, 163, **81,** 293, **83,** 15, 21
coastal configuration, relative effect **41,** 47, 66-7
equitable result **97,** 675
historic title and **97,** 675
Law of the Sea Convention (1982) **97,** 674-5
special circumstances, islands **97,** 675
Territorial Sea Convention (1958) **41,** 104, 133
unilateral application **41,** 108, 208-9
equilibrium, contractual, State contract **66,** 588, 590-1, 626-7
equitable execution 81, 719
equitable principles 41, 78, 104, **62,** 109, 115, 125, **71,** 85-6, 88-90, 111, 113, 120-2, 130, 184-5, 206, **81,** 263, 270-2, 287, 291, 337, **83,** 87, 88, 93, **89,** 522-3, **91,** 654, 663-77, **99,** 447. *See also* equity
customary international law **99,** 675-6
damages, application to **116,** 161, 249
delimitation by agreement, applicability to **99,** 517-19
delimitation, underlying principle of **41,** 62, 65, 76, 86, 87, 91, 109, 134, 141-51, 164, 193
distributive justice **81,** 271, 272
Diversion of Water from the Meuse **116,** 158, 247-8
equal division of overlap **41,** 82-3
equidistance and **41,** 109
equitable criteria, whether **99,** 587-8
Gulf of Maine **99,** 587-8
equitable result, need for **81,** 263, 359, 377
equity and **71,** 209
equity does not imply equality. *See* equity, equality and
equity looks to intent rather than form **99,** 593
equity, means of implementing **99,** 618-21
estoppel **99,** 587, 593
ex aequo et bono distinguished **89,** 522-3, 547
fairness **99,** 587, 588-9
inadimplenti non est adimplendum **76,** 715, 726
internationally recognized **80,** 581
just and equitable share **95,** 698
Law of the Sea Convention (1982) **83,** 93-4
maritime boundary, federal State **91,** 460-1
maritime delimitation **91,** 654, 663-77
limited to, whether **89,** 522-3
method **81,** 263
negotiated delimitation **41,** 86
no refashioning of geography **81,** 271
non-encroachment **81,** 271
normative character **81,** 271, 359
fundamental norm of international law **99,** 661, 671
praeter legem **41,** 138, 141, 144, 146, 151
proportionality **41,** 83. *See also* proportionality
result of **81,** 304
relevant/special circumstances, respect for **81,** 271
result **81,** 263
treaty interpretation **99,** 587
Truman Proclamation (1945) **41,** 62, 86, **81,** 391, **99,** 662

equitable remedies, injunction **86,** 649, **118,** 408, 410-12
equity **42,** 379, **54,** 115, **55,** 265, 266, 267, 268, 269, 334, 338-9, 381-2, **56,** 83, 173, 176-7, 185, 194, **67,** 53, 98-9, 102, 145, 149, 248-50, 292, 313, **71,** 132, 184, 194, 204-5, 209, **76,** 64-5, 337, **77,** 675-92, **78,** 408, **80,** 172. *See also* equitable principles; equitable result; equity; *ex aequo et bono*; justice; maritime delimitation
'absolute equity' **99,** 598
ex aequo et bono as **99,** 598-9
Orinoco Steamship Co. **99,** 231
overriding rules of law **99,** 599
African customary law **41,** 144
applicable law, parties' consent, need for **97,** 550, **99,** 568
Arbitral Commission on Property, Rights and Interests in Germany **42,** 372-3, 379, 387
arbitral tribunal, basis of jurisdiction, whether **80,** 613, 647
arbitration, applicability in **50,** 3, 18, 27-30, 38-9, 41
arbitration proceedings, in **82,** 82
balancing the equities **99,** 615-17
Anglo-French Arbitration **99,** 616
Helsinki Rules on the Uses of Waters of International Rivers (1966) **99,** 616-17, **116,** 248
Jay Treaty (1794) **99,** 616
North Sea **99,** 616
Tunisia–Libya **99,** 615-16
balancing-up of relevant/special circumstances **99,** 676
boundaries, land **97,** 430-1
Frontier Dispute **97,** 430
Libya/Chad **100,** 57
boundary dispute **113,** 85
causality, application of rules relating to **109,** 236
China **41,** 144
clean hands doctrine **76,** 64, 606, 627, 726-8, **81,** 570, 576, 580. *See also* failure to do *and* like and like *below*
forcible abduction/unlawful arrest **95,** 442
forum [non] conveniens **81,** 570, 576, 580
interim measures, compliance **95,** 113
provisional measures, compliance **95,** 113
common law and civil law systems **46,** 507
compensation **56,** 429
constructive trust **81,** 592-3
continental shelf, delimitation **41,** 76, 78-82, 142, 145-51, 163, 197, **54,** 24-5, 36, 60, 67, 100, 115, 123, 194-6
contra legem **41,** 141, 144, **80,** 472
corrective, as **41,** 143
costs **81,** 31, **113,** 485, 498
damages, moral injury **95,** 314
due process and **89,** 537-8
equality and **41,** 79, 107, 123-4, 144, 147, **67,** 56-7, 143, 248-50, 292, **80,** 535, **81,** 271, 351, **99,** 555-6, 559, 664, 681, **102,** 307
North Sea Continental Shelf **80,** 535
equality of parties **81,** 351
equidistance **41,** 36, 38, 39, 44, 46-7, 53, 65, 78-80, 106, 146, 147-9, 151-2, 153-5, 177, 178, 179-82, 183-4, 193-5, 197, 216, 227, **83,** 105-6
converging equidistance lines, in case of **41,** 46-7, 79-80

equitable execution **77,** 45-50, **80,** 188, 193, 195, 217
equitable interpretation
facts **99,** 617
rule of law **99,** 617
treaty **99,** 617
equitable result **62,** 115, 125-6
equivalence **81,** 316
ex aequo et bono distinguished, **67,** 53, 284-5, 287-8, 313, **71,** 209, **77,** 676
extradition and **79,** 421
failure to do **84,** 154-5. *See also* clean hands doctrine *above*; like and like *below*
finality **81,** 316
flexibility **99,** 636
force majeure, in case of **107,** 212
forum [non] conveniens and **81,** 563
fundamental norm of **81,** 323
gap, limited to **100,** 57
general principle of international law **40,** 172, 173
general principle of law **41,** 142-7, 155, **81,** 271, **99,** 600, 604-7
'derived from the specific nature of the international community' **99,** 605
'recognized by civilized nations' **99,** 605
general principle of morality **99,** 494
general rule of international law **77,** 675
good faith **41,** 86, **42,** 145 n. 2
Greek philosophy **41,** 143
Hindu law **41,** 144
implementation
balancing the equities. *See* balancing the equities *above*
equitable interpretation. *See* equitable interpretation *above*
equitable principles
application **99,** 620-1
choice **99,** 618-19
flexibility in application of rules **99,** 618-19
judicial discretion. *See* judicial discretion *below*
infra legem **41,** 146, **80,** 472, 534-5
intergenerational rights **106,** 63-4, **110,** 405-6, 452
Islamic law **41,** 144, 209, **62,** 175
judicial discretion **67,** 53-299, **71,** 205, **72,** 209, **99,** 586, 619-20
jus cogens/peremptory norm **99,** 585
just satisfaction, equitable basis of **60,** 203
justice and **41,** 78, 106, 107, 138, 146, 163-4, **80,** 534
avoidance of injustice **80,** 578, 581
general international considerations of and **77,** 456
general principles of **40,** 159, 163
Tunisia/Libya Continental Shelf **80,** 534
justice, emanation of **80,** 535, **99,** 419, 608-10, 611-12, **116,** 248
arbitration agreements **46,** 506
Barcelona Traction **99,** 608
distributive **99,** 613, 614-15
Tunisia–Libya **99,** 615
Free Zones of Upper Savoy and the District of Gex **99,** 608
individualized **99,** 613-14
Tunisia–Libya **99,** 613
North Sea **99,** 608

equity (*cont.*)
law and **41,** 78, 87-8, 97-8, 104, 138-9, 197-8, 228, **56,** 173, **62,** 175, 209, 218, **66,** 581-2, **71,** 105, 211-16, **81,** 322-3, **86,** 279, **99,** 559, 663-6. *See also* general principle of international law *and* general principle of law *above*
civil law concept **99,** 593-4
as corrective **99,** 594
praetorian law **99,** 593-4
common law concept **99,** 592, 593
Norwegian Shipowners' Claims **99,** 593
development of, as basis for **56,** 163, 164
Diversion of the Waters of the Meuse **41,** 143-4
emanation of **81,** 271, **99,** 592-4
equity *contra legem*
Barcelona Traction **99,** 601
Diversion of Water from the Meuse **99,** 602
equity *infra legem* **99,** 600-1
equity *praeter legem* **99,** 599-600
Libya/Chad **100,** 57
North Sea **99,** 600
ex aequo et bono distinguished. *See ex aequo et bono*
flexibility in application of **99,** 617-18
Frontier Dispute **99,** 664-5
Gulf of Maine **99,** 664
international law, whether part of **46,** 259, 506, 523-4, **99,** 584-5, 608-9
abuse of rights **99,** 585
fundamental change of circumstances **99,** 585
general principle of international law **40,** 172, 173
general rule of international law **77,** 675
good faith **99,** 585
jus cogens/peremptory norm **99,** 585
North Sea **99,** 584-5, 598
pacta sunt servanda **99,** 585
unjust enrichment **99,** 585
interpretation, method of **80,** 472
Fisheries Jurisdiction **80,** 472
predictability, need for **81,** 271, 357
Tunisia–Libya **99,** 663-4
law of the sea, importance of **99,** 626-7
liability of partners **81,** 708-9
like and like **81,** 324, **99,** 555-8. *See also* clean hands doctrine *and* failure to do *above*
mediation **82,** 585-6
Member States' liability for debts of international organization **80,** 613, 661
municipal and international law distinguished **99,** 564
natural resources, equitable sharing **99,** 614-15
navigational access **94,** 25
negotiations **56,** 173, 176-7
objectivity **41,** 142
parameters **71,** 210-11
praeter legem **41,** 138, 141, 144, 146, 151, **46,** 506, **80,** 472
'praetorian subjectivism' **83,** 92
procedure **105,** 342-3
proportionality. *See* proportionality, equity, check on

protection of shareholders in foreign company **46,** 222, 258-60, 365-6, 373, 433-4, 506, 523, 524
reasonableness, relation to **41,** 142-3, **71,** 211
refashioning of nature and **41,** 79-80
result rather than method **99,** 520-1
rights
  conflicting, reconciliation of **56,** 169-70, 171
  equitable adjustment of **56,** 172, 176-7, 181-2
sources
  customary international law **99,** 586, 603-4
    Diversion of Water from the Meuse **99,** 604
    North Sea **99,** 604
  general principle of law. *See* general principle of international law *and* general principle of law *above*
  international law **41,** 138-9, **62,** 175, 209, 215, **67,** 53, 98-9
  judicial decisions **99,** 586, 607
  State practice **99,** 610
  teachings of publicists
    Aristotle **99,** 607
    Grotius **99,** 607
  treaties **99,** 586, 602-3
    Agreement governing the Activities of States on the Moon and other Celestial Bodies (1979) **99,** 614
    Charter of Economic Rights and Duties of States (1974) **99,** 603
    Continental Shelf Convention (1958) **99,** 626, 627-8
    Convention on International Liability for Damage Caused by Space Objects **99,** 602-3
    International Covenant on Economic, Social and Cultural Rights (1966) **99,** 602
    International Telecommunications Union Convention (1982) **99,** 614-15
    Jay Treaty (1794) **99,** 603
    Law of the Sea Convention (1982) **99,** 602, 628-9
    OAU, Protocol of the Commission of Mediation, Conciliation and Arbitration **99,** 603
    UN Charter **99,** 609-10
Soviet law **41,** 144
State contract and **59,** 422-3
State immunity, jurisdiction, classification of act, applicable law **113,** 527
State practice **41,** 144-6
State succession and **48,** 21
  quasi-delictual obligations **45,** 26, 31
treaty interpretation and **40,** 457-9, **110,** 771
uncertainty **99,** 622-6
  absence of mechanisms for determining **99,** 623
  ad hoc approach **99,** 625-6
  changing rules **99,** 624
  results uncrystallized **99,** 624
  scope undefined **99,** 623-4
  subjective nature **81,** 322-3, 342
universality **99,** 641-6
unjust enrichment under. *See* unjust enrichment
uses of **67,** 53-299, **71,** 205, **72,** 209, **99,** 586, 599-600, 613-15, 619-20

equity (*cont.*)
basis for specific principles **99,** 614
fairness **99,** 614
justice, emanation of. *See* justice, emanation of *above*
method, as. *See* maritime delimitation, equity, as method
***erga omnes* principle**. *See also* opposability
adversarial proceedings and **116,** 126-7
environment **110,** 81-2, **116,** 126-7, 169
foreign investment, treatment of **46,** 514, 528
genocide **46,** 206, **115,** 39, 175, 218-19
good faith negotiation **110,** 223-4
health **110,** 83
human rights conventions **115,** 56-7
ICJ proceedings, third party intervention **70,** 263, 599, 637-9, **76,** 61-4, **81,** 363, **105,** 243-4, 272-3, 313-14, 385, 389-90, 392, 393
international organizations
international personality **77,** 604
privileges and immunities **116,** 468
judicial assistance obligations **110,** 699-700
maritime delimitation **41,** 50, 57
maritime jurisdiction **99,** 468
natural resources **105,** 283, 362
self-determination **105,** 270, 283, 343, 354-7, 362, 406-7
State responsibility and **57,** 532, **76,** 63-4, **110,** 81-2, 83
territorial status **49,** 167, **70,** 637-9, **105,** 389, **114,** 33-4, 48
torture **121,** 260
treaties
human rights **115,** 56-7
negotiation in good faith **110,** 223-4
unilateral undertaking **106,** 27
Eritrea
FAO Fisheries Infrastructure Development Project Report (1995) **119,** 451
Joint Yemeni–Eritrean Committee for Bilateral Cooperation, Treaty of 16 October 1998 **119,** 492-4
Memorandum of Understanding with Yemen of 15 November 1994 **119,** 488-91
Red Sea Islands. *See* Red Sea Islands
Eritrea/Yemen Arbitration Tribunal (1998). *See also* Eritrea/Yemen Arbitration Tribunal (1999); Eritrea/Yemen boundary; Red Sea Islands
Agreement on Principles (21 May 1996)
Arbitration Agreement (3 October 1996), primacy **114,** 29-30
interpretation
context **114,** 30
object and purpose **114,** 30
ordinary meaning **114,** 30
'respective positions of the two Parties' **114,** 30
applicable law
equitable principles **114,** 36
historic titles **114,** 35-6, 37-8
Islamic **114,** 42, 45, **119,** 448
maritime law, applicability to land boundaries **114,** 35-7
principles, rules and practices of international law applicable in the matter **114,** 35, 117
'without prejudice' clause **114,** 34

dispute
critical date **114,** 26-30
scope of dispute **114,** 26-30
applicable law **114,** 29-30
task
'award on territorial sovereignty' **114,** 34-5
common or divided sovereignty, possibility of **114,** 35
award which will 'allow the re-establishment and development of a trustful and lasting cooperation between the two countries' **114,** 137
definition of the scope of dispute **114,** 26

Eritrea/Yemen Arbitration Tribunal (1999)
applicable law, Law of the Sea Convention (1982) **119,** 457-8, 460-1
expert, designation **119,** 425
parties' arguments
fishing in the Red Sea **119,** 436-9
proportionality **119,** 432-3
proposed boundary line **119,** 426-30
sovereignty **119,** 431-2
pertinent factors. *See* relevant/special circumstances *below*
relevant/special circumstances. *See also* applicable law *above*
Tribunal's opinion on territorial sovereignty **119,** 457
task, delimitation of maritime boundaries **119,** 456, 464
two-stage nature of process, relevance **119,** 449-50, 475-81

Eritrea/Yemen boundary. *See also* Red Sea Islands
as determined by Tribunal **119,** 456-67
islands, relevance **119,** 445
median line **114,** 114, 131-2, **119,** 443-6, 453-65
absence of special factors requiring variation **119,** 464
equity **119,** 464
proportionality **119,** 465-6

erosion. *See also* accretion; alluvion; avulsion
avulsion distinguished **97,** 462
low-tide elevations **100,** 133
rivers **91,** 196, 458, **97,** 462
of title **97,** 594-5

espionage 42, 451, 465, 466, 468-9, **52,** 493, 503, **58,** 448, **83,** 190, 191
aerial **47,** 109-12
customary international law **94,** 74, 77, 78
equality of treatment, national acting within borders and non-national acting abroad **94,** 75
FRG/GDR Unification Treaty (1990) **94,** 76, 77
Geneva Convention (Protection of Civilian Persons in Time of War) (Convention IV) (1949) **83,** 190, 191
jurisdiction
lex loci delicti commissi **94,** 73
protective principle **94,** 74
liability to prosecution for acts carried out in third country **94,** 72-82
absence of human rights violations as mitigating factor **94,** 81
enforceability **94,** 75, 79
recommendation for legislation exempting **94,** 80-2
occupied territory, in **83,** 191
peacetime
customary international law **94,** 74

espionage (*cont.*)
Hague Regulations (1907), non-applicability **94,** 76
international law regulation **94,** 74, 75
lawful nature **94,** 74
right of prosecution **94,** 75
treaty regulation **94,** 74
political offence, whether **55,** 573
prevention of legitimate State interest **94,** 74-5
member of alliance, extension to **94,** 74
prisoners of war **42,** 451, 465, 466, 468-9, **52,** 503
State succession and **94,** 76-9
failure to agree treatment of espionage as breach of responsibility **94,** 81-2
time of war **52,** 503
establishment, freedom of. *See* freedom of establishment
Estonia (pre-1918)
applicable law **72,** 440-2
German occupation, effect of **72,** 444-5
Estonia (1918-40)
property post-1940
renunciation of Soviet claims **85,** 56
rights to **85,** 59
title **85,** 56-7, 60
Provisional Government, legislative enactments of **72,** 442
recognition, State (1919) **85,** 55
de facto and de jure, distinguishable, whether **85,** 59-60
UK **85,** 55, 57-8, 59, 62
USA **85,** 55
USSR **85,** 55
status **72,** 439, 441-2, **85,** 55
USSR's renunciation of sovereignty (1918) **72,** 439, 441-2
Estonia (1940-89)
annexation by USSR **85,** 55, 58
recognition
de facto **85,** 55, 56
de jure **85,** 55, 59
diplomatic mission in UK **85,** 55-6
diplomatic premises in UK, maintenance **85,** 62
diplomatic relations **85,** 56
occupation by Germany **72,** 444-5, **85,** 55
status **85,** 57, 61
estoppel. *See also* acquiescence; doctrine of acknowledgment; legitimate expectation; preclusion; prescription
acknowledgement
of child's birth **81,** 63, 65, 66, 70
of expropriation/nationalization **85,** 436, 463
acquiescence and **41,** 130, **71,** 131-2, **100,** 75-6, 79. *See also* acquiescence
of *alter ego* **71,** 131
distinction **83,** 69
acts amounting to
agreement following negotiations **97,** 466-7
agreement not to bring court proceedings **118,** 395, 400, 406-7, 410
conduct of parties **41,** 55-6, **63,** 56, **67,** 77, 299, **71,** 134, 136, **72,** 136, **81,** 445-6, **113,** 60, 192, **120,** 231
discontinuance of litigation **46,** 35-6

exhaustion of local remedies, failure to raise issue. *See* exhaustion of local remedies, estoppel
failure to challenge **91,** 286, **100,** 75-81
boundary demarcation **80,** 304-5, 306, 307
standing of party **120,** 249-50, 254-6, 315-16, 350-2
failure to protest **71,** 133-5, **113,** 119, 120, 219-23. *See also* acquiescence, protest
failure to raise issue
avulsion, failure to raise **97,** 466-7
legality **117,** 562
failure to warn of problems **89,** 623-4
official maps, publication of **38,** 77, 137
part performance **117,** 563
per rem judicatem **43,** 51, 57-8
signed agreement **37,** 187
simultaneous pursuit of alternative remedies **106,** 523
South Africa Mandate, acceptance as treaty **37,** 93
State succession, acts of predecessor **50,** 4
acts of private persons, responsibility of government for **46,** 35
Alaskan Boundary case **100,** 79
boundaries, successor State, acts of predecessor **50,** 4
breach of contract
approval of changes **106,** 609-12, 615
contributory fault **114,** 179
by agency **87,** 639
in case of reasonable belief in authorization **66,** 72-4, 131-2, 179, **77,** 155
collateral, requirements **72,** 660-2
fairness **79,** 382-3
contradiction between party's claims **113,** 131-4, **120,** 255
court's right to examine new facts **108,** 460
customary international law **100,** 75
definition **86,** 606-7, **113,** 129-30, 133
municipal law distinguished **38,** 77
Delagoa Bay Arbitration **100,** 79
diplomatic correspondence **38,** 77-9
diplomatic protection **46,** 359
duty of discovery **108,** 499-502
Eastern Greenland **80,** 556, **100,** 77
equitable principle **99,** 587
before the European Court of Human Rights **81,** 221, **86,** 337-88
failure to raise issue **56,** 341, **103,** 637-8
evidence, requirement to produce **79,** 64-5, 126
forclusion **80,** 556
foreign legislation, parties' knowledge of **81,** 438-40
general principle of international law **100,** 65-6
good faith and **55,** 5, **75,** 119-20, **83,** 69, **89,** 401, **106,** 523, **117,** 562, **120,** 230-1
Grisbadarna Arbitration **100,** 79
informal service of documents **103,** 365-6
international law
general principle of **38,** 76, **100,** 75-6
municipal law distinguished **69,** 595-6, **91,** 423
substantive rule of **44,** 266
international organization, staff circular **36,** 438, 442, 443
Island of Palmas **100,** 79

estoppel (*cont.*)
jurisdiction, relevance to **89,** 399-400
matter of law **105,** 578
parties' representations as to non-acceptance of **76,** 124-6, 175, 176
law
general principle of **41,** 130, 142, **113,** 133-4
substantive rule of **44,** 266
Muslim law **41,** 130
necessity **116,** 55
North Sea Fisheries **100,** 77-81
oppression/vexation and **118,** 412
preclusion distinguished **71,** 132, **83,** 69
procedural default **118,** 5, 6, 27-9, 33-4, 36, 40, 41
promissory, employment contract **84,** 441
reciprocity as basis **80,** 556
requirements
authorized statement **122,** 338-9
reasonable belief in authorization **66,** 72-4, 131-2, 179, **77,** 155
clear and unambiguous statement **122,** 338-9
conduct running counter to present claim **116,** 124-5
detriment/prejudice **41,** 112, **71,** 131-2, **75,** 119-20, **89,** 400-1, **97,** 239, **113,** 133, **116,** 124-5, **120,** 249-50, **122,** 338-9
knowledge **71,** 132, 135, **82,** 21
public **77,** 668
reliance upon representation **86,** 45, **97,** 239, **116,** 125
voluntary statement **122,** 338-9
res judicata and **68,** 614, **79,** 67
State, representation of and **89,** 12-13
State contract and **89,** 401, **117,** 562-3
State immunity, jurisdiction and **64,** 120-1, 135, **103,** 309
statutory limitation **103,** 550
tax credit, practice of payment to foreign government **103,** 335-6
Temple of Preah Vihear **38,** 76-7, **80,** 556, **100,** 78-9
territorial title **50,** 100, 410
acts falling short **52,** 221
treaties
acceptance of provisions **41,** 54-6, 129
applicability and **41,** 55, 129
compromis **120,** 231, 255
letter interpreting **105,** 55
reservation, possibility of and **41,** 55
termination for causes related to one's own breach **116,** 76, 94, 95, 221-2, 243
validity **44,** 203, 266, 285, **84,** 663 n. 3, 664, 665 n. 1
Ethiopia
expropriation measures (1975) **86,** 47-52
compensation **86,** 47
law of, Commercial Code **90,** 600
Art. 341, share transfers **66,** 482
territorial sea, primacy of International Law of the Sea Convention (1982) **119,** 458
ethnic cleansing. *See* genocide, ethnic cleansing
ethnicity, status as 'protected person' under Geneva Conventions (1949) and **122,** 58-60

EU. *See* European Union (EU)
Eurocontrol (European Organization for the Safety of Air Navigation). *See also* Air Navigation Safety Organization for Africa and Madagascar
'agent or instrumentality of foreign State' **107,** 324-8
charge-fixing
Member State's right to challenge **111,** 501-2
publication of charges distinguished **111,** 501-2
responsibility for, Consultative Economic Commission **111,** 501-2
EC competition rules, applicability **101,** 15-22, 25-9
employment contract
applicable law
administrative law **94,** 335-6
international administrative law **94,** 332-3
fonctionnaire international **94,** 336
unilateral nature **94,** 335-6
General Conditions of Employment
Art. 2 **94,** 336
Art. 92(1) **94,** 334, 336, 337, 338
Art. 93(1) **94,** 334, 336-8
immunity, jurisdiction **74,** 191-3
immunity, jurisdiction, waiver **94,** 333
seizure and detention of aircraft in settlement of bill **107,** 338-9
jurisdiction
ILO Administrative Tribunal **94,** 333, 334
accessibility **94,** 338
municipal courts **94,** 334, 336
diversity **94,** 336-7
tribunal, power to establish **94,** 338
legal status **74,** 192-3
privileges and immunities **107,** 322-46
agreement of parties determining factor **94,** 333
customary international law **94,** 338
Eurocontrol Convention, failure to prescribe **94,** 337
functional **94,** 333, 338, **101,** 18
sovereignty, transfer to **94,** 335, 337-8, **101,** 19-21, 25-9
jurisdiction and **94,** 337-8
staff contract claims **74,** 191-3
Staff Regulations
French text, primacy **94,** 335
'in the absence of a competent national jurisdiction' **94,** 334, 336-7
ordinary courts, ouster of jurisdiction **74,** 693
'personnel' **94,** 334
status **83,** 269, **94,** 332, 335
Statute
Art. 13(3)(a) **94,** 336
Art. 14 **94,** 338
United States, nexus **107,** 345-6
Eurofima
privileges and immunities **65,** 402-4
status **65,** 402-4
European Atomic Energy Community (Euratom)
Commission

European Atomic Energy Community (*cont.*)
delay in proceeding against defaulting government **48,** 217, 221
supply agreements, exclusive power to make **48,** 217-26
Cooperation Agreements, USA (1958) **48,** 224
Dragon project, UK Agreements on **44,** 410-11, 414, 419-22
Nuclear Material, Convention on the Physical Protection of (1980). *See* Nuclear Material, Convention on the Physical Protection of (1980)
officials
income tax and **44,** 409-22
status **60,** 502, 504, 509-10
recognition **60,** 502, 504, 509-10
supply agreements, Commission's exclusive right to make **48,** 217-26
transfer of powers to Euratom **48,** 222-3
treaty-making powers. *See* European Community treaties, treaty-making powers; nuclear energy exploitation; Nuclear Material, Convention on the Physical Protection of (1980)
European Atomic Energy Community Treaty (EAEC Treaty) (1957) 60, 502, 504, 507
amendment, proposal for **48,** 219
annual reports, duty to submit **48,** 219, 223
Art. 76, purpose **48,** 222
breach **48,** 217-26
competence, mixed **99,** 319-22
default, procedure for declaration of **48,** 220-2, 225
interpretation **60,** 502, 504
nuclear common market, community competence, exclusive **99,** 312, 314
ownership of nuclear material **99,** 316-18
ratification, French Constitution and **44,** 192-6
reservations, national requirements relating to access to nuclear material **99,** 314
safeguards, uncertainty relating to **99,** 315-16
European citizenship
national identities, preservation of **98,** 263
voting rights **98,** 263
European Coal and Steel Community (ECSC). *See also* European Coal and Steel Community Treaty (1951)
coal trade regulations, compatibility with European Convention on Human Rights (1950) **55,** 461-3, 467
decisions. *See* European Commission Decisions
dispute settlement procedures **47,** 411
external relations, authority to enter into **47,** 300
French steel industry (1966 measures) **47,** 406-11
independent legal order **93,** 521-2
Member States, duty of Cooperation **47,** 406
petroleum products **117,** 313, 329
transport rates rules, legislative status **44,** 292-4
European Coal and Steel Community Treaty (1951)
aims **55,** 481
coal export regulations, penalties for breaches **55,** 469
constitutional amendment, need for **93,** 521-2
discrimination, prohibition **55,** 461-7, 479
Treaty of Rome (1957), effect **99,** 216
European Commission
abuse of power **47,** 1-2, 5-7
acts of, effect **62,** 439-40

competence **44,** 393-402, **47,** 1-2, 7-9, **55,** 481, **59,** 6, **62,** 433, 443
competition rules **48,** 106-36
ensuring compliance with Community law **53,** 563
Euratom supply agreements **48,** 217-26
Regulations **59,** 400-2, 480-2
treaty-making power **47,** 279, **101,** 47-57, 63-7
Council and, duty of Cooperation **47,** 310
independent and impartial tribunal established by law, whether **111,** 135
judicial review of **47,** 280, 281, 289, 290-1, 305, 307-8, 406-11, **111,** 114-15
obligations, protection of Community's financial interests **113,** 404
procedural requirements, violation **47,** 1-2, 5, 8
European Commission Decisions
93/235/ECSC (ECSC/FRY trade) **117,** 308, 310, 313
16 December 1969 concerning the Gradual Harmonisation of Agreements concerning Commercial Relations between the Member States and Third Countries and the Negotiation of Community Agreements in this field (OJEC, L 326 of 29 December 1969) **77,** 437
29 September 1970 (OJEC, L 225 of 12 October 1970) **77,** 437
25 October 1971 (OJEC, L 248 of 9 November 1971) **77,** 437
10 September 1976 regarding Direct Elections to the European Assembly **74,** 527-9
2131/88/ECSC (anti-dumping duty on steel products 'originating in Yugoslavia') **117,** 340, 342, 355
applicability to the Former Yugoslav Republic of Macedonia **117,** 340-62
legal certainty and **117,** 348-51, 360-1
2177/84 (anti-dumping measures under GATT Article VI) **117,** 340-1, 354-5
2297/92/ECSC (amendment to Decision 2131/88/ECSC) **117,** 343, 347, 356
2424/88/ECSC (anti-dumping measures under GATT Article VI) **117,** 354-5
2767/86/ECSC (duties on products originating in Yugoslavia) **117,** 342, 355
annulment, grounds **47,** 1-2, 5-9
limitation period **48,** 112, 117, 119, 123, 126-7, 135-6
transfer of sovereignty, whether involving **74,** 528-9
validity **55,** 480
European Commission of Human Rights 62, 360-5, 375. *See also* European Convention on Human Rights (1950); European Court of Human Rights
admissibility **56,** 299, 323, 389-90, 392, 393, 394, 473-4, **61,** 297, **62,** 24-71, 299, **67,** 408-9, 459-60, 540, **68,** 73, 103, **71,** 307-9, 377, 401-4, **72,** 359, 397, 424, **73,** 426, 453, 469, 474, 489, 505, 525, 557, **74,** 369, **75,** 375-7, 380, 412, 479, 575, **78,** 203, 220, 238, 267, 318, 365, 374, **81,** 41, 82, 120, 164, 194, 219, 229. *See also* competence *below*; European Court of Human Rights, admissibility
abuse of procedure **62,** 37, 59-60
appeal against decision on **78,** 324
complaints not included in application **47,** 170-1, 172, 177, 179, 187-8
consideration of application, whether amounting to **71,** 308, **79,** 270, 271, 275
decisions of European institutions whose membership consists largely of Parties to Convention, European Patent Office **111,** 145-6
exhaustion of local remedies. *See* exhaustion of local remedies *below*; European Convention on Human Rights (1950), exhaustion of local remedies
grounds **81,** 219-20
manifestly ill-founded applications **71,** 307, 309
non bis in idem **62,** 34-5, 55, 63-4, 69, 80-1
power to determine **56,** 473
proceedings before organs of non-Party to Convention, European Communities **111,** 139-41

European Commission of Human Rights (*cont.*)
six-month rule **56,** 486-7, **62,** 59, **75,** 376-7, **79,** 269, 271, 275. *See also* time-limits *below*
continuing state of affairs **62,** 58-9
standing. *See* standing *below*
time-limits **62,** 35-6, 58-9, 76, 79-80. *See also* six-month rule *above*
commencement **62,** 35
continuing violation **62,** 58, 79-80
domestic remedies and **62,** 70, 80
United Nations, Human Rights Committee, effect of communication to **71,** 307-9
applications **56,** 419-20, **61,** 298, 299-300, 323, **62,** 9-11
individual **56,** 408, **74,** 475, **78,** 377-8, 381, 382-8
injured party **67,** 392, **70,** 318
inter-State **56,** 408, **62,** 55, 74, 80, 84, 87-8
abuse of procedure **62,** 82
domestic remedies and **62,** 76, 87
joinder **78,** 319
manifestly ill-founded **71,** 307, 309
substantial similarity of **62,** 34-5, 37-8, 44, 55-6, 63-4, 69, 81, **71,** 402
ultra petita rule **61,** 327-8, 380-1, 385
victim **61,** 298-9, 347-8, **67,** 410-11, 425-31, **68,** 73-6, 82, 84, 110-11
discontinuance of domestic proceedings **68,** 75-6, 84
mitigation of sentence **68,** 74-6, 82
prejudice, relevance of **68,** 74-6, 82, 110
Committee of Ministers, Report to **47,** 176
competence **56,** 395, **61,** 298-300, 323, **71,** 378-9
claim for compensation **41,** 294, 307
detention after Application filed **41,** 344, 351-2
ratione loci **62,** 27-34, 44, 55, 64-6, 70, 74-6, 85-7
treaties, other than European Convention on Human Rights (1950) **111,** 152, 158-9
duty to petitioner **41,** 445
ex officio examination of issue **71,** 377-9, 389-90, **78,** 285
jurisdiction, whether exceeds **71,** 378-9, 389-90
legal proceedings, whether **78,** 382-8
exhaustion of local remedies
absence of domestic remedy **93,** 615
Commission's duty to enquire **78,** 285
interlocutory injunction proceedings **100,** 426
need to raise defence in good time **92,** 283
fact-finding role **41,** 344, 345, **95,** 333-9, 354
findings, Court's right to make own assessment **108,** 460, **111,** 290-1, **120,** 50, 51
functions. *See* role *below*
'indications' not legal obligation **78,** 394
interim measures **78,** 374, 390-4. *See also* European Convention on Human Rights (1950), interim measures; Rules of Procedure, 36 (interim measures) *below*
binding force **108,** 317-18, 319-20
procedure **108,** 305
requirements
irreparable damage, relevance **108,** 317, 320
obstruction of effective exercise of right of petition **108,** 318, 320
prima facie case **108,** 317, 320
stay of execution **111,** 262
jurisdiction. *See* competence *above*; role *below*

jurisdictional immunity
members **41,** 438-51
Secretary **41,** 438-51
members
jurisdictional immunity **41,** 438-51
omissions, for **41,** 445
waiver **41,** 445
non-judicial character **45,** 132
observations **67,** 390-1, 439
opinions **67,** 409, 468, 490, 540, **71,** 377, 402, 419, **72,** 359, 397, 425, **73,** 425-6, 453, 469, 471, 474-5, 489, 505, 525, 528, 557, 639, **74,** 370, **75,** 412, 518-61, 575, 588-95, **78,** 202-3, 220, 238, 266-7, 285, 318
dissenting **75,** 557-61
petitions. *See* applications *above*
powers. *See* competence *above*; role *below*
proceedings **62,** 300, 334-5, **67,** 459-60, 490-1, 505-6, 516, 540, **68,** 73, 103-4, 138, **71,** 368, 376-7, 379, 396, 401-2, 414-15, 419, **72,** 324, 337, 359-60, 397, 424-5, **73,** 419-26, 453, 488-9, 505, 525, 556-7, 639, **75,** 479-80, 518-61, 575, **78,** 202-3, 220, 238, 266-7, 285, 318
'legal', whether **78,** 382-8
purpose **61,** 308-9
report of **45,** 127-9, 139
role **45,** 132, 140, 275, **56,** 349, 350, 369, 388-9, 395, 400, **75,** 377. *See also* competence *above*
assessment of compatibility of court's discretionary decision under Convention **96,** 616
European Court of Human Rights, reference to, preliminary objections, effect **45,** 118, 133
fact-finding. *See* fact-finding role *above*
petitions to the Secretary-General of the Council of Europe, to accept **78,** 377-8
review of application of national law by national courts **73,** 425
Rules of Procedure
36 (interim measures) **108,** 305-7, 342, **111,** 262
compliance **108,** 306, 313, 316-18, 319-20
termination of indication **108,** 307
sampling methodology **109,** 69-70
Secretary, jurisdictional immunity **41,** 438-51
standing
applicant government **62,** 9, 24-7, 37, 62, 67, 69, 71-4, 83-5
child of parent denied access **96,** 628
State application. *See* applications, inter-State *above*
State submissions **62,** 12-71, **73,** 419-21, 424, 471
request for **78,** 374
views **72,** 325, 337-8, 398, 401, **73,** 433-5, 447
European Community (EC).[v] *See also* European Coal and Steel Community (ECSC); European Community law; European Community treaties; European Court of Justice (ECJ); European Economic Community (EEC); European Economic Community Treaty (Rome) (1957); European Parliament; European Union (EU); fundamental rights within the EC/EU
act of government, immunity for, whether **96,** 220-1

[v] Including EEC, EC and EU arrangements, distinction being drawn only where there has been an identified change of law or practice.

European Community (EC) (*cont.*)
agricultural market **62,** 431-4, 440-1, 443
country of origin **62,** 97-8, 102-5
organization **62,** 99
refund system **62,** 92-5, 99, 102-6
anti-dumping measures **48,** 212-13
geographical ambit
change of name, effect **117,** 358-9
change of political boundaries, effect **117,** 346-7, 358-9
State succession and **117,** 346-7, 359-60
international law consequences **117,** 347
purpose **117,** 346
State debt, whether **117,** 347, 360
transaction between States, whether **117,** 347, 360
antitrust rules, enforcement **73,** 303-4, 312, 317, 333, 343-4, 353-5
Commission, acts of, Regulations, binding nature **59,** 484-5
common action in other organizations **47,** 294-5
common agricultural market. *See* agricultural market *above*
common commercial policy
broad concept **99,** 365
CFSP considerations **117,** 516-18, 540-2
common agricultural policy and **105,** 211-12
development aid **99,** 363-6
ECJ jurisprudence **99,** 362
non-restrictive interpretation **105,** 202
general economic policy as matter of national interest **99,** 366-8
international agreements on safety, whether **105,** 205-7
national measures and **100,** 283, **117,** 463-4, 540-2
Community authorization, need for **117,** 518, 530
effectiveness principle (*effet utile*) **117,** 520-1
flexibility in implementation of Security Council Resolutions **117,** 466-7
national measures and. *See also* uniform application, need for *below*
payments for exports to third countries and
economic sanctions and **117,** 518-28, 542-7
GATT provisions distinguished **117,** 520
political importance of subject-matter, relevance **99,** 367
price stabilization as instrument **99,** 362, 365
trade in services **105,** 202-7
commercial presence **105,** 204-5
consumption abroad **105,** 204-5
cross-frontier supplies **105,** 204-5, 207
natural persons within Community **105,** 204-5
UN trade embargo obligations and **117,** 388, 463-7, 492-4, 516-18, 550-1
Art. 228a basis **117,** 517-18
uniform application, need for **100,** 283-4, 298, 299-300. *See also* national measures and *above*
Uruguay Round **105,** 106-21, 202-12
common market
in coal **55,** 461-8, 473-5, 478
prohibition of internal import taxes **47,** 17
common transport policy
agreements with other States **47,** 283-6, 294-8

European Laying-up Fund for Inland Waterway Vessels, draft agreement (1957). *See* European Laying-up Fund for Inland Waterway Vessels, draft agreement (1957)
incomplete **105,** 214-15
International Convention as impediment **105,** 214-15, 216-17
Convention establishing freedom of navigation for non-EC member **99,** 284
community competence. *See also* competence *below*; European Commission; European-Community treaties, competence
co-extensiveness with Member States' authority under international law **120,** 626-7
'maritime waters coming within the jurisdiction of' a Member State **120,** 626
common commercial policy
commodity agreements **99,** 327-72
exclusive **99,** 214-16
financing by Member States, relevance **99,** 370, **105,** 198
financing from Community budget, relevance **99,** 352, 368-70
GATS **105,** 158-9
Member State responsibility for implementation, relevance **99,** 215
Natural Rubber Agreement (1979). *See* Natural Rubber Agreement (1979)
OECD Convention on harmonization of grant aid for exports **99,** 212-15
'without prejudice' Council decision on composition of delegation, relevance **99,** 352-3
common fisheries policy **113,** 344-81
conservation measures **113,** 365-7, 378-9
FAO Agreement to promote compliance with international conservation measures **113,** 351-5
fishing licences **113,** 379-80
registration and flagging of vessels **113,** 366-7, 379–80
common position, need for **113,** 368
continental shelf **120,** 626-7
external relations, functional relation with common rules within EC as basis **99,** 223, **105,** 213-15
FAO, Member State representation **113,** 344-9
fishery conservation **99,** 221-68
high seas **99,** 263
freedom of establishment. *See* freedom of establishment *below*
implied powers **105,** 121-47
powers of internal regulation **105,** 213-15, 216-17
inherent, whether **48,** 111, 116, 117, 119, 123
Law of the Sea Convention (1982) and **120,** 630-1
marine pollution **120,** 630-1
Member States' right to vote **113,** 368
obligation to co-operate **105,** 222-4, **113,** 380-1
problems arising from exercise, relevance **105,** 222-3
provisional allocation **113,** 364-5
retaliation measures **105,** 224
subsidiarity **105,** 173-4
'thrust of the issue' **113,** 368
treaties. *See* European Community treaties
treaty-making power. *See* European Community treaties, treaty-making power
WTO
implementation measures **105,** 159-60
joint participants **105,** 149-52, 186-91
Community institutions, sovereignty, extension by ECJ **93,** 447, 457-9

European Community (EC) (*cont.*)
competence. *See also* community competence *above*
Council of Ministers, primacy **93,** 489
mixed **105,** 153-4, 173-83, 187-91, **111,** 55-6, 110-11
obligation to co-operate **105,** 223-4
respect for fundamental rights, effect on **112,** 365
competition
abuse of dominant position **60,** 403, 405-7
applicable law, place of implementation **96,** 196
block exemption **48,** 141-2
concerted practices **48,** 106, 108, 123, 124, 127-34
concerted practices and **60,** 403-4, 407
customs duties and equivalent taxes. *See* customs duties and quotas *below*
distortion of trade within EC and **96,** 152-3
EC Free Trade Agreements and **96,** 19-92, 153-4, 199-200
cumulative **96,** 190-1
exclusive concession agreement **48,** 137-43
exclusive dealing contract **44,** 393-408, **45,** 460-1
extraterritorial application **48,** 106-44
foreign corporation and **63,** 117
impairment **48,** 140
individual's rights **62,** 401-7
information, right to **62,** 406-7, 413
legal remedies **62,** 404, 407
limits on **55,** 482-4
national laws and **44,** 393-402, **47,** 11-13
prohibited agreements, nullity **48,** 142
rules
limitation period **48,** 127
parties outside EC **96,** 152-3, 195-7
procedure **48,** 125-7
trade between Member States **48,** 134, 140, 141
Council of Ministers
Commission and, duty of Cooperation **47,** 310
Decisions. *See also* European Commission Decisions; European Council Decisions
as 'act of government' **96,** 222
form of **47,** 292-3
judicial review of acts of **47,** 280, 281, 289, 290-1, 305, 410
legal certainty, need for **47,** 410
time-limits **47,** 290, 307-8, 406-11
primacy **93,** 489
Regulations. *See* European Council Regulations
salaries, determination **56,** 576-7
Council Regulation (EC) No 3697/93 (withdrawal of tariff concessions in respect of Austria)
nature of measure **113,** 333-4
validity **113,** 298-338
countervailing charge **62,** 429, 432-4, 436-8, 443
customs duties and quotas **62,** 431, 435-7, 441
abolition **47,** 15-21
charges having equivalent effect **62,** 431, 436-7, 441-2, 445
Common Customs Tariff **53,** 158
customs duty, charge having equivalent effect **113,** 333-4

declaration, effect **93,** 433-4
democratic deficit
  European basis of politics and **98,** 210, 219
  lack of EC legislature **98,** 209, 211-12, 223, 224
  national parliaments, role **98,** 209, 223, 228-9, 245
  transparency of decision-making, need for **98,** 223-4
dependent territory, as non-member **105,** 196-7
deportation and **86,** 333
economic sanctions. *See also relevant European Council Regulations*
  basis, Art. 28a **117,** 517-18
  common commercial policy and. *See* common commercial policy, UN trade embargo obligations and *above*
environmental policy
  Convention on Biodiversity (1992) and **120,** 69
  environmental impact assessments (EIAs), directives 85/337/EEC and 97/11/EEC **120,** 629-30
  Habitats Directive. *See* Habitats Directive (92/43/EEC)
  precautionary principle **106,** 65-6
European Convention on Human Rights (1950) and **93,** 429, 433-4, 435, 615-22
  challenge in European Court of Human Rights **123,** 13, 22
external relations, responsibility for **47,** 278-311
fish quotas. *See* European Community (EC), fish quotas; European Economic Community (EEC) fisheries policy
fisheries licensing system **74,** 143, 145-8
fishing regulations **59,** 480-2, 484-8
fishing rights, Icelandic waters **55,** 374-5
foreign relations. *See also* European Union Treaty (Maastricht) (1992); Single European Act (1986)
  judicial review **96,** 213-23
    Member States' law **96,** 215-21
free movement of goods **60,** 406
free movement of workers **38,** 261-4, **40,** 289-92, **56,** 536, **60,** 252-3, 268-9, 271, 279, **62,** 390, 399, 409-11, 413
  directives relating to **62,** 393-7, 400-5, 410
  discretionary **62,** 391, 393-5, 399-401, 407, 412, 415
  extradition and **85,** 88-90
  individuals, procedural rights **62,** 391, 401
  limitations **62,** 391
    discrimination against foreigners and **62,** 395-7
    economic ends, not to serve **62,** 391, 406-7
    individual, personal conduct of, determining factor **62,** 393, 396, 398, 401, 406-7, 412-13
    judicial review and **62,** 391-414
    justified, whether **62,** 391, 395, 401-7, 412-16
    legislation, whether limited to **62,** 381, 399, 407, 412, 415
    national authority, at discretion of **62,** 391, 393-5, 399-401, 407, 412, 415
  public policy and **62,** 390-1, 399, 410
    economic ends **62,** 391, 406-7
  Regulation 38 **47,** 249-51
  territorial scope **62,** 391-2, 394, 397, 399, 405, 408
  trade union rights and **62,** 393, 396-9, 403, 406-7
    non-nationals' rights and **62,** 396-8
  Universal Declaration of Human Rights and **60,** 268

European Community (EC) (*cont.*)
free-at-frontier price **62,** 431-2
freedom of establishment **82,** 145
community competence **105,** 215-20
community preference **105,** 160-8
European Council's general programme **93,** 758-9
'establishment' **93,** 769
link with territory, need for **93,** 768-72
non-discrimination **93,** 42, 44, 83-4, 478-80
right to establish agencies **93,** 767, 771
residence requirement, effect **93,** 771
supply of services distinguished **93,** 770
third-country nationals **105,** 168-73
freedom of movement **81,** 147
extradition, effect on **114,** 419-21, 460-2
nationality requirement for public service **113,** 282-5
freedom to provide services (Art. 59)
freedom to receive services distinguished **93,** 479
qualifying activity **93,** 765
fundamental principles **62,** 394-6, 402
GATT, effect within **77,** 555-6
GDR and **62,** 99, 103
Protocol on Inner-German Trade **62,** 93, 97-8, 103
Guidelines on Recognition of New States in Eastern Europe and the Soviet Union (1991) **92,** 173-4, 179-80, 183, 187, 189, 208, 210
harmonization, legal systems **62,** 411
ILO, membership, exclusion from **99,** 379, 380, 388
immunity **77,** 98
immunity, jurisdiction, waiver **113,** 399-400
acknowledgment of receipt of attachment order **113,** 409
clear and unambiguous **113,** 399-400
duty of **113,** 404
international practice **113,** 399
individuals. *See* European Community law, individual
institutions. *See also* Council of Ministers *above*; European Commission; European Council
control of **62,** 395, 402, 412
intellectual property rights
Community competence **105,** 207-12, 220-2
harmonization of national laws **105,** 208-9
incomplete **105,** 220-1
international agreements relating to **105,** 207-12
EC treaties with non-Members **105,** 211-12
international law, subject of **48,** 116, 117, 119
international organizations
direct effect of non-Community law **99,** 288
enforcement mechanisms, potential conflict **99,** 289-91
membership of
common policy and **99,** 286-7
Member State participation in decision-making organs **99,** 286-7
parallel EC/Member State membership **99,** 285, 286-7
International Tin Council and, responsibility for acts of **96,** 225-30
judicial protection. *See* fundamental rights within the EC/EU

jurisdiction
  effects doctrine
    Art. 85 of Treaty of Rome **96,** 175-6, 179
    Beguelin **96,** 176
    competition law, applicability to **96,** 177
    Dyestuffs **96,** 176
    existence of infringement and jurisdiction distinguished **96,** 175-6, 186-7
    international law, conformity with, need for **96,** 177
    Walrave v. *Union cycliste internationale* **96,** 176-7
  Member States and
    demarcation **93,** 357
    independent competencies **93,** 532-5
    substitution of EC **96,** 179
  territorial **96,** 187, 196, **117,** 315
    aircraft found in territory of Member State **117,** 315
    ship found in territory of Member State **117,** 315, 330
Kompetenz/Kompetenz **98,** 229-35
law. *See* European Community law
legislative powers, residuary provision **47,** 286-7, 299, 310
levy **62,** 444
Luxembourg agreement (1966), 'very important national interests' **46,** 444
meat market. *See* agricultural market *above*
Member States. *See also* Council of Ministers *above*
  GATT, relation to **53,** 42-3, 46
  independent action, right of **123,** 337, 340
  joint action by, Community action distinguished **47,** 287, 293, 309
  legislation, possible effect on **78,** 463
    rights **62,** 401
  powers
    margin of appreciation **60,** 269, 272-3, 278-9
    right of entry **60,** 250-1, 256, 269, 271-3
  sovereignty, effect of membership **70,** 41
migrant workers **82,** 112, 114. *See also* free movement of workers *above*
monopolies
  Directive 5-1/72 **93,** 316-17, 324-8, 333-6
  non-discrimination **93,** 43, 45
movement certificates, issue
  cooperation between customs authorities, need for **100,** 273-4, 277-8, 297
  'customs authorities of the exporting State' **100,** 265, 273
  phytosanitary certificates distinguished **100,** 272-3, 284-5
  Turkish Republic of Northern Cyprus (TRNC) **100,** 263-303
    Commission practice **100,** 269-70, 282, 297
    dependability of procedures, relevance **100,** 266, 277, 285-6
    impediment caused by TRNC **100,** 267, 286
    impediment to export through Republic of Cyprus (ROC) **100,** 266, 271-2, 285-6
    impossibility of obtaining certificate from Republic of Cyprus (ROC) **100,** 266, 294
    Member State practice **100,** 270, 282-3, 297, 299
    obligation to accept **100,** 266
    recognition of TRNC, acceptance as **100,** 276, 284
    validity **100,** 266, 269-70, 295-300
nationality

European Community (EC) (*cont.*)
equality of treatment **92,** 370
right to determine
persons **93,** 785-6
ships. *See* European Community (EC), ships, nationality
natural law and **55,** 469, 481-4
new legal order **93,** 28, 30-1, 219-20, 224, 263, 361, 388-90, 520
contractual basis **111,** 62-3
European Parliament and **93,** 347
independence of national and EC systems **93,** 219-20, 361, 385, 396, 516, 520, 522, 524, 533-4, **98,** 248
international law, effect on precedence **100,** 142
jurisdictional implications **93,** 30-1, 38-9, 520-1
protection of individual **111,** 62-3
transfer of sovereign rights and **93,** 361, 555
New Zealand imports **74,** 260, 264, 269-70, 273
non-discrimination **93,** 580. *See also* European Community treaties,non-discrimination
difference of treatment by Member States distinguished **93,** 584-5
fish quotas **93,** 762-4
freedom of establishment **93,** 42, 44, 83-4, 478-80
monopolies **93,** 43, 45
nationality, ships **93,** 786
property rights **93,** 476-80
sexual **93,** 22, 623-8
ships, registration **93,** 762-3, 768-9, 786
officials
death duties **56,** 576-7
domicile for tax purposes **87,** 82-3
equality **56,** 570-1
privileges and immunities **56,** 570, 575-8
taxes **56,** 568-71, 575-8
Protocol on the Privileges and Immunities of the European Communities (1965) **87,** 82-3
payments between Member States and with third countries
liberalization under Treaty on European Union (1992) **117,** 521
national measures, requirements **117,** 521-2
phytosanitary certificates
issue, Turkish Republic of Northern Cyprus (TRNC) **100,** 264, 284-5, 291, 300-2
equality of standards, relevance **100,** 266-7, 271, 272, 277, 300-1
impediment caused by TRNC **100,** 267, 271-2
inconsistency of Commission practice **100,** 269-70, 282
Member State practice **100,** 270, 282
obligation to accept **100,** 266
validity **100,** 266, 269-70, 300-2
movement certificates distinguished **100,** 272-3, 284-5
uniformity of acceptance conditions, need for **100,** 301
policy, unanimity **47,** 285
powers, implied **47,** 299
presidency, violation of international law, statement as remedy **94,** 438
privileges and immunities **102,** 186-7
attachment order **113,** 385-411
contest in good time, need to **113,** 394, 396-7

interference with proper functioning of Community, need for **113,** 394-5, 397, 408
measure of constraint, whether **113,** 395, 396
measure of constraint
authorization, need for **113,** 394, 398, 408
relating to property or assets of the Community **113,** 395-6
national law, primacy **113,** 396-7, 408
need to claim, whether **113,** 408
Protocol on the Privileges and Immunities of the European Communities (1965), avoidance of effects under national law **113,** 396
uniformity, need for **113,** 397
property rights. *See* fundamental rights within the EC/EU, property, right to
proportionality, obligation to observe **98,** 245
public order/public policy/*ordre public*
free movement of workers **62,** 390-1, 399, 406-7, 410
quantitative restrictions or measures equivalent to **117,** 471-4, 526-8, 543-7
quantitative restrictions or measures equivalent to **47,** 18, **48,** 233-6
measures with equivalent effect **48,** 233-6
restrictions on exports to third countries **117,** 522-4
national marketing organization and **93,** 464-7
non-discrimination **93,** 109-10, 111, 112, 264, **117,** 470-4, 491-2
public policy exception **117,** 471-4, 526-8, 543-7
Regulation 2603/69 (Export Regulation) **117,** 522-4
applicability to measures having equivalent effect **117,** 522-8
Security Council sanctions and **117,** 470-4, 522-8, 545-6
trademarks, EC/Switzerland Free Trade Agreement (1973) **93,** 598-9, 600-1
veterinary and public health inspections **93,** 48-9, 438
reference price **62,** 429, 431-2, 437
Regulations. *See* European Council Regulations
residence
permit **62,** 392
territorial validity **62,** 392, 411, 414-16
right to **62,** 393-4, 400
territorial restriction **62,** 391-2, 394, 397, 399, 405, 407-9, 411, 414-16
ships. *See* European Community (EC), ships
social policy, community competence, Treaty of Rome (1957) **99,** 390-3
social security schemes
European Interim Agreement (1963) **56,** 533
migrant workers **53,** 598-600, 602-6
nationals of non-Member States **56,** 535
Staff Regulations, pensions **56,** 575-8
sovereignty. *See also* transfer of powers to *below*
Community institutions **93,** 18
extension by ECJ **93,** 447, 457-9
limited nature **93,** 458
Member States **87,** 354-5
State enterprise, competition provisions and **47,** 10-13
State responsibility. *See also* European Community law, breach, State responsibility
independent organization **93,** 590-1
status, inter-State institution **93,** 388, **102,** 186-7
trade regulations **55,** 478-80
trading activity, limitation **55,** 482-3
transfer of powers to **93,** 38, 39, 53, 219, 257-8, 390

European Community (EC) (*cont.*)
constitutionality **98,** 211-12
democratic legitimacy **98,** 213-15, 221-6
conferred by parliamentary approval **98,** 223, 225
majority voting and **98,** 222-3
opportunities for Member States to influence and **98,** 222
extension of rights to non-nationals distinguished **98,** 266, 268
limited and specific **98,** 221, 225-6, 229-30, 243. *See also Kompetenz/Kompetenz above*
national identities, preservation of **98,** 221, 245-6
national spheres of activity, need to retain **98,** 224-5, 241
parliamentary powers **98,** 208-9
rule of law, subject to **98,** 194
separation of powers and **98,** 211
sovereignty, effect on **98,** 225, 228
treaty, need for **98,** 230, 243
transport
social provision **47,** 279, 284-5, 289, 296, 298, 305
State protection of and aids to **45,** 458-9
treaties with non-Member States **47,** 283-4, 294-8, 304-5
treaties with non-Member States **47,** 278-311
concluded before accession/entry into force of Treaty of Rome (1957)
Art. 234 provisions **117,** 528, 548-9, 551
outstanding obligations **117,** 528-9, 547-9
permissive and compulsory provisions distinguished **117,** 548, 551
requirements, consistency with EC law **47,** 297
right to conclude **47,** 283-4, 285, 294-8, 304-5
treaties with non-Member States. *See also* European Community treaties
unilateral measures by Member State (Art. 224 of EEC Treaty)
common commercial policy, obstruction of **100,** 239
derogation from Community rules
fundamental **100,** 238
general **100,** 238
effect on peaceful resolution of dispute
competence to determine **100,** 242
relevance **100,** 242
political guidelines, departure from **100,** 239-40
protection of economic interests **100,** 238
request to suspend **100,** 225
requirements
consultations to minimize effects on common market **100,** 235
prejudice to fundamental interests of State **100,** 235
proportionality **100,** 234. *See also* European Community law, requirements, proportionality
'serious internal disturbances affecting . . . law and order' **100,** 235
'serious international tension . . . threat of war' **100,** 235-6
as United States of Europe **87,** 355
Vienna Convention on Diplomatic Relations (1961), applicability **102,** 186-7
Vienna Convention on the Law of Treaties (1969) and **117,** 407
Vienna Convention on the Law of Treaties between States and International Organizations (1986) and **117,** 407-8
wine market. *See* agricultural market *above*
Yugoslavia and. *See* Yugoslavia, Socialist Federal Republic (SFRY), Conference on (1991)

European Community (EC), fish quotas. *See also* European Economic Community (EEC) fisheries policy
derogation from principle of equal access **93,** 715-16, 762, 774-8, **99,** 224
freedom of establishment and **93,** 716, 717, 765-74
national implementation **93,** 628-9, 656-7, 706-7, 713-14, 716, 722, 775-8, **99,** 265-7
conformity with EC objectives, need for **93,** 716, 775-8, **99,** 266, 268
measure equivalent to quantitative restriction, whether **99,** 266-7, 268
proportionality, need for **93,** 778
real economic link. *See* real economic link *below*
non-discrimination and **93,** 762-4
real economic link
between vessel's fishing operations and population dependent on fisheries **93,** 713, 716, 728-9, 777-8
crew residence requirement **93,** 707, 713, 722
crewing condition (75EC nationals) **93,** 656, 713
residence and domicile requirement **93,** 727-9
sale of portion in quota State (landing test) **93,** 656
social security condition (subscription to quota State national insurance scheme) **93,** 656, 713
visiting test **93,** 656
registration of vessels. *See* European Community (EC), ships
right to participate in capital and **93,** 717
European Community (EC), ships
company compared **93,** 763
flags, grant of, right to determine **93,** 714-17
nationality
captain and master **93,** 768
companies **93,** 767
freedom of establishment and **93,** 765-8, 786
non-discrimination and **93,** 786
owners and operators **93,** 765-6, 767-8, 779, 789
residence and domicile requirement, combined effect **93,** 766
right to determine **93,** 722, 730, 759, 785-6
non-discrimination and **93,** 762-3, 768-9, 786
registration of fishing vessels
community competence **113,** 366-7
EC law, need for conformity with **93,** 589, 757, 758, 763, 783, 784
freedom of establishment and **93,** 758-9, 765-74, 785
habitual operation **93,** 774, 778
nationality. *See* nationality *above*
place of management, direction and control **93,** 773-4, 780, 787, 789
residence and domicile requirement
discrimination, whether **93,** 768-9
residence and domicile distinguished **93,** 770
European Community law 60, 403-7. *See also* European Community Law, direct effect
act of government, immunity for, whether **96,** 220-1
applicable law **93,** 534, 536
breach. *See* breach, applicable law *below*
compensation for breach or failure to implement
Community law, **111,** 67-8
measure **111,** 48, 95, 99-100, 101, 124-5, 129
EC legal system **93,** 534, 536

European Community law (*cont.*)
national courts, role **93,** 177-8, 446-7
State responsibility **93,** 176-7, **111,** 47, 100, 101
procedure **111,** 48, 50 n. 24, 92
substance **111,** 48, 50 n. 24, 53
validity **93,** 369-70, 386-403
Art. 177 reference. *See* European Court of Justice (ECJ), Art. 177 reference
bilateral treaties of Member States and **53,** 602, 604-5
binding effect **93,** 219-20, 399
breach
annulment of Commission decision **100,** 303
applicable law, damage caused by **93,** 172, 176-7
compensation. *See* compensation for breach or failure to implement *below*
criteria
complexity of situation **111,** 114
contribution of Community institution **111,** 117, 130
difficulty in interpreting or applying text **111,** 114
excusability of error of law **111,** 117, 130
good faith **111,** 130
margin of discretion **111,** 114-16, 117
date arising, failure to achieve required result **111,** 85, 95, 96, 101
defence, similar act by another Member State **100,** 161
evidence of, ECJ declaration of default **93,** 172, 180-1, 188, 202
interim measures. *See* interim measures (national) *below*; European Court of Justice (ECJ), interim measures
liability of Community institution **111,** 74-6
discretion and **111,** 74-6, 114-15
limitations on **111,** 74-6
national courts, role
characterization of breach **111,** 118
determination of facts **111,** 118
proceedings for
right to refrain from **100,** 161
sole responsibility of Commission **100,** 161
remedy. *See also* compensation for breach or failure to implement *below*
applicable law **93,** 176-7
appropriate measures to make good default **93,** 172, **111,** 60
choice **111,** 89-90
compensation for breach or failure to implement. *See* compensation for breach or failure to implement *below*
competence to determine **111,** 64-7
creation of **93,** 172, 176, **111,** 50, 64-6
effective remedy, right to **111,** 51, 91, 93, 100, 101, 109-10, 120-1, 128, 129
limitation *ratione temporis* **93,** 173, 190-2, 193-4, **111,** 93 n. 113, 95-6
national treatment, equality with **111,** 93, 100, 101, 120-1, 122, 124, 125, 129, **117,** 320, 334-5
proportionality and **117,** 319-21, 334-6
reimbursement of sums unduly paid **93,** 175
reinstatement of content of right **111,** 59-60, 67
setting aside national judgment **93,** 460
State responsibility **93,** 174-85
applicable law **93,** 176-7
causal link **93,** 328

courts, of **93,** 183-4
directly applicable EC law **93,** 174-9, 328
EEC Treaty as basis **93,** 200-1
fault, need for **93,** 329-31, 334-5
liability of Community institution as benchmark **93,** 186-7
margin of discretion as defence **93,** 190
national administrative act **93,** 330
non-directly applicable EC law **93,** 179-85
private undertakings **93,** 185
protection of individual **93,** 189
remedy, entitlement **93,** 328
uncertainty **93,** 173, 190-2
compatibility of national law **93,** 357, 388
conformity distinguished **93,** 323
EC obligation **93,** 389-90
measures implementing treaty **99,** 228-33
Council endorsement **99,** 233, 234
transitional **99,** 233, 234
presumption of **93,** 661
trial court, sole competence to determine **93,** 361
compatibility of treaties, North-East Atlantic Fisheries Convention (NEAFC) (1959), Art. 7(1) (amendment) (1970) **99,** 217-68
compensation for breach or failure to implement **93,** 171-92, 200-2, **111,** 39-130
action for repayment distinguished **93,** 183
applicable law. *See* applicable law, compensation for breach or failure to implement *above*
basis. *See also* applicable law *above*
Community law **111,** 53, 55
Humblet **111,** 51, 52
date *ab quo* **111,** 95-6, 126-7
date of judgment **111,** 127-8
direct effect of Community law, corollary to **111,** 110
Directive 89/665/EEC of 21 December 1989 **111,** 66
Directive 92/13/EEC of 25 February 1992 **111,** 66
essential element of 'making good' infringed right **111,** 60
Francovich **111,** 50-2, 55, 69-72
teachings of publicists **111,** 71-2
illegal act
'choice of economic policy', relevance **93,** 188
fault, need for **93,** 187-8, 329-31, **111,** 47
'wide discretionary power', relevance **93,** 188, **111,** 121, 129
interest **93,** 336
lawful and unlawful measures distinguished **111,** 87
measure **93,** 331, 335-6
Chorzów Factory **111,** 94
commensurate with loss **111,** 123, 125, 129
consequential damage **111,** 94
ex aequo et bono **93,** 172, 190
exemplary **111,** 100, 101, 125
interest on losses **111,** 94
lost profit **111,** 94, 124, 130
restitutio in integrum **111,** 94, 95
uniformity throughout Community, need for **111,** 94-5

European Community law (*cont.*)
mitigation of loss, obligation **111,** 89, 95, 98, 99
Council of Europe Recommendation R (84) 15 of 18 September 1984 **111,** 89
reasonable diligence **111,** 124
national law and **93,** 202, 328-9, **111,** 120, 125
obligation to make good damage caused by unlawful act **111,** 48-55
public interest considerations **111,** 87-8
purpose
implementation of Community law **111,** 52, 56, 58, 65, 90-1, 116
protection of individual **111,** 52, 56, 58, 63, 65, 67-8, 79, 116
rectification of infringement, relevance **111,** 52
requirements
actual damage **93,** 187, 201, **111,** 69, 71, 86-8, **113,** 400, 410
causal link **93,** 187, 201, 328, **111,** 47, 69, 71, 88, 116, 119, 121-2, 129, **113,** 400, 402-4, 410
clear rights created by directive **93,** 201, 328, **111,** 70, 116, 117, 121
Council of Europe Recommendation R (84) 15 of 18 September 1984 **111,** 77, 88 n. 98
fault **111,** 47, 71-2, 83-6, 101, 122-3, 129. *See also* fault *below*
illegal act. *See* illegal act *above*
infringement of Treaty provision having direct effect **111,** 70-1
manifest and serious breach **111,** 78-9, 80-3, 101, 115, 118-19
numbers affected, relevance **111,** 86-7
prior finding of infringement **111,** 81-2, 95, 126-7, 130
responsibility for determining whether met **111,** 86, 88, 119
sufficiently serious breach **111,** 77-8, 116, 117, 121, 126, 129, 130
superior rule of law for the protection of the individual **111,** 77-8, 79-80
unlawful conduct **111,** 69, 71, 77, **113,** 400-1, 410
unreasonable conduct **111,** 77
residual remedy, whether **111,** 54-5, 89-91
right of enforcement distinguished **93,** 183, **111,** 47, 48
uniformity throughout Community, need for **111,** 112
unlawful conduct of Commission, phytosanitary certificates issued by officials of Turkish Republic of Northern Cyprus (TRNC) **100,** 303
compliance, obligation **93,** 171, 172, 219, 318, 421
all State institutions **111,** 112
international law as basis **93,** 421
interpretation of national law and **93,** 453
confidentiality of proceedings, confidential transmission to interested parties **111,** 135-6
conflict with national law. *See also* primacy *below and* European Community law, direct effect
constitutional issue, whether **98,** 248-9, 250-1
discretionary power to grant exemptions from offending law, effect **93,** 767, 787-8, 789
interpretation avoiding **93,** 526-7
legal consequences
amendment of Constitution **93,** 31
continued validity of national law **93,** 534-5
implied repeal **93,** 526, 531, 534
legal certainty, need for **93,** 56-7, 58
power to determine **93,** 55-6

suspension of national law. *See* suspension of national law *below*
withdrawal from treaty **93,** 31
national courts' responsibility to resolve **98,** 195
non-application of national law **98,** 194
referendum **93,** 553
subsequent legislation **98,** 248-9
suspension of national law **93,** 177-9
automatic **93,** 51, 56, 73-4, 75
declaration of invalidity **93,** 51, 54, 56
unconstitutional, need for finding of **93,** 530-7
constitutional limitation **93,** 390
constitutional review, possibility **98,** 251
criminal law and **113,** 269
direct effect. *See* European Community law, direct effect
directive
64/221/EEC of 25 February 1964 **85,** 88-90, **86,** 333
92/43/EEC (Habitats Directive). *See* Habitats Directive (92/43/EEC)
94/22/EC (Hydrocarbons Licensing Directive) **120,** 628
binding effect, result to be achieved **93,** 181, 285
date of taking effect **93,** 473, 589-90
direct effect. *See* European Community law, direct effect, directive
primacy **93,** 135, 316, 320-4, 333
ECJ judgment and **93,** 537
fault. *See also liability entries below*
deliberate breach constituting **111,** 72 n. 62
duty of care, relevance **111,** 85
strict liability and **111,** 72 n. 63, 85
subjective factor **111,** 83-6
sufficiently serious breach constituting **111,** 122-3, 129
unlawfulness constituting **111,** 84
force majeure **93,** 381-3
absolute impossibility **93,** 381, 386
duty of care **93,** 381-2, 386
fundamental rights. *See* fundamental rights within the EC/EU
general principles of
Commission's obligation to act within a reasonable time in competition policy proceedings **113,** 277-8
legitimate expectation. *See* legitimate expectation *below*
proportionality **93,** 370, 431, **117,** 286-7
respect for fundamental rights **93,** 378, **111,** 140-1
right of parties to be heard **111,** 135
harmonization, international agreement as instrument **105,** 208-9
implementation **82,** 112
executive regulation **93,** 582
exercise of State power **93,** 393
grace period **93,** 564-5
Member State's discretion **111,** 76, 80-1
public policy and **117,** 473, 526-8, 543-7
national measures. *See also* European Community (EC), common commercial policy, national measures and
admissibility **93,** 526, 533-5
judicial review **93,** 526, **111,** 49-50, 93
need for **93,** 28

European Community law (*cont.*)
obligation to take effective **117,** 334-5
reasons underlying, need for **111,** 93 n. 113
permissible methods **93,** 572
individual **55,** 481-4, **93,** 220. *See also* European Community law, direct effect; right to invoke before national courts *below*
lever for implementation of Community law **111,** 56-8
protection of rights as prime objective **111,** 63
right derived from Treaty provision having direct effect on Member States **111,** 56, **117,** 438-9
as minimum guarantee **111,** 109
procedural matters **111,** 56
right to challenge on basis of customary international law **117,** 440-1
source of liability, relevance **111,** 79-80
interim measures (national) **93,** 686 n. 1. *See also* European Court of Justice (ECJ), interim measures
applicable law, nationals **93,** 698, 699
Art. 177 proceedings, effect on **93,** 703
balance of interests **93,** 716-17
compensation for loss suffered, need for **93,** 683, 790
effectiveness of judicial protection and **93,** 688-90, 695-6
presumptions
compatibility of national legislation **93,** 694-5
validity of EC law **93,** 663, 690-6
retroactivity and **93,** 687-9
stay of proceedings, whether **93,** 682
suspension of administrative act **93,** 692-3
suspension of primary legislation **93,** 692-3
international law **53,** 28-31, 37, 44-6, 48, **117,** 414-15
avoidance of conflict **100,** 148, 160
compliance with Security Council Resolution and **117,** 316
customary international law **117,** 440-1
incorporation into national law **100,** 142, 147
modification by Community law **100,** 142
national law distinguished **53,** 556, 564-5
precedence **100,** 142, 148, 180
interpretation. *See* European Community law, interpretation
judicial development **93,** 447, 457-9
judicial review **93,** 355-7, 386-403, 522-3, 524
of act of Community institution on basis of international law **117,** 423
Commission activity **111,** 114-15
compatibility of EC law distinguished **93,** 357
EC treaties **96,** 220-3
compatibility with Treaty of Rome **96,** 222
ex post facto **96,** 220
mixed agreement **96,** 222-3
political credibility of EC and **96,** 222
prior review procedure and **96,** 220-2
protection of third parties **96,** 222
inapplicability of rule, limited to **93,** 394, 395
national measures implementing **93,** 526
ordinary courts **93,** 536
protection of individual **93,** 357, **111,** 93

requirements **117,** 423
manifest error **117,** 441
legislative competence, EC organs **93,** 572
legitimate expectation
public interest and **117,** 428
treaty
individual's right to challenge Community actions and **117,** 424-7
measures prior to entry into force defeating its object and purpose **113,** 324, 334
termination and **117,** 426
liability. *See also* fault *above*
liability in connection with Iraq Law No 57 of 16 September 1990
actual and definitive damage, whether
definitive irrecoverability **117,** 386
definitive refusal to pay debts **117,** 383-5
applicant's failure to seek contractual remedies **117,** 385-6
causality
relevance of Regulation 2340/90 **117,** 386-8
relevance of Regulation 3155/90 **117,** 385-6
relevance of Security Council Resolution 661 (1990) **117,** 388
repeal of Law No 57, effect **117,** 384-5
unusual or special damage, whether **117,** 389-92
liability for lawful act
requirements
causal link **117,** 382, 385-6
unusual and special damage **117,** 384, 390-4
liability for unlawful act
compensation limited to fixed rate **117,** 396
failure to exercise discretion to provide for compensation **117,** 396-7
requirements
actual damage **117,** 396-7
causal link **117,** 382
limitation *ratione materiae* **93,** 523
national courts, role **93,** 49-50, 52, 56, 57, 59, 72, 73, 83-4, 174, 175, 176-7, 183-4, 188-96, 278, 542-7, 663-4, 685-6, 696-7, 698, 702-3
applicable law, EC law **93,** 177-8
applicable law, power to determine **93,** 446-7
Art. 169 infringement proceedings and **93,** 697
compatibility with Constitution, determination of **93,** 30, 184, 246-7, 257-8
sole competence of Constitutional Court, effect **93,** 50, 51-2, 59, 293
compatibility of national law, determination of **98,** 249, **117,** 529
compatibility of obligations under another treaty **117,** 549
effectiveness of Community law **98,** 249
finding of unconstitutionality, retroactive effect **93,** 54-5, 58, 74
implementation **93,** 237
interpretation in accordance with Community law **93,** 52
limitation on **98,** 249
resolution of conflict **98,** 195
review of European Community law **98,** 194
as national law **93,** 460, **98,** 248
national law and **44,** 399, 405-8, **47,** 11, **53,** 556, 564-5, **59,** 4-7, 487, **62,** 394, 400, 412. *See also* European Community law, direct effect
national measures. *See* implementation, national measures *above*

European Community law (*cont.*)
obligation to make good damage caused by unlawful act
basis
EC treaty system **111,** 51, 111
principles inherent in Community legal order **111,** 113
in case of directive not directly invocable in national courts **111,** 57
'in context of provisions of national law' **111,** 53, 92, 129
obligations
reciprocity **100,** 161
referendum, right to and **93,** 549-52
primacy **93,** 659, 681, 705, **123,** 15. *See also* conflict with national law *and* national law, as *above*; right to invoke before national courts *below*; European Community law, direct effect
Constitution **113,** 290-1
directive **93,** 135, 316, 320-4, 333
EEC Treaty (Rome) (1957) **93,** 27-32, 38-9, 214-23, 243-62, 446
effect on national law **93,** 438
fundamental rights and **93,** 391
Gibraltar **123,** 15
individual's right to rely on Community law having direct effect **111,** 109
overriding effect of EC law **93,** 438
pre-independence ordinance relating to French Metropolitan Territories **93,** 245-6
presumption of consistency **93,** 531
previous legislation **93,** 459-60, 531
implied repeal **93,** 29
primary and secondary national legislation, distinction, whether **93,** 178-9
referendum **93,** 523, 551-2, 553
Regulation **93,** 244-5, 308, 322, 427, 569, 572, 581-2
limited to, whether **93,** 217
rule part of national law **98,** 194
secondary EC law **98,** 195
single system **93,** 535
subsequent legislation **93,** 29-31, 44, 49, 51, 54, 72-3, 74-5, 459-60, 531-5
unwritten rule of primary EC law **98,** 194
protection **93,** 456
adequacy **93,** 357, 434-8
effectiveness **93,** 174-5, 200-1, 663, 685-6, 703
publication or notification of **47,** 281-2
Regulations. *See* European Council Regulations
requirements
communication to person concerned **113,** 335, 337
foreseeability **113,** 335
precision **113,** 335
proportionality **93,** 369, 370, 396-7, 431, **98,** 245, **117,** 286-92, 300-2, 321, 527-8, 547
EC Treaty and **93,** 370
general principle of EC law **93,** 370, 431, **117,** 286-7
national penalties and **117,** 320-1
retroactive effect **93,** 537, 663, 687-8
right to invoke before national courts **93,** 18-19, 53, 446, 456-7, 458, 473, 522, 554-6, 564, 576, 684-5, **98,** 195. *See also* primacy *above*; European Community law, direct effect
equality of EC and national rights **93,** 685-6

failure of State to implement law, relevance **93,** 140, 143, 144, 167-8, 196, 453-4, 456, 564
power of Commission and Member States to take juridical measures, relevance **93,** 19
public order and **93,** 284
venire contra factum proprium as basis **93,** 564, 656
scrutiny. *See also* judicial review *above*
Council of Ministers **93,** 523
ECJ **93,** 524-5
European Parliament **93,** 523
national parliaments **93,** 523
secondary legislation, international law, part of **93,** 320-1
Security Council obligations and **117,** 464, 528-9, 530, 547-9
sources
European Council practice **105,** 206-7, 209
general principles common to Member States **111,** 114
principles common to the laws of Member States **96,** 220
State liability. *See* State responsibility *below*
State responsibility **93,** 174-85, **111,** 39-130
applicable law **93,** 176-7
basis, EC Treaty **93,** 200-1
courts, of **93,** 183-4
directly applicable EC law **93,** 174-9, 328, **111,** 54-5, 56-9, 63-4, 109-10
for
failure to transpose directive in good time **111,** 130
incorrect transposition of Community directive into national law **111,** 130
national decision in breach of directly effective treaty provision **111,** 130
indivisibility of responsibility **93,** 183-4, **111,** 47, 60-7, 72-6, 112
legislative act **111,** 47, 60-7, 72-6, 96, 108, 129
remedy **111,** 64
unconstitutional legislation **111,** 61-2, 120
liability of Community institution as benchmark **93,** 186-7, **111,** 73-6, 114-15, 116
margin of discretion as defence **93,** 190
national administrative act **93,** 330
non-contractual liability **111,** 111
serious breach of superior rule of law for the protection of the individual **111,** 77-8
non-directly applicable EC law **93,** 179-85, **111,** 51
private undertakings **93,** 185
protection of individual **93,** 189
remedy, entitlement **93,** 328
requirements
fault **93,** 329-31, 334-5
precise obligation **111,** 81, 82, 96-9, 100, 101, 117
State responsibility under national law
imposing less strict conditions **111,** 120
as precedent **111,** 49
uncertainty **93,** 173, 190-2
status
foreign law, whether **93,** 522
independent **93,** 520, 524, 533-4
international law, whether **93,** 522
part of national law, whether **93,** 516, 522, 533-4
strict liability and **117,** 321
treaties concluded by Community as part of **117,** 440

European Community law (*cont.*)
uniform application, need for **62,** 413, **117,** 281, 333
validity
applicability, distinguishable, whether **93,** 392, 402-3
applicable law **93,** 369-70, 386-403
power to determine. *See* European Court of Justice (ECJ), jurisdiction, validity of EC law
presumption of **93,** 663, 690-6
respect for fundamental rights **117,** 287, 321
European Community law, direct effect 93, 218, 224, 263, 399, 520, 562, 563, 571. *See also* European Community law; European Community law, primacy; European Community law, right to invoke before national courts
administrative difficulties, relevance **93,** 121-2, 143
Art. 174 declaration of voidness
Art. 177 reference and **93,** 541-2, 545
national court proceedings, effect on **93,** 544-7
Decision **93,** 144-5, 589
66/532 **93,** 275
decisions of international organization and **99,** 288
derogation, right of and **93,** 551
direct application distinguished **93,** 563-4
directive **93,** 117, 137-8, 144-5, 272, 274-85, 443-61, 588-91
66/221 (public order measures) **93,** 275-6
68/31 (administrative services fee) **93,** 275
68/360 (free movement of workers) **93,** 276
76/207 (night work) **98,** 194-5
77/91 (Second Directive) **93,** 471-4
77/388 (Sixth Directive) (turnover taxes) **93,** 116-45, 285
80/987 (protection of employees in event of insolvency of employer) **93,** 151-203
80/1263 (model driving licence) **93,** 563-5
92/43/EEC (Habitats Directive) **120,** 656
application of principle to all directives **93,** 193, **111,** 57
protection against State's failure to implement **111,** 57 n. 36
decision compared **93,** 144-5, 452
extension of date for implementation, relevance **93,** 118-19
obligations and rights distinguished **93,** 119
regulation compared **93,** 444, 445-7, 451-8
separability **93,** 120
third party, effect on **93,** 141-3
EEC treaties. *See* European Community treaties, direct effect
EEC Treaty. *See* European Economic Community Treaty (Rome) (1957), direct effect
effectiveness doctrine **93,** 589
emergency measures, exception, whether **93,** 474
individual, protection of **111,** 79
full and uniform **93,** 189, 535, 684-5, 702, **111,** 59
implementing legislation, need for **93,** 55, 522-3
interim measures. *See* European Community law, interim measures (national); European Court of Justice (ECJ), interim measures
jurisdiction to determine **93,** 444-7
national court proceedings, effect on
certainty of law **93,** 545
uniform application of EC law **93,** 545, **111,** 59

public order/public policy/*ordre public* and **93,** 283-4
right of individual to invoke EC law **93,** 284
Regulations **47,** 249-50, **93,** 569-73, 581-2
570/86 (rules of origin) **93,** 580-2
1787/84 (ERDF) **93,** 571-2
requirements
choice of means of implementation, relevance **93,** 120, 135, 138-40, 166-9, 171, 199
competence of originating organ **93,** 571
effective transfer of right **93,** 445
express provision in constitutive treaty **93,** 571
identified beneficiary **93,** 165-6, 196-7
identified rights **93,** 166-9, 196, 551-2, 590
identity of person liable **93,** 196, 199
'minimum obligation' **93,** 169
negative obligation **93,** 42
no need for further intervention **93,** 41, 42, 120-1, 473, 522, 537, **98,** 195
unconditional and precise **93,** 41, 42, 119-20, 138, 140-1, 165-71, 193, 196-200, 473, 551-2, 590, **98,** 194, 195
subsequent developments in EC law and **93,** 445
transitional period, after **93,** 267
venire contra factum proprium distinguished **93,** 564, 565
European Community law, interpretation
aids
Commission opinion **100,** 282
context **117,** 283, 300, 348, 360
drafting history **120,** 635-6, 637, **122,** 558, 562-3, 564-5
Council Minutes **93,** 118
general principles of international law **120,** 635
international agreements and other international obligations **100,** 133, **120,** 630-1, 634-5
legal context **100,** 144
national legislation in related areas **120,** 631-2
practice under Community law **120,** 627-30, 636-7
preamble **122,** 563
Security Council resolution being implemented **117,** 281-5, 298-300, 316-17
context, 'the very nature of things' **120,** 626-7, 636
different language versions **117,** 281, 333-4
interpretation in light of all language versions **117,** 321, 335
different meaning attached to same expression **100,** 157
guidelines
lack of clarity **100,** 142
national courts' obligation to follow ECJ practice **122,** 562
legal certainty **117,** 286-7, 348-51, 360-1
legal conflict, avoidance **93,** 526-7, **120,** 636
literal in case of Regulation implementing Security Council Resolution **117,** 283, 546
object and purpose **100,** 144, **117,** 281, 298, 346, 358, **120,** 626-7, 636
proportionality **117,** 286-7, 300-2
purposive **122,** 556, 559
text as prime consideration **117,** 298, 358, **122,** 563, 564-5
parties' understanding

European Community law, interpretation (*cont.*)
Commission statements **120,** 635, 637
government statements **120,** 632, 637
phrases
'interest' **117,** 280-5, 299-301
'originating in Yugoslavia' **117,** 346
presumptions
conformity with principles of EC law **122,** 562
incorporation of international law **100,** 142
European Community treaties
applicable law **107,** 519-27, 532-3
international law **93,** 104
basis
powers under Treaty of Rome **108,** 253-4
Art. 235 (implied power to enable Community to carry out its functions) **108,** 254-5
implied **108,** 253-4
binding effect **93,** 103. *See also* compliance *below*
breach, jurisdiction, ECJ **100,** 190
Commission competence **100,** 220-1, **101,** 47-57, 63-7
Community legal system, integral part of **93,** 103, **99,** 321, **117,** 440
compatibility with Treaty of Rome (1957)
Art. 228 reference. *See* European Court of Justice (ECJ), Art. 228 reference
criteria, Community competence **99,** 211, 212-16
compliance. *See also* binding effect *above*
bona fide performance **93,** 104-5
choice of means **93,** 105, 285, 322-3
continued existence of incompatible legislation **93,** 285, 323
like product, need for
burden of proof **93,** 264-5
range of taxes for consideration **93,** 265-6
conclusion, date of Community's final consent **105,** 194
conflict with national law **93,** 601
Convention on Jurisdiction and the Enforcement of Judgments (1968), *in rem* action in sending State, exclusion **94,** 312
direct effect
aims and wording, relevance **93,** 81, 84, 106, 111, 112
denunciation, provision for, relevance **93,** 82, 105
derogation, provision for, relevance **93,** 82, 105
discretion and **93,** 84-5
EEC/Cyprus Association Agreement (1972) and Protocol (1977) **100,** 274-5, 294-5
clear, precise and unconditional obligation **100,** 274-5, 294-5
EEC/Greece Association Agreement (1961) **93,** 81
EEC/Portugal Free Trade Agreement (1977)
Art. 14 (quantitative restrictions) **93,** 81
Art. 21 (non-discrimination) **93,** 80-5, 102-7, 111
Art. 23 **93,** 112
Joint Committee role **93,** 84, 105
port wine, applicability to **93,** 107-8
EEC/SFRY Cooperation Agreement (1980) **117,** 429-30, 438-9
European Economic Area (EEA) Agreement (1991) **113,** 326-7
judicial enforcement, provision for, relevance **93,** 82, 105

Lomé Convention (1986) **107,** 524-5
method of conclusion, relevance **93,** 81
reciprocity, relevance **93,** 81, 82, 84
requirements
conformity with EC Treaty **113,** 326-7
precision **113,** 326-7
unconditional nature **113,** 326-7
Yaoundé Convention (1973) **93,** 81
dispute settlement, national courts, exclusion **107,** 527
EEC/Cyprus Association Agreement (1972) and Protocol (1977)
departure from rules
non-discrimination requirement and **100,** 268-9, 275-6, 277, 278-82, 297-8, 300-1
progressive implementation of agreement, prejudice to **100,** 276, 298
special situation of Cyprus, Republic of **100,** 293-4, 297
unilateral decision **100,** 283
direct effect **100,** 274-5, 294-5
intervention in affairs of Cyprus and **100,** 299
movement certificates. *See* European Community (EC), movement certificates
non-discrimination, *Namibia* principle distinguished **100,** 280-1, 299
phrases
'authorities empowered' **100,** 301
'the customs authorities of the exporting State' **100,** 300
'originating products' **100,** 265
EEC/Greece Association Agreement (1961) **62,** 429, 431, 436, 439, **93,** 81
objectives **62,** 433, 436
Protocol 14 **62,** 432, 436, 440
'treatment' **62,** 429, 431-2, 437
EEC/SFRY Cooperation Agreement (1980)
Decisions and Regulations in respect of. *See* European Council Decisions, 91/602/EEC (denunciation of EEC/SFRY Cooperation Agreement (1980)); European Council Regulations, 314/83 (implementation of EEC/SFRY Cooperation Agreement (1980)) *and* 91/586/ECSC, EEC, 3567/91 (imports of products originating in Bosnia-Herzegovina, Croatia, Macedonia and Slovenia)
direct effect **117,** 429-30, 438-9
mixed agreement **117,** 404
purpose **117,** 404
termination provisions **117,** 433, 434-5. *See also* European Council Regulations, 3300/91 (Suspension Regulation)
fundamental change of circumstances and **117,** 427-8, 432, 436-7, 442
establishment of judicial machinery **100,** 191, 196
European Economic Area (EEA) Agreement (1991). *See* European Economic Area (EEA) Agreement (1991)
European Economic Area (EEA) draft Agreement (1991). *See* European Economic Area (EEA) draft Agreement (1991)
European Laying-up Fund for Inland Waterway Vessels, draft Agreement (1976). *See* European Laying-up Fund for Inland Waterway Vessels, draft Agreement (1976)
Free Trade Agreements
application of Art. 85(1) of Treaty of Rome and **96,** 153-4, 181-92, 199-200
EEC/Switzerland (1973), Art. 13 (quantitative restrictions) **93,** 600-1
primacy **96,** 189-91
cumulative **96,** 190-1

European Community treaties (*cont.*)
ILO Convention 170 (chemicals at work). *See* International Labour Organization (ILO), Conventions, 170 (chemicals at work)
implementation, responsibility **99,** 308, 321-2
individual, rights, Lomé Convention (1986) **107,** 521-2, 527
interpretation
aids
context **113,** 328
subsequent practice **100,** 298, 299
aims and wording **93,** 81, 84, 106, 111, 112
EEC Treaty distinguished **93,** 80-3, 84, 107
guidelines
aims and wording **100,** 294
object and purpose **100,** 298
purpose **113,** 328
strict **100,** 300
identical provision in EC Treaty, extension of interpretation **113,** 327-36
'similarity' as community concept **93,** 110
Joint Committee, role **93,** 84, 105
judicial review **96,** 220-3
agreement with non-Member State **101,** 39-43, 61, **117,** 441
annulment, risks **96,** 222
compatibility with Treaty of Rome **96,** 222
ex post facto **96,** 220
legal certainty, need for **96,** 222
mixed agreement **96,** 222-3
political credibility of EC and **96,** 222
prior review procedure and **96,** 220-2
protection of third parties **96,** 222
non-discrimination
Namibia principle distinguished **100,** 280-1, 299
quantitative restrictions, like product, need for **93,** 109-10, 111, 112, 264
operation, legitimate interests of both parties **100,** 298
procedure, negotiation by Commission on basis of Council Mandate **99,** 320
treaty-making power **47,** 278-311
Commission competence **101,** 47-57, 63-7
community competence **99,** 212-15, 221-68
agricultural products **105,** 200-1
application on territory of Member States, relevance **99,** 223, 225-6
ECSC products **105,** 199-200
Euratom **99,** 306-22, **105,** 198-9
exclusive, whether **99,** 214-16, 222-4, 263-5, 389, 390-2
high seas **99,** 263
implementation of agreement and **99,** 308, 321-2
implied **99,** 261-3, 284, 388-9
legal personality **99,** 262
legislative difficulties, relevance **99,** 391
measures depriving Member States of competence **99,** 389
Member States operating according to Community Mandate **99,** 224, 388
necessary to meet Community objectives **99,** 284, 312-14, 389, 392
subject-matter determined by Community law as a whole **99,** 262-3, 308, 359
third-State opposition, relevance **99,** 223-4
WTO agreements **105,** 82-225

Member States
compatibility of proposed agreement with common market rules **99,** 225, 264, 265
duty to ensure participation of Community in agreement **99,** 265, 308
prior consultation, obligation **99,** 224, 226-7, 394
representing dependent territories **99,** 371, 393
transitional **99,** 227, 264, 389
Member State's domestic law, relevance **105,** 197-8
mixed competence **99,** 319-22, 390-2, 394
technical barriers to trade **105,** 90-1
unexercised community powers, in case of **99,** 225-7
uniform application, need for **93,** 103-4, 110, **100,** 300, 301
validity, effect of implementing Regulation in case of invalidity **117,** 440
Yaoundé I (1963) **53,** 155-6, 159-62
Yaoundé II (1973), unilateral character **93,** 81, 82
European Conference of Postal and Telecommunications Administrations (Pontresina) (1969), Recommendation T/TG. TPh7 **77,** 422
European Convention on Human Rights (1950) 37, 451, 455, **43,** 178-86, **51,** 429, 440, 444, 455, **91,** 80, 140. *See also* African Charter on Human and Peoples' Rights (1981); American Convention on Human Rights (1969); European Commission of Human Rights; European Court of Human Rights; International Covenant on Civil and Political Rights (ICCPR) (1966)
abuse of power **56,** 385, **86,** 343
abuse of rights, freedom of assembly/association and **122,** 417-18
access to courts **57,** 210, 212, 218, 219-20, 224-30, 238-40, 242-61, **60,** 172-3, **72,** 362-3, **75,** 505-9, 513, 517, 554-6, 585, **78,** 338-9, 342. *See also* civil rights and obligations; effective remedy before national authority *and* independent and impartial tribunal *below*
detention, in respect of **81,** 127-30
execution of judgments and **123,** 45-7
extent of right **78,** 334, **81,** 127-9, **111,** 158, **118,** 134-7, **123,** 37-8, 39-43, 64-6, 84-6
lawyer
communication with **78,** 340-2, 382-8
requirement to obtain **75,** 585
margin of appreciation **123,** 39, 64-6, 84-6
non-disclosure of evidence and **119,** 277, 307
State immunity, jurisdiction as procedural bar **123,** 38, 70-3, 81-2, **125,** 157-9
act of State doctrine and **89,** 242
general norm, relevance **89,** 105, 125, 126-7, 130, 149 n. 63, 175, 202
national security **89,** 231, 233-4
protection against abuse **89,** 231-4
parliamentary involvement **89,** 232-3
remedy, in respect of **89,** 111-12, 141, 181
administrative practice giving rise to breach, northern Cyprus **120,** 61-2, 64-5, 101-4, 106-8, 116, 122-3
aims **57,** 191
aliens. *See also* deportation *below*
immigration controls **92,** 315-16, 318-19
right of residence **86,** 336
amendment, by State practice **98,** 308-9
appeal, right of **72,** 321-2, 418-29, **78,** 60, **88,** 473-5, 647, **104,** 434-5
administrative body, from decision of **58,** 79, **78,** 207
competent court, from **56,** 379-80, **58,** 79
judicial decision **78,** 207
notification in native language **72,** 321-2, **74,** 413-16

European Convention on Human Rights (1950) (*cont.*)
oral argument, relevance **88,** 652
promptness, need for **78,** 207
applicability **45,** 118, 132. *See also* State responsibility *below*
dependent territories **75,** 582-3, **78,** 493, **123,** 18-19
Gibraltar **123,** 10, 18-19
'local requirements' **123,** 18-19
municipal courts **111,** 171
States not party **98,** 301
territorial **98,** 300-1
'within their jurisdiction'. *See* European Convention on Human Rights (1950), interpretation, phrases
applicant. *See* European Commission of Human Rights; European Court of Human Rights
arbitrary act **56,** 413-14, **89,** 207-8, 286-7
arbitrary detention **81,** 125-6, **111,** 485. *See also* detention *and* liberty of person, deprivation *below*
arrest **58,** 73, 231-2. *See also* detention *and* liberty of person, deprivation *below*
detention on suspicion and **41,** 301, 335
lawfulness **45,** 311, **58,** 79, **61,** 196-7, 198-9, 210-11, 263-4, 266
mentally ill person, detention of **67,** 472
military discipline, under **58,** 53-60, 71, 73-4
Northern Ireland, in **58,** 230-3, 280-1, 330
Articles 25 and 46 declaration. *See* European Court of Human Rights, Articles 25 and 46 declaration
birching. *See* corporal punishment *and* punishment *below*
breach
bar to criminal proceedings, whether **72,** 317-19, **86,** 532
continuing, time-limits and **62,** 58, 79-80
damages for. *See* just satisfaction (Art. 50 [41] of the European Convention on Human Rights (1950))
evidence of. *See* European Court of Human Rights, evidence
State responsibility. *See* State responsibility *below*
statutory provision as **96,** 613-14, 620
character
constitutional **57,** 294
law-making **57,** 294
child care
parental access **96,** 613
divorce, after **96,** 612-17, 620-3
inhuman or degrading treatment **96,** 617
interests of child **96,** 614, 615-17
civil rights and obligations
applicable law, domestic law **96,** 491, 552
autonomy of concept **58,** 400
claim under compensation agreement **48,** 159-62
contestation, need for **62,** 336-40, 343, 347-53, **68,** 111-12, 119-24, **71,** 419, 421-3, 432-5, **86,** 357-8, 366-7, 393, 424-6, 428-31, **92,** 241-2, 244, 248, **123,** 37-8, 61, 81-2
contestation de caractère civil **88,** 658
'criminal charge' distinguished **40,** 240, **41,** 343, 357, **58,** 84, **71,** 424-5, 431-3, **81,** 47
determination of by a court of law **57,** 214, **58,** 399, 400

direct interference **62,** 320-2, 338-9, 351-2
disciplinary proceedings and **62,** 336, 346-9, 355-9, 638-41, **71,** 421-4, 432-6, **78,** 354
discrimination complaint **123,** 70
dismissal from employment **96,** 580
dispute relating to **62,** 320-2, 336-40, 347-53, 355, 358, **71,** 419, 421-4, 432-6
domestic law
in **92,** 241
independence of **68,** 124
employment contract, locally engaged staff, diplomatic mission **123,** 62, 68-70
family life, respect for **74,** 446-7
fundamental freedoms distinguished **57,** 216
medicine, right to practise **62,** 320-2, 339, 346, 348-50, 351-3, 355, **71,** 423, 432-6
parental rights **92,** 241-4
paternity suit **81,** 67-8
'practical and effective' rights **68,** 106-7
preliminary question, whether **96,** 552
Court's duty to consider *proprio motu* **96,** 552
private life, respect for **81,** 68
procedural bar, State immunity, jurisdiction **123,** 38, 50-1, 61-2, 81-2
procedural delays **68,** 121
procedural guarantees **57,** 215, 225, 226-8
proceedings, legal right to institute **57,** 214-15, 230-1
profession, right to exercise **62,** 337, 351, 353
property rights as **68,** 111-12, 119-21, **75,** 504, 512-13
public interest and **68,** 124-5
relevant factors
analogies **86,** 362, 397
character of legislation **86,** 360, 395
compulsory nature of obligations **86,** 360, 395
contract of employment, connection with **86,** 361-2, 396, 409
'decisive for private rights and obligations' **96,** 491, 552
economic nature of right **86,** 361, 396
personal nature of right **86,** 361, 396
personal and property interest **96,** 491-2
State practice **86,** 359, 394
State responsibility **86,** 360-1, 393-7
remission of sentence, whether **78,** 353
social security benefits **86,** 358-63, 393-7
civil service, access to **88,** 553-4, 556-69
class/representative action **67,** 430
Commission and Court, division of powers and functions **56,** 391-3, 394
conscience, freedom of. *See* freedom of conscience *below and* freedom of conscience
conscientious objection. *See* freedom of conscience *below*; conscientious objection; International Covenant on Civil and Political Rights (ICCPR) (1966), conscientious objection
constitutional compatibility **115,** 642-55
Contracting Parties **62,** 41, 71-2, 83-4
Cyprus as **62,** 71-2, 83-4
role **68,** 75
corporal punishment **58,** 358, **72,** 324. *See also* punishment *below*
degrading, whether **58,** 353-5, 364
desirability **58,** 367

European Convention on Human Rights (1950) (*cont.*)
as deterrent **58,** 353
discrimination **58,** 358
humiliation, level of **58,** 353, 364
inhuman, whether **58,** 352
level of suffering **58,** 352
in Isle of Man **58,** 345-6, 348
justification **58,** 356-7
local requirements **58,** 355-8
juvenile **58,** 360, 362
nature of **58,** 354
public opinion **58,** 354
in Scotland **67,** 487-90, 492, 497
tawse **67,** 487
threat of as inhuman and degrading treatment **67,** 491-3
torture, whether **58,** 352
undesirability **58,** 367
corporation and **60,** 137
correspondence, respect for **41,** 282, **57,** 220-3, 230-9, **58,** 146-7, **72,** 363-72, **78,** 382, 383-8
interference with **57,** 235-7
espionage **58,** 448
'in accordance with the law' **72,** 363-8
justifiable **72,** 368-9
national security **58,** 448
'necessary in a democratic society' **58,** 447, 454, **72,** 369-72
northern Cyprus **120,** 89-90, 115
prisoners. *See* detention, correspondence, interference with *below*
public order/public policy/*ordre public* **58,** 448
terrorism and **58,** 448
costs. *See* just satisfaction (Art. 50 [41] of the European Convention on Human Rights (1950)), expenses *and* legal costs
court. *See also* independent and impartial tribunal *below*
duty to set up **45,** 159, 164
courts of cassation and **47,** 171, 176, 180-2
criminal legislation/judicial decision, retroactivity **44,** 127, 129-30, **57,** 177-9, **125,** 156
criminal proceedings
ne bis in idem, courts of same State, limitation to **111,** 152
nullum crimen/poena sine lege **121,** 212, **125,** 156
customary international law, evidence of **87,** 457
damages. *See* just satisfaction (Art. 50 [41] of the European Convention on Human Rights (1950))
death penalty
extradition. *See* extradition in case of death penalty *below*
non-Member State. *See* extradition in case of death penalty *and* obligation to refrain from act leading to *below*
obligation to refrain from act leading to **96,** 387-8, **98,** 307-9
breach as tort **96,** 387
NATO Status of Forces Agreement (1951) and **96,** 387-8
State practice **96,** 388
permitted, whether **98,** 307-9, 319-21, **100,** 689
State practice **98,** 308-9, **100,** 686
death row as inhuman or degrading treatment **98,** 307-12
age and mental state **98,** 311-12, **124,** 276, 277

conditions **98,** 310-11, **124,** 276-8
length of detention **98,** 310
defence **56,** 411-12, **58,** 104, 107, 108, **60,** 197. *See also* independent and impartial tribunal *and* legal assistance *below*
adequate time and facilities **43,** 180-1, **78,** 34, 39, 335-6
legal representation, right to **72,** 418-29, **73,** 470, 476
personal appearance **58,** 86, 99-100, 104
'practical and effective' **78,** 221
right to **72,** 418-29, **73,** 470, 476
speedy access **78,** 339
witnesses
right to call **43,** 178-9, **56,** 411
right to examine **78,** 336-7
degrading treatment. *See* inhumane or degrading treatment *below*
democracy as cornerstone **122,** 418, 422-3
denial of justice **57,** 218. *See also* denial of justice
deportation **92,** 373. *See also* aliens *above*; expulsion of alien *below*; deportation
compelling reasons of national security, risk of torture and **124,** 546
family life, respect for **92,** 366-9, **103,** 233, **108,** 422-3, 432-3, **111,** 169-70, 172, 192, 262-3
inhuman or degrading treatment **111,** 191, 266, 268-9
private life, respect for **111,** 172, 190-1, 193-4, 270-1
deprivation of property **75,** 383, 391, 414-28, 481-561, 581-2, 588-95, 612, 620-1. *See also* aliens *above*; expulsion of alien *below*; deportation
expropriation and construction permits amounting to **68,** 104-11, 116-18, 120-1
general interest and **75,** 589-91
individual joint owners, relations between **75,** 379
justified in public interest **75,** 415-19, 422, 424, 481-2, 486, 520-1, 525-31, 542, 559, 642
legitimate social objective **75,** 417-19, 422, 486, 531
need to rehouse refugees **120,** 65
rights of individuals, balancing of **68,** 108-10, **75,** 486, 520-1, 526-8, 559, 642
proportionality **75,** 591-4
as reprisal for expropriation of property by foreign State **47,** 412-17
State responsibility, need for **75,** 379-80
'subject to general principles of international law' **75,** 423-5, 435, 482-5, 515-17, 521-5
derogation **58,** 234, 237, 277-85, 293-4, 307, 329-31
conditions for **58,** 329-31
margin of appreciation. *See* margin of appreciation *below*
non-derogable provisions **122,** 446
procedure **58,** 329-30
destruction of rights **75,** 548
detainees, rights
correspondence, respect for **57,** 211, 220-3, 230-1, 233-7, **72,** 339-72, **78,** 338, 339-42, 343-4, 346-7, 380-8
complaints concerning, procedure **72,** 351-4
practice of authorities **72,** 354-8
rules concerning **72,** 342-51
freedom from discrimination **58,** 77-9, 285-8
judicial supervision **56,** 379
legal proceedings, institution **56,** 379-80, 382, **57,** 210, 230-1
private life, respect for **56,** 384, 398
reasons for arrest/detention **67,** 471-3

European Convention on Human Rights (1950) (*cont.*)
regular review **78,** 208
release pending trial. *See* release pending trial *below*
to challenge **58,** 71-9, 289, 699-700, **72,** 409
trial, right to **56,** 378-9, 401, 410, **67,** 545-9
detention. *See also* detainees, rights *above*
armed forces, members of **58,** 72-4, 94-5, 101-2, 107
conviction, after **41,** 303-4, 311
habitual offenders **67,** 540-9
without trial **67,** 545-9
inhuman or degrading treatment, whether **75,** 366-7
'lawful detention' **57,** 184-9, 190-2, 197-9, **58,** 75-6, 79, 94-5, 273-7, 280-1, 667-73, 674-7, **72,** 310-12, 314-16, **78,** 203-12, 243-5, 694-9, **95,** 339
'fulfilment of obligations prescribed by law' **73,** 394-5
habeas corpus proceedings **67,** 453-4, 468-71
judicial determination **58,** 676, 678, 695-9, **67,** 466-71, 545-9
public interest **40,** 187
wrongful conviction and **72,** 314-16
pending extradition **45,** 316-28
pending trial **43,** 180-1, **56,** 480-4, 487-8, 489-92, **57,** 194-7, **58,** 688-91, **72,** 309-13. *See also* provisional *below*
sentence, as part of **58,** 75-6, 107, 113
person of unsound mind **78,** 203-12, **81,** 121-6
conditions of detention, relevance **81,** 121-6
procedure **56,** 405
provisional **41,** 281-3, 284, **58,** 70, 73, 107, 275-6. *See also* pending trial *above*
rights, effect on **58,** 679-81
tax, for non-payment **40,** 241-2, 244-6
unlawful. *See also* 'lawful detention' *above*; liberty of person, deprivation *below*
dependence on breach of individual's own right **86,** 531
legal effects **56,** 409
remedy **56,** 416
remission of prison sentence **57,** 184-8, 197
vagrants **56,** 405-6
diplomatic protection compared **45,** 298-9, 302
disciplinary proceedings (fair trial requirement)
criminal charge **58,** 74, 81-2, 102, **62,** 321-2, 336, 341, 346-7, 352, 357-9, **78,** 324-8, 351-3
military **58,** 81, 101-2, 105-6, **73,** 395, 557-64, **78,** 227-53
nature of proceedings **62,** 320, 326, 336, 346-8, 353, 355-6, 358
prison **78,** 323-8
safeguards **71,** 423-9
sanctions **71,** 420
discrimination. *See* freedom from discrimination *below*
dispute, existence of **62,** 337-8
divorce, judicial separation distinguished **89,** 204-5
domestic courts. *See* municipal courts and *below*
domestic law. *See* municipal law and *below*
double jeopardy under **61,** 249
duty, negative **45,** 131, 151, 152-7, 227-8
education, right to **45,** 114, 118, 119-22, 128, 131, 138-231, **57,** 219
access to occupations **45,** 208, 213
discipline, ancillary function, whether **67,** 497-9, 504
family, measures affecting **45,** 163, 167, 173, 190, 224-5, **120,** 86

freedom from discrimination **58,** 145
UNESCO Convention against **45,** 156
language of **45,** 162, 165-6, 170, 172, 173, 190, 224, 227, **120,** 84-6, 114
morality, protection of **58,** 147-8
obligation to take action **45,** 150, 153, 170, 227
official recognition of studies **45,** 162, 173, 201-17, 225-6, 227
parental convictions, respect for **45,** 142, 147-9, **58,** 141, 142, 147-9
religious instruction and **67,** 495-7, 500-3, **72,** 324, **74,** 295-6
UK reservation **67,** 497, 502-3
sex education **58,** 126-34, 143-4
State regulation **67,** 498, 504
State schools, in **58,** 141
subsidies, withdrawal as punitive measure **45,** 177-9
teaching, freedom of **58,** 141, 143, 147, 149
EEC Treaty (1957) compared **62,** 391, 402
effective remedy before national authority **48,** 158, **62,** 22-3, 35, 56-7, 70, 77-8, 87-8, **72,** 373-6, **74,** 310, 325, 368-9, 381, 446, **81,** 96, 99-100, 101, 135-8, **82,** 89-90, **85,** 31, **86,** 335, **89,** 235-9, **92,** 246, 297, 347-8, **101,** 122-3. *See also* European Commission of Human Rights, local remedies rule; European Court of Human Rights, exhaustion of local remedies
absence of evidence **78,** 241-2
administrative practice giving rise to alleged breach **58,** 263, **71,** 302-3, **120,** 61, 62, 63-5, 101-4, 122-3
aggregation of ineffective remedies as **89,** 236-9, 241-2
availability **62,** 375, **86,** 345-6, **96,** 597
burden of proof **60,** 163, **96,** 597
criminal law provision, need for **81,** 98-9
critical date, developments subsequent to communication **45,** 271, 298-9, 301-2, **56,** 370-1
diplomatic privileges and immunities, relevance **111,** 158-9
doubts about availability **121,** 205
effectiveness **86,** 339-41
European Schools, relevance **108,** 641-2
exceptional or extraordinary remedies **60,** 166
failure to test **120,** 102-3, 104, 125
finding case time-barred **96,** 519
Greek Cypriots in northern Cyprus **120,** 94-6, 115, 120-2
inappropriate remedy **61,** 380-3
incorporation of Convention into municipal law, relevance **61,** 373-4, 378, 386-7, **68,** 75, **81,** 178-9
interim measures, non-availability against Crown, relevance **98,** 317
judicial authority, need for **89,** 238-9, 240-1
judicial review **98,** 316-17
asylum procedures **108,** 357-62, 422, 423-7, 430-2
just satisfaction proceedings and **86,** 348
justification for failure to provide, political solution, need for **120,** 66
legal advice against proceeding further **61,** 376-7, 385-6
legislative measures and **62,** 77
margin of discretion **108,** 358
official act, relevance **123,** 154
partial resolution, remedy offering **60,** 164-6, **61,** 371-2, 378
political solution as perceived prerequisite, relevance, **120,** 61-2, 66
reasonable chance of success, need for **56,** 371, **60,** 165, **61,** 372-4, 379-80, 384-6, **111,** 170-1

European Convention on Human Rights (1950) (*cont.*)
State Party's change of position before Convention institutions **111,** 205
relevance to alleged breach, need for **96,** 597
right to challenge legislation **75,** 432-3, 436-7, 508-9, 513, 516-17, 556-7
State immunity as bar to suit and **81,** 136-8, **91,** 301, **114,** 566-7, **119,** 372, 373, 376, 377-8, 383-5, **121,** 203-4, 208
statutory provision, sufficiency **96,** 596-7
sufficiency. *See* effectiveness *above*
time-limits and **62,** 79
Turkish Cypriots in northern Cyprus **120,** 109-10, 123
emigration, freedom of **74,** 300
enforcement **62,** 68. *See also* European Commission of Human Rights; European Court of Human Rights
European Court of Human Rights, role **89,** 260
international machinery **45,** 114, 120, 165, 219, 222
municipal courts **108,** 553
organs for **88,** 625, 626, 634
English common law, influence of **41,** 313-14
entry, freedom of **74,** 300-1
entry into force **51,** 240
equality of arms **41,** 316-17, 318, 335, 337, 357-8, **47,** 170, 175-6, 177, 179, 183, **58,** 97, 104, **86,** 363, 364, **96,** 561-2. *See also* European Court of Human Rights, equality of arms
applicability to conditions outside court's control **124,** 87
failure to provide copy of relevant report **96,** 619
release pending trial **45,** 277, 295, 296, 308, 315, **124,** 87 n. 85
time to prepare defence and **124,** 86
estoppel, passage of time **95,** 357
EU and. *See* fundamental rights within the EC/EU, European Convention on Human Rights (1950) and
European Coal and Steel Community (ECSC) coal regulations, compatibility **55,** 461-3, 467
European Union and. *See* fundamental rights within the EC/EU, European Convention on Human Rights (1950) and
evidence, Commission's role to evaluate **95,** 333-9, 354
exceptions **85,** 34-5
narrow interpretation **101,** 89
exhaustion of local remedies. *See* European Court of Human Rights, exhaustion of local remedies
expulsion of alien. *See also* deportation *above*
excluded by Art. 3, whether **111,** 271
exclusion compared **111,** 293
family life, respect for **108,** 312-13
freedom from discrimination **111,** 269
public policy and **99,** 7-11
risk of torture or inhuman or degrading treatment **108,** 308-12, 321, 353-7, 362-3, 414-17. *See also* Torture Convention (1984), non-refoulement to country of origin or any other country where risk of subjection to torture, substantial grounds for believing . . .
Convention on the Status of Refugees (1951) distinguished **108,** 411
fundamental right **108,** 355, 410, 439
expulsion of national **104,** 188-9
requirement to leave permanently **100,** 414

extradition. *See also* extradition in case of death penalty *below*; extradition
nationals **88,** 294, 295
permissibility **98,** 300, 305-6, 320-1
presence at hearing **40,** 208-10
suspension pending hearing **98,** 275, 313
extradition in case of death penalty **100,** 663. *See also* death penalty *above*
assurances that death penalty will not be carried out, need for **98,** 305-6, 320-1
extradition to another country with jurisdiction as alternative **98,** 312
extradition treaties **96,** 388
non-signatory State **78,** 389-94
fair hearing **47,** 169-88, **58,** 80-7, **60,** 169-77, **70,** 197, 315-23, **71,** 401, 418-36, **72,** 321-2, 362-3, 394-404, 418-30, **73,** 386-7, 395, 470, 476, 489-92, 505-11, 525-46, 557-9, 563-4, 639, **74,** 293-4, 457, **75,** 584-6, **78,** 214-25, 296-355, 382, **81,** 5-24, 25-8, **86,** 356, 363-6, 392, **92,** 244-5, 345. *See also* fair trial *below*
access to courts. *See* access to courts *above*
administrative and judicial proceedings distinguished **56,** 411
appeal, right of **86,** 365, **92,** 346
judicial review as **92,** 346-7
armed forces. *See* disciplinary proceedings (fair trial requirement), military *above*
cassation proceedings **47,** 171, 176, 180-2
expert
failure to appoint **96,** 555-8, 560-2
municipal court's responsibility to determine need **96,** 555, 558
as witness **92,** 294-5, 345
extradition **60,** 173
foreign judgments, enforcement of maintenance orders **47,** 189-93, 194-5
in absentia **71,** 418, 422
in camera **58,** 85, 97, 98, **71,** 418, **73,** 555
independent and impartial tribunal. *See* independent and impartial tribunal *below*
interpreter. *See* fair trial, interpreter *below*
judicial review and **68,** 113-14, 121-2, **92,** 245
lawyer, absence **96,** 601
length of proceedings **92,** 238, 240, 246, 257, 346
in case of future proceedings **121,** 211
contributory fault **107,** 60-1
criteria **107,** 60
eviction of diplomatic mission **111,** 158-9
limitations in respect of **57,** 219
military courts. *See* military courts
offer of settlement and **60,** 174-5
proceedings for enforcement of provisional foreign maintenance order **47,** 189-93
prompt hearing. *See also* prompt hearing *below*
relation to **70,** 197-200
public hearing. *See* public hearing *below*
right of appearance **86,** 363-4
waiver **60,** 175-7
wardship proceedings, whether **92,** 245
fair trial **40,** 187, 242, **41,** 281-306, 308-15, 316-60, **57,** 212, 225, **60,** 164, 169-71, 196, 197, **62,** 321-2, 326, 334, 337, 340, 343, 345, 348, 353-7, 359, **67,** 517, 519-25, **68,** 111-14, 119-25, 130-41, 160-73, **71,** 401, 418-36, **72,** 321-2, 394-404, 428-30, **73,** 386-7, 395, 470, 476, 489-92, 507-11, 525-46, 557-64, **81,** 45, **86,** 403, **95,** 340. *See also* fair hearing *above*
accused person, rights **60,** 169, 172-7, 196

European Convention on Human Rights (1950) (*cont.*)
administrative proceedings distinguished **73,** 525-31
armed forces **58,** 80-7, **73,** 395, 526, 557-64. *See also* military courts
case-file, access to **43,** 180-1
civil and criminal proceedings distinguished **57,** 259-60, **73,** 489-92, 505-11
'criminal charge'. *See* European Convention on Human Rights (1950), interpretation, phrases, 'criminal charge'
criminal proceedings **60,** 169-71, **73,** 386-7, 395, 557-64
defence. *See* defence *above*
disciplinary proceedings. *See* disciplinary proceedings (fair trial requirement) *above*
equality of treatment **81,** 195-8
evidence, withheld **67,** 519-25
freedom from discrimination, language and **58,** 484-5
independent and impartial tribunal. *See* independent and impartial tribunal *below*
interpreter **73,** 531-2
costs, entitlement **58,** 469-71, 706, **88,** 621-5, **100,** 334
free **58,** 484-5
judge
impartiality **68,** 130-41
public prosecutor, formerly **68,** 130-41
legal assistance. *See* legal assistance *below*
notification to accused **78,** 335
accusations, of, prompt **71,** 428-9
'charged with criminal offence' **72,** 398-9
'language which he understands', in **73,** 386-7, **74,** 413-16
lawyer of accused, to **78,** 221-3
native language **72,** 321-2
participation, right of **81,** 82-3
procedural decisions, applicability to **72,** 399-401
procedural guarantees **57,** 226-8
prosecution and defence, balance **43,** 178-9, **120,** 46-9
public hearing **105,** 614-15
consent **105,** 615
national security **105,** 614
private life **105,** 614
public morals **105,** 614
reasoned opinion, right to **121,** 312
'regulatory' offences **73,** 525-31, 533-46
rule of law **57,** 217
summary proceedings and **72,** 321-2
termination after prosecution, guilt, whether equivalent to finding of **67,** 519-25
transfer to another court **71,** 371-6, 386-7, 398-9, 407
ultimate control of judiciary, sufficient, whether **88,** 641, 643-4, 667-9
family life, respect for **45,** 114, 118, 119-22, 128, 137, 138-231, 371-6, **47,** 263-4, **51,** 236, **57,** 314, **61,** 270, 432, **72,** 573, **74,** 296, 446-8, **78,** 374, **81,** 67-8, **85,** 338, **89,** 175-6, 185. *See also* private life, respect for *below*
absence of compulsion **45,** 154
alien seeking to avoid deportation **123,** 597-8
arranged marriages and **61,** 263-5
burden of proof **111,** 295-6
child care
effect on family life **92,** 284

inhuman treatment, whether **92,** 294, 316-17
judicial consideration, right to **92,** 249, 303
justification for interference with **92,** 288-93
parental access **92,** 235, 292-3, 302-3, 314, 342-3
parent's right to be heard **92,** 236-8, 240, 248, 288
prohibition on removal from foster home **92,** 340-1
children, rights of **45,** 154-5
cohabitation, relevance **92,** 311-12, 341, 372-3
country of residence, right to choose **111,** 288
deportation and **92,** 366-9, **103,** 233, **108,** 422-3, 432-3, **111,** 169-70, 172, 181-5, 192. *See also* expulsion of alien and *below*
education, measures affecting family **45,** 163, 167, 173, 190, 224-5
environmental pollution, effect on **111,** 227-9
evidence of family life **111,** 182, 265-6
birth into marital union **111,** 286-7
critical date **111,** 289, 290-1
cultural background of family members **111,** 289
efforts to maintain family ties **111,** 287
expulsion of alien and **45,** 371-6, **108,** 312-13. *See also* deportation and *above*
failure to investigate disappearances and **120,** 59-60
family status, right to **89,** 178, 188-9
illegitimacy and **58,** 586-91, **89,** 179-82, 189
immigration controls and **81,** 165-70, **92,** 313-17, 318-19, **111,** 288-9
interference by public authority **111,** 287-8
'necessary in a democratic society' **92,** 288-93, **124,** 539
public safety **120,** 61
liberty of person, deprivation and **61,** 324-5
in northern Cyprus **120,** 86-91, 114
parents, rights of **45,** 154
paternity suit and **81,** 67-8, 70-1
prohibition on removal from foster home **92,** 340-1
property, denial of return or access to **120,** 60-3, 112
protection of minors **81,** 96
Protocol No 4 and **81,** 166-7
purpose of provision **81,** 71-2, 97, 168
right to found **61,** 262-3, 264, 265-6
family reunification, well-established right of abode, need for **111,** 281-2
forced or compulsory labour, definition **73,** 473-8. *See also* forced or compulsory labour, freedom from
ILO Conventions compared **73,** 472-5
forced or compulsory labour, freedom from **56,** 383, **74,** 303. *See also* forced or compulsory labour, freedom from
exceptions
military service **74,** 303
'normal civic obligations' **73,** 471, 475-8
meaning **73,** 473-8
ILO Conventions compared **73,** 472-5
'normal civic obligations' **73,** 471, 475-8
free elections
European Parliament elections
applicability of Art. 3 of Protocol 1 **123,** 14-16, 22-4
margin of appreciation **123,** 19-20
UK obligation to extend right to participate to Gibraltar **123,** 5-24

European Convention on Human Rights (1950) (*cont.*)
freedom of assembly/association **57,** 278, 286-8, **58,** 13, 14, 15, 16-17, 31, 91, **60,** 137, 141, **62,** 319, 321-2, 325, 328, 344-5, 354, 356-7, 360-1, 375-6, 378-9, 383-7, **71,** 429-30
abuse of rights and **122,** 417-18
closed shop agreement and **62,** 365-89. *See also* trade union, closed shop agreement
collective agreements, right to enter **58,** 31-2, 33
compulsion to join association and **62,** 319, 325, 328, 344, 361, 379-80, **75,** 60-2
interference **88,** 557, **122,** 419-20
'in accordance with the law'/'prescribed by law' **122,** 420, 421
legitimate aim **122,** 421
national security **122,** 421
necessary in a democratic society **122,** 421-4, **124,** 539
limits **58,** 14-15
northern Cyprus **120,** 80-2, 106-8, 114
peaceful assembly **58,** 31
political party
application to **122,** 415-29
choice of name **122,** 427
right to carry on activities **122,** 420
right to found **122,** 420
requirement to join professional association and **81,** 229
right not to join **62,** 361-2, 377-9, 384, 386-7
trade union rights and **57,** 279, 286-8, 297-8, **58,** 15, 33
freedom of belief **58,** 141, 142, 146, 147-9, 169. *See also* freedom of conscience *below*
freedom of choice **62,** 380, 384
freedom of conscience **58,** 146, 169, **62,** 375-6, 383, **73,** 383-5, **74,** 302-3
freedom of emigration **74,** 300. *See also* freedom of movement *below*
freedom of expression **40,** 188-90, **51,** 237-9, **58,** 87-91, **62,** 319, 321, 334-5, 361, 375-6, 380, 383, **72,** 373, 376, **73,** 382, 388, 395, 397-8, **78,** 396-402, **85,** 31-2, 34-5, 44-7, **88,** 524-30, 559, 585-90, 602-18, **89,** 234-5. *See also* correspondence, respect for *above*; freedom of opinion *below*
armed forces, in **58,** 87-90, **73,** 395-6
artistic expression **88,** 586
blasphemy laws and **87,** 434, 436
censorship of school books **120,** 78-80, 114
commercial advertising, whether within scope of Convention **81,** 221
commercial organization's right **101,** 153, 160-1
contempt of court and **78,** 396-402
content, relevance **101,** 115-16, 123, 133-4
correspondence and **72,** 373. *See also* correspondence, respect for *above*
damage to equipment for deployment of nuclear weapons as expression of opinion **122,** 512-13
democracy and **122,** 422-3
freedom from discrimination and. *See* freedom from discrimination, freedom of expression and *below*
freedom to impart information **73,** 382
freedom to receive information **89,** 235, 307, **101,** 128, 129-30, 152-4, 163
failure to account to families for missing persons **120,** 59-60
insulting Head of State **73,** 388
interference by public authority
ban on transmission **101,** 115-16, 128, 129-30

control of retransmission **101,** 116-18, 122
protection of freedom of expression as necessary objective **101,** 131
jurisdiction, retransmission **101,** 117-18, 125-8
licensing of broadcasting **73,** 397-8
military service and **73,** 383-5, **78,** 227-54, 256-74, 278-82
newspapers, prohibition on **120,** 80, 106
obscene publications. *See* obscene publications *below*
other conventions compared **75,** 44-8, 66-73
penalties, interference with **88,** 586, 588-9, 591-6
confiscation, permissibility **88,** 591-6
political opinion **58,** 176
prevention of disorder
military life and **58,** 89
'prevention of crime' and **58,** 89
public order/public policy/*ordre public* distinguished **58,** 88-9
prior restraint of publication **78,** 402
religious opinion **58,** 146
reporting methods for press to decide **107,** 42, 44
restrictions
administration of justice **78,** 397-402
law and order, protection of **73,** 395-6
maintenance of the authority of judiciary **88,** 605, 606
morals, protection of **73,** 382
'necessary in a democratic society' **73,** 382, 395, **75,** 44-5, **124,** 539
'pressing social need' **78,** 401-2
proportionality **122,** 512-13
respect for private life **88,** 533
retransmission
consent of broadcasting State, need for **101,** 139-63
technical developments, relevance **101,** 158-9, 161-2
standard, politician and private individual distinguished **88,** 527-8, 532-3
terrorism. *See* freedom of expression, terrorism and
unfair competition and **101,** 81-95
freedom from discrimination **45,** 114, 118, 119-22, 128, 131, 138-231, **49,** 101, **51,** 240, **56,** 385, **57,** 277-9, 281-3, 286-8, 290-304, **61,** 242-4, **68,** 21, 25-6, 28, **79,** 315-21, **81,** 96. *See also* freedom from discrimination
affiliation **58,** 581-3, 617
age **58,** 358
application of Convention and **58,** 611-13
armed forces
civilians and **58,** 87, 90, 101
ranks, between **58,** 77-9, 90, 101
arrest **58,** 285-8, 307
assistance, legal **58,** 584-5
association **58,** 16-17
bias **58,** 302
birth **58,** 578-9, 582-3, 586-7, 588-90, 597, 620
immigration controls and **81,** 177
as civil right **123,** 70
collective agreements **58,** 35
conscientious objection **78,** 251-2
corporal punishment **58,** 358
costs, interpretation **58,** 475-6, 484-5

European Convention on Human Rights (1950) (*cont.*)
denial of justice **58,** 182
detention **58,** 77-9, 285-8
education **58,** 145
UNESCO Convention against Discrimination in **45,** 156
effective remedy before national authority, right to **120,** 67
enjoyment of Convention rights **73,** 398, 425-6, 478-9, **75,** 374-5, 378
equality of treatment and **45,** 120, 156, 157-8, 164-5, 207, 230, **57,** 281-3, 287
fair hearing **58,** 77, 87, 290, 332, 484-5, 640
fair trial, language and **58,** 484-5
foreigner **58,** 484-5
interpretation costs **58,** 475-6, 484-5
freedom of expression and **107,** 39-45, 47-9
function of provision **45,** 131, 147, 225-76
human rights, in exercise of **73,** 398, 425-6, 478-9, **75,** 374-5, 378
independent obligations **45,** 159, 164
independent right, whether **81,** 67, 100, **121,** 205
inhuman treatment and **120,** 91-4, 115, 125
justified differential treatment **45,** 120, 156-8, 160, 164-5, 174, 180, 196, 199-200, 206, 209, 213, 215, 218-19, **58,** 337, 582-3, 584, 586, **75,** 424, 429-30, 483-4, 494, 500-4, 524-6, 542-7, **78,** 251-2, **79,** 301, 303, 306, 316-17, 319-20, 322
objective and reasonable **58,** 36, 78, 286, 579, 586, 588, 592, 600, 617
reasonableness **75,** 583-4
language **58,** 475-6, 484-5
legal assistance **58,** 584-5
legitimacy **58,** 578-9, 582-3, 586-7, 588-90, 597, 620
manifest abuse **58,** 182
marriage **58,** 582, 591-2, 597, 617
maternal affiliation, attribution of **58,** 581-3
mothers, married and unmarried **58,** 582, 591-2, 597, 617
nationality **58,** 484-5
nationality, deportation and **92,** 369-70
obligation to take action **45,** 156
patrimonial rights **58,** 588-9
peaceful enjoyment of possessions **120,** 67
personal characteristic **58,** 145
political opinion **58,** 169, 182
preferential treatment **58,** 13
private and family life **120,** 67
proceedings between military and civil **58,** 87, 90
property **58,** 640, 651
publications, seizure **58,** 181-2
racial **107,** 39-45, 47-9
immigration controls and **81,** 175-6
motive, relevance **107,** 45
transmission of another's remarks, responsibility for **107,** 39-45, 47-9
UN Convention on the Elimination of Racial Discrimination, relevance **107,** 38, 39-45, 47-9
religious **58,** 145, **87,** 435-6
religious broadcasting **47,** 198-203
sexual. *See* homosexuality, sexual discrimination *and* transsexualism *below*
status **58,** 87, 145, 349, 358, 578-9, 582-3, 591-2
terrorists, between **58,** 285-8, 332

trade unions, between **58,** 16-17, 35
members of, between **58,** 13
freedom of movement **61,** 311-12, 327, 328-32, 333, **71,** 257, **74,** 300-1, **77,** 534-5, **86,** 335. *See also* freedom of emigration *above*; liberty of person, deprivation *below*
residence, choice of **74,** 293
restrictions **77,** 535
travel outside national territory **77,** 535-6
freedom of opinion **62,** 380. *See also* freedom of expression *above*
freedom of the press **58,** 534-6. *See also* freedom of expression *above*
public
right to be informed and **58,** 148, 534, 535-6
right to inform **58,** 148, 534
restrictions **58,** 88-9, 172-7, 535-6
freedom of religion **47,** 198-203, 205-11, **61,** 320, 327, 334, 335-6, **92,** 296-7, 347
blasphemy laws and **87,** 433, 434-5
manifestation of religion in worship
'in community and with others' **73,** 420-1
right to **73,** 403, 407-8, 410-14, 420-6
restrictions, 'necessary in a democratic society' **73,** 407-8
restrictions on, freedom of movement as **120,** 77-8, 114, 124-5, 142
friendly settlement. *See* European Court of Human Rights, friendly settlement
general aim of parties **45,** 162, 209
general interest. *See* margin of appreciation *below*
general principles of international law and **75,** 423-5, 435, 482-5, 515-17, 521-5, **123,** 93
grievance
domestic courts, actions of and **68,** 74
existence of **68,** 73-6
grievance, existence of **68,** 73-6
domestic courts and **68,** 74
habitual offenders **67,** 540-9
detention without trial **67,** 545-9
home, respect for **75,** 576-81. *See also* family life, respect for *above*
denial of return or access to property in northern Cyprus and **120,** 60-3, 112-13
interference by public authority **75,** 577-81
'in accordance with the law' **67,** 411-12, **74,** 372-8, 383-91, **75,** 577-9, **120,** 62
'necessary in a democratic society' **75,** 580-1
political settlement, need for as justification **120,** 61-2
public safety **120,** 61
plans to make home **108,** 468-9
homosexuality **67,** 408, 418-19, 423, 426-8
age of consent **67,** 417-18
private life, respect for **67,** 409-18, 424-9, 431-7, **89,** 256-61
immigration controls, applicability to **111,** 291-2
immigration procedures **61,** 256, 257, 269-70
implementation
applicable law, Convention **108,** 421
different methods, consequences **81,** 183
obligation **81,** 48-9, **115,** 641-2
procedure, national discretion **104,** 446, **115,** 642-3
implementing legislation **72,** 297-8, 303, 374-6
absence **73,** 403, 410-11, **74,** 312, 325-6, 339-40, 357, 446

European Convention on Human Rights (1950) (*cont.*)
anticipated implementation **122,** 1, 436-9, 440-9, 453-9, 465-7
interpretation **78,** 326
incorporation of Convention into municipal law **68,** 75, **85,** 44, **88,** 555
anticipated implementation of legislation **122,** 1, 436-9, 440-9, 453-9, 465-7
effective remedy before national authority and **61,** 373-4, 378, 386-7, **68,** 75, **81,** 178-9
'in accordance with the law' and **124,** 539
independent and impartial tribunal **62,** 326, 342, 138-9, **71,** 401, 418-19, 425-6, **75,** 356-8, 362, 374, 377-8, 505-6, 550-1, 586, **77,** 439, **78,** 245-7, 249, 270-2, 290-1, 329-32, 354-5, **81,** 8-9, 41-9, **82,** 56, **86,** 363, **88,** 671-3
burden of proof **81,** 42
competent court **58,** 74-5, 95-7, 108-10, 275-6, 676, 678, 695-9, **67,** 468
established by law **62,** 342, **68,** 141-2, **75,** 506-7, 550-1
as autonomous concept **120,** 118
in unrecognized State **120,** 76, 118-19
European Commission, whether **111,** 135
evidence of **78,** 330-2
government report, effect of **75,** 356-7
impartiality **68,** 130-41, **71,** 401, 418-19, 425-6
presumption of **71,** 425
military court **58,** 75
military tribunal **58,** 75, **78,** 247, 249, **120,** 16, 105-6
objective test **121,** 333-4
right to hearing before **62,** 321, 326, 334-43, 345, 348, 354, 356, **68,** 119-20
content of rights distinguished **120,** 74-6
fact, question of **62,** 340-1
law **62,** 340-1
litigation by State in courts of another contracting State and **121,** 205
status as
administrative appeals board **86,** 363-5
administrative court with limited powers of review **96,** 580-2
Board of Prison Visitors **78,** 329, 350
court of appeal **81,** 47
courts in northern Cyprus **120,** 73-7, 113-14, 120-2, 141-2
Disabled Persons Board **96,** 581
immigration advisory panel **124,** 515-16
International Criminal Tribunal for the Former Yugoslavia **121,** 212
organs of medical association **62,** 325-8, 332-4, 358
Provisional Governor **96,** 581
treaty interpretation, in case of **107,** 61-2
individual's right to invoke **62,** 69, 73, **77,** 248, **93,** 226, **95,** 332. *See also* European Commission on Human Rights, applications, individual; European Court of Human Rights, individual
inhuman or degrading treatment **58,** 259, 264, 265-71, 316, 352, 353-9, 362-9, 592, 602, **61,** 249-50, 319, 327, 369, **67,** 491-3, **71,** 311-16, 347-53, 356-65, 419-20, **72,** 324, **81,** 96, 101, 177-8. *See also* inhuman or degrading treatment
assassination **99,** 9-10
balance of interests **98,** 302
death penalty in non-signatory State **78,** 389-94
death row. *See* death row as inhuman or degrading treatment *above*
deportation **111,** 191, 266, 268-9
derogation, excluded **98,** 302

detention **75,** 366-7
discrimination amounting to **120,** 91-4, 115, 125
environmental pollution **111,** 229
of family members in case of deportation giving rise to risk of torture **123,** 598
of family members in case of failure to investigate disappearances **120,** 58-9, 112, 131
freedom from **74,** 710-11
illegitimate family and **58,** 592-3
imprisonment, appropriate term **75,** 366-7
as international standard **98,** 302
interrogation methods **58,** 265-71, 304, 316, 324-6, 360
long imprisonment for war crimes **74,** 710-11, **75,** 366-7
refusal of parental access, whether **96,** 17
taking child into care, whether **92,** 294
threshold **108,** 311-12, 321, 355, 356
treatment of displaced persons **120,** 68
interim measures. *See also* European Commission of Human Rights, interim measures
absence of provision **108,** 315-16, 320
proposed Protocol **108,** 315-16
implied, whether **108,** 316-17, 320
international organizations, privileges and immunities, relevance **107,** 4-5, **118,** 132-7
judicial assistance, request for and **82,** 56
judicial process **56,** 411-13. *See also* fair hearing *above*
judicial review, effect on **112,** 385-7, 395-6, **114,** 421-2, 462-5
judicial role **88,** 672
jurisdiction
immunity, effect on **69,** 143
Parties' **62,** 12, 27-34, 44, 51, 54-5, 64-8, 74, 76, 86-7
just satisfaction (Art. 50 [41]). *See* just satisfaction (Art. 50 [41] of European Convention on Human Rights (1950))
legal aid, right to **111,** 208
legal assistance **57,** 220, 230-1, **58,** 86, 96, 99-100, 104, **60,** 196-9, **72,** 418-29
correspondence concerning, right of **78,** 382-8
free **72,** 419-29, **73,** 470, 476
lawyer of own choosing **58,** 86, 345, 346, **78,** 220-5, 335-6, 337-40, 343-4, 345, 346
speedy access **58,** 86, **78,** 339
legislation
as aid to interpretation **91,** 321
right to challenge **75,** 431-2, 512-13
right to hearing **75,** 431-2
liberty of person, deprivation **38,** 176, **40,** 245, **41,** 283, 297-8, 302, 313-15, **56,** 375, 378-9, 490, **57,** 215, **58,** 72, 73, 99, 274, 667-8, **61,** 310-18, 322-3, 333, **67,** 461, **72,** 309-16, 409, **78,** 238, 243. *See also* detainees *and* detention *above*
arbitrary **86,** 345
in armed forces **58,** 71-7
Art. 5 provisions, separability **111,** 209
compulsory residence and **61,** 311-13
mafiosi and **61,** 314-15, 331-2, 334
court, by **58,** 676, 678, 695-9, **67,** 461-2, 466-71, 540-5
definition **58,** 72
derogation **58,** 230, 234, 237, 239, 279-85, 307, 329, 330
detention on island, *mafiosi* in Italy **61,** 310-18
disciplinary unit, committal to **58,** 73, 107, 109

European Convention on Human Rights (1950) (*cont.*)
discrimination and **58,** 77-8, 285-8, 322, 337
as disguised extradition **86,** 346, **95,** 332-3
extrajudicial **58,** 274-7, 303
failure to carry out investigations into disappearances as **120,** 55-7, 112
family life and **61,** 324-5
following conviction by a competent court **58,** 75, 79, 107, 108, 275-6, 695, **67,** 462, 540-5
freedom of movement and **61,** 311-12, 327, 328-32, 333, 335-6, 339
habitual offenders **67,** 540-9
individual's right **95,** 332
inter-State liability **95,** 332
internment **58,** 272-7, 337
judicial guarantees **58,** 75, 107, 275-6, 694-9, 701-2
judicial review **67,** 466-71, 545-9
lawful detention with a view to deportation **86,** 346, **95,** 332-3, **108,** 417-20, 429-33
determination of lawfulness by advisory panel **104,** 437-8, **108,** 420-2
excessive length **108,** 417-19, 430, 433
procedure prescribed by law **108,** 419-22, 440-3. *See also* European Convention on Human Rights (1950), interpretation, phrases, 'in accordance with the law'/'prescribed by law'
'reasonably necessary' requirement **108,** 418, 437
lawful detention with a view to extradition **108,** 441, **111,** 206-10
applicant's dilatory conduct **111,** 209
applicant's failure to compel setting of time-limits **111,** 207
applicant's request for postponement **111,** 207-8
consent to extension of time-limit, implied **111,** 207
excessive length **111,** 207-8, 249-50
negligence of State authorities **111,** 250
State's obligation to expedite proceedings **111,** 207-8
lawfulness **58,** 97, 99, 276-7, 667, 669-71, 674-7, 701, **61,** 314-17, 334-5, 336-7, 339-40, **67,** 461-2, 464-6, 468-71, 541-5, **86,** 342-6
Convention, under **86,** 342, **95,** 331-2
municipal law, under **86,** 342
valid warrant **95,** 331-2
limitations **58,** 72, 75-6, 103, 671-3, 701, **67,** 465
mafiosi and **61,** 310-18, 331-2, 334
mentally ill person **58,** 658-63, 667-73, **67,** 462-71
military disciplinary training and **73,** 394-6
private life and **61,** 324-5
purpose other than that for which intended **111,** 250
restriction on freedom of movement distinguished **81,** 123-4
security, threat to **120,** 72-3, 113
State immunity as bar to suit and **121,** 203-4
statement of reasons **67,** 471-3
vagrants and **61,** 314-15, 331-2, 334
life, right to. *See also* death penalty *above*
alleged killings **120,** 53, 111
disappearances and **120,** 52-5
failure to investigate **120,** 55, 111-12
medical care, access to **120,** 71-2, 113, 140-1
obligation to take measures to protect and preserve **120,** 53-5
contribution to work of UN Committee on Missing Persons (CMP), relevance **120,** 52-3, 57, 131-2

margin of appreciation **58,** 278-9, 294, 306, 307, **68,** 108-10, 116-18, 124-7, **78,** 204, **88,** 526, 588, 595-6, 603, 614, **89,** 104-5, 138-41, 181, **92,** 236, 290, 303, 315, 319, 344, **101,** 86-8, 91-2, 121-2, **107,** 17. *See also* margin of appreciation; *and under individual rights*
balance of interests **101,** 94-5, **107,** 48, **123,** 52-3
individual/community as a whole **111,** 227, 229, 288, 293-4, **122,** 445-7, 480-1, 486-8
choice of means **107,** 17, **108,** 358
ECHR's competence to determine acceptability **118,** 134
nature of obligation, relevance **111,** 293-4
marriage, right of **72,** 297-8, **89,** 109, 121, 127-8, 141-6. *See also* family, right to found *above*
divorce, inadmissibility and **89,** 172-5, 185-8
freedom of conscience and **89,** 177
freedom from discrimination **58,** 582, 591-2, 597, 617
temporary restriction
human rights, abuse of, whether **89,** 195-206
legislative reform **89,** 199-200
transsexualism and **89,** 101-2, 109, 121, 127-8, 141-6, 153
mentally ill person **78,** 203-12
military service and **58,** 39-116
morals, absence of uniform European conception **88,** 589-90
municipal courts and
discontinuance of proceedings **68,** 74-6, 84
enforcement of Convention by **68,** 75-6, 135
fundamental procedural guarantees **38,** 174-90, **43,** 178-81, **45,** 315, 318, 452, **56,** 380-2
mitigation of sentences **68,** 74-6, 82
municipal law and **40,** 186, 238-43, 245-6, **57,** 191, 224, 550-5, **67,** 463, 550-5, **68,** 75, **73,** 382-8, 394-8, 403, 407-8, 410-14, **74,** 291-314, 322-6, 339-40, 357, 446-8, 457, 703, **78,** 234-7, **85,** 44-7. *See also* implementing legislation *above*
application by courts **78,** 372-8, **85,** 32
compatibility **56,** 409, **57,** 223, **78,** 338, **84,** 763, **89,** 196, **118,** 132-3
presumption of **47,** 129, 172, 186-7, **85,** 31
compliance with, obligation **86,** 344, **122,** 418-20
conflict **56,** 419-20, 424-6, **88,** 622
defence, whether **68,** 81
direct effect **38,** 177, **61,** 374, **71,** 257, 380, 403, **72,** 297-8, 303, 310, 376, **73,** 383, **74,** 303, 315, 325-6, 339-40, 357, 703, **85,** 46-7, **111,** 169, **115,** 644. *See also* implementation *above*
interpretation
aid to **86,** 368
responsibility for **86,** 344-5
modification of **68,** 340, **78,** 337-8, 340, **86,** 319-21
obligations under **85,** 31
part of, whether **85,** 31, **89,** 252
primacy. *See* primacy *below*
relevance **78,** 407, 415, 418
rights under, effect of Convention on **56,** 410
subsidiarity **111,** 171, **121,** 419
Namibia **103,** 94-5, 102
national authorities, freedom of choice **45,** 120, 122, 165, 219, 222
nature **57,** 250
necessity **88,** 596, 605

European Convention on Human Rights (1950) (*cont.*)
Northern Ireland and **58,** 230, 234, 237, 277-85
notice of **58,** 230, 234, 237
object **41,** 314, **57,** 191-2, 216-17, 229-30
European public order **103,** 650, **120,** 39, **123,** 115
reciprocal rights and obligations, whether **88,** 626, 633, 678
objects and methods of parties, review of **45,** 158
obligations
application of treaties concluded subsequent to Convention, effect **111,** 152
measures to secure rights under Convention **123,** 35-6, 115
nature **57,** 292, **62,** 62-3, 69, 72-3, **89,** 178, 179
positive nature **81,** 97-8, **111,** 293-4
representations on behalf of alien **123,** 596-8
respect for institutions **60,** 195
transfer of powers to international organization, effect **111,** 140-1, 145-6
obscene publications
discrimination and, seizure **58,** 181-2
freedom of expression and **58,** 171-80, **73,** 381-2
margin of appreciation **58,** 172, 174, 177
morals, protection of and **58,** 172-4
possessions, deprivation of and **58,** 180-2
seizure of, discrimination **58,** 181-2
peaceful enjoyment of possessions **60,** 17, 179, **73,** 480-1, **74,** 293, **75,** 428, 480-1, 520, 588-9. *See also* deprivation of property *above*
by Greek Cypriots in northern Cyprus **120,** 82-4, 114
control of use in public interest **117,** 287-8, 300-2
action in compliance with Security Council Resolutions **117,** 287-92, 301-3
denial of return or access to property in northern Cyprus **108,** 462-3, 467-8, 471-83, **120,** 63-5, 112-13
family life, respect for and **120,** 60-3, 112-13
freedom of movement distinguished **108,** 468, 488
historical and political context giving rise to **108,** 471-83, **120,** 125-35
home life, respect for and **120,** 60-3, 112-13
deprivation
control of use distinguished **108,** 468
justified in public interest **74,** 293
right to dispose of **120,** 83-4
interference with, justification
general interest **86,** 427
political settlement, need for **120,** 61-2
proportionality **86,** 427
public interest **74,** 293
reasonableness **75,** 588-9
protection, failure **120,** 84, 114
remuneration for services, applicability to **73,** 480-1
residential property accommodation order and **122,** 290-3
restrictions on. *See* interference with, justification *above*
right to exercise profession **86,** 426-7, 433
presumption of innocence **41,** 295, 314-15, 349, 351, **44,** 104, 106, **45,** 313, **56,** 490, **58,** 85, **60,** 177-8, **71,** 428, **72,** 394-404, **74,** 293-4, **78,** 329, 334-5, **81,** 198, **82,** 56, **100,** 333-4
burden of proof and **122,** 445-9, 476-80
'charged with a criminal offence' **72,** 398-9

civil rights, infringement of and **72,** 399
costs, apportionment of **72,** 399-404
extradition, applicability to **74,** 294
private prosecution **72,** 398-9
primacy **78,** 399, **86,** 120
balance of interests **96,** 388
direct effect of treaty, relevance **96,** 388
other treaties **96,** 387-8
previous legislation **38,** 176-80
prisoners. *See* detainees *and* detention *above*
private life, respect for **51,** 236, **57,** 220, 231-9, **58,** 146, 578, **73,** 396, **74,** 292, 296, 322, 324-5, 341-2, 371-91, **78,** 341. *See also* family life, respect for *above*
access to personal files and **89,** 300-7
deportation **111,** 172, 190-1, 193-4, 270-1
disclosure of medical reports in extradition proceedings **119,** 304, 316-17
fair trial and **105,** 614-15
homosexuality and **67,** 409-18, 424-9, 431-7, **89,** 256-61
interference by public authority **67,** 411-18, 431-7
'in accordance with the law' **67,** 411-12, **74,** 372-8, 383-91
legislation as **67,** 411, 425-9, 442
margin of appreciation **67,** 414, 417
proportionality **119,** 316-17
protection of morals **67,** 412, 417, 420-3, 433-7
protection of others **67,** 412-13
public interest **74,** 292
social need **67,** 413-18, 420-3, 424, 429, 433-7
unjust **67,** 409-18, 420-4, 433-7
liberty of person, deprivation **61,** 324-5
maintenance of secret record and **89,** 227-34
military discipline and **73,** 396
nature of right **67,** 431-3
in northern Cyprus **120,** 86-91, 114
police investigations **67,** 442-3
secret surveillance and **58,** 446-9, **120,** 89
seizure of materials as protective measure and **89,** 283-6
telephone-tapping **58,** 446, 461, 604, **74,** 321-2, 324-5, 341-2, 371-91
transsexualism and **89,** 103-9, 124-7
procedures, differing, common and civil law Parties **41,** 314, 344
proceedings under, 'legal', whether **78,** 382-8
prompt hearing **56,** 480-4, 487-8, 489-92, **71,** 376-9, 382-9, 404-8, **72,** 302-6, 317-19, **73,** 428, 453-7,489, 492-8, 505-9, 558-9, 563-4, **74,** 457, **78,** 238, 247-8, 249-50, 272, 285, 290, 332-3, 357-71, **92,** 238, 240
administrative proceedings **73,** 448-57
applicants, obstructive tactics of **68,** 80-1, 83
applicant's obligation to advance proceedings **96,** 530, 554, 588, 598
14 months **96,** 618
4 years **96,** 601
criminal proceedings **96,** 601
parental access cases **96,** 601
before 'officer authorized by law to exercise judicial power' **58,** 694-9, **78,** 238, 245-7, 269-72, 286-7, 289-90
advisory committee on internment **78,** 269, 287
breach as bar to proceedings **72,** 317-19

European Convention on Human Rights (1950) (*cont.*)
civil proceedings **73,** 492-8
complexity of case, relevance **45,** 300, 307, 312, 313, 325, **71,** 384, 406, **72,** 305, **78,** 366
conduct of parties, relevance **71,** 384, 406-7, **72,** 306, **78,** 209-11, 366-70
courts' workload, relevance **71,** 385, **72,** 306, **73,** 450-2, 455-6
criminal proceedings **68,** 77-86, **70,** 192-209, **71,** 376-9, 382-9, 401, 404-7, **72,** 302-6, 317-19
commencement **68,** 77-8, **71,** 382-3, 404-5, **72,** 302
determination **68,** 78-9, **71,** 383, 405-6
procedural bar, whether **72,** 317-19, **75,** 351-2
delayed prosecution **71,** 273-7, **72,** 302-6, 317-19
mental anguish **71,** 273-7, **72,** 302, 304-5, 319
delays attributable to State, limited to **96,** 554, 599, **99,** 25
fair hearing, relation to **70,** 197-200, 206-9
investigations, difficulty of **68,** 82
length of proceedings
reasonableness **68,** 80-4, **71,** 384-8, 406-8, **72,** 303-6, **73,** 453-7, 489, 492, **75,** 340, 348-58, 506, 551-4
relevant factors **71,** 406-7, **72,** 304-5
prompt control of detention distinguished **78,** 247-50
'reasonable time' **41,** 283, 284, 293-306, 308-15, 316-60, **45,** 232-3, 259-328, **62,** 297-9, 301, 310-17, **71,** 377, 378-9, 382-8, 404-8, **78,** 365, 370, **86,** 318, 398-402, **87,** 95
18 months **96,** 443
5 years **96,** 520, 523-33, 601
6 years **96,** 492-5
7 years **96,** 443-9, 472-4, 553-9, 598-600, 601-2
8 years **96,** 510-15
9 years **96,** 476, 519, 582-3, 601
10 years **96,** 459-63
12 years **96,** 602
court's duty to ensure prompt hearing **96,** 460, 530
delay in obtaining expert advice **96,** 461-2
divorce proceedings **96,** 519
relevant factors **41,** 309-10, 312, **57,** 194-7, **60,** 169, **71,** 371-9, 382-8, 398-401, 404-8, **72,** 303-6, **73,** 453-7, 489, 492-8, **75,** 348-58, 506, 551-4, **78,** 209-11, 366-70
absence of appellant **78,** 209-10
applicant's state of health **96,** 514-15
behaviour of judicial authorities **96,** 446-7, 494-5, 513-15, 519, 529, 531-3, 554-5, 589-90, 599-600
circumstances of case **96,** 459, 473, 492, 510, 513, 582, 587, 601
complexity of case **86,** 398-9, **96,** 444, 460, 493, 529, 530, 553, 582-3, 588, 598
courts' workload **68,** 83-4, **73,** 455-6, **86,** 400, **96,** 473, 519, 532-3, 554, 602
criteria **62,** 310-17
European standard of **45,** 313
exigencies of military life **78,** 249, 272
existence of alternative procedures **78,** 209
need to consult third State **99,** 25
parties' conduct **71,** 384, 406-7, **72,** 306, **78,** 209-11, 366-70, **86,** 399
practice in other Member States, relevance **96,** 513
state of case at commencement of period **96,** 473, 510, 529

relevant period **86,** 398
commencement of proceedings **96,** 443, 459, 587, 598
continuing **96,** 459
enforcement proceedings **96,** 529
entry of Convention into force **96,** 519, 601
judgment **96,** 443, 529, 587, 598
legal aid procedure **96,** 553
recognition of right of individual petition **96,** 473, 510, 529
remedial action, relevance **96,** 532, 554
State responsibility for acts and omissions of judicial authorities **96,** 515
action to remedy judicial procedure defects **96,** 473-4, 513, 519
delay in obtaining expert opinion **96,** 462
diligence in cases affecting civil status and capacity **96,** 519
mitigating factors **96,** 600
proper administration of justice **96,** 448, 474, 492, 495, 510-11, 532, 590, 601
provision of means to fulfil treaty obligations **96,** 515
termination of enforcement proceedings **96,** 510
prompt release **78,** 248
prompt trial. *See* prompt hearing *above*
property rights. *See* deprivation of property *and* peaceful enjoyment of possessions *above*
provisional detention. *See* detention, provisional *above*
public hearing **41,** 282, 284, 306-7, 316-18, 342, **57,** 60-1, **62,** 321-2, 326, 334, 343, 345, 353-4, 356-8, **71,** 419, 426-7, 430, **73,** 490-2, 505-11, 558-9, 563-4, **74,** 457, **78,** 332-3
absence, justification **73,** 508-9, 559, 563, **78,** 333-4
waiver **62,** 343, 353
public policy and, expulsion of alien, risk of assassination **99,** 7-8
public pronouncement of judgment **56,** 479, **73,** 489-92, 505-11, 558-63
absence, justification **73,** 491, 509, 560, 563
entirety of proceedings, examination in light of **73,** 491-2, 508, 558
form of publicity required **73,** 490-2, 509-10, 559-62
International Covenant on Civil and Political Rights (ICCPR) (1966) compared **73,** 492, 509, 560
literal interpretation not required **78,** 334
public right, private or civil right distinguished **62,** 355, 358
punishment **71,** 419-20
degrading **58,** 353-9, 362-9
circumstances **58,** 354-5
debasement, level of **58,** 353, 362
inhuman **58,** 352
juvenile, of **58,** 360
long imprisonment for war crimes, whether inhuman or degrading **74,** 710-11, **75,** 366-7
purpose **56,** 388-9, 392, **57,** 291, 293, **75,** 53
main **45,** 135
ratification, Fourth Protocol (1963) **61,** 329
Refugees, Convention on Status of (1951) and **108,** 440
release pending trial **41,** 316-18, 334, 335, 336-7, 342-3, 349-50, 357-8. *See also* prompt hearing *above*
absconding, risk of **41,** 305, 325, 326, 352-3, **45,** 263, 273, 276, 299, 305, 306, 308, 310, 315
equality of arms **45,** 277, 295, 296, 308, 315, **124,** 87 n. 85
expected punishment **45,** 321-8

European Convention on Human Rights (1950) (*cont.*)
gravity of offence **45,** 321-3
grounds for detention, relevance **45,** 264, 268-70, 300
means and end, proportionality **45,** 321
obstruction of enquiry by accused **45,** 326
repetition of offence, danger of **45,** 263, 272-3, 276, 277, 299, 305, 309-10, 311-12, 314-15
right to, **41,** 281-306, 308-15, 316-60, **45,** 232, 259-328, **70,** 203-6
security, amount **41,** 318, 329-30, 336, 348, 353-4
remedies **56,** 42, 425, **57,** 228, 256, 257
municipal courts **56,** 403
restitutio in integrum **56,** 497
right to **51,** 236-7
remedy for breach, international proceedings, limited to **115,** 643-4
remission, loss of, punishment, whether **78,** 327-8
reservations **38,** 174-80, **77,** 482. *See also* derogation *above*
definition **88,** 627-8, 641
interpretative declaration as **107,** 20, **123,** 383
non-interference with administrative procedure laws **107,** 11-12, 13-14
separability **123,** 290, 383
timing
ratification **107,** 18, 21
signature **107,** 18
torture/inhuman or degrading treatment (Art. 3) **108,** 355, 362, 410-11, 435
'extraterritorial' application **108,** 435
validity **88,** 678-9
'brief statement of the law concerned' **88,** 631-3, 634, 645-6, 669-70, **107,** 14, 18-19
burden of proof **103,** 650
'clear intention', need for **88,** 628, 643, 667-8
compatibility with object and purpose of Convention **88,** 668
contemporary jurisprudence and **88,** 668
content **88,** 666
essential basis for acceptance of obligations, whether **103,** 650
European Commission of Human Rights, competence to determine **88,** 625-7
European Court of Human Rights, competence to determine **88,** 626-7, 666-7
express provision, need for **103,** 646-7
general reservations **88,** 620-1, 643, 668-9
judicial review at time of making, need for **107,** 20-1
law currently in force, need for **107,** 13, 18, 19
'law then in force' **88,** 622
objection to, effect **107,** 20-1
'of a general character' **107,** 13, 18-19
purpose **88,** 663
ratification process **88,** 629-30, 641, 669
reaction of other States party **88,** 665
reaction of Secretary-General **88,** 665
rectification, possibility of **107,** 22
responsibility for determining **107,** 20-2
territorial restrictions on Art. 25 and 46 declarations **103,** 643-51
timing. *See* timing *above*
reserved domain **45,** 118, 119, 124, 131, 133, 135, 231
residence, freedom to choose **61,** 327, 328-32, **74,** 293

rights greater than in Convention **41,** 313
rights under **45,** 120, 156-8, 160, 164-5, 174, 180, 196, 199-200, 206, 209, 213, 215, 218-19, **58,** 14-15, 16, 32, 71-2, 75-6, 87, 88-90, 103, 148, 172-7, 181, 183-5, 281-4, 289, 290, 355-8, 523-36, 538, 540-1, 543, 548, 550-5, 582, 586-92, 667, 669-73, 701, **61,** 376-7, **62,** 361, 382, **72,** 368-9, **73,** 382, 395, **75,** 44-5, 424, 429-30, 483-4, 494, 500-4, 524-6, 542-7, **77,** 535, **78,** 251-2, 397-402, **79,** 301, 303, 306, 316-17, 319-20, 322
absolute, whether **81,** 84, **99,** 10, **124,** 275
aliens **111,** 170, 188
not to be deported **111,** 188
residence **111,** 188
civil rights and obligations. *See* civil rights and obligations *above*
equality of **122,** 446
freedom of choice in exercise of **62,** 361, 380, 384
individual **86,** 531, **93,** 613-15
jus quaesitum tertio **93,** 614-15
quod fieri debet infectum valet **93,** 613-14
interference with **57,** 219, **58,** 14-15, **81,** 222-9, **86,** 427. *See also* derogation *above*; European Convention on Human Rights (1950), interpretation, phrases, 'in accordance with the law'/'prescribed by law'; European Convention on Human Rights (1950), interpretation, phrases, 'necessary in a democratic society'
justification **62,** 361, 380-2, 385-6
nature of **60,** 196-7
rights under national law distinguished **45,** 227, 228
substance same for all parties **45,** 228-9, 230
waiver **81,** 83-4
burden of proof **81,** 83
scope **57,** 224-5
ratione personae **36,** 16-17, 308
self-determination **108,** 552-3
self-executing provisions. *See* municipal law and, direct effect *above*
separability **111,** 250
Art. 50 provisions **111,** 209
sex change, right to legal recognition of **61,** 369, 382-3
sexual discrimination **58,** 358
immigration controls and **81,** 171-5
paternity suit and **81,** 67-71
recruitment of locally engaged staff, diplomatic mission **123,** 66-7
slavery or servitude, prohibition, prolonged detention **120,** 55, 112
State responsibility
failure to rectify law **62,** 376-7
failure to rectify problem **111,** 228-9
following transfer of competence to European Community **123,** 13-14
Maastricht Treaty (1992), consequences **123,** 13-14
prompt hearing. *See* prompt hearing, State responsibility *above*
State responsibility for acts and omissions
in compliance with international obligations, execution of judgment of European Court of Justice **111,** 139-40
of judicial authorities **96,** 515
outside State's jurisdiction **98,** 299, 300-3, 404-6
direct result of own action **98,** 303, **123,** 35-6
foreseeable result of own action **98,** 301, 303
legal representation, lack of **98,** 313-14

European Convention on Human Rights (1950) (*cont.*)
statutory limitation **78,** 132-3
human right or fundamental freedom, whether **78,** 135
system established by, jurisdiction of institutions, limits **71,** 303, 378-9
tax, imprisonment for non-payment **40,** 241-2, 244-6
telephone conversations **58,** 446-54
margin of appreciation **58,** 448-9
safeguards **58,** 450-3
surveillance of **58,** 446
abuse **58,** 448-9
victim of **58,** 441-5, 460
telephone-tapping **58,** 446, 461, 604, **74,** 321-2, 324-5, 341-2, 371-91
text **57,** 226-7
thought, freedom of **62,** 361, 382, 384-5
religious broadcasting **47,** 198-203
torture **58,** 315, **71,** 300
administrative practices **58,** 263-4, 268-9
confession, extraction of as **58,** 267, 298
corporal punishment **58,** 352
definition **58,** 266, 297, 298-9, 304-5, 314-17, 326-8, 333-4, 335-6, 352, 360-1, **70,** 233-4, **121,** 264, **123,** 41
derogation **58,** 278-9, 294, 306, 307
inhumane or degrading treatment distinguished **121,** 264 n. 179
interrogation techniques **58,** 239-54, 265-7, 317-20, 326-9, 333-4, **71,** 295-303, 311
suffering, level of, relevance **58,** 267, 352, **121,** 264 n. 179
trade union
discrimination and **58,** 13, 16-17, 35
freedom to join **57,** 80, 296-8, **62,** 360-2, 369-74, 384
rights **57,** 279, 296-8, **78,** 405-21
consultation **57,** 285-7, 297-8, 305
form, to **57,** 296-8
freedom of assembly/association **57,** 279, 286-8, 297-8, **58,** 15, 33
nature of **57,** 285, 297-8
transsexualism **89,** 97-112, 118-53
marriage **89,** 101-2, 109, 121, 127-8, 141-6, 153
private life, respect for and **89,** 103-9, 110-12
registration of births and **89,** 106, 120-1, 125-6, 129, 152-3
certificate of current civil status and **89,** 107-8, 110-12
treaty nature **58,** 291
Turkey and
alleged breach **62,** 9-24, 33, 51-3
United Communist Party, dissolution and **122,** 429-30
UN, failure to provide claims procedures **45,** 447-8, 452
Universal Declaration of Human Rights, 1948 and **57,** 224, **60,** 137
vagrancy **56,** 376-8, 401-3, 404-5, 411
violation. *See* breach *above*
Zimbabwe **90,** 581-3, 585, **103,** 232-3
European Convention on Human Rights (1950), interpretation 57, 213, 224, 246-8, 251, 294, **58,** 70, 98, 354, 360-2, 415-16, 479-83, 524, 583, 590, 603, 605, 607, **61,** 309, 337-8, 339
aids

'any relevant rules of international law applicable in the relations between the parties' **108,** 461-2, **123,** 40, 65, 85, 108
context **57,** 227-9
Explanatory Report **88,** 294
municipal law **86,** 368
principles and practice of democratic States **45,** 165
State practice **86,** 368, 369, 374-5, 406, 412-13
subsequent human rights agreements **111,** 152
subsequent practice **75,** 484-5, **103,** 646, 647-8, **108,** 317, **123,** 108, 110. *See also* guidelines, subsequent changes, need to reflect *below*
travaux préparatoires. See travaux préparatoires, European Convention on Human Rights (1950)
applicable law, Vienna Convention on the Law of Treaties (1969) **86,** 370, **123,** 40, 65, 99-100, 108
good faith **57,** 217
guidelines **45,** 114
compatibility with UN Convention on Racial Discrimination **107,** 39
context **86,** 371-2, 409-10, **89,** 173, **103,** 646
military life **58,** 70, 98
Convention as a whole **45,** 155, 163-4, 229, **89,** 175-6, **98,** 308
effectiveness **45,** 158, **108,** 316, 319-20, **111,** 146, **124,** 168-9
eiusdem generis **57,** 257
human rights treaty status and **123,** 40, 65
intention of original signatories **103,** 645-6, **111,** 152, **123,** 22
international law, harmony with principles of **123,** 40, 108
liberal interpretation **78,** 334
as living instrument. *See* subsequent changes, need to reflect *below*
object and purpose **81,** 45, 48, **86,** 371-2, 409-10, **98,** 301, **103,** 646-7, 660-1, **123,** 108
objectives **88,** 627
ordinary meaning **45,** 119, 163, **89,** 173, **103,** 646
parties' intention **57,** 292-5, **86,** 370, **123,** 22
realities of situation **78,** 287
spirit **98,** 301
subsequent changes, need to reflect **81,** 72, **89,** 124, 143, 174, 236, **98,** 308, **103,** 645, **123,** 15, 22, 65, 110. *See also* aids, subsequent practice *above*
teleological **47,** 171, 182
multilingual nature **86,** 372-4
authentic languages, accordance with both **56,** 391, **58,** 524
English and French texts compared **45,** 120, 301, **57,** 214-15, 227, **58,** 524, **75,** 416
phrases
'affaire' **56,** 391
'after' **86,** 341-2
'arrest or detention with a view to deportation or extradition' **86,** 341-6
'brief statement of the law concerned' **88,** 631-3, 634, 645-6, 669-70, **107,** 14, 18-19
'charged with a criminal offence' **72,** 398-9, **81,** 82
'civil' **88,** 641, 658
'civil rights and obligations'. *See* civil rights and obligations *above*
'competent legal authority' **78,** 249
'conditions provided for by law, subject to' **75,** 425-61, 481-2, 525, 529-30
'correspondence' **70,** 183

European Convention on Human Rights (1950), interpretation (*cont.*)
'court' **58,** 96-7, **67,** 468
'criminal charge' **58,** 81-4, **60,** 170-1, **67,** 517-19, **71,** 424-5, 431-2, **73,** 395, 558-9, 563-4, **75,** 349, 532, **78,** 324-8, 351-3, **81,** 46, 47
details **41,** 360-5
disciplinary proceedings and **58,** 81-2, **62,** 321-2, 336, 341, 346-7, 352, 357-9, **78,** 324-8, 351-3
insignificant injury and fault **67,** 519-25
penalty determining factor **58,** 83
'regulatory' offences, whether **73,** 525-31, 533-46
'criminal matter' **88,** 647
'decided speedily by a court'
advisory panel, whether 'court' **108,** 420-2
exhaustion of local remedies, relevance **108,** 434
habeas corpus proceedings, whether 'court' **108,** 422
'right to effective remedy' distinguished **108,** 433-6
'determination of civil rights and obligations or of any criminal charge by a court of law' **47,** 171, 181-2, **57,** 214, **77,** 438-9, 445-8
'effective remedy before a national authority'. *See* European Court of Human Rights, effective remedy before national authority
'family' **89,** 175-6
'final decision' **86,** 340
'fundamental freedoms' **57,** 243-6
'general principles of international law, subject to' **75,** 423-5, 435, 482-5, 515-17, 521-5
'in accordance with the law'/'prescribed by law' **58,** 75-6, **72,** 363-8, **73,** 394-5, **74,** 372-8, 383-91, **75,** 577-9, **81,** 182, 222-4, **86,** 342, **89,** 228-30, 257-8, 284-7, **92,** 235, 236, 284-6, 314, 341-3, 367, **95,** 331, 333, 339, **96,** 614, 615, **101,** 93, **111,** 182
accessibility **58,** 524-7, **89,** 228-30, 286
certainty of unlawfulness, need for **101,** 132-3
constitutional provision **122,** 421
'decided by a national court' distinguished **108,** 420-2
executive regulation **101,** 130
foreseeability **58,** 523-9, **89,** 228-9, 286, **101,** 84-5, 120, **107,** 15
lawfulness not disputed **111,** 263
legislation implementing UN Convention on Racial Discrimination **107,** 39
legislation, need for **120,** 62
national law **86,** 342, **95,** 331
national law of State where act takes place **95,** 332
non-arbitrary requirement **92,** 285-6
precision of law, need for **92,** 285, 341, **101,** 156
predictability of law, need for **92,** 285, 342
rules of international law, accessibility **101,** 118-20
unpublished regulations **101,** 118-20, 124, 130, 155-6
unwritten law **58,** 523-4
'in community and with others' **73,** 420-1
'independent and impartial tribunal established by law'. *See* European Convention on Human Rights (1950), independent and impartial tribunal
'interference by public body' **81,** 222
'language which he understands' **73,** 386-7, **74,** 413-16
'law'
common law **89,** 284
professional rules **81,** 223

'lawful' **95,** 339
'lawful detention' **72,** 311-12, 314-16, **78,** 203-12, 243-5
'legal' **78,** 382-8
'legislature' **123,** 15, 22-4
'legitimate aim' **89,** 228, 257-8, 303, 310-11, **92,** 235, 236, 315, 318, **96,** 614
economic interests of the country **111,** 294
elimination of racial discrimination **107,** 43
interests of child **96,** 615-16
preservation of country's economic well-being **92,** 315
prevention of crime **92,** 367-8, 373
prevention of disorder **92,** 367-8, 373, **107,** 16, **111,** 182, 263
prevention of disorder in radio communications **101,** 120-1, 156-7, 161-2
protection of children **92,** 286, 343
protection of commercial interests **101,** 92, 93
protection of morals **58,** 172-4, 177, 183-4, 530, 544, **67,** 412, 417, 420-3, 433-7, **73,** 382, **88,** 589-90
protection of reputation or rights of others **101,** 85, **107,** 39, 47
protection of secrecy of telecommunications **101,** 157-9
State immunity, jurisdiction **123,** 40, 65, 68, 84-5, 86-93
'liberty', physical liberty **111,** 471
'national minority' **45,** 117-18, 129
'necessary in a democratic society' **45,** 122, 226, **47,** 171, 182, **58,** 447, 454, **72,** 369-72, **73,** 382, 388, 395-6, 407-8, **74,** 378-9, 391, **75,** 580-1, **81,** 182, 222, 225-9, 231-2, **88,** 525, 567-8, 586, 587-93, 594-5, 603, 604-6, 614, 617-18, **89,** 230-4, 257-61, 287-8, 305, **92,** 253-6, 303, 315-16, 318-19, 343-5, 368-9, 373, **96,** 614, **101,** 89
independent test, need for **89,** 305, 306-7, 311-12
'necessary' **89,** 288
parent's right to be heard. *See* European Convention on Human Rights (1950), family life, respect for
pressing social need **92,** 235-6, 286-7, 316, 368, **101,** 121, 132, 157, 163, **111,** 263-6
prevention of disorder **107,** 16-17, **111,** 183-5
proportionality **92,** 235-6, 287, 303, 316, 343-5, 368-9
protection of democracy **122,** 423
protection of health of child **96,** 616-17, 623
taking child into care **92,** 288-93
unfair competition and **101,** 93-5
'no-one shall be expelled' **100,** 414
'normal civic obligations' **73,** 471, 475-8
'officer authorized by law to exercise judicial power' **78,** 238, 245-7, 269-72, 286-7, 289-90
district prosecutor **86,** 321
'person charged' **70,** 194-6, 205-6
'practical and effective' rights **68,** 106-7, **78,** 221
'pressing social need' **78,** 401-2
'prevention of crime' **58,** 89
'prevention of disorder' **58,** 88-9
'proceedings' **56,** 379-80
'proportionate to the legitimate aim' **58,** 18, 36, 288, 535-6, 580, **62,** 361, 382, **81,** 69, 171, **88,** 527, 591, 594, **89,** 127, 258-60, 288-90, 305, **96,** 623, **101,** 86, 122, 132, **107,** 17, 22, 23, 43, 47, **111,** 171-2, **118,** 134-5, 136-7, **122,** 424, 429
between ends and means **45,** 165, 174, 200, 216-17, 222
criteria, need for **111,** 189

European Convention on Human Rights (1950), interpretation (*cont.*)
general and individual interest **89,** 104-5, 125, 127, 181, 302, 303, 304
measures in accordance with international law **123,** 40-3, 65, 68, 71-3, 84-93
public order/damage to family life **111,** 184-5, 189, 192, 265-6, 294-7
severity of punishment, relevance **107,** 44
'public interest' **45,** 160
'reasonable time' **41,** 306-7, 342, 348-9, 354-6, 359-60, **45,** 232-3, 259-328, **58,** 337, 582-3, 584, 586, **62,** 297-9, 301, 310-17, **68,** 77-80, **70,** 194, 197, 206-7, **71,** 376-9, 382-8, 389, 404-8, **72,** 303, **78,** 365, 370, **86,** 318, 398-402. *See also* European Convention on Human Rights (1950), prompt hearing, 'reasonable time'
'regulatory' offences **73,** 525-31, 533-46
'religion', 'faith' **115,** 653
'social origin', 'social status' **115,** 653
'subject to national laws' **89,** 202, 207
'unlawful detention' **86,** 531
'unsound mind' **78,** 203-12
'victim' **58,** 439, 441-5, 460, 476, 557, 615-16, 709, **60,** 167, **71,** 368, 376-7, 396, 403-4, 414, **72,** 324, 337-42, 359, 388, 409, 415, **73,** 428, 435, 462, 484, 500, 515, 547, 552, **74,** 324, 346, 380, **78,** 242-3, 267-8, **89,** 170-1, 253-6, 263-4
daughter of victim **92,** 348-9, 351-2
directly effected by act **101,** 113-14
lawyer of applicant **58,** 709
nationality irrelevant **46,** 221
next of kin of **72,** 359
prejudice suffered, relevance **71,** 404, **78,** 242-3, 267, **101,** 113
relative of disappeared persons **120,** 58-9
termination of infringement, relevance **111,** 225-6
'within their jurisdiction' requirement distinguished **123,** 114
'within their jurisdiction'
alien on territory **96,** 386-7
authorized agent of State abroad **95,** 330-1, 332
authorized agent of State bringing any other person within jurisdiction **95,** 330-1, 332
consular activity and **123,** 610-11
effective control of area as result of military action **103,** 642-3, 654, **108,** 465-7, 473, 484-7, **120,** 38-40, **123,** 112-13
European Patent Office decisions **111,** 145
extraterritorial acts **108,** 435, **123,** 103-16
family link, relevance **123,** 596
Gibraltar **123,** 12
Guantanamo Bay Naval Base detainees **123,** 610-11
jurisdictional responsibility, relevance **96,** 387
nationals in foreign country **95,** 330-1
NATO Operation Allied Force **123,** 103-16
in territory under control of USA **123,** 610-11
travaux préparatoires **123,** 100-1
wide interpretation **96,** 386
preamble **57,** 216, 255
preparatory work. *See travaux préparatoires,* European Convention on Human Rights (1950)
principles and rules of **73,** 472, 491, 507-8, 526-7, 543-6, 558, **75,** 416, 425, 434, 436, 483-5, 522-5, 529, **86,** 370, 374-5, 408, 410
Resolution of Committee of Ministers **41,** 315

responsibility
European Court of Human Rights **56,** 487, **86,** 344-5
municipal courts **86,** 344
travaux préparatoires **45,** 119, 131, 151, 152, 153-4, 155, 161, 228, **75,** 425, 434, 484, 524-5, 529, **81,** 72, **88,** 556, 565, **89,** 174
European Convention on International Commercial Arbitration (1961)
applicability **82,** 67
New York Convention on the Recognition and Enforcement of Foreign Arbitral Awards (1958) and **82,** 68
scope **82,** 67-8
enforceability of arbitral award **82,** 68
Geneva Convention on the Execution of Foreign Arbitral Awards (1927) distinguished **82,** 68
New York Convention on the Recognition and Enforcement of Foreign Arbitral Awards (1958) distinguished **82,** 68
European Convention on Mutual Assistance in Criminal Matters (1959)
breach
determination of **82,** 27-8
requirements **82,** 29
evidence, restitution
date of obligation **82,** 28-9
waiver **82,** 28-9
good faith and **82,** 28, 29
letters rogatory, obligation to execute 'in manner provided for by its law' **119,** 283-4
phrases
'as soon as possible' **82,** 28-9
'in manner provided for by its law' **119,** 283-4
State immunity and **82,** 51-2
European Convention for the Peaceful Settlement of Disputes (1957) 84, 268
compulsory jurisdiction of the ICJ and **84,** 269, 279, 293
deposit, need for **84,** 279
conciliation and **84,** 269
European Convention on State Immunity (and Protocol) (Basle) (1972) 64, 84, 100-1, **92,** 537
application **82,** 18, 21, 25
acts in forum State **94,** 346, **123,** 40, 80, 89
armed forces of defending State **121,** 201-2
armed forces **123,** 80
divergence of municipal law **82,** 33, 40
non-parties **65,** 419, 431, **82,** 21, 25, 40, **115,** 422, **116,** 532-3, 632, 658-61, **123,** 38-9
performance in forum State **101,** 383
piecemeal **82,** 33, 40
reluctance to ratify **123,** 82-3, 89
USA **114,** 517, 529
customary international law **64,** 362, **65,** 178, 419, 421-2, 431, **77,** 607-8, **78,** 116, **82,** 12-13, 21-2, 25, 40, **87,** 27, 32, **94,** 346, 347, **100,** 470, **101,** 383, **113,** 420, **114,** 517, 547, **115,** 422, 431, 432-4, **116,** 660-1, **119,** 378, **123,** 38-9, 89
regional **94,** 347
employment contract **87,** 27, **104,** 517, **116,** 632
customary international law **101,** 383
forum State jurisdiction **87,** 27

European Convention on State Immunity (*cont.*)
performance in forum State **101,** 383
habitual resident **82,** 21-2
non-national **82,** 21-2
foreign judgments
enforcement **82,** 40
recognition **82,** 33
implementation **82,** 33
in personam actions **64,** 107-8
Iran–US Claims Tribunal, non-applicability **94,** 325
non-party, application to **86,** 585, **115,** 422, **116,** 532-3, 631, 658-60
retroactive, whether **94,** 347
State agency/State-owned corporation/State entity, entitlement **82,** 12, 13
State immunity, execution/attachment
commercial purpose **113,** 420-1
effect on **65,** 155, 178-9, 430-1
restrictive tendency **65,** 422-3, **87,** 33-4
reversal of absolute immunity rule **113,** 420-1
safeguarding/conservatory measures **65,** 178
waiver **65,** 178, 431
State immunity, jurisdiction, classification of act **64,** 107-9, 232, **65,** 336, 421-2, 430-1, **77,** 607-9
status **113,** 420
European Convention on the Suppression of Terrorism (1978)
general principles of international law, conflict with. *See* terrorism, Conventions
Ireland and **79,** 105
European Council Decisions. *See also* European Commission Decisions; European Council Regulations
91/586/ECSC, EEC (Suspension Decision), provisions **117,** 405
91/602/EEC (denunciation of EEC/SFRY Cooperation Agreement (1980)) **117,** 406
European Council Regulations 62, 393
17/62 **73,** 304, 312, 317, 333, 343-4, 353-4
177/67 **62,** 90-6
213/85 (European Economic Interest Grouping) **77,** 76, **80,** 98
314/83 (implementation of EEC/SFRY Cooperation Agreement (1980)) **117,** 404
545/92 (import of products originating in Republics of Croatia and Slovenia and Yugoslav Republics of Bosnia-Herzegovina, Macedonia and Montenegro) **117,** 407
547/92 (implementation of Regulation 545/92) **117,** 407
990/93 (Yugoslav embargo: implementation of Security Council Resolutions) **117,** 275-7, 308-11, 326-7
application to aircraft leased from Yugoslav Airlines (JAT) **117,** 271-303
application to non-EC ship in international waters **117,** 307-37
obligation to prohibit entry into Yugoslav territorial sea **117,** 318-20, 332-5
when brought within Community territory **117,** 314-16, 331
force majeure and **117,** 318
implementation
Ireland **117,** 276-7
Italy **117,** 310, 327
rectification of error in Italian version of Regulation **117,** 319
proportionality and **117,** 286-92, 301-2, 319-21
1432/92 (as amended by Regulation 2015/92) (sanctions: Serbia and Montenegro)

provisions **117,** 462-3, 504-6, 522, 535-6, 543
partial implementation of UN sanctions Resolutions **117,** 467, 541-3, 545-6
2340/90 (implementation of Security Council Resolution 660 (1990) (unconditional withdrawal of Iraqi forces from Kuwait)) **117,** 367, **122,** 549-50
legality, failure to provide for compensation for effects of embargo **117,** 393-7
2603/69 (Export Regulation) **117,** 506
applicability to measures having equivalent effect to quantitative restrictions **117,** 522-8, 543-4
justification under Art. 11 **117,** 526-8, 543-7
3155/90 (implementation of Security Council Resolution 660 (1990) (unconditional withdrawal of Iraqi forces from Kuwait)) **122,** 550
3300/91 (Suspension Regulation)
provisions **117,** 406
validity **117,** 420-30, 438-43
consequences of invalidity **117,** 429-30
manifest breach of customary international law, whether **117,** 427-9, 442
3541/92 (Iraq and Kuwait embargo: implementation of Security Council Resolution 687) **122,** 551-8
Art. 1 **122,** 554-5
Art. 2 **122,** 555-8, 559-65
Art. 3 **122,** 555-6, 563-4
preamble **122,** 553-4, 563
3567/91 (import of products originating in Bosnia-Herzegovina, Croatia, Macedonia and Slovenia) **117,** 406-7
bilateral treaties, inconsistency with **47,** 297
date of incorporation into national law **93,** 28, 49
direct effect. *See* European Community law, direct effect, Regulations
implementation
in case of error in one or more language versions **117,** 319, 333-4
conflict between Regulation and national implementation measures, justification **117,** 493-4
international law and **77,** 391
interpretation. *See* European Community law, interpretation
legislative measure, whether **47,** 298, **93,** 29-30
national law, effect in **38,** 261-4
nature **56,** 535, **62,** 393-4
social provision in road transport **47,** 279, 284-5, 289, 296, 298, 305
social security schemes **56,** 533
treaty provision, simultaneous incorporation **93,** 28
UN obligations affecting common commercial policy and **117,** 388, 492-4
validity
compatibility with international law and **117,** 439-40
compatibility with Protocol on Privileges and Immunities of the European Communities (1957) **56,** 575-6
European Court of Human Rights 77, 438. *See also* European Commission of Human Rights; European Convention on Human Rights (1950)
abuse of process, political motivation in bringing application **103,** 637-8
acceptance of application by Commission
effect **56,** 369
facts subsequent to **45,** 232-3, 266, 270, 271-2, 277, 298, 300-1, 304
access to **57,** 250-1
individuals, by. *See* individual *below*

European Court of Human Rights (*cont.*)
administrative practice giving rise to breach, six-month rule **120,** 46, 111
admissibility **60,** 166-8, 192-4, **61,** 298-300, **78,** 238-41, 348, 365, **81,** 164-8, 198. *See also* European Commission of Human Rights, admissibility; exhaustion of local remedies; justiciability; *res judicata below*; standing
competence to determine **56,** 388-90, 391-3, 394-7
in case of party's non-participation in proceedings **120,** 34
'continuing violation' **120,** 132-3
exhaustion of local remedies. *See* exhaustion of local remedies *below*
friendly settlement. *See* friendly settlement *below*
interest, need for
legal **120,** 35-6, 111
material and moral **60,** 153, 167
new issues **71,** 378, 381-2, 389, 402-4, **98,** 314-15, **120,** 98-9
new material **45,** 264, 267
object, whether devoid of **60,** 166-8
as preliminary question **56,** 388-90
ratio temporis **60,** 192-4
six-month rule **45,** 124, 136, **56,** 367, 369, 399, **60,** 192, **120,** 46, 111
standing. *See* standing *below*
time-limits **86,** 335, 340
'within their jurisdiction' requirement distinguished **123,** 114
applicant
death of **60,** 153, 167
individual **57,** 219-20
personal attendance **88,** 532, 536, **89,** 115, 193, 245
status **60,** 167
Articles 25 and 46 declaration **108,** 324, 391
restrictions
temporal **103,** 651-3, **108,** 458
territorial **103,** 639-51, 658-60
separability **103,** 650-1, 656-7
burden of proof **60,** 195, **71,** 303
administrative practice giving rise to alleged breach **58,** 263-6, **120,** 49-50, 95-6
exhaustion of local remedies **60,** 163, **61,** 383-4, **120,** 50, 95
Chamber
constitution **60,** 152, 185, **71,** 369, 397, 414-15, **72,** 325-6, 337, 389, 409-10, 415, **73,** 447, 461-2, 485, 500-1, 514-15, 551-3, **74,** 322, 346-7, **75,** 400, 446, 565, **78,** 195-6, 214-15, 228, 277, 297, 357, **81,** 3, 34, 43, 60, 74-5, 87, 92, 109, 186, **86,** 316, 324, 352, 378, **88,** 536, 607, 648, **89,** 96, 115, 157, 245, 267, **95,** 341, **98,** 275, **111,** 163, 198, 214, 255, 274
ex officio member **45,** 123, 234, 278
jurisdiction, full court and **71,** 414, 436, **72,** 409, **73,** 462-3, 484-5, 500-1, 541-6, 547, 551-2, **74,** 346-7, **75,** 382-95, 401, 446
plenary court, relinquishment of jurisdiction to **98,** 275
Commission, relation to **56,** 394
competence. *See* jurisdiction *below*
compulsory jurisdiction. *See* jurisdiction, compulsory *below*
concurring opinion **81,** 131-2, 182-3, 232-4
costs. *See* just satisfaction (Art. 50 [41] of the European Convention on Human Rights (1950))
customary international law and **123,** 48-9

decisions **56,** 429, 495-6, 501-3, 505-6, **62,** 378
dispute (*contestation*) over right **96,** 490-1, 519. *See also* European Convention on Human Rights (1950), civil rights and obligations, *contestation*, need for
dissenting opinion **78,** 350, 353, **81,** 21-4, 132-8, 232
enforcement of foreign judgments **79,** 569
equality of arms
as essential element of fair trial **124,** 85-6
opportunity to present evidence **120,** 46-7, **124,** 87 n. 85
estoppel
exhaustion of local remedies, failure to raise issue. *See* exhaustion of local remedies, estoppel resulting from failure to raise issue *below*
issue determined by Commission **78,** 242
European Community acts. *See* European Community (EC), European Convention on Human Rights (1950) and
evidence
admissibility
Court's right to seek/consider new **108,** 310, 355, 460
subsequent to date of application **111,** 226
subsequent to event complained of **108,** 310, 355, 414
subsequent to proceedings in national courts **111,** 226
credibility **108,** 310-11
establishment of facts **120,** 50, 51, 69-71, 142. *See also* European Commission of Human Rights, fact-finding role
evaluation, equality of arms principle and **120,** 47, 95-6
failure to submit **86,** 402
proprio motu **108,** 310, 355, 414
standard of proof, 'beyond reasonable doubt' **58,** 264, **120,** 49-50, 70, 80, 99-101, 103-4
evidence of human rights conditions. *See* human rights, evidence of conditions
exhaustion of local remedies **60,** 162-6, **81,** 48, **86,** 335, 337-41, **88,** 554-6, **89,** 171-2, **102,** 278, **107,** 12, 37-8, **120,** 138-9, **122,** 446
'according to the generally recognized rules of international law' **120,** 138-9
alternative courses of action, relevance **111,** 223-5
burden of proof **60,** 163, **61,** 383-4, **120,** 50
compliance
competence to determine **56,** 368-9, 392, 395-6, 399-400
critical date **56,** 474-7
estoppel resulting from failure to raise issue **45,** 271, 275, 277, **56,** 341, 369-71, **60,** 162-3, 192-3, **61,** 302, 306, 371, **78,** 240, **86,** 337-8, **88,** 554, **96,** 579-80, **103,** 637-8
failure to exhaust remedies in another State **121,** 208, **123,** 86
failure to raise issue **45,** 271, 275, 277, **56,** 341, 369-71, **60,** 162-3, 192-3, 302, **61,** 302, 306, 371, **78,** 240, **88,** 554, **96,** 579-80, **103,** 637-8
flexibility **46,** 321-2, 323, **61,** 304, 323-4, 333, 375
liberty of person, deprivation and **108,** 434
non-recognition of controlling authority and **120,** 40-6, 111, 117-24, 136-7, 140
preliminary/procedural question, whether **45,** 274-5, 277, 309, **56,** 341, 392-3
merits, joinder **43,** 176
proceedings relating to same subject-matter, need to await outcome **111,** 224
purpose

European Court of Human Rights (*cont.*)
opportunity for State party to rectify situation **56,** 392, 487, **61,** 374-5, **111,** 225, **121,** 207-8
protection of national legal order **60,** 163
raising issue 'in substance', sufficiency **61,** 303-4
resort to appropriate courts, need for **61,** 305-6
State's duty to indicate remedies **60,** 162-3, **78,** 240-2
friendly settlement **60,** 166-7, **62,** 388-9, **81,** 105-6, **86,** 319, **96,** 520
absence of basis for **120,** 20
applicant's problem resolving itself **96,** 472
equitable nature **81,** 106, **92,** 252-3
fair trial, effect on **60,** 174-5
finding case time-barred **96,** 472
as just satisfaction
general interest **86,** 319-20, 321
individual interest **86,** 319, 321
as pardon **81,** 89-90
partial **81,** 235-6
procedure **62,** 73
parties' role **62,** 73
German, use of **88,** 515, 537
individual
appearance before **57,** 219-20
application by **57,** 251, 252, 254, 256
in abstracto review **81,** 195
application in respect of **57,** 219-20
as party to proceedings **56,** 477
protection of **89,** 150
right of petition **57,** 250, 292, **78,** 385
standing **56,** 496
judges
ad hoc **45,** 123
ex officio **56,** 442
judgment
compliance, Committee of Ministers of Council of Europe, responsibility **98,** 318
res judicata **81,** 27
jurisdiction **56,** 391, 400, **57,** 191, **60,** 162-3, 192. *See also* powers *below*
acceptance of Commission's application, effect **56,** 369
admissibility, determination of **56,** 473-4
Articles 25 and 46 declaration. *See* Articles 25 and 46 declaration *above*
basis, consent **45,** 118
breach of Convention, determination of **56,** 391
compensation **56,** 428, **57,** 191
complaints struck out by Commission **71,** 377
compulsory **60,** 152, 184, **72,** 337, 389, 415, **73,** 447, 462, 485, 501, 552, **74,** 346, **75,** 400, 446, 564, **78,** 256, 276, 296, **81,** 3, 34, 87, 92, 143, 186, 207, **86,** 315, **88,** 515, 536, 607, 648, **89,** 115, 157
critical date **103,** 658
continuing situation **108,** 460-1, 468, 472-8, 482-3, 487-8
dispute (*contestation*) over right. *See* dispute (*contestation*) over right *above*
effect of revolution on application of legislation **96,** 490

exhaustion of local remedies, determination of compliance with **56,** 368-9, 392, 395-6
forum prorogatum **45,** 133
in abstracto judgments **56,** 404-5, 409, **72,** 361, 402, **73,** 470, 507, **75,** 414, **120,** 105-6
interpretation and application of European Convention on Human Rights (1950) **56,** 394, 396, **88,** 554
issues arising after admissibility decision **120,** 107
issues not examined by Commission **120,** 57-8, 98-9, 116
issues not pursued by parties **120,** 57-8
issues raised by Commission *ex officio* **71,** 378-9, 389-90
just satisfaction proceedings **86,** 347-8, 403-4. *See also* just satisfaction (Art. 50 [41] of the European Convention on Human Rights (1950))
legislative measures, direction to State to take **96,** 476
national courts. *See* national courts *below*
national law. *See* national law *below*
practice of other International Courts **45,** 133
public policy and **86,** 320
ratione materiae **45,** 118, 129-35, **56,** 368
reservations, validity **88,** 626-7, 666-7
reserved domain and **45,** 132
review **45,** 120, 165
signatory State, over **88,** 675
temporal competence of Court and Commission distinguished **103,** 653
treaty interpretation, UN Convention on the Elimination of Racial Discrimination (1965) **107,** 42
victim, need for **56,** 404-5
jurisprudence, municipal courts, in **88,** 581
justiciability. *See also* admissibility *above*
modification of municipal law in preparation **89,** 171
legal representatives before **56,** 348-50
merits, interpretation and application of treaty as **88,** 554
national courts
anticipation of decision **96,** 496
assessment of evidence before **96,** 561, **101,** 88, 90
assessment of 'urgency' **111,** 240
review of
decisions **45,** 164, 168-9, 232, 277, 304, 314, **122,** 424
merits **96,** 490
national law
compatibility with Convention **118,** 132-3
interpretation **56,** 478, **81,** 99-100, **118,** 132-3
substance determining factor **81,** 131, 196
national authorities **107,** 15, **111,** 228
partial reference from findings of Commission **103,** 638-9
plenary court
exercise of jurisdiction **88,** 516
jurisdiction **89,** 97, 158
political question doctrine **108,** 478-9, 483, 485-7
powers. *See also* jurisdiction *above*
available remedies, establishment of **78,** 241
deferral of judgment **73,** 431

European Court of Human Rights (*cont.*)
evaluation of expediency of Commission reference **73,** 506
examination of
legislation *in toto* **75,** 414
question not raised before Commission **75,** 431
question raised following oral proceedings **75,** 582
uncontested allegation, investigation *proprio motu* **75,** 582
lack of power
municipal courts, annulment of judgment of **72,** 430
municipal legal regime, modification, review of **72,** 361-2
State party undertaking, obtention of **72,** 329
to remedy defects in State's case **86,** 338, 340
precedent **78,** 212, **81,** 45-8, **86,** 367-9, 405-7, **89,** 123-4, 131, 147-51, 179-80, 201-2
binding force **81,** 182-3
international judicial **56,** 486
preliminary issues **68,** 73-6
joinder to merits **68,** 76
preliminary objections **78,** 238-40, 267-8
State party, preliminary objections **71,** 377-82, 402-4
procedure **56,** 351-3, **57,** 205-6, **68,** 50-2, 90-2, 129-30, **71,** 369-70, 397-8, 414-16, 420, 436-8, **72,** 324-6, 337-9, 378-9, 388-90, 409-11, 415-17, 428-9, **73,** 447-8, 462-3, 484-6, 500-2, 514-16, 552-3, **74,** 346-9, **75,** 381-5, 400-1, 445-8, 564-6, **78,** 195-6, 214-25, 256-7, 267-8, 276, 296-7, 357-9, 374. *See also* preliminary issues *above*
appearance, right of **56,** 348-9, 350
Commission, reference to Court from **71,** 368-9, 396, 414, 436, **72,** 324, 337, 388, 409, 415, **73,** 447, 462, 484, 514-15, 546, 552, **74,** 322, 346, **75,** 382, 400, 445-6, 564, **78,** 195, 214, 227, 256-7, 276, 296
deferral of judgment, request for **73,** 429-32
language **81,** 61
lawyer of applicant, replacement at Court's insistence **71,** 376-7
preliminary objections, time-limits **56,** 371-2
request to strike case off list **60,** 166
restoration of case **81,** 90
witnesses
anonymity **120,** 47-8
'fairness' requirement **120,** 47-9
proceedings before, language of **41,** 286, 320, **45,** 235, 278-9
res judicata, resolution of Council of Ministers as **120,** 35-6
role **60,** 169
assessment of facts **108,** 310, 466
ICJ distinguished **103,** 648
municipal law, review of compliance with **89,** 285
Rules of Court (pre-1998). *See also* Rules of Court (1998), Rules of Court A *and* Rules of Court B *below*
2(3) **88,** 607, **89,** 211, **96,** 500, **111,** 163, 198
5(a) **123,** 4
9 **73,** 501
21 **72,** 337, 389, 415, **73,** 447, 462, 501, 515, 552, **74,** 347, **75,** 400, 446, 565, **78,** 199, 215, 228, 256, 257, 277, 297, 357, 358, **86,** 316, 324, 351, 352, 378, 418, **123,** 4
21(3)(b) **88,** 515, 536, 607, 648, **89,** 96, 115, 157, 193, 210, 245, 266, 267, 292, **95,** 341, **96,** 432, 454, 467, 480, 500, 522, 537, 565, 591, **98,** 275, **101,** 72, 100, 138, **103,** 626, **107,** 8, 26, 52, **108,** 288, 325, **111,** 163, 198, 214, 236, 255

21(4) **88,** 515, 536, 607, 648, **89,** 96, 115, 157, 193, 210, 245, 266, 267, 292, **95,** 341, **96,** 432, 454, 467, 468, 480, 500, 522, 537, 565, 591, **101,** 72, 100, 138, **103,** 626, **107,** 8, 52, **108,** 288, 325, **111,** 163, 198, 236
21(4)(b) **108,** 392, **111,** 255, 274
21(5) **88,** 536, 607, **89,** 96, 116, 158, 193, 245, 292, **95,** 341, **96,** 432, 454, 468, 480, 500, 522, 538, 565, 591, **101,** 101, 138, **103,** 626, **107,** 8, 26, **108,** 288, 325, 326, 392, **111,** 163, 198, 236, 274
21(6) **96,** 467, **108,** 450, **111,** 163, 274
22 **72,** 326, 337, 415, **73,** 429, 515, 548, **74,** 347, **75,** 565, **78,** 215, 256, 277, 297, 357-8, **86,** 378
22(1) **89,** 116, 211, **95,** 341, **96,** 432, 500, 538, 591, **107,** 53, **111,** 163, 198, 214
22(2) **111,** 214
23 **107,** 26
23(1) **88,** 607, **96,** 480
24 **72,** 326, 337, 415, **73,** 429, 548, 553, **74,** 347, **75,** 565, **78,** 297, 357-8, **86,** 378, **120,** 21
24(1) **88,** 607, **89,** 211, **95,** 341, **96,** 538, 564, 591, **103,** 627, **107,** 53, **108,** 326, **111,** 163, 214
24(2) **89,** 116, **96,** 480, **107,** 26
24(3) **108,** 451, **123,** 4
24(4) **123,** 4
26 **73,** 516, **78,** 196, **86,** 316
26(3) **88,** 532
27 **72,** 416, **73,** 448, 485, 502, 516, 553, **75,** 384, **78,** 229, 256, 277, 358, **86,** 352, 378
27(2) **96,** 480, **111,** 215
27(3) **88,** 537, **95,** 341, **96,** 454, 468, 480, **101,** 72, **111,** 215
28 **123,** 4
29 **73,** 448, 463, **75,** 384, 479
29(1) **123,** 4
30 **75,** 446, 587, **78,** 214, 228, 256, 357, **86,** 315, 324, 378, 418, **88,** 507, 515, 532, 536, 648, **89,** 96, 115, 157, 193, 210, 245, 266, 292, **95,** 340, **96,** 432, 454, 467, 479, 500, **98,** 275, **101,** 72, 100, 138, **103,** 626, **107,** 8, 26, 52, **108,** 288, 325, 392, **111,** 162, 198, 214, 235, 255, 274, **123,** 4
30(1) **96,** 537
33 **74,** 347, **75,** 565, **78,** 228, 277, 357, **86,** 315, 324, 351, 379, 418
33(3)(b) **89,** 157, **96,** 591
33(3)(d) **88,** 515, 532, 536, 607, 648, **89,** 96, 115, 157, 193, 210, 245, **95,** 340, **96,** 454, 467, 479, 500, 522, 537, 564, 591, **101,** 72, 100, **107,** 8, 26, 52, **108,** 288, 324, 391-2, **111,** 162, 198, 214, 235, 255, 274, **123,** 4
34 **103,** 626, 627, 658
36 **108,** 392
36(2) **108,** 392
37 **74,** 347, **75,** 446, 565, **78,** 228, 256, 277, **86,** 325, 352, 379, 418
37(1) **88,** 515, 536, 607, **89,** 96, 116, 158, 211, 245, 267, 292, **95,** 341, **96,** 433, 454, 468, 480, 500, 522, 538, 565, 591, **98,** 275, **101,** 72, 101, 138, **103,** 627, **107,** 8, 26, 53, **108,** 288, 325, 392, 450, **111,** 163, 199, 215, 236, 255, 274
37(2) **88,** 515, 536, **98,** 276, **107,** 26, **108,** 392
38 **74,** 347, **75,** 401, **78,** 228, 277, **86,** 352, **88,** 536, 607, **89,** 96, 193, 211, 245, 267, 292, **95,** 341, **96,** 454, 468, 480, 500, 591, **101,** 101, **103,** 627, **107,** 8, 26, 53, **108,** 289, 325, 392, 450, **111,** 163, 199, 215, 236, 255, 274
39 **88,** 532
40 **75,** 565

European Court of Human Rights (*cont.*)
41(1) **107,** 26-7
43 **78,** 357
44 **88,** 532
47 **75,** 582, **78,** 229, 239, 240, 256, 286
48 **72,** 409, **73,** 461, 463, 484, 500-1, 514-15, 551, **86,** 320, 366, 404
48(2) **81,** 89, **96,** 472
48(4) **81,** 90
50 **72,** 404, 410, 430, **75,** 394, 401, 446, **78,** 211, **86,** 352, 379, 418, **88,** 515, 536, 648, **98,** 275, **101,** 72, 101
50(3) **98,** 275
51 **73,** 457, 481, 496, 510, 532, 547, **101,** 138, **103,** 627, **107,** 27, **108,** 289
51(1) **108,** 392
51(2)(a) **103,** 627, **107,** 27, **108,** 392
51(2)(b) **103,** 627, **107,** 27, **108,** 392
52 **74,** 382, **75,** 510, **86,** 320, 366, 404
52(2) **81,** 19, 71, **88,** 593, **89,** 110, 184
52(3) **88,** 616
53 **74,** 382, **75,** 587, **78,** 224, **86,** 365
53(1) **81,** 105, **96,** 450
53(2) **95,** 354, **107,** 18, **108,** 318, 359, **111,** 290
53(3) **81,** 105
53(4) **81,** 106
55(2) **88,** 556
61(6) **103,** 627
74(2) **123,** 21
99 **123,** 4
Addendum 4 **78,** 278, **96,** 454, 538
Rules of Court (1998)
24 **123,** 75
28 **120,** 21
28(3) **120,** 21
28(4) **120,** 21
29(1) **120,** 21, **123,** 75
39 **121,** 210
52(1) **123,** 26, 55, 75
54(4) **123,** 27, 55, 75
55 **120,** 34
58(1) **120,** 21
59(2) **120,** 22, **123,** 27, 56
61(2) **123,** 56
64 **120,** 22
72 **123,** 26-7, 55, 75
74(2) **120,** 117
100(1) **120,** 21
Rules of Court A
21(4)(b) **122,** 407
21(5) **122,** 407
21(6) **122,** 407
24(1) **122,** 407
24(5) **122,** 407
27(3) **122,** 406
30 **122,** 406

32 **122,** 406
33(3)(d) **122,** 406
37(1) **122,** 407
38 **122,** 407
51 **122,** 407
51(2)(c) **122,** 407
51(3) **122,** 407
51(6) **122,** 407
Rules of Court B
21 **118,** 123
24(3) **118,** 124
24(4) **118,** 123
24(5)(a) **118,** 124
28 **118,** 124
28(2) **118,** 123
28(3) **118,** 123
29(1) **118,** 124
31 **118,** 123
61(3) **118,** 124
71 **118,** 124
99 **118,** 124
100(4) **118,** 124
sampling methodology **109,** 70
separate declaration **78,** 349
separate opinion **81,** 19-21
standing **56,** 348-9, **81,** 90, **89,** 253-5
actio popularis **89,** 254-5
amicus curiae role distinguished **103,** 638
individuals. *See* individuals *above*
national rules distinguished **89,** 235
recognition of government, relevance **103,** 636-7, **120,** 34-5
Republic of Cyprus in respect of northern Cyprus **120,** 34-5
'victim'. *See* European Convention on Human Rights (1950), interpretation, phrases, *victim*
State submissions **72,** 326, **73,** 329-31, 360-1, 380, 398, 401, 424, 426, 430-1, 433-5, 455, 457, 469-70, 489-90, 505-6, 525-6, 528, 557, **74,** 370, **75,** 386-7, 413, 575, **78,** 319
task
consideration of alleged breaches of Convention **92,** 249-51
development of law **89,** 139-40
time-limits. *See also* admissibility, six-month rule *above*
preliminary objections **56,** 371-2
victim, need for **56,** 404-5
European Court of Justice (ECJ)
admissibility. *See also* European Community law, judicial review
Commission's failure to act **96,** 224-6
difficulty of assessing conduct **96,** 223-4
liability without fault **96,** 225
merits distinguished **117,** 371-2
premature application **96,** 212-13
liability to be established at merits stage **96,** 212-13
requirements, sufficiency of information **117,** 371
Advocate General

European Court of Justice (ECJ) (*cont.*)
functions **47,** 185
Opinions, publication **99,** 205 n. 1, 354
applicable law **53,** 28-31, 37, 44-5
Community law **100,** 132
Art. 169/171 reference, purpose, establishment of basis of State responsibility **111,** 52
Art. 173 reference
Coreper decisions **113,** 359
dispute, need for **113,** 360-4
definition of subject-matter **113,** 393-6
fait accompli, in case of **113,** 359-60
legality of contested measure dependent on facts and law at time when adopted **113,** 322-3
measures having legal effect, definition by Council of its position affecting Community's external competence **113,** 358-61, 377-8
power to review agreement with non-member country **101,** 39-43, 61
Art. 177 reference **93,** 628, **111,** 10-11, 14-15, 102, **117,** 280, 293, 312, 325, 331, 344, 353, 357, 431, 510, 538
acte clair doctrine **93,** 279
admissibility **117,** 419-20
critical date **93,** 52
doubt, need for **93,** 279-80, **107,** 535
practical relevance, need for **93,** 17, 32, 51, 273-4, **117,** 420
subsequent repeal of offending law **93,** 57
application under national law **93,** 16-17
Art. 169 proceedings distinguished **93,** 37-8
Art. 174 proceedings and **93,** 541-2, 545
limitation *ratione temporis* **93,** 545-7
choice of questions, matter for national court or tribunal **93,** 17, 38, **101,** 15, 24-5
competence for referral, matter for national constitution **93,** 32
eligibility of company incorporated in unrecognized State **100,** 251-5
grounds of challenge to validity, relevance **117,** 438
interpretation of EEC Treaty **93,** 16-17, 261, 421, 422
examination of compatibility with national law distinguished **93,** 9, 37-8
need for uniform **93,** 18, 535, **113,** 287
reclassification of product for customs purposes **93,** 20
late intervention **100,** 246, 249, 254-7
obligation to avoid **93,** 146-7
preliminary ruling, binding effect **93,** 31, 421-2, 425, 446-7, 450-1, 459, 460, 537
question previously addressed **93,** 280-2, 416, 422-3
lack of clarity and **93,** 422
reasons, relevance **93,** 27
reformulation, power of **93,** 39
refusal to seek, arbitrary **93,** 422, 460
requirements **117,** 475, 490
doubt **117,** 494, 499, 500
urgency **100,** 249
withdrawal, notification by referring court, need for **93,** 52, 71
Art. 228(1) reference **99,** 207-16, 272-91, 327-73, 377-94, **100,** 169-97, 200-21
admissibility
binding international agreement, need for **99,** 210-11, 367-8, 387-8

competence according to Community as issue **99,** 387-8
possibility of Council action to overcome difference of view **99,** 358-60
non-contentious **99,** 212
preliminary ruling **100,** 190
timeliness
time-limit, whether **99,** 212
treaty negotiations at early stage **99,** 360-1
Art. 228(6) reference
admissibility
after signature **105,** 86-7, 194-5
prior to specific proposal **108,** 249-55
compatibility of agreement with Treaty of Rome, sufficiency of information, need for **108,** 252
competence of Community to conclude, decision of Council to open negotiations, relevance **108,** 250-2
purpose, prevention of subsequent legal dispute **108,** 249-50
competence, national law, in respect of **45,** 459
costs **48,** 143, 225, **93,** 21, 22, 33, 43, 45, 74, 111, 144, 202-3, 382, 703, 780, 788, **99,** 267, **100,** 148, 302, **101,** 29, **111,** 128, **113,** 276, 294, 338, 381, 410, **117,** 302, 336, 361, 443, 550
exceptional circumstances **100,** 164-5
intervening party **113,** 338
unsuccessful party **117,** 397
development of EC law and **93,** 457-9
dispute, essence **105,** 88-9
evidence
power to demand from State **110,** 633
States not party to proceedings **110,** 635
functions **60,** 259
judicial review **47,** 292, 305-6
fundamental rights, protection **98,** 216
Grand Chamber, relinquishment of jurisdiction to **103,** 627, **107,** 27, **108,** 392
individuals **47,** 1-9, **93,** 319, 343
interim measures. *See also* European Community law, interim measures (national)
Art. 225 action **100,** 233
Art. 169 breach distinguished **100,** 233, 240
impossibility of assessment prior to main hearing **100,** 233-4, 242
purpose, protection of Community interests **100,** 243-4
requirements
burden of proof **100,** 241
damage to Member State **100,** 240, 241, 243
damage to non-Member State **100,** 240, 241, 243, 244
non-prejudice to main proceedings **100,** 236-7, 243
prima facie case **100,** 234, 237, 239
serious and irreparable harm **100,** 242
urgency **100,** 234, 239-42, 243
international organizations and **60,** 508
Judge-Rapporteur, Report for Hearing, *Woodpulp* **96,** 154-73
judges, non-participation in other international tribunals **99,** 290-1
judgment **111,** 137
annulment of legislative or administrative act **93,** 318
applicable law, unwritten law **93,** 370
binding effect **93,** 277-83, 318, 361, 391-2, **100,** 180, 194

European Court of Justice (ECJ) (*cont.*)
all State organs **93,** 180
'decisions' **100,** 211
European Economic Area (EEA) and **100,** 219-20
national courts **93,** 216-17
national law, statements relating to **93,** 391
risk posed by provisions of draft EEA agreement (1991) **100,** 198
binding effect. *See also* Art. 177 reference, preliminary ruling *above*
Case 22/70 (*AETR*) **105,** 205-6, 214, 220
compliance **53,** 555, 563
choice of means **93,** 318
period of grace **113,** 294
second declaration **93,** 318
declaratory nature **93,** 318
consequences **93,** 182-3
execution **111,** 133-41
national court, organ of Community, whether **111,** 139-40
national court's duty to review underlying proceedings **111,** 141
individuals **93,** 319
judicial review **93,** 416-17
national courts
execution. *See* execution *above*
previous decision, effect on **93,** 438
review by **93,** 416-18, 424-6, **98,** 193, **111,** 137-8
obligation to comply **53,** 555, 563
Opinion 1/75 **105,** 200, 203
Opinion 1/76 **105,** 216-17, 220
Opinion 1/78 **105,** 197, 202
primacy **93,** 488
State responsibility, basis for **93,** 174, 180-1, 188, 202
temporal effect **112,** 357
judicial review **100,** 239
annulment of acts, consequences **47,** 307
Articles 36 and 224 distinguished **100,** 237
burden of proof **100,** 237
jurisdiction **59,** 3, **62,** 429, 440
Art. 177 reference. *See* Art. 177 reference *above*
basis **56,** 368
compatibility of EC law with national Constitution **93,** 389, 391
conflict, Tribunal of European Laying-up Fund for Inland Waterway Vessels **99,** 289-91
direct effect principle **53,** 30-1, 35, 37, 45, 47
European Schools **108,** 651
interpretation of Community treaties **100,** 190
exclusive nature **100,** 190
interpretation of EEC Treaty **93,** 16-17, 261, 420, 421, 422, 450-1
interpretation of European Convention on Human Rights (1950), connection with Community law, need for **113,** 269, 275, 276
interpretation of treaties not part of Community law **53,** 597, 602, 604-5
national courts. *See* European Economic Community Treaty (Rome)(1957), national courts, role
political questions **100,** 237, 243
Common Foreign and Security Policy **100,** 238

servants, disputes concerning **60,** 503, 508-9
under International Conventions, ratification, need for **98,** 218
validity of EC law **93,** 391, 403
national courts and **60,** 417-24, 426-7, 429. *See also* European Economic Community Treaty (Rome) (1957), national courts, role
duty to review underlying proceedings **111,** 141
organ of the Community, whether **111,** 139-40
reference from **44,** 395, 397, 403-8, **45,** 455-8, 461
review of decision by **117,** 282-5
national juridical system, incorporation within **93,** 418-22
preliminary rulings **60,** 250, 252, 257, 258-9, 270
discretion to refer to **60,** 417-24, 426-7, 429
procedure. *See also* Rules of Procedure *below*
pre-litigation procedure
length **113,** 285-7
purpose **113,** 286
right to act on own behalf **113,** 267-8
submissions by parties **55,** 480
written observations by interested parties **56,** 567
reference to
Commission, wording, relevance **105,** 195-6
discretionary **60,** 417-24, 426-7, 429
duty **48,** 233-6
national court **85,** 90
role, fundamental rights, protection **98,** 211-19
Rules of Procedure
37(1) **113,** 267
38(3) **113,** 267
44(1)(c) **117,** 371
58 **113,** 267
69(2) **100,** 161, **113,** 411
69(3) **100,** 161
83 **100,** 225
83(2) **100,** 234, 240, 242
85 **100,** 225
86(4) **100,** 234, 236
87(2) **113,** 338, **117,** 397
87(4) **113,** 338
91(1) **113,** 344
104(2) **113,** 268
107(1) **99,** 210, 273, 377, **100,** 170, 201, **108,** 231
107(2) **99,** 359, 388
108(2) **99,** 210, 273, 354, 377, **100,** 170, 201
114(1) **117,** 370
status, as national court **93,** 418-22, 450
Statute amendment **100,** 182
amendment of Treaty of Rome (1957), need for **100,** 195-6, 219-20
European Economic Area (EEA) Agreement (1991)
countervailing measures **113,** 331
directed at third countries **113,** 332
State aid distinguished **113,** 332-3
customs duties of a fiscal nature, customs duties on imports and exports and charges having equivalent effect distinguished **113,** 330-1

European Economic Area (EEA) Agreement (1991) (*cont.*)
derogation, admissibility **113,** 331
direct effect **113,** 326-7
draft Agreement. *See* European Economic Area (EEA) draft Agreement (1991)
EC Treaty
homogeneity **113,** 328-30
identity of provisions **113,** 330-1
EEC–Austria Free Trade Agreement (1972), primacy **113,** 324-5
free trade agreement, whether **113,** 328
interpretation, conformity with ECJ rulings prior to entry into force **113,** 330
European Economic Area (EEA) draft Agreement (1991) *See also* European Economic Area (EEA) Agreement (1991)
amendments to meet ECJ objections, text **100,** 201-10
Community law
autonomy **100,** 189-93, 219
uniform application **100,** 188-9, 191-2, 211
direct effect and primacy of Community law, promise of statutory provision of primacy, sufficiency **100,** 188
dispute settlement. *See also* judicial machinery *below*
arbitration **100,** 212
binding nature **100,** 212
interpretation of treaty excluded **100,** 220
classification of disputes **100,** 212-15, 217
interpretation of agreement **100,** 217
jurisdiction
Community **100,** 212-14
EFTA Surveillance Authority **100,** 214-15
need for **100,** 211-12
preferred method, political settlement in Joint Committee **100,** 212, 220
EEA Court
independence of ECJ **100,** 180
jurisdiction **100,** 190
participation of members of ECJ **100,** 179-81, 192-3
trespass on exclusive jurisdiction of ECJ **100,** 190-1
EEC Treaty distinguished **100,** 187, 189
EFTA Surveillance Authority, European Commission and, shared responsibilities **100,** 220-1
European Parliament observations **100,** 215
interpretation, ECJ, sole jurisdiction **100,** 212
judicial machinery
compatibility with EEC Treaty **100,** 169-97
EEA court. *See* EEA Court *above*
EFTA court
establishment **100,** 211, 216
jurisdiction **100,** 217
Joint Committee
dispute settlement, responsibility for **100,** 212, 220
effect on ECJ jurisprudence **100,** 218-19
interpretation or application of agreement **100,** 219
procés-verbal agréé ad article 105 **100,** 216, 219
legal certainty of provisions **100,** 215
purpose

settlement of disputes between Community and EFTA members **100,** 178
settlement of disputes within EFTA **100,** 178
uniformity of law within EEA **100,** 178, 216. *See also* uniformity of law within EEA *below*
text of relevant articles **100,** 170-7, 185-6
object, homogenous economic area applying EEC law **100,** 177
phrases
'contracting party' **100,** 189-90
'decisions', binding effect **100,** 211
precedent
binding effect of ECJ decisions **100,** 219-20
ECJ case-law, prior to EEA agreement, limited to **100,** 188
'reception' of new rulings **100,** 211
agreed minute by contracting parties **100,** 211, 212
declaration in Council minutes before conclusion of agreement **100,** 211, 212
uniformity of law within EEA
EFTA members' right to seek preliminary ruling, binding effect **100,** 178, 182-3, 193-4, 218, 220
exchange of information between ECJ, EFTA court and EFTA members' courts **100,** 211
Lugano Convention (1988) procedure **100,** 178. *see also* European Economic Area (EEA) Agreement (1991)
European Economic Community (EEC). *See also* European Community (EC)
accession
constitutionality
method **93,** 229-31
prospective legislation **93,** 229-31, 232
standing to challenge **93,** 229, 231, 232
direct effect **93,** 468
previous legislation automatically ineffective **93,** 468, 472
effect on existing law **93,** 575
implied repeal **93,** 468, 478
as customs union, prohibition of customs duties and charges **93,** 18-19, 20-1, 22
fishing rights, negotiating powers **82,** 669
privileges and immunities **81,** 718-19
Treaty of Rome. *See* European Economic Community Treaty (Rome) (1957)
European Economic Community (EEC) fisheries policy
applicable law, international law **100,** 141-2
balance of interests **100,** 145, 154, 156
baselines
ambulatory **100,** 134
conservation measures **100,** 129, 140, 141, 164
discriminatory, whether **100,** 137, 138-9, 140
incompatibility with provisions of Act of Accession (1972) **100,** 128
normal practice **100,** 127, 135, 140, 157
stability of fishing activity, incompatibility **100,** 145, 156
critical date **100,** 126, 127, 138
failure to indicate date **100,** 129, 140-1, 142, 157
Member State competence **100,** 126, 131-2
compatibility with international law, relevance **100,** 126, 131-2, 136-7, 140, 145, 153
retroactivity **100,** 136, 144, 150

European Economic Community (EEC) fisheries policy (*cont.*)
unilateral change affecting Community policy **100,** 126, 130-1, 140, 145, 154-6
Member State practice **100,** 160-2
multiple, risk of confusion **100,** 129, 135-6, 145-6, 162-3
enforcement, Member State obligation **100,** 163
equal access
derogation from
narrow interpretation **100,** 128, 139
respect for special fishing rights and fishing activities **100,** 125-6, 127, 139, 143
right to reserve coastal waters for local fishing **100,** 127
temporary **100,** 125, 127
London Convention (1964)
divergence of underlying philosophy **100,** 127, 143
priority **100,** 127, 128, 131, 133, 142-4, 158-60
Member State jurisdiction
basis for exercise **100,** 133-4
termination of exclusive right **100,** 128
method of designating area
geographical co-ordinates **100,** 129, 135, 141, 157-8, 163-4
'Shetland Area' **100,** 129, 135, 141, 157, 163-4
notification of national measures affecting **100,** 122-4, 152
clear indication of consequences **100,** 125
form **100,** 124, 125
timeliness **100,** 125
Regulations (EEC)
101/76 **100,** 121, 123-4, 125, 132, 138, 147
170/83 **100,** 121, 126, 127, 128-32, 133, 134-6, 138, 139-46, 148, 151, 152, 153-64
1094/86 **100,** 129
2141/70 **100,** 120-1, 128, 134, 138, 150
3094/86 **100,** 140
special fishing rights
abolition **100,** 128
'fishing activities' distinguished **100,** 126
European Economic Community law, interpretation, phrases, 'deliberate disturbance' **120,** 642-4
European Economic Community Treaty (Rome) (1957) 55, 483, **60,** 250, 403, 406-7, 409, 417. *See also* European Community treaties
aims, creation of unified economic area **53,** 25
applicability **59,** 2-5. *See also* national law and *below*
Gibraltar **123,** 6
international organization **101,** 15-22, 25-9
applicable law **93,** 557
Benelux Treaty (1958) and **113,** 291-2
bilateral treaties of Member States and **53,** 603, 604
breach
defence, provisions of treaty previously concluded **113,** 291
demographic situation **113,** 292-3
remedies
annulment **93,** 28
declaration of illegality **93,** 28
direct applicability of treaty and **93,** 6

finding of unconstitutionality **93,** 54-5
individual's right to **93,** 28-9
national courts, role. *See* national courts, role *below*
need for Art. 169-71 proceedings **93,** 32-3
restoration of rights **93,** 55
Community practice, relevance **105,** 206
competition. *See* European Communities, competition
constitutional amendment, need for **93,** 521
derogation
fundamental principles
European Convention on Human Rights (1950) compared **62,** 403
restrictive interpretation **62,** 210, 394, 396, 402, 410, 412
direct effect **47,** 10-13, 14-21, **48,** 212-13, **60,** 252-3, 257-8, 268-9, 276-7, **62,** 394, 410-13, **93,** 576. *See also* European Community law, direct effect; European Community treaties, direct effect
Art. 7 (discrimination on grounds of nationality) **117,** 470
Art. 7 (non-discrimination), fall-back **93,** 765
Art. 12 (customs duties and charges) **93,** 4, 6-9, 17-22
negative obligation, relevance **93,** 4, 6-9, 17-22, 223
Art. 27 (customs duties and charges/quantitative restrictions) **93,** 33, 42-3, 44-5
Art. 30 (quantitative restrictions) **117,** 470
Art. 48(3) (free movement) **93,** 22
Art. 52 (non-discrimination) **93,** 758-9
Art. 53 (freedom of establishment) **93,** 33, 41-2, 44
Art. 95 (non-discrimination) **93,** 83-4
Art. 119 (direct sexual discrimination) **93,** 22, 628, **112,** 356-7, 358
legal certainty and **93,** 8
Member State practice
Belgium **93,** 8
France **93,** 8
FRG **93,** 8-9
Italy **93,** 8
lack of uniformity **93,** 8-9
Luxembourg **93,** 554-6
Netherlands **93,** 8
obligations, limitation to Member States, effect **93,** 5-6
remedy for breach as indicator **93,** 6
requirements
clarifying legislation, relevance **93,** 22
clear and unambiguous provision **93,** 7, 19, 22
negative obligation **93,** 19, 22
no need for further intervention **93,** 19, 22-3
unconditional obligation **93,** 19, 22
retained legislative jurisdiction, effect **93,** 759
secondary legislation distinguished **93,** 576
discretion of national authorities **62,** 394-5, 401, 407, 412
ECJ role. *See* European Court of Justice (ECJ), Art. 177 reference
ECSC Treaty (1951), effect on **99,** 216
as EEC Constitution **93,** 523
equality of treatment **62,** 402, 406, 411, 415-16
establishment, right of **62,** 405
exercise of transferred power and extension distinguished **98,** 243
free movement of goods. *See* European Community (EC), free movement of goods

European Economic Community Treaty (Rome) (1957) (*cont.*)
free movement of workers. *See* European Community (EC), free movement of workers
freedom from discrimination
nationality and **62,** 397, 400, 411, 415-16
objective justification **117,** 491
UK implementation of Regulation 1432/92 and **117,** 467-70, 490-1
quantitative restrictions **93,** 109-10, 111, 112, 264, **117,** 470-4, 491-2
sexual. *See* sexual discrimination *below*
taxation **59,** 4
fundamental principles, derogation **62,** 394, 396, 402, 403, 410, 412
immigration authorities, discretion, limitations on **62,** 394
implementing legislation, interpretation, applicable law **93,** 450
import taxes. *See* European Communities, common market
incorporation into national law **93,** 581
individuals **93,** 576
Art. 93 (State aids) **93,** 40-1, 44
Art. 102 (distortion) **93,** 40, 44
direct effect **93,** 171-2, 557
rights under **59,** 3, **62,** 391, 395, 400-1, 406
interpretation **60,** 418, 424-5
applicable law, Community law **113,** 288
Art. 177 reference. *See* European Court of Justice (ECJ), Art. 177 reference
competence to perfect Treaty **98,** 243
ECJ role. *See* European Court of Justice (ECJ), Art. 177 reference
extensive **47,** 295, **60,** 300
guidelines
effectiveness **93,** 452, **98,** 243
European legal tradition **93,** 459
fundamental principles of Community legal system **111,** 111
general principles common to Member States **111,** 111
object and purpose **93,** 458. *See also* object and purpose *below*
protection of individual **93,** 452
implied powers **47,** 299
linguistic comparisons **47,** 291
methods of **74,** 579
national courts, role. *See* national courts, role *below*
restrictive **62,** 104
Treaty considered as a whole **47,** 304
UK legislation distinguished **93,** 634-5
judicial development **93,** 457-9
legal personality, international law, in **80,** 123
legislation, interpretation, as aid to **93,** 584-5
Member State's obligation to ensure fulfilment, garnishee order, admissibility **107,** 529-31
national courts, role
application of treaty **93,** 17, 21, 26-7
conflict with national law. *See* European Community law, primacy
national law and **47,** 10-13, **59,** 4
direct applicability, secondary legislation **60,** 252, 269-71, 277-8, **62,** 412
direct effect. *See* direct effect *above*
directive. *See* European Community law, directive
incompatibility **53,** 565
ratification, reception as result of **93,** 28

Regulation. *See* European Community law, Regulations
scope **62,** 103
object and purpose, establishment of new legal order **93,** 18, 458
obligations
limitation to Member States **93,** 5-6
towards non-Member States under previously concluded treaty **113,** 291
obligations under
responsibility for fulfilment of **53,** 562-4
submission of draft law insufficient **53,** 562
phrases
'agreements between Community and one or more States or international organization' **99,** 210-11, 367-8
binding effect, need for **99,** 211
within framework of international organization **99,** 367-8
'applied' **93,** 7
'charges having equivalent effect' **93,** 7-8
'effect' **96,** 175-6, 186-7
'national market organization' **93,** 464-7
'obligations with regard to customs duties' **93,** 9
'products originating in Community' (non-EC provenance) **93,** 576-7
'public service' **113,** 287-94
education **113,** 289-90
functional criterion **113,** 287-8
health **113,** 289
inland transport **113,** 289
national law, relevance **113,** 288
posts and telecommunications **113,** 289
research **113,** 289
utilities **113,** 289
powers and functions
delegated sovereign powers **80,** 123
jus missionis **80,** 123
jus tractatus **180,** 123
preliminary rulings under **60,** 250, 252, 257, 258-9, 270
discretion to refer **60,** 417-24, 426-7, 429
previous agreements and **93,** 759, **117,** 528-9, 530, 547-9
High Seas Convention (1958) **93,** 759-60
primacy **93,** 8, 557-8
Art. 177 ruling and **93,** 557
UN obligations **117,** 474-5
privileges and immunities
at common law **80,** 122, 180
customary international law **80,** 180
immunity from suit **80,** 54, 121-8, 149
inviolability of premises **80,** 127
privileges **80,** 127
Protocol on the Grand Duchy of Luxembourg (1957), possibility of derogation because of demographic situation **113,** 292
Protocol on Inner-German Trade and **62,** 93, 97-8, 103
public order/public policy/*ordre public* **62,** 391-416
public security **62,** 393-4, 399
reciprocity **93,** 389-400
Regulations. *See* European Council Regulations

European Economic Community Treaty (Rome) (1957) (*cont.*)
reservations, Art. 189 **93,** 39
sexual discrimination
applicable law **112,** 349
Council Directive 75/117/EEC of 10 February 1975 (equal pay) **112,** 349, 351
Council Directive 76/207/EEC of 9 February 1976 (equal treatment) **112,** 349-50, 382, 392-4, 396, 404-7, 411
family law issue outside EC Treaty, whether **112,** 353-4
gender discrimination distinguished **112,** 349-53, 392
P v. *S* **112,** 349-50
gender reassignment, *P* v. *S* **112,** 349-51
moral basis, relevance **112,** 354-6
sexual orientation **112,** 363-6, 392-3
Treaty of Amsterdam (1997) **112,** 365
travel concessions limited to co-habitee of opposite sex **112,** 352-3, 362-6
sovereign State
analogies with **80,** 123, 180
population, absence **80,** 123
territorial sovereignty, absence **80,** 123
sovereignty, limitations on **53,** 565
State trading monopolies, conformity with **45,** 455-8
status, sovereign State, powers and functions analogous to **80,** 123
uniform application, need for **93,** 53, 421, **113,** 287
European Economic Interest Grouping (EEIG) 77, 76, **80,** 98
European Fisheries Convention (1964) 41, 137
exclusive fishing zone (EFZ), delimitation **41,** 223
transitional provisions **41,** 101, 131
European Laying-up Fund for Inland Waterway Vessels, draft Agreement (1976)
analysis **99,** 273-6
compatibility with Treaty of Rome (1957) **99,** 272-91
decision-making powers **99,** 285
direct effect in EC Member States **99,** 288
parallel EC/Member State membership **99,** 285
amendment of Mannheim (1868) and Luxembourg (1956) Conventions, for purpose of **99,** 285
discrimination as between EC Member States **99,** 286-7
Member State participation in organs of Fund **99,** 286-7
transfer of Community powers to **99,** 288-9
EC common transport policy, compatibility **99,** 272-91
mixed EC/non-EC participation, problems **99,** 272-91
undermining of common policy **99,** 288
Tribunal
jurisdiction, conflict with ECJ jurisdiction, possibility of **99,** 289-91
membership, ECJ judges, exclusion **99,** 290-1
European Molecular Biology Laboratory (EMBL) 105, 8-74
European Organization for Astronomical Research in the Southern Hemisphere (ESO), officials, privileges and immunities **70,** 424-5
European Organization for Nuclear Research (CERN)
France, impact study relating to proposed operation in **82,** 88-9
Headquarters Agreement
dispute settlement, arbitration **102,** 214-15
legal status **102,** 213
lease of land to, cession of territory, whether **82,** 88

legal status **82,** 87-8, **102,** 213-15
agreements concerning, effect on immunity **82,** 87-8
Headquarters Agreement **102,** 213
European Organization for the Safety of Air Navigation. *See* Eurocontrol (European Organization for the Safety of Air Navigation)
European Parliament
democratic legitimacy, uniform electoral law, need for **98,** 224
Election of the Representatives of the European Parliament by Direct Universal Suffrage 1976 **123,** 10, 24
applicability **123,** 10
UK responsibility in respect of Gibraltar **123,** 13
as treaty **123,** 13
elections
overseas territories and **93,** 306-7, **123,** 5-24
right to stand **93,** 345-7
right to vote **93,** 344-7
European Convention on Human Rights (1950), applicability of free elections provisions **123,** 14-16, 22-4
European Union Treaty (Maastricht) (1992) **93,** 306-7, 345-7. *See also* powers *below*
importance **93,** 390, 401, 428, 432-3, 434-5
legislature, whether **98,** 211-12, **123,** 15, 16-18, 22-3
Gibraltar **123,** 16-18, 23-4
new legal order and **93,** 289, 347
powers
European Union Treaty (Maastricht) (1992) **93,** 347, **123,** 7-10, 17-18, 23
scrutiny of EC law **93,** 524-5
privileges and immunities, sovereignty, limitation on, reciprocity, need for **101,** 366-9
European Patent Office
decisions, European Convention on Human Rights (1950) and **111,** 145-6
human rights
procedural safeguards **111,** 146
protection equivalent to that provided for by the European Convention on Human Rights (1950) **111,** 146
European public law 46, 483, 486
European Schools
applicable law
constituent instrument **108,** 665, 667
international law **108,** 641, 651
jurisdiction over
absence of effective remedy before a national authority, relevance **108,** 641-2
European Community (EC) **108,** 641
European Court of Justice (ECJ) **108,** 651
municipal courts **108,** 641-2, 650-2, 666
legal protection, provision for **108,** 667-8
status
capacity to sue and be sued **108,** 651, 666
organ of international organization **108,** 641, 650-1, 666
'public institution'/'body'
effect on status as organ of international organization **108,** 641
transformation into, need for **108,** 652
Statute
6 **108,** 641, 650
6(3) **108,** 651, 666

European Schools (*cont.*)
7 **108,** 640
8 **108,** 640
12 **108,** 640
12(1) **108,** 641
12(4) **108,** 666-7
22 **108,** 640
23 **108,** 640
26(1) **108,** 647
26(4) **108,** 652
27 **108,** 651
28 **108,** 651
Statute (Personnel)
40(b) **108,** 668
45 **108,** 665, 668
tuition fees
admissibility **108,** 646-8, 650-3
legitimate expectation, whether **108,** 653
proportionality and **108,** 653
review by municipal court, admissibility **108,** 650-2
European Social Charter (1961) 45, 151
interpretation **58,** 15-16, 33
European Space Agency (ESA). *See also* European Space Research Organization (ESRO)
Appeals Board **118,** 130
compétence de la compétence **118,** 136
independence **118,** 136
dispute settlement provisions **118,** 129-30
immunity, jurisdiction **118,** 125-7, 128, 129, 133
waiver **118,** 126-7
legal status **118,** 129
privileges and immunities **118,** 129
purpose **118,** 129
Staff regulations **118,** 130
successor to ESRO, whether **118,** 125-7
European Space Operations Centre (ESOC) Agreement 118, 130-1
European Space Research Organization (ESRO). *See also* European Space Agency (ESA)
Appeals Board, competence **51,** 431
immunity, jurisdiction **74,** 693
officials, privileges and immunities **73,** 685-8
staff
contract of employment, claims **73,** 684-8, **74,** 693
Regulations, interpretation **51,** 431
status **73,** 686-7
Treaty of Rome (1957) and **51,** 431-2
European Union (EU)
amendments/extension
binding, whether **98,** 226, 231
constitutional review **98,** 226
Member State approval, need for **98,** 235
non-application **98,** 226, 231
procedure **98,** 235
ratification, need for **98,** 228

applicable law, Protocol on Privileges and Immunities of the European Communities (1957) **107,** 527-9
authority derived from Member States **98,** 228
Coreper
competence, 'preparing the work of the Council/carrying out tasks assigned to it' **113,** 359
decision-making powers **113,** 359, 375
decisions, Art. 173 reference **113,** 359
delegation of authority to **113,** 359
institution of Community, whether **113,** 375
Council Regulation, validity, backdating of publication **113,** 335-7
demographic considerations **113,** 292-3
European Commission, relations with non-Member States, applicable law **107,** 525-7
European Development Fund (EDF), payments to project contractors, Commission responsibility **113,** 401-5, 410
human rights, compatibility with Treaty of Rome **108,** 253-5
national identity, preservation, legitimate aim **113,** 290
reversibility, EMU and **98,** 212
status
economic community **98,** 227
State, whether **98,** 226
subsidiarity **98,** 243-5
binding principle **98,** 227
ECJ to monitor **98,** 244
as limitation of powers **98,** 244

European Union Treaty (Maastricht) (1992)
Common Foreign and Security Policy (CFSP). *See* Common Foreign and Security Policy (CFSP)
constitutional amendment, need for **93,** 340-53
Economic and Monetary Union (EMU) **98,** 186-7, 189
freedom of movement **98,** 188
voting rights for non-nationals **98,** 185-6, 263-4
constitutionality
democratic deficit **98,** 209
European Union provisions **98,** 219-20
fundamental rights within the Community. *See* fundamental rights within the Community
Kompetenz/Kompetenz **98,** 208-9
regions, infringement of powers **98,** 211
voting rights for non-nationals **98,** 211, 220
EC powers, extension of **98,** 214-15
environment, precautionary principle **106,** 65-6
European citizenship
right to stand in European Parliament elections **93,** 345-7
right to vote and stand as candidate in national elections **93,** 344-5
European Parliament. *See* European Parliament
free movement of persons **93,** 350-1
compatibility with national Constitutions **93,** 350-1
constitutional amendment, need for **98,** 188
unanimity rule **93,** 351
fundamental rights within the European Community. *See* fundamental rights within the European Community
intergovernmental cooperation

European Union Treaty (Maastricht) (1992) (*cont.*)
Common Foreign and Security Policy (CFSP). *See* Common Foreign and Security Policy (CFSP)
conversion to supranational competence, treaty amendment, need for **98,** 218
justice and home affairs. *See* justice and home affairs *below*
justice and home affairs
European Convention on Human Rights (1950) and **98,** 218
Geneva Convention on the Status of Refugees (1951) **98,** 218
reciprocity and **93,** 343
referendum, right to **98,** 212
right to stand as candidate in national elections, national sovereignty, compatibility with **98,** 265
Social Policy Protocol
indirect amendment of national law, whether **98,** 176-7
part of treaty, whether **98,** 172-5
annexation to Treaty of Rome (1957), relevance **98,** 172-3
legislative intention **98,** 173-5
Member State practice **98,** 172-3
sovereignty, threat to **98,** 212
voting rights for non-nationals
constitutional amendment, need for **98,** 185-6, 211, 220
right to stand as candidate in national elections, constitutional amendment, need for **98,** 263-70
evacuation 83, 142, 193. *See also* deportation; expulsion of alien
Evian Agreements (1962) 41, 21, 23, 257, 259, 269, 370, 375, 389, **44,** 39-41, **52,** 407-8, **72,** 54, 93, 219-20, 268, 589-90, **74,** 98-100
acquired rights **73,** 33-5, 37
assumption of obligations by Algeria **47,** 79-83, 104-6
contract **72,** 256
damages, provision for **62,** 207
debts **72,** 54-6, **73,** 34-5
French law, effect in **47,** 325-6
as international agreement **52,** 407-8, **72,** 589
interpretation **47,** 342-3
jurisdiction of French courts and **72,** 54-5, 57-8, 93
municipal law, relation to **72,** 589
nationality provisions **111,** 188-9
nationalization provisions **47,** 60-2, 119-26
compensation for **52,** 9-10, 407-8, **74,** 98-100
pension rights **73,** 37
social security funds **73,** 33-5
State succession **41,** 21, 23
tort liability **72,** 57-8, 268
trade union rights **72,** 589-90
evidence 54, 398-401, **68,** 587, 633, 645-51, **76,** 373-9. *See also* arbitral tribunal, evidence; arbitration, evidence; evidence of; extradition, evidence; United Kingdom, evidence; war crimes, evidence; *and under individual tribunals*
acquiescence as **50,** 28, 90-1
admissibility **46,** 272, **58,** 280, 304, 305, **79,** 77-8, 390, 434-5, 539-40
admissions **74,** 486-7
affidavit. *See* affidavit *below*
affirmation **78,** 505-12
audiotape **107,** 439-40

Court's right to seek/consider new **108,** 310, 355, 460
deceased witness **122,** 31
document obtained in breach of immunity **77,** 124-59
oral evidence based on such a document **77,** 134-5, 141, 143
where source non-justiciable **77,** 134
documentary **74,** 487-90
evidence not available to confirming Judge **108,** 148, 171-2
evidence not submitted by witness **122,** 30
evidence relating to acts not under indictment **121,** 224, 310-11
hearsay. *See* hearsay *below*
ILO Commission of Inquiry **36,** 377-9, 414
on oath **78,** 508-9
Security Council Resolutions **116,** 598-601
treaty interpretation **37,** 187, 190
videotape **109,** 511, **116,** 22
admission
admissibility **74,** 486-7
corroboration **42,** 463
defence not admission of facts **76,** 379
in diplomatic correspondence **50,** 469
statistical abstracts as **50,** 238, 260, 497, 513
aerial survey **38,** 26-7, 56-7
affidavit **64,** 180, **68,** 546, **69,** 228-39, 242-7, 263-8, **70,** 123, 505-7, **80,** 243, **105,** 612
deposition distinguished **44,** 244
extradition **44,** 232-5, **69,** 228-39, 242-7, 263-8
applicable law **87,** 315
lex fori **104,** 559
assessment. *See* evaluation *below*
authorizing legislation **87,** 315-16
bias
access to foreign materials **82,** 455-6
foreign government **82,** 453-5
boundary agreement **80,** 284
subsequent events **80,** 284
burden of proof. *See* burden of proof
circumstantial **46,** 333
Inter-American Court of Human Rights **109,** 154 n. 36
conduct **80,** 366
confession and corroboration **42,** 463
confidentiality **76,** 492
oral evidence **108,** 172-5
written evidence **108,** 172-5
consular immunity and **86,** 556
corroboration, need for, State practice **112,** 172-3
credibility **79,** 607-8, **108,** 310-11
critical date **76,** 373, **79,** 658
defence not admission of facts **76,** 379
delay in submitting, abuse of power, whether **85,** 107-8
depositions **37,** 244
affidavit distinguished **44,** 244
destruction of, ICJ provisional measures and **80,** 456, 458
difficulty of producing **83,** 477, 485-8
diplomatic correspondence **50,** 469

evidence (*cont.*)
diplomatic list **80,** 9-10
disclosure of documents. *See* disclosure of documents
disclosure, obligation **122,** 26-30, 31-5. *See also* disclosure of documents; General Agreement on Tariffs and Trade (GATT) (1947), Anti-Dumping Implementation Code (1980), obligations of confidentiality; Yugoslavia, International Criminal Tribunal for the Former (ICTY), evidence, disclosure, obligation
of expert evidence **121,** 228
in indictment **121,** 326, 328
non-disclosure **121,** 221, 223-4
as denial of access to courts **119,** 277, 307
to expert witnesses **121,** 227-8
disclosure as offence under law of foreign State **104,** 533-6, 580-7
applicable law, *lex fori* **104,** 555, 558
balancing the considerations **104,** 584-6, **108,** 629-30, 631
State immunity, jurisdiction **104,** 586
'just excuse' **104,** 534, 543, 559-61, 582-6, 588-90, 609-10, 628-9, **108,** 629-30, 631
oral evidence **104,** 557-8, 581
public interest **104,** 533, 535-6, 544
public policy **104,** 535-6
State practice **104,** 557, 558-9, 594-6, 625-7
'sufficient cause' **104,** 559-61, 582, 588-90, 609-10, 628-9, **108,** 623-32
documents
copy **43,** 337
discovery. *See* disclosure of documents *above*
UN Administrative Tribunal **54,** 365
effect of post-traumatic stress disorder **121,** 243-9, 321-2
electoral records **80,** 558
evaluation **76,** 65, 375-8, 412-16, 489
in absence of oral examination **121,** 83-4
arbitrator's discretion **106,** 448, 458
equality of arms principle and **120,** 47, 95-6
human rights tribunal **116,** 363
ILO Commission of Inquiry **36,** 413-19
inconsistencies **121,** 249-51
judicial discretion **105,** 609
oral evidence **116,** 363-4
transparency, need for **120,** 220
exclusion
by agreement **102,** 232
estoppel and **37,** 187
as irrelevant **121,** 314
executive certificate. *See* executive certificate/statement
expert. *See* expert, evidence
extradition. *See* extradition, evidence
fact-finding enquiry **76,** 656
failure to argue case **106,** 487, **121,** 27
failure to submit **46,** 389, **75,** 132-6, 138-42, **76,** 47-8, **86,** 402, **120,** 6, 7-8
false **76,** 606, 611, 725-6
'fishing expedition' **84,** 752
foreign official

examination of **101,** 353-8
public interest privilege **101,** 354-5
right to call **103,** 316-17
government gazetteer **50,** 255-6
hearsay **36,** 414, **76,** 376, **87,** 320, **107,** 438
best evidence rule **108,** 177
maps **50,** 108-10
person taking victim's statements **108,** 148, 175-9
improperly obtained **95,** 407
insufficient **76,** 574-9, **106,** 449-50
revolution, unnecessary damage by government forces **106,** 449-50, 462-3, 475
International Military Tribunals, exemption from technical rules **56,** 583-4
judicial notice. *See* judicial notice
late presentation **107,** 437-8, **124,** 75
legislation **80,** 68
maps. *See* maps
material not formally submitted **76,** 651-2
military courts **48,** 486-93
ministerial **76,** 377-8
negotiations
positions taken during, admissibility **102,** 22-3
with third parties **45,** 399
notice of, right to **121,** 309-10, 324
official publication **76,** 378
official statements **76,** 375-8, 658
opinion **76,** 376, **120,** 6
photographic **80,** 260, 264
power to demand from State
European Court of Justice (ECJ) **110,** 633, 635
Inter-American Commission on Human Rights **110,** 635-6
International Court of Justice (ICJ) **110,** 634-5
international law, compatibility with **110,** 637
Iran–US Claims Tribunal **110,** 636
remedy for failure to provide, adverse inference **110,** 635-6
press accounts **76,** 374-5, 387, 392, 394, 412-14, 651-2, 658-60, **79,** 39-40, 98, 607
presumptions **46,** 333, 381-5
privilege, claim of **73,** 302-6, 308-10, 312, 317-20, 323, 332-9, 343-8, 353-9
professional privilege **64,** 281-2, 287-90, 297-8
proprio motu **108,** 310, 355, 414
public knowledge **76,** 387
radar fix **69,** 82-4
redaction in case of outstanding hearings against other indicted persons **121,** 223
refusal, 'just excuse' **104,** 539, 543, 559-61, 562, 587-8, 599-600
requesting court's statement as to purpose, predisposition to accept **84,** 747
rules of **76,** 605, 658
international tribunals **36,** 377-9, **46,** 272, 313, 389
municipal law practice distinguished **120,** 220-1
Security Council Resolutions **103,** 408, **116,** 598-601
self-incrimination **104,** 540-6, 557, 581-3, 592-8, 625-9
absolute right **108,** 627-8
common law **104,** 582-3, 607, **108,** 627-8
enforced evidence, admissibility in foreign court **104,** 545-6, 562, 603-4

evidence (*cont.*)
extradition, refusal **104,** 541-2
First National Bank of Chicago **104,** 544-5
Frank **104,** 544-5
giving of evidence as offence **104,** 608-9, 628
In re Westinghouse Uranium Contract **104,** 626
judicial discretion **108,** 629-30
McRae **104,** 593-5, 625
offence against foreign law, relevance **104,** 609, 626-7, **108,** 625-9
rationale **104,** 627-8
Spencer **104,** 544, 594-5, 601-2
Two Sicilies **104,** 592-3, 625
signature **80,** 38
standard of proof **58,** 264, **76,** 657-65, **87,** 361
arbitral tribunal, Rules of Arbitration between Nations (1875) (*Institut de Droit International*) **106,** 448
balance of probabilities **108,** 635
ICJ **97,** 422
International Tribunal for the Law of the Sea (ITLOS) **120,** 255
'persecution or well-founded fear of persecution' **87,** 360-3, 473, 485-6, **104,** 101, **117,** 600, 603-6, 618-19
political offence **104,** 93
beyond reasonable doubt **58,** 264, **95,** 141-2, **112,** 85-8, 92, 96, 102, 122-4, 131, 140-1, 144, 146, 149, 255-6, **120,** 49-50, 70, 80, 99-101, 103-4, 222, **121,** 248, 307-8, **122,** 206-10
compelling reasons of national security **124,** 521-2, 526, 537-9, 547, 549-50
'evidence sufficient to support' **107,** 15
high civil balance of probabilities **124,** 521, 526-7, 535-6, 537-9, 547
international tribunals **109,** 151-2, 242-3, **110,** 750, **120,** 222
'not manifestly unfounded' **108,** 15-16
persecution or well-founded fear of persecution **117,** 600, 603-6, 618-19
prima facie case **106,** 448, **108,** 11-20
Convention for the Creation of an International Criminal Court for the Prevention and Punishment of Terrorism (1937) **108,** 14
draft Statute for an International Criminal Court (ILC 1994) **108,** 16-17
draft Statute for the Creation of an International Criminal Jurisdiction to Implement the Apartheid Convention (Ad Hoc Group of Experts 1981 Report) **108,** 15-16
International Criminal Tribunal for the Former Yugoslavia **108,** 11-20
International Tribunal for the Law of the Sea (ITLOS) **120,** 311
international tribunals **108,** 14-18
multiplicity of meanings **108,** 12
municipal courts **108,** 12-13
Nuremberg Charter (1945) **108,** 14-15
UN Committee on International Criminal Jurisdiction (1951 Report) **108,** 15
Versailles, Treaty of (1919) (war crimes tribunals) **108,** 14
reasonable grounds for believing **108,** 12, 43, 49-52, 55, 68, 89, 139, 156, 158, 163-6
reasonable suspicion **122,** 447-8, 459, 478-80, 481-2, 486-7
refugees **79,** 607
State responsibility for acts of irregular combatants **124,** 119
'sufficiently plausible' **110,** 750, 753, 767-8, 773-4
terrorist offences **122,** 447-8, 459, 478-80, 481-2, 486-7

tribunal's discretion **120,** 221-2
UNHCR *Handbook on Procedure for Determining Refugee Status* **79,** 609
well-founded **110,** 768, 773-4, 777, 780, **120,** 222-3
Statistical Yearbooks **80,** 302, 341-2
authority of publisher **80,** 341
subsequent absence of information **80,** 342
subsequent to event complained of **108,** 310, 355, 414
sufficiency **75,** 600, 605-6, **91,** 536-7, **107,** 436
failure to document **106,** 637-8, 655-6, 712-15, 731-2
taking abroad **84,** 731-54
documents held abroad, order to produce **73,** 299-363
examination of official **101,** 353-8
former **101,** 356-7
public interest privilege **101,** 354-5
foreign law enforcement, whether **84,** 749-51
Hague Convention on the Taking of Evidence Abroad in Civil or Commercial Matters (1970). *See* Hague Convention on the Taking of Evidence Abroad in Civil or Commercial Matters (1970)
taking at request of foreign State **86,** 173-4
conformity with local practice, need for **86,** 173-4
extradition distinguished **86,** 181
transcript of evidence, availability **86,** 174, 181
testimonial immunity, Head of State **101,** 506-7
transmission to third States, permissibility **86,** 167-8
treaties **80,** 52, 108, 141, **83,** 263
ad referendum **97,** 337-8
UN Compensation Commission. *See* United Nations Compensation Commission, evidence
video film **80,** 243
wishes relating to, applicable law distinguished **97,** 307, 554-6
witnesses **58,** 280, 304, 305
attendance **58,** 86, 97, 100, 104, 108, **121,** 16-17
costs of unnecessary **67,** 445
compellability **55,** 552-3, **118,** 351-2
credibility **112,** 177, **121,** 27-8
evaluation of evidence in case of non-attendance **121,** 83-4
examination of **58,** 86, 97, 100, 104, 108
judge's right to summon **104,** 389-93
notification of identity **121,** 222, 227, **122,** 27-8
objectivity **95,** 280, 281, 287-8, **118,** 71
probative value **58,** 280
protection of. *See* fair trial, protection of victims and witnesses
right to examine **121,** 313-14
anonymity and **105,** 624-6
victim as **112,** 173-4
evidence of. *See also* maps, evidence
acceptance of compulsory jurisdiction of ICJ **76,** 41-4, 111-14, 238-41, 495-7
ICJ Reports **76,** 303-5, 497
ICJ Yearbook **76,** 42-3, 67-70, 170-1, 175, 187-8, 194-9, 496-7
ratification **76,** 184-6, 194, 230-1, 238, 250-6, 278, 299-303
Act of Parliament **78,** 463
act of State
conduct **66,** 218-19, 233-6, 268

evidence of (*cont.*)
government agency minutes **66,** 314-15
official declaration **66,** 191, 260-7, 277
statement by Counsel **66,** 77, 217, 219-20, 236-8, 263
administration of territory **38,** 88-9
administrative practice giving rise to alleged breach **58,** 263-6, **120,** 49-50, 95-6, 101-4, 106-8, 142
agency **64,** 115-19, 137-9, 147-9, **80,** 46, 113
agreement **80,** 405-6, 412
aid **76,** 416-17
alien's intention to settle **99,** 43
armed conflict **108,** 49-50
status
ICRC **105,** 491-2
UN Resolutions **105,** 533
assets of honorary consul, purpose **82,** 7-8
bank account, use, international organization, certificate **78,** 116
bay, status
delimitation agreement **97,** 506, 511
practice of coastal States **97,** 506
boundary. *See also* boundaries, land, evidence of; Egypt–Israel Arbitration Tribunal (Taba), evidence; maps
absence of protest **77,** 667
maps **59,** 169-70, 202-3, 206, **77,** 664
boundary demarcation **94,** 11
compensation, provision for **78,** 681
conditions in applicant country **79,** 77-9, 448-50
consular status
absence of request for special residence permit **77,** 401
consular note **77,** 400
Ministry of Foreign Affairs' letter **77,** 401
continental shelf discontinuity **81,** 267, 268
contract, validity **121,** 23-8
contras
dependence on US **76,** 392-7
US control **76,** 397-401
US direction of strategy and tactics **76,** 394-6
control of bank **87,** 252-3
conviction **73,** 48-50
corporation
control **84,** 496-7, 518-21
ownership **83,** 466, 482-3, **84,** 496-502
value **83,** 477-9
corporation, nationality. *See* corporation, nationality
crime **55,** 510, 533, 541
crimes against humanity **108,** 65-6
authority of accused **108,** 119-28
destruction of property **108,** 165
destruction of sacred places **108,** 93-4
expulsion/deportation **108,** 94-5
indiscriminate attack **108,** 95, **122,** 136-7, 166-8
mass murder **108,** 59, 97-102

murder **108,** 163-5
plan or policy **108,** 102-12, **122,** 78-9
unlawful appropriation of property **108,** 93-4
unlawful detention of civilians **108,** 92-3
customary international law. *See* customary international law, evidence of
customary law **84,** 84
damage **55,** 175-6, **56,** 214, **57,** 196-7
debt **81,** 537
diplomatic immunity **61,** 502
diplomatic mission funds, certificate of head of mission **63,** 130-5, 321, **64,** 594-5, **74,** 173, 176, 179, 187-8, **82,** 8, **94,** 360, 361, **120,** 6
diplomatic relations **80,** 9-10, **84,** 250
diplomatic status. *See* diplomatic status, evidence of/requirements
discrimination **83,** 551, **112,** 114-23
dispute, contemporaneous written **56,** 326
divorce decree **53,** 589-90
embassy bank account, purpose. *See* embassy or consular bank account/funds, purpose/use, evidence of
enemy character, ships **40,** 474
expropriation/nationalization **83,** 465, 466-7, 470-3, 485-9
extradition agreement **87,** 316
foreign law **43,** 52-3, 59-60, 62, 74, **44,** 363, **53,** 17-18, **72,** 448-51, 458-65, **73,** 248-9, **78,** 518-19, 595, 597, **117,** 57, 581-2. *See also* foreign law, as fact
expert **72,** 448-51, 458-65, **73,** 238, 248-9, **78,** 518-19, 595, 597, **103,** 285-7
foreign judgment as **43,** 53-4, 55, 59-60, 74
genocide, intent
perpetration of acts intended to undermine group **108,** 134-5
political doctrine **108,** 134-5
Head of State, status **80,** 366, **103,** 584, 586, 587, **119,** 49, 56-7, 94, 100
health, state of **78,** 79
historic rights **41,** 125
human rights conditions. *See* human rights, evidence of conditions
identity **116,** 280
immunity of international officials, request for waiver **94,** 310
independence, independent participation in war **88,** 272
independence of tribunal **78,** 330-2
intention to be bound **80,** 38, 659-60
interim measures, prejudice **94,** 456-7
international criminal order **78,** 128-9
international law **52,** 79, **55,** 5, 294, **80,** 398, 403-4, 419, 421, 422-3
compatibility of municipal law, long-standing character **47,** 172, 179, 186-7
European Convention on State Immunity (and Protocol) (Basle) (1972) **64,** 362
principles of **77,** 238
UK courts, collective opinion of professors **77,** 76
US courts **77,** 210-11, 256
international legal personality
diplomatic relations **77,** 614
legal system **77,** 615
international organization
extent of immunity **80,** 35
Member States' liability for debts **80,** 140

evidence of (*cont.*)
membership
accession instruments **77,** 96
attendance at meetings **77,** 96
Foreign Office affidavit **77,** 96
practice
resolution **110,** 21-2
Secretary-General's Report **110,** 21-2
status, request to Ministry of Foreign Affairs **102,** 185
jus cogens/peremptory norm
multilateral treaties **124,** 364, 365-8
State practice **124,** 364
teachings of publicists **124,** 365
legal dispute **94,** 517, **97,** 471-2, 581-9
likely persecution **79,** 607-9
maintenance of diplomatic mission **80,** 9
manual of psychological warfare, responsibility for **76,** 400
marriage **107,** 438-9
maternal affiliation **58,** 580-4, 617
mens rea
law **104,** 380
superior orders **104,** 376-7
mental health **78,** 206
military intervention by Croatia on behalf of Bosnian Croats **108,** 151-4, **122,** 45-8
military manoeuvres **76,** 387
mining by US agency **76,** 379-82
mitigation of damages **78,** 673
nationality **41,** 357-65, **55,** 486, **61,** 389, 393, 397-8, 400-1
ambassador's letter **120,** 6
identity card **88,** 702
loss or deprivation of, visa requirement, relevance **77,** 386
'opinion' evidence **120,** 6
passport **49,** 504-6, **55,** 485, 486, **61,** 389, 393, 397-8, 400-1, **77,** 216, **83,** 466, **103,** 289
native title **125,** 356-62, 436-40
Nicaraguan cross-border attacks **76,** 420-1
Nicaraguan support of El Salvador guerrillas **76,** 412-17, 665
official nature of acts **77,** 612
political motivation **79,** 98-9
political offence **79,** 53
property
illegal acquisition **81,** 591-2
ownership **64,** 318, **81,** 587-9
public order/public policy/*ordre public*, Security Council Resolution **103,** 408-9
ratification **76,** 110-11, 115
reciprocity
resolution of GDR Council of State **77,** 441
statement by All-German Institute in West Berlin **77,** 441
recognition. *See* recognition, government, evidence of; recognition, State, evidence of
refugees
'persecution or well-founded fear of persecution' **79,** 614, 617-20, 623-4, 657-9, **87,** 441, 442, **90,** 8, **117,** 614-16

status **60,** 371-3
travel documents **77,** 579-80
rivers, names **38,** 94
role of foreign armed forces **88,** 10-12
official international bodies and **88,** 11, 21-2, 31
seizure **44,** 323-4, 349, 353
ships
enemy character **40,** 474
nationality **120,** 176-7, 224, 225-7
conduct of State of alleged nationality **120,** 228-9, 254-6, 314-15
ownership **65,** 25
registration, continuing validity **120,** 172-7, 209-13, 226-8, 242-3, 247-9, 252-4, 255-6, 304-16, 343-52, **125,** 298-300, 301-2, 304, 307-8, 315-16, 318-19
sovereignty **52,** 220-6, **59,** 61-74, **82,** 398. *See also* sovereignty, *effectivités*
allegiance **59,** 61, 73-4, 100, 120
overflights **76,** 385-7, **114,** 94, 108
special mission **80,** 420, **121,** 599-602
stability of revolutionary regime **82,** 387
State agency/State-owned corporation/State entity status **64,** 115-19, 137-9, 147-9, **81,** 540
certificate of head of diplomatic mission **63,** 130-5, 319, 321
control **103,** 511-12
State immunity, jurisdiction **66,** 60, 120, 223
certificate of head of diplomatic mission **64,** 458, 463, 467-8, 474, 594-5
executive certificate **64,** 35-6, 507-8, **80,** 21, **87,** 231-2, **102,** 172-3
nature of activity, use of commercial procedures, relevance **77,** 525
nature of contract **77,** 525
nature of funds
actual use **77,** 521-2
contract **77,** 521, 525
designation as public **77,** 520
statement of intention **77,** 519-20
State practice **53,** 342, **80,** 52, 67-8, 108, 135, 141, 173-6. *See also* State practice, evidence of
municipal legislation **41,** 135-6, 208-9, 211
statement at conference **81,** 277, **99,** 424
treaties **41,** 137, 158, 169-70, 213
UN resolutions **84,** 539
unilateral acts **41,** 119, 136, 158, 190, 208-9, 212-15
State responsibility **102,** 139, 143
acts of revolutionaries **106,** 449-50, 462-3, 475, 498
State liability for consequences of legal judgment **102,** 139, 143
statehood, attributes **77,** 626
State's intention to act as private person, arbitration clause **82,** 65
successor State, status as **83,** 22
survival of native title **112,** 610-13
taking of property **84,** 514-17
territorial limits of aboriginal rights **115,** 488-90
title. *See* title, evidence of
torture **116,** 311-14
torture/inhuman treatment, risk **108,** 267-8, 282, 373-5
travaux préparatoires, affidavit **68,** 592-3, 621-4
treaty **83,** 81-3

evidence of (*cont.*)
abrogation
absence from list of 'treaties which retain importance in practice' **77,** 436
absence of protest **77,** 436
absence of request for EEC Council approval **77,** 437
adhesion to, ministerial certificate **78,** 119
application **75,** 110-12
intention to be bound, conduct **41,** 54-6, 105, 111-12
meaning
expert **74,** 641, 645-6, 652, 665, 673, 680
extraneous **68,** 305-6, 392-4, 420
parties' intention to conclude **102,** 35
reservation, acceptance **77,** 605-6
validity **107,** 173-4
UCLA activity **76,** 383-5
value of property **82,** 198-9
waiver of Optional Clause reservation **76,** 543
war **87,** 274, 278-9
declaration of **87,** 274, **105,** 533
executive certificate/statement **87,** 183
expert **87,** 274
martial law, declaration of **87,** 274
war crimes **82,** 453-4
admissibility **104,** 386-9
commander's responsibility **122,** 152, 172-3, 186-8
superior/subordinate relationship **122,** 169-72
widespread and systematic nature of attack **122,** 152, 204-6
indiscriminate attack **108,** 49-52
individual responsibility **108,** 165-6
planned attack against civilians **122,** 127-30, 172-3
use of UN hostages as human shields **108,** 96
witnesses, judge's right to summon **104,** 389-93
war, state of
administrative regulations **67,** 617-18, 625
ceasefire **67,** 617
diplomatic relations, breaking off **67,** 623-4
emergency, declaration of **67,** 616-18
self-defence rights, invocation of **67,** 622-3
State broadcast **67,** 616-18
State legislation **67,** 615, 616-18
UN Secretary-General, statement of **67,** 619
well-founded fear of persecution **90,** 7-8
ex aequo et bono **41,** 37, 38, 50, 78, **52,** 123, **54,** 122, 207, **71,** 105, **81,** 271, 346-7, 391, **89,** 522
arbitral award **46,** 472, 506
arbitral tribunal, power to decide **41,** 164, **46,** 472, 506, **50,** 3, 18, **89,** 450
arbitration **99,** 479-81
equitable principles distinguished **89,** 522-3, 547, **99,** 562
equity distinguished **71,** 209, **77,** 676, **81,** 271, **97,** 542, **99,** 560-2, 586, 595-8, 665-6
non-application of law **99,** 561-2
ex gratia damages **106,** 499-500
exclusion by parties **97,** 306-7
ICJ
Art. 38 of Statute and **80,** 472

power to decide **41,** 50, **78,** 143-4, 163-5
parties' agreement **80,** 535
exceptio non adimpleti contractus. *See* contract, *exceptio non adimpleti contractus*
exchange, rate of, reasonableness **74,** 289
exchange contract 40, 13, 15, **41,** 231, 234, 237, **47,** 51, **66,** 173, **77,** 326
disguised monetary transaction **77,** 326-8, **118,** 573, 575
enforceability **75,** 130-4, 145-7, 159, **77,** 326-7, **118,** 567-78
conformity with foreign exchange control regulations, relevance **118,** 578
conformity with IMF Agreement (1945), relevance **72,** 544-5, **118,** 578
interpretation of concept **75,** 131-2
examination of correspondence **70,** 154-83
form, relevance **77,** 326
interpretation **72,** 544-5, 694-708, **77,** 326, **118,** 573-4
exchange controls 38, 138-40, 457, **40,** 9, 12-13, **41,** 230-9, **42,** 410, **43,** 208, **92,** 606-7. *See also* currency regulations; exchange rates; International Monetary Fund Agreement (IMF)
act of State **84,** 119, 120-1, 126-30
breach of contract **83,** 583
commercial activity, whether **84,** 192-3
contravention
enforceability of transactions **41,** 231-9, **75,** 130-6, 144-7, 159, **118,** 567-78
international arbitral tribunals, applicability to **75,** 132, 159
customary international law **84,** 122 n. 21
expulsion of alien and **82,** 202
extraterritorial effect **47,** 157-63
foreign court, application by **47,** 50-2, 162
in
Algeria **47,** 124, **52,** 11-14
Bulgaria **38,** 145
Cuba **38,** 138-40, 457
Czechoslovakia **47,** 158-63
France **52,** 11-14
transfers from Algeria **47,** 124
Germany (1938) **42,** 403, 406
Indonesia **40,** 9
Iran **75,** 128-35, 144-7
Mexico (1982) **84,** 109, 111, 112-13, 119, 120-1, 189, 190, 192-3, 198-200
Netherlands **47,** 46-52
Spain **46,** 182, 185, 233
Uganda **66,** 170-2
Zambia **70,** 159-64, 170-83
Zimbabwe **92,** 606-7
privacy of property and **70,** 154-83
regulations
bank circulars, whether **75,** 129-30, 145
capital transfers **75,** 130-1, 134, 146-7, 159
conformity with IMF Agreement **118,** 578
enforcement through extradition proceedings **78,** 505
sovereign activity **84,** 112, 113, 119, 120-1, 122 n. 21, **88,** 74
State responsibility for acts in relation to **117,** 240-1
as taking of property **84,** 198, **88,** 73 n. 1
transactions **84,** 121-6
workers' right to transfer of portion of wages **117,** 239-41
date of obligation **117,** 241-6

exchange of notes. *See* treaties, exchange of notes
exchange rates 59, 559-62. *See also* exchange controls
certificate of deposit, protection against exchange rate fluctuations **92,** 417-18
confiscatory **38,** 143
fixed par values **59,** 534-8
agreed par values distinguished **59,** 534, 589
alteration of **59,** 575-6
excludability of alien. *See also* aliens, admission
constitutionality of conditions **82,** 333-7
government minister **82,** 334
justiciability **82,** 333-5
member of foreign government **82,** 334
PLO Permanent Observer to UN **82,** 331, 334-6
right of **104,** 66
security, relevance **82,** 331
waiver **82,** 331, 335
constitutionality of conditions **82,** 333-7
executive discretion **82,** 331
security, relevance **82,** 331
widow of former President **82,** 334
exclusion of alien. *See also* deportation; deportation withhold/bar; excludability of alien; expulsion of alien
as act of State **92,** 502
burden of proof **95,** 538, **104,** 203-4
deportation distinguished **95,** 580
Gleneagles Accord (1977) **92,** 503-4, 507-9
justification
crimes against humanity **104,** 198
criminal record **95,** 573-4, **104,** 257-8
national security **123,** 595
war crimes **104,** 198
past behaviour, retroactive legislation **104,** 198
refouler **95,** 601, 607-8
right of **98,** 376-7
UK citizen, exemption **92,** 503
exclusive dealing contract, EEC Treaty and **44,** 393-408, **45,** 460-1
exclusive economic zone (EEZ) 55, 286, **56,** 192, **71,** 93, 110, 121, 154, 191, 194, 196-203, **74,** 142-8, **95,** 672. *See also* contiguous zone; exclusive fishing zone (EFZ)
200-mile limit **95,** 672, **99,** 462-3
basis **81,** 301
applicable law, customary international law **83,** 45, 86
baseline, outer edge of territorial sea **95,** 671
breadth **74,** 143-8
bunkering rights. *See* refuelling of fishing vessel *below*
claim, need for **81,** 264
Law of the Sea Convention (1982) **81,** 302, 303, **120,** 259-60
State practice **81,** 302
closing line **82,** 681
coastal State
duties, Law of the Sea Convention (1982) **81,** 303
rights **56,** 192
collision, jurisdiction **89,** 78-80
concept, evolution **82,** 606

continental shelf and. *See* continental shelf, EEZ and
customary international law **71,** 200, **74,** 144-6, **81,** 264, 330-1, 388, **82,** 642
customs laws, right to apply
  'customs law' **120,** 319-20
  Law of the Sea Convention (1982) **120,** 190-2, 245-6, 259-61, 265-9, 325
  necessity **120,** 190-2, 300-1
  public interest **120,** 190-1, 300-1, 326
  refuelling of fishing vessels **110,** 754-6, **120,** 189-92, 256-7, 322-7
delimitation **67,** 108-9, 240-2, **71,** 121, 191, 194, 198-202, 211, **83,** 49
  agreement, by **92,** 17-18
  equitable result **83,** 14, 16
  relevant/special circumstances **83,** 14, 16
  single boundary **71,** 143
    EEZ/continental shelf **92,** 66-7, 79, **99,** 463, 468, 477, 478, 484-5
developing States and **81,** 273
development of law relating to **74,** 145-8, **120,** 269
exclusive fishing zone (EFZ), equivalence **82,** 642, **99,** 462-3
extent
  200 miles **92,** 583-4
  territorial sea, effect on **92,** 583-4
fisheries agreements, obligation to conclude **92,** 18
fishing zones. *See* exclusive fishing zone (EFZ); fishing zones, EEZ and
foreign fishermen, access to, Law of the Sea Convention (1982) and **82,** 629-30, 658
foreign vessels
  hired by nationals **118,** 448-51
  permits, need for **118,** 449-50
innocent passage **120,** 295-6
islands
  entitlement **95,** 671, 684, **125,** 254
    contiguous zone, coterminous with **95,** 671, 684, 722-3
jurisdiction, over national, applicable law **101,** 447-8
Law of the Sea Convention (1982) **62,** 114, **71,** 121, 202, **81,** 264
  continental shelf and, confusion of concepts **99,** 474-6
  customs laws, application **120,** 190-2, 245-6, 259-61, 265-9, 325
  enforcement measures, right to take **125,** 211-15
  fisheries agreements, obligation to conclude **92,** 18
  imprisonment for breaches, prohibition **91,** 379-81
  status under **120,** 287-91
Mediterranean **81,** 254
purpose, natural resources, preservation **91,** 381
refuelling of fishing vessel
  activity ancillary to that of refuelled vessel **110,** 752, **120,** 263-4
    Convention for the Prohibition of Fishing with Long Driftnets in the South Pacific (1989) **110,** 752
  commercial activity, whether **120,** 192, 237-9
  customary international law **120,** 263-5
  customs legislation and **110,** 754-6, **120,** 189-92, 256-7, 268-9, 322-7
  freedom of navigation and **120,** 192, 237-9, 262-3, 279-81
  independent activity **110,** 752
  Law of the Sea Convention (1982) **110,** 752, **120,** 237-9, 256-7, 261-9
  non-fishing vessels distinguished **120,** 262
  public interest and **120,** 264-5, 300-1, 326
  State practice **110,** 752

exclusive economic zone (EEZ) (*cont.*)
remedies for breach, confiscation of vessels **118,** 450-1
rights
continental shelf **81,** 330
refuelling of fishing vessel, control of **110,** 751-6, 761, 771-3. *See also* refuelling of fishing vessel *above*
seabed **81,** 330
sovereign **82,** 627, 642
subsoil **81,** 330
water column **81,** 330
State practice and **81,** 265, 358, **120,** 292-5
status
area subject to 'specific legal regime' **120,** 287-8
Law of the Sea Convention (1982) provisions **120,** 287-91
sovereign area, whether **77,** 689, **120,** 287-8
territory, whether **83,** 66
superjacent waters, limited to **83,** 49 n. 18
treaties concluded before development of concept **83,** 85
Walvis Bay **91,** 375-8
exclusive fishing zone (EFZ) 55, 168-75, **82,** 602-70. *See also* exclusive economic zone (EEZ); fishing zones
Canadian
delegation of power to regulate **82,** 607
French metropolitan vessels, exclusion **82,** 607
French neighbouring islands, rights of **82,** 607
coastal State, inherent right to manage biological resources **82,** 612, 618, 627
delimitation **41,** 223
equal right of exploitation **82,** 617
establishment, purpose **82,** 628
jurisdiction **63,** 353, 601-3
exclusive **82,** 618, 627, 643
functional **82,** 626
regulatory right **82,** 656
licences **82,** 607, 652-7
Mediterranean **81,** 254, 302
preservation of stock **82,** 606
quotas **82,** 606
quasi-agreement **82,** 668-9
unilateral right **82,** 668-9
regulations, implied acceptance **82,** 619
sovereignty over **82,** 618, **120,** 623
limitations on **82,** 626
UK **120,** 618 n. 5, 623
UNCLOS I **82,** 605
UNCLOS II **82,** 605
executive abuse 118, 313-14
executive certificate/statement 64, 36-7, 541, **72,** 45, 54-5, 63-6, 237, 288, 659-60, 664, **75,** 679-83, 689-91, 694-8, **85,** 53, 57-8. *See also* executive authorization; executive discretion; executive power; United States of America (USA), State Department suggestions
binding on court, whether. *See* conclusiveness *below*
conclusiveness **38,** 149, 160-1, **55,** 48-9, 93-4, **67,** 612, 620, **69,** 213, 286-9, 294, **71,** 548-9, **72,** 45, 659-60, **73,** 14, 322, 358-9, 682, 700, **74,** 47-8, 75, 99, **75,** 21, 411, 680, 682, 695, **80,** 9, **82,** 421, 422, **87,** 182-3

consular privileges and immunities, entitlement **89,** 72
diplomatic agent, status **99,** 116
diplomatic protection, measures necessary to protect **121,** 511-12
foreign relations **44,** 44, 250-1
indemnity from suit **90,** 541-4
interpretation by courts **75,** 679-80, 682, 694-8
neutrality **87,** 183
private nature of transaction **63,** 11-12
recognition, government **80,** 4-6, 8, 9, **87,** 183, 241
recognition, State **41,** 15-20, **52,** 56, **63,** 30, **64,** 514-19, 522, 695-7, **86,** 643, **87,** 183, **122,** 535-6
in respect of purpose for which issued **108,** 528
responsibility for foreign relations **114,** 399-401
special rapporteur, privileges and immunities
Foreign Minister **121,** 377-80, 388-97
UN Secretary-General **121,** 375-7, 388-97, 412-13, 419-26, 431-3, 444-5
State immunity, jurisdiction **42,** 120-1, **64,** 594-5, **90,** 541-4, **98,** 10, **104,** 143 n. 7, **118,** 297. *See also* United States of America (USA), State Department suggestions (State immunity)
state of war **87,** 183
status as international organization **86,** 664, 666-7, 684, 685-6
territory, status of **49,** 484-5, 487-91, 496-7, **87,** 183
as to facts **108,** 528, **114,** 399-401
treaties
entry into force **44,** 216-17, 260, **55,** 48-9, **69,** 286-9, 293-4
validity **122,** 608, 614-15, 618-19
treaty interpretation **78,** 132, 135, **86,** 24-6, 28-9, 30, **96,** 103, **101,** 618, 621
deferential respect **82,** 312-13
effect **73,** 13-14, 20, 682, 704, **75,** 679-83, 690-1, 694-8
as evidence of
custom **70,** 391
diplomatic status **78,** 484
external act **55,** 48-9
Head of State, immunity, jurisdiction **65,** 14, **111,** 607, **118,** 297
issued by
ambassador/head of mission
effect **63,** 130-5, 321, **64,** 594-5, **82,** 8, **94,** 360, 361, **120,** 6
nationality **120,** 6
use of mission funds **63,** 130-5, 321, **74,** 173, 176, 179, 187-8, **82,** 8, **94,** 360, 361, **120,** 6
minister **65,** 9, 14, **121,** 378, 379, 413
judicial review **87,** 183
in respect of
bank account, use **82,** 2
civil war **74,** 22
consular agent, status **107,** 102, **108,** 526
diplomatic agent, status **101,** 378, **111,** 616
diplomatic mission
status **104,** 681
use of funds **74,** 173, 176, 179, 187-8
diplomatic privileges and immunities, taxation, exemption **108,** 524-5
diplomatic status **118,** 300
diplomatic mission, letter **63,** 321

executive certificate/statement (*cont.*)
immunity, jurisdiction and attachment distinguished **63,** 60
international organization, Director-General **78,** 116
neutrality **87,** 183
recognition, government **94,** 619-20, **125,** 632, 656, 657
registration of ship **125,** 301-2, 311-12
Southern Rhodesia, position of **39,** 66, 98-105, 160-1, 208-11, 282, 369
State succession **107,** 662
status of cultural institute **82,** 4
status of Mandate **82,** 481
treaty
adhesion to **78,** 119
UN Resolution, interpretation **78,** 136
war crimes, ministerial undertaking not to prosecute **75,** 340, 355-6, 362
situations calling for **41,** 466
matter involving international relations **74,** 22, 106-7
executive discretion 85, 39-52, **86,** 221-2. *See also* executive certificate/statement; executive power; judicial review, grounds, abuse of discretion
effect of
delay **87,** 331
improper purpose **86,** 228
perverse exercise **85,** 35
extradition, human rights, respect for in requesting State **100,** 428
foreign relations **95,** 614
limitations **87,** 331, 354-6
Anglo-Irish Agreement (1985) **87,** 331, 333, 354
Single European Act **87,** 354
treaty **85,** 39-52, 205-16
requirements
fairness **84,** 718
proportionality **85,** 33-4, 47, 51-2
purpose of legislation, respect for **85,** 212, **120,** 506, 512-13
rationality **87,** 331
reasonableness **85,** 32-3, 35, 41-4, 49-51, **87,** 331, **120,** 506, 512-13, 535
executive necessity 74, 223-7
executive power 87, 168, 176, 183, 188-9, 191
conclusion of treaty incompatible with **87,** 331
divestment of **87,** 331
establishment **83,** 228-30
executive statement. *See* executive certificate/statement
exequatur
arbitral award, enforcement. *See* arbitral award, enforcement, exequatur proceedings
consular, refusal to grant **40,** 224-7
treaty provisions **40,** 226
exhaustion of administrative remedies 88, 714. *See also* exhaustion of local remedies
exhaustion of established processes. *See* International Court of Justice (ICJ), admissibility
exhaustion of local remedies 45, 271, 275, 277, **46,** 200-3, **56,** 341, 369-71, **60,** 162-3, 192-3, 302, **78,** 240, 321-2, **84,** 349-50, **86,** 337-8, **88,** 554, **96,** 579-80, **103,** 637-8. *See also under individual tribunals*
alternative courses of action, relevance **111,** 223-5
appeal procedures **56,** 406-7, **69,** 173, 176, **71,** 361-3, **95,** 273
annulment and review of sentences **70,** 283-5, 292-4
appeal to higher administrative authority **46,** 201, 233-4

failure to appeal **75,** 375-6
inadequacy **118,** 266
procedural defects **46,** 202
time-limits **46,** 202, 235-6, 281-4
appeal against jurisdiction **46,** 201
unreasonably prolonged proceedings **70,** 292-4
applicable law **95,** 255-6, 272
arbitral tribunal, treatment of issue **102,** 231, 269-88
arbitration, acceptance of **102,** 282-6
arbitration and **54,** 315-17, **82,** 243, 247-8, 260-1, **96,** 278-9, **122,** 289, **124,** 14-17. *See also* compromissory clause, relevance *below*
diplomatic protection cases, limitation to **96,** 278-9
belief as to impartiality of courts, relevance **46,** 333
burden of proof **60,** 163, **61,** 383-4, **84,** 352, 353, **95,** 257, 271-2, **102,** 287, **120,** 50, 95, **123,** 135
compliance
competence to determine **56,** 368-9, 392, 395-6, 399-400
critical date **56,** 475-6, 486-7
compromissory clause, relevance **84,** 348. *See also* arbitration and *above*
conditional relief **70,** 283-5
customary international law **46,** 315-16, 475, **84,** 348, **96,** 278, **102,** 277, 281
diplomatic protection and **120,** 233, 318
denial of justice and **46,** 57, 316-21, **124,** 16-17, **125,** 140
diplomatic protection and. *See* diplomatic protection, exhaustion of local remedies and
direct injury to State **102,** 278-9
breach of treaty affecting individual **102,** 278-9
effective remedy, need for **71,** 361-4, 381, **74,** 368-9, **75,** 5, 7, **78,** 241-2, **92,** 477
administrative practice giving rise to alleged breach **58,** 263, **71,** 302, **120,** 61, 62, 63-5, 101-4, 122-3
doubts about availability **121,** 205
failure to test **120,** 102-3, 104, 125
internal channels, whether **72,** 375-6
judicial authority **72,** 374
nullity of proceedings and **46,** 280-1, 284, 321, 529
retroactive law making recourse to national courts futile **114,** 318
unreasonably prolonged proceedings **69,** 191, **71,** 361-4, **94,** 407, 408, 425, **96,** 630, 679, 702
US Department of Defense claims programme **123,** 136-8
estoppel
acceptance of arbitration **102,** 282-6
failure to raise issue **45,** 271, 275, 277, **56,** 341, 369-71, **60,** 162-3, 192-3, **61,** 302, 306, 371, **78,** 240, **84,** 349-50, **86,** 337-8, **88,** 554, **96,** 579-80, **103,** 637-8
exoneration from in case of
absence of jurisdictional link between victim and State causing damage **120,** 181-2, 183-4, 236, 330
inter-State disputes **54,** 323-5, **84,** 348-9, **120,** 182-3, 233-6, 250-1, 318
breach of Law of the Sea Convention (1982), whether **120,** 233-6
Italian–US Conciliation Commission claims **40,** 151, 153
just satisfaction proceedings **56,** 419-20, **86,** 348
legal advice against proceeding further **61,** 376-7, 385-6
expropriation and **41,** 386, 439, **84,** 527
extraterritorial jurisdiction, anti-terrorist legislation **104,** 147 n. 14, 178
failure to exhaust remedies in another State **121,** 208

exhaustion of local remedies (*cont.*)
failure to raise issue **45,** 271, 275, 277, **56,** 341, 369-71, **60,** 162-3, 192-3, 302, **61,** 302, 306, 371, **78,** 240, **88,** 554, **96,** 579-80, **103,** 637-8
federal State, in **95,** 501-2
flexibility **46,** 321-2, 323, **61,** 304, 323-4, 333, 375
general principle of international law **45,** 301-2, **46,** 125, 475, **56,** 368, **62,** 56, 76, 81, **95,** 255-6
international organizations
exhaustion of internal remedies **84,** 433-4
internal proceedings **113,** 488
investment guarantee programme and **44,** 91-2, 99-100
judicial system inoperable **107,** 459-60
jus cogens/peremptory norm, whether **56,** 486
liberty of person, deprivation and **108,** 434
NAFTA **122,** 289
before national authority **72,** 374-6
right to challenge legislation **75,** 432-3, 436-7, 508-9, 513, 516-17, 556-7
nationalization and **41,** 386, 394
non-recognition of controlling authority and **120,** 40-6, 76, 111, 117-24, 136-7, 140
political solution as perceived prerequisite, relevance, **120,** 61-2, 66
preliminary/procedural question, whether **45,** 274-5, 277, 309, **46,** 57, 125-6, 177, 316-17, **102,** 277
admissibility, question of **102,** 278
merits, joinder **43,** 176, **71,** 324
previous 'act of government' finding by national courts **115,** 260
proceedings relating to same subject-matter, need to await outcome **111,** 224
purpose **46,** 317, 323, **56,** 475-6
opportunity for State party to rectify situation **56,** 392, 487, **61,** 374-5, **96,** 705, **111,** 225, **121,** 207-8
protection of national legal order **60,** 163
raising issue 'in substance', sufficiency **61,** 303-4
resort to appropriate courts, need for **61,** 305-6
State immunity, jurisdiction and **65,** 389, **82,** 35
public law appeal and **82,** 35
State responsibility and **46,** 100-1, 200, 201, **54,** 324, **88,** 694, **89,** 533-5
ILC [Draft] Articles on State responsibility (1977/1980/1996/1998/2001) **54,** 324, **120,** 183, 329
State's duty to indicate remedies **60,** 162-3, **70,** 251, **71,** 358, **78,** 240-2
substantial identity of cause **84,** 352, 400
treaty obligation to arbitrate and **82,** 243, 247-8, 260-1, **102,** 282
expatriation 70, 343-4, **72,** 437-77. *See also* nationality, loss or deprivation of
Habsburgs **77,** 476
International Convention, effect of **70,** 343-4
international officials, additional expenses of **43,** 289
nationality **45,** 340-53, **60,** 239-40
voluntary act of **82,** 318
expert 85, 5, 484-556
Anglo-Italian Conciliation Commission **40,** 269, 283-8
appointment **83,** 14, 607-8, **85,** 393-4, 473
need for **116,** 404
Argentina–Chile Arbitral Tribunal (1966) **38,** 17, 27-8, 55-8, 96
Argentina–Chile Arbitral Tribunal (1994) **113,** 204-5, 216-19, 226-7, 323

costs **85,** 394, **107,** 46
disclosure of confidential evidence to **121,** 227-8
Eritrea/Yemen Arbitration Tribunal (1999) **119,** 401, 425
evidence **37,** 557, **62,** 112, 115-24, **68,** 546, **73,** 238, 248-9, **76,** 374, **78,** 408, 518-19, 595, 597, **80,** 398, 419, **105,** 15, **108,** 617. *See also* arbitral tribunal, expert; United Nations Compensation Commission, evidence, expert
best evidence rule **108,** 177
court expert and expert witness distinguished **81,** 188-98
disclosure of **121,** 228
field mission **38,** 17, 27-8, 55-8, 96
foreign law **83,** 254, **103,** 285-7
legislation, interpretation, translation **106,** 551
voir dire **117,** 155
ICJ
implementation of judgments and **81,** 455, 460, 485
use of **81,** 461-2
Iran–US Claims Tribunal **85,** 393-4, 411-14
Italian–US Conciliation Commission **40,** 427-8
limitations **85,** 589-90
role **85,** 624
weight of evidence **85,** 564-8
export association, agency or instrumentality of a foreign State **63,** 90 n. 24, 104, 175
export controls, proportionality **117,** 319-21, 527-8
export credit guarantees 44, 79-100, **46,** 443-4, **48,** 179
payment from foreign State under treaty
evidence of agreed date of payment to policyholders, need for **108,** 600, 610-11
interest on from agreed date of payment to policyholders, policyholders' right to interest **108,** 600
'recovery', whether **108,** 600, 618-20
recovery by insurers of sum in excess of entitled retention
balance to be held as trust, whether **108,** 600, 614-20
payment into consolidated fund, relevance **108,** 616, 617
debtor/creditor relationship, whether **108,** 617
export, right to 117, 524-5
expression, freedom of. *See* freedom of expression
expropriation/nationalization 53, 468-71, 475-83, **60,** 116, 117-19, 122-3, 124, 127, **61,** 45, **70,** 485-6, **71,** 13-36, **72,** 27, 482, 494, 554-6, 559-61, **73,** 235-47, 582-94, **75,** 272-330, 385-95, 408-28, 445-561, 588-95, 596-674, 705-22, **80,** 425-8, 429, 431-2, 433-9, **83,** 469-81, 532-53, **84,** 504-18, **85,** 437-50, **89,** 452-9. *See also* compensation for war-related events; confiscation; expropriation/nationalization, compensation; measure of damages/compensation including valuation of company/property/assets; property, rights; requisition; taking of property
as act of foreign policy **63,** 169
as act of State **62,** 199-200, 217, 220-4, **63,** 98-9, 152-5, 208-9, 317, 455, 456, **65,** 75, 290, **66,** 148-51, 240-1, 263-9, 292-315, 410, **69,** 9, **70,** 433-4, **77,** 175, 183, 186, 265, **79,** 573-81, 584-9, **80,** 432, **81,** 519, **82,** 133, 145, 146, **94,** 151, 193, **103,** 462-3, 469, **107,** 211-12. *See also* as sovereign act *below*
debt, right to repayment **87,** 512, **92,** 411
emigrant's property **82,** 49-50
enquiry into motives for **80,** 581 n. 28
foreign national's trademarks **42,** 41-4
taking of property of non-national abroad **41,** 10-12

expropriation/nationalization (*cont.*)
as *acta jure imperii* **94,** 317-18, **101,** 549
alien property **47,** 119-26, **48,** 175-86, **63,** 317, 455-6, **72,** 219-20, 230-3, **73,** 235-47, **74,** 153-6, **75,** 227, 290, 292, 296, 319, 371, 597-674
diplomatic protection **53,** 336-7
discriminatory taking **42,** 49-50
amicable settlement **56,** 184-5, 186, **57,** 561-2, **62,** 205
applicable law **71,** 29-30, **72,** 561, **73,** 243-4
customary international law **83,** 533
general principles of commercial law **86,** 259, 295
general principles of international law **86,** 259, 295
general principles of law **56,** 317, **85,** 391-2
international law **83,** 533, 547-8, **84,** 198, 540, **86,** 256, 295, **95,** 623
lex situs **92,** 474
municipal law of expropriating State **84,** 540, **89,** 453, **95,** 622-3, **121,** 177-8
treaty **85,** 391, **86,** 256
NAFTA (1992) **121,** 127, 178-9
arbitrability **62,** 150, 165, 179-80
arbitration clause, effect on **53,** 408-13, **62,** 177-8, 216
assets. *See also* of corporation assets *below*
contractual claim **79,** 588
title to **95,** 226
bank, foreign accounts, effect on **66,** 193-7, 250-5
as breach of concession agreement **63,** 166-9, 233-5, 475
as breach of contract **66,** 584, 592-3, 624-5, **83,** 551, **118,** 316-17
breach of contract distinguished **66,** 583, 592-3, 624-5, **67,** 337-8, **106,** 525-6, 716-17, **125,** 129-30
rate of interest dependent on **106,** 642, 643, 716-17
by duress **85,** 402
by legislation **40,** 185, **70,** 485-6, 492-3, **78,** 650-1, **83,** 530, 532, 540, 547-8, 552, **86,** 274, 275-6. *See also* requirements, legislation *below*
by occupying/administering power **48,** 175-7, **60,** 114-15, 116, 117, 118-19, 121, 122-3, 124-5, **94,** 47-8, 50, 51-2, 60, 61. *See also* compensation for war-related events, expropriation/nationalization by occupying/administering power
legality **94,** 51-2
State immunity, jurisdiction **48,** 175-7, **65,** 128-30, **94,** 47-8, 50, 51-2, 60, 61, **103,** 300-2, 354-5, 372-5, 387, 402-6, 414
compensation. *See* measure of damages/compensation including valuation of company/property/assets
compulsory purchase compared **75,** 486, 504
concession agreement, effect on **53,** 353, 462-3, **62,** 162-4, 170-81, 187-9
confiscatory **60,** 131, **62,** 196, **66,** 625-6
contract claim, status **79,** 588
contractual obligations and **56,** 272-3
contractual rights **106,** 627-9, **121,** 21
Amoco **106,** 629
Phillips **106,** 629
of corporation **53,** 470-1, **56,** 297-8, 299, 301-5, **71,** 14-36, **72,** 554-6, **73,** 237-47, 582-3, 585, 589-90, 592-3, **75,** 271-330, **78,** 678-82
dissolution as **116,** 579
effect on debt **42,** 155-7, **52,** 9
judgment debt **42,** 161-3
effect on trademarks **47,** 129-34

effective control **78,** 678
existence, effect on **44,** 65-6
split company **45,** 442-3
liability for debts **72,** 86-8
transfer of shares, relevance **84,** 503 n. 17
withdrawal of management of **45,** 442-3
of corporation assets **78,** 678-9, 680-2
assets of mother corporation **78,** 678-9, 680-2
corporation distinguished **84,** 518
debt owed to State and **66,** 409
effect on existence of corporation **44,** 65-6
effect on legal status **44,** 65-6
creditors' interests and, direct effect, need for **92,** 439-40
customary international law **83,** 541-4, 609
damages. *See* measure of damages/compensation including valuation of company/property/assets
date **40,** 94-6, 97-101, **42,** 158-61, 164-8, **83,** 466, 564, 609-11, **84,** 578, **85,** 392, 395, 398-411
critical date **108,** 660
debt
act of State and **87,** 512, **92,** 411
assets relating to **92,** 410-11
effect **41,** 267-71, 273-9, **42,** 155-7, **47,** 60-2, 63, 120-6, **48,** 82-3, **74,** 288-9, **79,** 584-9, **80,** 427
locus **79,** 586, 587-8
loss to creditor **40,** 171
right to collect **92,** 410-11
transfer to nationalized enterprise **48,** 82-3
definition. *See* expropriation/nationalization, classification as/de facto
of diplomatic premises **83,** 241
discriminatory. *See* expropriation/nationalization, legality, requirements, non-discrimination
disguised. *See* expropriation/nationalization, classification as/de facto
distinguished **62,** 185
Eastern Europe **62,** 186
effectiveness **62,** 165, 181, 199
employment contract, locally engaged staff, State agency, State immunity, jurisdiction and **65,** 44-6
enemy property, after cessation of hostilities **56,** 538
evidence of **83,** 465, 466-7, 470-3, 485-9
exhaustion of local remedies **41,** 386, 439, **84,** 527
expropriation and nationalization distinguished **60,** 118-19, 122-3, 126, **62,** 185
of external securities, premium on purchase of, relevance to compensation **92,** 587-618
extraterritorial effect **41,** 276, 373, **51,** 11-22, 98, **52,** 8-10, **53,** 468-9, **55,** 23-4, **65,** 60, **69,** 9, **70,** 470, **71,** 24, **72,** 27, 86-7, 559-61, **74,** 103, **75,** 277, 279, 288-9, 290, 293, 307, 315, 318-19, 325-30, 708-9, 715-16, **77,** 450, 548-9, **78,** 616-17, **79,** 576-8, 580, 586, **80,** 425-30, **82,** 131-48, **84,** 177-8, **94,** 60-1. *See also* recognition/enforcement *and* territorial limitation *below*; extraterritorial legislation; foreign law, recognition/enforcement, confiscatory legislation
absence **73,** 237, 239-41, 243-7
applicable law, *lex situs* **108,** 592
economic independence of foreign State, observance of **82,** 145
enforcement of title **94,** 193 n. 17

expropriation/nationalization (*cont.*)
Iraqi seizure of Kuwait Airways aircraft **116,** 585-6, **125,** 665-8, 708-9, 720-1
legal and illegal expropriation distinguished **82,** 139, 146
public policy and **72,** 561, **74,** 291-2, **79,** 577, 579, 580, **86,** 14
restricted **82,** 132-3
shares, acquisition of under private or public law, determining factor **82,** 146
'split' companies, legal status of **73,** 237, 239-41
in time of war **66,** 254-5
foreign judgment based on, execution **80,** 429
grounds. *See* expropriation/nationalization, legality
illegality. *See* expropriation/nationalization, legality
immunity in respect of. *See* State immunity, jurisdiction, classification of act, expropriation/nationalization
'interests in' **83,** 540-1
internal effect **69,** 9
international consequences **56,** 283
international law **89,** 453
violation **66,** 375-6
international obligations **56,** 279
international relations, effect on **53,** 470, 477-83
as international tort/wrong **62,** 162, 168, 182, 196-7, 203, 217, 224. *See also* expropriation/nationalization, legality
irreversibility **94,** 48, 52
of joint venture **67,** 374
judicial protection, withdrawal of **89,** 454
justification. *See* expropriation/nationalization, legality
of land
expropriation permits, effect **75,** 385-95
house occupation, prohibition **75,** 588-95
tenant's right of enfranchisement **75,** 408-28
of lapsed option **125,** 129-30
liability for, beneficiary companies **80,** 432
measures
Algeria **41,** 369, 371, 373, 384, 385, 390, 393-4, **47,** 119-26, 325-6, **48,** 82-3, **65,** 44-6, 84-5, **72,** 219-20, **80,** 433-9
Chile **59,** 378-83, 403-5, **65,** 58-60
compensation, whether obligation to pay **65,** 58-60
Congo (Brazzaville) **67,** 325-6, 329, 335-9, 366
Cuba **40,** 171, **42,** 41-2, 45, 48-9, 149-52, **43,** 20-1, **63,** 2, 188-9, **66,** 46, **80,** 568-70, 579-80, 582
intervention of property **42,** 41-2
Czechoslovakia **40,** 17-28, 94-7, **42,** 159-61, 162-4, 165-9, 170-2, 180-2, **47,** 31-9, **63,** 70-3
against German property **40,** 115, **44,** 67, **47,** 32, **55,** 23-4
Equatorial Guinea **88,** 695
Gabon **48,** 152-4
Hungary **65,** 17-19, 288-303, **72,** 85-8
Iran **63,** 454-7, **69,** 570, 584, 617, 627-8, **72,** 126-31, 227-33, 498-500, **75,** 596-674, **79,** 585-9
Libya **53,** 313-18, 408-13, 424-6, 437-8, 462-8, **60,** 129, **62,** 146-236, **63,** 166-9, 233-5
Mozambique **64,** 692-3

Poland **65,** 128-30
Tunisia **47,** 63-6
municipal law and **53,** 470, 484-6, 494-5
nationality, relevance **116,** 586-7
of nationals' property **53,** 470-1, **72,** 131, 498-500, **75,** 276-7, 290, 292, 314-15, 322, 408-28, 482-5, 511, 514-17, 521-5, 620, 705-8, **79,** 594, 598
international tort/wrong, whether **81,** 515
taking as **92,** 490
objectives **62,** 185-6
of oil concessions **63,** 166-70, 233-5, 475, **75,** 610, 637-8
ownership, interests sufficient to control **84,** 497, 499
of patent rights, extraterritorial effect **70,** 429-34
permanent sovereignty over natural resources and **83,** 24
of permits, loss caused by **75,** 385-95
of private rights **74,** 291-2, 320-1, **75,** 276-9
compensation, requirement of **73,** 82
procedure **118,** 317
'property' **83,** 539-41
of property rights **85,** 392, 434, 563-4. *See also* classification as/de facto, interference with property rights *above*
as public act **82,** 147
purpose. *See* objectives *above*
recognition/enforcement **63,** 98-9, **69,** 7-10, **75,** 272-330, **77,** 585-6, **78,** 679, **79,** 576-8, 579, **125,** 651-2. *See also* expropriation/nationalization, extraterritorial effect; foreign law, recognition/enforcement, confiscatory legislation
as act of State **77,** 450, 548-9, **78,** 679, 680-2
recognition and enforcement distinguished **82,** 132
remedies **84,** 543-6
compensation. *See* expropriation/nationalization, compensation
illusory **79,** 580, 581
restitution **84,** 544-5
acquisition by natural persons in good faith **94,** 50
'comparable' commercial undertaking **94,** 50
preferred remedy **94,** 50
restrictions on **94,** 50
remuneration, effect on **39,** 427-8
retaliatory **62,** 161, 165, 194
retroactive recognition of government, effect **84,** 177-8
right of **53,** 469-70, 477-83, 486, **75,** 480, 520-1, 705-7
rights and obligations
assumption **65,** 289-90, 295-303, **92,** 436
express assumption, need for **107,** 207, 210-11
situs, relevance **107,** 207, 211
extinction of **40,** 185, **65,** 301
sale of expropriated property **94,** 50
sequestration and **60,** 114-19, 122-3, 126
of shareholder rights **90,** 600
of shares **40,** 16-17, **67,** 329, 335-9, 374, **75,** 272-4, 282, 292-3, 296, 299-301, 307
as sovereign act **53,** 353, 418, 470, 484-6, 488, 494-5, **62,** 165, 185-8, 192, 196-200, 204, 206, 217, **63,** 169, 189, **80,** 432. *See also* act of State *above*
dominium eminens **41,** 10-12

expropriation/nationalization (*cont.*)
limitation of **62,** 192-6, 204
respect for contract, limitation on **62,** 192
stabilization clause. *See* stabilization clause
State contract **53,** 470, 477
administrative contract, effect on **53,** 477-9
as breach **53,** 325, 329, **62,** 147, 181-2, 187, 196-7, 203-7, 217, **66,** 583, 590-1, 626-7, **67,** 337-8
revocation, whether **89,** 468
State immunity, jurisdiction. *See* State immunity, jurisdiction, classification of act, expropriation/nationalization
State responsibility **83,** 565, 566, **95,** 620-3
at prompting of forum State **95,** 616-23
direct and substantial involvement, need for
benefit to State, need for **95,** 621-2
diplomatic persuasion as part of general policy **95,** 622
nature of involvement **95,** 621-2
stockholder claims **42,** 158-61
Suez Canal **62,** 206
territorial limitation **44,** 69, **45,** 436, 439, **94,** 60-1. *See also* extraterritorial effect *above*
applicable law, expropriating State **108,** 660
compensation, relevance **108,** 660
grounds for objection
intra vires **108,** 659-60
nexus with objecting State, need for **108,** 660
test **84,** 513
third party liabilities, State's right to compensation **66,** 595
Third World **62,** 186
as tort **82,** 155. *See also* as international tort/wrong *above*
of trademarks **61,** 45, 59, 83-5, **66,** 78-84, 93-101, 142-5
confiscation of foreign **42,** 41-4
ownership following **71,** 17, 23-5, 28-30, **73,** 583-5, **78,** 677-82
wartime **73,** 582, 588
UNGA Resolutions. *See* United Nations General Assembly Resolutions, 1803 (XVII) (Permanent Sovereignty over Natural Resources)
Vienna Convention on the Law of Treaties (1969) **83,** 25
wrecks and **87,** 523
wrongful and unlawful distinguished **62,** 204
expropriation/nationalization, classification as/de facto 56, 261-2, 313, 315, 317, 326, **59,** 375-6, **60,** 116-18, 122, 124, 127, **62,** 184-5, **82,** 143, **83,** 472, 539-40, 541-2, **89,** 453, **95,** 209-10. *See also* expropriation/nationalization, 'by' entries
acquisition of land for use by international organization **82,** 90
administration of foreign *bona vacantia* **41,** 266-7, 269, 270-1, 273-9
appropriation distinguished **66,** 148-9, **84,** 552, 556
bankruptcy proceedings **46,** 280, 448
breach of contract **53,** 325-6, 329, 355, **62,** 168, 181-2, 197, 199, 203, 217, **83,** 551, **118,** 316-17
building permit, failure to issue **95,** 210, **119,** 638-40, 655-6, 666-8
caveat lodged as part of divorce proceedings preventing repatriation of funds **103,** 452-3
compensation, relevance **106,** 629

'compulsorily acquired' **91,** 325
creeping **44,** 87, **66,** 584-5, **83,** 473, 545-7, **84,** 513, 540, **122,** 355-7
staged process **108,** 460, 478
currency depreciation, levies on gains from **44,** 149-56
currency regulations as **42,** 153-5, **66,** 12-21, 31-2, 33-4, 41-7, 72
denial of access to funds **85,** 408
deprivation and acquisition distinguished **92,** 607-8, 613, 614, 617
'deprived of' **91,** 325
development of concept **40,** 185
excessive taxation **56,** 322-3
export ban **121,** 181, 195
expropriation permits **68,** 92-4, 104-11, 116-18, 120-7
'expropriatory action' **56,** 261-2
expulsion **95,** 209-10
direct relationship between, need for **95,** 209-10
expulsion of alien **82,** 189-90, 211
forfeiture for crime distinguished **84,** 513
interference with operation of bank account **70,** 120-7
interference with property **68,** 104-11, 115-18, 125-7, **83,** 470, **85,** 390-3, 398-400, 403-5, 414-15, 454-9, 462-72
acts amounting to **116,** 558-9
acquisition **68,** 326, 349-51
combined effect of measures **68,** 116
damages for. *See* damages, for, interference with property
English law of conversion **116,** 541-6
forfeiture **78,** 597-632
Harvard Draft Convention on the International Responsibility of States for Injuries to Aliens **122,** 336
Iraqi law **116,** 547-56. *See also* Iraq, law of, RRC Resolution 369
legality **68,** 106, 108-10, 116-18, 125-7
'intervention of property' **42,** 41-2
judicial decision **75,** 375, 378-80, **89,** 454
loss of control **108,** 474
'measure tantamount to nationalization or expropriation' **110,** 595, **121,** 53-4, 55-7, 63-4, 122-3, 178-81
interference with business activity **122,** 335-7
modification of State economic system **75,** 601-2, 609-24
occupation by military authorities **67,** 374
permanent deprivation of ownership **121,** 122-3, 181
regulation distinguished **121,** 122-3, 178-80, **122,** 335
reparations **94,** 51
revolutionary events **85,** 450-5
sales at inadequate prices **85,** 407
sequestration of foreign property **60,** 114-15, 118, 121, 124-5
'taking' **82,** 143, **121,** 122
termination of contract **121,** 22-8
town-planning measures **68,** 106-7, 125-7
transfer of ownership to third party **89,** 454
wartime measures **41,** 12, **66,** 254-5
restrictions on **92,** 478
trademarks **73,** 582, 588
withdrawal of essential government support **106,** 629-30

expropriation/nationalization, compensation 53, 486, 488, 493, **56,** 300-8, **57,** 30, **62,** 221, 223, **63,** 455-6, **67,** 339-41, 375-6, **73,** 378-80, **80,** 426-7, 431, 433-9, **82,** 132, 135, 137, **83,** 542, **84,** 527, 529, 540 n. 35, 638, 656, **86,** 47, **91,** 261-2, **94,** 52, 60. *See also* claims settlement agreements; interest; measure of damages/compensation including valuation of company/property/assets
act of State doctrine and **92,** 435-6
annulment of arbitral award, effect **89,** 547, 548-9
award on agreed terms **83,** 490-500
Bill of Rights and **92,** 599, 617-18
BITs provisions **121,** 143
burden of proof **121,** 195
classical concept **62,** 165-6, 184, 196, 206, 218
customary international law **83,** 542-3, **86,** 300, **95,** 210
damages, entitlement **83,** 566, **84,** 516
damages, entitlement, punitive **83,** 567, **84,** 544-5, **89,** 343, **121,** 127 n. 53, 189, 192, 193
date due **84,** 656
discrimination, compensation by successor government for property confiscated under communist regime **115,** 265-76
distinguished from
breach of contract or tort **89,** 503
damages for breach of State responsibility **106,** 469, 480, 498-500
just satisfaction proceedings **89,** 617-18
double recovery **83,** 568, 622, **121,** 192, 195
in economically usable form **84,** 543
entitlement
cut-off date **89,** 624-5, 631-2
municipal court decision, effect **89,** 624-5
equitable **80,** 426, 431, **83,** 570-1, **92,** 602
failure to pay award of **82,** 46
GDR expropriations **94,** 48, 50, 80
general principle of international law **83,** 473, **86,** 457, **106,** 627
interest. *See* interest
liability
personal beneficiaries **91,** 262
State responsibility **91,** 262
lump sum agreements **83,** 625 n. 31, **84,** 525, 536-7, 654, 667 n. 1
method **83,** 571, **85,** 412-13, 485-7, 490-3, 509-70
at discretion of Tribunal **121,** 192-3
minority shares in new project **106,** 628
mitigation, international law **89,** 628
municipal law **95,** 210, **106,** 627, 727-30
need for **48,** 152-4, **53,** 317, **62,** 163-6, 183, 186-9, 194-8, 201, 204-7, 211, 217, **63,** 70-2, 152, 455-6, 561, **65,** 18, 60, 74-5, 79, 81, 85, 302-3, 448-9, **66,** 374-6, **72,** 85-8, **73,** 235, 237, 243-7, 583, 589-90, **74,** 103, 592-3, **75,** 711, 714, **77,** 450, **78,** 92-3, 187, 436, 680-2, **80,** 426, **106,** 625, 626-7, 628, **112,** 423, 554, 561, 634, 642, 715-16, **118,** 319, **121,** 126-7, 191
adequacy **47,** 34-5, **106,** 627-8, 630
breach of State contract for public purpose **83,** 562
extinction of native title **112,** 693-4
illusory **40,** 98, 101, **42,** 48-50
'on payment' **125,** 132
territorial principle **108,** 660, **121,** 193

non-expropriating State, by **80,** 434-5, 436, 438-9
non-payment **73,** 235-7
offer **90,** 600-1
offset, assets expropriated **95,** 226
payment
actual **83,** 612-13, **92,** 397
currency **89,** 509, 549-50
foreign currency, in **95,** 211, 229
convertible currency **95,** 229
date of conversion **95,** 229-30
exchange rate **89,** 646-7
US dollars **95,** 229
obligation **84,** 656
place **89,** 550-1
provision for **84,** 527 n. 14
repatriability **95,** 211, 229
possibility of **94,** 50, 58
possibility of restitution, relevance **94,** 66
power of courts to award **106,** 729-30
discretion as to amount **106,** 730
procedural defects as basis for **89,** 570-1
arbitral tribunal **89,** 618-22
denial of justice **89,** 619-22
international law **89,** 616-22
Draft Convention on the International Responsibility of States for Injuries to Aliens **89,** 616
European Convention on Human Rights (1950) **89,** 617-18
European Court of Justice (ECJ) **89,** 618
Restatement of Foreign Relations Law (Third) **89,** 616
as substantive wrong **89,** 618
municipal law **89,** 613-16
procedure for determining **62,** 208-15, **83,** 611
adequacy **83,** 549-50
arbitration **83,** 550
contractual provision **83,** 550
customary international law **83,** 550
nature of **83,** 550
responsibility for
courts **95,** 619
treaty provision **84,** 557 n. 14
State practice **83,** 550
promise **80,** 426
public and private interests, balance **92,** 597, 602
relevant factors
dispute settlement mechanism **83,** 613
facts subsequent to taking **83,** 625
financial capabilities of State **94,** 65-6
restitutio in integrum
as **83,** 475, 570, 577, 619, **89,** 632-3
distinguished **53,** 353
specific performance, alternative to **89,** 342
standard. *See* measure of damages/compensation including valuation of company/property/assets

expropriation/nationalization, compensation (*cont.*)
State responsibility rules, applicability **83,** 565-6
State succession, effect on right **74,** 98-100, **103,** 118-20
transfer of residual rights to joint venture company and **106,** 630
treaty provision **83,** 539-41, **86,** 49-52, 300
undertaking to pay, dishonoured **79,** 593, 595, 598
UNGA Resolution 1803 (XVII) (Permanent Sovereignty over Natural Resources) **83,** 474, 542, 613 n. 12
UNGA Resolution 3281 (XXIX) (Charter of Economic Rights and Duties of States) **83,** 474, 542, 613 n. 12
as unjust enrichment **92,** 436
unlawful taking. *See* expropriation/nationalization, legality; measure of damages/compensation including valuation of company/property/assets, in case of lawful expropriation/nationalization
US Foreign Claims Settlement Commission. *See* United States of America (USA), Foreign Claims Settlement Commission
valuation. *See* measure of damages/compensation including valuation of company/property/assets
expropriation/nationalization, legality 62, 179, 182, **83,** 611, **84,** 527, 528, 539-40
of acts of occupying power **94,** 51-2
of breach of basic rights **94,** 52, 56-7
of breach of contract and **83,** 561-3, 617
Certain German Interests in Upper Silesia **83,** 541
of confiscatory measure **82,** 139
determination of **77,** 548-9
court's competence to enquire into **65,** 302, **77,** 586, **79,** 576-8, 588
executive and legislative powers distinguished **118,** 314-15
of forestry conservation measures **48,** 179-86
freedom of movement and **118,** 321
human rights violations and **75,** 275, 279, 295-6, 305, 315, 319, 322, 385-95, 481-561, 588-95
relevance **84,** 527, 529, 540 n. 35, 656
relevant factors
compliance with UNESCO Convention for the Protection of the World Cultural and Natural Heritage (1975) **106,** 624-7, 657-9
inclusion of site on World Heritage Committee List **106,** 624-6
date **83,** 609
motivation **62,** 161, 165, 168, 194-5, **95,** 209
necessity **108,** 468, 481
requirements **53,** 317, **62,** 165-6, 183, 186-9, 194-8, 201, 204-7, 217. *See also* expropriation/nationalization, as international tort/wrong; expropriation/nationalization, compensation
compatibility with law **83,** 544-5, 547, 548, **112,** 423, **118,** 315
compensation. *See* expropriation/nationalization, compensation, need for
constitutionality **75,** 273, 286, 315
due process **121,** 126-7, 192
effective remedy **75,** 508-9, 512-13, 705-7, 715-16
formal act **84,** 511-13
good faith **89,** 622
legislation/government action **85,** 390, 425-6, 466, 608, **89,** 337-8, 468, 479, 599, **101,** 550, **121,** 54
non-arbitrariness **94,** 56

non-discrimination **62,** 151, 166, 184, 194-7, 207, 217, **66,** 584-5, **75,** 276-7, 279, 304-6, 319, 322, 429-31, 707-9, 716, 719, **77,** 450, **82,** 132, 137, 138, **83,** 530-1, 550-1, **84,** 199, 656, **89,** 337-8, **92,** 438, 439-40, **103,** 467-8, **121,** 126-7, 184, 192, **122,** 335
customary international law **83,** 550
evidence of **83,** 551
general principle of international law **62,** 194, **92,** 438
justified differential treatment **75,** 708-9
racial **82,** 139
public interest **75,** 415-19, 422, 424, 481-2, 486, 520-1, 526-31, 542, 612, 642, 705-7, **82,** 50
legitimate social objective **75,** 417-19, 422, **85,** 466-72, **118,** 317, 318-21
public order/public policy/ *ordre public* **75,** 274-6, 278-9, 287, 290, 296, 307, 313-14, 318-21, 325-30, **83,** 541, 542, 552-3, **94,** 60, **108,** 659-60
conformity with that of third State **77,** 548, 586, **79,** 577, 579, 580
public purpose **62,** 166, 183-5, 194, **66,** 584-5, **67,** 336-7, **83,** 541, 542, 552-3, **84,** 198, 656, **89,** 337-8, 468, **103,** 467-8, **106,** 626, **118,** 312-21, **119,** 620, **121,** 126-7, 192
avoidance of contractual obligations **83,** 552
customary international law **83,** 542
financial purpose **83,** 552
good faith **83,** 552
under municipal law **94,** 61, **106,** 627, 629
UNESCO Convention for the Protection of the World Cultural and Natural Heritage (1975) **106,** 624-7, 657-9, 733-4
expulsion of alien 38, 149-59, **41,** 380-3, 396-7, **42,** 205-32, **43,** 213-31, **44,** 179, 185, **45,** 371-6, **47,** 263-5, **53,** 521-3, 533-6, **59,** 460, 469, **61,** 431-3, 435-6, 437-42, **62,** 278-89, **68,** 160-73, **69,** 208-9, 211-15, 296-301, **70,** 358-9, 363-72, **71,** 451-509, **72,** 221-2, 419, 594-6, **73,** 613-56, **74,** 254, 260, 268-9, 425-48, **77,** 385-7, **78,** 187, **79,** 280-2, **82,** 149-78. *See also* deportation; deportation withhold/bar; displacement of people; excludability of alien; exclusion of alien; expulsion of national; extradition
as act of State **44,** 374, **45,** 106, **63,** 475, **64,** 426
as administrative act **63,** 51, **68,** 160-73
alien temporarily abroad **71,** 364
American Convention on Human Rights (1969) **95,** 322, 325, 326-7
appeal
procedure **69,** 211, 296-301, **79,** 280-2
right of **73,** 639, 641, **99,** 21
bona fide act, whether **70,** 371-2
burden of proof **70,** 372
choice of destination **43,** 213-18, **53,** 537-8
classification by race **42,** 205-7
collective **82,** 159, 170, 210, 218-19, **96,** 311-14
African Charter on Human and Peoples' Rights (1981) **96,** 312
customary international law **82,** 164-5, **96,** 312
European Convention on Human Rights (1950) **96,** 312
ILC draft **82,** 159
International Covenant on Civil and Political Rights (ICCPR) (1966) **96,** 311
Pact of San José (1964) **96,** 312
conduct **61,** 432-3, 436
constitutional rights and **71,** 454-5, 458-62, 480-1
constructive **82,** 163-4, 169-73, 214. *See also* methods *below*
corporation, breach of contract or expropriation as alternative **82,** 173

expulsion of alien (*cont.*)
criminal proceeding **77,** 446-7
Crown prerogative and **123,** 581, 590
damages **82,** 177-8, 197-203. *See also* measure of damages/compensation including valuation of company/property/assets, expulsion of alien
de facto **82,** 191
as degrading treatment **71,** 307
dependants **54,** 300-2
detention pending **88,** 250-1, 257-9
diplomatic agent **63,** 499, **99,** 110
distinguished **96,** 313
discretion **36,** 345-50, **71,** 497, 499, 505, **82,** 196
European Convention on Human Rights (1950). *See* European Convention on Human Rights (1950), expulsion of alien
exchange restrictions, legality **82,** 202
expropriation and **82,** 189-90, 211, **95,** 209-10
expulsion of national, distinction, whether **111,** 192-3
extradition and **43,** 213-18, **74,** 426, **77,** 339, 346-50
distinguished **55,** 14-16
family life, respect for **45,** 371-6, **61,** 440, 442, **108,** 312-13, **111,** 547
freedom of expression, compatibility with **71,** 459-61
following conviction **42,** 210-13, 226-9, **70,** 358-9, **71,** 236-8, **72,** 221-2, 419, 594-6, **74,** 254, 260, 268-9
completion of sentence abroad **74,** 260-1, 269, 271-2
completion of sentence, following **71,** 306-7
forced departure **85,** 405, 408-9
grounds **57,** 314, **71,** 454, 463-6, 470, 478, 480-1, 494-5, **94,** 423-4. *See also* requirements *below*
absence **71,** 451-4, 459, 470, 473, 478, 480
details, need for **73,** 643-51, 653, **74,** 428
national interest **69,** 211-15
national security **73,** 637-51, **74,** 438-41
right of appeal, absence **73,** 639-42
nationality **96,** 313-14
Nazi propaganda **51,** 237-8
political neutrality **74,** 429
political offence **61,** 95-101
public health, morals and safety **82,** 215
public interest **61,** 433, 435, 438, 439, 440-1
public order/public policy/*ordre public* **74,** 429-30, 434, 441, **82,** 215, 313, **96,** 310, **99,** 7-11
inherent power of receiving State **102,** 196-7
international officials **102,** 196-7
overriding consideration **99,** 7-8
prison sentence **99,** 25, 34
protection measures **99,** 10-11
risk of assassination if returned to own country, relevance **99,** 7-11
public policy as overriding consideration **99,** 7-8
security **82,** 215, 313, **95,** 325, **96,** 310, 311
termination of economic development agreement **96,** 309-10
UNHRC activity **94,** 426
hearing
absence **71,** 452-3

entitlement **71,** 454-8, 462-4, 467-78, 480-2, 488-90, 494-5, **73,** 621-6. *See also* representation rights *below*
International Covenant on Civil and Political Rights (ICCPR) (1966) **94,** 417-26, **95,** 322, 325, 326
judicial review **106,** 214
judicial role, whether **68,** 162-70
jurisdiction, arbitral tribunal **96,** 311
liberty of person, deprivation and **71,** 459, 465-6, 481-2
margin of appreciation **96,** 311, 313
marriage and **61,** 432
'measure capable of infringing the rights of shareholders or limiting rights of company to achieve objects', whether **96,** 315-16
member of visiting force **41,** 396-7
methods. *See also* constructive *above*
express order **82,** 196
implied order **82,** 196
indirect means attributable to State **82,** 159
legal order **82,** 159
unauthorized act of State **82,** 159
municipality, effect on existence of **44,** 61-3
national State, to **42,** 214-18
natural persons, doctrine limited to **82,** 173-4
procedure **43,** 213-31, **44,** 157-73, **61,** 435, **70,** 366-7, 371, **71,** 451-96, **73,** 620-6, 632-4, 637-56
defect, appeal against **72,** 594-6
natural justice, rules of **71,** 465-78, 487-92
urgency **47,** 264-5, **73,** 654-6, **74,** 425-48
professional life and **61,** 440, 442
public safety **70,** 367, 370-1
as quasi-judicial function **70,** 369-70
refouler **95,** 595, 600
refugees. *See* refugees, expulsion
representation rights **68,** 167-9, 171-3, 363-72, **69,** 21, **70,** 358-9
requirements. *See also* grounds *above*
accordance with law **95,** 325
of expelling State **94,** 425, **96,** 310, 314-15
administrative act **95,** 326
avoidance of unnecessary inconvenience **82,** 675
consular agent to be informed **82,** 675
customary international law **82,** 164-5, 197, 214, 215-16, 219
good faith **96,** 310
natural justice **71,** 454, 465-78, 487-92, **73,** 621-3, 633, 638, 645, 647
national security and **73,** 638-9, 645-51
non-arbitrary **82,** 214, **96,** 310
non-discrimination **82,** 214
non-impediment to enforcement of expulsion order **108,** 303
opportunity to submit reasons against **95,** 325
proportionality **61,** 442
family unity **111,** 547
individual and State interests **73,** 616-17, 630, 644
reasonable time **82,** 196-7, 219 n. 20
reasonableness **96,** 313
reasons **96,** 310, 313

expulsion of alien (*cont.*)
respect for person and property **96,** 310
right of review **94,** 420-4, 426, **96,** 310, 311
within reasonable time **94,** 426
right to residence and **82,** 219
treaty **82,** 164, 165, 197, 214-16, 219
residence permit
refusal **79,** 280
revocation distinguished **72,** 579-80
right of **71,** 455-6, 483-4, 492-4, **74,** 428-30, 432-3
South Tyrol, residents of **71,** 237-8
as sovereign activity **101,** 503, **111,** 188
State immunity, jurisdiction **63,** 51, 218, 474-6, 499, 589, **101,** 503
State practice **82,** 214
State responsibility **82,** 149-224
burden of proof **82,** 176-7, 214, 223, 224
Sudeten Germans from Eastern territories **44,** 53, **51,** 23-4, **78,** 187
sui generis nature of each case **82,** 158, 187-8, 210, 219-20
terrorist activity and **62,** 281-2, 284, **123,** 598-9
as tort **82,** 189, 211-13
UN draft Declaration on human rights of individuals who are not citizens of the country in which they live (1978) **82,** 164-5
unlawful arrest as **95,** 326-7
urgency **70,** 358-9, 363-4
woman married to citizen **41,** 380-3
expulsion of Jews, as murder **36,** 44
expulsion of national 111, 192-3, 194. *See also* nationals, entry/re-entry, right of
American Convention on Human Rights (1969) **104,** 188
European Convention on Human Rights (1950) **104,** 188-9
International Covenant on Civil and Political Rights (ICCPR) (1966) **104,** 188, **115,** 344-5
Magna Carta 1215 **123,** 575-9
obligation to prevent, whether **100,** 407
removal of population from colony **123,** 556-93
requirement to leave permanently **100,** 414
Universal Declaration of Human Rights (1948) **104,** 188
external affairs. *See* foreign relations
extinction of States. *See* states, extinction
extinction of title. *See* native title, extinction
extraditable offence 44, 174-6, 246-8, 257, **49,** 507-9, **51,** 328-31, 339, 348-60, **52,** 376-7, **55,** 531-2, **60,** 296, 298-9, 303-4, 312, 333, **69,** 217-18, 220-2, **72,** 65, 602-4, 610-12, 615-16, 621-3, 631-2, 637-9, **73,** 50-3, 658, **74,** 450-1, 456-7, 459-72, **78,** 502-5, 514-20, **84,** 57-9, **85,** 74, 130-43. *See also* political offence
assassination **86,** 180
capital punishment **74,** 456-7, **78,** 96-7, 100, 389-94
causing an explosion **100,** 424
intentional arson, whether **100,** 420
composite offence **87,** 150, 157
conspiracy **48,** 69-76, **73,** 50-2, **85,** 130-43, **104,** 5-6
import of narcotics, for **69,** 220-2
to hostage-taking **119,** 182-3
to murder **119,** 148, 184-8
to torture **119,** 148, 188-9, 190-2, 250

continuing criminal enterprise **87,** 145-53, 158, **90,** 413-15, **92,** 728, 730-2, **101,** 181-3
definition **87,** 147, 148, **101,** 177-8, 183
evidence of distinguished **87,** 148, 152
desertion **85,** 165
double criminality. *See* double criminality
drugs offence **87,** 145-52, 164, **88,** 241-6, **111,** 551-2
customary international law **99,** 170
drug-trafficking **99,** 170-1
Single Convention on Narcotic Drugs (1961) **99,** 170-1
'enumerative method' **73,** 52-3
equivalent act or omission **87,** 148
'essence of crime' **69,** 221, **78,** 518
'extradition crime' **41,** 400, **85,** 136, **119,** 2, 75-6, 93, 109, 139, 144-8, 181-2, 218-19, 249, 258
critical date **119,** 76, 109, 140, 145, 284-5
disappearances **119,** 285-6, 328
distinction **85,** 141, 143
'extradition offence' **125,** 531-2
extraterritorial offence **119,** 32
crime committed outside requested State **119,** 2, 32, 37-8
crime committed outside requesting State **55,** 97-8
jurisdiction of requesting State based on nationality of offender **119,** 2, 32, 38
jurisdiction of requesting State based on nationality of victim **119,** 38
torture **119,** 190
forgery **85,** 80
fraud involving political corruption **104,** 113-14
fraudulent acquisition of export grants or tax rebates **45,** 376-8
hostage-taking **119,** 76, 93, 147-8, 182-3
minimum period of imprisonment **72,** 622, **73,** 658, **74,** 450, 507
murder **69,** 247-9
by organized armed group **111,** 507
liability to prosecution and **88,** 287
nature **55,** 96-8
non-indictable offence **51,** 288
notional offence in extraditing country as test **101,** 191
offence 'within the jurisdiction of' **79,** 543
political offence. *See* political offence
presumption of **100,** 421, 618-19
procuring an offence **104,** 6
'relevant offence' **85,** 76-8
in requesting State, relevance **100,** 420
retroactivity. *See* double criminality, retroactivity
sexual offence **86,** 43-4
State succession and **85,** 143-5
substantial similarity **90,** 414
torture **119,** 76, 93, 150-1, 190, 249
treaty, defined by **79,** 391, 420, 426, 441, 446, 494, 542-4, **87,** 315, **100,** 419-23, 424, 618, **104,** 6
treaty concluded after agreement not to include **100,** 424
trial for other offences **70,** 3-15, **79,** 392, 451, **125,** 530-6
unlisted in extradition agreement **92,** 730-1, 733, **100,** 424
war crimes **79,** 391, 395

extradition 39, 433-52, **40,** 208-21, **41,** 397-406, **43,** 231-45, **44,** 174-89, **47,** 266-72, **48,** 187-90, **51,** 248-400, **55,** 8, **56,** 513-14, **60,** 283-9, 658-70, **72,** 636, **74,** 449-516, **77,** 331-5, 337-45, 346-50, 352-76, **78,** 95-101, 128-31, 501-5, 506-12, 514-20, **79,** 1-167, 386-547. *See also* deportation; deportation withhold/bar; double criminality; expulsion of alien; extradition agreement; forcible abduction/unlawful arrest; International Covenant on Civil and Political Rights (ICCPR) (1966); political offence; prisoners, transfer of persons sentenced abroad; refugees; *and under individual countries*
act of State. *See* act of State, extradition
admissibility of prosecution **77,** 395-6
agreement. *See* extradition agreement
agreement to. *See also* extradition agreement
acquired right **106,** 261
alteration of charge **69,** 217-18
appeal **60,** 323, **74,** 476-7, **87,** 161, **88,** 287-9. *See also* habeas corpus *and* judicial review *below*
admissibility **88,** 350-2, **104,** 106, 112, **106,** 309, **111,** 506-7
declaratory judgment suit **42,** 244-5
grounds
compatibility with international law **111,** 507-8
manifest error of fact **111,** 513
procedural irregularities **111,** 506-8
habeas corpus. *See* habeas corpus *below*
requesting State and accused, entitlement to different treatment **79,** 485
right of **79,** 462-7, 488-9, 498 n. 3, 539, **88,** 287-9
scope **79,** 420-2, 432, 442-3, 498 n. 3, 502-4, 539
standing **106,** 272
applicable law
armed conflict, laws of **104,** 68-76
assurances that death penalty will not be carried out, acceptability **106,** 302
European Convention on Extradition (1957) **119,** 31
evidence, requesting State **104,** 49
extraditing State **94,** 489, 592
general principles of international law **106,** 263
international public order/public policy/*ordre public* **106,** 263-8, 271-2
fundamental norm **106,** 263-8
municipal law **106,** 264
municipal/international law **125,** 534-6
procedure **45,** 379-80
treaty **106,** 263-4
armed forces in foreign countries **57,** 317-25
arrest
forcible abduction. *See* forcible abduction/unlawful arrest
of fugitive **60,** 336, 341-3, 350-1, 356-7
order, whether **43,** 231-4
provisional arrest **73,** 662-4, 668, 670, **87,** 323, 324-6
procedure **87,** 325-6
unlawful arrest, effect **77,** 333-5
arrest warrant **41,** 403, **44,** 184-5, **60,** 336-7, 341-2, 344-5, 350-1, 354, **86,** 218, **87,** 316-17
authentication **70,** 380-3, **79,** 69-73, 81, 83-4, **85,** 103
backing of **71,** 530-2, **79,** 81, 83
effect **79,** 88
multiple **119,** 39, 76-8
need for **72,** 201-9, **87,** 322-8, **88,** 274-5, **91,** 393

provisional **87,** 322-8, **88,** 364-9, **119,** 33-6, 92
relevance **87,** 317
validity **70,** 380-3, **79,** 69-73
asylum State, offence within **40,** 212-14
aut dedere aut punire/judicare **60,** 296, **87,** 166-7, **94,** 507, 534, **95,** 364, **106,** 237, 263, 267-8
customary international law **94,** 507, 521-2, 534, 551, 565
terrorism conventions **94,** 507-8
balance of interests **98,** 421
basis
comity. *See* comity *below*
reciprocity. *See* requirements, reciprocity *below*
treaty. *See* extradition agreement
between
British colonies **55,** 81-8
British Commonwealth, members of **77,** 344, **78,** 501-5, **80,** 13, 16-18, **88,** 270-6
France/Mauritius **87,** 312-20
Malawi/South Africa **52,** 84-6, **55,** 90, 92-5
Malaysia/Singapore **55,** 546, 549
British possession, to **42,** 51-8
civil claims, in respect of **55,** 505-6
comity **51,** 272, 274, **55,** 23-4, 35, **59,** 74, **74,** 480, **79,** 494, 546, **85,** 115-16, **87,** 164, **98,** 416, 420, **104,** 10, 115, **119,** 305-6
consultation with requesting State **119,** 308-9
committal proceedings compared **87,** 208-9
common law countries, statutory authority requirement **55,** 14-16, 24-7, **114,** 388
composite offence **87,** 150, 157
concurrent requests **100,** 660-2
bilateral agreement, relevance **100,** 660-1
European Convention (1957) **100,** 660-1
re-extradition and **100,** 661-2
relevant circumstances for choice **100,** 661-2
conditions in requesting State **87,** 162, **104,** 94-105
assurances regarding **104,** 102-3, 108
burden of proof **104,** 100-1
death penalty, in case of. *See* extradition in case of death penalty
fair trial. *See* fair trial, need for *below*
relevance **98,** 381, 416, **100,** 622
respect for fundamental rights and freedoms **111,** 508, 514, 521
responsibility for determining, executive **104,** 108
review **96,** 109, **104,** 101-5
court's duty, whether **104,** 97, 107-8
nationality, relevance **104,** 105
Soering **104,** 98-100
consent of accused **81,** 88
continuing criminal enterprise **87,** 145-53, 158
conviction for different offence **51,** 248, 366
courts, role **90,** 415, 685
cross-border offence. *See also* extraditable offence, conspiracy
crime partially committed in requested country **100,** 611-12
Extradition, European Convention on (1957) **100,** 612
effects doctrine **100,** 618
loss as determining factor **100,** 612, 613
customary international law **72,** 636, **74,** 457, 481-2, **78,** 98, 100, **92,** 686

extradition (*cont.*)
aut dedere aut punire/judicare **94,** 507, 534
death penalty and **78,** 98, 100, **124,** 326
motivation of requesting State **104,** 115
narcotics offences, extraditable offence **99,** 170
nationals **94,** 502, 522
political offence **59,** 474-6
as sovereign act **94,** 507
danger
assessment, matter for executive **79,** 438, 493 n. 1
exposure to and **79,** 82-3, 86, 438
definition **55,** 534, **78,** 129, **88,** 289-91, **119,** 30
delay **79,** 62, 69-73, 126-8, 389-90, 529
deportation distinguished **43,** 216-18, **77,** 339-41, 347, 349-50, **83,** 145-6, **86,** 226, 271, **88,** 254, **98,** 377, **104,** 47
detention, pending **45,** 316-28, **55,** 20, 32
discretion **55,** 511-12, 518-20, 575, **77,** 334-5, 343-4, 350, **80,** 16, 18, **88,** 293, **90,** 688 n. 20, **98,** 422, 423, **104,** 10, 47, 84, 544, **114,** 446-7, **119,** 38, 92, 108-9, 110-11, 249. *See also* obligation *below*
abuse of process **119,** 251
in case of death penalty **98,** 453, **124,** 304-5, 309-11
hardship **104,** 542
interests of claimants for compensation **119,** 277-8, 305, 326
interests of requesting State **119,** 277-8
'margin of appreciation' **106,** 265-8
medical condition **119,** 265-6, 318-24
fitness to stand trial **119,** 322-4, 328
possibility of trial in home State **119,** 326
as protection of accused **119,** 326-7
punishment, appropriateness **55,** 513
treaty obligations **104,** 78 n. 21, 96, **119,** 325
discrimination **79,** 127-8
disguised **45,** 97, 105-6, 107, **47,** 267-71, **77,** 338, **84,** 718, 719, **85,** 116, **86,** 216-17, 219-29, 346, **88,** 248-50, **92,** 657
extradition agreement, need for **51,** 319-23, 340-60, **78,** 128, 130, **88,** 251
non-renewal of passport **100,** 407
dispute relating to
arbitration, possibility of **106,** 247
failure to lay down procedure
European Convention (1957) **106,** 248
France–UK Extradition Agreement (1876) **106,** 248
double criminality. *See* double criminality
double jeopardy/*non bis in idem*, multiple extradition requests **104,** 62 n. 2, 82
duty **88,** 244-5
to refuse **100,** 612
to seek **94,** 345-6
equity and **79,** 421
European Convention (1957). *See* Extradition, European Convention on (1957)
European Convention on Human Rights (1950). *See* European Convention on Human Rights (1950), extradition
evidence **39,** 435, **44,** 240, 242, **51,** 339, 360-72, **55,** 510, 519, **60,** 323, 326, 331, 336-7, 340-1, 352-3, 357-8, **78,** 501-5, **87,** 148, 314
accomplice **79,** 442-6
uncorroborated **104,** 85

additional from requesting State **44,** 235-6
admissibility **78,** 505-12, **79,** 390, 434-5, 539-40, **85,** 94-108
generally recognized principle of international law, whether **79,** 83, 87
affidavit **44,** 232-5, **69,** 228-39, 242-7, 263-8
affirmation **78,** 508-12
applicable law, requesting State **104,** 49
assumption of validity **104,** 76-7, **119,** 258-60
authorizing legislation **87,** 315-16
burden of proof, political offence exception **104,** 91
charge, to support **55,** 532, 540
circumstantial **69,** 104-5
coerced **104,** 77-8, 85-6
conspirators **69,** 106-8
credibility, relevance **71,** 513-20, 523-8
disclosure of medical reports
assurance of confidentiality and **119,** 298-9
to human rights organizations **119,** 266-79
to requesting States **119,** 282-3, 284, 287-317
documentary **44,** 199-202
expulsion distinguished **73,** 43
extradition judge
alibis **72,** 610, 623, **74,** 462-71, 495
function **71,** 513, 516, 518-28, 532, **72,** 610-11, 623, 636-7
justifying **55,** 510, 519, 532, 540, **69,** 103-8, **78,** 505-12
law of requested State **104,** 21
on oath **78,** 508-9
oral **44,** 236
prima facie case. *See* requirements, prima facie case *below*
property in possession of accused at time of arrest **53,** 541-2
required **39,** 435, **44,** 240, 242
right of challenge **104,** 85
standard of proof **60,** 283-6, 288, 291-2, 294-5, 304-7, **69,** 101-2, **79,** 83-4, 392, 419, 433, 527, **88,** 348-50, **101,** 184-6, 187-90
treaty **101,** 188
sufficiency **71,** 511-29, **72,** 610
test for **71,** 512-13, 518-19, 522-3, 525-6
sworn or affirmed statements, need for **104,** 48, 49
to support request **87,** 213-14
weight **44,** 245-6
relevance **71,** 514-20, 522-8
'weighing'/'weighing up' distinguished **88,** 348-50
evidence of
conviction **73,** 48-50
crime **55,** 510
extraditable crime **55,** 504
foreign law **74,** 467-71, **90,** 413-15, **119,** 259-60, **122,** 615-18
nature of crime **55,** 510-11
warrant, validity **70,** 380-3, **79,** 69-73, 81, 83-4
exchange control legislation, enforcement through extradition proceedings **78,** 505
executive act **111,** 568
determination of fairness **111,** 569-70
executive responsibility **42,** 245, **79,** 436, 447-52, 458 n. 26, 487, 493, 501, 547, **87,** 168, 176, 188-9, 191, **96,** 109, **100,** 406, 615, **119,** 36, 38, **122,** 618, 664, **124,** 309-12

extradition (*cont.*)
expulsion
as **95,** 325, **100,** 407
distinguished **55,** 14-16
extraditable offence. *See* extraditable offence
extradition country **114,** 388-9
part of a country **114,** 389
fair trial, need for **87,** 161-2, **94,** 512-15, 593-5, **100,** 426, 429, 694, **107,** 174
additional charges **104,** 115-16
bail, right to **104,** 116
right to be adequately informed of charges **104,** 50
right to cross-examine **104,** 49-50
right to discovery **104,** 50, 116
fairness **79,** 166, 436, 481, 526-7, **87,** 400-7, **100,** 406, **119,** 293-317
as matter of law **119,** 313
representations and **119,** 307
requested State's right to take decision in case of international crime without consultation **119,** 301, 307-10
federal State **45,** 320, **48,** 188-90, **87,** 148, 150, 151-2, **90,** 675
local criminality **87,** 158
fiscal offences **45,** 376-8, **74,** 119-20
forcible abduction. *See* forcible abduction/unlawful arrest
foreign relations and **79,** 482 n. 6, 487, **87,** 164, **100,** 613, **119,** 72, 111, **124,** 311-12
foreign warrant, execution of **43,** 243-4
free movement of workers in the EC and **85,** 88-90
freedom of movement under Treaty of Rome (1957), effect **114,** 419-21, 460-2
fugitive criminal, definition **55,** 548, **60,** 296
general principles of extradition law, respect for fundamental rights and freedoms in Requesting State **111,** 508
general principles of international law and **87,** 209-10
amnesty in requesting State **106,** 264
guilt, relevance **87,** 167, **104,** 4
habeas corpus **55,** 509, 516, **79,** 386-95, 416, 418 n. 5, 421, 431, 436, 442-3, 463-7, 485-6, 493-533, 539-47, **84,** 61-2, **104,** 4, **124,** 453-9
as appeal **55,** 509, 516, **79,** 416, 421, 431, 436, 442-3, 485-6, 493-533, 539-47, **104,** 45, 81, 106, 112, **119,** 317-18, **122,** 671. *See also* judicial review *below*
scope **104,** 117
extension **104,** 80-2, 105-6, **124,** 453-9
Harvard Draft Convention on, political offenders **59,** 475
hearing, trial distinguished **69,** 236, 245-6, 266
Home Secretary's responsibilities. *See* United Kingdom, extradition, Home Secretary's responsibilities
Hong Kong/China **92,** 657
human rights, respect for in requesting State. *See also* conditions in receiving State *above*; extradition in case of death penalty
bilateral extradition agreement, presumed **100,** 410
executive discretion **100,** 428
inhuman and degrading treatment **100,** 426, 427-8
multilateral extradition agreement, accession to European Convention for the Protection of Human Rights (1950) as guarantee **100,** 410
request for measures to guarantee **100,** 427-8
request for supplementary information from requesting State **100,** 427

right of court in requested State to investigate **100,** 426, 429
right of individual petition under European Convention on Human Rights (1950) **100,** 426, 427, 429
individual's right of objection **87,** 189, **90,** 658, 671, 689
international criminal order and **106,** 238
judicial review **79,** 436, 487, **80,** 18, **87,** 146, 161, 168-9, **96,** 218, **98,** 378-9, 388, 418, 419-20, 423, **124,** 311-12, 321-2. *See also* appeal *and* habeas corpus *above*
annulment **100,** 670, 682
Bugdaycay **114,** 428-9
death penalty and **124,** 312, 321-2
grounds. *See also* scope *below*
abuse of power **111,** 556, 561-3, 568-70
lawful, fair and reasonable action, whether **119,** 275-8, 282-3
legality of executive action **111,** 556-7
new judge, need for **104,** 51, 62 n. 2, 78
political offence exception **104,** 62 n. 2
procedure **106,** 253
questions of fact **100,** 411
renewal of application following **106,** 252-3
requirements, exhaustion of alternative remedies **111,** 557, 563
scope **104,** 4, 45, 48, 81-2. *See also* grounds *above*
abstention from right to refuse **106,** 236
conditions in requesting State **104,** 81, 107-8, **106,** 241
constitutionality of executive action **104,** 81
de novo examination of questions of law **104,** 82, 93
finding of fact not clearly erroneous **104,** 48, 82, 93
jurisdiction of original judge **104,** 4, 45, 81
motivation of requesting State **106,** 241
offence within treaty **104,** 45, 81, 105
political offence exception **104,** 81
prima facie case **104,** 45, 81, 105, 107
procedural defects in extradition procedure **104,** 81
request for extradition **106,** 236
validity of extradition agreement **104,** 45
Soering **114,** 426-8
standing, requesting State **106,** 244-8, 260
jurisdiction **60,** 297, 309, **70,** 469-74, 485 n. 3, 493, 498-502, 531, **79,** 88, 387, 420, **85,** 98-9
extraditing State **60,** 317
'found' in the requested State **104,** 62-4, 82-3
illegal transfer from third country for sole purpose of extradition **104,** 62-4, **111,** 550-83
limitation to terms of request for **77,** 395-6
obligation to exercise **86,** 551-2
requesting State **60,** 326-30, **104,** 37, 78 n. 21, 83-4
right to exercise and **94,** 536-7
legal certainty **100,** 406
legality
court's power to enquire into **77,** 374-5, 395
determined by surrendering State **77,** 333, 395
if surrendering government unlawful **77,** 340, 344-5
prosecution, effect on **75,** 339-43
unlawful arrest, effect **77,** 333-4, 358-75

extradition (*cont.*)
liberty of person, deprivation, detention during proceedings **101,** 191-2
limitation period
for prosecution **43,** 243-4
for sentence **45,** 231-4
local criminality **87,** 157
margin of appreciation. *See* discretion *above*
military duty, breach of and **87,** 177
minimum standards of justice **79,** 79-82, 85-6, 166-7
motivation of requested State **86,** 224-8
motivation of requesting State **79,** 428, 450-1, 452, 482, **85,** 87, **104,** 114-15, **111,** 544-5
executive responsibility **79,** 452, **104,** 115
judicial responsibility **106,** 241
prosecution for race, religion, nationality or political opinion **79,** 83, **111,** 512-13, **119,** 110, 250
multiple charges **51,** 340-60
municipal law and **70,** 377-9, **87,** 151, 153, 154
relations between States
requested State/requesting State **70,** 375-9
requested State/third State **70,** 375-9
undertaking to apply in absence of treaty **87,** 176
nationals **38,** 134, **41,** 331, **51,** 281, **57,** 322, **60,** 295-7, 300, 316, **72,** 64, 201, 634, **73,** 657, **79,** 435-8, 494-5, 530, 533, **86,** 552, **87,** 163, 164-7, **88,** 291-7, **90,** 645, **94,** 345-6, 489, 501, 507, 517-18, 563-4, **95,** 363-4, **100,** 661-2, **117,** 86
alien integrated into national community **100,** 401-3, 431-2
customary international law **94,** 502, 522, 592
death penalty and **124,** 313, 314-15
Extradition, European Convention on (1957) **87,** 166, **100,** 401-3, 431-2
declaration defining nationality **100,** 402-3, 431-2
legislative implementation, need for **100,** 403
jurisdiction and **87,** 164-6
offence committed on high seas **56,** 513-17
requirements **60,** 303-4
reciprocity **87,** 165-6
uniformity of practice **60,** 296
natural justice and **51,** 248, **55,** 512, **69,** 243-7
naturalization, application for, relevance **111,** 513
nature **43,** 231-4, **55,** 35, 503
nexus, need for, conspiracy **104,** 5-6
object and purpose **55,** 505-6, **125,** 534
objection to
extraditing State **90,** 658
individual **87,** 189, **90,** 658, 671, 689
obligation **106,** 261-73, **117,** 85-6
European Convention on Extradition (1957) **111,** 557-8
occupied territories, from **83,** 146
of official of deposed government **81,** 623 n. 12
pardon, effect **51,** 331-9
passive personality principle **82,** 350-1, **104,** 83-4, **119,** 75-6
persecution, risk of **79,** 508 n. 15, 510 n. 19
political aspects **55,** 507
political offence. *See* political offence

procedure **55,** 32, 547, **60,** 336, 340-1, 345-6, 348-9, 354, **69,** 100-8, 224-37, 242-7, 263-8, **71,** 512, 521, 530-2, **73,** 42-3, 662-70, **74,** 293-4, 472-7, 482, 496, **77,** 395-6, **79,** 411-13, 471, 477, 543, **85,** 74-6, 139, 144-5, **87,** 146, 161-2, **98,** 282-6, 387-8, **119,** 33-6, **122,** 609-10. *See also* request for *and* requirements *below*; Extradition, European Convention on (1957), procedure
absence **88,** 266-7
appeal **79,** 394, 416-22, 431-8, 441-8, 460-75
applicable law **45,** 379-80
arrest. *See* arrest *above*; forcible abduction/unlawful arrest
authentication of documents **44,** 238-42
avoidance **95,** 393, 395, 399
completion, handover of person requested **100,** 407
courts and executive, division of competence **73,** 42
culpability, power to examine **100,** 614-15
defects in **69,** 224-7, 229, **79,** 69-73, 248, 418 n. 5, 434, **87,** 167-9
annulment **79,** 248
depositions. *See also* evidence, affidavit *above*
admissibility **41,** 398, 403-4, **44,** 184-5
magistrate, duty **69,** 236-7
representation of accused **69,** 228-37
extraditing State, determination by **90,** 660, 687
extraditing State, in
judicial review, exclusion **74,** 482, 496
nature of **78,** 515-18
fairness. *See* fairness *above*
formal documents **87,** 326-7
government taking court opinion **43,** 244-5
hearing
judicial nature **104,** 78 n. 22
purpose **104,** 4
importance **85,** 116
inter partes hearing **119,** 39-40
irregular **44,** 176-86
legal nature **119,** 254
ministerial signature, need for **111,** 507, **119,** 33
natural justice and **69,** 243-7
nature of **79,** 487, 498 n. 3
notification of offender **69,** 226, 247
presumption of innocence **74,** 293-4
reasons, need for **119,** 256
representations, admissibility **119,** 248, 318
request by diplomatic agent on behalf of ambassador **106,** 250, 254
requesting State, intervention of **39,** 434, 439, 445-6, **47,** 266-7
review of extradition warrant **119,** 38
time-limit **36,** 76-9, **60,** 337, 342-3, 351, **87,** 322-4, **91,** 388-9
extension **124,** 453-9
'reasonable' **124,** 453-9
urgency **73,** 662-3, 666-8
withdrawal of request **100,** 407
State practice **100,** 407
proceedings
criminal or civil **44,** 232
participation in as waiver of immunity **42,** 245-6

extradition (*cont.*)
proof of **70,** 9-10
protective measures, arrest as basis for **45,** 378-80
provisional detention **51,** 248, 324, **60,** 315-16, 318
public policy and **86,** 327, **88,** 245, **106,** 262, **111,** 521
death penalty, in case of **100,** 663, 668, 686
double criminality **100,** 685
punishment, discrepancy **88,** 242-6
purpose **88,** 289-90
self-interest of States **100,** 670
re-extradition to third State **70,** 375-9, **72,** 599, 629-32
concurrent requests and **100,** 661
customary international law **70,** 376-7
treaty practice **70,** 376-7
requirements **72,** 629, 631
consent of accused **72,** 630-1
consent of requested State **70,** 375-9, 629, 631, **72,** 599, **100,** 661-2
recognition of foreign law and **82,** 27
refusal. *See also* withdrawal of agreement *below*
act of State **106,** 235-43, 253, 263
final judgment in requested State **100,** 612
grounds. *See* refusal, grounds *below*
implied, failure to respond to request **106,** 253, 255
nationals. *See* nationals *above*
offence committed partly in requested State **100,** 611-12
reasons. *See* procedure, reasons, need for *above* refusal, grounds *below*
responsibility **106,** 240-1
safe haven, risk of creating **98,** 377-8, 380, 407-8, 422-3, 447, 519 n. 10, **100,** 670, 687, **124,** 342-3
sovereign or administrative act, distinguishable, whether **106,** 237-43
withdrawal of agreement distinguished **106,** 259-60
refusal, grounds
conditions in requesting State. *See* conditions in requesting State *above*
death penalty. *See* extradition in case of death penalty
effect on stability of country in which offences committed **119,** 111, 252
excessive penalty **55,** 512-13
Extradition, European Convention on (1957) **106,** 238
family life, effect on **79,** 126, 128
humanitarian considerations **119,** 111, 250, 252
international public policy. *See* international public policy *above*
motivation, relevance. *See* motivation of requested State *and* motivation of requesting State *above*
national interest **119,** 111, 252, 326
national security **106,** 263, **111,** 524
natural justice **55,** 512-13, **69,** 243-7, **98,** 388
necessity **106,** 266-7, 272
need for **106,** 238, 270-2, 273, **119,** 256
non-respect for fundamental rights and freedoms. *See* conditions in receiving State, respect for fundamental rights and freedoms *above*
political offence. *See* political offence
public policy. *See* public policy and *above*
threat to international peace and security **94,** 500
triviality of offence **55,** 512-13

UN model extradition treaty (1990) **106,** 262
'unjust or oppressive' **114,** 449-51
unlikelihood of fair trial **55,** 512-13
'relevant offences' **55,** 431, 433
'rendition' distinguished **101,** 287, 295
request for **55,** 16, 32, **59,** 477-8
imperfect **119,** 31
invalidity, effect **55,** 20-1
multiple
double jeopardy and **104,** 62 n. 2, 82
res judicata **104,** 82
standing of second requesting State **119,** 282-3
nature of **55,** 35
need for **119,** 32-3, 251-2
particulars of charge **55,** 539
standing **51,** 339, **55,** 24-7, 35
requested State
definition **79,** 451-2, 469-74, 499
undertaking not to prosecute for political offence **55,** 574-6
requirements **51,** 288, 312, 319, 324, 328, **55,** 534, **60,** 315-17, 323, 332, **72,** 65, 72, 598-604, 610-12, 616, 621-3, 629-32, 636-7, **74,** 450-72, **87,** 322, **104,** 22, 116. *See also* refusal, grounds *above*
arrest warrant. *See* arrest warrant *above*
authority to proceed **119,** 108-11, 146, 247-52, 318, 328-9
charges pending in requesting State **104,** 20
consent of requested State **72,** 599, 629, 631
constitution, compatibility **106,** 308-9
double criminality. *See* double criminality
extraditable offence. *See* extraditable offence
extradition agreement. *See* extradition agreement
fair trial. *See* fair trial, need for *above*
fairness. *See* fairness *above*
fairness of requesting State's judicial system, non-enquiry **114,** 627-8
good faith **55,** 507, **79,** 87-8, 99, 100, 108, **119,** 110, 251
jurisdiction of requesting State. *See* jurisdiction, requesting State *above*
ministerial authority **119,** 33
motivation, relevance. *See* motivation of requested State *and* motivation of requesting State *above*
non-re-extradition **114,** 642-5
'offence' under law of requested State **108,** 632
prima facie case **71,** 515, 520, 532, **79,** 83-4, 87, 99-100, 380, 391-2, 395, 419, 420, 427-8, 433, 443-6, 461, 477, 497, 527-8, **85,** 94-144, **86,** 218, **100,** 605-6, 608-9, 617-18, **101,** 184-5, **104,** 20-1, 22-37, 50-1, 76-8, 84-6, 117-18, **111,** 513, 579, 581, **114,** 633-8
Extradition, European Convention on (1957) **111,** 579
responsibility for determining **87,** 217
probable cause. *See* prima facie case *above*
proof of identity of person **104,** 20
proportionality **79,** 126, 128, 455 n. 21. *See also* political offence
reciprocity **44,** 173-5, **45,** 378, 380, **55,** 13-16, 32-3, 35, **60,** 296, **72,** 634, 636, **74,** 108, 166, 437-8, 454-5, 462, **79,** 88-9, **87,** 164-6, **98,** 416, 422, **100,** 613, **104,** 40, **106,** 241-2, **119,** 75-6
State practice **87,** 164-5

extradition (*cont.*)
request for. *See* request for *above*
serious offence **87,** 154
statutory authority **55,** 14-16, 24-7, **114,** 388
statutory basis **87,** 163
substantiation **87,** 316-20, 326-7, 328
waiver, **77,** 395-6, **90,** 664, 667-8
revocability **77,** 396
warranty of trial according to requesting State's laws **114,** 616, 630-1
res judicata
multiple extradition requests **104,** 82
non-applicability **79,** 389-90, 395, 418-20, 498 n. 3
responsibility **114,** 626-7
courts **100,** 403
executive. *See* executive responsibility *above*
review. *See* appeal *above*
security of extraditing State **98,** 420
sovereign act **77,** 333, 335, **88,** 267-8, **94,** 502, 521-2, 534, 589-90, 592
customary international law **94,** 502, 507
sovereignty, respect for and **55,** 86-7, **88,** 267-8, **90,** 660-1, **94,** 502, 507, 521-2, 534, 536-7, 589-90, 592, **95,** 364 n. 4
speciality **36,** 305, **44,** 174-6, **45,** 377, **48,** 187-8, **51,** 269-81, 340-65, **53,** 10, 13, 14, 16, **55,** 13-15, **60,** 311-12, 332, **69,** 217-18, **70,** 3-15, **72,** 599-604, **73,** 600, **79,** 95, 391, 451, 495, 546-7, **87,** 177-8, 189-90, 210, 211, **88,** 355-6, **90,** 657-9, **104,** 4, 10-11, **114,** 388
breach **90,** 684
conventional **83,** 76
customary international law **92,** 686, **125,** 535-6
enforcement of suspended sentence, admissibility **72,** 598-601, **73,** 659-60
extension of offences, by agreement **100,** 406, **104,** 10
fairness to individual **90,** 678, **104,** 39-40
forcible abduction contrasted **90,** 684
Hong Kong after reversion to China, risk of change **114,** 455-9, 632-3, 639
implied treaty provision **90,** 676, 682
individual's right to invoke **36,** 65, 77-8, **79,** 547, **90,** 659, 683, 684
legislative **83,** 76
limitation **92,** 689
offences committed after extradition **87,** 190
opportunity to return and **92,** 687-90
perpetual immunity **92,** 687-90
previous conviction, detention for **101,** 289-90
purpose **90,** 677-80
reason for rule **87,** 190
comity **104,** 10
risk of eventual surrender to third country **88,** 355-6
sovereignty, protection of **90,** 674, 678
treaty, means of enforcement **104,** 11
treaty rule **92,** 686, **101,** 286, **125,** 535-6
trial *in absentia* and **72,** 600
waiver by requested State **104,** 10
executive decision **104,** 11
State responsibility for acts following **98,** 374, **124,** 316-17
State succession and. *See* extradition agreement, State succession and

statutory limitation **79,** 494 n., 497, 526-7, 528-9, 530, **119,** 110
analogous offence **104,** 21-2
treaty provision **104,** 22
sui generis nature of proceedings **88,** 46-7
surrender, insistence on **94,** 421-2, 489, 490, 513
coercive measures **94,** 490, 522, 572-5, 592
Security Council endorsement **94,** 490, 513-14, 572-5, 589, 592
taking evidence at request of foreign State distinguished **86,** 181
terrorist offences **74,** 472-7, 498-504, 511-16, **79,** 52-3, 105, 131-2, 453-5, 478-81, 514-15, 517-18, 525, 531-2, **94,** 507, 521-2, 534, 551, 565. *See also aut dedere aut punire/judicare above*; Montreal Convention for the Suppression of Unlawful Acts Against Civil Aviation (1971), *aut dedere aut punire/judicare*; political offence
third State
crime committed in **74,** 454-5
to. *See* re-extradition to third State *above*
tortious acts **55,** 14
transfer of convicted prisoners and **92,** 552
transit of extradited person through third country **100,** 413-14
consent of third State, need for **100,** 413
enclave **100,** 413-14
treaties. *See* extradition agreement
trial *in absentia*
as bar to **86,** 327
convicted person **78,** 514-20
universal jurisdiction as alternative, preclusion by bilateral treaty **100,** 670-1
veiled. *See* disguised *above*
war crimes **72,** 607-14, **75,** 339, 343, **79,** 386, 391, 395, 511, **88,** 279-301
European Convention on Human Rights (1950), Protocol 4 **88,** 294-5
extraterritorial crimes, assumption of jurisdiction in respect of and **88,** 294
International Covenant on Civil and Political Rights (ICCPR) (1966) **88,** 293-4
withdrawal of agreement. *See also* refusal *above*
act of State **106,** 259-60
competence **106,** 260
failure to implement distinguished **106,** 259
reasons, need for **106,** 260-7
'reasons of fact and law' **106,** 261
'superior interests of State' **106,** 261
witnesses, compellability **55,** 552-3
extradition agreement 51, 378, **60,** 317-19, **72,** 621-6, 631, **75,** 108-13. *See also the Index to the Consolidated Table of Treaties*
absence **40,** 211-12, **55,** 16-19, 25-7, 32-3, **57,** 320-1, **87,** 209-10, 211
recognition of foreign judgment **78,** 107
absence of authority to enforce **42,** 233-8
ad hoc **88,** 266-7
administrative character, function of courts **48,** 187
application **74,** 118-20
assurances that death penalty will not be carried out **124,** 340-3
basis for **90,** 415
belligerent occupation, feasibility **83,** 194
breach **90,** 79-85, 652, 657-8, 661, 662, 671, 677-8
compliance, international relations, in interests of **79,** 395
conditions in signatory State, relevance **104,** 96, **124,** 322-3
subsequent change **104,** 96

extradition agreement (*cont.*)
conflict with other obligations **98,** 446, **104,** 95-6
conformity with international obligations, need for **95,** 325
courts' power to question acts of foreign State under **48,** 187-8
crime not in **55,** 97-8, 504
customary international law and **59,** 474, **70,** 376-7, **78,** 96
political offence **59,** 474-6
death penalty reservation **96,** 388, **100,** 671, 677, **124,** 324-5
definition **92,** 687
direct applicability **79,** 387
discretionary right to surrender, effect on **104,** 10, 78 n. 21, 96
double criminality and **75,** 108-13, **79,** 391, 395, **87,** 153-5
exceptions
military offence **104,** 37-8
political offence. *See* political offence
fiscal offence, applicability to **74,** 119-20
human rights, protection of **100,** 410
individual's rights under **45,** 95, **74,** 497, **86,** 531, **107,** 433, **114,** 599-600
informal understanding or arrangement **101,** 283-4, 286-7, 293
interpretation **85,** 139-40
general principles of international law and **87,** 151
liberal **104,** 115-16, **114,** 627
modern State practice and **72,** 631
principle of double criminality and **87,** 155
travaux préparatoires and **95,** 371 n. 15
legislation
applicability in absence of agreement **111,** 507
effect of agreement on legislation **124,** 453-8
municipal law and **43,** 238, **44,** 243, 273, **45,** 379, **70,** 3-15, **72,** 621, 624, 629, **74,** 504, 512, **87,** 154
statutory provision, need for **45,** 379-80, **72,** 65, 68, 71-2, **87,** 153
subsequent amendment **70,** 437, **87,** 151
need for **51,** 319-23, 340-60, **78,** 128, 130, **79,** 487, 494, **87,** 146-7, 148, 151, 153, 164, 314-15, **88,** 46-7, 251, **92,** 686, 690, **94,** 489, 592, **96,** 107, **104,** 10, 46-7, **106,** 309, **107,** 171-4, **117,** 85-6, **122,** 604, 664, **124,** 310, **125,** 534-6
occupied territory, feasibility **83,** 194
offence not included in **55,** 504
parties, whether limiting rights of **70,** 378-9
primacy **87,** 322
purpose **122,** 670-1, 677
reciprocity, relevance **88,** 291, 294-5, **119,** 75-6
relevance **88,** 244-5, 266-7, 289-90
'requested party' **79,** 451-2, 469-74, 499
self-executing **90,** 658, **95,** 366
US–HKSAR Extradition Agreement (1996) **122,** 679-80
special provision **104,** 115-16
speciality **79,** 395, 451
State practice **70,** 376-7, **72,** 66, 69, 73-4, 631
State succession and **52,** 84-5, **55,** 91, **68,** 5-6, **70,** 3-15, **72,** 65-74, **73,** 38-48, 53-4, **74,** 118-19, **79,** 387, 395, 415 n. 1, 417 n. 4, **85,** 143-5, **87,** 210-11, 316, **91,** 388, 389-90, **96,** 107-9, **104,** 46-7, **107,** 173-4, 176-7, **114,** 645-9
Hong Kong, reversion to China **104,** 46-7, **114,** 617, **122,** 604-19
Italy–UK Extradition Treaty (1873) **78,** 106-11
Liberia–UK Extradition Treaty (1892) **70,** 3-15

strict observance **40,** 210-11
termination **87,** 162, 163-4
UK–USA, extension to Hong Kong **87,** 321
validity, requirement of **79,** 420
extradition in case of death penalty 78, 95-101, **96,** 387-8, **106,** 299-304, 306-9, **111,** 521, **124,** 300-43
arbitrary sentencing **98,** 379
assurances that death penalty will not be carried out, Model Treaty on Extradition (1990) (Art. 4(d)) **98,** 376, **124,** 325
assurances that death penalty will not be carried out, need for **98,** 305-6, 320-1, 382-4, 386, 404-6, 407, 410, 417-18, 423, 424-5, 477, 478, **100,** 659-60, 663-4, **106,** 299-300, 302-3, 307-9, **124,** 304-5, 309-11, 312-17, 322-43
additional assurances **100,** 679-80, 682-5
applicable law **106,** 302
authority to give **106,** 314-15
binding nature **100,** 673, 693, **106,** 315
comity and **124,** 322-3, 341
court's role **106,** 303-4, 308
diplomatic note **106,** 300, 309, 314-15
executive responsibility **100,** 660, 673, 680-2, 683, 693-4, **106,** 303-4
extradition agreement provision
failure to obtain as breach of human rights **124,** 340-3
need for **100,** 659-60
Extradition, European Convention on (1957) **100,** 683, **124,** 325
failure to seek, reasonable and justifiable in a free and democratic society, whether **124,** 1403-5
federal State, in **100,** 681-2
International Covenant on Civil and Political Rights (ICCPR) (1966) **100,** 686-7
investigation into validity **100,** 677-85
judicial authorities **100,** 674, 683-5
legal certainty, need for **100,** 687-8
public policy reasons for not seeking **124,** 339
refusal to give **124,** 339
reparation for failure to observe **100,** 671
reservation, insufficient **100,** 664-5, 673-4
responsibility for determining acceptability **106,** 301-3, 307-9, 314
safe haven, risk of creating **98,** 380, 407-8, 422-3, **124,** 342-3
State practice. *See* State practice *below*
UNHRC resolutions **124,** 325-6
bilateral agreement to provide for same penalty as in requested State **100,** 671
cruel and unusual treatment, whether **98,** 374, 382, 386, 396-402, 417-18, **124,** 316
customary international law **78,** 98, 100, **124,** 326
as exile **124,** 304, 305-6
extradition agreement, death penalty reservation **96,** 388, **100,** 671, 677, **124,** 325
Extradition, European Convention on (1957). *See* Extradition, European Convention on (1957), death penalty
extradition to another country with jurisdiction as alternative **98,** 312
fundamental justice, breach of, whether **98,** 374-80, 381-3
right to life **100,** 660
judicial review **124,** 312, 321-2
Model Treaty on Extradition (1990) (Art. 4) **98,** 376, **124,** 325
nationals **124,** 313, 314-15

extradition in case of death penalty (*cont.*)
public policy and **100,** 663, 668
European **100,** 686
restriction on **78,** 96-7, 100
general principle of international law, whether **78,** 97, 389-94
safe haven, risk of creating **98,** 377-8, **100,** 670, 687
'shocking to the conscience', whether **98,** 377, 379, 382-3, 420-1, **124,** 304, 320-1
speciality principle leading to modification of request **100,** 671, 673
State practice
assurances that death penalty will not be carried out **100,** 674-8
Austria **100,** 676
bilateral agreements **100,** 677
Denmark **100,** 676
Extradition, European Convention on (1957) **100,** 674-5
Germany **100,** 675
Italy **100,** 676
Netherlands **100,** 675-6
Switzerland **100,** 676-7
United Kingdom **100,** 677
United States **100,** 677-8
Extradition, European Convention on (1957) 51, 328-39, **55,** 560, **72,** 621-5, **79,** 121-2
'accessory' extradition **72,** 622-3
applicability
aliens **111,** 267-8
between parties to **119,** 31
Hong Kong **106,** 249, 254
assurances that death penalty will not be carried out **100,** 683, **124,** 325
bilateral treaties, effect on **72,** 621, **74,** 496
compliance, choice of method **106,** 301-2
customary international law and **78,** 96
death penalty **106,** 299-300, 301-4
assurances that death penalty will not be carried out, need for **100,** 683, **124,** 325
Explanatory Report of the Council of Europe **106,** 302
restriction in case of **78,** 96, 97
double criminality **72,** 621-2, **74,** 451
critical date **74,** 451
exclusion of offences **72,** 621-3
extraditable offences **72,** 621-3
capital punishment **74,** 457
minimum period of imprisonment **72,** 622, **73,** 658, **74,** 450, 507
general principles of law and **78,** 97
Hong Kong, applicability to **106,** 249, 254
implementation, flexibility **119,** 325
Italian reservation **78,** 100
jurisdiction of requesting State, need to establish **82,** 52
European Convention on Mutual Assistance in Criminal Matters (1959) distinguished **82,** 52
municipal law, incorporation **72,** 621, **106,** 301-2, **119,** 2, 31
primacy of municipal law in absence of incorporation **119,** 324-5
mutual ratification, need for **100,** 660
ne bis in idem **71,** 234-5

obligation to extradite **106,** 237, 261-2, 267-9, **111,** 556-7
political offence **55,** 563-7, **72,** 623-6, **74,** 501-4
criteria, recourse to municipal law **72,** 624, **74,** 504
offences connected with **55,** 570-1, **74,** 501
prima facie case, need for **111,** 579
procedure
accusation case **119,** 255-6, 259
between non-parties to **119,** 146
between parties to **119,** 146
prosecution for race, religion, nationality or political opinion **79,** 83, 87
generally recognized principle of international law, whether **79,** 83
purpose, streamlining of process **119,** 254-5
ratification **79,** 121
reciprocity and **119,** 75-6
requested party's right to request supplementary information **119,** 180-1, 250, 256-7
Re Cuoghi **119,** 257
requesting party's rights, limited nature **119,** 294-5
reservations
'exceptionally serious consequences' **100,** 686
humanitarian considerations **106,** 262
'particular hardship' **100,** 431-2
'particularly serious offence' **100,** 621-2
sovereignty **106,** 262
'special circumstances' **106,** 262
speciality principle **53,** 10, 14
travaux préparatoires **55,** 564-7
extraterritorial jurisdiction. *See* extraterritorial legislation; jurisdiction, extraterritorial
extraterritorial legislation 54, 268, **56,** 56, **69,** 4-6, **71,** 24, 227-8, **72,** 27, 80-1, 86, 169-71, 179, 439-42, 556, 559-62, **73,** 228, 237, 239-41, 243-7, **77,** 450, 548-9, **78,** 461-2, 464, **82,** 244 n. 24, 344, 351, 353, 355 n. 24, **84,** 72-3, 116 n. 9, **85,** 276-300, **87,** 99-102, **90,** 622-41, **91,** 30, **98,** 379, 381, 388, 403, 417, 418, 423, **99,** 154-61. *See also* expropriation/nationalization, extraterritorial effect; legislation, territorial limitation; legislation, interpretation, presumption of territorial limitation
act of State, law founded on **78,** 599
alien exemption clause, effect **90,** 622, 626, 634-7
aliens on high seas **95,** 581-98
antitrust **46,** 340, **48,** 106-44, **56,** 32, **63,** 295, **66,** 279-86, 293, 343, 382-3, 490-7, 500-2, **72,** 79-80, **73,** 321, 337-8, 346-7, 357-8, **74,** 39-40, 48-54, 78-82
applicability
locally engaged staff on military base abroad **94,** 268
locally engaged staff of State bank **122,** 87-8
Australian states **51,** 39, **69,** 37, 55, 58, 110-26, **70,** 58-60, 66-8, 89-90, 101
bankruptcy proceedings **88,** 312-22
comity and **88,** 318
'between a [constituent] State and any place outside thereof' **90,** 623, 634
broadcasting regulation **61,** 184-5, **74,** 201-3
Canada, statutory provisions **69,** 93-8
characterization of action in England deciding factor **78,** 601
choice of law and **100,** 598-9
comity **91,** 97, **96,** 133-4, **100,** 586-7, 599, 601
conduct primarily in legislating State **100,** 522, 524-6
conflict of interests **100,** 585, 600

extraterritorial legislation (*cont.*)
conflict with law of third State, risk **95,** 589, **100,** 587, 601
constitutional provision for **82,** 351, 353, 355 n. 24, **118,** 642, **121,** 633
criminal **74,** 138-9, 195, **78,** 543, 597-8, 601-2, 615, 627-30
currency provision **77,** 450
discriminatory legislation **47,** 203-4, **90,** 622-41, **98,** 577, **107,** 601-2
effect in Antarctica **100,** 522-3, 526-7
effect within territory, basis of jurisdiction **72,** 79-80
employment by US companies of US citizens abroad **90,** 621-41
enemy property legislation **43,** 248
enforceability, relevance **78,** 464, 533-4, 542
enforcement abroad, right to **90,** 621
expropriation. *See* expropriation/nationalization, extraterritorial effect; expropriation/nationalization, territorial limitation
extraterritorial adjudication distinguished **100,** 597
fiscal and exchange control **41,** 230-9, **47,** 157-63, **78,** 505, 598, 605, 606, 607
fisheries conservation and management measures **123,** 351
fisheries protection **59,** 347-9, **70,** 110-16
foreign inland waters **59,** 347-9
foreign relations, relevance **95,** 598, 609-10, **100,** 497-503, 523, 524-5, 527-8, 529
goods shipped from foreign port **36,** 428-33
high seas, income earned on **74,** 206-9
human rights legislation **90,** 622-41, **123,** 611
implied by nature of offence **94,** 88, **99,** 157-8
Ireland, Republic of **59,** 347-9, **70,** 103-16
nationals abroad
jurisdiction over and **87,** 102, **100,** 541-2, **118,** 641-2
status and capacity **69,** 4-6
native title **125,** 380-1
organization existing only abroad **45,** 49-53
League of Nations Covenant and **37,** 33
'peace, order and good government', laws for **45,** 7-18, **70,** 58-60, 67, 90, 108-9
'political' law **78,** 603
political question doctrine **100,** 499
'possession' and **90,** 626, 636-7
possession of green turtles fished outside territorial sea **91,** 384-5
presumption against **84,** 695, **90,** 622, 630, 632, 634-5, **92,** 679, **94,** 235, **95,** 589, 609, **99,** 157, **100,** 498, 522, 523-5, 535-6, 597
prohibited effects in legislating country **87,** 101
protective principle and **87,** 101-2, **94,** 89-91, 95-6
public law **78,** 601, 603, 605-7
public policy and **69,** 4, **78,** 604, 607, 630
racial discrimination, advertisement for employment abroad **107,** 601-2
reasonable exercise **100,** 600-1
recognition distinguished **78,** 597
repeal of discriminatory legislation **47,** 203-4
requirements
clear intent **56,** 55-6, **82,** 351, 352, **90,** 624-5, 629, 630, 631-2, 633, 634, **94,** 235, **95,** 598, **96,** 132, 133-4, **99,** 154, 157, 159-61, **100,** 498-501, 524, 536, 539
clear language **90,** 63, 624-5, 629, 630, 631-2, 634
nexus **72,** 169-71, **87,** 102, **100,** 585, **118,** 549
revenue law **78,** 597-8, 599, 601, 602-3, 615, 627
South Africa, Republic of **69,** 131

sovereign immunity legislation and **72,** 169-71, 179
sovereignty, intrusion on **96,** 134
State-sponsored terrorism **121,** 633-4
Statute of Westminster 1931 **82,** 445-6
subrogation rights **69,** 4-6
substantial effects **100,** 585
Taking of Evidence Abroad Act, whether **84,** 751
tax haven **104,** 540-6, 555, 588-9, 601, **108,** 631
tax lien **38,** 112-20
taxation **71,** 220-1, **78,** 528-50
Trust Territory, applicability of laws to and **96,** 27, 30-1
war crimes **36,** 57-8

extraterritorial offence
conspiracy **48,** 69-76
counselling and procuring **79,** 94
crime committed prior to legislation **55,** 547
fraud **48,** 88-90
presumption against **85,** 126-7

extraterritoriality 57, 152-3, **60,** 14-15, 82-4, 112-13, 207, 260, **86,** 540-1. *See also* extraterritorial legislation; jurisdiction, extraterritorial
act of State. *See* act of State, extraterritorial effect; act of State, territorial limitation
consular premises **52,** 306-9, **55,** 385-6, 581-3
continental shelf **90,** 264
diplomatic agent, maintenance of normal residence in sending State **94,** 600
diplomatic mission **86,** 540-1
diplomatic premises **90,** 591, 592, **102,** 178, 179
inviolability distinguished **90,** 591 n. 9
sending State territory, whether part of **72,** 141, **90,** 589-90, 593-4, **94,** 351, 352
diplomatic privileges and immunities and **86,** 520
embassy or consular bank account/funds **65,** 9, **77,** 491-2
FAO Headquarters **101,** 392-3
Head of State **65,** 14-15, **103,** 585
legislation. *See* extraterritorial legislation
military base **90,** 592, **102,** 148
State immunity, jurisdiction **64,** 30-1, 39-40, **95,** 455
territorium as basis **86,** 540-1
UN Headquarters **96,** 77
visiting forces' shopping facilities **86,** 525

fair hearing 60, 164, 168-77, **69,** 243-7, **70,** 192-209, **71,** 482, **72,** 362-3, **73,** 395, 505-9, 558-9, 563-4, 639, **74,** 457, **75,** 584-6, **90,** 55-6. *See also* due process; European Convention on Human Rights (1950), fair hearing; fair trial; International Covenant on Civil and Political Rights (ICCPR) (1966), fair hearing; judicial impartiality
access to courts, right to. *See* access to courts
administrative power, challenge to **92,** 538-9
applicants for asylum and **92,** 653-6
armed conflict, relevance **106,** 281-2
deportation of aliens **73,** 639
enforcement of intellectual property rights **105,** 105-6
European Community (EC) **93,** 397, **111,** 135, 140-1
Geneva Convention Relating to the Status of Refugees (1951) **92,** 654-5
inaudita altera parte **105,** 105
international administrative tribunals, access to **116,** 649
natural justice and **90,** 56, 456, **92,** 654, 656, **118,** 491-8, 523-4

fair hearing (*cont.*)
nemo judex in sua [propria] causa/'no-one should be judge in his own cause' **43,** 480-6, **49,** 196, 259 n. 49, **57,** 238, **71,** 325, **118,** 489, 490-1, **119,** 120-4, 125-35
right to
be heard **74,** 431-2, 512-13, **78,** 642, 643-4, **118,** 496-501
legal counsel **106,** 282
criminal trial distinguished **107,** 449 n.
legal representation **118,** 354-5
United Nations Compensation Commission **109,** 512
fair trial 98, 659-60. *See also* European Convention on Human Rights (1950), fair trial; fair hearing; International Covenant on Civil and Political Rights (ICCPR) (1966), fair trial; Yugoslavia, International Criminal Tribunal for the Former (ICTY), fair trial
additional charges **104,** 115-16
amendment of Rules of Procedure, retroactive effect **110,** 679
Angola **118,** 535-6
appeal. *See also* European Convention on Human Rights (1950), appeal, right of; International Covenant on Civil and Political Rights (ICCPR) (1966), appeal, right of
legislation, need for **105,** 540
bail, right to **104,** 116
balancing interests of defence and prosecution **105,** 620-1, 636, 641-8, **120,** 46-9
Kostovski **105,** 623-4, 641-3
Ludi **105,** 644
Unterpertinger **105,** 643
belligerent occupation **83,** 191
burden of proof **98,** 548
charges
failure to distinguish between **107,** 442-3
right to be informed of **104,** 50, **121,** 308-9
choice of counsel **110,** 722
Constitution of court, right of election **82,** 458
cross-examine, right to **104,** 49-50
death penalty and. *See* death row as inhuman or degrading treatment
defence counsel, propriety of closing statement **98,** 547-8, 628-38
defence, right to, inviolable **101,** 369
delay **110,** 679
introducing war crimes legislation **98,** 576, **104,** 338
not attributable to the defence **121,** 221
post-charge **82,** 462-3, **104,** 402-3
pre-charge **82,** 460-2, **104,** 338, 402-3
deportation of aliens **74,** 446-7
derogation, armed conflict **105,** 622
disciplinary proceedings. *See* disciplinary proceedings (fair trial requirement)
equality of arms. *See* equality of arms
equality of parties. *See* equality of parties
evidence **69,** 170-6, 192. *See also* evidence
defence witnesses **69,** 192
withheld **69,** 170-6
expression of judicial opinion **100,** 333-4
extradition and. *See* extradition, fair trial, need for
'extravagant jurisdiction' **75,** 337-8, 374
as fundamental right **121,** 332
guilty plea **111,** 318-19
advantages **111,** 315, 392-3

common law basis **111,** 315, 317, 392
effect **111,** 318
presumption of innocence, effect on **111,** 332, 393, 394
promptness **114,** 324
requirements
prima facie case **111,** 394, 431-2, 436
unambiguous **111,** 314, 319, 331-3, 335, 374, 379-81, 385, 394, 432-6, 438-9
understanding of nature of charge and consequences **108,** 185-6, **111,** 313, 319, 321-31, 374, 393-4, 432
voluntary **108,** 185-6, **111,** 313, 318-21, 393, 432
identification procedures **107,** 440-1
improper calling of evidence **98,** 545-8, 577-8, 639-58
in absentia proceedings **110,** 722-3
International Military Tribunal for the Far East (Tokyo Tribunal) **105,** 475, 608-9
interpreter **73,** 531-2, **100,** 334
costs, entitlement **58,** 469-71, 706, **88,** 621-5, **100,** 334
free **58,** 484-5
joinder of cases **107,** 441-2
judicial impartiality. *See* judicial impartiality
jury, prejudice, risk of **94,** 514-15, 594-5
jury trial, right to **87,** 571-4
State immunity, jurisdiction and **63,** 245-51, 368-9, 438, 439-46, 546-9, 639-46, **72,** 95-100, 102-5, 109, **88,** 297, **107,** 354-8
lack of clarity in charge **98,** 575-6
legal aid **57,** 199, **58,** 630-1, **60,** 196-9, **79,** 270, 273, 276, **98,** 365, 368, **111,** 208
national security defence **110,** 668
non-disclosure of prosecution evidence. *See also* evidence, disclosure, obligation; evidence, disclosure as offence under law of foreign State
international tribunal's right to question conduct of defence lawyer **115,** 298-9
Nuremberg Tribunal **105,** 475, 608-9
oral hearing, right to, distribution of documents and **100,** 333-4
presumption of innocence. *See* presumption of innocence
prisoners of war, fair and impartial tribunal **99,** 167-8, **105,** 612
proceedings, international tribunal's right to question **115,** 297
prosecution's decision not to pursue certain counts **121,** 220
prosecution's negligent preparation of case, reopening of proceedings **121,** 223, 243-4, 248
protection of victims and witnesses **105,** 601-48, **122,** 31-2
anonymity **105,** 601-48, **120,** 47-8, **122,** 36
necessity **105,** 623
ratione materiae/*ratione temporis*/*ratione loci* **122,** 36
requirements **105,** 622-3
right to examine witnesses and **105,** 624-6
temporary **105,** 624, **122,** 36
balancing of interests **121,** 244-5, **124,** 88
limitation to protection requested **105,** 627
safe conduct **112,** 170
public hearing **105,** 430
reasoned opinion, right to **121,** 312-13
refusal to appear **100,** 334
right to
discovery. *See* disclosure of documents
effective representation **115,** 353-5

fair trial (*cont.*)
sexual offences, protection of victim, screened evidence **105,** 617-20
specific offence **82,** 456-8
specificity of charge, date and time of offence **112,** 170-1, **121,** 221
state of emergency, during **70,** 242-8, **123,** 155
State terrorism, in cases of **94,** 512-15, 568-9
translation **100,** 334
trial in national court **105,** 484-5
tribunal established by law. *See also under individual tribunals*
established in accordance with the rule of law **105,** 474-5
established by authorized institution **105,** 474
established by legislature **105,** 473-4, 564-5
European Convention on Human Rights (1950) **105,** 472, 563-5
general principle of law **105,** 472-3
International Covenant on Civil and Political Rights (ICCPR) (1966) **105,** 471-2, 563, 565
international tribunal **105,** 472-3
pre-established **105,** 475
unconstitutional removal of judge and **123,** 145-52
vagueness of legislation **104,** 337-8, 396-9
witnesses, right to examine, anonymity and **105,** 624-6
false imprisonment. *See* forceful abduction/unlawful arrest; liberty of person, deprivation
family life, respect for 57, 12, 314, **68,** 21, 28, **73,** 610-12, 617, **78,** 374. *See also* European Convention on Human Rights (1950), family life, respect for; International Covenant on Civil and Political Rights (ICCPR) (1966), family life, respect for
adultery and **72,** 578-9
burden of proof **92,** 311
burial grounds **118,** 264-78
cohabitation, relevance **92,** 311-12
'core' family, limitation to **72,** 573
customary international law **85,** 337-8
deportation. *See* deportation, family life, respect for; European Convention on Human Rights (1950), deportation, family life, respect for; International Covenant on Civil and Political Rights (ICCPR) (1966), deportation, family life, respect for
disappearances and **116,** 480, **120,** 59-60
EC **93,** 431
equality of rights **79,** 288
extradition and **79,** 126, 128
general principle of law **85,** 337-8, **111,** 538-9
International Covenant on Civil and Political Rights (ICCPR) (1966) **101,** 459-65, **103,** 232-3
military service abroad, whether threat to **73,** 610-12
nationality and **79,** 309, 323
privileges and immunities and **85,** 337-8
property, denial of return or access to **120,** 60-3, 112
right to found **68,** 28
rights **68,** 21, 28
Universal Declaration of Human Rights (1948) **85,** 338
family reunification 78, 186
Faroes, applicable law, traffic offences **91,** 280
fault
inhuman or degrading treatment, complainant **98,** 350, 353-4
need for

State responsibility **82,** 126-7, **93,** 329-31, 334-5
war crimes **98,** 595
unlawful arrest, relevance **86,** 530-2
FCN treaties. *See* Freedom, Commerce and Navigation (FCN) Treaty, Italy–USA (1948)
FDN (Fuerza Democràtica Nicaragüense) 76, 355
US aid to **76,** 387-96
Federal Republic of Yugoslavia (FRY). *See* Yugoslavia, Federal Republic (FRY)
federal State 51, 24. *See also* Rhodesia and Nyasaland, Federation of; union of States; United Arab Republic (UAR)
act of State **42,** 30-1, **61,** 74
applicable law **91,** 23, 585-7
boundaries. *See* boundaries, applicable law *below*
federal law **98,** 123
international law **57,** 77, 80, 374, **90,** 78-9, 375, 380, **91,** 460, **92,** 171
private international law, relations between constituent States **78,** 166-7
relations between foreign government and its ambassador **99,** 135
Statute of Limitations **95,** 639-43
tort, domicile of victim **101,** 527
balance of powers. *See* foreign relations, conduct, distribution of functions *below*
boundaries **57,** 28-38, **73,** 64, 79-80, **90,** 242-4, **91,** 445. *See also* territory *below*
applicable law **91,** 585-90
federal Constitution **86,** 187
international law **91,** 460, **92,** 171
confederation, at **90,** 271
equitable principles **91,** 460
low-water mark **90,** 242-4, 272
modification **86,** 187, 200, 202-3
permanent nature **91,** 197
prerogative power **86,** 190-2, 198, 200
river **91,** 190-204, 442-66
seaward **91,** 459
uti possidetis juris **92,** 171
variable nature **91,** 196-7
boundary dispute, jurisdiction **91,** 450, 459
Canadian Confederation, history **115,** 550-5
comity within **98,** 8
constituent States. *See also* Australia, constituent States; United States of America (USA), constituent States
characteristics, Bosnia-Herzegovina **115,** 130-2
constitutional balance **90,** 81
customary international law and **75,** 117-21, **90,** 198, 200-1
definition **101,** 483-4
diplomatic privileges and immunities **111,** 608-9
expulsion of international official, competence **102,** 197
extradition between **90,** 675
international personality **52,** 331, **68,** 238
legislative powers. *See* legislative powers, constituent State *below*
power to bind federal government **90,** 49-50
recognition **92,** 173-8
relations between **78,** 166-7
secession, de facto **115,** 578, 589, 595
sovereignty and **39,** 121-2, **51,** 191-2, **52,** 324
as State **111,** 608

federal State (*cont.*)
State immunity, entitlement. *See* State immunity, jurisdiction, entitlement, constituent State of federation
transfer of control of territory to federal authorities **90,** 78-9
treaties between
applicability of international law rules **90,** 78-9, 375, 380
boundary treaties **51,** 28-38, **73,** 64, 79-80, **91,** 445
justiciability **87,** 185
cultural and linguistic minorities, pursuit of collective goals **115,** 559-60
delimitation of powers between federal and State governments **57,** 78
dissolution
effect on treaties **52,** 86, **55,** 90-2
evidence of
loss of federal authority **92,** 166, 201, 202
non-recognition of claimant to succession **92,** 202
recognition of constituent State as separate legal entity **92,** 202
secession of constituent State **92,** 201, 202
unrepresentative nature of federal institutions **92,** 166
Yugoslavia **92,** 164-6, 200-5
double jeopardy, federal and State laws, interrelationship and **91,** 74, 82
enforcement of foreign judgment **103,** 570-1
extradition and **48,** 188-90
federal legislature, powers, inherent **68,** 316-17, 364, 382, 402-3, 446-7, 507-8
fiscal agreements. *See* treaties *below*
foreign relations **57,** 77, **80,** 374, **98,** 7-8, **121,** 509-12
defence distinguished **90,** 95-6
distribution of functions **68,** 200-1, 237-8, 252, **79,** 557-8
inter-State relations distinguished **98,** 8
inter-State trade **90,** 96
legislative powers **90,** 61, 73, 93, 96-7, 101, 104, 112
responsibility for **56,** 7, 18-19, **98,** 7-8, **121,** 509-12
federal government **98,** 7-8
Ruler of constituent State **118,** 297
treaties. *See* treaties *below*
GATT and **90,** 342
Head of State, immunity, jurisdiction **118,** 294-7
interaction between State and federal legislation **86,** 174-5
international law obligations
obligation to meet **101,** 287
federal authorities' responsibility **118,** 46
international personality **55,** 417, **68,** 200-1, 237-8, 252
constituent States **52,** 331, **68,** 238
interprovincial **84,** 690-2
jurisdiction
child care cases **92,** 620-35
elections to federal Parliament **103,** 245-58
exhaustion of State remedies **95,** 501-2
maritime claims liability **107,** 133-6
matters affecting federal government **101,** 265-6
matters affecting representatives of other countries **101,** 265
matters arising under treaty **101,** 262-5
primacy of federal appeal court **115,** 542
territorial **101,** 266-8

subject-matter jurisdiction distinguished **103,** 246-7, 256, 257-8
tort, domicile of victim **101,** 527
legislative powers **90,** 61, 73, 93, 96-7, 101, 104, 108-10, 111, 112, 135-6
airspace **90,** 253
concurrent, conflicting legislation **112,** 419-20, 706-9, 722-3
constituent State **91,** 72-3
continental shelf **91,** 210
customary international law **90,** 198
extraterritorial legislation **70,** 58-60, 66-8, 89-90, 101
international law, breach **90,** 208, 211
international law, conflict of subsequent legislation **90,** 210-11
power to bind federal government **90,** 49-50
source **90,** 208
territorial **91,** 13
territorial sea **91,** 210
treaties **90,** 199
continental shelf **91,** 210
determination
courts and **90,** 81, 83, 88, 91
criteria **90,** 81-2, 84-9
distribution **115,** 468, 557-9
federal **90,** 80-9, **91,** 72-3, 101
federal legislature's power to restrict State legislature **112,** 418-19, 424, 548, 706-21
fisheries outside territorial waters **101,** 173-4
just terms, need for **112,** 548
'peace, welfare and good government' **112,** 422
'people of any race for whom it is deemed necessary to make special laws' **112,** 702-5
source **90,** 208
territorial sea **91,** 210
waste lands, over **112,** 422, 452-4, 514-15, 577-8
membership **85,** 58
nature **39,** 122, 129, **44,** 8-25
Province, immunity, jurisdiction **63,** 70
representation, federal organs **115,** 154-7
reserved powers doctrine **68,** 241, 335-6, 370
sovereignty
duality **91,** 73, 101, **125,** 347-8
extraterritorial legislation and **91,** 72-3, 97-8, 101
State immunity, jurisdiction, entitlement
constituent States **52,** 330-1, **87,** 39-41, **111,** 608-10
act on behalf of State **111,** 608
State responsibility **118,** 46, **119,** 634, 639, 654-5
territorial sea **86,** 599-600
federation, effect **51,** 133-5, 159-63, 216
jurisdiction **70,** 58-60, 66-8, 89-90, 101, **90,** 242, **125,** 351-6
legislative powers **91,** 210
seabed and subsoil, ownership **125,** 460-3
sovereignty over **51,** 39-80, **69,** 36-41, 54-5, 58, 67, 71, 73-4, 77-88, 111, 113-19, 125, **70,** 58, 66, 68-9, 97, 100, **86,** 599-600, **90,** 242-3, 260, **125,** 347-51, 398-401
territory **91,** 413-15, 424. *See also* boundaries *above*
airspace, legislative powers **90,** 253
internal adjustments **86,** 185-208

federal State (*cont.*)
treaties **90,** 199
conclusion **52,** 330-1
constituent States, between. *See* constituent States, treaties between *above*
constitutional requirments, referendum **75,** 102-6
dissolution of federation, effect **52,** 86, **55,** 90-2
federal clause **68,** 200, 297-9, 303, 315, 342, 379, 395, 424, 455-6, 500
implementation **90,** 61, 73, 93, 96-7, 101, 104, 108-10, 111, 112, 135-6, **104,** 429, 496, **106,** 314-15
prior consultation with constituent State governments **101,** 249-50
transfer of powers exercised by constituent State **108,** 652
treaty-making power **52,** 330-1, **72,** 655-8, **83,** 157, **87,** 163-4
federalism 85, 264
Fiji, government of, recognition **80,** 2-10
Filfla 81, 280, 282-3, 352, 365, 401, 411
Finland
censorship **70,** 298-304
claim, sampling methodology **109,** 71 n. 14
conscientious objection
pardon, implication **94,** 395
right to decline military service **94,** 389-95, 397-9
continental shelf legislation **41,** 208
freedom of conscience. *See also* conscientious objection *above*
atheists **62,** 271-8
freedom of expression, censorship **70,** 298-304
human rights, alleged breach **62,** 271-8
International Covenant on Civil and Political Rights (ICCPR) (1966)
conscientious objectors and **118,** 139-45
municipal courts and **114,** 346-7
religious education and **62,** 271-7
judicial review, military disciplinary procedure **96,** 651
law of
Extraordinary Remedies in Administrative Affairs Act **94,** 398-9
Law 647/85 (Temporary Amendment to the Act on Unarmed and Civilian Service), compatibility with International Covenant on Civil and Political Rights **118,** 139-45
Law 42/1990 (Wilderness Act), purpose **114,** 333-8
Penal Code, sexual morality provision **70,** 298-304
Unarmed and Alternative Service Act 1969 **94,** 389, 398-9
military disciplinary procedure
compatibility with International Covenant for Civil and Political Rights (ICCPR) (1966) **96,** 650-60
judicial review **96,** 651
religious education **62,** 271-8
Sami rights
enjoyment of own culture
measures affecting **115,** 316-18
reindeer husbandry, effect of logging and road construction **115,** 316-18
Sweden, Arbitration Agreement (1926/1953) **46,** 169
Union of Free Thinkers **62,** 271-8
Finland, Gulf of
delimitation **41,** 160
USSR–Finland Boundary Agreement **41,** 208

fish. *See* lobsters; tuna, measures to protect
fisheries. *See also* European Community (EC), fish quotas; European Economic Community (EEC) fisheries policy; fishing zones
archipelagic states **56,** 194
boundaries, State succession and **83,** 37
boundary river, regulation **47,** 113-15
closing line **82,** 605, 639, 640
coastal States **55,** 316, **56,** 86, 132
natural resources **56,** 86, 132
preferential rights **55,** 171-5, 258-63, 265-8, 275, 333, **56,** 159, 164-7, 168-9, 220
conservation and management measures **55,** 206-7, **56,** 113, 118-19, 149-51, 160-1, 164-5, 170, 184, 191-2, 260-1, 275, 283-7, 303-4, 308-9, 322, 344, **82,** 606, 638, 641-2, 658, **99,** 463. *See also* Straddling Stocks and Highly Migratory Fish Stocks Agreement (1995)
definition **123,** 220-3, 237-40, 243, 259, 291-302, 311-15, 325-6
applicable law **123,** 271-2, 291-302, 303-4, 311-18, 325-9, 419-30, 448-52
'conservation' and 'management' distinguished **123,** 238
FAO Code of Conduct for Responsible Fisheries (1995) **123,** 297-8
development of concept **123,** 237-40
enforcement on the high seas **123,** 219-20, 225-6, 471-6
use of force **123,** 225-6, 346-7, 350-3
FAO Code of Conduct for Responsible Fisheries (1995) **123,** 295-8, 326-7
FAO Fishing Vessels Agreement (1993) **123,** 311, 312, 326
freedom of the seas and **123,** 219-27, 229-30, 269-72, 277-8, 354-9
high seas. *See* freedom of the seas and *above*
hot pursuit and **123,** 420-1
International Technical Conference on the Conservation of the Living Resources of the Sea (1955) **123,** 238
Kyoto Declaration (1995) **123,** 298
Law of the Sea Convention (1982), need for conformity with **82,** 628, 629-30, 642, **123,** 293-4, 316, 326-7, 428
legality, need for **123,** 252
Mediterranean **123,** 298-9
NAFO provisions. *See* NAFO (Future Multilateral Cooperation in the Northwest Atlantic Fisheries Convention) (1979)
right to take, definition distinguished **123,** 222
Santiago Conference on the Exploration and Conservation of the Marine Resources of the South Pacific (1952) **123,** 238-9
'special interests' and 'preferential requirements' **55,** 333
State practice **123,** 221-3, 297-300, 303-4, 314, 327
in territorial waters of foreign State **59,** 343-4, **63,** 602-3
UNCLOS I **123,** 300
UNCLOS III **123,** 293-4
contiguous zone and **55,** 345
continental shelf, continental shelf and **55,** 207, **56,** 134, 189
Danube **116,** 226
development of law relating to, increased concern for management **82,** 619
dispute
arbitration **56,** 165
capture and sinking of ship, war risk, whether **48,** 469-75
equitable apportionment, negotiations as basis **56,** 173, 176-7
European Economic Community **59,** 480-2, 484-8, **74,** 143, 145-8
foreign fishing boat

fisheries (*cont.*)
licence **91,** 394-5
tax on sale of fish, legality **91,** 394-7
green turtle, protection, jurisdiction **91,** 384-5
high seas
historic rights **55,** 333-4, **71,** 168
jurisdiction **55,** 146-8, 206, 207, 283, 343. *See also* conservation and management measures *above*
historic **81,** 302, **82,** 605
high seas **55,** 333-4, **71,** 168
Red Sea **114,** 137, **119,** 440, 447-53
jurisdiction **55,** 278, 281-7, 296, 301, 318-20, **59,** 352-3, **69,** 36-40, 54-5, 58, 67, 71, 73, 77-88, 110-26, **70,** 110-16, **71,** 366-8, **73,** 173-8, **74,** 143-8
coastal States **56,** 86, 132
declaration of, 'Santiago Declaration' (1952) **55,** 221-3
definition **56,** 186-7
determination by negotiation **56,** 157-9, 198, 206-7
extension **55,** 388, 396, **56,** 90, 109, 188-92
agreement **56,** 120
unilateral **55,** 4, 289-94, 300, 319-21, 331-2, 334, 372, **56,** 39, 83, 132-3, 139, 158, 188, 217
extent **55,** 293, 320-1, 330-2, **56,** 134, 188-92
basis **56,** 170
delimitation **55,** 331, **56,** 172
twelve-mile limit **55,** 392, 406, **56,** 109, 155, 162, 183
FRG–Iceland (1961) **56,** 78, 79, 84, 100-1, 103-8, 109-10, 121-2, 124, 130, 132-5, 149-50, 151, 157-9, 180, 198-9, 201, 206-7, 255-7
high seas **55,** 146-8, 206, 207, 283, 343
Iceland–UK (1961) **55,** 343, 346-8, 349, 356-7
Exchange of Notes (1961) **55,** 189-94, 209-15, 217, 219-27, 248-56, 307, 308, 323-5, 327, 328-9, 335-7, 341-3, 346, 348-53, 355, 357-8, 362-70, 383, 387-90, 399-406
interim agreement (1973) **55,** 379-81, 390-2, 395
Icelandic waters **55,** 374, 376-9
limits distinguished **55,** 357
NAFO (1979). *See* NAFO (Future Multilateral Cooperation in the Northwest Atlantic Fisheries Convention) (1979)
mutual fishing rights **74,** 144-8
natural resource of State **55,** 171, 219
negotiating rights, EEC **82,** 669
non-coastal States, historic rights **55,** 386
North East Atlantic Fisheries Convention (1959) **55,** 206, 303-4, 346, 371
denunciation, Netherlands **78,** 12
implementation, Netherlands **78,** 10-11
objects **56,** 118
quotas **78,** 10-11
individual **78,** 10-11
national **78,** 10-11
offshore waters **69,** 36-7, 55, 58, 77-88
preferential rights **55,** 171-5, 258-63, 265-8, 275, 333, **56,** 159, 164-7, 168-9, 170, 220
exclusive distinguished **56,** 167-8
protection legislation, extraterritorial effect **59,** 347-9, **70,** 110-16
quotas. *See* North East Atlantic Fisheries Convention (1959), quotas *above*

regulations
definition **82,** 617-22, 624, 629-30
fish processing plant, admissibility **82,** 629-30, 659
'fisheries laws and regulations' **110,** 772
'fishing' **82,** 648
'operations connected to fishing' **110,** 754
'fishing vessel' **82,** 621-2
'fishing waters' **108,** 634
'foreign fishing boat' **86,** 695
statement of policy, as **82,** 625, 626
undertaking to respect **82,** 602
rights
agreements, FRG/Iceland **56,** 78, 79, 84, 100-1, 103-8, 109-10, 121-2, 124, 130, 132-5, 155-7, 180, 198-9, 201
bilateral treaty, under **82,** 602-7
coastal States **55,** 171-5, 223-5, 258-63, 265-8, 275, 333, **56,** 86, 159, 164-7, 168-9, 220
conflicting interests, reconciliation **56,** 171, 176-7
drying rights **82,** 603
equitable adjustment **56,** 172, 176-7
filleting, 'fishing', whether **82,** 612, 618
international regulation **56,** 181
landing rights **82,** 643-4
preferential. *See* preferential rights *above*
reciprocity **82,** 606, 620
territorial sea **56,** 117, 189
treaty provision, non-discrimination **82,** 616-17, 626, 646-7, 657
sedentary **41,** 124, **71,** 170
territorial sea **55,** 208, 246, 321, **56,** 153-4, 189, 215-16
distinction **55,** 246, 258-9
treaty, absence of **88,** 685
fishing. *See* exclusive economic zone (EEZ), refuelling of fishing vessel; exclusive fishing zone (EFZ); fisheries; fishing zones; maritime delimitation, relevant/special circumstances
fishing practices 114, 137, **119,** 440-3, 447-53
fishing zones 55, 246-53, **62,** 115, **69,** 77-88, **71,** 92-110, 168-9, 188, 191, 194, **73,** 174-8, **74,** 142-8, **91,** 375-8. *See also* contiguous zone; exclusive economic zone (EEZ); exclusive fishing zone (EFZ); fisheries
12-mile limit **99,** 461-3
territorial sea extension, substitute for **99,** 461
50-mile limit, *Fisheries Jurisdiction* cases **99,** 462
200-mile limit **99,** 462-4
customary international law **99,** 462-3, **101,** 173
Law of the Sea Convention (1982) **99,** 463
adjacent to coast **92,** 678-82
200 miles, whether **92,** 682
applicable law
customary international law **99,** 495-6, 558
law applicable to EEZ **99,** 427
Law of the Sea Convention (1982) **99,** 427, 474
concept
development
European Fisheries Convention (1964) **99,** 462
pre-1950s **99,** 460-1

fishing zones (*cont.*)
UNCLOS I **99,** 461, 470
UNCLOS III **99,** 463
general recognition **99,** 461, 462
Law of the Sea Convention (1982), absence **99,** 463
legal, whether **99,** 463-4, 566
continental shelf distinguished **99,** 566
definition **59,** 355, **91,** 375, 376
delimitation **67,** 24, 65-6, 115-17, 146-7, 191-204, 241, **71,** 86, 89, 102-5, 110-11, 113-15, 125, 143-4, 167-71, 194-6, 211
applicable law. *See* applicable law *above*
criteria, equidistance/special circumstances **99,** 429-32
interim agreement **71,** 110-11
principles **55,** 339
relevant factors
conservation **71,** 85, 88, 125, 170, 211
geographical features **57,** 65
historical usage **57,** 65, **71,** 167-9
sedentary species **71,** 170
EEZ and **99,** 460-3
derived from, whether **99,** 566
distinction **99,** 462-3, 656
obligation to conserve fishing resources **99,** 463
establishment of **56,** 167, 176-7
European Fisheries Convention (1964) **59,** 352-3
exclusive. *See* exclusive fishing zone (EFZ)
extension **55,** 300
islands **62,** 115, **99,** 668
jurisdiction over **63,** 353, 601-3
overlapping
agreement not to exercise jurisdiction against vessels of other State, Australia–Indonesia Provisional Fisheries Arrangement (1981) **101,** 167-9
legislative powers **101,** 172-4
preferential **41,** 124
regulations, power to enforce **86,** 699-700
rights in, preservation **86,** 699
unilateral establishment **99,** 462, 463
Walvis Bay **91,** 375-8
flag desecration. *See* freedom of expression, flag desecration and
flag State. *See* high seas, jurisdiction, flag State; ships, jurisdiction, flag State
flags of convenience 54, 226-8, **77,** 414-16, **120,** 593-4
flight recorders. *See also* Chicago Convention on International Civil Aviation (1944), Annex 13 (accident and incident investigation)
disclosure of transcript **120,** 577-84
Fonseca Bay 83, 72-3
applicable law
evidence, wishes relating to distinguished **97,** 307-8, 554-6
general law of the sea **97,** 631
historic title **97,** 582-90
'peaceful and continuous exercise of State authority' **97,** 582
'rules of international law applicable between parties including, where pertinent, the provisions of the General Treaty of Peace [1980]' **97,** 278, 306-7, 473-4, 502, 550, 581-96

ex aequo et bono, exclusion **97,** 306-7
land and islands disputes, distinction, whether **97,** 582
'pertinence' for court to determine **97,** 307-8, 550
ratione personae restriction **97,** 550
uti possidetis **97,** 474, 505, 550-4, 582, 590-2
customary international law **97,** 550-2
defined by parties, whether **97,** 551
uti possidetis de facto distinguished **97,** 551
Central American Court of Justice (*El Salvador/Nicaragua*) (1917) **97,** 297, 505-20
closed sea **97,** 507
English translation **97,** 506-7
historic bay **97,** 507-13, 628 n. 1
challenge **97,** 663-73
Honduras, opposability **97,** 37
ICJ and
effect of ICJ decision on **97,** 630
interpretation or application by, whether **97,** 630
precedent **97,** 516-17
'subsidiary means for the determination of the rule of law' **97,** 517
Nicaragua, effect on **97,** 513, 516-17
res judicata, whether **97,** 37, 516-17
status of bay
evidence of **97,** 506, 511
proportional ownership **97,** 511
closing line
baseline **97,** 523
Central American Court of Justice (*El Salvador/Nicaragua*) (1917) **97,** 520
'coast' **97,** 523, 524
coastal States' practice **97,** 520
inner/outer gulf theory **97,** 520
maritime spaces outside
delimitation, possibility **97,** 524-5
El Salvador/Nicaragua territorial waters, exclusion **97,** 524
joint entitlement **97,** 524
territorial sea **97,** 522-4
tripartite presence **97,** 523
co-ownership **97,** 225, 511, 512-16, 628
absence of protest **97,** 517
administrative boundaries, absence **97,** 514-15, 517
agreement, need for **97,** 670
continued and peaceful exercise **97,** 515, 517
customary law **97,** 513
division, absence **97,** 515-16
as joint sovereignty **97,** 513-14
maritime belt, exemption **97,** 511, 521
maritime inspection belt, exemption **97,** 511, 513
maritime spaces outside closing line **97,** 524-5
State succession and **97,** 514-16
uti possidetis **97,** 517-18
sui generis nature **97,** 521
community of interests **97,** 518-19
continental shelf
agreement, need for **97,** 524

Fonseca Bay (*cont.*)
delimitation, possibility **97,** 524
inherent right **97,** 524
joint entitlement **97,** 524
definition **97,** 221-2, 502-4
delimitation
absence **97,** 515-16, 628, 629
applicable law, agreement on the basis of international law **97,** 631-2
Central American Court of Justice (1916) (*El Salvador/Nicaragua*) **97,** 223-6
El Salvador's acceptance **97,** 522
equidistance
equitable result **97,** 675
historic title and **97,** 675
Law of the Sea Convention (1982) **97,** 674-5
equidistance/special circumstances, islands **97,** 675
Honduras/Nicaragua Mixed Commission (1900) **97,** 222-3, 517-18, 521
limited extent **97,** 225-6
uti possidetis, relevance **97,** 518
ICJ
jurisdiction, whether **97,** 519
Nicaragua, effect of decision on **97,** 39-41
legal status, decision on as precondition for **97,** 519
possibility **97,** 631, 674
practical difficulties consequent on **97,** 518-19
passage and access, need for agreement **97,** 519-20
'States bordering an enclosed or semi-enclosed sea', relevance **97,** 676
El Salvador/Honduras, Cruz–Letona Convention **97,** 297
El Tigre **97,** 482-6
British occupation **97,** 483-4, 621-2
Honduran occupation **97,** 482-3, 485-6
El Salvador, acquiescence **97,** 482-3
El Salvador, protest **97,** 484-5
USA, sale to **97,** 484-5
exclusive economic zone (EEZ)
joint entitlement **97,** 524
proclamation, need for **97,** 524
historic bay **83,** 72-3, **97,** 224-5, 504-9, 628-32, 649-73
Central American Court of Justice (*El Salvador/Nicaragua*) (1917) **97,** 507-13, 628 n. 1
as closed sea **97,** 509, 512-13
declaration of status as **97,** 629-30
Gidel **97,** 509
Oppenheim (3rd edn) (1920) **97,** 664
State succession and **97,** 629-30
territorial rights **97,** 629
territorial waters within, possibility **97,** 524
UNCLOS I **97,** 664-5
history **97,** 505-9
Bryan–Chamorro Treaty (1914) **97,** 506
Reales Cédulas (1563/4), historic title, whether **97,** 585-9
titulos ejidales **97,** 560-4
innocent passage

gulf outside maritime belts **97,** 521
maritime belts, through **97,** 521
internal waters **97,** 511-12, 523-4
Honduras, acts of authority **97,** 622
'not territorial sea' **97,** 521
islands **97,** 297
El Salvador, claim
Central American Court of Justice (1916) **97,** 472-3
Constitution 1983 and **97,** 473, 521
historical title **97,** 475-6
'in accordance with the provisions of international law' **97,** 473
El Tigre. *See* El Tigre *above*
Honduras, claim, *effectivités* **97,** 476-8
Meanguera/Meanguerita. *See* Meanguera/Meanguerita *below*
terra nullius, whether **97,** 474, 481-2, 593
juridical bay **97,** 509
maritime belts
3-mile
exclusive jurisdiction **97,** 506, 508-9
territorial sea, whether **97,** 508
inspection belt **97,** 506, 511, 673
acquiescence **97,** 673
legal status **97,** 669-70
maritime spaces **97,** 496-534
Honduras/Nicaragua Delimitation Agreement (1900) **97,** 520-1
Meanguera/Meanguerita
Cruz–Letona Convention (1884) **97,** 487
El Salvador
absence of claims **97,** 627
acts of authority **97,** 488-90, 622
Honduran protest **97,** 491-3
El Salvador protest, Honduran failure to respond **97,** 488, 490, 495, 624-5
Honduran acts of authority, El Salvador protest **97,** 486-7
Honduras/Nicaragua Delimitation Agreement (1900) and **97,** 493-5
insular unity, whether **97,** 486, 495, 626
'island in dispute' **97,** 620-1, 622
agreement, need for **97,** 631
critical date **97,** 623
Meanguerita
'capable of appropriation' **97,** 486, 626-7
as dependency **97,** 486, 495, 625-7
terra nullius, whether **97,** 626, 627
uti possidetis (1821) **97,** 625
transfer of title **97,** 624-5
uti possidetis (1821) **97,** 596-622
documentary evidence **97,** 598-603, 605-7, 610-21
ecclesiastical jurisdiction **97,** 607-12, 618-20
resettlement of Indians **97,** 603-5
Zelaya–Castellanos Convention (1886) **97,** 487
overlapping jurisdictions **97,** 225
proportional ownership **97,** 511
rights in, basis, State succession **97,** 500

Fonseca Bay (*cont.*)
status
evidence of
Honduras/Nicaragua Delimitation Agreement (1900) **97,** 506, 511
practice of coastal States **97,** 506
open seas doctrine and **97,** 673-4
pluri-State **97,** 509-10
'internal waters' concept and **97,** 520-1
pre-1821 **97,** 669
territorial seas, sum of **97,** 649, 673-5
territorial sea
consensual basis **97,** 631
delimitation, agreement, need for **97,** 631
innocent passage, right of **97,** 506, 521
uso inocente **97,** 508-9
as internal waters **97,** 523
outside closing line **97,** 522-4
Food and Agriculture Organization (FAO). *See also* Uruguay Round, Agreement on Agriculture
Code of Conduct for Responsible Fisheries (1995) **123,** 295-8, 326
'conservation and management measures' **123,** 297-8
Credit Union **40,** 422-5
Director-General, rule-making powers **48,** 253
employment contract, claims under **71,** 240
expert, immunity of **71,** 563
Fishing Vessels Agreement (1993) **123,** 311, 312, 326
immunity, jurisdiction **71,** 241
representatives accredited to **71,** 567-9, 571-2
exercise of functions, limited to **71,** 568-9, 571-2
personality **87,** 6
applicable law **87,** 3
sovereign powers **87,** 6
privileges and immunities **87,** 3-10
acta jure imperii **87,** 6
applicable law **87,** 6
commercial acts **87,** 6
purpose of transaction **87,** 6
diplomatic missions as bench-mark **87,** 5
immunity from suit, Headquarters Agreement (Italy/FAO) (1950) **101,** 388-9
Member States' Constitutions as limiting factor **87,** 5
nature of transaction **87,** 6-7
organizational and administrative act, acquisition of premises **87,** 4
par in parem non habet jurisdictionem **87,** 7
food supply agency, agency or instrumentality of a foreign State **63,** 371, 376-7, 495-7, 569-72, **64,** 445-6, 447
force majeure **40,** 267, 272, 283, **41,** 142, **63,** 166, **71,** 666, 670, 680, **72,** 175-7, **78,** 12, **80,** 671, **82,** 160, 171, 551-3, **83,** 530-2, 554, 583, **86,** 268-70, 273-4, **93,** 381-2
absolute impossibility **93,** 381, 386
act of God, accession to independence **47,** 102-4
changed circumstances distinguished **86,** 270-1
contributory act and **96,** 318
duty of care **93,** 381-2, 386
effect **86,** 271

suspension of rights and obligations **83,** 531
termination of contract **82,** 549, **83,** 531-2
enforcement of EC Regulations and **117,** 318
government intervention as **64,** 199-202, 204, 205-7, 372-3. *See also* contract, breach, government action leading to, responsibility for; contract, frustration, government intervention as
State or State agency as party to contract and **64,** 199-202, 205-7
hostage crisis **84,** 570
impossibility of contract as result of Iraq's invasion of Kuwait **109,** 594, 595
liability of bank for loss of deposit in foreign branch **107,** 207-10, 216
loss to lie where it falls **107,** 216
non-renewal of funds by Congress **113,** 497-8
revolution, State responsibility **106,** 496
Rules of the Refined Sugar Association **64,** 199, 204, 205-7, 372-3
State contract and **63,** 166, 276, **72,** 175-7, **86,** 469-70
political turmoil **63,** 267
State responsibility and **82,** 551-3, **96,** 318, **106,** 496
termination of employment contract, State immunity, jurisdiction **107,** 370
threat, chemical weapons, deployment **106,** 398-9
tortious act, as defence **86,** 545
treaty law, law of State responsibility compared **82,** 549
force, prohibition on the threat or use of 55, 194, **61,** 543-4, 569-70, 577-9, 580-1, 589, **76,** 444-5, 452-3, 457, 485-8, 490, 719, **82,** 679-80. *See also* civil war; countermeasures; rebellion; revolution; terrorism; war
aid to insurgents **76,** 452-3
Charter of the Organization of American States **76,** 55, 637
customary international law **76,** 432-40, 485-8, 490-1, 517, 533, 864, **91,** 569
Declaration on Principles of International Law concerning Friendly Relations and Co-operation among States **76,** 435
deterrence as threat **110,** 475-6
economic coercion **91,** 569-71
economic pressure distinguished **91,** 571
falling short of armed attack **76,** 485
Hague Convention on the Limitation of Use of Force for Recovery of Debts (1907) **46,** 465-6
Helsinki Final Act (1975) **76,** 434
human rights, defence of **49,** 69
indirect **76,** 667-78
International Law Commission **76,** 638
measures short of **56,** 139
military manoeuvres **76,** 452
Montevideo Convention on Rights and Duties of States (1933) **76,** 434
nuclear weapons, possession **110,** 196-7
Sixth International Conference of American States (1928) **76,** 434
supply of arms **76,** 453
supply of funds **76,** 453
treaties and **61,** 553-4, 556-9
UN Charter **76,** 55, 637
UN practice **76,** 670-5. *See also* United Nations General Assembly (UNGA) Resolutions
Vienna Convention on the Law of Treaties (1969) **91,** 569
forced or compulsory labour, freedom from
Abolition of Forced Labour Convention (No 105) (1957), strike, right to **90,** 189
complaint of non-compliance, political character **36,** 392

forced or compulsory labour, freedom from (*cont.*)
economic development and **36,** 415-16, 418, 419-21, 423-4
Forced Labour Convention (No 29) (1930) **36,** 395, 405, 425
compliance
Liberia **36,** 352-427
staged **36,** 395-6
'forced or compulsory labour' **36,** 395
Geneva Conventions (1949) **83,** 137, 140-1, 148
Labour Inspection Convention (No 81)(1947) **36,** 419
military service as **74,** 303
prison work as **67,** 555-6
forced exile. *See* expulsion of national
forcible abduction/unlawful arrest 61, 192-3, 198-9, 200-1, 205, 208-11, 214, **68,** 10-14, 31, 45, **90,** 663-71, 673, 680-1, 683-5, 687, 688-90, 693-7, **91,** 474-5, 489 n. 1, 519-20, 531
abuse of process **95,** 406, **111,** 556, 561-3
arrest on foreign soil **61,** 192-3, 198-9, 200-1, 205, 208-11, 214, **68,** 10-14, 31, 45
breach of
comity **111,** 565
due process. *See* due process, violation *below*
individual's rights **111,** 565
international law **95,** 408, **103,** 214, **111,** 565
laws of foreign State **111,** 565
OAS Charter **90,** 661 n. 16, 665-6, 680
treaty **90,** 647, 661, 662, 671, 673, 680-1, **91,** 475, 519-30, **95,** 358, 360-8, **99,** 174-7, **107,** 433, **121,** 597
UN Charter **90,** 661 n. 16, 665-6, 680
clean hands doctrine **95,** 442
comity **95,** 403-4, 408
constitutional issue, whether **98,** 107 n. 11
court's power to enquire **95,** 383-416
customary international law **90,** 695
jurisdiction, effect on **86,** 529
deportation and **104,** 64 n. 4
domestic and international distinguished **90,** 675
due process, violation **90,** 645, 655-7, 662, **99,** 171-4
'shocking to the conscience' **104,** 63, 83
expulsion as **90,** 646, 663, **95,** 326-7, **104,** 62-4
extradition and **45,** 91-107, **104,** 62-4, **111,** 550-83
consent or acquiescence of extraditing State **90,** 662-5, 674, 691-2, **91,** 498. *See also* protest *below*
effect **91,** 498
ex post facto **90,** 680
extradition agreement, relevance **36,** 71-5, **111,** 487, 490, **121,** 597
in absence of extradition proceedings **45,** 91-2, 95-7
specific prohibition of forcible abduction, need for **107,** 433, **121,** 597
failure to observe extradition/deportation procedures **103,** 214-16, **111,** 562-3, 566
absence of authority to enforce extradition treaty **42,** 233-8
Bozano **111,** 486-7
Savarkar **103,** 215
Sinclair **103,** 215-16
Stocké **111,** 485-6
Youssef Said Abu Dourrah **36,** 75-6, **103,** 216

foreign relations, executive responsibility **104,** 63-4
from Swaziland **68,** 7-14
general principle of international law **90,** 677, 679-80, **95,** 366
human rights protection and **95,** 441
International Covenant on Civil and Political Rights (ICCPR) (1966) **95,** 326-7
international law, breach other than of treaty **91,** 519-20
jurisdiction, effect on **36,** 279, 304-8, **45,** 91-107, **61,** 192-3, 194-202, 210-11, 219, **68,** 9-14, 31, 45, **77,** 333-4, 359-76, **86,** 527-32, **88,** 265-8, **90,** 645-8, 652-67, 673, 674, 684-5, **91,** 474-5, 489 n. 1, 519-20, 531, **95,** 331, 349, 426-45, **103,** 208-18, **104,** 62-4, **107,** 433-46, **111,** 485-92, **118,** 642. *See also* arrest, illegal
abuse of power amounting to abuse of process, whether **111,** 556, 561-3
applicable law, *lex fori* **95,** 426
aut dedere aut punire/judicare **95,** 364
competence to determine **111,** 536, 557-63, 575-83
Atkinson **111,** 558-60, 576-7, 581-2
Bennett **111,** 556, 557-62, 564-6, 567-8, 577-83
bringing into/extradition from distinguished **111,** 560-1, 568, 581
consent of foreign government, effect **91,** 498
customary international law **68,** 10, 12-13, **86,** 529, **95,** 365, 367 n. 15, 378 n. 34
discretion to stay proceedings **95,** 390, 408-16, **103,** 209, 216-18
fault, relevance **86,** 530-2
Harvard Research Draft Convention on Jurisdiction in Respect of Crime **95,** 365, 377
Harvard Research Project (1935) **36,** 69-70, 73
individual's right to challenge **36,** 305-6, **95,** 404
jurisdiction based on subsequent event **107,** 446
kidnapping **45,** 90-107
Republic of the United Netherlands (1581-1795) **95,** 429-38
speciality doctrine **95,** 363
State practice **68,** 12-13, **95,** 349
armed forces, use of abroad **88,** 183-4
England **68,** 12
France **68,** 13
Israel **68,** 13
Union of South Africa **68,** 10-14
USA **68,** 12-13
treaty, contravention of **91,** 475, 519-30
evidence thus acquired **91,** 475
violation of international law **36,** 62-71, **86,** 529
other than of treaty **91,** 519-20
jurisprudence **95,** 390, 396-8, **103,** 212-14
Afouneh **36,** 61
Alvarez-Machain **95,** 397-8, **107,** 434-5, 445-6
Atkinson **111,** 558-60, 576-7, 581-2
Bennett **111,** 556, 557-62, 564-6, 567-8, 577-83
Brewster **36,** 63-4, **103,** 212
Donelly v. *Milligan* **36,** 71-2
Driver **95,** 385-6, 389-90, 411, 412, **103,** 212
Ebrahim **95,** 396
Eichman **36,** 23-4, 57-76, 304-8, **45,** 103
Elliott **36,** 60, **95,** 388-9, 406-7
Healey **95,** 410
Jolis **36,** 68
Katz **36,** 61

forcible abduction/unlawful arrest (*cont.*)
Ker-Frisbie **36,** 61, 65-6, 71, **90,** 645, 647, 655-7, 660, 661-2, 673-7, 692, **103,** 212-13, **107,** 433-5, **121,** 611
Lopez **36,** 67-8
Mackeson **95,** 383-4, 406-7, 410
Moevao **95,** 398, 405
Nelson and Brand **36,** 60
Noluli **95,** 426
Ramotse en 19 Ander **95,** 441
Rauscher **36,** 64-5
Reed **111,** 489
Robertson **95,** 440-1
Savarkar **36,** 62
Schmidt **111,** 489-90
Scott **36,** 62, **103,** 211-12
Sinclair **95,** 386-8
Susannah Scott **36,** 59-60, **95,** 386
Toscanino **95,** 396-7, 442-4, **103,** 213-14, **107,** 434-6, **111,** 488
Wilson **111,** 488-9
Yunis **111,** 488
jus cogens/peremptory norm, whether **107,** 435 n. 5
male captus bene detentus **45,** 104
preservation of friendly international relations **95,** 442
protest **45,** 92-3, **90,** 64, 647. *See also* extradition and, consent or acquiescence of extraditing State *above*
form **90,** 688-90, **95,** 361
need for **95,** 349
relevance **90,** 663-71, 673, 680-1, 683-5, 687, 693-7, **95,** 358, 366, 367 n. 15
withdrawal **90,** 690
relevant factors
coercion **111,** 567-8
motivation **107,** 444-5
physical force **103,** 214, **111,** 564-6
torture **107,** 435-6, 444-6
trickery **111,** 483-92, 566-8, 582-3
remedies **86,** 529-30
dependence on subsequent treatment **104,** 63
diplomatic channels **95,** 404
executive responsibility **95,** 367
foreign State **91,** 500
individual **86,** 530-2, **91,** 500
renunciation of entitlement **86,** 530
request for repatriation, need for, customary international law **90,** 695
return of kidnapped person **90,** 665, 671, 687-8, 693-6, **95,** 358, 361, 367-8
State practice **95,** 367 n. 15
Roman law **95,** 426-8
Roman-Dutch law **95,** 428-38
rule of law, breach **95,** 408
State practice **95,** 349
armed forces, use of abroad **88,** 183-4
State responsibility and **86,** 529-30, **90,** 645-6, 662, **95,** 332, 359-60, 424-5, **103,** 214
territorial integrity, breach **90,** 696-7, **95,** 368, 373-5, 378 n. 34. *See also* territorial sovereignty, breach *below*

territorial sovereignty, breach **90,** 648, 680, 696-7, **111,** 491-2
treaty, breach **90,** 647, 661, 662, 671, 673, 680-1, **91,** 475, 519-30, **95,** 358, 360-8
evidence thus acquired **91,** 475
treaty, contravention of **91,** 475, 519-30
evidence thus acquired **91,** 475
UN Charter, breach **90,** 661 n. 16, 665-6, 680
foreign affairs. *See* foreign relations
foreign arbitral award, enforcement. *See* arbitral award, enforcement; foreign judgment, enforcement
foreign assistance programme, State immunity in respect of **63,** 230, 344
'foreign country' 87, 549, 578, 100, 526, 531, 537-40, **100,** 553, **122,** 673-7
foreign enlistment 82, 318
foreign governments, inducement of acts of **57,** 25
foreign investment. *See* concession agreement; economic development agreement; investment; joint exploitation agreement; NAFTA (North American Free Trade Agreement); State contract
foreign judges. *See also* letters rogatory
cross-examination of fugitives by **71,** 223
foreign judgment
Iran–US Claims Settlement, General Declaration **81,** 575
res judicata, whether **94,** 365-6
foreign judgment, recognition/enforcement 60, 69-77, **70,** 431-4, **73,** 5, **78,** 600, **81,** 570, 637, **85,** 87, **91,** 314
agreement for
Algeria–France (1964) **80,** 428-30
expropriation, in case of **80,** 428-30
fair hearing, right to **47,** 194-5
France **47,** 63-6, **48,** 84-8
maintenance orders **47,** 189-93, 194-5
patent infringement **48,** 84-8
reciprocity **39,** 462-4
Sweden **62,** 225-8
Switzerland **62,** 228-36
United States **62,** 220-4
award in respect of fraudulent claim to compensation
private law matter **101,** 445-6
stay of execution in foreign court **101,** 445-7
bilateral agreement **101,** 445-7
court's power to amend judgment **106,** 279
effectiveness of judgment, relevance **106,** 279
res judicata **106,** 288, 292
validity of proceedings **106,** 288, 292
critical date, date of judgment **106,** 227
Enforcement of Judgments in Civil and Commercial Matters Convention (1968) **106,** 288
bankruptcy **101,** 348
'civil and commercial matters' **101,** 445-7
implementing legislation **107,** 497-9
'matters relating to tort' **103,** 205
purpose, harmonization of jurisdiction/remedies distinguished **107,** 497-8
European Convention on State Immunity (and Protocol) (Basle) (1972) and **82,** 33, 40
exequatur
need for **106,** 293

foreign judgment, recognition/enforcement (*cont.*)
State immunity **106,** 277-82, 288-91
expropriation without compensation **70,** 433-4
fair trial, relevance **106,** 288
federal State, in **103,** 570-1
foreign law, evidence of **43,** 53-4, 55, 59-60, 74
international law, need for conformity with
restraint order in aid of confiscation order made by foreign court, territorial jurisdiction and **122,** 518-24, 526-8
State immunity rules **65,** 202
maintenance orders **47,** 189-93
as political decision **78,** 107
public order/public policy/*ordre public* **70,** 431, 433, **73,** 5-6, **106,** 227-8, 288
reciprocity **65,** 204, **82,** 40
recognition of international organization **107,** 424-6
comity **107,** 424-6
State succession and **89,** 11-14
tax judgment **38,** 118, **42,** 114-18
treaty basis **65,** 204
State succession and **44,** 291-2
winding-up proceedings **77,** 30
foreign law. *See also* confiscation, legislation; expropriation/nationalization, extraterritorial effect; expropriation/nationalization, territorial limitation
as applicable law **104,** 183
conflict with domestic law **104,** 502-7
foreign State compulsion as defence **104,** 502-7, 601-4
choice of law, incorporation of foreign law distinguished **96,** 79
employment contract in accordance with, application of local law **82,** 22-3
enforcement. *See* foreign law, recognition/enforcement
evidence of **43,** 52-3, 59-60, 62, 74, **44,** 363, **72,** 448-51, 458-65, **73,** 248-9, **78,** 518-19, 595, 597, **84,** 84, **117,** 575
absence of **64,** 326, **125,** 692
books **103,** 285-7
expert **72,** 448-51, 458-65, **73,** 238, 248-9, **78,** 518-19, 595, 597, **103,** 285-7
extradition **74,** 467-71, **90,** 413-15, **119,** 259-60, **122,** 615-18
as fact **117,** 575-8, 581-2, 587, **125,** 692
interpretation **55,** 533, **78,** 595, 599, 609, 631, **117,** 575
US courts, by **66,** 189-91, 257-63, 266-7, 306-10, 323-4, 465-6
judicial notice **81,** 438-40
arbitral tribunal **117,** 575-7
ministers, presumed capacity **66,** 568
motives, judicial examination **66,** 204-6, 291-300, 314-15, 323-4, 349-50, 383-5, 388-98
recognition. *See* foreign law, recognition/enforcement
validity **42,** 22, 24, 25-6
foreign law, recognition/enforcement **52,** 8, 54, 57, 58, 66-7, **60,** 73-6, **66,** 69-71, 77, 96-9, 132-3, 169-72, 196, 215, 250-5, 357-8, 403, 455-6, **69,** 4-6, 9, **71,** 20, 38-9, **72,** 19-26, 33-5, 48, 449, 453-7, 459-60, 467-70, 474-6, **73,** 13-19, 22-5, 227-9, 237-9, 243-7, 589-90, 592-3, **78,** 464, 480, 597-607, 627, **88,** 307. *See also* act of State; political question doctrine
act of State and **64,** 344, **66,** 189-91, 257-63, 266-7, 306-10, 322-4, 465-6, **78,** 599, **88,** 306, **116,** 568-78
confiscatory legislation. *See* confiscatory legislation *below*

assistance in breach distinguished **104,** 536
in case of
illegal regime **72,** 33-5, 40, 48
unrecognized State/government **39,** 169-72, 235, 368, 370, 394, 396, **73,** 13-19, 22-5, 27, **75,** 678, 683-5, 694-6, **77,** 571, **82,** 409
characterization of action in England **78,** 601
civilized standards, falling below **88,** 307-8
comity and **42,** 22-3, **88,** 308, 310, **104,** 507, **108,** 592
confiscatory legislation **42,** 29-33, 410, 425-30, **43,** 61, **63,** 2-4, 98-9, **64,** 246-8, 694-5, **65,** 84-5, **72,** 18-27, 86-7, 449, 453-7, 459-60, 462, 467-70, 474-6, 559-61, **73,** 243-7, **74,** 153-6, **75,** 275-80, 299-308, **77,** 547-9, **78,** 598, 604-5, **79,** 573-81, **88,** 307, **108,** 591-2
enemy property **74,** 153-6
nationalization measures **47,** 31-9, **65,** 60
property in country of suit **88,** 307
contractual claim under impugnable foreign law **125,** 738–9
direct **75,** 280-2, 292, 298-308, 314, 320-1, 325-30
discriminatory law **64,** 246-8, 374-6, **88,** 307, 317
against nationals in time of war **108,** 591
racially discriminatory legislation **52,** 29
enforcement/recognition distinguished **78,** 597
extradition and **82,** 27
extraterritorial effect
Iraqi legislation in respect of Kuwait **125,** 607-8, 665-8
United States antitrust laws **74,** 39-40, 48-54, 78-82
fiscal, exchange control or revenue law **42,** 410, 425-9, **47,** 40-52, 57-8, **72,** 545, **75,** 280-3, 289, 290-1, 295-6, 299, 301, 304, 320-1, 325-30, **78,** 505, 597-8, 599, 601, 602-3, 605, 606, 607, 615, 627, **84,** 749-51, **104,** 536
guardianship decrees **42,** 26-9
human rights and **75,** 275-7, 279, 295-6, 305, 315, 319, 322, **108,** 554, 591
indirect **75,** 281-3, 290-2, 298-306, 314, 316, 320-1, 325-30
international law, need for conformity with **53,** 367, **57,** 11-12, **108,** 592, **125,** 633-8, 646-50, 680-5, 710-13
human rights law, whether limited to **125,** 633-8, 646-50, 680-5, 710-13, 718-22, 736-9
international organization, grant of immunity to **80,** 35
international public policy and **91,** 253, 254
judicial assistance and **82,** 27, **88,** 306-10, 320-2
judicial discretion **84,** 750, **88,** 308, 309
jurisprudence, *Luther* v. *Sagor* **64,** 264, **116,** 565-7, 587-9, **125,** 638-9
legal validity distinguished **78,** 464, 542, 553-4
morality of law, relevance **104,** 507
motivation of legislature
legislative history **88,** 308, 309
relevance **88,** 306, 307, 310
nationality laws **108,** 550-5
penal law **42,** 30, 410, 425-9, **48,** 84-5, 109, **64,** 246-8, 374-6, **75,** 274-5, 290-2, 295-6, 299, 300-4, 315-16, 325-30, 377-80, **78,** 597-8, 601-2, 615, 627-30, **88,** 307, **104,** 536
political law **78,** 603, **82,** 133
private international law and **78,** 597, **82,** 133, **88,** 307
private rights, protection of **72,** 19-26
public law **78,** 601, 603, 605-7

foreign law, recognition/enforcement (*cont.*)
protection of private interests **82,** 147
treaty provision **82,** 147
public policy and **42,** 429-31, 434, **52,** 61-2, **57,** 12, **63,** 3-4, **64,** 247-8, 375-6, **69,** 4-6, 9, **72,** 18-26, 453, 457, 467, 471, 474, **73,** 14, 228-9, 237-9, 244-7, 590, 592-3, **75,** 274-5, 277-80, 287, 290, 296, 299, 305-7, 314-16, 318-19, 321, 325-30, **78,** 604, 607, 630, **84,** 119, **104,** 536, **108,** 592-3, **116,** 556, 563-8, 595-8, **125,** 651-2, 665-8, 671, 727-8
context of legislation, relevance **125,** 668-70
international law and. *See* international law, need for conformity with *above*; jurisprudence
Oppenheimer v. *Cattermole* **116,** 564-5, 566, 568, **125,** 635-46, 656, 681, 684-9, 710-11, 718-19, 737-8
'Playa Larga' and 'Marble Islands' **116,** 567-8, **125,** 640-2
Princess Paley Olga v. *Weisz* **116,** 565-6, 588
Re Helbert Wagg & Co.'s Claim **116,** 567, 588, **125,** 633-4, 719
Williams v. *Humbert* **116,** 565, **125,** 642-3
racially discriminatory legislation **52,** 29
unrecognized government **39,** 169-72, 235, 368, 370, 394, 396
'recognition' **64,** 247-8
requisitioning measures **47,** 60-2
respect for **57,** 11-12
retroactive effect **71,** 38-9
retroactive legislation **92,** 477
revenue law. *See* fiscal, exchange control or revenue law *above*
State agency/State-owned corporation/State entity, status **65,** 81-2
State immunity and **42,** 22-3, **82,** 26-7
taking of evidence abroad, whether **84,** 749-51
unconstitutional law **88,** 308
validity under law of legislating State, relevance **125,** 674-6, 685-7
wartime measures **66,** 255
foreign maintenance orders, enforcement 47, 189-93
foreign policy. *See* foreign relations
foreign relations 56, 18, **82,** 289, 311-14, 324, 333-4. *See also* comity
act of State. *See* act of State, foreign relations
conduct of. *See* executive responsibility *and* responsibility for *below*
confidentiality and **96,** 348-58
balance of interests **96,** 351-4, 356-7
evidence, obligation to give, effect on **96,** 351, 354, 355, 356
obligation of person appointed by State to conduct foreign relations **96,** 350-8
rules of international organization **96,** 350, 356
constitutional conformity, need for **98,** 267
customary international law, compliance with **68,** 208-11, 223-4, 231-3, 250-1, 492-3
default judgment against foreign State and **84,** 144, **118,** 615-16, 617-18
definition **53,** 99
deportation and **86,** 332, 338
establishment of diplomatic relations, act of **100,** 327
evidence of **44,** 250-2
executive certificate/statement. *See* executive certificate/statement
executive orders, judicial review **74,** 38-9, 49, 78, 83
executive responsibility **57,** 26-7, **60,** 15, 40, **72,** 133-40, 143-50, 275-92, 655-8, **83,** 238, **104,** 64, **106,** 302, 303-4, 334-40, 351, 373-5, 380, 383-6, **107,** 288-9. *See also* prerogative, foreign relations; separation of powers

arbitrary exercise **106,** 380
attachment of foreign assets, nullification **72,** 274-82
compliance with international law **106,** 98-9, 385-6, **124,** 311-12
courts and **57,** 26, 77, 151, **63,** 17, 27-9, 31, 36-7, 40, 55-6, 218-19, 239-40, 247-8. *See also* United States of America (USA), Foreign Sovereign Immunities Act (FSIA) 1976/82, purpose, transfer of competence to courts ensuring uniformity of decision-taking and reduction of foreign policy implications
legislative encroachment **82,** 311-14
margin of discretion **106,** 395
private claims against foreign State, suspension **72,** 282-9
recognition of diplomatic status **73,** 682
recognition of foreign governments **72,** 655-6
treaties, conclusion **72,** 143-50, 275-6, 285-9, 655-8
expulsion and **104,** 63-4
executive responsibility **104,** 64
external affairs distinguished **68,** 216, 225, 450
extradition and **79,** 482 n. 6, 487, **100,** 613, **119,** 72
federal State. *See* federal State, foreign relations; *and under individual federal States such as the United States of America (USA)*
foreign commerce distinguished **96,** 134
geographical factors **68,** 197-8, 246, 307
heads of State, statements of **57,** 414
human rights restrictions and **101,** 404
international concern, topics of **68,** 201-2, 206-7, 217-18, 232, 235, 258, 308-11, 331-3, 373-8, 386, 394, 399, 414-17, 489, 492-8
international legal order and, arms export licence, refusal to issue **101,** 423-6
international relations, regulation **68,** 196, 198-9, 206-8, 225-6, 231, 258, 308-9, 311, 372, 387, 414-15, 451-2
international tribunal, decision of, conflict with **79,** 588
judicial restraint, acts between private individuals affecting foreign relations **96,** 216-17
judicial review **73,** 693-4, **74,** 38-9, 49, 78, 83, 96, 426, **80,** 402, 403, **84,** 717, 720, **87,** 348, **90,** 396-7, 686, **93,** 492-4, 497-8, 505-6, **96,** 213-23
diplomatic protection, exercise **107,** 469-81
discretionary powers **96,** 218
European Community (EC) **96,** 213-23
discretionary powers **96,** 218
prerogative and **96,** 216
scope, appropriateness of measures **106,** 395
justiciability **87,** 182, **89,** 7-8, **90,** 54, **98,** 178-9. *See also* political question doctrine
treaty-making power **87,** 182, 183, **90,** 54-5
legislature's role
legitimate failure to conclude treaty as infringement **106,** 336
political control, possibility of **106,** 375, 387, 388
right to co-determination **106,** 330-1
margin of discretion **96,** 216, **106,** 395
maritime exclusion zone, creation **74,** 95-6
means, executive's freedom to choose **106,** 336-8, 339
mutual legal assistance. *See* judicial assistance
NATO Treaty partners, relations between **73,** 610, 612, 674-5
peaceful co-existence **82,** 675-6
protectorates **71,** 44-5
publicity, restraint **82,** 676
racial discrimination **68,** 207-8, 223-4, 247-51, 386, 489

foreign relations (*cont.*)
reliability of State as international partner **96,** 352-4, 356-7
responsibility for **48,** 3-5, **53,** 20-2, 23, 532, 545-50, **56,** 7-10, 18-19, 525, **57,** 26, 77, 151, 425, **60,** 15, 19, 20-1, 40, **61,** 7, 11-13, 22-5, 447, 452-4, 657-8, **77,** 35, 200, 212-15, 230-4, 251, 252-6, **78,** 162-3, 192-3, **79,** 487, 499-502, 557, 572, 586, 588-9, **80,** 374, 402, 593, 595, **81,** 635, **82,** 289, 324, 333, **85,** 207, **87,** 163-4, 346-7, 700-1, **90,** 395-8, 685, **93,** 492-4, 496-500, 501-2, 506-8, **118,** 366-70
discretion **90,** 396-7
executive. *See* executive responsibility *above*
federal State. *See* federal State foreign relations; *and under individual federal States such as the United States of America (USA)*
judicial review **90,** 396-7
justiciability **89,** 7-8
Newfoundland **86,** 608, 611
protectorates **71,** 44-5, **118,** 426-7
right of suit to enforce laws and policies relating to **98,** 4-5, 11-12
scope **68,** 195-212, 215, 242, 245-58, 307, 331-3, 447-50, 488, 492-3
service on foreign ambassador and **80,** 374
sovereign equality and **93,** 497
sovereign rights **56,** 18
State immunity, jurisdiction and **63,** 218-20, 332, 451-2, 640-1, **82,** 18, **104,** 570, 612, 623, **107,** 357
treaty obligations, implementation **68,** 195-212, 215-42, 245-58, 307-16, 329-39, 372, 386-7, 396-8, 414-17, 449-56, 488-90, 498-9, **82,** 290
treaty-making power. *See* treaties, treaty-making power
USA, federal responsibility for **77,** 211-15
world heritage, preservation **68,** 311, 342, 372-8, 394, 399, 494-7
'foreign State' 84, 203-5, **85,** 98, 99-100, **90,** 599, 611 n. 5, **92,** 516, **104,** 280-2, **118,** 423, 425-7
foreign State, proceedings involving. *See also* act of State; Head of State; justiciability, foreign State; recognition, government; recognition, State; States; State immunity
action against
acts within own territory **103,** 476 n. 17
applicable law, international law **116,** 635
common law, possibility under **107,** 354-8
consent of forum government, need for
discretionary **92,** 533
merits distinguished **92,** 537-8
refusal, non-arbitrary **92,** 537, 538-9
Head of State, distinction, whether **92,** 520
liability to suit **92,** 536-7. *See also* State immunity, jurisdiction
human rights and **92,** 537
State agency distinguished **92,** 517-26
agencies. *See* state agency/State-owned corporation/State agency
agreement of State, need for **113,** 432
consent of forum government, need for **64,** 397-400, 411, 422, 425, 521-2, 537-8, 568-70, 618, **92,** 512, 514, 516-29, 533, 536, **118,** 423-4
waiver distinguished **64,** 573-4
counterclaim against
act of State doctrine **66,** 50-7, 75-8, 91, 104-24, 137-42, 212-45, 408-12, 427-33, 449, 458-9
assigned claim **66,** 407-12
compensation claim **66,** 50-7, 104-24, 137-42, 214-45, 408-12, 428-33

as equitable remedy to prevent evasion of liability **79,** 565
judgment
affirmative **66,** 91
restricted **66,** 110-12, 116, 141-2
currency regulations. *See* currency regulations
default judgment against. *See* default judgment against foreign State
due process, entitlement **107,** 341-2, **121,** 576, 597-9, 637-9
forum State's right to legislate for **64,** 502-3
Head of State. *See* Head of State
nexus with territory of foreign State, need for. *See* jurisdiction, nexus, in case of proceedings involving foreign State
notice of hearing, need for **107,** 637-8
'person', foreign State as **81,** 643
private right **64,** 497-8
procedural rules, applicability **107,** 631-2
recognition, need for **118,** 425-7
representation by
Attorney-General abroad **121,** 475-6
diplomatic agent **121,** 475-6
right of appeal in extradition hearing **107,** 176-7
right to appeal against alleged breach of international law or treaty **65,** 409-11, 427-8
right to sue and be sued **63,** 106-20, **64,** 502-3, 571-4, **65,** 437-8, **66,** 110, **106,** 244, 245-7, **116,** 630
foreign trade mission. *See* commercial/trade representation/mission
foreign trial, review **60,** 45-6
forestry conservation measures, expropriation, whether **48,** 179-86
forgery
government documents
export of cultural property, effect **118,** 580-92
forged currency compared **118,** 589-91
jurisdiction
currency notes abroad **48,** 69-76
documents abroad **48,** 90-3
passport **104,** 36-7
former Head of State. *See* Head of State, former
forum, choice of. *See forum [non] conveniens*; forum selection clause
forum [non] conveniens **60,** 67, **65,** 372, **66,** 287, 319-20, **74,** 40-2, 70-1, 75, 83-4, 86-7, **77,** 173, 184, 217, **79,** 555 n. 15, **81,** 559-80, 646, **83,** 252-4, **86,** 57, 64, 65-7, 101-6, **87,** 378, 381, 531, 536, 542, **98,** 147-8. *See also* jurisdiction, nexus
absence of alternative forum **81,** 563-4, 568, 572-3, 577-80, **103,** 358-60, **113,** 532-3
burden of proof **113,** 532-3
former Yugoslavia **104,** 163-4
applicable law and **64,** 564, **124,** 432
Bhopal gas leak disaster **118,** 457
commencement of proceedings, relative timing and **118,** 399-400
common law distinction between local and transitory actions **125,** 389-94
concurrent jurisdiction and **118,** 394
conditions for rejecting plea of **118,** 457
equitable basis **63,** 491, **81,** 563
ICSID **118,** 634-9
interference with affairs of foreign State and **124,** 568
jurisdiction presupposed **81,** 565
NAFTA **122,** 254

forum [non] conveniens (*cont.*)
place of conduct as determining factor **118,** 397-9
place of performance **64,** 541-2, 564-5
probability of effective outcome and **124,** 569
State immunity, execution/attachment and **124,** 569
State immunity, jurisdiction and **64,** 82-4, 88-9, 184-6, **103,** 518-19, **120,** 452-3, 461, **121,** 643
State-sponsored terrorism **121,** 643
stay of proceedings and **118,** 415-18
unclean hands and **81,** 570, 576, 580
forum prorogatum. *See* European Court of Human Rights, jurisdiction, *forum prorogatum*; ICSID (International Centre for the Settlement of Investment Disputes), arbitral tribunal, consent, *forum prorogatum*; International Court of Justice (ICJ), *forum prorogatum*
forum selection clause 68, 561-3, 568, 570, 574-5, 583-4, 589, 591, 596, 600, 603, 606-7, 609, 611-45, **70,** 493-4, **87,** 543-4. *See also* choice of law clause
administrative courts proceedings **125,** 83
ambiguity **68,** 644-5
arbitration clause as **68,** 563-4, 586-7, 591-4, 606-7, 609-10, 613, 628-9, **85,** 379, 417-18
binding, whether **68,** 615-24, 634-42. *See also* changed circumstances *below*
changed circumstances **68,** 565, 571, 576, 583-4, 591-3, 603-5, 612-24, 633, 635, 639-42. *See also* binding *above*; State succession and *below*
choice of 'homologue', validity **65,** 69
choice of law clause and **68,** 563-5, 613-14, 627-8
'competent courts', reference to **68,** 561-2, 575-6, 589-90, 600-1, 613, 626-8, 643-5
effective relief, possibility of **68,** 642
exclusive jurisdiction and **68,** 562-5, 568-72, 575-6, 580, 589-94, 596, 600-1, 613, 626-8, 643-5
NAFTA provisions **121,** 20
parallel claims by individual and government **125,** 90-1
Hague Convention on the Choice of Court (1964) **68,** 596
ICSID jurisdiction, effect on **125,** 6, 24-5
Lanco **125,** 24-5, 83-4
ITC contract **77,** 14
effectiveness **77,** 14
as nexus **65,** 391
private settlement procedures **68,** 591
scope **68,** 580-1, 596-7, 600-1, 613, 624-6, 644
separability **65,** 36, **68,** 565, 570-1, 576, 584, 591-2, 603-5, 619, 634-9
State succession and, change of legal system **118,** 528-39
stay of proceedings and **118,** 561
as waiver of immunity **63,** 357-8, 405-7, **65,** 35-6, 119, 333, 370, 400, **78,** 84, **87,** 40-1, 232, 235, 414-15, **92,** 447-8, **103,** 508
forum shopping 77, 189
Four Power rights and responsibilities. *See* Germany, Four Power rights and responsibilities; Germany, Democratic Republic (GDR), Four Power rights and responsibilities
France
abuse of power **86,** 334, 343
access to courts, refugees **70,** 356-8
acquired rights, agreement to extradite **106,** 261
acquisition of land for use by CERN
public utility, declaration of **82,** 87-8
Constitution, compatibility with **82,** 87-8

European Convention for the Protection of Human Rights (1950) **82,** 87-8
remedies of individual, effect on **82,** 89-90
act of government, judicial review **117,** 423
act of State **52,** 9-10
classification as
treaty, publication **106,** 238
treaty, suspension **106,** 208-11
domestic policy considerations
foreign armed forces, prohibition on stationing or transit **106,** 240
high seas, destruction of vessel **106,** 240
public service overseas **106,** 239-40
extradition, refusal **106,** 235-43
judicial assistance obligation, relevance **106,** 237, 240-2
separability from foreign policy **106,** 253
extradition, withdrawal of agreement **106,** 259-60
separability from foreign policy **106,** 260
foreign policy considerations **106,** 195, 196-7, 200-3
deregistration of Iraqi students following invasion of Kuwait **106,** 199-203
EU Council of Ministers, voting at **106,** 238
ICJ, submission of dispute to **106,** 239
margin of discretion in implementing treaty obligations, relevance **106,** 195, 201-2, 265-8
maritime exclusion zone, establishment **106,** 239
nuclear equipment, executive decision prohibiting export **106,** 194-7
nuclear tests, resumption **106,** 231-2
port regulation prior to war **106,** 238
protection of nationals **106,** 238
sale of weapons by private company to foreign State **106,** 220-1
suspension of technical cooperation with Iraq following invasion of Kuwait **106,** 201-2
treaty. *See* classification as, treaty *above*
judicial review, constitutional compliance **106,** 209
restrictive doctrine **106,** 195, 200-1, 202-3, 236
administrative tribunals, jurisdiction **47,** 235-6
admissibility **77,** 507, 513
execution, immunity **82,** 83
agricultural leases
aliens **44,** 141
refugees and **48,** 166-7
Yugoslav nationals **48,** 168
Algeria and. *See also* Evian Agreements (1962)
conflict, diversion of merchant ships **47,** 164
court decisions, effect in France **47,** 129
Declaration of Principles concerning Economic and Financial Cooperation (1962) **111,** 499-500
Economic and Financial Cooperation, Declaration on (1962) **48,** 61
French administrative decisions, review **44,** 43-6
Judicial Protocol (1962) **44,** 43-6, **47,** 78-83, 86, 94-7, 101-2, **48,** 60, 61
action by French national against Algerian company **47,** 127-9
interpretation **47,** 342-3
aliens **48,** 174. *See also* deportation *below*
access to courts **47,** 239-40
admission, readmission **44,** 139-40

France (*cont.*)
agricultural leases **44,** 141
commercial activity **47,** 248
discrimination against **62,** 404-5
extradition. *See* extradition *below*
false identity documents, public order and **86,** 334
family benefits **47,** 135
military service, liability for **47,** 235-6
political rights **72,** 589-90
privileged residents **45,** 365-70
residence permit **47,** 248
trade union rights **72,** 589-90
allegiance, Nationality Code **41,** 367
applicable law
contract, *lex loci contractus* **65,** 70
State's right of suit in foreign court dependent on **106,** 244-5, 246
arbitral award
annulment proceedings **86,** 481-92
award to have been rendered in France **82,** 96
grounds **86,** 490-1
arbitral award, enforcement **65,** 48-50, 52-3, 76-7, 79-80, 89-92, **113,** 445
applicable law, as determined by municipal law of contracting State **65,** 53
exequatur **65,** 48-50
distinguished **113,** 445
standing **65,** 53
jurisdiction, as determined by municipal law of contracting State **65,** 53
State immunity, jurisdiction, exequatur. *See* State immunity, arbitral award, enforcement *below*
arbitrary detention
statutory limitation, retroactive removal of **78,** 132-6
unstructured international crime and **78,** 129-30
arbitration, extradition dispute **106,** 247
arbitration clause
capacity to conclude, public order/public policy and **41,** 452-5, **48,** 329-30
as waiver of State immunity **65,** 48, 52-3, 89-92, 96, 98
arbitration procedures
provisional measures **89,** 34-5
merits, relevance **89,** 34-5
armed forces
applicable law **47,** 234
criminal acts committed abroad, liability for **74,** 245-56
arms trade, extradition **47,** 27-8
arrest warrant, execution. *See* jurisdiction, arrest warrant *below*
asylum **74,** 432
'laws and International Conventions incorporated into French law' **111,** 521
right of **45,** 94, 95-6
atmospheric nuclear tests **74,** 95-6
Baden, boundary treaties with **42,** 60
boundaries
Baden **42,** 60
inter-communal **42,** 59-61
Rhine **47,** 115-17
Switzerland, River Doubs **47,** 113-15

burden of proof, default judgment against foreign State, acceptance of judgment **65,** 87-8
Caisse International de l'Industrie **82,** 135
central/State-owned bank
  classification, private law as applicable law, relevance **65,** 65
  classification of act, affidavit in interests of public service **65,** 66-7
  classification as, separate legal entity test **65,** 55, 65-6
  as State agency **65,** 65-6
CERN, legality of acquisition of land for use by **82,** 86-90
China, Convention restoring leased territory (1945) **42,** 8-9
civil courts, competence **52,** 287
civil proceedings
  court's duty to ensure prompt hearing **96,** 598
  parties' responsibility for advancing **96,** 598
claims settlement agreements, extinction of claimant's rights against foreign State **65,** 50
comity, State immunity, execution/attachment **65,** 76-7
commercial/trade representation/mission
  diplomatic privileges and immunities **74,** 518-19
    recognition of State/government, relevance **65,** 56
  status, service of process as evidence of **65,** 56
Communal Administration Code **45,** 390
Comoros Islands, accession to independence **74,** 93-4
compensation
  expropriation by foreign State, for, effect on party's rights **80,** 438-9
  implied rejection of claim **89,** 17
  interest on **89,** 17
Compensation, Special Commission for distribution of **39,** 427-9, 465-6, **45,** 111-13, **47,** 166-8
compensation for war-related events
  losses arising out of military operations **48,** 467-9
  requisition of private property **72,** 237-8
    substitution of responsibility in post-war agreement **72,** 237-8
Congo (Brazzaville), Judicial Agreement (1960) **47,** 85-6
Conseil d'Etat
  jurisdiction **57,** 116-17
    continental shelf **57,** 147
Constitution 1946
  Preamble **111,** 521, **125,** 481
    customary international law **125,** 496, 499
  Art. 26 **88,** 203, 204, **93,** 254
  Art. 27 (treaties or agreements concerning international organization) **125,** 481
  Art. 28 (abrogation, modification or suspension of treaties) **88,** 203, 204, **93,** 29, 254, **106,** 207
  European Community law and **44,** 192-6, 399
  treaties **47,** 113-15, 312-27
Constitution 1958
  amendment, sovereignty, limitations **98,** 189
  Preamble **74,** 132, 525, 528, **78,** 128, **82,** 89-90, **93,** 342
  Art. 2 **74,** 528, **118,** 276
  Art. 3 (sovereignty) **74,** 529, **125,** 481
  Art. 5 (Presidential responsibility for treaties) **106,** 210
  Art. 17 **75,** 705-7
  Art. 21 (foreign policy, responsibility) **106,** 211

France (*cont.*)
Art. 22 **111,** 507
Art. 23 **74,** 529
Art. 24 **74,** 529
Art. 26 (immunity: members of Parliament) **125,** 482
Art. 28 (foreign policy, responsibility) **106,** 212
Art. 34 **75,** 706, **82,** 88, **89,** 20-2, **93,** 297
Art. 44 **88,** 203, 204, 207-9
Art. 53 (treaties or agreements concerning international organization) **74,** 84, 93, 687-8, **78,** 128, **82,** 88, **125,** 481
Art. 53(3) [1999] (recognition of jurisdiction of International Criminal Court) **125,** 490
Art. 54 (constitutional review of treaty) **74,** 527, **93,** 340, 342-3, 351, **98,** 183, 184, 185, **111,** 495-6, **125,** 477
Art. 55 (primacy of treaties) **72,** 688, **73,** 696, 700, **74,** 143, 145, 509, **77,** 501, **93,** 29, 236, 245, 263-4, 290-8, 304-5, 307, 341-2, **100,** 350, **106,** 207, 224-5, 227, 230, 262, **111,** 497, **125,** 481, 575
primacy of EC law, relevance **93,** 267, 320-1, 329-30
Art. 59 **111,** 497-8
Art. 60 (referendums) **98,** 190
Art. 61 **74,** 525, **93,** 251-3, 254-5, **111,** 497-8
Art. 62 **74,** 526
Art. 68 (immunity: President of the Republic) **125,** 482
Art. 68(1) (immunity: members of Government) **125,** 482
Art. 74 **89,** 20-2, **118,** 276
Art. 88 (amendment consequent on Maastricht Treaty) **98,** 185-6, 187-8
equality of burdens **72,** 219-20, 259-60
concept **47,** 326
French Community **44,** 26-8
treaties **45,** 96, 390, 456, 460, **47,** 322
application **48,** 1, 233
power to conclude **52,** 419-21
publication, need for **48,** 210-14
treaty suspension, absence of provision **106,** 207
Constitutional Council **52,** 419-20
res judicata **98,** 183, 184, 187
task
compatibility of Law with Constitution **111,** 498
compatibility of treaty with Constitution **93,** 344, 346, **111,** 498-500
constitutional review of treaties **98,** 189
determination of scope of treaty **93,** 342
constitutional review
referendums **98,** 190
treaties. *See* treaties, constitutional review *below*
consular immunity, jurisdiction, waiver, lease, cancellation clause **45,** 383-4
contiguous territories, Minquiers and Ecréhos **39,** 425-6
continental shelf **57,** 145-8
Continental Shelf Convention (1958), reservation **41,** 162, 205
contract
breach, government action leading to, responsibility for **106,** 194-7
definition **89,** 460, 465
pacta sunt servanda **89,** 495
performed abroad, right to sue on **48,** 171-4

public policy considerations **113,** 497
supply of gas, nature **80,** 438
corporation, jurisdiction over **73,** 579-80
costs
equity **113,** 485, 498
security for, aliens **47,** 239-40
time-limits **82,** 96
courts, municipal
application of foreign law **93,** 236, 239
competence **52,** 287
foreign act of State **47,** 53-6
OECD building **47,** 345-8
external trade regulation **93,** 262-3
EC directive **93,** 316, 320-4
foreign relations and **86,** 332
treaties
consideration of legality **47,** 53, 56
interpretation **74,** 99-100, 703-4
treaty interpretation **82,** 66
crimes against humanity. *See also* war crimes *below*
definition
Nuremberg Charter (1945) **100,** 349, 350
offence against ordinary law committed in certain circumstances **100,** 349, 350, 351
'heated' criminal reaction distinguished **100,** 356-7
international crime **78,** 128-9
extradition rules irrelevant **78,** 129
participation in common plan of extermination or persecution, separate offence, whether **100,** 334-6
persecution in name of State practising ideological supremacy **100,** 350-1, 363, 364
against opponents of policy **100,** 352
at instigation of officer of that State **100,** 363
on grounds of race or religion **100,** 352, 364
Nazi Germany **100,** 355-6
Vichy State **100,** 352-5
previous conviction on basis of same acts
acquittal **100,** 348
contacts with the enemy **100,** 347-9
reclassification **100,** 348-9
war crimes **100,** 332-3
prosecution, possibility of
municipal legislation **100,** 348
Nuremberg Charter (1945) **100,** 348
punishment of **74,** 700-4
resistance movements, protection **122,** 82
retroactivity, removal of right to non-retroactivity, statutory limitation **78,** 132-6
statutory limitation **78,** 136-7, 140, **100,** 333, 342
general principle of law recognized by community of nations **78,** 133
non-applicability to **78,** 132-6, **119,** 358
Nuremberg Charter (1945) **100,** 333
superior orders
ex proprio power of judge to ask **100,** 336
failure of defendant to raise point **100,** 337

France (*cont.*)
jury to be asked to consider **100,** 336-7
mitigation of punishment, limited to **100,** 336-7
terrorism distinguished **125,** 504
war crimes distinguished **78,** 137-40
criminal law
statutory limitation
derogation in respect of crimes at time of commission criminal according to general principles of law **78,** 134
retroactive removal of right to **78,** 132-6
criminal procedure
recours en référé **86,** 331-3
trial *in absentia* **78,** 518, **86,** 330
civil action inadmissible **78,** 137
public policy and **86,** 327
criminal responsibility, aiding and abetting **124,** 157
customary international law
Head of State, immunity, jurisdiction **125,** 495-510
requirements, constant and uniform practice **125,** 499
role, determination by municipal law **125,** 499
as source of law in absence of legislative or treaty provision **125,** 495
customs regulations, Free Zones of Gex and Upper Savoy **40,** 53-5
Czechoslovakia, payments agreement (1969) **47,** 163
death penalty, European Convention on Human Rights (1950), Additional Protocol No 6 (death penalty) **111,** 496-7
debt, order for attachment of assets, existence of asset, need for **82,** 72
declaration of public utility, effect **82,** 87-90
Declaration of the Rights of Man **74,** 525, **75,** 705-7, **78,** 128
Art. 3 (sovereignty) **125,** 481
decolonization process **80,** 484-6, 554-6
default judgment against foreign State
burden of proof **65,** 87-8
State immunity, jurisdiction, acceptance of judgment as waiver **65,** 87-8
deportation **86,** 329-30. *See also* refugees, non-refoulement
appeal
grounds **111,** 167, 179
review of proportionality **111,** 179
criminal law, punishment, whether **111,** 178
critical date, facts as at date of decision **111,** 178
discretion **111,** 170
European Convention on Human Rights (1950), applicability **111,** 168-9, 170-3
exempt persons **111,** 177-8
family life, respect for **111,** 169-70, 258
forcible **86,** 332, 336-7, 343-4
grounds, threat to public order/public policy/*ordre public* **111,** 167-8, 173, 176-7, 258
legislation relating to, retroactive effect **111,** 178
nationality and **111,** 172
non-compliance with order **86,** 343-4
order
indefinite duration **111,** 178
request for revocation, repeated **111,** 178
waiver **111,** 178
compulsory residence order **111,** 178

détournement de pouvoir **48,** 171
diplomatic agent
action on behalf of ambassador, validity **106,** 250, 254
protection, duty of **89,** 2-3
diplomatic immunity, jurisdiction **52,** 397
divorce proceedings **74,** 520-2
State immunity and, distinction **113,** 452, 465-6, 467-8, 471-2
diplomatic premises, inviolability, entry with consent of head of mission **113,** 480
diplomatic privileges and immunities, entitlement
commercial/trade representation/mission **74,** 518-19
family members **74,** 278-9, **77,** 496-7
international organizations, representatives and missions accredited to **74,** 278-9
UN delegates **47,** 275-7
nationals of receiving State **70,** 389-92
diplomatic protection, as exercise of State's own right **45,** 96-7
diplomatic relations, recognition of State/government, relevance **65,** 56
dispute settlement, methods, failure to make treaty provision **106,** 248
double criminality **44,** 181
equivalent act or omission **111,** 507
reclassification, possibility of **106,** 250-2, 254-5
drug-trafficking, jurisdiction **73,** 250-1, 699-704
EC
freedom of establishment **93,** 267
legislature, encroachment on **93,** 297
EC law
breach. *See* EC law, breach *below*
compatibility of national law, conformity distinguished **93,** 323
direct effect. *See* EC law, direct effect *below*
EC law, breach
compensation
interest **93,** 336
measure **93,** 331, 335-6
State responsibility
causal link **93,** 328
fault, need for **93,** 329-31, 334-5
national administrative act **93,** 330
remedy, entitlement **93,** 328
EC law, direct effect **93,** 263. *See also* EC law, primacy *below*
transitional period, after **93,** 267
EC law, primacy
directive **93,** 316, 320-4
EEC Treaty (Rome) (1957) **93,** 243-62
pre-independence ordinance relating to Metropolitan Territories **93,** 245-6
regulation **93,** 244-5, 308, 322
EC law, State responsibility
causal link **93,** 328
fault, need for **93,** 329-31, 334-5
national administrative act **93,** 330
remedy, entitlement **93,** 328
ECJ
judgment
binding effect **93,** 277-83
individuals **93,** 319

France (*cont.*)
Economic and Monetary Union (EMU), compatibility with Constitution **93,** 347-9
economic zone (EEZ) **74,** 142-8
ECSC, transport rates rules, legislation, whether **44,** 292-4
EEC Treaty (Rome) (1957), application of legislation contrary to **93,** 246-53, 290-307
Art. 55 of Constitution as basis **93,** 305-6
Art. 177 (EEC Treaty) preliminary ruling **93,** 324
constitutionality distinguished **93,** 252-3, 292-4, 330
EC directive **93,** 316, 320-4
interpretation of EC secondary legislation **93,** 323-4
loiécran theory **93,** 291, 294, 300
ordinary and administrative courts distinguished **93,** 247, 295, 296-7, 302-3, 307
State immunity, jurisdiction, research assistant **113,** 496-7
employment contract, locally engaged staff, diplomatic mission
classification of employment, medical staff **104,** 681, **116,** 623-4
diplomatic immunity, jurisdiction **113,** 452
medical staff **116,** 623-4
State immunity, jurisdiction
caretaker **113,** 493
security guard **113,** 451-2
employment contract, locally engaged staff, information/news agency, dismissal of government news agency journalist without special public service responsibilities **113,** 458-9, 492
employment contract, locally engaged staff, State agency
nationalization of employing company following independence **64,** 44-6
State immunity, jurisdiction
arbitration clause as waiver of right **113,** 497
research assistant **113,** 496-7
enemy property
cession by property administrator **73,** 582, 588
confiscation
compensation for **48,** 467-9
extraterritorial effect **44,** 490, 493
measures against **45,** 446, 489
environment, international considerations **72,** 13-14
equality, public burdens **47,** 23, **72,** 219-20, 259-60
equity, costs **113,** 485, 498
Eurocontrol charge-fixing
Member State's right to challenge **111,** 501-2
publication of charges distinguished **111,** 501-2
responsibility for **111,** 501-2
European Atomic Energy Agency, treaty constituting, breach **48,** 217-26
European Convention on Human Rights (1950)
Additional Protocol No 1, constitutional compatibility **111,** 498
Additional Protocol No 6 (death penalty), constitutional compatibility **111,** 495-6
applicability **74,** 302-3, 703, **100,** 333-4
municipal courts **111,** 171
direct effect **111,** 169
European Parliament
European Union Treaty (Maastricht) (1992), effect **93,** 347
independent legal order, part of **93,** 289

legal basis **93,** 346
right of EC citizens to vote and stand as candidates **93,** 345-7
European Union Treaty (Maastricht) (1992)
constitutional amendment, need for **93,** 340-53
Economic and Monetary Union (EMU) **98,** 186-7, 189
freedom of movement **98,** 188
voting rights for non-nationals **98,** 185-6
European citizenship
right to stand in European Parliament elections **93,** 345-7
right to vote and stand as candidates in national elections **93,** 344-5
free movement of persons **93,** 350-1
compatibility with Constitution **93,** 350-1
unanimity rule **93,** 351
fundamental rights **93,** 343
reciprocity and **93,** 343
exchange controls **52,** 11-14
transfers from Algeria **47,** 124
executive certificate/statement, conclusiveness **74,** 99
expropriation/nationalization. *See also* law of, Law of 11 February 1982 (nationalization) *below*
as act of State **65,** 75
declaration of public utility as **82,** 90
extraterritorial effect **41,** 373, **82,** 131-48
expropriation/nationalization, compensation **80,** 434-5, 438-9
requirement, whether **65,** 60
expropriation/nationalization, legality
requirements
compensation **65,** 60, **73,** 589-90, 592-3
non-discrimination **75,** 707-9, 716, 719
expulsion of alien **74,** 428-44
Algerian nationals **70,** 358-9
alien temporarily abroad **70,** 364
FRG, Convention of Establishment with (1956) **52,** 354
hearing, right to **70,** 363-4
judicial review **106,** 214
procedure **70,** 358-9, 363-4
urgent cases **47,** 264-5, 363-4, **70,** 358-9
extraditable offence
murder by organized armed group **111,** 507
political offence **111,** 508
extradition **45,** 91-3, 95-7, 99, 105, 107, **74,** 454-5, 506-9
administrative irregularities **79,** 248
annulment **79,** 248
agreement, death penalty reservation **100,** 671
agreement to, acquired right **106,** 261
appeal
compatibility with international law **111,** 507-8
manifest error of fact **111,** 513
procedural irregularities **111,** 506-8
standing **106,** 272
applicable law
general principles of international law **106,** 263
international public order/public policy/*ordre public* **106,** 264

France (*cont.*)
municipal law **106,** 264
treaty **106,** 263-4
conditions in requesting State, respect for fundamental rights and freedoms **111,** 508, 514
court, role **44,** 183
crime against humanity **78,** 128
definition **78,** 129
discretion, 'margin of appreciation' **106,** 265-8
disguised, violation of extradition treaty required **78,** 128, 129
dispute relating to
arbitration, possibility of **106,** 247
failure to lay down procedure **106,** 248
double criminality. *See* double criminality *above*
general principles of, amnesty in requesting State **106,** 264
international criminal order and **106,** 238
international public order/public policy/*ordre public* **106,** 263-8, 271-2
fundamental norm **106,** 263-8
judicial review
abstention from right to refuse **106,** 236
annulment **100,** 670, 682
conditions in requesting State **106,** 241
motivation of requesting State **106,** 241
procedure **106,** 253
renewal of application following **106,** 252-3
request for extradition **106,** 236
standing **106,** 244-8, 260
motivation of requesting State **111,** 544-5
judicial responsibility **106,** 241
prosecution for race, religion, nationality or political opinion **111,** 512-13
nationality, naturalization, application for, relevance **111,** 513
obligation
aut dedere aut punire/judicare **106,** 237, 263, 267-8
Extradition, European Convention on (1957) **106,** 237, 261-2, 267-9
prima facie case **111,** 513
procedure **47,** 266-72
ministerial signature, need for **111,** 507
request by diplomatic agent on behalf of ambassador **106,** 250, 254
public order/public policy/*ordre public* **106,** 262, **111,** 521
purpose, self-interest of States **100,** 670
refugees **111,** 508, 514-25
aut dedere aut punire/judicare, relevance **111,** 523
refusal. *See also* withdrawal of agreement *below*
act of State **106,** 235-43, 253, 263
distinguishable, whether **106,** 237-43
failure to respond to request **106,** 253, 255
national security **106,** 263, **111,** 524
necessity **106,** 266-7, 272
reasons, need for **106,** 238, 262, 270-2, 273
responsibility **106,** 240-1
withdrawal of agreement distinguished **106,** 259-60
requirements, reciprocity **106,** 241-2
trial *in absentia,* bar, whether **86,** 327

universal jurisdiction as alternative, preclusion by bilateral treaty **100,** 670
withdrawal of agreement. *See also* refusal *above*
act of State **106,** 259-60
competence **106,** 260
failure to implement distinguished **106,** 259
reasons, need for **106,** 260-7
extradition agreement
courts' power to question foreign State's acts under **48,** 187-8
individual's rights under **45,** 95
legislation, applicability in absence of agreement **111,** 507
extradition in case of death penalty **111,** 521
additional assurances **100,** 679-80, 682-5
assurances that death penalty will not be carried out, need for **100,** 663-4, 673-90
bilateral agreement to provide for same penalty as in requested State **100,** 671
public policy and **100,** 663, 668, 686
reservation, insufficient **100,** 664-5, 673-4
safe haven, risk **100,** 670, 687
speciality principle leading to modification of request **100,** 671, 673
Extradition, European Convention on (1957)
obligation to extradite **106,** 237, 261-2, 267-9
reservations
'exceptionally serious consequences' **100,** 686
humanitarian considerations **106,** 262
sovereignty **106,** 262
'special circumstances' **106,** 262
fair trial
expression of judicial opinion **100,** 333-4
interpreter **100,** 334
oral hearing, right to, distribution of documents and **100,** 333-4
refusal to appear **100,** 334
translation **100,** 334
faux **85,** 81
fisheries dispute, Nicaragua, capture and sinking of ship **48,** 469-75
fisheries jurisdiction, extension, French Guiana **56,** 194
fishing zones **74,** 142-8
force majeure, non-renewal of funds by Congress **113,** 497-8
forcible abduction/unlawful arrest **45,** 92-3
extradition agreement, relevance, in absence of extradition proceedings **45,** 91-2, 95-7
extradition and **45,** 91-107
jurisdiction, effect on **45,** 90-107
foreign confiscation, effect **47,** 132
foreign judges, cross-examination of fugitives by **71,** 223
foreign judgment, recognition/enforcement
Algeria, Agreement **80,** 429
critical date, date of judgment **106,** 227
exequatur **80,** 430
expropriation, in case of **80,** 428-30
public policy considerations **106,** 227-8
State succession and **89,** 11-14
treaty basis **44,** 291-2
treaty basis, State succession and **44,** 291-2
foreign law, recognition/enforcement **52,** 8

France (*cont.*)
confiscatory legislation **65,** 84-5
nationalization measures **65,** 60
State agency/State-owned corporation, status **65,** 81-2
foreign relations
conduct of, justiciability **89,** 7-8
judicial review **52,** 7, **72,** 13-14, 219-22, 238, **74,** 96
'foreigners', Andorrans, whether **39,** 412-13
forum selection clause
choice of 'homologue', validity **65,** 69
separability **65,** 36
free movement of workers **47,** 249-51
freedom of expression, anti-semitic remarks, prohibition **115,** 372-3
freedom of navigation **74,** 134
German occupation
court in occupied territory, judgment of **41,** 475-8
German decisions during **38,** 470-1
trading with the enemy **48,** 475-8
Germany
boundary
Baden **42,** 60
Rhine **47,** 115-17
cessation of hostilities with **40,** 434-5
Cooperation. *See* Institut Franco-Allemand de Recherche de Saint-Louis; Office Franco-Allemand pour la Jeunesse
liquidated property, law on **44,** 488
guarantor, State as (*solidarité nationale*) **80,** 435, 438
Head of State, former, immunity, jurisdiction
confiscation of assets in home State, relevance **65,** 37-8
Head of State in office distinguished **125,** 504
private acts **65,** 37-8
Head of State, immunity, jurisdiction. *See also* State immunity *below*
basis
customary international law **125,** 500-1
dignity of State **125,** 500
friendly relations, preservation of **125,** 500
functional **125,** 500
customary international law **125,** 495-510
jus cogens **125,** 496
treaty practice as evidence of **125,** 495-6, 502-3
diplomatic privileges and immunities, similarity of regime **125,** 500
international crimes **125,** 482
jus cogens/peremptory norm and **125,** 505-7
International Criminal Court (ICC) **125,** 497-8, 502-3
State responsibility for breach **125,** 507-8
State-sponsored terrorism **125,** 498, 507
supply of goods for birthday celebrations coinciding with national holiday **113,** 483-4
Head of State, recognition, Gaddafi **125,** 501
Hungary, compensation agreement (1950) **47,** 53-6
ICJ
compulsory jurisdiction, acceptance **106,** 248
consent to jurisdiction, need for **106,** 247-8

jurisdiction **57,** 472-88
optional clause, reservations **57,** 373, 376, 390-1, 521-2
India
cession of territories in **44,** 295-6, **49,** 485, 491
Pondicherry
transfer of administration of (1954) **49,** 485, 491
Treaty of Cession (1956) **49,** 485, 491
interest, date of commencement, date of final demand for payment **113,** 484
International Criminal Court (ICC), jurisdiction, terrorist crimes **125,** 497, 502-3, 505-6
International Criminal Court (ICC), Rome Statute (1998)
applicability, ratification/entry into force, relevance **125,** 490, 502
constitutional amendment, need for **125,** 477-90
ICC jurisdiction in case of amnesty/statutory limitation **125,** 488
investigation without presence of State Party on territory of that State **125,** 489
responsibility of Head of State, member of government or parliament **125,** 482
constitutional compatibility
principles applicable to criminal law and criminal procedure **125,** 483-6
sentencing, execution **125,** 489
Head of State, immunity, jurisdiction **125,** 497-8, 502-3
obligation to exercise criminal jurisdiction, Head of State immunity, relevance **125,** 497-8, 502-3
International Institute of Refrigeration Headquarters Agreement (1966). *See Consolidated Table of Treaties*
international law. *See also* treaties *below*
Constitution, conformity **78,** 129, 133
dualist theory **93,** 253-4
formal incorporation required **78,** 129
monist theory **93,** 296
municipal courts, obligation to raise *proprio motu* **65,** 76, 80-1
sources, judicial and arbitral decisions **106,** 266
transposition of municipal law to **65,** 34, 66
international officials, employment contract, State immunity, jurisdiction **113,** 439
international officials, immunity
execution/attachment **77,** 503
jurisdiction **74,** 690-3, **77,** 503
privileges and immunities **74,** 192-5, 690-3, 711-13, **77,** 503-4, 506-10
status **72,** 194, 711-13
international organizations, immunity, execution/attachment
execution measures as necessary preliminary **113,** 477
staff salaries **113,** 490
international organizations, immunity, jurisdiction
execution distinguished **113,** 439, **115,** 428
international organizations, immunity, jurisdiction, waiver, institution of proceedings for payment **113,** 477
international organizations, judicial review, Member State courts **111,** 501-2
international organizations, privileges and immunities
basis
constituent agreement **113,** 476
customary international law **113,** 477
headquarters agreement, UNESCO **113,** 490
international agreement **113,** 477
status agreement, WEU **113,** 488-9

France (*cont.*)
effective remedy, denial, European Convention on Human Rights (1950), primacy **113,** 489
functional **113,** 439
headquarters agreement and **113,** 439
conferring privileges and immunities on officials, relevance to Organization **113,** 439
international public order/public policy/*ordre public*, extradition, fundamental norm of international law **106,** 264-8
International Sanitary Regulations, direct applicability **48,** 231-2
Iran, Islamic Republic of, Iranian Atomic Energy Organization (IAEO), as instrumentality of Iran **113,** 455
Italy, Establishment Convention (1951) **39,** 467-8, **41,** 265-6
judicial assistance
international criminal order and **106,** 238
refusal, reasons, need for **106,** 238
judicial review
absolute liability for abnormal damage, in case of **96,** 218
act of State, constitutional compliance **106,** 209
administrative act
arbitrary act, need for **86,** 332
flagrant unlawfulness, need for **86,** 332
deportation **96,** 218
extradition **96,** 218
foreign relations **96,** 217-18
discretionary powers **96,** 218
malfunctioning of judicial system **96,** 595-6
remedy, whether **106,** 248
treaties
ratification, fact and form distinguished **106,** 209
suspension **106,** 209-10
jurisdiction **72,** 91-3. *See also* courts, municipal *above*
aliens, non-resident **41,** 259
arbitral award, annulment proceedings **82,** 96
arrest warrant
extradition proceedings, relevance **78,** 128-31
voluntary return to France **78,** 128-31
conservatory attachment **77,** 534
crimes against humanity **78,** 128-31
criminal **52,** 290, **73,** 250-1, 700-4
irregular apprehension **45,** 90-107
debt between aliens **77,** 534
defence rights to be assured **78,** 131
drug-trafficking **73,** 250-1, 699-704
extraterritorial, winding-up proceedings **65,** 84-5
forum rule in treaty, effect **72,** 91-3
fraud, extraterritorial elements **48,** 88-90
ICSID arbitration, provisional measures **82,** 80-3
international officials, employment contract **72,** 192-5, 711-13, **77,** 503-6
ne bis in idem principle **78,** 137
nexus, place of performance **65,** 70
over corporation **73,** 579-80
passive personality principle, immunity and **125,** 495, 496, 500-1

public funds, in respect of **80,** 437-8
sovereign power, exercise of, proceedings against company in forum State for breach of customs laws **113,** 449
State
dispute with former Head of State **113,** 449
foreign policy considerations **113,** 450
State contract **80,** 438
statute-barred
crimes against humanity **78,** 132-6
war crimes **78,** 136-7
subject-matter, *res judicata* **73,** 250-1
territorial **73,** 250-1, 699-704
treaty, limitation by **65,** 42-3
winding-up proceedings, in absence of establishment within the jurisdiction **65,** 85
jus cogens/peremptory norm
Head of State, immunity, jurisdiction **125,** 496
non-acceptance of doctrine **125,** 506-7
justiciability
diplomatic agent, protection of **89,** 2
diplomatic protection, request for **89,** 7-8
foreign relations question **89,** 7-8
export ban on nuclear equipment **106,** 193-7
outdated concept **106,** 200-1
Kuwait, State agency/State-owned corporation/State entity, Kuwait News Agency **113,** 458-9
law of **52,** 289-90. *See also* Constitution *and* criminal law *above*
Act of 16 fructidor of year III **86,** 332, 338
Act of 16/24 August 1790 **86,** 331, 338
Act of 29 October 1981 **86,** 343
Aliens (Conditions of Entry and Residence) Ordinance of 2 November 1945 **86,** 329, 343
Civil Aviation Code (1972) **73,** 701-2
Civil Aviation Code (1990), Art. R 134(1) **111,** 501-2
Civil Code **62,** 337, 368, 605, **67,** 332, **73,** 34, 572, **74,** 520-1
Art. 2 **107,** 129
Art. 3 **113,** 449
Art. 14 **47,** 127-9, **48,** 171-4, **65,** 42-3, 45, 85, **72,** 91-3, **113,** 458-9, 461, 483, 488
Art. 15 **113,** 458-9
Art. 154 (interest on judicial award) **113,** 484
Art. 340 (enforcement of foreign law, public policy) **106,** 227-8
Art. 1121 **67,** 340
Art. 1134 **67,** 337, **80,** 427
Art. 1149 **67,** 341
Art. 1150 **67,** 341
Art. 1153 **67,** 342-3
Art. 1154 **89,** 17
Art. 1174 **67,** 337
Art. 1315 **68,** 554
Art. 1351 **80,** 434
Art. 1354 **67,** 367
Art. 1356 **67,** 367
Arts. 1372-5 **85,** 465 n. 1

France (*cont.*)
Art. 1382 **80,** 431
Art. 1871 **67,** 337
Art. 2028 **67,** 342-3
Art. 2092 **80,** 429, **82,** 94, **113,** 486
Civil Procedure Code (New) **72,** 92, **74,** 691-2
Art. 2 **96,** 598
Art. 3 **96,** 598
Art. 12 **82,** 96
Art. 14 **80,** 438
Art. 16 **80,** 435
Art. 42 **77,** 534
Art. 46 **77,** 534
Art. 48 **65,** 97, **77,** 512, **89,** 34-5, **113,** 486
Art. 52 **65,** 97
Art. 74 **82,** 83, **113,** 496
Art. 75 **65,** 69
Art. 114 **77,** 497
Art. 123 **77,** 507
Art. 169 **47,** 153
Art. 373 **96,** 594
Art. 423 **65,** 76, 80
Art. 455 **80,** 429
Art. 627(1) **113,** 445, 449
Art. 668 **121,** 335 n. 255
Art. 688 **77,** 497, 508-9
Art. 693 **77,** 497
Art. 700 **77,** 500, 506, **106,** 220, **113,** 476, 487, 498
Art. 780 **96,** 594-5
Arts. 809-11 **65,** 79-80
Art. 910 **96,** 595
Art. 952 **65,** 90, 92
Art. 1074 **77,** 507, 508
Art. 1477(1) **113,** 444
Art. 1490 **86,** 494
Arts. 1498 ff **113,** 445
Arts. 1501 ff **82,** 96
Art. 1502 **86,** 483, 489, 490-1, 494
Art. 1502(5) **113,** 444
Art. 1504 **86,** 490-1, 494
Art. 1506 **86,** 494
debtor's property, attachment **47,** 161
unrepresented co-defendant, judgment, effect on **44,** 492
Commercial Companies (Law No 66-537 of 24 July 1966) **84,** 391
Constitutional Law No 92-554 of 25 June 1992 (European Union) **93,** 351-2
Copyright Law 1957 **44,** 493
Criminal Code 1810 (including amendments prior to 1994) **72,** 673, **74,** 468-9, 507-8, **85,** 81, 100, 405
Art. 59 **100,** 357
Art. 60 **100,** 357
Arts. 222-3 (rape) **121,** 270 n. 208
Art. 295 **100,** 357, 671
Art. 296 **100,** 357, 671

Art. 297 **100,** 357
Art. 302 **100,** 357
Criminal Code 1994
Art. 121-7 **124,** 157 n. 284
Art. 212-1 **119,** 353
Art. 212-2 (crimes against humanity: protection of resistance movements) **122,** 82
Art. 222(1) (torture) **125,** 574
Criminal Investigation Code, Art. 637 **78,** 132
Criminal Procedure Code 1958 (including amendments prior to 2000) **48,** 89-90, **73,** 250-1, 699-703, **74,** 518, **86,** 330, 337, 338
Amending Law of 10 June 1983 **78,** 137
Amending Law of 16 December 1992 (jurisdiction over offences committed outside French territory) **125,** 574
Art. 2(4) **78,** 136, 137
Art. 3 **78,** 136
Art. 4 **78,** 136
Art. 7 **78,** 136
Art. 24 **111,** 244
Art. 133 **78,** 130
Art. 135(1) **78,** 130
Art. 144 **78,** 131, 136
Art. 145 **78,** 131, 136
Art. 145-1 **111,** 243-4
Art. 148 **78,** 131, 136
Art. 310 (discretionary power of judge) **100,** 333, 334
Art. 319 **100,** 334
Art. 320 **100,** 334
Art. 328(2) (expression of judicial opinion) **100,** 333-4
Art. 344 **100,** 334
Art. 349 **100,** 334-6
Art. 356 **100,** 336-7
Art. 358 **100,** 336-7
Art. 573(3) **78,** 136
Art. 591 **78,** 128, 132
Art. 593 **78,** 128, 133, 136, **100,** 360
Art. 689(1) (jurisdiction in application of international conventions) **125,** 574, 576
Art. 689(2) (jurisdiction: Torture Convention) **125,** 574
Art. 689(3) (jurisdiction: terrorism) **106,** 263
Art. 689-2 **119,** 367
Art. D 288 **111,** 244
Art. D 289 **111,** 244
Art. D 507 **111,** 244
revision, action for **45,** 94-5, 101
Customs Code 1965 **72,** 672-4, **73,** 699-704
compatibility with EC law **93,** 263
Decree of 18 April 1939 (war materials, arms and munitions) **106,** 221
Decree of 2 November 1945 (entry of aliens into France) **106,** 214, **111,** 176-7
Decree of 23 May 1951 (armed forces' pension rights) **114,** 313
Decree (Berne International Convention (1952)) **65,** 43
Decree No 53-934 of 30 September 1953 **111,** 544
Decree of 13 April 1962 (Declaration on Economic and Financial Cooperation between France and Algeria) **106,** 223-4
Decree of 27 October 1967 (conservatory attachment of ships) **82,** 84

France (*cont.*)
Decree of 18 March 1970 (Franco-Spanish Treaty for the Recognition and Enforcement of Judgments) **89,** 7
Decree of 29 March 1971 (Vienna Convention on Diplomatic Relations (1961)) **113,** 471
Decree of 31 December 1971 (legal qualifications) **106,** 230
Decree No 74-360 of 3 May 1974 (publication of European Convention on Human Rights (1950)) **111,** 497-9
Decree of 12 October 1977 **82,** 88-9
Decree of 29 October 1981 (conditions of entry of aliens) **111,** 177, 190
Decree of 10 April 1984 (entry of aliens into France) **106,** 213-14
Diplomatic Privileges and Immunities Decree 1974 **42,** 243
Electoral Code, constitutional compatibility **111,** 498-9
Employment Code
Art. 122-14-4 **77,** 506
Art. L 511 **77,** 501
Entry and Residence of Aliens Ordinance 1945 **74,** 428-30, 438-44
Excise Code, import licence provisions **48,** 233-5
Expropriation Code **82,** 90
Extradition of Aliens Act of 10 March 1927 **86,** 327, **100,** 670
Art. 16 **100,** 689
Art. 21 **100,** 673
Extradition Law 1927 **74,** 454, 508-9, **106,** 240, 258, 268, **111,** 242-3, 506-8, 544
applicability in case of treaty provision **111,** 507
Art. 1 **78,** 128, **111,** 507
Art. 5 **111,** 508
Art. 16 **111,** 513
Art. 23 **78,** 129
Art. 25 **78,** 129
Art. 129 **78,** 129
political offence **45,** 96
Finance Law 1959 **73,** 37
Freedom of the Press Law (1881), Gayssot Act (1990) amending, legality **115,** 358-83
General Status of Members of the Armed Forces Law 1972 **82,** 588
International Mutual Assistance Law 1982, Art. 8 **100,** 675
Judicial Organization Code, Article L781-1 **96,** 595-6
Law of 20 April 1810 **80,** 429
Law of September 1940 (Appointment of Temporary Managers) **85,** 467-8
Law of 47-1707 of 4 September 1947 **80,** 484, 505, 557, 558
Law of 51-561 of 18 May 1951 (armed forces' pension rights) **114,** 313
Law of 25 July 1952 (Refugees) **111,** 515-16, 527, 537
Art. 5 (Refugee Appeals Commission) **111,** 515
Law of 3 April 1955 (Representation of the French State) **89,** 11-14
Law of 28 July 1960 (nationality) **111,** 179
Law of 26 December 1964 (London Agreement of 8 August 1945) **78,** 132, 133, 135, 143, **100,** 342, 348-9, 350
Criminal Code (maintaining contact with the enemy) distinguished **100,** 349
Military Justice Code (war crimes) distinguished **100,** 348-9
treaty text **78,** 132
Law of 20 December 1966 (nationality) **111,** 179
Law of 72-623 (Civil Aviation Code) 1972 **86,** 42
Law of 9 July 1973 (nationality) **111,** 179
Law of 73-1227 of 31 December 1973 (European Convention on Human Rights (1950) and Additional Protocols Nos 1, 3, 4, 5) **111,** 497-9

Law of 21 December 1974 (pension rights of non-French members of the armed forces) **114,** 318-19
Law of 24 May 1976 (tobacco monopoly) **93,** 314, 324-7, 332-6
Law of 10 July 1976 (nature protections), Art. 2 **82,** 88-9
Law of 7 July 1977 (European Parliament) **93,** 306-7
Law of 2 January 1978 **80,** 438
Law of 17 July 1978 **106,** 238
Law of 11 July 1979 **111,** 507
Law 79-387 of 11 July 1979 **79,** 248
Law of 11 February 1982 (nationalization)
Art. 1 **82,** 131
Art. 2 **82,** 131
Art. 4 **82,** 131, 137
Art. 5 **82,** 131, 137
Art. 11 **82,** 135
extraterritorial effect **82,** 131-48
Law of 2 March 1982 (decentralization) **82,** 90
Law of 7 January 1983 (decentralization) **82,** 90
Law of 20 April 1983 (Brussels Protocol relating to Collection of Route Charges(1981)) **111,** 501-2
Law of 22 July 1983 (decentralization) **82,** 90
Law of 25 January 1985, Art. 33 **113,** 476
Law of 31 December 1985 (European Convention on Human Rights (1950): Protocol No 6) **100,** 608, 663, 689
Law 86-825 of 11 July 1986 (Electoral Code). *See* Electoral Code *above*
Law of 17 July 1986 (New Caledonia) **89,** 20-2
Law of 16 July 1987 (Ratification of European Convention for the Suppression of Terrorism (1977)) **111,** 523
Law 87-1127 of 31 December 1987 **111,** 544
Law of 2 August 1989 (nationality) **111,** 190, 536, 538
Law of 2 January 1995 (ICTY Statute) **119,** 367
Military Justice Code, Art. 80 (war crimes) **100,** 349
Military Requisitions Law 1877 **44,** 39-41
National Service Code **74,** 303
Art. 19 **70,** 343-8
Art. 55 **70,** 341-2
Art. 124 **48,** 164
family links **70,** 341-2
Nationality Code **40,** 52, **41,** 367, **111,** 180
Order No 45-1708 of 31 July 1945 **111,** 544
Order of 2 November 1945 (as subsequently amended) (entry and residence of aliens) **111,** 536, 538, 547
Order of 21 July 1962 (nationality) **111,** 179
Ordinance of 7 November 1958 (Constitutional Council) **93,** 340, **111,** 497
Penal Code. *See* Criminal Code *above*
Prices Ordinance 1945 **44,** 395, 405
Public Health Code **73,** 250-1, 701-2
Republican Laws, Ordinance of 1944 re-establishing **41,** 475-7
Retirement Pensions Code **73,** 37
Social Security Code **73,** 35
accidents in course of employment **49,** 498-9
Trading with the Enemy Decree 1945 **48,** 476-8
War Damage Law **72,** 258-60
lease of land to international organizations, cession of territory, whether **82,** 88

France (*cont.*)
legislation. *See also* statutory limitation *and* treaties, implementing legislation *below*
implementation by courts in conformity with treaty obligations **115,** 378-80
retroactivity **74,** 455, 507, **78,** 132-6
supremacy, challenge to **93,** 298-9
territorial application
EC obligations and **93,** 236
primacy of treaties and **93,** 236, 239
taxation laws **93,** 236, 239
legislation, interpretation
aids, Art. 177 (EEC Treaty) preliminary ruling **93,** 324
guidelines, object and purpose **93,** 324-5
treaty-implementing legislation
Foreign Minister's interpretation conclusive **78,** 137
treaty as aid **78,** 132
lobster war, with Brazil **47,** 22-4
Maastricht Treaty (1992). *See* European Union Treaty (Maastricht) (1992) *above*
Madagascar, Judicial Cooperation Agreement (1960) **47,** 90-2, 97
Malagasy, Public Service Personnel Convention **40,** 247-9
Mandate, declaration re continuance of **37,** 152, 219, 320, 325, 330
matrimonial property **44,** 488
measure of damages/compensation including valuation of company/property/assets **75,** 711-22
expropriation/nationalization **82,** 137
military service **74,** 302-3
Monaco, War Damage Agreement (1954) **47,** 312, 315-16, 324
Morocco, responsibility for order in **47,** 21-2
nationality
acquisition, recognition of nationality **111,** 179-80
companies **39,** 430-1
criteria **72,** 567-8, 577, **73,** 573-4
competence of foreign court to determine **41,** 379-80
definition **73,** 566
Evian Agreements (1962) **111,** 188-9
loss or deprivation of **40,** 52
married women **44,** 131-3
retention of, Algerian resident in Morocco **41,** 366-8
nationalization of banks and financial institutions **75,** 705-22
constitutionality **75,** 705-22
naturalization **111,** 180
deportation and **111,** 180
necessity, extradition, refusal **106,** 266-7, 272
New Hebrides, Protocol on (1914) **57,** 116-17
New Zealand, *Rainbow Warrior* dispute **74,** 256-77
Niger, Judicial Agreements with **44,** 291-2
nuclear equipment, export ban
acte de gouvernement, whether **106,** 195, 196-7
basis
Opinion to Exporters **106,** 195, 197
Tripartite Agreement (1976) (France, USA, IAEA) **106,** 195
justiciability **106,** 193-7
nuclear tests **74,** 95-6, 265-6
resumption, act of State **106,** 231

statements on **57,** 405-7, 413-15, 424-31, 504-6, 518, 520, 570, 593-9
Treaty banning (1963), applicability **57,** 531-4
ordre public international **74,** 703-4
overseas territories
application of metropolitan law in **118,** 273-8
EC treaty, applicability to **93,** 289
part of territory of **93,** 289
passport, issue of **39,** 461
pension rights **73,** 36-8
petroleum import licensing system, EEC Treaty and **45,** 455-8
political offence
classification as
killing by organized armed group **111,** 508
terrorist offence **111,** 514
relevant factors, struggle for independence **111,** 508
Prize Court, competence **44,** 495-7
property
community of **42,** 164, 166-7
right of **48,** 170
proportionality
between means and legitimate aim **111,** 169-70
human rights **111,** 169-70
public interest, international considerations, definition by reference to **72,** 14
public order/public policy/*ordre public* **47,** 46, 50, 55-6, 58-9, 60-1, 65, 66, 67, 69, 71, 93, 120-2, 125, 128, 159-62, 218, 228-30, 233, **70,** 391, **72,** 92, 676, **73,** 34, 590, 592, **74,** 135, 507, **80,** 427, 431, 432
arbitration **41,** 373
arms trade **47,** 27-8
contract, validity of provisions contravening **113,** 497
executed treaty as *res judicata* **65,** 49-50
expropriation/nationalization, extraterritorial effect **41,** 373
extradition, conditions for **86,** 327
false identity documents and **86,** 334
foreign judgment, recognition/enforcement **106,** 227-8
international law obligations and **65,** 76-7
refugee, non-refoulement to country of origin **111,** 521
public utility
declaration of as expropriation/nationalization **82,** 90
immunity, jurisdiction **80,** 437-8
State immunity, effect on **82,** 88
recognition, State, declaratory theory **52,** 311
recognition, State/government **48,** 145, 148, **65,** 56
recognition/enforcement **80,** 425-8
refugees **44,** 133, **70,** 354-8, 408, 417-18, 432-44, **74,** 402-4
access to courts **70,** 356-8
'actions contrary to the purposes and principles of the UN', grave violations of human rights **111,** 529
agricultural leases **48,** 166-7
alien distinguished **111,** 537
Appeals Commission **74,** 433-44
powers **73,** 603-4
applicable law, law relating to aliens **111,** 536, 537
declaratory nature of grant of status **111,** 524-5

France (*cont.*)
definition, Refugees, Geneva Convention on the Status of (1951) and Protocol (1967) **111,** 523
expulsion, critical date **111,** 526
extradition **111,** 508, 514-25
non-refoulement rules, applicability **111,** 516-20, 524-5
family members, extension of rights of refugee to **111,** 533-43
absence of legislative provision **111,** 537
brothers/sisters **111,** 541
dependent parents or grandparents **111,** 534, 541
lawful residence, preliminary requirement **111,** 538
minor children **111,** 534, 541
mother of child of refugee **111,** 535
own fear of persecution, relevance **111,** 534, 535-7, 541
right not to be returned to country of origin **111,** 536
right to invoke European Convention on Human Rights (1950) **111,** 536
right to residence permit **111,** 536
spouse **111,** 533-43
family unity
expulsion **111,** 547
right of family members to join refugee **111,** 538
judicial review
administrative review **111,** 527
assessment of facts **111,** 542
exhaustion of administrative remedies, need for **111,** 516
legislative reciprocity **70,** 354-5
matrimonial property rights **52,** 338
mistaken recognition as nationals, effect **72,** 648-9
non-refoulement
extradition distinguished **111,** 516-20, 524-5
general principle of international law **106,** 264
Office for the Protection of Refugees **70,** 384-5, **74,** 408, 417-18, 433, 442
competence **70,** 384-5
'persecution', birth control policy **111,** 530-1
'persecution or well-founded fear of persecution'
burden of proof **111,** 547
relevant factors, attitude of public authorities **111,** 504-5
result of own abuse of human rights **111,** 529
State complicity **111,** 504-5
place of residence, right to choose **73,** 605-6
rights **72,** 587
cautio judicatum solvi **72,** 586-7
identity papers **111,** 537
protected conditions of residence **111,** 537
travel documents **111,** 537
'serious non-political crime'
murder by organized armed group **111,** 508
remedies **111,** 522-3
status
application for
entitlement to remain lawfully in country until status regularized or admission into another country obtained **111,** 527-8
unlawful presence, relevance **111,** 527

status, withdrawal
competent authority **111,** 515-16
grounds **111,** 515-16, 522
as *res judicata* **111,** 515-16
Refugees, Geneva Convention on the Status of (1951) and Protocol (1967)
interpretation **111,** 517-18
extradition/non-refoulement, distinction, whether **111,** 517-18
responsibility **111,** 539
obligation to respect **111,** 522
remedies
breach of treaty, reciprocal action **106,** 267
judicial review distinguished **106,** 248
'reparation or satisfaction within the meaning of international law' **106,** 248
repatriated nationals, legal protection **41,** 274
requisition, compensation for **72,** 237-8
res judicata **73,** 250-1
reserved domain **82,** 88
residence, territorial scope **62,** 393, 409
resistance forces
crimes against humanity and **122,** 82
injuries, war wounds, whether **47,** 463
restitution of stolen goods **44,** 458
Romania and
Compensation Agreement **44,** 102-3
Establishment Convention (1930) **48,** 172, 173
Senegal and, pension rights of former members of French armed forces **114,** 313-19
separation of powers
judicial/administrative, State immunity and **65,** 56
treaties, legislation, conflict **88,** 204-5, **93,** 249
service of process on diplomatic agent, procedural requirements **77,** 497, 508-9
service of process on foreign State or State agency
acceptance, as waiver of immunity **65,** 87
method, commercial/trade representation/mission of unrecognized State **65,** 56
shipping line as State agency/wholly-owned corporation **65,** 69-70
ships, State-owned, immunity, jurisdiction, carriers' liability **65,** 68-70
social security
legislation, EEC law and **48,** 236
stateless person **48,** 165-6
sovereignty
constitutional amendment and **98,** 189
rights, punishment **106,** 237
safeguarding of **74,** 528-9, 688
transfer of powers to international organization **93,** 342-3
International Criminal Court (ICC), Rome Statute (1998) **125,** 482-90
Soviet copyright, effect in **39,** 431-2
Spain
fishing rights **74,** 142-8
maritime delimitation **71,** 144, 150
standard of treatment of alien
equality **72,** 589-90
national treatment, treaty provision **45,** 366-70
States
equality, Head of State immunity and **125,** 500

France (*cont.*)
representation of **89,** 11-14
estoppel **89,** 12-13
successor State, power to determine **89,** 13
waiver of legal requirement **89,** 11-14
State agency/State-owned corporation/State entity
as agency of State **65,** 69, 84-5
classification
food manufacturing enterprise **65,** 74-5
national airline **77,** 511-13
shipping line **65,** 69-70
SNTR (Algeria) **65,** 84-5
State pension fund **65,** 71-3
classification as, Gaz de France **80,** 437-8
constituent links **113,** 446-7
control as test of independent status, appointment of managers **113,** 486
government news agency **113,** 458
instrumentality, Iranian Atomic Energy Organization (IAEO) **113,** 455
separate legal entity test **65,** 55, 59-60, 65-6, 69, **113,** 455, 458, 486
funding **113,** 455, 459
public service purpose **113,** 486
State immunity **47,** 153, **52,** 155, 316, 321, **77,** 511-13, 515-24
independent legal entity **77,** 513-14, 525-9, 533-4
State immunity, arbitral award, enforcement
exequatur **65,** 48, 52-3, **113,** 445
waiver of right to **113,** 443-4
State immunity, execution/attachment, applicability, winding-up proceedings **65,** 84-5
State immunity, execution/attachment, entitlement
national airline **77,** 511-13
recognition of State/government, relevance **52,** 310-14, **65,** 56
State agency/State-owned corporation/State entity **113,** 486-7
subrogation and **65,** 71-3
State-owned corporation **65,** 59-60
State immunity, execution/attachment, procedural aspects
applicable law, *lex fori* **65,** 72-3
authorization of court, need for **65,** 89-90
exequatur **65,** 52-3, **113,** 445
as jurisdictional measure **65,** 90-1
procedural irregularity **48,** 150
separation of powers and **65,** 56
State immunity, execution/attachment, purpose of proceedings
safeguarding/conservatory measures **65,** 79-82, 90-2, 96-8, 171-2, **89,** 33-6
likely outcome of eventual judgment and **77,** 512
as measure of constraint and legal violence **65,** 77
State immunity, execution/attachment, purpose/use of funds/assets **65,** 92
acquisition **65,** 56
burden of proof **89,** 36
commercial **89,** 35-6, **113,** 444
construction of nuclear reactor/enrichment of uranium **77,** 515-22, **113,** 455-6
contract governed by private law, relevance **113,** 456
contractual provision, relevance **89,** 35-6
determination of, appointment of expert **65,** 60, 81-2, 97

duty/right to examine **65,** 60, 81-2, **77,** 516
mixed **65,** 72-3
national airline **82,** 72-3
non-specific **65,** 56, 92, 97
ownership as test **77,** 520
property exclusively intended for industrial or commercial activity giving rise to proceedings **113,** 456
guarantee for repayment of loan **113,** 457
specific allocation of funds, need for **75,** 17-20, **77,** 516, **113,** 457
public services **65,** 81-2
State pension fund **65,** 71-3
State immunity, execution/attachment, theory/doctrine
absolute theory **65,** 56, 79-82, 89-92, 171-2
basis
comity **65,** 76-7
international public order/public policy/*ordre public* **113,** 444
State immunity, jurisdiction distinguished **65,** 52-4, 59-60
State immunity, execution/attachment, waiver
arbitration clause/agreement **65,** 48, 52-3, 98
clear and unequivocal communication, need for **65,** 77
waiver of immunity, jurisdiction and **65,** 49, 52-4, 97
State immunity, jurisdiction, acts of armed forces while on duty **42,** 135-6, 137-8
State immunity, jurisdiction, classification of act
affidavit in interests of public service **65,** 66-7
armed forces accommodation contract **42,** 123-4
attempt to ensure State-controlled body's performance under private contract **113,** 460-1
carriage of goods **65,** 68-70
construction of building for US administrators of Marshall Plan **44,** 76-8, **65,** 40
consul, official acts of **45,** 381-3
diplomatic premises, sale and repurchase **113,** 462-4
expropriation/nationalization **65,** 74-5, 84-5
foreign exchange control **65,** 65-6
gas-pipelines, cathodic protection **113,** 446-7
lease of building for use as State school **65,** 33-6
lease of premises for consular purposes **89,** 38-9
lease of premises for use as government tourist office **52,** 321, **65,** 62-3
medical secretary/nurse **113,** 469
military procurement, military equipment for use of armed forces **44,** 74
nature or purpose of transaction as determining factor, act rather than actor **65,** 72
personal injury outside forum State, customary international law **65,** 41-3
private person test **65,** 34-5, 40
public works contract **65,** 40, **113,** 447
railway construction **82,** 65
railways administration/operation **65,** 41-3
sale of commodities **65,** 59-60
supply of goods within framework of government decisions **113,** 486
supply of military equipment **44,** 74
tourism promotion **65,** 62
State immunity, jurisdiction, entitlement
recognition of State/government, relevance **52,** 310-14

France (*cont.*)
State agency/State-owned corporation/State entity, government news agency **113,** 458-9
State enterprise **80,** 437-8
State shipping line **65,** 69-70
State-controlled entity **77,** 531-2
court's right/duty to raise *proprio motu* **77,** 531-2
State-owned corporation **65,** 59-60
State immunity, jurisdiction, procedural aspects
applicable law, Vienna Convention on Diplomatic Relations (1961) **113,** 472
burden of proof, construction of houses for US visiting forces **42,** 123-4
court's right/duty to raise *proprio motu* **80,** 432, **113,** 479, 480
effective remedy, right to and, right of suit in 'defendant' State's courts. *See* right of suit in 'defendant' State's courts *below*
entitlement to raise, State concerned **113,** 465, 468, 479, 480
presumption of **113,** 468
right of suit in 'defendant' State's courts **106,** 244-8, 260
applicable law, relevance **106,** 244-5, 246, 260
availability of international remedy, relevance **106,** 247-8
nature or purpose of transaction as determining factor **106,** 246
State practice **106,** 245-7
State immunity, jurisdiction, theory/doctrine
basis
independence of States **65,** 34
international courtesy **65,** 34
law of 18 Ventose, Year II **45,** 382
State immunity, execution/attachment distinguished **65,** 49, 52-4, 97
State immunity, jurisdiction, waiver
clear and unequivocal communication, need for **65,** 87
execution and jurisdiction, need for separate waivers **65,** 49, 52-4, 97
implied
acceptance of default judgment **65,** 87-8
arbitration clause/agreement **45,** 83-5, **65,** 48, 52-3
forum selection clause **65,** 35-6
legal proceedings **106,** 245
submission to the jurisdiction as **65,** 35, 36
appearance as **65,** 52
State practice
as evidence of, generally accepted practice **125,** 503-4
State's right of suit in foreign court **106,** 245-7
State responsibility, treaty, application, loss arising **74,** 278-9
State responsibility for
defective mine-sweeping on the high seas **72,** 258-60
failure to observe international obligations **93,** 329
failure to protect nationals, failure to evacuate **52,** 6-7, **57,** 311-12
failure to publish treaty **72,** 238
Head of State immunity, breach **125,** 507-8
protection of nationals' interests, failure to provide diplomatic protection **72,** 219-22, 238, 266
unlawful act **93,** 329
State responsibility for acts and omissions during revolution
injury caused in operations to quell rebellion **72,** 57-8
insurgents and rioters **72,** 133-4, 267-9

State responsibility for acts and omissions of predecessor government, injury caused in operations to quell rebellion **72,** 57-8
State responsibility for breach of EC law. *See* EC law, breach *above*
State responsibility for breach of treaty, refusal of extradition for public policy reasons **106,** 267-8
State responsibility for contract
 action leading to breach **106,** 196, 197
 breach **72,** 254-62
 lawful termination **106,** 196, 197
State succession **72,** 54-8, **73,** 33-8
 foreign judgment, recognition/enforcement **89,** 11-14
 State contract **48,** 58-60
State-owned ships, commercial activity **65,** 39
State-sponsored terrorism, Head of State, immunity, jurisdiction **125,** 497-8, 507
stateless person **44,** 133
 social security **48,** 165-6
statutory limitation
 crimes against humanity. *See* crimes against humanity, statutory limitation *above*
 European Convention on Human Rights (1950) **78,** 132-6
  human right or fundamental freedom, whether **78,** 135
 retroactive removal of right to, arbitrary detention, whether **78,** 132-6
 war crimes **78,** 136-7, 140
steel industry, 1966 measures, EEC Treaty and **47,** 406-11
Switzerland, boundary, River Doubs **47,** 113-15
territory
 cession, lease of land to international organization, whether **82,** 88
 continental shelf **83,** 66
 EEZ **83,** 66
 overseas departments and territories, part of **93,** 289, 306
  elections to European Parliament and **93,** 306-7
terrorism
 crimes against humanity distinguished **125,** 504
 jurisdiction **86,** 42-3
Terrorism, European Convention for the Suppression of (1977)
 Law of Ratification of 16 July 1987 **111,** 523
 reservations, crimes committed prior to entry into force **111,** 523
terrorist acts, extradition for **74,** 453-4
terrorist offences, jurisdiction **86,** 42-3
trade union, rights, to strike **74,** 137-8
trademark infringement **73,** 582-9, 593
trademarks, *situs* **45,** 47-8
trading with the enemy laws **41,** 457-9
transport regulations, EEC Treaty and **45,** 458-9
treaties **54,** 315. *See also* treaty interpretation *below*
 act of State **106,** 208-11
 aliens' commercial rights **44,** 145-7
 anticipated implementation **78,** 97
 applicability
  date of challenge to decision under **106,** 248-9
  Hong Kong **106,** 249, 254
  Nuremberg Charter (1945) **100,** 333-7
  ratification/entry into force, relevance **125,** 490, 502-3
  territorial application **106,** 249

France (*cont.*)
breach, remedy, reciprocal action **106,** 267
conformity with Constitution **74,** 527-9, 686-8
constitutional amendment, need for **93,** 343, **98,** 189. *See also* European Union Treaty (Maastricht) (1992) *and* International Criminal Court (ICC), Rome Statute (1998) *above*
constitutional review
absence of ratification by another signatory, relevance **98,** 183-5
before legislative approval, admissibility **98,** 184
expert opinion on international issues, need for **98,** 183, 185
courts
consideration of legality **47,** 53, 56
interpretation **74,** 99-100, 703-4
cumulative **111,** 518
date of entry into force **106,** 249
ratification and publication, relevance **39,** 458-60
direct effect
clear provision, need for **119,** 365
Geneva Conventions (1949) **119,** 365
European Communities Amendment Treaty 1970, effect **52,** 419-21
fundamental change of circumstances
implied term of treaty **106,** 207
municipal law provision **106,** 207
non-contractual basis **106,** 207
suspension, ground for **106,** 206-7
Vienna Convention on the Law of Treaties (1969) **106,** 206-7
implementation, margin of discretion, relevance **106,** 195, 201
implementing legislation, need for **45,** 385-6, 489-90
regulation, prior legislation and **44,** 295-6
incorporation into municipal law, Nuremberg Charter (1945) **100,** 337
individual's rights **47,** 340-1
interpretation
agencies of **39,** 465-6
courts, powers of **73,** 700-1, 704, **74,** 99-100, 703-4
executive certificate/statement **72,** 589
Foreign Minister **44,** 297-8, **77,** 503
judicial review, absolute liability for abnormal damage, in case of **96,** 218
municipal law and **42,** 137
primacy. *See* primacy *below*
separation of powers **88,** 204-5
primacy **65,** 43, 45, **72,** 193-4, 589, 676, 688, **77,** 132, 501, **78,** 129, **88,** 203, 204-5, **93,** 29, 239, 307, **100,** 337, **106,** 261-2
administrative act **93,** 300
change of doctrine **93,** 253-4
compatibility, power to determine and **93,** 246-53, 291-5, 302-3, 307-8
constitutionality of conflicting legislation distinguished **93,** 252-3, 292
dualist doctrine, relevance **93,** 253-4
EC Treaty, distinction, whether **93,** 304-5
general principles of extradition law **106,** 264
human rights treaties **93,** 302-3
multilateral and bilateral treaties, distinction, whether **93,** 292-3, 303-4
pacta sunt servanda **93,** 342-3
reciprocity, relevance **106,** 224-5, 230

relative and contingent nature **93,** 292
repeal of existing law **88,** 225, **93,** 290
separation of powers **93,** 291, 295
subsequent legislation **88,** 204, **93,** 243-62, 290-5, 296
subsequent treaty **93,** 342-3, **111,** 169
territorial application of tax law and **93,** 236, 239
publication, need for **42,** 265-7, **45,** 385-6, 459-60, **65,** 49, **73,** 696, **82,** 66
correction of published text **48,** 209-11
suspension of treaty **106,** 211-13
ratification, fact and form distinguished **106,** 209
reciprocity
need for **106,** 224-5, 230
relevance **88,** 207-9, **93,** 8, 31, 236, 255, 263-4, 301-2, 343, 346, 347
responsibility for determining **106,** 224-5, 227
retroactive effect, elements on which treaty makes no provision **106,** 226-7
sovereignty, surrender, derogation, right of and **111,** 495-6
State responsibility to subjects for conclusion **41,** 480-2
suspension **106,** 206
act of government **117,** 423
act of State **106,** 208-11
courts **106,** 207-8
executive responsibility **106,** 207-8, 211
Head of State **106,** 210-11
as implementation of treaty **106,** 210
judicial review **106,** 209-10
municipal law, effect on **106,** 209, 212-13
notification through diplomatic channels **106,** 211-12
publication, need for **106,** 211-13
responsibility **106,** 210
treaty provision **106,** 206
termination, parties' agreement, need for **106,** 230
third parties
Japanese Peace Treaty **48,** 230-1
obligations **125,** 502-3
treaty-making power **39,** 456. *See also* conclusion *above*
compatibility with Constitution **52,** 419-21
USSR, recognition of and previously concluded treaties **47,** 240
treaties, State succession, France–Belgium Judicial Convention (1899) **113,** 483
treaty interpretation. *See also* treaties *above*
by arbitrator **82,** 66-7, 74-5
contrary to international public policy, whether **82,** 67
by Constitutional Court **111,** 499-500, 522, 539
by executive **82,** 66-7, 74-5, 84, **93,** 302, **107,** 56-7, 61-2, **111,** 500
by municipal courts **82,** 66, 84
definition of scope and effects distinguished **82,** 66
general principles of law **93,** 280
government interpretation
binding on arbitrator, whether **82,** 66-7
binding on court, whether **93,** 255
guidelines
literal interpretation **93,** 280
purpose and spirit **82,** 81-2, 84
responsibility, change of practice **107,** 56-7, 61-2, **111,** 499

France (*cont.*)
UN High Commissioner for Refugees, agreement with **42,** 241-3
UNESCO, representatives accredited to, immunity **74,** 278-9
unfair competition law **73,** 582-4, 586, 589-94
United Kingdom and, continental shelf delimitation **71,** 94, 101, 120, 151, 188
Universal Declaration of Human Rights, publication of **39,** 460-1
USA and
Air Services Agreement, interpretation **38,** 182-360
armed forces, liability for acts of **45,** 462-3
Cameroons and Togo, Agreements *re* (1923) **37,** 527
Vichy State
anti-semitism **100,** 354
Militia **100,** 355
practising policy of ideological supremacy, whether **100,** 352-5
Vienna Convention on Diplomatic Relations (1961), breach as basis for award of damages **113,** 471-2
Vietnam and
independence, agreement on transfer of (1949) **44,** 37-8
non-recognition **52,** 311-13
war
fisheries dispute with Nicaragua, capture and sinking of ship, whether act of **48,** 469-74
Suez operations, 1956, whether **48,** 467-8
winding-up proceedings **65,** 84-5, **73,** 33-5
Yugoslavia, compensation agreement **44,** 100-1
Franco-Italian Conciliation Commission 71, 641
Franco-German Mixed Arbitral Tribunal 71, 695
fraud, extraterritorial offence **48,** 88-90
free elections
European Parliament elections
margin of appreciation **123,** 19-20
right to participate in **123,** 5-24
free trade agreement, European Economic Area (AEA) Agreement (1991), free trade agreement, whether **113,** 328
Free Zones of Gex and Upper Savoy, special status **40,** 53-5
freedom of assembly/association. *See also* European Convention on Human Rights (1950), freedom of assembly/association; International Covenant on Political and Civil Rights (1960), freedom of association; trade union
abuse of rights and **122,** 417-18
EC **93,** 431
international official **38,** 427-31
political party
application to **122,** 415-29
choice of name **122,** 427
right to carry on activities **122,** 420
right to found **122,** 420
right to strike and **90,** 185, 186, 187, 199, 205-8, **94,** 248-59
right of workers to act in concert **94,** 249-50
strike, right to. *See* strike, right to
trade union **57,** 279, 286-8, 297-8, **58,** 14-16, 33, **68,** 31, 37, 39, **70,** 250-8, **73,** 389-90, **77,** 631-5, **78,** 405-21
freedom of association 73, 389-90, **90,** 548-9
freedom of belief. *See* European Convention on Human Rights (1950), freedom of belief
Freedom, Commerce and Navigation (FCN) Treaty, Italy–USA (1948)
alleged breaches **84,** 325, 326, 327, 328, 329, 352, 354-87

'arbitrary or discriminatory measures' **84,** 378-83, 423
compromissory clause **84,** 348
'constant protection and security of nationals' **84,** 369, 371, 401
corporation rights under **84,** 392-7
'corporations and associations' **84,** 370
expropriation/nationalization **84,** 369
'full and complete compensation' **84,** 426-7
'interests' **84,** 376-7
Italian company operating in Italy, protection of **84,** 396-8
'nationals' **84,** 370
prompt payment of just and effective compensation **84,** 401
'property' **84,** 370, 394
ratification process **84,** 403-6
'right to acquire, own and dispose of immovable property or interests' **84,** 383-7
'right to organize, control and manage' **84,** 356, 402
'rights' **84,** 377
standard of protection
international law **84,** 370, 371, 372
MFN **84,** 370, 371, 372
nationals **84,** 370, 371, 372, 373
Supplementary Agreement (1951)
integral part of FCN treaty **84,** 354, 402-3
purpose **84,** 354, 404-6
taking of property **84,** 373-83
freedom of communication
occupied territories, in **83,** 190-1
International Committee of the Red Cross, with **83,** 190-1
freedom of conscience 48, 28-30, **70,** 135-51, **71,** 497-9. *See also* conscientious objection; European Convention on Human Rights (1950), freedom of conscience; International Covenant on Civil and Political Rights (ICCPR) (1966), conscientious objection
emergent society, in **70,** 150
Jehovah's witnesses **70,** 135-51
national anthem, requirement to sing **70,** 135-51
national flag, requirement to salute **70,** 135-51
national unity and **70,** 147-8
religious ceremonies
refusal to participate in **70,** 135-51
'religious' nature of activity **70,** 138-42
restrictions, justification for **70,** 146-51
freedom of convictions. *See* freedom of conscience
freedom of establishment 44, 145-7, **47,** 245, 248, 249-50, **55,** 492, **61,** 425-6, **77,** 477, **82,** 145. *See also* aliens, abode, right of; expulsion of alien
commercial occupation **44,** 145-7
right to carry on **44,** 145-7
European Community and. *See* European Community (EC), freedom of establishment
FRG, in **61,** 424-7
legal practitioners **55,** 492
limitations **83,** 389
most favoured nation clause **45,** 367, 369
national treatment **61,** 425-7
prohibited occupations **45,** 366-70
residence permit **61,** 424
residency status and **82,** 675
salaried activity **47,** 245, 248, 249-50

freedom of expression 60, 141-7, 385-6, **70,** 154-83, 210-20, 298-304, **84,** 770-1. *See also* censorship; correspondence; European Convention on Human Rights (1950), freedom of expression; freedom of information
action to prevent or obstruct crime distinguished **122,** 625
blasphemy laws and **87,** 434, 436
broadcasting. *See* broadcasting
constitutional right **101,** 251-2
contempt of court and **78,** 396-402
corporation and **60,** 141
correspondence and **70,** 154-83, **72,** 373
damage to equipment for deployment of nuclear weapons as expression of opinion **122,** 512-13
discrimination **60,** 143
expulsion of alien, compatibility with **71,** 459-61
flag desecration and **122,** 569-601
'desecration' **122,** 585
freedom of speech as synonymous **122,** 595
International Covenant on Civil and Political Rights (ICCPR) (1966) **88,** 586
journalism **75,** 3-30, 33-75
compulsory licensing **75,** 4-30, 33-75
freedom of the press **75,** 13-30, 41-57, 66
nature of profession **75,** 9-12, 14-30, 42, 54-7, 63-5, 68-9
professional associations, compulsory membership **75,** 3-30, 35-6, 41-2, 48-57, 68-9
Talloires, Declaration of **75,** 25-6
limitations **88,** 556
respect for private life **88,** 521
respect for reputation **88,** 521, 524
obscene publications. *See* obscene publications
restrictions
justification
public interest **75,** 5, 10-11, 15, 17, 41-2, 44-6, 50-2, 54-7, **122,** 591, 596-600
public order/public policy/*ordre public* **70,** 210-20, **122,** 589-92
legitimacy **75,** 5-6, 11-30, 41-2, 44, 46, 48-57, 68-9
prior restraint of publication **78,** 402
rights and reputations of others and **79,** 343
right of reply **79,** 348, 349, 351
sedition and, violation of rights, whether **70,** 210-20
State immunity, jurisdiction and **82,** 309, 318
terrorism and **85,** 33, 34-5, 37-8, 39-40, 42-4, 48-9
test case, intention to promote and **122,** 626
freedom fighter. *See* liberation movements, 'freedom fighter'
freedom from detention, occupied territory, in **83,** 191
freedom from discrimination 91, 330-2. *See also* apartheid; equality; European Community (EC), non-discrimination; European Convention on Human Rights, freedom from discrimination; European Convention on Human Rights (1950), freedom from discrimination; expropriation/nationalization, legality, requirements, non-discrimination; International Covenant on Civil and Political Rights (ICCPR) (1966), freedom from discrimination
access to public service **94,** 428-32
African Charter on Human and Peoples' Rights (1981) **87,** 110
age **84,** 435, 438-9, 453
bilateral commercial treaty, employees 'of their choice' **101,** 619-23
Cuban measures against US property **42,** 49-50

currency conversion measures **42,** 153-4
deportation **61,** 241-5
deportation of protected person and **83,** 184
direct and intentional discrimination, need for **96,** 664
effective remedy before national authority, right to **120,** 67
English-speaking protestants in Colombia, treatment of **96,** 705-6
equality before the law and **37,** 465
equally unfavourable treatment **37,** 469
espionage, national acting within borders and non-national acting abroad **94,** 75
European Coal and Steel Community Treaty, **55,** 461-7, 479
extradition and **87,** 162
  as instrument of **98,** 454, 455-7, 459, 472
extraterritorial legislation, whether **98,** 577
fishing rights, treaty provision for **82,** 616-17, 626, 646-7, 657
general principle of law **83,** 652
geographic location and **82,** 447-53
homosexuality **67,** 408, 418-19, 423, 426-8
  age of consent **67,** 417-18
illegitimacy
  Convention on the Legal Status of Children Born out of Wedlock (1975) **88,** 216
    implementation **88,** 201-3
  succession, right of **88,** 217-20
inhuman treatment and **120,** 91-4, 115, 125
International Covenant on Civil and Political Rights (ICCPR) (1966). *See* International Covenant on Civil and Political Rights (ICCPR) (1966), freedom from discrimination
ILO Convention 111 (Discrimination in Employment) **43,** 319
justification for discrimination **96,** 362-3
legislation **90,** 622
  extraterritorial effect **90,** 622-41
membership of a particular social group and **124,** 482, 495-6
minorities and **92,** 186, 193
minorities treaties and **37,** 465-7
  State succession and **95,** 57-8
motive or intentions, relevance **37,** 450, 461
naturalization and **60,** 222
as norm **37,** 348, 350, 356-60, 366-84, 413, 450-71, 547-8, 552-3, 558, 573-8
occupied territory, application of law **47,** 472-6
peaceful enjoyment of possessions **120,** 67
Political Rights of Women Convention (1953) **47,** 196-7
prisoner of war **61,** 241-5
private and family life **120,** 67
public service appointments **47,** 196-7
racial. *See* racial discrimination
reasonableness and **37,** 464-77
religious **87,** 435-6
  hard-hat, requirement to wear **96,** 663-4
religious. *See* crimes against humanity, classification, religious persecution
sexual. *See also* married women; women
  African Charter on Human Rights and People's Rights (1981) **103,** 179
  customary law **87,** 107-20
  UN Charter **83,** 355
  Universal Declaration of Human Rights (1948) **87,** 110
State contract, liability for, repudiation **92,** 438-9

freedom from discrimination (*cont.*)
taking of property **84,** 326, 378-9
treaties. *See* minorities treaties *above*
unilateral amendment of conditions of service **83,** 652, 655
Universal Declaration of Human Rights (1948) **124,** 482, 496, 505
freedom from inhuman or degrading treatment. *See* American Convention on Human Rights (1969), inhumane treatment; European Convention on Human Rights (1950), inhuman or degrading treatment; inhuman or degrading treatment; International Covenant on Civil and Political Rights (1966), inhuman or degrading treatment
freedom of information
disclosure of information under the Chicago Convention (1944) relating to accidents and incidents **120,** 561-3
public interest privilege and **120,** 576-7
freedom of movement 60, 134-5, **71,** 257-8, **73,** 391-2
alien **60,** 252, 253, 268-9, 271, 279
alien husband, refusal of residence permit **103,** 230-4
children, restrictions on, effect on parent **103,** 164-7, 197
desirability **83,** 389
divided nation, in case of **100,** 383-4
exit visa, entitlement **73,** 391-2
public policy considerations **73,** 391-2
expropriation and **118,** 321
FRG–Poland Border Treaty (1990), effect **108,** 662
incompatibility of GDR border regime with international law **100,** 371
arbitrary deprivation of life **100,** 384-8
manifest violation **100,** 380, 392
national security **100,** 382
proportionality and **100,** 371, 379, 384, 387-8
public order/public policy/*ordre public* **100,** 382
limitations **83,** 389, **100,** 383
occupied territory, in **83,** 189-90, 191
passport. *See* passport
restrictions on **73,** 392
right to leave one's country
Czechoslovakia **74,** 410-11
GDR **100,** 380-7
International Covenant on Civil and Political Rights (ICCPR) (1966) **100,** 380-7
Netherlands **101,** 407-9
passport withdrawal **101,** 407-9
travel to foreign country **55,** 449-52
Universal Declaration of Human Rights (1948) and **83,** 458
freedom of navigation 74, 127-34, **76,** 463, 639, 714, **120,** 278-83, 286-7
definition
Oscar Chinn **120,** 235-6, 283
Wimbledon **120,** 283
duty to safeguard **73,** 165
EEZs and **95,** 677, 705, **120,** 287-95
environmental protection group, right of interference **101,** 434-5
public interest **101,** 434-5
freedom to fish distinguished **125,** 425
fundamental principle of international law **120,** 286
interference for safety reasons **74,** 95-6
Law of the Sea Convention (1982) **110,** 769, **120,** 223-4, 233-6, 278-81

as customary international law **95,** 705, **120,** 588
as part of the freedom of the high seas **120,** 279
refuelling of fishing vessel and **120,** 192, 237-9, 262-3
as right of individual **120,** 234-6
rivers. *See* rivers, freedom of navigation
territorial sea **125,** 350-1
common law **125,** 423-5
freedom of the press. *See also* freedom of association; freedom of expression; journalism
broadcasting service, obligation to maintain and **90,** 385-6
restrictions **60,** 142
freedom of religion 43, 188-91, **47,** 205-11, **73,** 401-26
blasphemy laws and **87,** 433, 434-5
freedom of the seas. *See* fisheries, conservation and management measures; freedom of navigation; high seas, freedom of
freedom of speech 82, 331-7. *See also* freedom of expression
terrorist organization and **82,** 307-14, **120,** 375-8
freight forwarding services, commercial activity **63,** 267, 276
French *Communauté* 83, 17, 51-2
autonomy of members **44,** 26-32
French Indo-China, independence, continuity of law **47,** 97-9
French Polynesia
burial grounds
failure to protect as breach of minority rights **118,** 277
family life, respect for and **118,** 264-78
non-application of metropolitan law **118,** 273-8
'indigenous tribunals', jurisdiction **118,** 266, 274
International Covenant on Civil and Political Rights (ICCPR) (1966), applicability **118,** 266-7, 276-7, 278
land disputes, settlement **118,** 266, 274
law of, Code of Civil Procedure, Art. 25 **118,** 267
French Union, Associated States 39, 410
Frente Sandinista de Liberación Nacional (FSLN) 76, 354
friendly settlement *See* European Court of Human Rights, friendly settlement; Inter-American Commission on Human Rights, friendly settlement procedure
fringe system. *See* reefs
frontier travellers, taxation **40,** 292-5
***frontière maritime* 71,** 92
frustration. *See* contract, frustration; treaties, frustration
fundamental change of circumstances. *See* boundaries, fundamental change of circumstances; treaties, fundamental change of circumstances
fundamental justice. *See also* Canada, Charter of Rights and Freedoms, s 7 (right to life, liberty and security/fundamental justice); death penalty, appeal to international bodies; fundamental rights within the EC/EU; *and individual human rights*
appeal, frustration **124,** 418-19
applicable law
international law **124,** 359
law of the forum **124,** 359
balance of interests **98,** 375, 379, **124,** 319-21, 338-40, 358-69, 382-3, 404, 416-17, 418
'reasonable limits' **124,** 382-3
right to stay of extradition or deportation pending consideration of case by international body **124,** 403-5, 407, 417-27. *See also* death penalty, appeal to international bodies
war crimes, retroactive/external jurisdiction and **98,** 572-7

fundamental rights
accused's right to silence **44,** 259
common law **118,** 374
fundamental rights within the EC/EU 55, 469, 470-1, 475-6, 480, 481-4, **62,** 396-7, 402, **93,** 343, 390-401, 437-8, 542-7
arbitrary act, freedom from **93,** 431
Art. 177 proceedings **93,** 542, 543-5
breach, effect on Act of Accession **93,** 424
breach by Community institution
national courts, role **98,** 216
national courts' role, general guarantee **98,** 216
codification, need for **93,** 390-1, 401, 428-9, 434-6
Common Foreign and Security Policy (CFSP), effect **98,** 217
complementary roles of ECJ and national courts **98,** 216, 218-19
constitutional traditions and **93,** 398, **117,** 292
continued validity of instrument of accession and **93,** 424
direct effect of EC law, relevance **93,** 392-3
double jeopardy/*non bis in idem*, avoidance **93,** 397, 431
EC and national practice, need for substantial similarity **93,** 435-6
EC Treaty, absence of provision **108,** 233, 253-4, **111,** 140
ECJ role **93,** 398, 616-21, **98,** 216-17, 218-19
absence of European Union jurisdiction **98,** 216-17
relevance to EC law, need for **93,** 616-21
EEC Treaty (Rome) (1957) **93,** 517
EU Treaty (Maastricht) (1992) **108,** 233-4, 254
European Convention on Human Rights (1950) and **93,** 398, 429, 432, 433-4, 435, 615-22, **117,** 287
accession
absence of negotiating Mandate **108,** 249-53
Commission's proposal **108,** 234-5
compatibility with Treaty of Rome **108,** 253-5
need for Treaty amendment **108,** 255
applicability
connection with Community law, need for **113,** 269, 275, 276
imprisonment for criminal offence **113,** 269, 274-6
challenge in European Court of Human Rights **123,** 13, 22
ECJ's competence to interpret **113,** 268-9
ECSC coal regulations, compatibility **55,** 461-3, 467
EEC Treaty (1957) compared **62,** 391, 402
protection equivalent to that provided by **111,** 140-1
European Patent Convention **111,** 146
respect for based on **111,** 141, **113,** 278
as general principle of law **108,** 255, **113,** 268, 278
social and home affairs, compliance with **98,** 218
European Parliament, need for **93,** 390-1, 401, 428, 432-3, 434-5
export, right to **117,** 524-5
fair hearing **93,** 397. *See also* judicial protection *and* legal hearing *below*
fair trial **111,** 135, 141
family life, respect for **93,** 431
freedom of association **93,** 431
freedom of economic activity **93,** 431
freedom from discrimination. *See* European Community (EC), non-discrimination
freedom of religion **93,** 431

general legal principle **93,** 397-8, 434, **112,** 365
constitutional traditions **93,** 429, 430-1
ECJ case-law **93,** 429-32, 433, 435
European Convention on Human Rights (1950) and **93,** 429, 433-4, 435, **117,** 286, 321
International Covenant on Civil and Political Rights (ICCPR) (1966), effect **112,** 365
national variations **93,** 543
inalienable **93,** 390-400, 536
judicial protection **93,** 398-9, 428, 431-2, 434, 436-7, 542-7
Art. 174 declaration of invalidity and **93,** 544-7
ECJ **93,** 398
national courts **93,** 398
legal certainty **93,** 397, 426, **117,** 286-7
retroactivity and **93,** 431
legal hearing **93,** 423-4, 428, 542. *See also* fair hearing *and* judicial protection *above*
expert assistance **93,** 428
liberty of person, deprivation, imprisonment for criminal offence **113,** 269, 274-6
Maastricht Treaty (1992), effect **98,** 217
national control of Community law and **98,** 209-10
national courts, role **93,** 536, 542-7, **98,** 216, 218-19
political declarations in respect of **108,** 234, **111,** 140-1
property, right to **93,** 431, **117,** 289-90
interference with in the public interest, proportionality **117,** 290-1, 300-2, 321
non-discrimination **93,** 476-80
proportionality. *See* European Community law, requirements, proportionality
protection **93,** 517, 524-5
confidence **93,** 397
ECJ role, absence of European Union jurisdiction **98,** 216-17
European Union Treaty (Maastricht) (1992) **93,** 343
reasoned decisions **93,** 431
respect for based on
international treaties **113,** 278
Member State practice **108,** 255, **111,** 141, **113,** 268, 278
sexual discrimination. *See* European Economic Community Treaty (Rome) (1957), sexual discrimination
Single European Act **108,** 233, 254
State obligation as source **93,** 200
territorial scope, expansion **98,** 215-16
unconstitutionality, finding of, retroactivity **93,** 50, 54-5, 58

Gabčíkovo/Nagymaros Project
applicable law
customary international law **116,** 223-4, 243
general treaties **116,** 224
treaties relating to the Danube **116,** 224
Treaty on Construction and Operation of Barrage System (1977) **116,** 223
environmental impact assessment **116,** 120-2, 242
environmental consequences **116,** 151-3, 186-90
Mutual Assistance Agreement (1977) **116,** 33-4
sustainable development and **116,** 97-120
acceptance of applicability of principle **116,** 99
Treaty on Construction and Operation of Barrage System (1977)
breach by Hungary **116,** 55, 135-6, 151-4, 167-72, 175-6, 185-98, 236-7, 241-3

Gabčíkovo/Nagymaros Project (*cont.*)
Czechoslovakia's right to implement 'provisional solution' **116,** 55-66, 172-4, 199-212, 214-23, 228-35, 236-40, 241-9. *See also* unilateral action under *below*
effectivités **116,** 135-41
environmental developments, provision for **116,** 76-7, 86-7, 122-4, 132, 133, 187-8
precautionary principle **116,** 161
obligation to reach negotiated settlement of dispute **116,** 85-9, 146-50, 177, 211-12, 226, 249-50
'related instruments' **116,** 37, 162-6, 180, 208
'socialist integration' and, effect of disappearance of COMECON **116,** 203-4
State succession and **116,** 78-82, 135, 224
termination
notice, effect **116,** 66-82, 95-6, 205-8, 213-14
premature **116,** 75-6, 94, 219-23
terms **116,** 29-33, 162-4
'treaty of a territorial character' **116,** 81, 134-6, 138-9
unilateral action under **116,** 63, 65, 136-43, 154-9. *See also* Czechoslovakia's right to implement 'provisional solution' *above*
works
acceleration **116,** 47
description **116,** 38-40
suspension **116,** 40-3
necessity **116,** 46-55, 168-9, 191-8
Gabon
Constitution (1961) **48,** 153
diplomatic immunity, jurisdiction, real/immovable property, dispute relating to, recovery of rent **89,** 44
expropriation/nationalization, draft Ordinance, constitutionality **48,** 151-4
law of
Law 7/65 of June 1965 (Warsaw Convention) **89,** 41
Law 48/61 (Vienna Convention on Diplomatic Relations (1961)) **89,** 44
garnishment 63, 215-27, 525-7
GATT. *See* General Agreement on Tariffs and Trade (GATT) (1947)
General Act for the Pacific Settlement of Disputes (1928)
applicability **57,** 447, 548-67
breach **57,** 501-2
continental shelf, disputes concerning and **60,** 582, 591-3, 625, 638
disputes between members, procedure governing **53,** 36, 43, 47
ICJ jurisdiction and **57,** 447, 472, 503, 546, 562-6
interim measures of protection and **60,** 525, 529, 534-5, 546, 557
League of Nations and **57,** 553-67
PCIJ, dissolution, effect **57,** 474-503, 555
reservations **60,** 580-7, 622-3, 629, 634-40
territorial status, disputes concerning and **60,** 580, 582-3, 587-93, 623-4
treaty in force, whether **60,** 529, 573-5, 621
desuetude and **60,** 529
UN Resolution concerning (1949) **46,** 167-8
General Agreement on Tariffs and Trade (GATT) (1947) 60, 646-9, **77,** 551-6
Agreement on Interpretation and Application of Articles VI, XVI and XXIII (Subsidies and Countervailing Duties) (1979), implementing legislation **90,** 334-65
Anti-Dumping Implementation Code (1980)
municipal law, effect in **107,** 93-8
obligations of confidentiality

'disclosure pursuant to a narrowly drawn protective order' **107,** 93-8
disclosure to accountant **107,** 97-8
disclosure to company lawyer **107,** 97
disclosure to employee **107,** 96
public interest **107,** 93-8
undertaking of confidentiality, terms **107,** 98-9
Art. XX exceptions
as balance between free trade and governments' right to regulate in interest of public values **121,** 142
NAFTA and **121,** 125, 142, 143, 156-7
narrow interpretation **121,** 138-9
countervailing duties
as economic sanction **107,** 119
interest, under or over-payment **107,** 295-6
judicial review, timeliness **107,** 291-4
material injury, relevance **107,** 281-3, 290-1
retroactive application **107,** 290-1
right to impose **107,** 107-21
direct effect **107,** 286, **117,** 425
dispute settlement
GATT Panels. *See* GATT Panels *below*
Uruguay Round. *See* Uruguay Round, Settlement of Disputes, Understanding on Rules and Procedures
EC implementing legislation **90,** 337 n. 7
economic reprisals, compatibility **60,** 646, 648-9
European Economic Community, effect within **77,** 556
evolving system **110,** 581
federal State, in **90,** 342
GATT Panels
binding on Member States, whether **107,** 285-9
North American Free Trade Agreement (1993) distinguished **107,** 288
individual and **107,** 112-13, **117,** 425
nature of provisions **53,** 35-7, 43, 46-7, **61,** 622-3, 624
North American Free Trade Agreement (1992) and. *See* North American Free Trade Agreement (NAFTA) (1992), GATT/WTO and
obligations, exceptions, narrow interpretation **110,** 577 n. 109
phrases, 'country under the Agreement' **107,** 281
Protocol of Provisional Application **56,** 554-5
standard of treatment
fair and equitable, procedural fairness **121,** 188
MFN clause and **60,** 647-8
national treatment **56,** 553-4
adverse effects on more than one investor, whether necessary **122,** 366
Alcoholic Beverages (Beer) **122,** 367-8
Asbestos case **122,** 366-7
Bananas dispute **122,** 363-6
internal taxes **56,** 554
Myers **122,** 368-9
US–Section 337 of the Tariff Act of 1930 **122,** 369-70
subsidy
countervailing duties. *See* countervailing duties *above*
export price set below prevailing world market price **107,** 112-20
financial burden borne directly or indirectly by government or public body **107,** 112-20

General Agreement on Tariffs and Trade (GATT) (1947) (*cont.*)
imports, material injury, need for **90,** 345-8, 352-65
'subsidy, bounty, reduction or remission of freight or other financial assistance' **107,** 111-21
Uruguay Round, redefinition **107,** 121
Treaty of Rome (1957) and **53,** 25, 32-7, 42-3, 46
Uruguay Round. *See* Uruguay Round
General Assembly. *See* United Nations General Assembly (UNGA)
general interest, legal recognition **37,** 419, 421-2, 511-21
general international law. *See* customary international law; international law, principles and rules
general principles of agency law, imputability of acts 107, 233
general principles of banking law, liability for loss **107,** 208, 217
general principles of commercial law 84, 552
general principles of company law 84, 293-5, 390-1, 392
treaty and **84,** 392
general principles of compensation 62, 176
general principles of EC law
proportionality **93,** 370, 431
respect for fundamental rights within the EC/EU **93,** 378
general principles of equity 84, 608, **99,** 599-600
general principles of expropriation/nationalization 56, 317
general principles of extradition law
amnesty in requesting State **106,** 264
legal system of requesting State **106,** 264
general principles of humanitarian law 76, 447, 448, 463-4
unconditional respect for fundamental human rights **108,** 46-7
general principles of international arbitration law
arbitral procedure **62,** 181-2
separability of arbitration clause **96,** 269
general principles of international civil service law 83, 650
general principles of international comity, immunity of international organizations **80,** 34
general principles of international law 41, 156-8, **66,** 560-1, 562, **70,** 501, 508, 519-22, 525, **72,** 440, 520, 531, 613, **77,** 35, 245, 269, 537, 581, 600, **79,** 83, 87, 105, 291-2, 366, **80,** 135, **82,** 139, **84,** 280, 297, **95,** 96. *See also* customary international law; international law, principles and rules
abuse of process **62,** 88-9
acquired rights **62,** 352-3, **89,** 497
importance of concept under traditional international law **46,** 484-5
act of State doctrine **36,** 46, **100,** 372
aliens, admission, sovereign right to refuse **90,** 25-6
as applicable law **89,** 329, 450, 521, 552
arbitral award, need for reasons **92,** 43
authorization and obligation distinguished **96,** 189
burden of proof, claimant **106,** 447
challenge to arbitral award **84,** 297
changing conditions, applicability under **110,** 355-6
Chorzów Factory **121,** 127-8
compétence de la compétence **105,** 461, **123,** 254
compliance **108,** 74
conflict **110,** 255-9
resolution, rules for **110,** 258, 509, 541
consent as basis of jurisdiction **62,** 620, **84,** 280, **106,** 543

Continental Shelf Convention (1958), Art. 6 **41,** 157
contract
  definition **89,** 463
  sanctity **62,** 10-11, 190-3
crimes against humanity **104,** 296
  absence of statutory limitation **78,** 135
  knowledge of illegality **104,** 321
customary international law and **41,** 157, **45,** 61, **61,** 180, **115,** 610
damages
  directly related **109,** 389
  fair compensation for loss suffered **109,** 389-90
  mitigation, obligation **109,** 388, 502, 618
damages, measure of **89,** 504
debtor's liability **80,** 132
debts of international organization, Member States' liability **80,** 52-3, 105, 106, 140, 172
double criminality **92,** 725-6
duty not to prejudice future decision of international tribunal **82,** 82
effective remedy, need for **98,** 331, **123,** 136
effects doctrine, intent **99,** 155
environmental protection **116,** 100-1
equality of **110,** 258
equality of States **65,** 191, **82,** 396-7
equity and **40,** 172, 173
estoppel **100,** 65-6
exhaustion of local remedies **45,** 301-2, **46,** 125, 475, **62,** 56, 76, 81, **95,** 255-6
expropriation/nationalization
  compensation **83,** 473, **86,** 457, **106,** 627
  non-discrimination **62,** 194, **92,** 438
expulsion of alien **82,** 159, 160
extradition **78,** 97, 131, **79,** 505, **90,** 677
  respect for fundamental rights and freedoms in requesting State **111,** 508
forcible abduction/unlawful arrest **90,** 679-80
freedom of the high seas **120,** 284, 588
freedom of navigation **120,** 286
general principles of law
  as **61,** 180, **115,** 610
  distinguished **53,** 452-3
generally recognized principles of law distinguished **45,** 60
good faith **120,** 510-11
Hague Conventions (1899/1947) **41,** 158
humanitarian principles **110,** 356, 533-4
inhuman or degrading treatment **98,** 510
interest **42,** 192, **84,** 529 n. 29
  reasonable rate **106,** 472
international claims **46,** 188
inviolability of embassy documents **86,** 150
judicial notice **123,** 492
jurisdiction over visiting forces **86,** 534
justiciability of disputes between foreign States **108,** 587
liability for debts of international organization **81,** 679-80, 699
Lotus principle ('what is not prohibited is allowed') **36,** 283-5, **110,** 220-1, 241-2, 339-40, 341-7, 376, 442-6, **115,** 590
mandamus **37,** 520-1

general principles of international law (*cont.*)
maritime delimitation, agreement as method **92,** 18
ne bis in idem **77,** 581
ne impediatur legatio **65,** 186, **70,** 400, **71,** 572, **77,** 493, **78,** 8, 103, **101,** 360
negotiate, duty to **41,** 202
non liquet and **110,** 272-3, 327, 339-40, 385-6, 507-31, 539-41, **111,** 345
non-refoulement **106,** 264, **111,** 520, 524, 538-9
nuclear weapons, legality **110,** 235
obligation to avoid prejudicing judgment **95,** 95-6
pacta sunt servanda **40,** 2, **86,** 457, **89,** 495-7, **100,** 100, **116,** 151-2, 233
as part of municipal law **66,** 560, **73,** 372, **95,** 471, 479, **102,** 140, 170, **117,** 582
political offence exception **79,** 505
power of Chamber of ICJ to determine **97,** 161
precise connotation **94,** 529
procedural economy **92,** 100
proportionality **99,** 535, 536-40
protection of national shareholders in foreign company **46,** 200
public conscience **110,** 356, 437-41
reciprocity **44,** 53
reparation for breach of treaty **118,** 102-3
res judicata **113,** 43
restitutio in integrum **109,** 28, **121,** 127-8
restrictive interpretation of jurisdiction **85,** 436
retroactivity, criminal offence **100,** 389
reversion doctrine **114,** 40, 115-17
self-defence **110,** 258
self-determination **91,** 230, **105,** 243, 270, 283, **115,** 581
source, human rights conventions **106,** 264-5
source of international law **104,** 335, **107,** 284-5
source of obligation **90,** 666 n. 25, **105,** 283-4
State agency, independence **107,** 379
State contract **62,** 170-6
State immunity, jurisdiction, employment contract **65,** 22
State immunity, jurisdiction, theory/doctrine. *See* State immunity, jurisdiction, general principle of international law
State responsibility **82,** 160, 551
damage caused by either side in military conflict **109,** 511
State succession and **91,** 344-54, 361, 366, 367
State rights **66,** 562
sustainable development **116,** 101-4
territorial integrity **90,** 680, **103,** 21, **115,** 483, 580, 582, 584-5
terrorist offences, jurisdiction **82,** 346-57
treaty, primacy **106,** 264
treaty interpretation, aid to **87,** 348
treaty rules as **80,** 678
uti possidetis juris **80,** 469, 470, 531, **92,** 171-2, **100,** 86-7
Vienna Convention on the Law of Treaties (1969) **82,** 612
war crimes **82,** 438-9, **104,** 296
knowledge of illegality **104,** 321
general principles of international relations, State immunity **82,** 4
general principles of judicial process 76, 373, 374
general principles of jurisdiction, consent as basis **62,** 620, 631
general principles of justice 41, 142-7

general principles of law 37, 455, 460, **40,** 262, 282, **41,** 139-41, **48,** 378, **53,** 366, 439, **70,** 508, 519, **77,** 31, 72, 613, **80,** 171, **81,** 40, **84,** 608
access to courts, right of **57,** 217-18
acquiescence **41,** 130
act of God **41,** 142
actio popularis **37,** 280-1
allegans contraria non audiendus est **50,** 410
applicable principles of international law distinguished **114,** 270
arbitration provisions **48,** 396-400
audi alteram partem **38,** 386, 404-5, 414-17, **54,** 401, **120,** 317
bona vacantia **49,** 231 n. 24
capacity **37,** 140-1
'common law' of international organizations **96,** 235
concession agreement **47,** 396, 399-400, 403
contract
frustration **49,** 147
impossibility **49,** 147
repudiation, compromissory clause and **48,** 397-400
sanctity **62,** 170-1, 176, 190-3
void or voidable **48,** 397
contract, breach
bones mores **106,** 705-6
duty of full disclosure **114,** 208-9, 269-71
international public order/public policy/*ordre public* **106,** 705-6
crimes against humanity, severity of penalty **108,** 193
damages for non-contractual liability, obligation to make good loss **111,** 48
decisions of international and administrative tribunals **96,** 235
declaratory judgment and specific performance distinguished **53,** 364-5
defence, right of **46,** 194, 196
denial of justice **57,** 217-28
derivation
international law **41,** 140
municipal law **41,** 140
'derived from the specific nature of the international community' **99,** 605
diplomatic protection **46,** 474, 495
double jeopardy/*non bis in idem* **124,** 191-3
due diligence **41,** 142
due process **89,** 537-8
equality **41,** 142
equidistance **41,** 31, 85, 138, 141, 184, 204
special circumstances **41,** 151
equity **41,** 142-7, 149, 152, 153, **81,** 271, **99,** 604-7
basis of, as **41,** 142
estoppel **41,** 130, 142, **113,** 133-4
expropriation/nationalization **56,** 317, **85,** 391-2
compensation **83,** 473
public utility **41,** 12
family life, respect for **85,** 337-8
family unity **111,** 538-9
faute **41,** 142
force majeure **41,** 142
frustration **49,** 147
gestion d'affaires **85,** 464-5

general principles of law (*cont.*)
good faith **89,** 385
indemnification of agent for unforeseeable injury **81,** 721, 723
interest **62,** 215
international civil service law **43,** 451
international law, and **53,** 452-3
international morality and **41,** 141, 142
judicial independence **46,** 328-9
jus cogens/peremptory norm and **83,** 26
just and equitable apportionment **41,** 50, 183-4
leading legal systems, relation to **53,** 467-8
lex mercatoria **53,** 447
liability of traders operating collectively **81,** 679
meaning **41,** 140
money judgment, obligation to pay at once **38,** 436
nationality, link concept **46,** 360
negotiate, duty to **56,** 138
nemo [debet esse] judex in propria sua causa **94,** 576, 595, **100,** 180
non-discrimination **83,** 652
non-misuse of rights **41,** 142
non-retroactivity **83,** 652
obligation to compensate **54,** 509
pacta sunt servanda **83,** 561-2, 613, **89,** 385, **96,** 266
presumption of innocence **118,** 85
private property, respect for **53,** 4
privity of contract **37,** 73
prize proceedings **40,** 476-7
property
right to **46,** 447
sanctity of **62,** 176
proportionality **83,** 652
'public order and good manners' **53,** 4
recognized by civilized nations. *See* general principles of law recognized by civilized nations
refugee, non-refoulement **111,** 538-9
reparation for breach of international obligation **95,** 314
res judicata **37,** 483, **89,** 559, 562
retroactive legislation **40,** 395
shareholder claims **46,** 474
State contract **56,** 275, 283
State responsibility **111,** 49
superior orders **108,** 188
territorial principle, Geneva Convention on the Protection of Civilian Persons in Time of War (1949) **48,** 482, 490
treaty
breach, right to terminate **49,** 37-8
interpretation **57,** 217, 304
tribunal established by law, right to **105,** 472-3
trustees, replacement of **37,** 306
unjust enrichment **41,** 142, 146, **44,** 449, 462, 471, **62,** 176
uti possidetis **83,** 58
general principles of law recognized by civilized nations 37, 456-7, **41,** 139-41, **80,** 135, **99,** 605

criminal law **121,** 269-72, **122,** 95
cultural diversity and **116,** 118-19
customary international law and **121,** 350-3, 361-4
'derived from the specific nature of the international community' **99,** 605
duress. *See* duress, general principle of law recognized by civilized nations
interpretation in accordance with local law **116,** 279
judicial impartiality **121,** 350-4
means for determining **121,** 269, 352-3
non liquet and **111,** 345, 440-2
rape **121,** 269-72
specific rules distinguished **111,** 345, 456-7
succession **116,** 279-80
universality, relevance **111,** 344-5, 440-1, **124,** 158-9
general principles of municipal law, State immunity **82,** 32, 33
general principles of private international law 57, 50-1, **62,** 143, 171
general principles of rule of law 53, 584, **57,** 217, **77,** 335
general principles of UN Charter 46, 477
general principles of vested rights 62, 176
general welfare. *See* public order/public policy/*ordre public*, general welfare
Geneva Conventions (1949) 74, 696-7. *See also* Geneva Convention (Treatment of Prisoners of War) (Convention III) (1949); Geneva Convention (Protection of Civilian Persons in Time of War) (Convention IV) (1949)
applicability
agreement of belligerent parties **105,** 443-4, 490-2, 509
Bosnia-Herzegovina **105,** 443-4, 490-2, 523-4, **108,** 149, 158-61, **112,** 184-200, **121,** 254-5
status of parties, effect on **112,** 188
crimes against humanity **112,** 210-11
geographical **105,** 486-9
'in all circumstances' **123,** 102
individual, private **104,** 156
internal conflict **105,** 449, 487-8, 508-11, 538, **108,** 45-6, **112,** 178-81, 202-3
Nicaragua **105,** 508
non-parties **88,** 49, 50
parties to conflict, insurgent military group **104,** 155-6
temporal **105,** 486-8
unilateral undertaking **105,** 509-11
Congo **105,** 509-10
FMLN (El Salvador) **105,** 510-11
Nigeria **105,** 510
Yemen **105,** 509
as codification **104,** 155-6
common Art. 3
applicability to members of armed forces who have laid down arms **122,** 81
breach as war crime **105,** 521-2
customary international law **122,** 68, 81
individual responsibility **122,** 70
rape **121,** 266
customary international law **121,** 267
torture **121,** 254-5, 256
customary international law **91,** 36, **105,** 442-3, 503, 506, 508-10, 586-7, **108,** 163, 465-6, **110,** 149-50, 207, 523, 530, **112,** 201, **122,** 68, **124,** 99 n. 113
extraterritorial jurisdiction **82,** 446-7

Geneva Conventions (1949) (*cont.*)
grave breaches **47,** 493, **105,** 442-4, 489, 496-9, 528-31, 536-8, 586-7, 596, **108,** 31, 44-5, 91, 130-2, 149, **112,** 178, 184-200, **122,** 23, 64-6. *See also* Yugoslavia, International Criminal Tribunal for the Former (ICTY), Statute
civilians, acts against **108,** 44-5, 91, 162-3
appropriation of property **108,** 91
deportation **108,** 31
detention **108,** 91
cruel treatment **112,** 250-1, 253
hostage-taking
'hostage' **122,** 73
UN hostages as human shields **108,** 91
human shields **108,** 91, **122,** 73
individual responsibility. **124,** 121 n. 175
internal conflict, applicability **105,** 538, 586-7
international conflict, need for **105,** 442-4, 494, 495-9, 596, **108,** 131-2, 149, **122,** 42-57, **124,** 99
jurisdiction, obligatory nature **36,** 38
'war crimes' **105,** 536, **108,** 44-5, 130-2
Hague Conventions (1899/1907), convergence **105,** 506, 517, 535-7
humanitarian law **105,** 500
implementing legislation, need for **123,** 604
individual, rights **99,** 176
inhuman treatment, as umbrella for other grave offences **122,** 65, 73
interpretation
guidelines
broad **108,** 159, 161
changed circumstances **125,** 566
jurisdiction, *aut dedere aut punire/judicare* **105,** 536
jurisprudence, absence **105,** 534-5
liberation movements, applicability to **88,** 49
municipal law
conflict with **41,** 421-6
part of **123,** 172
obligations, to respect and secure respect **105,** 449, 503
phrases
'each party to the conflict' **104,** 156
'grave breaches'. *See* grave breaches *above*
'of a nature to cause superfluous injury' **108,** 47
proportionality **108,** 48
sanctions, absence **105,** 536
state of war, need for, whether **88,** 49
Geneva Conventions (1949), First Additional Protocol relating to the Protection of Victims of International Armed Conflicts (1977) **74,** 696-7
applicability
international conflict **105,** 444, **108,** 44
nuclear weapons **110,** 209, 278
commanders
duty **122,** 110
failure to prevent crimes of subordinates **122,** 109-10
'had information' **122,** 109-10
crimes against humanity, applicability **112,** 211-12
customary international law and **88,** 50, 52-3, **104,** 91-2, **105,** 536-7, **110,** 209, 515, 530, **122,** 67, 70, 109-10, **124,** 99 n. 113

right to determination of status by competent tribunal **123,** 604
individual, rights **104,** 84
interpretation, French/English version, discrepancy **122,** 109-10
liberation movements, application to **74,** 696-7
political offence exception **104,** 87-8
rape **121,** 266
ratification **99,** 175 n. 32
failure **104,** 91-2
responsibility of commander **122,** 102-3, 109-10
Geneva Conventions (1949), Second Additional Protocol relating to the Protection of Victims of Non-International Armed Conflicts (1977)
applicability
geographical **105,** 488
internal conflict **108,** 44, **119,** 352
determination by trial judge **119,** 352
temporal **105,** 487-8
customary international law and **104,** 156 n. 8, **105,** 506, 514-15, 536-7, **108,** 163, **124,** 99 n. 113
as law or custom of war **108,** 45
Geneva Convention (Treatment of Prisoners of War) (Convention III) (1949) 58, 78, **60,** 212-13
applicability **52,** 502, 503, **83,** 218-23. *See also* status as prisoner of war, entitlement *below*
Bosnia-Herzegovina **122,** 63-4
international armed conflict **42,** 475
Noriega following US intervention in Panama (1989) **99,** 185-7
compensation for loss of earnings **61,** 235, 236
customary international law and **42,** 449, 472, 475
enforcement
individual, by **99,** 187-90, **123,** 607-8
legal action in courts of Detaining Power **99,** 188-90
protest to military authorities of Detaining Power **99,** 187-8
protest to Protecting Power **99,** 188
fair trial. *See also* legal representation, right to *below*
coerced confession **99,** 167-8
fair and impartial tribunal **99,** 167-8
humane treatment, constitutional provision against cruel and unusual punishment distinguished **99,** 192 n. 15
internment
according to nationality **99,** 169
civilian prison **99,** 190-4
detention distinguished **99,** 191
protection of Convention rights **99,** 192-4
interpretation
aids, Red Cross *Commentary* **99,** 170, 186, 191, **124,** 99-100
liberal **99,** 186, 193
most favourable to prisoner **99,** 192, 193-4
jurisdiction
deprivation, express provision, need for **99,** 170
double criminality requirement **99,** 170-1, **119,** 351
equivalency principle **99,** 168
ex post facto legislation **99,** 168-70
offences prior to capture **42,** 457, 472, **99,** 167, 168
legal representation, right to **123,** 607-8

Geneva Convention III (*cont.*)
legality requirement **119,** 351
phrases
'armed conflict' **42,** 463-4, 475, **52,** 498, **99,** 185-6
'belong . . . to a Party to the conflict' **124,** 99-100
'competent tribunal' **99,** 186-7
'fallen into the power of the enemy' **99,** 186
'part of [the] armed forces' of a Party to the conflict **124,** 99-100
'repatriated person' **83,** 220-3
purpose
humanitarian **99,** 171
protection of prisoners from abuse after capture **99,** 171
questioning, rules relating to **123,** 609-10
repatriation after cessation of hostilities, criminal proceedings pending **99,** 169-70
retroactive legislation and **91,** 49-50
status as prisoner of war, entitlement **42,** 442, 446-7, 451, 455-6, 472-3, **99,** 167 n. 22, 185, **123,** 173, 185-8, **124,** 99-100. *See also* applicability *above*
Algerian rebels **44,** 446-7
civilians **122,** 63-4, **123,** 166, 173, 187
evidence, absence **123,** 173
prisoners convicted of crimes **99,** 191-4
'protected prisoner of war' **42,** 444, 445-51, 455, 464-83
saboteurs in civilian dress **42,** 458-70, 483
transfer to third country **99,** 169
Geneva Convention (Protection of Civilian Persons in Time of War) (Convention IV) (1949) 47, 484, 485-6, 487-9, 490, **60,** 215. *See also* belligerent occupation, deportation; Geneva Conventions (1949) *for provisions common to the Conventions*
applicability
acts against civilian persons and property in Bosnia-Herzegovina **108,** 149, 158-61, **112,** 184-200
before establishment of stable occupation regime **123,** 174
assignment of place of residence, legality **125,** 548-60
deportation distinguished **125,** 549-50
imperative reasons of security **125,** 552-60
assignment of place of residence, legality. *See also* belligerent occupation, assignment of place of residence, legality
context **83,** 137, 138-9, 140-1, 142
customary international law **83,** 126, 138, 149, 154-5, 162, 186, 195, 196, **95,** 567, **125,** 547
deportation, permissibility **104,** 84
detention
detainee's right to appeal/be heard **123,** 175-8, 180, 187-8
ICRC right to visit **123,** 166-7
prisoner of war status distinguished **123,** 166, 172-4, 186-8
procedures **123,** 175
as security measure **123,** 174-5, 187-8
discretion **123,** 174-5
extradition, permissibility **104,** 84
general principles of law, and **48,** 482, 490
Hague Regulations (1907) and **83,** 191
interpretation in light of **83,** 185
hostage-taking **83,** 140, **122,** 73
individual, rights of **83,** 154, 186

internal conflict
applicability **95,** 567
asylum in case of flight from, right to **95,** 566-7
Israel, observance by **47,** 490-1
Israeli occupied territories, applicability **48,** 482, 489
local law, respect for **52,** 524-9
military court, appeal from **47,** 487-9, 497
object and purpose **83,** 142-3, **124,** 131-2
occupied territory, deportation from **83,** 129, 137-8, 140-2, 146, 185-97. *See also* belligerent occupation, deportation, prohibition
occupying power
obligations **83,** 137
powers **83,** 148
restrictions on **47,** 492
penal legislation **52,** 514-17
phrases
'armed conflict' **124,** 195-201
'deportations' **83,** 139, 140
'in any manner whatsoever ... in the hands of ... a Party to the conflict ... of which they are not nationals' **108,** 159-60, **112,** 185-200
'in the hands of', in territory under control of Power in question **112,** 185
'occupation' **108,** 160-1
'protected persons' **83,** 143, 144-5, 187, 193, 194, **105,** 497-8, **124,** 130-2
Bosnian civilian victims **108,** 159-60, **112,** 184-200, **124,** 130-2
Bosnian Muslims **122,** 58-63, 216, 248-9
Bosnian Serbs **105,** 494, **124,** 132
co-belligerency **122,** 60-3
critical date **112,** 185-6
diplomatic protection, relevance **124,** 131
diplomatic relations, relevance **122,** 61, 62-3
ethnicity and **122,** 58-60, **124,** 131-2
legality of presence, relevance **83,** 144-5
members of the armed forces *hors de combat* **112,** 203
Muslim detainees at Bosnian Serb detention camp **108,** 35, 132
nationality or domicile, relevance **83,** 146, **105,** 494, **112,** 188-200, 261-2, **122,** 58-9, **124,** 130-2
non-nationals **83,** 144
'persons taking no active part in the hostilities' **112,** 202-3, **122,** 71, 216
travaux préparatoires **124,** 130-2
'protected property', occupation, need for **108,** 160-1, **122,** 64
'regardless of their motive' **83,** 147, 148, 188
'within the occupied territory' **125,** 551-2
retroactive legislation **47,** 496-7
spies and saboteurs **83,** 190, 191
State responsibility, customary international law **112,** 188-9
Geneva Convention on the Continental Shelf (1958). *See* Continental Shelf Convention (1958)
Geneva Convention on the Execution of Foreign Arbitral Awards (1927)
continuing validity **82,** 70
European Convention on International Commercial Arbitration (1961) distinguished **82,** 68
Geneva Convention on the High Seas (1958). *See* High Seas, Geneva Convention on (1958)

Geneva Convention on the Status of Refugees (1951). *See* Refugees, Geneva Convention on the Status of
Geneva Convention on the Territorial Sea and Contiguous Zone (1958). *See* Territorial Sea and Contiguous Zone Convention (1958)
Geneva, Lake, boundaries **41,** 135, 149
Geneva Protocol (Prohibition of Asphyxiating, Poisonous or other Gases and Bacteriological Methods) (1925)
customary international law **110,** 530
'poisonous' **110,** 458-60
genocidal war 42, 439
genocide 77, 210, 220, **91,** 60, 61
act of State **36,** 48
Bosnia-Herzegovina, in
ethnic cleansing **95,** 66, 122, 149-50
target **95,** 152
flagrant conflict with moral law and spirit and aims of UN **95,** 66
Security Council Resolution 819 (1993) (ethnic cleansing) **95,** 66, 122
victims, 'Bosnian people' **95,** 123, 152, 163-4, 172
Chile, in **119,** 340-2
classification as
detention of civilians **108,** 91
ethnic cleansing. *See* ethnic cleansing *below*
failure to list site on World Heritage List **120,** 416
forced expulsion **104,** 187 n. 35, **108,** 135
forcible removal of aboriginal children **118,** 372-9
inhumane treatment **108,** 91, 134-5
murder **108,** 134
component elements **95,** 178
crime against humanity **36,** 41, **78,** 147, **119,** 229
distinguished **121,** 357
customary international law **118,** 330-1, 379, **119,** 106-7, **120,** 361
definition **119,** 338-42. *See also* Genocide Convention (1948), definition of genocide
distinguishing features **36,** 233
International Criminal Tribunal for the Former Yugoslavia, Statute **108,** 133
single act as **36,** 233, **115,** 240
Spain
'intent to destroy, in part or in whole, a national ethnic, racial or religious group' **119,** 339-40
'intent to destroy, in part or in whole, a national ethnic, social or religious group' **119,** 339
State as victim **95,** 63-4
UNGA Resolution No 96 (I) (1946) **36,** 32-3, **119,** 338
delictum juris gentium **95,** 178
ethnic cleansing
Bosnia-Herzegovina **95,** 66, 122, 149-50
constitutive intent **108,** 37, 134-5
northern Cyprus **120,** 110-11
policy, evidence of **108,** 112-19
sexual assaults **108,** 117-19
war crime, whether **95,** 150
General Assembly Resolution 96 (I) **95,** 38
Genocide Convention (1948). *See* Genocide Convention (1948)
individual responsibility **36,** 5-342. *See also* superior orders

campaign coordinated with government **107,** 459
domestic legislation **104,** 155
Nuremberg Charter (1945) **104,** 154
political/military authority **108,** 130
UNGA Resolution 96(I) **104,** 154
Jews, of **54,** 563. *See also* Jews, crimes against the Jewish people
jurisdiction **36,** 34, **57,** 38-9, 611, **118,** 369-70
civil **120,** 366
extraterritorial **119,** 336-7, 338. *See also* universal *below*
passive personality principle **119,** 56
possibility and obligation distinguished **119,** 336-7
universal **36,** 33-9, **82,** 348, **119,** 56, 70-1, 72, **120,** 361-2, 375-6, 391-405. *See also* extraterritorial *above*
jus cogens/peremptory norm **95,** 152, **103,** 616-17, **115,** 193-4, **120,** 366, 372, 377
means to prevent, right to
Genocide Convention (1948) **95,** 62-3, 123, 154, 159
right of self-defence **95,** 62-3, 122
Security Council Resolution 713 (1991) **95,** 63
native title, extinction **120,** 357, 374-5, 405-10
nuclear weapons
deployment **110,** 190, 451-2, 526-7, **111,** 585-90
research **111,** 585-90
obligation *aut dedere aut punire/judicare*, customary international law **120,** 361-5
obligation not to commit
erga omnes **46,** 206, **115,** 39, 175, 218-19
jus cogens/peremptory norm **118,** 376, **120,** 361
obligation to implement rule prohibiting **115,** 175-6
offence under municipal law, whether **119,** 338-42, **120,** 361-6, 373, 405
requirements
intent **36,** 233-4, **108,** 134-5, **110,** 190, 452
dolus specialis **95,** 178
evidence of **108,** 134-5
Revised and Updated Report on . . . the Prevention and Punishment of Genocide **95,** 162-3
self-defence **110,** 467
State responsibility, imputability **95,** 36-7
as terrorism **119,** 342-3
time of events constituting, relevance, events prior to legislation providing for jurisdiction **119,** 336-7
torture as part of **119,** 343
war crime, relative seriousness **121,** 357
Genocide Convention (1948). *See also* genocide; international crimes; terrorism; war crimes
accession
Dayton Agreements (1995) as basis **115,** 200-3
notification of succession **115,** 194-201
relevance **115,** 194-5
applicability
acts committed prior to coming into force of Convention **118,** 330, 372-9
critical date **115,** 30
Head of State **119,** 46, 65-6, 71, 85
nature of conflict, relevance **115,** 28, 174-5
Bosnia-Herzegovina, party to, whether **95,** 29-31
breach. *See also* responsibility for the prevention of genocide *below*

Genocide Convention (1948) (*cont.*)
individual **104,** 154-5, **115,** 45
private **104,** 154-5
punishment limited to, whether **95,** 160-1
Security Council Resolution 713 (1991) (Yugoslav arms embargo) **95,** 154-60
territorial jurisdiction, relevance **115,** 28-9, 176-82
codification/law-making treaty **36,** 34-5, **37,** 452
common interest of parties **37,** 583, 601
conduct directly contributing to genocide or genocidal activity **95,** 131
definition of genocide **36,** 30, **120,** 376-7
'acts committed with intent to destroy in whole or in part any identifiable group . . . distinguished by colour, race, religion or ethnic origin' **111,** 588, **119,** 339, **120,** 409
'acts committed with intent to destroy in whole or in part a national, ethnical, racial or religious group as such' **111,** 587-90
cultural genocide **118,** 361, 374, **120,** 409
'destruction of national ethnic, racial or religious group' **95,** 63, 149, 163-4, 172
'intent to destroy in whole or in part' **118,** 372-3, 376
dispute settlement provisions **37,** 83-4, 516, **115,** 22-35, 38-43, 44, 179-82, 193-4
reservations **119,** 335
retroactive, whether **115,** 204-5
humanitarian treaty, whether **115,** 184-5
ICJ and
'competent organ of the UN', whether **95,** 30
'dispute relating to the interpretation, application or fulfilment' **95,** 29-31, 131, 151, 171-2
individuals. *See also* breach, individual *above*
rights under municipal law **118,** 330
jurisdiction
appropriate international tribunal **95,** 161
competent tribunal of State in which act committed **115,** 44, **119,** 66, 335-6
effect on **36,** 36-9
extraterritorial jurisdiction **119,** 335-6
Geneva Conventions (1940) distinguished **36,** 38-9
ICJ **95,** 29-31, 38, 123, **115,** 42-3, 44-5
International Criminal Court (ICC) **115,** 42-3
international penal tribunal **115,** 43, 44, **119,** 66, 335-6
municipal courts **91,** 64, **95,** 161
obligation to legislate **91,** 63-4
organ of UN **115,** 43
States parties' right to exercise 'universal' where their law permits **119,** 334-6
territorial, whether **36,** 36-9, **95,** 182, **119,** 72
UN **95,** 182
means to prevent genocide, right to **95,** 62-3, 123, 154, 159
municipal law and
incorporation, need for **118,** 330, 373
where principles already part of law **119,** 355
object and purpose, protection of rights of individuals and groups of persons **115,** 39, 41-2
obligations
erga omnes nature **115,** 39, 218-19
jus cogens nature **115,** 193-4

dispute settlement provisions **115,** 193-4
non-derogable **115,** 62-3
prevention and punishment of genocide **95,** 65-6, 153-4, 161
distinct duties **95,** 161
limited to legislation within domestic sphere, whether **95,** 160-1
measures at inter-State level **95,** 161-2
preambular nature of obligation **115,** 39, 63
remedy for breach **115,** 39-40
territorial scope **115,** 28-9, 174, 176-82
reciprocal, whether **115,** 218-19
as part of municipal law **118,** 360-1, 373, 376, 379, **120,** 377
parties to
Bosnia-Herzegovina **115,** 23-5, 46-7
reservation in respect of, relevance **115,** 200-2
succession mechanism **115,** 23-7, 183-203
Federal Republic of Yugoslavia (FRY) **95,** 30, **115,** 23, 165-74
members of UN **115,** 24
recognition, relevance **115,** 25-7
ratification
Australia **118,** 360, 372, 376, **120,** 377, 391
Israel **44,** 229, 280
reservations
dispute settlement provisions **119,** 335
Reservations to the Convention on Genocide **36,** 33-4
rights, vested **115,** 63
State responsibility for the prevention of genocide **95,** 161-2, **115,** 29, 40-1, 44-5, 177-9, 180-2
act of ruler or public official **115,** 29, **120,** 48-9
active intervention outside territory **95,** 162-3
State practice **95,** 162-3
beyond territory **95,** 162, 181
occupied territory **95,** 162
State involved in conflict **95,** 162
State succession **115,** 23-5, 45-8, 52-66, 71, 183-203 . *See also* treaties, State succession, human rights conventions
gap, avoidance of **115,** 45-8, 64-5, 67-8
State/Head of State immunity **119,** 65-6
other than in State where act committed **119,** 66
genuine link, need for
diplomatic protection **46,** 253-7, 303, 315, 357-65, 379, 428, 455-6, 469
nationality of claims **46,** 520
ships. *See* ships, genuine link, need for
geographical error, boundaries, effect on **38,** 82-4, 86
German Debts, Tripartite Commission on 47, 433, 434-5, 436, 437, 443-4, 446-7, 450, 459
competence, disputes in respect of **47,** 450
German External Debts Agreement (1953)
Arbitral Tribunal
jurisdiction **47,** 421, 442, 446, 461
advisory opinion **59,** 523-7
dispute, need for **59,** 526-7
legal interest **59,** 526-7, 550-1

German External Debts Agreement (1953) (*cont.*)
bankruptcy **44,** 318-19
claims waived by 1947 Peace Treaties, effect on **44,** 317, 318-21
London Conference **47,** 433, 435, 446
negotiation, settlement of claims by **47,** 418, 420-2, 451-2, 457-61
right of individual to compensation for **41,** 480-2
scope **47,** 433-4
States allied to Germany, claims of less favourable treatment **44,** 320-1
travaux préparatoires **59,** 543-8, 558
German–US Mixed Claims Commission **47,** 418, 419, 420, 425, 434, 439, 440-2, 445
Germany[vi]
FRG–GDR Basis of Relations Treaty (1970)
recognition of GDR, whether **91,** 233
reunification and **91,** 232-3
unity of nationality and **91,** 231-3
German nationals
diplomatic protection abroad, constitutional obligation of FRG **78,** 192
diplomatic protection in the GDR
permanent residents of the GDR **78,** 159
travel from GDR to FRG, right of **78,** 157
German property abroad, Potsdam Agreement (1945) **51,** 403
inner-German border **78,** 168-9
inner-German relations **57,** 50, **74,** 299-300, **78,** 152-76
inter-zonal trade **45,** 37-46, **62,** 93-106, **78,** 162
Berlin Agreement (1951) **45,** 38
Frankfurt Agreement (1949) **45,** 38
Settlement Convention (1952/4) **45,** 37-8
legal competence **78,** 161
meaning of term after 1945 **40,** 5-6
'national question'. *See* Germany, Federal Republic of, 'national question'
nationality
citizenship of FRG
equivalence of under Basic Law **78,** 170-1
non-recognition **78,** 170-1
protection, FRG's duty of protection **78,** 170-2

[vi] Entries relating to Germany are distributed between the following headings:
Arbitral Commission on Property, Rights and Interests in Germany
Berlin
compensation for war-related events
Control Council Law No 10
German Debts, Tripartite Commission on
German External Debts Agreement (1953)
German–US Mixed Claims Commission
Germany, Democratic Republic (GDR)
Germany, Federal Republic (FRG)
Germany (for material relating to Germany as a whole following the end of World War II)
Germany, occupation (post-WWII)
Germany, occupation of Rhineland (post-WWI)
Germany (Reich) (for Germany until the end of World War II)
Nuremberg Charter (1945)
Nuremberg Tribunal
Potsdam Conference 1945
Tripartite Commission for the Restitution of Monetary Gold.

common nationality in FRG and GDR **57,** 50-1
Eastern Treaties and **78,** 185, 189-90
FRG–GDR Basis of Relations Treaty **78,** 157, 158, 170-2, 175
compatibility with FRG Basic Law **78,** 170-2, 175
Law concerning Citizenship of the German Democratic Republic 1967 **78,** 188
loss or deprivation of **80,** 683-90
Nationality and Citizenship Law 1913 **43,** 195-6, **78,** 188, 189
Oder–Neisse, territories east of. *See* Oder–Neisse, territories east of, nationality
Reich Nationality and Citizenship Law 1913 **78,** 188, 189
SS, recruitment into **44,** 443
unity of
applicable law **91,** 217-19
Basis of Relations Treaty and **91,** 231-3
deprivation **91,** 220
GDR citizenship and **91,** 216-35
public order/public policy/*ordre public* and **91,** 221, 224
unification commitment and **91,** 219, 221, 222-3
peace settlement
Declaration of 5 June 1945 regarding defeat of Germany **78,** 186
Eastern Treaties and **78,** 190-1
FRG–GDR Basis of Relations Treaty and **78,** 157
nationality questions and **78,** 191
outstanding **78,** 190
reservation of allied rights respecting **78,** 190-1
territorial question reserved to **78,** 186
permanent residents of, diplomatic protection **78,** 159
personal injuries litigation **73,** 502-5
reorganization **78,** 168
confederation, possibility of **78,** 168
reparations
World War I **59,** 504-6
value of ceded colonies **49,** 199
World War II **59,** 506-16, 552-60, 598-601
'sovereign intervention' **80,** 671
status, Eastern Treaties, effect of boundary provisions **78,** 190
trademarks, postwar registration, validity **59,** 490-4
Unification Treaty (1990). *See* Germany, Federal Republic (FRG), Unification Treaty (1990)
unity
Federal Republic, laws and organs of **78,** 156
reserved rights of allies and **78,** 156, 158
West Berlin and. *See* Berlin, Western Sectors
Germany, Democratic Republic (GDR). *See also* Germany; Germany, Soviet zone; Germany, Federal Republic (FRG); Germany (Reich)
border controls **71,** 252-8
border shootings
applicable law post-unification **100,** 372-3
defence
act of State doctrine **100,** 372
GDR law as interpreted at time **100,** 375-91
ignorance of law **100,** 371, 388, 391, 392
retroactivity **100,** 388-91
State immunity of GDR **100,** 373
superior orders **100,** 371, 389-90, 392-3

Germany, Democratic Republic (GDR) (*cont.*)
proportionality and **100,** 371, 379, 384-8
unlawful homicide, whether **100,** 370-1
conflict with FRG public order/public policy/*ordre public*, relevance **100,** 370, 380
illegality of border regime, relevance **100,** 370-1, 379-88, 391, 392
Constitution 1949, status of Germany **91,** 227
Constitution 1968
Art. 8 **100,** 382
Art. 30 **100,** 386
Art. 30(1) **100,** 386
Art. 30(2) **100,** 386, 387
Art. 33, organs of GDR, separate from State, whether **92,** 515-16
Art. 49 **100,** 386
Art. 51 **100,** 381
Art. 69 **80,** 366
Art. 71 **80,** 366
Art. 89(2) **100,** 386
Art. 90 **100,** 386
Art. 91 **100,** 389
Art. 96 **100,** 386
continuity of laws **94,** 170
Council of State, role **80,** 366
de jure authority in **43,** 25, 37, 39, 46, 48-9, 56, 69
Deutfracht Seereederei Rostock (DSR Lines), separate legal entity, whether **92,** 517-18, 527
diplomatic relations, effect of unification **115,** 616-17
emigration, prohibition **74,** 299-300
establishment **43,** 44, 47-8
expropriation/nationalization
compensation. *See* expropriation/nationalization, compensation *below*
responsibility of Federal Republic **94,** 59-67
restitution preferred remedy **94,** 50
acquisition by natural persons in good faith **94,** 50
'comparable' commercial undertaking **94,** 50
compensation as alternative. *See* expropriation/nationalization, compensation *below*
excluded by nature of property **94,** 50
restrictions on **94,** 50
sale of expropriated property **94,** 50
Soviet occupation **60,** 114-15, 116, 117, 118-19, 121, 122-3, 124-5
irreversibility **94,** 48, 52
land reform, for purpose of **94,** 51, 52, 55
Länder as beneficiaries **94,** 51
post-1949 expropriations distinguished **94,** 50, 51, 53, 54-6
reparations, as **94,** 51
Unification Treaty (1990) and **94,** 47-8, 50, 52
expropriation/nationalization, compensation
financial capabilities of State, relevance **94,** 65-6
GDR expropriations **94,** 50
proceeds from sale of property **94,** 50, 58
need for **94,** 52
possibility of **94,** 58
possibility of restitution, relevance **94,** 66
reserved to all-German parliament **94,** 48

expropriation/nationalization, legality
acts of Soviet and GDR authorities distinguished **94,** 51-2
Basic Law (*GG*) (FRG), relevance **94,** 59-60
breach of basic rights **94,** 52, 56-7
recognition of irreversibility as precondition for Germany **94,** 52
requirements
compensation **94,** 52. *See also* expropriation/nationalization, compensation *above*
non-arbitrariness **94,** 56
Four Power rights and responsibilities, reservation **90,** 407
freedom of movement
incompatibility of border regime with international law **100,** 371
arbitrary deprivation of life **100,** 384-8
manifest violation **100,** 380, 392
national security **100,** 382
proportionality and **100,** 371, 379, 384, 387-8
public order/public policy/*ordre public* **100,** 382
right to leave one's country
International Covenant on Civil and Political Rights (ICCPR) (1966) **100,** 380-7
Passport Law (*Passgesetz*) (1979) as defence **100,** 381-3
Germany, Federal Republic and. *See* Germany, Federal Republic (FRG), GDR and
Hague Convention on Civil Procedure (1905)
reapplication **77,** 441-3
Resolution of Council of State, sufficiency **77,** 442
immunity, jurisdiction **64,** 507-8, 519
International Covenant on Civil and Political Rights (ICCPR) (1966)
breach of obligations **100,** 380-1
individuals' rights under, relevance **100,** 380-1
'generally recognized rules of international law serving peaceful coexistence and Co-operation between peoples' **100,** 382-9
judicial review, reunification obligation **91,** 221-2
law of
Border Law (*Grenzgesetz*) 1982
Art. 18(2) **100,** 375
Art. 26 **100,** 369, 371, 376
Art. 26(2) **100,** 387
Art. 27 **100,** 369, 370-1, 376-80, 384-8
Art. 27(1) **100,** 371, 376, 377-8, 387
Art. 27(2) **100,** 369, 375, 376, 379-80, 387-8
Art. 27(5) **100,** 371, 376, 378
Civil Code, Art. 20 (right of State agency to sue) **94,** 181
Criminal Code (*StGB-DDR*) 1979
Art. 1(3) **100,** 375
Arts. 85-95 **100,** 389-90
Art. 95 **100,** 389-90
Art. 112 **100,** 371, 391
Art. 113 **100,** 371, 391
Art. 213 **100,** 370-2
Art. 213(3) **100,** 370-1, 375-6, 385, 387-8
Art. 258 **100,** 371
Art. 258(1) **100,** 391
Nationality Law (*Staatsbürgerschaftsrecht*) 1967 **91,** 218
Art. 3 **91,** 212
Passport Law (*Passgesetz*) 1979 **100,** 381, 383

Germany, Democratic Republic (GDR) (*cont.*)
life, right to, priority **100,** 376-80, 385-90
Military Government Law No 52, allied law, as **94,** 168-70
nationality
acquisition **91,** 221
common, whether **91,** 217-19, 221-35
identity card **91,** 217
naturalization **91,** 215
recognition **61,** 49, 51, 63-5, 70-2, 75-6, 146-7, 150-1, **64,** 505-6, 514-15, 518-19, **71,** 22, **72,** 61, 556, 558, 562, **90,** 406-7
Basis of Relations Treaty (1970) **91,** 234
de facto **61,** 64, 76, **64,** 517-19, **78,** 166
effects of non-recognition **43,** 23-79
of the FRG **71,** 20, **72,** 558
FRG–GDR Basis of Relations Treaty and **78,** 156, 158, 165-6
de facto recognition, as **78,** 166
UN membership **91,** 234
rule of law and **100,** 386-7
sovereignty **90,** 404-5
Soviet occupation **90,** 402-8
acts of GDR authorities attributed to occupying forces **94,** 554-6
beneficiary, relevance **94,** 55
specific endorsement **94,** 55
applicable law **90,** 405
occupation law **94,** 54-6, 168-70
authority in occupied territory **71,** 20, **72,** 554-5
Brezhnev Doctrine, intervention under **90,** 407
damage, compensation for **90,** 406
Eastern territories **78,** 184-5, 187
expropriation/nationalization, Soviet occupation. *See* expropriation/nationalization *above*
presence of foreign forces with consent distinguished **90,** 405-6
termination **90,** 403-8
Soviet Statement on relations between the Soviet Union and the GDR of 25 March 1954 **90,** 404
violation of rights **90,** 403-4
State agency/State-owned corporation/State entity, independent entity, as **94,** 181
statehood **78,** 156, 162, 166, **80,** 365
status **62,** 99, 103
Treaty concerning the Relations between the USSR and the GDR (1955) **90,** 404-5
Germany, Federal Republic (FRG). *See also* Germany; Germany, Democratic Republic (GDR); Germany (Reich)
act of State
civil law, absence of doctrine **100,** 372
general rule of international law, whether **100,** 372
sovereign activity, international law, under **115,** 613
administration of justice **73,** 504-5, 518-24, 526-9, 533-8
administrative proceedings in **58,** 382-95
admissibility **78,** 156, 159, 184
aliens
access to courts, legal person **65,** 224-5
admission, conditions for **73,** 571-3
applicable law **57,** 11-12

passport, conditions for issue **73,** 608-12
procedural rights **74,** 413-16
residence permit **74,** 398-401, 571-3
social security, entitlement **94,** 602
unlawful detention, compensation for **72,** 264-6
ambassador/head of mission
agrément, need for **115,** 616-17
State succession and **115,** 616-17
withdrawal to prevent abuses **115,** 611
powers
credentials, relevance **65,** 124
disposal of land on behalf of sending State **65,** 123-4
State immunity, jurisdiction, entitlement **115,** 613-14, **119,** 208-11
status, State agency **115,** 613-14
appeal rights
defence counsel **72,** 418-29
notification, in native language **72,** 321-2
applicable law
collisions at sea, International Regulations (1948) **65,** 107, **70,** 478-9
criminal acts committed abroad **94,** 73
GDR nationals detained for political reasons **100,** 373
offences committed in former GDR
acts committed by GDR **100,** 372-3
defence under GDR law **100,** 370-1, 380, 388, 390-1
FRG law **100,** 373-4
more lenient law **100,** 373, 375, 391-3
Unification Treaty (1990) provisions **100,** 374-5
property in west Berlin **65,** 112-13
arbitral award, USA–FRG Treaty of Friendship, effect on **53,** 17-19
armed forces, deployment
interim injunction, requirements **106,** 352
legislative consent, need for **106,** 323-52
collective security, agreement to treaty establishing **106,** 331-3, 347
declaration of state of defence as **106,** 349, 350
legislature's right of initiative **106,** 350-1
prior **106,** 326, 348, 349, 350
obligation
Basic Law (*GG*), effect of 1954 amendment **106,** 333-4
Basic Law (*GG*), effect of 1956 amendment **106,** 348
Basic Law (*GG*), effect of 1968 amendment **106,** 348
collective security system **106,** 326-34
Security Council Resolutions relating to Bosnia, participation in NATO/WEU implementing action **106,** 332-3
UN Mandate **106,** 350
UN Mandate, Somalia **106,** 326, 331-2
armed forces, stationing on FRG territory
Convention on the Presence of Foreign Forces in the FRG (1954) **106,** 380
sovereign activity, customary international law **106,** 394
armed forces, transfer of power of command to head of Government **106,** 349
arrest, illegal, protest, need for **95,** 349
asylum **73,** 410-11, **74,** 395-6, **80,** 676
conditions for **73,** 608-12, 615-16
fear of persecution **80,** 677, 680, 682

Germany, Federal Republic (FRG) (*cont.*)
motivation for offence **80,** 676
possible impediments
acts contrary to purposes and principles of UN **80,** 681
hijacking of aircraft **80,** 676, 679-80
offence completed in FRG **80,** 681
Bank Deutscher Länder, as successor to Reichsbank **44,** 453
Basic Law (*GG*) **60,** 205, 207-13, 222-3
Allied reservations **60,** 222-3, 224
amendment, Unification Treaty (1990) **94,** 57-8
application outside *Länder*, no longer within FRG's gift **78,** 169-70
area of application, sovereignty of FRG limited to **78,** 162
Art. 1(1) **100,** 397
Art. 1(2) **72,** 299, 420, **80,** 681, **106,** 362
Art. 2(1) **72,** 298, 420, **88,** 551, **93,** 426, 436-7, **106,** 362-3, **108,** 662-3, **115,** 603
Art. 2(2) (right to life) **106,** 360-2, 394-6, **115,** 603
Art. 3 **81,** 216
Art. 3(1) **72,** 265-6, 420, **80,** 672, **91,** 215, 220, 234, **94,** 64-5, 78-9, **108,** 663
justified difference of treatment **94,** 79-80
legislature, binding on **94,** 79
Art. 3(3) **74,** 424, **88,** 551, 552
Art. 5 **78,** 172, **81,** 215, 216, **88,** 554, 555, 556
Art. 6 **73,** 610, 612
Art. 6(1) **72,** 296-301, 420, 573
Art. 7(1) **108,** 653
Art. 8(1) **91,** 215, 234
Art. 9 **81,** 216
Art. 9(1) **91,** 215, 234
Art. 10 **78,** 172
Art. 11 **55,** 469, 482, **78,** 184, 190
Art. 11(1) **91,** 215, 234, **108,** 662
Art. 12 **81,** 216, **93,** 417-18
Art. 12(1) **88,** 551, 552, **91,** 215, 234, **93,** 426, 436-7
Art. 14 **55,** 469, 482, **70,** 433, **78,** 184, 190, **108,** 657 n. 1, 659, 661-2
Art. 16 **73,** 615-16, **78,** 161, 170-2, 190, **88,** 286
Art. 16(1) **91,** 215, 218, 220, 221-2, 234
Art. 16(2) **74,** 395-6, 426, 510, **80,** 678, 680
Art. 19(2) **72,** 298
Art. 19(4) **74,** 415-16, 495, 497, **90,** 398, **93,** 424-6, **108,** 667, **118,** 127
acts of foreign public authority and **65,** 130
legal hearing, right to **93,** 425
review of decisions of international courts **93,** 424-5
Art. 20 **72,** 317, **80,** 672, **106,** 396-7
Art. 20(2) **106,** 373-4, **108,** 667
Art. 20(3) **93,** 417, 426, 446, **115,** 603
Art. 23, FRG–GDR Basis of Relations Treaty and **78,** 169
Art. 23(1) **78,** 157
Art. 23(1) (amended) **98,** 206
Art. 23 (amended) **98,** 206, 214, 219, 228, 243, 245
Art. 24 **90,** 410
Art. 24(1) **93,** 355-6, 357, 361, 388, 390-1, 395-6, 399-403, 456, 457-60, **106,** 327, 338, 375-81, 387-8, 397-8, **108,** 652, 653

direct application of non-German law **93,** 426, 444-5
ECJ jurisdiction **93,** 451
strict construction, need for **93,** 445
Art. 24(2) **80,** 681, **106,** 326-34, 362, 379, 395-6
Art. 25 **45,** 60, **59,** 492-3, **65,** 103, 116, 120, 128-30, 141, 153, 159-60, 162-3, 166, 185, 191-2, 195-6, 202, 210, 222, **70,** 404, 431, **72,** 299, 440, 668, **73,** 244, 372, 687-8, **74,** 167-8, 372, 409, **80,** 370, **86,** 530, **90,** 694, **100,** 372, **106,** 362-3, 398, **114,** 505, **117,** 424
Art. 26(1) **80,** 681, **106,** 383, 398-9
Art. 32(1) **106,** 304
Art. 33(2) **88,** 552
Art. 33(3) **88,** 551
Art. 34 **108,** 673-4, **111,** 10, 40-1
Art. 38, Maastricht Treaty (1992), compatibility **98,** 208-9, 213-14, 219, 220-2
Art. 42(2) **106,** 350
Art. 45(a) **106,** 348-9, 386
Art. 45(b) **106,** 348-9
Art. 49(1) **106,** 371
Art. 52 (amended) **98,** 206
Art. 59 **73,** 693, **78,** 157
Art. 59(2) **80,** 678, **90,** 372, **93,** 420, 427, **108,** 651
Art. 59(2)(1) **106,** 334-47, 370, 372-5, 388, 397
Art. 67(1)(1) **106,** 387
Art. 78(1) **106,** 334
Art. 78(2) **106,** 334
Art. 79(3) **94,** 62 n. 3, **98,** 212, 220, 221-2, **100,** 397, **106,** 379
ex post facto rectification of injustice and **94,** 61
modification distinguished **94,** 58-9
Art. 80(1) **90,** 374, **108,** 653
Art. 80(a)(3) **106,** 349, 386
Art. 87(a) **106,** 333-4, 348-9, 386, 395-6
Art. 88 (amended) **98,** 206, 215
Art. 93(1) **78,** 156, **106,** 360
Art. 96 **86,** 391
Art. 100(1) **65,** 161, **93,** 394, 416, 419-22, 426, 429, 436, 460, **98,** 193
Art. 100(2) **65,** 118, 151, 159-63, 191, 196, 213, 220, 222, 225-8, 246, **93,** 394
Art. 101(1) **65,** 222, 225, **93,** 447, 450, **115,** 603
Art. 103(1) **65,** 222, 225, **72,** 420, **74,** 414-16, 495, **93,** 423-5, **115,** 603
Art. 103(2) **100,** 371, 388-91
Art. 115(1)(III) **106,** 349
Art. 115(a) **106,** 349, 350, 372, 384-5, 395-6
Art. 115(b) **106,** 349
Art. 116(1) **74,** 300, 398, **91,** 215, 217-19, 220, 221-4, 234
Art. 116(2) **72,** 297, 450-4, 459-66, 473, 476-7
Art. 123(1) **91,** 220
Art. 123(3) **94,** 56-8
Art. 143 **106,** 334
asylum **38,** 147
basic rights under
directly enforceable **94,** 58
legal entitlement remedy, need for **94,** 59-60
boundaries **44,** 56
continued existence of German people as basis **91,** 223-4

Germany, Federal Republic (FRG) (*cont.*)
correspondence, privacy **58,** 432-4
discrimination, prohibition of **57,** 12
duty to protect and care for all Germans **78,** 157
effectiveness, need for **91,** 224
entrenched provisions
amendment **98,** 210-11, 212, 219
referendum and **98,** 220
right to remedy/resist if endangered **98,** 210, 212, 220
equality **57,** 5-6
expropriation/nationalization **43,** 252
family life, respect for **57,** 12
federal Constitution, nature of **52,** 330
foreign law, application of **57,** 12
foreign relations, responsibility for **90,** 396
fundamental rights **43,** 249
GDR sovereign authority, relevance **91,** 223-4
hierarchy of provisions **80,** 681
'identity thesis' **78,** 158
individual rights, damage to, possibility of **78,** 192-3
international law. *See also* international law *below*
limitation by **80,** 679
interpretation, context **93,** 390
Länder / Bund relationship **57,** 2-3
legitimate interest, need for **90,** 394
nationality provisions. *See* Germany, nationality
Preamble **78,** 161, **80,** 681, **91,** 221
private property, protection of **57,** 5-6
Rechtstitel, cession **78,** 163
Reich, effect on **91,** 226
religious freedom **57,** 12
respect for family **45,** 373-6
'sole representation', right of **78,** 164
statelessness **43,** 195
territorial scope **91,** 223
transitional nature **91,** 222
treaties and municipal law **43,** 249
Berlin. *See* Berlin
Berufsverbot **88,** 530-69
bonos mores **72,** 444
boundaries
alterable by agreement **78,** 168-9
Basic law **44,** 56
area of application of **78,** 162
demarcation **74,** 122-3, **78,** 156
multiple recognition, scope for varying treaty regimes **78,** 168-9
central/State-owned bank
classification of act, letter of credit **65,** 133-7
classification as, separate legal entity test **65,** 134, 138
purpose/use of funds
cash and securities accounts **65,** 135
future use, relevance **65,** 135
chemical weapons, deployment

legality, defensive purposes **106,** 362-3
legislative consent, need for
collective security, agreement to treaty establishing **106,** 396-7
Convention on the Presence of Foreign Forces in the FRG (1954) **106,** 396-7
choice of law **80,** 383
civil service, *Berufsverbot* **88,** 530-69
claims, waiver by State **44,** 301-23, **45,** 436-45
collective security system
collective self-defence, distinction **106,** 329
definition **106,** 328
absence **106,** 328
inchoate state **106,** 340-1
legislative consent, need for
approval of constituent treaty as **106,** 331, 341, 346-7
prior **106,** 330
programme of integration, agreement to **106,** 381-7
NATO **106,** 330, 369
preservation of peace between members, limitation to **106,** 328
reciprocity of rights and obligations **106,** 329
sovereignty, surrender **106,** 329-30, 331-2
UN **106,** 329, 331
peacekeeping forces as part of **106,** 331, 346-7
WEU **106,** 369
collisions at sea, applicable law, International Regulations (1948) **65,** 107
Common Foreign and Security Policy (CFSP), fundamental rights within the EC, effect **98,** 217
competition, unfair **81,** 219
confiscation **61,** 170-3
Constitution. *See* Basic Law (*GG*) *above*
Constitutional Court (*BVerfG*). *See also* Constitutional Court (*BVerfG*) review *and* Constitutional Court Law (*BVerfGG*) *below*
Berlin, jurisdiction over **57,** 114-16, **78,** 175
executive and **78,** 160-1, 162-3
judgments, interpretation **78,** 174
judicial restraint **78,** 160
treaty interpretation **78,** 160, 161
Constitutional Court (*BVerfG*) review **43,** 6-8
acts by public authority **93,** 355, 392-3
implementation by State power **93,** 392-3
admissibility
exhaustion of ordinary remedies. *See* exhaustion of ordinary remedies rule *below*
foreign State, against **106,** 360-1
direct and current violation of constitutional right **98,** 213
EC law **93,** 355-7, 386-403
compatibility of EC law distinguished **93,** 357
inapplicability of rule, limited to **93,** 394, 395
ECJ judgment **93,** 416-17
European Union, amendments **98,** 226
exhaustion of ordinary remedies, injunction against/challenge to writ distinguished **111,** 136
foreign relations **106,** 395
fundamental rights, protection of **93,** 392-5
requirements

Germany, Federal Republic (FRG) (*cont.*)
infringement of personal rights **106,** 325-6, **118,** 127-8
judgment dependent on validity of norm **98,** 193
matter of general importance **118,** 127
supranational organization **93,** 351-7
treaties, scrutiny **43,** 9-10, 246-53, **78,** 160
Constitutional Court Law (*BVerfGG*) **73,** 693
Art. 32(1) **106,** 359
Art. 64 **106,** 331, 334
Art. 76 (No 1) **78,** 156
Art. 80 **65,** 159-60
Art. 84 **65,** 159-60
Art. 90 **93,** 355, 356, **106,** 360
Art. 90(1) **108,** 659, 661
Art. 92 **88,** 555
constitutional rights, primacy over other rules of law **72,** 297-300
consular agent
social security
entitlement **86,** 540, 541
FRG–Turkey Social Security Agreement (1960) **86,** 540-1
obligations **86,** 540
Vienna Convention on Consular Relations (1963) **86,** 541
continental shelf, unilateral acts **41,** 54-6, 129-31, 137, 155, 212-15, 221, 225-6
Continental Shelf Convention (1958), conduct relating to **41,** 54-6, 212-15
Continental Shelf Proclamation (1964) **41,** 56, 94, 112, 131, 138, 212-14, 221
contract
applicable law, place of performance **65,** 127
definition **89,** 462
conviction in error, imprisonment, legality **72,** 313-16
copyright
film score **65,** 145
State immunity, jurisdiction and **65,** 143-5
corporation
domicile, head office **65,** 203-4
seat, status as **65,** 203-4
courts, municipal **61,** 70-2. *See also* Constitutional Court *above*; jurisdiction; Labour Courts; Supreme Court *below*
Constitution, application of **57,** 5
judgment
law of Germany as a whole, effect **43,** 24, 52, 54-5, 62, 75
publication of, manner **73,** 504-5
criminal law
area of application
GDR **78,** 175
politically motivated crimes, protection of victims of **78,** 175
criminal proceedings, interpretation costs **58,** 469-70, 706
criminal responsibility, co-perpetration **124,** 156
critical date, expropriation/nationalization, date of expropriation/nationalization **108,** 660
customary international law **65,** 103-5, 116-17, 120-1, 128-9, 134-6, 141, 150, 153-5, 157, 159-64, 166-7, 175-7, 184-92, 195-6, 202, 207, 210, 213-14, 219-22, 226-9, 239, 241-5, **78,** 175

armed forces, stationing on foreign territory **106,** 394
diplomatic privileges and immunities
incorporation of receiving State into forum State, effect **115,** 615-16, 618
matters not covered by the Vienna Convention on Diplomatic Relations (1961) **115,** 611
diplomatic privileges and immunities, entitlement, third State, in **115,** 610-12
evidence of **65,** 166-7
as general principle of international law **61,** 180, **115,** 610
municipal law and **70,** 400-1, 404, **74,** 167-8, **93,** 361-2, **94,** 76
requirements
constant and uniform practice **115,** 610
general acceptance **45,** 61, **65,** 213-14, **115,** 610
opinio juris **115,** 610
damages
for breach of official duty **111,** 9-11
for breach of official duty, fault, relevance **108,** 673-4
debts of, acknowledgment of **59,** 507
default judgment against foreign State, State immunity, execution/attachment, waiver and **65,** 160
democratic legitimacy. *See* EC, transfer of powers to, democratic legitimacy *and* European Parliament, democratic legitimacy *below*
denial of justice **90,** 378
detention pending trial **72,** 309-13
diplomatic agent
breach of law
recall of diplomat **94,** 606
remedies **94,** 605-7
criminal offence, remedy, declaration as *persona non grata* **115,** 607
extraterritoriality, maintenance of normal residence in sending State **94,** 600
social security, entitlement **94,** 598-608
civil war in sending State **94,** 607
legal aid, entitlement **94,** 601
performance of functions, effect on **94,** 604-5
renunciation of diplomatic status **94,** 600, 607-8
requirement to work **94,** 600
sending State, responsibility of **94,** 600, 605
urgent distress **94,** 605, 606-7
Vienna Convention on Diplomatic Relations (1961), implications **94,** 600, 601, 603-6
social security obligations, employer **94,** 604
status, civil war in sending State, effect on **94,** 607
diplomatic immunity, jurisdiction
interference with functioning of mission and **65,** 109, 186-91
real/immovable property held on behalf of the sending State for the purposes of the mission, dispute relating to **65,** 109
State immunity and **115,** 605-6
distinction **65,** 109, **115,** 608-10, 613-14, **119,** 210
primacy **115,** 613-14
diplomatic mission
functions/'diplomatic activity'
bomb attack, assistance **115,** 600, 603
sale of land on behalf of sending State, whether **65,** 123-4

Germany, Federal Republic (FRG) (*cont.*)
diplomatic mission, special **80,** 389-424
diplomatic premises
extraterritoriality **65,** 112-13
immunity of **38,** 162-70
diplomatic privileges and immunities
abuse, measures to prevent **115,** 608, 611
agrément, dependence on **115,** 610, 611, 616-17
basis
foreign relations considerations **115,** 607
protection of own diplomats abroad **115,** 607
protection of sending State **115,** 609, 616, 617
criminal jurisdiction, serious violation of law **115,** 607
customary international law, State succession, incorporation of receiving State into forum State, effect **115,** 615-16, 618
functional **115,** 603, 605-7
act attributable to State **115,** 606
act illegal under sending State law **115,** 606
criminal act **115,** 606, 607
failure to prevent bomb attack **115,** 606
personal immunity distinguished **115,** 606, 609-10, 612-13
termination of status, after **115,** 600, 605-6, 612-13
incorporation of receiving State into forum State, effect
customary international law **115,** 615-16, 618
State practice **115,** 615-16
property **74,** 182
right of suit **94,** 601-2
Vienna Convention on Diplomatic Relations (1961) **94,** 601-2
State succession, incorporation of receiving State into forum State, effect **115,** 602, 614, 615-17
diplomatic privileges and immunities, entitlement
special mission **80,** 389-424
termination of diplomatic status, continuation after **115,** 600, 605-6, 609
third State, in **115,** 602
customary international law **115,** 610-12
effects doctrine **115,** 604-5
general principle of international law **115,** 602
Lateran Treaty (1929) as evidence against **115,** 612
recognition of judgment delivered by courts of receiving State **115,** 612
State practice **115,** 612
termination of mission, relevance **115,** 612-13
third State as successor State, relevance **115,** 602
diplomatic protection
discretion **90,** 395-8
German nationals **78,** 171-2, 175, 184-6
entitlement to FRG protection when within jurisdiction **78,** 171, 191
judicial review **90,** 395, 397, 398
occupation law and **90,** 397
discrimination, equalization of burdens **61,** 167-8, 178-9
double taxation agreements **72,** 216-17, 448-9, 457-8, **74,** 205-11
drug-trafficking, punishment of **74,** 167-8
Eastern Treaties for the Normalization of Relations with Poland and the USSR (1970) (Moscow and Warsaw Treaties) **73,** 692-4, **78,** 179-93. *See also* FRG–Poland Border

Treaty (1990) *and* FRG–Poland, Treaty for the Normalization of Relations (1970) (Warsaw Treaty) *below*
EC **62,** 99, 103
democratic deficit
European basis of politics and **98,** 210, 219
lack of EC legislature **98,** 209, 211-12, 223, 224
national parliaments, role **98,** 209, 223, 228-9, 245
transparency of decision-making, need for **98,** 223-4
fundamental rights within the European Community. *See* fundamental rights within the EC/EU *below*
jurisdiction, demarcation **93,** 357
Kompetenz/Kompetenz **98,** 229-35
proportionality, obligation to observe **98,** 245
transfer of powers to **93,** 390
constitutionality **98,** 211-12
democratic legitimacy **98,** 213-15, 221-6
limited and specific **98,** 221, 225-6, 229-30, 243. *See also Kompetenz/Kompetenz above*
national identities, preservation of **98,** 221, 245-6
national spheres of activity, need to retain **98,** 224-5, 241
parliamentary powers **98,** 208-9
rule of law, subject to **98,** 194
separation of powers and **98,** 211
sovereignty, effect on **98,** 225, 228
treaty, need for **98,** 230, 243
EC law **59,** 6-7
binding effect **93,** 399
compatibility **93,** 357, 388
EC obligation **93,** 389-90
trial court, sole competence to determine **93,** 361
conflict with national law
national courts' responsibility to resolve **98,** 195
non-application of national law **98,** 194
constitutional limitation **93,** 390
implementation as exercise of State power **93,** 393
judicial review **93,** 355-7, 386-403
protection of individuals **93,** 357
national courts' role, review of EC law **98,** 194
as national law **93,** 460
primacy **93,** 135, 427, 446
effect on national law **93,** 438
fundamental rights and **93,** 391
previous legislation **93,** 459-60
rule part of national law **98,** 194
secondary EC law **98,** 195
subsequent legislation **93,** 459-60
unwritten rule of primary EC law **98,** 194
protection of individual **93,** 456
adequacy **93,** 357, 434-8
right of individual to invoke before national courts **93,** 446, 456-7, 458
right to invoke before national courts **98,** 195
EC law, direct effect **93,** 135, 399, 443-61
directive

Germany, Federal Republic (FRG) (*cont.*)
76/207 (night work) **98,** 194-5
decision compared **93,** 452
regulation compared **93,** 444, 445-7, 451-8
jurisdiction to determine **93,** 444-7
requirements
effective transfer of right **93,** 445
no need for further intervention **98,** 195
unconditional and precise **98,** 194, 195
subsequent developments in EC law and **93,** 445
ECJ
Art. 177 preliminary ruling, binding effect **93,** 421-2, 425, 446-7, 450-1, **111,** 10-11
development of EC law and **93,** 457-9
effect of decision on previous national court decision **93,** 438
fundamental rights, protection **98,** 216
judgment, national courts, review by **93,** 416-17, **98,** 193, **111,** 137-8
jurisdiction, under International Conventions, ratification, need for **98,** 218
as 'statutory court' **93,** 418-22, 450
economic crime, delays in prosecution **68,** 50-86
Economic and Monetary Union (EMU)
automaticity **98,** 238
Bundestag/Bundesrat resolutions (December 1992) **98,** 207
as community of stability **98,** 235, 238-40
convergence criteria **98,** 236-8
watering-down, protection against **98,** 237-8
democratic deficit **98,** 214-15
European Central Bank
commitment to stability and **98,** 237, 239-40
independence **98,** 240-3
Member States' willingness, dependent on **98,** 236, 238
political union, inevitable, whether **98,** 240-1
reversibility of European Union and **98,** 212
separable, whether **98,** 240
economic ownership **42,** 363, 376
EEC Treaty (Rome) (1957)
exercise of transferred power and extension distinguished **98,** 243
implementing legislation, interpretation, applicable law **93,** 450
interpretation
competence to perfect Treaty **98,** 243
effectiveness **98,** 243
reciprocity **93,** 389-400
embassy or consular bank account/funds, immunity, execution/attachment
applicable law **65,** 188-9
economic position of State, relevance **65,** 153, 157, 158, 191
interference with functioning of mission/consulate and **65,** 152-3
embassy or consular bank account/funds, immunity, execution/attachment, purpose/use
account for use of separate legal entity **65,** 210-11
designation, conclusiveness **65,** 158, 190
diplomatic mission, expenses **65,** 185-91
right/duty to enquire into **65,** 153, 157-8, 160-1, 188-9
running of State's offices in forum State **65,** 115-19
emigration, freedom of **74,** 299-301, 410-11
employment contract, locally engaged staff, consulate
classification of employment, sovereign nature of consular acts **65,** 207-8

State immunity, jurisdiction **114,** 504-7, 510-12
applicable law clause, relevance **114,** 511-12
contract as waiver **114,** 512
State immunity, jurisdiction, theory/doctrine, customary international law **114,** 504-5
energy production, non-sovereign activity **80,** 382
entry, right of **74,** 300-1
equalization of burdens
Austrian expellees and resettled persons **65,** 12-13
individual's right to demand, FRG–Poland Border Treaty (1990) **108,** 661-2
'social State' and **108,** 661-2
espionage
equality of treatment, national acting within borders and non-national acting abroad **94,** 75
jurisdiction
lex loci delicti commissi **94,** 73
protective principle **94,** 74
liability to prosecution for acts carried out in third country **94,** 72-82
absence of human rights violations as mitigating factor **94,** 81
enforceability **94,** 75, 79
fairness **94,** 80
recommendation for legislation exempting **94,** 80-2
peacetime
customary international law **94,** 74
Hague Regulations (1907), non-applicability **94,** 76
international law regulation **94,** 74, 75
lawful nature **94,** 74
right of prosecution **94,** 75
treaty regulation **94,** 74
prevention of legitimate State interest **94,** 74-5
member of alliance, extension to **94,** 74
State succession and **94,** 76-9
failure to agree treatment as breach of responsibility **94,** 81-2
Unification Treaty (1990) **94,** 76, 77
European Convention on Human Rights (1950)
application **74,** 300-1
direct effect **72,** 297-8, 303
enforcement of provisions **72,** 302-6, 310-22
incorporation into municipal law **88,** 555
European Parliament
democratic legitimacy, uniform electoral law, need for **98,** 224
importance **93,** 390, 401, 428, 432-3, 434-5
legislature, whether **98,** 211-12
European Schools
applicable law
constituent instrument **108,** 665, 667
international law **108,** 651
jurisdiction over, municipal courts **108,** 641-2, 650-2, 666
status
capacity to sue and be sued **108,** 651, 666
organ of international organization **108,** 641, 650-1, 666
'public institution'/'body', transformation into, need for **108,** 652
tuition fees
admissibility **108,** 646-8, 650-3
legitimate expectation, whether **108,** 653

Germany, Federal Republic (FRG) (*cont.*)
proportionality and **108,** 653
review by municipal court, admissibility **108,** 650-2
European Space Agency (ESA)
immunity, jurisdiction **118,** 125-7, 128, 129, 133
immunity, jurisdiction, waiver **118,** 126-7
European Union (EU)
amendments/extension
binding, whether **98,** 226, 231
constitutional review **98,** 226
Member State approval, need for **98,** 235
non-application **98,** 226, 231
procedure **98,** 235
ratification, need for **98,** 228
authority derived from Member States **98,** 228
reversibility, EMU and **98,** 212
status
economic community **98,** 227
State, whether **98,** 226
union of States **98,** 227-8
subsidiarity **98,** 243-5
binding principle **98,** 227
ECJ to monitor **98,** 244
as limitation of powers **98,** 244
European Union Treaty (Maastricht) (1992)
constitutionality
democratic deficit **98,** 209. *See also* EC, democratic deficit *above*
European Union provisions **98,** 219-20
fundamental rights. *See* fundamental rights within the European Community *below*
Kompetenz/Kompetenz **98,** 208-9
Länder, infringement of powers **98,** 211
voting rights for non-nationals **98,** 211, 220
democratic deficit. *See also* EC, democratic deficit *above*
Economic and Monetary Union (EMU) **98,** 214-15
EC powers, extension of **98,** 214-15
Economic and Monetary Union (EMU). *See* Economic and Monetary Union (EMU) *above*
fundamental rights. *See* fundamental rights within the European Community *below*
intergovernmental cooperation
conversion to supranational competence, treaty amendment, need for **98,** 218
justice and home affairs. *See* justice and home affairs *below*
justice and home affairs
European Convention on Human Rights (1950) and **98,** 218
Geneva Convention on the Status of Refugees (1951) **98,** 218
referendum, right to **98,** 212
sovereignty, threat to **98,** 212
executive, Constitutional Court and **78,** 162-3
export ban, enforcement of **73,** 227-9
expropriation/nationalization. *See also* Germany, Democratic Republic (GDR), expropriation/nationalization
by occupying/administering power, State immunity, jurisdiction **65,** 128-30
compatibility with law of expropriating State, relevance **94,** 61
compensation. *See* expropriation/nationalization, compensation *below*

enforceability, public policy and **73,** 237-41, 244-7
foreign **61,** 173, **73,** 235-47
non-recognition **72,** 85-8
public order/public policy/*ordre public* **94,** 60
'split' companies
legal status **73,** 237-41
liability for debts **72,** 86-8
territorial limitation **94,** 60-1
grounds for objection **108,** 659-60
expropriation/nationalization, compensation **94,** 60
need for, territorial principle **108,** 660
expulsion of alien **45,** 372, 455
External Debts, Agreement on, Hungary, waiver of claims **45,** 439, 440
extraditable offence, fraudulent acquisition of export grants or tax rebates **45,** 376-8
extradition
Federal and State authorities **45,** 420
nationals **88,** 286-7
to **60,** 316-19, **70,** 375-9, **73,** 237-41, 510-16, **74,** 494-8
speciality principle **73,** 660
war criminals, of **72,** 607-14
extradition in case of death penalty **106,** 299-304
assurances that death penalty will not be carried out, need for **106,** 299-300, 302-3
responsibility for determining acceptability of assurances **106,** 301-3. *See also* responsibility for determining acceptability of assurances *below*
fair trial **72,** 317-19
family life, respect for **57,** 314, **72,** 573, **73,** 610-12, 617
Federal Antitrust Agency **57,** 115
fishing rights
Iceland, Exchange of Notes (1961) **56,** 78, 79, 84, 100-1, 103-8, 109-10, 121-2, 124, 130, 132-5, 149-50, 151, 155-7, 180, 198-9, 201
Icelandic waters, in **56,** 168, 176-7
forcible abduction/unlawful arrest
jurisdiction, effect on **90,** 684-5, **95,** 331, 349
State practice **95,** 349
remedy **90,** 695
request for repatriation, need for **90,** 695
return of kidnapped person **90,** 665, 671, 687-8, 693-6
foreign judgment, recognition/enforcement **70,** 431-4
international law, need for conformity with, State immunity rules **65,** 202
reciprocity **65,** 204
treaty basis **65,** 204
foreign law
evidence of **73,** 248-9
respect for **57,** 11-12
foreign law, recognition/enforcement **72,** 85-8, **73,** 227-9, 243-7
international law, need for conformity with **57,** 11-12
foreign relations
constitutional petition, limited scope **106,** 395
executive responsibility **106,** 302, 303-4, 334-40, 351, 373-5, 380, 383-6, 395
judicial review **73,** 693-4, **80,** 402, **96,** 215-16
legal limits **78,** 160
duty to avoid embarrassing Constitutional Court **78,** 161
political manoeuvre, room for **78,** 192-3

Germany, Federal Republic (FRG) (*cont.*)
legislature's role
legitimate failure to conclude treaty as infringement **106,** 336
political control, possibility of **106,** 375, 387, 388
right to co-determination **106,** 330-1, 378-9
margin of discretion **96,** 216
means, executive's freedom to choose **106,** 336-8, 339
responsibility for **78,** 162-3, 192-3, **80,** 374, 402, **90,** 395-8
discretion **90,** 396-7
judicial review **90,** 396-7
responsibility for. *See also* executive responsibility *above*
service on foreign ambassador and **80,** 374
forum selection clause, as waiver of immunity **65,** 119
France
cultural cooperation. *See* Institut Franco-Allemand de Recherche de Saint-Louis; Office Franco-Allemand pour la Jeunesse
Judicial Convention (1961) **44,** 134-5
expulsion procedure, effect on **44,** 135-9
freedom of expression **81,** 215, **88,** 556
flag desecration and **122,** 598-9
freedom of movement, FRG-Poland Border Treaty (1990), effect **108,** 662
freedom of the press, broadcasting service, obligation to maintain and **90,** 385-6
FRG–Poland Border Treaty (1990)
discriminatory, whether **108,** 663
Unification Treaty (1990) distinguished **108,** 663
freedom of movement, effect on **108,** 662
property rights in former German territories east of the Oder-Neisse **108,** 659-61
sovereignty, retroactive effect **108,** 660
FRG–Poland, Treaty for the Normalization of Relations (1970) (Warsaw Treaty) **78,** 186, 189
Approval Law **78,** 189
border settlement under **78,** 185
reunification of families, right to **78,** 186, 191-3
fundamental rights within the EC **93,** 390-401, 437-8
breach by Community institution, national courts' role **98,** 216
Common Foreign and Security Policy (CFSP), effect **98,** 217
complementary roles of ECJ and national courts **98,** 216, 218-19
Constitutional Court and **93,** 392-5, 436
direct effect of EC law, relevance **93,** 392-3
EC and **93,** 390-401, 427-38
breach by, effect on Act of Accession **93,** 424
codification, need for **93,** 390-1, 401, 428-9, 434-6
national practice, need for substantial similarity **93,** 435-6
Parliament, need for **93,** 390-1, 401, 428, 432-3, 434-5
ECJ role **98,** 216-17, 218-19
absence of European Union jurisdiction **98,** 216-17
EMU, German Mark, loss of right to **98,** 210, 215
as general legal principle
constitutional traditions **93,** 429, 430-1
ECJ case-law **93,** 429-32, 433, 435
European Convention on Human Rights (1950) and **93,** 429, 433-4, 435
inalienable **93,** 390-400
legal certainty **93,** 426. *See also* legal certainty *below*

legal hearing **93,** 423-4, 428
expert assistance **93,** 428
Maastricht Treaty (1992), effect **98,** 217
national control of Community law and **98,** 209-10
national courts' role **98,** 216, 218-19
proportionality **93,** 369, 370, 396-7, 426
protection **93,** 398-9, 428, 434, 436-7
territorial scope, expansion **98,** 215-16
garnishee order
foreign State
debts **57,** 152-3
service on **57,** 152-3
GDR and **57,** 29-51
basis of relations, UN Charter **78,** 166
Basis of Relations Treaty (1972) **78,** 152-76, **80,** 366, **90,** 406-7
amendment, possibility of **78,** 164
constitutionality **78,** 164-75
diplomatic protection and **78,** 170-2
Eastern Treaties and **78,** 165
effect on previously concluded agreements **78,** 165
freedom of assembly/association and **78,** 172
freedom of information and **78,** 172
freedom of political activity and **78,** 172
freedom of trade union activity and **78,** 172
interim settlement, whether **78,** 175
international law and **78,** 166
modus vivendi **78,** 164
peace settlement, absence of reservation as to **78,** 157
ratification **78,** 159-61
subsequent agreements to be covered by scrutiny process **78,** 165
termination clause, absence of **78,** 157, 164
time-limit, absence of **78,** 157, 164
UN Charter and **78,** 165
unity of nationality and **91,** 231-3
citizenship. *See* Germany, nationality, unity of
diplomatic relations, effect of unification **115,** 616-17
escape from, contract to assist, enforceability **74,** 298-301
foreign State, whether **78,** 162, **90,** 406-7, **91,** 234
'good-neighbourly relations' **78,** 168
inter-State relations, Permanent Representations **78,** 166
international law and **91,** 234
jurisdiction, in the GDR **61,** 75
legislation
recognition of **71,** 20
status of **74,** 299
non-recognition **72,** 558
offences committed in former GDR, applicable law **100,** 371-5, 380, 388, 390-3
previous agreements, effect on **90,** 407
recognition of **78,** 156
relations with **74,** 299-300
sovereign equality **78,** 168
'special relationship' **78,** 157, 165, 172
Permanent Representations, exchange of reflecting **78,** 166

Germany, Federal Republic (FRG) (*cont.*)
trade with **62,** 93-106, **78,** 162
treaties, succession to, Unification Treaty **115,** 614-15
Unification Treaty (1990). *See* Unification Treaty (1990) *below*
general principles of international law **80,** 678
customary international law as **61,** 180, **115,** 610
general principles of law as **61,** 180, **115,** 610
generally recognized principles of law distinguished **45,** 60
German nationals
diplomatic protection **78,** 171-2, 175, 184-6
entitlement to FRG protection when within jurisdiction **78,** 171, 191
good faith, employment relationships **118,** 136
human dignity, right to **100,** 397-400
constitutional right **100,** 396, 398
Länder, unwritten constitutional principle **100,** 397-8
probable death before conclusion of criminal proceedings and **100,** 396-400
human rights **51,** 240-8
alleged violation **62,** 297-8
balance of risk **106,** 365-6
breach, threat as **106,** 360-2
foreign State, assertability against **106,** 360, 361, 362
remedies for breach, constitutional complaint **106,** 360
Hungary, Peace Treaty with, incorporation of waiver clauses into German law **45,** 436-45
individual in international law **59,** 493, **70,** 404, **80,** 382
breach of treaty **95,** 331, 348
municipal courts, enforcement of rules in **65,** 162-3
rights **95,** 331, 348
unlawful arrest **95,** 331, 348
information centre, entitlement to immunity **63,** 171-2, 589
inheritance laws **57,** 50
interim measures
admissibility
foreign policy repercussions **106,** 352
international law repercussions **106,** 352
armed forces, injunction on deployment **106,** 352
purpose **94,** 602
prevention of act of force **106,** 359
prevention of hardship **106,** 359
International Covenant on Civil and Political Rights (ICCPR) (1966), application **74,** 300-1
international law **57,** 309-10, **61,** 168-9, 170, 173-8, 179-81, **80,** 403, 409, 413, 419. *See also* treaties *below*
courts, role **90,** 397-8
FRG–GDR Basis of Relations Treaty and **78,** 166
general rules
relating to right of asylum **80,** 678
status **80,** 678
municipal courts, creation by **45,** 81
municipal law and **44,** 155-6, **73,** 244, 372, 687-8, **93,** 8-9. *See also* Basic Law (*GG*), Art. 25 *above*
competence to determine whether **61,** 168-70, 179, 180-1, **70,** 400-1

general rules of international law **61,** 168-70
individuals **93,** 8, 394-5
treaty provisions as part of. *See* treaties, as part of municipal law *below*
primacy **94,** 603, **100,** 389
sources
judicial and arbitral decisions **115,** 610
teachings of publicists **115,** 610
State practice **78,** 175
international officials, immunity **70,** 414-18, **73,** 685-8
international organizations
jurisdiction over, municipal courts **108,** 651
'public authority', whether **118,** 127
transfer of sovereign rights to **93,** 395-6, 399, 426-9, 444
encroachment on national Constitution **93,** 390-1, 401, 427-8
subsequent developments in law of international organization, effect **93,** 445
turnover tax and **93,** 445-7
international organizations, immunity, jurisdiction, waiver, successor organization and **118,** 126
international organizations, privileges and immunities, basis, international agreement **118,** 126
Italy, agreement on compensation for persecutees (1962) **44,** 322-3
judge, disqualification for lack of impartiality, objective test **121,** 335
judicial assistance
in absence of agreement, comity **90,** 411
request for, whether required **65,** 197-8
judicial notice, State's social and political system **65,** 102
judicial review
diplomatic protection **90,** 395, 397, 398
foreign acts of State **100,** 372
foreign relations **90,** 396-7, **96,** 215-16
grounds, arbitrariness **90,** 398
legal rules, need for **96,** 215-16
legislature, over **93,** 416-17
Regierungsakte and justizfreie Hoheitsakte distinguished **96,** 215
jurisdiction. *See also* sovereignty *below*
administrative **73,** 372-3
armed forces, foreign **60,** 37-9, 43-4
basis for exercise of **72,** 440-1
concurrent **80,** 385
choice of law **80,** 383
proceedings already started **65,** 203-4
constitutional complaint **78,** 186-93
criminal **74,** 167-9. *See also* criminal law *above*
NATO forces **57,** 341
domestic connection requirement **73,** 246-7
effects doctrine **115,** 604-5
radioactive contamination **80,** 372-3
espionage
lex loci delicti commissi **94,** 73
protective principle **94,** 74
examination of foreign witness abroad
comity **90,** 410

Germany, Federal Republic (FRG) (*cont.*)
customary international law **90,** 410
Hague Convention on the Taking of Evidence Abroad in Civil or Commercial Matters (1970), application by analogy **90,** 410, 411
international law, compliance with rules of **90,** 410
treaty, in absence of **90,** 410, 411
garnishee order
debts of **57,** 152-3
service on **57,** 152-3
GDR **43,** 55, 58
GDR Head of State **80,** 365-6
high seas **72,** 212-14, **74,** 206-12
lex loci delicti commissi, espionage **94,** 73
NATO forces **57,** 341
nexus
bank account **65,** 137, 139
property within the jurisdiction **65,** 137, 139, 203
seat of corporation within the jurisdiction **65,** 203-4
Nuremberg Tribunal, implementation of decisions **90,** 392-5
passports **73,** 372-3, 609-10
protective principle, espionage **94,** 74
ratione materiae **80,** 372
situs **80,** 372-3, 380-2
effects doctrine **80,** 373, 380
ownership of property within the jurisdiction **80,** 380-1
treaty basis **80,** 381
social security legislation, status of Eastern territories for purpose of **78,** 190
sovereign act of third State **115,** 613
State enterprise, in respect of **80,** 385
subject-matter **73,** 241
taxation **74,** 206-12
territorial **65,** 126, **72,** 84-8, **73,** 227-51, **74,** 167-9
war crimes committed by German nationals **57,** 170-3
jus cogens/peremptory norm, requirements, State practice **65,** 166-7, **106,** 362-3
justiciability
foreign law **108,** 661
international measures, high standard required **78,** 158
Labour Courts
proceedings **62,** 302
prompt hearing **62,** 297-9, 301, 308-9, 311-17
Länder
Berlin. *See* Berlin
Constitution of, Basic Law (*GG*), relevance **100,** 397-8
human dignity, right to, unwritten constitutional principle **100,** 397-8
legislative powers **57,** 3
Maastricht Treaty (1992) as infringement of powers **98,** 211
status **44,** 314, **52,** 329-31
State immunity, jurisdiction and **87,** 39-41
treaties between, international law, applicability **90,** 375, 380
Länder / *Bund* relationship **57,** 2-3
law of
Administrative Court Rules (*VwGO*) **94,** 602

Art. 80(2)(1) **108,** 652
Art. 80(4) **108,** 653
Art. 173 **108,** 650
Administrative Courts Procedure Code (*VwGO*), Art. 98 **90,** 410
Administrative Procedure Code (*KOVVfG*)
Art. 40 **90,** 402
Art. 132 **88,** 550
Air Traffic Act (*LuftVG*)
Art. 6 **108,** 674
Art. 30(1) **108,** 674
Art. 33 **108,** 671-4
Art. 53 **108,** 671-4
Aliens Law 1965 **73,** 609-10, 615-16, **74,** 395, 398, 410, 571-3
Art. 14(1)(2) **80,** 677, 680-1
Aliens Police Ordinance **40,** 206, 290
EEC Regulation and **38,** 261-4, **40,** 289, 291
Arms Control Act **80,** 417
Asylum Ordinance 1953 **38,** 146, **40,** 202, 205
Basic Law provisions **38,** 147
Atomic Energy Act, Art. 25 **80,** 379-88
Bankruptcy Act **41,** 290, 291
Basic Law. *See* Basic Law (*GG*) *above*
Citizenship of the German Democratic Republic Law 1967 **78,** 188
Civil Code 1900 **61,** 51, 64, 65-9, 72, 74
Civil Code (*BGB*) **62,** 302, 307, **72,** 310, 313, 316, 645, 648, **73,** 237, 591, **74,** 299
Art. 17 **80,** 369, 372, 381
Art. 21 **80,** 369, 372, 381
Art. 23 **65,** 137-9, 227, **80,** 372, 380, 381, 387
Art. 32 **80,** 369, 372, 373, 380
Art. 114 **80,** 387
Art. 117 **80,** 386
Art. 118 **80,** 386, 388
Art. 199 **80,** 369
Art. 203 **80,** 371, 372, 375, 376
Art. 270 **80,** 369
Art. 271 **80,** 369
Art. 567 **80,** 369
Art. 568 **80,** 376
Art. 823 **108,** 673-4
Art. 839(1) (damages for breach of official duty) **111,** 9, 40-1
Art. 839(3) **108,** 675-6
good faith provisions **42,** 370
good faith provisions, acquisition of title **94,** 164-8
Introductory Law to (*ECBGB*) **72,** 443-4, **73,** 244, 246, **80,** 370
transfer of claims **42,** 4, 368
Civil Procedure Code (*ZPO*) **73,** 233, 238
Art. 12 **65,** 126
Art. 17(1) **65,** 203
Art. 18 **65,** 126
Art. 19 **65,** 130
Arts. 22-4 **121,** 335

Germany, Federal Republic (FRG) (*cont.*)
Art. 23 **65,** 126, 137, 138-9, 203-4, 227, **80,** 372, 380, 381, 387
Art. 38 **65,** 126
Art. 39 **65,** 126
Art. 114 **94,** 601
Arts. 158 ff **65,** 197
Art. 216 **65,** 130
Art. 286 **108,** 674-5
Art. 287 **108,** 676
Art. 314 **65,** 197
Art. 320 **65,** 197
Art. 328(1) **65,** 201, 203-4
Art. 363 **90,** 410
Art. 766 **65,** 225
Art. 793 **65,** 225
Art. 926 **65,** 201
Art. 936 **81,** 213, 214
Art. 944 **81,** 213, 214
Civil Service (Employment of Extremists) Decree 1972 **88,** 546
Co-determination Law **85,** 468-9
Commercial Code **73,** 586
Company Law (*Aktiengesetz*) **84,** 391
Compensation for Measures of Criminal Prosecution Law 1971 **72,** 264-7, 310
Compensation for Victims of Nazi Persecution Law
Art. 4(1) **74,** 420-2
Art. 160 **72,** 647-50, **74,** 281
Final Act **74,** 281-4, 420-2
Constitution 1867 **61,** 64, 65-6
Constitution of the Courts Law (*GVG*)
Art. 18 **65,** 195, **80,** 403, 423, **94,** 601, **118,** 126
Arts. 18-20 **65,** 160, **118,** 126, 128
Art. 19 **65,** 195, **80,** 403, 423, **118,** 126
Art. 20 **65,** 128-30, 134, 195, 202, 207-8, 213, **80,** 365, 397, 402, 403, 405, 409-10, 411, 413, 417, 423
Art. 20(1) **118,** 128
Art. 20(2) **108,** 650, **114,** 504, 505, 516, **118,** 126-7, 128, 133
Art. 25 **80,** 403
Constitutional Court Law (*BVerfGG*). *See* Constitutional Court Law (*BVerfGG*) *above*
Copyright Act
Art. 27 **65,** 144
Art. 89(3) **65,** 145
Corporation Tax Law **72,** 212, 215
Court Organization Law **73,** 687
Criminal Code (*StGB*) **72,** 302-4, 319, 633, 637-8, **74,** 167-9, 512-15
Art. 2(3) **100,** 370, 373, 375, 379, 391
Art. 3 **115,** 604-5
Arts. 3-7 **100,** 374
Art. 5(4) (applicable law) **94,** 73
Art. 5(6) **100,** 373
Art. 6(1) **80,** 679
Art. 7(1) **100,** 373, 374-5
Art. 9 **115,** 604-5

Art. 17 **100,** 371, 393
Art. 99 (espionage) **94,** 73-5
Art. 177 (rape) **121,** 270
Art. 212 **100,** 370, 391
Art. 213 **100,** 370, 372, 391
Art. 234(a) **100,** 374
Art. 241(a) **100,** 374
Art. 316 **80,** 679
Art. 424 **80,** 679
duress **47,** 468, 470-3
equality of treatment and **94,** 78-80
fraud and breach of trust **41,** 287, 290, 291
universality of law **80,** 679
Criminal Procedure Code (*StPO*) **72,** 305, 310, 312, 315, 319, 321-2, 418-23, 428-9, **73,** 519-23, 545
Art. 13 **80,** 365
Art. 134 **68,** 81
Art. 172 **86,** 537
Art. 206 **80,** 422
Art. 260(3) **100,** 396
detention pending trial **45,** 321-3
ECHR, incorporation of **68,** 75
Economic Crimes Act 1949 **73,** 518
Equalization of Burdens Act 1952 **43,** 4, **44,** 149-51, 170, **61,** 163, **65,** 12-13
Extradition Law (*DAG*) **44,** 175, **45,** 377-80, **70,** 375-9, **74,** 511-15, **80,** 679
Family Act 1965 **57,** 50
Federal Reparation Act **44,** 314, 317, 322
Federal Restitution Acts **42,** 378, **44,** 302, 303, 306, 313, 314, 316, 317-18, 321, 322, 340, 349
seizure, proof of **44,** 323-4, 349, 353
'subsequent acquirer' **44,** 349
Finance Law 1980 **90,** 394
Foreign Activities Decree (*Auslandstätigkeitserlass*) of 31 October 1983 **108,** 654-6
GDR, application in **115,** 600
General War Consequences Act 1957 **51,** 403-14
Geneva Convention on the Status of Refugees, Transformation Law **80,** 678
Hamburg Disciplinary Tribunals for the Medical Professions Act 1972 **81,** 217
Hamburg Veterinary Surgeons' Council Act 1964 **81,** 208-9, 217, 223
Rules of Professional Conduct **81,** 209, 223-4
Rules of Professional Conduct, compatibility with Basic Law **81,** 214-15
Income Tax Law (*EStG*) **72,** 212, 215, **74,** 205-11
Art. 34c(5) **108,** 655-6
Art. 34d(5) **108,** 655-6
Insurance Code (Reich) 1911 **86,** 390, 408-9
Insurance Law (*BVG*) **80,** 672
Introductory Law to the Criminal Code (*EGStGB*)
Art. 6 **100,** 380
Art. 315 **100,** 374-5
Art. 315(1) **100,** 375
Art. 315(4) **100,** 373, 374
Art. 351(1) **100,** 370, 373
Judicature Law (*GVG*). *See* Constitution of the Courts Act (*GVG*) *above*

Germany, Federal Republic (FRG) (*cont.*)
Law of 18 August 1961 (Status of Forces Agreement) **86,** 534
Law of 26 July 1965 (European Schools: Statute) **108,** 650-1
Law of 23 May 1972 (Moscow Treaty) **78,** 190
Notes of Three Powers, as integral part **78,** 190
Law of 6 June 1973 (FRG–GDR Basis of Relations Treaty) **78,** 158, 159
Law of 3 July 1975 (EMBL Headquarters Agreement) **105,** 24
Law of 17 July 1978 (European Schools: establishment) **108,** 650
Law Reorganizing Local Authorities **43,** 28, 38, 44, 65, 72
Legal Assistance in Civil Proceedings Order (*ZRHO*) **80,** 370
Legal Assistance in Criminal Matters (*IRG*)
Art. 8(1) **106,** 303
Art. 42(1) **106,** 300
Legal Status of Illegitimate Children Law, retroactive effect **71,** 38-9
Limited Companies Law (*AktG*), Art. 309 **80,** 386
Literary Copyright Act, Art. 52(1) **65,** 144
Military Criminal Code (*WStG*)
Art. 1(1) **100,** 391-2
Art. 5 **100,** 371
Art. 5(1) **100,** 391-2
Narcotic Drugs Law **72,** 417, 458-67, **74,** 167
Nationality Law 1969 **73,** 612
Pensions Law (*BVG*)
Art. 1 **90,** 402-4
Art. 5 **90,** 402-4
Post and Telecommunications Act, Restrictions on Secrecy of 1968 **58,** 432, 434, 435-6
Prisoners of War Indemnity Act **44,** 442, 445
Promotion of Employment Act **62,** 308
Provision of Labour (Temporary Staff) Act **118,** 136
Art. 1(1)(1) **118,** 128
Art. 1(9)(1) **118,** 128
Art. 1(10)(1) **118,** 128
Art. 1(10)(2) **118,** 128
good faith nature of relationships **118,** 136
Public Assistance Law (*BSHG*)
aliens, applicability to **94,** 602
Art. 2 **94,** 607
Art. 11 **94,** 606
Art. 123 **94,** 599-608
foreign diplomats, applicability to **94,** 599-608
Reduction of Workload in Civil Cases Act 1969 **73,** 504
Regulation of Open Property Issues Law (*VermG*) 1990 **94,** 50, 51
Regulations concerning Free Gifts **86,** 524
Removal of Obstacles to the Privatization of Commercial Undertakings and Promotion of Investments Law 1991 **94,** 50
Reservation of Evidence and Determination Law (*Beweissicherungs und Feststellungsgesetz*) **91,** 220
Road Traffic Act 1968-75 **73,** 517-31, 533-6, 544
'regulatory' offences **73,** 517-31, 533-46
Social Code (*SGB*) **90,** 402
Art. 5 **90,** 403

Art. 162 **90,** 406
Social Courts Act 1953 **86,** 391
Social Security Code (Reich) **86,** 539-41, 542
Social Security Law (*AVG*)
Art. 28 **80,** 668
'war' **80,** 670-3
Special Investments in the GDR Law 1990 **94,** 50
Trade Marks Law 1954 **71,** 17
Unfair Competition Act (*UNG*) 1909, freedom of expression, compatibility with **101,** 81-95
Unfair Competition Act (*UNG*) 1977 **81,** 211-12, **86,** 524
Art. 1 **81,** 214, 221, 223
freedom of expression, compatibility with **81,** 228
Unfair Dismissal Act **62,** 301-2
Use of Force by Members of the Armed Forces Law (*UZwGBw*)
Art. 15 **100,** 385
Art. 16 **100,** 379, 385
Use of Force by Prison Officers Law (*UZwG*), Art. 11 **100,** 379, 385
Veterinary Practitioners Act 1977 **81,** 217
Weapons Act **74,** 195
legal certainty, primacy **100,** 371
legal protection
requirements, judge as member of judicial body **108,** 667-8
right of **108,** 667-8
'legality of prosecution' principle **68,** 81
legislation, interpretation
aids, general principles of international law **100,** 382-3
in case of conflict with international law **57,** 2-3
critical date **90,** 406
guidelines
clear meaning **100,** 376
GDR practice **100,** 385-7
proportionality **100,** 371
phrases
'accident' **108,** 672-4
'act of war' **90,** 402
'acts of public authority' **93,** 355
'connection with the Second World War' **90,** 403
'Occupying Power' **90,** 403, 406, 407
'third party' **111,** 10, 41
relevant factors, law of third State **90,** 406
legislation, retroactivity **71,** 38-9
legislature, treaties, role in relation to **90,** 371-4
liability
absolute **80,** 383
Atomic Energy Act **80,** 383-4
choice of law **80,** 383
for sovereign activity **80,** 381-2
State enterprise, property belonging to **80,** 373
life, right to
chemical weapons deployment and **106,** 395-7
nuclear weapons deployment and **106,** 360-2

Germany, Federal Republic (FRG) (*cont.*)
Maastricht Treaty (1992). *See* European Union Treaty (Maastricht) (1992)
margin of appreciation, defence policy, acts of armed forces **108,** 674-5
marriage
foreign law, respect for **57,** 11-12
freedom of **72,** 297-301
protection of **57,** 314, **73,** 610-12, 617
medical profession **58,** 378-82
administrative proceedings relating to **58,** 382-95, 715
military service **59,** 323
definition **80,** 672-3
'national question'
FRG–GDR Basis of Relations Treaty and **78,** 167
reunification as **78,** 167
nationality **57,** 307-10
Basic Law (*GG*) **45,** 354, 355
Berlin (Western Sectors), citizens of **78,** 175
Nazi laws on
non-recognition of **72,** 454, 460-1, 470, 477
repeal, whether retroactive **72,** 460-1
rules governing **72,** 438-41, 449-55, 458-67
nationality of claims **74,** 282-4
nationals
domiciled in West Berlin **59,** 323
France–FRG Convention of Establishment **52,** 354
protection. *See* diplomatic protection *above*
NATO
accession to **45,** 390
criminal jurisdiction **57,** 341
State responsibility for acts and omissions of **108,** 675-6
naturalization **45,** 356, **60,** 220-2, 223, **74,** 394-7
discrimination and **60,** 222
Netherlands
Ems Estuary Agreements (1960/62) **41,** 81-2, 93, 95, 98, 102, 166, **43,** 252
Frontier Treaty (1960) **43,** 252
North-Rhine Westphalia, law of, Civil Servants Act **88,** 539, 543, 544, 548, 558
nuclear weapons, deployment
consent to, Convention on the Presence of Foreign Forces in the FRG (1954), sufficiency **106,** 370-1
legality, defensive purposes
customary international law **106,** 362-3
Non-Proliferation Treaty (1968) **106,** 376
legislative consent, need for **106,** 368-88
collective security, agreement to treaty establishing **106,** 369-70, 379
NATO 'Double Resolution' of 12 December 1979 **106,** 355-64, 370-88
sovereignty, surrender **106,** 375-87
collective security system, in context of **106,** 376-87
consultative rights, relevance **106,** 376, 378-9
Three Power rights and responsibilities, relevance **106,** 387
occupying power, jurisdiction over, in absence of right of suit in occupying/administering power's own courts **65,** 130
Oder–Neisse, territories east of. *See* Oder–Neisse, territories east of

Ostpolitik **78,** 164
police
agency of State, whether **65,** 198
State immunity, jurisdiction **65,** 196-8
State responsibility and **95,** 331
political asylum. *See* asylum *above*
political question doctrine, reasons for, absence of judicially discoverable and manageable standards **107,** 259
political union, EMU and **98,** 240-1
Portugal, Assets Agreement (1958) **51,** 401-29
prerogative
continental shelf/fishing zones, exploitation **106,** 372
diplomatic relations, termination **106,** 372
recognition of State **106,** 372, 374
territorial changes **106,** 374
treaties, denunciation **106,** 372
privileges and immunities. *See also* diplomatic privileges and immunities *and* international organizations, privileges and immunities *above*
GDR Head of State **80,** 365-6
prompt hearing **72,** 302-6, 317-19
property rights **51,** 401-14. *See also* Oder-Neisse, territories east of, property rights
proportionality
EC, obligation to observe **98,** 245
legislative interpretation and **100,** 371
public interest **73,** 609-17, 693-4
public order/public policy/*ordre public* **57,** 12, 50, **73,** 228-9, 237, 244-7, **74,** 400, 572
concept **72,** 571-3
exclusion, measures affecting German external assets **44,** 70
Rechtstitel, duty not to give up **78,** 163
recognition **61,** 51, 63-4, 72, 75, 76
law of **61,** 52-4, 64
referendum, right to
entrenched provisions of Constitution and **98,** 220
European Union Treaty (Maastricht) (1992) **98,** 212
refugees **74,** 395-7, **80,** 410-11, 675-82. *See also* asylum *above*
compensation for persecution **72,** 647-50
crime in country of refuge **40,** 206
Federal Office for Recognition of Foreign Refugees **80,** 676
persecution, compensation **72,** 647-50
protection of **57,** 326-7
unlawful entry **40,** 205
Reich
assumption of responsibility for debts **47,** 420, 432, 437, 449, **59,** 507
identity with **91,** 226, 230, **94,** 178
successor, whether **44,** 314, **59,** 492, **78,** 161-2, **88,** 287, **94,** 178-9
reparations
acts not attributable to compensating State **94,** 61-2
discretionary element **94,** 61-2
equalization of burdens **94,** 61-2
individual entitlement, whether **94,** 62-3
restitution laws **42,** 378, **44,** 302, 303, 306, 313, 314, 316, 317-18, 321, 322, 340, 349

Germany, Federal Republic (FRG) (*cont.*)
proof of seizure **44,** 323-4, 349, 353
'subsequent acquirer' **44,** 349
reunification **78,** 156, 162, 168. *See also* unification *and* unity *below*
confederation, possibility of **78,** 168
constitutional requirement **78,** 156, 162
constitutional step not open to FRG influence **78,** 170
right of **78,** 156
self-determination **78,** 156, 162
Schleswig-Holstein
law of, Provincial Charter (*LS*) 1949 **90,** 371
treaties, procedures **90,** 371-2
separation of powers
democratic requirement **106,** 372-3
foreign policy **106,** 373-5
transfer of powers to EC and **98,** 211
treaties, executive's rights **106,** 339-40
service of process abroad, responsibility for **80,** 372
service of process on foreign State or State agency **80,** 368-77
method
diplomatic channels **80,** 369, 372, 376
publication **80,** 371-2, 374, 375-7
through diplomatic channels **80,** 369, 372, 374, 376
through foreign ambassador/head of mission **80,** 368-71, 374-5, 376-7
Settlement Convention (1952/4) **43,** 4-5
compensation, exclusion **42,** 408, 489
discriminatory treatment **42,** 405-7
exemption from war taxes **44,** 317, 321
military government measures, German courts and **43,** 249
property requisitioned in occupied territory **42,** 488-90
reparations
acceptance of measures taken by allies (Chapter VI) **42,** 435
restoration of foreign rights and interests (Chapter X) **42,** 408, 489
rights reserved **44,** 462, 478
war charges and levies **43,** 4-5
ships, on high seas, jurisdiction over **72,** 212-14
ships, jurisdiction, flag State **72,** 212-14
ships, State-owned
immunity, arrest/attachment, applicable law **65,** 103
ownership, possession or control as test of status **65,** 102
social and political system of State, State immunity and **65,** 105
social security **86,** 390-2, 539-42
aliens
entitlement **94,** 602
motivation, relevance **94,** 602
residence requirement **94,** 602, 607
consular agent. *See* consular agent, social security *above*
foreign diplomat. *See* diplomatic agent, social security *above*
Social Security Insurance System **57,** 5-6
'sole representation' **78,** 164
FRG–GDR Basis of Relations Treaty and **78,** 164
sovereignty
area of exercise, 'area of validity of the Basic Law' **78,** 162

citizenship, attribution as sign of **78,** 188
jurisdiction as exercise of **60,** 43
Maastricht Treaty (1992), threat to **98,** 212
surrender to foreign State, nuclear weapons, deployment, agreement to **106,** 375-87
transfer of powers to Community. *See* EC, transfer of powers to *above*
transfer of powers to international organization
collective security system **106,** 329-30, 331-2, 379-80
collective security system, agreement to treaty establishing as consent **106,** 380
constitutional limitations. *See* Basic Law, ss 24(1) and 24(2) *above*
nature of organization, relevance **106,** 380-1
responsibility for determining whether **106,** 379
rights inalienable by organization **108,** 652-3
standard of treatment of alien
equality **72,** 264-6, **74,** 423-4
reciprocity **72,** 264-6
State agency/State-owned corporation/State entity
'agency or instrumentality of foreign State', ambassador **115,** 613-14
applicable law, *lex fori* **65,** 105-6
classification
NIOC **65,** 200, 202-3, 213, 218-24
police authority **65,** 198
tourist office **65,** 144
liability for acts of **80,** 385-7
separate legal entity test **65,** 202-3, 219-24, 227, 229, 232
separate legal identity test **80,** 385-7
State immunity **80,** 370-1, 372
tort **80,** 381-2
State immunity, execution/attachment, applicability
bank account, other than diplomatic or consular **65,** 190-1
funds held in private foreign bank **65,** 218-46
ownership and power of disposal, designation of account as determining factor **65,** 228-9
State immunity, execution/attachment, entitlement, commercial/trade representation/mission **65,** 210-11
State immunity, execution/attachment, procedural aspects
applicable law **65,** 118, 185, 188-9, 219-20, 243-4
lex fori **65,** 116, 220, 243-4
State practice **65,** 116
State immunity, execution/attachment, purpose of proceedings, safeguarding/conservatory measures **65,** 101, 133-7, 138-9, 181, 228-9, 239-45
State immunity, execution/attachment, purpose/use of funds/assets
diplomatic mission, expenses **65,** 151-9, 226-7
embassy building **65,** 111-14
future transfer to central bank for financing of State budget **65,** 218-24, 229-39, 243-6
future use, relevance **65,** 135, 176-7
impairment of functions test **65,** 112
non-specific **65,** 118-19, 189-90
ownership as test **65,** 220
private or commercial purpose **65,** 119
running of State's offices in forum State **65,** 115-19
sovereign purpose **65,** 184

Germany, Federal Republic (FRG) (*cont.*)
State immunity, execution/attachment, theory/doctrine
development of concept **65,** 153-6, 164, 175-7, 181-2, 184, 218-24, 226-9, 243-5
State immunity, jurisdiction
dependence on **65,** 135
distinguished **65,** 103
State practice **65,** 116-17, 153-7
State immunity, execution/attachment, waiver
clear and unequivocal communication, need for **65,** 160
forum selection clause **65,** 119
State immunity, jurisdiction, applicability, evidence, giving of **65,** 161
State immunity, jurisdiction, classification of act **65,** 120-2
armed forces, acts concerning, GDR **100,** 372-3
arms sales **65,** 122
commercial activities **114,** 504-7, 510-11
distinguishability from other non-sovereign rights **45,** 80
financial assistant **114,** 518-19
commission agreement **65,** 120-2, 125-7
consular activity **65,** 207-8
consular premises, lease or purchase **65,** 126
copyright material, use of **65,** 143-4
deployment of armed forces **90,** 410-11
diplomatic premises
mortgage interest on premises no longer used for diplomatic purposes **65,** 111-14
repair **45,** 58-9, 79-82, **64,** 272
expropriation/nationalization **65,** 128-31
interference with functioning of mission/consulate and **65,** 126, 152-3
legislative act **65,** 128-30
letter of credit **65,** 133-7
nature or purpose of transaction as determining factor **64,** 234, 318, **65,** 112, 121, 135-6, 143, **114,** 504-6, 517
police officer providing judicial assistance under bilateral treaty **65,** 195, 197-8
private law relationship **65,** 112, 121, 143-4, 214, 220
private person test **65,** 121, 136, 139, 211
summoning of witnesses **90,** 410
tourism promotion **65,** 144
State immunity, jurisdiction, entitlement
responsibility for determining, courts **45,** 59
State-owned corporation **65,** 202
State immunity, jurisdiction, procedural aspects
applicable law **80,** 382, **114,** 505
international law **45,** 59, 60-1, 80-1
lex fori **45,** 80-1, **65,** 105, 121, 126, 127, 128-9, 136-7, 142-3, 197
State practice, relevance **114,** 505, 517
burden of proof **114,** 507
court's duty to raise *proprio motu* **65,** 102-3
effective remedy, right to and **65,** 130
hearing, setting of date for as exercise of jurisdiction **65,** 130-1
State immunity, jurisdiction, theory/doctrine
absolute theory
customary international law **65,** 104

State-owned trading vessel and **65,** 104
basis
equality of States **65,** 157, **114,** 510
non-interference in the affairs of another State **65,** 154-5
par in parem non habet jurisdictionem **65,** 157
sovereignty **65,** 128, **114,** 506
unimpeded fulfilment of consular tasks **114,** 518-19
customary international law **45,** 61, **90,** 410
restrictive theory **114,** 505
development of concept **65,** 103-4, 120-1, 134-6, 141-3, 153-6, 164, 175-7, 181-2, 184, 195-6, 213-14, 218-24, 226-9, 243-5, **80,** 381
individual rights, effect on **65,** 191-2
public order/public policy/*ordre public* considerations **65,** 139
State practice **45,** 61-79, **65,** 120-1, 213-14
State immunity, jurisdiction, waiver **90,** 411
execution and jurisdiction, need for separate waivers **65,** 158
implied. *See also* submission to the jurisdiction as waiver
acceptance of service **65,** 198-9
submission to the jurisdiction as, challenge to jurisdiction **65,** 199
State practice
diplomatic privileges and immunities, entitlement, third State, in **115,** 612
nuclear weapons, deployment **106,** 362-3
State responsibility for
acts within GDR territory **94,** 59-60, 62
aliens
discrimination **72,** 265-7
reciprocity, relevance **72,** 265-6
breach of official duty **111,** 9-11
law infringing Constitution **111,** 41
unlawful interference **111,** 10, 41
third party particularly affected, need for **110,** 10, **111,** 41, 121
war reparations. *See* compensation for war-related events, German reparations
State responsibility for acts and omissions of police officer
junior **95,** 331
unauthorized acts **95,** 331
status, World War II, after **59,** 492
superior orders, GDR border shootings, retroactivity and **100,** 388-9
supranational organization, formal designation of organization, need for **93,** 356
Supreme Court decisions on Zeiss Foundation **43,** 53, 55-6, 59, 62, 77, 78
surveillance measures **58,** 432, 434-8
telecommunications **58,** 434
Switzerland, Agreement on German Equalization of Burdens Law **43,** 3, 4, **44,** 149-51
taxation, exemption, foreign State **88,** 681-3, **108,** 525
territorial questions, Eastern Treaties and **78,** 190
terrorist acts
extradition for **74,** 494-8, 509-16
punishment of **74,** 494
Three Powers, relations with. *See also* Settlement Convention 1952/4 *above*
Bonn–Paris Convention (1952/4) **58,** 434
Eastern Treaties and **78,** 190
final peace settlement, reservation of rights to **78,** 190
Finance Convention (1954) **47,** 115, 117

Germany, Federal Republic (FRG) (*cont.*)
treaties **59,** 490-4, **61,** 623, **80,** 678. *See also* Eastern Treaties for the Normalization of Relations with Poland and the USSR (1970), FRG–Poland Border Treaty (1990) *and* FRG–Poland, Treaty for the Normalization of Relations (1970) (Warsaw Treaty) *above*
amendment
interpretation as **106,** 338-9
legislative role, in absence of treaty of amendment **106,** 338, 345, 347
legislature, role of **90,** 373
NATO Council decisions **106,** 344-5
practice, by **106,** 338, 339, 345
preamble as trigger **106,** 338
treaty, need for **106,** 339
compliance, choice of method **106,** 301-2
constitutional conflict, excluded **78,** 160
Constitutional Court's scrutiny responsibility **43,** 250-1, **78,** 160, 161
FRG–GDR Basis of Relations Treaty and **78,** 160
GDR's knowledge of before Treaty's entry into force **78,** 174
constitutionality, encroachment on legal sphere of individual **94,** 54
content and scope, beyond judicial assessment **78,** 193
counter-denunciation, right of **90,** 380, 382-4
provision for, relevance **90,** 380
time-limit **90,** 380, 382-4
definition, agreement between subjects of international law intended to bring about international consequences **106,** 336-9, 342-3
denunciation **90,** 370-1, 373-4
balance of interests **90,** 379
counter-denunciation, right of. *See* counter-denunciation, right of *above*
customary international law, absence of rule **90,** 374-5
law-making act, whether **90,** 374
municipal law vacuum **90,** 373-4
special circumstances of treaty, relevance, **90,** 377-8
termination as between all parties **90,** 371, 374-82
withdrawal of denouncing party **90,** 381-2
direct effect in **78,** 184
elements **78,** 159-60
exchange of letters **106,** 346
form
oral agreement **106,** 336
relevance **106,** 336
GDR, with **78,** 152-76
general international law **78,** 166
inter-State treaty, whether **94,** 54
'relations *inter se*', significance **78,** 166
implementation, legislative responsibility **106,** 396-7
implementing legislation **78,** 189-90
need for **78,** 159
treaty dealt with as enacted law **78,** 174
Treaty Law published before Treaty initialled **78,** 174
validity in case of termination of treaty **90,** 384-5
incorporation into municipal law
ECHR **68,** 75
need for **59,** 6-7

obligation, whether **70,** 431-2
individuals under **78,** 184, 189, 192-3
express provision required **78,** 189
intention to conclude, need for **106,** 337-8, 343-5, 371
implicit **106,** 337-8, 343-4
interpretation. *See* treaty interpretation *below*
lacuna, completion
fundamental change of circumstances **90,** 379
as interpretation **90,** 378-9
legislative role
amendment **106,** 338, 345, 348
amendment to legislation, relevance of need for **106,** 347
budgetary matters **106,** 340
human rights **106,** 340
'non-political treaties' **106,** 335-6
political control **106,** 340
public international law matters **106,** 335-6
reserved matters **106,** 346
right of initiative **106,** 372-3
legislature, role of **90,** 371-4
conclusion of treaty and termination distinguished **90,** 372
modus vivendi, FRG–GDR Basis of Relations Treaty as **78,** 164
multilateral
non-parties and, application by analogy **90,** 410
third parties **65,** 103-4
municipal law and, conflict **57,** 2-3
NATO Council decisions **106,** 344
negotiating responsibility **90,** 372, **94,** 63-4
obligations
source **90,** 384
termination, in case of **90,** 385-6
obligations under **59,** 491-2
official statements and **78,** 164
operation, evidence of intentions **78,** 192
as part of municipal law **70,** 431, **90,** 694
obligation, whether **93,** 426
status **93,** 361-2
Petersberg Declaration (1992) **106,** 341
'political' treaty
fundamental departure from previous position **106,** 347
'treaty affecting existence of State, territorial integrity, its independence, its standing and potential weight' **106,** 336-7, 346
primacy **93,** 29-30
applicable law **93,** 426-7
international law, absence of rule **93,** 426-7
subsequent legislation **93,** 8-9
subsequent treaty **106,** 334
ratification
constitutional requirement **78,** 159
FRG–GDR Basis of Relations Treaty **78,** 159-61
responsibility **106,** 335
Reich, obligations of **59,** 492-3

Germany, Federal Republic (FRG) (*cont.*)
scrutiny **43,** 9-10, 246-53, **78,** 159-61
Basic Law and **78,** 160
entry into force before completion **78,** 161
GDR's knowledge of FRG's position **78,** 174
responsibility of Constitutional Court **78,** 160, 161
speed **78,** 160
State succession
ad hoc **115,** 615
agreement of all parties, need for **115,** 614
treaties concluded by the German Democratic Republic (GDR) **115,** 614
suspension, effect on reputation **94,** 68
termination, responsibility **106,** 335
termination clause, absence of **78,** 157, 164
time-limit, absence of **78,** 157, 164
transfer of powers exercised by *Länder* **108,** 652
treaty-making power **78,** 192-3
constitutional limitations **51,** 401-14, **73,** 692-4
executive **106,** 335-40
individual's power to influence **108,** 661-2
legislative role **106,** 335-6
prior legislative approval, need for **90,** 372-3
validity **90,** 382
Versailles, Treaty of (1919) **57,** 5-6
treaty interpretation
aids **78,** 159, 160
context and purpose **78,** 164, 189
municipal law **90,** 377
other treaties between parties **90,** 407
parliamentary proceedings **93,** 445-6
private law **90,** 378
subsequent practice **90,** 376, **106,** 370-1
travaux préparatoires **90,** 373-7
burden of proof **90,** 376
error, effect **90,** 383-4
guidelines
authentic languages equally authoritative **94,** 603
Basic Law as starting point **78,** 160, 174
brevity as indication of limited scope **78,** 189
identity of meaning of authentic language texts **94,** 603
maintenance of friendly relations **90,** 380, 384
non-authentic language **94,** 603
ordinary meaning **94,** 603
purpose **90,** 379, 380
sovereignty, preservation of **90,** 380
wording **90,** 407
limits **78,** 174
multilingual, parallel texts as interpreted under relevant national law as interpretative aid **108,** 651
obligation to accept **78,** 174
parties' intention **90,** 381, 407
phrases

'circumstances' **94,** 468-9, 522-3, 557-9
'domicile' **86,** 540
'exempt' **94,** 603-4
'services rendered for sending State' **94,** 604
'usual place of residence' **86,** 540-1
Preamble, essential to **78,** 167, 174
unification
'preservation' requirement **91,** 222
unity of nationality and **91,** 219, 221, 222-3
responsibility for, political organs **91,** 221-2
Unification Treaty (1990)
competence to conclude **94,** 57, 61
espionage, effect on **94,** 76, 77
expropriation by Occupying Powers **94,** 47-8, 50, 52, 60, 61
Four Power rights and responsibilities **94,** 51
FRG Basic Law (*GG*), amendment by **94,** 57-8
FRG law, applicability in former GDR **94,** 75-6. *See also* applicable law, offences committed in former GDR *above*
GDR acts, validity **100,** 372
Joint Declaration on the Regulation of Open Property Questions (15 June 1990)
constitutionality **94,** 56-7
equality of treatment, compatibility with **94,** 64-5
non-negotiability **94,** 53, 63-4
part of treaty, as **94,** 48
possibility of restitution, relevance **94,** 61
unenforceable nature of any original rights **94,** 61
suspension of application
property rights in eastern Germany, effect on **94,** 67-8
reputation of FRG, effect on **94,** 68
validity, accession of GDR to FRG and **94,** 50
unilateral declaration/undertaking, Declaration of Consent to deployment of nuclear missiles **106,** 370-5
unilateral undertakings
authority to give **106,** 371
binding nature **106,** 370-5
as legal clarification **106,** 371
legislative consent, need for **106,** 370-5, 388
unity. *See also* reunification *above*
Federal Republic, Letter of 19 June 1973 to Government of the GDR **78,** 156, 167
Letter of 19 June 1973 to Government of the GDR **78,** 156, 167
visiting forces, application of law and **86,** 524, 533-6
war
'defensive emergency' **106,** 348
'State of defence', transfer of power of command to head of Government **106,** 349
Germany, occupation (post-WWII) 59, 601, **61,** 42-5, 46 n. 15, 63, 75-6, 146, 151, **72,** 554-6, 559-61, **78,** 161. *See also* Control Council Law No 10; Germany, Democratic Republic (GDR), expropriation/nationalization, Soviet occupation; Germany, Democratic Republic (GDR), Soviet occupation
allocation of zones (1945) **43,** 25, 45-6, 67-8
applicable law **43,** 52, 58-9, 62, 75, **61,** 63-5. *See also* Control Council Law No 10
continuity of laws **94,** 168 n. 12

Germany, occupation (post-WWII) (*cont.*)
assumption of power by Allies **43,** 70
Declaration of (1945) **44,** 55
authority deriving from **94,** 169
Berlin. *See* Berlin
boundaries, demarcation **74,** 122
continued authority of *Länder* **94,** 178
costs
basis **90,** 394-5
imprisonment of war criminal **90,** 391
jurisdiction, relevance **90,** 394-5
Eastern zone, de jure authority in **43,** 25-6, 45-6
Four Power rights and responsibilities **78,** 161, 172, 190
continued existence of German State, evidence of **91,** 227
Eastern Treaties, effect **78,** 190
GDR, recognition of and **91,** 234
nuclear weapons, deployment **106,** 387
Nuremberg Tribunal and **90,** 392
occupation, termination and **90,** 407
reservation **90,** 407
suspension **94,** 51
termination **94,** 51
Unification Treaty (1990) and **94,** 51
USSR and **91,** 227
French occupation authorities, decisions of **41,** 478-80
'Germany as a whole'
applicable law **43,** 52, 58-9, 62, 75
Four Power responsibility for **78,** 158, 161, 163-4, 172
joint governing authority of occupying States **43,** 25-6, 40, 46, 69
imprisonment of war criminals **90,** 390-400
industrial enterprises, effect on ownership of **72,** 554-6, 560-1, 589-90, 592-3, **73,** 582-3
military tribunals in **91,** 48
nationals, protection of and **90,** 397
Occupying Powers. *See also* Four Power rights and responsibilities *above*
assumption of supreme authority, annexation, whether **91,** 225
foreign relations, responsibility for **91,** 225-6
international organizations and **91,** 225-6
governing authority **43,** 71
Law No 8 (Patents) **42,** 349-50, 362-8, 374-7, 381
French text, whether translation **42,** 375-6
interpretation, German concepts **42,** 362
objects of **42,** 363, 370-1, 374, 377
remedial *lex specialis* **42,** 378
Law No 59 (restitution) **42,** 38
legislation
definition **45,** 441
restitution, on **44,** 311
Nuremberg Tribunal, implementing of decision and **90,** 390-2
right to sue on Germany's behalf **94,** 172-3, 198
Oder–Neisse, territories east of. *See* Oder–Neisse, territories east of
patents
London Accord (1946) **41,** 459-61

sequestration **41,** 459-61
Polish Army in (1945), status **41,** 461-74
Potsdam Agreement (1945). *See* Potsdam Conference 1945
property transfers, prohibition **47,** 133
sequestration **61,** 44-5
patents **41,** 459-61
reparations distinguished **61,** 50 n. 21
Soviet zone
expropriation of industrial enterprises **71,** 14-15, 20, **72,** 554-6, 560-1, **73,** 582-3, 589-90, 592-3
responsibility for acts of authorities in **51,** 239, 244, 248
status, 1946 **47,** 133
subjugation theory **83,** 135
termination of occupation regime **45,** 37, 40
US Military Government in **81,** 512-13
courts **81,** 512
judicial review **81,** 513
law **81,** 511, 512-13
Thuringia, occupation forces, authority **94,** 168-70
Germany, occupation of Rhineland (post-WWI) 83, 135, 155
legislation
of occupied power, registration requirement **3,** 9-10
of occupying powers, incorporation, need for **3,** 9-10
Germany, occupation (WWII), Quadripartite Agreement (1972). *See* Berlin, Quadripartite Agreement (1972)
Germany (Reich)
allied occupation. *See* Germany, occupation (post-WWII)
Anschluss of Austria **44,** 335
nationality, effect on **45,** 353-7
Anti-Comintern Pact (1936) **44,** 335, 336
assets, claims to, Brussels Agreement (1947) **42,** 433-5
Berlin–Rome Axis (1936) **44,** 335
boundaries **44,** 55-6, 66. *See also* Germany, Federal Republic, boundaries
31 December 1937 **78,** 168, 186
demarcation **74,** 122, **78,** 156
Eastern treaties and **78,** 190
France
Baden **42,** 60
Rhine **47,** 115-17
rivers **47,** 115-17
inner-German **78,** 168-9
Basis of Relations Treaty **78,** 168-9
demarcation line **78,** 156
capitulation
Declaration of 5 June 1945 **56,** 46
effect **56,** 46-7, **78,** 161, **91,** 224-5
citizenship, deprivation by Nazi régime **72,** 449-77
confiscation of patents by allies, act of war **48,** 468-9
Constitution, Art. 45(3) (unilateral acts: consent of *Reichstag*) **106,** 372
continued existence **43,** 67, **44,** 302, 313, **56,** 46-7, **59,** 492, **61,** 63, **78,** 156, 161, 169, **91,** 224-5
assumption of supreme authority by Allied Powers and **91,** 225

Germany (Reich) (*cont.*)
Basic Law (FRG) **91,** 226
capitulation and **91,** 224-5
dissolution of Reich government and **91,** 225
dual State theory **94,** 179-80
FRG, creation of **91,** 230
GDR Constitution and **91,** 230
unity of nationality and **91,** 224-5
Control Council Law No 10. *See* Control Council Law No 10
Czechoslovakia, annexation of part of **47,** 31, 33
debts, assumption of liability by FRG **47,** 420, 432, 437, 449, **59,** 507
Denmark, Arbitration Convention 1926 **42,** 386
discriminatory legislation **66,** 23, 29-31, 51
division **43,** 52, 55, 58, 76, **44,** 55, **78,** 156
legal consequences **45,** 37-46
self-determination, need for **91,** 224
trade, effect on **62,** 90-104
treaties, effect on **74,** 114
enemy property legislation **42,** 349, 361, 376-7
Estonia, occupation of, legislative power, extent **72,** 444-5
exchange control legislation (1938) **42,** 403, 406
family reunification, FRG Declaration regarding **78,** 191
France
boundary, Rhine **47,** 115-17
cessation of hostilities with **40,** 434-5
FRG and **51,** 246, **59,** 492, **78,** 161-2
Reich, identity with **91,** 226, 230, **94,** 178
successor, whether **88,** 287, **94,** 178-9
GDR, successor, whether **94,** 178-82
law of
Law for the Reconstruction of the Reich 1934 **94,** 178
Nationality and Citizenship Law (*RuStAG*) 1913 **72,** 449-52, 455, 458-66, 470, **91,** 216, 217, 218, 223
Art. 25 **80,** 684
FRG, continuing validity in **91,** 220-1
Nuremberg Race Laws **36,** 82, 198
Patent Law 1936 **42,** 354, 359, 363, 365, 377, 381
Trademarks Law 1936 **47,** 130-1
Treaty of Versailles (1919) and **57,** 5-6
trust agreements **42,** 357-9
Zeiss Foundation Statute 1896/1905 **61,** 41-2, 51, 67
Mandates Commission, complaint to (1925) **37,** 74, 139
municipal corporations, continuity **44,** 57
Nazi laws, validity/recognition **36,** 22-3, 312, **72,** 449, 453-7, 459-61, 467-70, 474-6, 477
Nazi persecution
compensation, entitlement to **72,** 448, 457, 472, 647-50, **74,** 281-4, 420-4
political offence, whether **39,** 433-52
RSHA (Head Office for Reich Security), structure **36,** 85-6, 102-3, 171, 191, 216, 324-5, 330-1
SD, structure **36,** 85
South West Africa, surrender of **37,** 195, 543
surrender (1945) **42,** 37

effect on legal status **44,** 302, 313
treaties. *See also* Versailles, Treaty of (1919); Washington Debt Agreement *below*
obligations under **59,** 490-4
reapplication **91,** 226-7
USSR **45,** 74-5
outbreak of war with **44,** 336
treaties, jurisdiction provisions **45,** 74-5
war/hostilities, termination **42,** 142, **61,** 64, **81,** 512. *See also* Germany, peace settlement
France **40,** 434-5
Netherlands **42,** 421
Washington Debt Agreement (1930) **47,** 419, 420, 428
Ghana
diplomatic immunity, jurisdiction, waiver, consent of sending State, need for **60,** 378, 382-3
expropriation/nationalization, compensation, need for **95,** 210
government, change of **60,** 228-9
law of
Companies Law, registration of foreign investments in kind **95,** 226
Extradition Act 1960 **39,** 433-5, 440-1, 445
amendment 1966 **39,** 444
nationality and **60,** 228-9
Portugal, Forced Labour Convention, complaint regarding **37,** 84-5
revolution, consequences **60,** 231-6
status, change **90,** 459-60
UNCLOS I, statement **41,** 122
Gibraltar
British Nationality Act 1981 and **123,** 6
'defined domestic matters' **123,** 5-6
EC Treaty, applicability **123,** 6
European Community law, primacy **123,** 15
European Convention on Human Rights (1950), applicability **123,** 10
Protocol 1 **123,** 12
'within their jurisdiction' **123,** 12
European Parliament
elections, right to participate in **123,** 5-24
legislature, whether **123,** 16-18, 23-4
sovereignty **63,** 172
Gibraltar, Straits of, Morocco–Spain, Agreement (1967) **41,** 136
Gleneagles Accord (1977). *See* **apartheid, Gleneagles Accord (1977)**
Goa, Daman and Diu
applicable law
law of India **118,** 432-3
law of Portugal **118,** 431
conquest and annexation by India (1961) **46,** 484, **118,** 431, 432
India, relationship with, part of the Union of India, with effect from 20 December 1961 **118,** 432
law of
Goa, Daman and Diu (Administration) Act 1 (1962) **118,** 432
retrospective application **118,** 435
s 2(b) **118,** 435
s 4 **118,** 446
s 5(1) **118,** 435, 436, 439-46
Goa, Daman and Diu (Administration) Ordinance 1962 **118,** 432, 435

Goa, Daman and Diu (*cont.*)
Goa, Daman and Diu (Laws) Regulation No 12 (1962) **118,** 432
purpose **118,** 435
s 2(a) **118,** 435-6
s 4(2) **118,** 443
Indian law **118,** 432-3
effective date **118,** 435
Mines and Minerals (Regulation and Development) Act 1957 **118,** 432
s 5(2) **118,** 433
s 30 **118,** 433
Mining Concession Rules 1960 **118,** 432
24(3) **118,** 446
54 **118,** 434
Portuguese law **118,** 431
continuity **118,** 436-7, 439-46
legislation, interpretation, phrases, 'appointed day' **118,** 435
mining rights
after annexation by India **118,** 432-3
applicable law, Portuguese Colonial Mining Laws **118,** 431, 436-46
under Portuguese rule **118,** 431
gold clause
Aminoil concession **66,** 547-8, 610
anachronistic nature, legitimacy of measures to compensate for **101,** 591-615
good faith 41, 76, 86, 101, 117, **44,** 203, 266, 284, 285, **50,** 104, **53,** 494-5, **54,** 339, **56,** 173, 185, 271, **57,** 413, **58,** 543, **62,** 479, **71,** 119-20, 126, 132, 267, **76,** 55, 129, 131, 178, **77,** 661, **78,** 650, **84,** 306, 310. *See also* bad faith; equity
abuse of rights and **82,** 614
arbitration **84,** 592
'best efforts', relevance **102,** 295
bona fide representation of interests **118,** 491
compliance with recommendations of Inter-American Commission on Human Rights **123,** 546
concurrent jurisdiction **104,** 545
customary international law **65,** 282, 340-3
damages and **103,** 291-3, **125,** 705-6, 728-9
debts of international organization, Member States' liability for **80,** 140, 171, 613
employment relationships **118,** 136
equity and **41,** 145, **99,** 585
estoppel **55,** 5, **75,** 119-20, **83,** 69, **89,** 401, **106,** 523, **117,** 562, **120,** 230-1
expropriation for public purpose **83,** 552
extradition **55,** 507, **79,** 87-8, 99, 100, 108, **119,** 110, 251
foreign investment agreements **56,** 279
general principle of international law **120,** 510-11
human rights violations complaint, obligation to avoid adversely affecting situation of plaintiff **116,** 355
ICJ, acceptance of compulsory jurisdiction **106,** 178-9, 180, **123,** 244, 248, 258, 286-90, 324, 332-3, 383-5, 399-401, 411, 414-19, 436-7, 444, 447, 480, 481
immunity from suit and **81,** 114-15, 119-20, 130, 136-8
international agreement, basis of **56,** 280, 282-3
legal nature **86,** 279
legitimate expectation **113,** 324
litigation, in **46,** 143

Mandates system **37,** 79, 407, 448, 450
national security defence **110,** 728-9
negotiations **47,** 422, **56,** 173, 176-7, 185
third party involvement as evidence of **116,** 88
peaceful settlement of disputes and **84,** 254, 260-1
source of obligation, whether **84,** 260
State conduct and **83,** 82, 84
State contract and **83,** 554
State immunity, jurisdiction, basis for **64,** 688-9, **65,** 341-3, **104,** 545, 624, **113,** 433
State responsibility for breach of **82,** 670
taxation, mutual assistance **104,** 580
treaties. *See* treaties, good faith
treaty interpretation. *See* treaty interpretation, guidelines, good faith
UN Secretary-General's exercise of discretionary power **83,** 330, 455
unilateral acts and **41,** 117
unilateral amendment of conditions of employment **83,** 655
unlawful actions and **86,** 342-3
good offices 37, 89, **84,** 265, 268, 305. *See also* conciliation; mediation; negotiation
Contadora process **84,** 309
goodwill, compensation for **40,** 159, 161, 162
governing law. *See* applicable law
government. *See also* State
act of. *See* act of government
basis **85,** 285-6
change **86,** 3-4, 6-7
fundamental change of circumstances, whether **96,** 67
obligations of new government **96,** 67
recognized means in international law **39,** 25, 29, 49, 65, 87, 217, 218-19
de facto **90,** 500, 523. *See also* Kuwait, Iraqi invasion (1990), status following
constitutional amendment, effect **123,** 148-9
de jure distinguished **39,** 69-75, 78, 214, 222, 253-61, 280, 282, **53,** 61-6, **82,** 481
implied Mandate doctrine **70,** 18-34
acts in furtherance of rebellion **70,** 16, 21, 30
appropriate cases **70,** 30
authority for doctrine **70,** 22
civil war, applicability to **70,** 22, 30
following failure of rebellion **70,** 23
lawful government, policy of **70,** 21, 26, 28-30
legislative powers **55,** 54-5
scope **70,** 23-30
international law definition **39,** 214-15, 253-4, 386
judicial power, exercise of **39,** 354-5, **70,** 24. *See also* implied Mandate doctrine *above*
laws of, conflict between de facto and de jure sovereign authority **53,** 57-8
necessity and **70,** 24. *See also* implied Mandate doctrine *above*
State immunity of de jure Head of State and **103,** 585-8
validity of acts **49,** 208-9, **120,** 44-6
de jure **90,** 523
definition
'executive' **111,** 648-51, 667-71
police force, whether **111,** 646-53

government (*cont.*)
effectiveness **90,** 475-6
control of funds, need for **86,** 5
evidence of
international recognition **114,** 477-8
official dealings with **114,** 476-7
in exile, decrees of, recognition **42,** 409-36
immunity. *See* State immunity
implied Mandate. *See* de facto, implied Mandate doctrine *above*
legitimacy principle **90,** 475-6
negotiations between private parties, whether bound by **46,** 33-4, 139
obligations
parens patriae. See parens patriae
protection of constitutional rights **118,** 469-70
prerogative, exercise on foreign territory **42,** 123-4
recognition. *See* recognition, government
requirements
administrative control over territory **114,** 476-7
democratic **90,** 502, 516-17
effective **90,** 502, 512-20, 551-3
firmly established **90,** 502, 516, 520
public acceptance **90,** 502, 515-20, 553-5
revolutionary, absence of government distinguished **94,** 621
right to sue and be sued, recognition and **84,** 176-7
State distinguished **84,** 176, **122,** 661-3
State, equivalent to, whether **106,** 302, 308
successful revolution principle **90,** 478, 502, 511-20
necessity, doctrine of distinguished **90,** 505, 511-20
temporary breach of legal continuity distinguished **90,** 498
succession
contract, effect on **62,** 172-3
nationality, effect on **72,** 438-42
revolution, following **72,** 440-2
successor in interest, as **84,** 176
validity **90,** 473-520, 551-5
burden of proof **90,** 519-20
competence to determine **90,** 520-6
date of **90,** 482-3, 500, 508-11, 523
effectiveness **90,** 551-3
illegal seizure of power
judiciary, position of **90,** 520-6, 530-1, 554-5
king, continuity **90,** 554-5
reception of laws, relevance **90,** 475-6, 481-2, 500
judicial continuity **90,** 554-5
king, continuity **90,** 554-5
public acceptance **90,** 553-5
government acts. *See* act of State; State immunity, jurisdiction, classification of act, government activities
government, change, State succession distinguished **96,** 65, 66-7
government department. *See also* central/State-owned bank; State agency/State-owned corporation; State immunity, jurisdiction, entitlement, government department
central/State-owned bank **64,** 222
meaning **43,** 37

government procurement agency, agency or instrumentality of a foreign State **63,** 90, 175
Gozo 81, 283, 348, 349
Graeco-German Mixed Arbitral Tribunal 47, 418, 424
execution of awards **47,** 424
termination of German participation **47,** 419, 429
Great Lakes, status 94, 243-6
Greece
aliens
property
discrimination **93,** 477
EC membership and **93,** 476-80
Bulgaria, Caphandaris-Molloff Accord (1927) **47,** 420, 430
Constitution (1975)
s 28 **88,** 203, **93,** 464, 471-3, 477
text **93,** 462 n. 1
diplomatic premises, inviolability **65,** 254
EC and
freedom of establishment **93,** 468-9
mineral rights **93,** 468-9
national market organization in bananas **93,** 464-7
EC entry
direct effect **93,** 468
implied repeal of previous legislation **93,** 468, 472
EC law
primacy **93,** 464, 471-3, 477
scope of EEC Treaty, limited to **93,** 477-80
right to invoke before national courts **93,** 473, 478
EC treaties, as part of municipal law **93,** 472
German assets in, legislation concerning **47,** 419, 429
international law **65,** 252-5
municipal law and **65,** 252, 255
judicial review
act of government **96,** 218
treaty **96,** 218
judicial review, foreign relations **96,** 218
law of
BXH Law 1899 **65,** 252-4
Civil Procedure Code, s 26 **65,** 249, 252, 255
Compulsory Law No 1366/1938 (property rights in frontier areas) **93,** 476-80
Law 15/1938 (Emergency Law), State immunity, execution/attachment and **65,** 247-8, 251-2, 256
Law 2673/1953 of 4 February 1953 (ratification of Greece-USA agreement on immunity of property) **65,** 257
Law 1386/1983 (emergency financial measures)
EC law, compatibility with **93,** 471-4
emergency nature **93,** 474
Legislative Decree of 22 June 1970 (property rights in frontier areas) **93,** 476-80
Minerals Code, EC law, compatibility with **93,** 468-9
neutrality, World War, German breaches **47,** 418, 419, 428, 438
Olympic Airways **63,** 245-51
reparations against Eastern enemies (1930) **47,** 419, 428-9
salvage suits by non-nationals **42,** 187

Greece (*cont.*)
State contract, applicable law, municipal law of State party **65,** 264
State immunity, execution/attachment, procedural aspects, executive/ministerial authorization, need for **65,** 172, 247-8, 250-1, 252-3, 256
State immunity, execution/attachment, purpose of proceedings
safeguarding/conservatory measures **65,** 250-2, 256
as measure of constraint and legal violence **65,** 252
State immunity, execution/attachment, purpose/use of funds/assets, diplomatic premises **65,** 251-5
State immunity, execution/attachment, theory/doctrine
basis, foreign relations considerations **65,** 252
development of concept **65,** 172, 250
State immunity, jurisdiction, classification of act
diplomatic premises
lease **65,** 252-5
residential **65,** 257
military base, construction contract **65,** 262-4
private person test **65,** 256-7
State immunity, jurisdiction, entitlement
applicable law **65,** 252
NATO forces **65,** 262-4
State immunity, jurisdiction, procedural aspects, entitlement to raise, owner of diplomatic premises **65,** 247-8
State immunity, jurisdiction, theory/doctrine
basis
execution of judgment, difficulty **65,** 251
par in parem non habet jurisdictionem **65,** 255
development of concept **65,** 249-50, 255-7
State immunity, jurisdiction, waiver, implied, contract as **65,** 172, 253
treaties **88,** 203
Vienna Convention on Diplomatic Relations (1961), applicability **65,** 254
wartime emergency powers, State immunity, jurisdiction and **65,** 247-8, 251-2, 256
Greece–United States Friendship, Commerce and Navigation Treaty (1951), *travaux préparatoires* **101,** 618
Greenland
defamation **88,** 602, 609-11
freedom of expression **88,** 613-16
jurisdiction
Danish
applicable law **91,** 277, 278
sentence **91,** 278
visiting forces
customs and excise **91,** 271, 272
Danish nationals **91,** 263-75, 276-8
taxation **91,** 263-75
traffic offences **91,** 276-8
law of
Administration of Justice Act **88,** 612
Criminal Code
s 2 **91,** 277
s 4 **91,** 277
s 10 **91,** 277

Law No 5 (Income Tax) of 19 May 1979, s 3(7) **91,** 265-78
Penal Code **88,** 603, 609-11, 613
Traffic Law **91,** 277-8
legislation, interpretation
aids
legislative history **91,** 272-3
object and purpose **91,** 270, 274
treaties
applicability, non-metropolitan territory **91,** 271
multilateral and bilateral, interrelationship **91,** 271, 273
subsequent treaty
possible conflict **91,** 266-71, 272
primacy **91,** 270-1, 272, 273
treaties, State succession, obligation to respect existing treaties **91,** 270
treaty interpretation
guidelines, restrictive **91,** 272
multilingual **91,** 274-5
Greenpeace
damage to vessel by France, compensation for **74,** 259, 267-8, 274
regional organizations as distinct entities **101,** 434-5
Grenada
Constitution 1967 **90,** 500
Constitution 1973
amendment, referendum, need for **90,** 501
entrenched clauses **90,** 501
restoration **90,** 501
suspension **90,** 500
international armed conflict
detention of civilians **123,** 158-88
ICRC and **123,** 166-7
judiciary, continuity **90,** 50
law of
Act No 1 of 1985 (validation of legislation) **90,** 501, 504
effectiveness **90,** 501
Constitution. *See above*
People's Law No 4 (Supreme Court) 1979 **90,** 500, 501, 504
People's Law No 14 (Supreme Court) 1979 **90,** 500, 501, 504
People's Law No 84 (Appeals to Judicial Committee of the Privy Council) 1979 **90,** 500, 501
legislation, validation **90,** 501-2
necessity **90,** 500-5
People's Revolutionary Government (1979-83), status **90,** 500-4
Grotius 46, 490
obedience to usurper **39,** 113, 172, 256, 390, 396
positive and natural law **37,** 459
punishment **36,** 27-8, 51, 56
Guantanamo Bay Naval Base
detainees
consular protection **123,** 603, 605-10
legal representation, right to **123,** 606, 607-8
status **123,** 603-5
jurisdiction **123,** 603

guarantee 84, 601
guardianship decrees, recognition **42,** 26-9
Guatemala. *See also* Belize
ambassador, appointment
act of international courtesy **100,** 311, 325
Belize, of, validity **100,** 326-7
Belize, to
abandonment of territorial claim, whether **100,** 310, 312, 313-14
congressional approval, need for **100,** 330
constitutional importance **100,** 309, 310
recognition as State, whether **100,** 310, 313, 326
open to challenge, whether **100,** 311
procedural defects in claim **100,** 311
as political act **100,** 311, 326
validity
countersignature by minister invalidly appointed **100,** 323-4
failure to publish **100,** 308, 323
Belize, boundary, absence of agreement **100,** 314
Belize, claim to
abandonment of claim
appointment of ambassador **100,** 310, 312, 313-14
establishment of diplomatic relations **100,** 312, 313-14
constitutional **100,** 309-10, 320-3
executive powers to take steps to resolve situation **100,** 323
definitive agreement resolving situation
Congressional authority to determine whether definitive settlement **100,** 328, 329, 330
establishment of diplomatic relations, whether **100,** 312, 313, 330
popular consultation **100,** 309, 328, 330
recognition **100,** 313, 314
sovereignty, whether affecting **100,** 328
to national interests **100,** 310, 312
'part of its territory', abandonment **100,** 309
part of national heritage **100,** 309
Constitution (1825), Temporary Provisions, s 35 (territory) **100,** 320
Constitution (1945), Temporary Provisions, s 1 (Belize) **100,** 309, 321
Constitution (1956), Temporary Provisions, s 1 (Belize) **100,** 305, 321-2
Constitution (1965), Transitional and Final Provisions, s 1 (Belize) **100,** 305, 322-3
Constitution (1985)
s 121 **100,** 313
s 124 **100,** 313
s 149 **100,** 313
s 152 **100,** 313
s 171(1)(2) (congressional approval of treaties) **100,** 328
s 173 **100,** 310, 312
s 173(n) **100,** 310
s 183(o) **100,** 309, 326
s 183(p) **100,** 309, 326
s 183(s) (appointment of civil servants) **100,** 309, 323-4, 326
s 204 (precedence of Constitution) **100,** 327
Temporary and Final Provisions, s 19 (Belize) **100,** 309, 310, 313, 323, 324-8, 330

Constitution, Law Reforming (1855) **100,** 321
constitutional review, requirements, laws, regulations or provisions of general nature **100,** 312
continental shelf legislation **41,** 208
death penalty, reservation to American Convention on Human Rights **70,** 451-77
diplomatic relations
constitutionality **100,** 312-13
establishment
abandonment of territorial claim, whether **100,** 312, 313-14
definitive agreement for settlement of territorial dispute, whether **100,** 312
permitted by Constitution, whether **100,** 312-13
purpose, partner in negotiations **100,** 314
responsibility for **100,** 311-12, 326-7, 330
foreign relations, act of **100,** 327
foreign relations
establishment of diplomatic relations, act of **100,** 327
responsibility for, executive **100,** 312
law of
Additional Regulatory Law (1852) **100,** 321
Congressional Decree 174 of 11 October 1945 (UN Charter) **100,** 319
Congressional Decree 224 of 9 April 1946 **100,** 319
Judiciary, Law on, s 49 **100,** 329
Protection of Constitutional Rights, Law on **100,** 329
Republic of Guatemala, Law constituting (1851) **100,** 321
Republic of Guatemala, Law constituting (1879) **100,** 321
legislation, interpretation
aids, dictionary **100,** 324-5
phrases
'*acuerdo*' **100,** 325
'*definitivo*' **100,** 325
'*gestionar*' **100,** 325
'*hacer diligencias*' **100,** 325
'*realizar*' **100,** 325
'*resolver*' **100,** 324-5
margin of appreciation, legal control **100,** 313
recognition, State
abandonment of territorial claim, whether **100,** 313-14, 326, 330
bilateral agreement **100,** 314, 326
appointment of ambassador **100,** 308, 313, 316, 330
Belize
independence of Belize, relevance **100,** 326
official visit from **100,** 308
official visit to **100,** 308
unilateral act **100,** 314, 326, 330
validity **100,** 308
separation of powers **100,** 327-8, 329
rule of law and **100,** 328
sovereignty of people **100,** 328
treaties, popular consultation, need for **100,** 309, 310, 312, 330
Guernsey
constitutional position **75,** 570-1
EEC and **53,** 154-6, 159-62

Guernsey (*cont.*)
State control of housing **75,** 566-95
human rights violations and **75,** 575-95
Guinea
independence **44,** 48
law of
Customs Code **120,** 260, 319
s 1 **120,** 187-8
s 33 **120,** 188
s 34 **120,** 187-8
s 316 **110,** 775, 781
s 317 **110,** 775, 781
s 361 **120,** 187
s 363 **120,** 187
'customs law', whether **120,** 319-20
Decree of 6 January 1982 (Soguipêche) **82,** 80
Guinea-ization Act 1983 **82,** 80
Law regarding corporate entities of 1 September 1962 **63,** 536
Maritime Code (Law 94/007/CTRM of 25 March 1994)
s 1 **110,** 775, 781, **120,** 186, 187-8, 319-27
s 4 **120,** 186
s 6 **120,** 186
s 8 **110,** 781, **120,** 186
s 40 (exclusive economic zone (EEZ) rights) **110,** 754-5, 762-3, 775-7, 781-3, **120,** 186
Maritime Fishing Code (Law 95/13/CTRM of 15 May 1995) **110,** 754-5
classification **110,** 769-70, 776-7, 785
'fishing' **110,** 754
Penal Code
s 361 **110,** 775, 781
s 363 **110,** 775-6, 781
St Vincent and the Grenadines (*Saiga* dispute), factual background **120,** 167-70
Soguipêche
legal personality **82,** 80
State immunity, entitlement **82,** 80
SOTRAMAR **63,** 536-9
as mixed economy company **63,** 536
State immunity, jurisdiction, entitlement **63,** 536-9
State succession, judgment debt and **47,** 83-5
Guinea-Bissau
law of, maritime delimitation (straight baselines) 1985 **83,** 20, 110-11
maritime front **83,** 99-100
recognition by Portugal **83,** 17
State succession, clean slate theory **83,** 54
status, independence **83,** 17, 30
UN and **83,** 30
Guinea–St Vincent and the Grenadines (Saiga dispute). *See* International Tribunal for the Law of the Sea (ITLOS)
Gulf of Maine delimitation. *See* maritime delimitation
Gulf Oil Corporation 66, 548
gulfs
bays distinguished **69,** 42, 52, 61

closing line **69,** 35-6, 43-6, 53-7, 62-8, 71-3, **71,** 97, 164-5
offshore islands **69,** 35-6, 43-6, 53-4, 62, 64-5
Finland–USSR Boundary Agreement (1965) **41,** 160
Gabes **81,** 324, 396, 454-62, 485
Gulf of Mexico, Mississippi Sound **91,** 413-26
as internal waters **42,** 68-9, 74, 83-4, 86, **43,** 114-25, **69,** 43-6, 61-2, 66-7, **90,** 238, **91,** 431
Guyana
aliens, expulsion **71,** 451-96
Constitution **71,** 454-5, 459-62, 478-82
constitutional status **71,** 470
fundamental rights in **71,** 460, 465, 480-2
law applicable in **71,** 483
law of
Expulsion of Undesirables Ordinance **71,** 451-96
Guyana Independence Act 1966 **71,** 479, 481
Guyana Independence Order 1966 **71,** 481, 483
Immigration Ordinance **71,** 483-4
Gwalior, legislature **53,** 142-4
gypsies in northern Cyprus, alleged breach of rights 120, 103-4, 122-3, 125

habeas corpus 41, 313, **58,** 277, 648, **60,** 300, 303, 322-3, **61,** 256, **62,** 258-9, 261, 264, **67,** 453-5, **70,** 202, 250, 255, 258, 261-2, 329, 333, **71,** 530, **72,** 64, 68, 201, 204, **73,** 45, 54, **74,** 468, 481-2, **78,** 501, 507, 515, 518, **79,** 20, 22, 27-31, 46, 56, 57, 71, 142, 386, 394, 396, 424 n. 1, 474, **85,** 159-60, 165-6. *See also* American Convention on Human Rights (1969), habeas corpus
abrogation of right **85,** 160, 161
alien children awaiting adoption **95,** 490-2
amparo and **96,** 401-2, 413-14, 415
applicant outside jurisdiction **79,** 27-31, 41-4, 46-7, 48-9, **85,** 229-35, **119,** 393-8
asylum **38,** 155
in case of
detention by peacekeeping forces **119,** 393-8
detention of civilians during armed conflict **123,** 175, 185-6
colonies **85,** 231
de libero homine exhibendo **85,** 220, 229
disappearances **116,** 479-80
exhaustion of State remedies **95,** 502-3, **118,** 5
extradition and. *See* extradition, habeas corpus
failure to inform accused of rights under Vienna Convention on Consular Relations (1963) and **118,** 29-30, 33-7
foreign territory, on **85,** 229-34
grounds for **38,** 152-3
Honduras, effectiveness **95,** 273-6, 282-3
human rights violation and **79,** 182, 186
ICJ and **118,** 48
Inter-American Court of Human Rights, effective remedy, whether **95,** 273, 276
International Court of Justice (ICJ) **118,** 48
International Covenant on Civil and Political Rights (ICCPR) (1966) **62,** 241, 244-6, 249, 252, 255-6, 259, 262, 266, **71,** 323, 326, 330, 356, **79,** 182, 186, **118,** 258-9
as means to test validity of detention **119,** 393-4
non-availability **62,** 241, 244-5, 249, 252, 255-6

habeas corpus (*cont.*)
official detention, need for **95,** 490-2
Peru, ineffectiveness **116,** 479
protectorates **85,** 231
purpose **96,** 402
right of suspension **96,** 394-404, 413-15
scope of review **67,** 454
territorial limitation **95,** 492
UNGA Resolution 34/178 (1979) **123,** 175 n. 24
Habitats Directive (92/43/EEC)
applicability, 'in the European territory of the Member States to which the [EC] Treaty applies'. *See* 'European territory of the Member States to which the [EC] Treaty applies' *below*
Art. 174 [130r] of EC Treaty (Community environmental policy) as basis **120,** 623
cetaceans and *lophelia pertusa,* protection **120,** 626, 636-7
alternative measures **120,** 645
Art. 12 provisions **120,** 641-5
oil exploration as 'deliberate disturbance' **120,** 642-4
system of strict protection, whether requiring **120,** 642
'European territory of the Member States to which the [EC] Treaty applies'
applicability in **120,** 623-4, 625-37
comparison with
Conservation of Wild Birds Directive (79/409/EEC) **120,** 625
Convention on Biodiversity (1992) **120,** 628-9
directives 85/337/EEC and 97/11/EEC (environmental impact assessments) **120,** 629-30
'European territories for whose external relations a Member State is responsible' (EC Treaty) **120,** 625
'geographical area' (public procurement procedures directive (90/531/EEC)) **120,** 628
Hydrocarbons Licensing Directive (94/22/EC) **120,** 628
working condition on ships and offshore installations directive (95/21/EC) **120,** 628
implementation, UK. *See* United Kingdom, Conservation (Natural Habitats and of Wild Fauna and Flora) Regulations 1994
interpretation. *See also* 'European territory of the Member States to which the [EC] Treaty applies' *above*
aids
drafting history **120,** 635-6, 637
general principles of international law **120,** 635
international agreements and other obligations **120,** 630-1, 634-5
practice under Community law **120,** 627-30, 636-7
UK legislation in related areas **120,** 631-2
context, 'the very nature of things' **120,** 626-7, 636
'deliberate disturbance' **120,** 642-4
guidelines
legal conflict, avoidance **120,** 636
object and purpose **120,** 626-7, 636
parties' understanding
Commission statements **120,** 635, 637
government statements **120,** 632, 637
object and purpose
cetaceans and *lophelia pertusa,* protection, **120,** 626, 636-7

maintenance of diversity **120,** 623, 625-6
sustainable development **120,** 626
habitual offenders 67, 535-9, 541-5, **81,** 54. *See also* European Convention on Human Rights (1950), habitual offenders
detention **67,** 540-9
without trial **67,** 545-9
liberty of person, deprivation **67,** 540-9
punishment, effect on **81,** 54
habitual residence
employment contract, State immunity and **82,** 22
refugees and **99,** 3, **122,** 538-9
Hague Conference on Private International Law. *See* private international law, Hague Conference on Private International Law
Hague Convention on Civil Procedure (1905) 47, 239-40, **48,** 215-16
'nationals', corporation **44,** 134-5
reapplication by GDR **77,** 441-3
Hague Convention for the Pacific Settlement of Disputes (1907)
arbitration, definition **91,** 574-5
costs **105,** 67
Hague Convention for the Protection of Cultural Property in the Event of Armed Conflict (1954), customary international law **105,** 506
Hague Convention on the Taking of Evidence Abroad in Civil or Commercial Matters (1970)
'civil or commercial matter' **84,** 733-50
applicable law **84,** 739
certificate of diplomatic or consular agent **84,** 738, 746
civil law **84,** 743-5
common law **84,** 742-3
European Convention on Jurisdiction and the Enforcement of Judgments in Civil and Commercial Matters (1968) **84,** 745
fiscal matters **84,** 745
internationally acceptable definition **84,** 734, 745
public law, excluded, whether **84,** 734-5
US Restatement of Foreign Relations Law **84,** 748
discovery prior to trial **73,** 300-1, 306-7, 313-14, 323, 331, 351
reservations relating to **73,** 301, 314, 323, 331, 339, 351
examination of witnesses, application by analogy **90,** 410, 411
implementing legislation, need for **101,** 354, 357-8
letters rogatory **73,** 300, 306-7, 313, 323, 337
non-implementation, grounds for **73,** 322-3, 337, 358
Preliminary document No 3 **84,** 744-5
purpose **73,** 307
ratifications **73,** 313, 323, 339, 351
signature **73,** 307
Special Commission on Operation of **84,** 749
time-limits **68,** 633, 646-51
Hague Conventions (1899/1907)
applicability
conduct of hostilities **105,** 500-1
contracting parties, between **82,** 439
internal conflict **105,** 444
non-parties **91,** 123
where all belligerents parties **82,** 439

Hague Conventions (*cont.*)
Art. 3 offences
criminal nature **105,** 448-9
German Military Manual **105,** 449
Lieber Code (US Military Manual) **105,** 448-9
belligerent occupation
occupying power
obligations **83,** 137, 187, **96,** 58-9, 61
powers **83,** 136, 137, 148
civilian populations **91,** 124
compliance, sanctions, absence **105,** 535-6
crimes against humanity **105,** 500-4
customary international law **83,** 162, 163, **104,** 400-1, **105,** 447-50, 500, **110,** 150, 207, **122,** 65, **125,** 547
Geneva Conventions (1949), convergence **105,** 506, 517, 535-7
Geneva Convention on the Protection of Civilian Persons in Time of War (1949) and **83,** 185
humanitarian law **105,** 500-1
individual
responsibility **105,** 447, 448-9, **122,** 70
rights **96,** 58-9, **103,** 611
jurisdiction
obligation **105,** 449
right **105,** 449
'minimum yardstick' **105,** 447-8
opening of hostilities **42,** 37
prisoners of war
compensation for earnings as **61,** 235
employment, munitions manufacture **104,** 199
self-executing, whether **96,** 59
State immunity, jurisdiction **103,** 611
State immunity, security for costs **65,** 406
war crimes, retroactivity **104,** 400-1
Hague Regulations (1907) 91, 122
belligerent status **42,** 464, 466, **52,** 502
compulsory services **83,** 148
customary international law **83,** 163, 185, 194, **105,** 500, 504, **122,** 69
declaratory nature **53,** 3
espionage **52,** 502-3
in time of peace **94,** 76
Land Warfare
local law, respect for **52,** 513-17
powers of occupying powers **47,** 491
occupied territories **83,** 183-4
prohibitory nature **91,** 41
property
private **36,** 498, 501-2, **42,** 37-8, **53,** 3-4
public, seizure **40,** 429-34
rape **121,** 266
retroactivity and **91,** 48
scope, Geneva Conventions (1949) compared **105,** 500-1
torture **121,** 255

as treaty **83,** 160
UK, in **83,** 160-2
in World War II **53,** 3
Haiti
Banque Nationale de la République d'Haiti **63,** 42
concession, unilateral annulment **44,** 79-80, 84-5, 88-9, 99
USA, Inter-Governmental Guaranty Agreement **44,** 80-1, 91
harbours 42, 69-70, 80, 84, 97, **57,** 88-9, **59,** 210-11, 225-7
Hawaiian Kingdom. *See also* United States of America (USA), Hawaii
annexation, effect **119,** 584-5, 594, 597
Joint Resolution of 23 November 1993 **119,** 610-15
President Cleveland's message to the Senate and House of Representatives of 18 December 1893 **119,** 598-610
status as independent State in the 19th Century **119,** 581
hazardous activities. *See also* Bhopal gas leak disaster; waste disposal
claims procedure, recommendations **118,** 509-10
damage caused by
disaster fund, need for **118,** 509-10, 525-6
procedural reform, need for **118,** 526
damages, punitive **118,** 481-3, 511, 518
liability **118,** 479-83, 506-10
recommendations for control **118,** 504, 506-10, 526
head of government
Head of State distinguished **119,** 222
immunity, jurisdiction **80,** 21, **119,** 222
Head of State. *See also* diplomatic immunity, jurisdiction; diplomatic privileges and immunities; government; head of government; state; State immunity, execution/attachment; State immunity, jurisdiction
act of State and, private acts **57,** 31, **88,** 164-5, **99,** 163-5, **119,** 82
action against, consent of forum government, need for **92,** 520
action on behalf of subjects **118,** 590
as 'agency or instrumentality of foreign State' **103,** 589
allegiance owed to **52,** 72-3
applicable law
authority to act on behalf of State in international relations **115,** 103
functions. *See* functions, applicable law *below*
immunity **118,** 298
authority to act on behalf of State in international relations **115,** 34-5, 102-15
applicable law, international law **115,** 103
municipal law of own country, relevance **115,** 103
corporation owned by Head of State **101,** 506-8
definition
Convention on the Prevention and Punishment of Crimes against Internationally Protected Persons (1973) **99,** 162 n. 13, **102,** 202-3
customary international law **64,** 616-17, **99,** 162
'Ruler of a foreign State' **64,** 400-1, 412, 499-500, 570
dignity, protection of **73,** 388
as diplomatic agent **119,** 60-1
duty of protection **61,** 603, 604, 605-7, 612, 617, 619
evidence of status **80,** 366, **119,** 49, 56-7, 94, 101
suggestion of immunity letter **103,** 584, 586, 587
extraterritoriality **65,** 14-15, **103,** 585

Head of State (*cont.*)
family members on special diplomatic mission **81,** 606
functions **119,** 61-2. *See also* authority to act on behalf of State in international relations *above*; powers *below*
applicable law **119,** 61, 62, 97, 104-5
customary international law **119,** 61, 104-5, 193-6
international law **119,** 61-2, 104
municipal law of own country **119,** 61, 104-5
crimes against international law and **119,** 43-8, 61-70, 83-7, 97-9, 104-7, 155-6, 169-70
legality of act, relevance **119,** 62, 194-6, 224
murder **119,** 84
official nature of acts, relevance **119,** 103
subjects, duty to protect **43,** 166-75
torture **103,** 591-2, **119,** 4, 45, 47-8, 61-70, 97-100, 104, 151-7, 169-70, 204-18
as instrument of State policy **119,** 224
treaty-making power **44,** 220, 256, 279, **56,** 543
implied contract not to abuse power **81,** 617-18, 649
jurisdiction, extraterritorial, injunction against former **107,** 494-505
powers. *See also* functions *above*
action on behalf of State in international relations **95,** 26
Vienna Convention on the Law of Treaties (1961) **95,** 26
ICJ, seisure **95,** 26
private acts
act of State and **57,** 31, **88,** 164-5, **99,** 163-5, **119,** 82
capacity for **81,** 631
defamation and **88,** 164-5
immunity, jurisdiction. *See* Head of State, immunity, jurisdiction, private acts
proceedings involving
consent of central government, need for **64,** 397-400, 411, 422, 425, 480-2, 521-2, 537-8, 618
proceedings against State distinguished **64,** 413-15
as 'public official or person acting in that capacity' **119,** 71-2
Genocide Convention (1948) **119,** 70, 243-4
International Criminal Tribunal for the Former Yugoslavia (Statute) **119,** 71, 87, 162-3, 212, 243
Nuremberg Charter (1945) **119,** 71, 87, 162-3, 243
Rwanda, International Criminal Tribunal for (ICTR), Statute **119,** 71, 87, 162-3, 212, 243
Torture Convention (1984) **119,** 70-1, 92-3, 100, 151, 152, 156, 163, 164, 196-8, 213-14, 221-2
recognition **81,** 627
anticipated **104,** 161
breach of international law, right to challenge and **99,** 176
evidence of **115,** 35, 104-5
Gaddafi **125,** 501
immunity, jurisdiction and **99,** 161-3, **103,** 585-6, **113,** 512, 531, **119,** 349
Pinochet **119,** 56-7, 94, 100
responsibility, executive **99,** 161, **103,** 587, **104,** 142-3, **113,** 512, 531
State practice **80,** 366
UN **95,** 26
responsibility for international crimes. *See also* Head of State, former, immunity, jurisdiction; Head of State, immunity, jurisdiction

customary international law **119,** 200-1
Ruler. *See* Indian States, Rulers; Kutch, Rulers; Malaysia, Rulers
as State **64,** 397-401, 413, 497-8, 528, 570-2, 615-18, **65,** 14, **111,** 607, 609-10
testimonial immunity. *See* Head of State, immunity, testimonial
Vienna Convention on Diplomatic Relations (1961) **82,** 57, **111,** 606
Head of State, diplomatic privileges and immunities, entitlement 64, 671-2, **99,** 165-7, **111,** 607-8, **119,** 42-8, 60-1, 96-9, 102-3, 109, 210-11
personal, whether **64,** 400-1
time-limitation and **119,** 60-1, 89-90, 96-7
Vienna Convention on Diplomatic Relations (1961), application **119,** 42-8, 59-61, 89-90, 96-7, 102-3
by analogy **102,** 202-3
criminal proceedings **119,** 193
Head of State, execution/attachment, personal private property **64,** 438-9
Head of State, former
act of State and **81,** 619-28, **119,** 106-7
personal gain **81,** 623 n. 12, **119,** 82
conduct in office, applicable law **81,** 560-1, 572
injunction restraining from removing or dealing with assets **107,** 492-505
judicial relief against in foreign court **81,** 562, 564, 566-7
Vienna Convention on Diplomatic Relations (1961) and **119,** 59-61
Head of State, former, immunity, execution/attachment 82, 54-7
Head of State, former, immunity, income tax 53, 568-74, **64,** 406-7, 421, 483-9, 524-34
Head of State, former, immunity, jurisdiction 102, 200-5, **103,** 522-30, 555-8
arrest **119,** 61
change of law. *See* treaty exception *below*
confiscation of assets in home State, relevance **65,** 37-8
as courtesy **119,** 234
criminal proceedings **119,** 246-7, **121,** 572
customary international law **119,** 203-4, 208-11
customary international law **119,** 43-8, 62-70, 78-87, 99-100, 106-7, 203-4
ratione materiae **119,** 219, 236-7
as former diplomat **119,** 59-60, 89-90, 96-7, 102-3, 154, 160-1, 193, 196, 223-4, 245-7
genocide **119,** 72
Head of State in office distinguished **125,** 504
hostage-taking **119,** 72, 98
judicial assistance, Procedures for Mutual Legal Assistance Agreement (MLAA) (1986) **121,** 570, 575-6
official acts in exercise of functions **64,** 617, **119,** 2-3, 43-8, 55, 62-5, 79-83, 90, 103, 153-4, 161, 169-70, 193-6, 202-18, 234-47, 349. *See also ratione materiae below*
foreign relations **64,** 279
Hatch v. *Baez* **119,** 65, 81, 235
legislative activity **64,** 279
private acts **65,** 37-8, **119,** 79, **121,** 572
ratione materiae **119,** 223-4, 231, 240. *See also* official acts in exercise of functions *above*
customary international law **119,** 219, 236-7
Torture Convention (1984), effect **119,** 200-1, 215-16, 220, 231, 245
ratione personae **119,** 79, 96-9, 103
requirements, non-objection by present government **103,** 526
State no longer in existence **100,** 372-3
torture **119,** 45, 61-70, 97-100, 151-7, 219-21, 244-5, 250
Torture Convention (1984)

Head of State, former, immunity, jurisdiction (*cont.*)
exclusion **119,** 219-21, 245
as waiver **119,** 216-17, 221, 231-2, **125,** 504
treaty exception **119,** 68-70
acts prior to coming into force of treaty exception **119,** 68-70
acts prior to legislation implementing treaty exception **119,** 69-70
critical date **119,** 69-70, 140
need for **119,** 68-70
requirements **119,** 195-6
aut dedicare aut judicare provision regardless of nationality or place of offence **119,** 69
clear definition of crime against international law **119,** 69
convention to which requested and requesting States both party **119,** 69
provision for national jurisdiction to try former Head of State **119,** 69
strict interpretation **119,** 69, 72
waiver, Torture Convention (1984) as **119,** 216-17, 221, 231-2, 245, **125,** 504
Head of State, immunity
income tax **53,** 568-74, **64,** 406-7, 421, 483-9, 524-34, 617
testimonial **101,** 506-7
waiver, counterclaim as **101,** 507
Head of State, immunity, execution/attachment 64, 501-2, **91,** 260-3
customary international law **91,** 260
family members, entitlement **91,** 260-1
Head of State, immunity, jurisdiction 55, 423, **57,** 43, **64,** 79, 397-401, 406-7, 412, 415, 419-25, 524-30, 538, 571-4, 615-18, **92,** 520, 524, 526, **101,** 504-5, **106,** 504-5. *See also* Head of State, diplomatic privileges and immunities, entitlement
absolute theory **65,** 14-15, **87,** 237-8, **102,** 202, 203, **103,** 584-5, 592, **119,** 49, 80, 102, 222
legislation, affect on **103,** 588-92
act of State and, act in violation of international law **103,** 557, **119,** 106-7
acts committed abroad **119,** 60, 161, 236
acts committed in own country **119,** 60-1, 90, 203
acts committed within forum State **119,** 45, 56, 90, 194, 231, 237, 246
acts outside authority **104,** 125
basis **82,** 57, **103,** 585
customary international law **125,** 500-1
dignity of State **125,** 500
friendly relations, preservation of **125,** 500
functional **81,** 605 n. 1, 627, **119,** 59-70, **125,** 500
as Commander-in-Chief **80,** 22-3
common law **111,** 606, **113,** 531, **119,** 89-90
contract debt **64,** 79-80
crimes against humanity **119,** 45-8, 98-9
criminal proceedings **64,** 409, **80,** 365-6, **102,** 201-5, **103,** 590-2, **119,** 45, 58, 87-9, 96, 155, 162, 204-18
gravity of crimes, relevance **119,** 62, 84, 169
reasons for **80,** 366
cumulative nature **111,** 607
customary international law **64,** 409, 616-17, **99,** 161, 162, **102,** 201, 202, **103,** 585, **119,** 43-8, 62-70, 78-87, 99-100, **121,** 571-2, **125,** 495-510
ratione personae **119,** 219
treaty practice as evidence of **125,** 495-6, 502-3

de facto Head of State **99,** 162, **103,** 585-6, **121,** 595-6
Noriega **119,** 82-3
diplomatic privileges and immunities, similarity of regime. *See* Head of State, diplomatic privileges and immunities, entitlement
discretionary **102,** 203, **103,** 586
executive certificate/statement **65,** 14, **111,** 607, **118,** 297
extraterritoriality and **65,** 14-15
family member **81,** 605-6, **102,** 201
brother **121,** 587
rationale **81,** 607
wife **121,** 571
genocide **119,** 72
Genocide Convention (1948), applicability **119,** 65-6
other than in State where act committed **119,** 66
head of government distinguished **119,** 222
Hostages Convention (1979), applicability **119,** 65
ILC and **119,** 69, 72
international crimes **119,** 67-70, 83-7, 212-13, 223-33, 349, **125,** 505-7
international tribunals
International Criminal Court (ICC) **119,** 66-7, 155, **125,** 482, 497-8, 502-3
International Criminal Tribunal for the Former Yugoslavia (ICTY) **119,** 66, 71, 87, 155, 212, **125,** 497, 502
International Criminal Tribunal for Rwanda (ICTR) **119,** 46, 66, 155, **125,** 497, 502
International Military Tribunal for the Far East (Tokyo Tribunal) **119,** 66, **125,** 495
Nuremberg Military Tribunal **119,** 46, 66, 87, 98-9, 155
jurisdiction, effect of grant to municipal courts **119,** 155-6
justiciability **87,** 237-8, **119,** 73-4, 90-3
legality of act, relevance **119,** 62, 194-6, 224
marriage, breach of promise **64,** 444
official acts
in exercise of mandate **82,** 57
while in power **99,** 161, **102,** 201-3, **103,** 522-30, 556, 592, **119,** 41-9
personal entitlement **64,** 400-1, 412-13, 502-3
personal sovereign **64,** 103, 397-9, **87,** 237-8, **119,** 99
commercial acts **64,** 97-9
justiciability **87,** 237-8
real/immovable property, dispute relating to **64,** 98-9
trust fund cases **64,** 99
Pinochet proceedings, background **119,** 1-5
private acts **64,** 422-3, **87,** 237-8, **102,** 201, 202, **111,** 607-8, 609-10, **119,** 239, **121,** 596
breach of promise **64,** 444-5
personal sovereign **64,** 423, **87,** 237-8
supply of goods for birthday celebrations coinciding with national holiday **113,** 483-4
as privilege **64,** 448
ratione materiae **119,** 153-4, 156, 161, 172-3, 194-5, 200-1, 215, 223, 231, 239-42
Duke of Brunswick v. *King of Hanover* **119,** 63, 80-2
Torture Convention (1984), effect **119,** 200-1, 215-16, 220, 231, 245, **123,** 34-5
ratione personae **102,** 201-2, **119,** 79, 96-9, 161, 214, 222, 239
former Head of State distinguished **119,** 79, 96-9, 222-3
recognition, relevance **99,** 161-3, **103,** 585-6, **113,** 512, 531
responsibility for determining entitlement

Head of State, immunity, jurisdiction (*cont.*)
courts **121,** 572
executive **121,** 572
legislature **121,** 572
Ruler of State of Malaysian Federation **118,** 294-8
State immunity as basis **64,** 418
State immunity distinguished **64,** 397-401, 411, 413, 421-2, 495-8, 571-2, 615-18, **103,** 590, **111,** 607-8, **119,** 57, 62-5, 140, 152-7, 235. *See also* official acts *above*
State practice **119,** 67
State responsibility for breach **125,** 507-8
State-sponsored terrorism **121,** 642-3, **125,** 497-8, 507
statutory limitation, suspension **119,** 358
'trading within local limits of the Court' and **64,** 407, 425
treaty exception, Versailles, Treaty of (1919) **125,** 503. *See also* Head of State, former, immunity, jurisdiction, treaty exception; International Criminal Tribunal (ICC), Rome Statute (1998); International Military Tribunal for the Far East (Tokyo Tribunal); Nuremberg Military Tribunal; Rwanda, International Criminal Tribunal for (ICTR), Statute; Yugoslavia, International Criminal Tribunal for the Former (ICTY), Statute
waiver. *See* Head of State, immunity, jurisdiction, waiver
Head of State, immunity, jurisdiction, theory/doctrine
basis
comity **103,** 585, **119,** 45, 62, 97, **121,** 572-3, 642
foreign relations considerations **119,** 72-3
Head of State, immunity, jurisdiction, waiver
absence of objection by government **119,** 83
by de facto government **103,** 587-8
by government **103,** 586-7
by organ of successor government **102,** 203-5
by State, need for **119,** 79, 87
by successor government **103,** 555-6
counterclaim as **118,** 297-8
express **102,** 203-5, **121,** 571, 572-3
extending to execution, whether **118,** 298
initiation of proceedings **64,** 103
insurance contract **65,** 14-15
right to waive State and diplomatic immunity compared **121,** 572-3
submission to the jurisdiction as, revocation/withdrawal **65,** 15
submission to the jurisdiction. *See* submission to the jurisdiction as *above*
Head of State, inviolability of archives and documents 64, 293
bank records **86,** 162, 166-8
Head of State, jurisdiction, international crimes, *jus cogens*/peremptory norm and **119,** 155, 195, **125,** 469-71
headquarters agreements 85, 26-7 *See also* host agreements
African Reinsurance Corporation-Nigeria **86,** 659-60, 665
breach, closure of observer mission **82,** 235-44, 245-6, 247-50, 256-7
Convention on Privileges and Immunities of the Specialized Agencies of the UN (1947) and **101,** 390-3
direct effect **105,** 24
FAO–Italy (1950)
interpretation **101,** 388-94
legal personality **101,** 389
interpretation

applicable law
Vienna Convention on the Law of Treaties (1969) **105,** 21-2
Vienna Convention on the Law of Treaties between States and International Organizations (1986) **105,** 21-2
restrictive **105,** 21-2
legal personality determined by **102,** 211
privileges and immunities **107,** 185
tenancy agreement **101,** 360
purpose **81,** 705
self-executing, whether **86,** 659-60
treaty nature **82,** 233, 238, 285 n. 2
UN
breach **82,** 235, 236-44, 245-52, 254, 257, 258-9, 262-7, 269-71, 275-9, 293-4
common law extension **104,** 161
interpretation or application, obligation to arbitrate **82,** 230-82, 288-91
service of process, visitor **104,** 160-1
US security reservation **82,** 297 n. 31
waiver of privileges and immunities, whether **86,** 659, 661
health. *See also* World Health Organization (WHO)
nuclear weapons, relevance **110,** 84
obligations
active nature **110,** 84
erga omnes **110,** 83
right to **110,** 82-3
International Covenant on Economic, Social and Cultural Rights (1966) **110,** 83
Universal Declaration of Human Rights (1948) **110,** 83
State responsibility **110,** 82-4
Helsinki Final Act (1975)
force, prohibition on the threat or use of **76,** 434
implementation **77,** 252
individual's rights under **85,** 242-3
intervention in affairs of another State **76,** 441
legal obligations under **85,** 242-3
recognition, State, criteria **92,** 173, 190
renunciation of spouses **85,** 243
self-determination **115,** 163-4, 582, 585
self-executing, whether **85,** 242-3
State immunity, jurisdiction, waiver **85,** 242-3
treaties, obligations, to negotiate in good faith **110,** 214
treaty, whether **85,** 243
Hess, Rudolf, challenge to detention **90,** 390-400
Hickenlooper Amendment. *See* United States of America (USA), Hickenlooper Amendment
high seas. *See also* contiguous zone; continental shelf; exclusive economic zone (EEZ); exclusive fishing zone (EFZ); fisheries; fishing zones; High Seas Convention (1958); high seas, freedom of; high seas, jurisdiction; hot pursuit; inland waters; maritime waters; ships; territorial sea
applicable law **74,** 213-18, **123,** 439
collisions **70,** 478-9
submarine cables **74,** 213-18
collisions
applicable law **65,** 107, **70,** 478-9

high seas (*cont.*)
removal of wreck **74,** 199-200
common heritage of mankind/*res communis omnium* **56,** 116-17, 181, **57,** 459, **71,** 259, **125,** 422-3
definition
airspace **90,** 215-16
'all parts of the sea not included in the territorial sea or internal waters of a State' **55,** 206-7, 257, **56,** 118, 162, **63,** 353
'at sea' **78,** 573
contiguous zone as part of **71,** 261, **74,** 206, 210
waters above the continental shelf **123,** 211
'waters outside the territorial sea' **84,** 51
'waters subject to public use or constituting a whole with such waters' **55,** 145-8
NAFO Regulatory Area as **123,** 223-4, 279, 338
occupation
chank and pearl fisheries **90,** 326-8
effective **91,** 433-7
freedom of the high seas and **91,** 432-3
Judicial Regime of Historic Waters including Historic Bays 56 (UN Doc A/CN.4/143) (1962) **91,** 434 n. 14
requirements, acts attributable to State intended to assert exclusive authority **91,** 434, 436, 438
res communis omnium. See common heritage of mankind/*res communis omnium above*
responsibility for
prevention of interference with rights of other States **71,** 259-61
safety on **74,** 199-200, 240
sailing routes, upkeep **74,** 199-200
wrecks. *See* wrecks
High Seas Convention (1958) 55, 603, 608, **91,** 516-18. *See also* high seas
breach, remedies, compensation for damages **91,** 476
as codification **91,** 475
conservation of natural resources **82,** 627-8
flag States, duty to exercise jurisdiction **82,** 614
genuine link requirement **46,** 361, **93,** 729, 759, 760-1, 783-4, **120,** 179
hot pursuit **55,** 444-6, **77,** 591, 592, **91,** 515, 518-19
individuals and **71,** 259-60, **91,** 475-6
jurisdiction, flag State. *See* high seas, jurisdiction, flag State
municipal law and, primacy **91,** 475
non-parties and **91,** 475-6, 542
reservations **41,** 206
search and seizure by warship or other duly authorized ship or aircraft, prohibition **81,** 668 n. 10, **91,** 475, 516-18, 522 n. 20
applicability
crew and vessel from State not party to High Seas Convention (1958) **91,** 475-6
foreign merchant ship **91,** 516-17
foreign pleasure craft **91,** 517
stateless ship **91,** 475 n. 15, 490-1
exceptions
national ship despite flag **91,** 475
piracy **91,** 475
slave-trade **91,** 475
stateless ship **91,** 488-92
foreign merchant ship **91,** 516-17

foreign pleasure craft **91,** 517
State immunity, effect on **45,** 74
high seas, freedom of 40, 90, **55,** 257, 318, 332, 343, 445-6, **57,** 579, **77,** 589-90. *See also* high seas; High Seas Convention (1958); high seas, jurisdiction
artificial island as interference **71,** 259-61
coastal State obligations
customary international law **71,** 260-1, **74,** 199
obstruction, prevention of **71,** 259-61, **74,** 199-200
component elements **120,** 286-7
freedom of navigation. *See* freedom of navigation
Continental Shelf Convention (1958) and **41,** 116-17, 123, 128-9, 168
corollary of sovereignty in territorial sea **77,** 590
customary international law **41,** 69, 117, **77,** 590
flag State jurisdiction as corollary **120,** 588
freedom of communication **120,** 280-1
freedom of fishing **55,** 320, **56,** 162
general principle of international law **120,** 284, 588
Geneva Convention on the High Seas (1958) **77,** 590
global economy considerations **120,** 282, 291-2
interests of coastal States **77,** 590
Law of the Sea Convention (1982) provisions **120,** 279-83
prompt release provisions **125,** 191
limitations on
agreed conservation measures **55,** 118-19, 206-7, 208-9
historic rights **41,** 124
preferential fishing zones **41,** 124
reasonable regard to the interest of other States **56,** 184
sedentary fisheries **41,** 124
neutral ships **79,** 10
freedom of passage **79,** 9-10
exceptions **79,** 10
nuclear tests and **57,** 515, 535
private rights, creation of **71,** 259-60
res communis **55,** 204-5, 316, 332, **71,** 259-61
Security Council Resolution imposing sanctions and **117,** 316
stateless ship and **91,** 491
territorial sea and **55,** 327
unilateral extension **74,** 210
high seas, jurisdiction
artificial structure **54,** 234-40
British policy **91,** 529
broadcasting **101,** 412-18
broadcasting offences
European Agreement for the Prevention of Broadcasts transmitted from outside National Territories **101,** 413
State practice **101,** 414-15
UNCLOS III **101,** 414-15
conservation and management measures. *See* fisheries, conservation and management measures
criminal **38,** 120-32, **40,** 88-91, **45,** 4-18, **55,** 439, **69,** 162-3
drugs offences. *See* search and seizure, drug-trafficking *below*
enforcement of municipal law **74,** 201-12
customs legislation **91,** 525-7

high seas, jurisdiction (*cont.*)
fisheries regulation **55,** 146-8, 206-7, 343
revenue laws **40,** 88-91, **74,** 211-12
flag State **72,** 212-14, **77,** 589-90, **78,** 117-19, **91,** 515, 518, **101,** 413-18
as corollary to freedom of high seas principle **120,** 588
customary international law **91,** 524, **120,** 588, **123,** 356
exceptions. *See also* enforcement of municipal law *above*; fisheries, conservation and management measures
Convention relating to Intervention on the High Seas in case of Oil Pollution Casualties (1969) **120,** 589
customary international law **77,** 589-90
effects doctrine **42,** 144-5, **91,** 474, **120,** 590-3
Geneva Convention on the High Seas (1958) **77,** 538-9, 591
hot pursuit. *See* hot pursuit
infringement of coastal State's interests **77,** 590
Law of the Sea Convention (1982) **77,** 538, **120,** 588
measures necessary in case of grave and imminent danger to coastline **120,** 589
piracy **77,** 538-41
policing powers **77,** 538
safety at sea obligations **74,** 199-200, **120,** 593-9
search and rescue obligations **120,** 592-3
slave trade **120,** 588-9
High Seas Convention (1958) **101,** 415, 416
nationals on national ships, failure to carry cargo manifest **40,** 88-91
ship as part of flag State **74,** 206-8
UNCLOS III **101,** 414-15
waiver **84,** 211-13
foreign ship **74,** 211-12, **91,** 470-86
conspiracy **91,** 474
High Seas Convention (1958) **91,** 475-6
nationals on. *See* nationals on foreign ship *below*
safety at sea obligations **74,** 95-6, **120,** 593-9
foreigners on national ship **77,** 289
High Seas Convention (1958) **91,** 475-6
foreign ship **91,** 475-6
limitation of coastal state's, whether **91,** 524-30
national ship **91,** 474
nationals on foreign ship **77,** 285-92
nationals on national ship **51,** 230-2, **56,** 245
duty of protection **78,** 495
failure to carry cargo manifest **40,** 88-91
piracy. *See* piracy
protective principle **91,** 525
right of approach. *See* search and seizure *below*
search and seizure **42,** 390, **91,** 511-38, 542
as act of State, treaty provision **44,** 365-6
Algerian war **47,** 164
authority under national legislation **91,** 471-2
belligerent right **42,** 390
drug-trafficking **84,** 210, 214-15, **91,** 470-86
effects doctrine and **91,** 472-3
High Seas Convention (1958). *See* High Seas Convention (1958), search and seizure by warship or other duly authorized ship or aircraft, prohibition

military operation in peacetime, compensation **47,** 164
Miranda warnings **91,** 533
of national vessel **91,** 477-8
Pan-American Maritime Neutrality Convention **81,** 668 n. 10
protest, absence of **91,** 529-30
requirements
reasonable suspicion or probable cause **84,** 215-17, **91,** 478, 490, 497, 501-2, 519, 530-1, 535-6, 538
search warrant **91,** 477, 541
ship of same nationality as approaching warship **91,** 516-18
stateless ship **91,** 542
of stateless vessel **91,** 488-92
ships and nationals of forum State/equipment distinguished **101,** 414, 416
sinking of ship as civil wrong **79,** 15 n. 3
stateless ship **91,** 475 n. 15, 488-92, 542
submarine cables, damage to, applicable law **74,** 213-18
taxation, income earned on **74,** 207
US policy **91,** 524-7
vessel and crime distinguished **91,** 473
visit and search. *See* search and seizure *above*
waiver of objection by foreign State **84,** 211-12
high treason. *See* treason
hijacking of aircraft 60, 445, 447-8, **74,** 163-5, 447-8, **79,** 481, **80,** 674-80. *See also* Montreal Convention for the Suppression of Unlawful Acts Against the Safety of Civil Aviation (1971); terrorism
asylum, right of and **80,** 674-82
Chicago Convention on International Civil Aviation (1944) **48,** 434-5
crime against humanity, whether **80,** 679
diversion of Indian aircraft to Pakistan (1971) **48,** 331, 337, 348-9, 395, 411, 432, 453
International Conventions **82,** 348-9
international crime, whether **87,** 301
jurisdiction **71,** 230-1, **82,** 346-57, **87,** 299-300, 301-2, 303-5
Hague Convention for the Suppression of the Unlawful Seizure of Aircraft (1970) **87,** 299-300, 303-5, **88,** 180
location of aircraft **82,** 353
subsequent location of offender **82,** 353
universal **82,** 348-9, **88,** 181
USA **82,** 346-7, 353-7
liability of carrier for damage arising **89,** 26-9
necessity as defence **71,** 230
political offence, whether **80,** 680
punishment **74,** 163-5, **87,** 308-10
Hindu law
equity in **41,** 144
Mitakshara Law **49,** 372, 397
historic bays. *See* bays, historic; Fonseca Bay, historic bay
historic heritage, protection **82,** 26-7
historic rights 41, 124-5, **69,** 66, 73. *See also* title, historic
continental shelf
conflicting **67,** 65, 116-17, 123
delimitation and **67,** 55-6, 64-70, 115-17, 122-5, 129, 203-4
distinguished **67,** 67
interrelation **67,** 67, 116-17, 124-5, 203-4

historic rights (*cont.*)
evidence of **41,** 125
fishing **55,** 333-4, 386, **71,** 168, **82,** 605
Grisbadarna case **41,** 125 n. 1
Islamic law **41,** 125 n. 1
as relevant/special circumstances **41,** 151
historic title. *See* title, historic
historic waters 57, 77
Holy Places. *See* Jerusalem, East
Holy See. *See also* Roman Catholic Church
extradition, requirements, prima facie case **100,** 605-6, 608-9
immunity, jurisdiction **65,** 335-7, **78,** 121-3, **87,** 49-52, **100,** 605, 608-9
diplomats **71,** 537, 539
employment contract, nationality, relevance **65,** 335
Institute for Religious Works (IOR) **87,** 51-2
Pontificia Opera di Assistenza (POA) **65,** 334-7
Vatican Radio **78,** 121-3
Institute for Religious Works (IOR)
diplomatic status **82,** 51-2
immunity, jurisdiction **87,** 51-2
legal personality **87,** 49-50, **100,** 606-8
Italy and
extradition to **100,** 604-9
offences on Italian territory **100,** 605, 608
Lateran Treaty **75,** 335, **78,** 122
'exemption from interference' **87,** 50, **100,** 608, 609
purpose, protection of Italian State **87,** 51
reservation of sovereign powers **87,** 51
jurisdiction, central institutions of Catholic Church **100,** 605, 606-9
Lateran Treaty. *See* Italy and *above*
law of
Criminal Code, s 9 **100,** 606, 609
Criminal Procedure Code
s 635 **100,** 609
s 640 **100,** 609
s 641 **100,** 609
s 641(1) **100,** 606
s 641(6) **100,** 605
s 642 **100,** 609
s 646 **100,** 609
Law of 21 June 1969 **100,** 609
mediation role **82,** 678-83
'mission in the world' **78,** 122, **87,** 51
Papal Commission for the State of the Vatican City, Decree No 52 of 1 July 1969 **78,** 122
Poland, Concordat with (1925), termination **47,** 25
Pontificia Opera di Assistenza (POA)
immunity, jurisdiction **65,** 334-7
status **65,** 334-5
premises abroad, diplomatic immunity **78,** 121
privileges and immunities **102,** 170-3
status **65,** 335-6, **102,** 168-70
'foreign legal order' **87,** 51-2

international personality **65,** 335-6, **78,** 121-3
sovereignty **78,** 121-3, **102,** 169
treaty, as 'moral protector' **82,** 688
Vatican City distinguished **102,** 169
home, respect for. *See* European Convention on Human Rights (1950), home, respect for
homosexuality
armed forces **112,** 371-412
censorship based on **70,** 298-304
European moral standards **67,** 416-17, 422, 435
freedom from discrimination **67,** 408, 418-19, 423, 426-8
age of consent **67,** 417-18
gross indecency distinguished **67,** 429
margin of appreciation, protection of morals **70,** 298-304, **112,** 341, 343-4
persecution as 'member of particular social group' and **118,** 595-601, **124,** 486, 488-9, 508-9
private life, respect for **67,** 409-18, 424-9, 431-7, **89,** 256-61
public opinion **67,** 405-7, 415, 422, 435
Honduras
Continental Shelf Proclamation (1950) **41,** 118, 120
disappearances, State responsibility **95,** 296-9
Fonseca Bay
El Tigre, claim to
occupation of **97,** 482-3, 485-6, 580-1
recognition **97,** 580
'geographically disadvantaged State' **97,** 677-8
islands, claim to, *effectivités* **97,** 476-8
Meanguera/Meanguerita
absence of evidence **97,** 493
protest **97,** 488, 490, 491-3, 495
occluded, whether **97,** 631-2, 675
rights
continental shelf **97,** 631, 676
EEZ **97,** 631, 676
fishing in EEZ **97,** 677
innocent passage **97,** 675-6
joint sovereignty **97,** 631-2
maritime spaces **97,** 522
territorial sea **97,** 631, 676
habeas corpus, ineffectiveness **95,** 273-6, 282-3
human rights in
'disappearances'
evidence of **95,** 276-83
remedy **95,** 273-6
systematic manner **95,** 289-91
ICJ acceptance of compulsory jurisdiction **97,** 299
1948 Declaration **84,** 233-4
1960 Declaration **84,** 228, 231-2, 234-5, 237
1986 Declaration **84,** 232, 235-6
reservations **84,** 229, **97,** 299
Inter-American Court of Human Rights, contentious jurisdiction, recognition of **95,** 242, 243
property
alien's rights **97,** 335

Honduras (*cont.*)
Honduras' title to territory and **97,** 335
territory, definition, *King of Spain's Award* **97,** 553-4
Hong Kong. *See also* Hong Kong Special Administrative Region (HKSAR)
China–UK Joint Declaration on the Future of Hong Kong (1984)
entry into force **92,** 640
international treaty, whether **92,** 640
justiciability **92,** 640-4, 647, 649
municipal law, part of, whether
government's intentions, relevance **92,** 649
official declaration of status, relevance **92,** 642-3, 648-9
ratification, effect **92,** 642-3
rights enforceable in municipal courts, whether **92,** 640-4, 647-9
conspiracy
definition **84,** 44
English law, identity with **85,** 117
jurisdiction **84,** 43-50, 61-72
aliens, over **84,** 62-3, 69
courts, municipal
role
extradition **90,** 415
treaty interpretation **90,** 422-3
customary international law
municipal law and **92,** 655
non-refoulement **92,** 655
inconsistent municipal legislation **92,** 655
double criminality
conduct test **90,** 414-15
evidence of foreign law **90,** 413-15
Endangered Species of Wild Fauna and Flora, Convention on International Trade in (CITES) (1973)
phrases, 'exports' and 're-exports', distinction **90,** 424
'unworked or simply prepared' **90,** 419-22, 425-6
extraditable offence **84,** 57-9, **85,** 115
extradition **85,** 117-27. *See also* Hong Kong Special Administrative Region (HKSAR), extradition
arrest, provisional arrest **87,** 323, 324-6
arrest warrant, need for **87,** 322-8
China, after reversion to **104,** 46-7, **114,** 386-401, 407-66, **122,** 603-19
double criminality **114,** 616
motivation of requesting State **114,** 616
political offence provisions **114,** 617-18
where punishment before reversion impossible **114,** 613-49
competence in relation to **106,** 248
courts, role **90,** 415
disguised **92,** 657
double criminality. *See* double criminality *above*
evidence of extraditable offence
continuing criminal exercise **90,** 413-15
substantial similarity **90,** 414
Hong Kong/China **92,** 657
procedure
arrest. *See* arrest *above*
formal documents, necessary, whether **87,** 326-7

substantiation **87,** 326-7, 328
technical requirements, observance of **87,** 322
time-limit **87,** 322-4
speciality **114,** 617, 632-3
USA, to, United States of America (Extradition) Order 1976 **87,** 321
extradition agreement. *See also* Hong Kong Special Administrative Region (HKSAR), extradition agreement
need for **90,** 415
primacy **87,** 322
UK–USA, extension to Hong Kong **87,** 321, **122,** 604-5
warranty of trial according to requesting State's laws **114,** 616, 630-1
Extradition, European Convention on (1957), applicability **106,** 249, 254
fair hearing
applicants for asylum and **92,** 653-6
Geneva Convention Relating to the Status of Refugees (1951) **92,** 654-5
International Covenant on Civil and Political Rights (ICCPR) (1966) **92,** 656
natural justice, relevance **92,** 654, 656
Geneva Convention Relating to the Status of Refugees (1951), part of Hong Kong law, whether **92,** 654-5
high seas, waters outside territorial sea **84,** 51
International Covenant on Civil and Political Rights (ICCPR) (1966), part of Hong Kong law, whether **92,** 656
judicial review grounds
illegality **92,** 650
irrationality **92,** 650
legitimate expectation, disappointment of **92,** 650
procedural propriety **92,** 650
jurisdiction
conspiracy **84,** 43-50, 61-72
law enforcement officers of third State, over **84,** 70
law of
Animals and Plants (Protection of Endangered Species) Ordinance 1976 **84,** 52, 53, **90,** 417-18
s 60 **84,** 54
s 187 **84,** 54
Application of English Law Ordinance **92,** 643
Bill of Rights Ordinance (Cap. 383), freedom of expression **122,** 573
Chinese Extradition Ordinance 1889 **92,** 657
Criminal Procedure Ordinance
s 1 **84,** 51
s 19 **84,** 50-1
Dangerous Drugs Ordinance **85,** 125, 126-7
s 2 **84,** 59, 62
s 4 **84,** 58, 62, 63, 69, 73
s 39 **84,** 61
Dentists Registration Ordinance **85,** 127
District Court Ordinance, s 84 **84,** 51-2
English law, extension of **90,** 421
Extradition Act (UK) 1870, s 10 **84,** 64, 65, 72
Extradition (Hong Kong) Ordinance **85,** 114
Fugitive Offenders Act (UK) 1967 **84,** 65
Immigration Ordinance **92,** 652
Import and Export Ordinance, s 18 **84,** 52
international law, conflict, amendment, need for **90,** 422

Hong Kong (*cont.*)
Interpretation and General Clauses Ordinance **90,** 422
local circumstances, relevance **90,** 421
Magistrates Order **84,** 64
legislation
extraterritorial effect **84,** 72-3
validity **77,** 380-4
legislation, interpretation
aids
ambiguity, in case of **90,** 420-1
natural justice **92,** 656
guidelines
extraterritorial offence, presumption against **85,** 126-7
intention of legislature **90,** 421
plain meaning **90,** 420-1
treaty as aid **90,** 420-1, 422
natural justice
law, administration according to law **92,** 656
legislation, interpretation and **92,** 656
political asylum, applicability to **92,** 646, 654
New Territories
Chinese land tenure **77,** 378-9
Land Court **77,** 382-4
Peking Convention and **77,** 378, 381, 383
enforceability of in Hong Kong courts **77,** 380-4
precedent in municipal courts, *stare decisis* doctrine **84,** 69
public order/public policy/*ordre public* **84,** 48-9
refugees
fair hearing, right to **92,** 653-6
non-refoulement, customary international law, whether **92,** 655
treaties
applicability **77,** 380-4
applicability to
Extradition, European Convention on (1957) **106,** 249, 254
France–UK Extradition Treaty (1876) **106,** 249, 254
ICSID Convention (1965), 'Contracting State' **106,** 520, 585
China–UK Joint Declaration on the Future of Hong Kong (1984). *See* China–UK Joint Declaration on the Future of Hong Kong (1984) *above*
extension to, Sri Lanka/UK Bilateral Investment Treaty (1980) (Exchange of Notes of 14 January 1981) **106,** 422
implementing legislation, partial incorporation **90,** 424
justiciability **92,** 654-5
operation and enforcement, implementing legislation, need for **92,** 654-5
unequal **114,** 387
treaty interpretation
by municipal courts **90,** 422-3
guidelines, effectiveness **90,** 424, 426
uniformity, desirability **90,** 423
USA, to **87,** 321-8
Hong Kong Special Administrative Region (HKSAR). *See also* Hong Kong
applicable law
common law **114,** 396
treaty, international law **122,** 612-14

Basic Law 1990 **114,** 394-6
  fundamental rights under **114,** 445-6
  s 8 (legal system) **114,** 396, **122,** 606
  s 10(1) (regional flag) **122,** 581-2
  s 10(2) (regional flag) **122,** 581-2
  s 13 (responsibility for foreign relations) **114,** 395
  s 18 (legal system) **114,** 396, **122,** 580, 606
  s 19 (judicial power) **114,** 396, 424, **122,** 613
  s 27 (freedom of speech) **122,** 586, 595-7
  s 39 (incorporation of human rights conventions) **122,** 573, 586-7, 596
    Flag Ordinances, whether justified restriction on rights **122,** 573-7, 586-94, 596-601
  s 151 (relations with foreign States) **114,** 395, **122,** 606
  s 153 (international agreements: applicability) **114,** 395, **122,** 606
  s 157 (establishment of foreign missions) **114,** 395
extradition. *See also* law of, Fugitive Offenders Ordinance 1997 (Cap. 503) *below*
  Agreement for the Surrender of Accused and Convicted Persons between Australia and Hong Kong, applicability **114,** 392-4
    approval by China **114,** 393-4
  evidence of, foreign law **122,** 615-18
  HKSAR as 'foreign country' for purposes of US legislation **122,** 661-80
  procedure **122,** 609-10
  responsibility, executive **122,** 618
  speciality, risk of change **114,** 455-9, 632-3, 639
  surrender to China, possibility of **114,** 458-9
extradition agreement
  HKSAR–US Extradition Agreement (1996) **122,** 667-8, 678-9
    legislative history **122,** 678-9
    ratification, need for **114,** 626
    self-executing **122,** 679-80
    treaty status **122,** 678-9
  UK–US Extradition Agreement (1972), applicability **114,** 611-49
extradition arrangements between UK and HKSAR, delay in China's approval **114,** 424-5, 457-8
flag, respect for. *See* freedom of expression, flag desecration and *below*
foreign relations, responsibility, People's Republic of China **114,** 398-401
freedom of expression
  flag desecration and **122,** 569-601
    'desecration' **122,** 585
  freedom of speech as synonymous **122,** 595
Hong Kong pre-reversion to People's Republic of China, identity with **114,** 399
judicial notice, sacred nature of flag of People's Republic of China **122,** 573
law of
  Basic Law 1990. *See* Basic Law 1990 *above*
  Criminal Procedure Ordinance (Cap. 221), s 65C **122,** 569
  Fugitive Offenders Ordinance 1997 (Cap. 503)
    s 3(1) (application to foreign country or place, need for Ordinance triggering) **122,** 603-4, 607-9
    s 3(9) (conformity with Ordinance) **122,** 607-8
    s 3(12) (evidence of conformity with Ordinance) **122,** 608, 614-15
    s 3(14) (changes to extradition arrangements) **122,** 608, 618
    s 4 (extradition jurisdiction) **122,** 609
    s 5 (political offence exception) **122,** 609

Hong Kong Special Administrative Region (HKSAR) (*cont.*)
s 7(1)(a) **122,** 603
s 10(6)(b) **122,** 603, 609-10
Law on the National Flag (PRC), application **122,** 580-1
National Flag and National Emblem Ordinance (No 116 of 1997) (Cap. 1557) **122,** 57, 569, 580-1
compatibility with International Covenant on Civil and Political Rights (ICCPR) (1966) **122,** 571-7, 586-94, 596-601
Public Order Ordinance (Cap. 245) **122,** 569, 575
Regional Flag and Regional Emblem Ordinance (No 117 of 1997) (Cap. 1558) **122,** 569, 582-3, 596-601
compatibility with International Covenant on Civil and Political Rights (ICCPR) (1966) **122,** 571-7, 586-94
public order/public policy/*ordre public*, definition **122,** 589-92, 596-7
restrictions on rights
justification, public order/public policy/*ordre public* **122,** 588-92, 596-600
requirements, narrow and specific provision **122,** 597, 600-1
separation of powers, courts' obligation to follow approach chosen by legislature **122,** 600
status
international legal personality **114,** 397-8
subsovereign government **122,** 661-80
treaties. *See also* extradition agreement *above*; Hong Kong, extradition agreement
applicability, agreement of all parties, need for **114,** 621-2
applicable law. *See* applicable law, treaty *above*
capacity to conclude **122,** 678-9
continuity **114,** 619-20, **122,** 605-7
executive certificate/statement, conclusiveness **122,** 608, 614-15, 618-19
honorary consul/consulate. *See* consular privileges and immunities, honorary consul/consulate
host agreements. *See* headquarters agreements; World Health Organization Regional Office in Egypt, Agreement on privileges, immunities and facilities (1951)
hostage-taking 78, 1-3. *See also* diplomatic mission, receiving State's duty of protection; forcible abduction/unlawful arrest; Hostages Convention (1979)
act of State **119,** 96
conspiracy **119,** 182-3
customary international law **119,** 106-7
damages, claim for **81,** 545
definition, UK law **119,** 93, 147-8
extraditable offence **119,** 76, 93, 147-8, 182-3
Geneva Convention on the Protection of Civilian Persons in Time of War (1949) **83,** 140
international law, violation **81,** 545
Iran **61,** 538-41, 559, 561
lawfulness **61,** 562-3
State responsibility and **61,** 555-9, 561, 563-7, 568, 584-8
jurisdiction **82,** 346-57
Hostages Convention (1979) **82,** 350, **119,** 100
personal **82,** 353
universal **82,** 349
USA **82,** 346-7, 352-3
justifiable, whether **78,** 2-3

occupied territory, on **83,** 139-40
political offence, whether **79,** 481
punishment **78,** 2
purpose **78,** 2
reparation, duty to make **61,** 567-8
State responsibility **61,** 555-9, 561, 563-7, 568, 584-8, **72,** 250
as war crime **122,** 66, 73, 216-18, 224, 245
Hostages Convention (1979) 77, 236
applicability
'any offender whatsoever' **119,** 65
Head of State **119,** 65
aut dedere aut punire/judicare **119,** 65
State/Head of State immunity and **119,** 65, 72, 85, 96, 98, 100
hostilities. *See* armed conflict; civil strife; civil war; rebellion; revolution; war
hot pursuit 77, 588, 590-2
conservation and management measures distinguished **123,** 420-1
customary international law **77,** 591
delay in advancing claim **110,** 755, 766
Hague Codification Conference (1930) **77,** 591
High Seas Convention (1958) **55,** 444-6, **77,** 591, 592, **91,** 515, 518-19
customary international law and **77,** 591
Law of the Sea Convention (1982) **120,** 194-6, 234-5
requirements
authorized government vessel so marked **77,** 591, **120,** 257
commencement within territorial sea or contiguous zone **77,** 592, **91,** 518, **110,** 753, 755
daughter boat's presence in territorial sea **77,** 592
effects doctrine **120,** 276-7
continuity **110,** 753, **120,** 195
events within EEZ giving rise to **120,** 327-9
infringement of valid local laws **77,** 591, **120,** 195-6
'good reason to believe' **120,** 257
signal to stop **77,** 591, **91,** 518, **120,** 195, 257-8
'working as a team' **77,** 591-2
Security Council Resolution 820 (1993) (transhipment of commodities and products through FRY) and **117,** 317
hotel, operation of, commercial activity 63, 317
human dignity, right to 98, 398-402, **100,** 397-400
constitutional right **100,** 396, 398, **103,** 84
Geneva Convention (IV) **122,** 65
international humanitarian law and **121,** 264-5, 271
persecution of refugees and **90,** 151, 177
probable death before conclusion of criminal proceedings and **100,** 396-400
rape, oral penetration and **121,** 271
unwritten constitutional principle **100,** 397-8
human rights 42, 205-7, **43,** 178-86, **47,** 169-211. *See also* African Charter on Human and Peoples' Rights (1981); American Convention on Human Rights (1969); crimes against humanity; European Convention on Human Rights (1950); fundamental rights within the EC/EU; International Covenant on Civil and Political Rights (ICCPR) (1966); International Covenant on Economic and Social Rights (1966); life, right to; United Nations Human Rights Committee (UNHRC); *and individual rights*
aid and **87,** 668-9

human rights (*cont.*)
alien, breach by **89,** 73
applicability, individuals who are not citizens of the country in which they live **103,** 229
applicable law
compensation
applicable principles of international law **95,** 315, 319
treaty **95,** 315, 319
European Convention on Human Rights (1950) **58,** 601-8, 609-13, **103,** 94-5, 102, 233-4, **108,** 421
International Covenant on Civil and Political Rights (ICCPR) (1966) **103,** 232-3
legislative provisions of third State **103,** 94-6, 101, 102
reparations for breach **116,** 274-5, 410-11, 498, **118,** 103
arbitrary detention or imprisonment, preventive detention **101,** 304-5
armed conflict **105,** 500, 505-6, **123,** 135-6
arms dealing and **91,** 253-4
assault, freedom from **70,** 227-34
basis, human personality **95,** 287
breach
individual's responsibility, enforcement of law of State as defence **116,** 335-6
reparations/compensation **125,** 515-16, 518-19
need for new principles **116,** 444-8
threat as **106,** 360-2
broad interpretation **88,** 236-7
burden of proof **100,** 630-1
civil service, access to **88,** 553-4
compensation for violations. *See* damages, for, human rights violations; just satisfaction (Art. 50 [41] of the European Convention on Human Rights (1950))
concept
progressive **79,** 311, 312
undefined **37,** 364
Constitution, under **90,** 546
entrenchment **103,** 155
constitutional rights and **70,** 202-3
conventions compared **75,** 44-8, 66-73
corporal punishment **91,** 398-405
defence, reasonable punishment **91,** 399, 400, 402
degrading, whether **91,** 400, 401-2, 403
motive, relevance **91,** 402-3
public **91,** 399-405
corporate rights **60,** 137-41, **123,** 497-8
criminal proceedings, *ne bis in idem,* Brussels Convention (1987) **111,** 150-3
cruel and unusual treatment or punishment, preventive detention **101,** 305
denial
League of Nations Covenant **37,** 6
Mandate **37,** 6
derogation **90,** 454-9, **125,** 566-8. *See also* exceptions *below*
balance of interests of State and individual **125,** 548, 566-8
balance of risk **106,** 365-6, **108,** 370-5, 377-8
constitutional provision **103,** 143, 151-5, 159, 186-8
express provision, need for **103,** 155
non-derogable rights **110,** 456

in time of armed conflict, applicable law **125,** 548
direct applicability **79,** 372
domestic jurisdiction and **57,** 250, **79,** 363, **105,** 483
ECOSOC. *See* United Nations Economic and Social Council (ECOSOC), Human Rights Commission; United Nations Economic and Social Council (ECOSOC), Human Rights Sub-Commission
effective remedy, need for **91,** 298, 301
need for **100,** 654-6
El Salvador, in **87,** 668-9, **88,** 11 n. 6
enforcement **76,** 468-9
environment law and **110,** 441, **116,** 123-4
evidence of conditions
Amnesty International reports **108,** 404, 414-15
diplomatic reports **108,** 401-2, 403, 414-15, 436
National Human Rights Commission reports **108,** 402, 416
UN Special Rapporteur reports **108,** 403, 415
evidence of violation, single incident, relevance **116,** 316
evolution **96,** 426-7
exceptions. *See also* derogation *above*
common law **103,** 163
legitimate authority, need for **103,** 290
pre-existing legislation **103,** 157-9
strict interpretation **103,** 150, 228
foreign State, liability to suit and **92,** 537
free choice of employment **37,** 469
genocide. *See* genocide
health **110,** 82-4
honour and reputation, protection of **54,** 511
humanitarian law and. *See* international humanitarian law, human rights and
implementation, modalities, national discretion **104,** 446
incorporation into municipal law **101,** 246-52, **104,** 440, 486, **115,** 645
treaties **123,** 517-19, 529-30, **124,** 409-11
Indians in South Africa, treatment of **37,** 541
individual's rights **77,** 248. *See also* European Convention on Human Rights (1950), individual's right to invoke; International Covenant on Political and Civil Rights (1966), individual
inviolable **79,** 331-5
individuals who are not citizens of the country in which they live, UN Draft Declaration (1978) **82,** 164-5
international law and, nature of rules for protection of **46,** 406, 511
international obligations in respect of **49,** 69, **57,** 582
judicial assistance **86,** 182
judicial protection **37,** 555-6
immunity, execution/attachment and **101,** 369, 404-5
immunity, jurisdiction and **101,** 369
restrictions
foreign policy interest **101,** 404
public interest **101,** 404
jus cogens/peremptory norm **85,** 261-2, **104,** 486
legal proceedings, right to institute, foreign court as option **101,** 393
legal rights, whether limited to **112,** 434-5, 445, 636, **115,** 644-5
Universal Declaration of Human Rights (1948) **112,** 435

human rights (*cont.*)
limitations **55,** 482, **70,** 144, 147-8, 157, 169, 173-83, 210-20
communal benefit **70,** 173, 175-6
emergency regulations **70,** 178, 242-8
national unity **70,** 147-8
public interest **70,** 144, 157, 169
public order/public policy/*ordre public* **70,** 210-20
public safety **70,** 173-6, 177, 183
'reasonably justifiable in a democratic society' **70,** 147, 176, 178-82
minority grouping, right to choose **92,** 211
minority rights. *See* minority rights
multinational corporation and **118,** 465-6
municipal courts **91,** 301-2
European Court of Human Rights compared **71,** 303
functions **71,** 303
municipal law and **91,** 364
primacy **101,** 463-4
nationality and **46,** 221, 511, **60,** 207
right to choose **92,** 169
nuclear weapons, deployment **106,** 360-2, 405-6
passport, right to. *See* passport
penal legislation, retroactivity and **57,** 177-9
petition, right of **37,** 474
power of court to prevent abuse **100,** 634, 654-6
preventive detention
arbitrary detention or imprisonment **101,** 304-5
cruel and unusual treatment or punishment **101,** 305
privacy, right of. *See* private life, respect for
property, protection of. *See* property, protection of
property rights **112,** 434-5, 445, 636, 682-3
proportionality. *See* proportionality, human rights
protection of, basis for **46,** 475
purpose of law
protection of victim **95,** 286
reparation **95,** 286
racial discrimination. *See* racial discrimination
racial equality. *See* racial discrimination
recognition of State and **92,** 178, 181, 191, 192, 193-4
refugee status and **90,** 151
remedies for breach
constitutional complaint **106,** 360
right to **89,** 70
right to export **117,** 524-5
right to truth and information **116,** 480
self-determination and **92,** 168-9
right dependent on observance of **108,** 470-1
separation of powers and **103,** 280-1
'shocking to the conscience' test **98,** 377, 379, 382-3, 420-1, **104,** 63, 83, **124,** 304, 320-1, 353, 360-3
slavery. *See* slavery
standing, condemned prisoners **100,** 628-31
State responsibility, acts outside its jurisdiction **98,** 299, 300-3, 404-6, **103,** 638, 639-49, 654

State succession and **92,** 165, 166
State's obligation to ensure protection **104,** 485, **116,** 521-2
obligation to make representations to third State in respect of alien **123,** 595-9
obligation to make representations to third State in respect of national **123,** 606-9
summary execution, *jus cogens*/peremptory norm **104,** 185
trade union. *See* trade union
treaties
extraterritorial application **123,** 97-102
reciprocity, relevance **108,** 45
Martens Clause (customary international law: applicability in case of gaps) **108,** 46
State succession. *See* treaties, State succession, human rights conventions
UN Charter **85,** 241 n. 6, **87,** 456
under Constitution, foreign State, assertability against **106,** 360, 361, 362
United Nations Charter provisions. *See* United Nations Charter (1945), human rights
violations, evidence
burden of proof **71,** 303
medical **71,** 298-9
waiver **104,** 440
war, effect of laws and customs of **105,** 500, 505-6
non-combatants, death, injury or loss **123,** 135-6
workers' rights, international organizations, need for machinery to protect **77,** 576
Yugoslavia, in **92,** 178, 181, 191, 192, 193-4
human rights, jurisdiction
concurrent **95,** 272
extraterritorial **103,** 639-51, 658-60
human shields
as crime against humanity **122,** 83-4
as war crime **108,** 91, 96, **122,** 73, 224-5
humanitarian assistance 37, 83
intelligence information **76,** 459
lawfulness **76,** 458-9
humanity, crimes against. *See* crimes against humanity; international humanitarian law; war crimes
Hungary
Anti-Comintern Pact, accession to **44,** 336
armistice with Allied Powers **44,** 310
Austria, Cooperation Protocol (1934) **44,** 208
continued existence (1944) **44,** 340-1
expropriation/nationalization, compensation, property confiscated under communist regime, discriminatory, whether **115,** 265-76
France, compensation agreement (1950) **47,** 53-6
German invasion (1944) **44,** 327, 334, 337-40
Head of State (1920), powers **44,** 334
independence, German influence post-1938 **44,** 332-42
Italy, Cooperation Protocol (1934) **44,** 335
Jews
deportation to Germany **44,** 338-9, 341
persecution, laws and measures **44,** 324-33
property, disposition of **44,** 330-2, 342-9, 350-8
law of
Law 37 (1948) (regulation of State undertakings) **65,** 296, 298
Law 32 (1950) (assumption of responsibility for nationalized undertakings) **65,** 290, 297-8

Hungary (*cont.*)
Law IV (1959) (retroactive abolition of Act 32 (1951)) **65,** 290, 298-9
Law 11 (1960) **65,** 299
Law XXV (1991) (compensation for confiscation of property) **115,** 269-76
discriminatory, whether **115,** 274-6
Law LXXVIII (1993) (privatization of residential property), discriminatory, whether **115,** 274-6
nationality laws **43,** 192-3
nationalization measures **65,** 17-19, 288-303, **72,** 85-8
rights and obligations, assumption **65,** 289-90, 295-303
nationals, right to inherit from estates in USA **44,** 208
occupation **72,** 84-5
existence as State, effect on **44,** 302
expropriation of industrial enterprises **72,** 84-5
Peace Treaty (1947)
decisive texts **44,** 308, 310
reparation provisions **44,** 312
restitution claims, waiver **44,** 310-12
restoration of property, acts of French authorities in Austria **44,** 2-4
waiver of claims against Germany **44,** 301-23, **45,** 436-45
property, privatization of State-owned residential property, priority to tenants, fairness **115,** 276
refugees from, status **72,** 641-5
Romania, Treaty of Trianon **44,** 334-6
claims for revision **44,** 336
USA, declaration of war on **44,** 336
USSR, participation in war against **44,** 336
Vienna Award (1940) **43,** 192
Western Allies, secret agreement on bombing **44,** 336
Hurd Deep 71, 101, **83,** 101
Hyderabad
British Government, treaty with (1853) **49,** 411
status in international law **64,** 487-9
Hydro-Congo. *See* Congo, Popular Republic, Hydro-Congo
Hymans Report (1920) (Mandates) 37, 31, 59-60, 100, **37,** 122-3, 362, 524

Iceland 62, 108-25
continental shelf **55,** 171, **56,** 86, 131-2
fishing rights over **55,** 218-19
economic interests **55,** 382
extradition to, review of conditions **96,** 109
fisheries **56,** 166-7. *See also* fisheries jurisdiction *and* fishing zones *below*
conservation measures **55,** 245-53, 262, 299, 308-10, 341-3, 358-9, 405-6, **56,** 218, 220
dependence on **56,** 170
EEC, agreement with **55,** 374-5
exclusive rights over **56,** 86, 90
FRG, Exchange of Notes (1961) **56,** 78, 79, 84, 100-1, 103-8, 109-10, 121-2, 124, 130, 132-5, 149-50, 151, 180, 198-9, 201, 255-7
preferential rights **56,** 131-2, 149-50, 153-4, 155, 160-1, 163, 170, 176-7
Regulations (1972) **56,** 162
special interest **55,** 308-10

fisheries jurisdiction. *See also* fisheries *above*; fishing zones *below*
Althing Resolution 1948 **56,** 153
Althing Resolution 1959 **56,** 85, 103, 130-1, 155
Althing Resolution 1972 **56,** 310-11
claim to **55,** 343
extension **55,** 168-75, 185, 189, 218, 222, 241-2, 249-56, 262, 291, 310-11, 353, 355-7, 361-3, 371, 388-90, 400-6, **56,** 83, 103, 132-3, 154-5, 199-200, 216-17, 218, 220
'opposability to UK' **55,** 353, 355, 371, 387, 397
unilateral **56,** 86-7, 124-5, 129, 149-50, 155, 158, 169, 171, 176, 200
violation of international law, whether **55,** 271-3, 370, 385-90, 396, 397-8, 406
preferential treatment **55,** 356
Regulations (1972) **56,** 167, 171, 180-1
special situation **55,** 356
fishing zones. *See also* fisheries *and* fisheries jurisdiction *above*
50-mile limit, *Fisheries Jurisdiction* cases **99,** 462
dispute with UK **55,** 246-53
agreement with (1961) **55,** 191, 297-303
negotiations **55,** 190-4, 249-56
extension **55,** 300
law of
Law 33/1922 **65,** 260
Law on Territorial Sea, Continental Shelf and Economic Zone 1979 **66,** 111
ships, State-owned, immunity, jurisdiction, master **65,** 258-60
State agency/State-owned corporation/State entity, classification, ship's master **65,** 258-60
treaties, State succession **96,** 107-9
USA, military cargo trade **86,** 22-32
treaty regulating **86,** 23, 24-31, 32
ICSID Convention (Convention on Settlement of Investment Disputes between States and Nationals of Other States (1965))
ad hoc Committee
Arbitration Rules, applicability **125,** 48-51
disqualification of members, competence to determine **125,** 46-51
task/powers
annulment on grounds set out in Article 52 **125,** 79-82
appeal court distinguished **125,** 79-80
assessment of facts **125,** 95-6
discretion **125,** 81
partial annulment **125,** 81-2
appeal procedure, exclusion **89,** 562-3, **125,** 79-80
award, annulment. *See* arbitral award, annulment
breach, sanction, need for **114,** 266
diplomatic protection, waiver of and **89,** 521
entry into force
Argentina **125,** 18
France **125,** 18
Jamaica **114,** 149
United States **114,** 150
exequatur, simplified procedure **65,** 90-1
interpretation

ICSID Convention (*cont.*)
aids
BITs **124,** 26
context **114,** 266
generally recognized principles of international law **89,** 520
IBRD Report (executive Directors) **106,** 545
legislative history **89,** 562
travaux préparatoires **106,** 522, **114,** 286, **125,** 23-4
applicable law, customary principles of treaty interpretation **114,** 268, 286
competence, *ad hoc* Committee **114,** 286
'dispute', formal claim, need for **89,** 579
guidelines, effectiveness **114,** 268, 286
object and purpose **89,** 392
encouragement of inward investment for economic development **106,** 652-3
facilitation of dispute settlement **106,** 652
removal of investment disputes from municipal courts **82,** 81
phrases
'any claims', 'the' claim distinguished **89,** 578-9
'arbitration proceedings', annulment proceedings, whether **125,** 48-9
'Centre' **106,** 569
'Contracting State', Hong Kong **106,** 520, 585
'investment' **106,** 717-18
'national of another Contracting State' **89,** 321-4, **124,** 26-9
'rules'/'*principes*' **114,** 266
'within the framework of the Convention . . . where it applies' **106,** 552-3, 554-6
ratification
Jamaica **114,** 149
United States **114,** 150
State immunity, as waiver **89,** 358
travaux préparatoires **89,** 524
Art. 26 **82,** 81, **106,** 522
ICSID (International Centre for the Settlement of Investment Disputes), Additional Facility, NAFTA provision for **119,** 621 n. 4, **121,** 32, 38-9, **122,** 255
ICSID (International Centre for the Settlement of Investment Disputes), Additional Facility Rules (Arbitration)
2 **121,** 32, 34, 41
2(1) **121,** 39
3 **119,** 677
4 **125,** 114
4(2) **119,** 622-3, **121,** 10
6 **125,** 114
14 **125,** 114
15 **121,** 32
18 **121,** 33
21 **119,** 622
27 **125,** 111-12
28 **119,** 622
38(3) **121,** 14
39 **121,** 15
39(2) **125,** 109
40(4) **121,** 60
41(2) **125,** 105
43 **121,** 12-13

44(2) **125,** 108, 109
48(1) **119,** 632
48(2) **119,** 633
49 **119,** 677-8
53(1) **119,** 677, 678, 680
58 **119,** 680-1
municipal law obligations and **125,** 108-9
UNCITRAL Rules distinguished **121,** 197-8
ICSID (International Centre for the Settlement of Investment Disputes), Administrative and Financial Regulations
14(e)(3) **89,** 656-7
15(1) **114,** 158
25 **124,** 11
ICJ as model **89,** 52
ICSID (International Centre for the Settlement of Investment Disputes), arbitral tribunal. *See also* arbitral tribunal; arbitration; BITs (bilateral investment treaties); ICSID Convention (Convention on Settlement of Investment Disputes between States and Nationals of Other States (1965)); Iran–US Claims Tribunal; NAFTA (North American Free Trade Agreement) (1992), Arbitral Tribunal
amendment of claims, admissibility, in light of developments subsequent to original filing **119,** 631-3, 669-70
applicable law
'in accordance with such rules of law as may be agreed by the parties' **114,** 207-8
complementary to national law **114,** 270
corrective to national law **114,** 270
secondary status **114,** 270
law of the State party **118,** 625, 626
civil and commercial law applicable in the State party **114,** 208
arbitration agreement, effect **72,** 162
arbitration request **67,** 160, 322, 351, **72,** 155
arbitrator
appointment, ICSID, by **67,** 323, 352, **72,** 155, 159, **118,** 627, **124,** 10
resignation **114,** 144-5, **121,** 32-3
withdrawal **67,** 352
award. *See* arbitral award
competence, provisional measures **82,** 81
confidentiality of proceedings **119,** 622-3
consent **114,** 144, 149
agreement between defendant government and foreign-controlled company **114,** 163-6
arbitration clause in investment agreement **114,** 150, 161-2
as interpreted by signatory **114,** 247-8
BIT, entry into force and **124,** 33-5
broadening of basis **114,** 161
forum prorogatum **114,** 163, 248
forum selection clause, effect **125,** 6
implied derogation **114,** 162, 250-1
notification to ICSID, effect **114,** 150-1
ratione materiae, timing **114,** 163
subsequent agreement, effect **114,** 162-3, 166, 238-42, 263
unilateral withdrawal **114,** 150-1
written **114,** 150

ICSID, arbitral tribunal (*cont.*)
constituent subdivision or agency as party to the proceedings
designation, proceedings involving Contracting State itself **125,** 23-4, 83
exclusion *ratione materiae* **125,** 24
constitution **114,** 144-5, 159, **125,** 9-10
costs
Centre **125,** 39, 97
parties' costs, each to pay own **125,** 39, 97
relevant factors
complexity of issues **125,** 39
novelty/public importance of issues **125,** 39, 97, 163
exclusive remedy rule **82,** 81, 84, **89,** 328
exhaustion of local administrative or judicial remedies **124,** 13-18
BIT provision **124,** 14-17
condition of consent to jurisdiction **124,** 14-17
decision on merits requirement **124,** 15-16
political subdivision, failure to challenge in local courts **125,** 34-8, 66-9
subsequent resort to arbitration, right of ('fork-in-the-road') **124,** 15-17, **125,** 7, 67-8, 69-73. *See also* BITs (bilatreal investment treaties), exclusive remedy rule
forum conveniens, whether **118,** 635-9
function **67,** 322-3, 332, **72,** 155, 161-2
interim measures. *See* provisional measures *below*
jurisdiction. *See also* exhaustion of local administrative or judicial remedies *above*
basis, consent. *See* consent *above*
compétence de la compétence **118,** 627, 630-1, **124,** 12
dispute between Contracting State and national of another Contracting State **106,** 519, 520
legal entity which, because of foreign control, the parties have agreed should be so treated. *See* foreign-controlled legal entity *below*
ex aequo et bono **67,** 353, 358, 366, 375-83
foreign-controlled legal entity **114,** 163-6
change of nationality **114,** 164-5
critical date **114,** 165-6
ICSID arbitration clause as agreement **114,** 164
interpretation of concession agreement **125,** 7
interpretation of linked agreement with non-ICSID arbitration clause **114,** 218
linked agreement as aid to interpretation **114,** 263
legal dispute arising directly out of investment **106,** 519-20, **114,** 149
dispute relating to clearly identified matters, need for **124,** 34
'existence' **124,** 33-5
'investment' **106,** 717-18, **114,** 149
municipal courts, right to determine **118,** 634
preliminary issue **114,** 145-6, **124,** 12-13
tribunal's examination *proprio motu* **114,** 146
legal status **72,** 161
self-contained jurisdictional system **118,** 627-8
parties, failure to appear **63,** 539, **114,** 145, 146
precedent, decisions of another arbitral tribunal **119,** 639, 667-8
president, appointment, by Chairman of the Administrative Council **124,** 10-11, 155
procedure **67,** 323-5, 352-60, **72,** 159
default, conduct amounting to **67,** 354-5, 357-60
language **124,** 38
Motion for Directions **121,** 13-14

procedural order **67,** 360, **119,** 622-3
production of documents **67,** 359-60, **119,** 624, **121,** 13-14, 15
seat **114,** 159
statutory limitation and **124,** 57
submissions, on material produced during hearings **106,** 594
time-limits
extension **67,** 354-5, 357-60, **106,** 598, 599-600, **121,** 16, **125,** 8
failure to reply to claims **106,** 423
Tribunal's power to formulate own rules **106,** 584
witnesses. *See* witnesses *below*
written proceedings, additional **121,** 14-15
proper party, foreign investor in 'national' of another Contracting State **124,** 26-8
provisional measures **82,** 80-5, **124,** 7-9
burden of proof **124,** 7
domestic courts' right to order, parties' express consent, need for **124,** 7 n. 1
as extraordinary measure **124,** 7
purpose, preservation of rights in dispute **124,** 7
'recommend'/'order' **124,** 7
requirements
existing right **124,** 8
subject-matter of case, relationship with **124,** 8
remedies, powers relating to **118,** 637
seat **114,** 159, **122,** 255, **125,** 10
settlement **114,** 151 n. 4
stay of proceedings by national court **118,** 621-40
requirements
application by other party for stay **118,** 630
commencement of proceedings by party to Convention in national court **118,** 629
nexus between ICSID and national court proceedings **118,** 630-1
witnesses
attendance **121,** 16-17
contact with non-party **121,** 12-13
ICSID (International Centre for the Settlement of Investment Disputes), Rules (Arbitration) (1968/1984)
3 **106,** 513
3(1)(a)(i) **106,** 513
4 **106,** 513, **114,** 144, **124,** 37
5(1) **106,** 423
6 **106,** 423, **125,** 10, 47, 52-8, 59
6(1) **106,** 513, **114,** 159, **124,** 5, 11, 38
8 **114,** 145
9 **89,** 379, **125,** 47-8, 49-50
9(3) **125,** 47-8
13 **65,** 538, **114,** 145
13(1) **125,** 10
19 **124,** 40
20 **106,** 513, **114,** 159
26 **114,** 276
27 **89,** 350
32(3) **124,** 12, 39
34 **89,** 541
34(2)(a) **124,** 40-1
38 **124,** 36, **125,** 13

ICSID, Rules (Arbitration) (*cont.*)
38(1) **114,** 160, **124,** 43
38(2) **114,** 160, **124,** 43
39 **82,** 81, **89,** 404
39(1) 8, **89,** 404, **124,** 7
39(5) **124,** 7 n. 1
40 **89,** 576, 578, **106,** 623
41 **89,** 380
41(2) **106,** 568
41(3) **89,** 380, **124,** 12, 39, **125,** 11
41(4) **114,** 151, **124,** 40
46 **114,** 283-4
47 **89,** 350, **106,** 562, **124,** 36
47(1)(j) **114,** 310
48 **124,** 58
49(1)(d) **124,** 60
49(2) **89,** 525, **124,** 58-9
49(4) **124,** 60-1
50 **89,** 525, 528-9, **106,** 593
50(2) **125,** 59
52(2) **125,** 59
53 **114,** 310, **125,** 47, 59
53 [1968] **125,** 50
54(2) **89,** 518
55 **89,** 578, 579
lacunae **89,** 529
ICSID (International Centre for the Settlement of Investment Disputes), Rules (Conciliation) (1968/1984), 30(2) **106,** 568
ICSID (International Centre for the Settlement of Investment Disputes), Rules (Institution) (1968/1984)
1 **114,** 144, 158
2 **106,** 584, **114,** 158
4 **114,** 158
5 **124,** 9, 36
6(1) **114,** 144
7 **124,** 10, 1054
'Ihlen declaration' 37, 69, 78, 117, **50,** 377-9
illegal act. *See* international tort/wrong
illegitimate child
adoption by mother **58,** 571-93
affiliation **58,** 571-3
capitis deminutio **58,** 574
Convention on the Legal Status of Children Born out of Wedlock (1975) **58,** 574, 583
discrimination **58,** 578-9, 581, **88,** 216
family life **58,** 572, 580-4
family relations **58,** 584-6
inheritance **58,** 573, 591
possession, peaceful enjoyment of **58,** 591-2
property/patrimonial rights **58,** 586-90
status **58,** 604-6, **72,** 38-9
Legal Status of Children Born out of Wedlock, European Convention (1975) **89,** 180
succession **88,** 220, **89,** 218-19
voluntary disposition **58,** 573

Ilois. *See* British Indian Ocean Territory (BIOT), Ilois
IMF. *See* International Monetary Fund Agreement (IMF) (1944) (Bretton Woods Agreement)
immigration 81, 145-83. *See also* aliens; visa
appeals **81,** 154-6
controls, burden of proof **81,** 153
definition **45,** 334
discretion **95,** 607
discrimination and **81,** 149, 171-7
judicial review **85,** 212
Ministry of Foreign Affairs' role **85,** 207
national interest and **85,** 213
nationality laws and **81,** 145
procedures, inhuman or degrading treatment **103,** 181-2, 198
proceedings, *audi alteram partem* **68,** 171-3, **69,** 212-13, **70,** 369-72, **71,** 454, 480, 490, **87,** 128
removal of immigrant **61,** 252-4, 257
responsibility for **95,** 586, 588-9, 605-8, 610
spouse, rights of **81,** 149, 151-2, 153-4
visa application, misrepresentation of material fact **95,** 517-21, 525
work permit requirements **81,** 149
impartial tribunal. *See* independent and impartial tribunal
import restrictions
licences, EEC Treaty and **48,** 233-6
voluntary, as international agreements **61,** 7-9, 12, 13-15, 17-18, 21, 25
Inca civilization, sustainable development principle 116, 115
incommunicado detention. *See* American Convention on Human Rights (1969), detention incommunicado; detention, incommunicado; International Covenant on Political and Civil Rights (1966), detention, incommunicado
incorporation. *See* international law, municipal law and
indemnification. *See* compensation; compensation for war-related events; damages; just satisfaction (Art. 50 [41] of the European Convention on Human Rights (1950)); reparations
indemnity, international organizations, Member States, against **81,** 681-2, 722-5
independent and impartial tribunal 89, 81-2, **105,** 372, 437-8, 553
American Convention on Human Rights (1969) **89,** 81-2, **105,** 372
'competent, impartial and independent tribunal established by law' **105,** 472, 475-6, 563, 565
'established by law' **62,** 342, **68,** 141-2, **75,** 506-7, 550-1
as autonomous concept **120,** 118
in unrecognized State **120,** 76, 118-19
evidence of **78,** 330-2
impartiality **68,** 130-41, **71,** 401, 418-19, 425-6
presumption of **71,** 425
judicial impartiality. *See* judicial impartiality
objective test **121,** 333-6
right to hearing before **62,** 321, 326, 334-43, 345, 348, 354, 356, **68,** 119-20
content of rights distinguished **120,** 74-6
fact, question of **62,** 340-1
law **62,** 340-1
state of emergency and **96,** 400-1, 403, **123,** 155
status as
administrative appeals board **86,** 363-5
administrative court with limited powers of review **96,** 580-2

independent and impartial tribunal (*cont.*)
Appeals Council **62,** 341-2
Board of Prison Visitors **78,** 329, 350
court of appeal **81,** 47
courts in northern Cyprus **120,** 73-7, 104-6, 113-14, 116, 120-2, 141-2
courts in the Philippines **82,** 56
Disabled Persons Board **96,** 581
European Commission **111,** 135
Immigration and Refugee Board **118,** 247, 248-9
International Criminal Tribunal for the Former Yugoslavia **105,** 372, 437-8, 553, 612, **121,** 212
military tribunal **58,** 75, **78,** 247, 249, **116,** 387, **120,** 16, 105-6
organs of medical association **62,** 325-8, 332-4, 358
Prison Board of Visitors **78,** 329-32
Provisional Governor **96,** 581
Real Property Transactions Authority **81,** 15-18, 20-1
independent legal entity. *See* State agency/State-owned corporation/State entity
India. *See also* British India; India/Pakistan relations; Indian States
acquired rights, State succession **118,** 438-9
act of State
classification as, expulsion of alien **64,** 426
State succession, contractual obligations **45,** 19-24
territorial limitation, act in own State **64,** 426
Aitchison's Treaties **50,** 266, 419, 432, 498
aliens, detention, international obligations and **92,** 551-3
applicable law, multinational corporation **118,** 509
arbitrary laws, equality and **118,** 466-7
Atlas, origin of **50,** 155-6
Bangladesh, boundary demarcation. *See* Bangladesh, India, boundary demarcation; Pakistan, Islamic Republic
Baroda State Railway, separate legal entity, whether **92,** 518-20
BeruBari Union **53,** 182-3
territorial sovereignty **70,** 43-50
Bhopal gas leak disaster. *See* Bhopal gas leak disaster
Bombay Administration Reports **50,** 250-5, 419, 433
Bombay Government Resolutions, effect **50,** 302-3, 305-16, 417-18
boundaries, under British rule **50,** 80-105
British rule, boundaries under **50,** 80-105
citizenship
acquisition, intention to reside permanently, need for **45,** 330-9
Central Government to decide **53,** 522-3
competence of courts to determine **45,** 340-5
Constitution 1950 **45,** 329-39, 341, 344-65
intention to reside permanently **45,** 330, 332, 333-8
division of India, effect **45,** 335, 359
loss or deprivation of **45,** 348-9, 351, 361
possession of foreign passport **53,** 521, 524
comity, State immunity, jurisdiction **64,** 401
constituent States **53,** 141-8. *See also* Goa, Daman and Diu; Indian Native States; Indian States; Sikkim
Constitution 1950 **49,** 352, 354, 359, 361-4, 389-90, 429, 438, 464, 481, 484, 492, 494, **55,** 87-8

Amendment Acts
Nine (1960), in force, whether **92,** 559-61, 568-9, 576
Twelve (1962) **118,** 432
Twenty-six (1971) **118,** 428
Thirty-six (1975) **118,** 422-3, 428
Forty (1976) **92,** 583
Art. 1 **92,** 557, **118,** 423
Art. 1(3)(c) **118,** 432
Art. 14 **91,** 329-30, **118,** 466, 468, 484, 491, 493, 510, **125,** 521-2
Art. 15 **125,** 521
Art. 19 **118,** 467, 468, 510, **125,** 521-2
Art. 21 **118,** 466-9, 491, 493, 509, 510, **125,** 514-15, 521-2
Art. 22(5) **92,** 542, 543-4, 548-53
Art. 32 **92,** 547, **118,** 465, 468, **125,** 511, 515-16, 521-2, 524-6
Art. 37 **92,** 504
Art. 38 **118,** 472
Art. 39 **118,** 472
Art. 39A **118,** 472
Art. 42 **125,** 522
Art. 48A **118,** 509
Art. 51 **92,** 504, 528, **118,** 509, **125,** 523
Art. 51-A **125,** 522
Art. 73 **125,** 523
Art. 123(1) **118,** 432
Art. 133(1)(a) **118,** 431
Art. 133(1)(b) **118,** 431
Art. 136 **118,** 478
Art. 141 **125,** 526
Art. 142 **118,** 478
Art. 145(1) **92,** 504
Art. 226 **125,** 515-16
Art. 240 **118,** 432
Art. 245(1) **92,** 504
Art. 253 **92,** 504, **125,** 523
Art. 297 **92,** 583
Art. 372 **53,** 167, 171-2
Art. 372(1) **92,** 505, 507
Art. 394 **92,** 557
Boundary Agreement with Pakistan, implementation **53,** 182-3, 192-203
citizenship. *See* citizenship, Constitution *above*
commencement **53,** 186-8
continuance of existing law **53,** 144-6
development in accordance with changing international standards **118,** 509
foreign State, definition **53,** 97-100
freedom of movement **45,** 351
fundamental rights and freedoms, freedom of expression **70,** 212-13
preamble **118,** 472, 473
property
protection of rights **49,** 354, 462
succession to **49,** 422-44, 448, 461, 464-5
territory, inviolability **53,** 200-2
continuity of law **49,** 422-68, **53,** 170, 174-6, **55,** 87-8, **118,** 431, 436-46

India (*cont.*)
contract
effect of partition on **53,** 117-29
enforcement, by agent **64,** 536-7, 538
customary international law, municipal law and **92,** 505-7
Customs Line transactions **50,** 201-6
death penalty, delay in carrying out, relevance **98,** 352-3
definition, Interpretation Act 1889 **50,** 69
deportation, nationality and **45,** 346-52
detention
aliens
convicted prisoner distinguished **92,** 552-3
International Covenant on Civil and Political Rights (ICCPR) (1966) **92,** 551-2
International Covenant on Economic, Social and Cultural Rights (1966) **92,** 551-2
international obligations to be respected **92,** 551-3
Universal Declaration on Human Rights (1948) **92,** 551
purpose
breaking links of offender **92,** 551
prevention of criminal activity **92,** 551
reasons for, right to know in language understood by detainee **92,** 542-8
representation, right to make **92,** 248-51
delay in dealing with **92,** 249-51
transfer of detainee to home country to serve sentence
applicable law **92,** 552
length of sentence **92,** 552
preventive detention distinguished **92,** 552-3
Directive Principles of State Policy **118,** 472, 473
EEZ
extent
200 miles **92,** 583-4
territorial sea, effect on **92,** 583-4
foreign vessels
hired by nationals **118,** 448-51
permits, need for **118,** 449-50
remedies for breach, confiscation of vessels **118,** 450-1
effective remedy, need for **118,** 483-4
enclaves
Bangladesh/India Agreement providing for the Exchange of Enclaves (1974)
1982 Exchange of Letters as integral part **92,** 564
cession of territory, whether **92,** 535, 560-1, 564, 568, 569, 572-3
constitutional amendment, need for, whether **92,** 575-6
jurisdiction under **92,** 564-5, 574-5
notification in Official Gazette, need for, whether **92,** 575-7
ratification. *See* treaties, ratification *below*
sovereignty, effect on **92,** 567-8, 572, 576
right of access
customary international law, under **92,** 574
military, paramilitary and armed police **92,** 574
equality, arbitrariness and **118,** 466-7
evidence, taking of, abroad **84,** 741
evidence of, State immunity, jurisdiction, procedural aspects, executive certificate **64,** 507-8

exclusion of alien
act of State **92,** 502
Gleneagles Accord (1977) **92,** 503-4, 507-9
UK citizen, exemption **92,** 503
executive certificate/statement, conclusiveness, recognition, State **63,** 30, **64,** 515-19, 522
extraditable offence
'extradition offence' **125,** 531-2
trial for other offences **125,** 530-6
extradition
applicable law, municipal/international law **125,** 534-6
Extradition Act 1962 **78,** 109
speciality
customary international law **125,** 535-6
treaty rule **125,** 535-6
transfer of convicted prisoners and **92,** 552
United Kingdom **72,** 68, **78,** 106-11
extradition agreement
need for **125,** 534-6
State succession and **78,** 106-11
fair hearing
administrative power, challenge to **92,** 538-9
natural justice **118,** 491-8, 523-4
right to be heard **118,** 496-501
foreign State, proceedings involving. *See also* State immunity *below*
consent of forum government, need for **64,** 397-400, 411, 422, 425, 521-2, 537-8, **92,** 512, 514, 516-29, 533, 536, **118,** 423-4
discretionary **92,** 533
merits distinguished **92,** 537-8
refusal, non-arbitrary **92,** 537, 538-9
forum State's right to legislate for **64,** 502-3
private right **64,** 497-8
recognition, need for **118,** 425-7
right to sue and be sued **64,** 502-3
human rights and **92,** 537
immovable property in forum State, need for **92,** 536-7
State agency distinguished **92,** 517-26
GDR, recognition of **64,** 505-6, 514-15, 518-19
Goa, Daman and Diu. *See* Goa, Daman and Diu
good faith, *bona fide* representation of interests **118,** 491
government
obligations, protection of constitutional rights **118,** 469-70
salt monopoly **50,** 340
treaty-making power **53,** 192, 204
Governor-General, extraterritorial jurisdiction **38,** 4, 8
hazardous activities
damage caused by
disaster fund, need for **118,** 509-10, 525-6
procedural reform, need for **118,** 526
recommendations for control **118,** 504, 506-10, 526
Head of State
income tax, exemption **53,** 568-74, **64,** 406-7, 421, 483-9, 524-34
proceedings involving

India (*cont.*)
consent of central government, need for **64,** 397-400, 411, 422, 425, 448, 480-2, 521-2, 537-8
proceedings against State distinguished **64,** 413-15
'Ruler of a foreign State' **64,** 400-1
as State **64,** 397-401, 413, 497-8, 528
Head of State, diplomatic privileges and immunities, entitlement, personal, whether **64,** 400-1
Head of State, execution/attachment, personal private property **64,** 438-9
Head of State, immunity, execution/attachment **64,** 501-2
Head of State, immunity, jurisdiction **64,** 397-401, 406-7, 412, 415, 419-25, 538, **92,** 520, 524, 526
criminal proceedings **64,** 408-9
customary international law **64,** 409
personal entitlement **64,** 400-1, 412-13, 502-3
personal sovereign **64,** 397-9
private acts **64,** 422-3
private acts **64,** 422-3
as privilege **64,** 448
State immunity distinguished **64,** 397-401, 411, 413, 421-2, 495-8
'trading within local limits of the Court' and **64,** 407, 425
human rights
breach, reparations/compensation **125,** 515-16, 518-19
foreign State, liability to suit and **92,** 537
independence
continuity of law **53,** 144-6, **55,** 87-8, **118,** 431, 436-46
penal laws **118,** 444-5
extradition agreement **55,** 87-8
native States, position of **49,** 378-9
partition of territory **53,** 184
transfer of power from British Government **53,** 183-4
International Covenant on Civil and Political Rights (ICCPR) (1966)
applicability, detention of alien **92,** 551-2
enforceability, individual, by **92,** 507-8
implementing legislation, need for **125,** 515-19
reservations, compensation for victims of unlawful arrest or detention **125,** 518-19
international law
municipal law and **64,** 410-11
interpretation in light of **92,** 551-2
primacy **64,** 517, 519-22, **92,** 520, 521-3, 526-7
judge, disqualification, authorization to act in case of necessity **118,** 490
judicial independence, Beijing Statement of Principles of the Independence of the Judiciary in the LAWASIA region (1995) **125,** 524
Junagadh, status following termination of British protection **49,** 377, 379, 382, 384-8, 392-5
jurisdiction
concurrent **92,** 564-5, 574-5
sovereignty, effect on **92,** 565, 574-5
diplomatic premises, maintenance work
lex loci contractus **92,** 533
lex situs **92,** 533, 536
foreign ship
holder of national certificate of competency **92,** 584
outside territorial sea **92,** 584

lex loci delicti commissi **92,** 532
Teen Bigha **92,** 564-5, 574-5
territorial **92,** 536, 584
Kutch Administration Reports **50,** 240-4, 418, 433, 446, 495-6, 512
land, purchase by State, Customs Line transactions **50,** 201-6
law of
Agricultural Income Tax Act (Assam) 1949 **64,** 421
Agricultural Income Tax Act (Bengal) 1944 **64,** 531
applicability in Sikkim **118,** 424-5
Bhopal Gas Leak Disaster (Processing of Claims) Act 1985. *See* Bhopal gas leak disaster, Bhopal Gas Leak Disaster (Processing of Claims) Act 1985
British Statutes (Application to India) Repeal Act 1960 **84,** 741
citizenship, loss of, freedom of movement and **45,** 351
Citizenship Act 1955 **53,** 521, 524
Citizenship Rules **53,** 521, 524
Civil Procedure Code 1908 **84,** 741
gaps **64,** 438, 512
just, fair and reasonable **118,** 494-5
O I r 8 **118,** 496, 522
O I r 8(4) **118,** 496
O VII r 11 **64,** 396, 536
O XXIII r 1 **118,** 496
O XXIII r 3(b) **118,** 496-7
O XXIII r 33 **118,** 520
O XXIII r 38 **118,** 522
'Ruler of a foreign State' **64,** 400-1, 412, 499-500
s 84(1) (right of suit by State to enforce private rights) **64,** 497
s 86 (Ruler of a Foreign State: immunity, jurisdiction) **64,** 395-422, 447-8, 480-1, 486, 490-503, 506, 510, 519-23, 530-1, 537-8, **92,** 514, 516-29, 533, 536-9
s 86(1) (Ruler of a foreign State: immunity, jurisdiction) **64,** 397, 412-13, 415, 421, 495-503, 519-23, **118,** 425-503
s 86(2)(0) (consent of Central Government) **64,** 499, 537-8
s 86(2)(b) (institution of suit against ruler of a foreign State when trading within local limits of Court) **64,** 407, 425
s 86(3) (Ruler: immunity from arrest) **64,** 495, 499
s 86(4) (extension of s 86 provisions to certain categories of Officers) **64,** 499
s 87 (Ruler of a foreign State: right of suit) **64,** 413-15, 448, 486, 499, **86,** 395-422, **92,** 516, 524
s 87A (Head of State/State immunity) **64,** 397, 412-13, 499-501, **118,** 425-8
s 87B (Ruler of a former Indian State: immunity) **64,** 399-401, 494-5
Sikkim, applicability in **118,** 424-5
State immunity and **64,** 397-401, 412, 438, 447-8, 538, **118,** 423-7
Conservation of Foreign Exchange and Prevention of Smuggling Activities Act 1974
s 3 **92,** 541
s 11 **92,** 549
Constitution. *See* Constitution 1950 *above*
continuity of **53,** 144-6, **55,** 87-8
Contract Act, s 230 **64,** 536-7
Criminal Procedure Code
s 197A(2) (Ruler of former Indian State: immunity from criminal jurisdiction) **64,** 408-9
s 482 **92,** 581
Customs Act **92,** 541

India (*cont.*)
English common law as part of **53,** 167-8, 171-2, **64,** 406-7, 419-20
Extradition Act 1962 **78,** 109
s 2(c) ('extradition offence') **125,** 532
s 2(d) ('extradition treaty') **125,** 532
s 2(e) ('foreign State') **125,** 532
s 21 (trial for previous offence) **125,** 530-6
s 21 (trial for previous offence) (as amended 1993) **125,** 531, 532-3
Fatal Accidents Act 1846 **118,** 525
revision, need for **118,** 525
Foreigners Act 1946, s 3 **92,** 502-4
Foreigners Act **45,** 340-5, 346, 348, 350
Goa, Daman and Diu. *See* Goa, Daman and Diu *for laws relating to*
Income tax Act 1922 **64,** 421, 483-9, 524-34
Industries (Development and Regulation) Act, s 18A **118,** 493
Interpretation Act 1889 **50,** 69
Limitation Act 1963, request for consent to sue foreign government and **92,** 539
Maritime Zones of India Act 1981
purpose **118,** 449
s 3 **118,** 449
s 5 **118,** 448, 450
s 5(6) **118,** 448, 450
s 7 **118,** 448
s 10 **118,** 450
s 11 **118,** 450
s 12 **118,** 450
s 12(a) **118,** 449
s 12(b) **118,** 449
s 13 **118,** 30, 448
Maritime Zones of India Rules 1982
8(1)(q) **118,** 449, 450
16 **118,** 448
Merchant Shipping Act 1958
s 2 **92,** 580, 581, 584
s 21 **92,** 581-2
s 358 **92,** 580
s 363 **92,** 579-81, 584
Orissa Preventive Detention Act 1970 **92,** 503
Penal Code **52,** 376-7
s 375 (rape) **121,** 270 n. 209
Protection of Human Rights Act 1993 **125,** 527
Punjab Restoration of Jagirs Act 1957 **49,** 336-8, 346-7
Representation of the People Act 1951, s 90(2) **118,** 495
Sea Customs Act 1878 **78,** 599-600
sedition **70,** 215-16
States Merger (West Bengal) Order 1949 **92,** 558
Territorial Waters, Continental Shelf, Exclusive Economic Zone and other Maritime Zones Act 1976
s 2 **92,** 582
s 3 **92,** 582-3
s 5 **92,** 583 n.
s 7 **92,** 583 n.
Terrorist and Disruptive Activities (Prevention) Act 1987 **125,** 531

legislation
binding effect on Government **53,** 165-71, 174-7
territorial limitation **92,** 584
validity
reasonableness **118,** 464-5, 484-5
remedies in case of invalidity **118,** 477
restrictions on fundamental rights **118,** 464-7
validity of implementation distinguished **118,** 476, 489, 511-12, 519
legislation, interpretation
aids, legislative history, parliamentary proceedings **118,** 490
guidelines
consistency within Statute **64,** 400-1
effectiveness **118,** 488
expressio unius est exclusio alterius **64,** 421
intention of legislature **118,** 488
plain language **92,** 517
restrictive **92,** 517
phrases
'claimant' **118,** 461, 490
'claims' **118,** 461, 478
'claims', monetary claims, limitation to **118,** 470
'foreign State' **92,** 516, **118,** 423, 425-7
'Indian ship' **92,** 581-2
'Ruler' **92,** 516-17
'shall also be liable to confiscation' **118,** 450
presumption of conformity with international obligations **64,** 421, **92,** 526
liability, hazardous activities **118,** 479-83, 506-10
life, right to, police operations, death during **125,** 511-18
maps and documents, inspection of for arbitration **50,** 17
maritime jurisdiction[s], separate concepts **92,** 583-4
measure of damages/compensation including valuation of company/property/assets, ability to pay **118,** 500
Merger Agreement, Miraj and Bombay **49,** 474
multinational corporation
enforcement of judgments **118,** 526
UN Code of Conduct for Transnational Corporations (1986), implementation **118,** 508-9
nationality **49,** 504-6
native States. *See* Indian Native States
natural justice
claims settlement and **118,** 468, 523-4
exercise of government power and **92,** 538-9
fair hearing **118,** 491-8, 523-4
nemo judex in sua propria causa principle **118,** 489, 490-1
necessity, disqualification of judge, authorization to act **118,** 490
parens patriae **118,** 471-6, 485-6, 521-3
Pondicherry, France, cession **49,** 484-96
Proclamation of Queen Victoria (1858) **50,** 68, 74, 382, 401-3, 411, 459, 465, 466, **60,** 71
recognition, State
de facto/de jure distinguished **64,** 517-19
evidence of, executive certificate/statement, conclusiveness **63,** 30, **64,** 515-19, 522
revenue settlements **49,** 345

India (*cont.*)
Rulers. *See* Indian States, Rulers
salt monopoly **50,** 340
servitudes, self-imposed restraint, as **92,** 574
Shipping Corporation of India **63,** 364-9, 639-46
Sikkim. *See* Sikkim
South Africa, Indians in, treatment of **37,** 540-1
sovereignty
British assumption of **49,** 336-9
as bundle of rights **92,** 573
limitations on **92,** 566-8, 574, 576
customary **92,** 574
enclave, right of access to **92,** 567-8, 576
powers, promotion of subjects' interests **118,** 475-6
State agency/State-owned corporation/State entity
classification
food supply agency **64,** 445-6, 447
national airline **64,** 432, 433-4, 436, 447, 454, 474
Register of Shipping **92,** 512
shipping line **64,** 537-8
as government department **64,** 436-7
State Bank
government functions of officials **63,** 83-4
nature of operations **63,** 83-5
as State agency **63,** 82-5, 88-91
State immunity, jurisdiction, applicability
in own courts, foreign State immunity distinguished **64,** 423-4
in own courts as standard **92,** 536
State immunity, jurisdiction, classification of act **92,** 527-8
anti-terrorist measures **125,** 512-15
commercial activities **64,** 424-5
State immunity, jurisdiction, entitlement
agent of foreign State **92,** 523
government department **64,** 436-7
recognition of State/government, relevance **64,** 512-15
Register of Shipping **92,** 512
republican State **64,** 398, 401, 415, 500-1, 572
State agency/State-owned corporation/State entity **92,** 517-20, 523, 524-6, 527
determination of status as, preliminary matter **92,** 527
State immunity, jurisdiction, procedural aspects
applicable law, forum State **118,** 424-6
consent of forum State, relevance. *See* foreign State, proceedings involving, consent of forum government, need for *above*
effective remedy, right to, arbitration between forum government and government sued, recommendation for **92,** 539
entitlement to raise, joinder of State, relevance **64,** 438-9, 474-5
in personam actions, commercial activity **64,** 423, 425
need to plead **118,** 424
preliminary issue, whether **64,** 510-12, **92,** 529
procedural bar **118,** 424
State immunity, jurisdiction, theory/doctrine
absolute theory **92,** 521

acta jure imperii/acta jure gestionis distinguished, difficulty **64,** 402, 406, 424
basis **64,** 409-10
comity **64,** 401, **92,** 512
dignity of foreign State **92,** 534
equality of States **92,** 534, 538
non-intervention in affairs of another State **92,** 538
par in parem non habet jurisdictionem **64,** 401-2, 416
reciprocity **64,** 409-10, 426-8
customary international law **92,** 533-4
development of concept **64,** 402-6
role of English law and **64,** 406-7, 438-53, 455-74
general principle of international law **92,** 512
Head of State immunity distinguished **64,** 399-400, 411, 413-15, 422
international law, modification **92,** 520, 521-3
State immunity, jurisdiction, waiver
authority, need for **64,** 478-9
clear and unequivocal communication, need for **64,** 453
implied, failure to raise immunity promptly **118,** 424, 427-8
submission to the jurisdiction as **64,** 396-7, 428-9, 449-53, 475-8, **118,** 427
conditional appearance **64,** 438, 454-5, 478
State responsibility for acts and omissions of police officer **125,** 511-18
State succession
continuity of law **49,** 422-68, **53,** 144-6, 170, 174-6, **55,** 87-8, **118,** 431, 436-46
contractual obligations **45,** 19-24, **53,** 183-4
Declaration of automatic succession (1956) **78,** 109
India Extradition Act 1962 **78,** 109
India Independence (International Arrangements) Order 1947 **78,** 109
India Independence (Rights, Property and Liability) Order 1947, contract, effect on **53,** 183-4
India–Pakistan Devolution Agreement (1947) **78,** 109
to vassal States **50,** 4, 81, 215, 412, 422, 500
status during period of transition from British rule **84,** 205
Survey of **50,** 109, 113-23
authority of **50,** 121, 421-2, 431, 466, 479, 485-6
functions and methods **50,** 114-15, 117-19, 122-3, 428-31, 485
history **50,** 117
maps, distribution of **50,** 123-6, 421, 431
Osmaston's Survey 1937-8 **50,** 134-50, 445, 482-5, 493
pre-Survey maps **50,** 126-34, 478
Teen Bigha
Bangladesh, exercise of rights relating to **92,** 561, 572-6
jurisdiction **92,** 564-5, 574-5
lease in perpetuity **92,** 562-5, 571, 575-6
sovereignty over **92,** 561, 565, 572
territorial sea
breadth, 12 miles **92,** 582-4
EEZ, extension, effect on **92,** 583-4
power of government to amend in accordance with international law and State practice **92,** 582-3
territory
annexation. *See* Goa, Daman and Diu
cession
constitutional amendment, need for **92,** 573

India (*cont.*)
of French territories in **44,** 47, 395-6
to Pakistan **53,** 197-201
inviolability, constitutional provisions **53,** 200-2
lease in perpetuity **92,** 562-5, 571, 575-6
servitudes, self-imposed restraint, as **92,** 574
treaties
amendment, unimplemented agreement **92,** 569
Bangladesh/India Agreement providing for the Exchange of Enclaves (1974). *See* enclaves, Bangladesh/India Agreement providing for the Exchange of Enclaves (1974) *above*
enforceability, individual, by **92,** 504-8
estoppel, private law expression, use of, as **92,** 571
extradition, Italy **78,** 106-11
heads of government, between, treaty nature **92,** 570-1
implementation, obligation, whether **92,** 504
implementing legislation, need for **92,** 508, 558-9, 575-7, **125,** 518-19
as part of municipal law **92,** 504-8, **125,** 523
continuity of British law and **92,** 504-5
ratification
absence, effect **92,** 565-6
conduct, by **92,** 570-1
requirement **92,** 565-6, 570-1
United Kingdom **72,** 68, **78,** 106-11
power of executive **53,** 192, 204
treaties, State succession, extradition treaties. *See* extradition agreement, State succession and *above*
treaty interpretation
aids
international law **92,** 571
private law analogy **92,** 571
guidelines
object and purpose **92,** 571-2
terms of agreement **92,** 571
phrases, 'lease in perpetuity' **92,** 571-2
Union of. *See also* Indian States
Covenants forming, treaty character **49,** 375
formation **118,** 422
Goa, Daman and Diu. *See* Goa, Daman and Diu
merger of Indian States **45,** 19-24, **53,** 189
Sikkim and. *See* Sikkim
Versailles Peace Conference, status at **37,** 529
women
discrimination in the field of employment, Elimination of all Forms of Discrimination against Women, Convention on (1979) **125,** 524-6
sexual harassment, measures to prevent **125,** 521-9
Guidelines and Norms (1997) **125,** 526-9
relevant international instruments **125,** 524-6
relevant legislation **125,** 522-3
India/Pakistan relations 50, 150, **70,** 43-4, 46
BeruBari Union, transfer to Pakistan
deprivation of citizenship and property without compensation, whether **92,** 560
effected, whether **92,** 559-61, 569-70

boundaries **53,** 182-3, 185-204, **70,** 43-4
demarcation **53,** 182-3, 185, 194-204, **70,** 43-4, 46
boundary dispute, India–Pakistan Boundaries Disputes Tribunal **53,** 187-8
cease-fire and arbitration agreement (1965) **50,** 2, 14-16, 22, 217, 341, 388, 470
foreign States, whether **53,** 96-101
hostilities. *See* state of war *below*
India–Pakistan Devolution Agreement (1947) **78,** 109
India–Pakistan Ministerial Level Conference on Western Border Issues (1960) **50,** 50, 469
Indian maps and documents, inspection of for arbitration **50,** 17
Nehru–Noon Agreement (1958) **70,** 43-4, 46
constitutional amendment, need for **92,** 559
as dispositive treaty **70,** 44, 46
effect **53,** 194-201
implementing legislation, need for **92,** 558-9
modification **92,** 569
overflights
agreement (1966) **48,** 332, 335, 424-5, 432, 436-8
suspension of rights (1971), dispute concerning **48,** 331, 337, 347, 453
partition **38,** 3-9
effect on contract **53,** 117-29
Rann of Kutch arbitration **50,** 1-521, **70,** 39
state of war **40,** 472-80, **67,** 615-29
cease-fire and arbitration agreement (1965) **50,** 2, 4-16, 22, 217, 341, 388, 470
declaration of **71,** 709, 711
enemy aliens, effect on **53,** 117-29, 609-12, 616-27
existence of **67,** 615-29
responsibility for determining **71,** 711-12
prize law **40,** 472-80
termination **71,** 710-11
Tashkent Declaration (1966) **48,** 332, 337, 436, **67,** 623-4, 628
Indian Native States. *See also* India, constituent States; Indian States
accession, to India or Pakistan **50,** 76-80, 463
cession of Crown territory to **50,** 85-9, 102-3, 175, 402-5
Government of India, relationship with **49,** 405-6
status **50,** 68-73, 76-7, 80, 92-9
Indian Princely States. *See* Indian Native States; Indian States
Indian States. *See also* India; Indian Native States
British Crown, relationship with **64,** 529
continuity of State **49,** 387, 455
Covenants forming United States
effect **49,** 425-6
personal nature of privileges under **64,** 484-5
treaty character **49,** 375
Gwalior, legislature of **53,** 142-4
international personality **64,** 487-9, 526-7, 529-30
law of **53,** 143-8
merger **45,** 19-24, **53,** 189, 569-74
Bombay–Miraj **49,** 474
Kathiawar States **49,** 430, 479
Patiala–East Punjab **49,** 338, 433-4, 449-50, 453, 459
Rajastan States **49,** 349, 351, 440-2, 450-3, 457
Saurashtra States **49,** 380, 460, 480

Indian States (*cont.*)
tort liability **49,** 365-9
uniqueness **49,** 458
Rulers **64,** 571-4, 615-18
derecognition **118,** 428
as 'foreign State' **64,** 421, 422, 615-18, **118,** 425-6
immunity, jurisdiction **64,** 420, 524-5
immunity, taxation **53,** 568-74, **64,** 421, 483-9, 524-8
comity **64,** 421
international personality and **64,** 526-7, 529-31
mediatized **49,** 344
State distinguished **64,** 414-15
status of descendants of **49,** 336-49
status as Head of State **64,** 528-31, 618
treaties with **50,** 54-6, 59-63, 218, 270, 398-401, 424, 425, 459, 464, 465, 470, 477
status **64,** 414-15
individual in international law 36, 286, 305, **42,** 195-238, **43,** 178-245, **46,** 405, 505-6, **47,** 169-274, **48,** 155-90, **51,** 237-9, **54,** 323-4, **62,** 391, 401, **65,** 278-9, 302-3, **69,** 190-2, **71,** 283, 288-90, 586, **77,** 221-4, 245-8, 617, **88,** 88, **91,** 117-18, **99,** 66. *See also* aliens; claims settlement agreements, State control over claims; extradition; Hague Conventions (1899/1907), individual; human rights; nationality; refugees; treaties, individual rights; Yugoslavia, International Criminal Tribunal for the Former (ICTY)
breach by **86,** 94, **103,** 528-9, 530, **104,** 144-6, 147-8, 151-7
acting in concert with foreign State **104,** 158
acting outside authority **104,** 125 n. 8
genocide. *See* genocide
Minister of Defence **104,** 171-3, 174-5
piracy. *See* piracy
slavery **104,** 152, 153
torture. *See* torture
war crimes. *See* war crimes
direct rights and duties **45,** 61
EEC Regulations **47,** 1-9
existence **106,** 406-7
Helsinki Final Act(1975) **85,** 242-3
human rights law **77,** 248
ICJ **54,** 398, 435, **85,** 254, 255-62
international economic law **53,** 457-60
international tribunals **37,** 57, 170, 171, 403, 420, 501
internationally enforceable right **79,** 347
jus cogens/peremptory norm **85,** 259-62
justiciability **104,** 144-6
laws of war and **42,** 480
liquidators **71,** 268-9
municipal courts, enforcement of rules in **65,** 162-3, **77,** 207-11, 215-16, 249
PCIJ, proposed access to **37,** 57
prize law **77,** 245
property rights **56,** 18
protection of **62,** 400-1, 406
relations with foreign State **104,** 144
relations with international tribunal. *See* Yugoslavia, International Criminal Tribunal for the Former (ICTY), individual, duty of compliance

relations with own State **88,** 88-9, 92, **104,** 144
remedy under, whether
transboundary pollution **86,** 582
unlawful arrest **86,** 530-2
right to claim under **80,** 382
rights **87,** 184
access to ports **81,** 515
against governments **77,** 179
ship's seaworthiness **81,** 515
to challenge waiver of sovereign rights **105,** 576-7
Road Traffic Convention, rights under **47,** 328-33
State as link **88,** 90
State responsibility. *See* State responsibility, imputability, individual, attribution of responsibility to
State succession and **92,** 165, 166
States and **59,** 461
treaties and. *See* treaties, individuals
Treaty of Rome (1957) **62,** 391, 395, 400-1, 406, 409
trustees for bondholders **71,** 268-9
UN **105,** 567-9
action on behalf of States **105,** 568-9
UN Charter **85,** 241-2
UN Human Rights Committee **77,** 248
UN Resolution, enforcement **77,** 199
war, challenge to legality of **42,** 393-401
war crimes **77,** 221-2

Indonesia
administrative act, procedural irregularities, effect **89,** 613-16
contract
definition **89,** 461-2, 464
pacta sunt servanda **89,** 494
damages **89,** 504, 629
mitigation **89,** 628
due process **89,** 537-8
exchange control laws **40,** 9
expropriation/nationalization
compensation for **89,** 467
courts, responsibility for **89,** 454
law relating to **89,** 390-1, 453, 467
of plantations (1959) **42,** 39
requirements **89,** 628
law of
BKPM Chairman's Decree 01/1977 **89,** 470, 493-4, 534, 536, 600-13
Civil Code **89,** 461, 465, 494-5, 504, 538, 615, 635, 636
Decree 21/1973 (Principal Rules of Capital Investment Procedure) **89,** 479-80
Decree 54/1977 **89,** 470, 493, 536-7, 627
Decree 63/1969 **89,** 479-80
Foreign Capital Investment Act **66,** 388-95
Law 1/1967 (Foreign Capital Investment Law) **89,** 390-1, 393, 412-14, 452-3, 465, 467, 479-80, 484-6, 489, 509, 542, 543, 545, 550, 600, 607
Bank of Indonesia, role **89,** 607-8
Law 6/1968 **89,** 484-6
Malaysia, state of hostilities with **42,** 441-70, **52,** 498

Indonesia (*cont.*)
nationalization of property of Dutch nationals, compensation arrangements **74,** 285-9
Netherlands
nationals of, measures affecting property **40,** 7-15
Round Table Conference Agreements and Union Statute (1949), Indonesian denunciation **70,** 439-40
Union Statute **40,** 11
PM Jakarta Lloyd **63,** 541-9
State oil company (Pertimina) **63,** 74-6
Industrial Bank of Cuba. *See* Cuba, Industrial Bank of Cuba
Industrial Development Authority, agency or instrumentality of a foreign State 63, 616
industrial property 70, 431-2
information, right to. *See also* freedom of expression
competition **62,** 406-7, 413
missing persons **120,** 59-60. *See also* disappearances
inherent powers. *See also under individual organizations and tribunals*
Certain Expenses of the United Nations **110,** 626
Effects of Awards of Compensation made by the United Nations Tribunal **110,** 625-6
expulsion of alien, international official **102,** 196-7
implied powers distinguished **110,** 698 n. 27
judicial determination necessary for exercise of jurisdiction **110,** 704
jurisdiction
compétence de la compétence **105,** 460-1, **110,** 625-6
revision **102,** 579-81
penalties, power to impose **110,** 698
procedure, determination **105,** 30
Reparations for Injuries Suffered in the Service of the United Nations **110,** 624-5
requirements
effective functioning **110,** 624-7, 630-2
necessity **110,** 627 n. 37
inheritance rights, non-resident aliens **42,** 1-8
inhuman or degrading treatment 85, 151. *See also* corporal punishment; crimes against humanity, classification; European Convention on Human Rights (1950), inhuman or degrading treatment; International Covenant on Civil and Political Rights (1966), inhuman or degrading treatment; International Covenant on Civil and Political Rights (ICCPR) (1966); Rwanda, International Criminal Tribunal for (ICTR), Statute; Yugoslavia, International Criminal Tribunal for the Former (ICTY), Statute
cause of action **104,** 187
changing standard **100,** 630
customary international law. *See also jus cogens*/peremptory norm *below*
definition, lack **95,** 635
universal practice, absence **95,** 635
death penalty **98,** 381, 398-402, 407
method of execution, relevance **98,** 379-80
prosecution for non-capital charges while on remand **124,** 269-70
death row. *See* death row as inhuman or degrading treatment
definition **70,** 225
clear criteria, absence **104,** 186-9
Torture Convention (1984), US reservation **104,** 186-7
detention involving. *See* detention, inhuman treatment or torture, whether involving
distinguished **91,** 401-3
failure of State to investigate prison conditions **115,** 298

food, deprivation **114,** 330
forced exile **104,** 187-9
humanity and respect for inherent dignity of person distinguished **114,** 330
immigration procedures **103,** 181-2, 198
jus cogens/peremptory norm **104,** 185-9
clear criteria **104,** 185-6
lesser penalty to prevail **98,** 576
medical treatment, lack **114,** 330
non-refoulement. *See* Torture Convention (1984), non-refoulement
proportionality **98,** 396-7, 399, 408
recreational facilities, denial **114,** 330
requirements, discrimination **104,** 187-9
Torture Convention (1984), failure to prescribe penalty **104,** 186 n. 33
torture. *See* torture
'well-founded fear of persecution' **104,** 189 n. 38
whipping
adult offenders **90,** 581-5
juvenile offenders **90,** 585
injunction. *See also* Mareva injunction
comity and **118,** 415
equitable remedy, whether **86,** 649, **118,** 408, 410-12
foreign State, against. *See* State immunity, execution/attachment, purpose of proceedings, safeguarding/cautionary measures; stay of proceedings
stay of proceedings distinguished **118,** 408-9, 414-15
injury
direct and indirect **46,** 411, 426, 470-1
to right or interest **46,** 210, 212
'interest' **46,** 212, 299-300
inland waters. *See also* internal waters
definition, California **42,** 86-102
force majeure **82,** 696
Great Lakes **94,** 243, 245-6
internal waters distinguished **94,** 243
international boundary, effect on status **94,** 243-6
right of passage, treaty provision **82,** 696-9
innocent passage 41, 124, **73,** 182-3, 283-6, **76,** 445. *See also* territorial sea
access to high seas as part of common heritage **125,** 423
activities prejudicing 'innocence' **120,** 295-6, **125,** 421
archipelagic internal waters **97,** 509
beaching of salvaged vessel **101,** 437-8
customary international law **84,** 84, **125,** 420
EEZ **120,** 295-6
exclusion of limited areas **125,** 421-2
former high seas enclosed by straight baselines **97,** 509
historic bay, in **97,** 508-9
internal waters, exclusion, relevance **91,** 425-6
juridical bay **97,** 509
Law of the Sea Convention (1982) **97,** 509
pluri-State bay **97,** 509
previous authorization, need for **91,** 500-1
straits
fisheries regulations, respect for **81,** 602
pollution regulations, respect for **82,** 602

innocent passage (*cont.*)
territorial sea **97,** 506, 521, **125,** 349-50, 420-3
clarification, need for **84,** 86
coastal State legislation and **84,** 75, 83
customary law **84,** 84
necessity and **84,** 76
right, whether **84,** 80, 85, 86
uso inocente **97,** 508-9
Territorial Sea and Contiguous Zone Convention (1958) **91,** 500, **101,** 437-8
warship **91,** 500
other ships distinguished from, whether **91,** 500
insolvency. *See* bankruptcy; bankruptcy proceedings; service of process out of the jurisdiction, insolvency/insolvency-related proceedings
Institut de Droit International
arbitration, standard of proof **106,** 448
double criminality, Oxford Resolutions (1880) **87,** 151, 156
employment contract, State immunity, jurisdiction **113,** 433
extradition, Oxford Resolutions (1880) **87,** 151, 156
law of the sea, bays **97,** 652
Mandates, resolution on (1931) **49,** 135-6, 205
natural resources, Resolution on Pollution of Rivers and Lakes (1979) **108,** 358
Resolution on the Recognition of New States and Governments (1936) **108,** 358
State immunity, execution/attachment, restrictive theory **45,** 78, **65,** 182, 391
State immunity, jurisdiction
employment contract **113,** 433
good faith and **113,** 433
personal injury in forum State **123,** 90
State immunity, jurisdiction, theory/doctrine, restrictive theory **45,** 78
Institut Franco-Allemand de Recherche de Saint Louis
immunity, jurisdiction **72,** 711-13
staff contract claim **72,** 711-13
Staff Regulations, ouster of jurisdiction of ordinary courts **72,** 711-13
Institute of International Law resolutions **72,** 485, 520-8, 531, 537, 547, **75,** 195, 230, 233, 252, 255, 262, 264, 266
discrimination between armed forces and civilian populations (Edinburgh 1969) **110,** 450
Immunity of Foreign States (1954) **38,** 167, **45,** 78
war, effect on treaties (Helsinki 1985) **96,** 305
Institute for Religious Works (IOR). *See* Holy See, Institute for Religious Works (IOR)
insurance
'act of war', civil war **44,** 439-41
applicable law, life insurance **38,** 138-41
civil commotion, definition **74,** 33-4
civil war, definition for insurance purposes **44,** 439-41, **74,** 7-8, 23-8, **82,** 108-9
as commercial activity **63,** 457
diplomatic immunity, effect **40,** 222-3
excepted perils **74,** 7-8, 21-35
expropriation in Cuba, effect on contract **42,** 149-52
FC & S Clause **78,** 564, 566
letters of mart **78,** 576
life insurance, applicable law **38,** 138-41
piracy **78,** 568-75
Declaration of Paris (1856) and **48,** 471, 473

'pirates, rovers and thieves' **78,** 567-8
riot endorsement **74,** 6-7, **78,** 576-7
transfer of claim against tortfeasor **47,** 29
war risks
association **78,** 564-6
fisheries dispute, capture and sinking of ship as **48,** 469-75
open cover, applicability **78,** 684-95
insurance company, as 'agency or instrumentality of a foreign State' **63,** 454, 456-7
insurance policy
'civil war, insurrection or rebellion' **107,** 507-16
burden of proof **107,** 507
export credit guarantees. *See* export credit guarantees
'war risk' clause **82,** 107-9
insurrection. *See* civil strife; civil war; revolution
inter fauces terrae **42,** 63, 66-7, 75-7, 80, **45,** 63, 66-7, 75-7, 80, **69,** 55-7, 59, **73,** 199, 201, 215, 218, 224-5, **90,** 238, 273-4, 307-11, 322-9
Inter-American Commission on Human Rights **62,** 247, 250, 261, 264-5, **75,** 3-4, 6-30, **76,** 423, 468, 718, **78,** 49
admissibility
complaints against States not party to Convention **123,** 133-5, **124,** 270-2, 285, 294-5
decisions on **67,** 585-8, 592-3, **75,** 7-9
declaration of, need for **95,** 245-6
challenge by State **95,** 246
exhaustion of local remedies. *See* exhaustion of local remedies *below*
request by Commission for information as evidence of **95,** 245-6
reviewability by Court **67,** 587-8
statement of facts tending to establish violation of guaranteed rights, need for **123,** 134-5, 160-1
applicable law **123,** 167-71
American Declaration of the Rights and Duties of Man (1948) **123,** 167-9, 184-5
Geneva Conventions (1949) **123,** 184
international humanitarian law **123,** 169-71, 184
other relevant international obligations **123,** 169-70
competence. *See* jurisdiction *and* powers *below*
compulsory jurisdiction, death penalty reservation **123,** 512-13
conclusions of **75,** 6-13
dissenting opinions **75,** 13-30
evidence, power to demand from State **110,** 635-6
exhaustion of local remedies **75,** 7-8, **123,** 135-8
burden of proof **123,** 135
in State against whom petition not lodged **123,** 138 n. 3
exhaustion of procedures **95,** 249
expenses, entitlement to reimbursement **116,** 294
explanation of vote **67,** 589
friendly settlement procedure **95,** 249
compulsory, whether **95,** 246-7
failure to reach **95,** 249-50, **123,** 542-3
parties to **95,** 304
termination of judicial proceedings following **95,** 253
functions **67,** 585-8, 592-3, **70,** 455-6
individuals, applications by **67,** 569-70, 586-7, **75,** 8, 37-9, 65, **124,** 285, 292, 294
jurisdiction
advisory opinion requests **67,** 562-4

Inter-American Commission on Human Rights (*cont.*)
extraterritorial acts **123,** 168
matters relating to fulfilment of obligations of State parties **116,** 384, **123,** 183-4
recognition of **75,** 6-7
on-site investigation, compulsory, whether **95,** 247-8
petitioner, residence requirements **75,** 8
postponement of decision **95,** 241
powers **75,** 8, 38
investigation, Cooperation of State, need for **95,** 286
procedural objections **70,** 455
review of domestic law **75,** 7-8, 24
compliance with Convention, limitation to **123,** 150-1
preliminary hearing, compulsory, whether **95,** 248
procedural objections, power to rule on **70,** 455
procedures
purpose **67,** 586-7, 592-3, 595, 598-9
time-limits (Article 51) **123,** 544, 546-8
waivability **67,** 586-7, 592-3, 595, 598-9
recommendations. *See also* American Convention on Human Rights (1969), reparations; Inter-American Court of Human Rights, judgment
failure to comply **123,** 552-3
good faith obligation to comply **123,** 546
information to Commission within 60 days of measures taken **95,** 241
punishment of those responsible **95,** 241
suspension of procedural effects **95,** 252
thorough and impartial investigation to determine responsibility **95,** 241
time-limits for implementation, reinstatement **95,** 252
'weight and respect', effect limited to **98,** 347, **123,** 544, 553-4
Regulations
1 **123,** 182
32 **123,** 134
32(a) **123,** 133
32(b) **123,** 133
32(d) **123,** 133
34(1)(c) **95,** 245-6
34(3) **95,** 245-6
34(5) **124,** 286
34(7) **124,** 286
35 **95,** 245-6, **123,** 134
36 **95,** 245-6
37 **123,** 138 n. 3
37(1) **123,** 135
37(3) **95,** 257, **123,** 135
38 **123,** 133
39 **123,** 133
41 **95,** 246, **123,** 134
42 **95,** 240, 248, 286, 298
42(2) **95,** 253
43 **95,** 248
44 **95,** 247
44(3) **124,** 286
45 **95,** 246
45(1) **95,** 301

45(2) **95,** 247, 303
45(3) **95,** 303
50 **116,** 274, 298
50(1) **95,** 261, 306
50(2) **95,** 261, 306
51 **124,** 294
52 **123,** 134, 161
53 **123,** 161, 165, 188
54 **95,** 252, **123,** 178, 188
55-9 **95,** 247
59(9) **95,** 241
report
Art. 50 report
reconsideration **95,** 241-2, 251-2
requirements **95,** 251
resolution as **95,** 251
Art. 51 report, where application filed with Court **95,** 250, 253-4
failure to reach friendly settlement, following **95,** 249-50
publication **95,** 250
request for information, failure to reply within reasonable time, presumption of truth of allegations **95,** 240, 286, 298
Resolutions
22/86 **95,** 241-2, 251-3, 254
30/83 **95,** 240-1, 242, 251-3
Art. 50 report, as **95,** 251
reconsideration **95,** 241, 242
Statute
Art. 1 **123,** 133-4
Art. 20 (States not party to Convention) **123,** 134, 138 n. 3
submission of case to, UNHRC examination and **68,** 44, **69,** 187-8, **70,** 251-3
termination of proceedings
friendly settlement, following **95,** 253
presentation of case to Court **95,** 253
publication of Article 51 report **123,** 546-9, 552-3
withdrawal of case **79,** 171, 184, 221, 222, 237, 239
Inter-American Conference for the Maintenance of Continental Peace and Security (Rio de Janeiro) (1947) 84, 272
Inter-American Conference on Problems of Peace and War (1945) 76, 691, **84,** 271
Inter-American Court of Human Rights 75, 33-75
admissibility
complaints imputable to States not party to Convention **124,** 270-2
decisions on **75,** 36-40, **79,** 289-94, 328, 339-42, 352-6, 358, 362-6, 374
exhaustion of domestic remedies. *See* exhaustion of local remedies *below*
request for advisory opinion. *See* advisory opinion *below*
advisory jurisdiction **67,** 561-2, 596-609, **70,** 451-65, 476-7, **75,** 36-9, **79,** 285-325, 326-35, 338-77, **116,** 329-33
acceptance by State party **70,** 454, 456-65
as alternative judicial method **96,** 409
contentious jurisdiction
relation to **70,** 456-65, **75,** 38-9, **116,** 329, 333
risk of interference with **116,** 258-9
ICJ advisory jurisdiction compared **70,** 462
jurisdictional objections, joinder to merits **70,** 454-9

Inter-American Court of Human Rights (*cont.*)
jurisdictional preconditions, applicability **70,** 454, 456-65
procedure **70,** 454-9
amicus curiae **79,** 327, 339, **116,** 306, 324
Art. 64(1) and (2) of Convention distinguished **79,** 290, 339, 361-2, 375
discretionary **79,** 290, 341
jurisdiction and merits combined **70,** 454-9
notice **79,** 290
observations **79,** 327, 338-9
purpose **70,** 456-8, 461-4, **79,** 291-3
refusal to exercise **70,** 461, **116,** 259
scope **67,** 596-609, **79,** 292, 362-3
American Declaration of the Rights and Duties of Man (1948) **96,** 422-4, 428-9
draft legislation **79,** 290-3
hypothetical situation **96,** 409
interpretation of Constitution **79,** 290
interpretation of Convention **70,** 451-77, **116,** 329
interpretation of Convention, reservations **70,** 465
advisory opinion **67,** 561-2, 596-609, **75,** 40-75
binding force **70,** 460, **75,** 38
concerning freedom of expression **75,** 38-9, 65
request for **70,** 451, 461-3, **79,** 285-6, 326-8, 338-9, **116,** 252-60
context **70,** 464
discretion to decline **79,** 293, 328, **96,** 423-4
reformulation **79,** 353-6, 357, 359
right to seek **79,** 289, **96,** 394
Inter-American Commission **96,** 394, **116,** 325-32
Member State **96,** 408, 422, **116,** 329
appeal court, whether **95,** 243
application to, extension of time-limit for, effect on State's procedural rights **95,** 252-3
applications, retention **67,** 589
burden of proof
person making allegations **95,** 284
refutation of evidence **95,** 287
Commission and
freedom to decide independently of **95,** 243
non-representation **96,** 419
competence **67,** 562, 584, 588-9, 590-1, 596-609
concurring opinion **116,** 387, 444-50, 521-6
contentious jurisdiction **67,** 584, 588-9, 596, 600
acceptance **116,** 296 n. 3, 307, 340 n. 3
advisory jurisdiction distinguished **70,** 456-65, **116,** 333-5
jurisdictional objections **70,** 456, 459-65
recognition of **75,** 6-7, 37-8, **95,** 242, 243, 261
scope, hypothetical situation **116,** 335
costs and expenses. *See* American Convention on Human Rights (1969), costs and expenses
dissenting and concurring opinion **79,** 356-77
dissenting opinion **79,** 305-7, 352-6, **116,** 318-19, 386-7, 442-4
domestic jurisdiction and **79,** 296
effective remedy, need for **95,** 324, **123,** 136
amparo **95,** 273
appeal **95,** 273
cassation **95,** 273

failure to achieve desired result **95,** 273
habeas corpus
danger to those invoking **95,** 273, 276
partiality **95,** 273
persons held clandestinely **95,** 273, 276
powerlessness **95,** 273, 275-6
measures constituting **95,** 315
partiality **95,** 273
presumptive finding of death based on disappearance **95,** 272-3
US Department of Defense claims programme **123,** 136-8
evidence
admissibility **116,** 394-5, 400-2, 404-5, 495-8
at reparations hearing **116,** 406-8, 498-9, 503, **118,** 90, 93-102, 106-8
failure of State to submit brief, effect **118,** 103-5
circumstantial **95,** 285, **109,** 154 n. 36, **116,** 311, **118,** 72
evaluation **95,** 287, **116,** 363-75, 402-3, 404, 496, **118,** 71-2
victim's evidence **116,** 407-8
failure to submit **95,** 276, 286
caused by State's failure to cooperate **116,** 310-11
human rights and criminal law distinguished **95,** 286
media reports
government statements **95,** 288
Nicaragua **95,** 288
non-objection to **95,** 287
oral **116,** 363-4, 406
signature, need for, annex to document **116,** 497-8
standard of proof **116,** 495
submission by fax **116,** 394
supplementary, Court's right to request **116,** 495
timeliness **95,** 286, **116,** 394, 405, 496-7
justification for late submission **116,** 405
witnesses
objectivity **95,** 280, 281, 287-8, **118,** 71
where held incommunicado **118,** 72
exhaustion of local remedies
absence of rules in the American Convention on Human Rights (1969) **95,** 256
admissibility requirement **95,** 255-8, **116,** 375
timeliness of objection **95,** 256-7
applicable law
'generally accepted principles of international law' **95,** 255-6, 272
procedure **95,** 256
substance **95,** 256
burden of proof **95,** 257, 271-2
exhaustion of remedy **95,** 272
existence of remedy **95,** 272
'disappearances', evidence of absence or ineffectiveness of remedy **95,** 258
effective remedy, need for. *See* effective remedy, need for *above*
exception to, existence as breach of Convention **95,** 257, 272
'interpretation or application of [the] Convention' **95,** 255
merits and **95,** 255, 257, 258, **116,** 471
waiver **95,** 256
expenses, entitlement to reimbursement **116,** 294
expert
evidence **116,** 408-10, **118,** 101-2

Inter-American Court of Human Rights (*cont.*)
falling outside 'expert' category **116,** 410
need for appointment of expert **116,** 404
functions **67,** 590, 599-600
establishment of facts **116,** 308
role of Inter-American Commission on Human Rights distinguished **116,** 308
implementation, supervision **95,** 319
individuals, applications by **67,** 586-7, 592-3, **116,** 334-5
information, sufficiency **79,** 377
Inter-American Human Rights Commission, referral from **67,** 589
judges
ad hoc **95,** 238
recusal **95,** 238, 261
judgment
binding nature **116,** 375, **123,** 554
implementation **95,** 305-6
applicable law **95,** 305
payment of compensation in instalments **95,** 319
supervision by Court **116,** 439, **118,** 119, 120
timescale **95,** 319, **116,** 439, 519-20, **118,** 118
trust fund **116,** 439
ratio decidendi, whether part of **95,** 315
jurisdiction. *See also* advisory jurisdiction, contentious jurisdiction *and* competence *above*
admissibility, decisions on **95,** 243
advisory. *See* advisory jurisdiction *above*
advisory opinion. *See* advisory opinion *above*
'all matters relating to the interpretation or application of [the] Convention'
compétence de la compétence **95,** 243
sole judicial organ **95,** 243, **116,** 308
verification of procedural norms **95,** 243
'all matters relating to the interpretation or application of [the] Convention or other treaties concerning protection of human rights in the American States' **96,** 394, 408
compétence de la compétence **95,** 243, **123,** 554
interpretation of Convention provisions on procedure **95,** 243
determination of reparations **118,** 92
Inter-American Commission on Human Rights, views of **67,** 582
interpretation of treaties **67,** 596-609, 639
limitations **67,** 599-602, 607-8
justiciability **79,** 296
merits
abstention on **79,** 357
dissent on preliminary issues, effect **79,** 357
notice **79,** 290
observations **79,** 338
powers, review of domestic law **79,** 340, 352-6, **116,** 255-60, 324-7
preliminary objections, joinder to merits **95,** 270
procedure **67,** 560, 581-93, 595-6, **95,** 265-6. *See also* Rules of Procedure *below*
closed hearing **95,** 265-6
equality of parties **95,** 266
established by President of Court **95,** 238-9
failure of claimant to appear **116,** 414-15
formalities, relevance **95,** 244, **116,** 412-14, 497
appointment of representatives **116,** 412-14, 501-2

municipal courts' procedure, relevance **95,** 285, **116,** 413, 497, 502
timeliness, need for **95,** 266
provisional measures **95,** 266-70
in case no longer pending **123,** 547-9
discontinuance **118,** 70-1
emergency meeting of Court **95,** 267
government to
extend urgent measures to family **118,** 70
investigate and punish **95,** 267
report steps taken **95,** 268-9
take measures to guarantee safety **95,** 267
take measures to make clear individual's right to appear before Court **95,** 269
take measures to prevent infringement of rights of those appearing before Court **95,** 267
where State remains in breach of Convention **123,** 552-3
request for information, extension of time-limit **95,** 269-70
Rules of Procedure. *See also* procedure *above*
15 **79,** 357
23 **95,** 268, **116,** 414, 437-8, 519
24(1) **116,** 354
24(4) **116,** 355
26 **118,** 65
26(1) **95,** 261, **116,** 302
26 ff **116,** 347, 456, **118,** 62
27(3) **95,** 238
29(2) **118,** 65
30(3) **95,** 238
37 **95,** 280, 281, 287
38(1) **118,** 71
41(2) **116,** 305
43 **116,** 394-5, 405, 495
44 **116,** 495
45(1) **95,** 258
46 **116,** 404
47 **116,** 404
49 **79,** 339
49(2) **96,** 407
51 **79,** 286, 339
52 **52,** 338, **79,** 327, **96,** 393, 406, 419, **116,** 254
54(1) **116,** 324
55(1) **116,** 437
separate opinion **79,** 308-25
standing **67,** 591
Statute
Art. 1 **95,** 261
Art. 10 **95,** 238
Art. 19 **121,** 332
Art. 19(2) **95,** 238, 261
urgent measures. *See* provisional measures *above*
Inter-American Defense Board, as *amicus curiae* **63,** 162
Inter-American Development Bank
as *amicus curiae* **63,** 162, 338
immunity, jurisdiction **42,** 138-43

Inter-American Development Bank (*cont.*)
immunity, jurisdiction, waiver **63,** 95
Inter-American Institute of Legal Studies 84, 266-80
interest 40, 169-74, **42,** 192, **46,** 287, **57,** 312, **61,** 345, 358, **62,** 169, 182, 210, 215-16, 218, **66,** 613, **67,** 342-3, 379-80, **69,** 654-6, 659-63, **71,** 610, 625, 675, **72,** 492, 724, **75,** 386-7, 607, 625-6, 648, **78,** 669, 673, **82,** 202-3, **83,** 481, 566, **84,** 139, 529 n. 29, 537, 576, 588, 671, **86,** 309-13, 472, **88,** 734, 736, 742-3, 745, **89,** 351, 511, 635
applicable law **89,** 511
choice of law clause, determined by **106,** 642-3
express provision in contract **86,** 310
general principles of **86,** 310
municipal law of Contracting State **106,** 641, 642
relevant principles of international law **84,** 529 n. 29
trade usage **86,** 310
arbitral awards **69,** 659-63
arbitral tribunal's jurisdiction **86,** 309-13
collective interest of UN Members **37,** 182-3, 539-42
compensation awards **42,** 189-94
on compensation for expropriation/nationalization **119,** 644
compensatory indemnity, in lieu of **62,** 144, 215
compound **106,** 641-3, **124,** 57
countervailing duties, under- or over-payment **107,** 295-6
damages, on **88,** 734, 745, **89,** 351, 511, 635
applicable law **89,** 511
damages, part of **69,** 659, **106,** 472
date **85,** 602
date of commencement **40,** 173-4, **62,** 215-16, **67,** 342-3, 379, **69,** 654-6, **86,** 311, **89,** 511
date of award **106,** 642, 730, **124,** 57
date of final demand for payment **113,** 484
date of request for arbitration **106,** 472
date of wrong **106,** 641, 643-4
integral part of calculation of compensation **89,** 568-9
integral part of decision **89,** 568-9
date of termination **40,** 173-4, **69,** 656, **86,** 311
date of payment of award **106,** 644, **124,** 57
ex aequo et bono **67,** 379, **96,** 329, 330
expropriation/nationalization/taking of property **42,** 190-4, **86,** 310
general principle of international law **42,** 192, **84,** 529 n. 29
reasonable rate **106,** 472
general principle of law **62,** 215
independent cause of action, whether **86,** 311, 312
Islamic law **62,** 215, **86,** 310
legal, in non-material matters **37,** 83-8, 99, 100, 103-4, 166, 180-2, 265-6, 267, 273, 412-21, 425-6, 583, 585-6, 599-600
legally protected **46,** 499-502, 524
loss of profit and **120,** 200
as part of value of property **122,** 523-4, 525-6
post-judgment **94,** 330, **96,** 332
interest as part of award distinguished **106,** 644, 716-17
pre-judgment **94,** 229-30
delay in prosecuting claim **94,** 229-30
enrichment **94,** 229

principal, relationship to **106,** 642
purpose **42,** 192
compensation for breach of Community law **93,** 336
compensation for delay **95,** 211
rate **42,** 193-4, **62,** 210, 215-16, **67,** 342, 375, **69,** 660, 662, **85,** 601-3, 617-19, **86,** 311, **95,** 319, **105,** 56, 63
5% **106,** 642-3
10% **106,** 472
agreed by parties **117,** 564
compensation for breach of contract and expropriation distinguished **106,** 642, 643
London Interbank Offered Rate (LIBOR) **95,** 230, **124,** 57
reasonable **75,** 607, 625-6, 648
Alabama **106,** 472
general principle of international law **106,** 472
variable **120,** 200
restitutio in integrum, general principle of international law **109,** 28
right distinguished **46,** 370, 410, 411, 425-6, 429-30, 445, 451, 498-502, 513-15, 523, 527
simple **89,** 648, **106,** 642
State liability for **42,** 189-94, **70,** 234
usury **62,** 215
intergenerational rights 106, 63-4, **110,** 405-6, 452
Stockholm Declaration on the Human Environment (1972) **106,** 63-4
Intergovernmental Committee for European Migration 77, 573-7
privileges and immunities **77,** 573-7
interim measures. *See* provisional measures *and under individual tribunals*
interim relief. *See also* provisional measures
Bhopal gas leak disaster **118,** 458
internal armed conflict
applicability of
Geneva Conventions (1949) **95,** 567, **105,** 449, 487-8, 508-11, 538, **108,** 45-6, **112,** 178-81, 202-3
Geneva Conventions (1949), Second Additional Protocol relating to the Protection of Victims of non-International Armed Conflicts (1977) **105,** 444, **119,** 352
Hague Conventions (1899/1907) **105,** 444
ICTY Statute **108,** 162, **121,** 253-4, 292-3, **122,** 40, 67
asylum in case of refugees from **95,** 566-7
in Chile **119,** 352
classification as a threat to international peace and security **105,** 466-7
crimes against humanity, customary international law **105,** 504-24, **108,** 45-6
grave breaches of the laws and customs of war, customary international law **105,** 528-31, 538, **108,** 162-3
war crimes, individual responsibility **105,** 520-4, 537-8
internal conflict. *See* civil strife; civil war; internal armed conflict; rebellion; revolution
internal waters 69, 55-7, 59, **77,** 404-5, **90,** 307-11, **91,** 413-15. *See also* Australia, South Australia, internal waters; bays; contiguous zone; inland waters; lakes; rivers; straits; territorial sea
areas of sea on landward side of territorial sea baseline **94,** 242-3, **119,** 459
'sea' **94,** 242
artificial accretions **42,** 98
artificial installations **90,** 238
bays and gulfs as **42,** 68-9, 74, 83-4, 86, **43,** 114-25, **69,** 43-6, 61-2, 66-7, **90,** 238, **91,** 431

internal waters (*cont.*)
pluri-State **97,** 520-1
claim **91,** 419, 421, 422
'contiguous dry lands' **90,** 277-8
customary international law **91,** 415
definition **91,** 413, 414, 431, 514 n. 9, **94,** 242-5, 342-5
US Submerged Lands Act **42,** 86-102
Delaware Bay **91,** 418 n. 4
delimitation **41,** 107-8, 135, **97,** 661-2
disclaimer **91,** 423-5
Fonseca Bay. *See* Fonseca Bay, internal waters
harbours **42,** 69-70, 80, 84, 97, **57,** 88-9, **59,** 210-11, 225-7
inland waters, whether **90,** 273-4, **94,** 243
innocent passage, exclusion, relevance **91,** 425-6
inter fauces terrae **42,** 63, 66-7, 75-7, 80, **90,** 238, 273-4, 307-11, 322-9
international headlands **90,** 324-5
King's Chambers **90,** 308-11
Law of the Sea Convention (1982) **97,** 662
limits **91,** 515 n. 9
Mississippi Sound, whether **91,** 413-26
Nantucket Bay, whether **91,** 429-38
neutrality and **90,** 308
proprietary rights **90,** 289
common law rule **90,** 324, 325
seaward edge **91,** 416, **119,** 459
Solent **90,** 323
Solway Firth **90,** 324-5
sovereignty over **51,** 139, **91,** 415
straight baselines **42,** 90-3
straits as **90,** 322-4
Territorial Sea and Contiguous Zone Convention (1958) **91,** 415-16, 431
definition **91,** 431
territorial waters, whether **97,** 508, 521, 523
international administrative tribunals. *See also* Asian Development Bank Administrative Tribunal; International Labour Organization Administrative Tribunal; International Labour Organization Administrative Tribunal (ILOAT); International Labour Organization (ILO) Conventions; League of Arab States Administrative Tribunal; NATO Appeals Board; United Nations Administrative Tribunal; United Nations Administrative Tribunal (UNAT); World Bank Administrative Tribunal
competence, non-observance of terms of appointment, complaint **43,** 276
disclosure of documents **43,** 260-4, 269, 326-7, 335, 415, 422
duty to create **116,** 645-6
corollary of international organizations' absolute immunity of from jurisdiction **116,** 648
evidence, copy documents **43,** 337
jurisdiction
distance of headquarters from place of work, relevance **116,** 647
independence of tribunal, relevance **116,** 647
membership, *nemo judex in re sua* **43,** 480-6
natural justice principles, applicability **68,** 165-7
oral hearings **43,** 307, 308, 318, 320, 373
procedure **43,** 316-17, 318, 320, 329
revision of judgments **43,** 480-91

International Air Transport Association (IATA) 75, 99-106
fares structure **74,** 61-3, 66-9, 74
fiscal immunity, Switzerland **75,** 99-106
officials, non-nationals **75,** 103
status **75,** 105
'public international organization' **75,** 105
'quasi-governmental organization' **75,** 105-6
International Amateur Athletics Federation
membership
China, admission **74,** 107-8
Taiwan, exclusion **74,** 107-12
rules
interpretation **74,** 108-12
'country' **74,** 109-11
international armed conflict. *See also* armed conflict; internal armed conflict; war
civil war distinguished **80,** 668-9
classification as
applicable law
international humanitarian law **124,** 98-101
rules relating to State responsibility **108,** 155-6, **124,** 98
attributability of acts to State **124,** 103
Bosnia-Herzegovina. *See* Bosnia-Herzegovina
combatants 'belonging to a Party to the conflict' test **42,** 476-8, **124,** 99-100
direct involvement of another State, relevance **108,** 150-4, **122,** 43-57, 245-50
ICRC involvement **105,** 491-2, **122,** 44-5
objective decision **122,** 44
Security Council statements **105,** 492-3, **124,** 115 n. 155
as required nexus
for applicability of laws and customs of war **105,** 528-31
application of the laws and customs of war, customary international law **105,** 528-31
Geneva Conventions (1949), First Additional Protocol relating to the Protection of Victims of International Armed Conflicts (1977) **105,** 444, **108,** 44
Geneva Conventions (1949), universal jurisdiction **105,** 496-7
ICTY jurisdiction **105,** 444-50, 485-526, 528-31, 581-3, 592, 596, **108,** 131, **122,** 20
ICTY Statute
Article 2 **108,** 131, 149, **112,** 178-201, 261-76, **122,** 20, **124,** 96-8
Article 3 **121,** 253-4, 292-3, **122,** 40, 67
war crimes **105,** 452, 525-6, **108,** 35-6, 131-2
international assemblies, recommendations, effect 77, 420-3
international associations. *See also individual associations*
legal status **75,** 105-6
membership **74,** 107-12
admission **74,** 107-8
exclusion **74,** 108-12
rules, interpretation **74,** 108-12
International Atomic Energy Agency (IAEA)
officials, immunity, taxation **38,** 453-6, **71,** 574-6
representatives to, privileges and immunities **70,** 414-18
International Bank for Reconstruction and Development (IBRD). *See also* World Bank Group
as *amicus curiae* **63,** 162, 338
immunity, jurisdiction, statutory basis **63,** 88

International Bank for Reconstruction and Development (IBRD) (*cont.*)
South Africa, aid to **49,** 85
International Carriage of Goods by Road Convention (1956). *See* Carriage of Goods by Road, Convention on (1956)
International Catholic Migration Commission (ICMC), privileges and immunities **102,** 151-62
International Centre for Advanced Mediterranean Agronomic Studies (CHEAM) 77, 602-9, **78,** 87-90, 113-16
Bari Institute (IAM) **78,** 87-90, 113-16
CHEAM, relationship **87,** 34, 36
employment contract, immunity, jurisdiction
staff as integral part of decision-making organization **87,** 20
trade union activities distinguished **78,** 88
immunity, execution/attachment **87,** 31-7
privileges and immunities, restructuring of organization, trade union rights and **87,** 37-8
immunity, execution/attachment **78,** 114-16
Paris Agreement (1977), Italian reservation reinstating customary law **77,** 607-8, **78,** 88
privileges and immunities **77,** 604-9
absolute immunity **87,** 32
determined by customary international law **78,** 88
foreign State, model **78,** 88, 90, 114-15
jurisdiction **78,** 114
Staff Regulations **78,** 87
International Centre for the Settlement of Investment Disputes (ICSID). *See* ICSID (International Centre for the Settlement of Disputes)
International Chamber of Commerce (ICC). *See also* arbitral tribunals; arbitration
Arbitration Rules
arbitral award, annulment **82,** 96
arbitration agreement, terms of reference distinguished **86,** 482, 491
waiver of right of appeal **86,** 483
arbitrator, role **67,** 627-8
Court of Arbitration **68,** 606
jurisdiction **67,** 614-29
documentary credit rules, Uniform Customs and Practice **63,** 183, 398, 406, 555, 557, 575, **65,** 133
Rules of Arbitration **65,** 446, 451
Art. 2(4) **80,** 604
Art. 8(5) **77,** 522-3
Art. 11 **80,** 617
Art. 13 **80,** 605
Art. 24(2) **65,** 98, **77,** 522-4
State immunity, execution/attachment, acceptance as waiver **63,** 566, 635, **65,** 59-60, 96-8, **77,** 523
Uniform Customs and Practice for Documentary Credits (1974 revision) **77,** 324, **79,** 550 n. 3
International Civil Aviation Organization (ICAO) 75, 100. *See also* International Civil Aviation Organization (ICAO), Council
aims and objectives **48,** 435
Council. *See* International Civil Aviation Organization (ICAO), Council
legal personality **48,** 417
Member States, non-discrimination between **48,** 417, 435
President, rights **48,** 455-6

Rules for Settlement of Differences **48,** 331, 341, 357-8, 359, 360-1, 365-7, 368, 370, 376, 378, 379, 382, 406-7, 421, 422-4, 427, 431-2, 447-9, 457, 460
interpretation **48,** 424
Secretary-General, legal opinion **48,** 368, 408
International Civil Aviation Organization (ICAO), Council
decisions
appeals from **48,** 331-465
suspensory effect **48,** 365, 367, 368
time factor **48,** 364
definition **48,** 423, 488-9
procedural irregularity **48,** 333, 335, 355-6, 357-8, 361, 384-7, 420-4, 439-41, 443-9, 457-65
validity **48,** 452-5
procedural **48,** 341-2, 375, 448
dispute settlement
applicable law **48,** 442
jurisdiction **48,** 333, 337, 339, 342-3, 347-56, 369-71, 376-7, 387-400, 410-20, 432-9, 450-6, 457
procedure
equity **48,** 421
time for members to seek instructions **48,** 460-3
voting **48,** 384-6, 421-2, 440, 443, 445-7, 458, 459, 464
Rules for Settlement of Differences **48,** 331, 341, 357-8, 359, 360-1, 365-7, 368, 370, 376, 378, 379, 382, 406-7, 421, 422-4, 427, 431-2, 447-9, 457, 460
treaty provision
adverse admission, risk **48,** 340
jurisdictional clauses, interpretation **48,** 413, 450-1
separability **48,** 332, 339-40, 348, 350-1, 390, 413-14, 419
unilateral suspension of treaty, effect **48,** 339-40, 390, 413-14, 432, 434
functions, Chicago Convention **48,** 412
ICJ, appeal to **48,** 331-47, 357, 359, 362-9, 372-6, 378-87, 402-10, 426-32, 443-5, 454-7
interim measures **48,** 368
jurisdiction
complaints
appealability **48,** 426-30
equity and **48,** 344-5, 384, 427
dispute settlement **48,** 333, 337, 339, 342-3, 347-56, 369-71, 376-7, 387-400, 410-20, 432-9, 450-6, 457
limitations on **48,** 391, 412-13
quasi-judicial functions **48,** 360-1, 439, 451, 455, 457-8
preliminary objection, lack of reasons **48,** 370, 423, 441, 443-4, 453-5, 459, 465
International Civil Service Commission
functions
coordination of UN agencies **69,** 314, 318, 372, 444-5, 523
repatriation grants **69,** 318, 326-7, 363, 372, 397-8, 412-21, 435-42, 453-4, 466, 507-27, 538-9
staff members, decisions affecting **69,** 314, 439
transitional arrangements, institution of **69,** 436-7, 453, 507, 509-10, 527, 538-9
repatriation grants, reports on **69,** 317-19, 321, 326-7, 372, 412-21, 434, 466, 500-7, 538
reports, promulgation **69,** 415-16
Statute

International Civil Service Commission (*cont.*)
Art. 10 **69,** 416, 436
Art. 11 **69,** 414, 417-18, 436
UNGA Resolution 33/119, interpretation **69,** 318-19, 326-7, 363, 397, 415-18, 436-8, 441-2, 453-4, 466, 518-27, 539
General Assembly reaction **69,** 518-27
international civil service law 43, 451
International Coffee Agreement (1962) 62, 422-8
limited duration **62,** 423, 427
quotas **62,** 422-8
pro rata 425-8
system of adjustment **62,** 425-6
selective system **62,** 422-3, 425, 428
International Coffee Council 62, 422-8
law relating to **62,** 422, 424
nature of **62,** 424
international comity. *See* comity
International Commission for North-west Atlantic Fisheries (ICNAF) 71, 110
International Commission for the Study of Communication Problems (1980), journalists, compulsory licensing **75,** 23
International Committee of the Red Cross (ICRC)
civilian detainees, right to visit **123,** 166
customary international law and **105,** 511, 529
International Criminal Tribunal for the Former Yugoslavia, establishment **105,** 529
occupied territory
deportations, attempt to prevent **83,** 139-40
hostage-taking, attempt to prevent **83,** 139-40
protected persons, right to communicate **83,** 190-1
Twentieth International Conference **76,** 459
international community, will of 37, 454
international conference, legal effect of attendance at 41, 111-12
International Conference of American States (Bogotá) (1948) 84, 289
International Council of Monuments and Sites (ICOMOS) 68, 274, 426
International Court of Justice (ICJ),[vii] **admissibility 37,** 99-100, 183, 276, 591, **46,** 23, 52, 55, 122, 126, **57,** 387, 408, 422, 434-8, 450-5, 503-16, 529, 541-2, 567-8, 569, 593-601, **76,** 140-52, 157, 553-80, 618-30, **81,** 480, **84,** 230, 245-62, 281, 300, 327, 348

[vii] International Court of Justice (ICJ) entries are distributed between the following headings:
International Court of Justice (ICJ), admissibility
International Court of Justice (ICJ), advisory jurisdiction
International Court of Justice (ICJ), advisory opinion
International Court of Justice (ICJ), advisory opinion, request for
International Court of Justice (ICJ), Chamber
International Court of Justice (ICJ), compulsory jurisdiction, acceptance
International Court of Justice (ICJ), compulsory jurisdiction, acceptance, interpretation
International Court of Justice (ICJ), compulsory jurisdiction, acceptance, reservations
International Court of Justice (ICJ), consent to jurisdiction
International Court of Justice (ICJ), contentious proceedings
International Court of Justice (ICJ), 'dispute'
International Court of Justice (ICJ), evidence
International Court of Justice (ICJ), *forum prorogatum*
International Court of Justice (ICJ), intervention of third State
International Court of Justice (ICJ), intervention of a third State, 'interest of a legal nature

action against single member of Trust Territory Administering Authority **97,** 22-6, 66
municipal law analogies **97,** 54-5, 56-7, 66
compliance, relevance **76,** 148-9, 430-1
conditional agreement not to challenge **102,** 65-6
continuing conflict **76,** 146-9, 501, 621-4
critical date **84,** 250, 255, **97,** 20-2, **117,** 22-4, 48-9, 54, 65-8, 104-6
nationality of claims **117,** 66
enforceability of judgment, relevance **105,** 360, 415-16
evidence, sufficiency **76,** 574-9
exhaustion of established processes **76,** 149-52, 155-7, 164-5, 226-7, 267, 340-1, 471, 500, **84,** 348
request for interpretation of judgment and **81,** 448-9, 465
failure to plead **99,** 652-3
international dispute, need for **115,** 34
jurisdiction distinguished **57,** 368-9, 381-2, 447, 567-8, **76,** 553, **102,** 84, **117,** 87
as legal question **84,** 261
legitimate object, need for **105,** 358-9
merits and **57,** 503, 508, **97,** 29
precedent **56,** 129
public presentation of position, right to **106,** 15, 46-7, 102
Security Council Resolutions and **117,** 21-4, 26-7, 44-5, 48-9, 52-7, 63-7, 87-90
Security Council responsibility **76,** 142-7, 574-9
self-defence **76,** 618-20
termination of Trusteeship, effect **97,** 17-20
third party interests **76,** 141-2, 168-9
useful purpose, need for **105,** 359-60

International Court of Justice (ICJ), advisory jurisdiction 54, 390, 392-5, 396-7, 404, 496, **62,** 548, 562
abuse of process **49,** 294, **110,** 319. *See also* legal question, need for, motivation, relevance *below*

which may be affected by the decision' as requirement
International Court of Justice (ICJ), judge
International Court of Justice (ICJ), judge *ad hoc*
International Court of Justice (ICJ), judgment
International Court of Justice (ICJ), jurisdiction
International Court of Justice (ICJ), justiciability
International Court of Justice (ICJ), merits
International Court of Justice (ICJ), precedent
International Court of Justice (ICJ), preliminary objections
International Court of Justice (ICJ), procedural issues
International Court of Justice (ICJ), provisional measures
International Court of Justice (ICJ), in relation to other tribunals and dispute settlement procedures
International Court of Justice (ICJ), request for an examination of the situation
International Court of Justice (ICJ), request for correction of judgment
International Court of Justice (ICJ), request for interpretation of judgment
International Court of Justice (ICJ), revision of judgment
International Court of Justice (ICJ), Rules of Court
International Court of Justice (ICJ), Security Council and
International Court of Justice (ICJ), Special Agreement
International Court of Justice (ICJ), status and functions
International Court of Justice (ICJ), Statute
International Court of Justice (ICJ), third States and.

International Court of Justice (ICJ), advisory jurisdiction (*cont.*)
appellate proceedings distinguished **54,** 455
contentious proceedings distinguished **54,** 475, **59,** 89, 129, 160, **69,** 367, 425-6, 469-70, **85,** 314, 316, **105,** 304-5, **110,** 186, 234
Convention on Privileges and Immunities of United Nations (1946), Section 30 **121,** 421-2
Eastern Carelia doctrine **49,** 13, 92, 146, 161-3
equality of parties **46,** 133, **69,** 349-50, 367, 386, 391-2, 471
exercise of **59,** 160
flexibility **83,** 363
hypothetical question **62,** 460-73, **110,** 100-2, 186-7, 321-3, 362
judicial character **49,** 120, 163, 321, **54,** 395, 397, 402, **59,** 38, 45, 90, 155, **62,** 472, 484-5, 509, 548, 578, **69,** 345-6, 349-51, 363-4, 367, 385-9, **85,** 315-16, **110,** 106, 127, 187, 319, **121,** 460-1, 463
judicial propriety **59,** 99, 160
as judicial review **54,** 390-5, 397, 398-401, 408, 473-8
judgment of international tribunal, grounds **54,** 455-6
legal question, need for **59,** 37, 94, 121-2, 126, 133-5, 157, **82,** 244-5, 254, **83,** 334, **85,** 312, 313-14, **110,** 12-14, 48, 183-4, 247-50
amendment of law, request for **110,** 250
Charter *travaux préparatoires* and **110,** 248
compatibility with relevant principles and rules of international law **110,** 184
formulation of question **110,** 140-2
identification of obligations under international law **110,** 13-14
legal dispute distinguished **59,** 89
Member State obligations, determination **110,** 36-7, 45, 49-51, 67-8
motivation, relevance **62,** 469-71, 483-4, 494, 549, **110,** 14, 78, 184, 187, 284, 300, 318
political implications, relevance **49,** 93, 117, 160-1, **110,** 13-14, 47, 77, 78, 89, 95-6, 103, 161-2, 184, 285-6, 300
within scope of activities of requesting organ **83,** 315-16, 363, 364, 422-3, **110,** 14-24, 27, 29, 49-109, 128-48, 159, 160-1, 249-50, **121,** 422-3
procedural issues **49,** 16, 118, 142, 161-2, 165-7, 300-1, 303, 306
evidence **59,** 45-6, 159
future intentions of States **69,** 458
interested parties, participation **59,** 45-6, 89, 129-30
oral hearings **54,** 402, **69,** 337, 350, 367, 391-2
preliminary questions **49,** 315-16, **59,** 121-4, 128-9
Rules of Court **49,** 16, 118, 142, 161-2, 300-1
standing, individual **83,** 315
stay of proceedings in municipal court **121,** 419-20, 468-9
purpose **54,** 448-9, **59,** 163, **110,** 126
requirements. *See also* legal question, need for *above*
consent of interested parties **59,** 37, 39-42, 98-9, **85,** 315-19, **110,** 320
dispute, existence of **59,** 155, 161, **82,** 232-3, 237-48, 254
importance of question **110,** 132
UN Administrative Tribunal judgments, review. *See* United Nations Administrative Tribunal, review of judgments by ICJ
International Court of Justice (ICJ), advisory opinion. *See also* International Court of Justice (ICJ), advisory jurisdiction; International Court of Justice (ICJ), advisory opinion, request for
appeal decision compared **69,** 367-8, 374, 381, 389, 425-8, 447, 464-5, 470-2, 483, 492
authoritative interpretation, whether **62,** 550-2

binding, whether **49,** 211-12, **54,** 395, 402, 465, **59,** 138-9, **85,** 315-16, **110,** 521, **122,** 642
under the Convention on Privileges and Immunities of United Nations (1946), Section 30 **121,** 422, 433, 450, 461, 468-9, 471
clear statement of law, need for **110,** 250, 399-400
Court's powers **62,** 508, 549
findings of fact **110,** 349
endorsement of legal axiom **110,** 282-3, 300, 317
General Assembly, acceptance by **37,** 569, **49,** 101
on interpretation of Agreement of 25 March 1951 between WHO and Egypt **62,** 457-581
judgment distinguished **59,** 155
judicial propriety **110,** 322
legal effect **59,** 84-5, 99, **69,** 347-8, 469-70
on legality of use of nuclear weapons
application in Scotland **122,** 642-51
UNGA request **110,** 177-542, **122,** 642-51
WHO request **110,** 6-163
lowest common denominator **62,** 491
Mandate
effect on status **49,** 151, 211-12
revocation and **49,** 140
merits **110,** 38-9
PCIJ and **110,** 320
precedent **37,** 185, 239, 417, 431, 487, 569, **105,** 304-5
purpose, authoritative legal opinion **110,** 126, 521
reasoning, need for **110,** 284-5, 290-1
scope **69,** 347-8, 469-70
on special rapporteur, immunity, jurisdiction **121,** 408-63, 468-71
time-limits **85,** 305-6, 339
value **110,** 521-2
probative **49,** 141
International Court of Justice (ICJ), advisory opinion, request for 54, 445, 461, 516, **59,** 95, **62,** 458, 469-71, 483, 547-9, 552, **81,** 231
admissibility **59,** 125
competence to determine **110,** 29-33, 157-60, 187
parallel consideration in another forum **110,** 96-7, 162, 183
discretion to decline **49,** 17, 92, 118, 134, 146, 160, 291-8, **54,** 499, **62,** 548, 562, 575-6, **69,** 345-8, 358, 388-9, 443, 447, 457-8, **83,** 363, **110,** 282, 319-20, 323-4, **121,** 457-61
in case of ambiguity **121,** 461
compelling reason, need for **54,** 403, 450-1, 476-8, 499, **69,** 358, 386-8, 390, 400, 458, 464, 471, **83,** 316, 363, **85,** 317-19, **110,** 27-9, 38, 43, 46-8, 67, 93, 94-5, 111, 127, 160, 185-6, **121,** 423, 463
effect on situation, relevance **110,** 26, 97-9, 127, 500
effect on treaty negotiations, relevance **110,** 99-100, 187, 323
generality of question **110,** 102
hypothetical question. *See* International Court of Justice (ICJ), advisory jurisdiction, hypothetical question
jurisdiction as preliminary requirement **110,** 13, 24, **121,** 423
law-making, need to avoid **110,** 103-4, 187, 509, 510
motivation for request, relevance **121,** 461
non-judicial nature of process as basis **110,** 319-20
partial nature of opinion, relevance **110,** 26, 188

International Court of Justice (ICJ), advisory opinion, request for (*cont.*)
political considerations, relevance **49,** 5, 13, **83,** 363
precedent **110,** 104, 107, 320-2
priority, considerations of **85,** 339-40
procedural irregularities **69,** 353-9, 387-8, 390-5, 400-8, 412, 421-2, 451, 458-64
restrictive approach **83,** 403
sovereignty, interference with **110,** 104-6, 161
Statute **83,** 315
UN Charter **83,** 315
where underlying presumptions prejudge outcome **49,** 291-3
formulation by 'authorized' body **121,** 424-6, 443-4, 455, 458-61
in pendente dispute between States and **49,** 14-15, 118-19, 129, 142, 161-7, 299-300, 303-6, 316-20
interpretation **59,** 149-52, **69,** 359-61, 365-6, 381-2, 403, 425, 451, 462-3, 471, 490-2, **82,** 231, **121,** 429
ambiguity **110,** 283, 317
discrepancy between texts **83,** 319, **110,** 188, 248, 282
establishment of intentions **83,** 327-8, 364
interpretation. *See also* reformulation by Court *below*
irregularities in **69,** 400-8, 412, 451, 462-3
object **59,** 87, 91
reformulation by Court **62,** 460, 470-3, 484-5, 495, 550-1, 562-5, 577-8, 581, **69,** 361, 404, 449-52, **83,** 327-9, 362, 364, **110,** 128, 130-2, 139-43, 247-8, 283
Application for Review of UNAT Judgment No 273 **110,** 130-2
refusal. *See* discretion to decline *above*
standing **54,** 392, 496
due authorization, need for **110,** 11-12, 23-4, 48, 159, 182-3
ECOSOC (UNGA Resolution 89(I)) **121,** 420-1
General Assembly **59,** 35, 43-4, 86-7
'any questions or any matters' within scope of Charter **110,** 183, 250
disarmament **110,** 183
limitation to matters on which it can take binding decisions **110,** 183
progressive development of international law **110,** 183
specialized agency distinguished **110,** 183, 232, 250
threat or use of force **110,** 183
individual **83,** 315
international organization **62,** 548-52, 562, **69,** 358-9, 388-9, 447, 458-9
non-governmental organization **110,** 285-6
specialized agency **110,** 11-24, 26, 121, 137-9, 249-50
subsidiary body of ECOSOC **85,** 314
WHO **62,** 452, 458, 469, **110,** 6-163
subsidiary organ of UN **54,** 496-7, 518
travaux préparatoires **83,** 364
validity
General Assembly's views, relevance **110,** 97
majority resolution **110,** 51-2, 157-60, 284-5, 291, 317
minority State's right to challenge before Court **110,** 51-2
International Court of Justice (ICJ), Chamber 71, 65-74, 79, 90, **81,** 397
ad hoc judge, power to appoint. *See* International Court of Justice (ICJ), judge *ad hoc*
as arbitral procedure **97,** 181-3, 268
Chamber for Environmental Matters **106,** 131
Chamber of Summary Procedure **97,** 198
change of Mandate **97,** 156, 158, 163, 498

competence **61,** 546-9, **70,** 685
  determination of general principles of international law **97,** 161
  dispute settlement **61,** 549, 570, 574, 592-3
competence to determine composition of Chamber
  Chamber **97,** 155, 157, 158
  full Court **97,** 155-6, 160-1, 163
  observations of parties **97,** 155, 164-8, 198
competence to determine incidental issues **97,** 155, 208-10
  ELSI **97,** 155
  Frontier Dispute **97,** 155
composition **71,** 65-8, 71-4, 79, 90, **97,** 143-53
  change of Chamber **97,** 156, 158, 162-5
  consultation of parties. *See* consultation of parties *below*
  discretionary right of Court **71,** 72
  nationality of judges **71,** 65-8, 71-4
  parties, powers of selection **71,** 65-8, 71-4
  time-limits **71,** 65-8, 71-4
Constitution **97,** 139-42, 274-5
  impartiality, need for **97,** 142
consultation of parties
  amendment of Rules and **97,** 173
  composition **97,** 141, 164, 167, 188-9, 191-203
  consent of parties **97,** 142
  Gulf of Maine **97,** 173-4
  independence of judge, threat to **97,** 196-7
  intervening State **97,** 164
  number of judges **97,** 163, 186-8, 255
  Statute, compatibility with **97,** 174
  Washington Commission of Jurists **97,** 185-8
as deprivation of
  right of access to full Court **97,** 167-8, 169
  right to judicial hearing **97,** 172
diversity, Chamber, composition and **97,** 197-8
establishment **84,** 323-4
full court and
  binding effect on **97,** 160
  equivalent of **97,** 160, 167, 207-8
  limitation on powers of **97,** 159, 163-4
  part of **97,** 142
  procedure, retained right to determine **97,** 160-1, 168, 211-12
  transfer of jurisdiction from **97,** 160-1, 169
'globally representative' requirement and **97,** 197-8
judgment
  status **71,** 68-9, **80,** 479
  third party review **71,** 69
opposition to **97,** 180-2
procedural reform, need for **97,** 161, 166 n. 1, 211-13
request to form **71,** 65-8, 71-4, 79
request to full Court, propriety **97,** 158-9, 206-8, 211-12
Statute and Rules, compatibility with **71,** 65-8, 71-4
tenure **97,** 200-3
  effect on validity of Chamber **97,** 202-3
  extension **97,** 193-203
  parties' wishes as determining factor **97,** 200-2

International Court of Justice (ICJ), Chamber (*cont.*)
validity **97,** 204-6
withdrawal of case, right to **97,** 142, 166, 173
International Court of Justice (ICJ), compulsory jurisdiction, acceptance 46, 146, **70,** 573, 584, 673-4, **76,** 40-6, 109-23, 184-8, 207-21, 228-35, 244-56, 274-5, 329-33, 366, 495-9, 512-17, 551-2, **85,** 260, 261, **106,** 149, 155. *See also* International Court of Justice (ICJ), consent to jurisdiction
amendment. *See* modification/replacement *below*
binding character **76,** 115-18, 120-4, 280-1, **123,** 375-6
by
Canada (10 May 1994) **123,** 200-481
El Salvador **97,** 299, 300-1
France **106,** 248
Honduras **97,** 299
text **123,** 200-1
clarity, need for **76,** 161, **84,** 279
collective **84,** 239, 279, 290, 295. *See also* multiple *below*
deposit of instruments, need for **84,** 279
conduct of parties as evidence of **76,** 120-2, 124-6, 194, 199-200, 496
consensual nature **46,** 146
critical date **76,** 127, 174, 257, 264
deposit with UN Secretary-General **123,** 386-7, 403
disputes between States, limitation to **97,** 13
El Salvador/Honduras General Treaty of Peace (1980), effect **97,** 300-1
form **76,** 123-4, 186-7
good faith and **106,** 178-9, 180, **123,** 244, 248, 258, 286-90, 324, 332-3, 380, 383-5, 399-401, 411, 414-19, 437, 444, 447, 480, 481
Nicaragua **123,** 383
implied **76,** 68-9
intervention of third State and **70,** 584-5, 671-4, 677-8, 683, 685-6, **97,** 254-5
modification/replacement **76,** 70-3, 126-32, 176, 219-20, 256-64, **84,** 238, 240-1, **123,** 200-1, 214-15, 217-18, 220, 247-8, 268-71, 275, 284-5
multiple **84,** 269, 291-2, 295-6. *See also* collective *above*
termination, unilateral **84,** 296
PCIJ system distinguished **76,** 114-15
philosophy **123,** 263-6
reciprocity, need for **76,** 44, 46, 72, 109-10, 124, 127-8, 130-2, 152, 177, 222, 259-60, 333-8, **106,** 155-6, 178-9, 180, **123,** 376, 441
registration of treaty as **84,** 279
rejection of compulsory jurisdiction by drafters of Statute **70,** 584-5, 588
reservations. *See* International Court of Justice (ICJ), compulsory jurisdiction, acceptance, reservations
scope **37,** 275-6, 283-4, 295
separability **76,** 180, **123,** 231-2, 252, 290-1, 382-3
ILC Draft Articles on the Law of Treaties **123,** 382
State practice **76,** 71-2, 127, 258-64
termination **46,** 146, **76,** 44-5, 126-32, 176, 211-14, 217-19, 221-4, 333-8
notice of **76,** 178-9, 205-6, 327-9, 335-6
transferability to ICJ **76,** 116-17, 321
treaty character **37,** 117
treaty or convention conferring
European Convention for the Peaceful Settlement of Disputes (1957) **70,** 609
need for parties to be party to same treaty or convention **70,** 609

Optional Protocol to Vienna Conventions on Diplomatic and Consular Relations concerning the Compulsory Settlement of Disputes **61,** 519-20, 550-4, 576-8, **118,** 11-13
Trust Territory, applicability to **97,** 12-14
UN publication, relevance **76,** 42-3, 67-70
unilateral application under **99,** 572-8, 648-52
unilateral nature **46,** 146, **123,** 212-13, 317-18, 376, 384, 388
validity **76,** 115, 172-3, 188
International Court of Justice (ICJ), compulsory jurisdiction, acceptance, interpretation
in accordance with international law **123,** 325, 378-9, 403-4, 419-30, 438-79, 481
relevant rules of international law applicable between the parties **123,** 411, 425, 426
vital interests, relevance **123,** 404-5
compatibility with international law, presumption of **123,** 228-9
context **123,** 423
contra proferentem **123,** 213, 215, 404
declaration as a whole **123,** 260-2, 325, 401-4, 423, 441
effectiveness **123,** 215, 220, 223, 235-6, 261, 404-6, 425, 446-8
government press release **123,** 433-4
intention of State at time of declaration **123,** 214-15, 220, 224-5, 235-6, 292-3, 328-9, 377-8, 409, 410-14, 481
Aegean Sea Continental Shelf **123,** 215
legislation **123,** 409, 423-4, 430
parliamentary proceedings and **123,** 215, 217-18, 224-5, 328-9, 430-3, 443-4
underlying intention **123,** 385-9, 411-12, 444-6, 478, 479
literal **123,** 385
mutuality of consent and **123,** 213, 317-18, 376-7
narrow, effect **123,** 253-4, 262-3
natural and reasonable **46,** 172, **123,** 214-15, 216, 222-3, 224, 226, 236, 262, 325, 377-8, 409
object and purpose **123,** 411, 419-25
objective nature **123,** 414
optional nature of consent, relevance **123,** 378-9
ordinary meaning **123,** 411, 429-30
previous declaration, relevance **123,** 213-15, 403, 434-6, 440
restrictive interpretation of reservation **123,** 213-15
subsequent practice **123,** 424-5
textual **123,** 328-9, 377-9, 385-7, 413-14
Anglo-Iranian Oil Company **123,** 214, 377-8, 409
grammar **123,** 214, 445
treaty interpretation, relevance **123,** 214, 244, 317-18, 385, 411
treaty related to subject-matter of declaration and **123,** 436-7
International Court of Justice (ICJ), compulsory jurisdiction, acceptance, reservations **57,** 373, 376, 390-1, 496, 521-2, **76,** 109, 132-6, 155, 159-61, 165-9, 176-80, 200-6, **85,** 261, **106,** 155. *See also* compulsory jurisdiction, acceptance
agreement to have resort to some other method **92,** 38, **97,** 12-14
'arising after' **92,** 38
'automatic' (self-judging) **123,** 227, 229-31, 258, 383, 405, 426
'Commonwealth reservation' **97,** 94
compatibility with international law, relevance **123,** 211-12, 215-17, 219-23, 225-7, 230, 242-4, 246-7, 251, 254-8, 284-5, 323-4, 379-82
ordre public international **123,** 284
proportionality and **123,** 256

International Court of Justice (ICJ), compulsory jurisdiction (*cont.*)
Right of Passage over Indian Territory **123,** 215
violation of fundamental norm of international law **123,** 255-8, 266, 380-1
violation of UN Charter **123,** 380-1
as definition of terms of consent **123,** 213-14, 255
'disputes arising out of or concerning' **123,** 218-19, 227, 476-9
domestic jurisdiction **76,** 133, **123,** 246
doubt about legality of position as reason for **123,** 216, 230, 247, 324, 418
history **76,** 210-15, **123,** 245-50, 379
as integral part of declaration accepting jurisdiction **123,** 212, 213, 217, 230-1
multilateral treaty reservation **76,** 132-6, 160-1, 165-9, 179-81, 265-6, 313-27, 365-8, 486, 508, 512, 516-17, 526-33, 535-45, 549-53, 630-40, 863-70
effect on jurisdiction clause of a treaty **76,** 873
effect where analagous rule of customary international law coexists with treaty **76,** 428, 430
reservation as to nature of jurisdiction, admissibility **97,** 501
Schulz letter. *See* International Court of Justice (ICJ), compulsory jurisdiction, acceptance, reservations, modification/replacement
treaty reservations compared **123,** 407
as unilateral act **123,** 214, 216, 235-7, 246, 317-18
Vandenberg Amendment. *See* multilateral treaty reservation *above*
waiver **76,** 367-8, 542-4
International Court of Justice (ICJ), consent to jurisdiction 46, 158, 161, **55,** 195-6, **56,** 79-80, 83, 84, 135, 220-1, **57,** 374-81, 508, 547, 562, 611, **70,** 539, 545, 551-2, 564, 567-9, 574, 584-8, 591, 595, 597, 602, 621-2, 648, 656, 668-9, 671-2, 677, 679, 682-3, **76,** 223-4, 517, 863, **80,** 482, **81,** 468, **84,** 264, 280, **92,** 38, **95,** 130, **97,** 27, 96-7
common **102,** 68-9
compromissory clause **56,** 107-8, 123, 199-201, **84,** 348. *See also* International Court of Justice (ICJ), Special Agreement; Mandate, South West Africa, compromissory clause; Mandates, compromissory clause
dispute settlement convention distinguished **84,** 267-8
'matters specially provided for . . . in treaties and conventions in force' **102,** 33
compulsory jurisdiction. *See* International Court of Justice (ICJ), compulsory jurisdiction, acceptance; International Court of Justice (ICJ), compulsory jurisdiction, acceptance, interpretation; International Court of Justice (ICJ), compulsory jurisdiction, acceptance, reservations
evidence of **102,** 104-6
Head of State's letter in another forum **115,** 31-2
standard of proof **102,** 103-6
Head of State's authority, relevance **115,** 34-5
implied **97,** 498-9
conduct in proceedings **115,** 33
request for provisional measures **115,** 33-4
statement of position **106,** 16, 17
need for **37,** 111, **62,** 634, **106,** 139, 142, 247-8
PCIJ and. *See* International Court of Justice (ICJ), in relation to other tribunals and dispute settlement procedures, PCIJ
request for an examination and **106,** 17
requirements
express provision **97,** 498. *See also* implied *above*
'unequivocal indication . . . of a voluntary and undisputed acceptance' **95,** 59-60, **102,** 104-6, 109, 111-12, 113, **115,** 33-4

scope **37,** 164-5
Special Agreement. *See* International Court of Justice (ICJ), Special Agreement
withdrawal **123,** 323. *See also* compulsory jurisdiction, acceptance, modification/replacement *above*
International Court of Justice (ICJ), contentious proceedings 84, 264
General Act for the Pacific Settlement of Disputes (1928) **60,** 572-80, 597, 621
Greece–Turkey, Brussels Communiqué (1975) **60,** 598-603, 606, 609-10, 615, 640-1
judicial proceedings distinguished **59,** 89, 129
jurisdiction **54,** 391, 560-1, **60,** 537-8, 540, 542, 552-3, **70,** 572, 585, **71,** 91-3, **84,** 264
consensual basis **59,** 162, **84,** 269
limited object **62,** 641-2, 647-8
South West Africa **49,** 3, 122, 166
Special Agreement **71,** 91-3
International Court of Justice (ICJ), 'dispute' 57, 464-5, 505, 509-14, 530, 574-5, **76,** 147, 360-1, 554-73, **84,** 246, 269, 300-1, **106,** 171-2, 190-1
additional, means of bringing **70,** 552, 667
admissibility, as problem of **97,** 575, **105,** 376
amendment of claim **97,** 34, **123,** 208-9
claim (*petitum*) and **102,** 94-5, **123,** 308-11, 348-56, 361-6
classification as. *See also* legal character *below*
'a disagreement on a point of law or fact, a conflict of legal views or interests between two persons' **37,** 10
'any dispute whatever' **37,** 24-5, 50-3, 88, 98, 103, 167, 169, 275, 404
international dispute between States **115,** 70-1
negotiations as necessary preliminary **123,** 240-1
'which cannot be settled by negotiation' **37,** 25-8, 53-6, 89-91, 104, 167-9, 174-6, 291-2, 357, 428-9, 480, 486, 565
cognizance of **61,** 517, 521-2, 545-6
conflict of interests distinguished **97,** 575-6, 577
context **61,** 517, 521, 544, 546
critical date **97,** 472
date arising **82,** 248, 254, 257, 261-72, 275-6, 277, 278-81
enactment of legislation **82,** 270, 275-6
implementation of legislation **82,** 270-2
definition **59,** 87-9, **82,** 245, **105,** 376-7
request to intervene and **97,** 234-5, 238
standing **105,** 248-59
disagreement relating to performance of treaty obligations **115,** 27-30
breach of treaty distinguished **115,** 42
infringement of rights of State, need for **115,** 38-42
discontinuance **61,** 593-5
dissolution of union of States **91,** 306
evidence of **94,** 517
argued claims **97,** 471-2, 579-80
failure to resolve legal controversy **97,** 486-7
existence of
absence of defence **82,** 246-7
determination by Court **57,** 416
intervening State and principle parties, between **70,** 549, 551, 554, 567, 613-14, 662, 667, 681-2
objective matter **82,** 245-7, 267, **97,** 574, **105,** 240-1, 272
unilateral assertion **82,** 245-7, 267, **117,** 52-3

International Court of Justice (ICJ), 'dispute' (*cont.*)
failure to agree issues **97,** 227-8, 239-41, **100,** 13-14, **102,** 58, 116, 118
intervention, distinct dispute, introduction of **70,** 567, 571, 582-3, 586, 613-14, 621-2, 628, 636-7, 646-7, 649-52, 654-6, 660, 667, 676-7, 679, 682-4, 693
jurisdiction, as problem of **97,** 575
legal character **57,** 455, 464-5, 472, 479, 483, 505, 509-14, 530, 548-51, 562-3, 574-6, **62,** 452. *See also* classification as *above*
'any question of international law' **123,** 321
'existence of any fact which would constitute a breach of international law' **123,** 321
need to indicate **123,** 361-2
legislation independent of application as basis **84,** 247, **123,** 364-6, 373-4
maritime delimitation. *See* maritime delimitation, ICJ and
mootness **57,** 415-16, 420-3, 596-601, **123,** 227-8, 240-1, 335-6, 372-3
need for **37,** 10, 52, 81-2, 98-9, 165, 176-7, **53,** 417-18, **57,** 404-5, 415-16, 422-4, 434, 468, 575, **97,** 470-1, 574-7
between States **55,** 151
political character **41,** 165, **57,** 433, 442, 509-12, **62,** 472, 479, 483, 548-51, 562-3, 574-6, 581, **110,** 227-8
preliminary matter **37,** 10, 177, 180, 575, 580
recent assertion of title **97,** 485-6
requirements. *See also* whole dispute to be submitted *below*
declaration of **82,** 276
express difference of views **37,** 10-11, **105,** 241
precise nature of claim to be specified in application **97,** 32-4, **102,** 20-1, **123,** 208-10, 274, 282, 307-8, 348-50
settlement **61,** 549, 570, 574, 592-3
Australia/Nauru (1993) **97,** 111
Passage through the Great Belt (Finland v. *Denmark)* **105,** 649-50
statements of parties **57,** 518
'subject of dispute', determination
by applicant **123,** 208-9, 363, 481
by Court **123,** 209-11, 272-84, 318, 366-75, 390-1
in case of proceedings instituted by application **123,** 308
equality of parties and **123,** 390-1, 481
parties' differing views (*Fisheries Jurisdiction* (*Spain* v. *Canada*)) **123,** 207-8, 242, 251, 272-8, 291, 319-23, 348-74
as tripartite operation **123,** 272-3, 275-7, 282, 371-3
title as cause of action **123,** 274-5, 291, 356-9, 438-43, 476-9
Continental Shelf (Libya/Malta) **123,** 357-8
Fisheries Jurisdiction cases **123,** 358
Nationality Decrees in Tunis and Morocco **123,** 441-2
validity of claim, relevance **97,** 472
whole dispute to be submitted **102,** 21-2, 23, 90-1, 93-6, 106, 112-13, 115-16, 120
'all the disputed matters' distinguished **102,** 84
Court's invitation to submit whole dispute **102,** 22, 23, 27-8, 31-2
North Sea Cases **123,** 321
Qatar v. *Bahrain* **123,** 283, 306-7
Right of Passage over Indian Territory **123,** 322
separability of elements **123,** 321-2, 362-3
International Court of Justice (ICJ), evidence 54, 398-401, **59,** 155, **67,** 18, **80,** 468-9
admissibility **37,** 553
depositions **37,** 244

negotiations, positions taken during **102,** 22-3
videotape **116,** 22
Advisory Opinion, probative value **49,** 141
in advisory proceedings **59,** 45-6, 159
burden of proof **55,** 294, **70,** 501, **75,** 137-8
desirability of placing facts on record **95,** 141
documentation, after closure of written proceedings **97,** 490
EC mediator **95,** 89
expert **71,** 83, **97,** 124 nn. 8 and 9
appointment **80,** 551-2
on behalf of Parties **80,** 564-5
assistance of **37,** 557, **71,** 80, 92
survey, request for **81,** 460-1, **97,** 277-8, 315
failure to seek **81,** 472
merits stage, distinction, whether **95,** 140-1
government statement **95,** 80-1, 89, 91
independent **95,** 89-90, 141
absence **95,** 91
Helsinki Watch **95,** 89
UN officials **95,** 89
UN resolutions **95,** 141
UNHCR official **95,** 89
US Bureau of Refugees Program Director **95,** 89
US Senate Committee on European Affairs **95,** 89
joinder of parties and **97,** 66-7
Nicaragua **97,** 67
judicial notice **46,** 323, **95,** 141
international law **56,** 152
Nicaragua **95,** 141
UN decisions **105,** 264, 392-3
media reports **95,** 75-6, 89, 177
difficulty of communication, relevance **95,** 76, 142
Nicaragua **95,** 76
US Diplomatic and Consular Staff in Tehran **95,** 75-6
nationality of corporation **70,** 501, 510-11, 519
negotiations, positions taken during, admissibility, customary international law **102,** 22-3
notoriety **95,** 178-9
on-site inspections **37,** 243, 461, **97,** 277-8, 315, **116,** 23
power to demand **110,** 634-5
presumptions, rebuttability **80,** 483, 532
provisional measures stage **95,** 75-6, 139-42, 175-7
need to avoid pre-judgment of facts **95,** 77-8, 89
refusal to receive **49,** 212-13, 306
rules of **110,** 360
absence **95,** 75
standard of proof
balance of probabilities **97,** 422
beyond reasonable doubt **95,** 141-2
substantial credibility **95,** 78
translation **84,** 347, 357-8, **97,** 321 n. 1
Yugoslav State Commission for War Crimes and Genocide **95,** 79-80, 82-3, 91
delay in presenting **95,** 82-3

International Court of Justice (ICJ), ***forum prorogatum*** **95,** 59-60, 134-9
Anglo-Iranian Oil Company **95,** 72-3, 137-8
consensual basis **95,** 71-2, **99,** 482
clear intention, need for **95,** 72-3
conduct of parties **95,** 134-9
parties' intention **95,** 72-3
Corfu Channel **95,** 73
Jan Mayen **99,** 482
jurisdictional basis, need for **95,** 135-9
proprio motu measures, relevance to **95,** 139
provisional measures based on **95,** 165-6
request for measures going beyond agreed jurisdiction **95,** 59-60, 72, 135-9
unilateral commencement of proceedings **95,** 130, **102,** 33-4, 103, **115,** 45, 49-51
International Court of Justice (ICJ), intervention of third State 37, 103, 539, **46,** 454, 503, **57,** 395-7, **62,** 601-4, 632, **67,** 17, **70,** 593, 623-4, **76,** 74-103, 505-6, 646-8, **81,** 404-10, **84,** 284-5, **97,** 27-8, 103, 154-213. *See also* International Court of Justice (ICJ), intervention of third State, 'interest of a legal nature which may be affected by the decision' as requirement; International Court of Justice (ICJ), third States and
ad adjuvandum. See supporting intervention *below*
ad excludendum. See competing intervention *below*
admissibility **70,** 585, 605, 612, 638, 647, 652, 664, **76,** 75, 77, 78, 79
amount of detail required **97,** 251, 259-65
basis
interpretation of **76,** 93-100
convention **62,** 611, 639
ICJ Statute **76,** 98-9
optional clause declaration **76,** 100-1
UN Charter **76,** 95
by parties to convention to be interpreted **62,** 622, 624, 637
competing intervention **70,** 596
consent to jurisdiction requirement and **70,** 584-5, 671-4, 677-8, 683, 685-6, **97,** 254-5
discretionary powers of Court and **62,** 621, 635, 640, 643, **70,** 538, 554, 557, 571, 582, 603, 615, 617, 635, 641-2, 664-5, 678, 680
effect of
on intervening State **62,** 619-20, 627-9, 634-5, 636, 647
on principal parties **62,** 628-9, **70,** 554, 594-6
El Salvador v. *Nicaragua* **105,** 265-7
erga omnes norm as issue **105,** 243-4, 272-3, 313-14, 385, 389-90, 392, 393
estoppel **70,** 613
'genuine' **70,** 552, 565, 619-20, 649, 653, 660, 667-8
geographical scope **70,** 593-4
grounds for **62,** 618, 622, 625-6, 629, 634-7
hearing on declaration of **76,** 75, 77, 78, 79, 81, 89-92, 505, 647
interested parties, right to appear **56,** 98
intervening party **70,** 542, 566, 577, 579, 620, 628, 666, 676
judge *ad hoc*, right to nominate **62,** 615
joinder of parties
audi alteram partem **97,** 60
binding force of decision limited to parties **97,** 28-9, 64, 100, 109
consensual basis of jurisdiction and **97,** 59, 65, 68, 106-97
Corfu Channel **97,** 97
Land, Island and Maritime Frontier Dispute **97,** 27, 62-3, 102-4
Libya–Malta (Intervention) **97,** 61-2, 168

Monetary Gold **97,** 26, 28, 29, 55, 59-67, 68-9, 97-8, 236-7, 243, 345
municipal law analogies **97,** 96-7
Nicaragua **97,** 27, 60-1, 99-102
optional clause declaration of non-participating party and **97,** 55-6
proprio motu power to order **97,** 27, 59
judgment, binding effect **97,** 525-6, 535-6, 646-7
consent of other parties, need for **97,** 526, 632
reciprocity **97,** 526
jurisdiction stage **76,** 74, 103, 647
jurisdictional link between parties and intervening State, need for, whether
Libya/Malta **97,** 253
Tunisia/Libya **97,** 253
non-party intervener **62,** 617, 627-8, 639-40, 644, 646, 648, **70,** 567-9, 571-7, 583, 634, 665-6, 676
notification. *See* International Court of Justice (ICJ), procedural issues, notification to third States (Art. 63 of UN Charter) *below*
objection to **76,** 79, 88-90
Order, need for **97,** 159
principles and rules of international law, interpretation of and **62,** 611, 639-40, 642, 643, **70,** 633-5
procedure **70,** 646-8
economy of means **70,** 555, 576, 621-2, 636, 663
incidental issue **70,** 614-16, 618, 647-51, 659, 662, 668, 672, 675, 685, **97,** 155, 156-7, 158, 162, 209-10, 255, **106,** 23
pleadings of principal parties, provision of **70,** 562, 679
purpose **62,** 618-22, 624, 626-8, 641, 647-8, **70,** 541-2, 548, 550, 552, 560, 565, 573, 577-8, 581-2, 593, 595-6, 605-6, 608, 610, 612, 618, 628, 636, 640, 646, 650, 675, 681, **81,** 404-5
interest of a legal nature distinguished **70,** 610
protection of legal rights **97,** 249-51
protection of State's interests **81,** 258, 349, 363, 401-2
protection of third States **70,** 555, 563, 623, 677
to inform Court of legal rights **97,** 249-52
refusal **81,** 257-8, 404-5
remedy **70,** 617
request for examination of the situation and **106,** 14, 28-9, 110-11
requirements **62,** 616, 620, 635. *See also* International Court of Justice (ICJ), intervention of a third State, 'interest of a legal nature which may be affected by the decision' as requirement
conformity with ICJ Statue **62,** 621-2, 628, 644
failure to meet **76,** 83, 101
jurisdictional link between parties and intervening State **62,** 617, 619-21, 623-4, 627-9, 631, 633, 649, **70,** 537, 543, 545, 547, 551-3, 556, 557, 561, 563, 564-6, 568-70, 571-5, 577-8, 584, 586, 588, 591, 593, 596-7, 601, 602, 604-6, 608-9, 614-16, 618, 620-3, 626, 628, 647-8, 656, 660, 669, 672, 673-8, 681-2, **97,** 252-6
intervening State as non-party **62,** 611, 636, 639
intervening State as party **62,** 611, 624, 633-5, 636-7
precise object of intervention **97,** 249-52
specific elements of case as basis **62,** 626
right of **70,** 632, 673, **76,** 92-103, 136, 142
scope **70,** 619-20, 623, 626-7, 637
separability of issues **105,** 390-2
Special Agreement and **62,** 628, **70,** 553, 592, 678

International Court of Justice (ICJ), intervention of third State (*cont.*)
standing **70,** 618
State responsibility for own acts, relevance **105,** 311-13, 415
status of State requesting **97,** 156
admissible arguments **97,** 497-8
limited to aspects of case in which 'legal interest which may be affected' exists **97,** 237, 256-7
new dispute, permissibility **97,** 254-5
party, whether **97,** 255-7, 497-8, 525, 632
right to be heard **97,** 166, 257, 526
to take procedural situation as found, whether **97,** 156, 211-13, 497
Statute of Court and **70,** 569, 572, 575, 587, 600-1, 603, 628-35, 673, 685
strictly limited **70,** 678-9, 682-3, 685
supporting intervention **70,** 596
UN law as issue **105,** 392, 393
validity of treaty with third party as issue **105,** 241-3, 245, 263-4, 265-7, 273-4, 394-6
unilateral acts of one party **105,** 395-6
International Court of Justice (ICJ), intervention of third State, 'interest of a legal nature which may be affected by the decision' as requirement 37, 88, 99, 100, 103-4, 166, 180-2, 240, **57,** 536, **62,** 615-18, 621, 635, 640, 645, **70,** 537, 539, 554, 565, 568-9, 572, 578-83, 600-1, 603, 605-8, 610-13, 615, 624-6, 635, 637-8, 640, 646, 650-3, 655, 660, 662, 677, 683, 697-8, **97,** 27-8, 156, 210, 227-8, 235-49, 257, 259-62, 276
'affected by the decision' **62,** 618-19, 622-3, 628, 635, 640, 642-3, 645-9, **70,** 540, 552, 564, 572, 601, 603, 610-11, 639, 642, 649, 658, 660-4, 666-7, 669-70, 673, 678-80, 684-5, 688, **76,** 133, 135-7
direct effect **97,** 240
burden of proof **97,** 238-9, 244, 245-6
development of legal principles and rules **62,** 617, 619-22, 628, 640, 642-3, 647
evidence of **70,** 661-2, 679
general principles and rules, interest in **97,** 245, 247-8, 259
geographical location, relevance **62,** 618, 628
juridical character **97,** 49-50, 95
navigational rights, interest in **97,** 246
object of intervention distinguished **70,** 610, 667
observance of Mandate obligations **37,** 24-5, 50-2, 82-9, 98-100, 103-4, 108-9, 166-7, 250-84, 289-95, 298, 400-12, 416, 418-30, 433, 478, 480, 539-42, 546, 572-3, 583-7, 591-602
previous judicial decision to which party **97,** 242, 243
principles and rules of international law, clarification of **70,** 640, 642
reasoning of Court, whether **62,** 618, 620-2, 628, 645
recognition of interest by other parties **97,** 239-40, 242-3
requirements **70,** 538, 564, 569, 572, 574, 610, 634, 678, 680, 682
assertion of claim **97,** 242-3
precise definition **97,** 43-4, 239, 246
right to argue case **106,** 80-1
security interests **97,** 246
sovereign rights **70,** 687-8
protection of **70,** 539-40, 549-50, 552, 555, 561, 566, 571, 575-7, 583, 608, 612-13, 627, 636-7, 651-7, 678, 683, 686, 688
recognition of **70,** 548-50, 552, 560-1, 567, 571, 575-7, 579-80, 583, 595-6, 612-13, 627, 636-7, 651-6, 661, 683
Special Agreement, disputed interpretation and **97,** 239
subject-matter of decision, whether **70,** 677, 684

taking into account coast of third State **97,** 245-6, 262-3
'very subject-matter of the decision' **97,** 26-7, 28, 63-4, 68-9, 235-40, 243, **105,** 243, 245-6, 254, 261, 271, 297-8, 384-6
'very subject-matter of dispute' distinguished **97,** 243
International Court of Justice (ICJ), judge
abstention, right of **110,** 323
acting president, powers **71,** 70-9
ad hoc. See International Court of Justice (ICJ), judge *ad hoc*
'election by secret ballot' **97,** 195-6
'independent' **97,** 196-7
creation of Chambers and **97,** 196-7
judicial caution **95,** 141
judicial discretion **99,** 447, 559-65, 586
judicial error **76,** 504-5
judicial power, alienation, municipal law analogies **97,** 193-4, 199
judicial propriety **59,** 99, 160, **60,** 605-6, **76,** 77, 78, 492-4, 570-9
political considerations **105,** 398-9
judicial restraint, unilateral submission to Court and **99,** 572-8, 651
nationality **71,** 65-8, **76,** 71-4, 493, 862, **81,** 427
nationals of parties **56,** 149, **117,** 11
objections to **49,** 8-9, 120, 128, 299, 313-14
participation in drafting of texts later before Court **49,** 9, 120, 128, 313-14
Presidency, exercise by national of party to case **117,** 11, 32
questions by **37,** 353, 551, 563, **67,** 18, **71,** 65-9, 79, 83
request for information **46,** 91
tenure **97,** 200-3
Statute **97,** 201
International Court of Justice (ICJ), judge *ad hoc* 56, 99, **59,** 27-8, 34, 91, 123-4, **60,** 526, 527, 542, **67,** 17, **71,** 65-8, 70, 79, **81,** 249, 427
absence **57,** 614
applicable law
judge *ad hoc* **97,** 152
Statute **97,** 152
appointment **94,** 452, **95,** 53, **97,** 144, **102,** 11, 49
Application of Genocide Convention **115,** 11
arbitral practice, as **97,** 153
Cameroon v. *Nigeria* **106,** 152
competence **97,** 147-53
East Timor **105,** 234
Fisheries Jurisdiction (Spain v. *Canada)* **123,** 197-8
Frontier Dispute **97,** 147
Gabčíkovo–Nagymaros Project **116,** 22
Gulf of Maine **97,** 147, 173-4
Libya/Malta **97,** 149
Order, need for **97,** 147-8
priority of decision on **49,** 15, 16, 315-16
refusal **49,** 5, 9, 15-17, 57-8, 118-20, 129-31, 140, 142-3, 298-307, 315-21
right of. *See* nomination *below*
death. *See* replacement following death *below*
equality of parties and **106,** 16, **117,** 37
impartiality, duty of **95,** 127, **97,** 166
independence **97,** 165
jurisdiction as precondition **106,** 15

International Court of Justice (ICJ), judge *ad hoc* (*cont.*)
nomination by
Chamber **97,** 161, 164
intervening party **62,** 615, **97,** 158
parties **71,** 65-8, 70, 79, **97,** 147-53, **117,** 10
ICJ practice **117,** 32-6
PCIJ practice **97,** 150, 177-85, **117,** 31-2
'parties in the same interest' **117,** 11, 30-42
purpose **95,** 127, **106,** 142-3, **115,** 236
replacement following death **97,** 144, 146-53, 218, **102,** 50
standing-down procedure **97,** 147, 189-91
application to Chamber proceedings **97,** 191
ELSI **97,** 189-90
Frontier Dispute **97,** 190
Gulf of Maine **97,** 189
right to dispense with **97,** 190
International Court of Justice (ICJ), judgment 55, 361
applicability **57,** 574, 598
basis **106,** 12, 16, 22-3, 28, 34, 41-2, 53-5
right to select **37,** 253, 471
unilateral undertaking by party **106,** 17, 19, 118-19, 120
binding force **37,** 114, 168, 270, 417-18, 431-2, 479, 480, 482-6, 569, 571, **46,** 359, 394, 441, **62,** 618, 620, 627-8, 637-9, **67,** 33-4, 95, 136-40, 314, **70,** 542, 555, 566, 577-8, 581, 585, 598-9, 616, 622, 628, 630-3, 663, **71,** 68-9, 80, 81, **76,** 489-90, **81,** 257, 348, 451-2, 455-6, 459, 461, 480-2. *See also* International Court of Justice (ICJ), precedent
Art. 41 of Statute, ambiguity **95,** 115-17
Aegean Sea Continental Shelf **95,** 95
Art. 41 of Charter as procedural provision **95,** 96-7
Art. 59 of Statute **95,** 121
Art. 60 of Statute **95,** 121
Electricity Company of Sofia and Bulgaria **95,** 95, 97 n. 1
extra-judicial writings **95,** 104
gravity of subject matter **95,** 97
ICJ jurisprudence **95,** 102-3, 116-17
'indication', significance **95,** 96, 97-8, 104, 106
inherent authority of tribunal as basis **95,** 94-7
obligation to avoid prejudicing judgment **95,** 95-6, 97
obligation to comply with decisions of Court **95,** 101-2
'order' as mechanism **95,** 100-1
'ought', significance **95,** 98-9
'power' of Court, relevance **95,** 101-2, 117
'principle of institutional effectiveness' **95,** 94
'provisional measures' **95,** 99-100
'shall', significance **95,** 117
urgency, relevance **95,** 117-18
in case of decisions on jurisdiction **123,** 480-1
Chamber decision **97,** 160-1
intervening State **97,** 525-6, 535-6
municipal courts **82,** 480
municipal law analogies **105,** 260
need for **97,** 65-6
parties to case, limited to **97,** 28, 66, **99,** 455, **105,** 268, 311

request for interpretation and **81,** 450
stipulation in Special Agreement **71,** 80, 91
third party review **71,** 69
third States and **70,** 539, 544, 546, 554-6, 575-6, 597-9, 616, 623, 627, 634, 638-9, 664, 677, 686-9, **76,** 539, **81,** 257, 350-1, 406, **97,** 28-9, 59-65, 68-9, 93-5, 96-7, 98, 101, 210, **100,** 32, **105,** 268, 311
enforcement procedures, absence **97,** 57
limitation to parties **105,** 268, 311
power to restrict **81,** 260
compensation, acts *pendente lite* **56,** 197
compliance **81,** 451-2, **85,** 261. *See also* implementation *below*; International Court of Justice (ICJ), provisional measures, compliance
alternative solution **81,** 451-2
jus cogens/peremptory norm and **85,** 235-6
obligation **76,** 490, 508-9, **81,** 451-2
individual **94,** 498
UN Charter **85,** 255
consequences **37,** 140-1, 164, 479, 480-7, **57,** 598
correction. *See also* International Court of Justice (ICJ), request for correction of judgment
for *erreur matérielle* **81,** 431
judgment as means **81,** 431
decisions of Special Chamber
status **71,** 68-9
third party review **71,** 69
declaratory **57,** 457-66, 597-8, **84,** 307-9, **116,** 84-5
applicability **57,** 466
legal effects **57,** 465-6
objects **57,** 486
purpose **57,** 459
right to **37,** 266-7, 480
self-standing, whether **84,** 264, 266, 274, 276-7, 279-80
dispositif **70,** 686
function and scope **37,** 276, 417, 483
divided court **37,** 297, 432, 477, 559
effective legal application **57,** 574-5
effects
on intervening States **62,** 618-19, 629, 633-7, 639, 642-3, **70,** 546, 554-6, 562, 574-5, 578, 582, 598, 606, 608, 620-1, 627, 634, 637, 641, 658, 686
prior **46,** 40-1, 76, 78, 80, 87, 159. *See also* binding force *above*; International Court of Justice (ICJ), precedent
enforcement/implementation **81,** 451-2. *See also* compliance *above*
agreement **81,** 725-7
expert role **81,** 455, 460, 485
individual's right **85,** 254, 255-62
equitable requirement **41,** 138, 163
ex aequo et bono **37,** 443-4, **41,** 50, 78, 143-4, 163-4, **71,** 105, 207
exhaustiveness, desirability **46,** 335-7
existing law, limited to **53,** 483, **56,** 163, 183, 191
finality. *See* binding force *above*
as guide **41,** 115
interlocutory
admissibility **102,** 31-2, 92-3
Free Zones of Upper Savoy and the District of Gex **102,** 92-3

International Court of Justice (ICJ), judgment (*cont.*)
international law
conformity with, need for **94,** 575
as statement of **53,** 498-9
interpretation **67,** 33-4, 139-40
academic publication **106,** 44
in accordance with precedent **110,** 328
avoidance of unreasonable or absurd result **106,** 58
context **106,** 53, 54
implied term **106,** 58
interdependence of legal grounds **110,** 215, 328
object **106,** 53
official publication of Court **106,** 44, **115,** 439-40
ordinary meaning **106,** 53
interview regarding **76,** 513-14, 648-9
jurisdiction, going beyond **81,** 308-9
legal nature **81,** 322, **84,** 246
legislative judgment **37,** 234, 269, 281, 312, 338, 408, 443, **41,** 185
meaning and scope **81,** 447, 456, 463, 474
multilateral conventions, influence on **62,** 125
nature of **59,** 139
non liquet **41,** 148, **110,** 211-13, 216, 219-22, 225-6, 229-31, 232-5, 328-9, 339-40, 385-6, 507-31, 532, 533, 539-41
obiter dicta, effect **105,** 389, **110,** 279, 327
object of claim and **57,** 588
obligation to avoid prejudicing
binding force of provisional measures and **95,** 95-6, 97, 121
general principle of international law **95,** 95-6
general principle of law recognized by civilized nations **95,** 96
Norm-Grundsatz **95,** 96
operative section, basis of judgment distinguished **106,** 53
orders **57,** 460
parties' arguments, relevance **94,** 472
per incuriam **37,** 295, **53,** 583, 584, **78,** 590
premature disclosure **57,** 418
prescriptive **116,** 84-5
provisional measures and **55,** 393-4, **95,** 95-6, 97, 121
ratio decidendi. See reasons *below*
reasons **81,** 453, **106,** 53-4, **110,** 233-4
need for **37,** 417-18, 483, **99,** 455, 459, 483, **110,** 533-5
as source of law **49,** 163-4
unsatisfactory **99,** 482-5, 496-7, **120,** 301
request for interpretation. *See* International Court of Justice (ICJ), request for interpretation of judgment
request for revision. *See* International Court of Justice (ICJ), revision of judgment
res judicata. See binding force *above*; International Court of Justice (ICJ), precedent
review, possibility of **81,** 480-1
scope **62,** 636, **70,** 556, 571, 627, 647
silence, interpretation of **81,** 308-9
subsequent legal development and **56,** 174-5
validity, attitude of parties, relevance **76,** 358
International Court of Justice (ICJ), jurisdiction 41, 91, **56,** 174-5, **57,** 382, 385, 456, 469, **60,** 538, **62,** 549-50, 619-20, **70,** 537-8, 542-3, 545, 570-1, 574, 585-7, 597-8, 609,

615, 620, 625, 634, 647-9, 655, 669, 671-4, 677, **76,** 362-3, 450, 495-9, 550-3, 640-6, 862-4. *See also* International Court of Justice (ICJ), compulsory jurisdiction, acceptance; International Court of Justice (ICJ), consent to jurisdiction
absence of formal request **97,** 486
acceptance **46,** 41, 46-7, 146, 158, 159, 161, 162, 164
'clear and unequivocal' **46,** 169-71
acquiescence in **48,** 338
caution as to **48,** 359
admissibility and **37,** 99-100, 276, 486, **110,** 107-8
agreement as part of treaty **55,** 211
appeal provisions, interpretation **48,** 360
basis **55,** 169, 188-9, 277, 361, 372, **57,** 379-83, **62,** 609, 614, 619-20, 631, 634, **70,** 588, 662, 667, 681-2
additional grounds **95,** 56-7
alternative **57,** 503
arbitral award, annulment proceedings **92,** 37-8, 56, 68-9
failure to invoke **95,** 32
international law **54,** 477
'matters specially provided for . . . in treaties and conventions in force' **102,** 33, 36, 85
Minorities Treaty (St Germain-en-Laye) (1919) **95,** 57-8, 132-3
Nuremberg Charter **95,** 132
protection against **70,** 574
specification **76,** 137-40
'State accepting the same obligation' **84,** 236
treaty or convention in force. *See* treaty or convention in force conferring *below*
boni judicis est ampliare jurisdictionem **56,** 197
burden of proof **37,** 115, 164, **84,** 230-1, **123,** 211
case title **76,** 654-5
collective self-defence **76,** 361
compensation claims **56,** 221-2
compétence de la compétence **55,** 187-8, **105,** 292, 299-300, **123,** 211, 283-4, 323, 332-3, 479
critical date **37,** 481, 541, **76,** 257, 260, 338, **117,** 64
denial of **56,** 83
determination of **54,** 443, 478, 493, **55,** 98, **56,** 114, **57,** 437, 469, 545, 613-15
as exercise of **54,** 505
discretionary power **57,** 599-600
dispute, need for. *See* International Court of Justice (ICJ), 'dispute'
equality of States **70,** 551, 565, 567, 569, 588, 590, 593-4, 669
ex aequo et bono **81,** 346-7
Art. 36(1) declarations and **99,** 481
Art. 36(2) declarations and **99,** 480
Art. 38(2), drafting history **99,** 595-8
contra legem, whether **99,** 598
equity, relevance **97,** 542
parties' consent, need for **97,** 549-50, **99,** 480, 481-2, 561-2, 595
existence and exercise distinguished **97,** 472, 576, 577
factual issues **49,** 167-8
fin de non-recevoir **37,** 10, 100, 183, 416
full exercise of **81,** 255
General Act for the Pacific Settlement of Disputes (1928) and **57,** 447, 472, 503, 546, 563-6
genocide cases **115,** 42-3

International Court of Justice (ICJ), jurisdiction (*cont.*)
human rights, in respect of **57,** 448
incidental **70,** 545, 585, 614, 616, 670, 672, 684
inherent **57,** 404-5, 466-7
international law as basis **54,** 477
effect **56,** 80
interpretation or application of treaty **76,** 139, 157, 163-4, 226, 340-1, 469-70, 645, 873, **84,** 348, **94,** 490, 493-4, 516-18, 563-4, 579-80, 581-3, **95,** 129-31, 151, 171-2, **117,** 47, 48, **118,** 11-12, 16-17, 44, 45
dispute as to whether treaty applicable to case **117,** 15-16, 53
'interpretation or application', distinguishable, whether **82,** 261, 269, 276-7, 611
interpretation of UN Charter **94,** 539, **117,** 60-2, 75-6, 107
existence of relevant substantive rules of law **95,** 12
intuiti personae **70,** 590
invocation as unfriendly act **94,** 583
issues not raised in submissions **37,** 346, 352-3, 471, 594, **76,** 137-8, 226, **81,** 308-9
judicial review, judgments of international tribunals. *See* International Court of Justice (ICJ), status and functions, judicial review
judicial role and **57,** 404-5
judicial settlement agreement and **55,** 169, 194
legal question **84,** 231
reparation, failure to seek and **37,** 593, 596
limitation **56,** 182, **62,** 629, **70,** 585, 594, 673
consent of parties **56,** 186
lack of political will **95,** 130-1
lack of primacy **97,** 57
merits and. *See* merits, jurisdiction and *below*
misuse of power, determination of **54,** 491
municipal law analogy, interlocutory judgment **102,** 31-2
'negative answer' **92,** 110, 115, 125
optional. *See* International Court of Justice (ICJ), compulsory jurisdiction, acceptance; International Court of Justice (ICJ), consent to jurisdiction
pleadings in respect of **56,** 94-6
preconditions **81,** 449
principal **70,** 585-6, 588
proprio motu **48,** 338, **76,** 79, 447, 468, 504, 579
ratione materiae **70,** 589, **95,** 27
Convention in force between parties **95,** 29-31
ratione personae **70,** 589, 593, **95,** 27-9
Bosnia-Herzegovina **95,** 27-9
compromissory clause **95,** 29
non-party to Statute **95,** 29
ratione temporis, critical date **115,** 30
reciprocity **70,** 551, 567, 588-90, 592, 618, 656, 669-70
refusal to accept **55,** 353
Northern Cameroons **80,** 481
reasons, need for **80,** 481
reparation, determination of **76,** 476-7
restrictive interpretation **94,** 557, **106,** 179-81, **115,** 42-3
avoidance of **82,** 281-2, **105,** 378-80
Security Council and. *See* International Court of Justice (ICJ), Security Council and
Special Agreement. *See* International Court of Justice (ICJ), Special Agreement
standard of proof **106,** 90, 95-6, 97

State sovereignty and **56,** 85
States party to the Statute and **56,** 128
submission to **55,** 195-6
executive function **85,** 254
territorial dispute **105,** 385
treaty or convention in force conferring **76,** 137-40, 155-62, 239, 868, 869, **84,** 290, 292, 293
Genocide Convention (1948), Art. IX **115,** 22-35, 38-43, 44, 179-82
Mandate **37,** 115-19, 164-5, 184
Mandate, South West Africa **37,** 42-9, 77, 79, 92, 95-7, 115, 129-36, 564, 565
Montreal Convention for the Suppression of Unlawful Acts Against the Safety of Civilian Aviation (1971) **94,** 489, 491, 493-4, 533-6, **117,** 14-22, 44-7, 61-5
Nicaragua–US Treaty of Friendship, Commerce and Navigation **76,** 137-40, 155, 161-2, 163-5, 172, 225-7, 242-3, 266-8, 339-48, 469, 580-3, 640-6, 720, 872-4
optional clause declaration distinguished **37,** 117, **46,** 146
Pact of Bogotá (1948) **76,** 240-1, 300-1, **84,** 228, 229, 231-3, 237-45. *See also* Pact of Bogotá (1948), ICJ and
reservations **57,** 562-3
Special Agreement. *See* International Court of Justice (ICJ), Special Agreement
Treaty of Saint-Germain-en-Laye (1919) **115,** 32-3
UN Administrative Tribunal judgments, review of. *See* United Nations Administrative Tribunal (UNAT), review of judgments by ICJ
UN resolution, determination of validity **94,** 515, 524-5, 526-7, 537-40, 585-99, **105,** 296
unilateral application **85,** 260, **95,** 31-3, 58-9, 132
International Court of Justice (ICJ), justiciability 37, 111, 120, 353, 434, 445-8, 547-9, **61,** 546, **76,** 360-1, 500-4, 555-80, 627-30, 696
International Court of Justice (ICJ), merits
advisory opinion, in case of **110,** 38-9
antecedent question *re* standing **37,** 251
anticipation of decision on merits **110,** 38-9
avoidance of prejudicial statements on **48,** 337-8
definition, *Anglo-Iranian Oil Co.* **97,** 42
jurisdiction and **57,** 434, **76,** 364-5, **105,** 284-5, **110,** 36
distinguished **55,** 178, 180-2, **56,** 102
international law, relevance at two stages distinguished **123,** 216-17, 221, 243-4, 252, 253-8, 269-72
participation in merits stage in case of objection to jurisdiction **76,** 510-11
pleaded separately **56,** 95-6
preliminary objections and merits, joinder **37,** 110, **46,** 52-7, 64-5, 75, 93, 108, 110-12, 120, 124, 126, 174-7, 231-2, 284-7, 442, 461, 530, **117,** 69-70, 109-10
International Court of Justice (ICJ), precedent 62, 549-51, 562-5, 575, 578, **71,** 101-2, 115, 120, 134-7, 162, 187-9, 192, 201, 205-6, 208, 210, **76,** 258, **81,** 409
advisory opinion **37,** 185, 239, 417, 431, 487, 569, **105,** 304-5, **110,** 104, 107, 320-2
arbitral decisions **85,** 347
binding, whether **99,** 501
Central American Court of Justice, decision **97,** 517
consistency, desirability **46,** 78, 80, 159, **99,** 486
context of decisions **71,** 187, 216
departure from own jurisprudence **49,** 273 n. 63, 279, 321
European Court of Human Rights **85,** 347-8
influence, reasons, need for **99,** 455
interpretation of judgment **110,** 328

International Court of Justice (ICJ), precedent (*cont.*)
judgment **71,** 93-4, 102, 115, 120, 124, 135, 162, 187-9, 192, 201, 205-6, 208, 210, 643, 657, 695-6, **76,** 258
previous proceedings relating to same dispute **97,** 64-5, 66
reversal of decision **97,** 174, 203-4
Aerial Incident **97,** 204
test of reasonableness **105,** 302-4
International Court of Justice (ICJ), preliminary objections 46, 22-3, 108-12, **48,** 338, 367, 371, 421, **55,** 180-2, 187, 195, **56,** 95, 102, **57,** 449, **76,** 160-1, 169, 180, 322, 362-5, 529, **81,** 483
1946 and 1978 Rules of Court distinguished **97,** 38-9, **123,** 267
in absence of jurisdiction **106,** 17, 21, 31
abuse of rights under Statute or Rules of Court **115,** 35
Barcelona Traction **78,** 641, **97,** 39, 40
decision on, finality **37,** 270-1, 289, 294, 296, 431-2, 482, 594-7
determination at preliminary stage, preference for **97,** 38-9
Nicaragua **97,** 39-40
procedure **123,** 333-8
purpose **115,** 166
ratione temporis **46,** 23, 25, 50-1, 172-4
requirements
exclusively preliminary character **97,** 38, **116,** 51-2, **117,** 24-7, 44-7, 55, 68-9, 87-8, 102-4, 106, **123,** 227, 232, 253, 267, 291, 308-10, 480
Nottebohm **97,** 41
Nuclear Tests Cases **123,** 309
possibility of effective judgment **117,** 55-6
presumption of legal obligation **97,** 40-3
value to Court **115,** 35
waiver **81,** 449, 467-8
International Court of Justice (ICJ), procedural issues 54, 495-6, **55,** 335. *See also* International Court of Justice (ICJ), Rules of Court
abuse of process **84,** 246, **97,** 22, **105,** 358, **110,** 319
absence of objection **110,** 238
political exploitation **37,** 541-2, 577
pressure groups **110,** 237-8
adversarial nature of proceedings **57,** 587
agent, appointment **57,** 545
agreement *inter partes* on facts **37,** 349
applicable law **67,** 30-1, 40, 53, 96-102, 127-8, 140-9, **76,** 358-9, 372, 426-31, 446, 530, 537, 538, 542-4, 551, 584, 674, 868, **80,** 472-3, 479-80
corrective justice **55,** 305-6
equity **71,** 211-16. *See also* equity
jura novit curia **76,** 358
jus standi **46,** 408
municipal law **84,** 409
Special Agreement and **80,** 479-80, **97,** 152, 498-9, 644-5
UN law **105,** 387, 392, 393
application instituting proceedings **55,** 168-9, **57,** 443
amendment, Additional Application as **106,** 149-52
effect **37,** 292
new **46,** 19-20, 25, 114
statement of facts and grounds, need for **123,** 349
withdrawal and lapse **46,** 474

arguments
  averments distinguished **37,** 352-3
  not raised by parties **46,** 256-7, 258, 358
audi alteram partem **57,** 410, 585, **76,** 652, **97,** 60, **106,** 47
  subsequent statements of parties, effect **57,** 585, **76,** 652
claims before
  arguments distinguished **55,** 373
  for
    damages **57,** 513, 596-7
    declaration. *See* International Court of Justice (ICJ), judgment, declaratory
  limitation to those formulated by parties **46,** 211
composition
  objection to **37,** 243
  universality of Court **71,** 73
confidentiality of proceedings **57,** 438-41, **116,** 240
  premature disclosure **57,** 438-51
consolidation of proceedings **110,** 8-9, 140, 179
costs **54,** 469-71
Court's power to determine **95,** 114, **97,** 142, **106,** 21, 42, 45, 121, **123,** 255
Court's power to transfer procedural powers to third parties **97,** 175-6
critical date **37,** 481, 541
cultural diversity and **116,** 106
Deputy Registrar, privileges and immunities **94,** 309-13
discontinuance of proceedings **46,** 20, 24, 28-37, 59-60, 127-44, **71,** 67, **118,** 20-1
  by agreement **46,** 30-1, 59-60, 112, 127-30, 139
  conditional **46,** 60, 141, 143
  final character of **46,** 114-16
  municipal law compared **46,** 131
  notice of, significance **46,** 32-3, 113, 133-4
  objection, respondent's right of **46,** 31, 34-5
  reasons for **46,** 31, 59-60
  renunciation of cause of action and **46,** 29, 32-7, 59-60, 92-3, 114-20, 127-44
  Rules of Court **46,** 30-1, 33, 35, 59-60, 89, 112-14, 128-32
  as ultimatum to Court **71,** 72-4
documentation, surfeit **95,** 54-5
equality of parties **54,** 435-6, 485-7, **76,** 60-1, 488, 658-9, 662, **95,** 55, **97,** 37-8
  Chamber proceedings **97,** 37-8
  equal opportunity to present case **54,** 435-6
  individuals, representation of **69,** 349-50, 367, 386, 391-2
  non-appearance and **57,** 436
  UN Administrative Tribunal judgments, review of **69,** 349-51, 367, 386-8, 393-4
equity and **81,** 322-3, 346-7, 357, **99,** 582, 583, 584-6
fairness to parties **76,** 654-5
formalism, need to avoid **37,** 551, **97,** 57-9, **106,** 33, 60, 136, **110,** 360, **115,** 25-7
  defect of form **76,** 90, 152, 165
  substance to prevail **105,** 268-9
functions of Court **55,** 337
haste **76,** 648
importance **84,** 263
joinder of actions **41,** 35, 48, 107, 182-3, 196, **55,** 240-1, **56,** 148, 205
  identity of decision, whether necessary **41,** 48
  'parties in the same interest' distinguished **117,** 37-41
joinder of parties **37,** 539-40

International Court of Justice (ICJ), procedural issues (*cont.*)
'very subject-matter of the decision' **97,** 26-7, 28, 63-4, 68-9, 235-40, 243
judges' written notes, need for **123,** 337-8
justice and **57,** 423
litis contestatio **55,** 337
merits distinguished **57,** 510
municipal law analogies **97,** 54-5, 56-7, 176-7, 184-7
non-appearance of party, effect **54,** 398-401, **55,** 244, 353, **56,** 95, 102, 151-2, **57,** 377, 379-80, 385, 435-7, 517, 543-4, **60,** 619, 633-4, **61,** 517, 521, 544-6, **76,** 357-9, 367, 376, 378, 412, 488, 578-9, 648-54, 655, 862-3, **85,** 261, **97,** 22-9, 58, 103-4, 236-7, 243
deprivation of rights **97,** 61, 64
equality of parties and **57,** 436
'indispensable parties' rule **97,** 59
interested parties **56,** 98
Monetary Gold **97,** 236-7
provisional measures and **55,** 151, 163, 187-8, 232-3, 361-2, **56,** 78-9, **57,** 362, 378
notification to third States (Art. 63 of UN Charter) **76,** 92-3, 95-9, **81,** 427
oral hearings
desirability **97,** 166, 167
need for **115,** 227, 236, 237-8
provisional measures and **118,** 44, 51-2
reopening **57,** 584-5, 586-8
review of UN Administrative Tribunal judgments **83,** 417-28
Order of Court
authoritative text **71,** 70
for compensation **57,** 598
declaration appended **71,** 71
dissenting opinion **71,** 72-4
injunction **57,** 599
modification **56,** 143
parties' submissions **57,** 546
amendment **37,** 471, 563, 587, **56,** 202, **97,** 34, 402-3, **102,** 83
Certain Phosphate Lands in Nauru **123,** 350, 370-1
Nicaragua **123,** 281
arguments distinguished **117,** 41
interpretation **37,** 351-3, 551
joint or separate acts, by **102,** 22
maps, status **97,** 421
non-intervening parties **46,** 455
post-hearing **76,** 373
public availability **117,** 11
reformulation, Court's role **97,** 578, **123,** 209-11, 279-85, 303, 304-10, 319-22, 363-75
Libya/Chad (Territorial Dispute) **123,** 209, 304-5
Nuclear Tests Cases **123,** 210, 279-81, 305-6, 309-10, 367-70, 372
Right of Passage over Indian Territory **123,** 209-10, 283, 306, 372
reformulation, Court's role. *See also* International Court of Justice (ICJ), 'dispute', 'subject of dispute', determination
pleadings **57,** 460-2, **71,** 82-90. *See also* parties' submissions *above*
amendment **37,** 471, 563, 587
availability **67,** 18-19, **71,** 83
to public **81,** 250, **105,** 234, **116,** 22
to third State **81,** 250

external documents **57,** 378
jurisdiction **55,** 180-2, **56,** 94-6
memorial/counter-memorial
dealing exclusively with jurisdiction of the Court **37,** 357
definition **56,** 94, 95
limitation at request of Court to jurisdictional issues **55,** 180-2
modification, freedom of **46,** 36
publication. *See* availability *above*
practical experience as basis **97,** 202 n. 1
preliminary proceedings **57,** 508, 542-3, **59,** 121-4
dispute, ascertainment of existence of **57,** 434, **59,** 123-4
preliminary questions **80,** 480
President's casting vote **110,** 218
privileges and immunities, Deputy Registrar **94,** 309-13
proper parties
East Timor **105,** 276-9, 315-16
failure to arraign all 'proper' parties **105,** 315-17
States **105,** 276
public hearing **110,** 8-9, 140, 179
regulation of **57,** 567
removal of case from Court's list **46,** 20, 28, 31, 59, 112, 130, 137
Reply, complaints in **37,** 397
Rules of Court. *See* International Court of Justice (ICJ), Rules of Court
safeguards **46,** 54
seisin **70,** 570-1, 574. *See also* parties' submissions *above*; International Court of Justice, jurisdiction
administration of justice distinguished **71,** 191
following request for arbitration **117,** 15
jurisdiction distinguished **102,** 56-8, 64-5, 101-3, 113
parties' agreement on method, need for **102,** 61-2, 64-5, 78, 96-101
Special Agreement, by **71,** 92
unilateral **102,** 33-6, 39, 46, 64, 89-90, 96-103, 110, 113-14, 115-18
Application for Revision and Interpretation of the Judgment of 24 February 1982 (Tunisia v. *Libya)* **102,** 102
Corfu Channel **102,** 102-3
forum prorogatum. See International Court of Justice (ICJ), *forum prorogatum*
German Interests in Upper Silesia **102,** 102
United States Diplomatic and Consular Staff in Teheran **102,** 102
separate or dissenting opinion
distinction **110,** 241, 326
effect **122,** 649
international law, contribution to **46,** 490-1
nature **37,** 477-8, 481
Order of Court **71,** 72-4
purpose **62,** 509, **81,** 346
right to give **37,** 285-9, 294, 432-3, 560
scope and limits **46,** 238, 288, 338, 458, 530-1
standing **37,** 50-4, 81-9, 99, 100, 103-4, 108-9, 166-7, 250-84, 289-95, 298, 400-12, 416, 418-30, 433, 478, 480, 539-42, 546, 572-3, 583-7, 591-602, **46,** 499, 500, **76,** 184-8, 222, 224, 270-1, 274-311
Administering Power **105,** 397-8
'another Member of the League' **37,** 17, 19-20, 23, 28, 37, 46-7, 48-50, 52-3, 71-9, 96, 136-65, 199-210, 213, 238, 298, 300-5, 572
at time of dissolution of League **37,** 20

International Court of Justice (ICJ), procedural issues (*cont.*)
applicants as agents for General Assembly **37,** 539-42
direct concern, need for **37,** 50-3, **105,** 396-7
individual **54,** 392, 398, 435, **85,** 258, **118,** 49
customary international law **94,** 575-6
enforcement of judgments **85,** 254, 255-62
representation **69,** 349-50, 367, 386, 391-2
'Member of the League of Nations' **37,** 17
suspension of proceedings **46,** 115, 135, 138, 142
time-limits **46,** 204-5, 287, 395, **76,** 513, **81,** 427
delays **57,** 443-7
for memorial/counter memorial **55,** 180-1
for written observations and submissions on preliminary objections **56,** 91-3, 94, 95
for written pleadings **57,** 435-6, 444, **71,** 67-8, 82
title of cases, neutrality **94,** 516
UN Secretary General and **61,** 546-9
what not prohibited, allowed **95,** 114
International Court of Justice (ICJ), provisional measures 48, 368, **55,** 151, 160-7, **60,** 524-36, 538, 540, 552-3, **61,** 513-27, **80,** 450-9, **92,** 9-29
additional, need for new facts **95,** 55
admissibility and jurisdiction, relation to **57,** 443
applicability to both parties **76,** 55, 56-61
armed force, reason for request **80,** 456
assurance that right will not be infringed **94,** 456, 463, 476
negotiated settlement, obstacle to **95,** 169-70, 175, 182
basis **57,** 381, 383-4
forum prorogatum **95,** 165-6
binding force **95,** 83-5, 92-104
enforceability distinguished **95,** 84, 92-3, 96, 118
Nicaragua 83
non-compliance with previous measures and **95,** 85
PCIJ **95,** 83-5
Bosnia-Herzegovina **95,** 18-183
acts on territory of, responsibility for **95,** 41, 168, 181
background **95,** 143-8
Bosnia-Herzegovina and FRY responsibilities distinguished **95,** 64-5, 69-70, 168-9
clarification of rights for use at UN **95,** 62, 63, 123
compliance with ceasefire **95,** 166
Cooperation with UN agencies **95,** 166
declaration of illegality of annexation or incorporation **95,** 152-3
free movement of those wishing to leave Bosnia-Herzegovina **95,** 166
FRY to desist from efforts 'to partition or dismember, annex or incorporate . . .' **95,** 151-2
FRY to desist from 'providing any type of support . . .' **95,** 151
humanitarian relief (UNPROFOR) **95,** 164
means to prevent genocide **95,** 39, 62-3, 122, 123, 153-60, 163-4, 165
non-commission of genocide by armed units or organizations and persons subject to FRY control **95,** 39, 41-2
non-discrimination **95,** 166
non-supply of arms **95,** 165
prohibition of ethnic cleansing **95,** 165

release of ethnic prisoners **95,** 166
respect for Geneva Conventions (1949/1977) **95,** 166
burden of proof, requesting party **95,** 62
ceasefire, observance of **80,** 457, 459
cessation of restriction of access to ports **76,** 53
change in circumstances **55,** 236
compensation for injury caused by **94,** 467
compliance **95,** 77-8
'clean hands' doctrine **95,** 113
failure **95,** 83-6
fresh request, dependence on **95,** 111-15, 124
fresh request, relevance to **95,** 110-15, 129-30
obligation **76,** 478, **95,** 67
reaffirmation **95,** 67-8
refusal **118,** 54-5
reparation for non-compliance **95,** 85-6
Contadora process and **76,** 49-52
Court's discretion **94,** 522-3, 531-2, 557-60, 571-3, 576, 593, **95,** 85, 113, 115
Court's freedom of choice **92,** 25, 28-9
Court's function and **80,** 468
Court's inherent power **95,** 112, 113-15, 124
international law, under **95,** 124
Statute, under **95,** 113-14
Court's right to act *proprio motu* **80,** 452-3, 456, **92,** 25, **95,** 37, 65, 85, 115
without oral hearings **118,** 44, 51-2
damages, in respect of **57,** 596, **76,** 477-8
proof of **55,** 175-6
death penalty and **118,** 4-21, 39-55
'decision', whether **95,** 101-2
'*pour statuer d'urgence*' **95,** 101
declaratory judgment **95,** 123
early decision, desirability **94,** 463, 476
encouragement to negotiate **92,** 29, **94,** 458, 461-2, 464-5, 476-7
enforceability
Anglo-Iranian Oil Co **95,** 92-3
binding force distinguished **95,** 84, 92-3, 96, 118
Fisheries Jurisdiction **95,** 103
Free Zones of Upper Savoy and Gex **95,** 103, 116
Nuclear Tests **95,** 102
Polish Agrarian Reform **95,** 103
Security Council, decision relating to, relevance **95,** 93
Security Council, role **95,** 119-24
supervisory force, absence **95,** 85-6
US Diplomatic and Consular Staff in Tehran **95,** 118-19
equality of parties **94,** 476, 556, **95,** 94, 97
exceptional nature **94,** 467
exhortation to do what is being done **95,** 164
expiry **56,** 212
extension **56,** 141-3
failure of party to appear, effect **55,** 151, 163, 187-8, 232-3, 361-2, **56,** 78-9, **57,** 362, 378
fresh request **95,** 110-15
Anglo-Iranian Oil Co **95,** 110

International Court of Justice (ICJ), provisional measures (*cont.*)
compliance with previous order, need for **95,** 111-15, 124
'existence of circumstances' **95,** 130
new facts, need for **95,** 129-30
Nicaragua **95,** 110, 112
future obligations, limited to **95,** 31, 65
General Act for the Pacific Settlement of Disputes (1928) and **60,** 525, 534-6, 538, 540, 542-5, 557, 560-1
ICJ Statute **60,** 525, 530, 532, 534, 536, 542, 557
'incidental proceedings', whether **60,** 536, 550, **95,** 127-8
interim judgment distinguished **95,** 73-4, 102, 129-30
Chorzów Factory **95,** 74, 129
need to avoid **95,** 180-2, **118,** 18, 49
US Diplomatic and Consular Staff in Tehran **95,** 129
judgment of Court, part of **95,** 118
judicial decision, whether **95,** 85
jurisdiction **55,** 169-75, **57,** 362-7, 370-3, 386-8, 404, 539-40, 544, **76,** 65-73, **80,** 454, 455
parallel action by parties **80,** 456
legal rights
freedom from external interference **95,** 35
freedom from genocide **95,** 35
freedom from use or threat of force **95,** 35
human rights **95,** 35
measures to prevent genocide **95,** 62-3
physical survival as people and State **95,** 35
right of self-determination **95,** 35
merits and **55,** 173, **56,** 80, 84-5, 89, 161, **57,** 362, 370, 380, 383-4, 402-3, **60,** 536, **80,** 458, **92,** 13-14, 17-18, 19-23, **94,** 468, 497, 516, 524
modification
'indication' and 'measures' distinguished **95,** 85
new facts, need for **95,** 55
nature **56,** 84, **57,** 383-4, 609-10
new facts **94,** 461, **95,** 55, 59, 129-30
as obstacle to settlement **95,** 169-70, 175, 187
Operation Allied Force **123,** 99
order for **55,** 165-6, **56,** 76-82, **57,** 360-7
modification **55,** 230-1, 232-5
pendente lite **56,** 173
legal position preserved **94,** 457, 460, 476
obligation to avoid prejudice **94,** 461
postponement **57,** 609-10, 611, 615
preliminary decision on merits compared **56,** 88
premature filing of application, relevance **95,** 31
Presidential power to take advance measures **94,** 490, 492
priority hearing **94,** 533
prospect of early decision and **94,** 463, 476
provisional nature **95,** 107, 128-9, **118,** 14, 45
purpose **55,** 233-5, **56,** 80, **57,** 364-5, 370, 375, **60,** 536, 538
Anglo-Iranian Oil Company, Interim Protection **92,** 22, 27
avoidance of destruction of evidence **80,** 457, 458
avoidance of irreparable damage **60,** 536-7, **92,** 17, 25-7, **94,** 490, 493, 522, 555-6, 567-8, 592-3, **95,** 34, 60, **118,** 17, 19. *See also* requirements, risk of irreparable harm or damage *below*

Denunciation of Treaty of 2 November 1865 between China and Belgium **92,** 20-1, 27
Fisheries Jurisdiction **92,** 21-2, 27
preservation of rights in dispute **60,** 530, 531-2, 536-7, **76,** 48, 52, 60, 477, **92,** 19, **94,** 454, 455-6, 491, 521, **95,** 34, 37, 60, 94, 172, **118,** 7-8, 13, 19-20, 45, 49
prevention of aggravation or extension of dispute **80,** 456, **92,** 19, **94,** 490, 553-4, 556, 559, 595, **95,** 38, 39, 60
ratione temporis **56,** 88
reaffirmation **95,** 67-8
reason for, need to give **95,** 173-5
request for **55,** 174, **56,** 77, 79, 144-5, **60,** 527-8, 542, 556-7, **76,** 35-73
generous interpretation **94,** 501
withdrawal **57,** 609, 611, 615
requirements **56,** 89, **57,** 364-6, 537, 542, 558, **60,** 530-2
balance of parties' rights **95,** 41-2, **118,** 10
connection with dispute before Court **92,** 14-15, 19-23, 27-8, **118,** 17, 49
evidence of prejudice **94,** 456-7
existence of legal dispute **94,** 563-4
'if circumstances so require' **95,** 64-5, 77-8, 88-91
ineffectiveness of reparation **95,** 67
jurisdiction undisputed **94,** 453
likelihood of consistency with decision on merits **92,** 22-3, 24, **95,** 74
necessity **118,** 20
non-anticipation
decision on admissibility **95,** 38, 67
decision on merits **92,** 29, **94,** 467-8, 469-74, **95,** 37, 38, 41, 73-4, 89, 128, 142-3
remedy **95,** 129
non-interference with parties' right to argue case **95,** 38, 65, 67, 128
non-prejudicial to decision on merits **95,** 180, **118,** 17-18, 45
participation of affected States **76,** 50
precision **94,** 523, 531-2
prima facie case **94,** 455, 466-74, 475, 493-4, 521-2, 563, 564-5, 575
prima facie jurisdiction on merits **60,** 536-7, **76,** 45, 72-3, **94,** 453, 468-9, 491, 493-4, 534, 536, 557, 563, **95,** 27, 55-6, 57, 59, 60, 62, 151, **118,** 11, 17, 43-4
respect for sovereignty **76,** 53, **118,** 19
risk of irreparable harm or prejudice **56,** 88, **60,** 528-32, 537, 548-9, 558, **80,** 455, **118,** 45, 49
timeliness of request **94,** 506, 519-20, 565-7, **95,** 82-3, **118,** 44, 51-2
urgency. *See* urgency *below*
within scope of merits **94,** 501-2, 555, **95,** 34, 35, 64
review of **56,** 141-3
revocation, new facts, need for **95,** 55
status quo, maintenance of **80,** 459
Statute **60,** 525, 530, 532, 534, 536, 542, 557
third parties, directed towards **95,** 62, 63
treaty
call to desist from breach **94,** 490, 492
declaration of breach **94,** 489, 492
declaration of compliance **94,** 489, 492
UN, notice to **80,** 551
urgency **94,** 455, 457, 463, 475-6, 495-6, 522, 565, 593, **118,** 45, 49
effect on consideration of issues **95,** 128-9, 178
Nuclear Tests **95,** 128-9
postponement of hearing and **95,** 24
risk of negation of rights **95,** 142-3

International Court of Justice (ICJ), provisional measures (*cont.*)
withdrawal of armed forces **80,** 450-9
International Court of Justice (ICJ), in relation to other tribunals and dispute settlement procedures. *See also* International Court of Justice (ICJ), Security Council and; Permanent Court of International Justice (PCIJ)
arbitration and
arbitral decisions, obligation to uphold **92,** 97, 99
distinguished, Permanent Court of Arbitration (PCA) **85,** 340, **91,** 306, **97,** 177-8
pre-selection of judges **97,** 177-85
similarity of approach **80,** 141
municipal courts and **84,** 368, 379, 409
PCIJ
advisory opinion and **110,** 320
Charter, Protocol of Signature **76,** 45-6, 66-7, 110-12, 115, 172-3, 184-6, 229-32, 244-6, 276-80, 495
compulsory jurisdiction system distinguished **76,** 114-15
continuity **37,** 76, **76,** 189-94, 247, 282-7
interpretation of Statute compared **97,** 149-50
judge *ad hoc* **97,** 150, 177-85, **117,** 31-2
succession to **57,** 373, 476, 493, **76,** 111-13, 118-19, 172-3, 189-94, 228, 232-8, 296-7
transfer of jurisdiction **37,** 16-17, 48, 75, 76, 92, 112, 114-15, 136-7, 142, 202, 209-10, 237, 313, 414, 565, 573, **46,** 38-51, 62-4, 77-88, 97-108, 145-72, **48,** 338-9, 404-5
Permanent Court of Arbitration distinguished (PCA) **85,** 340, **91,** 306, **97,** 177-8
International Court of Justice (ICJ), request for an examination of the situation
admissibility, *Nuclear Tests* **106,** 10-143
continuity of case, need for **106,** 11, 15-16, 22-3, 44-5
change in law, relevance **106,** 20-1
'if basis of judgment were to be affected' **106,** 11-12, 19-20, 24, 26-8, 36-7, 41, 46, 59, 98-100, 115-20. *See also* International Court of Justice (ICJ), judgment, basis
legal dispute as originally defined **106,** 34-6
new scientific evidence, relevance **106,** 19-20, 50-1, 61-3
preservation of rights **106,** 59-60
correspondence of complaints **106,** 47-50
entry in Court's General List **106,** 24
'in accordance with the provisions of the Statute' **106,** 17, 21, 23, 24-5, 45-6, 90-1
jurisdictional base **106,** 96-7
as at time of original application **106,** 12, 14, 37, 91
contemporary **106,** 23
denunciation of treaty conferring jurisdiction **106,** 15-16, 59-60, 116-18
Nottebohm **106,** 37
original judgment **106,** 121-2
limitation period **106,** 42, 44, 91, 121
limitation to analysis of previous judgment **106,** 27
provision under Statute **106,** 22
request for interpretation distinguished **106,** 21, 22, 25, 42, 120
request for revision distinguished **106,** 21, 22, 25, 42-3, 97-8, 120
special procedure **106,** 25-6, 42-3, 44, 60, 121
International Court of Justice (ICJ), request for correction of judgment 81, 427, 430-1
admissibility **81,** 427-30, 453-4, 463, 480
Court's power **81,** 430, 431

International Court of Justice (ICJ), request for interpretation of judgment 81, 427-53, 462-3, 469-78, 480-5
admissibility **81,** 427-30, 436, 447-53, 462-3, 469-78, 480-5
binding force of judgment as limitation **81,** 450
decisive fact **81,** 440-7, 473-4, 479
dispute, existence of **81,** 450-1, 455
exhaustion of alternative procedures, need for **81,** 448-9, 465
new fact **81,** 436-7, 481-2
basis
agreement of parties **81,** 447-9, 465-8
Statute **81,** 447-9, 465, 467
purpose **81,** 452, 456
revision, as request for **81,** 474, 478
unilateral **81,** 460-1
International Court of Justice (ICJ), revision of judgment 76, 512, **81,** 430
new facts **37,** 483, 487-8
International Court of Justice (ICJ), Rules of Court 46, 128, **48,** 366-7, 371
6(4) **94,** 492
7 **97,** 148
13 **118,** 8, 43
13(1) **117,** 11, **118,** 8
13(2) **118,** 21
17 **71,** 64-71, **84,** 347, **97,** 143, 164
17(2) **84,** 324, **97,** 141, 142, 147, 150, 159, 173-5, 199, 274
26(1) (1972 Rules) compared **97,** 173-4
17(3) **97,** 150-1, 195
17(4) **97,** 150-1, 200-3
18 **71,** 64, **84,** 348
26(b) **106,** 24, 28
31 **80,** 464, **84,** 226, **100,** 10, 11, **102,** 11, 119, **105,** 284, **115,** 206, 212, **116,** 15, **123,** 197, 198
31(3) **102,** 11
31(5) **117,** 11, 37-41
32 **117,** 31, **118,** 8, 43
32(1) **118,** 8
34(2) **41,** 35
35 **71,** 68, 79, **97,** 143
35(3) **97,** 144, **117,** 11
35(4) **97,** 146, 151, **115,** 237
35(5) **97,** 146, 148, 151
36 **117,** 31
36(2) **115,** 237
37 **110,** 11
37(1) **117,** 30
37(2) **117,** 30
38 **76,** 427, **102,** 21
38(1) **102,** 32, 33-4, 46, 90, 112, **123,** 348
38(2) **97,** 33-4, **123,** 208, 348-9
38(4) **94,** 491, **95,** 24, **100,** 10, **118,** 8, 42
38(5) **102,** 34, **106,** 17, 23
39 **102,** 21
39(1) **100,** 9, **102,** 33, 46, 90
39(2) **102,** 99

International Court of Justice (ICJ), Rules of Court (*cont.*)
41 **92,** 24, 29
42 **71,** 82, **76,** 38, **80,** 463, **92,** 10, **94,** 452, 491, **95,** 24, **97,** 218, 274, **100,** 10, **106,** 152, **116,** 22, **118,** 9
43 **84,** 226, **94,** 491, **95,** 24, **115,** 11, **117,** 10, **118,** 9
44 **102,** 119, **115,** 206
44(2) **41,** 35
44(3) **105,** 234
45 **115,** 206
46(2) **100,** 10, **102,** 99
49(2) **115,** 216
51 **84,** 347
51(3) **97,** 320 n. 1
53 **80,** 464
53(1) **97,** 219, 228, 239
53(2) **81,** 427, **97,** 277, **99,** 409, **100,** 11, **102,** 12, **105,** 234, **115,** 12, **117,** 11, **123,** 198
54 **84,** 226, **92,** 31
56 **80,** 464, **97,** 490, **99,** 409, **102,** 12
56(1) **116,** 22
56(2) **100,** 11, **115,** 237, **116,** 22
56(3) **102,** 12
56(4) **105,** 234, **123,** 198
57 **97,** 277
58 **76,** 579, **80,** 464
58(2) **100,** 11
60 **76,** 108
61(4) **102,** 12
62 **46,** 28, 54, 109
62(3) **37,** 4
66 **97,** 277-8, 315, **116,** 15-16, 23
66(3) (1972) **106,** 18
67 **97,** 277-8, 315, **115,** 237
68 **46,** 30-1, 89, 112-14, 128
69 **46,** 20, 27-31, 33, 35, 89, 112-14, 128, **84,** 226
69(2) **117,** 10
69(3) **94,** 491, **117,** 10
70(2) **97,** 277
72 **84,** 226, **100,** 11, **102,** 12, **116,** 14
73 **76,** 35, 37, **80,** 451-2, 453, **84,** 226, **92,** 9, 17, **94,** 452, 486, 554, 568, **95,** 112, **106,** 148, 152, 156, 167, 172, **118,** 4, 7, 39, 41, 44, **123,** 99
73(2) **94,** 491, **95,** 24, 51, 173, 174, **106,** 153, 175, **118,** 42
74 **76,** 35, 37, 648, **92,** 9, 10, 31, **94,** 486, 554, 568, **95,** 24, 112, 128, **106,** 148, 172, **118,** 4, 7, 39, 41, 51
74(1) **94,** 533, 565
74(2) **95,** 101, **106,** 181
74(3) **94,** 453, 491, **95,** 53, 55, **106,** 153-4, **118,** 9
74(4) **94,** 492, **95,** 51, **106,** 18, **118,** 43
75 **76,** 37, 61, **80,** 452-3, **92,** 24-5, 28, 29, **95,** 112, **106,** 148, 172, 188, 190-1, **118,** 4, 7, 39, 41, 43
75(1) **94,** 461, **95,** 51, 52, 65, 115, 139, **118,** 39, 45, 51-2
applicability in case of request for interim measures **118,** 51
75(2) **94,** 523, **95,** 37, 115, **106,** 159, 171

75(3) **94,** 461, **95,** 55, 130
76 **80,** 459, 464, **95,** 55, 112
76(1) **95,** 101
76(3) **95,** 101
78 **76,** 37, **95,** 86
79 **76,** 136, 159-60, 180, 266, 273, 322-4, 529, 536, **97,** 9, **106,** 17, **115,** 237, **117,** 24-7, 68-70, **123,** 333-8
79(1) **106,** 47, **115,** 12, 35, 210, **117,** 24, 54
79(3) **97,** 10, **106,** 152, **117,** 10
79(5) **123,** 308-9
79(6) **117,** 69, **123,** 267, 308-9, 391
79(7) **97,** 38, **102,** 29, **106,** 47, **115,** 166, 237, **117,** 25-7, 44-7, 49-50, 55, 102-4, **123,** 227, 232, 253, 291, 309
62(5) (1946 Rules) distinguished **97,** 38-9, **123,** 267
79(8) **84,** 324
80 **84,** 282-3, **115,** 206, 216-19, 223-9, 237-8, 244-5
80(1) **115,** 212, 216, 218, 224-6, 234, 245
80(2) **115,** 216, 218, 234
80(3) **115,** 212, 214, 226-8, 234, 235-6, 238
81 **97,** 211
81(1) **97,** 195, 228, 233
81(2) **97,** 228, 229-30, 232-3, 256, 259
81(2)(a) **70,** 537, 605
81(2)(b) **70,** 537, 541, 573, 605-6, 610, 681
81(2)(c) **70,** 537, 541, 573, 605, 609, 645, 675, 681
82 **97,** 210
83 **97,** 210, 211
83(1) **97,** 155, 219
84 **84,** 284, **97,** 210, 211
84(2) **97,** 220
85 **97,** 210, 211, 257, 294
89 **118,** 20
89(2) **118,** 21
89(3) **118,** 21
90 **97,** 158, 210
92 **71,** 61, 82, **80,** 464
97 **105,** 8 n. 1, 67
98 **81,** 100, 427, 430
98 ff **81,** 483
104, **62,** 459, **69,** 337, **83,** 304
106, **62,** 459, **85,** 306, **110,** 9, 180
authority, Statute distinguished **110,** 724
Court's competence to make **46,** 127, **62,** 617, **95,** 115
discontinuance of proceedings **46,** 30-1, 33, 35, 59-60, 89, 112-14, 128-32
revision/amendment **62,** 625
1972 **76,** 136, 180, 323-4, 363-5
Statute, consistency with **97,** 185-200
travaux préparatoires **70,** 570

International Court of Justice (ICJ), Security Council and 60, 533, 537, 540, 548, 554-5, 559, **61,** 547-50, **76,** 51-2, 142-7, 573-4, 621-7. *See also* International Court of Justice (ICJ), in relation to other tribunals and dispute settlement procedures
Chapter VII action, ICJ role **94,** 550, **95,** 123-4, **117,** 106-8
'collateral examination' **105,** 552

International Court of Justice (ICJ), Security Council and (*cont.*)
effect on jurisdiction **117,** 21-2
interim measures
enforcement
Anglo-Iranian Oil Co **95,** 119
Art. 34/35 action **95,** 119, 124
Art. 94 action **95,** 119-20
interference with exercise of Security Council powers, whether **94,** 494-8, 523, 573-4
to prevent action within Security Council **94,** 495-6
judicial review. *See* United Nations Security Council, judicial review
Namibia **105,** 550-2
parallel exercise of functions **60,** 540-1, 559, **94,** 503-5, 509-10, 516-23, 542-3, 552-3, 561-2, 583-90, **105,** 360-1, 382, **110,** 97, **117,** 54
conflicting decisions, risk of **94,** 511-12, 517-18, 526-7, 542, **117,** 58-60, 73, 77-8, 99
fact-finding Commission **61,** 546-50
Nicaragua **94,** 503-5, 512, 543, 562, **95,** 34, **117,** 71-2
US Diplomatic and Consular Staff in Tehran **94,** 503-4, 512, 543, 561-2
reference to ICJ, duty, whether **94,** 525-6
renvoi of issues to **49,** 117
Resolution
admissibility, effect on **117,** 21-4, 26-7, 44-5, 55-6, 63-7
adopted in knowledge of impact on Court's deliberations **94,** 501, 527
as change of circumstances **94,** 498, 508, 510, 556-7
effect **117,** 21-2, 35
jus cogens/peremptory norm, conflict with **95,** 159-60
not addressed to parties in proceedings **95,** 159-60
request for parties' views on implications **94,** 497
retroactive effect **94,** 524
validity, Court's power to pronounce on **94,** 515, 524-5, 526-7, 537-40, 585-99
Security Council's lack of standing **117,** 77-8
International Court of Justice (ICJ), Special Agreement **71,** 65-74, 79-82, 90-2, 118, 145, 189-98, **80,** 481, **81,** 255, 306, 406-7, 409, **85,** 260, **97,** 470
applicable law
appointment of judge *ad hoc* **97,** 152
normal rules of treaty interpretation **97,** 498-9, 644-5
Bahrain–Qatar, efforts to conclude **102,** 36-46, 61-2, 87-90
bilingual texts **71,** 92
binding on court, whether **41,** 116, **71,** 92-4, 99, 190-8
Burkina Faso/Mali **80,** 450, 461-4
Canada–USA **71,** 64-74, 79-82, 90, 91, 118, 145, 189-98
extension of delimitation area, provision for **71,** 69, 82, 91
frontière maritime, meaning **71,** 92
text **71,** 79-82
transmission to UN **71,** 82
Chad–Libya (1989) **100,** 7-10, 13, 14
Chamber, provision for **97,** 140-1
Denmark–FRG **41,** 30, 32-5, 37, 40, 48, 116, 167, 179, 195-8, 200, 201
deposit with UN Secretariat **97,** 140, 218
'determine the legal situation of the islands' (Fonseca Bay) **97,** 470-2, 576-81, 632-46
El Salvador/Honduras (1986)
appointment of judge *ad hoc* **97,** 152

English text **97,** 272-4
Spanish text **97,** 215-18, 470, 499
entry into force **71,** 65, 82
evidence provisions **71,** 81-2
form, simplicity **102,** 99
FRG–Netherlands **41,** 30, 32-5, 40, 48, 116, 167, 179, 195-8, 200, 201
Hungary/Slovakia (1993), text **116,** 19-22, 167, 168, 172, 175, 176
interpretation **41,** 116, **81,** 255, 406-7, 409
agreed translation, difference of meaning **97,** 470
Chamber, by **97,** 470, 581, 633
restrictive **97,** 644
'to determine the legal situation of the island and maritime spaces' **97,** 35, 498-502, 632-46
intervention of third State and **62,** 628
jurisdiction, basis **41,** 91, **80,** 481, **81,** 255, 306, 406-7, 447-9, 465-8
legal effect **71,** 80-191
Libya–Malta **81,** 247-9
obligation to negotiate implied **67,** 137-8
possibility under **99,** 480
question raised by Court **71,** 65-9, 79
questions raised by Court, replies, effect given to **71,** 69, 79
redefinition of question **80,** 483
Statute and Rules, compatibility with **71,** 65-74
technical provisions **71,** 81, 92
termination provisions **71,** 67
as ultimatum to Court **71,** 72
title
disagreement as to **97,** 140
provisions of agreement, effect on **97,** 140
translation into official language of Court
by Registry **97,** 140, 221, 274
by UN Secretariat **97,** 140
failure to provide agreed **97,** 140
title **97,** 140
Tunisia–Libya **67,** 14-17
interpretation **67,** 31-4, 101, 139-40, 272-6
International Court of Justice (ICJ), status and functions 41, 148, 196-7, **46,** 337, **55,** 383-4, **56,** 161, 185-6, 209, **57,** 598-9, **60,** 554-5, **62,** 618-19, **67,** 30-3, 40, 53, 71, 80, 93-6, 128-9, 136-49, 246-8, 272-4, **70,** 587
adjudication of issue submitted by parties **102,** 29-30, 92-3, **105,** 299-302, 380-1, **106,** 85
administration of justice based on law **106,** 37-8
appeal court **94,** 538, **118,** 13, 16, 19, 45, 48. *See also* United Nations Security Council, judicial review
ICAO Council, appeals court **48,** 331-47, 357, 359, 362-9, 372-6, 378-87, 402-10, 426-32, 443-5, 454-7
UN Administrative Tribunal judgments. *See* United Nations Administrative Tribunal (UNAT), review of judgments by ICJ
basis **54,** 516-17
boni judicis est ampliare jurisdictionem **102,** 106-7
broad interpretation of **106,** 38
changing character **37,** 578
clarification of law **110,** 500

International Court of Justice (ICJ), status and functions (*cont.*)
conciliation **102,** 32, 46
contribution to the working of, UN system **62,** 551-2
as *cour de cassation* **92,** 56, 75-6, 97
as court of justice **97,** 171-2, **105,** 378-80, **110,** 106
advisory opinion **110,** 106
declaration, development and maintenance of international law **106,** 139-40
declaratory **49,** 62
determination by parties **41,** 37-8
development of international law **105,** 274-5, **106,** 81-4, 140, 142, **110,** 229-31, 243, 500, 521-2
development of UN law **105,** 382
direction to Parties to negotiate **56,** 172, 176-7
dispute settlement **56,** 184, **57,** 512
in accordance with international law **80,** 534
international legal disputes **41,** 156, **118,** 13, 19, 45
on legal basis **81,** 340
peaceful settlement of disputes **92,** 97, **102,** 93, 118-19
duty to
apply law **46,** 176
sub specie legis ferendae **53,** 483
establish facts **76,** 655-7
facilitate settlement **76,** 487
fulfil task **80,** 484
promote peace **76,** 487
dynamic development of international law **94,** 575
General Assembly and **82,** 260
guidance in application of law **81,** 254, 476, 483
habeas corpus proceedings **118,** 48
integrity of Court, Court as guardian **97,** 171-2, **123,** 262-3
international law, development by **41,** 141, 174, 185, **46,** 76, 238, 422
International Tin Council bankruptcy, in respect of **77,** 99
interpretation **56,** 209-10
judicial **55,** 234, 254-5, 272-3, 275, 278, 338-9, **57,** 459, **59,** 94, **62,** 452, 472, 484-5, 509, 548, 550, 562-3, 575-6, 581, **117,** 52-3
declaratory judgments **57,** 533
interpretation of parties' submissions **57,** 407-8
judicial legislation **37,** 234, 269, 281, 312, 338, 408, 443, **41,** 185
limitations **37,** 111, 282, 338, 443
review of judgments of international tribunals **54,** 478
settlement of disputes **57,** 415-16
'supervision' **37,** 120
judicial character **54,** 395-7, **57,** 467-8, 475-8, 482-3
judicial process **55,** 306, 577-9, **61,** 569-70
use of force and **61,** 543-4, 569-70, 577-9, 580-1, 589
judicial review
judgments of international tribunals **54,** 475-8, 487, 498
nature of **54,** 489, 491
powers of **49,** 35, 95, 122-3, 133, 141
jura novit curia **55,** 314
justice **56,** 184
municipal law and, interpretation, ICJ role **84,** 353
negotiations, duty to encourage **61,** 574

oral proceedings **54,** 398-401, 435-6, 473-5, 485-7, **56,** 214, **71,** 87-90
powers **56,** 181-2, 468, **57,** 392, **60,** 618-19, **70,** 570-1. *See also* International Court of Justice (ICJ), jurisdiction
alienation, power of **97,** 193-4, 199
developing **95,** 105-7
implied **97,** 192-3
investigation, of **54,** 485-7
limited **95,** 105-7
compatibility with Statute **97,** 185, 192-3, 198-200, 205-6
duty to preserve judicial character of Court **97,** 183-5, 193, 205-6
misuse, determination of **54,** 491
as principal judicial organ of UN **82,** 260, **84,** 246, **85,** 339-40, **94,** 402, 503, 505, 509, 517, 527, 528, 537-8, 562, 579, 583-4, 586, 595, **97,** 198, 205, 208, **110,** 106-7, 185
independence **94,** 540-2
significance **49,** 13, 17, 133, 162-3, 170
refinement of law **81,** 340, 346
refugee, determination of status **87,** 133
review of judgments of ILO Administrative Tribunal **38,** 436-7, 438
role, legislative **110,** 243, 322, 375
settlement of disputes and **61,** 549, 570, 574, 592-5
in absence of settled rules of international law **94,** 464-5
exhortation to **94,** 531, 581-2, **95,** 175, 183
preferred method **94,** 458, 461-2, 476-7
interested third parties, involvement of **94,** 462
presumption of failure **94,** 464, 518-19, 535
Special Agreement and **67,** 31-4, 71, 94-6, 136-40, 246, 272-4, **80,** 468, 534, 550-1, **81,** 254-8, 306, 308, 447-9
specificity **81,** 308
statement of existing law **110,** 187, 389-90, 503
supervisory, ICAO Council **48,** 346, 360, 392, 409
treaty interpretation **55,** 382-3, **68,** 634-5, **118,** 13
Competence of General Assembly for Admission to UN **41,** 116
UN system
contribution to working of **83,** 360, **105,** 382, 392
participation in activities of **69,** 358-9, 388-9, 447, 458-9
UN system, contribution to working of **105,** 382, 392
International Court of Justice (ICJ), Statute. *See also the Consolidated Table of Treaties*
Articles 36(1) and (2) compared **84,** 290, 293-9
interpretation **46,** 43-6, 86, 98-102, **70,** 569, 572, 575, 587, 600-1, 603, 628-35, 673, 685
acceptance of practice by Member States **95,** 107
comparison of English and French versions **95,** 98-100, 101, **97,** 151
development of powers of Court **95,** 106-7, **105,** 317-18
dictionary **95,** 98
inconsistency of language **97,** 149
PCIJ usage **97,** 149-50
restrictive **46,** 157-8, 161
travaux préparatoires **95,** 98, 99-100, **105,** 317-19
objects and purpose **46,** 82, 83, 88, 147-50
relevant UN practice **46,** 166-8
party to, effect of becoming **46,** 153-4
phrases
'affected' **97,** 251-2

International Court of Justice (ICJ), Statute (*cont.*)
'appoint' **97,** 149-53
'cases' and 'disputes' **37,** 176, 179
'chosen' **97,** 149-53
'declarations . . . still in force' **76,** 68-70, 117-23, 281-311
'if circumstances so require' (Art. 41) **94,** 468-9, 522-3, 557-9, **95,** 64-5, 77-8, 88-91
'indicate' **95,** 97-8, 106
'legal dispute' **84,** 246
'[matters specially provided for . . .] in treaties and conventions in force' **57,** 492-4, **84,** 269, **102,** 33, 36, 85
'number' **97,** 191-3, 199-200
'ought' **95,** 98-9
'parties in the same interest' **117,** 11, 30-42
joinder of actions distinguished **117,** 37-40
plurality of respondents/applicants, relevance **117,** 40-1
'power' **95,** 100
'provisional measures' **95,** 98-9
'State accepting same obligation' **84,** 236
'subject of dispute', PCIJ *travaux préparatoires* **123,** 307-8. *See also* International Court of Justice (ICJ), 'dispute', 'subject of dispute', determination
ratification **76,** 42-6, 66-7, 184-6
travaux préparatoires **70,** 570, 600, 663, 668
written statements **54,** 387, 402, 485
International Court of Justice (ICJ), third States and 41, 195-6, **76,** 61, **80,** 480-4, **84,** 282-7, **95,** 62. *See also* International Court of Justice (ICJ), intervention of third State; International Court of Justice (ICJ), judgment, binding force
Ambatielos **105,** 308
Certain Phosphate Lands in Nauru **105,** 245-6, 271, 297, 309-10, 384-5, **119,** 510, 589-90, 591
consensual basis of jurisdiction and **105,** 241-3, 248, 260-3, 270
acceptance of compulsory jurisdiction and **105,** 248
intervention in case distinguished **105,** 248
Corfu Channel **105,** 262-3, 305-8
East Timor **119,** 590, 592
effect of Court's decision on, effect and judgment distinguished **105,** 261-3, 296, 363-4, 383-4
Monetary Gold **80,** 484, **105,** 254, 260-3, 270-3, 297-310, 318-19, 364, 382, 384-6, 391-2, **119,** 588-92, 594-7
Nicaragua **105,** 390-1
non-participation of third State, relevance **105,** 386-90
power to restrict jurisdiction **81,** 260, 349, 406-9
protection of rights **62,** 632, **70,** 555, 563, 623, 677, **105,** 310-11, 383
legal interests distinguished **119,** 592
Libya–Malta (Intervention) **97,** 168
undertaking not to adversely affect **97,** 168
international courtesy 82, 73
appointment of ambassador **100,** 311, 325
comity and **64,** 13-17, 39, 49, **80,** 399
State immunity, jurisdiction and **91,** 302
International Covenant on Civil and Political Rights (ICCPR) (1966) 37, 357, 454, **47,** 205, 207, 208, 258-9, **88,** 556, 558. *See also* African Charter on Human and Peoples' Rights (1981); American Convention on Human Rights (1969); European Convention

on Human Rights (1950); expulsion of alien; International Covenant on Economic, Social and Cultural Rights (1966); United Nations Human Rights Committee (UNHRC)
aliens, expulsion
in accordance with law of expelling State **62,** 278, 281-5, **94,** 425
lawful, whether **62,** 278-9, 281-5
conditions for **62,** 284, **71,** 316, 320-3, 349, 359, 361-5
right of review **94,** 420-4, 426
within reasonable time **94,** 426
UNHRC activity **94,** 426
appeal, right of **69,** 177-82, 192-3, **70,** 242-8, 250-8, 260-6, 282-3, 286, 289-90, 294-6, **71,** 316, 320-3, 328, 349, 359, 361-5, **78,** 59-62, **104,** 424, 426-36, **105,** 454
'according to the law' **70,** 242-3, 247-8
application for special leave to appeal, sufficiency **104,** 432-6
delays, workload of tribunal **71,** 321-2
during arbitrary detention **71,** 316, 321, 328, 349, 361
emergency regulations **70,** 242-8
prompt hearing and **69,** 176-7
applicability. *See also* State responsibility *below*
detention of alien **92,** 551-2
persons within jurisdiction of State party **98,** 486, **118,** 195
signatory State, non-acceptance of Human Rights Committee and **86,** 119
time of war **110,** 189-90
arbitrary act
conformity with provisions, aims and objectives of Covenant, need for **112,** 340-1, **115,** 342-3
test
proportionality **115,** 348-9
reasonableness **115,** 342-3
arbitrary detention, freedom from **59,** 442-3, **68,** 31, 35, 36, 38-9, **69,** 192, **70,** 256, **71,** 312, 316, 319, 321, 325-31, 347-53, 355-6, 361, 363, 365, **78,** 26, 27, **79,** 182-6, 189, 191-2, **94,** 414
unfair trial distinguished **118,** 291
arrest
arbitrary **62,** 257-8, **118,** 291
on foreign territory **68,** 38-40, 45-7
illegal **62,** 240-1, 248, 253, 259-60, **68,** 31, 35, 39, 45, **118,** 208, 291
asylum, refusal of request for **79,** 280-2
fair hearing **79,** 282
bilateral agreements, consistency with Covenant, need for **98,** 445, 500
binding on all persons, whether **96,** 372-3, 390
capital punishment **78,** 25
child care
interest of child **96,** 633-4
denial of parental access and **96,** 634-5
statutory criteria, need for **96,** 634, 636-7
parental access
after divorce **96,** 631-7
compatibility of legislation **96,** 636
interest of child **96,** 634-5
child rights **101,** 459-65, **117,** 628-34, 638-9
clemency. *See* remedies, clemency *below*
compensation for violations. *See* remedies, compensation *below*

International Covenant on Civil and Political Rights (ICCPR) (*cont.*)
conscience, freedom of **62,** 271-7
conscientious objection **94,** 394, 395, 444-5
absence of provision **94,** 399, 445
discrimination **94,** 444-5, **118,** 142-5
pardon, implication **94,** 395
right to decline military service **94,** 389-95, 397-9, **118,** 142
automatic, whether **94,** 395
conscript's right of appeal **94,** 444-5
national authorities' power to determine **94,** 394
torture **94,** 410, 443
investigation by State, need for **94,** 442
convicted persons
appeal rights **70,** 242-8
'according to the law' **70,** 242-3, 247-8
rights **69,** 176-7, 180-2
sentencing changes, retroactive benefit **70,** 306-13, **71,** 339-45
correspondence, freedom from arbitrary or unlawful interference with **69,** 180-2
censorship **78,** 51, 52, 53
courts, right to protection of **62,** 286-7
criminal law, retroactivity **91,** 49
customary international law **104,** 432
evidence of **87,** 457
death penalty
accordance with the law, need for **98,** 367, 368-9, **115,** 354
excluded, whether **98,** 334, 434, 445-6, 447, 501-4, 511, **114,** 366-7, 371, 372-4
'most serious crimes' **114,** 366-7
extradition. *See* extradition, death penalty in case of *below*
inhuman or degrading treatment. *See* inhuman or degrading treatment, death penalty *below*
mitigating factors, age **124,** 327-8
obligation not to reintroduce **114,** 374, 377-8, 379-80
extradition as instrument for **98,** 457, 458-9, 471, 504-5, 517-18, 519
plea bargaining, relevance **114,** 368
Second Optional Protocol (1989) **98,** 394-5, 445, 446, **124,** 326
violations of Covenant and **98,** 334, 367, 368-70, **118,** 261
death row as inhuman or degrading treatment **98,** 447-8, **114,** 368, 375-7, 381-2, **115,** 297-8, **118,** 257-8
three-year delay in hearing appeal **115,** 297-8
defence
adequate assistance **78,** 78-80
adequate time and facilities for preparation **78,** 34, 39, **79,** 268, 276, **98,** 366, **118,** 259-60
documents **79,** 118, 259-60, 273, 276
degrading treatment or punishment **62,** 257, 260, **71,** 307, 360-1, **79,** 178-9
deportation
decision in accordance with law **115,** 330, 337
family life, respect for **115,** 337, 341
inhuman or degrading treatment, whether **115,** 330
derogation by States party, possibility of **62,** 241-5, 247, 254, 256, 260, 262, 269, **107,** 70-1. *See also* reservations *and* restrictions on rights *below*
detainees, rights **69,** 177-82, 192, **70,** 250-8, 260-6, **71,** 311-16, 320-31, 347-53, 356-65, **79,** 182-6. *See also* detention *below*; fair trial, charges *below*

appeal. *See* appeal, right of *above*
correspondence, freedom from arbitrary or unlawful interference with **69,** 180-2
censorship **78,** 51, 52, 53
defence. *See* defence *above*
freedom from
ill-treatment **62,** 241, 244-7, 256-8, 260
racial harassment **69,** 177-8
humane treatment **69,** 177-8
judicial review **96,** 659-60
legal representation. *See* legal representation *below*
medical attention **69,** 192-3, **70,** 258, 294, **79,** 237, 239, 257
military detention, applicability to **96,** 654, 659-60
prompt appearance before a judge **118,** 258
'prompt' **118,** 258
prompt notification of charges **62,** 247, 254, **69,** 192, **70,** 255-7, 261, **118,** 258
'prompt' **118,** 258
reasons for arrest/detention **62,** 241, **79,** 185, 186, 192
release on completion of sentence **71,** 312, 314-15, 360-1, 363
conditional upon leaving the country **71,** 356, 363
segregation from convicted persons **69,** 177-80
detention. *See also* detainees, rights *above*; fair trial *below*
alien **92,** 551-2
conditions of **62,** 241-6
incommunicado **62,** 242, 246-8, 253, 255-8, 260-1, **68,** 31, 36, 46, **70,** 256, 258, 260-1, 282, 286, 289-90, 295-6, **71,** 311-13, 347, 355-6, 363, 365, **78,** 34, 35, **79,** 183, 186, 214, 218, 224, 232, 259, 260. *See also* solitary confinement *below*
inhuman treatment or torture, whether involving **62,** 241, 244-7, 256-8, 260, **71,** 311-13, 315-16, 347-53, 356-65, **78,** 52, 78-9, 80, **79,** 191-2, 204-5, 207-8, 209, 210, 214, 224, 225, 232, 235-6, 239, 241, 257-60
'lawful detention' **62,** 241-3, 245, 256-7, 260
legal representative **71,** 313
legality, challenge to **71,** 353, 356, 365, **79,** 189, 259, 260
mentally ill person
lawfulness **67,** 462-71
review procedures **67,** 466-71
provisional release order, following **71,** 312, 316
solitary confinement **69,** 192, **78,** 51. *See also* incommunicado *above*
without charge **62,** 241-6
without trial **62,** 256, 260
effective remedy, duty to provide. *See* United Nations Human Rights Committee (UNHRC), effective remedy, need for
enforceability, by individual **92,** 507-8
entry into force, continuing violation and **62,** 243-4, 258
entry to one's own country, deportation or expulsion, relevance **115,** 335, 340
equality **91,** 329-32
before the courts **62,** 248
before the law **62,** 294-5, **71,** 307, **79,** 281, **118,** 144-5
Court's role, avoidance of involvement in policy assessment **96,** 343
education **96,** 371
International Covenant on Economic, Social and Cultural Rights (1966) distinguished **96,** 361
reports to Human Rights Committee
Canada **91,** 331

International Covenant on Civil and Political Rights (ICCPR) (*cont.*)
Mauritius **91,** 331
sexual **62,** 294
social security **96,** 361, **118,** 158-63
spouses following divorce **96,** 633
equality of arms **115,** 664-5, **118,** 259, **124,** 85-6
applicability to conditions outside court's control **124,** 87
as essential element of fair trial **124,** 85-6
legal aid and **124,** 572
expulsion **95,** 322
in accordance with the law **95,** 325, **98,** 464-5
administrative act, need for **95,** 326
as extradition **95,** 325
national **104,** 188, **115,** 344-5
national security **95,** 325
unlawful arrest, as **95,** 326-7
extradition
in accordance with the law **98,** 464-5
admissibility **98,** 433
arbitrary **98,** 447
conditions in receiving State, relevance **98,** 512-13
covered by Covenant, whether **98,** 448-50, 464-5, 486, 514-15, **114,** 361-2, 369
deliberate omission **114,** 373-4
discretion **98,** 446-7, 468
in case of death penalty **98,** 453
expulsion distinguished **98,** 434, 465, 514-15
abolition of death penalty in extraditing State, relevance **98,** 502
fair trial, relevance **98,** 447
foreseeable and necessary consequences resulting in violation of Covenant **114,** 361-2, 366-71
lawfulness of request for **79,** 249
nationals **88,** 293-4
safe haven, risk of creating **98,** 447, 519 n. 10
UN Human Rights Committee's loss of jurisdiction, relevance **114,** 377
extradition in case of death penalty **98,** 444-8, **100,** 686-7, **114,** 372-4, 379-81
assurances that death penalty will not be carried out, need for **98,** 446-7, 451, 468-71, 502-3, 506, 516, **114,** 362, 367-8, 381
discretion **98,** 453
equality of treatment **98,** 454, 455-7
extradition agreement obligation **98,** 446, 453-4
reintroduction of death penalty, whether **114,** 374, 377-8, 379-80
right of appeal, relevance **114,** 376-7
fair hearing **92,** 656. *See also* fair trial *below*
failure to complain at time **118,** 249
immigration review proceedings **69,** 169-70
right to **62,** 248, 255, 261-2, 266, 290
fair trial **57,** 253, **59,** 436, **62,** 246-7, 253, 255, 262, 266, **68,** 32-9, 45-6, **69,** 186-92, **70,** 242-8, 254-5, 257, 282-96, **71,** 307, 319-21, 325-31, **79,** 236, 278, 281. *See also* detainees, rights *and* fair hearing *above*
charges
joinder **79,** 274
right to be informed of **78,** 25, **79,** 271, 275, **118,** 259
rights of detainee distinguished **118,** 259

common trial **78,** 59, 61
competent tribunal, right to **62,** 246, 248-9
death sentence cases
arbitrariness **98,** 370
special relevance, whether **98,** 369-70
defence. *See* defence *above*
delay **78,** 78, 80
due process **78,** 27
failure to complain at time **118,** 260
forced confessions **68,** 32, 39, **70,** 290, 296
in absentia **69,** 192, **78,** 24
in camera **70,** 257, 283, 286
legal aid **79,** 270, 273, 276, **98,** 365, 368
legal representation. *See* legal representation *below*
military courts and **69,** 186, 189, 191-2, **70,** 242, 244-6, 254-5, 257, 283-4, 286, **71,** 319-21, 325-30
non bis in idem **70,** 242, 245-6, **115,** 365
non-disclosure of prosecution evidence **115,** 298-9
presence at trial **62,** 266, **70,** 283, 285, **98,** 366-7, **118,** 260-1
res judicata **70,** 242, 246
sentence exceeding statutory maximum **71,** 319, 321
state of emergency, during **70,** 242-8
witnesses
absence **118,** 259
examination **79,** 268, 271, 272
failure to call **98,** 332, 366, **118,** 260
family life, respect for **62,** 189-91, 287, 293-4, **68,** 21, **96,** 633, **101,** 459-65, **103,** 232-3
burial grounds **118,** 264-78
cultural values distinguished **118,** 278
deportation. *See* deportation, family life, respect for *above*
family, right to found **62,** 285, 287, 289, 291
forced and compulsory labour **73,** 491
freedom of association **75,** 59-65, **79,** 248
definition **75,** 59-60, 64-5
public interest and **75,** 60
freedom of departure from any country **70,** 236-40, **78,** 70, **79,** 198, 199-200
freedom of emigration **74,** 301, **78,** 70
freedom of entry **74,** 301, **78,** 70
freedom of expression **62,** 245, 254, **75,** 44-5, 47, 66-8, 72, **79,** 243-4, 248, 260, **88,** 586, **114,** 324, 330
anti-semitic remarks **115,** 372-3
censorship of correspondence **78,** 51, 52, 53
censorship of media **70,** 298-304
public morals and **70,** 298-304
public order/public policy/*ordre public* and **62,** 245, 254
restrictions **62,** 245, 254, **115,** 372-3
right to use language of choice **118,** 182-3
freedom from discrimination **87,** 110
access to public service **94,** 428-32
burial grounds, non-application of metropolitan law in French Polynesia **118,** 273-4, 275
civilian service alternative to military service **118,** 142-5
differentiation based on reasonable and objective criteria **114,** 319

International Covenant on Civil and Political Rights (ICCPR) (*cont.*)
change of nationality **114,** 319
differences in economic, financial and social conditions **114,** 319
possibility of abuse of pension rights **114,** 319
extraditability and **114,** 380
extradition as instrument of **98,** 454, 455-7, 459, 472, 518
invidious discrimination **94,** 432, **96,** 666
legitimate aim **96,** 666
nationality, 'other status' **114,** 318-19
pension rights **114,** 315, 318-19
political opinions **114,** 325
racial **107,** 37
in respect of property rights **115,** 265-76, **118,** 193-5, 239
sexual **62,** 285-8, 290, 293-6, **68,** 21, 25, **87,** 11
social security provisions **118,** 149-51, 158-63
Sikh headwear **96,** 666
war pensions legislation **118,** 234-5
freedom of movement **68,** 38-9
banishment **94,** 414
passport as means **78,** 70
passport, need for **78,** 70
restrictions **78,** 70, **114,** 325, 330
narrow interpretation **100,** 381-2, 383
provided by law **100,** 381-2, **101,** 408
public order **100,** 381-2, **101,** 408
public security **100,** 382, **101,** 408
right to leave own country **100,** 381-5, **101,** 407-8
absence of reasons **100,** 383
passport, withdrawal **101,** 407-9, **114,** 325, 330
right of appeal, relevance **100,** 383
Single Convention on Narcotic Drugs (1961), obligations under **101,** 408-9
freedom of opinion **62,** 245, 247, 254-5, 271-7
freedom of religion **62,** 274
freedom of thought. *See* freedom of opinion *above*
government's waiver of compensation for unlawful treatment of prisoners of war **118,** 221, 233
habeas corpus **62,** 241, 244-6, 249, 252, 255-6, 259, 262, 266, **71,** 323, 326, 330, 356, **79,** 182, 186, **118,** 258-9
honour and reputation **118,** 238, 239
implementation, national measures as primary means **115,** 659
implementing legislation, need for **101,** 247-50, 300-4, **104,** 428-30, **124,** 396, 404-5, 413-15, **125,** 515-19
accession to First Optional Protocol, relevance **104,** 430
right of application to UN Human Rights Committee and **124,** 417-27
right to invoke before municipal courts and **114,** 346
scheduling to Act, effect **104,** 430
individual
right of complaint to Human Rights Committee **101,** 250-1, 464-5, **124,** 396
right to secure criminal prosecution **118,** 168, 208, 291
inhuman or degrading treatment **68,** 31-2, 35-7, 39, **69,** 177-8, **78,** 52, 78-9, 80, **79,** 178-9, 190-2, 204-5, 207-8, 209, 210, 214, 224, 225, 232, 241, 257-60, 281
burden of proof **98,** 510
death penalty, method, relevance **98,** 379-80, 450-1, 503-4, 505, 506-7, 509-12, 513-14, 518, 519, **114,** 369, 378

death row. *See* death row as inhuman or degrading treatment *above*
delay in notification of stay of execution **98,** 344
deportation **115,** 330
deprivation of liberty as **96,** 657-8
detention involving. *See* detention, inhuman treatment or torture, whether involving *above*
failure of State to investigate prison conditions **115,** 298
general principle of international law **98,** 510
prolonged judicial proceedings, death penalty, in case of **98,** 334, 367-8, 434, **114,** 368-9, 375
uniform standard, absence **98,** 510
interim measures
non-extradition of author **114,** 362
prevention of irreparable damage to authors **114,** 339
interpretation
aids
context **70,** 309-10, 312
object and purpose **70,** 313
guidelines
autonomous meaning of terms **70,** 312
independence of national systems **70,** 312
liberal **114,** 373-4
liberty of individual **70,** 308, 310
object and purpose **98,** 368, 369, 451
ordinary meaning **98,** 368
responsibility **70,** 300, 306-13, **71,** 340-5, **124,** 425
judgment, publication of **73,** 491, 509, 560
judicial review, right to, liberty of person, deprivation **96,** 659-60
legal aid, 'interests of justice' **79,** 276
legal representation **62,** 241-2, 245, 249, 253, 255, 256, 261-2, 264, 266, **70,** 257, 283-4, 286, 289-90, 295-6, **79,** 205, 210, 216, 218, 232, 259-60, 268, 273, 274, **118,** 258-9
communication with counsel **79,** 241, 259
correspondence with counsel **78,** 338, 339-42, 343-4, 346-7, 380-8
counsel nominated by State **98,** 332-3, 366
death sentence cases **98,** 366-7, **118,** 260-1
detention of **71,** 313
effective **115,** 353-5
'of his own choosing' **68,** 32, 34-5, 37, 39, 45, **69,** 192, **70,** 257, 283-4, 286, 289-90, 295-6, **78,** 24, 34, 53, 220-5, 335-6, 337-40, 343-4, 345, 346, **79,** 183-4, 186, 232, 273, 276
replacement of at court's insistence **71,** 376-7
legislation, as aid to interpretation **91,** 321, 329, 330-1, **104,** 430-1
legitimate aim **96,** 648
protection of workers **96,** 666
liberty of person, deprivation **59,** 436, **62,** 241-2, 244-5, **68,** 31-9, 45-6, **69,** 192, **78,** 26, 27, 34-5, 128-31, **79,** 249
abduction **78,** 51
arbitrary detention. *See* arbitrary detention *above*
arrest **111,** 471
arbitrary **111,** 484-5
right to be informed promptly of reasons for **114,** 330
corporal punishment, need for, whether **96,** 655
extradition **79,** 244, 248, 249-50

International Covenant on Civil and Political Rights (ICCPR) (*cont.*)
military detention, whether **96,** 655, 658-9
obligation to protect **118,** 155
period of detention **96,** 655, 657
physical and mental effects **96,** 657
presumption in favour of **70,** 308, 310
security of person. *See* security of person *below*
solitary confinement **96,** 655, 657
life, right to **70,** 260-6, 268-81, **71,** 359-60, 364-5, **94,** 387, **100,** 380-1, **125,** 515-19
arbitrary deprivation, applicable law **110,** 190
death penalty and **98,** 451, 454-5, 516-17
delay in carrying out death penalty and **98,** 367
derogation, possibility **98,** 451-3, 454-5
disappearances **118,** 155-6, 207-8
extradition in death penalty cases **98,** 460
GDR border shootings and **100,** 380-1
measures to ensure **94,** 442-3
margin of appreciation **70,** 298-304
marry, right to **62,** 289, 291, 293
minorities **68,** 21, 26-8
consultation with minority representatives, relevance **115,** 317
enjoyment of own culture **115,** 316-18
aboriginal Indians in Canada **96,** 702-4
Arhuaco Community in Colombia **118,** 287
context, to be seen in **96,** 646-7
cumulative effect of measure affecting **115,** 318
economic and social activities **96,** 703
exploitation of natural resources and **96,** 703-4
historical inequities **96,** 703
interests of society as a whole **96,** 704
preservation intact **96,** 704
Sami in Sweden **96,** 646-8
failure to protect burial grounds **118,** 277
French Polynesia **118,** 277
membership of minority **68,** 26-7
natural resources, right to dispose of freely **96,** 704
self-determination. *See* self-determination *below*
miscarriage of justice
compensation **94,** 394-5
pardon, effect **94,** 395
multiple infringements **68,** 28
municipal law and **91,** 329-31
effect on **112,** 491
implementing legislation, need for. *See* implementing legislation, need for *above*
responsibility for determining consistency **91,** 329-31
national security defence, *in camera* proceedings **110,** 674 n. 248
obligations
cooperation with Human Rights Committee **114,** 323, 329, 330
effective protection of rights **118,** 275
entry into force as critical date **118,** 189
continuing violation **115,** 268-9, 285
existing legislation to conform **96,** 361
implementation **96,** 361

investigation of alleged violations of human rights **118,** 208, 291-2
investigation in good faith of allegations against it **114,** 324, 330, **118,** 154-5
provision of effective and enforceable remedy for violation **115,** 299, 355, **118,** 195, 227-35, 291-2
provision to Human Rights Committee of all information at its disposal **114,** 330
offenders, rights of. *See* convicted persons *above*
Optional Protocol (First) (1966)
Covenant, relation to **107,** 72
denunciation **123,** 513-14, 527
object and purpose **107,** 72
reservations. *See* reservations, admissibility, Optional Protocol (First) (1966) *below*
treaty, whether **107,** 72
Optional Protocol (Second) (1989)
death penalty **98,** 394-5, 445, 446, **124,** 326
extradition **114,** 373
object and purpose **107,** 73
reservations. *See* reservations, admissibility, Optional Protocol (Second) *below*
part of Hong Kong law, whether **92,** 656
participation in conduct of public affairs **96,** 711-12
applicable law, national law **96,** 712
direct participation **96,** 712
passport
identity and travel documents as **78,** 70
unjustified refusal **78,** 70-1
penal legislation, retroactivity **62,** 247-8, 255
penalty heavier than at time of offence **101,** 303-4
people, definition **79,** 266
phrases
'competent, impartial and independent tribunal established by law' **105,** 472, 475-6, 563, 565
'convicted of a crime' **104,** 447, 448
'court', supervisory military officer **96,** 659-60
'crime', civil contempt **104,** 432-3, 447, 448
'family'
broad interpretation **118,** 274-5, 277
kinship link, relevance **118,** 274-5
parent/child relationship **96,** 634, 636
'has been examined' **79,** 271
'his own country' **115,** 330-1, 335-6, 337-49
'country of nationality' distinguished **115,** 335, 346
failure to acquire nationality, relevance **115,** 336-7, 343-4, 347-8
stateless person **115,** 335
'in accordance with procedure established by law' **111,** 484-5
'least possible physical and mental suffering' **98,** 503-4, 509-12, 513-14
'penalty' **70,** 306-13, **71,** 338-45
parole, forfeiture **70,** 306-13, **71,** 338-45
'people', Optional Protocol, relevance **96,** 702
'privacy' **118,** 278
'review by a higher tribunal according to law' **104,** 433-6, 449
'sex', sexual orientation **112,** 341-3, 393-4
'suit at law', refugee proceedings **118,** 246-7
'victim'. *See* United Nations Human Rights Committee (UNHRC), complainant; United Nations Human Rights Committee (UNHRC), victim

International Covenant on Civil and Political Rights (ICCPR) (*cont.*)
'within its territory' **123,** 102, 115
political rights **62,** 286, 290, 296, **70,** 257-8, **79,** 243-4, 249
deprivation of **62,** 266, 268, 270-1
entitlement under national law to stand for Presidency **94,** 414
freedom of opinion **94,** 414
reasonable restrictions **62,** 266, **66,** 268-9, 271
presumption of innocence **62,** 248, **71,** 307, **118,** 85, **122,** 445
primacy **98,** 446, 453-4
private life, respect for
burial grounds, failure to protect **118,** 278
consensual homosexual activity in private **112,** 340-2
criminalization as health/moral measure, proportionality **112,** 341, 343-4
interference on discretionary grounds **112,** 343
non-enforcement of offending measures **112,** 340-2, 343
prompt hearing **62,** 241-2, 245, 247, 255-6, 262, 266, **69,** 176-7, 192, **70,** 254, 296, **71,** 353, 356, 361, 365, **79,** 186, 192, 209, 210, 218, 233, 241, 260, 271, 275, 276, **118,** 258
administrative delays **69,** 173, 175-7
appeal procedures, effectiveness **69,** 176
right to **69,** 173, 175-7, 192, **71,** 353, 356, 361, 365
prompt trial **68,** 32, 36, 39, 46, **69,** 192, **70,** 256, **94,** 410, **114,** 324, 330
delay due to authorities' oversight **98,** 333-4
property rights **115,** 268, **118,** 189
discrimination in respect of compensation by successor government for expropriation under communist regime **115,** 265-76, **118,** 193-5
discrimination in respect of compensation by successor government for expropriation under pre-communist regime **118,** 239, 240
protection of **91,** 321
proportionality **96,** 648
provisions, States, whether restricted to **69,** 190-2, **78,** 39
public hearing **62,** 246, 248, 255, 261-2, 266
public life
restrictions **62,** 254-5
right to participate in **62,** 246-7, 249, 253-4, 286, 289-90, 292, 295-6
purpose
mechanism for adoption at national level **105,** 565
universality of human rights **96,** 658
relationship to other International Conventions **112,** 406
religious education **62,** 271-8
remedies **68,** 39, 241-3, 246-7, 255, 257, 260, 262, 266, 846, **78,** 80
appropriate **118,** 150
avoidance of future violations **79,** 179, 186, 192, 260, **114,** 325, 331, **115,** 355, **118,** 172, 209, 275, 292
clemency **78,** 39
commutation of death sentence **98,** 334, **115,** 354, **118,** 261
compensation **62,** 246, **70,** 266, 279, 286, **71,** 316, 353, 365, **78,** 27, 53, 192, 233, 260, **79,** 179, **94,** 410, 415, **95,** 314, **114,** 325, 331, **115,** 299, **118,** 172, 195, 208, 292
measure **118,** 209
discretionary where Covenant not part of municipal law **104,** 436-40
effective **78,** 39, 71, 80, **79,** 186, 192, 200, 233, 241, **94,** 410, 426, 443, **96,** 660, 703, **114,** 319, **118,** 156, 172

expedition of criminal proceedings **118,** 209
investigation of violations **94,** 410, 443, **118,** 156, 171-2
offending legislation
amendment **118,** 183
repeal **112,** 342, 344
restitution of property **118,** 195
review **118,** 195
protection from harassment **118,** 209
release from detention **98,** 368
State representations to avoid death penalty **98,** 504, 506
steps to ensure non-repetition **94,** 410, 415, 426, 443, **96,** 660
reservations. *See also* restrictions on rights *below*
admissibility **107,** 68-76
broadly formulated **107,** 71-2
burden of proof **107,** 71
Danish **71,** 307-9
Italian **78,** 56-62
non-derogable provisions of Covenant **107,** 70-1
Norwegian **79,** 270-1, 275
object and purpose test **107,** 69-71, 74-5
obligation to ensure and respect rights **107,** 70
obligation to implement Covenant **107,** 70
obligation to provide remedies in case of breach **107,** 71-2
obligations vis-à-vis Human Rights Committee **107,** 71-3
Optional Protocol (First) (1966) **107,** 72-3
Optional Protocol (Second) (1989) **107,** 73
right to determine own political status **107,** 70
via reservation to First Optional Protocol (1966) **107,** 72
compensation for victims of unlawful arrest or detention **125,** 518-19
interpretative statement distinguished, limitation *ratione temporis* **107,** 72-3
objection to, effect **107,** 74
provision for, Optional Protocol (Second) (1989) **107,** 73
requirements
explanation of failure to conform to Covenant **107,** 75-6
precision **107,** 75-6
preservation of autonomous nature of Covenant **107,** 75
preservation of integrity of Covenant **107,** 75
transparency **107,** 75
in respect of Art. 27 **118,** 266, 276, 277-8
review, need for regular **107,** 76
separability **107,** 75
timing **107,** 73
validity, responsibility for determining **107,** 73-6
residence rights **68,** 27-8
restrictions, reasonable and objective justification **68,** 27-8
restrictions on rights **62,** 295, **68,** 37-8, **78,** 32, **79,** 247
author's failure to comply with law as result of State's own action **118,** 194
courts' interpretation of law in compliance with treaty obligations, relevance **115,** 378-80
justification
public order disturbances **70,** 247, 271-3, 278-9, **71,** 320, 329, **122,** 574-7, 588-92, 596-600
state of emergency **62,** 267, 269-70, **78,** 31-2

International Covenant on Civil and Political Rights (ICCPR) (*cont.*)
'state of siege' **70,** 241-3, 247, 278-9, **71,** 320, 329
prompt security measures **62,** 244-5, 260
proportionality **62,** 254
requirements
compliance of law with provisions of Covenant **115,** 372
conformity with aims and objectives of Covenant **115,** 372, 374, 380-1
legitimate purpose **115,** 372
narrow and specific provision **122,** 597, 600-1
necessity **62,** 269-70, **115,** 373, 374-7, 378-9, 380-3, **122,** 574-7, 588, 592-3
proportionality **115,** 376-7, 380-1
provision by law **115,** 372, 380-1, **122,** 588
reasonable and objective criteria **118,** 143, 144, 145, 150, 194, 234
retroactive legislation **91,** 49, 80, 140
act criminal according to general principles of law at time committed **98,** 574-5, **105,** 449-50
right of entry **78,** 70
right to take part in the conduct of public affairs **114,** 325
security measures **68,** 37-8
security of person, arrest and detention, whether limited to **114,** 324-5
self-determination **92,** 168
individual's right to challenge **96,** 645-6, 705-7
self-executing, whether **86,** 116, 119-20, **100,** 381
sexual discrimination. *See* discrimination, sexual *above*
State responsibility
acts outside its jurisdiction **68,** 38-40, 45-7, **98,** 433
defence of conditions in third State **98,** 512-13
foreseeable result of own action **98,** 445, 465-8, 470-1, 486, 500-1, 504, 507-8, 509, 516
hypothetical events **98,** 502
adoption of challenged legislation **96,** 647
for disappearances **79,** 179
State succession, Czech Republic **118,** 185 n. 2
strike, right to **94,** 253-4
non-prejudice of ILO guarantee **94,** 254
summary execution **95,** 634
torture **59,** 443, **62,** 240-2, 244, 256-7, 261, 264, **69,** 192, **78,** 51, 52, **79,** 178-9, 214, 231, 257-60, **118,** 170-2, 208, 291, **123,** 33, 41, 42
conscientious objection and **94,** 410, 442, 443
deportation to country where risk of **124,** 365-6
travaux préparatoires, death sentence **98,** 368-70, 451
violations **71,** 316, 331, 353, 365, **79,** 178-9, 186, 191-2, 199-200, 209-10, 217-18, 224-5, 232-3, 241, 260
continuing **62,** 243-4, 258, 266, **94,** 406, **115,** 268-9, 285
continuing effects **68,** 21, 25-6, **70,** 295, **79,** 247, 249
duty to investigate
State **94,** 410, 414, 442
UNHRC **94,** 386
investigation of **70,** 265-6, 296
duty on States party **71,** 351, 364, **79,** 179, 190, 224, 256-60
measures to prevent **94,** 410, 415, 442, 443
preceding entry into force of Covenant **62,** 241-4, **68,** 21, 25, **70,** 295, **71,** 313, 351-3, 357, **79,** 227-8, 231-2, 247, 249, 278, 279
subsequent execution of prison sentence **79,** 249

remedies. *See* remedies *above*
request for extradition **79,** 249
'views' of United Nations Human Rights Committee with regard to **71,** 316, 331, 345, 353, 365, **79,** 169, 181, 188, 194, 218, 220, 227, 233
waiver of rights **104,** 445-6
International Covenant on Economic, Social and Cultural Rights (1966) 110, 83. *See also* International Covenant on Civil and Political Rights (ICCPR) (1966)
detention of alien **92,** 551-2
direct effect **96,** 340-3, 362, 363, 372-3, 390-1
draft **37,** 357, 454
equality
destruction of existing equality **96,** 341
discrimination, need for **96,** 351-2
pay **96,** 340-3, 390-1
near-identity of positions, need for **96,** 343
patent inequality, need for **96,** 341-3
perpetuation of inequality **96,** 362-3
destruction of existing equality distinguished **96,** 341
legislation, as aid to interpretation **91,** 321
self-determination **92,** 168
strike, right to **94,** 252-3
in conformity with national law **94,** 253
non-derogation and **94,** 253
public service in **94,** 253
essential services, limited to **94,** 258
international crimes 91, 48. *See also* crimes against humanity; genocide; international criminal law; international humanitarian law; international tort/wrong; terrorism; war crimes
applicable law
international law **91,** 43, 118-19
conformity with international law, need for **91,** 118-19
lex fori **104,** 181-4, 191-2
classification as
torture **119,** 149-50, 155-6, 199-201, 217
Torture Convention (1984), relevance **119,** 229-30
customary international law **91,** 121, **119,** 65-70
definition **120,** 362
instigation of State authorities, need for **119,** 226-7, 243
scale, relevance **119,** 217, 229, 250
extradition, requested State's right to decide without consultation **119,** 301
forum, right to choose **105,** 441
Head of State, immunity, jurisdiction **119,** 43-8, 61-70, 83-7, 97-9, 104-7, 155-6, 169-70, 212-13, 223-33, 349, **125,** 495-510
jurisdiction **91,** 40-4, **119,** 139
extraterritorial jurisdiction and **120,** 398-9
immunity from/right of distinguished **119,** 69
right to challenge, State **105,** 440-1, 480
treaty as basis **120,** 398-9
universal. *See* universal jurisdiction *below*
legislation, retroactive **91,** 48, **120,** 363
critical date **91,** 50
procedural provisions distinguished **119,** 336-7, 350-1
'ordinary' crime **105,** 483
separation of powers and **91,** 92-3

international crimes (*cont.*)
State responsibility, breach **110,** 81-2
statutory limitation
Control Council Law No 10 **119,** 357
customary international law **119,** 358
European Convention on the Non-Applicability of Statutory Limitation to Crimes against Humanity and War Crimes (1974) **91,** 35, **119,** 357-8
UN Convention on the Non-Applicability of Statutory Limitations to War Crimes and Crimes against Humanity (1968) **79,** 405, **119,** 357-8
universal jurisdiction **91,** 40, 121-2, **105,** 485, **119,** 67, 229-33, 243, 350, **125,** 579-80
breach of *jus cogens*/peremptory norm, need for **119,** 229
as breach of UN Charter **119,** 344-5
creation of international tribunals as evidence against **119,** 364
effectiveness, need for **119,** 325-6
as element of offence **91,** 121
gravity, relevance **119,** 229
non-universal **120,** 398-9
presence of offender, relevance **119,** 350, 367
relevance to classification as **119,** 156
International Criminal Court (ICC). *See also* International Criminal Court (ICC), Rome Statute (1998)
jurisdiction
complementarity **125,** 486-8
amnesty, effect **125,** 488
statutory limitation, effect **125,** 488
most serious crimes of concern to the international community **119,** 212-13
terrorist crimes **125,** 497, 502-3, 505-6
International Criminal Court (ICC), Rome Statute (1998). *See also* International Law Commission (ICJ), Draft Statute for an International Criminal Court (1994); Yugoslavia, International Criminal Tribunal for the Former (ICTY)
aiding and abetting **121,** 288. *See also* common purpose *below*
acting with a common purpose distinguished **121,** 279-80, 320, **122,** 99 n. 310, **124,** 155-6
applicability
Head of State **119,** 67, 212-13
ratification/entry into force, relevance **125,** 490, 502-3
common purpose **124,** 155-6. *See also* aiding and abetting *above*
constitutional amendment, need for **125,** 470-90
ICC jurisdiction in case of amnesty/statutory limitation **125,** 488
investigation without presence of State Party on territory of that State **125,** 489
responsibility of Head of State, member of government or parliament **125,** 482
crimes against humanity **122,** 77
definition **119,** 354
deportation or forcible transfer of civilians **122,** 88
discrimination **124,** 180
mens rea **122,** 90-1
war crimes distinguished, relative seriousness **124,** 232, 256
widespread or systematic attack **122,** 80
customary international law and **121,** 283-4, **124,** 155-6
continuing development for purposes other than Statute **124,** 156 n. 282
Head of State immunity **119,** 66-7, 155, **125,** 482, 497-8, 502-3
judicial assistance, investigation without presence of State Party on territory of that State **125,** 489

mens rea **122,** 90-1
intent and knowledge **121,** 288, **122,** 99 n. 315
obligation to exercise criminal jurisdiction, Head of State immunity, relevance **125,** 497-8, 502-3
phrases, 'wilfully causing great suffering', rape **121,** 266 n. 192
principles applicable to criminal law and criminal procedure, compatibility **125,** 483-6
responsibility of commander, effective control test **122,** 103
responsibility of Head of State, member of government or parliament **125,** 482
sentencing, execution **125,** 489
State or organizational objective **122,** 80
status **121,** 283, **124,** 155-6
opinio juris **124,** 156
torture, definition **123,** 49
international criminal law. *See also* international crimes; international tort/wrong
conventions **71,** 246
development **71,** 246-7
extradition rules, relevance **78,** 129
nature **36,** 289-97
as international law **119,** 355
primacy **119,** 355
UN resolutions **71,** 246
international criminal order
establishment **106,** 238
extradition and **106,** 238
international criminal procedure
international tribunals, specificity **111,** 390-1
municipal law analogies, relevance **111,** 390
International Criminal Tribunal for Rwanda (ICTR). *See* Rwanda, International Criminal Tribunal for (ICTR)
International Development Agency (IDA). *See* World Bank Group
international development law
UN Development Decade (Resolution 1710 (XVI)) **106,** 654-5
UN Resolution 1803 (XVII) **106,** 655
international economic development, law of **46,** 340
international economic law 46, 453
International Finance Corporation (IFC) 77, 87-8. *See also* World Bank Group
personality **77,** 88
international humanitarian law 76, 446-9. *See also* crimes against humanity; Geneva Conventions (1949); international crimes; international law; war, laws and customs; war crimes; Yugoslavia, International Criminal Tribunal for the Former (ICTY), Statute
armed forces and **88,** 10-13
customary international law **110,** 209-10, 223, 444, 514-15, 533-4, **122,** 68
definition, *Fundamental Rules of International Humanitarian Law Applicable in Armed Conflicts* (1978) **110,** 149
Geneva Conventions (1949) and **76,** 447-9
human rights law and **123,** 169, 182-8
jus cogens/peremptory norm **110,** 208, 223-4, 446-7, 523-4
as legal regime **110,** 393-4
Manual of Psychological Operations in Guerrilla Warfare **76,** 463-4, 490, 525, 722-3, 872
multicultural basis **110,** 428-32, 449
non-international conflicts **76,** 447-8

international humanitarian law (*cont.*)
nuclear weapons, applicability to **110,** 149, 194-5, 206-13, 216, 222-3, 251, 255-6, 258, 261, 270-2, 386, 426-7, 478-9, **122,** 646-7, 653-4
purpose
'conciliation of the necessities of war with the laws of humanity' **110,** 394
legal requirements of conduct **110,** 538
protection of human dignity **121,** 264-5
protection of persons *hors de combat* **111,** 378, **121,** 265
requirements
nexus with armed conflict **112,** 183-4, **119,** 351-2, **121,** 291-2, **122,** 39-42, 653-4
internal armed conflict **119,** 351-2
self-defence, applicability to **110,** 195, 223, 225-6
sovereignty and **110,** 445-6
United Nations Charter (1945), effect **110,** 440-1
violations, encouragement of **76,** 464, 722-3
International Institute of Refrigeration. *See also* Headquarters Agreement (1966) *in the Consolidated Table of Treaties*
employment contract, applicable law **77,** 503, 505-6
Implementing Regulations
Preamble **77,** 503
Art. 27 **77,** 505
Art. 28 **77,** 502, 504
Art. 29 **77,** 502, 504-5
Art. 32 **77,** 501, 505
Art. 33 **77,** 505
Chapter VII **77,** 504
Chapter VIII **77,** 504
Protocol, Art. 12 **77,** 502
International Labour Organization Administrative Tribunal (ILOAT)
abuse of process **40,** 311-12, 328, 329-30
accessibility **94,** 338
acts challengeable before **48,** 293-5, 296-7
admissibility **48,** 280-95
exhaustion of other remedies **48,** 292, 295
time-limits **48,** 240-1, 275, 278, 280-3, 298-304
arbitral jurisdiction **38,** 421-2, 427
competence. *See* jurisdiction *below*
composition **40,** 304-5, 307-8, 309, 310, 312, 314, 318, 325, 327, 329, 333
costs **38,** 402, 434-8
doubt as to jurisdiction **43,** 459-62
decisions
comments on, publication of **40,** 315, 317-18, 319
finality **38,** 396, 436, 438, **48,** 305-7
review **40,** 303-6, 332, 333
by ICJ **38,** 436-7, 438, **54,** 498, 502
grounds **54,** 487-9
discretionary powers, review of **40,** 413
duty to ascertain law **40,** 319
intervention by third parties **38,** 435-6
joinder of actions **40,** 321-2, 324-5
judgments. *See* decisions *above*
jurisdiction **54,** 485-6
arbitral **38,** 421-2, 427

execution of judgment **38,** 435
ratione personae **38,** 379-80, 387-9, 426, 433, **40,** 422-5, **43,** 448, 450-1, **48,** 305-7
review of exercise of discretionary powers **48,** 354-61
UN Joint Staff Pension Fund **43,** 323
UNESCO Staff Association **38,** 382
pleadings, disclosure to third parties **40,** 323, 325-6, 328
procedure
caractère contradictoire **38,** 436
submission of evidence **38,** 409
remedies, compensation in lieu of specific performance **48,** 320
Statute
Art. XII **83,** 417-18
review of decision **54,** 494
time-barred claim **38,** 401-2
UN Administrative Tribunal, proposed fusion with **69,** 444-5
UNESCO Appeals Board, reference back to **43,** 468-70
United Nations Administrative Tribunal (UNAT), merger recommendation **83,** 360
International Labour Organization (ILO) 71, 240. *See also* Asian Development Bank Administrative Tribunal; International Labour Organization Administrative Tribunal (ILOAT); International Labour Organization (ILO) Conventions; United Nations Administrative Tribunal (UNAT); World Bank Administrative Tribunal
Commission of Inquiry
compliance with recommendations **36,** 427
discretion **36,** 394-5
evidence
admissibility **36,** 377-9, 414, **37,** 414
evaluation **36,** 413-19
hearsay evidence **36,** 414
judicial role **36,** 369, 374, 390, 392-3
Member States' obligation to place information at disposal of **36,** 379
prima facie case **36,** 394-5
procedure **36,** 355-8, 365, 368-71, 373-7
visit to country of alleged breach **36,** 379, 411-12
witnesses **36,** 370, 373-7
Committee of Freedom of Association
interpretation of conventions, role **94,** 256
public sector right to strike **94,** 256-8
essential services, limitation to **94,** 258
Constitution
Art. 4(1) **99,** 378
Art. 12(2) **99,** 387
Art. 15(5)(d) **99,** 387
Art. 19(2) **99,** 378
Art. 19(5)(b) **99,** 378
Art. 19(5)(c) **99,** 378, 381
Art. 19(5)(d) **99,** 378, 383
Art. 19(6)(b) **99,** 378
Art. 19(6)(c) **99,** 378
Art. 19(8) **99,** 379, 391
Arts. 22-34 **99,** 379
Art. 26 **36,** 352
Art. 27 **36,** 379

International Labour Organization (ILO) (*cont.*)
complaints procedure **37,** 84, 86, 407, 512, 514, 541-2
as law-making treaty **37,** 451
revision **46,** 168
'standards' established by **37,** 365, 367
text (extracts) **36,** 354-5
EC
failure to implement undertakings, responsibility, Member State **99,** 380
membership **99,** 379, 394
participation in negotiations **99,** 379-81
employee entitlements on termination of employment **109,** 382-4
governing body members
immunity, jurisdiction, scope **75,** 76-8
status **54,** 502, **75,** 76-8
Headquarters Agreement **40,** 301
International Labour Conference (1978) **90,** 207-8
Recommendations
municipal law and **90,** 212-13
status **90,** 212-13
review procedures **69,** 369, 404, 407, 443-4, 477, 487-9
Statute
Art. VI **69,** 488
Art. XII **69,** 366, 470, 477-8, 481, 487-9
revision **46,** 168
strike, right to, Covenants Concerning Freedom of Association and Protection of Right to Organize (1945) **94,** 254-8
trade union and **62,** 386
International Labour Organization (ILO) Conventions. *See also* International Labour Organization (ILO)
81 (Labour Inspection Convention (1947)). *See* forced or compulsory labour, freedom from
107 (Indigenous and Tribal Populations (1957)), recommendation for ratification by Liberia **36,** 425-6
169 (Indigenous and Tribal Peoples in Independent Countries (1989)) **116,** 279
170 (chemicals at work)
analysis **99,** 381-3
EC competence **99,** 377-94
complaint of non-compliance, right of **36,** 391-2
deposit **37,** 80, 81
Discrimination in Employment **43,** 319
forced labour. *See* forced or compulsory labour, freedom from
implementation
choice of means **36,** 398-9, 401
competent national authority **99,** 378
duty to make effective **36,** 403-5, 421
reports on **36,** 388-9, 394, 409-11, 422, 424, 425
interpretation
commission of inquiry **94,** 256
Committee of Experts **94,** 256
Committee on Freedom of Association **94,** 256
ICJ **94,** 256
procedure for adoption **99,** 378
ratification, rights in absence of ratification by other party **36,** 391
tripartite consultation **99,** 378-9, 389

international law. *See also* comity; customary international law; equity; general principles of international law; international courtesy; international criminal law; international tort/wrong; treaties
act of State doctrine and **43,** 12-18, **57,** 26, 29
actio popularis **57,** 515
administrative law **54,** 469
Afro-Asian influence **46,** 464
Anglo-American law, relation to **54,** 323-4
applicability
between enterprises of different countries **47,** 28-30
between non-sovereign States **50,** 395-8
between Paramount Power and vassal **50,** 3, 28, 39, 70-1, 90-9, 102, 214, 247, 395-8, 401, 411-12, 464
within federal State **57,** 110, **59,** 218-27
as applicable law **84,** 20, 31, 170, 198, 529, 540
arbitral tribunal **82,** 627
expropriation/nationalization **83,** 527-8, 533, 559, 565
State immunity questions **84,** 20, 31
applicable principles and rules **78,** 649
basis
consent **80,** 108, **92,** 527, **110,** 241-2, **115,** 192
customary international law **110,** 235, **115,** 192
force, rules relating to **46,** 483
survival of mankind **110,** 330-1, 541
binding force
basis
consent **87,** 455
customary international law **87,** 455
conditions for **72,** 72-3
breach. *See also* State responsibility
in abstract, possibility of **79,** 359-61, 364
acquiescence **90,** 662-5, 691-2
admission **77,** 275
applicable law
international law **53,** 480-1, **104,** 181-3, **116,** 332-3
municipal law **104,** 181-3
defence
municipal law **100,** 381, **108,** 72-5, 650, 718, **116,** 332-3, **117,** 561, **121,** 22-3
Georges Pinson **108,** 74
Polish Nationals in Danzig **108,** 74
diplomat, offence against **36,** 293
erga omnes obligation **105,** 354-7
establishment of **79,** 9-10
extradition and **79,** 479-80, 511-12, 515, 519, 529
failure to legislate **79,** 359-61
exhaustion of domestic remedies and **79,** 364
failure to pass implementing legislation **121,** 258-60
hostage-taking **81,** 545
improper assumption of jurisdiction as **77,** 532
individual responsibility. *See also* war, laws and customs, individual liability; war crimes, responsibility
offence under municipal law **82,** 516-17
municipal law jurisdiction based on **81,** 499-500, 591, **103,** 530, **104,** 125-9

international law (*cont.*)
municipal proceedings and **45,** 94, 95-6, 102, 104
national of acting State, in case of **81,** 515
nationality of victim, relevance **77,** 172, 178, 185
private support for rebel forces, whether **80,** 590-2
racial discrimination as **68,** 209-11, 221-2, 236
remedies. *See* remedies
as sovereign act **103,** 528-9
sovereignty, violation of **74,** 258, 266-7
State action, need for **104,** 156-7
State immunity and **77,** 265-7, **79,** 6-7, 8, 9-13
universality of offence and **81,** 499, 591
war **56,** 583
changing circumstances **83,** 135
codification. *See also* customary law, treaties and other international instruments reflecting
impossibility **104,** 335
and progressive development **41,** 147, 218
UNGA and **110,** 226
commerce and **46,** 511, 529-30
compliance
absence of means to secure **91,** 130
choice of means **104,** 194, **105,** 24-5, 350-3, **110,** 642, **123,** 216-17
customary international law **105,** 24
good faith **105,** 24, **110,** 146-7, **116,** 332-3
level of **106,** 139
machinery to ensure **82,** 636, 637-8
municipal law as defence **94,** 515
nationality law **57,** 309-10
obligation of **110,** 146-7, 668
implementing agency in absence of binding legislation **120,** 601-2
preservation of international standing **113,** 433
presumption of **84,** 293, **110,** 756, 764-5
public interest considerations **57,** 11-12, **107,** 93-8
reciprocity and **99,** 197, **118,** 31
States' interest in **37,** 83
conflict of rules, resolution, complementary **99,** 502
consensual nature **55,** 277, **64,** 126
treaty, need for **110,** 246
contemporary, *uti possidetis* and **80,** 471-2, 535
contract **84,** 258-9
enforceability under **77,** 328
courts, municipal. *See* municipal courts *below*
definition **80,** 107
derogation **41,** 71, 76
by agreement **99,** 503-4, 561-3. *See also jus cogens*/peremptory norm
by treaty **71,** 220, **74,** 283-4, 400, **110,** 726-7
jus cogens/peremptory norm **83,** 25
municipal law restrictions **71,** 222-6
desiderata
certainty **81,** 340
clarity **81,** 340
consistency **81,** 419
predictability **81,** 340, 419
stability **81,** 340

development
by international courts **41,** 141, 174, 185, **46,** 76, 238, 422
by international organizations **37,** 453-5, 553
by municipal courts **66,** 112, **119,** 67
cultural diversity and **116,** 105-20
equality of States and **41,** 140
new trends **46,** 460-9, **67,** 30-1, 40-2, 101-2, 152-4, 240, 276-8, 290-1, 313
political and legal factors **37,** 411-22
progressive **55,** 273, 330, **119,** 67
treaty interpretation and **82,** 619
dualist theory **85,** 257, 258, **119,** 69
EC law, whether **93,** 320-1
economic, applicability to individuals **53,** 457-60
enforcement **59,** 469
comity and **84,** 174
equitable principles. *See* equitable principles
erga omnes rules, adversarial proceedings and **116,** 126-7
establishment **80,** 52-3, 132-41. *See also* sources *below*
difficulty **84,** 121-2
European character **41,** 139, 208
European Communities, law of and **53,** 28-37, 44-6, 48, **77,** 391
evidence of. *See* evidence of, international law
evolving nature **113,** 419
expansion **68,** 220-1
extradition in case of death penalty, assurances that death penalty will not be carried out, need for **98,** 435
federal State, in **90,** 198, 199, 200-1, 208, 211
applicability between members of **57,** 110, **59,** 218-27
flexibility **105,** 542
fundamental norms **55,** 296, **77,** 172. *See also jus cogens*/peremptory norm *below*
'approximate application' **116,** 60, 61, 62, 71, 136-7, 202, 243
public policy exception to extradition obligation **106,** 264-8
rights of individual **69,** 190-2, **92,** 165, 166
rights of people and minorities **92,** 165, 166
gaps **41,** 137-8, 139, 141, 144, 174, 188, **46,** 305, **79,** 366, **84,** 538 n. 18, **91,** 683, **107,** 291-4
death penalty and **78,** 98, 100
equity *praeter legem* and **99,** 599-600
inadmissibility **80,** 135
Islamic law and **64,** 625-32
lege deficiente, recurritur ad consuetudinem, et deficiente consuetudine, recurritur ad rationem naturalem **80,** 134
political offenders **59,** 474-6
general character **59,** 4
general rules of **61,** 622, **62,** 472, 476, 542, 544, 546, 573, **72,** 214, 440, 561
conflict of treaty with **61,** 623-4, **79,** 105
definition, rules of customary international law complemented by internationally recognized principles of international law **61,** 180
frequency of rule, relevance **79,** 9
mutuality of interest required **79,** 9
pacta sunt servanda **61,** 623, 624
prescription **76,** 175
Vienna Convention on the Law of Treaties (1969) **79,** 291-2

international law (*cont.*)
human rights and **57,** 448, 582
ICJ
basis of jurisdiction **54,** 477
role in developing **81,** 340
imperfect nature of **49,** 214
implementation. *See also* treaties, operation and enforcement
arbitral award, payments under **77,** 199
municipal court's responsibility **77,** 328
municipal law, in **77,** 188
obligations, method of meeting not prescribed **77,** 207
political matter **117,** 46
sanctions authorized **77,** 223
inconsistency **83,** 135
Indian States, applicability between **50,** 27, 39, 213
international commercial law, whether **96,** 134
international legal order, whether **101,** 422-4
international personality. *See* subjects *below*
interpretation
minimization of disputes **41,** 228
municipal and international courts **40,** 70
object and purpose **121,** 289-91
responsibility
executive **77,** 503
municipal courts **77,** 503, 586
intertemporal nature **59,** 186, **83,** 32
Islamic law and **62,** 175, 191, **64,** 626-32, 650, **114,** 42, **119,** 448
jus cogens. See jus cogens/peremptory norm
laches. *See* gaps *above*
lacunae. *See* gaps *above*
Latin American influence **46,** 464-9
law of nations, meaning under US law **77,** 217-18
law, whether **104,** 329
legal order established by **89,** 73
legislation
interpretation in accordance with **94,** 291
vagueness of international law, relevance **104,** 397-8
lex specialis **67,** 31
limited role **77,** 246-7
maritime delimitation as part of **55,** 257
matter of law for judge **98,** 557, 571
ministerial action, compatibility, authority to determine **83,** 237, 238, 243
morality and **46,** 460
multilateral trade agreements, whether **96,** 134
GATT **96,** 134
Uruguay Round Negotiations **96,** 134 n. 45
municipal courts. *See also* municipal law and *below*
application by **53,** 545-6, **80,** 90, 144, 150, **82,** 385-6, **104,** 397, **113,** 418, **115,** 545-6, **124,** 359
breach as cause of action **104,** 127-8, 176-84
international adjudication, relevance **107,** 480
judicial obligation to observe norms **94,** 252
national view of international law and **91,** 62-3, **117,** 587-8

principles established by ICJ **94,** 366-7
unincorporated law **107,** 473-4
creation by **45,** 81, **80,** 109, **81,** 680, 715, **104,** 189
binding effect on other States or International Courts **115,** 545
interpretation of international law **40,** 70
obligation to raise *proprio motu* **65,** 76, 80-1
role **90,** 397-8
as source **48,** 398-400, **64,** 577-8, **74,** 182-3, 481-2, 603, 641, 663, 674-5, **82,** 25, **83,** 541, **101,** 401, **104,** 329, **108,** 12-13, 17, **110,** 350-2, **115,** 545
courts of another country **64,** 180-1, 238-40, 316-18, 362
treaty interpretation if no question of public international law **77,** 503
unenforceability of contract under international law, duty to raise *proprio motu* **77,** 327
municipal law and **38,** 134, **43,** 3-11, **51,** 1-10, **55,** 5, **64,** 15, 89-90, 127-8, 142, 152, 169, 410-11, 600, 670, 711, **65,** 30-1, 252, 255, 354, 397, 429, 437, **69,** 149-50, 153-4, **74,** 167-8, **77,** 32, 94-6, 172, 187, 469, 553-5, 563-6, **78,** 129, 131, **79,** 7, 9-17, 87, 105, 363, 399-406, 546, **80,** 52-3, 102, 105-7, 132-41, 403, 409, 413, 419, 574, **81,** 499-500, 714, **82,** 260, 277, 292, 295, **84,** 20-1, 30-1, **85,** 255-62, **86,** 585-6, **87,** 5, 6, 26, 35, **88,** 48, 707, **90,** 129, **91,** 500, **93,** 8-9, **103,** 427, **104,** 147, 159, 334, **116,** 638
application under **56,** 476, **77,** 314-20
arbitral proceedings, interrelationship in **89,** 594
common principles **80,** 574
compatibility, presumption of **80,** 102
competence to determine whether part of **61,** 168-70, 179, 180-1, **70,** 400-1, **117,** 590
concurrence with **77,** 563-6
concurrent jurisdiction **80,** 383
conflict **44,** 109, 117, 203, 269-70, 275, 288, **45,** 26, **52,** 297, **53,** 11-13, 15-16, **64,** 673, 711, **79,** 292, **90,** 337-8
amendment, need for **90,** 422, **101,** 8
attempts to resolve **82,** 236-8, 263-4, 265-8, 271-2, 275-6
conformity, presumption of **82,** 262-3, **87,** 34, **90,** 129
consistency, assumption of **36,** 24-5, **108,** 590
declaratory of **80,** 124
direct application **70,** 431-2
dualist theory **93,** 253-4, **111,** 389, **113,** 418
effect of breach **91,** 478-9
effect on statutory language **91,** 352
enforcement under **79,** 401-3
entrenchment **104,** 198-9
foreign State, justiciability **44,** 1-2
general principles of international law in completion of **66,** 560, **67,** 338-9, 366, **73,** 372, **102,** 140, 170, **117,** 582
general rules of international law **61,** 168-70, 601, **117,** 583
harmonisation, desirability **69,** 71-2
implementation in **74,** 311-13, 339-40, 357, **77,** 188, **79,** 345
inconsistency **82,** 235, 236-44, 245-52, 254, 257, 258-9, 262-7, 269-71, 275-9
incorporation, need for **59,** 460-1, **64,** 127-8, **103,** 610 n. 1, **104,** 443
independence of two systems **84,** 380
individuals **93,** 8, 394-5
inheritance, non-resident aliens **42,** 1-8

international law (*cont.*)
institutions and concepts of **46,** 207-11, 240, 246, 407-10, 428, 446, 495, 509, 512, 517
inter-State disputes **91,** 311-14
interpretation in accordance with **94,** 291
jurisdiction and **79,** 15, 401-6
legislation in breach of **90,** 208
legislation, need for **113,** 418
legislative powers, limitations on **91,** 30
lex posterior derogat priori **77,** 551, 554
long-standing law
compatibility with international law **87,** 34
evidence of compatibility with international law **47,** 172, 179, 186-7
monist theory **39,** 457, **85,** 258, **93,** 296
municipal law in international law **46,** 408, 446, **53,** 480-1, **70,** 596-7, **91,** 361, 368, **115,** 121-3
pacta sunt servanda and **59,** 5
primacy. *See* primacy *below*
recommendations of international assemblies **77,** 421-3
renvoi to **46,** 446-7, 452, 509, 512, 522-3, **106,** 454, **116,** 653
resolutions of international organizations **91,** 409
retroactivity and **91,** 43-4, 47-8
rights of nationals and **87,** 5, 32
transformation doctrine **64,** 127-8, 142, 151, 169, **80,** 132
unlawfulness, interrelationship **91,** 353-4
mutual legal assistance **75,** 123
legal nature **75,** 84-5
nature of **57,** 392
new situations **69,** 581, 594
new States and **46,** 461, 462, 482-4, 504, 505
obligations. *See also* international obligations
creation of **57,** 412
customary international law **90,** 198, 199-202, 694, **105,** 350-3
incorporation of principles into municipal law **91,** 354
municipal law enforcement **79,** 341, 345, 346, 347, 350-1, 364, 366, 367, 368, 400, 402-3
nature of **79,** 359, 368-9
pressure groups, relevance **82,** 636
redress of violation **104,** 180 n. 21
respect for **90,** 648
unenforceable and **37,** 280
unwritten **90,** 648
personality. *See* subjects *below*
policy considerations, relevance **111,** 366-8, 395, 429
South West Africa Cases **111,** 367
policy instrument **57,** 295
precedent in international tribunal and **57,** 301, **104,** 99
precedent in municipal courts and **64,** 88-90, **81,** 409, **104,** 616-17, **111,** 422
stare decisis doctrine **64,** 15-20, 89-90, 127-8, 140-6, 150-3, 169-70, 217-19, 549-50, 705-6, 714-15
primacy **36,** 24-5, 280-1, **40,** 74, **43,** 1-2, **46,** 408, 446, **64,** 519-22, **82,** 139, **86,** 43, **88,** 181, **89,** 329, 521, **93,** 210-11, **123,** 490-1
customary international law **45,** 25-6

international law **61,** 180-1, **82,** 252-3, 259, 260, 277, **93,** 209-14, **94,** 603, **120,** 600
municipal law **36,** 280-1, **43,** 1-2, **59,** 467-8, **82,** 399-400, **88,** 181
principles and rules **41,** 37, 38, 49-83, 104, 148-9, 185, 201, **60,** 39, 46-7, **71,** 580-1, 640-3, 653, 655-8, **72,** 73, 141-2, 148, 231, 235, 265, 440, 456, 469-70, 654, **73,** 177, 282-3, 687-8, **76,** 60, 62, 135, 318, 441, 549, 686. *See also* continental shelf delimitation, principles and rules applicable to; general principles of international law; *jus cogens*/peremptory norm
Continental Shelf Convention (1958) **41,** 36, 37, 38, 104
customary international law as **82,** 548
distinguished **71,** 115-17
equitable principles **67,** 30
equitable result **81,** 340
evidence of, Continental Shelf Convention **41,** 220
proportionality **81,** 276
countermeasures **72,** 250-1
private international law and **46,** 229, **81,** 681, **82,** 139, 140. *See also* private international law
private law
concepts and **37,** 32, 38, 73, 228, 401, 418-19, 436, 439, 456
methods of interpretation and **37,** 444
procedural justice **91,** 479
proof of. *See* evidence of, international law
reciprocity, principle of **44,** 53
regional, States with liberal economies **46,** 451
remedies. *See* remedies
renvoi to municipal law. *See* municipal law and, *renvoi* to *above*
retroactivity **82,** 441
rights under
enforcement procedures, relevance **97,** 57
nature of **79,** 359-61
obligation as corollary **105,** 349-50, 356
reasonableness in enjoyment of **82,** 614, 631, 658
Roman-Dutch law and **84,** 20-1, 30-1
rules of. *See also* principles and rules of *above*
absence of machinery for determining **90,** 397
federal State, system compared **90,** 397-8
basis of ICJ jurisdiction, whether **95,** 132
self-determination, right to **59,** 138-9
Socialist States and **46,** 482 n. 43
'soft law' **106,** 654-5
sources **36,** 450-60, **37,** 366-9, 450-60, **55,** 324, 335, **56,** 180, 188, 194-5, **71,** 117-18, **88,** 87 n. 13, **107,** 284-5, **113,** 418-19, **119,** 236
arbitral decisions. *See* judicial and arbitral decisions *below*
case-law. *See* judicial and arbitral decisions *below*
company practice **66,** 605-7
consent of States **53,** 4
conventions. *See* treaties, source of international law
customary international law. *See* customary international law
definition **77,** 245
development and **36,** 289-91
equity. *See* equity, sources
executive or legislative acts **88,** 48

international law (*cont.*)
general practice accepted as law. *See* State practice
general principles recognized by civilized nations. *See* general principles of law recognized by civilized nations
general rules of law **62,** 472, 542, 544, 573
hierarchy **62,** 546, **74,** 214-15, **91,** 129-30
ICJ judgments. *See* judicial and arbitral decisions, ICJ judgments *above*
ICJ Statute, Art. 38 **87,** 456, **94,** 575
Institute of International Law Resolutions **72,** 520-8, 531, 537, 547, **75,** 195, 230, 233, 252, 255, 262, 264, 266
international commission **91,** 125
judicial and arbitral decisions **37,** 487, **46,** 76, 238, 422, 489, **62,** 109, 126, 172, 175, 178, 180, 189, 192, 510, 576, 623-5, 637-9, **70,** 501, 519, **71,** 120, 129-30, 640-3, 653, 655-8, **72,** 485-6, 504-20, 525-37, 547-9, **75,** 191-4, 199-200, 211, 216, 242-4, 617-20, 631, 634, **77,** 174, 198, 269, 524, 658, **79,** 9, 10, **80,** 53, 135, 138-41, 423, **81,** 273, 346, 680, 715, **82,** 25, 214, **86,** 667, **87,** 66, **88,** 48, 741, **91,** 126-7, 131, **94,** 575, **96,** 267-8, 277, **105,** 498-9, **106,** 266, 454-7, 491-4, **115,** 610, **119,** 237
ICJ **49,** 163-4, **53,** 498, **70,** 519, **71,** 93-4, 102, 115, 120, 124, 135-7, 162, 181, 183-5, 188, 192, 201, 205-6, 208, 210, 642
international and administrative tribunals **96,** 235, 250
lack of **77,** 247
municipal courts. *See* municipal courts, as source *above*
uniformity, need for **74,** 482, 603, 641, 663
legislation **80,** 135
long-standing policy, requirements for **82,** 625-6
in municipal law **39,** 259
municipal law analogies **32,** 228, **37,** 32, 38, 73, 228, 401, 418-19, 436, 439, 456, **46,** 229, 240, 248, 495, **84,** 390, **85,** 340, **105,** 342. *See also* general principles of law
alienation of judicial power **97,** 193-4, 199
bona vacantia **49,** 231 n. 24
conformity with object and purpose of international rules **111,** 388
explicit reference, need for **111,** 388
intervention *ad excludendum* **70,** 596
joint and several liability **97,** 52-3
limitations on **110,** 696-7, 698, **111,** 387-92, 395-6, 440
methods of interpretation **37,** 444, **49,** 256
procedure **97,** 54-5, 56-7, 176-7, 184-7
reference necessarily applied **111,** 388
reparations **116,** 445-8
'ripe for consideration' **110,** 696-7
treaty interpretation **49,** 256
validity of contract and of parties' conduct distinguished **105,** 315
municipal legislation **91,** 126, 128, 131, **101,** 401, 402
natural law **37,** 458-9
NGOs **88,** 32
opinio juris. See opinio juris
reason and justice **80,** 132
special international law **71,** 127-9
conduct of parties **71,** 130-9
treaties **71,** 127-30
State papers **80,** 135

State practice. *See* State practice
'subsidiary means for the determination of the rules of law', arbitral tribunal, advisory opinion **96,** 715
teachings of publicists **40,** 75, **41,** 88, 118, **45,** 78-9, **46,** 490-1, **53,** 546, **62,** 172, 186-7, 192, **64,** 576-8, 603-8, **72,** 486-7, 523-5, 530-1, 548, **74,** 103, 635-8, 642, 652-3, 655, 662-3, 665-6, 674-5, **75,** 94, 192-4, 199-200, 211, 216, 242-4, 621-4, 631, **77,** 174, 198, 206, 256, 269, 524, **78,** 108, 674, **79,** 9, 10, 411, **80,** 53, 106, 108, 135-8, **81,** 273, 316, 330, 715, **82,** 12-13, 16-17, 25, 214, 346-7, **83,** 58, 247, **84,** 23, 289, 300-1, 303, 526, 534, 695-6, **86,** 667, **87,** 242-3, 263, **88,** 628, 653, 708-9, 741, **90,** 661 n. 14, **91,** 125, 131, 425, **92,** 102, 139-40, **94,** 617, 622, **95,** 95-7, **104,** 151, 397-8, **106,** 302-3, 454, 457-8, 491-4, **107,** 565-6, **110,** 458, **111,** 338, **115,** 610, **119,** 237-8
Aristotle **99,** 607
Grotius **99,** 607
Kelsen **103,** 22, 50-72, 73-4
limitations **104,** 320-3, **107,** 565
use in adversarial process **107,** 565
travaux préparatoires. See travaux préparatoires
treaties. *See* treaties, source of international law
UN Charter **37,** 577
UN decisions **82,** 479, **94,** 509
UN Declarations **46,** 476
UN resolutions **53,** 484-95, **62,** 189, **66,** 435-7, 588, 601-2, **75,** 609-10, 617-18, 632-3, 637, 639
UNESCO Declarations **73,** 228-9
UNHCR *Handbook on Procedures and Criteria for Determining Refugee Status* (1979) **107,** 588
usages and practices **86,** 511, 516, **104,** 151
writings of jurists. *See* teachings of publicists *above*
sovereignty and **106,** 138-9
State sovereignty as basis of **76,** 467
statutory interpretation and **36,** 280-1, **40,** 1-3
statutory limitation and **79,** 404
subjects **51,** 1-10, **53,** 457-60, **59,** 80, 181, **85,** 273, **88,** 87, **102,** 169. *See also* individual in international law
EEC **48,** 116, 117, 119
federal State **55,** 417, **68,** 25, 200-1, 237-8, **104,** 296
constituent States **52,** 331, **68,** 238, **87,** 39-41
German Reich **78,** 161-2
Holy See. *See* Holy See, status
Indian States **64,** 487-9, 527, 529-30
individuals. *See* individual in international law
international organizations. *See* international organizations
liberation movement **79,** 25-6
liquidators **71,** 268-9
minorities. *See* minorities
Namibia **49,** 58, 104
'nations' **87,** 353
Order of Santa Maria Gloriosa **77,** 622-6
organized political entity **77,** 221, 235
Ruler of Indian Princely States **64,** 529-31
separate legal entity **59,** 80
Sovereign Order of Malta **65,** 309-10, 323-4, **77,** 613-15

international law (*cont.*)
Association of the Italian Knights of **77,** 613-15
States **53,** 457-60, **77,** 221-4, 245-8, **81,** 514-15, **88,** 213, **91,** 352
acting against own nationals **104,** 144
trust territory **61,** 94, 96-9, 107-8, 125-6, 132
trustees for bondholders **71,** 268-9
United Nations **49,** 284, 330-1
substantive and non-substantive **48,** 390, 392
taxation **40,** 257
teleological approach **46,** 295, 301, **49,** 173, **74,** 579, 611, **77,** 175, 206, 218, 241-5. *See also* treaty interpretation, guidelines, teleological
transposition of municipal law to **65,** 34, 66, 76
treaties. *See* treaties
treaty interpretation and **87,** 348, 353
uncertainty **80,** 52, **83,** 134-5, 164, **91,** 130
absence of authority to determine **91,** 130
universality **41,** 139, **46,** 482-3
universality of law and **74,** 168-9, 482, **79,** 402
usages, binding force **91,** 67
validity **90,** 382
violation. *See* breach *above*
International Law Association (ILA)
Declaration of Oxford (1932) **62,** 183
Declaration of Vienna (1926) **62,** 183
Draft Articles on State Immunity (1982) **65,** 237-8, 245, **79,** 569
effects doctrine **96,** 186-7
Helsinki Rules **41,** 104
river basins **41,** 104
Resolution on State immunity (1952) **45,** 77
river basins, Helsinki Rules **41,** 104
Seoul Declaration on the Progressive Development of Principles of Public International Law relating to a New International Economic Order (1986) **83,** 474
International Law Commission (ILC) 65, 186, **67,** 104-5, 171-80, 195-204, 224, **71,** 120, 124, 140, 147
arbitration and **82,** 273
Model Arbitral Rules (1958). *See* arbitration, Model Arbitral Rules (ILC) (1958)
Committee of Experts (1953) (continental shelf) **41,** 63-5, 133, 146, 148, 149, 151, 160, 170, 204, 226, **67,** 77, 178-80, 195-204, 224, **71,** 140, 147, **81,** 392, **86,** 619-20
continental shelf delimitation **41,** 31, 62-6, 67, 91, 105, 109, 146, 148, 151, 171, 202-4, 220
special circumstances **41,** 148, 216
customary international law, role in developing **41,** 84
Draft Articles on Arbitral Procedure **62,** 148, 180-1
Draft Articles on Diplomatic Intercourse and Immunities (1978) **65,** 186-7, **78,** 6 n. 1
Draft Articles on International Liability for Injurious Consequences Arising out of Acts Not Prohibited by International Law (1994) **106,** 127, 130
Draft Articles on Jurisdictional Immunities of States and Their Property (1991). *See also* Report on the Jurisdictional Immunities of States and their Property *below*
Art. 11 (employment contracts) **104,** 518
employees appointed under public/administrative law **123,** 60, 66, 67-8, 69-70
Art. 12 (act or omission occurring in forum State if author in that territory at time) **123,** 80-1, 89-92

binding effect **113,** 420
counterclaims **115,** 241-2
customary international law **123,** 90-2
embassy or consular bank account/funds **113,** 423
immunity from execution of assets for commercial purposes **113,** 420
Draft Articles on the Law of Sea (1956), Art. 29 ('genuine link' requirement) **120,** 179
Draft Articles on the Law of Treaties **37,** 66, 67, 71, 116, **44,** 261-2, 267-8, 277, 278-9, 285-6, **70,** 442, **76,** 434, 533, 716
Report (Brierly) **37,** 67-8, 73
Report (Lauterpacht) **37,** 68
separability of declaration accepting ILC compulsory jurisdiction **123,** 382
[Draft] Articles on State Responsibility (1977/1980/1996/1998/2001) **54,** 324, **56,** 283-4, **76,** 522, 711, **82,** 159, 213, 549-50, **84,** 422-3, 424, 669 n. 2, **89,** 457-8, **91,** 360
Art. 1 (internationally wrongful act entailing responsibility of State) **110,** 654-5
Art. 3 (municipal/international law, role) **125,** 89-90
Art. 4 (acts of judicial authorities) **125,** 130
Art. 5 (acts of State organ) **110,** 708, **124,** 105 n. 129
Art. 6 **96,** 320
Art. 7 (acts of territorial government entity) **124,** 105 n. 130, 110 n. 140, 111
Art. 8 (private persons or groups acting on behalf of State) **108,** 155, **124,** 108
Art. 8(a) (private persons or groups acting on behalf of State) **82,** 193
Art. 8(b) (exercise of authority in absence of government) **82,** 193
Art. 10 **82,** 201
Art. 10 (*ultra vires* acts of State organ) **124,** 110, 110 n. 139, 111
Art. 11 (group of individuals not acting on behalf of State) **110,** 716
Art. 13 (treaty obligation) **125,** 131
Art. 14 **82,** 159, 549-50, 565
Art. 14(1) (act of continuing character/causing continuing loss) **125,** 128
Art. 15 **82,** 159, 160, 175-6, 191, 215-16, 219
Art. 17 **82,** 550
Art. 19 (environment) **110,** 81
Art. 21(1) (obligation of result) **110,** 712 n. 64
Art. 22 **124,** 16 n. 5
Art. 25 **82,** 567, **96,** 323-4, **116,** 140-1, 183
Art. 27 (aid or assistance to another State for commission of internationally wrongful act) **76,** 318-19
Art. 27(2) **97,** 50-1
Art. 31 **82,** 551, 553-4, **96,** 318
Art. 33 **82,** 551, 554, **96,** 318, **116,** 48-50
Art. 33(1) (necessity) **116,** 191
Art. 41 **116,** 63, 140
Arts. 47-50 **116,** 64
cessation **82,** 572, **96,** 320-1
collective expulsion **82,** 159
compensation for economic harm caused by wrong **121,** 128, 191
conduct of territorial government entity **119,** 634
countermeasures **116,** 228, 232-3
customary international law, whether **96,** 319, 321
distress **82,** 552, 553-4, 581
'extreme peril' **82,** 553-4, **116,** 48-55
necessity distinguished **82,** 554
exhaustion of local remedies **54,** 324, **120,** 183, 329
joint and several liability **97,** 50-1

International Law Commission (ILC) (*cont.*)
liability for suit **97,** 53-4
necessity **82,** 554-5, 569, **96,** 318, **116,** 48-50, 191-2
political subdivision **125,** 22
preclusion of wrongfulness
force majeure **82,** 551-3, **96,** 318
fortuitous event **82,** 551
revolutionary movements **82,** 160-1, 175-6
State agency **124,** 29-30, 105 nn. 129 and 130
time factor **82,** 565, **96,** 323-4
Draft Articles on State Succession to Treaties **72,** 67, 69-70, 73-4, **73,** 46, 54
Art. 15 **72,** 67, **73,** 46-7
Art. 23 **72,** 69-70, 73-4, **73,** 46, 54
Draft Code of Offences against the Peace and Security of Mankind (1949/1976/1989/1996) **76,** 638, 671, **119,** 211-12. *See also* International Criminal Court (ICC)
aiding and abetting **121,** 283, 284, 287
crimes against humanity **119,** 217
discrimination, need for **124,** 180
'other inhumane crimes' **122,** 90
'grave breaches', 'war crimes' **105,** 536
Head of State responsibility **119,** 211, 212, 218, 226
'murder' **122,** 83
'persecution' **122,** 86
State responsibility **115,** 178-9
status **121,** 283
war crimes
nexus **105,** 452, 525, **111,** 344, **119,** 148, 163, 226
relative seriousness **124,** 231-2
wilful infliction of serious mental or physical injury and great suffering **122,** 90
Draft Continental Shelf Convention **81,** 374
equidistance **99,** 505, 507-10
obligation to seek arbitration **99,** 480-1
Draft Declaration on the Rights and Duties of States, primacy of international law **93,** 209
Draft Statute for an International Criminal Court (1994)
act of a serious nature inflicted on human being **112,** 252
Art. 18 **112,** 215-16, 252
Art. 19 (widespread or systematic violations) **108,** 17
Art. 26 (attendance of witnesses) **110,** 637
Art. 26(3) (*subpoenas*) **110,** 637, 639-40
Art. 27 **108,** 17
Art. 27(1) **108,** 16
Art. 27(2) **108,** 16
Art. 33 **108,** 16-17
Art. 35 **108,** 16
Art. 46 (sentencing) **112,** 310
crimes against humanity, widespread or systematic violations **108,** 17, **112,** 214-17, **122,** 76, 78 n. 380, 79-80
Draft Statute for an International Criminal Court (1996), crimes against humanity, responsibility **112,** 221
equidistance and **41,** 170, 204, 226
Head of State immunities and **119,** 69, 72

jurisdiction, extraterritorial **96,** 185
law of the sea, codification **41,** 218-19
Model Rules on Arbitral Procedure **76,** 571, **92,** 104, 125, 132-3, 140-1
Report on the Jurisdictional Immunities of States and their Property (1991), express waiver, need for **119,** 167
Report on the Jurisdictional Immunities of States and their Property (1999), *jus cogens*/peremptory norm violation **123,** 31-2, 42
Report on Multiple Nationality (1954) **72,** 529, **75,** 256-7
role **41,** 84
codification **41,** 157
development distinguished **41,** 218-19
State immunity, codification of **45,** 76
State succession, State property, archives and debts **96,** 728
Tokyo Session (1964) **52,** 293, 297
treaties, reservations **88,** 634
International League for Human Rights 79, 194
international leases. *See also* Hong Kong
restoration of leased property
concession, effect on **42,** 8-9
Sovereign Base Area, Cyprus, Republic of **41,** 25-8
international legal order 101, 442-4
arms sales
refusal of export licence **101,** 423-4, 451-2
effect on economy of supplying country, relevance **101,** 452
reprocessing in intermediary country **101,** 451-2
'development or impairment of' **101,** 428-9, 442-4, 450-2
freedom of international trade and **101,** 420-6, 428-9
international law, whether **101,** 422-4
judicial review, role **101,** 428-9
pursuit of good relations **101,** 423-4, 428-9
strategic scientific equipment, refusal of export licence **101,** 428-9
International Maritime Consultative Organization (IMCO), Resolution A.375(X) of 14 November 1977 (Malacca Straits) **84,** 81
International Military Tribunal for the Far East (Tokyo Tribunal)
crimes against humanity **119,** 68
requirements, discrimination **124,** 1128
fair trial **105,** 475, 608-9
Head of State, immunity, jurisdiction **119,** 66, **125,** 495, 503
war crimes
definition **91,** 46
rape **121,** 266-7
responsibility of commander, obligation to prevent **122,** 105-7
superior orders **91,** 57
International Military Tribunals. *See also* belligerent occupation; crimes against humanity; International Military Tribunal for the Far East; Nuremberg Tribunal
evidence, exemption from technical rules **56,** 583-4
jurisdiction, basis, constituent instrument **91,** 46
International Monetary Fund Agreement (IMF) (1944) (Bretton Woods Agreement) 38, 140, 456-8, **44,** 473-4, 484, **47,** 46, 49-52, 58, 60, 68. *See also* Arab Monetary Fund (AMF); exchange controls; exchange rates; international monetary system; World Bank Group
act of State and **84,** 125 n. 27
approval of discretionary function **84,** 125

International Monetary Fund Agreement (IMF) (*cont.*)
Articles of Agreement **72,** 544-5, 693-708, **74,** 686-8
amendment **74,** 686-8
procedure for **74,** 687
application **52,** 12-13
Czechoslovakia, whether party to **48,** 229-30
debt rescheduling **88,** 65
devaluation **59,** 534-5, 586-8
implementing legislation (UK) **41,** 230, 232, 233, 237, **72,** 693, 696, **77,** 323, 326-9, **80,** 68, **83,** 269, **85,** 12, 20, **118,** 570
insurance contract, application to **42,** 151
interpretation
binding nature **84,** 124 n. 6
IMF's authoritative role **84,** 124-5
phrases, 'current international transactions' **84,** 122, 123-4
Member States
quotas, increases in **74,** 686-8
sovereignty, protection of **74,** 688
object and purpose **47,** 50-1, **72,** 693, 696, 698, 700-1, 704-5, 708
parity, changes in **74,** 687-8
presumption of conformity with **84,** 124, 126 n. 8
reparations and **42,** 410, 431-2
withdrawal from, effect **66,** 134-5
international monetary system. *See* Arab Monetary Fund (AMF); exchange controls; exchange rates; International Monetary Fund Agreement (IMF) (1944) (Bretton Woods Agreement); World Bank Group
international obligations. *See also* compliance; State responsibility; treaty, obligations
basis, *pacta sunt servanda* **57,** 528
binding nature **57,** 518-19
parties' intention **57,** 518-19
statement of intention **57,** 518-19
consent of States **68,** 557
continuing violation, State responsibility for **49,** 6, 44, **116,** 139-41, 215-19
creation
policy statements **49,** 253
undertakings **68,** 300-6, 339-42, 421-4, 454-6
unilateral declaration of States **57,** 412-17, 455, 518-20, 593-7
duty to comply **77,** 553
erga omnes. See erga omnes principle
European Commission on Human Rights 'indications' as **78,** 394
executive instruction, effect on **44,** 322
general and specific distinguished **57,** 582
long-term engagement, frustration **49,** 147-8
method of meeting not prescribed **77,** 207
municipal enforcement, powers of courts **74,** 311-13, 339-40, 357
not to kill, wound or kidnap **76,** 397
policy statements, binding undertakings, whether **49,** 253
proof of existence **68,** 556-7
reciprocity **77,** 441-3
termination **37,** 543-4
wording **68,** 300-6, 339-42, 378-9, 388-96, 419-24, 454-6, 497-8
international officials 38, 265-456, **39,** 469-93, **40,** 296-425, **42,** 273-347, **43,** 260-500, **47,** 348-95, **48,** 236-328. *See also* International Labour Organization Administrative

Tribunal (ILOAT); League of Arab States Administrative Tribunal; NATO officials/employees; NATO Status of Forces Agreement (1951); United Nations Administrative Tribunal (UNAT); United Nations Staff Rules and Regulations; World Bank Administrative Tribunal; World Bank Group
accident, compensation for **38,** 446-8, **39,** 470, 472-4
acquired rights **69,** 310-16, 322-3, 328, 329-30, 341, 362, 366, 373-4, 397, 410-11, 439-42, 466, 508-10, 516-17, 522, 533-5, 537-9, 541, 544-8, 552-3, 559-61, **83,** 655, **96,** 235
compensation for infringement **69,** 323, 364-5, 411, 541, 553
continuation of employment, to **42,** 326, 329-30
illegal practices as source of **69,** 452, 545-8
public purpose **69,** 329-30
transitional rule as source of **69,** 322-3, 372-4, 398-9, 410-11, 425, 453-4, 467, 527-8, 544-8
UN practice, effect of **69,** 316, 321, 325, 362-3, 374, 432-5, 441, 451-2, 466-7, 513-14, 538, 544-5
unilateral amendment **38,** 450-3
violation **48,** 252-3
administrative decision
due process **45,** 492-8
nature of **43,** 273-4, 311, 322
quashing, effect **43,** 364
administrative documents, rectification **40,** 361, 366
as aliens **102,** 196-7
allocation of work, discretionary powers **45,** 487-91
allowances. *See also* repatriation grant *below*
assignment allowance **43,** 290-302
education grant **40,** 309-11, **43,** 287-90, **69,** 533-4
installation allowance **38,** 356
appeals
audi alteram partem **69,** 356
due process **40,** 337, 338
expenses **43,** 286
internal remedies **43,** 275
procedure **43,** 451, 462
time-limits **40,** 335-44, 414-18, **43,** 269, 281, 294, 357-8, 359-60, 426-7, 448, 451, 463-6
agreement to waive **40,** 337-8, 340, 343-4
Appeals Boards, procedure **43,** 281, 283, 297, 298, 300, 336
appointment, procedure **38,** 309-11
assignment to lower grade work **43,** 277-84
ban on entry to headquarters **83,** 346
breach of contract, whether **83,** 346
certificate of service **40,** 331-4, 366, **42,** 293, 297-8
classification of **38,** 443-5
posts, discretionary powers **43,** 447-70
compensation **83,** 291
breach of contract **40,** 352-4
damage to professional reputation **54,** 410-16, 453, 466-9
delay in settling claim **38,** 319, 369, 376
ex aequo et bono **38,** 423
illegal decision, prejudice caused by **43,** 456
improper failure to renew contract **48,** 320

international officials (*cont.*)
measure
deprivation of employment **96,** 250
difficulty of obtaining other work **96,** 250
loss of pension **96,** 250
moral injury **96,** 250
moral injury **43,** 395, 399
non-renewal of contract **36,** 486, 494-5
procedural delay **40,** 384-5, **43,** 411, 421-2
rescission of decision and **96,** 250
sickness **42,** 299-303
specific performance and **96,** 250
termination of employment. *See* termination of employment, compensation or damages for *below*
competition for vacancy **40,** 418-22
complaint, reply by person responsible **43,** 362-3
conditions of employment **52,** 465-6
harmonization **42,** 343-7
unilateral amendment **38,** 427-38, 450-3, **40,** 319-20, 387-96, **42,** 331-43, **43,** 486-95, **48,** 249-53
challenge, time-limit **38,** 429-33
corpus juris **83,** 649, 650
defamatory statements **48,** 296-7
as diplomatic agents **102,** 175, **105,** 48-56
distinction **102,** 193-4, 195
equality of treatment **102,** 193-4
disability attributable to service, claim **40,** 474, 476, 478, 482, **45,** 464-77
due process **38,** 368, 370, 373-5, **40,** 375, 382, 386
disability pension **38,** 358-76, **40,** 367
ex gratia offer **40,** 372, 375, 377
disciplinary measures **40,** 323-6, 404, 405-7, **48,** 236-43
discretionary power **43,** 388
procedure **43,** 270
disciplinary proceedings
administrative review **43,** 385
defence, opportunity for **43,** 380
independent investigation **43,** 385
discretionary powers **48,** 243-9, 254-61, 279
allocation of work **45,** 487-91
assignment to lower grade work **43,** 277-84
classification of posts **43,** 447-70
disciplinary measures **43,** 388
judicial review **38,** 384-5, 400-1, 415
renewal of fixed term appointment **40,** 413, **43,** 398, 408, 431, 438, 452
suspension of recruitment **40,** 353
termination of employment **43,** 283-4, 328-30, **47,** 367-8
transfer **43,** 264-71, 275, 277
dismissal
compensation **43,** 364
conditions of **43,** 378
judicial review **43,** 363
misconduct, for **39,** 480-93, **43,** 361-93
serious misconduct, for **48,** 236-43

statement of reasons **43,** 383-93
summary **47,** 388-95, **48,** 236, 238, 242-3, 256, 260-1
grounds for **38,** 410, **40,** 330
natural justice and **48,** 239
rescission **38,** 268-76, 413
restitutio in integrum **38,** 270, 273, 274
serious misconduct, for **38,** 267-76, 389-90, 407-13
due process
administrative decision **45,** 492-8
appeals **40,** 337, 338
conversion of probationary appointment **36,** 469, 470-1
disability attributable to service, claim **38,** 368, 370, 373-5, **40,** 375, 382, 386
elements
fair and balanced scrutiny of qualifications **96,** 236
performance appraisal **96,** 236
policy discretion and **96,** 237-8
right to **96,** 235-8
termination of employment **38,** 285, 286, 289, 350, **43,** 379, 381-2, 390, **47,** 356-72
employees **77,** 574-6, 631-5
clerical **77,** 573
manual **77,** 573-4
officials, whether **38,** 420-7
trade union rights **77,** 634, **78,** 88-9
employer
classification of decisions **48,** 293-7
misuse of authority **48,** 259-60, 279
evaluation of service
periodic reports **54,** 356, 363, 366, 368-70
prejudice **54,** 370
ex post facto decisions **40,** 405-6, 407
examination for post **40,** 420-1
expatriation, additional expenses of **43,** 289
expert distinguished
Committee on the Elimination of All Forms of Discrimination against Women **85,** 321
Committee on the Elimination of Racial Discrimination **85,** 321
International Civil Service Commission **85,** 321
International Law Commission (ILC) **85,** 321
UN Advisory Committee on Administrative and Budgetary Questions **85,** 321
UN Human Rights Committee **85,** 321
expulsion **102,** 196-7
headquarters agreement, special procedure **102,** 197
international agreement, relevance **102,** 197
family, travel expenses **43,** 287
financial claims, delay, equity **43,** 290-1, 294, 297, 299-300
fixed-term appointment. *See also* permanent appointment *and* short-term contract *below*
conversion into career appointment **83,** 285, 288, 291, 380-6
conditional **96,** 235
expectancy of **83,** 285, 287, **96,** 235, 240-1. *See also* 'legal expectancy' of further UN service *below*
extension distinguished **83,** 286, 287
review **96,** 246

international officials (*cont.*)
conversion into indefinite **43,** 439-47, 448-56, **48,** 261-70
expiry **54,** 355, 365
non-renewal **36,** 486, 491-3, **43,** 393-439, **54,** 355, 365, 425-6
appeal/judicial review **43,** 398, **54,** 356
remedies **36,** 386, 494-5
obligation to reassign **54,** 366, 367, 370
probation as **83,** 290, 385, 439
renewal **38,** 273, 318, 335-43, **40,** 355-66, 412-14, **42,** 287-98
discretionary **40,** 413, **43,** 398, 408, 431, 438, 452
expectancy of **83,** 286, 287
right of **42,** 294-5, 297, **54,** 451-3
secondment as **36,** 481, 486-91
General Assembly Resolutions 53/210, 37/126, 38/232, 957 (X), 1803 (XVII) *and* 3281 (XXIX). *See* United Nations General Assembly (UNGA) Resolutions
good faith **43,** 400, 405, 410
government of, relations with, relevance **83,** 287-8, 349-51, 407, 410-13. *See also* nationality *below*
grading of posts **42,** 343-7
grants, regulations governing entitlement **69,** 312-13, 362, 373, 375-6, 397-9, 455, 533
home leave, entitlement **43,** 303-11, **69,** 536-7
host State, law of, duty to respect **102,** 175
ignorantia legis neminem excusat **48,** 284-6
illegal decision, compensations for prejudice caused **43,** 456
inquiry, persons reporting on complainant **43,** 437
investigation procedure **48,** 271-4
irregular procedures **48,** 257-8, 279
judgments of international tribunals, right to challenge **54,** 503
judicial procedure and administrative remedies **38,** 265-7
judicial protection **54,** 475, **83,** 317-18, **101,** 393-4
judicial review
grounds
arbitrariness **96,** 238, 247
failure to observe correct procedures **96,** 238
improper motivation **96,** 238
unreasonableness **96,** 238
non-renewal of contract **38,** 384-5, 400-1, 415, **43,** 398
law, sources of **38,** 330
leave
accrued, payment for **43,** 411-14, 416, 418, 420-1
home
entitlement to **43,** 303-11
special leave and **54,** 355, 360, 363-4
'legal expectancy' of further UN service **83,** 285, 287, 292, 312, 319-20, 322-3
married women, residential status **48,** 249-53
medical examination **42,** 281, 287
questionnaire **38,** 321-2, 333, **40,** 367-95
challenge to questions **40,** 358-9, 361-2, 364-6
independent medical board **40,** 368, 373, 378-80, 384
medical reports, disclosure to third party **38,** 368, 373
military service, refusal to perform, integrity and **43,** 453-6
misconduct
dismissal for. *See* dismissal *above*; summary dismissal *below*

duress **48,** 237-8, 240-1
Investigating Officer, role **43,** 372, 375, 376, 378, 381
investigation, representations of official **43,** 379-80, 381
written warning **43,** 394
money paid by mistake, recovery of **43,** 290, 293, 299
moral injury, compensation **43,** 395, 399
nationality. *See also* government of *above*
change of, implications **83,** 218, 322-3, 348-9, 352, 379, 387-90, 404-7, 408, 458-9
national of receiving State **91,** 246-8
locally engaged staff distinguished **91,** 248
oral promises, reliance on **43,** 400-5, 407, 409
outside activities **38,** 377-9
private business activities **43,** 413, 419-20
overtime **40,** 321-3
pension fund
challenge, right of **38,** 429-33
contributions, withdrawal **40,** 387
enrolment in **48,** 299-303
ICAO and **36,** 436
participation in **43,** 311-24, 460-1
validation of previous service **36,** 434-45
pensionable service, reinstatement in **40,** 388-96
pensions
children's benefit **43,** 324-7
retirement **38,** 427-31
valuation of service for **43,** 311-24
widow's **38,** 431-4
performance appraisal
exchange of views **96,** 248
future steps **96,** 236, 242-3
general practice accepted as law **96,** 236
written provision, relevance **96,** 237
personal observation, need for **96,** 244-5, 248
senior staff **96,** 248
written **96,** 236, 237, 241-9
periodic reports on **42,** 280-5, 288, 299-300, **43,** 470-8
permanent appointment
termination **36,** 445-53
duty to find alternative post **36,** 447, 448, 449, 451-2
health reasons **36,** 471-80
reasons, need for **36,** 450
remedies **36,** 433-56
permanent resident status **43,** 303-11
personal files **43,** 438
posts
abolition **48,** 275-80
classification **48,** 275-80
prejudice of superior **54,** 507
private business activities **43,** 413, 419-20
probationary appointment
conversion to fixed term **38,** 335, 338-9
due process **36,** 469, 470-1
termination **36,** 466-71, **38,** 280-90, 339-41, 386, 419, **47,** 382-8

international officials (*cont.*)
probationary period **42,** 299-302
procedural delay, compensation for **40,** 384-5, **43,** 411, 421-2
procedural irregularity
failure to correct **40,** 385-7, 404, 408
review of rescission of decision **47,** 353-4
promotion **43,** 283, 305, 439, 441-2, 446, 447, 471-2
publication of report criticizing views of **43,** 271-7
'reasonable consideration' for career appointment **83,** 285, 288, 319-21, 323, 324-5, 330, 331, 337-8, 341-4, 347-8, 352, 354-5, 365-6, 376, 377, 384, 385-6, 391, 396-8, 403, 408, 423-5, 428, 433-8, 442-3, 450-7, 458
legal question **83,** 337-8
'reasonableness' **83,** 337-8, 386, 391
recruitment, suspension of, discretion as to **40,** 353
redundancy, vacant posts and **48,** 243-9
religious convictions, right to **40,** 298-9, 300
remedy, judicial or arbitral, right to **48,** 326-7
repatriation grant **43,** 463-8
acquired right, whether **69,** 310-12, 318-19, 322-3, 326-30, 340, 362-4, 397-8, 410-11, 415, 425, 440-2, 452, 466, 508-10, 516-17, 559-61
'earned', whether **69,** 322-3, 364, 432, 452-3, 467, 503-4, 511, 514, 519, 541-4
evidence of repatriation **69,** 315-30, 339-41, 362-3, 370, 382, 409-21, 432-8, 441, 451, 453-5, 504-5, 507-8, 517, 524-7, 541, 545, 551-4
loss of entitlement **69,** 543
purpose **69,** 314-15, 324-5, 339, 362-3, 370, 431-2, 442, 465-6, 493-4, 497, 499-504, 541
relocation, dependence on **69,** 315-29, 339-40, 362-3, 370-1, 409-21, 432-5, 510-11, 514-17, 520-7, 540-5, 551-4
Secretary-General, role **69,** 316-17, 363, 370-3, 397, 431, 439-41, 454, 511, 513, 515, 538, 541-7, 553
sick official **38,** 322-3, 325, 328, 332
transitional provisions **69,** 319-23, 326-7, 339-40, 372-3, 397-9, 410, 415-19, 435-8, 453-4, 466-7, 505, 517-18, 526-8, 537, 539-51
UN practice, effect of **69,** 316, 325, 362-3, 374, 432-5, 441, 451-2, 466-7, 513-14, 538, 544-5
residence, change of, relevance **83,** 459
residence rights **54,** 251-2
residential status, married women **48,** 249-53
resignation **48,** 271-80
duress, under **38,** 377-9, **43,** 262, 264
forced **43,** 262, 264
retirement **43,** 495, 498-9
review system, procedural requirements **47,** 355
right of association **38,** 427-31
right of fair comment **38,** 410, 412
salaries
double taxation **56,** 572
equality **56,** 572
increments
annual **42,** 280-5
reinstatement **40,** 403, 405, 409-11
withhold **40,** 403-11, **45,** 481-6
scales **48,** 261-70, **54,** 362
strikes, deduction from **38,** 448-50

secondment **83,** 366-7, 380-1, 456-8
conflict with UN Charter provisions on independence of UN Secretariat **83,** 457
extension or conversion to career appointment
agreement of all parties, need for **83,** 285-6, 288, 294-5, 322, 323, 345, 381-6, 413, 414, 434, 435, 436, 439-40, 442, 449-50, 452-3
ICJ, asked to clarify **83,** 316-17
'legal impediment to' **83,** 319-21, 324-5, 330-1, 333-4, 343, 347, 352, 366
as fixed-term contract **36,** 481, 486-91
lawfulness of requirement for **83,** 414-17
security investigation **40,** 398
sexual discrimination **51,** 432-50
SHAPE, employees, exemption from taxation **91,** 243-9
short-term contract. *See also* fixed-term appointment *above*
conversion to fixed term appointment **38,** 343-58
Pension Fund and **43,** 311-24
renewal, abuse of power **38,** 276-80
sick leave **38,** 321-2, 326, 328, 329, 368, **40,** 306-8
illness due to Administration **40,** 327-8
imposed **38,** 326-8, 330-2
sickness, compensation for **42,** 299-303
'special contractual obligations' owed to **69,** 312, 314, 328-9, 454-5, 466, 528-37, 541
special leave **83,** 453
special rapporteur. *See* special rapporteur
staff association
elections to **38,** 381-3
employees, status of **40,** 422-5
Staff Regulations and Rules **69,** 313, 370-1, 398
general principles of law **43,** 451
incorporation into municipal law **69,** 312-13, 362, 397, 455, 533, 546-7, 558
jurisdiction and **72,** 711-13, **74,** 191-2, 690-3
staff representatives, rights and duties **38,** 407, 410
status **72,** 194, 199, 711-13, **73,** 684-7, **74,** 191-3, 690-3
determination **88,** 723-6
diplomatic mission member, equivalence **77,** 507, 508, 509
evidence of, inclusion of name on list **88,** 726
implicit **88,** 726
Provision of Operational and Executive Personnel (OPAS) **88,** 723-6
UN employment, whether **88,** 723-6
State practice **105,** 55-6
UNFICYP, member of as organ of UN **77,** 474
UNHCR Representative in Belgium **77,** 417-19
status ante quo, restoration of **38,** 269, 270, 272-6, 334
statutory rights **83,** 654-5
strikes, deduction from salary **38,** 269, 270, 272-6, 334
summary dismissal. *See* dismissal, summary *above*
suspension from duty **43,** 393-400
without pay **48,** 236, 238, 241-2
taxation. *See also* international officials, exemption from taxation; taxation
assessment of income for tax purposes **94,** 320
equality of States and **36,** 459
pensions and annuities **94,** 320
taxpayer in receiving State, whether **102,** 192-3
technical assistance expert
host State and

international officials (*cont.*)
demand for withdrawal by **42,** 303, 305-7, 310
jurisdiction **42,** 315
status, diplomatic staff distinguished **42,** 310, 315-16
termination of employment **39,** 469-80, **40,** 328, 330, 335-9, **42,** 299-302, 303, 307-20, 321-31, **44,** 423-5, 431
abolition of posts **42,** 321-31, **43,** 332-56, 438-9
appeals against **43,** 279-80, 283-4, 328-61
audi alteram partem **38,** 386, 404-5, 414-17, **40,** 416, 418, **42,** 303, 315, 317, 319, **43,** 367-82, **47,** 377-82
compensation or damages for **36,** 453-6, **38,** 314-16, 318, 395-7, 401, 417-20, **43,** 339, 359-61, 426, 434, 488-90, 491-4, 495-9, **85,** 635, 670
irregular **42,** 320-1
lawful **43,** 339, 359-61, 426, 434
continued employment on different terms **43,** 498
definition **36,** 454, 455, 456
disciplinary powers **43,** 264
discretionary powers **43,** 283-4, 328-30, **47,** 367-8
judicial review **38,** 384-5, 400-1, 415
discrimination, nationality **43,** 330-2
documents, non-disclosure of **38,** 403-5
due process **38,** 285, 286, 289, 350, **43,** 379, 381-2, 390, **47,** 356-72, **83,** 687
health reasons **48,** 286-92
improper motive **38,** 285, 286, 289-90
'in the interests of the Organization' **38,** 288, 397-402
notice **43,** 356-9
official's break with government and **83,** 287
permanent appointment. *See* permanent appointment *above*
probationary employment **36,** 466-71, **38,** 280-90, 339-41, 386, 419, **47,** 382-8
procedures
error of fact **39,** 476-80
privileged statements **47,** 370
reasons
failure to give **40,** 416, 418, **47,** 348-56
later change **38,** 311-20
relocation of NATO Headquarters **43,** 496-7
unsatisfactory performance **36,** 467, **96,** 237
remedies **36,** 453-6, **38,** 395-7, 401, 417. *See also* compensation *above*
secondment, effect **38,** 291-302
security of tenure **96,** 248-9
seniority, relevance **42,** 322, 325, 326-7, 328-9
unsatisfactory performance **38,** 391-5, 403-6, **39,** 474-5, **43,** 328-30, **47,** 377-82
waiver of claim **38,** 383-4
written warning **38,** 391-5
time-limits **38,** 439-43
transfer **48,** 254-61, 281
appeal against **43,** 261-2, **48,** 264-71, 274-7
decision, *audi alteram partem* **43,** 267
as disciplinary measure **43,** 267, 268, 270
from post to post **40,** 312-15
to another organization **45,** 487-91
travelling expenses **43,** 287, 463-8, **48,** 321-3, 327-8
UN, staff challenging decisions of organization, provision of counsel **47,** 360

UN Secretary-General and. *See* United Nations Secretary-General, UN officials and
undertaking to consider for continued employment **43,** 423-34
Universal Declaration of Human Rights (1948) and **43,** 375, 376, **83,** 458
Vienna Convention on Diplomatic Relations (1961), applicability **77,** 454-7, 508, **102,** 194
waiver of claim **38,** 383-4
working conditions, safety and health **43,** 278, 282
international officials, employment contract 51, 433-7, **69,** 312, 362, 397, 455, 533, 546. *See also* international officials
agreement of official's government, whether need for **83,** 286, 288
amendment **69,** 312-13, 532-3
acquiescence in **43,** 486-95
acquired rights, respect for **69,** 313-14, 320-3, 329-30, 341, 362, 373-4, 410-12, 437, 467, 510, 522, 541, 544, 547
rights, of **43,** 486-95
unilateral **38,** 427-38, 450-3, **40,** 319-20, 387-96, **42,** 331-43, **43,** 486-95, **48,** 249-53
applicable law **77,** 503, 505-6, **88,** 688, 689, 690, **91,** 245, 247, **115,** 425, **116,** 645
administrative law **94,** 335-6
general principles of law **84,** 449
host State **94,** 325-6
international administrative law **94,** 332-3
international civil service law **116,** 645
lack of uniformity if disputes submitted to municipal jurisdiction **116,** 645
breach **54,** 466-7
anticipatory **40,** 344-54
compensation **40,** 352-5
claims **73,** 684-8, **74,** 191-3, 690-3
as commercial act **63,** 343-6
contractual norms, reliance on **69,** 397
denial of justice **116,** 649
disputes relating to
arbitration clause, obligation to include **94,** 329
organization as final authority **94,** 325, 327, 329-30
remedy
absence **94,** 326
enforcement **94,** 325
settlement preferred method **94,** 325
special procedure **94,** 329-30
duty station **48,** 258
failure to observe terms **43,** 276, **83,** 376, 377
fixed-term. *See* fixed-term appointment *below*
formation **38,** 302-9, 387-9, **40,** 344-51, 396, 400-2, **43,** 400, 406, 408, 411
offer **84,** 448-9
parties' intention **84,** 449
procedures, applicant's knowledge of **84,** 450-1
immunity, jurisdiction **63,** 192-4, 338-46, **71,** 240-1, **72,** 192-5, 197-200, 711-13, **73,** 684-8, **74,** 191-3, 690-3, **86,** 656-9, 690, **113,** 439, **115,** 425
administrative tribunals as remedy **99,** 101 n. 56, **116,** 645-6
clerical employees **77,** 575
customary international law **71,** 240-1, **77,** 574
European Convention on State Immunity (and Protocol) (Basle) (1972), relevance **77,** 607-9
fonctionnaire international **94,** 336

international officials, employment contract (*cont.*)
Institute Manager **114,** 541-51
internal organization **77,** 573-7
manual workers **77,** 575-6, **87,** 7, 18, 227
multiple employment practices and **99,** 97-8, 100-1
national of receiving State **77,** 607, **114,** 547-8
oral agreement **94,** 325-6, 328, 330
permanent integration into organization's organic structure **65,** 337, **114,** 551
permanent staff **87,** 27
staff as integral part of decision-making organization **87,** 20, 27-8, 36
State immunity compared **77,** 607-9, **114,** 551
tasks of organization distinguished **86,** 690
termination **114,** 552
translation and interpreting services **94,** 326, 328, 330
implied **38,** 298, 300, **83,** 286, 288, 312
interpretation, multilingual texts **43,** 497
jurisdiction **72,** 192-5, 711-13, **77,** 503-6
host State **94,** 328
express provision for, need for **116,** 646
ILO Administrative Tribunal **94,** 333
international administrative tribunal
distance of Headquarters from place of work, relevance **116,** 647
independence of tribunal, relevance **116,** 647
sole **116,** 647
monthly **43,** 411-22
novation **43,** 495-9
oral promises relating to **48,** 261-70
personnel action forms as part of **69,** 529
proper law of **43,** 456-8
renewal **48,** 243-9, 307-20
'chain contracts', legality **116,** 654
legitimate expectancy of **48,** 311-20
rights **83,** 654-5
special obligations **69,** 312, 314, 328-9, 454-6, 466, 528-37, 541
specific performance **48,** 320
compensation in lieu of **47,** 372
supplementary terms **69,** 312, 314, 328-9, 454-5, 466, 528-37, 541
termination. *See* international officials, termination of employment
trade union activities, employment distinguished **78,** 88
unilateral nature **94,** 335-6
international officials, exemption from taxation 38, 453-6, **44,** 409-22, **56,** 522-3, 569-71, **70,** 407-12, 420-5, **71,** 574-6, **73,** 2-3, **75,** 87-8, 100-6, **83,** 648, 656-70, **94,** 320
articles for personal use **105,** 48-56
customs duties **62,** 466, 507
death duties **56,** 572-3
deductibility for tax purposes of interest paid to **102,** 193-4
first and second category officials distinguished **75,** 87-8
fiscal equality as basis **36,** 459, **94,** 320
income tax **36,** 457-65, **44,** 409-22, **56,** 522-3, 569-71
national of receiving State **91,** 243-9
privately owned car used partially for official purposes **105,** 56-7, 67
social security tax. *See* international officials, privileges and immunities, social security
surtax on housing subsidy **102,** 175-6
taxpayer in receiving State, whether **102,** 192-3

international officials, immunity, execution/attachment **77,** 503
international officials, immunity, jurisdiction. *See also* international officials, privileges and immunities
acts performed in official capacity **41,** 438-51, **113,** 507, 518 n. 3, **121,** 402-4
civil jurisdiction **70,** 414-19, **71,** 538, 563, **72,** 199-200, 664-5, **73,** 684-8
counterclaim **77,** 455-6
custody proceedings **77,** 454-7
criminal jurisdiction **71,** 538, 567-9, 571
divorce proceedings **77,** 507, 510
functional basis **77,** 509, **101,** 360, **102,** 175, 196
illegal acts **113,** 507, 521
maintenance order **42,** 273-80
motivation, relevance **113,** 507
official functions and **72,** 199, **73,** 685, **77,** 508, 509
private acts **42,** 241-3, **70,** 414-19
real/immovable property, dispute relating to **94,** 311-13
property held on behalf of sending State **94,** 312-13
senior officials **75,** 90-6
tenancy agreement, property right distinguished **101,** 360
traffic offences **75,** 90-6
waiver **40,** 296-301, 302-3, **70,** 419, **77,** 454-7, 509
change of nationality and **83,** 288, 350, 504
head of organization's agreement, need for **77,** 454, 456, 508, **94,** 310, **101,** 360
request for as evidence of immunity **94,** 310
retroactive, whether **72,** 665
international officials, privileges and immunities **52,** 391-5, **56,** 570, 575-8, **71,** 562-3. *See also* international officials, exemption from taxation; international officials, immunity, jurisdiction
Convention on Privileges and Immunities of Specialized Agencies (1947) **83,** 657
diplomatic agent, equivalence **77,** 454-7, 496-7, 508, 509, **94,** 309-10, **101,** 360, **113,** 506
local law, duty to comply with **40,** 324
service of documents **77,** 508-9
social security
obligation **102,** 184-8
return of contributions **36,** 457-65, **102,** 184-8
voluntary payments **102,** 187-8
special rapporteur. *See* special rapporteur
taxation. *See* international officials, exemption from taxation
UN officials **73,** 687
expert **71,** 562-3
insurers of, whether immunity covers **71,** 563-4
Vienna Convention on Diplomatic Relations (1961) **77,** 454-7, 508
international officials, privileges and immunities, entitlement
Deputy Registrar of ICJ **94,** 309-13
expert **71,** 562-3, **77,** 130, 139
family and dependents **71,** 568
IAEA HQ Agreement **77,** 456-7
UNIDO HQ Agreement **77,** 456-7
wife **72,** 664-5
former official **113,** 506-7
individual capacity, in **72,** 199
junior and senior officials distinguished **71,** 538, **75,** 87-8

international organizations[viii]
acts of **62,** 549
legality **62,** 484-5, 488-9

[viii] See also the following:
African Reinsurance Corporation
Air Navigation Safety Organization for Africa and Madagascar
Alexander Sanitary Bureau
American Law Institute
Arab Monetary Fund (AMF)
Arab Organization for Industrialization
East African Community
Eurocontrol (European Organization for the Safety of Air Navigation)
Eurofima
European Atomic Energy Community (Euratom)
European Coal and Steel Community (ECSC)
European Community (EC)
European Economic Area (EEA) Agreement (1991)
European Economic Community (EEC)
European Organization for Astronomical Research in the Southern Hemisphere (ESO)
European Organization for Nuclear Research (CERN)
European Parliament
European Patent Office
European Space Agency (ESA)
European Space Research Organization (ESRO)
European Union (EU)
Food and Agriculture Organization (FAO)
General Agreement on Tariffs and Trade (GATT) (1947)
International Atomic Energy Agency (IAEA)
International Catholic Migration Commission (ICMC)
International Centre for Advanced Mediterranean Agronomic Studies
International Civil Aviation Organization (ICAO)
International Institute of Refrigeration
International Labour Organization (ILO)
International Law Commission (ILC)
International Patents Institute
International Refugee Organization
International Rice Research Institute (IRRI)
International Tin Council (ITC)
Italian–Latin American Institute
NATO
Organization of African Unity (OAU)
Organization of American States (OAS)
Organization for Economic Cooperation and Development (OECD)
Organization for European Economic Cooperation (OEEC)
Organization of Petroleum Exporting Countries (OPEC)
Pan Arab Regional Health Organization
Pan-American Sanitary Organization
United Nations
United Nations Development Agency
United Nations Educational, Scientific and Cultural Organization (UNESCO)
United Nations Relief and Works Agency for Palestine Refugees in the Near East
United Nations Truce Supervision Organization (UNTSO)
World Bank Group
World Health Organization (WHO)
World Trade Organization (WTO).

advisory opinion, request for. *See* International Court of Justice (ICJ), advisory opinion, request for, standing, international organization
as agency **77,** 89-94, **80,** 46, 53, 110-21, 177-9, **81,** 715-18
Member States' liability for debts and **80,** 110-16, 176-9, 661
aims of organization
organization and administration **77,** 575
indistinguishable from functions **78,** 88-9
applicable law **77,** 52, 53, 634, **80,** 138, 611, 657, **81,** 682, 699-700, 711
administrative law **94,** 335-6
banking facilities **80,** 27
capacity to sue/be sued **107,** 423-4
customary international law **107,** 423-4
domicile **107,** 423-4
competence, constituent instrument **110,** 14
constituent instrument **80,** 101, 610, 611, 657, 658, **96,** 235, **110,** 14
international law **80,** 101, 658
contract **80,** 101
debts, liability for **80,** 102, 104, 138-41, 612-16
general principles of international law
'common law' of international organizations **96,** 235
decisions of international and administrative tribunals **96,** 235, 250
independence of municipal laws of Member States **108,** 586-7, 591
international law **80,** 101, 102, 104
law of host State **94,** 325-6
legal personality **80,** 104
municipal law of host State **94,** 325-6
personality
administrative law **94,** 335-6
international administrative law **94,** 332-3
international law **94,** 324, 327
status **80,** 611
arbitral award, enforcement **77,** 14, 162
arbitration clause, capacity to conclude **80,** 659
'assets and property', money and credits **78,** 115
banking facilities, applicable law **80,** 27
bankruptcy proceedings **77,** 21-41, 43-55
winding-up. *See* winding-up *below*
'capacities', whether corollary **80,** 153
capacity **62,** 544
limitations **62,** 473-4, 539
'capacity . . . to institute legal proceedings' **101,** 389-90
capacity to sue/be sued
applicable law **107,** 423-4
distinction, whether **101,** 389-93
executive decision to deny **107,** 426-8
privileges and immunities distinguished **79,** 595-6, **101,** 389-90, **107,** 423-4
recognition of judgment of foreign court respecting **107,** 424-6
waiver **107,** 428
character **62,** 473
classification of activities
activities in pursuit of purposes of organization **105,** 42
activity and mode of performance distinguished **107,** 612
payment, relevance **105,** 44, 47, 68

international organizations (*cont.*)
provision of meals and living accommodation
for staff **105,** 44, 68
for visiting scientists **105,** 43
provision of working accommodation for visiting scientists **105,** 42, 43, 68
rent of accommodation for director-general **105,** 46-7, 68-9
research **105,** 42
restrictive interpretation **105,** 44
commercial activities, supervision of personnel, whether **72,** 199
common law of **62,** 466, 474, 478, 492, 510, 515-22, 544, 546-8, 552, 558-9, 569-70, 572, 579. *See also* customary practice of *below*
competence. *See also* functions *below*
applicable law, constituent instrument **110,** 14
compétence de la compétence **110,** 22-3
ICJ power to review **110,** 22-3, 29, 157-8
implied **110,** 19, 137-8, 624-6
essential for functions **105,** 568-9, **110,** 137
overlapping. *See* speciality *below*
speciality **110,** 18-19, 26, 46, 88-90, 132-7
'within scope of its activities' **110,** 14
interpretation of constitution **110,** 22, 27-8
constituent instrument. *See* constitution (international organization)
contract
applicable law **80,** 27, 71
arbitration clause, requirement **77,** 14, **81,** 683-4
forum selection clause **77,** 14
repudiation **81,** 683
applicable law **77,** 44, 51
corporation distinguished **77,** 28, **78,** 88
creation, *acta jure imperii* **81,** 722
customary international law **71,** 240-1, **78,** 88
customary practice of **60,** 508. *See also* common law of *above*
customs duties **62,** 507
debts, liability for **77,** 1-168, **80,** 52-3, 138-42, 152, 158, 159, 171, 612-16
applicable law **80,** 613
concurrent **81,** 699, 708-10
constituent instrument and **80,** 141, 165, 170, 172
exclusion **80,** 144-6, 173-6
general rule of international law **80,** 52-3, **81,** 679-80, 699
indemnification of organization **80,** 170, **81,** 682, 714-15
intention of founding States **80,** 141, 165, 170
international law and municipal law, under, whether to be distinguished **80,** 52, 53
Member States. *See* Member States, liability for debts *below*
policy decision **81,** 682, 684
secondary liability **80,** 159-60
decisions of
appeal from **48,** 409
revocation of mistaken **43,** 463, 467
definition **80,** 33-4, 65-6, **102,** 157-8
development **80,** 65-8
Rhine Commission (1815) **80,** 66

diplomatic missions compared **87,** 5, 23
diplomatic protection by **40,** 297-8, 301
disclosure of documents **43,** 260-4, 269, **77,** 166
discretionary power
  abuse of, Member State, pressure by **43,** 448-53
  self-imposed policy limitation **43,** 287-90
dispute settlement **81,** 683
estoppel, staff circular **36,** 438, 442, 443
expulsion provisions, League of Nations Covenant **49,** 50
foreign legal body distinguished **83,** 222, 255-6, 263, 270-1
functioning **62,** 542-4, 551
functions
  defined by treaties establishing **62,** 487, 495, **77,** 577
  executive and judicial distinguished **49,** 289
  modification, practice **49,** 272
grading of posts, harmonization between organizations **42,** 343-7
Headquarters Agreements. *See* headquarters agreements
host State
  contractual, whether. *See* host agreements, contractual, whether
  legal status **62,** 510, 540-1, 543-5, 553, 569
  obligations **62,** 477-81, 513, 539, 546
    accordance of 'full facilities' for performance of Member State functions **99,** 142
    financial advantage, avoidance **105,** 22, 47
    respect for status of organization **105,** 30-1
  relationship with **62,** 473, 477-9, 490-2, 495, 509-11, 513, 537-42, 553-5, 571-3, 577-9
  special regime **62,** 476, 542, 559
  technical assistance expert
    abolition of post **43,** 332-9
    demand for withdrawal by **42,** 303, 305-7, 310
    jurisdiction **42,** 315
immunity, jurisdiction, permanent staff **77,** 606-7
internal regulations **62,** 553
  interpretation **54,** 502
interpretation, applicable law, Vienna Convention on the Law of Treaties (1969) **110,** 142-3
judicial review, Member State courts **111,** 501-2
legal personality. *See* personality *below*
liability for acts of organization or its agents **121,** 433
  settlement process **121,** 433
Member States. *See also under individual organizations*
  arbitral clause, whether bound by **80,** 610, 612-16, 657, 659-60
    equity and **80,** 661
  as **80,** 152-3
  collective will **62,** 495
  common interest **62,** 549
  determined by instruments of accession **77,** 31, 96
  indemnification, obligation **80,** 170-1
  individual will **62,** 495
  liability for debts **80,** 46, 47, 52, 56, 90-121, 138-42, 171, 224, 612-16, 661, **81,** 676-725

international organizations (*cont.*)
evidence of **80,** 140
exclusion or limitation of **80,** 56, 67-8, 141, 143, 145
express warning **80,** 67
general rule of international law **80,** 52-3, 132
good faith **80,** 140
international and municipal law, under, whether to be distinguished **80,** 52, 53
municipal institutions, practice **80,** 141
obligations **62,** 31, 74-7, 477-81, 513, 539, 546, **68,** 209-11, 222, 239, **77,** 22, 31, 44
breach, determination, responsibility for **110,** 36-8
relationship with **62,** 463, 485-6, 495, 511, 579-80, **77,** 36
rights **62,** 488, 490
voting **62,** 488
status within **62,** 495
voting rights **62,** 488
membership, EC/EC Member States. *See* European Community (EC), international organizations, membership of
missions to, Switzerland **75,** 77
municipal law
comity and **80,** 93
subjection to **85,** 25-6
'nationalization' **80,** 611-12, 636
nature **62,** 542, **77,** 36, **80,** 66
objectives **62,** 488
obligations **62,** 54, 477-81, 513, 539
functioning, to ensure **62,** 489
officials. *See* international officials
organization, municipal court competence in respect of **77,** 634, **78,** 89
organs **62,** 485
judicial control by **62,** 496
judicial control of **54,** 396, **62,** 484-5
political nature of **54,** 396
subsidiary
establishment **54,** 352-3
powers **54,** 446-8
participation in **62,** 84
personality **37,** 116, 263, 293, 522, 523, **63,** 340, **77,** 16, 74-7, **80,** 90-7, 160-1, 616, **86,** 686-9, **87,** 6, **115,** 426. *See also* capacity to sue/be sued *above*; status *below*
applicable law **87,** 3
administrative law **94,** 335-6
international administrative law **94,** 332-3
international law **94,** 324, 327
autonomy **80,** 658
capacities of juridical person **83,** 261
constituent instrument as determining factor **77,** 623, **82,** 112
European Communities, European Economic Interest Groupings **77,** 76
evidence of **83,** 263
headquarters agreement, host State's obligations under **80,** 161
international legal personality, acceptance of permanent delegation as recognition of **116,** 648-9
Member State legislation, territorial, whether **83,** 252, 263

members, continuing liabilities **77,** 74-7
multiple **83,** 251-2, 262, 263, **85,** 7, 28
multiplicity **108,** 581
municipal law and **77,** 77, **81,** 708, 709, 711-12
incorporation **81,** 706-7
non-governmental organization **77,** 624
objectives, relevance **80,** 95
Order of Santa Maria Gloriosa **77,** 622-7
Reparation for Injuries Suffered in Service of United Nations case **80,** 132, 161-2, 170
requirements **77,** 623-4
sovereign, whether **77,** 17
State administration, analogous to **77,** 634
State compared **62,** 487, 539, **102,** 211-12
subject of international law, whether **62,** 495, 539, 552
Switzerland, in **83,** 258
test
behaviour of Member States **87,** 26
binding effect of decisions of Members **96,** 228
constitution **87,** 25, 26
existence of administrative tribunal **87,** 24
independence of Member States **87,** 23, **96,** 228
international personality **87,** 24
private law rules, relevance **96,** 228
ratification of HQ Agreement, relevance **87,** 26
sovereign powers **87,** 6, 23
territory **87,** 23
treaty-making power **80,** 95
piercing the corporate veil **80,** 138, 172, 616
political organ, judicial review of judgments **54,** 396
powers. *See* competence *above*
privileges and immunities. *See* international organizations, privileges and immunities
proper law of **77,** 35, 52-3
international law **77,** 634
property. *See* international organizations, privileges and immunities
proposal to, rejection of, implication **49,** 26
'public authority', whether **118,** 127
publication of report criticizing official's views **43,** 271-7
'quasi-governmental' organizations compared **75,** 105
'receiving State', jurisdiction **77,** 631-5
recognition **85,** 5, 8-9, 12, 20-3
conferral of corporate status distinguished **85,** 5, 10
customary international law **83,** 248
enforcement of rights and obligations, objective **83,** 255
grant of privileges and immunities distinguished **83,** 249
justiciability of treaties and **82,** 249, **83,** 249, 263
matter of constitutional law **77,** 28
membership **94,** 622
need for, whether **83,** 247, 249-50, **107,** 422
obligation, whether **83,** 247, 248, 249-50
recognition of governments and **62,** 38, 42, 69, 72, 84
regional office. *See* host agreements; World Health Organization Regional Office in Egypt, host agreement

international organizations (*cont.*)
representatives accredited to. *See* diplomatic privileges and immunities, entitlement, international organizations, representatives accredited to
resignation or expulsion, effects **37,** 53-4
resolutions
customary law and **37,** 453, 553. *See also* United Nations General Assembly (UNGA) Resolutions
interpretation
practice **110,** 145-6
Vienna Convention on the Law of Treaties (1969) **110,** 142-3
minority State's right to challenge **110,** 51-2
municipal law, part of, whether **91,** 409
validity
form and substance distinguished **110,** 22-3, 29
Secretariat's views, relevance **110,** 35
rights and duties
determined by constituent instrument **80,** 161, 170
purposes and functions, dependence on **80,** 170
seat. *See also* ICSID (International Centre for the Settlement of Investment Disputes), arbitral tribunal, seat; World Health Organization Regional Office in Egypt, seat, transfer
privileges and immunities, relevance **87,** 25
territorial, absence **102,** 212
secretariat
merger of branches of **43,** 272
role **62,** 489
Secretary-General, discretionary powers, staff appointments **42,** 313-14, 316, 328
service of process on **63,** 61-2, 288
out of the jurisdiction **77,** 98, **80,** 26-30, 59
special rapporteur. *See* special rapporteur
specialized agencies. *See* specialized agency
staff. *See* international officials
status **62,** 473, 495, 539, **72,** 161-2, 193-4, 197, 199, **73,** 686-7, **74,** 191-3, 690-3, **75,** 105-6, **77,** 74-5, 624, **78,** 88-90, **80,** 61, **85,** 8-9, 12, 20-3, 24-6, 28-9. *See also* personality *above*
applicable law. *See also* basis *below*
domicile **108,** 582-5, 586
international law **108,** 586-94
basis. *See also* applicable law *above*
constituent agreement **105,** 21, 67
headquarters agreement **102,** 211, **105,** 67
international agreement **102,** 211-12
international law **81,** 707
legislation conferring juridical personality **83,** 252, 266
recognition by executive **83,** 247, 250, 268-9
recognition by foreign country **83,** 247, 249-50, 256, 263, 266, 271-2
evidence of, request to Ministry of Foreign Affairs **102,** 185
foreign legal body distinguished **83,** 222, 255-6, 263, 270-1
independent entity **81,** 698-9, 702, 703-8, 712, **96,** 227-8
international law
as basis **80,** 65-6
on plane of **80,** 70
municipal courts, role **77,** 35, **83,** 24, 251

sui generis **83,** 261
UK not party to constituent instrument **83,** 250, 258, 265
'visitor from . . . outer space' **83,** 261
Steering Committee on Tax Problems of International Organizations Respecting Methods of Tax Reimbursement **83,** 659, 667
succession **43,** 459, **49,** 214, 217, 232 n. 25
League of Nations and UN **37,** 39, 202, 207, 208, 213-14, 227, 233, 310-15, 441, 544
principle of **37,** 202, 208, 313, 316, 441
tenancy agreement
arbitration clause, validity **101,** 361-3
rent increase, enforceability **101,** 362
territorial seat, absence **102,** 212
transfer of sovereign rights to **93,** 395-6, 399, 426-9, 444
encroachment on national Constitution **93,** 390-1, 401, 427-8
subsequent developments in law of international organization, effect **93,** 445
turnover tax and **93,** 445-7
treaty creation **63,** 162-3, **77,** 28
UK not a member and no permanent establishment, status **83,** 266, 268-9
UK not a member and no UK establishment, members' rights and obligations **83,** 269
ultra vires acts **62,** 487
voluntary submission of question to, implications **49,** 252-3
voting system
essential characteristic **49,** 276
Member States' rights **62,** 488
winding-up
effect
breach of treaty **77,** 30-2
extraterritorial **77,** 30
termination of organization **77,** 32
jurisdiction of Member States **77,** 21-41
receiver, appointment of **77,** 45-56
international organizations, archives **77,** 13, 30-1, 113-68, **80,** 214, 222-3
definition **77,** 116-20, 128-9, 137-9
copy of document **77,** 129
information **77,** 124, 134-5
'official' **77,** 116-17, 131-5, 144
premises as **77,** 13, 30-1, 116
third party, held by **77,** 129-30, 138, 151-6
trading documents of international organization **77,** 129, 138
inviolability **77,** 113-68
authorized disclosure **77,** 156
breach by Member State **77,** 132
confidentiality distinguished **77,** 142
documents of representative or expert **77,** 123
erroneous disclosure **77,** 156
meaning **77,** 131-2
Member States' own documents **77,** 153
published documents **77,** 127, 133
purpose **77,** 142, 154
universal obligation **77,** 132, 154
Vienna Convention on Diplomatic Relations (1961) **77,** 131, 140

international organizations, archives (*cont.*)
waiver **105,** 62
winding-up as breach **77,** 30
international organizations, exemption from taxation 75, 102-3
applicable law, host State **105,** 45, 48
customs duties, official activities **105,** 47-8
direct **105,** 41
indirect **105,** 41
official purchase of goods or services **105,** 42, 44, 47
official sale of goods or services **105,** 42, 44-5, 46
unofficial purchase of goods or services **105,** 41, 44, 47
unofficial sale of goods or services **105,** 42, 45
use of goods and services for official purposes **105,** 42, 45-6
use of goods and services for unofficial purposes **105,** 41, 46
international organization **38,** 453-6, **71,** 574-6, **75,** 99-106
living accommodation **105,** 43-4
procedure **105,** 61-2, 69-70
residence of director-general **105,** 46-7
service charges **105,** 41
international organizations, immunity, *ratione materiae* **80,** 123-4
international organizations, immunity, execution/attachment 63, 341-2
execution measures as necessary preliminary **113,** 477
exequatur as preliminary step **115,** 429
headquarters and assets, distinguishability **101,** 389-93
'jurisdiction', whether **78,** 114-15
UN Compensation Fund **109,** 581
waiver, seizure and detention of aircraft in settlement of bill **107,** 338-9
waiver, need for **115,** 428, 429
international organizations, immunity, execution/post-judgment attachment 78, 113-16
nature of assets as test **115,** 428-9
staff salaries **113,** 490
international organizations, immunity, jurisdiction 63, 92-5, 162-3, 286-98, 340-1, **71,** 240-1, **78,** 114, **107,** 179-82. *See also* international officials, employment contract, immunity, jurisdiction; international organizations, exemption from taxation; NATO Status of Forces Agreement (1951), State immunity, jurisdiction, entitlement; United Nations, immunity, jurisdiction
absolute immunity
Convention on Privileges and Immunities of the United Nations (1946) **113,** 501, 520
erga omnes nature **116,** 648
undertaking to establish administrative tribunal as corollary **116,** 648
absolute theory **63,** 162-3, **102,** 211-12, **113,** 505, **116,** 647-8
alternative remedies, relevance **118,** 136
capacity to sue and be sued distinguished **79,** 595-6, **101,** 389-90, **107,** 423-4
classification of act
act in pursuit of aims of institution **87,** 8-9
act within scope of tasks **94,** 329
construction work on headquarters building **47,** 345-95
employment contract **63,** 344, **77,** 573, 575-7
oil, price-fixing by OPEC **63,** 288-94
declaration of public utility, effect **82,** 87-8
European Convention on Human Rights (1950) and **118,** 132-7
execution distinguished **78,** 114-15, **113,** 439, **115,** 428

functional theory **87,** 8
human rights offences, official acts and **107,** 609-13
labour law of host State **102,** 151-62
liability for compensation for damage distinguished **121,** 433
nature of transaction **87,** 6-7
arbitration and non-waiver clause, effect **87,** 9-10
presumption in favour of **77,** 37
restrictive theory **63,** 93-5, **77,** 577, 607-9, **87,** 7-8
State immunity compared **63,** 92-5, 163, 194, 339, **77,** 609, **78,** 88, 89, 115-16, **86,** 687, **94,** 325, **113,** 437, 501
customary international law **107,** 319 n. 3, 324 n. 10
waiver **42,** 139-42, **63,** 93, 95, 162-3, **77,** 114, 120-1, **81,** 707, **86,** 661-7, 668, 673, 676-90, **89,** 91-2, **94,** 333, 338, **115,** 425
avoidance of defences which might imply **77,** 114
by board of directors **86,** 690
by executive body or executive chairman **77,** 130
by representative of Member State **77,** 130
contractual claims **77,** 14
Convention on the Privileges and Immunities of the UN (1946) **77,** 11
customary international law
burden of proof **86,** 666
counterclaim **86,** 666
estoppel compared **86,** 681
express **86,** 673, 679, **89,** 91-2, **99,** 95, 96
Head of State agreement **86,** 668
headquarters agreement, signature as **86,** 659, 661
implied. *See* waiver, implied *below*
limitation to suit **77,** 6
presumption against **107,** 181
statutory **63,** 162-3, 340
submission to the jurisdiction as **86,** 668
conditional appearance **86,** 661, 666, 683, 685, 687, **107,** 323 n. 9
disclaimer **107,** 184-5
successor organization and **118,** 126
timeliness **86,** 677-8, 687-8
to secure tax exemption **105,** 62
treaty provision **63,** 162
waiver, implied
arbitration clause **80,** 33, 36, **102,** 212-13, 214-15
Articles of Agreement **99,** 96-103
bank facility letter **77,** 3-7, 10-12, 17-18
choice of forum clause **114,** 545-6
choice of law clause **114,** 543, 545-6
contract for dining facilities **99,** 102 n. 67
institution of proceedings for payment **113,** 477
knowledge and intent, need for **107,** 182
tenancy agreement **101,** 362-3
treaty undertaking not to permit racial discrimination **113,** 501
international organizations, inviolability of premises 62, 554, **101,** 228
waiver **77,** 120-1
international organizations, privileges and immunities 42, 138-43, **52,** 466, **77,** 113-68, **80,** 29-30, 33-6, **87,** 3-10. *See also* consular privileges and immunities; diplomatic privileges and immunities; International Tin Council, privileges and immunities; State immunity; *and under individual organizations*

international organizations (*cont.*)
act of State and **80,** 34
commercial transactions, applicability to **80,** 34
alternative remedy, need for **102,** 160-1, **114,** 553-4. *See also* international administrative tribunals, duty to create
ad hoc arbitration **102,** 212-13
applicable law **87,** 6
customary international law **114,** 547-8
European Convention on State Immunity (and Protocol) (Basle) (1972) **114,** 547-8
headquarters agreement **105,** 21-2
international law **105,** 22
law relating to States **114,** 544
NATO Status of Forces Agreement (1951) **114,** 548
treaty reservation **114,** 550-1, 553
basis **89,** 91
avoidance of partiality and interference **102,** 160
basis and functions **116,** 647
constituent agreement **107,** 185
non-Member State, in **113,** 476
customary international law **113,** 477
headquarters agreement **107,** 185
UNESCO **113,** 490
international agreement **102,** 212, **105,** 42, **113,** 477, **118,** 126
international personality **87,** 26
par in parem non habet jurisdictionem **87,** 7, 23, 26
status agreement, WEU **113,** 488-9
treaty **77,** 577
implementing legislation **77,** 17, 605
classification of act
construction contract **63,** 93-5
interpretation **77,** 608-9
organization and administration **71,** 241, **77,** 575-6, **81,** 707, **87,** 6-10
purpose **87,** 6
tenancy agreement **87,** 7, 9, 18
commercial activities **72,** 193-5, 199, **77,** 37, **80,** 30
common law **86,** 672
constitutive Agreement, absence of provision **94,** 337
criteria
aims of organization, acts in pursuit of **87,** 8-9
intention of parties **94,** 333
organizational and administrative act **87,** 4
customary international law **94,** 329, 338, **105,** 21, **107,** 423-4, **114,** 551, **116,** 647
date of commencement **107,** 2
diplomatic privileges and immunities as benchmark **87,** 5
disclosure of foreign assets **77,** 166, 168
East African Currency Board **43,** 154-61
effective remedy, denial, European Convention on Human Rights (1950), primacy **113,** 489
employment practices **113,** 501-2, 504-8
establishment *jure imperii* or *jure gestionis* **80,** 137
European Commission of Human Rights, members of **41,** 445
expert
diplomatic agent, 'like to' **77,** 130

to extent necessary to carry out functions **77,** 130, 139
functional **77,** 130, 139, 577, **87,** 7, **94,** 324, 333, 338, **99,** 97-101, **101,** 360, **102,** 160, **113,** 439
commercial activities, relevance **114,** 549
employment practices **107,** 612, **113,** 501-2, 504-8
General Assembly, entitlement **113,** 501
governing body members, scope **75,** 76-8
headquarters agreement and **86,** 659-60, **101,** 388, **105,** 21-2, **107,** 185, **113,** 439
conferral of privileges and immunities on officials, relevance to Organization **113,** 439
host State
consent, need for **94,** 329
obligations
to inform relevant national authorities of entitlement **105,** 22-31, 67-8
to provide single organization to oversee **105,** 26-31, 68
outside **80,** 29
inherent right, whether **87,** 23, 24-5
limitation by statute **63,** 162-3
Member States' Constitutions as limiting factor **87,** 5, 35
nature of transaction, tenancy agreement **87,** 7, 9
peacekeeping operations, operation of logistics and supply base **113,** 519-20
political question **102,** 157
Privileges and Immunities of the Specialized Agencies, Convention on (1947). *See Consolidated Table of Treaties*
property **63,** 93
purpose, protection from interference by individual governments **118,** 134-5
racial discrimination **113,** 500-3
ratione personae **80,** 123-4
recovery of documents **77,** 131, 156
seat of organization, relevance **87,** 25
sovereignty, transfer of and **94,** 337-8
special rapporteur. *See* special rapporteur
specialized agency **77,** 577
State practice **105,** 42, 55-6
'suit and legal process' **77,** 3, 4, 167
things done in course of official duties **77,** 168
trade union rights **78,** 88-90
translation and interpreting services, essential role, need for **94,** 329-30
UK not a member and no permanent establishment **83,** 269
UN Compensation Commission **109,** 556-7
UN Compensation Fund **109,** 555, 580-1
immunity from suit **109,** 581
UN Compensation Fund Escrow Account, immunity from suit **109,** 581
international organizations, privileges and immunities, entitlement
FSIA **63,** 94-5, 163
Members **77,** 98
presence in US for UN meeting **107,** 460
representative of Member State **77,** 129, 130, 495-7, **81,** 707
visitor to organization **104,** 159-61
international organizations, State immunity, jurisdiction, international personality, relevance **78,** 114
International Patents Institute, employees, jurisdictional immunity **70,** 419
international public order/public policy/*ordre public* **50,** 104
apartheid and **91,** 369

international public order/public policy/*ordre public* (*cont.*)
applicable law and **91,** 241
arms dealing and **91,** 253-5
contract contrary to, enforceability **106,** 705-6
expropriation/nationalization
compensation, measure of **82,** 137
recognition of and **82,** 132, 136-7
extradition **106,** 263-8
fundamental norm of international law **106,** 264-8
jus cogens/peremptory norm and **91,** 254
'to ensure respect for the general principles of law recognized by civilized nations' **91,** 254
treaty, interpretation by arbitrator and **82,** 66-7, 74
international public policy/*ordre public international* 47, 159-62, 228-30, **74,** 703-4, **78,** 135, **80,** 426-7
absence of protest **67,** 64
arms trade **47,** 27-8
compulsory jurisdiction, acceptance, reservations **123,** 284
International Refugee Organization 79, 621-2
certificate, validity of **61,** 496
international relations. *See also* foreign relations
effectiveness, principle of **83,** 26
fundamentals of **62,** 192
imputation of bad faith to friendly government **52,** 366
International Rice Research Institute (IRRI), privileges and immunities **102,** 153-62
International Sanitary Bureau 43, 459
International Sanitary Regulations, direct applicability **48,** 231-2
International Telecommunications Union (ITU), Convention (1965), South West Africa, application to **49,** 305. *See also* telecommunications
International Telegraph and Telephone Consultative Committee, Fourth Plenary Assembly (Mar del Plata) (1968), Opinion E.231 77, 422
International Tin Agreements. *See* International Tin Council (ITC); *and the Consolidated Table of Treaties*
International Tin Council (ITC) 77, 1-168, **85,** 9-10, 24-5. *See also* United Kingdom, law of, International Organizations Act 1968 *and* International Tin Council (Immunities and Privileges) Order 1972; *and* International Tin Agreements *and* ITC–UK Headquarters Agreement *in the Consolidated Table of Treaties*
activities, *jure imperii*, whether **80,** 145
applicable law 77, 54, 634
law of place of Headquarters 77, 52
none 77, 53
arbitral award, enforcement **80,** 34, 96, 120
arbitration clauses, failure to include as breach of Headquarters Agreement **80,** 121
archives and premises 77, 13, 30-1, 113-59
'information' 77, 124
inviolability 77, 113-68
documents of representative or expert 77, 123
waiver 77, 120-1, 130, 134, 157-8
winding-up as breach 77, 30
capacity to
be sued 77, 164
contract 77, 13, 89, **81,** 678, 703
hold property 77, 50, **81,** 703

institute legal proceedings **81,** 703
sue **80,** 195
members **77,** 50
confidentiality of proceedings
action against single Member State, relevance **96,** 353-4
ITC Rules as basis of obligation **96,** 350
Constitution **77,** 68-73
Headquarters Agreement (1972) **77,** 70-1
International Organizations Act 1968 (UK) **77,** 71-2
International Tin Agreement (6) (1982) **77,** 68-70
International Tin Council (Immunities and Privileges) Order 1972 (UK) **77,** 72
interpretation, Member States' courts powers **77,** 53
contract, applicable law **77,** 44, 51
debts
agency theory **80,** 110-16, 176-9
applicable law **80,** 101-2, 104
concurrent **80,** 97-9, 148
contract under municipal law, in respect of **80,** 146
direct **80,** 143
exclusion or limitation of **80,** 56
general rule of international law, as **80,** 52-3, 105, 106
international and municipal law, under, whether to be distinguished **80,** 52, 53
Member States' liability **80,** 46-7, 52, 53, 90-121, 131-2, 135-52, 161-80, **81,** 676-725
agency theory **81,** 700, 715-19
applicable law **81,** 699-700
concurrent **81,** 699, 709-10, 714-15
general rule of international law **81,** 679-80, 699
functions, economic and commercial **77,** 114, 137
Headquarters Agreement. *See also the Consolidated Table of Treaties*
arbitration clauses, requirement for **80,** 121
breach **80,** 121, **81,** 703-5
interpretation **80,** 143-4
privileges and immunities **81,** 694
history **80,** 68-74, **81,** 684-93, **96,** 205-10
immunity, jurisdiction, waiver **77,** 114, 120-1, **81,** 707
arbitration clause as **80,** 33, 36
International Tin Agreements. *See also Consolidated Table of Treaties*
justiciability in UK courts **77,** 54
judgment against, to be met from own funds **77,** 50
Member States
debts, liability **81,** 676-725, **96,** 228
definition **81,** 687
independence **77,** 50
obligations **77,** 22, 31, 44
relationship **77,** 129-30
determination by Member States' courts **77,** 53, 54
determination by treaty **77,** 52, 54
partnership **77,** 52
right of indemnity from **77,** 51
determined by ITA **77,** 53
unacceptable conduct **80,** 47
objectives **77,** 12, 22

International Tin Council (ITC) (*cont.*)
personality **77,** 68-94, 98, 113-14, 125, 137, 148-9, 152, 164-5. *See also* capacity to *above*; status *below*
separate from members **77,** 44-5, 50, 98, 152
privileges and immunities **77,** 1-168
arbitral award, enforcement **77,** 14, 162
basis, Headquarters Agreement **81,** 694
burden of proof **77,** 119-20
commercial activities **77,** 37
documents **77,** 113
immunity, execution/attachment. *See* arbitral award, enforcement *above*
immunity from suit **80,** 29-30, 33-6, 96, 120, 187-90
'jurisdiction and execution' **77,** 6, 37
Mareva injunction **77,** 1-8, 165-6
officials **80,** 214-15, 222
'suit and legal process' **77,** 3, 4, 167
proper law of. *See* applicable law *above*
remedy for breach **80,** 121
Rules
Economic and Price Review Panel
composition **77,** 126
confidentiality of documents **77,** 126
Rule 12 **77,** 126
Rule 16 **77,** 126
Rule 19 **77,** 126
Rules of Procedure
binding on third parties, whether **96,** 350
continued application **96,** 348
direct effect **96,** 348
publication, effect **96,** 350
service of process on **80,** 26-9
status **81,** 696. *See also* capacity to *and* personality *above*
agency **77,** 89-94, 99, **80,** 46, 53, 110-21, 177-9, **81,** 700, 715-19
contract excluding possibility **77,** 93
basis
Headquarters Agreement **81,** 703
international law **80,** 52, 57
treaty establishing **80,** 52, **81,** 705
body corporate **77,** 3, 25, **80,** 41-5, 131, **81,** 677-8, 681, 703
capacity and **80,** 92, **81,** 705
collective trading name **81,** 698-9, 703-8
diplomatic mission distinguished **77,** 118
independent legal entity **80,** 51, **96,** 227-8
binding effect on Members of Council's decisions **96,** 228
Chairman as organ of ITC **96,** 227
independence of Council **96,** 228
international law **80,** 92, 131
international organization under International Organizations Act 1968 (UK) **77,** 3
'mixed entity' **80,** 52, 97-9, 103
municipal law, under **81,** 678, 705, 708, 712
organization **77,** 52
reasons for choice of **80,** 44, 93
waiver, implied, bank facility letter **77,** 3-7, 10-12, 17-18

winding-up. *See* international organizations, winding-up
international tort/wrong 62, 162, 168, 182, 196-7, 202-3, 217. *See also* international crimes
abuse of rights **46,** 498
Alien Torts Statute (US), under **77,** 207-8
child custody, breach of rules not **77,** 182
counterfeiting of foreign securities **77,** 218
detention, prolonged and arbitrary **77,** 210
disappearances **95,** 634-5
genocide. *See* genocide
human rights violations **77,** 210
illegal seizure of alien **77,** 182
inhuman and degrading treatment **95,** 635
international criminal law
development **74,** 168-9
treaties **74,** 164, 168-9
jurisdiction, claim arising under municipal law, need for **99,** 65-7, **104,** 127-9, 178-84
murder by State authorities **95,** 634
murder or disappearance of individuals **77,** 210
official act **95,** 633
passport abuse **77,** 216, 222
piracy. *See* piracy
private act **95,** 633
racial discrimination. *See* racial discrimination
requirements for, State involvement **77,** 210, 220
seaworthiness doctrine, breach **77,** 182
slavery or slave trade **77,** 210, 220
specific facts, need for **95,** 633
State responsibility **89,** 535, **104,** 158
summary execution **77,** 220
systematic racial discrimination **77,** 210
torture if committed by State official **77,** 174, 217, 220, 224
torture of wounded non-combatant civilian **99,** 78-9
international trade agreements. *See also* European Union (EU); General Agreement on Tariffs and Trade (GATT) (1947); NAFTA (North American Free Trade Agreement) (1992); Uruguay Round; World Trade Organization (WTO)
purpose, regime differing from multilateral regime **110,** 596
revision, difficulty **121,** 135
scope **121,** 141-3
withdrawal, difficulty **121,** 134-5
International Tribunal for the Law of the Sea (ITLOS)
burden of proof **120,** 220-1, 311
soundness of allegation **110,** 780
costs **117,** 125, **120,** 202-3, 208-9, 237
as court of law **117,** 185
equality of parties, Tribunal's verification of nationality **120,** 342
evidence
burden of proof. *See* burden of proof *above*
evaluation, transparency, need for **120,** 220
standard of proof
balance of probabilities **120,** 255
'beyond reasonable doubt' **120,** 222
prima facie case **120,** 311

International Tribunal for the Law of the Sea (ITLOS) (*cont.*)
'sufficiently plausible' **110,** 750, 753, 767-8, 773-4
Tribunal's discretion **120,** 221-2
well-founded **110,** 768, 773-4, 777, 780, **120,** 222-3
expert evidence, *voir dire* **117,** 155
Guidelines concerning the Preparation and Presentation of Cases before the Tribunal, paragraph 10 **110,** 742
individuals and. *See* standing, individual *below*
institution of proceedings **120,** 157-61
judge *ad hoc*, appointment **117,** 155
judgment
binding effect. *See also* Law of the Sea Convention (1982): Part XV (settlement of disputes), prompt release, binding effect; Law of the Sea Convention (1982): Part XV (settlement of disputes), provisional measures, binding effect
facts **110,** 750
law **110,** 750
obiter dicta, effect **110,** 771-3
revision. *See* revision of judgment *below*
translation into Spanish where written pleadings in English or French **125,** 185-6
legal profession, role **125,** 305-7
preliminary objections, joinder to merits **120,** 339
revision of judgment, grounds, decisive new fact **120,** 351
Rules. *See* International Tribunal for the Law of the Sea (ITLOS), Rules of the Tribunal
separate opinion, Resolution on the Internal Judicial Practice **120,** 251
standing
failure to challenge **120,** 249-50, 254-6, 315-16, 350-2
flag State **125,** 178-9, 206, 295-301, 302-4
critical date **125,** 313-15, 319
'genuine link' requirement **120,** 177-80
individual **120,** 233-6
legal interest, need for **120,** 353
nationality of owner of ship and **120,** 330, 352
registration of ship and **120,** 172-7, 215-18, 251-4, 339, 340
stateless ship **120,** 351-3
Statute. *See Consolidated Table of Treaties*, Convention on the Law of the Sea (10 December 1982), Annex VI (Statute of the International Tribunal of the Law of the Sea)
submission to Tribunal
amendment **117,** 122
date **117,** 115
International Tribunal for the Law of the Sea (ITLOS), Rules of the Tribunal
9 **117,** 153, **125,** 282
45 **110,** 742, **125,** 168, 228, 281, 282
52(2)(a) **110,** 741
59 **120,** 160
60 **120,** 160
63(1) **120,** 162, **125,** 169
63(2) **120,** 162, **125,** 169
64(3) **120,** 162, **125,** 169
64(4) **125,** 185-6
67(2) **110,** 743, **117,** 117, 154, **120,** 164, **125,** 169, 229, 282
68 **110,** 742, **117,** 114, 154, **120,** 162, **125,** 169, 282
71 **120,** 162, **125,** 170, 283
72 **110,** 742, **120,** 162, **125,** 168, 228, 280

73 **125,** 168, 228, 282
75(2) **117,** 122, **120,** 166, **125,** 172, 232, 285
76 **110,** 743, **117,** 114, 154, **120,** 162
77(1) **117,** 123
86 **120,** 164
88(1) **120,** 339
89 **117,** 113, 151
89(1) **117,** 115, **120,** 160
89(5) **117,** 124, 127-8, 164, 187-9
90 **117,** 113, 151
94 **117,** 167, **120,** 160, 161
95(1) **117,** 124, 125, 126-7, 164, 167
95(2) **117,** 124, 128, 164
96 **120,** 335
97 **120,** 335
97(1) **120,** 171-2, 338
110 **110,** 747, **125,** 179, 241
110(2) **110,** 748
111 **125,** 179, 241
111(2) **125,** 210
111(2)(b) **125,** 184
111(2)(c) **125,** 210
111(4) **110,** 741, 742, **125,** 168, 227, 280
112(1) **110,** 749
112(3) **110,** 741, 749, **125,** 168, 227, 280
112(4) **110,** 749
113 **110,** 767, **125,** 188-9, 243
compatibility with Convention **125,** 188-9
113(1) **110,** 768, 781, **125,** 188
113(2) **110,** 757, **125,** 179, 185, 213, 248-9
113(3) **110,** 758, 761, **125,** 185, 188
114 **125,** 185
125(2) **110,** 760, **120,** 207
127 **120,** 351
international tribunals[ix]
admissibility **56,** 369

[ix] See also the following:
Arbitral Commission on Property, Rights and Interests in Germany
Argentina–Chile Tribunal (1904)
Argentina–Chile Tribunal (1966)
Argentina–Chile Tribunal (1994)
Asian Development Bank Administrative Tribunal
Badinter Commission (Yugoslavia)
Chile–USA International Commission (Letelier and Moffitt)
claims settlement tribunals
Court of Arbitration for Sport (Ad Hoc Division: Sydney Olympic Games)
Egypt–Israel Arbitration Tribunal (Taba)
Eritrea/Yemen Arbitration Tribunal (1998)
Eritrea/Yemen Arbitration Tribunal (1999)
European Commission of Human Rights
European Court of Human Rights
European Court of Justice (ECJ)
European Economic Area (EEA), EEA Court

international tribunals (*cont.*)
advisory report, decision on unilateral claim distinguished **54,** 326
applicable law, international law **56,** 152
application to **59,** 521-3
awards
binding force **45,** 500-2
competence **54,** 462-5
failure to provide adequate relief **54,** 459-60
implementation **77,** 199
review by ICJ **54,** 475-8, 487, 498
right of challenge **54,** 464
ultra vires **54,** 465
claims settlement tribunals. *See also* claims settlement tribunals
agreements establishing **46,** 420-1
decisions of, authority **46,** 421
competence. *See also* jurisdiction *below*
boundary lines, to draw **54,** 188
rectification of error **54,** 174
compétence de la compétence. See arbitral tribunal, *compétence de la compétence*; jurisdiction, *compétence de la compétence*

German Debts, Tripartite Commission on
German External Debts Agreement (1953), Arbitral Tribunal
German–US Mixed Claims Commission
ICSID (International Centre for the Settlement of Investment Disputes), arbitral tribunal
Inter-American Commission on Human Rights
Inter-American Court of Human Rights
International Chamber of Commerce (ICC)
International Civil Aviation Organization (ICAO), Council
International Court of Justice (ICJ)
International Criminal Court (ICC)
International Labour Organization Administrative Tribunal (ILOAT)
International Military Tribunal for the Far East (Tokyo Tribunal)
International Tribunal for the Law of the Sea (ITLOS)
Iran–US Claims Tribunal
Iraq–Kuwait Boundary Commission (UN)
Italian–US Conciliation Commission
just satisfaction (Art. 50 [41] of the European Convention on Human Rights (1950))
Law of the Sea Convention (1982): Annex VII (settlement of disputes)
NAFTA (North American Free Trade Agreement) (1992), arbitral tribunal
New Zealand, Waitangi Tribunal
Nuremberg Tribunal
Permanent Court of Arbitration (PCA)
Permanent Court of International Justice (PCIJ)
Racial Discrimination, UN Committee on the Elimination of
Rwanda, International Criminal Tribunal for (ICTR)
Tripartite Commission for the Restitution of Monetary Gold
UNCITRAL (United Nations Commission on International Trade Law)
United Nations Administrative Tribunal (UNAT)
United Nations Committee on the Elimination of Racial Discrimination
United Nations Compensation Commission
United Nations Human Rights Committee (UNHRC)
US–UK Arbitral Tribunal (Heathrow Airport User Charges)
World Bank Administrative Tribunal
Yugoslavia, International Criminal Tribunal for the Former (ICTY).

costs **54,** 432, 469-71
decision
reasoning and *dispositif* distinguished **54,** 163-77
res judicata, whether **54,** 167-71
declaratory judgments **54,** 318-19, **57,** 590
damages, subsequent claim **57,** 464
dispute, existence **48,** 453
dissolution of union of States, disputes arising from **91,** 307
duty not to prejudice future decisions of **82,** 82
equality of parties **54,** 485-7
error
procedural **54,** 428-30, 512
competence to rectify **54,** 174
evidence, admissibility **36,** 377-9, **46,** 272, 332
functions **62,** 350-1
boundary disputes, settlement of **57,** 21
government and foreign company, between **40,** 158-64
individuals' right of recourse **77,** 564, 566
judgment
reasons **54,** 430-1, 513-14
review **54,** 462-5, 473-8
by ICJ **54,** 434, 437, 489
grounds for **54,** 454-6, 463-5
judicial interpretation **55,** 384
judicial role **54,** 467-8
jurisdiction **54,** 35, 343
'actual controversies' **54,** 327
burden of proof **48,** 457
consensual nature **57,** 508, **119,** 67
determination of, exercise of, whether **54,** 505
exhaustion of local remedies. *See* exhaustion of local remedies
failure to exercise **54,** 408-27, 443, 467
justice **56,** 186
mass processing **109,** 252-3
methods, judicial exchange of views **83,** 332
municipal jurisdiction, effect on **77,** 566
national security defence. *See* national security defence, international tribunals
negotiated settlement, guidance to parties for **47,** 423, 460-1
objectives, dispute settlement **55,** 277
precedent **57,** 301
procedural irregularities, illegalities, whether **48,** 463-4
standard of proof **109,** 151-2, 242-3
statutory limitation. *See* statutory limitation, international tribunals
treaty interpretation **56,** 487
Tribunals
Greco-Bulgarian Mixed Arbitral Tribunal **78,** 653
Indo-Pakistan Boundaries Disputes Tribunal **53,** 187-8
Shanghai, International Mixed Court **40,** 84-5
International Union for the Conservation of Nature and Nature Resources (IUCN) 68, 272-8, 426
international waters
equity and **99,** 616-17, **116,** 248
rights and obligations **91,** 515 n. 9

international wrong. *See* international tort/wrong
internment. *See also* Geneva Convention (Treatment of Prisoners of War) (Convention III) (1949), internment
enemy aliens, right to sue, effect on **53,** 620
Northern Ireland **58,** 213-19, 233-6
refugees **60,** 209-10, 213-16
interpretation, *acta jure imperii* **77,** 609
interpretation in international law. *See also* arbitral award, interpretation; contract, interpretation; European Community law, interpretation; legislation, interpretation; treaty interpretation
categories of instrument distinguished **113,** 44-5
judicial role **113,** 45
Jus nature methodo scientifico pertractatum (Christian Wolff) **113,** 44
intertemporal law 37, 455, **50,** 453, **80,** 472-3, **83,** 32
boundary dispute, relevance **100,** 39
effect on applicable law of changing values **112,** 480-1, 546-7, **116,** 122-4, 129-35
historic rights and **59,** 185-6
new scientific evidence, relevance **106,** 19-20, 50-1, 61-3
tempus regit factum **59,** 186
title **114,** 46, 115
treaty implementation **116,** 124
treaty interpretation **49,** 21, **75,** 671-4, **77,** 657, 673, **83,** 45, **92,** 153-4, 157-8
Vienna Convention on the Law of Treaties (1969) **116,** 123
intervention in affairs of another State 59, 383-8, **74,** 168, **76,** 440-4, 457-69, 490-1, 533, 602-3, 717
counter-intervention. *See* countermeasures *below*
countermeasures **76,** 444, 461, 464-8
Cyprus, in, EC **100,** 299
decolonization, in support of **76,** 684-6
double standard **76,** 607
economic pressure **76,** 403-4, 459-60
genocide, to prevent, State practice **95,** 162-3
Helsinki Final Act (1975) **76,** 441
humanitarian assistance **36,** 296, **37,** 83, **76,** 458-9, **91,** 125
military **44,** 337
prohibited
Corfu Channel case **76,** 440-1
customary international law **76,** 441-4, 460, 517, 533, 639, 685, 868
Havana Convention on the Rights and Duties in the Event of Civil Strife (1928) **76,** 436
Montevideo Convention on the Rights and Duties of States (1936) **76,** 441
Additional Protocol relative to Non-intervention **76,** 870-1
Organization of American States, General Assembly Resolution AG/RES.78 and AG/RES.128 **76,** 441
support of opposition whose intention is to overthrow Government **76,** 458, 603
UNGA Declaration on the Inadmissibility of Intervention in the Domestic Affairs of States and Protection of their Independence and Sovereignty **76,** 441
UNGA Declaration on the Principles of International Law concerning Friendly Relations and Cooperation among States **76,** 436, 440, 441, 442
rights arising from **105,** 389
supply of arms **76,** 441
intimidation, military manoeuvres **76,** 387, 452
Intourist. *See* Union of Soviet Socialist Republics (USSR), Intourist

investment. *See also* BITs (bilateral investment treaties); ICSID Convention (Convention on Settlement of Investment Disputes between States and Nationals of Other States (1965)); Multilateral Agreement on Investment (MAI); NAFTA (North American Free Trade Agreement) (1992); standard of treatment of alien; Uruguay Round; World Trade Organization (WTO)
applicable law
choice of law, admissibility **106,** 722-7
municipal law of Contracting State **106,** 722-7
in companies with nationality of host State **46,** 427, 433
definition **106,** 717-18, **121,** 18, 110-13, 135-8, 139-40
company, shares in stock of company and any form of participation in company **124,** 27
inward flow of capital for economic development **106,** 653, 654
US Investment Guaranty Program **44,** 94-5, 98
export of earnings **46,** 230
foreign capital, failure to transfer **106,** 731-2, 734-5
government guarantees **56,** 278-9
arbitration **56,** 258-330
host State's duty to consult, investor/home State distinguished **121,** 186
investor
approval, need for **106,** 620-3
evidence of **106,** 620-3
host State's duty to consult **121,** 186-8
host State's relations with **46,** 419-24, 444
protection **60,** 40, 45-6
loss of, damages recoverable **44,** 92-9
national incorporation requirement **46,** 366
nationals, by, State economic interests **46,** 220, 370-3, 439, 443-4, 451, 453, 505, 523
as part of national wealth **46,** 220, 370-3, 439, 444, 451, 453, 515, 523
as property right **46,** 66, 300-1
protection of **60,** 34-5
State interests, as **46,** 220, 370-3, 439, 443-4, 451, 453, 505, 523
treatment by host State **46,** 206, 220, 340, 347, 351-2, 366, 442, 447-8, 508, 510, 512, 513
investment disputes. *See* arbitration; contract, applicable law; ICSID Convention (Convention on Settlement of Investment Disputes between States and Nationals of Other States (1965)); ICSID (International Centre for the Settlement of Investment Disputes); International Chamber of Commerce (ICC)
Iran. *See also* Iran, Islamic Republic
applicable law, contract **47,** 404
arbitral award, State-owned company and foreign private company, validity **47,** 396-405
contract, applicable law **47,** 404
marriage **57,** 12
Saudi Arabia, Agreement on off-shore areas **41,** 97, 102-3
State immunity, Railway Administration **52,** 316
Iran, Islamic Republic. *See also* Iran; Iran–US Claims Tribunal
Abu Musa, sovereignty claims **66,** 177, 330-8
Air Force **63,** 262-83
arbitration, refusal to participate in **96,** 268-9
arbitration laws **68,** 563-4, 628
Atomic Energy Organization (IAEO) **77,** 515
Bank Melli Iran **63,** 425-34
Bank Omran **63,** 347-50

Iran, Islamic Republic (*cont.*)
Bimeh Merkazi Iran (Central Insurance of Iran) **63,** 454-8
Civil Aviation Department, State immunity **63,** 212-14
Constitution **84,** 603-4
Art. 44 **69,** 617, 627-8, **71,** 691
Art. 150 **82,** 192 n. 7
Principle 139 **78,** 649-50
consular immunity, breaches of **61,** 556-7, 558-9, 561-2, 563
Continental Shelf Convention (1958), reservation **41,** 205
controlled entity **84,** 602-5
State General Gendarmerie **84,** 597-9
corporation, succession **69,** 576, 578-9, 581, 593-4
contractual obligations, liability for, de facto succession **69,** 581, 592-6, 618
diplomatic privileges and immunities, breaches of **61,** 556-7, 558-9, 561-2, 563
exchange control **75,** 128-35, 144-7
expropriation/nationalization **63,** 454-7, **69,** 570, 584, 617, 627-8, **79,** 585-9
alien property **72,** 227-33, **75,** 596-674
debt, effect on **79,** 585-9
nationals' property **72,** 126-31, 498-500
'Fidelity Affidavits' **69,** 576-7, 588
hostage-taking **61,** 538-41, 559, 561
lawfulness **61,** 562-3
reparation, duty to make **61,** 567-8
State responsibility and **61,** 555-9, 561, 563-7, 568, 584-8
Iran Power Generation and Transmission Company **63,** 409-16, 498-511
Iranian Atomic Energy Organization (IAEO), instrumentality of Iran **113,** 455
judicial changes **68,** 617-18, 620-1, 641
jurisdiction **70,** 487, 493-4, **71,** 636-49, 669
exclusion in favour of Iran–US Claims Tribunal **75,** 160
exclusive **68,** 562-5, 568-72, 575-6, 580-7, 589-94, 596-7, 600-1, 609-10
Kavir, instrumentality of Iran **81,** 553-4
law of **62,** 605
Agency law **69,** 598-9
Appointment of Temporary Managers Law 1979 **84,** 508, 628 n. 5
Attraction and Protection of Foreign Investment Act 1955 **83,** 557, 562, **84,** 622
Bill for Appointment of Temporary Managers 1979 **85,** 389, 390, 463-7, 608
Civil Code **47,** 404, **57,** 12, **71,** 658, 680, 682, **72,** 542, 548, 721, **75,** 265, **85,** 464, 476 n. 1
Art. 9 **84,** 665
Art. 224 **86,** 257
Art. 225 **86,** 257
Art. 438 **84,** 608
Art. 656 **69,** 599
Art. 658 **69,** 598
Art. 660 **69,** 629, 636
Art. 990 **84,** 614
Civil Procedure Code **71,** 646, 649, 679, **85,** 426, 432-3, 465, 472
Art. 3 **86,** 257
Art. 356 **68,** 554
Art. 635 **68,** 564
Art. 649 **78,** 674
Art. 657 **68,** 564, 610
Art. 662 **68,** 564
Art. 665 **68,** 564, 610

Art. 740 **78,** 666
cancellation **68,** 618, 620-1
Civil Responsibility Law 1960, Art. 8 **84,** 608
Commercial Code **71,** 697, **72,** 499, 541, **75,** 137, 139, **84,** 597-9, 652, **85,** 433, 552
Art. 20 **84,** 597
Art. 118 **78,** 666
Art. 126 **71,** 621-2
Art. 135 **78,** 666
Art. 136 **84,** 635
Art. 357 **71,** 622
Art. 583 **84,** 597
Art. 589 **84,** 597-8
cancellation **68,** 618, 620-1
Companies Law **79,** 585
Confiscation of Pahlavi Properties Decree 1979 **85,** 404
Constitution. *See* Constitution *above*
Development of Petrochemical Industries Act 1965 **83,** 557, 562
Direct Taxation Act **85,** 546-8
Labour Code **78,** 665
Law concerning the Appointment of Temporary Managers **79,** 585
Law No 7/2571 of June 1970 **84,** 643 n. 3
Law No 6738 of 26 March 1958 **84,** 515
Law No 8780 of 16 April 1958 **84,** 515
Monetary and Banking Law 1972 **72,** 544, **75,** 130, 144
Nationalization Act 1951 **96,** 268
Nationalization of Insurance Enterprises Law 1979 **75,** 599, 641, **84,** 503 n. 17, 512, 649, 668, 669
Nationalization of Oil Industry Act 1951 **83,** 547, 552
Penal Code **66,** 152-8
Petroleum Act 1957 **47,** 140, 145, 397, **65,** 219, 220, **96,** 268
Protection and Development of Iranian Industries Law 1979 **72,** 227-8, 734
Protection and Development of Iranian Industries Law 1980 **84,** 503, 514
Art. 1 **84,** 512
Clause A **84,** 512
Clause C **84,** 510, 511, 545, 554, 604
Reduction of Rental Housing Units Act **85,** 589
Registration of Properties Code **85,** 465
Single Article Act 1980 **78,** 645-8, 650-1, 656, **83,** 575-6, 609, **86,** 240, 299-300, **96,** 268
compensation under **83,** 548-9, 612
as expropriation. *See* as nationalization *below*
Iran–US Claims Settlement Declaration, effect on **70,** 485-6, 492-3, **78,** 650-1
as nationalization **70,** 485-6, 492-3, **78,** 650-1, **83,** 530, 532, 540, 547-8, 552, **86,** 274, 275-6
statute of limitations **78,** 666
'legal authorities', courts, whether identical with **68,** 580-1, 629-30, 644-5
Majlis **68,** 618, 623, **70,** 487-8, 493-4, **78,** 646-51, 656
married women, property rights **71,** 658-9
National Iranian Oil Company (NIOC) **63,** 306-10
as government-controlled entity **47,** 139-49, **65,** 200, 202-3, 213, 218-24, **66,** 177, **69,** 570, 575-6, 592
immunity, execution/attachment **65,** 200, 213-14, 218-25, 245
immunity, jurisdiction **47,** 139-49, **56,** 213, **65,** 202
State agency/State-owned corporation/State entity **69,** 576, 592

Iran, Islamic Republic (*cont.*)
Oil Service Company of Iran, relation to **69,** 569, 575-602
alter ego **69,** 578, 600-1
control **69,** 569, 575-6, 578, 582, 585, 600-1
employer–contractor **69,** 576-7, 600
estoppel and **69,** 595
law determining relationship **69,** 576, 578-9, 581, 593-6
principal–agent **69,** 569, 576-7, 582-3, 596-601
service contract (1973) **69,** 573-5
State organ **47,** 138-49
succession **69,** 569, 578-83, 588-96, 602
nationality, loss or deprivation of **72,** 542, 548
nationalization of insurance companies, value of shares **75,** 599-601, 603-7, 641-3
nationalization measures **83,** 530, 532, 540, 547-8, 552, **84,** 512, **86,** 274, 275-6
nuclear energy exploitation **65,** 94-7
cooperation agreement, termination **65,** 94-5
oil, nationalization of industry **69,** 570, 584, **70,** 485-6
Oil Service Company of Iran
NIOC and. *See* NIOC, Oil Service Company of Iran, relation to *above*
object of company **69,** 572, 576, 585, 600
ownership **69,** 572
Organization for Investment and Economic and Technical Aid (IOIETA) **77,** 515
revolutionary changes **68,** 617-18, 620-1, 641
shipping industry, expropriation/nationalization **69,** 617, 627-8
Star Line Iran Company
government controlled agency, whether **69,** 623-5, 627-8
Star Line Shipping Company Inc., relation to **69,** 618
State agency/State-owned corporation/State entity, whether **69,** 617
sustainable development principle **116,** 114
treaties, breaches of **61,** 556-7, 558-9, 561-2, 563
United States of America
Claims Settlement Declaration. *See* Iran–US Claims Settlement Declaration
Claims Tribunal. *See* Iran–US Claims Tribunal
USA. *See* United States of America (USA), Iran
Iran–US Banking Agreements (1981) 68, 527-58
Iran–US Claims Settlement Declaration 62, 582-607
Art. II **78,** 652, 654
Art. III **78,** 675
Art. III(1) **68,** 520
Art. III(2) **68,** 518
Art. V **68,** 542-3, 545-6, 618, 621, 635
Art. VI **68,** 535
Art. VI(1) **68,** 561-614 *passim*
Art. VI(2) **68,** 619
Art. VI(3) **68,** 540
Art. VI(4) **68,** 621. *See also* forum selection clause
'any disputes' **68,** 581, 596-7, 600-1, 613, 624-6, 644
Art. V and **68,** 635
'binding contract' **68,** 570-1, 581-3, 591-4, 603-5, 612-24, 634-9
Iranian courts, exclusive reference to **68,** 561-2, 575-6, 589-90, 600-1, 613, 626-8, 633, 643-5
promissory notes, claims based on **68,** 568-9, 624-5
'specific provision' **68,** 562-3, 575-6, 584-5, 590-1, 600-1, 633, 643-5

claims
exclusion **70,** 492, **71,** 602, 607-8, 614-21, 629-30, 651-4, 659-62, 668-9, 690-1, 694-7, **72,** 241, 483-9, 496-8, 502, 532-3, 719-20, 727-32, **75,** 156, **78,** 655, 665, **86,** 248-9
ownership, 'ownership interests sufficient to control corporation' **72,** 728-32
corporation, nationality **69,** 603, 606, 621-2, 632
counterclaims
jurisdiction over **71,** 637-8, 641-8, **75,** 607, **78,** 667, 669
subject matter of claim, relation to **70,** 127
description **96,** 6
government controlled entities **69,** 570, 575-6, 592, 617, 623-6, 631
burden of proof **69,** 625
government liability **69,** 626
interpretation **68,** 521, 542-3, 592-3, 604-5, 612, 615-16, 619-24, 633-9, **75,** 602-3, 629-30, 665-7. *See also* treaty interpretation
by Claims Tribunal **71,** 637-40, 643-6, 648, 652-5, 659-60, 673, 690-1, 694-700, **72,** 241, 251-2, 483-9, 496-8, 502, 532-5, 719-20, 727-32, 734, **75,** 179-268
jurisdiction **68,** 521
task of Tribunal **75,** 187
nature **75,** 187, 221-3
nullification of attachments of Iranian assets **72,** 274-82, 482, 488, 536, **75,** 157-8, 196, 199, 215
suspension of claims distinguished **72,** 282
objectives **75,** 187-8, 196, 199-200, 205, 213-14
ordinary courts, exclusion of jurisdiction **72,** 128-9, 135-40, 276, 289-90, 487-8, **78,** 654-5
other treaties compared **75,** 186, 189-90, 212-13, 238
phrases
'corporation' **72,** 728-32
'entities controlled by Iran' **71,** 607-8, 615-20, 669, 691, 694-700, **72,** 241, 251-2, 719, 734, **75,** 156, **78,** 665
'Iran' **69,** 568-9, 592, 600, 617, **70,** 123, 518, **71,** 607-8, 691, 694
'measures affecting property rights' **71,** 629-30, 652-5, 657-61
'nationals of Iran or US' **72,** 483-9, 497-8, 532-5, 719, **75,** 182-6, 188, 196, 198-200, 211-14
prohibition of other litigation **75,** 154-5, 157-8, 160, 185
counterclaims, effect on **71,** 637-8, 643-6, 648
taking without just compensation **81,** 550-1
third States, duty not to frustrate **75,** 173
transfer of Iranian assets **72,** 276-7, 279
travaux préparatoires **68,** 531, 533, 535-6, 543, 550, 554-6, 592-3, 605-6, 621-4, 637-9, **70,** 521
treaty status **68,** 545, **75,** 154
US nationals, definition **69,** 603, 605, 621-2, 632, **70,** 123, 499
Iran–US Claims Tribunal 62, 582-94, 595-607
act of State and **84,** 503 n. 17, 653, 666 n. 2
adversary proceedings **70,** 509
Algiers Accords. *See also* Iran–US Claims Settlement Declaration; Iran–US General Declaration
individual's rights, effect on **96,** 10-11
President's power to conclude **96,** 10-11
self-executing, whether **96,** 8

Iran–US Claims Tribunal (*cont.*)
applicable law **82,** 214, **84,** 510-11, **86,** 256
customary international law **84,** 510-11
general principles of commercial law **84,** 552
general principles of law **72,** 721-2, **75,** 155, 190, 222-3
Iran–US Treaty of Amity (1955) **83,** 473, 483, **84,** 510-11, 524, 552, 663-7, **86,** 256
indirect claims **84,** 557 n. 14
municipal law **75,** 183, 189-90, 202-4, 215-16, 221-3
principles and rules of international law **86,** 256
relevant rules of international law **72,** 483, 547, **75,** 155, 182, 188, 219-20
arbitrators
absence, effect **69,** 620-1, 629, 635-7, 663, **71,** 612-14, 626, **78,** 670-5
appointing authority **68,** 520-1
designation by Permanent Court of Arbitration (PCA) **68,** 521
challenge **62,** 581-94, **68,** 515-22
procedure **68,** 518
concurring opinions **72,** 226, 234-5, **78,** 672-5
validity **72,** 234-5
deliberations
adequacy **71,** 612, 626-7
confidentiality **69,** 628, 631-4, 658, **71,** 627, **72,** 234
disqualification **68,** 515-22
dissenting opinions **78,** 639-75
equitable discretion **72,** 247
explanation **78,** 670-2
impartiality **68,** 519-20, 522, **72,** 234-6, **75,** 194-5, 197, 267-8, **78,** 641
neutrality. *See* impartiality *above*
refusal to sign award **69,** 619, 629-31, 634-5, 638, 658, 661, **72,** 492, 500
resignation **69,** 620, 630-1, 638-41, 662, **71,** 612-13, **78,** 670-3, 674
UNCITRAL Rules **68,** 515-22
award
on agreed terms **68,** 530-3, 652-4, **72,** 225-6, **83,** 490-500, 629-38
duties of Tribunal **68,** 530-3
standards applicable **68,** 531-3
'without prejudice' **68,** 652-4
Algiers Accords, provisions under **96,** 8
binding nature **69,** 619-20, 628-31, 634-7, 663, **71,** 611-12, 625-7, **75,** 155, 157, 180, **84,** 616, 617
arbitrator's absence, effect **69,** 620-1, 629, 635-7, 663
compensation **78,** 667-9
compliance, obligation, whether **96,** 8
correction **84,** 662
currency of payment **75,** 606, 627, 643-51
damages **69,** 620-1, 654-6, 660-3, **71,** 608-11, 670-7, **78,** 637-9, 672-3
basis of assessment **75,** 599-625, 631-43, 663-4
mitigation **78,** 673
enforcement
against Iran **96,** 8
in favour of Iran **96,** 8
US courts, by **96,** 5
interest **69,** 618-21, 653-6, 659-60, **71,** 610, 625, 675, **72,** 492, 724, **75,** 607, 625-6, 648, **78,** 669, 670, 673
rate **69,** 618-21, 653-6, 659-60

as just satisfaction **84,** 495
'made in foreign State', whether **96,** 9, 11-12
partial **69,** 651
payment, Security Account **71,** 611, 624, 678, **72,** 226, 492, 724, **75,** 649-50
precedent, as. *See* precedent *below*
primacy, ordinary courts and **71,** 638-49
recognition **75,** 156-7, 166-73
New York Convention and **75,** 166-7
refusal to sign **85,** 605, 623-4
signature **84,** 591-2, 616, 617, 662
absence **78,** 671-2, 674-5
refusal by arbitrator **71,** 611-12, 625-7, **72,** 492, 500
validity **78,** 657
absence of signature **78,** 674-5. *See also* binding character *above*
non-signature and **84,** 616, 617
burden of proof **85,** 414
controlled entity **84,** 605
mitigation of damages **78,** 673
restriction on sovereignty **78,** 650 n. 2
Case No A/18 **84,** 616, 617
Chamber
autonomy **86,** 313
excess of authority **78,** 641-3
choice of law clause **78,** 665
claims
alleged expulsion
failure to compensate **82,** 213
losses to property or property interests **82,** 213
State responsibility **82,** 213
alternative **85,** 425-7, 436-8, 561-2
amendment **69,** 603, 605-6, 610-13, **84,** 652
substitution of claimant **69,** 606, 610-13
bank account, right to payment from **70,** 123-6
bank drafts **71,** 605-11
basis **68,** 614
contract **85,** 426
diplomatic protection **75,** 182-4, 190, 202, 224-33, 264
dishonoured cheque **75,** 128-90, 202, 227-8, 230, 264
individual rights **75,** 186, 189-90, 202, 227-8, 230, 264
breach of contract **71,** 634-49, 664-82, 689-93, 700-3, **72,** 240-52, **78,** 668, 669, 672-3, **83,** 517, 530, **86,** 249, 250, 286-9, 305
force majeure and **71,** 666, 670, 680
continuity **84,** 491-2, 502-4
continuous ownership **70,** 499, 502, 521-3, **85,** 368
corporation, against, liquidation, effect **71,** 608, 698
corporation, by. *See* corporation, nationality
deadline **69,** 606-9
Tribunal delays **69,** 608-9
debt **72,** 240-52
definition **70,** 123-4, 126, **78,** 653-4
delay in bringing, statutory limitation and **78,** 666
destruction of property in military action **71,** 601-2, 652-3
direct **84,** 585-8

Iran–US Claims Tribunal (*cont.*)
dishonoured cheque **72,** 480-2, 491-2, 539-40, 543-5, 717-24
dual nationals **72,** 480-549, **75,** 170-268
exchange control contravention, effect **75,** 130, 132-6, 144-7, 158-9
exclusion **84,** 652-3
expropriation/nationalization **75,** 597-674, **83,** 517, 530, **84,** 503
extinction, US embassy hostages' **72,** 134, 137-40, 143-50
government agency, against, service of claim **69,** 568, 622-3, 631
indirect **84,** 492, 504, 549-84
change to direct **84,** 504
Treaty of Amity, applicability **84,** 557 n. 14
invoice **84,** 579-82
Iranian nationals, against **84,** 616
Iranian nationals, by **70,** 518, **71,** 601-2, 675-7
lease, under **72,** 240-52
frustration of purpose **72,** 243-6, 249-51
'measures affecting property rights'
failure to provide protection **71,** 652-4, 657-61
proximate cause of injury, whether **71,** 629-30
municipal court claims, relevance **85,** 378-9
nationality of claim **70,** 521
nationality of claimant. *See* corporation, nationality
outstanding at date of Declaration **70,** 488-9, 494-5, **78,** 655
ownership of **71,** 607, 668, **72,** 241, 719-20, 728-32, **75,** 129, 135, 598-9
political **71,** 630
Principle 'B' and **78,** 653-5
quantum meruit **71,** 675
recovery of undelivered goods **86,** 249, 250, 286, 304
repayment of investments **86,** 249, 304
security measures, cost of **71,** 673
taking of property **72,** 227-33, 494, 498-500
tort **71,** 601-2, 652-3, 655-62
transfer to foreign subsidiary **84,** 502 n. 16
unjust enrichment **72,** 720, **75,** 128, 147-50, 159
US corporation, by **75,** 597-674
US Iranian Assets Control Regulations, frustration of contract by **72,** 241-7
US nationals
against **62,** 598-607
by **70,** 119, 122-3, 499-526, **71,** 604-8, 614-15, 629-31, 633-7, 651-4, 657-62, 664-75, 689-93, 700-3, **72,** 225-8, 240-1, 717-18
wrongful death, dependants' rights **71,** 651-4, 657-61
composition **69,** 620, 629, 635-41, 663
concurring opinion **83,** 608-28
controlled entity **70,** 518, **84,** 515, 602-5
costs **69,** 618, 656-7, 660, **70,** 127, **71,** 610, 630-1, 677, **72,** 247, 252, 492, 500, 724, **75,** 134, 608, 626, **78,** 670, 673, **82,** 162, 203, 224, **83,** 481, **84,** 588-9, 601, 638, 661, **85,** 557, 603, 622-3
arbitration **84,** 588
expert **85,** 394
legal **84,** 588, 671-2
waiver **83,** 638
counterclaims **72,** 240, **75,** 607, **78,** 667, 669, **85,** 413-14, 554-6. *See also* jurisdiction, counterclaims *below*

breach of contract **83,** 598-601, 604-7
for completion of project **85,** 409-62
jurisdiction **83,** 602-4, 607, 628
late filing **85,** 379, 418
non-delivery of goods **83,** 601-4
tax liabilities **83,** 591-8, 628
diplomatic protection, relevance **84,** 493, 494, 666
discretion **85,** 589-90
employment contract
absence of remedy **94,** 326
applicable law, municipal law of host State **94,** 325-6
disputes relating to
settlement preferred method **94,** 325
Tribunal as final authority **94,** 325, 327, 329-30
jurisdiction, municipal courts **94,** 328
oral agreement **94,** 325-6, 328, 330
translation and interpreting services, *acta jure imperii* **94,** 326, 328, 330
estoppel **84,** 607-8, **85,** 436, 463
European Convention on Human Rights (1950), applicability **107,** 4-5
evidence **68,** 587, 633, 645-51
admissibility, post-hearing **71,** 685-6
affidavit **68,** 546, **70,** 123, 505-7
burden of proof **70,** 500-1, 507-11, 519-21, 525-6, **71,** 679, 684, 693, 701, **75,** 133-8, **78,** 650 n. 2, 673, **82,** 160, 202, 223, 224, **83,** 477
actori incumbit onus probandi **68,** 554
cheques, authenticity **71,** 683-4
contract, authenticity **71,** 682-3, 691-3
control of corporation by State **71,** 607-8, 615-20, 668-9, 691, 694-700, **72,** 241, 251-2, 719, 734
difficulty of producing **83,** 477, 485-8
failure to produce, inferences from **71,** 678-9, 691, 699-700, **72,** 233, 729, **75,** 134-6, 140-1, 605-6
inadequacy **71,** 678, 682-4, 691, 693, 699-703
insufficient **82,** 162, 202
judicial notice **70,** 524-5
nationality of claimants **70,** 499-526, **71,** 607-8, 614-15, 668, 690-1, **72,** 727-30
official statistics **70,** 504, 523
power to demand from State **110,** 636
presumption. *See* public documents, inference from *below*
public documents, inference from **70,** 501-2, 504-5, 509-10, 523-5
rebuttal evidence **70,** 501, 519-20, 525-6
sufficiency **72,** 498-500, 728-32
taking of property, regarding **72,** 498-500
time-limits **68,** 633, 646-51
underlying transaction **75,** 132-6, 138-42
evidence of
change of control **85,** 403-4
expropriation/nationalization **83,** 465, 466-7, 470-3
nationality **83,** 466
nationality of claimants **85,** 377-8
ownership of corporation **83,** 482-3, **84,** 496-502
value of corporation **83,** 477-9
exchange control regulations

Iran–US Claims Tribunal (*cont.*)
examination of **75,** 128-35, 144-7
expulsion of alien and **82,** 203
exhaustion of local remedies **83,** 515-16, **84,** 653, 662 n. 2
expert **85,** 484-556
appointment **83,** 607-8, **85,** 393-4, 473
costs **85,** 394
evidence **68,** 546, **70,** 506
limitations **85,** 589-90
role **85,** 624
weight of evidence **85,** 564-8
expulsion of alien **82,** 149-224
function **72,** 488, 501, 522, 532, **75,** 182, 207, 211, 259, **84,** 494, 538 n. 18
evaluation of legal and factual assumptions **84,** 571
General Declaration
act of State doctrine, under **81,** 567, 575, 576
Art. II **85,** 378-9, 423, 433-4, 435, **86,** 248, 312, 313
interest **84,** 671
interim measures **71,** 635-49
interlocutory award **78,** 651, **85,** 359
International Monetary Fund Agreement, application **75,** 132
judicial notice **85,** 559
jurisdiction **82,** 154-5, 188-90, 211-13, **83,** 465-9, 482-5, 514-17, 598, **84,** 492-504, 597-9, 602-5, 630, 650-3. *See also* proceedings, status of *below*
admission, effect **68,** 593
Algiers Declarations
interpretation **68,** 521, **86,** 309
supplementation of terms **68,** 551
arbitrators, challenge to **68,** 521
award on agreed terms **68,** 530-3, 652-4
basis **75,** 168-73
consent of States **78,** 640
claims outstanding at date of Declaration **70,** 488-9, 494-5, **78,** 655, **86,** 247-8
Claims Settlement Declaration **83,** 515, 516, 517, 534
filing before court, necessary, whether **86,** 248
concurrent **70,** 492-3
continuity of claims **84,** 651
contract annulment, effect of **70,** 484-9, 491-5
contractual assignments, relevance **83,** 515
corporation organized under law of Iran **84,** 496
counterclaims **71,** 637-8, 641-8, **75,** 607, **78,** 667, 669, **83,** 602-3, 607, 628
subject matter of claim, relation to **70,** 127
determination of **69,** 569-70, 575, 583-4, 603, 605-6, 608-9, **70,** 122-7, 491-5, 499-526, **71,** 601-2, 607-8, 614-21, 629-30, 633-49, 654, 659-62, 667-9, 690-1, 694-7, **72,** 225, 241, 483-9, 496-8, 719-20, 727-32, **78,** 639-40, 665, **86,** 243-9
due functioning of Tribunal **68,** 521
exceeded **78,** 642
exclusion, acts of popular movements **82,** 154, 213
exclusion of claims. *See* Iran–US Claims Settlement Declaration, claims, exclusion
exclusive, whether **71,** 637-8, 641-9, **72,** 128-9, 134, 138, 289-90, 487-8, **75,** 157-8, 160
expropriation/nationalization **84,** 652, 666
expulsion of alien, as expropriation **82,** 189, 211

forum selection clause, effect **68,** 561-5, 567-72, 575-6, 580-7, 591-4, 596-7, 600-1, 603-5, 609-10, 611-45, **70,** 493-4, **71,** 636, 648, 669
Full Tribunal
'important issue' **75,** 654-5
interpretation of Claims Settlement Declaration **75,** 179-268
interest, award of **86,** 309-13
Iran, claims against **69,** 583, 592
Iran–US Treaty of Amity (1955), application **75,** 602, 615, 628-30, 651-74
lex specialis, whether **75,** 602, 614, 628, 651-2, 674
Iranian courts, exclusive jurisdiction **70,** 487, 493-4, **71,** 636-49, 669
Iranian nationals, over **84,** 616
law of seat of Tribunal and **75,** 165-8
Majlis' position **70,** 485, 487-8, 491-4, **78,** 646-51, 655
merits distinguished **78,** 639-41
National Iranian Oil Company, claims against **69,** 569-70, 583, 592
unjust enrichment **69,** 570, 583
nationality of claimant. *See* corporation, nationality
nationalization. *See* expropriation/nationalization *above*
nullified oil agreements **78,** 639-57. *See also* Iran, Islamic Republic, law of, Single Article Act 1908
obligation to arbitrate, relevance **83,** 515
'other measures affecting property rights' **84,** 653, 666, **122,** 337
outstanding claims before US courts
discrepancy **85,** 378-9
suspension **72,** 134, 276-7, 388, 482, **75,** 157-8, 197
termination **72,** 134, 276-7, **75,** 154-5, 185, 196, 199, 215
preliminary objections, suspension of proceedings **78,** 639-41
presumption of absence **78,** 655-6
procedure for determining **86,** 243-9
'property rights', tort affecting **82,** 188-90, 212
restrictive interpretation **68,** 562, **78,** 655, **85,** 436
self-determination **68,** 621 n. 26
tort **82,** 154-5, 188-9
legal personality, international law, under **94,** 324, 327
membership **68,** 516-18, 520-1
municipal courts and
conflict with decision of, effect on foreign relations **79,** 588
multiple litigation, risk of **84,** 493-4
nationality of claimants. *See* corporation, nationality
nature **72,** 532, **75,** 184, 186, 205-6, 220-4
Netherlands Government and, responsibility for acts of **107,** 4
parties' rights **78,** 641-4
pleadings
amendment **69,** 603, 605-6, 610-13
errors in **69,** 608
powers
limits **75,** 260-1, 266-7
Tribunal Rules **71,** 642-3
precedent **68,** 614
inconsistent awards of municipal courts **71,** 640-1
international case-law **85,** 400
previous awards as **72,** 496, 732, 734
Presidential Order No 1 **68,** 647-8, **86,** 313

Iran–US Claims Tribunal (*cont.*)
Para. 6(a) **69,** 609
Presidential Order No 10 **78,** 671
privileges and immunities
agreement, in absence of **94,** 327
date of commencement **107,** 2
European Convention on State Immunity (and Protocol) (Basle) (1972), non-applicability **94,** 325
functional **94,** 324
Iran/Netherlands/US Agreement (1981) **94,** 324, 327
retroactive effect **94,** 324
procedure
absence of parties **68,** 648-51
amendment of claims, admissibility **75,** 129, 147-8, 165
awards on agreed terms **68,** 530-3, 652-4
class actions. *See* representative claims, admissibility *below*
delays **78,** 675
'exaggerated formalism' **69,** 607, 613
formalism, avoidance of **84,** 652
'important issue', raising of its own motion **75,** 654-5, **78,** 640
irregularities **69,** 620-1, 624-7, 629-32, 635-41, 658-9, 663
composition of Tribunal **69,** 635-41
deliberations **69,** 620-1, 640, 658-9, 663
evidence, regarding **69,** 624, 627
jurisdiction, merits **78,** 639-40
late filing **85,** 379, 417-18
law governing **75,** 156
Memorial filed after hearing **68,** 646-51
municipal courts, proceedings before, stay, power to request **71,** 635-49
Procedural Guideline No 1 **68,** 647
prompt decision, right to **71,** 686-7, **78,** 675
related cases **85,** 560 n. 1
reopening of hearings **71,** 685
representative claims, admissibility **72,** 732-4
right to be heard **78,** 642, 643-4
time-limits, extension of **68,** 646-51
proceedings, status of
Dutch law **75,** 156-7, 165-8
English law **75,** 168-73
international law **75,** 168-73
Iranian law **75,** 160, 168
United States law **75,** 157-8, 168
proper claimant **86,** 243-7
individual member of consortium **86,** 244-5
proper forum, whether **85,** 379, 417-18
proper parties **83,** 516-17
proper respondent **85,** 379, 425-6, 562
purpose **72,** 134, 488, 501
quorum **68,** 521
Rules **78,** 672, 673
Art. 15, Note 51 **71,** 636
Art. 19 **70,** 495, **75,** 652
Art. 20 **69,** 603, 606, 610-12, **75,** 129, 149

Art. 24(1) **71,** 679, 684, **75,** 137
Art. 24(3) **72,** 732
Art. 25(6) **71,** 686
Art. 26(1) **71,** 642-3, 647
Art. 29 **71,** 665, 685
Art. 31
Note 2 **69,** 628, 633-4, 658
Note 41 **69,** 634-5, 685, **71,** 627
Art. 31(1) **69,** 636
Art. 32(1) **71,** 665
Art. 32(2) **75,** 181
Para. 1 **69,** 650
Para. 4 **69,** 658, 660, 663
Art. 34(1) **72,** 226, 233, 235
Art. 38 **69,** 656, 660, **72,** 252, **75,** 626
Art. 40 **69,** 656, 660, **71,** 602, **72,** 252, **75,** 626
Introduction, Art. 3 **69,** 635
UNCITRAL Rules and **69,** 660, **70,** 520, **71,** 642, **75,** 155-6, 194, 197
Rules of Procedure
19 **85,** 379
25 **85,** 552 n. 22
26 **85,** 558, 564, 565 n. 37
27 **85,** 394, 488-9, 566
30 **84,** 652
31 **85,** 395
32 **84,** 591
34 **83,** 493, 632
36 **84,** 662
38 **84,** 588
40 **84,** 588, **85,** 622
41 **85,** 394
sampling methodology **109,** 69
seat **75,** 156, 165
Security Account **83,** 482, 490, 634, **84,** 589, 590, 661
settlement of claims **68,** 530-3, **75,** 652-4
agreement between parties **72,** 225-6
sovereignty and **78,** 640, 650 n. 2, 654-5
standing **83,** 514-15
State immunity, jurisdiction **81,** 567, 575, 576, **84,** 666 n. 2
State submissions **75,** 182-7, 206-7
US Enabling Act **75,** 228, 264
US nationals, claims by, through foreign subsidiary companies **69,** 603, 605-13, 616-17
Iran–US Escrow Agreement. *See* Iran–US Banking Agreements
Iran–US General Declaration. *See also* Iran–US Claims Tribunal, Algiers Accords; Iran–US Claims Settlement Agreement
Art. II(1) **83,** 517
Art. IV **86,** 309
Art. V **83,** 533, **86,** 255-6, 309, 311
Art. VII **85,** 368, 377-8, 417, 422, 423, 428, 435, **86,** 244, 249
Art. VII(2) **83,** 465, 540
continuity of claim **84,** 491-2
description **96,** 6

Iran–US General Declaration (*cont.*)
enforcement of judgments **81,** 575
estoppel **85,** 436
General Principle B **68,** 620-1, 636-7, **69,** 610, **78,** 652-5, 657
interpretation **68,** 535-7, 544-7, 550-8. *See also* treaty interpretation
by Claims Tribunal **71,** 637-40, 643, 661, 673
'Iran' **84,** 597-9, 650
Iranian assets, transfer provisions **68,** 526-8
nationality of claimant **84,** 490, 494
objectives **68,** 620, 635-6
Para. 6 **68,** 548
Para. 7 **68,** 535, 543-8, 550, 654, **85,** 604
object and purpose **68,** 545-6, 555
Para. 11 **68,** 632
Para. 17 **68,** 521, 535
phrases
'such claims' **85,** 378-9
'whether or not filed with any court' **85,** 378-9
Principle B **84,** 493, 495, 666 n. 2
security funds **68,** 526-7. *See also* Iran–US Security Account
transfer of assets **68,** 526-7
State immunity under **81,** 567, 575, 576
treaty status **68,** 545
Undertakings **68,** 527
Iran–US Security Account 68, 527-58, **69,** 619, 623, 626, 631, 656
banking fees **68,** 529, 537-41, 543
indemnification of Depository Bank **68,** 529, 541-2
interest **68,** 529, 534-7, 542-58
ownership claims **68,** 534-7, 552-4, 556, 558
Iran–US Treaty of Amity (1955) 68, 640, **86,** 256
as applicable law **84,** 510-11, 524, 552, 557 n. 14
breach **83,** 533, 536
customary international law and **84,** 510-11, 524, 532, 535-6, 666
dual nationals **72,** 483, **75,** 183, 186
entry into force **72,** 230-1, 250-1, **75,** 199
fundamental change of circumstances and **83,** 533, 536-7
individuals' rights under **63,** 456
'interest in property' **83,** 540-1, **84,** 557 n. 14
interpretation **75,** 628-9, 671-4
Iran–US Claims Tribunal, application by **75,** 602, 615, 628-30, 651-74
Iranian nationalization programme, applicability to **75,** 599, 628
nationalization under **83,** 539-41
as part of municipal law **84,** 665
partial suspension **83,** 536
'property' **83,** 539-42
self-executing **63,** 456
termination **84,** 663-5
travaux préparatoires **63,** 434, **83,** 557 n. 14, **84,** 533-4, 557 n. 14
validity **75,** 653-71, **83,** 533, 534-8, **84,** 524, 530-1, **86,** 256
violations. *See* breach *above*
waiver of State immunity, whether **63,** 270-3, 280-2, 347, 430, 433-4, 454-5, 456-7, 502-4, 506-7, 510, 514-19, **72,** 123, 127, 178, 189, **81,** 554, 556, **101,** 551-2

Iranian Oil Consortium (1954) 46, 374-5
Iraq
aliens, access to courts **106,** 292-3
Constitution
Art. 18 (ownership of real property) **109,** 391 n. 328
Art. 58 (Presidential powers) **116,** 554
Continental Shelf Declaration (1958) **41,** 136
damages, for, usurpation of property in absence of damage **125,** 690-1
Egyptian workers' right to transfer of dollar portion of wages
date of obligation **117,** 241-6
delays over transfer **117,** 243-6
entitlement to recover funds excluded from UN Compensation Commission's jurisdiction **117,** 246, 252
international agreements **117,** 240
long-standing practice **117,** 240
measures to clear backlog **117,** 243
trade embargo/assets freeze and **117,** 250-2
Kuwait and. *See* Iraq–Kuwait boundary; Iraq–Kuwait Boundary Commission (UN); Kuwait, Iraqi invasion (1990)
law of
Civil Code
applicability to public corporation **116,** 554
Arts. 192-201 **116,** 547-56, **125,** 690
Arts. 211-17 **116,** 550-6
Art. 215(2) **116,** 554-5
Constitution. *See* Constitution *above*
Discipline of Public Servants Law, applicability to public corporation **116,** 554
Labour Code **109,** 384-8
Art. 12 **109,** 384
Art. 32 **109,** 384
Arts. 36-7 **109,** 384
Arts. 41-3 **109,** 384
Art. 67 **109,** 387
Art. 68 **109,** 387
Art. 72 **109,** 387
Art. 73 **109,** 387
Law 57 of 16 September 1990
EC liability to compensate for damage suffered **109,** 374-95. *See also* European Community (EC), liability in connection with Iraq Law No 57 of 16 September 1990
freezing of assets **117,** 367
jurisdiction of Kuwaiti courts **106,** 281, 292, **109,** 365
retroactive effect **117,** 367
petroleum exports
immunity from attachment or other legal action **109,** 581
monitoring **109,** 581-2
payment due to UN Escrow Account **109,** 581
pricing **109,** 581-2
property
interference with **116,** 547-56
burden of proof **116,** 553
real property, foreign nationals and **109,** 391 n. 328

Iraq (*cont.*)
sanctions against. *See* sanctions, Iraq
State responsibility, banks' foreign exchange operations **117,** 240-1
Iraq–Kuwait boundary. *See also* Iraq–Kuwait Boundary Commission (UN)
Anglo-Ottoman Convention (1913) **94,** 11
demarcation, noticeboard **94,** 11
Exchange of Letters (Prime Minister of Iraq/Ruler of Kuwait) (1932) **94,** 11
Exchange of Letters (Ruler of Kuwait/British Political Agent Kuwait/British High Commissioner Iraq) (1923) **94,** 11
history **94,** 11-13
maps **94,** 11-12, 13-16
unreliability **94,** 21-2
Iraq–Kuwait Boundary Commission (UN). *See also* Iraq–Kuwait boundary
composition **94,** 6, 8-9
demarcation principles **94,** 13
mapping, need for new **94,** 13-14
organization of work **94,** 10
participation **94,** 9
Iraq **94,** 9
rules of procedure **94,** 8-9
Security Council Resolutions
687 (1991) **94,** 3-9
773 (1992) **94,** 6, 10, 28
833 (1993) **94,** 41
task, demarcation
maintenance **94,** 40
physical **94,** 40
terms of reference **94,** 7-8
Ireland, Republic of
act of State, absence of doctrine **96,** 220
Aer Lingus, State agency, whether **92,** 456 n. 2, 457
Aer Linte, State agency, whether **92,** 457
applicable law, general principles of international law **95,** 471, 472, 473, 479
armed rebellion, political offence, relevance to **79,** 149-50
British Crown, rights and obligations, implicit devolution **78,** 438
burden of proof
delay, justification **79,** 167
deprivation of constitutional rights **79,** 142
political offence **79,** 53, 59, 92, 116, 117, 132-3
standards of justice, failure to meet **79,** 82, 85, 164, 166
citizenship
domicile requirement **45,** 336
entitlement **87,** 337
Constitution 1937 **53,** 10-13, 15
Preamble **79,** 162
Art. 2 **79,** 147, 162, **87,** 345, 349, 352
Art. 3 **79,** 147, 162, **87,** 349, 350, 352
Art. 6 **79,** 147, 156, 157, 160, 161, **93,** 491, 510
Art. 6.1 **79,** 140, 162
Art. 6.2 **79,** 140
Art. 15.4.1 **79,** 67
Art. 15.6 **79,** 120, 122, 156

Art. 26 **79,** 149, 160
Art. 26(2) **93,** 511
Art. 28(2) **87,** 347, 354, **93,** 505-6
Art. 28.3.3 **79,** 97, 149
Art. 29 **53,** 552-3, **87,** 353
Art. 29(3) **95,** 471, 479, **104,** 703, **123,** 80
Art. 29(4) **87,** 347, 354, **93,** 484, 486-8, 490, 501-2, 505
Art. 29(5) **87,** 355, **93,** 497-8, 499, 509
Art. 29(6) **93,** 490, 497-8
Art. 29.1 **79,** 162
Art. 29.2 **79,** 162
Art. 29.3 **79,** 87
Art. 39 **79,** 120, 122, 156
Art. 40 **79,** 64, 71, 72, 73, 76, 77, 137-8
Art. 40.1 **79,** 68, 150
Art. 40.3 **79,** 86
Art. 40.4.2 **79,** 71
Art. 41 **88,** 318, **89,** 161-2
breach of rights, 'matter relating to tort' **103,** 325
interpretation **70,** 107, 112-13
laws repugnant to **70,** 104, **79,** 67-8
legislation, assumption of compatibility with **87,** 348
burden of proof **87,** 348, **93,** 487
political Cooperation with other States and **93,** 493-5
Third Amendment (EEC Accession) **93,** 486
amendments to EC treaties within scope of Community objectives **93,** 484-7, 489
courts, municipal, standing
common good **87,** 346, 356-7
common informer **89,** 250-1, 252
infringement of individual rights, need for **93,** 511, 512-13
treaties and **87,** 347
violation of the Constitution **87,** 345-6, **93,** 485-6
criminal law **55,** 251
disclosure of documents
extraterritorial **103,** 320, 321
State immunity, jurisdiction and **103,** 319-21
divorce **58,** 630, 645-6, **89,** 161-3
foreign divorce, recognition **89,** 162-3, 176-7
reform **89,** 166-7
EC Council of Ministers, primacy **93,** 489
ECJ judgments, primacy **93,** 488
EEC Regulation 990/93 (Yugoslav embargo: implementation of Security Council Resolution 820 (1993)), applicability to aircraft leased from Yugoslav Airlines (JAT) **117,** 280-4
emergence **59,** 346-7
employment contract, locally engaged staff, diplomatic mission, State immunity, jurisdiction, commercial purposes of mission **95,** 473
European Convention on Human Rights (1950) and **89,** 252
as part of municipal law **89,** 252
European Union (EU), constitutional amendment, need for **93,** 495
evidence

Ireland, Republic of (*cont.*)
admissibility **79,** 77-8
affidavit **79,** 78
disclosure of documents. *See* disclosure of documents *above*
foreign official, right to call **103,** 316-17
evidence of, conditions in Northern Ireland **79,** 77-9
executive discretion, limitations
Anglo-Irish Agreement (1985) **87,** 354
Single European Act **87,** 354
extraditable offence, political offence **55,** 559, 563-7, 572, 576-7, **79,** 52-3, 58-69, 92-5, 96, 100-9, 113-23, 130-3, 146-63
extradition
delay **79,** 62, 69-73, 126-8
discrimination **79,** 127-8
double criminality **55,** 518-21, 533-8, 539, 540-2
exposure to danger and **79,** 82-3, 86
fairness **79,** 88-9
good faith **79,** 89, 99-100, 108
military law, offence under **79,** 96
minimum standards of justice **79,** 79-82, 85-6
political offence, absence of statutory provision **79,** 105
prima facie case **79,** 99-100, 161
procedure **55,** 530-1
backing of warrants **79,** 81, 83-5
defects in **79,** 69-73
proof of crime **55,** 533, 541
proportionality **79,** 126, 128
reciprocity **79,** 88-9, 108
revenue offence **79,** 96
speciality **79,** 95
UK, to **55,** 520, 525-7, 531-2, 537, 539, 560, **79,** 52-167
arrest warrant, validity **70,** 380-3, **79,** 69-73
Extradition Act 1965 **53,** 9-13, 14-15, 541, **55,** 515-17
purpose **55,** 520, 526-7
s 3 **79,** 70, 92
s 11 **79,** 96
s 11(2) **79,** 87
constitutionality **79,** 75-7, 81-2, 84, 85-9
s 42(2) **79,** 152
s 43 **79,** 51, 72, 145
s 44(2) **79,** 152
s 45 **79,** 70
s 45(1) **79,** 76
s 47 **79,** 52, 56, 78
s 48 **79,** 51
s 50 **79,** 51, 56, 57-8, 62-3, 76, 91, 92, 95, 96, 100, 107, 110, 113, 116, 117-18, 120, 121, 130, 139, 146, 150, 152
s 11 compared **79,** 96
s 50(1) **79,** 111
s 50(2) **79,** 51-3, 58, 60, 68, 69, 73, 93, 100, 107, 111, 117, 118, 130, 146, 150, 152-67
s 54 **79,** 54, 70
s 54(1) **79,** 144

s 55 **79,** 70-2
s 55(i) **70,** 380-3, **79,** 145
Sections 41-55 **79,** 51, 62, 64, 70, 75-7, 81-2, 84, 85-9, 96, 108, 113
Extradition, European Convention on (1957) **55,** 560
ratification **79,** 121
extraterritorial offences, counselling and procuring **79,** 94
fisheries jurisdiction **59,** 352-3
foreign relations **87,** 346-7, **93,** 492-4, 496-500, 501-2
consultation with foreign power, admissibility **93,** 502-3, 506-8
non-binding arrangement **93,** 500, 507, 508
treaty obligation **93,** 506-8
curtailment of sovereign powers, admissibility **93,** 502-3, 506-8
judicial review **87,** 348, **93,** 492-4, 497-8, 505-6, **96,** 220
responsibility for, courts **87,** 346-7
Gaeltarra Eireann **63,** 613-14, 619-21
general principles of international law, as part of municipal law **95,** 471, 479
homosexuality **89,** 248-64
illegitimate child
status, Legal Status of Children Born out of Wedlock, European Convention on (1975) **89,** 180
succession **89,** 218-19
Industrial Development Authority of Ireland **63,** 613-14, 617-19
international disputes, pacific settlement **87,** 353
international law
European Convention on the Suppression of Terrorism, incompatibility with **79,** 105
municipal law and **79,** 87
conflict **53,** 11-13, 15-16
Ireland as a whole
claim to **87,** 350-2
political nature **87,** 350-1
right to legislate for **87,** 350-1
judicial review, foreign relations **93,** 492-4, 497-8, 505-6, **96,** 220
judicial separation **58,** 631, 637
jurisdiction
criminal, extradition **79,** 88
enforceability, of judgment, relevance **95,** 476
extraterritorial **79,** 85, 88-9
nationals, acts committed abroad **70,** 103-16
residents, acts committed abroad **70,** 110-16
legislative **59,** 354
Northern Ireland, offences committed in **70,** 103-16
Justice of the Peace, Universal Declaration of Human Rights **53,** 552-3
law of
Constitution. *See* Constitution 1937 *above*
Constitution (Consequential Provisions) Act 1937 **89,** 249-50
Criminal Justice (Administration) Act 1924 **89,** 249
Criminal Law Amendment Act 1885 **89,** 248-53
Criminal Law (Jurisdiction) Act 1976 **70,** 103-9
s 2 **79,** 95
s 3 **79,** 95
s 20(4)(b) **79,** 95
Schedule **79,** 97

Ireland, Republic of (*cont.*)
Criminal Procedure Act 1967 **89,** 250-1
European Communities (Prohibition of Trade with the Federal Republic of Yugoslavia) (Serbia and Montenegro) Regulations 1993 **117,** 276-7
Extradition Act 1965. *See* Extradition Act 1965 *above*
Foyle Area (Control of Netting) Regulations 1966 **70,** 110-16
Foyle Fisheries Act 1952 **70,** 110-16
Gaeltacht Industries Act 1957 **86,** 78, 80
Government of Ireland Act 1920 **59,** 346-7, 360-1, **79,** 524
Industrial Development Authority Act 1950 **86,** 78, 80
Offences Against the Person Act 1861 **89,** 248-53
Offences Against the State Act 1939 **79,** 82
Penal Servitude Act 1891 **89,** 249
sovereignty, surrender of **87,** 354, 356
Status of Children Bill 1986 **88,** 219-20, **89,** 171, 180
Succession Act 1965 **88,** 218
Universal Declaration of Human Rights, whether part of **53,** 552-3
legal aid **58,** 630-1
legal training, need for **79,** 145-6
legislation
competence **59,** 354
extraterritorial effect **70,** 103-16
presumption of validity **79,** 85
territorial limits. *See* extraterritorial effect *above*
legislation, interpretation **79,** 161-3
guidelines, teleological approach **117,** 282-3
legislation, interpretation aids, legislative history **79,** 97
legislation, interpretation guidelines
compatibility with Constitution **87,** 348
Constitution, conformity with **79,** 120, 157, 161
'may' to mean 'shall' **79,** 97
ordinary meaning **79,** 146, 161
reciprocity with UK legislation, whether required **79,** 92
strict, extraterritorial **103,** 320
legislative power, delegation **70,** 113-14
Leictron Teoranta **63,** 613-14
marriage. *See also* divorce *above*
divorce **58,** 630, 645-6
judicial separation **58,** 631, 637
nullity **58,** 630
unmarried couples, legal status **89,** 163-4
nation
rights of **87,** 350
State distinguished **87,** 349-50, 353
national emergency **79,** 97, 148-9
penal servitude
constitutionality **79,** 108
Universal Declaration of Human Rights and **53,** 552-3
political offence
burden of proof **79,** 53, 59, 94-5, 116, 117
classification as
escape from prison **79,** 59, 61-2, 63-5, 73, 163
murder **79,** 92-5

treason **79,** 150
violence, relevance **79,** 150-2
as common law offence **79,** 100
definition/requirements **79,** 52, 58-9, 61, 62, 92, 101-7, 114-17, 120-3, 131-2, 146-63
government policy, attempt to change by violent means **79,** 150-2
'pure'/'relative' **79,** 97, 100, 121, 163
extraditable offence **55,** 559, 563-7, 572, 576-7, **79,** 52-3, 58-69, 92-5, 96, 100-9, 113-23, 130-3, 146-63
extradition and, possibility of prosecution for **79,** 93-5, 99-100, 133
incidence test
escape from detention **79,** 107, 122, 123, 133
'political incidence' test/*Castioni* **79,** 92, 99-100, 102
relevant factors **79,** 107, 115, 116, 163
armed rebellion **79,** 149-50
reunification
constitutional imperative **79,** 147
means of achieving **79,** 147-8
Rules of the Superior Courts
Order 11 **103,** 326
Order 12, Rule 26 **103,** 323
Order 31, Rule 29 **103,** 319-21
Order 39 **79,** 78
Order 40 **79,** 72
separation of powers **79,** 147, **87,** 437, **93,** 491-5, 510-13
Single European Act (1986)
Constitution, compatibility with **87,** 347, **93,** 485-513
Cooperation of Member States within WEU/NATO framework **93,** 501
preservation of neutral status and **93,** 509
EC court of first instance **93,** 488
European Union as aim **93,** 491, 500, 504-5, 507, 508
foreign policy provisions (s. III)
amendment of EC Treaty, whether **93,** 509
constitutional amendment, need for **93,** 485-513
formalization of European Political Cooperation (EPC) practices and procedures **93,** 508-9
political union **93,** 490
separate status **93,** 495
sovereignty, surrender **93,** 500, 505, 506-8, 509
fundamental rights and **93,** 489
'necessitated by the obligation of membership of the Communities', whether **93,** 486, 490, 499
original aims and objectives of EC and **93,** 488-9
qualified majority voting **93,** 488
ratification, challenge **93,** 485-6, 511, 512-13
courts' role **93,** 491-5, 509-13
derogation, absence of provision for **93,** 506-7
timing **93,** 484, 485-6, 498, 499, 510
referendum, need for **87,** 357, **93,** 503
treaty nature **93,** 503
sovereignty, surrender
Anglo-Irish Agreement (1985) **87,** 356
Single European Act (1986) **87,** 356, **93,** 500, 505
State agency/State-owned corporation/State entity, responsibility for **86,** 78-80

Ireland, Republic of (*cont.*)
State immunity, jurisdiction, applicability
constitutional rights, infringement, general principle of international law **103,** 316-17
disclosure of documents **103,** 319-21
waiver **103,** 321
Employment Appeals Tribunal **95,** 473, 481-2
State immunity, jurisdiction, classification of act
driving embassy car **95,** 469-82
police officer not directly controlled by government **103,** 323-5
service contract, commercial purpose of mission **95,** 473
tort
shooting by British soldier in Republic **103,** 312-15, **121,** 201-2, **123,** 76-93
State practice **103,** 315, 316
State immunity, jurisdiction, theory/doctrine
absolute theory **95,** 477-8, 481
basis
comity **95,** 476
par in parem non habet jurisdictionem **95,** 476
reciprocity **103,** 315, 316, **121,** 202
teachings of publicists **95,** 476
general principle of international law **95,** 471, 472, 473, 479, **123,** 80, 82-3
restricted **95,** 472-3, 479-80
State property, alienation **70,** 114-15
territorial sea, control of **59,** 347-8
treason, as political offence **79,** 150
treaties **53,** 552-3
compatibility with Constitution, assumption of **87,** 349
conclusion
constitutional constraints **93,** 492, 497-8, 502, 506
good faith **93,** 499
power of **93,** 492-4, 496-500
form
communiqué **87,** 347
head of government agreement **87,** 346
incorporation into municipal law **93,** 498
judicial review **87,** 347-8
obligations, constitutional invalidity, effect **93,** 499-500
ratification, need for **93,** 499-500
charge upon public funds **93,** 498, 499, 511-12
referendum, need for **93,** 503
registration **87,** 347
Sunningdale Agreement, whether **93,** 498-9
treaty interpretation
guidelines
general principles of international law **87,** 348
international law determining factor **87,** 348, 353
Vienna Convention on the Law of Treaties (1969) **87,** 348
USA and, Treaty of Friendship and Commerce (1950) **42,** 196
Islamic law 62, 605
arbitration **62,** 178
contract **62,** 189-92
sanctity of **53,** 461-2, **62,** 190-3
custom **62,** 174

divorce under, recognition **74,** 531-56
equity **41,** 144, 209, **62,** 175
estoppel **41,** 130
Hanafi School **62,** 175
historic rights **41,** 125 n. 1
interest **62,** 215, **86,** 310
international law and **62,** 175, 191, **64,** 625-32, 650, **114,** 42, **119,** 448
lucrum cessans **62,** 202
Maliki School **62,** 174-5, 185, 202
natural law **64,** 629-31
property **62,** 184-5
limitations **62,** 184
as residuary source of law **64,** 625-32
restitution and **53,** 495-7, **62,** 198
retroactivity **62,** 171
sources **62,** 174-6, 193, **64,** 628-9
sovereignty **114,** 42, 45, **119,** 448
Sunni School **62,** 174
treaties **62,** 193
pacta sunt servanda **64,** 631
islands 41, 110, 216, **62,** 114-15, 125-6, **67,** 55-7, 81-2, 84, 86-7, 92, 143, 256-9, 263-4, 293-8, **71,** 97, 111, 113-14, 149, 155, 163-4, 214, **77,** 679, **81,** 273, 282, 411, 443, 459, 460
Abu Musa. *See* Abu Musa
arising *de novo* **43,** 109-10
artificial, State territory, whether **80,** 686-7
average distance curve and **83,** 107
baselines **59,** 300, **67,** 256-9, 264, 293-8, **81,** 393
as basepoints **81,** 280, 282-3, 295
Eritrea–Yemen **119,** 455-6
bays, at entrance to, territorial sea delimitation and **69,** 35-6, 43-5, 53-4, 62, 64-5, 68-9
Bijagos Archipelago **83,** 109, 110, 111
case-law **83,** 112-13
Channel Islands. *See* Channel Islands
coastal **83,** 110
coastal configuration and **83,** 109
coastal direction and **83,** 109, 112
coastal length and **83,** 109, 113
coastal projection and **81,** 308, 310-13, 350, 411
contiguous zone **62,** 125
continental shelf **67,** 293
continental shelf, entitlement **64,** 336, **91,** 673, 674-7, 774-7, **95,** 665-6, **99,** 437, 668
Anglo-French Arbitration **95,** 721
inherent **91,** 675-6
Law of the Sea Convention (1982) **91,** 673, **95,** 666, **99,** 468-9
Libya/Malta **95,** 722
political status, relevance **95,** 665-6, 702, 703-4, 720
relevant/special circumstances and **91,** 674-7
Territorial Sea and Contiguous Zone Convention (1958) **95,** 666
Darnley Island. *See* Australia, Darnley Island
definition **57,** 64, **69,** 81, 85, **99,** 667

islands (*cont.*)
platforms and man-made structures distinguished **100,** 507
dependent and independent distinguished **81,** 274, 374, 395, 414
EEZ **62,** 114, 125
entitlement, Law of the Sea Convention (1982) **99,** 468-9
Law of the Sea Convention (1982) **62,** 114
effect
equity **83,** 112, **99,** 551
half **71,** 164, **81,** 309, 371, 396-7, 399-401, **83,** 112, 113, 114, **99,** 440-1
partial **67,** 82, 92, 143-4, 296-8, **83,** 112, **99,** 638-9
quarter **83,** 113
variable **99,** 638-9
El Tigre. *See* Fonseca Bay, El Tigre
evidence of, territorial sea/EEZ claims **100,** 507
Filfla. *See* Filfla
fishing zones **62,** 115, **99,** 668
Fonseca Bay. *See* Fonseca Bay, islands
Gozo **81,** 283, 348, 349
Isle of Man. *See* Isle of Man
islets. *See* islets
Jan Mayen. *See* Jan Mayen
Jersey. *See* Jersey
Johnston Atoll, whether **100,** 507
Kerkennah. *See* Kerkennah Islands
Kermadec Islands. *See* New Zealand, Kermadec Islands
Law of the Sea Convention (1982) **62,** 114-15
leap-frogging **119,** 462-3
low-water elevations **69,** 81, **83,** 110-11, 112
mainland, as part of **59,** 287-8, 290-3, **69,** 43-5, 53, 62, 64-6, 68-9
natural barriers **69,** 45, 53, 55, 61-2, 65, 68
relevant factors **69,** 44
Malta. *See* Malta; Maltese Islands
maritime delimitation and **62,** 126, **67,** 55-7, 81-2, 84, 86-7, 92, 143, 256-9, 263-4, 293-8, **71,** 97, 111, 113-14, 149, 155, 163-4, 214, **81,** 273, 282, 411, 443, 459, 460, **83,** 95, 99, 109-13
Abu Musa **66,** 177, 330-8, **91,** 663-77
baselines and. *See* baselines *above*
coastal projection, radial **81,** 308, 310-13, 350, 411
continental shelf, entitlement **95,** 665, 684
dependent and independent, distinction **81,** 274, 395, 414
EEZ, entitlement **95,** 671, 684
enclave solution **62,** 126, **95,** 668, 686, 712
Red Sea Islands **119,** 455-6, 463
equality of States **95,** 665
equity, radial effect **99,** 551
half-effect **71,** 164, **81,** 309, 371, 396-7, 399-401, **91,** 677
Law of the Sea Convention (1982) **62,** 114-15
partial effect **67,** 82, 92, 143-4, 296-8
political status, relevance **95,** 665, 666
proportionality. *See* proportionality *below*
regional practice **91,** 677
as special circumstance **41,** 216, **91,** 665, **95,** 702-3, **97,** 675, **99,** 491, 558, 667-71

State practice **91,** 665, **99,** 638-9
Meanguera/Meanguerita. *See* Fonseca Bay, Meanguera/Meanguerita
as minor geographical features **81,** 282, 368-9
Minquiers and Ecréhos. *See* Minquiers and Ecréhos
Nantucket **81,** 400
natural prolongation and **99,** 546-7
Okinawa Islands. *See* Okinawa Islands
Palmas **41,** 126
Penguin Island. *See* Cape Colony, Penguin Island
portico doctrine. *See* title, appurtenance *below*
proportionality **81,** 395-7
between islands **99,** 452-3, 659-60
Eritrea/Yemen **119,** 454-5
islands and mainland coast **99,** 548-50
Rann of Kutch **50,** 177-92
Red Sea Islands. *See* Red Sea Islands
as relevant circumstance **41,** 110, 216
Rio Grande Banks **83,** 110, 111
rivers, in. *See* rivers, boundary
rocks
Jan Mayen, whether **99,** 667
entitlement to maritime jurisdiction **99,** 667
Law of the Sea Convention (1982) **99,** 637, 667
status, habitability as basis **99,** 637
Ryukyu Islands. *See* Ryukyu Islands
St Pierre and Miquelon. *See* St Pierre and Miquelon
Scilly Isles. *See* Scilly Isles
Seal Island. *See* Seal Island
seasonal habitation **114,** 92-3
sovereignty over **59,** 343
median line principle **50,** 35-41, 178, 180-2, 189, 194-5, 208-13, **114,** 114, 131-2, **119,** 443-6, 453-65
shore, proximity **50,** 178, 180-2, 184-5, 189, 192, 208-13, 512, 516
special circumstance **97,** 675, **99,** 491, 558, 667-8
Jan Mayen, whether **99,** 432-3
State practice **83,** 112
straits, in **62,** 126
territorial sea **57,** 64, 74-5, **62,** 114, 125, **69,** 81
breadth **91,** 674, **119,** 463
chain of islands **119,** 463
channels between islands, whether **42,** 101
enclave principle **62,** 126, **119,** 462-3
entitlement **91,** 673-4, **119,** 462-4
effect on equidistance line **91,** 674
Law of the Sea Convention (1982) **62,** 114, **119,** 463
median line **119,** 463
overlapping **119,** 462-4
Territorial Sea Convention (1958) **69,** 81
title
appurtenance **114,** 48, 119, 124, 125
proximity and **41,** 126
territorial sea, within **114,** 123-4
unity **114,** 119-20

islands (*cont.*)
Uncohomo **83,** 110, 111, 112
Ushant. *See* Ushant
Isle of Man
corporal punishment **58,** 344-6, 348, 352
European Convention on Human Rights (1950) and **58,** 343, 355-8
international relations and **58,** 347
local requirements in **58,** 355-8
relationship with UK **58,** 347, **86,** 159
status **86,** 159
as territory of UK **58,** 346-7
treaty-making power **86,** 159
islets 67, 55-7, 81-2, 293-8, **71,** 156, 163-4, **83,** 110, **119,** 459-61
as relevant/special circumstance **41,** 49, 178, 194, 227, **67,** 55-7, 81-2, 293-8
Israel
aliens, right to appoint foreign counsel **47,** 251
civil proceedings, Hague Conventions, parties to **48,** 485, 492
courts, municipal
evidence **83,** 170
classified **83,** 180-1
jurisdiction, court's duty to examine *proprio motu* **36,** 20
witnesses, right to call **83,** 182
Criminal Code Ordinance
conspiracy **36,** 230-2
jurisdiction provisions **36,** 21
customary international law, municipal law and **83,** 149, 150-1, 153-4, **119,** 227
Declaration of the Establishment of State **36,** 52-3
displacement of people, as breach of human rights **125,** 547-8
Egypt
boundary. *See* Egypt–Israel Arbitral Tribunal (Taba); Egypt–Israel boundary
Peace Treaty (1979). *See* Egypt–Israel Peace Treaty (1979)
extradition **51,** 331-9
Extradition, European Convention on (1957) **87,** 166
nationals, of **87,** 162-3, 166
United States, from **79,** 538-47
extraterritorial legislation, war crimes **36,** 57-8
foreign law, anti-Jewish, repeal **47,** 203-4
freedom from discrimination **87,** 162
general principles of international law **36,** 25
Geneva Conventions (1949), interpretation, changed circumstances **125,** 566
Hague Regulations (1907), applicability in **83,** 194
international law **52,** 69, **83,** 150. *See also* customary international law *and* general principles of international law *above*; treaties *below*
primacy, municipal law **36,** 24-5, 280-1
Jerusalem. *See* Jerusalem, East
Jewish law, application to Jews outside Israel **47,** 213-14
jurisdiction
crimes against humanity, protective principle **36,** 49-50, 52, 57
extraterritorial
crimes against humanity **36,** 20-40, **79,** 544-6
crimes against the Jewish people **36,** 20-40, **79,** 544-6
war crimes **36,** 20-40, **79,** 544-6

protective principle, crimes against humanity **36,** 49-50, 52, 57
religious courts **48,** 93-106
universal **36,** 20-40, **79,** 545-6, **120,** 367-71, 395-7
law of
Administration and Law Order (No. 1) 1967 **48,** 64, 67, 94
Advocates Law 1961 **47,** 204, 252, 254-62
Air Navigation (Security in Civil Aviation) Law 5737-1977 **83,** 154
Antiquities Ordinance (West Bank Region) 1967 **48,** 63-8
Basic Law: the Judiciary 1984, s 15 **83,** 181
Crime of Genocide (Prevention and Punishment) Law 5710-1950 **83,** 154
Defence (Emergency) Regulations 1945 **48,** 486, 492
Geneva Convention (Protection of Civilian Persons in Time of War) (1949) , compatibility with **83,** 126-8, 136-8, 147, 185-97
Regulation 85 **83,** 175
Regulation 108 **83,** 169, 170, 174, 187
Regulation 111 **83,** 182-3
Regulation 112 **83,** 166, 170, 171, 181, 183, 194
Regulation 114 **83,** 182-3
Regulation 122 **83,** 182-3
Designation of Areas Order 1967 **48,** 67, 94
Evidence Law (New Version) 5731-1971 **83,** 170, 179-80
Extradition Law 5714-1954 **83,** 194, **87,** 162, 163, 166
evidence required **44,** 246, 272
extraditable offences **44,** 246-8
legal background **44,** 273
Genocide, Law for Prevention and Punishment of, 1950 **36,** 39
Immunity and Rights (International Organizations and Special Missions) Law 5743-1983 **83,** 154
International Organizations (Status) Law 5740-1980 **83,** 154
Interpretation Order (Judea and Samaria Region) (No 130) 5727-1967 **83,** 183-4
Interpretation Ordinance 1945 **44,** 210-14, 217, 221-2
Law and Administration Ordinance 1948 **44,** 198, 202, 207, 209-13, 218-20, 227, 231, 249, 255, 263, 270
Law and Administration, Proclamation No 2, 1967 **47,** 473, **48,** 487, 488, 490, 492
Legal Assistance to Foreign States Law 5716-1956 **44,** 258-9, 268
Legal Capacity and Guardianship Law 5722-1962 **47,** 206, 207, 210
Nazi and Nazi Collaborators (Punishment) Law 1950 **36,** 20-1, 22, 25, 30, 58, 78-9, 179, 184, 273
crime against humanity **36,** 239-52, 274-6, 288
crime against the Jewish people **36,** 20-40, 227-39, 273-4
international law, conformity with **36,** 23-32, 287-9, 315-16
scope *ratione personae* **36,** 279
superior orders defence **36,** 255-6, 314-15, 323
war crimes **36,** 275
Offences Committed Abroad (Amendment of Enactments) Law 5738-1978 **87,** 163
Penal Code 5737-1977 **87,** 160
Penal Code (Offences Committed Abroad) (Consolidated Version) 5733-1973 **87,** 163
Principles of Criminal Liability Order **48,** 481

Israel (*cont.*)
Prohibition of Acts of Incitement and Hostile Propaganda Order **83,** 175
Sale (International Sale of Goods) Law 5731-1971 **83,** 154
Security Provisions Order 1967 **47,** 485, 488, 496-7, **48,** 478-85, 487, 488, 492
Succession Law 1965 **48,** 94, 95, 98, 99-101, 103, 104
Transition Law 1949 **44,** 198, 220, 227-8, 249, 255, 263, 270, 282, 288
United Nations Privileges and Immunities Ordinance 1947 **44,** 213
legislation, interpretation **47,** 480
aids
context **83,** 130
legislative history **83,** 131
structure of legislation **83,** 131
guidelines
purpose **83,** 129-30
text **83,** 129
judicial discretion **83,** 129
presumption of conformity with international law **36,** 24-5, 280-1, **52,** 79-82
legislation, retroactive
crimes against humanity **36,** 20-40, 55
territorial limitation **36,** 279
military commanders, Supreme Court's jurisdiction respecting orders of **47,** 495
military courts, rules of evidence **48,** 486-93
nationality, acquisition **48,** 162
non-recognition, notarial acts, effect on **40,** 40-2
occupied territory. *See* Israel, occupied territory
Palestine, continuity of law of **44,** 218, 226-7
religious education, law concerning **47,** 205-11
state succession **78,** 108
Switzerland, Extradition Convention (1958), whether in force **44,** 197-290
treaties
individuals and **83,** 152, 186
law-making treaties **83,** 149
legislation, need for **83,** 149-63
ratification, law on **44,** 197-290
self-executing **83,** 156
treaty-making power **83,** 156
position under Mandate **44,** 256, 270
UK practice, relevance **83,** 160
treaty interpretation
aids, context **83,** 146, 184
guidelines
general principles of international law **83,** 146 n. 1
liberal **83,** 184, 191
object and purpose **83,** 146, 184
selectiveness in applying principles **83,** 147
unilateral act of government, binding nature **83,** 195-6
United States, extradition from **79,** 538-47
Treaty (1962) **48,** 188-90, **51,** 340-60, **79,** 441-58, 470, 541-5, 547
West Bank, occupation
courts **52,** 526-9
right of audience **42,** 484-7
local law, respect for **52,** 515-16
Yom Kippur War **63,** 166

Israel, occupied territory. *See also* law of, Law and Administration Ordinance 1967 *above*; Jerusalem, East
applicable law
fundamental principles of administrative law **125,** 547
Geneva Conventions (1949) **83,** 149-63, 194-6
humanitarian provisions **83,** 195-6, **125,** 547
Geneva Convention (Protection of Civilian Persons in Time of War) (Convention IV) (1949) **48,** 482, 489, **125,** 548-60
customary international law **125,** 547
Geneva Convention on the Protection of Civilian Persons in Time of War (1949) **48,** 482, 489
human rights, derogation **125,** 548
international humanitarian law **125,** 546-8
local law, respect for **52,** 515-16
assignment of place of residence, legality **125,** 539-68
deportation distinguished **125,** 549-50
as deterrent **125,** 557, 562, 564, 566
discretionary power of military commander, 518-19
for imperative reasons of security (Geneva Convention IV) **125,** 552-60
proportionality **125,** 555-7
standard of proof **125,** 555
as preventive measure **125,** 554-5
'reasonable' test **125,** 559-60
Security Provisions (Judaea and Samaria) Order (No 378), 5730-1970 **125,** 542-3
'within the territory subject to belligerent occupation' **125,** 551-2
courts
Jerusalem **52,** 81-2
military **47,** 476-7, 484-9, 492-4, 496, 499
West Bank **52,** 526-9
deportation from **83,** 125-97
former emergency laws, continuance **47,** 476-84, 486-7
human rights
derogation
applicable law **125,** 548
balance of interests of State and individual **125,** 548, 566-8
Judea and Samaria **83,** 164
assigned place of residence, legality **125,** 539-68
Gaza as 'within the occupied territory' **125,** 551-2
orders assigning **125,** 543
validity of Defence (Emergency) Regulations 1945 **83,** 127
law relating to
Defence (Emergency) Regulations 1945 **83,** 127
Security Provisions (Gaza Strip) (Amendment No 87) Order (No 1155), 5762-2002 **125,** 542-3
Security Provisions (Judaea and Samaria) Order (No 378), 5730-1970 **125,** 541-3
'imperative security reasons' requirement **125,** 542-3, 558
Security Provisions (Judaea and Samaria) (Amendment No 84) Order (No 510), 5762-2002 **125,** 542-68
West Bank and Gaza Strip as single territorial unit **125,** 551-2
Israel–Palestine Interim Agreement **125,** 551-2
Israel/Jordan relationship, state of war **42,** 475, **48,** 485

Israeli Commission of Enquiry into events at Shatilla and Sabra refugee camps, responsibility of commander **122,** 111
Italian Somaliland, Administration of, Italy and 40, 37-40
Italian–Latin American Institute (IILA). *See* Italy, Italian–Latin American Institute (IILA)
Italian–US Conciliation Commission
death of claimant **40,** 120
decisions
binding force **45,** 500-1
request for clarification **45,** 500-1
jurisdiction **40,** 151
inter-governmental disputes **40,** 257
issues of domestic law **40,** 133, 447-8
Italy
act of State **78,** 93
relevant factors, public interest/good **65,** 281-2
State immunity, jurisdiction and **65,** 281-2
admissibility **78,** 96-8, 121-3
affiliation, law of **71,** 570
AGIP, USA, State immunity and **63,** 18-21
Albania, union with **40,** 29-32, 35
aliens, status, in accordance with international law **78,** 98
ambassador/head of mission, status, State organ **65,** 269-70, 307
Anti-Comintern Pact (1936), accession to **44,** 335
appeal, right of **78,** 59-62
arbitration, jurisdiction clause, validity **71,** 588-9
Armistice 1943
Allied Military Command, powers **40,** 469-70
occupying powers, powers **40,** 468-9
Berlin–Rome Axis (1936) **44,** 335
citizenship
African territories **40,** 196-7
Law No 555 **71,** 448, 570, 572
loss of **71,** 570-3
civil proceedings
Court's duty to ensure prompt hearing **96,** 460
parties' responsibility for advancing **96,** 460
remedial action **96,** 601
request for ruling on jurisdiction as evidence of existence of action **87,** 17
commercial/trade representation/mission, State immunity, jurisdiction **65,** 283
common purpose **124,** 157 n. 286
foreseeability **124,** 157 n. 286
compensation claims, nationality of, Royal Decree **77,** 566
compensation for war-related events, private property, loss or damage to, United Nations nationals, entitlement **77,** 563-6
Constitution 1947
compatibility with prior laws **78,** 98
Constitutional Court's competence to determine **78,** 98
equal rights **40,** 198
phrases, 'right of victim of a crime to see the offender punished' **101,** 369
s 1(2) **78,** 104
s 2 (inviolable human rights) **78,** 102, 103, **87,** 61, **101,** 369
s 3 **87,** 32, 35
s 3(1) **78,** 99, 102, 103

s 7 **78,** 122
s 10 (incorporation of international law) **65,** 168, 266, 268, 274, 278, 282, 292, 309, 314, 322, 326, 340, **71,** 233-5, 536-7, 590, **77,** 557, 573, 581, 600, **78,** 96, 98, **87,** 5, 6, 34, 35, 45, 54, 61-2, **101,** 308, 365, 378, 402, 405
s 10(1) **65,** 305, **78,** 92, 103, 111, 121
s 10(2) **78,** 102, 103
s 11 (treaty-implementing legislation) **78,** 102, **93,** 30, 430-7, 517, **101,** 365-9
EC aims and objectives, relevance **93,** 517, 518-21, 525
s 24 (judicial protection) **93,** 543, 547, **101,** 369, 403-4
s 24(1) **78,** 102, 103
s 25 **77,** 558
s 26 (extradition: death penalty) **106,** 307
s 26(2) **78,** 98
s 27 (right to life) **106,** 308, 309
s 27(4) **78,** 99
s 34 **77,** 564
s 34(1) **78,** 102
s 36 **77,** 619
s 65 **71,** 371
s 80 **71,** 592-3
s 87 **71,** 592-3, **78,** 104
s 102 **87,** 61
s 113 **96,** 215
Title VI **78,** 104
Constitutional Court, fundamental rights, protection of **93,** 342-7
consular agent
functions
administration of international hospital **101,** 371-5
applicable law, municipal law of receiving State **101,** 372
bilateral agreement **101,** 373
commercial relations **114,** 564-5
lease of consular premises **101,** 382
purchase of goods for consulate **101,** 382
consular immunity, jurisdiction, functional, interference with functions as test **101,** 384
consular privileges and immunities **71,** 579-83, **77,** 582-4, 593-8, 610-12
basis, sovereign nature of consular activity **101,** 372-3, 375
entitlement, national of receiving State **101,** 382-5
functional, customary international law **101,** 372, 382, 383
official acts, employment contract **77,** 595-7
Vienna Convention on Consular Relations (1963), bilateral agreement, precedence **101,** 373
continental shelf delimitation **70,** 593-6, 611, 638, 651-2, 665, 684, 687
contract
fiduciary **40,** 141-2
formation, place of **87,** 13, 16, 18
simulated **40,** 131-2, 133-5, 139-40
corporation, single shareholder **40,** 142-3
courts, municipal
Constitutional Court, competence **78,** 59, 98
publication of judgments **73,** 488-9, 491-2
criminal procedure
contumacia **81,** 80-1, 88
late appeal **81,** 81

Italy (*cont.*)
latitante **81,** 80-1
nullity **81,** 81
criminal proceedings **71,** 371-9, 382-8, 398-401, 404-8
appeal, right of. *See* appeal, right of *above*
common trial **78,** 59, 61
defence, inadequacy **78,** 220-3
delays in **71,** 385-401, 404-8
transfer to another court **71,** 371-6, 386-7, 398-9, 407
trial *in absentia* **78,** 515
customary international law **65,** 302-3, 317, 321-2, 326, 335, 339-43, **74,** 167-8, **78,** 92, 103-4, 121
evidence of, need for **87,** 31
municipal law and **71,** 536-7, 590-1, **78,** 92, 103-4, 121, **101,** 403
change of municipal law as consequence of change in customary law **101,** 403, 405
constitutional provisions. *See* Constitution 1947, s 10 (incorporation of international law) *above*
defection to Western allies (1943) **44,** 337
diplomatic agent, status, executive certificate **101,** 378
diplomatic immunity, jurisdiction
civil jurisdiction **78,** 102-4
judicial remedy, denial of right to **78,** 103
real/immovable property, dispute relating to
lease, whether **101,** 378-9
recovery of rent **78,** 102-4
State immunity and **87,** 5
State immunity, distinction **65,** 307
diplomatic mission, status, organ of sending State **65,** 269-70
diplomatic premises, inviolability
forcible eviction **101,** 361
residence of member of mission, eviction order **101,** 361
diplomatic privileges and immunities
Constitution, compatibility with **78,** 102-4
fundamental institution of international law **78,** 104
private acts **71,** 536-9, **78,** 103
public acts attributable to State **78,** 103
purpose **78,** 103
right of suit, consent of sending State, need for **65,** 269-70
standard of treatment of alien, equality **78,** 103
State, beneficiary, whether **87,** 5
diplomatic protection, as preferred method **65,** 278-9
discriminatory and racial legislation **40,** 130, 197, 198
EC
fundamental rights within the EC/EU
national courts, role **93,** 536
protection **93,** 517, 524-5
jurisdiction, independent competencies **93,** 532-5
law. *See* EC law *below*
EC law **53,** 556-9, 562-5
applicable law, EC legal system **93,** 534, 536
conflict with national law
continued validity of national law **93,** 534-5

implied repeal **93,** 526, 531, 534
interpretation avoiding **93,** 526-7
referendum **93,** 553
unconstitutional, need for finding of **93,** 530-7
ECJ judgment and **93,** 537
implementation, national measures, admissibility **93,** 526, 533-5
judicial review **93,** 522-3, 524. *See also* national courts, role *below*
ordinary courts **93,** 536
limitation *ratione materiae* **93,** 523
national courts, role **93,** 49-50. *See also* judicial review *above*
implementation **93,** 237
national measures implementing, admissibility, judicial review **93,** 526
obligations, referendum, right to and **93,** 549-52
part of law of, whether **53,** 556-9, 562-5
primacy **93,** 333, 355
presumption of consistency **93,** 531
previous legislation **93,** 531
referendum **93,** 551-2, 553
subsequent legislation **93,** 531-5
right to invoke before national courts **93,** 522
scrutiny
EC Council of Ministers **93,** 523
ECJ **93,** 524-5
European Parliament **93,** 523
national parliaments **93,** 523
status
foreign law, whether **93,** 522
independent **93,** 520, 524, 533-4
international law, whether **93,** 522
part of national law, whether **93,** 516, 522, 533-4
EC law, direct effect **93,** 55, 520, 522-3
requirements, no need for further intervention **93,** 522
ECSC Treaty (1951), constitutional amendment, need for **93,** 521-2
EEC Treaty (Rome) (1957)
constitutional amendment, need for **93,** 521
as EEC Constitution **93,** 523
employment contract, academic appointment in respondent State
State immunity, jurisdiction
non-State school **65,** 305-8
State school **87,** 53-6
employment contract, locally engaged staff, commercial/trade representation/mission
classification of employment
act of appointment, relevance **65,** 313-15
non-official nature **65,** 283
private law nature of relationship **65,** 283, 315, 342
State immunity, jurisdiction **65,** 282, 313-15
employment contract, locally engaged staff, consulate
classification of employment
administrative and technical **65,** 342
commercial secretary **101,** 376
employee performing tasks essential to proper functioning of consulate **101,** 376
consular immunity, jurisdiction
restrictive immunity **101,** 384

Italy (*cont.*)
voluntary retirement of employee, relevance **101,** 384-5
State immunity, jurisdiction, nature of functions of employee as test **65,** 345-6
employment contract, locally engaged staff, cultural institute, State immunity, jurisdiction, archivist/secretary **65,** 325-8, **114,** 538-9
employment contract, locally engaged staff, diplomatic mission
classification of employment, managerial role **65,** 329-30
State immunity, jurisdiction **87,** 43-7, **116,** 630
applicable law clause, relevance **114,** 528
dismissal **114,** 531, 557-8
driver/interpreter **114,** 533
financial aspects **114,** 530-1, 533, 535-6, 566
nationality of employee, relevance **114,** 533
permanent clerical duties and **87,** 46-7
secretary and technical officer **114,** 531
sovereign functions of embassy and **87,** 43, 45, 46-7
telephonist **114,** 557-8
employment contract, locally engaged staff, information office/news agency
private law nature of relationship **65,** 284
State immunity, jurisdiction
challenge to grading **114,** 524
financial aspects **114,** 522-4
public service responsibilities of employee, relevance **65,** 284-7, **113,** 458-9, 492
employment contract, locally engaged staff, public broadcasting network, State immunity, jurisdiction, forum selection clause as waiver **87,** 40-1
employment contract, locally engaged staff, Sovereign Order of Malta
State immunity, jurisdiction **65,** 309-12
in relation to administrative staff **65,** 312
espropriazione **84,** 374, 376
European Convention on State Immunity (and Protocol) (Basle) (1972) **87,** 27
expert, evidence **78,** 515
export tax, artistic work, EEC Treaty and **47,** 14-21
expropriation/nationalization
as act of State **65,** 290
legality, determination of, court's competence to enquire into **65,** 302
rights and obligations
assumption **65,** 289-90, 295-303
extinction of **65,** 301
extradition **78,** 95-101
administrative nature of decisions relating to **78,** 95-6
agreement, need for **106,** 309
appeal, admissibility **106,** 309
death penalty
European Convention on Extradition **78,** 96, 97, 100
offences punishable by **78,** 95-101
restrictions on extradition **78,** 95-101
legislative act required **78,** 96
nationals **100,** 661-2
political crimes **78,** 98
requirements, constitution, compatibility **106,** 308-9
speciality **78,** 104
extradition agreement
implementation, draft treaty **78,** 97-8

State succession and **78,** 107-11
India **78,** 107-11
reactivation **78,** 107-8
extradition in case of death penalty **106,** 306-9, 311-15
assurances that death penalty will not be carried out, need for **106,** 307-9, 313-15. *See also* responsibility for determining acceptability of assurances *below*
responsibility for determining acceptability of assurances **106,** 307-9, 314
extradition treaties
France (1870) **78,** 95-7
constitutionality **78,** 99, 101
implementation
administrative matter **78,** 95-6
legislative act required **78,** 96
India
applicability of UK–Italy agreement **78,** 107-11
existence of **78,** 107
extraterritoriality, FAO Headquarters **101,** 392-3
fair trial, defence, right to, inviolable **101,** 369
fiscal immunity **65,** 321-4
Food and Agriculture Organization, immunity **71,** 240-1
foreign divorce, recognition of **40,** 29-35
foreign judgment, recognition/enforcement **78,** 106-11
requirements **78,** 106
treaty, limitation **71,** 48-9
foreign law, recognition/enforcement, confiscatory legislation **77,** 547-9
foreign relations, judicial review **96,** 214
forum selection clause, as waiver of immunity **65,** 333
freedom of expression, flag desecration and **122,** 598-9
FRG, agreements on compensation for persecutees (1961) **44,** 322-3
fundamental rights within the EC/EU
Art. 177 (EEC Treaty) proceedings as protection **93,** 542, 543-5
EC and **93,** 542-7
general legal principle, national variations **93,** 543
inalienable **93,** 536
judicial protection **93,** 542-7
Art. 174 declaration of invalidity and **93,** 544-7
legal hearing **93,** 542
unconstitutionality, finding of, retroactivity **93,** 50, 54-5, 58
Geneva Conventions on the Law of the Sea (1958), implementation **71,** 259-61
Germany
declaration of war against (1943) **40,** 67, 71, 72
invasion by, export of monetary gold **44,** 457
good faith, State immunity, jurisdiction, basis for **65,** 341-3
Hague Regulations (1907), as municipal law **40,** 430, 431
headquarters agreement, privileges and immunities **101,** 360
historical heritage, protection of **82,** 26-7
Holy See and. *See* Holy See, Italy and
human rights
legal proceedings, right to institute
foreign court as option **101,** 393
immunity, execution/attachment and **101,** 369, 404-5
immunity, jurisdiction and **101,** 369
restrictions

Italy (*cont.*)
foreign policy interest **101,** 404
public interest **101,** 404
interim measures, State immunity **101,** 401
International Centre for Advanced Mediterranean Agronomic Studies. *See* International Centre for Advanced Mediterranean Agronomic Studies
International Covenant on Political and Civil Rights (1966)
reservation **78,** 57-8, 59, 60-2
implementing laws covered by **78,** 61
international law **40,** 61, 88, 90, 91
customary international law. *See* customary law *above*
interpretation **74,** 177, 182-3, **78,** 99-100
municipal courts **77,** 586
legislation, conformity with **71,** 233, **77,** 557, 581, 600
municipal law and **78,** 104, **87,** 5, 6, 26, 35, 62
general principles of international law **78,** 96, 103-4
incorporation doctrine **77,** 553-5, 563-6
treaty codifying customary international law **78,** 96, 103-4
obligations, to be respected **77,** 596
sources, municipal legislation **101,** 401, 402
violation of Constitution excluded **78,** 105
international officials, employment contract, immunity, jurisdiction
Institute Manager **114,** 541-51
permanent integration into organization's organic structure **65,** 337
international officials, judicial protection, right to **101,** 393-4
international officials, jurisdiction, tenancy agreement **101,** 360
international officials, privileges and immunities
diplomatic agent, equivalence **101,** 360
functional basis **101,** 360
international organizations
diplomatic mission compared **87,** 5, 23
personality, test
existence of administrative tribunal **87,** 24
independence of Member States **87,** 23
international personality **87,** 24
ratification of HQ Agreement, relevance **87,** 26
sovereign powers **87,** 23
territory **87,** 23
tenancy agreement
arbitration clause, validity **101,** 361-3
rent increase, enforceability **101,** 362
international organizations, immunity, execution/attachment **78,** 115-16
international organizations, immunity, execution/attachment, theory/doctrine, 'jurisdiction' distinguished **78,** 114-16
international organizations, immunity, jurisdiction **78,** 114
capacity to sue and be sued distinguished **101,** 389-90
waiver
choice of forum clause **114,** 545-6
choice of law clause **114,** 543, 545-6
tenancy agreement **101,** 362-3
international organizations, privileges and immunities **77,** 573-7, 602-9
absolute immunity **87,** 32

acta jure imperii **87,** 6
alternative remedy, need for **114,** 553-4
applicable law **87,** 6
customary international law **114,** 547-8
law relating to States **114,** 544
NATO Status of Forces Agreement (1951) **114,** 548
reservation to treaty establishing **114,** 550-1
treaty reservation **114,** 550-1, 553
basis
international personality **87,** 26
par in parem non habet jurisdictionem **65,** 309, **87,** 7, 24
classification of act
employment contract **77,** 573, 575-7
interpretation **77,** 608-9
organization and administration **71,** 241, **77,** 575-6, **87,** 6-10
commercial activities **87,** 6
customary international law **77,** 574, **114,** 551
diplomatic mission compared **87,** 5, 23
employment contract
national of receiving State **114,** 547-8
permanent integration into organization's organic structure **114,** 551
State immunity distinguished **114,** 551
termination **114,** 552
functional **101,** 360
commercial activities, relevance **114,** 549
headquarters agreement and **101,** 388
headquarters and assets, whether distinguishable from organization **101,** 389-93
Member States' Constitutions as limiting factor **87,** 5
nature of transaction **87,** 6-7
organizational and administrative act, acquisition of premises **87,** 4
personality **87,** 6
applicable law **87,** 3
sovereign powers **87,** 6
purpose **87,** 6
representatives accredited to **71,** 567-9, 571-2
seat of organization, relevance **87,** 24
State immunity, basis **78,** 88, 90, 114-15
treaty provision, relevance **87,** 25
intervention proceedings. *See also* International Court of Justice (ICJ), intervention of third State
request for permission to intervene **70,** 535, 554, 557, 675
effect **70,** 554, 575
sources
custom **78,** 103
decisions of municipal courts **78,** 103
doctrine **78,** 103
State practice **78,** 103
teachings of publicists **78,** 108
Italian Social Republic, legislation **40,** 128-9, 150, 157
Italian–Latin American Institute (IILA)
international organization, whether **87,** 22-8
personality **87,** 22-3

Italy (*cont.*)
privileges and immunities **87,** 22-8
test **87,** 23, 25-6
sovereignty **87,** 22-3
jurisdiction
aliens, legal person **65,** 265-6
civil obligations of non-nationals **87,** 12-13, 16, 18
applicable law **87,** 13
compétence de la compétence, waiver **105,** 461
competence to determine **78,** 91
concurrent **77,** 557-8, 563-6, **78,** 119
criminal **71,** 567-9, 571, 579-83, **78,** 117-19
evidence obtained abroad **71,** 222-6
ne bis in idem **71,** 232-5
international organization, structure **78,** 115
municipal courts
Conciliation Commission, effect **77,** 566
subsumption by international courts **77,** 566
nexus
injury in the forum State **65,** 269
loan payable in forum State **65,** 266
State immunity, precedence **78,** 91
personal **77,** 586, 589
protective principle **77,** 590-1
requirements, extradition agreement **78,** 106
ships
Convention for the Unification of Certain Rules relating to Penal Jurisdiction in Matters of Collision or Other Incidents of Navigation (1952) **78,** 119
foreign, in territorial sea **78,** 118
foreign, outside territorial sea **77,** 589-92
foreign territory, whether **78,** 117-18
Geneva Convention on the Territorial Sea and Contiguous Zone (1958) **78,** 118
national **77,** 589
shipwreck **78,** 117-19
territorial **77,** 586, 589
treaty, limitation by **65,** 48-9
visiting forces **77,** 600-1, 617-20
waiver, by individual in employment contract with foreign government **65,** 285
law of
Bankruptcy Act 1942
Art. 5 **84,** 364
Arts. 160 ff **84,** 336
Civil Code
Art. 25 **65,** 281
Art. 826(2) **82,** 26
Art. 840 **77,** 548
Art. 1176 **87,** 13, 18
Art. 1180 **101,** 405
Art. 1398 **87,** 12
Art. 1705 **87,** 12
Art. 1782 **87,** 18
Art. 1834 **87,** 18
Art. 2043 **84,** 352-3

Art. 2350 **84,** 391
Art. 2351 **84,** 391
Art. 2446 **84,** 330, 335
Art. 2447 **84,** 335
Art. 2450 **84,** 335, 359
Art. 2909 **87,** 23
possession and title, *bona fide* third parties **44,** 458
Civil Code Preliminary Provisions
Art. 22 **101,** 379
Art. 27 **71,** 224-5
Art. 31 **71,** 570
Civil Procedure Code **73,** 488, 491
Art. 2 **65,** 285, **71,** 595, **87,** 10
Art. 4 **65,** 265-6, 269, 276, 281, 305-6, 319, 332, **77,** 586, **78,** 91, 93, **87,** 2, 12-14, 16, 18-19
Arts. 4-5 **87,** 23
Arts. 34-6 **121,** 335
Art. 37 **71,** 536
Art. 41 **65,** 344, 347, **87,** 17
Art. 48(2) **65,** 347
Art. 55 **71,** 380-1, 403
Art. 74 **71,** 380-1, 403
Art. 99 **96,** 460
Art. 100 **77,** 617
Art. 102 **77,** 617
Art. 115 **96,** 460
Art. 175 **96,** 460
Art. 329 **87,** 23
Art. 360 **77,** 617, **87,** 23, 24
Art. 367 **65,** 344-7
Art. 409 **77,** 618
Art. 482 **77,** 584
Art. 553 **78,** 115
Art. 700 **65,** 345
Art. 796 **77,** 615
Art. 943 **77,** 586
Art. 980 **77,** 550
Art. 1777 **77,** 546, 586
Constitution 1947. *See* Constitution 1947 *above*
Constitutional Court Law, Art. 28 **96,** 215
Criminal Code 1978 **72,** 622
Art. 2 **77,** 559, **79,** 248
Art. 3 **77,** 557, 559, 589, **79,** 248, **87,** 52
Art. 4 **77,** 589, 590
Art. 6 **77,** 557, **78,** 96
Art. 7(2) **78,** 107
Art. 7(5) **78,** 118-19
Art. 8 **78,** 118
Art. 9 **78,** 117-18, **87,** 49
Art. 10 **87,** 49
Art. 10(2) **78,** 100
Art. 11 **71,** 233-5, **77,** 581
Art. 12(1) **78,** 107

Italy (*cont.*)
Art. 12(2) **78,** 107
Art. 13 **78,** 96
Art. 81 **71,** 398-9
Art. 88 **78,** 198, 205
Art. 110 **87,** 49, **124,** 157 n. 286
Art. 116 **124,** 157 n. 286
Art. 157 **71,** 374
Art. 160 **71,** 374
Art. 202 **78,** 201
Art. 204 **78,** 201, 204
Art. 206 **78,** 198, 202
Art. 207 **78,** 199, 201-2
Art. 208 **78,** 200, 205
Art. 222 **78,** 198, 201, 203
Art. 254 **87,** 49
Art. 328 **71,** 380-1, 403
Art. 368 **71,** 398-9, 409-10
Art. 519 **121,** 270 n. 208
in contumacia **78,** 515-16, 519
Criminal Code (Rocco) 1931 **78,** 515
Criminal Procedure Code 1913
Art. 427 **78,** 218
Art. 635 **78,** 96, 199, 201
Art. 640 **78,** 200, 202
Art. 641 **78,** 202
Art. 652 **78,** 107
Art. 662 **78,** 99
Art. 674(1) Nos 2 and 4 **78,** 106
Criminal Procedure Code
Art. 13 **106,** 308
Art. 45 **71,** 375
Art. 48 **71,** 399, 406
Art. 49 **78,** 59, 61
Art. 55 **71,** 374
Art. 56 **71,** 374-5
Art. 60 **71,** 398-9
Art. 65 **71,** 401
Art. 152 **71,** 376
Art. 157 **71,** 376
Art. 166 **71,** 375-6
Art. 169 **81,** 79
Art. 170 **81,** 77
Art. 171 **81,** 79
Art. 173 **81,** 80, 88
Art. 185 **81,** 81
Art. 201 **81,** 78-9
Art. 245 **87,** 49
Art. 268 **81,** 80, 88
Art. 269 **71,** 381
Art. 298 **71,** 381
Art. 389 **71,** 372, 399
Art. 413 **71,** 375

Art. 439 **71,** 373
Art. 485 **78,** 198
Arts. 497-501 **78,** 515, **81,** 80, 88
Art. 499 **81,** 80
Art. 524 **87,** 42
Art. 531 **87,** 52
Art. 606 **106,** 312
Art. 663 **106,** 306
Art. 666 **106,** 307
Art. 668 **106,** 307, 309
Art. 698 **106,** 312
Art. 3014 **87,** 49
prompt hearing and **96,** 601
Extraordinary Tax Decrees 1947 **40,** 437, 439-40
Law 2248 of 20 March 1865 **84,** 338
Law 379 of 11 August 1897 (Italy–San Marino Extradition Convention) **78,** 95
Law of 27 May 1919 **87,** 52
Law 1263 of 15 July 1926 (execution measures against foreign State) **65,** 167, 271-3, 293, **87,** 31, 34, 61, 64-8, **101,** 400, 402-3
Law of 3 March 1934 (bankruptcy) **84,** 344-5, 351
Law of 28 May 1936 (State immunity, execution/attachment) **65,** 294
Law 23 of 4 January 1938 (Sovereign Order of Malta) **77,** 622
Law 546 of 16 May 1947 (FAO Constitution) **87,** 3
Law of 15 June 1949 (Italy–USA FCN Treaty) **84,** 353
Law 465 of 1 August 1949 (Treaty of Washington) **77,** 632
Law 908 of 1 December 1949 (Peace Treaty) **77,** 565
Law 295 of 5 April 1950 (implementation of GATT) **77,** 552, 553, 554
Law 11 of 9 January 1951 (FAO Headquarters Agreement) **87,** 4, 5
Law 1740 of 24 July 1951 **77,** 573
Law 645 of 20 June 1952 **79,** 243, 247
Law 848 of 20 June 1952 (European Convention on Human Rights (1950)) **79,** 246
Law 1177 of 30 July 1952 (France–Italy Cultural Agreement (1949)) **87,** 55
Law of 11 March 1953 (Constitutional Court) **93,** 31
Law 244 of 25 March 1953 (ICEM Agreement) **77,** 573
Law 1335 of 30 November 1955 (NATO Status of Forces Agreement) **65,** 294, 318, **77,** 557-8, 568-70, 599-601, 617-18, 632
Law 1338 of 30 November 1955 (Paris Protocol) **77,** 632
Law 298 of 7 March 1957 (Italy–UK Consular Convention) **77,** 541, **101,** 373, 381
Law 1203 of 14 October 1957 (ratification of EEC Treaty), constitutional validity **93,** 516-26, 547
Law of 1 August 1960 (Italy–USA FCN Treaty) **84,** 355, 398
Law 1658 of 8 December 1961 (Territorial Sea and Contiguous Zone Convention) **78,** 118
Law 20 of 25 January 1962 **78,** 56, 59, 61
Law 932 of 13 July 1965 (Paris Agreement) (Bari Centre) **78,** 87, 113, **87,** 33
reservation to treaty, integral part **78,** 114
Law 794 of 4 October 1966 (Italian–Latin American Institute (IILA)) **87,** 22
Law 875 of 4 October 1966 (France–Italy Cultural Agreement (1949)) **87,** 55
Law 804 of 9 August 1967 (Vienna Convention on Diplomatic Relations (1961)) **77,** 594, **87,** 5, **101,** 371-5, 378
Art. 2, constitutionality **78,** 102-4
Law 482 of 2 April 1968 **79,** 251-2
Law 300 of 20 May 1970 (Workers' Charter) **65,** 339-43, **77,** 632, 634, **87,** 37

Italy (*cont.*)
Art. 28 **78,** 87
Law of 30 December 1970 (fees for veterinary and public health inspections)
compatibility with EC law **93,** 49
repeal **93,** 51-2
Law 112 of 12 February 1974 (Vienna Convention on the Law of Treaties) **77,** 631
Law 1307 of 7 November 1975 **77,** 553
Law 88 of 25 October 1977 (Penal Jurisdiction in Matters of Collision) **78,** 119
Law 638 of 11 November 1983 **79,** 251-3
Law 230 of 15 May 1993 (implementation of EC Regulation 990/93 (Yugoslavia: sanctions)) **117,** 310-11
confiscation of goods, acceptability **117,** 321, 333-6, 337
strict liability and **117,** 321
Navigation Code **78,** 119
Art. 2 **77,** 559, 589, 590
Art. 5 **77,** 560
Art. 8 **77,** 560
Art. 12 **77,** 590
Art. 1235 **77,** 560
Art. 1237 **77,** 560
Patent Act, Industrial Property Convention and **70,** 429-34
Presidential Decree No 3 of 10 January 1957 **77,** 596
Presidential Decree No 2083 of 18 September 1962 (Paris Agreement) **77,** 617, 631, 632
Presidential Decree No 120/67 (EEC Regulation 120/67), validity **93,** 529-37
Presidential Decree of 26 October 1983 **87,** 58
Provisions on the Law in General
Art. 22 **77,** 547, 549
Art. 25 **77,** 560
Art. 32 **77,** 547
Regional Basic Law of 13 May 1968 **84,** 362
Royal Decree 5726 of 30 June 1870 (France–Italy Extradition Treaty) **78,** 98
constitutionality **78,** 99, 101
Royal Decree 1295 of 25 March 1873 (UK–Italy Extradition Treaty) **78,** 107-8
Royal Decree 3181 of 13 December 1923 (Austria–Italy Extradition Treaty) **78,** 96
Royal Decree 1559 of 19 July 1924 (Italy–Czechoslovakia Extradition Treaty) **78,** 96
Royal Decree of 6 January 1928 (Brussels Convention (1926)) **65,** 293
Royal Decree 1611 of 1933 **87,** 58
Royal Decree 1938 (requisition) **77,** 566
Royal Decree of 6 March 1939 (Hague Convention, 1899), expropriation under **77,** 459
Statuto albertino, Art. 5 **78,** 96
Trade Code, de facto companies **40,** 122
legal aid **60,** 188-90
legislation, Government Report on Delegated Legislation **87,** 61
legislation, interpretation **78,** 99-100
aids, *travaux préparatoires* **77,** 555
ambiguity **77,** 555
guidelines, *lex posterior derogat priori* **77,** 554
phrases, 'foreigner' **65,** 265-6
presumptions, conformity with international law **71,** 233, **77,** 555
treaty-implementing legislation, interpretation **77,** 567-70
liberty of person, deprivation **78,** 195-212

detention of *mafiosi* on island **61,** 310-18
margin of appreciation **78,** 204
mentally ill person **78,** 195-212
mafiosi
regulation of **61,** 294-7, 310-18, 331-2, 334
lawfulness **61,** 310-20
Mandates System **37,** 546
medicine, right to practise **71,** 448-9
mines, law **40,** 266-7, 268
minors, status **71,** 570-2, 580
nationality
access to liberal professions and **71,** 448-9
acquisition, foreign wife **48,** 250
dual nationality **71,** 579-80
minors **71,** 570-2, 580
NATO officials/employees, State immunity, jurisdiction **65,** 317-20
occupation of, law governing **40,** 430, 433
Paris Agreement (International Centre for Advanced Mediterranean Studies), reservation **78,** 87, 88
parliamentary immunity, waiver **71,** 371, 385
Peace Treaty (1947)
'arrangement' in lieu of compensation **40,** 106, 107, 109
claims under
continuity of nationality **77,** 566
nationality of company **45,** 109-10
stateless person **77,** 566
'UN nationals who hold, directly or indirectly, ownership interests in corporations or associations which are not UN nationals' **45,** 109-10
compensation **45,** 500-2, **77,** 563-6
Conciliation Commissions **77,** 566
municipal courts and **77,** 566
procedure **44,** 459, 461-6
copyright claim **40,** 427-8
drafting **44,** 474-5, 484
entry into force (Netherlands) **44,** 452, 464, 469
equal rights provision **40,** 198
Free Territory of Trieste under **77,** 628
implementing legislation **77,** 563-6
individuals' rights under **77,** 563-6
Libya, provisions on **49,** 51
renunciation of rights **40,** 191, 193
local remedies and treaty claims **40,** 151, 153
'loss by reason of injury or damage' **40,** 146-7
loss in Italy **40,** 155-6
loss of profit **40,** 261, 264, 267, 273, 276, 281-2
nationality provisions **40,** 192-4
'owner' and 'successor' **40,** 450, 461
pillage, claims for **40,** 261, 264, 267, 269, 271, 281-2
'property', mining concession **40,** 261, 262, 266-7, 277-81
'property, rights and interests' **40,** 278-9
restitution provisions **40,** 255, 257, 441, 461, **44,** 448-85
limits of obligation **44,** 480
looted property and monetary gold **44,** 448-50, 477-9, 482-3

Italy (*cont.*)
monetary gold, good faith transactions **44,** 458
shareholders' claims **40,** 144-6
tax exemption provisions **40,** 149, 152, 154-7, 250-9, 436-63
time-limits **40,** 152
'treated as enemy' **40,** 117, 126-9, 149-52, 157
Trieste, provisions concerning **40,** 46-8
UK, Exchange of Notes on tax provisions **40,** 438
USA Memorandum (1957) **40,** 117, 126-9, 262, 276
waiver of claims **40,** 64, 69-73
war damage
assessment **40,** 147, 164-8, 262, 283
compensation for **40,** 103-11, 129, 457-8
Penal Code. *See* Criminal Code *above*
post-war legislation on abandoned property **40,** 431-2
privileges and immunities, Italian Knights of the Sovereign Order of Malta **77,** 612-13
Protocol on Participation in Monetary Gold Pool (1947) **44,** 476
public order/public policy/*ordre public* **77,** 586
public property, inalienability **40,** 433-4
public safety **79,** 248
Red Sea Islands. *See* Red Sea Islands, Italian jurisdiction
referendum
EC obligations and **93,** 549-52
as legislative act **93,** 552
Refugees, Geneva Convention on the Status of (1951) and Protocol (1967), reservations, refugees as result of events in Europe, limitation to **99,** 4, 15-16
Repubblica Sociale Italiana (RSI), status **111,** 414 n. 73
requisition **84,** 339, 354-8, 365-8, 398, 409-10
damages **84,** 409
right to control and manage, effect on **84,** 356, 368, 414
right to life **78,** 99
separation of powers **77,** 557-8, 586
legislative conflict with EC law and **93,** 49
sequestration laws **40,** 265, 271
ships, jurisdiction, flag State **78,** 117-19
social security contributions, nationals abroad **71,** 220-1
South Tyrol
Austrians in, treatment of **96,** 706
terrorism in **71,** 237-8, 243-7, 286-93
UNGA Resolutions **71,** 287-9, 291
sovereignty
limitation, treaty specifically to assure international peace and justice **78,** 102
limitations on, privileges and immunities of members of European Parliament **101,** 365-7
transfer of powers to international organization
constitutional limitations **93,** 517, 518-21, 525, **101,** 365-7
EEC Treaty (Rome) (1957) **93,** 517, 518-21
equality of States and **93,** 520
national legislative powers, effect on **93,** 531-2
reciprocity, need for **101,** 367-9
Trieste **40,** 43-50
standard of treatment of alien, equality **78,** 98, 99-100

State agency/State-owned corporation/State entity
applicable law
law of State of creation **65,** 300-1
lex fori **65,** 266-7
classification
agricultural cooperative **65,** 266-7
ambassador **65,** 307
commercial/trade representation/mission **65,** 314-15
cultural institute **40,** 60-3, **65,** 325-8
government department **65,** 307
government information office **65,** 284-5
national airline **87,** 65-8
nationalized undertaking **65,** 295-303
status, applicable law **114,** 564
State contract, private law nature of **65,** 267
State immunity, execution/attachment, entitlement
national airline **87,** 65-8
State corporation, public purpose, need for **87,** 66
State immunity, execution/attachment, procedural aspects
competence to determine **65,** 271-2
effective remedy, right to and, payment by forum State of debt **104,** 405
executive/ministerial authorization, need for **65,** 271-3, **87,** 34, 66-8
separation of powers and **87,** 58, 61
State immunity, execution/attachment, purpose of proceedings
enforcement of judgment **87,** 60
interim measures **101,** 401
State immunity, execution/attachment, purpose/use of funds/assets
aircraft used for commercial purpose **87,** 68
bank balances **87,** 60-2
burden of proof **87,** 36
cash **87,** 31
commercial activities **87,** 60, 62, 68
mixed **87,** 36
non-specific **87,** 61
private, protection dependent on reciprocity **101,** 402-5
public activities of embassy **87,** 62
purpose **87,** 60-2
sovereign **87,** 62, 66
staff salaries **87,** 36
State immunity, execution/attachment, theory/doctrine
absolute theory **87,** 66
effective reintroduction of doctrine **101,** 404
customary international law **87,** 62, 65
restrictive **101,** 401
human rights and **101,** 404-5
reciprocity, need for **65,** 271-3, 293, **87,** 34, 61, 67, **101,** 401-5
restrictive **87,** 34, 65-8
uncertainty as to limits **65,** 167-8, **87,** 59-60, 66, 67
State immunity, jurisdiction, acts of diplomatic agent **78,** 103
State immunity, jurisdiction, applicability, real/immovable property, dispute relating to **87,** 18
State immunity, jurisdiction, classification of act
academic appointment, non-State school **65,** 304-6

Italy (*cont.*)
commercial activities **87,** 13
private law relationship **87,** 13, 14, 17-18
consular premises, lease or purchase **65,** 274-5
cultural relations, promotion **65,** 327-8
customary international law and **65,** 294
diplomatic mission, driving embassy car **65,** 269
diplomatic premises, lease **65,** 332-3
expropriation/nationalization
as act of State and **65,** 290
contractual obligations assumed by State **65,** 295-303
financial undertaking **101,** 400-1
hospital operation **65,** 311, 324
legislative act **65,** 295-6, 299-303
nature or purpose of transaction as determining factor **40,** 76
equality of parties as test **40,** 75-6
nature of property right distinguished **65,** 311
occupying forces, supply of materials to **40,** 64-9
private law relationship **65,** 266-7
private person test **65,** 305-6, 332-3
public works contract **65,** 263-4
sale of goods **87,** 13
sale of property **87,** 13
social security provision in contract and **65,** 311-12
trade promotion **65,** 314-15, 345-6
traffic accident **65,** 268-70
State immunity, jurisdiction, entitlement
constituent States **87,** 39-41
government department **65,** 307
Holy See. *See* Holy See, immunity, jurisdiction
public broadcasting company **87,** 39-41
State agency/State-owned corporation/State entity **87,** 13
cultural institute **87,** 46, **114,** 538-9
government information agency **114,** 522-4
State immunity, jurisdiction, procedural aspects
applicable law **40,** 65-6
bilateral agreement **114,** 538
customary international law **40,** 66
international law **40,** 61
effective remedy before national authority and **114,** 566-7
preliminary issue, whether **40,** 62
State immunity, jurisdiction, theory/doctrine
absolute theory **87,** 32, 35
customary international law **87,** 54
acta jure imperii **87,** 35, 45
acta jure imperii/acta jure gestionis distinguished
difficulty **65,** 294
relevance **87,** 44, 54-5
basis
good faith **65,** 341-3
independence of States **87,** 35, 55
non-intervention in affairs of another State **114,** 528-31

par in parem non habet jurisdictionem **65,** 274, 281, 306, **78,** 92, **114,** 538, 557, 567
reciprocity **87,** 55
sovereignty **65,** 266
customary international law **78,** 92, **87,** 17, 54
absolute doctrine **87,** 54
confidentiality of action **114,** 523
restrictive doctrine **87,** 17
development of concept **65,** 281, 292-4, 339-40, **114,** 530
teachings of publicists **65,** 273-4
restrictive **78,** 92, **87,** 27
customary international law **87,** 54-5
restrictive theory, uncertainty regarding **87,** 32-3
State immunity, jurisdiction, waiver, implied
forum selection clause **65,** 333, **87,** 40-1
recognition of debt founding private law relationship **65,** 276-8
State succession. *See* treaties, State succession *below*
statehood, requirements/evidence of, territory **65,** 309
stateless person, New York Convention on the Status (1954), implementation **71,** 448-9
statelessness **40,** 192, 195
treaties
codifying customary international law, automatic incorporation of customary content **78,** 103-4
constitutional requirements **71,** 591-3
right to challenge **93,** 518
direct effect **77,** 554, 566
implementation, unratified treaty **78,** 97-8
implementing legislation **71,** 259-61, 448-9, 591-3, **77,** 553, 565, 566
constitutionality **78,** 98
court's duty to establish *proprio motu* **78,** 107
executive act **78,** 95-6
need for **77,** 553-4, 564, **78,** 96
subsequent legislation, effect **78,** 98-9
unratified treaty **78,** 97-8
incorporation into municipal law, implementing legislation, sufficiency **77,** 553, 564
individuals and **77,** 554, 564, **84,** 353
obligations, nature of **77,** 563-5
primacy **93,** 8
subsequent legislation **93,** 29, 30
ratification, binding nature of executive statement **78,** 97-8
ratification, relevance **71,** 592-3, **87,** 27, **101,** 383
reactivation **78,** 107-8
reciprocity **93,** 519
reservations **71,** 449, **78,** 100, 114-15
retroactive effect **71,** 588-9
customary international law as substitute **101,** 390
self-executing **84,** 353
simplified form **71,** 592-3
sovereignty, surrender. *See* sovereignty, surrender *above*
termination **71,** 595-6
unratified treaty, need for legislation **78,** 97-8
treaties, State succession **78,** 107-11
validity **78,** 107-11

Italy (*cont.*)
treaty interpretation
aids, subsequent practice **101,** 242, 390, 391
guidelines
purpose **101,** 390
restrictive **101,** 379
multilingual, discrepancy between texts **101,** 389-90
phrases
'capacity . . . to institute legal proceedings' **101,** 389-90
'real action relating to real immovable property' **101,** 378-9
Trieste, sovereignty over **40,** 43-50
war, Ethiopia, in, sanctions **44,** 335
war crimes, common purpose, post-WWII cases **124,** 150-4
war damage, succession taxes on payment for **40,** 447
Yugoslavia, Agreement delimiting Adriatic (1967) **41,** 122
Ivory Coast
Constitution, Art. 75 **96,** 376
extradition from **73,** 670
law of
Criminal Procedure Code **73,** 670
Extradition Law **73,** 670
nationals training as fishermen, commercial transaction, whether **63,** 9-11
treaties, applicability
declaration by colonial power, need for **96,** 378
'overseas territory' **96,** 379
treaties, State succession **96,** 376-9
conduct of parties **96,** 379
Constitution **96,** 376
notification by depository **96,** 379
notification of succession **96,** 377, 378, 379

Jamaica
aluminium
exploitation
production costs **56,** 300-5
State contract **56,** 262, 276-7
State contract, renegotiation **56,** 265
applicable law **72,** 204-8
arrest, powers of **72,** 202-9
bauxite mining
concessionary agreement **74,** 220-37
production levy **74,** 220-3, 227-37
taxes **56,** 280-1
Constitution 1962 **56,** 318, **72,** 68, 72, **73,** 47, **74,** 220-3, 228-32
Art. 17(1) (torture/inhuman or degrading treatment), delay in carrying out death sentence, whether **98,** 347-56
Art. 17(2) (torture/inhuman or degrading treatment), delay in carrying out death sentence, whether **98,** 347-56, **124,** 293
Art. 25 (fair trial) **98,** 332
Art. 25 (rights of individual) **98,** 332, 354
death penalty
delay in execution
breach of Constitution, whether **98,** 344-5, 347-56

Inter-American Commission on Human Rights, appeal to **98,** 355-6
UNHCR, appeal to **98,** 355-6
inhuman or degrading treatment, whether **98,** 350-6
appeals procedure, relevance **98,** 350-5
fault of complainant, relevance **98,** 350, 353-4
reference to Privy Council, duty of promptness **98,** 340-2, 343
death row as inhuman or degrading treatment **98,** 350, **118,** 257-8
English law, application of **72,** 204-8, **73,** 45-53, 275-6
extradition from **72,** 64-74, 201-9, **73,** 45-55
fair trial **118,** 251-61
independence, accession to, treaty obligations, effect on **72,** 64-74, **73,** 45-8, 53-4
inhuman or degrading treatment, death row. *See* death row as inhuman or degrading treatment *above*
jurisdiction
criminal **73,** 180-5, 275-95
personal **72,** 201-9
law of
Bauxite Act 1974 **56,** 267-8, 320-3, **74,** 220-37
Bauxite Industries Act 1967 **74,** 224-6
Constitution. *See* Constitution 1962 *above*
Dangerous Drugs Act **73,** 50, 52-3, 180, 183, 275-6, 284, 286-7
Extradition Law 1942 **72,** 68, 71-3, 203
Interpretation Act **72,** 205
Mining Act 1974 **74,** 220-3, 227
Territorial Sea Act 1971 **73,** 182-3, 275-6, 283-5, 289, 293-5
mining laws and regulations **56,** 263, 268-9
National Bauxite Commission **74,** 234-6
natural resources
exploitation
Guaranty Agreements **56,** 277-8
objective **56,** 264
public order/public policy/*ordre public* **56,** 318
rights **56,** 264
remedies, commutation of death sentence **98,** 354-5, 356, **118,** 261
territorial sea, innocent passage **73,** 182-3, 283-6
UK–USA Extradition Treaty, applicability to Jamaica **72,** 65-74, **73,** 45-8, 53-4
Jan Mayen 62, 113-15, 117, **99,** 437, 452-3, 667-71
establishment of fishing zone **62,** 115
island, whether **99,** 667
maritime jurisdiction, entitlement **99,** 667
single boundary, fishing zone/continental shelf **99,** 424-6, 447, 484-5, 495-7, 566-70, 653-7
as special circumstance **99,** 432-3
Japan
aliens, treatment of **55,** 456
Anti-Comintern Pact (1936) **44,** 335
Burma, Union of, succession to property situated in Japan **53,** 152
central/State-owned bank, as State agency **65,** 65-6
Constitution 1947
freedom to travel **55,** 446-52, 456
passports **55,** 447
due process **55,** 445
fisheries

Japan (*cont.*)
law
aims and purposes **55,** 145-8
application **55,** 145-8
sovereignty over **59,** 343, 344
foreign relations
China **55,** 451
North Korea **55,** 457-8
freedom of expression, flag desecration and **122,** 599
government, US as successor to **61,** 99, 101
high seas, definition, 'waters subject to public use or constituting a whole with such waters' **55,** 145-8
international law and **55,** 445
jurisdiction
criminal **54,** 3-4
personal **54,** 218-21, 222-3
Korea
Peace Treaty, nationality, effect on **53,** 519
sovereignty over **54,** 3-5
Kunashiri Island and **55,** 148
law of
Commercial Code **84,** 391
Fisheries Law **59,** 342, 343
Law for the Conservation of Aquatic Resources **59,** 342, 343
Law for the Extradition of Fugitives from Justice 1964 **55,** 473-4
Nationality Law 1899 **53,** 516
Nationality Law 1950 **53,** 517
Passport Law **55,** 446, 448-52
Penal Code 1947
Art. 1 **54,** 216
Art. 3 **54,** 218-21, 222-3
Art. 177 (rape) **121,** 270 n. 207
Mandated islands. *See* Japanese Mandated Islands
nationality **53,** 515-17, 520
China, Peace Treaty with, effect **53,** 515-17
Peace Treaties, effect on **53,** 519
nationals
freedom to travel to foreign country **55,** 446-52, 456
Okinawa inhabitants, whether **54,** 217-23
passports, refusal to issue **55,** 446-7
protection in foreign country **55,** 450-2
Okinawa Islands. *See* Okinawa Islands
passports, refusal to issue, nationals **55,** 446-7
Peace Treaty (1951)
appropriation by Allies of Japanese property **44,** 490-4
prisoners of war, absence of compensation for ill-treatment **118,** 211-22, 224-35
renunciation of claims to property under control of Allies **44,** 493
seizure of shares in Allied companies **38,** 460, 463, 467
political offenders **59,** 476-7
Potsdam Declaration and **53,** 5-8
Ryukyu Islands. *See* Ryukyu Islands
territorial sovereignty **54,** 216

Tokyo bonds, Peace Treaty and **48,** 230
treaties, municipal law and **55,** 445
USA
Peace Treaty (1952) **54,** 216-17, 218-21
Treaty *re* Pacific Islands **37,** 545
World War II, Instrument of Surrender **53,** 152
Japanese Mandated Islands 37, 546
Trusteeship Agreement for **54,** 216-21, **61,** 91-100, 117, 123-4, 133, 139-40, **84,** 203, **87,** 549 n. 6, 559-60, 563, 567, 578, 598-9, 606-7, **96,** 25-6, 27, 35-7
Jay Treaty, aboriginal peoples, rights under **104,** 208-10
Jehova's Witnesses, freedom of conscience **70,** 135-51
Jerba Island 67, 56-7, 78, 81, 126, 263, 265, 277, 291, 293-4, 307, 309, 311
Jersey
Carriage of Goods by Road (CMR) Convention (1956), applicability **86,** 152-60
status **86,** 154-6, 158-60
relationship with UK **86,** 15
State, whether **86,** 155-6
treaty-making power **86,** 156, 159
Jerusalem, East
courts **52,** 81-2
Israeli occupation/annexation **47,** 472-6, **48,** 63-8, 94, 98, **52,** 80-2
Protection of Holy Places Law **47,** 473-4
status **47,** 472-6, **48,** 63-8, 93-106
Jews
crimes against the Jewish people **36,** 20-40, 41-2, 227-39, 273-4, **79,** 544-6
as crime against humanity **122,** 84-6
legislation, retroactive **36,** 20-40
discrimination against **70,** 260, 692-8
anti-Jewish legislation in Poland, repeal, **47,** 203-4
employment **54,** 563, 597
emigration, prevention **36,** 194-8
establishment of the State of Israel and **36,** 52-3
expulsion as murder **36,** 44
Final Solution, responsibility for **36,** 235-7
genocide **54,** 563
German treatment of as war crime **55,** 551
Jewish law, application to Jews outside Israel **47,** 213-14
non-German nationals in Germany **36,** 119-20, 192
Operation Groups and **36,** 151, 153, 177-9, 261-2
persecution of in Europe **36,** 81-215
sterilization **36,** 200-2, 238-9
Wannsee Conference **36,** 109-12, 171, 175, 228, 330
'war' against **36,** 255, 264
Johannesburg principles on National Security, Freedom of Expression and Access to Information (1995) 124, 533
joint exploitation agreement 81, 254, 294. *See also* concession agreement; delimitation agreements, maritime; joint exploitation of maritime resources; joint venture agreements; natural resources; State contract; *and the Index to the Consolidated Table of Treaties*
Bahrain–Saudi Arabia (1958) **41,** 102, 145
Denmark–UK (1965) **41,** 81, 95 n. 1, 98
Ems Dollard (1960) **41,** 166
Supplementary Agreement (1962) **41,** 155
Iran–Saudi Arabia **41,** 97-8, 102-3

joint exploitation agreement (*cont.*)
Kuwait–Saudi Arabia (1965) **41,** 102
joint exploitation of maritime resources
Eritrea/Yemen **119,** 445-6
Joint Yemeni–Eritrean Committee for Bilateral Cooperation, Treaty of 16 October 1998 **119,** 492-4
Memorandum of Understanding of 15 November 1994 **119,** 488-91
Gulf of Maine
entrepreneur contract **62,** 131
joint venture **62,** 130
production sharing contract **62,** 130
service contract **62,** 130
Jan Mayen **62,** 126-36
La Bretagne **82,** 672-3, 676, 681-2
North Sea **41,** 81-2, 88, 98, 103, 152, 166
oil **67,** 314-17, **119,** 445-6
overlapping area **41,** 82, 83, 88, **119,** 445-6
State practice **119,** 445-6
joint venture agreements 62, 130, 135, **67,** 361, **72,** 154, 161
expropriation/nationalization **67,** 374
government interference **67,** 368-74
protectionist measures **67,** 370-1
tax preference **67,** 370
Jordan. *See also* Israel, occupied territories; Israel/Jordan relationship; Mandate, Trans-Jordan
East Jerusalem. *See* Jerusalem, East
law of
Antiquities Law 1966 **48,** 63-8
Companies Law 1964 **80,** 98
Constitution 1952 **83,** 128
Criminal law 1960 **48,** 479
Criminal Procedure Code **48,** 487, 492
Defence Law, extension to West Bank **47,** 476-84
Law and Administration, Proclamation No 2, 1967 **48,** 64-6, 68
Popular Front for Liberation of Palestine, measures against **42,** 477-8
West Bank
Defence Law, extension to **47,** 476-84
East Bank, unification **47,** 478
journalism. *See* freedom of expression, journalism
judge, disqualification. *See also* judicial impartiality
authorization to act in case of necessity **118,** 490
delay in raising **118,** 349-50
psychological incapacity to try accused **36,** 319
judgments. *See also* foreign judgment, recognition/enforcement
enforcement of, multinational corporation, against **118,** 526
ultra petitio **48,** 420
judicial assistance 74, 118-20, **75,** 84-5, 123, **82,** 27-9, **88,** 124. *See also* European Convention on Mutual Assistance in Criminal Matters (1959); Hague Convention on the Taking of Evidence Abroad in Civil or Commercial Matters (1970); Yugoslavia, International Criminal Tribunal for the Former (ICTY), judicial assistance; Yugoslavia, International Criminal Tribunal for the Former (ICTY), Statute, 29 (cooperation and judicial assistance)
applicable law **81,** 603, **82,** 55, **117,** 100, **121,** 571
comity and **86,** 182, **90,** 411

in absence of agreement **90,** 411
crimes against humanity, UNGA Resolution 3074 (1973) **91,** 35, **108,** 207, **119,** 99
courts, municipal and **57,** 167-8
customary international law, duty to comply with request **110,** 645-6
diplomatic status, for determination by requesting State **83,** 57
double criminality, need for **65,** 408, **82,** 57
duty of **86,** 182
equality of relationship **110,** 718
European Convention on Human Rights (1950), proceedings in requesting State and **82,** 56
extraterritorial jurisdiction and **75,** 84-5, 123
fiscal offence **65,** 408-9
France/Vietnam **47,** 266-7
Head of State, former, recovery of assets from **82,** 54-7
disclosure of documents **102,** 199-205
disclosure of information **107,** 501-3, **121,** 569-77
injunction restraining removal or dealing with **107,** 492-505
Head of State immunity and, Philippines–USA Procedures for Mutual Legal Assistance Agreement (MLAA) (1986) **121,** 570, 575-6
human rights and **86,** 182
International Criminal Court (ICC), Rome Statute (1998) **125,** 488-9
international criminal order and **106,** 238
International Criminal Tribunal for the Former Yugoslavia **110,** 645, 718
limitation **88,** 306-10
foreign law, recognition/enforcement **88,** 306-10
Montreal Convention for the Suppression of Unlawful Acts Against the Safety of Civil Aviation (1971) **94,** 489, 556, 562, 564, 577
refusal
proportionality and **82,** 52
reasons, need for **106,** 238
serious and intolerable harm to person affected **101,** 454
treaty basis **101,** 454-5
request for, whether required **65,** 197-8
Scheme relating to Mutual Assistance in Criminal Matters within the Commonwealth (1986/1990) ('Harare Scheme') **111,** 615, 653-4
State immunity and **65,** 195, 197-8, **82,** 51-2
taking evidence abroad **44,** 258-9
taxation
customary international law **104,** 579
good faith **104,** 580
treaty, in absence of **82,** 55, **90,** 411
Trusteeship System and **37,** 155-61, 164
'judicial authority'
Justice of the Peace **79,** 144-6, 167
UNHRC **115,** 657, 660-5, **124,** 574-6
judicial control of arbitration. *See* arbitration, judicial control of
judicial discretion **77,** 334-5, 343-5, 358-76, **78,** 679-80, **79,** 499, **84,** 750, **99,** 560-5, 681
act of State and **63,** 187, **81,** 519, 528, 653-4, **103,** 516, 548 n. 22
equity and **67,** 53-299, **71,** 205, **72,** 209, **99,** 586, 599-600, 619-20
evidence
evaluation **105,** 609
self-incrimination **108,** 629-30

judicial discretion (*cont.*)
State immunity and **104,** 539, 561, 586
foreign law, recognition/enforcement **84,** 750, **88,** 308, 309
ICJ **99,** 447, 559-65, 586
interim measures **94,** 522-3, 531-2, 557-60, 571-3, 576, 593
jurisdiction **77,** 334-5
legislation, interpretation **83,** 128, 129, **122,** 446
maritime delimitation **99,** 560-5
nobile officium **56,** 513, 517, **122,** 622
stay of proceedings **118,** 533-9
for forcible abduction/unlawful arrest **95,** 390, 408-16
judicial economy 82, 275, **117,** 57, **121,** 146
prosecution decision not to pursue certain counts **121,** 220
judicial impartiality 68, 132-5, 140, **77,** 130-41
appearance of bias **119,** 120-4, 127-35, **121,** 333-42, 353-4
Amnesty International Charity Limited, relationship with **119,** 113-35
reasonable person test **121,** 336, 337-40
bias and **43,** 220-1
customary international law **121,** 350-3, 362-4
disqualification for lack of **121,** 329-43
burden of proof **121,** 338
contemporaneity of potential conflict, relevance **121,** 336-7
delay in raising **121,** 330-1
grounds for automatic **121,** 336
judge's obligation to withdraw distinguished **121,** 330
general principle of law recognized by civilized nations **121,** 350-4
nemo judex in sua [propria] causa/'no-one should be judge in his own cause' **119,** 120-4, 125-35
presumption of **121,** 333, 337-8
'real danger' **119,** 124, 132
'real suspicion' **119,** 130, 132
judicial independence 56, 405, **81,** 43-5, **96,** 486
Beijing Statement of Principles of the Independence of the Judiciary in the LAWASIA region (1995) **125,** 524
general principle of law **46,** 328-9
investigating judge **81,** 43-5
unconstitutional removal as breach of right to fair trial **123,** 146-52
judicial investigation, observance of general welfare treaties **37,** 85, 111
judicial notice 46, 323, **79,** 25, 156, 386, 446 n. 9, 453, 509, **85,** 559
customary international law **122,** 627-9
definition **94,** 234-5
diplomatic protest **90,** 696
foreign law **81,** 438-40
arbitral tribunal **117,** 575-7
general principles of international law **123,** 492
International Court of Justice (ICJ) **95,** 141
UN decisions **105,** 264, 392-3
international events **87,** 182
international law **56,** 152, **64,** 143, 704-5
Iran–Iraq conflict, facts relating to **99,** 83 n. 1
legislation **87,** 315-16
Nicaragua **95,** 141
political turmoil **63,** 276

sacred nature of flag of People's Republic of China **122,** 573
Security Council Resolutions **116,** 599, 601
service of process **107,** 365
social and political system of State **65,** 102
sources of indisputable accuracy
atlases **94,** 235
dictionaries **94,** 235
encyclopaedias **94,** 235
maps **94,** 235
status of foreign government **64,** 513
treaties **41,** 6, **43,** 120, **64,** 33-4, 44-5, **123,** 491-2
judicial process, requirements 54, 396, 397
judicial propriety 59, 99, 160, **60,** 605-6, **76,** 77, 78, 492-4, 570-9
advisory opinion, refusal **110,** 322
psychological capacity **36,** 319
judicial protection. *See also* American Convention on Human Rights (1969), judicial protection
EC **93,** 398-9, 428, 431-2, 434, 436-7, 542-7
right to have judgment enforced
express refusal **113,** 416
on ground recognized by law **113,** 416, 427-8
properly reasoned **113,** 416
limitations
legislative **113,** 416
proportional **113,** 416
reasonable **113,** 416, 427
State immunity and **113,** 415-18, 426, 427-9
alternative remedies **113,** 429
right to judicial enforcement of rights **113,** 431
judicial restraint 96, 219, **115,** 574-5
act of State and **64,** 264, 279-80, 292-3, 344-51, **119,** 74, 92, **124,** 563-4, **125,** 645, 650-7
foreign relations, acts between private individuals affecting foreign relations **96,** 216-17
ICJ, unilateral submission to court, in case of **99,** 572-8, 651
judicial review 48, 158, **78,** 373, 391, 394, 424, 467, **79,** 436, 487, 645, 647, 657, 662, 663-4, **85,** 32-3, 34, 35, 38, **88,** 14. *See also* constitutional petition; refugees, judicial review; separation of powers
act of State. *See* act of State, judicial review
act threatening life or liberty **96,** 219
acts by public authority **93,** 355, 392-3
implementation by State power **93,** 392-3
administrative act **86,** 332, 411
administrative claims **80,** 22 n. 7
appeal and **85,** 50, 192-3, **92,** 231-2, **114,** 418, 452
arbitral award **56,** 329-30, **86,** 483, **119,** 648-82. *See also* arbitral award, review
Constitution (State) **105,** 544-6
criminal proceedings **88,** 653-4
decision of local authority relating to a child in care **92,** 230-2
deportation **96,** 218
development of concept **84,** 768
diplomatic protection **90,** 395, 397, 398, **96,** 215, 219-20, **116,** 609-22
directives approved by Parliament **84,** 761
discretionary nature **84,** 718-19, **117,** 649, **123,** 574-5

judicial review (*cont.*)
EC. *See also* European Community law, judicial review
compliance with directives **120,** 646-56
public interest **120,** 655-6
effective remedy, whether **98,** 316-17, **106,** 248, **108,** 357-62, 422, 423-7, 430-2, **124,** 515-16, 531-2, 540-1
entry permit **85,** 212
entry of property on World Heritage List **90,** 122
European Commission, acts of **47,** 280, 281, 289, 290-1, 305, 307-8, 406-11
European Convention on Human Rights (1950) and **112,** 385-7
executive acts in occupied territory **81,** 513
executive certificate/statement **87,** 183
export licence, refusal **90,** 570
extradition. *See* extradition, judicial review
failure to establish prima facie case and **88,** 9, 28, 30
foreign acts of State. *See* act of State
foreign relations. *See* foreign relations, judicial review
fundamental rights, protection of **93,** 392-5
general principles governing **54,** 398
grounds
abuse of discretion **88,** 16, 17-19, **117,** 628
abuse of power **111,** 556, 561-3, 568-70
abuse of process **111,** 566
arbitrariness **86,** 332, **90,** 398, **96,** 238, 247
bad faith **92,** 231
change in applicant's personal circumstances **114,** 419
denial of natural justice **91,** 186-7, **117,** 645
error of law **91,** 187-8, **114,** 415-25, **117,** 597, 600, 644-5
international obligation, failure to construe correctly **91,** 188
failure to consider relevant circumstances **92,** 231
failure to give reasons **108,** 652
failure to observe correct procedures **92,** 231, **96,** 238
illegality **84,** 766, **90,** 453, **92,** 231, 650, **111,** 556, **114,** 453, 464
flagrant unlawfulness **86,** 332
improper exercise of power **85,** 194-5
improper motivation **96,** 238
insufficiency of evidence **85,** 192-4
irrationality/unreasonableness **84,** 766, 769, **85,** 195, **90,** 56-7, 140, 142-4, 152, 158, 164-5, 177-80, 453, 579, **92,** 650, **96,** 130, 131, 238, **112,** 387, 389-91, 395, 399-403, 407-9, **114,** 414, 449, 452, 464-5, **118,** 600, **124,** 353-8, 388, 470-1
legitimate expectation, disappointment of **92,** 650
partiality **84,** 768-9, 778
procedural impropriety **84,** 766, **90,** 453-4, **92,** 650, **114,** 418-19
proportionality **84,** 766-7
ultra vires **92,** 231
unfairness **124,** 467-70
ICJ advisory opinion as. *See* International Court of Justice (ICJ), advisory opinion
implementation of treaty **90,** 227
international official, non-renewal of contract **38,** 384-5, 400-1, 415, **43,** 398
international officials **96,** 238, 247
legality of government actions, limited to **98,** 169
legislation **93,** 416-17, **96,** 360, 367-71
conformity with treaty **96,** 367-9

European Convention on Human Rights (1950) and **96,** 369
fundamental principles of law **96,** 36
growing power of executive and **96,** 368
secondary **93,** 632
draft Order in Council **93,** 632-4, 636-9
limited purview **90,** 145, **117,** 606
malfunctioning of judicial system **96,** 595-6
margin of discretion **96,** 219
matters relating to trial on indictment, consent to prosecutions **122,** 440-2, 450-3, 468-71, 472, 475-6, 491-5
military disciplinary proceedings **96,** 651
national security **112,** 382-9
nature of **54,** 489, 491
non-statutory body **114,** 583-6
parties, inherent jurisdiction concerning **100,** 251
passport, refusal **84,** 716-17, 720
political question doctrine and. *See* political question doctrine
powers of reviewing body **117,** 609, 623-5
remission to tribunal **117,** 608, 623-5
prerogative and **84,** 717, 718-19, **90,** 34, 35, 50-5, **123,** 605-6
procedural fairness **124,** 419
restrictions on grounds of public order/public policy/*ordre public* **62,** 391-414
Security Council Resolutions, ICJ **94,** 525, 538, 585-7
standard **124,** 353-8, 388-90
standard of review **88,** 19, 25-30, **90,** 672, **96,** 129-30. *See also* grounds *above*
standing **93,** 485-6, 636
infringement of individual rights, need for **93,** 511, 512-13
'legitimate expression' **90,** 451-2
'sufficient interest' **90,** 451, **119,** 279-80
human rights groups **119,** 279-80
supranational organization **93,** 351-7
taxation **91,** 326-8
transfer of persons sentenced abroad **84,** 722, 725
treaties **87,** 330-3, 347-8, **96,** 219, 339, 360
absolute liability for abnormal damage, in case of **96,** 218
compatibility with international law **106,** 404
implementation **90,** 227
implementing legislation **108,** 645-6
ratification, fact and form distinguished **106,** 209
suspension **106,** 209-10
validity of legislation **90,** 536-45
judicial role 59, 94
abuse of process and **95,** 390-5, 401, 407-8
activities abroad **95,** 403-4, 408
comity **95,** 403-4, 408
examining magistrate **95,** 393-5, 412-16
application of general principles to particular situations **110,** 442-3, 540
development of international law **41,** 141, 174, 185
indirect incorporation of customary international law/treaty distinguished **104,** 472, **120,** 372, 399-405
indirect incorporation of treaty distinguished **104,** 472
lex ferenda **41,** 68, **53,** 468, 483, **55,** 283, 284, **56,** 279, **57,** 512, **58,** 419, **67,** 171-2, **73,** 572, **81,** 382, **92,** 65

judicial role (*cont.*)
executive acts, supervision **95,** 392-3, 399-406, 409-10
forensic process **95,** 390, 405, 407-8
implementation of treaties **108,** 508
law enforcement **39,** 230
judicial settlement. *See also* arbitration; conciliation; ICSID (International Centre for the Settlement of Investment Disputes); International Court of Justice (ICJ); Iran–US Claims Tribunal; Permanent Court of Arbitration (PCA); Permanent Court of International Justice (PCIJ)
conciliation and **84,** 269-74
judiciary
bad faith, allegations of **46,** 323-4, **121,** 24
continuity **90,** 50
legal limits on jurisdiction, relevance **46,** 530
wrongful acts, State responsibility for. *See* State responsibility for acts and omissions of, judicial authorities
jurisdiction 61, 229-32, **84,** 687-700, **87,** 393. *See also* arbitral tribunal, competence; *forum [non] conveniens*; maritime jurisdiction[s]; State immunity, jurisdiction; *and under individual courts and tribunals*
aboriginal Indians in Canada
interjurisdictional immunity **115,** 520-1
jurisdiction over land distinguished **115,** 520
aboriginals in Australia **86,** 210-14
acquisition. *See also* attachment, jurisdiction, as basis for; forcible abduction/unlawful arrest, jurisdiction, effect on
burden of proof **107,** 188
forcible abduction/unlawful arrest **54,** 232
sequestration **66,** 149-60
service on consular agent **63,** 149
voluntary return **107,** 187-95
act of State. *See* act of State
acts committed abroad
requirements
actionability if committed in forum State **118,** 406
unjustifiability by law of place where committed **118,** 406
acts committed abroad. *See also* criminal, acts committed abroad *below*
adjudicative and enforcement jurisdiction, distinguishability **107,** 644-58
admiralty. *See* admiralty jurisdiction
admissibility distinguished **121,** 67-70
advisory. *See* Inter-American Court of Human Rights, advisory jurisdiction; International Court of Justice (ICJ), advisory jurisdiction; Permanent International Court of Justice (PCIJ), advisory jurisdiction; Yugoslavia, International Criminal Tribunal for the Former (ICTY), jurisdiction, advisory
advisory opinion, decision subject to suspension by executive **104,** 142-3
aircraft **88,** 181, **107,** 390. *See also* foreign aircraft *below*; hijacking of aircraft, jurisdiction
crime committed on **40,** 209
airport. *See* airports, jurisdiction
airspace **40,** 92-3, 346, **54,** 316-17, **77,** 280, 484
above the high seas **90,** 215-16
aliens
abroad **38,** 133-6, **74,** 157-9, 167-9, 194-6, 706-7, **77,** 279, **85,** 279-300, **90,** 639, **104,** 125-7
resident **101,** 345

between **88,** 81 n. 3
admiralty jurisdiction **98,** 19 n. 6
in case involving foreign State **63,** 393-8
conspiracy **84,** 57-9
contract between **77,** 413-16
criminal. *See* criminal *below*
debt between **77,** 534
foreign official acting under State authority, anti-terrorism legislation **104,** 146-8
foreign State, claim against **72,** 129-31
legal person **65,** 265-6
limitations **46,** 423, 528
member of firm carrying on business in country **101,** 346
ne bis in idem principle **71,** 232-5, **75,** 106, 338-40, 354
present in country **101,** 345-6
at time of transaction **101,** 345
involuntarily present **85,** 283, 290-1. *See also* forcible abduction/unlawful arrest, jurisdiction, effect on
resident, acts committed abroad **125,** 574
resident in country **101,** 345
tax lien **38,** 112-20
terrorist offences **74,** 163-5, **94,** 488-9, 521
tort claim against **72,** 91-3
tort claim by **61,** 121-3
acts committed abroad **77,** 171-81, 484-5
foreign seaman **54,** 224-9
war liabilities **61,** 164, 166, 173-8
wardship proceedings **43,** 168
alien abroad **41,** 239, 240, 247, 250, 254-6
allegiance as basis for **41,** 239, 240, 247, 250, 254-6, **42,** 109-12, **43,** 168, **54,** 268-73, 281-91, **92,** 630-5
allegiance of non-citizens **43,** 166-75
alternative forum with exclusive jurisdiction, absence of **77,** 534
appeal, inherent **105,** 540
applicable law
distinguished **106,** 476-7
ICSID Convention **106,** 555
municipal law **106,** 577
need to apply **106,** 500
powers under municipal law and international law distinguished **123,** 421-2, 444
relevance **91,** 40, 43, 294, 300, 316
arbitration, duty of, effect on jurisdiction of domestic courts **82,** 288-91
armed conflict, legality of participation in, municipal courts **42,** 393-401
armed forces abroad **40,** 86-7, **41,** 20, **49,** 498-503, **56,** 229-33, **60,** 42-3, **77,** 279, 557-8, **85,** 157-8, 161, 163-4, 173-4, **86,** 501-2, **88,** 710. *See also* belligerent occupation, jurisdiction; NATO Status of Forces Agreement (1951)
authority over British forces in Korea **41,** 20
extraterritorial **79,** 38
official duties, acts unconnected with **77,** 557-8
US Forces in Japan **56,** 229-33
waiver **85,** 174, 180
availability of evidence and **88,** 121, 123-4
bankruptcy
foreign company **46,** 189, 191-2, 235, 277-80, 459

jurisdiction (*cont.*)
subsidiaries, attachment of property of **46,** 192-3
basis **72,** 440
Barcelona Traction **96,** 178
compromis d'arbitrage **43,** 492
domicile **54,** 225, **80,** 369
effectiveness of judgment **55,** 7-10
international law **96,** 177-9
breach **104,** 125-9, 147-8
Lotus **96,** 177-9
sovereignty **96,** 177-9
boni judicis est ampliare jurisdictionem **56,** 197
burden of proof **107,** 346, **123,** 211
collusion **63,** 102
central/State-owned bank, dispute relating to agreement with foreign commercial bank **96,** 736, 737
child care cases
federal State, in **92,** 620-35
prerogative jurisdiction **92,** 624-6, 630-2
presence of child within jurisdiction, necessary, whether **92,** 635
statutory **92,** 623
civil **73,** 227-51, 298-364
collisions at sea
Convention for the Unification of Certain Rules relating to Penal Jurisdiction in Matters of Collision or Other Incidents of Navigation (1952) **78,** 119
foreign ship in territorial waters **78,** 118-19
comity and **60,** 97-8
alien, to be construed in favour of **80,** 29
commission of war crime/crime against humanity as condition precedent **98,** 528, 531, 564-5
jury responsibility to determine, whether **98,** 553-6, 561-6
whether to be established pre-trial or pre-judgment **98,** 566-71
common law **90,** 297-9
company name **72,** 557-60
compensation for damage caused by offence committed abroad **91,** 240-2
compétence de la compétence **48,** 374, 408, 409, 450, **55,** 187-8, **90,** 610, **105,** 292, 299-300, 460-3, 553-5, 571, **106,** 542-5, **123,** 211, 391. *See also* arbitral tribunal, *compétence de la compétence*
decisions by other courts in same matter, relevance **106,** 544-5
general principle of international law **105,** 461, **123,** 254
inherent power **105,** 460-1, **120,** 241
limitation, express provision, need for **105,** 461
matter *sub judice* in another forum **106,** 529
Nottebohm **105,** 553, **123,** 254-5
parties' interpretation of unilateral consent, relevance **106,** 542, 558, **123,** 211
primary jurisdiction distinguished **105,** 459, 462
rules of procedure **123,** 255
waiver **105,** 461
competence distinguished **105,** 457
compulsory. *See also* European Court of Human Rights, jurisdiction, compulsory; International Court of Justice (ICJ), compulsory jurisdiction, acceptance
absence of in international system **49,** 158
'conciliation or arbitration', need to distinguish, whether **106,** 556, 569-70, 571-2, 585-6

concurrent **57,** 166, **60,** 37-8, **63,** 447 n. 2, **77,** 557-8, 563-6, **80,** 385, **82,** 104-5, **84,** 676, **86,** 37, 42, **92,** 564-5, 574-5, **106,** 529, **117,** 85
absence of rule governing **106,** 529
choice of law and **80,** 383
drug-trafficking **86,** 551-2
exercise for determination between sovereign States **84,** 213
good faith and **104,** 545
international and municipal courts, primacy **101,** 4-9
international trade **96,** 185
NATO Status of Forces Agreement (1951) **91,** 240-2
primary
delay **86,** 537
non-exercise **86,** 537
proceedings already started **65,** 203-4
sovereignty, effect on **92,** 565, 574-5
stay of proceedings. *See* stay of proceedings
treaty provision **82,** 104-6
visiting forces **86,** 534
confiscated property, State of incorporation **78,** 91-3
conflict, failure to object **96,** 197
connecting factors. *See* nexus *below*
consent
ambiguity **106,** 577, 587-8
declaration of intent, whether **106,** 574, 577
as legislative provision **106,** 576
general principle of international law **106,** 543
interpretation, restrictive, whether **106,** 543-4
notification to ICSID of kinds of disputes which might be submitted, whether **106,** 543, 571
Preamble to ICSID Convention **106,** 520, 543
presumption of **106,** 543, 577
pursuit of alternative remedy as recognition that consent lacking **106,** 521
ratification of ICSID Convention, whether **106,** 543
written, need for **106,** 520-2, 555, 567-9, 578-9
ad hoc **106,** 555-6
promotional literature as offer **106,** 567-9, 577-82
single instrument, relevance **106,** 521, 569
conspiracy **69,** 100-1, 106-8, **78,** 503-5, **84,** 43-50, 61-72, 675-6, 682, 683-4, **85,** 117-26
agent as perpetrator of crime **84,** 47-50
alien, over **57,** 119, **84,** 43-50, 61-72
extraterritorial offence **48,** 69-76
foreign ship on high seas **91,** 474
initiated abroad **52,** 290, **57,** 119
public order/public policy/*ordre public* **84,** 48
to commit crime abroad **41,** 261-5, **84,** 43-6, **101,** 180-1, **104,** 307, **114,** 595-6
contentious. *See* European Convention on Human Rights (1950), civil rights and obligations, *contestation,* need for; Inter-American Court of Human Rights, contentious jurisdiction; International Court of Justice (ICJ), contentious proceedings
contiguous zone **89,** 79
continental shelf **57,** 147, **60,** 525, 556
contract between aliens **77,** 413-16
contractual agreement to exclude **88,** 689

jurisdiction (*cont.*)
- contractual obligation **87,** 376
- coroner's **78,** 551-63
  - purpose **78,** 563
- over corporation **46,** 340-1, **73,** 572, 575-6, 579-80
  - non-resident **63,** 42
  - *siège administratif* **41,** 393
  - *siège social* **41,** 391
- counterclaim **106,** 718
  - against diplomat **77,** 455-6
- courts. *See* courts, municipal, jurisdiction
- crimes against humanity. *See* crimes against humanity, jurisdiction
- criminal **73,** 180-5, 250-95, 366-71, 699-704, **75,** 336-40, **84,** 678-87. *See also* extradition
  - acts committed abroad **78,** 551-63, **86,** 559-61
    - agent **48,** 90-1
    - aliens **36,** 279, 283-7, **38,** 122-3, **42,** 143-5, **47,** 136-7, 267, 270, **54,** 268-77, 281-5, **72,** 129-31
    - applicable law **86,** 560-1
    - armed forces **77,** 279
    - double criminality **86,** 560-1
    - nationals **41,** 261-5, **42,** 146-8, **43,** 176-7, **47,** 267, 270, **54,** 268-77, 281-5, 321-2, **71,** 230-1, **73,** 253-73, **74,** 157-9, 167-9, 194-6, 706-7, **78,** 559, **86,** 559-61, 589, 591
    - non-resident alien, by **82,** 346-57
    - private prosecution, requirement for in place of commission, relevance **86,** 560-1
    - time-barred in place of commission, relevance **86,** 560-1
  - aliens **47,** 136-7, **54,** 268-77, 281-5, **71,** 232-8, **73,** 366-73
    - conspiracy initiated abroad **57,** 119
  - assassination attempt **72,** 615-17
  - bigamous marriages **71,** 227-8
  - border control offences **71,** 252-8
  - completion of offence **77,** 280, 484, **78,** 503, **84,** 679, 696
  - connecting factors. *See* nexus *below*
  - conspiracy. *See* conspiracy *above*
  - continuing offence **84,** 680-1, 684, 685-6, 688, 691
  - contract law analogy **84,** 692
  - credit card abuse **86,** 562-3
  - crimes against humanity. *See* crimes against humanity, jurisdiction
  - drug-trafficking. *See* drug-trafficking *below*
  - effects doctrine. *See* effects doctrine *below*
  - evidence obtained abroad **71,** 222-6
  - extraterritorial **45,** 51, **48,** 478, 482-3, **60,** 97. *See also* acts committed abroad *above*
  - foreign embassy **52,** 306-9
  - foreigners. *See* aliens *above*
  - fraud. *See* fraud *below*
  - gravamen of offence **84,** 675, 678, 680, 681, 682-3, 687, 690, 693-4, 696
  - high seas. *See* high seas
  - international law and **36,** 283-7
  - *lex loci delicti commissi* **59,** 327-34, 336-40, **77,** 179, **79,** 5, 7
    - relevance **77,** 484

'linking point', need for **36,** 50-5, 304
location of crime **55,** 106, 112-14, 117-21, 123-4, 135-8, 141-3, 431-7, **57,** 119-20, 143, **88,** 339
attempt **87,** 410-12
corruption **88,** 347-8
false accounting **88,** 346-7
presentation of cheque **88,** 341-3, 344-5
single *situs* **84,** 681
situs of single element of crime **84,** 678
telex, despatch **88,** 340-2, 343-4
telex, receipt **88,** 345
theft **88,** 340-6
murder **72,** 610-14, **78,** 559, **79,** 544
internationally protected persons **79,** 544
nature of offence as determining factor **84,** 678, 681
ne bis in idem **71,** 232-5, **84,** 697-8, **86,** 537-8
offences committed outside State **69,** 130-2
personal **77,** 179, 591
political offence. *See* political offence
preparatory acts **69,** 132-3
protective principle. *See* protective principle *below*
reciprocal **60,** 37, 43
rogatory letters **71,** 222-6
ship in port **43,** 176-7, **57,** 164-6
submission of offender **69,** 130-2
substantial links **84,** 679
territorial airspace **77,** 280, 484
terrorist offences. *See* terrorism, jurisdiction
treason, merger of other offences **71,** 244-6
venue, relevance **84,** 677, 684
war crimes **72,** 610-14, **78,** 129, 131
death, in case of **78,** 551-63
debt, enforcement **87,** 514
decision respecting, nature of **48,** 342-3, 359, 379, 384, 406, 449, 450
decline of, unambiguous rule required **78,** 8
'deemed to have been committed' within territory **98,** 533-6, 614-20, **104,** 302, 304-10, **123,** 202-3, 225-6
creation of new offence distinguished **98,** 570-1, **104,** 304-6, 307-8, 358-9
double criminality requirement **98,** 535-7, 617-20
provisional 'deeming' **98,** 568-9
retroactivity, avoidance **104,** 399
definition **50,** 446-7, **105,** 457-8
adjudicative and enforcement powers distinguished **77,** 4-8
Alcom case **77,** 5
designation of alternative court
inappropriate **77,** 496
possibility of **77,** 558
'designation of competent court' and **86,** 567, 577-8
detainees on foreign territory **85,** 229-35
diplomatic agent, sending State's diplomats, over **89,** 71
diplomatic mission, locally engaged staff, home State **82,** 20
diplomatic premises. *See* diplomatic premises

jurisdiction (*cont.*)
direct effect in forum State, need for. *See* nexus *below*
disclosure of assets outside **80,** 214, 222
divorce proceedings, refugees **70,** 356-8, **72,** 642-5, **74,** 533-56
domestic. *See* domestic jurisdiction
drug-trafficking **73,** 250-1, 699-704
concurrent **86,** 551-2
obligation to exercise **99,** 157
extradition, request for, relevance **86,** 551-2
personal **86,** 551-2, 589, 591
protective principle **84,** 214-15
transit-lounge **88,** 261-2
duty of court to examine competence **36,** 20
EC Convention concerning Jurisdiction and Enforcement in Civil and Commercial Matters (1968) **82,** 136
ecclesiastical courts in Morocco after independence **45,** 53-6
EEC, in respect of **80,** 126-7
EEZ
collision **89,** 78-80
national of forum State, applicable law **101,** 447-8
effective service and **92,** 627-8
effectiveness doctrine. *See* enforceability of decisions *below*
effects doctrine **48,** 106, 108-10, 114-16, 117-19, 121-3, 140, **61,** 188, 194-8, 221-3, **63,** 150, 185-6, 402-5, 457, 637-8, **66,** 63, **72,** 80, 169-71, 179, **73,** 265-6, 271-2, **74,** 48, **81,** 500, **84,** 99-100, 116-17, 676, 678-9, 685-6, 690, **86,** 544-5, 654, **99,** 154-6, **115,** 604-5. *See also* United States of America (USA), Foreign Sovereign Immunities Act (FSIA) 1976/82, 28 USC 1605(a)(2) (commercial activity exception), 'that causes a direct effect in the United States'
absence of rule against **96,** 187
Alcoa **96,** 181
applicable law **86,** 544-5
balancing of judicial interest **96,** 183-4
comity **96,** 182, 183, 187, 197
commercial activities having direct effect in forum State **104,** 613-14
expropriation/nationalization, failure to pay compensation **63,** 457
conspiracy **99,** 155
direct effect **96,** 186
effect as element of offence **96,** 179, 186
Horlogerie Suisse **96,** 181
indirect effect **96,** 186
intended **96,** 182, 186, **99,** 155-6
International Law Association (ILA) (1972) **96,** 186-7
Laker Airways **96,** 183
Lotus **96,** 177-9
Manningtree Mills **96,** 182-3
qualified effect **96,** 185-7
competition law, applicability to **96,** 185-6
radioactive contamination **80,** 372-3
separable elements of crime distinguished **114,** 596, 599
substantial and foreseeable result **81,** 501, **96,** 182, 186
Timberlane **96,** 182
trend towards **84,** 16

embassies abroad **90,** 590-3
torts committed by foreign State in **90,** 590-3
employment contract **88,** 688-90
academic appointment in respondent State **65,** 5-6
host State **94,** 328
enforceability of judgment, relevance **55,** 7-10, **85,** 229, 231, 233, **86,** 566, 567, 568-9, 570, 573, 574, **88,** 121, 124-5, **91,** 315, **95,** 476, **103,** 3-4, **107,** 642-58
enforcement
blocking legislation **96,** 180
extraterritorial. *See* extraterritorial *below*
prescription distinguished **96,** 179-80
imposition of fine, classification **96,** 180
espionage **94,** 73
lex loci delicti commissi **94,** 73
protective principle **94,** 74
European Convention on Human Rights (1950) violation **77,** 438
European Convention on Jurisdiction and the Enforcement of Judgments **80,** 372
European Convention on the Law Applicable to Contractual Obligations (1980) **87,** 97, 99
European Schools. *See* European Schools, jurisdiction over
evidence. *See* evidence
examination in bankruptcy **88,** 312-22
exclusion
classification of State activity **86,** 577
Security Council Resolution **103,** 158-9
treaty, by **90,** 601-2
exclusive **60,** 37, 41
exclusive fishing zone (EFZ) **82,** 618, 626
execution, fines as **48,** 115, 118, 122
execution as **78,** 114-16
exemptions. *See also* diplomatic privileges and immunities; international officials, privileges and immunities; international organizations, immunity, jurisdiction; State immunity
foreign armed forces **69,** 137-9
UN forces **69,** 141-4
exercise of
fishing licences **83,** 20
fixing of date for hearing, whether **65,** 130
permits for exploration/exploitation **83,** 20
protests **83,** 20
exhaustion of local remedies. *See* exhaustion of local remedies
extent **54,** 268, 282-4
extradition **77,** 395-6, **85,** 98-9
nationals, of and **87,** 164-6
extraterritorial **57,** 152-3, **61,** 187, 188, 217, 221-3, 226, 229, 231-2, **62,** 44, 51-5, 74-5, 85-6, **77,** 202, 250, 277-83, **79,** 85, 88-9, 543-5, **84,** 688, **87,** 376-7, **103,** 524-30. *See also* territorial *below*; extraterritorial legislation; fisheries, conservation and management measures; legislation, interpretation, presumption of territorial limitation; service of process out of the jurisdiction
airport transit zone **77,** 484
aliens abroad. *See* aliens, abroad *above*

jurisdiction (*cont.*)
American Convention on Human Rights (1969) **123,** 168
anti-terrorism legislation **83,** 351-7, **104,** 146-7
appearance in court to raise State immunity **123,** 113
broadcasting from beyond territorial sea **61,** 184-5, **74,** 201-3
burden of proof **36,** 57
civil right **87,** 380
over colonies following accession to independence **71,** 220-1
conditions for **77,** 217
conflicting jurisdiction **96,** 185
conservation measures **123,** 256-7
crimes against humanity **36,** 20-40, **79,** 544-6, **104,** 298-9, **119,** 227
crimes against the Jewish people **36,** 20-40, **79,** 544-6
customary international law **96,** 185
death penalty, relevance **114,** 598-600
'deemed to have been committed' within territory. *See* 'deemed to have been committed' within territory *above*
effects doctrine. *See* Constitution *above*
enforcement **96,** 180
  injunction against foreign State **86,** 581
European Convention on Human Rights (1950) **123,** 109-16
examination of foreign witness abroad
  international law, compliance with rules of **90,** 410
  treaty, in absence of **90,** 410, 411
exceptional nature. *See* presumption against *below*
expropriation/nationalization. *See* expropriation/nationalization, extraterritorial effect; expropriation/nationalization, territorial limitation
extradition of national and **88,** 294
foreign company abroad **71,** 220-1
fraud **48,** 88-90
fundamental rights, breach, whether **98,** 573-4
Geneva Conventions (1949) **119,** 365
Governor-General of India **38,** 4, 8
habeas corpus writ **79,** 27-31, 41-4, 46-7, 48-9
  enforcement **79,** 46, 47
human rights **103,** 639-51, 658-60, **123,** 109-16
injunction against former Head of State **107,** 494-505
injunction, grant **74,** 161
international law, enforcement **77,** 202, **79,** 546
judicial assistance and **75,** 84-5, 123
legislate, right to and **91,** 531, **94,** 86, **121,** 494 n. 6
legislation conferring, interpretation **114,** 596-7
legitimate interests, need for **96,** 185
letters rogatory. *See* letters rogatory
limitation
  acquiescence **91,** 71
  conflicting obligations **96,** 185, 197
Lockerbie trial in the Netherlands **117,** 666-91
objection by foreign State, relevance **99,** 157
offence planned in forum State **114,** 590, 594-9, 605-6
offences against ship of forum State **98,** 532
outside territorial sea **55,** 7-10

past conduct
persons at the time nationals **91,** 73, 162
persons at the time non-nationals **91,** 14
piracy **98,** 532, **104,** 307
presumption against **77,** 279, 281, 283, **123,** 109-10, 111-13
property, execution on **77,** 491
purpose **124,** 22-3
reasonableness, need for **99,** 156-7
general acceptance **99,** 157
importance to regulating State **99,** 157
security, threat to **91,** 473
serious and universally condemned offences, limited to **99,** 156-7
subpoena, right of **61,** 231-2, **90,** 638
territorial sovereignty and **86,** 544, **119,** 77
terrorist offences **82,** 139, **121,** 633-4
Torture Convention (1984) **100,** 471, **103,** 526-30, **104,** 180, **107,** 449-51, 546, **119,** 40, 70-1, 76, 85, 100, 139-40, 150, 156, 230-1, **123,** 34
obligation to exercise **104,** 184 n. 25
visiting forces **79,** 38
war crimes **82,** 443-7, **104,** 298-9
winding-up proceedings **65,** 84-5, **77,** 30
'extravagant' assertion of human rights as violation **75,** 374, 377-8
fairness and **79,** 14
federal State. *See* federal State, jurisdiction
fisheries. *See* fisheries, jurisdiction
forcible abduction. *See* forcible abduction/unlawful arrest, jurisdiction, effect on
foreign aircraft **71,** 230-1, **73,** 702-4
'air commerce' **86,** 37, 40
anti-terrorism conventions **86,** 37-40
in distress **82,** 363-70
flag State **73,** 702
landing, need for **77,** 282, 283
outside airspace **86,** 35-6, 37-43
place of landing **86,** 35-6, 38, 42
sexual offences **86,** 35-6, 37, 38
place of landing **86,** 35-6, 38, 42
scheduled stop **86,** 35-6
unscheduled stop **86,** 39
place of registration **86,** 42
sexual offences **86,** 35-6, 37, 38
'special aircraft jurisdiction' **86,** 35-6, 37-9, 40-1
territorial airspace, outside **77,** 283, **87,** 299-300
territorial airspace, within **77,** 279-80
foreign courts within State **48,** 102, 104-6
foreign enterprises with territorial contact **46,** 340-1
foreign investment, protection of **60,** 34-5
foreign proceedings, injunction against **74,** 40-2, 70-7, 83-7
foreign ships. *See* ships, jurisdiction, foreign ship
former colonial power, actions against **89,** 16
forum, implied choice, choice of law clause **107,** 350
forum [non] conveniens. See forum [non] conveniens
forum rule in treaty, effect **72,** 79-81, 91-3

jurisdiction (*cont.*)
fragmentation, avoidance **82,** 82
fraud
extraterritorial elements **48,** 88-90
place of commission **86,** 562-3
genocide. *See* genocide, jurisdiction
Germany, FRG and GDR, confined to own territory **78,** 169
Harvard Research Project (1935) **82,** 348
high seas. *See also* high seas, jurisdiction
drugs offence **84,** 210
hijacking of aircraft. *See* hijacking of aircraft, jurisdiction
Holy See, central institutions of Catholic Church **100,** 605, 606-9
hostage-taking **82,** 346-57. *See also* terrorist offence *below*
hot pursuit. *See* hot pursuit
human rights, concurrent **95,** 272
ICJ. *See* International Court of Justice (ICJ), jurisdiction
ICSID arbitration, provisional measures **82,** 80-5
improper assumption of, breach of international law **77,** 532
in personam **90,** 560, 562
independent territory, over **78,** 452-3
inherent
appeal **105,** 540
compétence de la compétence **105,** 460-1, **120,** 241
interests of forum State **84,** 104
international crime **91,** 40-4. *See also* terrorist offence *and* universal *below*
International Criminal Tribunal for the Former Yugoslavia. *See* Yugoslavia, International Criminal Tribunal for the Former (ICTY), jurisdiction
international law
governed by **79,** 11-12
rules on **46,** 279
violation of **72,** 127, 130-1, 143, **79,** 546
international military tribunals, defeated power **90,** 392-5
international and national, harmonization, local remedies rule **46,** 373
international officials **77,** 417-19, 454-7
international officials, employment contract **72,** 192-5, 711-13, **77,** 503-6
host State **94,** 328
ILO Administrative Tribunal **94,** 333
international organizations
conditions of service **77,** 609
internal organization, competence of Member States' courts **78,** 115
international organizations, over, municipal courts **108,** 651
international tort/wrong **77,** 172, 181-2, 210-11, 269
claim arising under municipal law, need for **99,** 65-7, **104,** 127-9, 178-84
nationality of parties, relevance **77,** 172
judicial discretion **77,** 334-5
jury role in determining **98,** 553-7, 561-6, 601-2, 619-26, **104,** 303, 308-9, 310-11, 317, 355-6
international and domestic elements, distinguishable, whether **98,** 623-6
international elements **104,** 327-30
justiciability distinguished **60,** 16, 40-1, **66,** 112, 160-2, 293, 396-7, **99,** 46 n. 1, **105,** 463, **107,** 257 n. 1
lack of, denial of justice, relevance **46,** 346, 528, 530
law enforcement officers abroad **84,** 70

legislation as consent **106,** 521, 540-3, 545-62, 568, 576-7
bilateral treaties, conclusion, evidence of absence of general consent, whether **106,** 559
declaration of intent **106,** 576-7
interpretation
international law applicable to unilateral declarations **106,** 543
original language to determine, whether **106,** 547-8, 572-3
parties', whether governing **106,** 542
principles of statutory interpretation **106,** 543
treaty rules **106,** 542-5, 570, 587
mandatory, whether **106,** 546-9, 561
municipal law as fact **106,** 541-2
as offer requiring acceptance **106,** 570-1, 578, 582, 585, 653
self-executing, whether **106,** 576
separate agreement, need for **106,** 552-6
translation
agreed by parties for use in arbitration proceedings **106,** 545-6
variations **106,** 572-6
unilateral act **106,** 542, 570-1
international obligation, whether **106,** 542
letters rogatory. *See* letters rogatory
lex fori **48,** 93, 100
lex loci delicti commissi **59,** 327-34, 336-40, **60,** 60, **77,** 179, **79,** 5, 57, **92,** 532. *See also* applicable law
espionage **94,** 73
limitations, constituent instrument **105,** 458
loss of jurisdiction after commencement of proceedings **103,** 4
marine pollution **94,** 232-7
marriage **72,** 297-300
meanings **41,** 249
multilateral conventions, Hague Convention for the Suppression of the Unlawful Seizure of Aircraft (1970) **87,** 299-300, 303-5, **88,** 180
mutual legal assistance and **75,** 84-5
nationality **79,** 294, 301, **82,** 347, **84,** 3, 7-8
customary international law **84,** 10-11
NATO Status of Forces Agreement (1951) **82,** 114
restrictive application **84,** 7
territorial principle, avoidance of conflict with **84,** 7, 11
nationals abroad **55,** 145-8, **62,** 75, 86, **63,** 244-51, **70,** 103-16, **71,** 243-58, **72,** 203, **73,** 253-73, **74,** 158-9, 194-6, 201-3, 706-7, **75,** 337, 341, 353, 362, 367, **77,** 279, **78,** 69, **81,** 500, **84,** 676, **87,** 300, 371, 531, **88,** 298-301, **90,** 621-41, **99,** 154 n. 4, **117,** 85. *See also* personal *below*; State responsibility for, failure to protect nationals
crime against **40,** 87-8, **61,** 228-30, **78,** 559
in embassy **61,** 224-6
crime committed in foreign waters **59,** 343-4
crime committed on high seas **40,** 88-91
crimes against humanity **74,** 706-7
entry, control of **43,** 130-40
in exile **38,** 458
freedom to travel **43,** 126-30
injury to **63,** 213-14, 323-8, **92,** 445-7, 451-4
murder or manslaughter **78,** 559, **119,** 55, 184
property abroad **56,** 530

jurisdiction (*cont.*)
nationals, over, applicable law **101,** 447-8
NATO Appeals Board **52,** 465-6
ne bis in idem **71,** 232-5, **77,** 581, **78,** 137
nexus **63,** 398, **69,** 116-19, 122, 124-5, **70,** 58-60, 67, 89-90, **80,** 373, **82,** 23, 26, 33, 37, 40, 48, 138, 346 n. 1, **84,** 112, 678, 695, 698, 699-700, **87,** 102, **90,** 565, 594, 602-3, **98,** 7, 17, 34-5, 90-2, **101,** 516-18, **108,** 499. *See also* effects doctrine *above*; *forum [non] conveniens*
'act performed in the US in connection with a commercial activity elsewhere' **63,** 618-19, **92,** 378-80, **100,** 550-1, **103,** 441-2
advertising campaign **103,** 465, 466, 468
agency or instrumentality of foreign State **98,** 90-2
agreement to arbitrate in forum State **63,** 538
applicable law **64,** 219, **101,** 347, **124,** 83
arbitration clause **65,** 449-50
bank account **63,** 150-1, 152, 187, 374-5, 399-400, **65,** 7, 137, 139, **86,** 65, **98,** 98-100, **101,** 516, **103,** 441
between act and grievance **63,** 400-1, **92,** 457-8, **103,** 440
in case of proceedings involving foreign State **62,** 229, 234-5, **65,** 168-9, 233, 332, 360-2, 389, 391, 393, 399-401, 420, 424-5, 430, 432-4, 449-50, **75,** 123-4, **78,** 91, **82,** 26, **107,** 340-6, **116,** 639
immovable property in forum State, need for **92,** 536-7
causal connection **103,** 440, 478, 485, 488-9, 515-16, 609
commercial activities in forum State **84,** 90-5, 99-100, 115-17, **90,** 602, **96,** 185, **103,** 439-43, 465-7, 488-9
commercial/trade representation/mission **103,** 568
continuous and systematic/enduring relationship, need for **63,** 241, 322-3, 373-6, 496-7
contract of employment concluded in forum State **65,** 379-80
contract governed by foreign law **63,** 459, 463-5
contract negotiated abroad **63,** 459, 463-5
contractual payment **98,** 42, 89-90, 97, **100,** 517-19
crash of foreign-owned plane abroad **98,** 23-5
loss of aircraft **98,** 25
suffering of pilot's family **98,** 24-5
criminal investigations **121,** 640-1
debt, *situs* **98,** 98-100, **103,** 545-6
demand for payment in US **86,** 72
destination of aircraft **98,** 74
diplomatic relations **121,** 640-1
'direct effect in the United States' **63,** 133, 168-9, 182-6, 212-14, 240-4, 295, 324, 356, 377, 402-8, 459, 462-6, 489-92, 496, 522-4, 538-9, 562-4, 598, 619-20, 637-8, **72,** 169-71, 179, **79,** 560, **86,** 59, 63-4, 72, **92,** 445-7, **107,** 229, 230-2, 234-7, 251 n. 26, 265, 334-8
diminution of New York as world financial leader **107,** 235
failure to pay **121,** 494
payment through agent **107,** 265
'doing business in' **38,** 114, **63,** 212-13, 322-3, 324-5, 400-1, 496-7, 520-1, **96,** 76-8, **98,** 145
duty **98,** 134-5
employment contract **98,** 135
employment contract, diplomatic mission
national of sending State **116,** 663

non-national of sending State **116,** 667-8
enforcement of arbitral award and **62,** 234
expropriation/nationalization **63,** 596-8
extraterritorial legislation **92,** 445
failure to pay **121,** 494
failure to transfer funds **92,** 466-7
federal State, within **98,** 42, 92
financial loss **98,** 89, **103,** 443, 466-7, **107,** 230-2, 236-7, 335-8
nationality, relevance **98,** 89
seat of corporation **107,** 237
foreseeable effect **92,** 460-1, **98,** 88, 97 n. 2, 146, **100,** 517, **101,** 550-1, **103,** 443-4, 489, 515-16, **107,** 334
forum selection clause **65,** 391
freezing-out of forum State directors **101,** 550-1
import and sale of goods **63,** 636-8
in rem jurisdiction and **64,** 234, 323
injury in the forum State **63,** 323-8, **65,** 269
injury to nationals inflicted abroad **63,** 213-14, 611-12, **92,** 445-7, 451-4. *See also* suffering following injury overseas *below*
suffering **103,** 608-9
issue of negotiable promissory notes **98,** 115-17
issue of ticket in forum State **92,** 458 n. 3, **98,** 46-7
'legally significant acts' test **98,** 133, **107,** 335-6
letter of credit governed by foreign law **63,** 491
letter of credit payable in forum State **63,** 377, 403-8, 460-5, 491, 562-4
repudiation abroad **63,** 402, 403, 491, 563
loan payable in forum State **64,** 219, **65,** 266, 424-5
loss of grain purchased through forum State's aid programme **63,** 611
loss and suffering of families of deceased **98,** 23-5, 75
mail, use of **63,** 619-20, **86,** 65
'minimum contacts' **63,** 150, 168-9, 185, 204-5, 213-14, 234-5, 240-4, 266-7, 361-2, 372-7, 399-402, 461-6, 491-2, 496, 516-18, 520-1, 564-6, 571-2, 618-20, 626, 647-8
place of injury test distinguished **63,** 491
mortgagee, loss of value of pledge **98,** 35-6
nationality of company suffering loss, relevance **98,** 97
nationals abroad. *See* nationals abroad *above*
nature and purpose of transaction **101,** 349
non-UN activities **96,** 77-8
origin of obligation **82,** 48
participation in aid programme **63,** 230, **86,** 60-1
payment
of compensation **115,** 417
on guarantee **103,** 443-4
of pensions using local infrastructure **103,** 608
of profits **103,** 467
for reservations **103,** 466
through agent **107,** 265
personal jurisdiction and **79,** 14, **121,** 588
in case of foreign State **63,** 57-8, **84,** 112 n. 5, **103,** 546-8, **107,** 340-6
place of business **101,** 349, **107,** 350-1
place of incorporation **107,** 350
place of injury **63,** 491-2

jurisdiction (*cont.*)
place of performance **65,** 70, 379-80, 400-1, **107,** 235, **113,** 529-60
previous visit by ship on which death occurred **98,** 164-6
'principal office' **90,** 648
property within the jurisdiction **65,** 7, 15, 17-18, 19, 137, 139, 203, 204, 450, **101,** 347, 349. *See also* possession of heritable [real] property within the jurisdiction *below*
ratione loci **62,** 27-34, 44, 55, 64-6, 70, 74-6, 85-7, **82,** 103, 121, **86,** 566, 567, 570, 573, 574, 577, 578, 580-2
real and substantial connection **124,** 432-3
registered office **115,** 416
relevance in case of waiver of immunity **63,** 406-7, **79,** 555 n. 15
representation by agent **98,** 146, 155
residence **101,** 349
sale of air ticket **63,** 449-50
seat of corporation within the jurisdiction **65,** 203-4
servicing of aircraft **98,** 75
settlement negotiations **103,** 441-2
shares
in company based in forum State **124,** 556, 568
nationals' possession of foreign shares **81,** 500-2
signature of treaty **113,** 550
sovereign contacts **121,** 640-1
State immunity, execution/attachment and **65,** 135, 168-9, 233, 389, 391, 393, 399-401, 420, 424-5, 430, 432-4, 449-50
State immunity, jurisdiction and **78,** 91
effect on immunity in related matters **103,** 518
subject-matter jurisdiction, need for **103,** 445, 453, 462, 528-30, 612
State-sponsored terrorism, nationality of forum State **121,** 639-41
substantial contact **100,** 563-4, **101,** 550-1
substantial effect **63,** 205-6, 491, 522-4, 636-8, **92,** 460-1, 466, **98,** 88, 97 n. 2, **100,** 517, **103,** 443
suffering following injury overseas **103,** 608-9, **124,** 436. *See also* injury to nationals inflicted abroad *above*
telex, overseas transaction by **63,** 241-3, 496, 620
tort and contract distinguished **63,** 323-4, **107,** 236, **124,** 433
transaction affecting control of bank **121,** 588
transaction as a whole **98,** 18-19
UN Permanent Observer's non-UN activities **96,** 77-8
wages claim by foreign seamen based on legislation of forum State **63,** 629-32
non-nationals **87,** 542
Nuremberg Tribunal **82,** 438, 440
objection to, failure to consider **106,** 652
offer
legislation as **106,** 570-1, 578, 582, 585
promotional literature as **106,** 567-9, 577-82
origin of obligation, place of performance **82,** 48
ouster **72,** 128-9, 135-40, 276, 289-90, 487-8, 711-13, **74,** 191-3, 690-3
passive personality principle **36,** 304, **82,** 348, 349-51, **86,** 44, **88,** 181
extradition based on **82,** 350-1, **104,** 83-4, **119,** 75-6
genocide **119,** 56
immunity and **125,** 496, 500-1
terrorist acts **82,** 350-1, 353, **88,** 181, **121,** 612, 640
torture **119,** 363

passports **73,** 372-3, 609-10, **78,** 69, 70-1, **79,** 198
permanent representative of defendant State, absence of **86,** 566, 581
personal **39,** 327, **51,** 230-2, **54,** 232, **55,** 118, **60,** 53, 62-6, 74, **61,** 219-21, 225-6, 229, 231-2, **66,** 133-5, 196-7, 251-3, 489-502, **71,** 242-58, **77,** 288-92, 586, 589, **79,** 14-15, **82,** 288, 352, **86,** 41, 559-61, 562-3, **87,** 532-3, **90,** 602-3, **98,** 117
agency or instrumentality of foreign State **90,** 603, **98,** 42-3, 91-2
court's power to refuse **86,** 44
drug-trafficking **86,** 551-2, 589, 591
due process requirement **63,** 257-8, 612, **98,** 146-7, **121,** 495
federal State **69,** 161
foreign branches of bank **45,** 96, 102, 105
foreign State, over **63,** 62, 77-80, 148-52, 185, 207-8, 239-43, 266, 322-3, 334-7, 421, 478, 489, **86,** 89, **90,** 602-3, **103,** 546-8, **107,** 642-58
service of process by mail as means of acquisition **63,** 226-7
national ships in foreign port **43,** 176-7
nationals abroad. *See* nationals abroad *above*
nexus. *See* nexus *above*
over foreign State. *See* United States of America (USA), Foreign Sovereign Immunities Act (FSIA) 1976/82, 28 USC 1330(b) (personal jurisdiction over foreign State)
residents **70,** 110-16
subject-matter distinguished **69,** 95
tort **72,** 115-18
piracy. *See* piracy
political question, *Certain Expenses* **105,** 463
ports **38,** 159, **43,** 176-7, **55,** 440-1, **57,** 164-6
colonial **55,** 441-2
possession or control **90,** 560, 561-2
possession of heritable [real] property within the jurisdiction **107,** 642-58
consular use, relevance **107,** 643-58
nature of title, relevance **107,** 646-8, 653-5
prescriptive, nationals' property abroad **42,** 31
presence on territory **77,** 283, 333, 343, 363, 365, 374-6, **79,** 174, 177, **87,** 299-300, 303-5
alleged offender **42,** 108-11, **57,** 142-4, **82,** 354
involuntary **85,** 283, 290-1, **86,** 41, **103,** 209-16
forcible abduction. *See* forcible abduction/unlawful arrest, jurisdiction, effect on
'is found' **82,** 353, 354, 356 n. 25, **88,** 180, 182
'presence in' **94,** 488-9, 521, 565, 578
seat of organization **103,** 3
voluntary **86,** 41
prisoners of war **99,** 166-70
as procedural matter **104,** 177, **107,** 137-44, **119,** 336-7, 350-1, **125,** 573
proceedings in defendant's home State, possibility of
bias **86,** 566
certification, need for **86,** 568, 574
unreasonable or impossible **86,** 567, 574, 577
product liability, corporation with foreign subsidiaries **46,** 340-1
proper law of contract **87,** 531
relevance **87,** 383, 385, 393, 396-8
proprio motu duty to raise **77,** 429, **125,** 574
protected State, in **42,** 51-8
protective principle **36,** 304, **42,** 145, **48,** 115, **70,** 103-9, **77,** 484, 589-91, **82,** 348, 351 n. 14, **84,** 214-15, **87,** 101-2, **90,** 593 n. 11, **91,** 525

jurisdiction (*cont.*)
crimes against humanity **36,** 49-50, 52, 57
drug-trafficking **86,** 214-15
espionage **94,** 74
existing State, limitation to **36,** 54-7
foreign policy and **87,** 101
strictly construed **82,** 351 n. 14
terrorist offence **94,** 501, **104,** 83, 181
protectorates, protecting State **71,** 40-7
public order/public policy/*ordre public* and **46,** 201, **125,** 574
quasi in rem **63,** 145-8, 187, 252-60, 349, 564, **103,** 444-5
real/immovable property, dispute relating to
applicable law **91,** 310-12
dispute between States **91,** 294, 296, 299, 302, 308, 315-16
outside State boundaries **48,** 93, 100
situs **91,** 294, 299, **125,** 339-40
EEC Convention on Jurisdiction and the Enforcement of Judgments (1968) **94,** 312
reasonable exercise **84,** 103-4
burden of defence **84,** 103-4
conflict with sovereignty **84,** 104
efficiency **84,** 104, 105
receiving in third country **86,** 653-4
recognition and **61,** 75-6
refugees, divorce **70,** 356-8, **72,** 642-5
religious courts
Israel **48,** 93-106
Morocco **45,** 53-6
requirements, nexus. *See* nexus *above*
res judicata **90,** 560, 564-5
residence of plaintiff, relevance **123,** 30-1
residence, relevance **78,** 536, 549
aliens resident in country **101,** 345
'ordinarily resident' **41,** 239, 240, 246-7, 254
residents **78,** 50-1
acts committed abroad **70,** 110-16
responsibility for determining **114,** 591-4, 605-6
river, foreign ship **48,** 77-81
search and seizure of alien's property abroad **85,** 276-300
warrant, need for **85,** 297-8
shares, cancellation **72,** 18
ships. *See* flag ship jurisdiction; ships, jurisdiction
sovereign act of third State **115,** 613
Sovereign Base Areas (Cyprus) **41,** 25-8
waters of **88,** 238-9
sovereign power, exercise of
dispute with former Head of State **113,** 449
proceedings against company in forum State for breach of customs laws **113,** 449
sovereignty and **48,** 101, 111, **91,** 39, 117, 119, **92,** 674-5, **105,** 440-1, 443, 497, 575-9
co-extensive, whether **49,** 386-7
exercise of jurisdiction and **57,** 115-16, **71,** 224-5
standard of proof **104,** 311, **114,** 591-4, 605-6
standards for decision and **88,** 121, 123

stateless infant **41,** 239-56
States, dispute between. *See also* foreign State, proceedings involving; State immunity, jurisdiction
foreign policy considerations **113,** 450
forum, absence of alternative forum **91,** 298, 299, 301, 316
international law as applicable law, relevance **91,** 294, 300, 316
municipal courts **91,** 307
State succession, dispute arising from **91,** 307
Status of Forces Agreement, under **49,** 498-503, **77,** 557-8, 617-20
waiver **77,** 558
statutory limitation. *See* statutory limitation
subject-matter. *See also* United States of America (USA), jurisdiction, Foreign Sovereign Immunities Act (FSIA) 1976/82, jurisdiction over foreign State or instrumentality, as basis for
consent, relevance **103,** 611
effects doctrine. *See* effects doctrine *above*
enforcement of foreign arbitral award **103,** 565
nationality as basis **81,** 500
personal distinguished **69,** 95
res judicata **73,** 250-1
submission to court **92,** 628-9
subpoena
right of **90,** 638
served abroad **61,** 231-2
taxation **71,** 220-1, **74,** 206-12, **75,** 82-4, **78,** 528-50
technical assistance expert, host State **42,** 315
Teen Bigha **92,** 564-5, 574-5
territorial **36,** 233-4, 237, 255-6, 260, 268, 270, 302, **38,** 125, 133-6, **44,** 309, 312, **45,** 6, 16, **47,** 119-63, **51,** 233-4, **52,** 290, **54,** 268-77, **57,** 114-17, 119, 130, 152-3, **60,** 56-7, 58-61, 82-9, 95, 96-9, 104-5, 108, **65,** 126, **66,** 59-60, 195-7, 250-5, 279-86, 319-20, 382-3, **69,** 7-10, 100, 106-8, 110-26, 130-2, **70,** 58-60, 66-8, 89-90, 101, 103-16, 433-4, **71,** 220-42, **72,** 30, 80-1, 84-8, 91-3, 214, 440, 672-6, **73,** 227-373, 663, 699-704, **74,** 152, 167-9, 482, **77,** 217, 279-83, 450-1, 586, 589, **78,** 503-5, **80,** 26, 28, 30, **82,** 347, **84,** 677, 687, 688-9, 693, **85,** 229-30, **86,** 519, 529, 653-4, **87,** 371, 380-2, **88,** 238-9, 251, **91,** 35, 531, **92,** 536, 584, **98,** 531-2, 610-14, **103,** 3-4, **104,** 309-10, 352-3. *See also* extraterritorial *and* nexus *above*; *forum [non] conveniens*
acts begun abroad **96,** 177
air services **54,** 316-17, 346
aircraft. *See* aircraft *above*
airport. *See* airports, jurisdiction
American Banana case **96,** 180-1
attempt to commit offence abroad **73,** 253-73
avoidance of infringement on third State **84,** 698
basis
avoidance of infringement on third State **104,** 326
comity **104,** 326, 327-8
efficacy of prosecution **36,** 302-3, **104,** 326
sovereign integrity **104,** 353, 617-18
bigamy committed abroad **74,** 157-9
Calvo Clause **46,** 465-8, **66,** 319-20, **124,** 23
causation and **60,** 58
comity and **60,** 82-3, **73,** 265-6, **84,** 677, 684-6, 694-5, 698-9
connection **60,** 75

jurisdiction (*cont.*)
conspirators **69,** 100, 106-8
constitutional limits **55,** 145-8
construction of legislation **69,** 7-10, 110-26, 131
constructive **87,** 303
criminal **84,** 690-8, **85,** 117, **88,** 25, **104,** 294, **125,** 310-17. *See also* criminal *above*
cross-border offences **80,** 681
declining importance **84,** 50
'deemed to have been committed' within territory. *See* 'deemed to have been committed within the territory' *above*
diplomatic and consular premises **52,** 306-9, **55,** 585-6
discretionary **42,** 104-7
ecclesiastical courts, Morocco after independence **45,** 53-6
effects doctrine. *See* effects doctrine *above*
'essential link' **60,** 58
exceptions **86,** 519
extradition **55,** 431-7
extradition procedure abroad **74,** 482
false representations made abroad **73,** 254-7, 261-5, 269-70
fisheries **73,** 173-8, 366-8
foreigners. *See* aliens *above*
forgery produced abroad **73,** 369-71
forum rule in treaty, effect **72,** 79-81, 91-3
habeas corpus **95,** 492
in personam jurisdiction **104,** 621
in rem jurisdiction **104,** 621
industrial property, protection **93,** 595, 596
inheritance **42,** 103-4
international commerce, applicability **96,** 184-5
judicial doctrine **84,** 677
kidnapping **61,** 192-3, 194-9, 210-11, 214, 219
lakes, riparian States **75,** 82-4
letter posted abroad **73,** 256-7, 260-1, 264-5, 269-71, 371
limits of jurisdiction **46,** 325, **47,** 119-54, **48,** 69-105, **74,** 157-61
embassy, crime committed in **42,** 112-14
offence outside territorial sea **38,** 120-32
locus delicti **60,** 60
Lotus principle **36,** 57, **123,** 356, 410
maritime zones. *See* exclusive economic zone (EEZ)
non-exercise, comity and **88,** 262, **104,** 326
objective territorial principle **60,** 96-9, 104-5, 108, **61,** 188, 221-3
objective territoriality **48,** 109, 114-15
offence committed outside State **69,** 130-2
offence on international train **82,** 104-6
place of terrorist incident **94,** 565
presumption of territoriality. *See* 'deemed to have been committed' within territory *above*
protective principle **70,** 103-9
restraint order in aid of confiscation orders made by foreign court **122,** 518-24, 526-8
retroactive application of legislation authorizing **122,** 521-3, 528

restrictive application **84,** 17
service of process out of the jurisdiction and. *See* service of process out of the jurisdiction
special admiralty or maritime jurisdiction **63,** 353
special maritime and territorial jurisdiction **91,** 474
State immunity and **63,** 372-3, **64,** 86, **65,** 419-20, 438, **81,** 548 n. 7, **84,** 170, **90,** 589-91, **95,** 455, **103,** 470, **104,** 570, 576, 577, 612, 617-19, **119,** 236
State sovereignty and **63,** 88
subject-matter jurisdiction distinguished **103,** 246-7, 256, 257-8
subjective **60,** 82-9
acts completed abroad **96,** 177. *See also* effects doctrine *above*
telephone conversation and **60,** 58, 66
territory, definition **72,** 141-2
torture **107,** 449-51
transit-lounge **88,** 261-2
territorial sea. *See* territorial sea, jurisdiction
territory, title to and **50,** 329-87, 446-63, 501-19, **90,** 292-6
tort **72,** 115-18, 130-1, **74,** 124-7. *See also* nexus *above*
double actionability **116,** 541-2, **125,** 675, 685-90, 713-14, 722-8, 729-39
damages **125,** 690-1, 714
location of act **84,** 99-100, 116
trespass to foreign land **73,** 17-24, 27-30
torture. *See* torture, jurisdiction
transit, persons in **82,** 359-75
treaty. *See also* NATO Status of Forces Agreement (1951)
breach as bar **90,** 676
deprivation, express provision, need for **99,** 170
limitation by **65,** 42-3, 48-9, **74,** 47, 73, **91,** 520-2
UN Compensation Commission. *See* United Nations Compensation Commission, jurisdiction
universal **57,** 119, **74,** 168-9, **77,** 210, 217, **79,** 545-6, **80,** 679, **82,** 348-9
abuse of process and **91,** 152
acquiescence **91,** 144
admiralty **78,** 570
applicable law, international law **91,** 40-4, **104,** 183 n. 25
attack on neutral ship in international waters **79,** 7, **81,** 662
aut dedere aut punire/judicare **36,** 302-3
breach of international law distinguished **91,** 40
civil law and **79,** 7
compatibility of municipal and international law, need for **91,** 48, 50-1, 61-2, 118-19, 150-1
court, need for **91,** 40
crimes against humanity **36,** 26-9, 40, 298-304, **91,** 119-21, **104,** 313, **119,** 67, 212-13, 228-9, 357, 360
International Criminal Tribunal for the Former Yugoslavia (ICTY) **103,** 619
crimes against internationally protected person **77,** 274, **79,** 544
customary international law **81,** 662
exclusive jurisdiction, relevance **105,** 441
extradition and **100,** 670-1
general principle of international law **82,** 349, **94,** 502
Geneva Conventions (1949) **36,** 38
international conflict, need for **105,** 496-7
genocide **36,** 33-9, **82,** 348, **119,** 56, 72, 336-7, **120,** 361-2, 375-6, 391-405

jurisdiction (*cont.*)
hostage-taking **82,** 348-9
hostis humani generis **77,** 184, 187, **91,** 40, 41, 42, **103,** 428, **121,** 258
incorporation of customary international law/treaty, need for **120,** 371-3, 391-405
international crimes **91,** 40, 121-2, **105,** 485, **119,** 67, 229-33, 243, 350, **125,** 579-80
jus cogens/peremptory norm **103,** 618-19, **104,** 193, **125,** 576
legislate, obligation to **91,** 63
municipal law, application of and **91,** 48, 50-1
piracy **82,** 444-5, **91,** 40-1
aircraft **82,** 348-9
requirements
appropriate court **91,** 40
identified international law **91,** 40
presence of offender **82,** 348-9, **87,** 299-300, 303-5, **94,** 565, **119,** 350, 367
retroactivity and **91,** 48-51
right of **91,** 39
sovereignty and **105,** 497, **120,** 371-2
system of law, need for **91,** 40, 151
abuse of process and **91,** 152
federal State, in **91,** 40, 151
variability **91,** 152
terrorism **80,** 679, **82,** 348-9, 445, **88,** 181, 182, **94,** 501-2, 504-5, 564-5, **119,** 342
torture **100,** 471, **107,** 546, **119,** 2, 70-1, 76, 85, 149-50, 155-6, 229-31, 343, **121,** 258, 262
treaty as basis **82,** 348, **94,** 501-2
war crimes **36,** 29, 40, 294, 298-304, **91,** 39-51, 119-21, **104,** 299-300, **105,** 485, **119,** 227-8, **120,** 367-71
unlawfully brought within the jurisdiction **87,** 180-1
circumvention of provisions of extradition agreement **87,** 181
usurpation of
foreign company, in relation to **46,** 325, 528
State responsibility for **46,** 191-2, 204, 318, 320, 324, 327-34, 439, 530
venue **90,** 603-4, 638
distinguished **114,** 592, 597-8
violations of international law, nexus with US law **77,** 217
visiting forces **85,** 163-4, 173-4, **86,** 501-2. *See also* armed forces *above*; NATO Status of Forces Agreement (1951)
concurrent **86,** 534
customary international law **86,** 534
general rules of international law **86,** 534
integrated forces distinguished **86,** 534
international forces distinguished **86,** 534
waiver **85,** 174, **86,** 534
effect on concurrent jurisdiction **86,** 534
receiving State **86,** 534
sending State **86,** 534
withdrawal of **86,** 534
waiver **60,** 49
ad hoc **84,** 211-12
armed forces **85,** 174, 180
bilateral agreement **84,** 211
by individual in employment contract with foreign government **65,** 285
visiting forces. *See* visiting forces, waiver *above*

waiver of other remedies **106,** 521-2
war crimes. *See* war crimes, jurisdiction
warship. *See* warship, jurisdiction
winding-up proceedings, in absence of establishment within the jurisdiction **65,** 84-5, **77,** 30
'within their jurisdiction'. *See* European Convention on Human Rights (1950), phrases, 'within their jurisdiction'
jurisdiction *aut dedere aut punire/judicare*. *See aut dedere aut punire/judicare*
Jurisdiction and the Enforcement of Judgments in Civil and Commercial Matters Convention (1968). *See* foreign judgment, recognition/enforcement, Jurisdiction and the Enforcement of Judgments in Civil and Commercial Matters Convention (1968)
jurisdictional clauses. *See* arbitration agreement; arbitration clause; dispute settlement, treaty provision; forum selection clause; ICSID Convention (Convention on Settlement of Investment Disputes between States and Nationals of Other States (1965)); International Court of Justice (ICJ), compulsory jurisdiction, acceptance
jury trial. *See* fair trial, jury trial, right to; United States of America, Foreign Sovereign Immunities Act (FSIA) 1976, jury trial, right to and
***jus cogens*/peremptory norm** **37,** 458, **41,** 60, 71, 113, 175, 209, 222, **43,** 3, 8, **46,** 478, 499, **52,** 134, 166, **53,** 479, 481, 482, **65,** 166-7, **66,** 587-8, **76,** 325, 434-5, 487, 533, **83,** 25, 26, 49, 534-5, **85,** 259-62, **87,** 31
arbitrary detention **104,** 185
arms dealing **91,** 254
aut dedere aut punire/judicare **94,** 552, 565
basis
consent **103,** 471, 617
custom **83,** 26
customary international law **103,** 471, 616
general principles of law **83,** 26
multilateral treaties **115,** 192
colonial powers' right to alienate territory, limitation on **83,** 25-7
convictio juris **92,** 98, **105,** 274
crimes against humanity **119,** 355
criteria. *See* requirements *below*
definition
Committee of US Citizens in Nicaragua **103,** 609
as higher form of customary international law **124,** 442
Restatement of Foreign Relations Law (Third) **103,** 609, 616
Vienna Convention on the Law of Treaties (1969) **103,** 470, 615-16, **107,** 391
derogation **83,** 25, **115,** 164-5, **124,** 365
disappearances **104,** 185
effectiveness principle, effect on **115,** 119-20
equidistance rule as **41,** 175
equity, principle of **99,** 585
evidence of
multilateral treaties **124,** 364, 365-8
State practice **124,** 364
teachings of publicists **124,** 365
exclusion of derogation by agreement **83,** 25
forcible abduction/unlawful arrest **107,** 435 n. 5
genocide **95,** 152, **103,** 616-17, **115,** 193-4, **120,** 366, 372, 377
[Draft] Articles on State Responsibility (1977/1980/1996/1998/2001) **95,** 158
Vienna Convention on the Law of Treaties (1961) **95,** 158
Head of State, immunity, jurisdiction **119,** 155, 195, 197, **125,** 496, 505-7

***jus cogens*/peremptory norm** (*cont.*)
Holocaust **103,** 615-21
human rights **85,** 261-2, **103,** 617, **104,** 486
ICJ judgments, compliance **85,** 259-62, 273
ICTY Statute **124,** 181
incorporation doctrine and **120,** 371-3, 391-405
inhuman or degrading treatment **104,** 185-9
international humanitarian law **110,** 208, 223-4, 446-7, 523-4
intervention in third State **95,** 182
jus de non evocando **105,** 441
maritime delimitation **99,** 477, 503-4, 568
equidistance **41,** 175
non-acceptance of doctrine **125,** 506-7
non-recognition of forceful occupation of territory **105,** 403
nuclear weapons, threat or use of **110,** 329-30, 374, 446-7
primacy
customary international law **95,** 158, **103,** 471-2, **125,** 506-7
treaty **95,** 158, **103,** 471-2, **125,** 506-7
prohibition
aggression **82,** 417
apartheid **82,** 417
genocide **118,** 376, **120,** 361
racial discrimination **82,** 417
'recognized by international law' **91,** 353, 354
requirements **85,** 260-2
appropriate subject-matter **110,** 524
clear criteria **104,** 184, 185
non-derogability **104,** 184
State practice **65,** 166-7, **106,** 362-3
universality **104,** 184, 185-9
under international law **104,** 186
reservation to treaty and **88,** 677
right of self-determination **82,** 417, **83,** 24
Security Council Resolution and **95,** 158-9
validity **95,** 159, 165
effect of invalidity **95,** 159
self-determination **105,** 243, 270, 283, 329, 334-8, 350, 362
slavery **103,** 616-17
sovereignty over natural resources **83,** 24
State immunity, jurisdiction and **64,** 597, **103,** 473-5, **107,** 541-4, **113,** 433, **119,** 67, 225, **123,** 32, 41-3, 50-1
implied waiver **103,** 609-10, **113,** 537-40, 547-8
States, creation of and **82,** 417-18, 419
summary execution **104,** 185
terrorist act **107,** 391-2
torture **103,** 421-2, 427-31, 472-5, **104,** 184-5, **107,** 541-4, **119,** 85, 86, 149, 200, 206-7, 214, 244, 310-11, **120,** 385-6, **121,** 257-8, 260-2, **123,** 33-4, 41-3, 49-53, **124,** 363-6
obligation to provide civil remedy against foreign State for acts committed outside the forum State **124,** 441-3
treaties and **43,** 8-9, **83,** 15, 24-30, 534-5
exclusion of derogation by agreement **83,** 25
slave-trading agreement **116,** 278
uncertainty **85,** 261

UNESCO Convention for the Protection of the World Cultural and Natural Heritage (1975), obligation to preserve listed properties **106,** 658-9
universal jurisdiction **103,** 618, **104,** 193, **125,** 576
Vienna Convention on the Law of Treaties (1961) **85,** 260, **95,** 158, **103,** 470, 615-16
jus sanguinis **71,** 579, **72,** 504, 507, **75,** 187, 203, 235, 237, 259
jus solis **72,** 504, **75,** 203, 235, 237
just satisfaction (Art. 50 [41] of the European Convention on Human Rights (1950)) **56,** 424-5, 427, 428-31, **57,** 190-4, 197-9, 223, **58,** 91-2, **60,** 161, 179-80, 200-3, **61,** 309, 320-1, 345, 347-58, **62,** 345, 362, 383, **70,** 315-40, **71,** 388. *See also* compensation; costs; damages; remedies; reparation
admissibility of claims **81,** 236-7
agreement, by **57,** 184-6, **67,** 393-4, 476-9, **71,** 391-3, 437
equitable nature **67,** 393, 479, **70,** 332, **71,** 393
mentally ill applicant **67,** 479
applicability **67,** 392
applicant, injured party **61,** 347-8, **67,** 392
argument, need for **108,** 469
basis **81,** 86
equitable **81,** 102, **96,** 450, 464, 476, 517, 534, 560, 584
breach of international obligation **82,** 576-7
apology **82,** 576
declaration of unlawfulness **82,** 576
nominal damages **82,** 576
punishment of responsible individual **82,** 576
change of law **67,** 441
adequacy **67,** 441
compensation **45,** 319, **51,** 239-44, 247, 248, **56,** 419-23, 424-6, 427, 428-31, 499, 501-4, 507-10, **57,** 190-2, **60,** 161, **61,** 320-1, **72,** 309-19, 325-33, 377-86, 404-8, 430-2, **73,** 435-45, 457-8, 548-9, **74,** 381-2, **78,** 211, 224-5, 252-3, 370-1
partial satisfaction by national law **56,** 419-26, 429-31
compensation following death of applicant **70,** 326, 330, 333
compensation for damage caused and application for release distinguished **78,** 240-1
compensation for deprivation of property
margin of appreciation **75,** 417, 422, 486-7, 492-3, 511, 527-31, 559
measure **75,** 422-6, 435, 486-504, 511-12, 518-25, 532-47, 558-61, 642-3
inflation and **75,** 493-5
international law standard, applicability **75,** 423-5, 435, 482-5, 514-17, 521-5, 642
valuation of property, reference period **75,** 488-95, 499-500, 511, 535-40, 558-60
nationals and non-nationals distinguished **75,** 423-5, 435, 482-5, 514-17, 521-5, 642
right to **75,** 421-2, 434, 485, 510, 612, **120,** 65
compensation for injuries to individuals **56,** 419-23
compensation for unlawful detention **45,** 319, **56,** 409, 425, 432-3, **57,** 184-8, 197, **72,** 313-16, **78,** 252-3, 291-2
competence of Court **70,** 318-19
costs. *See* expenses *and* legal costs *below*
creditors in bankruptcy, payment of compensation to **56,** 499, 501-4, 506-10
damage caused by violation **61,** 348, **72,** 329-33
damage caused by violation, cost necessarily incurred distinguished **70,** 319
damages. *See* damages
death of applicant following **70,** 325-33
expenses **70,** 332
legal costs **70,** 326, 331-2
legislative reform **70,** 326, 328

just satisfaction (*cont.*)
equitable basis **60,** 203
exhaustion of local remedies **56,** 419-20, **86,** 348
expenses **56,** 433, **60,** 200, **61,** 348-9, 352-6. *See also* legal costs *below*; costs
'actually, necessarily and reasonably incurred' **67,** 443-5, **70,** 320, **72,** 328-30, 331-2, 338-9, 383-4, 405, **73,** 435, 440, 458, 548, **122,** 432-3
additional legal services **70,** 339
unpresented bills **70,** 331-2
evidence of necessity **70,** 337
legal. *See* legal costs *below*
loss of earnings **70,** 323, **72,** 406-7
'reasonably incurred' **75,** 393-4
subsistence **70,** 317, 323, **71,** 409-10, **72,** 407
supplementary **67,** 445
travel **70,** 317, 323, **71,** 409-10, **72,** 327-8, 384-5, **123,** 20-1
failure to seek **111,** 266
injured party **61,** 347-8, **86,** 403
instruments of
annulment of deportation order, court's competence **111,** 266
annulment of professional disciplinary sanctions **70,** 316, 318-19, **71,** 437-9
court's finding **107,** 45-6, 63, **108,** 428, **111,** 186
deduction of detention pending trial **78,** 252-3, 273-4, 291-2
disciplinary sanctions, annulment **70,** 318-19, **71,** 437-9
finding of breach **61,** 349, **70,** 319-20, **72,** 329-30, 380-1, 405, 431, **78,** 211, 235, 347, **81,** 180, **89,** 206, 261-2, **122,** 430-1
fines, reimbursement **70,** 320
friendly settlement. *See* European Court of Human Rights, friendly settlement
government declaration **67,** 440-1
judgment **84,** 495, **86,** 403, **98,** 318
legislative amendment **88,** 676, **89,** 205, **96,** 476
legislative reform **70,** 326, 328, **71,** 409-10, **72,** 361-2, **78,** 75, 393-4
scope of case, whether within **71,** 409
order assuring parental rights **92,** 255-6
interest **70,** 339-40, **73,** 445, **75,** 386-7, **122,** 432, **123,** 21
on damages sought from government **96,** 496
lost **78,** 370
interpreter's fees **58,** 469-71, 706, **73,** 548
legal costs **61,** 348-9, 352-7, 359, **70,** 316, 320-2, 330-2, 338-9, **71,** 392-3, 409, 438, 440, **72,** 327-8, 330, 383-6, 405-8, 412-13, 431-2, **73,** 429-30, 436-45, 457-8, 548, **75,** 392-4, **78,** 211-12. *See also* expenses *above*
bringing case to ECHR **96,** 518
claims accepted in part **70,** 321-2
domestic **70,** 320-1, 330-2
equitable basis **70,** 322-3, **78,** 224, 348, **123,** 21
'fair proportion' **70,** 322, **78,** 348
individual applicants **56,** 433
legally aided applicant **67,** 394, **70,** 330-2, 337-40, **71,** 393
object of proceedings **70,** 320-1
payment by third party **67,** 443, **70,** 339
requirement to exhaust local remedies and **70,** 321
unenforceable against applicant **67,** 444
measure
loss **60,** 200

lost opportunities **81,** 86, **96,** 450, 517
reasonableness **61,** 352, 357
necessity **67,** 441
non-pecuniary loss **60,** 179, 180, 200-2, **70,** 317, 319, 338, **71,** 409-10, 438, **72,** 326-7, 329-30, 332-3, 405, 411-12, 430-1, **73,** 429-30, 434-5, 457-8, **75,** 386, **78,** 211, 224, 273-4, 291-2, 346-7, **81,** 86, 102, 179-80, 202, 236-7, **89,** 182-3, 190, 202, 205, 308, **111,** 186
deprivation of liberty **111,** 251
distress and anxiety **111,** 231
excessive length of detention **111,** 251
fear and distress **67,** 440-1, 442
mental distress **70,** 328-30, 333
death of applicant, effect **70,** 330, 333
police investigations **67,** 442-3
prolonged uncertainty **96,** 450, 475-6, 496, 517, 559, 583
reputation and honour **96,** 329, 330
unlawful detention **60,** 200-2
participation of judge dissenting on substance **78,** 349-50
pecuniary loss **60,** 179, 180, **70,** 317, 319, 337, **71,** 409-10, **72,** 326-7, 329-30, **73,** 429-30, 432-3, 435-45, 458, 548, **75,** 386, 389-91, **78,** 211, **81,** 18-19, 201-2, **89,** 182, 192, 308
bank commission on precautionary entry in land registry **96,** 533
effect on applicant's chance of proving causal link **96,** 559
increased costs incurred **96,** 463-4
inflation **96,** 533
interest and **96,** 533
mitigation **96,** 475
reparation for damage **111,** 230
termination of infringement, effect **111,** 225-6
rate of exchange, date of judgment **111,** 232
repayment
expenditure incurred **88,** 531
improper fine **88,** 530, 675-8
request for **60,** 161, 179
requirements, causal link between treaty violation and damage **70,** 318-19, 329, **73,** 433, 440, **78,** 211, 345
reservation **68,** 84, **71,** 389, 391, 430, **72,** 325, 377-8, 410, **73,** 428, 532, **74,** 381-2, **75,** 383, 587
restitutio in integrum. See restitutio in integrum
settlement, effect **61,** 346, 350-2
standing **81,** 85-6
unfair hearing **81,** 21-2
justice. *See also* equity; natural justice
administration of
equality of parties. *See* equality of parties
requirements **54,** 475
Aristotle on **37,** 463, **46,** 297
continental shelf delimitation and **81,** 391-2
corrective and distributive **55,** 305-6
distributive. *See* maritime delimitation, distributive justice
equity and. *See* equity, justice, emanation of
failure of **54,** 492
error in procedure **54,** 428-30, 456, 506-7

justice (*cont.*)
fundamental principles of, obligation to give notice of possible prosecution **92,** 677
inherent jurisdiction **100,** 250
international standard **56,** 18, **60,** 47
judge's role **118,** 504
jurisdiction, acceptance of **105,** 378-9
legal basis, need for **81,** 400-1
maritime delimitation **81,** 365, 391-2, 400
settlement of disputes, basis for **56,** 186
justiciability 60, 16, 40-1, **77,** 77, 94-8, 99, 132, 133, 134, 218-20, **79,** 35-6, 48-9, 296, **84,** 299-300, **87,** 181-8, 661-70. *See also* act of State; admissibility; International Court of Justice (ICJ), justiciability; judicial review; political question doctrine
act of State and. *See* act of State, justiciability and
advisory jurisdiction
hypothetical question **115,** 546
legal nature of question **115,** 546-7
comity **108,** 576, **111,** 598-9, 602-3
Constitution, interpretation **87,** 184
decision based on political judgement, foreign State's adherence to treaty **114,** 422-3, 425-6, 429-33, 450-1
definition **105,** 435
diplomatic agent
acts of **48,** 3-4
protection of **89,** 2
diplomatic protection, request for **89,** 7-8
excludability of aliens **82,** 333-5
fact-finding, problems of and **87,** 662-5, 702
foreign law **108,** 661. *See also* foreign law, recognition/enforcement
foreign relations **77,** 226, 231-2, **87,** 182, 185, 515, 664, **88,** 122, **89,** 7-8, **90,** 54, **98,** 178-9, **107,** 288-9, **118,** 366-9. *See also* foreign relations, responsibility; political question doctrine
exercise of consular relations **123,** 608-9
export ban on nuclear equipment **106,** 193-7
interference in domestic affairs of another State **123,** 605-7
treaty-making power **87,** 182, 183, **90,** 54-5
foreign State
breach of treaty **108,** 576, 594-6
disputes between **64,** 339-43, 348-51, **108,** 574-7, 587-91, 594-6, 613
general principle of international law **108,** 587
government act, in domestic courts **86,** 461
Head of State, immunity, jurisdiction and **87,** 237-8, **119,** 73-4, 90-3
imprecise or ambiguous question **115,** 548-9
individual in international law **88,** 88, **104,** 144-6
relations with foreign State **104,** 144
relations with own State **88,** 88-9, 92, **104,** 144
international law, State as link **88,** 90
judicial notice and. *See* judicial notice
jurisdiction distinguished **60,** 16, 40-1, **66,** 112, 160-2, 293, 396-7, **99,** 46 n. 1, **105,** 463, **107,** 257 n. 1
law of evidence and **87,** 182
legal problem, limited to **115,** 575-6
legislature's role **119,** 96

municipal law
modification in preparation **89,** 171
primacy **88,** 181
national security **122,** 638-40, **123,** 609-10
nature of issue determining factor **80,** 86-7, **123,** 605-6
nuclear weapons, declaration of threat or use of as breach of international law **118,** 346-8
nuclear weapons, deployment **122,** 638-40
outdated concept **105,** 463, **106,** 200-1
political question doctrine. *See* foreign relations *above*; political question doctrine
preliminary question **107,** 257
prerogative act **84,** 720, **90,** 34, 50
private law principle **119,** 78
protection of national abroad **47,** 21-2
recognition **104,** 456
remedy, need for **85,** 255, **104,** 159
ripeness of dispute **87,** 692-4, 703-5
Security Council actions. *See* United Nations Security Council, judicial review
separation of powers and **85,** 253-4, **87,** 664, 675-9, 688, 700, 701
'special damages' **72,** 381-3
treaty, breach, adequate satisfaction **73,** 435
undertakings from party in breach **72,** 329, 430
State immunity, jurisdiction and **80,** 124, 164, 205, **119,** 78
subject-matter **80,** 372
substantive issue **119,** 78
territorial **80,** 372
effects doctrine **80,** 373
treaties. *See* treaties, justiciability
UN Charter, Preamble **95,** 109

Kathiawar, United States of, formation 49, 430, 479
Kellogg–Briand Pact (1928) 42, 398
Kenya
arbitral award, enforcement, State succession and **45,** 33-6
extradition
procedure **55,** 509
Uganda, between **55,** 511
jurisdiction
criminal **55,** 141-3
forgery of documents abroad **48,** 90-3
law of
Extradition Contiguous and Foreign Countries Act **55,** 508-9, 511
Kenya Independence Order in Council 1963 **45,** 34-5
Official Secrets Act 1968 **51,** 414-23
State agency/State-owned corporation/State entity
government department, separate legal entity distinguished **103,** 239-41
separate legal entity, Ministry of Defence Claims Commission (UK) **103,** 239-41, 242-3
State succession
arbitral award, enforcement **45,** 33-6
Convention on Arbitral Awards **45,** 33-6
Kerguelen Islands, EEZ, entitlement **125,** 254

Kerkennah Islands 67, 56-7, 81-2, 86, 92, 126, 143, 149, 262, 277, 291, 293-8, 307-11, **81,** 397, 459, 460, 485, **83,** 112
kidnapping. *See* forcible abduction/unlawful arrest
Kiel Canal, Versailles Treaty provisions **37,** 72, 516, 600
Knights of Malta. *See* Sovereign Order of Malta
Koran 62, 171, 174, 184, 191, 193
Korea. *See also* Korea, Democratic People's Republic of; Korea, Republic of
  division of **41,** 19
  independence, recognition by Japan **54,** 4
  status, under Japanese rule **54,** 3
  USA, trading with the enemy legislation **42,** 15-16, 20
Korea, Democratic People's Republic of
  existence, date of coming into **41,** 19
  non-recognition **52,** 68-9, **55,** 455
    effect **41,** 15-20
  status **52,** 72-6
Korea, Republic of
  adoption procedure **66,** 165
  Armistice Agreement (1953) and **41,** 19
  existence, date of coming into **41,** 19
Korean war
  British armed forces, authority of British government over **41,** 20
  civil war, whether **41,** 19
Krajina. *See* Croatia, Serbian Krajina
Kutch
  Administration Reports **50,** 240-4, 418, 433, 446, 466, 495-6, 512
  boundary
    1885 Resolutions **50,** 297-303, 480, 488, 493
    Thar Parkar District, 1876 Resolution **50,** 290-7, 487-8
  India, accession to (1947), validity **50,** 331
  Rann and **50,** 392, 495
  Rulers
    sovereignty **50,** 473
    treaties with British **50,** 54-6, 59-63, 218, 270, 398-401, 424, 425, 459, 464, 465, 470, 477
  Sind
    boundary
      coterminous **50,** 276-85, 479-80, 481, 499, 512, 514
      definition, 1935 **50,** 321-8, 422
      rectification (1914) **50,** 21, 23, 289, 304-16, 416, 417-18, 431, 438-42, 466, 468, 474, 487, 489
    wars with **50,** 393-5
  State of, authority to speak for **50,** 415
  status under British control **50,** 54, 59-63
Kuwait
  Aminoil concession
    'Abu Dhabi Formula', application to **66,** 555, 572-82, 620-1
    administrative contract **66,** 588-91
    Arbitration Agreement **66,** 532-5, 559, 561
    arbitration clause **66,** 593-4
      choice of law clause **66,** 520, 560-1
    colonial nature **66,** 587
    'confidential letter' (1961) **66,** 550

Draft Agreement (1973) **66,** 552
provisional implementation **66,** 553, 566-7
status **66,** 566-71, 615-20
expropriation/nationalization, validity **66,** 582-93
gold clause **66,** 547-8, 610
negotiation clause **66,** 550, 563-6
nature of duty **66,** 565-6, 578
operating conditions **66,** 550
original terms **66,** 547-8
'reasonable rate of return' **66,** 52-3, 578, 582, 608-13
royalty rate. *See* 'Abu Dhabi Formula' *above*
stabilization clause **66,** 548, 550, 586-91, 621-7
nationalization and **66,** 589-90, 623-5
permanent sovereignty over natural resources, effect **66,** 587-8
Supplemental Agreement (1961) **66,** 549-50
termination, compensation in case of **66,** 601-14
business practices **109,** 403-4
rent-a-permit **109,** 412, 413-15
Constitution
Art. 18 (private ownership), compensation for expropriated property **66,** 550-1
Art. 21 (sovereignty over natural resources) **66,** 51, 587
stabilization guarantees, effect on **66,** 587
Art. 31 (torture) **123,** 32
Art. 152 (concession agreements) **66,** 551
international law, municipal law and, general principles of international law **66,** 560, 601
law of
Civil Code (Law 67 of 1980), Art. 53 **109,** 384
Commercial Code 1980, Art. 23 **109,** 404
Commercial Companies Law (Law 32 of 1969) **109,** 404
Constitution. *See* Constitution *above*
Decree Law 124 **66,** 532, 558-9, 624-5
validity **66,** 582-94
Labour Code (Law 38 of 1964) **109,** 384
Art. 28 **109,** 384
Art. 38 **109,** 387
Art. 52 **109,** 385
Art. 54 **109,** 387
Law 19, 1973 (Conservation of Petroleum Resources) **66,** 554
oil concessions. *See also* Aminoil concession *above*
expropriation/nationalization **66,** 554, 558, 577
progressive **66,** 584-5
real property
Amiri Decree of August 1976 **109,** 393
foreign nationals and **109,** 393
Law 74 of 1979 **109,** 393
State agency/State-owned corporation/State entity, Kuwait News Agency **113,** 458-9
Kuwait, Iraqi invasion (1990)
Iraqi legislation relating to
as breach of international law **125,** 671-2
RCC Resolution 55 (Security Council Resolution 686: repeal of RCC resolution relating to Iraq), retroactive effect **116,** 601-6, **125,** 631-2, 655-6

Kuwait, Iraqi invasion (*cont.*)
RCC Resolution 369 (dissolution of Kuwait Airways Corporation and transfer of assets)
extraterritorial effect **125,** 607-8, 665-8
jurisdictional validity **116,** 587
justiciability in UK courts **125,** 653-7, 709-10, 718-22
recognition by UK **116,** 554-7, 562-8, 578-601, **125,** 680-5, 709-13
text **125,** 627-8
State immunity, jurisdiction
Iraq **125,** 656-7
Iraqi Airways Co. (IAC) **125,** 656-7, 678, 741-2
status following
continuance as State **116,** 581
Iraq as de facto government **116,** 579-87
effective control **116,** 586
international recognition **116,** 586, **125,** 658-65
stability **116,** 586
Security Council Resolutions 661 and 662, effect **116,** 581
Kuwait Oil Company 66, 548, 554, 577
Kuwait–Saudi Arabia Neutral Zone 66, 532, 547
division **66,** 547
Kyoto Declaration (1995), fisheries conservation and management measures **123,** 298

Labrador. *See* Canada, Labrador
laches. *See* international law, gaps
lakes
boundaries **41,** 135, 149, **50,** 391-2
Constance, jurisdiction over **75,** 82-4
riparian landowners, rights **74,** 122-3
riparian States
condominium theory **75,** 83
jurisdiction **75,** 82-4
status
freshwater **94,** 242-6
Great Lakes **94,** 242-6
inland waters **94,** 245-6
international boundary, effect **94,** 243-6
land
aliens, ownership **48,** 169-71
disposition and ownership, law governing **44,** 57
purchase by State, Indian Customs Line transactions **50,** 201-6
landing rights (air) 40, 92-3, **78,** 521-6
landing rights (fisheries) 82, 643-4
landlocked States
continental shelf **81,** 315
right of transit **82,** 369
Laos, independence, acquisition of **39,** 405-9
Lapps. *See* Finland, Sami rights; Sweden, Sami
Lateran Treaty. *See* Holy See, Italy and
Latin American States, international law on State responsibility and **46,** 464-9, 495
Lausanne, Treaty of, exemption from property levies **44,** 154
law
as body of rules **114,** 269
characteristics **49,** 354-7, 402-3

existence in any society **39,** 239-42, 345
function **39,** 333, **118,** 352
fundamental principles of, freedom from discrimination **51,** 440
interpretation, voluntarism and subjectivism **37,** 437, 443-4
legitimacy of **79,** 335
meaning
American Convention on Human Rights **79,** 326-35
statutory and non-statutory distinguished **79,** 327-35, 341, 345-6, 373, 376
morality and **41,** 143
nature and purpose **37,** 30, 267, 425
nature, refashioning of and **41,** 79-80
politics and **37,** 446-7
reason as source of **39,** 207
rules/principles, distinction **114,** 269
social substratum **37,** 454
law of conflicts. *See* private international law
law of the sea. *See also* contiguous zone; continental shelf; continental shelf delimitation; exclusive economic zone (EEZ); exclusive fishery zone (EFZ); fishing zones; high seas; inland waters; internal waters; islands; lakes; Law of the Sea Convention (1982); maritime delimitation; maritime jurisdiction[s]; maritime waters; rivers; seabed and subsoil; territorial sea
development **81,** 357-61, **92,** 67
equity, difficulty of defining as result **99,** 624-5
recent phenomenon **83,** 36
equity, role **99,** 626-7
Law of the Sea Convention (1982) 62, 114-15, 125, **70,** 607, 611, 640-1. *See also* Continental Shelf Convention (1958); High Seas Convention (1958); law of the sea; maritime delimitation; Territorial Sea and Contiguous Zone Convention (1958)
applicability
before entry into force **83,** 86-7, **95,** 701, **99,** 452
before ratification **91,** 379, **95,** 701
States not party to **119,** 457, 460-1
arrest of ships. *See also* Law of the Sea Convention (1982): Part XV (settlement of disputes), Art. 292 (prompt release) proceedings
use of force **120,** 196, 274
Art. 292 (prompt release) proceedings. *See* Law of the Sea Convention (1982): Part XV (settlement of disputes), Art. 292 (prompt release) proceedings
balance between rights of coastal State and freedom of navigation **120,** 223-4
Art. 292 (prompt release) proceedings **110,** 769
bays
applicable law **97,** 504
as internal waters **97,** 661
pluri-State **97,** 504
coastal states, disputes relating to sovereign rights **119,** 552-3, 563
commission on the Limits of the Territorial Sea, role **95,** 674-5, 701, 723
compliance, conduct within the Commission for the Conservation of Southern Bluefin Tuna as evidence of **117,** 161
conciliation, exclusion from compulsory procedures and **99,** 481
consensus, significance **71,** 121
conservation and management measures **82,** 628, 629-30, 642, **123,** 293-4, 316, 326-7, 428
continental shelf **81,** 281
breadth **70,** 607, 611
definition **81,** 383, 388

Law of the Sea Convention (*cont.*)
delimitation **71,** 121-2, 188, 192, 193-4, 199, 201-2, 204, 210, **72,** 121, **91,** 670
equitable result **81,** 307
distance, title and **81,** 296-7
EEZ, assimilation to **71,** 121-2, 201-2, **92,** 65, **99,** 467-8
existing law, relation to **71,** 121, 188, 192, 202, 210
fisheries agreements, obligation to conclude **92,** 18
islands, political status, relevance **95,** 666
measurement, on surface of water **81,** 302-3
natural prolongation, title and **81,** 329
Convention for the Conservation of Southern Bluefin Tuna (1993) and. *See* tuna, measures to protect, Convention for the Conservation of Southern Bluefin Tuna (1993)
customary international law **81,** 261-2, 264, 287, 300, 351, **82,** 629, 642, **83,** 86-7, **92,** 66, **97,** 504, **99,** 499, 655, **119,** 458
continental shelf **81,** 262
EEZ **81,** 264
evidence of, whether **95,** 701, **99,** 476
fishing zones **99,** 495-6
flag State jurisdiction on the high seas **120,** 588
freedom of navigation **95,** 705, **120,** 588
islands, rocks, distinction **99,** 452
declaratory nature **55,** 205-6, **71,** 121, 202
delimitation **55,** 257
detention of vessel
on the basis of laws and regulations within meaning of Art. 73(2). *See* Law of the Sea Convention (1982): Part XV (settlement of disputes), detention of vessel on the basis of laws and regulations within meaning of Art. 73(2)
notification to flag State **110,** 757
disputes under. *See also* International Tribunal for the Law of the Sea (ITLOS); Law of the Sea Convention (1982): Part XV (settlement of disputes)
action to prevent aggravation, waiver of claims and **117,** 123
compulsory procedures entailing binding provisions
agreement of all parties to dispute, need for **119,** 553, 561-5
conciliation and **99,** 481
limitations (Art. 297) **119,** 552-3, 562-5
subsequent treaty practice **119,** 553-4, 561
disputes affecting coastal states rights **119,** 552-3, 563
failure to choose means of settling under Art. 287 **117,** 152
obligation to exchange views (Art. 283), 'no settlement has been reached' and **119,** 550-1
distance **83,** 103
drafting **99,** 474-6
EEZ. *See* exclusive economic zone (EEZ)
entry into force **83,** 43
equidistance, territorial sea **83,** 14, 15, **97,** 674-5
equitable principles/equidistance **83,** 93-4
equitable result. *See* maritime delimitation, equitable result *below*
European Community (EC) competence and **120,** 630-1
existing bilateral agreements, effect of **82,** 614, 629
fisheries jurisdiction **56,** 217
flag State, obligation to exercise jurisdiction **82,** 614, **120,** 179-80, 251-2
genuine link requirement **120,** 178-80, 252
hot pursuit **120,** 194-6

implementation
implementing legislation, conformity with Convention **110,** 765, **120,** 260
rules enacted by States, international organizations and international conferences **120,** 236-7
innocent passage **97,** 509
internal waters **97,** 662
interpretation. *See* Law of the Sea Convention (1982), interpretation
as legal framework for law of the sea activity **123,** 293-4, 316, 326, 428
low-tide elevations **83,** 110-11
maritime delimitation
agreement, procedural rule **81,** 373
equitable principles **81,** 317
equitable result **81,** 262, 317, 322, 373
methods **81,** 262-3, 317, 328, 372-3, 380
unilateral delimitation **81,** 373
natural resources **82,** 629-30, 642
'economic needs of coastal fishing community' **82,** 629, **119,** 442 n. 18
navigational access **94,** 25
non-living resources **81,** 303
notification of laws, need for **120,** 327
obligations
in case of parallel or implementation treaties **119,** 548-9, 560-1
conformity with coastal State laws **120,** 236-7
to conclude fisheries agreements **92,** 18
to cooperate to ensure conservation of migratory species **117,** 161, 168
to exercise jurisdiction **82,** 614, **120,** 179-80
parties, UN Council for Namibia **91,** 379
policy and **46,** 477-8
port State powers **120,** 596
reefs **119,** 460
refuelling of fishing vessel **110,** 752, **120,** 237-9, 256-7
remedies
detention of vessel. *See* detention of vessel *above*
imprisonment **110,** 778
reparations **120,** 199
right of review under **83,** 42-3
rights
not attributed under **120,** 192, 238, 297-8
of State and ship/individual distinguished **120,** 233-6
status **81,** 261-2, 300-1, 357, 372
third parties and **82,** 629
travaux préparatoires **110,** 770, 786
aid to interpretation **119,** 563-5, **120,** 240
excluded provisions, status **120,** 245-6, 325
violation
economic nature **91,** 380
remedies
forfeiture of fish **91,** 383
forfeiture of ship **91,** 381-3
imprisonment **91,** 379-81
penalty **91,** 380-2
Law of the Sea Convention (1982), interpretation
aids

Law of the Sea Convention, interpretation (*cont.*)
parallel texts **119,** 561
structure of treaty **119,** 562-3
subsequent treaty practice **119,** 553-4, 561
Art. 73, uncertainties **125,** 308
by ICJ **70,** 641
context, related agreement **119,** 559-60
guidelines
authentic languages, identity of meaning **125,** 256-8
effectiveness principle **120,** 235
object and purpose **119,** 563, 565
interrelationship of ss 1, 2 and 3 of Part XV **119,** 552, 562-3
phrases
'economic needs of coastal fishing community' **82,** 629, **119,** 442 n. 18
'entails a binding decision' **117,** 184
'fisheries laws and regulations' **110,** 772
'geographically disadvantaged State', Honduras **97,** 676
'in order to achieve an equitable solution', legal concept, whether **99,** 476
'States bordering on enclosed or semi-enclosed sea', Fonseca Bay **97,** 676
revision distinguished **120,** 246
travaux préparatoires. See travaux préparatoires below
Law of the Sea Convention (1982): Part XV (settlement of disputes)
abuse of process **119,** 554
admissibility. *See also* exhaustion of local remedies
accurate use of term **125,** 258
conformity with requirements of Art. 292 of the Law of the Sea Convention (1982) **110,** 749-57
nationality of claims issues **120,** 184-5
objections to
at preliminary/merits phases distinguished **120,** 172, 241-2, 255, 333-9
objections to jurisdiction distinguished **120,** 171-2
right to raise **120,** 171-2, 239-42, 333-9
agreement to seek settlement by peaceful means of own choice (Art. 281(1)) **119,** 550-1
Convention for the Conservation of Southern Bluefish Tuna (1993), Art. 16 provisions as **119,** 549-51, 557-65
arbitral tribunal (Annex VII). *See also* International Tribunal for the Law of the Sea
constitution **117,** 191, **119,** 511-12
ICSID role **119,** 512
procedure, determination of **117,** 191
role **117,** 171
arbitration as default procedure **117,** 162, 182-4
Art. 292 (prompt release) proceedings **110,** 741-86
Art. 286 (dispute concerning interpretation or application of Convention) proceedings distinguished **110,** 770-1
Art. 290 proceedings (provisional measures) distinguished **110,** 768
Art. 290(5) proceedings compared **110,** 771
as autonomous proceeding **125,** 193, 195, 244
balance between rights of coastal State and freedom of navigation **110,** 769, **125,** 210-12
binding effect **110,** 749-50
concurrent proceedings in national courts, avoidance **125,** 207-9
delay in initiating **125,** 207-9

detention of vessel on the basis of laws and regulations within meaning of Art. 73(2) **110,** 769-70, 774-7, 778-85, **125,** 182-5, 195-6, 199-205, 211-12, 242-8
declaration of non-compliance, need for **125,** 188-90, 205, 216, 258-61
detention/arrest of ship, as response to **125,** 190-1
dispute, relevance **125,** 309-10
exhaustion of local remedies, need for **125,** 181-2, 198-9, 207
limited nature of proceedings **110,** 770-1, 773-4, 786, **125,** 309-10
municipal court proceedings and **125,** 197-9. *See also* exhaustion of local remedies, need for *below*
facts, determination by municipal courts **125,** 251-4, 255-6
penalties for EEZ violations (Art. 73(3)), relevance **125,** 181-2
preliminary proceedings, whether **110,** 749-50, 760-1, 768, 774
prompt notification of arrest or detention (Art. 73(4)), relevance **125,** 181-2
purpose/basis of provision **125,** 190-1, 205-7, 211-12, 217
Explanatory Statement by Secretary **125,** 194
freedom of the high seas **125,** 191
reasonable bond or financial security, relevance **110,** 756-7, 786, **125,** 182-5
time limit for application, whether **125,** 179-80
compulsory procedures entailing binding provisions
agreement to seek settlement by peaceful means of own choice (Art. 281(1)) and **119,** 551-4
obligation to seek peaceful settlement **119,** 563-6
dispute
arising under both UNCLOS (1982) and Convention for the Preservation of Southern Bluefin Tuna (1993) **119,** 546-9, 557-65
parties' arguments **119,** 536-44
UNCLOS (1982) as sole basis of jurisdiction **119,** 554
disagreement relating to performance of treaty obligations **119,** 546-9
existence as objective matter to be determined by Tribunal **119,** 546-7
as single dispute **119,** 550
termination of dispute, effect **119,** 545-6
estoppel
compromis **120,** 231, 255
conduct of parties **120,** 231
failure to challenge standing of party **120,** 249-50, 254-6, 315-16, 350-2
good faith and **120,** 249-50
requirements, detriment/prejudice **120,** 249-50
exhaustion of local remedies
Art. 292 (prompt release) proceedings. *See* Art. 292 (prompt release) proceedings, exhaustion of local remedies; Law of the Sea Convention (1982): Part XV (settlement of disputes)
inter-State disputes **120,** 182-3, 233-6, 250-1, 318
breach of Law of the Sea Convention (1982), whether **120,** 233-6
jurisdictional link between victim and State causing damage **120,** 181-2, 183-4, 236, 330
provisional measures and **117,** 133
'where this is required by international law' **120,** 182-3
exhaustion of procedures for amicable dispute settlement, provisional measures and **117,** 160, 190
jurisdiction
acceptance of submission to Tribunal **117,** 116
Agent, need for authorization according to Rules **110,** 748
agreement to alternative procedure with binding effect (Art. 282) and **119,** 529

Law of the Sea Convention: Part XV (*cont.*)
basis
Agreement (1998) (Guinea–St Vincent and the Grenadines) **117,** 113-15, **120,** 158-9, 170, 332-8
Art. 297(1) **117,** 122, **120,** 170
compétence de la compétence **120,** 241
disagreement as to **117,** 122, **120,** 170
dispute concerning the interpretation or application of the Law of the Sea Convention (1982)
'dispute' **117,** 161, 163
limitation to inter-State disputes **120,** 235
dispute. *See* dispute *above*
exclusion of compulsory measures entailing binding provisions, Convention for the Conservation of Southern Bluefin Tuna (1993) dispute provisions as **119,** 557-65
failure to submit question of release from detention to another court within 10 days of detention **110,** 748, 780
lack of, effect on provisional measures **119,** 554-5
merits. *See* merits *below*
municipal law
compatibility with Convention **120,** 188-9, 213-14, 236-7
interpretation **120,** 227, 252-3
nationality, verification **120,** 341-2
ownership, relevance **110,** 748-9
parties to Convention, over **110,** 748
prima facie **117,** 160-2
provisional measures Order and **117,** 123-4, 133-4
refusal, resulting injustice **120,** 217-18, 232, 316-17
specific provisions for prompt release of vessels, need for **110,** 770, **125,** 250-1
Tribunal's obligation to examine basis **125,** 297
merits
incidental to prompt release proceedings **110,** 750, 761
municipal courts, determination by **110,** 749-50, 770, 776, 780, **125,** 251-4, 268-72, 304-5
restraint in considering **110,** 750, **125,** 261-2
standard of proof, relevance **110,** 750, 774, **125,** 260-1, 263-4, 271-2
prompt release of vessels and crews. *See also* reasonable bond or financial security *below*
Art. 286 (dispute concerning interpretation or application of Convention) proceedings **110,** 771
Art. 290(5) proceedings **110,** 771
Art. 292 proceedings. *See* Art. 292 (prompt release) proceedings *above*
classification of legislation justifying detention
presumption of legality of State's action **110,** 756, 776-7
responsibility for **110,** 768-9, 776-7, 785
Tribunal's freedom of decision **110,** 756, 762-7, 768-9
detaining State's failure to comply with Convention **110,** 761-2, 780
justifying factors **120,** 198, 299
discretion of Tribunal **125,** 200, 207
incidental proceedings distinguished **110,** 750
legality of arrest, relevance **110,** 753, 761
burden of proof **110,** 761
procedures for ensuring **110,** 749

proceedings limited to **110,** 749-50
responsibility for failure to post **110,** 757
provisional measures
adequacy of scientific information, relevance **117,** 168-9, 173
arbitral tribunal and
decision of tribunal as critical date **117,** 171, 178
establishment of tribunal **117,** 162-3
Art. 290 proceedings **117,** 113-47, 151-94
action pending constitution of arbitral tribunal **117,** 162, 191
Art. 290(1) and 290(5) proceedings distinguished **117,** 180
'in the circumstances' **117,** 135-6
procedural nature **117,** 134-5
urgency **117,** 134-5, 139
binding effect **110,** 750, **117,** 131
compliance with
obligation **117,** 126, 131
reporting obligation **117,** 124, 125, 126-7, 128
convenience of parties, relevance **117,** 172
exhaustion of local remedies **117,** 133
exhaustion of procedures for amicable dispute settlement **117,** 160, 190
ICJ/PCIJ provisions distinguished **117,** 130, 135-6, 139-40, 188-9
irreparability of damage, relevance **117,** 112-13, 141, 146, 147 n. 67, 170-1, 178
non-State parties and **117,** 131 n. 4, 138
Order of 11 March 1968 (Guinea–St Vincent and the Grenadines), text **117,** 122, **120,** 158-9
Order of 27 August 1999 (Australia and New Zealand v. Japan), text **119,** 525-9
pending arbitration **119,** 523-30
purpose
preservation of the rights of the parties **117,** 136-40, 143, 163, 172, 175-6
preservation of the *status quo pendente lite* **117,** 130-1, 177
preservation of subject-matter of review **117,** 143
prevention of aggravation or extension of dispute **117,** 143-5, 146, 147
prevention of harm to the marine environment **117,** 131, 146, 163, 171, 175-7, 178-80
recommendation for action distinguished **117,** 127-9
requirements
balancing of Parties' rights **117,** 139-40, 147
clarity and precision **117,** 194
continuing purpose **117,** 123
prima facie jurisdiction **117,** 122, 133-4, 160, 181-4, **119,** 529
right of party to requested measures **117,** 136-9
urgency **117,** 140-1, 171, 177-80, 189-93
subsequent finding that tribunal lacks jurisdiction, effect **119,** 554-5
third parties and **117,** 140
Tribunal's right
discretionary nature **117,** 132, 134
to determine **117,** 124, 128, 164
to prescribe **117,** 125-7
ultra petita **117,** 144, 187-9
urgency, substantive and procedural distinguished **117,** 147
reasonable bond or financial security **110,** 750-1, 752, 756-8, 786
applicable law

Law of the Sea Convention: Part XV (*cont.*)
international law **125,** 217
municipal law of detaining State **125,** 193, 258-9, 262
Art. 292 (prompt release) proceedings, relevance **110,** 756-7, 786, **125,** 182-5
standard of treatment of aliens distinguished **125,** 192
bank guarantee
cash or banker's draft, acceptability **125,** 205, 248-9, 262
practice relating to **125,** 262
determination as responsibility of Tribunal **125,** 196
margin of appreciation **125,** 258-9
need for **110,** 757, **125,** 182-3
offset **110,** 758
posting with Tribunal, need for parties' agreement **125,** 185
reasonable in overall balance of amount, form and nature of bond or financial security **110,** 757-8, **120,** 299-300, **125,** 183-4, 210-11, 243-7, 248-9, 260-1
release **120,** 201-2
relevant factors
accused's circumstances **125,** 200
conservation considerations **125,** 197, 201-2, 259-60, 264-5
consistency **125,** 193, 266
Convention as a whole **125,** 200
enforcement of national fisheries laws and regulations **125,** 197, 202-4, 211-12, 217-19, 245
gravity of offence **125,** 183-4, 203-4, 245, 254-5, 259, 266-7
illegal fishing in area **125,** 196
penalties imposable in national court **125,** 183-4, 202-3, 213-15, 245-6, 258-9
proportionality **125,** 193, 266
value of catch and gear **125,** 184, 246-8, 261-2
value of ship **125,** 183, 184, 210, 218-19, 260, 266, 269-70
speediness of procedures in national courts, relevance **125,** 199
suffisante **125,** 256-8
terms **125,** 185
title of proceedings **119,** 513
League of Arab States
Administrative Tribunal. *See* League of Arab States Administrative Tribunal
status **116,** 645
international legal personality, acceptance of permanent delegation as recognition of **116,** 648-9
League of Arab States Administrative Tribunal
access to **116,** 649
costs **116,** 649
jurisdiction
distance of Headquarters from employee's place of work, relevance **116,** 647
employment contract disputes, sole **116,** 647
independence of tribunal, relevance **116,** 647
legal representation **116,** 649
League of Nations. *See also* United Nations (UN)
abstention **49,** 176 n. 1 *and* 2
Board of Liquidation **37,** 328, **49,** 237
Codification Committee **37,** 67
Covenant. *See* League of Nations Covenant
de facto existence **37,** 439
dissolution

effects **57,** 479, 491
on Mandates **37,** 14-24, 37-9, 74, 75, 77, 96, 114, 157, 204-39, 301, 320, 324-32, 339-45, 430, 433-4, 437-42
on Members' rights **37,** 269, 304, 401
nature of **37,** 139, 202, 304, 406
transfer of power to United Nations **57,** 478-9
dissolution resolutions **37,** 19-22, 39, 54, 78, 97, 132, 151, 152, 159, 162, 218-19, 222, 234, 235, 301, 325-9, 340, 366, 405-6, 415, 439, 570
establishment **37,** 30
expulsion clause **37,** 263, **49,** 50
immunity of officials **71,** 538
legal interests of League and Members **37,** 596
legal personality **37,** 116, 263, 293, 522, 523
Mandates and. *See* Mandates, League of Nations and
Members
aggregation **37,** 593
expulsion **49,** 50
Mandatories' duties, interest in observance of **37,** 24-5, 33, 37, 46, 49-50, 51, 72, 104, 181, 241-2, 255, 257-84, 293, 400-12, 418-30, 507, 510-11, 517, 573, 579-80, 597-600
rights of **37,** 259
Membership, Declarations concerning **37,** 80
organs of, action through **37,** 257, 258
personality
aggregation of members **37,** 593
organized international community **37,** 438
Protocol for the Pacific Settlement of International Disputes (1924) **84,** 291
treaty-making capacity **37,** 122, 134, 135
UN, transfer of functions to **37,** 16-17, 118, 154-5, 157, 160, 202, 206-39, 310-12, 314, 324-5
UN General Assembly
assumption of Council's functions (1946) **37,** 20, 114, 406
functions **37,** 352-3
Mandates system, Resolution for Continuance of (1946) **37,** 19-24, 151-4, 222, 344, **49,** 25, 28-9, 185-7, 200, 236-9, 245
unanimity rule **37,** 18-19, 23-4, 146-7, 149, 200, 208, 209, 264, 278, 308, 310, 311, 343-4, 360, 402, 421, 441, 532, 565, 592, 596, **49,** 39, 49, 189-97, 218, 259, 262, 263, 275-8
League of Nations Council
as arbitral tribunal **91,** 575
composition **37,** 532
decisions, Mandatories and **49,** 258-9
Mandatory
competence to create 'standards' for **37,** 360-2
decisions of Council and **49,** 258-9
PCIJ judgments of and **37,** 169, 513
resolutions
effect **37,** 12, 63, 64, 66, 68, 81, 107, 118, 124, 134, 260, 387-8
treaty nature **37,** 224, 235
treaty registration, regulations for **37,** 80-1
League of Nations Covenant
amendment **37,** 241-2
Art. 22

League of Nations Covenant (*cont.*)
compromise, result of **37,** 196, 206, 228, 309
UN Charter, Art. 73 and **37,** 161-2
Mandates
Art. 22 **37,** 161-2, 330-1, 333-4, 341, 345-6, 493-4
Declaration and **37,** 199-200
provision **49,** 5, 18, 24, 192, 196, 200, 201, 202
President Wilson's draft, Mandates provisions **49,** 37-8
territorial guarantees **37,** 77
treaties, registration of **37,** 45, 79-81
leases, international
restoration of leased property, concessions, effect on **40,** 8-9
Sovereign Base Areas, Cyprus, Republic of **41,** 25-8
Lebanon. *See also* United Nations Interim Force in the Lebanon (UNIFIL)
disturbances (1975-6) **74,** 14-21, 27-8, 32-5
civil war, whether **74,** 23-8
history **74,** 9-21
insurance contract, effect on **74,** 7-8, 21-35
Mandate. *See* Mandate, Lebanon
legal aid
ECHR proceedings **81,** 180, **89,** 309
effective remedy and **98,** 365, **120,** 104
entitlement
alien **72,** 418-29
diplomatic agent **94,** 601
equality before the law **124,** 572
fair trial and **57,** 199, **58,** 630-1, **60,** 196-9, **79,** 270, 273, 276, **98,** 365, 368, **111,** 208
Judicial Committee of the Privy Council **124,** 563-4
obligation to provide **115,** 664-71
prompt hearing and **96,** 553
separation proceedings **58,** 639, 641
territorial limitation **124,** 575-6
legal assistance. *See also* European Convention on Human Rights (1950), legal assistance
courts, whether identical with **68,** 580-1, 629-30, 644-5
legal certainty
European Community law **93,** 397, 426, **117,** 286-7, 348-51, 360-1
extradition **100,** 406
legal fiction, teleological application **46,** 295, 301
legal hearing, right to. *See also* fair hearing; fair trial
EC **93,** 423-4, 428, 542
legal norms 37, 446
legal personality 86, 354. *See also* international law, subjects; international organizations, personality
American Battle Monuments Commission **115,** 440
Australian Federal Police **111,** 628-9
Belgian Congo **45,** 25, 29
existence and capacity, whether distinct **80,** 42
failure to accord as breach of treaty obligation **80,** 150-1, **81,** 681, 703-4
intention to confer **80,** 93
international organizations **80,** 90-7, 151-62
objectives, relevance **80,** 95
legal capacity and **80,** 41-2, 43, 94-6
tests, treaty-making power **80,** 95

trade union **80,** 43, **81,** 707
unincorporated committee established by statute **80,** 42-3
legal principles, validity 46, 478
legal protection
requirements, judge as member of judicial body **108,** 667-8
right of **108,** 667-8
legal representation. *See also* European Convention on Human Rights (1950), legal assistance; International Covenant on Civil and Political Rights, legal representation
freedom of choice **70,** 185-91, 204
denial of employment permit **70,** 185-91
government's assumption of responsibility for
Bhopal gas leak disaster **118,** 464-526
conflict of interest **118,** 488-90
Guantanamo Bay Naval Base detainees **123,** 603, 607-9
prisoners of war **123,** 607-9
legal system, conditions for existence **39,** 345-6
legislation. *See also* foreign law; legislation, interpretation; treaties, implementing legislation
air transport agreements, implementing legislation **87,** 372-8, 381-9, 392-3
anti-terrorist **82,** 311
application before entry into force, discretion not to prosecute **122,** 436-9, 440-9, 453-9, 465-7
British Commonwealth, within **69,** 94, 114-15, **86,** 604
Statute of Westminster 1931 **69,** 94
challenge to, burden of proof **98,** 397
constitutionality **79,** 555-60, **103,** 295-7, 298, **112,** 695-729
competence to determine **78,** 61
overinclusiveness **121,** 523-5, 530-1, 538-41
proposed amendments, review by international tribunal **79,** 285-325
underinclusiveness **121,** 525-6, 541-4
context of operation, relevance **112,** 695-6
Council of Europe, laws of Member States and **58,** 583
court procedure and **40,** 445
criminal
ad hominem **44,** 115
invading enemy forces **40,** 452, 456-7
retrospective, human rights **44,** 108-9, 116
customary international law and **85,** 258-9
delegated, *ultra vires*, separability **44,** 20
dependent territory, law of mother country and **88,** 271
emergency **79,** 478-9
repeal **47,** 483, 487
repeal of other laws by **47,** 481
entrenchment **78,** 462
European Communities membership, possible effect on **78,** 463
'existing law' **85,** 137, **90,** 458
extraterritorial. *See* territorial limitation *below*; extraterritorial legislation
federal State. *See* federal State, legislative powers
foreign relations, law relating to, classification **90,** 81-2, 84-9
Government, binding effect on **53,** 165-71, 174-7
implementation
by broadcasting authority in conformity with treaty obligations **115,** 407
treaty as guide **90,** 27
treaty, obligation to take into account **117,** 647-9

legislation (*cont.*)
independence and, continuance of law of colonial power **87,** 314
international law and **87,** 298
declaratory of **80,** 94
interpretation. *See* legislation, interpretation
legality of, foreign court's right to determine **119,** 92
limitations on, international law, relevance **91,** 30, **104,** 452-6
nationality **79,** 287-9, 297-300, 303-5
Parliamentary powers **55,** 547
powers
executive **91,** 328-9
taxation law **91,** 326
trust territory **87,** 550
preamble
aid to interpretation. *See* legislation, interpretation, aids, preamble
effect **103,** 140-1
proportionality to purpose and object **90,** 84, 112-13
purpose, peace, order and good government **70,** 58-60, 67, 90, 108-9, **91,** 75, 99, 146-7, 162, 326, **123,** 587-91, 592-3
recognition. *See* foreign law, recognition/legislation
repeal
emergency legislation **47,** 483, 487
implied **48,** 73-6, **79,** 5-6, **81,** 665, **122,** 664
by treaty **36,** 397-9, **88,** 225, 228, **93,** 290
EC law **93,** 526, 531, 534
retroactivity. *See* legislation, retroactive
separability **103,** 122-4
State succession, evolution, scope for **86,** 650
subordinate law-making **90,** 121-2, 136-7
tax statute, colourable device, whether **91,** 320, 326, 327-9
territorial application **86,** 548, **92,** 584, **93,** 595, 596. *See also* extraterritorial legislation
EC obligations and **93,** 236
imported goods **93,** 596
primacy of treaties and **93,** 236, 239
taxation laws **93,** 236, 239
territorial limitation **48,** 482, **92,** 584, **103,** 3-4
legislation extending beyond territorial sea **120,** 629, 631-2
subsequent territorial changes **103,** 3-4
treaties and. *See also* treaties, operation and enforcement
implicit repeal **36,** 397-9, **88,** 225, 228, **93,** 290
separation of powers **88,** 204-5, **93,** 249, **104,** 428-9, 706
unlawful government, validity
American Civil War cases **39,** 121, 125-33, 137-40, 365-8, 388-90, 394-6, **90,** 487-90
belligerent occupation distinguished **90,** 486
Cyprus, in **90,** 492-3
Grenada, in **90,** 500-5
international relevance **90,** 490, 491
Nigeria, in **90,** 494-6
Pakistan, in **90,** 491-2, 496-500
requirements
preservation of just rights of citizen **90,** 485, 511
public policy, conformity with **90,** 485, 494, 511

reasonably required for orderly running of country **90,** 485, 487-91, 493-4, 498-500, 505-11
retrospective acknowledgement **90,** 490-1
Rhodesia, in **90,** 493-4
validity **55,** 546, **90,** 535-49
clarity of intention **112,** 422
conflict with international obligations **115,** 410-12
constitutionality. *See* constitutionality *above*
courts' competence to determine **55,** 546
declaration of invalidity, vacuum as result **103,** 167-8
inaccurate declaration of existing law, effect on previous judicial decisions **112,** 431
incorporation of common law **112,** 723-6
invalidity of single clause, effect **112,** 726
judicial process, interference with **112,** 422-3
judicial review **90,** 536-45
reasonableness **118,** 464-5, 484-5
remedies in case of invalidity **118,** 477
restrictions on fundamental rights **118,** 464-7
under international law **64,** 344, 351
unlawful government. *See* unlawful government, validity *above*
vagueness **104,** 397-8
validity of implementation distinguished **118,** 476, 489, 511-12, 519
legislation, confiscatory. *See* confiscation, legislation; foreign law, recognition/enforcement, confiscatory legislation
legislation, interpretation 47, 480, **48,** 73-6, **59,** 219-27, 252-4, **60,** 4-5, 7, **69,** 14-15, 18-21, 25-8, 110-26, 131, **78,** 14-17, 99-100, **79,** 161-3, 463-7, 555-60, **80,** 14-16, 44, 52, 57, 65, 69, 72, 88-9, **87,** 610, **88,** 296. *See also* legislation; treaties, municipal law and; treaties, primacy
absence of clear provision **80,** 52
absence of contrary indication **80,** 44
absence of explicit language **79,** 499
aids **78,** 15
absence of enforcement mechanisms **90,** 627
administrative interpretations **90,** 627-8, 629-30, 631, 632, 639-41
ambiguity, in case of **90,** 420-1, **91,** 321, 330, **96,** 131, **107,** 365, 402-3
Art. 177 (EEC Treaty) preliminary ruling **93,** 324
context **83,** 130, 131, **86,** 196, **87,** 389, **90,** 357, **91,** 29, 258, **92,** 680, 696, **104,** 304, 305, **108,** 530, **115,** 393-5, 405, 406
aboriginal rights, legislation relating to **125,** 413
at time of drafting **121,** 508
dictionary **92,** 668, 678-9, 680, **96,** 131, 136-7, **100,** 324-5, 534, 551, **103,** 191, 193-4, **122,** 372 n. 67
earlier legislation **78,** 554-8, **86,** 155
EC norm **93,** 584-5
EEC Treaty (Rome) (1957) **93,** 584-5
European Convention on Human Rights (1950) **91,** 321
executive intention **85,** 157, 159
expert, translation **106,** 551
explanatory note **42,** 421
foreign constitutions **91,** 321, 329-30
general principles of international law **100,** 382-3
grammar **103,** 191

legislation, interpretation (*cont.*)
implementing regulation **106,** 551
International Covenant on Civil and Political Rights (ICCPR) (1966) **91,** 321, 329, 330-1, **100,** 387
International Covenant on Economic, Social and Cultural Rights (1966) **91,** 321
international law **79,** 630, **85,** 181-2, **91,** 500
judicial and arbitral decisions **90,** 584, 585
municipal courts of another country **79,** 669, 674-5, **94,** 251, 271
League of Nations resolutions **79,** 694
legislative history **63,** 342-3, 385-7, 450-2, **69,** 27, **72,** 688, **77,** 211-15, 249-51, 290-1, **78,** 686-8, 694, **79,** 5, 7, 12-13, 97, 381, 463, 551, 555, 566, 567-8, 606, 618-25, 631, 636-8, **81,** 175, 546, 547-8, 577, 663, 664, 683, **83,** 131, **84,** 91, 99, 100, 116, 155, 157, 171, 172, 173, 210-12, **85,** 157, 172, 175-6, 279, 285, 294, **86,** 7, 36-40, 567, 634-5, **87,** 494, 552, 612, **88,** 84, 186, **89,** 54, 69, 364, 365, **90,** 590-1, 595, 631, 632, 635-6, 639, 641, **91,** 272-3, 498-9, 532 n. 41, **92,** 387, 395, 419, 451-2, 465, 466, 486, **94,** 91 n. 12, 92-3, **95,** 590-2, **96,** 131, **98,** 174-5, **99,** 3, 86, **100,** 254, **101,** 423, 474-5, 512, 513, 543-4, 567, **103,** 146, **104,** 147, 158, 176, 178, 304, **106,** 557, 576, 577, **107,** 312, 313, 316-17, 365, 402-3, 420-1, **115,** 392-3, **118,** 490, **119,** 154, 161, **120,** 485-6, **122,** 676-9. *See individual statutes under country headings for references to the legislative history of specific legislation. Entries at this point are limited to discussion (as opposed to citing) of legislative history as an aid to interpretation*
ambiguity, relevance **96,** 131, **107,** 365, 402-3
location in text **95,** 586 n. 17, 588-90, 608
marginal note **86,** 194-5, **90,** 458, **91,** 330, **103,** 123
ministerial statement **92,** 600, 604-5, 607, **125,** 374-6
natural justice **92,** 656
non-binding statements by UNHCR **79,** 638
official commentary **100,** 402-3
official declaration **66,** 191, 260-7
official report **103,** 145-6
other national legislation **79,** 569, **122,** 675-6
parallel legislation **79,** 569, **88,** 681, **101,** 423, **103,** 179-80, **104,** 304
parliamentary proceedings **39,** 283, **86,** 203-4, **90,** 338, **125,** 374-9
preamble **86,** 194-5, 201, **92,** 681, **101,** 423, **103,** 141, 194
previous legislation **84,** 737, 745
promotional literature **106,** 560-1, 577-81
purposes and provisions of enabling act **87,** 369, 394
State practice **90,** 590, 591
structure of legislation **83,** 131, **86,** 122, **104,** 555, **107,** 648
teachings of publicists **90,** 584
textbook **90,** 228
title of chapter **44,** 228
title of statute **85,** 172, 173, **103,** 123
long title **78,** 841, **80,** 72, **118,** 313
travaux préparatoires. See legislative history *above*; treaty *travaux préparatoires below*
treaty. *See* treaty as aid *below*
UNHCR *Handbook on Procedures and Criteria for Determining Refugee Status* (1979) **88,** 8-9, 30, 31, **92,** 698, 704, **95,** 551
Universal Declaration of Human Rights (1948) **91,** 321
ambiguity **78,** 481, 554-6, 559-60, 626, **86,** 36, 196, **90,** 420-1, **91,** 321, 330, **96,** 131, **103,** 191, 195, **107,** 365, 402-3
absence of **82,** 109, 424
applicable law **84,** 739, 745-6

by international tribunals **40,** 70
'boiler plate' language **90,** 623-4
civil law interpretation, acceptability **84,** 739, 742
Commonwealth practice **84,** 740-1, 742-3
comparative study of principles **93,** 212
Constitution, special rules **91,** 351, 363-6
contemporaneity **90,** 628
critical date **90,** 406
customary international law rules **104,** 181
different statute, relevance **84,** 203 n. 2
foreign legislation **78,** 595, 599, 609, 631
gaps, filled by analogy **104,** 189-92
general and special clauses **39,** 267-8
guidelines
a verbis non est recendendum **106,** 587
absurdity, avoidance **85,** 179-80, **96,** 132, **112,** 722-3
actual language **91,** 347-8, 349
aliens, presumption in favour of **79,** 629
ambiguity, to be resolved in favour of alien **79,** 629
clear language **84,** 148, 155, 172, 173, **91,** 68, **95,** 605, **96,** 130, 131, 135, **99,** 160-1, **103,** 428-9
clear meaning **91,** 367, **100,** 376
common sense **99,** 86, 87
consistency between common and civil law usage **84,** 734
consistency between primary and subordinate legislation **77,** 37, **90,** 628
consistency between related legislation **64,** 391, **112,** 697 n. 192
consistency within Statute **64,** 400-1, 570-1, 574-5
contemporary meaning **99,** 87, **100,** 514
disjunctive treatment of phrase **103,** 93
effectiveness **88,** 272-3, **91,** 363, **106,** 574, 587, **107,** 644-5, 650-1, **118,** 488
eiusdem generis rule **70,** 233, **78,** 615
every provision to have meaning **90,** 260-1
every word to have meaning **115,** 405
expressio unius est exclusio alterius **38,** 263-4, **64,** 421, **103,** 136, 151, 152-6, 171-2, 184-8, 194-5, **107,** 400-1
foreign relations, avoidance of embarrassment **90,** 592
'forever speaking' principle **88,** 275
GDR practice **100,** 385-7
generalia specialibus non derogant **90,** 547
'identical language' rule **96,** 137-9
implied provision **91,** 24
intention of legislature
changing practice **98,** 396
clearly expressed **78,** 686, **79,** 630-1, **118,** 313, **121,** 633-4
'person', State as **63,** 107-20
judicial interpretation, avoidance **83,** 134
language of Statute **87,** 612-13, **90,** 590-1, 639, 641, **101,** 564, **107,** 377
later legislation, primacy **81,** 705, **82,** 296, **90,** 577
leges posteriores priores contrarias abrogant. See later legislation, primacy *above*
liberal **41,** 434, **91,** 11, 29, 70, 72, 146, 161, 350, 363-6, **118,** 321
construction of tax law **87,** 553
marginal notes **44,** 228
motive, relevance **82,** 213
natural meaning. *See* ordinary and natural meaning *below*

legislation, interpretation (*cont.*)
object and purpose **78,** 613, 625-6, **83,** 128, 129-30, **84,** 112, **86,** 164, 167, 202, 204, 450, **87,** 389, 549, **88,** 298, **91,** 29, 69-70, 270, 274, **92,** 680, 696, **96,** 141-2, **104,** 555, **115,** 404-5, **122,** 675-6, **125,** 412, 416-17
amelioration of injustice, relevance **125,** 371, 406-7
EC directive **93,** 324-5
ordinary grammatical meaning **106,** 547, **115,** 406-7
ordinary and natural meaning **64,** 189, 190, **78,** 546, 555-7, **79,** 146, 161, 617-18, **84,** 766, **86,** 166-9, **87,** 148, 181, **88,** 316, **92,** 598, **100,** 534, 551, **101,** 273, **104,** 589, **118,** 314, **122,** 446, 472-3
legislation intended to promote justice and **125,** 372-3
penal legislation to be interpreted restrictively **92,** 679
perverse conclusion, avoidance of **90,** 342
plain language **81,** 676, **82,** 353, **92,** 517, **95,** 529-30, 538 n. 3, 586, 587, **96,** 130-5, **103,** 526, **104,** 158, 182, 555, **107,** 390, 400-1
plain meaning **87,** 396, 442, 512, 552, **90,** 69, 225-6, 227, 228, 357, 420-1, 595, 623, 628, **122,** 672-3
plain and ordinary meaning **79,** 693, **80,** 149
plain and unambiguous **80,** 44, 184
policy coherence **90,** 594, 595
potential application **79,** 308, 309
powers of legislature **87,** 389
principle of double criminality **87,** 151
proportionality **100,** 371
purpose. *See* object and purpose *above*
purposive **91,** 347, 350, 363-4
reasonable **99,** 91
reasonable and logical **79,** 568
reciprocity with legislation of third State **79,** 92
restrictive **82,** 314, 318, **92,** 517
in case of fundamental rights **77,** 481
penal statute **88,** 272
singular to include plural **104,** 265
sovereignty, avoidance of conflict with **90,** 626-7
Statute as a whole **78,** 599-601, **82,** 308, **85,** 172, **86,** 164, 202, **90,** 259, 626, 635, **100,** 533, **107,** 648, **115,** 404-5
including amendment **121,** 631
strict **78,** 505, **85,** 244
extraterritorial legislation **103,** 320
substance rather than form **112,** 445
teleological approach **40,** 70, **87,** 114, **117,** 282-3
text **83,** 128
treaty rules **106,** 542-3
validity, presumption of **79,** 85
intention of legislature **44,** 125, **63,** 21, 69, 75-6, 80, 86-7, 90, 103, 108-13, 124, 153, 175-6, 185, 194, 206-7, 208-51, 256, 270, 281, 291, 309, 325, 336, 345, 349, 353, 396-7, 418, 422, 441-2, 450, 503, 506, 518, 520, 527, 534, 543-8, 564, 572, 576, 581, 587, 599, 610, 627, 631, 642, 651, **77,** 481-2, **90,** 421, 592, 593, **94,** 95, **95,** 609, **96,** 130-5, 144-7, **104,** 524, 589, **107,** 134-5, 164-6, 403, 649-51, 653, **108,** 530-4, **112,** 431, 432, 440-1, **115,** 398-9, **118,** 488
parliamentary proceedings as evidence of, language of Statute, preference for **125,** 416-17
joint legislation, legal concepts of all signatory States **42,** 363, 374-5

lenity principle **86,** 36
multilingual texts
 official language, preferred text, whether **87,** 500
 original language to determine, whether **106,** 547-8, 572-3
need for **83,** 131
new circumstances and **91,** 499
penal legislation **78,** 543
phrases, 'transaction or occurrence' **63,** 316
presumption against
 arbitrary deprivation of property **112,** 440-4
 expropriation without compensation **112,** 440-4
 extinction of native title **112,** 550-1
 extraterritorial effect. *See* presumption of territorial limitation *below*
 interference with rights of individuals **87,** 285
 penal nature **84,** 763
 retroactivity **84,** 763, **91,** 105, **107,** 140-1, 143, **112,** 442, **122,** 523
presumption of conformity with comity **64,** 575, 579, 633
presumption of conformity with Constitution **79,** 120, 161, **87,** 348, **104,** 295, **118,** 314
presumption of conformity with customary international law **118,** 373-4, **119,** 87, **124,** 437
presumption of conformity with EC law **93,** 661
presumption of conformity with foreign law **90,** 627, 637, 639
presumption of conformity with international human rights law **101,** 458-65, **125,** 440
presumption of conformity with international law **36,** 24-5, 280-1, **45,** 17, **52,** 79-82, **54,** 268, **64,** 311-12, 575-6, 579-80, 632-3, **77,** 265, **79,** 12, **81,** 664, **84,** 215, **86,** 43, **88,** 180-1, **90,** 215-16, 632-3, **95,** 610, **100,** 597-9, **101,** 288-9, 566-7, **103,** 428, 619, **104,** 513, 517, **115,** 395, **118,** 373-4, **119,** 234, **122,** 676
 in case of apparent conflict **57,** 2-3, **120,** 601-5, **124,** 437-8
 implementation in accordance with subsequent changes in international law **64,** 576, **120,** 603-4
 vagueness of international law, relevance **104,** 397-8, **120,** 573
presumption of conformity with international obligations **64,** 421, **70,** 4, 6, 15-16, **80,** 156-9, **81,** 703-4, **82,** 493-4, **85,** 31-2, **86,** 43, 164-5, **92,** 526, 687, 696, 708, 731, 734, **103,** 161-2, 179, **104,** 471, 513, 517, **107,** 115, **115,** 662-3, **120,** 572-3
 clear meaning of legislation and **80,** 157, **118,** 374-5
 law of the sea **120,** 599-605
 legal personality, conferment of **80,** 151, 154
presumption of conformity with legal obligations **123,** 258-60, 328
presumption of conformity with treaty **40,** 1-3, **41,** 431-2, 435-6, 447, **43,** 121, 124, **63,** 281, **68,** 208, 224, 235-6, 242, 258, 307, 312-16, 338-9, 349, 373, 427-34, 453, 457-60, 499-500, **73,** 615-16, **74,** 340, 537, 541, 543, 552, **77,** 37, 464, 555, **84,** 762, 763, **87,** 302, **90,** 335, 339-40, 360, 578, **94,** 93-4, **96,** 132, **101,** 275-6, 303-4, 567-9, **107,** 281-9, 498, **115,** 378-80, 407-10, **117,** 639-40, **122,** 676, **124,** 472
 ambiguity, in case of **107,** 281
 in case of apparent conflict **86,** 167, **90,** 342, **124,** 457-8
 constitutional conflict **107,** 284
 derivative obligations **107,** 284-8
 effect to be given to **87,** 318
 legislative intent, relevance **82,** 291-3, 395, **107,** 284
 relevance **91,** 329-30
 Treaty of Waitangi (1840) **120,** 482

legislation, interpretation (*cont.*)
presumption of human rights protection, interference with **91,** 347-51, 363-6, **101,** 245-51, **118,** 377-9, **120,** 414
presumption of lawful conduct **87,** 276
presumption of State immunity **104,** 524-5, 619
customary international law **120,** 572-3
presumption of territorial limitation **38,** 122, **43,** 150, **63,** 87-8, **77,** 151, 281, 283, **78,** 528-50, **84,** 72, 695, **85,** 126-7, **87,** 113, 375, 376-8, 379-80, 381-2, 388-91, 392, 395, 397, **88,** 181, 317, **90,** 622, 630, 632, 633, 634-5, **92,** 679, **94,** 235, **95,** 589, 609, **99,** 157, **100,** 498, 522, 523-5, 535-6, 597, **101,** 341-50, **104,** 524-5, 540-1, 555, **114,** 596-7
basis of rule **87,** 381
foreign relations as basis for **121,** 634
non-applicability to foreigners for acts abroad **104,** 555
presumption of validity **70,** 146, 168-9, 218-19, **90,** 69, **91,** 362
intra vires **90,** 205
validation of unauthorized act **112,** 441
relevant factors, law of third State **90,** 406
responsibility
courts **95,** 548 n. 6, **120,** 484
national **117,** 575
executive **66,** 191, 260-7, **79,** 626-8, 631-6, **120,** 484
implementing party **106,** 414-15
judicial **114,** 400
rules of
determined by judiciary **83,** 128-9
peculiar to each system **83,** 128
subsequent legislation, relevance **44,** 123-4
terminology
changing meaning **80,** 89, 92-3, 155-61
differences of **80,** 14
identity of **80,** 157-8
territorial limits **69,** 93-8, 110-26, 131, **78,** 528-50
treaty as aid **40,** 2, **41,** 1-10, **60,** 115-18, 122-3, 125, 127, 358-60, 364-5, 471, 473-4, 477, 487, **64,** 191-3, **71,** 249, **77,** 77-8, **78,** 132, **79,** 621-4, **80,** 157, **81,** 701, 703, 713, **84,** 737, 740, 763-4, 771, 772-3, 774, **85,** 214, **87,** 85-6, 474, 475, **90,** 225-8, 335, 340, 420-1, 422, 578, 585, **91,** 321, 329, 330-1, **93,** 610-13, **94,** 92-5, 251-2, **95,** 586, 592-6, 599, **98,** 251, **101,** 188, 209-10, 301-5, 423, **104,** 494-5, **107,** 87-8, **119,** 59-60
in case of ambiguity **41,** 7-8, **64,** 191-2, **84,** 763-4, 774-5, **101,** 209-10, 301-4, 354, **107,** 89, 115-18, **121,** 397-400
expressly accorded meaning of treaty **101,** 210
foreign text **101,** 210-11
French text **84,** 740
'having the force of law' **64,** 390-1, **101,** 210
language of treaty
correspondence with **91,** 134-6, **101,** 188, **103,** 568-9, **110,** 754-5, 764-5
divergence **104,** 634-5
'drawn into' legislation **101,** 210, **104,** 638
unincorporated treaty **41,** 7-8, **111,** 635
ratification and **103,** 177-8
signature and **103,** 177
travaux préparatoires **74,** 634-6, 638, 642-8, 650, 654-6, 660-2, 666-8, 674-5, 682, **90,** 225, 226-7, 228, 343, **95,** 587, 596-8, **104,** 236-7, 258

public and accessible record, need for **78,** 686
unincorporated treaty **64,** 189, **80,** 88-9, **90,** 578-9, **103,** 159, 160-1, 177-8, 400, **104,** 264-5, 430-2, 471, 482-3, 704, **108,** 637, **111,** 281, 635, **115,** 663, **118,** 376, **124,** 363, 437-8
language of treaty **41,** 7-8, **111,** 635
unratified treaty **90,** 578
treaty interpretation distinguished **83,** 133-4, 135, **107,** 87
preamble **119,** 59
treaty-implementing legislation **41,** 1-10, 426-36, **68,** 261-2, **71,** 249, **72,** 4-9, **78,** 132, 137, 325, 326, **90,** 334-65, **118,** 373
applicable law **101,** 210-11, 242, 313-14, 322
consistency with customary international law **119,** 161
language compared **80,** 69-71
language of treaty, use of **90,** 342-4
treaty as aid **74,** 536-8, 541, 543, 552, **77,** 31, 381, **88,** 206, **90,** 225-8, **94,** 251-2, **124,** 437
war-time legislation **42,** 421-2
legislation, retroactive 44, 108-30, **55,** 546, 547, 548, **57,** 177-9, **61,** 78, **62,** 170-1, **71,** 222-6, **72,** 443, 460-1, **74,** 455, 507, 642, 648, **78,** 132-6, **79,** 381, 411, **82,** 315, 430-1, **84,** 155-7, 707-8, **86,** 499, **87,** 298, 302, 434-5, 617, **90,** 232-3, **91,** 16, 20, **117,** 475-82. *See also* retrospective distinguished *below*; legislation, retrospective
African Charter on Human and Peoples' Rights (1981) **91,** 141
American Convention on Human Rights (1969) **91,** 80, 140
anti-terrorist legislation **121,** 611 n. 4, 631-2, 645
bill of attainder **91,** 16, 17, 83-6, 107-9
Canadian Commission of Inquiry on War Criminals (Deschnes Commission) (1986) **91,** 49
clear intention **107,** 143
Control Council Law No 10 **91,** 48
crimes against humanity **36,** 20-40, 55-7, 281-3
crimes against the Jewish people **36,** 20-40
criminal legislation **44,** 127, 129-30
critical date, acquired right, relevance **107,** 128-9
definition **107,** 166-7
deportation and **79,** 381, **111,** 178
economic sanctions **117,** 475-7, 498
effect **79,** 603
enforcement in foreign State **92,** 477
European Convention on Human Rights (1950) **91,** 80, 140
exclusion of alien for past behaviour **104,** 198
express provision **123,** 503-4
extraterritorial effect, extension of jurisdiction distinguished **82,** 432, 443
fairness, minimum standards of and **91,** 89
fishing regulations **123,** 503-4
general principle of international law **91,** 141
general principle of law **91,** 80, 156-7
Geneva Convention (Prisoners of War) (1949) **91,** 49-50
Geneva Convention on the Protection of Civilian Persons in Time of War (1949) and **47,** 496-7
'henceforth' **103,** 614
International Covenant on Civil and Political Rights (ICCPR) (1966) **91,** 49, 80, 140
act criminal according to general principles of law at time committed **98,** 574-5
international crimes **91,** 48, **120,** 363
critical date **91,** 50

legislation, retroactive (*cont.*)
procedural provisions distinguished **119,** 336-7, 350-1
international law and **36,** 281-2, **71,** 38-9, **79,** 411
legislation authorizing restrain order in aid of confiscation orders made by foreign court **122,** 521-3, 528
legislation implementing Torture Convention (1984) **119,** 230
natural justice and **36,** 22-3
nulla poena sine [precia] lege [penale] **86,** 499, **91,** 50
presumption against **84,** 763, **91,** 105, **107,** 140-1, 143, **112,** 442
procedural legislation **104,** 177, **107,** 137-44, **119,** 336-7
public interest, protection of **91,** 141-2
purposes of legislation, relevance **107,** 143
retrospective distinguished **82,** 432-3, **91,** 166, **98,** 574
separation of powers and **91,** 18, 77-86, 89-91, 107-9
sovereignty and **91,** 105
State immunity legislation **63,** 75, 129 n. 1, 151-2, 155, 212-14, 256-7, 302-4, 478-9, 634-5, **64,** 225, 226, 269, 270, 271, 311-12, 619-23, 651-3, **84,** 142, 146-8, 172, 175, 183-5, **103,** 563-4, 565, 605-7, 614-15, **104,** 412, **107,** 268, **119,** 193
territorial limitation **36,** 279
test of acceptability, offensiveness **91,** 142-3
torture **104,** 176-8
treaty implementation, Brussels Convention on Limitation of Liability for Maritime Claims (1976) **107,** 128-30, 133, 137-45
Treaty of Waitangi Act 1975 (New Zealand) **120,** 487
trial, provision for, relevance **91,** 81, 96
Universal Declaration of Human Rights and **44,** 129-30
universality of crime and **91,** 143, **120,** 394-5
validation of administrative act distinguished **91,** 16
war crimes **36,** 20-40, 43-4, **88,** 297
legislation, retrospective, clear intention **82,** 433-4
legislative discretion 86, 123
legitimate expectation. *See also* acquired rights; estoppel; European Community law, legitimate expectation
consultation as alleviation **117,** 481
death penalty, non-implementation while petition to Inter-American Commission on Human Rights in train **124,** 289-90, 294-5, 297-8
'legal expectancy' **83,** 285, 287, 292, 312, 319-20, 322-3
legal rule distinguished **104,** 474
ministerial statement of future intentions **122,** 442, 450
procedural fairness **104,** 473-6, 481
distinction **104,** 481-3, 491-4
notice, need for **104,** 475, 486-7, 491-4
public interest and **117,** 428, **119,** 278
requirements
certainty of expectation **117,** 479-81
knowledge of **104,** 483
reliance on policy **117,** 499
standing **104,** 474-5
stay of deportation pending consideration by international body **124,** 411-12
treaty
intention to incorporate **122,** 440-2, 450, 456-9, 467
measures prior to entry into force defeating its object and purpose **113,** 324, 334, **117,** 426

ratification and **104,** 473-5, 480-1, 483-4, 487, 494-8, 704-6, **122,** 440-2
right of individual under ratified but unincorporated treaty **117,** 640, **123,** 520-1, 527-30, **124,** 397-8
termination, non-precipitate **117,** 426
Lesotho
aliens
Minister of Interior's discretionary powers **70,** 365-72
residence requirements **70,** 368
Attorney-General, right of representation abroad **121,** 475-6
Bophuthatswana, recognition, government, *in mediis rebus* **103,** 27
burden of proof, revolution, legal validity of regime **103,** 77
Constitution 1959 **90,** 432-3
Constitution 1965 **90,** 433-5, 437, 455-6
Constitution 1966 **90,** 436-8, 465-6, 529-30
creation of ministers **39,** 418-19
customary law **103,** 36
entrenched clauses **90,** 437, 539, 547
executive power **103,** 36
human rights and **90,** 550
judicial power **103,** 36-7
judicial review under **90,** 449-52, 539-60
standing **90,** 450-2
legislative authority **103,** 35-6
s 2 **103,** 33
ss 4-22 **103,** 33
s 15 **90,** 451
s 20 **90,** 445, 449-50
s 21 **90,** 440
s 33 **90,** 443
s 34 **90,** 443
s 40 **103,** 33
s 42 **103,** 33
s 43 **103,** 33
s 55 **103,** 33
s 63 **103,** 33
s 67 **103,** 33
s 68 **103,** 33
s 71 **103,** 34
s 72 **103,** 34
s 73 **103,** 34
s 76 **90,** 465
s 76(4) **103,** 34
s 80 **103,** 34
s 122 **90,** 466
s 139 **90,** 444
supremacy **90,** 539
suspension **90,** 438, 439, 440, 441, 445, 529, 549, **103,** 37
Constitution
Lesotho Order 1970 as **90,** 549
Lesotho Order 1973 as **90,** 549
Lesotho Order (No 2) 1986 as **90,** 549-50
Parliament Act 1983 **90,** 549-50
will of the people, reflection of **90,** 550-1

Lesotho (*cont.*)
written, need for **90,** 549-51
Constitution (Suspension) Order 1970 **103,** 37, 47
continuity of law **90,** 458-61
coup d'état (1970) **90,** 438-44
coup d'état (1986) **90,** 446-8
coup d'éat (1990) **103,** 41-72
customary law **90,** 443-4, **103,** 36
designation of king **90,** 436
'existing law', whether **90,** 443-4
role of king **90,** 443-4
executive power, Constitution 1966 **103,** 36
Geneva Convention on Refugees (1951), accession to **39,** 415-24
government
validity **90,** 473-520, 551-5
effectiveness **90,** 551-3
judicial continuity **90,** 554-5
king, continuity **90,** 554-5
public acceptance **90,** 553-5
High Court Rules
8(22)(c) **90,** 449
50 **90,** 452
history, 1966-1992 **103,** 33-41
human rights
association, right of **90,** 548-9
Constitution and **90,** 550
derogation **90,** 454-9
judicial power, Constitution 1966 **103,** 36-7
judicial review
Constitution, under **90,** 449-52
grounds
illegality **90,** 453
irrationality **90,** 453
procedural impropriety **90,** 453-4
standing
'legitimate expression' **90,** 451-2
'sufficient interest' **90,** 451
king, role of
abolition of monarchy **103,** 47
Constitution 1965 **90,** 437, **103,** 45-6
Constitution 1966 **90,** 436-7, 445, **103,** 35-7, 46-7
continuity **90,** 554-5
coup d'état (1970) and **90,** 441-4
customary law **90,** 443-4
Lesotho (No 2) Order 1986 (No 3) **90,** 446-8
Lesotho Order 1973 **103,** 47
Lesotho Order 1986 (No. 2) **103,** 40-1, 48-9
Office of King Order 1970 **103,** 49
Parliament Act 1983 **90,** 446, **103,** 47-8
law of
Adaptation of Existing Laws (No 9) **90,** 458
Aliens Control Act 1966 **39,** 415, 417-22, **55,** 68-75
Audit Act 1973, s 12 **121,** 479-80

Basutoland Order 1965 **103,** 45-6
Bill of Rights **90,** 433-4
Chieftainship Amendment Order 1970 (No 29) **90,** 441, 443
Citizenship Act 1968 **90,** 442
Constitution. *See* Constitution *above*
Constitution (Suspension) Order 1970 (No 2) **90,** 439, 528-9
Continuation of the State of Emergency Order 1970 (No 59) **90,** 441
continuity of British law **90,** 457-61, 464-5
Court of Appeal Act 1978 **90,** 530-1
Court of Appeal and High Court Order 1970 (No 17) **90,** 443, 530
customary law. *See* customary law *above*
Customs and Excise Act 1973 **121,** 480
Electoral Act 1968 **90,** 446
Electoral (Amendment) Act 1984 **90,** 446
Emergency Powers Act 1966 **90,** 440
Emergency Powers Order 1970 (No 3) **90,** 440
Emergency Regulations 1970 (No 50) **90,** 439-41
General Amnesty Order 1986 (No 2) **90,** 448, 556
General Election (Invalidation) Order 1970 (No 4) **90,** 441
General Interpretation Proclamation 1942 (No 12) **90,** 443-4
High Court Act 1967 **90,** 442
High Court Act 1978 **90,** 530-1
Human Rights Act 1983 (No 24) **90,** 445, 448, 450, 451, 545-8, **124,** 539
  derogation **90,** 547
  entrenched provisions, whether **90,** 547, 549
  Lesotho (No 2) Order 1986 and **90,** 547
  revocation **90,** 547
  Suspension of Political Activities Order 1986 and **90,** 548-9
Indemnity Order 1987
  Human Rights Act 1983 and **90,** 545-8
  Indemnity Act (UK) and **90,** 540-2, 548
  judicial review **90,** 536-9
  Lesotho Order 1986 and **90,** 535-6, 540
  period of immunity **90,** 548
  validity **90,** 533-48, 555
Independence Order 1966 **55,** 72-3
Interpretation Act 1977 **90,** 440
  s 34(1)(a) **103,** 32
Judicial Service Commission Act 1983 **90,** 445
Judicial Service Commission Rules 1969 **90,** 444, 445
Legal Notice 1970 (No 35) **90,** 440-1
Lesotho Citizenship Order 1971 (No 16) **90,** 444
Lesotho Highlands Development Authority Order 1986 (No 23) **90,** 553
Lesotho law **90,** 432
Lesotho Order 1966
  customary law, under **90,** 444
  suspension **90,** 442-3
Lesotho Order 1970 **103,** 37-8
Lesotho Order 1970 (No 1) **90,** 438-44, 528-9
  amendment **90,** 442
  as Constitution **90,** 549
Lesotho Order 1973 **90,** 444-5, 529, **103,** 38, 47-8
  as Constitution **90,** 549

Lesotho (*cont.*)
Lesotho Order 1986 (No 1) **90,** 446-7, 448, **103,** 39
s 4 **103,** 31
s 6 **103,** 31
s 7 **103,** 31
s 9(1) **103,** 31
s 9(2) **103,** 31
Lesotho Order 1986 (No. 2)
king, role of **103,** 40-1, 48-9
Military Council, composition **103,** 40
s 1 **103,** 31
s 4 **103,** 40
s 6(1)(b) **103,** 32
Lesotho Order 1990 **103,** 41-2
Lesotho Order (No 2) 1986 (Order No 3 of 1986) **90,** 447-8, 530, 535
assumption of rights and responsibilities of previous government **90,** 551
as Constitution **90,** 549-50
role of king **90,** 446-8
supremacy **90,** 540
validity **90,** 530-1, 552-3
Ministers of State Order 1971 (No 34) **90,** 444, 448
Office of King Order 1970 (No 51) **90,** 441-2, 444, **103,** 47
Offices of Chief Order 1970 **90,** 444
Parliament Act 1983 **90,** 446, 448, 549, **103,** 39, 47-8
as Constitution **90,** 549-50
repeal **103,** 39
Police Medals Act 1969 **90,** 442
Public Service Order 1970 (No 2) **90,** 444, 445
repeal **90,** 446, 448
Royal Lesotho Defence Force Act 1980 (No 13) **90,** 462-3
Societies Act 1966 **90,** 451
Suspension of Party Political Activities Order 1986 (No 4) **90,** 448, 450, 548-9
Human Rights Act 1983 and **90,** 548
validity **90,** 548, 555
legislation, interpretation, aids, marginal note **90,** 458
legislative authority, Constitution 1966 **103,** 35-6
legislative powers, British Crown **90,** 434
Paramount Chief
king, designation as **90,** 436
powers
Constitution 1959 **90,** 433, **103,** 43-4
Constitution 1965 **90,** 433-5, **103,** 44-6
phrases
'Act of Parliament' **90,** 458
'existing law' **90,** 458
recognition, government
applicable law, constitutional law **103,** 59-62, 74
burden of proof **103,** 77
democratic regime **103,** 66, 75-6
in mediis rebus **103,** 27
judicial acceptance **103,** 68
obligation, whether **103,** 72-9, 81
popular acceptance **103,** 66, 71, 75-6

requirements
effective government acquiesced in **103,** 52-6, 66-72, 73-9
permanency **103,** 71
responsibility for, courts, pre-revolutionary **103,** 72, 77-8
retroactive **103,** 57, 80
revolution
claim to have seized power, relevance **103,** 50
competing regimes, relevance **103,** 50, 69-70
constitutional deviation distinguished **103,** 41-72
definition, illegitimate change of legal order **103,** 51-4, 69
fundamental change, need for **103,** 49-50
internal **103,** 64-5
judiciary, status **103,** 72
Kelsen's theory **103,** 50-72, 73-4
reception of previous laws **103,** 51
State necessity **103,** 42, 54, 57-8, 63
violence, relevance **103,** 51
State immunity, jurisdiction, applicability, in own courts, good faith **90,** 540-1, 542
status
applicable law **90,** 454-5
Roman-Dutch law **90,** 454
South African common law **90,** 454
British Commonwealth, membership **90,** 467-72
British Crown, position of **90,** 454-72
independence **90,** 435-8
qualified, whether **90,** 465-7
visiting forces, rights **90,** 461-4
letter of credit
amendment
as act of State **63,** 190
as commercial activity **63,** 152, 185-6, 491, 562-4, 594-5
breach, anticipatory, act of State, whether **63,** 154
definition **106,** 411 n. 1
exchange contract **66,** 173
executory nature **106,** 415
function and operation **63,** 375
immunity in respect of. *See* State immunity, jurisdiction, classification of act, letter of credit
property, interest in **106,** 414-15
repudiation, locus **66,** 171-2
letters rogatory 71, 222-6, **73,** 299-363, **81,** 603
European Convention on Mutual Assistance in Criminal Matters (1959), obligation to execute 'in manner provided for by its law' **119,** 283-4
Hague Convention on the Taking of Evidence Abroad (1970). *See* evidence, Hague Convention on the Taking of Evidence Abroad (1970)
non-implementation, grounds for **73,** 322-3, 337-8, 346-7, 358
pre-trial discovery **73,** 300-2, 307-8, 313-17, 323-32, 340-3, 351-3
restrictions on **73,** 301-2, 314, 331-51
privilege, claim of. *See* evidence, privilege, claim of
liability. *See also* measure of damages/compensation including valuation of company/property/assets, causality
causality, varying requirements **125,** 715-16
fault **54,** 509-10, **77,** 409

liability (*cont.*)
faute **41,** 142, **111,** 64 n. 47
faute de service **65,** 66
faute personelle **65,** 66-7
faute quasi délictuelle **75,** 147
foreseeable consequences **77,** 409
hazardous activities **118,** 479-83, 506-10
intent **77,** 409
limitation **52,** 424-6, 428-30, 432, 433-5, 439-40, **77,** 424, 426
applicable law **87,** 558-9
venue **87,** 551-2, 559
recklessness **77,** 409, **101,** 322-4, 330
Rylands v. *Fletcher* **118,** 479-81, 506-7
Universal Postal Convention **77,** 424, 426
Warsaw Convention on International Carriage by Air (1929) **77,** 409
LIAMCO. *See* Libya, LIAMCO and
libel. *See* defamation
liberation, wars of. *See* colonies, decolonization; national liberation movements
Liberia
aboriginal rights **36,** 381-2
Constitution 1847
treaty-making power **36,** 397, 399-400
Constitution 1984 **89,** 338
contract
binding force **89,** 339
breach, damages for **89,** 339
property right **89,** 339
due process **36,** 382, 386, 397, 401
as flag State **74,** 206-8
Forced Labour Convention (No 29) (1930), compliance **36,** 352-427, **37,** 541-2
Indigenous and Tribal Peoples in Independent Territories Convention (No 107) (1957) and **36,** 425-6
law of
Code of Laws 1956 **36,** 380-1, 384, 385, 396, 402, 421, 588, **89,** 338-9, 343
difficulty of establishing **36,** 384-6
Foreign Relations Law, treaties **36,** 382, 386, 397, 400
Investment Incentive Code 1966/1973 **89,** 340
labour legislation **36,** 362-3, 380-6, 396, 406-9, 413, 419, 421-2
treaties
implementing legislation, need for **36,** 389, 397-9, 402
primacy in case of conflict **36,** 382
non-application of legislation **36,** 403-4
repeal of legislation **36,** 386, 388, 397-9, 421
subsequent legislation **36,** 386-8, 399-405
publication/promulgation, need for **36,** 382
treaty-making power, legislative sanction, need for **36,** 397, 400
liberty of person, deprivation 60, 211, **71,** 459, 465-6, 481-2. *See also* arbitrary detention; crimes against humanity, civilian population, acts against as requirement; detainees, rights; detention; European Convention on Human Rights (1950), liberty of person, deprivation; habeas corpus proceedings; International Covenant on Civil and Political Rights, liberty of person, deprivation
burden of proof **79,** 39

compensation for **70,** 233-4, 692-8
victims of national socialist persecution **70,** 692-8
detention during extradition hearings **79,** 244, 248, 249-50, **101,** 191-2, **108,** 441, **111,** 206-10, 249-50
failure to carry out investigations into disappearances as **120,** 55-7
false imprisonment **70,** 227-34
damages **70,** 233-4
notification of charges **70,** 227-32
State immunity in respect of **63,** 474-5
Geneva Conventions (1949) **123,** 172
habitual offenders **67,** 540-9
internment and **60,** 209-16
protective custody **79,** 32-6
State immunity as bar to suit and **121,** 203-4
Libya
citizenship, 'Italian Libyan citizens' **40,** 191-9
concession agreement. *See* oil concessions *below*
continental shelf
delimitation **70,** 553, 594, 687
dispute
Libya **71,** 93-4, 102, 115, 120-1, 137, 150-1, 153, 181, 183, 188-9, 199
Malta **70,** 534-5, 539
Special Agreement with Malta **70,** 544, 592, 607, 618
Special Agreement with Tunisia, compared **70,** 544
continuity of State **62,** 172-3
expropriation/nationalization **53,** 351-3, 356, 476-83, **63,** 166-9, 233-5, **66,** 198-206, 289-300, 340-6, 362-76, **77,** 548-9. *See also* oil concessions, expropriation *below*
arbitration agreement, effect on **53,** 408-13
foreign oil companies
arbitration proceedings **53,** 302-5
breach of contract, whether **53,** 325, 329
decrees **53,** 313-18, 397-8, 424-6, 437-8
oil concessions, effect on **53,** 362-6
Prime Minister's statement **62,** 164, 195, 208
sovereign act, whether **53,** 418
expropriation/nationalization, compensation
need for **65,** 79
undertaking to pay **62,** 163, 165, 208
General National Maritime Transport Company (GNMTC) **63,** 215-27, **77,** 531
immunity **77,** 531-2
independence
interim arrangements **71,** 220-1
social security contributions, collection of **71,** 220-1
international law, conformity of municipal law **53,** 461-2, **62,** 173-5, 191, 198, 209, 217
Islamic law. *See* Islamic law
law of
Civil Code
s 812(2) **77,** 547
s 840 **77,** 548
s 1777 **77,** 546
Concession No 65 Nationalization Law 1971 **77,** 544, 548

Libya (*cont.*)
Labour Code 1970, Art. 40 **109,** 383 n. 301
Law 42, 1973 **66,** 291, 340, 362, 366
Law 66 of 1 September 1973 **62,** 162-3, 165, 196, 201, 208, 223, **77,** 586
Petroleum Law 25, 1955 **53,** 318-22, 394-8, 423, 476-7, **62,** 151-2, 172-6, 178, 185, **66,** 188, **77,** 547, 548, 585
Petroleum Regulations 1955 **81,** 438-9
Resolution of Council of Ministers of 28 March 1968 **81,** 431, 434-5, 436, 438
LIAMCO and, Deeds of Concession **62,** 156-7
lucrum cessans **62,** 202
Minister of Petroleum, status **53,** 415-16
National Oil Corporation **63,** 166-9, 215-17, 224, 242
oil concessions **62,** 151, 155-60, 169-70, 229
amendment **62,** 152-5, 176, 223
Deeds of Concession **53,** 314, 319-22, 324, 327, 422-3, 437-8
expropriation/nationalization **75,** 371, 610, 637-8
terms **62,** 155-60
oil, title to **62,** 151, 161-2, 164, 185, 195, 197, 199
property **62,** 183
public corporation, General Publications Averiting (sic) Distribution Company (GPADC) **87,** 12
recognition, government **96,** 94-5
interim government **96,** 92, 94
National Patriotic Reconstruction Assembly Government (NPRAG) **96,** 94-6
restitutio in integrum **53,** 331-2, 495-7
UNGA Resolutions (1949) **49,** 51
Libyan Producers Agreement 1971 as antitrust violation 66, 200-7, 291-300
Lieber Code (US Military Manual, 163)
Hague Conventions (1899/1907), criminal nature of Art. 3 offences **105,** 448-9
rape **121,** 266, 342 n. 293
torture **121,** 155
life, right to 70, 260-6, 268-82, 466-7, **71,** 359-60, 364-5. *See also* American Convention on Human Rights (1969), life, right to; death penalty; European Convention on Human Rights (1950), life, right to; International Covenant on Civil and Political Rights (ICCPR) (1966), life, right to
chemical weapons deployment and **106,** 395-7
death penalty, extradition and **100,** 660
disappearances and **118,** 155-6, 207-8, **120,** 52-5
nuclear tests **115,** 255-62
nuclear weapons deployment **106,** 360-2, **110,** 189-90, 456-8, 527-8
police operations, death during **70,** 268-81, **125,** 511-18
law enforcement requirements, proportionality **70,** 279
Lima Declaration on Guidelines on Auditing Precepts (1977) 104, 575
Limburg, secession from The Netherlands 39, 117-18, 240
limitation of liability. *See* liability, limitation
limits 41, 63, 83, **83,** 30, 58-60. *See also* boundaries
boundaries compared **77,** 662-4, 670, **81,** 294, 328, **119,** 456
line or zone **77,** 662-4, 670
liquidators
status
as trustees for bondholders **71,** 269
under international law **71,** 268-9

winding-up
effect **77,** 29-30
enforcement distinguished **77,** 40
extraterritorial **77,** 3
Lithuania
aliens, rights, rights and freedoms of citizen **115,** 653-4
Constitution 1938
restoration **115,** 622-3
s 2 **115,** 642
s 3 **115,** 642
s 4 **115,** 642
s 6 **115,** 646
s 7 **115,** 644
s 12 **115,** 642
s 20(2) **115,** 648-9
s 20(3) **115,** 649-50
s 23 **115,** 633, 635
s 26(4) **115,** 650-1
s 29 **115,** 652-3
s 32 **115,** 653-4
s 46 **115,** 629
s 47 **115,** 628
s 48(5) **115,** 647-8
s 54 **115,** 628, 633
s 102 **115,** 636
s 138 **115,** 644, 645
European Convention on Human Rights (1950)
constitutional compatibility **115,** 642-55
Art. 4 (forced or compulsory labour) **115,** 646-8
Art. 5 (prompt hearing) **115,** 648-50
Art. 9 (freedom of religion) **115,** 650-1
Art. 14 (discrimination) **115,** 651-3
Protocol 4, Art. 2 (freedom of movement) **115,** 653-4
implementation
obligation **115,** 641-2
procedure, national discretion **115,** 642-3
municipal law and, direct effect **115,** 644
human rights, legal rights, whether limited to **115,** 644-5
independence, declaration of **115,** 622
law of
Civil Code, s 606 **115,** 643
Civil Procedure Code, s 482 **115,** 643
Law on International Agreements of the Republic of Lithuania 1991, s 12 **115,** 644
Law on Land Reform 1990 **115,** 635-6
Law on the Legal Status of Foreigners in the Republic of Lithuania 1991 **115,** 654
Law on the Procedure and Conditions of the Restoration of the Rights of Ownership to Existing Real Property 1990 **115,** 626-7
Law Appending and Amending 1993 **115,** 627-8
Law on the Provisional Basic Law of the Republic of Lithuania 1990 **115,** 623-4
Law on the Reinstatement of the 12 May 1938 Constitution 1990 **115,** 622-3

Lithuania (*cont.*)
effect on other laws in force prior to 15 June 1940 **115,** 625
property rights **115,** 623-37
property, public good **115,** 628-9, 634, 635
property rights
continuity **115,** 624-6
restoration **115,** 626-37
compensation for non-restoration **115,** 626-7
limitations on **115,** 629-36
standard of treatment of alien, equality **81,** 8, **115,** 653-4
treaties
implementation
means, choice **115,** 642
obligation **81,** 49, **115,** 641
municipal law and, part of, whether **115,** 644
primacy
civil matters **115,** 643
criminal matters **115,** 643-4
litigation, dynamic effect **62,** 355
Litvinov assignment 42, 32, 203, **84,** 162-4, 165, 175, 176, 177-8, 180 n. 11, 181
loans
inter-governmental, currency in specie **44,** 456
multiple currency exchange rate guarantee **59,** 534-8, 559-62, 565-7
as State contract **89,** 485-6, 489
lobsters
livestock, whether **91,** 200-10
lobster war (France/Brazil) **47,** 22-4
protection legislation **71,** 108-9
local government, 'agency or instrumentality of a foreign State', whether **63,** 368
local remedies, exhaustion of. *See* exhaustion of local remedies
***Lockerbie* trial in the Netherlands 117,** 664-89
London Agreement on External Debts (1953)
compensation **61,** 236
Poland and **61,** 236-7
looted property. *See also* crimes against humanity, classification as, wanton destruction and plunder of property not justified by necessity
Bretton Woods Agreement (1944), measures to protect **42,** 431-2
good faith of acquirer **44,** 473-5, 483-4
Italian Peace Treaty (1947) provisions **44,** 448-50, 477-9, 482-3
neutral States **44,** 474
restitution claims **44,** 448-85
***lophelia pertusa*, protection**. *See* Habitats Directive (92/43/EEC), cetaceans and *lophelia pertusa*, protection
***Lotus* principle ('what is not prohibited is allowed') 36,** 283-5, **110,** 220-1, 241-2, 339-40, 341-7, 376, 442-6, **115,** 590
low-water mark
at spring tide **94,** 366-7
as baseline **69,** 79-80, 85-8, **73,** 176-8, 193-4, 199-200, 205, 216-17, **81,** 485, **90,** 238, **91,** 416, 660-1, **94,** 25, **100,** 118, 149, **119,** 458
federal State boundaries **90,** 242-4, 272
river boundary and **91,** 452

lucrum cessans. *See* measure of damages/compensation including valuation of company/property/assets, *lucrum cessans*

Luxembourg

access to courts, refugees **119,** 365
act of government **96,** 218
aliens, Consultative Commission for **73,** 655-6
applicable law, visiting forces, NATO Status of Forces Agreement (1951) **91,** 283
Berufsverbot **88,** 562-3
Constitution, Art. 24 **88,** 563
Constitutional Law 1956, primacy of international law **93,** 210 n. 57
crimes against humanity, jurisdiction
  customary international law **119,** 363-4
  universal **119,** 366-7
customary international law, requirements, constant and uniform practice **119,** 364
EC law, right to invoke before national courts **93,** 554-6
expulsion of alien **73,** 652-6
extradition **73,** 666-9
  cross-border offence
    crime partially committed in requested country **100,** 611-12
    loss as determining factor **100,** 612, 613
  duty, to refuse **100,** 612
  foreign relations and **100,** 613
  procedure, culpability, power to examine **100,** 614-15
  reciprocity, need for **100,** 613
  refusal
    final judgment in requested State **100,** 612
    offence committed partly in requested State **100,** 611-12
  responsibility, executive **100,** 615
foreign relations, extradition and **100,** 613
international law, primacy **93,** 210-11
judicial review
  act of government **96,** 218
  foreign relations **96,** 218
jurisdiction
  criminal **73,** 366-71
  fisheries **73,** 366-8
  over corporation **73,** 575-6
  passive personality principle, torture **119,** 363
  territorial **73,** 366-71
law of
  Law of 13 March 1870, s 2 **100,** 615
  Law of 20 May 1953 (Geneva Convention on the Status of Refugees (1951)) **106,** 317-18
  Law of 22 June 1963 (State officials' remuneration), compatibility with EC law **93,** 554-6
  Law of 26 July 1986 (minimum income), applicability to aliens **106,** 317-18
  Civil Code **73,** 572, 575
  Companies Law 1915 **73,** 573-4
  Criminal Code **119,** 364
  Criminal Investigation Code **119,** 364
  Criminal Procedure Code **73,** 370-1
  Education Act **88,** 562-3

Luxembourg (*cont.*)
Extradition Law 1870 **73,** 666-8
Nationality Law 1968 **73,** 570-1
Penal Code **73,** 368, 370
Prosecution of Crimes Committed Abroad, Law on, 1879 **73,** 367
legislation, interpretation
phrases
'pay' **93,** 555
'public relief and assistance' **106,** 318
'wage' **93,** 555
nationality
corporation **73,** 572-5
option **73,** 569-70
opinio juris, deliberate practice, need for **119,** 364
refugees **73,** 672-3
access to courts **119,** 365
sovereignty, transfer of powers to international organization, EEC Treaty (Rome) (1957) **93,** 555
standard of treatment of alien, equality, minimum wage legislation **106,** 317-18
Torture Convention (1984), direct effect **119,** 363, 365
treaties
direct effect
clear provision, need for **119,** 363, 365
parties' intention **119,** 363
Torture Convention (1984) **119,** 363, 365
primacy, conflict **101,** 618, **106,** 317-18
visiting forces
applicable law, NATO Status of Forces Agreement (1951) **91,** 283
compensation for damage caused by **91,** 283-8
consent, need for
absence of protest **91,** 286
estoppel **91,** 286
general **91,** 285, 286
implied **91,** 284, 285-6
sovereignty and **91,** 283-4, 285-6

Maastricht Treaty (1992). *See* European Union Treaty (Maastricht) (1992)
Macedonia, former Yugoslav Republic of (FYROM) 92, 182-7
Constitution 1991 **92,** 184, 186-7
Amendment I, text **100,** 226
Amendment II, text **100,** 227
Art. 3, text **100,** 226
Art. 49, text **100,** 226
EC aid, Common Foreign Policy (CFP), whether **100,** 241
European Commission Decision 2131/88/ECSC and. *See* European Community Decisions, 2131/88/ECSC
Greek sanctions
competence, EC Member State **100,** 231
link with EC commercial policy, relevance **100,** 231
unilateral measures under EEC Treaty, admissibility **100,** 225-41. *See also* European Community (EC), unilateral measures by Member State (Art. 224 of EEC Treaty)
'Macedonia', acceptance of name **92,** 187, **100,** 229

minorities, undertaking to protect rights **92,** 184, 185-6
recognition
criteria **100,** 229
Greek refusal **100,** 230
succession
date **96,** 721
'originating in Yugoslavia', applicability to **117,** 348-51, 359-61
successor to Yugoslavia, whether **92,** 184, 185, **117,** 347
UN Security Council Resolution 817 (1993) **100,** 230
Madagascar (Malagasy Republic)
Constitution, treaties, ratification **40,** 248
detainees, rights
conditions of detention **78,** 34, 35, 36, 39
defence, preparation **78,** 34, 39
diplomatic immunity, jurisdiction
immovable property, dispute relating to **40,** 80-1
State immunity and **40,** 80-1
exit visa, restrictions **73,** 391-2
expulsion of alien
grounds **94,** 423-4
responsibility of Ministry of Interior **94,** 423
right of challenge **94,** 420, 426
right of review **94,** 420-4, 426
freedom of movement
exit visa, entitlement **73,** 391-2
public policy considerations **73,** 391-2
independence **44,** 29-32
insurance legislation **71,** 563-4
international officials, privileges and immunities **71,** 562-3
Investment Code
Art. 23 **65,** 53
Art. 24 **65,** 53
Art. 25 **65,** 53
Art. 27 **65,** 53
law of
Act No 62-006 of 6 June 1962 **94,** 420, 425
Criminal Code
s 83 **78,** 31
s 112 **78,** 31
ss 114 ff **78,** 31
Criminal Procedure Code
s 112(2) **78,** 31, 32
s 550 **78,** 34
s 551 **78,** 34
Decree No 75-112 MD of 11 April 1975 **78,** 31
privileges and immunities, international officials **71,** 562-3
public order/public policy/*ordre public* **73,** 392
State immunity, jurisdiction
classification of act, diplomatic premises, encroachment on neighbour's land **40,** 80-1
need to plead **40,** 82-3
waiver, Vienna Convention on Diplomatic Relations (1961) **40,** 82-3
trade union rights **73,** 389-90

Madagascar (Malagasy Republic) (*cont.*)
treaties
enforcement **73,** 390
as part of municipal law, obligation to comply with **73,** 390
ratification **40,** 248
UN mission in **71,** 562-3
mafiosi**, regulation in Italy 61,** 294-7
compulsory residence **61,** 314-15, 331-2, 334
detention on island **61,** 310-18
lawfulness **61,** 310-20
Maghreb, 14th century meaning **41,** 21, 23
mail. *See* correspondence
Malacca Straits
IMCO Resolution A.375(X) of 14 November 1977 **84,** 81
internationalization **84,** 81
safety of navigation **84,** 81
Malagasy Republic. *See* Madagascar (Malagasy Republic)
Malawi
allegiance, duty of **54,** 264-90
citizens **54,** 290
Constitution **42,** 460
human rights **54,** 267, 282
s 15 **54,** 289
extradition
Fugitive Offenders Act (England) 1881, applicability **53,** 108-11
Rhodesia and Nyasaland–South Africa, Extradition Agreement (1963), applicability **52,** 84-6, **55,** 90-5
human rights, constitutional provision **54,** 267, **116,** 282
jurisdiction **54,** 289
law of
Constitution Act **1966**. *See also* Constitution *above*
continuity of existing laws **53,** 179-80
Fugitive Offenders Act (England) 1881, applicability **53,** 108-11
Geneva Conventions Act 1962 **42,** 442, 443, 446-7, 454-6
Internal Security Act **42,** 442, 443-4, 451-3, 454-7, **116,** 443-4
Malawi Citizenship Act 1966 **54,** 268-9
Malawi Independence Order 1964
status of courts **53,** 179-80
validity of existing legislation **53,** 110-11
Penal Code **55,** 96
s 40 **54,** 266, 281-3
legislation, interpretation, presumptions, conformity with international law **54,** 268
Rhodesia and Nyasaland, succession **55,** 90-5
status **55,** 90-2, 95
treason, definition **54,** 266, 281-3
Malaysia
applicable law **80,** 27
comity, diplomatic privileges and immunities **121,** 379
common law, relevance **86,** 643, 648, 650
Constitution **55,** 84-7, 547
s 4 **55,** 85

s 32(1) **87,** 237
s 74 **55,** 84-5, **84,** 78, 84
s 159 **55,** 84-5
s 160(2) **87,** 233
s 181 **118,** 295-6
s 181(2) **87,** 237-8
continental shelf legislation **41,** 208
continuity of law **55,** 84-7, 91-3
courts, municipal, standing **80,** 28, **93,** 485-6
customary international law, indirect incorporation through UK law **84,** 84, 85
customary law, evidence of, need for **84,** 84
diplomatic agent, protection **87,** 221
diplomatic immunity, jurisdiction **87,** 214
criminal **87,** 214
diplomatic immunity, jurisdiction, waiver **87,** 214-22
agreement to authenticate document, whether **87,** 218, 219-20
conditional **87,** 215
customary international law **87,** 216
evidence, giving of, whether **87,** 222
implied **87,** 215, 220, 221, 222
limited **87,** 215
Vienna Convention on Diplomatic Relations (1961) **87,** 216
withdrawal **87,** 216-17, 218
diplomatic mission, purposes, ownership of residences **87,** 236
diplomatic premises
definition
residence of head of mission **87,** 236
residence of members of mission **87,** 236
extraterritoriality **87,** 230-1
inviolability **87,** 220-1
service of process and **87,** 230-1
ownership, foreign sovereign, by **87,** 236
diplomatic privileges and immunities
absolute theory **87,** 235
arrest, immunity **87,** 214, 217-18
disturbance of internal order **87,** 221
basis, comity **121,** 379
courts
jurisdiction to determine **121,** 380-2, 384-8
responsibility for determining **121,** 379, 396
diplomatic agent, definition **87,** 214, 221
evidence, obligation to give, whether **87,** 214, 215-16, 217, 218, 219
functional, nature of act as determinant **121,** 380
inviolability, arrest. *See* arrest, immunity *above*
restricted immunity **87,** 235-6, **121,** 375
service of process **87,** 230-1
substituted service **87,** 230-1
diplomatic privileges and immunities, entitlement, special rapporteur **121,** 395
double criminality **55,** 546-7
equitable remedy, injunction as **86,** 649
evidence, confession and corroboration **42,** 463
executive certificate/statement

Malaysia (*cont.*)
conclusiveness, special rapporteur, privileges and immunities **121,** 377-80, 388-97, 419-26, 431-3, 444-5
issued by
minister **121,** 378, 379, 413
UN Secretary-General **121,** 375-7, 388-97, 412-13, 419-26, 431-3
extradition
evidence to support request **87,** 213-14
prima facie case, responsibility for determining **87,** 217
Singapore **55,** 546, 549
foreign relations, role of Ruler **118,** 297
Geneva Convention on the Territorial Sea and Contiguous Zone (1958), partial incorporation **84,** 84
ICJ advisory proceedings
acceptance of advisory opinion as binding **121,** 468-71
stay of proceedings in municipal court **121,** 419-20, 468-9
Indonesia and, hostilities **42,** 441-70, **52,** 498
injunction, breach of criminal law, against **86,** 649-50
innocent passage **84,** 75, 76, 80, 85-6
conflict with municipal law **84,** 85
international officials, privileges and immunities, functional basis **121,** 372-3
law of
Carriage by Air Act **84,** 84
Civil Law Act 1956 **86,** 643, 648, 650
Commonwealth Fugitive Criminals Act 1969
double criminality **55,** 548
'fugitive criminal' **55,** 546-7
procedural nature **55,** 546-7
retrospective application **55,** 546, 548
Constitution. *See* Constitution *above*
Courts of Judicature Act 1956 **87,** 233
s 3 **87,** 238
Courts of Judicature Act 1964 **87,** 218
s 23 **80,** 28, **121,** 381
Criminal Procedure Code **42,** 453, 461, **86,** 650
s 9 **87,** 215
s 323 **87,** 213
Diplomatic and Consular Privileges Ordinance No 53 1957
s 3 **87,** 235
s 9 **87,** 236
s 66 **87,** 224, 230
Diplomatic Privileges (United Nations and International Court of Justice) Order 1949
s 12 **121,** 372, 392, 393, 394
whether in force **121,** 404
Diplomatic Privileges (Vienna Convention) Act 1966 **87,** 214, 218, 219, 222, 232, 235, **121,** 372
s 2 **87,** 235
Schedule, Art. 31 **87,** 235-6
Emergency (Criminal Trials) Regulations 1964, constitutionality **42,** 460-2
Emergency (Essential Powers) Act **42,** 461
Emergency (Essential Powers) Ordinance No 7 of 1969 **84,** 78, 84
Emergency (Essential Powers) Ordinance No 11 of 1969 **84,** 78
English law **87,** 233-4

application of **86,** 643, 648, 650
evolution of, possibility **86,** 650
Evidence Act 1950 **84,** 84, **87,** 215
s 3 **87,** 209
s 5(2) **87,** 210
s 9 **87,** 208, 215
s 10 **87,** 207, 217
Extradition (Thailand) Order 1960 **87,** 210
Fisheries Act 1963/1979 **84,** 75, 76, 77, 84-5, 86
Fisheries (Maritime) Regulations 1967 **84,** 75, 76
International Organizations (Privileges and Immunities) Act **121,** 372
s 7 **121,** 377, 392, 393-4
Interpretation Act 1967 **87,** 234
Interpretation and General Clauses Ordinance 1948 **42,** 461-2, **87,** 234
legislation
Parliamentary powers **55,** 547
validity
courts' competence to determine **55,** 546
courts' competence to rule on **55,** 546
legislation, interpretation
phrases
'fugitive criminal' **55,** 546-7
'jurisdiction' **87,** 230-1
'maritime waters' **84,** 78
treaty as aid, in case of ambiguity **121,** 397-400
legislation, retroactive **55,** 546, 548
liability, strict **84,** 78
Parliament, legislative powers **55,** 547
Rulers
State immunity, jurisdiction **118,** 294-8
status **118,** 294-7
sovereign independence **118,** 297
Rules of High Court 1980
O 6 r 6224 **87,** 230, 231
O 11 **87,** 224, 230, 231
Selangor. *See* Selangor
service of process on foreign State or State agency **87,** 230-1
on diplomatic premises **87,** 230-1
diplomatic privileges and immunities and **87,** 230-1
State immunity, jurisdiction and, substitute service **87,** 231
statutory requirements **87,** 230-1
service of process out of the jurisdiction, as exercise of extraterritorial jurisdiction **80,** 26-30
Singapore
extradition **55,** 546, 549
relation to **55,** 410-11
special rapporteur
costs of proceedings in respect of **121,** 404-5, 413-14, 433, 448, 471
as expert on mission **121,** 374, 375-6, 427-8, 433
Foreign Minister's certificate, conclusiveness **121,** 377-80, 388-97, 413
UN Secretary-General's certificate, conclusiveness **121,** 375-7, 388-97, 412-13, 419-26, 429-30, 444-5
functions

Malaysia (*cont.*)
statement to commercial magazine, whether within **121,** 373, 400-1, 428-31, 445-7, 453-7, 461-2
UN Secretary-General's right to determine whether act within **121,** 376, 391-7, 419-26, 429-30, 431-3, 461-2
immunity, jurisdiction, waiver
acceptance of service **121,** 373-4
conditional appearance **121,** 373-4
privileges and immunities
defamation proceedings **121,** 369-405
diplomatic privileges and immunities distinguished **121,** 395
functional **121,** 375-6, 396
as preliminary question **121,** 379-82, 383-405, 432-3, 448-9, 456-7, 461-2
State immunity
absolute theory **86,** 646-7
civil and criminal jurisdiction distinguished **86,** 643
comity **86,** 651
commercial activity, acts of customs officer, whether **86,** 643, 644-6, 651
common law **86,** 643, 647-8
restrictive theory **86,** 643
development of **86,** 646-7
restrictive theory **86,** 643-7
common law **86,** 643
status, independent federation **55,** 84-7
Supreme Court Rules, Order 11 **80,** 26-30
territorial sea, delimitation **84,** 78-9
treaties, incorporation, need for **84,** 84
treaties, State succession **87,** 210-11
exchange of aides-mémoires and **87,** 210
United Nations, Privileges and Immunities Convention (1946), incorporation into municipal law **121,** 397
Vienna Convention on Diplomatic Relations (1961)
'private immovable property' **87,** 236
restricted immunity **87,** 235-6
Mali. *See also* Burkina Faso/Mali boundary dispute
law of, Law No 82-39/AN-RM of 26 March 1982 **111,** 545
malicious damage 122, 629-30
necessity as defence **22,** 631-8
Malta 81, 412, 414
continental shelf
delimitation **70,** 687
dispute with Libya **70,** 534-5, 539
Special Agreement with Libya **70,** 592, 607, 618
continental shelf, delimitation
Libya
dispute with **70,** 534-5, 539
Special Agreement **70,** 592, 607, 618
Malta, Sovereign Order of. *See* Sovereign Order of Malta
Maltese Islands 81, 282, 368, **83,** 113
***mandamus* 63,** 24, 31-2,**78,** 551, **79,** 467-8
general principles of international law **37,** 520-1
Mandates 37, 360-2, 534, **49,** 5, 22-33, 62-3, 99-101, 114, 121, 136, 181-9, 213, 220, 258-9, 332. *See also* mandated territories; Mandates Commission; Mandatory; *and individual Mandates*

'another member of the League' **37,** 17, 19-20, 23, 28, 37, 46-7, 48-50, 52-3, 71-9, 96, 136-65, 199-210, 213, 238, 298, 300-5, 572
'any dispute whatever' **37,** 24-5, 50-3, 88, 98, 103, 167, 169, 275, 404
'beneficiaries' **37,** 548-50, 584
categories
'A', 'B' and 'C' Mandates
differences **49,** 22, 265-6
Frontiers, Memorandum on **80,** 318
'B' Mandates, drafting **37,** 499-506
'B' and 'C' Mandates **49,** 59
'integral portion' clause **49,** 265-6
'C' Mandates **37,** 23, 34, 253, 255, 263, 277, 283, 419-20. *See also* Mandate, South West Africa
drafting **37,** 57-8, 170, 419-20, 499-506, 523-7
missionary clause **37,** 504, 507
'Open Door' provision **37,** 58, 60, 73, 88, 242, 499, 507, 518-19
ownership in all but name **49,** 267
compromissory clause **37,** 148, 150
compromise nature **37,** 440, 528
compromissory clause **37,** 150, 172-3, 199-200, 255, 261, 265, 269-74, 276-7, 282-4, 402. *See also* Mandate, South West Africa
importance of inclusion **37,** 36-7
ultra vires, whether **37,** 46, 49, 95
'conduct' provisions. *See* Mandate, South West Africa, 'conduct' provisions
definition **37,** 66, 118, 121
drafting **37,** 57-8, 170-4, 197-8, 260-1, 403, 408, 419-20, 499-511, 523-7
essential principles **37,** 11, 28, 29, 33, 44, 49, 75, 94, 122, 146-51, 205, 253, 257-8, 279, 402, 412, 425, 434-7, 445, 518, 567, 592
equality principle **37,** 460, 518-19
personal and real elements **37,** 30, 435
functioning **37,** 277-80, 402
institutional basis **37,** 260, 436-7, 570
interpretation
applicable principles **37,** 453, 455
by Mandates Commission **37,** 549
Covenant of the League of Nations and **37,** 199-200
standards **37,** 552, 569, 573
teleological **37,** 498
judicial protection **37,** 17-19, 25, 35, 36-7, 46, 52-5, 75, 100, 102, 105, 108-9, 120, 122, 146-51, 158, 169, 172, 199, 299-301, 402-7, 414, 420-3, 430, 508, 565, 586, 593, 602
PCIJ
advisory jurisdiction **37,** 19, 37
contentious jurisdiction at behest of Member of League **37,** 19, 37, 47-8
League of Nations and **37,** 521-34, 597-9
administrative supervision and control **37,** 17-19, 32-3, 34-5, 37, 44, 94, 102, 120, 204, 229, 231, 232, 312, 405, 407, 414, 421, **49,** 52, 198
continuance of Mandates after dissolution of League **37,** 15, 20-4, 28, 37-41, 77, 95-6, 442, **49,** 5, 22-33, 62-3, 99-101, 114, 121, 136, 181-9, 213, 220, 332. *See also* Mandatory, obligations, continuance after dissolution of League
Council
approval **37,** 13, 35-6, 44, 46, 59-61, 63-4, 66, 124-8, 135, 197, 524-5
competence to create 'standards' **37,** 360-2
compromissory clause as *ultra vires* **37,** 46, 49, 95

Mandates (*cont.*)
decisions, binding on Mandatory, whether **49,** 258-9
definition of scope and authority of Mandatory **37,** 32, 35-6
functions in relation to **49,** 18-20, 254-9
Mandates Commission reports and **37,** 18, 361, 402
revocation **49,** 6, 154-69
supervision **37,** 200, 360-2, 387-8, 402, **49,** 218-19, 259
establishment of Mandates **37,** 31
as Party to Mandates **37,** 14, 38, 42
Resolution for continuance of (1946) **49,** 25, 28-9, 185-7, 200, 236-9, 245
Secretariat's role **37,** 534
Mandate Agreements, function **37,** 34, 35-6, 81, 119
Mandates Commission. *See* Mandates Commission
nature of institution **37,** 14, 36, 43, 64, 71, 95-6, 114, 144-5, 228, 260, 436-8, 442, **49,** 96-8, 105, 147, 192-3, 197-206, 267
common features **37,** 253
duration **37,** 38
perpetuity **37,** 438
temporary **37,** 34
as a system **37,** 33-4
nature of instrument **49,** 36-7. *See also* treaty character *below*
administrative instrument of League **37,** 45, 47
bona fide contract **37,** 436
declaration or agreement **37,** 35-6, 44-6, 81, 93, 94-5, 121
parallel unilateral declarations **37,** 34, 435
part of Covenant **37,** 33-4
part of Treaty of Versailles (1919) **37,** 33-4
unilateral contract **37,** 34
object and purpose **37,** 29-30, 50, 51, 94, 228, 445-7, 519, 558, 567, 592, 601, **49,** 5, 18, 197, 204
for benefit of territories 'inhabited by peoples not yet able to stand by themselves . . .' **97,** 23
exploitation of phosphate deposits **97,** 23-4
promotion of well-being of inhabitants. *See* Mandatory, obligations
ultimate goal **37,** 470, 553
origin **37,** 11, 29, 56, 94, 119, 122, 257, 401, 420
bilateral agreement **37,** 31, 35
Hymans Report (1920) **37,** 31, 59-60, 100, 122-3, 362, 524
as part of municipal law of mandatory, whether **82,** 472-3, 481-5, **84,** 478, 490-4
parties to
League **37,** 14, 38, 42, 48, 72, 93, 116 n. 1, 132, 135, 435
Mandatory **37,** 13, 34, 38, 48, 93, 116 n. 1, 130, 435
Members of League **37,** 72, 93, 126, 133-5, 261
legal right or interest in observance of mandate **37,** 24-5, 49, 51
population of territory **37,** 32, 38, 51, 130, 435
Principal Allied Powers **37,** 12-13, 65, 77, 130-3, 435
United Nations **37,** 435
petitions procedure **37,** 399, 474, 531, 533, 571
Principal Allied Powers
continuing rights and obligations **37,** 31-2
as party to **37,** 12-13, 67, 77, 130-3, 435
reversionary interest **37,** 545-6

reporting obligation **82,** 470
revocability **49,** 38, 63, 98-9, 121, 135-6, 152-3, 200-6, 213, 254-69, 325-8
'sacred trust of civilization' **37,** 11, 15, 29-33, 119, 204, 228-9, 237, 257, 267-8, 277, 279, 420-1, 435, 511, 558, 564, **49,** 18-19, 21, 51, 52, 95-6, 136, 197, 200
legal incidents **37,** 268, 567, 574
legal nature **37,** 51, 228, 401
legal obligations **37,** 33, 86, 94, 412
responsibility of Members for fulfilment **37,** 33, 35, 37, 46, 50, 51, 104, 200, 259, 262, 268, 402-3
protection of own interests **37,** 25
protection of well-being of inhabitants **37,** 11, 25, 29-33
'securities for performance of this trust' **37,** 17-19, 119-20, 148, 199, 204, 205, 229, 241-2, 258-9, 277, 279, 280, 299, 306, 401, 445, 527-8, 553, 565, 570. *See also* judicial protection *and* League of Nations, administrative control and supervision *above*
Smuts proposal **37,** 196, 518, 528
'special interests' provisions **37,** 167, 254-5, 262, 266, 274, 276, 283, 427, 547, 564, 592-3, 596
'Tanganyika clause' **37,** 87, 102, 173-4, 277, 420, 506-11
termination **37,** 496, **80,** 263. *See also* Mandate, South West Africa, termination
League Board of Liquidation report **37,** 328
unilateral, League of Nations Council **49,** 6, 254-69
transfer
to League **37,** 29
to Mandatories **37,** 121-2
treatment 1945-46 **37,** 154-61
treaty character **37,** 12-14, 28, 35-6, 44, 47, 66, 67-71, 93-5, 107, 115, 116-29, 135, 435, 564, **49,** 200, **82,** 473-4
bilateral agreement as origin **37,** 31, 35
law-making treaties compared **37,** 435
parties **37,** 13-14, 32, 34, 38, 42, 48, 72, 93, 116 n. 1, 126, 130-5
relevant factors
'Declaration' (*exemplaire*), description as **37,** 13-14
deposit with League of Nations **37,** 13-14, 36
'instrument' (*acte*), description as **37,** 13
publication **37,** 14, 36, 45, 47
registration **37,** 14, 36, 45
transmission to signatories of Peace Treaty with Germany **37,** 13-14
Trusteeship system and **37,** 410, 412, **49,** 240-2, 249, 253, **97,** 24
ultimate goal **37,** 470, 553
Mandate, Iraq
subsequent treaties **37,** 132 n. 1
Iraq–UK **37,** 132 n. 1
treaty form **37,** 121, 129, 260
Mandate, Lebanon, termination **37,** 20
Mandate, New Guinea, Australian Mandate **55,** 57-60
Mandate, Palestine 60, 209, 213
Aqaba, status (1925) **80,** 260
boundaries
Egyptian frontier
Annual Reports to League Council **80,** 261-2
delimitation of Palestine frontiers and **80,** 260-1, 262
fixed nature **80,** 263, 323

Mandate, Palestine (*cont.*)
recognition as definitive frontier, implied **80,** 261
failure to establish at time of entry into force **80,** 260
dissolution of League of Nations and **37,** 224, 320, 494-6, 546
part of law of Palestine **44,** 334, 335-6, 340
termination **80,** 263
territory 'not to be ceded, leased or placed under control of foreign Power' **80,** 260
treaty-making provisions **44,** 198, 207-8
Mandate, Ruanda-Urundi, 'open-door' clause **37,** 73, 301
Mandate, South West Africa. *See also* Namibia; South Africa, South West Africa
annexation and **49,** 5, 18, 20, 23, 33
applicable law, South Africa, law of **37,** 358, **52,** 28-9
Balfour Draft **37,** 31, 44, 46, 61, 63, 101, 123, 198, 240, 526
basis, agreement of Powers **37,** 64
breach
adoption of measure objected to by Permanent Mandates Commission/Council **37,** 18-19
remedies **82,** 473
South Africa **37,** 347-400, 444-77, **49,** 211
commercial matters, preferential rights **49,** 25
compromissory clause. *See also* disputes; Mandates, compromissory clause
'another Member of the League' **37,** 17, 19-20, 23, 28, 37, 46-7, 48-50, 52-3, 71-9, 96, 136-65, 199-210, 213, 238, 298, 300-5, 572
at time of dissolution of League **37,** 20
'any dispute whatever' **37,** 24-5, 50-3, 88, 98, 103, 167, 169, 275, 404
'which cannot be settled by negotiation' **37,** 25-8, 53-6, 89-91, 104, 167-9, 174-6, 291-2
continuance after dissolution of the League of Nations **2,** 201, 203, 227, 228, 343, 564, 571, 573, 596, **37,** 15, 17-24, 46-7, 54, 77, 144-65, 201, 203, 227, 228, 343, 564, 571, 573, 596
South Africa's membership of UN, relevance **37,** 43-4
PCIJ optional clause and **37,** 47
ultra vires League Council, whether **37,** 46, 49, 95
'conduct' provisions **37,** 167-9, 253-6, 259, 261, 262, 266, 277, 279-80, 426, 427, 518, 564, 592-3, 596
continuance after dissolution of the League of Nations **37,** 20-4, 28, 37-41, 42-4, 54, 71, 252, 285, 339-40, 430, 433-4, 437-42, 479, 481, 485, 487, 493, 542-6, 570-1, 575, 596-7, **49,** 285, **82,** 476-7. *See also* lapse *below*
definition **37,** 66, 118, 121
deposit in League archives **37,** 81, 94, 129
disavowal of **49,** 290
discrimination **37,** 358
criticism, Mandates Commission **37,** 413
draft Convention **37,** 58-60, 197
drafting **37,** 55-9, 61, 63, 66, 101-2, 170-4, 197-8, 240, 276, 299, 403-4, 408, 419-20, 496-511
effect of dissolution of PCIJ **37,** 140-1, 201, 203
entrenched rights **82,** 472-3, 482-3
in force, whether **37,** 42-9, 77, 79, 92, 95-7, 115, 129-36, 564, 565
dissolution of League of Nations, relevance **37,** 15-24
legal effect, date of **37,** 127-8
form **37,** 36, 44, 61, 63, 66, 93-5, 107, 121, 124-9, 135, 362. *See also* treaty character *below*

implied terms **37,** 307, 309, 311, 358, 366
individual's rights under **82,** 472-3
institutional character **37,** 33, 36, 43, 64, 71, 95-6, 114, 144-5, 228, 260, 436-8, 442, 564, 570, 597
interpretation
  literal meaning **37,** 275
  standards **37,** 552, 569, 573
judicial protection. *See* compromissory clause *above*
lapse **37,** 228, 247, 249, **49,** 5, 22-3, 28-33. *See also* continuance *above*
legal effect, date of **37,** 127-8
literal meaning **37,** 275
missionaries, rights **37,** 72, 73-7, 172, 229, 254, 277, 598
modification **37,** 61, 95, 126, 128, 132, 200, 230, 246, 249, 340, 358, 399-400, 401, 476-7, 522, 571, 596
nature of instrument. *See* treaty character *below*
need for **37,** 17-19, 46-7, 75, 146-51, 200-1, 204, 229, 277-81, 284, 343, 602
obligations, enforcement
  judicial responsibility, whether **82,** 474
  League of Nations' responsibility **82,** 473
PCIJ
  dissolution, effect **37,** 140-1, 201, 203
  optional clause and **37,** 36, 47, 66, 198
phrases, 'relating to interpretation or application of the Mandate' **37,** 357-9, 366
purpose **37,** 150, 172-3, 199-200, 242, 299, 602
reporting obligations **49,** 211, 215, 219-23, 239, 246, 249-50, 260-1, 286, **82,** 470
repudiation, South Africa **49,** 37, 151
revocation by General Assembly **52,** 29
  requirements, necessity **49,** 329
rights conferred by **37,** 270-7
scope **37,** 50-4, 88, 98, 100-4, 115, 150, 164, 167-74, 198
South Africa
  authority **82,** 477
  law of, application **37,** 358, **52,** 28-9, **82,** 469-99
  Parliament, legislative competence **52,** 40-1, **82,** 487-8
    limitations on **82,** 483
  sovereignty, limitation on **82,** 480
  validity of acts **82,** 475, 478-9
    municipal law, under **82,** 475, 478-9
'special interests' provisions **37,** 167, 254-5, 262, 266, 274, 283, 427, 547, 564, 592-3, 596
termination **37,** 36-40, 95, 103, 104-6, 117, 122, 123, 131, 136, 153-5, 158, 178-9, 210, 215, 253, 279-80, 290-1, 295-7, 305, 322-30, **49,** 4, 6, 36-40, 61, 63, 95, 103, 104-6, 117, 122, 123, 131, 136, 153-5, 158, 178-9, 210, 215, 253, 279-80, 289, 290-1, 295-7, 305, 322-30, **52,** 30
  agreement, need for **82,** 476-7
  fundamental breach leading to **82,** 474
  General Assembly Resolution 2145 **82,** 475, 478, 480, 488, 490
  international domain, in **82,** 478
  unilateral
    South Africa **82,** 476-7
    United Nations **82,** 476, 478, 481
terms and effect **52,** 36-9, 41-2, **82,** 470-1

Mandate, South West Africa (*cont.*)
treaty character **37,** 12-14, 28, 35-6, 44, 66, 67-71, 93-5, 107, 115, 116-29, 135, 564, **49,** 200, **82,** 473-4
bilateral agreement as origin **37,** 31, 35
parties **37,** 13-14, 32, 34, 38, 42, 48, 72, 93, 116 n. 1, 126, 130-5
relevant factors
'Declaration' (*exemplaire*), description as **37,** 13-14, 35-6, 44-6
deposit with League of Nations **37,** 13-14
'instrument' (*acte*), description as **37,** 13
publication **37,** 14, 36, 45, 47
registration **37,** 14, 36, 45
transmission to signatories of Peace Treaty with Germany **37,** 13-14
UN Council for South West Africa, administering authority, whether **82,** 480
unilateral character **37,** 142, 164, 198
validity **37,** 46, 64, 95
Walvis Bay, treatment as part of **82,** 470, 494-8
Mandate, Syria, termination **37,** 20
Mandate, Togo and Cameroons, drafting **37,** 62-3, 507, 527
Mandate, Trans-Jordan, termination **37,** 20, 496
mandated territories
allocation of colonial possessions by Principal Allied Powers **37,** 29, 31, 35, 56-7, 59, 61, 62, 64, 65, 94, 121, 123, 197, 198, 524-5, 545
applicable law, law of Mandatory **37,** 34, 358, **52,** 28-9, **82,** 469-99
boundaries
approval by Principal Allied Powers or League Council **80,** 261
Foreign Office (UK) Memorandum **80,** 261, 318
inhabitants
legal capacity **37,** 32-3, 34
petitions from **37,** 227, 233, 245, 246, 249, 334, 399, 414, 472, 474, 571
rights **37,** 32, 72, 231, 232, 402, 435, 472, 548, 571, **49,** 23, 104
self-determination **37,** 34, 245, 248, 413, 471-4, 558
nationality of inhabitants **37,** 387-8, 472, **79,** 472, 690-4
League of Nations resolution **79,** 690-4
as non-self-governing territory **37,** 144, 161-4, 231, **49,** 239, 240, 249, 250-2, 286
Permanent Mandates Commission **80,** 318
self-determination **37,** 7, 245, 248, 413, 471-4, 558
territorial sovereignty **37,** 30, 34, 61, 121 n. 1, 409, 440, 570, **87,** 606
Trusteeship System and **37,** 155-61, 164, 216, 230
Mandated Trust Territories. *See also* Mandate, South West Africa; Mandate system; Namibia
State succession. *See* Namibia, State succession
treaties, applicability **91,** 379
Mandates Commission 49, 19, 223, 241, 260, **80,** 318
Bondelzwarts rebellion and **37,** 532-3
boundary agreement, South Africa-Portugal **37,** 409
Caprivi area, report on **37,** 391
competence to create 'standards' **37,** 362-3
composition **37,** 441, 531
functions **37,** 18, 258, 361, 363, 402, 531
Germany, complaint (1925) **37,** 74
League, dissolution and **37,** 205. *See also* League of Nations, dissolution
UN General Assembly, proposed Committee **49,** 34, 186, 223, 235-6
Mandatory 60, 209, 213

breach of Mandate **37,** 18-19, 347-400, 444-77, **49,** 211
determination of **37,** 110-11
declaration of continuance of administration (1946) **37,** 21, 74, 76, 78-9, 151-4, 162, 269, 325, 330, 406, 414, 570
addressees **37,** 406
discretionary powers **37,** 354-5, 472, 473-4
exercise, reviewability **37,** 553-9
League Council **37,** 533
veto in **49,** 49, 189-97, 218, 262, 263, 267
Mauritius and **60,** 209, 213
nature of interest
agent or trustee for League **37,** 32, 257
legal title **37,** 59, 96, 228, 543, 564
obligations **37,** 11, 15, 56, 65-6, 198, 228, 229, 245, 248, 404, 436, 508-9, **52,** 39, 42, **55,** 57, 59-60. *See also* rights *below*
annual reports **37,** 15, 18, 64, 198, 205, 213, 224, 227, 231, 233, 236, 241, 245-6, 249, 250, 258, 306, 308, 336, 401, 404, 414, 421, 503, 569, 570, 572, **49,** 211, 215, 219-23, 239, 246, 249, 260-1, 286
novation **49,** 217, 223, 227 n. 18, 243, 246, 257
breach, determination of **37,** 110-11
continuance after dissolution of League **37,** 21, 43, 245, 247, 248, 323-45, 415, 433, 439-44, 481, 570. *See also* Mandates, League of Nations and, continuance of Mandate after dissolution of the League
owed to Members severally **37,** 24-5, 33, 37, 49-50, 65, 77, 181, 241-2, 255, 257-84, 400-12, 508, 510-11
promotion of well-being of inhabitants **37,** 11, 173, 205, 229, 245, 248, 347-51, 354-6, 404, 406, 412-13, 419-20, 436, 444-77, 518, 548-59, 574, 585-6, **49,** 77-8, 168, 212
substantive and adjectival **37,** 404, 427-8
supervision and control by League of Nations **37,** 15, 33, 250, 312, 334, 360, 392-3, 401, 416, 439-44, 474, 553, 564, 569, 570-1, 572. *See also* Mandates System, 'securities for performance'
three classes **37,** 406
to conclude Trusteeship Agreement **37,** 23, 40-1, 43-4, 54, 155-61, 233, 304, 329, 442, **49,** 333-4
Palestine and **60,** 209
powers **52,** 39, 42
discretionary **37,** 34, 56, 64-6, 198, 228, 229, 245, 248, 404, 436, 508-9
legislative **37,** 34
restrictions on **49,** 199
revocation, necessity as basis **49,** 329
Principal Allied Powers, draft treaties with **37,** 31, 123
rights **37,** 34, 228, 337-8, 412, 435-6, 440, 564, **49,** 124
dependence on obligations **37,** 11, 15, 34
to administer Mandate **49,** 124
UN membership, consequences **37,** 453, 455, 461
maps 50, 17, 77, 690-1, **81,** 485. *See also* boundaries, evidence of; boundaries, land, evidence of
accuracy **113,** 106-7
admission against interest **114,** 99-100
colour **114,** 96
'best evidence' rule **50,** 109-10
boundaries, error **38,** 60, 76-9, **50,** 106, 111, 167, 477, 485

maps (*cont.*)
cartographic unity **113,** 118
charts, officially recognized
lack **73,** 176-8
large scale, Territorial Sea Convention (1958) **43,** 116, 122-3
dependence on accompanying documentation **113,** 106-7
description in words **50,** 325-6, 327, 407, 423, 443, 466
disclaimer of territory, as **91,** 424
discrepancy with text of agreement **106,** 663-73, 687-8
distribution **50,** 123-6, 421, 431
evidence **50,** 4, 7, 23, 25, 101-2, 105-13, 420, 423, 485, 515, **52,** 165, 182, 198-206, 208-20, 229-30, **59,** 169-70, 202-3, 206, **69,** 70-1, **77,** 664, **80,** 254, 268, 287, 289, 291, 292, 293, 295, 300-1, 324, 333-4, 350-1, 486-92, 532, 535-8, 544-50, **100,** 30
hearsay character **50,** 108-10
inter-temporal **50,** 27, 388, 389-91, 463, 470, **52,** 206, 208-20
official and non-official **50,** 106-7, 110, 112-13, **52,** 203-5
primary or original **50,** 110
value
corroborative **97,** 466, **100,** 32
Frontier Dispute **97,** 466
hearsay character **50,** 108-10
inter-temporal **50,** 27, 388, 389-91, 463, 470, **52,** 206, 208-20
official and non-official **50,** 106-7, 112-13, **52,** 203-5
primary or original **50,** 110
evidence of
arbitrator's jurisdiction **113,** 114, 118, 119-22, 178
boundaries, land. *See* boundaries, land, evidence of, maps
exercise of territorial jurisdiction **113,** 79
geographical knowledge **113,** 183-4
title to territory **80,** 486, 562, **91,** 629-30, 632-4, 648, **97,** 327-30, **114,** 97
'approximate tentative international boundary' **114,** 102-3
exercise of jurisdiction and **50,** 176-7, 515
federal authorities' competence **91,** 634
geodesic arcs **77,** 690
inspection for arbitration **50,** 17
Iraq–Kuwait boundary **94,** 11-12, 13-16
jurisdiction and **50,** 176-7, 515
loxodromic system **77,** 690
Mercator projection **83,** 46-7
official
binding on State **50,** 111, 125, 323, 420-2, 443, 485, 514
as official description of territory **50,** 21, 105-6, 111, 120-1, 125, 165, 167, 169-70, 174, 175-6, 420-2, 514-15
as official description of territory **50,** 21, 105-6, 111, 120-1, 125, 165, 167, 169-70, 174, 175-6, 420-2, 514-15
orientation **81,** 370, 475
pecked lines, significance **113,** 68-9, 77, 105-6, 112-13, 167-9, 181, **114,** 98
preparation **94,** 13-16
Red Sea Islands. *See* Red Sea Islands, maps
relevance **113,** 51-5, 58, 100, 104-5
approval by ruler, in absence of **114,** 96
supportive value **114,** 96-7
unpublished **114,** 102-3

reliability **91,** 629-30, **94,** 11-12, 21-2, **97,** 540
scale 77, 690, **80,** 287, 295, 300, **81,** 252, 459, **113,** 215-23
glacial area, relevance **113,** 224-6
Territorial Sea Convention (1958) **43,** 116, 122-3
significance of choice **83,** 46-7
title, evidence of. *See* title, evidence of
treaty interpretation and **52,** 198-203, 229-30
value **80,** 486-90
world geodesic ellipsoid WGS72 **77,** 690
***mare clausum* 41,** 86, 107-8, **57,** 82
Mareva injunction 64, 222-5, **77,** 1-8, 165-6, 492, **80,** 216, 219-20, **87,** 414-18
extraterritorial effect **107,** 500-1
fiduciary obligation of disclosure **120,** 421-7, 439-40
international organizations, privileges and immunities **77,** 1-8, 165-6
State immunity, execution/attachment and **64,** 222-5, **77,** 1-8, 492, **87,** 414-18
undertaking in damages and **120,** 421-7, 438-46, 455-7
margin of appreciation 58, 72, **60,** 269, 272-3, 278-9, **68,** 108-10, 116-18, 124-7, **78,** 204, 294, **79,** 301, 302, 303, **81,** 70-1, 129, 171, 173, 232. *See also* European Convention on Human Rights (1950), margin of appreciation; proportionality
access to courts **123,** 39, 64-6, 84-6
act of State **89,** 242
'best efforts' **102,** 294
choice of means **58,** 15-16, 34, 173, 449, 579, 584, 639, 670
correspondence, interference with **58,** 448-9
defence policy, acts of armed forces **108,** 674-5
derogation **58,** 278-9, 294, 306, 307
diplomatic protection **107,** 480
European Court of Human Rights, supervision by **58,** 174, 543
free elections **123,** 19-20
freedom of association **94,** 250
freedom of expression **58,** 89, 172, 174, 177, 184, 185, 543-8
good faith **58,** 543
human rights implementation **104,** 446-7
legal control **100,** 313
military discipline and **52,** 89, **58,** 72, 89
national authorities **58,** 173-4, 179, 306, 529, 541, 543-8, 556, 614, **122,** 480-1
national courts **58,** 529
private life, interference with **67,** 414, 417
protection of morals **58,** 173-4, 179, **67,** 414, 417-18, 420-3
homosexuality **70,** 298-304
public opinion **67,** 415
requirements
good faith **58,** 543
legitimate aim **58,** 89, 177, 185, 523-4, 527-9
proportionality **58,** 18, 36, 174, 179, 185, **67,** 414, 417. *See also* proportionality
scope **58,** 530
secret surveillance and **58,** 448-9
social need **67,** 414, 417-28
telephone conversations **58,** 448-9
treaties, termination **117,** 427
treaty obligations **107,** 93-8
unfair competition and **81,** 219, 226
margin of discretion. *See* margin of appreciation

marine pollution **72,** 2-3, 112, 116-18
discharge of radioactive waste **87,** 87-90
customary international law **106,** 20
European Community (EC) competence **120,** 630-1
innocent passage and **82,** 602
jurisdiction **94,** 232-7
oil discharge
failure to keep records **94,** 232-7
failure to report **94,** 232
prevention, unilateral action, right of **120,** 596-9
treaties
Convention relating to Intervention on the High Seas in case of Oil Pollution Casualties (1969), measures by non-flag State **120,** 589
Law of the Sea Convention (1982), coastal State powers **120,** 598-9
London Convention on the Prevention of Marine Pollution by the Dumping of Wastes (1972)
implementing legislation **100,** 507
land-based disposal of radioactive waste, preference for **87,** 89-90
packaging **87,** 89-90
'platforms or other man-made structures at sea' **100,** 507
self-executing **100,** 507
'trace' **87,** 85-7
Oslo Convention on Marine Pollution (1972), prior consultation procedure **87,** 86-7
Pollution of Sea by Oil, International Convention for the Prevention of (1954) **60,** 457, 459-60, 475, 478
enforcement **60,** 457, 460, 466
maritime archaeological sites. *See* wrecks
maritime area **81,** 252-4, 259-60, 292, 347-51, 361-3, 443
definition **95,** 660, 711-15
delimitation **71,** 95-100. *See also* maritime delimitation, limits of delimitation
'coastal wings' **71,** 99, 207
relevant features **71,** 99-100
Guinea/Guinea-Bissau **81,** 347
Gulf of Maine **71,** 95, 99-100 **81,** 347, 397-9
historic title **42,** 101-2
'in dispute' **67,** 27-8, 34-5, 54-5, 75, **83,** 87-8. *See also*'of concern' *below*
equal division **71,** 127, 140, 147-8, 150, 154, 158-61, 202, 206, 208-9
subdivision **67,** 75-6, 79-81, 86-8
Jan Mayen **99,** 412-13, 415-16, 446
limitation
claims of third States **81,** 313, 345, 347-9, 350-1, 361-3
opposite coasts, need for **81,** 308, 312-13
marginal area **41,** 52, 62. *See also* overlapping area *below*
'maritime spaces' **97,** 499-500
'maritime waters' **84,** 78
'of concern' **67,** 27-8, 35, 54-5, 242-5. *See also* 'in dispute' *above*
overlapping area **41,** 66, 82, 83, 88-9, 95, 96, 102-4, 111, 114, 152, 165-6
by agreement **41,** 82, 87
claims and entitlement distinguished **99,** 432, 478-9, 495-6, 672, 681
effect on whole area **99,** 545-6
equal division **41,** 82, 83, **99,** 449, 544-50
fishing zones

agreement not to exercise jurisdiction against vessels of other State, Australia–Indonesia Provisional Fisheries Arrangement (1981) **101,** 167-9
legislative powers **101,** 172-4
islands, territorial sea **119,** 462-4
joint exploitation of maritime resources **41,** 82, 83, 88, **119,** 445-6
limitation to **81,** 304, 328, 345, 390, **99,** 415, 469
relevant area distinguished **99,** 484, 672
proportionality and **81,** 304, **99,** 544-50
proportionality and. *See* proportionality, maritime delimitation
relevant **95,** 711-15, **99,** 552
legal significance **99,** 415
territorial waters as part of **81,** 324
Tunisia–Libya **81,** 347
maritime belt. *See* territorial sea
maritime claims liability
Brussels Convention on the Limitation of Liability for Maritime Claims (1957)
abrogation by 1976 Convention **107,** 127
as between States party to 1976 Convention **107,** 143
common law rights, effect on **107,** 126-9
denunciation **100,** 480
effective date **107,** 133
subsequent validity **100,** 482, 488
incorporation into municipal law **100,** 476-7
Brussels Convention on the Limitation of Liability for Maritime Claims (1976)
applicability
critical date **107,** 124-30, 132-3, 137-46
person for whom shipowner or salver is responsible **107,** 124, 130-1, 144
constitution of limitation fund **107,** 125, 128-9
customary international law **107,** 142-3
entry into force **100,** 480
Australia **107,** 133, 143
implementing legislation, Australia **107,** 124-46
procedural, whether **107,** 137-44
purpose
constitution of limitation fund. *See* constitution of limitation fund *above*
limitation of liability of shipowner **107,** 142-3
standardization of rules relating to limitation of liability **107,** 124-5
retroactive effect **100,** 483-8, **107,** 142-3, 145-6
transitional arrangements, absence **107,** 127
right to apply for limitation decree, acquired right, whether **107,** 128-9
maritime delimitation 77, 675-92, **82,** 681-2, **83,** 87-119. *See also* continental shelf; continental shelf delimitation; Eritrea/Yemen Arbitration Tribunal (1998) *and* (1999); exclusive economic zone (EEZ); fisheries, boundaries; fishing zones; law of the sea; Red Seal Islands; territorial sea
adjacency **67,** 54, **71,** 123-5, **95,** 662
19th century concept **86,** 187-8
in absence of **81,** 309
coasts **83,** 117
continental shelf **41,** 86, 174, **67,** 54
title **81,** 338
Continental Shelf Convention (1958) **41,** 173-4
continental shelf delimitation, coastal opening, need for **81,** 273

maritime delimitation (*cont.*)
definition **92,** 678-82
distance and, *North Sea* **41,** 59-60, 61, 63, 65-6, 87, 115, 126-7, 152, 173, 189-90, 193
domination of sea by land through coasts and **41,** 81
equidistance and **41,** 115, 126-7, 189-90, 193
historical evidence **95,** 662-3
legal phenomenon, 'neighbouring States' **41,** 220 n. 1
natural prolongation, expression of **41,** 86, 174
sectors doctrine and **41,** 89-90, 127
title and
Gulf of Maine **71,** 123, **123,** 355
Jan Mayen **123,** 356
North Sea **41,** 189
spheres of influence **41,** 127
adjacent States, between **67,** 42, 56, 81, 100, 129-30, 287, **70,** 553, 611-12, 641-2, **71,** 85, 88, 118, 150-2, 158-60, 164, 208-9
low-water mark **94,** 12
thalweg **94,** 12
adjacent waters, control of
islands, relevance **77,** 679
need for **77,** 676
agreement. *See* basis, agreement *below*
applicable law **41,** 53, 75-6, 85, 132, 201, **67,** 30-1, 36-7, 52, 85, **70,** 684, **83,** 42-3, 83-7, 91
Continental Shelf Convention (1958) **99,** 424, 425-6, 427-8, 473-4, 488-9, 499-500, 657, 660, 673
single boundary **99,** 425, 496, 568
customary international law **83,** 87, **91,** 656, **99,** 438, 473-4, 657, 660, 666, 672
continental shelf **99,** 438, 473-4, 657, 660, 666, 672
non-parties to 1958 Conventions **91,** 656, 658-9
delimitation by agreement, equitable principles **99,** 517-18
fishing zones
customary international law **99,** 495
Law of the Sea Convention (1982) **99,** 473-4
Law of the Sea Convention (1982) **83,** 42-3
fishing zones **99,** 473-4
prior to entry into force **83,** 86
negotiated delimitation **41,** 75-6, 85, 201
precedent **99,** 430
single boundary **95,** 663, **99,** 425-7, 496
Continental Shelf Convention (1958) **99,** 425, 496, 568
State practice **99,** 432
Territorial Sea and Contiguous Zone Convention (1958) **83,** 85-6
single boundary **95,** 663
third party claims **67,** 35
apportionment **41,** 32, 51-2, 80, 97, 115, 141, 148, 149, 151, 152, 165-6, 174, 178-82, 184, 185, 187-8, 193-4, 196, 199-200, 228, **67,** 246-8, 306. *See also* distributive justice *below*
distinguished **83,** 117-18, **95,** 696-7, **99,** 434-5, 527-9, 564
arbitrary **99,** 484-5
baselines. *See* baselines
basis

agreement **41,** 104, **67,** 177-83, **71,** 93, 118-21, 126-7, 194, 202, **81,** 299. *See also* methods, agreement *below*
non-self-governing territory **105,** 344-5
consensual **41,** 104
equitable principles **41,** 65, 76-7
equity and law **41,** 76
bays, Bay of Fundy **71,** 95-7, 149, 152, 163, 180-5
bilateral nature **41,** 179, 190
binding norms
Law of the Sea Convention (1982) **62,** 115
States and **41,** 71, 76, **62,** 115
North Sea **41,** 71, 76
Browns Bank **71,** 86, 111, 146
by agreement **67,** 177-83, **71,** 93, 118-21, 126-7, 194, 202
claims
entitlement distinguished **99,** 495-6
maximalist **99,** 469, 494-5
claims of parties, significance **71,** 203
closed sea **41,** 86, 107-8. *See also* bays, closed sea; continental shelf delimitation, closed sea
coastal front. *See* coastal front
coasting trade **71,** 167-9, 180-1
coastline. *See* coastline
coasts. *See* coasts
compromise between parties to dispute **71,** 180, 203, 209, 216
conduct of parties **67,** 76-7, 91, **71,** 81, 86, 89, 130-9, **83,** 81
conservation of natural resources and **71,** 88, 95, 125, 170
constitutive nature **41,** 51, 78-9, 82, 115, 190-1
continental margin. *See* continental margin
Continental Shelf Convention (1958). *See* Continental Shelf Convention (1958)
continuity of shelf. *See* rift zones
criteria. *See also* relevant/special circumstances *below*
adjacency. *See* adjacency *above*
agreement/equidistance/special circumstances **41,** 156, 167, 177, 202, 456
agreement/equitable principles/relevant circumstances **81,** 295, 381
agreement/international law/equitable principles/equidistance/special circumstances **81,** 382
agreement/international law/equitable result **41,** 62, 76-7, **62,** 115
appurtenance **41,** 58-61, 81
cut-off effect. *See* non-encroachment *below*
distance **41,** 120-2, **67,** 242
proportionality and **62,** 125
equidistance/relevant circumstances, customary international law **99,** 426
equidistance/special circumstances **41,** 49, 66-7, 109-10, 151, **81,** 280, 328, 357, 372-95, **99,** 498-527. *See also* Continental Shelf Convention (1958), Art. 6(1); equidistance
1953 Committee of Experts **99,** 522-3
Anglo-French Arbitration **81,** 376-8
Continental Shelf Convention (1958) **41,** 49, 70
customary international law **81,** 375, 401
equitable principles/relevant circumstances distinguished **99,** 512, 522
equity and **81,** 361, 378, 391-5
fishing zones **99,** 429-32

maritime delimitation (*cont.*)
governmental consultation **99,** 523-4
Jan Mayen **99,** 427-9, 456, 496-7
Law of the Sea Convention (1982) **81,** 359
need for equitable result and **99,** 519-22
North Sea **81,** 375-6, **99,** 510-11
Second Report on the High Seas (1951) **99,** 522-3
single shelf **81,** 390-1
special circumstances as exception **99,** 506-12, 524-5, 674
UNCLOS I **81,** 374-5
UNCLOS III **81,** 380-2
equitable **71,** 119
equitable principles/equitable result **95,** 706
equitable principles/equitable result/equidistance **83,** 87
equitable principles/relevant circumstances **81,** 270, 278, 279, 297
customary international law **99,** 512
equidistance/special circumstances distinguished **99,** 512, 515-16
equitable principles/relevant circumstances/equitable result **81,** 270, 279, 280, 288, 289, 299, 338, **95,** 663
equitable result **41,** 193, **62,** 125
exploitability **41,** 222-3, **81,** 261
feasibility **99,** 451
geographical **62,** 111, 112
geological **62,** 111, 112
Gulf of Maine **99,** 510
just and equitable share **41,** 30, 32, 36-7, 38, 39, 50-2, 59, 61, 92, 93, 96, 99, 100, 148, 151, 183, 199
appurtenance theory as basis **41,** 52, 59
macrogeographic **83,** 97 n. 57
morphological **62,** 109, 116
natural prolongation. *See* natural prolongation *below*; continental shelf, natural prolongation
non-encroachment. *See* non-encroachment *below*
precision, need for **81,** 352
proportionality. *See* proportionality, maritime delimitation
proximity **41,** 59, 60
'reasonable' **41,** 89, 108, 216
relevant factors, relevance **95,** 706
special circumstances/equidistance, relevant circumstances/equitable principles compared **99,** 671
technical norm **41,** 106, 109, 113, 165 n. 1
customary international law **71,** 115-27, **81,** 261-2, **91,** 653, 654, 656, 658-9. *See also* principles and rules applicable to *below*; relevant/special circumstances *below*
as applicable law. *See* applicable law *above*
equitable principles/relevant circumstances **99,** 512
single boundary **99,** 568, 657
cut-off effect. *See* non-encroachment *below*
de facto delimitation **71,** 107, 137-8
declaratory nature **41,** 51-2, 217
deepest water line **71,** 111, 114-15, 143
definition **41,** 51-2
delimitation agreement and subsequent dispute distinguished **83,** 85
determination of boundary distinguished **92,** 152, **97,** 499, 635-8, **99,** 570, 571-2, 575-6, **119,** 456, 464

land boundaries distinguished **80,** 482, **99,** 576
determination of the legal situation of the maritime spaces distinguished **97,** 498-502
dispute
avoidance **71,** 85, 88, 125
crystallization **71,** 107-8
distance principle **67,** 242, **71,** 123-5, 180. *See also* methods, distance *below*
distributive justice **41,** 183, 184, 227, **46,** 297, **81,** 391-2, **99,** 486-8. *See also* apportionment distinguished *above*
equal division **81,** 304, 322, 323, 351, 390
Gulf of Maine **99,** 487
Libya–Malta **99,** 488
North Sea **99,** 486-7
Tunisia–Libya **99,** 487
ecological aspects **71,** 86, 89, 100, 102-5, 113-14, 143, 146, 153-4
natural boundaries **71,** 103-4
economic zones **95,** 677
applicable law **95,** 677
freedom of navigation **95,** 677, 705
customary international law **95,** 677
overlap, relevance **95,** 676-7
EEZ. *See* exclusive economic zone (EEZ), delimitation
enclaves and **62,** 126, **77,** 680, 682, **95,** 668, 686, 712, **119,** 455-6, 463
equal division **71,** 127, 140, 147-8, 150, 154, 158-61, 202, 206, 208-9, **99,** 449, 543-58
adjustments **71,** 154-5, 206
distance between opposite coasts **99,** 550-5
equidistance and **99,** 546
Gulf of Maine **99,** 548
North Sea **99,** 547
resources **41,** 99-100, 102-3
treatment of like with like **99,** 555-8
equality
equidistance method, result of **99,** 550-5
Anglo-French Arbitration **99,** 549-50
equality of States and **83,** 117-18
equidistance. *See* equidistance/special circumstances *above*; equidistance
equitable **67,** 37, 39-40, 70, 144-9, 248-50, 255, 262. *See also* criteria, just and equitable share *above*
equitable apportionment distinguished **67,** 246-8, 306
natural prolongation and **67,** 39-40, 51-2, 70, 96-8, 144-9, 248-50, 255, 262
equitable principles **67,** 36-7, 40, 42, 47, 51-3, 85, 96-9, 141-3, 177, 186-90, 230, 239, 248-50, 255, 274-5, 284-93, **71,** 85-6, 88, 90, 111, 113, 120-2, 130, 184-5, 206. *See also* equitable principles
equitable result, relation to **67,** 52-3
geographical scope **67,** 96-7
natural prolongation and **67,** 40, 96-7
non-encroachment **67,** 112-13
relevant/special circumstances, consideration of **67,** 42, 53, 98-9, 102, 248-9
equitable result **67,** 42, 47, 51, 52-3, 69, 72, 75, 77, 88, 97, 100, 141-9, 275, 311, 313, **71,** 85, 88, 90, 105, 117, 119, 121-2, 126-7, 139-40, 143-8, 150, 153, 160, 166-71, 192-3, 195-6, 204-6, 208, 215, **77,** 675, **81,** 284, 287, 317, 318, 322, 443, 454, **83,** 14, **92,** 66. *See also* equitable delimitation *and* equitable principles *above*
balanced cut-off, need for **95,** 688
choice of method, relevance **99,** 520-1
as common objective **99,** 430

maritime delimitation (*cont.*)
Continental Shelf Convention (1958) **99,** 627
criteria. *See also* equitable principles *above*
adjustments **71,** 145-6, 154-5
appropriateness **71,** 140, 195-6
auxiliary **71,** 155, 162
ex aequo et bono solution, exclusion **77,** 676
ICJ, selection by **71,** 139-40
justice, sense of **77,** 676
other delimitations to be taken into account **77,** 677, 684
equitable principles, possibility of conflict **99,** 590-1
Eritrea/Yemen **119,** 454-5
ex aequo et bono, exclusion **77,** 676
flexible concept **83,** 117
fundamental norm **81,** 322, **83,** 91, 93, 94, 103, 114, **95,** 693, 698, 718-20, **99,** 426
Gulf of Maine **99,** 591-2
judicial discretion and **99,** 560-5
justice **77,** 676
Law of the Sea Convention (1982) **81,** 307, 391, **99,** 476, 590, 592, 628-9
Libya–Malta **99,** 591
need for **81,** 287, **91,** 676, **99,** 437, 447, 453, 479, 590-2, 612, 628-9
North Sea **99,** 591
other delimitations to be taken into account **77,** 677, 684
primacy **81,** 262, 270-1, **99,** 519-22, 665, 676
relevant/special circumstance as **81,** 322-3
responsibility for determining whether, court/parties **99,** 520, 659
Tunisia–Libya **99,** 591
Tunisia–Malta **99,** 592
verification **83,** 114
equitable solution. *See* equitable delimitation, equitable principles *and* equitable result *above*; equity *below*
equity **41,** 62, 65, 76, 86, 87, 91, 141-51, 193, 228, **59,** 239-41, **62,** 109, 115, 125, **67,** 98-9, 102, 144-6, 149, 248-53, 284-5, 313, **71,** 132, 184, 194, 204-5, 209-16, **83,** 88, 91, **91,** 654, 662-3, 665, **92,** 161, **99,** 579-626, **100,** 57. *See also* equity
Anglo-French Arbitration **95,** 666
balancing the equities **95,** 697-8, **99,** 615-17
Anglo-French Arbitration **99,** 616
distinguished **95,** 698-9
ex aequo et bono distinguished **95,** 698
Helsinki Rules on the Uses of Waters of International Rivers (1966) **99,** 616-17
Jay Treaty (1794) **99,** 616
North Sea **99,** 616
Tunisia–Libya **99,** 615-16
balancing-up of relevant/special circumstances **81,** 444, **99,** 676
choice of relevant/special circumstances **99,** 621-2
disadvantages **83,** 92
distance and **95,** 695
equidistance **95,** 698
geography and **95,** 688
Jan Mayen **99,** 488
Libya/Malta **95,** 666
as method **41,** 52, **99,** 586, 611, 676

multiple stage process. *See* multiple stage process *below*
multiple stage process **99,** 586, 621-2
decision-taking **99,** 622
identification of area of dispute **99,** 621
test of result. *See* test *below*
natural inequalities **67,** 56-7, 143, 248-50, 292
prevailing principle **81,** 391, **113,** 82
proportionality. *See* proportionality, maritime delimitation
as result **83,** 91, 93, **99,** 520-1
result **41,** 52
subjective nature **81,** 357
test **81,** 414
arithmetical **81,** 287
equitable principles/relevant circumstances **81,** 279
relevant circumstances **81,** 280, 414-15
of result **99,** 586, 611-12, 622, 676
result and methods **83,** 93, 94
variability between different jurisdictions **92,** 66
whole area of delimitation, in relation to **91,** 662-3
estoppel **71,** 107, 131-7. *See also* estoppel
ex aequo et bono **71,** 105, 209, **77,** 676
exclusive economic zone. *See* exclusive economic zone (EEZ), delimitation
existing rights, effect on **41,** 101
extension of boundary line **71,** 69, 82, 91
extension of coastal front **71,** 125
flexibility of approach **71,** 184-5
Fonseca Bay. *See* Fonseca Bay
foreign exploitation **67,** 117
freedom of navigation **95,** 677, 705
customary international law **95,** 677
fundamental norm of international law. *See* principles and rules applicable to, fundamental norm of international law *below*
geographical features **67,** 47, 55-6, 75, 79-82, 85-6, 100, 125-32, 143-5, 250-3, 263-4, 291, 293-8, **71,** 85-6, 89, 95-100, 105, 123, 127, 145-7, 149-50, 154-5, 180, 201-2, 206-7, **81,** 299, 353, 392, **95,** 660-3, 675, 699, **99,** 630, 676. *See also* coasts
abandonment **95,** 700
exaggerated consequences **71,** 183
minor features **71,** 98, 156, 159
political aspect **71,** 154. *See also* land boundaries *below*
primary consideration **71,** 105, 122-3, 154, 160
special features **71,** 86
Georges Bank **71,** 86, 89, 99-100, 102-13, 131-5, 138, 142, 144, 146, 149, 167-8, 170, 180, 200, 214
German Bank **71,** 86, 89, 143, 146
Gulf of Maine
basin **71,** 86, 103, 143
Canadian lines **71,** 111, 114, 147-52, 158
Canadian submissions **71,** 84, 87-8, 114-15
Cape Cod **71,** 95-8, 111, 113-14, 149, 152
US lines **71,** 111, 114-15, 143-7, **72,** 111
US submissions **71,** 85-90, 114-15
historic rights **41,** 101, **59,** 231-3, 264-73, **67,** 55-6, 64-70, 115-17, 122-5, 129, 203-4. *See also* historic rights

maritime delimitation (*cont.*)
historic title. *See* relevant/special circumstances, historic title *below*
historical usage **71,** 167-9, 180-1
ICJ and **67,** 30-3, 53, 71, 80, 93-6, 128-9, 136-49, 152-4, 246-8, 272-4, **70,** 539, 553, 578-9, 581-2, 592, 595-6, 598, 607, 637-40, 650-2, 654, 661, 664, 680, 683-4, 687, **99,** 470-82, 571-2, 577-8
agreement of parties, need for **99,** 459
between third States **81,** 256, 348-9
Court's discretion **71,** 139-40, 205, 209
demarcation distinguished **97,** 301-2, 335, **99,** 424, 445-6
determination of applicable law **81,** 254-7, 287, 483
determination of priority between continental shelf and EEZ **99,** 482
determination of relevant factors **99,** 482
discretion of court **71,** 139-40, 205, 209, **99,** 447, 453, 455
finality of Court's decision **68,** 189, **71,** 68-9, 80, 91, 189
'indication of geographic points on lines susceptible of defining frontier' **97,** 301-2
indication of line **81,** 308, **99,** 446, 479, 570, 571-2, 575-6
indication of method **81,** 256, 287, **99,** 479, 570, 571-2
jurisdiction, need for **97,** 519
limits of delimitation **71,** 80, 88, 90-3, 99. *See also* starting point of delimitation *below*
negotiations as dispute **99,** 477, 571-2, 577-8
precedent. *See* International Court of Justice (ICJ), precedent
task **67,** 30-3, 53, 71, 80, 93-6, 128-9, 136-49, 152-4, 246-8, 272-4, **71,** 80, 90-4, 105, 189-90, 215, **81,** 245-419, 425-85
third State's rights, effect on **71,** 92
islets **67,** 55-7, 81-2, 293-8, **71,** 156, 163-4, **81,** 280, **119,** 459-61
joint exploitation **71,** 201-2
jurisdiction
distinguished **90,** 238, 296
divisibility **92,** 79
jurisdiction of coastal State, effect on **71,** 94
just and equitable share. *See* criteria, just and equitable share *above*
land boundaries **67,** 57-9, 77-8, 86, 249, 264, 301-3, **71,** 86, 89, 100, 114, 140, 161, 180
land delimitation compared **41,** 160, 176
lateral equidistance line. *See* equidistance, lateral line
lateral line. *See* equidistance, lateral line
laterally adjacent States. *See* adjacent States *above*
law of
applicability to land boundaries **114,** 37
common law of **41,** 66-7, 159-61
continental shelf and territorial sea **41,** 159-61
Finland–USSR delimitation agreement **41,** 160
criteria, equitable principles/relevant circumstances/equitable result **81,** 346
development by courts **41,** 141, 174, 185, **81,** 346, **99,** 527
evolution **41,** 138-9, **71,** 117, 120-7, 129-31, 141, 187-9, 191, **79,** 184-5
equality of States and **41,** 140
recent trends **67,** 30-1, 40-2, 101-2, 152-4, 240, 276-81, 290-1, 313, **71,** 121
norms
equitable principles/relevant circumstances/equitable result. *See* criteria, equitable principles/relevant circumstances/equitable result *above*
equitable result. *See* equitable result *above*
equity. *See* equity *above*

identity for negotiated and third party delimitations **81,** 271, 359
lack **81,** 346, **99,** 477
uncertainty **81,** 322
Law of the Sea Convention (1982). *See* Law of the Sea Convention (1982), maritime delimitation
legal concept **41,** 164 n. 1, 165, **77,** 676, 687, **99,** 442, 477, 479
length of boundary **71,** 141
length of coastlines. *See* coastline, length of coastline
limits of delimitation **71,** 80, 88, 92-3, 99. *See also* starting point of delimitation *below*
customary international law and **91,** 515
limits distinguished **41,** 63, 83
lobster protection legislation **71,** 108-9
'long distance delimitation'. *See* length of boundary *above*
low-tide elevations **67,** 55, 57, 81-2, **71,** 156, 159
baseline adjustment **67,** 259-60, 262, 264, 293-8
Mandate Agreements and **37,** 34, 81, 119
Mandates Commission. *See* Mandates Commission
maps. *See* maps
median line. *See* equidistance
methods **71,** 85, 88, 127, 139-42, 146-8, 153, 156-8, 160, **77,** 675-92
agreement **82,** 686-7, **92,** 17-18. *See also* negotiated *below*
carte blanche **99,** 476-7, 479, 517-19
equity, relevance **99,** 517-18
evidence of **99,** 416-24
general principle of international law **92,** 18
jus cogens/peremptory norm, relevance **99,** 477
amplification effect **41,** 47, 66-7, 78-9
appropriateness **71,** 141-2, 146-7, 156
arbitration **41,** 63, **83,** 20
arcs of circles **95,** 686
average distance curve **83,** 107-8
azimuth prolonged and raised to superjacent water column **83,** 16, 21
bisector of angle **83,** 107, 113, 114
choice
by Court **71,** 139-41, 156-8
court's right **95,** 670
freedom of **41,** 79, 82, 83, 89, 135, **71,** 148, **77,** 681, **83,** 104
parties' right **99,** 445
combination **67,** 72, 75-6, 81, 86-8, **71,** 85, 142, 146, 158
admissibility **95,** 715-20
distorted effect **95,** 720
conciliation, Law of the Sea Convention (1982) **99,** 474-5
deepest water line **71,** 111, 114-15, 143
disputes settlement procedures **99,** 571
distance **77,** 686
enclave. *See* radial projection *below*
equal division. *See* equal division *above*
equidistance. *See* equidistance
equitable criteria, relation to **71,** 156, 160
equitable principles and **41,** 79
equity, relevance **99,** 517-18, 589-90
practical methods compared **99,** 589
extension of coastal front **71,** 125

maritime delimitation (*cont.*)
extension of land boundary **41,** 63, 64, **91,** 460, 461
façade **77,** 684
frontal projection **83,** 98, **95,** 668, 671-3, 685-8, 712-15, 716-18
breadth of coastal opening **95,** 672, 699
right-angled coast **95,** 686 n. 8
geometrical **99,** 505
equitable basis, whether **99,** 589 n. 3
geometrical construction **71,** 95-8, 149, 156, 161, 164-5, 206-7
isodistance **83,** 108-9
land boundary, extension of **41,** 63, 64
main waterway **52,** 185
median curve **83,** 106-7
natural prolongation **81,** 277, 289. *See also* continental shelf, natural prolongation
negotiated. *See* negotiated *below*
parallels of latitude **77,** 684, **83,** 21
perimeter **77,** 684
perpendicular
adjustments **71,** 86, 90, 113-14, 145-6
bisection of angle between perpendiculars **71,** 160
to baseline **91,** 460-1
to coast **71,** 140, 146-7, 160
to general line of coast **41,** 64, 181, **71,** 86, 90, 113-15, 140, 144, 146-7, 160
to gulf closing line **71,** 165
to land boundary **41,** 64, 181
prejudgment of excluded **77,** 681
priority **77,** 681, 686
projection of land frontier **83,** 43
prolongation of land territory **77,** 676
prolongation of territorial sea boundary **83,** 43
proportionality. *See* proportionality, maritime delimitation
radial projection. *See* radial projection *below*
radiation **83,** 98
region as a whole as basis **77,** 683
rhumb line **91,** 653, 656, 663
sectors **41,** 150, 181
single boundary delimitation **71,** 128-30, 148, 153, 156-8, 160
single method for all delimitations in same area **99,** 445
special circumstances **71,** 160
thalweg **41,** 204
modus vivendi **67,** 117-25, 147-8, 298-301, **71,** 131, 137-8
multilateral **41,** 65
Nantucket Island **71,** 95, 97, 111, 113-14, 149
natural boundary **71,** 86, 89, 101-3, 115. *See also* Northeast Channel *below*
natural prolongation **41,** 83, **71,** 120, **81,** 277, 289. *See also* continental shelf, natural prolongation
single boundary, in case of **95,** 665
nature and concept **49,** 96-8, 105, 147, 192-3, 197-206, 267
negotiated **41,** 62, 64, 65, 71, 76, 86, 90, 105, 156, 162, 175, 177, 188, 191-2, 202, 204, 216, **71,** 108-14, 119-20, 126, **83,** 20. *See also* method, agreement *above*
applicable law **41,** 75-6, 85, 201
constitutive, whether **41,** 190-1

duty to reach **41,** 71, 76-7, 91, 106, 109, 148, 149-50, 199, 201, **71,** 119-20, 126
Law of the Sea Convention (1982) **62,** 115
meaning **41,** 76
equidistance as starting point **41,** 223
equitable principles **41,** 62, 76-7
equitable result, verification, right to **83,** 42-3
guidelines **41,** 83
rules governing **41,** 75-6, 80, 85, 88, 90
non-encroachment **41,** 61, 77, 83, 86, 104, **67,** 112-13, 187-8, 311, **71,** 85, 88, 125-6, 140, **81,** 311, 321, 454, **95,** 667-8, 671, 672, 688-9, **99,** 432
balanced cut-off **95,** 688
cut-off effect **41,** 49, 50, 61, 228, **67,** 109-10, **71,** 126, 140, 155, 162, **77,** 680
equidistance **41,** 61
equitable principles **67,** 112-13
frontal projection and **95,** 717
high seas **41,** 116, 128-9
Libya/Malta **95,** 667-70
natural prolongation and **41,** 61, 89, **67,** 109-15
avoidance of cut-off **95,** 668, 695
navigational rights **95,** 699
North Sea Continental Shelf **95,** 667
ports **67,** 114-15, 128-9
security **95,** 695-6, 699
Northeast Channel **71,** 86, 89, 101-4, 108, 111, 114-15, 143, 146, 170
natural boundary, as **71,** 86, 89, 101-4
Nova Scotia peninsula **71,** 86, 89, 95-8, 100, 111, 145, 149, 152, 158, 160-4
object and purpose **49,** 5, 18, 197, 204
opposability **41,** 47-9, 50, 84, 179, 181, **56,** 164
opposite States, between **70,** 611-12, 641-2, **71,** 118, 121, 124, 150-2, 158, 161-4
origin **37,** 29, 56, 94, 119, 122, 257, 401, 420
partition, whether necessary consequence **99,** 675
peninsula, effect. *See* Cape Cod *and* Nova Scotia peninsula *above*
pertinent factors. *See* relevant/special circumstances *below*
political operation **71,** 104. *See also* land boundaries *above*
precedents **71,** 93-4, 101-2, 115, 120, 124, 129-30, 135-7, 141, 151, 153, 162, 181, 183-5, 187-9, 192, 201, 205-6, 208, 210, 212
context of decisions **71,** 187, 210
predictability, need for **99,** 432
principles and rules applicable to **70,** 539, 541, 554, 578, 580-1, 596, 608, 611, 639-40, 664, 684, 687, **71,** 80, 85, 90, 94, 105, 115-27, 130, 153, 155, 166, 187-204, **91,** 654
binding norms
Law of the Sea Convention (1982) **62,** 115
North Sea **41,** 71, 76
States, on **41,** 71, 76, **62,** 115
fundamental norm **70,** 122-3, 126-7, 130, 153, 155, 166, 194, 205, **71,** 122-3, 126-7, 130, 153, 155, 166, 194, 205
equitable result and **81,** 322, **83,** 91, 93, 94, 103, 114, **95,** 693, 698, 718-20, **99,** 426
practical means of implementation **70,** 554, 578, 581-2, 608, 639-40
prolongation of land territories **77,** 676
proportionality. *See* proportionality, maritime delimitation
proximity. *See* adjacency *above*

maritime delimitation (*cont.*)
purpose **83,** 65
radial projection **81,** 308, 310-13, 350, **95,** 668, 686, 712
arcs of circles **95,** 686-7
cannon-shot rule **95,** 686
closed sea, in **81,** 310-13, 345
equality of States and **81,** 310
State practice **81,** 310-13, **95,** 686
recent trends **67,** 30-1, 40-2, 101-2, 152-4, 240, 276-81, 290-1, 313, **71,** 121
Red Sea Islands. *See* Red Sea Islands
redistributive effect **41,** 51, 52
regional **77,** 683-5
relevant area. *See* maritime area
relevant coast **67,** 54-7, 75, 253-60
relevant/special circumstances **41,** 37, **62,** 126-7, **67,** 47-8, 53-86, 98-9, 102, 115-17, 125-30, 248-9, 275-6, 290, 293, 313, **71,** 85-6, 88-90, 114, 122, 127, 141-2, 146, 153, 155, 198, 203, 206, 210, **83,** 14
absence, agreement between parties **99,** 420-1
adjacency of States **67,** 56, 81, 88, 100, 126-7, 129-30, 287, **77,** 676
admissibility **41,** 178
distorting effect, need for **41,** 49
'any other pertinent factors' **119,** 456-7
assimilation of two concepts **99,** 430, 672
balancing-up **81,** 272, 444, 454
basepoints, choice. *See* basepoints
bathymetry **67,** 55, 73
as check on equity **83,** 114, **95,** 675
coastal configuration. *See* coastal configuration
coastline **67,** 55-6, 75, 79-82, 85-6, 100, 125-32, 255-6, 291, 293-5
general direction **41,** 83
coasts. *See* coasts
comprehensive consideration, need for **99,** 588-9, 628, 634-5
concessions **67,** 64, 76-7, 80-1, 86, 91, 147-8, 261, 298-300
conduct of parties **67,** 76-7, 86, 91
continental shelf
continuity **67,** 56-7
nature **77,** 685
Continental Shelf Convention (1958) **99,** 430
continental shelf and fishing zone distinguished **99,** 447
control of adjacent areas, necessity **77,** 676
culture **99,** 442
customary international law **41,** 66, **95,** 703 n. 4, **99,** 430, 489, 678
cut-off effect **67,** 55-6, 109-10, 125-7
defence **81,** 274
delimitation of area **81,** 443
discontinuities. *See* rift zones
distance **83,** 101, 103, **95,** 696-9
Law of the Sea Convention (1982) **83,** 103
distorting effect and **41,** 49
economic **41,** 81-2, 88, 228, **62,** 111, 112, **67,** 55, 70, 296, **77,** 688-9, **81,** 273, 344, 391, **95,** 675, 696-7, 699, **99,** 678-9
Eritrea/Yemen **119,** 440-1
Gulf of Maine **99,** 637-8
impermanent nature **77,** 689

EEZ **81,** 265
environmental **71,** 85, 89
equality of States **95,** 665-6
equidistance and **81,** 270, 367-9
equidistance, linked to **99,** 430, 634-5, 674
equitable result. *See* equitable result *above*
equity in choice **83,** 95, 96-7
equity of distance, as check on **41,** 194
equity of equidistance, check on **41,** 194
'fact necessary to be taken into account in the delimitation process' **99,** 430
fishing practices **81,** 273
  Eritrea/Yemen **119,** 441-3, 447-53
fishing rights **67,** 116, **95,** 675-7, 697
  bilateral agreement **95,** 676
  quotas **95,** 676, 704
  reciprocity **95,** 675-6, 704
fishing zone **81,** 302, 443
future delimitations **81,** 285
genesis, UNCLOS I **99,** 430
geographical context **41,** 88, 106, 109-10, **81,** 272, 282, 283, 284, 288, 289, 368-9, 413, 414, 419
geographical features. *See* geographical features *above*
geology **41,** 80, 81, 83, **67,** 55-6, 73, 85, 106, 110-11, **71,** 100, 115, 154, **81,** 288, **83,** 101, 102, 103. *See also* continental shelf, natural prolongation
geomorphology **67,** 57, 85, 106, 110-11, **71,** 100-2, 115, 143, **81,** 292, 293, **83,** 101, 102, 103
  discontinuities **67,** 57, 105, 110-11
geophysical character **81,** 288
harsh inequities **41,** 110
historic rights **67,** 55-6, 64-70, 115-17, 122-5, 129, 203-4
historic title **41,** 101, **59,** 231-3, 264-73
historic waters **41,** 151
historical particularities **67,** 55
ILC **41,** 151
inherent unity **99,** 430-1, 456, 670-1
interrelationship of maritime areas **77,** 676
island status **81,** 273, 344
islands **41,** 216, **67,** 55-7, 81-2, 84, 86-7, 92, 143, 256-9, 263-4, 293-8, 311, **97,** 675, **99,** 491, 558, 667-8
  continental shelf and **91,** 674-7
  distorting effect **99,** 668
  Jan Mayen, whether **99,** 432-3, 667-71
islets **41,** 49, 178, 194, 227, **67,** 55-7, 81-2, 293-8
land boundary **67,** 57-9, 77-8, 86, 249, 264, 301-3, **77,** 682, **81,** 443
landmass **41,** 181, **81,** 272-3, 353, 391, **95,** 701-2
legal concept, whether **99,** 473
legal situation **41,** 151
legislative acts **67,** 56-62
limit **81,** 272
  absence **99,** 629-31
  de facto **81,** 443
  Helsinki Rules on the Uses of Water of International Rivers (1961) **99,** 630
  Libya–Malta **99,** 629
low-tide elevations **67,** 55, 57, 81-2, 259-60, 262, 293-8, 311

maritime delimitation (*cont.*)
macrogeography **41,** 161, **81,** 376, 393-5
maritime boundaries **67,** 58-64, 90-1
meridians **81,** 370
narrow interpretation **41,** 228
natural boundary **83,** 101
natural prolongation **67,** 51
natural resources. *See* natural resources, maritime delimitation and
navigation channels **41,** 110-11, 216
opposite States **67,** 55-6, 88
opposite States **67,** 55-6, 88
parties' conduct **67,** 77, **81,** 443, **99,** 640, 669
non-aggravation of dispute **99,** 443
previous agreement **99,** 442-5
petroleum concessions **81,** 443
petroleum fields **67,** 56, 70-1, 311-12
physical structure **41,** 83
political **81,** 391
population **81,** 391, **99,** 441-2, 636-7, 677
status of rocks and **99,** 637
priority **71,** 105, 110-11, 115, 128, 141-2, 144
proportionality. *See* proportionality, maritime delimitation
protuberance **41,** 49, 178
regional characteristics **77,** 676
relationship between features **99,** 557-8
relevance **81,** 41
relevant circumstances as wider concept **99,** 489, 515-17, 557, 669
relevant economic positions **81,** 273
rift zones. *See* rift zones
seabed structure **41,** 61, 153, **83,** 104, **95,** 665, 668
security **77,** 689, **81,** 273, 274, 344-5, **95,** 695-6, **99,** 442-3, 639
control of adjacent areas **77,** 676, 689
equitable consideration **81,** 274
proximity to coast and **81,** 274, 284
Truman Proclamation (1945) **81,** 274
social **95,** 697, **119,** 441-2
social justice **81,** 391-2
socio-economic **99,** 441-2, 669, 677-8, 681
State practice, variability **99,** 638-9
subsequent delimitations **81,** 353
technical requirements **41,** 88
Territorial Sea Convention (1958) **99,** 430
test of equity, as **81,** 280, 284
third States **67,** 55-7, 84, 87, 242-5, 305-6
island States **67,** 55-7, 84, 87, 242-5, 305-6
title and **83,** 91, 94, 103
treaty **41,** 151
UNCLOS III **99,** 430
undefined **99,** 430-2
unilateral delimitation **77,** 677
rift zones. *See* rift zones
river basin **41,** 93, 103
Helsinki Rules **41,** 103
rocks **71,** 156, 159

scope **71,** 80
Scotian shelf **71,** 86, 89, 103
Seal Island **71,** 163-4
single boundary **62,** 126, **71,** 94, 103-4, 110-11, 115, 118, 122, 123, 128-30, 139, 141-2, 144, 148, 153, 180, 189-204, 209, **83,** 42-3
all-purpose, Red Sea Islands **119,** 457-8
applicability
seabed **95,** 675, 700, **99,** 566
superjacent waters **95,** 675, 700, **99,** 566
applicable law **99,** 425-7, 496
bilateral agreement relating to continental shelf, relevance **95,** 677, 700
Continental Shelf Convention (1958), applicability **71,** 118-20, 128-30 **95,** 663-4, 700, **99,** 425, 496, 568
customary international law **99,** 568, 657
delimitation, practical methods **71,** 128-30, 148, 153, 156-8, 160
EEZ delimitation and **71,** 154
EEZ/continental shelf **92,** 66-7, 79
possible, whether **99,** 463, 468, 477, 478, 484-5
equidistance/special circumstances method. *See* equidistance/special circumstances *above*
equitable criteria **71,** 153-4, 160
equitable result **71,** 197, 200, 203
fishing zone/continental shelf
Jan Mayen **99,** 424-6, 447, 484-5, 495-7, 566-70, 653-7
possible, whether **99,** 566-70
international law, absence of rule against **95,** 663, **99,** 568-9
jurisdiction of coastal States **71,** 94
Law of the Sea Convention (1982) **99,** 477, 655-6
as legal concept **71,** 190, 198
legal justification **71,** 94, 191-204
natural boundaries **71,** 103-4
parties' agreement, relevance **99,** 425, 478, 565, 568-9, 655-6, 672
implicit **99,** 569
priority **99,** 496
reasonable solution, whether **71,** 197
seabed, relevance **95,** 665, 668, 700, **99,** 657
simplicity of boundary line **71,** 157
socio-economic factors **71,** 86, 89, 99-100, 104-5, 125, 167-71, 187-8, 198
historical developments **71,** 167-9, 180-1
State practice **99,** 656
superimposition of rights **99,** 656
treaty provision, applicability to subsequent maritime delimitation **83,** 43-5
unique, whether **95,** 700, **99,** 424-5, 566, 654-6, 672-3
sovereign rights, effect on **71,** 92, **77,** 678. *See also* relevant/special circumstances *above*
special circumstances **41,** 30, 37, 38-9, 49, 64, 65, 71, 106, 109-11, 148, 151-2, 161-2, 177-8, 192-4, 197, 216, 226, **62,** 111-12, 115, 125-7, **67,** 100, 116, 180-3, 186, 190, 276, **71,** 105, 108, 111, 113-14, 124, 129, 140, 143, 149-50, 157, 160, 189-91, 195, 197. *See also* relevant/special circumstances *above*
starting point **71,** 92-3, 159-60, 190, 214
outer edge of territorial sea **41,** 87, 189, 190-1, **81,** 441-2, 461, **83,** 113, **90,** 238
State practice **67,** 72, 82, 111, **81,** 261-2
sui generis nature of each case **77,** 676, **81,** 287
technical report **95,** 680-2

maritime delimitation (*cont.*)
territorial limits, minor features **71,** 98, 156, 159
territorial sea **56,** 137, **57,** 61, 62, 65, **66,** 33, **73,** 174-8, 193-4, 199-200, 205, 216-17
adjacent States, between **41,** 47, 63, 64, 66, 75, 91, 134-5, 158-61, 163, 167, 223, 224. *See also* territorial sea, delimitation
artificial structure, effect **57,** 59, 102-5
by courts **69,** 57-8
equidistance and **41,** 46, 47, 66-7, 75, 163
extension of **71,** 140
Grisbadarna **41,** 159 n. 2
indented coastline **57,** 64
landmarks **57,** 60
low water mark **57,** 83-8
methods **41,** 163
river mouths **57,** 60-4
straight coastline **57,** 63-4
straits **57,** 64-5
unilateral **48,** 470, 472, 474
thalweg **77,** 664, 667, 670, 691, **94,** 12
third States **67,** 35, 55-7, 84, 87, 242-5, 305-6, **119,** 459, 465
intervention proceedings. *See* International Court of Justice (ICJ), intervention of third State
island States **67,** 244-5
rights, effect **71,** 92
title
claims distinguished **99,** 481, 495-6
distinguishable, whether **81,** 262, 328-9, 405-10, **99,** 468-9, 528-9, 657-60, 672, 675
relevance **81,** 257, 260, 262, 267-8, 275, 278-9, 329
treaties **71,** 85, 88, 117-22, 127-30, 197, **77,** 677. *See also* boundary treaties, maritime; Continental Shelf Convention (1958); Law of the Sea Convention (1982); *and Index to the Consolidated Table of Treaties*
applicability **77,** 677
unification of rights **71,** 198-9
unilateral **41,** 164, 191, 208, **67,** 148, 312-13, **77,** 677, **81,** 299
opposability **71,** 119, **99,** 518-19
recognition **77,** 677
unitization **67,** 315-17
unity of shelf. *See* rift zones
uti possidetis juris, applicability **92,** 153
water column **71,** 102-5, 109-10, 153-4, 157
natural boundaries **71,** 103-4
unity and continuity **71,** 102-4
maritime delimitation, proportionality, between coastal lengths, disproportion **81,** 282, 284, 288, 413
maritime exclusion zone 74, 95-6
maritime front 83, 100, 116
maritime jurisdiction[s] 62, 126. *See also* maritime delimitation; maritime space
basis
coastline **99,** 442
territorial sovereignty **95,** 669, 701
differences between **41,** 66-7, 159
effectiveness as criterion **83,** 64
interruption by territory of third State **83,** 89-90

third State territory as enclave **83,** 90-1
unity of jurisdiction **83,** 90
interruption by territory of third State. *See also* maritime delimitation, enclaves and
jus cogens/peremptory norm **99,** 477, 503-4, 568
limited nature **83,** 58-9
opposability, *erga omnes* **99,** 468
overlapping, absence of rules governing **99,** 481
overlapping jurisdictions, Fonseca Bay **97,** 225
protest against exercise of **83,** 19, 20
right and exercise distinguished **83,** 49
separate concepts **92,** 583-4
continental shelf and fishing zones **99,** 566
single boundary. *See* maritime delimitation, single boundary
single regime, whether **41,** 127, **119,** 457-8. *See also* maritime delimitation, single boundary
territorial jurisdiction distinguished **83,** 58-9, 64
maritime law
Continental Shelf Convention (1958) **41,** 69
customary law and **41,** 69
technical norms and **41,** 176
maritime rights
coasts. *See* coasts
continental shelf. *See* continental shelf
superimposition **41,** 128
territorial sovereignty and **41,** 127-8
maritime space, as territory **83,** 70-1
maritime torts, State immunity, jurisdiction **63,** 533
maritime waters. *See also* contiguous zone; continental shelf; exclusive economic zone (EEZ); high seas; inland waters; internal waters; lakes; rivers; straits; territorial sea
definition **84,** 78
maritime zone
Law of the Sea Convention (1982), red Sea **119,** 452
right to establish
Convention on the Conservation of Antarctic Marine Living Resources **108,** 636-7
customary international law **108,** 637
South Georgia and South Sandwich Islands, Proclamation of 7 May 1993 **108,** 634
territorial claim, whether **108,** 637
marriage. *See also* divorce; European Convention on Human Rights (1950), marriage, right to; married women; matrimonial property
arranged **61,** 261-6
illegal immigration and **61,** 261-6
breach of promise, Head of State immunity, jurisdiction **64,** 444
definition **103,** 231
evidence of **107,** 438-9
expulsion and **61,** 432
family, right to found **61,** 262-6
formalities
applicable law, *lex loci celebrationis* **41,** 467, 471-2
members of occupying forces **41,** 461-74
freedom from discrimination **58,** 582, 591-2, 597, 617
freedom of **58,** 593, 607, 630-1, **61,** 262-6, **72,** 297-301, 579
judicial separation **58,** 631, 637
nationality and **42,** 235, **53,** 515-17

marriage (*cont.*)
discrimination between sexes **79,** 299, 303-4
family unity and **79,** 303, 309
Native rights, effect on **37,** 589
naturalization and **41,** 381
nullity **58,** 630
protection of
deportation of alien and **73,** 617, **78,** 374
military service abroad and **73,** 610-12
refugee status and **111,** 540, 541, 542
proof of marriage, need for **111,** 540, 541, 542-3
right of **62,** 289, 291, 293, **72,** 298
divorce, inadmissibility and **89,** 172-5, 185-8
freedom of conscience and **89,** 177
temporary restriction
human rights, abuse of, whether **89,** 195-206
legislative reform **89,** 199-200
transsexualism and **89,** 101-2, 109, 121, 127-8, 141-6, 153
separation **58,** 630-1
fair hearing and **58,** 635-8, 653-8
family life, respect for **58,** 641
legal aid and **58,** 639, 641
unmarried couples, legal status **89,** 163-4
married women. *See also* women
discrimination against women married to aliens **62,** 286-7, 290, 294-5
domicile **118,** 302
international officials, residential status **48,** 249-53
nationality **41,** 380-3, **44,** 131-3, 141-3, **73,** 568, **79,** 297-9, 303-5
Elimination of all Forms of Discrimination against Women, Convention on (1979) **79,** 299
Nationality of Married Women, Montevideo Convention on (1933) **79,** 299, 303-4
property rights **71,** 658-9
Marshall Islands
Constitution, Art. 11(4) **87,** 580
detainees, rights, legal representation **87,** 579
government as legal personality **64,** 566
judicial system **64,** 563
State immunity, jurisdiction **64,** 546-9, 563
status **64,** 546-8, 565, **84,** 203-5, **87,** 577-8
'foreign country' **87,** 578
free association **87,** 578, 581, 654
independent entity **87,** 581
recognition **64,** 565, **87,** 581
US Status of Forces Agreement (1982) **87,** 581
Martens Clause (customary international law: applicability in case of gaps) 108, 46, **110,** 124, 153-4, 207, 210, 251, 261, 355-61, 399, 514
customary international law norm **110,** 355-60, 433-7
public conscience and **110,** 359-60, 437-41
variation of wording
Geneva Conventions (1949) **110,** 358-9, 433-4
Geneva Conventions (1949), First Protocol (1977) **110,** 356
Hague Conventions Respecting the Laws and Customs of War on Land (1899) **110,** 355-8, 433-4

martial law
basis
defence of State **87,** 261, 270, 271
necessity **87,** 261-3, 270
dependence on **87,** 261-2
determination of **87,** 261
evidence of **87,** 261
limitation of powers **87,** 262
prerogative **87,** 261, 275
civil commotion and **87,** 270
common law **87,** 276
definition **81,** 627 n. 23
rebellion and **87,** 270
South Africa, in **87,** 261-76
as suspension of law **87,** 260, 275
matrimonial property 73, 672-3, **74,** 113-15, 531, 548
enemy property, legislation on and **44,** 487-8
Mauritania
independent State, emergence as **59,** 145, 181
Western Sahara
claims over **59,** 75-80, 82-4, 130
relation to **59,** 96-8, 120, 131-2, 136-9, 181, 188-9, 192-3
Mauritius
aliens
deportation **62,** 286, 288, 291-2
naturalization **62,** 288, 290-1
residence status **62,** 287-8, 290-2, 294
women married to, discrimination **62,** 286-7, 290, 294, 295
British Mandatory government and **60,** 209, 213
Chagos Archipelago. *See* British Indian Ocean Territory (BIOT); Chagos Archipelago
Constitution 1968
European Convention on Human Rights (1950) and **44,** 127
expression **70,** 210-20
fair hearing **70,** 192-209
inhuman treatment, freedom from **70,** 221-6
permitted restrictions **70,** 210-20
prompt hearing **70,** 192-209
fair hearing **70,** 192-209
freedom of expression **70,** 210-20
fundamental rights and freedoms **70,** 204-5
enforcement **70,** 204-5
inhuman or degrading treatment, freedom from **70,** 221-6
interpretation **70,** 193, 201, 207, **91,** 321, 329-30, 331-2
permitted restrictions **70,** 210-20
prompt hearing, right to **70,** 192-209
property rights, protection of **91,** 320, 321-2
s 1 **91,** 321, 322
s 2 **91,** 327
s 3 **91,** 321, 322, 325, 326, 332
s 7(1) **70,** 221-6
s 8 **91,** 321, 322-3, 325-6
s 10(1) **70,** 192-209
s 12(1) **70,** 210-20

Mauritius (*cont.*)
s 16 **91,** 321, 323-4, 332
s 17 **91,** 332
s 20 **91,** 336
s 31 **91,** 321, 324, 326
s 45 **91,** 321, 324, 326
s 47 **91,** 326
s 54 **91,** 321, 324, 326
s 81 **107,** 177
s 103 **91,** 321, 324, 326
supremacy **91,** 327, 330
torture, freedom from **70,** 221-6
criminal law
presumption of innocence **44,** 104-8
retroactive **44,** 108-30
Dependencies and Colony **44,** 120-1
deportation **62,** 286, 288, 290-3, 296
discrimination against women married to aliens **62,** 286-7, 290, 294, 295
electoral districts, legality **44,** 104-8
equality **91,** 329-32. *See also* discrimination against women married to aliens *above*
identity of treatment distinguished **91,** 330-2
International Covenant on Civil and Political Rights (ICCPR) (1966) **91,** 329-31
report to Human Rights Committee **91,** 331
European Convention on Human Rights (1950) and **91,** 321
evidence
applicable law **87,** 315
authorizing legislation **87,** 315-16
extradition agreement, existence of **87,** 316
hearsay **87,** 320
extraditable offence, treaty, defined by **87,** 315
extradition
agreement, need for **87,** 314-15
arrest warrant **87,** 316-17
conditions in requesting State, fair trial, provision for **107,** 174
evidence **87,** 314
authorizing legislation **87,** 315-16
France, to **87,** 312-20
agreement, existence of **87,** 314
procedure
arrest. *See* arrest warrant *above*
substantiation **87,** 316-20
extradition agreement, State succession and **87,** 316, **107,** 173-4, 176-7
freedom from discrimination **91,** 330-2. *See also* equality *above*
Governor, delegation of powers **51,** 25-7
effect after independence **51,** 25-7
human rights violations **62,** 289-96
immigration **62,** 286-8, 290-3, 296
independence **51,** 25
effect on previous delegation of powers **51,** 25-7
International Covenant on Civil and Political Rights (ICCPR) (1966) **91,** 329
judicial notice, Order in Council, of **87,** 315-16
judicial review, taxation **91,** 326-8

law of
  Bankruptcy Ordinance 1888
    s 4 **87,** 314-15
    s 9 **87,** 312
    s 11 **87,** 317-18
    s 12 **87,** 312
    s 19 **87,** 318, 320
    s 30 **87,** 319-20
  Campement Sites Tax Act (No 32) 1983 **91,** 318-32
    constitutionality **91,** 318-32
  Constitution. *See* Constitution *above*
  Crown Lands Act **91,** 328
  Emergency Powers (Arrest and Detention of Suspected Persons) Regulations 1972 **70,** 221-6
  Extradition Act 1970 **107,** 176-7
    s 2 **107,** 173
    s 3(1) **107,** 172
  Extradition Acts (UK) 1870-1935 **107,** 172
  Ilois Trust Fund Act 1982 **91,** 334-40
  Income Tax Act
    s 11(1) **91,** 319
    s 111 **91,** 327
  Interpretation Act (UK) 1889 **91,** 330
  Interpretation and General Clauses Act 1974, s 7 **87,** 315
  Mauritius Independence Order 1968 **87,** 314
    s 5 **87,** 315, 316
  Pas Géometriques Act **91,** 328
  Penal Code, s 283, constitutionality **70,** 210-20
  Privilege of Treasury Act **91,** 326
  Registration Duty Act **91,** 327
  UK law, continuance in force **87,** 314
legislation
  purpose, peace, order and good government **91,** 326
  tax statute, colourable device, whether **91,** 320, 326, 327-9
legislation, interpretation
  aids
    ambiguity, in case of **91,** 321, 330
    European Convention on Human Rights (1950) **91,** 321
    foreign constitutions **91,** 321, 329-30
    International Covenant on Civil and Political Rights (ICCPR) (1966) **91,** 321, 329, 330-1
    International Covenant on Economic, Social and Cultural Rights (1966) **91,** 321
    marginal notes **91,** 330
    treaties **91,** 321, 329, 330-1
    Universal Declaration of Human Rights (1948) **91,** 321
  Interpretation Act (UK) 1989 **91,** 330
  phrases
    'campement site' **91,** 332
    'compulsorily acquired' **91,** 325
    'deprived of' **91,** 325
  presumption of conformity with treaty obligations **87,** 318
  taxation statute **91,** 327-8

Mauritius (*cont.*)
legislative power
executive **91,** 328-9
taxation law **91,** 326
Mandatory government and **60,** 209, 213
nationality, Chagos Archipelago **91,** 336
property rights
compulsory taking, prohibition **91,** 320, 321-9
taxation as **91,** 321, 325-6. *See also* taxation *below*
European Convention on Human Rights (1950) **91,** 321
International Covenant on Civil and Political Rights (ICCPR) (1966) **91,** 321
lease, government undertaking to protect from future taxes **91,** 327-9
Universal Declaration of Human Rights (1948) **91,** 321
sedition. *See* law of, Penal Code, s 283 *above*
State responsibility for acts of predecessor government **91,** 339-40
State responsibility for, displacement of people **91,** 339-40
taxation
constitutional constraints **91,** 326-9
as deprivation of property **91,** 325
enforcement of legislation, as **91,** 325-6
discriminatory, whether **91,** 320
executive powers **91,** 326, 328
judicial review **91,** 326-8
legislation, colourable device, as **91,** 320, 326, 327-9
ministerial discretion **91,** 327
reasonable justification in democratic society, whether **91,** 320, 325-8
as rent increase **91,** 320
treaties
consistency of law with, relevance **91,** 329-30
individuals, rights under **91,** 337-40
as part of municipal law **91,** 329, 330-2
reservations, evidence of **107,** 173-4
right of action under **91,** 340
validity, evidence of **87,** 316
treaties, State succession **87,** 316
reciprocity, need for **107,** 173
Mayotte, Island of. *See* Comoros Islands
Meanguera/Meanguerita. *See* Fonseca Bay, Meanguera/Meanguerita
measure of damages/compensation including valuation of company/property/assets **40,** 158-73, **53,** 353, **56,** 175-6, **59,** 404-5, **61,** 345, **62,** 208-10, 211-12, **66,** 435-40, 581, 601-2, 605, 609, **67,** 340-4, 375-9, **70,** 337-8, **72,** 230-3, 327-33, 379-86, 404-13, 430-2, **73,** 435-45, 457-8, 503, 548, **74,** 258-9, 267, 271, **75,** 386, 390-4, 422-5, 452-79, 486-504, 505-7, 511-12, 514-17, 521-5, 532-47, 549-56, 558-61, 599-643, 663-4, 711-22, **77,** 190-1, **78,** 252-3, 668, 672-3, **82,** 123, **83,** 577, 586, **84,** 521-46, 557-76, 653-5, 656, 669-72, **85,** 393-5, 411, 562-4, 606, 607-12, **88,** 738, **89,** 596-9, 627-8, 656. *See also* damages, punitive
ability to pay **118,** 500
actual value **95,** 211
added value **86,** 472
adequate **59,** 390, **83,** 474, **84,** 540, **89,** 337-8, 467, 468, **92,** 587-8, 593, 596-600, 601-7, 609, 617, **106,** 480
Aminoil **83,** 475-6, 611
Amoco (US–Iran) **106,** 470
applicable law **85,** 562, 563, **89,** 343

customary international law **84,** 523, 552
general principles of international law **75,** 423-5, 435, 482-5, 513-17, 519-25, 599-603, 614-16, 641-3
general principles of law **83,** 473
generally accepted accounting principles **56,** 297-8, 299, 301-5
treaty provision **84,** 523, 524, 557, 653-5, **119,** 641
appropriate **62,** 188, **66,** 435-9, 601-2, **75,** 609-14, 624, 627, 633-41, **83,** 474-5, **84,** 523, 526, 540, 657
balance sheet **96,** 327-8
benefit to wrongdoer **125,** 701-2
book value **75,** 600, 624, 641, 712-13, 719-20. *See also* net book value *below*
book value minus accumulated depreciation **109,** 595, 596
building materials
deterioration **95,** 226
diversion **95,** 224-6
value at time of importation **95,** 226
bundling of costs and **119,** 643
burden of proof **82,** 198
business losses **109,** 416-17
castle and grounds **40,** 166-8
causality **89,** 500-3, 505, 595, 629, 630, **125,** 693-4, 696-8, 716. *See also* liability
changes in value, allowance for **75,** 491-3, 560, 712, 717-20
Chorzów Factory. See Chorzów Factory principle of reparation for wrong
common law **89,** 504
comparable sales **84,** 560-2
compensation for expropriation/nationalization and other situations distinguished **121,** 127, 180, 190, 191-2, 194-5
compensation for illegal expropriation and damages for breach of State responsibility distinguished **106,** 469, 480, 498-500
concession reserves **62,** 205
consequential damage **46,** 21
Contract of Guaranty **44,** 92-9
contract as performed **86,** 285-6
contractual rights **83,** 568
'convenient and equitable' **62,** 207
corporeal properties **83,** 568, 586
costs incurred
burden of proof **106,** 655, 731
expenses in connection with development of project **106,** 637, **116,** 90, 175, 177
failure to document sufficiently **106,** 637-8, 655-6, 712-15, 731-2
investment **106,** 636
lease of replacement aircraft **125,** 741
cumulative **109,** 296, 308, 311, 331, 372, 429, **121,** 128-9
currency of payment **75,** 606, 627, 643-51
date of conversion **75,** 606, 627, 643-7, 649-51
current assets **62,** 211
customary international law **83,** 473, 565, **84,** 523, 524-5, 527, 529, 535-43, 653, 654-5
evolution **84,** 538-43, 656-7
damage suffered by individual **46,** 276
damnum emergens **40,** 263, 272, 281-2, **53,** 347, **54,** 509, **62,** 201, 211, 217, **67,** 341, **83,** 567, 568, 577, 587, 619, **84,** 528, 574, **86,** 471, **89,** 342-4, 504, 630-1, **96,** 323. *See also* lost profit *and lucrum cessans below*
date **84,** 657

measure of damages/compensation including valuation of company (*cont.*)
departure/relocation costs **109,** 289-91
depreciation **95,** 230
deprivation of employment **96,** 250
difficulty of obtaining other work **96,** 250
discount factor **109,** 330
discounted cash flow (DCF) **83,** 572-4, 575-84, 624-5, **85,** 494-506, 569, 609-12, **86,** 471-2, **89,** 506-7, 635-6, 648, **95,** 228, **106,** 469, **109,** 596
in absence of evidence of future profits **119,** 641-2
discount rate **85,** 588
flexibility **89,** 636
rejection **106,** 633-5
discretionary **109,** 389
dockyard equipment and installations **40,** 158-64
economic losses **121,** 191, 195-6
economic value **62,** 203
effect of expropriation, relevance **84,** 516, 558, **85,** 409-10, **89,** 633, **92,** 591, 592, 602, 603, 613, 614, **96,** 324
effective **84,** 401
equilibrium between reciprocal obligations **114,** 219-21, **116,** 90, 159-60, 226-7, 249-50
abuse of rights and **116,** 240
equitable **62,** 209-10, 212, 218, **66,** 581, **75,** 391. *See also* fair *below*
equitable discretion **85,** 589-90
estimated profitability **62,** 205, 207
evidence of **84,** 524-6
lump sum agreement **84,** 524-6, 654, 667 n. 1
exclusive licence, value of **62,** 205
expulsion of alien **82,** 177-8, 190, 197-202
forced sale of property **82,** 197
forfeited deposit **82,** 201-2
loss of property **82,** 201-2, **96,** 329
loss of salary and employment benefits **82,** 199-200
failure to mitigate, effect **116,** 64
fair **75,** 449-51, 500, 514-15, 519, 613, 638, 640, **83,** 474, 611
fair actual value **84,** 537, **125,** 694-6
fair compensation for loss directly suffered **109,** 389-90
fair market value **62,** 166, 205, 207, **75,** 602-3, 614-16, 624, 631, 634, 642, **85,** 490-2, 542-5, 569, 606, 610, 611, 612-15, **95,** 211, 228, **106,** 469, **121,** 126-7, 192. *See also* market value *below*
definition **85,** 490-1, 608
effects of taking **84,** 522, 533, 558, 574, **85,** 491-2, **121,** 127
fair value distinguished **121,** 192, 195
fair and reasonable **84,** 556
fixed assets **62,** 211
foreseeable damage **89,** 505, 506, 629, 630
direct and natural compared **125,** 703-6, 740-1
full **75,** 601-2, 609, 615-20, 624-5, 634-7, 639, 641, **84,** 523, 527, 528, 529, 536, 540-1, 653, 657-8, **89,** 505
full and complete **84,** 426-7
full equivalent **83,** 473, 565-6, 619-22, **84,** 522, 534-5, 557, **85,** 563, 607, 610-11, 617 n. 15
full monetary equivalent **92,** 597, **121,** 191
full value **106,** 465

furniture, art objects and paintings **40,** 166-8
going concern value **66,** 439-40, **83,** 476, 568, 572, 577, 578, 589-90, **84,** 653, 659-61, 669-70, **92,** 409, **106,** 468, 469-70
good faith, relevance **103,** 291-3, **125,** 705-6, 728-9
goods, for customs purposes **41,** 1-13
goodwill **83,** 479-81, **84,** 653, 655, 658, **106,** 469-70
government actions, relevance **84,** 570, 654, 657, 658-9
imprecision **85,** 589-90
incorporeal assets **44,** 100-1
inflation, allowance for **66,** 609-13, **75,** 451, 493-5, 712, **89,** 637-46, 647, 649-57
injury **92,** 441
insurance coverage **84,** 652
intangible values **83,** 568, 586
interest on award **78,** 370
international law standard **66,** 605, 606, **75,** 423-5, 435, 482, 514-17, 599-603, 609-25, 631-43, 663-4, **84,** 526
international nature of offence, relevance **77,** 190
investment **95,** 228-9, **119,** 642-3
  retroactive effect **96,** 324
Iran–US Treaty of Amity (1955) **63,** 454-5, **83,** 473, 476
juridical settlements **84,** 536-7
just **75,** 558, 612-13, 663-4, 711-13, 716-21, **83,** 474, 564, 571, 609, **84,** 401, 537, 557 n. 14, 653, 654, **85,** 563, 602, 606
just price **83,** 567
lawfulness of taking, relevance **62,** 202, 204-5, 207, **83,** 564, 565-71, 584, 619, **84,** 544-5, **85,** 608, 611, **86,** 299, **92,** 397, **94,** 60, **103,** 467-8, **121,** 127, 179, 192
  Aminoil **83,** 565, 570-1
  limitations on **83,** 566-7
  lost profit **62,** 204-8
legal and audit costs **106,** 638-9
  incurred in proceedings before another tribunal **106,** 638-9
legitimate expectations **86,** 285-6
liability, relevance **118,** 470, 481-2
Liamco **83,** 570
liquidation value **84,** 585-6
loss **89,** 627-8
loss of capital **121,** 192
loss of financial support **88,** 734, 735, 736, 743-4
loss of opportunity **62,** 214, **119,** 641
loss of pension **96,** 250
loss of support **109,** 330
lost earnings **96,** 329, 330, **109,** 596
lost income **88,** 734-5, 742
lost profit **46,** 187, **67,** 341-2, 375, **83,** 476, 564, 568, 618, **84,** 401, 522, 574-6, 653, 655, 658, **85,** 506-30, 576-84, **89,** 345-9, 629, 630-1, 635, **95,** 228, **96,** 323, 326-7, **106,** 467-71, 499, 734-5. *See also damnum emergens above and lucrum cessans below*
  in case of lawful expropriation/nationalization **62,** 204-8
  difficulty of calculation, relevance **106,** 499
  evidence of **95,** 228
  future prospects distinguished **83,** 568
  supervening illegality **106,** 634-5
  US investment guaranty programme **44,** 94
lost reputation **89,** 350

measure of damages/compensation including valuation of company (*cont.*)
lucrum cessans **53,** 347, **54,** 509, **62,** 201-9, **67,** 341, 343, 375, **83,** 568, 569, 570, 578, 589, 622, 624, **86,** 471, **89,** 434, 498-500, 504, 630, **106,** 469, 734. *See also damnum emergens and* lost profit *above*
dies ad quem **83,** 570
future profits distinguished **83,** 568-9
Islamic law **62,** 202
relevant period **106,** 634-5
market value **62,** 211-12, **75,** 386, 389, 391, 422, 479, 486, 719, **83,** 572, 574-5, **84,** 540, **92,** 597, 598, 602-3, 610, 618. *See also* fair market value *above*
in absence of **40,** 162
objectivity **83,** 574
value of shares on Stock Exchange **92,** 598
willing buyer/seller basis **75,** 478, 603-4
method of determining **62,** 212-16
moral injury. *See* damages, for, moral injury
nationals and non-nationals distinguished **72,** 230-3, **75,** 423-5, 482-5, 514-17, 521-5, 530
net asset value **92,** 409-11
net book value **62,** 164, 208, **66,** 605, 609, **83,** 575, 577, 584-8, 627, **84,** 401, 523, 655, 659-60, 670, **89,** 506, 634-5. *See also* book value *above*
net profit **62,** 203
net value **46,** 198
nexus with territory of expropriating State, relevance **121,** 193
non-pecuniary loss. *See* damages, for, non-pecuniary loss
offset **85,** 476
project costs **85,** 530-42, 546, 584-8
taxes **85,** 546-8, 574-5
partial **84,** 528, 654
disadvantages to developing countries **84,** 668
payment. *See* compensation claims agreements, payments under as property of State; expropriation/nationalization, compensation, payment
personal property loss **109,** 345-50
political and economic conditions **83,** 480-1, **84,** 558, 658, 670-1
premium paid for purchase of foreign securities **92,** 587-618
price/earnings method **109,** 596
professional expectations **58,** 716, 719
prompt **83,** 549-50, **84,** 401, 654, 667, **92,** 397, 599
prompt, adequate and effective **63,** 455-6, 595, **66,** 434-40, **75,** 423, 482, 519, 599, 609, 631, 634-7, 641-3, **83,** 474, 475 n. 14, **84,** 523, 528, 538 n. 18, 543, 653, **92,** 397, **95,** 211
customary international law **95,** 211
'prompt' **92,** 397
prompt and just **83,** 549, **92,** 397
prompt, just and effective **84,** 401, **86,** 49-52
property within forum **92,** 477
purchase option values **84,** 566-7
real property, tax valuations **42,** 170
reasonable **66,** 375
reasonable businessman **85,** 472-8, 485-550, 562-601
reasonable time **84,** 654
reference period, choice of **75,** 449-53, 477-8, 488-95, 499-500, 511, 535-40, 558-600, 712-13, 716-19

remediation costs **119,** 643
rent losses **109,** 401-2
mitigation **109,** 402
period of compensation **109,** 401-2
repairs to real property **109,** 400-1
replacement value **83,** 575, **84,** 562-3, **109,** 595
restitutio in integrum **83,** 565, 570, 572, 577, 619, **84,** 426-7, 541, **95,** 228
bilateral treaties **95,** 228
customary international law **95,** 228
risk factor **83,** 582, 583, **89,** 632-4, 648, 651-2
seized cash **82,** 200
State practice **84,** 524-5, **111,** 94-5
statistical model **109,** 346-50
subsequent events, relevance **84,** 657, 658
Topco **83,** 475
transparency **89,** 633
treaty provision **83,** 539-41, 564
as *lex specialis* **75,** 602, 615, 628, 651-2
'true' **40,** 175, 183, **84,** 540
UN Resolutions 1803, 3171, 3201 and 3281. *See* United Nations General Assembly (UNGA) Resolutions
unauthorized bribe **82,** 200-1
United Nations Compensation Commission, discounted cash flow (DCF) **109,** 596
unjust enrichment **62,** 213, **83,** 564, 578, 627, **84,** 523, 638, **92,** 436
US Foreign Claims Settlement Commission **42,** 190, 191, 193-4
value at time of taking
full **84,** 401
plus interest **83,** 473
value of concession at midpoint in expropriation process **62,** 210
value of investment **106,** 639-41
value of shares **41,** 394, **62,** 205, **75,** 452-79, 486-504, 511-12, 514, 532-47, 599-601, 603-7, 641-3, 711-22, **106,** 467-8
absence of market and **106,** 467, 635-6
applicable law **106,** 467
arbitration, provision for **75,** 452-8, 505-7, 549-56
changes in value, allowance for **75,** 451, 476-7, 493-4, 560, 712
inflation, allowance for **75,** 451, 476-7, 493-4, 560, 712
quoted and unquoted shares distinguished **75,** 452-3, 477-9, 487-9, 532-42, 559, 711-13, 716-21
reference period, choice of **75,** 451-3, 477-8, 488-95, 499-500, 511, 535-40, 558-60, 712-13, 716-19
distorting effect of nationalization plans **75,** 489, 492, 511, 535, 711, 718, 721
vehicle **109,** 356-9
Motor Vehicle Valuation Table (MVV Table) **109,** 357-8, 359, 461
wrongful arrest of ship, damage or loss to ship and persons concerned with operation **120,** 200-1, 250-1. *See also* damages, punitive
median line. *See* equidistance
mediation **37,** 89, **84,** 265, 268, 272, 273, 305. *See also* Burkina Faso/Mali boundary dispute, OAU Mediation Commission
Contadora process **84,** 309
dissolution of union of States, disputes arising from **91,** 306, 307

mediation (*cont.*)
'equitable and principled' **82,** 585-6
Holy See **82,** 678-83
third party as essential element **91,** 645
mediatized rulers 49, 344
medicine, right to practise 58, 401-3, 414-15, 417, 421
disciplinary proceedings **62,** 319, 321-2, 325-8, 332-4, 358, **71,** 415-36
professional conduct, whether **62,** 324-8, 358
Mediterranean
conservation and management measures **123,** 298-9
EEZs **81,** 254
exclusive fishing zones (EFZ) **81,** 254
Memel dispute, parties to 37, 540
Memel Territory, Statute, treaty character 37, 68
mentally ill person 78, 204
capacity **58,** 662-3
compulsory detention, trade union activity respecting **81,** 113-16
detention **58,** 667-73, 675-8, **67,** 465, 470
emergency measures **67,** 463, 465, 470
judicial review **67,** 466-71
regular **67,** 466-8, 470
lawfulness **67,** 462, 464-71
minimum conditions **67,** 462, 465-6
recall into custody, arrest, whether **67,** 472
review procedures **67,** 466-71
rights **58,** 679-82, **67,** 461-6, 471-3
treatment **58,** 673
mercenaries
definition **74,** 490-1
employment contract, State immunity and **64,** 668-72
punishment **74,** 484-92
merger of States. *See* States, creation, merger of States; union of States
Mexican Claims Commission 70, 501, 519
Mexico
AeroMexico **63,** 447-52
attorney-general, authority **66,** 260-3, 267
Banco Nacional de Fomento Cooperativo **63,** 360-2
Continental Shelf Declaration (1945) **41,** 113, 118, 158
environmental protection measures
fair and equitable treatment under NAFTA, whether **119,** 634-8
responsibility for **119,** 634-8
exchange control regulations of 12 August 1982 **84,** 109, 111, 112-13, 119, 120-1, 189, 190, 192-3, 198-200
extradition, nationals, of **90,** 691
federal State, State responsibility **119,** 634, 639, 654-5
law of
Ecological Decree (San Luis Potosi) (20 September 1997), as measure tantamount to expropriation/nationalization **119,** 640, 655-6, 671-3
Extradition Law 1975 **90,** 691
General Ecology Law (LGEEPA) 1988, constituent State responsibilities under **119,** 645-6
Petroleum Law 1927 **66,** 188

nationalization of banks **84,** 109-10, 190
occupation by France **46,** 465 n. 8
oil compensation commissions **66,** 266
oil concessions
expropriation/nationalization **66,** 147-50, 186-92, 260-3, 269
British protest **46,** 371, 431
Petroleos Mexicanos, State agency/State-owned corporation/State entity **66,** 149-50
treaties, as part of law of **121,** 62-3
USA, Payne–Warren Agreement **66,** 88-9, 263-5
treaty status **66,** 263-5
Micronesia, Federated States of. *See also* Marshall Islands; Northern Mariana Islands; Palau
status, free association **87,** 654
migrant workers, EC law **82,** 112, 114
military aircraft, responsibility for actions of **88,** 58-60
military assistance, contract to provide, legality
international law **117,** 563
municipal law provisions of State party and **117,** 561
military base
extraterritoriality **90,** 592, **102,** 148
State immunity. *See* State immunity, jurisdiction, classification of act, military base
military courts. *See also* military tribunal
appeal from **47,** 487-9, 497
applicable law **91,** 240
war crimes **91,** 47-8
evidence **48,** 486-93
fair trial **69,** 186, 189, 191-2, **70,** 242, 244-6, 254-5, 257, 283-4, 286, **71,** 319-21, 325-30, **73,** 557-64, **116,** 378-80
jurisdiction **54,** 528-9
criminal **62,** 264, **70,** 242-8, **71,** 311, 315, 320-1, 323, 325-30, 347-53, 356-65
foreign soldier **119,** 350
territorial extent **47,** 485
occupying power
jurisdiction **48,** 478-85
civilian infiltrators **47,** 484-7
war crimes, applicable law **91,** 47-8
military discipline. *See* armed forces, military discipline
military equipment. *See* armed forces, military equipment
military government. *See* belligerent occupation, military government; Egypt–Israel Peace Treaty (1979), military government, effect on; Germany, US Military Government in; Trieste, Free Territory of, Allied Military Government
military intimidation 76, 387, 452
military necessity. *See also* self-defence, limitations on exercise of/requirements, necessity
enemy property, destruction **56,** 542
military occupation. *See* belligerent occupation
military organization, uniform, relevance **88,** 187-8
military personnel. *See* armed forces
military service. *See also* armed forces
aliens **42,** 195-6
relief from **42,** 195-6
avoidance
asylum, claim to and **73,** 608-12
NATO obligations and **73,** 610, 612

military service (*cont.*)
conscientious objections **71,** 497-9, **73,** 383-5, 675-6, **74,** 302-3, **78,** 14-17, 230-2, 236, 250-9
integrity of international official **43,** 453-6
compulsory, Oder–Neisse, territories east of **78,** 188
conscientious objections **71,** 497-9, 675-6, **73,** 383-5, **74,** 302-3, **78,** 14-17, 230-78
forced or compulsory labour, freedom from and **74,** 303
South West Africa, liability of non-Whites **82,** 469-99
sovereignty **88,** 8, 21
military tribunal. *See also* International Military Tribunal for the Far East (Tokyo Tribunal); military courts; Nuremberg Tribunal; Rwanda, International Criminal Tribunal for (ICTR); Yugoslavia, International Criminal Tribunal for the Former, jurisdiction
applicable law **91,** 240
national law **111,** 342-4, 400-1
occupied Germany
Control Council Law No 10 **36,** 39-41, **111,** 343-4, 398 n. 12, 400-1, 407
law of defendant **111,** 401, 407-8
lex loci delicti commissi **111,** 401, 407-8
national law **111,** 342-4, 400-1, 406-7
procedural matters **111,** 406-7
ICTY as **105,** 612
independent and impartial tribunal **58,** 75, **78,** 247, 249, **116,** 387, **120,** 16, 105-6
international tribunal **111,** 342
national court **111,** 342-4
mine-laying **76,** 56, 380-2, 586-7, 603, 712-15, 870-1
basis of obligations **76,** 714
breach of territorial sovereignty **76,** 445-6
Corfu Channel **76,** 446, 714, 870
customary international law **76,** 463
duty to notify **76,** 446, 714, 879
Hague Convention No VIII (1907) **76,** 446, 713
Nicaragua–US Treaty of Friendship **76,** 875
self-defence **76,** 870-1
territorial sovereignty, breach **76,** 445-6
mines and minerals 71, 106-9, 132, 137-8, 169-71
applicable law, Goa **118,** 431, 436-46
bauxite mining **74,** 220-37
definition **77,** 304-7
maritime delimitation and **71,** 131, 137-8
offshore rights **73,** 193-5, 199-200, 215-16
mining enterprise, agency or instrumentality of a foreign State, whether **63,** 90, 104, 134, 174-8, 230, 290, 292, 344, 449, 588, 617
ministerial acts
bona fides, burden of proof **70,** 372
State's international obligations and **44,** 322
minorities. *See also* International Covenant on Civil and Political Rights (ICCPR) (1966), minorities; minority rights
continuation of obligations to **37,** 544
English-speaking protestants in Colombia **96,** 705-6
identity under international law **92,** 168
Indians. *See* Canada, aboriginal Indians in
Lapps. *See* Finland, Sami rights; Sweden, Sami
League of Nations, continuance of regime after dissolution **37,** 543-5

membership **68,** 19-20
Minorities Treaty (St Germain-en-Laye) (1919)
applicability
Federal Republic of Yugoslavia **95,** 58
'inhabitants of the Kingdom' **95,** 133
people of Herzegovina **95,** 58, 133
ICJ jurisdiction, basis for **95,** 57-8, 132-3
PCIJ, right to bring proceedings **95,** 133
all Members of the League of Nations **95,** 133
State succession and **95,** 57-8
nationality, right to choose **92,** 169
recognition of State and **92,** 174, 176, 180-1, 185-6, 210-11
residence **68,** 26-8
Sami. *See* Finland, Sami rights; Sweden, Sami
self-determination, right to decide community **92,** 168-9, 211
South Tyrol, treatment of Austrians in **96,** 706
special status areas **92,** 210-11
autonomy **92,** 211
demilitarization **92,** 211
State succession and **92,** 165, 166
treaties
community interest in **37,** 86, 273
compromissory clauses **37,** 83, 86, 101, 273, 274, 300, 407, 421, 512, 514-15
non-discrimination norm **37,** 465-7

minority rights
constitutional principle **115,** 566-8
enjoyment of own culture **115,** 316-18
measures affecting
consultation with minority representatives, relevance **115,** 317, 516, 534
cumulative effect **115,** 318
threshold **115,** 316-18
reindeer husbandry, logging and road construction **115,** 316-18
fair treatment **62,** 382
freedom from discrimination **92,** 186
language, protection **92,** 186, 191
'national identity', protection **92,** 185-6, 191
protection, customary international law **68,** 208-11, 221-2, 236
residence rights **68,** 26-8
respect for human rights, Convention of the Conference on Yugoslavia of 4 November 1991 (draft) **92,** 168-9, 176
self-determination. *See* self-determination

Minquiers and Ecréhos
contiguity of France and England **39,** 425-6
prescription **97,** 480-1

Miraj
Bombay, merger with **49,** 474
East India Company, Treaty with (1819) **49,** 470

misrepresentation, State immunity in respect of **63,** 585, 597, 618-19

misuse of power. *See* abuse of power

mitigating circumstances. *See* Yugoslavia, International Criminal Tribunal for the Former (ICTY), mitigating circumstances

Mixed Arbitral Tribunals. *See* international tribunals

mixed contract. *See* concession agreement; State contract

Mocambique. *See* Mozambique
modus vivendi **67,** 63-4, 77-8, 88-91, 117-25, 147, 300-1, **71,** 131, 137-8, **78,** 137
maritime delimitation **67,** 117-25, 147-8, 298-301, **71,** 131, 137-8
treaties **78,** 164
Monaco, France, War Damage Agreement (1954) **47,** 312, 315-16, 324
monetary gold
Declaration by USA, UK and USSR (1944) **44,** 473, 475
definition **44,** 448, 467-9
restitution provision, Italian Peace Treaty **44,** 448-85
Tripartite Commission for the Restitution of. *See* Tripartite Commission for the Restitution of Monetary Gold
monetary reform
compensation for losses due to **44,** 102-3
'taking' of property, whether **42,** 153-5
money. *See* Arab Monetary Fund (AMF); International Monetary Fund Agreement (IMF) (1944) (Bretton Woods Agreement); World Bank Group
money-laundering, measures to prevent **86,** 160-8
monist theory 39, 457, **85,** 258, **93,** 296
Monroe Doctrine, *uti possidetis* and **100,** 83
Montego Bay Convention. *See* Law of the Sea Convention (1982)
Montreal Convention for the Suppression of Unlawful Acts Against the Safety of Civil Aviation (1971) 74, 164, **77,** 235, **86,** 39, 41
applicability, State terrorism **94,** 512, 520
application and interpretation, dispute relating to
arbitration 'within [*dans*] six months of date of the request'
delay mandatory, whether **94,** 501, 591-2, **117,** 15
failure to agree to **94,** 493-4, 578-9, 591, **117,** 15
meaning **94,** 519-20
existence of dispute **94,** 533-4, **117,** 15-22, 61-5, 79-81, 96-102
ICJ role **94,** 490, 493, 518, 536, 551-2, 582, **117,** 14-22, 44-7, 48, 51-4
protection of treaty rights **94,** 521
negotiations, preferred method **94,** 493, 518
aut dedere aut punire/judicare **94,** 487-9, 578, **117,** 83-4, 86
customary international law **94,** 521-2, 551, 555, 565, 592
law of extraditing State as applicable law **94,** 489, 521-2, 592
non-extradition of national **94,** 489, 521-2, 592
extradition
absence of extradition agreement **94,** 488-9, 534, **117,** 99-100
refusal, permissibility **94,** 507-8, 521-2, 555, 592
request for **117,** 98-9
fair trial, feasibility **94,** 512-15, 593-5
surrender, insistence on **94,** 489, 490, 521-2, **117,** 101-2
coercive measures **94,** 490, 522, 572-5
interim measures against, request for **94,** 491
Security Council Resolution 731 (1992) **94,** 570. *See also* United Nations Security Council Resolutions, 731 (1992) (Lockerbie bombing) *and* 748 (1992) (Lockerbie bombing)
Security Council Resolution 748 (1992) **94,** 496-8, 500-1, 511-12, 513-14, 528, 530. *See also* United Nations Security Council Resolutions, 748 (1992) (Lockerbie bombing)
customary international law
aut dedere aut punire/judicare **94,** 521-2, 551, 555, 565, 592
extradition **94,** 521-2
surrender, insistence on **94,** 489, 490, 521-2

judicial assistance, duty to provide **94,** 489, 556, 562, 564, 577
'afford' **117,** 100-1
applicable law **117,** 100
basis for interim measures **94,** 556
jurisdiction, concurrent. *See aut dedere aut punire/judicare above*
obligations
aut dedere aut punire/judicare. See aut dedere aut punire/judicare above
judicial assistance. *See* judicial assistance, duty to provide *above*
measures to establish jurisdiction **117,** 97-8
offences against aviation, sole convention relating to, whether **94,** 487
phrases
'any person' **94,** 520
'within [*dans*] six months of date of the request'. *See* application and interpretation, arbitration 'within [*dans*] six months of date of the request' *above*
rights under general international law distinguished **94,** 501-2
moral damages. *See* damages, for, moral injury
morality, law and **41,** 143, **69,** 200
morals
education in **58,** 147-8
European standards **58,** 173, **67,** 422
homosexuality **67,** 416-17, 422, 435
freedom of expression and **58,** 172, 177, 183-4, 530, 544
margin of appreciation and **58,** 173-4, 179, **67,** 414, 417-18, 420-3
obscenity and **58,** 172
private life, respect for and **67,** 412, 417, 420-3, 433-7
Morocco
administrative authorities, acts of, French courts and **44,** 35
ecclesiastical courts, jurisdiction after independence **45,** 53-6
expropriation/nationalization, land **48,** 4-5
France, responsibility **47,** 21-2
law of, Law (Dahir) No 1-81 **67,** 279
nationality, Algerian residents **41,** 366-8
termination of protectorate
ecclesiastical courts, jurisdiction **45,** 53-6
status of pasha **44,** 31
territorial limits **59,** 105-9, 120, 144-7, 166
treaties, State succession **39,** 453-6
Western Sahara
claims over **59,** 59-74, 82-4, 126, 130, 144-7, 152-4, 166
relation to **59,** 96-8, 101-2, 104-19, 131-2, 136-7, 144-7, 150, 164-81, 188-91
mortmain 87, 50
Moscow Conference of Foreign Ministers, Communiqué, treaty character **37,** 68-9
Moselle, freedom of navigation **74,** 134-6
most favoured nation (MFN) treatment 47, 240, 243, 245, **48,** 168, 170, **56,** 552-4, **77,** 435, **106,** 441, 442, 446, 452, 487-90, **124,** 18-26. *See also* standard of treatment of alien; Uruguay Round, Agreement on Trade–Related Aspects of Intellectual Property Rights (TRIPS); Uruguay Round, General Agreement on Trade in Services (GATS)
customary international law **106,** 488-9, 490-1
dispute settlement, application to, public policy considerations **124,** 23-4
eiusdem generis rule **124,** 20-1, 23
GATT and **60,** 147-8, 647-8
national treatment provisions **56,** 553-4
Germany–Switzerland Equalization of Burdens Agreement (1952) **44,** 149-51
NAFTA (1992) **110,** 577, **121,** 55 n. 15

most favoured nation (MFN) treatment (*cont.*)
trades and professions, exercise of **44,** 145-7
treatment of aliens and **45,** 367, 369, **47,** 240, 243, 245, **84,** 370, 371, 372, **106,** 441, 442, 487-91
treatment of foreign investors/treatment sought for its own nationals abroad equation **124,** 23
movables, possession and title **44,** 458
movement, freedom of. *See* freedom of movement
Mozambique
armed conflict
civil war, rebellion or insurrection, whether **107,** 507-16
external support, relevance
Rhodesia **107,** 511-12
South Africa **107,** 512-14
expropriation/nationalization, nationalization measures **64,** 692-3
law of
Decree Law 2 of 1975 **87,** 241, 244-8
Decree Law 29 of 1975 **64,** 692-4
Decree Law 53 of 1975 **87,** 241
recognition **64,** 697
State succession and **64,** 691-2, 694
Multilateral Agreement on Investment (MAI)
criticisms of proposal for **121,** 144-5
governments' right to regulate in the public interest and **121,** 144-5
multinational corporation
applicable law **46,** 230-1, **47,** 28-30, **118,** 509, 526
diplomatic protection **46,** 442, 457
enforcement of judgments **118,** 526
human rights and **118,** 465-6
problems **46,** 469
UN Commission on Transnational Corporations **118,** 508
Code of Conduct for Transnational Corporations (1986) **118,** 508-9
Munich Agreement (1938), validity 44, 50, 55
municipal courts. *See* courts, municipal
as source of international law. *See* international law, municipal courts, as source
municipal law. *See also* European Community law; foreign law, recognition/enforcement; international law, municipal law and; legislation; treaties, operation and enforcement; treaties, primacy; *and under individual countries*
contract constituting exception to **83,** 556
as fact **106,** 570
German Interests in Upper Silesia **106,** 541
human rights conventions, effect on **91,** 364
international law and. *See* international law, municipal law and; treaties, municipal law and
municipality, legal identity, change of sovereignty, effect **44,** 50-70
Murray Islands 112, 413-661, **118,** 329-30
annexation, 1879 **112,** 422, 481-2, 556, 606-8
beneficial ownership, whether conferring **112,** 477-81, 492-504, 535-47
extinction of native title **112,** 509
applicable law **112,** 422, 446, 453, 482, 521-2, 554, 571
Queensland **112,** 422
Crown land, whether **112,** 519, 553, 601, 621, 622
history **112,** 448-52, 469-76, 542-6, 550-4, 576-90
identity as distinct people **112,** 437, 445, 506-7

jurisdiction, exercise in accordance with customs of Meriam people **112,** 507-8
native title, extinction **112,** 509
occupation, exclusive right of Murray Islanders **112,** 506
property rights **112,** 419-20
survival, legislative denial **112,** 424-5
reservation **112,** 509-10, 515, 553, 621
'settled colony' **112,** 477
trust. *See* reservation *above*
Muslim law. *See* Islamic law
mutual assistance. *See* judicial assistance
mutual legal assistance. *See* judicial assistance

NAAEC (North American Agreement on Environmental Cooperation) (1993)
as aid to interpretation of NAFTA (1992) **121,** 148
Commission for Environmental Cooperation **121,** 109
objectives **121,** 109
as precondition for conclusion of NAFTA (1992) **121,** 148
NAFO (Future Multilateral Cooperation in the Northwest Atlantic Fisheries Convention) (1979)
Canada–EC agreement relating to (1995) **123,** 205-7, 241
'conservation and management measures' **123,** 222, 436-7
use of force **123,** 474
jurisdiction **123,** 223-5
coastal States **123,** 234-5, 292-3
Fisheries Commission **123,** 234, 292-3
flag State in NAFO Regulatory Area **123,** 436-7
object and purpose **123,** 294-5
objection procedure **123,** 342-3
Regulatory Area **123,** 233-4
as high seas **123,** 223-4, 270, 279, 338, 350
jurisdiction. *See* jurisdiction *above*
NAFTA (North American Free Trade Agreement) (1992)
applicability
continuing wrong **125,** 127-33
investments existing on entry into force or made thereafter **125,** 127-33
Arbitral Tribunal. *See* NAFTA (North American Free Trade Agreement) (1992), Arbitral Tribunal
Basel Convention on the Control of Transboundary Movements of Hazardous Wastes and Their Disposal (1989) and
implementation, obligation to choose measures least inconsistent with NAFTA **121,** 109, 150-1
primacy **121,** 108 n. 36, 109, 150-1
bilateral agreements related to, Canada–USA Free Trade Agreement (FTA) (1988). *See* Canada–USA Free Trade Agreement (FTA) (1988) *below*
breach
compensation for. *See* compensation for breach *and* expropriation/nationalization, compensation *below*
inconsistent legislation as **119,** 633, 653-4
locus of breach and place where damage incurred distinguished **122,** 285-6
obligations under another treaty as defence **121,** 109, 125
Canada–USA Free Trade Agreement (FTA) (1988) **110,** 554-5
GATT *Working Party Report on the Free-Trade Agreement between Canada and the United States* **110,** 582-3
incorporation of provisions into NAFTA **110,** 559, 595-7, 599

NAFTA (North American Free Trade Agreement) (*cont.*)
effect on provisions **110,** 583-4
limitation on **110,** 597
minimum volume of imports **110,** 597
non-tariff barriers **110,** 597
rewording, need for **110,** 584
tariff reduction **110,** 597
tariffs resulting from tariffication **110,** 597
Uruguay Round rights and obligations replacing earlier rights and obligations **110,** 596-7
interpretation, object and purpose of NAFTA, conformity with **110,** 596
objectives, preservation of GATT protection **110,** 596
official statements following conclusion **110,** 582
'retain their respective rights and obligations under customary international law' **110,** 580
'retain their rights and obligations . . . under [the GATT] and agreements negotiated under the GATT' **110,** 559, 579
entry into force of provision **110,** 579
rights and obligations created subsequent to entry into force of NAFTA **110,** 579-89
temporal application **110,** 579-89
Uruguay Round obligations, obligation to incorporate **110,** 582 n. 121
compensation for breach
applicable law
applicable international law **121,** 190
NAFTA **121,** 126, 190, 191-5
cumulative **121,** 128-9
determination as two-stage process **121,** 136-8
expropriation. *See* expropriation/nationalization, compensation *below*
payment to investor (Art. 1116) and enterprise (Art. 1117), need to distinguish **125,** 134-5
punitive damages **121,** 127 n. 53, 189, 192, 193
diplomatic protection distinguished **125,** 132
environment. *See* objectives, balance between NAFTA free trade obligations and protection of environment *below*
exempted measures **122,** 305
expropriation/nationalization
compensation. *See* expropriation/nationalization, compensation *below*
contractual rights **121,** 21
creeping **122,** 355-7
customary international law and **122,** 336-7
Iran–US Tribunal mandate distinguished **122,** 337
'measure tantamount to nationalization or expropriation' **110,** 595, **121,** 53-4, 122-3, 178-81
building permit, failure to issue **119,** 638-40, 655, 666-8
interference with business activity **122,** 335-7
regulation as **121,** 122-3, 178-80, **122,** 335
'tantamount' **121,** 123, **122,** 337
non-discrimination, relevance **122,** 335
property interest, access to market as **122,** 334-5
expropriation/nationalization, compensation
interest **119,** 644
lawfulness of taking, relevance **121,** 126-7, 191, 192, **125,** 132
'on payment' **125,** 132

measure
actual investment **95,** 228-9, **119,** 642-3
applicable law **121,** 127
bundling of costs and **119,** 643
effects of taking, relevance **121,** 127
fair market value **119,** 641-2, **121,** 192
loss of opportunity **62,** 214, **119,** 641
remediation costs **119,** 643
method
at discretion of Tribunal **121,** 192-3
discounted cash flow (DCF), in absence of evidence of future profits **119,** 641-2
other breaches distinguished **121,** 127, 180, 190, 191-2, 194-5
expropriation/nationalization, legality, requirements
compensation **121,** 126-7, 191
due process **119,** 620, **121,** 126-7, 192
non-discrimination **119,** 620, **121,** 126-7, 184, 192
public purpose **119,** 620, **121,** 126-7, 192
GATT/WTO and **110,** 555-7
Art. XX exceptions **121,** 142, 143, 156-7, 172-4
obligation to incorporate Uruguay Round obligations into Canada–USA Free Trade Agreement **110,** 582 n. 121
preservation of rights and obligations **110,** 554-5, **121,** 125
created subsequent to entry into force of NAFTA **110,** 579-89
TRIMS compared **121,** 141-2
WTO Agreement on Agriculture **110,** 547-99
interpretation. *See* NAFTA (North American Free Trade Agreement) (1992), interpretation
municipal law, as part of **121,** 62-3
notice of arbitration, as public document **125,** 107
objectives **121,** 105-6, 281
balance between NAFTA free trade obligations and protection of environment **121,** 105-10, 116, 133-4, 152-3
Art. 1114, relevance **121,** 153
'expanded and secure market . . . consistent with environmental protection and conservation' **121,** 105
governments' right to regulate in interest of public values, effect on **121,** 145-6, 178-80
conflict between Chapters 3 and 7, primacy **110,** 597-8
due process before impartial tribunal **122,** 348
principles and rules defining, national treatment **110,** 577
public policy considerations **121,** 168-74. *See also* expropriation/nationalization, requirements for legality *above*
transparency **110,** 577, 586, **119,** 635, 653, 665-6
obligations
Chapter 11, relationship with
Chapter 3 **121,** 123-4, 171-4
Chapter 12 **121,** 123-4
cumulative **121,** 123-5, 128-9, 173
exceptions
application to federal State or local governments **119,** 634
narrow interpretation **110,** 577 n. 109
host State's duty to consult **121,** 186-8

NAFTA (North American Free Trade Agreement) (*cont.*)
to ensure all necessary measures are taken to give effect... by State and provincial governments' **119,** 634
performance requirements **121,** 120-2, 175-8, **122,** 323-30
damages, effect on **121,** 177-8, 194
measures applied in an arbitrary or unjustifiable manner **121,** 177
settlement of disputes. *See also* ICSID (International Centre for the Settlement of Investment Disputes), Additional Facility, NAFTA provision for; NAFTA (North American Free Trade Agreement) (1992), Arbitral Tribunal; UNCITRAL (United Nations Commission on International Trade Law), Rules
consultation and negotiation, obligation **122,** 287, 289
standard of treatment
in accordance with [customary] international law **119,** 663-5, **121,** 55, 183, **122,** 379-80, 682
'customary' as acceptable gloss **125,** 141-51
applicability, issues other than treatment by courts **125,** 139-41
fair and equitable **119,** 634-8, 654-5, **121,** 55, 120, 183, **122,** 379-402, **125,** 145-51
additional to minimum standard, whether **122,** 380, 382-4, 682
customary international law **125,** 147-51
procedural fairness **121,** 185-8, **122,** 401-2
transparency **115,** 664-6, **119,** 633, 635, 638, 653
full protection and security **121,** 55, 183, **122,** 379
State immunity for intentional tort and **125,** 150-63
MFN **110,** 577, **121,** 55 n. 15
minimum international standard **119,** 662-4, **121,** 21-2, 118-20, 182-90
breach of treaty and **121,** 183-4
failure to provide national treatment and **121,** 120, **122,** 323
good faith, relevance **121,** 189
treatment superior to that of nationals **121,** 182-3
minimum standard **121,** 21-2, 118-20, 182-90
'most favorable'/'no less favorable'/'best' **122,** 360-2
national treatment **110,** 577, **119,** 662, **121,** 55 n. 15, 114-18, 153-75, **122,** 263, 322-3
adverse effects on more than one investor, need for **122,** 358-60
adverse effects on non-national, need for **121,** 159, 167-8, 184
de facto/de jure distinguished **122,** 370
discriminatory remarks before entry into force of NAFTA **125,** 129-30
disproportionate damage, whether necessary **122,** 362-71
minimum standard and **121,** 120, **122,** 323
non-discrimination on grounds of nationality **122,** 373-4
non-tangible interests **125,** 140-1
State responsibility, State enterprise **121,** 47-8
Uruguay Round and. *See* GATT/WTO and *above*
WTO and. *See* GATT/WTO and *above*
NAFTA (North American Free Trade Agreement) (1992), interpretation
aids
context
annexes **119,** 633
preamble **119,** 633
trade liberalization background **110,** 576-7
OECD practice **121,** 116-17
other treaties
between all parties in connection with conclusion of treaty **119,** 633

BITs (bilateral investment treaties) **119,** 664, **121,** 139-40, 183, **122,** 381-2
inconsistency of language **110,** 577
NAAEC **121,** 148, 180
non-involvement of all parties **110,** 577
parliamentary proceedings **121,** 140
State practice **121,** 122
travaux préparatoires **122,** 328
WTO case law **121,** 115-16, 124, 138-9, 141-3, 155, 173-4, 183
applicable law
applicable rules of international law **110,** 575-6, **121,** 119
Vienna Convention on the Law of Treaties (1969) **121,** 51, **122,** 328, **125,** 123
guidelines
avoidance of unintelligible, absurd or unreasonable result **122,** 384
effectiveness **121,** 65, 67
object and purpose **110,** 575, **119,** 633, 653-4, **121,** 105-6, 179, **122,** 288-9, 327, 348, 383
ordinary meaning **110,** 576, **119,** 663-5, **121,** 106, 179, **122,** 328, 372, 383, **125,** 123
in context **121,** 106
parties' intention **122,** 360, 382-3
plural usage **122,** 359-60
primacy of 'another Chapter' in case of inconsistency with Chapter 11 **121,** 106, 171-4
strict/liberal **122,** 328-9, 348
treaty as a whole **121,** 119, 183
phrases
'alleged breach' **121,** 54-7
'commercial arbitration' **119,** 657-9
'enterprise', ownership or control **121,** 111-13
'events giving rise to a claim' **122,** 288-9
'expansion, management, conduct [and] operation' of investment, implementation of treaty **122,** 358
'investment' **121,** 18, 110-13, 135-8
'enterprise' as **121,** 136-7, **122,** 304
loan to an affiliate **121,** 136
'investment dispute' **122,** 304-8
'investments of investors' **122,** 358-60
'investor[s] of a Party'. *See* NAFTA Tribunal, standing
'like circumstances' **121,** 115-17, 154-9, **122,** 371-8
'measure' **121,** 53, 63-6, **122,** 283-5, 310
bilateral treaty **122,** 310, 372 n. 69
measures implementing treaty **122,** 310, 372
unenacted bill **122,** 283-5
'measure tantamount to nationalization or expropriation'. *See* NAFTA (North American Free Trade Agreement) (1992), expropriation/nationalization
'measures relating to an investment' **121,** 114, 138-41
'of another party' **122,** 308
'relating' **122,** 308-10
'or any successor agreement' **110,** 581 n.115
'shall be in writing' **121,** 50-1
'state or province' **119,** 634
'with respect to the measure' **121,** 57-8
presumption, consistency between provisions **121,** 124
responsibility, Free Trade Commission (FTC) **122,** 682

NAFTA (North American Free Trade Agreement) (1992), interpretation (*cont.*)
binding, whether **125,** 143
Chapter 11 interpretations (31 July 2001) **125,** 141-51
NAFTA (North American Free Trade Agreement) (1992), Arbitral Tribunal
admissibility. *See also* conditions precedent *below*
consent 'in accordance wih the procedures set out in this Agreement', effect **125,** 123-4
appeals tribunal, whether **121,** 23, 64-5
applicable law
applicable rules of international law **119,** 633, 653, **121,** 38, 106, 190, **122,** 279-80
Vienna Convention on the Law of Treaties (1969) **122,** 279
ICSID Additional Facility Rules as amended by NAFTA (1992) **119,** 621-2, **121,** 32, 632
municipal law **121,** 197-8
NAFTA (1992) **119,** 633, 653, **121,** 38, 106, **122,** 278, 280
UNCITRAL rules **121,** 198, **122,** 264, 280, 294 n. 2, 351
arbitrator
challenge to **121,** 80
resignation **121,** 80
award
publication, desirability **121,** 135
review by courts of place of arbitration **119,** 646-82
burden of proof **110,** 560, 561, 577-8
jurisdiction **121,** 52-3
conditions precedent **121,** 9. *See also* admissibility *above*; jurisdiction *and* standing *below*
consent to arbitration **121,** 40, **122,** 281-2
investment as **122,** 314
consent and waiver **122,** 273-4, 290-1, 313-15
failure to comply, effect **125,** 123-4
waiver of right to initiate or continue domestic proceedings. *See* waiver of right to initiate or continue domestic proceedings *below*
confidentiality
Crown privilege **121,** 81, 196-8, 349-51, **122,** 403
public access to documents
exceptions **122,** 282
permissibility **122,** 681-2
solicitor–client relationship **122,** 351-2
consolidation of claims **122,** 344
costs
absence of fault on part of unsuccessful party **121,** 49
arbitration costs **121,** 49
bad faith and **125,** 163
claimant to meet **122,** 293
contributory fault of successful party **121,** 28
enforceability, relevance **121,** 28
novelty/public importance of issues **125,** 163
parties' own **121,** 49
Tribunal, unsuccessful party **125,** 163
unfamiliarity of proceedings, relevance **121,** 28
decision, binding on Member State, whether **107,** 288
denial of justice
exhaustion of local remedies and **125,** 140

serious departure from previous jurisprudence/new rule **125,** 153-5
failure to consider retrospective application of new rule **125,** 156
disclosure of documents **122,** 339-42, **125,** 105, 107-10
freedom of information legislation and **125,** 108-9
notice of arbitration as public document **125,** 107
Order and Interim Decision **125,** 108
dispute
consultation or negotiation, obligation **122,** 287-8, 289
identification **110,** 551-2, 574-5
tariffication obligation arising out of Uruguay Round **110,** 574-5
equality of parties, withhold of documents and **122,** 351, 403
estoppel **122,** 337-9
evidence
evaluation of written in absence of oral examination **121,** 83-4
failure to argue case **121,** 27
witnesses. *See* witnesses *below*
witnesses, tribunal's right to call/evaluate **125,** 107
exhaustion of local remedies, denial of justice and **125,** 140
judicial economy **121,** 146
jurisdiction. *See also* conditions precedent *above*
admissibility distinguished **121,** 67-70
appeals from decisions of municipal courts. *See* appeals tribunal, whether *above*
breach of contract **121,** 21
burden of proof **121,** 52-3
enforcement of Art. 1121 waiver **121,** 39-40
enjoinder of application of measure **122,** 301
interpretation in accordance with object and purpose of NAFTA **122,** 280-1
investment dispute **122,** 304-8
joinder to merits **121,** 11-12, 19, **125,** 104-5
liberal interpretation **122,** 348
measure breaching Art. 116(1) obligation leading to loss or damage, need for **122,** 272-3, 282-4, 306-8
as preliminary question **121,** 59-60, **122,** 280
procedural issues distinguished **122,** 281-2
resort to domestic tribunal, effect **121,** 20
violation of Chapter 11, Part A obligation, need for **121,** 19-20, 23-4
language of proceedings **122,** 270-1
Model Rules of Procedure for Chapter Twenty Pursuant to Rule 35 on the Availability of Information ('Model Rules') (13 July 1995) **110,** 549
4 **110,** 552
20 (timetable) **110,** 550
22 **122,** 255
33 (burden of proof: inconsistency of measure under Agreement) **110,** 561, 577-8
text **110,** 561 n. 34, 577
34 (burden of proof: exception under Agreement) **110,** 557-8, 560
text **110,** 560 n. 28, 577
notice of intention to submit claim **121,** 38, **122,** 273, 288-90
description of provisions alleged to have been breached **122,** 273, 315-16
Panel, constitution **110,** 549
parallel proceedings, exclusion. *See also* waiver of right to initiate or continue domestic proceedings *below*
Mexican Annex 1120.1 **121,** 62-3, 70-2
reasons for **121,** 63-7

NAFTA (North American Free Trade Agreement) (1992), Arbitral Tribunal (*cont.*)
place of arbitration **122,** 252-9. *See also* arbitration, place of arbitration
designation by tribunal **122,** 258-9, 268-9
forum [non] conveniens **122,** 254, 255-9
NAFTA, Art. 1130(b) **122,** 253, 255 n. 7, 258-9
neutral forum **122,** 258-9
UNCITRAL Notes on Organizing Arbitral Proceedings **122,** 254, 256-9, 317. *See also* UNCITRAL (United Nations Commission on International Trade Law), Notes on Organizing Arbitral Proceedings
UNICTRAL Rules, Art. 16(1) **122,** 253-4, 258
precedent **121,** 145-6
procedural history (Mondev) **125,** 113-20
procedure. *See* ICSID (International Centre for the Settlement of Investment Disputes), Additional Facility Rules (Arbitration); Model Rules of Procedure for Chapter Twenty Pursuant to Rule 35 on the Availability of Information ('Model Rules') (13 July 1995) *above*; UNCITRAL (United Nations Commission on International Trade Law), Rules
revision/amendment of claim **122,** 291-2, 347-9
six-month rule **122,** 273, 288-90
standing. *See also* third party submissions *below*
attempt to assert on behalf of third party **125,** 137-9
'investment owned or controlled directly or indirectly' **125,** 133-5
Barcelona Traction distinguished **125,** 133-4
failure/expropriation of investment, relevance **125,** 134-5, 138-9
investment/trade in goods, distinction **122,** 283, 305, 308, 309-10
'investor[s] of a Party' **121,** 18, **122,** 304, 306
investment, need for **121,** 110-13
'on behalf of an enterprise' **121,** 38, **122,** 311, **125,** 135-7
'on behalf of itself' **121,** 110-14, **125,** 135-7
investor's right to bring direct complaint **121,** 133, 144
Chapter 11 and Chapter 20 dispute settlement provisions distinguished **121,** 144
joinder to merits **121,** 11-12, 19
nationals of signatory State, limitation to **121,** 19
preliminary question **121,** 10
task
examination of application of customs duties **110,** 552
findings and determination as provided under Art. 2016 of NAFTA (1992) **110,** 552
precise interpretation of NAFTA **121,** 146
recommendations for resolution of dispute **110,** 552
terms of reference, determined by Parties **110,** 552
third party submissions **119,** 625-6, **122,** 270-1, 346, 348
time-limits **122,** 312-15
burden of proof **122,** 312, 313
extension, Panel's Report **110,** 550
knowledge of breach and knowledge of damage as trigger **122,** 312-13, **125,** 137
waiver, relevance **122,** 313
waiver of right to initiate or continue domestic proceedings **121,** 34-7, 39, 41-9, 50, **122,** 311
by investment **122,** 314-15
consent to arbitration as **122,** 290-1, 314-15
enforceability by Tribunal, relevance **121,** 39-40
entry into force **121,** 41
as extinction of right **121,** 41, 58-9
formal requirements **121,** 34-7

clear and express commitment **121,** 41, 50-1
delivery to disputing party **121,** 42-3, 48-9
as determined by NAFTA **121,** 42-3
failure to comply with **121,** 48-9
inclusion in submission of claim to arbitration **121,** 41, 42-3, 48-9
lack of specificity **121,** 50-1
need for compliance **121,** 41-2
purpose **121,** 42
writing **121,** 42-3, 45
notice of intention to file claim as **121,** 9-10, 34-5
party's subsequent conduct, relevance **121,** 43-9, 51-3, 58-9, 60-2, 67
effect on admissibility **121,** 68-70
precondition, whether **122,** 313-15
in respect of alleged breaches other than of NAFTA **121,** 45-8, 51-2, 57
breach of municipal law obligations **121,** 54-7, 183
measure amounting to **121,** 53-4
parallel proceedings **121,** 46, 52, 59-67. *See also* parallel proceedings, exclusion *above*
retroactive **122,** 311, 315
separability of claim and **121,** 69-70
time-limits **122,** 311
time-limits for submission of claim and **122,** 313-15
unilateral nature **121,** 41
'with respect to the measure' **121,** 57-8
witnesses
credibility **121,** 27-8
evaluation of evidence in case of non-attendance **121,** 83-4
Namibia. *See also* Mandate, South West Africa; South West Africa
act of State **91,** 343-4
annexation by South Africa **49,** 80-1
applicable law, human rights, European Convention on Human Rights (1950) **103,** 94-5, 102
Constitution 1990
Art. 1 **91,** 376-7, 378
Art. 8(2)(b) (torture, inhuman of degrading treatment) **103,** 84, 93-104
Art. 10 **103,** 101-2
Art. 16 **91,** 369, **103,** 118, 120, 121
Art. 24(3) **103,** 93
Art. 25(1)(a) **103,** 126-7
Art. 25(1)(b) **103,** 102
Art. 78 **91,** 349
Art. 124 **91,** 349
Art. 131 **91,** 348
Art. 138 **91,** 346, 349
Art. 140 **91,** 344, 345, 346-57, 359-70, 377-8, **103,** 110-11
Art. 140(1) **103,** 111
Art. 140(3) **103,** 111-12, 115-24
Art. 141 **91,** 346, 349
Art. 143 **91,** 346, 349
Art. 144 **103,** 110
Art. 145 **91,** 344, 345-6, 351, 352-7, 366-70, **103,** 110
Constitution
interpretation

Namibia (*cont.*)
broad **103,** 116
human rights as underlying consideration **103,** 84
property rights, protection of **103,** 118-20
corporal punishment
inhuman or degrading, whether **103,** 93-101
arbitrary **103,** 94, 97, 104
attack on dignity **103,** 94, 97, 103
demeaning to State **103,** 94, 97
impersonal **103,** 94, 97
international consensus **103,** 94-6
irrational **103,** 94, 97
judicial organs of State **103,** 84-92
adult offenders **103,** 94-7
juvenile offenders **103,** 97-100, 103-4
method, relevance **103,** 98-100
motive, relevance **103,** 97-8
schools **103,** 92-3, 100-1, 103-4
authority delegated by parent **103,** 101
costs, failure to abandon case **103,** 124-6
delict
definition **91,** 344, 347
State responsibility for unlawful acts of predecessor government **91,** 343-57, 359-70
European Convention on Human Rights (1950) **103,** 94-5, 102
expropriation/nationalization, compensation, State succession, effect on right **103,** 118-20
fishing zone **91,** 375-8
human dignity, right to, constitutional right **103,** 84
human rights, interpretation of Constitution, entrenchment **91,** 348
international law, municipal law and **91,** 354
effect on international law **91,** 361
recognition of municipal law by international law **91,** 368
unlawfulness, interrelationship **91,** 353-4
international legal personality **49,** 58, 104
law of
Animals Protection Act 71 of 1962, s 2 **103,** 91
Children's Act 33 of 1960 **103,** 90
Constitution **1990**. *See* Constitution 1990 *above*
Criminal Code, Art. 287 **91,** 380
Criminal Law Amendment Act 8 of 1953
s 1 **103,** 90
s 2 **103,** 90-1
Criminal Procedure Act 51 of 1977
s 112 **103,** 84-5
s 276 **103,** 85
s 290(2) **103,** 85
s 292 **103,** 85-6
s 293 **103,** 86
s 294 **103,** 86
s 295 **103,** 87
s 302 **103,** 87
s 308 **103,** 87

s 309 **103,** 87
s 321 **103,** 87
Defence Act 44, 1957 **91,** 355
Magistrates' Courts Act 32 of 1944, s 92 **103,** 87
Prisons Act 8 of 1959
s 36 **103,** 88
s 37 **103,** 88
s 48 **103,** 88-9
s 54 **103,** 89
s 56 **103,** 89
Prisons Regulations, Regulation 100 **103,** 89-90
Proc R348 of 1967
s 3 **103,** 91
s 4 **103,** 91-2
South African law, incorporation. *See* State succession, continuity of law *below*
State Repudiation (Cultura 2000) Act 1991
constitutionality **103,** 114-24
text **103,** 112-14
Supreme Court Act 15 of 1990, s 15(2) **103,** 83
Territorial Sea and Exclusive Economic Zone Act 1990 **91,** 374, 378
legislation, interpretation
aids
marginal note **103,** 123
title of statute **103,** 123
constitution, special rules **91,** 351, 363-6
guidelines
actual language **91,** 347-8, 349
clear meaning **91,** 367
disjunctive treatment of phrase **103,** 93
effectiveness **91,** 363
liberal **91,** 350, 363-6
purposive **91,** 347, 350, 363-4
phrases
'any action', lawful action, limited to, whether **91,** 347, 361-6
'any law in force' **91,** 277
'existed under international law' distinguished **91,** 352-5
'fishing zone' **91,** 375, 376
'recognized by international law' **91,** 367-9
'territorial waters' **91,** 376
'torture or cruel, inhuman or degrading treatment or punishment' **103,** 93
presumption of human rights protection **91,** 347-51, 363-6
presumption of validity **91,** 362
legislation, separability **103,** 122-4
national struggle, legitimacy **49,** 59
peoples of, history **49,** 75-9
plebiscite, proposal for **49,** 10-11, 47-8, 54-5, 112, 169
property
as chose-in-action **91,** 350-1, 369-70
right to
expropriation without compensation **103,** 118-20
State succession and **103,** 118-20
remedies
amendment of defective legislation **103,** 126-7

Namibia (*cont.*)
declaration
unconstitutionality **103,** 102
unlawfulness **103,** 102
Security Council Resolutions, effect on **49,** 41, 103-4, 106, 117, 121, 123-6, 133, 137, 179
South Africa
annexation de facto by **49,** 80-1
continued presence in, consequences **49,** 3-335
South African administration, acts of
taxation **49,** 209
validity **91,** 356, **103,** 107-27
State immunity, jurisdiction, as procedural bar **91,** 355
State responsibility for acts and omissions of official **91,** 366
State responsibility for acts and omissions of predecessor government **91,** 343-57, 359-70
acquired rights **91,** 344-7, 350-1, 359-60, **103,** 121-2
conquered State **91,** 345, 367
contractual liabilities **91,** 345-6
declaration of unconstitutionality, need for **103,** 114-16
delict **91,** 343-58
disclaimer **91,** 352-3
Hawaiian Claims (1925) **91,** 367
human rights, conflict with **91,** 350
lawfulness of acts under international law, relevance **91,** 347, 352-5, 361-7, 368-9
Lighthouses Arbitration (1956) **91,** 353, 368
merger **91,** 367
municipal law, liability under **91,** 361
national liberation movements **91,** 360-1
pre-succession State liability, relevance **91,** 371
proper party **91,** 358-9
repudiation **103,** 107-19
legislation, need for **103,** 120, 122
uncompleted acts, whether limited to **103,** 115-17
Robert E Brown Claim (1923) **91,** 367
State succession
acquired rights
continuing liability of successor government **103,** 121-2
international law, rule of, whether **91,** 344-54
continuity of law **91,** 346, 350, 361, 368, 377-8
international law, role **91,** 354-5
invalidity of previous administration and **91,** 356
rights and obligations, acceptance of **91,** 349, 351, 354-5, 368
municipal law, as part of municipal law **91,** 354
repudiation **91,** 354, 365
State responsibility. *See* State responsibility for acts and omissions of predecessor government *above*
taxation, validity under double taxation agreement **49,** 209
territory **91,** 376-7
'recognized by the international community through the organs of the UN' **91,** 378
Walvis Bay, whether. *See* Walvis Bay

UN Economic Commission for Africa, in **49,** 58
UN Security Council Resolutions
435 (1978) **85,** 233
439 (1978) **85,** 233
UN Settlement Plan **85,** 228, 232-3
Walvis Bay. *See* Walvis Bay
narcotic drugs. *See* drug-trafficking
nation
rights of **87,** 350
State distinguished **87,** 349-50, 353
national airline as agency or instrumentality of a foreign State. *See* State agency/State-owned corporation/State entity, classification, national airline
national defence, meaning **57,** 521
national heritage
historic wrecks **70,** 59-60, 67, 99-100
protection of, enforcement of legislation **78,** 607-36
national interest
comity and **83,** 265
EC and **69,** 211-15, **99,** 366-8
extradition **119,** 111, 252, 326
immigration **83,** 265
National Iranian Oil Company. *See* Iran, Islamic Republic of, National Iranian Oil Company
National Labor Relations Board. *See* United States of America (USA), National Labor Relations Board
national liberation movements 77, 236. *See also contras*; Palestine Liberation Organization(PLO); Palestine, Popular Front for the Liberation of
army, status **79,** 25-6, 36-7
as visiting force **79,** 26, 36-7
'freedom fighter' **79,** 26
Geneva Convention relating to Armed Conflict (1949/1977), applicability **88,** 49
Portuguese-Guinea, in **83,** 27-30
recognition **46,** 478
army as visiting force **79,** 36-7
lawfulness and **46,** 478
State responsibility **124,** 115-16
for acts and omissions of predecessor government **91,** 360-1
treaties, relevance to **83,** 15, 26, 27-30, 39
unlawful possession of arms and **91,** 407-11
national security defence. *See also* deportation, compelling reasons of national security and; refugees, non-refoulement, compelling reasons of national security; Yugoslavia, International Criminal Tribunal for Former, national security defence
admissibility, responsibility for determining **110,** 668-76, 723-8
ministerial affidavit **110,** 729-80
separation of powers **110,** 670
State practice
Australia **110,** 672, 728
Austria **110,** 728 n. 104
Canada **110,** 672
former Yugoslavia (SFRY) **110,** 672
New Zealand **110,** 728
Pakistan **110,** 672

national security defence (*cont.*)
relevance **110,** 670
UK **110,** 672
USA **110,** 670-1
correspondence, respect for and **58,** 447-8
customary international law **110,** 726-7
evidentiary privilege **110,** 661-2
fair trial **110,** 668
good faith **110,** 728-9
International Covenant on Civil and Political Rights (ICCPR) (1966), *in camera* proceedings **110,** 674 n. 248
international tribunals. *See also* Yugoslavia, International Criminal Court for Former (ICTY), national security defence
Chapter VII obligations and **110,** 666-7
criminal tribunal, special nature **110,** 666-8
European Court of Human Rights, *Cyprus* v. *Turkey* **110,** 725
European Court of Justice (ECJ) **110,** 669
The Observer and the Guardian v. *United Kingdom* **110,** 663
ILO Administrative Tribunal
Ballo case **110,** 725
McIntire v. *FAO* **110,** 725 n. 98
Inter-American Court of Human Rights, *God'nez Cruz Case* **110,** 662-3, 725
International Court of Justice (ICJ), *Corfu Channel* **110,** 662, 668, 669, 724, 725
US–German Mixed Claims Commission, *Sabotage* cases **110,** 724-5
interruption of telecommunications **83,** 227
Preparatory Committee on the Establishment of an International Criminal Court **110,** 663-4
safeguards **110,** 666, 674, 728-30, 731-6
editing of documents **110,** 729
good faith, relevance **110,** 728
in camera proceedings **110,** 674 n. 248, 729
return of documents **110,** 729
scrutiny by single judge **110,** 729
transcript of proceedings **110,** 729
translation to be provided by State Party **110,** 729
State practice
Australia **110,** 666
Austria **110,** 665-6
Canada **110,** 664
Costa Rica **110,** 665
France **110,** 665
FRG **110,** 665
New Zealand **110,** 666
Pakistan **110,** 664-5
UK **110,** 665
USA **110,** 664
terrorism and **58,** 448
national treatment. *See* most favoured nation (MFN) treatment; standard of treatment of alien, national treatment
national waters. *See also* inland waters; internal waters
definition **73,** 201-4, 215, 224-5

inter fauces terrae **73,** 199, 201, 215, 218, 224-5
straits, ownership of land covered by **73,** 191-225
national wealth, foreign investments as part of **46,** 220, 370-3, 439, 444, 451, 453, 515, 523
nationality **41,** 366-83, **42,** 43, 187-97, **47,** 211, **55,** 489-91, 493-4, **59,** 460-5, 468, **72,** 437-549, **73,** 566-94, **84,** 610-16. *See also* citizenship; Germany; Germany, Democratic Republic (GDR); Germany, Federal Republic of; refugees, stateless person; stateless person
acquisition **41,** 379-80, **48,** 162-4, **53,** 515-17, **60,** 205-8, 220-3, 225-6, 242, **61,** 406-7, **72,** 438, 481, 495, 542, 548, **73,** 566, **75,** 201, **91,** 221. *See also jus sanguinis below*
automatic **79,** 298
birth **79,** 689-94. *See also jus solis below*
coupled with descent. *See* descent, coupled with birth *below*
child fostered abroad **70,** 341-2
declaration, by **70,** 341-2, **79,** 295
descent **103,** 148, 183, 192-3
coupled with birth **103,** 281-8
right of women to transmit citizenship through descent **103,** 133-7, 141-62, 170-2, 174-80, 183, 185-8, 192-7, 202
guardianship **103,** 148
identity card **91,** 217
intention of individual **57,** 309-10
intention to reside permanently, need for **45,** 330-9
jus communicationis **71,** 580
jus sanguinis **71,** 579, **72,** 504, 507, **75,** 187, 203, 235, 237, 259
jus solis **72,** 504, **75,** 203, 235, 237
legality **70,** 695-6
marriage **79,** 298, **86,** 129-30
discrimination between sexes **79,** 299, 303-4
family unity and **79,** 303, 309
meaning **68,** 154, 156
naturalization. *See* naturalization
recognition of nationality **111,** 179-80
retroactive **70,** 694-5
territorial **103,** 148
transfer of sovereignty and **53,** 519
Algerians resident in Morocco **41,** 366-8
allegiance and **52,** 72-3, **53,** 525-6, **54,** 268-77, 284, **92,** 631, **103,** 148
American Convention on Human Rights (1969) **79,** 296-7
American Declaration of the Rights and Duties of Man (1948) **79,** 294-8
annexed territory, imposition on inhabitants of **47,** 33
Anschluss of Austria, effect **45,** 353-7
applicable law **45,** 80, **59,** 460-1, 467-8, **72,** 452-3, 455-8, 471, 474-5, **73,** 574-80
Constitution **103,** 148, 149
customary law **103,** 146-8
international law **43,** 192-4, **57,** 309-10, **79,** 294, **103,** 148
lex loci **108,** 550-1
Cyprus, Republic of **108,** 550-6
municipal law **79,** 295, 296
municipal law of country according **108,** 496-7
Australian citizens, as British subjects **69,** 161-3
British citizenship **81,** 152

nationality (*cont.*)
Chagos Archipelago **91,** 336
change of
becoming stateless as **120,** 9
international officials **83,** 218, 322-3, 348-9, 352, 379, 387-90, 404-7, 408, 458-9
involuntary, effect on claims **46,** 275
loss leading to statelessness as **120,** 9
change of sovereignty, effect. *See* State succession and *below*
citizenship
as **60,** 225-6, 244-6
distinguished **54,** 268, 279-80, **75,** 182-6, 188, 196, 198-200, 211-14, **103,** 147-8, **120,** 6
'citizenship of convenience' **46,** 362
claims. *See* nationality of claims
concept, municipal and international law **46,** 296
corporation. *See* corporation, nationality
customary international law
connection, need for **91,** 224
self-determination **91,** 231
territorial limitation **91,** 224, 330
definition **73,** 566, **75,** 182-6, 188, 194, 196, 198-200, 211-13, 257
deportation and **92,** 369-70, **103,** 282, 288, 297
deprivation. *See* loss or deprivation of *below*; stateless person
'designated' national **66,** 355-7
determination of **55,** 487
diplomatic protection and. *See* diplomatic protection; nationality of claims
discrimination **61,** 242-3, 245
right of women to transmit citizenship through descent **103,** 133-7, 141-62, 170-2, 174-80, 183, 185-8, 192-7, 202
domicile and **79,** 287, 309, **85,** 7
dominant. *See* dual nationality, dominant and effective
dual. *See* dual nationality
Eastern Treaties (1970) and **78,** 185, 189-90
EC membership and **93,** 785-6
effective link **43,** 192-4, **79,** 295-6, 303
effectiveness, need for **48,** 163-4, **72,** 484-9, 497-8, 501-19, 522-9, 535-49, **73,** 568, **75,** 185-8, 191-4, 202-4, 206, 220, 229, 234-58, 262, 265, **91,** 224. *See also* dual nationality, dominant and effective
election **57,** 308-10, **72,** 455, 477
emigration, effect of **72,** 438-41, 469-70, 489-91, 496-8
enemy State **60,** 211
entry, right of and **61,** 392, 397, 400-1, 404
ethnicity and **122,** 58-60
Evian agreements (1962) **111,** 188-9
evidence of **41,** 357-65, **55,** 486, **61,** 389, 393, 397-8, 400-1
ambassador's letter **120,** 6
identity card **88,** 702
loss or deprivation of, visa requirement, relevance **77,** 386
passport **49,** 504-6, **55,** 485, 486, **61,** 389, 393, 397-8, 400-1, **77,** 216, **83,** 466, **103,** 289, **120,** 304
expatriation **45,** 340-53, **60,** 239-40
extradition and. *See* extradition, nationals

extraterritorial legislation, effect **43,** 192-4, **72,** 439-42
family life, respect for and **79,** 309, 323
forfeiture **103,** 284-8
German–Persian Establishment Convention (1929) **60,** 205-6
Gibraltar **123,** 6
government, change of, effect **72,** 438-42. *See also* State succession and *below*
grant of **43,** 193-4
Hague Codification Conference on **60,** 206
human rights. *See also* right to *below*
  relevance **77,** 172, 178, 185
independence, effect of **41,** 392-3. *See also* State succession and *below*
International Covenant on Civil and Political Rights (ICCPR) (1966), relevance under **78,** 49
international officials, change of, implications **83,** 218, 322-3, 348-9, 352, 379, 387-90, 404-7, 408, 458-9
investment, right to and **89,** 484-5, 542-3
jurisdiction. *See also* jurisdiction, nationality
  NATO Status of Forces Agreement (1951), under **82,** 114
legal capacity and **79,** 294
legislation **79,** 287-9, 297-300, 303-5
  non-recognition **72,** 449, 453-7, 459-61, 467-70, 474-6
loss or deprivation of **47,** 274, **48,** 162-4, **55,** 498-9, 501, **60,** 205-8, 231, 235-7, **68,** 145-58, **70,** 341-4, 693-6, **72,** 437-42, 449-77, 542, 548, **74,** 705-7, **75,** 201, **79,** 297, **83,** 388. *See also* State succession and *below*
  acquisition of
    another nationality **43,** 194-6
    foreign citizenship **68,** 145-58
  arbitrary **79,** 294-5
  burden of proof **77,** 386
  conditions for **75,** 337-8, 358
  deprivation of civic rights amounting to **120,** 6-8
  enemy aliens **72,** 449-77
  evidence of, visa requirement, relevance **77,** 386
  failure to claim nationality **70,** 693-6
  persons living abroad **72,** 438-42, 449-77
  prevention of **79,** 297
  proof of **77,** 386
  racial grounds **45,** 353-7, **72,** 449-77
  as result of International Convention **70,** 343-4, 693-4
  statelessness. *See* stateless person
  under foreign law **44,** 131-3
  Universal Declaration of Human Rights (1948) **83,** 458
Malawi, in **54,** 290
mandated territories **37,** 387-8, 472, **79,** 472, 690-4
marriage, effect **53,** 515-17
married women **41,** 380-3, **44,** 131-3, 141-3, **73,** 568, **79,** 297-9, 303-5
  Elimination of all Forms of Discrimination against Women, Convention on (1979) **79,** 299
  Nationality of Married Women, Montevideo Convention on (1933) **79,** 299, 303-4
medicine, right to practise and **71,** 448-9
minorities and **92,** 169

nationality (*cont.*)
minors **71,** 570-2, 580
multiple **72,** 529
naturalization. *See* naturalization
nullification **43,** 194-6
Okinawa Islands, nationals of **54,** 217-23
Olympic Charter **120,** 2-10
option **45,** 357-65, **70,** 341-2
time-limit for exercise **73,** 569-70
patriality **59,** 455, **61,** 391-2
certificate of **61,** 393, 397-8, 400-1
Peace Treaties and
China–Japan (1953) **53,** 515-17
Italy (1947), 'Italian Libyan citizens' **40,** 190-9
Korea–Japan (1952) **53,** 519-20
personal law, whether **103,** 156-7
political rights dependent on **79,** 294, 295
principles of **53,** 86
recognition, State, non-recognition, effect **108,** 555-6, **122,** 536-41
regulation
act of sovereignty **79,** 301, 318, **111,** 189
municipal and international law, respective roles **79,** 294, 295
reinstatement **84,** 614
renunciation **60,** 242-5, **70,** 343-4, **72,** 490, 497, 542, **75,** 201-2
State discretion and **72,** 438, 490, 497, 542
residence and **118,** 642
meaning of **60,** 225-6
retention, permission for **84,** 613-14
right to **60,** 207, **92,** 365
American Declaration of the Rights and Duties of Man (1948) **79,** 294
international law **79,** 294
Universal Declaration of Human Rights (1948) **79,** 294
right to determine **93,** 722, 730, 759, 785-6, **111,** 189
persons **93,** 785-6
Romania, North Transylvania, inhabitants of **43,** 191-4
ships. *See* ships, nationality; stateless ships
single **83,** 389
Southern Rhodesia **78,** 492
State discretion and **72,** 438, 490, 497, 542, **79,** 295
State succession and **43,** 191-4, **49,** 504-6, **53,** 515-17, 519, **54,** 217, **72,** 438-42, **73,** 566, **79,** 301, 318, **108,** 550
stateless person. *See* stateless person
States, rights of and **45,** 436, 443, **120,** 8-9
subject distinguished **40,** 195, 197
treatment as alien **84,** 613
Universal Declaration of Human Rights **79,** 294
nationality of claims 40, 117-29, 148-58, **42,** 182-6, **46,** 207, 226, 261, 267, **47,** 166-8, **72,** 488, 650, **77,** 463-6. *See also* diplomatic protection
acquisition of nationality after claim arises **72,** 650, **74,** 281-4, **79,** 598, **120,** 228-9
'Austrian person' defined for purpose **77,** 429-32
Distribution Law (Poland) **77,** 429
Property Treaty with Poland **77,** 429
burden of proof **46,** 262-3, 376, 442, 456-7

change of nationality **40,** 153-5, **46,** 275
continuity of **42,** 182-6, **46,** 267-8, 273-7, 315, 363, 367, 376-8, 402, 403, 442, 519, **72,** 720, **77,** 429, 465-6, **79,** 598
corporation, nationality. *See* corporation, nationality
critical date **77,** 431-2, 465, 466
customary international law **117,** 66
derogation by treaty **74,** 282-4
diplomatic protection and **72,** 488, 650, 728-32, **74,** 283-4, **75,** 182-4, 189-90, 202-3, 224-65
entitlement determined by treaty **77,** 464
shareholders in foreign company **72,** 728-32
dual nationality. *See* dual nationality, claims, effect on
effective nationality test. *See* dual nationality, dominant and effective; nationality, effectiveness, need for
foreign nationals, claims of, settlement **74,** 259, 267-8, 274
genuine link, need for **46,** 520
Peace Treaty with Italy (1947), 'UN nationals who hold, directly or indirectly, ownership interests in corporations or associations which are not UN nationals' **45,** 109-10
shareholder claims **46,** 261-73, 309-10, 315, 376, 442
ships, relevance of rule in cases concerning **120,** 184-5
successor in title, continuity of nationality, need for **77,** 429-32
UN Compensation Commission. *See* United Nations Compensation Commission, nationality of claim
nationalization. *See* expropriation/nationalization
nationalized industries. *See* State agency/State-owned corporation/State entity
nationals. *See also* diplomatic protection
allegiance to sovereign, duty **52,** 72-3
claim against own State **52,** 5-7, **85,** 262-3, 265, 273, **121,** 182-3
'State' action, need for **85,** 265-9
tortious act **85,** 271-3
tortious omission **85,** 269-71
discrimination **60,** 211, 215-18
entry/re-entry, right of **59,** 455-7, 460, 468, 469, **74,** 300-1, **104,** 266-7. *See also* expulsion of national
extradition. *See* extradition, nationals
international official, summary dismissal **48,** 239
jurisdiction over. *See* jurisdiction, nationals abroad *and* personal
natural law and **46,** 484
personal sovereignty over **54,** 222-3
property abroad
claims for losses **56,** 544
legislative jurisdiction **42,** 31
protection of. *See* diplomatic protection
standard of treatment **103,** 618, **121,** 182-3
State obligation towards **104,** 485
human rights **104,** 485
State responsibility and **85,** 470
subjects, definition **52,** 74
treatment as, possibility **98,** 268-9
native title. *See* Australia, native title; Canada, aboriginal title; Murray Islands, native title; Papua New Guinea, land titles; United States of America (USA), native title
NATO. *See also* NATO Appeals Board; NATO officials/employees; NATO Status of Forces Agreement (1951)

NATO (*cont.*)
Council decisions, binding, whether **106,** 345, 377
'Double Resolution' of 12 December 1979 (Cruise/Pershing Missiles) **106,** 355-64, 370-88
Headquarters, removal from France **43,** 331, 496
member's action on behalf of, attributability to NATO **106,** 376-7
obligations of members
choice of means **106,** 377
military service, avoidance of and **73,** 610, 612, 674-5
Operation Allied Force
European Convention on Human Rights (1950), applicability **123,** 97-117
provisional measures, request for **123,** 99
State responsibility for acts and omissions of **108,** 675-6
status
coalition of States **82,** 112
collective security system **106,** 330, 369, **123,** 99
inter-governmental organization **106,** 377, 388
subject-matter of agreement determining factor **82,** 112
UN Charter, Art. 51 as basis **106,** 329
NATO Appeals Board
admissibility of appeals **43,** 479, 486-7
competence. *See* jurisdiction *below*
composition **44,** 430
partiality **43,** 482, 484-6
costs **43,** 360-1, **44,** 428-9, 432. *See also* expenses *below*
expenses, complainant's **43,** 458, 490-1, 494-5, 499. *See also* costs *above*
indemnity for loss of job **44,** 427-8
judgment, rectification **44,** 425-7
jurisdiction **44,** 426
compromis d'arbitrage **43,** 492
ratione personae 456-8
review of Member States' decisions **44,** 423-5
rehearing, petition for **44,** 427-8, 430-2
security clearance **44,** 423-4
security, deposit of **43,** 479, 486-7
NATO officials/employees. *See also* international officials; NATO Appeals Board
Civilian Personnel Regulations
appeals expenses **43,** 286, 364-5
applicability as evidence of status **77,** 620
Complaints Committees, function **43,** 366
discretion, duty to exercise **43,** 363-4
local civilian labour **43,** 457
nationality of staff **43,** 331
Provident Fund **43,** 489-90, 492-4
reinstatement in functions of post **43,** 285
State immunity, jurisdiction, waiver, NATO Status of Forces Agreement (1951) **86,** 627-39
status, conventions governing **82,** 112
termination of appointment
due to relocation of NATO Headquarters **43,** 496-7
French staff **43,** 330-2
grounds for review **43,** 363

NATO Status of Forces Agreement (1951) 42, 124, 135-7, **60,** 37, 48. *See also* NATO; NATO officials/employees; visiting forces
applicability
territorial **94,** 365
visiting forces on service in contracting State **94,** 365
bilateral agreements and, precedence **91,** 270-1, 272, 273, **94,** 290-1
categorization under
'a force' **91,** 284-5, **100,** 434
'civilian component' **65,** 318-20, **91,** 244, 246, 247, **100,** 434, 437, 443, **119,** 377
'civilian workers' distinguished **82,** 113-14
'local civilian labour' distinguished **65,** 319, **77,** 633
national of receiving State **65,** 319-20
permanent post, need for **77,** 620
'local personnel' **91,** 245
'third party' **100,** 435-7, 443, 445-6, 448
damage caused by visiting forces or member of
civil remedy against receiving State **86,** 535
liability of sending State **77,** 398-9
damage caused by visiting forces or member of, compensation
applicable law, law of receiving State **69,** 5-6
Belgium–USSR agreement (1989) **91,** 287-8
damage caused by crash of foreign military aircraft **91,** 284-5, 287
where one State responsible **91,** 284
indemnification provisions **69,** 5-6
performance of official duty and **91,** 284-5
procedure for determining **91,** 287-8
North Atlantic Council, role **91,** 287
responsibility for **91,** 283-8
personal liability **69,** 137-9
receiving State **77,** 398-9
entry of Member State's forces into territory of another
consent, need for
general **91,** 285, 286
implied **91,** 284, 285-6
European Convention on Human Rights (1950), precedence **96,** 387-8
jurisdiction **52,** 465-6, **60,** 37-8, 42. *See also* State immunity, jurisdiction *below*
bilateral agreement **82,** 114
building regulations **86,** 533-5
concurrent **82,** 113-14, **86,** 537, **91,** 240-2
criminal **57,** 341, **77,** 557
custody pending trial **87,** 91-2
exhaustion of criminal process **86,** 537-8
judicial decision **86,** 538
military legal authorities, decision of **86,** 538
individual members, limited to **86,** 534-5
local civilian labour **77,** 600
members of force or civilian component **82,** 113-14
tort **96,** 382-3
nationality, relevance **65,** 319, **82,** 113, 114
non-criminal **77,** 557
primary **86,** 537
non-exercise **86,** 537

NATO Status of Forces Agreement (*cont.*)
unreasonable delay **86,** 537
priority **77,** 557
sale of cars **86,** 524-5
sending State **69,** 137-9
criminal **77,** 557
territoriality, reconciliation with **77,** 557
trade union matters **77,** 634, 635, 735
justiciability **100,** 462-3
'local civilian labour'
jurisdiction **77,** 600, 618-20
applicable law **77,** 600
technicians under contract **82,** 114
municipal law and
French law, effect in **45,** 389-90, 462
implementing legislation **100,** 434, 440, 442, 444, 454, 461
incorporation, effect **100,** 434, 453, 457, 461-3
ratification, need for **94,** 290
Preamble, enforceability **91,** 283-4, 285
privileges and immunities
entitlement, local civilian labour **82,** 113-14
social security contributions **82,** 113-14
tax exemption **82,** 113-14, **91,** 243-9
proper claimant, member of visiting forces against own State **100,** 434-7, 440-64
proper defendant, Ministry of Defence **100,** 434
purpose
balance of interest between sending and receiving States **82,** 113
modification of absolute sovereignty rule **100,** 445
reconciliation of interests of receiving States and the Organization **65,** 318
receiving State
jurisdiction. *See* jurisdiction *above*
law of
civil responsibility **57,** 346
competition law, applicability **86,** 524-5
duty to respect **86,** 524, 535
enforcement **86,** 535
obligations of private nature **82,** 113-14
rights under **39,** 45-7, **60,** 39
liability for damage caused by member of force or civilian component **49,** 499-503, **77,** 398-9, **86,** 535
obligation to return to sending State, death penalty and **96,** 386-9
servicemen, claims against **49,** 498-503
sovereignty and **91,** 283-4, 285-6
State immunity, jurisdiction **65,** 294
absolute theory **100,** 445, 447-52, 455, 460-1
construction contract **65,** 263, 266
employment contract. *See* State immunity, jurisdiction, employment contract *below*
personal injury to member of force **100,** 441, 444-52, 455-64
tort **94,** 365
treaty as waiver **86,** 628, 633, **94,** 271, 290, **100,** 445, 448-9, 460-1
State immunity, jurisdiction, employment contract
as commercial activity **65,** 627-39
force or civilian component **82,** 113-14

local civilian labour **65,** 317-20, **77,** 600, **86,** 627-39
State responsibility for acts of visiting serviceman
receiving State **96,** 381-3
sending State **96,** 381-3
tort **96,** 381-3
Supreme Headquarters Allied Powers in Europe (SHAPE). *See* Supreme Headquarters Allied Powers in Europe (SHAPE)
tax exemption, competition law and **86,** 524-5
trade union rights **77,** 631-5
NATO Status of International Military Headquarters Protocol (Paris Protocol) (1952)
'civilian component' **91,** 244, 246, 247
'international civil servants' **91,** 244, 245
NATO, Status of the Organization, National Representatives and International Staff (1951), diplomatic privileges and immunities
members of delegations to **48,** 204-8
officials **70,** 422
natural boundaries. *See* boundaries, natural
natural justice 57, 238, **68,** 162-73, **78,** 416. *See also* justice
administrative act and **68,** 165-7, 171-3, **70,** 365-72
aliens, admission **90,** 20, 25
audi alteram partem rule **53,** 370-2, **68,** 162-73, **69,** 213, **70,** 265-6, 369-72, **71,** 454, 480, 490
civil proceedings. *See also* due process *below*
fairness of proceedings **118,** 491-8
claims settlement and **118,** 468
deportation procedure **43,** 219-24
detriment to individual as essential element **90,** 35, 49-50, 51, 53, 54
due process and **87,** 400, 406. *See also* civil proceedings *above*
economic sanctions, change of policy and **117,** 482
executive's expression of view concerning probable outcome of inquiry **107,** 490
exercise of government power and **92,** 538-9
expulsion of alien **52,** 344-5, 349-50, **71,** 454, 465-78, 487-92, **73,** 621-3, 633, 638, 645, 647
extradition proceedings **55,** 512, **69,** 243-7, **98,** 388
fair hearing **90,** 56, 456, **92,** 654, 656, **118,** 491-8, 523-4
judicial review and **91,** 186-7, **117,** 645
law, administration according to law **92,** 656
legislation, interpretation **92,** 656
legislation, retroactive **36,** 22-3
nemo judex in sua propria causa principle **118,** 489, 490-1
political asylum, applicability to **92,** 646, 654
victim's right to punish **36,** 51
natural law 37, 457-9, 463, **41,** 58-61
acquisition of territory, survival of existing interests **112,** 524
denial of justice and **46,** 333
equality and **37,** 464
international law, source of **37,** 458-9
Islamic law **64,** 629-31
knowledge of illegality of act **104,** 321
median line concept **50,** 38, 209
natural justice and **46,** 484
necessity, doctrine of **39,** 115, 170
nuclear weapons and **110,** 246

natural law (*cont.*)
positive law and **41,** 183
racial equality **49,** 67
self-defence **110,** 240
State immunity and **84,** 174
State's right to survival **110,** 223
natural prolongation. *See* continental shelf, natural prolongation; maritime delimitation, natural prolongation
natural resources 81, 527, **83,** 15, 24-5. *See also* environment; marine pollution; nuclear energy exploitation; UNESCO Protection of the World Cultural and Natural Heritage Convention (1972)
applicable law, EC law **120,** 625
common heritage of mankind **83,** 90
conservation. *See also* fisheries, conservation and management measures
filleting at sea and **82,** 634-6
Hague Conference (1930) **82,** 627
High Seas Convention (1958) **82,** 627-8
law of the sea and **82,** 606, 638, 641-2, 658
Law of the Sea Convention (1982) **82,** 628, 629-30, 642
territorial jurisdiction and **123,** 256-7
continental shelf **41,** 51, 84, 85-8, 92-104, **51,** 227-8, **55,** 323, **56,** 137, **81,** 303, 383
Law of the Sea Convention (1982) **81,** 303
Continental Shelf Convention (1958)
definition **56,** 119
exploitation **56,** 119
fish **56,** 119
continental shelf delimitation **81,** 273, 344, 391
EEZ and **91,** 381
equal division **41,** 99-100, 102-3
equitable apportionment **41,** 228
equitable sharing
Agreement governing the Activities of States on the Moon and other Celestial Bodies (1979) **99,** 614
Helsinki Rules on the Uses of the Waters of International Rivers (1966) **99,** 615
International Telecommunications Union Convention (1982) **99,** 614-15
Lac Lanoux Arbitration **99,** 615
Resolution on Pollution of Rivers and Lakes (*Institut de Droit International*) (1979) **99,** 615
equity and **41,** 87-8
exploitation **41,** 51, 63, 81-2, 83, 84, 85-8, **56,** 264, 318
right to **62,** 169, 187
sovereign right, whether **65,** 220
export licence, grant
commercial activity, whether **80,** 584-6
sovereign activity **80,** 584-6
expropriation, justification for, UNESCO Convention for the Protection of the World Cultural and Natural Heritage (1972) **106,** 624-7, 657-9, 733-4
fisheries, as **55,** 171, 219, **56,** 132
GATT Art. XX(g) and **121,** 171-2
Habitats Directive. *See* Habitats Directive (92/43/EEC)
High Seas Convention (1958) **82,** 627-8

international Cooperation **90,** 579
joint exploitation. *See* joint exploitation of maritime resources
maritime delimitation and **41,** 87, 92-100, 151-2, 216, 227, 228, **81,**273, 344, 391, **83,** 16, 24, **95,** 676, 677, 704-5. *See also* joint exploitation ofmaritime resources
conservation **71,** 88, 95, 125, 170
fishing resources **95,** 676, 704-5, **99,** 438-41
equitable access **99,** 447, 483, 493-4, 497, 679
ice, relevance **99,** 639
mineral resources **71,** 106-9, 132, 137-8, 169-71, **95,** 677, **99,** 438
oil concessions, relevance **114,** 110-14, 126, **119,** 443-6
minority, right to dispose of freely **96,** 669-73
non-self-governing territory's rights
compensation for loss **105,** 417
general principle of international law **105,** 294
obligation to protect **105,** 294-5, 338-41, 417
Administering Power **105,** 321-2
offshore mineral rights. *See also* oil
continental shelf **90,** 238
ownership **90,** 238
right to exploit **90,** 238, 239
right to legislate for **90,** 238, 239
inland waters **90,** 238
straits between Vancouver and British Columbia **90,** 269-330
territorial sea **90,** 238
ownership **90,** 238-9
patrimonial sea, rights in respect of **56,** 137
rights of State in respect of **56,** 264-5
sovereignty over **53,** 484-6, **56,** 90, 136, 137, 264-5, **62,** 178, 185-9, 196, 229, **63,** 291-3, 455, **65,** 60, 82, **66,** 187, 344, 436, 551, 587, **80,** 584-6, **81,** 527, **82,** 627, 642, **84,** 527, **105,** 338-40
agreements, respect for and **62,** 189
compensation for taking of property and **84,** 527
customary international law **84,** 540
erga omnes right **105,** 362
jus cogens/peremptory norm of international law, whether **66,** 587-8, **83,** 24
alienation of territory and **83,** 24
nationalization of assets and **83,** 24
trends **62,** 189
United Nations General Assembly Resolutions
1515 (XV) (Permanent Sovereignty over Natural Resources) **105,** 338
1803 (XVII) (Permanent Sovereignty over Natural Resources) **46,** 496, **56,** 279, **62,** 187-9, 192, 201, **63,** 291, 455, **65,** 214, **66,** 435-6, 588, 601-2, **73,** 244, **75,** 514, 609-10, 617-18, 633-5, 637, 639, 641, **83,** 2 n. 1, 474, 542, 613 n. 12, **84,** 525-7, 539-40, 665 n. 1, **105,** 338-40
2158 (XXI) (Permanent Sovereignty over Natural Resources) **83,** 3 n. 2, 24
3171 (Permanent Sovereignty over Natural Resources) **84,** 538
3201 (S-VI) (Declaration on the Establishment of a New Economic Order) **84,** 525, 538
3281 (XXIV) (Charter of Economic Rights and Duties of States) **84,** 525, 538, 540, 657, 664 n. 1
legal nature **84,** 540
special circumstance, as **41,** 93, 110, 151-2

natural resources (*cont.*)
title to **62,** 185. *See also* oil, title to
UNESCO Protection of the World Cultural and Natural Heritage Convention (1972)
customary international law, codification of **106,** 658-9
jus cogens/peremptory norm, whether **106,** 658-9
listing under, declaratory effect **106,** 659
unity of deposits **41,** 81-2, 88, 95, 102, 152
Vienna Convention on Succession of States (1978) **83,** 15
natural rights 70, 202. *See also* fundamental rights; human rights
Natural Rubber Agreement (1979)
analysis **99,** 354-8
economic objectives **99,** 355-6
International Rubber Council tasks **99,** 358
structure **99,** 356-7
EC common commercial policy, mixed agreement, whether **99,** 346-72
naturalization 60, 205-6, 208, 222, **61,** 406-7, **62,** 288, 290-1, **71,** 442-6, 507, **73,** 612, **74,** 394-7, **91,** 215, **111,** 180
conscientious objectors **69,** 196-201
consent and **43,** 193-4
denaturalization
wilful concealment of a material fact **95,** 507, 534
clear evidence, need for **95,** 514-15, 525, 527-8
'material' **95,** 512-13, 516-21, 523, 524-8
mitigating circumstances, admissibility **95,** 513-14, 521-2, 530 n. 11
visa application, applicability to **95,** 516-21, 525, 528
wilful misrepresentation **95,** 515-16
deportation and **111,** 180
discrimination **60,** 222
draft exemption, effect of claim to **42,** 195-7
effect **56,** 561
eligibility **71,** 443-6
criminal offences and **71,** 443-6
foreign public opinion, relevance **71,** 446
entitlement
refugees **74,** 396-7
spouses **60,** 222, **73,** 612
former nationality, effect on **72,** 449-52, 455, 461-2, 471-2, 489-90, 497-8, 542, 548
marriage and **41,** 381
oath of allegiance **69,** 196-201
requirements **79,** 287-8, 308-10, 691, 693
revocation **79,** 539
strict compliance with conditions, need for **95,** 515
unfriendly act **60,** 221
Nauru
Administering Authority
Australia, role
delegation of powers to **97,** 45, 72
General Assembly endorsement **97,** 45
Mandate, under **97,** 105
Nauru Independence Act 1967 **97,** 47
phosphate industry, competence of government and **97,** 48-9
treaties, application **97,** 47

Trusteeship Agreement as basis **97,** 44-9, 105-6
unity of British crown doctrine and **97,** 43
UK and New Zealand, role
commercial **97,** 46-7
legal interest, whether **97,** 49-50
partner governments **97,** 106, 108-9
right to consultation **97,** 46-7, 49-50
British Commonwealth, status within **97,** 94
British Phosphates Commission, assets, entitlement **97,** 29-34
Constitution, rehabilitation of worked-out phosphate lands **97,** 90-1
dispute between Administering Authority and inhabitants
claim, need for transfer to Nauru **97,** 89
delay **97,** 90-1
jurisdiction
General Assembly **97,** 13
good faith **97,** 90-1
UN, limited to **97,** 72, 89
UN Trusteeship Council **97,** 13
possibility of pre-independence **97,** 89
termination of trusteeship, as settlement of dispute **97,** 13
ICJ
Australia/Nauru Settlement Agreement (1993) **97,** 111
compulsory jurisdiction, acceptance, reservation **97,** 12
rehabilitation of worked-out phosphate mines
1965 discussions **97,** 71-6
Constitution of Nauru and **97,** 90-1
Davey Committee (1965-7) **97,** 19, 74, 79-80, 82-3
evidence of dispute **97,** 19-20
joint responsibility **97,** 107-9
UN Visiting Mission (1965) **97,** 18-19
UNGA Resolutions
226 (XXI) **97,** 80
2111 (XX) **97,** 19, 78-9
waiver of claim to **97,** 13, 14-17
Head Chief's pre-independence discussions **97,** 15-17, 79-89
Nauru Island Phosphate Industry Agreement (14 November 1967) **97,** 13, 14-15
reservation of claim, need for **97,** 78
resettlement of inhabitants, possibility of **97,** 73-4
Trusteeship
participation of Nauru people in administration **97,** 72
termination **97,** 17-20, 85-9
General Assembly Resolution 2347 (XXII) **97,** 18, 20, 87, 88-9
rehabilitation of worked-out phosphate lands and **97,** 18-19
Trusteeship Council Resolution 2149 (S-XIII) **97,** 84
UN responsibility **97,** 72
Nauru Trusteeship Agreement 37, 537, 538
naval deserters, return, enforcement of treaty **42,** 232-8
naval vessels. *See* ships, State-owned; warship
naval warfare 79, 1-17. *See also* neutrality
contraband **44,** 395-8
diversion, right of **38,** 472-3
enemy merchant ship, capture and removal from occupied territory **42,** 390
letters of marque and reprisal **85,** 280

naval warfare (*cont.*)
neutral ship in international waters, attack on, State immunity and **81,** 661-9
universal jurisdiction, whether **81,** 622
visit and search
Algerian conflict **47,** 164
neutral merchant ships **38,** 471-4
Nazis. *See* Germany (Reich), Nazi laws, validity/recognition *and* Nazi persecution
ne bis in idem **75,** 106, 338-40, 354, **77,** 557, 581, **78,** 137
Extradition, European Convention on (1957) and **71,** 234-5
general principle of international law, whether **77,** 581
law and order, need to preserve **52,** 61
municipal law, application to **71,** 232-4
territoriality principle, relation to **71,** 233-4
'Near East' 38, 217-21, 228-43
necessity 39, 68, 71, 72, 111-21, 124-36, 167, 169-76, 234, 360-3, 368, 388-90, 400-5, **52,** 59-60, 63, **55,** 54, **70,** 22, 24, 30. *See also* distress; duress; self-defence, limitations on exercise of/requirements, necessity
act of State distinguished **81,** 519
action to prevent or obstruct crime and **122,** 631-2
American Law Institute Penal Code **122,** 638
argument based on **37,** 46-7, 146-51, 199-201, 204, 229, 277-81, 284, 443
belligerent occupation **90,** 485-6
deportation **83,** 142
civil war and **70,** 22, 30
common law **118,** 490
Constitution, justification for departure from **70,** 26-7
crimes against humanity/war crimes **36,** 340-1, **104,** 331, 333, 367, 381, **108,** 165-6
criminal law defence **90,** 483-4, **101,** 278-80, **122,** 631-8
customary international law **116,** 49-50, 191, **120,** 191-2
damage to alien **85,** 470
definition **111,** 417, **116,** 49, 191
destruction of enemy property **56,** 542
desuetude **110,** 495
disqualification of judge, authorization to act **118,** 490
Dudley and Stephens **111,** 444
EEZ jurisdiction and **120,** 191-2, 300-1
estoppel **116,** 49, 55
executive necessity **74,** 223-7
expropriation of foreign ship, in case of famine **82,** 555
extradition, refusal **106,** 266-7, 272
hijacking **71,** 230
historical origin **110,** 495
'implied Mandate' **70,** 22, 24, 30, **90,** 505, 508
inherent powers **110,** 627 n. 37
innocent passage and **84,** 76
inviolability of diplomatic premises **102,** 179
Mandate, Mandatory's power of revocation and **49,** 329
martial law **87,** 261-3, 270
neutrality, violation **110,** 239-40
non-violence and **122,** 627
nuclear weapons, possession and deployment, whether giving rise to **122,** 509-12, 625-7, 655-6, 658
protection of victims and witnesses **105,** 623

rebellion, acts in aid of **39,** 126, 132, 137-42, 146-9, 177, 367, 369
requirements
absence of alternative **102,** 179, **116,** 48, 50, 53-4, **122,** 633
close relationship to actor **122,** 635
danger to person or property **102,** 178-9
Draft Code of Offences against the Peace and Security of Mankind (1949/1976/1989/1996) **116,** 48-50, 192-3
duress **122,** 633-5
essential interest to State **116,** 49, 50, 191-8, **120,** 191-2
ecological preservation **116,** 50
grave and imminent peril **116,** 48-55, 192-5, 197-8, **120,** 191-2, **122,** 632-3, 656
proportionality **102,** 179, **110,** 195, 377, 534-7, **122,** 635, 636
prospect of success **122,** 636, 658
responsibility for determining **116,** 49
Roman–Dutch law and **39,** 111
self-defence **76,** 437, 456-7, 475, 603-5, 627-30, 643-4, **110,** 195, 257, 258, 260, 326
State responsibility and **82,** 554-5, **106,** 441, 450-1, **116,** 46, 48-50, 192-3, 197-8
distress distinguished **82,** 554
test case, desire to provoke **122,** 625, 626, 656
treaties and
breach **116,** 72, 168-9, 191-2, 207-8
non-performance **96,** 316-18, **116,** 72
responsibility for breach and consequences of breach distinguished **116,** 192
suspension **116,** 48, 191-8
termination **116,** 72, 168-9
unconstitutional acts, legitimization **103,** 22, 26
unlawful government, validity of laws and
American Civil War cases **39,** 121, 125-33, 137-40, 365-8, 388-90, 394-6, **90,** 487-90
belligerent occupation distinguished **90,** 486
municipal law
Cyprus, in **90,** 492-3
Grenada, in **90,** 500-5
international relevance **90,** 490, 491
Nigeria, in **90,** 494-6
Pakistan, in **90,** 491-2, 496-500
retrospective acknowledgement **90,** 490-1
Rhodesia, in **90,** 493-4
requirements
preservation of just rights of citizen **90,** 485, 511
public policy, conformity with **90,** 485, 494, 511
reasonably required for orderly running of country **90,** 485, 487-91, 493-4, 498-500, 505-11
Vienna Convention on Diplomatic Relations, breach, defence, as **71,** 230, 254, 558
war **91,** 52-3, 54, 68, 134
negligence, actions for against foreign State **63,** 212-14, 244-51, 319-33, 352-3, 380-90, 421-3, 436-46, 464, 474-6, 529-34, 634-8, 639-46
negotiation 55, 266-7, 276-7, 302, 312, 378, 395, **57,** 184-6. *See also* arbitration; conciliation; diplomacy; diplomatic channels; dispute settlement; good offices; mediation
avoidance of prejudicial acts during **82,** 674
Beagle Channel Dispute **82,** 672-3
collective **37,** 27, 55, 89, 174-5, 181
within UN **37,** 27, 89, 166, 174-5, 181
with Concert of Europe **37,** 89

negotiation (*cont.*)
Contadora process **84,** 248, 251-62
deadlocked **37,** 27, **66,** 592
direct **84,** 265, 306
dispute settlement through **82,** 25-8, 250-2, 258, **116,** 86-8
dissolution of union of States, disputes arising from **91,** 306, 307
duty **41,** 76-7, 86, 109, 111, 114, 149-50, 177, 185, 199-201, 202, **44,** 418, **49,** 149-51, 333-5, **54,** 338-41, **71,** 119-20, 126, **81,** 462, **116,** 86-7
customary international law **41,** 86
NAFTA **122,** 287, 289
nature **66,** 565-6, 578
Railway Traffic between Lithuania and Poland **41,** 77
to conclude **94,** 318
effect **52,** 225
equitable principles and **41,** 86
exchange of views distinguished **47,** 420-1, 459
good faith **47,** 422, **56,** 173, 176-7, 185
ICJ's duty to encourage **61,** 574
judicial settlement as alternative **41,** 77
Free Zones of Upper Savoy and Gex **41,** 77
maritime delimitation **71,** 108-14, 119-20, 126
meaning **37,** 167-8, 175, 486
meaningful **47,** 422, 453-4
obligation. *See* duty *above*
oral, exchange of notes, equivalent of **47,** 444
pactum ad contrahendum **44,** 418, **47,** 422, 453, **81,** 452, **106,** 554
pactum de negotiando **47,** 418, 422, 438-9, 453, 457, 460-1
Peace Treaty, disputes regarding **80,** 240
prerogative function **112,** 742
provisional agreement, binding, whether **97,** 542
relevance **67,** 77
statements during
acquiescence, whether **97,** 542
binding, whether **94,** 320, **97,** 321-2, 542, **99,** 424, 454-5
neighbourship
control of pollution **82,** 613
customs areas **82,** 613
fishing rights **82,** 639
frontier workers **82,** 613
legal concept, whether **82,** 665
'neighbours' **82,** 613
shared river basin **82,** 613
treaty **82,** 664-70
voisinage **82,** 613, 614, 639, 665
Nepal
Royal Nepal Airline Corporation Act 2014 SY **64,** 434, 435, 436
Royal Nepal Airline Corporation, status **64,** 432, 433-4, 436, 447, 454, 474
Netherlands
accountants, regulation **86,** 421, 424-7, 429, 430-1
Advisory Board on Conscientious Objectors **78,** 230, 258
air transport agreements, Canada/Netherlands (1974)
'air services' as 'scheduled services' **96,** 335
'designated airlines' **96,** 335-6

directly binding on individuals, whether **96,** 336
failure to object to proposed tariffs, effect **96,** 336-7
aliens
access to courts **73,** 600-2, **74,** 116-17, **79,** 281
admission, power to refuse, intention to settle **99,** 42
asylum, request for **79,** 280-1
fair hearing **79,** 282
intention to settle
burden of proof **99,** 43
public order and **99,** 43
residence permit **74,** 448
humanitarian reasons and refugee status distinguished **99,** 5-6, 31-2
request for as evidence of intention to settle **99,** 43
right of residence **92,** 310-12
spouse **92,** 310-12
applicable law
collisions at sea, Netherlands–USSR Agreement on Merchant Shipping (1969) **65,** 365-7
foreign civil aviation companies operating on territory, bilateral air transport agreement **96,** 334-6
State immunity, jurisdiction, forum State **94,** 376
succession *mortis causa* **94,** 372
tort, place of alleged tort **94,** 365-7
treaty, terms of treaty **96,** 341
arbitral award, enforcement, Recognition and Enforcement of Foreign Arbitral Awards Convention (New York). *See* New York Convention on the Recognition and Enforcement of Foreign Arbitral Awards (1958) *below*
arbitral award, qualification as **65,** 359
arbitration agreements, legal requirements **75,** 156-7, 166
arms dealing, foreign relations, refusal to issue export licence and **101,** 423-6
asylum **79,** 280-2
Booty Agreement with UK (1946) **40,** 464, 467
broadcasting, jurisdiction **101,** 413-18
broadcasting outside territorial waters, control of **74,** 201-3
burden of proof, family life, respect for **92,** 311
central/State-owned bank
as State agency **65,** 350-3
status, relevance **65,** 350-4
child care, parental access
divorce, after **96,** 607-17, 620-3, 625-37
interests of child **96,** 621-2
choice of law clause, contract, strike on board ship in port **87,** 97
conscientious objection. *See also* law of, Conscientious Objection to Military Service Act *below*
conscript's right of appeal **94,** 444-5
non-discrimination **94,** 444-5
Constitution 1887, s 59 **73,** 39
Constitution 1922, s 58 **73,** 40
Constitution 1947
s 6(1) **74,** 706
s 58 **74,** 426
s 59 **73,** 39
s 66 **40,** 134, **74,** 3

Netherlands (*cont.*)
s 77 **74,** 710
s 198, deletion **78,** 15
s 199, deletion **78,** 15
Constitution 1972
s 65 **87,** 71
s 66 **87,** 71, **88,** 203, **93,** 4, 8, 558-9
Constitution 1983
s 68 **96,** 354, 355
s 93 **96,** 341, 350, 390
s 94 **96,** 341, **99,** 33, 34, **106,** 403
s 120 **96,** 367-9, **106,** 403
consular archives, inviolability **94,** 372
documents belonging to estate of national **94,** 372
consular privileges and immunities, functional **94,** 371-3
improper performance, relevance **94,** 372
consulate, as 'seat' of State/government **65,** 373
continental shelf legislation **41,** 95
contract
applicable law
European Convention on the Law Applicable to Contractual Obligations (1980) **87,** 97, 99
principal place of business of party required to effect performance **87,** 99, 100
Uniform Act governing the International Sale of Goods **87,** 99
breach, maritime claim **96,** 377
definition **89,** 462
European Convention on the Law Applicable to Contractual Obligations (1980), customary international law, whether **87,** 97, 99
courts, municipal
competence of **78,** 3, 6
foreign relations **78,** 3
jurisdiction **78,** 9
limitations under international law **47,** 144
crimes against humanity, punishment of **74,** 704-13, **75,** 336-68
criminal procedure. *See also* law of, Army and Air Force Code of Procedure *below*
mental handicap and **81,** 94-6, 98-102
Czechoslovakia, Agreement for Settlement of Financial Matters (1964) **74,** 103-4
death duties **56,** 568
detention **78,** 231-4
compensation **78,** 234-5
declaratory judgment of unlawfulness **78,** 235
material loss only **78,** 235
diplomatic immunity, jurisdiction
real/immovable property, dispute relating to
action in sending State, excluded **94,** 312
held on behalf of sending State **94,** 312-13
reasons for exception **94,** 311-12
diplomatic immunity, jurisdiction, waiver, State, by **94,** 340-1
diplomatic premises
duty to protect **94,** 306-7, 349-50
motives of accused, relevance **94,** 306-7, 350

part of territory of sending State, whether **94,** 351, 352
recognition as such, executive responsibility **94,** 349
diplomatic privileges and immunities, entitlement, third State, in **94,** 340-1
diplomatic privileges and immunities, international officials, applicability to **94,** 309-10
diplomatic protection
claims of nationals, lump sum settlements **73,** 378-80, **74,** 285-9
discretion **94,** 345
legal obligation, whether **100,** 413-14
international law **94,** 344-5
municipal law **94,** 345
national 'entrapped' by foreign State **94,** 345
Parliament, role **94,** 345
diplomatic relations, break
China, People's Republic, threat **101,** 425
reduction to Chargé d'Affaires status distinguished **101,** 425
discrimination, justification **96,** 362-3
double criminality, punishment, relevance **100,** 410-11
EEC Treaty (Rome) (1957)
applicable law **93,** 557
individuals, direct effect on **93,** 557
primacy **93,** 8, 557-8
Art. 177 ruling and **93,** 557
emergency. *See force majeure below*
employment contract, academic appointment in respondent State
applicable law, relevance **65,** 380
jurisdiction, contract concluded in forum State **65,** 379-80
State immunity, jurisdiction
in case of employment by foreign ministry **65,** 380
nationality of employee, relevance **65,** 379-80
State school **65,** 378-80, **94,** 314-15
employment contract, locally engaged staff, consulate
privileges and immunities of employee distinguished **65,** 373
State immunity, jurisdiction **65,** 372-4, **94,** 356
employment contract, locally engaged staff, diplomatic mission
applicable law, receiving State **94,** 353
dismissal **94,** 353-4
State immunity, jurisdiction
locally engaged embassy clerical worker **94,** 353
medical insurance, duty to ensure, whether **94,** 356
nationality of employee, relevance **94,** 353
Ems estuary
Agreements with the FRG (1960/62) **41,** 81-2, 93, 95, 98, 102, 166, **43,** 252
territorial status **74,** 125-6
environment, Greenpeace, regional organizations as distinct entities **101,** 434-5
equality
education
Elimination of Discrimination in Education, Paris Convention (1960) **96,** 371
European Convention on Human Rights (1950) **96,** 371
International Covenant on Civil and Political Rights (ICCPR) (1966) **96,** 371
transitional rules **96,** 371-2
European Convention on Human Rights (1950) **73,** 382-8, 394-8, **74,** 282-6, 391, 446-8, **75,** 340, 348-58, 362, 366-7, **78,** 234-7, **92,** 312-19

Netherlands (*cont.*)
inhuman or degrading treatment, assassination **99,** 9-11
margin of appreciation, expulsion of alien **99,** 7-8
rights, absolute, whether **99,** 10
supremacy **78,** 234
exchange control legislation **47,** 46-52
exchange of notes, effect **74,** 118-20
expulsion of alien **74,** 425-6, 444-8, **79,** 280-1
grounds
measures to protect **99,** 10-11
public policy overriding consideration **99,** 7-8
methods, public policy, risk of assassination and **99,** 7-11
expulsion of national, requirement to leave permanently **100,** 414
extraditable offence
causing an explosion **100,** 420, 424
presumption of **100,** 421
in requesting State, relevance **100,** 420
treaty, defined by **100,** 419-23, 424
extradition **73,** 39-43, 658, **74,** 450-3, 456-8, 472-7, 498-505
disguised, non-renewal of passport **100,** 407
double criminality. *See* double criminality *above*
duty to seek, whether **94,** 345-6
Extradition, European Convention on (1957)
declaration defining nationality **100,** 402-3
legislative implementation, need for **100,** 403
reservations, 'particular hardship' **100,** 431-2
fair trial, need for **100,** 426, 429
fairness **100,** 406
human rights, respect for in requesting State
bilateral extradition agreement, presumed **100,** 410
executive discretion **100,** 428
inhuman and degrading treatment **100,** 426, 427-8
multilateral extradition agreement, accession to European Convention for the Protection of Human Rights (1950) as guarantee **100,** 410
request for measures to guarantee **100,** 427-8
request for supplementary information from requesting State **100,** 427
right of court in requested State to investigate **100,** 426, 429
right of individual petition under European Convention on Human Rights (1950) **100,** 426, 427, 429
judicial review, questions of fact **100,** 411
legal certainty **100,** 406
legality **75,** 339, 343
nationals
alien integrated into national community **100,** 401-3, 431-2
Extradition, European Convention on (1957) **100,** 401-3, 431-2
Extradition, European Convention on (1957), declaration defining nationality **100,** 402-3, 431-2
procedure, completion **100,** 407
responsibility, executive **100,** 406
speciality, extension of offences, by agreement **100,** 406
transit of extradited person through third country **100,** 413-14
consent of third State, need for **100,** 413
enclave **100,** 413-14

withdrawal of request **100,** 407
State practice **100,** 407
extradition treaties, application **74,** 118-20
family life, respect for. *See also* child care *above*
burden of proof **92,** 311
cohabitation, relevance **92,** 311-12
force majeure **78,** 12
forcible abduction/unlawful arrest
jurisdiction, effect on **86,** 527-32
Republic of the United Netherlands (1581-1795) **95,** 429-38
foreign judgment, *res judicata*, whether **94,** 365-6
foreign judgment, recognition/enforcement **73,** 5
fraudulent claim to compensation, stay of execution in foreign court **101,** 445-7
foreign law, recognition/enforcement, confiscatory legislation, enemy property **74,** 153-6
foreign nationalization, recognition of **74,** 103
foreign relations
confidentiality and **96,** 348-58
balance of interests **96,** 351-4, 356-7
evidence, obligation to give, effect on **96,** 351, 354, 355, 356
obligation of person appointed by State to conduct foreign relations **96,** 350-8
rules of international organization **96,** 350, 356
reliability of State as international partner **96,** 352-4, 356-7
responsibility for **78,** 3
foreign State, international obligation towards, duty to respect **94,** 358, 359, 360
forum selection clause, as waiver of immunity **65,** 370-1
freedom of movement, restrictions
provided by law **101,** 408
public order **101,** 408
public security **101,** 408
freedom of navigation **74,** 127-34
duty to safeguard **73,** 165
environmental protection group, right of interference **101,** 434-5
public interest **101,** 434-5
international rivers **73,** 164-5
FRG
Agreement on delimitation of continental shelf (1964) **41,** 29, 37, 46, 89, 90, 130-1
Ems Estuary Agreements (1960/2) **41,** 81-2, 93, 95, 98, 102, 166, **43,** 252
Extradition Treaty (1896) **44,** 174-6
Financial Treaties (1960/2) **43,** 246-53
Frontier Treaty (1960) **43,** 252
state of war with, termination **42,** 421
gold looted by German occupant, restitution claims **44,** 448-85
high seas
jurisdiction, nationals and broadcasting equipment on board foreign ship **101,** 412-18
submarine cables, damage to, applicable law **74,** 213-18
hijacking of aircraft, punishment **74,** 163-5
hostage-taking, punishment **78,** 2
purpose **78,** 2
ICJ, Deputy Registrar, privileges and immunities **94,** 309-13
immigration policy **92,** 310-12

Netherlands (*cont.*)
in camera proceedings **58,** 59
individual in international law, existence **106,** 406-7
Indonesia
Round Table Conference Agreements and Union Statute (1949) **40,** 11
treaties, Indonesian denunciation **70,** 439-40
innocent passage, beaching of salvaged vessel **101,** 437-8
International Covenant on Civil and Political Rights (ICCPR) (1966)
binding on all persons, whether **96,** 372-3, 390
equality
courts' role **96,** 343
education **96,** 371
International Covenant on Economic, Social and Cultural Rights (1966) distinguished **96,** 361
social security **96,** 361
freedom of movement, restrictions **101,** 407-9
obligations
existing legislation to conform **96,** 361
implementation **96,** 361
International Covenant on Economic, Social and Cultural Rights (1966)
direct effect **96,** 340-3, 362, 363, 390-1
equality
destruction of existing equality **96,** 341
discrimination, need for **96,** 351-2
patent inequality, need for **96,** 341-3
pay **96,** 340-3, 390-1
perpetuation of inequality **96,** 362-3
international law **65,** 352-4, 360-2, 368, 381. *See also* treaties *below*
customary international law **96,** 377-8
development **96,** 377-8
expert opinion, desirability **96,** 378
ICJ judgment **94,** 366-7
international legal order
arms sales
refusal of export licence **101,** 423-4, 451-2
reprocessing in intermediary country **101,** 451-2
judicial review, role **101,** 428-9
pursuit of good relations **101,** 423-4, 428-9, 452
strategic scientific equipment, refusal of export licence **101,** 428-9
international officials, exemption from taxation **70,** 407-12, 420-5, **73,** 2-3, **94,** 320
international officials, immunity, jurisdiction **70,** 419
real/immovable property, dispute relating to **94,** 311-13
international organization, immunity
acta jure imperii, translating and interpreting services **94,** 326, 328, 330
customary international law **94,** 329
employment contract
enforcement of remedy for breach **94,** 326
oral agreement **94,** 325-6, 328, 330
functional **94,** 324, 329
host State, in, consent, need for **94,** 329
international organizations, privileges and immunities, jurisdiction **74,** 192-3
International Tin Council (ITC)

confidentiality of proceedings
action against single Member State, relevance **96,** 353-4
ITC Rules as basis of obligation **96,** 350
Rules of Procedure
binding on third parties, whether **96,** 350
continued application **96,** 348
direct effect **96,** 348
publication, effect **96,** 350
Iran–US Claims Tribunal. *See also* Iran–US Claims Tribunal
status of proceedings **75,** 156-7, 166-8
judicial assistance, refusal
serious and intolerable harm to person affected **101,** 454
treaty basis **101,** 454-5
judicial restraint **96,** 219
judicial review
act threatening life or liberty **96,** 219
legislation **96,** 360, 367-71
Charter of the Kingdom **96,** 369-71
conformity with treaty **96,** 367-9
European Convention on Human Rights (1950) and **96,** 369
fundamental principles of law **96,** 367-8
growing power of executive and **96,** 368
margin of discretion **96,** 219
treaties, compatibility with international law **106,** 404
treaty **96,** 219, 360
jurisdiction
criminal **74,** 163-5
extraterritorial, injunctions, grant of **74,** 161
National abroad, over, extraterritorial effect of legislation and **87,** 102
nexus **87,** 102
in case of proceedings involving foreign State **62,** 234-5, **65,** 361-2
contract of employment concluded in forum State **65,** 379-80
place of performance **65,** 379-80
personal **74,** 194-6
piracy **73,** 374-5
protective principle **87,** 101-2
foreign policy and **87,** 101
law of. *See also* Constitution *above*
Act of 15 May 1829/26 April 1917 (jurisdiction), Art. 13(a) **94,** 314
Act of 6 April 1875 (conclusion of treaties)
Art. 1 **100,** 421
Art. 2 **100,** 421
Act of 16 December 1959 (Brussels Protocol) **93,** 4
Act of 28 June 1962 (Registration of Accountants) **86,** 421
Act of 8 April 1971 (statutory limitation) **87,** 95
Act of 13 December 1972 (Certified Accountants) **86,** 419, 424-7, 430-1
Administrative Decisions Appeals Act
Art. 8(1) **101,** 443
Art. 11(1) **94,** 361
Administrative Jurisdiction of Mandatory Corporations Act, Art. 5 **101,** 420-6, 429, 452
Aliens Act 1965 **73,** 674-6, **74,** 405, 426, 445-7, 473-4, **92,** 310-11

Netherlands (*cont.*)
Art. 11(5) **99,** 24
Art. 14 **99,** 34
Art. 15 **99,** 34
Art. 15(1) **99,** 4, 5
Art. 15(2) **99,** 24
Art. 15(3) **99,** 35
Art. 21(1)(b) **99,** 7-8
Art. 29 **99,** 2
Art. 30 **99,** 2
Art. 34(1) **99,** 2-4
Appeals Act 1955 **86,** 354-5
Appropriation of Enemy Property Law 1951 **74,** 154
Army and Air Force Code of Procedure 1903 **58,** 53
Army and Air Force Code of Procedure 1978 **78,** 231
Art. 4 **78,** 231, 259, 279
Art. 5 **78,** 231, 259
Art. 7 **78,** 231, 232, 236, 237, 243, 244, 259-60, 263, 264, 266, 279, 280, 283, 284
Art. 11 **78,** 232, 236, 237, 260, 263, 264, 266, 283, 287
Art. 12 **78,** 260
Art. 13 **78,** 249, 279
Art. 14 **78,** 232, 244, 260, 263, 264, 266, 280, 283, 284
Art. 15 **78,** 232
Art. 29 **78,** 234, 262, 282
Art. 31 **78,** 233, 263, 280
Art. 33 **78,** 233, 237, 264, 266, 284
Art. 34 **78,** 233, 249, 283
Art. 48 **78,** 234, 262, 282
Art. 62 **78,** 234, 282
Art. 78 **78,** 234, 262, 282
Art. 121 **78,** 283
Art. 126 **78,** 233, 262, 281
Art. 135 **78,** 283
Art. 151 **78,** 233, 280
Art. 156 **78,** 233, 280
Art. 161 **78,** 262, 282
Art. 219 **78,** 281
Art. 276 **78,** 233-4, 262, 282
Art. 278 **78,** 234
Art. 290 **78,** 234, 282
Art. 297 **78,** 234, 262, 282
Art. 368 **78,** 234, 262, 282
Art. 370 **78,** 234, 262, 282
Bailiffs' Regulations **94,** 358-60
Broadcasting Act, licensing under **73,** 397-9
Charter for the Kingdom
Art. 49 **96,** 369-71
judicial review of legislation **96,** 369-71
Civil Aviation Act **96,** 335
Civil Code **73,** 379
Art. 14 **65,** 373
Art. 161(1) **96,** 608, 636

Art. 161(5) **96,** 608, 613
Art. 623(1) **75,** 156-7, 166
Art. 1401 **65,** 376
breach of International Covenant on Civil and Political Rights, whether **96,** 613-14, 620-1, 636
Civil Code Amendment Act 1969 **96,** 613-14
Civil Code Amendment Act 1979 **96,** 614
Civil Code, Book I
Art. 125 **94,** 352
Art. 378 **81,** 96
Art. 1401 **81,** 98, **94,** 356
Art. 1407 **81,** 98
Civil Code, Book II **86,** 354
Civil Procedure Code
Art. 92 **94,** 352
Art. 94 **94,** 352
Art. 125(b) **94,** 375
Art. 191 **96,** 351, 354, 355, 356
Art. 254 **87,** 79, 91
Art. 256 **87,** 81
Art. 289 **78,** 235
military claims under **78,** 235, 239
Compulsory Education Act **74,** 296
Compulsory Military Service Act 1922 **78,** 14-17. *See also* Conscientious Objection to Military Service Act *and* military service *below*
amending Act of 1 August 1959 **78,** 15
Art. 27 **78,** 14
Art. 28 (duration of basic training) **78,** 15
Art. 29 (duration of refresher training) **78,** 15
Art. 33, interpretation **78,** 15-17
circumstances on the spot, relevance **78,** 16
UN peacekeeping operations **78,** 17
Conscientious Objection to Military Service Act
Advisory Board on Conscientious Objectors **78,** 230, 236, 258
Art. 4 **78,** 230, 236, 258
Art. 7 **78,** 230
Art. 8 **78,** 230
Art. 10 **78,** 230
Military Decree of 31 July 1970 **78,** 230, 258, 278
procedure under **78,** 230, 259-62, 278
Conscription Act 1912 **78,** 16
Council of State Act
Art. 77(4) **96,** 349
Art. 80 **94,** 358, 361
Art. 107 **96,** 349-50
Criminal Code **73,** 374, 382, **74,** 195-6, 452, 500-3, **75,** 337-9, 344-6, 354
Art. 1(2) **78,** 12
Art. 8 **94,** 340
Art. 70 **87,** 95
Art. 96(2) **100,** 425
Art. 98 **96,** 354
Art. 138 **94,** 306
Art. 157 **100,** 424

Netherlands (*cont.*)
Art. 180 **121,** 270 n. 213
Art. 184 **101,** 448
Art. 242 **121,** 270 n. 211
Art. 282 **94,** 306
Art. 350 **94,** 306
change in law under **78,** 12
hijacking of aircraft, provisions concerning **74,** 163-4
Criminal Procedure Code **75,** 340, 358
Art. 12 **81,** 94, 101
Art. 64(1) **81,** 95, 96
Arts. 89 ff **78,** 234
Art. 163 **81,** 94
Art. 164 **81,** 94
Art. 239 **81,** 95, 99-100
Art. 242 **81,** 95
Art. 244 **81,** 95
Art. 245 **81,** 95
Art. 246 **81,** 95
Art. 247 **81,** 95
Art. 248 **81,** 95-6, 99
Art. 249 **81,** 95
Art. 445 **81,** 95
Arts. 512-19 **121,** 335 n. 255
Art. 552(K) **101,** 454
gaps **81,** 99, 102
Military Code and **78,** 231, 234
Enemy Property Decree 1044 **40,** 464-7
Enemy Property Order **43,** 247
European Patent Office Protocol on Privileges and Immunities (1973) **94,** 320
Extradition Act 1967 **73,** 38, 42-3, 658, **74,** 293-4, 426, 450-3, 473-6, 503-4
Art. 4 **100,** 402-3
Art. 5(1) **100,** 424
Art. 5(2) **100,** 424
Art. 11 **100,** 421
Art. 30(2) **100,** 411
Extraordinary Penal Law (war crimes) **36,** 43-4
Extraordinary Penal Provisions Decree 1943-71 **74,** 704-7
Art. 4(2) **75,** 337, 353
Art. 27(a) **75,** 337-8, 341-2, 344-7, 354, 359
Firearms Act **74,** 194-5
Fisheries Act 1963
amending Act of 8 June 1977 **78,** 12
Art. 4 **78,** 10
Sea Fisheries Regulations 1971 **78,** 10
General Disablement Benefits Act, sexual discrimination **96,** 360-3
General Provisions of Legislation Act 1829
Art. 13 **65,** 354
Art. 13(a) **94,** 310, 352, 364, 375
General Widows' and Orphans' Act (*AWW*)
compatibility with International Covenant on Civil and Political Rights (ICCPR) (1966) **118,** 158-63
retroactive benefits under **118,** 158-63

Harmonization Act, equality **96,** 371-3
Health Insurance Act 1913 **86,** 354, 355, 371
Housing Act 1947 **74,** 291-3
Import and Export Act
  Art. 1(1) **101,** 451, 452
  Art. 2 **101,** 420-6, 428
Import and Export of Amphetamines Decree 1972 **74,** 449
Income Tax Act 1964 **94,** 320
Indonesia Distribution Act 1969 **74,** 285-6, 289
Inland Waterways Act **74,** 3
International Covenant on Economic, Social and Cultural Rights Act, direct effect of Covenant **96,** 391
Judicial Review of Administrative Decisions Act (*Wet AROB*) **74,** 476, **99,** 2-4
Judiciary Organization Act, Art. 39 **94,** 375
Kingdom Act of 26 April 1956 **78,** 15
Kingdom Act of 23 August 1956 **78,** 15
Labour Relations, Extraordinary Decree **94,** 242, 326
Limitation of Sole and Plaice Catches Decree 1976 **78,** 10-11
Marine Pollution Act **87,** 85
Military Code. *See* Army and Air Force Code of Procedure *above*; Military Penal Code *below*
Military Discipline Act 1903 **58,** 53-60, **73,** 395-6
  appeal **58,** 59
  disciplinary proceedings under **58,** 53-60
  provisional arrest **58,** 58, 76
Military Penal Code **58,** 53, **74,** 195
  Art. 147 **58,** 68
  Art. 150 **78,** 264, 265, 283, 284
Military Service Act. *See* Compulsory Military Service Act *above*
Nuclear Energy Act **87,** 87
Open Government Act, foreign relations and **96,** 348-58
Opium Act, Art. 3 **101,** 407
Passport Regulations 1952
  Art. 70 **101,** 407-9
  Art. 73 **101,** 407-9
  Art. 87 **101,** 407-9
Primary Education Act **74,** 295-6
Restoration of Legal Rights, Royal Decree concerning 1944 **72,** 17-26
Road Traffic Act **74,** 196
Royal Decree of 4 January 1946 (London Charter of the International Military Tribunal (1945)) **87,** 94-5
Scheduled Air Transport Tariffs Decree **96,** 335
Sea Fisheries Regulations 1971. *See* Fisheries Act 1963, Sea Fisheries Regulations 1971 *above*
Social Security Organization Act 1952 **86,** 354
Special Employment Relationships Decree (*BBA*) 1945
  Art. 2 **65,** 374, 379
  Art. 6 **65,** 372-4, 379
State Taxes General Act **73,** 2-3, **94,** 320
  Decree for the implementation of **87,** 78
Succession Law 1956 **56,** 567, 575
Telegraphs and Telephone Act 1904 **74,** 201-18
Wealth Tax Act 1964 **87,** 83

Netherlands (*cont.*)
legal personality **86,** 354
legislation, compatibility with treaty **94,** 320
legislation, interpretation **42,** 421, **78,** 14-17
aids
history **78,** 15
legislative history **96,** 370, **99,** 3, **101,** 423
ministerial statement **96,** 370-1
official commentary **96,** 370, **100,** 402-3
opinion of Government **78,** 15
opinion of Parliament **78,** 15
parallel legislation **101,** 423
subsequent practice **96,** 371
European Convention on Human Rights (1950), supremacy **78,** 234
guidelines
nature **96,** 371-2
scope **96,** 371-2
test **96,** 370
phrases
Art. 1401 **78,** 235, 239
auditeur-militair **78,** 233-4, 245-7, 262, 269-71, 281-3, 285, 287-9
'detention under' **78,** 231-3, 243-5, 259-62, 279-85
'international legal order' **101,** 442-4
'international legal order', 'development or impairment of' **101,** 428-9, 442-4, 450-2
'normal times' **78,** 16
officier commisaris **78,** 233-4, 238, 262, 271-2, 281-3, 285, 289-90
'service outside Europe' **78,** 15-17
'statutory legislation' **101,** 448
treaty as aid **87,** 85-6, **101,** 423
legislation, retroactive, Extraordinary Penal Law (war crimes) **36,** 43-4
liberation, currency captured during **40,** 463-7
Lockerbie trial **117,** 664-89
mental handicap **81,** 94-6, 98-102
mentally ill person, detention **58,** 658-63
military service **73,** 383-5, 394-5, **74,** 194-5. *See also* Compulsory Military Service Act *above*
consent of conscripts, need for **78,** 15-17
'normal times' **78,** 16, 17
'other exceptional circumstances' **78,** 15-16
tasks, relevance **78,** 16
'war or threat of war' **78,** 15
outside Europe **78,** 15-16
mutual legal assistance **74,** 118-20
nationality
loss or deprivation of **74,** 705-7
conditions for **75,** 337-8, 353
married women **73,** 568
NATO Status of Forces Agreement (1951)
applicability
territorial **94,** 365
tort by visiting serviceman **96,** 381-3

visiting forces on service in contracting State **94,** 365
privileges and immunities, individual members of the Forces, tort **94,** 365
negotiations, good faith obligation to conclude, whether **94,** 318
New York Convention on the Recognition and Enforcement of Foreign Arbitral Awards (1958)
applicability, non-parties **65,** 358
applicable law, need for reference to specific State **65,** 358-9, 362-3
award, enforcement, limitation to award made within territory of another contracting State **65,** 358-9
award, recognition **86,** 493-5
reservations, limitation to awards made in another Contracting State **65,** 358-9
North-East Atlantic Fisheries Convention
denunciation **78,** 12
municipal law, effect on validity of **78,** 12
recommendations under, implementation **78,** 10-11
nuclear weapons, deployment
consent to, control remaining with US, relevance **106,** 406
human rights and **106,** 405-6
legality, defensive purposes **106,** 405-6
occupation, share certificates issued during **47,** 58-60
passport, withdrawal, right to leave one's own country and **101,** 407-9
political offence
classification as
bomb attack on bar used by opposing group **100,** 423
offence while escaping from prison **100,** 423, 425
definition/requirements
absence/lack of precision **100,** 421, 422
political character **100,** 420-3, 425-6
treaty at time of conclusion **100,** 422-3
proportionality and **100,** 423
relevant factors
effect directly related to political objective **100,** 423, 425
motivation **100,** 422
'special category status' **100,** 423, 426
prisoners, transfer of persons sentenced abroad **94,** 346
public order/public policy/*ordre public* **73,** 5, **74,** 103
expulsion of alien **99,** 7-11
measures to protect **99,** 10-11
overriding consideration **99,** 7-8
protection measures **99,** 10-11
risk of assassination if returned to own country, relevance **99,** 7-11
railway authority, agency of State, whether **65,** 355
refugees **73,** 42-3, 674-7, **74,** 405-6
constitutional rights **99,** 33-4
country of first refuge
economic conditions, relevance **99,** 19-20
failure to establish refugee status and **99,** 37
non-party to Convention as **99,** 20
obligation to apply for refugee status in **99,** 4, 15-16, 19-20
observation of Convention obligations, need for **99,** 15, 20, 21
de facto refugees distinguished **99,** 13
non-refoulement

Netherlands (*cont.*)
adequacy of protection **99,** 15-16, 19-20
commission of serious crime **99,** 33-4
written undertaking, need for **99,** 20-1
'persecution or well-founded fear of persecution'
apartheid **99,** 12-13
conscientious objection **99,** 13
political activity, continuity, need for **99,** 13
political motivation, leaving intelligence service **99,** 7-8
political motivation, leaving Secret Service **99,** 7-8
social group membership **99,** 3
relocation requirement **99,** 5-6
detrimental economic and social impact, relevance **99,** 3-4
relevance **99,** 5-6
Representative of UN High Commissioner **74,** 406
residence
relocation requirement. *See* relocation requirement *above*
right to choose place of **99,** 4
status
appeal against decision respecting **99,** 2-3
de facto refugees distinguished **99,** 13
requirement to relocate, detrimental economic and social impact, relevance **99,** 3-4
residence permit on humanitarian grounds distinguished **99,** 5-6, 31-2
status, refusal **79,** 281
appeal, right of **99,** 2-3
Refugees, Geneva Convention on the Status of (1951) and Protocol (1967)
equality in State of habitual residence **99,** 3
self-executing, whether, 'binding on anyone' **99,** 3
Republic of the United Netherlands (1581-1795)
external sovereignty **95,** 425
forcible abduction/unlawful arrest, jurisdiction, effect on **95,** 429-38
internal sovereignty **95,** 429
States General, powers **95,** 429
Restoration of Civil Rights, Council for, Securities Division, competence **42,** 324-424
Rhine
freedom of navigation **74,** 127-34
Police Regulations, territorial scope **74,** 139-40
right to leave own country, Single Convention on Narcotic Drugs (1961), obligations under **101,** 408-9
rivers, freedom of navigation **73,** 164-5
Schöffer Commission **75,** 356-7
service of process, Convention on the Service Abroad of Judicial and Extra-judicial Documents in Civil and Commercial Matters (1965) **94,** 363-4
service of process on foreign State or State agency
applicable law, forum State **94,** 364
refusal to accept, effect **94,** 364
State immunity and **94,** 364
ships, State-owned
applicable law, Netherlands–USSR Agreement on Merchant Shipping (1969) **65,** 365-7, 369
immunity, arrest/attachment
appointment of representative in forum State and **65,** 366-7

domicile, choice of and **65,** 366-7
Netherlands–USSR Agreement on Merchant Shipping (1969) and **65,** 365-7
immunity, jurisdiction, waiver, Netherlands–USSR Agreement on Merchant Shipping (1969) and **65,** 368-9
social security **86,** 354-6, 358-63
civil right, whether **86,** 358-9, 361-3
France, Convention with (1950) **48,** 236
public law right, whether **86,** 359-61
South Africa and, boycott of, 1980 Paraplegic Games **87,** 69-72
sovereignty, violation, remedy **94,** 348
standard of treatment of alien, equality **73,** 599-600
Standing Consultative Committee for Alien Affairs **79,** 280
State agency/State-owned corporation/State entity
classification
NIOC **47,** 139-49
police authority **65,** 381-2
separate legal entity test **65,** 355
State immunity, arbitral award, enforcement **65,** 171, 357-60, 362-3, 365-7
exequatur proceedings, compromise agreement and **65,** 364
State immunity, execution/attachment, applicability, funds held in private foreign bank **94,** 368-9
State immunity, execution/attachment, purpose of proceedings, safeguarding/conservatory measures, likelihood of compliance with judgment and **65,** 376
State immunity, execution/attachment, purpose/use of funds/assets
evidence of purpose **94,** 360, 361
public activities of embassy **94,** 359-60
relevance **65,** 376
State immunity, execution/attachment, theory/doctrine, customary international law **94,** 358-9
State immunity, jurisdiction, classification of act
academic appointment, State school **65,** 378-80
act in territory of forum State **94,** 346
customary international law **94,** 346
concession agreement **47,** 139-41, 147-9
diplomatic premises, lease **65,** 370-1
expropriation/nationalization **94,** 317-18
monetary policy **65,** 353
nature or purpose of transaction as determining factor **94,** 347
police, entrapment by **94,** 346, 347-8
police power, exercise of, abuse amounting to tort **65,** 381-2, **100,** 552-4, 555-8, **124,** 435
private law relationship **65,** 371-2, 376
private person test **65,** 361, **94,** 315, 352-3, 365
railway construction **65,** 357-8, 361
sale of onions **65,** 371-2
tort **65,** 376
State immunity, jurisdiction, entitlement, officials **94,** 364-5
State immunity, jurisdiction, procedural aspects, need to plead **65,** 381
State immunity, jurisdiction, theory/doctrine, customary international law, European Convention on State Immunity (and Protocol) (Basle) (1972) **94,** 346
State immunity, jurisdiction, waiver
implied, forum selection clause **65,** 370-1

Netherlands (*cont.*)
objection to default judgment **94,** 317
submission to the jurisdiction as, appearance as **65,** 377
State immunity, taxation, assessment **94,** 320
State responsibility for
acts and omissions of
undercover agent **94,** 347-8
visiting serviceman **96,** 381-3
defective mine-sweeping **74,** 239-40
State succession **73,** 39-42
Supreme Military Court, appointment to **58,** 59
Surinam. *See* Surinam
telephone tapping **74,** 391
territorial sea, baseline, low-water mark at spring-tide **94,** 366
terrorist acts
extradition for **74,** 472-7, 498-504
punishment **74,** 695-8, **78,** 2
treaties. *See also* Constitution, Art. 66 *above*
amendment, parties' conduct **96,** 337
conclusion, procedure **96,** 338-9
continued application, declaration regarding **74,** 119
direct effect
binding on all persons, need to be **96,** 372-3
clear provision, need for **96,** 341, 372, 391
date of legislation intended to implement, relevance **96,** 363
International Covenant on Economic, Social and Cultural Rights (1966) **96,** 340-2, 372-3, 390-1
nature and content **96,** 341, 390-1
obligation to take progressive steps and **96,** 391
parties' intention **96,** 372-3
'shall be agreed upon between [individuals]', significance **96,** 336
'shall come into effect on the expiration of the period' **96,** 336
structural context for implementation **96,** 341-2
terms of treaty, determined by **96,** 341
implementing legislation **78,** 10, 12
need for **87,** 86
individual, rights **106,** 406
initialling, effect **96,** 338-9
municipal law and
EEC Treaty. *See* EEC Treaty (Rome) (1957) *above*
subsequent legislation **100,** 422-3
primacy
balance of interests **96,** 388
direct effect, relevance **96,** 388, **99,** 35
European Convention on Human Rights (1950) **96,** 387-8
reservations, restrictive interpretation **100,** 432
retroactive effect, Netherlands-USSR Agreement on Merchant Shipping (1969) **65,** 369
self-executing **93,** 5, 8, 29, 558
'binding on anyone' **99,** 3
Geneva Convention Relating to the Status of Refugees (1951) **99,** 3, 34
Netherlands-USSR Agreement on Merchant Shipping (1969) **65,** 366
signature, initialling distinguished **96,** 338-9

supremacy of **78,** 234
termination **74,** 114-15
treaty-making power
executive **96,** 339
judicial review **96,** 339
legislature **96,** 339
treaties, State succession **74,** 116-17
treaty interpretation
aids
ECJ decisions **101,** 445-6
exchange of notes **100,** 420, 424
legislation **100,** 421-3, 424
phrases
'civil and commercial matters' **101,** 445-7
'National' **100,** 402-3
'no-one shall be expelled' **100,** 414
'*notamment*'/'for example' **100,** 431-2
'transit' **100,** 413-14
UK
continental shelf delimitation agreement (1965) **41,** 90
exploitation of single geological structures under North Sea **41,** 81, 95 n. 98
UNIFIL
assignment of conscripts **78,** 16
absence of legal basis **78,** 17
Vienna Convention on Diplomatic Relations (1961), as customary international law **94,** 310
war, laws and customs, enforcement **87,** 93-5
war crimes. *See also* crimes against humanity *above*
applicable law
international law **91,** 45
municipal law **91,** 44-5
Land Warfare Regulations, breach as **87,** 94-5
'murder of civilian population of or in occupied territory' **87,** 94-5
statutory limitation **87,** 94-5
war with Germany, termination **42,** 421
wartime decrees, recognition **42,** 409-36
wrecks, removal costs, liability for **74,** 124-7, 199-200
neutrality. *See also* naval warfare; neutralization
attack on neutral ship **79,** 10, 12
as piracy **79,** 10
attack on neutral ship in international waters, tortious liability **81,** 661-9
breach **79,** 9-10
German violation of Greek during WWII **47,** 418, 419, 428, 438
remedies **79,** 10
customary international law **110,** 210-11
economic consequences **49,** 86-8
internal waters and **90,** 308
Lend-Lease and **49,** 83
necessity **110,** 239-40
neutral corporation, seizure of property **54,** 542
neutral merchant ships
capture **40,** 472-80
visit and detention **38,** 471-4

neutrality (*cont.*)
neutral persons, commercial domicile **40,** 478
neutral States
looted property, legislation on **44,** 474
monetary gold, transactions with belligerents **44,** 449, 475, 479-81
nuclear weapons and **110,** 210-12, 239-40, 256, 258, 337-9, 413-14, 451, 466-7, 514
intent **110,** 451
obligations **49,** 83-9
rights in time of war **79,** 10
Declaration of Paris (1856) **79,** 10
Geneva Convention on the High Seas (1958) **79,** 10
judicial decisions **79,** 10
self-defence **110,** 466-7
Switzerland **71,** 280-1, 443-6
territorial integrity **110,** 256, 337-9, 413-14
violation, necessity **110,** 239-40
UN Charter and **49,** 82
neutralization. *See also* neutrality; war
Magellan Straits **82,** 687
New Caledonia, attainment of independence, consultation of people **89,** 19-22
New Guinea, Mandate. *See* Mandate, New Guinea
new international economic order, ILA declaration (Seoul, 1986) **83,** 474
New International Economic Order. *See* United Nations General Assembly (UNGA) Resolutions, 3201(S-V) (Declaration on the Establishment of a New Economic Order)
new situations 69, 581, 594
New South Wales. *See* Australia, New South Wales
New York Convention on the Recognition and Enforcement of Foreign Arbitral Awards (1958) 62, 220-5, **82,** 68
applicability
award, annulment **82,** 96
non-parties **65,** 358, **82,** 68
States **65,** 357
applicable law
need for reference to specific State **65,** 358-9, 362-3
parties' right to choose **96,** 12
arbitration agreement
Head of State's power to conclude **96,** 10-11
filing of claim as endorsement **96,** 11
individual's rights, effect on **96,** 10 n. 9
written, need for **96,** 10
Algiers Accords **96,** 10
award
date **103,** 568-70
definition **96,** 9
permanent arbitral tribunal, by **96,** 9
finality **82,** 70
foreign State, made in, award of international tribunal, whether **96,** 9, 11-12
award, annulment, applicability **82,** 96
award, enforcement
arbitral agreement, beyond scope of **96,** 17-19
pleading error, relevance **96,** 18
award according to law of specific State, need for **65,** 358-9, 362-3
defences

burden of proof **94,** 221, **96,** 12 n. 13, 17
excess of powers **94,** 224-7, **96,** 17
fraud **94,** 221-4
public policy, violation **94,** 227-8, **96,** 12
limitation to award made within territory of another contracting State **65,** 358-9
specific performance, necessary, whether **96,** 20-1
award, finality, burden of proof **82,** 68
award, recognition **86,** 493-5
implementing legislation **96,** 9, **103,** 568-9, 578
interpretation, object and purpose **86,** 495
reservations
limitation to awards made in another contracting State **65,** 358-9
non-application to awards preceding ratification **82,** 68
State immunity and **65,** 357-9, **103,** 563, 565-7, 577-80
travaux préparatoires **71,** 588-9, **86,** 494
New Zealand
access to courts, arbitration clause and **118,** 634
act of State, State immunity, jurisdiction and, distinction **104,** 618
administrative law, general principles of **90,** 577
admiralty jurisdiction
foreign ship, action *in rem* against **64,** 552-61
sister ship jurisdiction **90,** 559
State immunity and **64,** 552-61, **90,** 558-67
aliens
residence permit, cancellation, permit procured by fraud, forgery, false, misleading or concealment of information **117,** 644-5
review of procedure **68,** 161-2
applicable law
disclosure of documents an offence against foreign law, *lex fori* **104,** 554, 558
private international law and **104,** 554, 558
property, immovable, *lex situs* **104,** 612
property, moveable, *lex situs* **104,** 612
arbitration clause, interpretation, phrases, 'arising under' **118,** 631-4
Australia, parallel policy **90,** 569, 579
Chicago Convention on International Civil Aviation (1944)
Annex 13, as part of municipal law **120,** 569-72
implementation, ad hoc approach **120,** 565-9. *See also* law of, *Civil Aviation Acts, Regulations and Rules below*
as part of municipal law **120,** 563-9
legislation, need for **120,** 568-9
child rights
family interests distinguished **117,** 639
immigration and **117,** 638-9
International Covenant on Civil and Political Rights (ICCPR) (1966) **101,** 459-65, **117,** 628-34, 638-9
UN Convention on the Rights of the Child (1989) **101,** 458-60, **117,** 628-35, 638-9
comity
foreign law, breach **104,** 536, **108,** 632
State immunity, jurisdiction **104,** 517
common law
self-incrimination **104,** 582-3, 607
State immunity **104,** 510, 514, 520-2, 524-5
absolute theory **104,** 524-5

New Zealand (*cont.*)
Cook Islands **79,** 685-94
costs **80,** 10
courts, municipal
recognition of governments and **80,** 8-10
standing, representation of persons protected under the Treaty of Waitangi (1840) **120,** 470, 535
UK courts, equivalence **88,** 275-6
customary international law
Council of Europe/OECD Convention on Mutual Administrative Assistance in Tax Matters (1988) **104,** 579
taxation, exemption, judicial assistance **104,** 579
deportation, rights of child under international conventions and **117,** 645-9
diplomatic channels, as remedy, State immunity, jurisdiction and **104,** 580, 622
diplomatic relations, Fiji **80,** 5-6
disclosure of documents, State immunity, jurisdiction **104,** 536-40, 556-8, 606, 611-25
dispute settlement, international investment policy, relevance of changing practice **118,** 637-9
employment contract, locally engaged staff, consulate, applicable law, *lex fori* **104,** 514
employment contract, locally engaged staff, diplomatic mission
applicable law, locally engaged embassy staff **104,** 523
State immunity, jurisdiction, State practice **104,** 523-4
State practice, variation **104,** 517-18
employment contract, locally engaged staff, office of Governor of British colony, applicable law, law of sending State **104,** 525
employment contract, State immunity, jurisdiction
Governor of British colony **104,** 513-14
nationality of employee **104,** 517, 520
State practice **104,** 523-4
employment contract, State immunity, jurisdiction, procedural aspects, applicable law, receiving State **104,** 520
Endangered Species of Wild Fauna and Flora, Convention on International Trade in (CITES) (1973) **90,** 572, 576, 578
European Convention on State Immunity (and Protocol) (Basle) (1972), employment contract **104,** 517
evidence
applicable law, *lex fori* **104,** 559
disclosure as offence under law of foreign State **104,** 533-6, 580-7
applicable law **104,** 555, 558
balancing the considerations **104,** 584-6, **108,** 629-30, 631
'just excuse' **104,** 534, 543, 559-61, 582-6, 588-90, 609-10, 628-9, **108,** 629-30, 631
oral evidence **104,** 557-8, 581
public interest **104,** 533, 535-6, 544
public policy **104,** 535-6
State practice **104,** 557, 558-9, 594-6, 625-7
'sufficient cause' **104,** 559-61, 582, 588-90, 609-10, 628-9, **108,** 623-32
self-incrimination **104,** 540-6, 557, 581-3, 592-8, 625-9
absolute right **108,** 627-8
common law **104,** 582-3, 607, **108,** 627-8
enforced evidence, admissibility in foreign court **104,** 545-6, 562, 603-4

extradition, refusal **104,** 541-2
First National Bank of Chicago **104,** 544-5
Frank **104,** 544-5
fundamental right **108,** 627-8
giving of evidence as offence **104,** 608-9, 628
In re Westinghouse Uranium Contract **104,** 626
judicial discretion **108,** 629-30
McRae **104,** 593-5, 625
offence against foreign law, relevance **104,** 609, 626-7, **108,** 625-9
rationale **104,** 627-8
Spencer **104,** 544, 594-5, 601-2
Two Sicilies **104,** 592-3, 625
executive Council members, powers **68,** 171
executive discretion
limitations on, treaty **85,** 205-16
requirements
purpose of legislation, respect for **85,** 212, **120,** 506, 512-13
reasonableness **120,** 506, 512-13, 535
expulsion of alien **68,** 160-73, **74,** 260, 268
extradition **77,** 331-5
arrest, unlawful arrest, effect **77,** 333-5
arrest warrant, need for **88,** 274-5
discretion **104,** 544
hardship **104,** 542
UK, to **88,** 270-6
extraterritorial legislation **45,** 4-18
'peace, order and good government', laws for **45,** 7-18
family life, respect for, International Covenant on Civil and Political Rights (ICCPR) (1966) **101,** 459-65
flight recorders. *See also* Chicago Convention on International Civil Aviation (1944)
disclosure of transcript **120,** 577-84
forcible abduction/unlawful arrest, jurisdiction, effect on **77,** 333-4
foreign armed forces
crimes committed by
punishment of **74,** 245-56, 268-9, 271-3
superior orders as defence **74,** 250-1, 260-1
foreign law
as applicable law, conflict with municipal law **104,** 601-4
assistance in breach distinguished **104,** 536
foreign law, recognition/enforcement
fiscal **104,** 536
penal law **104,** 536
public policy **104,** 536
forfeiture under Customs Acts
automaticity **78,** 597, 620-6, 632
date of transfer of ownership **78,** 609, 623-6, 631
penal nature **78,** 601-2, 629
forum [non] conveniens
applicable law and **64,** 564
ICSID **118,** 634-9
place of performance **64,** 541-2, 564-5
stay of proceedings and **118,** 634-9
France, *Rainbow Warrior* dispute **74,** 256-77

New Zealand (*cont.*)
freedom of information, public interest privilege and **120,** 576-7
general principles of international law, State immunity, jurisdiction **104,** 516
High Court Rules
310 **104,** 575
311 **104,** 575
R477 **90,** 560
homosexuality, persecution as 'member of particular social group' and **124,** 486, 488
human rights, municipal law, primacy of human rights **101,** 463-4
ICSID Convention (1965), implementing legislation **118,** 626-7
immigrants, Ministry of Foreign Affairs and **85,** 207
International Convention on the Elimination of All Forms of Racial Discrimination (1965), municipal law and **85,** 205-16
obligations **85,** 205-16
part of, whether **85,** 205
State practice **85,** 210
International Covenant on Civil and Political Rights (ICCPR) (1966)
implementation, national measures as primary means **115,** 659
individual, right of complaint to Human Rights Committee **101,** 464-5
international law **85,** 214
compliance, obligation of implementing agency in absence of binding legislation **120,** 601-2
precedent **104,** 616-17
primacy, international law **120,** 600
treaties. *See* treaties *below*
International Law Commission (ILC), Draft Articles on Jurisdictional Immunities of States and Their Property (1991), Art. 11 (employment contract) **104,** 518
judicial discretion **77,** 334-5, **108,** 629-30
evidence, giving of, State immunity, jurisdiction **104,** 539, 561, 586
judicial review
discretionary nature **117,** 649
entry permit **85,** 212
export licence, refusal **90,** 570
grounds
denial of natural justice **117,** 645
error of law **117,** 644-5
unreasonableness **90,** 579
non-statutory body **114,** 583-6
jurisdiction. *See also* admiralty jurisdiction *above*
concurrent, good faith in exercise **104,** 545
effects doctrine, commercial activities having direct effect in forum State **104,** 613-14
in personam **90,** 560, 562
possession or control **90,** 560, 561-2
res judicata **90,** 560, 564-5
territorial
in personam jurisdiction **104,** 621
in rem jurisdiction **104,** 621
sovereign integrity **104,** 617-18
State immunity and **104,** 612
justiciability, foreign relations **85,** 213
Kermadec Islands
annexation **86,** 191, 198, 204
validity **86,** 196

law of
Acts Interpretation Act 1924 **79,** 690, **88,** 272
s 5 **78,** 613, 625, 635
s 5(j) **104,** 534
Admiralty Act 1973 **90,** 559
s 4 **90,** 558
s 5 **90,** 558, 560
Admiralty Rules 1975, Rule 11(7) **90,** 560
Air Navigation Act 1931 (Paris Convention on Aerial Navigation (1919)) **120,** 563, 569
'enabling' effect **120,** 563-4
Aliens Act 1948
s 14 **68,** 164, 168
s 15 **68,** 164-5
applicability, Cook Islands **104,** 502-7
Arbitration Act 1908 **118,** 627
s 5 **118,** 629, 630
Arbitration (Foreign Agreements and Awards) Act 1982, s 4 **118,** 629
Arbitration (International Investment Disputes) Act 1979 **118,** 626-7
s 8 **118,** 629-30
s 37 **118,** 627
s 62 **118,** 627
Aviation Crimes Act 1972 **120,** 566
Bill of Rights 1990
s 18 **104,** 603-4
s 23(4) **108,** 627
s 25(d) **104,** 582, **108,** 627
British Nationality and Status of Aliens (in New Zealand) Act 1923, s 14 **79,** 686, 691-4
British Nationality and Status of Aliens (in New Zealand) Act 1928
purpose **79,** 687
s 3 **79,** 687, 692
s 6 **79,** 688-9
s 7 **79,** 686-94
Schedule 1 **79,** 688
Carriage by Air Act 1967 (Warsaw Convention) **120,** 566
Citizenship Act 1977, s 13 **79,** 685
Citizenship (Western Samoa) Act 1982 **79,** 694
Civil Aviation Act 1948 (Chicago Convention (1944)) **120,** 563, 569
scope **120,** 564
Civil Aviation Act 1964 **120,** 563, 569
Civil Aviation Act 1990 **120,** 563
'giving effect to Chicago Convention', whether **120,** 566-7
s 4(2A) (flight over high seas) **120,** 566
s 14(2)(a) (administration of participation in international aviation conventions) **120,** 566-7
s 28 (power to make rules for implementation of obligations under Chicago Convention) **120,** 567
s 33(1)(a) (consistency of aviation rules with ICAO standards 'to extent adopted') **120,** 567
s 36(1)(a) (power to incorporate international texts into New Zealand law) **120,** 567
'to ensure compliance with obligations under international aviation agreements' **120,** 566

New Zealand (*cont.*)
Civil Aviation (Investigation of Accidents) Regulations 1953, Annex 13 of the Chicago Convention (1944) **120,** 569
Civil Aviation (Investigation of Accidents) Regulations 1978
Annex 13 of the Chicago Convention (1944) **120,** 569-70
s 23 (accidents in New Zealand to foreign aircraft) **120,** 569
s 24 (accidents to New Zealand aircraft outside New Zealand) **120,** 570
Civil Aviation Regulations 1953 **120,** 563
21A (flight over high seas) **120,** 565
implementation of Chicago Convention and **120,** 564-5
Civil Aviation Rules **120,** 563
Civil Procedure Code
Rule 48(b)(iii) **64,** 541-2, 564
Rule 49 **64,** 541-2, 564-5
Commerce Act 1986
object and purpose **118,** 636-7
s 27 **118,** 623-4, 628-40
s 54 **104,** 600
s 111(b) **118,** 623
Commissions of Inquiry Act 1908 **104,** 533
applicability in Cook Islands **104,** 502-7
s 4C **104,** 502-7, 534, 553, 575-6, 598
s 4D **104,** 534, 553, 598-9, **108,** 624-5
s 6 (immunities of witnesses) **104,** 534, 553, 560, 581, 588, 599, 607, **108,** 624, 630
s 9 **104,** 506-7, 553, 559-61, 588, 607, 610
s 9(1) ('without sufficient cause') **104,** 543, **108,** 625, 630
s 9(2)(b) **104,** 599
s 13A **104,** 534, 554, 559-61, 583-4, 588, **108,** 630
s 13A(1)(b) ('any just excuse') **104,** 534, 539, 543, 610
s 13B **104,** 534
s 13C **104,** 534
Commissions of Inquiry Amendment Act 1995 **104,** 534
Conservation Act 1987 **90,** 570, 574-5, 577
'principles of the Treaty of Waitangi' **120,** 541
Constitution Act 1852 **45,** 5, 7-11, 14-16, **88,** 271, 272
Constitution Amendment Act 1947 **45,** 7-9, 14-15
Constitution Amendment Act 1970 **88,** 272
Constitution Amendment Act 1973 **88,** 272
Consular Privileges and Immunities Act 1971 **68,** 176-80
Continental Shelf Act 1964 **43,** 113
Cook Islands Act 1915 **79,** 690
ss 340-7 (extradition) **104,** 542
Crimes Act 1961 **45,** 5-7, 11-18, **74,** 244, 248
s 352(1) ('just excuse') **104,** 539, 560, 561, 600
Customs Act 1913 **78,** 597, 611
s 47 **78,** 621
s 251 **78,** 611, 621, 622, 623
s 252 **78,** 611
s 253 **78,** 611
s 254 **78,** 623
s 255 **78,** 622
s 259 **78,** 622

s 262 **78,** 622
s 264 **78,** 622
Customs Act 1966 **78,** 597, 612-13
s 272 **78,** 623
s 273 **78,** 624
s 274 **78,** 622, 623, 626
s 275 **78,** 622
s 277 **78,** 623
s 278 **78,** 622
s 282 **78,** 622
s 283 **78,** 622
s 286 **78,** 622
s 287 **78,** 622
Diplomatic Privileges and Immunities Act 1968, s 22 **80,** 5
Diplomatic Privileges and Immunities (ICAO) Order 1959 **120,** 563, 566
District Courts Act 1947 **104,** 600
Employment Contracts Act 1991
extraterritorial effect **104,** 524-5
s 3(1) **104,** 519
s 3(2) **104,** 519
State immunity, effect on **104,** 519, 524-5
Evidence Act 1908
s 4 (self-incrimination) **104,** 582
s 481 (prohibition of disclosure to foreign authorities) **104,** 507, 557
Evidence Amendment Act (No 2) 1980 **104,** 539
Extradition Act 1965 **88,** 276
Fugitive Offenders Act (UK) 1881, applicability **88,** 270-6
Fugitive Offenders Amendment Act 1976 **77,** 332, **88,** 276
Historic Articles Act 1962 **78,** 594-636
forfeiture under **78,** 594-639
penal law, whether **78,** 601-2, 627-30
public law, whether **78,** 603-7, 630
revenue law, whether **78,** 602-3, 627
s 5 **78,** 594, 596-636
s 12 **78,** 595, 596-636
Immigration Act 1964 **68,** 171-3, **74,** 252, 254, 268, **85,** 205-6, 209-16
s 14(5) **79,** 686
s 20 **117,** 644-9
s 20(1)(b) **117,** 642
Immigration Act 1987 **101,** 457, 464
Immigration Amendment Act 1991 **101,** 458
Income Tax Act 1976, s 293(2) **104,** 572-3
International Air Services Licensing Act 1931 **120,** 563, 566
Judicature Act 1908
s 56 **104,** 560, 600, **108,** 625
s 61A **120,** 480
s 64 **120,** 476
Judicature Amendment Act 1972, s 8 **120,** 469, 470, 473-4, 480, 514
Legal Services Act 1991 **115,** 665-71
s 19(1) **124,** 572-6
s 19(1)(e)(5) **124,** 573-6
s 19(1)(j) **124,** 573-4
Legislative Council Abolition Act 1950 **88,** 272

New Zealand (*cont.*)
Maori Antiquities Act 1908, s 6(3) **78,** 620
Maori Community Development Act 1962
s 17 **120,** 465 n. 11
s 18 **120,** 470
Maritime Transport Act 1994
conformity with international law **120,** 599-605
failure to make international law binding on Maritime Safety Authority **120,** 600
as implementation of maritime conventions **120,** 595
'pleasure ship', whether including foreign ships **120,** 602-5
s 2(1) **120,** 603
s 5 **120,** 600, 601
ss 6-16 **120,** 603
s 19 **120,** 603
s 20 **120,** 603
s 21(1) **120,** 588, 589-91, 601-5
ss 23-6 **120,** 603
s 28 **120,** 603
s 29 **120,** 603
ss 31-3 **120,** 603
s 32 **120,** 602
s 55 **120,** 603
s 172 **120,** 602, 603
s 192(1) **120,** 603
s 397 **120,** 603
s 461 **120,** 603
New Zealand (Appeals to the Privy Council) Order 1910
Rule 2(a) **117,** 637-8
Rule 2(b) **117,** 638-40
Official Information Act 1987 **90,** 569
Privacy Act 1993
s 21(1)(b) **117,** 643
s 27(1)(c) **117,** 643
s 29(1)(f) **117,** 643
Radiocommunications Act 1989 **120,** 563
Reciprocal Enforcement of Judgments Act 1934 **90,** 559
Royal Titles Act 1974 **88,** 272
Samoa Act 1921 **79,** 690
State-Owned Enterprises Act 1986 (SOEA). *See* State-Owned Enterprises Act 1986 (SOEA) *below*
Statute of Westminster Adoption Act 1931 **88,** 271
Statute of Westminster Adoption Act 1947 **88,** 272
Summary Proceedings Act 1957
Annex 13 of the Chicago Convention (1944) and **120,** 573-6
public interest privilege and **120,** 576-7
s 38 **104,** 600
s 39 **104,** 560, 600
s 198 (search warrants) **120,** 554, 573-6
Takeovers Act 1993, s 44 **104,** 600
Transport Accident Investigation Commission (TAIC) Act 1990
public interest privilege and **120,** 576-7
s 4 (purpose of Commission) **120,** 571

s 14(2) (participation of foreign organizations in investigation) **120,** 571
s 14(3) (investigation by persons other than the Commission) **120,** 571-2
Treaty of Waitangi Act 1975. *See* Treaty of Waitangi Act 1975 *below*
Undesirable Immigrants Exclusion Act 1919 **85,** 205, 212, 214
War Pensions Act 1954, discriminatory, whether **118,** 231, 234-5
Wildlife Act 1953 **90,** 569, 570-4, 577-8
Wildlife Regulations 1955 **90,** 573-4
League of Nations resolutions and **79,** 694
legal aid
Judicial Committee of the Privy Council **124,** 563-4
territorial limitation **124,** 575-6
UNHRC, obligation to provide **115,** 664-71, **124,** 571-7
legislation
enforceability
by English courts **78,** 597-607, 614-20, 627-30
extraterritoriality **78,** 614
implementation
treaty, conflict with **90,** 572, 578
treaty, obligation to take into account **117,** 647-9
legislation, interpretation
Acts Interpretation Act 1924 **88,** 272
aids
League of Nations resolutions **79,** 694
legislative history **120,** 485-6
structure of legislation **104,** 555
guidelines
effectiveness **88,** 272-3
'forever speaking' principle **88,** 275
intention of legislature **104,** 524, 589
later legislation, precedence **90,** 577
object and purpose **104,** 555
ordinary and natural meaning **104,** 589
plain language **104,** 555
plain meaning **79,** 693
restrictive, penal statutes **88,** 272
phrases
'bird' **90,** 572
'British possession' **79,** 688
'in His Majesty's dominions' **79,** 691, 692
'in the same manner in all respects . . . for all purposes as part of New Zealand' **79,** 691, 692-4
'interest of the State enterprise' **120,** 507
'just excuse' **104,** 539, 543, 559-61, 562, 587-8, 599-600
'natural-born British subjects' **79,** 689
'officer of an international or foreign company' **104,** 555-6
'principles of the Treaty of Waitangi' **120,** 487-93, 494, 500-2, 511-13, 521-2, 525-6, 531-3, 541-50
'privileges and immunities' **104,** 560, 588
'proceedings in respect of any matter to which the proceedings pursuant to the Convention relate' **118,** 630-1
'purposive' **78,** 613, **79,** 625-6
'reasonable excuse' **104,** 588, 600
'sufficient cause' **104,** 543, 559-61, 562, 587-8, 600

New Zealand (*cont.*)
United Kingdom Interpretation Act 1889 **79,** 688
'within His Majesty's allegiance' **79,** 692
presumption of conformity with international human rights law **101,** 458-65
presumption of conformity with international law
in case of apparent conflict **120,** 601-5
implementation in accordance with subsequent changes in **120,** 603-4
law of the sea **120,** 599-605
vagueness of international law, relevance **120,** 573
presumption of conformity with international obligations **104,** 513, 517, **115,** 662-3, **120,** 572-3
presumption of conformity with treaty obligations **90,** 578, **117,** 639-40
Treaty of Waitangi (1840) **120,** 482
presumption of State immunity **104,** 524-5, 619
customary international law **120,** 572-3
presumption of territorial limitation **104,** 524-5, 540-1, 555
non-applicability to aliens for acts abroad **104,** 555
recognition, by English courts **78,** 615-16, 627
responsibility
courts **120,** 484
English courts **78,** 595, 609, 631
executive **120,** 484
treaty as aid **85,** 214, **90,** 578-9, **115,** 663
legislation, retroactive, Treaty of Waitangi Act 1975 **120,** 487
legitimate expectation, treaty, right of individual under ratified but unincorporated treaty **117,** 640
Lima Declaration on Guidelines on Auditing Precepts (1977) **104,** 575
Mandate territory
declaration *re* continuance of **37,** 220, 320, 325, 330, 336
status **79,** 690-4
Maori Council. *See also* Waitangi Tribunal *below*
functions **120,** 465 n. 11, 535
State-Owned Enterprises Act 1986, consultation on implementation **120,** 492-3, 495, 513
standing to represent interests of persons protected under Treaty of Waitangi **120,** 470, 535
national heritage, protection of **78,** 607
nationality **79,** 685-94
Cook Islands **79,** 685-94
natural-born British **79,** 691, 693
Mandate territory **79,** 690-4
natural-born **79,** 689-94
Western Samoans **79,** 685-94
natural-born British, whether **79,** 689-94
natural justice, judicial review remedying possible defects **117,** 645
natural resources. *See* Endangered Species of Wild Fauna and Flora, Convention on International Trade in (CITES) (1973) *above*
naturalization, residence requirement **79,** 691, 693
participation agreements
dispute settlement clause **118,** 625-6, 631-4
'dispute under the agreement', effect of subsequent legislation, whether **118,** 631-4
subsequent legislation, effect **118,** 623-4, 631-9

unfair competition and **118,** 622-36
precedent in municipal courts, *stare decisis* doctrine, international law and **64,** 549-50
prisoners of war
compensation for unlawful treatment, Peace Treaty with Japan (1951) **118,** 233
disability pension rights **118,** 233, 234-5
private international law
applicable law and **104,** 554
foreign State compulsion **104,** 562, 601
public interest privilege
class/representative action **120,** 576-7
investigation of air accidents and **120,** 576-7
public policy, State immunity, jurisdiction **104,** 606-7, 611, 620, 622, 624-5
recognition, government **80,** 2-10
recognition, State, responsibility, executive **104,** 568
Refugee Status Appeals Authority **114,** 573-5
judicial review **114,** 583-6
refugees
'internal flight' possibility, relevance **114,** 577-80, 582-3
international obligations in respect of family, relevance **114,** 582, **117,** 628-35
judicial review by non-statutory body **114,** 583-6
judicial review grounds
error of law **114,** 579-80, 581-3
unreasonableness **114,** 579, 581-3
'membership of a particular social group', homosexuals **124,** 486, 488
protection, State's ability to undertake, relevance, relocation and **114,** 581-3
status, burden of proof **114,** 577
remedies
declaration of entitlement to export licences **90,** 579-80
employment contract, law of sending State **104,** 525
service of process out of the jurisdiction
balance of convenience **64,** 541, 562-6
foreign State or State agency **64,** 540, 562-6
ships, State-owned
commercial activity, effect on immunity **64,** 553-60
immunity, jurisdiction
cargo **64,** 555-61
in rem action **64,** 552-61
ownership, possession or control as test of status **64,** 555-60
South Rhodesian officials, recognition of acts of **48,** 33-40
sovereign status **45,** 9
State agency/State-owned corporation/State entity, classification, Government Auditor **104,** 574-6, 605
State immunity, execution/attachment, purpose/use of funds/assets, property in hands of State bailee **104,** 569
State immunity, jurisdiction, applicability
disclosure of documents
confidentiality of financial information **104,** 556-7
proportionality **104,** 580, 621-2
tax haven **104,** 536-40, 556-8, 606, 611-25
evidence, giving of, judicial discretion **104,** 539, 561, 586
immovable/real property, disputes relating to **104,** 612
property, dispute relating to **104,** 575, 612, 621

New Zealand (*cont.*)
transactions involving industrial or intellectual property **104,** 612
State immunity, jurisdiction, classification of act
act contrary to fundamental principle of justice **104,** 577, 623
employment contract **104,** 519-24
government audit **104,** 575-6
guarantee of charter **90,** 564, 565-6
nature or purpose of transaction as determining factor **104,** 614-16
mixed, dominant element **90,** 566
private person test **104,** 612-13
profit, relevance **104,** 615
promissory note dealings **104,** 537-8
repair to commercial vessel **64,** 545, 565-6
sale of, tax credits **104,** 538-40, 569-74, 605-7, 614-16
tort
European Convention on State Immunity (and Protocol) (Basle) (1972) **104,** 577
ILC Draft Articles on State immunity (1991) **104,** 577
Letelier **104,** 577-8
State practice **104,** 577
violation of international law **104,** 578
'iniquity factor' **104,** 539-40, 606-7
State immunity, jurisdiction, entitlement, State agency/State-owned corporation/State entity, Government Auditor **104,** 574-6, 605
State immunity, jurisdiction, procedural aspects
effective remedy, right to and, diplomatic channels as **104,** 580, 622
entitlement to raise, private parties **104,** 621
in personam actions **64,** 565-6, **104,** 621
responsibility for determining, executive decision as alternative **104,** 580
State immunity, jurisdiction, theory/doctrine
acta jure imperii, acta jure gestionis distinguished **104,** 537, 570-1
basis
comity **104,** 517, 557, 570, 576, 586, 616, 624
dignity of foreign State **104,** 510, 616, 623
dignity of sovereign **90,** 564, 565
equality of States **104,** 516, 570, 616
foreign relations considerations **104,** 570, 612, 623
good faith **104,** 624
independence of State **104,** 510, 570, 616, 623
international law **104,** 517, 576
international order **104,** 616, 624
public policy **104,** 516, 576
reciprocity **104,** 570, 616
sovereignty **104,** 509, 557, 586, 623
State personality **104,** 576
common law **104,** 510, 514, 520-2, 524-5
general principle of international law **104,** 516, 517-18, 570, 616-17
international law, flexibility **104,** 611
legislation
desirability **64,** 550-1
divergence **104,** 517-18
public order/public policy/*ordre public* considerations **64,** 105, **65,** 139, **88,** 711, **104,** 516, 576, 606-7, 611, 620, 622
restrictive **104,** 611-16

development of **104,** 517
I° Congreso del Partido **104,** 510, 520
Littrell **104,** 510
Sengupta **104,** 521
restrictive theory **90,** 562-4, 566
State practice
employment contract **104,** 523-4
statutory provision, limitation as precedent **104,** 517-18
territorial jurisdiction/sovereignty and **104,** 570, 576, 577, 612, 617-19
State immunity, jurisdiction, waiver, defence as **90,** 561
State immunity, taxation **104,** 538, 571-4, 605, 615
State-Owned Enterprises Act 1986 (SOEA)
18 December 1986, significance **120,** 472, 473-4, 483, 548-50
implementation, consultation with Maori Council, recommendation for **120,** 492, 495, 513
interpretation, *travaux préparatoires* **120,** 485-6
legislative history, inadequacy of scrutiny **120,** 486
long title **120,** 463 n. 6, 477, 504
as preservation of right of remedy against past breaches of Treaty of Waitangi (1840) **120,** 522
'principles of the Treaty of Waitangi', primacy **120,** 494, 512-13, 531-3
recommendations of Waitangi Tribunal and **120,** 487
s 4 (State-owned enterprise objectives) **120,** 474, 504
s 6 (Ministers' responsibilities to House of Representatives) **120,** 504
s 7 (agreements with Crown in respect of non-commercial activities) **120,** 504
s 8 (industrial relations) **120,** 504
s 9 (Treaty of Waitangi)
as added protection against s 27(2) risks **120,** 483-7
application to Crown land **120,** 484
burden of establishing considerations in regard to particular issues **120,** 475
as constitutional guarantee **120,** 485, 541
Crown acting reasonably and in good faith **120,** 491
as principle operating in conjunction with s 27 **120,** 474, 484, 504, 507-8, 525, 530-1, 547-50
'principles of the Treaty of Waitangi' **120,** 487-93, 494, 512-13, 518-19, 521-2, 541-50
as response to Waitangi Tribunal's comments, **120,** 480, 497-8
safeguard machinery, need for **120,** 492-3, 513, 550
screening process, Crown's obligation **120,** 474-5, 496, 512, 525-6, 534
text **120,** 464 n. 8, 470, 482, 527
transfers of land inconsistent with, examples **120,** 480-1, 502-4, 515-17, 548-50
s 23 (transfer of Crown assets to State enterprises) **120,** 496
text **120,** 464 n. 7, 477-8, 536
s 23(1) (effect of other legal provisions on Crown's freedom of action) **120,** 505, 506-7, 513-14, 517, 527
discretion, limitations on **120,** 506, 512-13, 526
s 23(4) (effect of other legal provisions) **120,** 517
s 23(10) (transfer of leasehold interests administered by Minister of Forests) **120,** 496, 517
s 27 (Maori land claims)
as response to Waitangi Tribunal's comments **120,** 480, 497-8
as specific provision for application of general principle in s 9 **120,** 484, 506-8, 547-50

New Zealand (*cont.*)
text **120,** 464 n. 9, 470-1, 482-3, 517-18, 527-8, 538-9
s 27(1) (land subject to pre-1986 Waitangi Tribunal claim) **120,** 472, 473-4, 486, 492, 507-8, 524-5, 548
s 27(2) (Crown's right to resume ownership in light of Waitangi Tribunal's findings) **120,** 472-3, 486-7, 492, 507-8, 524, 525-6, 533-4, 548
s 27(3)(b) (compensation), 'interest of the State enterprise' **120,** 507-8
s 29(1) (definitions) **120,** 528
s 29(3) (effect of other legal provisions on Crown's freedom of action) **120,** 474, 525-6, 528
text **120,** 471
statutory power to transfer land, interim relief **120,** 469-76, 480, 493, 496
status **88,** 273-4
'British possession' **88,** 274
independence, evidence of, participation in Vietnam War **88,** 272
'part of Her Majesty's Dominions' **88,** 271, 273-4
self-governing colony **88,** 271
stay of proceedings
arbitration proceedings, statutory provisions, variations **118,** 629
discretion **118,** 631, 634-7
ICSID reference **118,** 621-40
requirements **118,** 629-31
taxation, judicial assistance
customary international law **104,** 579
good faith **104,** 580
territorial sovereignty, violation **74,** 249, 258, 262, 266-7
territory
Cook Islands **79,** 685-94
Western Samoa **79,** 685-94
terrorist acts **74,** 250-6
punishment **74,** 254-6
treaties
authoritative text, as contained in legislation **120,** 518, 523, 543
conclusion, executive act **85,** 211
continuity **80,** 5
good faith, Treaty of Waitangi (1840) **120,** 501-2, 508-9, 510-11, 513, 534
implementing legislation, need for **85,** 211, **120,** 563
Treaty of Waitangi (1840) **120,** 482, 495, 500, 520-1, 546-7
incorporation into municipal law **80,** 5
legislation, interpretation and **90,** 578-9
need for **85,** 205
municipal law and, conflict **90,** 572
operation and enforcement **90,** 572
ratification, legislation, interpretation and **90,** 578
unincorporated, evidence of international law **104,** 579
treaty interpretation
aids, opinions of Waitangi Tribunal **120,** 478, 488-9, 523, 541, 543-5
guidelines
parties' intention, at time of conclusion **120,** 499
spirit and purpose **120,** 544-5
multilingual, discrepancy between texts **120,** 489-90, 499-502, 519-20, 543-6
Treaty of Waitangi (1840)
as Bill of Rights **120,** 482

breach **120,** 472
duty to remedy **120,** 491, 494, 522
established complaints of **120,** 534
conclusion **120,** 498, 545-6
implementing legislation, need for **120,** 482, 495, 500, 520-1, 546-7
interpretation
effectiveness principle **120,** 482
in light of subsequent developments **120,** 482
parties' intention, at time of conclusion **120,** 499
spirit and purpose **120,** 544-5
Waitangi Tribunal's authority **120,** 478, 523, 541, 543-5
object and purpose **120,** 509
principles
duty to consult **120,** 492, 495, 500, 511
duty to remedy breaches **120,** 491, 525-6
literal text distinguished **120,** 489-90
primacy in interpretation of legislation **120,** 487-93, 494-5, 512-13, 518-19
protection of property of Maori **120,** 521-2
relationship between parties
fiduciary **120,** 491, 494, 532
guarantee of protection **120,** 501-2, 509-10, 532-3
obligation to act reasonably and in good faith **120,** 501, 508-9, 510-11, 513, 534
partnership **120,** 490-1, 511, 532, 534
solemn compact **120,** 501, 509
representation of persons protected under, Maori Council **120,** 470
text
authoritative nature of texts scheduled to Treaty of Waitangi Act 1975 **120,** 518, 523, 543
English 'reconstruction of the literal translation' **120,** 489-90
English version as scheduled to Treaty of Waitangi Act 1975 **120,** 519-20, 529, 541-2
Maori and English versions, discrepancy **120,** 489-90, 499-502, 519-20, 543-6
Maori version as scheduled to Treaty of Waitangi Act 1975 **120,** 542-3
treaty, whether **120,** 499
Treaty of Waitangi Act 1975
Crown dealings, extension to **120,** 512
description of Act **120,** 463 n. 5
interpretation, aids, opinions of Waitangi Tribunal **120,** 488-9
long title **120,** 497, 522-3, 536
preamble **120,** 499, 522-3
retrospective effect **120,** 487
s 4 **120,** 523
s 6 **120,** 472, 474, 497, 523, 524, 539-40
s 6(1) **120,** 472
s 6(3) **120,** 497, 514, 540
s 6(4) **120,** 497, 540
s 8 **120,** 497
Waitangi Tribunal. *See* Waitangi Tribunal *below*
Treaty of Waitangi Amendment Act 1985, s 3 **120,** 539
Treaty of Waitangi (Fisheries Claims) Act 1992, violation of International Covenant on Civil and Political Rights (1966), whether **124,** 571
UNHRC

New Zealand (*cont.*)
'administrative tribunal or judicial authority', whether **115,** 657, 660-5
legal aid, obligation to provide **115,** 664-71, **124,** 571-7
Vienna Convention on Privileges and Immunities (1961), incorporation into municipal law **80,** 5
Waitangi Tribunal. *See also* Maori Council *and* Treaty of Waitangi Act 1975 *above*
establishment **120,** 478, 497
functions **120,** 497, 523, 526-7, 539-41
interpretation of Treaty of Waitangi (1840) and **120,** 478, 488-9, 523, 541, 543-4
recommendations
Crown's right not to act on **120,** 478, 512, 524
s 9 of State-Owned Enterprises Act 1986 and **120,** 487
scope **120,** 478
State-Owned Enterprises Bill, comments on **120,** 478-80
status **120,** 478
Western Samoa **79,** 685-94
Newfoundland. *See* Canada, Newfoundland
news agency. *See* press agency
Nicaragua
Banco Central de Nicaragua **63,** 585-9
structure and functions **63,** 590-1
confiscatory legislation **79,** 573-81
ICJ, acceptance of compulsory jurisdiction **84,** 231, 236-7
law of
Decree No 3/1979 (Somoza assets) **79,** 574, 579-80, **92,** 472
Decree No 10/1979 (Law of National Emergency) **79,** 574, 579-80, **92,** 473
Decree No 38/1979 (Clarification of Decree No 3) **79,** 575
Decree No 172/1979 (Suspension of the Application of Decree No 38) **79,** 575, **92,** 473 n. 4
Decree No 282/1980 (Judicial Status of Persons whose Assets have been Intervened) **79,** 575-6, 579-80, **92,** 473 n. 4
Decree No 422/1980 (Confiscation of Assets) **79,** 576, 580, **92,** 473 n. 4
OAS, Consultation of Ministers of Foreign Affairs **76,** 465-6, 520, 718
Niger, France, Judicial Agreements with **44,** 291-2
Nigeria
Biafra
Biafran forces, status **52,** 495-6
civil war, diplomatic premises, effect on **52,** 383
judicial proceedings in rebel territories **70,** 18-34
lawful government, policy of **70,** 21, 31-3
judiciary in rebel territories, position of **70,** 21, 30-2
secession from, diplomatic premises, effect on **52,** 383
Central Bank **63,** 63-6, 140-5, 150, 155, 391-408, 460-6, 553-68, 574-83
as department of government/State **64,** 134, 136-9, 146-9, 222
functions **63,** 150, **64,** 116-19, 134, 147-8
restrictions on private banking activities **64,** 119
as separate legal entity **64,** 134, 222
as State agency **63,** 65, 150-1, **64,** 115-19
Constitution 1963, nationality **103,** 283, 284
Constitution 1979
deportation **103,** 280
s 6 (jurisdiction) **103,** 281
s 7 (nationality) **103,** 283

s 12 **86,** 678
s 33 (fair hearing) **103,** 296-7
s 38 (deportation) **103,** 280, 288, 291
s 42 **103,** 281, 282, 296-7
Constitution, amendments, validity **90,** 494-6
damages
exemplary **103,** 294-5
for passport, improper withdrawal **103,** 291-5
deportation
criminal law, punishment, whether **103,** 292
nationality and **103,** 282, 288, 297
diplomatic immunity, jurisdiction
State immunity and **103,** 310
distinction **103,** 309
dual nationality, avoidance **103,** 284-8
estoppel, State immunity, jurisdiction **103,** 309
expert, evidence, foreign law **103,** 285-7
fishing dispute, capture and sinking of French ship **48,** 469-75
foreign law, evidence of
books **103,** 285-7
expert **103,** 285-7
freedom of movement, passport, entitlement **103,** 290-1
general principles of international law, State immunity, restrictive theory **103,** 303-11
human rights, exceptions, legitimate authority, need for **103,** 290
international organizations. *See also* international organizations, immunity, jurisdiction *and* international organizations, privileges and immunities *below*
African Reinsurance Corporation **86,** 656-9
headquarters agreement **86,** 659-60
self-executing, whether **86,** 659-60
waiver of immunity, whether **86,** 659, 661
personality **86,** 686-9
international organizations, immunity, jurisdiction **107,** 179-82
waiver **86,** 661-7, 668, 673, 676-90
board of directors, by **86,** 690
conditional appearance **86,** 666, 683, 687
counterclaim **86,** 661, 685
customary international law, burden of proof **86,** 666
customary international law, counterclaim **86,** 666
estoppel compared **86,** 681
headquarters agreement, signature as **86,** 659, 661
intention, need for **107,** 182
presumption against **107,** 181
requirements, express **86,** 673, 679
requirements, Head of State agreement **86,** 668
submission to the jurisdiction **86,** 668
timeliness **86,** 677-8, 687-8
international organizations, privileges and immunities
commercial transaction **86,** 664, 673-9
employment contract **86,** 656-9, 690
State immunity compared **86,** 687
law of
Central Bank of Nigeria Act 1958/1962/1969 **64,** 116-18, 147-8

Nigeria (*cont.*)
Constitution. *See* Constitution *above*
Diplomatic Immunities and Privileges Act 1962, s 18 **107,** 181
Diplomatic Privileges (African Reinsurance Corporation) Order 1985 **86,** 603, 665, 667, 672, 684, 688
Diplomatic Privileges and Immunities Act 1967 **86,** 661-2, 664-5, 666, 667, 669-75, 676, 677, 680, 683-5, 688
Evidence Law
s 56 (foreign law) **103,** 285
s 112 (foreign law) **103,** 285
Fundamental Rights Enforcement Procedure Rules 1979 **103,** 280
time-limits **103,** 287
Immigration Act 1963
s 12 **103,** 288
s 18(3) **103,** 288
Lagos State (Civil Procedure) Rules **86,** 657, 681
sedition **70,** 216-17
Tribunals of Inquiry Act 1966, validity **103,** 295-6, 298
legislation, constitutionality **103,** 295-7, 298
measure of damages/compensation including valuation of company/property/assets, good faith, relevance **103,** 291-3
nationality
deportation and **103,** 282, 288, 297
forfeiture **103,** 284-8
native title, radical and beneficial native titles distinguished, *Amodu Tijani* **112,** 497-8, **125,** 332
necessity **90,** 494-6
passport
entitlement, freedom of movement **103,** 290-1
evidence of nationality **103,** 289
remedies
apology **103,** 294-5
declaration
nationality **103,** 282
return of passport **103,** 291
separation of powers, human rights and **103,** 280-1
State immunity, jurisdiction, classification of act
diplomatic premises, construction contract **103,** 310
nature or purpose of transaction as determining factor **103,** 310
State immunity, jurisdiction, procedural aspects, estoppel and **103,** 309
State immunity, jurisdiction, theory/doctrine
basis
dignity of foreign State **103,** 310
independence of State **103,** 310
general principle of international law **103,** 303-11
State responsibility for acts and omissions of diplomatic agent **103,** 310
territorial sea **48,** 469, 472, 474
treaties
implementing legislation, need for **86,** 678-9
third parties, enforcement by **86,** 679
nobile officium **56,** 513, 517, **122,** 622
non bis in idem. *See* double jeopardy/*non bis in idem*

non liquet **37,** 459, **41,** 148, **76,** 571, **80,** 308, 347, **106,** 721, **110,** 211-13, 216, 219-22, 225-6, 229-31, 232-5, 328-9, 339-40, 385-6, 507-31, 532, 533, 539-41, **111,** 345
non-aligned countries, Conferences
declarations **49,** 64
resolutions on self-determination **46,** 485
non-governmental organization (NGO)
advisory opinion, pressure to request **110,** 285-6
officials, ILO Administrative Tribunal and **38,** 380
personality **77,** 623
non-intervention. *See* intervention in affairs of another State
Non-Proliferation Treaty (1968). *See* nuclear weapons, deployment, Non-Proliferation Treaty (1968)
non-self-governing territory
Administering Power
exclusive authority, whether **105,** 244-5, 263-5, 276-7, 329-30, 413
physical control, relevance **105,** 320-1, 418
renunciation of role **105,** 413-14
right of representation **105,** 322-3, 417
status
defined by UN Charter **105,** 410
demise **105,** 257-9, 277, 319-34
consultation **105,** 363, 381, 416
UN as medium **105,** 279
continental shelf
coastal power, Administering Power **105,** 251-4
title **105,** 251-4, 344-5
independence, grant of, powers of UN General Assembly **49,** 273
international law concerning **49,** 5, 21
natural resources, entitlement
duty to protect **105,** 294
general principle of international law **105,** 294
sovereignty **105,** 410-14
status
determined by UN **105,** 413, 417
ICJ and **105,** 276-9
territorial integrity **105,** 381
treaties, opposability after independence **105,** 418
treaty-making power **105,** 246, 263-5, 319, 344-5, 416-17
UN competence **105,** 322, 326-30, 413, 417
norms, legal and cultural **37,** 446
North American Free Trade Agreement (NAFTA) (1992). *See* NAFTA (North American Free Trade Agreement) (1992); NAFTA (North American Free Trade Agreement) (1992), Arbitral Tribunal
North Atlantic Treaty Organization. *See* NATO
North Pacific Fur Seal Convention **41,** 103
North-East Atlantic Fisheries Convention (1959). *See* fisheries, North-East Atlantic Fisheries Convention (1959)
Northeast Channel **71,** 86, 89, 101-4, 108, 111, 114-15, 143, 146, 170, **83,** 102
northern Cyprus. *See* Cyprus, Turkish Federated State; Cyprus, Turkish Republic of Northern Cyprus (TRNC)
Northern Ireland
administration of justice
arrest in **58,** 231

Northern Ireland (*cont.*)
Diplock courts **79,** 479, 481, 482
fairness **79,** 79, 80-1, 481-2
Anglo-Irish Agreement (1985)
direct rule, relevance to **87,** 357-8
interim nature **87,** 354
judicial review **87,** 330-3
legal consequences **87,** 352, 353
registration **87,** 347
Republic of Ireland and **87,** 332-3
Constitution, compatibility with **87,** 337
right of consultation **87,** 331-2
sovereignty **87,** 356
termination, absence of provision for **87,** 354
text **87,** 338-44
treaty status **87,** 333, 346
Anglo-Irish Intergovernmental Conference
international nature **87,** 333
UK law, contravention of, whether **87,** 333
armed conflict, existence of **79,** 97, 480-1, 525-6
citizen of Great Britain, equality of treatment **87,** 331-2
conditions in **79,** 524
evidence of **79,** 77-9
constitutional position **67,** 403-4
counselling and procuring, common law offence **79,** 95
courts, municipal. *See* Diplock courts *below*
definition **87,** 351
degrading treatment in **58,** 265-71, 304, 316, 360
detention in **58,** 214, 222-3, 226
Diplock courts **79,** 479, 481, 482
discrimination, terrorists and **58,** 285-8, 332
emergency powers **79,** 77-8
emergency situation in **58,** 208-30
European Convention on Human Rights (1950), derogation **58,** 230, 234, 237, 277-85
extradition from **71,** 530-4
fisheries jurisdiction **59,** 346-7, 350, 355
homosexuality, law on **67,** 401, 439
enforcement **67,** 407-8
public opinion **67,** 405-7, 415, 422, 435
purpose **67,** 412
reform **67,** 439
proposals **67,** 404-7
UK law compared **67,** 410-13, 415, 435-6
inhuman treatment in **58,** 320-3, 333
internment **58,** 213-19, 233-6
interrogation in
degrading treatment, whether **58,** 265-71, 304, 316, 324-6, 360
five techniques **58,** 249-56, 265-6, 298, 317-20
inhuman treatment, whether **58,** 320-3, 333
torture, whether **58,** 265-7, 317-29, 333-4
law of

Backing of Warrants (Republic of Ireland) Act 1965 **71,** 530-3
Criminal Jurisdiction Act 1975
s 6(2) **79,** 94
s 6(3) **79,** 94
s 11 **79,** 94
Criminal Law Act Northern Ireland 1967 **79,** 81
counselling and procuring **79,** 94
extraterritorial offences **79,** 94
Emergency Provisions Act. *See* Northern Ireland (Emergency Provisions) Act 1973 *below*
Fisheries Act 1966 **59,** 346-8
Fisheries Limits Act 1964 **59,** 350
Northern Ireland Constitution Act 1973, s 12 **87,** 332-3
Northern Ireland (Emergency Provisions) Act 1973 **58,** 236-8, **79,** 479, 482, 524
s 6 **79,** 80
Northern Ireland (Emergency Provisions) Act 1978 **79,** 77, 79, 479, 482
s 8 **79,** 80
s 11 **79,** 81
Northern Ireland (Miscellaneous Provisions) Act 1932 **59,** 354
Prevention of Terrorism Act 1974 **79,** 525
Special Powers Act 1971 **58,** 230-4, **79,** 524
legislation, competence **59,** 346-8, 360-2
fisheries **59,** 346-8
liberty, extrajudicial deprivation of **58,** 230-8, 274-7
minority, rights of, Republic of Ireland and **87,** 356-7
political offences, classification as, membership of proscribed organization **79,** 97
prerogative power **87,** 332-3
Provisional IRA, organization of **79,** 478, 497
relevance to finding of political offence **79,** 478, 481
territorial sea **59,** 355-7, 360-5
terrorists, discrimination and **58,** 285-8, 332
torture **58,** 265-7, 317-29, 333-4

Northern Mariana Islands
Constitution 1978, Art. 1(8) **87,** 569
Covenant (1975) **87,** 560
s 101 **87,** 568
s 105 **87,** 569
s 201 **87,** 569
s 302 **96,** 37
s 402(b) **87,** 548, 549-52
s 501 **87,** 567, 568-9
s 505 **87,** 507 n. 16
s 1003(b) **87,** 550-1
fair trial, jury trial and **87,** 571-4
jurisdiction, US courts **96,** 38
law of
Pacific Islands Trust Territory, applicability to **96,** 37
Public law No 1-21 **87,** 547
US law **96,** 37-8
State immunity **87,** 548-9, **96,** 38
US, of **96,** 40-1, 42

Northern Mariana Islands (*cont.*)
status **87,** 548, 551-2
'foreign country' **87,** 548-9
independent entity **87,** 552
self-governing commonwealth **87,** 568
sovereignty **87,** 551-2
US law, applicability **87,** 561-2, 563, 568
Norway
administration of justice **79,** 27, 270
joinder of charges **79,** 274
provision of documents **79,** 273, 274-5, 276
continental shelf legislation **41,** 208
evidence, affirmation **78,** 507-12
fisheries jurisdiction, delimitation **57,** 65
fishing zone, Jan Mayen, establishment of **62,** 115
freedom of expression, flag desecration and **122,** 599
jurisdiction
criminal **71,** 553-61
exemptions recognized by international law **71,** 555, 557, 560-1
passive personality principle **86,** 44
law of
civil and commercial matters, classification **84,** 746-7
Criminal Code 1902 **78,** 511, **86,** 44
s 63 **79,** 270, 274
s 91 **71,** 554
s 168 **78,** 509, 512
s 233 **71,** 554-5
Criminal Procedure Code 1981 **79,** 270, 273
s 5 **71,** 553-5, 560-1
s 99 **79,** 273, 274
s 186 **78,** 509
s 238 **71,** 553-5, 560-1
s 411 **71,** 553, 559-60
Law Courts Act **84,** 748
public law, fiscal matters **84,** 764
Road Traffic Act 1965 **79,** 269, 270, 271
Royal Decree of 23 May 1980 **62,** 115
Statistics Act 1907 **79,** 269, 271
privileges and immunities, diplomatic premises, inviolability **71,** 553-61
Norwegian Trough 41, 41, 50, 61, 88, 187, **83,** 101
novation, Mandatory's reporting obligations and **49,** 217, 223, 227 n. 18, 243, 246, 257
Novosti Press Agency. *See* Union of Soviet Socialist Republics (USSR), Novosti Press Agency
nuclear bombing 42, 440
nuclear disarmament. *See also* nuclear tests; nuclear weapons, deployment
obligation to negotiate in good faith
customary international law **110,** 223-4, 231, 260, 531
Non-Proliferation Treaty (1968) **110,** 213-15, 217, 235, 279, 530
non-signatories **110,** 279
nuclear energy exploitation. *See also* nuclear installations
cooperation agreement **65,** 94-8
injunction proceedings against foreign State **86,** 576-8, 580-2

public activity, whether **63,** 103-4, **65,** 97-8, **77,** 517, **86,** 569, 577
State immunity, jurisdiction and **63,** 103-4, **65,** 98, **77,** 517, **86,** 569, 577
transboundary pollution **86,** 565-70
rights relating to
individual **86,** 582
State, vested in **86,** 569, 582
nuclear equipment, export ban. *See also* nuclear energy exploitation; nuclear installations; nuclear tests; nuclear weapons, deployment
acte de gouvernement, whether **106,** 195, 196-7
basis
Opinion to Exporters **106,** 195, 197
Tripartite Agreement (1976) (France, Pakistan, IAEA) **106,** 195
justiciability **106,** 193-7
nuclear installations. *See also* Chernobyl nuclear accident; nuclear energy exploitation; nuclear equipment; Nuclear Material, Convention on the Physical Protection of (1980)
liability in respect of **80,** 384-8
Nuclear Material, Convention on the Physical Protection of (1980)
analysis **99,** 298-306, 308-10
implementation of Convention
mixed competence **99,** 321
part of EC law **99,** 321
compatibility with European Atomic Energy Community Treaty (1957) **99,** 295-322
coincidence of subject-matter **99,** 311
EC membership, whether necessary **99,** 311, 313, 316
EAEC Treaty safeguards **99,** 315-16, 319
implementation of Convention **99,** 319-20
nuclear common market responsibility **99,** 312-14
ownership of EAEC nuclear material **99,** 316-18, 319
transfer of powers to EAEC **99,** 319
nuclear common market, compatibility with **99,** 312-14, 319
nuclear tests. *See also* nuclear disarmament; nuclear equipment; nuclear weapons, deployment
atmospheric tests **74,** 95-6
international law, whether violation of **57,** 415, 424, 431-4
environmental impact assessment (EIA), need for. *See* environment, environmental impact assessment (EIA), need for
legality **106,** 101
Nuclear Test Ban Treaty (1963), opposability to non-parties **57,** 432
precautionary principle **106,** 12, 20-1
radioactive waste
marine environment and **106,** 67-8, 100-1
territorial sea **106,** 67
Rio Declaration on Environment and Development (1992) **106,** 68
resumption, act of State **106,** 231
threat of catastrophic accident, whether **115,** 262
threat to life, whether **115,** 255-62
nuclear weapons, deployment. *See also* nuclear disarmament; nuclear equipment; nuclear tests
acceptability to international community **110,** 331-7, 348-52, 353
applicable law **110,** 147-54, 189-93
customary international law. *See* customary international law *below*
Geneva Conventions (1949), Protocol I (1977) **110,** 209

nuclear weapons, deployment (*cont.*)
Geneva Protocol (Prohibition of Asphyxiating, Poisonous or other Gases and Bacteriological Methods) (1925) **110,** 458-62, 530
Genocide Convention (1948) **110,** 526-7
genocide, customary international law relating to **110,** 190
International Covenant on Civil and Political Rights (ICCPR) (1966) **110,** 189-90, 527-8
international humanitarian law **110,** 149, 194-5, 206-13, 216, 222-3, 251, 255-6, 258, 261, 270-2, 386, 426-7, 478-9, **122,** 646-7, 653-4
international instruments relating to poisoned weapons **110,** 198
law of armed conflict **110,** 193, 251, 271-2, 362-3, 386
treaties relating to **110,** 198-203, 238, 386, 477
Hague Regulations (1907) **110,** 462
reservations **110,** 258, 259, 366
UN Charter **110,** 193, 194-7, 269-70, 384, 386, **122,** 644-5
consent to. *See also* legislative consent, need for *below*
control remaining with US, relevance **106,** 406
Convention on the Presence of Foreign Forces in the FRG (1954), sufficiency **106,** 370-1
State responsibility **110,** 147
cruise missiles in Europe, justiciability **99,** 45-53
customary international law **110,** 202, 203-13, 235, 238-42, 525
authorization of threat or use **110,** 197, 216, 327, 339-40, 346, **122,** 502-6
equipment used in connection with, individual's right to take action against **122,** 651-2, 657-8
persistent objector rule **110,** 264-5, 330, 363, 365, 370, 437
prohibition on use **110,** 202, 203-5, 216, 242, 246-7, 327, **122,** 502-6, 645, 650-1
treaty reservations **110,** 213
definition **110,** 193-4, **122,** 644
Paris Accords (1954) **110,** 148
'poison or poisoned weapons' **110,** 198
Treaty of Tlatelolco (1967) **110,** 148-9
deterrent. *See* possession *below*
Effects of Nuclear War on Health and Health Services (WHO Management Group) **110,** 18
equality of States and **110,** 272-3
equipment used in connection with, individual's right to take action against
customary international law **122,** 651-2, 657-8
duress **122,** 509
necessity **122,** 509-12, 625-7, 652, 655-6, 658-9
genocide, whether **110,** 190, 451-2, 526-7, **111,** 585-90
human rights and **106,** 360-2, 405-6, **110,** 456-8
European Convention on Human Rights (1950) **106,** 405-6
internal use **110,** 197
justiciability **118,** 346-8, **122,** 638-40
cruise missiles in Europe **99,** 45-53
legal regime
consolidation, need for **110,** 245-6
evolving **110,** 245-6
legality
advisory opinion, request for
UNGA **110,** 177-542
WHO **110,** 6-163

burden of proof **110,** 236, 349
counter-arguments
absence of authorization **110,** 245
General Assembly's hostility to **110,** 245
non-use since 1945 **110,** 245
customary international law. *See* customary international law *above*
defensive purposes **110,** 194-7, 213, 216, 238
customary international law **106,** 362-3, 406
Non-Proliferation Treaty (1968) **106,** 376, 405
reservations **110,** 259
deterrence policy **110,** 213, 227-8, 233, 234-6, 241, 257-9, 264, 273-9, 335-7, 488-92
environmental protection and **110,** 124-6, 154-7, 191-3
evidence of
absence of objection to treaty reservations **110,** 540
assurances of nuclear Powers **110,** 540
declaration of legality, absence **110,** 245
deterrence policy **110,** 540
Institute of International Law (Edinburgh 1969) **110,** 350
Non-Proliferation Treaty (1968) **110,** 264, 350, 361
UNGA Resolutions **110,** 223-4, 265-7, 332, 340-1, 349-50, 360, 437-8, **122,** 645-6
internal war **110,** 494
Lotus principle ('what is not prohibited is allowed') **110,** 220-1, 241-2, 339-40, 341-7, 376, 442-6
'materials', radiation, whether **110,** 460-2
non-deployment, implications **110,** 245, 528-9
non-discriminatory nature **110,** 122-4, 212, 222-3, 261, 270-1, 406, 449-50, 466, 514
Martens Clause (customary international law: applicability in case of gaps) **110,** 124, 355-61
post-battle obligations and **110,** 123
poisoned weapon, whether **110,** 198
principles and rules of international law
compatibility with **110,** 235
exception to **110,** 245
prohibition, whether **110,** 216, 238, 242, 442-6
treaty **110,** 198-203, **122,** 645
proportionality **110,** 195, 239, 260, 261, 270-1, 326, 398-9
reprisals **110,** 278, 339, 387, 524-5
State practice **106,** 362-3, **110,** 245-7, 261, 262-3
statement of, absence **110,** 245
tactical weapons **110,** 496-500
treaty provision **110,** 246, 438-9, 530
implying contrary **110,** 263-8, 313-14, 318, 364-70, 385, 484-5, 486, 530
Non-Proliferation Treaty (1968). *See* Non-Proliferation Treaty (1968) *below*
UN Charter principles **110,** 384
UNGA attitude **110,** 245
WHO Constitution **110,** 157
legislative consent, need for **106,** 368-88. *See also* consent to *above*
collective security, agreement to treaty establishing **106,** 369-70, 379
NATO 'Double Resolution' of 12 December 1979 **106,** 355-64, 370-88
natural law and **110,** 246
neutrality, relevance **110,** 210-12, 239-40, 256, 258, 337-9, 413-14, 466-7, 514

nuclear weapons, deployment (*cont.*)
Non-Proliferation Treaty (1968)
interpretation, UN Charter, Art. 51 and **106,** 376, 405
legality of nuclear weapons, recognition **110,** 264-5, 486-8
nuclear and non-nuclear Powers, balance **110,** 262-4, 308-9, 314, 367
non-nuclear Powers' renunciation of right of self-defence **110,** 368
nuclear Power assurances **110,** 265-7, 312-14, 319, 370-4, 540
obligation to negotiate in good faith for nuclear disarmament **110,** 213-15, 217, 235, 279, 530, **122,** 647-8
non-signatories **110,** 235, 279
unequal treaty **110,** 312
possession
distinguished **110,** 264, 283, 398, **122,** 640
individual's right to take action against equipment, self-defence **122,** 508-9
as threat of force **110,** 196-7, 283, **122,** 641-2, 644-5, 650-1, 654-5
sovereign rights, surrender **106,** 375-87
collective security system, in context of **106,** 376-87
consultative rights, relevance **106,** 376, 378-9
request for Advisory Opinion **110,** 104-6
Trident missiles, action relating to in Scotland **122,** 621-59. *See also* equipment used in connection with, individual's right to take action against *above*
World Health Organization (WHO) and. *See* World Health Organization (WHO), advisory opinion on legality of nuclear weapons, right to request; World Health Organization (WHO), nuclear weapons, relevance
***nullum crimen sine lege* 36,** 42-4, 279, 281-3, **39,** 438-9, **71,** 283, **91,** 43, 48, 50, **105,** 447, 449-50, 452, 525-6, 588, **108,** 195-6, 206, **111,** 395, 429, **122,** 68, 76
Nuremberg Charter (1945) 42, 398, 437, **72,** 609, **74,** 701-3, **75,** 334, 359-60, 362, **76,** 620-1, **77,** 221-2, **78,** 129, 131, **82,** 438. *See also* war crimes, aiding and abetting
common plan or conspiracy, consideration by Tribunal limited to waging aggressive war **121,** 274 n. 217
crimes against humanity **72,** 609, **74,** 359-60, 362, 701-3, **75,** 344, **77,** 221-2, **78,** 136, 137-8, 143-4
aiding and abetting **122,** 93
as an extension of jurisdiction **124,** 230-1
armed conflict, need for **112,** 207-8
definition **36,** 48-9, **78,** 131, **91,** 57-8, 60, 126-7, **100,** 349, 350, 363, **105,** 451, 524-5, **119,** 67, 68, 353, **122,** 74
discrimination, need for **124,** 178
individual responsibility **82,** 438, **104,** 154, **112,** 205-6, 225-36, **119,** 148, **121,** 256-7
persecution of Jews **122,** 84-7
war crimes, nexus **105,** 451, **112,** 205, **119,** 226
crimes against peace **78,** 131
customary international law, subsequent adoption of Charter as **111,** 342
declaratory nature **36,** 39-40, 295, **82,** 440
obligations of UN Member States to punish or send back suspects **78,** 129
deportations from occupied territory **83,** 141
Head of State immunity **119,** 46, 66, 87, 98-9, 155, **125,** 497, 503
individual responsibility **82,** 438, **104,** 154, **112,** 205-6, 225-36, **119,** 148, **121,** 256-7
Head of State **119,** 162-3, 211, 243
legality **119,** 148
UN Resolution 95(I) and **36,** 296-7, 311, 317, **78,** 131, **82,** 440, 441, **119,** 67, 99, 148

Nuremberg Tribunal, limitation to **36,** 48-9, **95,** 132
participation in common plan of extermination or persecution **100,** 335-6
knowledge of existence, need for **100,** 335
penalty **108,** 193
purpose, deterrence/retribution **108,** 202
State immunity **79,** 12, 511-13, **119,** 46, 66
statutory limitation **100,** 333
superior orders **91,** 6-7
mitigation of punishment, limited to **100,** 336-7
torture, omission **121,** 255
UN General Assembly Resolution 95(1) **82,** 440, **100,** 333
war crimes **78,** 131
definition **105,** 445
individual's responsibility **77,** 221-2
pre-existing **91,** 48-9
Geneva Conventions (1949) **91,** 46
Hague Conventions (1907) **91,** 46
retroactivity **104,** 322, 400-2, **105,** 569-70
universal jurisdiction **91,** 46-7
Nuremberg Tribunal
decisions
basis, Four Power rights and responsibilities for Germany as a whole **90,** 392
enforcement
FRG **90,** 392-5
responsibility for **90,** 390-5
FRG jurisdiction and **90,** 390-2
legality **90,** 392
UN Charter, Art. 107 and **90,** 392
establishment **90,** 390
fair trial **105,** 475, 608-9
ICJ jurisdiction, as basis for **95,** 32
jurisdiction **82,** 438, 440
basis **79,** 545-6
World War II, limited to **105,** 445-6
prisoner, release of, grounds
humanitarian **90,** 392, 396-7
illegality of judgment **90,** 392, 397
procedure, *ad hoc* nature **110,** 638
status
international tribunal **91,** 60
joint tribunal **119,** 225
occupation court **91,** 60, **119,** 225
Nyasaland. *See* Malawi; Rhodesia and Nyasaland, Federation of

OAS. *See* Organization of American States (OAS)
OAU. *See* Organization of African Unity (OAU)
obligations, protection of rights guaranteed by constitution **118,** 471
obscene publications. *See also* obscenity
discrimination and, seizure **58,** 181-2
freedom of expression and **58,** 171-80, **73,** 381-2
margin of appreciation **58,** 172, 174, 177
possessions, deprivation of and **58,** 180-2
protection of morals and **58,** 172-4

obscene publications (*cont.*)
seizure of, discrimination **58,** 181-2
obscenity 58, 162-4, 165-8, **88,** 575-80, 582. *See also* obscene publications
penalties **88,** 580-4
occupation. *See also* belligerent occupation; Germany, occupation; high seas, occupation; territory, acquisition
concession agreement, validity **40,** 111-13
foreign territory in time of peace
contractual liability of occupying power **101,** 556-61
treaty terminating occupation, effect **101,** 561
Ryukyu Islands **101,** 556-61. *See also* Ryukyu Islands
Namibia **49,** 79-80, 208
sovereignty and **87,** 603
terra nullius and **67,** 190, **100,** 82-4, 98
transfers during, invalidation **40,** 111, 112
western provinces of China (Boxer Rebellion) **46,** 465 n. 8
occupying power 90, 403. *See also* belligerent occupation; Germany, occupation (post-WWII)
authority **61,** 43, 64, 75-6, **62,** 12, 39, 42-7, 49, 50, 57-8, 61, 64, 70, 74, 79, 86-7
enforcement **48,** 489
definition **90,** 403, 406, 407
armed forces, use of **90,** 403
exercise of supreme authority **90,** 403
expropriation/nationalization. *See* expropriation/nationalization, by occupying/administering power; Germany, Democratic Republic (GDR), expropriation/nationalization, Soviet occupation
functions
administrative **40,** 471, **41,** 478-80, **77,** 628-30, **78,** 161, 186-7
delegation **43,** 23, 32, 37-9, 40, 41, 44, 46-7, 67-9, 70-1
judicial **41,** 475-8, **48,** 478-85
legislative **42,** 484-7, **48,** 482-5, 486-93
jurisdiction in absence of right of suit in occupying/administering power's own courts **65,** 130. *See also* belligerent occupation, jurisdiction
Nuremberg Tribunal, implementation of decision and **90,** 390-2
obligations
damages **70,** 697-8
Hague Conventions (1899/1907) **96,** 58-9, 61
mandatory, whether **96,** 61
public order, maintenance **52,** 518-20, **83,** 136, 137, 185, 187, **96,** 61
to inhabitants **42,** 482, 483
powers **39,** 364-5, 397, **52,** 525-7
maintenance of security **83,** 136, 137, 187
sovereignty **40,** 468, 469, 470, **61,** 675-8
State responsibility. *See* belligerent occupation, State responsibility for acts in occupied territory; State responsibility/liability of Iraq for 'any direct loss, damage . . . as a result of Iraq's unlawful invasion and occupation of Kuwait'
Oder–Neisse, territories east of 78, 184-93
administration by Poland **65,** 128-30
Auctochthonen **78,** 188
boundary questions **78,** 186-7
compulsory resettlement **78,** 188
diplomatic protection of Germans in **78,** 185-6
dual nationality **78,** 188

elections, right to vote **78,** 188
expulsion from **78,** 187
family reunification **78,** 186
FRG
Eastern Treaties **78,** 184-96
FRG–Poland Border Treaty (1990) **108,** 659-61, 663
foreign territory, social security provisions and **78,** 193
renunciation of any claim to **78,** 185
military service, introduction of compulsory **78,** 188
nationality
Auctochthonen **78,** 188
diplomatic protection and **78,** 185-6
GDR Law concerning Citizenship of the German Democratic Republic 1967 **78,** 188
Germans, Eastern Treaties and **78,** 185-6
Poland and **78,** 185-6
Law of 9 January 1951 **78,** 188
USSR and **78,** 188
Poland
administration by **65,** 128-30
compulsory military service **78,** 188
confiscatory legislation **65,** 128-30, **78,** 187
elections, right to vote **78,** 188
nationality and **78,** 185-6
property rights **78,** 184-5
confiscation **78,** 187
compensation, without **65,** 128-30, **78,** 187
de facto **78,** 187
legality **65,** 128-30, **78,** 185
USSR **78,** 187
Eastern Treaties, effect **78,** 185, **108,** 659-61, 663
protection by FRG **78,** 184-5
Soviet–Polish rule
effectiveness **78,** 184-5
sphere of influence **78,** 187
status **78,** 186-7
OECD. *See* Organization for Economic Cooperation and Development (OECD)
offenders' rights, sentencing changes, retroactive benefit **70,** 306-13, **71,** 339-45
Office Franco-Allemand pour la Jeunesse
Appeals Commission, ordinary courts, ouster of jurisdiction **72,** 193-4
immunity, jurisdiction **72,** 193
staff contract claims **72,** 192-5
status **72,** 193-4
Office of Human Resources Management. *See* United Nations, Office of Human Resources Management
official secrets, disclosure in course of duties **107,** 99
oil
ECSC and **117,** 313, 329
exploration and production in the Atlantic Frontier area (UK). *See also* Habitats Directive (92/43/EEC); United Kingdom, Conservation (Natural Habitats and of Wild Fauna and Flora) Regulations 1994
licensing process, right of challenge under the EC Habitats Directive **120,** 646-56
delay **120,** 650-6
public interest **120,** 655-6

oil (*cont.*)
natural resources, risk to
cetaceans **120,** 640-1, 645
lophelia pertusa **120,** 637-40
within UK continental shelf/EFZ outside territorial sea **120,** 623
'good oilfield practice' **63,** 596-9, **66,** 552
Middle Eastern, general trends **66,** 563-4, 572-3
nature of obligation **66,** 597-9
valuation of assets **66,** 609, 613
joint exploitation. *See* joint exploitation of maritime resources
nationalization by Libya **63,** 166-9, 233-5
participation agreement. *See* participation agreements
price-fixing, commercial activity, whether **63,** 288-94
production cut, commercial activity, whether **63,** 257
State-owned corporation. *See also* Iran, Islamic Republic, National Iranian Oil Company (NIOC)
as agency or instrumentality of a foreign State **63,** 166-8, 233, 302-10
title to **62,** 151, 161, 164, 181, 185, 195, 197, 199
Oil Service Company of Iran. *See* Iran, Islamic Republic of, Oil Service Company of Iran
Okinawa Islands
inhabitants, Japanese nationals, whether **54,** 217-23
sovereignty over **54,** 216, 218-21, 222-3
status **54,** 215, 216-18, 221, 222
Peace Treaty (1951) **54,** 216-17, 218-21
Olympic Airways. *See* Greece, Olympic Airways
Olympic Charter
nationality **120,** 2-10
Rules
3(1) **120,** 9
9(1) **120,** 9
46, Bye-law (change of nationality) **120,** 3-10
74 **120,** 5
stateless person's right to compete **120,** 8-10
OPEC. *See* Organization of Petroleum Exporting Countries (OPEC)
Operation Allied Force. *See* NATO, Operation Allied Force
opinio aequitatis **81,** 340
opinio juris **37,** 559, **41,** 58, 71-5, 89, 105, 114, 118, 135, 136-7, 158, 170-1, 186, 209-11, 214, 221, **46,** 361, 479-80, 503, **55,** 324-5, 335, **56,** 191, **59,** 138, **62,** 233, **66,** 605-7, **70,** 402, **71,** 126, 550, **75,** 610-14, 633-4, 637, 639, **76,** 431-2, 433-6, 440, 442-3, 445, 493, 518, **77,** 225, 492, **80,** 173, 419, **105,** 498-9, 530, 588, **125,** 499
compensation, standard **83,** 475
criminal responsibility of individual for breach of humanitarian law **105,** 522-3
declaration of international conference **76,** 434
deliberate practice, need for **119,** 364
duress **66,** 606, **111,** 341-2, 440
emerging **110,** 268
evidence of **91,** 128
UN Resolution **110,** 205, 268-70, 349-50
General Assembly Resolution **76,** 434
ICC (Rome) Statute (1998) **124,** 156
illegality as bar to development **110,** 329-30, 363-4, 365, 374
Lotus **41,** 74

natural law and **41,** 58
need for **110,** 259, 373-4
relevant factors
codification **41,** 58
multilateral convention, influence **41,** 58
State practice **41,** 58
repetition of principles **110,** 246-7, 269-70, 300
as requirement for formation of customary international law **81,** 261, 301, 340, **84,** 525, 540, **91,** 37, 116, 123, 124, **115,** 610
States' views, relevance **110,** 359-60
unratified treaty **46,** 361
war crimes, individual responsibility **105,** 537-8
opposability. *See also erga omnes* principle
boundaries **41,** 108, **80,** 482-5
fisheries jurisdiction, extension **55,** 353, 355, 371, 387, 397
maritime delimitation **41,** 47-9, 50, 84, 179, 181, **56,** 164
travaux préparatoires, to States not party to original negotiations **59,** 545, 563-4
treaties **57,** 432, **67,** 61-2, 64, 76, 79, 132, 148, **83,** 19, 22, 39, 50, 79, 85
non-self-governing territory after independence **105,** 418
nullity distinguished **83,** 80
unilateral declaration/undertaking **46,** 362, 363, **71,** 119
optional clause. *See* International Court of Justice (ICJ), compulsory jurisdiction, acceptance
oral hearings, right to. *See* intervention, hearing on declaration of *and* oral proceedings *above*
Organization of African Unity (OAU)
Cairo Resolution (1964) **67,** 59, 91, 124, **77,** 657
uti possidetis and **77,** 657
Charter, territorial integrity **50,** 407-8, **77,** 657
Mediation Commission. *See* Burkina Faso/Mali boundary dispute, Mediation Commission
resolution, municipal law, part of, whether **91,** 409
South West Africa, oral statement to ICJ **49,** 9
Organization of American States (OAS) 62, 153, 186, **63,** 92-5, 162-3, 337-46, **76,** 436, 441, 465-6, 520, 694-5, 718. *See also* American Convention on Human Rights (1969); Inter-American Commission on Human Rights; Inter-American Court of Human Rights
Charter **37,** 455
Consultation of Ministers of Foreign Affairs, Ninth Meeting (1964) **76,** 694-5
General Assembly Resolution
of 21 April 1972 **76,** 436
AG/RES. 78 **76,** 436, 441
AG/RES. 128 **76,** 441
human rights legislation **67,** 602-9
immunity, jurisdiction **63,** 92-5, 162-3, 338-46
permanent observers **63,** 93-4
permanent observers, immunity, jurisdiction **63,** 93-4
Protocol of Buenos Aires (1967) **63,** 94
Seventeenth Meeting (23 June 1979), Resolution on Nicaragua **76,** 465-6, 520, 718
Organization for Economic Cooperation and Development (OECD)
Administrative Tribunal, jurisdiction
private dispute between heirs of former employee **110,** 601
review of legality of decisions of Organization **110,** 605
Conference on the Reorganization of **44,** 417

Organization for Economic Cooperation and Development (OECD) (*cont.*)
coordinated salary-fixing
Decision of OECD Council **110,** 605-6
variations in different organizations, admissibility **110,** 605-6
Draft Convention for the Protection of Foreign Property **84,** 516, 669 n. 2
Art. 1 **106,** 484-5
'fair and equitable treatment' **106,** 484-5, **122,** 382
'most constant protection and security' **106,** 484-5
headquarters building, jurisdiction of municipal courts in respect of work on **47,** 345-8
International and Multinational Enterprises, Declaration of 21 June 1976, 'like situations' **121,** 116-17
Multilateral Agreement on Investment (MAI)
criticisms of proposal for **121,** 144-5
governments' right to regulate in the public interest and **121,** 144-5
Pension Scheme Rules, Art. 51, salary variations between organizations and **110,** 606
Privileges and Immunities, Convention on **44,** 410, 411-12, 414, 417
Staff Provident Fund, fraudulent withdrawal, liability **110,** 601-2
Staff Regulations. *See* Organization for Economic Cooperation and Development (OECD), Staff Regulations
status under French law **47,** 347
Organization for Economic Cooperation and Development (OECD), Staff Regulations
acquired rights, salary variations between organizations **110,** 606
Annex I
Art. 13 (budgetary constraints affecting salaries)
linguistic differences **110,** 605-6
travaux préparatoires **110,** 605-6
good faith in applying **110,** 606
Annex VI (Staff Provident Fund), Rule 12 **110,** 601-2
Organization of Petroleum Exporting Countries (OPEC)
Geneva Agreements **66,** 551-2, 554
price setting
'Abu Dhabi formula' **66,** 554-5, 572-3
as act of State **80,** 34
commercial activity **66,** 416-17
US antitrust violation **66,** 414-21
Teheran Agreement **66,** 551-2, 554
Orissa, creation as Governor's Province (1935) **50,** 324, 326
Ostpolitik **78,** 164
Ottoman Bank, nationality and corporate seat **47,** 216-32
overflights. *See* airspace, overflight rights; India/Pakistan relations, overflights; sovereignty, foreign military aircraft, overflights
ownership 77, 544, 547-50, 585-6. *See also* applicable law, ownership; title
acquisition of title **77,** 547-9
date **77,** 548
expropriation measures and **77,** 585-6, **78,** 681
animo rem sibi habendi **77,** 547
deprivation of **58,** 180-2
discrimination **58,** 182
differing legal concepts **42,** 363, 375
equitable **78,** 681

Pacific Islands Trust Territory
authority, UN **96,** 27

government, agency of US government, whether **96,** 27-9
history and structure **96,** 25-7
law of
Northern Mariana law, Trust Territory government base in Saipan, relevance **96,** 37
US law, specific extension, need for **96,** 27, 30-1
State succession, responsibility for acts of previous government **61,** 100-1
status **84,** 203
termination **87,** 654
territory or possession of US, 'like' **96,** 29-30
Trusteeship Agreement **96,** 27
Pact of Bogotá (1948)
arbitral procedure agreement under **84,** 228, 229, 277, 302
Articles XXXI and XXXII, interrelationship **84,** 264-5, 267-9, 281, 290, 301-5
Contadora process. *See* Contadora process
denunciation **84,** 242, 292
El Salvador **97,** 299
exhaustion of local remedies and **46,** 467
ICJ and **84,** 273-4, 281
acceptance of compulsory jurisdiction, whether **84,** 228, 229, 231-3, 237-45, 264, 266, 276-7, 279-80, 288-92, 294, 301-2
amendment by unilateral Declaration under ICJ Statute **84,** 239, 295-6
restrictions on **84,** 239-40
exhaustion of local remedies and **64,** 467
failure of negotiated settlement, mutual manifestation **84,** 248, 249-50, 306-7
unilateral application to Court under **84,** 228, 237, 293
unsuccessful conciliation procedures precondition of resort to, whether **84,** 228, 229, 243-5, 261-2, 266, 268, 269, 277, 281, 299-305
individuals, rights **96,** 50
interpretation **84,** 242-3, 264-79
discrepancy between texts **84,** 244, 249-50, 268
parties' intention **84,** 300
travaux préparatoires **84,** 274-9
legal disputes **84,** 267, 281, 302
negotiation under **84,** 309
non-legal disputes **84,** 267, 281
pacific settlement under **84,** 265
phrases
'direct negotiation' **84,** 248-9
'Pacific procedure' **84,** 255, 260, 281-2, 309
conclusion **84,** 255, 260
freedom of choice **84,** 279
'special procedure' **84,** 254, 260, 307, 309-11
Contadora process, whether **84,** 281, 306-7
preceding dispute, exclusion **84,** 297, 298
reservations **84,** 233, 240-1
applicability to ICJ Statute, Art. 36(2) declarations **84,** 296-9
ex post facto **84,** 294
review **84,** 291
pacta sunt servanda **48,** 412, 415, **50,** 397, 401, 402, 465, **53,** 332-3, 462, **56,** 139, 283, **59,** 5, **61,** 623-4, **62,** 190-2, 196, 217, **65,** 452, **66,** 590, **68,** 416, 554, **76,** 584, **80,** 482, **82,** 550, 571, 680, **83,** 554, 561-2, **86,** 457, 458, 460, 462, **87,** 153, **89,** 494, 495-7, **90,** 690, **93,** 342, **94,** 563, **106,** 552, 570, **107,** 285, **117,** 409, 426. *See also* contract, *pacta sunt servanda*; treaties, *pacta sunt servanda*

pacta sunt servanda (*cont.*)
arbitration clause/agreement **65,** 452
customary international law **65,** 452-3, **117,** 409, 426, 441
Pakistan, Islamic Republic. *See also* British India; India/Pakistan relations; Pakistan/Bangladesh relations
arbitration, definition, 'suit' **64,** 580-4
boundaries, independence, demarcation **53,** 184
burden of proof, State immunity, jurisdiction **64,** 597
citizenship law **45,** 358, 363-4
commercial/trade representation/mission
applicable law, *lex loci contractus* **64,** 592-4
State immunity, jurisdiction **64,** 590-3
status, applicable law **64,** 590-4
Constitution 1947, amendments, validity **90,** 491-2, 500
Constitution 1962
Art. 24 **66,** 255
Art. 30 **67,** 616
continuity of law, Tribal Areas in India, application of laws of **38,** 3-9
contract, partition of India, effect **53,** 131-7
courts, municipal, jurisdiction **66,** 196-7
customary international law, State immunity, jurisdiction **64,** 597-607
diplomatic privileges and immunities, entitlement, commercial/trade representation/mission **64,** 590-2, 596
diplomatic privileges and immunities, treaty exception, trade agreement **64,** 590-4
East Pakistan Development Corporation, effect of dissolution **65,** 446-8
East Pakistan Fertilizer Development Corporation
as *alter ego* of government **63,** 54
immunity **63,** 52-6
enemy aliens
capacity to sue **71,** 710
definition **53,** 609, 616, 622, 623-4
evidence of, State immunity, jurisdiction, certificate of head of diplomatic mission **64,** 594-5
executive certificate/statement, conclusiveness, State immunity, jurisdiction **64,** 594-5
foreign State, proceedings involving
consent of forum government, need for **64,** 568-70, 573-4, 618
waiver distinguished **64,** 573-4
right to sue and be sued **64,** 571-4, 615-18
Head of State
income tax, exemption **64,** 617
as State **64,** 570-2, 615-18
Head of State, former, immunity, jurisdiction, official acts in exercise of functions **64,** 617
Head of State, immunity, jurisdiction, State immunity distinguished **64,** 616-17
income tax, exemption, Head of State **64,** 617
independence
boundaries, demarcation **53,** 184
partition of India, effect on contract **53,** 131-7
Islamic law, as residuary law of **64,** 625-32, 650
jus cogens/peremptory norm **64,** 597
law of

Arbitration Act 1940 **64,** 568, 580-2
citizenship law **45,** 358, 363-4
Civil Procedure Code 1908
1859, 1861, 1877 and 1882 compared **64,** 609-24
arbitration proceedings and **64,** 580-4
'Ruler of a foreign State' **64,** 570
s 20 **66,** 196-7
s 83 **53,** 609, 616, 622, 623-4, **71,** 709-10
s 84(1) (right of suit by State to enforce private rights) **64,** 570, 574, 616
s 86 (Ruler of a Foreign State: immunity, jurisdiction) **64,** 568-72, 574-85, 653
s 86(1) (Ruler of a foreign State: immunity, jurisdiction) **64,** 580-3
s 86(2)(b) (institution of suit against ruler of a foreign State when trading within local limits of Court) **64,** 581
s 87 (Ruler of a foreign State: right of suit) **64,** 570-1
State immunity and **64,** 580-4
State immunity and, personal nature **64,** 618
'suit' **64,** 580-4
Criminal Code, s 375 (rape) **121,** 270 n. 209
Diplomatic and Consular Privileges Ordinance 1972 **64,** 596, 651
Diplomatic Immunities (Commonwealth) Countries Representatives Act 1957 **64,** 581
Diplomatic and Privileges Act 1972 **64,** 596
Domestic Violence and Matrimonial Proceedings Act 1976 **124,** 492
Emergency Powers Ordinance 1955, effect **90,** 492
Foreign Exchange Regulations Act 1947 **41,** 230, 234, 235-6, 238, **118,** 576
Islamic law, as residuary law of **64,** 625-32, 650
Laws (Continuance in Force) Order 1977 (No 1) **90,** 499-500
Muslim Family Laws Ordinance 1961 **74,** 533-47, 554-5
Pakistan Independence (Rights, Property and Liabilities) Order 1947, India-Pakistan Devolution Agreement 1947 **53,** 132
Public Demands Recovery Act, s 23 **71,** 708
State Immunity Ordinance **1981**. *See* State Immunity Ordinance 1981 *below*
trademarks legislation **71,** 23-35
UN Privileges and Immunities Act 1948 **64,** 581
legislation, interpretation
guidelines, consistency within Statute **64,** 570-1, 574-5
presumption of conformity with comity **64,** 575, 579, 633
presumption of conformity with international law **64,** 575-6, 579-80, 632-3
implementation in accordance with subsequent changes in international law **64,** 576
legislation, retroactive, State immunity legislation **64,** 619-23, 651-3
Muslim Bank, branches, legal status **66,** 194-5
nationals, UK and **61,** 267-75
necessity **90,** 492-3
Sind, as successor to **50,** 4, 81, 379, 412, 422, 495, 500
State agency/State-owned corporation/State entity
classification, commercial/trade representation/mission **64,** 590-3
separate legal entity test, trade representation (USSR) **64,** 590-2
State immunity **64,** 632. *See also* State Immunity Ordinance 1981 *below*
State immunity, execution/attachment, theory/doctrine
development of concept **64,** 576-80, 614-32, 633-50
restrictive theory **65,** 230

Pakistan, Islamic Republic (*cont.*)
State immunity, jurisdiction, classification of act
commercial activities **64,** 607-8, 650-3
nature or purpose of transaction as determining factor **64,** 607
State immunity, jurisdiction, entitlement
commercial/trade representation/mission **64,** 590-3
executive certificate/statement, conclusiveness **64,** 594-5
republican State **64,** 572
State immunity, jurisdiction, procedural aspects
burden of proof **64,** 597
consent of forum State, relevance. *See* foreign State, proceedings involving, consent of forum government, need for *above*
State immunity, jurisdiction, theory/doctrine
absolute theory, customary international law **64,** 597-607
basis
comity **64,** 595
equality of States **64,** 595
reciprocity **64,** 595
State immunity, jurisdiction, waiver
treaty provision **64,** 593-4
trade agreement **64,** 590-4
State Immunity Ordinance 1981
retroactive, whether **64,** 619-23, 651-3
s 5 (State immunity: commercial transaction and contracts to be performed in Pakistan) **64,** 619, 651-2
s 5 (State immunity: exceptions to s 5(1)) **64,** 619
States, legal personality and **64,** 571-2, 615-18
trademarks legislation **71,** 23-35
Vienna Convention on Diplomatic Relations (1961)
applicability, commercial/trade representation/mission **64,** 596
incorporation into municipal law **64,** 596
war with India. *See* India/Pakistan relations
Waziristan, whether included in **38,** 3-9
women as a 'particular social group' **124,** 477-511
Pakistan/Bangladesh relations 63, 53, 56, **66,** 194-7, **70,** 43-4
Palau
administrative responsibility, exercise **87,** 560
Compact of Free Association (1986) **87,** 600, 603, 654-6
Art. I **87,** 605
sovereign immunity **87,** 615-17
Joint Resolution 1681. *See* United States of America (USA), Code (USC), 48 USC
State immunity, as procedural bar **87,** 616
Covenant **87,** 560
independence from US courts **87,** 561-2, 563
law of
National Code **87,** 636
National Government Private Borrowing Act (RPPL 1-20) **87,** 610-13, 635, 642-3, 651
National Government Private Borrowing Act (RPPL 1-54) **87,** 610-13, 634-5, 642, 643, 651-2
National Government Private Borrowing Act (RPPL 2-10) **87,** 610
US law, applicability **87,** 562, 653-6

legislation, interpretation **87,** 610
aids
language of Statute **87,** 612-13
legislative history **87,** 612
plain meaning **87,** 612
President, powers **87,** 610-13
waiver of State immunity **87,** 616-17
sovereignty over **87,** 563-4, 606
State immunity
waiver **87,** 615-17, 633-5, 642-3
suspension **87,** 634-5
status **87,** 558, 559-64
'foreign country' **87,** 564, 600-7, 648-57
sovereign **87,** 599-600, 601, 654-7
dormant **87,** 605-6
partial **87,** 551-2, 564, 602
temporary **87,** 605-6

Palestine
Emergency Regulations 1945, continuance **47,** 476-84, 486-7
law of, Mandate part of **44,** 333-4, 335-6, 340
Mandate. *See* Mandate, Palestine
Order in Council, religious courts, provision concerning **48,** 102, 105
UK reference to UN **49,** 253
UN Special Committee Report **37,** 221, 224-5, 331-2, 336, 341

Palestine Liberation Organization (PLO). *See also* Palestine, Popular Front for the Liberation of
as agent of Libya **77,** 250
diplomatic privileges and immunities **82,** 286, 288
diplomatic relations **82,** 286
suit, right of and **96,** 74-5
international responsibility **77,** 205, 220, 234
international status **77,** 220, 234-5, 250-1
piracy **82,** 317
State immunity, jurisdiction **96,** 73-4
State, whether
foreign relations, capacity to establish **96,** 74
permanent population, lack **96,** 74
recognition **82,** 286, 332
territory, lack **96,** 74
Tashkent Declaration 1966 **67,** 623-4, 628
UN and
Headquarters Agreement, applicability to **82,** 294 n. 27, **96,** 74
observer status **77,** 234, **82,** 233, 234, 235-6, 237, 242, 248-9, 255-7, 261-4, 286
State immunity, jurisdiction and **96,** 74
USA, in **82,** 233-4, 235-50, 255-9, 261-72, 275-80, 285-8, 293-5, 304-18, 331-7. *See also* United States of America (USA), law of, Anti-Terrorism Act 1987
abuse of UN observer status, evidence of, whether **82,** 297, 313
agency of **82,** 304 n. 3, 308-10, 314
establishment of office **82,** 304-5, 311
constitutionality **82,** 308
expending funds from **82,** 304, 311

Palestine Liberation Organization (PLO) (*cont.*)
information office, right to **82,** 318
jurisdiction over
'doing business in New York' requirement **96,** 76-8
non-UN business **96,** 77-8
Keyes Declaration **82,** 332-3
Permanent Observer to UN
excludable alien **82,** 331, 334-6
State immunity, jurisdiction **96,** 74
receipt of anything of value from, prohibition
constitutionality **82,** 307-8
travel expenses **82,** 304-5
terrorist organization **82,** 304, 317
Palestine, Popular Front for Liberation of. *See also* Palestine Liberation Organization (PLO)
members, prisoner of war status, entitlement **42,** 470-83
Pan American Health Organization. *See* Pan American Sanitary Organization
Pan American Sanitary Organization 62, 461, 522
as *amicus curiae* **63,** 162
International Sanitary Bureau, successor to **43,** 459
staff disputes, appeals procedure **43,** 460-2
status **72,** 197, 199
WHO and **43,** 459-62
Pan-American Union, Inter-American Juridical Committee. *See also* Pact of Bogotá (1948)
Draft American Treaty Relating to Peaceful Procedures (1944) **84,** 270
arbitration **84,** 270, 272-4
mediation **84,** 270
negotiation **84,** 270
Draft Inter-American Peace System (1947) **84,** 299-300
arbitration **84,** 272-4
conciliation **84,** 271, 273-4
diplomatic channels **84,** 274
good offices **84,** 273
investigation **84,** 273-4
judicial settlement **84,** 271, 273, 274
mediation **84,** 270-1, 273-4
Draft Treaty for the Coordination of Inter-American Peace Agreements (1944) **84,** 270
Pan Arab Regional Health Organization 62, 499, 522, 524
Panama
Banco Nacional de Panama (BNP), central bank, whether **86,** 13
Constitution, Art. 170 (executive branch) **99,** 161
Panama Canal Zone
Code **51,** 282-8, 372-4
sovereignty over **56,** 51
recognition, government, US **96,** 46-54, **99,** 161-3
US intervention (1989)
political question doctrine **99,** 177-83
State responsibility for, failure to restore and maintain public order **96,** 57-61
USA, Isthmian Canal Convention (1902) **51,** 281, 282
Papua New Guinea
Constitution, s 200 **117,** 558-9

land titles **71,** 40-7, 51-6
Land Titles Commission **71,** 41, 51, 56
jurisdiction **71,** 51, 56
military assistance
contract with Sandline to provide
applicable law **117,** 568-72
legality **117,** 558, 562-3, 569-72
provisions **117,** 554-5
repudiation **117,** 556
Paraguay
Constitution 1967, Art. 50 **77,** 188
law of
Civil Code 1985
Art. 1102 **77,** 188
Art. 1103 **77,** 188
Art. 1112 **77,** 188
Penal Code 1883, Art. 337 **77,** 188
Paramount Power, boundaries, decisions of, binding nature **50,** 28
parens patriae **92,** 624, 630, **118,** 471-6, 521-3
definition **118,** 471, 472
Indian concept **118,** 471
limitation to proceedings abroad **118,** 475
prerogative and **118,** 472
requirements **118,** 472-3
pari passu clause, function **59,** 539
Paris Convention for the Protection of Industrial Property (1934), municipal law, direct effect **70,** 431-2
parks maintenance, public law act, whether 63, 327
parliamentary immunity, waiver 71, 371, 385
participation agreements
dispute settlement clause **118,** 625-6, 631-4
'dispute under the agreement', effect of subsequent legislation, whether **118,** 631-4
unfair competition and **118,** 622-36
partnership 78, 681, **80,** 92, 97-9, 100, 144, 145
assets abroad, ownership **40,** 20-1, 25-6
characteristics **46,** 291, 293, 472
legal personality **47,** 33
Czech law **40,** 18, 20
Italian law **40,** 18, 20
Scotland, in **81,** 679, 709
passport
abuse of as international law violation **77,** 216, 222
alien's, conditions for issue **73,** 608-12
allegiance and **55,** 492, 494
citizenship, possession of foreign passport and **53,** 521, 524
diplomatic
diplomatic status, whether conferring **99,** 165-6
discretionary power **99,** 166
diplomatic protection and **43,** 128, 135, 182-3
discretionary power **84,** 717-18
entitlement **103,** 290-1
freedom of movement **103,** 290-1

passport (*cont.*)
evidence of
diplomatic status **99,** 110, 166, **119,** 78
family relationship **109,** 156
nationality **49,** 504-6, **55,** 485, 486, **61,** 389, 393, 397-8, 400-1, **77,** 216, **83,** 466, **103,** 289, **120,** 304
as exit permit **43,** 126-30
false, deportation and **79,** 380
forged **104,** 36-7
border controls infringements **71,** 252-8
freedom of movement, necessary for **77,** 535-6
grant, act of State **66,** 492-3
identity and travel document as substitute **78,** 70
issue of **39,** 461
act of State **63,** 317
jurisdiction concerning **73,** 372-3, 609-10, **78,** 69, 70-1, **79,** 198
nationality and **49,** 504-6, **55,** 485, **61,** 389
nature and function **39,** 128, 135, **55,** 447
property of government **87,** 179
refusal **55,** 446-7
citizen resident abroad **70,** 236-40, **78,** 70-1
grounds, liability to arrest **84,** 718, 719
judicial review **84,** 716-17, 720
nationals **55,** 446-7
public order/public policy/*ordre public* **78,** 70
reasons, need for **84,** 719-20
remedies, absence of injury **84,** 719, 720
for travel to restricted area **38,** 102-11
unjustified **78,** 70-1, **79,** 200
retention by consul, right to recover **113,** 512-13
right to **60,** 134, 145
nature of **60,** 133-4
for South Sinai **80,** 693
State immunity, jurisdiction and **63,** 317
travel document, whether **79,** 195-6, 200
'United Kingdom passport' **43,** 130-40
withdrawal, right to leave one's own country and **101,** 407-9
patents
act of State and **66,** 492-3, **70,** 429-34
decisions respecting, exequatur **48,** 84, 86-7
forfeiture, extraterritorial effect **70,** 429-34
German patents, confiscation by allies
act of war **48,** 468-9
restoration **42,** 348-80
territoriality **48,** 84-8
trust agreement relating to **42,** 353-6, 363
Union of Paris for Protection of Industrial Property and **48,** 84, 86
Patiala, East Punjab States, **49,** 338, 433-4, 449-50, 453, 459
patriality. *See* nationality, patriality
patrimonial rights
of illegitimate child **58,** 587-90
discrimination **58,** 588-9

disposition **58,** 580, 586
family life, respect for and **58,** 587
intestacy and **58,** 586-7
of unmarried mother **58,** 591-2, 620-1
discrimination **58,** 591-2
disposition **58,** 591
patrimonial sea 55, 175, 221, 322, 329, **56,** 90
natural resources, rights over **56,** 137
peace, crime against 80, 681
peace treaties. *See also* Austria, State Treaty (1955); Egypt–Israel Peace Treaty (1979); Germany, peace settlement; Hungary, Peace Treaty (1947); Italy, Peace Treaty (1947); Japan, Peace Treaty (1951)
ex-enemy property, treatment of **42,** 204
Declaration of 5 June 1945 regarding defeat of Germany **78,** 186
territorial questions reserved to **78,** 186-7, 190
Soviet–Polish Treaty of 16 August 1945 **78,** 187
interpretation **40,** 459
nationality and **53,** 414-17, 519
penal character **44,** 320
performance **40,** 436-63
restitution provisions **44,** 448-85
reparation provisions, shareholder claims **46,** 478, 479
stateless person, right to claim **77,** 566
termination of war, relevance to **40,** 434-5
waiver of claims
Hungarian claims against Germany **44,** 301-23, 436-45
Peace Treaty with Italy (1947) **40,** 64, 69-73
WWI **82,** 439
peaceful assembly. *See* European Convention on Human Rights (1950), freedom of assembly/association
peaceful co-existence 82, 675-6
peaceful enjoyment of possessions. *See* European Convention on Human Rights (1950), peaceful enjoyment of possessions; expropriation/nationalization; property, possessions, peaceful enjoyment of; taking of property
peaceful settlement of disputes. *See* arbitration; conciliation; Contadora process; diplomatic channels; dispute settlement; good offices; mediation; negotiation; Pact of Bogotá (1948), pacific settlement under
peacekeeping operations. *See* United Nations peacekeeping operations
PEMEX (Petroleos Mexicanos). *See* Mexico, PEMEX (Petroleos Mexicanos)
penal servitude, slavery, whether 53, 552-3
pensions, freedom from discrimination **114,** 313-19, **118,** 149-51
people
minority distinguished **79,** 264-5
Namibia, history of peoples of **49,** 75-9
requirements **80,** 687-8
adequate territory, need for **80,** 687-8
community life **80,** 687
permanent residence **80,** 687
self-determination
collective right, whether **79,** 263, 264-5, 266
consultation of **89,** 19-22
sovereignty, inherent right/will **49,** 58, **90,** 450, 482-3, 514-20

peremptory norm. *See jus cogens*/peremptory norm
Permanent Court of Arbitration (PCA) 78, 657 n. 3, **84,** 537
designation of appointing authority **68,** 521
fact-finding role **119,** 597-8
ICJ distinguished **85,** 340, **97,** 177-8
jurisdiction
dissolution of union of States, disputes arising from **91,** 306
ICJ compared **85,** 340, **91,** 306, **97,** 177-8
Optional Rules for Arbitrating Disputes between Two Parties of which Only One is a State **119,** 582-3
non-contractual disputes **119,** 582
where neither party a State **119,** 582-3
Permanent Court of International Justice (PCIJ) distinguished **85,** 340
Permanent Court of International Justice (PCIJ). *See also* International Court of Justice (ICJ); Permanent Court of Arbitration (PCA)
abuse of competence
Customs Regime between Austria and Germany **92,** 94
Free Zones of Upper Savoy and the District of Gex **92,** 94
advisory jurisdiction, purpose **62,** 551
advisory opinion
consent of interested parties, need for **110,** 320
Eastern Carelia **110,** 320
effect **37,** 19
Agent, declaration by, effect **37,** 78
amendment of claim, *Société Commerciale de Belgique* **97,** 34
applicable law **37,** 81
arbitration, compulsory and **84,** 272-4
boundaries, uncertainty, effect, *Monastery of Saint Naoum* **41,** 62
Chorzów Factory, unilateral acts **80,** 534
competence, 'interest of a legal nature' **37,** 240
compulsory jurisdiction, acceptance **37,** 47, **46,** 40, 63, 77, 81, 85, 150-1, **57,** 554. *See also* International Court of Justice (ICJ), compulsory jurisdiction, acceptance
General Treaty of Inter-American Arbitration (1929) **84,** 301
termination **84,** 292
dispute, need for **122,** 417
Dissenting Opinions, Resolution on **37,** 286
dissolution **37,** 75
effects **46,** 38-51, 62-4, 77-88, 96-108, 145-72
dispute settlement treaties and **46,** 166, 168-9, **49,** 180, **57,** 479, 493
Eastern Greenland
estoppel **80,** 556
parties' rights, effect of incidents on **80,** 456
equity **71,** 211
part of international law, *Diversion of Water from the Meuse* **41,** 104
functions **57,** 476
immunity of officials **71,** 538
individuals, proposed access to **37,** 57
interim relief **71,** 642
interpretation of judgments, dispute as to **81,** 450-1
judgment, consequences of **37,** 140-1
jurisdiction
basis, consent **84,** 280
sources **37,** 70

League organs and **37,** 421, 546
negotiate, duty to
Free Zones of Upper Savoy and Gex **41,** 77
Railway Traffic between Lithuania and Poland **41,** 77
officials, taxation exemption **73,** 2-3
Permanent Court of Arbitration (PCA) distinguished **85,** 340
practice **62,** 563, 578-9
provisional measures, legally binding whether, *Acts and Documents concerning the Organization of the Court* **95,** 83-5
Rules of Court (1922)
39 **115,** 247
40 **115,** 223, 247
Special Agreement, registration **37,** 80
standing **37,** 513-14
League of Nations **37,** 19, 46
League of Nations Council **37,** 19
Statute
Art. 38 (*ex aequo et bono* jurisdiction), *travaux préparatoires* **99,** 595-8
travaux préparatoires **70,** 570, **85,** 340
Permanent Mandates Commission. *See* Mandates Commission
permanent sovereignty over natural resources. *See* natural resources
persecution. *See also* crimes against humanity, classification as, persecution; refugees, 'persecution or well-founded fear of persecution'; war crimes, classification as, persecution
definition **79,** 381
Persian Gulf States, Qatar, status 42, 51-8
persona non grata **61,** 565, 566, **80,** 403, 418, **115,** 443-5, 607
personal law, definition 103, 156-7
personality. *See* international law, subjects
Pertamina. *See* Indonesia
Peru
American Convention on Human Rights (1969), accession to **116,** 340 n. 3, 347
Compania Pervana de Vapores SA **63,** 436-46, 541-9
Constitution 1979, Art. 235 **116,** 321 n. 2, 323
Constitution 1993, Art. 140 **116,** 323
Continental Shelf Proclamation (1947) **41,** 118, 120
disappearances **116,** 476-7
legislation typifying **116,** 519
habeas corpus, ineffectiveness **116,** 479
high seas, claim to sovereignty over 200 miles **41,** 120-2, 123
human rights violations **116,** 347-87
law of
Amnesty Law 1995 **116,** 435-6
compatibility with American Convention on Human Rights (1969) **116,** 523-6
Decree-Law No 25.475 (terrorism), compatibility with international law **116,** 355, 379, 434-5
Decree-Law No 25.659 (treason), compatibility with international law **116,** 379, 434-5
Notary Law No 26.002 **116,** 412-14
public corporation, Banco de la Nación **87,** 17
Petroleos Mexicos. *See* Mexico, Petroleos Mexicos
petroleum. *See* oil
Philippines
comity, State immunity, jurisdiction **64,** 666

Philippines (*cont.*)
Commission on Good Government **81,** 584, 625, **82,** 54
Constitution 1935, Art. II(3) **64,** 655, **88,** 707, 710
Constitution 1973
Art. II(3) **64,** 655
Art. VII **81,** 626, **82,** 57
Head of State. *See* Head of State immunity *below*
Constitution 1986, Art. III (17) **121,** 573-4
Constitution 1987
Art. II(2) **102,** 139, 170
Art. II(18) **102,** 159-60
Art. III(8) **102,** 160
Art. VIII(3) **102,** 160
Art. XVI(3) **102,** 139-40
continental shelf legislation **41,** 208
courts, municipal, independence and impartiality **82,** 56
diplomatic privileges and immunities, State immunity and, distinction **102,** 172
evidence of, State immunity, jurisdiction, executive certificate **102,** 172-3
executive certificate/statement, State immunity, jurisdiction **102,** 172-3
expropriation/nationalization, Executive Orders
No 1 **81,** 482, 584, 597
No 2 **81,** 584, 597, 625
Nos 1 and 2, whether **81,** 597
extradition from, US military base **57,** 316, 321-4
extraterritoriality, military base **102,** 148
foreign forces, jurisdiction **88,** 710
general principles of international law, State immunity **102,** 138-40
Head of State immunity
during and out of office distinguished **81,** 632
official acts in exercise of mandate **82,** 57
Holy See
privileges and immunities **102,** 170-3
status **102,** 168-70
sovereignty **102,** 169
Vatican City distinguished **102,** 169
Independence Treaty (1946) **46,** 481
International Catholic Migration Commission (ICMC), privileges and immunities **102,** 151-62
international law
as part of municipal law **64,** 655, **88,** 707, **102,** 139, 170
general principles of international law **102,** 140, 170
subjects **102,** 169
international officials, immunity **52,** 395
international organizations, definition **102,** 157-8
international organizations, immunity, jurisdiction, waiver, submission to proceedings **107,** 184-5
international organizations, privileges and immunities
alternative remedy, need for **102,** 160-1
basis
avoidance of partiality and interference **102,** 160
constituent agreement **107,** 185
headquarters agreement **107,** 185

functional **102,** 160
labour law of host State, immunity from **102,** 151-62
political question **102,** 157
International Rice Research Institute (IRRI), privileges and immunities **102,** 153-62
jurisdiction, foreign forces **88,** 710
law of
Act 3083 (governmental immunity) **102,** 140
Civil Code 1950, Art. 2180 **102,** 144
Civil Code (Spain) 1889
Art. 1554 **88,** 707
Art. 1560 **88,** 707
Decree of 28 February 1986 **82,** 54
Labour Code 1974
amendments (Republic Act No 6715) **102,** 163-4
Art. 243 **102,** 160
Art. 246 **102,** 160
Omnibus Rules implementing **102,** 155-6
Republic Act No 213 (competition policy) **88,** 715-16
Tariff and Customs Code 1957 (Republic Act No 1937) **52,** 391
occupation **88,** 706-9
'Republic of Philippines', status **88,** 709
political question doctrine, international organizations, privileges and immunities **102,** 157
Presidential Commission on Good Government, member, State immunity of **92,** 484-90, 491
presumption of innocence **82,** 56
specialized agency
definition **102,** 158
International Catholic Migration Commission (ICMC) **102,** 156
State immunity, jurisdiction, acts of
agent **64,** 115, 658
armed forces abroad
personal liability **64,** 656-7, 659-60
termination of logging licence for security reasons **64,** 655-61
State immunity, jurisdiction, applicability, in own courts **88,** 711
State immunity, jurisdiction, classification of act
construction contract, naval base **102,** 123-31
disposal **102,** 170-3
drugs control **102,** 143-4
military base
barber's shop **102,** 146-7
games room attendant **102,** 148
restaurant, availability to public **102,** 145
restaurant, profit, relevance **102,** 145
supply of lumber **64,** 665-7
nature or purpose of transaction as determining factor **102,** 126, 171
naval base, construction contract **102,** 123-31
profit, relevance **102,** 145, 146-7, 171-2
State immunity, jurisdiction, entitlement
Head of State. *See* Head of State immunity *above*
visiting forces **102,** 140-2

Philippines (*cont.*)
State immunity, jurisdiction, procedural aspects, exhaustion of administrative remedies **88,** 714
State immunity, jurisdiction, theory/doctrine
basis
dignity of foreign State **102,** 128-9
par in parem non habet jurisdictionem **102,** 139
public order/public policy/*ordre public* **88,** 711
sovereignty **102,** 128-9, 131
restrictive theory, customary international law **102,** 170
State immunity, jurisdiction, waiver
implied
contract **102,** 128, 140, 142-3
legal proceedings **102,** 140
proper authority **102,** 144
treaty **102,** 129-31
Philippine–US Military Bases Agreement (1947) **64,** 657
signature of contract **88,** 712, 714
statutory **102,** 140, 144
submission to the jurisdiction, challenge to jurisdiction **102,** 148
State responsibility for acts and omissions of
armed forces **64,** 659-60
termination of activity in military base for security reasons **64,** 659-60
judicial authorities **102,** 139, 143
trade union, right to form, privileges and immunities of international organization and **102,** 151-62
treaties
executive agreements
distinction, whether **88,** 715-16
validity **88,** 715
ratification, legislature, by **88,** 715
visiting forces, extraterritoriality **102,** 148
philosophical convictions
definition **67,** 495-6
right to hold **58,** 141, 142, 146-7
pillage 40, 261, 264, 267, 269, 271, 281-2, **42,** 35, 38, **122,** 72
piracy 36, 26-7, 292, 298-300, **73,** 374-5, **77,** 210, 222, 223, 243, 537-41. *See also* privateering
attack on neutral ship as **79,** 10
Declaration of Paris (1856) and **48,** 471, 473
definition **56,** 245-9, 250-1, 254, **77,** 243. *See also* requirements *below*
Geneva Convention on the High Seas (1958) **77,** 539-41, **78,** 569
'for private ends' **77,** 539-41, **78,** 571
insurance contract, for the purpose of **78,** 569, 573, 574
municipal law **56,** 252-3, **78,** 569-75
passengers who mutiny **78,** 573
rioters from the shore **78,** 573
General Treaty of Peace (Trucial States) (1820) **91,** 559
individual, responsibility for **104,** 152, 153
insurance and **78,** 569, 573, 574
Declaration of Paris **48,** 471, 473
jurisdiction **73,** 374-5, **77,** 538-41, **78,** 568-74, **91,** 40, 41
municipal law **78,** 569-75

universal **82,** 444-5, **91,** 40-1
jus gentium **78,** 569-70, 572, 574
PLO **82,** 317
requirements
'at sea' **78,** 573-4
force **78,** 568, 574, 575
intention **78,** 575
high seas **56,** 255, 256, **78,** 568, 570-1
theft **78,** 568, 570, 574
attempt at **78,** 574
territorial waters and **56,** 254, **78,** 568-74
tort, whether **123,** 502
USA **77,** 174, 243
war, act of distinguished **91,** 559
within foreign jurisdiction **78,** 574
within foreign port **78,** 571
Pitcairn
applicable law, English rules of equity and statutes of general application **104,** 511-12, 515
Commissioner's secretary, employer, Crown **104,** 512-13
courts, establishment **104,** 511-12
State immunity in respect of, entitlement
Crown **104,** 513
Governor on Crown's behalf **104,** 513
status, British colony **104,** 511, 515
plebiscite, Namibia, proposal for **49,** 10-12, 47-8, 54-5, 112, 169
plunder. *See* crimes against humanity, classification as, wanton destruction and plunder of property not justified by necessity; pillage
Poland. *See also* Oder–Neisse, territories east of
anti-Jewish legislation, repeal, effect in Israel **47,** 203-4
applicable law, Rules of the Refined Sugar Association **64,** 196
army, status in Germany (1945) **41,** 461-74
boundaries, adjustment by treaty **71,** 586-7
compensation, for loss of property **71,** 586-7
Concordat (1925), termination **47,** 25
confiscation of Austrian property **47,** 412-17
cultural institute in
diplomatic status **82,** 2-5
as State agency **82,** 4
diplomatic immunity, jurisdiction, entitlement
cultural institute **82,** 2-5
non-appearance **82,** 2-5
diplomatic mission, cultural institute, part of, whether **82,** 3
employment contract, locally engaged staff, cultural institute, State immunity, jurisdiction, librarian **82,** 3-5
executive certificate/statement **82,** 2
force majeure
government intervention as **64,** 199-201, 204, 205-7
Rules of the Refined Sugar Association **64,** 199, 204, 205-7
FRG and. *See* Germany, Federal Republic (FRG), Eastern Treaties for the Normalization of Relations with Poland and the USSR (1970) (Moscow and Warsaw Treaties); Germany, Federal Republic (FRG), FRG–Poland Border Treaty (1990); Germany, Federal Republic of, FRG–Poland, Treaty for the Normalization of Relations (1970) (Warsaw Treaty)

Poland (*cont.*)
law of
Civil Procedure Code 1979
Art. 3(2) **82,** 3
Art. 1111 **82,** 2, 3
Art. 1143 **82,** 2, 3
Decree of 8 March 1946 (nationalization measures) **65,** 129
Decree of 1956 (Protection of National Frontiers) **47,** 118
Labour Code 1974
Art. 2 **82,** 52
Art. 6 **82,** 2, 3
Law of 9 January 1951 **78,** 188
Law of 5 November 1974 (sugar exports) **64,** 198, 199
partition, courts of partitioning powers, judgments **47,** 107-8
Polski Linie Oceanicze Gdynia **63,** 541-9
private international law in **51,** 424-9
public order/public policy/*ordre public* **52,** 29
Roman Catholic Church, legal personality **47,** 24-5
Rules of the Refined Sugar Association
as applicable law **64,** 196
export licences, duty to obtain **64,** 202-3
force majeure **64,** 199, 204, 205-7, 372-3
ships, floating island theory **47,** 118
State agency/State-owned corporation/State entity, classification, cultural institute **82,** 2-5
State immunity, jurisdiction, theory/doctrine, basis, reciprocity **82,** 4
treaties, individual rights under **71,** 586
USA, Claims Agreement (1960) **42,** 183-6
interest on awards **42,** 189-94
Vienna Convention on Diplomatic Relations (1961), applicability, States/State entities **82,** 3
police
agency of State, whether **65,** 198, 381
State immunity, jurisdiction and **63,** 327, 352-3, **65,** 195, 196-8, 381-2, **100,** 552-4, 555-8, **124,** 435
State responsibility for. *See* State responsibility for acts and omissions of, police officer
police investigations
private life, respect for **67,** 442-3
wrongful detention, whether **67,** 442
police power, revolution, State responsibility 106, 496-7
political asylum. *See* asylum; refugees, non-refoulement
political offence 40, 214-21, **45,** 96, 97, **51,** 271-2, 312-19, 366-400, **52,** 379, **55,** 431, 476-7, 553, 563-7, 570-4, **59,** 473-6, **60,** 361, **61,** 434-5, **69,** 250-62, 268-75, **70,** 5, **71,** 236-7, 530-4, **72,** 612-13, 615-17, 623-6, 631, 634, 637-8, **74,** 474-6, 480-2, 495-516, **79,** 52-3, 58-69, 92-5, 96, 100-9, 113-23, 130-3, 146-63, 244, 390, 395, 428, 435, 441, 446-7, 469-74, 478-82, 493-4, 495, 497-533, **85,** 84-7, **86,** 180, **104,** 38-42, 64-76, 86-94, **114,** 388, 631-2
burden of proof **79,** 53, 59, 94-5, 116, 117, **104,** 93, 94
classification as **80,** 17-18. *See also* definition *below*
anarchism **72,** 620, 625-6, **79,** 455-6, 480 n. 4, 508, 514
applicable law, requested State **104,** 56, 67
armed conflict **79,** 149-50, 453-4
acts in furtherance of aims of, evidence of **79,** 98
consensus in favour of, need for **79,** 478 n. 2

definition **79,** 480
assassination **63,** 388-9
attempt on Head of State **72,** 615-17
attacks on third parties **69,** 261
bomb attacks on **72,** 620-6, **74,** 511-16
bar used by opposing group **100,** 423
civil airport **107,** 562-90
civilians travelling by commercial bus **104,** 64-76
bomb-making, Extradition, European Convention on (1957) **100,** 621
by offender **69,** 270
emergency legislation, offences under **79,** 478-9
escape from detention **55,** 572-4, 577, **59,** 61-2, 63-5, 73, 482
offence connected with political offence **79,** 163, 498
espionage **55,** 573
fraud involving political corruption **104,** 113-14
government authority, attacks on **69,** 261
government policy, attempt to change **69,** 272
guerrillas, robbery for funds to train **40,** 220-1
hijacking **80,** 680
hostage-taking **79,** 481
illegal export to East bloc country **72,** 634, 637-8
incidence test **79,** 450, 498, 509-10, 513-16, 521-6, **104,** 40-2, 65, 86-90, 93, 94, 112-13, 667, **107,** 154-8, 161-2, 566-70
kidnapping **74,** 502-3, 515
killing by organized armed group **111,** 508
killing and injuring of innocent bystanders **107,** 165-8
logistical support outside territory **100,** 619-22
murder **55,** 554, **71,** 530-3, **72,** 612-13, 615-17, **74,** 498, 503-4, 511-14, **79,** 92-5
mass murder **39,** 433-52
mass wartime executions **72,** 612-13, **79,** 542-3
Nazi treatment of Jews, approval of **40,** 214-18
offence
by official while suppressing rebellion **104,** 38-42
connected with political offence **55,** 560, 566, 570-4, 576-7, **74,** 501, **100,** 619, 620
jure gentium **40,** 221
ordinary offence with political motivation **100,** 620-1, **104,** 86, **107,** 153, 161
outside country of uprising **79,** 519, 530
outside the jurisdiction **100,** 619-22
of a political character **86,** 172, 178-9, **100,** 420-3, 425-6, 619-20
political motive **69,** 260, 270-1
political organization. *See* political organization *below*
'pure' political **104,** 86
while escaping from prison **100,** 423, 425
within the jurisdiction **88,** 45-7
political motive **69,** 260, 270-1
political organization. *See* political organization *below*
'pure' and 'relative' distinguished **55,** 571
sectarian attack **79,** 132-3
skyjacking **79,** 519
terrorist offence **79,** 52-3, 105, 131-2, 453-5, 478-81, 514-15, 517-18, 525, 531-2, **104,** 79, 87-93, **107,** 160-1, 163-4, 166-7, **111,** 514
political by definition **104,** 92
torture **121,** 262

political offence (*cont.*)
violation of international law **79,** 479-80, 511-12, 515, 519, 529
violent conduct if peaceful means available **79,** 480 n. 4
war crimes **55,** 553, **79,** 511, **86,** 179-81, **105,** 482
definition, political character **40,** 220
definition, requirements **55,** 554-7, 568, **60,** 362-3, **71,** 532-3, **79,** 52, 58-9, 61, 62, 92, 101-7, 113-23, 131-2, 146-63, 452, 453, 461, 479-82, **85,** 84-7, **104,** 666-72. *See also* classification as *above*; relevant factors *below*
absence **107,** 153 n. 1
broad **100,** 421, 422
'connected with' **79,** 116, 123
customary international law and **74,** 481-2
international law **79,** 121, **86,** 180
lack of precision **79,** 58, 92, 121, 446, 505
treaty, time of conclusion **100,** 422-3
UNHCR *Handbook on Procedures and Criteria for Determining Refugee Status* (1979) **104,** 670, **107,** 163, 577, 588
UNHCR office in Canada **107,** 164
delicta communia **100,** 422
double jeopardy **104,** 62 n. 2
European Convention on the Suppression of Terrorism (1977) **104,** 87, **107,** 564
evidence **60,** 362-4, 366, **69,** 249-50, 259-62, 268-73
burden of proof **104,** 93, 94
circumstances in requesting State **79,** 449-50, 453
implied admission of guilt **69,** 270-1
insufficiency of **71,** 533-4
standard of proof, balance of probabilities **104,** 93
expulsion for **61,** 433-6
extradition and **45,** 96, 97, **80,** 16-17, **85,** 84-7, **119,** 250
judicial review **80,** 18
extradition judge, role **69,** 251-9, 273-5
fear of persecution for **72,** 631, **74,** 474-6, **79,** 93-5, 99-100, 133
First Additional Protocol to the Geneva Conventions (1977) **104,** 87
general principle of international law **78,** 97, 131, **79,** 505
on high seas **55,** 555
historic development **79,** 493, 504-15
judicial review, power to review **104,** 81
jurisprudence
Atta **107,** 586
Cheng **107,** 566-70, 583
Eain v. *Wilkes* **107,** 584
Gil **107,** 588
Littlejohn **107,** 569, 584
McMullen **107,** 586-7
Meunier **107,** 566-7, 581-2
justification **79,** 505
avoidance of unfair trial **79,** 505
legitimacy of political crimes **79,** 505
non-intervention **79,** 505
law and order, maintenance of, where requesting State's interest transcends **79,** 482
liability to prosecution for **79,** 100
occupied territory, in **86,** 171, 176-7
partisans, against **86,** 176

officials, acts by **79,** 512 n. 24, 529
'political' character **55,** 569
'political incidence' test **79,** 92, 390, 452, 506-26, 529
political organization
existence of **79,** 506-7
membership of **79,** 513 n. 26, 523
nature of **79,** 480, 481
political uprising **79,** 497, 500
by indigenous people **79,** 519, 525-6
definition **79,** 452, 453
evidence of **79,** 453, 524-6
existence of **79,** 518-20, 522-6, 529, 530
in furtherance of **79,** 497, 508, 523, 529
war as **79,** 509 n. 17
proportionality and **79,** 506, 507, **100,** 423, **104,** 670-2, **107,** 164, 167, 559-60, 570-2, 577-8
dominant motive **107,** 571
McMullen **107,** 571
need for **72,** 612-13, 616, 625-6, **74,** 504
proscribed organization, membership **79,** 97, 453, 454
'pure' **79,** 59, 97, 100, 446, 447 n. 24, 505-6
espionage **79,** 505
sedition **79,** 505
reasons for exception
changed context **104,** 40, 88, 90, **107,** 557, 562-4
non-intervention in internal affairs of another country **104,** 39, 40
protection against authoritarian regime **104,** 39
protection against unfair trial and punishment **104,** 39
refugees and **74,** 441, **77,** 580, **99,** 33-4, **104,** 658-72, **107,** 572-3
'relative' **79,** 59, 97, 100, 121, 446, 457 n. 24, 505-6
criteria **79,** 506-8
relevant factors **86,** 171-3, 175-6
accused's connection with place of offence **104,** 66 n. 8
acts within framework of struggle for independence **111,** 508
damage to political institutions **100,** 620-1
effect directly related to political objective **100,** 423, 425, **104,** 669, **107,** 160, 165-7
'ideological self-preservation' **79,** 507 n. 14
incidence test. *See* acts incidental to violent uprising *above*
legality under international law
law of armed conflict **104,** 90, 93
military rules of engagement **104,** 68-9, 90
likelihood of movement's success **79,** 481, 498, 515, 521, 523
membership of
paramilitary group **79,** 523
proscribed group **79,** 95, 453, 454
terrorist organization **74,** 498-500, 504, 511-16. *See also* proscribed organization, membership *above*
motivation **40,** 216, 218-19, **55,** 561, **79,** 52, 98-9, 107, 116, 132-3, 163, 390, 435, 453, 454-5, 482, 497, 506, 509, 514, 523, **100,** 422, **104,** 65-8, 86, 89, **107,** 557, 577
nature of
offence **79,** 107, 116, 163, 390, 480, 509
organization on whose behalf offence committed **79,** 480, 481

political offence (*cont.*)
requesting State **79,** 116
non-civilian injury **79,** 52, 59
paramilitary group
commission by **79,** 59, 523
existence of **79,** 53
place of offence **79,** 480-1, **86,** 179, **100,** 619-22, **104,** 66 n. 8
within geographical area of uprising **79,** 523-6, 529-30, 532
political activity, arising out of **79,** 53, 60-1
political legitimacy **79,** 515, 516-17
political movement, existence of **79,** 506-7
prevailing circumstances at time of offence **79,** 61, 99-100, 102, 390, 424, 435, 448, 480, 508
proportionality. *See* proportionality and *above*
Quinn v. *Robinson* **107,** 585
'regarded by the requested party' **107,** 572
Schtraks **107,** 566, 582
standards of reasonable and civilized people **79,** 52, 99, 132, 480
State, direct offence to **79,** 506
status of offender **79,** 480, 497, 523
status in prison **79,** 60-1
'special category status' **100,** 423, 426
status of victim **79,** 107, 390, 456-7, 481, 498, 514, 522, 523, 531, **104,** 89-90, 94
civilian representatives of government **79,** 480-1
struggle for power **72,** 612, 616, 625-6, 637, **74,** 501, 504, 508, 511
tactic previously used **104,** 66 n. 8
terrorism **79,** 52-3, 105, 131-2, 453-5, 478-81, 514-15, 517-18, 525, 531-2
use of violence **79,** 480
responsibility for determining whether **79,** 446-52, 462, 469-74, 482 n. 6, 493-533, **104,** 38 n. 22, 87
executive certificate/statement, conclusiveness **104,** 87, 163
conformity with international/national norms **104,** 87
separation of powers **107,** 451
superior orders **39,** 434, 437, 451-2, **86,** 180-1
treason **79,** 150, 505
undertaking not to prosecute for **55,** 574-6
UNGA Resolution 61 (1985) **104,** 87
war and **79,** 509 n. 17, 520, 529
political question doctrine 66, 111-13, 119, 306, 333-8, 396-7, **77,** 225-7, 232, 252, 256, 270-1, **80,** 22, 590, **81,** 566-7, 637 n. 11, **85,** 252, 253-5, **87,** 185-6, 515, 662, 675, 676, 677-9, 687-9, 699-703, **88,** 57-9, 125-6, **118,** 345. *See also* act of State; justiciability; prerogative
acts and omissions of State organs, warship **99,** 84
clarification of legal framework for democratic decisions **115,** 547
Constitution as basis **94,** 100, 109, 112-13, 117-21, **99,** 61
contras in Nicaragua **99,** 58-91
control of State's assets abroad **86,** 18
criteria **66,** 239, 333-8, 397
European Court of Human Rights **108,** 478-9, 483, 485-7
foreign relations questions and **82,** 290
historical development **94,** 101-6
immunity of State vessel **94,** 105

implementation of law **94,** 126-7
internal affairs, relevance in **94,** 109-10
nationalization measures in course of war **94,** 109-10
international organizations, privileges and immunities **102,** 157
justiciability **42,** 393-401, 438, **63,** 72, 317, **66,** 111-13, 119, 306, 333-8, 396-7, **77,** 225-7, 232, 252, 256, 270-1, **80,** 22, 590
maintenance of forces abroad, properly authorized, whether **94,** 114, 120
military operation **99,** 84-5
prisoner of war status **99,** 187
reasons for
absence of judicially discoverable and manageable standards **64,** 351, **94,** 110-11, 114, 126, **99,** 49-51, 53, 62-72, 77-8, 84-5, 181, **104,** 162, **106,** 361-2, **107,** 257-8, 259, **114,** 628-9, **116,** 588-94, **125,** 650-2, 653-5
confidentiality **94,** 110, 114
difficulty in handling relevant information **94,** 110, 114, **96,** 75
foreign policy considerations **104,** 162-3, **107,** 258
hierarchy, whether **99,** 49
international effects **94,** 110, 114, **99,** 52, 72-4, 79
outdated **105,** 463
policy decision, need for **104,** 162
responsibility of another branch of government **96,** 75-6, **99,** 48-9, 53, **104,** 162, **107,** 258, 259
recognition of foreign government **86,** 3-4, 5-7, 12, 18, **94,** 102, 103-4
recognition of foreign State **96,** 48
remedy, existence of alternative
complaint to executive agency **107,** 259-60
judicial review **107,** 260
remedy sought, relevance **99,** 49 n. 8, 51-3, 85
removal of judges by de facto government **123,** 149-50
requirements, legal criteria **96,** 217
self-defence **94,** 114
separation of powers and **94,** 109, 115-16, 117-20, **99,** 61, 177, 180, **123,** 147
State Department suggestions **66,** 336
state of exception **123,** 149-50
State immunity, jurisdiction **63,** 71-3, 317
State succession questions and **63,** 55
State immunity, jurisdiction, classification of act, violation of international law **103,** 557-8
state of war **94,** 113-14
termination **94,** 106
test **94,** 107-8, 124-5
treaty interpretation **90,** 685-6
US intervention in Panama (1989) **99,** 177-83
war, matters relating to **99,** 90-1
political refugees. *See* refugees, definition, political refugee
political responsibility 82, 473
political rights
definition **72,** 589-90
deprivation of **70,** 250, 257-8
entitlement of aliens to **72,** 589-90
nationality and **79,** 294, 295
political turmoil
as *force majeure* **63,** 276

political turmoil (*cont.*)
judicial notice of **63,** 276
political union, EMU and 98, 240-1
pollution. *See* environment, pollution; marine pollution; nuclear energy exploitation
Pondicherry, France, cession 44, 295-6, **49,** 484-96
pornography. *See* obscene publications
Porter Convention (The Hague) (1907) 46, 465-6
ports
blockade. *See* blockade
free access **77,** 514-15, **81,** 515
rule of comity **77,** 182
jurisdiction **38,** 159, **43,** 176-7, **55,** 440-1, **57,** 164-6
colonial **55,** 441-2
flag State **120,** 593-9
control of crew **38,** 159, **43,** 176-7
vessel in distress **82,** 362-3, 366-7
foreign ship **54,** 228, **57,** 164-6, **91,** 384-5
port State powers. *See* port State powers *below*
non-encroachment principle **67,** 114-15, 128-9
port State powers
after departure of ship **120,** 596
Law of the Sea Convention (1982) **120,** 596
customary international law, protection of State interest **120,** 596
enforcement on high seas of safety legislation going beyond generally accepted requirements of international law **120,** 593-9
Minimum Standards in Merchant Ships Convention (1976) **120,** 593-6
regional memoranda of understanding **120,** 595-6
Safety of Life at Sea Convention (1974) **120,** 594-6
ship in, jurisdiction **91,** 384-5
Portugal
applicable law, foreign State, proceedings involving, action against, international law **116,** 635
civil proceedings **78,** 359-70
delays **78,** 359-70
courts' duty to ensure speed and fairness **96,** 511-12
Constitution 1933 **83,** 30-2, 39
judicial independence **96,** 486
reparation for infringement of fundamental rights within the EC/EU **96,** 486
Constitution 1976 **78,** 368
Art. 8(1) **116,** 628, 635
Art. 8(3) (direct application of acts of international organizations) **93,** 563, 570-2
Art. 21 **96,** 486-7
Art. 115 (primacy of law) **93,** 572
Art. 168(1) (regional authorities), European Regional Development Fund (ERDF) and **93,** 568-73
regulatory power
EC law as basis **93,** 572
need for *lex anterior* **93,** 572
customary international law
municipal law and **116,** 627-8
requirements, general acceptance **116,** 628-32
democracy, restoration of **78,** 363
diplomatic agent, obligations, respect for laws and regulations of receiving State **116,** 633

diplomatic immunity, jurisdiction, State immunity and, overlap **116,** 628-9
diplomatic premises, inviolability, extraterritoriality distinguished **116,** 632
EC law
  legislative competence, EC organs **93,** 572
  primacy **93,** 569, 572
  right to invoke before national courts **93,** 564
    venire contra factum proprium as basis **93,** 564, 656
EC law, direct effect **93,** 562, 563, 571
  direct application distinguished **93,** 563-4
  regulation **93,** 569-73
  requirements
    competence of originating organ **93,** 571
    express provision in constitutive treaty **93,** 571
  venire contra factum proprium distinguished **93,** 564, 565
employment contract, locally engaged staff, diplomatic mission
  immunity, jurisdiction
    classification of act **116,** 633
    customary international law **116,** 628-33
    diplomatic and State immunity, overlap **116,** 628-9, 633
    inviolability of premises, relevance **116,** 632
    Vienna Convention on Diplomatic Relations (1961), relevance **116,** 628-9, 632
  immunity, jurisdiction, waiver **116,** 633, 636
  jurisdiction **116,** 631
  State immunity, jurisdiction, European Convention on State Immunity (and Protocol) (Basle) (1972) **116,** 632
foreign State, proceedings involving, action against, applicable law, international law **116,** 635
freedom of expression, flag desecration and **122,** 599
Fundo de fomenteo de exportacao, as State agency **82,** 102
law of
  Administrative and Fiscal Tribunals Act, compatibility with Constitution **96,** 220
  Civil Code 1966, Art. 501 **96,** 491
  Civil Procedure Code 1939 (including amendments in 1961, 1995 and 1996)
    Art. 159 **78,** 360
    Art. 167 **78,** 360
    Art. 264(1) **96,** 510
    Art. 266 **96,** 511
    Art. 484 **96,** 488
    Art. 485 **96,** 488
    Art. 486 **96,** 488
    Art. 490 **96,** 488
    Art. 661(2) **78,** 362
    Arts. 783-800 **78,** 359
  Colonial Mining Laws, application in Goa, Daman and Diu **118,** 431
  Criminal Code 1982 (including amendments in 1995 and 1998), Art. 17(1) (*mens rea*) **93,** 565
  Decree of 26 February 1958 (grant of concession to Esso) **83,** 18
  Decree of 27 June 1967 (Guinea-Bissau straight baselines) **83,** 77
  Decree-Law 48.051 of 21 November 1967 **96,** 486, 491
  Decree-Law 119/82 **88,** 209, 304, 307
  Decree-Law 353-H/77 **88,** 303
  Decree-Law No 37:538 of 2 September 1948 (*Fundo de fomenteo de exportacao*) **82,** 102

Portugal (*cont.*)
Law 3/74 of 14 May 1974 **96,** 486
Organic Law on Overseas Provinces 1953/1955 **83,** 39
Resolution (Council of Ministers) No 44/86 (Application to Portuguese Territory of the European Regional Fund), constitutional validity **93,** 568-73
Road Traffic Act, Art. 68 **78,** 359
Road Traffic Code
compatibility with EC law **93,** 561-6
summary action **96,** 511
nationals, international driving licence for use in home country **93,** 561-3, 565
South Africa, Angola-South West Africa boundary **37,** 409
South West Africa, boundary agreement with South Africa **49,** 199
State immunity, jurisdiction
administrative act **96,** 220
legal liability, effect on **116,** 633
State practice, lack of consensus **116,** 628-9
State responsibility, jurisdiction, civil liability basis **96,** 491
State responsibility for acts and omissions during revolution **96,** 490
State responsibility for acts and omissions of
private administration **96,** 487, 491
public administration **96,** 487, 491
State responsibility for non-contractual liability **96,** 486-8
territory
alienation **83,** 30
determination of limits **83,** 30
treaties
approval, need for **83,** 30-1
colonies, extension to **83,** 75-6
domestic procedures **83,** 78
publication/promulgation, need for **83,** 39
treaty-making power **83,** 30-4
delegation **83,** 31
UN Charter **83,** 34
positive law, natural law and **41,** 183
positivism 37, 458-9, 460
possessions, right to peaceful enjoyment of. *See* property, peaceful enjoyment of possessions
post. *See* correspondence
Potsdam Conference 1945 56, 540, **78,** 186-7
Potsdam Agreements
cession of confiscated assets to Soviet Union **72,** 84
German Property Abroad (1945) **51,** 403
confiscation of German patents **48,** 468
restoration of property **44,** 4-5
transfers of German population **44,** 65
as violation of US Constitution **56,** 543
Potsdam Declaration, application to Japan **53,** 5-8
power of attorney
legalization **40,** 19
revocability **66,** 197
practice of States. *See* State practice
precautionary principle. *See* environment, precautionary principle

precedent in international tribunals 57, 301. *See also* European Economic Area (EEA) draft Agreement (1991), precedent; International Court of Justice (ICJ), precedent; Iran-US Claims Tribunal, precedent; Yugoslavia, International Criminal Tribunal for the Former (ICTY), precedent
arbitral decisions **71,** 94, 101, 120, 129-30, 139, 187, 192, 201, 205-6, 208, 210, 212, 641-2, 655-6, 658-9, 695-6
arbitral tribunals **83,** 70, **119,** 639, 667-8
State's right to change position **83,** 69-70
Central American Court of Justice decision, ICJ and **97,** 517
European Court of Human Rights **56,** 486, **78,** 212, **81,** 182-3, **86,** 367-9, 405-7, **89,** 123-4, 131, 147-51, 179-80, 202, **90,** 92-3
Iran–US Claims Tribunal. *See* Iran–US Claims Tribunal
Italian–US Conciliation Commission **45,** 500-1
jurisdiction, decisions by other courts in same matter, relevance **106,** 544-5
municipal court decisions **104,** 99, **106,** 485-6
precedent in municipal courts
development of law and **87,** 417
ECJ decision **107,** 118-19
GATT Committee on Subsidies and Countervailing Measures **107,** 119
international arbitral award **108,** 537
international law and **64,** 88-90, 128, 152-3, 549-50, 705-6, **71,** 640-1, **81,** 409, **104,** 616-17, **111,** 422
municipal courts in other countries **107,** 140-1
South African courts, South West Africa and **82,** 483-5
stare decisis doctrine **53,** 583, **64,** 15-20, 89-90, 212-15, **84,** 69, 683, **90,** 527
international law and **64,** 16, 89-90, 127-8, 140-6, 150-3, 169, 212-15, 549-50, 705-6
preclusion 48, 340, **52,** 221. *See also* acquiescence; doctrine of acknowledgment; estoppel; prescription
estoppel distinguished **71,** 132, **83,** 69
international proceedings **46,** 256-7, 265-6
preferential rights. *See* fisheries, preferential rights
preferential treatment 58, 13. *See also* freedom from discrimination
prerogative. *See also* United Kingdom, prerogative
armistice agreement **83,** 160
boundaries **86,** 190-2, 198, 200
constitutional basis **118,** 367
continental shelf/fishing zones, exploitation **106,** 372
dependent territories and **86,** 191, 199-204
diplomatic relations
negotiation **112,** 742
termination **106,** 372
foreign relations **84,** 717, **107,** 469-73, **118,** 367
judicial appointment **123,** 146
judicial review and **84,** 717, 718-19, 720, **90,** 34, 35, 50-5, **123,** 605-6
justiciability and **84,** 720
legislative provision, State immunity, power to override **108,** 534
martial law and **87,** 261
parens patriae and **118,** 472
political question doctrine. *See* political question doctrine
recognition of State **106,** 372, 374
territorial changes **106,** 374, **123,** 557-8
treaty denunciation **106,** 372

prerogative (*cont.*)
treaty interpretation **107,** 56-7
treaty-making power **44,** 208, 368, 371, **77,** 33, 389, **81,** 676, 700-1, **84,** 717, **87,** 333, 347-8, **98,** 175-6, **108,** 611, **124,** 413, 419
prescription 41, 101, **50,** 381-4, **59,** 210, 232, **75,** 117, 120, 466. *See also* acquiescence; boundaries, prescription; doctrine of acknowledgment; estoppel; preclusion
acquisition of title **41,** 101
critical date **75,** 120
Grisbadarna **41,** 101
high seas, rights on **41,** 124
historic bays **91,** 418
Island of Palmas **97,** 479-80
occupation distinguished **91,** 432
protest
absence **97,** 488-91
diplomatic note **97,** 484-5
requirements
absence of protest **91,** 450, 451
acquiescence **114,** 52
animus occupandi **114,** 52
continuous and open exercise of authority **91,** 418, 420, 421 n. 10, 448-51, **97,** 479-80, 583, 592-4
constructive notice **91,** 449
policing **91,** 451
taxation **91,** 449, 451
desert and inhospitable area **100,** 97
effectiveness, evidence of **97,** 485
non-active nature of doctrine **91,** 448-9
passage of time **91,** 450
length **91,** 418 n. 3
possession **91,** 448
terra nullius. See terra nullius, need for *below*
terra nullius, need for **97,** 480-1
Minquiers and Ecrehos **97,** 480-1
treaty provision as bar **114,** 52
uti possidetis and **97,** 480, 481
valid concept, whether **97,** 593-4
press, freedom of. *See* freedom of the press
press agency, State agency, whether **63,** 130-2, **64,** 445, 462-4
presumption of innocence 44, 104, 106, **71,** 307, **72,** 394-404, **82,** 56, **121,** 245. *See also* American Convention on Human Rights (1969), presumption of innocence; European Convention on Human Rights (1950), presumption of innocence; International Covenant on Civil and Political Rights (ICCPR) (1966), presumption of innocence; Universal Declaration of Human Rights (1948), presumption of innocence
burden of proof and **81,** 198
general principle of law **118,** 85, **122,** 445-9
guilty plea, effect **111,** 332, 393, 394
terrorism **122,** 445-9, 476-80
price fixing, EEC competition law and 48, 106-36
prisoners. *See also* detainees, rights; detention; liberty of person, deprivation; prisoners of war
Convention on the Transfer of Sentenced Persons (1983)

Articles 10 and 11 distinguished **84,** 726-7
delays in sentencing State, effect **84,** 728-9
Explanatory Report **84,** 727
interpretation **84,** 722-9
phrases
'adapt the sentence' **84,** 725-9
'for a similar offence' **84,** 726
remission
applicable law **84,** 728
relevance **84,** 728-9
sentence
continued enforcement **84,** 725
conversion **84,** 725, 727
transfer of persons sentenced abroad
bilateral conventions **84,** 723
consent of prisoner **84,** 723
consent of sentencing State **84,** 723
existence of offence in administering State **84,** 723
travaux préparatoires **84,** 727
multilateral conventions **84,** 723. *See also* Convention on the Transfer of Sentenced Persons (1983) *above*
prisoners of war. *See also* detainees, rights; Geneva Convention (Treatment of Prisoners of War) (Convention III) (1949); prisoners
Algerian rebels **44,** 446-7
deserter, status as **42,** 448
Detaining Power, nationals of **42,** 441-57
difference of treatment by Allied Governments of Japanese and German prisoners of war, discriminatory, whether **118,** 234
disability pension rights **118,** 222, 234-5
doctors as **45,** 2
Geneva Convention (1949). *See* Geneva Convention (Treatment of Prisoners of War) (Convention III) (1949)
irregular forces **42,** 476-8
legal representation, right to **123,** 607-9
levée en masse **42,** 476
munitions manufacture, employment in
Hague Conventions (1907) **104,** 198
war crime **104,** 199-200
PPFL, members of **42,** 470-83
repatriation **57,** 608
delay in **44,** 441, 443
stateless person **44,** 443
right to sue **53,** 620
saboteurs in civilian dress **42,** 458-70, **52,** 501, 502-4
as spies **42,** 451, 465, 466, 468-9, **52,** 503
status **52,** 501-4
allegiance, relevance **42,** 441-57, 477-8
burden of proof **88,** 50, **99,** 185-6
delay in release, effect **44,** 441-5
doubt as to **42,** 442, 446-7, 451, 455-6, 472-3
entitlement **42,** 470-83
private enemy individual **83,** 220

prisoners of war (*cont.*)
requirements
'armed conflict' **99,** 185-6
arms carried openly **43,** 478-9, **88,** 49
distinctive sign **88,** 49
operation in accordance with the laws of war **42,** 479, **88,** 49
organized command **88,** 49
responsibility for determining
competent tribunal **99,** 186-7, **123,** 603-5
political question, whether **99,** 187
proprio motu **99,** 185
traitors **42,** 448
uniform, significance **42,** 467, 478, **52,** 503-4
unlawful treatment, compensation for, Peace Treaty with Japan (1951) and **118,** 211-22, 224-35
privacy, right to. *See* private life, respect for
private international law **47,** 225-6, **62,** 143, 171-2, 178, **77,** 457
agency **69,** 576, 597-8
antitrust claims **66,** 284-6
applicable law **86,** 544, **91,** 241, **104,** 554, 558
recognition, State **108,** 530, 536-7
State contract **62,** 169
violation of international law **77,** 186, 188
choice of law, rules **77,** 187
common law rules **125,** 396-8
contract **66,** 195-7
expropriation/nationalization, recognition, *lex rei sitae* as determinant **82,** 139
federal State **77,** 85
foreign court, competence **52,** 82-3
foreign legislation
application **52,** 58
categorization **78,** 596
foreign State compulsion **104,** 562, 601
Hague Conference on Private International Law
avoidance of conflict rule formulation **84,** 745
officials, privileges and immunities **70,** 420-1
international law
municipal law and, application in case of conflict **80,** 102, 103
relevance to **46,** 229
jurisdiction
arbitration agreements **75,** 166-8
arbitration proceedings **75,** 168-73
cheques **75,** 136-7
contract, between foreign employer and employee **77,** 415
forum selection clause. *See* forum selection clause
nexus **66,** 320, **72,** 24-5, **74,** 213-14, **75,** 123-4
'most significant contacts' **66,** 43, 133, 171-2, 195-7
justiciability **119,** 78
law governing. *See* applicable law
lex loci rule **66,** 115
locus, aviation disaster **107,** 389-90
'most significant contacts' **66,** 43, 133, 171-2, 195-7

nexus **66,** 320
personal status, alteration of, retroactive, whether **72,** 443, 460-1
principles of **57,** 50-1
procedural law, determination of **74,** 692
property, characterization **47,** 74
public international law and **81,** 681, **82,** 139, 140
purpose, protection of private interests **82,** 133
recognition of
foreign law. *See* foreign law, recognition/enforcement
international law entities **83,** 241, 242, 247, 248-9, 261-2, 263, 264-5, **85,** 14, 16
renvoi. See renvoi
rule superior to, need for, public policy of forum **82,** 139
rules, whether mandatory **66,** 466
statutory limitation **79,** 407-11
succession, property **56,** 8
tortious liability principle **52,** 299
private life, respect for 51, 236, **57,** 220, 231-9, **58,** 146, 578, **61,** 324-5, 327, **67,** 409-18, 420-6, 428-37, **73,** 396, **74,** 292, 296, 317-19, 322, 324-5, 333-6, 341-2, 371-91, **78,** 341, **89,** 49, 73-7. *See also* European Convention on Human Rights (1950), private life, respect for; International Covenant on Civil and Political Rights (1966), private life, respect for
burial grounds, failure to protect **118,** 278
definition **67,** 431
deportation **111,** 172, 190-1, 193-4, 270-1
diplomatic immunity and **89,** 49-59
disclosure of medical reports in extradition proceedings **119,** 304-5, 316-17
fair trial and **105,** 614-15
freedom of expression and **88,** 521
homosexuality and **67,** 409-18, 424-9, 431-7, **89,** 256-61
armed forces and **112,** 371-412
consensual homosexual activity in private **112,** 340-2
criminalization as health/moral measure, proportionality **112,** 341, 343-4
interference by public authority **67,** 411-18, 431-7
on discretionary grounds **112,** 343
'in accordance with the law' **67,** 411-12, **74,** 372-8, 383-91
legislation as **67,** 411, 425-9, 442
margin of appreciation **67,** 414, 417
proportionality **119,** 316-17
protection of morals **67,** 412, 417, 420-3, 433-7
liberty of person, deprivation **61,** 324-5
military discipline and **73,** 396
non-enforcement of offending measures **112,** 340-2, 343
in northern Cyprus **120,** 86-91, 114
police investigations **67,** 442-3
privacy of
business diary **88,** 237
telephone directory **88,** 237
search of premises **88,** 232-8
business premises **88,** 235-8
waiver of right to warrant **88,** 233
secret surveillance
abuse **58,** 449
public authority, by **58,** 446-9

private life, respect for (*cont.*)
surveillance techniques **91,** 496-7
telecommunications, interception/interference with **58,** 434-8, 441-5, 446-54, 461, 604, **61,** 193-4, 202-3, 205, **74,** 307-91, **85,** 299 n. 14
transsexualism **89,** 103-9, 110-12
private parties, negotiations between, effect on governments **46,** 33-4, 139
private rights, continuity 62, 172
privateering. *See also* piracy
abolition, insurance policies, effect on **48,** 471, 473
privileges and immunities. *See* arrest warrant against Minister of Foreign Affairs of third country for violations of international humanitarian law; consular privileges and immunities; diplomatic privileges and immunities; diplomatic relations; Head of State, immunity; international officials, privileges and immunities; international organizations, privileges and immunities; NATO Status of Forces Agreement (1951), privileges and immunities; special rapporteur; State immunity; universal jurisdiction
Privy Council (UK), appeals jurisdiction 90, 500, 501, **117,** 637-40
applicable law **123,** 526, 549
legal aid and **124,** 563-4
promptness of reference, need for **98,** 340-2, 343
validity of decision **98,** 566
prize law
India-Pakistan war **40,** 472-80
neutral ships, detention of **38,** 471-4
torture **81,** 591
prize proceedings
applicable law **40,** 473, 476-7
competence **44,** 495-7, **81,** 664-6
individual's rights **77,** 245
judgment, acquisition of title and **40,** 476-7
State immunity in **79,** 6, 11
procedural fairness. *See also* due process; fair hearing; fair trial; standard of treatment of alien
deportation **124,** 378-83, 390-1, 411-12
fundamental justice and **124,** 378-83, 390-1
judicial review **124,** 419
legitimate expectation **104,** 473-6, 481
distinction **104,** 481-3, 491-4
notice, need for **104,** 475, 486-7, 491-4
procedure. *See also under individual tribunals*
ad hoc nature **110,** 637-8
amicus curiae brief **63,** 162, 338, **64,** 211, 355, 365, **75,** 34, 50, 678, 688, **78,** 554, **79,** 327, 339, 402-3, 504, **103,** 638, **108,** 146, **110,** 618, 680, 681, **116,** 306, **118,** 301, **121,** 228-9, 330
basis, purpose of tribunal **110,** 638
class/representative action, for equitable relief **118,** 332
evidence. *See* evidence
foreign State, applicability to **107,** 631-2
in camera proceedings, national security defence **110,** 674 n. 248, 729
municipal law practices, appropriateness in international tribunals **108,** 12-13, 17
orders. *See subpoena duces tecum below and* Yugoslavia, International Criminal Tribunal for the Former (ICTY), orders
subpoena ad testificandum **88,** 318

subpoena duces tecum **73,** 301, 332, 338, 342, **88,** 318. *See also* Yugoslavia, International Criminal Tribunal for the Former (ICTY), orders, *subpoena duces tecum*
common/civil law procedure **110,** 637, 656
England
challenge to **110,** 658-9
Scotland **110,** 629
international tribunals
European Court of Justice (ECJ) **110,** 657-8
Iran–US Claims Tribunal **110,** 657
Rwanda, International Criminal Tribunal for (ICTR) **110,** 640 n. 94
as order compelling attendance of witness **110,** 637-40
penalty for non-compliance, relevance **110,** 649 n. 135, 694-7, 704-7
requirements
reasonableness **110,** 657, 704
relevance **110,** 656-9
specificity **110,** 658, 703-4
State immunity and **122,** 32-5
State practice **110,** 628-30, 656-9
Canada **110,** 629
Costa Rica **110,** 629
England **110,** 629, 657, 658
France **110,** 630
Germany **110,** 630
Malaysia **110,** 657
Pakistan **110,** 629
Spain **110,** 630
USA **110,** 628-9, 656-7, 658
Yugoslavia (SFRY) **110,** 629
time-limits
applicability to State **107,** 628-32
failure to reply to claims **106,** 423
tribunal's right to determine **107,** 72-3
procés-verbal, legal effect **37,** 69
process, service of. *See* service of process
profession, commercial advertising, restriction on, freedom of expression and **81,** 208-34
professional associations 75, 17-30, 33-6, 42, 50-7, 59-62. *See also* freedom of assembly/association; freedom of expression
professional privilege 64, 281-2, 287-90, 297-8
waiver **64,** 290, 306
prompt hearing 70, 192-209, 254, 256, 261, 296, **87,** 95, **96,** 525-8. *See also* European Convention on Human Rights (1950), prompt hearing; International Covenant on Civil and Political Rights (ICCPR) (1966), prompt hearing
court's workload **96,** 526
damage to plaintiff's interests, need for **96,** 526
death penalty and. *See* death row as inhuman or degrading treatment
delayed prosecution **71,** 273-7
mental anguish **71,** 273-7
war crimes **75,** 340, 348-58
ECHR jurisprudence **96,** 526
natural right to **70,** 202
normal delay as 'norm' **96,** 526-7

prompt hearing (*cont.*)
prioritization of cases **96,** 526
prompt trial, waiver of right to 121, 222
proof. *See* evidence
proper law. *See* applicable law
proper party, joinder, at request of other party 106, 623-4
property. *See also* confiscation; enemy property; expropriation/nationalization; Oder–Neisse, territories east of, property rights; ownership; State immunity, execution/attachment; taking of property; title
abandonment **42,** 35
access to market **122,** 334-5
aliens, rights of. *See* aliens, property
applicable law, *lex situs*. *See* applicable law, property
charterparty, beneficial ownership, whether **64,** 188-94
classification as **83,** 539-41, **84,** 557 n. 4, **85,** 411-12, 563-4
concession **62,** 189, 201, 217
contract right **62,** 221, 224, **84,** 196, 197, **85,** 392, 598
currency **118,** 590
debt repayment, right to **92,** 439
debt/chose in action **64,** 78-9, **91,** 350-1, 369-70
future or contingent interest **106,** 414-15
inheritance of estate **58,** 591-2, 609, 620
interest in aircraft leased from Yugoslav Airlines (JAT) **117,** 280-5, 299-300
interest in as ancillary right, customary international law **85,** 598
interest in blocked account **63,** 427-9
'property, rights and interests' **40,** 278-9, **46,** 212, 299-300, 308
incorporeal assets **44,** 100-1
public good **115,** 628-9, 634, 635
under international law **40,** 277
compulsory transfer/purchase **75,** 479, 486, 504. *See also* deprivation of *below*; expropriation/nationalization
between individuals **75,** 408-28
individuals, compensation, adequacy **75,** 423-5
conversion, damages for **116,** 559-62, **125,** 693-706
of deceased nationals, consular protection **56,** 530
deprivation of. *See also* European Convention on Human Rights (1950), deprivation of property *and* peaceful enjoyment of possessions
tenant's right of enfranchisement **75,** 408-28
derelict **56,** 45-6
destruction of **58,** 181, 186
disposition and **58,** 591-2, 609, 620
of emigrant, expropriation as act of State **82,** 49-58
enemy. *See* enemy property
Estonian. *See* Estonia, property of
forfeiture and **58,** 181
indirect ownership **84,** 385
industrial **70,** 431-2
intangible **84,** 197
interference with. *See* expropriation/nationalization, classification as/de facto, interference with property
lease of
commercial activity **63,** 588
restoration of leased property

concession, effect on **42,** 8-9
Sovereign Base Area, Cyprus, Republic of **41,** 25-8
letter of credit **106,** 414-15
matrimonial property
refugees' rights,
applicable law **73,** 672-3
recognition in country of refuge **52,** 338
Romania, in **47,** 272-4
moveable, title **44,** 458
native title, whether **112,** 525-6, 611-12, **125,** 333-4
'no property or interests in property', definition, responsibility **106,** 414-15
occupation **54,** 244-6
France, restitution **44,** 2-5
Hungarian property, acts of French authorities **44,** 2-4
ownership distinguished **86,** 599
patrimonial rights and **58,** 587-93
payment on cheque **88,** 87
peaceful enjoyment of possessions **58,** 180-1, 186-7, 587, 591-2, 598, **60,** 179, **73,** 480-1
aboriginal claims of wrongful dispossession and **120,** 534-5
telephone tapping and **74,** 316-17, 356
privacy, exchange control enforcement and **70,** 154-83
private
expropriation/nationalization **62,** 185
military damage to, responsibility for **54,** 244-6
military occupation of, responsibility for **54,** 244-6
privatization of State-owned residential property, priority to tenants, fairness **115,** 276
property right, claim to compensation for expropriation/nationalization **107,** 60
protection of, failure by State **48,** 4-5
real/immovable
applicable law **42,** 164, 166-7
cuius est solum **62,** 183
dispute relating to, State immunity, jurisdiction. *See* State immunity, jurisdiction, real/immovable property, dispute relating to
domicile, requirement for **82,** 46
foreign nationals and **109,** 391 n. 328, 393
right to indemnification **84,** 93-4
res communis, dissolution **41,** 188
right to **56,** 18, **62,** 183
political negotiations and **85,** 59, 62
protection under international law **46,** 66
State succession and **103,** 118-20
expropriation without compensation **103,** 118-20
rights **58,** 592, **84,** 90-4
absolute, whether **68,** 125
acquisition **81,** 6
alien. *See* alien, property
arbitrary deprivation **112,** 435-6, 445, **115,** 624
as 'civil right' **68,** 111-12, 119-20
continuity **115,** 624-6
contract, enforcement of **87,** 619
general interest and **68,** 108-10, 116-18, 124-7

property (*cont.*)
general principle of law **46,** 221
guaranteed, whether **58,** 592
as human right **91,** 321, **112,** 435-6, 445, 636, 682-3, **115,** 624, **117,** 287-9
of illegitimate child **58,** 586-90
Ilois in British Indian Ocean Territory (BIOT) **123,** 561
International Covenant on Civil and Political Rights (ICCPR) (1966) **115,** 268, 274-6
investment as **46,** 66, 300-1
mentally ill person **58,** 667, 679-82
method of acquisition
aliens **82,** 43
public law **82,** 26
relevance **82,** 145
nature of **62,** 183-5, 196, 206
protection **78,** 184-5
restoration
compensation for non-restoration **115,** 626-7
limitations on **115,** 629-36
territorial dispute, effect **66,** 178
of unmarried mothers **58,** 591-3
sanctity **62,** 176
seizure and **58,** 180-6
shareholders, assets of company **84,** 370, 385-6
situs **88,** 67, 73-4
succession **56,** 8
tangible **84,** 197
title
illegal export, effect **118,** 592
lex situs **78,** 599
town-planning and **68,** 104-18, 124-7
of transferred population, obligation to compensate **65,** 12-13
trends **62,** 184
unlawful taking. *See* expropriation/nationalization, legality
use of **58,** 180, 186, 592, 609-11
user restrictions **68,** 93-4, 104-11, 112-18, 126-7
Property Treaty (1945) (Austria-Czechoslovakia), effect on status of former Czech bank **77,** 451
proportionality **58,** 18, 36, 174, 179, 185, **79,** 301, 303, 306, 316-17, 319-20, 322, 455 n. 21
arbitrary act and **100,** 384-5, **115,** 348-9
belligerent occupation, assignment of place of residence **125,** 555-7
between ends and means, unilateral amendment of conditions of employment **83,** 652, 655
between means and legitimate aim **107,** 17, 22, 23, **110,** 192-3, 239, 352-3, 468, **111,** 169-70. *See also* European Convention on Human Rights (1950), margin of appreciation; European Convention on Human Rights (1950), interpretation, phrases, 'proportionate to the legitimate aim'; margin of appreciation
responsibility for determining **110,** 352-3
civil and political rights, restrictions on **62,** 254
compulsory jurisdiction, reservations **123,** 256
countermeasures **116,** 61, 65, 143, 215, 221, 229, 231
customary international law **110,** 195

death row, measures prescribing time-limits for appeal to international bodies **123,** 516, 531-2
defence interests **91,** 64-5
war and peace distinguished **91,** 65
deportation and **74,** 616. *See also* expulsion and *below*
EC law. *See* European Community law, requirements, proportionality
enjoyment of right under international law **82,** 631
export controls **117,** 319-21, 527-8
expulsion and **61,** 442, **73,** 616-17, 630, 644. *See also* deportation and *above*
extradition **79,** 126, 128, 455 n. 21. *See also* political offence *below*
freedom of movement, restriction on **100,** 371, 379, 387-8
GDR border shootings **100,** 371, 379, 384-8
homosexuality, criminalization as health/moral measure **112,** 341
human rights, restrictions on and **81,** 69, 171, **92,** 235-6, 287, 303, 316, 343-5, 368-9, **111,** 169-70, **117,** 292. *See also* fundamental justice, balance of interests
inhuman or degrading treatment **98,** 396-7
irrationality as **84,** 766-8, 776
judicial assistance, basis for refusing, whether **82,** 52
law enforcement requirements **70,** 279
legislation
interpretation **100,** 371
purpose and object and **90,** 84, 112-13
margin of appreciation and **89,** 258-60, 288-90
maritime delimitation. *See* proportionality, maritime delimitation
necessity and **90,** 484, 508, **102,** 179, **110,** 192-3, 377, 534-7
nuclear weapons, deployment **110,** 195, 239, 260, 261, 270-1, 326, 352-3, 377, 398-9, 464-6
penalties **88,** 583-4
political offence **72,** 612-13, 616, 625-6, **74,** 504, **100,** 423, **104,** 670-2, **107,** 164, 167, 559-60, 570-2, 577-8. *See also* extradition *above*
dominant motive **107,** 571
private life, respect for, interference by public authority **119,** 316-17
punishment and **90,** 584-5
refugees, non-refoulement **104,** 665-6
reprisals **110,** 196, 278
restrictions on human rights and **86,** 427
self-defence **110,** 194-5, 260, 326, 377, 468-9, 532-3, 534-7
self help **54,** 338-41, 343-4
treaties, reciprocal breach **116,** 221-2
war crimes/crimes against humanity, defence **108,** 46-7, 48, **122,** 177
war reparations **72,** 250-1, 613-14
proportionality, maritime delimitation **41,** 46, 50, 61, 82, 83, 86, 150, 195, 227, **62,** 125, **67,** 34, 36, 55, 64, 68-71, 84, 130-2, 251-3, 305-8, **70,** 594, 611, **71,** 85, 88, 140, 149-50, 161-4, 180-5, 208, 211-12, **81,** 69, 71, 129, 225-9, 232, 275-8, 303-6, 317-24, 410-19, **83,** 91, **84,** 762, 766-7, **85,** 33-4, 47, 51-2, **99,** 527-58
adjacent States, relevance to delimitations between **81,** 342, 416, **99,** 539
Anglo-French Arbitration **81,** 304-5, 417, **119,** 465
application **67,** 84, 86, 131-2, 253
apportionment and **41,** 151
bays **71,** 163, 181-5
basepoints and **81,** 280
between coastal length and surface areas **41,** 46, 50, 61, 82, 86, 150

proportionality, maritime delimitation (*cont.*)
disputed area, whether limited to **41,** 46, 50, 61, 82, 86, 150, **71,** 208
equity and **67,** 68-9, 84, 131-2, 145, 251-3, 308
internal waters **67,** 64, 69, 84, 131-2, 251-3, 307-8
relevant coasts **67,** 54-5, 68-9, 84, 86, 131, 251-3, 307-8
status of concept **71,** 150, 211
territorial sea **67,** 64, 69, 84, 131-2, 307-8
variations **67,** 84, 307
between coastal lengths **81,** 275, 278, 281, 282, 284, 285, 288, 289, 291, 292, 304, 305, 309-10, 316-24, 325, 349-50, 364-6, 376, 399, 401, 413, **83,** 117, 119, **95,** 662, **99,** 535, 543-58, 640-1, 669
adjacent **99,** 539
opposite coasts **99,** 433-7, 449, 483, 484, 488-94, 497
Eritrea/Yemen **119,** 465-6
Gulf of Maine **99,** 492-3
Libya/Malta **99,** 493
North Sea **99,** 491-2, 535, 537-8
relevant **99,** 539, 676
special circumstance **99,** 436-7
between coastal lengths and areas of continental shelf **81,** 278, 285, 289, 304, 320, 321-2, 401, **99,** 540-3
determination of relevant areas **81,** 285
Libya/Malta **99,** 542
between coastal lengths and landmass **81,** 281, 285-7, 305-6, 341, **99,** 640
between coastal lengths and maritime area **83,** 97-8, 114, **95,** 668-9, 678, 690-3, 719-20
difficulty of establishing **95,** 691-3
between coastlines **77,** 687-8
between islands **99,** 452-3, 659-60
between islands and mainland coast **99,** 548-50, 552-5
between surface areas **77,** 683, 687
continental shelf entitlement **81,** 277
as criterion **81,** 276-7, 314, 370
cut-off effect and **81,** 321, **99,** 538
difficulty of determining **81,** 285, 343, 364, **99,** 436
disproportion, avoidance **41,** 195, **99,** 543, 551-2, 641, **119,** 465-6
coastal lengths **81,** 282, 284, 288, 413
distance and **62,** 125
distance between coasts and **81,** 333
equidistance method, result of **81,** 366
equitable **67,** 68-71, 145, 251-3
equitable principles and **41,** 83, **67,** 86, **81,** 275-7, 304, 342, **99,** 536, 538
equitable result, need for **81,** 321, **83,** 114, **99,** 433, 437, 454, 641
equity, check on **81,** 275, 276, 277, 281, 285-7, 288, 306, 315-21, 342-3, 364-5, 366-7, 414-15, 416, **95,** 667-8, 669-70, 691, **99,** 433-4, 539-43, 640-1, 676-7
Libya/Malta **95,** 669-70, 677-8
Tunisia/Libya **95,** 691
France–Spain Agreement (Bay of Biscay) **81,** 321
as 'function of equity' **81,** 342
geographical factors **99,** 484
Gulf of Maine **81,** 417
irregularities **81,** 393-5
islands
400 miles from mainland **99,** 551

between **99,** 452-3, 659-60
mid-sea islands **119,** 454-5
'just and equitable share', as **81,** 304
justice and **99,** 641
land mass **77,** 687-8
limited applicability **81,** 304-5
overlapping areas **81,** 304, **99,** 544-50
method of delimitation, as **81,** 277, **99,** 542-3, 676, **119,** 465-6
distinguishable, whether **95,** 693
natural prolongation and **99,** 529-38
North Sea **81,** 275-7, 305, 366-7, **99,** 536-8, **119,** 465
opposite States, relevance to delimitations between **81,** 321, 366-7
population **99,** 484
power to generate maritime zones and **83,** 91, 116
precision, need for **81,** 281-2, 364
principle of international law, whether **81,** 276-7, 304, 341, **99,** 535, 536-40
principle or rule relating to delimitation, whether **41,** 86
protection of environment and **90,** 97
reasonable degree of **83,** 117
refashioning of nature and **81,** 276-7
relevant area **81,** 324, **83,** 118-19
relevant/special circumstances **41,** 82, 83, 216, **67,** 36, 68-9, 84, 86, 130-2, 305-8, **81,** 281, 312-18, **83,** 117, **99,** 641, 669-70, 674, 676-7
Anglo-French Arbitration **99,** 670
Libya/Malta **99,** 541, 669-70
Tunisia/Libya **99,** 539-40
State practice **81,** 275, 277
test of
flexibility **81,** 320-1
inaccuracy **81,** 343, 365
third State claims and **81,** 285, 364, 365
title, relevance to **83,** 114
treaties
obligations and **90,** 67
purpose and **90,** 97
Tunisia/Libya **81,** 417
UNCLOS III **81,** 317
protected States 42, 51-8
protection
diplomatic archives **61,** 525, 556-9, 562
diplomatic premises **60,** 385, 387, **61,** 525, 556-9, 562
national abroad, right to **60,** 210-11, 215-18. *See also* diplomatic protection
seizure of assets, compensation for **42,** 204
protectorates 71, 40-7
act of State and **71,** 42, 46-7
Bohemia and Moravia, German protectorate **70,** 694, 696
British
Brunei **55,** 490, 493
jurisdiction **51,** 1-10
nature of **71,** 40-7
legislation, power of Crown under **71,** 47
foreign relations **71,** 44-5, **118,** 426-7
inhabitants, status **71,** 44-6

protectorates (*cont.*)
jurisdiction
protecting State
nature of **71,** 40-7
of **71,** 40-7
land, acquisition by protecting State **71,** 40-7, 51-6
act of State **71,** 42, 46-7
annexation **71,** 51-6
applicable law **71,** 47, 54-6
as exercise of jurisdiction **71,** 44
purchase **71,** 41-3
legitimate inequalities **79,** 301, 303, 306, 316-17, 319-20, 322
powers of protecting State **71,** 40-7
proclamation of protectorate **71,** 44-5
protecting State, relationship to, foreign State **118,** 422-3
sovereignty **71,** 44-7
State immunity, jurisdiction, protecting State in protectorate **118,** 422-8
consent of forum State, relevance **118,** 423
general principle of international law **118,** 423
State, recognition, right of **118,** 426-7
State responsibility for protection of individuals **44,** 1-2, 32-3, **70,** 696
termination, Morocco. *See* Morocco, termination of protectorate
treaties, as parties to **39,** 453, 456-8
protest
acquisition of title and **91,** 612, 620-5, 627, 631, 648-9
element of dispute **37,** 178, 179, 181
failure to, effect **50,** 413-15, 496
opposability, relevance **67,** 63-4
provisional measures **71,** 642-9, **77,** 544-50, **93,** 657-65, 681-703. *See also* arbitration, interim measures; European Community law, interim measures (national); European Convention on Human Rights (1950), interim measures; ICSID (International Centre for the Settlement of Investment Disputes), arbitral tribunal, provisional measures; injunction; Inter-American Court of Human Rights, provisional measures; International Court of Justice (ICJ), provisional measures; Iran–US Claims Tribunal, interim measures; Law of the Sea Convention (1982): Part XV (settlement of disputes), provisional measures; Mareva injunction; State immunity, execution/attachment, purpose of proceedings, safeguarding/conservatory measures; United Nations Human Rights Committee (UNHRC), interim measures
admissibility **106,** 158
extraterritorial. *See* extraterritorial *below*
foreign policy repercussions **106,** 352
international law repercussions **106,** 352
liberal **106,** 186-8
limited, PCIJ **106,** 185-6
non-parties to arbitration agreement **119,** 578
restricted, ICJ **106,** 186
armed forces, injunction on deployment **106,** 352
as attachment **82,** 72
balance of convenience **93,** 719-31
binding force **106,** 184, **108,** 317-18, 319-20
enforceability distinguished **106,** 184
international practice **108,** 317
compensation for loss suffered, preclusion **93,** 683, 705-6, 719-20

EC law, compatibility with **93,** 790
Court's discretion **106,** 164, 175, 183, **117,** 141
Court's freedom of choice **106,** 159
Court's right to act *proprio motu* **106,** 183, 188, 189
EC law as issue **93,** 659-65, 681-703
duty to predict ECJ decision **93,** 706
obligation **93,** 664, 680, 697-9
power **93,** 664, 680, 697-8
effective remedy before national authority, non-availability against Crown, relevance **98,** 317
effectiveness of judicial protection and
EC **93,** 688-90
German/Polish Mixed Arbitration Tribunal (29 July 1924) **93,** 689 n. 1
Italy **93,** 689 n. 1
extraterritorial **107,** 492-505
Mareva injunction **107,** 500-1
monetary and proprietary claim distinguished **107,** 499-500
third parties, effect on, *Babanaft* **107,** 503-5
time-limit **107,** 502
hardship, relevance **93,** 726
human rights treaties **108,** 316-17
injunction restraining ex-Head of State from removing or dealing with assets, outside the jurisdiction **107,** 492-505
judicial review, time-limits **106,** 413
jurisdiction and **106,** 158
legal dispute compounded by supervening armed conflict and **106,** 164, 168, 171-2
mediation to resolve problem, effect on Court's jurisdiction **106,** 157
merits and **106,** 158, 165
military measures, admissibility **106,** 163, 164, 171-2, 184-5
precautionary principle. *See* environment, precautionary principle
presumption of validity of legislation and **93,** 721, 725-6
purpose
compliance with obligation to maintain international peace and security **106,** 164, 168, 191, **117,** 130, 145
preservation of
environment **117,** 146
evidence **106,** 158, 160, 189-90
rights in dispute **106,** 13-14, 156-7, 161-2, 164, 165, 184-8, **117,** 130-1, 136
subject-matter of review, suspension of *subpoena duces tecum* **110,** 685
prevention of
act of force **106,** 359
aggravation or extension of dispute **106,** 14, 157-8, 185-8
dissipation of assets **104,** 129-33
hardship **106,** 359
requirement to
assist fact-finding mission **106,** 160
conserve evidence **106,** 160, 168
observe cease-fire agreement **106,** 159, 163, 164, 168
refrain from action by armed forces which might prejudice rights **106,** 159, 163, 164, 168
requirements
clarity **106,** 158, 163, 166, 168
clear evidence **106,** 161-2, 174-5, 182, 184-5

provisional measures (*cont.*)
connection with dispute before Court **106,** 23, 28
impossibility of remedy by way of compensation or reparation **106,** 161
irreparable damage, relevance **106,** 158, 161-2, 164, 165, 188-9, **108,** 305, 317, 320, **117,** 141, 142-3, 170-1
non-prejudice to merits **106,** 18, 61, 158, 165, 183-4
possibility of implementation **106,** 172, 184-5
prima facie case **106,** 61, 156, 164, 359, **108,** 317, 320
prima facie jurisdiction **106,** 96, 156, 178-81
Interhandel **106,** 180-1
Jurisdiction and Enforcement of Judgments in Civil and Commercial Matters Convention (1968), effect **107,** 496-9
reasons for request **106,** 175-6
relevance to real subject-matter of dispute **106,** 161-2
time-limitation **108,** 305
urgency **106,** 13, 14, 157, 161, 164, 181-2, **117,** 140-1
Agreement Relating to the Conservation and Management of Straddling Fish Stocks and Highly Migratory Fish Stocks (1995) **117,** 171 n. 3, 180
Application of the Convention on the Prevention and Punishment of the Crime of Genocide **106,** 182
Passage through the Great Belt **106,** 181-2
retroactive effect **93,** 687-9
State immunity **101,** 401
stay of proceedings, concurrent jurisdiction, pending decision **106,** 529-30, 651-2
UN fact-finding mission, relevance **106,** 158-9
UNHRC **115,** 256, 306
psychological warfare, Manual of 76, 400-3, 490, 525, 722-3, 872
public health legislation, drug-trafficking, territorial scope **71,** 248-50
public interest 62, 183, **79,** 395, **85,** 32-3
default judgment and foreign State **84,** 144
deprivation of property in **75,** 415-19, 422, 424, 481-2, 486, 520, 525-31, 559, 705-7
disclosure of confidential information and **119,** 275-7, 299-306, 310, 312
expropriation/nationalization **82,** 50
human rights and **70,** 144, 147-8, 157, 169, 173-83, 210-21
implementation of Security Council Resolutions **117,** 292-3, 301-2, 317, 321, 392-3
judicial review of compliance with EC directive **120,** 655-6
legitimate expectation and **117,** 428
necessitus publica major est quam privata **90,** 485
refuelling of fishing vessel in EEZ **120,** 264-5, 300-1, 326
rights of individual, balancing of **75,** 486, 520, 526-8, 559, 642, 705-7
strict liability and **117,** 321
public interest privilege 64, 285, 290-2, 298-306
balance of interests **64,** 291, 305
class/representative claim to **120,** 576-7
communications between States **64,** 285, 291-4, 297-306
disclosure of documents **64,** 285, 290-2, 298-306
balance of interests **64,** 291, 305
evidence
foreign official, public interest privilege **101,** 354-5
taking abroad, examination of official **101,** 354-5
freedom of information **120,** 576-7

investigation of air accidents and **120,** 576-7
public knowledge. *See* evidence, public knowledge
public law
fiscal matters **84,** 746
variety of definition **84,** 743-5
public morals. *See* margin of appreciation, protection of morals
public order/public policy/*ordre public* **46,** 195, 201, **47,** 27-8, 159-62, 228-30, **53,** 170, 367, **57,** 50-1, **58,** 88-9, 448, 582, **60,** 173, **62,** 245, 254, **69,** 4-6, 9, **70,** 391, 431, 433, **72,** 61-2, 92, 636, 676, 684, **73,** 34, 392, 590, 592, **74,** 47-9, 56, 75, 103, 135, 400, 507, 572, 703-4, **75,** 131, **77,** 502, 548, 549, 571, 586, **78,** 70, 311, 405-6, 407-8, 414, 418-21, **79,** 333, 408, 412, **80,** 429, 430, 435, 439. *See also* international public policy/*ordre public international*; public interest; public safety
act of State and **119,** 106
annulment of arbitral award **80,** 634
arbitration, capacity of State to submit to **48,** 330
arbitration clause, State's acceptance of **41,** 452-5, **48,** 329-30
breach of contract, justification for **83,** 562
colonization and **78,** 425
compatibility of act with international law, court's right to consider **116,** 571-2
contract, validity of provisions contravening **113,** 497
contract in violation of foreign law **48,** 230
definition **72,** 571-3, **122,** 589-92, 596-7
determined by law **96,** 310
economic considerations, relevance **72,** 572
individual and State interests, balancing **72,** 571-3
Siracusa Principles (1984) **122,** 590-1
enforcement of foreign law **84,** 119
evidence of, Security Council Resolution **103,** 408-9
exchange controls and **75,** 131, 279
executed treaty as *res judicata* **65,** 49-50
expropriation. *See* expropriation/nationalization, legality, requirements, public order/public policy/*ordre public*
expulsion of alien **74,** 429-30, 434, 441, **82,** 215, 313, **96,** 310, **99,** 7-11
international officials **102,** 196-7
inherent power of receiving State **102,** 196-7
overriding consideration **99,** 7-8
prison sentence **99,** 25, 34
protection measures **99,** 10-11
risk of assassination if returned to own country, relevance **99,** 7-11
extradition and **88,** 245
in case of death penalty **124,** 339
conditions for **86,** 327
extraterritorial effect of legislation **54,** 268
false identity documents and **86,** 334
fishery regulation and **82,** 658
foreign judgments, recognition/enforcement and **70,** 431, 433, **73,** 5-6, **106,** 227-8, 288
foreign law, recognition/enforcement. *See* foreign law, recognition/enforcement, public policy and
free movement of workers **62,** 390-1, 399, 406-7, 410
freedom of expression and **122,** 589-92
freedom of movement, exit visa, refusal **73,** 392
French concept **52,** 9-10
'general welfare', integral part of **79,** 333

public order/public policy (*cont.*)
international law obligations and **57,** 295, **65,** 76-7, **117,** 560
jurisdiction and **46,** 201, **65,** 28, 40
jurisdiction in respect of conspiracy **84,** 48
MFN treatment and **124,** 23-4
nationalization. *See* expropriation/nationalization, legality, requirements, public order/ public policy/*ordre public*
necessity and **52,** 62
occupying power, obligation to maintain **83,** 136, 185, 187
political policy distinguished **78,** 419
private international law subject to **82,** 139
quantitative restrictions or measures equivalent to **117,** 471-4, 526-8, 543-7
reciprocity **78,** 607, 620
recognition, expropriation/nationalization **48,** 82-3, **65,** 60
refugee, non-refoulement to country of origin **111,** 521
rule of law **78,** 419
sedition and **70,** 214-19
State immunity and **64,** 105, **65,** 81, 139, 393, **88,** 711, **104,** 516, 576, 606-7, 611, 620, 622
trading with the enemy **53,** 617-21, 624
travel abroad by nationals, restrictions on **73,** 392
treaty obligations and **107,** 93-8, **121,** 168-74
public policy. *See* public order/public policy/*ordre public*
public purpose, expropriation and. *See* expropriation/nationalization, legality, requirements, public purpose
public safety 79, 248
public services. *See* European Economic Community Treaty (Rome) (1957), phrases, 'public services'
public ships. *See* ships, State-owned
Pufendorf
eminent domain/*dominium eminens* **41,** 12
obedience to usurper **39,** 118-19
punishment. *See also* crimes against humanity, punishment; European Convention on Human Rights (1950), punishment; Yugoslavia, International Criminal Tribunal for the Former (ICTY), penalty
degrading or inhuman. *See* inhuman or degrading treatment
object **36,** 27-8, 51, 56
Punjab, law of, Resumption of Jagirs Act 1957 **49,** 336-8, 346-7

Qatar, status 42, 51-8
quantitative restrictions. *See also* European Community (EC), quantitative restrictions or measures equivalent to
import licences, EEC Treaty and **48,** 233-6
quotas, cotton goods from Pondicherry to French overseas territories **44,** 295-6
***quantum meruit* 63,** 103, **71,** 675, **79,** 584
quasi in rem jurisdiction. *See* jurisdiction, *quasi in rem*
quasi-contractual obligation
money paid under mistake
criteria for recovery **66,** 75-7
situs of obligation **66,** 76-7, 137-8, 215-16, 218, 233
repudiation, act of State **64,** 266, **66,** 77, 138-9, 215-20, 232-6, 240-1, 448-9
Quebec. *See* Canada, Quebec
Queensland. *See* Australia, Queensland

race *See also* racial discrimination; racial harassment
aliens, expulsion of and **42,** 205-7
concept **68,** 437-9
racial discrimination 46, 206, **49,** 67, **57,** 178-9. *See also* race; racial harassment
aggrieved person. *See* person aggrieved *below*
air carriage **56,** 27-9
apartheid **49,** 4, 6, 47, 68-75
customary international law **68,** 208-11, 221-2, 236
equality before the law, other persons enjoying denied rights, need for **112,** 424-7, 446-7, 455-6, 683-5
extinction of native title **125,** 433
compensation, failure to pay **112,** 693-4
international concern **68,** 207-8, 221-4, 247, 388
International Covenant on Civil and Political Rights (ICCPR) (1966) **107,** 37
international law violation **68,** 209-11, 221-2, 236, **77,** 210
international organizations, privileges and immunities **113,** 500-3
international peace **68,** 236
occupation of land **68,** 264-5
repeal of discriminatory legislation, effect in other States **47,** 203-4
standard of non-discrimination **37,** 348, 350, 358, 359-66, 369-84, 413, 450-71, 552, 559, 573-8
transfer of lease **68,** 191-2, 213
treaties. *See also* freedom from discrimination, minorities treaties and; Racial Discrimination, International Convention on the Elimination of All Forms of (1965)
in context of **47,** 439, 440, 445
treaty interpretation and **68,** 210
UN Charter **68,** 209-10, **107,** 37
Universal Declaration of Human Rights (1948) **107,** 37
Racial Discrimination, International Convention on the Elimination of All Forms of (1965) 68, 186-7, 213, 223-4, 235-6, 240, 258, 489, 497, **107,** 37
draft **37,** 357, 454-5, 576
equality before the law **112,** 425-7
discrimination deriving from **112,** 426
other persons enjoying denied rights, need for **112,** 424-7, 446-7, 455-6, 683-5
'special and concrete measure' **112,** 426-7, 517-18, 641, 654-5, 656
equality before tribunals **112,** 318-27
bias of juror **112,** 327
legal rights, whether limited to **112,** 434-5, 445
municipal law and **85,** 205-16
part of, whether **85,** 205
standing ('person aggrieved') **68,** 192-3, 224-5, 236-7, 259-65
obligations under **85,** 205-16
operation and enforcement **112,** 424, 445, 456, 654-5
State practice **85,** 210
Racial Discrimination, UN Committee on the Elimination of
admissibility **112,** 322
competence, municipal law, interpretation **112,** 327
decisions **85,** 209-10
remedies, recommendation for action to eliminate racial bias in jury proceedings **112,** 327
Rules of Procedure, 91 (admissibility) **112,** 322
status **85,** 208
racial harassment 69, 177-8

railway authority
agency of State, whether **47,** 241, 242, **65,** 42, 232, 355, 397-8
immunity, jurisdiction **42,** 355, 397-8, **56,** 316, **65,** 42, 355, 358, 360-1, 402-4
treaty obligations, compensation for loss of income as result of **44,** 292-4
Rajastan, United States of 49, 349, 351, 440-2, 450-3, 457
Rann of Kutch
as broad belt of boundary **50,** 21, 24, 127, 224, 273, 389, 435-6, 476-7
historical background **50,** 41-80
islands, jurisdiction over **50,** 177-92
Kutch
entity belonging to **50,** 236-70
entity surrounding **50,** 224-9
Sind **50,** 229-31
natural characteristics **50,** 2-3, 20, 30-41, 212, 217, 352, 386, 390, 391, 470
as no-man's land **50,** 287-9, 330, 340, 344, 463, 479
occupation, whether capable of **50,** 6, 386, 511
roads in, construction and maintenance **50,** 334-8, 502
as separate legal entity **50,** 217-24, 478-9
rape in time of war
aiding and abetting. *See* torture, aiding and abetting
customary international law **121,** 266-7
definition of rape
absence in international law **121,** 268-9
aggravating factors **121,** 270-1
Akayesu **121,** 269
element of force, need for **121,** 270
Furundžija pre-trial brief **121,** 268
general principle of law recognized by civilized nations as determining factor **121,** 269-72
ICTY **121,** 272
oral penetration, whether **121,** 271-2
as serious manifestation of sexual assault **121,** 268, 272
ICTY Statute. *See* Yugoslavia, International Criminal Tribunal for the Former (ICTY), Statute, 3 (violation of the laws or customs of war)
treaties and other instruments prohibiting
African Charter on Human and Peoples' Rights (1981) **121,** 267 n. 196
American Convention on Human Rights (1969) **121,** 267 n. 196
Bosnia and Herzegovina municipal law **121,** 266
Control Council Law No 10 **121,** 266
European Convention on Human Rights (1950) **121,** 267 n. 196
Geneva Conventions (1949) **121,** 266
First Additional Protocol (1977) **121,** 266
Hague Regulations (1907) **121,** 266
International Covenant on Civil and Political Rights (ICCPR) (1966) **121,** 267 n. 196
International Military Tribunal for the Far East (Tokyo Tribunal) **121,** 266-7
Lieber Code (US Military Manual, 1863) **121,** 266
SFRY municipal law **121,** 266
as war crime **121,** 266-7, 341-2
ratification. *See* treaties, ratification
real property. *See* property, real/immovable
reason, as source of law **38,** 207
rebellion 70, 18-34, **74,** 32-3. *See also* revolution

change of constitution by **53,** 71-2, 77-8
rebel government, laws of **55,** 51, 53-5
acquisition of property **53,** 151-2
status **53,** 150-1
rebus sic stantibus. *See* treaties, fundamental change of circumstances
recidivists. *See* habitual offenders
reciprocity **72,** 265-6, **75,** 656
diplomatic immunity and **60,** 385
recognition. *See also* arbitral award, enforcement; evidence of; expropriation/nationalization, recognition/enforcement; foreign judgment, recognition/enforcement; foreign law, recognition/enforcement; international organizations, recognition; New York Convention on the Recognition and Enforcement of Foreign Arbitral Awards (1958); recognition, government; recognition, State
aboriginal people
government **79,** 262
State **79,** 262
act of State. *See* act of State, recognition of
acts of foreign government. *See* act of State, recognition of
belligerent **80,** 669-70
applicability of laws and customs of war **105,** 446
need for **80,** 668
boundaries **50,** 90, 100-1, 409-15, 464, 466, 495, **80,** 283, 332, 351-2
civil war in foreign State **74,** 22
de facto, treaty as **78,** 166, 170
of diplomatic envoys **64,** 695-6
of diplomatic premises **94,** 349
diplomatic relations and **49,** 45, 209, **62,** 69, 84
disclaimer **80,** 336
of embassy, executive responsibility **94,** 349
forceful occupation of territory
collective, East Timor **105,** 406
criteria, 'prevailing factual situation' **105,** 409
de facto **105,** 238, 341
de jure **105,** 239, 341
delimitation of continental shelf as **105,** 239
effect, validation of effective control **105,** 406
non-recognition, obligation **105,** 403-6
jus cogens/peremptory norm of international law **105,** 403
responsibility, executive **104,** 456, **107,** 256-9
Stimson doctrine **105,** 403
treaty
applicable to **105,** 238-9, 341-3, 374, 401-6
capable of application to **105,** 245, 374, 402-3
foreign criminal convictions **66,** 152-8
guardianship decrees **42,** 26-9
Head of State. *See* Head of State, recognition
implied, diplomatic or consular relations **49,** 45, 209
justiciability **104,** 456
liberation movement **79,** 36-7
army as visiting force **79,** 36-7
Mandatory, right to administer Mandate **49,** 124
Muslim divorce **74,** 531-56
non-recognition doctrine

recognition (*cont.*)
flexibility **49,** 156
treaty-relations and **49,** 124
UN Charter **49,** 4, 6
illegal situation **49,** 4, 6
obligation **49,** 155-6
UN Charter, non-recognition of illegal situation **49,** 4, 6
par in parem relationship **80,** 125
refugee. *See* refugees, recognition as
revolutionists, State responsibility and **106,** 493, 495
sovereignty **59,** 67-73
territory
acquisition **71,** 297-300, 497-502, **73,** 58-61, 99-120, 139, 146
claims **66,** 336-8
treaties and **96,** 86-9
Trust Territories **64,** 565
unrecognized de facto authority, Geneva Convention on the Treatment of Prisoners of War (1949) **44,** 446-7
withdrawal **55,** 64-6
Recognition and Enforcement of Foreign Arbitral Awards Convention (New York) (1958). *See* New York Convention on the Recognition and Enforcement of Foreign Arbitral Awards (1958)
recognition, government 39, 210-13, 219-22, 291-369, **40,** 58, 446-7, **42,** 32-3, 203, **43,** 49, 69-70, **47,** 240, **52,** 72-3, 75, **73,** 12-27, **74,** 101, 106, **77,** 571, **80,** 2-10, 669, **90,** 553-4. *See also* recognition; recognition, State; revolution
aboriginal government **79,** 262
absence of government **94,** 619, 620
revolutionary government distinguished **94,** 621
absence of sovereign authority **94,** 202
access to courts and **87,** 587-9, **94,** 207-8, 213-15, **96,** 52, **108,** 504
act of State and **77,** 220, **98,** 65
ambassador, appointment **86,** 18, **107,** 258
applicable law
constitutional law **103,** 21-2, 59-62, 74
international law **84,** 204
burden of proof **103,** 77
change of practice, *Republic of Somalia* **116,** 581-5
China, People's Republic of **55,** 64, **84,** 153
effect **96,** 85-7
China (Taiwan) **74,** 106, 111, **82,** 405
withdrawal **55,** 64
Ciskei, Republic of, effects of non-recognition **75,** 679-80, 682-5, 690
conditional **98,** 5-6
criteria. *See* requirements *below*
Cyprus, Turkish Federated State. *See* Cyprus, Turkish Federated State
Cyprus, Turkish Republic of Northern (TRNC). *See* Cyprus, Turkish Republic of Northern (TRNC)
de facto/de jure distinguished **43,** 49, 69-70, **53,** 79, **72,** 15, 20, 37, **73,** 12, 15, 20, **80,** 669
relevance **80,** 4, 7
whether **82,** 385-6, **90,** 473-4, 479, 531-4
democratic regime **103,** 66, 75-6

different levels of **80,** 5
diplomatic relations **80,** 9-10, **84,** 177, 204, **87,** 586-7
distinguished **94,** 214
status as head of diplomatic mission **84,** 204
effect **62,** 25, 72-3, 76, 84-5, **72,** 456-7, 655, **84,** 176-7, 179 n. 11
nullification of obligations of predecessor government **84,** 180
right to sue and be sued **84,** 176, **96,** 94, **116,** 581
territorial and extraterritorial distinguished **84,** 181
effective control and **73,** 15-18, 24-5, **80,** 7-9
emir, of **91,** 612
European Court of Human Rights, relevance to proceedings **103,** 636-7
evidence of
executive certificate/statement **94,** 619-20, **125,** 632, 656, 657, 658-65. *See also* responsibility for, executive *below*
rebuttable, whether **94,** 619-20
UN recognition **94,** 621
in exile **44,** 58, **79,** 36-7
extradition and **77,** 340, 344-5
formal acts, need for **80,** 5, **87,** 74, 587
consequences **80,** 7-10
French revolutionary **82,** 404
implied **62,** 84-5, **68,** 5-6, **80,** 9-10
interference in internal affairs, whether **96,** 50
interim government **94,** 615-16
constitutional successor, whether **94,** 621
effective government, whether **94,** 618-21
establishment by international conference **94,** 618, 621
international conference, establishment of interim government, relevance **94,** 618, 621
judicial acceptance **103,** 68
legal considerations **94,** 617, 621
legal counsel, right to appoint and **96,** 51-2
legitimacy
finding of distinguished **90,** 534
necessity **103,** 22, 26
'successful revolution' doctrine **103,** 22-6
Kelsen **103,** 22
Libya **94,** 213-15, **96,** 94-5
interim government's right of suit **96,** 92, 94
National Patriotic Reconstruction Assembly Government (NPRAG) **96,** 94-6
Mandatory, whether **87,** 586
Marshall Islands **84,** 204
municipal courts, role **75,** 680, 682, 697-8
municipal law, in **90,** 473, 479, 480, 520, 527-9
international law distinguished **90,** 473, 531-4
New Zealand practice **80,** 2-10
non-recognition, effects **39,** 210-13, 219-22, 291, 369, **47,** 72-4, **49,** 157, **73,** 13-20, 22-5, 27
enforcement of arbitral award **94,** 213-15
foreign policy exception **86,** 9
legal standing **86,** 8, 12
legislation **82,** 409, **116,** 586-7
obligatory consequences **49,** 124-7, 139

recognition, government (*cont.*)
State agency/State-owned corporation/State entity, right to sue **94,** 204, 206-9
North Korea **52,** 68-9, **55,** 455
obligation, whether **103,** 72-9, 81
Panama **96,** 46-54
political expediency **82,** 403, **94,** 214, 617, 621-2
political question **86,** 3-4, 5-7, 12, 18
premature, *in mediis rebus* **103,** 27
property, right to and **96,** 48-9
applicable law
act of State doctrine and **96,** 49
lex fori **96,** 49
recognition of laws distinguished **39,** 212
recognition of State distinguished **94,** 620, **108,** 529-30, **116,** 580. *See also* recognition, State
difficulty **94,** 621
relevance **80,** 7, 10
requirements **82,** 404, 410
acquiescence of population **103,** 24-6
constitutional and revolutionary governments distinguished **94,** 621
constitutionality **94,** 622, **116,** 582-3
continuing control of territory **94,** 617, 622
democratic regime **103,** 25-6
effective control of territory **94,** 617, 620-1, 622, **103,** 22, 24-6, **116,** 582-3, 586
effect of loss on constitutional government **94,** 621-2
effective government acquiesced in **103,** 52-6, 66-72, 73-9
formal act, cessation of practice **108,** 529-30
governmental dealings, relevance **116,** 582-5
international obligations, relevance **116,** 585
international recognition **94,** 622, **116,** 582-3, 586
permanency **103,** 71
popular acceptance **103,** 66, 71, 75-6
stability **116,** 586
responsibility for **42,** 33
act of State, relevance **99,** 74 n. 8
courts, role **86,** 6, 12, **87,** 74, 586, 587, **94,** 617, **116,** 579-85
pre-revolutionary **103,** 72, 77-8
executive **64,** 694-7, **86,** 4, 5, 12, 17, **87,** 586, 587, **94,** 617-20, **96,** 48, 49-50, 94, **98,** 5-7, **99,** 161, **103,** 586, 587-8, **114,** 474, **122,** 672
legislative **94,** 102
retroactive **82,** 384-5, 387, 411, **84,** 177-8, 180, 182 n. 14, **103,** 24, 57, 80
extraterritorial effect of nationalization and **84,** 177-8
revolutionary government
absence of government distinguished **94,** 621
successor government, whether **94,** 621
Sierra Leone **114,** 475-8
Somalia **94,** 615-26
Spanish **80,** 669
State immunity and. *See* State immunity, execution/attachment, procedural aspects, recognition of State/government, relevance; State immunity, jurisdiction, procedural aspects, recognition of State/government, relevance
State practice

British practice **43,** 49, 69-70, **80,** 5, 6
change **80,** 4-10, **87,** 587, **94,** 207, 214, 616-20, **116,** 579-85, **125,** 658-9
state of war, compatibility with non-recognition **82,** 405
'to be inferred from nature of dealings' **94,** 616-17
treaties, effect on **96,** 86-9
Uganda **39,** 3, 32
UN, by **94,** 621-2
as evidence of status **94,** 621
unconstitutional change and **80,** 7-10
USSR **42,** 32, 203, **47,** 240, **82,** 404-5, **84,** 162-4
withdrawal **94,** 201-2
continuation of diplomatic relations **96,** 86
recognition, State 48, 30-40, **66,** 107-8, 335-8, **68,** 3-6, **72,** 30-51, **73,** 12-27, **74,** 106, 111, **75,** 679-85, 690-8, **78,** 156, 158, 165-6
abandonment of territorial claim as **100,** 313-14, 326, 330
bilateral agreement **100,** 314, 326
aboriginal people as **79,** 262
acceptance of movement and phytosanitary certificates **100,** 276, 284
Algeria **75,** 81
applicable law
lex fori **122,** 534-5
private international law **108,** 530, 536-7
public international law **108,** 530
appointment of ambassador **100,** 308, 313, 316, 330
The Arantzazu Mendi **116,** 579-80
arbitrary **82,** 403
Belize
independence of Belize, relevance **100,** 326
official visit from **100,** 308
official visit to **100,** 308
unilateral act **100,** 314, 326, 330
validity **100,** 308
China, People's Republic of **82,** 403
China (Taiwan) **74,** 106, 111
collective
Belgium **82,** 420
Czechoslovakia **82,** 420
Greece **82,** 420
Poland **82,** 420
State practice **82,** 420
constituent state of federation **92,** 173-8. *See also* Bosnia-Herzegovina; Croatia; Macedonia; Slovenia; Yugoslavia, Federal Republic of (FRY)
constitutive theory **39,** 159, 290, **77,** 623, **104,** 152 n. 2, **108,** 536-40, **115,** 589. *See also* declaratory theory *below*; statehood, requirements/evidence of
absence of uniformity **82,** 412
criticism of **82,** 405-12
Institut de Droit International Resolution on the Recognition of New States and Governments (1936) **108,** 358
Montevideo Convention on the Rights and Duties of States (1933) **108,** 537
corporate status, recognition of and **100,** 253-4
courts and executive **43,** 35, 72
criteria

recognition, State (*cont.*)
absence of territorial claims **92,** 174-5, 177, 186
bilateral treaty
good relations **100,** 229
inviolability of frontiers **100,** 229
EC Guidelines on Recognition of New States in Eastern Europe and the Soviet Union (1991) **92,** 173-4, 179-80, 183, 187, 189, 208, 210
free elections **92,** 211
name of State, acceptance of **92,** 187, **100,** 229
removal of protection from 'National' in third country **100,** 229
respect for
Charter of Paris (1990) **92,** 173, 190
dispute settlement procedures **92,** 174, 184-5, 192
Helsinki Final Act (1975) **92,** 173, 190
human rights **92,** 176-7, 180-1, 184, 185, 190
inviolability of frontiers **92,** 174, 184, 186, 191
minority rights **92,** 174, 176, 180-1, 185-6, 190, 208
non-use of force **92,** 208
nuclear non-proliferation agreements **92,** 174, 184, 191
security and regional stability commitments **92,** 174
UN Charter **92,** 173, 190
Restatement of Foreign Relations Law (Second) (1965) **115,** 97-8
will of people **92,** 178
referendum **92,** 178
de facto/de jure distinguished **39,** 158, 159-60, 214-15, **64,** 517-19, **72,** 44-5, **75,** 679, 681, 693-8
declaratory theory **41,** 16, **52,** 311, **77,** 623, **82,** 400-12, **92,** 164-5, 201, 208. *See also* constitutive theory *above*
diplomatic relations, relevance **62,** 69, 84, **108,** 519, 538
discretionary **92,** 208
effect **43,** 69, **55,** 64-6, **92,** 201
Egypt (1922) **80,** 259-60
evidence of **64,** 507-8, 517-19, 695-7
diplomatic relations. *See* diplomatic relations, relevance *above*
executive certificate/statement
conclusiveness **43,** 41-2, 45, 49, 56, 68-9, 71, **52,** 56, **63,** 30, **64,** 514-19, 522, 695-7
State immunity, for purposes of **108,** 519
government to government contacts, UK/northern Cyprus **108,** 544-5
ex-colony **83,** 17
GDR **64,** 505-6, 514-15, 518-19, **71,** 20, 22, **72,** 61, 556, 558, 562, 655, **78,** 156, 158, 165-6
by India **64,** 507-8, 517-19
FRG–GDR Basis of Relations Treaty (1970) **91,** 233
UK position **43,** 23-79
UN membership **91,** 233-4
governments of and **80,** 9
implied
acceptance of courts as 'established by law' **120,** 76, 118
treaty **115,** 200
intervention in judicial review proceedings by company **100,** 252-4
Israel **82,** 405
legal norms. *See* political act, whether *below*

legality of State, effect on **115,** 165, 201-2
legislation, conflicting **108,** 539-40
membership of international organization **92,** 201, 202
Mozambique **64,** 697
non-recognition, duty of **49,** 155-6, **120,** 44-5
non-recognition, effect **39,** 159, 161, 165, 226-7, **40,** 40-2, **41,** 15-20, **43,** 23, **68,** 4-5, **72,** 33-5, 40, 42-4, 47-51, **75,** 679-85, 690-8, **82,** 420
administrative contacts **108,** 519
application of laws of **43,** 23-79
commercial obligations **108,** 534
legislation, expropriation of property **108,** 462, 468, 474-5, 503-5
Namibia principle **122,** 536-9
North Korea **52,** 68-9
PLO **82,** 286
conditions **82,** 332
political act, whether **108,** 529-30, **115,** 96-102, 589-91
recognition, government distinguished **108,** 529-30
relevance **82,** 402-3
nationality, power to confer **108,** 555-6, **122,** 536-41
private matters **49,** 46, **108,** 462, 534, **120,** 43-6, 118-19
refugees for purposes of Geneva Convention (1951) **122,** 533-45
representatives, diplomatic status **108,** 520-1, 527
responsibility for violation of international law **104,** 158
reversal of acts, possibility **108,** 478-9
taxation, exemption **108,** 525-40
validity of acts **108,** 477-8, 503-5, 534, **120,** 40-6, 76, 111, 117-24, 135-7, 139, **122,** 536-8
responsibility **82,** 333
executive **63,** 30, **64,** 694-7, **85,** 6, 10, **104,** 568, **108,** 504
retroactive effect, legitimization of secession **115,** 589-90, 595
Rhodesia **39,** 159, 161, 165, 226-7, **52,** 56, **68,** 4-6
following declaration of independence **72,** 33-51
role **41,** 15-20, **52,** 73-4, 311-12
State immunity and. *See* State immunity, execution/attachment, recognition of State/government, relevance; State immunity, jurisdiction, recognition of State/government, relevance
statehood, need for **52,** 73-5
Taiwan **74,** 106
Transkei **82,** 376 n. 1
Vietnam, Democratic Republic **65,** 56
withdrawal **55,** 64
Red Cross. *See* International Committee of the Red Cross (ICRC)
Red Sea, Saudi Arabian claims **41,** 122
Red Sea Islands
appurtenance, title and **114,** 48, 119, 124, 125
British Admiralty (BA) Charts **119,** 458, 460
Dahlak Islands **119,** 459-61
as integral part of coastal configuration **119,** 459-60
straight baselines and **119,** 460-1
delimitation
coastal median line **114,** 36-7, **119,** 443-6, 453-65
enclave solution **119,** 455-6, 463
geodetic line **119,** 464-5

Red Sea Islands (*cont.*)
single all-purpose line **119,** 457-8
Eritrean claims **114,** 11-16, 23-6
Haycocks **114,** 124-6
historic fishing regime
entitlement to engage in artisanal fishing **119,** 450-3
freedom of access **119,** 451-2
Memorandum of Understanding between Eritrea and Yemen (1994) **119,** 451-2
guano and mineral extraction **119,** 451
perpetuation **114,** 137, **119,** 441-3, 447-53
in absence of agreement **119,** 452
res communis **114,** 40-2, **119,** 450
historic title, Eritrean claim, succession through Italy **114,** 116-17, 128-9, **119,** 451
historic title, Yemeni claim
evidence of
1492 expedition to control smuggling **114,** 71
continuity **114,** 115
Ottoman rule, relevance **114,** 115-16, **119,** 448
generality **114,** 71-3
history **114,** 31-4, 37-60
Italian jurisdiction **114,** 48-51
Jabal al-Tayr/Zubayr Group **114,** 134-7, **119,** 461
jurisdiction
divided **114,** 33-4, 43-5, 134
Imam of Yemen **114,** 39
Italy **114,** 48-51, 54-7
Kamaran, as basepoint **119,** 461-2
maps
1872-1918 **114,** 99
1924-39 **114,** 99
supportive value **114,** 96-7
1950-92 **114,** 99-100
1992-5 **114,** 100
accuracy, colour **114,** 96
approval by ruler, need for **114,** 96
Petroconsultants **119,** 443-5
pre-1872 **114,** 95-6, 99
Shell map (1976) **114,** 102
UN map of 1950 **114,** 97
Mohabbaks **114,** 122-4
Negileh Rock **119,** 460
oil concessions
Ethiopia/Eritrea **114,** 110-14, 126, **119,** 443-6
International Petroleum/Amoco Production Sharing Agreement (1988) **114,** 111-14
Yemen
BP Production Sharing Agreement (1990) **114,** 107-8
concession blocks (1990-) **114,** 110
Hunt Oil Company Offshore Production Sharing Agreement (1984) **114,** 106-7
Shell Petroleum Agreement (1974) **114,** 101-3
Shell Seismic Survey (1972) **114,** 101
Tomen–Santa Fe Seismic Permit (1974) **114,** 103-6
Total Production Sharing Agreement (1985) **114,** 108-9

Red Sea lights. *See* Red Sea lights
reefs as basepoints
islands north of Kamaran **119,** 462
Negileh Rock **119,** 460
sovereignty. *See also* title *below*
continental shelf rights distinguished **114,** 106-7
evidence of
airstrip in active use **114,** 109, 132, 133-4
criminal or civil jurisdiction **114,** 90-1
customary law arbitration **114,** 90-1
fishing vessel arrests **114,** 75-8, 86
geodetic station **114,** 89
landing parties **114,** 87-8
legislative acts **114,** 74-5
licensing of activities on islands **114,** 89-90, 113-14, 133-4
licensing of activities in offshore waters **114,** 78
military post **114,** 88
naval and coastguard patrols **114,** 80-5, 129-30
notices to mariners **114,** 79-80
overflight **114,** 94, 108
permission to cruise/land **114,** 78-9
private fishing activity **114,** 85-6
search and rescue operations **114,** 80, 86
seasonal habitation **114,** 92-3
shrines and holy places **114,** 89
fishing regime, compatibility **114,** 139, **119,** 447-53
Italy **114,** 52, 55-7, 96-7
maintenance of lighthouse **114,** 91, 129, 135-6
oil concessions **114,** 100-14, 126, 131-2, 136, **119,** 443-6
Ottoman Empire **114,** 33, 42-3, 46, 115-17
military occupation as basis **114,** 46
renunciation **114,** 39, 51, 115-16
right of alienation **114,** 46, 115
public claims to
Eritrean Constitution (1952) **114,** 70
Eritrean Constitution (1955) **114,** 70
Eritrean Constitution (1987) **114,** 70
Eritrean Constitution (1997) **114,** 70
Ethiopian Federal Crimes Proclamation (1953) **114,** 70
Ethiopian Maritime Order (1953) **114,** 70
Ethiopian State of Emergency Order (1970) **114,** 70
UN Resolution approving Eritrean Constitution (1952) **114,** 70
Yemen communication to Ethiopian Embassy of intention to conduct aerial survey (1973) **114,** 70-1
seismic survey **114,** 105, 133
status
indeterminate **114,** 40, 51-60, 115-16, 136-7, **119,** 445
preservation **114,** 52-8
Italy/United Kingdom Agreement and Protocols (1938) **114,** 55-7
registration, relevance **114,** 56
'parties concerned' **114,** 51, 67
Red Sea lights, relevance **114,** 63-70
Rome Conversations (1927) **114,** 52-3

Red Sea Islands (*cont.*)
Treaty of Lausanne (1923) **114,** 33-4, 39, 40, 47-9, 59, 115-16
acquisitive prescription, possibility of **114,** 51, 52
Treaty of Peace with Italy (1947) **114,** 59
Treaty of Sèvres (1920) **114,** 46-7
UN Draft Eritrean Constitution (1949) **114,** 59-60
title. *See also* historic title, Eritrean claim *and* historic title, Yemeni claim *above*; sovereignty
appurtenance **114,** 48, 119, 124, 125
interruption of chain **114,** 40
reversion **114,** 40, 46, 47, 51, 115-17
standard of proof **114,** 137
territorial sea, within **114,** 123-4
uti possidetis **114,** 32-4
Yemeni claims **114,** 16-23, 38-9, 57-8
exclusive economic zone (EEZ) **114,** 67-8
historic title **114,** 71-3, 115-17
Zuqar–Hanish group **114,** 127-34, **119,** 464
Red Sea lights
history **114,** 60-9
Convention concerning the Maintenance of Certain Lights (1930) **114,** 62-3
Lighthouse Convention (1962) **114,** 65-9
London Conference (1989) **114,** 135-6
status of Red Sea Islands and **114,** 63-70, 88-90, 91
protest, relevance **114,** 68-9
factors affecting **114,** 83-5, 102-3, 108, 112-13, 136
reefs, Law of the Sea Convention (1982) **119,** 461, 462
referendum
democratic, whether **115,** 565
EC law, primacy and **93,** 523, 549-52, 553
legality **115,** 135-46
as legislative act **93,** 552
need for **87,** 357
procedure **115,** 135-46
right to, entrenched provisions of Constitution and **98,** 220
Single European Act (1986), need for **93,** 503
treaties, ratification **93,** 503
refinancing agreement, choice of law clause **118,** 603
Refined Sugar Association, Rules
406 (applicable law) **64,** 249-50, 376-7
as applicable law **64,** 196
export licences, duty to obtain **64,** 202-3
force majeure **64,** 199, 204, 205-7, 372-3
refugees 72, 443, 580-7, 624, 633-50, **73,** 42-3, 596-8, 603-6, 615-16, 628-34, 671-7, **74,** 281-2, 395-7, 401-11, 417-18, 432-44, 474-6, 506-7, **79,** 612-40, **92,** 663-70, 693-719. *See also* asylum; Refugees, Geneva Convention on the Status of (1951) and Protocol (1967); stateless person
access to courts **44,** 143-4, **48,** 171-4, **70,** 356-8, **72,** 586-7, 642, **111,** 537, **119,** 365
appeal against refusal of refugee status and **99,** 2-3
reciprocity and **48,** 173
agricultural leases **48,** 166-7
Appeals Commission, recourse to **73,** 603-5, **74,** 433-44. *See also* United Kingdom, Special Immigration Appeals Commission (SIAC)
applicable law, law relating to aliens **111,** 536, 537

burden of proof **92,** 705, 718, **104,** 233
cautio judicatum solvi and **72,** 587, **73,** 676-7
compensation **61,** 241
conscientious objectors **40,** 202-4
constitutional rights **99,** 33-4, **124,** 358
country of first refuge **74,** 405-6, 418
economic conditions, relevance **99,** 19-20
failure to establish refugee status and **99,** 37
non-party to Convention as **99,** 20
obligation to apply for refugee status in
2 years' residence **99,** 4
3 years' residence **99,** 19-20
9 months' residence **99,** 4
adequate protection against refoulement, need for **99,** 15-16, 19-20
requirements
close link **99,** 19
observation of Convention obligations **99,** 15, 20, 21
right of return to **69,** 203-4, **77,** 580, **79,** 656
UNHCR Executive Committee Recommendation (1979) **99,** 19
country of residence, relevance **73,** 597, **122,** 534
Cyprus, Republic of **62,** 52-3
definition **39,** 416, **55,** 70-1, 75-8, **57,** 325-7, **70,** 385, **71,** 498, **72,** 580-1, 643-4, **73,** 596, 674-7, **74,** 402, 404-6, 418, 506-7, **79,** 615, 618, 621-3, 635, 639, 646, 661-2, **85,** 186, 187-8, **87,** 195, 441, 466, 474, **88,** 6, 16, **90,** 4-6, 16, 27, 28-31, 145, 155-6, 163, 175, **92,** 667-8, **104,** 226, 246, 258, 265, **107,** 149, **124,** 413
in Australia **90,** 28-9, 159-60, 175, **117,** 597, 603-5
in Canada **104,** 226, 246, 258, 265, **107,** 149, **124,** 413
de facto refugee **99,** 13, 31-2
flexible **90,** 28-9
history **79,** 621
international obligations in respect of family, relevance **114,** 582
International Refugee Organization (IRO) **90,** 175
political refugee
distinction, whether **90,** 5
recognition by UN High Commissioner **68,** 31
Refugees, Geneva Convention on the Status of (1951) and Protocol (1967) **39,** 146-8, **79,** 615, 619, 621-2, 646, 661-2, **87,** 133, 195, **90,** 159-60, 172, **111,** 523, **117,** 595, 601-3, **124,** 491-2, 504
UNHCR *Handbook on Procedures and Criteria for Determining Refugee Status* (1979) **90,** 145
in USA **87,** 482, 493
well-founded fear of persecution as **87,** 466
deportation **73,** 596, 598, 615-16, 628-34, **74,** 432-44. *See also* expulsion *below*
appeals procedure **74,** 433-44, **79,** 612, 616-18, 635, **85,** 184-208
national security and **74,** 438-40
urgency, cases of **74,** 435-8, 443-4
deportation withhold/bar. *See* deportation withhold/bar
divorce, jurisdiction over **70,** 356-8, **72,** 641-5
dual nationality, relevance **104,** 229, **122,** 534
economic migrants **104,** 250
expulsion **69,** 202-4, 208-9, **70,** 361-2, **73,** 42-3, 615-16, 628-33, **74,** 433-44, **79,** 623, 645-64, 668, **87,** 122-9
appeal, right of **74,** 433, 436-9, 443-4

refugees (*cont.*)
critical date, date of order **111,** 526
danger to security **73,** 615-16, 629-31
discretion, exercise of **71,** 497, 499
due process requirement **74,** 433, 436-7
family unity **111,** 547
fear of persecution **71,** 497, 501
hearing, right to **74,** 433, 435-8, 443-4, **87,** 128-9
judicial review **79,** 645, 663-4
'national security or public order' **74,** 441, **79,** 651
non-refoulement **79,** 613, 616, 623-4, 638
opportunity to seek admission to another country **73,** 629-31
procedures **77,** 386
reasonable period to seek admission elsewhere **77,** 287
refugee status
'national security or public order' **79,** 651
prior to determination of **69,** 208-9, **79,** 651, 663
temporary admission **79,** 651
removal on ground of illegal entry distinguished **79,** 648
representation, right to **87,** 124
lawful presence in country of refuge, need for **87,** 129
residence permit, non-extension as **77,** 579, 580
third country
risk of further deportation **79,** 657-9
to **79,** 651-9
travel documents, restriction on **69,** 202-4
unlawful presence in expelling country **70,** 361-2, **79,** 650
extradition **72,** 634-6, **73,** 42-3, **74,** 474-6, 506-7, **111,** 508, 514-25
aut dedere aut punire/judicare, relevance **111,** 523
country of origin, to **111,** 516-22
incompatibility with purpose of Geneva Convention for the Protection of Refugees (1951) **111,** 520
international organizations, practice **111,** 520
State practice **111,** 518-20
exemption from **44,** 187-9
extradition **72,** 636
national treatment **44,** 187-9, **74,** 474-6, 506-7
non-refoulement rules, applicability **111,** 516-20, 524-5
Protocol on the Status of (1967) **51,** 372-4
public order/public policy/*ordre public* and **72,** 636
status
claim to and **74,** 473-7, 506-7
priority of extradition request **74,** 474
relevance **100,** 619
third country without risk **111,** 516
fair hearing, right to **92,** 653-6
family members, extension of rights to **111,** 533-43
brothers/sisters **111,** 541
dependent parents or grandparents **111,** 534, 541
lawful residence, preliminary requirement **111,** 538
member of a family unit **117,** 600, 610
minor children **111,** 534, 541
mother of child of refugee **111,** 535

own fear of persecution, relevance **111,** 534, 535-7, 541
right not to be returned to country of origin **111,** 536
right to invoke European Convention on Human Rights (1950) **111,** 536
right to residence permit **111,** 536
spouse **111,** 533-43
co-habitee **111,** 540
divorce **111,** 540
marriage after acquisition of refugee status **111,** 540, 541, 542
proof of marriage, need for **111,** 540, 541, 542-3
of same nationality **111,** 534, 539, 540, 542
State practice **111,** 539-40
withdrawal of refugee status, effect **111,** 540
family unity
continuing validity of original assessment, need for **111,** 289
expulsion, proportionality **111,** 547
family members, extension of rights of refugee to. *See* family members, extension of rights of refugee to *above*
right of family members to join refugee **111,** 538
freedom of movement **73,** 605-6
place of residence, restrictions on **73,** 605-6
general principles, non-return to country of origin **111,** 520, 524
hearing of evidence, foreign relations and **87,** 128
history of protection **74,** 432-3
illegal entry or presence, imposition of penalties on account of **44,** 147-9, **74,** 432, 439
'internal flight' possibility, relevance **114,** 577-80
international obligations in respect of family, relevance **114,** 582, **117,** 628-35
International Refugee Organization. *See* International Refugee Organization
internment **60,** 209-10, 213-16
judicial review
administrative review **111,** 527
assessment of facts **111,** 542, **117,** 606, 623
decisions relating to status **79,** 662, **90,** 20, 21-31, 140-80, **91,** 175, 176
exhaustion of administrative remedies, need for **111,** 516
expulsion **79,** 645, 663-4
grounds **117,** 617
abuse of discretion **117,** 628
error of law **114,** 579-80, 581-3, **117,** 597-8, 618-19, 620-3
failure to exercise jurisdiction **117,** 606
unreasonableness **114,** 579, 581-3, **117,** 620
non-statutory body **114,** 583-6
standard, 'not over-zealous' **117,** 613-14, 619
maintenance and rehabilitation **53,** 135-6
matrimonial property rights
law governing **73,** 672-3
recognition in country of refuge **52,** 338
'membership of a particular social group' **87,** 493-5, **92,** 695-9, 708-12, 715-16, **95,** 573, **104,** 246-58, **118,** 595-601
birth control policy constituting **117,** 602, 609-10
causal relationship, need for **124,** 489-90, 497-500, 504
cohesiveness, need for **124,** 483-7, 488, 496, 502-3, 507-10
common victimization **104,** 248-51
criminals, exclusion **104,** 256-8

refugees (*cont.*)
discrimination as link **104,** 251-6
Eritrea **99,** 3
evidence of persecution **87,** 495-6
existence of group independently of persecution, need for **124,** 483, 488-9, 497, 502, 507, 509-10
group persecution **88,** 7, 20, 24, 31, 33-5
homosexuals **118,** 595-601, **124,** 486, 488-9, 508-9
INLA **104,** 230-1, 259-60
'Refugees, Women and International protection' (1985) (UNHCR Executive Committee) **124,** 497
sex **95,** 573
Tamils in Sri Lanka **99,** 30-1
terrorist groups, exclusion **104,** 230, 256-8
UNHCR *Handbook on Procedures and Criteria for Determining Refugee Status* (1979) **92,** 698, 717, **118,** 597
women **104,** 263-4
in Pakistan **124,** 477-511
youth **95,** 573
naturalization, entitlement **74,** 396-7
non-refoulement. *See also* Torture Convention (1984), non-refoulement to country of origin or any other country where risk of subjection to torture
as adequate protection **99,** 15-16, 19-20
appeal, procedures **108,** 347-8
in case of non-Convention refugees **108,** 351-2
compelling reasons of national security **108,** 370, 381-2, 435-7
balance against danger to refugee, need for **108,** 370-5, 377-8, 382-4, 406, 410-11, 435-7
compassionate circumstances **108,** 382-4
conviction of serious crime, need for **124,** 371
proportionality **108,** 371
terrorist activity **108,** 370
threat to security of another State, relevance **124,** 371
'conducive to the public good' **108,** 368-70, 377, 409-11
country of destination, relevance **107,** 555-6, 578
'country or territory to which there is reason to believe he will be admitted' **122,** 544
customary international law, whether **92,** 655, **124,** 367-8
extradition distinguished **107,** 152-4, 161, 167, 555, 562, 575, 576, 580, **111,** 516-20, 524-5
diplomatic and jurisdictional guarantees **111,** 517
general principle of international law **106,** 264
judicial review **108,** 348-50
effective remedy, whether **108,** 357-62, 423-7
'persons considered not to be deserving of international protection' **107,** 563
proportionality **104,** 665-6
UNHCR *Handbook on Procedures and Criteria for Determining Refugee Status* (1979) **104,** 666
public order/public policy/*ordre public*
commission of serious crime **99,** 33-4
danger to security of country **107,** 572-3
right of asylum, whether **107,** 555, 560, **108,** 353, 443

safe third country alternative **108,** 440, 443
written undertaking, need for **99,** 20-1
'persecution'
birth control policy **111,** 530-1, **117,** 617
denial of employment **90,** 177
denial of fundamental rights or freedoms **90,** 142
discrimination as **118,** 600
disregard of human dignity **90,** 151, 177
evidence of **79,** 614, 617-20, 623-4, 657-9
ideology **88,** 13 n. 3, 28
injurious action and oppression **87,** 364
military service evasion. *See* 'persecution or well-founded fear of persecution', military service evasion *below*
race **90,** 29, **92,** 668, 670
refusal to join non-governmental group **95,** 560
religious belief **92,** 668, 670, **95,** 554, **99,** 37
selective harassment **90,** 176
serious harm, need for **124,** 506
serious punishment, penalty or disadvantage **117,** 601
substantial economic disadvantage **95,** 540-1
'persecution or well-founded fear of persecution' **71,** 498-9, 501, **72,** 581, 585, **73,** 615-16, 674-7, **74,** 402, 405-6, 410, 418, 474-5, 506-7, **79,** 613, 616-20, 623-41, 657, 662, **85,** 186-8, **88,** 6-7, 20-5, **90,** 141, 142-5, 149-50, 161-2, 172-7, **91,** 177, **95,** 548 n. 4
apartheid **99,** 12-13
burden of proof **88,** 7, **90,** 7, **95,** 564-5, **108,** 379-80, **111,** 547
changed circumstances **90,** 151, 156-7, 158-9, 162-4
conscientious objection **71,** 498-9, **95,** 550-6, 558-60, **99,** 13
non-governmental group, refusal to join distinguished **95,** 560
political belief **95,** 555
UNHCR *Handbook on Procedures and Criteria for Determining Refugee Status* (1979) **95,** 551, 555
conscientious objections **71,** 498-9
Convention reason, need for **117,** 601-2, 616-17, **124,** 504, 510
critical date **87,** 363, **90,** 141, 144, 150-1, 156-7, 163-4, 178-9
damage to foreign relations resulting from finding of **90,** 149
ECOSOC Report (1950) **87,** 442, 469 n. 10
evidence of **87,** 441, 442, **90,** 8, **117,** 614-16, 622
applicant's responsibility to provide **90,** 7
exile **90,** 143
extended family **95,** 565-6
extortion **95,** 540-1
freedoms, acceptable restrictions on distinguished **118,** 598-9
general conditions of political unrest **95,** 565
member of FIS if returned to Algeria **107,** 560-2, 576
'membership of a particular social group'. *See* 'membership of a particular social group' *above*
military service evasion **104,** 269-77
military action internationally condemned **104,** 273-7
penalties for **88,** 7-13, 21, **104,** 273
political objection **88,** 8-9, 24-5
political offence, whether **99,** 36-7

refugees (*cont.*)
role of military **88,** 10-13
UNHCR *Handbook on Procedures and Criteria for Determining Refugee Status* (1979) **99,** 36-7, **104,** 270
ordinary meaning **87,** 364
past persecution **95,** 542-3
'persecution'. *See* 'persecution' *above*
political activity **99,** 31, 37
continuity, need for **99,** 13
political motivation
leaving intelligence service **99,** 7-8
leaving Secret Service **99,** 7-8
political opinion **87,** 486-8, **90,** 142-3, **95,** 540-2, **99,** 24, **104,** 260-3
actual belief **104,** 261
implied **104,** 261, **117,** 603-4
public authorities
attitude, relevance **111,** 504-5
intentions, relevance **104,** 274
quality of life **87,** 364
relevant factors. *See also* political motivation *above*
attitude of public authorities **111,** 504-5
denial of admittance to home territory **104,** 267
disproportionately heavy sentence **99,** 26, 37
First *Ad Hoc* Committee on Statelessness and Related Problems (1950) **104,** 240
intentions of authorities **99,** 30-1, **104,** 274
motivation **95,** 553-4, 556
physical assault **95,** 541 n. 6
punishment as key **88,** 9, **95,** 559
relocation and **114,** 581-3
State's ability to protect **104,** 228-9, 231, 232, 234-6, 239-42
UNHCR *Handbook on Procedures and Criteria for Determining Refugee Status* (1979) **104,** 240-1, 267
unwillingness distinguished **104,** 239-42
requirements
action directed at individual **90,** 30-1, 176
acts by non-governmental group **90,** 5-6
arrest **87,** 196, 491
Convention reason. *See* Convention reason, need for *above*
discrimination **95,** 550-1, **99,** 36-7, **117,** 616
government's knowledge or belief **95,** 559
identification of reasons, UNHCR *Handbook on Procedures and Criteria for Determining Refugee Status* (1979) **104,** 260
independent corroboration **87,** 488
political profile prior to departure **117,** 598-600
State complicity **92,** 669-70, 698-702, 712-13, 715, **104,** 228, 231, 236-9, 241-2, **111,** 504-5
UNHCR *Handbook on Procedures and Criteria for Determining Refugee Status* (1979) **104,** 237
in respect of future behaviour which can be avoided **118,** 599-600
responsibility for determining **87,** 196-7, **88,** 23, 26-7
discretion **87,** 441, 442

result of own abuse of human rights **111,** 529
spouse **111,** 529
standard of proof **87,** 360, 364, 466, 505-6, **95,** 548, **117,** 622
change, whether **87,** 466, 470, 473, 481
clear probability **87,** 377, 441, 466, 467, 470, 473-4, 482-3, 491, 499, **90,** 162, **95,** 549-50, 554-6, 559, 564
well-founded fear distinguished **95,** 530
State responsibility and **88,** 11, 23, 31
private acts **95,** 540-1
threat to life or freedom **71,** 500, **72,** 635, **73,** 615, 628-30, **79,** 616, 623, **87,** 472, 484, 485, 495-9, **90,** 151, 165, 179-80, **95,** 542
UNHCR *Handbook on Procedures and Criteria for Determining Refugee Status* (1979) **90,** 29, 150-1, 156, 165, 172-3
variety of interpretation **90,** 173
violation of human rights **90,** 151
well-founded fear **57,** 325-7, **79,** 613, 616-20, 623-41, 657, 662, **87,** 194, 359, 363-4, 440-3, 466, 467, 472 n. 18, 473, 482-3, 493, 503-4, 505-6, **104,** 236
assumed belief **95,** 542, 555, 556
balance of probabilities test **87,** 360-3, 473, 485-6, **104,** 101, **117,** 600, 603-6, 618-19
clear probability **79,** 614, 617-20, 623-41
genuine fear **95,** 539, 553
good reason to fear **90,** 175
likelihood of realization **90,** 143, 149-50, 174, 176
'more likely than not' **95,** 549, 556
objective test **87,** 194, 440, 466-7, 497, 505-6, **90,** 149, 156, 175-6, **95,** 540-2, 553, 565, **117,** 602-3
personal effect **95,** 572
possibility of error in determining **117,** 605-6
probability test **84,** 711
real chance **90,** 143, 150, 157, 158, 174, **117,** 602-7, 613-14, 620, 623
real and substantial risk **90,** 143
reasonable chance **84,** 710, 711, **90,** 150, 173, **95,** 539, 565
'reasonable person' test **88,** 20, 32 n. 11, 36
self-created **91,** 178-9
serious possibility **90,** 174
State's ability to protect **104,** 242-6
subjective **90,** 149, 156, 164, **92,** 697, **95,** 540, 572
substantial grounds for thinking **84,** 710, 711-12
prolonged imprisonment, risk of **71,** 497-9
receiving State, second, obligations of **79,** 656, 657-9
recognition as **60,** 371-2, **88,** 6, 16
minor child with own right to consular protection **74,** 408
political, UN High Commissioner **68,** 31
relevance **90,** 163, 172
recognition as national of State of residence, mistake, effect **72,** 648-9
Refugees, Geneva Convention on the Status of (1951) and Protocol (1967), relevance **90,** 27
renvoi **69,** 209
residence
relocation requirement **99,** 5-6

refugees (*cont.*)
detrimental economic and social impact, relevance **99,** 3-4
relevance **99,** 5-6
right of **92,** 710
right to choose place of **73,** 605-6, **99,** 4
residence permit
family members, right to **111,** 536
refusal to renew
as expulsion **77,** 579, 580
public order justification **77,** 580
rights **61,** 496-7, **72,** 587, 635, 642, **74,** 281-2
identity papers **111,** 537
political persecution **74,** 404-6, 410-11, 418
protected conditions of residence **111,** 537
'serious non-political crime' **104,** 658-72, **107,** 149-68. *See also* political offence
asylum, ground for refusal **104,** 658-72
burden of proof **104,** 663-5
'*crime grave de droit commun*' **107,** 149, 561
degree of criminality, relevance **107,** 167-8, 556-7, 571
murder by organized armed group **111,** 508
in own country, remedies **111,** 522-3
political offence exception as model **107,** 580
terrorism **104,** 663-72, **107,** 562-90, **111,** 514-16
standard of treatment
equality with nationals
access to courts **111,** 537
education **111,** 537
labour legislation **111,** 537
public relief **111,** 537
social security **111,** 537
equality in State of habitual residence **99,** 3
equality of treatment, public relief and assistance, minimum wage legislation **106,** 317-18
MFN
right of association **111,** 537
right to paid employment **111,** 537
national treatment **44,** 71, **73,** 597, **74,** 474-6, 506-7
extent of entitlement **72,** 587, 634-6, 642-5, 648-9
extradition **44,** 187-9
mistaken recognition as national, effect **72,** 648-9
not less favourable than normally available to aliens **44,** 140-5
right to housing **111,** 537
self-employment **111,** 537
treatment not less favourable than normally available to aliens, acquisition of property **111,** 537
stateless person compared **71,** 506
status **54,** 541, **57,** 326-7, **60,** 370, **61,** 496-7, **70,** 385, **87,** 128-9, 194-7, **91,** 175-9
'actions contrary to the purposes and principles of the UN', grave violations of human rights **111,** 529
aliens **55,** 71, 75-9, **111,** 537-8
appeal against decision respecting **79,** 644-64, **99,** 2-3
admissibility **77,** 418-19
stay of proceedings and **99,** 18

application for
  entitlement to remain lawfully in country until status regularized or admission into another country obtained **111,** 527-8
  failure to follow procedure **69,** 208-9
  unlawful presence, relevance **111,** 527
burden of proof **114,** 577
claim to **73,** 674-6, **74,** 408, 417-18, **79,** 652
  executive, question for **39,** 154-5
  illegal entry and **43,** 212-13, **79,** 649-50
competence to accord **77,** 418, **79,** 622, 635
conditions for **70,** 384-7, **71,** 498-9, **72,** 643-5, 648-9
critical date **87,** 136-7
date of acquisition **70,** 384-7
date arising **90,** 21-2, 27, **91,** 175
date of claim, relevance **99,** 3
  subsequent events, relevance **99,** 24-5
delay in claiming, effect **74,** 405
determination **85,** 186, 188, 191-5, **87,** 482
  binding on third country, whether **99,** 23, 25-6
  matter for country of refuge **79,** 622, 638, **87,** 127-8, 132-3, 141
  procedures **87,** 127-9, 132-3, 134, **91,** 171, 172
  responsibility **87,** 138-40, 141-2, **90,** 163, 172
effect **60,** 371-3
entry permit, relevance **90,** 27-8, 155, 159, 160, 168, **91,** 176
error of law, possibility **90,** 20, 24-5, 27-31
evidence of **60,** 371
  travel documents **77,** 579-80
expulsion and **43,** 229-31
extradition and **100,** 619
ICJ as ultimate arbiter **87,** 133
judicial review of decisions relating to **79,** 662, **90,** 20, 21-31, 140-80, **91,** 175, 176
justiciability **79,** 662
loss **73,** 597, **74,** 281-2
political asylum **71,** 497-8, 501-2
political status **60,** 211
preferential immigrant **87,** 472, 476
procedures for determining **79,** 652-9
  clearly identified authority **79,** 649
  permission to remain in country pending decision **79,** 649
  reasonable time to appeal **79,** 649
  UNHCR *Handbook on Procedures and Criteria for Determining Refugee Status* (1979) **79,** 649
recognition, relevance **90,** 163, 172
refugees '*sur place*' **57,** 327, **72,** 650, **91,** 177-9
request, need for **90,** 178
requirement to relocate, detrimental economic and social impact, relevance **99,** 3-4
resettlement following flight, effect **70,** 348-53, 361
residence permit on humanitarian grounds distinguished **99,** 5-6, 31-2
right of re-entry to third State, effect on **77,** 580
rights under Convention dependent on **87,** 129
second receiving State, obligations **69,** 207-9, **79,** 656, 657-9
serious intention to claim **73,** 597

refugees (*cont.*)
statutory basis **85,** 185, 188
visit to State of origin, effect **72,** 581, 585
withdrawal **72,** 580-1, 585
children, effect on **72,** 585
circumstances justifying **72,** 581, 585
competent authority **111,** 515-16
family members, effect on **111,** 540
grounds **72,** 581, 585, **74,** 402-3
grounds, changed circumstances **111,** 515
grounds, serious non-political crime **111,** 515-16, 522
as *res judicata* **111,** 515-16
status of children, effect on **72,** 585
status, refusal
judicial review/appeal **85,** 192-203, **90,** 20, 21-31, **91,** 175, 176, 181-9, **99,** 2-3
reasons for, right to **87,** 131-2, 140
temporary visa **73,** 598
travel documents **72,** 641, 643
effect of **69,** 203-4, **77,** 579
UNHCR, relevance of views concerning **99,** 15-16
United Nations High Commissioner for Refugees. *See* United Nations High Commissioner for Refugees (UNHCR)
unwillingness to avail oneself of protection of national authorities **92,** 669-70, 701-6, 714-19
dual nationality and **92,** 704-6, **104,** 230, 232-3, 264-7
UNHCR *Handbook on Procedures and Criteria for Determining Refugee Status* (1979) **92,** 704-5, 714-15
protection of national State, primacy **104,** 239, 250
right to live in country, relevance **92,** 704-6, 716-18
USA, in **88,** 5-36
voluntary re-availment of protection of country of nationality **74,** 402-3
work permit, revocation, unjustified **77,** 580
Refugees, Geneva Convention on the Status of (1951) and Protocol (1967) 40, 202-7, **43,** 182-6, 213, **44,** 71, 140-4, 147-9, 187-9, **48,** 166-7, 171-4, **51,** 372-4, **55,** 69-78, **69,** 202-4, 206-9, 297-301, **77,** 417, 418, 579, **79,** 613, 619-24, 628-9, 638, 639, 645-7, **87,** 468-70. *See also* refugees
accession to, Lesotho **39,** 415-24, **55,** 71-5
acquired rights **72,** 443
appeal procedures, UNHCR's right to review **108,** 442
applicability
critical date **124,** 496
mass flight **95,** 595, 603
persons receiving protection from UN agency **99,** 28
voluntary relinquishment of protection **99,** 28
asylum, withhold of deportation distinguished **79,** 616 n. 6
automatic **79,** 625
authoritative texts **95,** 601-2
breach, Kenya **79,** 657-9
cautio judicatum solvi **72,** 586-7, **73,** 676-7
compliance with **79,** 616, 628, 637, 667
Cyprus, Turkish Republic of Northern (TRNC) and **122,** 530-45
definition. *See* refugees, definition

European Union (EU), justice and home affairs, compliance with **98,** 218
'events occurring before 1 January 1951' **40,** 203, **72,** 643-5, **73,** 677
exceptional measures against person, property or interest of foreign national, waiver in Peace Treaty with Hungary and **45,** 444
exceptions, security reasons **95,** 601-2
Extradition, European Convention on (1957) and **74,** 474
extradition law, compatibility **104,** 258
extraterritorial application **95,** 582, 586, 592-8
  high seas **95,** 599-600
  UNHCR *Handbook on Procedures and Criteria for Determining Refugee Status* (1979) **95,** 604 n. 8
families of refugees
  absence of provision **111,** 533, 535-7, 539
  Final Act of the Conference of Plenipotentiaries **111,** 533-4, 539
Hong Kong, part of Hong Kong law, whether **92,** 654-5
implementation **69,** 297-301, **73,** 603-4, 615-16, 627, 677, **74,** 395, **79,** 616, 618-20, 628, 637, 645-7, 649-50, 651, 662, **88,** 7 n. 3
implementing legislation **87,** 467-8, 480 n. 2, **91,** 175
individual's right to invoke before national courts **93,** 226
interpretation **72,** 643-4, **79,** 638
  aids
    Conference of Plenipotentiaries (1950) **111,** 517-18
    preamble **124,** 481-2, 495, 505
    specialist international conferences **111,** 518
    State practice **114,** 578
    teachings of publicists **111,** 518
    UNHCR *Handbook on Procedures and Criteria for Determining Refugee Status* (1979) **91,** 178, **99,** 28, **114,** 578, **118,** 598
  extradition
    bilateral agreements, independence **111,** 517-18
    non-refoulement, distinction, whether **111,** 517-18
  guidelines
    eiusdem generis **124,** 401, 486, 487-8
    purposive **122,** 358, 540-1, **124,** 486-7
    text **111,** 517
    uniformity **122,** 540
  responsibility **111,** 539
  social changes, need to reflect **124,** 502
legislative reciprocity **70,** 354-5
matrimonial property regime **52,** 338
'membership of a particular social group', *travaux préparatoires* **124,** 481-2, 494-5
municipal law and **69,** 300-1, **72,** 642, **80,** 678-9, **87,** 132, 141, **91,** 175. *See also* implementing legislation *and* individual's right to invoke before national courts *above*
national treatment **73,** 597
nationality/without nationality distinction **122,** 540-1
naturalization **74,** 395-6
obligations
  other contracting parties as sole beneficiaries **87,** 132, 136
  to respect **111,** 522
personal status, applicable law **72,** 642, **73,** 672-3
phrases

Refugees, Geneva Convention on the Status of (*cont.*)
'actions contrary to the purposes and principles of the UN'. *See* refugees, status, 'actions contrary to the purposes and principles of the UN'
'administrative detention' **108,** 439, 443
'as a result of events occurring before 1 January 1951' **114,** 571-3
'assisted the enemy in persecuting civilians' **95,** 508, 518-19
'country of first refuge'. *See* refugees, country of first refuge
'country of former habitual residence', status as State, relevance **122,** 538-9, 541-3
'expel or return (refoulement)'
'exclusion' **95,** 601, 607-8
expulsion **95,** 595, 600
presence in host country, need for **95,** 593, 596-8, 599-605, 608
'*refouler*' **95,** 594, 600-5
'repulse' **95,** 594, 600
'membership of a particular social group'. *See* refugees, 'membership of a particular social group'
'refugees *sur place*' **57,** 327, **72,** 650, **91,** 177-9
good faith, need for **91,** 178-9
'serious non-political crime'. *See* refugees, 'serious non-political crime'
'voluntarily assisted enemy forces . . . in their operations' **95,** 508, 518-19
procedures **87,** 127-9, 132-3, 134
Protocol (1967) **79,** 619-20, 621-4, 628
effect **72,** 645
entry into force **72,** 645, **73,** 677
preferential immigrant **87,** 472, 476
purpose **87,** 136
right to asylum and right not to be deported distinguished **79,** 613
purpose
definition, recognition and protection of refugee **111,** 520
eradication of discrimination **124,** 482, 495-6
return of refugee to country of origin, compatibility **111,** 520
qualifying date **72,** 643-4, 649
removal of **72,** 645
reservations, refugees as result of events in Europe, limited to **99,** 4, 15-16
retroactive effect, whether **72,** 443
return **73,** 42
self-executing, whether **95,** 585 n. 14
'binding on all persons' **99,** 3, 34
travaux préparatoires **79,** 676-7, 681-3, **90,** 174-5, **95,** 587
'membership of a particular social group' **124,** 481-2, 494-5, 502, 505
UN purposes and principles, conduct contrary to **71,** 279-84, 286-93
evidence of **71,** 280-2
high treason **71,** 277-84, 290
motivation **71,** 289-93
terrorism **71,** 286-93
UN, preceding establishment of **71,** 281-3
regional arrangements 76, 55, 149-52, 505-7
regional health organizations. *See* Pan American Sanitary Organization; Pan Arab Health Bureau; World Health Organization Regional Office in Egypt
regional international law 50, 213, **76,** 518
Latin American influence **46,** 464-9
need to complement **123,** 171
States with liberal economies **46,** 451

regions, Maastricht Treaty (1992) as infringement of powers **98,** 211
reinsurance as commercial activity 63, 454-5
relevant circumstances. *See* maritime delimitation, relevant/special circumstances
religion
discrimination on grounds of **58,** 145
Religious Intolerance, Draft Treaty for Prevention of **47,** 206
exemption from trade union membership, ground for **62,** 360, 370, 373
freedom of. *See* freedom of religion
Statehood, element of **59,** 115
religious belief, lack of, acquisition of citizenship and **43,** 187-91
religious courts
Israel, jurisdiction **48,** 93-106
Morocco, jurisdiction after independence **45,** 53-6
religious education 62, 271-8
minors **47,** 205-11
remedies. *See also* compensation; compensation for war-related events; damages; declaratory award; European Community law, breach, remedies; European Economic Community Treaty (Rome) (1957), breach, remedies; injunction; International Covenant on Civil and Political Rights (ICCPR) (1966), remedies; just satisfaction (Art. 50 [41] of the European Convention on Human Rights (1950)); provisional measures; reparations; *restitutio in integrum*; Vienna Convention on Consular Relations (1963), breach, remedies; Yugoslavia, International Criminal Tribunal for the Former (ICTY), penalty
absence of injury **84,** 719, 720
administrative and judicial distinguished **59,** 393
adverse inference **110,** 635-6
allied shareholders in enemy companies **46,** 478, 518
alternative, possibility of **106,** 521-3, 530
amendment of defective legislation **103,** 126-7
apology **74,** 258, 266, 271, **82,** 516, 519, 576-7, 586, **103,** 294-5
applicable law **82,** 548
appropriate termination package **83,** 715
breach of international law, individual's entitlement **84,** 530-2, **86,** 347-8, 530-2, 582, **96,** 329-30
breach of treaty
compensation **91,** 476
discretionary **104,** 436-40
reciprocal action **106,** 267
restoration of treaty **117,** 414, 439-40
commutation of death sentence **98,** 334, **115,** 354
corollary to right **79,** 563, 569-70
costs, adjustment **105,** 66
costs and damages, relationship **54,** 469-71
damages. *See* damages
declaration of **84,** 307-9, 326, 327
breach of international obligations **84,** 307-9, 326, 327, **96,** 329, **105,** 418, **106,** 13, **118,** 6, **120,** 199, 201
breach of treaty **82,** 570, 571, 575-7, 578-9, 580
entitlement to export licence **90,** 579-80
failure to observe Statute or Rules, reported to Security Council **110,** 704-7, 730
failure to observe Tribunal Rules **110,** 704-7
invalidity of law **118,** 477
legal or equitable right **118,** 586-92
accrued cause of action, need for **118,** 587-92

remedies (*cont.*)
nationality **103,** 282
return of passport **103,** 291
unconstitutionality **103,** 102
unlawfulness **103,** 102
of nuclear tests without prior environmental impact assessment (EIA) **106,** 13
declaratory relief
requirements **117,** 608
third party, effect on **102,** 527
definition **59,** 392
detention on isolated military facility **82,** 519, 584-90
'for a minimum of three years'/*pour une période minimale* **82,** 584-90
diplomatic channels
forcible abduction/unlawful arrest **95,** 404
State immunity, jurisdiction, in case of **102,** 173, 182, **104,** 580, 622
diplomatic protection as **79,** 570 n. 4
effective measures to remedy violations **94,** 410, 426, 443, **96,** 660, 703
employment contract, law of sending State **104,** 525
establishment of good relations fund **82,** 578, 579, 580
expropriation/nationalization. *See* expropriation/nationalization, remedies
extinction of native title
declaration **112,** 548, 554-5, 627, 636
equitable **112,** 549
injunction **112,** 555, 622
finding of breach distinguished **53,** 364
finding of contempt **110,** 639, 722, 730
forcible abduction/unlawful arrest
dependence on subsequent treatment **104,** 63
diplomatic channels **95,** 404
request for repatriation, need for, customary international law **90,** 695
return of kidnapped person **90,** 665, 671, 687-8, 693-6
forged document in absence of accrued cause of action **118,** 586-92
hierarchy **106,** 527-8, 544, 546-7, 549-52, 561, 574-5
ICSID, powers relating to **118,** 637
in absentia proceedings **110,** 722
interim award **76,** 477
international law, breach
foreign State **91,** 501
civil remedy **104,** 153, 159, 180
individuals **91,** 501
retaliation **101,** 403
international tort/wrong, for **46,** 197-9, 509-10
investigation of violations **94,** 410, 443
invitation to reach agreement to free transfer of shares/liabilities **106,** 471, 473
judgment as **95,** 315
judicial or arbitral, international official's right to **48,** 326-7
judicial review distinguished **106,** 248
just satisfaction. *See* just satisfaction (Art. 50 [41] of the European Convention on Human Rights (1950))
justiciability and **85,** 257
Law of the Sea Convention (1982) violation
forfeiture of fish **91,** 383

forfeiture of ship **91,** 381-3
imprisonment **91,** 379-81
penalty **91,** 380-2
lawfulness of State's behaviour and **65,** 302-3
need for **115,** 576, 643
ubi jus ibi remedium **115,** 643
neutrality, breach of, for **79,** 10
offending measures
cessation **107,** 287
compensation **107,** 287
recommendation to bring into conformity **107,** 287
suspension **107,** 287
political process as **115,** 576
publication of judgment **83,** 698-9
recognition of statehood as **79,** 263
recommendation for action to eliminate racial bias in jury proceedings **112,** 327
recommendation to negotiate treaty **110,** 213-15, 223-4, 242-3
reimbursement of taxes improperly levied **105,** 56
release from detention **98,** 368
'reparation or satisfaction within the meaning of international law' **106,** 248
repeal of offending legislation **112,** 342, 344
rescission of contested decision **83,** 687-8, 698-9
responsibility for **80,** 592-3
restoration. *See restitutio in integrum*
return of kidnapped person **90,** 665, 671, 687-8
request for, necessary, whether **90,** 688 n. 22, 693-6
willingness of receiving State to accept repatriation **90,** 671, 690
self help, proportionality **54,** 338-41, 343-4
separate decision on, relevance **102,** 527, 575
specific performance **53,** 335, **54,** 370, **89,** 342
compensation in lieu of **48,** 320, **96,** 250
nemo potest praecise cogi ad factum **54,** 509
declaratory judgment distinguished **53,** 364-5
as *restitutio in integrum* **82,** 570, 571
State immunity, jurisdiction and **87,** 233
State representations to avoid death penalty **98,** 504, 506
statement of adverse inference **89,** 622
steps to ensure non-repetition **94,** 410, 415, 426, 443, **96,** 660
termination of employment
compensation **85,** 635, 670
rescission of contested decision **85,** 670
specific performance **85,** 670
third party claim **104,** 189-92
trade issues, assistance over **82,** 517
trade undertakings **74,** 259-60, 269-70, 273
treaty disputes, claims for **48,** 433
unlawful deportation, for **84,** 347-8
waiver **106,** 521-2
waiver of State immunity and **80,** 591-2
war damage. *See* war damage, remedies
withdrawal of attachment **84,** 589
workmen's compensation **83,** 691, 715

remedies (*cont.*)
World War I, value of ceded colonies **49,** 199
renvoi **41,** 198, **47,** 227, **69,** 209, **80,** 283
most favoured nation clause **106,** 452
refugees **69,** 209
renvoi fixe **116,** 131
renvoi mobile **116,** 131
to customary international law **106,** 458
to municipal law **46,** 446-7, 452, 509, 512, 522-3, **106,** 454, **116,** 653
to Security Council **49,** 117
reparations *See also* American Convention on Human Rights (1969), reparations; *Chorzów Factory* principle of reparation for wrong; claims; compensation for war-related events; damages; expropriation/nationalization; just satisfaction (Art. 50 [41] of the European Convention on Human Rights (1950)); taking of property
general principle of international law **95,** 314, **118,** 102-3, **120,** 199
general principle of law **95,** 314
Law of the Sea Convention (1982) **120,** 199
municipal law analogies as basis **116,** 445-8
responsibility for determining, ICJ **76,** 476
seriousness of breach **82,** 565
State responsibility. *See* State responsibility, breach, reparations
territorial infringement **74,** 253, 256, 258-60, 266-74, **76,** 476
treaty practice regarding **74,** 154
repatriation grants. *See* international officials, repatriation grant
reprisals **54,** 338-41, 343-4, **61,** 665-7, **72,** 249-51, 609, 613-14. *See also* countermeasures; retorsion
definition **36,** 391-2
Naulilaa Incident **123,** 475
duty to arbitrate and **54,** 338-41
grounds for **54,** 319-20, 338-41
overfishing **123,** 475-6
international organization, complaint to as **36,** 391-2
legality **110,** 225, 339, 387, 492-4, 512
customary international law **110,** 278
Declaration concerning Principles of Friendly Relations and Cooperation among States (UNGA Resolution 2625 (XXV)) **110,** 492
non-discrimination **110,** 524
nuclear weapons, deployment **110,** 278, 339
proportionality **110,** 196, 278
State practice **110,** 278
unnecessary suffering **110,** 524-5
proportionality, requirement of **72,** 250-1, 613-14
public administration of foreign property as **47,** 412-17
State responsibility **61,** 569-70, 667
trade sanctions **74,** 259-60, 264, 269-70
war crimes, defence **104,** 331, **108,** 46-7
Republika Srpska. *See* Bosnia-Herzegovina, Bosnian Serbs (Srpska)
requisition **84,** 339, 354-8, 365-8, 398, 409-10. *See also* compensation for war-related events; expropriation/nationalization; taking of property
belligerent occupation
materials **40,** 67, 69
private property **41,** 480-2, **42,** 488-90
right of **88,** 707-9

compensation for **56,** 525-6, **72,** 237-8, **84,** 409
definition **106,** 465
right to control and manage, effect on **84,** 356, 368, 414
ship **56,** 525-6, **64,** 101-2
res derelicta. *See* wrecks, derelict (*res derelicta*)
res judicata
amnesty, relevance **119,** 343-4
arbitral award. *See* arbitral award, *res judicata*
extradition, multiple extradition requests **104,** 82
operative part of judgment **113,** 43-4, 62
essential elements in reasoning **113,** 44, 62
previous conviction on basis of same acts
acquittal **100,** 348
reclassification **100,** 348-9
principle of international law **113,** 43
residence, meaning **68,** 150
resident status, departure from country, effect, membership of unlawful organization and **118,** 641-2
responsibility. *See* State responsibility
restitutio in integrum **38,** 270, 273, 274, **46,** 197-8, 397, 399, 525, **53,** 330-7, 338-42, 345-8, 349-53, 495-509, **56,** 421, 425, 428-31, 497, **57,** 197-8, **58,** 113, 717, **60,** 202, **61,** 321, **62,** 147, 169, 181-2, 197-200, 204-5, 217, **66,** 604-5, **75,** 386, 609, 618-19, 634-5, **81,** 29, 54, 55, 201, **82,** 570-4, **83,** 475, 566, 571, 572, 619, **89,** 475, 632-3, **90,** 665, **116,** 89-90
as alternative to damages **44,** 458, 460, 471, 479, 485, **94,** 463, 476, **96,** 321
annulment of law, as **81,** 201
availability **53,** 346
breach of contract **53,** 363
breach of State responsibility **96,** 321
compensation as alternative **96,** 321
Chorzów Factory **83,** 566, **116,** 276, 506, **121,** 127, 190, 191
compensation and **46,** 197-9, **53,** 347, 348, 505-9, **94,** 463, 476, **95,** 314, **116,** 275-6
death penalty and **118,** 17
declaratory judgment distinguished **53,** 364
definition **83,** 566
damages, payment of **95,** 314
reparation of damage caused **95,** 314
restoration of prior situation **95,** 314
diplomatic protection, inability to exercise **118,** 6-7
European Court of Human Rights, judgment, as **81,** 54, 202
foreseeability, relevance **89,** 633
illegal expropriation/nationalization **83,** 566-71, 572, 577, 619
impossibility **116,** 481, 507
infringement of legal right, need for **94,** 457, 461
international official, summary dismissal of **38,** 270, 273, 274
loss during war or civil disturbance not attributable to the State **106,** 480
loss of life plan and **116,** 433, 447
justification for inclusion **116,** 448-50
as measure of damages/compensation **83,** 565, 570, 572, 577, 619, **84,** 426-7, 541, **95,** 228
bilateral treaties **95,** 228
customary international law **95,** 228

restitutio in integrum (*cont.*)
pardon as **81,** 201, 202, 210
provisional measures and **94,** 457
rehearing as **81,** 29
release as **81,** 29
specific performance, as **82,** 570, 571
cessation of illegal activity distinguished **82,** 571-2, 584
ILC draft **82,** 572
termination of obligation, after **82,** 573, 579
State, against **89,** 475, 537
unlawful deportation **86,** 347-8
restitution. *See also restitutio in integrum*
claims for, action for detinue and **44,** 319
monetary gold, compensation in lieu **44,** 458, 460, 471, 479, 485
Namibia, restitution of property to people **49,** 208
property taken from occupied France **44,** 2-5
'restraint of princes' 78, 584
contract and **78,** 584
restraint of trade. *See* antitrust legislation; competition, restraint of trade; General Agreement on Tariffs and Trade (GATT) (1947); restrictive practices
restrictive practices. *See also* antitrust legislation; competition; European Economic Community Treaty (Rome) (1957), restrictive practices; General Agreement on Tariffs and Trade (GATT) (1947)
agreement, applicable law, place of implementation **96,** 196
retaliation, seizure of foreign assets **42,** 204
retirement benefits, contractual, non-payment **42,** 157-8, 169-72
retorsion 70, 402, **72,** 134, 249-51. *See also* reprisals
retroactivity. *See also* crimes against humanity, retroactivity; foreign law, recognition/enforcement, retroactive; foreign law, recognition/enforcement, retroactive legislation; legislation, retroactive; recognition, government, retroactive; recognition, State, retroactive effect; war crimes, retroactivity
treaties, implementing legislation, prior to **100,** 485-7
reunification of families 78, 186, 192
Réunion
Criminal Code, Art. 131-6(10) **125,** 291
Criminal Procedure Code
Art. 142 (security) **125,** 175, 176-7, 236, 238-9, 290
Art. 471 **125,** 291
Law No 66-400 of 18 June 1966 (sea fishing and marine exploitation)
Art. 2 **125,** 176, 235, 236, 237, 289, 290
Art. 4 **125,** 176, 178, 236, 237-8
Law No 83-582 of 5 July 1983, Art. 3 (seizure of vessels) **125,** 175-6, 221 n. 3, 236-7, 274, 290
revolution. *See also* Head of State, former; rebellion
civil war distinguished **107,** 507, 516
claim to have seized power, relevance **103,** 50
competing regimes, relevance **103,** 50, 69-70
established government in power **103,** 266
Constitution, change of following **39,** 48-50, 65, 81-90, 157-8, 163, 215-19, 385-7
constitutional deviation distinguished **103,** 41-72
courts, jurisdiction to pass upon **39,** 213-14, 259
definition

illegitimate change of legal order **103,** 51-4, 69, **115,** 590
organized and violent uprising intended to overthrow government **107,** 507
dependent territories, in, effect on legal order **39,** 65, 89, 92-3, 165, 219, 878
external support, relevance **107,** 511-15, 516
force majeure, whether **63,** 276
Ghana. See Ghana, revolutionary regime
government, powers **60,** 231, 233-4, 236
insurance policy and **107,** 507-16
internal **103,** 64-5
judges, duty **39,** 230-2
judiciary, status **103,** 72
Kelsen's theory **103,** 50-72, 73-4
Mozambique. *See* Mozambique, armed conflict
nationality and **60,** 231, 235-7
parliamentary sovereignty and **60,** 231-5
rebellion/insurrection, distinguishability **107,** 507-8, 516
reception of previous laws **103,** 51
recognition, government. *See* recognition, government
regime
legal validity **82,** 385-6. *See also* recognition, government
effective government acquiesced in **82,** 385, 387
evidence of **82,** 387
'firmly established' **82,** 385-7
interim government, whether **82,** 385-6
retroactive **82,** 384-5, 387
requirements
fundamental change **103,** 49-50
manifesto **107,** 514
spontaneous internal uprising **107,** 511-14, 516
coercion, relevance **107,** 515-16
violence **103,** 51
revolutionary movement, capacity to conclude contract **103,** 266-7
State necessity **82,** 384, **103,** 42, 54, 57-8, 63
State responsibility. *See* State responsibility for acts and omissions during revolution
validity of laws and administrative act **39,** 366-70, 389, 394
Rhine 101, 39-43, 431-2
bridges in Alsace-Lorraine, maintenance **47,** 115-17
Central Commission for Navigation of **80,** 66
opinion, interpretation by courts **74,** 129
Police Regulations 1954 **74,** 140
territorial scope **74,** 139-40
freedom of navigation **72,** 681-9, **74,** 127-34
'Rhine navigation' 74, 139-40
Rhodesia and Nyasaland, Federation of
'Government' **44,** 8-9, 14, 17, 25
Immigration Act 1954 **44,** 8-12, 14-22
separate identity of members **44,** 8-25
Rhodesia, Republic of. *See also* Rhodesia and Nyasaland, Federation of; Southern Rhodesia; Zimbabwe
Constitution, s 30(3) (extraterritorial legislation) **118,** 642
Declaration of Independence, following **68,** 3-6
authority of courts **70,** 26-30

Rhodesia, Republic of (*cont.*)
extraterritorial legislation
constitutional provision for **118,** 642
nationals abroad **118,** 641-2
forcible abduction/unlawful arrest, jurisdiction, effect on **118,** 642
law of
Law and Order (Maintenance) Act
s 37(1) **118,** 641-2
s 52(2)(d) **118,** 641-2
Roman Dutch law **39,** 242, 383
nationality, residency and **118,** 642
recognition **68,** 3-5
resident status, departure from country, effect, membership of unlawful organization and **118,** 641-2
rift zones 41, 61, 153, **67,** 50, 105-6, 111, 114, **71,** 101-2, 108, **81,** 266-9, 277-8, 299-300, 330, **83,** 101-3
200 miles limit, relevance **81,** 267
Aruba Trough **83,** 101 n. 60
as boundary line **81,** 267, 308
continental margin distinguished **81,** 389
Escarpment Fault Zone **81,** 266, 299
evidence of **81,** 269
Hurd Deep **67,** 50, 111, **71,** 101, **81,** 292, 298, **83,** 101
Linosa Trough **81,** 266
Malta Channel **81,** 266
Malta Trough **81,** 266
natural prolongation and **81,** 266-9, 277-8, 330
North East Channel **71,** 101-2, **81,** 298, **83,** 102
Norwegian Trough **67,** 105, **81,** 292, 385, **83,** 101
Pantelleria Trough **81,** 266
Pelagian Block **81,** 266
relevance **81,** 268-9
State practice **67,** 111, **81,** 337, **83,** 101
Timor Trough **81,** 293
Tripolitanian Furrow **67,** 48-50, 57, **83,** 102
Zira Ridge **81,** 292
Zuwarah Ridge **81,** 292
Rio Declaration on Environment and Development (1992). *See* environment, Rio Declaration on Environment and Development (1992)
Rio Grande Banks 83, 110, 111
riots, marine insurance and **78,** 576-7
risk
contract **106,** 657-8, 732-3
damages, measure **106,** 647
notion du risque **106,** 657
rivers. *See also individual rivers*
avulsion
applicable law, as, burden of proof **97,** 463
boundaries, effect on. *See* boundary *below*
rule of
international law **97,** 463
Roman law applicable to private property **97,** 463
Spanish colonial law **97,** 463

baselines, effect on **59,** 281
basin, apportionment of waters of **41,** 93, 94, 95, 98, 103
boundary **38,** 87, 92-7, **41,** 133, 204, **51,** 27-30, **74,** 126, **91,** 190-204, 442-66, **97,** 298
accretion, effect **91,** 196, 453-4, 458, 464
ad medium filum aquae **41,** 204, **91,** 195, 452, 456
avulsion, effect **51,** 28-30, **91,** 196, 454, 457-8, 464, **97,** 462-4
critical date **97,** 462-4
erosion/accretion distinguished **97,** 462
estoppel and **97,** 466
in case of two or more channels **38,** 93-7
changes. *See also* accretion *and* avulsion *above*; erosion *below*
engineering works, caused by **91,** 457-8
erosion **91,** 458
Doubs (Franco-Swiss) **47,** 113-15
El Salvador/Honduras. *See* El Salvador–Honduras land boundary, rivers as
erosion and accretion **91,** 196
fisheries regulation **47,** 113-15
Franco-German **47,** 115-17
Franco-Swiss **47,** 113-15
in India **50,** 94
islands **91,** 422-6
arising after dispositive treaty, effect **91,** 451-4
right-angle principle **91,** 455-6, 462-3
tri-equidistance **91,** 456, 462-3
joint jurisdiction over **74,** 126
low-water mark **91,** 452
regulation **47,** 113-15
thalweg **38,** 97, **41,** 204, **77,** 664, 667, 672-3
changes **91,** 194-204
common law principles **91,** 195, 196
course
definition **91,** 193-4, 196-7, 199
evidence of **97,** 462-8
maps, old **97,** 465-6, 467
parties' conduct **97,** 466-7
Danube. *See* Danube
divided
both channels as river **91,** 197-8
main channel as river **91,** 193, 198
erosion **91,** 196
freedom of navigation **72,** 681-9, **73,** 164-5, **74,** 127-38
Act of Mannheim (1922) **101,** 431-2, 439-43
diversion of traffic, legality **74,** 130-4
for
purpose of trade **101,** 431
'transport of goods and persons' **74,** 128
port safety regulations and **101,** 431-2
restrictions, justification
public order/public policy/*ordre public* **74,** 135
right to strike and **74,** 137-8
security **74,** 132-4
Rhine Boatmen's Certificate Scheme and **101,** 439-43

rivers (*cont.*)
unilateral modification to scheme **101,** 441-2
riparian States, duties **73,** 165
obstacles, removal **73,** 165, **74,** 127-9, 135-6
jurisdiction **74,** 124-7
ship on foreign **48,** 77-81
maritime delimitation, baselines and **59,** 241-2, 281
mouth
choice, by ICJ **97,** 468-9
location in absence of headland **91,** 454-5, 459
names, evidence of **38,** 94
non-navigable **41,** 204
non-navigational uses of international watercourse
Convention on the Law of the Non-Navigational Uses of International Watercourses (1997) **116,** 65, 244
right to equitable and reasonable share of resources **116,** 63, 65, 89, 158-61, 175, 202, 211-12, 221-2, 224-5, 243-8
territorial status **74,** 125-6
treaty regulating **74,** 124-6
wrecks on, removal costs, liability for **74,** 124-7
Road Signs and Signals, Geneva Protocol (1949) 40, 235-7
Road Traffic Convention (1949) 40, 235-8. *See also* Carriage of Goods by Road Convention, (1956); Road Signs and Signals, Geneva Protocol (1949)
individual's rights **47,** 328-33
municipal regulations, effect on **70,** 438-9
rocks. *See* islands, rocks
rogatory letters. *See* letters rogatory
Roman Catholic Church, legal personality **47,** 24-5. *See also* Holy See
Roman law, forcible abduction/unlawful arrest, jurisdiction, effect on **95,** 428-38
Roman-Dutch law
applicability **39,** 242, 383
common law
in South Africa **82,** 484, **95,** 426, 442
in South West Africa **82,** 484
de libero homine exhibendo **85,** 220, 229
flexibility **39,** 207
Grotius' contribution **39,** 116
international law, part of, whether **84,** 20-1, 30-1
jus gentium, part of **39,** 116
necessity doctrine **39,** 111
promulgation of laws, need for **39,** 67, 106, 239, 384
Rhodesia, common law of **39,** 242, 383
treason **82,** 393
Romania
act of State, expropriation of emigrant's property **82,** 49-50
Arbitration Commission **74,** 561-2, 567-9
Austria, Financial Treaty (1964) **48,** 157, 159, 160-1, 175-8
Bessarabia, occupation by USSR **44,** 336
commercial/trade representation/mission, State immunity, jurisdiction **65,** 313-15
ECOSOC Sub-Commission on Human Rights, special rapporteur, availability **85,** 308-13, 327-30, 332-3, 336, 342-3
exchange rates, confiscatory **38,** 143

expropriation/nationalization, emigrant's property **82,** 49-50
France, Compensation Agreement (1959) **44,** 102-3, **47,** 166
Hungary, territory awarded to (1940) **44,** 336
law of, Decree No 223 of 3 December 1974 (expropriation of emigrants' property) **82,** 46, 49
matrimonial property laws **47,** 272-4
nationality of inhabitants of North Transylvania **43,** 191-4
occupying powers, expropriation by **48,** 175-7
property of emigrant, expropriation as act of State **82,** 49-58
property, real, domicile, requirement for **82,** 46
property of transferred population, obligation to compensate **65,** 12-13
share transfers, law regarding **48,** 476
State agency/State-owned corporation/State entity **63,** 58-9, 237-44
State entities, immunity, entitlement **72,** 184-90
State trading enterprise
liability for each other's debts **82,** 94
separate entities, whether **82,** 94
Terra **63,** 237-44
United Nations Privileges and Immunities Convention (1946), reservations **85,** 310-12, 315, 316-17, 341-2
USA
Release of Assets, Agreement on (1960) **43,** 210
Vinexport **63,** 58-9
Rome Statute. *See* International Criminal Court (ICC), Rome Statute (1998)
Roumania. *See* Romania
Ruanda–Urundi. *See* Mandate, Ruanda–Urundi
Rubber Agreement. *See* Natural Rubber Agreement (1979)
rule of law
definition **115,** 563-6
constitutionalism distinguished **115,** 564-5
GDR **100,** 386-7
Ruler. *See* Head of State; Indian States, Rulers; Kutch, Rulers; Malaysia, Rulers
Russia. *See* Union of Soviet Socialist Republics (USSR)
Russian Federation, State agency/State-owned corporation/State entity, privatized company, Sevrybokholodflod **107,** 662-6
Rwanda, International Criminal Tribunal for (ICTR)
evidence, corroboration, need for **124,** 92
penalty, factors determining, gravity of offence **121,** 358
procedure, *subpoena duces tecum* **110,** 640 n. 94
Rwanda, International Criminal Tribunal for (ICTR), Statute
Art. 3 (inhumane acts)
applicability to former combatants **122,** 81
presence of non-civilians, relevance **122,** 81-2
widespread or systematic attack against any civilian population **122,** 77, **124,** 233
Art. 6 (individual responsibility) **119,** 46, 66-7
Art. 6(2) (individual responsibility: action in official capacity), customary international law **121,** 257
Art. 23(1) (penalty: general practice in courts of Rwanda) **124,** 220 n. 25
crimes against humanity
definition **119,** 217, 353
war crimes distinguished, relative seriousness **124,** 233

Rwanda, International Criminal Tribunal for, Statute (*cont.*)
death penalty **124,** 326
Head of State immunity **119,** 66, 71, 87, 155, **125,** 497-8, 502
Head of State responsibility **119,** 162-3, 212, 243
rape, definition, *Akayesu* **121,** 269
Ryukyu Islands
occupation in time of peace **56,** 230
Civil Administration Courts **56,** 231-2
Japanese residual sovereignty **101,** 556
US armed forces, status **56,** 231
agents of US government **101,** 558-61
US occupation courts, jurisdiction **42,** 146-8
status **42,** 146, **56,** 231

Saar, Franco-German Treaty (1956) **46,** 481
saboteurs 52, 503
in civilian dress, prisoners of war, whether **42,** 458-70, **52,** 501, 502-4
St Lawrence River, International Joint Commission for
capacity
functions **73,** 168, 171-2
immunity from suit **73,** 172
competence **73,** 167-72
St Pierre and Miquelon 95, 650-725. *See also* Channel Islands
Channel Islands distinguished **95,** 663
competence of court **95,** 673-5
continental shelf, entitlement **95,** 665, 684
description of area **95,** 658-60
EEZ, entitlement **95,** 671, 684
enclave solution **95,** 668, 686, 712
Treaty of Versailles (1783)
contemporary effect **95,** 667, 722
in force, whether **95,** 666-7
St Vincent and the Grenadines
law of, Merchant Shipping Act **120,** 174, 176, 209-19, 226-8, 232-3, 242-4, 247-50, 252-4, 302-14, 343-4
ships, registration **120,** 172-7, 209-19, 232-3, 242-5, 247-50, 252-4, 301-17, 340-51
sale of goods, statutory warranty, imported goods **43,** 140-53
salvage. *See also* wrecks
abandoned ship in international waters
derelict, whether **56,** 46
ownership **56,** 45-6
claims, against US Government **42,** 186-9
maritime lien in respect of **70,** 80-1
Salvage and Assistance at Sea, Convention for Unification of Law on (1910) **60,** 482
salvor
meaning **70,** 77-8
rights **70,** 77-85, 88-9, 95-6
Sami. *See* Finland, Sami rights; Sweden, Sami
sanctions 61, 658-61. *See also* countermeasures; European Community (EC), unilateral measures by Member State (Art. 224 of EEC Treaty)
customary international law **49,** 287
'economic situation caused thereby' **109,** 617
European Court of Human Rights **58,** 271, 308, 344, 520-1

Iraq
ban on satisfaction of claims made by persons in Iraq in respect of contract affected by **122,** 548-65
compensation for losses due to **109,** 584, 593-4
lifting **109,** 578, 582
obligation, whether **105,** 353-4
Rhodesian **52,** 2-3, **53,** 66, 86, 92
Santa Maria Gloriosa, Order of 77, 621-6
international status **77,** 623-6
Saramacas
applicable law **116,** 278
compensation for human rights violations
distribution **116,** 277-82, 289-90
tribe entitlement **116,** 285-6
customary law
determination of successors **116,** 279-80
recognition by Suriname **116,** 278
evidence of identity **116,** 280
family structure **116,** 279
Foundation for the Administration of Compensation for Human Rights Violations **116,** 292-3
territorial jurisdiction
applicable law **116,** 286
breach, recourse to Suriname courts **116,** 286
Saudi Arabia
continental shelf, Royal pronouncement (1949) **41,** 164
Iran, Agreement on off-shore areas **41,** 97, 102-3
Red Sea, claims to **41,** 122
Saurashta, United States of, formation **49,** 380, 460, 480
Scheldt River, freedom of navigation **73,** 164-5
Schleswig-Holstein, cession to Denmark, inhabitants' rights, effect on **57,** 5-6
scientific relations, development, diplomatic activity, whether **63,** 172
Scilly Isles 81, 380, **83,** 112
Scotland. *See also* Union of England and Scotland
courts, municipal. *See also* United Kingdom, law of, Criminal Procedure (Scotland) Act 1995
Lockerbie trial in Netherlands **117,** 664-89
standing, citizen intervener **122,** 636-8
criminal jurisdiction, offences in England **42,** 112-14
customary international law, judicial notice **122,** 627-9
European Convention on Human Rights (1950)
EC law, part of, whether **93,** 615-22
Art. 177 (EEC Treaty) reference, possibility of **93,** 617-22
individual's rights **93,** 613-15
European Human Rights Commission petitions **93,** 615
quod fieri debet infectum valet **93,** 613-14
as part of municipal law **93,** 607-15
Scotland Act 1998 and **122,** 476
fishing rights **59,** 482-3
freedom of expression
action to prevent or obstruct crime distinguished **122,** 625
test case, intention to promote and **122,** 626
ICJ advisory opinion, binding, whether **122,** 642

Scotland (*cont.*)
international law, municipal law and **41,** 11-12
judicial discretion, *nobile officium* **56,** 513, 517, **122,** 622
judicial notice, customary international law **122,** 627-9
justiciability
national security **122,** 638-40
nuclear weapons, deployment **122,** 638-40
law of. *See also* Union of England and Scotland
actio popularis **59,** 487
civilian writers and **41,** 11-12
Representation of the People (Scotland) Act 1832 **124,** 584, 595
Representative Peers (Scotland) Act 1847 **124,** 595
Representative Peers (Scotland) Act 1851 **124,** 595
Roman-Dutch law basis **41,** 11-12
Scottish Representative Peers Act 1707 **124,** 594-5
Statute Law Revision (Scotland) Act 1964 **124,** 595
Act of Parliament of Scotland ratifying and approving the Treaty of Union with England 1707 and **124,** 580, 583
Tokyo Convention Act 1967 **56,** 254, 256
legislation, interpretation, treaty as aid **93,** 610-13
malicious damage **122,** 629-30
necessity
action to prevent or obstruct crime and **122,** 631-2, 636, 652, 658-9
criminal law defence **122,** 631-8
non-violence and **122,** 627
nuclear weapons, possession and deployment, whether giving rise to **122,** 625-7, 655-6, 658
requirements
absence of alternative **122,** 633
close relationship to actor **122,** 635
duress **122,** 633-5
grave and imminent peril **122,** 632-3, 656
proportionality **122,** 635
prospect of success **122,** 636, 658
test case, desire to provoke **122,** 625, 626, 656
nuclear weapons, deployment
equipment used in connection with, individual's right to take action against
customary international law **122,** 651-2, 657-8
necessity **122,** 625-7, 652, 655, 658
justiciability **122,** 638-40
possession
distinguished **122,** 640
as threat of force **122,** 641-2
partnership in **81,** 679, 709
separation of powers **81,** 676
piracy **56,** 253, 256
precedent in municipal courts, English case-law **93,** 609, 613
public and private rights distinguished **59,** 483-4
treaties
implementing legislation, need for **93,** 608
individuals. *See* third party *below*
jus quaesitum tertio. See third party *below*
third party

class, in favour of **93,** 614
parties' intention **93,** 614
Union with England, history **124,** 588-9
sea, law of. *See also* bays; contiguous zone; continental shelf; continental shelf delimitation; exclusive economic zone (EEZ); exclusive fishing zone (EFZ); fisheries; high seas; inland waters; innocent passage; internal waters; lakes; law of the sea; maritime delimitation; rivers; seabed and subsoil; straits; territorial sea
codification, 1958 **74,** 144-6
customary international law **74,** 144-6
evolution **74,** 145-6
UNCLOS (1974) **74,** 145
sea warfare. *See* naval warfare
seabed and subsoil 51, 179, **77,** 307-21. *See also* continental shelf
Arabian Gulf **64,** 336-8
common heritage of mankind **83,** 90, **99,** 466
continental shelf
co-existence of rights **86,** 601
distinguished **86,** 601
part of territory, as **91,** 209-10
EEZ **81,** 330
high seas **91,** 424
international seabed area **83,** 90
maritime delimitation and **64,** 336, **83,** 104, **95,** 665, 668, 700
ownership **43,** 94-5, 99-101, 104, 106, 112, **51,** 120-33
common law **125,** 398-401, 427, 433-6
federal State and **125,** 460-3
inter fauces terrae **43,** 106, 108
native title **125,** 427-9, 433-6, 449-50
outside territorial sea **77,** 315, 316, 318-20
straits **73,** 191-225
territorial sea **43,** 104, 106-10, **125,** 350, 354, 433-6
res nullius, whether **82,** 601
single boundary, applicability **95,** 675, 700
relevance **95,** 665, 668, 700
sovereignty, internal/territorial waters distinguished **77,** 404-5
structure, maritime delimitation and **83,** 104, **95,** 665, 668
territorial sea **77,** 315, 316, **91,** 413-15, 422 n. 12, 429 n. 1
federal State **90,** 242-3, 260
rights over **90,** 241-4
territory, whether part of **73,** 316-17, **80,** 686, **91,** 209-10, 413-15, 422 n. 12, 429 n. 1
wrecks, whether distinguishable from **70,** 69-70
Seal Island 81, 399, **83,** 113
Sealand, Duchy of, status 80, 683-8
seaman
breach of contract, appropriate forum **42,** 104-7
discharge in foreign port **41,** 416-20
search without warrant 70, 154-83
secession. *See also* self-determination
applicable law, municipal law **115,** 133-46, 580, 590
corporate seat, effect on **52,** 488, 491
of dependent territories and part of existing State distinguished **115,** 188-91
'effectivity' principle **115,** 589-91. *See also* States, creation, effectiveness principle
Limburg from the Netherlands **39,** 117-18, 240

secession (*cont.*)
referendum **115,** 570-1, 592-3
right of constituent part of a federal State
amendment to Constitution, need for **115,** 135-7, 568-9, 574
applicable law
international law **115,** 546, 579
municipal law **115,** 590
Bosnia-Herzegovina **115,** 130-57
complementary rights of federal government and other provinces **115,** 571-3
de facto **115,** 578, 589, 595
international law, under **115,** 579-91
legitimacy
recognition **115,** 576, 593
refusal to negotiate, effect **115,** 576-7
referendum **115,** 570-1, 592-3
unilateral **115,** 568-95
self-determination distinguished **115,** 584
State succession distinguished **115,** 116-17
territorial integrity **115,** 150-3, 162-4, 580, 582, 584-5
secret surveillance. *See also* correspondence
abuse **58,** 448-9
margin of appreciation **58,** 448-9
private life, respect for
abuse **58,** 449
public authority, by **58,** 446-9
target, right to be informed **58,** 452-3
telephone-tapping **58,** 446, 461, 604, **74,** 321-2, 324-5, 341-2, 371-91
when permitted **58,** 449
Security Council. *See* United Nations Security Council
security interests. *See also* deportation, compelling reasons of national security and; refugees, non-refoulement, compelling reasons of national security; self-defence, essential security interests
belligerent occupation, deportation **83,** 142, 185, 189
expulsion of alien and **82,** 215
sedentary fisheries 41, 124
sedition
criteria **70,** 211-12, 214-20
freedom of expression and **70,** 210-20
public order and **70,** 214-19
seditious libel 87, 436-8
Selangor
Constitution **118,** 295-6
Ruler, State immunity, jurisdiction **118,** 294-8
self-defence 61, 570, 593-5, 667
The Caroline **74,** 269
collective self-defence **76,** 85-6, 452-7, 509-10, 587-92, 603-7, 684, 687-96, 719
justiciability **76,** 85-6, 361
place of measures **76,** 684, 703-7
request for assistance by attacked State **76,** 438-40, 454-5, 510, 688, 690
requirements. *See* requirements *below*
vicarious defence distinguished **76,** 879-80
covert actions **76,** 708
customary international law **76,** 437, 678, 681-2, 686

environment **110,** 467
essential security interests **76,** 450-1, 475, 875
general principle of international law **110,** 258-9, 366
genocide **95,** 62-3, 122, **110,** 467
right to prevent **95,** 62-3, 122
inherent right **76,** 428, 485, 589-90, 676, 686, 707
Inter-American Treaty of Reciprocal Assistance (1947) **76,** 691-5
international humanitarian law and **110,** 195, 223, 225-6
justified **110,** 252-3
responsibility for determining whether **110,** 509
'survival of the State' **110,** 251-2, 510-11, 521
limitation on exercise of/requirements
armed attack **76,** 437-8, 454, 456, 510, 690, **110,** 463-70, 512-13
attempt at peaceful settlement **76,** 698
customary international law **110,** 195, 225-6
primacy **110,** 254
environmental considerations **110,** 528
international humanitarian law **110,** 195, 223, 251-3
lawfulness **110,** 251, 253, 510-13
necessity **76,** 437, 456-7, 475, 603-5, 627-30, 643-4, **110,** 195, 257, 258, 260, 326, 377
non-discrimination **110,** 466
over-formality to be avoided **76,** 879
promptness **76,** 702-3
proportionality **76,** 437, 456-7, 603-4, 633-4, **110,** 194-5, 260, 326, 377, 464-6, 468-9, 512, 532-3, 534-7
report to Security Council of measures deemed necessary **76,** 439, 455-6, 486-7, 695-6, 707-11, **110,** 512
Art. 51 of UN Charter, procedural nature **76,** 710
customary international law and **76,** 711
unnecessary suffering **110,** 464
mine-laying **76,** 870-1
natural law **110,** 240
neutrality and **110,** 466-7
nuclear weapons, deployment **110,** 213, 216, 240-2, 251-4, 256-60, 267, 366-70, **122,** 647
non-nuclear Powers' renunciation of right **110,** 368
Nuremberg Charter (1945) **76,** 620-1, 696
right and means distinguished **110,** 368-70
salus reipublicae extrema lex **87,** 260, 261, 268, 271, 272-3, 281
sovereign right **110,** 255, 256, 356-9, 476, 510
State practice **76,** 703-7
Tokyo Tribunal **76,** 696
UN Charter **76,** 369-70, 428, 436-7, 589-92, 681-2, 693, 878, **95,** 122, **110,** 194-7, 216, 240-2, 256-7, 267
deterrence policy and **110,** 234, 241, 257-9, 273-9, 335-7, 475-6
vital security interests distinguished **110,** 326, 488-9
self-determination 46, 478, 485-6, **49,** 5, 55, 59, 62-5, **74,** 92-4, **83,** 15. *See also* secession; self-preservation; State succession; United Nations General Assembly Resolutions, 1514 (XV) (Declaration on the Granting of Independence to Colonial Countries and Peoples) *and* UNGA Resolution 2625 (XXV) (Declaration on Principles of International Law concerning Friendly Relations and Cooperation among States in accordance with the UN Charter)

self-determination (*cont.*)
annexation and **49,** 81
Bandung Conference 1955 **46,** 485
Bophuthatswana **82,** 416
customary international law **105,** 266, 270, 335, 346, **108,** 553
obligations, international community **105,** 346, 351
division of Germany, need for **91,** 224, 225, 230-1
European Convention on Human Rights (1950) **108,** 552-3
exercise of, former legal ties, effect **59,** 92, 139
general principle of international law **105,** 243, 270, 283, **115,** 581
Helsinki Final Act (1975) **115,** 163-4, 582, 585
implications, undefined **92,** 168
International Covenant on Civil and Political Rights (ICCPR) (1966) **92,** 168, **105,** 335, 346, **115,** 581, 585
International Covenant on Economic, Social and Cultural Rights (1966) **92,** 168, **105,** 335, 346, **115,** 581, 585
jus cogens/peremptory norm of international law **83,** 24, **105,** 243, 270, 283, 329, 334-8, 350, 362, **115,** 146-7, 202
erga omnes **105,** 270, 343, 354-7, 362, 406-7
sovereignty over natural resources and **105,** 362
third party sovereignty, recognition, relevance **105,** 341-5
liberation from foreign domination **59,** 116-17
limitations, tribal and cultural divisions **49,** 53
mandated territory, inhabitants **37,** 7, 245, 248, 413, 471-4, 558
minorities. *See* minorities
multi-ethnic State, in **115,** 121, 133-4
non-self-governing territories and **59,** 162
northern Cyprus, right to **108,** 470-1, 553
obligations
international community **105,** 249, 338, 346-57, 362, 416
customary international law **105,** 346, 351
treaty **105,** 346
UN Resolutions **105,** 346-9, 362
respect for human rights **108,** 470-1
'people' **115,** 147, 583
consultation **59,** 191, **89,** 19-22
municipal law, under **115,** 147
Quebec **115,** 594
Yugoslavia **115,** 123-30, 143
principle of **50,** 412
process of liberation. *See also* liberation movements
date of commencement **83,** 15, 30
resolutions of Conferences of non-aligned countries **46,** 485
right
colonial people **115,** 585-6, 594-5
definition **59,** 97-8
force used to frustrate **49,** 79
international law, whether part of **59,** 138
oppressed people **115,** 586, 594-5
'people' **79,** 264-5, **115,** 580-8, 594-5
people denied right of self-expression **115,** 586-8, 594-5
within existing State **115,** 582-5

'within the framework of sovereignty' **105,** 408-9
secession distinguished **115,** 584
territorial integrity and **79,** 264, 265
tribal society **49,** 53, **79,** 262, 263
UN Charter **91,** 230-1, **105,** 335-8, 346, **115,** 581
UN Study on the Right of Self-Determination **79,** 264
UNGA Resolution 2158 (XXV) (Declaration on Principles of International Law concerning Friendly Relations and Cooperation among States in accordance with the Charter of the UN) **105,** 337-8, **115,** 581-2
uti possidetis juris and **80,** 471, **92,** 168
Versailles Peace Conference and **37,** 29
self-executing treaties. *See* treaties, self-executing
self-governing colony, non-interference in affairs of **39,** 65, 71, 79, 93, 105, 191-2, 196, 238-9, 375, 385
self-preservation 69, 157-8. *See also* self-determination
Senegal
aliens, 'Senegalization' **78,** 85-6
Constitution 1976
Art. 6 **125,** 571
Art. 36 **78,** 85
Art. 79 (treaties: primacy) **125,** 575, 578, 579-80
crimes against humanity, jurisdiction, absence of provision **125,** 573
discrimination, worker's right to invoke treaty **78,** 85
extradition from **73,** 662-4
international law and. *See* treaties *below*
jurisdiction
aliens, acts committed abroad **125,** 574
as procedural matter **125,** 573
proprio motu duty to raise **125,** 574
public order/public policy/*ordre public* and **125,** 574
law of. *See also* Constitution *above*
Criminal Code 1999
Art. 4 **125,** 573
Art. 288 **125,** 571-2, 578-9
Art. 295-1 **125,** 573, 578-9
Criminal Procedure Code
Art. 77 **125,** 573
Art. 130 **125,** 573
Art. 669(7) **125,** 571-2, 574, 578
Extradition Act 1971 **73,** 662-3
Law 86-26 of 16 June 1986 (Torture Convention) **125,** 571, 578
Law 96-16 of 28 August 1996 (amendment of criminal code provisions on torture) **125,** 573
pension rights of former members of French armed forces **114,** 313-19
'Senegalization' **78,** 85-6
Ministerial Circular No 1781 of 31 March 1970 **78,** 85
employer's responsibility for loss under **78,** 85
labour courts, right of recourse to **78,** 85
political directive **78,** 85
status
autonomy within French *Communauté* **83,** 17, 52
French Mali, part of **83,** 17

Senegal (*cont.*)
independence **83,** 17
sovereignty **83,** 17
torture, jurisdiction, creation of offence in implementation of Torture Convention (1984) distinguished **125,** 573-4, 579-80
Torture Convention (1984)
implementing legislation, need for **125,** 577-9
part of the law of, whether **125,** 575-7
treaties
courts' duty to establish existence **78,** 85
as part of municipal law **125,** 575-7
worker's right to invoke treaty **78,** 85
Warsaw Convention, Hague Protocol to and **45,** 386-9
separation of powers 39, 350, 354, **48,** 115, 118, 122, 123, **77,** 35, 557, **79,** 147, **80,** 591 n. 5, 592-3, 595, **81,** 519, 576, 676, **85,** 264, **86,** 122-3, **87,** 61, 68, 168, 347, 470, 664, 691, 700, 701, **91,** 75, 77, 138, **93,** 244, 632-4, 636-9, **100,** 327-8, 329, **107,** 288-9
act of State and **63,** 187, 567 n. 38, **77,** 226, 230-3, **79,** 6, 446-51, 499-502, 586, 596-7, **81,** 519, 525, 528, 536, 595, 619-20, 625, 636 n. 9, 645, 654, **84,** 119 n. 14, **86,** 48, **88,** 66, 73, 97, 99, 119-20, 121-3, 125-6, **92,** 389, 496, **98,** 65, 108-9, **99,** 162, 165
bill of attainder and **91,** 18
courts' obligation to follow approach chosen by legislature **122,** 600
democratic requirement **106,** 372-3, **123,** 146
deportation and **124,** 544-6
due process and **123,** 516-17
exceptions
contempt of parliament, power to punish **91,** 91
international crimes **91,** 92-3
military tribunals **91,** 91
speciality **104,** 11
foreign policy **106,** 373-5
human rights and **103,** 280-1
judicial/administrative, State immunity and **65,** 56
justiciability and **85,** 253-4
legislative conflict with EC law and **93,** 49
legislative procedures, role of courts **93,** 231, 232
national security defence, admissibility **110,** 670
political offence **107,** 451
political question doctrine and. *See* political question doctrine, separation of powers and
recognition **104,** 457
retroactive legislation and **91,** 18-19, 77-86, 89-91, 107-9
rule of law and **100,** 328
sovereignty of people **100,** 328
State immunity, execution/attachment and **65,** 56, **87,** 61, 68
State immunity, jurisdiction and **63,** 28-9, **99,** 162
transfer of powers to EC and **98,** 211
treaties
executive's rights **106,** 339-40, **123,** 526
legislation, conflict **88,** 204-5, **93,** 249
validity and **104,** 453-6, 706
treaty interpretation **107,** 61-2
United Nations **105,** 473-4

sequestration. *See also* confiscation; expropriation/nationalization
bankruptcy and **87,** 172-6
as basis for jurisdiction **66,** 149-60
belligerent occupation and **61,** 44, 45, **88,** 709
confiscation distinguished **88,** 709
enemy property **42,** 198-205
patents **41,** 459-61
Italy, law in **40,** 265, 271
of ownerless property in Algeria **47,** 60-2
reparations distinguished **61,** 50 n. 21
Serbia, Yugoslavia (SFRY) as successor to **73,** 39-41, **79,** 387, 394, 395
service of default judgment out of the jurisdiction, requirements **118,** 615-17
service of process. *See also* Yugoslavia, International Criminal Tribunal for the Former (ICTY), service of indictment
service of process at UN headquarters
UN Headquarters Agreement **104,** 159-61
designated representative of UN member **104,** 160
transit to and from airport **104,** 160
visitor to UN **104,** 160-1
service of process on diplomatic agent, procedural requirements **77,** 497, 508-9
service of process on diplomatic mission 42, 239-41, **63,** 21-3, 60-2, 124-7, **80,** 369, 372, 374, 376
service of process on foreign company or company based outside the jurisdiction 80, 118-19, **103,** 360-3, 393-5
applicable law, forum State **96,** 78-80
dissolved company **103,** 567-8
informal by agreement, estoppel **103,** 365-6
method, legal notice in foreign State **46,** 283-4
out of the jurisdiction, nexus, need for **101,** 350-1
service of process on foreign State or State agency 63, 264-8, 288, 388, **77,** 64, 99, **80,** 367-77, **84,** 138-9, **90,** 602. *See also* United States of America (USA), Foreign Sovereign Immunities Act (FSIA) 1976/82, 28 USC 1608
acceptance or acknowledgment, as waiver of immunity **65,** 87, 198-9
applicable law
forum State **94,** 364, **106,** 280
law of State where process to be served **106,** 281
break of diplomatic relations, effect **63,** 414-15
comity and **90,** 459
Convention on the Service Abroad of Judicial and Extra-judicial Documents in Civil and Commercial Matters (1965) **94,** 363-4
date of
certified or signed receipt or other proof **63,** 413-16
handing to postal authorities **115,** 420
transmission of diplomatic note **63,** 413, **115,** 420
default judgment **63,** 198, 287-8, 296-7, 382, 389-90, 397-400, 421, **84,** 143, 166-8, **107,** 264, 265-7, 268, 365, **118,** 603-19, **121,** 606, 624. *See also* default judgment against foreign State
action to set aside will **64,** 673-4
agency or instrumentality distinguished **107,** 365
as 'process' **118,** 615-17
requirements **118,** 605-19
failure to comply with, effect **118,** 615-18

service of process on foreign State or State agency (*cont.*)
leave of court **118,** 605
service out of the jurisdiction, requirements **118,** 615-17
diplomatic immunities and **87,** 230-1
ex parte proceedings **108,** 560-2
extraterritorial. *See* out of the jurisdiction *below*
foreign corporation distinguished **63,** 149
garnishee order **65,** 22
government representative, by **103,** 365
Hague Convention relating to Civil Procedure (1954) **80,** 371
reservation **80,** 369
judicial notice **107,** 365
method
agreed agent **118,** 603-15
agreed alternative **118,** 605
ambassador/head of mission **42,** 239-41, **63,** 23, **80,** 368-71, 374-5, 376-7, **92,** 395
diplomatic immunity and **63,** 23
foreign policy grounds for refusal **80,** 374, 376
as representative of State **80,** 368-71, 374-5, 376-7
appointment of agent to accept
unilateral change **118,** 603-15
waiver of immunity, whether **63,** 356-7
consular channels **63,** 97, 264, 266, 372, 377, **64,** 365
courier **106,** 280-1
court's power to determine **106,** 280-1
delivery to mission to UN **63,** 60-2, 124-7, 136-7
diplomatic agent **103,** 363-5, 396-7
diplomatic channels **63,** 413, **64,** 272, **65,** 8, **80,** 369, 372, 374, 376, **84,** 138, **103,** 363-5, 396-7, **104,** 686-9, **106,** 280-2, **115,** 420, **120,** 450-1
commercial/trade representation/mission of unrecognized State **65,** 56
friendly relations, effect on **63,** 23
specification of alternative means, effect **118,** 609, 615-16
through embassy in forum State **65,** 413, 415-16
diplomatic premises **63,** 21-3, **87,** 230-1
diplomatic immunity and **42,** 239-41, **63,** 21-3, 124-5, 254 n. 1, **77,** 497, 508-9, **87,** 230-1, **102,** 182
service on ambassador distinguished **63,** 21-3
government representative **103,** 365
informal by agreement, estoppel **103,** 365-6
publication **65,** 415-16, **80,** 371-2, 374, 375-7
registered post **63,** 21-3, 46-8, 179-80, 232, 254 n. 1, 264, **115,** 420, 440-1, **121,** 624 n. 1
to Ministry of External Relations **63,** 21-3, 381
service on lawyer **63,** 22
State-owned corporation **63,** 60-2
substitute form of service **63,** 411-16, **87,** 231
telex **63,** 415-16, 551
through agreed agent **118,** 603-15
unilateral change **118,** 603-15
visiting government officials **63,** 70
mission to UN as State for purposes of **63,** 125

out of the jurisdiction **63,** 412-15, **64,** 540-2, 562-4, **80,** 59
as act of public authority on foreign territory **65,** 415
act within jurisdiction, need for **100,** 469
insolvency/insolvency-related proceedings **124,** 557-70
refusal to accept **65,** 1, 5, 8, 387-8, 413, **94,** 364, **108,** 560-3
ex parte proceedings **108,** 560-2
on grounds of prejudice to sovereignty or security **65,** 11
refusal to provide legal assistance distinguished **65,** 11
return of document, effect **84,** 138, **121,** 624 n. 1
requirements
acknowledgement of receipt **63,** 198, **94,** 261-2, 263-4, **118,** 605
actual notice **107,** 365
adequate notice **107,** 314-15
official language of foreign State **63,** 136, **79,** 389, **84,** 143, **104,** 686
proper service **118,** 605
'substantial compliance' **107,** 364-5
timeliness **63,** 410-11
service on agency or instrumentality distinguished **106,** 280-1
State immunity, jurisdiction and **40,** 79-80, **79,** 594, **80,** 370-1, **84,** 138, 143, **87,** 230-1, **90,** 602, **94,** 261, 364, **103,** 564, **104,** 686-9, 690, 691, **107,** 312, 363-6
acknowledgement of receipt, need for **94,** 261-2
mandatory nature of rules **104,** 688-9, **107,** 313-15
plea after **40,** 79-80, 82
State and State agency distinguished **107,** 311-17
State-owned corporation **63,** 254, 631, **80,** 367-77
State-owned ship **63,** 626, 631
on master **63,** 626, 631
Vienna Convention on Diplomatic Relations (1961) and **102,** 182
service of process on international organization 63, 61-2, 288
out of the jurisdiction **77,** 98, **80,** 26-30, 59
service of process out of the jurisdiction 38, 133-6
balance of convenience **64,** 541, 564
consistency with the law of the place where service is to be made **63,** 412-13
as exercise of extraterritorial jurisdiction **69,** 93-8, **80,** 26-30, 59, **98,** 150, **120,** 450-2
foreign State or State agency **63,** 412-15, **64,** 540, 562-4, **80,** 59
as act of public authority on foreign territory **65,** 415
act within jurisdiction, need for **100,** 469
insolvency/insolvency-related proceedings
leave, need for **124,** 558
'serious issue to be tried', requirements **124,** 566-9
'whole subject matter of a claim relates to property located within the jurisdiction' requirement **124,** 559, 564-6
international organization **77,** 98, **80,** 26-30, 59
jurisdiction over alleged offence, relevance **69,** 96
nexus, need for **101,** 350-1
statutory authority **120,** 450-2
servitudes 50, 387, 459, 468. *See also* historic rights
self-imposed restraint **92,** 574
Settlement Agreement, *Passage through the Great Belt (Finland* v. *Denmark)* **105,** 649-50
settlement of disputes. *See* dispute settlement

Settlement of Investment Disputes Convention (1965). *See* ICSID Convention (International Convention for the Settlement of Investment Disputes)
sex change, right to, legal recognition of **61,** 369, 382-3
sexual discrimination. *See* European Convention on Human Rights, transsexualism; European Convention on Human Rights (1950), sexual discrimination; European Economic Community Treaty (Rome) (1957), sexual discrimination; freedom from discrimination, sexual; homosexuality; International Covenant on Civil and Political Rights (ICCPR) (1966), political life, respect for
Seychelles
extradition
arrest warrant, need for **91,** 393
Italy–UK Extradition Treaty (1873), applicability **91,** 388, 389-90
procedure, time-limits **91,** 388-9
extraterritorial legislation, possession of green turtles fished outside territorial sea **91,** 384-5
fisheries, foreign fishing boat
licence **91,** 394-5
tax on sale of fish, legality **91,** 394-7
jurisdiction, green turtle served on board vessel in port **91,** 384-5
law of
Control of Fishing Decree 1979 **125,** 261
Extradition Ordinance (Mauritius) **91,** 387, 389, 391-3
Fishery Limits Act **91,** 395-7
Green Turtles Protection Legislation 1968 **91,** 384-5
legislation, interpretation, phrases, 'taking of fish' **91,** 396
precedent
European Court of Human Rights **91,** 400-1
foreign courts **91,** 400-1
ships, jurisdiction, in port **91,** 384-5
State succession, continuity of law **91,** 391-2
treaties, State succession **91,** 388, 389-90
Shanghai, International Mixed Court 40, 84-5
SHAPE. *See* Supreme Headquarters Allied Powers in Europe (SHAPE)
shareholders. *See also* corporation; shares
assets of company **84,** 370
deprivation of rights **72,** 227-30, 494, 498-500, **73,** 236, 239-40
direct rights **84,** 391
economic identity with corporation **46,** 306-7, 450
equal treatment of **46,** 297
expropriation/nationalization, extraterritorial effect and **82,** 142
foreign company
diplomatic protection of **46,** 23, 26, 55-6, 64-75, 94-5, 121-5, 180, 188, 199-200, 205-25, 240-57, 289-315, 342-4, 365-75, 378-94, 402-4, 405-16, 418-38, 446-53, 470-6, 489, 491-507, 509-10
in, beneficial owners **46,** 73, 309, 389, 392-3
nationality, proof of **46,** 363, 378-94, 439, 456-7
nominee holders **46,** 309
preponderance of national holding **46,** 302
general interest, right to act in **82,** 136
individual rights and rights for common purpose of company **46,** 299, 307, 499
nationality of, nominee or trustee holders **46,** 182, 199, 267-73, 309-10
nominee, principals, position of **46,** 182, 199, 267-73, 389, 527

ownership of company and **82,** 133-4, 142
position and rights **46,** 207-10, 241-5, 290-3, 297, 299-309, 342, 409, 412, 430, 445, 448-9, 470-1, 496-7, 501-2, 509, 519
suit on behalf of company **37,** 426, **84,** 391
territoriality and **82,** 133
shares. *See also* corporation; measure of damages/compensation including valuation of company/property/assets, value of shares; nationalization/expropriation, shares; shareholders
acquired rights **82,** 141-3
applicable law, cancellation of **72,** 18
bearer **42,** 417-20
ownership **46,** 383-5, 387, 435-6
State responsibility to holders **46,** 435, 437
cancellation of
applicable law **72,** 18
by court, in foreign company **46,** 192, 279, 325
jurisdiction **72,** 18
as nexus **81,** 500-2, **124,** 556, 568
locus, State of issuing company **82,** 140
nature of **42,** 411, **46,** 300
possession of, 'mediate and constructive' **46,** 183, 192, 193, 325, 331
situs **42,** 412-17, 419, **47,** 67, 70, **66,** 481-3
trading with the enemy legislation, shares held abroad **42,** 415-19, 435
trustee and nominee holders distinguished **46,** 389
Sharjah
as independent State **64,** 340-1
territorial sea **66,** 176-85, 330-8
Sherman Act. *See* United States of America (USA), law of, Antitrust (Sherman) Act 1890
shipping, embargo as act of State **63,** 187-90, 491
shipping line as State agency/wholly-owned corporation 63, 78, 90, 104, 175, 220-1, 256, 330-3, 365, 417-19, 443, 495, 532, 606, 625, 639-40, **65,** 102-7, **69,** 69-70, **81,** 540-1, **103,** 575-6
commercial activity **63,** 629
ships. *See also* European Community (EC), ships; jurisdiction, foreign ships
abandoned
international waters, ownership **56,** 45-6
res derelicta, whether **56,** 46
arrest. *See also* high seas, jurisdiction, search and seizure; hot pursuit; Law of the Sea Convention (1982): Part XV (settlement of disputes), prompt release of vessels and crews; ships, State-owned, immunity, arrest/attachment
compensation, Law of the Sea Convention (1982) **120,** 198-201, 234-6, 250-1
due process considerations **125,** 313
grounds
Arrest of Seagoing Ships Convention (1952) **52,** 450-1, 454-61, **72,** 3-9
breach of customs laws in EEZ **120,** 190-2, 256-7, 259-61
State-owned ships. *See* ships, State-owned
termination, effect on prospects of recovery **96,** 378
use of force **120,** 196-7, 258
Agreement Relating to the Conservation and Management of Straddling Fish Stocks and Highly Migratory Fish Stocks (1995) **120,** 196-7
customary international law **120,** 196-7

ships (*cont.*)
Law of the Sea Convention (1982) **120,** 196, 274
Arrest of Seagoing Ships Convention (1952)
applicability, contract of sale and purchase **96,** 377
draft amendments, applicability **96,** 377
grounds **52,** 450-1, 454-61, **72,** 3-9
attachment. *See* arrest *above*; ships, State-owned, immunity, arrest/attachment
confiscation, prohibited trading **44,** 365
crew, contract for provision of as commercial transaction **63,** 9-12
flag. *See also* registration *below*
obligation to fly **91,** 475, 517
right to determine right to **93,** 707, 714-17, **101,** 415, 416-17
domicile **93,** 717
residence **93,** 717
flag State obligations
High Seas Convention (1958), effective jurisdiction **82,** 614, **120,** 179
international law **82,** 614, **93,** 716
Law of the Sea Convention (1982) **82,** 614, **93,** 720, **120,** 228-9, 251-2, **125,** 303-4, 319-20
flag State status
burden of proof **125,** 295-7
critical date **125,** 313-15, 319
flags of convenience **54,** 226-8, **77,** 414-16
Minimum Standards in Merchant Ships Convention (1976) **120,** 593-4
genuine link, need for **123,** 500. *See also* nationality *and* registration *below*
Agreement Relating to the Conservation and Management of Straddling Fish Stocks and Highly Migratory Fish Stocks (1995) **120,** 180
Agreement to Promote Compliance with International Conservation and Management Measures by Fishing Vessels on the High Seas (1993) **120,** 180
customary international law **93,** 729
effective implementation of flag State duties as purpose **82,** 614
Law of the Sea Convention (1982) **120,** 179-80
UN Convention on Conditions for the Registration of Ships (1986) **120,** 179-80
High Seas Convention (1958) **46,** 361, **93,** 729, 759, 760-1, 783-4, **120,** 179
ILC Draft Articles on the Law of the Sea (1956) **120,** 179
Law of the Sea Convention (1982) **120,** 178-80, 252
nationality **46,** 360-1, **120,** 178-80
registration **93,** 729, 759, 760-1, 763, 783-4
UN Convention on Conditions for the Registration of Ships (1986) **120,** 179-80
undefined **93,** 763
jurisdiction. *See* ships, jurisdiction
liability for actions of, citation of State as 'civilly liable' **120,** 197-8
merchant ship, definition **91,** 519
nationality **69,** 161-2. *See also* registration *below*
absence of legal requirements **77,** 416
burden of proof **120,** 176-7
captain and master **93,** 768
companies **93,** 767
constitutive act, need for **120,** 224. *See also* registration, relevance *below*
evidence of **120,** 176-7, 224, 225-7, **123,** 501-2, **125,** 310-12
conduct of State of alleged nationality **120,** 228-9, 254-5, 314-15

freedom of establishment and **93,** 765-8, 786
genuine link, need for **46,** 360-1
High Seas Convention (1958) **120,** 179
ILC Draft Articles on the Law of the Sea (1956) **120,** 179
Law of the Sea Convention (1982) **120,** 178-80
Law of the Sea Convention (1982) **120,** 175, 214-15, **125,** 297-300
non-discrimination and **93,** 786
owners and operators **93,** 765-6, 767-8, 779, 789
question of fact **120,** 176, 252
registration, relevance **40,** 474, **69,** 162, **93,** 714-17, **120,** 175, 210-11, 224, 249, 251-2, 301-17, **125,** 298-300
nominal **42,** 104-7
residence and domicile requirement, combined effect **93,** 766
right to challenge **120,** 230-2, 317, 341-2, 350-1
Tribunal **125,** 297, 316
right to determine **93,** 722, 730, 759, 785-6
State's exclusive jurisdiction **120,** 175, 214-15, 243-4, 251-2, 340-2
nationality of claims rule and **120,** 184-5, 228-9
navigation facilities in waters under jurisdiction of third State **82,** 682, 688
non-discrimination and **93,** 762-3
oil rig, whether **94,** 455
ownership, evidence of **65,** 25
refuelling. *See* exclusive economic zone (EEZ), refuelling of fishing vessel
registration. *See also* flag *above*
burden of proof **120,** 311
change of ownership, relevance **120,** 254, 304-10, 350
criteria, choice of
customary international law **93,** 761-2
divergent practice **93,** 761
flag State's right to determine **120,** 175, 214-15, 244, 251-2, 314, 341-3
Law of the Sea Convention (1982) **93,** 729, 761-2, **120,** 251-2, 254-5
UN Convention on Conditions for Registration of Ships (1986) **93,** 761-2
EC membership and **93,** 714-17, 729-30
European Community, within **113,** 366-7
evidence of continuing validity **120,** 172-7, 209-13, 226-8, 242-3, 247-9, 252-4, 255-6, 304-16, 343-52, **125,** 298-300, 301-2, 304, 307-8, 310-12, 315-16, 318-19
fishing vessels. *See* registration of fishing vessels *below*
genuine link, need for
customary international law **93,** 729
High Seas Convention (1958) **93,** 729, 759, 760-1, 783-4
undefined **93,** 763
nationality requirement. *See* nationality, registration and *above*
nexus, need for **82,** 614
provisional, problems arising from practice **120,** 218-19, 232-3, 256, 330
State's sole competence **82,** 614, 666, 668, **120,** 243-4
registration of fishing vessels
EC law, need for conformity with **93,** 589, 757, 758, 763, 783, 784
freedom of establishment and **93,** 758-9, 765-74, 785
habitual operation **93,** 774, 778
nationality. *See* nationality *above*
place of management, direction and control **93,** 773-4, 780, 787, 789
residence and domicile requirement

ships (*cont.*)
discrimination, whether **93,** 768-9
residence and domicile distinguished **93,** 770
requisition **56,** 525-6, **64,** 101-2
sister ships
arbitral award, enforcement **90,** 559
State immunity, arrest/attachment and **64,** 175, 231
stateless. *See* stateless ship
territory, part of, whether **36,** 57, **40,** 90, **43,** 176-7, **47,** 118, **63,** 611 n. 8, **72,** 212-16, **74,** 206-12, **77,** 560, **91,** 98-9, **123,** 356, 410
warship. *See* warship
wrecked. *See* salvage; wrecks
ships, jurisdiction. *See also* high seas, jurisdiction, flag State; stateless ship
applicable law
employment contract **87,** 97
lex loci **87,** 97
coastal State **87,** 96-7
in case of strike on board ship **87,** 97
where legal order of State affected **87,** 97
flag State **42,** 145, **54,** 227-9, **57,** 164-6, **72,** 212-14, **74,** 206-12, **77,** 289, 538, 539, 560, 589-90, **78,** 117-19, **84,** 676, **90,** 633, **91,** 515, 518
aircraft **73,** 702-4
customary international law **91,** 524, **120,** 588, **123,** 356
inland waters **78,** 119
ports **120,** 593-9
control of crew **38,** 159, **43,** 176-7
Minimum Standards in Merchant Ships Convention (1976) **120,** 593-4
Safety of Life at Sea Convention (1974) **120,** 594-6
ship as territory of flag State **43,** 176-7, **63,** 611 n. 8
territorial sea exceptions
Geneva Convention on Territorial Sea and Contiguous Zone (1958) **78,** 118
infringement of coastal State's interests **78,** 118
request for assistance **78,** 118
risk to navigation **78,** 118
foreign ship **72,** 212-14, **87,** 370, **91,** 470-86
conspiracy **91,** 474
contiguous zone **74,** 211-12, **120,** 276-7
customary international law **91,** 524
effects doctrine **91,** 474
foreign crew against foreign owners **65,** 24
holder of national certificate of competency **92,** 584
national on foreign ship in foreign waters **77,** 289, 539
obligations arising on **77,** 560
outside territorial sea **84,** 210-18, **92,** 584
waiver of objection by flag State **84,** 211-12
in port **54,** 228, **57,** 164-6, **63,** 628, 630-1, **91,** 384-5
vessel in distress **82,** 362-3, 366-7
on river **48,** 77-81
safety at sea obligations **120,** 593-9
taxation of national **72,** 211-17
territorial sea **57,** 164, **73,** 182-3, 275-95
concurrent **57,** 164-6

crime not covered by local law or treaty **77,** 559-61
customary international law **77,** 559-60
interference with life on shore criterion **77,** 560-1, **120,** 276-7
high seas. *See* high seas, jurisdiction
national on national ship
in foreign port **43,** 176-7
in foreign territorial waters **78,** 118-29
police assistance **87,** 97
State-owned. *See* ships, State-owned
stateless ship **91,** 475 n. 15, 488-92, 542

ships, State-owned
admiralty jurisdiction. *See* admiralty jurisdiction, State immunity and
applicable law, Netherlands–USSR Agreement on Merchant Shipping (1969) **65,** 365-7, 369
'beneficially owned as respects all the shares therein' **64,** 188-93
classification as
fishing vessels **63,** 15
ownership, possession or control as test. *See* ownership, possession or control as test of status *below*
collision involving **63,** 14-15, 605-12, **64,** 179, **65,** 101-7, 365-7
commercial activity, effect on immunity **42,** 125-34, **63,** 13-15, 546-7, 603-10, **64,** 17-18, 24-5, 74, 97-110, 168, 175-80, 182, 232-3, 237, 313, 403-4, 417, 456-7, 542-4, 553-60, **65,** 24-6, 39, 102-5, 177-8, 259-61, 293, 365, 368-9, **66,** 222-4, **72,** 100, 107
charter as **63,** 640
European Convention on State Immunity (and Protocol) (Basle) (1972), classification of act **64,** 107-8
immunity, arrest/attachment **63,** 14-15, 24-32, 40, 215-17, 219-27, 252-60, 416, 624-6, **64,** 184-6, **65,** 101-4, 177-8, 293, 365-7, **66,** 222-4, **72,** 100, 104, 107, **82,** 94
acquisition by State subsequent to cause of action **65,** 24-5
applicable law **65,** 103
arbitration agreement, relevance **82,** 84
Brussels Convention on Immunity of State-owned Ships (1926) **42,** 129, 187-8, **64,** 103, 108-9, 232-3, 312, 313, **65,** 165, 177, 293-4
claims for non-payment of wages **65,** 23-6
commercial activity and. *See* commercial activity, effect on immunity *above*
domicile, choice of and **65,** 366-7
jurisdictional and post-judgment attachment distinguished **63,** 15
loss of *in personam* remedy in case of wrongful **63,** 224-7
Netherlands–USSR Agreement on Merchant Shipping (1969) and **65,** 365-7
requirement to post counter-security **63,** 416-19
sister ships **64,** 175, 231
treaty undertaking to enforce judgment and **65,** 366-7
warship. *See* warship
immunity, arrest/attachment, purpose of proceedings, safeguarding/conservatory measures. *See* safeguarding/conservatory measures *below*
immunity, enforcement of maritime lien **63,** 24-32, 40, 77-80, 215-27, 257, 416-19, 532-4, 620, 629
immunity, jurisdiction **42,** 125-34, **48,** 84-5, **55,** 419, 420, **64,** 460, **65,** 177-8, 259-61, 293-4, 368-9
Brussels Convention on Immunity of State-owned Ships (1926) **45,** 73-4, **65,** 104, 177, 293
nature of ship/nature of act **64,** 182

ships, State-owned (*cont.*)
cargo **64,** 555-61, **65,** 368-9
carriers' liability **65,** 68-70
commercial activity and. *See* commercial activity, effect on immunity *above*
in rem action **64,** 91-110, 416-17, 552-61
master **65,** 258-60
merchant ships **40,** 84-5
ship confiscated in course of war **64,** 97
immunity, jurisdiction, waiver, Netherlands–USSR Agreement on Merchant Shipping (1969) and **65,** 368-9
ownership, possession or control as test of status **64,** 99-100, 104, 110, 170-4, 183-4, 188-94, 326, 327-8, 330, 439-40, 555-60, **65,** 25, 102, 105
charterparty **64,** 188-94
confiscated ship **64,** 170-4
evidence of **64,** 170-4, 175, 318, 324-5
public purpose, relevance **63,** 546-7, **64,** 100, 101, 109, 168, 233, 554
safeguarding/conservatory measures **65,** 25-6
Brussels Convention on Immunity of State-owned Ships (1926) **65,** 165, 177, 294
ownership, relevance **65,** 25-6
service of process on **63,** 626, 631
trading vessel. *See* commercial activity, effect on immunity *above*
Sierra Leone
Constitution 1961, challenge in English courts **42,** 11-26
extradition agreement, State succession and, Liberia-UK Extradition Treaty (1892) **70,** 3-15
government, recognition **114,** 475-8
grant of land to settlers **42,** 12, 14, 17
independence **55,** 53
law of. *See also* Constitution 1961 *above*
Extradition Act 1962 **70,** 3-15
Prohibition of Transfers of Assets Decree 1967 **55,** 51
National Reformation Council, effect of legislation **55,** 53-4
nationality **55,** 485
UK treaty obligations, succession to **70,** 3-15
UN peacekeeping operations **119,** 389-98
custody or control of rebel leader **119,** 389-98
habeas corpus proceedings in UK and **119,** 386-98
Sierra Leone Company 42, 14-15
Sikkim
immunity, jurisdiction, India **118,** 422-8
India, relationship with
foreign State **118,** 422-3
part of the Union of India
after 26 April 1975 **118,** 422, 428
prior to 26 April 1975 **118,** 422
protectorate **118,** 422
law of, Indian law, applicability **118,** 424-5
State, recognition, right of **118,** 426-7
Sind
boundaries of. *See* Kutch, Sind, boundary
British India, as part of **50,** 54, 426-7, 465

Governor's Province, creation (1935) **50,** 321-8, 422, 468, 490-2
Great Rann, extension into **50,** 20, 516-17
Indian States, boundary **50,** 19, 21-5
Singapore
Constitution 1963, s 105(1) **55,** 84-5
Geneva Convention on the Treatment of Prisoners of War (1949) **52,** 499-501
law of, Independence Act 1965 **55,** 410
State Immunity Act 1979, restrictive theory and **65,** 230
State immunity, jurisdiction, applicability, State succession and **55,** 409-11, **75,** 125
State succession, State immunity, jurisdiction and **55,** 409-11, **75,** 125
status **55,** 78-80, 411
Single European Act (1986). *See also* European Economic Treaty (Rome) (1957); European Union Treaty (Maastricht) (1992)
compatibility with national constitutions **93,** 485-513
Cooperation of Member States within WEU/NATO framework **93,** 501
preservation of neutral status and **93,** 509
EC court of first instance **93,** 488
European Union as aim **93,** 491, 500, 504-5, 507, 508
foreign policy provisions (s. III)
amendment of, EC Treaty, whether **93,** 509
constitutional amendment, need for **93,** 480-513
direct effect, political union **93,** 490
formalization of European Political Cooperation (EPC) practices and procedures **93,** 508-9
separate status **93,** 495
sovereignty, surrender **93,** 500, 505, 506-8, 509
fundamental rights and **93,** 489
'necessitated by the obligation of membership of the Communities', whether **93,** 486, 490, 499
original aims and objectives of EC and **93,** 488-9
political union **93,** 490
qualified majority voting **93,** 488
ratification, challenge **93,** 485-6, 511, 512-13
courts' role **93,** 491-5, 509-13
derogation, absence of provision for **93,** 506-7
timing **93,** 484, 485-6, 498, 499, 510
treaty nature **93,** 503
Siracusa Principles (1984) 122, 590-1
slave trade. *See also* slavery
freedom of the high seas and **120,** 588-9
individual, responsibility for **104,** 152, 153
treaties
validity **116,** 278
visit and search **120,** 589
slavery. *See also* slave trade
penal servitude, whether **53,** 552-3
prohibition **53,** 552-3
prolonged detention as **120,** 55, 112
protection from **46,** 206
Slovakia
diplomatic protection **70,** 696-8

Slovakia (*cont.*)
nationality **70,** 694-7
sovereignty **70,** 696-8
State succession and **116,** 81-2
Slovenia 92, 188-94
Constitution 1991 **92,** 190, 191
human rights, undertaking to protect **92,** 191, 192, 193-4
minorities, undertaking to protect **92,** 191, 192
succession, date of **96,** 721
smuggling 77, 588-92
Smuts proposal, Mandates System **37,** 196, 518, 528
social and political system of State
judicial notice **65,** 102
State immunity and **65,** 105
social security 86, 354-6, 358-63
aliens
entitlement **94,** 602
motivation, relevance **94,** 602
residence requirement **94,** 602, 607
applicable law
entitlement, usual place of residence **86,** 540, 541
obligations, place of employment **86,** 540, **102,** 188
place of employment **86,** 540
cession of territory (Schleswig-Holstein), effect on **57,** 5-6
civil or public law right **86,** 358-63, 366
civil right **86,** 358-9, 361-3, 369, 394
diversity of European practice **86,** 359, 369, 394
public law right **86,** 359-61
consular agent. *See* consular agent, social security
contributions, income tax, whether **36,** 459, 460, 461-5
diplomatic agent. *See* diplomatic agent, social security
freedom from discrimination **118,** 149-51, 158-63
interference with rights as taking of property **42,** 170-2
international officials. *See* international officials, privileges and immunities, social security
State immunity **63,** 195-6
State succession, collection of contributions **71,** 220-1
stateless person **48,** 165-6
socialist States. *See also* COMECON
international law and **46,** 482 n. 43
State immunity, jurisdiction **82,** 32
sole jurisdiction. *See* forum selection clause, exclusive jurisdiction and
solitary confinement 69, 192, **70,** 221-6, **78,** 51, **96,** 655, 657. *See also* detainees, rights; detention, incommunicado
Solomon Islands
Constitution 1978
s 2 **91,** 400
s 7 **91,** 399, 400
supremacy **91,** 400
human rights
corporal punishment **91,** 398-405
degrading, whether **91,** 400, 401-2, 403
motive, relevance **91,** 402-3

public **91,** 399-405
reasonable punishment, defence, as **91,** 399, 400, 402
Teachers' Handbook **91,** 400, 401, 403-4
degrading or inhuman treatment distinguished **91,** 401-3
law of
Constitution. *See* Constitution 1978 *above*
Criminal Code
s 35 **91,** 405
s 226 **91,** 400, 402
s 228 **91,** 402
Criminal Procedure Code, s 282 **91,** 398
Somalia, recognition of government **94,** 615-26
sonic boom. *See* airspace, infringement
SOTRAMAR. *See* Guinea, SOTRAMAR
sources of international law. *See* international law, sources
South Africa. *See also* South West Africa
air carriage, race discrimination and **56,** 27-9
aircraft in distress, Lesotho Airways Corporation/South African Civil Aviation Authorities agreement **82,** 370-5
apartheid. *See* apartheid
arms embargo **49,** 83-4, 88
arrest, legality, persons in transit **82,** 359-75
attachment
jurisdiction, as basis for **64,** 669-72, 675-83, 686, 691, 697-8, 710, 715-16
requirements
evidence of ownership **64,** 680-1
prima facie cause of action **64,** 697-8, 711
Bantustan policy, territorial integrity of country and **82,** 418
boycott of
1980 Paraplegic Games **87,** 69-72
European Convention on Human Rights (1950) and **87,** 70
legality **87,** 69-72
withdrawal of grant for games as **87,** 69-72
UN Charter, Art. 2(7) and **87,** 69-70
UNGA Resolution 2625 (XXV) (Declaration on Principles of International Law concerning Friendly Relations and Cooperation among States in accordance with the UN Charter) **87,** 69-70
burden of proof
jurisdiction, acquisition **107,** 188
ownership of property **64,** 680-1
Ciskei. *See* recognition, Ciskei, Republic of
citizenship. *See* nationality *below*
common law, Roman-Dutch law **95,** 426, 442
conscription **87,** 281
campaign against **87,** 281-4
Constitution Act 32 of 1961
s 7(3)(d) (diplomatic representatives, recognition) **64,** 697
s 59 **82,** 482, 490
Constitution Act 110 of 1983, s 97 **82,** 486
Constitution Fifth Amendment Act 101 of 1980, s 35 **82,** 486
consular immunity, jurisdiction, traffic offences, honorary consul **52,** 98-405
consular privileges and immunities, honorary consul/consulate, traffic offences **52,** 98-405

South Africa (*cont.*)
costs **82,** 375, 477, 498
enforceability, relevance **103,** 5
jurisdiction, termination, relevance **103,** 4-5
courts, municipal
decision of, binding on South West African courts, whether **82,** 483-5
ICJ decisions, binding, whether **82,** 480
jurisdiction
ouster, martial law, by **87,** 260, 261, 263-4
validity of legislation **82,** 490-1
customary international law
establishment **82,** 370-4
municipal law and **64,** 670, **82,** 479
defamation
protectable interest, non-trading corporation **87,** 281
reasonable apprehension of injury, need for **87,** 284-5
diplomatic agent, recognition, need for, responsibility for **64,** 696
diplomatic immunity, jurisdiction, entitlement derived from municipal law **82,** 365-6
Diplomatic Privileges Act 71 of 1951, s 2(1) (diplomatic representatives: recognition) **64,** 696
diplomatic privileges and immunities, security and **82,** 364-6
economic sanctions **49,** 84-5
employment contract, mercenary in Congolese army, State immunity, execution/attachment **64,** 668-72
employment discrimination **66,** 304-10
extraditable offence, punishment, discrepancy **88,** 242-6
extradition
narcotics offences **88,** 242-6
to Rhodesia **68,** 3-6
extradition agreement, State succession and
South Africa–Southern Rhodesia Treaty (1965) **68,** 3-6
Switzerland–UK Extradition Treaty (1880) **75,** 108-13
extraterritorial legislation effect **69,** 131
fishing zone
extent **91,** 376
South Africa distinguished **91,** 376
forcible abduction/unlawful arrest
applicable law, *lex fori* **95,** 426
clean hands doctrine **95,** 442
human rights, protection of and **95,** 441
jurisdiction, effect on **68,** 10-14, **69,** 150-8, **95,** 426-45
preservation of friendly international relations **95,** 442
Roman law **95,** 426-8
Roman-Dutch law **95,** 428-38
South African jurisprudence
common law **95,** 439-42
Noluli **95,** 426
Ramotse en 19 Ander **95,** 441
Robertson **95,** 440-1
State responsibility **95,** 424-5
from Swaziland **68,** 7-14

US jurisprudence, *Toscanino* **95,** 442-4
Foreign State Immunities Act 1981
restrictive theory and **65,** 230
s 2(1) **121,** 475
s 3(1) (waiver) **121,** 476-7
foreign State, proceedings involving
representation by
Attorney-General outside own country **121,** 475-6
diplomatic agent **121,** 475-6
Government, status **87,** 243-4
Head of State, diplomatic privileges and immunities, entitlement **64,** 671-2
independence, treaties and **75,** 108-13
international law
judicial notice **64,** 704-5
municipal law and **55,** 5, **64,** 670, 711, **69,** 149-50, 153-4
conflict **64,** 673
primacy **82,** 478-9
treaties. *See* treaties *below*
UN resolutions **82,** 479-80
Johannesburg Principles on National Security, Freedom of Expression and Access to Information (1995) **124,** 533
judge
disqualification for lack of impartiality, 'reasonable man' test **121,** 335
impartiality, presumption of **121,** 338
judicial notice, international law **64,** 704-5
jurisdiction **68,** 7-14
acquisition
burden of proof **107,** 188
voluntary return **107,** 187-95
aircraft in distress, passengers in transit **82,** 359-75
enforceability of decision, relevance **103,** 3-4
forcible abduction/unlawful arrest and. *See* forcible abduction/unlawful arrest, jurisdiction, effect on *above*
loss of jurisdiction after commencement of proceedings **103,** 4
magistrates courts **69,** 130
presence of party, seat of organization **103,** 3
Supreme Court **69,** 90
Supreme Court Act 59 of 1959 **95,** 439-40
territorial **103,** 3-4
law of
Abuse of Dependence Producing Substances and Rehabilitation Centres Act 41 of 1971 **88,** 242
Act 32 of 1961 **103,** 3
Act 42 of 1925 **82,** 491
Act 44 of 1950 **82,** 490
Act 49 of 1919 **82,** 491
Act 62 of 1962 **82,** 490
Act 83 of 1967 **82,** 490
Air Services Act 1949 **103,** 2
s 10 **103,** 4-5
Carriage by Air Act 17 of 1946 **87,** 291, 292
Criminal Procedure Act 51 of 1977 **82,** 361, **95,** 424

South Africa (*cont.*)
codification of common law, whether **95,** 439
s 39 **95,** 439
Criminal Procedure Act 56 of 1955, s 154 **69,** 130-4
Criminal Procedure Act 1977
Namibia, applicability **91,** 374, 375
s 106(1) **107,** 187
Crown Liability Act 1, 1910
South Africa, applicability **91,** 365, 370, 371
South West Africa, applicability **91,** 365, 371, 375
Defence Act 44 of 1957 **82,** 469-99, **87,** 270, 275, 279, 281, 285-6
s 2 **82,** 486, 489, 494, 495-6
s 3 **82,** 494
s 7 **82,** 486
s 21 **82,** 498
s 35 **82,** 498
s 62 **82,** 489, 497
s 66 **82,** 489, 495
s 67 **82,** 489
s 68 **82,** 498
s 138 **82,** 495
s 153 **82,** 486, 495
Diplomatic Immunity Act 71 of 1951 **82,** 365-6
s 2 (immunity from civil and criminal jurisdiction: persons entitled) **64,** 671-2
Diplomatic Privileges Act 71 of 1951. *See* Diplomatic Privileges Act 71 of 1951 *above*
Extradition Act 67 of 1962, s 12 **88,** 241
Extradition Act 1962 **52,** 409-13, **55,** 96
Foreign State Immunities Act 1981. *See* Foreign State Immunities Act 1981 *above*
General Law Amendment Act 62 of 1966 **82,** 472
Internal Security Act 74 of 1982 **87,** 275
National States Constitution Act 21 of 1971 **82,** 394
Police Act 7 of 1958 **82,** 361
Police Act 1958, s 6(6) **107,** 190
Proc R131 of 1980 (Administrator-General's powers to administer Defence Act (South Africa)) **82,** 469-99
Proc R202 of 1977 **82,** 494
Railway Management Proclamation 20, 1920, South West Africa, applicability **91,** 365, 371
Republic of Ciskei Constitution Act 1981 **75,** 678, 688, 695
Republic of South Africa Constitution Act 1961 **52,** 33-5, 37-8
Reserve Bank Act 29 of 1944 **87,** 253
Sea Fisheries Act 58, 1973, Namibia, applicability **91,** 374, 375-8
Separate Representation of Voters Act 46 of 1951 **82,** 482
South Africa Amendment Act 1956 **82,** 482
South African Citizenship Act 1919 **37,** 472
South African Citizenship Act 1949 **68,** 145-58
South West Africa, applicability. *See* Namibia, State succession, continuity of law
South West Africa Constitution Act 39 of 1968

s 1 **82,** 492
s 37 **82,** 486
s 38 **82,** 492, 494
South West Africa Mandate Act 49 of 1919 **37,** 530, **52,** 40, **82,** 471-2
Status of Bophuthatswana Act 89 of 1977 **82,** 394, 418
Status of Ciskei Act 1981 **75,** 678, 683, 688-9, 695-6, **80,** 8, **82,** 422
Status of Transkei Act 100 Of 1976 **82,** 378
Suppression of Communism Act 1950 **39,** 416, 423, **52,** 30
Supreme Court Act 59 of 1959
s 19(1)(a) **95,** 439
s 19(3) **95,** 439
Territorial Waters Act 87, 1963 **91,** 375
South West Africa, applicability **91,** 376
Territorial Waters Act 1963 **55,** 5
Terrorism Act 83 of 1967 **68,** 9-10, **82,** 360-2, 374-5, 472, 481-2
Union Nationality and Flags Act 1927 **55,** 497
legislation
application in South West Africa **82,** 489, **103,** 3-4
based on apartheid **49,** 73
identity of **82,** 495-6
territorial limitation, subsequent territorial changes **103,** 3-4
legislation, interpretation **68,** 145-58
aids, context **68,** 156-8
guidelines
conformity with international obligations **82,** 493-4
intention of legislature **68,** 151, 154-8
literal construction **68,** 155-6
phrases
'causes arising' **95,** 439
'time of war' **87,** 275
presumption against interference with rights of individuals **87,** 285
presumption of lawful conduct **87,** 276
Malawi, foreign or associated State, whether **52,** 91
Namibia. *See also* South West Africa *below*
continued presence in, legal consequences **49,** 3-335
de facto annexation **49,** 80-1
de facto government of **49,** 139
obligations in respect of **49,** 109, 123, 138, 285-6
occupation
aggression **49,** 79-80
restitution of public property to people **49,** 208
nationality
loss or deprivation of **55,** 498-9, **68,** 145-58
South African Citizenship Act 1949 **68,** 145-58
'Union national' **55,** 497-9
Union Nationality and Flags Act 1927 **55,** 497
Parliament
legislative powers over South West Africa **52,** 40-1, 43
representation of SW Africa **37,** 388-91, 472-3
resolution on SW Africa (1947) **37,** 333-4, 341
PCIJ, acceptance of 'optional clause' **37,** 47-8, 76
Portugal

South Africa (*cont.*)
Agreement on Angola-SW Africa boundary **37,** 409
boundary agreement (1926) **49,** 199
precedent in municipal courts, *stare decisis* doctrine, international law and **64,** 705-6, 714-15
provinces, territorial sea **69,** 89-90
recognition, government, responsibility, executive **64,** 694-7
recognition, State **68,** 4-6
evidence of, executive certificate/statement, conclusiveness **64,** 696-7
responsibility, executive **64,** 694-7
Rhodesia **68,** 4-6
service of process on foreign State or State agency, default judgment, action to set aside will **64,** 673-4
ship or aircraft in distress
immunity, jurisdiction **82,** 362-8
security and **82,** 364-8
South West Africa
basis of authority over **37,** 338, **49,** 31, 207-8
belligerent occupation of **37,** 195
incorporation (1945)
1945 statement **37,** 211-12, 414
1946 statements **37,** 219, 330, 332, 414
Indians, treatment of **37,** 540-1
Mandate
breach **37,** 481-2
continuance of (1947) **37,** 226, 334, 341
continuance, declaration (1946) **37,** 21, 74, 76, 78-9, 151-4, 156, 219, 234, 324, 330, 332-3, 414, 415
continuance, non-acquiescence **37,** 156, 315, 317, 319, 321, 327, 488
continuance, recognition **49,** 29
disavowal **49,** 290
failure to submit to supervision of **49,** 40, 206
lapse **37,** 228, 543
repudiation **49,** 37, 151
statements of intention regarding **49,** 244-6, 248
Mandatory status after dissolution of League **37,** 75
official acts concerning, validity **49,** 46
proposed incorporation (1946) **49,** 30, 247
termination of reporting to UN on **49,** 30-1
United Kingdom, agreements with (1919) **37,** 31, 46
State agency/State-owned corporation/State entity
as agency of State **64,** 679-80
as government department **64,** 681-2
as organ of State **64,** 681-2
State immunity **84,** 29-30
State immunity, execution/attachment, applicability to, property in possession or control of foreign State **64,** 680-1
State immunity, execution/attachment, entitlement, State agency/State-owned corporation/State entity **64,** 681-2
State immunity, execution/attachment, purpose of proceedings, jurisdictional, employment contract, mercenary in Congolese army **64,** 668-72
State immunity, execution/attachment, purpose/use of funds/assets, public purpose, money held on behalf of government for payment to mercenaries **64,** 670-1

State immunity, execution/attachment, theory/doctrine, development of concept **64,** 684, 698-706
State immunity, jurisdiction, applicability, action to set aside will **64,** 673-4
State immunity, jurisdiction, classification of act
diplomatic premises, construction contract **64,** 687-8
expropriation/nationalization **64,** 706
investigation into customs fraud **121,** 476-81
State immunity, jurisdiction, entitlement, legal interest in proceedings **121,** 478-80
State immunity, jurisdiction, procedural aspects
in personam actions **64,** 704
legality of act, relevance **121,** 478-80
State immunity, jurisdiction, theory/doctrine
basis
dignity of foreign State **64,** 688-9
good faith **64,** 688-9
development of concept **64,** 711-15
restrictive theory, basis **64,** 699
State responsibility, imputability, authorization of acts **95,** 425
territorial sea **69,** 89-90
breadth **91,** 376
South West Africa distinguished **91,** 376
terrorist, definition **82,** 361
transit across, right of, whether **82,** 368-75
Transkei Republic, criminal procedure **69,** 131-2
treaties
authority to conclude **52,** 411-12
conclusion, executive act **52,** 426
implementing legislation, necessity for **52,** 426
implicit, requirements **82,** 370-4
municipal law and, clear intention of legislature to supersede **82,** 493-4
UN Commission on the Racial Situation in the Union of South Africa **85,** 209
unitary State **82,** 397
Walvis Bay area **37,** 371-2, 394
South China Sea, Traffic Separation Scheme **84,** 79-80, 81-2
South Georgia and South Sandwich Islands
applicable law
procedural matters, law of the Falkland Islands **108,** 633
substantive matters, law of South Georgia and South Sandwich Islands **108,** 633
burden of proof, fishing in prohibited zone, legitimacy **108,** 635
evidence, standard of proof, balance of probabilities **108,** 635
law of
Fisheries (Conservation and Management) Ordinance 1993
s 2 **108,** 634
s 3 **108,** 634
s 5(1) **108,** 633-8
s 5(3) **108,** 634-5
Fishing (Maritime Zone) Order 1993
s 3(1) **108,** 634
s 3(2) **108,** 634
s 4(1) **108,** 634-8
s 4(2) **108,** 634
legislation, interpretation
aids, unincorporated treaty **108,** 637

South Georgia and South Sandwich Islands (*cont.*)
phrases
'fishing waters' **108,** 634
'the specified area' **108,** 634
Maritime Zone
Proclamation of 7 May 1993 **108,** 634
right to establish
Convention on the Conservation of Antarctic Marine Living Resources **108,** 636-7
customary international law **108,** 637
territorial claim, whether **108,** 637
South Molucca, independence **78,** 1-3
South Tyrol. *See* Austria, South Tyrol; Italy, South Tyrol
South Vietnam. *See* Vietnam, Democratic Republic of
South West Africa. *See also* Mandate, South West Africa; Namibia; South Africa, South West Africa
administration as integral part of South Africa **37,** 354, 355, 361, 389, 472-3, 485, 553
annexation by South Africa (1918)
British decision **37,** 195
objection to **37,** 18-19, 153, 155, 212, 315, 321, 329, 330, 332, 385-93, 414-15, 472, 473
annexation proposal (1946), international recognition **49,** 247
apprenticeships **37,** 589
Bondelzwarts rebellion **37,** 532
boundary, Angola **37,** 409
Caprivi area **37,** 391, 473-4
census classification groups **37,** 589, 600
citizenship **37,** 387-8, 472
conquest by South Africa **37,** 543
contract of service, offences connected with **37,** 589
courts, municipal, South Africa Supreme Court, decisions of, binding, whether **82,** 483-5
education in **37,** 375-6, 381, 383, 590
executive certificate/statement, status of South West Africa Mandate **82,** 481
freedom of movement of other Africans **37,** 600
Germany. *See also* Versailles, Treaty of (1919)
surrender by **37,** 195, 543
history **37,** 370-4
ICJ and
advisory opinion (1950) **37,** 113-15, 155, 161, 181, 227-39, 337-44, 405, 431, 439, 440, 442, 481, 487, 542-3, 569, 580, **49,** 3, 27-8, 34, 35, 122, 130, 135, 154, 180, 190, 211, 223-5
advisory opinion (1971) **49,** 262 n. 53
contentious proceedings **49,** 3, 122, 166
Judgment (1966), General Assembly attitude to **49,** 291
international status **37,** 6, 7, 248, 308, 384-93, 433, 472, 473
International Telecommunication Convention (1965), application to **49,** 305
job reservation **37,** 589
land policy **37,** 377-80, 474
law of
AG 105 of 1 August 1980 **82,** 486

Constitution Act 39 of 1968, s 38 **82,** 486, 497
Proc 180 of 1977 **82,** 469
Proc 181 of 1977 (Administrator-General's powers to make law by proclamation) **82,** 469
Proc 198 of 1980 (extension of liability for military service to non-whites) **82,** 469-99
Proc 222 of 1981 **82,** 484-5
Proc R101 of 1985 **82,** 488
South African legislation, applicability **91,** 355, 371, 375
South West Africa Amendment Act 1949 **37,** 472-3
South West Africa Constitution Act 1925 **37,** 413
legislation, interpretation, common law of South Africa and **82,** 484
Legislative Assembly **37,** 413, 550, 589
local government **37,** 589
Mandate. *See* Mandate, South West Africa; South Africa, South West Africa
marriage, effect on Native rights **37,** 589
military bases **37,** 7, 245, 248-9, 393-9, 475-6, 481
military training **37,** 475
mining licences **37,** 589
Native Affairs, Administration **37,** 391-2
'Native' missionaries **37,** 600
'Native' trade union **37,** 589
negotiations regarding, South Africa and UN **49,** 34-5
non-discrimination **35,** 590, **37,** 369-84
pass laws **37,** 590
petitioners from **37,** 368-9
Police Zones, restrictions on Natives **37,** 589
population **37,** 370-3
1919 **37,** 548
Regiment Windhoek **37,** 395
self-government in **37,** 380, 530
South Africa
de facto government **82,** 480-1
sovereignty **82,** 480-1
South African Parliament, representation in **37,** 388-91, 472-3
status, *erga omnes* **49,** 167
UN General Assembly, Committees **37,** 55, 181
UN supervision, consent to **49,** 243-53
uniqueness **37,** 212, 216, 219, 570
Southern Bluefish tuna. *See* tuna, measures to protect
Southern Rhodesia 72, 33-5
allegiance
effect of Declaration of Independence **39,** 326-9, 340
to UK **39,** 253, 260
citizens, allegiance to UK **53,** 88-9
Constitution 1961 **39,** 375-7, **52,** 50-1, 52, 58, 59, **53,** 55-66, 69-75, 76, 81-6, 88, 91-3, **55,** 51-3, **72,** 36, 42-3, 47, 49-50, **78,** 492, 498, **82,** 399
amendment **39,** 341, 347, 349, 377, **53,** 81-6
Declaration of Rights **39,** 143, 177, 178, 283, 347, 376, **85,** 151
Governor, discretion of **39,** 62, 75, 79, 94, 133, 143, 194, 349
Queen, position of **39,** 348
restriction of rights under **39,** 141, 178

Southern Rhodesia (*cont.*)
suspension after 1965 **39,** 105, 165-6, 234, 235, 241, 275-6, 343
unconstitutional delegated legislation **39,** 264
unilateral repudiation, effect **39,** 93, 342
Constitution 1965 **39,** 62, 152-4, 187, 199-201, 340, 342, 344, **52,** 52-8, **53,** 60, 63, 72, 73-6, **72,** 37, 42-3, 48, 50
creation of new State **39,** 159
Declaration of Rights **39,** 143, 177, 178, 201, 269
entrenched clauses **39,** 200, 349
legality **39,** 64, 65-6, 77-8, 80, 94, 96, 150, 156-66, 340, 342, 344, 350, 380
Officer Administering the Government **39,** 62, 63, 75, 96-7, 143, 153, 199-200
proclamations of emergency **39,** 63, 70, 76, 143-4, 151, 156, 178, 187-8, 261-5, 283-4, 347, 371
Rhodesian Government, status **53,** 59-66, 72, 74-9, 91-3
Constitution 1969 **72,** 50
legality **52,** 55, 59
continuity of law **39,** 384
courts, municipal
authority after unilateral declaration of independence **39,** 235-8, 336, 352-3, **52,** 67, **53,** 75, **72,** 33-6, 40, 43-5, 47-51
competence, to determine status of Rhodesian Government **53,** 56-9, 61-4, 73-5
status **53,** 55-9, 62-6
de facto republic **39,** 339
Declaration of Independence 1965 (UDI) **39,** 62, 63, 75, 77, 152, 156, 271, 342, 350, 378, **48,** 31, 32, **53,** 84-6, 90, **55,** 52, **72,** 33, 35, 42, 47, 50-1, **77,** 344, **78,** 492
allegiance, effect on **39,** 326-9, 340
authority of courts after. *See* courts, authority after unilateral declaration of independence *above*
constitutional response **39,** 337-8
constitutional validity **52,** 51-2, 54-5
de facto government and **72,** 42
effect on, existing laws **72,** 37-9, 47
Government of Rhodesia. *See* Government after Declaration of Independence *below*
revocation **72,** 33, 40
status of Government after **53,** 69-75, 76, 80-1
UK legislation, effect **52,** 53
UN sanctions and **72,** 33, 42
validity following
divorces **72,** 37-8
extradition **77,** 340, 344-5
Fugitive Offenders Act 1881 **77,** 344
subsequent legislation **72,** 33-5, 40, 48
European Convention on Human Rights (1950), applicability **78,** 492
external powers, before Declaration of Independence **39,** 196-7, 278, 289
extradition agreement, South Africa **52,** 409-13
extraterritorial legislation, effect **71,** 227-8
Government after Declaration of Independence **39,** 63-4, 69-70, 78-9, 106-9, 350-1, 388
effective control by **39,** 136, 150, 168, 203, 205, 223-9, 276-7, 279, 282, 328, 336, 343, 347, 351
powers **39,** 261, 270, 336

status **39,** 72, 94, 106, 109, 111, 120, 154-5, 176, 201, 276, 346, 350, 352, 378, 392, 398-400, 402-3
Governor's Directive, November 1965 **48,** 36, 37
habeas corpus, procedure **39,** 184-5
High Court **39,** 343-4, 349, 351
human rights, prompt trial **71,** 273-7
illegal detention in **78,** 491-500
illegal regime
acts of officials **48,** 30-40
detention by **78,** 491-500
British Government's duty to protect from **78,** 491-500
UK attitude towards **48,** 32-3, 35
independence, Security Council Resolution on right to (1965) **46,** 448
judges **39,** 94-6, 154, 162, 203-4, 224, 229-38, 276, 335-7, 338, 344, 351, 353, 357, 368, 397-400
salaries **39,** 399
judges appointed before and after unilateral declaration of independence distinguished **72,** 32, 38, 40
judges appointed under 1961 Constitution **53,** 69-75
jurisdiction, criminal
bigamy **71,** 227-8
extraterritorial **51,** 233-4
law applicable after Declaration of Independence **39,** 238-61, 328, 347, 350
Emergency Powers Act and Regulations **39,** 265-9, 288-9, 347-8, 371-3, 377, 380, 382, 392, 401-2
Preservation of Constitutional Government Act **39,** 350
Southern Rhodesia Act 1965 **52,** 52-3
Southern Rhodesia Citizenship and British Nationality Act 1949 **39,** 326, 385, 393
Trading with the Enemy Act 1939 **52,** 480-1, 483-5
law of. *See also* Constitution 1961, Constitution 1965 *and* Constitution 1969 *above*
Administration of Estates Act **48,** 35
Law and Order (Maintenance) Act **85,** 151
s 71 **85,** 152, 153
Magistrates Courts Act **51,** 233-4
nationals, protection of **78,** 491-500
non-recognition, effects **39,** 159, 161, 165, 226-7, **52,** 56, 59, 62, **72,** 33-51
Parliament, authority after unilateral declaration of independence **72,** 34-6, 40, 48, 50
Roman-Dutch law, common law and **39,** 242, 383
sanctions
effects **39,** 225-8, 342
measures to circumvent, legality **39,** 140
UN Resolution 253 **52,** 2-3, **53,** 66, 86, 92
sovereignty over **52,** 56
after UDI **72,** 33-6, 40, 42-4, 47-51
law and order, implied Mandate to maintain **72,** 33-45
responsibility and jurisdiction **78,** 493, 497-8
revolution, acquisition by **39,** 61-405
international law, relevance **39,** 291-2
status of usurping government **53,** 55-66, 80-1
statehood, significance of UN Resolution **39,** 209
status **53,** 69-75, 76, 80-1, **55,** 53

Southern Rhodesia (*cont.*)
semi-independence prior to 1965 **39,** 69, 71, 79, 133, 164, 191-9, 209, 260, 270, 289, 324, 342, 343, 385-6
trademarks, transfer **52,** 476-81, 482-5
UK, constitutional relationship with **39,** 64, 191, 253, 260, 275, 289, 340-2, 349
sovereign. *See* Head of State
sovereign equality of States. *See* States, equality
sovereign immunity. *See* State immunity
Sovereign Order of Malta
Constitutional Charter **77,** 615
employment contract, locally engaged staff, State immunity, jurisdiction **65,** 309-12
immunity, taxation **65,** 323
Italian Knights of **77,** 613-15
immunity **77,** 613-15
Magisterial Tribunals **77,** 615
Maltese Code **77,** 615
Order of Santa Maria Gloriosa compared **77,** 623, 625
State immunity, jurisdiction, employment contract, locally engaged staff **65,** 309-12
State immunity, jurisdiction, entitlement **65,** 309-11, 323-4, **77,** 613-15
status **65,** 309-11, 323-4, **77,** 614-15, 622
sovereignty 61, 92, 93, 107, 111, **76,** 445, 464-8. *See also* eminent domain/*dominium eminens*; statehood; territorial integrity; territory
acquisition **39,** 280, 301
act of State doctrine and **56,** 38-9, **57,** 26, 38, **79,** 586, **81,** 519, 525-6, 527, 595, 622, 654-6, **111,** 595
airspace. *See* airspace, sovereignty over
arbitration and. *See* arbitration, sovereignty and
atmospheric nuclear tests and **74,** 95-6
belligerent occupation and. *See* belligerent occupation, sovereignty
border controls. *See* border controls
British Commonwealth, membership of and **90,** 467-8
bundle of rights, as **92,** 573
change of. *See also* State succession
effect on contracts **62,** 172
effect on municipal law **52,** 80
efficacy of change principle **53,** 56-7, 65, 66, 73, 74, 76-81
municipality, legal identity and **44,** 50-7
characteristics **36,** 309, **39,** 134, 197-9, 327, **51,** 106, 116-74, **52,** 306, **57,** 375, 391-2, **63,** 291, **84,** 117. *See also* rights/powers *below*
as bundle of rights **92,** 573
ephemeral concept **87,** 603-4
independence of authority **55,** 418-19
indivisibility **53,** 83, 87, 89
territory as basis **52,** 293, 297
identity of concepts **95,** 695
compliance with orders of international tribunal **110,** 648-9, 699, **121,** 361
constitutional amendment and **98,** 189
crimes against humanity and **91,** 130-1, **105,** 497
de facto governments. *See* government, de facto
de facto/de jure **39,** 86, 164, 221, 229, 281, 338, **87,** 604, 607, 654-6
definition **87,** 551
Corfu Channel **82,** 415
Duff Development Corporation v. *Government of Kelantan* **116,** 590

Island of Palmas **82,** 395-6
majestas **82,** 392-3, 395, 399, 420, 423, 424, **90,** 456
dual. *See* joint/dual *below*
in EEZ **82,** 642
effectivités **97,** 311, 540-1, 557-9, 567, **116,** 135-41
airstrip in active use **114,** 109, 132, 133-4
colonial and State distinguished **97,** 557
criminal or civil jurisdiction **114,** 90-1
customary law arbitration **114,** 90-1
fishing vessel arrests **114,** 75-7, 86
geodetic station **114,** 89
intentional display of authority **59,** 59-67, **114,** 69, 94
continuous basis **114,** 69, 75
landing parties **114,** 87-8
licensing of activities on islands **114,** 89-90, 113-14, 133-4
licensing of activities in offshore waters **114,** 78
lighthouse, maintenance **114,** 29, 63-70, 88-91, 135-6
military post **114,** 88
nature of territory, relevance **114,** 69, 118
size of population, relevance **114,** 69
naval and coastguard patrols **114,** 80-5, 129-30
notices to mariners **114,** 79-80
oil concession **81,** 527, **114,** 101-14, 126, 131-2, 136
overflight **76,** 385-7, **114,** 94, 108
peaceful basis **114,** 69, 75
civil war, relevance **114,** 69, 76
permission to cruise/land **114,** 78-9
private fishing activity **114,** 85-6
relevance in absence of evidence **100,** 96-8
search and rescue operations **114,** 80, 86
seasonal habitation **114,** 92-3
seismic survey **114,** 105, 133
shrines and holy places **114,** 89
standard of proof **114,** 118
uti possidetis, priority **97,** 622-3
elections, right of non-national to stand **98,** 265
environmental integrity and **57,** 578-82
equality of States to conduct foreign relations and **93,** 497
European Community. *See* European Community (EC), sovereignty
evidence of **59,** 61-74, **82,** 398
allegiance **59,** 61, 73-4, 100, 120
exercise of governmental authority. *See effectivités above*
legislative acts regulating activity **114,** 69, 73-4
public claim **114,** 69-73
State structure **59,** 61-2
exclusive fishing zone (EFZ), limitations **82,** 626
exercise of **88,** 274. *See also* Kuwait, Iraq invasion (1990), status following
enjoyment of distinguished **53,** 481-2, **105,** 411-13
on foreign territory **38,** 118, 134, **46,** 192, **72,** 214, **73,** 243-4, 265, 357-8, **78,** 615, 616
letters rogatory and **73,** 321-2, 337-8, 346-7, 357-8
service of legal notices **46,** 283-4
extraterritorial effect of legislation and **82,** 133, **91,** 72-3, 97-8, 101, **96,** 134

sovereignty (*cont.*)
federal State **39,** 121-2, **91,** 72-3, 97-8, 101
airspace **90,** 253
constituent States **51,** 191-2, **52,** 324
duality **91,** 73, 101
extraterritorial legislation and **91,** 72-3, 97-8, 101
territorial sea. *See* territorial sea, sovereignty over
fishing regime, compatibility **114,** 139, **119,** 447-53
forcible abduction/unlawful arrest. *See* forcible abduction/unlawful arrest, territorial sovereignty, breach
foreign military aircraft, overflight
consent, need for
absence of protest **91,** 286
estoppel **91,** 286
general **91,** 285, 286
implied **91,** 284, 285-6
NATO Status of Forces Agreement (1951) **91,** 283-4, 285
freedom of the seas and **74,** 210
habeas corpus writ and **79,** 29
high seas, airspace **90,** 215-16
in/over
Berlin, Western Sectors **52,** 287-8, **57,** 115-16
colonies. *See* colonies, sovereignty
continental shelf **56,** 85, 131, **77,** 689
Estonia **72,** 439, 441-2, **85,** 55, 57-8, 59-60, 62
Germany, GDR **90,** 404-5
Germany (post-WWII) **78,** 162
Gibraltar **63,** 172
Gulf emirates **91,** 641, 681, 690
India, British rule and **50,** 471-2
mandated territories **37,** 30, 34, 61, 121, 409, 440, 472, 570, **87,** 606
non-self-governing territory **59,** 162, **105,** 410-14
Okinawa Islands **54,** 216, 218-21, 222-3
Panama Canal Zone **56,** 51
patrimonial sea **55,** 221
Southern Rhodesia. *See* Southern Rhodesia, sovereignty over
territorial waters. *See* territorial sea
territory occupied in time of peace **87,** 603
Trust Territories. *See* Trust Territories, sovereignty
incidents likely to aggravate dispute, whether affected by **80,** 456
Eastern Greenland case **80,** 456
independence and **94,** 589
distinguished **83,** 17
members of French Community **44,** 26-8
interference with, obligation under international law to refrain from **116,** 589-95
internal **95,** 429
external distinguished **39,** 197-9, 220-1, 278, 280, 290-1, **90,** 456-7, 470
habitual obedience **90,** 519
legislation **55,** 54-5, 86, **82,** 396
parliamentary sovereignty **78,** 466, 476-8, **90,** 470-2
internal waters **91,** 415
international agreements. *See* treaties *below*

international courtesy **82,** 73
international and municipal law, conflict between, effect on **53,** 11
Islamic law **114,** 42, 45, **119,** 448
joint/dual
  bays **97,** 513-14
  federal State **91,** 73, 101
jurisdiction **57,** 115-16, **71,** 224-5, **105,** 440-1, 443, 497, 575-9
  ability to exercise and **91,** 39, 117, 119, **118,** 19
  co-extensive, whether **49,** 386-7
  concurrent jurisdiction, effect on **92,** 565, 574-5
  distinction **114,** 33-4, 51
  jus de non evocando **105,** 439
laws and customs of war and **105,** 505-6
legal order of foreign State, respect for **72,** 299, **73,** 243-4
legal ties distinguished **59,** 94
limitations on **57,** 392, **61,** 96, 99, 129, **62,** 233, **87,** 551-2, 564, **92,** 566-8, 574, 576
  arbitration and **62,** 165, 178, **78,** 640, **122,** 280-1
  competing jurisdictions **110,** 343, 375-6
  customary **92,** 574
  enclave, right of access to **92,** 567-8, 576
  external restraints **82,** 393
  good neighbourliness principle **110,** 455-6
  international humanitarian law **110,** 445-6
  international law **123,** 380
  Lotus principle ('what is not prohibited is allowed') **36,** 283-5, **110,** 188-9, 220-1, 241-2, 343-6, 376, 444-6
  mandatory universal jurisdiction **105,** 497, 575-8
  nationality, determination of **111,** 189
  privileges and immunities of members of European Parliament **101,** 365-7
  restrictive interpretation **46,** 487
  rights of other States **56,** 171
  Security Council measures relating to peace and security **110,** 648-9, 667
  sovereignty of other States **55,** 127, 130, 145
  treaty **56,** 272, 273, 283-4
    specifically to ensure international peace and justice **78,** 102
  treaty interpretation, presumption against **37,** 121-2, **45,** 395, 407, 411, 424, 426, **78,** 654, **83,** 133, **90,** 380, **92,** 688
  UN Charter **110,** 344-6
  uti possidetis **83,** 67
military service laws and **88,** 8, 21
natural resources, over. *See* natural resources, sovereignty over; UN General Assembly (UNGA) Resolutions, 1803(XVII) (Permanent Sovereignty over Natural Resources)
obligations, defence **97,** 595
occupation, in time of peace, residual **101,** 556
overflight charges as exercise of **82,** 73
parliamentary **78,** 466, 476-8
patrimonium and **43,** 108
people, inherent right/will **49,** 58, **90,** 450, 482-3, 514-20
  people under tutelage **49,** 59
personal limits **54,** 217-21
personal supremacy and **44,** 308

sovereignty (*cont.*)
Protection of the World Cultural and Natural Heritage Convention (1972) and **90,** 97
protectorates and **71,** 44-7
re-establishment of **44,** 58
recognition and **59,** 67-9, **82,** 478-9
treaties **59,** 67, 71-3
respect for **90,** 660-1
collaboration between States and **71,** 225
cross-examination of fugitives by foreign judges **71,** 224-6
extradition **55,** 86-7, **88,** 267-8, **90,** 660-1, **94,** 502, 507, 521-2, 534, 536-7, 589-90, 592, **95,** 364 n. 4
speciality **90,** 674, 678
extradition agreement **90,** 660-1
obligation **94,** 589
speciality and **90,** 661
restitutio in integrum and **62,** 198, 217
resulting from revolution **53,** 71-2, 77-8
retroactive effect of FRG–Poland Border Treaty (1990) **108,** 660
retroactive legislation and **91,** 105
rights/powers **56,** 83
acquisition of foreign territory **53,** 202-3
action to regain control of territory **106,** 494-8
admission of alien, refusal **90,** 25-6
alienation/cession of territory **53,** 201-2, 203, **82,** 396, 397, 419, **114,** 46
applicable law **112,** 508
attribution of citizenship **78,** 188
communication with foreign State **55,** 34
competence and powers, distinction, whether **93,** 218-19
conduct of foreign relations **55,** 48-9
continental shelf rights distinguished **114,** 106-7
control of alien **101,** 503, **111,** 188, 265, 269, 292
criminal policy **111,** 190
currency issue **111,** 593, 595, 598-9, 602-3
designation as State organ **110,** 710, 712
incidents likely to aggravate or extend dispute, effect **106,** 157
licensing of foreign vessels **82,** 631
promotion of subjects' interests **118,** 475-6
punishment **106,** 237
regulation of commerce **56,** 38
regulation of telecommunications **77,** 422
territorial integrity **110,** 526, **115,** 152
treaties **56,** 18, **77,** 464
treaty limitation **82,** 646
trial of nationals or persons within jurisdiction **105,** 575-9
waiver **62,** 178
individual's right to challenge **105,** 576-7
international crime **105,** 440-1
Security Council Chapter VII action **105,** 576
safeguarding of, IMF rules **74,** 688
security
nuclear weapons **110,** 104-6
right to determine requirements **110,** 104-6
self-defence **110,** 255, 256, 356-9

spheres of interest, reservation of **80,** 260
stabilization clause and **83,** 562
State contract and **56,** 272, 273
State immunity and **63,** 372-3, **64,** 86, **65,** 419-20, 438, **81,** 548 n. 7, **82,** 18, 32, 37, 102, 120, **84,** 21-2, 170, 707, **90,** 589-91, **95,** 455, **103,** 470, **104,** 570, 576, 577, 612, 617-19, **119,** 236
  bankruptcy petition **94,** 368-9
State responsibility for acts of subjects **59,** 168
territorial
  boundary disputes and **91,** 586-7
  as modern Western concept **114,** 45, 116, 137
third-party obligations affecting, treaties and contracts contrasted **78,** 470
threat to, Maastricht Treaty (1992) **98,** 212
transfer of **53,** 482
  effect on occupation **70,** 42-6
transfer of powers to another State, nuclear weapons, deployment, agreement to **106,** 375-87
transfer of powers to international organization **43,** 2, **93,** 342-3. *See also* European Community (EC), transfer of powers to
  collective security system **106,** 329-30, 331-2, 379-80
  constitutional amendment/legislative consent, need for
    collective security system, agreement to treaty establishing **106,** 380
    International Criminal Court (ICC), Rome Statute (1998) **125,** 470-90
    subsequent development of organization, relevance **106,** 380-7, 388
  constitutional limitations **93,** 517, 518-21, 525, **101,** 365-7, **106,** 326-34, 338, 362, 375-81, 387-8
  direct elections to European Assembly **74,** 528-9
  equality of States and **93,** 520, **101,** 368
    Security Council veto **101,** 368
  Eurocontrol (European Organization for the Safety of Air Navigation) **94,** 335, 337-8, **101,** 19-21, 25-9
  federal State, powers exercised by constituent State **108,** 652
  national legislative powers, effect on **93,** 531-2
  nature of organization, relevance **106,** 380-1
  nuclear weapons, deployment, agreement to **106,** 375-87
  reciprocity, need for **101,** 367-9
  responsibility for determining whether, court **106,** 379
  rights inalienable by organization **108,** 652-3
  Security Council **110,** 634
transferability **78,** 471
treaties, effect **53,** 474-6, 565, **70,** 41, 44, 696-8
  restrictive interpretation and **41,** 284, 295, 303
UN Charter
  domestic jurisdiction **105,** 479-84, 576, 578-9
  surrender **105,** 439, **106,** 329
usurpation **52,** 56
  attempt to regain control, effect on de facto sovereignty **53,** 66-9, 74-5, 77-81
  capacity of courts to determine status of new regime **53,** 55-6, 74-5, 87-8
  status of de facto government **53,** 55-6, 64, 77-80
violation **74,** 249, 258, 262, 266-7
  burden of proof **105,** 480
  entrapment of national by foreign State **94,** 348
  proceedings before international tribunal as **75,** 5, 8

sovereignty (*cont.*)
right to plead, individual **105,** 479-80
violation, remedies, EC Presidential statement **94,** 348
violations of international law and **73,** 243
Yugoslavia, International Criminal Tribunal for the Former (ICTY), Statute **110,** 648-9, **121,** 361
Spain 63, 172
act of State, immunity, abrogation **96,** 219-20
administrative decisions, remedies against **46,** 201, 233
aliens, labour law, application to **88,** 688, 689-90
applicable law, employment contract **88,** 688, 689, 690
asylum
refusal, grounds, need to state **86,** 507
right of **86,** 506-7
illegal entry, subsequent to **86,** 507
late application **86,** 506-7
violation of norms relating to, procedure for determining **86,** 506
bankruptcy laws **46,** 183, 189, 192-6, 234-6, 281-4, 439, 458
Belgium, Treaty of Conciliation, Judicial Settlement and Arbitration (1927) **46,** 19, 36-7
denial of justice **46,** 197, 200
jurisdictional clauses **46,** 23-6, 37, 38, 48-51, 188, 315, 354-5
PCIJ, effect of dissolution **46,** 38-40, 47-51, 105-6, 145-72
burden of proof, existence of loan **124,** 54
civil proceedings
court's duty to ensure prompt hearing **96,** 530
parties' responsibility for advancing **96,** 530
colonial territories, status **59,** 42
compensation, unjust enrichment as **88,** 702
Constitution 1978
primacy **98,** 260
s 9 **86,** 520, 522
s 9(3) **119,** 337
s 10(2) (fundamental rights, interpretation) **93,** 584-5
compatibility with EC law **93,** 584-5
s 13 **86,** 506
s 13(2) (voting rights)
compatibility with Maastricht Treaty (1992) **98,** 254-70
text **98,** 252
s 14 **86,** 522, **88,** 696
s 15 (right to life) **111,** 220
s 17(1) (freedom of person) **111,** 220
s 18 (private and family life) **111,** 220
s 19 (freedom of movement/choice of residence) **111,** 220
s 24 **86,** 511, 515
s 24(1) (right to enforcement of judgment) **113,** 414, 416, 422
s 24(2) **96,** 526
s 25 **119,** 337
s 45 (protection of the environment) **111,** 220, 221, **124,** 51
s 53 **86,** 506
s 93 (conclusion of treaties)
basis for extension to non-national of right to stand as candidate in municipal elections **98,** 266
breach of Community law and **98,** 248-9

indirect amendment of Constitution, scope for **98,** 267-8
text **98,** 247 n. 1
s 95 (treaties: constitutional review), text **98,** 252 n. 1
s 96 (treaties: primacy) **119,** 336
s 96(1) (treaties as part of law) **88,** 682, **119,** 335
constitutional status of EC law **98,** 249
Genocide Convention (1948) **119,** 335
text **98,** 247 n. 2
s 97 **88,** 685
s 106 **88,** 692
s 117(3) (enforcement of judgments) **113,** 416
s 140 **86,** 503
constitutional review
acts of Community **98,** 250-1
acts of national public authorities, limited to **98,** 250-1
declaration of constitutional compatibility of treaty
binding effect **98,** 260-1
legal nature **98,** 261
procedure **98,** 259-61
consular privileges and immunities, State immunity and, distinction **113,** 419, 422
denial of justice, right of action and **86,** 515
diplomatic immunity, jurisdiction
immunity from law distinguished **86,** 521-2
State immunity and, distinction **113,** 419, 422
diplomatic immunity, jurisdiction, waiver **86,** 520-1, 522
express **86,** 520
general **86,** 520
retroactive, whether **86,** 520
diplomatic privileges and immunities
basis
extraterritoriality **86,** 520
sovereignty of sending State **86,** 520
purpose, functional **86,** 520
diplomatic privileges and immunities, entitlement
family members **71,** 545-6
personal **86,** 510-11
State **86,** 510-11
Vienna Convention on Diplomatic Relations (1961) **86,** 509-10
drugs offences, 'narcotic', definition **86,** 498
EC
accession, effect on existing law **93,** 575
non-discrimination, difference of treatment by Member States distinguished **93,** 584-5
State responsibility, independent organization **93,** 590-1
transfer of powers to, extension of rights to non-national distinguished **98,** 266, 268
EC law
compatibility of national law, trial court, sole competence to determine **98,** 249
conflict with national law
constitutional issue, whether **98,** 248-9, 250-1
subsequent legislation **98,** 248-9
constitutional review, possibility **98,** 251
constitutional status **98,** 248-9
implementation, executive regulation **93,** 582

Spain (*cont.*)
national courts' role
compatibility of national law **98,** 249
to ensure effectiveness of Community law **98,** 249
as national law **98,** 248
primacy **93,** 581-2
national courts' role, limitation on **98,** 249
right to invoke before national courts **93,** 576
EC law, direct effect
decision **93,** 589
directive **93,** 588-91
regulation **93,** 581-2
EEC Treaty (Rome) (1957)
direct effect **93,** 576
secondary legislation distinguished **93,** 576
incorporation into municipal law **93,** 581
individuals **93,** 576
interpretation, 'products originating in Community' (non-EC provenance) **93,** 576-7
legislation, interpretation, aid to **93,** 584-5
embassy or consular bank account/funds, immunity, execution/attachment **113,** 423-5
absolute immunity, whether **113,** 427-9
amount involved, relevance **113,** 428
ILC Draft Articles on Jurisdictional Immunities of States and Their Property (1991) **113,** 423
State practice **113,** 423-4
employment contract, locally engaged staff, diplomatic mission
State immunity, jurisdiction **86,** 510, 511, 515-16, **113,** 432-4
nationality of employee, relevance, national of sending State **86,** 509-11
European citizenship
national identities, preservation of **98,** 263
voting rights **98,** 263
European Convention on Human Rights (1950) and **46,** 447
European Convention on State Immunity (and Protocol) (Basle) (1972), status **113,** 420
European Union Treaty (Maastricht) (1992)
constitutional amendment, need for
right to stand as candidate in national elections **98,** 263-70
voting rights for non-national **98,** 263-4
right to stand as candidate in national elections, national sovereignty, compatibility with **98,** 265
exchange control regulations **46,** 182, 185, 233
application **46,** 189, 190, 348, 354
expropriation of companies
constitutionality **75,** 273, 286
recognition by English courts **75,** 272-300
extradition procedure **69,** 225-6
foreign companies, law governing **46,** 193
foreign relations, constitutional conformity, need for **98,** 267
France
maritime delimitation **71,** 144, 150
mutual fishing rights **74,** 142-8
genocide
Chile, in **119,** 340-2

definition **119,** 338-42
'intent to destroy, in part or in whole, a national ethnic, racial or religious group' **119,** 339-40
'intent to destroy, in part or in whole, a national ethnic, social or religious group' **119,** 339
jurisdiction
extraterritorial **119,** 336-7, 338
passive personality principle **119,** 56
possibility and obligation distinguished **119,** 336- 7
universal **36,** 33-9, **82,** 348, **119,** 56, 336-7
as terrorism **119,** 342-3
time of events constituting, relevance **119,** 336-7
events prior to legislation providing for jurisdiction **119,** 336
torture as part of **119,** 343
Genocide Convention (1948)
incorporation into municipal law **119,** 335
jurisdiction
competent tribunal of State in which act committed **119,** 335-6
extraterritorial jurisdiction **119,** 335-6
international penal tribunal **119,** 335-6
States parties' right to exercise 'universal' where their law permits **119,** 334-6
reservations, dispute settlement provisions **119,** 335
Gibraltar and **63,** 172
Head of State, former, immunity, jurisdiction, official acts in exercise of functions **119,** 349
international crimes, universal jurisdiction, as breach of UN Charter **119,** 344-5
international law
evolving nature **113,** 419
municipal courts, application by **113,** 418
municipal law and
dualist theory **113,** 418
legislation, need for **113,** 418
sources **113,** 418-19
International Law Commission (ILC), binding effect **113,** 420
judicial protection, right to have judgment enforced
express refusal on ground recognized by law **113,** 416, 427-8
express refusal properly reasoned **113,** 416
limitations **113,** 416
State immunity and **113,** 415-18, 426, 427-9
judicial review, diplomatic protection **96,** 219-20
jurisdiction
contractual agreement to exclude **88,** 689
employment contract **88,** 688-90
territorial **86,** 519
exceptions **86,** 519
universal
genocide **36,** 33-9, **82,** 348, **119,** 56, 336-7
torture **119,** 343
visiting forces **86,** 501-2
law of
Civil Code 1889 **88,** 707
Civil Code 1978 **86,** 498, 520, 521, 522

Spain (*cont.*)
Art. 1(5) **88,** 682, 689, 690, **119,** 335
Art. 8 **71,** 545
Art. 35 **46,** 193
Art. 64 **71,** 545
Art. 1214 **88,** 695, **124,** 54
Art. 1262 **124,** 56
Art. 1445 **46,** 195
Art. 1449 **46,** 195
Art. 1461 **46,** 195
Art. 1462 **46,** 195
Civil Procedure Code 1881 (as amended)
Art. 114 **46,** 195
Art. 300 **46,** 194
Art. 408 **46,** 237
Art. 755 **46,** 237
Art. 903 **46,** 237
Art. 918 **46,** 237
Art. 919 **46,** 194
Art. 1167 **46,** 194
Art. 1236 **46,** 195
Art. 1240 **46,** 195
Arts. 1266-74 **46,** 195
Arts. 1291-4 **46,** 195
Art. 1319 **46,** 194
Art. 1321 **46,** 236
Art. 1322 **46,** 195
Art. 1326 **46,** 234
Art. 1330 **46,** 236
Art. 1331 **46,** 194
Art. 1342 **46,** 194
Art. 1354 **46,** 194
Art. 1358 **46,** 195
Art. 1363 **46,** 196
Art. 1512 **46,** 195
Art. 1513 **46,** 195
Art. 1796 **46,** 235
Commercial Code 1829 **46,** 193, 194, 195, 234
Commercial Code 1885 **46,** 116, 174, 192, 193, 194, 195
Art. 54 **124,** 56
Compulsory Expropriation Law **88,** 700
Constitutional Court Law 1979 **111,** 221
Criminal Code 1983 **84,** 722
Art. 23 **86,** 499
Art. 24 **86,** 499
Art. 102 **86,** 501
Art. 104 **86,** 501
Art. 137 *bis* **119,** 339-40, 341
Art. 344 **84,** 498, 499, **86,** 497, 498, 499
Art. 347 *bis* **111,** 222
Art. 457 **86,** 501
Art. 458 **86,** 501
Criminal Code 1995, Art. 607 **119,** 340

Criminal Prosecution Law 1944, Art. 849 **86,** 521
Decree 2414/1961 **111,** 221
Decree No 1870 of 27 July 1968 (labour law) **88,** 688, 689
Employment Contracts Law **88,** 704-5
Execution and Attachment Law (*Ley de Expropriacion Forzosa*) **86,** 502, 503
General Taxation Law 1963 **88,** 682
Judicial System Law (*Ley de Regimen Juridico*) **86,** 502
Jurisdiction Law **88,** 699
Labour Courts Procedure Law **86,** 511
Labour Proceedings Law **88,** 688, 704
Law 700/62 (Single Convention on Narcotic Drugs) (1961) **86,** 498
Law of 20 December 1963 (Equatorial Guinea: special administrative status) **88,** 693
Law 49/68 (Equatorial Guinea: independence) **88,** 693
Law 44/71 (introduction of genocide into Criminal Code) **119,** 339
Law 62/78 (protection of fundamental rights) **86,** 506, **111,** 221
Law 7/83 **75,** 273, 286-7, 313, 316
Law 23/86 (legal organization of chambers of agriculture), compatibility with EC law **93,** 584-5
Law 30/92 of 27 November 1992 (Public Administrations and Common Administrative Procedure) **124,** 45-6
Law 6/97 of 14 April 1997 (State commercial organizations) **124,** 46
Law 1/99 of 5 January 1999 (capital venture entities) **124,** 46
Legal Framework of the State Administration **88,** 692-3, 694, 695, 700
Local Administrative Law (*Ley Regimen Local*) **86,** 503
Local Government Regulation Law **88,** 681
Organic Law on the Judiciary 1870 **86,** 519
Art. 333 **71,** 545
Art. 334 **71,** 545
Art. 336 **119,** 337
Organic Law on the Judiciary 1985 **86,** 511, 515-16, 519, 520
Art. 21(2) **113,** 418-22
Art. 23(2) **119,** 336, 343-4
Art. 23(4) **119,** 336-7, 338, 341, 342, 343, 344-5
Art. 197 **119,** 333
non-retroactivity **119,** 336
procedural nature **119,** 336-7
retroactive effect **86,** 499
Royal Decree 30 December 1976 (taxation) **88,** 681-2
Royal Decree 342/1979 of 20 February 1979 **86,** 506
Royal Decree 1654/80 of 11 June 1980 (legal disputes involving the State abroad) **86,** 510, 511, 515
Royal Decree 2/1983 **75,** 273, 286-7
Royal Decree 1302/1986 of 28 June 1986 (environmental impact assessment) **124,** 51
legislation, interpretation, aids
EC norm **93,** 584-5
EEC Treaty (Rome) (1957) **93,** 584-5
parallel legislation **88,** 681
legislation, retroactive **86,** 499
international crimes, procedural provisions distinguished **119,** 336-7
procedural legislation **119,** 336-7
nationality, evidence of, identity card **88,** 702
nationals

Spain (*cont.*)
protection of **88,** 686, 694, 696
acts or omissions causing loss **88,** 686, 689-90
treatment as, possibility **98,** 268-9
prompt hearing **96,** 525-8
Constitution **96,** 525-6
court's workload **96,** 526
damage to plaintiff's interests, need for **96,** 526
ECHR jurisprudence **96,** 526
normal delay as 'norm' **96,** 526-7
prioritization of cases **96,** 526
relevant period, total time taken by trial **96,** 526-7
remedial steps, relevance **96,** 528
public order/public policy/*ordre public* **46,** 195
res judicata, amnesty, relevance **119,** 343-4
sovereignty, right of non-national to stand in municipal elections and **98,** 265
State agency/State-owned corporation/State entity
'employee'/'official' distinguished **124,** 59-60
public business entities/State commercial corporations distinguished **124,** 45-6
SODIGA **124,** 28-33, 45-8
State immunity, applicable law, international law **113,** 418-26
State immunity, execution/attachment
State practice
Anglo-Saxon jurisdictions **113,** 421, 428-9
civil law jurisdictions **113,** 421
usages and practices of international law **86,** 511, 516
State immunity, execution/attachment, applicability, bank accounts other than diplomatic or consular **113,** 425-6
State immunity, execution/attachment, procedural aspects
applicable law, *lex fori* **113,** 425-6
right to have judgment enforced and **113,** 414-18, 426, 427- 9
State immunity, execution/attachment, purpose of proceedings, debt recovery **82,** 39-45
State immunity, execution/attachment, purpose/use of funds/assets **113,** 420-2, 425-6
burden of proof **113,** 428
consular premises **113,** 423
diplomatic premises **113,** 423
European Convention on State Immunity (and Protocol) (Basle) (1972) **113,** 420-1
ILC Draft Articles on Jurisdictional Immunities of States and Their Property (1991) **113,** 420
property exclusively intended for industrial or commercial activity giving rise to proceedings **113,** 420-1, 426
sovereign purpose **113,** 419-20, 423
State practice, inconsistent practice **113,** 420
State immunity, execution/attachment, theory/doctrine
reciprocity, need for **86,** 511, 516
restrictive **113,** 422
treaty provision **86,** 511, 516
State immunity, jurisdiction, European Convention on State Immunity (and Protocol) (Basle) (1972) **86,** 514-15
State immunity, jurisdiction, classification of act, purchase of goods or services **113,** 435
State immunity, jurisdiction, entitlement, government department **52,** 318-21
State immunity, jurisdiction, procedural aspects
applicable law

Vienna Convention on Consular Relations (1963) **113,** 419, 422
Vienna Convention on Diplomatic Relations (1961) **113,** 419, 422
presumption in favour of **86,** 515
State immunity, jurisdiction, theory/doctrine
basis
reciprocal independence **86,** 514
sovereignty **113,** 422
legislation **86,** 515
restrictive **86,** 510
general principle of international law **113,** 419
State practice, source of international law **113,** 418, 419
State responsibility, obligation to anticipate problems **88,** 685
State responsibility for acts and omissions of
local authority employee **86,** 503
police officer, disclosure of document provided by member of visiting forces **86,** 501-3
State responsibility, breach, defences, *force majeure* **86,** 502
State responsibility, procedural aspects
burden of proof **86,** 502
exhaustion of local remedies and **88,** 694
limitations on liability **88,** 695
proceedings to establish, time-limits **88,** 694, 695-7
requirements
damage of economic value **86,** 502
direct result of public service operation **86,** 502
State-sponsored terrorism **119,** 343
taxation, exemption, foreign State **88,** 681-3
terrorism
definition/requirements
intention to subvert constitutional order **119,** 342
organized group **119,** 342
jurisdiction, universal **119,** 342
time of events constituting, relevance, events prior to legislation providing for jurisdiction **119,** 336-7, 342
time-limits **88,** 694, 695-7, 699-700
dies a quo **88** 695, 696
torture
as element of genocide **119,** 343
jurisdiction, universal **119,** 343
treaties
applicability **86,** 506, **88,** 682
constitutional amendment, need for **98,** 260, 261, 262-3, 269, 270
constitutional review
before legislative approval **98,** 260
implementing legislation **98,** 260
fundamental change of circumstances **88,** 685
implementation, subsequent agreement, by **88,** 690
implementing legislation, absence **86,** 506
incorporation into municipal law, publication, by **88,** 681, 682, 688
municipal law and
aid to interpretation **98,** 251
conflict, constitutional issue, whether **98,** 249
constitutional status **98,** 248-9, 250-1
part of law, whether, Annexes, publication, need for **86,** 499

Spain (*cont.*)
publication in official bulletin, need for **86,** 499
source of international law **113,** 418-19
source of law **86,** 497-8
treaty interpretation, phrases, 'individual' **88,** 682
UN, admission to **46,** 39, 46-7, 50-1, 105, 148, 153, 160
Vienna Convention on Diplomatic Relations (1961) **86,** 509-10
Wages Guarantee Fund, EC directive 80/987 (insolvency of employers) and **93,** 590-1
Special Agreement. *See* International Court of Justice (ICJ), Special Agreement
special envoys, diplomatic privileges and immunities **48,** 205-8
special rapporteur 121, 395
costs of proceedings in respect of **121,** 404-5, 413-14, 433, 448, 471
as expert on mission **121,** 374, 375-6, 427-8, 433
Foreign Minister's certificate, conclusiveness **121,** 377-80, 388-97, 413
UN Secretary-General's certificate, conclusiveness **121,** 375-7, 388-97, 412-13, 419-26, 429-30, 444-5
functions **121,** 372-3
obligation to remain within **121,** 433, 441-2
statement to commercial magazine, whether within **121,** 373, 400-1, 428-31, 445-7, 453-7, 461-2
tortious act **121,** 400
UN Secretary-General's right to determine whether act within **121,** 376, 391-7, 419-26, 429-30, 431-3, 461-2
immunity, jurisdiction, waiver
acceptance of service **121,** 373-4
conditional appearance **121,** 373-4
privileges and immunities **85,** 312, 323-4. *See also* diplomatic privileges and immunities; international officials, privileges and immunities; international organizations, privileges and immunities
in country of permanent residence **85,** 312, 323-4, 331
defamation proceedings **121,** 369-405
diplomatic privileges and immunities distinguished **121,** 395
functional **121,** 375-6, 396
as preliminary question **121,** 379-82, 383-405, 432-3, 448-9, 456-7, 461-2
status as
determination by organization **85,** 325, 343
role of national State **85,** 325, 333, 335, 336, 342-3
speciality. *See* extradition, speciality; international organization, speciality
specialized agency. *See also individual agencies*
advisory opinion, right to request. *See* International Court of Justice (ICJ), advisory opinion, request for, standing, specialized agency
competence **62,** 483-5, 487, 511
Constitution, interpretation, guidelines, overall UN system **110,** 19-21, 46
definition **102,** 158, **110,** 19-20
functions **62,** 485
International Catholic Migration Commission (ICMC) **102,** 156
objectives **62,** 485
structure **62,** 485
speech, freedom of. *See* freedom of expression
sphere of influence
adjacency as basis of title and **41,** 127
boundary dispute, relevance **100,** 39
hinterland doctrine **100,** 83-4

spies. *See* espionage
sport. *See* Court of Arbitration for Sport (Ad Hoc Division: Sydney Olympic Games); Olympic Charter, Rules
Sri Lanka
administrative practice, torture **71,** 302-3
Constitution 1978
fundamental rights
application out of time **71,** 298
evidence of infringements **71,** 298-9
executive action, violation by **71,** 300-3
freedom from torture. *See* s 11 *below*
s 11 **71,** 295
s 13(6) **87,** 298
s 126 **71,** 298, 300
s 157 (incorporation of treaties) **106,** 429, 477, 479, 491, 500
validity of legislation and **87,** 301
criminal procedure **87,** 305
defects in judgment **87,** 298-9, 302-3
joinder of actions **87,** 299, 301, 305-7
preliminary enquiry, need for **87,** 300
sentencing **87,** 308-10
Hague Convention for the Suppression of the Unlawful Seizure of Aircraft (1970), 'inquiry into the facts' **87,** 300, 307-8
jurisdiction
foreign aircraft, territorial space, outside **87,** 299-300
national, over **87,** 300
'presence in' **87,** 299-300, 303-5
territorial, constructive **87,** 303
law of
Constitution. *See* Constitution 1978 *above*
Criminal Code 1833 **87,** 308-9, 314-29
s 296 **87,** 309
s 343 **87,** 309
s 394 **87,** 297, 301
Criminal Procedure Act 1979
s 128(3) **87,** 302
s 145 **87,** 307-8
s 175(1) **87,** 305
s 203 **87,** 305
s 279 **87,** 302
s 283 **87,** 298, 303
Criminal Procedure (Special Provisions) Law No 15 of 1978 **87,** 300
Evidence Ordinance, s 9 **87,** 301-2
Offences against Aircraft Act No 24 of 1982
s 2 **87,** 300, 301
s 12(2) **87,** 308
s 17 **87,** 302
s 17(1) **87,** 297, 299, 301
s 18 **87,** 310
s 19(1) **87,** 297, 299-300, 303, 304-5
s 19(3) **87,** 297, 299-300, 303, 304-5
s 20 **87,** 307
s 21(2) **87,** 308

Sri Lanka (*cont.*)
Prevention of Terrorism (Temporary Provisions) Act 1979 **71,** 297
legislation, interpretation
multilingual, official language, preferred text, whether **87,** 300
phrases, 'present in' **87,** 299-300, 303-5
legislation, retroactive **87,** 298, 302
State, nation distinguished **87,** 349-50, 353
sustainable development principle in **116,** 107-13
Tamil Tigers, 'combat action' **106,** 450, 485-6
terrorism **124,** 348-9
jurisdiction **87,** 299-300, 301-2
torture in **124,** 348-9
treaties, as part of municipal law **106,** 429, 477
Sri Lanka/UK Bilateral Investment Treaty (1980)
Hong Kong, extension to (Exchange of Notes of 14 January 1981) **106,** 422
standard of treatment of alien, customary international law **106,** 441, 479-83, 486-7
stabilization clause 53, 455-7, **56,** 275, **62,** 159, 164, 170, **66,** 548, 550, 586-91, 621-7, **67,** 335-9, **83,** 558-60, 623 n. 30, **86,** 258, 295-9, **89,** 340
applicable law, effect on **53,** 455-7
expropriation/nationalization and **53,** 479, **66,** 589-90, 623- 5, **67,** 335-9, **83,** 562
standard of treatment of alien 88, 87-9
in accordance with [customary] international law **119,** 663-5, **121,** 55, 183, **122,** 379-80
applicability
courts **89,** 619
issues other than treatment by courts **125,** 139-41
physical protection and protection of investments distinguished **125,** 147
applicable law
customary international law **106,** 443-4, 446, 452-4, 479-80, 483, 484-5
treaty provision as **106,** 441, 443
inter-State relations as basis **46,** 400, 416, 429
international law **46,** 406-8, 510, **84,** 370, 371, 372
treaty provision **84,** 372, **106,** 440-53
customary international law and **106,** 441, 443
NAFTA provision. *See* NAFTA (North American Free Trade Agreement) (1992), standard of treatment
'protection and security by international law' **106,** 441, 442-6, 452, **121,** 55, 183
arbitrary **84,** 326
'constant protection and security of national' **84,** 369, 371, 401
'degree of security reasonably expected' **106,** 458
due diligence **106,** 443-6, 452-4, 480, 484, 494, 496
presumption of compliance **106,** 492, 498
preventive measures, obligation **106,** 457-8
'equal footing'
access clause **82,** 660
equal treatment **82,** 662
national treatment **82,** 624, 660-4
reciprocity **82,** 661-2, 663
State practice **82,** 660-1
'without discrimination' **82,** 616

equality **45,** 370, **71,** 307, **73,** 599-600, **74,** 423-4, 428, **77,** 464, 465, 466, **78,** 85-6, 98, 99-100, **79,** 412, **81,** 8, **85,** 283-4, **115,** 653-4
minimum wage legislation **106,** 317-18
fair and equitable **119,** 634-8, 654-5, **121,** 55, 120, 183, **122,** 379-402
additional to minimum standard, whether **122,** 380-4, 682
BITs **119,** 663-4, **121,** 185, **122,** 381-4
customary international law **125,** 136-9
OECD Draft Convention on the Protection of Foreign Property **106,** 484-5, **122,** 382
procedural fairness **121,** 185-8, **122,** 401. *See also* deportation, procedural fairness
customary international law **121,** 187
treaty provisions **121,** 186-7
transparency **115,** 664-6, **119,** 633, 635, 638, 653, **124,** 54
UNCTAD *Fair and Equitable Treatment* (1999) **122,** 381 n. 105
full protection and security **121,** 55, 183, **122,** 379
State immunity for intentional tort and **125,** 150-63
individual's status in international law and **125,** 147-8
jurisprudence
Blumenkson **106,** 493
ELSI **106,** 444, 483, **125,** 151-2
Home Insurance Company **106,** 456
Kummerow **106,** 455
Neer **125,** 147-8
Sambiaggio **106,** 443-4, 455, 483
Spanish Zone of Morocco claims **106,** 454-8
United States Diplomatic and Consular Staff in Tehran **106,** 484
Upton **106,** 493
Victor A. Ermerins **106,** 456
Law of the Sea Convention dispute settlement provisions distinguished **125,** 192
MFN **110,** 577, **121,** 55 n. 15
minimum international standard **46,** 423, 427-8, 495, **85,** 460, **106,** 453, 484-5, **119,** 662-4, **121,** 21-2, 118-20, 182-90
breach of treaty and **121,** 183-4
failure to provide national treatment and **121,** 120
good faith, relevance **121,** 189
treatment superior to that of nationals **121,** 182-3
minimum standard **63,** 455, **88,** 89, **121,** 21-2, 118-20, 182-90
customary international law **83,** 533
'most constant protection' **106,** 442, 483-5
'most favorable'/'no less favorable'/'best' **122,** 360-2
most favoured nation clause, customary international law **106,** 484-5, 488, 490-1
national treatment **46,** 495-6, **56,** 552-7, **61,** 172, 425-7, **74,** 399, 414, 572, **84,** 326, 370, 371, 372, 373, **110,** 577, **121,** 55 n. 15, 114-18, 153-75
access to courts **44,** 300, **45,** 365-70, **111,** 537
adverse effects on non-national, need for **121,** 159, 167-8, 184
compensation for failure to accord **121,** 190-4
customary international law **106,** 487
de facto/de jure distinguished **122,** 370
disproportionate damage, whether necessary **122,** 362-71
EC law, remedy for breach **111,** 93, 100, 101, 120-1, 122, 124, 125, 129, **117,** 320, 334-5
effect on more than one investor, whether necessary **122,** 358-60

standard of treatment of alien (*cont.*)
GATT **56,** 553-4
minimum standard and **122,** 323
NAFTA (1992). *See* NAFTA (North American Free Trade Agreement) (1992), standard of treatment, national treatment
National Treatment for Foreign-Controlled Enterprises (OECD) (1993) **122,** 372 n. 73
refugees **44,** 71, 187-9, **72,** 587, 634-6, 642-5, 648-9, **73,** 597, **74,** 474-6, 506-7
trading leases **47,** 240-3
treaty provision **45,** 366-70
non-discrimination **54,** 546, **61,** 167-8, 178-9, **72,** 265-6, **84,** 326, **106,** 495. *See also* equality *above*
extent of entitlement **72,** 264-7, 576-7, 579, 587, 589-90, 594-5
on grounds of nationality **122,** 373-4
objective **106,** 458
OECD Draft Convention on the Protection of Foreign Property **106,** 484-5
reciprocity **72,** 264-6, **84,** 386-7
State practice **106,** 457
strict liability **106,** 442-6, 474, 483-4
standard of treatment of nationals 88, 87-9, **103,** 618, **121,** 182-3
***stare decisis* doctrine**. *See* precedent in municipal courts, *stare decisis* doctrine
States. *See also* recognition, State; statehood
agent or instrumentality of. *See* United States of America (USA), Foreign Sovereign Immunities Act (FSIA) 1976/82, agency or instrumentality of a foreign State
annexation
effect, right to determine **119,** 584-5, 594
Hawaiian Kingdom **119,** 584-5, 594, 597
assets in foreign State, control of **86,** 15-19
central bank, liability **86,** 13
change of government and **86,** 3-9
disposition, public interest and **86,** 19
disposition of public interest and **86,** 19
political question doctrine and **86,** 18
title **86,** 17, 18
capacity to sue **63,** 106-20, 294, 298, 395
capitulation, effect **78,** 161
characteristics. *See* statehood, requirements/evidence of
classification
Cyprus, Turkish Republic of Northern (TRNC) **108,** 467
'unrecognized foreign State' **108,** 540-5
East Timor **87,** 74-6
EEC **80,** 123
Germany
Länder **87,** 39-41
special nature of two Germanies **78,** 155-6, 165-7
Germany, Democratic Republic (GDR) **78,** 165-6, 169
Germany (Reich) **78,** 161, 169
Holy See. *See* Holy See, status
Jersey **86,** 155-6
Sovereign Order of Malta. *See* Sovereign Order of Malta, status
communication with
designated authority **110,** 641-3, 717-18
exclusive means, whether **110,** 642-3

government official **110,** 641-3
individual, right of communication with **110,** 642-3, 710-12
diplomatic channels **110,** 711
State Agent before Tribunal **110,** 711
confederation. *See* federal State
continuity. *See* State succession, continuity of State
contract. *See* State contract
country, distinguishability **86,** 152-60, **100,** 532-40, **114,** 396-9, **117,** 346
sovereignty, relevance **100,** 533-4, 540
creation
applicable law
international law **115,** 117-20
municipal law **115,** 121-3
armed struggle **82,** 394
effectiveness principle **115,** 118-20. *See also* secession, 'effectivity' principle
evolution **82,** 394
legality, recognition, effect **115,** 165
merger. *See* merger *below*
regrouping **82,** 394
revolution **82,** 394
self-determination. *See* self-determination
unification **82,** 394
criminal sanctions, possibility **110,** 698
de facto **84,** 205
diplomatic immunity, entitlement **86,** 510
dismemberment. *See also* dissolution *below*; State succession
Belgium and Congo **47,** 75-8
France/Algeria **47,** 79-83, 86-9, 94-6, 99-106
French Indo-China **47,** 97-9
Poland **47,** 107-8
dissolution. *See also* dismemberment *above*; State succession
alteration in territorial status, effect **91,** 226
dispute relating to
international nature **91,** 305-7
settlement, method **91,** 305-7
reduction of territory **91,** 226, 230
requirements **91,** 226, 230
sovereign decision of constituent members **91,** 304, 305
duties **53,** 172-3, 176-7
protection of nationals abroad **60,** 210-11, 215-18
emergence. *See* State succession
equality **46,** 496, **62,** 602, **82,** 396-7, **91,** 307
customary international law, formation **41,** 140, **110,** 228, 476
development of international law and **41,** 140
general principle of international law **65,** 191, **82,** 396-7
Head of State immunity and **125,** 500
ICJ proceedings **97,** 37-8
Chamber **97,** 210
international organizations **105,** 21, 30, 65-6, 67
maritime delimitation **83,** 117-18
continental shelf **41,** 140, **81,** 274-5, 412, 414
equidistance **81,** 274-5
islands **95,** 665

States (*cont.*)
proportionality and **83,** 117-18
radial projection of coasts and **81,** 310
relevant factor **95,** 665-6
nations **50,** 412
nuclear weapons, deployment **110,** 472-3, 476-8, 526
Security Council veto **101,** 368-9
State agency, independence **107,** 379-80
State immunity and. *See* State immunity, execution/attachment, theory/doctrine, basis; State immunity, jurisdiction, theory/doctrine, basis, equality of States
surrender of sovereignty to international organization and **93,** 520, **101,** 368
taxation of international officials **36,** 459
to conduct foreign relations **93,** 497
UN and **44,** 375, 377, **65,** 191
establishment
change of entity's status **84,** 204-5
State succession and, Marshall Islands **84,** 204
termination of trusteeship **84,** 204-5
existence of, civil strife **48,** 6-8
extinction
nationality, effect on **72,** 439
State succession and **94,** 180
federal. *See* federal State
federation, members of, relations between **78,** 166-7
formation, *jus tractatus* and **83,** 26
genocide, victim of, whether **95,** 63-4
government official as **110,** 641-3, 653
governments
as **106,** 302, 308
distinguished **84,** 176
Head of State as. *See* Head of State, as State
independence. *See also* colonies, independence, accession to
legal and economic **46,** 463
military intervention and **44,** 337
State immunity and **64,** 31, 39, 49, 58, **65,** 34, **82,** 18, 102, 120, **86,** 514, **87,** 35, 55, **95,** 452, **103,** 310, **104,** 510, 570, 616, 623
strong foreign influence, Hungary after 1938 **44,** 332-42
international obligations towards, duty to respect **94,** 358, 359, 360
legal interests, non-material matters **37,** 83-8, 99, 100, 103-4, 166, 180-2, 265-6, 267, 425-6, 513-21, 573, 583, 585-6, 599-600
legal personality and **64,** 413, 571-2, 615-18, **87,** 653, **88,** 682-3
loss of territory, effect **74,** 563, 566
merger. *See also* State succession, merger of States
Bombay/Miraj **49,** 474
sovereignty of former ruler, effect on **53,** 571
obligations, respect for interests of third States **95,** 698
occupation, administrative, effect **78,** 186-7
organization, lack of **78,** 161
personal union **40,** 30, 32, 35
personality **51,** 11-24, **53,** 167-8, 172-3, **68,** 3-6
political subdivision of. *See* State agency/State-owned corporation/State entity, classification

powers and functions
jus missionis **80,** 123
jus tractatus **80,** 123
recognition. *See* recognition, State
relatio inter pares **77,** 625-6
relations between **55,** 510
religion **59,** 115
representation of **89,** 11-14
estoppel **89,** 12-13
power to determine **89,** 13
successor State **89,** 13
successor State, power to determine **89,** 13
waiver of legal requirement **89,** 11-14
rights and duties
annulment of contract **83,** 554
conclusion of contract with foreign corporation **83,** 552
distribution of decedent's estate **56,** 6-7, 11
enforcement of **57,** 582-3
international organization headquarters, acceptance/refusal **62,** 473
legal protection of **71,** 230, 255-7
pollution control **57,** 533-5
subrogation **69,** 4-6
territorial sovereignty **57,** 576
towards other States **56,** 212, **57,** 533-4
secession. *See* secession
security interests, competence to determine **57,** 428-9
status
right to determine **119,** 584-5, 594, 597
unilateral change **49,** 258
suspension of status as **91,** 313
'territory' distinguished **114,** 398
loss of territory, relevance **115,** 172-3
separate legal system, relevance **114,** 398
unitary **82,** 397
of United States, definition **101,** 483-4
unity principle **53,** 415-16
State administration, nationalization, whether **41,** 266-7, 269, 270-1, 273-9
State agency/State-owned corporation/State entity. *See also* State department; State enterprise; State responsibility
abuse of corporate form **79,** 565
agency or instrumentality of a foreign State. *See* United States of America (USA), agency or instrumentality of a foreign State
as agency of State **64,** 679-80, **65,** 69, 84-5, **79,** 568
alter ego theory **52,** 327-8, **63,** 54, 59, **64,** 64-7, 115-19, 133-4, 137-9, 147-9, **66,** 110, 114, 426, 448, 457, 507-12, 516, **71,** 694, **86,** 78 n. 2, **90,** 616, **103,** 508, 509-11, **107,** 249-51, 254. *See also* separate legal entity test *below*
applicable law **82,** 11, **87,** 244, **90,** 612-14, **114,** 564
international law **80,** 574, **90,** 612, **124,** 29
law of chartering State **90,** 612
law of State of creation **52,** 324, **65,** 81, 105-6, 300-1, **107,** 312
law of State of incorporation **80,** 573
lex fori **64,** 65-6, 138, **65,** 266-7, **80,** 573 n. 11, **90,** 612

States agency/State-owned corporation/State entity (*cont.*)
attribution of activities of other State entities **98,** 92
attribution of acts to government **86,** 449, 451-5
as 'citizen of a State' **63,** 443
classification as **63,** 90
AGIP, USA Inc. **63,** 18-21
agricultural cooperative **65,** 266-7
ambassador **65,** 307, **104,** 412, **115,** 613-14
armed forces **101,** 558-61, **107,** 311-17
air force **63,** 263, 266-7, 278
art museum **86,** 12
bank
acting at request of State **104,** 280-2
applicable law **87,** 244
controlled by State, performance of commercial banking operations as determining factor **82,** 92
evidence **87,** 252-3
Bosnian Croats, agents of Croatia, whether **108,** 155-8, **122,** 48-57, 245-7
British Rail International **63,** 5-12
central/State-owned bank. *See* central/State-owned bank, as State agency
Chilean Copper Corporation **65,** 59-60
City of London Corporation **63,** 46-8
city official **66,** 163-7
civil aeronautics board **64,** 665-6
commercial/trade representation/mission **48,** 148-50, **64,** 590-3, **65,** 210-11, 314-15, **82,** 102
community action agencies **63,** 104
Compania Anonima Venezolane de Navegación **63,** 416-19
compensation tribunal **66,** 266
Corporacion de Mercadeo Agricola (CMA) **64,** 677-82
Corporacion Venezolana de Fomento **63,** 301-4, 478-80
criteria. *See* separate legal entity test *below*
critical date for determining, date of action **98,** 143, **107,** 362
cultural agency **86,** 635-7
cultural institute **40,** 60-3, **65,** 325-8, **82,** 2-5, **86,** 635-7, **87,** 46, **114,** 538-9
treaty basis **82,** 4
development corporation **52,** 322-8
economic development agency **63,** 175, 302
electricity company **63,** 334
Eurocontrol **107,** 324-8
Eurofima **65,** 402-4
export association **63,** 90, 104, 175
food manufacturing enterprise **65,** 74-5
food supply agency **63,** 371, 376-7, 495-7, 569-72, **64,** 445-6, 447
foreign corporation, piercing the veil **63,** 233-5
'foreign State or political subdivision' **81,** 540, **84,** 597
distinguished **103,** 239-41, **107,** 311-17, 365, 377
'organ thereof' **107,** 375-8
foreign trade enterprise **63,** 205-8, **72,** 184, 186-7
Government Auditor **104,** 574-6, 605
government department **65,** 307
Ministry of Finance **87,** 415

separate legal entity distinguished **103,** 239-41
government information office **65,** 284-5
government news agency **113,** 458
government procurement agency **63,** 90, 104, 175
individual acting in official capacity **113,** 527-8
industrial development authority **63,** 616
insurance company **63,** 454, 456-7
international organization **107,** 414-15
Iranian Atomic Energy Organization (IAEO) **113,** 455
local government **63,** 368
merchant marine **63,** 532
military commander **66,** 148-9, 209-10, 219, 234
mining enterprise **63,** 90, 104, 134, 174-8, 230, 290, 292, 344, 449, 588, 617, **72,** 105, **73,** 234
Ministry of Defence Claims Commission (UK) **103,** 239-41, 242-3
mixed economy company under laws of Guinea **63,** 536
municipal highways authority **64,** 64-9
municipality **44,** 63-4
national airforce. *See* armed forces *above*
national airline **63,** 90, 104, 175, 195-6, 245-51, 344, 447, 448, 449, 469, **64,** 432, 433-4, 436, 447, 454, 474, **66,** 58-60, **77,** 511-13, **79,** 564-6, **86,** 16-17, 18, 573, **87,** 65-8, **98,** 44-6, 49-54, 71-2, **103,** 352-5
national airports authority **107,** 229, 230, 233
nationalized undertaking **65,** 295-303
official newspaper **98,** 84
oil corporation **47,** 138-49, **63,** 166-8, 233, 309, **103,** 427-500
Gulf Oil Corporation **66,** 548
Libyan National Oil Corporation **63,** 166-8, 233, 309
NIOC **47,** 139-49, **65,** 200, 202-3, 213, 218-24
Petroleos Mexicanos **66,** 149-50
organization created by treaty with sovereign State membership **107,** 324-8
permanent mission to international organization **63,** 125
police authority **65,** 198, 381-2
Pontificia Opera di Assistenza (POA) **65,** 334-5
preliminary matter **92,** 527
press agency **63,** 130-2, **64,** 445, 462-4
privatization/commercialization policy and **124,** 46
privatized company **107,** 662-6
public business entities/State commercial corporations distinguished **124,** 45-6
railway authority **47,** 241, 242, **65,** 42, 232, 355, 397-8
rebuttable presumption **124,** 29
Register of Shipping **92,** 512
Republika Srpska, armed forces, agents of Federal Republic of Yugoslavia (FRY), whether, **112,** 188-200
Securities and Exchange Commission (SEC) **64,** 48-51
shipping line **63,** 78, 90, 104, 175, 220-1, 256, 330-3, 356, 365, 416-19, 443, 495, 532, 606, 625, 639-40, **64,** 537-8, **65,** 69-70, 102-7, **69,** 617, **72,** 96-7, **81,** 540-1, **103,** 575-6
ship's master **63,** 626, 631, **65,** 258-60, **66,** 219
SIACONGO **67,** 372
SNTR (Algeria) **65,** 84-5
State controlled bank **106,** 278

State agency/State-owned corporation/State entity (*cont.*)
State corporation. *See also* state trading enterprise *below*
in process of privatization **103,** 575-6
State pension fund **65,** 71-3
State trading enterprise **64,** 201-2, **82,** 94, **103,** 563, **106,** 563. *See also* State trading enterprise
State-controlled bank **106,** 278-80
steel company **63,** 90, 174-8
subdivision of government **66,** 63-7
Taiwan **98,** 66
tourist office **65,** 62, 144, 434-5
tourist organization **63,** 320-2
transport organization **63,** 90, 104, 175
United States Information Service (USIS) **65,** 284-5
Vinexport **63,** 58-9
wholly owned commercial bank **107,** 263
wholly owned and controlled company **107,** 239-40, 362
workers' organization **63,** 103-4
'commercial activity' **63,** 588, 617
commercial transactions, engagement in **55,** 425, 427
constituent links **113,** 446-7
consulate, 'organ of a foreign State or political subdivision thereof' **101,** 482, 489
control as test of independent status **63,** 176, **69,** 623-5, **71,** 607-8, 615-20, 668-9, 691, 694-700, **72,** 241, 251-2, 719, 734, **80,** 384-8, **82,** 92, **98,** 53, **107,** 376. *See also* State responsibility, imputability, effective/de facto control test
49% share **107,** 663-6
97% share **63,** 19, 20
appointment of managers **113,** 486
appointment of managers by government of predecessor State **107,** 666
'controlled entity' **71,** 695-7, **78,** 665
evidence of **103,** 511-12, **112,** 189-200, 268-76, **122,** 48-57, 245-7
ship's certificate **107,** 662
counterclaim against **66,** 407-12, 427-33, 456-9, 510-12
critical date, change of status after cause of action or institution of legal proceedings **98,** 143, **107,** 362
debts
liability for each other's **82,** 94, **98,** 54
liability for State, independent personality and **82,** 92
designation of company as a constituent subdivision of the State **114,** 160
'employee'/'official' distinguished **124,** 59-60
evidence of. *See* evidence of, State agency/State-owned corporation/State entity status
expropriation/nationalization **59,** 378-83
force majeure, government intervention as, right to rely on **64,** 201-2, 205-7
frustration, government intervention as, right to rely on **64,** 250-4, 377-9
as government department **63,** 49-52, 213, **64,** 201-2, 436-7, 446, 464, 467-8, 473, 681-2, **89,** 36, **98,** 16, 23, **103,** 239-1
'interventors' **66,** 218, 233, 235
jurisdiction over **63,** 42, 50, 302-4, 334-7, 541-6, 624-38, 647-54
legal standing. *See* separate legal entity test *below*
liability for
acts of Government **66,** 506-12, **80,** 572, 576, 578
each other's debts **82,** 94

obligations of controlling body **107,** 248-9
obligations of State **106,** 278-80
local subsidiary of, jurisdiction over **63,** 647-54
as organ of State **64,** 681-2
separate legal entity test **47,** 138-49, **63,** 90, 103, 130, 167, 625, **64,** 208, **65,** 59, 69, 81, 85, 96-7, 106-7, 134, 138, 202-3, 213, 219-24, 227, 229, 232, 296-301, 355, 397-8, 402-3, 422-3, 427, 429-30, 434-5, **77,** 519, 527, **79,** 564-6, 595, **80,** 570-2, 575-8, **82,** 11-13, 94, **86,** 484, **87,** 104-5, **90,** 611-16, **94,** 182-3, **101,** 546-9, **103,** 352, 368, 400, **107,** 312, 316-17, 375-6, 379-80, **113,** 455, 458, 486. *See also alter ego* theory *above*
broad interpretation **107,** 375
burden of proof **80,** 577, **101,** 547, **103,** 496-500, 510
characteristics **80,** 575-6
commercial autonomy **64,** 201-2, 208, 379
control. *See* control as test of independent status *above*
discretionary power **87,** 242, 253-4
financial autonomy **80,** 575, **87,** 242, 254
destination of profits **103,** 509-10
funding **64,** 174, **103,** 509-10, **113,** 455, 459
fraud or injustice **98,** 54
legal standing **86,** 9, 13, **94,** 182-3
retroactive **94,** 182
lifting the veil **65,** 422-3
nature of functions **64,** 66, **80,** 580 n. 27, **87,** 242, 244-6, 251-2, 253, **124,** 30-3, 47-8
'organization of the State' **64,** 201, 207-8
ownership **98,** 53, 54, **124,** 31
majority ownership **63,** 167, 174-6, 302, 334, 437, **81,** 540, **84,** 111, **88,** 82, **98,** 53, 120-2, 132, **103,** 509-10, **107,** 375, 376-8
ownership of assets **87,** 242, 243, 254
piercing the corporate veil **79,** 595, **80,** 574, 578, **124,** 29
presumption of **98,** 53-4, 91-2, **101,** 546, 553, **103,** 496, 510, **107,** 252, 379-80
comity **107,** 379-80
equality of States **107,** 379-80
general principle of international law **107,** 379-80
sovereignty **107,** 379-80
principal activity governed by private law **77,** 527
property ownership system as determinant **63,** 104
property, powers to hold and sell property **80,** 575
public service purpose **113,** 486
recognition
burden of proof **79,** 566
comity and **80,** 576
right to sue/be sued **64,** 66, **80,** 575, **107,** 312
structure **64,** 66, **124,** 45-6
trade representation (USSR) **64,** 590-2
service of process on **63,** 60-2, 254, 356-7
sovereign authority **66,** 218-19
as State entity **72,** 241, 251-2, 719, 734
State gendarmerie **84,** 597-9, 602-5
purchase of housing for **84,** 603

State agency/State-owned corporation/State entity (*cont.*)
State immunity, execution/attachment. *See* State immunity, execution/attachment, entitlement, State agency/State-owned corporation
State responsibility distinguished **63,** 59
successor, liability **103,** 564, 567-8
unrecognized government, of **86,** 13
right to sue **94,** 204, 206-9
warship. *See* warship
State aids EEC Treaty provisions **48,** 212-13
State contract. *See also* concession agreement; cooperation agreement; economic development agreement; joint exploitation agreement; stabilization clause
abrogation **56,** 273
act of public power, whether **82,** 95
arbitration clause, relevance **82,** 95
administrative contract **53,** 463-8
civil contract distinguished **53,** 467-8
nationalization, effects on **53,** 477-9
principles **53,** 324
stabilization clause, effect **53,** 465-7
alteration **62,** 154, 159, 191. *See also* variation agreement *below*
contrarius consensus 191.
stabilization clause **62,** 159, 164, 170
unilateral **62,** 147, 191
for aluminium exploitation **56,** 262, 276-7
amendment **53,** 423-4
annulment **83,** 554
grounds
illegality under municipal law **106,** 608
misrepresentation **106,** 616-19
applicable law **41,** 455, **53,** 441-50, **56,** 271, **62,** 171-6, 201, 217, **86,** 457, **89,** 460-1, 463, 465, 494, 503
choice of law. *See* choice of law clause *below*
common principles **62,** 168, 172-5, 191, 198-9, 201-9, 217
customary international law **95,** 207
EEC Draft Convention on State contract (1972) **53,** 445
general principles **53,** 452-3, **56,** 283, **62,** 172-6, 199, 209-18
law of the parties **62,** 196
municipal law of State party **53,** 460-1, **65,** 264, **89,** 461, 463, **95,** 207
conflict with **96,** 265-6
subsequent legislation **96,** 265-6
parties' right to choose **53,** 460-1, **62,** 178, 190, 196
private international law **62,** 169
public international law **53,** 448-50, **62,** 170-3, **89,** 463, **117,** 560-1
stabilization clause, effect **53,** 455-7
approval, need for **106,** 620-3, 667
arbitral award relating to, enforcement **82,** 92
autonomy of parties **53,** 442, 445, **62,** 173, 190, 196, 217
award, enforceability **74,** 561-9
binding nature **56,** 282, **62,** 173, 190-2, 196-7, 217, **89,** 466, **125,** 154-5
pacta sunt servanda **89,** 496
breach **56,** 271, 315, **67,** 335-41, 367-74, **72,** 156, 175, 184, 240-7, 726, **89,** 333-5, 340

applicable law **56,** 271
determination of, remedies distinguished **53,** 346
effect **53,** 325
continuity **53,** 363, 365
on innocent party **53,** 346
nationalization as **53,** 325, 329, **62,** 147, 181-2, 187, 196-7, 203-7, 217, **66,** 583, 590-1, 626-7, **67,** 337-8
public policy as defence **83,** 562
fair compensation sole remedy **83,** 562
restitutio in integrum **53,** 330-7, 338-42, 345-8, 349-53, 495-509
revocation of licence as. *See* revocation *below*
specific performance **53,** 335
categorization, relevance **83,** 559
change of government, fundamental change of circumstance, whether **96,** 67
choice of law clause **53,** 441-50, 451-2, 454, **62,** 169, 171-5, 190, 200, **117,** 559-60. *See also* applicable law *above*
applicable law **53,** 443
binding nature **53,** 443-4
compliance, duty of **89,** 335-7
conditions, retroactive **89,** 470-1
contractual equilibrium **66,** 588, 590-1, 626-7
definition **53,** 438-41, **56,** 274-5, **117,** 560
'delocalization' **56,** 275. *See also* 'internationalization' *below*
'denationalization' **106,** 430
dispute relating to
interpretation **62,** 176, 179
performance **62,** 176, 179
duty to respect **83,** 561, **101,** 557-61
enforcement **62,** 171
equality of parties **62,** 171
equity and **59,** 422-3
estoppel **89,** 401, **117,** 562-3
failure to raise legality issue **117,** 562
part performance **117,** 563
executive necessity **74,** 223-7
expropriation/nationalization **53,** 470, 477
administrative contract, effect on **53,** 477-9
as breach **53,** 325, 329, **62,** 147, 181-2, 187, 196-7, 203-7, 217, **66,** 583, 590-1, 626-7, **67,** 337-8
revocation, whether **89,** 468
financial guarantees **67,** 326-7, 329-30, 333-4, 361, 369, **72,** 174-7, **74,** 221-7
force majeure **63,** 166, **72,** 175-7
foreign and national parties on same basis **83,** 562
frustrated contract legislation, applicability **75,** 372-80
frustration **62,** 213, **72,** 243-7, 249-51
good faith **83,** 554, 559
governing law. *See* applicable law *above*
Institute of International Law, Provisional Report on Agreements between a State and a Foreign Private Person **53,** 443
intangibility clause. *See* stabilization clause
'internationalization' **53,** 446-50, 452-7. *See also* 'delocalization' *above*
agreement to arbitrate, effect **53,** 454-5

State contract (*cont.*)
meaning and scope **53,** 457-61
interpretation, parties' conduct **89,** 645
investment
amount **89,** 487, **95,** 205-6
time-limit **95,** 206
application to project **95,** 22
burden of proof **89,** 489-90, 542
calculation **89,** 488-92, 541-5
capital basis, change to **95,** 205-6
foreign currency denominated
building materials **95,** 224-6
evidence of **95,** 224
travel and communication expenses **95,** 224
in kind
forfeiture **95,** 226
registration, need for **95,** 226
loan as **89,** 485-6, 489
local currency, in, source of funds, relevance **95,** 227
nationality and **89,** 484-5, 542-3
period **89,** 487-8
letters of credit **72,** 174-7, 184-5, 241, 726
liability for debts, State agency with independent personality **82,** 92
mineral concession and **59,** 425
ministerial consent for shutdown of operations **74,** 234-7
municipal law and **56,** 271
parliamentary privilege **53,** 446, **56,** 271
nationalization. *See* expropriation/nationalization *above*
nature of **89,** 494
contract, whether **89,** 334, 459-69, 496-7
unilateral administrative act **89,** 460, 466, 468, 496
non-performance **62,** 198, 201
non-tangibility clause **96,** 266
pari passu clause, function **59,** 539
parties
applicable law and **53,** 460-1, **62,** 178, 190, 196
intention **62,** 171, 178-9
Ministry of Finance as State **87,** 415
obligations **56,** 265, **62,** 170, 178-9, 181-2, 196-7, 211, 217
rights **62,** 159, 170, 179
status and capacity **53,** 458-60
private contract distinguished **89,** 334
private law nature of **62,** 169, **65,** 267
production levy, effect **74,** 220-2, 227-37
proper law. *See also* applicable law *above*
definition **62,** 171
relevant/special circumstances **62,** 193
renegotiation **56,** 265
renegotiation clause **83,** 559-60
repudiation. *See* revocation *below*
revocation **66,** 292, 343-6, 583, 592-3, 624-5, **74,** 561-2, **82,** 79, **89,** 467-514, 516-17, 599-623

arbitration clause, effect on **62,** 178
breach, for **89,** 333-5, 340, 467
automaticity **89,** 340
compensation for **89,** 468-9, 498-511
damages for, entitlement
bad faith and **89,** 610
'tainted background' **89,** 602-3, 610, 622, 623
justification **89,** 469, 475-93, 538-9, 546
bad faith of private party **89,** 613
estoppel **89,** 482
insufficiency of investment **89,** 483-93, 541-7
non-fulfilment of obligations. *See* non-fulfilment of obligations *below*
public interest **89,** 468, 479, 494, 503
waiver **89,** 482
misrepresentation, estoppel **95,** 205-6
nationalization, whether **89,** 468
non-discrimination and **92,** 438-9
non-fulfilment of obligations **89,** 468, 479-80, 488
assignment of interest **89,** 476-83
remedied **89,** 482-3
notice, need for **89,** 333-5, 340, 370-475, 483, 494, 536-7, 546
procedure **89,** 467-9, 470-5
applicable law **89,** 469
rectification, possibility of **89,** 602
State responsibility and **89,** 457, 493-8
unilateral **62,** 147, 181, 191
unlawful
international law, under **89,** 613-16
municipal law, under **89,** 613-16
procedural irregularities **89,** 661-3
right to conclude **62,** 190
sanctity **62,** 170, 190-3
sovereignty and **53,** 439, **56,** 272, 273
State immunity **82,** 64-5
State responsibility and **83,** 554, **89,** 493-8
contract concluded on behalf of State **117,** 562
international law, under **89,** 495-8
municipal law, under **89,** 493-5
State succession
executed contract **96,** 65
executory contract **96,** 65
status regarding contract concluded by State-controlled entity **83,** 556-7, 562
supply **82,** 64
tax concessions **74,** 220-32
termination. *See* revocation above
treaties compared **53,** 447-9, 474
treaty distinguished **83,** 561-2
validity
parties' conduct **95,** 206
right to conclude **62,** 190, **83,** 552
ultra vires **56,** 282
variation agreement. *See also* alteration *above*

State contract (*cont.*)
duress, effect on validity **66,** 569-71, 615-16
quid pro quo, failure of **66,** 568-9, 616-20
status **66,** 566-9, 615-20
voluntary nature **59,** 428
state of emergency. *See also* emergency legislation
determination of **54,** 539
effective remedy and **96,** 412
fair trial **70,** 242-8
independent and impartial tribunal **96,** 400-1, 403
International Covenant on Civil and Political Rights (ICCPR) (1966), derogations **62,** 267, 269-70, **78,** 31-2
State succession and **96,** 66
State enterprise. *See* State agency/State-owned corporation/State entity
State entity. *See* State agency/State-owned corporation/State entity
State immunity.[x] *See* act of State; consular immunity, jurisdiction; consular privileges and immunities; diplomatic premises; diplomatic privileges and immunities; embassy or consular bank account/funds, immunity, execution/attachment; European Convention on State Immunity (and Protocol)(Basle) (1972); foreign State, proceedings involving; Head of State, immunity; Head of State, immunity, jurisdiction; international organizations,

[x] With the restrictive doctrine now long established, it seems inappropriate to continue to index material under the subheadings 'absolute' and 'restrictive' immunity, not least as the entries under these headings have tended to duplicate one another as the court recapitulates the history of sovereign/State immunity. Current *ILR* indexing practice, applied retroactively as far as practicable, is to ascribe such material to 'development of concept' and to retain the 'absolute'/'restrictive' headings only on occasions, such as the unexpected application of one or other principle, where the treatment in the text seems to demand it. A similar change has been made in respect of such concepts as '*acta jure gestionis*'/'*acta jure imperii*' where the appearance of one has almost invariably been accompanied by the appearance of the other, and where the assiduous inclusion in the index of all uses of these terms has led to excessively long strings of page references. It is now the practice (again applied retrospectively so far as is practicable) to index such material under the neutral 'classification of act' or 'purpose/use of funds/assets'.

Material relating to State immunity is indexed principally, loosely categorized, under the following main headings. It is also indexed, where relevant, in parallel entries under individual countries, and, where appropriate, as a subheading to other main heading:

State immunity, arbitral award, enforcement
State immunity, headings: execution/attachment, applicability
State immunity, execution/attachment, entitlement
State immunity, execution/attachment, procedural aspects
State immunity, execution/attachment, purpose of proceedings
State immunity, execution/attachment, purpose/use of funds/assets
State immunity, execution/attachment, theory/doctrine
State immunity, execution/attachment, waiver
State immunity, jurisdiction, acts of
State immunity, jurisdiction, classification of act
State immunity, jurisdiction, entitlement
State immunity, jurisdiction, procedural aspects
State immunity, jurisdiction, theory/doctrine
State immunity, jurisdiction, waiver.

Reference should also be made to: act of State; consular immunity, jurisdiction; consular privileges and immunities; diplomatic premises; diplomatic privileges and immunities; embassy or consular bank account/funds, immunity, execution/attachment; foreign State, proceedings involving; Head of State, immunity; Head of State, immunity, jurisdiction; international organizations, privileges and immunities; service of process on foreign State or State agency; ships, State-owned.

privileges and immunities; service of process on foreign State or State agency; ships, State-owned
State immunity, arbitral award, enforcement 62, 220-5, 229-36, **65,** 48-50, 52-3, 76-7, 79-80, 89-92, 170-1, 233, 364, **77,** 14, **89,** 358, **103,** 561-71, **113,** 445
exequatur proceedings **65,** 48, 52-3, 357-64, **113,** 445
compromise agreement and **65,** 364
New York Convention on the Recognition and Enforcement of Foreign Arbitral Awards (1958), State immunity, jurisdiction. *See* New York Convention on the Recognition and Enforcement of Foreign Arbitral Awards (1958), State immunity, jurisdiction
voluntary submission to and recognition of binding force distinguished **77,** 522-3
waiver
agreement for recognition and enforcement of arbitral awards **103,** 577-80
consent to ICSID jurisdiction **89,** 358-9, **106,** 521-2, **113,** 443-4
waiver of right to **113,** 443-4
State immunity, execution/attachment, Iraqi petroleum exports, immunity from attachment or other legal action **109,** 581
State immunity, execution/attachment, applicability. *See also* State immunity, execution/attachment, purpose/use of funds/assets
bankruptcy/winding-up proceedings **65,** 84-5
effect on performance of diplomatic functions **94,** 368-9
as infringement of sovereignty **94,** 368-9
default judgment **64,** 70-6, **92,** 425-6
failure to comply with requirements for service **118,** 615-18
comity and **118,** 616
right to raise jurisdictional immunity **64,** 73-4, **92,** 425-6
funds held by Tripartite Commission for the Restitution of Monetary Gold (1946) **63,** 71-3
funds held in private foreign bank **47,** 157-63, **65,** 168-71, 218-46, **94,** 368-9
funds of nationalized bank held by central/State-owned bank **63,** 1-4
garnishee order on earnings of embassy employee **65,** 21-2
property in hands of State bailee **64,** 440-1, 464-6, **104,** 569
property in possession or control of foreign State **64,** 680-1
ships. *See* ships, State-owned, immunity, arrest/attachment
State-owned ship. *See* ships, State-owned, immunity, arrest/attachment
State immunity, execution/attachment, entitlement
commercial/trade representation/mission **65,** 210-11
national airline **77,** 511-13, **86,** 573, **87,** 65-8
recognition of State/government, relevance **52,** 310-14, **65,** 56
State agency/State-owned corporation/State entity **63,** 309-10, **64,** 222-5, 680, 681-2, **65,** 59-60, 80-2, 84-5, 95-9, 134-6, 210-11, 214, 218-45, 271, 414, 429, 432-5, 436-8, **72,** 121-3, 174, 182, 184-6, 189, **77,** 512-13, **86,** 79, **113,** 486-7
as open question **65,** 422-3
public purpose, need for **87,** 66
subrogation and **65,** 71-3
State immunity, execution/attachment, procedural aspects
applicable law
lex fori, State practice **65,** 116
purpose/use of funds/assets. *See* State immunity, execution/attachment, purpose/use of funds/assets
authorization of court, need for **65,** 89-90
blocking/freezing as attachment **63,** 427-9, 505, **81,** 646
competence to determine **65,** 271-2

State immunity, execution/attachment, procedural aspects (*cont.*)
connection between property and claim, need for **65,** 174, 177, 242-3, **79,** 566
connection with judgment debt **79,** 566
property 'on which claim based' requirement **79,** 566-9
economic position of State, relevance **65,** 153, 157, 158, 191, 221, 223
effective remedy, right to and **79,** 570, **113,** 414-18, 426, 427-9
enforcement of judgments, European Court of Human Rights **79,** 569
payment by forum State of debt **104,** 405
remedies, diplomatic protection **79,** 570 n. 4
executive/ministerial authorization, need for **65,** 167, 169, 172, 247-8, 250-1, 252-3, 256, 271-3, 293, 428, **87,** 34, 66-8
exequatur **65,** 52-3, **106,** 277-82, **113,** 445
applicability to **106,** 277-8
as jurisdictional measure **65,** 90-1, **106,** 278-9
safeguarding/conservatory measures **65,** 26
pre- and post-judgment distinguished **63,** 270, 309-10, 347-50, 417-18, **92,** 402-3, **101,** 401
presumption in favour of **77,** 493-4, 525
procedural irregularity **48,** 150
procedure, merits and jurisdiction distinguished **87,** 415, 416
separation of powers and **65,** 56, **87,** 61, 68
State immunity, execution/attachment, purpose of proceedings
conservatory measures. *See* safeguarding/conservatory measures *below*
debt recovery **82,** 39-45
debt repayment from blocked account **63,** 425-35
enforcement of judgment **62,** 234, **63,** 25-35
tort judgment **79,** 563
interim measures. *See* safeguarding/conservatory measures *below*; Mareva injunction
jurisdictional **63,** 347-50. *See also* attachment, jurisdiction, as basis for
distinguished **63,** 349-50, 500 n. 4, **92,** 404
employment contract, mercenary in Congolese army **64,** 668-72
payment of costs **65,** 413-16
preventive measures. *See* safeguarding/conservatory measures *below*
safeguarding/conservatory measures **65,** 27-8, 79-82, 90-2, 96-8, 101, 133-7, 138-9, 165, 167-8, 171-2, 177-83, 250-2, 256, 376, 391, 405-7, **77,** 492-3, 515-25, **89,** 33-6, **101,** 401
Alcom case **77,** 493-4
customary international law and **65,** 167-8, 228-9, 239-45, 252-3
injunction **63,** 457
Iranian assets in USA **63,** 500-11
likelihood of compliance with judgment and **65,** 376
likely outcome of eventual judgment and **77,** 512
as measure of constraint and legal violence **65,** 77, 252
as measure of execution, Hague Conventions (1899/1907) **65,** 406
preliminary ruling on **77,** 534
security for costs **65,** 405-7, **103,** 550-1
State-owned ship. *See* State-owned ship, safeguarding/conservatory measures
State immunity, execution/attachment, purpose/use of funds/assets 47, 142, 148, 157-63, **50,** 146, **65,** 92, 176, **77,** 518-19, **87,** 60-2, **89,** 35-6, **113,** 420-2, 425-6, 444
acquisition and use distinguished **98,** 9-12
acta jure imperii concept, relevance **65,** 405
administrative assets **65,** 232, 397, 402, 435
aircraft used for commercial purposes **77,** 511-13, **87,** 68

applicable law **65,** 118
  lex fori **65,** 72-3, 116, 184-5, 188-9, 219-20, 243-4, **113,** 425-6
  Vienna Convention on Diplomatic Relations (1961) **106,** 296-7
assets held 'in the name of and on behalf of the State, its ministries . . . or State entities' **65,** 434-5
blocked assets **63,** 427-9
burden of proof **87,** 36, **89,** 36, **98,** 12, **102,** 206-7, **106,** 290-1, **113,** 428
cash **87,** 31
commercial activity **72,** 107, 658-60, **74,** 174-9, 184-8, **77,** 518, 527, 533
construction of nuclear reactor/enrichment of uranium **77,** 515-22, **113,** 455-6
consular premises **107,** 239-42, 642-58, **113,** 423
contract governed by private law, relevance **113,** 456
contractual provision, relevance **89,** 35-6
critical date **65,** 393
cultural and educational centre for foreign workers **82,** 39-45
cultural institute **86,** 573
debt **82,** 41, 72-3
determination of, appointment of expert **65,** 60, 81-2, 97
diplomatic functions **77,** 492-4
diplomatic mission, expenses **63,** 526-7, **65,** 76-7, 151-9, 185-91, 226-7, 236
diplomatic premises **65,** 111-14, 251-5, **98,** 4, 9, 11-13, **113,** 423
  immovable property exception, whether **98,** 49
  residential **102,** 206-8
duty/right to examine **65,** 60, 81-2, **77,** 516, 525
evidence of
  diplomatic note **102,** 206, 207, **106,** 290-1
  reasonableness of holdings for declared purpose **106,** 290-1, 292
film depicting Head of State **65,** 28
foreign exchange reserves **63,** 16-17, **64,** 146, **82,** 35-6
future transfer to central bank for financing of State budget **65,** 218-24, 229-39, 243-6
future use, relevance **65,** 135, 176-7, 221, 376
governmental purpose. *See* sovereign purpose *below*
ILC Draft Articles on Jurisdictional Immunities of States and Their Property (1991) **113,** 420
impairment of functions test **65,** 112
military activity, property for use in **63,** 265, 280-2
  under control of military authority **63,** 268, 272-3, 280
mixed **52,** 336, **63,** 524-7, **65,** 72-3, 85, 219-20, **86,** 570, **87,** 36
national airline **82,** 72-3, **86,** 573
nature of property **77,** 518
nexus, need for. *See* connection between claim and property *above*
non-specific **65,** 92, 97, 118-19, 189-90, 392, **87,** 61
other than diplomatic or consular **65,** 190-1, 493, **113,** 425-6
ownership and power of disposal, designation of account as determining factor **65,** 228-9
ownership as test **65,** 220, **72,** 107, **77,** 520
patrimonial assets (*patrimoine privé*) **65,** 232, 250, 402, 414-15, 435
pension funds **65,** 72-3, 233-4
private **65,** 182, 183, **82,** 35, 36
  diplomatic service **82,** 41
  promissory note, IBRD **82,** 36
private assets, protection dependent on reciprocity **101,** 402-5

State immunity, execution/attachment, purpose/use of funds/assets (*cont.*)
private or commercial purpose **65,** 119
promotion of image of Head of State **65,** 28
property exclusively intended for industrial or commercial activity giving rise to proceedings **65,** 184, **113,** 420-1, 426, 456
guarantee for repayment of loan **113,** 457
specific allocation of funds, need for **77,** 516, 517-20, **113,** 457
public activities of embassy **87,** 62, **94,** 359-60
public purpose **65,** 219-23, 226-9, 242-5, 250, 376, 392, 402-4, 415, 427, 430, 435. *See also* sovereign purpose *below*
money held on behalf of government for payment to mercenaries **64,** 670-1
sovereign purpose distinguished **82,** 42
State pension fund **65,** 71-3
public services **65,** 81-2
purchase of arms **65,** 391-2
railway equipment **82,** 44
relevance **65,** 376
running of State's offices in forum State **65,** 115-19
shares **65,** 402-4, 414-15
shipping fees **89,** 359-60
sovereign purpose **65,** 184, **82,** 34-5, **87,** 62, 66, **113,** 419-20, 423. *See also* embassy or consular bank account/funds
central bank funds **82,** 35-6
designation as, need for **82,** 35, 36, 52
embassy bank account. *See* embassy or consular bank account/funds
State practice **82,** 44
staff salaries **87,** 36
State practice **101,** 402
inconsistent practice **113,** 420
State immunity, execution/attachment, theory/doctrine
absolute doctrine, effective reintroduction
designation of use/purpose by State **77,** 520
overuse of foreign affairs considerations **101,** 404
act of State and **77,** 521, **89,** 359 n. 11
basis **106,** 277
enforcement of awards/judgments against foreign State **87,** 60
equality of States **65,** 452
foreign relations considerations **65,** 252
international courtesy **65,** 56, 76-7, 80, 171, 174
international public order/public policy/*ordre public* **65,** 393, **113,** 444
respect for sovereign independence **65,** 419, **77,** 519
treaty, Vienna Convention on Diplomatic Relations (1961) **102,** 208
customary international law **74,** 180-2, **78,** 116, **87,** 62, 65, **94,** 358-9, 369
bankruptcy proceedings **94,** 369
Basle Agreement (1977) **78,** 116
development of concept **42,** 20, **63,** 430-1, **64,** 224-5, 226, 684, **65,** 116-17, 135, 150, 152-6, 164, 166-78, 181-5, 218-24, 226-45, 250, 391-2, 398-9, 402, 414-15, 419-22, 428, 430-2, 435, 449, **74,** 180-1, 517-19, **77,** 511-13, **87,** 34, 65-8, **101,** 401, **106,** 290-1, **113,** 422
Asia–African Legal Consultative Committee Report (1960) **65,** 181
German International Law Association and **65,** 155, 182-3, 190
Harvard Law School Study Report (1932) **65,** 182, 187

ILA Draft Articles on State Immunity (1982) **65,** 237-8, 245, **79,** 569
Institut de Droit International **45,** 78, 182, 391
teachings of publicists **65,** 238-9
uncertainty as to limits of restrictive theory **87,** 59-60, 66, 67
freezing/blocking of assets as negation of **63,** 504-9
human rights and **101,** 404-5
reciprocity, need for **65,** 271-3, 293, **86,** 511, 516, **87,** 34, 61, 67, **101,** 401-5
restrictive theory, bilateral treaties and **65,** 179-80
State immunity, jurisdiction
dependence on **64,** 223, **65,** 135, 430-1
distinguished **52,** 311-15, **63,** 60, 266 n. 13, 500 n. 4, **64,** 74, **65,** 49, 52-4, 97, 103, 116-17, 154, 164-6, 233, 250-1, 391-2, 420-1, **79,** 569-70, **99,** 143
State immunity, execution as bar to jurisdiction, whether **107,** 642-58
State practice **65,** 3-7, 116-17, 213-14, **77,** 492-3
Anglo-Saxon jurisdictions **113,** 421, 428-9
civil law jurisdictions **113,** 421
treaty provision **63,** 510, **65,** 177-81, 211, 430-2, **86,** 511, 516
absence of **65,** 28, 104, 116, 227, 430-1
bilateral treaties **65,** 179-80
Brussels Convention on Immunity of State-owned Ships (1926) **42,** 129, 187-8, **64,** 103, 104-5, 108-9, 232-3, 312, 313, **65,** 165, 177, 293-4
European Convention on State Immunity (and Protocol) (Basle) (1972) **65,** 155, 178-9, 422-3, 430-1
Geneva Convention on the High Seas (1958) **65,** 177-8
Geneva Convention on the Territorial Sea (1958) **65,** 177-8
usages and practices of international law **86,** 511, 516
wartime emergency powers **65,** 169, 428
State immunity, execution/attachment, waiver 63, 309-10, 347-50, **65,** 49, 52-4, 119, 174, 190, 230-1, 239-40, **72,** 121-3, 174, 182, 184-90, **87,** 416
acceptance of ICC Rules of Arbitration as **63,** 566, 635, **65,** 59-60, 96-8, **77,** 522-4
arbitration clause/agreement as **65,** 52-3, 98
express provision **63,** 526, **96,** 292, 294
Canadian State Immunity Act 1982 and **65,** 230-1
consent to ICSID jurisdiction as **106,** 521-2, **113,** 443-4
European Convention on State Immunity (and Protocol) (Basle) (1972) **65,** 178, 431
express/clear and unequivocal communication, need for **65,** 77, 160, **72,** 121-3, 188-90, **77,** 5-6, 522, **92,** 403-5
forum selection clause as **65,** 119
lease, failure to notify status when signing as **106,** 295-6
post-/pre-judgment attachment distinguished **63,** 309-10, **92,** 402
State agency/State-owned corporation/State entity
'and its agencies', entity distinguished **98,** 52-4
waiver by State **107,** 240
treaty provision **63,** 267-8, 269-72, 280-2, 347, 429-30, 433-4, 510, 514-19, **65,** 181
express provision, need for **63,** 270-2, 430, 503
Iran–US Treaty of Amity (1955) **63,** 503, 516
waiver of immunity, jurisdiction and **65,** 49, 52-4, 97, 251, **72,** 664-5, **75,** 522, **77,** 3-7, 522, 524, **87,** 415, 416, **92,** 404
State immunity, jurisdiction, acts of
agent **64,** 115, 658
private person acting as **113,** 514-15
outside scope of authority **113,** 514

State immunity, jurisdiction, acts of (*cont.*)
armed forces, tort, shooting by British soldier in Republic of Ireland **103,** 312-15, **121,** 201-2, **123,** 76-93
armed forces abroad **52,** 334-5, **85,** 157-8, 164, 169, 534-5, **102,** 140-2, **104,** 696-704. *See also* armed forces, acts concerning *below*; State responsibility for acts and omissions of, armed forces
as agents of sending State **52,** 334
personal liability **64,** 656-7, 659-60
applicable law, customary international law **100,** 455-7, 461-3
common law **119,** 371, 373, 374-5, 380, 381-2
judicial decision **86,** 538
military legal organs **86,** 538
receiving State **86,** 534
sending State **86,** 534
shooting by British soldier in Republic of Ireland **103,** 312-15, **121,** 201-2, **123,** 76-93
termination of logging licence for security reasons **64,** 655-61
tort **104,** 696-704
waiver, effect on concurrent jurisdiction **86,** 534
while on duty **42,** 135-6, 137-8
withdrawal of **86,** 534
commercial/trade representation/mission **82,** 116-18
customs officers **86,** 643, 644-6, 651
diplomatic agent **78,** 103, **82,** 117
ambassador/head of mission **99,** 133-4, **104,** 412
Vienna Convention on Diplomatic Relations (1961), effect on previous jurisprudence **82,** 117
general in successful revolutionary forces, *Underhill* v. *Hernandez* **119,** 82
local government **63,** 46-8, 368
official
in official capacity **101,** 501-2, 504, **103,** 523-5, **104,** 175
outside scope of authority **57,** 157-8, **104,** 123-5, 175-6
police officer providing judicial assistance under bilateral treaty **65,** 195, 197-8
State agency/State-owned corporation/State entity. *See* State immunity, jurisdiction, entitlement, State agency/State-owned corporation/State entity
State immunity, jurisdiction, applicability
admiralty actions, foreign ships. *See* admiralty jurisdiction; ships, State-owned
arbitral proceedings **53,** 308-9, 433-4, **65,** 449, 451-3
constitutional rights, infringement, general principle of international law **103,** 316-17
counterclaim arising out of the same subject matter **63,** 311-17, **66,** 242, 243, **94,** 152 n. 2
counterclaim anticipating main suit distinguished **92,** 396
cross-claim distinguished **98,** 17, 20-1
extension of waiver to **120,** 432-40, 442-6, 457-9
criminal proceedings **98,** 153, **119,** 58, **124,** 433-4
civil jurisdiction distinguished **86,** 643, **119,** 205, 208, 217-18, 222, 226, 234-6, 239, **123,** 42, 45-52
disclosure of documents **43,** 260-4, 269, 326-7, 335, 415, 422, **64,** 280-5, 287-94, 298-306, **84,** 173, **98,** 108, **99,** 162, **102,** 233-8, **103,** 319-21, **104,** 536-40, 556-8, 606, 611-25, **107,** 251-3, 254
confidentiality of financial information **104,** 556-7
proportionality **104,** 580, 621-2

tax haven **104,** 536-40, 556-8, 606, 611-25
waiver **103,** 321
evidence, giving of **65,** 161, **91,** 408
judicial discretion **104,** 539, 561, 586
Iran–US Claims Tribunal. *See* Iran–US Claims Tribunal, State immunity, jurisdiction
negligent deployment of military aircraft **88,** 59-60
in own courts **63,** 548, **80,** 591, **81,** 114-15, 119-20, 130, 136-8, **88,** 57-9, 711, **92,** 536, **101,** 560, **107,** 355, 356-7
acts committed abroad **80,** 22 n. 7
for acts of officials/public servants **80,** 23, **81,** 137-8
intentional tort **125,** 150-63
combatant activities in time of war **80,** 22 n. 7
discretionary acts by officials **80,** 22 n. 7
foreign State immunity distinguished **64,** 423-4, **125,** 157-9
good faith **90,** 540-1, 542
intentional tort, protection and security of protection and **125,** 150-63
national security questions **88,** 58-9
native title, protection and **112,** 549
negligent failure to warn civilian aircraft **88,** 59-60
rationale **125,** 159-60
State practice **125,** 160-1
Vienna Convention on Consular Relations (1963) **118,** 54, 55
prize proceedings **79,** 6, 11
property, dispute relating to **64,** 119, **77,** 157-8, **104,** 575, 612, 621, **111,** 651-2. *See also* real/immovable/property, dispute relating to *below*
contract debt/chose in action **64,** 77-80
damage or loss of tangible property caused by act or omission in forum State **103,** 375-6, **111,** 664
industrial or intellectual property **104,** 612
possession or control of property and **64,** 440-1
property for private purpose **64,** 88
property for public use **42,** 128-34, **55,** 419-23
property seized following illegal annexation **125,** 656-7, 678, 741-2
real/immovable property, dispute relating to **63,** 179-80, 206, 230, 278-80, 608, **64,** 61-2, 85, 417, **65,** 30-1, 256-7, **82,** 41-2, **84,** 88, 89, 90-4, **87,** 18, **91,** 296, 300-1, 302, 308, 310-12, **101,** 494, **103,** 453, **104,** 612, **107,** 198-9. *See also* property, dispute relating to *above*
annulment of contract **65,** 30-1
breach of planning regulations **107,** 198-9
diplomatic premises. *See* State immunity, jurisdiction, classification of act, diplomatic premises
salvage cases **79,** 11
specific performance, claim for **87,** 233
monetary claim distinguished **87,** 233
State succession and **55,** 409-11, **63,** 55, **75,** 125
Holocaust **103,** 600-1
pending actions **65,** 439-41
trust funds, action relating to **64,** 85, 99, 119-20, 417
winding-up/bankruptcy proceedings, duty to give embassy preferential treatment **101,** 333-7
State immunity, jurisdiction, classification of act 64, 238-40, 576-9, 697, 712, 738. *See also* employment contract
academic appointment

State immunity, jurisdiction, classification of act (*cont.*)
non-State school **65,** 304-6
State school **65,** 378-80, **87,** 53-6, **94,** 314-15
university **65,** 6-7, **107,** 369-70
acquisition and use distinguished **98,** 12-13
act contrary to fundamental principle of justice **104,** 577, 623
act *hostis humani generis* **103,** 428
act or omission in respect of discretionary function **63,** 383-8, 598, **84,** 99, 100-2, **90,** 592, **101,** 494-5, 504, 532, **107,** 199-201, 222-3
planning/operations distinction **98,** 129
act in territory of forum State **94,** 346, 347-8, **103,** 424-5
decisions of international tribunals relating to **124,** 444-6
State practice **124,** 443-4
acta jure imperii, definition **57,** 150, **103,** 372, 397-8
acta jure imperii/*acta jure gestionis* distinguished **63,** 59, 450-1, **82,** 37, **84,** 35-8, **87,** 44, 54-5, **91,** 297, 310, **101,** 192-201. *See also* nature and purpose of act as determining factor *below*
private person involvement, relevance **82,** 26-7
action to set aside will **64,** 673-4
acts in own territory **63,** 389, **81,** 548, **100,** 470-3
aerial bombardment **80,** 22-3, **87,** 682-3
affidavit in interests of public service **65,** 66-7
aid programme, participation in **86,** 60, 71, 635
aid to rural areas, contract for advice on **92,** 426-30
air navigation charges **107,** 328-34
air service **77,** 511-13
aircraft, diversion of **79,** 568. *See also* foreign aircraft *below*
aircraft engine, overhaul **92,** 457
airport operation **64,** 738
anti-terrorist measures **125,** 512-15
appointment of national airline pilot **101,** 198-201
appointment under public/administrative law **123,** 60, 66, 67-8, 69-70
civil servant **101,** 200-2
armed forces, acts concerning **63,** 51, 57, 218, 265, 344, **80,** 23. *See also* State immunity, jurisdiction, acts of, armed forces; State responsibility for acts and omissions of, armed forces; *and 'military' entries below*
deployment **90,** 410-11
employment **63,** 344
State no longer in existence **100,** 372-3
training, foreign personnel **63,** 422
arms sales **65,** 122
assassination **63,** 388-9, **81,** 63, 378-9, 554, **101,** 527-32
attempt to conceal facts from Head of State **113,** 527-8
attempt to ensure State-controlled body's performance under private contract **113,** 460-1
bank guarantee **77,** 533
breach of tenancy agreement **84,** 18-38
building works **82,** 41
car carrying mail on public road **40,** 74-8
carriage of goods **65,** 68-70, 368-9
carriage of grain for resale or free distribution **63,** 50-2
caveat lodged as part of divorce proceedings **103,** 452
certificates of deposit **88,** 72-3
civil servants, employment of **63,** 230, 344

commercial activities **63,** 587, **64,** 85-6, 89, 104, 106-8, 168-9, 175-82, 271-2, 316-18, 424-5, 516, 607-8, 650-3, 682-3, **66,** 9, 22, 222-7, 237, **72,** 112-14, 127-8, 163-71, 178-9, 654, **79,** 567, **80,** 53, 58, **86,** 59-61, 70-1, 89-98, 628-32, 633-9, **87,** 13, 201, 232, 236-8, 416, 525-36, 542, **90,** 602, **92,** 527-8, **103,** 439-44, 506, 513-15, 543-6, 607-9
act in private capacity **113,** 528
'based upon' **86,** 91-2, **107,** 378
'commercial purposes' **104,** 682-3
'commercial transaction' **107,** 603
definition **86,** 59 n. 2, 60, **98,** 18, 58
deliberately unclear **98,** 61
distinguishability from other non-sovereign rights **45,** 80
embassy and **64,** 271-2, 686-8, **65,** 420-1
as jurisdictional element **98,** 155, 158-9
merchant ship **84,** 708
nexus. *See* jurisdiction, nexus
'regular course of commercial conduct' **63,** 133-4, 240-1, 292, 343-4, 398, 399-402, 449 n. 4, 521-2, 610-12, **73,** 532, **98,** 18, 146
sovereign activity, foreign exchange dealings **88,** 83-7
substantial contact, need for **92,** 465-6
test **84,** 706
Vienna Convention on Diplomatic Relations (1961) and **64,** 596
commercial air traffic operated by national airline **63,** 195-6
commercial purposes distinguished **55,** 420-3
commission agreement **65,** 120-2, 125-7, 399-401
concession agreement **47,** 139-41, 147-9, **63,** 166-9, 233-4, **89,** 357
confiscation **63,** 595, 597, **64,** 179, 181
construction of building for US administrators of Marshall Plan **44,** 76-8, **65,** 40
consular activities **45,** 381-3, **57,** 154-9, **65,** 207-8, **98,** 128-31, **101,** 489-96, **114,** 504-7, 510-11
financial assistant **114,** 518-19
consular premises
lease or purchase **65,** 126, 274-5, **89,** 38-9, **101,** 491-2
use as **53,** 550
contract **72,** 173-81, 184-5
breach **64,** 326-30, 359, **84,** 114, **103,** 515
carriage of goods by sea **84,** 706-8
concert performances **63,** 22-31
kidney transplants for nationals **101,** 514-18
termination **64,** 235-6, 319-23, **107,** 368-70
force majeure, relevance **107,** 369
motive, relevance **107,** 369
to be performed in forum State **107,** 603
tortious interference with **63,** 169, 230, 387, 619-21
conversion **63,** 597, 619-21, **64,** 179, 236, 240-1, 320-3, 324-8, 330
copyright material, use of **65,** 143-4
as criminal **124,** 433-4
cultural relations **63,** 171-2, 229-32, 589
cultural relations, promotion **63,** 171-2, 229-32, 589, **65,** 327-8
currency controls, implementation **84,** 192-3
customary international law and **65,** 136, 184-5, 214, 243, 294, 322
damage to or loss of property **90,** 232
debt for services rendered **64,** 85

State immunity, jurisdiction, classification of act (*cont.*)
defamation **63,** 464, 590
by State press agency **63,** 132-5
demurrage **63,** 137-61, 494-7, 553-7, 569-72, **65,** 138
deportation **63,** 474, 589. *See also* expulsion of alien *above*
development programme **98,** 59
developments in law relating to **114,** 530
diplomatic activity **57,** 156-8, **63,** 51, 57, 171-2, 218, 231, **64,** 233, **65,** 187-8, 210-11
contract designed to embarrass government friendly to forum State **57,** 154-9
diplomatic agent, employment of **63,** 230, 344, 527
diplomatic immunity and. *See* diplomatic privileges and immunities, State immunity and
diplomatic involvement, relevance **65,** 390
diplomatic mission
communications **82,** 19
driving embassy car **65,** 269, **95,** 469-82
repair **82,** 18-19, 40, 41
diplomatic premises **40,** 80-1, **64,** 366-7, 388-92, **72,** 141-3, 658-60
action relating to immovable property, whether **98,** 4, 9, 11-3
construction contract **63,** 37-8, **64,** 271-2, 687-8, **84,** 25, **103,** 310
encroachment on neighbour's land **40,** 80-1
lease **63,** 230, 388, **64,** 60-2, 70-6, **65,** 252-4, 332-3, 370-1, 383-4, 386-7, 390, **75,** 122-4, 125, **82,** 18-19, **87,** 232-3, 236, **91,** 297
mortgage interest on premises no longer used for diplomatic purposes **65,** 111-14
operating naval chancery **107,** 198, 199-201
purchase **65,** 112, 257, **84,** 25-6, 27-9, 36-8, **87,** 236
repair **45,** 58-9, 79-82, **63,** 230, 588, **64,** 272, **84,** 35, **99,** 138
residential **65,** 257, 390-1, **102,** 207
sale and repurchase **113,** 462-4
diplomatic protection, relevance **88,** 740
dismissal for national security reasons **94,** 283
disposal **102,** 170-3
drugs control **102,** 143-4
economic relations, development of **63,** 172
electricity poles, transaction concerning **84,** 707, 708
embargo on shipping **63,** 187-90, 491
emigrant's property **82,** 46-50
employment contract, locally engaged staff. *See employment contract headings*
employment contract. *See* employment contract
employment of
architect for construction of pavilion at exhibition **64,** 2-20, 22, 25-8, 45-6
exhibition organizer **75,** 78-80
manual labour **82,** 120
official to work on foreign territory **78,** 121-3
essential sphere of State action and **65,** 197, 214, 220
establishment of Office for Management of Public Debt (recovery of compensation in respect of expropriation of private property) **115,** 417-18
exploitation of natural resources **80,** 584-6
hydro-electric development **92,** 659-61
hydrocarbons **77,** 527
oil-drilling **72,** 113-18
export promotion **98,** 59-61
export/import control **121,** 494

expropriation/nationalization **63,** 51, 96-8, 152-5, 166-9, 188-9, 218, 317, 454-6, 475, 500, 592-6, 599, 692-3, 697, **64,** 235, 706, **65,** 18-19, 58-60, 74-5, 84-5, 128-31, 299-303, 448-9, **72,** 127-31, **78,** 92-3, 594-5, 600, **79,** 594-5, **80,** 431-2, **82,** 47-50, 146, **92,** 398, **94,** 317-18, **101,** 549-50, **115,** 417
as act of State and **65,** 290
by occupying/administering power **48,** 175-7, **65,** 128-30, **94,** 47-8, 50, 51-2, 60, 61, **103,** 300-2, 354-5, 372-5, 387, 402-6, 414
'commercial activity in the United States', need for **107,** 229-30, 232-3, 237, 247-51
presumption of **107,** 232-3
contractual obligations assumed by State **65,** 295-303
direct effect in forum State, need for **63,** 233-5
emigrant's property **82,** 46-50
in occupied/administered territory **65,** 128
presence of property in forum State, need for **107,** 247 n. 10
property seized in occupied territory **65,** 128-30, **103,** 373-5, 380-2, 387, 405-6
in violation of international law **78,** 594-5, 600, **86,** 94 n. 7, **92,** 490, **103,** 452-3, 467-9, **113,** 549
expulsion of alien **63,** 51, 218, 474-6, 589, **101,** 503. *See also* deportation *above*
false imprisonment **63,** 474-5
film, agency contract for distribution of **64,** 56-8
film, lease of **65,** 431-2
financial undertaking **101,** 400-1
suspension of foreign debt repayment, relevance **101,** 400-1
foreign aircraft. *See also* aircraft *above*
removal to third country **103,** 354-5, 372-5, 403-6, 414
seizure and detention **107,** 331-4
seizure in occupied territory **103,** 354, 372, 380, 402-6
foreign assistance programme **63,** 230, 344
foreign exchange control **63,** 590-5, **65,** 65-6, 349-53, 423-4, **84,** 112, 113
foreign exchange reserves **63,** 16-17
functional test **64,** 53-5
gas-pipelines, cathodic protection **113,** 446-7
government audit **104,** 575-6
Lima Declaration on Guidelines on Auditing Precepts (1977) **104,** 575
government building, construction of **63,** 230, 344
government policy, involvement in **98,** 60
government tourist office, lease of premises for **52,** 321, **65,** 62-3
guarantee of charter **90,** 564, 565-6
Holocaust, successor government **103,** 600-2
hospital operation **65,** 311, 324, **100,** 556-8
hostage-taking **107,** 299-302
for profit **107,** 299-302
humanitarian relief **113,** 520
immigrants' centre **82,** 38-45
immigration controls **79,** 568
information centre, maintenance of **63,** 171-2, 231
insurance contract **63,** 454, **65,** 268-9
interference with functioning of mission/consulate and **65,** 126, 152-3
internal administrative act **63,** 51, 57, 218, **96,** 220
international exhibition, participation in **64,** 21-2, 28
international organization, construction of building for **63,** 95
investigation into customs fraud **121,** 476-81

State immunity, jurisdiction, classification of act (*cont.*)
investment in US corporation **63,** 205, 230, 588
joint control of funds for education institution **104,** 413-17
partial control, relevance **104,** 417
judicial act **103,** 549-50
judicial assistance **82,** 51-2
jus cogens/peremptory norm violation **103,** 472-5, 526, **107,** 541-4, **113,** 433, **119,** 67, 225, **123,** 32, 41-3, 50-1
crimes against humanity **103,** 615-21
implied waiver **103,** 610, **113,** 537-40, 547-8
torture. *See* torture *below*
kidnapping **79,** 568, **87,** 204, **101,** 503
law enforcement **124,** 434-5
lease agreement **101,** 491-2
legal suit **98,** 35
legislative act **63,** 51, 57, 218, **65,** 12, 128-30, 295-6, 299-303, 448-9
legislative attempts at **119,** 374-5
letter of credit **63,** 63-6, 137-61, 182-90, 347-50, 371-8, 391-408, 460-6, 481-93, 562-5, 575-6, 594-5, **64,** 132, 139-46, **65,** 133-7, 421, **121,** 492-4
libel **63,** 132-5, 464, 590, **64,** 445
in official newspaper **63,** 132-5, **98,** 83-4, 90 n. 10
loan agreement **65,** 233, 423-5, **98,** 42
between commercial banks **65,** 423-4
for refurbishment of diplomatic premises **99,** 138
management contract **48,** 149, **52,** 310-15
medical office **104,** 682-3
medical secretary/nurse **113,** 469
military base **90,** 592, **119,** 371
barber's shop **102,** 146-7
bowling alley **120,** 606-11
civilian clothing hire service **52,** 332-5
construction contract **65,** 262-4, **102,** 123-31
cultural base distinguished **94,** 288-9
games room attendant **102,** 148
medical facilities **100,** 441, 444-52, 455-64
operation **94,** 283, **113,** 520
restaurant, availability to public, relevance **102,** 145
restaurant, profit, relevance **102,** 145
supply of lumber **64,** 665-7
support staff **94,** 271-91, 303-5
training and education contract **119,** 370-6, 380-3
military procurement
cement for military purposes **63,** 64-6, 154-5, 182-90, 490-1, 559-61, **64,** 132-3
footwear **63,** 388, 561
meat **63,** 44
military equipment for use of armed forces **44,** 74, **63,** 43-5, 63-6, 230, 280-2, 344, 368, 388, 560-1, 588
provisions for military purposes **63,** 43-5, 63-6, 154, 230, 344, 560, 588
supplies used also for civilian purposes **63,** 42-5
military supplies, to occupying forces **40,** 64-9
milk production plant **82,** 34
misrepresentation **63,** 585, 597, 618-19

monetary policy **65,** 353
nationalized industries **65,** 69, 74-5, 177-80, 202-3, 213, 218-19, 266-7, 296-303, 355
natural resource, exploitation **80,** 584-6
natural resources, exploitation **65,** 98. *See also* oil production *below*
nature of legal relationship as determining factor **82,** 17-18, 19, 26, 48, 102, 120
nature or purpose of transaction as determining factor **40,** 75-6, **45,** 80, **63,** 66, 154-5, 180, 206-7, 210, 230-1, 344, 352, 462, 526-7, 560-1, 588-9, 618, **64,** 234, 235-6, 313, 314-15, 318, 327, 358-61, 404-5, 607, **65,** 112, 135-6, 143, 390, 401, 431, **77,** 518, 608, **80,** 585, **82,** 120, **84,** 35, 36, 114, 138, **86,** 91 n. 4, 93-4, 586, 630, **88,** 82, **92,** 426, 428, **94,** 274, 275-83, 297-9, 302-3, 347, **98,** 35, 60-1, 83, 121-2, **100,** 464, 515-16, 558-9, **101,** 195, 199-200, 491-2, 503, 512-13, 515-16, **102,** 126, 171, **103,** 310, 354, 373-5, 380-2, 384-6, 402, 404, 416-17, 513, 514-15, 544, **104,** 614-16, **106,** 277, **107,** 198, 299-301, 329-30, 378, **113,** 520, **114,** 505, 516-17, **124,** 434-5, 561-3
  act rather than actor **52,** 313, **65,** 72, **98,** 107
  common law **94,** 276-8
  contract **64,** 180-2
  distinction, whether **98,** 58-9, **103,** 514-15
  equality of parties as test **40,** 75-6
  legislation **94,** 278-80
  mixed, dominant/essential element **90,** 566, **98,** 68
  nature of property right distinguished **65,** 311
neutral ship in international waters, attack on **79,** 3-7, 9-17, **81,** 661-9
nuclear energy exploitation **63,** 103-4, **65,** 98, **77,** 517, **86,** 569, 577
official article in government publication **63,** 133-4
offset of loss from nationalization **92,** 396
oil, price-fixing by OPEC **63,** 288-94, **66,** 416-17
oil production **63,** 290, **65,** 214. *See also* natural resources, exploitation
  contract for **65,** 214
  cut **63,** 522
overflight charges **82,** 73
ownership of real property **63,** 179-80
parks, maintenance of **63,** 327
passport, issue of **63,** 317
personal injury **72,** 95, 103, 140-3
  attributability to defendants **87,** 204
  caused by tort **99,** 143
personal injury in forum State **65,** 2, **87,** 201, 203-4, **90,** 232, **123,** 80-1, 87, 89-92, **124,** 436-41
  customary international law **123,** 89-92
  European Convention on State Immunity (and Protocol) (Basle) (1972) **123,** 31, 40, 80, 89
  ILC Draft Articles on Jurisdictional Immunities of States and Their Property (1991) **123,** 80-1, 89-92
  private acts, limitation to **104,** 283-4
  Torture Convention (1984) and **124,** 436-41
  transit stop in third country **104,** 283-4
personal injury outside forum State, customary international law **65,** 41-3, **123,** 40
personnel supervision **72,** 199
police, entrapment by **94,** 346, 347-8
police department, operation of **63,** 327
police enforcement of fisheries legislation **63,** 352-3
police officer not directly controlled by government **103,** 323-5

State immunity, jurisdiction, classification of act (*cont.*)
police power, exercise of, abuse amounting to tort **65,** 381-2, **100,** 552-4, 555-8, **124,** 435
power generation **63,** 104
presumption against sovereign nature of act **63,** 50-2
prisoners of war, hiring as slave labour **103,** 607-8
private acts **90,** 231-2, **94,** 364-5
impossibility in certain cases **98,** 106-7, 108
private law act appertaining to core of State authority **65,** 185
private law relationship **65,** 6, 12, 112, 121, 143-4, 214, 220, 266-7, 371-2, 376, **87,** 13, 14, 17-18, **94,** 347
private person test **63,** 290-1, 560, 588, **64,** 179-80, 241, 360-1, **65,** 34-5, 40, 121, 136, 139, 171, 211, 256-7, 332-3, 361, 390-1, 398-400, 423, 431-2, **94,** 273, 274, 275, 290, 303-5, 315, 352-3, 365, **98,** 42, 121, 145, **100,** 515, 516, 553-4, 555-6, 561-2, 565, **101,** 492, 513, 515, **103,** 401, 452, 464-5, 488, 513, 544, 545, **104,** 612-13, **107,** 332-4, 370, **115,** 421, 433, **121,** 492-3
princeps in alterius territorio privatus **65,** 305
production of nuclear power **86,** 569
promissory note dealings **104,** 537-8
public loans **63,** 51, 57, 218, 230-1
public relations, maintenance of **63,** 171-2
public works contract **65,** 40, 263-4, 324, **82,** 64-5, **92,** 661, **113,** 447
purchase of
bullets **63,** 388
foodstuffs **63,** 371-7, 495-7, 560, 569-72, 588
furnaces possibly for nuclear weapons production **106,** 277
goods or services **101,** 513, **106,** 277, **113,** 435
grain for humanitarian or State use **63,** 50-2, 57
purpose of transaction. *See* nature or purpose of transaction as determining factor *above*
railway construction **65,** 357-8, 361, 399-400, **82,** 65
railways administration/operation **42,** 355, 397-8, **56,** 316, **65,** 42, 355, 358, 360-1, 402-4
recruitment of locally engaged staff **123,** 65-6, 67-8, 69-70
recruitment of staff to work in third country **100,** 549, 551, 555, 559
refinancing of bonds **100,** 513-17, 518-19
reinsurance contract **63,** 454
relationship with private individual outside territory **82,** 18, 22
relevant factors **65,** 420, 431
fair value **100,** 516
motivation **113,** 527
nature of funds **77,** 494
nature or purpose of transaction. *See* nature or purpose of transaction as determining factor *above*
place **100,** 463-4
position of parties **77,** 608
profit **63,** 422, **79,** 568, **101,** 493, 516, **102,** 145, 146-7, 171-2, **103,** 464, **104,** 615, **120,** 610
provision for immunity from taxes **92,** 428-30
public purpose **82,** 42
social security provision in contract **65,** 311-12
use of non-official agents **107,** 299-300
repair to commercial vessel **64,** 545, 565-6

reparations to Holocaust victims **113,** 548-9
responsibility for determining **91,** 297
sale of
bonds **84,** 138, 142 n. 4, 171, 172
certificate of deposit **84,** 113-15
commodities **65,** 59-60
deposit certificate by State-owned bank **92,** 416
golf carts **63,** 205-7
goods **65,** 371-2, **87,** 13
property **87,** 13
shares **65,** 401
tax credits **104,** 538-40, 569-74, 605-7, 614-16
scientific relations, development of **63,** 172
scientific research programme **63,** 39-40
securities legislation, enforcement **64,** 48-51
security provision **63,** 416-19
service contract, commercial purpose of mission **95,** 473
shares, transfer following reoganization of banking sector **124,** 559-63
shipping services **63,** 267
shooting by British soldier in Republic of Ireland **104,** 699-700
sovereign activity, general public purpose **94,** 299-300
sovereignty **103**, 20, **111,** 633-4
State concert society, contract with **63,** 230, 344, 526-7
State school, lease of premises for **65,** 33-6
State secrets and **82,** 20
'strictly political or public acts' **63,** 57, 171-2
summoning of witnesses **90,** 410
supply and delivery of fishing vessel for training purposes **63,** 9-12
supply of goods within framework of government decisions **113,** 486
territorial sea, extension of **63,** 317
terrorist act **79,** 568, 570, **107,** 391-2, **113,** 539. *See also* State-sponsored terrorism
State sponsor of terrorism, designation as and **113,** 542, **121,** 611-12, 630
tort **63,** 169, 212-14, 229-31, 244-51, 320-9, 340-3, 384-90, 422-4, 440-2, 464, 474-6, 533-4, 588-90, 597-9, 601, 618-21, 632-8, 639-46, **65,** 376, **72,** 112, 114-15, 118, **79,** 563, **84,** 88, 89, 94-5, 98, 99-100, **88,** 82, 90-1, **101,** 493-6
abuse of police power **100,** 552-4, 555-8, **124,** 435
commercial activity distinguished **63,** 598, **90,** 594, **100,** 551-4, 556-60, **103,** 375, 517-18, **107,** 396-404, **124,** 434-5
detention in hotel room **113,** 513-14
in embassy abroad **90,** 589-90, 592-3
European Convention on State Immunity (and Protocol) (Basle) (1972) **104,** 577, **123,** 80
general principle of international law **104,** 700-4
ILC Draft Articles on State immunity (1991) **104,** 577
intentional **107,** 223-4, **125,** 150-63
interference with private use and enjoyment of land **107,** 199
Letelier **104,** 577-8, **121,** 486
locus, relevance **90,** 587, 589-90, 593-5, **101,** 503-4, **103,** 453, **107,** 302, 389-90, **113,** 549-50
nature of conduct, relevance **107,** 200
nexus, need for **84,** 90-5, 99-100
public act **63,** 386-8

State immunity, jurisdiction, classification of act (*cont.*)
respondeat superior **107,** 307
scope of employment **101,** 493-4, 526-32, **121,** 483-7
act incident to employment **101,** 528
applicable law **101,** 493-4, 526-32
benefit to employer **101,** 528
criminal act **107,** 200, **113,** 514
driving self for medical treatment during duty hours **107,** 307-8
off-duty driving **63,** 422-3
policy judgement, need for **107,** 200-1
reasonably foreseeable **101,** 528
respondeat superior **101,** 493-4, 526-32
violation of defendant State's own law, relevance **101,** 531
State practice **103,** 315, 316, **104,** 577, 700-4
taking of property, whether **92,** 490
territorial jurisdiction **90,** 590, **103,** 470
terrorist act. *See* terrorist act *above*
torture. *See* torture *below*
torture **100,** 470-1, **103,** 421-32, 469-75, **104,** 123-5, **107,** 541-4, **119,** 45, 47-8, 85-7, 205-8, **123,** 29-30
customary international law **124,** 443
tourism promotion **65,** 62, 144, 427, 435
trade promotion **65,** 210-11, 314-15, 345-6
trade union rights, exercise of **65,** 342-3
trading in open market, one-off disposal of diplomatic property distinguished **87,** 238
traffic accident **65,** 268-70, **68,** 386-7, **107,** 199
translation and interpreting services **94,** 326, 328, 330
transportation of people for public purpose **98,** 121-2
treaty obligation to pay compensation **65,** 12-13
Tripartite Commission for the Restitution of Monetary Gold (1946) **63,** 71-3
union certification procedure **94,** 274-91
union certification proceedings **94,** 274, 275-6, 283-90, 304-5
violation of international law **64,** 182-3, 241, 323, **72,** 127, 130-1, 143, **77,** 265-7, **79,** 6-7, 8, 9-13, 16-17, 594, **84,** 193, **87,** 530, 682, **88,** 82, 83-7, **90,** 599-601, **92,** 490, **100,** 470-1, **103,** 427-31, 452-3, 467-9, 528-30, **104,** 578, **106,** 427-31, 452-3, 528-30, **113,** 549, **118,** 34-5, **119,** 224-9, 241-2. *See also jus cogens*/peremptory norm violation *above*
general principles of international law **103,** 526
'iniquity factor' **104,** 539-40, 606-7
torture. *See* torture *above*
wine, distribution by State agency **63,** 58-60
State immunity, jurisdiction, entitlement. *See also* United States of America (USA), State Department suggestions (State immunity)
activity of State outside area of sovereign authority **65,** 128-30
applicable law **65,** 252
British Rail International **63,** 5-7
burden of proof. *See* State immunity, jurisdiction, procedural aspects, burden of proof
central bank. *See* central/State-owned bank
colony **44,** 72-3
commercial/trade representation/mission **64,** 590-3, 651-2, **65,** 1, 55-6, 177, 179-80, 210-11, 283, 313-15, **99,** 103-12
constituent State of federation **52,** 322-8, 330-1, **55,** 413-17, **87,** 39-41, **111,** 608-10
acts 'in the exercise of sovereign authority' **111,** 608, 610

Attorney-General **95,** 457
division of executive **95,** 457
cultural institute **40,** 60-3, **65,** 325-8, **82,** 4, **87,** 46
Custodian for Enemy Property **56,** 228
denial of by executive **121,** 596
diplomatic agent **114,** 495
discretion as to **98,** 144
European Community (EC) **64,** 131-2, 144-5, **80,** 58, 121-8
executive certificate/statement, conclusiveness **42,** 120-1, **64,** 594-5, **90,** 541-4, **98,** 10, **104,** 143 n. 7, **111,** 606, **118,** 297
executive role **84,** 151, 170, **92,** 485, 487-8
foreign minister **81,** 604, 606
Government Auditor **104,** 574-6, 605
government department **52,** 318-21, 324-5, 327-8, **55,** 424, 426, **63,** 90, 104, 175, **64,** 436-7, **65,** 1, 307, **84,** 703, **89,** 36, **94,** 263, **98,** 16, 23
control of **55,** 426
Department of Civil Aviation (Iran) **63,** 213-14
evidence of status, consular certificate **92,** 514-15
government information agency **113,** 458-9, **114,** 522-4
guarantor of municipality loan **47,** 157
head of foreign government **81,** 604, 606. *See also* Head of State, immunity, jurisdiction
members of official party **81,** 604
Holy See. *See* Holy See, immunity, jurisdiction
individual **119,** 221-2
misrepresentation of authority **94,** 367
official acts **92,** 484-8, **101,** 501, **104,** 175-6
acts on behalf of Head of State **113,** 527
personal immunity of foreign sovereign. *See* Head of State, immunity, jurisdiction
private acts **92,** 491-2
private individual **82,** 26, 38, 138
ultra vires acts **92,** 491-2, **104,** 175-6
information centre **63,** 171-2, 231, 589
international organizations, representatives and missions accredited to **75,** 78-80
legal interest in proceedings **121,** 478-80
legal question **84,** 165
members of official party **81,** 604
mining company **63,** 134, 230, 292, 344, 449, 588
Ministry of Defence Claims Commission (UK) **103,** 236-43
monarchical State. *See* Head of State, immunity, jurisdiction
municipality, loan guarantee **47,** 155-7
nationalized oil company **103,** 435-6, 483-90, 495-500
officials **63,** 68-70, **87,** 202, 205, **94,** 364-5, **98,** 106-9, **104,** 282
illegality of act **95,** 460-2, **98,** 108, 129-31
official receiver **90,** 230-3
scope of duties **87,** 203, **95,** 459
State agency **95,** 457-60
oil drilling company **72,** 113, 115
personal holding company **121,** 587
PLO in USA **96,** 74
political subdivision **63,** 46-8, 68-70
City of London **63,** 46-8
Presidential Commission on Good Government (PCGG) (Philippines) **103,** 508, 509-13
protecting State in protectorate **118,** 422-8

State immunity, jurisdiction, entitlement (*cont.*)
provincial government **55,** 413-17
public broadcasting company **87,** 39-41
recognition of State/government, relevance **52,** 310-15, **64,** 512-15, **65,** 56, **84,** 182-3, **88,** 40, **108,** 519
Register of Shipping **92,** 512
republican State **64,** 398, 401, 415, 418-19, 500-1, 572
in respect of secondary or concurrent liability **80,** 53, 120
responsibility for determining **79,** 4, 12, 14, **87,** 524
courts **45,** 59, **84,** 153, **121,** 596
Ruler of State of Malaysian Federation **118,** 294-8
sovereign entity without territory **65,** 323, 335
Sovereign Order of Malta **65,** 309-11, 323-4, **77,** 613-15
sovereign status, dependence on **84,** 708
standard of proof **104,** 413-14
State agency/State-owned corporation/State entity **40,** 59-63, **55,** 425-7, **63,** 74-6, 90, 104, 134, 167 n. 2, 174-8, 195-6, 205-8, 233-4, 245-51, 292, 302-4, 334-7, 371-7, 391-407, 436-52, 473, 514, 541-6, 588-9, 617, 624-38, 647-54, **64,** 48-51, 65, 115, 536-8, **65,** 42, 44-6, 59-60, 75, 202, 213, 219, 299-303, 355, 422-3, **66,** 59-60, **72,** 165, 178, 184-7, **82,** 11-13, 34-5, 37-8, 80, 102-3, **84,** 190, **86,** 59 n. 3, 77-80, **87,** 13, **90,** 611-16, **92,** 517-20, 523, 524-6, 527, 659-61, **98,** 16, 22-6, 49-54, **101,** 193-201, **103,** 352-4, 370-5, 387-8, 399-402, 417-19. *See also* State agency/State-owned corporation/State entity, classification as
act at request or instruction of State **103,** 401-2
act in exercise of sovereign authority **103,** 401-2, 414-15, 417-19
bank **104,** 280-2
action as agency of State, need for **43,** 163-5, **52,** 333-5, **55,** 424, 427, **63,** 59
AGIP, USA **63,** 18-21
authorization of act, need for **63,** 276 n. 5
central/State-owned bank. *See* central/State-owned bank, immunity, execution/attachment
compliance with law, whether conferring derivative immunity **63,** 474-5, **84,** 114-16
employment contract, national of sending State **107,** 378-9
individual **92,** 484-90
joint conduct **86,** 59 n. 3, 80
liability and immunity distinguished **103,** 510
nature of immunity distinguished **103,** 414-15
organ of government **52,** 316, 325-8, **88,** 711
press agency **63,** 132-5
punitive damages, liability for **86,** 79
restricted **82,** 11-13, **124,** 559-63
State compared/distinguished **64,** 64-9, **86,** 59 n. 3, 77-80
'circumstances such that a State ... would have been so immune' **103,** 400-1, 418-19
State-controlled entity **92,** 660-1
tort **103,** 388
State shipping line **42,** 39-41, **63,** 220-7, **65,** 69-70, **72,** 103, 105-9, **87,** 103-5, **103,** 576-80
State-owned ships. *See* ships, State-owned
trade agreement, effect **64,** 592-4
trust territory. *See* Trust Territories, State immunity, jurisdiction, entitlement
State immunity, jurisdiction, procedural aspects
admissibility, question of **84,** 708
appeal/judicial review

denial of evidentiary hearing **107,** 305-6
public law appeal **82,** 47
time-limits
extension **104,** 650-5, 678
time-limits **65,** 393
applicable law **40,** 65-6, **65,** 105, 184-5, 197, 208, 220, 243, 294, **80,** 382, **113,** 527
bilateral treaty **82,** 25, 32, 48, **114,** 538
customary international law **40,** 66, **82,** 25, **100,** 455-7, 461-3, **119,** 233-4
defendant State **82,** 26-7
equity **113,** 527
European Convention on State Immunity (and Protocol) (Basle) (1972) **82,** 18, 21, 25
Swiss law, divergence from **82,** 33, 40
USA and **114,** 517, 529
general principles of municipal law **82,** 32, 33, 40, 48
international law **40,** 61, 74, **45,** 59, 60-1, 80-1, **82,** 44, **84,** 20, 31, 170, **86,** 577, **91,** 295, 311-14, **113,** 418-26, 527, **114,** 505
relevance **91,** 311-14
lex fori **45,** 80-1, **65,** 105, 121, 126, 127, 128-9, 136-7, 142-3, 197, **82,** 44, **94,** 353, 376, **114,** 505, 517, **118,** 424-6, **119,** 233-4
State practice, relevance **114,** 505, 517
sending State **94,** 268, **103,** 538-9
Vienna Convention on Consular Relations (1963) **113,** 419, 422
Vienna Convention on Diplomatic Relations (1961) **113,** 419, 422, 472
burden of proof **63,** 220-1, 266, 280, 473, 579-80, 583, 588, **64,** 11, 21-2, 28-9, 35-6, 75, 80, 113, 119, 463-4, 468-9, 474, 597, **77,** 63-8, 263-5, **79,** 15, **80,** 585, **87,** 525, **89,** 36, **90,** 611, **92,** 395, 397-8, **98,** 41-2, 144-5, 156-7, 163-4, **101,** 489, 501, **103,** 403, 424, 425, 442-3, 451, 463-4, 468-9, 488, 512, 538-9, 555, 568, 576, 607, **107,** 230, 306, 378, 397-8, **113,** 545-6, **114,** 507
construction of houses for US visiting forces **42,** 123-4
good arguable case against, need for **100,** 467-8, 471, 473-4
immunity of independent legal entity **77,** 527
non-appearance of defendant **77,** 263, 264
waiver **106,** 581
as cause of action, preceding statutory provision **87,** 202, 204, 205
consent of forum State, relevance. *See* foreign State, proceedings involving, consent of forum government, need for
court's right/duty to raise *proprio motu* **65,** 102-3, 157-8, **77,** 64, 263, **79,** 557 n. 20, **80,** 432, 585, **84,** 26, **104,** 143, 655, 678, **113,** 479, 480, **115,** 431, **116,** 644, 645, 670, 673-4
critical date
assertion of claim of sovereignty **84,** 707
cause of action **94,** 262
issue of writ **84,** 703, 707, 708
default judgment. *See also* non-appearance, effect *below*
evidential requirement **107,** 265-6
impossibility of performance **107,** 267
setting aside **84,** 161-85, **118,** 603-19
waiver and **65,** 87-8, **94,** 317
defence, whether **63,** 43 n. 7, **86,** 460, 462, **92,** 422-3, **103,** 438
mistaken belief in entitlement **107,** 268
effective remedy, right to and **65,** 31, 130, **81,** 136-8, **91,** 301, **114,** 566-7, **119,** 372, 373, 376, 377-8, 383-5, **121,** 203-4, 208, **123,** 73, 86, 87-8, 93

State immunity, jurisdiction, procedural aspects (*cont.*)
diplomatic channels as **64,** 179, **102,** 173, 182, **104,** 580, 622, **113,** 434
right of suit in 'defendant' State's courts. *See* right of suit in 'defendant' State's courts *below*
Employment Appeals Tribunal **95,** 473, 481-2
enforceability of judgment, relevance **84,** 105, **86,** 568-9, 570, **95,** 476
entitlement to raise **81,** 594
bank holding affected funds **104,** 416-17
joinder of State, relevance **64,** 438-9, 474-5
owner of diplomatic premises **65,** 247-8
private parties **104,** 621
State concerned **113,** 465, 468, 479, 480
estoppel and **103,** 309
evidence
oral hearing, need for **107,** 307
standard of proof **77,** 63-8
facts **107,** 306-7
jurisdiction **107,** 306-7
executive/ministerial authorization, relevance **65,** 9, **87,** 34, 66-8
exhaustion of administrative remedies **88,** 714
exhaustion of local remedies **65,** 389, **82,** 35
foreign law, recognition/enforcement and **42,** 22-3, **82,** 26-7
forum [non] conveniens and **64,** 82-4, 184-6, **84,** 104-5, **103,** 518-19, **120,** 452-3, 461, **121,** 643
hearing, setting of date for as exercise of jurisdiction **65,** 130-1
immunity from jurisdiction and liability distinguished **86,** 629, **103,** 336-7, **116,** 633, **120,** 432
in personam actions **55,** 419, 422, **64,** 98-9, 101, 107-8, 114-15, 130-1, 146, 168-9, 175-82, 210, 216-19, 231, 232, 269-71, 319, 403-5, 417-19, 423-4, 565-6, 704, **104,** 621
commercial activity **64,** 423, 425, 542-5
European Convention on State Immunity (and Protocol) (Basle) (1972) **64,** 107-8
real action relating to private immovable property **64,** 365-7, 390
in rem/personal actions distinguished **55,** 418-23, **63,** 151, 220, 222-4, 289, 335-6, **64,** 96-9, 108-9
public property and **55,** 419-23
interim measures. *See* State immunity, execution/attachment, purpose of proceedings, safeguarding/cautionary measures
interlocutory review, admissibility **98,** 73
international tribunals, proceedings before and **86,** 510
jury trial and **63,** 245-51, 368-9, 438, 439-46, 541-9, 639-46, **107,** 354-8
legality of act, relevance **119,** 224, **121,** 478-80
method of challenge **77,** 265
need to plead **40,** 82-3, **64,** 73-4, **65,** 381, **77,** 264-5, **84,** 117 n. 10, **95,** 464-5, **118,** 424
nexus, need for. *See* jurisdiction, nexus
non-appearance, effect **63,** 421-2, **64,** 293, **65,** 374, **77,** 114-15, 263, 264, **84,** 168, **104,** 416-17, 655, 678, **111,** 606-7, 630, **116,** 672-3. *See also* default judgment *above*
as admission of allegations **124,** 430-1
reasonable misunderstanding **98,** 85-8
preliminary issue, whether **40,** 62, **64,** 510-12, **65,** 7, **80,** 53, 119, 179, **82,** 26, **92,** 529, **107,** 306, 378-9, **115,** 417
merits distinguished **90,** 589, **100,** 515-17

presumption against **64,** 148-9
presumption of **77,** 265, 493-4, **84,** 167, 169, 193, **86,** 515, **103,** 445-6, **107,** 396, **113,** 468, 545
good arguable case against, need for **100,** 467-8, 471, 473-4
as procedural bar **64,** 32, **84,** 26, **87,** 201, 233, 616, **91,** 355, **94,** 305, **118,** 424, **119,** 57-73, 78, **123,** 38, 50-1, 61-2
access to courts and **123,** 38, 70-3, 81-2, **125,** 157-9
effect on cause of action **65,** 451, **86,** 138
procedure for establishing **79,** 557 n. 20
responsibility for determining, executive decision as alternative **104,** 580
right of suit in 'defendant' State's courts **103,** 601, **106,** 244-8, 260
administering authority of occupied territory **65,** 130
applicable law, relevance **106,** 244-5, 246, 260
availability of international remedy, relevance **106,** 247-8, **113,** 434
nature of act as determining factor **106,** 246
State practice **106,** 245-7
unreasonable or impossible **86,** 567, 574, 577, 578, 580-2
separation of powers and **63,** 28-9, 35-6, **99,** 162
service of process and. *See* service of process on foreign State or State agency, State immunity, jurisdiction and
State department suggestions. *See* United States of America (USA), State Department suggestions, State immunity
subpoena duces tecum order **122,** 32-5
State immunity, jurisdiction, theory/doctrine
absolute theory
agreement by parties to apply **64,** 64
antecedent right, whether **84,** 173-5
China **84,** 152
common law **87,** 234, 237-8, **104,** 524-5
customary international law **40,** 65, **64,** 141-2, 597-607, **65,** 104, **87,** 54, **116,** 627-8
international goodwill and **91,** 309
NATO Status of Forces Agreement (1951) and **100,** 445, 447-52, 455, 457, 460-1
opposability **84,** 152
State-owned trading vessel and **64,** 108-9, **65,** 104
USSR and **91,** 296
act of State and. *See* act of State, State immunity, jurisdiction and
acta jure imperii/*acta jure gestionis* distinguished
contract, form **82,** 65
difficulty **45,** 58-9, **64,** 180, 402, 406, 424, **65,** 294, 398-9
immunity, execution/attachment, relevance to **65,** 405
I° Congreso del Partido **104,** 537, 570-1, **111,** 667-8
Kuwait Airways **104,** 537, 570-1
Vienna Convention on Diplomatic Relations (1961), relevance **82,** 117
basis
avoidance of burden of litigation **103,** 486
avoidance of impairment to government activities **84,** 102
comity. *See* comity, State immunity, execution/attachment; comity, State immunity, jurisdiction
dignity of foreign State **64,** 49, 58, 135, 178-9, 313-14, 633, 688-9, **84,** 21-2, **86,** 638, **90,** 611-16, **92,** 534, **94,** 282-3, **102,** 128-9, **103,** 310, **104,** 510, 616, 623
dignity of sovereign **90,** 564, 565
diplomatic privileges and immunities **64,** 418

State immunity, jurisdiction, theory/doctrine (*cont.*)
equality of States **64,** 595, **65,** 30, 157, 191, 281, 321, 326, 340, 352-3, **77,** 16, 577, **82,** 4, 102, 120, **86,** 629, **92,** 534, 538, **104,** 516, 570, 616, **107,** 381, **111,** 632, **114,** 510, **119,** 223
execution of judgment, difficulty **40,** 77-8, **64,** 84, **65,** 251
extraterritoriality **64,** 30-1, 39-40, **95,** 455
foreign relations considerations **63,** 35, 218-20, 332, 451-2, 546-7, 640-1, **82,** 18, **104,** 570, 612, 623, **107,** 357
good faith **64,** 688-9, **65,** 341-3, **104,** 545, 624
Institut de Droit International **113,** 433
independence of States **64,** 31, 39, 49, 58, **65,** 34, **82,** 18, 102, 120, **86,** 514, **87,** 35, 55, **95,** 452, **103,** 310, **104,** 510, 570, 616, 623
international courtesy **64,** 49, 58, **65,** 34, 255, 321, **91,** 302
international goodwill **91,** 309
international law **82,** 120, **104,** 517, 576, **111,** 632
international order **104,** 616, 624
lèse majesté **87,** 238
mutual recognition **87,** 237
natural law **84,** 194
non-interference in the affairs of another State **64,** 219-20, **65,** 154-5, **92,** 538, **113,** 432, **114,** 522-4, 528-31, 565-6, **119,** 222, 223
par in parem non habet jurisdictionem **53,** 433, **55,** 583, **62,** 233, 401-2, 416, 493, 516, 633, 650, **65,** 157, 255, 274, 281, 306, 309, 317, 321, 326, 340, **77,** 604, 633, **80,** 125, **87,** 7, 35, **91,** 298, 302, 538, **95,** 476, **102,** 139, 538, 557, 567, **116,** 629, **119,** 161, 172, 174, 222, 374, **123,** 40
'perfect equality and absolute independence of States' **77,** 16
prevention of international conflicts **82,** 18
protection of prerogative **98,** 108
reciprocity **64,** 409-10, 426-8, 595, **82,** 4, **87,** 55, 237, **94,** 291, 305, **103,** 315, 316, **104,** 570, 616, 695, 703, **107,** 403, **111,** 632, **113,** 432, **121,** 202
sovereignty **52,** 312, **65,** 128, 266, **82,** 18, 102, 120, **84,** 21-2, **102,** 128-9, 131, **104,** 509, 557, 586, 623, **111,** 632, **113,** 422, 433, **114,** 506
sovereignty of forum State **82,** 18
State immunity legislation as sole basis. *See* legislation, as sole basis *below*
State personality **104,** 576
unimpeded fulfilment of consular tasks **114,** 518-19
common law **63,** 644, **86,** 643, 647-8, **87,** 234, **94,** 276-8, **104,** 510, 514, 520-2, 524-5, **107,** 354-8, **111,** 606
absolute theory **87,** 234, 237-8, **104,** 524-5
restrictive theory **86,** 643
customary international law **38,** 163-4, **45,** 61, **64,** 594-5, 597-607, **77,** 604, **78,** 92, 116, 121, **81,** 604-5, **82,** 25, 27, 37, **86,** 510, **87,** 17, **90,** 410, **91,** 295, **92,** 533-4, **119,** 378, **123,** 38-9
confidentiality of action **114,** 523
employment contract **113,** 432-3, **116,** 628-33, **123,** 71-2
European Convention on State Immunity (and Protocol) (Basle) (1972) **115,** 422, 432-4
personal injury in forum State **123,** 89-92
personal injury outside forum State **123,** 40
visiting forces **100,** 455-7, 461-3
definition **66,** 105-7, 109-10, 416
development of concept **40,** 74-5, **42,** 126-8, **45,** 61-79, **63,** 11, 217-18, 248, 288-9, 437, 450-2, 501, 530, 640-1, 645, **64,** 3-20, 21-2, 29-32, 36-43, 52-9, 60-2, 87-9,

103-8, 109, 129-32, 140-5, 148-51, 168-70, 216-20, 232, 312-14, 402-7, 422-3, 438-53, 455-74, 492-3, 520-1, 524-5, 542-5, 549-50, 553-4, 576-80, 597-608, 614-32, 633-50, 682-3, 698-706, 711-15, **65,** 30, 103-4, 120-1, 134-6, 141-3, 150, 153-6, 158, 164, 175-7, 181-2, 184, 195-6, 213-14, 218-24, 226-9, 243-5, 249, 281, 292-4, 314, 322, 326, 335-6, 339-43, 389, 398, 401, 431, **72,** 100-1, 112, 199, 287, **77,** 5, 11, 16, 493, **79,** 4, 11, 552-4, 567, **80,** 381, **82,** 32, **84,** 20-4, 27, 29-31, 142, 147, 150-2, 169-71, 173-6, 183, 191, 703-6, **86,** 628-9, 646-7, **87,** 17, 32, 35, 54-5, 200, 524, **90,** 231, **91,** 309, **92,** 484-5, 521, **94,** 276-80, 297-310, 375-6, **95,** 369-70, 452-5, 470, 477- 8, 481, **98,** 8-9, **100,** 446-7, 461-2, **102,** 170, **103,** 437-8, 461-2, **104,** 517, **113,** 433, **114,** 505, 527, 535, **115,** 434, **116,** 628-9, **119,** 238-9, **120,** 428-9
Africa and Asia **64,** 647-8
civil law **64,** 642-6
codification. *See also* United States of America (USA), Foreign Sovereign Immunities Act (FSIA) 1976/82
Asian–African Legal Consultative Committee (1957/1958) **45,** 76-7
Bustamante Code of Private International Law **65,** 30
Committee of Experts for the Progressive Codification of International Law (1926) **45,** 76
Harvard Law School Study Report (1932) **45,** 77, 157, **64,** 601, **65,** 143, 157
ILA Resolution (1952) **45,** 77, **64,** 601
Institut de Droit International **45,** 78, **65,** 143, **113,** 433, **123,** 90
Vienna Convention on Diplomatic Relations (1961), relevance **45,** 76-7
Paris Administrative Headquarters Agreements (1919/1920) and **45,** 73
precedent, effect on **64,** 16, 89-90, 140-6, 150-3, 169, 212-15, **87,** 416-17
role of English law in India and **64,** 406-7
Soviet Union and Eastern Europe **64,** 646-7
teachings of publicists **65,** 274-5, **95,** 476
European Community (EC) **64,** 131-2, 144-5
Lomé Convention (1975) and **64,** 121
general principle of international law **62,** 233, **65,** 30, **78,** 116, **82,** 32, 33, **86,** 584, **92,** 512, **95,** 471, 472, 473, 479, **102,** 138-40, **103,** 303-11, 474, **104,** 516, 655, 695, 696, **119,** 204-5, 238-42, **123,** 80, 82-3
absence **104,** 517-18, 570, 616-17
as between protectorate and protecting State **118,** 423
liability for tort **104,** 700-4
general principle of municipal law **82,** 32, 33, 40, 48
Head of State immunity distinguished **64,** 399-400, 413-15. *See also* Head of State, immunity, jurisdiction
individual rights, effect on **63,** 26, **65,** 191-2, **82,** 18, 20, **94,** 291
freedom of speech **82,** 309, 318
liberty of person, deprivation of and **121,** 203-4
international law
flexibility **104,** 611
modification **92,** 520, 521-3
legislation **86,** 515
desirability **64,** 550-1
diversity **95,** 452, **101,** 196, **104,** 517-18, 700-4, **120,** 430, 432, **124,** 446
retroactive, whether. *See* legislation, retroactive, State immunity legislation
as sole basis **63,** 220, 444-5, 644, **79,** 4-5, 12, 14, 564, **81,** 663, 668-9, **84,** 90, 169, 171, **87,** 682-3, **98,** 30, 66-7, 73-4, 114, 152-3, **103,** 445, 450, 517-18, 537-8, 589, 605, **104,** 123, **107,** 197, 230, 246-7, 264-5, 339, 357-8, 374, 396, **113,** 545, **119,** 160, **121,** 587, 629, **124,** 438
as legitimate aim **123,** 40, 65, 68, 84-5, 86-93

State immunity, jurisdiction, theory/doctrine (*cont.*)
natural law **84,** 194
non-justiciability as alternative **80,** 124, 164, 205, **119,** 73-4, 78
political question doctrine and **63,** 71-3, 317
as privilege **63,** 506
public order/public policy/*ordre public* considerations **64,** 105, **65,** 139, **88,** 711, **104,** 516, 576, 606-7, 611, 620, 622
balance of interests **104,** 624-5
ratione materiae **80,** 123-4, **119,** 153, 173-4, 223-33
ratione personae **80,** 123-4, 206, **119,** 153, 173-4, **123,** 43
restrictive theory **82,** 26, 32-3, 37-8, 48-9, 102, 120, **84,** 22-4, 32, 33, 171, 703-4, 706, **86,** 510, 585-6, 628-31, 643-7, **87,** 27, 201, 524, **90,** 562-4, 566, **92,** 484-5, 661, **94,** 299-300, **95,** 452-5, 470, 472-3, 479-80, **103,** 237-8, **104,** 611-16, **107,** 329-30, 403-4, **116,** 662
basis
certainty in commercial transactions **64,** 179-80
equality before the law and **64,** 42
protection of litigation rights **64,** 313-14, 699, **84,** 100
common law **86,** 643
general principle of international law **103,** 303-11, 474, **104,** 516, 655, 695, 696, **113,** 419, **123,** 93
Government of Canada **104,** 695-7
ILC **91,** 297-8
international organizations, application to **63,** 340-3
Littrell **104,** 510, 699
retroactive effect **84,** 142
Sengupta **104,** 521
uncertainty regarding **87,** 32-3
State immunity, execution/attachment distinguished. *See* State immunity, execution/attachment, State immunity, jurisdiction, distinguished
State practice **45,** 61-79, **62,** 232, **63,** 561, **64,** 129-30, 136-7, 237-40, 602, 635-50, **65,** 120-1, 213-14, 419-21, **81,** 548, **91,** 297-8, **116,** 639
acts in territory of forum State **81,** 548, **82,** 44, **124,** 443-4
employment contract **104,** 523-4, **113,** 432-3
lack of consensus **64,** 126-7, 144-5, **95,** 469-70, **116,** 628-32, 658-9
legislation. *See* legislation *above*
right of suit in 'defendant' State's courts **106,** 245-7
tort **103,** 315, 316, **104,** 700-4
Tate letter. *See* United States of America (USA), Tate letter
teleological approach **79,** 11
territorial jurisdiction/sovereignty and **63,** 372-3, **64,** 86, **65,** 419-20, 438, **81,** 548 n. 7, **84,** 170, **90,** 589-91, **95,** 455, **103,** 470, **104,** 570, 576, 577, 612, 617-19, **119,** 236. *See also* basis, extraterritoriality *above*
State immunity, jurisdiction, waiver 84, 168, **86,** 61-2, 584, **87,** 201, 204-5, **90,** 411, **103,** 239-40
in absence of **82,** 120
amendment of claim, effect **107,** 598-9
authority, need for **64,** 478-9, **102,** 144, **104,** 646, 679-80, **111,** 653, 671
bill of lading as **86,** 62
burden of proof **106,** 581
by head of diplomatic mission **86,** 678
by Head of State **86,** 668
by State enterprise **72,** 127

by treaty. *See* treaty provision *below*
clear and unequivocal communication, need for **64,** 453, **65,** 87
contractual **86,** 61, **87,** 232, 233-4, 414
express term **86,** 584-5
interdependent contracts **92,** 448
restrictive interpretation **87,** 416
counterclaim as **56,** 529, **63,** 301, 304, 607-8, **66,** 109-10, 123-4, 411-12, 429, **77,** 454, **78,** 5, 8, **82,** 80, **101,** 507, **118,** 297-8
counterclaim, extension to **120,** 432-46, 457-9
disclosure of documents **103,** 321
effect of waiver by one State agency on immunity of another **92,** 488-90
exception to immunity, whether **107,** 357-8
exclusion by Constitution **116,** 629-30
execution and jurisdiction, need for separate waivers **65,** 49, 52-4, 97, 158, 251, **72,** 664-5, **75,** 522, **77,** 3-7, 522, 524, **87,** 415, 416, **92,** 404
express **80,** 168-9, 644, **86,** 584-5, 628, 678, **94,** 271, **96,** 292, 294, **99,** 135, **103,** 555, 556, **106,** 577, 581, **107,** 620-1, **111,** 652-3
Civil Aviation Board permit, provision **98,** 45-6, 74
ILR Report on the Jurisdictional Immunities of States and their Property (1991) **119,** 167
Vienna Convention on Diplomatic Relations (1961) **40,** 82-3
foreign State as plaintiff **84,** 178-9
forum selection clause as **63,** 357-8, 405-7, **65,** 35-6, 333, 370-1, 391, 400, **78,** 84, **87,** 232, 235, 414-15, **92,** 447-8, **103,** 508
human rights treaties 77, 268-9
Universal Declaration of Human Rights (1948) **103,** 475
implied **64,** 135, **81,** 554, **86,** 73-5, **87,** 541 n. 2
acceptance of applicable law for contract **86,** 61-2
acceptance of applicable law in respect of ships in port **63,** 40
acceptance of default judgment **65,** 87-8, **94,** 317
acceptance of provision of law of State **86,** 73-4
acknowledgement of receipt of complaint **92,** 424
adjudication provision **86,** 62
agreement for recognition and enforcement of arbitral awards **103,** 577-80
agreement to arbitrate in third country **63,** 198, 405-7, 519-20, 537-8, 635, **72,** 159-63, **103,** 565-7, 570-1
arbitral award, judgment confirming **98,** 33
arbitration clause/agreement **41,** 452-5, **42,** 177-8, **45,** 83-5, **47,** 150-1, **61,** 105-6, **62,** 223, 228, 234-5, **63,** 197-8, 357-8, 405-7, 462, 519-20, 537-8, 566, 645, **65,** 48, 52-3, 89-92, 96, 383-4, **77,** 267, 523-4, **78,** 84, **80,** 33, 36, 644-5, **82,** 74, **87,** 414-15, **89,** 358, **92,** 426 n. 8, **103,** 576-80, **113,** 550-1
charterparty **41,** 452-5, **57,** 149, 151
arbitration proceedings, submission to **106,** 561-2, 577
bankruptcy claim **107,** 339 n. 57
bill of lading **63,** 356-7
choice of law clause **63,** 40, 198, 405-7, 520, 537, **87,** 232, 235, 414-15, **94,** 271, **101,** 490-1, **107,** 349-52, **113,** 538, **114,** 511, **120,** 614-16
in manual of employment **120,** 614-16
Civil Aeronautics Board (USA) permit, acceptance of **63,** 195-6
commercial dealings **64,** 97, **80,** 644, 646
contract as **63,** 422, **65,** 172, 253, **88,** 712, 714, **102,** 128, 140, 142-3, **114,** 512
counterclaim as, withdrawal, relevance **77,** 455-6
extradition proceedings, participation in **42,** 245-6

State immunity, jurisdiction, waiver (*cont.*)
failure to raise immunity promptly **63,** 405, **92,** 416, **101,** 543-4, **103,** 539-43, 547-8, **118,** 424, 427-8
guarantee of satisfaction in case of liability **107,** 390-1, **113,** 540-1
insurance contract **65,** 14-15
inter-State military training contract **63,** 421-2
judgment in forum court, invocation as defence **98,** 33-4
jurisdictional legislation **96,** 40-1, 42, 58
jus cogens/peremptory norm violation **103,** 610, **113,** 537-40, 547-8
lease **52,** 320-1
letter to court **113,** 546
liability for suit provision **103,** 500-2
narrow interpretation **63,** 321-2
objection to default judgment **94,** 317
parallel **107,** 380-1
participation in aid programme **86,** 61
recognition of debt founding private law relationship **65,** 276-8
relationship to legal proceedings **113,** 538-40
service of process
acceptance or acknowledgment **64,** 366, **65,** 87, 198-9
appointment of agent for **63,** 356-7
undertaking in damages **120,** 432-40, 455-7
undertakings to court **111,** 652-3, 664-5
waiver of jurisdiction in third State **98,** 32
knowledge and intent, need for **63,** 422, **101,** 491 n. 6, 544, **103,** 610, 620, **111,** 671, **113,** 538-9
limitation to actions in own courts **63,** 48
membership of international organization **80,** 164-5, 168-9
narrow interpretation **103,** 577
nexus, relevance in case of **63,** 406-7, **79,** 555 n. 15
personal defendants, extension to **120,** 446-50, 460-1
provisional measures, claim for compensation for allegedly wrongful attachment **82,** 80
related action **103,** 570-1
restrictive interpretation **63,** 503-4, **107,** 380, 390
statutory **63,** 162-3, 340, **80,** 22-3, 591, **86,** 483, **99,** 85-6, 91, **100,** 535, 539-40, **102,** 140, 144
adoption of Crown Proceedings Act 1963 (UK) **63,** 352-3
narrow interpretation **100,** 535, 539-40, **101,** 490, 491
submission to the jurisdiction as **63,** 520, **64,** 34, 36, 39, 46, 449-53, 475-8, **65,** 172, 250, 438-40, **66,** 56, **77,** 16, 267, 454-5, **84,** 38, **103,** 355-6, 377-9, **104,** 679, **107,** 603, 620-2, **111,** 664, **118,** 427
action to stay proceedings **87,** 205, **95,** 462-4, **103,** 356, 379, 382
appearance as **40,** 81-3, **63,** 223, **65,** 35-6, 52, 374, 377, **103,** 356, 366-7, 376-9
challenge to jurisdiction **64,** 34, 35-6, 396-7, 428-9, **65,** 199, **102,** 148, **103,** 377-9, 382, 388-90, **104,** 689-90
conditional appearance **63,** 606-7, **64,** 438, 454-5, 478, **87,** 231-2, **101,** 472-5
criminal proceedings **103,** 476-8
'deemed submission' **104,** 680
defence **86,** 482, **90,** 561
forum [non] conveniens claim **103,** 378-9, 389-90
initiation of proceedings **42,** 46-7, **64,** 103, **98,** 114-15, **102,** 140, **106,** 245
insurance contract **65,** 14-15
non-justiciability claim **103,** 378-9

notice of appearance **104,** 680, **107,** 620-1
person signing contract **104,** 680
revocation/withdrawal **65,** 15
submission to own courts distinguished **103,** 451
timing **87,** 416, **101,** 472-5
time of **87,** 234-5
treaty provision **45,** 73-5, **63,** 510, **64,** 42-3, 593-5, **65,** 177-81, 399, 430-1, **72,** 178-9, **77,** 263, 267-8, 631, **81,** 554, 556, 668, **85,** 240-3, **86,** 90, **87,** 105, **101,** 551-3, **102,** 129-31, **103,** 475-6, **107,** 222
absence of **65,** 103, 141, 195, 399, 418-19, 430-1
bilateral treaties **65,** 179-80
Brussels Convention on Immunity of State-owned Ships (1926) **45,** 73-4, **64,** 648-9, **65,** 104, 177, 293
Chicago Convention on International Civil Aviation (1944) **64,** 648-9
conflict with legislation conferring immunity, need for **107,** 388
critical date **107,** 388, **113,** 541
European Convention on State Immunity (and Protocol) (Basle) (1972). *See* European Convention on State Practice (and Protocol) (Basle) (1972)
express provision, need for **119,** 166-9, 170
FRG–USA Treaty of Friendship, Trade and Navigation (1956) **45,** 74
Geneva Convention on the High Seas (1958) **64,** 649, **65,** 177-8
Geneva Convention on the Territorial Sea (1958) **64,** 649, **65,** 177-8
Geneva High Seas Convention (1958) **45,** 74
Hague Conventions (1899/1907) **103,** 611
Helsinki Final Act (1975) **85,** 242-3
Iran–US Claims Settlement Declaration **81,** 567
Iran–US Treaty of Amity (1955). *See* Iran–US Treaty of Amity (1955), waiver of State immunity, whether
NATO Status of Forces Agreement (1951) **86,** 628, 633, **94,** 271, 290, **100,** 445, 448-9, 460-1
Philippine–American Military Bases Agreement **64,** 657
Security Council Resolution **107,** 387-8
Torture Convention (1984) **119,** 165-75, 196-9, 201, 216-17, 219-21, 231-2, 245
trade agreement **64,** 590-4
treaty of establishment **98,** 31-2
Treaty of Versailles (1919) **45,** 73
UN Charter **85,** 240-2, **103,** 476, **113,** 541
USSR treaties (1920-1960) **45,** 74-5
Warsaw Convention (1955) **98,** 74
Warsaw Convention on International Carriage by Air (1929) **64,** 648-9
US Foreign Claims Act **80,** 22
withdrawal **63,** 526, **65,** 15, **107,** 592, 599, **113,** 538
written **82,** 33, **104,** 633-6, 643-6
diplomatic correspondence **107,** 620-1
solicitor's letter to employer prior to employment contract **104,** 633-6, 643-6
unilateral undertaking **104,** 645
State immunity, procedural aspects, punitive damages, liability for **63,** 79, 205-6, 236, 418, 579, **79,** 554 n. 12, 558 n. 22, **86,** 79, **101,** 526, **103,** 550, **107,** 316
State immunity, taxation 104, 538, 571-4, 605, 615, **108,** 525. *See also* Head of State, immunity, income tax
assessment **94,** 320
local rates

State immunity, taxation (*cont.*)
consular/diplomatic premises **53,** 545-50
educational institute **68,** 681-3
property held by public corporation for public use **43,** 162-5
real estate **63,** 179-80, **65,** 547
social security contributions **63,** 195-6
unemployment insurance **63,** 195-6
unenforceability as basis for **53,** 547-50
State liability. *See* State responsibility
State necessity. *See* necessity
State practice. *See also* customary international law; *opinio juris*
acts, words distinguished **84,** 539
'appreciable section of the community' **110,** 228, 262
arbitration clause, severability **62,** 178
arbitrator, withdrawal **78,** 674
armed conflict, international and internal, distinction **105,** 498-9
aut dedere aut punire/judicare obligation **119,** 86
bilateral investment treaties **84,** 525, 540
breach of treaty, protest, effect **90,** 693
broadcasting from outside territory, jurisdiction **101,** 414-15
Chicago Convention on International Civil Aviation (1944), implementation of Annex 13 **120,** 561-2
civil or public law classification **86,** 359, 369
collective self-defence **76,** 703-7, 865
compensation
lump sum agreements **84,** 525, 536-7, 654, 667 n. 1
obligation to pay **62,** 201
standard of **62,** 206, **66,** 605-7, **84,** 564-5
concession contract **41,** 136
conscientious objection **95,** 552-3
conservation and management measures **123,** 221-3, 297-300, 303-4, 314, 327
constitutive treaty and **83,** 153
consular access, notification of right to **118,** 10
continental shelf **41,** 81-2, 85-6, 88, 105, 109, 133-7, 158, 190, **62,** 125, **67,** 170, 173
continental shelf delimitation **41,** 206-11, **54,** 132-3, **62,** 125, **81,** 261-2, 379
delimitation line, terminal point **81,** 310-13
discontinuities **67,** 111, **81,** 337
equidistance **67,** 72, **81,** 270, 274-5, 293, 298, 339-40, 359
proportionality **81,** 277
contract, definition **89,** 461
courts' duty to keep in step with **77,** 17
criminal responsibility of individual **105,** 522-3
common purpose **124,** 139, 156-9
customary international law, evidence of **41,** 72-5, 85, 114, 118, 133-7, 158, 169-71, 190, 209, 221, **57,** 63-4, 433, **70,** 376-7, 402-4, **71,** 121, 536, 550, 559, 581, **91,** 116, 124, **104,** 329, 335
death penalty **98,** 308-9
detention, house arrest **108,** 76-8
diplomatic privileges and immunities
entitlement, third State, in **115,** 612
functional **78,** 103
double jeopardy/*non bis in idem* **124,** 191-3

duress. *See* duress, State practice
EEZ **67,** 108, **74,** 144-6, **81,** 265, 302, 358, **82,** 642
  refuelling of fishing vessel **110,** 752, 754-6, **120,** 189-92, 237-9
  sovereignty, economic **82,** 642
embassy or consular bank account/funds, immunity, execution/attachment **113,** 423-4
employment contract, variation **104,** 517-18
employment legislation, employee entitlements on termination of employment **109,** 382-8
equidistance. *See also* continental shelf delimitation, equidistance, State practice
  modification of **41,** 227
equity **41,** 144-5
equity, source of **99,** 610
European Community law, European Council practice **105,** 206-7, 209
evidence, corroboration, need for **112,** 172-3
evidence of **53,** 342
  draft multilateral agreement **101,** 414-15
    comments on **105,** 588
    UN **105,** 512, 530
  EU declaration **105,** 513, 514, 517-18
  generally accepted practice **125,** 503-4
  judicial and arbitral decisions **105,** 588, **125,** 503-4
  jus cogens/peremptory norm **124,** 364
  legislation **80,** 68, 135, **105,** 522, 588
  Manifesto of the Chinese People's Liberation Army (1947) **105,** 508
  military manual **105,** 498, 510, 515-16, 521-2, 588, **110,** 447-8, **111,** 397, 408-9
  municipal institutions, practice regarding **80,** 141
  municipal legislation **41,** 135-6, 208-9, 211
  practice of international organization **105,** 588
  State contract, whether **41,** 136
  State papers **80,** 135
  statement
    at conference **81,** 277, **99,** 424
    in Parliament **105,** 507
  treaties **41,** 137, 158, 169-70, 213, **80,** 52, 67-8, 108, 173-6, **105,** 498-9, 588
  UN Resolutions **84,** 539, **105,** 329, 511-14, 522-3, **110,** 507
  unilateral acts **41,** 119, 136, 158, 190, 208-9, 212-15
exclusive fisheries zone **55,** 285-7, **56,** 188, 191, 193-5
execution against foreign State **77,** 492-3
expropriation/nationalization, procedure for determining compensation **83,** 550
expulsion of alien **82,** 214
extradition, assurances that death penalty will not be carried out **100,** 407, 674-8
extradition treaties **70,** 376-7, **72,** 66, 69, 73-4, 631, **73,** 39-42, 47-8, 54, **79,** 83
family members, extension of rights of refugee to **111,** 539-40
humanitarian law **105,** 520-4
inconsistent **46,** 489
International Convention on the Elimination of All Forms of Racial Discrimination (1965) **85,** 210
international law, conflict **110,** 261
international organizations
  Member States' liability **80,** 52, 67-8, 173-6
  positions taken in **46,** 476, 477
  transfer of seat **62,** 495
  treaties *ex post facto* **80,** 108

State practice (*cont.*)
intervention outside territory **76,** 442-3
to prevent genocide **95,** 162-3
inviolability of diplomatic premises, prevention of demonstration **101,** 231-2, 243-4
islands **83,** 112
joint exploitation of maritime resources **119,** 445-6
jurisdiction
extent **81,** 549
fisheries **56,** 216
riparian States **75,** 82-4
trial by 'natural' judge **105,** 484-5
law of the sea and **41,** 63, **74,** 145-6
limitation as precedent **101,** 196, **110,** 696-7, 698, 709-10, 712, 713-14
location of diplomatic mission in capital **99,** 108
maritime delimitation **81,** 261-2. *See also* continental shelf delimitation *above and* territorial sea delimitation *below*
applicable law **99,** 432
harbour works **91,** 662
relevant/special circumstances **99,** 638-9
single boundary **99,** 656
mass claims processing **109,** 252-4
national interest, determination of **62,** 194
nuclear weapons, deployment **106,** 362-3, **110,** 261, 262-3, 330
deterrence theory **110,** 262
penalty, purpose **108,** 202-4
'poison or poisoned weapons' **110,** 198
prior consultation procedure before discharge of potential pollutants **87,** 87
treaty interpretation and **87,** 154
punitive damages **88,** 741
recognition, collective **82,** 420
requirements
constant and uniform usage **55,** 280, 285-7, **62,** 209, **94,** 77. *See also* uniform and regular *below*
continuity **41,** 209, 219
frequency **41,** 209
generality. *See* uniformity *below*
immemorial usage **41,** 219
sufficiency **41,** 72, 105, 106, 212
uniformity **41,** 72, 73, 105, 209, 212, 219, **46,** 504
resistance from opposing parties **46,** 490
sampling methodology **109,** 68-76
self-defence **76,** 703-7
self-determination **49,** 64-5
as source of international law **67,** 163, **77,** 174, 206, **113,** 418, 419
State immunity. *See* State immunity, execution/attachment, State practice; State immunity, jurisdiction, State practice
State immunity in own courts **125,** 160-1
State responsibility, standard of protection **106,** 457
State succession **73,** 601
State's right of suit in foreign court **106,** 245-7
sustainable development principle **116,** 102-4
territorial dispute **91,** 594
territorial sea delimitation **57,** 63-4

torture **77,** 178, 206, 269
treaties **74,** 154
constitutive **83,** 153
denunciation **90,** 372
pacta sunt servanda **62,** 192
State succession **75,** 108-13, **83,** 54, **115,** 186-92
validity in case of known conflict with municipal law **78,** 175
treaty interpretation **72,** 630-1, 643-4, 687, **75,** 182, 185-6, 191-2, 198, 202-3, 208-9, 219, 259
aid to **82,** 660, **86,** 368, 370, 374-5, 406, 408, 412-13, **95,** 366, **103,** 647-8, **106,** 500
unilateral undertakings, legislative consent, need for **106,** 371-2
war crimes **82,** 440
individual responsibility **105,** 537-8
obligation to seek out and prosecute **91,** 36-7, 116
retrospectivity **82,** 434-5
war, laws and customs **105,** 506-24
chemical weapons **105,** 518-19
war reparations **74,** 154
weapons, legality **110,** 197
State representatives, authority of **70,** 48-9, 486, 492-3
restrictions on
internal laws of fundamental importance **70,** 486, 493
knowledge of other States **70,** 48-9
specific restriction **70,** 486, 492-3
State responsibility.[xi]
State responsibility for
aid or assistance to another State for commission of internationally wrongful act **76,** 318-19
aid or assistance to insurgents **76,** 387-403
bad faith, agents **91,** 296

[xi] Material relating to State responsibility is indexed under the following main headings (and, where relevant, in parallel entries under individual countries) and as a subheading to other main headings:
belligerent occupation, State responsibility for acts in occupied territory
environment, environmental impact assessment, State responsibility for effects
European Community (EC), liability for lawful act
European Community law, State responsibility
European Convention on Human Rights (1950), State responsibility
International Covenant on Civil and Political Rights (ICCPR) (1966), State responsibility
International Law Commission (ILC), [Draft] Articles on State Responsibility
State responsibility for (for material which does not fall into any of the identified categories)
State responsibility for acts and omissions in compliance with international obligations
State responsibility for acts and omissions during revolution
State responsibility for acts and omissions outside State's jurisdiction
State responsibility for acts and omissions of predecessor government
State responsibility, breach
State responsibility for breach of treaty
State responsibility for contract
State responsibility, imputability
State responsibility, law relating to
State responsibility, procedural aspects
State responsibility/liability of Iraq for any direct loss, damage . . . as a result of Iraq's unlawful invasion and occupation of Kuwait.

State responsibility for (*cont.*)
breach of European Community law. *See* European Community law, State responsibility
breach of official duty **111,** 9-11
compensation for war-related events **40,** 103-11, **94,** 61-2
individual's right to compensation **41,** 480-2, **56,** 537-56
substitution of responsibility in post-war agreement **72,** 237-8
crimes against humanity, customary international law **121,** 257
criminal acts **74,** 253, 258
ILC Draft Code of Offences against the Peace and Security of Mankind (1976) **115,** 178-9
damage caused by
closure of consular post **89,** 89
military aircraft **91,** 283-8
strike **74,** 135-8
visiting forces **91,** 287-8
performance of official duty and **91,** 284-5
debts **72,** 240-52, 480-3, 491-2, 539-45, 717-24
arising from dismissal of foreign national from employment with State monopoly **39,** 427-9
in the Belgian Congo **45,** 24-32, **47,** 75-8, **48,** 20-5, **82,** 124
liability of State agency **82,** 92
public corporation, of **87,** 12, 103-4
defective mine-sweeping on the high seas **72,** 258-60, **74,** 239-40
delays in civil proceedings **78,** 369
depth charges dropped in peacetime **74,** 240
denial of acquired rights, pension rights **42,** 169-72
denial of justice **75,** 375, 378-80, **89,** 451, **121,** 24
disappearances **79,** 179, **95,** 296-9, **118,** 207-8, 290-1
displacement of people **91,** 339-40
economic injury deriving from permissible regulation **84,** 513
exercise of authority over territory to which State has no title **49,** 6
expropriation. *See* expropriation/nationalization, State responsibility
expulsion of aliens **82,** 149-224
failure to foresee consequences of acts of nationals **88,** 685
failure to monitor and control activity **86,** 569
failure to observe international obligations **56,** 180-1, **57,** 507, **93,** 329, **95,** 296-9, 300
failure to prevent attack **82,** 170-1
failure to prevent nationals' interference with rights of other States in the contiguous zone **71,** 260-1
failure to protect against damage from wrecks **89,** 2-3
failure to protect aliens **56,** 271, **71,** 651-4, 657-61, **82,** 170-1, 201, 219, **106,** 441-64
customary international law **82,** 219
Draft Convention on the International Responsibility of States for
Injuries to Aliens (1961) **71,** 657, 662, **72,** 229, 519-20, 529, **84,** 516
'taking of property' **85,** 398-9, 402 n. 1
reciprocity, relevance **72,** 265-6
failure to protect diplomatic premises **61,** 525, 556-9, **82,** 125-7, **89,** 2-3, **123,** 502-3, **124,** 116-17
justification **61,** 563-7
failure to protect individuals in protectorate, German Reich/Slovakia **70,** 696
failure to protect nationals, failure to evacuate **52,** 6-7, **57,** 311-12

failure to warn of mines **76,** 713-14
financial information provided by State agency **124,** 48-50
forcible abduction/unlawful arrest **86,** 529-30, **90,** 645-6, 662, **95,** 332, 359-60, 424-5, **103,** 214
Head of State immunity, breach **125,** 507-8
health **110,** 82-4
hostage-taking **61,** 555-9, 561, 563-7, 568, 584-8, **72,** 250, **124,** 116-17
human rights violations **116,** 317
incarceration in government prison **100,** 469
incitement to commit offence **76,** 722-3
injury to interest or right **46,** 210, 212
international crime **110,** 81
international tort/wrong **89,** 535, **104,** 158
  investment dispute compared **89,** 535
'internationally wrongful act' **110,** 654-5
intervention in Panama (1989), failure to restore and maintain public order/public policy/*ordre public* **96,** 57-61
lawful act **86,** 557
legislation **62,** 376-7
  wrongs connected with **72,** 261-2
legitimization of wrongful act **89,** 458-9, 534-5
loss arising from grant of diplomatic immunity **74,** 278-9
non-contractual liability **96,** 486-8
nuclear power station, accident **86,** 569
nuclear weapons deployment **110,** 147
persecution **95,** 540-1
political persecution **88,** 11, 23, 31
prevention of genocide **95,** 36-7, 161-3, 181, **115,** 29, 40-1, 44-5, 177-9, 180-2
  Genocide Convention (1948). *See* Genocide Convention (1948), State responsibility for the prevention of genocide
proper administration of justice **96,** 448, 462, 473-4, 492, 495, 510-11, 515, 532, 590, 601
protection of foreign investment **89,** 457, 516, 531, 532-3
  UNGA Resolution 3281 (XXIV) (Charter of Economic Rights and Duties of States) **89,** 533
protection of nationals' interests, failure to provide diplomatic protection **72,** 219-22, 238, 266
public order disturbance **89,** 18
racial persecution **70,** 692-8
safety of airspace **89,** 30-1
social security **86,** 360-1
State terrorism. *See* State-sponsored terrorism, State responsibility
taking or interference with property **40,** 94-102, **41,** 266-79, **42,** 158-61, **47,** 31-9, 60-2, 63-6, 120-6, 129-34, **66,** 12- 19, 31-4, 42-7, 183-5, 358-60, 424, 433-40, 481-3, 516, 582-94, **70,** 119-28, **71,** 266-9, 601-2, 677, **72,** 150-2, 227-33, 291-2, 494, 498-500, **74,** 222-37, **75,** 379-80
  interference with pension rights **42,** 169-72
  revocation or annulment of concession agreement **44,** 79-100, **70,** 484-9, 491-5
torture **104,** 143-6, 157, **121,** 257
transboundary nuclear pollution **86,** 565-70
transfer of funds on authority of State agency **124,** 53
treatment of non-resident shareholders **46,** 422

State responsibility for (*cont.*)
treaty in breach of international law, joint responsibility of parties **116,** 169
Tunisia/France **44,** 1-2, 32-3
unjust enrichment **72,** 721-4
unlawful act **86,** 557, **93,** 329
illegality under municipal law **106,** 608-9
violation of foreign sovereignty **69,** 153
war
breach of the laws and customs of **76,** 722-3
loss during war or civil disturbance not attributable to State **106,** 480, 487-94, 498-500
losses arising out of military operations **48,** 467-8
war crimes **108,** 155-6, **124,** 98
assimilation of civilians to State officials **124,** 119-21
reprisals **61,** 569-70, 667
wrecks **89,** 5
destruction of **89,** 5
wrongful act, countermeasure as. *See* countermeasures, lawfulness
State responsibility for acts and omissions in compliance with international obligations 111, 139-40
execution of judgment of European Court of Justice **111,** 139-40
State responsibility for acts and omissions contrary to rights of another State 56, 179
State responsibility for acts and omissions during revolution 61, 555-6, 559, 560-1, **85,** 401-2, 450-4, **96,** 490, **106,** 441. *See also* State responsibility for, aid or assistance to insurgents
acts prior to establishment of government **82,** 160, 174
acts of revolutionaries, evidence of **106,** 449-50, 462-3, 475, 498
authorization **82,** 162
contract **103,** 266-7
counter-insurgency activities **106,** 457-64, 494-8
customary international law **106,** 491-4
damage incidental to **82,** 216
endorsement by new legislature **103,** 266-7
failure to provide proper standard of protection **106,** 457-9
negligence, relevance **106,** 458
force majeure **106,** 496
government forces or authorities **106,** 441, 450
caused unnecessarily **106,** 441, 493-8
evidence, sufficiency **106,** 449-50, 462-3, 475, 498
wanton destruction **106,** 491, 493-8
injury caused in operations to quell rebellion **72,** 57-8
insurgents and rioters **72,** 133-4, 267-9
mobs **82,** 216, **85,** 401-2
national liberation movements. *See* State responsibility for acts and omissions of, national liberation movements
opponents of **82,** 176
overthrown government remaining in control of situation **82,** 160
police power **106,** 496-7
preventive measures, obligation **106,** 457-64, 494-8
revolutionary forces **106,** 441
murder **71,** 661-2
recognition, relevance **106,** 493, 495
successful **76,** 716, **82,** 160, 176, 191, 215

revolutionary movement **82,** 155
supporters **82,** 161, 174-6
State responsibility for acts and omissions of. *See also* State responsibility, imputability
administrative authorities **46,** 191, 204, 324, 327
exhaustion of remedies and **46,** 200-1
agency **90,** 660
another State **56,** 540, **105,** 311-13, 314
agents of third State **90,** 646-7
armed forces **54,** 244-6, **62,** 50, 75, **63,** 422-3, **74,** 253, 258, 260, 266, 269-70, **88,** 187-8, **89,** 11-14, 456-9, 531-3, 548, 571, 594-9, **124,** 100-1. *See also* State immunity, jurisdiction, acts of, armed forces abroad; State immunity, jurisdiction, classification of act, armed forces, acts concerning
air force officers shooting down plane illegally **121,** 612
commercial enterprise acting on behalf of **89,** 455-6
during armed conflict **99,** 87-9
irregular combatants. *See* State responsibility, imputability, effective/de facto control test
low-level flights **108,** 674-6
margin of appreciation **108,** 674
NATO forces **108,** 675-6
off-duty soldier **63,** 423
rents paid by armed forces abroad **88,** 711-12
termination of activity in military base for security reasons **64,** 659-60
visiting serviceman **96,** 381-3
central/State-owned bank. *See* central/State-owned bank, State responsibility
consular agent **86,** 556-7, **99,** 125
diplomatic agent **86,** 547-50, **87,** 59, **103,** 310
executive **74,** 135-8
federal State **118,** 46, **119,** 634, 639, 644-5
former colonial power **89,** 11-14
former colony **82,** 124
FRG within the GDR **94,** 59-60, 62
government minister **84,** 634, 642-5
conclusion of contract on behalf of State **117,** 562
judicial authorities **46,** 191-2, 204, 318, 320, 324, 327-34, 439, **75,** 375, 378-80, **89,** 451, 502-3, **102,** 139, 143, **118,** 46, **121,** 22-3, 432-3, 449-50
denial of justice. *See* for denial of justice *below*
disavowal of courts at international level, relevance **121,** 23
in federal State **118,** 46
legitimization of wrongful act **89,** 458-9, 534-5
proper administration of justice. *See* European Convention on Human Rights (1950), prompt hearing, State responsibility
legislature, unconstitutional legislation **111,** 61-2
local government authority **121,** 20
employee **86,** 503
members of family of Head of State **100,** 469, 473
militants **61,** 555-6
military aircraft **88,** 58-60, **91,** 283-8
national liberation movements **91,** 360-1, **124,** 115-16
acts of predecessor government **91,** 360-1
effective/de facto control test **124,** 115-16
neutral territory, collateral damage **110,** 338-9, 451
occupying authorities

State responsibility for acts and omissions of (*cont.*)
Hague Convention (1907) **96,** 58-9, 60
US intervention in Panama (1989) **96,** 57-61
occupying power. *See* belligerent occupation, State responsibility for acts in occupied territory
official **62,** 74-5, 85-7, 240-2, 244-8, 251-2, **81,** 136-84, **91,** 366, **100,** 469. *See also* State responsibility, imputability, effective/de facto control test
administrative practices **71,** 300-3, **120,** 122
consistent with State's policies **121,** 636
Nicaragua test **124,** 104-7
safety of airspace above airport **89,** 30-1
torture **121,** 257
ultra vires act **82,** 201, **95,** 296, **106,** 608-9, **119,** 205, 207, 639, **124,** 109-11. *See also* State responsibility, imputability, authorization, relevance
unlawful acts **71,** 300-3
police officer **70,** 227-34, 268-81, **125,** 511-18
disclosure of document provided by member of visiting forces **86,** 501-3
junior **95,** 331
outside scope of authority **90,** 663, **95,** 331
political subdivision **84,** 545 n. 40, **125,** 22-4, 27-38
bad faith **125,** 29-32, 69-71
compliance with obligations, action to ensure **125,** 34-8, 66-7
standard of liability, relevance **125,** 26-7, 65 n. 17, 67
prison officers **103,** 426
private administration **96,** 487, 491
private bank **124,** 52-4
private persons or groups **46,** 199, 225, **82,** 159-62, **95,** 297, 540-1
acting on behalf of State **82,** 193, **95,** 332, **124,** 108-11
as agents **124,** 109
Bosnian Croats **108,** 155-8, **122,** 48-57, 245-7
Bosnian Serbs **112,** 188-200, **124,** 114-15
breach of international obligation while **124,** 109
as attribute of sovereignty **59,** 168
control. *See* State responsibility, imputability, effective/de facto control test
as de facto State organ or agency **124,** 103, 108-51
criteria **112,** 191-200
customary international law **112,** 188-200
war crimes trials **124,** 119-20
[Draft] Articles on State Responsibility (1977/1980/1996/1998/ 2001) **82,** 193, **124,** 108
exercise of authority in absence of government **82,** 193
government officials refusing to carry out instructions **110,** 716
implied or express approval or instructions, need for **82,** 201, **124,** 107, 109-19
rationale for attribution **124,** 108, 110-11
torture **104,** 143-6
public administration **96,** 487, 491
receiving State **61,** 556-7, 562
revolutionary forces. *See* State responsibility for acts and omissions during revolution
security forces, outside armed combat **106,** 441
State agency. *See* State organ *below*
State bank. *See* central/State-owned bank, State responsibility
State corporation **86,** 295
State employees **70,** 232-5

State organ **64,** 322, **80,** 384-8, **84,** 376, **86,** 78-9, 80 n. 4, **110,** 708, **124,** 48-50
abroad **86,** 547-50
acts on behalf of State and private acts distinguished **84,** 558
aliens, failure to protect **71,** 651-4, 657-61
applicable law **86,** 549-50
clandestine operations, death and damage caused in **74,** 253, 256, 258, 262
contravention of instructions **82,** 201
contravention of municipal law **95,** 296, 299
customary international law **124,** 105 n. 129
de facto State organ or agency. *See* private persons or groups *above*
dependants, rights of **71,** 651-9
designation of individual as **110,** 710, 712
destruction of property during rescue mission **71,** 601-2, **125,** 702-3
[Draft] Articles on State Responsibility (1977/1980/1996/1998/2001) **124,** 105 nn. 129 and 130
execution of law necessary feature **86,** 549
failure to control **82,** 200
identity of perpetrator unknown **95,** 296
illegal act **124,** 111
instrument of State, responsibility of State **83,** 556-7, 559-60
international law **71,** 655-8
motivation, relevance **95,** 296
NAFTA provisions **121,** 47-8
official act **82,** 201, **95,** 296, **124,** 105-6
official orders, relevance **95,** 299
respondeat superior doctrine **63,** 621
Revolutionary Guards in Iran as **82,** 193-5, **124,** 112-13
safety of airspace above airport **89,** 30-1
State immunity distinguished **63,** 59
unauthorized bribe **82,** 200-1
wrongful death **71,** 654-8
Turkish Republic of Northern Cyprus (TRNC) **103,** 638, 639-49, 654, **108,** 466, 485, **120,** 36-40, 111, 133-5, **124,** 114
private individuals **120,** 39-40
undercover agent **94,** 347-8
workers' syndicate **84,** 631-2, 642
State responsibility for acts and omissions outside State's jurisdiction 62, 44, 50-1, 55, 74-5, 85-6
area 'under control' **108,** 465-6, 473, 485, **120,** 38-40, 111
death penalty **98,** 402-7, 417, **124,** 316-17
deportation to country where risk of subjection to torture **124,** 361-3
direct result of own action **98,** 303, **123,** 35-6
following extradition **98,** 374, **124,** 316-17
foreseeable result of own action **98,** 301, 303
human rights violation **98,** 299, 300-3, 404-6, **103,** 638, 639-49, 654, **120,** 38-40
lawfulness of military intervention, relevance **108,** 466, 481
legal representation, lack of **98,** 313-14
respect for other States **98,** 417-18
State organ **86,** 547-50
US officials in Antarctica **100,** 530-44
State responsibility for acts and omissions of predecessor government 89, 11-14, 18, **91,** 339-40, 343-57, 359-70. *See also* State succession, rights and obligations
acquired rights **91,** 344-7, 350-1, 359-60
possibility of abolition **91,** 345

State responsibility for acts and omissions of predecessor government (*cont.*)
administrative responsibility shared with successor State **88,** 58-60, 701-2
change of government **95,** 299
conquered State **91,** 345, 367
contractual liabilities **91,** 345-6
debts incurred in the Belgian Congo **45,** 24-32, **47,** 75-8, **48,** 20-5
declaration of unconstitutionality, need for **103,** 114-16
delict **91,** 343-57
amendment of claim **91,** 357-8
substitution of defendant party **91,** 356-7
disclaimer **91,** 352-3. *See also* repudiation *below*
enforcement of judgments **89,** 11-14
espionage, failure to agree treatment of **94,** 81-2
Hawaiian Claims (1925) **91,** 367
human rights, conflict with and **91,** 350
injury caused in operations to quell rebellion **72,** 57-8
lawfulness of acts under international law, relevance **91,** 347, 352-5, 361-7, 368-9
Lighthouses Arbitration (1956) **91,** 353, 368
merger **91,** 367
municipal law liability **91,** 361
national liberation movements **91,** 360-1
pre-succession State liability, relevance **91,** 371
proper party **91,** 358-9
repudiation **103,** 107-19
legislation, need for **103,** 120, 122
uncompleted acts, whether limited to **103,** 115-17
Robert E Brown Claim (1923) **91,** 367
State responsibility, breach
cessation, duty **96,** 320-1
customary international law **96,** 321
waiver of right to **96,** 321-2
continuing wrong **49,** 6, 44, **116,** 139-41, 215-19
continuity from time of act to finding of illegality **95,** 299, **96,** 323-4
ILC [Draft] Articles on State Responsibility. *See* International Law Commission (ILC), [Draft] Articles on State Responsibility (1977/1980/1996/1998/2001)
contractual and tortious liability, distinction, whether **82,** 551
defences
force majeure **82,** 549, **86,** 502, **96,** 318, **106,** 496
contributory act and **96,** 318
municipal law **125,** 22, 89-92
national security
constitutional provision **106,** 497-8, 500
customary international law **106,** 497-8
treaty provision **106,** 497-8
necessity **82,** 554-5, **106,** 441, 449-51, **116,** 48-50, 192-3, 197-8
self-defence **76,** 711-12
reparations **74,** 253, 256, 258-60, 266-74
apology **74,** 258, 266, 271
for breach of treaty **82,** 551, **116,** 86-90
for damage suffered in riot **54,** 244-6
distinguished **125,** 132
double **46,** 451, 502-3, 505, 525

duty to make **46,** 451, 502-3, 505, 525, **61,** 567-8, **116,** 276-7, 410-11, 498-9, **118,** 103, **121,** 127-8, 191
for failure to protect diplomatic premises **61,** 559, 567-8, 571-2, 578-80
fault and **54,** 466-9
for international tort/wrong, damage, need for **82,** 569-70
punitive damages **63,** 38
restitutio in integrum **96,** 321
compensation as alternative **96,** 321
satisfaction distinguished **46,** 466
trade undertakings **74,** 259-60, 269-70, 273
requirements
breach of international law **99,** 131
causal relationship **82,** 220-1, **93,** 328, **96,** 323, **117,** 246-50, **124,** 113 n. 151
damage of economic value **86,** 502
direct result of public service operation **86,** 502
due diligence, absence **103,** 426
fault **82,** 126-7, **93,** 329-31, 334-5
proximate cause **71,** 630, **109,** 235-6
wrongful act, preparatory actions distinguished **116,** 63, 66, 75-6, 139-43, 179-84, 204-5, 215
State contract, unilateral termination **89,** 457, 493-8
State responsibility for breach of treaty 102, 362-3
abuse of discretion by State agency
failure to act for reasons incompatible with treaty **102,** 358
non-culpable ignorance of **102,** 357
acts on own territory prior to **116,** 63, 65, 75-6
American Convention on Human Rights (1969) **95,** 296-9
applicable law **116,** 47, 48, **125,** 89-92
continuity of improper action, need for **102,** 385
duty of reparation **82,** 551, **116,** 86-90
failure to intervene **102,** 439, 443
failure to investigate **95,** 296, 300, **102,** 358, 373, 374-5, 376, 378-9, 380, 396-7, 398, 416, 419, 426-7, 428-9, 438, 441-3, 445-6
serious investigation, need for **95,** 297
State, by **95,** 297-8
failure to pass implementing legislation **121,** 258-60
torture **121,** 259-60
failure to prevent **61,** 556, 561-2, 563, **95,** 296-9
justifiable belief in appropriateness of action **102,** 357
legislation inconsistent with obligations **70,** 257-8, 268-81, 298-304, 306-13
loss arising from **89,** 8
mitigation of damage as justification **116,** 63, 154
necessity as defence. *See* necessity
non-performance, *force majeure* **96,** 318
refusal of extradition for public policy reasons **106,** 267-8
treaty in force at time of alleged breach, need for **125,** 129-32
State responsibility for contract
breach **42,** 173-8, **62,** 197-201, **63,** 166-9, 233-5, **70,** 484-9, 491-5, **72,** 240-52, 254-6, **86,** 295-6, **99,** 131
action leading to breach **106,** 196, 197
good faith **82,** 670
State contract **83,** 554

State responsibility for contract (*cont.*)
during revolution **103,** 266-7
employer's termination of expelled alien's **82,** 220
interference with **63,** 167-9, 233-5, **74,** 222-37
lawful termination **106,** 196, 197
liabilities of predecessor government **91,** 345-6
non-payment of contractual retirement benefits **42,** 157-8
State responsibility, imputability 61, 555-6, 559-61, 563, **76,** 384-5, 387, 398-9, 452, 490, 521-2, 665-6, 870-1, **77,** 436, **79,** 364-5, **82,** 159-62, 169-70, 213, **84,** 556, 631-4, 637-8, **86,** 78-9, **89,** 454-9. *See also* acts and omissions *and* 'for' *entries above*
acquiescence of State **95,** 297
armed conflict, applicability of rules relating to State responsibility **108,** 155-6, **112,** 188-200, **124,** 98
attribution as essential feature of State responsibility **125,** 23, 65
authorization of act, relevance **69,** 153, **82,** 162, **95,** 540-1, **101,** 527-32
burden of proof **82,** 194, 223, 224
degree of control. *See* effective/de facto control test *below*
due diligence, lack of **82,** 159, 201
effective/de facto control test **82,** 194-5, **101,** 545. *See also* State responsibility for acts and omissions of, private persons or groups
agency test **124,** 104-7, 200-1
Bosnian Croats **108,** 155-8, **122,** 24-7, 48-57
Bosnian Serbs **112,** 194-200, 268-76, **124,** 1, 121-30, 195-201
crimes against humanity **112,** 220-2
direction, control, organization or enforcement of acts, need for **122,** 50-1, 54-7, **124,** 102-3, 115-30
evidence of
command and control **112,** 194-6, **124,** 114-15
economic or military assistance **124,** 116 n. 157
payment of salary **112,** 193, 196, **124,** 122
staffing **112,** 194, 196
standard of proof **124,** 119
Geneva Conventions (1949) **112,** 275
irregular combatants **124,** 99-130, 149-72
Stephens **124,** 112
Yeager **124,** 112
Nicaragua **112,** 268-75, **122,** 49, **124,** 102-3, 195-201
overthrown government remaining in control of situation **82,** 160
State practice, national liberation movements **124,** 115-16
identification of actors **82,** 191-3
individual, attribution of responsibility to **124,** 121. *See also* State responsibility for acts and omissions of, private persons or groups; State responsibility, imputability, effective/de facto control test
customary international law **110,** 707, 710, 712
functional immunity **110,** 707-8
Eichmann **110,** 708
Rainbow Warrior **110,** 707-8
The Caroline **110,** 707 n. 50
State's right to designate individual as State organ **110,** 710, 712
Iran–US Claims Tribunal **124,** 117-18
Nicaragua for aid to El Salvador rebels **76,** 417-20, 665, 722
requirements

causal relationship **82,** 220-1, **93,** 328, **96,** 323, **117,** 246-50, **124,** 113 n. 151
proximate cause **71,** 630, **109,** 235-6
respondeat superior **101,** 527-32
revolution. *See* State responsibility for acts and omissions during revolution
treaty provision **106,** 441
United States for acts of
contras **76,** 387-403, 522-5, 723, 870-2, **124,** 102-3, 107, 116, 195-201. *See also* evidence of, *contras*
UCLAs **76,** 379-85, **124,** 104-5, 107, 117
United States Diplomatic and Consular Staff in Teheran **124,** 116-17
use of government transport **100,** 469
State responsibility, law relating to. *See also* International Law Commission (ILC), [Draft] Articles on State Responsibility (1977), 1980, 1996 *and* 1998
applicable law, forum State **94,** 348
customary international law **82,** 213, 215, 219, 548
for actions of diplomatic agents **87,** 59
crimes against humanity **121,** 257
de facto organ or agent **112,** 188-9
Head of State **119,** 200-1
individual, attribution to **110,** 707, 710, 712, **112,** 224-7, **121,** 257
national security **106,** 497-8
revolution **106,** 491-4
State organ **124,** 105 n. 129
erga omnes nature **57,** 532, 582, **76,** 63-4, **110,** 81-2, 83
general principle of law **111,** 49
general principles of State responsibility **82,** 551
international law **46,** 509, 511
Latin American and Afro-Asian influence **46,** 464-9
obligation of conduct **84,** 422-3
obligation of result **84,** 422-3
OECD Draft Convention on the Protection of Foreign Property **84,** 516, 669 n. 2
Organtheorie **77,** 472-4
quasi-contractual obligation as basis for responsibility **52,** 7
Vienna Convention on the Law of Treaties (1969) **82,** 549-50, **117,** 409
State responsibility in occupied territories. *See* belligerent occupation, State responsibility for acts in occupied territory
State responsibility, procedural aspects
burden of proof **82,** 33, 160, 162, 176-7, 202, 214, 223, 224, **86,** 502, **106,** 447-9
evidence of **102,** 139, 143, **103,** 426, 432
State liability for consequences of legal judgment **102,** 139, 143
exhaustion of local remedies **46,** 100-1, 200, 201, **54,** 324, **88,** 694, **89,** 533-5, **120,** 183, 329
waiver **89,** 533-4
treaty **46,** 421
government, change of **62,** 172-3
individual's right to remedy **42,** 8-9, **71,** 316, 331-53, 365, 554, 558, **86,** 569, 572, **95,** 332, **111,** 49
joint responsibility, treaty in breach of international law **116,** 169
joint and several liability
Corfu Channel **97,** 51-2
ILC [Draft] Articles on State Responsibility (1977/1980/1996/1998/ 2001) **97,** 50-1

State responsibility, procedural aspects (*cont.*)
municipal law analogies **97,** 52-3
limitations on liability **88,** 695
balance between interests of State and individual **111,** 49
proceedings to establish, time-limits **88,** 694, 695-7
recognition and **77,** 205, 220, **106,** 493, 495
transfer of powers to international organization, effect on **111,** 140-1
State responsibility/liability of Iraq for 'any direct loss, damage . . . as a result of Iraq's unlawful invasion and occupation of Kuwait' 109, 288-9, 507. *See also* United Nations Compensation Commission, causality
accident resulting from military action **109,** 170-1
acquis (Security Council Resolution 687 (1991)) **109,** 506-7
costs of Allied Coalition Forces **109,** 622
death or injury caused by Iraqi soldier during the occupation **109,** 143
departure or relocation costs, of temporary or exceptional nature **109,** 289
deterioration of pre-existing illness **109,** 171
environmental damage or depletion of natural resources **109,** 506-8
failure to transfer dollar portion of Egyptian workers' wages **117,** 246-50
firing of oil wells **109,** 508-11
allied bombing **109,** 511
general principle of international law **109,** 515
guidelines, need for **109,** 562
heart attack **109,** 172-3
illness or death related thereto **109,** 146-7
injuries suffered in refugee camps **109,** 147
injury or death related to authorities other than Iraqi **109,** 147-8, 173
entitlement to compensation under general principles of law **109,** 148
entitlement to payment out of Compensation Fund **109,** 148
lack of medical care **109,** 145-6, 171
loss of income, place of employment, relevance **109,** 373, 379-80
stress related illness **109,** 171-2
traffic accident **109,** 317, 329
accident during evacuation or flight **109,** 169-70
accident involving Iraqi military vehicle **109,** 144
accident resulting from military action **109,** 144
critical date **109,** 144
place of accident, relevance **109,** 144-5
State rights. *See* States, rights
State succession. *See also* territory, changes in; treaties, State succession, boundary treaties
accession to independence. *See* colonies, independence, accession to
acquiescence and **80,** 500
acquired rights **73,** 33-5, 37
international law, rule of, whether **91,** 344-54
administrative act, responsibility for **51,** 25-7, **69,** 30
agreement
equitable arrangement, need for **96,** 722, 725, 726, 731
need for **92,** 205
possibility of **96,** 722
Algeria. *See* Algeria
annuity, liability to pay **49,** 374-6
applicable law, international law **91,** 354-5, **92,** 165, 166, 205, **94,** 180
arbitral award, enforcement **45,** 33-6

assets **75,** 81
Austria, pre-1938 treaties **38,** 135
Belgian Congo. *See* Belgian Congo
bonds **47,** 75-8
boundaries, respect for **50,** 82, **77,** 657, **80,** 284, 440-563, **91,** 579-80. *See also uti possidetis*
acts of predecessor, estoppel **50,** 4
fisheries **83,** 37
OAU Charter **77,** 657
recognition of State and **92,** 174, 184, 186
Vienna Convention on Succession of States in Respect of Treaties (1978) **83,** 61, **91,** 579-80
British crown, rights and obligations **78,** 438-47, 451-2, 467-8
central/State-owned bank
agency of successor States, whether **96,** 735
disintegration and **96,** 735
distribution of assets following succession, applicable law **96,** 736
compensation for war-related events. *See* compensation for war-related events, State succession
concession agreement **44,** 37-8, **48,** 58-9, **66,** 87
continuity of law **41,** 389, **87,** 314, **90,** 458-61, **91,** 346, 350, 361, 368, 377-8, 391-2, **103,** 266-7, **118,** 534, 538
Algeria **47,** 101-2, 103-4, 106, **48,** 61-2
Angola **118,** 534, 538
Bahamas **85,** 133-9
Congo, Popular Republic of **44,** 434
Congo, Republic of **69,** 29-30
Czech Republic **118,** 238
dependent territory **90,** 458-61
evolution, scope for **86,** 650
French Indo-China **47,** 97-9
Goa, Daman and Diu **118,** 431, 436-46
India **49,** 422-68, **53,** 144-6, 170, 174-6, **55,** 87-8, **118,** 431, 436-46
Lesotho **90,** 458-61
liability in consequence **49,** 468-83
Malaysia **55,** 84-7, 91-3, 547
merger of States **53,** 141
occupied territory, in **94,** 170
Pakistan, Islamic Republic **38,** 3-9
penal laws **118,** 440-1
private contract and **47,** 102-4
Seychelles **91,** 391-2
Southern Rhodesia **39,** 384
Togo **65,** 440
Western Sahara **88,** 705
continuity of State
Algeria **75,** 81
Anschluss of Austria **45,** 356
civil strife **48,** 6-8
constitutional changes, effect **74,** 563, 565-6
Cyprus, Republic of **48,** 6-8
Czechoslovakia **44,** 57-9

State succession (*cont.*)
dissolution of Federation, effect **55,** 91-2
Germany (Reich) **43,** 67, **44,** 302, 313, **56,** 46-7, **59,** 492, **61,** 63, **78,** 156, 161, 169, **91,** 224-5
co-existence with successor 'States' **78,** 161-2, 169
Indian States **49,** 387, 455
Libya **62,** 172-3
Romania **74,** 563, 565-6
continuum juris **80,** 473, 560
contractual obligations **44,** 37-8, **45,** 19-24, **47,** 102-4, **48,** 58-60, **53,** 119-29, 136-7, 183-4, **69,** 25-30, **72,** 256, **75,** 125, **78,** 107-11, **82,** 125
attorney's fees **41,** 20-4
executed contract **96,** 65
liability **96,** 65
termination **96,** 65
executory contract, termination **96,** 65
termination
executed contract **96,** 65
executory contract **96,** 65
corporate seat, effect on **52,** 488-91
counterclaims arising out of the same transaction **84,** 182
criminal law **54,** 3-5
customary international law and **75,** 125
Czechoslovakia. *See* Czechoslovakia, State succession
date
Bosnia-Herzegovina **96,** 721-2
Croatia **96,** 721
Macedonia **96,** 721
Slovenia **96,** 721
slow disintegration of State, in case of **96,** 721
Vienna Convention on State Succession in Respect of State Property, Archives and Debts (1983) **96,** 720
Vienna Convention on State Succession in Respect of Treaties (1978) **96,** 720
de facto **88,** 702
debts **48,** 25, **72,** 54-6, **73,** 33-5, **89,** 618-19, **92,** 205
assumption of responsibility for **47,** 420, 432, 437, 449, **59,** 507
civil servant, retirement grant **48,** 8-20
judgment **47,** 83-5, **48,** 21, 23
local and sovereign distinguished **47,** 76-8
definition
attainment of independence **96,** 65
change of government distinguished **96,** 65
closing of borders, relevance **96,** 66
declaration of state of emergency, relevance **96,** 66
military coup, relevance **96,** 66
partial takeover by another State **96,** 65
renaming of State, relevance **96,** 66
replacement of responsibility for international relations **92,** 165
suspension of constitution, relevance **96,** 66
total absorption by another State **96,** 65
dependent territory, continuity of law **90,** 458-61, **118,** 534, 538
diplomatic privileges and immunities, effect on. *See* diplomatic privileges and immunities, State succession

dismemberment of States **45,** 25, 32
  Belgium and Congo **47,** 75-8
  France/Algeria **47,** 79-83, 86-9, 94-6, 99-106
  French Indo-China **47,** 97-9
  Poland, partition **47,** 107-8
disputes, peaceful settlement **92,** 174, 184-5, 192, 205
EC anti-dumping duties and **117,** 347, 359-60
entities involved, partial States **83,** 41
equitable agreement, need for **48,** 21, **92,** 204, **96,** 725, 726, 731
espionage, failure of merged States to agree treatment of **94,** 81-2
Estonia. *See* Estonia
estoppel, acts of predecessor **50,** 4
evidence of, executive certificate/statement **107,** 662
expropriation/nationalization, compensation **74,** 98-100, **103,** 118-20
extradition. *See* extradition agreement, State succession and
fiscal assets **44,** 51, 57
foreign judgment, recognition/enforcement **44,** 291-2, **89,** 11-14
former colonial power. *See also* Belgian Congo
  enforcement of judgments against **89,** 14, 16-18
  jurisdiction in actions against **89,** 16
  representation of **89,** 13
former State, extinction **94,** 180
fundamental obligations of international law, obligation to respect **92,** 165, 166, 204
German Reich. *See* Germany (Reich), FRG and; Germany (Reich), GDR and
grants
  land **49,** 376-96
  land revenues **49,** 336-49
  maintenance **49,** 396-421
  retirement grant to civil servant **48,** 8-20
  tax exemptions **49,** 349-65
hiatus, whether **91,** 368
International Law Commission Draft Articles **73,** 46-7, 54, **75,** 110-13
international organizations, membership, termination **92,** 205
international practices or customs **53,** 151
invalidity of previous administration and **91,** 356
Israel **78,** 108
judgment debts **47,** 83-5, **48,** 21, 23
judgments of courts of predecessor **44,** 47-9, **47,** 85-97, **72,** 54-5
  effect **53,** 179-80
  Japanese courts in Korea **54,** 3-5
  liability under **47,** 83-5
  partitioning of Poland **47,** 107-8
  right of appeal **52,** 78-82, **54,** 3-5
jurisdiction **52,** 80-2, **72,** 54-5, 57-8
  over State-controlled corporations **47,** 152-5
  pending actions **44,** 42-7, **47,** 104-6, **48,** 61-2
law, continuity. *See* continuity of law *above*
legislation, evolution, scope for **86,** 650
loan agreement with private parties and **87,** 80-1
merger of States **94,** 81-2. *See also* States, creation, merger; union of States
  claims against ruler **45,** 19-24
  continuity of law **53,** 141

State succession (*cont.*)
Mozambique **64,** 691-2, 694
municipality, effect on legal identity **44,** 50-70
nationality **108,** 550
nationality of claims **46,** 275
obligations. *See* rights and obligations *below*
officials, quasi-delictual liability **45,** 24-32
Pakistan–Bangladesh **70,** 43-4, 46
partial or universal **49,** 457-8
pensions **69,** 29-30, **73,** 36-8
principles governing **75,** 125
private rights **49,** 370-421, 468-83, **51,** 24, **66,** 194-7
property **53,** 151-2
rebel governments, rights **53,** 150-2
in third State **53,** 151
requisitioned before independence **44,** 39-41
territory of successor State **94,** 180-1
third countries, in **92,** 205
public corporation, liabilities of **48,** 40-58
quasi-delictual liability for wrongful acts of officials **45,** 24-32
rebellion, effect on property in third State **53,** 151
recognition as trigger **94,** 180
responsibility for determining, executive **107,** 256-9
rights and obligations **52,** 81-2, **74,** 98-100, **84,** 137. *See also* contractual obligations *and* debt *above*; State responsibility for acts and omissions of predecessor government
acceptance of **47,** 79-83, 104-6, **48,** 59, **91,** 349, 351, 354-5, 368
municipal law, as part of **91,** 354
acquired rights, continuing liability of successor government **103,** 121-2
annulment **84,** 162
date of transfer **96,** 723
enforceability **84,** 182
expropriation of property of departed institutions **107,** 211
legislation in third State, applicability **107,** 664-6
recovery of property embezzled by previous Head of State **107,** 492-505
repudiation **84,** 178, 179-85, **91,** 354, 365
effect on rights **94,** 181
unjustified enrichment **94,** 181
undertaking by predecessor government, immediately prior to take-over **107,** 210-11
Russian Federation, successor to USSR, whether **107,** 661-6
Sierra Leone **70,** 3-15
social security, collection of contributions **71,** 220-1
State immunity, jurisdiction
Holocaust **103,** 600-1
pending actions **55,** 409-11, **65,** 439-41
State property, archives and debts. *See* State succession, State property, archives and debts
State responsibility and. *See* State responsibility for acts of predecessor government
status, India during transition from British rule **84,** 205
successor, status as, conduct as evidence of **83,** 22
Surinam **87,** 79-81
territorial sea, rights to **90,** 242-3
torts **48,** 21, **49,** 365-9

treaties. *See* treaties, State succession
Trust Territory, assets allocated to Administering Authority **97,** 29-34
universal, whether **49,** 457-8
Upper Volta **78,** 108
uti possidetis. See uti possidetis
Vienna Convention on State Succession in Respect of State Property, Archives and Debts (1983) **83,** 61
as customary international law **92,** 164, 204
Vietnam, Socialist Republic, as successor to South Vietnam **75,** 125
Yugoslavia **92,** 204-5
applicability of Minorities Treaty (St Germain-en-Laye) (1919) **95,** 57-8
applicability of Security Council Resolution 713 (1991) **95,** 155-6
State succession, State property, archives and debts 49, 439, **63,** 53, 56
agreement
binding on third States, whether **96,** 725, 726
equitable arrangement, need for **96,** 725, 726, 731
customary international law
case-by-case application **96,** 728
immovable property on territory of successor State **96,** 731
dispute relating to, peaceful settlement, obligation **96,** 732, 736
dissolution of predecessor State, Vienna Convention on State succession in Respect of State Property, Archives and Debts (1983) **96,** 728
equity
equitable proportions distinguished **96,** 728
immovable property, compensation **96,** 731
Vienna Convention on State succession in Respect of State Property, Archives and Debts (1983) **96,** 728
war damages, relevance **96,** 728-9
offset, possibility of **96,** 728
immovable property on territory of successor State
compensation **96,** 732
customary international law **96,** 731
locus in quo **96,** 731
origin or financing of property, relevance **96,** 731
international agency, decision of, third State, obligation to implement **96,** 726
movable property
division **96,** 731-2
origin or financing of property, relevance **96,** 732
Vienna Convention on State succession in Respect of State Property, Archives and Debts (1983) **96,** 731-2
previous ownership, determination, applicable law, national law in force at date of succession **96,** 732
protective measures **96,** 725-6
refusal to cooperate
breach of obligation **96,** 725, 726
non-forcible countermeasures, right to take **96,** 725, 726
third State, in, obligation of third State to take action **96,** 725, 726
State territory. *See* territory
State trading enterprise. *See* State agency/State-owned corporation/State entity
State-controlled entity. *See* State agency/State-owned corporation/State entity
State-owned organization. *See* State agency/State-owned corporation/ State entity
State-owned ships. *See* ships, State-owned

State-sponsored terrorism 74, 250-6, **77,** 224, 236, **119,** 343
act of State doctrine and **121,** 642
applicable law **121,** 632-3
classification as
'extrajudicial killing' **121,** 612, 634-6
suicide bombing **121,** 634-6
financial assistance in support of terrorist activities **121,** 636
shooting-down of plane 18 miles from coast **121,** 606-18
terrorist act by or on behalf of foreign State **121,** 630, 634
extraterritorial legislation **121,** 633-4
forum [non] conveniens **121,** 643
Head of State, immunity, jurisdiction **121,** 642-3, **125,** 497-8, 507
jurisdiction
extraterritorial **121,** 633-4
requirements **121,** 611-13
act within scope of office, agency or employment **121,** 634, 636
designation as **113,** 542, **121,** 611-12, 630, 634
occurrence outside foreign State **121,** 612
offer of arbitration **121,** 634
terrorist act by or on behalf of foreign State. *See* classification as *above*
victims as nationals of forum State **121,** 612, 634, **123,** 32, 47-8
Montreal Convention for the Suppression of Unlawful Acts Against the Safety of Civilian Aviation (1971), applicability **94,** 512, 520
obligation to renounce **94,** 517
prompt compensation, demand for **94,** 494, 514, 557, 569-70
Security Council responsibility **94,** 517, 520, 524
State responsibility **74,** 258, **94,** 514, 569, 580
act of agent or official consistent with State's policies **121,** 636
act of air force pilot **121,** 612
imputability, need for **94,** 569, 580
obligation to renounce **94,** 517
Security Council responsibility **94,** 517, 520, 524
statehood 41, 16-17, **44,** 62. *See also* recognition, State; sovereignty; States
allegiance **59,** 120
associated Statehood, Cook Islands **104,** 503
attributes. *See* requirements/evidence of *below*
Bosnia-Herzegovina **115,** 71-102
Bosnian Serbs (Srpska) **104,** 157-8
capacity to enter into relations with other States **82,** 415-17
Cook Islands **104,** 503-4
date of attainment **39,** 290, 405-11, **87,** 603-4
definition. *See* requirements/evidence of *below*
determination by international law **82,** 398
evidence of. *See* requirements/evidence of *below*
federal State, States within **115,** 77
negotiation with entity, relevance **82,** 404
not fully sovereign State **39,** 324
proclamation of independence and **87,** 74
requirements/evidence of **52,** 14-17, 75, 311, **61,** 73-4, **62,** 45, **77,** 220, **80,** 685, **84,** 176, **86,** 155-6, **87,** 586, 650, **104,** 146 n. 12. *See also* sovereignty, *effectivités*
communication with other States **55,** 341
currency **104,** 158
defined territory **82,** 402, **96,** 73-4, 88, **104,** 158, **108,** 542, **115,** 71-2, 74-80

effective existence **52,** 311
effective government **80,** 685, **82,** 399, **96,** 73, **104,** 158, 504, **108,** 542, **115,** 72, 79-94
exclusive territorial jurisdiction **52,** 15-25, **77,** 221
government to government contacts, UK/northern Cyprus **108,** 544-5
imperium **77,** 624
inhabitants, relevance **82,** 401-2
international organization, membership of **87,** 599, 653, 655
law-making and enforcement authority **39,** 275, 279, 290, **104,** 503
legal personality **64,** 413, 571-2, 615-18, **87,** 653, **88,** 682-3
Montevideo Convention on Rights and Duties of States (1933) **82,** 400-1, **94,** 621
national flag **87,** 599, 603
national postal system **87,** 599, 603
nationals, power to create **39,** 325
organized political authority, relevance **92,** 165
people **80,** 685, 687-8. *See also* permanent population *below*
definition **80,** 687-8
permanency **87,** 75
permanent population **77,** 624, **87,** 74, **92,** 165, **96,** 73, 74, 88, **108,** 542, **115,** 72-4. *See also* people *above*
organized as political entity **77,** 624
power over national **87,** 653
power to
administer territory **87,** 603, 653
conclude peace **87,** 603, 653
conclude treaties **86,** 155-6, **87,** 599, 603, 653, 655
conduct foreign relations **87,** 655
control aliens **87,** 599, 603
declare and wage war **87,** 603, 653
enter into relations with other States **52,** 27, **104,** 503-4, **108,** 542-3, **115,** 72
implement international obligations **96,** 74
maintain diplomatic relations **87,** 603, 604, 653, **96,** 73, 74, 88
make international law **87,** 653-4, 655
negotiate **86,** 155-6
recognition **41,** 18-19, **52,** 73-5, **82,** 402-3, **87,** 656, **96,** 88, **108,** 545, **115,** 71, **118,** 425-7. *See also* recognition, State, constitutive theory
unrecognized State as 'foreign State' for legislative purposes **108,** 527-8, 556-7
Restatement of the Foreign Relations Law of the United States (Revised) (Tent. draft 2) **82,** 401
Restatement of the Foreign Relations Law of the United States (Second) (1965) **115,** 97-8
Restatement of the Foreign Relations Law of the United States (Third) **104,** 157-8
separate legal entity test **77,** 624, **108,** 542-5, **115,** 79
sovereignty **115,** 73
stable and effective authority **87,** 74-5
territory **62,** 539, **65,** 309, **77,** 614, **80,** 685-7, **82,** 399, 402, **92,** 165
continuous, necessary, whether **82,** 413
UN Resolutions **39,** 209
uncertainty of international law regarding **82,** 410
stateless person **40,** 19, 31, 192, **43,** 192, 195-6, 449, 493, **47,** 212-15, **55,** 488, **70,** 695-6, **71,** 448-9, 504-9, **72,** 438-42, 457, 464, 546, **79,** 298, 324. *See also* nationality, loss or deprivation of; refugees; stateless ship
access to courts **44,** 143-4

stateless person (*cont.*)
claims under Peace Treaty **77,** 566
date *a quo* **120,** 7
definition **71,** 508, **77,** 385, **120,** 8
de facto/de jure **120,** 8, 9
loss of nationality requirement **77,** 386
New York Convention on the Status of (1954) **77,** 386
UN Human Rights Commission Resolution on stateless persons (1947) **120,** 8
diplomatic protection **46,** 362, **109,** 577-8
expulsion **61,** 440-1 **71,** 504-9
discretion **71,** 505-9
right of **71,** 507
French law **44,** 133
'his own country' **115,** 335
infant, jurisdiction over **41,** 239-56
liberal profession, access to **71,** 448-9
New York Convention on the Status of (1954) **41,** 247, 255, **47,** 212-15, **48,** 165-6
definition **77,** 386
implementation **71,** 448-9, **77,** 385-6
obligations **71,** 506-9
Olympic Games, right to compete in **120,** 8-10
personal law of **47,** 212
prisoners of war, repatriation **44,** 443
refugee compared **71,** 506
social security **48,** 165-6
status **71,** 506-9
travel document **41,** 240, 242, 247, 252, 255-6
UN Human Rights Commission Resolution 1947 (stateless persons) **120,** 8
Universal Declaration of Human Rights (1948) **40,** 195
stateless ship 91, 475 n. 15, 488-92, 542, **120,** 340
Agreement Relating to the Conservation and Management of Straddling Fish Stocks and Highly Migratory Fish Stocks (1995) **120,** 244 n. 36
freedom of high seas and **91,** 491
High Seas Convention (1958) and **91,** 475 n. 15, 490-1
jurisdiction **91,** 475 n. 15, 488-92, 542
Law of the Sea Convention (1982) **120,** 244 n. 36
protection, State of nationality of owner **120,** 330, 351-2
search and seizure **91,** 542
statutory limitation 66, 211, **79,** 404-11
applicable law **79,** 404, 407-11, **81,** 533 n. 2
federal State, in **95,** 639-40
lex loci commissi **95,** 639-41
lack of uniformity **95,** 641
arbitral award, enforcement **103,** 564, 568-9
Charter of the International Military Tribunal **78,** 132
civil and criminal distinguished **79,** 405-6
crimes against humanity **78,** 132-6, 140, **100,** 333, 342
Control Council Law No 10 **119,** 357
customary international law **119,** 358
European Convention on the Non-Applicability of Statutory Limitation to Crimes against Humanity and War Crimes (1974) **91,** 35, **119,** 357-8
France **100,** 333, 342, **119,** 358
date *a quo*

duty of estoppel **108,** 499-502
good faith requirement **108,** 506-7
due diligence, need for **108,** 501-2
equitable tolling **95,** 641-3
estoppel **103,** 550
European Convention on Human Rights (1950) **78,** 132-6
extradition and **36,** 76-9, **43,** 231-4, 243-4
fees, recovery of **78,** 666
flexibility **95,** 641
ICSID proceedings and **124,** 57
International Covenant on Civil and Political Rights (ICCPR) (1966) **78,** 135
international crimes
European Convention on the Non-Applicability of Statutory Limitation to Crimes against Humanity and War Crimes (1974) **91,** 35, **119,** 357-8
UN Convention on the Non-Applicability of Statutory Limitations to War Crimes and Crimes against Humanity (1968) **79,** 405, **119,** 357-8
international tribunals, municipal statutes of limitation and **78,** 666, **124,** 57
International Criminal Court (ICC), jurisdiction **125,** 488
private international law rules, government interest test **79,** 409
public policy and **79,** 408
retroactive removal **78,** 132-6
arbitrary detention, whether **78,** 132-6
suspension during period of immunity **119,** 358
torture **104,** 192, **121,** 262
violation of international law **77,** 271-2
war crimes **78,** 136-7
statutory right or privilege 44, 12-13, 15-17, 22-5
stay of proceedings 78, 391-2, **80,** 618. *See also forum [non] conveniens*; provisional measures, stay of proceedings
abuse of process and **118,** 409-10, 414, 418-19
agreement not to sue, relevance **118,** 390-1, 395-6, 410
in case of forcible abduction/unlawful arrest **95,** 390, 608-16
comity **106,** 529, **118,** 413
discretion **106,** 529, **118,** 631, 634-7
forum selection clause
'just and proper' exception **118,** 532-3, 535-6, 537
relevance in case of change of legal system **118,** 528-39
ICSID reference **118,** 621-40. *See also* ICSID (International Centre for the Settlement of Investment Disputes), stay of proceedings by national court
injunction distinguished **118,** 408-9, 414-15
power to order in courts of another State **118,** 381-420
in absence of nexus **118,** 549
antitrust legislation and **118,** 542-65
applicable law, *lex fori* **118,** 551
avoidance of injustice **118,** 394-6
concurrent and sole jurisdiction distinguished **118,** 394, 550, 561-2
frivolous and vexatious proceedings **118,** 549-50
greater suitability of foreign court **118,** 395
in personam nature of order **118,** 560, 565
injunction prohibiting foreign proceedings **74,** 40-2, 54-8, 70-7, 83-7
oppressive proceedings **118,** 400-1, 418-19, 564-5
prevention of distortion of domestic policy **118,** 395, 396-401
relevant factors **118,** 384-6

stay of proceedings (*cont.*)
treble damages proceedings **118,** 397-8, 400-1, 406, 412-13
unconscionable conduct **118,** 548-60
where foreign court only forum **118,** 550
steel company, agency or instrumentality of a foreign State **63,** 90, 104, 174-8
stockholder claims 42, 158-61, 178-80
Stockholm Declaration on the Human Environment (1972). *See* environment, Stockholm Declaration on the Human Environment (1972)
Straddling Stocks and Highly Migratory Fish Stocks Agreement (1995)
arrest of ships, use of force **120,** 196-7
'conservation and management measures' **123,** 220-3, 259, 299, 311-15, 325-6
use of force **123,** 471-2
customary international law **117,** 180, **123,** 471
dispute settlement provisions **119,** 556
genuine link, need for **120,** 180
Law of the Sea Convention (1982), and **123,** 316, 326
provisional measures **117,** 171 n. 3, 180
travaux préparatoires **123,** 311-14, 327
straits 69, 35-7, 41-4, 53-4, 59-73
bays, relation to **69,** 54
boundaries **90,** 278-81, 296
mid-channel **90,** 328-9
definition **52,** 170, **57,** 75-7
Gibraltar, Morocco–Spain Agreement (1967) **41,** 136
Great Belt (Finland/Sweden) **94,** 451-77
customary international law **94,** 460
innocent passage. *See also* right of passage *below*
fisheries regulations, respect for **82,** 602
pollution regulations, respect for **82,** 602
international **42,** 95
internationalization **84,** 81
islands in **62,** 126
land covered by, ownership **73,** 191-225
mineral resources, jurisdiction and proprietary rights distinguished **90,** 271, 276
neutralization, Magellan **82,** 687
right of passage **94,** 460. *See also* innocent passage *above*
bridge as infringement **94,** 454, 455-6
oil rigs and drill ships **94,** 454, 455-6
'reasonably foreseeable ships' **94,** 454
structures more than 65 metres in height **94,** 455
safety of navigation **84,** 81
State territory, whether **69,** 43-6, 61-2, 66-7
in territorial sea **57,** 64-5
Torres Strait. *See* Australia, Torres Strait
Strategic Trust Territory. *See* Palau; Trust Territories, Strategic Trust Territory
strike, right to 58, 15-16, **74,** 137-8
Abolition of Forced Labour Convention (No 105) (1957) **90,** 189
conformity with domestic law **90,** 187, **94,** 253-4
customary international law **90,** 200, 211-12
freedom of association and **90,** 185, 186, 187, 199, 205-8, **94,** 251-8
ILO Convention concerning Freedom of Association and Protection of Right to Organize (1948) **90,** 185-7, 195-8, 205, **94,** 254-8

International Covenant on Civil and Political Rights (ICCPR) (1966) **94,** 253-4
International Covenant on Economic, Social and Cultural Rights (1966) **90,** 187-9, 199-200, 205, **94,** 252-3
International Labour Conference (1978) **90,** 207-8
lawfulness, ILO standards and **87,** 97
public service, in **90,** 183-213, **94,** 248-59
compulsory arbitration **94,** 257
essential services, limitation to **94,** 258
State immunity and **94,** 285-6, 305
Treaty of Versailles, Part XIII (1919) **90,** 184-5, 198-9, 205
Universal Declaration of Human Rights (1948) **90,** 199, 205
Suarez, obedience to usurper **39,** 114, 257
subject-matter jurisdiction. *See* jurisdiction, subject-matter
subjugation 83, 135
acquisition of territory **37,** 543
Hague Regulations (1907) and **83,** 135
submarine cables
Conception Bay **43,** 105
damage, liability for **74,** 213-15
applicable law **74,** 213-18
submarine mines, taxation of, local authority boundaries **42,** 62-85
subordinate legislatures, legislative competence **69,** 225
subpoena duces tecum. *See* procedure, *subpoena duces tecum*; Yugoslavia, International Criminal Tribunal for the Former (ICTY), orders, *subpoena duces tecum*
subsidiarity. *See* European Union (EU), subsidiarity
subsoil. *See* seabed and subsoil
succession. *See also* State succession
applicable law
general principles of law recognized by civilized nations **116,** 279-80
interpretation in accordance with local law **116,** 279-80
mortis causa **94,** 372
Sudan
extradition **74,** 479-92
jurisdiction, territorial **74,** 482
law of
Armed Forces Rules 1958 **74,** 480, 484
Penal Code **74,** 480-5
'waging war', meaning **74,** 483-4
mercenaries, punishment **74,** 484-92
State succession, *coup d'état*, whether **96,** 65-7
Sudeten Germans, expulsion from Eastern territories **44,** 53, **51,** 23-4, **78,**187
Suez Canal Company, expropriation/nationalization **46,** 474
Suez operations (1956), war, whether **48,** 467-8
sugar. *See* Refined Sugar Association
summary judgment, act of State and **63,** 456
superior orders 104, 332-4, 367, 378, **108,** 186-9
crimes against humanity **36,** 253-62, 313-19, 339-40
criminal responsibility and **74,** 250-1, 260-1
Dover Castle **104,** 372-3
duress compared. *See* duress, superior orders compared
Einsatzgruppen case **104,** 375
ex proprio power of judge to raise **100,** 336

superior orders (*cont.*)
failure of defendant to raise point **100,** 337
GDR border shootings
breach of criminal law, relevance **100,** 371
retroactivity and **100,** 388-9
general principle of law **108,** 188
history **104,** 369-74
human rights violations **116,** 335-6
jury responsibility **100,** 336-7, **104,** 382-4
Llandovery Castle **104,** 372-3
mens rea, evidence of **36,** 259-70, **104,** 376
mitigating circumstance **36,** 256, **100,** 336-7, **108,** 186-9, 197-200
moral choice test **104,** 333, 374-6, 381-2, **108,** 187-9, **111,** 454-5
Nuremberg Charter (1945) **104,** 297
political offence, extradition **39,** 434, 437, 451-2
R v. *Smith* **104,** 371
rank, relevance **108,** 188, 199-200
requirements
Kafr Qassem **104,** 374
manifest illegality **36,** 256-8, **104,** 373-4, 381
public interest **36,** 314-15
reasonable belief that order was lawful **104,** 333, 380-1
reasonable to assume knowledge that act was war crime/crime against humanity **104,** 333
Torture Convention (1984) **119,** 150, 152
war crimes **36,** 256-7, 313-19, 339-40, **39,** 438, **42,** 437, **47,** 464-6, **52,** 495, **61,** 668, **72,** 610, **74,** 250-1, 260-1, **82,** 451-3, **91,** 10, 26-7, 54-7, 92, 136-8, 150, **98,** 598-9
act of State and **39,** 438
burden of proof **98,** 599
customary international law **91,** 92-3
International Commission for Penal Reconstruction and Development **91,** 55-6
International Military Tribunal for the Far East (Tokyo Tribunal) **91,** 57
Manual of Military Law (Australia) (1941) **91,** 54-5, 93, 137
Manual of Military Law (Australia) (1944) **91,** 56, 93, 137
Manual of Military Law (UK) (1929) **91,** 55, 93
Nuremberg Charter (1945) **91,** 56-7
Rules of Land Warfare (US) (1940) **91,** 55, 93
Supreme Headquarters Allied Powers in Europe (SHAPE)
employees
exemption from taxation **91,** 243-9
status **91,** 244-9
locally engaged staff **91,** 246-8
national of receiving State **91,** 248
employment contract, applicable law **91,** 245, 247
Surinam. *See* Suriname
Suriname
American Convention on Human Rights (1969), accession to **116,** 261 n. 2, 296 n. 3, 307
Convention concerning Indigenous and Tribal Peoples in Independent Countries (1989) (ILO Convention 169) **116,** 279
Guyana, boundary with **48,** 77
human rights in **116,** 264-317
measures to protect **116,** 316

violations by military personnel **116,** 316-17
registry offices, insufficiency **116,** 280
Saramacas. *See* Saramacas
separate legal entity test
declaration of **87,** 80
treaty commitments, declaration regarding **74,** 116-17
status
autonomous **87,** 80
Charter for the Kingdom of the Netherlands 1954 **87,** 80
'Kingdom affairs' **87,** 80-1
sovereign **87,** 80-1
surveillance. *See* secret surveillance
sustainable development principle. *See also* development; environment
conventions and international instruments reflecting **116,** 102-4, 169-70
Bergen Declaration on Sustainable Development (1990) **116,** 102-3
Dublin Declaration on the Environmental Imperative (1990) **116,** 102 n. 14
European Conservation Strategy (Council of Europe) (1990) **116,** 103
Habitats Directive (92/43/EEC) **120,** 626
Stockholm Declaration on the Human Environment (1972) **116,** 101
customary international law **116,** 101-4
development of principle **116,** 101-4
cultural diversity and **116,** 105-20
Gabčíkovo/Nagymaros Project **116,** 97-120, 169-70
in
Africa **116,** 113-14
China **116,** 114-15
Inca civilization **116,** 115
Iran **116,** 114
Sri Lanka **116,** 107-13
as reconciliation of conflicting principles of development and environmental law **116,** 99, 169-70
State practice **116,** 102-4
suzerain, vassal States and, acquiescence **50,** 99-100, 104, 246, 398
Swaziland
arms, unlawful possession, membership of national liberation movement as defence **91,** 407-11
law of
Arms and Ammunition Act 1964 **91,** 409
OAU resolutions, whether part of **91,** 409
State immunity, jurisdiction, applicability, evidence, giving of **91,** 408
Union of South Africa, Extradition Treaty **68,** 8
Sweden
administrative act, judicial review **68,** 101, 113, 120
aliens, International Covenant on Civil and Political Rights (ICCPR) (1966) and **62,** 278-85
arbitrability **62,** 225-6
arbitral award, enforcement **65,** 233
arbitral proceedings, application of Swiss law to **65,** 499-500
child care
administration **92,** 278-9
care order
appeal against **92,** 281
implementation **92,** 279-80, 338-9

Sweden (*cont.*)
termination or variation **92,** 280-1
ECHR and **92,** 281-303, 335-49
parental access **92,** 280
prohibition on removal and **92,** 343, 346-7
prohibition on removal **92,** 336-8
voluntary care **92,** 274-8, 335-6
claim, sampling methodology **109,** 71 n. 14
Constitution 1975
Chapter 2(3) **89,** 216
Chapter 11(6) **89,** 220
Chapter 11(7) **89,** 222
Chapter 12 **89,** 222
ethnic minorities, protection **96,** 640
criminal procedure **58,** 688-92
detention pending trial **58,** 689-90
diplomatic immunity, jurisdiction, waiver, arbitration clause **78,** 84
District Attorney's powers **58,** 691-2
European Convention on Human Rights (1950) and, amendments to law resulting from **86,** 319-21
expulsion of alien **62,** 278, 280-1
requirements, non-impediment to enforcement of expulsion order **108,** 303
freedom of information **89,** 224-6
German assets in, liquidation **44,** 474, 479, 484, 485
governmental acts, appeals **68,** 101-2, 113-14
human rights, alleged violation **62,** 285
land expropriation permits **68,** 96-8, 104-11, 115-18, 122-7
human rights violations and **75,** 385-95
law of
Aliens Act 1954, terrorism and **62,** 280-1, 283-5
Aliens Act 1980 **108,** 303
Art. 3 (asylum) **108,** 303-4
Aliens Act 1989 **108,** 303
Aliens Ordinance 1980 **108,** 303
Art. 33 (residence permits) **108,** 304-5
Aliens Ordinance 1989 **108,** 303
Building Act 1947 **68,** 92, 95-100
Child Welfare Act 1960 **92,** 274-5, 280
Civil Liberty Act 1972 **68,** 103
Constitution. *See* Constitution 1975 *above*
Expropriation Act 1917 **68,** 92, 96-8, 107, 122-3
Expropriation Act 1972 **68,** 96-8, 109, 122-3
Foreign Arbitration Agreements and Awards Act 1929 **62,** 225, **65,** 452
Freedom of the Press Act 1766 **89,** 224
General Criminal Register Act 1963 **89,** 224-5
Instrument of Government. *See* Constitution 1975 *above*
Judicial Procedure Code 1983
European Convention on Human Rights (1950) and **86,** 319-21
s 13 **121,** 335 n. 255
s 14 **121,** 335 n. 255
Parental Code **92,** 338-9, 346-7
Personnel Control Ordinance 1969 (as variously amended) **89,** 216-20

'law', whether **89,** 228-30
Reindeer Husbandry Act 1971
Art. 12 **96,** 646-8
compatibility with International Covenant on Civil and Political Rights (ICCPR) (1966) **96,** 646-8
purpose **96,** 641, 647
Restrictions on the Right of Access to Public Documents Act 1937/1974 **89,** 224-6
Service of Process Act **62,** 226
Social Services Act 1980 **92,** 326, 330-1, 335-8, 341-2
Social Services Ordinance 1981 **92,** 281
Special Provisions on the Care of Young People Act 1980 **92,** 276-8, 280
Supervision Act 1975 **89,** 220
minorities
objective ethnic criteria for determining membership, need for **96,** 648
Sami. *See* Sami *below*
national security, police register **89,** 216-17
access to information **89,** 217-20
supervisory control **89,** 220-4
reopening of proceedings **68,** 102
Sami
compatibility of legislation with International Covenant on Civil and Political Rights (ICCPR) (1966) **96,** 646-8
right to self-determination **96,** 643
sameby, right to membership **96,** 638-48
service of process **62,** 225-6
State immunity, jurisdiction, waiver, implied, arbitration clause/agreement **65,** 383-4
State liability, exhaustion of available remedies and **89,** 226
Supreme Administrative Court, appeal to **68,** 101-2, 113-14
town-planning procedures **68,** 92-103
appeal **68,** 100-2, 113-14
access to courts, whether amounting to **68,** 113-14
civil rights and **68,** 120
construction prohibitions **68,** 98-100, 104-11, 115-18
expropriation permits **68,** 96-8, 104-11, 115-18, 122-7
Parliamentary Ombudsman, views **68,** 99-100, 110
public authorities, liability **68,** 103
Switzerland
access to courts, refugees **72,** 641-5
act of State, relevant factors, public interest/good **65,** 281-2
administration of justice, measures to improve **73,** 450-2
airport noise and pollution, damages for **73,** 448-50
aliens
acquisition of property **82,** 43
constitutional rights **72,** 575-9, 594-6
procedural rights **72,** 594-6
residence permit **72,** 571, 577-8
humanitarian grounds, relevance **111,** 282
settlement permit distinguished **111,** 281-2
Allied Powers, Financial Agreement 1946 **44,** 484
applicable law
arbitration, agreement, exclusion of national law **102,** 215

Switzerland (*cont.*)
corporation, name **72,** 557-60, 563-5
employment contract, locally engaged staff, diplomatic mission, municipal law of receiving State **82,** 22-3
social security obligations, place of employment **102,** 188
arbitral award, enforcement **65,** 233
dependence on qualification as award **65,** 359
public order/public policy/*ordre public* and **72,** 61-2
arbitral award, qualification as (516 CPC of Vaud) **65,** 359
arbitral proceedings **47,** 399, 403
appeal
arbitrariness **80,** 649-50, 661, 664
breach of right to be heard **80,** 648-9
competence, improper assumption of **80,** 639-40
grounds **80,** 662. *See also* appeal proceedings *above*
irregular constitution of tribunal **80,** 638-9
appeal proceedings **80,** 622-66
applicable law **80,** 632-3
eligibility **80,** 661, 663, 665
request for annulment **80,** 633
Concordat. *See* law of, Intercantonal Arbitration Concordat (*IAC*) *below*
nullity of award
non-arbitrable subject **80,** 634
public order/public policy/*ordre public* **80,** 634
arbitration, applicable law, seat of arbitration **65,** 449-50
arbitration clause
judicial control by host State, exclusion **102,** 212-13, 214-15
waiver of immunity of international organization, whether **102,** 212-13, 214-15
asylum, conditions for **72,** 583-5
attachment, purpose of funds, sovereign **82,** 9
cantons
dispute between, customary international law and **75,** 117-21
referendum requirement **75,** 101-2
treaties, approval of **75,** 101-2
cartel legislation, territorial scope **72,** 79-80
central/State-owned bank
classification as, separate legal entity test **65,** 422-3
purpose/use of funds, diplomatic relations **82,** 35
State immunity, execution/attachment, nature of underlying relationship as determining factor **65,** 423-4
claims settlement agreements **46,** 371, 451-2
Constitution 1874
Art. 4 **65,** 437, **72,** 575-9, 594-6, 670, **102,** 194, 208
Art. 54 **89,** 198-9
Art. 69 **72,** 583
Art. 102(1)(8) **65,** 409, 411, 428
Art. 102(8) **102,** 186
Art. 113 **65,** 409, 410, 427-8, **89,** 196
fundamental rights **72,** 684
consular employee, fiscal liability **75,** 97-8
consular immunity, execution/attachment
honorary consul/consulate **82,** 7-10
private residence **82,** 6

Vienna Convention on Consular Relations (1963) **82,** 9-10
consular immunity, execution/attachment, entitlement, honorary consul/consulate, funds in private bank account **82,** 7-10
courts, municipal
evidence out of time **82,** 41
interpretation costs **88,** 621-5
jurisdiction
compatibility of Constitution and treaty, power to determine **89,** 196
Federal Court **62,** 231
public law **82,** 47
treaties, breach of and **82,** 27-8
withdrawal of arbitral award from docket, effect **82,** 69
criminal law
judicial review **88,** 653-4
penalties
confiscation **88,** 580-2, 584
destruction of obscene object **88,** 582-3
proportionality **88,** 580, 583-4
criminal procedure, Police Board **88,** 653-7, 671-3
critical date, State immunity, execution/attachment, purpose/use of funds/assets **65,** 393
customary international law
diplomatic mission, status **102,** 181-2
Head of State, immunity **102,** 201, 202
municipal law and **102,** 201
debt, service of process out of the jurisdiction and **65,** 413-16
defamation proceedings **72,** 391-402
diplomatic channels, as remedy, State immunity, jurisdiction and **102,** 182
diplomatic immunity, jurisdiction
restricted immunity **116,** 666
State immunity and **102,** 182
State as party to dispute **102,** 181-3
diplomatic immunity, jurisdiction, waiver
failure to appear **102,** 182
failure to exercise right of appeal **102,** 182
diplomatic mission
administrative and technical staff **116,** 640
agent of sending State **102,** 181-3
lease, breach, diplomatic channels as remedy **102,** 182
lease, sending State as contracting party **102,** 182
status
agent of sending State **102,** 181-3
customary international law **102,** 181-2
independence of sending State **102,** 181-2, 207
diplomatic premises
duty of host government to protect **102,** 180
extraterritoriality **102,** 178, 179
inviolability
illegal occupation **102,** 179
service of writ as breach **102,** 182
diplomatic privileges and immunities, entitlement
European Community (EC) **102,** 186-7
illegal occupant of diplomatic premises **102,** 179-80
termination of diplomatic status, relevance **102,** 183

Switzerland (*cont.*)
diplomatic protection, corporation **46,** 371
dispute settlement, international organization, in respect of, need to make provision **102,** 212-13, 214-15
divorce jurisdiction **72,** 641-5
domicile
corporation **72,** 355-63
taxation and **72,** 668-70
double criminality, judicial assistance and **65,** 408, **82,** 57
embassy or consular bank account/funds, immunity, execution/attachment
allocation for sovereign purpose **116,** 528
allocation for specific purpose **102,** 208
difficulty of distinguishing **116,** 527-9
diplomatic service **82,** 7
mixed use **116,** 528-9
in name of honorary consul **82,** 7-10
separability **82,** 8-10
employment contract, consulate, immunity, jurisdiction, chauffeur **116,** 662
employment contract, international organization, applicable law, international civil service law **116,** 645
employment contract, locally engaged staff, diplomatic mission
applicable law, Federal Department of Foreign Affairs Directive **82,** 22, 240
employee's right to institute proceedings against employing State **116,** 638
employee's right to institute proceedings against employing State, waiver of plaintiff's diplomatic immunity **116,** 638
jurisdiction **116,** 638, 640
Rules governing Diplomatic and Consular Employment of 24 November 1967 **82,** 22-3
State immunity, jurisdiction **116,** 639-42
interpreter/translator **116,** 665-8
national of sending State **113,** 432
termination
acte de gouvernement **116,** 655, 674-5
enquiry into reasons for **116,** 654-5
employment contract, mission to international organization, applicable law, receiving State law **116,** 653
employment contract, mission to international organization, immunity, jurisdiction, telephonist **116,** 637-42
employment contract, State immunity, jurisdiction, test, sovereign nature of functions of employee **116,** 658, 666, 671
European Community (EC)
diplomatic privileges and immunities **102,** 186-7
status, inter-State institution **102,** 186-7
Vienna Convention on Diplomatic Relations (1961), applicability **102,** 186-7
European Convention on Human Rights (1950) **89,** 196
reservations **88,** 621-33, 657-9, 662-71
European Court of Human Rights, case-law in municipal courts **88,** 581
European Organization for Nuclear Research (CERN)
Headquarters Agreement
dispute settlement, arbitration **102,** 214-15
legal status **102,** 213
legal status **102,** 213-15
Headquarters Agreement **102,** 213

evidence of
assets of honorary consul, purpose **82,** 7-8
embassy or consular bank account/funds, purpose, diplomatic note **102,** 206, 207
international organization, status, request to Ministry of Foreign Affairs **102,** 185
exhaustion of local remedies, State immunity and **65,** 389, **82,** 35
expropriation/nationalization, without compensation, non-recognition **72,** 27, 556, 561
extradition **72,** 598-601, 607-39
concurrent requests **100,** 660-2
bilateral agreement, relevance **100,** 660-1
re-extradition to third State **100,** 661-2
relevant circumstances for choice **100,** 661-2
double criminality **72,** 610-11
Extradition, European Convention on (1957), mutual ratification, need for **100,** 660
function of judge **72,** 610-11, 623
obligation, *aut dedere aut punire/judicare* **106,** 263
re-extradition to third State **72,** 629-32
concurrent requests and **100,** 661
reciprocity **72,** 634, 636
refugees **72,** 634-6
refusal
aut dedere aut punire/judicare **106,** 263
public order/public policy/ *ordre public* **106,** 262, 269
speciality principle **72,** 599-601
extradition in case of death penalty
assurances that death penalty will not be carried out, need for **100,** 659-60
extradition agreement, need for **100,** 659-60
right to life **100,** 660
extraterritorial effect of legislation **72,** 27, 556, 559-62
extraterritoriality, diplomatic premises **102,** 178, 179
family reunion, well-established right of abode, need for **111,** 281-2, 285, 289
Federal Court, jurisdiction **62,** 231
Federal Department of Justice and Police, Sequestration of Assets of Foreign States Circular of 26 November 1967 **82,** 22-3
federal State, constituent States, expulsion of international official, competence **102,** 197
foreign judgment, enforcement **62,** 228-36
foreign law, recognition/enforcement **72,** 19-24
confiscatory legislation **72,** 18-27, 559-61
extradition and **82,** 27
judicial assistance and **82,** 27
public law **82,** 147
public policy and **72,** 19-26
foreign State, immunity. *See* State immunity *below*
foreign State, proceedings involving
admissibility **62,** 229
nexus, need for. *See* jurisdiction, nexus, in case of proceedings involving foreign State *below*
right of suit **65,** 437-8
right to appeal against alleged breach of international law or treaty **65,** 409-11, 427-8
standing **65,** 397, 409-11
forum selection clause, as nexus **65,** 391
France, boundary with, River Doubs **47,** 113-15

Switzerland (*cont.*)
freedom of expression **88,** 581-2
freedom of navigation, international rivers **72,** 681-9
GDR, non-recognition, effect **72,** 61, 556, 558, 562
Head of State, definition, Convention on the Prevention and Punishment of Crimes against Internationally Protected Persons (1973) **102,** 202-3
Head of State, former, immunity **102,** 200-5
Head of State, immunity, jurisdiction
absolute **102,** 202, 203
criminal **102,** 201-5
customary international law **102,** 201, 202
family members **102,** 201
official acts while in power **102,** 201-3
private acts **102,** 201, 202
ratione personae **102,** 201-2
Vienna Convention on Diplomatic Relations (1961), application by analogy **102,** 202-3
willingness of receiving State to accord **102,** 203
Head of State, immunity, jurisdiction, waiver
express **102,** 203-5
organ of successor government, by **102,** 203-5
headquarters agreement, legal personality determined by **102,** 211
inheritance law **42,** 103
International Labour Organization (ILO), Headquarters Agreement **40,** 301
international law **65,** 388, 397-8, 418-22, 427-9, 437, 449, **116,** 638
customary international law **82,** 25
international officials
alien **102,** 196-7
as diplomatic agent **102,** 175
distinction **102,** 193-4, 195
equality of treatment **102,** 193-4
exemption from taxation, surtax on housing subsidy **102,** 175-6
expulsion **102,** 196-7
headquarters agreement, special procedure **102,** 197
international agreement, relevance **102,** 197
host State, law of, duty to respect **102,** 175
immunity, jurisdiction **72,** 664-5, **75,** 90-6
social security
obligation **102,** 184-8
return of contributions **102,** 184-8
voluntary payments **102,** 187-8
taxation
deductibility for tax purposes of interest paid to **102,** 193-4
taxpayer in receiving State, whether **102,** 192-3
Vienna Convention on Diplomatic Relations (1961), applicability **102,** 194
international officials, privileges and immunities
fiscal **75,** 85-9, 100-6
functional **102,** 175, 196
personality **83,** 258
status
acceptance of permanent delegation as evidence of **116,** 648-9
determination of **75,** 100-2
Federal Decree concerning **75,** 102

headquarters agreement **102,** 211
international agreement **102,** 211-12
international personality **116,** 648-9
request to Ministry of Foreign Affairs as evidence of **102,** 185
State distinguished **102,** 211-12
territorial seat, absence **102,** 212
international organizations, immunity, jurisdiction, waiver, implicit, arbitration clause **102,** 212-13, 214-15
international organizations, privileges and immunities
absolute immunity **102,** 211-12
alternative remedy, need for, *ad hoc* arbitration **102,** 212-13
fiscal **75,** 85-9, 99-106
international agreement as basis **102,** 212
Permanent Mission to **75,** 77, 100
Israel, Extradition Convention (1958) **44,** 197-290
judicial assistance **82,** 27-9. *See also* law of, International Mutual Assistance in Criminal Matters Law (*EIMP*) *below*
applicable law **82,** 55
diplomatic immunity, relevance **82,** 57
double criminality, need for **65,** 408
European Convention on Mutual Assistance in Criminal Matters (1959) **82,** 27-9
European Convention for the Protection of Human Rights (1950), proceedings in requesting State and **82,** 56
Head of State, former, recovery of assets from, disclosure of documents **102,** 199-205
judicial proceedings, intention to institute sufficient **82,** 55-6
jurisdiction **82,** 26
arbitral award, annulment **82,** 68-9, 70
connecting factors **72,** 24-5
forum rule **72,** 79-81
fraud **72,** 598-601
ne bis in idem **75,** 106
nexus **75,** 124, **82,** 23, 26, 33, 37, 40
arbitration clause **65,** 449-50
in case of proceedings involving foreign State **62,** 229, 234-5, **65,** 168-9, 233, 361-2, 389, 391, 393, 399-401, 420, 424-5, 430, 432-4, 449-50, **82,** 26, **107,** 340-6, **116,** 639
employment contract, locally engaged staff, diplomatic mission, national of sending State **116,** 663
employment contract, locally engaged staff, diplomatic mission, non-national of sending State **116,** 667-8
enforcement of arbitral award and **62,** 234
forum selection clause **65,** 391
loan payable in forum State **65,** 424-5
place of performance **65,** 400-1
State immunity, execution/attachment and **65,** 168-9, 233, 389, 391, 393, 399-401, 420, 424-5, 430, 432-4, 449-50
riparian State, Lake Constance **75,** 82-4
territorial **72,** 80-1
industrial property, protection **93,** 595, 596
State immunity and **65,** 419-20, 438
law of. *See also* Constitution *above*
Acquisition of Property Law 1983, Art. 7 **82,** 43
Administration of Justice Act, Art. 100(b)(3) **111,** 281

Switzerland (*cont.*)
Administrative Proceedings Act (*LPA*) 1968
Art. 71 **65,** 428
Art. 73(1) **65,** 410
Army (Constitution of Courts and Criminal Procedure) Act 1889 **73,** 554-6, 559, 562
Cartels, Law on **72,** 79-80
Civil Code (*ZBG*) 1907 **72,** 79-80
Art. 8 **102,** 207
Art. 84 **65,** 281
Art. 103 **89,** 197
Art. 150 **89,** 195-206
Art. 151 **89,** 199
Civil Procedure Code (*ZPO*)
arbitration under **47,** 399, 403
Art. 17(3) **80,** 657
Art. 24 **80,** 620, 647
Art. 25 **80,** 648
Art. 59(1) **65,** 405
Civil Relations of Persons Established or Resident in Switzerland (*NAG*) **72,** 641
Code of Obligations 1881 **80,** 612
Code of Obligations (*CO*/*OR*) 1911 **80,** 139, **84,** 391
Arts. 181 ff **80,** 609
Art. 336 **116,** 654, 674
Art. 337(c) **116,** 675
Art. 481 **65,** 423
Arts. 764 ff **80,** 612
Art. 868 **80,** 656
Constitution of the Courts Act (*OJ*). *See* Judicature Act (*OJ*) *below*
Criminal Code (*StGB*) **72,** 391, 396, 622, 631-2, 637-8
Art. 21 **79,** 425
Art. 34(1) **102,** 178
Art. 34(2) **102,** 178-9
Art. 58 **88,** 580-2
Art. 204 **88,** 575-80, 582-3, 587-93
Art. 261 **88,** 575, 583
Arts. 312-17 **82,** 57
Art. 342 **102,** 179
Art. 345 **88,** 642, 653
universal jurisdiction **106,** 263
Criminal Procedure Code
Art. 98 **88,** 622
Art. 220 **102,** 179
Art. 245 **88,** 631
Criminal Procedure Code (Neuchâtel) **88,** 621
Criminal Procedure Code (Zurich) **72,** 392-3, 396-7
Debt Claims and Bankruptcy Law (*LP*) 1889
Art. 17 **65,** 413
Art. 19 **102,** 208
Art. 36 **65,** 388-9
Art. 66(4) **65,** 415-16
Art. 109 **82,** 34
Art. 271 **82,** 47
Art. 271(3) **102,** 208

Art. 271(4) **65,** 396
Art. 272 **82,** 47
Debt Collection against Local Authorities Law 1947
Art. 7 **65,** 402, 435
Art. 9 **65,** 402, 435, **82,** 44
divergence from **82,** 33, 44
Equalization of Burdens Agreement, Law on (*LAG*) **43,** 3, 4, **44,** 149-51
European Convention on Extradition, Decree approving, 1966 **72,** 621-4
Expropriation Act 1930 **73,** 449-50
Extradition Law **72,** 610, 612, 621, 624, 629-30, 634, 636, 639
Art. 1 **72,** 639
Art. 2 **72,** 634
Art. 10 **72,** 612, 615, 624
Federal Order of 23 March 1961 **82,** 43
General Law on Public Taxes 1887 (*LCP*)
Art. 7 **75,** 101-5
Art. 68(c) **102,** 193
Intercantonal Arbitration Concordat (*IAC*)
Art. 4 **80,** 656
Art. 6 **80,** 635, 656, 660
Art. 8 **80,** 656
Art. 24 **80,** 617, 620, 647
Art. 36 **80,** 633-4
Art. 36(a) **80,** 638-9
Art. 36(b) **80,** 639, 650
Art. 36(d) **80,** 648, 649
Art. 36(f) **80,** 649
Art. 36(i) **80,** 649
Art. 37 **80,** 633
Art. 39 **80,** 650
International Mutual Assistance in Criminal Matters Law (*EIMP*) **106,** 262, 269
Art. 1 **82,** 11, 55-6, 57, 64
Art. 2 **82,** 56
Art. 18 **102,** 200
Art. 37(1) **106,** 263
Art. 37(2) **100,** 659
Art. 40(2) **100,** 661
International Organizations, Federal Decree concerning **75,** 102
Introductory Act to the Jurisdictional Statute (*EGJN*)
Art. IX (text) **116,** 529-30
Art. IX(2) **116,** 527-9
Art. IX(3) **116,** 528
Judicature Act (*OJ*) 1943 **72,** 79, 397, 577, **73,** 450-2, 455, **75,** 100-1, **89,** 196
Art. 33(1) **116,** 673
Art. 63 **89,** 196
Art. 63(2) **102,** 207
Art. 81 **102,** 207
Art. 84 **65,** 388, 397, 437, **75,** 101-6, **82,** 35, 39, 47
Art. 84(1)(a) **65,** 410
Art. 84(1)(c) **65,** 397, 409-10, 427-8, 429, 437
Art. 84(1)(d) **65,** 397, 429, 437
Art. 88 **82,** 48
Art. 89(1) **65,** 393

Switzerland (*cont.*)
Art. 91(2) **80,** 656
Art. 96(1) **65,** 411
Art. 103(a) **102,** 186
Art. 104(c) **102,** 197
Art. 156(1) **65,** 413
Jurisdiction of Labour Tribunals (*LJP*)
Art. 1(1) **116,** 645
Art. 1(2) **75,** 78-80, **116,** 638
Art. 50 **75,** 79
Law on the Organization of the Judiciary, Art. 84 **65,** 397, 409-10, 428-9, 437
Local Authorities Act 1956 **88,** 653
Military Criminal Code **73,** 554
Military Criminal Procedure Act 1979 **73,** 556, 562
Municipal Decisions Act 1969 (Vaud) **88,** 652, 653-7, 674-5
Old Age Pensions Law (*LAVS*)
Art. 1(2) **102,** 186, 188
Art. 12(3) **102,** 186
Order Limiting the Number of Aliens of 6 October 1986
Art. 13(f) **111,** 276, 279-80, 284
Art. 36 **111,** 280, 284
Art. 38 **111,** 284
Art. 39 **111,** 284
Postal Services Law **72,** 682-9
Private International Law Law (*LDIP*) of 18 December 1987 **116,** 653, **120,** 5
Art. 176(2) **102,** 215
ss 176 ff **102,** 215
Procedural Code of Vaud, Art. 516 **82,** 63, 69
Residence and Establishment of Aliens Law 1931 (*LSEE*) **72,** 595
Art. 3 **102,** 197
Art. 4 **72,** 577, **111,** 283
Art. 4(1) **102,** 197, **111,** 277-8
Art. 5(1) **111,** 282
Art. 6(1) **111,** 282
Art. 9 **72,** 575, 578
Art. 10 **102,** 197
Art. 16 **111,** 283
Art. 17 **111,** 283
Art. 17(2) **111,** 278, 281
Art. 18 **72,** 578
Art. 21 **72,** 583, 585
Art. 22 **79,** 425
Art. 25(f) **102,** 196
Art. 148 **79,** 425
Art. 251 **79,** 425
Road Traffic Law, diplomatic immunity and **75,** 92-3
Terms of Employment of Employees of the Confederation and PTT Organization of 24 November 1967 **82,** 22
Trade Mark Protection Act (*MSchG*), territorial application **93,** 595, 596
League of Arab States, status **116,** 645
legislation, territorial limitation **93,** 595, 596
imported goods **93,** 596
legislation, interpretation

phrases
'origin' (trademarks) **93,** 596
'taxpayer in Switzerland' **102,** 191-2
treaty as aid **111,** 281
marriage
temporary restrictions on
human rights, abuse of, whether **89,** 195-206, 207
legislative reform **89,** 199-200
military disciplinary proceedings **73,** 554-62
necessity
inviolability of diplomatic premises **102,** 179
requirements
absence of alternative **102,** 179
danger to person or property **102,** 178-9
proportionality **102,** 179
neutrality **71,** 280-1, 443-6
Nufenen Pass boundary dispute **75,** 115-21
obscenity **88,** 575-80, 582
penalties **88,** 580-4
political offence **72,** 612-13, 615-17, 624-6, 631, 634, 637-8
postal services monopoly, commercial river traffic **72,** 685-9
presumption of innocence **72,** 394-404
private prosecution **72,** 390-404
costs, apportionment of **72,** 391-404
period of limitation **72,** 391
proportionality, necessity and **102,** 179
public order/public policy/*ordre public* **72,** 61-2, 636, 684
expulsion of alien, international official **102,** 196-7
publication of judgments, manner of **73,** 556, 562
reclamation of property seized in occupied territories, Decree on, 1945 **44,** 474
recognition, States, Algeria, Popular Democratic Republic of **75,** 81
refugees
access to courts **72,** 641-5
extradition **72,** 634-6
status, withdrawal **72,** 580-1, 585
service of process on foreign State or State agency
diplomatic channels, through embassy in forum State **65,** 413, 415-16
diplomatic premises, inviolability and **102,** 182
method, publication **65,** 415-16
out of the jurisdiction, as act of public authority on foreign territory **65,** 415
Vienna Convention on Diplomatic Relations (1961) and **102,** 182
shareholders, protection of **46,** 380, 452
social security
applicable law, obligations, place of employment **102,** 188
international officials
obligation **102,** 184-8
return of contributions **102,** 184-8
voluntary payments **102,** 187-8
South Africa, extradition practice **75,** 108-13
standard of treatment of alien, equality **72,** 576-7, 594-6
State agency/State-owned corporation/State entity
classification
railway authority **65,** 397-8

Switzerland (*cont.*)
tourist office **65,** 434-5
separate legal entity test **65,** 397-8, 427, 429-30, 434-5
lifting the veil **65,** 422-3
State immunity
European Convention on State Immunity (and Protocol) (Basle) (1972) **82,** 18, 21, 25
Federal Council Message of 27 May 1981 **82,** 7, 21
Swiss law, divergence from **82,** 33, 40, **116,** 660-1
immigrants' centre **82,** 38-45
real property **82,** 41-2
State immunity, classification of act, *acta jure gestionis*/*acta jure imperii* distinguished **82,** 34
State immunity, execution, attachment, theory/doctrine, wartime emergency powers **65,** 169, 428
State immunity, execution/attachment, entitlement, State agency/State-owned corporation/State entity, as open question **65,** 422-3
State immunity, execution/attachment, procedural aspects, executive authorization, need for **65,** 169, 428
State immunity, execution/attachment, purpose of proceedings
debt recovery **82,** 41-2, 46-50
payment of costs **65,** 413-16
safeguarding/conservatory measures **65,** 391, 405
security for costs, whether measure of execution **65,** 405-7
State immunity, execution/attachment, purpose/use of funds/assets
assets held 'in the name of and on behalf of the State, its ministries ... or State entities' **65,** 434-5
burden of proof **102,** 206-7
critical date **65,** 393
cultural and educational centre for foreign workers **82,** 39-45
evidence of **102,** 206, 207
non-specific **65,** 392
patrimonial assets (*patrimoine privé*) **65,** 402, 414-15, 435
public purpose **65,** 392
purchase of arms **65,** 391-2
railway equipment **82,** 44
shares **65,** 402-4, 414-15
State immunity, execution/attachment, theory/doctrine
acta jure imperii concept, relevance **65,** 405
basis
international public order/public policy/*ordre public* **65,** 393
respect for sovereign independence **65,** 419
treaty **102,** 208
development of concept **65,** 168-70, 172, 181, 184, 231-3, 391-2, 398-9, 402, 414-15, 419-22, 428, 430-2, 435, 449
diplomatic premises, residential **102,** 206-8
State immunity, jurisdiction, dependence on **65,** 391-2, 420-1, 430-1
State immunity, execution/attachment, waiver, European Convention on State Immunity (and Protocol) (Basle) (1972) **65,** 431
State immunity, jurisdiction, territorial jurisdiction/sovereignty and **65,** 419-20, 438
State immunity, jurisdiction, applicability, property right derived from public law **82,** 26-7
State immunity, jurisdiction, classification of act

acta jure imperii/*acta jure gestionis* distinguished, private person involvement, relevance **82,** 26-7
commission agreement **65,** 399-401
diplomatic involvement, relevance **65,** 390
diplomatic premises **75,** 122-4, 125
lease **75,** 125
residential **65,** 390-1, **102,** 207
employment of exhibition organizer **75,** 78-80
film, lease of **65,** 431-2
loan agreement, between commercial banks **65,** 423-4
nature or purpose of transaction as determining factor **65,** 390, 401, 431
private person test **65,** 390-1, 398-400, 423, 431-2
railway construction **65,** 399-400
railways administration/operation **65,** 402-4
tourism promotion **65,** 427, 435
State immunity, jurisdiction, entitlement
constituent States **52,** 330-1, **55,** 413-17
international organizations, representatives and missions accredited to **75,** 78-80
private individual **82,** 26, 38, 138
provincial government **55,** 413-17
State immunity, jurisdiction, procedural aspects
appeal, time-limits **65,** 393
appearance, need for **116,** 672-3
applicable law
bilateral treaty **82,** 25, 32, 48
customary international law **82,** 25
forum State **82,** 44
general principles of international law **82,** 32, 33
general principles of municipal law **82,** 32, 33, 40, 48
international law **82,** 44
law of defendant State **82,** 26-7
connection with Swiss territory, need for. *See* jurisdiction, nexus *above*
court's right/duty to raise *proprio motu* **116,** 644, 645, 670, 673-4
exhaustion of local remedies **65,** 389, **82,** 35
foreign law, recognition/enforcement and **82,** 26-7
preliminary issue, whether **82,** 26
State immunity, jurisdiction, theory/doctrine
acta jure imperii/*acta jure gestionis* distinguished, immunity, execution/attachment, relevance to **65,** 405
basis, *par in parem non habet jurisdictionem* **82,** 37
development of concept **65,** 340, 389-91, 430-2, 449, **116,** 662
restrictive theory **82,** 26, 37-8, 48-9
State practice **65,** 419-22, **116,** 639
State immunity, jurisdiction, waiver
submission to the jurisdiction as **65,** 438
treaty provision **65,** 181
absence of **65,** 399, 418-19, 430-1
State immunity, procedural aspects, public law appeal **65,** 393, **82,** 47
taxation, exemption, international officials, deductibility for tax purposes of interest paid to **102,** 193-4
taxpayer in receiving State, whether **102,** 192-3
treaties

Switzerland (*cont.*)
breach, responsibility for determining, European Convention on Mutual Assistance in Criminal Matters (1959) **82,** 27-8
breach, State's right to challenge in foreign court **65,** 409-11, 427-8
compatibility with Constitution, power to determine **89,** 196
direct effect **93,** 597-8, 600-1
clear and precise provision, need for **93,** 600-1
EC/Switzerland Free Trade Agreement (1973) **93,** 600-1
gaps, principles of treaty law **100,** 661
good faith and **82,** 28, 29
individuals
obligations **93,** 597-8
right to appeal against breach **65,** 409-11
municipal law and
legislative sanction, need for **72,** 683
need for amendment **100,** 660
ratification, effect **72,** 682-3
primacy **72,** 669, **100,** 660, 661, **106,** 262
ratification, relevance **100,** 660
violation, jurisdiction of Swiss courts **65,** 427-9
treaty interpretation **72,** 683-9, **82,** 28-9
aids
context **93,** 600
object and purpose **93,** 600
travaux préparatoires **93,** 600
wording **93,** 600
parties' intention **93,** 600
phrases, 'measures of equivalent effect' **93,** 600
UN officials, fiscal immunity **75,** 85-9
Vienna Convention on Diplomatic Relations (1961)
applicability
by analogy and special agreement **102,** 186
European Community (EC) **102,** 186-7
Head of State **102,** 202-3
international officials **102,** 194
signatory State **102,** 187
bilateral agreement, validity **102,** 187-8
European Community (EC), applicability **102,** 186-7
Head of State, applicability **102,** 202-3
Vietnam, Socialist Republic of, South Vietnam as successor to **75,** 125
wartime emergency powers, State immunity, jurisdiction and **65,** 169, 428
WHO, immunity, jurisdiction **75,** 90-6
Syria
Foreign Trade Organization **63,** 569-72
Mandate. *See* Mandate, Syria
SYRIAMAR **63,** 495-7

Taba dispute. *See* Egypt–Israel Arbitration Tribunal (Taba) (1979)
tacit agreement. *See* acquiescence
Taiwan
International Amateur Athletics Federation, exclusion from **74,** 107-12
non-recognition **74,** 106
State immunity, entitlement **98,** 66-7

status **98,** 65, 66
taking of property 87, 514, 515, 617. *See also* compensation for war-related events; confiscation; expropriation/nationalization
classification as
annulment of debt **42,** 155-7, 161-3
compensation award, revocation **42,** 163-4
currency conversion **42,** 153-5
espropriazione **84,** 374, 376
exchange control **84,** 198, **88,** 73 n. 1
executive agreements for preclusion of claims **81,** 545
extinction of nationals' compensation claims **72,** 150-2, 291-2
failure to render contractually required assistance **84,** 554
forestry conservation measures **48,** 179-86
governmental abrogation of contract **87,** 617-20, 634
justification **87,** 618
interference with rights **84,** 635-8
pension rights **42,** 170-2
interference with use, enjoyment or disposal **84,** 374
requisition **84,** 374, 375-7
taxation **91,** 215-16, 320, 321
unreasonable interference **70,** 124
definition **66,** 12-16, 21, 33-4, 42-7, 210, **70,** 124. *See also* classification as *above*
espropriazione/expropriation distinguished **84,** 556
evidence of **84,** 514-17
legality **62,** 182, 198, 202, 221, 224, **84,** 544, 545
of nationals, international law and **88,** 87-90, 92
presumption of **84,** 513
State responsibility **84,** 631-4, 637-8
Talloires Declaration (1981) 75, 25-6
Tamil Tigers, as terrorist organization **123,** 595, **124,** 375-8
Tanganyika, common law, reception of **87,** 116
'Tanganyika clause' 37, 87, 102, 173-4, 420, 506-11
Tanzania
Constitution 1977
amendment, 1979 **103,** 249-50
Bill of Rights, incorporation **87,** 110, 119
invalidation of discriminatory laws **87,** 110-13
jurisdictional provisions **103,** 248-58
s 13 **87,** 119
s 30 **87,** 110-13
s 38 **103,** 250
s 83 **103,** 250-1, 254-5, 257
s 115(2) **103,** 249, 254-5, 257
Constitution (Consequential, Transitional and Temporary Provisions) Act 1984, s 5 **87,** 113-19
courts, municipal, customary law, modification **87,** 113-16, 118-19
customary law
modification by courts **87,** 113-16, 118-19
sexual discrimination under **87,** 107-20
jurisdiction
effects doctrine **86,** 654
federal, elections to Federal Parliament **103,** 245-58
receiving in third country **86,** 653-4

Tanzania (*cont.*)
territorial **86,** 653-4
subject-matter jurisdiction distinguished **103,** 246-7, 256, 257-8
law of
Civil Procedure Code **86,** 653
Constitution. *See* Constitution *above*
Declaration on Customary Law, Rules of Inheritance **87,** 118-29
Elections Act 1985 **103,** 250-1, 252, 253-8
Elections (Election Petitions) Rules 1970, Rule 4 **103,** 245
Grundnorm **87,** 116
Law Reform (Fatal Accidents and Misc. Provisions) 1968 **87,** 111
Penal Code, jurisdiction **86,** 653, **103,** 246-7
legislation, interpretation
conformity with Constitution **87,** 113-16
guidelines, individual's rights, promotion of **87,** 113
teleological **87,** 114
Rules of Court, need for **87,** 111-12
sexual discrimination **87,** 107-20
territorial sea, delimitation **41,** 136
Trusteeship Agreement **48,** 26-30
tariff, definition **110,** 551 n. 4
Tashkent Declaration (1966) 48, 332, 337, 436, **67,** 617-18, 622
TASS Agency 63, 130, 132-5
Tate letter. *See* United States of America (USA), Tate Letter
tax haven
Cook Islands regime **104,** 548
extraterritorial legislation **104,** 540-6
legitimacy **104,** 534-6, 547-8, 620-1
tax judgments, enforcement 38, 118, **42,** 114-18
taxation. *See also* diplomatic privileges and immunities, taxation, exemption; double taxation; international officials, exemption from taxation; jurisdiction, taxation; tax judgments
in breach of Mandate, Namibia **49,** 209
church dues **38,** 454-5
confiscatory **56,** 322
constitutional constraints **91,** 326-9
death duties as part of **56,** 572-3
as deprivation of property **91,** 321, 325
enforcement of legislation as **91,** 325-6
discriminatory, whether **91,** 320
domicile, relevance **72,** 669, **74,** 206, 209
double taxation conventions **87,** 83
official of European Community (EC) **87,** 82-3
exchange of information, Council of Europe/OECD Convention on Mutual Administrative Assistance in Tax Matters (1988) **104,** 578-9
executive powers **91,** 326, 328
exemption
Agents-General (Commonwealth) **108,** 525-6
basis, fiscal equality **36,** 459, **94,** 320
burden of proof **108,** 548-9
consular. *See* consular privileges and immunities, taxation, exemption
death duties **56,** 572-3
diplomatic. *See* diplomatic privileges and immunities, taxation, exemption

foreign State **88,** 681-3, **108,** 525
enforceability of claim for **53,** 547-50
estoppel **103,** 335-6
non-recognition, effect **108,** 512-57
real estate **63,** 179-80
tax credit, entitlement **103,** 332-6, 337-9
treaty arrangement **108,** 528-9
Head of State **64,** 421, 483-6, 524-34, 617
comity **64,** 421
international organization. *See* international organizations, exemption from taxation
State-owned corporation, unemployment insurance **63,** 195-6
frontier travellers **40,** 292-5
high seas, income earned on **74,** 207
immunity. *See* exemption *above*
income tax
continental shelf, recovery **78,** 528-50
exemption **36,** 457-65, **44,** 409-22, **56,** 522-3, 569-71
Head of State **64,** 406-7, 421, 483-6, 524-34, 617
international law rules **40,** 237
judicial assistance
Council of Europe/OECD Convention on Mutual Administrative Assistance in Tax Matters (1988) **104,** 579
customary international law **104,** 579
good faith **104,** 580
judicial review **91,** 326-8
legislation, colourable device, as **91,** 320, 326, 327-9
level
determination of **56,** 322
excessive **56,** 322
expropriatory, whether **56,** 322-3
lump sum compensation, liability on **74,** 285-6
ministerial discretion **91,** 327
production levy, tax, whether **74,** 228-34
reasonable justification in democratic society **91,** 320, 325-8
as rent increase **91,** 320
social security. *See* social security
State acquisition distinguished **68,** 350, 441-2, 472-81
State sovereignty and **44,** 413
tax haven. *See* tax haven
territorial principle **38,** 118, **42,** 114-18, **71,** 220-1, **78,** 528-50
telecommunications. *See also* telephone-tapping
interception **58,** 434-8, 441-5, 446-54, 461, 604, **61,** 193-4, 202-3, 205, **74,** 307-91, **85,** 299 n. 14
abuse **58,** 448
confidentiality, right of **74,** 319-22, 336-9, 356
European Convention on Human Rights (1950) **74,** 324-5, 339-41, 357, 371-91
grounds, prevention and detection of crime **74,** 351-90
lawfulness **58,** 477
of legal counsel **74,** 391
margin of appreciation and **58,** 448-9
'metering' **74,** 367-8, 379-81
private life, respect for **74,** 317-19, 322, 324-5, 333-6, 341-2, 371-91

telecommunications (*cont.*)
remedies under municipal law **74,** 307-15, 329-40, 343-6, 355-6
right of property and **74,** 316-17, 356
victim **58,** 441-5, 460
interference by public authority **58,** 447
International Telecommunications Union **77,** 422
interruption **83,** 227-30
reserved to competent executive organs **83,** 237
State security and **83,** 227
sovereign right to regulate **77,** 422
telephone-tapping 74, 307-90
confidentiality **74,** 319-22, 336-9, 356
privacy, right of **74,** 317-19, 333-6
television programmes, censorship, human rights and **40,** 188-90
terra nullius. *See* territory, *terra nullius*
territorial disputes. *See* territory, dispute
territorial integrity 79, 263, 264. *See also* sovereignty; territory
general principle of international law **103,** 21, **115,** 483, 580, 582, 584-5
Genocide Convention (1948), relevance **95,** 151-2, 163-4
importance **115,** 580, 582, 584-5
inviolability **83,** 64
neutrality and **110,** 256, 337-9
non-self-governing status and **105,** 381
secession **115,** 150-3, 162-4, 580, 582, 584-5
self-determination and **115,** 162, 583
sovereign right **110,** 526
UN Charter **115,** 161-2
violation, protest, need for **90,** 696-7
territorial jurisdiction. *See* jurisdiction, territorial
territorial nexus 69, 58, 116-19, 122, 124-5, **70,** 58-60, 67, 89-90
offshore waters **69,** 117-18, 124
territorial rights, Security Council competence **49,** 284
territorial sea 51, 81-217, **77,** 307-21, 404-5. *See also* bays; contiguous zone; continental shelf; exclusive economic zone (EEZ); exclusive fishing zone (EFZ); fishing zones; high-seas; inland waters; internal waters; rivers; straits; Territorial Sea and Contiguous Zone Convention (1958)
Abu Musa. *See* Abu Musa, territorial sea
applicable law
common law **125,** 334-42
international law **90,** 254, 257
baselines. *See* baselines
bays **57,** 59, **71,** 181. *See also* bays, closing line
breadth **38,** 131, **41,** 91, 163, **55,** 3-4, 257, 281, 320-3, 330-2, 354, **56,** 162-3, 188, **74,** 210-12, **90,** 238, **91,** 376
3 miles **43,** 84, 86, 90-1, 99, 104, **73,** 194-5, 205, 217, 219, 280-1, **74,** 207, 209-11, **82,** 681, 687, **91,** 515
12 miles **55,** 221, 320-3, 325-6, 327-8, **73,** 177, 181, 275, 284, 295, **74,** 143-5, 148, **82,** 602, **92,** 582-4
opposability to neighbouring and third States distinguished **82,** 687
broadcasting
from outside **61,** 184-5, **74,** 201-3
from within **43,** 80-93
Strasbourg Agreement (1965) **74,** 201-3

claims to **55,** 208
need for **86,** 599-600, 615
coastline. *See* coastline
common, Fonseca Bay **83,** 72-3
contiguous zone and **55,** 205, **74,** 207, 209-12
continental shelf
distinguished **41,** 64, 75, 91
extension of rules to **41,** 64
delimitation **41,** 153
continental shelf and, title to, separable, whether **86,** 600
creeks **69,** 50
Crown prerogative **43,** 81, 86, 88, 92, 116, 117-18, 120, **112,** 500-1, 557, **125,** 398-400
customs jurisdiction distinguished **90,** 254
declaration of
Crown prerogative **43,** 84, 116, 117-18
international law and **43,** 84, 87, 88
definition **43,** 80-93, **59,** 483
delimitation **56,** 137, **57,** 61, 62, 65, **64,** 336-43, **66,** 33, **73,** 174-8, 193-4, 199-200, 205, 216-17, **83,** 43
adjacent States, between **41,** 47, 63, 64, 66, 75, 91, 134-5, 158-61, 163, 167, 223, 224
Arabian Gulf **64,** 336-8
artificial structure, effect **57,** 59, 102-5
by courts **69,** 57-8
equidistance **41,** 46, 47, 66-7, 75, 163
Law of the Sea Convention (1982) **83,** 14
extension of **71,** 140
Grisbadarna case **41,** 159 n. 2
indented coastline **57,** 64
landmarks **57,** 60
Law of the Sea Convention (1982) **83,** 14
low-water mark **57,** 83-8
methods **41,** 163
prolongation of land boundary **83,** 43
river mouths **57,** 60-4
straight coastline **57,** 63-4
straits **57,** 64-5
unilateral **48,** 470, 472, 474
dependent territories **90,** 243, 305-6
dispute
act of State and **64,** 279-80, 292-4, 348-51
justiciability **66,** 335-7
economic interests **69,** 66, 72
EEZ and **74,** 144-5, 148, **92,** 583-4
evolution of law **90,** 244-7, **125,** 347-51
Air Navigation Convention (1919) **90,** 245
Hague Codification Conference (1930) **90,** 245-6, 254
International Law Commission (ILC) **90,** 245-7
Territorial Sea and Contiguous Zone Convention (1958), customary international law, codification **90,** 247
extension **55,** 327-8
act of State **63,** 317, **66,** 182

territorial sea (*cont.*)
compatibility with international law, unilateral measure, whether **100,** 155
unilateral declaration, freedom of the seas and **74,** 210
fisheries jurisdiction and **55,** 326, **56,** 153-4, 162-3, 189, 215-16, **90,** 327
fishing rights **55,** 3, 204-5, 327, **59,** 485, **125,** 350-1
foreign conservation measures **59,** 343-4
freedom of navigation **125,** 350-1
common law **125,** 423-5
gulfs. *See* gulfs, closing line
high seas, relation to **55,** 204-5, 327
historic evidence **69,** 43, 45, 49-52, 56, 59, 69-70
historic rights **69,** 66, 73
historic title **59,** 231-3, 264-73
Indian jagirs **49,** 336-49
innocent passage. *See* innocent passage
internal waters distinguished **77,** 311, 404-5
islands. *See* islands, territorial sea
jurisdiction **41,** 67, 158, **43,** 80-93, 101, **59,** 342, 343, 360, **72,** 3-9, 216, **73,** 173-85, 216-17, 223-5, 275-95, **74,** 206-12
admiralty jurisdiction. *See* admiralty jurisdiction
common law and **125,** 334-42, 366-7, 380-407, 455-9
crimes committed outside **38,** 120-32
criminal **78,** 118-19
federal State. *See* federal State, territorial sea
foreign nationals on foreign vessel **63,** 603
law enforcement by foreign State over own ship **91,** 408-502
low-water mark, property beyond **42,** 62-85
nationals in foreign **55,** 145-9
source **90,** 238
statutory basis **125,** 388-9, 401-3
lakes, riparian States **75,** 82-4
maritime belt **51,** 39-87, 89-94
jurisdiction **51,** 217-24
measurement. *See* baselines
municipal law, determining factor, whether **90,** 241-2, 244
native title and **125,** 327-468
exclusive rights, claim to **125,** 355, 357-64, 367, 419-21
traditional laws and customs as basis **125,** 357-62
public rights of fishing, navigation and innocent passage, relevance **125,** 351, 362-4, 418-26, 436, 466-7
nuclear waste **106,** 67
outer limit, as starting point for maritime delimitation **41,** 87, 189, 190-1, **81,** 441-2, 461, **83,** 113, **90,** 238
ownership. *See* property rights in *above*
patrimonial sea and **56,** 90
piracy **78,** 568-74
power of government to amend in accordance with international law and State practice **92,** 582-3
property rights in **42,** 81-3, **86,** 599-600, **90,** 296
jurisdiction distinguished **90,** 276
ownership **86,** 599, **90,** 300
ownership of seabed and subsoil **43,** 104, 106-10, **125,** 350-1, 354, 433-6, 449-50

recognition by other States, need for **90,** 241
rights and duties **55,** 208
airspace, over **90,** 241
of central authority **77,** 405
coastal States **56,** 117
continental shelf distinguished **56,** 119
jus regale **90,** 243
prerogative **90,** 243
recognition by other States and **43,** 95, 112
State succession and **90,** 240-1
seabed and subsoil. *See also* property rights in *above and solum below*
rights over **70,** 58, 66, 69, **77,** 315, 316, **90,** 241-4, **91,** 413-15, 422 n. 12, 429 n. 1
sovereignty over
Crown in right of the Commonwealth **90,** 242
Crown in right of the Island of Newfoundland **90,** 260
federal State **70,** 58, 66, 69, **90,** 242-3, 260, **125,** 347-51
State succession and **90,** 242-3
solum **51,** 178, **90,** 243, 248, 254-5, 271, 277, 320. *See also* seabed and subsoil *above*
Sovereign Base Areas (Cyprus) and **88,** 238-9
sovereignty over **41,** 67, 158, **55,** 316-17, **56,** 116-17, **57,** 83, **76,** 445, **86,** 601, **90,** 241, **91,** 515
federal State. *See* federal State
starting point. *See* baselines
territorial waters claimed . . . *titre de souverain* **97,** 508
territorial waters distinguished **97,** 657 n. 1
territory, whether **77,** 311-19, 404-5, **83,** 78, **90,** 243, 246-8, 290-2, 317, **91,** 209-10
admiralty jurisdiction, relevance **90,** 292-6
customary international law **90,** 246
as extension of **41,** 127, **56,** 116
internal waters distinguished **77,** 315
part of the realm **77,** 308-10
seabed **91,** 413-15, 422 n. 12, 429 n. 1
status **77,** 307-21
Trust territory **61,** 98-9, 123-5, 126-7
uncertainty **90,** 241-2
usage of waters **69,** 66
Territorial Sea and Contiguous Zone Convention (1958) 51, 46, 47, 90, 112, 167-8, 175, 182, 183, 187-9, **74,** 210
baselines **41,** 163, **59,** 225-7, 242-3, 275, 280, **69,** 44, 63-8, 72, 79-81, **73,** 174-8, 217
economic interests **41,** 153 n. 1
rivers, effect **59,** 241-2, 281
bays, definition **42,** 78, **43,** 119-25, **59,** 273, 278
charts
large scale **43,** 116, 122-3
officially recognized, lack **73,** 176-8
coastal States
responsibility, private acts **71,** 259-61
rights **56,** 116-17
coastline
artificial construction **57,** 92
definition **57,** 108

Territorial Sea and Contiguous Zone Convention (1958) (*cont.*)
harbours **57,** 92, **59,** 218-20, 225-7
contiguous zone **56,** 189
definition **56,** 117
fisheries jurisdiction and **56,** 189
customary international law **69,** 63, 72, **73,** 177-8, 195, 214
delimitation **55,** 344
equidistance principle **41,** 104, 133, **59,** 239-41
equity and **59,** 239-41
evidence **59,** 194, 275-6
historic title **59,** 231-3
historic waters **59,** 264-9
median line **59,** 218-20, 229, 240
definition **59,** 226
relevant/special circumstances **59,** 236-41
rivers, effect **59,** 241-4
denunciation **83,** 85-6
equidistance **83,** 14, **95,** 663-4
government ships used commercially **45,** 74
harbour works **91,** 662
individuals' rights under **71,** 259-60
inland waters. *See* internal waters *below*
innocent passage **73,** 182-3, 283-6
warship, other ships distinguished from, whether **91,** 500
internal waters **91,** 415, 431
definition **42,** 87, 89-92, **57,** 92
'low-tide elevation' **43,** 80, 83, 91, 115-16, 124-5
low-water mark **43,** 123-4, **59,** 284
'opposite' and 'adjacent' **41,** 223, 225
relevant/special circumstances, historic title **41,** 101
straight baselines **81,** 254, 485
determination of **59,** 256-64
territorial sea
definition of **72,** 213
sovereignty over **55,** 204, 344
UK Territorial Waters Order 1964 **43,** 120-1
territorial waters. *See* territorial sea
territory 51, 28-32, **54,** 216, **73,** 57-163. *See also* boundaries; internal waters; sovereignty; territorial sea; title
abandonment **38,** 89, **59,** 171
acquiescence and **50,** 4, 90, 95, 99-105, 246, 381, 383, 448, 452, 474, 495-500
acquisition **40,** 50-3, **42,** 59-61, **71,** 51-6, **72,** 440, **91,** 424. *See also* alluvion, avulsion *and* erosion *below*
accretion **91,** 453-4, 458, 464
inland waters **50,** 35, 37-8, 41, 390
act of State **55,** 59-60, **73,** 119-20, 152, 156-7
justiciability **112,** 481-2, 513, 521, 523, 535-8, 642, 670
acts of jurisdiction **52,** 220-6
alluvion **74,** 122-3
ancient title. *See* historic title *below*
annexation. *See* annexation
applicable law, international **112,** 482, 521
armistice agreement **114,** 46, 58

avulsion **91,** 454, 457-8, 464. *See also* accretion *and* alluvion *above*; erosion *below*
belligerent occupation **114,** 46
cession. *See* cession *below*
colonization, grant, need for **90,** 281-4
conquest **37,** 543, **48,** 63-8, **73,** 107-8, 143, 149, 153, 162, **86,** 212
  critical date **39,** 101-3
  Goa **46,** 484, **118,** 431-46
  South West Africa **49,** 33, 111-12, 201
discovery and occupation **71,** 51, **73,** 60, 62, 103-10, 127, 132, 138, 144, 149, 151, 162, **91,** 430, **112,** 520-1, 569
  title of occupants, effect on **73,** 60, 62, 65-87, 103-27, 138, 144, 149, 151, 162
erosion **91,** 458. *See also* accretion *and* avulsion *above*; rivers, avulsion
exploitation **91,** 434-7
Fonseca Bay islands, whether **97,** 474, 481-2, 593
'forcible seizure followed by unilateral assertion of title' **95,** 153
historic title. *See* title, historic
immemorial possession **59,** 59-67, 171-2, **73,** 57-9, 77-83, 87-99, 138, 145, 157-8, 162
inhabited territory. *See* inhabited territory *below*
invasion **50,** 393
Island of Palmas **97,** 593
Mandates **55,** 59-60
municipal act, need for **90,** 264
naming of places **97,** 628 n. 1
native title. *See* Australia, native title; Canada, aboriginal title; Murray Islands, native title; Papua New Guinea, land titles; United States of America (USA), native title
occupation **46,** 465 n. 8, 484, **59,** 56-7, 140-1, **71,** 51-6, **73,** 58-60, 65, 79-127, 138, 141, 151, 153, 162, **86,** 211, 212-13, **91,** 430
  adverse possession **38,** 89
  continental shelf **67,** 168-75, 215, 313
  Rann of Kutch, whether capable of **50,** 6, 386, 511
  uti possidetis de facto **97,** 479
'peaceful and continuous exercise of State authority'. *See* prescription
recognition **71,** 297-300, 497-502, **73,** 58-61, 99-120, 139, 146
requirements
  intent **50,** 382, 448-9, 459, 460
  legislation **90,** 240
secession. *See* secession
settlement, **112,** 520
survival of existing interests **112,** 498-9, 508-15, 522-34, 551, 557-602, 641
  Adeyinka Oyekan v. *Musendiku Adele* **112,** 524, 526-7, 560-1
  Administration of Papua and New Guinea v. *Daera Guba* **112,** 525
  Amodu Tijani **112,** 524, 525-6, 528, 533, 559-60, 609, 611-12
  enforcement **112,** 533-4, 549-50, 652-3
  evidence of **112,** 610-13, 671-80
  justiciability **112,** 508, 523, 609-10, 670-1
  natural law **112,** 524
  presumption of **112,** 671-80
  private property rights, limitation to **112,** 610-11
  Re Southern Rhodesia **112,** 524, 525, 562-3, 609
  requirements, recognition **112,** 501-4, 523, 540, 558-61, 563-76, 580, 585, 590-1, 608-10
  St Catherine's Milling and Lumber Co. v. *R* **112,** 565-6

territory (*cont.*)
terra incognito **73,** 115, 132
terra nullius. See terra nullius below
waste and vacant land. *See* annexation, waste and vacant land
acquisitive prescription. *See* prescription
administering power
annexation precluded **77,** 628
assignment of territory as objective **77,** 628
belligerent occupation, deriving from law of war **77,** 629
occupying powers as **77,** 628
rights distinguished **77,** 628
administration, evidence of **38,** 88-9
aircraft **71,** 230
airspace. *See* airspace
alienation
colonial power, by, contrary to *jus cogens*/peremptory norm of international law, whether **83,** 24, 25-7
delimitation distinguished **83,** 30
limitation on powers of **83,** 24, 30
aliens, protection of **79,** 28
annexation. *See* annexation
Antarctica. *See* Antarctica
applicable law **112,** 523
intertemporal law **114,** 46, 115
method of acquisition, relevance **112,** 482, 521-2
traditional laws and customs **112,** 504-8, 529
continuous practice, need for **112,** 505-6, 514
artificial structure, whether **80,** 685-7
attribution, boundary delimitation and **80,** 468-9
Vienna Convention on the Law of Treaties (1969) **80,** 468
Vienna Convention on Succession of States in respect of Treaties **80,** 468
bays **51,** 230-2
boundaries. *See* boundaries
boundary disputes and
demarcation and allocation of territory distinguished **94,** 28, 40, **100,** 49-50
interrelationship **91,** 586-7, **100,** 13-14, 25, 37
cession **40,** 50-2, **42,** 59-61, **56,** 51, **57,** 5, **70,** 38-50, **73,** 62-3, 66-8, 73-4, 81, 100, 106-8, 110-12, 126, **82,** 418, 602-4, **91,** 424
boundary demarcation as **70,** 43-50
of British territory **50,** 85-9, 102-3, 175, 325, 402-5, 465-6
constitutional amendment, need for **92,** 573
executive, powers **70,** 43-50
in India. *See* India, territory, cession
inhabitants' rights **49,** 389, 393, 395, 408-13
lease of land to international organization, whether **82,** 88
legislative sanction, need for **70,** 43, 46-50
municipal law requirements **70,** 48-9
pension rights **57,** 5-6
physical possession of land and **70,** 39, 44-6
private rights, effect on **49,** 389, 393, 395, 408-13, **70,** 39-41, **118,** 431, 436-46
Schleswig-Holstein **57,** 5-6

sub modo **49,** 197, 201
temporary, effect **90,** 256
treaty, ratification **49,** 484-96
changes in **77,** 628-30
effect on
nationality **40,** 50-1, 191-9, **43,** 191-4, **72,** 438-42
private rights **49,** 389, 393, 395, 408-13, **70,** 39-41
treaties **74,** 563-6
Security Council, competence **49,** 284
civilian administrative authority **77,** 629
claim to
assertions of distinguished **50,** 6
conflicting **50,** 5, 6
critical date **50,** 27, 388, 389-91, 463, 470
demarcation agreement **90,** 280, 311-16, 329
lighthouse, erection of **114,** 63-70, 129
navigation agreement **90,** 280-1
part of national heritage **100,** 309
recognition of **66,** 336-8, **90,** 280-1
restrictive interpretation **50,** 514
concept, derivation of **51,** 89
contiguity and. *See* contiguity principle
continental shelf. *See* continental shelf, territory, whether part of
critical date **38,** 79-80
definition **72,** 141-2, 213
development of **120,** 635
internal waters **77,** 311
King of Spain's Award **97,** 553-4
land, inland waters and territorial sea, limitation to **120,** 635
seabed and subsoil, territorial waters, inside and outside distinguished **77,** 316-17
territorial sea **77,** 307-21
delineation **74,** 93
dependent territories **90,** 245
dispute **77,** 629
act of State and **64,** 280, 292-4, 303, 343-4, 348-51, **66,** 180-5, 334-8
critical date **59,** 55
General Act for the Peaceful Settlement of Disputes (1928) **60,** 580, 582-3, 587-93, 623-4
jurisdiction, municipal courts **57,** 21-2
justiciability **64,** 339-43, 348-51, **108,** 574-7, 587-91, 594-6, 613
property rights, effect on **66,** 178, 334
division of, legal consequences **45,** 37-46
effectiveness, need for **97,** 557, **100,** 37
equitable distribution **50,** 213
erosion, avulsion distinguished **97,** 462
extent, determined by Paramount Power **50,** 404
extent, low-water mark **90,** 239-40, 244, 276-7
federal State **91,** 413-15, 424
dependent territories, power to adjust **86,** 185-208
internal adjustments **86,** 185-208
fishing rights on high seas and **55,** 147-8

territory (*cont.*)
high seas, seabed **91,** 424
incorporation. *See* annexation *above*
independence and **48,** 3-5
infringement of
atmospheric nuclear tests **57,** 514, 573, 576-84
environment, injury to **57,** 578-84
inhabited territory **112,** 482-8. *See also terra nullius below*
terra nullius, assimilation to **112,** 483, 486-8, 493-4, 542, 571-6, 607-8
human rights, compatibility with **112,** 490-1
internal waters. *See* internal waters
intertemporal law **50,** 453, **59,** 186
invasion **50,** 393
lakes. *See* lakes
lease in perpetuity **92,** 562-5, 571, 575-6
'legal ties' **59,** 57-8, 81, 92-4, 97, 152
loss
extinction of rights
by exercise of sovereignty by colonial power **73,** 59-61, 65-72, 76-7, 100-3, 117-19, 138, 141, 151-3, 156-7, 162
by treaty **73,** 73-4, 106-8, 111-12, 138
mandated territories **37,** 30, 34, 61, 121, 309, 440, 570
maritime belt **51,** 39-87
maritime rights dependent on **83,** 116
military courts, jurisdiction and **47,** 485
native title. *See* native title
natural disaster, effect of **50,** 425, 476
nature **59,** 182
'no-man's land' **50,** 287-9, 330, 340, 344, 463, 479
occupation, *terra nullius* **100,** 98
overseas departments and territories, part of **93,** 289, 306
elections to European Parliament and **93,** 306-7
peace settlement, questions reserved to **78,** 186-7
peaceful possession and display of authority **50,** 6, 7
permanent occupation, incapable of **50,** 6, 386, 511
possession, requirement of **50,** 511, 513
'proclaimed waters' **51,** 86
reclaimed territory, whether **80,** 686
recognition and **50,** 90, 100-1, 409-15, 464, 466, 495, **59,** 67-73
religion as element of **59,** 115
renunciation **50,** 5, 7, 500, 513, 515-16, **77,** 629
restrictions on, treaty-making power of European Communities **47,** 278-311
retroactive **77,** 630
rights and duties
exclusive **50,** 500
property and control **49,** 386
variation in **50,** 5
sans maître. See terra nullius below
seabed, whether **77,** 316-17, **80,** 686, **91,** 209-10, 413-15, 422 n. 12, 429 n. 1
secession. *See* secession
servitudes **50,** 387, 459, 468. *See also* historic rights
self-imposed restraint **92,** 574

sovereignty, identity of concepts **77,** 628, **95,** 695
status
critical date **114,** 32
erga omnes
treaty provision **114,** 33-4, 48
UN decision **105,** 389
evidence of, government internal memoranda **114,** 31-2
straits. *See* straits
submerged land, whether **80,** 686
terra nullius **49,** 76, **50,** 6, **59,** 56-7, 91-2, 102-4, 130, 140-1, **67,** 168-72, **73,** 138, 141, 145, 157, 162, **80,** 562, **86,** 205, 210-12, **91,** 642, **97,** 303, 474, 481, 482. *See also* inhabited territory *above*
Advisory Opinion on Western Sahara **112,** 489-90, 607-8
assimilation to inhabited territory **50,** 6, **59,** 102-3, **73,** 138, 141, 145, 157, 162, **86,** 210-12, **97,** 474
Chad/Libya border area **100,** 37, 52-9
continental shelf **67,** 168-74
definition **59,** 56-7, 91-2, 103, **112,** 490
Fonseca Bay
islands, whether **97,** 474, 481-2, 593
Meanguerita, whether **97,** 626, 627
Gulf emirates **91,** 642
inhabitation by tribes having social and political organizations **100,** 52-3
Island of Palmas **97,** 593
municipal law, relevance of concept **86,** 212
occupation **100,** 98
constructive **100,** 82-4
notional **67,** 170
prescription **97,** 480-1
rejection of concept **112,** 642
submarine areas **67,** 168-74
uti possidetis and **97,** 303, **100,** 82-4
territorial sea, whether. *See* territorial sea, territory, whether
territorial waters. *See* territorial sea
territorium, meaning **86,** 540
title. *See* title
undetermined, Trieste **40,** 43-50
unlawful arrest as bar to proceedings and **86,** 529
usage **50,** 6, 512
violation
abduction of fugitive **36,** 62-4, 67-71, **45,** 91, 96, 102
apology as reparation for **74,** 258, 266, 271
explosion caused by foreign agent **74,** 249, 258, 262, 266-7
extent **76,** 445
mine-laying **76,** 445-6, 462
UN Charter **74,** 258, 262
water boundaries **51,** 28-39
terrorism **62,** 280-1, 283-5, **74,** 250-6, 453-4, 494, 498-504, 511-16, 695-8. *See also* hijacking of aircraft; hostage-taking; *mafiosi*, regulation in Italy; piracy; political offence; terrorism, Conventions
arrest of suspects **69,** 157-8
asylum, right to and **80,** 679-80

terrorism (*cont.*)
aut dedere aut punire/judicare **88,** 296-7, **94,** 487-8, 507-8, 534, 551, 556, 564-5, **107,** 564-5
customary international law **110,** 702
classification as, suicide bombing **121,** 634-6
correspondence, respect for and **58,** 446-54
definition/requirements **74,** 252, **77,** 235-7
'atrocity' **107,** 573-4
crimes against humanity distinguished **125,** 504
difficulty of **107,** 576, **124,** 373-5
in domestic law **124,** 373-5
indiscriminate violence **107,** 574-5, 578, 581-90
intention to subvert constitutional order **119,** 342
'international terrorism' **121,** 635-6
League of Nations Draft Convention for the Prevention and Punishment of Terrorism (1937) **107,** 563, 575, 576
organized group **74,** 494, 498-504, 511-16, 695-8, **119,** 342
Terrorism, International Convention for the Suppression of the Financing of Terrorism (1999) **124,** 374
terrorist **82,** 361
terrorist act
'accident at work', whether **91,** 257-8
compensation for **91,** 257-8
'use of violence for political ends' **104,** 663, 665
deportation and, compelling reasons of national security **108,** 379, **124,** 348-51, 360-3, 367-78, 520-2, 525
diplomatic mission, protection against. *See* diplomatic mission, receiving State's duty of protection
discrimination and **58,** 285-8
expulsion of alien and **62,** 281-2, 284, **123,** 598-9
extradition for **74,** 472-7, 498-504, 511-16, **79,** 52-3, 105, 131-2, 453-5, 478-81, 514-15, 517-18, 525, 531-2, **94,** 507, 521-2, 534, 551, 565
freedom of expression and. *See* freedom of expression, terrorism and
hijacking of aircraft. *See* hijacking of aircraft
human rights and **116,** 377-80
intent
burden of proof **88,** 187
hostage-taking **88,** 181
jurisdiction, hijacking **88,** 182
relevance **88,** 186-7
international law, whether violation of **77,** 224-5, 252
jurisdiction **71,** 236-7, 243-7, **72,** 620-6, **74,** 163-5, **82,** 346-7, 355, **86,** 42-3, 179, 180, 279, 280, **87,** 299-300, 301-2, 303-5, **94,** 501, 565
aliens **74,** 163-5, **94,** 488-9, 521
anti-terrorism conventions **82,** 350, **86,** 37-40
customary international law **94,** 507-8, 521-2, 551, 555, 565, 592, **110,** 702
extraterritorial **104,** 146-7
forum State, committed for benefit of **71,** 243-7
obligation to establish **94,** 487-9, 578
passive personality principle **88,** 181, **121,** 612
political character **71,** 236-7, 246-7
territorial **94,** 501, 565
place of incident **94,** 565

presence of suspect **94,** 565
universal **80,** 679, **82,** 348-9, **88,** 181, **94,** 501-2, 504-5, 564-5, **119,** 342
jus cogens/peremptory norm **107,** 391-2
legislation **82,** 235, 236-44, 245-52, 254, 261-7, 269-72, 275-7, 278, 279-80, 285, 286-8, 299, 311, **83,** 154
liberation movements and **77,** 236
liberty of person, deprivation and **58,** 272-5
political offence and. *See* political offence, classification as, terrorist act
presumption of innocence **122,** 445-9
punishment **74,** 254-6, 454-5, 494, 695-8, **77,** 224
retroactive legislation **121,** 611 n. 4, 631-2. *See also* time of events constituting, relevance *below*
as 'serious non-political crime' **104,** 663-72, **107,** 562-90
State immunity, jurisdiction. *See* State immunity, jurisdiction, classification of act, terrorist act
State-sponsored terrorism. *See* State-sponsored terrorism
superior orders as defence **74,** 164-5, **88,** 187-9
support for, Iran **96,** 7 n. 4
Terrorism, European Convention for the Suppression of (1977), reservations, crimes committed prior to entry into force **111,** 523
terrorist act, act of war, whether **91,** 257-8
time of events constituting, relevance. *See also* retroactive legislation *above*
events prior to entry into force of the European Convention for the Suppression of Terrorism (1977) **111,** 523
events prior to legislation providing for jurisdiction **119,** 336-7, 342
UN Declaration on Principles of International Law Concerning Friendly Relations and Cooperation Among States in Accordance with the UN Charter **77,** 236
war, laws and customs and **77,** 224-5, **91,** 257-8
terrorism, Conventions
ambit **86,** 41-2
Convention for the Suppression of Terrorist Bombing (1997)
aiding and abetting, acting with a common purpose distinguished **124,** 154-5
travaux préparatoires **124,** 155
European Convention on the Suppression of Terrorism (1978) **77,** 236, **80,** 680
asylum, right to and **80,** 680
general principles of international law and **79,** 105
political offence **104,** 87, **107,** 564
Hague Convention for the Suppression of the Unlawful Seizure of Aircraft (1970) **74,** 164, **77,** 236, **80,** 679-80, **86,** 38-9, **88,** 180
asylum, right to and **80,** 679-80
'inquiry into the facts' **87,** 300, 307-8
operation and enforcement **88,** 182
implementing legislation **86,** 37-40
ambit **86,** 37-40, 41
limited to offences under conventions, whether **86,** 37-40, 41
International Convention for the Suppression of the Financing of Terrorism (1999), definition of terrorism **124,** 374
jurisdiction, concurrent **86,** 37, 42
Montreal Convention (1971). *See* Montreal Convention for the Suppression of Unlawful Acts Against the Safety of Civilian Aviation (1971)
New York Convention (1973) **61,** 516, 519, 554, **77,** 236
Tokyo Convention (1963) **77,** 236, **86,** 37
UN Draft Convention on the prevention and suppression of terrorism **79,** 517

terrorist organization
deportation for membership of **124,** 375-8
freedom of speech and **82,** 307-14, **120,** 375-8
political offence and **74,** 498-500, 504, 511-16
whether **88,** 187-8
PLO **82,** 304, 317
Tamil Tigers **123,** 595, **124,** 375-8
Texas. *See* United States of America (USA), Texas
Thailand, law of
Civil Code **74,** 553-4
Conflict of Laws Act **74,** 554
thalidomide 58, 501-8
thalweg
bays **91,** 421-2
definition **94,** 17
land boundary **38,** 97, **77,** 672-3, **83,** 18, 119, **94,** 17-18, 21
rivers **38,** 97, **41,** 204, **77,** 664, 667, 672-3
straight lines, method **94,** 17
thought, freedom of. *See* European Convention on Human Rights (1950), freedom of belief
threat of force. *See* force, prohibition on the threat or use of
time-limits. *See also* International Court of Justice (ICJ), procedural issues, time-limits; Iran–US Claims Tribunal, procedure, time-limits
effect on cause of action **86,** 560-1
title. *See also* ownership; sovereignty; territory
acquiescence **97,** 321-5, 335-6, 338, 482-3
acquisition **77,** 547-9. *See also* evidence of *below*
acquiescence
continuous, peaceful exercise of sovereignty. *See* jurisdiction, acts of *below*
Grisbadarna **91,** 622-3
Island of Palmas **91,** 623
Norwegian Fisheries **91,** 623
protest, absence **91,** 612, 620-5, 627, 631
Temple of Préah Vihéar **91,** 623
date **77,** 548
desert areas **91,** 589, 622, 624
expropriation measures and **77,** 585-6, **78,** 681
adjacency. *See* maritime delimitation, adjacency, title and
ancient **91,** 429-38. *See also* historic *below*
basis, discovery and occupation **91,** 432
historic title compared **91,** 432, 434
occupation and **91,** 432, 434
basis
legal rule linking territorial sovereignty and maritime rights **83,** 116
Royal Decree **97,** 305
State succession **97,** 305
bays
'county waters' doctrine and **91,** 430-3, 437-8
discovery and occupation **91,** 430
exploitation **91,** 434-7
as cause of action **123,** 123, 291, 274-5, 356-9, 438-43, 476-9
claim
distinguished **99,** 481, 495-6

modification **91,** 648, 649-51
consolidation **46,** 484 n. 52, **50,** 105, 385
continental shelf. *See* continental shelf, title
Court's decision, declaratory **80,** 468
definition
delimitation, whether limited to **80,** 468
as evidence of existence **80,** 469, **123,** 319-21, 353-4
as source of right **80,** 469, **123,** 319-21, 353-4, 439
effective exercise, need for **97,** 594-5
erosion **97,** 594-5
establishment of, better prevails **80,** 284, 287
evidence of **97,** 474-80, 557-9. *See also* sovereignty, *effectivités*; statehood, requirements/evidence of
absence **97,** 432
administrative act **97,** 312-13
agreements, conclusion of **91,** 604-6
allegiance of tribesmen **91,** 588, 601, 636-48, 690-1
alliance and **91,** 637, 644, 648
variable concept **91,** 589
alliance **91,** 637, 644, 648
ambiguity **97,** 479
basis of title distinguished **97,** 304-5, 314-15
Frontier Dispute **97,** 304-5, 314-15
best evidence rule **50,** 109-10, **97,** 591
burden of proof **91,** 651, 686
census **97,** 488-9, 622
conduct of parties **91,** 611-25, 630-4, 684-6
independence, after **97,** 315, 316-17, 475-83, 495, 559
protest **91,** 612, 620-5, 627, 631, 648-9
construction of buildings **91,** 630-1
critical date, relevance **97,** 591-2
digging of wells **91,** 645-6, 650-1
documentary **97,** 304-5, 439-41, 474-5, 598-603, 605-7, 610-21
official **97,** 557-8
priority **97,** 378, 559
resettlement of indigenous people **97,** 603-5
title deeds to commons. *See titulos ejidales below*
value **91,** 590, 618
ecclesiastical jurisdiction **97,** 607-12, 618-20
permanent church, need for **97,** 478
sparsely populated territory **97,** 478
education **97,** 313, 439-41, 490, 622
effective control **91,** 588, 600-11, 644-6, 649-52, **97,** 305, 312-17. *See also* jurisdiction, acts of *below*
greater degree of control as test **91,** 685-6
time, length **91,** 624-5, 685
elections **97,** 622
Frontier Dispute **97,** 557
health services **97,** 489-90
historic title **91,** 603
insufficiency **97,** 495
judicial appointments **97,** 488, 622
jurisdiction, acts of and. *See* jurisdiction, acts of and *below*

title (*cont.*)
land grants to individuals **97,** 310, 314
land registry **97,** 489, 622
maps **80,** 486, 562, **91,** 629-30, 632-4, 648, **97,** 327-30
contemporary scaled plan **97,** 333
federal authorities' competence **91,** 634
reliability **91,** 629-30, **97,** 540
marginal areas **97,** 475
military appointments **97,** 488, 622
military control **97,** 313
movable property, transfer **97,** 314
national, presence **97,** 312, 334-5, 559
native settlements, boundaries between **97,** 309-11, 334
negotiations, agreed position **97,** 321-2
occupancy **115,** 498
occupation **91,** 589
oral histories **115,** 453, **125,** 360-2
ownership of property **91,** 589, 606-7
parties' conduct **97,** 337-8
police authority **97,** 313
post-independence grant of title **97,** 311
postal services **97,** 489, 622
public utilities **52,** 220-6, **97,** 312, 313-14, 489, 622
registration of births and deaths **97,** 314, 338-9, 489, 622
sovereign activity **52,** 220–6, **97,** 479
survey reports **97,** 322, 325-34, 567-70, 572-3
map **97,** 327-30
overlapping jurisdictions, avoidance **97,** 330, 331
survival of native title **112,** 610-13
taxation **97,** 488, 622
titulos ejidales **97,** 305, 308-11, 560-5
as act of sovereignty **97,** 539, 540-3
effect on **97,** 564
evidentiary value **97,** 564-5
importance **97,** 484, 538-40
property rights, limited to **97,** 564
uti possidetis principle **97,** 303, 304
validity **91,** 602-3, 614, 618, 650
good faith acquisition **94,** 164-8
historic **50,** 447-52, 469, **97,** 583-90. *See also* ancient *above*; historic rights; historic waters
continuity and lapse of time, need for **114,** 35-6
critical date **97,** 589
evidence of, effective display of authority **50,** 448, 512
historic bays **42,** 88, 95-7, **57,** 64-5, **59,** 264-73, **69,** 63, 66, 72-3, **114,** 35
international law title, whether **97,** 587, 588-9
maritime areas **41,** 124, **42,** 101-2
maritime delimitation and **41,** 101, **59,** 231-3, 264-73, **67,** 55-6, 64-70, 115-17, 122-5, 129, 203-4
nomadic lands **114,** 39-40
original colonial title, whether **97,** 585-8
possession, relevance **114,** 35-6

Red Sea Islands. *See* Red Sea Islands, historic title
territorial sea **59,** 231-3, 264-73
uninhabited island outside historic waters **114,** 40
illegal, tainted, whether **95,** 153
jurisdiction, acts of and. *See also* evidence of *above*
cattle grazing and grazing taxes **50,** 352-75, 380, 387, 456, 460, 462, 468, 503-4, 507-11
civil **97,** 312, 489, 622
continuous **91,** 624
'reasonable time' **91,** 624-5
continuous, peaceful exercise of **50,** 331, 380, 381, 383, 385, 448, 459, 511, 518
criminal **97,** 313, 338, 489, 622
critical date **50,** 331, 454
customs collection **50,** 349-52, 455, 460, 461, 504-5
economic development **91,** 619-21
local or provincial authority, of **50,** 383, 451
mediation **91,** 645
military control **50,** 341, **91,** 608-11, 626-7, 629, 643
peaceful **91,** 624
police authority **50,** 344-7, 455, 458, 462, 505-7, **91,** 607, 613-19, 627-8, 631-2
private individuals, acts of **50,** 339, 386, 449-50, 458, 459, 460, 468, **91,** 606
protest, absence of **91,** 612, 620-5, 627, 631, 648-9
public **91,** 624
religious tax (zakat) **91,** 588, 690-1
salt, acts concerning use of **50,** 339-41, 454, 457, 460, 462, 502
sparsely populated areas **91,** 624
survey operations **50,** 342-4, 452, 462
taxation **50,** 461
territorial title and **50,** 329-87, 446-63, 501-19
trial of criminal cases **50,** 347-9, 455-6, 506
Latin America, Spanish crown **97,** 481, 561
maritime delimitation and **41,** 51, 52, **80,** 468-9, **97,** 335
delimitation distinguished **81,** 257, 260, 262, 267-8, 275, 278-9, 328, 329, **83,** 94, 103, **99,** 468-9, 528-9, 657-60, 672, 675, **123,** 357-8
maritime inspection belt **97,** 673
native title. *See* Australia, native title; Canada, aboriginal title; Papua New Guinea, land titles; United States of America (USA), native title
natural prolongation and **99,** 532
natural resources **62,** 185
negotiations, position taken during as **97,** 542
occupation, based on **49,** 33, 112-13
oil **62,** 151, 161, 164, 181, 185, 195, 197, 199
in Papua New Guinea **71,** 40-7, 51-6
possession, title prevails over **80,** 319, 470
proportionality, relevance **83,** 114
protest in absence of, relevance **114,** 47
Red Sea Islands. *See* Red Sea Islands, title
reversion doctrine **114,** 40, 115-17
continuity, need for **114,** 115
intervening alternative sovereignty **114,** 115
successor in, continuity of nationality, need for **77,** 429-32

title (*cont.*)
territory, seizure by force and **95,** 152
unsettled territory **91,** 635-6
uti possidetis juris, freezing of title **80,** 473
validity, intertemporal law **114,** 46, 115
waiver **97,** 325
Togo
accession to independence **65,** 439-40
continuity of law, Togo **65,** 440
courts, municipal, jurisdiction **73,** 364
international law **65,** 440
law of
Decree of 22 February 1958 (Togo: competence) **65,** 440
Employment Code **73,** 364
Law of 5 March 1958 (Togo: courts) **65,** 440
State immunity, jurisdiction, applicability, State succession and, pending actions **65,** 439-41
State succession, State immunity, jurisdiction **65,** 439-41
Togo and Cameroons. *See* Mandates, Togo and Cameroons
Tokyo Tribunal. *See* International Military Tribunal for the Far East (Tokyo Tribunal)
Tonga, Privy Council, validity of decision **90,** 566
Torres Strait 68, 194, **86,** 186, 189-90, 202, 204
tort
actio personalis moritur cum persona **118,** 525
applicable law. *See* applicable law, tort
armed conflict and **121,** 254-7
conversion **116,** 541-6
damages for **116,** 559-62, **125,** 693-706
definition **125,** 687-90, 714
nationalization measures, whether **62,** 196-7, 217
State immunity, jurisdiction. *See* State immunity, jurisdiction, classification of act, tort
torture 59, 443, **61,** 191-3, 209-10, 214, **62,** 240-2, 244, 256-7, 261, 264, **68,** 31-9, **69,** 192, **70,** 52, 214, 221-34, 250, 256, 257-66, 288-91, 295-303, 311, 315, 356-7, **77,** 171-92, **78,** 51, **79,** 169-79. *See also* crimes against humanity, classification as; deportation, to country where risk of subjection to torture; European Convention on Human Rights (1950); inhuman or degrading treatment; International Covenant on Civil and Political Rights (ICCPR) (1966); Torture Convention (1984); Torture, Inter-American Convention to Prevent and Punish (1985)
act of State **119,** 96
administrative practice **58,** 263-4, 268-9, **71,** 300-3
aiding and abetting **121,** 273-91. *See also* war crimes, aiding and abetting
co-perpetration **121,** 294, 295, 319-21
knowing presence **121,** 322-3
limited applicability **121,** 291
moral support **121,** 295
perpetration distinguished **121,** 289-91, 320
amnesty, UNHRC General Comment No 20 **121,** 261 n. 172
armed conflict and **121,** 254-7
humiliation as objective **121,** 264-5
necessary elements. *See also* humiliation as objective *above*
intentional act or omission **121,** 264
nexus with armed conflict **119,** 148-9, **121,** 264, 328

official involvement **121,** 264
relevant objective **121,** 264, 294
severe pain or suffering whether physical or mental **121,** 264, 318-19
classification as
corporal punishment **58,** 352
delay in carrying out death sentence **98,** 347-56
disappearances **118,** 291, **119,** 285-6, 328
presumption of **118,** 156
extraction of confession **58,** 267, 298
inhuman or degrading treatment **104,** 189, **121,** 264 n. 179, **123,** 536
interrogation techniques **58,** 239-54, 265-7, 317-20, 326-9, 333-4, **71,** 295-303, 311
police acts **70,** 227-34
sexual assault **109,** 439
common law **119,** 189
conspiracy **119,** 148, 183-4, 188-9, 190-2
as crime **121,** 140
as crime against humanity **108,** 29-30, 37, **119,** 229, **121,** 255-6
as cruel and unusual punishment **124,** 360-1
customary international law **103,** 472-5, **104,** 153, 177, **119,** 106-7, **121,** 318
aiding and abetting **121,** 273-89, 322-3
Nicaragua **121,** 256
UN Declaration on the Protection of All Persons from Being Subjected to Torture **104,** 153
war crimes distinguished **100,** 471
damages, measure **70,** 233-4
definition **109,** 438-9
Canadian criminal law **124,** 358
critical date **119,** 328
customary international law **121,** 263-4
Declaration on the Protection of all Persons from being subjected to Torture and Other Cruel, Inhuman or Degrading Treatment or Punishment **121,** 263 n. 177
European Convention on Human Rights (1950) **58,** 266, 297, 298-9, 304-5, 314-17, 326-8, 333-4, 335-6, 352, 360-1, **70,** 233-4, **121,** 264, **123,** 41
intentional infliction of severe pain or suffering **119,** 328
Inter-American Convention to Prevent and Punish Torture (1985) **121,** 263-4
International Criminal Court (ICC), Rome Statute (1998), torture **123,** 49
psychological pressure **104,** 100
Restatement of Foreign Relations Law (Third) **103,** 470-1
suffering, level of, relevance **58,** 267, 352, **121,** 264 nn. 179 and 180
torture in armed conflict. *See* armed conflict and *above*
Torture Convention (1984). *See* Torture Convention (1984), definition
UK criminal law **103,** 426, **119,** 2-3, 70-1, 93, 183-4, **121,** 93
UN Special Rapporteur **121,** 264
rape **121,** 265
UNHRC General Comment No 20
level of suffering, relevance **121,** 264 n. 180
rape **121,** 265
US law **104,** 156-7, 176 n. 12, 178 n. 15
as element of genocide **119,** 343
erga omnes obligation **121,** 260
evidence of **116,** 311-14
extraditable offence **119,** 76, 93, 150-1, 190, 249

torture (*cont.*)
as function of Head of State **103,** 591-2, **119,** 4, 45, 47-8, 61-70, 97-100, 104, 151-7, 169-70, 204-18
as instrument of State policy **119,** 224
Head of State, former, immunity, jurisdiction **119,** 45, 47-8, 61-70, 97-100, 151-7, 219-21, 244-5, 250
implementing mechanisms
European Committee against Torture **121,** 257 n. 164, 265
UN Special Rapporteur **121,** 257 n. 164
implementing mechanisms. *See also* United Nations Committee against Torture
as international crime **119,** 149-50, 199-201
scale, relevance **119,** 217, 250
Torture Convention (1984), relevance **119,** 229-30
universal jurisdiction, relevance **119,** 156
as international wrong if committed by State official **77,** 174, 217, 220, 224
jurisdiction
creation of offence in implementation of Torture Convention (1984) distinguished **125,** 573-4
extraterritorial **100,** 471, **107,** 546, **119,** 70-1, 76, 85, 190
incorporation of customary international law/treaty, need for **120,** 304-5
obligation to exercise **121,** 258-62
passive personality principle **119,** 85, 363
universal **100,** 471, **107,** 546, **119,** 2, 70-1, 76, 85, 149-50, 155-6, 229-31, **121,** 258, 262
jus cogens/peremptory norm **103,** 421-2, 427-31, 472-5, **104,** 184-5, **107,** 541-4, **119,** 85, 86, 149, 200, 206-7, 214, 244, 310-11, **120,** 385-6, **121,** 257-8, 260-2, **123,** 33-4, 41-3, 49-53, **124,** 363-6
obligation to provide civil remedy against foreign State for acts committed outside the forum State **124,** 441-3
nationality of victim, relevance **77,** 178
as political offence **121,** 262
prize law and **81,** 591
rape. *See* rape in time of war
responsibility
aiding and abetting **121,** 273-91. *See also* aiding and abetting *above*
individual **104,** 157, **121,** 256-7, 261-2, 294
for act committed in foreign State **121,** 261-2
criminal liability **121,** 262
military commander **104,** 172
State. *See* State responsibility *below*
State immunity, jurisdiction **100,** 470-1, **103,** 421-32, 469-75, 555-7, **104,** 123-5, **107,** 541-4, **119,** 45, 47-8, 85-7, 205-8, **123,** 29-30
Torture Convention and. *See* Torture Convention (1984), State immunity, jurisdiction *ratione materiae* and
State immunity, jurisdiction, theory/doctrine, customary international law **124,** 443
State practice **77,** 178-9
State responsibility **104,** 143-6, 157, **121,** 257
statutory limitation **104,** 192, **121,** 262
treaties and other instruments prohibiting. *See also* implementing mechanisms *above*; Torture Convention (1984)
American Declaration of the Rights and Duties of Man **77,** 173
Control Council Law No 10 **121,** 254-5

Geneva Conventions (1949) **121,** 254-5, 256
Second Additional Protocol (1977) **121,** 254-5, 256
Hague Regulations (1907) **121,** 255
International Covenant on Civil and Political Rights (ICCPR) (1966). *See* International Covenant on Civil and Political Rights (ICCPR) (1966), torture
Lieber Code (US Military Manual, 1863) **121,** 155
obligation to implement **121,** 259-60, 261
UN Declaration on the Protection of All Persons from Being Subjected to Torture **58,** 298-9, **77,** 173, 187, 224, 235, **123,** 33
Universal Declaration of Human Rights (1948) **58,** 298, **77,** 173, 273, **123,** 32, 41, 42
as violation of international law **103,** 426-7, **104,** 144, 153, 156-7
as violation of right to life, security and liberty **124,** 352
of wounded non-combatant civilian, international tort/wrong **99,** 78-9

Torture Convention (1984)
customary international law and **119,** 198, **121,** 263-4, 318, **123,** 41, 42
definition **103,** 425-6, **104,** 176 n. 12, **107,** 546, **119,** 70, 183, 196-7, **121,** 262-5, **123,** 33, **124,** 358
action 'by a public official or other person acting in an official capacity' **119,** 2-3, 70-2, 92-3, 100, 150, 152, 156, 163, 188, 244-5, **124,** 438-9
Head of State and **119,** 70-1, 92-3, 100, 151, 152, 156, 164, 196-8, 213-14, 220-1, 244-5
'for the purposes of this Convention' **121,** 263
Draft Convention (E/CN.4/L 1576) **77,** 224
extraterritorial jurisdiction. *See* universal jurisdiction *below*
Head of State, former, immunity, jurisdiction
Convention as exclusion **119,** 219-21, 245, **123,** 34-5
Convention as waiver **119,** 216-17, 221, 231-2, 245, **125,** 504
Head of State, former, immunity, jurisdiction *ratione materiae* and **119,** 200-1, 215-16, 220, 231, 245
Head of State, immunity, jurisdiction *ratione materiae* and **119,** 200-1, 215-16, 220, 231, 245, **123,** 34-5
municipal law and
direct effect **119,** 363, 365, **125,** 575-7
implementing legislation
need for **125,** 577-9
retroactive, whether **119,** 230
non-refoulement to country of origin or any other country where risk of subjection to torture **108,** 268, **119,** 163-4, **121,** 258, **124,** 367-8. *See also* refugees, non-refoulement
deportation **124,** 366-7
substantial grounds for believing . . . danger of being subjected to torture/inhuman treatment **108,** 266-8, 281-3, 355, 362-3, 414-17, **124,** 358, 380, 389
critical date **108,** 411-12
evidence **108,** 267-8, 282, 373-5
fundamental right **108,** 355, 362-3, 410, 439
government's assurances **108,** 375, 378, 416, 436-7
pattern of gross, flagrant or mass violations of human rights **108,** 266-7, 282
personal risk, need for **108,** 267, 282, 355, 356, 362-3, **124,** 358
real foreseeable risk **108,** 267, 308-12, 321, 356, 436-7
'receiving' State not party to Convention, relevance **108,** 267-8, 283
obligations
assistance in connection with criminal proceedings **123,** 44

Torture Convention (1984) (*cont.*)
aut dedere aut punire/judicare **119,** 70-1, 85, 150, 151, 164
civil remedy for act outside forum **124,** 436-7, 438-41
as assertion of jurisdiction over acts of foreign State in own territory **124,** 439-41
reservations **124,** 440
creation of criminal offence **119,** 150, 164, 197-8, 215
effective measures to prevent torture **119,** 163, 215, **123,** 33, **124,** 439
establishment of extraterritorial jurisdiction. *See* universal jurisdiction *below*
non-refoulement to country of origin or any other country where risk of subjection to torture. *See* non-refoulement to country of origin where risk of subjection to torture *above*
private right of action **103,** 526-8
reservations **103,** 526-8
civil jurisdiction in respect of acts outside the forum State **124,** 440
State immunity, jurisdiction *ratione materiae* and **119,** 85, 163-75, 196-9, 201, 216-17, 219-21, 231-2, 245
civil proceedings **123,** 42, 44-52
exclusion **119,** 165-6, 170-5, 245
as waiver **119,** 166-9, 196-9, 201, 216-17, 231-2, 245
superior orders **119,** 150, 152
torture as extraditable offence **119,** 150-1
travaux préparatoires **119,** 170, 171-4
universal jurisdiction **100,** 471, **103,** 526-30, **107,** 449-51, 546, **119,** 70-1, 76, 100, 139-40, 150, 164, 230-1
limitations **123,** 44-5
dependence on waiver of immunity **119,** 156, 214-15
passive personality principle **119,** 85, 363, 364
tort committed outside territory, legislation **124,** 439-41
Torture, Inter-American Convention to Prevent and Punish (1985), definition **121,** 263-4
tourist office
agency of State, whether **65,** 62, 144, 427, 434-5
immunity, jurisdiction **65,** 62, 144
tourist organization, agency or instrumentality of a foreign State **63,** 321-2
town-planning 68, 108-10, 116-18
trade. *See* competition; economic relations; European Economic Community (EEC); FCN treaties; General Agreement on Tariffs and Trade (GATT) (1947); Germany, interzonal trade; international trade; NAFTA (North American Free Trade Agreement) (1992); trademarks; trading with the enemy; Uruguay Round; World Trade Organization (WTO)
trade name. *See* trademarks
trade representatives. *See* commercial/trade representation/mission
trade union 57, 278-9, 281. *See also* European Convention on Human Rights (1950), freedom of assembly/association; strike, right to
closed shop agreement. *See also* refusal to join trade union *below*
British Rail **62,** 365, 369-72
definition **62,** 365
dismissal for not joining **62,** 365-72
exemptions **62,** 367-8, 370, 373
religious grounds **62,** 360, 370, 373
existing employee **62,** 360-2, 366, 370, 373
lawfulness **62,** 360-89
'post-entry' shop **62,** 365

'pre-entry' shop **62,** 365, 367
collective agreements **58,** 32
consultation, right to **57,** 285-7, 297-8, 305
debts, liability for **80,** 46
discrimination and **58,** 13, 16-17, 35
employment contract and trade union activities distinguished **78,** 88
free movement of workers and **62,** 393, 396-9, 403, 406-7
freedoms **58,** 14-16
action **58,** 15, 33
assembly and association **57,** 279, 286-8, 297-8, **58,** 14-16, 33, **68,** 31, 37, 39, **70,** 250-8, **73,** 389-90, **77,** 631-5, **78,** 405-21
restrictions, public policy and **78,** 405, 408, 414, 418-19
GDR–FRG Basis of Relations Treaty (1972) and **78,** 172
International Labour Organization (ILO) and **62,** 386
membership **58,** 34. *See also* closed shop agreement *above*
freedom to join **57,** 280, 296-8
NATO Status of Forces Agreement (1951) and **77,** 634, 735
nature of **57,** 285, 297-8
occupational interests, protection of **58,** 15-16, 33-5
political boycott, prohibited **82,** 309
public authorities and **57,** 271-5
refusal to join trade union **62,** 360-2, 372-4
dismissal because of **62,** 360-2, 366-8, 373-4, 379
existing employee **62,** 360-2, 372-4
lawfulness **62,** 368
religious grounds **62,** 360, 370, 373
right to form, privileges and immunities of international organization and **102,** 151-62
rights **57,** 279, 296-8, **78,** 405-21
aliens **72,** 589-91
consultation **57,** 285-7, 297-8, 305
Evian Agreements (1962) **72,** 589-90
formation **57,** 296-8
nature of **57,** 285, 297-8
participation in **57,** 280, 296-8
alien **72,** 589-91
protection of **73,** 389-90
to strike **58,** 15-16, **74,** 137-8
South West Africa, 'Native' trade union **37,** 589
State as employer **58,** 14-15, 32-3
status **80,** 43, 154, **81,** 707
trademarks. *See also* Uruguay Round, Agreement on Trade-Related Aspects of Intellectual Property Rights (TRIPS)
appellation of origin distinguished **55,** 46
concurrent user **71,** 26
EC/Switzerland Free Trade Agreement (1973), quantitative restrictions and **93,** 598-9, 600-1
enemy company
rights in **54,** 532-3
war, effect **52,** 475-81, 483-5
expropriation/nationalization **42,** 41-4, **61,** 45, 59, 83-5, **66,** 78-84, 93-101, 142-5. *See also* wartime confiscation *below*
ownership following **71,** 17, 23-5, 28-30, **73,** 583-5, **78,** 677-82
infringement **73,** 582-9, 593

trademarks (*cont.*)
action for **73,** 583-4, 587-9, 593
where occurring **66,** 85-6
injunction relief **66,** 87-91
international registration, renewal **40,** 19
Madrid Agreement for the Registration of (1891)
registration **59,** 491, 493
war and **59,** 492
nationalization of company, effect **47,** 129-34
'origin' **93,** 596
ownership **73,** 582-9
expropriation/nationalization, following **71,** 17, 23-5, 28-30, **73,** 583-5, **78,** 677-82
transfer of domicile, effect **71,** 23-36, **73,** 584-5
protection
applicable law **40,** 22, 28
territorial principle **93,** 595-7
registration **59,** 491
effect **47,** 33, 37-8
situs **45,** 47-8, **47,** 129-30, 132, **66,** 97
trade name, protection of **47,** 38-9
transfer **40,** 24, 25
validity, formal and substantive **40,** 18-19, 23
wartime confiscation **73,** 582, 588. *See also* expropriation/nationalization *above*
trading with the enemy 41, 457-9, **54,** 579, 581, 602-3. *See also* Australia, law of, Trading with the Enemy Acts 1939/57; Southern Rhodesia, law applicable after Declaration of Independence, Trading with the Enemy Act 1939; United States of America, Trading with the Enemy Acts
benefit to the enemy **52,** 477, 483-5
contract with enemy company **48,** 475-8
control of enemy property **74,** 153-5
Trans-Jordan, Mandate. *See* Mandate, Trans-Jordan
transit
custom **82,** 371-5
customary international law **82,** 369-71
extradited person **100,** 413-14
foreign armed forces **106,** 240
immunity, jurisdiction **82,** 362-8
security and **82,** 364-8
jurisdiction **82,** 359-75
airports and **72,** 673-6, **73,** 661, 663, 702-4, **77,** 484
land passage, facilitation **82,** 682-3
right of **82,** 368-75
privilege **82,** 369
ship in waters under jurisdiction of third State **82,** 682, 696-9
Transkei
costs **82,** 387
criminal procedure **69,** 131-2
law of
Constitution Act 15 of 1976 **82,** 377, 378
Decree 1/1988 **82,** 377, 378, 379-83
Decree 2/1988 **82,** 382
recognition **82,** 376 n. 1

regime, legal validity **82,** 386-7
retroactive **82,** 387
revolution **82,** 382-7
regime, status **82,** 383-7
separate legal entity test **82,** 378-82
transnational corporation. *See* multinational corporation
transport organization, agency or instrumentality of a foreign State **63,** 90, 104, 175
transsexualism 89, 97-112, 118-53
human rights and **61,** 369, 382-3
marriage **89,** 101-2, 109, 121, 127-8, 141-6, 153
private life, respect for and **89,** 103-9, 110-12
registration of births and **89,** 106, 120-1, 125-6, 129, 152-3
certificate of current civil status and **89,** 107-8, 110-12
Transvaal, annexation **39,** 101
travaux préparatoires. *See also* legislation, interpretation, aids, legislative history; treaties, drafting
absence **106,** 445
GATT *Working Party Report on the Free-Trade Agreement between Canada and the United States* **110,** 582-3
American Convention on Human Rights (1969) **67,** 566-7, 598-9, 606-7, **79,** 348-9, 351, 367-8, 369
Art. 2 **79,** 350-2, 367-8, 369-70
Art. 4 **70,** 468-9
Art. 14(1) **79,** 348-9
Art. 64 **67,** 598-9, 606-7
arbitral award **38,** 89-90
Brussels Convention on Immunity of State-owned Ships (1926) **64,** 182
Brussels Convention on the Limitation of Liability of Owners of Sea-going Ships (1957) **70,** 446-7
Canada–France Agreement on Fishing in the Gulf of St Lawrence (1972) **82,** 612, 623-4, 644-5
circumstances of conclusion **102,** 35-6, 87
rejection of a party's position, significance **110,** 585
classification as
delegate's remarks on the record **95,** 603-4
diplomatic texts **77,** 657
draft text **100,** 68-9, **102,** 62-3, **110,** 591
ex post facto UN study of language used in convention **77,** 15
explanation of votes **41,** 227
minutes of negotiations **59,** 545-6, **74,** 634-6, **82,** 644-5, **100,** 95, **105,** 56
negotiating proposal **82,** 634, **110,** 590-1, **113,** 84
oral statements during negotiations **56,** 218, 219, **77,** 657
in official capacity **59,** 544
parliamentary proceedings **77,** 657, **84,** 403-6, **123,** 430, **125,** 145-6
acceptance of compulsory jurisdiction of ICJ and **123,** 224-5
procés-verbal of negotiations **77,** 657
statements in Security Council **105,** 446, 493, 501-2, **112,** 209, **124,** 181-4
treaties concluded by other parties **45,** 395, 407
subsequent accession to **59,** 545, 563-4
compromissory clauses **55,** 104-10, 190-4, **76,** 347, 645
Convention for the Suppression of Terrorist Bombing (1997) **124,** 155
Convention on the Transfer of Sentenced Persons (1983) **84,** 727

travaux préparatoires (*cont.*)
European Convention on Human Rights (1950) **45,** 119, 131, 151, 152, 153-4, 155, 161, 228, **75,** 425, 434, 484, 524-5, 529, **81,** 72, **88,** 556, 565, **89,** 174
Art. 1 **123,** 100-2, 110-11
Art. 6(1) **86,** 372-4, 410-12
Art. 8 **45,** 131, 163, **58,** 141
Art. 11 **62,** 377-8
Art. 12 **89,** 174
Protocol (First)
Art. 1 **58,** 180, 621, **75,** 425, 434, 484, 524-5, 529
Art. 2 **45,** 131, 150-2, 161, 163, 228, **67,** 495-7, 500-2
Art. 3 **123,** 22
Protocol (Fourth) **88,** 556-7
Protocol (Seventh) **88,** 556-7
evidence of
affidavit **68,** 592-3, 621-4
declaration by negotiator **68,** 637
excluded provisions, status **120,** 245-6, 325
France–Libya Treaty of Friendship and Good Neighbourliness (1955) **100,** 26-7
France–Portugal Convention for the Delimitation of Possessions in West Africa (1886) **77,** 657, 658
France–USA Air Transport Services Agreement (1946) **38,** 235-43
General Act (1928), reservations, Rapporteur's letter to Greek Foreign Minister recommending **59,** 585-6
Geneva Convention IV (1949) **124,** 131
Geneva Convention on the Status of Refugees (1951) **79,** 676-7, 681-3, **90,** 174-5, **95,** 587, **104,** 237, **124,** 481-2, 494-5, 502, 505
Geneva Conventions (1958)
Continental Shelf (1958) **67,** 38, **99,** 489-90
Art. 1 **67,** 104-5
Art. 6 **41,** 134, 147-8, 190, 226-7, **67,** 115-16, **81,** 379
Territorial Sea and Contiguous Zone (1958) **43,** 124-5
Greece–United States Friendship, Commerce and Navigation Treaty (1951) **101,** 618
Guinea-Bissau–Senegal Arbitration Agreement (1985) **92,** 48, 156-7
Hague Convention on the Conflict of Nationality Laws (1930) **72,** 438, **75,** 189
ICJ Statute
Art. 36 **105,** 317-19
Art. 36(5) **72,** 282-6, **76,** 134, 174, 189-92, 247, 296
Art. 62 **62,** 624, **70,** 551, 570, 600-2, 663, 668
Art. 63 **70,** 629-31, **76,** 93
ICSID Convention (1965) **89,** 524
Art. 26 **82,** 81, **106,** 522
ICTY Statute **124,** 183-4
International Covenant on Civil and Political Rights (ICCPR) (1966) **114,** 374
interpretation, aid to
absence of relevant material **62,** 424, **90,** 174-5
admissibility **64,** 182
ambiguity, relevance **37,** 190-2, 598-9, **55,** 189-90, **56,** 104, **74,** 425, **93,** 600, **95,** 162, **96,** 142, **100,** 72, **101,** 603-7, **102,** 97-9, **110,** 576, 591-2, **120,** 240, **123,** 109, **124,** 184
common understanding of parties, need for **40,** 256, **59,** 545, **68,** 592-3

as confirmation **38,** 235-43, **59,** 543, **62,** 476, **100,** 26-7, **101,** 324-5, 331, **102,** 62, 97, **110,** 576, **123,** 111
knowledge of material facts during drafting **47,** 455
limitations on **37,** 497, 499, **74,** 636, 644-5, 647, 656, 662, 667-8, 675, **82,** 634, **84,** 240, **102,** 62-3, 77-80, 99, **114,** 286
opposability to States not party to original negotiations **59,** 545, 563-4
as supplementary means **124,** 440
value **123,** 100
contradictory nature of **100,** 72, **102,** 72-3, 77, 80
Vienna Convention on the Law of Treaties (1969) **74,** 655, 660-2, 668, 673, **77,** 658, **124,** 183-4, 440
customary international law **124,** 183-4
Iran–US Claims Settlement Declaration (1981) **68,** 531, 535-6, 592-3, 621-4, 637-9, **70,** 521, **75,** 208-9
Iran–US General Declaration, (1981) **68,** 554-6, **70,** 521, **75,** 208-9
Iran–US Treaty of Amity (1955) **63,** 434, **83,** 557 n. 14, **84,** 533-4
Italy–USA Treaty of Friendship, Commerce and Navigation (1948) **84,** 403-6
Law of the Sea Convention (1982) **110,** 770, 786, **119,** 563-5
aid to interpretation **119,** 563-5, **120,** 240
excluded provisions, status **120,** 245-6, 325
League of Nations Covenant **37,** 308
London Agreement on German External Debts (1953) **59,** 543-8, 558
Mandate **37,** 167, 169-74, 200, 308
Mexico–USA Extradition Treaty (1978) **95,** 364, 371 n. 15
NATO Status of Forces Agreement (1951) **77,** 570
New York Convention on the Recognition and Enforcement of Foreign Arbitral Awards (1958) **71,** 588-9, **86,** 494
Norddeutscher Rundfunk State Treaty (1955) **90,** 374-7
Nuremberg Charter **91,** 60
Pact of Bogotá (1948) **84,** 240-1, 244, 267
PCIJ Statute **85,** 340, **105,** 317-19
Art. 59 **62,** 638-9, **70,** 631-3
Art. 62 **62,** 632, 634-6, **70,** 571, 600-2
Art. 63 **62,** 638-9, **70,** 633
Rhine Navigation Convention (1879) **72,** 683
Straddling Stocks and Highly Migratory Fish Stocks Agreement (1995) **123,** 311-14, 327
Torture Convention (1984) **119,** 170, 171-4
Treaty of Peace (Italy) (1947) **40,** 256, 277
UN Administrative Tribunal (UNAT) Statute **83,** 398-9, 401-3, 425-6, 438
Art. 2 **69,** 555
Art. 11 **69,** 465-6, 468, 474-87
UN Charter **76,** 624
Art. 80 **37,** 211, 232
UNCITRAL Rules **68,** 533, **69,** 629 n. 3
UNESCO Protection of the World Cultural and Natural Heritage Convention (1972) **68,** 303-6, 392, 420-1
UNGA resolutions **83,** 294-5, 474
Vienna Convention on Consular Relations (1963) **86,** 556
Vienna Convention on Diplomatic Relations (1961) **71,** 550, 558, 559, **99,** 106-9
Art. 31(1)(c) **107,** 455
Vienna Convention on the Law of Treaties (1969) **71,** 550, **83,** 132-3

travaux préparatoires (*cont.*)
Art. 75 **67,** 566-7
contested provisions **102,** 69
restrictive use **82,** 634
Third Report on the Law of Treaties **102,** 69-72
Warsaw Convention (1929) **96,** 119-21
Hague Protocol (1955) **74,** 634-6, 642-5, 647, 650, 654-6, 660-2, 666-8, 674-5, 682, **77,** 407-9
WHO–Egypt Headquarters Agreement (1951) **62,** 475-6, 488-9, 569
Yugoslavia, International Criminal Tribunal for the Former (ICTY), Statute, interpretation **105,** 446, 493, 501-2, **112,** 209, **124,** 181-4
travel document. *See* passport
treason 82, 390-4
allegiance and **54,** 268-73, 281-91, **82,** 392-3
de facto sovereign, to **39,** 309, 359, 388
internal and external sovereignty distinguished **82,** 393
Bacon on **39,** 314
definition **54,** 266, 281-3
English Statutes of 1351/1495 **39,** 71, 242-53, 293, 303, 304, 307, 334, 353, 359, 388, **74,** 28
foreign State, acts against **71,** 243-7, 443-5
Foster on **39,** 312-13, 323, 334
Hale on **39,** 246-8, 307-9, 323
Hawkins on **39,** 245, 246, 248, 311-12, 323, 334
as political offence **79,** 150, 505
requirements
Roman-Dutch law **82,** 393
treasure trove 61, 671-3
treaties 39, 408-9, **40,** 228-95, **41,** 421-37, **42,** 249-72, **43,**246-59, **44,** 192-358, **48,** 209-28, **61,** 200-2, 205, 211-12, 215, 237-8, 623-4. *See also* European Community treaties; Headquarters Agreements; international organizations, constituent instrument; treaty interpretation; *and under individual countries, individual treaties and the Consolidated Table of Treaties*
abrogation. *See* termination *below*
accession to **37,** 66, **39,** 455, **55,** 74-5
exchange of notes **70,** 4, 7-8, 12-13
notification of succession **115,** 194-201
acquired rights, effect on **101,** 561
act of State **70,** 41-2, **106,** 208-11
duty of State to legislate **70,** 432
action based on, State responsibility for **44,** 33-4
action invoking and action outside distinguished **48,** 333, 350, 389
ad referendum, as evidence **97,** 337-8
adjudication clauses, necessity for **37,** 146
administrative act **93,** 300
adoption **85,** 12
amendment **40,** 47-8, **46,** 159, **50,** 423, **57,** 341, **59,** 524-5. *See also* revision *below*
by multilateral convention **99,** 170
change of name **96,** 88-9
change of obligations, need for **96,** 89
executive act **85,** 211
interpretation as **106,** 338-9
legislative role **90,** 373

in absence of treaty of amendment **106,** 338, 345, 347
NATO Council decisions **106,** 344-5
parties' agreement **101,** 614
preamble as trigger **106,** 338
subsequent practice **45,** 319, **79,** 437, **96,** 337, **101,** 49-51, 66, 597-601, **106,** 338, 339, 345
acquiescence **101,** 600
subsequent treaty **57,** 481
treaty, need for **106,** 339
American Law Institute Draft **37,** 67
annexes
as part of 'context' **121,** 106
ratification and **72,** 676
status **72,** 675-6
annulment. *See* termination, annulment *below*
applicability **86,** 506, **88,** 682. *See also* municipal law and *and* operation and enforcement *below*
after termination **59,** 525
Carriage of Goods by Road (CMR) Convention (1956) **86,** 556
courts, by **86,** 51, 52
critical date, date of challenge to decision under **106,** 248-9
denial of justice **84,** 398
dependent territory **86,** 155-6
good neighbourly relations **83,** 45
international law and **59,** 493
loss arising from **59,** 493, **74,** 278-9
non-metropolitan territory **91,** 271
non-party. *See* third parties and *below*
ratification/entry into force, relevance **36,** 391, **47,** 92, **125,** 490, 502-3
security **83,** 45
temporary incompetence of party **59,** 492
territorial application **106,** 249
Trust Territory **97,** 47
applicable law
implementing legislation, treaty interpretation rules **101,** 210-11, 242
international law **77,** 54, 55, **78,** 166, **122,** 612-14, **123,** 315-16
obligations
State responsibility rules **82,** 547-51, **116,** 47, 48
treaty **82,** 547-51, **116,** 85
operation and enforcement, municipal law **118,** 33
reservations, Vienna Convention on the Law of Treaties (1969) **107,** 69, 74
as specified by treaty **46,** 512
validity, municipal law of State party **44,** 260, 269, 282-8, **83,** 32
arbitral tribunals, establishment by **75,** 154-5, 169, **77,** 642-7
arbitration agreements. *See* arbitration agreement
associated documents. *See* corpus, elements of *below*
authoritative text, as contained in legislation **120,** 518, 523, 543
balance of interests **62,** 423, 427
Berlin
clause **78,** 157
extension to **78,** 157, 172
binding force
exchange of notes **74,** 118-20

treaties (*cont.*)
understanding between States regarding application **72,** 216-17
bona fides **68,** 204-6, 212, 220, 231-2, 252, 416
boundaries and **50,** 406, **78,** 169
legislative sanction, need for **70,** 43, 46-50
boundary agreements. *See* boundary treaties; treaties, State succession, boundary treaties; treaties, State succession, treaties of a territorial character; *uti possidetis*
breach **76,** 470-6, 584-7, 720-2, 874, **90,** 652, 657-8
admission **118,** 10, 12, 15
anticipatory **94,** 566-7
applicable law
determination of obligation **82,** 548, **116,** 47-8
remedies **82,** 548
bar to jurisdiction, whether **90,** 676
basis of rights, whether **47,** 439
before entry into force **70,** 295-6, **123,** 141, 141 n. 1
compensation for **56,** 201-2
consequences **48,** 217, 221-2, 333, 413-16, 433-4
continuous **82,** 544, 559, 563, 565, 566, 567, **116,** 139-41, 215-19
damages for **61,** 532-3, 567-8, **84,** 325, 326, **91,** 476, **93,** 329
absence of injury **84,** 329
declaration of **84,** 326
determination of **82,** 27-9
administrative authorities **82,** 28
economic pressure **76,** 472, 474
effect on rights of party in breach **116,** 63, 207-8
essential security interests **76,** 875
failure to agree on means of implementation **116,** 74-5
forcible abduction/unlawful arrest as **90,** 671
inconsistent legislation as **82,** 235, 236-44, 245-52, 254, 257, 258-9, 262-7, 269-71, 275-9, **116,** 332-7
as internationally wrongful act **116,** 63
interpretation and **82,** 269
intersecting violations. *See* reciprocal *below*
jurisdiction clause, effect on **82,** 269
justification **48,** 224-5, **61,** 563-7, **82,** 543-5
breach by other party **116,** 179-83, 220-2
impossibility of performance **116,** 72-3
municipal law **36,** 389, **41,** 341, **77,** 631, **82,** 233-50, 252-3, 544-5, **93,** 499-500, **105,** 25, 29-30, **119,** 633-4, 653-4, **121,** 107, **124,** 415
necessity. *See* necessity, treaties and
provisions of treaty previously concluded **113,** 291
loss arising from, State responsibility for **89,** 8
manifest **82,** 269
material **82,** 551, 559, 564, 565, 579, **116,** 75
definition **82,** 564
Vienna Convention on the Law of Treaties (1969) **82,** 564, **116,** 70-1, 206, 230
municipal courts and **42,** 263, 440-1, **77,** 327
notice of, need for **82,** 29
obligations under another treaty as defence **121,** 109, 125
official act **95,** 375-7
prima facie **82,** 543

private act **95,** 375-7
protest
form **90,** 659
need for **90,** 659, 661, 693
State practice **90,** 693
timeliness **90,** 696
reciprocal **116,** 90, 143-4. *See also* termination, grounds, reciprocal breach *below*
proportionality **116,** 221-2
remedies for individuals against the State **71,** 316, 331-53, 365, 554, 558
reparation
seriousness of breach and **82,** 565
State responsibility for **82,** 551, **116,** 89-90
response determined by executive **79,** 438 n. 27
State responsibility. *See* State responsibility for breach of treaty
State's right to challenge in foreign court **65,** 409-11, 427-8
termination of treaty **49,** 5-6, 36-7, 203, 256, 328-9, **82,** 568, **87,** 163, **116,** 74-6, 221
types of **42,** 440-1
codification of existing law **55,** 584, **70,** 391, **71,** 119-21, 568, 571-2, 580-1, **76,** 486, 487, 864-5. *See also* customary international law, treaties and other international instruments reflecting
application to non-signatories **77,** 401, 657, 658, 659
where not yet in force **46,** 361, **77,** 659
colonial territories, extension to **83,** 75-6
compatibility with EC law. *See* European Community law, compatibility of treaties
compliance **79,** 358, 486, 616, 628, 637, 645-7, 649-50, 651, 662, 667, **82,** 673, 683. *See also* enforcement; implementation *and* obligations *below*; European Community treaties, compliance
arbitral tribunal's guidance on **102,** 496
duty to ensure respect by national **82,** 637
good faith **102,** 497
'moral protection' of Holy See **82,** 688
obligation **59,** 493, **62,** 190-3, 487, 507, 554, **103,** 175-9, **118,** 15
not to defeat purpose of treaty **100,** 70
compromis **87,** 348-9, 357
conclusion. *See* legislature, role; treaty-making power; *and* validity *below*
conflict **90,** 572
consensual nature **37,** 185
consideration doctrine **37,** 67
constitutional compatibility **89,** 53-4, 55, 69, 70, **108,** 646, **115,** 642
constitutional amendment, need for **93,** 343, **98,** 260, 261, 262-3, 269, 270. *See also* European Union Treaty (Maastricht) (1992), constitutional amendment, need for
constitutional review. *See* constitutional review, need for *below*
constitutionality of conflicting legislation distinguished **36,** 400, 421, **93,** 252-3, 292
encroachment on legal sphere of individual **94,** 54
human rights protection **104,** 95-6
power to determine **89,** 196
primacy **89,** 53-4, 55, 69, 70
constitutional requirements **44,** 264-8, 283-7, **47,** 25, 312-27, **48,** 1, **51,** 401-29, **52,** 419-21, **70,** 43, 46-50, **71,** 591-3, **72,** 655-7, **73,** 2-3, 39-41, 696, 700, **74,** 509, 524-9, 686-9, **75,** 99-106, **78,** 95-6, 97, 160, 170-5, **83,** 30-4, **87,** 348, **93,** 492, 497-8, 502, 506, **98,** 176, **102,** 18-19
knowledge of other party, need for **44,** 254, 263-4, **70,** 48-9, **78,** 174-5, 646-9

treaties (*cont.*)
ratification by another signatory, relevance **98,** 183-5
constitutional review, need for
before legislative approval **98,** 184
expert opinion on international issues, need for **98,** 183, 185
implementing legislation **98,** 260
constitutional status **38,** 176-80, **77,** 446, **98,** 248-9, 250-1
continuity **80,** 5
contract
analogies with **49,** 256
compared **68,** 423-4
effect on **45,** 386-8
conventional rules and declaratory provisions **41,** 31, 68
corpus, elements of **78,** 159-60, 190
scrutiny
covered by **78,** 159-60
third party documents and **78,** 190
status **78,** 160, 190
cumulative **111,** 518
customary international law. *See also* customary international law, treaties; customary international law, treaties and other international instruments reflecting
co-existence of identical rule **99,** 503
later custom to prevail **99,** 503
primacy **43,** 8
Vienna Convention on the Succession of States in respect of Treaties (1978) **115,** 185-92
date of conclusion, final consent of party **105,** 194-5
declarations accompanying ratification **110,** 200-3
objection, absence **110,** 200, 241, 540
declaratory and constitutive distinguished **83,** 153
resolution of international conference, relevance **83,** 153
as defence **44,** 368, 381, 385
definition **42,** 268-9, **76,** 96, **93,** 631, **101,** 564-9, **104,** 211-15, **122,** 673. *See also* form *below*
agreement with aboriginal peoples distinguished **104,** 210-15
Jay Treaty (1794) **104,** 210-15
agreement between subjects of international law intended to bring about international consequences **106,** 336-9, 342-3
approval as treaty, need for **96,** 424
contract **81,** 676, **95,** 371 n. 3, **96,** 87
between sovereigns **107,** 454, **122,** 673
designation, relevance **37,** 13-14, **99,** 210-11
understanding between entities subject to international law with binding effect **99,** 210-11
Vienna Convention on the Law of Treaties (1969) **96,** 424
Vienna Convention on the Law of Treaties between States and International Organizations or among International Organizations (1986) **96,** 424, **101,** 63
denunciation **62,** 536, 544-5, 560, 570, **71,** 311-16, 319-31, 338-53, 355-65, 377, 386, 389, 402, 410, 419, 430, 554, 558, **72,** 324, 359-60, 377, 404, 409, 429, 432, 669, **73,** 428, 457-8, 481, 496, 510, 531-2, 561, **74,** 47, 56, 307, 381-3, **75,** 58-9, 383, 575, 587, 595, **78,** 12, **79,** 438 n. 27, **82,** 327, **83,** 85-6, 537-8, **84,** 242, **90,** 370-1. *See also* revision *and* termination *below*
in absence of provision for **83,** 87

by agreement **47,** 240
counter-denunciation, right of **90,** 380, 382-4
balance of interests **90,** 379
provision for, relevance **90,** 379
time-limit **90,** 380, 382-4
customary international law **90,** 374-5
domestic remedies **74,** 307, 311-15
effect **90,** 373-4
on implementing legislation **78,** 12
law-making act, whether **90,** 374
on municipal law **78,** 12
termination as between all parties **90,** 371, 374-82
effective date **107,** 133
municipal law vacuum **90,** 373-4
necessity **71,** 558-9
relevant/special circumstances **62,** 270, **90,** 377-8
requirements
notice **62,** 476, 479, 498, 508, 520
prescribed form **96,** 308
undermining object and purpose as **76,** 583-4, 874-6
unfriendly acts **76,** 477
unilateral **62,** 488-90, 508, 511, 514, **70,** 439-40
withdrawal of denouncing party **90,** 381-2
dependent territory
application to **75,** 582-3, **86,** 152-6
extension to **45,** 429-30
power to conclude **86,** 155-6
depository
functions **42,** 262
League of Nations **37,** 13, 36, 47
parties to treaty, responsibility for determining **96,** 377, 379
powers **115,** 183-4
derogation. *See also* European Convention on Human Rights (1950), derogation; International Covenant on Civil and Political Rights, derogation by States party, possibility of
express provision, need for **70,** 551
possibility of **107,** 70-1
strict interpretation **70,** 551
desuetude. *See* termination, desuetude *below*
diplomatic relations, break, effect
existing treaties **96,** 303, 304-5
Vienna Convention on the Law of Treaties (1969)
absence of need for diplomatic relations, in **96,** 303, 304, 308
conclusion of new treaties **96,** 303
existing treaties **96,** 303
United States Diplomatic and Consular Staff in Teheran **96,** 305
direct effect **48,** 212-13, **60,** 252-3, 257, 268-9, 276-7, **69,** 142-3, **70,** 435-6, **71,** 257, 259, 386, **73,** 303-4, 343, 353, 383, 700, 704, **74,** 3, 45, 303, 312, 315, 325-6, 339-40, 357, 446, 703, **75,** 5-6, 8-9, 23-4, 566, **77,** 198, 199, 237-9, 376-84, 392-3, **79,** 368-71, 399-401, 486, **81,** 701-2, **83,** 227, 228, **93,** 597-8, 600-1. *See also* self-executing *below*; European Economic Community Treaty (Rome) (1957), direct effect
applicable law, terms of treaty **96,** 341
binding on all persons, need to be **96,** 372-3

treaties (*cont.*)
clear provision, need for **93,** 600-1, **96,** 341, 372, 391, **117,** 425-6, **119,** 363, 365
criteria
nature and content **96,** 341, 390-1
structural context for implementation **96,** 341-2
date of legislation intended to implement, relevance **96,** 363
EC/Switzerland Free Trade Agreement (1973) **93,** 600-1
GATT **107,** 286, **117,** 425
human rights law and **79,** 372
International Covenant on Economic, Social and Cultural Rights (1966) **96,** 340-2, 372-3, 390-1
nature and content **96,** 341, 390-1
obligation to take progressive steps and **96,** 391
parties' intention **96,** 372-3, **119,** 363
implementing legislation as evidence **96,** 391
'shall be agreed upon between [individuals]', significance **96,** 336
'shall come into effect on the expiration of the period' **96,** 336
structural context for implementation **96,** 341-2
terms of treaty, determined by **96,** 341
Torture Convention (1984) **119,** 363, 365
Treaty of Rome (1957) **60,** 252-3, 257-8, 268-9, 276-7, **62,** 394, 410-12
dispute settlement provision **85,** 310, 315
draft, international law, evidence of **94,** 375-6
drafting **84,** 274-9
proposals made during, binding, whether **44,** 475
duration **62,** 423, 427. *See also* treaties, State succession, duration of treaty, relevance
absence of provision **78,** 164
indefinite, intention to allow for future developments **82,** 628-9, 631
limited, boundary establishment, relevance **100,** 36, 96, 100
duress. *See* validity, duress *below*
East India Company, with Indian Rulers **50,** 54-6, 59-63, 218, 270, 398-401, 424, 425, 459, 464, 465, 470, 477
effect and fact distinguished **81,** 702, 716
emendation. *See* amendment *above*; revision *below*
enforceability **68,** 300-1
enforcement. *See* operation and enforcement *below*
entry into force **45,** 89, **56,** 543-4, **71,** 106, 121, **74,** 696, **92,** 640, **100,** 480
applicability and **77,** 401, 657, 658, 659, **78,** 97-8, 100, **94,** 407-8, **100,** 485-7
'a different intention' **100,** 486-7
customary international law **100,** 485-7
Vienna Convention on the Law of Treaties (1969) **100,** 486-7, **123,** 141 n. 1
constitutional procedures
before completion of **78,** 161
responsibility for consequences **78,** 161
date **106,** 249
agreed date **69,** 286, 288-9, 293-4
Vienna Convention on the Law of Treaties (1969) **107,** 143
executive certificate/statement, conclusiveness **44,** 216-17, 260, **55,** 48-9, **69,** 286-9, 293-4
municipal and international law distinguished **88,** 203
ratification, need for **39,** 458-60, **45,** 86-90, **57,** 341, **69,** 287-8, 293-4, **70,** 42-3
reservations and **67,** 564-71
signature, on **83,** 34

Vienna Convention on the Succession of States in respect of Treaties (1978) **115,** 186, 191
estoppel, private law expression **92,** 571
European Union (EU). *See* European Community treaties
as evidence **83,** 263
evidence of
abrogation
absence from list of 'treaties which retain importance in practice' **77,** 436
absence of protest **77,** 436
absence of request for EEC Council approval **77,** 437
adhesion to, ministerial certificate **78,** 119
application **75,** 110-12
embassy statement **96,** 108
executive intentions **96,** 107-8, 112
existence, ministerial statement **69,** 288
incorporation into law **96,** 108
listing in *Treaties in Force* **96,** 108
meaning
expert **74,** 641, 645-6, 652, 665, 673, 680
extraneous **68,** 305-6, 392-4, 420
reservation, acceptance **77,** 605-6
State conduct **83,** 81-3, **96,** 108
exchange of notes **74,** 118-20, 262-3, **82,** 602, **102,** 17, 34-5, 85, **105,** 54-6, **106,** 346
binding force **74,** 118-20
effect on **74,** 118-20
oral negotiations, equivalent to **47,** 444
treaty interpretation and **74,** 118-20
executive agreement **72,** 133-50, 275-7, 285-9, 655-8, **77,** 389-94
constitutional authority for **72,** 143-50, 285-9, 655-7
direct effect **77,** 392-3
enforcement by executive in municipal courts **72,** 136-40, 655-8
municipal law, effect in **77,** 392-4
nature **77,** 389-92
treaty status **101,** 563-9
Vienna Convention on Treaties and **77,** 390
executive, role **90,** 372-3
existence, responsibility for determining
court *proprio motu* **78,** 107
Minister of Justice **78,** 107
Expo 67 Rules and Regulations, whether **64,** 33-4
extension
Berlin **78,** 152, 172
by analogy **77,** 633-4
Hong Kong **106,** 422
extradition. *See* extradition agreement
federal State. *See* federal State, constituent States, treaties between; federal State, treaties
form. *See also* definition *above*
agreed minute **86,** 694, 697, **100,** 211, 212, **102,** 17-19, 23, 29, 35-6, 86-90, 120
implementing provisions unspecified **102,** 29
minutes of meeting distinguished **102,** 18
signature by head of delegation **108,** 601
'arrangement' **82,** 613

treaties (*cont.*)
communiqué **87,** 347
draft **102,** 34, 85
communiqué or *procés-verbal* **37,** 68-9
conventions **76,** 96-7
declaration **37,** 68, **76,** 100-1, 126, 132, 172-3, 257, **78,** 60
Declaration (*exemplaire*) **37,** 13, 93
Declaration to Council of League of Nations **37,** 68
exchange of letters. *See* exchange of notes *above*
exchange of notes. *See* exchange of notes *above*
executive agreement. *See* executive agreement *above*
formal declaration before conclusion of treaty **100,** 211, 212
head of government agreement **87,** 346
Ihlen Declaration **37,** 69, 78, 117
implementing regulation **101,** 585-7
implicit agreement, requirements **82,** 370-4
informal **62,** 507
Iran–US Claims Settlement Declaration **68,** 545, **75,** 154
letter **78,** 160
Mandate. *See* Mandate, treaty character
memorandum **78,** 160
memorandum of understanding **102,** 351-3
minutes of meeting **83,** 89
modus vivendi **78,** 164
neighbours, arrangement between **82,** 664-70
oral agreement **37,** 67, 69, 116-17, **106,** 336
parties' right to choose **62,** 507
press statement **60,** 598, 600, 602-3, 609-10, 615, **99,** 111
Protocol Note **78,** 171
recommendations of international assemblies distinguished **77,** 420-3
record of political understanding distinguished **102,** 19-20
relevance **82,** 285 n. 2, **83,** 66, 67, **101,** 44-53, 63-4, **102,** 17, **106,** 336
Resolutions of League of Nations Council **37,** 224, 235
simplified **71,** 592-3, **83,** 30, 51
Munich Agreement (1938) **83,** 66
terminology, relevance **37,** 13, 67-71, 94, 116
undertaking at conference **37,** 117
unilateral undertaking. *See* unilateral declaration/undertaking
Vienna Convention on the Law of Treaties (1969) **101,** 565
fraud **83,** 534
FRG–GDR treaties **78,** 152-76
inter-State, whether **94,** 54
special nature of **78,** 164, 166
frustration **37,** 74, 75, 77, 145
full powers, relevance **44,** 204-5, 214-16, 248-50, 261, **108,** 601
fundamental change of circumstances **55,** 198-202, 210-13, **56,** 84, 111-12, 113, 134, **60,** 591-3, 627, **62,** 193, 207, **75,** 665-8, **76,** 331-2, **82,** 549, 670, **83,** 533, **84,** 663, **88,** 685, **116,** 73-4
basis
implied term of treaty **106,** 207
non-contractual **106,** 207
change of government, whether **96,** 67

circumstances as essential basis of consent to treaty **116,** 69, 74, **117,** 426, 441-2
contemplated by parties, whether **56,** 125. *See also rebus sic stantibus* clause *below*
continental shelf **60,** 591-3, 627
customary international law **117,** 409-10, 425-6, 441
economic conditions **116,** 73
environmental developments **116,** 74, 210
equity, principle of **99,** 585
foreseeability **62,** 193, 207, **116,** 74
impossibility of performance, need for **117,** 428
Iran–US Treaty of Amity (1955) **83,** 533, 536-7
legal circumstances **55,** 197-8, 199-200, 213, **56,** 109
limited applicability **116,** 74, **117,** 426
municipal law provision **106,** 207
political conditions **116,** 73, 210
private person's right to assert against view of parties to treaty **101,** 596, **117,** 427
rebus sic stantibus clause **46,** 485
State succession **83,** 71
suspension, ground for **106,** 206-7, **117,** 427-8
uncertainty of rule **117,** 425-6
Vienna Convention on the Law of Treaties (1969) **83,** 536, **106,** 206-7, **116,** 73-4, **117,** 408-9, 410, 425-6, 436-7, 442
Yugoslavia, breakup **117,** 427-8, 432, 436-7, 442
general international law **44,** 155
general principles and **84,** 392
general rules of international law, part of **61,** 623-4
general and special distinguished **53,** 4
good faith **37,** 45
applicability of multilateral treaty before entry into force **83,** 86
applicability of multilateral treaty before incorporation **124,** 413-14
avoidance of measures before entry into force which would defeat object and purpose **113,** 322-3, **116,** 215
customary international law **113,** 322-3
compliance **82,** 637, **84,** 295, **102,** 310, 497
conclusion **93,** 499
in violation of international law **83,** 34
effectiveness as principle of **37,** 203
operation and enforcement **82,** 28, 29, 542-4, 550, 562, 563, 565-6, 580, 583, **116,** 87-8, 137-8, 153, 214-15, **124,** 413-14
procedural principles **116,** 75
termination **116,** 219
notice **116,** 223
Treaty of Waitangi (1840) **120,** 501-2, 508-9, 510-11, 513, 534
Vienna Convention on the Law of Treaties (1969) **116,** 88, 121, 153
Harvard Draft on Law of **37,** 67
headquarters agreement. *See* headquarters agreements
Hong Kong. *See* Hong Kong, treaties; Hong Kong Special Administrative Region (HKSAR), treaties
host agreement. *See* host agreements
human rights treaties. *See* human rights, treaties; treaties, State succession, human rights conventions
humanitarian, Genocide Convention (1948), whether **115,** 184-5

treaties (*cont.*)
ICJ Statute as **76,** 98-100
implementation. *See also* operation and enforcement *below*
choice of means **36,** 398-9, **90,** 77, 111, **100,** 487, **106,** 301-2, **107,** 87, **108,** 75, **115,** 642
executive responsibility **101,** 586, 592, 601
federal State **104,** 429, 496, **106,** 314-15
judicial role **108,** 508
legislation. *See* implementing legislation *below*; legislation, interpretation, treaty-implementing legislation
legislative responsibility **104,** 495, **106,** 396-7
margin of discretion, *acte de gouvernement* and **106,** 195, 201
means
speciality rule **104,** 11
to be identified **102,** 29
obligation **81,** 49, **92,** 504, **115,** 641
State practice, relevance **101,** 258
subsequent agreement, by **88,** 690
implementing legislation **43,** 120-1, 246-53, **53,** 192-4, **71,** 249, 448-9, 591-3, 595, **72,** 4-9, 374-5, **73,** 300, 306, 390, 603-4, 615-21, 627, 677, 679, 686, **74,** 395, 432-3, 496, 526, 532, 536-8, 541, 543, 552, 563, 577, 586-7, 610, 615, 632, 649, 660, 685-8, 703, **80,** 68-71, 155-61, **86,** 111-12, 153, 156. *See also* incorporation into municipal law, legislature's role *and* municipal law and *below*
absence. *See* unincorporated *below*
applicability in respect of third party **36,** 431-2
duty of State to legislate **69,** 79-80, 85-8, 142-3, 296-301, **70,** 431-2, **71,** 591-3, **72,** 66, 68, 71-2, 217, 261-2, 297-8, 303, 310, 375, 655-7, 683, 693, **79,** 347, 373, 376
effect **51,** 429
effectiveness **100,** 487
entry into force of treaty before **71,** 121, **78,** 97
evidence of purpose **90,** 334-5, 360
federal State **104,** 430, 495-6
imprecision of treaty provisions **77,** 553
need for **36,** 389, 402, 408, 422, 425, **39,** 460-3, **40,** 180, 181, 232, 233, 235, 245, **41,** 421-6, **42,** 233-8, 265-71, **44,** 255, 291-2, **45,** 385-6, 389-90, **47,** 214, 312-27, **48,** 209-11, **51,** 2, 414-23, **52,** 415-17, 426, **69,** 79-80, 86-8, 142-3, 296-301, **70,** 431-2, **71,** 591-3, **77,** 553, 563-5, **78,** 346-7, **80,** 166-8, **81,** 681, 701, 713-14, **83,** 149-63, **85,** 6, 211, **86,** 697-9, **87,** 86, **88,** 211-14, **89,** 85-7, **90,** 209, 338-9, 657, **91,** 522, **92,** 508, 558-9, 575-7, **93,** 608, **101,** 208-9, 248-9, 300-1, 312, 313, 354, 357-8, **104,** 216-18, 219, 232, 428-30, 470-1, 483, 704-6, **108,** 637, **120,** 563, **123,** 491, 517-19, 526-30, **124,** 363, 396-8, 404-5, 410-11, 413-15, 420-3. *See also* direct effect *above*; incorporation *and* self-executing *below*
Geneva Conventions (1949) **123,** 604
human rights treaties **123,** 517-19, 529-30, 604, **125,** 518-19
international organization, instruments constituting **81,** 678
separation of powers **104,** 429
Treaty of Waitangi (1840) **120,** 482, 495, 500, 520-1, 546-7
presumption of conformity **40,** 1-3, **41,** 5, 7-8, 10, 431-2, 435-6, 447, **43,** 121, 124, **52,** 419-21, 457, 460, **63,** 270-2, 503, **70,** 4-6, 9, 14-15, **72,** 688, **73,** 411, 413, **78,** 338, **79,** 621-4, **84,** 762, 763, **89,** 196
presumption of constitutionality **78,** 98
purpose **80,** 92-3, 155

regulations 'necessary or convenient' to give effect to, limitations on **101,** 212-17, 218-25, 232-5, 238-9, 254
reservation, effect **78,** 100, 114-15
scheduling to Act, effect **104,** 430, 496-7
separability from treaty **45,** 2-3
source of obligation **77,** 26, 617-18, **101,** 262-4, **104,** 215, **123,** 518
sufficiency **77,** 553, 564
unincorporated **86,** 506
validity **90,** 60-115
subsequent legislation, effect **70,** 437, **78,** 98-9, **87,** 151
implied agreement **38,** 253, 258, 259-60
implied terms **37,** 192, 193, 194-5, 205, 207, 211, 215, 221, 222, 230, 232, 307, 421
'environmental' treaties **116,** 121
impossibility of performance **46,** 156, **82,** 549
ground for termination **116,** 68, 72-3
'permanent disappearance or destruction of an object indispensable for the execution of the treaty' **116,** 68, 72-3
where result of party's breach of treaty **116,** 73
justification for non-performance **82,** 549, **116,** 72-3
requirements **116,** 72-3
inconsistent laws and. *See* municipal law and, inconsistency *below*
incorporation into municipal law **44,** 319, 322, **69,** 142-3, 296-301, **79,** 367-73, 667, **80,** 128, **82,** 479, **83,** 232, **85,** 205, **87,** 292, 456, **89,** 81-2, 85-7, **93,** 498. *See also* implementing legislation *above*; municipal law and *and* unincorporated *below*
automatic **71,** 591-3
effect **89,** 82
human rights treaties **123,** 518
legislation, interpretation and **90,** 578-9, **103,** 149, 160-1, **107,** 166-70
need for **47,** 214-15, **59,** 6-7, **104,** 443
obligation, whether **70,** 431-2, **93,** 426
partial **90,** 424
publication, by. *See* publication, need for *below*
ratification, by **99,** 187
Indian Rulers
Kutch **50,** 54-6, 59-63, 218, 270, 398-401, 424, 425, 459, 464, 465, 470, 477
with, East India Company **50,** 54-6, 59-63, 218, 270, 398-401, 424, 425, 459, 464, 465, 470, 477
individuals, rights **40,** 175-84, 232, 234, 235, **45,** 1-2, 27, 317, 319, **47,** 10-13, 14-21, 328-41, 486, 493, **53,** 577-8, 580-2, 584, **56,** 543-5, 562, **59,** 3, **61,** 134-8, 139-41, 200, 204, 206, 210-12, 215, 622-4, **64,** 737-8, **66,** 497-8, **71,** 259-60, 586, 593, **72,** 376, **74,** 3, 56, 136, 312, 325-6, 339, **77,** 554, 564, **78,** 184-5, **79,** 343, 347, 399-401, 485, **81,** 514, 676, 701, 710, **83,** 151-2, 154, 186, **84,** 212-13, 215, 353, 666, **87,** 126-7, **88,** 226, **90,** 658-60, 674, 683-5, 686, **91,** 337-40, **93,** 225-6, **95,** 498, **104,** 84, **106,** 406. *See also* American Convention on Human Rights (1969), individuals; European Convention on Human Rights (1950), individual's right to invoke; International Covenant on Civil and Political Rights (1966), individual
appeal against breach **65,** 409-11
assertion of fundamental change of circumstances **101,** 596, **117,** 427
challenge to procedural legality **117,** 428-9
challenge to validity of treaty **107,** 77-80
claims settlement agreement **107,** 59-60, **108,** 612, 619
codification of customary international law **91,** 476

treaties (*cont.*)
compensation agreement **91,** 334-40
customary international law **117,** 425
derivative **90,** 659, 674, **91,** 476
direct effect, relevance **93,** 171-2, **117,** 424-5
disposed of by **45,** 436-45
dispute settlement procedure **107,** 489
EEC Treaty (Rome) (1957) **59,** 3, 484-5, **62,** 391, 395, 400-1, 406, 409, **93,** 40-1, 44
effect on **81,** 701
enforcement **63,** 456, **77,** 199, 617, **81,** 676, 681, **82,** 65-6, **86,** 52, **92,** 504-8, **100,** 507, **123,** 607-8
incorporated treaty **99,** 187-90
European Convention on Human Rights (1950) **93,** 226
extradition agreement **86,** 531, **87,** 189, **90,** 658, 671, 689, **107,** 433
GATT (1947) **107,** 112-13
Geneva Convention on the Status of Refugees (1951) **93,** 226
Hague Conventions (1899/1907) **103,** 611
human rights treaties **107,** 74
infringement **44,** 368, 386, 388
justiciability **104,** 215-18
Lomé Convention (1986) **107,** 521-2, 527
non-self-executing treaty **42,** 12, 17-18, **103,** 530
Pact of Bogotá (1948) **96,** 50
ratification, relevance **70,** 42
remedies **91,** 476
specific provision required **78,** 189
State as agent for **42,** 17-18, **104,** 218-19
UN Charter **96,** 50
unincorporated treaty **80,** 87, 167-8, **85,** 46-7, **100,** 457, **104,** 429, 447, 471, **120,** 414, **123,** 607-8, 609-10
international agreements as **68,** 545
international law **48,** 415
in breach of, joint responsibility of parties **116,** 169
conflict with rules of **61,** 623-4, **79,** 105
distinguished from **77,** 207
source of. *See* source of international law *below*
subsequent changes in, provision for **116,** 76-7, 122-4, 132, 133, 187-8
treaty dependence on **48,** 415
International Law Commission (ILC)
Brierly Report **37,** 67-8, 73
Draft Articles on the Law of Treaties. *See* International Law Commission (ILC), Draft Articles on the Law of Treaties
Lauterpacht Report **37,** 68
international organizations. *See* constitution (international organization)
interpretative declarations **84,** 240-1
investment protection provisions **46,** 221
judicial development **93,** 457-9
judicial notice **41,** 6, **43,** 120, **64,** 33-4, 44-5, **123,** 491-2
judicial review. *See* judicial review, treaties
jurisdiction, limitation on **91,** 520-2
jurisdiction clause **56,** 107-8, 199-201, **57,** 500, **72,** 79-81, 91-3

adjectival nature **37,** 272, 276
interpretation **37,** 115, 117, 164, 292-3
termination of treaty, effect **56,** 123
jus cogens/peremptory norm **83,** 15, 25, 534-5
exclusion of derogation by agreement **83,** 25
jus quaesitum tertio. See third parties *below*
jus superveniens **71,** 587
justiciability **81,** 717, **83,** 249, 259, 263, **85,** 19, **92,** 640-4, 647, 649. *See also* unincorporated treaty, justiciability *below*
contract incorporating terms **83,** 263
implementing legislation **83,** 263
treaty-making power **87,** 182, 183, **90,** 54-5
language **77,** 691
lapse. *See* termination, lapse *below*
law-making **37,** 451, **58,** 524, **83,** 149, 154, 162. *See also* declaratory and constitutive distinguished *above*
legal relations of co-nationals, effect on **70,** 442
legislature's role **36,** 397-9, **70,** 40-3, 46-50, **90,** 371-4, **106,** 335-6. *See also* implementing legislation *above*
amendment, power of **53,** 576, 582, 584, **106,** 338, 345, 348
amendment to legislation, relevance of need for **106,** 347
budgetary matters **106,** 340
conclusion of treaty and termination distinguished **90,** 372
human rights **106,** 340
implementation **104,** 495
'non-political treaties' **106,** 335-6
political control **106,** 340
prior legislative approval, need for **42,** 249-59, **90,** 372-3
public international law matters **106,** 335-6
reserved matters **106,** 346
right of initiative **106,** 372-3
role **90,** 371-4
legitimate expectation. *See* unincorporated treaty *below*; legitimate expectation, treaty
lex specialis **75,** 602, 615, 628, 651-2, **77,** 574, 577
Lomé Convention (1975), State immunity, jurisdiction and **64,** 121
loophole, as deliberate feature **82,** 273, 281
modification. *See* amendment *above*; revision *below*
modus vivendi **78,** 164
most favoured-nation clause
exemption from war taxes **43,** 4-5
retroactive effect **39,** 467-8
multilateral. *See also* customary international law, treaties and other international instruments reflecting
acquiescence in **41,** 129, 130, 211
amendment, by two parties to *inter se* **48,** 424, 432, 436-8
applicability
accession and **41,** 54
parties to **41,** 56-7
ratification **41,** 54
applicability before entry into force **99,** 427
between ratifying parties **83,** 86
when reflecting customary international law **83,** 86

treaties (*cont.*)
bilateral and, interrelationship **72,** 621, **91,** 271, 273
equality of parties **47,** 439, 440, 445, 460
interpretation. *See* treaty interpretation, multilateral treaties
jus cogens/peremptory norm, creation of **115,** 193
'legislation' **37,** 497
nature of **70,** 442
parties' interest in observance of **37,** 84-7, 166, 600-1
reservations **42,** 260-3
third parties **65,** 103-4, **83,** 162-3
applicability by analogy **90,** 410
effect on **57,** 43-4. *See also* opposability *below*
invocation by **82,** 611
municipal law and **40,** 447, **42,** 8-9, 237, **43,** 1-2, **44,** 117, 130, 142, **47,** 10-13, 14-21, **48,** 152-4, **53,** 18-19, 552-3, **55,** 59, 445, **56,** 1-2, **61,** 184-5, 237, 622- 3, 624, 626, 628-30, 639, **62,** 244-5, 270, 274, 277, 280-1, 283-5, 286-8, 290-3, 296-7, 391, 394, 396, 410-12, **84,** 775-8, **104,** 428-30. *See also* direct effect *and* incorporation into municipal law *above*; unincorporated treaty *below*
aid to interpretation, as. *See* legislation, interpretation, treaty as aid
clear intention of legislature to supersede, need for **96,** 132-3
constitutional requirements. *See* constitutional requirements *above*
derogation from **72,** 92
direct effect. *See* direct effect *above*
EEC Treaty. *See* EEC Treaty (Rome) (1957)
force of law **44,** 292-4
as guide to implementation of **90,** 27
implementing legislation. *See* implementing legislation *above*; legislation, interpretation, treaty-implementing legislation
inconsistency **40,** 247-9, **41,** 421-6, **43,** 238, **45,** 28, 31, **57,** 2-3, **82,** 235, 236-44, 245-52, 254, 257, 258-9, 262-7, 269-71, 275-9, **84,** 85, **86,** 164, 167
Administration's attempts to resolve **82,** 236-8, 263-4, 265-8, 271-2, 275-6
constitutional issue, whether **98,** 249
interpretation as remedy **82,** 237-8, 292, 295-8, 304, 322, 326
remedy on international plane **84,** 771
judicial notice **82,** 398, 399
need for amendment **82,** 254, **100,** 660
obligation to exercise powers in conformity with **124,** 472
ratification law and Statute distinguished **93,** 223-4
renvoi **46,** 512
self-executing. *See* self-executing *below*
statutory approval, effect **101,** 250
subsequent legislation, effect of reference to **77,** 397-9
subsequent treaty, effect **40,** 231, 233, 237, 244, **77,** 469, **82,** 241-3, 246, 250, 258-9, 263-7, 275-6, 277, 278-9, 291
transformation. *See* implementing legislation *above*
treaty as source of **44,** 292-4, **47,** 25
nationality provisions, corporation **46,** 357
neighbours, arrangement between **82,** 664-70
non-performance
change of economic policy **96,** 319-20
distress **82,** 549, 581-3
force majeure **82,** 549, **96,** 318
fundamental change of circumstances **82,** 549

jus cogens/peremptory norm, emergence of new rule **82,** 549
necessity **96,** 316-18
Vienna Convention on the Law of Treaties (1969) **96,** 317-18
nullity. *See* validity, nullity distinguished *below*
obligations **61,** 237-8, **62,** 479, 490, **90,** 51, 65-7, 73, 75. *See also* international obligations
anticipated **90,** 71
avoidance of measures in advance of entry into force which would defeat object and purpose **113,** 322
'best efforts' **102,** 291-5, 309, 310-11
absolute duty, whether **102,** 294
complaint, relevance **102,** 293, 486
continuous duty to take active steps **102,** 293-4, 392, 486, 490-1
expediency **102,** 295
foreseeability, relevance **102,** 447
good faith, relevance **102,** 295
margin of appreciation **102,** 294
policy considerations, relevance **102,** 295, 486
reasonable belief in adequacy **102,** 294, 302, 486-7, 490
reasonable time-limit **102,** 294-5
standard, third party assessment, need for **102,** 295
statutory power, whether sufficient **102,** 293, 302
timeliness **102,** 312
unconditional interest of own **102,** 294, 488
wrong ends, relevance **102,** 295, 302-3
changed circumstances **68,** 553
claims settlement agreement, individual's rights. *See* individuals *above*
consistency with multilateral convention **98,** 445
contract law compared **68,** 423-4
date arising **82,** 28-9
duration **82,** 545, 566-8, 583-90
incorporation into another treaty, effect **110,** 583-5
margin of appreciation **107,** 93-8
mutual **62,** 477-8
nature of **77,** 563-4, **79,** 343, 616, 628, 638
obligation of conduct, **102,** 290, 295-7, 298, 303, 386, 480-2, 483, 490
implementing legislation **108,** 74-5
political intent distinguished **68,** 300-1, 378-9
power to override
standing **60,** 395
UN Charter **60,** 394, 397
UN Security Council Resolution **60,** 394
US Congress **60,** 396-7
proportionality and **90,** 67-8, 76-8, 89-90
respect for **59,** 493, **68,** 518, 522
right distinguished **110,** 592-4
source **90,** 384
suspension **46,** 106, 156-7, 162-5
termination, in case of **90,** 385-6
unilateral **90,** 680
third parties, written acceptance **110,** 700
to negotiate in good faith
customary international law **110,** 223-4
Declaration on Friendly Relations between States (1970) **110,** 214, 217

treaties (*cont.*)
erga omnes character **110,** 223-4
Helsinki Final Act (1975) **110,** 214
Non-Proliferation Treaty (1968) **110,** 213-15, 217, 235, 279
undertaking to negotiate in good faith **110,** 213-15
Vienna Convention on the Law of Treaties (1969) **110,** 214
'under customary international law', evolving nature **110,** 580
under parallel treaties **19,** 548-9, **119,** 555-6, 559-61
effect of implementing treaty on framework convention **119,** 548-9
waiver **82,** 29
wording **68,** 300-6, 339-42, 378-9, 388-96, 419-24, 454-6, 497-8
operation and enforcement **48,** 392, **56,** 533-4, **60,** 45-7, **61,** 153-4, 205, 212, 623-4, **67,** 564-71, 581-93, **71,** 118, 127-30, 196, **81,** 676, **82,** 104-6, **90,** 61, 73, 93, 96-7, 101, 104, 108-10, 111, 135-6, 572. *See also* compliance *and* municipal law and *above*
applicable law, intertemporal law **116,** 124
application, completion of constitutional procedures, anticipation **78,** 97
choice of means **84,** 770
compliance. *See* compliance *above*
diplomatic channels **84,** 740
enforceability **79,** 400
federal State, responsibility for **90,** 61, 73, 101, 104, 108-10, 111, 112, 135-6
foreign judgment, recognition/enforcement **82,** 40
good faith. *See* good faith *above*
international plane **79,** 344, **90,** 657
interpretation distinguished **82,** 633
municipal courts **90,** 657-8, **108,** 553. *See also* treaty interpretation, by municipal courts
non-acceptance of enforcement mechanism, effect **86,** 119
parliamentary approval, need for **77,** 425
in advance of conclusion of treaty **77,** 425
parties to, sole right **86,** 679
piecemeal **82,** 33, 40
rebus sic stantibus **75,** 655, 665
recognition and **62,** 62-3, 69, 73, 84
request of foreign State for **81,** 676, 681
responsibility for **82,** 290
several treaties covering same ground **82,** 67-8
Special Commission on Operation of Hague Convention on the Taking of Evidence Abroad **84,** 749
standing to challenge **60,** 395, **90,** 658
State practice, State succession **75,** 108-13
third parties, effect on **67,** 185-9, **71,** 130
understanding between States regarding application, binding on courts, whether **72,** 216-17
violation. *See* breach *above*
opposability **57,** 432, **67,** 61-2, 64, 76, 79, 132, 148, **83,** 19, 22, 39, 50, 79, 85
non-self-governing territory after independence **105,** 418
nullity distinguished **83,** 80
Optional Clause declarations as **37,** 117, **76,** 126, 129, 131, 132, 221, 257, 331, 333
oral agreements **37,** 67, 69, 116-17

pacta sunt servanda **48,** 412, 415, **53,** 332-3, **57,** 528, **61,** 623-4, **62,** 190-2, 196, 217, **65,** 452, **66,** 590, **68,** 416, 518, 522, 554, **76,** 110, 584, **82,** 680, **100,** 100, **107,** 69, **116,** 77, 130, 151-3, 233, **117,** 408
'approximate application' theory and **116,** 60, 61, 71, 136-7, 202, 207, 243
customary international law **117,** 409, 426, 441
equity, principle of **99,** 585
as general principle of international law **40,** 2
good faith principle **117,** 564
Islamic law **64,** 631-2
primacy **93,** 342-3, **117,** 426
State practice **62,** 192
Vienna Convention on the Law of Treaties (1969) **53,** 332-3
as part of municipal law **81,** 513, **84,** 665, **90,** 198, 199-202, 215, 217, 672, **91,** 329, 330-2, **92,** 640-4, 647-9, **94,** 252, **95,** 592, **98,** 8, **106,** 429-30, 477, **115,** 644, **118,** 33-4, **125,** 523. *See also* implementing legislation *above*
government's intentions, relevance **92,** 649
obligation to comply with **61,** 468-9, **73,** 390
obligation, whether **93,** 426
official declaration of status, relevance **92,** 642-3, 648-9
ratification, relevance **104,** 428
status **93,** 361-2
partial continuance **37,** 145
parties
'*al-tarafan*' **102,** 59, 110, 113, 116-17
autonomous State as **83,** 52-3
change of name **96,** 88-9
determination
depository power's responsibility **96,** 377, 379
EC treaty **101,** 44-5
diplomatic recognition, need for, whether **96,** 88
discretionary powers **62,** 490
'Party', government, whether **106,** 302, 308, 314-15
protectorates **39,** 453, 456-8
signatory's error as to, relevance **96,** 379
sovereign powers **87,** 348
need for, whether **96,** 88
States, whether limited to **115,** 100
temporary incompetence **59,** 492
performance **60,** 45-7
formation of obligation distinguished **70,** 42
Petersberg Declaration (1992) **106,** 341
'political' treaty
fundamental departure from previous position **106,** 347
treaty affecting 'existence of the State, its territorial integrity, its independence and its standing and potential weight' **106,** 336-7, 346
popular consultation, need for **100,** 309, 310, 312, 330
primacy **36,** 428-33, **65,** 43, 45, **72,** 193-4, 589, 676, 688, **73,** 704, **77,** 132, 501, **78,** 129, 399, **87,** 82-3, **88,** 201-6, 217, 221-2, 225, 226, **89,** 53-4, 55, 69, 70, 82, **90,** 338, 340, 343-5, 358, **93,** 8, 29-30, 207-14, 220-4, 239, 307, **100,** 337, **106,** 261-2
amendment of treaty **88,** 205-6
applicable law **93,** 426-7
balance of interests **96,** 388

treaties (*cont.*)
basis **88,** 205
change of doctrine **93,** 253-4
civil matters **115,** 643
compatibility, power to determine and **93,** 246-53, 291-5, 302-3, 307-8
conflict **101,** 618, **106,** 317-18, **107,** 87
constitutional compatibility **89,** 53-4, 55, 69, 70
constitutionality of conflicting legislation distinguished **93,** 252-3, 292
criminal matters **115,** 643-4
customary international law **43,** 8, **108,** 539
direct effect, relevance **96,** 388, **99,** 35
dualist doctrine, relevance **93,** 253-4
EC Treaty, distinction, whether **93,** 304-5
'equal in stature and force' to **99,** 141
European Convention on Human Rights (1950) **96,** 387-8
general principles of extradition law **106,** 264
human rights treaties **93,** 302-3
international law **82,** 252-3
absence of rule **93,** 426-7
leges posteriores priores contrarias abrogant, applicability **82,** 296
multilateral and bilateral treaties, distinction, whether **93,** 292-3, 303-4
pacta sunt servanda **93,** 342-3, **117,** 426
previous legislation **93,** 213, 224
relative and contingent nature **93,** 292
repeal of existing law **36,** 386, 388, 421, **88,** 225, 228, **93,** 290
self-executing **93,** 234
separation of powers **93,** 291, 295
subsequent legislation **36,** 386-8, 399-405, **72,** 80, 676, 687-8, **74,** 134, 525, **86,** 118, 122, **88,** 204-6, **93,** 8-9, 213, 221-3, 243-62, 290-5, 296, **100,** 422-3
non-application of legislation **36,** 403-4, **93,** 290
subsequent treaty **38,** 176-80, **78,** 65, **91,** 270-1, 272, 273, **93,** 342-3, **106,** 334, **111,** 169
in case of conflict **91,** 266-71, 272
territorial application of tax law and **93,** 236, 239
treaty **47,** 92-3, **70,** 3-15, **72,** 80, 193, 589, 621, 629, 642, 657, 669, 676, 687-8, **74,** 3-4, 134, 146, 371, 509, **75,** 4-6, 8, 24, **77,** 391-2, 431-2, 501, **83,** 152, 218, 226, **86,** 112, 113-14, 693-4, 697-9, **100,** 660, 661
reciprocity, need for **86,** 115-16, 119
private rights. *See* individuals, rights *above*
promulgation, need for **39,** 456-7. *See also* publication *below*
protocols, part of, whether
annexation to another treaty, relevance **98,** 172-3
parties' intention **98,** 172-5
public and private interests distinguished **82,** 66, 74
publication, need for **37,** 69, **39,** 456-7, **40,** 180, **42,** 254, 265-7, **44,** 195, 291-2, 295-6, **45,** 385-6, 459-60, **47,** 113-14, **48,** 213-14, **65,** 49, **73,** 696, **77,** 425-7, **82,** 66, **83,** 15, 18, 39-41, **115,** 426. *See also* promulgation *above*
annexes **86,** 499
colonial territory, in **83,** 75
contracting State, in **77,** 425-7, **86,** 499
correction of published text **48,** 209-11
effect **36,** 382, **72,** 675, **86,** 693-4

language of **83,** 80
contracting State **77,** 425-7
matter for international law **83,** 41
registration compared **37,** 14, 45, **83,** 41
relevance where rights unaffected **82,** 66
secrecy distinguished **83,** 40
suspension of treaty **106,** 211-13
ratification **43,** 246-53, **44,** 192-6, **48,** 211, 213-14, **51,** 423-9, **71,** 592-3, **73,** 313, 323, 339, 351, 403, 410, 601-3, 692-4, **74,** 302, 339, 432, 518, 521, 536-7, 541, 552, 563, 601, 615, 660, 696, **76,** 186-7, 229-31, 278-80, **78,** 4, 7, **86,** 24, 25, **88,** 223-4. *See also* unratified treaty, applicability *below*
annexes, status following **72,** 676
binding nature of executive statement **78,** 97-8, **86,** 24-6, 28-9, 30
by exchange of notes **69,** 293-4
constitutional requirements **42,** 264-5, **44,** 192-6
foreign State, notice of **44,** 254, 263-4
declaration appended to, effect **71,** 128
declaration of intention to observe principles **104,** 706
international community **104,** 466, 474, 483, 495
national community **104,** 466, 474, 495
disincentive **91,** 476
effect on
customary international law **41,** 112, 186, 206-7, 212
municipal law **72,** 262, 682-3, **76,** 676, **92,** 642-3, **94,** 290, **120,** 362
presumed validity of executive action **72,** 657
entry into force and **39,** 458-60, **45,** 86-90, **57,** 341, **69,** 287-8, 293-4, **70,** 42-3
executive responsibility **90,** 210, **106,** 335, **123,** 520-1
ILO conventions **36,** 391, **37,** 80
implicit authorization to State agencies to act in accordance with **91,** 500-1, **104,** 484, 704-6
incorporation as result of **93,** 28, **104,** 428, 484
intention **41,** 112
international and municipal law distinguished **44,** 277-82, **47,** 319, 321, 323
judicial review, fact and form distinguished **106,** 209
legislation **42,** 259-63, **69,** 141-2
amendment of treaty **69,** 142, 159-61, 166
legislation, interpretation **90,** 578, **104,** 704
meaning **47,** 312
municipal courts and **42,** 250-1, **48,** 210, **78,** 160, 161
nature **44,** 253-5, 276-7
need for **44,** 276, **52,** 410-13, **56,** 240, **87,** 347, **93,** 499-500, **100,** 660
charge upon public funds **93,** 498, 499, 511-12
referendum, need for **93,** 503
non-objection to, effect **62,** 84
procedure determined by States party **88,** 223, 228
provision for, effect **70,** 42-3
relevance **41,** 54, 112, 186, 206-8, 212, **64,** 239-40
requirements **83,** 34
reservations, subject to **67,** 564-71
unauthorized signature, as validation of **44,** 231-2, 290
reactivation **74,** 119, 564, **78,** 107-8

treaties (*cont.*)
reapplication. *See* treaties, State succession, reapplication
rebus sic stantibus. See fundamental change of circumstances *above*
reciprocity **82,** 675, **86,** 115-16, 119, **88,** 210, **90,** 690, **93,** 8, 31, 236, 255, 263-4, 301-2, 343, 346, 347, 519, **100,** 71-2, **106,** 224-5, 230, **114,** 629
failure to observe as breach **79,** 438 n. 27
human rights treaties, relevance **108,** 45
judicial review **106,** 224-5
need for **106,** 224-5, 230
responsibility for determining **106,** 224-5, 227
recognition, relevance **96,** 86-9, **105,** 238-9, 245, 341-3, 374, 401-6
de facto **78,** 166
non-recognition and **49,** 124
recommendations of international assemblies distinguished **77,** 420-3
referendum, need for **93,** 503, **100,** 309, 310, 312, 330
registration **44,** 198, 203, 206-7, **83,** 18, 41-2, **87,** 347
acceptance of compulsory jurisdiction of ICJ and **84,** 279
Mandates **37,** 14, 36, 45
parties' intention, evidence of **102,** 35, 85
protest against **102,** 35, 86-7
publication compared **37,** 14, 45, **83,** 41
purpose of requirement **37,** 14
treaties concluded
before 10 January 1920 **37,** 14
League of Nations **37,** 14
unregistered treaty **37,** 14, 36, 45, 79-81, 129, 135-6, 235, 328-9, **48,** 337
admissibility before arbitral tribunal **83,** 41
State succession and **100,** 96
validity, effect on **37,** 45, **102,** 19, 35, **114,** 53, 56
remedies for breach **62,** 246, **80,** 121, 173, **90,** 671
annulment **93,** 28
apology **118,** 17
damages. *See* damages
declaration of illegality **93,** 28
direct applicability of treaty and **93,** 6
discretionary **104,** 436-40
finding of unconstitutionality **93,** 54-5
individual's right to **93,** 28-9
initiation of dispute settlement procedure **116,** 230
international **90,** 657
municipal courts, role. *See* municipal courts, role *below*
negotiated solution respecting objectives of treaty **116,** 86-7, 146-50, 177, 211-12, 226, 249-50
reciprocal action **106,** 267, **114,** 219-21, **116,** 90, 159-60, 226-7
rectification of irregularities **116,** 85-9, 146-9
restoration of rights **93,** 55, **116,** 225-6
termination of treaty **116,** 74-6, 230, 236
where obligations overtaken by events **116,** 86
renewal **57,** 562
repudiation, compromissory clause and **48,** 397-8, 419
reservations **57,** 494-7, 562, 563, **71,** 307, 449, **72,** 684, **73,** 301, 314, 323, 331, 339, 351, **78,** 87-90, **81,** 376, **84,** 233, 240-1. *See also* European Convention on Human Rights

(1950), reservations; International Covenant on Civil and Political Rights (ICCPR) (1966), reservations
acceptance by other parties **67,** 564-71, **77,** 605-6
admissibility **41,** 69. *See also* validity *below*
broadly formulated **107,** 71-2
customary international law, in respect of **107,** 69-71, **110,** 213
fundamental norms, in respect of **107,** 69-71
human rights treaties **107,** 69-71, 588
object and purpose test **70,** 469-70, **77,** 605-6, **107,** 20-1, 69-70, 73-5, **110,** 200, 241
applicable law, Vienna Convention on the Law of Treaties (1969) **107,** 69, 74
codifying treaties and **41,** 205-6
customary international law and **41,** 68-70, 71-2, 105-6, 107, 109, 113, 137, 162, 204-5, 222, 225, **77,** 606, **84,** 240
declaration accepting compulsory jurisdiction. *See* International Court of Justice (ICJ), compulsory jurisdiction, acceptance, reservations
declaratory provisions **41,** 68-9, 107, 113, 137, 162, 175, 186, 204, 222
definition **57,** 494-5, **70,** 465
EEC Treaty (Rome) (1957) **93,** 39
effect **41,** 70, **63,** 608, **67,** 564-71
other reserving States, on **41,** 70
events preceding ratification **82,** 68, 70
as evidence of international law **104,** 186-7
evidence of, expert **107,** 173-4
General Act for the Peaceful Settlement of Disputes (1928) **60,** 580-7, 622-3, 629, 634-40
Hague Convention relating to Civil Procedure (1954) **80,** 369
indirect **85,** 341-2
International Law Commission (ILC) **88,** 634
interpretation. *See* treaty interpretation, reservations
interpretative declaration distinguished **84,** 240-2, **107,** 20, 68-9
form, relevance **107,** 68-9
limitation *ratione temporis* **107,** 72-3
party's intention **107,** 68
jus cogens/peremptory norm and **41,** 175
League of Nations **88,** 634
multilateral treaties **42,** 260-3
Pan-American Union **88,** 634
provision for, effect **41,** 55
reasons for allowing **41,** 204-5
reciprocity **57,** 559
recognition of State, prevention of implied **115,** 200-1
requirements
compatibility with purpose **41,** 70, 175, **67,** 564-71
legal effect on treaty obligation **107,** 69-70
precision **107,** 75-6
preservation of autonomous nature of treaty **107,** 75
preservation of integrity of treaty **107,** 75
prohibition on, relevance **107,** 69
provision for **107,** 73
reciprocity, relevance **107,** 74
timeliness. *See* timeliness *below*

treaties (*cont.*)
transparency **107,** 75
restrictive interpretation **100,** 432
review, need for regular **107,** 76
scope **70,** 453, 465, 469-77
separability **103,** 650-1, 656-7, **107,** 75, **123,** 382-3
successive, effects **57,** 492, 497-501
timeliness **84,** 398, **85,** 341-2
accession **107,** 73
post-ratification **84,** 294
ratification **84,** 240, **107,** 18, 21, 73
signature **107,** 18
Torture Convention (1984) **103,** 526-8
validity. *See also* admissibility *above*
burden of proof **103,** 650
effect of invalidity **77,** 606
judicial review at time of making, need for **107,** 20-1
objection, relevance **110,** 259, 262, 366, 540
rectification, possibility of **107,** 22
responsibility for determining **107,** 20-2, 73-6
Vienna Convention on the Law of Treaties (1969) **107,** 20-1
Vienna Convention on the Law of Treaties (1969) **57,** 494-5, **70,** 471, **77,** 605
retroactive effect **71,** 588-9, **83,** 131, **100,** 483-8, **107,** 142-3, 145-6
context **107,** 142-3
customary international law and **101,** 390, **105,** 588, **107,** 143
elements on which treaty makes no provision **106,** 226-7
implementing legislation, prior to **100,** 485-7
intention **107,** 142-3
Iran/Netherlands/US Agreement (1981) **94,** 324
Netherlands–USSR Agreement on Merchant Shipping (1969) **65,** 369
Refugees **72,** 443
Vienna Convention on the Law of Treaties (1969) **100,** 486-7
revision. *See also* amendment *above*
denunciation/termination distinguished **62,** 475, 478, 490, 498, 507-8, 512, 521, 536, 545-6, 560, 570
interpretation distinguished **37,** 142, 160, 189-90, 193, 195, 204, 281-2, 443, **83,** 45, **110,** 722, **116,** 132, 137, **120,** 246
revolutionary government, competence **76,** 716
rights **56,** 166-7, **83,** 259, **90,** 601-2, **91,** 340
balance **82,** 615
harmonization of **82,** 614
individuals. *See* individuals, rights *above*
reciprocal **82,** 614
restraint in exercise of **82,** 614, 631, 658
review **83,** 42-3
Law of the Sea Convention (1982) **83,** 42-3
waiver **82,** 28, 29, **90,** 693
rule of international law, equivalent to **82,** 47
sanctity **62,** 192-3
scrutiny **43,** 9-10, 246-53, **78,** 159-61
elements covered **78,** 160
entry into force before completion **78,** 161
responsibility for consequences **78,** 161

ratification law as **78,** 159
speed **78,** 160
secret **77,** 253
unpublished distinguished **83,** 40
self-executing **40,** 183, 189, 228-9, 231, 233, 236-8, 239-42, 244, **47,** 10-13, **60,** 47, **61,** 139-41, **66,** 497-8, **68,** 199-200, 216, 227, **73,** 2, **79,** 309-401, **83,** 156, **84,** 213, 353, 398, **86,** 116, 119-20, **88,** 210-14, 224-5, 226-8, 229, **93,** 4-9, 29, 558. *See also* direct effect *and* implementing legislation *above*
Basle Convention on the Control of Transboundary Movements of Hazardous Wastes and Their Disposal (1989) **100,** 507
'binding on anyone' **99,** 3
creation of corporation **85,** 9
executory agreement distinguished **90,** 657
existing legislation, effect on **91,** 521, 530 n. 35, **122,** 679-80
extradition agreement **90,** 658, **95,** 366
Geneva Convention on the High Seas (1958), whether **91,** 522-30
Geneva Convention on the Protection of Civilian Persons in Time of War (1949) **95,** 498
Geneva Convention on the Protection of Civilian Persons in Time of War (1949), First Additional Protocol (1977) **104,** 91
Geneva Convention on the Status of Refugees (1951) **99,** 2, 3, 34
individuals' rights **93,** 225-6, **95,** 613-14
Iran–US Treaty of Amity (1955) **63,** 456
limitations on **91,** 523
London Convention on the Prevention of Marine Pollution by Dumping of Wastes and other Matter (1972) **100,** 507
multilateral treaties **91,** 528-9
Netherlands–USSR Agreement on Merchant Shipping (1969) **65,** 366
OAS Charter **90,** 665
partially **91,** 530 n. 35
power to determine whether **91,** 522, **95,** 614
primacy **93,** 234
Refugees, Geneva Convention on the Status of (1951) **95,** 498
requirements **91,** 523, 524, **95,** 614
complete and precise provision **90,** 686 n. 17, **93,** 225
mutuality **91,** 524, 528-9
non-infringement of law **93,** 226
parties' intention **93,** 225-6
reciprocity **93,** 105
subsequent legislation, effect **101,** 595-6
Torture Convention **125,** 575-7
UN Charter **90,** 665
Universal Declaration of Human Rights (1948) **95,** 498
US-HKSAR Extradition Agreement (1996) **122,** 679-80
Vienna Convention on Consular Relations (1963) **118,** 31
separability **37,** 71, 414, **46,** 81, 105-6, 154-6, **83,** 44, **99,** 188
dispute settlement. *See* dispute settlement, treaty provision, separability
reservations **103,** 650-1, 656-7, **107,** 75
signature **73,** 307
ad referendum **41,** 112
authority of ambassador to sign **44,** 202, 204-5, 215, 216
effect **41,** 186, 211-12, 221, **44,** 215-16, 253, 275, **71,** 591, **83,** 34
unconnected treaty, on **41,** 131

treaties (*cont.*)
full powers, need for **108,** 601
source of international law **37,** 451, **53,** 4, **59,** 529, **71,** 117-18, 197, **75,** 189-92, 228-34, **77,** 198, **80,** 53, 108, 135, 141, 173, **81,** 715, **87,** 455, 456, **88,** 48, **90,** 585, **104,** 335, **113,** 418-19
codification **72,** 520-5
consensus **77,** 174
customary international law. *See* customary international law, treaties and other international instruments reflecting
maritime delimitation **41,** 90, 116-17
overriding general principles **77,** 600
Paquete Habana case **77,** 174
superior **76,** 533
UN auspices, under **77,** 658
unratified **73,** 229
primacy **108,** 535
treaty interpretation distinguished **104,** 471
source of judicially measurable and manageable standards **99,** 68
sovereignty, effect on **53,** 473, **70,** 41, 44. *See also* sovereignty, transfer of powers to international organization
derogation, right of and **111,** 495-6
limitation of **53,** 565
stability **46,** 484
State, extinction of and **66,** 359
State contract, compared **53,** 447-9, 474, **62,** 193
State practice, as evidence of **70,** 391, **72,** 66, 69, 73-4, 193-4, 631, 643-4
extradition treaties and **73,** 39-42, 47-8, 54
weight of **72,** 644
State responsibility, to nationals for conclusion of **41,** 480-2
status as **92,** 640
Act of Union between England and Scotland 1706/1707 **124,** 579-80, 582, 583-4, 589-92
international law as applicable law, need for **123,** 315-16
Sunningdale Agreement, whether **93,** 498-9
suspension **106,** 206, **116,** 47-8. *See also* denunciation *above*; termination *below*
act of government **117,** 423
act of State **106,** 208-11
applicable law **116,** 47, 48
effect on reputation **94,** 68
human rights treaties during civil war **115,** 62
implementation of treaty, as **106,** 210
judicial review **106,** 209-10
municipal law, effect on **106,** 209, 212-13
notification through diplomatic channels **106,** 211-12
partial **83,** 536-7
publication, need for **106,** 211-13
rebus sic stantibus. See fundamental change of circumstances *above*
responsibility
courts **106,** 207-8
executive **106,** 207-8, 211
Head of State **106,** 210-11
parallel **106,** 210

treaty provision **106,** 206
war, as result of **91,** 390
termination **48,** 217-26, **60,** 529, **62,** 452-3, 475, 478, 490, 533-6, 560, 570-1, **82,** 551, **84,** 530-1, 663-5, **116,** 175-7. *See also* denunciation *and* suspension *above*
abrogation **57,** 26, **77,** 435-6
by later treaty **44,** 317
absence of provision **87,** 354, **116,** 71-2
intentional omission **116,** 71-2
by implementing legislation, amendment **87,** 162
by legislation **47,** 25
by mutual consent **62,** 511, 514, 537, 541-2, 553
by parties' conduct **83,** 533-4, 537, **96,** 87
by subsequent legislation, presumption against **101,** 595
by subsequent treaty **57,** 473-5, 492, **82,** 68, **107,** 127
as between States party to subsequent treaty **107,** 143
by treaty of equivalent status **123,** 183
clause, absence of **78,** 164
contracting party
dismemberment **74,** 114-15
extinction **73,** 41
desuetude **57,** 482-4, 561, **60,** 529, **70,** 440, **77,** 438. *See also* lapse *below*
General Act for the Peaceful Settlement of Disputes (1928) **57,** 479, 493, **60,** 529
effect on
compromissory clause **48,** 397-8, 419, **56,** 123
pre-existing rights **84,** 665
reciprocal obligations **116,** 95-6
related agreements **116,** 208
responsibility for breach **82,** 568
rights and obligations created by implementation of treaty prior to termination **116,** 211, 224
executive responsibility **82,** 290, **96,** 87, **106,** 335
fulfilment of objects **56,** 123-4
grounds **57,** 549-50
breach **48,** 333, 348, 349-51, 352-3, 411, 413-16, 419, 433-4, **49,** 5-6, 36-7, 203, 256, 328-9
breach by other party **84,** 663-4, **87,** 163, **116,** 74-6, 172, 205-8, 220-2
breach by other party of another treaty or rule of international law **116,** 74
change of circumstances. *See* fundamental change of circumstances *above*
fundamental change of circumstances. *See* fundamental change of circumstances *above*
impossibility of performance. *See* impossibility of performance *above*
loss of *animus contrahendi* **116,** 95
necessity. *See* necessity, treaties and
reciprocal breach **116,** 77, 85, 95, 207-8
implied **77,** 436-8
lapse **57,** 526. *See also* desuetude *above*
partial **46,** 155-6, 162, **48,** 217, 219, 222
margin of appreciation **117,** 427
obligations of parties **62,** 478, 495-6, 508, 513-14, 541
partial **37,** 145, **46,** 155-6, 162, **48,** 217, 219, 222
parties' intention to allow for future developments and **82,** 629, **116,** 76-7, 86-7
PCIJ, dissolution of and **57,** 479, 493

treaties (*cont.*)
premature **82,** 321-8, **116,** 75-6, 94, 219-23
requirements
notice **62,** 476, 478-9, 508, 541, **84,** 663-4, **116,** 207, 222-3, **117,** 409, 428-9, 442-3
parties' agreement **106,** 230, **116,** 77, 153
Vienna Convention on the Law of Treaties (1969) **117,** 409, 429, 437, 442-3
right of **76,** 178, 221, 263
effect of own breach **116,** 76, 94, 95, 221-2, 243
suspension. *See* suspension *above*
transitional period **62,** 536
war **40,** 19, **48,** 418, **71,** 595-6, **74,** 118-19, 563
withdrawal from **57,** 432-3
grounds for **57,** 479
territorial. *See* treaties, State succession, treaties of a territorial character
third parties **37,** 72-3, 140, 166, 451, **41,** 31, 47-8, 55, 112-13, 168, 217, 218, **46,** 159, **61,** 237, **82,** 681-2, **83,** 538-9, **86,** 582, 585, **105,** 53, **115,** 422, **116,** 532-3, 632, 658-61, **123,** 38-9
acquiescence **74,** 146
application to **37,** 72-3, 140, 166, 451, **42,** 188, **82,** 21, 25, 40, **115,** 422, **116,** 532-3, 632, 658-61, **123,** 38-9
as beneficiaries **37,** 72-3, 140, 166, 451, **44,** 302, 314-15
class, in favour of **93,** 614
customary international law **96,** 725
duty not to frustrate **75,** 173
effect on **41,** 31, 47, 55, 112-13, 168, 218, **48,** 215-16, 230-1, **67,** 599, 607, **70,** 391, 435-6, **73,** 229
enforcement by **86,** 678-9
evidence of current State practice **70,** 391
nationals of third States **70,** 435-6, **72,** 231, 668-70, **73,** 601-2, **74,** 3-4, 146, 497
obligations **96,** 725-6, **125,** 502-3
written acceptance **110,** 700
pacta tertiis neque nocent neque prosunt **37,** 72-3, 75, 79, 140, 166, 451, **41,** 31, 47, 55, 112-13, 114, 116, 168, 218, **44,** 188, **70,** 575, 595, 599, 616, 686-7, **78,** 110, 584, **80,** 660, **81,** 701, **96,** 725-6
parties' intention **93,** 614
State succession and **78,** 110-11
stipulation pour autrui **67,** 340, **82,** 93
Vienna Convention on the Law of Treaties (1969) **96,** 725
title, relevance **97,** 140
translation **80,** 254, 255, 302
lack of authentic **80,** 253
treaty-making power **39,** 456, **40,** 237, **42,** 250-9, **52,** 415-17, 419-21, 426, **53,** 203-4, **70,** 43-50, **78,** 192-3, **81,** 676, 700-1, **83,** 156, **93,** 222, 492-4, 496-500
absence of provision for **62,** 475, 512-13, 536, 560, 565, 570
as act of State **81,** 700-1
constitutional limitations **51,** 401-14, **52,** 419-21, **70,** 42, 46-50, **73,** 692-4, **87,** 348, **98,** 176, **102,** 18-19
knowledge of other States, whether within **70,** 48-9
dependent territories **86,** 155-6
East Timor **105,** 246, 263-5, 319, 344-5, 416-17
European Community. *See* European Community treaties, treaty-making power

executive **87,** 126, **106,** 335-40, **108,** 637
federal State **52,** 330-1, **83,** 157, **87,** 163-4
Head of State **44,** 220, 256, 279, **56,** 543
individual's power to influence **108,** 661-2
individual's right to challenge executive **70,** 39-41
Jersey **86,** 156, 159
justiciability **87,** 182, 183, **90,** 54-5
legislative role. *See* legislature, role *above*
negotiating responsibility **90,** 372, **94,** 63-4
non-self-governing territory **105,** 246, 263-5, 319, 344-5, 416-17
prerogative **44,** 208, 368, 371, **77,** 33, 389, **81,** 676, 700-1, **84,** 717, **87,** 333, 347-8, **98,** 175-6, **108,** 611, **124,** 413, 419
prior legislative approval, need for **90,** 372-3
sovereignty and **56,** 18, **77,** 464, **83,** 27
Vienna Convention provisions **70,** 49
trusteeship agreements. *See* Trusteeship agreements
UN Resolutions **84,** 665 n. 1, **107,** 387-8
unequal **46,** 481, 485, **100,** 60-1. *See also* Canada, aboriginal Indians in, treaties; New Zealand, Treaty of Waitangi (1840)
Non-Proliferation Treaty (1968) **110,** 312
unilateral action under **116,** 55-66, 136-43, 154-9, 162-74, 199-212, 214-23, 228-35, 236-40, 241-9
unilateral declaration. *See* unilateral declaration/undertaking
unilateral suspension, compromissory clauses and **48,** 339-40, 390, 413-14, 432, 434
unilateral undertaking. *See* unilateral declaration/undertaking
unincorporated treaty
breach, discretionary remedy for **104,** 436-40
contract, use in **81,** 701
courts' right to apply **85,** 44, **104,** 428-32, **122,** 442-4
courts' right to interpret **64,** 182, **81,** 701, **107,** 484-9
courts' right to use as evidence **100,** 462-3
effect **80,** 87, **81,** 701, **86,** 699, **90,** 28, **100,** 455-6, **108,** 611
evidence of international law **104,** 579
obligation of passive compliance **103,** 178
private rights and obligations **100,** 457
State-sponsored terrorism and **121,** 612
enforceability **73,** 403, 410-11, **74,** 312, 325-6, 339-40, 357, **90,** 657-8
as evidence of factual background **108,** 613
individual rights before national courts **80,** 87, 167-8, **85,** 46-7, **104,** 429, 447, 471, **108,** 612-14
intention to incorporate, legitimate expectation and **122,** 440-2, 450, 456-9, 467
justiciability **80,** 52, 57, 86-90, 102-4, 111-12, 148, 177, 203-5, 208, **81,** 700-2, 703, 710, 713-15, 716, 719, 724, **100,** 462-3
legislation, aid to interpretation of. *See* legislation, interpretation, treaty as aid, unincorporated treaty
obligation of compliance **103,** 178, **119,** 407-8
terrorist conventions **86,** 37-40
treaties conferring immunity **100,** 456-7, 461-3
union of States, Covenants forming, treaty character **49,** 375
unratified treaty
as aid to interpretation **100,** 64-5, **103,** 177

treaties (*cont.*)
application of **56,** 240, **57,** 341, **70,** 426-7, **71,** 121, **77,** 457, **83,** 86, **122,** 442-3, 453-60
codifying treaty, effect **46,** 361
delay in ratification **41,** 207
failure to ratify **41,** 206, **57,** 341
effect **69,** 287-8, 293-4, **70,** 391-6, **92,** 565-6
relevance of treaty **100,** 54-5, 57, 93, **101,** 383, **104,** 91-2, **114,** 63
rights of other party **36,** 391
as source of international law, *Paquete Habana* case **73,** 229
temporary injunction to prevent ratification **73,** 692-4
USA boundary treaties **51,** 28-38, **73,** 64, 79-80, **91,** 445
inter-State **51,** 28-38, **73,** 64, 79-80
validity **83,** 19, 533-4. *See also* treaty-making power *above*
ambiguity **102,** 39
amendment of implementing legislation, effect **87,** 151, 163-4
applicable law, municipal law **44,** 260, 269, 282-8, **83,** 32, **116,** 124
authority to conclude, need for **44,** 55
breach of international obligation in negotiating, relevance **105,** 266, 314-15
changed circumstances **56,** 134
continuing **82,** 681, **96,** 107-9
corruption **106,** 706
critical date **83,** 534
Cyprus/UK, Treaty of Establishment (1960) **108,** 552
derecognition of party to **96,** 86-9
duress **44,** 55, **55,** 194, 214, **56,** 107, 139, **83,** 533, 534
executive certificate/statement, conclusiveness **122,** 608, 614-15, 618-19
fraud **83,** 533, 534, **106,** 706
full powers, relevance **44,** 204-5, 214-16, 248-50, 261, **108,** 601
inequality of parties. *See* unequal *above*
intention to conclude, need for **106,** 337-8, 343-5, 371
implicit **106,** 337-8, 343-4
NATO Council decision as **106,** 344
jurisdictional clauses and **48,** 332, 339-40, 348, 350-1, 390, 413-14, 419
jus cogens. See jus cogens/peremptory norm *above*
municipal courts, competence **70,** 38-43
non-enforceability, effect **77,** 52
nullity distinguished **83,** 80
parties' intention, relevance **102,** 18-19, 87
presumption of **78,** 161, 164
prior legislative approval, need for **42,** 249-59, **90,** 372-3
publication. *See* publication, need for *above*
ratification, relevance. *See* ratification *and* unratified treaty, applicability *above*
reciprocity, relevance **88,** 206-16
compliance procedures, relevance **88,** 211
responsibility for determining **88,** 207, 222
registration and. *See* registration *above*
reservations. *See* reservations, validity *above*
secret agreement **100,** 96
several treaties covering same ground **82,** 68
standing to challenge **83,** 34
individuals **70,** 39-40, **107,** 77-80

subsequent conduct **83,** 80, 83-4
treaties concluded by colonial State in respect of dependent territory while process of liberation in train **83,** 26-30, 38-9
violation of internal law, relevance **78,** 60, 647
conflict with fundamental provision **76,** 132, **78,** 646-9
'manifest'/within the knowledge of other State requirement **44,** 254, 263-4, **70,** 48-9, **78,** 174-5, 646-9, **83,** 3 n. 2, 30-4, 39, 40, **105,** 30
presumption of official regularity **98,** 6-7
standing of individuals regarding **70,** 39-40
violation. *See* breach *above*
waiver of immunity and **63,** 267-8, 269-72, 280-2, 347-50, 433-4, 503-4, 514-19
waiver of rights, restrictive interpretation **50,** 62
waiver of terms **67,** 585-7
revocability **67,** 587
war
effect **37,** 71, **40,** 19, **44,** 318, **48,** 418, **59,** 492, **71,** 595-6, **74,** 118-19, **96,** 305
multilateral treaties **74,** 564
separability and **37,** 71
winding-up of international organization, effect on **77,** 30
withdrawal **62,** 475-6, 484, 488
notice, obligation to give **62,** 476
treaties, State succession 39, 408-9, 415-24, 453-6, **53,** 159, **55,** 71-5, **66,** 359-60, **70,** 3-15, **71,** 48-9, **72,** 61-2, 65-74, **73,** 38-55, 601, **74,** 114, 116-17, **75,** 100-13, **77,** 657, **78,** 107-11, **79,** 387, 395, 415 n. 1, 417 n. 4, **85,** 143-5, **87,** 210-11, **91,** 388, 389-90. *See also* Germany, Federal Republic (FRG), treaties; Germany (Reich), treaties
aboriginal Indians, treaties with **78,** 436, 467-8
ad hoc approach **115,** 615
agreement of parties to continuance
exchange of notes **85,** 143-4, **87,** 212, **96,** 112
need for unanimity **52,** 409-13, **114,** 621-2, **115,** 614
annexation of territory as protectorate, Madagascar (Malagasy Republic) **11,** 77-8
arbitral tribunal's competence to determine validity of pre-existing treaty **83,** 21-2
automatic **115,** 185-91
Indian Government's Declaration (1956) **78,** 109
Vienna Convention on the Succession of States in respect of Treaties (1978) **115,** 185-92, **116,** 79-80
autonomy of colony at time of signature, relevance **83,** 52-3
Bosnia-Herzegovina. *See* Bosnia-Herzegovina, treaties, State succession
boundary treaties **83,** 35-9, **116,** 81, 134-5. *See also* treaties of a territorial character *below*; *uti possidetis*
breach of treaty concluded by predecessor government **76,** 422-6, 464-6
case by case (Nyerere doctrine) **78,** 110
Tanganyika **78,** 110
challenge to validity of treaty, grounds for **83,** 22
clean slate theory **73,** 41, 46-8, 53, **75,** 110-11, **78,** 107-8, **83,** 22, 35, 37, 54-5, **85,** 143, **96,** 108, 376, **115,** 54-6
boundary agreements, exclusion **100,** 96
change of rule **96,** 376
customary international law **83,** 54
human rights conventions **115,** 56-66
limitations of doctrine **83,** 55 n. 21

treaties, State succession (*cont.*)
State practice **83,** 54
conduct of parties **73,** 39-42, 48, 54, 601, **75,** 108-13, **85,** 144
predecessor State **83,** 83-4
successor State **83,** 15, 16, 19, 20, 38, 44
statement of intention to remain bound **96,** 112, **115,** 23
continuity of entity **96,** 108
continuity of States **74,** 563, 565-6
customary international law **107,** 173
Vienna Convention on the Succession of States in respect of Treaties (1978) **115,** 185-92, **116,** 79-80
de facto succession **115,** 158
de jure **115,** 158-61
decolonization and **95,** 30
dependency becoming independent colony **91,** 388, 389-90
devolution agreement **78,** 110
third parties, applicability to **78,** 110-11
duration of treaty, relevance **83,** 38-9, 73-4, **100,** 36, 96, 100
evidence of treaty in force **87,** 316, **96,** 107-9
exceptio non adimpleti contractus **54,** 319-20, **77,** 439
extradition agreement. *See* extradition agreement, State succession and
federation, dissolution **52,** 86, **55,** 90-2
fundamental change of circumstances **83,** 71
Geneva Convention on the Status of Refugees (1951) **39,** 415-24, **55,** 73-5
Genocide Convention (1948) **115,** 23-5, 46-8, 52-66, 183-203
Hong Kong. *See* Hong Kong, treaties; Hong Kong Special Administrative Region (HK-SAR), treaties
hostilities, during **48,** 337, 339, 348, 394, 413
validity, from date of notification **77,** 439
human rights conventions **115,** 52-3, 184-5
confirmatory nature **115,** 58
customary international law as basis **115,** 59
erga omnes nature **115,** 56-7
gap, avoidance **115,** 60-1, 64-6, 67-8
general principles of human rights and humanitarian law and **115,** 58-9
principle of continuity **115,** 61-2
res inter alios acta **115,** 62
stability, protection of **115,** 60-1
State sovereignty, relevance **115,** 57-8
Indian Independence (International Arrangements) Order (14 August 1947) **78,** 109
International Covenant on Civil and Political Rights (ICCPR) (1966), Czech Republic **118,** 185 n. 2
legality of creation of successor State, relevance **115,** 115-16, 157-74
Vienna Convention on the Succession of States in respect of Treaties (1978) **115,** 158-61
Minorities Treaty (St Germain-en-Laye) (1919) **95,** 57-8
multilateral treaties **115,** 190-1
municipal legislation giving effect to **45,** 33-6
non-endorsement **83,** 78-9
notification of succession **95,** 30
date of effectiveness **95,** 31

instrument of accession as **95,** 31
obligation to respect existing treaties **91,** 270
pacta tertiis neque nocent neque prosunt **78,** 110
publication, relevance **83,** 40, 78, 79-80
reapplication **77,** 436-8, **91,** 226-7
Germany (Reich) **91,** 226-7
peace treaty **91,** 390
treaty, need for **77,** 441-2
reciprocity requirement **72,** 61, **87,** 316, **107,** 173
registration, relevance **100,** 96
res inter alios principle **115,** 62
rights
review of treaty **83,** 42-3
to choose whether or not to retain treaties **83,** 26, 27
Russian Federation **107,** 661-2
Protocol to the UK–USSR Treaty of Merchant Navigation (1968) **107,** 662
separate legal entity test **52,** 86-8, **85,** 143, **87,** 316
devolution agreements **96,** 376
Slovakia **116,** 81-2
State practice **115,** 186-92
subsequent practice **60,** 448
succession of dependent territory and secession of part of State distinguished **115,** 189-90
successive **48,** 215-16, **56,** 532-4
suspension **47,** 240
tabula rasa. See clean slate theory *above*
termination
by predecessor State **96,** 108, 112
prior to succession, assumption of responsibilities by successor State **116,** 224
third parties and **78,** 110-11
treaties concluded by the GDR **115,** 614
treaties of a territorial character. *See also* boundary treaties *above*; *uti possidetis*
customary international law **116,** 81
treaties concerning water rights or navigation on rivers **116,** 81, 134
Treaty of Saint-Germain-en-Laye (1919) **115,** 32-3
uti possidetis. See uti possidetis
Vienna Convention on the Law of Treaties (1969) **117,** 409-10
Vienna Convention on the Succession of States in respect of Treaties (1978)
customary international law **92,** 164, 204, **115,** 185-92
entry into force **115,** 186, 191
interpretation, ILC Commentary **91,** 579-80
sovereignty over natural resources **83,** 15
Vienna Conventions. *See* Vienna Convention on the Law of Treaties (1969); Vienna Convention on the Succession of States in respect of Treaties (1978)
Warsaw Convention **39,** 408-9, 453-6
treatment of aliens. *See* standard of treatment of alien
treaty interpretation 39, 465-7, **40,** 250-9, **41,** 437, **43,** 254-9, **44,** 297-301, **48,** 222-3, 227-8, 411, **54,** 317, **56,** 208, **58,** 524, 583, 590, **59,** 530, **61,** 337-9, 415, 417, 639- 40, 642-4, **62,** 74, 86, **69,** 142, 288, 302-3, **71,** 338-45, **76,** 117-24, **78,** 386, **79,** 543-5, **84,** 124-5, 533-5, 722-9, **85,** 82, **90,** 383-4
as act of State **107,** 56
agreement of a special type, applicability of general rules **45,** 421
aids

treaty interpretation (*cont.*)
amendment of treaty **102,** 73-7, 117
'any relevant rules of international law applicable in the relations between the parties' **108,** 461-2, **121,** 361, **123,** 40, 65, 108
applicable principles of international law **95,** 368-9
at time of interpretation **121,** 360-1
banking usages **68,** 536, 543, 546-7, 550-2, 555-6
circumstances of conclusion **82,** 612, 644, **84,** 403-6, **92,** 119, **100,** 21, **102,** 64
commentaries **74,** 581, 619, 622, 625, 637, 642, 652-3, 655, 662-3, 665-6, 674-5
common usage **38,** 218, **62,** 475, **82,** 620, **106,** 440, 443, 445
Constitution of State party **106,** 479
context **37,** 188, 337, **38,** 228-9, **57,** 227-9, **59,** 534-40, 556-8, **61,** 640, **68,** 615-16, 620, 634, **70,** 309-10, 312, 584-5, 671-2, **72,** 683, **77,** 408, 673-4, **78,** 164, 189, 652, **79,** 292, 329, 334, **82,** 587, 589-90, 612, 620-1, **83,** 142, 144, 146, 147, 188, 542, **84,** 266, 267, 269, 726, **86,** 155, **89,** 173, **90,** 682, **91,** 522, 524, **92,** 108, 112-16, 118, 151, 687, **93,** 600, **95,** 371, **96,** 118, 398, **97,** 499, 638-41, **99,** 142, 418, **100,** 186, 187, **101,** 242, **107,** 135-6, 454, **110,** 579, 588, 770, **114,** 30, 372. *See also* other treaties *and* other treaties concluded by parties *below*
annexes to treaty **119,** 633, **121,** 106
change of **102,** 61-2
circumstances prevailing at time of conclusion **116,** 132
consistency of interpretation, need for **77,** 633
diplomatic correspondence **100,** 61, 62
draft text **110,** 591
exchange of notes **100,** 420, 424
juridical system in force at time of interpretation **123,** 169-70
legal **95,** 371
preamble **97,** 639, **119,** 633, **121,** 106
previous obligations **102,** 59
related agreement **41,** 133-4, **97,** 499, 638-9, **119,** 559
sentence as **97,** 499
statements in Security Council, relevance **124,** 181-4
text and agreements in connection with conclusion of treaty **124,** 440
text of article under consideration **82,** 620-1
text of other articles in treaty **45,** 409, **102,** 59, **120,** 271, 274-5
trade liberalization background **110,** 576-7
treaty as a whole. *See* guidelines, treaty as a whole *below*
variation of meaning in accordance with **121,** 115-16
customary international law **75,** 182, 185-6, 191-2, 198, 202-3, 208-9, 219, 259, **81,** 376-7, **82,** 548-51, **83,** 541, 618-19, **87,** 348, **92,** 125, 160, **95,** 365, **97,** 502, **101,** 309, 310-15, 379, **106,** 441, **119,** 196
dictionary **82,** 660, **95,** 594, 600, **96,** 119, **97,** 636
executive statement **44,** 29, 30-1, 38, 40, 45, 297-8, 446, 489, **45,** 83, 85, 111-13, 366, 367, **47,** 87-8, 90-2, 121, 125-6, **52,** 407-8, **72,** 54-5, 237, 589, **73,** 701, 704, **74,** 47, 99, 428, 573, **78,** 132, 135, **79,** 542
Explanatory Report **88,** 215, 294
general principles of international law **65,** 162, **87,** 153-5, **92,** 724-5. *See also* international law *below*
general principles of law **93,** 280
generally recognized principles of international law **89,** 520
government guidelines **99,** 119
hierarchy **82,** 633

ILC Commentary **91,** 579-80
incorporating obligations **110,** 583-5
international law **92,** 571
international manual **88,** 21, **104,** 237
interpretive note **40,** 2
judicial and arbitral decisions **38,** 89, **62,** 350-1, 471, 484-5, 510, 548-50, 563-5, 576-9, 638-9, **91,** 177, **104,** 238-9, **106,** 443, **121,** 361-2
ECJ **101,** 445-6
foreign **74,** 594-5, 598, 603, 611, 619-20, 636-8, 641-2, 654-6, 663, 666, 674-5
WTO **121,** 115-16, 124, 138-9, 141-3, 155, 173-4, 183
language of treaty **70,** 678
legislation **69,** 142, **81,** 701, 703, 713, **86,** 159, **100,** 421-3, 424, **101,** 390
subsequent **107,** 455 n. 7
legislative history **89,** 562
maps **52,** 198-203, 229-30, **77,** 664, 669-70, 691
memorandum to treaty **74,** 399
memorandum of understanding **102,** 353
municipal law **89,** 42, **90,** 377. *See also* treaty interpretation, by municipal courts
recourse to **70,** 433-4, **72,** 311, **77,** 407-8, **78,** 174-5
municipal law analogies **37,** 228, **62,** 605
official statement **110,** 582
opinions of Waitangi Tribunal **120,** 488-9
other treaties **62,** 422, 474, 476, 478, 492, 510, 544, **72,** 534-5, 571-2, 686-7, **73,** 472-5, 491, 509, 560, **74,** 474, 572-3, **75,** 44-8, 66-73, 212-15, 236-8, **79,** 351-2, 368, **84,** 266, **86,** 159, **124,** 23
analysis by negotiators **106,** 485, 488-9, 500
covering same subject matter **38,** 218-21
draft **106,** 485
inconsistent language **110,** 577, 584
multilateral **101,** 117-18, 481
not involving all parties **110,** 577
previous **106,** 440, 443
other treaties concluded by parties **81,** 407, **90,** 407, **100,** 25-6
in connection with conclusion of treaty **119,** 633
contemporaneous **100,** 25-6, **119,** 411-12, **121,** 148, 180
opposability to third State **100,** 32
previous **82,** 617, 660, 662, **100,** 436-7
unratified **100,** 64-5
parliamentary proceedings **93,** 445-6, **99,** 419, **100,** 66-8, 437, **121,** 140
failure to reflect parties' common intention **82,** 98
parties' conduct **106,** 477, **110,** 584-5
in parallel negotiations **110,** 584-5
parties' construction **59,** 517-19, **91,** 452-3, **95,** 582 n. 10, **96,** 121-2, **99,** 142
agreed interpretation annexed to treaty **44,** 319-21
at time of accession **95,** 582 n. 10
contemporaneous **37,** 101, 104, 148, 164, 185, 190, 192, 557, 576, **46,** 151, **96,** 103
reasonable **99,** 142, **101,** 577
practice of international organizations **121,** 115-17
preamble **52,** 132, **57,** 216, **62,** 474, 498, **72,** 685, **78,** 167, **124,** 481-2, 495, 505
principles and rules of international law **106,** 440, 443
private law analogy **90,** 378, **92,** 571

treaty interpretation (*cont.*)
protocol **44,** 300-1
ratification process **77,** 669, **84,** 403-6, 414, **95,** 371 n. 15, **96,** 103, **99,** 108-9
State practice **62,** 623-5, **71,** 697, **72,** 630-1, 643-4, 687, **76,** 693, **82,** 292-4, 660, **84,** 242-3, **86,** 368, 370, 374-5, 406, 408, 412-13, **87,** 154, **92,** 725, **95,** 366, **103,** 647-8, **106,** 500
divergent interpretation **74,** 594-5, 598, 603, 611, 619-20, 641-2, 654
modern **75,** 185-7, 191-4, 229
statement by Foreign Minister **39,** 465-6
statement by official at meeting of advisory body **125,** 597
structure of treaty **77,** 663, 672, **83,** 144, **93,** 18, **119,** 562-3
subsequent agreement **59,** 541-3, **77,** 666
subsequent exchange of letters **48,** 175-7
subsequent interpretation **96,** 121-2
subsequent legal developments **49,** 21
subsequent practice **37,** 190-1, 206, 211, 213, 230, 315, 335, 497, **38,** 227-8, 245-6, **45,** 395-6, 407, 418-19, 426, **52,** 145, 186-201, 223-6, 230, **54,** 335, 346-7, **59,** 541-3, 574, **60,** 448, **62,** 426, 623, **75,** 484-5, **77,** 663, 666-8, 674, **82,** 292-3, 616-17, 629, **90,** 376, **95,** 364, 371 n. 15, **97,** 501-2, 635, 642-5, **99,** 419, **101,** 242, 390, 391, 600-1, **103,** 646, 647-8, **106,** 370-1, **108,** 317, **110,** 576, 591-2, **123,** 108. *See also* developments subsequent to conclusion of treaty and *below*
in absence of ambiguity **97,** 502
creation of right/obligation **108,** 317
implementation of another treaty as evidence of **97,** 502, 639, **99,** 419, **101,** 390-1, 393
international organizations **11,** 15
Vienna Convention on the Law of Treaties (1969) **97,** 502
subsequent related agreements **40,** 449
subsequent technological developments **74,** 216
subsequent treaty practice **70,** 448, **101,** 124, **106,** 440, **110,** 576, **119,** 553-4, 561
treaties between the same parties **81,** 407, **100,** 30-2, 33-4, 72-4, **105,** 25-6, 43, 52-5
supplementary means **70,** 466, 471
Arts. 31 and 32 of Vienna Convention (1969), interrelationship **123,** 100, 109, **124,** 440
in case of ambiguity or uncertainty **110,** 591
teachings of publicists **91,** 177-8, **100,** 436, **104,** 237-8
Commentary on treaty **110,** 786
tenor of treaty **70,** 447-8
title **96,** 397, **97,** 140
translation **75,** 349, 352
travaux préparatoires. See travaux préparatoires
treaties with third States **45,** 396, 420, 425
UN interpretative statement **82,** 294
UNESCO Recommendation passed contemporaneously **68,** 305-6, 392-4, 420
UNGA Resolution defining Aggression **76,** 679
UNHCR *Handbook on Criteria for Determining Refugee Status* **90,** 145, **91,** 178
unincorporated treaty **108,** 613, **114,** 484
unratified treaty **100,** 64-5, **103,** 177
wording. *See* guidelines, language of treaty *below*
ambiguity **76,** 624, **77,** 672

applicable law **79,** 291-2, **84,** 533
customary international law **70,** 442, **75,** 182-6, 198, **78,** 8
as codified by Vienna Convention on the Law of Treaties **100,** 478
customary principles of interpretation **114,** 268, 286
general international law **37,** 103, 184
general principles of international law **57,** 217, 304, **62,** 475-6, 479, 568, **68,** 543, **75,** 416, **79,** 291-2, 310
international law **101,** 313, 602, **104,** 432, 447, **106,** 437-8, **110,** 575
Vienna Convention on the Law of Treaties **110,** 478, 575-6
law in force at time of conclusion **116,** 130-1
'fixed reference' (*renvoi fixe*) **116,** 131
'mobile reference' (*renvoi mobile*) **116,** 131
law in force at time of interpretation **96,** 426. *See also* developments subsequent to conclusion of treaty and *below*
municipal law **104,** 86
municipal rules of construction **45,** 428, 431
principles and rules of treaty interpretation **45,** 393-5
ICJ jurisprudence **37,** 191-2, 337
arbitration agreement **92,** 45-9
Art. 177 (EEC Treaty) reference. *See* European Court of Justice (ECJ), Art. 177 reference
authoritative **62,** 548-51, **84,** 124-5
autonomous interpretation **70,** 312, **73,** 527, 538-9
bilingual. *See* multilingual *below*
burden of proof **90,** 376
context **90,** 407
by arbitral tribunal **62,** 606
by arbitrator **82,** 66-7, 74-5
contrary to international public policy, whether **82,** 67, 74
private interest, in respect of **82,** 66
by European Court of Justice (ECJ) **70,** 407-10
by executive **77,** 503, **90,** 681, 685, **93,** 302, **99,** 102-3, 119, **107,** 56-7, 61-2, **108,** 613, **111,** 500
benefits **107,** 61-2
binding, whether **107,** 56
unincorporated treaty **108,** 613
by international tribunal **124,** 425-6
by municipal courts **40,** 51, 70, **47,** 53, 56, 79, 81-3, 90-2, 121, 125-6, 342-4, **70,** 39-41, **73,** 700-1, 704, **74,** 47, 99-100, 144, 311-13, 339-40, 357, 703-4, **75,** 5-6, 8, **77,** 31, 503, 553, **82,** 66, **90,** 129, 422-3, 685
binding effect on third State **77,** 31
Channel Tunnel agreements **119,** 409-11, **125,** 591, 592-3
reference to executive **44,** 29, 30-1, 38, 40, 45, 297-8, 446-7, 489. *See also* executive statement *above*
terms incorporated into contract **108,** 613
third States, effect on **77,** 31
codifying conventions **71,** 118, **78,** 8-9, 652
conflicting **67,** 607-8
conformity. *See* uniformity *below*
declaration of nullity distinguished **83,** 44
declarations accepting compulsory jurisdiction of ICJ. *See* International Court of Justice (ICJ), compulsory jurisdiction, acceptance, interpretation
derogation provision **70,** 551

treaty interpretation (*cont.*)
developments subsequent to conclusion of treaty and **49,** 20, **57,** 477-8, **75,** 671-4, **92,** 79, 91-2, **95,** 364, 371 n. 15, **100,** 422-3, 447-9. *See also* intertemporal *below*; intertemporal law
contemporary law **95,** 667
intention to allow for **116,** 76-7, 122-4, 132, 133
indefinite duration of treaty **82,** 628-9
legal **82,** 617, 619
notification to ICJ **100,** 74-5
relations between parties **82,** 617
disputes, to reduce possibility of **41,** 228
double taxation agreement **45,** 427-35
EEC Treaty (Rome) (1957). *See* European Court of Justice (ECJ), Art. 177 reference
equitable principles of **99,** 587
equity, relevance **110,** 771
error of fact or law **101,** 210
estoppel **77,** 668
exception clauses **41,** 178
executive certificate/statement, conclusiveness **72,** 589, **86,** 24-6, 28-9, 30, **96,** 103, **101,** 618, 621
express terms **49,** 20, **62,** 603
function **71,** 215
gaps, completion **37,** 442, 443, **62,** 474-5, 510-11, 560, 565, 570, 623-4, 632-3, 649, **77,** 665, 670, **79,** 366
customary international law, recourse to **72,** 502
deliberate omission **62,** 377-8
fundamental change of circumstances **90,** 379
interpretation as **54,** 345-9, **90,** 378-9
principles of treaty law **100,** 661
government interpretation, binding nature **93,** 255, **96,** 103, **101,** 576, 618, 621, **104,** 87
Grotius **49,** 172
guidelines
a contrario **62,** 600, **70,** 587-8
a pari **70,** 587
absence of provision **95,** 363, 364
avoidance of implied term **92,** 122, **119,** 170
avoidance of unintelligible, absurd or unreasonable result **40,** 454, **48,** 419, **60,** 459-60, 465, 471, 475-6, **77,** 674, **82,** 589, **122,** 384
broad interpretation **72,** 644-5, 683-4, 699-700, 706, **74,** 594, 598, 660, 664, 672, 693-4, **75,** 67, **120,** 9
'broad principles of general acceptation' **104,** 447
change of policy **95,** 378 n. 35
chapeau as umbrella **122,** 76
'circumstances of conclusion', supplementary means of interpretation **97,** 500
clear language **37,** 238, 499, 550, **44,** 419, **74,** 144, 552, **75,** 188, 218, **95,** 587, 599, **99,** 526, **101,** 574, 577, 579, **106,** 438, 451
conflict between annex and treaty **47,** 422, 451
consistency **83,** 184
with other treaties **77,** 633, **93,** 80-3, 84, 85, 107, 112
within treaty **83,** 133
constitution, compatibility **104,** 96, **108,** 646
context. *See* aids, context *above*

contra proferentem **45,** 395, 407, 411, 424, **68,** 558, **75,** 210, 216, 218, 261, **84,** 493, **102,** 97
contract law **92,** 731
customary international law, provision deviating from **40,** 117, 127
effectiveness **45,** 431, **59,** 570, **62,** 422, 424, 428, 551-3, 558, **68,** 619, **82,** 589-90, **90,** 423-4, 426, **92,** 121-2, **93,** 452, 627, **94,** 535, **97,** 500, 645, **100,** 24-5, **102,** 60, 100, **106,** 440, **114,** 268, **120,** 235, **121,** 65, 67
avoidance of redundancy **62,** 603, **68,** 620, 634-5, 637
every element of treaty to be given effect **106,** 439, 446
useful effect **75,** 183
words to be given some meaning **110,** 590
eiusdem generis **57,** 257, **71,** 652, 659-60, **74,** 484, 536, 552, 585, 588, 602, 610, **78,** 572, **90,** 188, **124,** 486, 487-8, 501
emendation **52,** 157-61
European legal tradition **93,** 459
exception from rule **57,** 190-1, **62,** 428, **99,** 511-12, 517
exceptiones sunt strictissimae interpretationis **41,** 178
expressio unius est exclusio alterius **45,** 433, **54,** 316-17, **87,** 151
fairness **106,** 440, 443, 445
finality of boundaries **91,** 453
formalism, avoidance **83,** 135
general international purpose **90,** 162
general meaning **85,** 82
generalia specialibus non derogant **52,** 142, **105,** 56, **106,** 481-2, 486, 550
Admissions Case **106,** 482
Payment of Various Serbian Loans Issued in France **106,** 482
good faith **47,** 422, 451, **57,** 217, **59,** 569, **62,** 568-9, 605-6, **72,** 533, 683, **75,** 202, 206, 208-9, 217-19, **77,** 661, **79,** 357, **82,** 644, **96,** 397, **97,** 645, **100,** 20-1, 69-72, **105,** 24-5, **123,** 415-16, **124,** 15
balance of reciprocal obligations, presumption of **100,** 70-2
pacta sunt servanda and **100,** 69
UN Charter **100,** 69-70
Vienna Convention on the Law of Treaties (1969) **87,** 153, **100,** 69-71, **101,** 379, **114,** 372, **124,** 15
grammatical structure **40,** 449, 451, 461, **41,** 301, **44,** 302, **45,** 409, 423, **102,** 307
punctuation **77,** 672
hierarchy **92,** 111
human rights, protection **101,** 245-6, **104,** 95-6, **115,** 344
human rights treaty status and **123,** 40, 65, 604
implicit assumptions **90,** 682
'in conformity with applicable laws and regulations' **84,** 356-7
independence of each provision **114,** 379-80
'integral' **84,** 402-3
integration principle **37,** 192, 337, **68,** 620. *See also* treaty as a whole *below*
international law
determining factor **87,** 348, 353
in the light of **83,** 133. *See also* aids, general principles of international law *above*
'written in' **106,** 446
internationally acceptable meaning **84,** 734, 745
language of treaty **68,** 300-6, 339-42, 378-9, 388-96, 419-24, 454-6, 497-8, **83,** 132, **90,** 682, **91,** 522, **93,** 18, 81, 84, 106, 111, 112, 600, **95,** 363
variation **96,** 118

treaty interpretation (*cont.*)
liberal **43,** 239, 242, **74,** 578-9, 611, 670, 674, **83,** 184, **85,** 140, **104,** 473, **107,** 454, **108,** 159, 161, **114,** 373, 627
'historical approach' and **83,** 189
literal **37,** 51, 79-80, 111, 167, **40,** 70, 449, 451, 461, **45,** 425, 426, **48,** 359, 379, 405, **61,** 640-3, **83,** 144, 146, 147, 191, 192, **93,** 280, **94,** 520, **101,** 601-2. *See also* ordinary meaning *below*
as living instrument. *See* subsequent changes, need to reflect *below*
maintenance of friendly relations **90,** 380, 384
minimization of risk of dispute **41,** 228
multilingual texts **122,** 109-10
natural and ordinary meaning **41,** 126, 131, 227, **52,** 157, **82,** 548-50, 612, 616, 620, 621, 644, **92,** 45-6, 54, 77, 78, 111-13, 160
absence of **38,** 228-31
normal legal meaning **69,** 303
object and purpose **47,** 422, 451, **49,** 20, **57,** 229-30, 293, **59,** 540-1, 549-50, 552-6, 569, **61,** 415, 417, 420-1, **62,** 74, 361, 422, 424, 429, 433-4, 438, 441, 474, 476, 480, 490, 498, 506, 556, 600, 606, **67,** 566-71, **68,** 536-7, 545-6, 555, 615-16, 635, **70,** 313, 447-8, 466, 471, **72,** 533, 683, 685, 694, 698, 700-1, 704-5, 708, **73,** 491, 509, 543, 560, **74,** 552, 588, 608, 624, 650, 670, 672, 674, **75,** 67, 187-8, 196, 208-10, 523, **76,** 118, 247, 286, 346, 873-4, **77,** 407-9, 661, 665, **78,** 652, 654, **79,** 292, 329, 334, **82,** 615, **83,** 132, 142-3, 146, 147, 184, **84,** 267, 279, 404-6, **85,** 321, **86,** 495, **90,** 379, 380, 682, **92,** 108, 112, 122-7, 151, 159-60, 571-2, 687, **93,** 18, 85, 458, 600, **95,** 253-4, 371, 586-7, **96,** 397, **97,** 634-5, 639, 645, **99,** 418, **100,** 21, 60-4, 186-7, **101,** 242, 314, 390, 598, **102,** 60, 62, **103,** 646-7, 660-1, **104,** 433, **105,** 25, 43, **106,** 445, **107,** 420-1, **110,** 575, 576, 588, 770, **114,** 30, **119,** 633, 653-4, **121,** 105-6, 179, **122,** 288-9, 327, 348, 383. *See also* spirit and purpose *below*
ancillary clauses **99,** 369
boundary treaties **100,** 62
Chorzów Factory **92,** 123
clash of purposes **82,** 615
conflicting objectives **110,** 368
of implementing legislation **103,** 578
interest reipublicae ut sit finis litium **92,** 124-5
Law of the Sea Convention (1982) **119,** 563, 565
motivation of parties distinguished **38,** 220-1, **100,** 62
ordinary international meaning **78,** 509, **85,** 321
ordinary meaning **37,** 17, 24, 167, 188, 192, 201, 337, 499, **38,** 218, 229-30, **40,** 451-3, **41,** 126, 227, **45,** 119, 163, 395, **75,** 210, 212-13, 217-18, 259, 423, 483, 523, **79,** 292, 329, 334, 343, 469, **81,** 329, **82,** 548-50, 612, 616, 644, **84,** 494, **85,** 139, **87,** 153, **89,** 173, **95,** 600, **97,** 499, 634, **100,** 21, 186, **101,** 242, **102,** 62, 111, 117, 293, **103,** 646, **104,** 483, **105,** 25, **106,** 438-9, 443, 445, **107,** 454, **110,** 576, 588, 772, **114,** 30, 372, **119,** 663-5, **120,** 334, **121,** 106, 179, **122,** 328, 372, **125,** 123
in context **47,** 422, **77,** 661, **121,** 106, **122,** 383
equity and **40,** 457-9
plain language **95,** 162, **119,** 565
plain meaning. *See* ordinary meaning *above*
plural usage **122,** 359-60
presence or absence of provision **77,** 665, 670
primary meaning **72,** 697-9

protection of individual **93,** 452
purposive **122,** 358, 540-1, **124,** 486-7
reasonable **74,** 216
reasonable meaning **83,** 133
reasonable result **102,** 60, 77
respect for reciprocal nature of treaty **75,** 183
restrictive **37,** 121-2, **38,** 243, **40,** 256, 458-9, **41,** 284, 295, 303, 308-9, **45,** 396, 418, 423, **62,** 104, 357, 394, 402, 412, 445, 558, 632, 649, **68,** 543, 557-8, **70,** 524, **71,** 653, **72,** 533-4, **74,** 552, 573, 599, **75,** 67, 183, 216-18, 436, **78,** 654, **82,** 98, **83,** 133, 134, **84,** 301, 377, 493, **91,** 272, **92,** 93, **101,** 379
derogation provision **70,** 551
exceptional provisions **40,** 146
redundancy **84,** 301
rules generally accepted by municipal legal systems **82,** 620
rules of statutory interpretation **100,** 435
simplicity **91,** 453, 465-6
social changes, need to reflect **89,** 124, 127, 143, 174, 236, **103,** 645, **124,** 502
spirit and purpose **37,** 17, 76, 337, 408, **62,** 354, **70,** 593, **72,** 443, **82,** 81-2, 84, **92,** 160, **94,** 520, **106,** 445, **120,** 544-5. *See also* object and purpose *above*
spirit and terms **44,** 472
subsequent changes, need to reflect **81,** 72, **89,** 124, 143, 174, 236, **98,** 308, **103,** 645, **123,** 15, 22, 65
teleological **37,** 111, 141-2, 186, 189-90, 192, 194, 195, 203, 281, 408, 430, 442, **38,** 219, 220, 240, **40,** 70, **41,** 284, 303, **43,** 241, **46,** 476, 477, **47,** 171, 182, **49,** 174-5. *See also* international law, teleological approach; object and purpose *above*
terms **57,** 226-7, **62,** 474, 543, 554, 556, 565, **76,** 179
Competence of General Assembly for Admission to UN **41,** 116
terms of agreement **92,** 571
text **90,** 407, **96,** 102, 103, 117, **99,** 142, 524, **102,** 295-6, **110,** 770, 771-2, 786, **114,** 619
treaty as a whole **38,** 228-9, **45,** 394, 405, 434, **47,** 457, **48,** 106, **82,** 621, 665, **89,** 175-6, **97,** 499, 638, 639, **100,** 71-2, **106,** 439-40, 445-6, **110,** 576, **113,** 82, **119,** 411-12, **121,** 119. *See also* integration principle *above*
uniformity **72,** 699-700, **74,** 578-9, 581, 587-8, 594, 601, 603, 611, 615, 619-20, 641, 655-6, 663, 671, **77,** 408, **79,** 669, **107,** 119, 130, 581, **119,** 196, **122,** 540, **124,** 501-2
prior consultation procedure **87,** 86-7
ut res magis valeat quam pereat. See effectiveness *above*
Vienna Convention on the Law of Treaties (1969) **87,** 348
history. *See travaux préparatoires*
ICJ and **92,** 118
inclusio unius est exclusio alterius **49,** 201
individual rights and, most favourable interpretation **75,** 48
International Law Commission Draft Articles on the Law of Treaties **70,** 442
international organizations
constitutions **37,** 497, 540, **62,** 471, 547, 549, 553, 575
Member States' courts' power **77,** 53
international organizations, privileges and immunities, relevance **107,** 4-5
international tribunals, by **56,** 487
intertemporal **49,** 21, **75,** 671-4, **77,** 657, 673, **83,** 45, **92,** 153-4, 157-8
jurisdictional clauses **37,** 115, 117, 164, 292-3

treaty interpretation (*cont.*)
jus cogens/peremptory norm provisions **46,** 486
lacunae. *See* gaps *above*
language **62,** 427, 579
object and intent **78,** 509
law-making **41,** 284, 303, **58,** 524
legal connotations **77,** 662
legal operation **83,** 44
legislation, interpretation distinguished **83,** 133-4, 135
legislative history. *See travaux préparatoires*
methods **49,** 172-5
multilateral **37,** 498, **41,** 431-2, **43,** 257, 258
against drafting party **47,** 438, 444
bilateral distinguished **37,** 498
multilingual **38,** 454, **41,** 283-4, 298, 303, 309, 311, 427, 430-2, 435-6, **43,** 124, 185, **45,** 120, 301, 407-11, 423, **57,** 214-15, 227, **58,** 173, 180, **59,** 105, 529, 548-50, **62,** 623, 633, **67,** 598-9, **70,** 446, 478-9, **71,** 92, **75,** 416, **76,** 69, 117-18, 174, 189-94, 233-5, 237, 249-50, 283-6, **77,** 567-70, **82,** 630 n. 16, 647-8, **84,** 244, 249-50, 268, 377, **86,** 155-6, 157-8, 372-4, **91,** 274-5, **96,** 117-19
ambiguity **74,** 589, 594, 602, 607, 609, 632, 641, 650, 652, 657, 661, 663, 670, 673-4, 678-81, **78,** 626
compatibility of both texts, objective **77,** 568-9
authentic languages
equal authority **94,** 603, **95,** 601 n. 5, **125,** 595
identity of meaning, presumption of **125,** 256-8
to prevail **104,** 209-10
contra proferentem **59,** 549
customary international law **94,** 603
dictionaries, use of **74,** 641, 645, 651-2, 665, 673, 680
contemporaneous **77,** 662-3
discrepancy between texts **92,** 24 n. 1, **96,** 397, **101,** 389-90
Geneva Protocols (1949), First Additional Protocol (1977) **110,** 109-10
Pact of Bogotá (1948) **84,** 244, 249-50, 268
Treaty of Waitangi (1840) **120,** 489-90, 499-502, 519-20, 543-6
drafting language, priority **59,** 529-30, 583-5, **96,** 119
English and French texts compared **45,** 120, 301, **57,** 214-15, 227, **58,** 524, **75,** 416
expert evidence of meaning, necessity for **74,** 590, 593-4, 600, 608, 641, 645, 651-2, 673, 680
foreign language text
primacy **74,** 632, 641, 645, 650, 660, 663, 670-1, 673, 676, 679
recourse to **74,** 552, 583, 586, 589-90, 600, 602, 607-10, 620, 632, 641, 650-4, 665-6, 669-71, 673, 676-81
interpreters, use of **74,** 652, 680
lowest common denominator **59,** 549, 582
non-authentic language **94,** 603
identity of meaning **94,** 603
parallel texts as interpretative aid **101,** 65-6, 323, 324, 325, **119,** 561
relevant national law, relevance **108,** 651
reconciliation **56,** 486
shared expectations of parties **96,** 118-19
Vienna Convention on the Law of Treaties (1969) **94,** 603, **104,** 209-10
municipal law, private law terms **69,** 303
new situation **71,** 117

paragraphs of same article **44,** 477-8, 482
parties' conduct **76,** 119, 170
concessions outside agreement **45,** 403, 404, 407, 426-7
parties' intention **37,** 142-3, 185-7, 194, 203, 204, 225, 228, 230, 307, 337-9, 408, 437, 439, 442, 443, **38,** 246, **40,** 454, **63,** 271-3, **70,** 676, **82,** 659, **83,** 132, 184, **90,** 381, 407, **91,** 465, 522, **92,** 54, 78, 93, 100, 116-22, **93,** 600, **97,** 500, **101,** 314, 577, 618, **102,** 294, 295, 297, **107,** 454, **110,** 588-9, **114,** 372-3, **122,** 360
aids to establishing **37,** 187, 190
circumstances of conclusion **77,** 669, 673-4
Constitution **97,** 500-1
context **110,** 580-1
maps **52,** 229-30
municipal law **77,** 465
negotiating position **110,** 587
parliamentary proceedings **60,** 118, 123, 125, **82,** 98, **110,** 587-8
preamble **57,** 216, **92,** 118-19
ratification documentation **77,** 669
statements by parties **52,** 162-3, **56,** 218, 219
subsequent practice **56,** 562, **77,** 666-8
text **97,** 645, **102,** 117, **110,** 580-1
travaux préparatoires. See travaux préparatoires
at time of conclusion **38,** 234-5, **78,** 654, **82,** 624, **83,** 132-3
according to contemporary applicable law **116,** 130-1
Treaty of Waitangi (1840) **120,** 499
in case of agreement based on compromise **37,** 206
change of mind, presumption against **102,** 97-8
common **82,** 98, **102,** 68
'converging will' **75,** 188, 211
ex post facto, relevance **92,** 118-19
express **62,** 507
failure to produce evidence **122,** 382-3
honest performance **40,** 178
implied **62,** 475, 479, 507
'mental reservation' by one party **45,** 396, 418
one party's view **56,** 562, **79,** 371
original signatories **103,** 645-6
presumed **74,** 579-80, 599-600, 609-10, 620, 639
primacy **116,** 88
special meaning of term **120,** 335
tacit **75,** 113
phrases. *See under individual treaties*
preparatory work. *See travaux préparatoires*
presumption against
parties' change of mind **102,** 97-8
racial non-discrimination **68,** 210
sovereignty, limitation on **37,** 121-2, **45,** 395, 407, 411, 424, 426, **78,** 654, **83,** 133, **90,** 380, **92,** 688
presumption of
balance of reciprocal relationship **100,** 70-2
brevity as indication of limited scope **78,** 189
consistency between provisions **121,** 124
municipal jurisdiction, subsumption of **77,** 566
stability of boundaries **100,** 42-3, 47-8

treaty interpretation (*cont.*)
previous practice **43,** 124, 125
principles and rules of
amorphous nature **87,** 153
ICJ jurisprudence **92,** 151
regional treaties, universal treaties compared **75,** 47, 72-3
relevant/special circumstances **62,** 428
reservations **70,** 453, 465, 469-77, **71,** 308-9, **78,** 60-1
context **70,** 470
object and purpose **70,** 469-70, 471, **77,** 605-6, **78,** 60-2, **107,** 20-1, 69-70, 73-5, **110,** 200, 241
ordinary meaning **70,** 470
same rules apply **79,** 292
responsibility. *See also* 'by' entries *above*; right of *below*
change of practice **107,** 56-7, 61-2, **111,** 499
conclusiveness of Order in Council **93,** 632, 635
Constitutional Court **111,** 499-500, 522, 539
fair hearing, effect on **107,** 61-2
separation of powers, relevance **107,** 61-2
restrictions on **79,** 291, 357
revision distinguished **37,** 142, 160, 189-90, 192, 193, 195, 204, 281-2, 443, **83,** 45, **110,** 772, **116,** 132, 137, **120,** 246
scope and effects distinguished **82,** 66, 74-5
selectiveness in application of principles of **83,** 147
sovereignty, limitation on **37,** 121-2
Special Agreement, normal rules to apply
UN Conference on the Law of Treaties **97,** 644
Vienna Convention on the Law of Treaties (1969) **97,** 644-5
specialis derogant generalibus **62,** 600-1
supplementation of terms **68,** 551
international organizations **62,** 475-6, 480, 487-8, 490, 495, 510
systematic **44,** 483, 485
title **52,** 131
travaux préparatoires. See travaux préparatoires
underlying rules **71,** 119
unilateral **97,** 555, **105,** 43
Treaty of Waitangi (1840). *See* New Zealand, Treaty of Waitangi (1840); New Zealand, Treaty of Waitangi Act 1975
treble damages action. *See* damages, punitive
Trident missiles. *See* nuclear weapons, deployment
Trieste, Free Territory of
Allied Military Government, powers **40,** 44-8, 50
Memorandum of Agreement (1954) **77,** 629
Osimo Treaty (1975) **77,** 628
Peace Treaty with Italy (1947) **77,** 628
rights over
administrative **77,** 628-9
belligerent occupying power **77,** 629
retroactive **77,** 630
sovereign **40,** 43-50, **77,** 629-30
Trinidad and Tobago
American Convention on Human Rights (1969)
denunciation **123,** 513-14, 527

ratification **123,** 512-16
Constitution 1976
as continuance of earlier Constitutions **123,** 527
human rights and **90,** 546, **123,** 542
rights created after coming into force of jurisdiction **123,** 517-18, 519
s 4(a) (due process). *See* due process *below*
s 4(a) (right to life). *See* death penalty *below*
s 5(2)(b) (cruel or unusual treatment or punishment). *See* death row as inhuman or degrading treatment *below*
s 14 (remedies for breach of Constitution) **123,** 526
Privy Council role **123,** 526
death penalty
appeal to international bodies
constitutional right **123,** 516-21, 525-32, 549-51
suspension of execution during **123,** 540-9
commutation
breach of constitutional rights and **123,** 524
reinstatement following appeal **123,** 524-5
Instructions relating to applications [to Inter-American Commission and UN Human Rights Commission] from persons under sentence of death **123,** 513-16, 531-2
proportionality **123,** 516, 531-2
reference to Privy Council, applicable law **123,** 526
death row as inhuman or degrading treatment
conditions of detention **123,** 523-4, 533-4, **124,** 277-8
delay before trial **123,** 521-3, 533
delay caused by appeal, relevance **123,** 521-3
repeated reading of death warrant **123,** 550-1
time-limits **124,** 268-9
due process
access to international appellate bodies as right under municipal law **123,** 518-19, 530-1, 551-4
on grounds not provided for under Constitution **123,** 531
applicable law **123,** 527, 530
right to complete legal processes **123,** 518-19
rule of law and **123,** 516-17
separation of powers and **123,** 516-17
Inter-American Court of Human Rights, compulsory jurisdiction, death penalty reservation **123,** 512-13
International Covenant on Civil and Political Rights (ICCPR) (1966) and Optional Protocol
accession to **123,** 512
denunciation **123,** 513-14, 527
legitimate expectation, treaty, ratification and, right of individual under ratified but unincorporated treaty **123,** 520-1, 527-30
personal liberty, failure to bring promptly before a competent court **123,** 542
separation of powers
due process and **123,** 516-17
treaties **123,** 520-1, 526
treaties
implementing legislation, need for **123,** 517-19, 526-30
ratification, executive responsibility **123,** 520-1
Tripartite Commission for the Restitution of Monetary Gold 44, 448-9, 453, 455, 457, 459, 461, 466-70, 471-2, 483, 484

Tripartite Commission for the Restitution of Monetary Gold (*cont.*)
gold, control of, governmental action, whether **63,** 71-2
individual's right to demand payment from **63,** 71-3
State immunity, execution/attachment in respect of gold held by **63,** 71-2
Tripolitanian Furrow 83, 102
Trucial States. *See also* United Arab Emirates (UAE)
boundary disputes between **57,** 21
status **57,** 24, 31, 34-6
Truman Proclamation (1945) 41, 62, 77, 82-3, 86, 113, 118, 119, 127 n. 1, 128, 145, 150, 158, 164, 167, 220, **51,** 139-40, **64,** 336, **67,** 36, 85, 114, 117, 167, 177, **71,** 105-6, 120, 138-9
Canadian reaction **71,** 106, 138-9, **74,** 145, 210
customary law, declaratory of **41,** 77
equitable principles **41,** 62, 86, **81,** 391, **99,** 623
relevant/special circumstances and **81,** 274
trust, holding of sovereign in during colonial period **50,** 471
Trust Territories. *See also* Marshall Islands; Northern Mariana Islands; Pacific Trust Territory; Palau; Trusteeship; Trusteeship Agreement; Trusteeship agreements; Trusteeship system
Administering Authority
Administrator, independent legal personality, whether **97,** 25, 46
exclusive authority of single member to administer **97,** 18, 25, 45-50
as joint authority **97,** 24-6, 93, 106-9
joint and several liability, whether **97,** 25, 50-3
Trusteeship Agreement determining factor **97,** 41, 45-6, 47
'partner governments' **97,** 106-9
rights and duties **61,** 91, 98, 100-1, 123-5, 129-30, 133-9
State immunity, jurisdiction **61,** 91
task
governmental function, whether **96,** 28
nurture towards self-government **96,** 2, 28
Administration and Administering State, relationship between **40,** 37-40
authority over. *See also* sovereignty *below*
limitation **87,** 567-8, **96,** 28
vested in UN **96,** 27
dispute relating to
jurisdiction
General Assembly **97,** 13
UN, limited to **97,** 72, 89
UN Trusteeship Council **97,** 13
termination of Trusteeship and **97,** 13, 20
government as agency of Administering Authority **61,** 106-9, 111-12, 123-5, 127, 133-4, **96,** 27-9
inhabitants
resettlement **97,** 73-4
right to participation in administration **97,** 72
jurisdiction **87,** 549, 550-2, **96,** 38
law of, US laws, applicability **96,** 37-8
specific extension, need for **96,** 27, 30-1
legislation and Agreement, conflict **48,** 26-30
legislative power **87,** 550. *See also* law of *above*
objectives of system **97,** 71-2

rehabilitation of worked-out phosphate lands
discharge of obligation, termination of Trusteeship **97,** 20
discussions relating to **97,** 72-91
UN, within **97,** 79-91
reservation of claim, need for **97,** 78
reservation of rights, need for **97,** 20, 89
transfer of claim to former Trust Territory, need for **97,** 89
Trusteeship Agreement as basis of obligation **97,** 49
waiver of claim **97,** 13, 14-17
clear and unequivocal communication, need for **97,** 14
express **97,** 15
implied **97,** 14-15, 78
pre-independence **97,** 14, 15-17
separate legal entity test **40,** 38
sovereignty **61,** 92-4, 95-6, 98-9, 107-12, 123-8, **64,** 547-8, **87,** 563-4, 578, **96,** 29-30. *See also* authority over *above*
quasi **96,** 28, 37-8
State immunity, jurisdiction, entitlement **61,** 28-30, 93-100, 126, 128-9, 132, 133, 138, **64,** 546-9, 563
Administering Authority **61,** 91
government **61,** 91, 94, 99, 100
Northern Mariana Islands **87,** 548-9, **96,** 38-9
US government **96,** 40-1, 42
State immunity, jurisdiction, waiver **87,** 615-17, 633-5
status **61,** 94, 96-9, 107-8, 125-6, 132, **64,** 546-8, 565, **84,** 203-5, **87,** 548, 551-2, 558, 559-64, 577-8
'foreign country' **87,** 578, **96,** 37
free association **87,** 578, 581, 654
government of **61,** 93, 94, 99, 118, 123, 125-6, 132-3
independent entity **87,** 552, 581
recognition **64,** 565, **87,** 581
self-governing commonwealth **87,** 568
sovereignty. *See* sovereignty *above*
State of US distinguished **87,** 551
termination **87,** 654
agreement, by **87,** 547, 605-6
UN approval, need for **87,** 606, 607
territory or possession of US, 'like' **96,** 29-30, 37, 38
US laws, applicability **87,** 561-2, 563, 568
Strategic Trust Territory **37,** 149, 208, **87,** 606. *See also* Palau
Security Council and **87,** 606-7
termination of Trusteeship
breach of Trusteeship, effect on **97,** 17-20
date of, General Assembly resolution **97,** 18
as discharge of obligations **97,** 20
settlement of dispute **97,** 13, 20
treaties, applicability to **97,** 47
trustee
rights to trust property **46,** 107
tests of conduct **37,** 555
Trusteeship. *See also* Trust Territories; Trusteeship Agreements; Trusteeship system
termination **40,** 36-7, **44,** 36-7, **49,** 206, 273

Trusteeship Agreements. *See also* Japanese Mandated Islands, Trusteeship Agreement for; Trust Territories; Trusteeship; Trusteeship system
breach, termination of Trusteeship, estoppel, whether **97,** 17-20
compliance, UN responsibility to ensure **97,** 72
conclusion **49,** 33-4, 182, 187, 237, 243
drafting **37,** 536-9
individual's rights under **81,** 514
judicially enforceable rights under **96,** 38-9
monetary damages, right to **96,** 38-9
jurisdictional clauses **37,** 282-3, 410, 536
legal character **97,** 44
legal nature **37,** 130
legislation, conflict with **48,** 26-30
liability of Administering Authority, determined by **97,** 41
limitations imposed by **87,** 567-8, 606-7
non-discrimination norm **37,** 454
obligation to negotiate **37,** 23, 40-1, 43-4, 54, 155-61, 233, 304, 329, 442, **49,** 333-4
obligations
nature of **61,** 124-5, 129-30, 133-8
rehabilitation of worked-out land **97,** 49
parties, Security Council **87,** 605, 606-7
revocation clause, absence **49,** 268
rights, nature **61,** 91, 92, 99-100, 118, 129-30, 134-8, 139-41
termination **40,** 36-7, **44,** 36-7, **87,** 549, 560, 563, 654, **96,** 36
as treaty **96,** 38
Trusteeship system 37, 39-41, 54, 64, 155, 208-9, 434. *See also* Trust Territories; Trusteeship agreements
annual reports **37,** 410
ICJ and **37,** 201
mandated territories and **37,** 155-61, 164, 304, 329, 441, 572
Mandates system, as successor to **37,** 441
objectives **49,** 3, 23, 25, 182
Temporary Trusteeship Committee **37,** 214, 215, 317-18, 489
Trusteeship Council
composition **37,** 311, 441
creation **37,** 157
functions **37,** 282
recommendations **37,** 364
SW Africa, discussions **37,** 333
UN, Member of, rights **37,** 283
UN General Assembly
powers **37,** 149, 208, 282, 410-11
recommendations **37,** 364, 410
Trusteeship Territories, US strategic trusteeship **37,** 536
tuna, measures to protect 117, 163-4, 168-9, 179-80, 185-6, 191-3
Convention for the Conservation of Southern Bluefin Tuna (1993) **117,** 161-2, 182-4
dispute settlement provisions (Art. 16)
agreement to alternative dispute settlement procedure with binding effect (UNCLOS Art. 282), whether **119,** 529
Antarctic Treaty (1959) compared **119,** 552

parallel methods **119,** 555-6, 559-61
'peaceful means of settlement' under **119,** 550-2
EFP (Experimental Fishing Programme) **119,** 515-21, 545-6, 547
exclusion of compulsory procedures entailing binding provisions, whether **119,** 551-4, 557-65
Law of the Sea Convention (1982) **117,** 161-2, 182-4, **119,** 521-4, 546-9
continuing obligations under UNCLOS **119,** 548-9, 560-1
UNCLOS obligations extending beyond CCSBT **119,** 549
TAC (total allowable catch) **119,** 515, 517
Japanese attempts to increase **119,** 519-21, 547
text **119,** 515-24

Tunisia
conquest **46,** 465 n. 8
French courts in, abolition **44,** 33-4
French protectorate **44,** 1-2
law of
Fishery Control Decree 1951 **67,** 60-1
Law 62-35 (1962) **67,** 60-1
Law 63-49 (1963) **67,** 61, 67
Law 73-49 (1973) **67,** 67, 132, 308-9
Nationality Code **48,** 162-3
Libya, continental shelf delimitation **71,** 93-4, 102, 115, 120-1, 137, 151-5, 163, 181, 183, 188-9, 199
nationalization measures **47,** 63-6
riots, 1952/6, compensation law **44,** 33
separate legal entity test **39,** 460
State responsibility for protection of individuals **44,** 1-2, 32-3
territorial sea **67,** 60-4, 67-8, 131-2, 203, 308-11

Turkey
Armenian massacres, representations **37,** 83
central/State-owned bank, classification as, separate legal entity test **65,** 422-3
Constitution 1961
treaty-making power **42,** 250-9
Constitution 1982
Art. 2 **122,** 411
Art. 3(1) **122,** 411
Art. 6 **122,** 411
Art. 10(1) **122,** 411
Art. 14(1) **122,** 412
Art. 66(1) **122,** 412
Art. 68 **122,** 412
Art. 69 **122,** 412-13
Cyprus, northern part of. *See also* Cyprus, Turkish Federated State; Cyprus, Turkish Republic of Northern (TRNC)
authority in **62,** 12, 45-7, 57-8, 61, 64, 70, 74, 79
occupation by **73,** 11, 15-17, 19, 27
domestic remedies, effectiveness **62,** 22-3, 56-8, 77-8, 87-8
in Europe, whether **99,** 16
human rights, alleged violation **62,** 9-24, 33, 51-5, 59-62
jurisdiction, scope **62,** 3, 32-4, 44, 51, 54, 75, 85-6
law of
Banking Law 1958 **47,** 231-2

Turkey (*cont.*)
Commercial Code 1956 **47,** 230-1
Law 2820 (regulation of political parties)
s 78 **122,** 413
s 80 **122,** 413
s 81 **122,** 413
s 90(1) **122,** 414
s 96(3) **122,** 414
s 101 **122,** 414
s 107(1) **122,** 414
Makina ve Kimya Endustrisi Kurumu **63,** 634-8
minorities, continuance of obligations to **37,** 544
NATO Treaty, implementing treaties **42,** 255, 258-9
Ottoman Bank **47,** 216-32
'Public Law of Europe' and **46,** 483
treaties
conclusion, legislative approval **42,** 249-59
ratification, constitutional requirements **42,** 264-5
Turkiye Garanti Bankasi AS
State immunity, entitlement **65,** 422-4
status **65,** 422-4
United Communist Party of Turkey (TBKP), dissolution, compatibility with European Convention on Human Rights (1950) **122,** 408-32
Turkish Federated State of Cyprus. *See* Cyprus, Turkish Federated State
Turkish Republic of Northern Cyprus (TRNC). *See* Cyprus, Turkish Republic of Northern (TRNC)
tutelage
Roman law **49,** 204
change of guardian **49,** 189
self-interest, absence of **49,** 198

Uganda
Constitution 1966
fundamental rights and freedoms, detainees, rights **70,** 231-2
s 10(2) **70,** 231
s 21(6)(a) **70,** 232
validity **39,** 16-31, 46-50
contract, capacity to conclude, revolutionary movement **103,** 266-7
courts, municipal, role, interpretation of law **103,** 265
diplomatic privileges and immunities, customs duties, goods imported for embassy use **48,** 191-205
electoral law **51,** 1-10
habeas corpus, procedure **39,** 3-9
law of. *See also* Constitution *above*
contract law, common law of England **103,** 265
Criminal Procedure Act, s 30 **70,** 230
Customs Tariff Act 1968 **48,** 193-205
Decree 19 of 1972 **70,** 233
East African Customs Management Act **48,** 193, 198, 202, 205
Emergency (Powers of Arrest and Search) Regulations 1969 **70,** 227-34
Exchange Control Act **66,** 170-2
Expropriated Properties Act 1982 **107,** 465

Legal Notice 1/86 (legalization of revolution), liability for acts of previous government **103,** 266
Ministerial Detention Order, challenge in courts **70,** 231
Penal Code, s 117 (rape) **121,** 270 n. 209
Properties and Businesses (Acquisition) Decree 1972 (Decree No 32) **64,** 211, 219-20
Uganda Citizenship Ordinance 1962 **59,** 463-6
nationality, Uganda Citizenship Ordinance 1962 **59,** 463-6
revolution (1966) **39,** 1-3, 45-6
revolution (1986), competing regimes, relevance, established government in power **103,** 266
State responsibility for acts and omissions during revolution
contract **103,** 266-7
endorsement by new legislature **103,** 266-7
State succession
appointment of Boundary Commissioner **51,** 1-8
continuity of law **103,** 266-7
status, previous legal provisions, effect **51,** 1-8, 25
Umm al Qaiwain (UAQ)
continental shelf **64,** 336-8
as independent State **64,** 341
sovereign status **81,** 524
territorial sea **64,** 336-8, **66,** 176-85, 330-8
UNCITRAL (United Nations Commission on International Trade Law)
Model Law of International Commercial Arbitration (Model Law)
commercial arbitration, definition **119,** 657-9
need for
adoption by parties to dispute **119,** 585
incorporation into domestic law **119,** 585
remission proceedings **125,** 473
Model Law on International Credit Transfers (1992) **117,** 242
Notes on Organizing Arbitral Proceedings
place of arbitration **122,** 254, 255-6
availability and cost of support services **122,** 257
convenience of parties and arbitrators **122,** 256-7, 259
existence of multilateral or bilateral treaty on enforcement of award **122,** 256 n. 8
location of subject matter in dispute and proximity of evidence **122,** 257-8, 259
suitability of law on arbitral procedure **122,** 255-6, 259
UNCITRAL (United Nations Commission on International Trade Law), Rules 62, 587-94, **68,** 515-22, 619, 643-4, **70,** 508, 520, 523, 525
1 **119,** 577
3 **122,** 291
4 **121,** 80
6 **68,** 517
7 **68,** 517
8 **68,** 517
9 **68,** 517-18
10 **68,** 517-18
11 **68,** 517-18
12 **68,** 517-18

UNCITRAL, Rules (*cont.*)
12(1) **121,** 80
13 **121,** 80
15 **68,** 633 n. 4, **85,** 427, **122,** 351
15(1) **119,** 572, 578, 579
16(1) **122,** 253, 258
17 **95,** 189
18 **121,** 80, **122,** 291-2
19 **121,** 80
20 **95,** 204, **122,** 292
21 **85,** 437
21(1) **68,** 621 n. 26
21(2) **68,** 619, 635, 647
21(4) **68,** 612, **122,** 280
24 **68,** 649, **95,** 207
25 **68,** 633 n. 4
26 **71,** 642
28(3) **122,** 350, 351
31 **68,** 650
32 **69,** 624-6, 658, **119,** 580-1
32(1) **119,** 579
32(2) **95,** 222
33(1) **119,** 578
34 **68,** 530-3, 653
36 **95,** 37
37 **95,** 222
38 **95,** 230, **121,** 129
38-40 **95,** 211
40 **95,** 211, **121,** 129
41 **117,** 557
as applicable law **119,** 571-2, 582, 583-6
dispute involving State **119,** 586
NAFTA (North American Free Trade Agreement) (1992), Arbitral Tribunal **121,** 198, **122,** 264, 280, 294 n. 2, 317, 351
need for adoption by parties **119,** 585-6
non-contractual dispute **119,** 586
ICSID Additional Facility provisions distinguished **121,** 197-8
legal dispute, need for **119,** 578
treaty, whether **76,** 95-6
UNCLOS I. *See* United Nations Conference on the Law of the Sea (First) (UNCLOS I)
UNCLOS III. *See* United Nations Conference on the Law of the Sea (Third) (UNCLOS III)
unconditional surrender. *See* war, unconditional surrender
UNCTAD. *See* United Nations Conference on Trade and Development (UNCTAD)
unequal relationships. *See also* treaties, unequal
validity **50,** 412
UNESCO. *See* United Nations Educational, Scientific and Cultural Organization (UNESCO)
UNESCO Protection of the World Cultural and Natural Heritage Convention (1972) **73,** 229
customary international law **106,** 658-9
jus cogens/peremptory norm, whether **106,** 658-9
dispute procedures, absence **68,** 299-300, 394

federal clause **68,** 297-9, 303, 315, 342, 379, 389, 395, 424, 455-6, 496-7, 500
international obligations, effect on **68,** 342, 379, 388, 395, 424, 456
indigenous people's rights under **120,** 415
individual's right to invoke before national courts **120,** 414, 415
interpretation **68,** 303-6, 339-42, 389-96, 419-24, 454
aids
contemporaneous Recommendation **68,** 305-6, 392-4
travaux préparatoires **68,** 303-6, 392, 420-1
natural resources
customary international law, codification of **106,** 658-9
jus cogens/peremptory norm, whether **106,** 658-9
listing under, declaratory effect **106,** 659
obligations **90,** 65-71, 73, 75, 87-8, 128-9, 131, 133, 134, 136
identification of areas for protection **90,** 67, 102, 104, 112, 125-6, 134, **120,** 412-13
imprecise **90,** 94
interim protection **90,** 67, 103, 104
legal duty, whether imposing **68,** 299-306, 315, 339-41, 378-9, 388-96, 398, 414, 419-24, 427, 454-6, 495-8, **120,** 414
property rights, protection of **68,** 299, **90,** 66
proportionality in meeting **90,** 67
protection of identified property **90,** 128-9, 131, 133, 134, 136, **120,** 411-12
statement of political intent **90,** 66
phrases
'buffer zone' **90,** 70-1, 104-5
'cultural heritage' **68,** 275, 298, **73,** 228-9, **90,** 40, 62, 63
'identified property' **68,** 281, 431-4, 457-8, 469-70, **90,** 42, 51, 120-1, 126-8, 136-7, **120,** 412-13
'natural heritage' **68,** 275, 298
'protected area' **90,** 60, 74, 114
'qualifying area' **90,** 62, 74, 79-80
provisions **68,** 290-8
purpose **90,** 110
proportionality and **90,** 97
sovereignty, avoidance of encroachment on **90,** 97, 133
State sovereignty, respect for **68,** 299, 396
World Heritage List **68,** 293-4, 299, 341, 374, 390, 425, 455, 496, **90,** 35, 43-4, 47-8, 129-30, 133, 136-7
criteria **68,** 425-6, **90,** 40-4, 129-30
economic factors **90,** 64
discriminatory, whether **90,** 68-70
duty of care **120,** 416
effect **90,** 130-1, **120,** 413-14
forestry management, effect on **90,** 68-70, 99-100, 113-14, 123-4
justiciability of listing **120,** 413, 416
mining interests, effect on **90,** 44-53
responsibility for decision **120,** 413
unfair competition. *See* competition
unforeseen events 62, 193, 207
UNHCR. *See* United Nations High Commissioner for Refugees (UNHCR)
Unhocomo Island 83, 110, 111, 112
UNHRC. *See* United Nations Human Rights Committee (UNHRC)
UNIFIL. *See* United Nations International Force in the Lebanon (UNIFIL)

Uniform Customs and Practice (ICC). *See* International Chamber of Commerce (ICC), Uniform Customs and Practice (ICC)
unilateral declaration/undertaking 37, 67-8, 72, 117, 119, 328, **57,** 405-7, 409, 412-17, 455, 518-20, 593-7, **67,** 59-62, 76-7, 89, 132, 148, 172-3, 312-13, **82,** 633-4, 637, **101,** 585. *See also* International Court of Justice (ICJ), compulsory jurisdiction, acceptance, unilateral nature
authority to give **106,** 371
binding nature **41,** 117, 129-32, **83,** 195-6, **100,** 56, **105,** 52-5, **106,** 370-5
Nuclear Tests **106,** 19
commitment to accept unilateral submission of dispute to ICJ **95,** 33
customary international law, evidence of **41,** 117-18
Declaration of Consent to deployment of nuclear missiles **106,** 370-5
effect **57,** 412-13, 467-8, **76,** 76, 177, 464-7, 718-19, **77,** 441-2, **78,** 191
erga omnes **106,** 27
third parties and **50,** 5
ICJ proceedings, outside **106,** 27
'Ihlen declaration' **50,** 377-9
integral part of treaty, relevance **106,** 371
interpretation **41,** 131
as legal clarification **106,** 371
legal consequences **80,** 477-8
Chorzów Factory **80,** 534
intentions **80,** 478
Nicaragua **80,** 478
Nuclear Tests **80,** 478
legislative consent, need for **106,** 370-5, 388
customary international law **106,** 371-2
State practice **106,** 371-2
opposability **46,** 362, 363, **71,** 119
oral, desirability of written confirmation **99,** 20
Rhodesia, Unilateral Declaration of Independence (UDI) **68,** 3-6
right to modify **84,** 296
State practice, evidence of **41,** 119, 136, 158, 190, 208-9, 212-15
Vienna Convention on the Law of Treaties (1969) **106,** 371
Union of England and Scotland
Act of Parliament of Scotland ratifying and approving the Treaty of Union with England 1707/Act of Union with Scotland Act 1706 **59,** 481-2
amendment by Parliament of Great Britain, right of **124,** 579-80
Art. III **124,** 582
amendment **124,** 580
devolution and **124,** 580
Art. V **124,** 589
Art. XVIII **124,** 583
Art. XXII
amendment, inevitability **124,** 584
entrenched, whether **124,** 580-1, 590-2, 593
legislation (House of Lords Bill 1999) removing right of hereditary peers to sit in Lords and **124,** 578-99
Peerage Act (UK) 1963 and **124,** 579-80, 583, 589, 595-6
provision for Scottish peers to sit in House of Lords of United Kingdom **124,** 579
repeal of Article XXII of Act of 1707 by Statute Law Revision (Scotland) Act 1964 **124,** 580, 583

representative status of elected peers **124,** 584-5, 594-5, 596-9
text **124,** 593
Art. XXIII **124,** 597
assent of Queen Anne to Scottish Act, relevance **124,** 582
differing dates of adoption of Gregorian Calendar and **124,** 588-9
Statute Law (Repeals) Act 1993 **124,** 596
as common market **124,** 597-8
history **124,** 581-6, 588-9
negotiation and signature of articles of union (22 July 1706) **124,** 582, 588
personal union **124,** 588
treaty in international law relating to, whether **124,** 580, 582, 583-4, 589-92
Union with Scotland (Amendment) Act 1707 **124,** 595
Union of Soviet Socialist Republics (USSR)
abolition of nobility **72,** 439-45
aliens, rights **42,** 3-4
Bessarabia, occupation of **44,** 336
boundaries, Gulf of Finland, Agreements **41,** 160
citizenship **72,** 440
commercial/trade representation/mission
applicable law, *lex loci contractus* **64,** 592-4
status
diplomatic mission **64,** 591
private merchant **64,** 591-3
State organ **64,** 592-3
treaty provision **64,** 590-3
Constitution 1936
Art. 6 **64,** 537-8
Art. 126 **63,** 132
copyright, effect abroad **39,** 431-2
Council of People's Commissars
Decree No 11 **66,** 210-11
Decree No 245 **66,** 210-11
courts, municipal, separate legal entity test **86,** 566, 567, 574
Culture, Ministry of **63,** 229-32
debt securities, uncollectability **84,** 164
diplomatic privileges and immunities
commercial/trade representation/missions **64,** 590-2, **65,** 179-80, 187
violation **77,** 274-5
equity **41,** 144
FRG, Eastern Treaties **78,** 184-93
GDR. *See also* German Democratic Republic (GDR), Soviet occupation
agent of, whether **43,** 23, 32, 37-9
recognition of **43,** 32, 40, 44, 47, 57, 68-9, 71
Hungary, occupation of, expropriation of industrial enterprises **72,** 84-5
international law, breach, admission of **77,** 275
Intourist **63,** 320-30
jurisdiction provisions in treaties with Germany **45,** 74-5
Kunashiri Island, sovereignty over **59,** 343
law of. *See also* Constitution 1936 *above*
Civil Code 1922, aliens' rights **42,** 3-4
Civil Law Principles 1962, aliens' rights **42,** 4
Criminal Code **77,** 274

Union of Soviet Socialist Republics (USSR) (*cont.*)
Diplomatic and Consular Representations of Foreign States on the Territory of the USSR Statute 1966 **77,** 274
Merchant Shipping Act **65,** 106-7
Trade Delegations and Commercial Agencies of the USSR 1933, status and functions of trade delegations **64,** 590, 593-4
League of Nations, expulsion **37,** 208
Mandates, statement on supervision of (1947) **37,** 336
membership **85,** 58
Merchant Fleet, immunity, jurisdiction **40,** 84-5
nationality
de facto and de jure **72,** 438
loss or deprivation of **72,** 437-42, **83,** 388
nationalization measures, application by foreign courts **47,** 72-4
obligations
enforceability **84,** 182
repudiation **84,** 178, 179-85
Potsdam Agreements, cession of confiscated assets **72,** 84
press agencies **63,** 129-34
real property, ownership rights **42,** 7
recognition **84,** 162-4
by USA **42,** 32, 203
effect **84,** 176-7, 179 n. 11
nullification of obligations of predecessor government **84,** 180
territorial and extraterritorial distinguished **84,** 181
non-recognition, effect **74,** 101
retroactive **84,** 177-8, 182 n. 14
right to sue and be sued, relevance **84,** 176
revolutionary government
powers **72,** 440-2
service of process on **63,** 232
shipping line, status **64,** 537-8, **65,** 69-70, 102-7, **87,** 103-5
ships
commercial use of **65,** 102, 104-5, 368-9
immunity **63,** 39-40, **65,** 101-5, 259-61, 365-6
State agency/State-owned corporation/State entity
classification
commercial/trade representation/mission **64,** 590-3
shipping line **64,** 537-8, **65,** 69-70, 102-7, **87,** 103-5
State Concert Society **63,** 229-32
State corporation
legal personality, evidence of **87,** 104-5
regulations governing **87,** 105
State immunity, jurisdiction
commercial activities and **64,** 595
treaty provision, dependence on **64,** 594-5
State immunity, jurisdiction, entitlement, State agency/State-owned corporation/State entity **72,** 165
State immunity, jurisdiction, theory/doctrine
basis, reciprocity **64,** 595
development of concept **64,** 646-7, 705
State immunity, jurisdiction, waiver, treaty provision **64,** 593-4
transboundary nuclear pollution, responsibility for **86,** 565-70, 572-4

treaties
primacy **77,** 274
suspension **47,** 240
Turkey, Commercial Agreements with **42,** 264-5
union of States 51, 24, **91,** 302-4, 305, 306-7. *See also* dispute settlement, dissolution of union of States, disputes arising from; federal State; Indian States, merger; State succession, merger of States; States, creation, merger; Union of England and Scotland
Albania/Italy **40,** 29-32, 35
alliance **91,** 312
dissolution **91,** 306, 307
establishment **91,** 306
sovereign decision of constituent members **91,** 305
evidence of **91,** 307
acceptance of treaty obligations **91,** 313
UN membership **91,** 313
fusion distinguished **91,** 312-13
personal
Denmark/Iceland **91,** 304
Norway/Sweden **91,** 304-5
real distinguished **91,** 304
real **91,** 303-4, 312
alliance distinguished **91,** 312
personal distinguished **91,** 304
single external personality **91,** 303-4, 307
secession distinguished **91,** 313
United Arab Emirates (UAE)
Arab Monetary Fund. *See* Arab Monetary Fund (AMF)
boundaries **91,** 550-71
applicable law **91,** 585-90
consent, need for **91,** 566-71
Dubai/Sharjah **91,** 549-701
duress and **91,** 568-71
economic coercion **91,** 569-71
Louth Agreement (1910) **91,** 604-6
protest and **91,** 612, 620-5, 627, 631, 648-9
seabed **91,** 570-1
Tripp decisions **91,** 563-5, 583
arbitral, whether **91,** 571-80, 585, 681-3
binding nature **91,** 5, 578-9, 583, 585. *See also res judicata*, whether *below*
consensual, whether **91,** 566-71
implementation **91,** 585
justification *a postiore* **91,** 577
legal status **91,** 566-80, 583-5
res judicata, whether **91,** 572. *See also* binding nature *above*
UK, role **91,** 558-65
unilateral imposition **91,** 567
Constitution 1971 **83,** 257-8, 267
s 96 **91,** 586
treaties **85,** 4-5
emirates
emir, recognition of **91,** 612
international status **91,** 567
federal State **91,** 585-7, 593

United Arab Emirates (UAE) (*cont.*)
General Treaty of Peace (1820) **91,** 559-60
historical survey **91,** 558-65
law of
Constitution. *See* Constitution 1971 *above*
Federal Decree No 35 (1977) (Arab Monetary Fund) **83,** 257-8, 267, **85,** 5, 7, 10, 24
treaties
binding nature, procedures **83,** 257-8, 267, 270
Constitution **85,** 4-5
part of law, whether **83,** 269-70
publication, need for **83,** 270
United Arab Republic (UAR)
creation **64,** 395, 411-12
status **91,** 302-4, 312-14
successor to Egypt, whether **64,** 409, 427
United Kingdom
abuse of power, delay in producing evidence **85,** 107-8
abuse of process
breach of bargain **95,** 392, 406
evidence improperly obtained **95,** 407
extradition **119,** 251
forcible abduction and **95,** 406, **111,** 556, 561-3
forensic process, whether limited to **95,** 405-6
improper purpose **118,** 591-2
injustice and **95,** 406
judicial role **95,** 390-5
access to courts
non-disclosure of evidence and **119,** 277, 307
reasonable cause of action, need for **118,** 345-8, 362-4, 586, 591
act of State **44,** 359-92, **64,** 254-60, **66,** 108, 210-11, 228, **87,** 185-6
act committed abroad **64,** 343-4. *See also* territorial limitation *below*
British subjects outside British territory **44,** 364-70, 374, 379, 387-9, 391, **64,** 259
immunity in own courts **121,** 202
act of individual officer, ratification **44,** 370
act involving own nationals **44,** 364-70, 374, 379, 387-9, 391, **57,** 39-40, **64,** 259, **70,** 42
acta jure imperii/*acta jure gestionis* distinguished, relevance of distinction **64,** 258
applicability
high seas **64,** 264
territorial dispute **64,** 280, 292-4, 303, 343-4, 348-51
basis, equality of States **64,** 260-1
burden of proof **64,** 264-5, 380-1
classification as
breach of contract **64,** 266
hostage-taking **119,** 96
public act **64,** 383
quasi-contractual obligation, repudiation **64,** 266
torture **119,** 96
commercial activities **81,** 722, **103,** 358
common law doctrine **119,** 94
court's right to raise *proprio motu* **64,** 267
criminal law and **44,** 387

as a defence **64,** 380-1, **103,** 408
definition **44,** 368-9, 371, 373, 383-4, **119,** 74
foreign policy considerations **116,** 574-8
international organizations, acts of Member States **80,** 164-5
judicial abstention and **103,** 409-10
judicial restraint **64,** 279-80, 344-51, **119,** 74, 92, **124,** 563-4, **125,** 645, 650-7
jurisprudence
Buttes Gas and Oil Co. v. *Hammer* **64,** 257-8, 261-2, **111,** 594, 595-6, 597, 601, 603, **116,** 556, 568-70, 575-8, **119,** 63, 74, 91, 95, **125,** 639-40, 655-7, 683-4, 709-10, 718
Duke of Brunswick v. *King of Hanover* **64,** 255-6, 345-6
I° Congreso del Partido **64,** 258, **111,** 594, 596-7, 602
Kamachee Boye case **64,** 265, 346
Luther v. *Sagor* **64,** 256-7, 263, 264, **116,** 565-7, 570-1, 587-9, **125,** 638-9
Princess Paley Olga v. *Weisz* **64,** 257, **116,** 570-1, 588
justiciability and **80,** 124, 177, 201-2, 205, **81,** 700-1, 721-2, **83,** 259, **103,** 406-10, **116,** 568-78, 594, **119,** 73-4, 90-3, 95-6, **125,** 633-57, 709-10, 718-22
as preferred term **119,** 78
nationality, relevance **125,** 633-57
public policy and **64,** 266, **119,** 106-7
recognition **116,** 568-78
compatibility with international law, courts' competence to examine **116,** 571-2, 589-91, 595
non-cognizance rule **44,** 384, 387-8, 389
recognition of foreign law and **64,** 344, **88,** 306, **116,** 568-78
relevant factors
level of decision **64,** 381
motivation **64,** 381
public interest/good and **64,** 200-1, 206-7, 208
requirements, authorization **64,** 381
sovereign activity **111,** 603
State immunity, jurisdiction and **64,** 254-60, **80,** 124, 164, 205, **103,** 356-8, **119,** 73-4, 240
distinction **57,** 39, **63,** 153, 187-9, **64,** 255, 258, 260
territorial limitation **64,** 259, 382, **119,** 95-6
act within own territory **125,** 633, 650
waiver, possibility of **64,** 266-7
administrative law, discretionary powers, exercise in furtherance of purpose for which granted **117,** 486-9
admiralty jurisdiction **55,** 440-1, **77,** 66, **78,** 570-2, 685, 689-94, **90,** 293-6
basis **72,** 3-4
foreign ship, action *in rem* against **64,** 186-93, 234, **72,** 2-10
universality **78,** 570
agency
authority of **80,** 46
evidence of **80,** 46, 113
implied **80,** 43-4
international organization, whether **80,** 46, 53, 110-21, 177-9
undisclosed principal **80,** 115-16
State immunity and **80,** 120
Air Council, status **81,** 706
air transport, international, regulation of **74,** 45-87

United Kingdom (*cont.*)
airports, landing fees, sanctions for non-payment **78,** 521-6
aliens **86,** 222. *See also* refugees *below*
arranged marriages **61,** 261-6
British Nationality Act 1948. *See* law of, British Nationality Act 1948 *below*
illegal entry **61,** 251-60, 261-6, **79,** 645, 649-50
refugee status and **79,** 648
Immigration Act 1971. *See* law of, Immigration Act 1971 *below*
Immigration Rules. *See* law of, Immigration Rules *below*
judicial review **79,** 647
nationality, deprivation of, non-recognition **72,** 449, 453-7, 459-60, 467-70
Pakistani nationals **61,** 267-75
right of entry **79,** 648, 660-1, 663
executive power to determine **79,** 663
temporary admission **79,** 651
war burdens and **61,** 164, 166, 173-8
allegiance
Blackstone on **39,** 248, 314-16, 323, 388
British passport holders **55,** 492, 494
Hume on **39,** 316-17
ambassador/head of mission, status, agent of sending State **64,** 442-4
Amnesty International Charity Limited, effect of relationship with on impartiality requirement **119,** 113-35
Anglo-Egyptian Agreement on Compensation 1971
interpretation **60,** 115-18, 123, 125
Hansard and **60,** 118, 123, 125
'Anton Pillar' order
audi alteram partem and **89,** 281
execution **89,** 271-2, 274-7
procedure **89,** 270-1
remedies **89,** 272-3
respect for private life and **89,** 283-9
applicable law **60,** 61-2
choice of forum clause and **118,** 528-39
colonies **72,** 204-8, **123,** 583-4
contract
place where account kept **114,** 472
Rome Convention on the Law Applicable to Contractual Obligations **114,** 472
corporation
domicile **116,** 579
lex fori **85,** 20, 23
place of incorporation **81,** 710-11, **114,** 473
European Commission and non-Member States, relations between **107,** 525-7
Head of State, functions. *See* Head of State, functions, applicable law *below*
International Tin Council (ITC)
constitution **80,** 101-2, 104
contract **80,** 71
debts, liability for **80,** 102
property, *lex situs* **78,** 599, **108,** 592
recognition, State
lex fori **122,** 534-5
private international law **108,** 530, 536-7
refinancing agreement, choice of law clause **118,** 603

stay of proceedings, law of forum **118,** 551
Arab Monetary Fund
recognition **83,** 249, 250
obligation, whether **83,** 248
status **83,** 247-52, 255-72
Arab Monetary Fund Agreement (1976), effect in **83,** 266-7
arbitral award, enforcement **74,** 561-9, **75,** 169-74, **80,** 223
international organization **80,** 57, 120, 213
arbitral tribunal, compensation commission distinguished **103,** 358-60
arbitration. *See also* arbitral award, enforcement *and* arbitration clauses *below*
judicial control of **78,** 582-3
res judicata and **75,** 161-4, 172-5
arbitration clauses, international organization, failure to include **80,** 121
armed forces, homosexuality **112,** 371-412
arranged marriages **61,** 261-6
assets
disclosure of **80,** 213-24
outside the jurisdiction **80,** 214, 222
government undertakings as **80,** 207-8
asylum **79,** 645-64
discretionary **118,** 600
in case of country in breach of European Convention on Human Rights (1950) **118,** 600-1
refusal
degree of criminality, relevance **107,** 556-7, 571
judicial review **79,** 645, 663-4
'serious non-political crime'/'*crime grave de droit commun*' **107,** 561
terrorism **104,** 663-72, **107,** 562-90
right of **79,** 668
Australia, colony of. *See also* Australia
Royal Proclamation 1770 **73,** 138, 144-5, 147, 148, 152, 157
sovereignty over, exercise of **73,** 138, 141, 144-9, 151-3, 156-64
Australia, relationship to **69,** 14-15, 21-3, 161-3, **70,** 100
bank, confidentiality **86,** 167
bankruptcy proceedings. *See also* law of, Insolvency Act 1986; law of, Insolvency Rules 1986 *and* service of process out of the jurisdiction
jurisdiction, aliens **101,** 338-51
power to require person to appear for examination **88,** 312-22
comity and **88,** 316
resident abroad **88,** 313-14, 316-19
power to require person to submit to examination abroad **88,** 319-22
State's entitlement to preferential treatment **101,** 336-7
bays, fishing rights, title and **90,** 301-5
belligerent occupation, expropriation/nationalization, State immunity, jurisdiction **103,** 354-5, 372-5, 387, 402-6, 414
blasphemy **87,** 419-38
freedom of expression and **87,** 434, 436
freedom of religion and **87,** 433, 434-5
historical development **87,** 423-32
Indian Penal Code **87,** 432
Law Commission Working Paper No 79 **87,** 430-1
Law Commission Working Paper No 145 **87,** 432
non-Christian religions **87,** 421-38

United Kingdom (*cont.*)
bona vacantia **85,** 60, 62
Booty Agreement (1946) (Netherlands) **40,** 464, 467
British Columbia, colony of. *See also* Canada, British Columbia
Act concerning Government of 1858 **73,** 190, 207, 221
Confederation of Canada, entry into **73,** 69-72, 78, 80, 191-2, 204, 213-14
Royal Proclamation 1763 **73,** 58, 61-2, 65, 112-17
sovereignty over, exercise of **73,** 59-65, 67-72, 78-83, 112-17, 120-6, 188-92, 205-12, 214-15, 218-25
British Protected States **55,** 490, 493
British Rail, closed shop agreement **62,** 365, 369-72
British subjects **55,** 497-9
British Telecommunications Act 1981 **74,** 352, 360
burden of proof **81,** 724-5
act of State **64,** 264-5, 380-1
diplomatic immunity, jurisdiction, waiver **111,** 623
persuasive/evidential burden distinguished **122,** 478-80, 482-3, 497-8
presumption of innocence and **122,** 445-9, 476-88, 497-8
State immunity, jurisdiction **103,** 403, 424
taxation, exemption **108,** 548-9
Burma, independence of **53,** 150-2
central/State-owned bank
classification of act, transfer of shares following reoganization of banking sector **124,** 559-63
as department of government/State **64,** 119, 134, 136-9, 146-9, 222
functions **64,** 116-19, 147-8
mixed private/public **64,** 136, 147
as organ of government **64,** 133-4
purpose/use of funds
funds held for its own account **64,** 224-5
monetary **64,** 119
as separate legal entity **124,** 559-61
as State agency **64,** 115-19
State immunity, execution/attachment **124,** 553-6, 569
immunity, jurisdiction and **64,** 135
Mareva injunction **64,** 222-5
period of exposure between transfer of central bank role and transfer of assets/shares **124,** 553, 554
State immunity, jurisdiction, dependence on **64,** 223
US/UK law distinguished **64,** 224-5, 226
State immunity, execution/attachment, waiver. *See* waiver of immunity from execution/attachment *below*
State immunity, jurisdiction **124,** 556
State immunity, execution/attachment and **64,** 135
State immunity, jurisdiction, classification of act. *See* classification of act *above*
status, evidence of, ambassador/head of mission certificate **64,** 137
waiver of immunity from execution/attachment
compatibility with central bank status **124,** 554
reference to applicable legal system, relevance **124,** 554
in respect of bank having lost central bank status **124,** 554
Channel Islands. *See* Channel Islands
Channel Tunnel Act 1978

extracts **119,** 404, **125,** 586
s 1(1) (purpose) **119,** 407
s 11 (implementation of international arrangements) **119,** 406, 407-8, **125,** 586-7
'international arrangements' **119,** 404, **125,** 586-7
obligation to give directions consistent with Treaty and Concession **119,** 407-8
s 15(1) (applicable law) **125,** 587
s 15(3) (applicable law: Arbitration Acts) **125,** 587
s 15(4) (applicable law: Arbitration Acts) **125,** 587
s 16(3)(b) (directions relating to protection against acts of violence) **125,** 587
s 20 (objection to directions) **125,** 587-8
s 49(1) ('international arrangements') **125,** 586-7
Channel Tunnel (Security) Order 1994 (Part III)
Art. 14 **119,** 405
Art. 16(1)(b) **119,** 405
Art. 16(2)(b) **119,** 405
validity of directions under **119,** 400-16, **125,** 582-601
competence of UK courts to determine **119,** 409-11, **125,** 591, 592-3
charterparty, beneficial ownership, whether **64,** 188-94
Chicago Convention on International Civil Aviation (1944)
as part of municipal law **124,** 471-5
legislation, interpretation in conformity with **124,** 472-4
obligation to exercise powers in conformity with **124,** 472
child care
adoption **92,** 233
care order **92,** 226
appeal against **92,** 226
termination or variation **92,** 226
care proceedings **92,** 225
ECHR and **92,** 233-56
local authority decisions relating to, judicial review **92,** 230-2
parental rights **92,** 242-4
access **92,** 231, 243
place of safety order **92,** 224-5
supervision order **92,** 225
voluntary care **92,** 224, 227
parental rights resolution **92,** 227-9
reception into care **92,** 227
wardship **92,** 224, 229-30
choice of law clause, agreement between State entities **124,** 567
Ciskei, Republic of
non-recognition, effects **75,** 679-85, 690-8
standing before English courts **75,** 678-80, 684-5, 687, 690, 696
citizenship
'British' **81,** 152
'British Dependent Territories' **81,** 152
'British Overseas' **81,** 152
City of London Corporation, immunity **63,** 46-8
civil aviation
provisional suspension or variation of certificate **124,** 462-75
irrationality/unreasonableness **124,** 470-1

United Kingdom (*cont.*)
unfairness **124,** 467-70
civil war, attitude of judiciary **39,** 330-3
claim, sampling methodology **109,** 74-5
claims settlement agreement, implementation machinery **107,** 472
claims settlement agreements, payments under as property of State **108,** 612-14, 618-20
closed shop agreement. *See also* trade union *below*
British Rail **62,** 365, 369-72
definition **62,** 365
dismissal for not joining **62,** 365-72
exemptions **62,** 367-8, 370, 373
religious grounds **62,** 360, 370, 373
existing employee **62,** 360-2, 366, 370, 373
lawfulness **62,** 360-89
legal status **62,** 360, 365-9
'post-entry' shop **62,** 365
'pre-entry' shop **62,** 365, 367
colonial ports, jurisdiction in **55,** 441-2
colonies
applicable law **72,** 204-8, **123,** 583-4
constitutional conventions and usages **53,** 87
governors of, authority **43,** 137
legislative powers **69,** 114-15, **84,** 72-3, **123,** 584-91
Magna Carta 1215 and **123,** 576-9
sovereignty over **52,** 50
comity **64,** 260
bankruptcy proceedings, power to require person to appear for examination **88,** 316
extradition, consultation with requesting State **119,** 308-9
forcible abduction/unlawful arrest, judicial enquiry into **95,** 403-4
foreign currency, circulation **111,** 593, 598-9, 602-3
justiciability **108,** 576, **111,** 598-9, 602-3
national interest and **83,** 265
pronouncement on legality of act of third State **123,** 605
State immunity, jurisdiction **64,** 279-80
common law
counselling and procuring, offence at **79,** 95
Crown prerogative **52,** 415-17, **53,** 169-71, 174-6
definition **79,** 25
jurisdiction and, local and transitory actions distinguished **125,** 389-94
State immunity, jurisdiction **107,** 542, **111,** 606
employment contract, locally engaged staff, diplomatic mission **64,** 357-63
State immunity, jurisdiction, acts of, armed forces abroad **119,** 88-90, 371, 373, 374-5, 380, 381-2
territorial sea, applicability in **125,** 334-42, 389-94, 455-9
torture **119,** 189
common law offence **120,** 401-3
common purpose **124,** 158. *See also* conspiracy *below*
Commonwealth (1641-60) **39,** 308-9, 332-3
Commonwealth Telecommunications Organization **77,** 15
companies. *See* corporation *below*
compensation for war-related events
destruction of property as military operation **41,** 11-12

expropriation/nationalization **41,** 11-12
confidentiality, telephone-tapping **74,** 319-22, 336-9, 356
confiscation, extraterritorial **78,** 616-17, 618
Conservation (Natural Habitats and of Wild Fauna and Flora) Regulations 1994
complete and lawful implementation of EC Habitats Directive, whether **120,** 641-4
'European marine site', territorial sea, limitation to **120,** 621, 623-4, 642
as implementation of EC Council Directive 92/43/EEC ('Habitats Directive') **120,** 618
conspiracy **57,** 43, 45, 119-28, 129-39, 142-4. *See also* common purpose *above*
jurisdiction **84,** 43-8, 682, 683-4, **85,** 117-26
torture **119,** 148, 183-4, 188-9, 190-2, 250
'constable' **86,** 164
Constitution
conventions **53,** 82-3, 87
executive and judiciary, relationship **52,** 48, 66
reality and theory distinguished **53,** 82-4, 87, 91
rights, abrogation by executive **123,** 579-84
constitutional monarchy **39,** 197-9
consular access
arrest of national
customary law and **123,** 608
legal representation, right to require **123,** 608-9
Vienna Convention on Consular Relations (1963) **123,** 608
contempt of court doctrine **78,** 396-402
applicability **78,** 397-402
administrative and judicial bodies distinguished **78,** 397-402
valuation court **78,** 395-402
origin **78,** 400-1
term misleading **78,** 402
continental shelf
defined **77,** 313-14
as extension of territorial sea **86,** 602
'part of' UK, whether **78,** 538
rights in, vested in Crown **77,** 314-16
contract **78,** 583-91. *See also* exchange contract *below*
breach, government action leading to, responsibility for **64,** 196-203, 319-20
frustration. *See also force majeure below*
date of **64,** 252-4, 373-4
government intervention as **64,** 250-4, 372-9
State agency/State-owned corporation, right to rely on **64,** 250-4, 377-9
legislation **75,** 372-80
war and **78,** 583-91
performance, collateral guarantee of continuing legality under law of place of **64,** 376-7
third party obligations **81,** 716-17
contract, interpretation
phrases
'civil war' **107,** 507
'insurrection' **107,** 507
'rebellion' **107,** 507
Convention on the Means of Prohibiting and Preventing the Illicit Import, Export and Transfer of Ownership of Cultural Property (1970)
'cultural property' **118,** 582

United Kingdom (*cont.*)
as part of municipal law **118,** 582-3
corporal punishment in schools, parental right, violation of **72,** 324
corporation. *See also* partnership *below*
definition **103,** 362-3
domicile
nationality and **85,** 7
place of incorporation **85,** 6
place of registration **85,** 6
foreign
recognition **85,** 6, 10-11, 13, 14, 20, 23-4
right to sue **85,** 10-11
incorporation in unrecognized State, relevance **100,** 251-4
Foreign Corporations Act 1991 **100,** 252-4
liability of members **81,** 681, 708-9
mixed entities **81,** 679
personality **77,** 80-2
common law **77,** 80
separate from that of members **77,** 80-2
courts, municipal
appointment of receiver **77,** 45-50
assumed reluctance of foreign State to use **83,** 238
Attorney-General, intervention by **52,** 47-8
'British court', Rhodesian courts after UDI 1965, whether **72,** 32, 35-7, 40, 42, 44-6, 50-1
enforcement of foreign judgment. *See* foreign judgment, enforcement *below*
European Court of Human Rights decisions, binding effect **78,** 399
executive and **52,** 48, 66
executive certificate/statement, and **75,** 680, 682, 697-8
functions
administration of justice according to the law **78,** 407
application of law **78,** 463, 476
determination of public policy **78,** 419
legislative **57,** 134-5
international law, application by **80,** 90, 144, 150, 201
jurisdiction **60,** 91, 103, 104, 108, **80,** 18
Canadian Indians' property rights **78,** 423-53
civil or commercial matters **84,** 735-51
Constitution of independent country **78,** 464-5
criminal **57,** 119-21, 126-8, 129-31
development **39,** 358
domestic legislation as basis **84,** 740
effect in Canada of Royal Proclamation of 1763 **78,** 435
foreign legislation, determination of legality **64,** 219-20, **119,** 92
inherent **77,** 163, 165
interpretation of non-binding international instrument **79,** 649
justiciable issues on basis of law **78,** 435
obtaining of evidence for use abroad **84,** 737, 742
winding-up of international organization **80,** 184-6
legislation, powers in respect of **59,** 351, 358, 485-6
legislature and **53,** 57, 82-4, 358, **84,** 761-2
recognition
acts of foreign government **57,** 39

governments, of **61,** 53-4, **75,** 679-80, 698
role
Divisional Court **80,** 18
Magistrates' **80,** 18
standing, Ciskei **75,** 678-80, 684-5, 687, 690, 696
CPR
6.19(2) **124,** 556, 558
6.20(10) **124,** 558-9, 564-6
crimes against humanity **91,** 129
customary international law **119,** 106-7
Head of State immunity, jurisdiction **119,** 45-8, 98-9
criminal jurisdiction. *See* jurisdiction, criminal *below*
criminal law
attempt as offence **87,** 409-10
location of offence **87,** 410-12
extraterritoriality **60,** 97, 98
location **57,** 131-3
territorial principle. *See* jurisdiction, criminal *below*
criminal offence, place of commission **78,** 502
criminal proceedings, effect on immunity **119,** 88
Crown. *See also* Crown rights and obligations, prerogative *and* State immunity, jurisdiction, in own courts *below*
divisibility **123,** 569-75
immunity from suit **63,** 548, **81,** 114-15, 119-20, 130, 136-8
for acts of public servants **81,** 137-8
good faith and **64,** 573
State immunity compared **64,** 573-4
money due from **80,** 194-5
Crown Colony, legislative power, Colonial Laws Validity Act, validity under **77,** 381, 382
Crown rights and obligations
breach, without remedy **78,** 493-6
enforceability **78,** 493-6
'imperfect' **78,** 495, 496
legal duty, whether **78,** 493-6
protection
inroads of sea **78,** 495
nationals on British ships on high seas **78,** 495
situs **84,** 435, 437, 468
transfer
Australia **78,** 438
Canada **78,** 439-48, 467-8
implied **78,** 438-9, 468-9
Ireland **78,** 438
unity and divisibility of **78,** 425, 429, 431, 433, 443-4
Southern Rhodesia **78,** 496-8
Statute of Westminster and **78,** 432-3
'usage and practice' **78,** 431, 468
currency
issue
comity **111,** 593, 598-9, 602-3
holding/disposal in foreign country distinguished **111,** 592-603
ownership, outside country of issue **111,** 600

United Kingdom (*cont.*)
customary international law **64,** 126, 127-8, 131-2, 140-4, 152-3
as aid to interpretation of legislation implementing treaty **119,** 161
crimes against humanity **119,** 106-7
evidence of, legislation **64,** 311-12
genocide **119,** 106-7
Head of State, immunity, jurisdiction **119,** 44-8, 62-70, 78-87, 99-100, 104-5, 219
Head of State, responsibility for international crimes **119,** 200-1
hostage-taking **119,** 106-7
municipal law and **64,** 600, **83,** 238, **102,** 201, **117,** 424, **119,** 78-9, 87, **120,** 397-8, **122,** 505-6
action to prevent breach of customary international law as defence to criminal charge **122,** 507-8
change of municipal law as consequence of change in customary law **108,** 535-6
criminal offence, direct creation **122,** 506-7
transformation doctrine **120,** 362-5, 378-86, **122,** 506-7
universal recognition/UK consent requirement **122,** 505-6
recognition, State **108,** 535-6
State immunity, jurisdiction **100,** 455-7, 461-3, **119,** 233-4, 378, 384, **123,** 38-9
torture **119,** 106-7
war crimes distinguished **100,** 471
treaties, primacy **108,** 539
customs officer, powers **86,** 164
customs statute, interpretation, reference to treaty **41,** 1-10
Cyprus, Republic of
agreement for restoring civil peace (1963) **44,** 359, 361, 371
Truce Force in **44,** 361-2, 370
Cyprus, Turkish Federated State
non-recognition, effect **73,** 12-27
representative in London, status **73,** 12-13, 20
Czechoslovakia, compensation agreement, trustee claims **42,** 180-1
damages
for
conversion of property **116,** 559-62, **125,** 693-706, 739-41
usurpation of property in absence of damage **125,** 690-1, 739-40
requirements, nexus **116,** 559-62
death penalty, wrongful conviction and **124,** 334-6
debts, liability for
club **80,** 46
international organization **80,** 46, 47
partnership **80,** 45
trade union **80,** 46
unincorporated association **80,** 45
default judgment against foreign State
effective date **118,** 618
foreign relations and **118,** 117-18, 615-16
'process', whether **118,** 615-17
setting aside, grounds, breach of State immunity, jurisdiction **118,** 607-8, 615-18
definition **69,** 20
Great Britain **77,** 306, 307

territorial waters, whether part of **77,** 310, 313-18
United Kingdom **77,** 306
continental shelf **78,** 538
territorial sea **77,** 310-13
denial of justice **75,** 375, 378-80
dependent territories **86,** 193-4
legislative powers
concurrent **86,** 191
extraterritorial **86,** 191, 198-9, 205, 207
deportation **73,** 636-51, **78,** 372-5, 393-4
appeal
'conducive to the public good' and **73,** 639, 641, **124,** 515, 532
independent advisory panel **108,** 381, 420-2, **115,** 515
procedure **108,** 367
right of **124,** 540-2
Special Immigration Appeals Commission (SIAC) **124,** 513-18. *See also* Special Immigration Appeals Commission (SIAC) *below*
standing **124,** 515
stay of deportation pending **124,** 515
compelling reasons of national security and **108,** 370, 381-2
action directed/targeted at deporting State, need for **124,** 521-2, 523-5, 532-5, 543, 548-9
balance of interests **108,** 370-5, 377-8, 406, **124,** 517, 526-7
compassionate circumstances **108,** 382-4
defence of the realm and **124,** 535
matter of law/fact **124,** 544-5
responsibility for determining **124,** 519-22, 523-8, 535-6, 537-9, 544-9
risk of torture and **124,** 546
standard of proof **124,** 521-2, 526, 537-9, 547, 549-50
terrorist activity **108,** 379, **124,** 520-2, 525
'conducive to the public good' **71,** 456-7, 460-2, 480-2, 485-7, **73,** 637, 639, 641, **108,** 368-70, 377, 409-11, **124,** 514-15. *See also* compelling reasons of national security and *above*
appeal **73,** 639, 641, **124,** 515, 532
foreign relations considerations **124,** 520, 545
mutual exclusivity of 'conducive to the public good' grounds **124,** 520, 525, 534-5, 537, 548-9
proportionality **108,** 371
stay of deportation pending European Commission proceedings **78,** 372-5
deserter, handing-over, visiting forces, limited to, whether **85,** 158
detainees, rights, humane treatment, interrogation techniques **71,** 301-3
diplomatic agent
Head of State as **119,** 60-1
Police Liaison Officer **111,** 616, 661
dual status **111,** 635, 636-7
status, executive certificate/statement **111,** 616
status in forum State, recognition of, need for **94,** 614
diplomatic archives
internal embassy document
functions of mission, relating to **86,** 138
voluntary disclosure **86,** 145
diplomatic archives, inviolability
internal embassy document **86,** 132-51

United Kingdom (*cont.*)
absolute privilege and **86,** 37-46
diplomatic immunity and **86,** 145-6
Diplomatic and Consular Premises Act 1987
s 1 **83,** 234-5, 236, 238
s 2 **83,** 235, 236
s 3 **83,** 236
Diplomatic Immunities Act 1952 **41,** 407, 409, 410, 412, 413
Diplomatic Immunities (Commonwealth Countries and Republic of Ireland) Act 1952 **88,** 397, **90,** 463
diplomatic immunity, jurisdiction
alternative forum, desirability **114,** 484-5
enforcement of covenant proceedings **64,** 364-7, 385-93
legal liability distinguished **64,** 392-3, **114,** 494
matrimonial jurisdiction **78,** 485
State immunity and **64,** 391, **87,** 415, 416, **111,** 632-4, **119,** 222
diplomatic privileges and immunities as basis of State immunity **64,** 419
distinction **107,** 636, 639-40, **111,** 606, **114,** 495
diplomatic immunity, jurisdiction, waiver **86,** 146-7
authority, need for **86,** 147, 151, **111,** 623, 634, 643, 656-7, 663, **114,** 481-3, **120,** 448-50
burden of proof **111,** 623
by lawyer on behalf of client **111,** 628, 657
Children Act 1989 and **114,** 483
compatibility with claim of inviolability of documents **86,** 146-7, 150-1
counterclaim **111,** 639-41, 658-9
defence, as part of **86,** 135-6, 147, 148, 151
express **111,** 626-8, 642-5, 656-8
initiation of proceedings **111,** 637-41, 658-9, **120,** 448-50
International Conventions relating to children's rights, effect **114,** 483-4
knowledge and intent **111,** 643, 656
parallel proceedings **111,** 658
retrospective **111,** 645
separate waivers for jurisdiction and execution **111,** 645
submission to the jurisdiction as **111,** 642, 656-7
undertaking to court by diplomatic agent **111,** 623, 641-2, 656-8
writing **111,** 643
diplomatic immunity, jurisdiction, waiver, implied, clear and unequivocal communication **111,** 645
diplomatic mission
administrative and technical staff **64,** 357, 361-2
'member'
diplomatic status, relevance **107,** 635-7
entitlement to privileges and immunities, relevance **104,** 642
locally engaged staff **104,** 637-43, **107,** 639-40
nationality, relevance **104,** 643, **107,** 639-40
notification of appointment, relevance **104,** 637-8, 642-3, 681
staff of medical office **104,** 680-1, **107,** 635-40
status, emanation of sending State **103,** 364-5
diplomatic premises
definition
residence of member of mission **64,** 365-7, 390-1

'used for purposes of [maintaining] a diplomatic or consular mission' **64,** 367, 388-92
duty of host government **83,** 234-43
to sell **83,** 236
handing over of keys to host government by disaffected embassy staff, effect **83,** 240-1
inviolability
damages, action for and **64,** 393
residence of member of diplomatic mission **64,** 365-7, 390-1
protection
customary international law **83,** 237
sale as fulfilment **83,** 237, 240
status
dependence on use as such **108,** 563-4
loss **83,** 236, 239
loss of inviolability **83,** 239
Vienna Convention on Diplomatic Relations (1961) **83,** 236-7, 239
Diplomatic Privileges Act 1708 **41,** 409-10, 412, 414, **78,** 486, **86,** 667, 669, **88,** 424
dependent territories, application to **86,** 669
waiver under **78,** 486
Diplomatic Privileges Act 1964 **41,** 407-16, **52,** 371, 379-81, 384-5, 386-8, **73,** 13, **74,** 187, **77,** 7, 12, **78,** 484-90, **80,** 222, **83,** 237, **86,** 147, 678, **87,** 415, 416, **88,** 326, 397, 408-9, **111,** 606-10, **119,** 160-1, 223
acts committed in own country **119,** 60-1, 90, 203
executive certificate/statement **88,** 384-6
'generally recognized principles of international law' and **119,** 62
Head of State **111,** 606, **119,** 42-8, 59-60
'subject to any necessary modifications' **119,** 59-60, 89-90, 96-7, 102-3, 154, 160-1, 193, 196, 223-4, 245-7
Head of State, former **119,** 59-60, 89-90, 96-7, 102-3, 154, 160-1, 193, 196, 223-4, 245-7
international officials, 'official duties' **80,** 222
interpretation
in conformity with customary international law **119,** 161
in light of Vienna Convention on Diplomatic Relations (1961) **64,** 390-1
'premises of the mission' **64,** 391-3
s 1 **78,** 485, **111,** 629, **119,** 42, 59, 89
s 2 **64,** 365, **78,** 485, **119,** 42, 59, 168-9, 203
s 2(1) **111,** 629
s 2(3) **111,** 630, 633-4, 643
s 2(5) **111,** 656
s 3 **87,** 414
s 3(1) **111,** 632
s 4 **88,** 396, **111,** 616
s 24 **77,** 128
Schedule 1 **119,** 78, 203
Art. 1 **107,** 635-6, **111,** 629
Art. 24 **64,** 293
Art. 29 **111,** 629, **119,** 203, 245
Art. 31 **78,** 485, **111,** 629, 656, **119,** 42, 203, 245
Art. 31(c) **111,** 635-6
Art. 32 **111,** 630, 656
Art. 32(2) **111,** 641-2, 658-9, **119,** 168-9

United Kingdom (*cont.*)
Art. 32(3) **111,** 637-42
Art. 32(4) **77,** 7
Art. 39 **78,** 485-6, **119,** 245-6
Art. 39(2) **111,** 636-7, 659-61
State immunity and **111,** 606
subsequent treaties, effect **114,** 483-4
Vienna Convention on Diplomatic Relations (1961), implementation. *See* Vienna Convention on Diplomatic Relations (1961), implementation *below*
Diplomatic Privileges (Extension) Act 1944 **77,** 11, 88, **80,** 69, 89, 94, **81,** 683, 694-5, 705, **83,** 247, 248, 249, 269, **85,** 20
declaratory of common law **83,** 247
Diplomatic Privileges (Extension) Act 1946 **77,** 11, 88, **80,** 69, 95, 157-8
Diplomatic Privileges (Extension) Act 1950 **80,** 70, **81,** 695, 705
Diplomatic Privileges (Extension) Acts 1944/50 **80,** 68, 151, 153
diplomatic privileges and immunities
basis, reciprocity **86,** 140
courts' right/duty to raise *proprio motu* **78,** 489, **86,** 147
civil jurisdiction **78,** 485
termination of diplomatic status and **78,** 485-90
distinction **87,** 415, **119,** 61
functional **111,** 636, 660-1
burden of proof **111,** 636
termination of status, after **119,** 153
receiving State, agreement, need for **88,** 324-8
third State, inviolability in **88,** 326-7
diplomatic privileges and immunities, entitlement
family members 'forming part of household' **114,** 481
Head of State **111,** 607-8, **119,** 42-8, 59-61, 96-9, 102-3, 109. *See also* Diplomatic Privileges Act 1964 *above*
termination, permanent departure **111,** 636, 660-1
termination of diplomatic status, relevance **114,** 495
diplomatic protection
exercise of State's own right **108,** 611-12
agent or trustee, whether **108,** 612, 613
exhaustion of local remedies and **116,** 614-15
deficient or ineffective local machinery **107,** 472-3
margin of appreciation **107,** 469-73, 480
judicial review **116,** 609-22
non-intervention in the affairs of another State **116,** 614, 615-16, 618, 620-2
diplomatic relations
break, Cambodia, whether **83,** 239-40
recognition, State/government, relevance, distinguished **108,** 538
diplomatic representations, bond and share holders, on behalf of **46,** 345-6, 371
diplomatic status
evidence of/requirements, diplomatic passport **119,** 78
foreign office certificate **78,** 484
stayed action, revival of **78,** 486-9
termination **78,** 485-90
disclosure of documents
comity and **64,** 280
non-disclosure as denial of access to courts **119,** 277, 307

professional privilege **64,** 281-2, 287-90, 297-8
waiver **64,** 290, 306
public interest privilege **64,** 285, 290-2, 298-306
balance of interests **64,** 291, 305
communications between States **64,** 285, 291-4, 297-306
State immunity, jurisdiction **64,** 280-5, 287-94
dominions
applicability of UK legislation **69,** 13-15, 17-23, 161-3, **70,** 70-2, 90-1, 98-100
Australian states **69,** 14, 161
double criminality **78,** 501-5, **85,** 79-87
comparable offence **78,** 503, **85,** 80-4
conspiracy **78,** 503-5
critical date, commission of offence **119,** 41, 55, 146-7, 159-60, 175-6, 182, 189-93, 202, 214, 250, **120,** 364-5, 367, 384-5
determination of
on basis of law as set out in request **119,** 259-60
evidence of foreign law **119,** 259-60
magistrate's power **78,** 503
jurisdiction, relevance **88,** 338-9
specification of charges **88,** 352-5
subsequent legislation, relevance **85,** 82
theft **78,** 501-3, **85,** 83-4
double taxation agreements **72,** 448-9, 457-8
drug-trafficking
money laundering, measures to prevent **86,** 160-8
Single Convention on Narcotic Drugs (1961), implementing legislation. *See* law of, Drug-trafficking Offences Act 1986 *below*
duress, nuclear weapons, possession and deployment, whether **122,** 509
EC
freedom of movement, extradition and **85,** 88-90
privileges and immunities **81,** 718-19
Undertaking to finance supplementary budget, ancillary treaty, whether **93,** 630-41
EC law
amendment, Parliamentary approval, need for **98,** 175-7
compatibility, presumption of **93,** 661
growing influence **85,** 34
implementation
conflict between Regulation and national implementation measures, justification **117,** 493-4
discretion **117,** 473
public policy and **117,** 471-4, 492, 526-8, 543-7
primacy **93,** 659, 681, 705
UN obligations and, possibility of conflict **117,** 474-5
validity, presumption of **93,** 663
EC law, direct effect **73,** 303-4, 343, 353
interim measures. *See* provisional measures, EC law as issue *below*
national courts, role **93,** 663-4, 685-6, 696-7, 698, 702-3
Art. 169 infringement proceedings and **93,** 697
protection, effective **93,** 663, 685-6, 703
regulations, individuals, applicability to **59,** 484-5
ECJ
Art. 177 reference **85,** 90, **111,** 14-15, 45

United Kingdom (*cont.*)
conditions on intervention **100,** 257
eligibility of company incorporated in unrecognized State **100,** 251-5
late intervention **100,** 246, 249, 254-7
requirements **93,** 628, 664, **107,** 535, **117,** 475, 490, 499, 500
urgency **100,** 249
EEC. *See also* law of, European Communities Act 1972 *below*
legal personality, international law **80,** 123
powers and functions
delegated sovereign powers **80,** 123
jus missionis **80,** 123
jus tractatus **80,** 123
privileges and immunities
common law **80,** 122, 180
immunity from suit **80,** 54, 121-8, 149
inviolability of premises **80,** 127
privileges **80,** 127
sovereign State
analogies with **80,** 123
population, absence of **80,** 123
territorial sovereignty, absence of **80,** 123
status, sovereign State, powers and functions analogous to **80,** 123
treaty establishing, incorporation **80,** 128
EEC Treaty (Rome) (1957)
direct effect, Art. 119 (non-discrimination) **93,** 628
interpretation, UK legislation distinguished **93,** 634-5
effective remedy before national authority
judicial review **98,** 316-17, **124,** 515-16, 531-2, 540-1
asylum procedures **108,** 357-62, 422, 423-7, 430-2, **124,** 515-16, 531-2, 540-1
State immunity as bar to suit and **119,** 372, 373, 376, 377-8, 383-5
Egypt
independence, recognition of **80,** 259
termination of protectorate 1922 **80,** 259-60
reservation of areas of interest **80,** 260
embassy or consular bank account/funds, immunity, execution/attachment **87,** 417
employment contract, locally engaged staff, consulate, waiver of immunity, choice of law clause in manual of employment **120,** 614-16
employment contract, locally engaged staff, diplomatic mission
State immunity, jurisdiction **64,** 354-63, **107,** 603-4
common law **64,** 357-63
dismissal **64,** 360-1
presumption of **120,** 616
State immunity, jurisdiction, theory/doctrine, customary international law **64,** 357-63
enemy alien, access to courts **83,** 162
entry, right of **61,** 270, 392, 397, 404, 428-9
equitable execution **77,** 45-50, **81,** 719
equity **78,** 408
liability of partners **81,** 708-9
estoppel
informal service of documents **103,** 365-6
State immunity, jurisdiction and **64,** 120-1, 135
tax credit, practice of payment to foreign government **103,** 335-6

Euratom, Dragon Project, Agreements on **44,** 410-11, 414, 419-22
Eurocontrol, status **83,** 269
European Agreement relating to Persons participating in Proceedings of the European Commission and Court of Human Rights **78,** 383-4, 386
European Community treaties
'Community treaties' **93,** 631
direct effect **107,** 523-5
European Convention on Human Rights (1950) **84,** 763-4
application by courts **73,** 403, 407-8, 410-14, **78,** 372-8, 382-8, **85,** 32
Southern Rhodesia and **78,** 493
breach, refugees, asylum, relevance **118,** 600-1
enforcement **112,** 403-4, 409-10, **114,** 421-2
municipal courts **108,** 553
executive discretion **85,** 31
incorporation into municipal law. *See also* United Kingdom, law of, Human Rights Act 1998
anticipated implementation of Human Rights Act 1998 **122,** 1, 436-9, 440-9, 453-9, 465-7
'in accordance with the law' and **124,** 539
support for **85,** 47
inhuman or degrading treatment, of family members in case of deportation giving rise to risk of subjection to torture **123,** 598
interim measures under **78,** 390-4
legal obligation, not **78,** 394
judicial review, effect **112,** 385-7, 395-6, **114,** 421-2, 462-5
municipal law and. *See also* incorporation into municipal law *above*
compatibility **78,** 338, **84,** 763, 771, **85,** 31, 34, **122,** 445-9, 453-60, 474-6, 483-8
impact on **78,** 418
interpretation **78,** 326, 376, 386
justiciability under **78,** 407
modification of **78,** 337-8, 340
same as **78,** 415
status **73,** 403, 410-11, 413, **74,** 311-14, 325-6, 339-40, 357, **78,** 375-7, 399, **85,** 31, 44, 47
obligations
representations on behalf of alien **123,** 596-8
to secure rights within jurisdiction **85,** 31
European Convention on State Immunity (and Protocol) (Basle) (1972). *See* State Immunity Act 1978, European Convention on State Immunity (and Protocol) (Basle) (1972) and *below*
European Court of Human Rights decisions
applicability **85,** 32
binding effect **78,** 399
European Union Treaty (Maastricht) (1992)
Common Foreign and Security Policy (CFSP), transfer of prerogative powers, whether **98,** 177-9
Social Policy Protocol
indirect amendment of national law, whether **98,** 176-7
part of treaty, whether **98,** 172-5
evidence **77,** 113-14
admissibility **77,** 113, **78,** 507-12
extradition proceedings **85,** 94-108

United Kingdom (*cont.*)
foreign affidavit **64,** 180
Security Council Resolutions **116,** 598-601
when archival immunity violated **77,** 124-59
affirmation **78,** 508-12
'to affirm' distinguished **78,** 511
assistance to foreign courts in obtaining **73,** 299-363
burden of proof **77,** 63-4, 119-21
delay, abuse of power, whether **85,** 107-8
disclosure of documents. *See* disclosure of documents *above*
discovery **77,** 166-7
pre-trial **73,** 300-2, 307-8, 313-17, 323-32, 340-3, 351-3
restrictions on **73,** 301-2, 314, 331, 351
of foreign law **78,** 518-19, 595, 597
improperly obtained **95,** 407
on oath, need for **78,** 508-9
privilege, claim of **73,** 302-6, 308-10, 312, 317-20, 323, 332-9, 343-8, 353-9
professional privilege **64,** 281-2, 287-90, 297-8
requesting court's statement as to purpose, predisposition to accept **84,** 747
standard of proof **87,** 360, 361, 363-4, **88,** 348-50
compelling reasons of national security **124,** 521-2, 526-7, 537-9, 549-50
high civil balance of probabilities **124,** 521, 526-7, 535-6, 537-9, 547
Prevention of Terrorism (Temporary Provisions) Act 1989 **122,** 447-8, 459, 470-80, 481-2, 486-8
State Immunity Act 1978 **77,** 63-8
taking of abroad **84,** 731-54
transmission to third States, permissibility **86,** 167-8
witnesses, compellability **55,** 553
evidence of
Act of Parliament **78,** 463
public policy, Security Council Resolution **103,** 408-9
exchange contract **40,** 13, 15, **41,** 231, 234, 237, **47,** 51, **66,** 173, **77,** 326-9
disguised monetary transaction **77,** 326-8, **118,** 573, 575
enforceability **75,** 130-4, 145-7, 159, **77,** 326-9, **118,** 567-78
conformity with foreign exchange control regulations, relevance **118,** 578
conformity with IMF Agreement (1945), relevance **118,** 578
interpretation **72,** 544-5, 694-708, **77,** 326, **118,** 573-4
exclusion of alien, justification, national security **123,** 595
exclusive fishing zone (EFZ) **120,** 618 n. 5, 623
sovereignty over **120,** 623
executive certificate/statement **75,** 679-83, 689-91, 694-8, **78,** 424, 436
conclusiveness **73,** 321-2, 358-9, **74,** 22, 47-8, 75
recognition, State **64,** 514-15, **122,** 535-6
in respect of purpose for which issued **108,** 528
in respect of recognition, government **125,** 632, 656, 657
diplomatic mission, status **104,** 681
Estonia, recognition of **85,** 57-8
Head of State, immunity **111,** 607
State immunity, jurisdiction **111,** 606
executive discretion **85,** 39-52. *See also* judicial review *below*
effect of
delay **87,** 331

perverse exercise **85,** 35
European Convention on Human Rights (1950) **85,** 39-52
limitations, Anglo-Irish Agreement (1985) **87,** 331, 333
reasonableness **85,** 32-3, 35, 41-4, 49-51
requirements
proportionality **85,** 33-4, 47, 51-2
rationality **87,** 331
reasonableness **87,** 331
executive powers. *See also* prerogative *below*
conclusion of treaty incompatible with **87,** 331
divestment **87,** 331
need for fairness **84,** 718
exhaustion of local remedies, diplomatic protection. *See* diplomatic protection, exhaustion of local remedies and *above*
expert, evidence **78,** 408, 518-19, 595, 597
export credit guarantees. *See* export credit guarantees
expropriation/nationalization
aircraft and shipbuilding industries **75,** 448-561
compensation, valuation **75,** 452-8, 486-504, 532-47, 558-60
corporation, dissolution as **116,** 579
extraterritorial effect, Iraqi seizure of Kuwait Airways aircraft **116,** 585-6
nationality, relevance **116,** 586-7
occupying powers, by, State immunity, jurisdiction **103,** 354-5, 372-5, 387, 402-6, 414
property seized in occupied territory, State immunity, jurisdiction **103,** 373-5
recognition/enforcement **125,** 651-2
expulsion of alien
Crown prerogative and **123,** 581, 590
illegal entry **79,** 648
expulsion of national, Magna Carta 1215 **123,** 575-9
expulsion of refugee. *See* refugees, expulsion *below*
extraditable offence **79,** 101-5, **84,** 58, **85,** 74, 130-43
conspiracy **85,** 130-43
to hostage-taking **119,** 182-3
to murder **119,** 148, 184-8
to torture **119,** 148, 188-9, 190-2, 250
drugs offence **111,** 551-2
'extradition crime' **41,** 400, **85,** 136, **119,** 31, 75-6, 93, 109, 139, 144-8, 181-2, 218-19, 249, 258
critical date **119,** 45, 76-7, 109, 140, 284-5
disappearances **119,** 285-6, 328
distinction **85,** 141, 143
extraterritorial offence
crime committed outside requested State **119,** 2, 32, 37-8
jurisdiction of requesting State based on nationality of offender **119,** 2, 32, 38
jurisdiction of requesting State based on nationality of victim **119,** 38
torture **119,** 190
hostage-taking **119,** 76, 93, 147-8, 182-3
Indian Penal Code, application **52,** 376-7
'relevant offence' **85,** 76-8
torture **119,** 76, 93, 150-1, 190, 249
extradition **51,** 248-70, 288-319, 360-72, 374-400, **74,** 459-72, **77,** 346-50, 352-76, **78,** 389-94, 506-12, 514-20. *See also Extradition Acts and Fugitive Offenders Acts below*

United Kingdom (*cont.*)
appeal **79,** 465 n. 10
admissibility **88,** 350-2
applicable law, requesting State **87,** 408
arrest warrant, provisional **87,** 401-2, **88,** 364-9, **119,** 33-6, 92
aut dedere aut punire/judicare **95,** 364
comity, consultation with requesting State **119,** 308-9
crimes committed on the high seas **56,** 515-16
definition **119,** 30
disclosure of medical reports
assurance of confidentiality and **119,** 298-9
to human rights organizations **119,** 266-79
to requesting States **119,** 282-3, 284, 287-317
discretion
abuse of process **119,** 251
fitness to stand trial **119,** 322-4, 328
interests of claimants for compensation **119,** 277-8, 305, 326
interests of requesting State **119,** 277-8
medical condition **119,** 265-6, 318-24
possibility of trial in home State **119,** 277-8, 305, 326
as protection of accused **119,** 326-7
treaty obligations **119,** 325
disguised **77,** 338, 350, **84,** 718, 719
double criminality. *See* double criminality *above*
EC law, freedom of movement under and **85,** 88-90
evidence
admissibility **78,** 507-12
assumption of validity **119,** 258-60
standard of proof **88,** 348-50
'weighing' and 'weighing up' distinguished **88,** 348-50
executive act **111,** 568
determination of fairness **111,** 569-70
fairness **87,** 400-7, **119,** 293-317
as matter of law **119,** 313
representations and **119,** 307
requested State's right to take decision in case of international crime without consultation **119,** 301, 307-10
Federal Republic of Germany (Extradition) (Amendment) Order 1978 **85,** 94, 97-8
Federal Republic of Germany (Extradition) Order 1960 **56,** 513, **85,** 94, 95
to Fiji **80,** 11-18
foreign relations and **119,** 72, 111, 252
freedom of movement under Treaty of Rome (1957), effect **114,** 419-21, 460-2
habeas corpus **56,** 515-16, **119,** 317-18, **124,** 453-9
extension **124,** 453-9
Home Secretary's responsibilities **119,** 36, 38
discretionary nature of powers **80,** 16, 18, **114,** 446-7, **119,** 38, 92, 108-9, 110-11, 248. *See also* discretion *above*
personal nature **114,** 433-6, 440-2, 453
treaty basis **119,** 277-8
Hong Kong after reversion to China **114,** 407-66
from Ireland **55,** 560, **79,** 49-167

judicial review
abuse of power **111,** 556, 561-3, 568-70
Bugdaycay **114,** 428-9
exhaustion of alternative remedies, need for **111,** 557, 563
lawful, fair and reasonable action, whether **119,** 275-8, 282-3
legality of executive action **111,** 556-7
Soering **114,** 426-8
jurisdiction **85,** 98-9
applicable law **87,** 408
determination of **87,** 407-12
illegal transfer from third country for sole purpose of extradition **111,** 550-83
lay adjudication **77,** 348, 350
motivation of requesting State **85,** 87
prosecution for race, religion, nationality or political opinion **119,** 110, 250
nationals **95,** 363-4
offence committed on high seas **56,** 513-17
obligation, European Convention on Extradition (1957) **111,** 557-8
political offence. *See* political offence, extradition *below*
procedure **56,** 515, **85,** 74-6, 139, 144-5, **98,** 282-6, **119,** 33-6
arrest. *See* arrest warrant *above*; forcible abduction/unlawful arrest *below*
avoidance **95,** 393, 395, 399
evidence **85,** 94-108, 144
Extradition, European Convention on (1957), between parties to. *See* Extradition, European Convention on (1957) *below*
legal nature **119,** 254
order to proceed **87,** 402, 403-7
reasons, need for **119,** 256
representations, admissibility **119,** 248, 318
specific charges, need for **87,** 400-7
warrant, authentication **85,** 103
proceedings, leave to intervene **119,** 69
refusal, grounds
effect on stability of country in which offences committed **119,** 111, 252
humanitarian considerations **119,** 111, 250, 252
national interest **119,** 111, 252, 326
'unjust or oppressive' **114,** 449-51, **118,** 564
relevant and comparable offence **88,** 373-7
request for
imperfect **119,** 31
need for **119,** 32-3, 251-2
standing of second requesting State **119,** 282-3
requirements
authority to proceed **119,** 108-11, 146, 247-52, 318, 328-9
good faith **119,** 110, 251
ministerial authority **119,** 33
prima facie case **111,** 579, 581
review of extradition warrant **119,** 38
Scotland, application in **56,** 516
speciality **72,** 602-4, **88,** 355-6
Hong Kong after reversion to China, risk of change **114,** 455-9
risk of eventual surrender to third country **88,** 355-6
statutory limitation and **119,** 110

United Kingdom (*cont.*)
stay of, European Commission proceedings and **78,** 389-94
Sweden and Norway (Extradition) Order 1873 **78,** 508
treaties. *See* extradition agreement *below*
United States of America (Extradition) Order 1935 **85,** 134
United States of America (Extradition) Order 1976 **84,** 57, **85,** 79, **87,** 321, **124,** 454
Extradition Act 1845 **85,** 96
Extradition Act 1866 **85,** 96-7
Extradition Act 1870 **51,** 249, 250-61, 290-2, 296-9, 306-8, 360-5, 374, 378-9, 384-91, 397-400, **56,** 514-17, **71,** 532-3, **74,** 459-71, **79,** 58, **85,** 98-9, **88,** 371-3
application in Jamaica **72,** 65-72, 202, 208-9
Bahamas, applicability in **85,** 129-45
'criminal matter' **55,** 552
double criminality, critical date **119,** 146-7, 176, 182, 189-93, 202, 250
evidence required **44,** 246
'extradition crime'. *See* extraditable offence, 'extradition crime' *above*
Fugitive Offenders Act 1967 distinguished **85,** 77, 78
'political offences' **55,** 552
s 2 **72,** 68, **78,** 517, **85,** 97, 134, 143
s 3 **79,** 103, **80,** 17, **85,** 87-8, 89-90
s 3(1) **79,** 101
s 5 **85,** 138
s 7 **85,** 75, 93, 103-7, 131-3, 139, 145
ss 7-10 **85,** 134-6
s 8 **85,** 75, 93, 131, 133, 145, **87,** 322-3, 327, **124,** 453-9
s 8(2) **87,** 324-6, 401
s 9 **87,** 402-3, 408
s 10 **78,** 510, 511, 516, **85,** 75, 93, 99, 103, 115, 131, **87,** 327, 400, 402-3, 408, **111,** 572-3
s 11 **78,** 389, 390, **85,** 99, **111,** 573
s 14 **78,** 508, 510, **85,** 95, 97, 98-9, 101-3
s 15 **85,** 95, 99, 102
s 17 **85,** 137
s 19 **72,** 603-4
s 20 **85,** 78, **87,** 327, 400, 402-3, 408
s 26 **78,** 516, 517, **85,** 83, 126, **87,** 408
Schedule 1 **87,** 400, **119,** 146-7
Schedule 2 **87,** 402
separation of powers **87,** 168
statement of charges under **88,** 352
Extradition Acts 1870-3, Seychelles, applicability **91,** 387-92
Extradition Acts 1870-1932 **73,** 45-53, **80,** 13
Extradition Acts 1870-1935 **87,** 314, 322, 401, **90,** 413, 415
extension to Hong Kong **84,** 57, **85,** 114-15
Extradition Act 1873
s 3 **84,** 58
s 4 **78,** 508-9, 511, 512
s 5 **84,** 739
s 8 **85,** 137
Extradition Act 1879 **86,** 224
Extradition Act 1932 **85,** 138, 141

Extradition Act 1989 **107,** 564, **119,** 139, 288, 308
as implementation of European Extradition Convention (1957) **95,** 404, **119,** 30, 254-5
Act as applicable law **119,** 324-5
s 1 **119,** 109, 246
s 1(1) **119,** 31, 144-5, 181
s 2 **119,** 2, 31-2, 41, 109, 144-5
s 2(1) **119,** 31, 190-1
s 2(1)(a) **119,** 37-8, 41, 76, 145, 177, 181-2, 184-5, 187, 258
s 2(1)(b) **119,** 2, 38, 55, 75, 92, 93, 181-2, 185, 187
s 2(2) **119,** 32, 41, 188
s 2(3) **119,** 2, 32
s 2(3)(a) **119,** 38, 55
s 2(3)(b) **119,** 38
s 2(3)(c) **119,** 38, 145
s 4(1) **119,** 32, 189
s 6 **111,** 574, 581, **119,** 109, 110, 249
s 6(1) **111,** 568
s 6(1)(a) **107,** 580, **119,** 110, 250
s 6(1)(c) **119,** 110, 250
s 6(1)(d) **119,** 110, 250
s 6(2) **111,** 568
s 6(3) **111,** 568
s 6(4) **95,** 404, **114,** 455
s 6(4)(b) **119,** 176
s 6(5) **119,** 176
s 6(9) **111,** 568
s 7 **111,** 551, 574, **119,** 77, 157, 256, 264, 281, 318
s 7(1) **119,** 32, 115
s 7(2) **119,** 33
s 7(2)(b) **119,** 146, 257
s 7(4) **111,** 551, 557, **119,** 33, 108-9, 178, 201-2, 248, 251, 286, 327, 329, 330
s 7(5) **119,** 146, 250
s 8 **111,** 574, **119,** 33-4
s 8(1)(b) **111,** 550, **119,** 1, 33-4, 53, 75, 77, 113, 176-7
s 8(3) **119,** 34, 146
s 8(4) **119,** 30, 34, 37, 53, 77
s 9 **111,** 574, 581, **119,** 251
s 9(1) **119,** 35
s 9(4) **111,** 579, **119,** 35
s 9(5) **119,** 35
s 9(6) **119,** 35
s 9(7) **119,** 35
s 9(8) **111,** 557, 577, **119,** 35, 36, 178, 189-90, 202, 249, 260, 284
s 9(8)(a) **119,** 146, 325
s 9(9) **119,** 35
s 10 **119,** 35-6
s 11 **111,** 574-5, **114,** 408, **119,** 36, 304
s 11(1) **111,** 557
s 11(3) **111,** 557, 568-70, 575, 577, 581, **119,** 251, 326
s 12 **111,** 575, 582, **119,** 36, 39, 92, 100, 108, 109, 110-11, 249, 251, 252, 265, 273, 276, 277, 278, 284, 293-4, 295, 297, 306, 310-17, 325

United Kingdom (*cont.*)
s 12(1) **114,** 407-8, 425-36, 446-7, **119,** 324
s 12(2) **114,** 409-10
s 12(2)(a) **119,** 324, 326
s 12(2)(a)(ii) **114,** 410, **119,** 110, 250-1, 294
s 12(2)(a)(iii) **119,** 110, 253
s 12(5) **119,** 28, 111, 251-2, 281
s 13 **111,** 560, 575, **119,** 36, 295
s 13(2) **119,** 294
s 13(4) **111,** 557
s 13(6) **111,** 557, 569, 581, **119,** 36, 294
s 15 **111,** 579
s 16 **119,** 39
s 16(1) **111,** 581
s 18 **95,** 404
s 18(2) **119,** 295
s 22 **119,** 295
s 22(4) **119,** 182
s 22(6) **119,** 182, 189
s 24 **119,** 110, 250
Schedule 1, para 20 **119,** 147
speciality **95,** 404
text (ss. 1-14) **119,** 6-20
extradition agreement. *See also* Extradition, European Convention on (1957) *below*
interpretation **85,** 139-40
legislation, effect of agreement on legislation **124,** 453-8
reciprocity, relevance **119,** 75-6
State succession and **85,** 143-5
Extradition, European Convention on (1957) **119,** 108, 248
Extradition Act 1989 as applicable law **119,** 324-5
incorporation into UK law **95,** 404, **119,** 2, 30, 31, 180-1, 254-5. *See also* Extradition Act 1989 *above*; Extradition Act 1989 *and* law of, European Convention on Extradition Order 1990 *below*
absence **119,** 324-5
obligation to extradite **111,** 556-7
prima facie case, need for **111,** 579
procedure, accusation case **119,** 255-6, 259
procedure between non-parties to **119,** 146
procedure between parties to **119,** 146
requested party's right to request supplementary information **119,** 180-1, 250, 256-7
Re Cuoghi **119,** 257
requesting party's rights, limited nature **119,** 294-5
Extradition (Hong Kong) Ordinance **84,** 57, **90,** 413, 415
extraterritorial legislation **78,** 461-2, 464, 559, 561, **80,** 34-5, **91,** 30
bankruptcy proceedings **88,** 312-22
enforceability **78,** 464, 533-4, 542
international comity and **88,** 318
federal State
constituent States
as State **111,** 608
State immunity, jurisdiction **52,** 322-8, **111,** 608-10
fisheries jurisdiction **59,** 352-3
fishing rights

historic rights, Icelandic waters **55,** 387, 397-8
Icelandic waters **55,** 263-9
force majeure
government intervention as **64,** 199-202, 204, 205-7, 372-3
State or State agency as party to contract and **64,** 199-201, 205-7
forcible abduction/unlawful arrest
breach of
comity **111,** 565
individual's rights **111,** 565
international law **111,** 565
laws of foreign State **111,** 565
circumvention of extradition arrangements **111,** 566
comity **95,** 404-5
court's power to enquire **95,** 383-416
extradition and **111,** 550-83
failure to observe extradition/deportation procedures **111,** 562-3, 566
international law, breach **95,** 408
jurisdiction, effect on **45,** 103
abuse of power amounting to abuse of process, whether **111,** 556, 561-3
bringing into/extradition from distinguished **111,** 560-1, 568, 581
competence to determine **111,** 557-63, 575-83
discretion to stay proceedings **95,** 390, 408-16
individual's right to challenge **95,** 404
New Zealand jurisprudence
Elliott **95,** 388-9, 406-7
Healey **95,** 410
Moevao **95,** 398, 405
Sinclair **95,** 386-8
Susannah Scott **95,** 386
relevant factors
coercion **111,** 567-8
physical force **111,** 564-6
trickery **111,** 566-8, 582-3
remedy, diplomatic channels **95,** 404
rule of law, breach **95,** 408
South African jurisprudence, *Ebrahim* **95,** 396
UK jurisprudence
Driver **95,** 385-6, 389-90, 411, 412
Mackeson **95,** 383-4, 406-7, 410
US jurisprudence **95,** 390, 396-8
Alvarez-Machain **95,** 397-8
Toscanino **95,** 396-7
foreign judgment, recognition/enforcement **60,** 69-77, **78,** 600, **85,** 87
applicable law, Enforcement of Judgments in Civil and Commercial Matters Convention (1968)/municipal law **107,** 497-9
bank guarantee, foreign State, **107,** 503
characterization of action in England deciding factor **85,** 69-70
Enforcement of Judgments in Civil and Commercial Matters Convention (1968)
harmonization of jurisdiction/remedies distinguished **107,** 497-8
implementing legislation **107,** 497-9
restraint order in aid of confiscation order made by foreign court, territorial jurisdiction and **122,** 518-24, 526-8
foreign law

United Kingdom (*cont.*)
evidence of **78,** 518-19, 579, 595
absence of **64,** 326, **125,** 692
as fact **125,** 692
relevance **85,** 23
foreign law, recognition/enforcement **66,** 44, **75,** 271-330, **78,** 597-607, 614-20, 627
act of State and **64,** 344, **78,** 599, **88,** 306, **116,** 568-78
characterization of action in England deciding factor **78,** 601
civilized standards, law falling below **88,** 307-8
comity **88,** 308, 310, **104,** 507, **108,** 592
confiscatory legislation **64,** 246-8, **72,** 449, 453-7, 459-60, 467-70, 474-6, **78,** 598, 604-5
contractual claim under impugnable foreign law **125,** 738-9
discrimination against nationals in time of war **108,** 591
discriminatory law **64,** 246-8, 374-6, **88,** 307
enforcement distinguished **78,** 597
expropriation/nationalization **78,** 604, **108,** 591-2
extradition proceedings as means of **78,** 505
extraterritorial effect, United States antitrust laws **74,** 39-40, 48-54, 78-82
fiscal, exchange control or revenue law **78,** 505, 597-8, 599, 601, 602-3, 605, 606, 607, 615, 627, **84,** 749-51, **88,** 321
infringement of human rights **108,** 554, 591
international law, need for conformity with **108,** 592
human rights law, whether limited to **125,** 633-8, 646-50, 680-5, 709-13, 718-22, 736-9
interpretation **78,** 595, 609
Statute, whether to be considered as a whole **78,** 599-601
judicial discretion and **88,** 308, 309
jurisprudence, *Luther* v. *Sagor* **64,** 264, **116,** 565-7, 587-9, **125,** 638-9
motivation of legislature **88,** 306, 307, 310
nature of, for determination by English court **78,** 628
obtaining evidence from abroad, whether **84,** 749-51
penal law **60,** 76, **64,** 246-8, 374-6, **78,** 597-8, 601-2, 615, 627-30, **88,** 307
'political' **78,** 603
private international law and **78,** 596, **88,** 307
public law **78,** 601, 603, 605-7, 615-19, 627
public policy and **64,** 247-8, 375-6, **78,** 604, 607, 630, **108,** 592-3, **116,** 56, 556, **125,** 637-46, 651-2, 665-8, 671, 727-8
context of legislation, relevance **125,** 668-70
'recognition' **64,** 247-8
recognition distinguished **78,** 597, 615
unconstitutional law **88,** 308
validity under law of legislating State, relevance **125,** 674-6, 685-7
Foreign Office certificate **52,** 69, 73-4, **73,** 12-13, 20
foreign relations
default judgment against foreign State and **118,** 615-16, 617-18
extradition and **119,** 72
judicial restraint, acts between private individuals affecting foreign relations **96,** 216-17
judicial review **74,** 38-9, 49, 78, 83
diplomatic protection, exercise **107,** 469-81
prerogative and **96,** 216
justiciability **98,** 178-9

responsibility for, executive **83,** 238
foreign State. *See also* State immunity *and* State Immunity Act 1978 *below*
notice of hearing, need for **107,** 637-8
procedural rules, applicability **107,** 631-2
forfeiture of property **78,** 609-11, 629
forgery, government documents, forged currency compared **118,** 589-91
forum [non] conveniens **83,** 252-4
absence of alternative forum **103,** 358-60
interference with affairs of foreign State and **124,** 568
probability of effective outcome and **124,** 569
State immunity, execution/attachment and **124,** 569
State immunity, jurisdiction and **64,** 82-4, 88-9, 184-6
forum selection clause
State succession and, change of legal system **118,** 528-39
stay of proceedings **118,** 561
France, continental shelf delimitation **71,** 94, 101, 120, 129, 151, 188
freedom of association. *See also* trade union *below*
principle of English law **78,** 414
European Convention on Human Rights (1950) **78,** 413-14
freedom of expression **85,** 34-5, 48-9
administration of justice and **78,** 397, 399
contempt of court and **78,** 396-402
exceptions, necessary and proportionate **85,** 35
prior restraint of publication **78,** 402
public interest and **85,** 32
terrorism and **85,** 34-5, 37-8, 42-4, 48-9
freedom of information, access to personal records files
consent of contributor **89,** 303, 304, 306, 311
private life, respect for and **89,** 293-313
public interest in maintenance of candid files **89,** 304
retrospective right **89,** 311
freedom of religion **73,** 403, 407-8, 410-14
Fugitive Offenders Act 1881 **41,** 400, **42,** 52-8, **51,** 292, **53,** 104-11, **55,** 81-2, **72,** 68, 203, **77,** 332, 344, **79,** 161, **88,** 270, 273-4
history **88,** 271
s 2 **53,** 103-8
s 10 **111,** 573
Fugitive Offenders Act 1967 **51,** 312-19, **52,** 371, 378, **55,** 431-2, **73,** 52, **79,** 676, **84,** 65, 683, **87,** 404, 405, **111,** 569
additional evidence **44,** 236-7
discretionary powers **80,** 16
evidence **44,** 246
evidence under **88,** 348-50
Extradition Act 1870 distinguished **85,** 77, 78
political offence **55,** 431
s 1 **88,** 370
s 3 **85,** 76-7
s 3(1) **88,** 338-9, 363
s 4(1)(c) **87,** 361-2
s 4(3) **88,** 355-6
s 5 **85,** 77, **88,** 362, 365, 370
s 5(1) **88,** 363

United Kingdom (*cont.*)
s 5(2) **88,** 353, 363
s 5(3) **88,** 363
s 6 **85,** 77, **88,** 363-4
s 6(1) **88,** 358, 359, 370
s 7 **88,** 337, 363, 365, 370
s 7(2) **88,** 371, 376
s 7(4) **88,** 362, 399
s 7(5) **88,** 331, 338-9, 358, 380
s 8 **88,** 331, 337
s 8(3) **88,** 401, **111,** 573-4
s 11 **88,** 337, 401
s 29 **85,** 99
Schedule 1 **78,** 502, **80,** 12-13, 14
s 2 **80,** 12-13, 14-15
s 3 **78,** 502-3, **80,** 15
s 4 **80,** 12, 15, 16, 18
s 5 **80,** 12, 18
s 7 **78,** 501-5, **80,** 12, 18
s 8 **80,** 17, 18
s 14 **80,** 15
s 19 **80,** 14, 15
Schedule 2 **79,** 660
para. 9 **79,** 645, 647, 650
para. 21 **79,** 651
Schedule 3 **80,** 128
s 1 **77,** 96
s 2 **80,** 123
s 4 **80,** 128
statement of charges under **88,** 352-5
Fugitive Offenders (Designated Commonwealth Countries) (No 3) Order 1970 **80,** 13
GDR, recognition **43,** 23-79, **71,** 22
Geneva Conventions (1949), implementing legislation, need for **123,** 604
Geneva Convention (Treatment of Prisoners of War) (Convention III) (1949), enforcement, individual, by **123,** 607-8
genocide. *See also* Genocide Act 1969 *below*
customary international law **119,** 106-7
definition **111,** 587-90
Head of State, immunity, jurisdiction **119,** 72
nuclear weapons
deployment **111,** 585-90
research **111,** 585-90
Genocide Act 1969 **111,** 587, 589
Head of State and **119,** 46, 72, 85
incorporation of Genocide Convention (1948) **119,** 46, 65-6, 72
'constitutionally responsible rulers', omission **119,** 46, 72, 85
Genocide Convention (1948)
applicability, Head of State **119,** 46, 65-6, 71, 85
State/Head of State immunity **119,** 46, 65-6, 71, 85
good faith
Crown's immunity from suit and **81,** 114-15, 119-20, 130, 136-8
extradition **119,** 110, 251

government
  definition
    'executive' **111,** 648-51, 667-71
    police force, whether **111,** 646-53
  evidence of
    international recognition **114,** 477-8
    official dealings with **114,** 476-7
Guernsey, constitutional position **75,** 570-1
habeas corpus **56,** 515, **61,** 256, **78,** 501, 507, **80,** 12, **85,** 73-90
  applicant outside jurisdiction **119,** 393-8
  in case of detention by peacekeeping forces **119,** 393-8
  deportation compared **85,** 86-90
  extradition and. *See* extradition, habeas corpus *above*
  as means to test validity of detention **119,** 393-4
Hague Convention on the Taking of Evidence Abroad in Civil or Commercial Matters (1970), implementation. *See* law of, Evidence (Proceedings within the Jurisdiction) Act 1975 *below*
Hague Regulations (1907), applicability in **83,** 160-2
head of government, immunity, jurisdiction **119,** 222
Head of State
  action on behalf of subjects **118,** 590
  as diplomatic agent **119,** 60-1, 246
    State Immunity Act 1978 and **119,** 245-6
  Diplomatic Privileges Act 1964 and **111,** 606, **119,** 42-8, 59-61
  evidence of status as **119,** 49, 56-7, 94
  functions
    applicable law **119,** 61, 62, 97, 104-5
    applicable law, international law **119,** 61-2, 104
    applicable law, municipal law of own country **119,** 61, 104-5
    crimes against international law and **119,** 43-8, 61-70, 83-7, 97-9, 104-7, 155-6, 169-70
    customary international law **119,** 61, 104-5, 193-6
    illegal act **121,** 62
    murder **119,** 84
    official nature of acts, relevance **119,** 103
    torture **119,** 4, 45, 47-8, 61-70, 97-100, 104, 151-7, 169-70, 204-18
  Genocide Act 1969 and **119,** 46, 72, 85
  as 'public official or person acting in that capacity' **119,** 70-2, 92-3, 100, 151, 152, 156, 162-3, 164
  responsibility for international crimes, customary international law **119,** 200-1
  as State **111,** 607, 609-10
  State Immunity Act 1978 and **119,** 58-60, 89, 94-5
Head of State, diplomatic privileges and immunities, entitlement **111,** 607-8, **119,** 42-8, 60-1, 96-9, 102-3
  time-limitation and **119,** 60-1, 89-90, 97
  Vienna Convention on Diplomatic Relations (1961), application, criminal proceedings **119,** 193
Head of State, former
  act of State and **119,** 106-7
  State Immunity Act 1978 and **119,** 58-61, 89-90
Head of State, former, immunity, jurisdiction
  arrest **119,** 61

United Kingdom (*cont.*)
as courtesy **119,** 234
criminal proceedings **119,** 246-7
customary international law **119,** 203-4, 208-11, 219
customary international law **119,** 43-8, 62-70, 78-87, 99-100, 106-7, 204
ratione materiae **119,** 219, 236-7
official acts in exercise of functions **119,** 4, 43-8, 55, 62-5, 79-83, 103, 153-4, 161, 169-70, 193-6, 202-18, 234-47
foreign relations **64,** 279
legislative activity **64,** 279
private acts **119,** 79-83
ratione materiae **119,** 223-4, 231, 240
customary international law **119,** 219, 236-7
Torture Convention (1984), effect **119,** 200-1, 215-16, 220, 231, 245
ratione personae **119,** 79, 96-9, 103
torture **119,** 45, 61-70, 97-100, 151-7, 219-21, 244-5, 250
Torture Convention (1984), exclusion **119,** 219-21, 245
treaty exception **119,** 68-70
acts prior to legislation implementing treaty exception **119,** 69-70
critical date **119,** 69-70, 140
requirements **119,** 69-70, 72, 195-6
strict interpretation **119,** 69, 72
Head of State, former, immunity, jurisdiction, waiver, Torture Convention (1984) as **119,** 216-17, 221, 245
Head of State, immunity, jurisdiction
absolute theory **119,** 49, 102
acts committed abroad **119,** 60-1, 161, 236
acts committed in own country **119,** 60-1, 90, 203
acts committed within forum State **119,** 45, 56, 90, 194, 231, 237, 246
common law **111,** 606, **119,** 88-90
contract debt **64,** 79-80
crimes against humanity **119,** 45-8, 98-9
criminal proceedings **119,** 45, 58, 87-9, 96, 155, 162, 204-18
gravity of crimes, relevance **119,** 62, 85, 169
cumulative nature **111,** 607
customary international law **119,** 44-8, 62-70, 78-87, 99-100, 104-5
ratione personae **119,** 219
executive certificate/statement **111,** 607
genocide **119,** 72
Genocide Convention (1948), applicability **119,** 65-6
head of government distinguished **119,** 222
hostage-taking **119,** 4
Hostages Convention (1979), applicability **119,** 65
international crimes **119,** 67-70, 83-7, 212-13, 223-33
jurisdiction, effect of grant to municipal courts **119,** 155-6
justiciability **119,** 73-4, 90-3
legality of act, relevance **119,** 62, 194-6, 224
official acts, while in power **119,** 41-9
personal sovereign
commercial acts **64,** 97-9
private acts **64,** 422-3, **87,** 237-8
real/immovable property, dispute relating to **64,** 98-9

trust fund cases **64,** 99
Pinochet proceedings, background **119,** 1-5
private acts **119,** 239
ratione materiae **119,** 153-4, 156, 161, 172-3, 194-5, 200-1, 215, 231, 239-42
Duke of Brunswick v. *King of Hanover* **119,** 63, 80-2
Torture Convention (1984), effect **119,** 200-1, 215-16, 220, 231, 245, **123,** 34-5
ratione personae **102,** 201-2, **119,** 79, 96-9, 161, 214, 222, 239
former Head of State distinguished **119,** 79, 96-9, 222
State immunity and **119,** 57, 62-5, 140, 152-7, 235
State immunity as basis **64,** 418
State immunity distinguished **64,** 616-17
Head of State, immunity, jurisdiction, theory/doctrine, basis, foreign relations considerations **119,** 72-3
Head of State, immunity, jurisdiction, waiver, by State, need for **119,** 79, 87
Head of State, inviolability of archives and documents **64,** 293
High Seas Convention (1958), implementing legislation **78,** 530
high treason. *See* treason *below*
homosexuality, law on **67,** 400-3, 435-6
England and Wales **67,** 401-2
Northern Ireland **67,** 400-1
Scotland **67,** 403
Hong Kong. *See* Hong Kong; Hong Kong Special Administrative Region (HKSAR)
hostage-taking. *See also* law of, Taking of Hostages Act 1982 *below*
act of State **119,** 96
customary international law **119,** 106-7
definition, Taking of Hostages Act 1982 **119,** 93, 147-8
extraditable offence **119,** 76, 93, 147-8, 182-3
Hostages Convention (1979)
applicability, Head of State **119,** 65
State/Head of State immunity and **119,** 65, 72, 85, 96, 98, 100
House of Lords
jurisdiction to rescind or vary an earlier order **119,** 120
non-representative status of members **124,** 585
human rights
alleged violation of **62,** 359-89
interference with
'in accordance with the law' **124,** 539
'necessary in a democratic society' **124,** 539
State's obligation to ensure protection
obligation to make representations to third State in respect of alien **123,** 595-9
obligation to make representations to third State in respect of national **123,** 606-9
Hungary, declaration of war on **44,** 336
Iceland, fishing dispute **55,** 246-56
Immigration Advisory Service **79,** 652
immigration controls **81,** 145-83. *See also relevant legislation under* law of *and* Special Immigration Appeals Commission (SIAC) *below*
appeals **81,** 154-6
Commonwealth citizens, working holiday rule **81,** 149
discretionary powers **81,** 148, 153
entry clearance **81,** 150
Immigration (Procedure) Rules 1972 **81,** 154-6
nationality laws and **81,** 145

United Kingdom (*cont.*)
non-patrial husband or fiancé **81,** 149, 152, 153
non-patrial wife or fiancée **81,** 151-2, 153-4
sanctions **81,** 154
'settled in the UK' **81,** 149
UK ancestry rule **81,** 149
work-permit requirements **81,** 149
income tax
assessment, maintenance orders **42,** 274-80
recovery, continental shelf and **78,** 528-50
indemnity, international organization, Member States against **80,** 201-2, 206, 208, **81,** 722-5
direct claim against Member States distinguished **80,** 205
individual in international law, rights **77,** 32
injunction, statutory provision **77,** 46, **80,** 194, 214, 216-18, **93,** 718, **107,** 501, **118,** 412 n. 71
insolvency/insolvency-related proceedings. *See* law of, Insolvency Act 1986; law of, Insolvency Rules 1986 *and* service of process out of the jurisdiction, insolvency/insolvency-related proceedings *below*
insurance contract. *See also* marine insurance *below*
excepted perils **74,** 7-8, 21-35
Interception of Communications White Paper 1980 **74,** 351-2, 359-66
interest, as part of value of property **122,** 523-4, 525-6
internal waters **43,** 114-25, **90,** 307-11
inter fauces terrae **90,** 307-11
King's Chambers **90,** 308-11
neutrality and **90,** 308
International Convention relating to the Arrest of Seagoing Ships (1952)
implementation **78,** 686, 689
travaux préparatoires **78,** 686, 687, 693
international crimes
classification as
torture **119,** 149-50, 155-6, 199-201, 217
Torture Convention (1984), relevance **119,** 229-30
definition
instigation of State authorities, need for **119,** 226-7, 243
scale, relevance **119,** 217, 229, 250
Head of State, immunity, jurisdiction **119,** 67-70, 83-7, 212-13, 223-33
jurisdiction **119,** 139
immunity from/right of distinguished **119,** 69
universal jurisdiction **119,** 67, 229-33, 243
effectiveness, need for **119,** 325-6
international law **59,** 460-1, 467-8, 469, **64,** 130-1, 140-4, 152-3, **77,** 314-20. *See also* treaties *below*
compatibility of ministerial action, authority to determine **83,** 237, 238, 243
compatibility with municipal law
bad faith **83,** 239
judicial review **83,** 231
court's duty to apply **80,** 90, 144, 150, 201
proprio motu **77,** 327
dualist theory **85,** 257, 258, **119,** 69

establishment of **80,** 52-3, 132-41. *See also* sources *below*
evidence of, collective opinion of professors, admissibility **77,** 76
implementation of obligations, political matter **117,** 482
incorporation, need for **59,** 460-1, **64,** 89-90, 127-8, **77,** 32, 94-6, **78,** 376-7, 393-4, **80,** 132-3
judicial notice **64,** 143
lacuna, admissibility **80,** 135
municipal courts
application by, international adjudication, relevance **107,** 480
creation by **81,** 680, 715
relevance **85,** 23
unincorporated law **107,** 473-4
municipal law and **80,** 52-3, 102, 105-7, 132-3, **81,** 714, **103,** 427, **117,** 560, 581, 582, 590. *See also* primacy *below*
customary international law. *See* customary international law *above*
established rule, need for **80,** 132-3
transformation doctrine **80,** 132
precedent in municipal courts **64,** 88-90
stare decisis doctrine **64,** 16, 89-90, 140-6, 150-3, 169, 212-15, 549-50
primacy, municipal law **59,** 467-8
private international law distinguished **81,** 681
sources **119,** 236. *See also* treaties, source of international law *below*
customary law **80,** 173
general principle of law recognized by civilized nations **80,** 135
judicial and arbitral decisions **80,** 53, 135, 138-41, **119,** 237
judicial and arbitral decisions, municipal courts of another country **64,** 180-1, 238-40, 316-18, 362
legislation **80,** 135
reason and justice, supplementary **80,** 146
State papers **80,** 135
State practice **80,** 173-6
teachings of publicists **80,** 53, 106, 108, 135-8, **81,** 715, **83,** 247, **107,** 565-6, **119,** 237-8
usage **80,** 135, 173
treaties. *See* treaties *below*
unenforceable contract **77,** 327
International Monetary Fund Agreement (IMF) (1944) (Bretton Woods Agreement). *See also* law of, Bretton Woods Agreements Act 1945 *and* Bretton Woods Agreements Order in Council 1946 *below*
incorporation into UK law **72,** 693, 696, 702
International Oil Pollution Compensation Fund **77,** 15
international organizations
as agency **81,** 715-18
applicable law **81,** 682, 699-700, 711
classification of activities, activity and mode of performance distinguished **107,** 612
constituent instrument. *See also* law of, International Tin Council (Immunities and Privileges) Order 1972 *below*
enforcement **81,** 717, 724
implementing legislation **81,** 712
contract
arbitration clause, need for **81,** 683-4
repudiation **81,** 683

United Kingdom (*cont.*)
debts, liability for **80,** 46, 52-3, 152, 158, 159, **81,** 676-725
concurrent **81,** 699, 708-10
exclusion **80,** 144-6, 173-6
general rule of international law **80,** 52-3, **81,** 679-80, 699
indemnification of organization **80,** 170, **81,** 682, 714-15
intention of founding States **80,** 141, 165, 170
international law and municipal law distinguished **80,** 52, 53
members **80,** 46
policy decision **81,** 682, 714-15
secondary liability **80,** 159-60
development of **80,** 65-8
constituent instruments **80,** 67
implementing legislation **80,** 68-71
State practice **80,** 67-8
dispute settlement **81,** 683
Headquarters Agreement, purpose **81,** 705
immunity, jurisdiction, waiver **81,** 707
implementing legislation **80,** 68, 69-71, 89, 92-3, 155-61
consistency **80,** 68
language compared **80,** 69-71, 89, 92-3, 155-61
Member States, obligations to indemnify **80,** 170
municipal law, subjection to, comity and **80,** 93
status
absence of action **85,** 12, 20
applicable law, domicile **108,** 582-5, 586
corporation **85,** 12
establishment in UK **85,** 20
incorporation into municipal law **81,** 706-7
independent entity **81,** 698-9, 702, 703-8, 712
international law as basis **80,** 65, **81,** 707, **108,** 586-90
legal capacities of body corporate **85,** 20
legal personality, need for **85,** 8-9
'mixed entity' **80,** 52, 97-9, 103
municipal law, under **81,** 708, 709, 711-12
right of suit **85,** 28-9
treaty, relevance **85,** 12, 20, 24
UK non-member **85,** 8-9, 12, 20
uniformity, absence of **85,** 12
international organizations, privileges and immunities
classification of act, organization and administration **81,** 707
functional, employment of staff **107,** 612
human rights offences, official acts and **107,** 609-13
UK not a member **83,** 269
international organizations, privileges and immunities, entitlement, representatives of Member States **81,** 707
International Tin Council (ITC) **83,** 250-2, 262-3, 270-1, **85,** 9-10. *See also* law of, International Organizations Act 1968 *and* International Tin Council (Immunities and Privileges) Order 1972 *below*; International Tin Council (ITC)
Iran–US Claims Tribunal
proceedings, status **75,** 165-73
res judicata and **75,** 161-4, 172-5
Ireland, Republic of

extradition from **79,** 49-167
foreign State, whether **87,** 331-2
relationship with **59,** 346-7
Irish Free State Constitution Act (1922) **79,** 29-30
Isle of Man. *See* Isle of Man
judicial assistance
Head of State, former, recovery of assets from
disclosure of information **107,** 501-3
injunction restraining removal or dealing with **107,** 492-505
limitation **88,** 306-10
enforcement of foreign law **88,** 306-10, 320-2
Scheme relating to Mutual Assistance in Criminal Matters within the Commonwealth (1986/1990) ('Harare Scheme') **111,** 615, 653-4
judicial decision, expropriation, whether **75,** 375, 378-80
judicial discretion **84,** 750
foreign law, recognition/enforcement **88,** 308, 309
legislation, interpretation **122,** 446
stay of proceedings **118,** 533-9
for forcible abduction/unlawful arrest **95,** 390, 608-16
judicial impartiality
appearance of bias **119, 119,** 120-4, 127-35
Amnesty International Charity Limited, relationship with **119,** 113-35
nemo judex in sua [propria] causa/'no-one should be judge in his own cause' **119,** 120-4, 125-35
objective test **121,** 334
'real danger' **119,** 124
'real suspicion' **119,** 130
judicial notice **83,** 250
international law **64,** 143
Security Council Resolutions **116,** 599, 601
status of foreign government **64,** 513
treaty **41,** 6
judicial restraint
act of State and **64,** 279-80, 344-51, **119,** 74, 92, **124,** 563-4
foreign relations, acts between private individuals affecting foreign relations **96,** 216-17
judicial review **78,** 373, 391, 394, 424, 468, 551, **79,** 645, 663-4, **80,** 18, **85,** 32-3, 34, 35, 38
aliens
illegal entry, removal for **79,** 647
refoulement **79,** 652
refugee status **79,** 662
refusal of entry **79,** 648, 661, 663
appeal distinguished **85,** 50, **92,** 231-2, **114,** 418, 452
asylum application **79,** 657
'civil proceedings' **78,** 391
decision of local authority relating to a child in care **92,** 230-2
development of concept **84,** 768
diplomatic protection **116,** 609-22
directives approved by Parliament **84,** 761
discretionary **84,** 718-19, **123,** 574-5
effective remedy, whether **98,** 316-17, **124,** 515-16, 540-1
European Convention on Human Rights (1950) and **112,** 385-7
foreign relations **84,** 717, 720

United Kingdom (*cont.*)
prerogative and **96,** 216
grounds
abuse of power **111,** 556, 561-3, 568-70
abuse of process **111,** 566
bad faith **92,** 231
change in applicant's personal circumstances **114,** 419
due impartiality, lack **84,** 768-9, 778
error of law **114,** 415-25
failure to consider relevant circumstances **92,** 231
failure to observe correct procedures **92,** 231
illegality **84,** 766, **92,** 231, **111,** 556, **114,** 453, 464
irrationality/unreasonableness **112,** 387, 389-91, 395, 399-403, 407-9, **114,** 414, 449, 452, 464-5, **118,** 600, 601, **124,** 470-1
procedural impropriety **84,** 766, **114,** 418-19, 451-2
proportionality **84,** 766-7
ultra vires **92,** 231
unfairness **124,** 467-70
legality of government actions, limitation to **98,** 169
matters relating to trial on indictment, consent to prosecutions **122,** 440-2, 450-3, 468-71, 472, 475-6, 491-5
national security **112,** 382-9
parties, inherent jurisdiction concerning **100,** 251
prerogative powers, exercise of **84,** 717, 718-19, **123,** 605-6
secondary legislation **93,** 632
draft Order in Council **93,** 632-4, 636-9
standing **93,** 636
'sufficient interest' **119,** 279-80
transfer of persons sentenced abroad **84,** 722, 725
judicial role
abuse of process and **95,** 390-5, 401, 407-8
activities abroad **95,** 403-4, 408
examining magistrate **95,** 393-5, 412-16
executive acts, supervision **95,** 392-3, 399-406, 409-10
forensic process, limited to, whether **95,** 390, 405, 407-8
jurisdiction. *See also* justiciability *below*
adjudicative and enforcement jurisdiction, distinguishability **107,** 644-58
admiralty. *See* admiralty jurisdiction *above*
aliens **59,** 326
member of firm carrying on business in country **101,** 346
present at time of transaction **101,** 345
present in country **101,** 345-6
resident in country **101,** 345
British ship on high seas **56,** 245, 254
alien **77,** 289
British subject **77,** 289
British ship not on high seas, British subject **77,** 289
Canadian Indians' property rights **78,** 423-55, 470
civil **73,** 298-363
colonies **123,** 569-75, 591-2
common law **90,** 297-9
'conduct' crime **77,** 280
Constitution of independent country **78,** 464-5

coroner's **78,** 551-63
criminal **59,** 336-40, **84,** 43-8, 678-87, **85,** 117-26
  attempt **87,** 410-12
  completion of offence **84,** 679
  continuity of offence **84,** 680-1, 684, 685-6
  crimes committed abroad **41,** 263
  extraterritoriality **60,** 97, 98
  fraud **72,** 602-4
  gravamen of offence **84,** 678, 680, 681, 682-3, 687
  high seas, definition **55,** 440
  jurisdiction **84,** 43-8
  location of crime **88,** 339-48
  nationals abroad **73,** 253-74, **78,** 559
  nature of offence as determining factor **84,** 678, 681
  nexus **84,** 678, 699-700
  place of commission **78,** 503, 600-1
  single *situs* **84,** 681
  situs of single element of crimes **84,** 678
  substantial links **84,** 679
  territorial **55,** 112-14, 117-21, 123-4, 130, 135, 137, **84,** 677, **85,** 117
EEC **80,** 126-7
effects doctrine **84,** 676, 678-9, 685-6
  Government Memorandum **48,** 119-20
enforceability of decision, relevance **107,** 642-58
examination in bankruptcy **88,** 312-22
extradition **85,** 98-9, **88,** 338-9
extraterritorial. *See also* United Kingdom, presumption of territorial limitation, legislation, interpretation
  alien abroad **77,** 279, 281
  criminal law **60,** 97, 98
  injunction against former Head of State **107,** 494-505
  lawful authority, justification or excuse under *lex loci delicti commissi* **119,** 71
  national abroad **77,** 279
  Torture Convention (1984) **100,** 471, **107,** 546, **119,** 70-1, 76, 85, 150, **123,** 34
extraterritorial offence, counselling and procuring **79,** 94
fisheries **59,** 352-3
forcible abduction and **95,** 363-8
foreign aircraft
  landing in UK required **77,** 283
  outside territorial airspace **77,** 280
  in territorial airspace **77,** 280
foreign law, enforcement. *See* foreign law, recognition/enforcement *above*
foreign ship on high seas, British subject **77,** 284-92
immunity from. *See* privileges and immunities *below*
international organization
  expert **77,** 132
  Member States' relations with **77,** 133
  third States' relations with **77,** 133
Law Commission Working Paper No 29 **85,** 124
nationals abroad, murder or manslaughter **78,** 559, **119,** 55, 184
nexus
  applicable law **64,** 219, **101,** 347

United Kingdom (*cont.*)
in rem jurisdiction and **64,** 234, 323
loan payable in forum State **64,** 219
nature and purpose of transaction **101,** 349
place of business **101,** 349
possession of heritable [real] property within the jurisdiction. *See* possession of heritable [real] property within the jurisdiction *below*
property in country **101,** 347, 349. *See also* possession of heritable [real] property within the jurisdiction *below*
residence **101,** 349
shares in company based in forum State **124,** 556, 568
offences committed abroad
alien **77,** 279
members of the armed forces **77,** 279
nationals abroad **78,** 559
Parliament, intention of **60,** 97, 108
piracy **78,** 568-74
ports, colonial **55,** 441-2
possession of heritable [real] property within the jurisdiction
consular use, relevance **107,** 643-58
nature of title, relevance **107,** 646-8, 653-5
presence in territory as basis **77,** 283, 374-6, **78,** 533, 535-7, 558
residence, relevance **78,** 536, 549
alien resident in country **101,** 345
plaintiff **123,** 30-1
tax **78,** 528-50
territorial **73,** 253-73, 298-363, **77,** 283, 288, **78,** 503-5, 528-50, 558, 559, 561-3, 614-20
avoidance of infringement on third State **84,** 698
comity and **84,** 677, 684-6, 698-9
judicial doctrine **84,** 677
restraint order in aid of confiscation orders made by foreign court **122,** 518-24, 526-8
State immunity and **119,** 236
Territorial Waters Jurisdiction Act 1878. *See* law of, Territorial Waters Jurisdiction Act 1878
tort committed abroad
double actionability **116,** 541-2, **125,** 675, 685-90, 713-14, 722-8, 729-39
double actionability, damages **125,** 690-1, 714
trespass to foreign land **73,** 17-24, 27-30
universal, international crimes **119,** 67, 229-33, 243
visiting forces **79,** 22-5, 37-8
jus cogens/peremptory norm
Head of State immunity, jurisdiction and **119,** 155, 195, 197
State immunity, jurisdiction and **103,** 421-2, 427-31, **107,** 541-4, **119,** 225, **123,** 32, 50-1
torture **103,** 421-2, 427-31, **107,** 541-4, **119,** 85, 86, 200, 206, 214, 244, 310-11, **120,** 385-6
justice, inherent jurisdiction **100,** 250
justiciability **80,** 66, 86-90, 199-210, **84,** 687. *See also* jurisdiction *above*
act of State **80,** 124, 177, 201-2, 205, **81,** 700-1, 721-2
comity **108,** 576, **111,** 598-9, 602-3

Crown's duty of protection in dependent territory **78,** 491-500
decision based on political judgement, foreign State's adherence to treaty **114,** 422-3, 425-6, 429-33, 450-1
foreign relations **98,** 178-9
foreign State. *See also* act of State, applicability, territorial dispute
breach of treaty **108,** 576, 594-6
disputes between **64,** 339-43, 348-51, **108,** 574-7, 587-91, 594-6, 613
Head of State, immunity, jurisdiction and **119,** 73-4, 90-3
legislature's role **119,** 96
national security **123,** 609-10
nature of issue determining factor **80,** 86-7, **123,** 605-6
prerogative powers, exercise of **84,** 720
State immunity and **80,** 124, 164, 205, **119,** 78
substantive issue **119,** 78
treaty-making power **87,** 183
unincorporated treaty **80,** 52, 57, 86-90, 102-4, 111-12, 148, 177, 208, **81,** 700-2, 703, 710, 713-15, 716, 719, 724
landlord and tenant, tenant's right of enfranchisement **75,** 408-28
compensation, valuation **75,** 423-5, 435
law of
Access to Personal Files Act 1987 **89,** 299, 305, 311
Access to Personal Files (Social Services) Regulations 1989 **89,** 298-9, 305
Act for the Government of Vancouver Island and the Colony of British Columbia 1866 **90,** 271, 285-92
Act to define the Boundaries of British Columbia and to provide for the Government of the said Colony 1863 **90,** 285
Act to provide for the Government of British Columbia 1858 **90,** 284-5
Act of Union 1707. *See* Union of England and Scotland, Act of Parliament of Scotland ratifying and approving the Treaty of Union with England 1707/Act of Union with Scotland Act 1706
Adaptation of Enactments Act 1922, s 6 **79,** 167
Administration of Justice Act 1956 **52,** 450-1, 454-6, **72,** 3-9
'beneficially owned as respects all the shares therein' **64,** 188-93
s 1(1) **78,** 685, 686
s 1(1)(d)-(r) **64,** 177-8
s 1(1)(g) **64,** 176
s 1(1)(h) **64,** 176
s 1(1)(n) **64,** 88
s 3(4) **64,** 177, 186-94, 231
s 8(1) **78,** 691
s 47(2) **78,** 684-6, 688-93
Administration of Justice Act 1960, s 1(2) **84,** 725-6
Administration of Justice Act 1961 **85,** 93
Administration of Justice Act 1970 **89,** 295
Administration of Justice (Miscellaneous Provisions) Act, s 2 (2) **95,** 412
Admiralty Offences Act 1844, **77,** 290
Admiralty Offences (Colonial) Act 1849 **48,** 79, **77,** 290
Adoption Act 1976 **89,** 120
Agriculture (Miscellaneous Provisions) Act 1954 **87,** 370
s 11 **77,** 278
Air Force Act 1955 **90,** 463, 464
Air Navigation Act 1920 **90,** 252

United Kingdom (*cont.*)
Air Navigation Order 1976 **78,** 523-6
Air Navigation Order 1980 **78,** 523
s 59(1) **107,** 482, 484, 490
s 80 **107,** 482
Air Navigation Order 1985. *See also* civil aviation, provisional suspension or variation of certificate *above*
incorporation of Chicago Convention on International Civil Aviation (1944), whether **124,** 471-5
s 62(1) (provisional suspension or variation of certificate) **124,** 462-75
Aircraft and Shipbuilding Industries Act 1977 **75,** 450-79, 487-561, 612
Airports Act 1986
s 30(3) **102,** 281, 286-8
s 85(4) **102,** 281
Airports Authority Act 1975
s 1(1), **78,** 521
s 2 **78,** 523
Alberta Act 1905 **78,** 450
Aliens Acts 1909/14 **38,** 156, **43,** 176
Aliens Order 1919 **71,** 457
Aliens Order 1953 **71,** 485
discretion of Home Secretary **52,** 340-5, 347-8, 349, 351-3
extension of landing permit **52,** 352
visiting forces and **41,** 396-7
Aliens Restriction Act 1914 **86,** 222
Aliens Restriction Act 1919 **52,** 340-1, 347-8, **71,** 584
Aliens Restriction (Consolidation) Order 1916 **86,** 222
Allied Forces Act 1940 **79,** 22, 23-5, 38, 39
Arbitration Act 1889 **80,** 187
Arbitration Act 1950 **74,** 562-8
Arbitration Act 1979
appeal under **78,** 582-3
s 1(3) **78,** 579
Arbitration (Foreign Awards) Act 1930 **74,** 563, 565
Arbitration (International Investment Disputes) Act 1966 **75,** 167
Army Act 1955 **90,** 463, 464
Asian Development Bank (Privileges and Immunities) Order 1974 **77,** 89
Asylum and Immigration Appeals Act 1993 **104,** 658-9, **107,** 561-2
s 8(1) **104,** 659, **122,** 531, 543
s 8(2) **122,** 543, **124,** 500
s 8(4) **107,** 579
s 9(1) **104,** 659
Asylum and Immigration Appeals Act 1999
s 69(2) **122,** 543
s 69(3) **122,** 543
Atomic Energy Authority Act 1954 **44,** 409
Australia Act 1986 **91,** 12, 97
Australian Colonies Act 1861 **86,** 188, 194, 206
Australian Constitutions Acts 1850 **51,** 47, 177
Aviation and Maritime Security Act 1990 **107,** 565
Backing of Warrants (Republic of Ireland) Act 1965 **51,** 366
Bahamas Extradition Act 1926 **85,** 137
Bahamas Islands (Constitution) Act 1963 **85,** 137-8

Bahamas Islands (Constitution) Order 1973 **85,** 137, 138
Banking Act 1979 **77,** 2
Bankruptcy Act 1869 **87,** 390-1
Bankruptcy Act 1883 **80,** 187, **84,** 679, **88,** 314
Bankruptcy Act 1914 **72,** 32, 35, 40-1, 44, 46-7
s 25 **88,** 312-22
s 122 **88,** 313, 314
s 123 **88,** 313, 314, 319
s 132 **88,** 316, 322
Bankruptcy Rules 1952
Rule 86 **88,** 313
Rule 86 (amended) **88,** 313, 314, 319
Basutoland (Constitution) Order in Council 1959 **90,** 355, 432, 435
Basutoland Order 1965 **90,** 433-5, 436, 455, 458
Bechuanaland Protectorate and Swaziland Court of Appeal Order in Council 1954 **90,** 458
Bill of Rights 1688, s 1(9) **77,** 123
Bills of Exchange Act 1882, s 30 **118,** 577
Births and Deaths Registration Act 1953 **89,** 98, 100-1, 119-21
Boarding-out of Children Regulations 1955 **89,** 294, 310
Bretton Woods Agreements Act 1945 **41,** 230, 232, 233, 237, **77,** 326, **80,** 68, **83,** 269, **85,** 12, 20, **118,** 570
Bretton Woods Agreements Order in Council 1946 **77,** 323, 326-9, **85,** 12, **118,** 570
British Nationality Act 1948 **39,** 326, 385, 393, **44,** 374, **61,** 400, **78,** 492, **81,** 145
British protected person, definition **55,** 490, 493-4
s 1 **80,** 13
s 1(2) **92,** 634
s 39(6) **124,** 514
Schedule 4 **124,** 514
British Nationality Act 1981 **80,** 13, 14, **81,** 152
Gibraltar and **123,** 6
s 6 **81,** 153
s 11(1) **81,** 152
British Nationality and New Zealand Citizens Act 1948, s 16(3) **79,** 685
British Nationality and Status of Aliens Act 1914 (Imperial) **79,** 686-7
s 1 **79,** 691-4
s 2 **79,** 691-4
s 8 **79,** 688, 691-4
British Nationality and Status of Aliens (in New Zealand) Act 1923, s 14 **79,** 686, 691-4
British Nationality and Status of Aliens (in New Zealand) Act 1928
purpose **79,** 687
s 3 **79,** 687, 692
s 6 **79,** 688-9
s 7 **79,** 686-94
Schedule 1 **79,** 688
British North America Acts. *See* Canada, British North America Acts
British Settlements Acts 1887/1945 **42,** 11, 15, 16, 19, 24-5, **44,** 113, 116, **104,** 511, 515, **123,** 585-7
Broadcasting Act 1981
consolidation, as **84,** 771
reserve powers **84,** 765-6
s 2 **85,** 36

United Kingdom (*cont.*)
s 3 **85,** 36
s 4 **85,** 36, 40-1
s 4(1) **84,** 762, 765-6, 774, 778
s 29(2) **84,** 766
s 29(3) **84,** 754, 762, 766, 770, 771, 773, 774-5, **85,** 31-2, 36, 37, 38-9
s 29(4) **84,** 766
Broadcasting Authority Act 1960, s 31(1) **84,** 764-5
Building Societies Act 1874 **77,** 82
Burma Independence Act 1947, s 4.1 **78,** 451
Carriage by Air Act 1932 **41,** 428-36, **43,** 254-9, **74,** 632, 640, 649, 671, **87,** 367, 388, 392
s 4 **87,** 368, 372, 381-2, 385, 389, 393
Carriage by Air Act 1961 **41,** 428-36, **43,** 254-9, **74,** 632, 639, 640, 645, 649, 657, 660, 663, 671, 675-7, 682, **87,** 337-8, 367
s 1 **87,** 353, 367-8, 393
s 1(1) **87,** 353, 385, 392
s 1(4) **87,** 353
s 9 **87,** 385
s 10 **87,** 369-70, 372, 375-6, 377-8, 382, 389, 392
s 10(1) **87,** 368, 386, 393
s 10(2) **87,** 368
Schedule **87,** 386-7
Carriage by Air Act (Non-international Carriage) (UK) Order 1952 **87,** 368, 376-8, 389
Carriage by Air Acts (Application of Provisions) Order 1967 **87,** 367, 369, 378, 383, 387-9, 394, 396-8
Carriage by Air and Road Act 1979 **74,** 637-9, 642, 647-9, 667, 682
Carriage of Goods by Road Act 1965 **74,** 577, 581, 587, 591, 596, 601, 605, 609, 613, 615, 679, **86,** 153-60
Carriage of Goods by Road (Parties to Convention) (Amendment) Order 1980 **86,** 158
Carriage of Goods by Sea Act 1924 **74,** 581
Carriage of Goods by Sea Act 1971 **74,** 582, 624
Child Abduction and Custody Act 1985, declaration of wrongful removal **114,** 497-501
Child Care Act 1980 **92,** 224
Children Act 1948 **92,** 227
Children Act 1975 **92,** 224, 233
Children Act 1989, diplomatic privileges and immunities, relevance **114,** 480-5
Children and Young Persons Act 1969 **92,** 224, 225-6
Citizenship of Southern Rhodesia and British Nationality Act 1963 **78,** 492
Civil Aviation Act 1971 **74,** 72-3
Civil Aviation Act 1982 **80,** 68, 158, **83,** 269, **86,** 43
s 1(1)(c) **124,** 462
s 60 **124,** 462
Civil Aviation (Eurocontrol) Act 1962 **80,** 68, 158
Civil Evidence Act 1968 **73,** 309, 312, 317, 333, 343, 353, **108,** 626, **116,** 599-600
Civil Jurisdiction and Judgments Act 1982 **84,** 745
s 25(1) **107,** 496
s 25(2) **107,** 496-7, 501-2
Coal Industry Nationalisation Act 1946 **77,** 315
Coal Mines Act 1911 **77,** 311

Colonial Boundaries Act 1895 **51,** 47, 182, **86,** 191, 197, 198, 202, 204, 205, 206, 207, 605, **123,** 557
Colonial Courts of Admiralty Act 1890 **48,** 79, **51,** 46, 47, 77
Colonial Laws Validity Act 1865 **38,** 124, **39,** 341, **44,** 111, 118, **73,** 112, 283, **77,** 380, **86,** 200, **90,** 250, 468,**123,** 585
s 2 **123,** 576
s 3 **123,** 576
Colonial Letters Patent Act 1863 **86,** 197
Common Fund for Commodities (Immunities and Privileges) Order 1981 **77,** 89
Commonwealth of Australia Act 1900 **51,** 47, **86,** 192, 196-7, 208
Commonwealth Immigration Act 1962 **43,** 131-3, 135, 139, 166-7, 168-70, 172-5, 176
passports **78,** 436
Commonwealth Secretariat Act 1966 **80,** 68, 158
Companies Act 1948, s 407 **78,** 529
Companies Act 1985 **77,** 21-41, **81,** 679, **85,** 5
s 537 **77,** 20
s 561 **80,** 221
s 665 **77,** 27, 28, 31, 34-5, **80,** 183, 184-6
ss 665-74 **80,** 184
s 671 **77,** 27, 28, 31, 34-5
s 674 **77,** 27, 29
s 716 **80,** 97
Company Directors Disqualification Act 1986 **77,** 99
Conservation (Natural Habitats and of Wild Fauna and Flora) Regulations 1994. *See* Conservation (Natural Habitats and of Wild Fauna and Flora) Regulations 1994 *above*
Consular Relations Act 1968 **88,** 397
Consular Relations Act 1972 **74,** 187
Contagious Diseases (Animals) Act 1878, **77,** 282
Continental Shelf Act 1964 **43,** 113, **77,** 305, 313, **86,** 602
'designated areas' **78,** 530, 538
s 1 **77,** 314-15
s 1(1) **77,** 320, **120,** 618, 623
s 1(3) **77,** 315
s 1(5) **77,** 315
s 1(7) **77,** 316, **120,** 623
Cook Islands Act 1915 **79,** 690
Cornwall Submarine Mines Act 1858 **43,** 107
Council of Europe (Immunities and Privileges) Order 1960 **41,** 438-40, 443-4, 446, 448-51
County Courts Admiralty Jurisdiction Act 1868 **78,** 690
County Courts Admiralty Jurisdiction Amendment Act 1869, s 6.2, **78,** 685, 689, 693
Courts Act 1971 **78,** 307, **88,** 275
Courts (Emergency Powers) Act 1914 **80,** 188
Criminal Appeal Act 1968 **57,** 118-19, **73,** 262
Criminal Attempts Act 1981 **87,** 409
s 1 **87,** 410
s 1(4) **87,** 409-10
Criminal Damage Act 1971 **74,** 460, **77,** 286
s 1(1) **77,** 285, 288
Criminal Evidence Act 1965 **74,** 489

United Kingdom (*cont.*)
Criminal Justice Act 1988 **87,** 401
retroactive, whether **119,** 230
right of appeal from High Court **122,** 518-21, 524-5
s 4(6) **87,** 406
s 71 **122,** 525-6
s 71(4) **122,** 526
s 74(1) **122,** 526
s 74(1)(a) **122,** 520
s 74(1)(b) **122,** 520
s 74(10) **122,** 520, 526
s 76 **122,** 522, 526
s 77 **122,** 516, 518-21
s 96 **122,** 521-2, 526, 527
s 96(1)(a) **122,** 527-8
s 96(2) **122,** 525-6, 527
s 97 **122,** 527
s 102(4) **122,** 522, 526, 527-8
s 102(7) **122,** 520
s 134 **100,** 471, **119,** 2-3, 40, 46, 70-1, 76, 106, 139, 144, 151, 160, 182, 188, 192, 201, 214, 220, 230-1, 246, 258, 327, 329, 330
s 134(1) **103,** 426, **119,** 76, 93, 183, 188
s 134(3) **119,** 183-4, 188, 258
Criminal Justice Act 1988 (Designated Countries and Territories) 1991 (as amended 1994) (DCO) **122,** 516
enforcement proceedings under, whether criminal cause or matter **122,** 516, 518-21, 524-5
retrospectivity **122,** 521-3
Criminal Justice (International Cooperation) Act 1990 **119,** 283-4
s 7(4) **111,** 615, 659
Criminal Justice and Public Order Act 1994
s 82(1) **122,** 474
s 146 **112,** 373-4
s 146(4) **112,** 375-6
Criminal Justice (Scotland) Act 1980 **85,** 106
Criminal Law Act 1967, s 3(1) **111,** 587, 588-9
Criminal Law Act 1977
s 1 **119,** 189
s 1(4) **119,** 184-5, 189, 190
s 5 **119,** 184
Criminal Law Amendment Act 1885 **67,** 400-1
Criminal Law Jurisdiction Act 1975
s 6(2) **79,** 94
s 6(3) **79,** 94
s 11 **79,** 95
Criminal Procedure (Scotland) Act 1887 **56,** 252
Criminal Procedure (Scotland) Act 1995
s 123(1) **122,** 621-3
s 123(5) (Lord Advocate's power of reference on questions of law without affecting acquittal) **122,** 624
Crown Lands Resumption Ordinance **77,** 379
Crown Proceedings Act 1947 **44,** 363, 374, **52,** 326, **73,** 129, **80,** 71, 188, **81,** 136, 707

s 10 **100,** 435, 437
s 21 **78,** 391-2
s 40 **78,** 433, 436, 494, 496
Crown Proceedings Act 1987 **100,** 451-2, 455
Customs and Excise Act 1952 **57,** 122, 129, **74,** 576, 582, 584, 588, 596, 600, 604, 610, 679
acts committed abroad **57,** 144
ss 47-56 **78,** 610
ss 275-80 **78,** 610
Schedule 7, para. 1 **78,** 610
Customs and Excise Management Act 1979 **78,** 620
Customs Laws Consolidation Act 1876 **78,** 620
s 106 **78,** 610
s 130 **78,** 610
s 138 **78,** 610
Cyprus Act 1960 **73,** 12
applicability to Cyprus as a whole **108,** 549
renunciation of all power in respect of Cyprus, Republic of **112,** 741
s 1 **112,** 737, 741
Dangerous Drugs Act 1965 **57,** 121, 122, 133-4, 140-1, **73,** 270
Diplomatic Privileges Acts. *See Diplomatic Privileges Acts above*
Diseases of Animals Act 1894, s 22 **77,** 282-3
Diseases of Animals Act 1950 **87,** 379
s 20 **77,** 282
s 23 **77,** 281-3
s 78(1)(v) **77,** 278, 281
District Court (Temporary Provisions) Act 1923 **79,** 145, 167
Divorce Reform Act 1969 **74,** 553
Documentary Evidence Act 1868, s 2 **87,** 315
Domicile and Matrimonial Proceedings Act 1973 **74,** 547, 551, 553
Drug-trafficking Offences Act 1986
s 27 **86,** 162, 163, 164, 167
s 29 **86,** 164
s 38 **86,** 163, 164, 167
search warrants under **86,** 163
Education Act 1944 **73,** 402, 406-7, 409-14, 417-19, 425
Emergency Provisions Act 1973 **79,** 524
Employment Act 1980 **62,** 368
s 4 **78,** 408
Employment Appeal Tribunal Rules 1993, appeals out of time **104,** 650-5, **107,** 628-32
Employment Protection Act 1975, s 53 **78,** 408
Employment Protection (Consolidation) Act 1978
crown employment overseas **104,** 512
s 23 **78,** 408
Endangered Species (Import and Export) Act 1976 **90,** 417, 423
European Bank for Reconstruction and Development (Immunities and Privileges) Order 1990, validity **107,** 612-13
European Communities Act 1972 **73,** 303, 309, 317, **74,** 658, **77,** 96-8, **84,** 763
s 2(1) **107,** 533
s 3(2) **107,** 533
European Communities (Definition of Treaties) (Third ACP-EEC Convention of Lomé) Order 1985 **107,** 533

United Kingdom (*cont.*)
European Convention on Extradition Order 1990 **119,** 31-2, 181, 254, 265, 324
para. 3 **111,** 574, 579, **119,** 249
para. 12 **119,** 33
para. 12(2)(b) **119,** 40
para. 13 **119,** 33, 40
para. 16 **119,** 34
European Parliamentary Elections Act 1978, s 6 **98,** 171
Evidence Act **73,** 48-50
Evidence by Commission Act 1859/1885 **84,** 739
Evidence (Foreign, Dominion and Colonial Documents) Act 1933 **86,** 155
Evidence (Proceedings in Other Jurisdictions) Act 1975 **73,** 300, 305-63
s 9(4) **101,** 354-8
Evidence (Proceedings within the Jurisdiction) Act 1975 **84,** 733
legislative history **84,** 737-8
previous legislation **84,** 737
purpose, codification **84,** 737-8, 739
purpose, implementation of the Hague Convention on the Taking of Evidence Abroad in Civil or Commercial Matters (1970) **84,** 737
s 1 **84,** 735-6
s 5 **84,** 747
s 9 **84,** 733, 741-2, 746-7
UK, applicability within **84,** 742
Explosive Substances Act 1883, extraditable offences and **100,** 419
Export Guarantees and Overseas Investment Act 1978
s 1 **108,** 600, 616
s 12 **108,** 600, 616
Extra-Provincial Jurisdiction Order 1949 (Indian Tribal Areas) **38,** 7
Extradition Acts. *See* Extradition Acts *above*
Family Law Reform Act 1969 **92,** 229
Fatal Accidents Act 1976 **87,** 366
Federal Council of Australia Act 1885 **51,** 49, 66, 82
Fertilizer and Feeding Stuffs Act 1926, imports, application to **43,** 140-3
Fiji Independence Act 1970 **80,** 13
Finance Act 1955 **77,** 34
Finance Act 1961 **72,** 473
Finance Act 1973, s 38 **78,** 529, 531, 539, 543, 545, 548, 549
Finance Act 1974, s 21 **78,** 531
Firearms Act 1968 **60,** 79-80, 82-3
comity and **60,** 82-3
extraterritorial application **60,** 82-3
Firearms (Northern Ireland) Act 1969 **79,** 461
Fishery Limits Act 1964 **59,** 483, **120,** 618 n. 5
s 1(1) **120,** 623
Fishing Boats (European Economic Community) Designation Order 1983 **100,** 122, 152
Fishing Boats (France) Designation Order 1964 **100,** 130
Foreign Compensation Acts 1950/1969 **60,** 115, 120
Foreign Compensation (Egypt) Order 1971 **60,** 115-16, 119
Foreign Corporations Act 1991 **100,** 252-4, **108,** 534
Foreign Jurisdiction Act 1890 **42,** 12, 15, 52-8, **44,** 198, 207, 208, 221, 225-6, 227, 230, **51,** 9-10, **53,** 104-6
Indian (Foreign Jurisdiction) Order 1902 **50,** 206

Foreign Jurisdiction Acts, effect on protectorates **71,** 43-4, 47
Foreign Tribunals Evidence Act 1981
s 1 **84,** 738, 739
s 2 **84,** 738-9
Forgery and Counterfeiting Act 1981, s 15 **84,** 725
Fugitive Offenders Acts. *See Fugitive Offenders entries above*
Geneva Conventions Act 1957 **41,** 421-6, **83,** 159, 160-1
Genocide Act 1969. *See* Genocide Act 1969 *above*
Ghana (Consequential Provisions) Act 1960 **90,** 459-60
Government of India Act 1833 **50,** 66, 68, 84
Government of India Act 1858 **50,** 66, 68, 84
Government of India Act 1870 **38,** 5-7
Government of India Act 1915 **50,** 325, 326
Government of India Act 1935 **38,** 5-7, **49,** 351, 359, 390, 395, 413, 414-15, 417, **50,** 19, 67, 76, 78, 85, 190, 321, 323, 324, 416, 422, 468, 490
Government of Ireland Act 1920 **59,** 346-7, 360-1, **79,** 524
Government of New South Wales and Van Diemens Act 1842 **86,** 200
Guardianship of Minors Act 1971 **92,** 229
Habeas Corpus Act 1679 **85,** 159, 160, 161, 164
Habeas Corpus Act 1816 **67,** 454, **85,** 59
Habeas Corpus Act 1862 **79,** 27, **85,** 231
area of application **79,** 27
Health and Social Services and Social Security Adjudication Act 1983 **92,** 232, 243
Homosexual Offences (Northern Ireland) Order 1982 **67,** 439
Hong Kong Act 1985 **92,** 643
Hong Kong Royal Instructions **77,** 382
House of Lords Bill 1999, Act of Union with Scotland 1706/1707 and **124,** 578-99. *See also* Union between Scotland and England, Act of Parliament of Scotland ratifying and approving the Treaty of Union with England 1707/Act of Union with Scotland Act 1706
Human Rights Act 1998
interpretation of legislation, new approach **122,** 446, 472-3
legitimate expectation arising from **122,** 440-2, 450, 456-9, 467
s 3(1) **122,** 446, 453, 460, 465, 473, 475, 495-8
s 3(2)(b) **122,** 496
s 4 **122,** 446, 465
s 4(2) **122,** 496
s 4(4) **122,** 465, 496
s 4(5) **122,** 496
s 4(6)(a) **122,** 465
s 6(1) **122,** 465, 496
s 6(2) **122,** 465, 496
s 6(6) **122,** 496
s 7 **122,** 466
s 7(1) **122,** 465
s 7(1)(b) **122,** 441, 455, 467, 472, 491, 495-8
s 12 **122,** 446
s 13 **122,** 446
s 22 **122,** 466
s 22(2) **122,** 466, 490
s 22(3) **122,** 441
s 22(4) **122,** 440-2, 449, 455, 458, 466-7, 472, 495-8
territorial limitation **123,** 611

United Kingdom (*cont.*)
Hydrocarbons Licensing Directive Regulations 1955 **120,** 628
Immigration Act 1971 **57,** 176-9, **60,** 253, **61,** 254, 257-9, 269, 272, 274, 392, 397, 399-401, **71,** 505-6, 509, **78,** 372, **81,** 145-6, **84,** 774, **90,** 23
Part II **79,** 649
racial discrimination **57,** 178-9
s 1(1) **79,** 660
s 1(2) **81,** 146
s 3 **85,** 186
s 3(1) **79,** 660, **81,** 146
s 3(2) **79,** 660, 671, **81,** 146-7
s 3(3) **81,** 146
s 3(5) **108,** 380-1
s 3(5)(b) **108,** 366, 404, **124,** 514-15, 531, 540-5
s 3(6) **108,** 380
s 4 **88,** 408, 415-17
s 4(1) **79,** 647, 660, **81,** 146
s 4(2) **79,** 660
s 6 **88,** 417-18
s 8(3) **88,** 408, 409-11, 420, 423
s 11(1) **79,** 651
s 13 **108,** 347
s 13(1) **79,** 648
s 13(3) **79,** 650, 663
ss 13-21 **79,** 660-1
s 14(1) **79,** 648
s 15 **79,** 648
s 15(1) **108,** 405
s 15(1)(a) **124,** 515, 531
s 15(2) **124,** 515
s 15(3) **108,** 367, 381, 405, **124,** 515-16, 523, 525, 531, 534, 537, 540-2, 543, 548-9
s 16(2) **79,** 663
s 17 **79,** 648, **108,** 347
s 17(5) **79,** 648
s 19 **108,** 348
s 19(1) **124,** 516, 541
s 20 **104,** 658-9, **108,** 348
s 23 **108,** 347-8
s 24 **71,** 505-6
s 26(1) **79,** 650
Immigration Appeals Act 1969 **43,** 176, **73,** 639, **81,** 154
s 13 **81,** 154
s 14 **81,** 154
s 15 **81,** 154
s 19(1) **81,** 155
s 19(3) **81,** 155
s 20(1) **81,** 155
Immigration Appeals (Procedure) Rules 1984 (SI 1984/2041) **108,** 347-8
Immigration and Nationality Act 1952, s 1101 **85,** 186
Immigration Rules **61,** 269, 270, 272, 397, 400, **71,** 498-9, 507, 509, **73,** 641, 646-7, 649, 651, **81,** 146-8
conflict with treaty obligations and **79,** 662

EC national and **81,** 147
Irish national and **81,** 147
legal status **81,** 147-8
Statement of Changes in (1983) **79,** 646-50, 662, 667, 671
Immigration Rules 1980 **81,** 148-52
discriminatory, whether **81,** 171-7
Immigration Rules 1982 **81,** 152-3
Immigration Rules 1983 **81,** 153-4
paragraph 134 **87,** 359, 362-3
Imperial Defence Act 1888 **51,** 52
Import, Export and Customs Powers (Defence) Act 1939
Export of Goods (Control) Order 1981 **78,** 611
s 3 **78,** 611
s 9 **78,** 611
Income and Corporation Taxes Act 1970
s 181 **78,** 531, 546
s 204 **78,** 528-50
s 205 **78,** 532
s 246 **78,** 531, 539, 541, 549
s 482 **78,** 541
Income and Corporation Taxes Act 1988
s 1 **103,** 336, **108,** 524
s 19 **108,** 524
s 20 **103,** 331-2
s 231 **103,** 332-5
s 232 **103,** 338-9
Income Tax Act 1952 **73,** 309, **90,** 463
Income Tax Acts **72,** 450
Indemnity Act 1920 **90,** 540-2, 548
India (Consequential Provisions) Act 1949 **90,** 459-60
India Independence Act 1947 **49,** 378, 413, 473-4, **50,** 14, 19, 27, 67, 76-7, 80-1, 82, 323, 388, 463
boundary provisions **92,** 556-7
Pakistan territories **38,** 5
s 7 **78,** 431
India Independence (International Arrangements) Order 1947 **78,** 109
India Independence (Rights, Property and Liability) Order 1947 **53,** 183-4
Indian Councils Act 1861 **50,** 190
Indian (Foreign Jurisdiction) Order 1937 **38,** 5
Indictable Offences Act 1848 **51,** 294, 310
Industrial Courts Act 1919 **78,** 398
Industrial Relations Act 1971 **62,** 366-7
s 5 **78,** 407-8, 414
s 65 **78,** 408
Industrial Tribunals Rules of Procedure 1985, Rule 3 **107,** 620-2
Insolvency Act 1986 **77,** 54
discretion to decline jurisdiction **124,** 558, 569
discretion to give priority to embassy **101,** 336-7
s 238 **124,** 554, 556
s 238(2) **101,** 339, 342-4
s 238(3) **101,** 342
s 239 **101,** 342-3
s 240 **101,** 343

United Kingdom (*cont.*)
s 241 **101,** 343
ss 339-42 **101,** 343
s 411 **124,** 557
s 412 **124,** 557
s 423 **124,** 551, 554, 555-9, 568-9
ss 423-5 **101,** 343, **124,** 556-7
Insolvency Rules 1986
7.2 **124,** 557
7.3 **124,** 557
12.12 **101,** 350-1
International Development Association Act 1960 **80,** 68
International Finance Corporation Act 1955 **80,** 175-6
International Organizations Act 1968 **77,** 3, 12, 25, 78, 88, 137, 148, **81,** 695, **83,** 249, 259, 266, 268, **85,** 20, 26, 28
s 1 **81,** 695, 707, 709
s 1(6) **107,** 612-13
s 1, Part 1 **77,** 127
International Organizations (Immunities and Privileges) Act 1950 **41,** 438-40, 442, 443, 445, 446, 448-51, **77,** 78, 88, **80,** 68, 70, 151
International Sugar Organization Act 1973 **83,** 269, **85,** 20
International Tin Council (Immunities and Privileges) Order 1956 **77,** 87, **80,** 153, **81,** 695
International Tin Council (Immunities and Privileges) Order 1961 **77,** 87
International Tin Council (Immunities and Privileges) Order 1972 **77,** 3-18, 25, 30-1, 36-9, 40, 43-6, 86-9, 98, 114, 127-31, 137, 162, **80,** 33, 34-5, 41, 88, 127, 151-5, 163-5, 167-9, 222, 302, **83,** 264, 265
International Tin Agreement, breach of, whether **81,** 681, 703-4
ITC's status under **77,** 44-5, 78, 82, 139, 162, **81,** 677-8, 702-15
purpose **81,** 677-9, 704
s 1 **81,** 713
s 2 **77,** 115, 137, 138, **81,** 713
s 4 **77,** 128, **80,** 93-4, 101, 131, **81,** 613, 707, 711, 712
s 5 **77,** 86, 87, 115, 127, **80,** 43-4, 93-4, 101, 131, 147-8, **81,** 677, 696, 703, 707, 709, 711
s 6 **77,** 3, 4, 6, 8, 10, 12-18, 40, 86, 87, 127, **80,** 120, 187, **81,** 707, 709, 711
s 6(1)(a) **77,** 14-16, 115, 120
s 6(1)(c) **77,** 14, 39
s 7 **77,** 138-43
s 7(1) **77,** 115, 117, 120, 127, 130, 145, 146-59
s 7(2) **77,** 128
s 14 **77,** 128, 130, **81,** 713
s 14(1) **77,** 120-1
s 14(1)(b) **77,** 115-16, 122, 139
s 17 **77,** 120-1, 128
s 17(b) **77,** 115-16, 122
Interpretation Act 1889 **90,** 456
India **50,** 69
Interpretation Act 1978 **77,** 39, 163
Iraq and Kuwait (United Nations Sanctions) (Amendment) Order 1990 (SI 1990/1651) **122,** 550
Iraq and Kuwait (United Nations Sanctions) (Amendment) Order 1990 (SI 1990/1768) **122,** 550

Ireland Act 1949, s 2 **87,** 331
Irish Free State (Agreement) Act 1922 **79,** 29
Irish Free State Constitution Act 1922 **85,** 230
Joint Stock Companies Act 1844 **80,** 98, 148
s 25 **81,** 709, 710
Joint Stock Companies Act 1848 **77,** 54, **80,** 98, 148
s 25 **77,** 81
s 66 **77,** 81
Judicature Ordinance 1985, applicability to locally engaged staff of British missions abroad **104,** 525
Land Court (New Territories) Ordinance 1900 **77,** 382-4
Land Registration Act 1925, *ex parte* proceedings **108,** 558-63
Larceny Act 1861 **74,** 460, 468, **85,** 81-2
Larceny Act 1916 **78,** 502
Law Reform (Frustrated Contracts) Act 1943 **75,** 372-80
Law Reform (Miscellaneous Provisions) Act 1934 **87,** 366
Leasehold Reform Act 1967 **75,** 402-28
Lesotho Independence Act 1966 **90,** 435-8, 455, 457-61, 466
Lesotho Independence Order 1966 **39,** 420, 421, **90,** 436, 437-8, 457, 463
s 2 **90,** 472
s 5 **90,** 465-7
Limitation Act 1980 **83,** 237, 240, 241
s 3 **125,** 705
s 4 **125,** 705
Limited Liability Act 1855 **80,** 98
Local Authority Social Services Act 1970 **89,** 297
Local Government Act 1949 **86,** 203-4
Lord Brougham's Act 1850 **78,** 508, 510
Magistrates Courts Acts 1952 **51,** 294, 311
applicability to colonies **123,** 575-9
Magna Carta 1215 (and subsequent endorsements) **62,** 183, **63,** 47, **123,** 516-17, 528-9, 575-9
colonies, application to **123,** 576-9, 586
expulsion of national **123,** 575-9
legislative status **123,** 576
Marine Insurance Act 1906 **74,** 681, **78,** 573-5
Schedule 1, Rule 8 **78,** 574
Schedule 1, Rule 9 **78,** 577
Maritime Conventions Act 1911 **74,** 677
Matrimonial Causes Act 1973 **74,** 531, 539, 549, **89,** 101-2, 121, **92,** 229
Matrimonial Homes Act 1967 **74,** 533
Mauritius Independence Act 1968 **51,** 26
Mental Health Act 1959 **78,** 383
lawfulness **67,** 462-4
s 60 **81,** 111, 118
s 65 **81,** 111, 133
s 65(1) **81,** 118
s 65(1)(c) **81,** 112
s 66 **67,** 450-3, 462-4
s 99 **81,** 113
s 141 **81,** 114, 115, 119-21, 127-8, 129-30, 131, 136-8
Merchant Shipping Act 1651/1660 **120,** 224
Merchant Shipping Act 1854 **87,** 389, **90,** 323

United Kingdom (*cont.*)
s 267 **77,** 291
s 503 **87,** 370
s 504 **87,** 370
Merchant Shipping Act 1894 **48,** 80-1, **51,** 59, **55,** 439, **69,** 12-13, 17, 23, 161-2, **70,** 60-1, 70-2, 90-1, 98-100, **77,** 312, **107,** 132 n. 36, 140 n. 57
application, Australian territorial sea **70,** 70-2, 90-1, 98-100
British ship on high seas, jurisdiction over **56,** 249, 253
colonies **70,** 70, 90
retroactive effect **70,** 96, 98
s 11 **77,** 288, 291
s 511 **77,** 287, 291
s 511(1) **77,** 311
s 544 **77,** 287
s 686(1) **77,** 284, 286-92
s 687 **77,** 287-8, 291
St Vincent and the Grenadines ships **120,** 225
Schedule 22 **77,** 288
UK, whether limited to **70,** 70-1, 90-1
Merchant Shipping Act 1906 **41,** 416-20
Merchant Shipping Act 1958
application, Australian states **69,** 13-15, 17-23
application, dominions **69,** 13-15, 17-23
compensation provision, scope **69,** 13-15, 17-21
Merchant Shipping Act 1988
amendment to comply with EC law **93,** 717
compatibility with EC law **93,** 652-4, 707, 714-18, 722, 764-74
Merchant Shipping Amendment Act 1855, s 21 **77,** 288, 290-1
Merchant Shipping Amendment Act 1862 **107,** 132 n. 36
Mineral Exploration and Investment Grants Act 1972 **77,** 316-17
s 1(1) **77,** 316
s 1(8) **77,** 316
Mines (Working Facilities and Support) Act 1923, s 18(3) **77,** 312
Mining Industry Act 1920 **77,** 311
s 1 **77,** 311
Ministry of Fuel and Power Act 1945 **77,** 312-13
s 1(1) **77,** 313
s 6(1) **77,** 313
s 7(1) **77,** 313
Misuse of Drugs Act 1971 **85,** 14, 137, 138
s 22 **86,** 164, 167
s 36 **86,** 163, 165, 166
Mortmain and Charitable Uses Act 1888, s 1 **78,** 610
National Coal Board (Additional Powers) Act 1966 **77,** 316-17
s 1(1) **77,** 316
National Health Service Act 1977
s 3 **81,** 115, 118, 130, 131, 138
s 4 **81,** 118
Nationality Act 1981, s 37(1) **108,** 549
Naval Discipline Act 1957 **90,** 463, 464
s 138(1) **112,** 374
negative resolution procedure **81,** 147, 152

New South Wales Act 1823 **92,** 633
New Territories Order in Council 1898 **77,** 380-1
New Territories Land Court Ordinance 1900 **77,** 382-4
Ordinances under **77,** 380-4
New Zealand Constitution Act 1852 **88,** 271, 272
Northern Ireland Constitution Act 1973, s 12 **87,** 332-3
Northern Ireland (Emergency Provisions) Act 1973 **79,** 479
s 6 **79,** 80
Northern Ireland (Emergency Provisions) Act 1978 **79,** 77, 78, 79, **85,** 36
Review of operation of (Baker Report) **79,** 478
s 8 **79,** 80
s 11 **79,** 81
Oaths Act 1838 **78,** 510, 511
Offences against the Person Act 1828 **78,** 559
Offences against the Person Act 1861 **67,** 400-1, **73,** 52, **74,** 158, **77,** 288, **79,** 461, **119,** 189
s 4 **119,** 184-5
s 9 **119,** 38, 55, 184
s 18 **119,** 189
Offences against the State Act 1939, s 30 **79,** 124
Offences at Sea Act 1536 **77,** 290
Offences at Sea Act 1799 **77,** 290, **84,** 51
Offences at Sea Acts 1536-1894, legislative history **77,** 290-1
Offshore Petroleum Production and Pipelines (Assessment of Environmental Effects) Regulations 1999 **120,** 629-30
Oil and Undersea Pipeline Act 1975 **85,** 469
Palestine Act 1948 **44,** 219
Parliament Act 1911 **78,** 463
Parliament Act 1949 **78,** 463
Parliamentary Commissioner Act 1967
s 10 **78,** 317
s 12 **78,** 317
Parliamentary Papers Act 1840 **77,** 123-4
s 1 **77,** 123
s 2 **77,** 123
Partnership Act 1890 **80,** 45, 92, 97-8
s 4 **81,** 679, 709
Patents Act 1949 **52,** 69-70
application for extension **41,** 15-20
non-recognized State, applicability **108,** 527-8
Peerage Act 1963 **124,** 579-80, 583, 589, 595-6
Perjury Act 1911 **89,** 102, 121
Petitions of Right Act 1860 **78,** 444
Petroleum (Production) Act 1918 **77,** 307
Petroleum (Production) Act 1934 **77,** 304, 305, 318
s 1(1) **77,** 307, 308, 317, 319, 321
s 1(2) **77,** 319
s 2 **77,** 307
s 3 **77,** 307, 315
s 5 **77,** 307, 315
s 6 **77,** 307
s 8, repeal **77,** 313

United Kingdom (*cont.*)
s 11(1) **77,** 307
s 11(3) **77,** 307
Petty Sessions (Ireland) Act 1851 **79,** 108
Police Act 1964 **74,** 309, 369
Police Act 1996, s 88(1) **111,** 662
Police and Criminal Evidence Act 1984 **86,** 162, 163, **88,** 337-8
Post Office Act 1969 **74,** 330-2, 336, 352-5, 360, 375-7, 380
Post Office (Protection) Act 1884 **74,** 331, 353-5, 368
Practice Note (Chancery: Deposition) 1984 **78,** 466
Practice Statement of July 1966 (precedent) **78,** 399
Prevention of Corruption Act 1906, s 1 **88,** 348, 373
Prevention of Fraud (Investments) Act 1958 **60,** 91-2, 102-3, 107
Prevention of Terrorism Act (Temporary Provisions) 1976
s 1 **79,** 111
s 1(3) **79,** 119
s 12(1)(b) **79,** 81
Prevention of Terrorism (Temporary Provisions) Act 1974 **79,** 525
Prevention of Terrorism (Temporary Provisions) Act 1982 **85,** 36
Prevention of Terrorism (Temporary Provisions) Act 1989 **104,** 266-7
compatibility with European Convention on Human Rights (1950) **122,** 445-9, 453-60, 474-6, 483-8
s 16A **122,** 436-9, 489-98
s 16A(4) **122,** 447, 450, 453-6, 472-6, 481-8
s 16B **122,** 442, 445-9, 491-2
s 19(1)(aa) **122,** 437, 438, 463, 489, 493, 495
standard of proof **122,** 447-8, 459, 478-80, 481-2, 486-8
Prison Act 1952 **57,** 209, **72,** 342
s 6 **78,** 307
s 47 **78,** 305-6, 326
Prison Rules 1964 **72,** 342-51
Orders and Instructions under **72,** 348-51
prisoners' correspondence and **72,** 343-51
Prison Rules 1964, amended **78,** 299, 305-6, 307-20, 380-8
disciplinary proceedings **78,** 306-12
Orders and Instructions under **78,** 310-12
'party to any legal proceedings' **78,** 382-8
prisoners' correspondence and visits under. *See* prisoners' correspondence and visits, control of *below*
Private International Law (Miscellaneous Provisions) Act 1995 **125,** 679-80
s 10 **125,** 722-3
s 11 **125,** 727, 730
s 11(1) **125,** 686-7
s 12 **125,** 727, 730
s 14(3)(a)(i) **125,** 686-7, 727-8
Proclamation of Queen Victoria 1858 **50,** 68, 71, 74, 382, 401-3, 411, 459, 465, 466
Protection of Trading Industries Act 1980 **74,** 38, 44, 50-8, 75, 78-85
Protection of Trading Interests (United States Antitrust Measures) Order 1983 **74,** 38, 49-58, 80-5
Quebec Act 1774 **73,** 112
Queensland Constitution Act 1867 **86,** 200, 202
Race Relations Act 1976. *See* Race Relations Act 1976 *below*

Recognition of Divorces and Legal Separations Act 1971 **55,** 581, **74,** 532-47, 550-6
'divorce obtained by judicial or other proceedings' **74,** 533-47, 551-6
Refugee Act 1980 **85,** 186
Registration of Business Names Act 1916 **81,** 677
'relevant offence' **41,** 397-406, **55,** 431, 433, **78,** 502
Repatriation of Prisoners Act 1984 **84,** 722-5
objective **84,** 723
s 1 **84,** 723
s 3 **84,** 723
Resident Magistrates Acts 1887-91 **73,** 276-7, 282-3, 288, 290-4
Restoration of Order in Ireland Act 1920 **79,** 29, 42, **85,** 230,**119,** 387-9
Royal Charter 1670 (Rupert's Land) **78,** 437
Royal and Parliamentary Titles Act 1927 **77,** 306
Royal Proclamation 1763 (Indians in Canada) **78,** 423-4, 426-8, 435
effect **78,** 426-8
entrenched **78,** 473
'force of law' **78,** 473
status **78,** 473
transfer of obligations under **78,** 468
Sale of Goods Act 1893 **43,** 141, 143, 148, 149, **74,** 585, 588
Scotland Act 1998, s 29(2)(d) **122,** 476
Sea Fish (Conservation) Act 1967, EC membership and **93,** 656
Sea Fisheries Act 1883 **51,** 82
Secession Law 1990 **85,** 58
Security Service Act 1989, s 1(2) **124,** 532
Serbia and Montenegro (United Nations Sanctions) Order (1992 No 1302). *See* Serbia and Montenegro (United Nations Sanctions) Order (1992 No 1302) *below*
Sex Discrimination Act 1975 **84,** 772-3, **89,** 102, 122
compatibility with EEC Treaty (1957) **93,** 622-8
s 1(1) ('sex discrimination') **123,** 57
s 4(1) ('victimization') **123,** 58
s 6 (circumstances) **123,** 58
Sexual Offences Act 1956 **67,** 401-2, **74,** 460, **121,** 270 n. 212
Sexual Offences Act 1967 **67,** 401-2, **89,** 102, 122
s 1(7) **112,** 373, **121,** 270 n. 212
Sierra Leone (Constitution) Order in Council **42,** 11-13, 16, 18-26
Sierra Leone Independence Act 1961 **42,** 12, 16, 18, 20, 21, 24
South Africa Act 1909 **90,** 469
Southern Rhodesia Act 1965 **39,** 65, 71, 72, 93, 105, 155, 201-2, 241, 271, 341, 378, 384-6, 390, 402-3, **48,** 31, 32-4, 38, 39, **72,** 42, 47
s 1 **78,** 491-2, 497
s 2 **78,** 497
s 3 **78,** 497
Southern Rhodesia (Annexation) Order 1923 **39,** 375
Southern Rhodesia Constitution, Letters Patent, 1923 **78,** 491
Southern Rhodesia (Constitution) Act 1961 **39,** 340-1, 375
Southern Rhodesia (Constitution) Order 1965 **39,** 273-6, 350, 379-80, 384-6, 391, 402-5, **48,** 31, 32-4, 38, 39, **53,** 52-5, 69, 72-9, 82-6, 91-3, **72,** 34, 47-8, **78,** 491, 492, 497-8
Southern Rhodesia constitutional amendment Act 1964 **72,** 36-51
sovereign immunity of Member States, effect on **80,** 152-3
Special Immigration Appeals Act 1997 **124,** 513, 516-17

United Kingdom (*cont.*)
compliance with European Convention on Human Rights (1950) and **124,** 516, 541-2
s 1 **124,** 516, 538
s 2 **124,** 516
s 2(1)(b) **124,** 528
s 2(1)(c) **124,** 529, 541, 548
s 4 **124,** 538-9
s 4(1) **124,** 516, 541, 545
s 5 **124,** 517
s 6 **124,** 517
s 7 **124,** 517, 527, 532, 543
Schedule I **124,** 538
Special Powers Act 1971 **79,** 524
State Immunity Act 1978. *See* State Immunity Act 1978 *below*
State Immunity (Merchant Shipping) (Union of Soviet Socialist Republics) Order 1978, applicability to Russian Federation **107,** 661-6
Statement of Changes in Immigration Rules (1983) **108,** 346
Statement of Changes in Immigration Rules (1990) **108,** 366, 370, 377, 382-4, 405, 406
Statement of Changes in Immigration Rules (1994), Rule 334 **107,** 556, 562
Statute Law Revision Act 1953, s 1 **78,** 462
Statute Law Revision (Scotland) Act 1964. *See* Scotland, law of, Statute Law Revision (Scotland) Act 1964
Statute of Westminster 1931 **39,** 238, 239, 324, 384, **43,** 111, **45,** 5, 7-8, 10-11, 14-15, **51,** 47, 183, **69,** 13-14, 17, 21, 115, 161, **70,** 68, **86,** 199, 607, 608, 611, **88,** 271, **90,** 240-1, 243, 250, 468-72
declaratory of existing law, whether **78,** 462
effect **87,** 269
s 2 **78,** 473
s 3 **69,** 115, **78,** 473
s 4 **69,** 13, 17, **78,** 458, 465-6, 473-4, 476-82
s 7 **78,** 442, 458, 473, 474, 477-82
s 8 **78,** 473
s 9 **78,** 473
s 9(2) **69,** 13
s 11 **69,** 14
Statutes of 1351 and 1495 **39,** 71, 242-53, 293, 303, 304, 307, 318-20, 334, 353, 359, 388
Summary Jurisdiction Acts **51,** 293, 294, 299, 300, 310
Suppression of Terrorism Act 1978 **79,** 105, 479, **87,** 410, **107,** 564
extraditable offences and **79,** 105, **100,** 419, **119,** 184, 250
s 1 **119,** 110, 250
s 4 **119,** 40, 184
s 4(1) **107,** 564-5, **119,** 186
s 4(1)(a) **119,** 187
s 4(1)(b) **119,** 187
Supreme Court Act 1981 **75,** 317
s 16 **122,** 518
s 18(1)(a) **122,** 518-21
s 20(1) **78,** 690, 691
s 25 **80,** 216-17
s 29(3) **122,** 439-40, 450-3, 468-71, 491-5

s 31(6) **120,** 646
s 37 **93,** 718
s 37(1) **77,** 46, **80,** 194, 214, 216-18, **107,** 501, **118,** 412 n. 71
s 151(1) **118,** 303
Supreme Court of Judicature Act 1873, s 25(8) **77,** 46, **118,** 412 n. 71
Supreme Court of Judicature (Consolidation) Act 1925 **72,** 4, 9, **78,** 383, **89,** 268
s 22 **78,** 686, 689
s 45 **77,** 46
s 45(1) **118,** 412 n. 71
Taking of Hostages Act 1982 **85,** 98
Head of State and **119,** 46, 96, 147-8, 160
incorporation of Hostages Convention (1979) **119,** 96
s 1 **119,** 40, 65, 72, 76, 96, 106, 148, 182-3
Taxes Management Act 1970 **73,** 305, 309
s 98 **78,** 531, 538, 544
s 100 **78,** 544
Telegraph Acts 1863/9 **74,** 331-2, 353-5, 368
Television Act 1954 **84,** 772
Territorial Sea Act 1987 **100,** 136-7, 138
s 1 **100,** 122, 151
s 1(1)(a) **100,** 122
s 1(1)(b) **100,** 122
s 1(4) **100,** 122, 151
s 1(5) **100,** 151
Territorial Waters (Amendment) Order in Council 1979 **100,** 122
Territorial Waters Jurisdiction Act 1878 **43,** 81, 82, 85-7, 88, 90, 92, 100, 102-3, 111, **51,** 43-6, 48, 73-4, 109, 155, 157, 179-80, **56,** 345, **73,** 223-5, 275, 277, 279, 283, 288-93, **77,** 310, 312, **90,** 239-40, 277, 292-7, **125,** 349
s 2 **77,** 310
s 7 **77,** 310
Territorial Waters Order in Council 1964 **43,** 80-93, 115, 117, 118-25, **77,** 318, **100,** 122, 138, 151-2
Theft Act 1968 **59,** 336-40, **73,** 253-5, 259-61, 264, 267-9, **74,** 460, 462, **85,** 74, 82
British ships, extension to **69,** 162-3
s 3(1) **88,** 344
s 8 **78,** 575
s 15 **78,** 502
s 15(1) **79,** 118
s 17(1) **88,** 347
Tokyo Convention Act 1967 **56,** 254, 256
Torts (Interference with Goods) Act 1977 **125,** 688
s 3 **125,** 699
s 5 **125,** 699
Trade Marks Act 1940 **71,** 24-34
Trade Union Act 1871 **80,** 43, 154
Trade Union and Labour Relations Act 1974 **62,** 367-8, **73,** 402, 410
s 5 **78,** 408, 414
Trade Union and Labour Relations (Amendment) Act 1976 **62,** 368, 372-4
s 1 **78,** 408
Transit of Animals (General) Order 1973 **87,** 379
Art. 3(3) **77,** 278, 280, 282
Art. 5(2) **77,** 277-83
Art. 11 **77,** 278

United Kingdom (*cont.*)
Treason Acts 1351/1495 **39,** 71, 242-53, 293, 303, 304, 307, 334, 353, 359, 388, **74,** 28
Tribunals of Enquiry (Evidence) Act 1921 **78,** 401
Unemployment Insurance Act 1920 **78,** 398
Unfair Contract Terms Act 1977 **78,** 416
Union with Ireland Act 1800, s 6 **87,** 331-2
Union with Scotland (Amendment) Act 1707 **124,** 595
United Nations Act 1946, s 1 **117,** 461-2, 484-6, 494-5
United States of America (Extradition) Act 1933 **90,** 461, 463
United States of America (Visiting Forces) Act 1942 **79,** 22
Visiting Forces Act 1952 **79,** 22, 25, 39, 40, **100,** 434, 440, 442, 444, 454, 461
s 8(2) **100,** 454-5
s 9 **100,** 434
s 10(1) **119,** 377
s 13 **85,** 158
Visiting Forces (British Commonwealth) Act 1933 **79,** 22
State succession and **90,** 461-4
War Crimes Act 1991 **91,** 129, **104,** 302
War Damage Act 1965 **44,** 382
War Precautions Act 1914 **86,** 223
Whaling Industry (Regulations) Act 1934 **120,** 635
Winding-Up Acts 1848-9 **77,** 54
Wireless Telegraphy Act 1949 **43,** 80, 82, 83-5, 87-91, 114, 116, 117, **74,** 335, 339
Zambia Independence Act 1966 **90,** 461
Zanzibar Act 1963 **90,** 461
legal personality **77,** 80-5, **80,** 90-7, 151-62
corporation. *See* corporation *above*
existence and capacity, whether distinct **80,** 42
failure to accord
breach of UK treaty obligations **80,** 150-1, **81,** 681, 703-4
intention to confer **80,** 93
legal capacity and **80,** 41-2, 43, 94-6
quasi-corporation **77,** 84-5
trade union **77,** 83-5, **81,** 707
legal representation, prisoners of war **123,** 607-9
legislation. *See also* treaties, implementing legislation *below*
absence of clear provision **80,** 52
absence of contrary indication **80,** 44
application in Jamaica **72,** 204-8, **73,** 45-53
courts' powers in respect of **59,** 351, 358, 483-6
delegated legislation **81,** 147
enforceability **78,** 464, 533-4, 542
entrenchment **78,** 462
'constituent instrument' **78,** 462
international law, declaratory of **80,** 94
limitations on, international law, relevance **91,** 30
nationals abroad, murder by **78,** 559
primary and subsidiary, whether distinguishable **80,** 67, 94
repeal, effect on common law **78,** 414
tax, extraterritorial enforceability **78,** 533-4, 542
territorial limitation **78,** 528-50, 561
legislation extending beyond territorial sea **120,** 629, 631-2

rule of construction **78,** 533, 540
validity
effect of European Communities Act 1972 **78,** 463
under international law **64,** 344, 351
legislation, interpretation **69,** 14-15, 18-21, **77,** 33-40, 279-83, **80,** 14-16
absence of clear provision **80,** 52
absence of contrary indication **80,** 44
aids
Cabinet documents **77,** 79-80
context **77,** 291-2, **87,** 389, **108,** 530
departmental documents **77,** 79-80
earlier legislation **78,** 554-8, **84,** 737, 745, **86,** 155
generally recognized principles of international law **119,** 62
later legislation **81,** 705
legislative history **77,** 290-1, **81,** 683, **98,** 174-5, **100,** 254, **119,** 154, 161
long title **78,** 481, **80,** 72
purposes and provisions of enabling act **87,** 369, 394
structure of legislation **107,** 648
ambiguity **78,** 481, 554-8, 559-60, 626, 685-6, 694
treaty as aid. *See* treaty as aid, in case of ambiguity *below*
applicable law **84,** 739, 745-6
area of effectiveness **77,** 279
Commonwealth practice and **84,** 740-1, 742-3
crime, conduct and result crimes distinguished **77,** 280
first impression paramount **77,** 15-16, 86
guidelines
civil law interpretation, acceptability **84,** 739, 742
clear language **103,** 428-9
consistency between common and civil law usage **84,** 734
consistency between primary and subordinate legislation **77,** 37
consistency between related legislation **64,** 391
effectiveness **106,** 574, 587, **107,** 644-5, 650-1
eiusdem generis **78,** 615
extradition statute **78,** 505
fair and reasonable **77,** 281
general words **77,** 33-4
Human Rights Act 1998, new approach **122,** 446, 472, 497-8
intention of legislature **77,** 79, 291, **107,** 649-51, 653, **108,** 530-4
object and purpose **77,** 281, **78,** 625-6, **86,** 164, 167, **87,** 389
ordinary and natural meaning **64,** 189, 190, **78,** 555-7, **84,** 766, **86,** 166-9, **88,** 316, **122,** 446, 472-3
plain meaning **81,** 676, **87,** 396
plain and ordinary **80,** 149
plain and unambiguous **80,** 44, 184
powers of legislature **87,** 389
purpose **83,** 128
restrictive **78,** 505
Statute as a whole **86,** 164, **107,** 648
text **83,** 128
wide to meet unknown future requirements **77,** 37
words as they stand **78,** 479
New Zealand legislation **78,** 597-607, 614-20, 627-30
penal legislation **78,** 543

United Kingdom (*cont.*)
phrases
'action, suit or proceeding' **84,** 739, 740
'ancillary' **77,** 97
'any person' **88,** 316-19, **101,** 339, 341-51
'appearance in proceedings' **103,** 366-7
'archives' **77,** 116, 128-9
'as such' **111,** 587-90
'association' **80,** 184
'between States' **103,** 355, 376
'British possession' **42,** 52, **79,** 688, **85,** 136, **88,** 274, **91,** 390-1
'British settlement' **123,** 586
'British subject' **43,** 130-4, **81,** 145, **92,** 634
'capacity' **77,** 164, **80,** 72
'circumstances such that a State ... would have been so immune' **103,** 400-1, 418-19
'citizen of UK and Colonies' **43,** 130-4
'civil or commercial matter' **84,** 738, 739, 741-5
'commercial purposes' **104,** 682-3
'commercial transaction' **103,** 353, 370-1, 400-1, 413-15
'Commonwealth citizen' **81,** 145, **108,** 545-56
'Commonwealth country' **80,** 14
'Commonwealth subject' **92,** 634
'Community treaties' **93,** 631
'company' **80,** 184
'concerning'/'involving' **107,** 497-8
'constable' **86,** 164
'corresponding law' **86,** 163, 165-6
'country' **86,** 155, **108,** 549
'criminal cause or matter' **122,** 516, 518-21, 524-5
'criminal matter' **55,** 552
'divorce obtained by judicial or other proceedings' **74,** 533-47, 551-6
'drug-taking' **86,** 163
'employment at an establishment in Great Britain' **107,** 601-2
'entered into by the State' **80,** 120, 149, 180
'every British court elsewhere' **88,** 320
'existing law' **85,** 137
'facilities' **80,** 72
'falls to be performed' **80,** 180
'force of law' **78,** 473
'foreign State', unrecognized State **108,** 521-40, 556-7
'habitually resident' **114,** 498
'in the exercise of sovereign authority' **111,** 608, 610
'in a foreign State' **85,** 98, 99-100
'in His Majesty's dominions' **53,** 103-4, **79,** 691, 692
'in the same manner in all respects ... for all purposes as part of New Zealand' **79,** 691, 692-4
'international organization' **80,** 89, 151, 153
'jurisdiction and execution' **77,** 37
'legal capacities of a body corporate' **77,** 86-9, **80,** 41-5, 57, 65, 69, 93-6, 131, 151, 154-62
'legal policy' **78,** 399, 401, 418
'legal proceedings' **78,** 382-8
'like' inviolability **77,** 117, 138

'manifest ambiguity' **78,** 557
'matter' **84,** 738, 762, 764-5, 774
'may' **86,** 164, 166
'member of a mission' **104,** 636-43
'mines and minerals' **77,** 304-7
'mischief' **80,** 152, 154
'natural-born British subjects' **44,** 374, 391, **79,** 689
'official' **77,** 116-17, 131-5, 144
'official activities' **80,** 167-8
'only of . . . claiming immunity' **103,** 377-9, 388-90
'ordinary and natural' meaning **78,** 546
'ordinary wide meaning' **78,** 691
'other similar person' **103,** 394-5
'oversea company' **103,** 360-3
'parts of Her Majesty's Dominions' **88,** 273-4
'patrials' **81,** 145-6
'political offences' **55,** 552
'prior written agreement' **104,** 632-6
'privileges' **87,** 415, 416
'professional or commercial activity' **111,** 635-6
'relevant offence' **41,** 397-406, **55,** 431, 433, **78,** 502, **85,** 76-8
'retained' **86,** 164, 166-8
'separate entity' **103,** 352, 368, 400
ship, 'belonging to' **77,** 288-92
'sovereign authority' **103,** 353, 370-5, 401, 417-18
'suit and legal process' **77,** 37-8, **80,** 187
'taking any step in the proceedings relating to the merits' **103,** 367
'treaty' **93,** 631
'treaty ancillary to any of the Treaties' **93,** 634-5, 638, 639-41
'unincorporated body having members other than States' **80,** 207
'victim' **122,** 497-8
'whether of a commercial, industrial, financial, professional or similar character' **103,** 419
'within His Majesty's allegiance' **79,** 692
'writ or other document' **118,** 615-17
presumption against
breach of international law **77,** 33-4, 78
conferment of legal personality **80,** 151, 154
expropriation by Crown without compensation **77,** 318
jurisdiction, grant of **77,** 33-5
penal nature **84,** 763
retroactivity **84,** 763, **122,** 523
presumption of conformity with comity **64,** 575, 579, 633
presumption of conformity with customary international law **119,** 87
presumption of conformity with EC law **93,** 661
presumption of conformity with international law **64,** 311-12, 579-80, **103,** 428, **119,** 234
presumption of conformity with international obligations **41,** 5, **78,** 386, 399, 418, **80,** 156-9, **81,** 703-4, **85,** 31-2, **86,** 164-5
clear meaning of legislation and **80,** 157
presumption of conformity with treaty **77,** 37, **79,** 650, **84,** 762, 763, **85,** 31-2, **107,** 498, **124,** 472
in case of apparent conflict **86,** 167, **124,** 457-8

United Kingdom (*cont.*)
presumption of territorial limitation **77,** 151, 281, 283, **78,** 529, **87,** 375, 376-8, 379-80, 381-2, 388-91, 392, 395, 397, **88,** 317, **101,** 341-50
presumptions, rebuttable **77,** 281
technical meaning **78,** 556
terminology
changing meaning, possibility of **80,** 89, 92-3, 155-61
differences of **80,** 14
identity of **80,** 157-8
treaty as aid **41,** 1-10, **77,** 77-8, **80,** 157, **81,** 701, 703, 713, **84,** 737, 740, 771, 772-3, **119,** 59-60
in case of ambiguity **41,** 7-8, **64,** 191-2, **77,** 381, **84,** 763-4, 774-5, **101,** 354
'having the force of law' **64,** 390-1
language of incorporated treaty **103,** 400
preamble **119,** 59
travaux préparatoires **74,** 634-6, 642-5, 647, 650, 654-6, 660-2, 666-8, 674-5, 682, **78,** 686
unincorporated treaty **41,** 7-8, **64,** 189, **78,** 480, **80,** 88-9, **103,** 400, **111,** 635
treaty interpretation distinguished **78,** 509, **85,** 140, **100,** 435
treaty-implementing legislation, treaty as aid **74,** 536-8, 541, 543, 552, **77,** 31, 77-9, 116-17, **78,** 386, 399, 418, 510, 525
legislation, retroactive **87,** 434-5, **117,** 475-82
bill of attainder **91,** 17
Criminal Justice Act 1988 **119,** 230
economic sanctions **117,** 475-7, 498
legislation authorizing restrain order in aid of confiscation orders made by foreign court **122,** 521-3, 528
State Immunity Act 1978 **64,** 225, 226, 269, 270, 271, 311-12, **119,** 193
legitimate expectation. *See also* estoppel *above*
consultation as alleviation **117,** 481
Human Rights Act 1998 and **122,** 440-2, 450, 456-9, 467
ministerial statement of future intentions **122,** 442, 450
public interest and **119,** 278
requirements
certainty of expectation **117,** 479-81
reliance on policy **117,** 499
treaty
intention to incorporate **122,** 440-2, 450, 456-9, 467
ratification **122,** 440-2
letter of credit, immunity in respect of **64,** 132, **69,** 139-46
letters rogatory
European Convention on Mutual Assistance in Criminal Matters (1959), obligation to execute 'in manner provided for by its law' **119,** 283-4
execution of **73,** 299-363
liberty of individual, restrictions, contract, validity to be upheld **78,** 407
Maastricht Treaty (1992). *See* European Union Treaty (Maastricht) (1992)
mandamus **78,** 551
Mandate
conclusion of Trusteeship Agreements **37,** 329
continuance of **37,** 152, 219, 320, 323-4, 330, 331
Mareva injunction. *See* Mareva injunction
margin of appreciation. *See* proportionality *below*

marine insurance. *See also* insurance contract *above*
FC&S clause **78,** 564, 567-8
piracy and **78,** 568-75
'pirates, rovers and thieves' **78,** 567-8
riots **78,** 576-7
measure of damages/compensation including valuation of company/property/assets
benefit to wrongdoer **125,** 701-2
causality **125,** 693-4, 696-8
fair actual value **125,** 694-6
foreseeable damage, direct and natural compared **125,** 703-6, 740-1
good faith, relevance **125,** 705-6, 728-9
mentally ill person **81,** 109-38
compulsory detention **67,** 450-2, **70,** 326-8, **81,** 118-20, 121-4
trade union activity respecting **81,** 113-16
Home Secretary, role **67,** 451-3, 462-4, 471
recall into custody, notification of reasons **67,** 453, 471-3
Muslim divorce, recognition of **74,** 531-56
national security **73,** 637-51
nationality **59,** 469-70
'British' and 'Commonwealth' subjects, same, whether **92,** 634
British protected persons **59,** 454, 462
naturalization. *See* naturalization *below*
patriality **59,** 455, **61,** 392, 397, 398, 404, 428-9
recognition, State, non-recognition, effect **108,** 555-6, **122,** 536-41
Rhodesia, citizens of, status **39,** 196, 278, 325-6, 385
rules governing **72,** 452-3, 455-6, 458-60, 471-2
nationals
act of State doctrine and **44,** 364-70, 374, 379, 387-9, 391, **57,** 39-40, **64,** 259, **70,** 42
expulsion from foreign State, right of re-entry **59,** 455-7
NATO Status of Forces Agreement (1951)
implementing legislation **100,** 434, 440, 442, 444, 454, 461
justiciability **100,** 462-3
municipal law, effect on, incorporation into municipal law **100,** 434, 453, 457, 461-3
phrases
'a force' **100,** 434
'third party' **100,** 435-7, 443, 445-6, 448
proper claimant, member of visiting forces against own State **100,** 434-7, 440-64
proper defendant, Ministry of Defence **100,** 434
purpose, modification of absolute sovereignty rule **100,** 445
State immunity and **100,** 441, 444-52, 455-64
treaty as waiver **100,** 445, 448-9, 460-1
natural justice **78,** 416
naturalization **72,** 449-52, 455, 461-2, 471-2
Nazi nationality laws, non-recognition **72,** 449, 453-7, 459-60, 467-70, 474-6
necessity **39,** 135, 175-6
nuclear weapons, possession and deployment, whether giving rise to **122,** 509-12. *See also* Scotland, necessity
Northern Ireland. *See* Northern Ireland
nuclear weapons, deployment
equipment used in connection with, individual's right to take action against
duress **122,** 509
necessity **122,** 509-12

United Kingdom (*cont.*)
individual's right to take action against equipment
necessity. *See also* Scotland, nuclear weapons, deployment
self-defence **122,** 508-9
oil. *See* oil, exploration and production in the Atlantic Frontier area (UK)
ontology. *See* legal personality *above*
Pakistan nationals and **61,** 270
Parliament
Irish fisheries, powers in respect of **59,** 346-8, 349
legislation for dominions **69,** 13-15, 17-23, 161-3
Australian states **69,** 13-15, 17-23, 161-3
supremacy doctrine **69,** 21
ultra vires, capacity to act **78,** 460, 476
Parliamentary Commissioner for Administration **78,** 317
parliamentary proceedings, impeachment of **77,** 123-4
parliamentary sovereignty **52,** 415-17, **53,** 82-4, 87, 89, **59,** 351, **78,** 465, 478
legislative **55,** 117-19, 127, 130, **59,** 358
power to bind itself **78,** 465
power to surrender **78,** 461, 465-6, 476
treaties and **41,** 7
partnership **80,** 92, 97-9
Scotland **80,** 100, 144, 145, **81,** 679, 709
passport
discretionary power **84,** 717-18
refusal
grounds, liability to arrest **84,** 718, 719
judicial review **84,** 716-17, 720
reasons, need for **84,** 719-20
remedies, absence of injury **84,** 719, 720
'United Kingdom passport' **78,** 436
piracy **78,** 564-75
marine insurance purposes **78,** 568-75
pleadings, striking out **75,** 276-7, 308-12, 322-5
political offence **79,** 101-5
asylum, association with **79,** 103
classification as
anarchism **79,** 101-2
bomb attack on civil airport **107,** 562-90
Suppression of Terrorism Act (1978) provisions **119,** 110, 250
definition/requirements, absence/lack of precision **79,** 101-3
extradition and **80,** 16-17, **85,** 84-7, **119,** 250
determination as **80,** 17-18
judicial review **80,** 18
proportionality and **107,** 559-60, 570-2, 577-8
dominant motive **107,** 571
reasons for exception, changed context **107,** 557, 562-4
relevant factors
motivation **107,** 557
prevailing circumstances at time of offence **79,** 102
'special category status' **100,** 423, 426
political question doctrine, reasons for, absence of judicially discoverable and manageable standards **116,** 588-94, **125,** 650-2, 653-5

political uprising in, whether **79,** 522-6
power to require person to appear for examination, bankruptcy proceedings, comity and **88,** 316
precedent in municipal courts
development of law and **87,** 416-17
international arbitral award **108,** 537
possibility of not following **78,** 399
stare decisis doctrine, international law and **64,** 16, 89-90, 127-8, 140-6, 150-3, 169, 212-15, 549-50
prerogative **52,** 415-17, **53,** 169-71, 174-6, **77,** 33, **87,** 331-2
boundaries and **86,** 190-2, 198, 200
British forces abroad and **44,** 359, 363, 381
British Indian Ocean Territory (BIOT) **123,** 557-8, 585-6, 590, 591-2
colonies and **43,** 130-40, **44,** 110, 113, 117, 127-8, **123,** 557-8, 585-7, 590, 591-2
conclusion of armistice agreements **83,** 160
conduct of war **83,** 160
dependent territories and, limitations **86,** 191, 199-204
diplomatic immunity, grant of **77,** 33
expulsion of alien and **123,** 581, 590
foreign relations **84,** 717, **107,** 469-73
judicial review **84,** 717, 718-19, 720
justiciability and **84,** 720
legislative provision, State immunity, power to override **108,** 534
non-payment of taxes **87,** 118
scope **44,** 389-90
territorial sea **43,** 81, 86, 88, 92, 116, 117-18, 120
treaty-making power **44,** 208, 368, 371, **77,** 33, **81,** 676, 700-1, **84,** 717, **87,** 333, 347-8, **98,** 175-6, **108,** 611
jurisdiction, effect on **77,** 33
presumption of innocence, terrorism **122,** 445-9, 476-80
Prison Board of Visitors **78,** 307-12, 323-4, 329-37
independence and impartiality **78,** 329-32
proceedings
'criminal' **78,** 350, 351-5
'legal' **78,** 315
review of **78,** 310-12
Prison Rules 1964 **84,** 728
prisoners' correspondence and visits, control of **57,** 209-10, **78,** 382-8
complaints concerning
procedure for **72,** 351-4, **78,** 316-18, 341-2
remedies, effectiveness **3,** 373-6
human rights violations and **72,** 362-72
practice of authorities **72,** 354-8
'prior ventilation' rules **78,** 339-40
rules concerning **72,** 342-51
prisoners' rights. *See also* prisoners' correspondence and visits, control of *above*
legal advice **57,** 210-16
visiting **57,** 211
prisoners, transfer of persons sentenced abroad **84,** 722-9. *See also* law of, Repatriation of Prisoners Act 1984 *above*
bilateral conventions **84,** 723
consent of prisoner **84,** 723

United Kingdom (*cont.*)
consent of sentencing State **84,** 723
existence of offence in administering State **84,** 723
multilateral conventions **84,** 723
privacy, right of
scope **74,** 317-19, 333-5
telephone-tapping **74,** 317-19, 333-6
Younger Report (1972) **74,** 319-20, 335, 337
private international law, entities under international law, recognition **83,** 247, 248-9, 251, 252, 261-2, 263, 264-5
private life, respect for
disclosure of medical reports in extradition proceedings **119,** 304-5, 316-17
homosexual orientation, armed forces and **112,** 371-412
interference by public authority, proportionality **119,** 316-17
Privy Council. *See* Privy Council (UK), appeals jurisdiction
procedure
amicus curiae brief **64,** 211, 355, 365
foreign State, applicability to **107,** 631-2
professional privilege **64,** 281-2, 287-90, 297-8
waiver **64,** 290, 306
prompt trial **70,** 198, 202, 208
property
classification as, debt/chose in action **64,** 78-9, **91,** 350-1, 369-70
title
illegal export, effect **118,** 592
lex situs **78,** 599
proportionality **84,** 762, 766-7, **85,** 33-4, 47, 51-2
diplomatic protection **107,** 480
irrationality **84,** 766-8, 776
political offence, dominant motive **107,** 571
private life, respect for, interference by public authority **119,** 316-17
protectorates
dominions distinguished **53,** 104
relation to **71,** 40-7
provisional measures **93,** 657-65, 681-703. *See also* Mareva injunction
balance of convenience **93,** 719-31
compensation for loss suffered, preclusion **93,** 683, 705-6, 719-20
EC law, compatibility with **93,** 790
EC law as issue **93,** 659-65, 681-703
duty to predict ECJ decision **93,** 706
obligation **93,** 664, 680, 697-9
power **93,** 664, 680, 697-8
effective remedy before national authority, non-availability against Crown, relevance **98,** 317
extraterritorial
Mareva injunction **107,** 500-1
monetary and proprietary claim distinguished **107,** 499-500
time-limit **107,** 502
hardship, relevance **93,** 726
injunction restraining ex-Head of State from removing or dealing with assets, outside jurisdiction **107,** 492-505
presumption of validity of legislation and

primary legislation **93,** 726
secondary legislation **93,** 721, 725-6
requirements, prima facie jurisdiction **107,** 496-9
third parties, effect on, *Babanaft* **107,** 503-5
public interest **85,** 32-3
disclosure of confidential information and **119,** 275-7, 299-306, 310, 312
judicial review of compliance with EC directive **120,** 655-6
public interest privilege **64,** 285, 290-2, 298-306
balance of interests **64,** 291, 305
communications between States **64,** 285, 291-4, 297-306
public law
penal **85,** 69
revenue **85,** 69
public order/public policy/*ordre public* **52,** 47-8, 61-2, **72,** 453, 457, 467, 471, 474, **73,** 14, **74,** 47-9, 56, 75, 567-9, **75,** 274-5, 278-80, 290, 296, **78,** 311, 405-6, 407-8, 414, 418-21
act of State doctrine and **64,** 266, **119,** 106
colonization and **78,** 425
compatibility of act with international law, court's right to consider **116,** 571-2
EC law, implementation **117,** 471-4, 492, 526-8, 543-7
enforcement of foreign legislation. *See* foreign law, recognition/enforcement, public policy and *above*
evidence of, Security Council Resolution **103,** 408-9
international law and **117,** 560
part of the law **78,** 419
political policy distinguished **78,** 419
reciprocity and **78,** 607
quasi-contractual obligation, repudiation, act of State **64,** 266
Race Relations Act 1976, applicability
advertisement in UK for employment abroad **107,** 601-2
'employment at an establishment in Great Britain' **107,** 601-2
international organizations **107,** 605-13
receiver, appointment of **77,** 45-56
equitable execution, as **80,** 193, 195, 217
rights of debtor **77,** 54
recognition
corporate status, recognition of and **100,** 253-4
intervention in judicial review proceedings by company **100,** 252-4
recognition, government **75,** 679-85, 690-8
change of practice **116,** 579-85, **125,** 658-9
Republic of Somalia **116,** 581-5
China (Taiwan) **74,** 106, 111
effect, right to sue and be sued **116,** 581
non-recognition, effect **43,** 23-79, **52,** 56, 62, 68-9
legislation **116,** 586-7
North Korea **52,** 68-9
practice **39,** 215
recognition of State distinguished **116,** 580
requirements
constitutionality **116,** 582-3
effective control of territory **116,** 582-3, 586
formal act, cessation of practice **108,** 529-30

United Kingdom (*cont.*)
international obligations, relevance **116,** 585
international recognition **116,** 582-3, 586
stability **116,** 586
UK government's dealings, relevance **116,** 582-5, 586
responsibility, executive **114,** 474
role of courts **75,** 679-85, 698
Sierra Leone **114,** 475-8
recognition, State **75,** 679-85, 690-8
applicable law, *lex fori* **122,** 534-5
The Arantzazu Mendi **116,** 579-80
China (Taiwan) **74,** 106, 111
constitutive theory **108,** 536-40
Estonia **85,** 55, 57-8, 59-60, 62
executive decision **85,** 6, 10
legislation, conflicting **108,** 539-40
legislation establishing Republic of Ciskei, non-recognition, effects **75,** 678, 683-5, 695-6
non-recognition, effect **52,** 56, 62, 68-9, **73,** 12-27
administrative act **108,** 534
commercial obligations **108,** 534
nationality, power to confer **108,** 555-6, **122,** 536-41
private matters **108,** 534
North Korea **52,** 68-9
political act, whether **108,** 529-30
practice **85,** 59-60
refinancing agreement, choice of law clause **118,** 603
Refined Sugar Association, Arbitration Rule 406 (applicable law) **64,** 249-50
refugees **71,** 497-503, **79,** 645-64, 666-83
country of residence, relevance **73,** 597, **122,** 534
definition **79,** 667, 671, **124,** 491
dual nationality, relevance **104,** 229, **122,** 534
expulsion. *See also* non-refoulement *below*
prior to determination of status **79,** 651, 663
to third country **79,** 651-9
'membership of a particular social group'
causal relationship, need for **124,** 489-90, 497-500, 504
cohesiveness, need for **124,** 483-7, 488, 496, 502-3, 507-10
existence of group independently of persecution, need for **124,** 483, 488-9, 497, 502, 507, 509-10
women in Pakistan **124,** 477-511
nationality/without nationality distinction **122,** 540-1
non-refoulement **79,** 645-64
in case of non-Convention refugees **108,** 351-2
country of destination, relevance **107,** 555-6, 578
'country or territory to which there is reason to believe he will be admitted' **122,** 544
extradition distinguished **107,** 555, 562, 576, 580
right of asylum, whether **107,** 555, 560
'persecution'
discrimination as **118,** 600
injurious action and oppression **87,** 364
ordinary meaning **87,** 364

quality of life **87,** 364
serious harm, need for **124,** 506
standard of proof **87,** 360, 363-4
well-founded fear **87,** 359, 363-4
'persecution or well-founded fear of persecution' **85,** 186
balance of probabilities **87,** 360-3
Convention reason, need for **124,** 504, 510
critical time **87,** 363
evidence of **79,** 657-9, 677
objective test, whether **79,** 669-70, 671-83
'persecution'. *See* 'persecution' *above*
United States judicial decisions compared **79,** 669-70, 672-6, **118,** 598
'well-founded' **79,** 657, 662
'serious non-political crime', asylum, ground for refusal **104,** 658-72
status, determination of
appeal against **79,** 644-64
competence **79,** 622, 635, 673, 678
procedures **79,** 652-9
UNHCR *Handbook on Procedures and Criteria for Determining Refugee Status* **79,** 648-9, 681-2
unlawful presence **79,** 650
Refugees, Geneva Convention on the Status of (1951) **79,** 645-7, 649-50, 651, 662
incorporation into municipal law
for practical purposes **79,** 671
Statement of Changes in Immigration Rules **108,** 372
as part of municipal law **79,** 667
remedies, declaration of legal or equitable right **118,** 586-92
accrued cause of action, need for **118,** 587-92
remission of sentence, right, whether **78,** 327-8
requisition, ship **64,** 101-2
res judicata **75,** 161-4, 172-5
Rhodesia, sovereignty over **39,** 64-5, 71, 80, 92-3
riot **78,** 576-7
elements of **78,** 576
Royal Commissions on Criminal Law **39,** 249-50, 318-20
Rules of the Supreme Court (RSC)
O 2
r 1 **108,** 561-2
r 2 **64,** 186
O 5, r 3 **108,** 561
O 11 **64,** 187, **77,** 64-8, **80,** 59, 119, 122, **88,** 318
r 1 **75,** 371-2, **107,** 496-9, **123,** 30-1, **124,** 558, 564-6
r 7 **103,** 363, 396
r 9 **107,** 499
O 11(1) **100,** 466-74
O 11 r 4 **77,** 66
O 12 **104,** 687
r 8 **64,** 186, 365, **80,** 122, **103,** 366, 410
O 13, r 7A **104,** 687, **118,** 605-19
O 15
r 6(2) **100,** 250
r 16 **74,** 311-14, **78,** 498
O 18 **80,** 122

United Kingdom (*cont.*)
r 19 **75,** 296, 308, 322-5, **77,** 73, **78,** 458, **85,** 63
O 24
r 2 **64,** 297
r 9 **64,** 297
r 10 **64,** 297
O 25, r 11 **64,** 300
O 29 **89,** 2, 269
r 1 **77,** 165
O 32, r 5 **108,** 562
O 33, r 3 **75,** 323-5
O 38, r 3 **77,** 113
O 39
r 2 **88,** 320
r 3 **88,** 305, 308, 309
O 41, r 5 **77,** 64, 113, 135
O 48 **77,** 162-7, **80,** 44, 213-24
r 1 **77,** 162-3
O 49 **74,** 180, **107,** 520-2
O 50, r 1 **108,** 562
O 51 **80,** 194
O 53 **90,** 451, **100,** 249
r 3 **78,** 389, **100,** 250
r 3(2) **79,** 659
r 4(1) **120,** 646
r 9 **100,** 250
r 50 **90,** 452
O 65, r 3 **103,** 361, 363, 393-5
O 77 **80,** 194
r 16 **77,** 44
O 81 **80,** 92, 97
O 93, r 12 **108,** 561
Scotland. *See* Scotland
seabed and subsoil, ownership, common law **125,** 398-401, 427, 433-6, 449-50
Security Council obligations
implementation **117,** 461, 497-8
primacy, EC law **117,** 464, 529-30, 547-9
sedition **70,** 214
seditious libel **87,** 436-8
object of offence **87,** 437-8
separation of powers **93,** 244, 632-4, 636-9
deportation and **124,** 544-6
Serbia and Montenegro (United Nations Sanctions) Order (1992 No 1302)
compatibility with EC law **117,** 462-75, 489-94, 511-31, 534-51. *See also* European Community (EC), common commercial policy
effectiveness **117,** 527-8
proportionality **117,** 527-8, 547
quantitative measure or measure having equivalent effect **117,** 522-8
implementation
consultation, need for **117,** 480-2, 499
exercise of discretionary powers in furtherance of purpose for which granted **117,** 486-9
failure to consult **117,** 481-2

fairness **117,** 477-9, 499
legitimate expectation and **117,** 479-81, 499
rationality **117,** 482
validity of change of policy under United Nations Act 1946 **117,** 484-6
validity under Art. 10 of the Order **117,** 486-9
nature of powers in respect of medical and humanitarian goods **117,** 455-61, 466
provisions **117,** 495-6, 507
relevance **117,** 484
retroactive application **117,** 475-82, 498
service of default judgment out of the jurisdiction, requirements **118,** 615-17
service of process on foreign company or company based outside the jurisdiction **80,** 118-19, **103,** 360-3, 393-5
informal by agreement, estoppel **103,** 365-6
out of the jurisdiction, nexus, need for **101,** 350-1
service of process on foreign State or State agency **77,** 99
act within jurisdiction, need for **100,** 469
default judgment
as 'process' **118,** 615-17
requirements **118,** 605-19
ex parte proceedings **108,** 560-2
government representative, by **103,** 365
method
agreed agent **118,** 603-15
agreed alternative **118,** 605
consular channels **64,** 365
diplomatic channels **64,** 272, **103,** 363-5, 396-7
specification of alternative means, effect **118,** 609, 615-16
unilateral change **118,** 603-15
out of the jurisdiction, insolvency/insolvency-related proceedings **124,** 557-70. *See also* service of process out of the jurisdiction *below*
refusal to accept **108,** 560-3
requirements
failure to comply with, effect **118,** 615-18
leave of court **118,** 605
official language of foreign State **104,** 686
proper service **118,** 605
service of process on international organization, out of the jurisdiction **77,** 98, **80,** 59
service of process out of the jurisdiction, insolvency/insolvency-related proceedings
'land situate within the jurisdiction'/'property located within the jurisdiction' distinguished **124,** 565
leave, need for **124,** 558
'serious issue to be tried', requirements **124,** 566-9
'whole subject matter of a claim relates to property located within the jurisdiction' requirement **124,** 559, 564-6
sex
definition **89,** 102, 121-2
non-discrimination, EC and **93,** 623-8
ships, sister ships, State immunity, arrest/attachment and **64,** 175, 231
ships, State-owned
classification as, ownership, possession or control as test. *See* ownership, possession or control as test of status *below*
collision involving **64,** 179
commercial activity, effect on immunity **64,** 97-110, 542-4

United Kingdom (*cont.*)
immunity, arrest/attachment **64,** 184-6
sister ships **64,** 175, 231
immunity, jurisdiction
in rem action **64,** 91-110, 416-17
ship confiscated in course of war **64,** 97
ownership, possession or control as test of status **64,** 99-100, 104, 110, 170-4, 183-4, 188-94, 326, 327-8, 330, 439-40, **65,** 25
charterparty **64,** 188-94
confiscated ship **64,** 170-4
evidence of **64,** 170-4, 175, 318, 324-5
Southern Rhodesia. *See* Southern Rhodesia
sovereign immunity. *See* State immunity *below*
sovereignty
EEC membership, effect **70,** 41
exercise of **88,** 274
parliamentary. *See* parliamentary sovereignty *above*
Special Immigration Appeals Commission (Procedure) Rules 1998 **124,** 541
7 (communication to appellant) **124,** 517
10(1) (statement of case) **124,** 518, 542, 548
23(1) (record of determination and reasons) **124,** 527
Special Immigration Appeals Commission (SIAC)
amicus, at appeal **124,** 522-3
closed session **124,** 517, 522-3, 529
composition **124,** 538-9
establishment **124,** 513
protection of sensitive information **124,** 527. *See also* closed session *above*
reasons for determination, need for **124,** 527
closed evidence **124,** 527, 530, 536
role **124,** 514-17
restraint, need for **124,** 547-8
review of facts **124,** 516, 520, 526-7, 532, 538-9
Rules of Procedure. *See* Special Immigration Appeals Commission (Procedure) Rules 1998 *above*
special advocate **124,** 517, 522-3
standing, 'any party . . . on any question of law material' **124,** 517, 527, 532
State agency/State-owned corporation/State entity
classification
applicable law, *lex fori* **64,** 138
government department, Ministry of Finance **87,** 415
national airline **103,** 352-5, 370-5, 387-8, 399-402, 417-19
State trading enterprise **64,** 201-2
control as test of independent status, appointment of manager by government of predecessor State, relevance **107,** 666
frustration, government interventions as, right to rely on **64,** 250-4, 377-9
separate legal entity test **103,** 352, 368, 400, **107,** 312, 316-17
commercial autonomy **64,** 201-2, 208, 379
legal personality **64,** 208
'organization of the State' **64,** 201, 207-8
State contract, parties to, Ministry of Finance as State **87,** 415
State Immunity Act 1978 **64,** 225, **80,** 58, 71, 116-20, 164, 205, **81,** 707, **87,** 66, **119,** 193. *See also* law of, State Immunity (Merchant Shipping) (Union of Soviet Socialist Republics) Order 1978 *above*

applicability
  civil proceedings **123,** 49-51
  criminal proceedings **119,** 58, 88-9, 96, 162, 208
  federal State **111,** 608-10
  Head of State **119,** 58-60, 89, 94-5
  Head of State, former **119,** 58-61, 89-90, 223-4, 245-7
  States **119,** 58
  visiting armed forces **119,** 370-85
attachment of property, certificate of use, need for **74,** 179, 187-8
burden and standard of proof **77,** 63-8
classification of act **119,** 374-5
common law, effect on **103,** 331, **107,** 542, **119,** 88-90, 371, 373, 374-5, 380, 381-2, **124,** 559
criteria for immunity **77,** 518
customary international law and **19,** 203-4, **64,** 224, **100,** 470-1, **119,** 88-9, 193, 219, 222, 224
Diplomatic Privileges Act 1964 and **64,** 391, **87,** 415, 416, **119,** 89-90, 96-8, 102-3, **123,** 59
European Convention on State Immunity (and Protocol) (Basle) (1972) and **100,** 470, **123,** 31, 38-9
international law, conformity with **119,** 242
jurisdiction, effect on **107,** 642-58
model legislation, as **65,** 230
new law, whether **64,** 270, 271
object and purpose **107,** 651-2
  protection of State property **107,** 658
Part I (proceedings in the UK by or against other States) **119,** 78, 87-9, 154, 193, 205-6, 284, 369
  s 1 (general immunity from jurisdiction) **77,** 63, 64, **80,** 119, **87,** 417, **101,** 335, **111,** 630, **118,** 605, 607-8, **119,** 42, 47, 58, 94-5, 206, **120,** 616
  s 1(1) (immunity from jurisdiction) **87,** 414, **100,** 447, 470-1, **103,** 331, 424, 427-31, **104,** 632, **107,** 540, **111,** 606, **119,** 58, 85-6, 88, 168, 205, 239, **123,** 29, 58
  s 1(2) (immunity in case of non-appearance) **64,** 293, **77,** 114-15, **104,** 655, 678, **111,** 606-7, 630
  s 2 (exceptions to immunity) **74,** 183, **87,** 414, **103,** 376-9, 402, **104,** 632, 643, 689, **107,** 540, **111,** 630-1, **118,** 607-8, **120,** 613
  s 2 (1) (submission to the jurisdiction) **104,** 679, **107,** 603, 620-2, **111,** 664
  s 2(2) (submission after dispute has arisen or by prior written agreement) **104,** 633, 635, 644-6, **119,** 168, **120,** 614-15
  s 2(3) (submission to the jurisdiction) **103,** 355-6, 377-9
  s 2(3)(a) (institution of proceedings) **111,** 554
  s 2(3)(b) (intervention or step in the proceedings) **80,** 119, **104,** 679, 690, **107,** 620-2, **111,** 661
  s 2(4) (non-application of s 3(b)) **103,** 355-6, 377-9, 388-90, **104,** 679, 689-90
  s 2(4)(a) (intervention for purpose of claiming immunity) **120,** 613-14
  s 2(4)(b) (intervention for purpose of asserting interest in property) **64,** 293
  s 2(5) (submission in ignorance of entitlement to immunity) **104,** 679
  s 2(7) (authority to submit to proceedings) **104,** 679-80
  s 3 (exceptions to immunity) **74,** 174-80, 184, 187, **77,** 63-4, 67, 73-4, 93, **81,** 696, **103,** 353, 370-1, 400-1, 413-15, **107,** 540, **111,** 631, 633, **119,** 94, 370, 379-80

United Kingdom (*cont.*)
s 3(1) (exceptions to immunity) **64,** 234, **103,** 387, **107,** 603, **119,** 373-4
s 3(1)(a) (commercial transaction) **77,** 73, **80,** 118, 119-20, 149, **101,** 336, **103,** 376, **119,** 383, **124,** 561
s 3(1)(b) (contract falling to be performed in UK) **64,** 388, 389, **80,** 53, 118, 119, 148-9
s 3(2) (exceptions to s 3(1)(b)) **103,** 355, 375
s 3(3) ('commercial transaction') **78,** 616, **80,** 53, 58, **103,** 371, **104,** 682, **107,** 603
s 3(3)(c) (transaction or activity entered into otherwise than in exercise of sovereign authority) **103,** 376, 414, 416, 419, **119,** 383
s 4 (employment contracts) **111,** 631, **120,** 613
s 4(1) (employment contracts) **64,** 355, **104,** 636, 641, 681, 682, **123,** 58
s 4(2) (employment contracts: exceptions to s 4(1)) **104,** 682, **123,** 58
s 4(2)(a) (employment contracts: national of State concerned) **64,** 355
s 4(3) (establishment maintained in the UK for commercial purposes) **104,** 682-3, **123,** 48
s 4(4) (UK law requiring proceedings to be brought in UK court) **107,** 603
s 5 (exceptions) **100,** 447, 460, 470, 471-4, **103,** 375-6, 424, 431-2, **107,** 540, **123,** 29-30, 89
s 5(b) (damage to or loss of tangible property) **111,** 651-2, 664
s 6 (ownership, possession and use of property) **74,** 186-7
s 6(1) (interest in, possession or use of immovable property) **64,** 366-7, 385, 388-92, **87,** 233
s 6(3) (jurisdiction relating to estates, winding up of companies or administration of trusts) **101,** 335-6
s 6(4) (ownership, possession and use of property: proceedings against person other than State) **77,** 67
s 7 (patents, trademarks) **77,** 67, **104,** 632
s 8 (membership of bodies corporate) **80,** 206-7
s 9 (waiver: arbitration agreement) **81,** 696
s 10(2) (ships used for commercial purposes) **64,** 542
s 11 (rates and taxes) **103,** 331
s 12 (service of process) **64,** 272, **77,** 64, 67, **80,** 118-19
s 12, proceedings relating to matters occurring before 22 November 1978 **64,** 272
s 12(1)(service through FCO and Ministry of Foreign Affairs) **103,** 363, 365, 396-7, **104,** 687, 690, **108,** 561, **111,** 631, **118,** 605, 607, 608, 615-16
s 12(2) (time-limits for appearance) **104,** 690, **118,** 605, 608
s 12(3) (appearance in the proceedings: service and) **103,** 366-7
s 12(4) (default judgment) **118,** 605, 608
s 12(5) (transmission of default judgment) **118,** 608, 615, 617-18
s 12(6) (service of process: alternative means) **103,** 366, **118,** 605, 607, 609, 616-17
s 13 (penalties) **74,** 174, 177, 179-80, 183, 185, **77,** 7, **87,** 415, **107,** 656-7
s 13(2) (specific performance; enforcement process) **111,** 631
s 13(2)(a) (specific performance) **64,** 367, **87,** 414, 415, 417, **111,** 652-3
s 13(2)(b) (enforcement process) **87,** 414, 415, 417
s 13(3) (waiver of enforcement measures) **111,** 631
s 13(4) (waiver of immunity, enforcement: European Convention on State Immunity) **87,** 417
s 13(5) (head of diplomatic mission: consent to process/certificate of use) **65,** 244-5
s 13(6)(b) (enforcement of arbitration award) **107,** 648-56, 657-8
s 14 **74,** 175, 178, 180, 183, **111,** 631-2, 646, **119,** 58, 61, 193
s 14(1) ('State') **103,** 400, **111,** 646, 664, 665-71, **119,** 41, 94-5, **124,** 560-1

s 14(1)(a) (sovereign or Head of State in public capacity) **111,** 607, 646, **119,** 100, 239
s 14(1)(b) (government of foreign State) **111,** 646
s 14(1)(c) (government department) **111,** 646
s 14(2) (separate entity) **64,** 234, **78,** 616, **103,** 352-5, 368, 370-5, 383, 387-8, 397, 413-15, **111,** 646, 664, 665-71, **124,** 561
s 14(2)(a) (separate entity in exercise of sovereign authority) **103,** 414-19, **111,** 608-10, **124,** 561
s 14(2)(b) (separate entity in circumstances in which State would have been immune) **103,** 377, 400-6, 414, 418-19, **111,** 608
s 14(3) (separate entity other than central bank or other monetary authority) **103,** 377
s 14(4) (property of central bank or other monetary authority) **119,** 58
s 14(5) (constituent territories of federal State) **111,** 609
s 14(6) (constituent territories of federal State) **111,** 608
s 16 **74,** 187, **87,** 416, **104,** 636, 649, 681, 686-7
s 16(1) **111,** 632, **119,** 154
s 16(1)(a) (members of a mission or consular post) **64,** 357, **104,** 513, 636-43, 654-5, **107,** 635-7, **120,** 613, **123,** 59
s 16(1)(b) (title or possession of property for purposes of diplomatic mission) **64,** 367, 388-92, **87,** 233, 236
s 16(2) (visiting armed forces) **100,** 447, **119,** 88, 370-2, 373-4, 379-81, 383, **120,** 611
s 16(3) (Nuclear Installations Act 1965) **119,** 88
s 16(4) (criminal proceedings) **119,** 58, 88, 95, 102, 168, 205
s 16(5) (taxation) **103,** 331, **119,** 88
s 17 **74,** 175, 179, 180, 186-7
s 17(1) **104,** 682
Schedule 1, Part 1 **77,** 115
Part III (miscellaneous and supplementary) **119,** 59-70, 78, 193
s 20 (Diplomatic Privileges Act 1964) **119,** 4, 55-6, 59, 60, 89-90, 96-9, 168, 203
s 20(1) **119,** 3, 6, 42, 43, 45, 59, 102-3, 154, 160-1, 168-9, 193, 203-4, 222, 223-4, 245-7
s 20(1)(a) **119,** 219
s 20(5) (Diplomatic Privileges Act 1964: sovereign or Head of State) **119,** 193, 239
s 21 (certificate of Secretary of State: conclusiveness) **111,** 606
s 21(a) ('State', 'constituent territory', head or government of State) **111,** 606, 607-10, **119,** 57, 193
s 22 ('court') **104,** 641
s 22(1) ('court') **107,** 603
s 23(3) (non-retroactive effect) **119,** 42, 193
s 23(3)(b) (non-retroactive effect: transactions entered into before coming into force of Act) **64,** 355-6
phrases
'armed forces' **119,** 370-1
'commercial purposes, use for' **74,** 174-9, 184-7
'entered into by the State' **80,** 120, 149, 180
'falls to be performed' **80,** 180
'government' **111,** 646-53, 667-71
'in his personal capacity' **119,** 94-5
'proceedings relating to' **64,** 356
'sovereign authority' **111,** 666-7
'unincorporated body having members other than States' **80,** 207

United Kingdom (*cont.*)
procedural and jurisdictional provisions distinguished **107,** 649-58
proceedings concerning employment of members of a mission **123,** 70
ratione personae nature of immunity **119,** 95
retroactive, whether **64,** 225, 226, 269, 270, 311-12, **119,** 193
secondary liability and **80,** 53, 120
as sole source of law **119,** 160
text (extracts) **119,** 20-2
visiting forces, applicability to **100,** 447, 449, 460, **120,** 610-11
waiver of immunity
implied **119,** 168-9
submission to jurisdiction **77,** 5, **119,** 168-9
State immunity, execution/attachment, central/State-owned bank. *See* central/State-owned bank, State immunity, execution/attachment *above*
State immunity, execution/attachment, procedural aspects, merits and jurisdiction distinguished **87,** 415, 416
State immunity, execution/attachment, purpose of proceedings
safeguarding/conservatory measures. *See* provisional measures *above*; Mareva injunction
State immunity, execution/attachment, purpose/use of funds/assets, commercial purpose **87,** 417
State immunity, execution/attachment, theory/doctrine
development of concept **74,** 180-2
judgment affecting rights in immovable property, bar to jurisdiction, whether **107,** 642-58
State immunity, jurisdiction, dependence on **64,** 223
State immunity, execution/attachment, waiver **87,** 416
waiver of immunity, jurisdiction, effect **87,** 415, 416
State immunity, jurisdiction, acts of
agent **64,** 115
armed forces, common law **119,** 371, 373, 374-5, 380, 381-2
State immunity, jurisdiction, applicability
acts in own territory **100,** 470-3, **107,** 544
acts in territory of forum State **103,** 424-5, **107,** 544
disclosure of documents **64,** 280-5, 287-94
in own courts
for act of State abroad **121,** 202
foreign State immunity distinguished **64,** 423-4
property, dispute relating to **64,** 119, **111,** 651-2. *See also* real/immovable property, dispute relating to *below*
contract debt/chose in action **64,** 77-80
damage or loss of tangible property caused by act or omission in forum State **103,** 375-6, **111,** 664
possession or control of property and **64,** 440-1
property for private purpose **64,** 88
property seized following illegal annexation **125,** 656-7, 678
real/immovable property, dispute relating to **64,** 85, 417. *See also* property, dispute relating to *above*
diplomatic mission **64,** 366-7, 388-92
trust funds, action relating to **64,** 85, 99, 119-20, 417
winding-up order in bankruptcy, duty to give embassy preferential treatment **101,** 333-7

State immunity, jurisdiction, classification of act
acts *hostis humani generis* **103,** 428
commercial activities **80,** 53, 58, **87,** 416, **107,** 603
confiscation **64,** 181
contract
breach **64,** 359
termination **64,** 235-6, 319-23
contract to be performed in forum State **107,** 603
conversion **63,** 597, **64,** 179, 236, 240-1, 320-3, 324-8, 330
debt for services rendered **64,** 85
diplomatic activity **64,** 233
diplomatic premises, construction contract **64,** 271-2
expropriation/nationalization **64,** 235
property seized in occupied territory **103,** 373-5, 380-2, 387, 405-6
foreign aircraft
removal to third country **103,** 354-5, 372-5, 403-6, 414
seizure in occupied territory **103,** 354, 372, 380, 402-6
jure imperii and *jure gestionis* distinguished **80,** 71
legislative attempts at **119,** 374-5
letter of credit **64,** 132, 149-64
military base
bowling alley **120,** 606-11
medical facilities **100,** 441, 444-52, 455-64
training and education contract **119,** 370-6, 380-3
military medical facilities **100,** 449-52, 457-60, 463-4
military procurement, cement for military purposes **64,** 132-3
nature or purpose of transaction as determining factor **64,** 235-6, 313, 314-15, 318, 327, 358-61, 404-5, **100,** 464, **103,** 354, 373-5, 380-2, 384-6, 402, 404, 416-17, **124,** 561-3
contract **64,** 180-2
private person test **64,** 179-80, 241, 360-1, **103,** 401
tort, commercial activity distinguished **103,** 375
torture **100,** 470-1, **103,** 421-32, **107,** 541-4, **119,** 45, 47-8, 85-7, 205-8
transfer of shares following reoganization of banking sector **124,** 559-63
violation of international law **64,** 182-3, 241, 323, **100,** 470-1, **103,** 427-31, **119,** 106-7, 224-9, 241-2, **123,** 29-30
jus cogens/peremptory norm violation **103,** 421-2, 427-31, **107,** 541-4, **119,** 225, **123,** 32, 50-1
State immunity, jurisdiction, entitlement
diplomatic agent **114,** 495
EC. *See* EC *above*
executive certificate/statement, conclusiveness **111,** 606
federal State **52,** 324-6, 327
constituent States **52,** 322-8, **111,** 608-10
government department **52,** 327-8
individual **119,** 221-2
police force **111,** 646-53
State agency immunity distinguished **103,** 414-15
State agency/State-owned corporation/State entity **103,** 399-402
act in exercise of sovereign authority **103,** 401-2, 414-15, 417-19
act on instruction of State **103,** 401-2
tort **103,** 388

United Kingdom (*cont.*)
State immunity, jurisdiction, procedural aspects
applicable law
customary international law **100,** 455-7, 461-3, **119,** 233-4, 384
forum State **119,** 233-4
burden of proof **64,** 113, **103,** 403, 424, 425
cause of action, effect on **86,** 138
default judgment, setting aside **118,** 603-19
effective remedy, right to and, diplomatic channels as **64,** 179
immunity from jurisdiction and liability distinguished **103,** 336-7
in personam actions **55,** 419, 422, 428, **64,** 98-9, 101, 107-8, 114-15, 130-1, 146, 168-9, 175-82, 210, 216-19, 231, 232, 269-71, 319, 403-5, 417-19, 423-4, 565-6, **104,** 621
commercial activity **64,** 423, 542-5
real action relating to private immovable property **64,** 365-7, 390, 392-3
State Immunity Act 1978 and **64,** 269-70
in rem/personal actions distinguished **64,** 96-9, 108-9
non-appearance, effect **64,** 293, **77,** 114-15, **104,** 655, 678, **111,** 606-7, 630
preliminary issue, whether **80,** 53, 119, 179
presumption against **64,** 148-9
presumption of, good arguable case against, need for **100,** 467-8, 471, 473-4
procedural bar **119,** 57-73, **121,** 78
State immunity, jurisdiction, theory/doctrine
absolute theory **64,** 169, 232, 312, 422-3, **65,** 213
customary international law **64,** 141-2
NATO Status of Forces Agreement (1951) and **100,** 445, 447-52, 455, 457, 460-1
act of State and. *See* act of State, State immunity, jurisdiction and *above*
acta jure imperii
definition **103,** 372, 397-8
I° Congreso del Partido **111,** 667-8
place **100,** 463-4
sovereignty and **111,** 633-4
basis
comity **64,** 135, 279-80
dignity of foreign State **64,** 135, 178-9, 313-14
diplomatic privileges and immunities **64,** 418
equality of States **111,** 632, **119,** 222
execution of judgment, difficulty **64,** 84
international law **111,** 632
non-interference in the affairs of another State **64,** 219-20, **119,** 222
par in parem non habet jurisdictionem **80,** 125, **119,** 161, 172, 174, 222, 374
reciprocity **64,** 427-8, **111,** 632
sovereignty **111,** 632
civil and criminal jurisdiction distinguished **119,** 205, 208, 217-18, 222, 226, 234-6, 239
common law **107,** 542, **111,** 606, **119,** 88-90, 371, 373, 374-5, 380, 381-2
development of concept **42,** 126-8, **64,** 38-42, 60-2, 103-8, 129-32, 140-5, 148-51, 168-70, 216-20, 232, 312-14, 406-7, 438-53, 455-74, 492-3, 542-5, 576-80, 598-608, 634-40, 699-706, **100,** 446-7, 461-2
precedent, effect on **64,** 16, 89-90, 140-6, 150-3, 169, 212-15, **87,** 416-17
International Organizations (Immunities and Privileges of the International Tin Council) Order 1956, effect **80,** 152-3, **81,** 707
non-justiciability as alternative **80,** 124, 164, 205, **119,** 78

ratione materiae **80,** 123-4, 206, **119,** 223-33
ratione personae **80,** 123-4, 206, **119,** 153, **123,** 43
restrictive theory **64,** 50-1, 84-6, 150-3, 169-70, 177, **65,** 229-30
common law **64,** 308, 323-4, 327
purpose, certainty in commercial transactions **64,** 179-80
purpose, protection of litigation rights **64,** 313-14
territorial jurisdiction/sovereignty and **64,** 86, **119,** 236
State immunity, jurisdiction, waiver
action to stay proceedings **103,** 356, 379, 382
arbitration clause **87,** 414-15
authority, need for **111,** 653, 671
choice of law clause **87,** 414-15
in manual of employment **120,** 614-16
contractual **87,** 414, 416
diplomatic correspondence **107,** 620-1
execution and jurisdiction, separate waivers, need for **87,** 416
express **80,** 168-9, **111,** 652-3
forum [non] conveniens claim **103,** 378-9, 389-90
implied
arbitration proceedings, submission to **106,** 561-2, 577
service, acceptance or acknowledgment **64,** 366
knowledge and intent **111,** 671
membership of international organizations **80,** 164-5, 168-9
NATO Status of Forces Agreement (1951) **100,** 445, 448-9, 460-1
non-justiciability claim **103,** 378-9
notice of appearance **107,** 620-1
step in proceedings **103,** 356, 366-7, 376-9
submission to the jurisdiction as **80,** 164, 168-9, **103,** 355-6, 377-9, **104,** 679, **107,** 603, 620-2, **111,** 664
challenge to jurisdiction **103,** 377-9, 382, 388-90
timing **87,** 416
treaty provision, Torture Convention (1984) **119,** 166-75, 196-9, 201, 216-17, 231-2, 245
undertakings to court **111,** 652-3, 664-5
State practice, treaties as evidence **80,** 52, 173-6
State, recognition, diplomatic relations distinguished **108,** 538
State responsibility for acts and omissions of
government employees **100,** 469
members of family of Head of State **100,** 469, 473
misfeasance in public office **111,** 13-14, 45
prison officers **103,** 426
State organ **64,** 322, **124,** 48-50
State responsibility, breach
damages
administrative remedies, whether precluding **111,** 44
Bourgoin v. *Minister of Agriculture, Food and Fisheries* **111,** 13-14
civil liability rules **111,** 44
economic loss, need for **111,** 44
misfeasance in public office **111,** 45, 121
State responsibility, imputability
incarceration in government prison **100,** 469
use of government transport **100,** 469
State responsibility, procedural aspects, evidence of **103,** 426, 432

United Kingdom (*cont.*)
State responsibility, requirements
due diligence, absence **103,** 426
duty of care **111,** 13-14, 44
knowledge of invalidity of act **111,** 13
knowledge of likely injury **111,** 13
State succession
rights and obligations, legislation in third State, applicability **107,** 664-6
Russian Federation, successor to USSR, whether **107,** 661-6
statehood, requirements/evidence of, unrecognized State as 'foreign State' for legislative purposes **108,** 527-8, 556-7
stateless person **71,** 504-9
stay of proceedings **78,** 391-2
applicable law, *lex fori* **118,** 551
forum selection clause **118,** 561
'just and proper' exception **118,** 532-3, 535-6, 537
relevance in case of change of legal system **118,** 528-39
power to order in courts of another State
in absence of nexus **118,** 549
antitrust legislation and **118,** 542-65
concurrent and sole jurisdiction distinguished **118,** 550, 561-2
frivolous and vexatious proceedings **118,** 549-50
in personam nature of order **118,** 560
injunction prohibiting foreign proceedings **74,** 40-2, 54-8, 70-7, 83-7
oppressive proceedings **118,** 564-5
unconscionable conduct **118,** 548-60
Suez operations (1956), war, whether **48,** 467-8
taxation, exemption
burden of proof **108,** 548-9
foreign State
estoppel **103,** 335-6
recognition, relevance **108,** 512-57
tax credit, entitlement **103,** 332-6, 337-9
liability to collect **78,** 536-41
liability to pay **78,** 536
residence and **78,** 533
'tax presence' **78,** 535-7
taxation statute **91,** 327-8
telephone-tapping **74,** 307-90
Birkett Report (1957) **74,** 319-20, 328, 351-4, 363-6, 375-6
European Convention on Human Rights (1950) **74,** 324-5, 339-41, 357, 371-90
warrants for **74,** 308-18, 329-32, 351-66
White Paper (1980) **74,** 351-2, 359-66
territorial sea
Crown prerogative **43,** 81, 86, 88, 92, 116, 117-18, 120, **112,** 500-1, 557, **125,** 398-400
jurisdiction
common law and **125,** 334-42, 389-94, 455-9
statutory basis **125,** 388-9, 401-3
Minquiers and Ecréhos **39,** 425-6
property rights in, ownership of seabed and subsoil **43,** 104, 106-10
rights
colonies, in respect of **90,** 243

Crown in right of Commonwealth **90,** 243
jurisdiction, ownership distinguished **90,** 299-301, 306
jus regale **90,** 243
prerogative **90,** 243
solum. *See* seabed and subsoil *below*
seabed and subsoil **77,** 312, 315-20, **90,** 243, 254-5
inside and outside territorial sea distinguished **77,** 316-17
territory, whether **90,** 243-8, 296-8
admiralty jurisdiction, relevance **90,** 292-6
internal waters distinguished **77,** 311
part of the realm **77,** 308-10
status **77,** 307-21
territory
acquisition, specific act, need for **90,** 240, 299
continental shelf **78,** 538
definition
internal waters **77,** 311
land, inland waters and territorial sea, limitation to **120,** 635
seabed and subsoil, territorial waters, inside and outside distinguished **77,** 316-17
territorial sea **77,** 307-21
extent
common law and international law distinguished **90,** 277, 329
low-water mark, to **90,** 239-40, 244, 276-7, 320-1
territorial sea. *See* territorial sea, territory, whether *above*
terrorism
definition/requirements, 'atrocity' **107,** 573-4
jurisdiction **86,** 43
presumption of innocence **122,** 445-9, 476-80
title, adverse possession **83,** 237
tort
applicable law, *lex loci delicti commissi* **125,** 679-80, 722-7
conversion **116,** 541-6
damages for **116,** 559-62, **125,** 693-706
definition **116,** 558-9, **125,** 687-90
torture
act of State **119,** 96
classification as, disappearances **119,** 285-6, 328
common law **119,** 189
conspiracy **119,** 148, 183-4, 188-9, 190-2, 250
crime, whether **121,** 140
customary international law, incorporation into municipal law **120,** 385-6
definition
action 'by a public official or other person acting in an official capacity' **119,** 2-3, 71-2, 92-3, 100, 152, 183-4, 188, 244-5
Criminal Justice Act 1988 **103,** 426, **119,** 2-3, 70-1, 93, 183-4, 188, **121,** 93
critical date **119,** 328
intentional infliction of severe pain or suffering **119,** 328
Torture Convention (1984) **103,** 425-6, **107,** 546, **119,** 70, 150
extraditable offence **119,** 76, 93, 150-1, 190, 249
as function of Head of State **103,** 591-2, **119,** 4, 45, 47-8, 61-70, 97-100, 104, 151-7, 169-70, 204-18
as instrument of State policy **119,** 224

United Kingdom (*cont.*)
Head of State, former, immunity, jurisdiction **119,** 45, 47-8, 61-70, 97-100, 151-7, 219-21, 244-5, 250
as international crime **119,** 149-50, 155-6, 199-201
scale, relevance **119,** 217, 250
Torture Convention (1984), relevance **119,** 229-30
universal jurisdiction, relevance **119,** 156
jus cogens/peremptory norm **103,** 421-2, 427-31, **107,** 541-4, **119,** 85, 86, 200, 206, 214, 244, 310-11, **120,** 385-6
State immunity, jurisdiction **100,** 470-1, **103,** 421-32, **107,** 536-51, **119,** 45, 47-8, 85-7
Torture Convention (1984), incorporation into UK law **108,** 372, **119,** 2-3, 70, 140
universal jurisdiction **100,** 471, **107,** 546, **119,** 2, 70-1, 76, 85, 150
violation of international law **103,** 426-7
Torture Convention (1984)
Head of State, former, immunity, jurisdiction
Convention as exclusion **119,** 219-21
Convention as waiver **119,** 216-17, 221, 231-2
Head of State, former, immunity, jurisdiction *ratione materiae* **119,** 200-1, 215-16, 220, 231, 245
Head of State, immunity, jurisdiction *ratione materiae* and **119,** 200-1, 215-16, 220, 231, 245, **123,** 34-5
'public official or other person acting in an official capacity', Head of State and **119,** 70-1, 92-3, 100, 151, 152, 156, 164, 196-8, 213-14, 220-1, 244-5
State immunity, jurisdiction *ratione materiae* and **119,** 85, 163-75
exclusion **119,** 165-6, 169-75, 245
as waiver **119,** 166-9, 196-9, 201, 216-17, 231-2, 245
universal jurisdiction **100,** 471, **103,** 526-30, **107,** 449-51, 546, **119,** 70-1, 76, 100, 139-40, 150, 164, 230-1
dependence on waiver of immunity **119,** 156, 214-15
trade union. *See also* closed shop agreement *above*
Bridlington principles **78,** 409-21
legally enforceable contract, whether **78,** 409
expulsion from **78,** 415, 416
freedom to join, closed shop agreement **62,** 369-72
public policy and **78,** 405-6, 407-8, 414, 418-21
refusal to join trade union **62,** 360-2, 372-4
dismissal because of **62,** 360-2, 366-8, 373-4, 379
existing employee **62,** 360-2, 372-4
lawfulness **62,** 368
religious grounds **62,** 360, 370
right to join **78,** 405-21
rules, contract, whether **78,** 415-16
status **80,** 43, 154, **81,** 707
Trades Union Council, Disputes Committee **78,** 411-12
transsexualism **89,** 97-112, 118-53
marriage **89,** 101-2, 109, 121, 127-8, 141-6, 153
private life, respect for and **89,** 103-9, 110-12
registration of births and **89,** 106, 120-1, 125-6, 129, 152-3
certificate of current civil status and **89,** 107-8, 110-12
travaux préparatoires, interpretation, aid to
admissibility **64,** 182
as confirmation **101,** 324-5, 331

treason
Bacon on **39,** 314
Coke on **39,** 306
Hale on **39,** 246-8, 307-9, 323
Hawkins on **39,** 245, 246, 248, 311-12, 323, 334
Statutes of 1351/1495 **39,** 71, 242-53, 293, 303, 304, 307, 318-20, 334, 353, 359, 388
treaties. *See also* legitimate expectation, treaty
aboriginal Indian treaties **78,** 429-31, 466-72. *See also* Canada, aboriginal Indians in, treaties
collateral warranties and **78,** 466-7
international treaties, whether **78,** 436
State succession and **78,** 436, 467-8
status **78,** 467, 472
adoption **85,** 12
EC Treaties **84,** 763
European Convention on Human Rights (1950) **84,** 763
judicial **84,** 772
applicability to non-party, evidence of customary international law **108,** 537
breach
courts' power **74,** 311-13, 339-40
remedy **74,** 307, 311-15, 343-6, 355-6
compliance **79,** 667
as contracts **81,** 676
Convention on the Transfer of Sentenced Persons (1983) **84,** 722
implementation **84,** 722-5. *See also* law of, Repatriation of Prisoners Act 1984 *above*
definition **93,** 631
direct effect **81,** 701-2, **84,** 772
effect and fact of distinguished **81,** 702, 716
enabling legislation. *See* implementing legislation *below*
enforcement **81,** 676
municipal courts **108,** 553
request of foreign State for **81,** 676, 681
request of individual for **81,** 676, 681
as evidence **83,** 263
form, agreed minute, signature by head of delegation **108,** 601
guidelines
language, object and intent **78,** 509
ordinary international meaning **78,** 509
purpose and objective **79,** 681
reference to French text **78,** 626
travaux préparatoires **79,** 676-7, 681-3
implementation **84,** 725-7
choice of means **84,** 770
implementing legislation **74,** 532, 536-7, 541, 543, 552, 563, 577, 586-7, 601, 615, 632, 649, 660, **77,** 3-18, 25, 30-1, 36-9, 40, 313-15, 318, 319-21, 324-9, **79,** 645-7, 649-50, 651, 662, 671-83, **80,** 68-71, 155-61
applicable law **101,** 322
customary international law as aid to interpretation **119,** 161
'general nature and effect' of treaty, relevance **77,** 79
international organization, instruments constituting **81,** 678
need for **77,** 380, **80,** 166-8, **81,** 681, 701, 713-14, **83,** 156-62, **85,** 4-5, 6, 7, **101,** 354, 357-8, **123,** 604

United Kingdom (*cont.*)
purpose **80,** 92-3, 155
incorporation into municipal law **52,** 415-17, **83,** 238. *See also* adoption *and* implementing legislation *above*; primacy *and* unincorporated *below*
European Convention on Human Rights (1950) **122,** 440-2
Treaty of Rome (1957) **80,** 127
individuals, rights **42,** 12, 17-18, **81,** 676, 701, 710
effect on **59,** 484-5, **74,** 45, 56, 312, 325-6, 339, 357, **77,** 95, 380, **81,** 701
Lomé Convention (1986) **107,** 521-2, 527
payment under claims settlement agreement **108,** 612
unincorporated treaty **123,** 607-8, 609-10
international organizations, instruments constituting **80,** 66, 67-8
implementing legislation **80,** 68-71
intentions of founding Members, determination of **80,** 141
interpretation and enforcement, courts' power **77,** 31, 35, 79
Ireland, with **87,** 331-2, 333
joint communiqué **87,** 333
judicial review **87,** 330-3
justiciability **77,** 73, 94-8, **83,** 249, 259, 263, **85,** 19
contract incorporating terms **83,** 263
implementing legislation **83,** 263
incorporated treaties **83,** 263
Lomé Convention (1975), State immunity, jurisdiction and **64,** 121
municipal law and
effect in **87,** 71
obligation to exercise powers in conformity with **124,** 472
unincorporated treaty. *See* unincorporated treaty *below*
operation and enforcement **85,** 9
as part of municipal law, Geneva Convention on the Status of Refugees (1951) **79,** 667
patriation. *See* adoption *above*
primacy, customary international law **108,** 539
protocols, part of, whether **98,** 172-5
ratification, relevance **83,** 159
signature, full powers, need for **108,** 601
source of international law **80,** 53, 108, 135, 141, 173, **81,** 715
primacy **108,** 535
statute and **41,** 421-6
termination **74,** 563-6
treaty-making power **41,** 423-4, **52,** 415-17, **81,** 676, 700-1
as act of State **81,** 700-1
limitation **87,** 348, **98,** 176
prerogative **44,** 208, 368, 371, **77,** 33, **81,** 676, 700-1, **84,** 717, **87,** 333, 347-8, **98,** 175-6, **108,** 611
unincorporated treaty
contract, use in **81,** 701
courts' right to apply **85,** 44
courts' right to interpret **64,** 182, **80,** 88, **81,** 701, **107,** 484-9
courts' right to use as evidence **100,** 462-3
effect **77,** 32, 77, 94-5, 377-84, **80,** 87, **81,** 701, **100,** 455-6, **108,** 611
evidence of factual background **108,** 613
evidential value **80,** 52

justiciability **80,** 52, 57, 86-90, 102-4, 111-12, 148, 177, 203-5, 208, **81,** 700-2, 703, 710, 713-15, 716, 719, 724, **100,** 462-3
legitimate expectation and **122,** 440-2, 450, 456-9, 467
obligation of compliance **119,** 407-8
private rights and obligations **80,** 87, 167-8, **85,** 46-7, **100,** 457, **108,** 612-14
treaties conferring immunity **100,** 456-7, 461-3
unratified treaty, application of **122,** 442-3
treaty interpretation **72,** 693-708, **74,** 576-682, **79,** 671-83, **84,** 725-7, **85,** 139-40
aids
customary international law **119,** 196
legislation **81,** 701, 703, 713
other related treaties **119,** 411-12
other treaties concluded by parties **100,** 436-7
parliamentary proceedings **100,** 437
statement by official at meeting of advisory body **125,** 597
teachings of publicists **100,** 436
unincorporated treaty **108,** 613, **114,** 484
authentic languages, equal authority **125,** 595
by executive **107,** 56-7, **108,** 613
by municipal courts
Channel Tunnel agreements **119,** 409-11, **125,** 591, 592-3
terms incorporated into contract **108,** 613
conclusiveness of Order in Council **93,** 632, 635
developments subsequent to conclusion of treaty and **100,** 447-9
guidelines
avoidance of implied term **119,** 170
effectiveness **93,** 627
purposive **122,** 358, 540-1
rules of statutory interpretation **100,** 435
treaty as a whole **119,** 411-12
uniformity **107,** 581, **119,** 196, **122,** 540, **124,** 501-2
multilingual, parallel texts as interpretative aid **101,** 65-6, 323, 324, 325
phrases
'a real action relating to private immovable property' **64,** 365-7, 392-3
'treaty ancillary to any of the Treaties' **93,** 634-6
reference to French text **86,** 156, 157-8
Trucial States and **57,** 24, 34-6
trust law, *Benjamin* order **85,** 60
UN, status **80,** 95
UN obligations, implementation by virtue of Art. 1 of the United Nations Act 1946 **117,** 461-2, 484-6, 494-5
unfair dismissal **62,** 360-2, 365-75, 379
claim for **73,** 402-26
unincorporated association, liability of members **80,** 45
United States, extradition from **79,** 4-534
Vancouver Island, colony of
Act of Union with Colony of British Columbia 1866 **73,** 190-1, 209, 219, 221
Confederation of Canada, entry into **73,** 69, 191
sovereignty over, exercise of **73,** 65-7, 69, 104, 124-5, 189-91, 206, 218-19
Venezuela, Gulf of Paria, Treaty on Submarine Areas of (1942) **43,** 112-13
Vienna Convention on Diplomatic Relations (1961)

United Kingdom (*cont.*)
implementation **83,** 237, **111,** 606, 629-30, 634, **119,** 3, 42, 59, 161, 196, 245-7
as part of municipal law **88,** 326
'professional or commercial activity' **111,** 635-6
war
contract, effect on **78,** 583-91
Suez operations, whether **48,** 467-8
war damage, France, agreement with (1946) **48,** 1-2
wardship jurisdiction **43,** 168-76
stateless infant **41,** 239-56
warship, immunity, jurisdiction **64,** 232-3
winding-up order, international organization, in respect of **80,** 57, 183-90
winding-up proceedings
effect **77,** 29-30
enforcement, whether **77,** 40
extraterritorial **77,** 30
United Mexican States. *See* Mexico
United Nations. *See also* United Nations Charter (1945); United Nations Committee on Human Rights (UNCHR); United Nations General Assembly (UNGA); United Nations Secretary-General; United Nations Security Council
ad hoc Committee on Seabed **41,** 115, 129, 146
Administrative Instruction ST/A1/262 **69,** 308-9, 319, 327, 339, 372, 417
Administrative Instruction ST/A1/269 **69,** 309-10, 312, 325, 340, 355, 362, 372-3, 419-20
administrative law. *See also* administrative law; International Labour Organization Administrative Tribunal (ILOAT); international officials; United Nations Administrative Tribunal (UNAT); World Bank Administrative Tribunal
need for improvement **83,** 359-60, 363-4, 392-4
admission to **74,** 92-3
as *amicus curiae* **63,** 338
claims against
by company, arbitration **44,** 433-7
Congo operations **45,** 446, 450, 452, 453-4
individuals **69,** 141-5
as collective security system **106,** 329, 331
peacekeeping forces as part of **106,** 331, 346-7
Committee on Relations with Host Country **82,** 235, 262
Congo operations, Agreement with Belgium settling claims resulting from **45,** 446, 450, 452, 453-4
Consultative Committee on Administrative Questions, repatriation grants, reports on **69,** 315-16, 325, 371, 432-3, 435, 494-7, 499-502, 511, 538, 541
Council for Namibia **49,** 60, 297
General Assembly. *See* United Nations General Assembly (UNGA)
general practice of Organization **49,** 12
Headquarters, international enclave **82,** 285
internal administrative law **54,** 477
Korea, forces in **41,** 20
League of Nations and
similarity to **37,** 441, 443
succession to **37,** 202, 207, 208, 213-14, 227, 233, 310-15, 441, 544
acceptance of 'sacred trust' **49,** 179
automaticity **37,** 39

South West Africa, termination of Mandate for **49,** 4, 6, 36-40, 61, 63, 95, 103, 104-6, 117, 122, 123, 131, 136, 153-5, 158, 178-9, 210, 215, 253, 279-80, 289, 290-1, 295-7, 305, 322-30
supervisory body for Mandates **49,** 6, 63, 100-2, 122, 180-9, 214, 217-25, 232-5, 254-5
validity of resolutions **49,** 12, 35, 103, 119, 121, 133-5, 141, 153, 170-2, 174, 178-9
voting, 'important questions' **49,** 178
transfer of assets, agreements on **37,** 328
transfer of functions from **37,** 118, 154-5, 157, 160, 202, 206-39
legal capacity **45,** 446
legal personality **80,** 94-5, 160-1
consequences **37,** 182
organized international community **37,** 441, 443, 569, 572
sovereign power, whether **45,** 448, 453
subject of international law, whether **49,** 284
'super-State' **49,** 330-1
legal question, dispute between Member States, whether **49,** 166
legal status, State, whether **44,** 375, 377
Mandates
consent to modification **37,** 476-7
San Francisco Conference discussion **37,** 156, 206, 213, 215, 227, 232, 316-20, 340, 488-93
mandate system
powers relating to, derived nature **49,** 254
'sacred trust', acceptance of **49,** 179
South West Africa mandate, termination **49,** 4, 6, 36-40, 61, 63, 95, 103, 104-6, 117, 122, 123, 131, 136, 153-5, 158, 178-9, 210, 215, 253, 279-80, 289, 290-1, 295-7, 305, 322-30
successor to League of Nations
supervisory body, as **49,** 6, 63, 100-2, 122, 180-9, 214, 217-25, 232-5, 254-5
validity of resolutions **49,** 174-5, 178-9
supervision of **37,** 323
Member States
Administrative Tribunal decisions, challenge to **69,** 342-4, 346-9, 357, 368, 384-6, 389-90, 423-5
difference of opinion between, legal question, whether **49,** 166
obligations **68,** 208-11, 222, 239
human rights **68,** 209-11, 222, 239
non-recognition of illegal situation **49,** 155-6
to make armed forces available to UN **78,** 17
war, in respect of **67,** 619-20
representation **49,** 107
privileges and immunities **47,** 275-7
representatives, status **37,** 52, 55
war between, presumption against **67,** 619-20
membership, Yugoslavia **95,** 27-9
mission to
'agency or instrumentality of a foreign State' **63,** 125
'foreign State' **63,** 125
service of process on **63,** 61-2
negotiations within **37,** 89, 166, 174-5, 181
Office of Legal Affairs' opinion on **69,** 319, 321, 326-7, 415, 466, 510-16, 520

United Nations (*cont.*)
observer status, 'invitees' **82,** 255, 262, 263, 285-6
Office of Human Resources Management **83,** 441
organs
definition **54,** 392
judicial and political, roles **49,** 117
judicial review. *See also* United Nations Security Council, judicial review
Expenses Advisory Opinion **105,** 430-1
Lockerbie **105,** 430-1
Namibia Advisory Opinion **105,** 430-1
resolutions, validity of **54,** 496
structure **105,** 543-4, 548-9
PLO status. *See* Privileges and Immunities Convention *above*; Palestine Liberation Organization (PLO), UN and
powers
advisory opinions, to request **54,** 393, 397
'essential' **69,** 349
establishment of subsidiary organs **54,** 392, 446-8, 518
quasi-legislative **49,** 140
regulation of staff **54,** 447-8
principles and purposes **59,** 48-50
privileges and immunities. *See* United Nations, privileges and immunities; United Nations, Privileges and Immunities Convention (1964)
publications, authority of **76,** 65-70, 112-14, 119-20, 170-1, 194-9, 238, 251-6, 299-305, 497
Regional Arrangements **76,** 149-52, 505-6
Rhodesia
resolutions **39,** 209, **53,** 253
statehood **39,** 209
revolution, competence to consider **39,** 338
sanctions **53,** 66, 86, 92
role **62,** 549
Security Council. *See* United Nations Security Council
special agreement, need for **106,** 346-7
United Nations Administrative Tribunal (UNAT). *See also* United Nations Staff Rules and Regulations; World Bank Administrative Tribunal
applicable law **83,** 438-9
UN Charter, provisions of **83,** 336-7, 425-6
principles distinguished **83,** 337
UN Staff Rules and Regulations **83,** 336, 342, 425-7, 447
UNAT jurisprudence **83,** 447
UNGA resolutions **83,** 342
applications, admissibility
administrative remedies **38,** 265-7
frivolous applications **43,** 470, 475-6
time-barred **38,** 340-1
Appointments and Promotions Board **83,** 339, 342, 448
awards. *See* judgment *below*
Committee on Applications for Review of Administrative Tribunal Judgments **54,** 393-5, 398, **69,** 368-70, 404-8, 442-5, 457-8, 472-87, **83,** 304, 314, 361, 424
competence **54,** 449, 464, 518-19
composition **54,** 478-80, 498, **69,** 351, 387, 460-2
equality of parties **69,** 350-1, 356-8, 386-8, 391, 393, 443, 461

functions **54,** 478-80, 498
quasi-judicial **54,** 396-7, 447-8, 478-84, **69,** 346, 351, 357, 393, 443, 461
judgments, review of. *See* review of judgments by ICJ *below*
judicial process, respect for **69,** 351, 357-8, 385-7, 391
Member State applications **69,** 342-4, 346-9, 357, 368, 384-6, 389-90, 423-5
Secretariat, whether impinging on authority of **69,** 348-9, 385-6, 423-4
staff member, effect on performance of duties **69,** 349
third-party interventions as **69,** 346-7, 384-6, 423-4
as organ of UN **54,** 395, 396, 447-8, 479-80
political character **54,** 498, **83,** 317, 363, 393, 420
procedure **54,** 436-7, 478-80
applications **69,** 355-7, 401-3
irregularities **69,** 353-9, 387-8, 390-5, 400-8, 443, 458-64
representation of parties **69,** 350-1, 356-8, 388, 391, 393, 462
rules **69,** 353-9, 402-3
quasi-judicial nature **83,** 393, 420
request for ICJ advisory opinion **54,** 387, 390-5, 396-7, 398-401, 403, 408, 444-7, 478-84, 497, 518-19
formulation **83,** 371-4, 420
role **83,** 419-21
competence. *See* jurisdiction *below*
composition **54,** 396, 425-6, 435, 445, 446-7, 545-6, **69,** 361-3, 400, 459-60
costs **40,** 384
documentary evidence, discovery **40,** 367, 374, 375, 377, 378, 397, 399-400, **54,** 365
frivolous applications **43,** 470, 475-6
functions **54,** 396, 425-6, 435, 445, 446-7, 454-5, **83,** 337-8
General Assembly
relation to **54,** 447-8, 462-5
Resolution 34/165, immediate effect, whether denied by Tribunal **69,** 355, 359, 365-6, 374-5, 380, 395-9, 408, 410-11, 442, 448-56, 468, 551-4
ILO Administrative Tribunal (ILOAT), merger, recommendation for **69,** 444-5, **83,** 360
as independent body **83,** 362
judgment
binding nature **69,** 425
compensation **54,** 415-24, 466-9, 508-10
confirmation of **54,** 375, 377
costs **54,** 419-21, 469-71
finality **83,** 362
interpretation **36,** 455-6, **47,** 376
UN Secretary-General **83,** 332-3
review. *See* review of judgments by ICJ *below*
revision **47,** 372-6
application for, time-limits **54,** 377
grounds **54,** 377-9
settlements **54,** 375-6
as judicial body **54,** 425, 462-5, **83,** 362
jurisdiction **54,** 373-7, 462-5, 466-9, **69,** 342, 374-6, 379, 387-8, 397, 402, 442, 456, 467-8, 472-4, 555-61, **83,** 361. *See also* competence *above*
claims against employing government **88,** 726
errors of law and **69,** 376, 387
failure to exercise, **54,** 408-24, 427, 437-42, 456-60, 467-9, 476, 487, 492-3, 505
FAO staff **43,** 322-3
interpretation of decisions **36,** 455-6

United Nations Administrative Tribunal (UNAT) (*cont.*)
legal issues **83,** 284, 312, 377
Member State, actions of **83,** 346, 356
ratione personae **48,** 321-7
resignation under duress **38,** 278
review of discretionary act of UN Secretary-General **83,** 292-3, 367
'staff member' **38,** 302, 306-8, **40,** 344, 349-51, 396, 399, 400-2
to order action within organization's discretionary power **43,** 377
waiver of officials' immunities **38,** 330
wrongful acts by UN officials **38,** 327, 328-30
legal counsel, obligations **54,** 378
choice of legal submissions **54,** 379
municipal court decision as *res judicata* **43,** 470-8
preliminary measures **88,** 725
application for **54,** 351-3
preliminary questions, joinder to merits **42,** 296
procedure
questions to parties **43,** 391
remand for correction of **38,** 375, **43,** 367, 375, 376, 382
proceedings, oral **54,** 377
remedies
compensation **54,** 370
specific performance **54,** 370
review of judgments by ICJ **54,** 462-5, 473, 482. *See also* Committee on Applications for Review of Administrative Tribunal Judgments *above*
advisory opinion **54,** 374, 377, **83,** 304-459
effect **69,** 347-8, 392, 469-70
as appellate court **83,** 374-5
Charter obligations, compatibility of procedure with **69,** 344, 348-9, 446-51, 455-8
competence of court **69,** 342-5, 366-70, 425-8, 447, 457-8, 468-92, 559-61, **83,** 315, 318, 361, 364, 393
equality of parties **69,** 349-51, 367, 386-8, 393-4
formulation of request for advisory opinion distinguished **83,** 420-1
grounds **54,** 387-90, 476, 480-1, 501, 503-7, 510-13, **69,** 355-6, 360-1, 378, 401-8, 412, 463, 472-87, 554
error in judicando **54,** 504
error of law concerning UN Charter **69,** 341-2, 366-70, 374-5, 379-80, 387, 396-9, 402, 404-8, 412, 428-31, 443-61, 465, 468, 472-4, 480, 482-7, 491-2, 554-61, **83,** 314, 318-19, 335-57, 361, 371, 372, 374, 379, 392, 395, 399, 403-16, 425-37, 444, 446-59
error in procedendo **54,** 504
error in procedure occasioning failure of justice **54,** 428-33, 456, 492-3, 503-7, 510-13, **69,** 351-3, **83,** 314, 335, 361, 362, 371, 372, 387, 444
excess of competence **69,** 342, 374-6, 379, 387-8, 397, 402, 442, 456, 467, 472-4, 555-61, **83,** 361, 371, 444
failure of justice **54,** 503-7
failure to exercise jurisdiction **83,** 314, 321-3, 326-7, 328-30, 335, 361, 362, 369, 371, 372, 387, 391, 392, 423, 444-6
inadequacy of compensation as failure to exercise jurisdiction **54,** 458-9
'occasioning failure of justice', relevance **83,** 351
judicial process requirements **69,** 345-6, 349-51, 367, 385-7, 463-4
Member State applications **69,** 342-4, 346-9, 368, 384-6, 389-90, 423-4, 485, 561
merits **69,** 366-9, 374, 381, 425-7, 430-1, 446-7, 465, 468, 470-92, 556, 560

oral proceedings **83,** 417-18
second-tier court, need for **83,** 394, 563-4
Secretary-General, impact on authority of **69,** 328-9, 386, 423-4
task of Court **69,** 344, 366-70, 381, 389, 425-8, 447, 458, 465, 470-2, 489-92, **83,** 318-19, 352, 364-5, 367, 375-6, 392-3, 400-3, 407-8, 421-2
judicial review **83,** 402
proprio motu **83,** 387
UNGA Resolution 957 (X) **83,** 374
staff challenge to decisions, provision of counsel **47,** 360
Staff Regulations and Rules, application of **69,** 312-23, 340-1, 361-5, 369-73, 376, 397-9, 409, 439-40
Art. 6.1 **69,** 352, 460
validity of rules applied **69,** 439-40
Statute
Art. 2 **69,** 375-6, 455, 473, 546, 548, 550, 555-6
travaux préparatoires **69,** 555
Art. 3.1 **69,** 352, 459-60
Art. 6 **69,** 352, 459-60
Art. 11 **54,** 387, 390-5, 396-7, 398, 407-8, 434, 444-7, 462-5, 473-80, 485, 487-93, 496, 500-7, 516, **69,** 337-8, 341-5, 347-50, 352-4, 356, 359-60, 365-9, 379-80, 384-5, 387, 392-4, 401-8, 424, 426, 428, 443, 446-7, 460-1, 463, 470-92, 554, 557, 560, **83,** 304, 314-15, 327, 328, 337, 351, 361, 363, 364, 371, 398-9, 401, 417-18, 419-21, 444
interpretation **40,** 401
travaux préparatoires **69,** 465, 468, 474-87
travaux préparatoires **83,** 398-9, 401-3, 425-6, 438
UNEF, local employees, standing **48,** 321-7
United Nations Charter (1945) 52, 1, 2. *See also Consolidated Table of Treaties*
Act of Chapultepec and **76,** 691-2
amendment, need for **95,** 115-16
judicial measures **105,** 439-40, 474, 570
applicable law, UN Administrative Tribunal (UNAT) **83,** 336
armed force, permissibility **71,** 288-9, 292-3
Art. 73, role **37,** 161-2, 330-1, 333-4, 341, 345-6, 493-4
Art. 80
implied terms **37,** 230-2
interpretation **37,** 214-15, 230-4, 237
purpose **37,** 232-4, 237
Arts. 55 and 56, Mandates, application to **37,** 364-5, 366
Art. 2(4) (prohibition on use of force), Art. 51 (self-defence) and **110,** 194-7, 216, 327-8
Art. 3, conflict of obligation **81,** 468
breach, South West Africa, in respect of **49,** 61, 79-80
Chapter X
breach by UN organs, effect **37,** 331
scope **37,** 41, 330-1, 341
Chapters XI, XII and XIII, Mandates, interpretation **37,** 359, 360
customary international law
Art. 2(4) **110,** 247
evidence of **85,** 241 n. 6
respect for **117,** 58
deterrence policy and **110,** 234, 241, 257-9, 273-9, 335-7, 475-6
dispute
definition **49,** 144-6

United Nations Charter (1945) (*cont.*)
judicial settlement **57,** 492
negotiations **55,** 395
obligation to settle by peaceful means **71,** 287, 291-2
situation distinguished **49,** 12
domestic jurisdiction **105,** 439, 441, 479-84, 576, 578-9
Dumbarton Oaks Conference (1944) **46,** 485
enforcement measures **49,** 155
equity, application of **99,** 609-10
expulsion provision **49,** 122, 273, 290
force, effect on treaties **55,** 194
general principles of international law, respect for **117,** 58
good neighbourliness **110,** 455-6
human rights **71,** 288-9, 292-3, **77,** 175-6, **85,** 241 n. 6, **87,** 456
expulsion of alien **42,** 205-7
legal obligation **37,** 451-2
promotion of **37,** 450-2
racial discrimination **107,** 37
sexual discrimination **83,** 355
implementation **83,** 425
implementing legislation, need for **52,** 2-3
individuals **85,** 257
obligations **52,** 2-3, **71,** 283, 288-90
rights **77,** 237-9, **81,** 514, **85,** 241-2, **96,** 50
international humanitarian law, effect on **110,** 440-1
interpretation **54,** 392-4
aids
drafting history **37,** 70, 211, 227, 232, 315
general practice of the Organization **49,** 12, 174
San Francisco formula **49,** 141, 170, 174
Art. 2(7) **46,** 487-8
Art. 80 **37,** 314-15
evolutionary **117,** 77
guidelines
broad and liberal **49,** 175
effectiveness principle **49,** 331
liberal **83,** 410
literal **94,** 528, **105,** 470
spirit **94,** 528
teleological **46,** 476, **49,** 174-5
phrases
'decision' **95,** 101-2, 120-1
'these measures' **105,** 470
'threat to peace and security' **105,** 466
'undertake' **95,** 101-2
responsibility
General Assembly **37,** 40
ICJ **117,** 58-60
UN organs **46,** 487
UNGA Resolution **110,** 269
legal obligations under **85,** 241-2
Mandate
Art. 73 **37,** 161-2, 330-1, 333-4, 341, 345-6, 493-4

Arts. 55 and 56, application to **37,** 364-5, 366
effect on **37,** 40, 231, 237, 573
implied amendment **37,** 231, 237
implied term, supervision of Mandates **37,** 312-15
mandatories
accountability obligations **49,** 225-31
interpretation **49,** 180-9, 228-31
powers of Security Council **49,** 177
safeguard clause for Mandates **49,** 23-7, 36, 114
non-discrimination principle **49,** 101
non-self-governing territories
definition **49,** 187-8
mandated territories **37,** 155, 161-4, 220-1, 223, 226, 330-1, 333, 491, 494
'sacred trust' **37,** 39
organs of UN, limitation on competence **49,** 269-85
Pact of Bogotá (1948) and **76,** 369-70
Preamble, justiciability **95,** 109
principles of **71,** 288-9, 581
priority over other treaties **49,** 89, **117,** 50, 58, 316, 474-5, 529, 549
purposes and principles of Organization
equal rights and self-determination **83,** 26
provisions distinguished **83,** 337
Security Council duty to respect **94,** 528
reservations, acceptability **37,** 43
resistance, right of **71,** 292-3
self-defence (1945). *See* self-defence, UN Charter, Art. 51
self-executing, whether **83,** 425, **85,** 257
sovereign equality of States and **44,** 375, 377, **65,** 191
sovereignty
delegation of powers to UN **105,** 432
duty of non-interference **116,** 590-1
surrender **105,** 439, **106,** 329
State immunity, jurisdiction, treaty exception **103,** 476
subsequent legislation affecting **85,** 256-8
temporary trusteeship committee, proposal for **37,** 214, 215, 317-18, 489
as treaty **76,** 95-6, **85,** 240-1, **103,** 476
trusteeship system. *See* Trusteeship system
UN officials
geographical consideration **83,** 403-4
paramount considerations in employment of **83,** 294, 346-53, 386-7, 426, 428
competence **83,** 403
efficiency **83,** 403
integrity **83,** 403
sole consideration distinguished **83,** 348, 387
voting, reservations **49,** 324
United Nations Commission on Human Rights, Resolutions
20 (XXXVI) (Working Group on Enforced or Involuntary Disappearances) **95,** 291
1997/12 (death penalty) **124,** 325-6
1998/8 (death penalty) **124,** 325-6
1999/61 (death penalty) **124,** 325-6
2000/65 (death penalty) **124,** 325-6
United Nations Commission on International Trade Law (UNCITRAL). *See* UNCITRAL (United Nations Commission on International Trade Law)

United Nations Commission on the Racial Situation in the Union of South Africa 85, 209
United Nations Commission on the Status of Women (UNCSW)
participation in as ground for disqualification as judge **121,** 329-30, 337-42
representatives, official status **121,** 338-9
United Nations Committee against Torture 121, 257 n. 164
admissibility
absence of objection **108,** 281
agreement not to contest **108,** 272
exhaustion of local remedies. *See* exhaustion of local remedies *below*
matter not being examined under another international procedure **108,** 266, 281
exhaustion of local remedies **108,** 261, 266
Rules of Procedure, Rule 108 **108,** 272
structure **108,** 268 n. 1
United Nations Committee on the Elimination of Racial Discrimination. *See* Racial Discrimination, UN Committee on the Elimination of
United Nations Committee on Missing Persons (Cyprus) (CMP)
communication of information to **120,** 51
competence **120,** 27, 55
contribution to as discharge of obligations to protect life/liberty **120,** 52-3, 57, 131-2
establishment **120,** 24, 131-2
United Nations Compensation Commission
applicable law
banking practice **109,** 365
Commissioners' obligation to develop applicable legal principles **109,** 408-9
criteria established by Governing Council for particular categories of claims **109,** 15, 47, 58, 67, 224, 408-9, 563
decisions of Governing Council where pertinent **109,** 15, 47, 58, 67, 133, 224, 225, 251, 450, 467, 471
employee entitlements on termination of employment
applicable Kuwaiti/Iraqi legislation **109,** 384-5
ILO legislation **109,** 382-4, 385
Libyan expulsion of Egyptians and Tunisians (1985) **109,** 383-4
State practice **109,** 382
family member, definition, national law of claimant **109,** 139
generally accepted actuarial principles **109,** 330
municipal law of Kuwait/Iraq, importance **109,** 384 n. 303
relevant principles and rules of international law **109,** 67, 133, 224, 251, 450, 467, 471, **117,** 240, 242
causality **109,** 235, **117,** 247-9
Rules of Procedure **109,** 225, 450, 467, 471
Security Council Resolutions
687 (1991) **109,** 15, 47, 58, 67, 133, 224, 467, 471, 506-7
where relevant **109,** 15, 67, 133, 251
UNCITRAL Arbitration Rules **109,** 563
Category 'A' claims (fixed amounts in respect of departure from Kuwait between 2 August 1990 and 2 March 1991)
amounts claimable **109,** 18
claim forms. *See* Claim Form 'A' *below*
departure patterns **109,** 32-6
discrepancy between number of awards and claims reported **109,** 101 n. 5
instalment 1 **109,** 1-46
corrections **109,** 663

guidelines for exclusion **109,** 25
guidelines for inclusion **109,** 21-2
recommendations **109,** 43-6, 625-8
instalment 2 **109,** 46-56
corrections **109,** 663
guidelines for inclusion **109,** 49
recommendations **109,** 53-6, 639-42
instalment 3 **109,** 57-64
corrections **109,** 664
guidelines for inclusion **109,** 60
recommendations **109,** 63-4, 642-3
instalment 4 **109,** 64-93
corrections **109,** 664
guidelines for exclusion **109,** 76
guidelines for inclusion **109,** 76-7
recommendations **109,** 90-3, 644-7
sampling methodology **109,** 78-90
instalment 5 **109,** 94-9
corrections **109,** 665
recommendations **109,** 96-9, 625-6
sampling methodology **109,** 95-6
instalment 6 **109,** 99-117
recommendations **109,** 114-17, 660-6
sampling methodology **109,** 102
'most urgent' **109,** 15
Category 'B' claims (serious personal injury or death)
discrepancy between number of awards and claims reported **109,** 174, 187
instalment 1 **109,** 129-61
recommendations **109,** 157-60, 622-4
sampling methodology **109,** 132-3
instalment 2: part one **109,** 162-82
recommendations **109,** 174-82, 631-5, 647
instalment 2: part two **109,** 184-93
recommendations **109,** 187-93, 635-9, 647
instalment 3 **109,** 195-204
recommendations **109,** 200-4
mental pain and anguish **109,** 141-3
Category 'C' claims (individual claims up to US 100,000)
admissible claims **109,** 226-7
mental pain and anguish **109,** 227, 292, 299-304, 390-1
application phase **109,** 258
C1 (damages arising from departure or detention) **109,** 222, 256 n. 115, 269-305
accommodation costs **109,** 279
critical date **109,** 287-8
food costs **109,** 279
methodology **109,** 269-77, 298, 459-61
relocation costs **109,** 279
transportation costs **109,** 278-9
C2 (personal injury) **109,** 222, 256 n. 115, 305-20
C3 (death of claimant's spouse, child or parent) **109,** 222, 256 n.115, 320-32
C4 (personal property losses) **109,** 223, 256 n. 115, 332-59
methodology **109,** 461
vehicle claims **109,** 350-9, 461

United Nations Compensation Commission (*cont.*)
C5 (loss of bank accounts, stocks, securities) **109,** 223, 256 n. 115, 359-66
bank accounts in Iraq **109,** 365-6
bank accounts in Kuwait **109,** 363-4, 461-2
Eighth Report of Executive Secretary **109,** 365
methodology **109,** 461-2
pre-invasion obligation, whether **109,** 364 n. 285, 365
C6 (loss of income, unpaid salaries or support) **109,** 223, 256 n. 115, 366-91
claimants' difficulty in calculating monthly income **109,** 373-5
definition of 'support' **109,** 375-6
employment related losses **109,** 381-2
methodology **109,** 462-4
place of employment, relevance **109,** 373, 379-80
presence as evidence of employment **109,** 379
C7 (real property losses) **109,** 223, 256 n. 115, 391-402
location of property, relevance **109,** 402
standard of proof **109,** 398-9
C8 (individual business losses) **109,** 223, 256 n. 115, 402-17
instalment 1 **109,** 410-11
Egyptian claims **109,** 451 n. 8, 478, **117,** 199-266
instalment 1 **109,** 214-447
corrections **109,** 668
limitations **109,** 260-1
recommendations **109,** 418-24, 656-9
instalment 2 **109,** 448-65
claims amenable to expedited processing, limited to **109,** 452-3, 464-5
corrections **109,** 669
recommendations **109,** 465, 656-9
instalment 3 **109,** 466-70
Kuwaiti/Egyptian claims **109,** 468-9
recommendations **109,** 469-70, 659-60
instalment 4 **109,** 470-8
recommendations **109,** 474-8, 629-31, 666-9
loss, need to establish **109,** 285-7
methodology, need to develop **109,** 451
'most urgent' **109,** 222, 450
precedent phase **109,** 257-8, 452
sampling methodology **109,** 251-2, 254, 258-60, 452, 456-61
Category 'E' claims (corporations), public sector enterprise, environmental damage claim **109,** 500-3
Category 'F' claims (environmental damage or depletion of natural resources) **109,** 502, 506-8
causality **109,** 234-6. *See also* State responsibility, liability of Iraq for 'any direct loss, damage . . . as a result of Iraq's unlawful invasion and occupation of Kuwait'
bank account losses **109,** 365
burden of proof **109,** 148, 289, 379-80
death **109,** 328-9
lack of medical treatment **109,** 329
equity and **109,** 236
evidence of **109,** 156-7
death certificate **109,** 329
Governing Council Decision No 1 **117,** 246-7

place of employment outside Kuwait/Iraq **109,** 373, 379-80
presumption of **109,** 316-17
relevant principles and rules of international law **109,** 235, **117,** 247-9
Claim Form 'A'
'A' Claim Form Data Capture System (DCS) **109,** 17-18
Instructions for Claimants **109,** 265, 283 n. 136
Claim Form 'B'
'B' Claim Form Data Capture System (DCS) **109,** 456
Instructions for Claimants **109,** 266
Claim Form 'C'
ambiguities **109,** 255, 281, 298, 314, 330, 410
correction of errors **109,** 256, 264-5, 411
Instructions for Claimants **109,** 223-4, 283 n. 136
real property losses, definition **109,** 391
Claim Form 'D', Instructions for Claimants **109,** 267
classification of claims
legal implications **109,** 502, 507-8
loss of support **109,** 375-6
materials for repair of real property **109,** 395 n. 338
mental pain and anguish **109,** 295
public sector enterprise, claim for environmental damage **109,** 500-3
reallocation **109,** 142-3, 160, 169, 180, 191, 201, 295, 376, 402, 413
Secretary-General's Report (S/22559) **109,** 561-2
standard of proof and **109,** 314
commissioners, task **109,** 557
compensation. *See also* Decision 8 (ceilings for mental pain and anguish) *below*
contract
Iraq as party **109,** 594
Iraq not party **109,** 594-5
cumulative, mental pain and anguish **109,** 296
currency **109,** 622
distribution
costs **109,** 620-1
government responsibility **109,** 620-2
time-limits **109,** 621
for. *See also entries under* Category 'C' claims *above*
Allied Coalition Forces, costs **109,** 622
burial expenses **109,** 329
capital expenditure **109,** 521-6, 534-7
common costs **109,** 525-6, 531, 549-60
contract losses **109,** 594-5. *See also* contract *above*
departure/relocation costs **109,** 289-91
employment benefits and allowances **109,** 387
firefighting/support services **109,** 527-9, 538-40
firefighting/support services of own team **109,** 532
freight costs **109,** 540-1
legal costs **109,** 531, 549-60
loss of bearer instruments **109,** 366
loss of support **109,** 329-31
loss of tangible assets **109,** 595
losses dependent on continuation of past practice **109,** 595
losses relating to income-producing properties **109,** 596
management costs **109,** 537-8

United Nations Compensation Commission (*cont.*)
medical expenses **109,** 317-18
non-availability of dollar portion of workers' wages **117,** 238-50
pay in lieu of notice **109,** 385-6
post-capping costs **109,** 529
remuneration for duration of employment contract **109,** 385
rent losses **109,** 391, 401-2
repair costs **109,** 358-9, 400-1
sanctions-related losses **109,** 584
severance allowances **109,** 387-8
temporary staging area **109,** 543-4
unpaid remuneration **109,** 386
measure
compensation in full **109,** 15, 47, 58, 66, 94
directly related **109,** 389
fair compensation for loss suffered **109,** 389-90
lost profit **109,** 594
restitutio in integrum **109,** 28, 244
substantial interim relief **109,** 15, 47, 58, 66, 94
mitigation of losses
applicability to all types of business losses **109,** 618
control of oil-well fires **109,** 502-3
loss of employment **109,** 376, 388-9
offset **109,** 587. *See also* mitigation of losses *above*
compensation previously paid **109,** 614
residual value of capital equipment **109,** 521-3
partial payment, outstanding obligation, whether **109,** 563
payment
procedures. *See* Decision 17 (priority of payment and payment mechanism Guiding Principles) *below*
prompt **109,** 91, 99, 117
valuation. *See* valuation *below*
Compensation Fund (Security Council Resolution 692 (1991))
administration **109,** 555-6
entitlement to payment out of, in case of injury or death related to authorities other than Iraqi **109,** 148
financing **109,** 558-60, 574
Iraq's contribution **109,** 558
privileges and immunities **109,** 555, 580-1
Escrow Account **109,** 555, 580-1
immunity from attachment **109,** 581
immunity from suit **109,** 581
shortfall **109,** 563, 564, 582, 583
special account of UN **109,** 555
composition **109,** 15
correction of decision **109,** 101 n. 5, 102, 111-14, 186-7, 202, 473, **117,** 264-5
cross-filing **109,** 106
multiple family claims **109,** 186-7
costs **109,** 557, 564
incurred for work on behalf of Commission **109,** 578
currency of payment
rate of exchange **109,** 548-9
critical date **109,** 242-6

US dollar **109,** 243
death claim
causality. *See* causality, death *above*
critical date **109,** 328-9
death of new-born **109,** 141
eligibility. *See* standing, death claim *below*
evidence of death
death or burial certificate **109,** 150-1, 155-6, 327-8
martyr's certificate **109,** 155-6
presumption of death **109,** 137-8, 328-9
Decision 1 (criteria for expedited processing of urgent claims) **117,** 201
circumstances creating presumption of directness of loss **117,** 246-7
para. 1 **109,** 15, 17, 225-6
paras. 10-13 (payment of fixed amounts) **109,** 571
para. 13 ('one family (consisting of any person and his or her spouse, children and parents')) **109,** 138-9
para. 14 (compensation for actual losses) **109,** 279
paras. 14-16 (claims up to $100, 000) **109,** 572
para. 15 (standard of proof) **109,** 236, 239
para. 17 (Iraqi nationals: dual nationality) **109,** 106-7
para. 18 (circumstances directly linked to Iraq's invasion and occupation of Kuwait) **109,** 145, 234, 279-80, **117,** 238
para. 19 (submission of claims by Government) **109,** 130, 247 n. 87, 577-8
text **109,** 569-73
Decision 2 (arrangements for ensuring payments to Compensation Fund), text **109,** 574
Decision 3 (personal injury and mental pain and anguish) **109,** 140, 292, 295-6, 310-11, 325
paras. 1-3 (serious personal injury) **109,** 575
text **109,** 574-6
Decision 4 (individual business losses) **109,** 407
text **109,** 576-7
Decision 5 (expedited processing of urgent claims), text **109,** 577-8
Decision 6 (ensuring payments to Compensation Fund)
States' obligations **109,** 582
text **109,** 578-82
Decision 7 (criteria for processing of claims of individuals not otherwise covered)
expedited processing, need for **109,** 584, 586
paras. 16-29 (payments in respect of direct damage or injury to corporations) **109,** 500-1, 585-8
paras. 30-9 (claims of governments and international organizations) **109,** 588-9
para. 35 (environmental damage and depletion of natural resources) **109,** 500-3
text **109,** 583-91
Decision 8 (ceilings for mental pain and anguish) **109,** 296, 311, 325, 428-30
Category 'A' (death of spouse, child or parent) **109,** 428
Category 'B' (serious personal injury) **109,** 428
Category 'C' (sexual or aggravated assault) **109,** 429
Category 'D' (witness to intentional death or torture) **109,** 429
Category 'E' (detention) **109,** 429
Category 'F' (forced hiding) **109,** 429
Category 'G' (deprivation of resources threatening survival) **109,** 429
cumulative **109,** 296, 308, 311, 331, 372, 429
employment related claims **109,** 372
length of detention **109,** 298, 300, 304

United Nations Compensation Commission (*cont.*)
modifying factors **109,** 318-20, 440-4
aggravating circumstances **109,** 442
aggravation due to lack of medical care **109,** 442
burn injuries **109,** 442
dependence on others for subsistence **109,** 442
dependents **109,** 444
gravity of injury **109,** 442
inability to follow previous employment **109,** 442, 444
intentionality of actions **109,** 442
loss of fertility **109,** 442
new as opposed to pre-existing condition **109,** 442
repeated incidents **109,** 443
significant disfigurement to face or genitals **109,** 442
text **109,** 591-3
Decision 9 (business losses: types of damage and valuation) **109,** 407-8, 416
'economic situation caused thereby' **109,** 617
para. 6 (trade embargo losses) **109,** 616-18, **117,** 238, 251-2
para. 8 (contracts) **117,** 238
text **109,** 593-6
Decision 10 (Rules of Procedure). *See* Rules of Procedure *below*
Decision 11 (eligibility for compensation of members of the Allied Coalition Armed Forces) **109,** 136
text **109,** 612
Decision 12 (time-limits: extension) **109,** 137, 230-1
text **109,** 612-13
Decision 13 (avoidance of multiple recovery), text **109,** 613-14
Decision 15 (compensation where trade embargo also cause)
para. 6 (circumstances directly linked to Iraq's invasion and occupation of Kuwait) **109,** 234, 408, **117,** 238, 250-2
text **109,** 615-18
Decision 16 (awards of interest) **109,** 27-9, 52, 62, 78, 96, 116-17, 549, **117,** 265-6
text **109,** 618-19
Decision 17 (priority of payment and payment mechanism Guiding Principles)
para. 2 (initial payment) **109,** 50
text **109,** 619-20
Decision 18 (distribution of payments), text **109,** 620-2
Decision 19 (costs of Allied Coalition Forces), text **109,** 622
Decision 20 (Category 'B' claims, instalment 1). *See* category 'B' claims, instalment 1 *above*
Decision 21 (multi-category claims) **109,** 51, 61, 77
text **109,** 622-4
Decision 22 (Category 'A' claims, instalment 1). *See* category 'A' claims, instalment 1 *above*
Decision 23 (deadline for filing of individual claims), text **109,** 628
Decision 24 (multi-category departure claims), text **109,** 628-9
Decision 25 (Category 'C' claims, instalment 1). *See* category 'C' claims, instalment 1 *above*
Decision 26 (Category 'B' claims, instalment 2: part two). *See* category 'B' claims, instalment 2: part two *above*
Decision 27 (Category 'B' claims, instalment 2: part one). *See* category 'B' claims, instalment 2: part one *above*

Decision 28 (Category 'A' claims, instalment 2). *See* category 'A' claims, instalment 2 *above*
Decision 29 (Category 'A' claims, instalment 3). *See* category 'A' claims, instalment 3 *above*
Decision 30 (deadline for filing of corporate/government claims), text **109,** 628
Decision 31 (Category 'A' claims, instalment 4). *See* category 'A' claims, instalment 4 *above*
Decision 32 (Category 'B' claims, instalment 2: parts one and two). *See* category 'B' claims, instalment 2: part one *and* part two *above*
Decision 33 (Category 'A' claims, instalment 5). *See* category 'A' claims, instalment 5 *above*
Decision 34 (Category 'B' claims, instalment 3). *See* category 'B' claims, instalment 3 *above*
Decision 35 (review of claims under Art. 38) **109,** 492
  text **109,** 655
Decision 36 (Category 'C' claims, instalment 2). *See* category 'C' claims, instalment 2 *above*
Decision 37 (Category 'C' claims, instalment 3). *See* category 'C' claims, instalment 3 *above*
Decision 38 (Category 'A' claims, instalment 6). *See* category 'A' claims, instalment 6 *above*
Decision 39 (Category 'C' claims, instalment 4). *See* category 'C' claims, instalment 4 *above*
Decision 40 (Well Blowout Claim), text **109,** 669-70
detention/forced hiding
  coercion, need for **109,** 299-300
  'detention' **109,** 299
  evidence of **109,** 299, 300
  length of detention **109,** 298, 300, 304
    reasonable assumption regarding **109,** 304
  'manifestly well-founded fear'
    member of Kuwaiti royal family, armed forces or government **109,** 303
    member of medical profession or media **109,** 303
    national of country targeted by Iraq **109,** 302
    presumption of **109,** 303-4
    shown cause **109,** 303
  restrictive interpretation **109,** 299-300
Escrow Account
  establishment **109,** 578-9
  payments into **109,** 579-80
establishment, UN Security Council competence **109,** 672
estoppel, second presentation of claim **109,** 505
evidence. *See also under individual headings*
  absence **109,** 151-2, 173-4
    request for documentation **109,** 180-1, 186, 191, 196-9
  Arrival/Departure Records **109,** 19-20, 22, 53, 62
    diplomatic records **109,** 37
    evacuation records **109,** 37
    evidentiary value **109,** 38-41, 53, 62-3
    government records **109,** 37-8
    immigration/customs records **109,** 37
    refugee camp rosters **109,** 38
    residence lists **109,** 38

United Nations Compensation Commission (*cont.*)
travel records **109,** 37
birth certificate **109,** 156
burden of proof **117,** 260
Category 'C' claims
bank records **109,** 240, 380, 398
contract **109,** 240, 263, 376
employee identification card **109,** 263, 377
employment documentation **109,** 377, 380
expatriate employment patterns **109,** 381
newspaper article **109,** 240
photographs **109,** 240
previous formal statement of income **109,** 377
professional correspondence **109,** 240
published pay scales **109,** 381
real property records **109,** 240, 263, 398
receipts/invoices **109,** 240
certificate of inheritance **109,** 156
circumstantial **109,** 154, 242, 264, 286-7, 297
claim form **109,** 237-8
claimants' statements **109,** 149-50, 152, 157, 239, 263, 342, 377, 381, 399
evidentiary value **109,** 149-50
death or burial certificate **109,** 150-1, 155-6, 157, 238, 327-8
evidentiary value **109,** 151
family registration record **109,** 156, 238
government certificate **109,** 298
identity documents **109,** 149, 173-4, 238-9, 262-3
inventory **109,** 342
marriage certificate **109,** 156
martyr's certificate **109,** 155-6
medical documentation **109,** 151, 157
injury caused by pollution from burning oil wells **109,** 154-5
need for **109,** 153-4
non-contemporaneous **109,** 152
sexual assault **109,** 154
torture **109,** 153-4
party's obligation to provide **117,** 260-2
passport **109,** 156, 238
dual nationality **109,** 167
presence as evidence of employment **109,** 379, 412
standard of proof. *See* standard of proof *below*
travel documentation **109,** 281
videotapes of explosives on well-heads **109,** 511
witness statements **109,** 150, 157, 239-40, 263, 343, 377, 381, 399
evidentiary value **109,** 150, 239-40
family member **109,** 297
evidence, expert
employment law **109,** 251
mass claims processing **109,** 251
medical **109,** 164, 184, 251, 313, 327, 391
panel of psychiatric experts
appointment **109,** 430

composition **109,** 430-4
statistical procedures **109,** 67, 251, 449
fair hearing, need to ensure **109,** 512
family claim **109,** 138-9, 175-7, 185, 231-3
ceiling, application **109,** 175-7, 185
consolidation **109,** 175-7
correction of decision **109,** 186-7
family relationship
evidence of **109,** 239, 319, 327
birth certificate **109,** 156
certificate of inheritance **109,** 156
failure to provide **109,** 196-9
family registration record **109,** 156
marriage certificate **109,** 156
passport **109,** 156
Governing Council
guidelines for conduct of its work **109,** 568-9
Member States' obligation to cooperate **109,** 569
structure and composition **109,** 556
task **109,** 220-1, 557
headquarters **109,** 557
hostage-taking. *See* detention/forced hiding *above*
interest. *See also* Decision 16 (awards of interest) *above*
'A' claims **109,** 27-9, 52, 62, 78, 96, 116-17
'C' claims **109,** 465, 470
date *ab quo* **109,** 27-8, 117
date of invasion **109,** 29, 52, 62, 78, 96, 246-7
date of loss **109,** 549, **117,** 265
judicial tribunal, whether **109,** 512, 560
investigative role **109,** 512
jurisdiction
concurrent **125,** 657
guidelines, need for **109,** 561
critical date
2 August 1990 **117,** 238, 241-2
'A' claims **109,** 26, 50, 61
'B' claims **109,** 134-5
burden of proof **109,** 134, 227-8
'C' claims **109,** 227-8, 285
evidence of departure within relevant period **109,** 109-11
place of loss, relevance **109,** 143, 144-5, 228-9
pre-invasion obligations **109,** 364 n. 285, 365, 561, **117,** 246
'debt' or 'obligation' **117,** 239-41
ratione personae
Iraqi national **109,** 25, 106-7, 135, 229
member of Allied Coalition Armed Forces **109,** 136, 167-8, 229
member of Kuwaiti Armed Forces **109,** 136
member of Kuwaiti resistance **109,** 136
non-Iraqi member of Iraqi Armed Forces **109,** 185
person identified by national claim number only **109,** 168
person not listed on claim form **109,** 168
verification of claims **109,** 562-3

United Nations Compensation Commission (*cont.*)
liability of Iraq for 'any direct loss, damage . . . as a result of Iraq's unlawful invasion and occupation of Kuwait'. *See* State responsibility/liability of Iraq for 'any direct loss, damage . . . as a result of Iraq's unlawful invasion and occupation of Kuwait'
mental pain and anguish. *See also* Decision 3 (personal injury and mental pain and anguish) *above*
admissibility as Category 'C' claim **109,** 227, 292, 299-304, 390-1
bibliography **109,** 444-6
Category 'A' (death of spouse, child or parent), suddenness of event, relevance **109,** 437
Category 'B' (serious personal injury), permanency of condition, relevance **109,** 438
Category 'C' (sexual or aggravated assault)
sexual assault, characteristics **109,** 438-9
torture, characteristics **109,** 438-9
classification **109,** 142, 314
mental injury distinguished **109,** 142-3
contributory factors, relevance **109,** 437
death of family member **109,** 331
detention for less than three days with threat to life **109,** 300-1
detention for more than three days **109,** 299-300
employment related, requirements **109,** 390-1
Expert Report **109,** 424-47
expert advisers **109,** 446-7
forced hiding **109,** 301-4
'mental disorders', International Classification of Diseases, 10th revision **109,** 435-6
presumption of **109,** 318
remedies
compensation **109,** 436
moral assistance to victims **109,** 436
rehabilitation **109,** 436
witnessing torture **109,** 318-20
inflicted intentionally **109,** 320, 332
nationality of claim
corporation, State of incorporation or organization **109,** 587
Iraqi dual national
date of acquisition of second nationality, relevance **109,** 107, 167
effectiveness, relevance **109,** 107
evidence of dual nationality **109,** 167
good faith, need for **109,** 106-7, 167
individual review **109,** 107
Panel ('A' claims), appointment **109,** 16
Panel ('B' claims), appointment **109,** 129
Panel ('C' claims)
appointment **109,** 221
task
assessment of losses **109,** 224
determination of causality **109,** 224
Panel (Egyptian claims) **109,** 451 n. 8, 478
Panel (Well Blowout Claim)
recommended compensation **109,** 550-1
task
causality **109,** 511

verification of claimed costs **109,** 511, 520-47
precedent as between Panels **117,** 253, 266
privileges and immunities **109,** 556-7
procedure
additional written submissions **117,** 210
complex claim, presentation by individual **109,** 583, 589
Egyptian Workers' Claims
Memorandum of Understanding of 17 June 1993 **117,** 202-3, 254-5, 260
Procedural Order No 1 **117,** 206-9
Procedural Order No 2 **117,** 206-8
following establishment of jurisdiction **117,** 253-4
government responsibility for filing claim
appointment of special representative **109,** 577-8, 584
consolidated claim **109,** 560-1
corporation, State of incorporation or organization **109,** 587
persons without government to pursue **109,** 577-8, 584
'observers under protest' **109,** 492-3
oral proceedings **117,** 206, 208-11
simple and expedited **109,** 250-61, 341, 450
claims amenable to, priority **109,** 452
claims on behalf of corporation **109,** 586
Criteria for Expedited Processing of Urgent Claims. *See* Decision 1, para. 1 *above*
fairness, need for **109,** 117, 252, 255, 256-7
fast-track distinguished **109,** 468
requests for additional information, need to avoid **109,** 226
Secretary-General's Report (S/22559) **109,** 561-2
verification of claim. *See* verification of claim *below*
withdrawal from proceedings **109,** 493
Rules of Procedure **117,** 694
6 (claim forms and language) **109,** 247, **117,** 202
7(1) (computer format of 'A' claims) **109,** 17
7(2) (format of non-'A' claims) **109,** 468, 473
11(1) (receipt of claims) **109,** 247
13 (filing receipt) **109,** 247
14(1) (verification that formal requirements met) **109,** 23-4, 130-1
14(1)(c) (nationality of claims) **109,** 135, 229, 238 n. 65
15 (claims not meeting formal requirements) **109,** 247
16, 203, (Executive Secretary's reports to Governing Council) **117,** 204-5, 694
16(1) (Executive Secretary's reports to Governing Council) **109,** 23-4, 131, 248, 280, 365, 372-3, 397, 404, 467, 489
16(2) (Executive Secretary's reports to Governing Council: circulation) **109,** 489
16(3) (Executive Secretary's reports to Governing Council: governments' comments) **109,** 24, 131, 326, 363, 409, 472
18(1) (nomination of commissioners) **109,** 16, 129, 221
28 (constitution of panels) **109,** 221
30 (confidentiality) **109,** 671-2
30(1) (confidentiality of Panel proceedings) **109,** 622 n. 1, 625 n. 1, 639 n. 1, 642 n. 1, 644 n. 1, 647 n. 1, 650 n. 1, 656 n. 1, 659 n. 1, 660 n. 1, 662 n. 3, 666 n. 1, 668 n. 2, **117,** 694 n. 1
30(2) (confidentiality of Panel proceedings) **109,** 16, 129, 164, 184, 250
31 (applicable law) **109,** 15, 47, 58, 133, 224, 250, **117,** 237, 242
32 (submission of claims to panels) **109,** 16, 24, 132, 249, 251, 449, 450, 466, 467, 471, 472, **117,** 200, 204

United Nations Compensation Commission (*cont.*)
32(1) (submission of claims to panels) **109,** 15, 129, 218
32(3) (reallocation of claims) **109,** 160, 169, 180, 191, 201, 413
33(2) (panels: place of work) **109,** 16, 164, 184, 250, 449
34 (assistance by the Executive Secretary) **109,** 132, 250, 494
35 (evidence) **109,** 19, 236, 362, 396, 472
35(1) (claimant's responsibility for submission of documents) **109,** 148
35(2)(a) (standard of proof: 'A' claims) **109,** 19, 48, 59, 67-8, **117,** 260
35(2)(b) (standard of proof: 'B' claims) **109,** 148
35(2)(c) (standard of proof: reasonable minimum) **109,** 27 n. 2, 236
36 (additional information) **109,** 226
36(b) (expert advice) **109,** 449
37 (review of claims) **109,** 108
37(a) (verification of claims: matching) **109,** 20, 66, 95, 101
37(b) (verification of claims: sampling) **109,** 20, 66, 67, 95, 101, 131, 165, 226, 341
37(c) (procedure for arriving at recommendation) **109,** 226
37(d) (time-limits) **109,** 226
37(e) (panels: reports) **109,** 15, 43, 53, 58 n. 2, 63, 66, 90, 94, 96, 114, 129, 157, 158, 163, 174, 184, 200, 218, 418, 449, 464, 466, 471, **117,** 200, 254, 266
38(d) (complex claims) **109,** 489-90
38(e) (Panel reports) **109,** 489, **117,** 237
40 (decisions) **109,** 623
40(5) (confidentiality of decisions) **109,** 622 n. 1, 625 n. 1, 639 n. 1, 642 n. 1, 644 n. 1, 647 n. 1, 650 n. 1, 656 n. 1, 659 n. 1, 660 n. 1, 662 n. 3, 666 n. 1, 668 n. 2, **117,** 694 n. 1
41 (correction of decision) **109,** 101 n. 5, 102, 111, 186-7, 202, 473, **117,** 264-5
41(1) (correction of decision) **117,** 255-6
text **109,** 597-611
sampling methodology **109,** 76-7, 95-6, 250, 251-2, 254, 258-60, 378-9, 426-7, 452, 456-61
assessment of sample claims **109,** 83-5
country-specific **109,** 79, 165
criteria for determination of sample **109,** 79-80
extrapolation **109,** 87-90
randomness **109,** 83
review and assessment of claims **109,** 85-7
sample size **109,** 80-3
supporting evidence **109,** 90
secretariat, task **109,** 558
Secretary-General's Report (S/22559), text **109,** 554-64
serious personal injury
'B' and 'C' claims distinguished **109,** 310
'seriousness', relevance **109,** 310-11
death claim distinguished **109,** 141
Decision 3 **109,** 575-6
definition **109,** 140-1
mental pain and anguish distinguished **109,** 141-3, 169
miscarriage, abortion or stillbirth **109,** 141
stress related illness **109,** 171-2
standard of proof
'A' claims **109,** 18-20, 48, 67-8, 151-2
'B' claims **109,** 148, 151-7
'C' claims **109,** 151-2, 236-43, 450

'C7' claims **109,** 398-9
gradation **109,** 237, 436-7
need to determine **109,** 225, 328, 397
classification of claim, relevance **109,** 314
loss of income **109,** 380-1
presumption in favour of claimant **109,** 300, 303-4, 344-5
'reasonable minimum . . . appropriate under the particular circumstances' **109,** 237-43, 264, 284-7, 327, 362-3, 411, **117,** 260
business practices in Iraq and Kuwait **109,** 241, 343, 416
circumstances in Kuwait and Iraq **109,** 240-1, 282, 315-16, 343-4
effect of being taken hostage or forced to hide **109,** 316
loss of rent **109,** 401
national claims programme **109,** 242, 255
real property, value **109,** 397-8
retention of documents, usual practice **109,** 343
socio-economic characteristics of claimant **109,** 241, 255, 282
serious personal injury caused by **109,** 152-5
pollution from burning oil wells **109,** 154-5
sexual assault **109,** 154
torture **109,** 153-4
standing
corporation **109,** 587
death claim
family member **109,** 138-9
units within family **109,** 139
where more than one wife **109,** 139
family claim. *See* family claim *above*
heir to potential claimant **109,** 185
individual business losses **109,** 233
public sector enterprise **109,** 503-5
claim deemed to be on behalf of government **109,** 505
third party claim. *See* third party claim *below*
status **109,** 556-7
subsidiary organ of Security Council **109,** 15, 218
third party claim
detained or missing person **109,** 136-7, 168, 229-31, 304
seriously injured person
award to injured person **109,** 140, 177
exceptional circumstances **109,** 139-40
executor of estate of deceased person in case of obligation arising before death **109,** 140, 168-9
legally entitled person **109,** 130, 233
time-limits **109,** 585, 591
claims on behalf of detained person **109,** 137
extension, Well Blowout Control Claim **109,** 492
importance **109,** 225-6
torture
definition **109,** 438-9
sexual assault as **109,** 439
witnessing intentional infliction of death or torture **109,** 443
valuation. *See also* measure of damages/compensation including valuation of company/property/assets
book value minus accumulated depreciation **109,** 595, 596

United Nations Compensation Commission (*cont.*)
business losses **109,** 416-17
departure/relocation costs **109,** 289-91
discount factor **109,** 330
discounted cash flow (DCF) **109,** 596
loss of support **109,** 330
lost earnings **109,** 596
market value **109,** 596
personal property loss **109,** 345-50
price/earnings method **109,** 596
rent losses **109,** 401-2
mitigation **109,** 402
period of compensation **109,** 401-2
repairs to real property **109,** 400-1
replacement value **109,** 595
statistical model **109,** 346-50
vehicle **109,** 356-9
Motor Vehicle Valuation Table (MVV Table) **109,** 357-8, 359, 461
verification of claim **109,** 264-6, 562-3
Arrival/Departure Records. *See* evidence, Arrival and Departure Records *above*
competence of Commission. *See* jurisdiction *above*
cross-filing, avoidance **109,** 105-6, 166-7, 265-7, 282-3
binding nature of 'A' claim **109,** 51-2, 61-2, 77-8, 117 n. 10
correction of decision **109,** 106
need for guidance **109,** 26-7
formal requirements, preliminary check **109,** 24-5, 102-4, 247, 262-4
business loss caused by invasion **109,** 415-16
existence of incorporated business **109,** 412-13
identity of claimant **109,** 262-3
loss of personal property caused by invasion **109,** 344-5
loss of real property caused by invasion **109,** 399-400
loss of vehicle caused by invasion **109,** 355-6
ownership of business **109,** 413-15
ownership of personal property **109,** 342-4
ownership of real property **109,** 390-9
ownership of vehicle **109,** 354-5, 461
presence or residence in Iraq or Kuwait **109,** 263-4, 284-5, 299
value of loss **109,** 345-6
individual review **109,** 20, 48, 102, 108-11, 132-3, 252, 341
bank account losses in Iraq **109,** 365
burial expenses **109,** 329
in case of countries submitting less than 100 claims **109,** 79 n. 29
in cases where no compensation is awarded **109,** 166
claims with evidence falling outside sample **109,** 108
claims without supporting evidence **109,** 108
departure outside jurisdictional period **109,** 108
employment related support claims **109,** 390
instalment 1 'C7' claims **109,** 398, 452
Iraqi dual nationals **109,** 102, 107
jurisdictional problems **109,** 452
multiple claims **109,** 452
personal injury or death **109,** 452
jurisdictional period. *See* jurisdiction, critical date *above*

matching **109,** 20-1, 41-3, 48, 53, 59, 62
multiple recovery, avoidance **109,** 25-6, 50, 60-1, 77, 104-5, 267-9, 465, 469-70, 474, 477-8, 593
compensation from non-Fund sources **109,** 268-9
detailed record of payments **109,** 26, 60-1, 478
duplicate claims **109,** 267-8, 477, **117,** 264
governments to provide information about claims against Iraq in municipal courts **109,** 613
Iraq to provide information about claims against it in municipal courts **109,** 613
public sector enterprise claim deemed to be on behalf of government **109,** 505
rent-a-permit **109,** 413-15
post-capping costs **109,** 530
reallocation. *See* classification of claim, reallocation *above*
sampling methodology. *See* sampling methodology *above*
Well Blowout Control Claim **109,** 485-551
United Nations Conference on International Organization 77, 587-9
United Nations Conference on the Law of the Sea (First) (UNCLOS I)
conservation and management measures **123,** 293-4
equidistance/equitable principles **81,** 301, 317
natural prolongation **81,** 386
United Nations Conference on the Law of the Sea (Third) (UNCLOS III) 55, 258, 273, **56,** 181, **71,** 121
codification and progressive development of maritime law **56,** 163
conservation and management measures **123,** 293-4
delimitation methods, failure to agree **81,** 317
equidistance/special circumstances **81,** 374-5, 382
functions **56,** 182
Informal Composite Negotiating Text (ICNT) **81,** 381, 383
Informal Single Negotiating Text (ISNT) **81,** 381, 383
landmass **81,** 273
method of work **71,** 191-2
purpose **55,** 334
Revised Single Negotiating Text (RSNT) **81,** 381, 383
United Nations Conference on Trade and Development (UNCTAD)
Resolutions
88(XII) **75,** 633
93(IV) (Integrated Programme for Commodities) **99,** 327-9, 349-51
United Nations Council for Namibia, travel document **79,** 20, 32
United Nations Council for South West Africa, as Administering Authority **82,** 480
United Nations Development Agency 51, 433-8
United Nations Economic and Social Council (ECOSOC). *See also* international officials; World Bank Group
Human Rights Commission **85,** 306-7, 323
Mandate **85,** 306-7, 323
Resolutions
1947 (stateless persons) **120,** 8
1983/32 **85,** 32
1985/12 **85,** 307, 309, 323, 332
1985/13 **85,** 307
1987/112 **85,** 307
1988/02 **85,** 309
1988/37 **85,** 305, 310-12, 330
1989/37 **85,** 305, 312, 330

United Nations Economic and Social Council (ECOSOC) (*cont.*)
1989/45 **85,** 313, 324
refugees, *ad hoc* Report (1950) **87,** 442
Resolutions
11(II) (UNCSW) **121,** 338
1946/5(1) **85,** 305, 306
1979/38 **95,** 291
1987/102 **85,** 309
1989/75 **85,** 305, 312, 313, 317, 327
Subcommission for the Prevention of Discrimination and Protection of Minorities Resolution 5B(XXXII) **95,** 291
United Nations Educational, Scientific and Cultural Organization (UNESCO) 77, 507-10
Appeals Board, jurisdiction, erroneous decision as to **43,** 468-70
Communication Problems, International Commission on (1980) **75,** 23
Convention against Discrimination in Education **45,** 156
officials, status **77,** 509
privileges and immunities **77,** 507-10
recommendation on cultural and natural heritage **68,** 305-6, 392-4
representative accredited to
immunity **74,** 278-9
wife, extension to **74,** 278-9
Staff Association, ILO Administrative Tribunal and **38,** 382
World Heritage Committee **68,** 272-8
United Nations Emergency Force (UNEF)
boundary markers **80,** 265
disbandment **80,** 266
establishment **80,** 265
local employees, UN Administrative Tribunal, standing **48,** 321-7
United Nations Force in Congo, damage from wrongful acts **45,** 446-55
United Nations Force in Cyprus (UNFICYP) 73, 15
Commander
commanders of national contingents distinguished **77,** 473-4
contradictory orders **77,** 471-4
component forces, national discipline **44,** 377
criminal jurisdiction over members of **44,** 376
Cyprus, Status of Forces Agreement **44,** 362, 375
financing of **44,** 376
members of
criminal jurisdiction over **44,** 376
responsibility for acts of **77,** 473-4
status **77,** 472-4
organ of UNFICYP **77,** 474
peace negotiations under auspices of **73,** 16
Regulations
Point 5a **77,** 473
Point 6 **77,** 473
Point 12 **77,** 473, 474
Point 17 **77,** 473
Point 18 **77,** 473
Point 21a, b and d **77,** 473
Point 25 **77,** 473
status **44,** 359-60

United Nations General Assembly (UNGA)
advisory opinion of ICJ, request for **59,** 183-6
competence
judicial decision-making **49,** 39, 270, 289-91
range **49,** 103, 215, 226-7, 270-3
Decisions
36/457 **83,** 382
40/465 **83,** 360
Declarations
nature **77,** 177, 238, 247-8
status **46,** 476, 485
Fourth Committee **37,** 55, 181, 216, 333, 334
Human Rights of Individuals who are not Citizens of the Country in which they Live, Draft Declaration (1978) **82,** 164-5
ICJ and **82,** 260
advisory opinion, request for **59,** 183-6
recommendation for reference to **49,** 322
judicial body, whether **69,** 554
judicial role **54,** 393
League of Nations functions, transfer to **37,** 118, 154–5, 157, 160, 202, 206-39, 310-12, 314, 324-5, 441, 544
Resolution on **37,** 217-18, 322, 326-7, 328
Mandated territory
authority in respect of, basis **49,** 51, 102, 136, 153-4
supervisory functions **37,** 155, 157, 216, 326, 415–16, 441, 443, 474, 490, 571, 572
Mandates, functions in respect of **49,** 26-7, 29, 34, 63, 100-3, 153, 180-9, 190, 215, 221, 254, 261
powers
conferred *ab extra* **49,** 274, 275
create standards for Mandatory **37,** 363-4, 577-8
delegation of **37,** 56
executive **49,** 271, 274, 289
implied **49,** 40, 271
legislative **110,** 269
suspension or expulsion of Members **49,** 273, 290
Trust Territories **37,** 149, 208, 410-11
privileges and immunities, entitlement **113,** 501
recommendations, significance **37,** 568-9
Resolutions. *See* United Nations General Assembly (UNGA) Resolutions
responsibility, promotion of purposes of UN **49,** 174
Rules of Procedure
Rule 39 **69,** 353
Rule 103 **69,** 354
Secretary-General and **69,** 313-14, 316-17, 370-3, 398, 424, 439-40, 454, 545-7, 553, 555
Staff Regulations and Rules, authority over **69,** 311-14, 320-3, 329–30, 341, 355, 365-6, 370-1, 374, 383, 395-8, 402, 410-11, 424, 431-42, 448, 451, 455, 466-7, 509-10, 522, 532-3, 539-40, 543, 546-55, 557-61
SW Africa cases
'interest' in **37,** 539-42
partition of, rejection **37,** 56
SW Africa, Committees on **37,** 55, 181, 473

United Nations General Assembly (UNGA) (*cont.*)
task, progressive development and codification of international law **110,** 226
Trusteeship Agreements, invitation to conclude **37,** 216–17, 235, 321-2
United Nations Administrative Tribunal and **54,** 447-8, 462-5
voting **37,** 23, 149, 209, 284, 311, 410, 441
United Nations General Assembly (UNGA) Resolutions
3 (I) **82,** 441
13 (I) **36,** 461-5
14 (I) (assumption of certain League functions) **49,** 233-5
31/6a (Bophuthatswana) **82,** 388 n. 1
31/141 **69,** 317, 413
32/105N (Transkei independence) **82,** 376 n. 1
33/119 **69,** 308, 318, 320, 326, 339, 363, 371-4, 397-8, 415, 421, 435-8, 453, 466, 492, 507-9, 518-27, 538, 545, 558
interpretation by International Civil Service Commission **69,** 318-19, 326-7, 363, 397, 415-18, 421, 436-8, 441-2, 453-4, 466, 518-27, 539
33/165 (treatment of South African conscientious objectors as refugees) **99,** 12 n. 2, 13
33/173 **95,** 291
34/165 **69,** 309, 311-12, 320-6, 328, 341, 354-5, 359, 362, 364-6, 371-5, 380-2, 395-9, 402, 408, 410, 419, 430, 436, 438, 442, 448-52, 454-6, 466-8, 492, 524-7, 539-40, 547, 551-61
Administrative Tribunal, application by **69,** 320-3, 372-5, 393-9, 410-11, 455-6, 540-1, 548-54, 555-61
immediate effect **69,** 355, 359, 365-6, 374-5, 380-1, 395-9, 408, 410-11, 442, 448-56, 468, 551-4
retroactive effect **69,** 311-12, 320-4, 364, 373-4, 381-2, 411, 442, 453-4, 539-40
34/178 (1979) (habeas corpus) **123,** 175 n. 24
35/210 (personnel questions) **83,** 381-2
36/233 (International Civil Service Commission Report) **83,** 382
37/126 (UN officials) **83,** 285, 288, 289, 292, 294–5, 312, 328, 333, 336, 337, 340, 342, 343, 347-8, 354, 365, 378, 381, 385, 386, 391, 396, 398, 422-3, 426-7, 432, 433, 437, 439, 441, 443, 450, 451, 455, 458
binding on Secretary-General, whether **83,** 292, 323, 340-1, 399-400, 438
'every reasonable consideration' **83,** 312, 324, 340, 439
implementation **83,** 441
38/10 (1983) **76,** 50
38/232 **83,** 290, 339, 378-9, 381, 385
42/210B (UN Headquarters Agreement) **82,** 231, 234, 235, 236, 239-40, 242, 256, 257
42/229A (UN Headquarters Agreement) **82,** 231, 233, 239, 242, 249, 260
42/229B (UN Headquarters Agreement) **82,** 230-2, 233, 239, 240-1, 242, 264, 265
42/230 (UN Headquarters Agreement) **82,** 243, 259, 260
47/37 (protection of the environment in times of armed conflict) **110,** 192
47/168 (establishment of Department of Humanitarian Affairs) **110,** 135-6
49/75 K (WHO Resolution 46/60) **110,** 23-4, 177-9
text **110,** 177-9
95 (I) (Nuremberg Tribunal) **36,** 296-7, 311, 317, **78,** 131, **82,** 440, 441, **119,** 67, 99, 148, 211, 226
obligation to seek out and prosecute **91,** 35
96 (I) (genocide) **36,** 32-3, 48, 296-7, **119,** 338
117 (II) (general principles of international law) **36,** 47-8
169 (II) (UN Headquarters Agreement) **82,** 231, 239
170 (II), obligation to seek out and prosecute **91,** 35
217A (II) **57,** 177-9, 224, 252, 254

264 (revocation of South West Africa Mandate) **91,** 379
289 (IV) (independence of Libya) **49,** 51
290 (IV) (Essentials of Peace) **76,** 671
380 (V) (Peace through Deeds) **76,** 671
395 (V) (Racial Discrimination) **49,** 74
428 (V) (Statute of the Office of the UN High Commissioner for Refugees) **77,** 418
470 (V) **69,** 314, 339, 370, 431, 497
590 (VI) **69,** 315, 398, 409
626 (VII) (Right to Exploit Freely Natural Wealth and Resources) **62,** 187, 192
648 (VII) **80,** 652
888 (IX) **69,** 446-7
957 (X) (UNAT Statute) **83,** 374-5, 417
973 A (X) **36,** 461-5
973 C (X) **36,** 461-5
1386 (XIV) (Declaration of the Rights of the Child) **77,** 238, 247. *See also* child rights, UN Convention on the Rights of the Child (1989)
1514 (XV) (Declaration on the Granting of Independence to Colonial Countries and Peoples) **46,** 464, 478, 484, 485, 488, **49,** 21, 64, **59,** 46-54, 97-8, 139, 183-4, 186-7, **79,** 263, **80,** 554, **83,** 26
  legal effect **59,** 138
1515 (XV) (Permanent Sovereignty over Natural Resources) **105,** 338
1541 (XV) **87,** 560 n. 7, 600
1710 (XVI) (Development Decade) **106,** 654-5
1803 (XVII) (Permanent Sovereignty over Natural Resources) **46,** 496, **53,** 475, 484-90, **55,** 396-7, **56,** 279, **62,** 187-9, 192, 201, **63,** 291, 455, **65,** 214, **66,** 435-6, 588, 601-2, **73,** 244, **75,** 514, 609-10, 617-18, 633-5, 637, 639, 641, **83,** 2 n. 2, 24, 52, 474, 542, 613 n. 12, **84,** 525-7, 539-40, 665 n. 1, **89,** 337-8, 466, **105,** 338-40
  compensation for expropriation **106,** 655
  customary international law, whether **84,** 540
1904 (XVIII) (Declaration on the Elimination of All Forms of Racial Discrimination) **49,** 74
2131 (XX) (Declaration on the Inadmissibility of Intervention in the Domestic Affairs of States and the Protection of the Independence and Sovereignty) **46,** 485, **76,** 671
2145 (XXI) (South West Africa Mandate) **82,** 475, 478, 480, 488, 490
2158 (XXV) (Declaration on Principles of International Law concerning Friendly Relations and Cooperation among States in accordance with the Charter of the UN) **63,** 291, **83,** 26, 74, **105,** 337-8
2340 (XXII) **67,** 207
2444 (XXIII) (respect for human rights in armed conflicts) **105,** 511-12, **108,** 45–6, **110,** 348
2625 (XXV) (Declaration concerning Principles of Friendly Relations and Cooperation among States) **49,** 64, 105, 107, **65,** 191, **75,** 669, **76,** 434, 435-6, 467, 670, 674-5, **77,** 176, 236, 238, **79,** 263, **87,** 69-70, **91,** 231, **92,** 172, **110,** 146-7, 492
2675 (XXV) (Basic Principles for Protection of Civilian Populations in Armed Conflicts) **77,** 238, **105,** 512-13, **108,** 45-6, **123,** 169 n. 8
2712 (XXV), obligation to seek out and prosecute **91,** 36
2749 (XXV) **67,** 207
2750 C (XXV) **67,** 207
2849 (XXVI) (environment) **110,** 80-1
3059 (torture) **119,** 149
3074 (XXVIII) (international cooperation in relation to war crimes/crimes against humanity) **108,** 207, **119,** 99
  obligation to seek out and prosecute **91,** 35, **119,** 357, 366-7

United Nations General Assembly (UNGA) Resolutions (*cont.*)
3103 (XXVIII) (Basic Principles of the Legal Status of the Combatants struggling against Colonial and Alien Domination and Racist Regimes) **77,** 224
3106 **63,** 291
3171 (XXVIII) (Permanent Sovereignty over Natural Resources) **66,** 436, **75,** 633-4, 639, 669, **84,** 538
3201 (S-V) (Declaration on the Establishment of a New Economic Order) **53,** 485-6, 488-95, **63,** 291, **66,** 436, **75,** 634, 639, **84,** 525, 538
3232 (XXIX) (judicial settlement of legal disputes) **94,** 583
3237 (XXIX) (PLO observer status) **77,** 234, **82,** 233, 234, 235, 238-9, 242, 261-2, 263
3281 (XXIV) (Charter of Economic Rights and Duties of States) **53,** 485-95, **62,** 188, 192, 201, 209, **63,** 291, **66,** 436-7, **75,** 610, 637, **83,** 476, 542, **84,** 525, 538, 540, 657, 664 n. 1, 665 n. 1, **85,** 471-2, **89,** 533
legal nature **84,** 540
3314 (XXIX) (14 December 1974) (Definition of Aggression) **76,** 437, 672, 678-80, 724, **77,** 224
expression of customary international law **76,** 674-5, 724
3452 (XXX) (Declaration on the Protection of all Persons from being subjected to Torture Convention) **58,** 298-9, **77,** 176-7, 187, 224, 235, **107,** 540-1, **119,** 149
definition of torture **121,** 263 n. 177
3453 (torture) **119,** 149
3845 (XXX) (East Timor) **105,** 285-7
4139 (13 December 1985) **88,** 11 n. 6, 31 n. 8
application of **69,** 372-5, 395-9, 410-11, 455-6, 548-54, 555-61
customary international law and **36,** 297, **37,** 367-9, 559, 568, 577, **82,** 479, **105,** 331, **108,** 45-6, **110,** 204-5
requirements **110,** 269-70
'decides', significance **83,** 384, 438
determination of a situation, as
authority **49,** 65, 101, 153, 329
legal effect **49,** 220 n. 9, 271, 273, 274, 277–8
effect **49,** 220 n. 9, 271, 273, 274, 277-8, **55,** 397, **59,** 138, **82,** 475, **83,** 292, 323, 384, **84,** 526, 539
binding **105,** 245, 387-8
colonial issues **105,** 387-8
consent to, of **76,** 434
declaratory **84,** 540 n. 29
erga omnes character **105,** 389-90
international law, source **36,** 297, **82,** 479
municipal law, in **52,** 2, **87,** 71
repetition, relevance **110,** 300, 308, 318
retroactive **69,** 311-12, 320-4, 364, 373-4, 381-2, 411, 442, 453-4, 539-40
subsequent legislation **36,** 463
enforcement **77,** 254
individual's right **77,** 199
evidence of *opinio juris* **110,** 205, 268-70, 349-50, 482-3
implementation by Secretary General **69,** 313-21, 370-3, 424, 439-40, 454, 545-7, 553, 555
individual
conduct, regulation by **71,** 289
right of enforcement, **77,** 199

interpretation **59,** 149, 183, **69,** 381, 396
'appreciation' **110,** 370-3
ICJ **105,** 264, 295-6
'national income taxes' **36,** 464
natural meaning **36,** 464, **110,** 247
structure **110,** 247
subsequent developments and **36,** 464
judicial notice of **82,** 418, **105,** 264
lapse **105,** 330-2
legal effect. *See* effect *above*
legal nature **37,** 127, 284, 410-12, 559, **53,** 484-95, **62,** 189, **67,** 619
legislative **110,** 483
limitations **69,** 381, 396
normative value **110,** 204-5
obligation to consult **105,** 279
source of international law, whether **75,** 609-10, 617–18, 632, 637, 639
staff contract, in breach of **69,** 383
staff relations, regulating **36,** 461-5, **69,** 549, 557, 559
State practice, evidence of **84,** 539
travaux préparatoires **83,** 294-5, 474
treaties, effect on **84,** 665 n. 1
validity, presumption of **49,** 12, 174-5
United Nations General Assembly (UNGA) (South West Africa Mandate), Resolutions, 2145 (XXI) **49,** 178-9, 321-30, **52,** 29
United Nations High Commissioner for Refugees (UNHCR) 73, 628, 632, **77,** 385, 386. *See also* refugees; Refugees, Geneva Convention on the Status of (1951) and Protocol (1967)
delegates of, jurisdictional immunity **42,** 241-3
Handbook on Procedures and Criteria for Determining Refugee Status **79,** 609, 622, 638, 648-9, **87,** 493 n. 4, 494, **88,** 8-9, 30, 31, **90,** 29
legislation, aid to interpretation **88,** 21, 30
military service, evasion of **88,** 8-9, 21, 31
non-binding **79,** 638, 648-9
local representatives, status **69,** 207
municipal administrative authority, whether **69,** 207
political refugee status
certificate of **77,** 385, 386
recognition of **68,** 31, **69,** 207
'Refugees, Women and International Protection' (1985) (conclusion No 39 (XXXVI)) **124,** 497
Representative in Belgium **77,** 386
competence to accord refugee status **77,** 418
status **77,** 418-19
State succession and **55,** 73-5
Statute of **72,** 649
UN General Assembly Resolution regarding **77,** 418
views of **72,** 644
United Nations Human Rights Committee (UNHRC) 62, 240, 243, 246, 256. *See also* International Covenant on Civil and Political Rights (ICCPR) (1966); International Covenant on Economic, Social and Cultural Rights (1966)
abuse of right of submission **96,** 703
'administrative tribunal or judicial authority', whether **115,** 657, 660-5, **124,** 574-6

United Nations Human Rights Committee (UNHRC) (*cont.*)
admissibility **59,** 439, **62,** 241, 243, 247, 249-50, 252, 256, 258, 265, 269, 272-7, 281, 286, 287-8, **68,** 33-4, **69,** 169-70, 187-8, **70,** 237, 239-40, 243, 251-3, 262, 276, 292, 294, 300, 307-9, **71,** 347, 350-1, 357-8, **78,** 31, 35, 36, 48-50, 57-9, 66, 69, 75-7, **79,** 172, 184, 190, 194, 196, 198, 205, 206, 213, 215, 216, 221-2, 229-30, 231-2, 237, 239-40, 244-50, 251-3, 255-6, 262-6, 269, 270-1, 275-6, 278-9, 281-2. *See also* complainant *and* individual's right of complaint *below*
actio popularis **62,** 285-6, 288, 293, **96,** 706
'being examined under another procedure of international investigation or settlement' **69,** 187-8, **70,** 251-3, **71,** 307-9, 324, 357, **79,** 221, 222, 237, 239, 270, 271, 275, **94,** 380, 383-4, **96,** 630, 645, **98,** 362-3
Amnesty International **94,** 383
Inter-American Commission on Human Rights **94,** 380, 383, **98,** 329
International Commission of Jurists (ICJ) **94,** 383
International Committee of the Red Cross (ICRC) **94,** 380, 383
prior consideration under another procedure **96,** 630
UNHRC Special Rapporteur **94,** 380, 383
citizens resident abroad, communication from **70,** 239–40
Committee's duty to spell out arguments for consideration at merits stage **96,** 702
complainants abroad **71,** 314-15, **79,** 172, 174, 177, 181, 194, 202, 230, 235, 254
continued application of legislation **118,** 238, 240
continuing effects **115,** 268-9, 285
exhaustion of local remedies. *See* exhaustion of local remedies *below*
extradition. *See* International Covenant on Civil and Political Rights (ICCPR) (1966), extradition
identity of complaint before international and municipal tribunal **79,** 246
Inter-American Commission and **62,** 247, 250, 261, 264-5, **68,** 44, **118,** 167-8
late objection **94,** 425, **118,** 270-1
legislation subsequent to complaint, relevance **118,** 182
'manifestly ill-founded' **96,** 645
ratio materiae **79,** 249, 250, 263
ratio temporis **79,** 246, 278, **94,** 406-7
reasonable substantiation of complaint **94,** 431
reconsideration of decision **118,** 271
reliance on authors' information **118,** 270-1
resolution of complaint **94,** 391
possibility of **94,** 407
State's acceptance, relevance **115,** 306
State's failure to challenge **115,** 297
State's failure to comment on **118,** 189, 238
'subject to the jurisdiction' **79,** 174, 198, 229
sufficiency of evidence **115,** 352-3
violations preceding entry into force of International Covenant on Civil and Political Rights (ICCPR) (1966) **62,** 241-4, **68,** 21, 25-6, **71,** 313, 351-3, 357, **79,** 227-8, 231-2, 245, 249, 278, 279, **94,** 406, 407-8, **118,** 221, 234
burden of proof **94,** 442
complainant. *See also* victim *below*
authorization **79,** 265
benefit already obtained **70,** 313
child of parent denied access **96,** 629
child of victim **70,** 253, 362, **79,** 235, **94,** 436
family members **78,** 21-2
family of victim **79,** 243

individual authorized to act on behalf of group, whether **79,** 264-5
parent of victim **79,** 202
personally affected, whether. *See* 'victim' *below*
spouse of victim **70,** 262, **79,** 181, 254
duties, good faith examination of all complaints **94,** 386
effective remedy, need for **62,** 246, 274, **94,** 392–3, **98,** 365-6, **118,** 154, 178-9, 234-5
absence of legal aid, relevance **98,** 365
administrative or disciplinary remedies **118,** 207, 286-7, 290
appeal, adequacy **118,** 266
availability **96,** 679
complainant misled **94,** 393
constitutional motion bound to fail **98,** 331-2, 355-6
critical date, developments subsequent to communication **115,** 364-5
delay in bringing criminal proceedings **70,** 272-6, **118,** 201
doubts about effectiveness **115,** 364-5
exceptional or extraordinary remedies **62,** 246-7, 251-3, **70,** 284, 293-4, **94,** 392-3
general principle of international law **98,** 331, 366
habeas corpus **62,** 249, 258
lack of independent judiciary **70,** 272-6, 284-5, **96,** 412
legislative changes falling short **115,** 178-9
prerogative of mercy **71,** 339-40
reasonableness **94,** 398-9
establishment **59,** 434
evidence **70,** 255-8, 262-6, 276-9, 286, 294-6, **71,** 315, **79,** 170-1, 174-7
absence of opportunity to rebut **98,** 346
burden of proof **70,** 256-8, 265-6, 286, 294, **71,** 364, **79,** 224
insufficient **79,** 186, **94,** 414
State submissions, failure to provide. *See* State submissions, failure to provide *below*
exhaustion of local remedies **59,** 446-7, **62,** 243, 247, 250, 258, 273-4, 287, **70,** 237, 243, 253, **78,** 36, 50, 76-7, **79,** 172, 182-3, 184, 186, 189, 190, 192, 196, 198, 205, 208-9, 213-14, 215, 217, 222, 229, 230, 237, 239, 255, 256, **94,** 379-80, 403, 406, 444-5, **98,** 329, 363, 499-500, **118,** 286, **124,** 396, 401, 413-14. *See also* admissibility, 'being examined under another procedure of international investigation or settlement' *above*
burden of proof **94,** 407
change of law **96,** 630
changed practice in respect of treatment of principles of Covenant **114,** 346-7
dismissal of identical case in national courts **115,** 365
dismissal of petition for leave to appeal **115,** 297
doubt about effectiveness **118,** 248
effective remedy, need for **124,** 573
unreasonably lengthy procedures **71,** 361-4
failure to complain about trial before Special Criminal Court **115,** 285-6
failure to seek judicial review **115,** 286
non-objection by State party **114,** 360-1
preliminary/procedural question, whether, merits, joinder **71,** 324, **94,** 405-6
presumption of right, need for **94,** 429
previous 'act of government' finding by national courts **115,** 260
purpose
opportunity for redress **96,** 705
opportunity for State party to rectify situation **96,** 705
retroactive law making recourse to national courts futile **114,** 318
State's duty to indicate remedies **70,** 251, **71,** 358

United Nations Human Rights Committee (UNHRC) (*cont.*)
unreasonably prolonged proceedings **94,** 407, 408, 425, **96,** 630, 679, 702
extradition in case of death penalty **124,** 325-6
findings of fact **71,** 315-16, 328-9, 351-3, 363-4. *See also* views *below*
allegations in general terms **70,** 240-6, **79,** 200, 209
binding, whether **112,** 365
State evidence, in absence of **68,** 36-7, **78,** 51
submissions from State party, in absence of **70,** 238-40, 264-6, 286, 294-6, **71,** 351, 353, **79,** 178, 190-1, 209, 240-1, 259
General Comment
binding, whether **107,** 65 n. 1
Consensus Statement of Human Rights Committee adopted on 30 October 1980 **107,** 65 n. 1
No 20 (torture) **121,** 258, 261 n. 172, 264 n. 180, 265
No 24 (ICCPR reservations) **121,** 260 n. 170
individual opinions **71,** 308, **79,** 260, **118,** 144, 151, 240, 276
individual's right of complaint **62,** 241, 243, 246, 256-7, 261-2, 268, 272-4, 279, **77,** 248, **78,** 48-9, **105,** 440
authorization **79,** 265
before incorporation of Covenant **124,** 413-27
on behalf of group **79,** 264-5
national of State not party to ICCPR and Optional Protocol (1966) **124,** 285
in respect of violation of company's rights **118,** 182
standing **69,** 191-2, **79,** 263-5
interim measures **115,** 256, 306
compensation as effective remedy, relevance **115,** 331
irreparable damage, need for **115,** 331
non-binding nature of request **124,** 395, 398-9, 401-2, 404-8, 425-6
request to State to take **96,** 680
stay of deportation **124,** 395, 398-9, 401-2, 425-6
stay of extradition proceedings **98,** 448, 471-2, 487, 504, 518
suspension of death sentence **98,** 325, 326, 360
International Criminal Tribunal for the Former Yugoslavia and **105,** 440
judicial institution, whether **112,** 365, **124,** 406-7
jurisdiction **62,** 272, 278-9, 282-5, 286, **79,** 264
basis **124,** 576
conformity with national law, review **96,** 655, **124,** 413
continuing **96,** 707
evaluation of facts and evidence as presented in national courts **115,** 297, **118,** 259
interpretation of Covenant **70,** 300, 312-13, **79,** 266, 271, **124,** 425-6
ratione loci **98,** 433, 486
where State not party to Optional Protocol **98,** 501
ratione materiae **98,** 433, 444, 486
requested remedy outside **79,** 263
reservation to Optional Protocol, effect **71,** 307-9
reservations affecting, admissibility **107,** 71-3
reservations to Covenant, determination of validity **107,** 72-6
review of municipal courts' findings of fact **79,** 258–9
review of national courts
evaluation of facts **96,** 634, 635, **98,** 356, 434-5, 501, **124,** 403
exercise of discretion **96,** 635-6
instructions to jury **98,** 366
right to question conduct of trial **115,** 297

right to question defence lawyer's conduct **115,** 298–9
consultation with accused **115,** 354
legal aid, obligation to provide **115,** 664-71, **124,** 571-7
membership **79,** 168 n. 1, 219 n. 1
national legislation, review of **70,** 302, **79,** 252
nationality, relevance **78,** 49, **114,** 312 n. 1
powers
acts within jurisdiction of State party **78,** 49
communication with victim **69,** 188-92
procedure **59,** 439, 446, **62,** 241-6, 248-55, 257-60, 262-6, 268-71
audi alteram partem [auditur est altera pars] **70,** 265-6, **79,** 177
evidence **69,** 191-2
interim measures **70,** 250
joinder of cases **94,** 384
merits, joinder **118,** 271
requests for information. *See* requests for information *below*
right to determine **107,** 72-3
Rules of Procedure. *See* Rules of Procedure *below*
State submissions, failure to provide. *See* State submissions, failure to provide *below*
requests for information **69,** 169, 187, **70,** 237-8, 242, 251, 253, 261-2, 270, 273, 276, 283, 285, 291-2, 294, 300, 307, **71,** 313-21, 324, 330-1, 340, 350-1, 357-8, **78,** 21-3, 32-3, 48, 50, 66, 77, **79,** 172-3, 182, 190, 196, 198, 205, 206, 207, 213, 215-16, 221, 222, 229, 230, 240, 255, 256, 263, 269
date of conclusion of proceedings **94,** 422
death certificate **94,** 380, 383, 436
inadequacy **94,** 386
failure to respond **78,** 32-3, 36, 50-1, **94,** 386, 413, 442, **118,** 154-5, 266
information and observations on admissibility **94,** 380, 412
investigations undertaken **94,** 440
medical report **94,** 380, 383
reasons for expulsion **94,** 422-3
report of inquiry into death **94,** 380, 383, 436
time-limits, non-compliance with **71,** 351, **78,** 37, **79,** 190, 240, 259
Rules of Procedure
85 **94,** 400 n. 1
85 (composition of Committee) **114,** 312 n. 1, **115,** 356 n. 1
86 (interim measures) **96,** 683, **98,** 325, 326, 471-2, 487, **114,** 362, **115,** 256, 325, 331, **124,** 401-2, 405
87 (admissibility) **94,** 399, 430, 445, **96,** 645, 652, **98,** 329, **114,** 315, 360, **115,** 261, 285, 330, **118,** 238, 248
88(2) **94,** 384
90(a) **118,** 179
91 (information and observations on admissibility) **94,** 398, 403, 412, 428, 436, **96,** 628-9, 639, 643, 652, **98,** 325, 326, 360, **114,** 314-15, 336, **115,** 324-5, **118,** 155, 177, 189, 238
93(4) **96,** 680, 699, **98,** 435, **118,** 170, 270
94(3) **118,** 144, 151
standing **79,** 252, 265. *See also* complainant *above*; 'victim' *below*
State submissions **62,** 243, 250, 258, 270, **70,** 242-4, 251-2, 254-5, 271-4, 283-5, 292-3, 300-1, 307-10, **71,** 313-14, 321-2, 324, 327-30, 340-3, 349, 357-9, **78,** 31-2, 66-7, 77-8, **79,** 173, 196-7, 199, 206-9, 213-14, 216, 223, 229, 231, 237-9, 240, 245-7, 263-4, 269-73, **94,** 403-5, 419-21, 428-9, 436-9, **96,** 639-43, 652-5, 665-6, 673-8, 683-4, 685, 686-7, 689-93, 697, 710

United Nations Human Rights Committee (UNHRC) (*cont.*)
duty to investigate allegations of violations of Covenant **94,** 410
failure to provide **71,** 351, 363-4, **78,** 32-3, 36, 50-1, **79,** 177-8, 185, 190-1, 208, 240, 259, 260
substantiation of complainant's allegations assumed **94,** 386-7, 409-10, 414, 442
general statement, sufficiency **94,** 409, 410, **118,** 171
incomplete **68,** 36-7, 45
time-limits, expiry of **62,** 251, **68,** 44, **69,** 189, 192, **70,** 276, 294
State's failure to cooperate **114,** 323, 324, 329, 330
status as judicial body **115,** 657, 660-5, **124,** 490
victim **70,** 302, **79,** 179, 252-3, **98,** 503, 508-9, **112,** 333
'actually affected' **114,** 339, **115,** 261-2, 372
as complainant **62,** 273-4, 277, 286-8, 292-3, 296-7, **70,** 302, 313, **79,** 179, 252-3, 265
date of entry into force of Optional Protocol, relevance **114,** 314-16
group of individuals **96,** 702, 705-6
joinder to merits **98,** 487, 499, 500, 508
non-enforcement of offending legislation **112,** 333, 343
possible future events **98,** 465-7
'prospective victim' **114,** 370, 372, 376
right of self-determination, individual **96,** 645-6, 679-80
views. *See also* findings of fact *above*
inadequacy of information **98,** 460-4
misleading information, effect **98,** 343, 345
non-binding nature **124,** 404-8, 421-2
'weight and respect' **98,** 347
United Nations, immunity, jurisdiction 45, 446, 452-3, **53,** 589-90, **69,** 141-4. *See also* international organizations, immunity, jurisdiction
arbitration, effect on **44,** 437
conditional, whether **69,** 142
Convention on Privileges and Immunities of the United Nations (1946) **113,** 501, 520
European Convention on Human Rights (1950), effect **69,** 143
limited, whether **69,** 143
private law claims **69,** 141-2
UN Charter, Art. 105, effect **69,** 143
United Nations Interim Force in the Lebanon (UNIFIL)
conscientious objection and **78,** 14-17
nature of task **78,** 16
obligation to make armed forces available **78,** 17
prior request from Security Council, need for **78,** 17
request from UN Secretary General, sufficiency **78,** 17
United Nations Joint Appeal Board, delay in considering case, compensation **54,** 371-2
United Nations Joint Staff Pension Board 88, 722-3
United Nations Office of Technical Cooperation 75, 86
officials, fiscal immunity **75,** 85-9
submissions of parties **68,** 20, 22-5, 36-7
interpretation **68,** 36-7
United Nations peacekeeping operations 78, 16
as implementation of Charter **106,** 331, 346-7
integration of national contingents into UN system **106,** 331-2

legality, Somalia **113,** 521
non-combat participation **106,** 347
as part of collective security system **106,** 331, 346–7
powers **49,** 6, 41, 138, 216, 282, 330
Sierra Leone **119,** 389-98
custody or control of rebel leader **119,** 389-98
habeas corpus proceedings in UK and **119,** 386-98
UNFICYP, creation **44,** 359, 362, 375
United Nations Pension Fund 71, 240, **75,** 89
competence
determination of status **88,** 723
entitlement to benefit **88,** 723-6
Regulations, 'service' **88,** 725
United Nations, privileges and immunities. *See also* international officials, privileges and immunities; special rapporteur, privileges and immunities; United Nations, Privileges and Immunities Convention (1946)
basis **45,** 446, 453, **121,** 436-7
functional nature **85,** 312, 321, 323, 346
Member State missions and representatives **99,** 141-2
officials **70,** 407-12
privileges and immunities of national officials distinguished **121,** 438-9
representatives accredited to **47,** 275-7, **71,** 567–9, 571-2
representatives sent by **47,** 275-7
uniformity of application, desirability **121,** 439-40
United Nations, Privileges and Immunities Convention (1946) 42, 243, **51,** 172, **69,** 141, 241-3
applicability
application distinguished **85,** 318, 327, 335, 344-8
experts **71,** 538, 563, **121,** 374-8
forces **69,** 141-4
insurers **71,** 563-4
in country of permanent residence **85,** 317, 322-3, 344-8
expert **85,** 319-25
family members **85,** 337-8
national State, in **85,** 322-3, 344-8
special rapporteur **85,** 312, 323-4, 331
difference relating to interpretation or application
between States party **85,** 316
between States party and UN **85,** 316
dispute settlement provisions **45,** 447-8, 451, **85,** 310, 315, **121,** 414-16
consent, need for **85,** 315-16
reservations **85,** 316
sections 29 (disputes of private law character) and 30 (interpretation or application of Convention) distinguished **121,** 457-8
Member State missions and representatives **99,** 142
obligations
incorporation into municipal law **121,** 397
notification to judicial authorities of findings of UN Secretary-General **121,** 431-3, 449-50, 451
of result **121,** 462
to be 'in a position under its own law to give effect to terms' **121,** 431
to ensure respect for Convention obligations **121,** 451-2
phrases, 'experts on mission' **85,** 320-1, 333-5, 344, **121,** 374, 375-6, 427-8, 432-3

United Nations, Privileges and Immunities Convention (1946) (*cont.*)
reservations **85,** 315, 316-17, 322, 341-2
effect **85,** 317
right to leave State of nationality or residence **85,** 344-8
special rapporteur **121,** 369-405
United Nations Relief and Works Agency for Palestine Refugees in the Near East, financial basis, relevance for staff contract **42,** 328
United Nations Secretariat, Medical Director, powers **38,** 324-6, 328, 331, 333, 372
United Nations Secretary-General
authority
privileges and immunities, determination of right to **121,** 375-7, 388-97, 412-13, 419-26, 429-30, 440-1, 444–5, 458-9
review procedures, effect **69,** 348-9, 385-6, 423-4
disciplinary power, judicial review **38,** 270, 271, 274
General Assembly, relationship to **69,** 313-17, 370-3, 398, 424, 439-40, 454, 545-7, 553, 555
independence from Member States, obligation to maintain **83,** 244-6, 290, 313, 347, 351-2, 356-7, 409, 414-17, 449, 450-1, 455, 456, 458-9
secondment, conflict **83,** 457
powers, International Criminal Tribunal for the Former Yugoslavia **105,** 555, 559-60
responsibilities, parties to multilateral treaties, determination of **115,** 169-74, 183-4
settlement of disputes by **74,** 256-77
agreement for reference to **74,** 256-7, 264-5
ruling
binding force **74,** 257, 261, 274-7
interpretation, recourse to arbitration **74,** 261, 270, 273-4, 276
UN officials and
discretionary powers **83,** 291, 292-3, 313, 347, 351-2, 356-7, 409, 414-17, 449, 450-1, 455, 456, 458-9
arbitrary exercise **83,** 330, 344
burden of proof **83,** 438
good faith **83,** 330, 455
implementation **83,** 454
official's change of nationality **83,** 387–90
reasonable consideration of rights and obligations of staff **83,** 455
regulations as limitation **83,** 450
review **83,** 427, 443
standard **83,** 455
sole competence **83,** 427
United Nations Administrative Tribunal (UNAT)
function distinguished **83,** 337-8
interpretation of judgment, relevance **83,** 332-3
United Nations Security Council
abstention, effect **49,** 5, 12, 107, 143-4, 175-6
advisory opinion of the ICJ, request for, drafting **49,** 129-31
arms embargo, South Africa **49,** 83-4
ceasefire declaration before **71,** 711
Chapter VI action
creation of subsidiary organ **105,** 438-9
dispute settlement **94,** 543, 570-1
ICJ, role **94,** 549-50
recommendations
binding, whether **94,** 548-50

limitations on **94,** 548-9
voluntary contribution of armed forces **106,** 331-2
Chapter VII action **95,** 154-5
Art. 41 measures ('measures not involving the use of force')
exhaustive, whether **105,** 467, 469
Member State action, whether limited to **105,** 469-70
classification of situation as a threat to international peace and security **94,** 515, 525-6, 543, 559, **105,** 560-1, **117,** 77
discretion **94,** 543, **105,** 466
internal conflict **105,** 466-7
justiciability **105,** 528, 561
measures to restore peace **105,** 436-7
consent of party affected **95,** 157
discretion **105,** 429, 467, 471, 546-7, 560-3
ex post facto determination of inadequacy, relevance **105,** 436, 471
establishment of International Criminal Tribunal for the Former Yugoslavia **105,** 427-40, **110,** 620-3
ICJ role **94,** 550, **95,** 123-4
municipal law, effect in **103,** 358-60
primacy of obligations **110,** 667
Resolution 687 (1991) (Iraq's liability for direct loss, damage or injury as result of occupation of Kuwait) **109,** 506
Resolution 692 (1991) (UN Claims Commission and Compensation Fund) **109,** 506 n. 15
sovereignty and **105,** 439, 441, 481, 576, 578–9, **110,** 648-9, 726-7
consent, relevance **110,** 649
Yugoslav arms embargo. *See* United Nations Security Council Resolutions, 713 (1991) (Yugoslav arms embargo)
China, representation in **49,** 107
decisions
non-abstention of parties to dispute **49,** 13, 178
obligation to comply with **49,** 4, 6, 42-4, 126, 140, 155, 283
powers **49,** 42, 108, 126, 140, 176, 282-3
dispute settlement **60,** 533-4, 537, 554-5, 559
dispute or situation **49,** 12, 108
economic sanctions, South Africa **49,** 84-5, 126
general principles of international law, duty to respect **94,** 529
ICJ and, **60,** 533-4, 537, 554-5, 559, **61,** 547-50, **76,** 51-2, 142-7,
individuals
imposition of criminal liability **105,** 439, 567-9
right to challenge **105,** 439
State's waiver of jurisdiction, right to challenge **105,** 576
interim measures
enforcement action distinguished **105,** 469
power to indicate **95,** 120
domestic jurisdiction limitation **105,** 469
international law, duty to respect **94,** 500, 528-9, 544-8, 589
judicial measures, admissibility **105,** 432-40, 554-5, 560-3, **110,** 623
Art. 40 measures (interim measures) distinguished **105,** 468-9
Art. 41 measures ('measures not involving the use of force') distinguished **105,** 469
Art. 42 measures (military measures) distinguished **105,** 468
Charter amendment, need for **105,** 439-40, 474, 570
Effect of Awards **105,** 437-8

United Nations Security Council (*cont.*)
establishment of tribunal, delegation of powers, whether **105,** 470-1
General Assembly, role **105,** 439-40
judicial review **94,** 515, 524-5, 526-7, 537-40, 585-99, **95,** 157-9, **105,** 428-9, 433-6, 458-63, 528, 546-8, 549-52, **117,** 70-8, 106-8. *See also* International Court of Justice (ICJ), Security Council and
compliance with findings **105,** 555
Lockerbie **105,** 430-1, 435, 549-50, 552
travaux préparatoires **117,** 74-7
Mandates and **49,** 281-5, **60,** 617-18
powers **49,** 215, 253
powers
arbitrary exercise **105,** 561-7
binding effect **105,** 467
characterization of situation as a threat to international peace and security **117,** 77
Charter *travaux préparatoires* **94,** 524, 544-8, **105,** 429, **117,** 108
'collective' measures **105,** 470
legislative nature **117,** 59-60
limitations **94,** 515, 548
Charter **105,** 429, 432-3, 435-6, 465-6, 467
maintenance of international peace and security **94,** 503, 518, 543, 579, **117,** 93
peacekeeping operations **78,** 16
to order sanctions **49,** 288
Presidential Statement on Bosnia-Herzegovina of 8 August 1996 **108,** 140-1
purposes of UN, responsibility for promotion of **49,** 174
Resolutions. *See* United Nations Security Council Resolutions
responsibility, promoting purposes of UN **49,** 174
Rhodesia, sanctions **52,** 2-3
rights of sovereign State, infringement **94,** 543-8
sanctions
arms embargo **49,** 83-4
power to order **49,** 288
Resolution 748 (1992) **94,** 510, 523
Rhodesia **52,** 2-3
South Africa **49,** 84-5, 126
threat of **94,** 490, 495, 523
treaty obligations, effect on **94,** 511
use of force **94,** 490, 512, 573-4
self-determination **71,** 288-9, 292-3
'situation', right of non-member to participate in discussion **49,** 5, 12, 108
South Africa
arms embargo **49,** 83-4
economic sanctions **49,** 84-5, 126
sovereignty and **74,** 258, 262, **110,** 634, 667
Strategic Trust Territory and **87,** 606-7
subsidiary organ
delegation of powers to **110,** 622-3
flexibility of concept **110,** 622
separate legal entity test **110,** 623
United Nations Compensation Commission **109,** 15
Yugoslavia, International Criminal Tribunal for the Former **105,** 459-60, 562-3, 568, **110,** 620-3, 634, 642, 646, 666-7, 676
terrorism **94,** 508, 549, 562, 579

State terrorism **94,** 517, 524, 579, 580-1
treaties
incompatible with **46,** 466
registration **48,** 337
trusteeship
agreement **87,** 605
termination, role **84,** 203-5
Trusteeship system. *See* Trusteeship system
UN Charter, duty to respect **94,** 528-30, 544-8, 582, 585, **105,** 433
customary international law distinguished **94,** 530
ICJ role **94,** 530
Universal Declaration of Human Rights and **60,** 642
veto, right of **49,** 259 n. 49
equality of States and **101,** 368
voting, Trust Territory **37,** 149, 208
wars of aggression **42,** 398
United Nations Security Council Resolutions
143 (1960) (Congo) **105,** 348
145 (1960) (Congo) **105,** 348
146 (1960) (Congo) **105,** 348
171(II) (interpretation of Charter) **94,** 586
186 (1964) (The Cyprus Question) **48,** 8
242 (1967) **47,** 485, 486
255 (1968) (Non-Proliferation Treaty (1968)) **110,** 374
276 (1970) (South West Africa) **82,** 475, 478, 480
301 (Namibia: dealings with South Africa) **95,** 612-14
self-executing, whether **95,** 612-14
384 (East Timor) **105,** 285-7, 325, 347, 349, 354
389 (East Timor) **105,** 285-7, 325, 347, 350, 354
402 (1976) (Bophuthatswana/Transkei independence) **82,** 376 n. 1, 388 n. 1
407 (1977) (Bophuthatswana/Transkei independence) **82,** 376 n. 1, 388 n. 1
425 (1978) (UNIFIL) **78,** 16, 17
435 (1978) (South West Africa) **82,** 475
457 (1979) (US hostages in Iran) **61,** 590
461 (1979) (US Hostages in Iran) **61,** 591
530 **76,** 50
541 (1983) (TRNC: illegality of secession) **100,** 268, **108,** 454, 461, 553, **120,** 23-4, 36-7, **122,** 532-3, 542
550 (1984) (Turkish Republic of Northern Cyprus) **100,** 268, **108,** 454, 461, 553, **120,** 23-4, 36-7
575 (4 March 1964) **77,** 473
660 (1990) (unconditional withdrawal of Iraqi forces from Kuwait) **117,** 366, **122,** 549, **125,** 628-30, 720
661 (1990) (trade embargo following Iraq's non-compliance with Resolution 660 (1990)) **117,** 366-7, **122,** 549-58, **125,** 630, 720
662 (1990) (Iraq's annexation of Kuwait) **125,** 630, 720, 721
670 (1990) (Iraq: sanctions) **125,** 630
674 (1990) (Iraq: sanctions) **125,** 630
678 (1990) (Iraq: enforcement of resolutions) **125,** 630
686 (1990) (Iraq: demand for rescission of action relating to Kuwait) **125,** 631
687 (1991) (Iraq–Kuwait Boundary Commission) **94,** 3-9, **103,** 358-60, **105,** 563. *See also* 687 (1991) (Iraq's liability for direct loss, damage or injury as result of occupation of Kuwait) *below*

United Nations Security Council Resolutions (*cont.*)
municipal jurisdiction, effect of establishment of Compensation Commission **103,** 358-9
prior rights and obligations, effect on **106,** 289-90
sovereignty of Iraq, effect on **106,** 290
687 (1991) (Iraq's liability for direct loss, damage or injury as result of occupation of Kuwait) **109,** 15, 143, **117,** 241-2, **122,** 350-6. *See also* 687 (1991) (Iraq–Kuwait Boundary Commission) *above*
as applicable law **109,** 15, 47, 58, 67, 133, 224, 467, 471, 506-7, **117,** 237-8
Chapter VII powers, exercise of **109,** 506
para. 16 (Iraq's debts and obligations prior to 2 August 1990) **109,** 561
para. 19 (claims procedure) **109,** 560-2
para. 22 (lifting of sanctions) **109,** 578, 582
para. 29 (protection against exposure to unjustified Iraqi claims) **122,** 551-5, 564
text **109,** 553-4
692 (1991) (UN Claims Commission and Compensation Fund)
Chapter VII powers, exercise of **109,** 506 n. 15
text **109,** 564-5
706 (1991) (Iraqi petroleum sales: proceeds), text **109,** 673-6
712 (1991) (Iraqi petroleum sales: proceeds), text **109,** 676-8
713 (1991) (Yugoslav arms embargo) **117,** 273
applicability to Bosnia-Herzegovina **95,** 155-6
breach of Genocide Convention (1948), whether **95,** 154-60
context of adoption **95,** 155
equality of parties **95,** 156
reaffirmation **95,** 156
self-defence, denial of right to **95,** 63
724 (1991) (Yugoslavia: Sanctions Committee) **117,** 274–5
731 (1992) (Lockerbie bombing) **94,** 494-6, 508, 525, 537–8, 549-50, 571, 580-2, **107,** 387-8, **117,** 15, 53, 90-3
Mandatory, whether **94,** 570
748 (1992) (Lockerbie bombing) **94,** 496-8, 500-1, 511-12, 513-14, 528, 530, **107,** 387-8, **117,** 93-4
effect on ICJ jurisdiction under Montreal Convention **117,** 21-4, 26-7, 44-5, 55-7, 63-7, 94-5
endorsement of demand for compensation **94,** 514
use of force **94,** 512
757 (1992) (Yugoslavia: sanctions) **105,** 533, **117,** 271-3, 307, 494-5, 502-4, 535
discretionary nature **117,** 460-1
EC and. *See* European Council Regulations, 1432/92 (as amended by Regulation 2015/92) (sanctions: Serbia and Montenegro)
implementation in UK **117,** 450, 456-61, 484-9, 495-6, 529. *See also* United Kingdom, Serbia and Montenegro (United Nations Sanctions) Order 1992; United Kingdom, Serbia and Montenegro (United Nations Sanctions) Order (1992, No 3102)
evidence of nature of goods in question **117,** 489
measures against abuse of humanitarian exceptions **117,** 451-82, 497-9, 537-8
771 (1992) (Yugoslavia: abuses of international humanitarian law) **105,** 492-3, **124,** 115 n. 155
773 (1992) (Iraq–Kuwait Boundary Commission) **94,** 6, 10, 28
777 (1992) (Yugoslavia) **95,** 27-8
778 (1992) (Iraqi petroleum exports: proceeds), text **109,** 678-81
780 (1992) (International Criminal Tribunal for the Former Yugoslavia: Committee of Experts) **108,** 64

787 (1992) (Yugoslavia: transshipment through FRY of economically vital products) **117,** 273
788 (1992) (Liberia: application of international humanitarian law) **105,** 513
794 (1992) (Somalia: application of international humanitarian law) **105,** 514
808 (1993) (International Criminal Tribunal for the Former Yugoslavia) **95,** 66, 122, **105,** 436-7, 528
Secretary-General's Report **121,** 360
814 (1993) (Somalia: application of international humanitarian law) **105,** 514
819 (1993) (ethnic cleansing) **95,** 66, 122
820 (1993) (transshipment of commodities and products through FRY) **117,** 273-4, 307-8. *See also* European Council Regulations, 990/3 (Yugoslav embargo: implementation of Security Council Resolutions)
applicability to acts in international waters **117,** 307-37
applicability to aircraft leased from Yugoslav Airline (JAT) **117,** 271-303
enforcement and penalties for violation distinguished **117,** 317-18
hot pursuit under **117,** 317
obligation to prohibit entry to Yugoslav territorial sea **117,** 316-18, 330-3
827 (25 May 1993) (International Criminal Tribunal for the Former Yugoslavia) **95,** 66, **101,** 8, **108,** 64, **121,** 339. *See also* Yugoslavia, International Criminal Tribunal for the Former
context **105,** 490
failure to identify basis for Tribunal **105,** 468
innovatory nature **105,** 434-5
obligation of compliance with Statute **108,** 74
obligation to cooperate with Tribunal **108,** 74-5, **110,** 647
833 (1993) (Iraq–Kuwait Boundary Commission) **94,** 41
859 (1993) (international war crimes tribunal) **95,** 66, 122
883 (1993) (Lockerbie bombing) **117,** 93-4
effect on ICJ jurisdiction under Montreal Convention **116,** 46-7, **117,** 21-4, 26-7, 54-7, 63-7, 94-5
972 (1995) (Liberia: application of international humanitarian law) **105,** 513
984 (1995) (Non-Proliferation Treaty (1968), extension) **110,** 370-4, 469
986 (1995) (Iraqi petroleum exports), text **109,** 682-6
993 (1993) (Georgia: application of international humanitarian law) **105,** 514
1001 (1995) (Liberia: application of international humanitarian law) **105,** 513
1031 (1995) (International Criminal Tribunal for the Former Yugoslavia), obligation to cooperate with Tribunal **110,** 647
1037 (1996) (Eastern Slavonia) **111,** 478-9
1132 (1997) (Libyan embargo) **110,** 756
binding force **49,** 6, 43-4, 108-10, 126, 137, 138, 331, **94,** 500, 508, 509-10, 524, 540, 548, 550, 556-7, 570-1, 584-5, **105,** 346-9, **106,** 329, **117,** 48-9
European Community (EC) **117,** 282
Chapter VI and Chapter VII action distinguished **94,** 509, 525-6, 548-9, 570-1, 574-5, 580-2, 584
clarification, need for **94,** 560
compliance **94,** 498, 511, 530, 533, 544, 571, 584, **105,** 362, **116,** 593-4, **117,** 455
European Community **117,** 316, 388
customary international law and **105,** 346, 354
effect **52,** 2-3
on non-Member States **49,** 127, 139, 209
validity **49,** 35, 104, 107, 119, 121, 133-5, 141, 143, 170-2, 174
Eichmann **36,** 58, 307
as evidence **103,** 408, **116,** 598-601

United Nations Security Council Resolutions (*cont.*)
ICJ and. *See also* International Court of Justice (ICJ), Security Council and, Resolution
ICJ's duty to draw conflict to Security Council's attention **95,** 159, 165
potential conflict **94,** 527-32
implementing legislation **110,** 650-1
judicial notice **116,** 599, 601
jus cogens/peremptory norm and **95,** 158-9
effect of conflict **95,** 159
primacy over other international obligations **94,** 498, 500, 511, 512, 530, 543-4, 550
EC law **117,** 464
public interest and **117,** 290-1, 301-2, 317, 321, 392-3
retroactive effect **94,** 498, 524
right to take action, basis of **49,** 127
self-executing, whether **106,** 289, **107,** 388-9
parties' intent **95,** 614
treaty, whether **107,** 387
validity
excess of power **94,** 588
possible invalidity **94,** 497, 515, 524-6, 528-30, 585-6
presumption of **94,** 511, 529-30, 533, 574-5
United Nations Staff Rules and Regulations 83, 343, 446-7. *See also* international officials; United Nations Administrative Tribunal (UNAT)
acquired rights, respect for **69,** 311-14, 320-3, 329-30, 341, 365-6, 373-5, 383, 397-8, 410-11, 439-42, 451-2, 466, 509-11, 532-3, 534, 539-40, 543, 547, 552-4, 559-61
Annex IV **69,** 310, 315-16, 320, 339, 363, 365, 370, 372, 409, 431, 452, 511-12, 514, 539, 541-3, 558, 598
assignment allowance **54,** 371
change of residence **83,** 459
General Assembly powers **69,** 313-16, 370-1, 374, 383, 398, 439, 446, 543, 546-61
interpretation, ICJ and **83,** 362-3
obligations **54,** 425
compliance **36,** 452
periodic reports on officials **54,** 356, 363, 365, 366, 368-70
Regulations
1 **83,** 456
1.2 **36,** 489-90, **69,** 543
3.3 **36,** 461-5
4 **83,** 427, 432, 433, 447, 448-9, 451-2, 455
4.2 **83,** 426, 432, 433, 451, 455
5.2 **54,** 360-1, 362, 363, 370, 371
9.1 **36,** 469-71
9.4 **69,** 310, 315-16, 320, 339, 363, 370, 372, 409, 511-15, 539
11.2 **69,** 558
12.1 **69,** 311, 313, 329, 341, 362-4, 366, 372-4, 396-9, 410-11, 452-3, 455, 466, 534, 544, 547, 554, 559
'relating to provisions of Charter' **83,** 425-6
relation between **69,** 313, 370-1, 398
rule-making authority **69,** 313, 316-17, 341, 370-3, 397-8, 423-4, 439-41, 454, 511, 513, 518, 538, 545-7, 553, 555, 557
Rules
101, 1 **69,** 397
103(c) **54,** 371

104, 7 **69,** 433, 441, 516-17, 536, 558
104, 12 **83,** 286, 287, 293, 322, 323, 339, 378, 380, 381, 434, 452-3
104, 13 **83,** 339
104, 14 **36,** 470-1, **83,** 339
105, 2 **83,** 453
105, 3 **69,** 536
107, 4 **69,** 515
109, 1 **36,** 454
109, 5 **69,** 315, 320, 322-3, 339-40, 363-5, 370, 372-4, 395, 397-9, 409-21, 425, 498, 507, 511-15, 517-20, 527, 539, 541, 543-7, 558
amendments **69,** 320-2, 339-40, 372, 397-9, 410, 412-21, 437-8, 453-4, 517-18, 547
110, 4 **54,** 371
112, 2(a) **69,** 313, 341, 362, 364, 373-4, 410-11, 437, 455, 544
scope and purpose **69,** 313
Secretary-General, functions **36,** 469-70, **69,** 313, 316-17, 341, 370-3, 397-8, 423-4, 439-41, 454, 511, 513, 515, 538, 545-7, 553, 555, 557
special leave **54,** 360-1, 362, 363, 370, 371
staff contract, incorporation into **69,** 312-13, 362, 397, 455, 533, 546
subsistence allowance **54,** 359, 361, 363, 371
suspension from duty **54,** 371
United Nations Sub-Commission on Prevention of Discrimination and Protection of Minorities 79, 264
United Nations Truce Supervision Organization (UNTSO) 80, 264
United States of America (USA)
access to courts. *See also forum [non] conveniens below*
accreditation
diplomatic mission, special **121,** 601-2
diplomatic privileges and immunities and **99,** 165
requirements
agreement/*agrément* of receiving State **99,** 166
full-time diplomatic activity **99,** 165-6, **121,** 602 n. 4
non-immigrant visa **121,** 602 n. 4
residence in capital **99,** 165
acquiescence **61,** 56
treaty amendment **101,** 600
act of State **51,** 11, **57,** 336-7, **61,** 55, 73–5, 77-8, **63,** 95-9, **77,** 175, 183, 186, 218-20, 226, 232–3, **79,** 499-502, 573-81, 584-9, **81,** 511, 515, 595, **82,** 309, **84,** 90, 109, 110, 117-20, **86,** 47-52, **88,** 95-100, 117-26, 163-5. *See also* Hickenlooper Amendment *below*
applicability
acts within own territory **63,** 475-6, **64,** 263-4, **113,** 529, **121,** 496, 642
administrative agencies **66,** 306-10
belligerent State, acts of **66,** 50-8
State courts **66,** 306-7
territorial dispute **64,** 348-51, **66,** 180-5, 334-8
applicable law **84,** 127, 193-4
authorization of action, need for **88,** 117-18, **104,** 163
military officers **88,** 117
balance of considerations **66,** 112-24, 231, 342, 419-20
basis **87,** 512, 515-16, **88,** 97
avoidance of embarrassment to legislature **84,** 194
choice of applicable law, as **88,** 119

United States of America (USA) (*cont.*)
comity **66,** 105-8, 160-1, 189, **84,** 130, 195, **88,** 65, 97, 99, **92,** 389, 474
difficulty of extraterritorial enforcement **92,** 474
foreign policy considerations. *See* foreign policy considerations *below*
respect for sovereignty **88,** 99
sovereign independence **92,** 496-7
burden of proof **66,** 11, 27-8, 327, **81,** 519, 593–4, 597, 637, **101,** 533, **103,** 469
classification as. *See also* expropriation/nationalization, as act of State *below*
antitrust claims **57,** 27-8, **63,** 198–211, **66,** 204-6, 276-9, 291-300, 327-8, 349-50, 383-5, 388-95, 417-20, **80,** 34, **81,** 517, 519-21, 526
commercial debt, repudiation **66,** 220-2, 233-6
confiscation of property in forum State **63,** 595 n. 10
crimes against humanity **66,** 50-8
drug-trafficking **119,** 65, 82-3
sale of airline tickets abroad **121,** 496 n. 10
terrorist act **121,** 642
collection of extraterritorial debt and **92,** 478
commercial activities **66,** 149-50, 220-2, 226-32, 237-40, 263, 315-16, 343, 384-5, 391, 419-20, 449, **81,** 518, 527, **84,** 119-21, 195 n. 5, **86,** 49, **88,** 74, **94,** 151, **103,** 508, **121,** 496
State department view **66,** 226-9
confiscation. *See also* Hickenlooper Amendment *below*
intangible property **87,** 512
property within USA **66,** 62, 69-70, 93-101, 132-3, 172, 194-7, 215, 250-5, 357-8, 403, 455-6
constitutional protection **79,** 580
counterclaim against foreign State **66,** 50-7, 75-8, 91, 104-24, 137-42, 212-45, 408-12, 427-33, 449, 458-9
affirmative judgment **66,** 91, 241-5
restricted judgment **66,** 110-11, 116, 141-2
State department criteria **66,** 116, 141
court judgments and **88,** 118
criterion, acts by foreign State in own territory **98,** 65, 108
currency regulations **66,** 12-13, 41
customs and tax laws, inquiry into and **92,** 476
debt **103,** 549
situs **81,** 535, 536-7
declaration of invalidity of foreign act, need for **88,** 97-100
definition **66,** 9-12, 24, 54, 95, 105, 112-13, 119, 129, 148, 153, 160-1, 181, 209-10, 217, 249, 260, 276, 292, 298, 306, 322, 327, 342, 349, 357, 363, 366, 383, 390, 397, 402, 410, 417, 427, 477-8, 491, **81,** 518-19, 645
deposed government, acts of former officials of **81,** 595
disclosure of documents and **92,** 389-91
discretionary nature of doctrine **63,** 187, **81,** 519, 528, 653-4, **103,** 516, 548 n. 22
Dunhill doctrine **86,** 48-9
evolution **81,** 519
exceptions
act in violation of international law **103,** 474-5
Bernstein exception. *See* Bernstein exception *below*
corruption **81,** 527-8
international law, violations **66,** 41, 367
ministerial act of foreign government **81,** 518-19
private acts **81,** 630-3

repudiated act of State **66,** 385
unjust enrichment **66,** 138, 448
exchange control **84,** 119, 120-1
executive certificate of non-applicability, need for **92,** 435-6
extraterritorial effect **61,** 55, **79,** 576-8, 580, 586, **84,** 126-30, **88,** 67, 68
asset, *situs* **88,** 67, 73-4
compatibility with US law **81,** 597
flexibility **88,** 164
Foreign Corrupt Practices Act 1977 and **81,** 527-8
foreign criminal conviction **66,** 152-8
foreign government, ousted, acts of **66,** 50-8
foreign law, recognition/enforcement **66,** 189-91, 257-63, 266-7, 306-10, 322-4, 465-6
foreign law requirements **66,** 10, 269, 401
foreign officials applying own law **84,** 193-4
foreign policy considerations **66,** 13, 35-6, 50-8, 95-100, 106-23, 138-9, 161, 181, 221-8, 243, 250-3, 276-7, 284, 296-7, 306-10, 315, 322-3, 335-8, 342, 419-20, 493-7, **88,** 68, **92,** 390, 435, 474, **98,** 65, **101,** 533, 534, **103,** 516, 548
act within territory of foreign State **121,** 496
counterclaim as set-off and **92,** 437
expropriation, standard of compensation and **92,** 435-6
foreign States
compulsion **66,** 58-60, 277-9, 327-8, 492-3
insignificant involvement **66,** 388-95
motives **66,** 204-6, 291-300, 314-16, 323-4, 349-50, 383-5, 388-95, 397-8, **81,** 520-1, 526-7
FSIA and **84,** 118 n. 12
governmental compulsion distinguished **81,** 519
Head of State
act in violation of international law **103,** 557
private acts **99,** 163-5, **121,** 588
Head of State, former **81,** 619-28
basis **81,** 623
personal gain **81,** 623 n. 12
judicial abstention and **88,** 121
judicial restraint **64,** 292-3
jurisdiction and **62,** 223-4, **66,** 147-51, 160-2
jurisprudence
First National Bank v. *Banco Nacional de Cuba* **125,** 645-6
Kirkpatrick v. *Environmental Tectonics* **111,** 601, 602, **119,** 74, 91, 95-6, **125,** 646
Oetjen v. *Central Leather Co.* **64,** 256, 346-7, **116,** 588, **119,** 92
Sabbatino **42,** 31, 35-6, **57,** 29, **64,** 259, 347, **86,** 48, **111,** 597-8, **119,** 73, **125,** 643-5
Underhill v. *Hernandez* **64,** 256-7, 346-7, **111,** 596
justiciability and **82,** 323-4, **88,** 119, **92,** 496, **99,** 163
legality of actions, relevance **104,** 163
limitation
Foreign Assistance Act 1961 **88,** 126
Foreign Sovereign Immunities Act (FSIA) 1976/1982 **88,** 126
military operation, ally's assistance as **80,** 21-2
motivation, relevance **92,** 496-7
non-appearance, effect **66,** 162
official act, need for **92,** 496, **99,** 163

United States of America (USA) (*cont.*)
participation in law suit and **88,** 118
political asylum and **88,** 22-3, 32-3
political offence and **79,** 511-13
political question and **66,** 111-13, 119-20, 306, 333-8, 396-7, **87,** 515
private acts **81,** 630-3, **113,** 528
Head of State **88,** 164-5
rationale **66,** 13, 50-7, 98-100, 106-24, 138-9, 150, 181, 204, 221-3, 226-9, 238-9, 249, 252-3, 276-9, 296-8, 306-7, 315, 322-3, 327, 363, 367-8, 383-4, 390-4, 417-18, 427, 480, 491
recognition of effect, *situs*, relevance **107,** 211-12
recognition, government, relevance **98,** 65, **99,** 74 n. 8
relevant factors, legality of actions **121,** 642
scope **66,** 114-24, 140-1, 181-2, 189-91, 204-6, 252-3, 291-300, 314-16, 323-4, 349-50, 371-3, 388-95, 397-8, 417-20
federal determination **66,** 9, 148, 371
relevant considerations **66,** 100, 118-20, 225
separation of powers and **63,** 567 n. 38, **79,** 6, 446-51, 586, 596-7, **86,** 48, **88,** 66, 73, 97, 99, 119-20, 121-3, 125-6, **92,** 389, 496, **98,** 108-9, **99,** 162, 165
set-off against foreign State. *See* counterclaim, against foreign State *above*
sovereign activity **103,** 508
State immunity, execution/attachment **89,** 359 n. 11
State immunity, jurisdiction and **63,** 99, 317, **66,** 105-6, 120, 123, 222-3, 237-9, 411-12, 418-19, **79,** 6-7, 596-7, 599, 601-2, **84,** 118 n. 12, 126, **86,** 49, **88,** 81, 193, 198, **99,** 163, 165, **101,** 532, **103,** 548-9, **119,** 73
distinction **121,** 496
status of parties, relevance **84,** 195
territorial limitation **66,** 23, 53, 77, 95-6, 98-9, 106, 129, 132, 148-9, 173, 196, 209-11, 250-5, 292, 309-10, 328, 357-8, 402-3, 455, 468, 481-3, **87,** 512–15, 516, 518, **88,** 89 n. 17
cause of action **66,** 357-8
taking of property on own territory **88,** 73
wartime exception **66,** 254-5
treaty exception **86,** 47-8
treaty or other unambiguous agreement **66,** 121, 268, 345, 479-80, **81,** 625 n. 12, 632 n. 4, **84,** 121-6, **86,** 47-8
unambiguous agreement, need for **86,** 49-52
treaty rights and **57,** 337
unjust enrichment **66,** 448, **79,** 597
waiver, counterclaim **84,** 179 n. 9
Administering Authority, as **61,** 106-7, 108-9, 111-12
admiralty jurisdiction. *See* Foreign Sovereign Immunities Act (FSIA) 1976/82, 28 USC 1605(b) (admiralty jurisdiction: enforcement of maritime lien) *below*
admissibility, exhaustion of local remedies. *See* exhaustion of local remedies *below*
aerial espionage, over China **47,** 109-12
agency, imputability of acts
general principle of agency law **107,** 233
of principal **107,** 233
to principal **107,** 233
agency or instrumentality of a foreign State **80,** 572, **81,** 540-1, 553-4, **84,** 111 n. 3, **86,** 59 n. 3, 77-80, **88,** 82, **103,** 523-4, 564, **104,** 280-2, **107,** 233
alter ego theory **66,** 426, 448, 457, 507-12, 516, **71,** 694, **90,** 616, **103,** 508, 509-11, **107,** 249-51, 254

applicable law **80,** 573-4, **90,** 612-14
  international law **90,** 612
  law of chartering State **90,** 612
  lex fori **90,** 612
broad interpretation **107,** 375
classification as
  Agency for International Development **63,** 230, 344
  Air Force **63,** 263, 266-7, 278
  armed forces **107,** 312-17
  central/State-owned bank **63,** 65, 90, 104, 150, 175, 347, 360, 391, 425, 460, 490, 496, 558-61, 575, 587, **84,** 109-10, **92,** 483, **107,** 263, **121,** 491
  economic development agency **63,** 175, 302
  electricity company **63,** 334
  Eurocontrol **107,** 324-8
  export association **63,** 90 n. 24, 104, 175
  food supply agency **63,** 371, 376-7, 495-7, 569-72, **64,** 447
  government department **63,** 49-52
  government procurement agency **63,** 90, 175
  Head of State **103,** 589
  Industrial Development Authority **63,** 616
  merchant marine **63,** 532
  mining enterprise **63,** 90, 104, 134, 174-8, 230, 290, 344, 449
  mission to international organization **63,** 125
  mixed economy company under laws of Guinea **63,** 536
  national airline **63,** 90, 104, 175, 195-6, 245-51, 344, 447, 448, 449, 469, **64,** 447, 454, **66,** 58-60, **79,** 564-6, **86,** 16-17, 18, 573, **87,** 65-8, **98,** 44-6, 49-54, 71-2, **103,** 352-5
  shipping line **63,** 78, 90, 104, 175, 220-1, 256, 330-3, 356, 365, 416-19, 443, 495, 532, 606, 625, 629, 639-40, **103,** 576-80
  ship's master **63,** 626, 631, **66,** 219
  State shipping company **63,** 78
  steel company **63,** 90, 104, 174-8
  tourist organization **63,** 321-2
  transport organization **63,** 90, 104, 175
  wholly owned commercial bank **107,** 263
immunity, execution **80,** 577
incorporation under laws of United States **107,** 253-4
independence **90,** 603, 611-16, **101,** 546-9, **107,** 375-6, 379-80
President's power to determine **98,** 66
separate legal entity test **98,** 53, 54, **107,** 312, 316-17
  applicable law **90,** 612-14
  attribution of activities of other State entities **98,** 92
  burden of proof **101,** 547, **103,** 496-500, 510
  fraud or injustice **98,** 54
  presumption of **98,** 53-4, 91-2, **101,** 546, 553, **103,** 496, 510, **107,** 379-80
State responsibility **86,** 78, 80 n. 4
Taiwan **98,** 66
test **98,** 53, 54, **107,** 312, 316-17
  control **103,** 509-10
  destination of profits **103,** 509-10
  funding **103,** 509-10
  majority ownership **63,** 167, 174-6, 302, 334, 437, **81,** 540, **84,** 111, **88,** 82, **98,** 53, 120-2, 132, **103,** 509-10, **107,** 375, 376-8

United States of America (USA) (*cont.*)
wholly owned and controlled company **107,** 239-40, 362
Agency for International Development
as agency or instrumentality of a foreign State **63,** 230, 344
contract of guaranty **48,** 179-86
air transport, international
Air Transport Agreements
France (1946), interpretation **38,** 182-260
South Africa (1947) **52,** 424-8, 436-42
carriage of goods **52,** 428, 438-42
regulation of **74,** 45-87
antitrust legislation, application to **74,** 46-59, 64-5, 68-9, 73-87
Alaska, boundaries, fixing of **73,** 64, 79-80
Alien Property Custodian **54,** 552, 572, 574, **61,** 48-9
Alien Tort Claims Statute 1789 (28 USC 1350) **72,** 130-1, **77,** 173, 174–84, 240-5, **79,** 4-7, 8, 10-12, 14-15, **80,** 21, 588, 590-1, **81,** 499, 510, 511, 512, 591, 662, 664, **87,** 681, **95,** 489 n. 13, **99,** 66, **103,** 526-8, 530, 556-7
applicability, non-US national **107,** 459 n. 2
cause of action, whether **95,** 630, 631-2, 639 n. 10, **104,** 127-9, 178-84, **107,** 449-51
abatement on death **104,** 129
applicable law, relevance **95,** 639 n. 10
individual's rights. *See* individual's rights *below*
effect on existing remedies **81,** 662
federal jurisdiction and **104,** 125-7
violation of international law **104,** 128–9, 143-6, 151-8
Filartiga **107,** 449-51
genocide **104,** 154-5, **107,** 459-60
individual's rights **107,** 449-51, 459
international law basis **77,** 179, 240, **81,** 499-501, 664, **107,** 450-1
developing concept **81,** 662, **95,** 631
international common law tort **95,** 631, 632-5, **104,** 144-5, **107,** 450
lex fori as applicable law **95,** 499, **104,** 181-4, 191-2
treaties, breach of **81,** 510-12
jurisdiction under **77,** 173, 174, 185, 186-7, 200-2, 205-18, 222, 228, 262, 268-71, **79,** 4-7, 8, 10-12, 14-15
act or omission, in USA **79,** 5
damage arising in USA, for **79,** 5
international law, wrong under **77,** 181, 200, 249, **79,** 10-12
legislative history **77,** 211-15, 249-51, **79,** 5–6
prize law and **81,** 664-5
torture claims under **81,** 591
requirements
alien suit **107,** 450
tort **107,** 450
violation of international law. *See* international law basis *above*
sovereign immunity and **79,** 3-7, 8, 10-12
State action, need for **104,** 154, **107,** 459
State activity, application to **80,** 590-1
State immunity, jurisdiction, exception to, whether **103,** 469 n. 13, 525-6, **113,** 551
State immunity, jurisdiction, waiver, whether **96,** 58, 61
Tel-Oren **107,** 450
third party claim **104,** 189-92
torture **104,** 143-6, 156-7, **107,** 450, **121,** 615

Torture Victim Protection Act, effect on **104,** 154
waiver of State immunity, whether **80,** 22, 591
war crimes **104,** 155-6
aliens. *See also* Alien Tort Claims Statute 1789 *above*
access to courts **54,** 227-9, **63,** 108, 393-7, 564, 574-5, 577-8, 580-2, **77,** 212
admission
discretionary **95,** 486, 500
judicial review **95,** 487
temporary pending determination of status **95,** 486, 500
asylum, right to **53,** 533-6
children awaiting adoption
access to record **95,** 487-8, 492-3
constitutional rights **95,** 487
custody **95,** 498
habeas corpus **95,** 490-2
interests of child **95,** 498, 503
claim for personal injuries **54,** 227-9
Constitution
protection when abroad **80,** 592
rights under **82,** 315 n. 24, **87,** 449–50
illegal entry **87,** 491
international organizations, employees of **54,** 251-2
legalization of status **79,** 614 n. 3
military service obligations **56,** 563
'non-immigrant treaty trader' **54,** 259-63
obligations while resident in USA **54,** 227-9
permanent resident status **54,** 254
property, jurisdiction over **53,** 589-90
Salvadorans in US
burden of proof **95,** 573-4
criminal conviction, effect **95,** 573-4
temporary protected immigration status **95,** 573
status, parole **95,** 486, 500
treatment of **56,** 15
US law, limitation of applicability by treaty **82,** 293
visa application, misrepresentation of material fact **95,** 516-21, 528
ambassador/head of mission
ambassador to UN, bilateral ambassador distinguished **99,** 130, 135
duty to control actions of members of mission **121,** 486
functions **56,** 521-3
powers
conclusion of treaties **99,** 130-1
conclusion of treaties, contract distinguished **99,** 136 n. 1
to bind sending State **99,** 130
to bind sending State, authorization, need for **99,** 130-1
to bind sending State, reasonable reliance on apparent authority **99,** 131, 133, 136-8
special envoy as **99,** 116
status, agent of sending State **99,** 130-4, 136-8
American Convention on Human Rights (1969), expulsion of national **104,** 188
AMTRAK, foreign government corporation compared **63,** 250
antitrust. *See also* law of, Antitrust (Clayton) Act 1914 *and* Antitrust (Sherman) Act 1890 *below*
act of State and. *See* act of State, classification as, antitrust claims *above*

United States of America (USA) (*cont.*)
Antitrust Guide for International Operations (1977) **96,** 182
damages, proof of **57,** 28
foreign governments, acts of **57,** 25-7
Foreign Sovereign Immunities Act (FSIA) 1976 and **63,** 201-3, 205-6, 294-7
foreign State compulsion **66,** 276-9, 327-8, 492-3
jurisdiction
effects test **66,** 279-86, 490-1, 500
limitations **57,** 25
public interest **66,** 492, **81,** 520
remedies **63,** 108
restraint of trade **57,** 20
substantial and foreseeable effect, need for **96,** 182
antitrust legislation. *See also* law of, Antitrust (Clayton) Act 1914 *and* Antitrust (Sherman) Act 1890 *below*
enforcement **73,** 318-23, 335-8, 345-7, 356-9, **74,** 43-59, 64-5, 68-9, 73-87
extraterritorial effect **48,** 110, 114-15, 118, 119, **56,** 32, **63,** 295, **66,** 279-86, 293, 343, 382-3, 490-7, 500-2, **73,** 321, 337-8, 346-7, 357-8, **74,** 39-40, 48-54, 78-82
stay of proceedings and **118,** 542-65
applicable law **81,** 533 n. 2
act of State **84,** 127, 193-4, **88,** 119
Antarctica **100,** 533-5, 540-2
bankruptcy proceedings **107,** 345
choice of law
federal law **98,** 123
lex fori **108,** 498
contract
place of conclusion **94,** 142
place of performance **94,** 142
custody of children **95,** 498-500
Hague Convention Concerning Powers of Authorities and the Law Applicable in Respect of the Protection of Infants (1971) **95,** 499
Hague Convention Regarding Guardianship of Infants (1902) **95,** 499
lex fori **95,** 499
nationality **95,** 499-500
diplomatic privileges and immunity, Vienna Convention on Diplomatic Relations (1961) **107,** 454-5
expropriation/nationalization
expropriating State **95,** 622-3
international law **95,** 623
lex situs **92,** 474
extradition, evidence, requesting State **104,** 49
foreign law **104,** 183
injuries suffered in civil war in foreign State **99,** 64-5, 67
international crime
international law **91,** 43, **99,** 66-7, **104,** 181-3
lex fori **104,** 181-4, 191-2
international law
adoption by federal courts and **96,** 16 n. 3
coastline, determination of **91,** 431
inter-State boundary disputes **91,** 460
State succession **94,** 180

judicial assistance **81,** 603, **121,** 571
lex situs **84,** 127
place of injury **98,** 124
political offence, classification, requested State **104,** 67
relations between foreign government and its ambassador, federal State, in **99,** 135
service of process, *lex fori* **96,** 78, 79-80
State immunity, jurisdiction, sending State **103,** 538-9
State succession, international law **94,** 180
State-sponsored terrorism **121,** 632-3
tort, *lex loci delicti commissi* **108,** 498-9
transfer of personal property
dominant interest **94,** 171
lex situs **94,** 171
treaty implementation, municipal law **118,** 33
treaty interpretation, international law **101,** 602
Vienna Convention on Diplomatic Relations (1961) **107,** 454-5
arbitrability **62,** 223
arbitral award
date **103,** 568-70
definition, recognition and enforcement, for purposes of **96,** 9
foreign State, made in, Iran–US Claims Tribunal, whether **96,** 9, 11-12
specific performance, need for **96,** 20-1
arbitral award, enforcement **53,** 18-19, **62,** 220-5, **65,** 236, **72,** 154-71, **89,** 356-60, **94,** 221-31
defences **94,** 221-8, **96,** 12
Iran–US Claims Tribunal. *See* Iran–US Claims Tribunal
jurisdiction, requirements
arbitration agreement **96,** 10
commercial relationship **96,** 9
foreign element **96,** 9
foreign State, made in **96,** 9
legal relationship **96,** 9
national tribunal, emanation from. *See* foreign State, made in *above*
licence to seek, need for **94,** 215-19
New York Convention on the Recognition and Enforcement of Foreign Arbitral Awards (1958) **62,** 220-5, **94,** 221, **96,** 5, 12
non-recognition of government and **94,** 213-15
President's power to bar **94,** 217-18
procedure **103,** 569-70
State immunity, jurisdiction. *See* State immunity, arbitral award, enforcement *below*
as violation of national law **96,** 19-20
alternative satisfaction **96,** 20
arbitral award, interpretation, effectiveness **96,** 19
arbitral tribunal, failure to appear **63,** 536-7, 539
arbitrary detention **87,** 448-60
aliens **87,** 451-60, **95,** 633
customary international law **87,** 455-60, **95,** 633
human rights and **87,** 455-60, **95,** 633, **104,** 185
as international tort/wrong **95,** 633
jus cogens/peremptory norm **104,** 185
prolonged detention of national **95,** 633-4
arbitration, UN Headquarters Agreement **82,** 230-82

United States of America (USA) (*cont.*)
arbitration agreement
Algiers Accords, whether **96,** 10
Presidential power to conclude **96,** 10-11
individual's rights, effect on **96,** 10-11
armed conflict. *See* war *below*
armed forces
in China, jurisdiction over **40,** 86-7
criminal jurisdiction abroad **40,** 86-7, **57,** 316–18, 321-5, 341
in France, claims arising out of acts of **45,** 462-3
humanitarian law, offences against
evidence of **104,** 173 n. 4
responsibility **104,** 171-3, 174-5
immunity **52,** 333-5
arrest **82,** 338, 341, 342, **90,** 645-8. *See also* law of, Posse Comitatus Act *below*
illegal. *See also* forcible abduction/unlawful arrest *below*
constitutional issue, whether **98,** 107 n. 11
use of forces **82,** 338-43
international waters, in **82,** 338
non-regulatory, proscriptive or compulsory **82,** 342-3
use of military aircraft to transport **82,** 341
asylum **79,** 508 n. 15, 612-40, **87,** 472, 479-80, 488, 491. *See also* law of, Immigration and Nationality Act 1952 *and* Refugee Act *below*
burden of proof **79,** 615 n. 3, 620, 623, 628 n. 32, 633, 638, **95,** 538, 572
Immigration Act 1990, effect **95,** 573-4
class/representative action **95,** 574
country of first refuge, relevance **88,** 16
deportation withhold distinguished **87,** 475-7, 481, 482, 496, **95,** 549, 581, 582 n. 11
discretionary **79,** 612, 615, 623, 635, **95,** 539 n. 4, 543 n. 10, 549, 559, 572, 581, 604 n. 8
internal armed conflict, flight from, duty to offer **95,** 566-7
international officials **83,** 288, 387-90
permanent residence **83,** 388
judicial review, evaluation of conformity with evidence **95,** 564
past persecution, sufficiency **95,** 542-3
prima facie case **88,** 9, 28, 30, **95,** 542
standard of proof **88,** 28
procedure **79,** 616, 619-20, **88,** 16-17
refugees outside territory **95,** 581-98
interception on high seas **95,** 581-98
requirements for **79,** 633 n. 2, 640 n. 8
status, permanent resident **95,** 549
withhold of deportation distinguished **79,** 616 n. 6, 617-20, 623-41
attachment
discretionary nature **63,** 307
freezing of assets distinguished **81,** 646
grounds
arrest before judgement as alternative **63,** 277
burden of proof **63,** 280, 308-10
risk of removal of property from jurisdiction **63,** 277-8, 348
jurisdiction, as basis for, post-judgment attachment distinguished **63,** 307-8, 348-9

requirements
defendant outwith the jurisdiction **63,** 277-8, 348
impossibility of service within the jurisdiction **63,** 277, 278-9
timely implementation **63,** 253-5
timely service implementation **63,** 410-11
Austro-Hungarian Bank, funds repaid to **71,** 267-9
bank deposit, cause of action, date arising **81,** 533
bankruptcy proceedings
applicable law **107,** 345
creditor, international organization as **107,** 416-18
'right to payment', enforceability, relevance **107,** 417-18
banks, national, foreign branches, legal identity **66,** 447-8, 469-70
baselines, straight **91,** 416, 431 n. 9
bays
ancient title **91,** 429-38
closing line **91,** 414 n. 1
10 miles **91,** 421
historic bays **91,** 417-18
Vineyard Sound **91,** 429
as internal waters **91,** 431
measurement **57,** 66, 71-4
title
bays doctrine and **91,** 430-3, 437-8
discovery and occupation **91,** 430
exploitation **91,** 434-7
Bernstein exception **42,** 38, **66,** 50-8, 106-23, 140-1, 221, 226-9, 237, 342, 428-30, 458-9, 478-9, 515, **81,** 511, 518, **84,** 173, 179, **86,** 48, **98,** 65-6
Board of Immigration Appeals **79,** 379, 380
procedural regulations, interpretation **79,** 382
statutory ambiguity to be resolved in favour of **79,** 629
Bosnia-Herzegovina, Bosnian Serbs (Srpska)
recognition **104,** 146, 152 n. 2
responsibility for acts of **104,** 144-6
boundaries
acquiescence **91,** 448. *See also* prescription *below*
inter-State **42,** 87-8, **51,** 28-38, **57,** 92, **59,** 200-45, 258-64, **73,** 64, 79-80, **91,** 445
islands arising after dispositive treaty, effect **91,** 451-4
boundaries, water
delimitation **57,** 92
determination of **59,** 258-64
Louisiana–Texas dispute **59,** 200-45
boundary dispute, jurisdiction **91,** 450, 459
broadcasting, regulation, outside territorial sea **61,** 184-5
burden of proof **54,** 573, 579, 581-2, 602-3, 606–7, **63,** 638
act of State **81,** 519, 597, 633, 635, **101,** 533
agency or instrumentality of a foreign State, independence **101,** 547, **103,** 496-500, 510
agency relationship **90,** 611
attachment, grounds for **63,** 280, 308-10
availability of alternative forum **84,** 105
default judgment, entitlement **63,** 382, 389-90
displaced persons **95,** 508

United States of America (USA) (*cont.*)
exhaustion of State remedies **118,** 28
extradition, conditions in requesting State **104,** 100-1
fear of persecution **88,** 7
Head of State, public nature of acts **99,** 164
IMF, disapproval of exchange controls **84,** 124 n. 25
independence of State entity **80,** 577
judicial review, request for **88,** 19
jurisdiction **107,** 346
legislation, interpretation **90,** 623
political offence exception **104,** 91, 93
Salvadorans in US **95,** 573-4
service of process in language of foreign State **79,** 389, **84,** 143
standard **91,** 430
State immunity, entitlement **80,** 585
State immunity, execution/attachment, purpose **98,** 12
State immunity, jurisdiction. *See* State immunity, jurisdiction, procedural aspects, burden of proof *below*
California
aliens
employment of **53,** 528-31
property, rights of succession to **53,** 532
Business and Profession Code
s 16720 **81,** 524
s 17045 **81,** 524
Civil Code **83,** 468
s 2224 **81,** 618
Civil Procedure Code, s 483.010 **81,** 646
Constitution **79,** 411
retroactive legislation **79,** 411
corporation law **83,** 465, 466
inland waters **57,** 59-77
baselines **42,** 92-3
bays **57,** 59
definition **42,** 86-102
harbours **57,** 59
historic waters **57,** 77
low-water mark **57,** 60
Monterey Bay **42,** 94
river mouths **57,** 60
Santa Barbara Channel, whether bay **42,** 94-5
Probate Code **56,** 15-20
discrimination, whether **56,** 16
foreign relations and **56,** 20
non-resident aliens, rights of **42,** 1-8
statutory limitation **79,** 407-11
Cameroons and Togo, treaties in respect of **37,** 527
cause of action, Foreign Sovereign Immunities Act (FSIA) 1976, whether **63,** 578-80
central/State-owned bank
as agency or instrumentality of a foreign State **63,** 65, 90, 104, 150, 175, 347, 360, 391, 425, 460, 490, 496, 558-61, 575, 587, **92,** 483, **107,** 263, **121,** 491
classification of act
commercial purpose **89,** 364-5

sale of certificates of deposit **92,** 416
definition **86,** 8-9, 12, 13
purpose/use of funds
funds held for its own account **64,** 224-5, **92,** 402-3
mixed use **63,** 527, **89,** 365
State immunity, execution/attachment **89,** 364 n. 4
assets of nationalized bank **63,** 1-4
central and State-owned bank distinguished **92,** 416
State immunity, jurisdiction, sovereign activity, central bank's sale of currency **98,** 59
waiver of immunity from execution/attachment **92,** 402–3
certiorari **79,** 422, 438, 458, 468, 534
child care, custody
applicable law **95,** 498-500
grandparent's right **95,** 498-500
Chile, intervention in internal affairs of **59,** 383-8
choice of law **84,** 104-5. *See also* applicable law *above*
choice of law clause, failure to include **101,** 518
church, status
incorporation, relevance **108,** 496-7
separate legal entity **108,** 496-7
citizenship **56,** 558-60, 562
alien, resident, rights and duties **54,** 227-9
application for **56,** 563
by marriage **42,** 235
constitutional provisions **53,** 525
naturalized citizens **56,** 558-60, 561
draft exemption, effect of claim to **42,** 195-7
residence **56,** 562
Civil Aeronautics Board (CAB)
Economic Regulations **54,** 310, 326, 336, 342-3
foreign air transportation decisions, judicial review **63,** 30 n. 7
civil proceedings. *See also* Federal Rules of Civil Procedure; law of, Administrative Procedure Act *below*
Federal Arbitration Act **66,** 200
'notice of suit' **63,** 125, 136, 212-13, 222, 226-7, 413-15, 513, 520
removal of cases from State to Federal Courts. *See* Foreign Sovereign Immunities Act (FSIA) 1976/82, 28 USC 1441(d) (foreign State: removal of civil action to federal court)
service of process. *See* service of process *below*
summary judgment, motion for **63,** 77-80
civil war
extradition and **104,** 73-4
injuries to US national, right of civil action in US court **99,** 58-79
laws and customs of war, applicability **104,** 73-4
claims
assignment **84,** 163
Litvinov Assignment **84,** 162-4, 165, 175, 176, 180 n. 11, 181
sampling methodology **109,** 72-4
State control over **84,** 93
claims programme of Department of Defense, as effective remedy **123,** 136-8
claims settlement agreements, extinction of claimant's rights against foreign State **72,** 133-40, 143-50, **84,** 90, **94,** 219-20
arbitration, offer of and **95,** 623

United States of America (USA) (*cont.*)
change of applicable law and **94,** 220
payment by government of less than full claims and **84,** 163
State responsibility **95,** 617, 623
Clayton Act 1914. *See* law of, Antitrust (Clayton) Act 1914 *below*
coastline
definition **91,** 413-14
low-water mark **91,** 414, 431
Code (USC)
5 USC 702. *See* law of, Administrative Procedure Act *below*
7 USC 1691 ff **86,** 57
8 USC 1103 **87,** 471 n. 13
8 USC 1105 **87,** 491
8 USC 1158 **87,** 481, 482, 491, 496, 497, 503
8 USC 1182 **87,** 449, 451, 453, 455, 468
8 USC 1182(a)(28)(F) **82,** 331
8 USC 1182(d)(3) **82,** 331
8 USC 1182(d)(6) **82,** 331, 334, 335
8 USC 1223 **87,** 448
8 USC 1225 **87,** 449, 451
8 USC 1227 **87,** 451, 452
8 USC 1231 **87,** 491
8 USC 1252 **87,** 453
8 USC 1253 **87,** 453, 464, 465, 467, 481, 484, 491, 492, 493-4
8 USC 1481 (oath of allegiance to foreign government) **82,** 318
9 USC 201-8. *See* law of, Federal Arbitration Act *below*
10 USC 371-8 **82,** 340, 341
10 USC 375 **88,** 184
10 USC 2631 (Cargo Preference Act 1910) **86,** 22-4, 28, 30, 32
11 USC 101(5) **107,** 417
11 USC 101(10) **107,** 417
11 USC 502(b) **107,** 418
11 USC 1109 **107,** 416
12 USC 94 **81,** 533
12 USC 632 **86,** 4-9, 12-14, 17-19
14 USC 7 **81,** 667 n. 7, **90,** 628
14 USC 89 **84,** 213, 217, 219
14 USC 89(a) **91,** 472, 475, 478, 489-90, 498-500, 530-1
15 USC 1 **81,** 524, **100,** 568-9, 574-6, 585, 595-6, 597
15 USC 1-7 **118,** 404 n. 37
15 USC 2 **81,** 518, **100,** 579 n. 2
15 USC 13 **81,** 524
15 USC 72. *See* law of, Antidumping Act 1916 (15 USC 72) *below*
15 USC 78 **84,** 193
15 USC 78ii(b). *See* law of, Securities Exchange Act 1934 *below*
15 USC 78(dd). *See* law of, Foreign Corrupt Practices Act 1977 *below*
15 USC 1011-113. *See* law of, McCarran–Ferguson Act *and* Robinson–Patman Act (15 USC 13 ff) *below*
15 USC 1127. *See* law of, Lanham Act *below*
15 USC 1311-14. *See* law of, Antitrust Civil Process Act *below*
15 USC 2052. *See* law of, Consumer Product Safety Act *below*
16 USC 1801-1882. *See* law of, Fishery Conservation Act 1976 *below*
18 USC 2 **99,** 152

18 USC 2(a) (procuring an offence) **104,** 6
18 USC 7(0) (special maritime and territorial jurisdiction) **90,** 593 n. 11
18 USC 7(3) (special maritime and territorial jurisdiction: places acquired by and under jurisdiction of US), embassy abroad **61,** 225-6, **81,** 548-9, 667 n. 7
18 USC 7(5) (American-owned aircraft) **86,** 35
18 USC 7(7) (offences against US nationals) **86,** 35
18 USC 32. *See* law of, Destruction of Aircraft Act *below*
18 USC 37, ss 792-9 (espionage) **82,** 313 n. 15
18 USC 40, ss 841-7 (explosives) **82,** 313 n. 15
18 USC 81, ss 1651-61 (piracy) **82,** 313 n. 15
18 USC 105, ss 2151-7 (sabotage) **82,** 313 n. 15
18 USC 109(a) **104,** 188 n. 25
18 USC 115
  s 831 (nuclear materials) **82,** 313 n. 15
  ss 2381-91 (treason, sedition and subversive activities) **82,** 313 n. 15
18 USC 351/1751 (kidnapping and assassination of leading figures) **82,** 313 n. 15, **94,** 87-92
  extraterritorial effect **94,** 88-92
18 USC 371 **82,** 346
18 USC 401 **88,** 38
18 USC 959 (foreign enlistment) **82,** 318
18 USC 1116 (murder of foreign official or internationally protected person), extraterritorial effect **94,** 92-6
18 USC 1117 (conspiracy to violate 18 USC 1116) **94,** 96-7
18 USC 1201 (statute of limitations) **104,** 22
18 USC 1203 (Hostage-taking Act). *See* law of, Hostage-taking Act (18 USC 1203) *below*
18 USC 1341 **79,** 427, **81,** 616, 643, 650, 651
18 USC 1343 **79,** 427, **81,** 616, 643, 650, 651
18 USC 1385. *See* law of, Posse Comitatus Act *below*
18 USC 1961 **81,** 615, 617, 643, 650, 651
18 USC 1962. *See* law of, Racketeer Influenced and Corrupt Organizations Act *below*
18 USC 2032 **87,** 580
18 USC 2241 **86,** 35
18 USC 2311 ff. *See* law of, National Stolen Property Act 1934 *below*
18 USC 2314 **81,** 616, 650, 651
18 USC 2315 **81,** 616, 643, 650, 651
18 USC 2331 (terrorist acts abroad against US national) **82,** 313 n. 15, **104,** 83
18 USC 2441. *See* law of, War Crimes Act 1996 (18 USC 2441) *below*
18 USC 3161 **86,** 44
18 USC 3181 (extradition) **79,** 424 n. 1, 442, **122,** 604, 661, 662, 669
18 USC 3182 (extradition) **79,** 528
18 USC 3184 (jurisdiction, extradition cases) **79,** 387, 415-17, 420, 424, 432, 436, 441, 442, 447, 464, 466, 467, 473, 474, 477, 493, 497, 499, **90,** 685, **104,** 62, 82, **122,** 604, 661-5, 668-79
  extradition to subordinate territory and **122,** 661-80
18 USC 3186 **79,** 436
18 USC 3190 (evidence, extradition cases) **79,** 434, **104,** 49
18 USC 3231 (jurisdiction over military personnel) **99,** 167-8
18 USC 3281-2 **79,** 405
18 USC 3500. *See* law of, Jencks Act *below*
18 USC 3731 **87,** 577
19 USC 1401 **84,** 211

United States of America (USA) (*cont.*)
19 USC 1504(a) **107,** 279
19 USC 1514(a) **107,** 291
19 USC 1516a(a)(2) **107,** 272, 280
19 USC 1671(b) **107,** 281, 290-1
19 USC 1675 **107,** 279
19 USC 1701 **81,** 667 n. 7, **90,** 628
19 USC 1709 **84,** 211 n. 1
19 USC 2503(a) **107,** 281
19 USC 2503(c) **107,** 281
19 USC 2601 ff. (UNESCO Convention on Cultural Property implementation). *See* law of, Cultural Property Implementation Act 1983 *below*
21 USC 321. *See* law of, Federal Food, Drug and Cosmetic Act (21 USC 32) *below*
21 USC 846 **91,** 471, 511
21 USC 952 **99,** 157-8
21 USC 955 **84,** 214
21 USC 959 **99,** 152, 157
21 USC 963 **84,** 214, **91,** 471, 474, 511, **99,** 152
22 USC 254(a-e) **88,** 40
22 USC 254(d) (diplomatic immunity) **99,** 105-6, **113,** 531
22 USC 288. *See* law of, International Organizations Immunities Act (IOIA) *below*
22 USC 2370. *See* Hickenlooper Amendment *below*
22 USC 2691 **82,** 331
22 USC 5001-116. *See* law of, Comprehensive Anti-Apartheid Act 1986 *below*
22 USC 5701-32. *See* law of, Hong Kong Policy Act 1992 (22 USC 5701-32) *below*
22 USC 5721(b) **114,** 619 n. 18
23 USC 1292(b) (certification of appropriateness for appeal) **60,** 53, **121,** 583
26 USC 991-7 **86,** 93 n. 6
28 USC 517 **87,** 588
28 USC 636 **96,** 84
28 USC 1291 (appeal) **81,** 504, 553, **87,** 570, **107,** 361, 395
28 USC 1292 **81,** 504
28 USC 1292(a)(1) **95,** 484, 487
28 USC 1333 **81,** 662, 665, 666
28 USC 1334(b) (civil proceedings under title II) **107,** 415-16
28 USC 1335 **81,** 665
28 USC 1337 **81,** 499, 665
28 USC 1338 **81,** 665
28 USC 1343 **101,** 480, 483-4
28 USC 1343(3) **95,** 488
28 USC 1346 **81,** 550
28 USC 1351 **101,** 480-2
28 USC 1361 **81,** 545
28 USC 1367 **103,** 508, 517-18, **107,** 460
28 USC 1367(a) (supplemental jurisdiction) **113,** 530–1
28 USC 1367(c) (supplemental jurisdiction) **104,** 149
28 USC 1391 **84,** 97, 109-10, 135, 146, 149, **90,** 589, 604, **107,** 316
28 USC 1391(a) **113,** 532
28 USC 1391(f) **87,** 540, 543 n. 4, **107,** 313, 384-5, **113,** 532
28 USC 1391(f)(4) **77,** 262, **121,** 624, 633
28 USC 1404 **81,** 574
28 USC 1406 **86,** 81
28 USC 1446(b) **87,** 544

28 USC 1447(c) **87,** 598
28 USC 1491 **81,** 550
28 USC 1581(c) **107,** 272, 280
28 USC 1604 (immunity of foreign State from jurisdiction: exceptions), 'subject to existing international agreements' **63,** 267-8, 289, 309, 353, 421 n. 2, **84,** 240-5
28 USC 1631 **81,** 551
28 USC 1782(a) (assistance to foreign and international tribunals) **81,** 603, **121,** 574-6
28 USC 1927 **87,** 682
28 USC 1983 **95,** 488
28 USC 2106 **81,** 503
28 USC 2241 **79,** 474, **87,** 448
28 USC 2254 **118,** 32, 34
28 USC 2501 **81,** 551
28 USC 2680 **87,** 549
28 USC 2680(h) (assault committed by official other than law enforcement officer) **121,** 485-6
28 USC 3071 **82,** 352 n. 15
29 USC 51 ff. *See* law of, Americans with Disabilities Act 1990 *below*
29 USC 151-68. *See* law of, National Labor Relations Act (NLRA) *below*
29 USC 185 **81,** 591
29 USC 401 ff. *See* law of, Labor-Management Reporting and Disclosure Act 1990 *below*
29 USC 621 ff. *See* law of, Age Discrimination in Employment Act (ADEA) 1967 *below*
29 USC 2001-6. *See* law of, Federal Employers Liability Act (FELA) *below*
42 USC 1983 (appeals jurisdiction) **103,** 485, **104,** 147, **118,** 32, 35
42 USC 4321-47. *See* law of, National Environmental Policy Act (NEPA) *below*
43 USC 1301 ff. *See* law of, Submerged Lands Act 1953 *below*
46 USC 814. *See* law of, Shipping Act *below*
46 USC 1902 **84,** 216
46 USC 1903 **84,** 210-13
46 USC App 688. *See* law of, Transportation Safety Act 1974 *below*
48 USC 183 **87,** 551
48 USC 183(a) **87,** 556
48 USC 185 **87,** 556
48 USC 1424(a) **87,** 570
48 USC 1424(b) **87,** 570
48 USC 1561 **87,** 571 n. 17
48 USC 1616 **87,** 571 n. 17
48 USC 1681 **87,** 548, 552, 613, 634, 635, 646, 649-50, 652, **96,** 26
48 USC 1694a(b) **87,** 548, 549-52
48 USC 1694c(b) **87,** 570
49 USC App 1301 **88,** 40
49 USC App 1461(a) **82,** 323-4
49 USC App 1472 **86,** 35, 38
49 USC App 1472(i)-(o) (hijacking and piracy) **82,** 313 n. 15
50 USC 1541-8. *See* War Powers Resolution *below*
legislative history **87,** 615-16
comity **81,** 521. *See also* international law *below*
choice of law as **100,** 599
constituent States, between **98,** 8
constitutional restrictions distinguished **84,** 174
definition **107,** 425

United States of America (USA) (*cont.*)
extradition **104,** 10, 115
foreign judgment, recognition/enforcement, recognition of international organization **107,** 424-6
piercing the corporate veil **103,** 500
State immunity, execution/attachment **65,** 174
common purpose, Pinkerton doctrine **124,** 158 n. 289
community action agencies, as 'agency or instrumentality' of Federal Government **63,** 104
compensation of citizens from foreign assets **42,** 203, 204
Concurrent Resolution process **82,** 313
Congress, powers. *See also* foreign relations, responsibility for *below*
commerce, regulation **82,** 327, 355 n. 24, **90,** 625
legislative jurisdiction **60,** 57, 59-60, 62-3
to declare war **42,** 395, 397, **60,** 16
to raise armies **42,** 436-7
treaties, denunciation **82,** 327
conspiracy **91,** 480-5, 502-4, 532-3, 534-5
constituent States
boundaries **42,** 87-8, **51,** 28-38, **57,** 92, **59,** 200-45, 258-64, **73,** 64, 79-80, **91,** 445
Geneva Conventions on the Law of the Sea 1958, applicability **59,** 218-27
water, delimitation **59,** 200-45, 258-64
'country', whether **100,** 532-40
sovereignty, relevance **100,** 533-4, 540
courts of
application of foreign law **43,** 198, 202, 210
application of international law **59,** 218-27
extradition between **90,** 675
immunity **90,** 635
legislation
aliens, bequests to non-resident **43,** 197-212
effect on other States **59,** 229
legislative powers **53,** 530-1
national State, whether distinction intended **56,** 59
sovereignty of **39,** 121-4
territorial waters, rights in respect of **57,** 98-101
territory
Acts of Admission and **91,** 417, 422 n. 12
historic bays **91,** 413
navigable waters, land under **91,** 413
territorial sea (3-mile limit) **91,** 413-15, 422 n. 12
testamentary disposition of property, power over **56,** 16
Constitution **56,** 232, **77,** 197, 251
I (bills of attainder) **42,** 32, **81,** 597, 664, **82,** 311, 315 n. 22, 318, 351, **84,** 215, **90,** 625
I (regulation of offences against law of nations) **63,** 383, **79,** 411
I(8) **87,** 661, 687, 689, 694, 698, 699, **88,** 58
I(8)(10) (authority to legislate in respect of offences against international law) **91,** 43, **121,** 505, 506, 533, 551, 572
I(9)(3) **91,** 17
I(10)(1) **91,** 17
II **72,** 145, **86,** 25, **87,** 586
II(2) **80,** 22, **88,** 58, **99,** 90, **101,** 563-79, **107,** 258

II(3) **107,** 258
III **79,** 555-60, **81,** 513-14, 541, 545-6, 652, **82,** 289, 317, **84,** 215, **87,** 586, 654, 687, 694, 699, **99,** 48, 61, **101,** 468-70, **107,** 413
'arising under' clause **63,** 578-83, **104,** 126-7, 193-4
Foreign Diversity Clause **42,** 146-8, **63,** 394-5, 564, 574-5, 577-8, 580-2, **72,** 127-31, 137-40, 180, 198, 273, 288, **79,** 550-2, 555-60
State immunity and **103,** 528-30
III(2) (political question doctrine) **88,** 40, 56, **94,** 100, **99,** 123
IV **87,** 654
IV(2) (inter-State extradition) **104,** 97
IV(4) (recognition of governments) **94,** 102, **99,** 62
V (self-incrimination) **108,** 627
VI **84,** 665, **90,** 672
VI(2) (federal statutes) **43,** 16, **72,** 657, **95,** 592 n. 35
VII (trial by jury), State immunity, jurisdiction and **63,** 245-51, 368-9, 438, 439-46, 541-9, 639-46, **72,** 95-100, 102-5, 109, **107,** 354-8
acts committed on high seas, jurisdiction over **81,** 664
aliens abroad **80,** 592
aliens, rights **87,** 449-50, **91,** 477, 491, 535, **104,** 129 n. 12
Amendments
First **56,** 242, **57,** 26, **66,** 310, **77,** 190, **82,** 198, 307-14, 331, 335-7, **94,** 250, **121,** 513-14, 530-1, 532-3, 543-7, 551-62
Fourth **74,** 318, 335, **84,** 215-17, **88,** 233-8, **90,** 647
Fourth, high seas, applicability to **84,** 215-16
Fourth, international law and **91,** 479
Fourth, searches and seizures **91,** 476-9, 491-2, 497-8, 501-2, 535-6, **99,** 174 n. 28
Fifth **38,** 139, **42,** 32, **43,** 16, 199, **54,** 243-5, **56,** 11-12, 236, 240-2, 333, 334, 338-9, **60,** 57, 63, **63,** 566, **66,** 98, 359, **72,** 151-2, 198, 291, **73,** 305-6, 310, 312, 318-20, 323, 333-8, 345-8, 355-7, **79,** 419 n. 7, 521, 580, **81,** 597, 603, **87,** 449-50, 578, 579, 580, 617-20, 705-6, **88,** 90-1, 184, **90,** 590 n. 5, 652, 657
Fifth (self-incrimination clause) **121,** 573-6, **124,** 192
Sixth **79,** 389, **88,** 184
Seventh (jury trial) **63,** 249, 330, 369, 439-40, 546-9, 639, 644-6, **72,** 95-100, 102-5, 109
Eighth **87,** 449-50
Ninth **56,** 22, **118,** 34-5
Tenth **56,** 22, **87,** 551 n. 18
Eleventh **90,** 635, **118,** 54
Thirteenth **88,** 44
Fourteenth **42,** 32, **56,** 7, 12-13, 15-18, **63,** 566, **66,** 359, **72,** 116, 198, **81,** 597, **87,** 571-4, 580, **90,** 675, **91,** 329-30
applicability **56,** 231-2
non-resident aliens **56,** 15
Trust Territory **87,** 566, 567, 571-4
appropriation of Treasury funds, standing to challenge **94,** 129-33
civil rights, protection of **56,** 22
corporation and **60,** 138
declaration of war, power of **42,** 393-401
denial of passport **38,** 100-11
due process. *See* Fifth Amendment *above and* due process *below*
excludable alien **87,** 449-50
extraterritorial legislation **82,** 351, 353, 355 n. 24, **121,** 633

United States of America (USA) (*cont.*)
fair trial **60,** 39, 42-4, 49
federalism **81,** 576
foreign agent's rights **82,** 308-10
foreign power and **82,** 308-9
foreign relations under **42,** 395, **43,** 17, 198-211, **53,** 20-2, 23, **56,** 7, **72,** 143-50, 277-92, 657-8, **77,** 212, 251
President's powers **42,** 201, **44,** 279
fundamental rights and freedoms **60,** 16, 20-3
speedy trial **70,** 197-9, 203
immigration, quota system **42,** 246
international law **56,** 240, **77,** 174, **84,** 150, **121,** 515, 532-5
interpretation **37,** 497
context at time of drafting **121,** 508
as a whole **82,** 308
jurisdictional questions under **86,** 41
Just Compensation Clause
direct and substantial government involvement, need for **95,** 620–3
extraterritorial **95,** 620
liberty, right to travel **43,** 128
non-resident aliens **42,** 202, **56,** 231-2
protection of property **56,** 333, 334, 526, 540, 541-2
search and seizure on the high seas **91,** 472
separation of powers. *See* separation of powers *below*
sequestration of alien's assets **42,** 198-205
standing **99,** 173-4
supremacy of **60,** 42-3, 47
Supremacy Clause **77,** 173
treaties **42,** 437, **56,** 543, **81,** 576, **121,** 533-5
violation of
Potsdam Agreement (1945), whether **56,** 543
power to decide **56,** 23
war, power to declare **56,** 22-3
constitutionality
court's obligation to seek to sustain **82,** 298
locus standi, threat of persecution, need for **82,** 306
standing **82,** 305-6
personal stake, need for **82,** 306-7, **94,** 123-31
constructive trust, equity, principle of **81,** 592-3
consular access, Vienna Convention on Consular Relations (1963). *See* Vienna Convention on Consular Relations (1963) *below*
consular agent **61,** 583-4, 598-600
acts attributable to sending State, Foreign Sovereign Immunities Act (FSIA) and **99,** 125
diplomatic agent distinguished. *See* diplomatic privileges and immunities, consular distinguished *below*
functions **99,** 123-4
bilateral agreement **101,** 469-70
'in accordance with the laws of the receiving State' **99,** 124-5
protecting interests of sending State and its nationals **99,** 123-4
representation of national in court **101,** 468-70, 479 n. 3
social, economic and political policy, grounded in **98,** 128-9

'subject to practices and procedures obtaining in receiving State' **101,** 470, 479 n. 3
Vienna Convention on Consular Relations (1963) **101,** 469-70, 479 n. 3
wrongful act **101,** 482-3, 494-5
consular archives, inviolability **61,** 555-7, 559-60
consular immunity, jurisdiction, official acts **56,** 530
consular premises
immunity, local rates **53,** 545-9
inviolability **61,** 448-60, **107,** 240-2
consular privileges and immunities
functional **99,** 123
responsibility for determining whether **99,** 123
wrongful act **101,** 481-2, 493-5
Vienna Convention on Consular Relations (1963) **99,** 123-5
bilateral agreement, precedence **101,** 373, 480
consulate
'mission', whether **107,** 240-1
'organ of foreign State or political subdivision thereof' **101,** 482, 489
contiguous zone
customs protection **91,** 524-6
jurisdiction, Territorial Sea and Contiguous Zone Convention (1958) **91,** 515
continental shelf claims **71,** 105-6, 108-9
contract
agency by estoppel **87,** 639
applicable law
place of conclusion **94,** 142
place of performance **94,** 142
choice of law clause **87,** 635-6
depecage **87,** 636
duty to respect **101,** 557-61
fraudulent misrepresentation **87,** 636-9, 643-5
interpretation, reconciliation of conflicting clauses **87,** 543-4
mistake **87,** 640
State contract. *See* State contract *below*
substitute **63,** 156-7
unilateral **37,** 67
contract, interpretation
aids, context **107,** 216
guidelines
clear language **107,** 216
consistency with applicable law **107,** 208, 218
corporation
debts, liability for
enforceability of award **96,** 17
fraudulent intent **96,** 16-17
jurisdiction over, non-resident **63,** 42-5, 50, 117, **73,** 579–80
overseas investments
compensation for loss of **56,** 297-8, 299, 301-5, 327-8
protection of **59,** 313, 383-8, 391-400, 412-14, 423-4
piercing the corporate veil **80,** 578, 581, **81,** 501, **96,** 16-17
agency or instrumentality of a foreign State **107,** 240
comity **103,** 500

United States of America (USA) (*cont.*)
correspondence
foreign and domestic distinguished **56,** 236-7, 239-42
non-mailability, determination of **56,** 238-42
Postmaster General, powers **56,** 238-9, 240-2
transport of, constitutional protection in respect of US nationals **56,** 241
costs, equitable **92,** 478
counterclaim against foreign State
as act of State **66,** 50-7, 75-8, 91, 104-24, 137-42, 212-45, 408-12, 427-33, 449, 458-9
security, need for, US and non-US actions compared **63,** 417-18
countermeasures **61,** 542-4
lawfulness of **61,** 569-70, 589, 593-5
treaties and **61,** 550-4, 576-9
Court of Claims
jurisdiction **72,** 151, 291-2
transfer of case to **81,** 551
courts, municipal. *See also* foreign relations, responsibility for *and* separation of powers *below*
acts of foreign State. *See* act of State *above*
competence, foreign law **79,** 576-8
consolidated actions **66,** 243
counterclaims, 'opposing party' requirement **66,** 431-3
Court of Military Appeals **60,** 652-5
decisions of, recourse to by UK courts **79,** 669, 674–5
diplomatic objectives, determination of **57,** 157
district, original jurisdiction **63,** 75
diversity jurisdiction **42,** 150, **77,** 204, 211-15
equitable discretion **87,** 662, 669, 675-9, 691-2
executive, relationship with. *See* foreign relations, executive and courts, relationship *below*
expropriation and **61,** 49-51, 60-2, 75-7
extradition, role **90,** 685
extraterritorial powers **81,** 649
foreign currency debts, conversion rules **66,** 471-3
foreign judgments and **60,** 37-9, 44-6
foreign legislation, interpretation **66,** 189-91, 257-63, 266-7, 323-4, 465-6
foreign policy and **63,** 17, 112, 332, 506, 510-11
Foreign Sovereign Immunities Act (FSIA) 1976. *See* Foreign Sovereign Immunities Act *below*
foreign State in, encouragement **92,** 429-30
in pari delicto **66,** 203
international organization, jurisdiction over **63,** 92–5, 162-3
international tribunals and **77,** 203
jurisdiction **42,** 27-8, **56,** 225, 227. *See also* jurisdiction *below*
28 USC 1331. *See* Foreign Sovereign Immunities Act (FSIA) 1976/82, 28 USC 1331 (federal jurisdiction) *below*
28 USC 1343(3) **95,** 488
42 USC 1983 **95,** 488
Immigration and Nationality Act **95,** 489
international boundary disputes **57,** 21
Trust Territories, appeal from **87,** 569-70
laches **61,** 55-6, **66,** 83

letters rogatory **57,** 167-8
military occupation, basis **81,** 512-13
missing parties **66,** 180
non-residents, comity and **81,** 571
political protest, forum for **80,** 23-4
political question doctrine **56,** 23, 24
powers **56,** 22, **57,** 167-8
presentation of case **87,** 554
procedures **80,** 21 n. 2
protest, forum for **87,** 682
standing **87,** 662, 670, 690-1, 699 n. 1
recognition and **61,** 50-1, 60-1, 64-5
remedies **57,** 24-5
standing
agent **66,** 321-2
attorney **66,** 464-7
capacity distinguished **107,** 418-19
confiscated business, former owners **66,** 94-8, 254-5, 354
consul **101,** 468-70
corporation, foreign **66,** 93, 97-101
foreign State **63,** 106-20, 294, 298, 395, **66,** 110
international organization, bankruptcy proceedings **107,** 416-18
principal **66,** 321-2
shareholder **66,** 354
treaty enforcement **90,** 658
treaty rights **90,** 683-5
undisclosed principal **107,** 266-7
supervisory powers **90,** 666, 686
war crimes, competence to determine **56,** 583
Criminal Code. *See* United States of America (USA), law of, National Security Act
criminal procedure
conspiracy **91,** 480-5
evidence, sufficiency **91,** 480, 486
foreign judges, cross-examination of fugitives by **71,** 222-6
instruction to the jury **91,** 506-7
Jencks Act **91,** 505-6
procedural default **118,** 5, 6, 27-9, 33-4, 36, 40, 41
voire dire **91,** 504-5, 507-8
critical date
cause of action **94,** 173-4, 194-7
date arising **94,** 173-7
State immunity, jurisdiction, treaty exception **107,** 388
unreasonable delay **94,** 174-7
Cuba
cessation of trade with **42,** 42
nationals claims against **42,** 204
sanctions and **61,** 657
travel restrictions **43,** 126-30
Custodian of Enemy Property **54,** 572
customary international law **79,** 401-3, 411
asylum
international conflict, flight from **95,** 567
jus cogens/peremptory norm, absence **95,** 567

United States of America (USA) (*cont.*)
enforceability **79,** 402
evidence of **79,** 411
statement of international official **95,** 567
treaty reflecting **95,** 567
UN Declarations **77,** 177
extradition, motivation of requesting State **104,** 115
judicially measurable and manageable standards, as source of **99,** 67
municipal law and, due process rules **104,** 92
President's authority to override **95,** 378 n. 34
private action in tort, basis for **99,** 65-7
private acts, application to **80,** 590-1
requirements
jus cogens. See jus cogens/peremptory norm *below*
persistent objector rule **103,** 471
torture **103,** 472-5
customary international law, treaties and other international instruments reflecting
evidence of **95,** 567
Geneva Convention on the Protection of Civilian Persons in Time of War (1949) **95,** 567
UN Charter **103,** 476
Universal Declaration of Human Rights (1948) **103,** 475
customs
19 CFR **81,** 657
customs waters **91,** 526 n. 28
distinguished foreign visitor for purposes of **81,** 657
damages **84,** 139
for genocide **107,** 460
for injury to feelings (solatium) **121,** 647-50
interest **84,** 139
for pain and suffering **121,** 646-7
punitive
Civil Liability for Acts of State Sponsored Terrorism Act 1996 **121,** 614, 645, 650-2
extra-judicial killing **121,** 616-17
Foreign Sovereign Immunities Act (FSIA) 1976 and. *See* Foreign Sovereign Immunities Act (FSIA) 1976/82, 28 USC 1606 (State liability: exclusion of punitive damages) *below*
genocide **107,** 460
purpose **121,** 614-16
State-sponsored terrorism **121,** 614-18, 643-5, 650-2
torture **121,** 615-16
treble damages action. *See* law of, Antitrust (Clayton) Act 1914 *and* Antitrust (Sherman) Act 1890 *above*
for State-sponsored terrorism
compensatory **121,** 613-14, 645-50
liability of foreign State **121,** 643-5
liability of officials acting within scope of functions **121,** 644
punitive **121,** 614-18, 643-5, 650-2
for suffering of hostages **81,** 545
date *a quo*, statutory limitation **108,** 499-502
death penalty
habeas corpus proceedings **118,** 26-37
Washington, Revised Code **124,** 308, 315

wrongful conviction and **124,** 331-4
debt
attachment of assets of public corporation **87,** 242-56
confiscation, act of State doctrine and **87,** 512
enforcement jurisdiction **87,** 514
situs, relevance **87,** 514, 517-18
expropriation/nationalization **92,** 410-11
act of State and **92,** 411
obligation of original debtor to repay **92,** 410-11
seizure of assets, creditors' rights and **81,** 538
situs **81,** 535, 536-7, **87,** 511-19, **92,** 410-11
creditor's presence **87,** 516-17
currency of loan **92,** 410
domicile of debtor **94,** 151 n. 17, 193 n. 17
enforcement jurisdiction **87,** 514, 517-18
jurisdiction over debtor **107,** 212
liability for, piercing the corporate veil **96,** 16-17
location of borrowers **92,** 410
multiple **87,** 513, 515, 518
place of loan **92,** 410
place where deposit held **107,** 212 n. 5
power to collect **92,** 475
State immunity and **103,** 544-6
declaratory judgment, as *res judicata* **81,** 550-1
declaratory relief **81,** 545
defamation **88,** 106-9, 116-61
applicable law **88,** 166
government official, of **88,** 126-9
Head of State **88,** 164-5
libel-proof defence **88,** 109-13
official report privileges **88,** 166-75
applicability to foreign governments **88,** 166-75
special damages, relevance **88,** 113-15
default judgment against foreign State. *See also* Foreign Sovereign Immunities Act (FSIA) 1976/82, 28 USC 1608(e) (default judgment) *below*
burden of proof **63,** 382, 389
foreign relations and **84,** 144
defence expenditure, taxation, France, agreement with **48,** 213-14
Department of State. *See* State department *below*
deportation **54,** 251-7, **79,** 379-82, 428 n. 11. *See also* asylum *above*; deportation, with-hold/bar; exclusion of alien *and* extradition *below*
appeal **79,** 603-9, **88,** 5-36
scope **79,** 606-7
deportability, illegal entry **87,** 480, 491
discretion **104,** 84
to country of citizenship **104,** 83
due process violation, whether **104,** 83
forcible abduction **104,** 64 n. 4
imprecise term **87,** 475
judicial review **87,** 482 n. 8. *See also* appeal *above*
nature **79,** 381
punishment, whether **79,** 381
political nature of decision **88,** 28

United States of America (USA) (*cont.*)
procedure **87,** 481
withhold. *See* deportation withhold/bar, grounds *below*
deportation withhold/bar **87,** 464-77, 479-88
asylum distinguished **87,** 475-7, 481, 482, 496, **95,** 549, 558-9, 581, 582 n. 11
eligibility, need for **95,** 574
burden of proof **95,** 572, 574
clear probability **87,** 496
objective test **87,** 499
deportation to specific country **95,** 549, 581, 604 n. 8
extended voluntary departure **95,** 568
grounds
compelling reasons of national security **79,** 605
persecution **79,** 380, 381, 502, 605-9
persecution by government or by group government unable to control **79,** 605, 607-9
persecution for political beliefs **79,** 605
persecution, well-founded fear **87,** 473, 483-8
threat to life or freedom **79,** 502 n. 8, 505 n. 11, **87,** 472, 496, 499
Mandatory **95,** 543, 549, 558
refugees **79,** 612-20, 623-9, 632-9
standard of proof **87,** 472
detainees, rights, legal representation **87,** 578-83
diplomatic agent
conduct in foreign countries **56,** 520-1
ranking, sending State, responsibility of **99,** 116
special envoy, as head of Mission **99,** 116
status
determination responsibility of executive **113,** 531-2
diplomatic licence plates, relevance **99,** 111
diplomatic passport, relevance **99,** 110, 166
diplomatic visa, relevance **99,** 111, 112 n. 19, 166-7
evidence of, diplomatic lists **99,** 111
executive certificate, conclusiveness **99,** 116
receiving State's right to refuse **99,** 106-12
training, State's duty **107,** 222, 223-4
diplomatic archives, inviolability **61,** 526, 557
diplomatic immunity, jurisdiction **42,** 393
employment of domestic staff **107,** 453-6
diplomatic immunity, jurisdiction, waiver **84,** 168, 178-9, **88,** 40
express **81,** 602
institution of legal proceedings **99,** 116-17
need to know of status **99,** 116-17
diplomatic mission
capital, location in as requirement **99,** 108
commercial/trade representation/mission, status as, jurisdictional nexus **103,** 568
diplomatic premises distinguished **99,** 107-9
functions/'diplomatic activity'
campaign to embarrass government friendly to host State **57,** 154-9
export promotion **98,** 59-60
head of mission. *See* ambassador/head of mission *above*
size, receiving State's right to determine **99,** 112

diplomatic premises
definition
residence of member of mission **98,** 10
'used for purposes of maintaining a diplomatic or consular mission'. *See* 'used for purposes of maintaining a diplomatic or consular mission' *below*
duties of host government
dignity interest **121,** 535-8
implementing legislation, constitutionality **121,** 506-66
security interest **121,** 535, 540-3
duty of host government to prevent any disturbance of the peace of the mission or impairment of its dignity
foreign relations considerations **121,** 504-5, 506-9
freedom of expression and **60,** 385-6, **101,** 243-54, 256, 257, **121,** 503-63
measures necessary to meet obligation, executive statement, conclusiveness **121,** 511-12
protection of local government and political figures distinguished **121,** 513
immunity, taxation **57,** 336, **98,** 3-12
inviolability **61,** 525-6, 556-9, 583-4
extraterritoriality distinguished **90,** 591 n. 9
seizure, lawfulness **61,** 560-4
'used for purposes of maintaining a diplomatic or consular mission', burden of proof **98,** 12
diplomatic privileges and immunities **56,** 519-21, 525, **61,** 525, 538-40, 543-4, 555-9, 561-4, 569-70
abuse of **56,** 520-3
accreditation/presentation of credentials and **99,** 165
basis
efficient performance of diplomatic functions **107,** 455
foreign relations considerations **107,** 456, **121,** 507
protection of own diplomats abroad **107,** 456
consular distinguished **53,** 549-50, **99,** 109
discretionary **84,** 173
duty-free importation **56,** 519-23
family members, as employees of embassy **121,** 483-4
FSIA and **99,** 198, **103,** 589-90
functional **99,** 115
historical development **84,** 142, 150-2, 169-71
Judiciary Act 1789 **77,** 243-4
presumption of **84,** 167, 169, 191
property, immunity of. *See* embassy or consular bank account/funds, immunity, execution/attachment *below*
property taxation **72,** 654-62
purpose **72,** 656
receiving State, agreement, need for **88,** 40
recognition of sending State, need for **88,** 40
regulations **56,** 520-4
restrictive **84,** 171, 172
State, beneficiary, whether **98,** 6, **99,** 120
State immunity distinguished **89,** 363
diplomatic privileges and immunities, entitlement
commercial/trade representation/mission **99,** 103-12
diplomatic status granted after commencement of suit **99,** 114-16

United States of America (USA) (*cont.*)
Head of State **99,** 165-7
international organizations, privileges and immunities, benchmark, Member State representatives and missions **99,** 141-3
location of office in mission premises, relevance **99,** 109-10
membership of diplomatic mission, need for **99,** 105-11
special advisor to special mission **121,** 600-2
termination of diplomatic status, relevance **99,** 109-10, 119-21
diplomatic protection
disposal of private claims **90,** 588, 589
national other than diplomatic agent under death penalty **118,** 54
victim of Holocaust **103,** 600 n. 3, 614
diplomatic relations
executive responsibility for establishing **82,** 333-4
as nexus required for jurisdiction **121,** 640-1
diplomatic representations, US shareholders in foreign companies **46,** 184-5, 350-3, 372
diplomatic status, evidence of/requirements, special mission, member **121,** 599-602
disappearances **104,** 185
disclosure of documents, CIA involvement, relating to **107,** 441
displaced persons
burden of proof **95,** 508, 512, 522, 528-9
definition, International Refugee Organization, Constitution (1946) **95,** 508
determination of status **95,** 508-9
non-eligibility
assisting enemy in persecuting civilians **95,** 508
burden of proof **95,** 512, 522, 528-9
evidence of **95,** 510-12
involuntarily assisting enemy forces **95,** 530-5
voluntarily assisting enemy forces in operations **95,** 508
District of Columbia Code **86,** 96
long-arm provision, 'doing business in' **63,** 212-13, 324-5, 401
Section 22-1115
'congregation' clause **121,** 503, 521-2, 527-8, 538-41, 547-50, 552, 560-3
constitutionality **121,** 502-66
'display of placard' clause **121,** 503, 518-20, 527-8, 551-60, 563, 566
diversity jurisdiction. *See* Foreign Sovereign Immunities Act (FSIA) 1976/82, 28 USC 1332(diversity jurisdiction) *below*
double criminality **79,** 390-1, 392, 426-7, 495, 510, 542-3
determination, extradition court **104,** 48
equivalent act or omission, 'substantially analogous' **104,** 48
jurisdiction, relevance **104,** 5-6
need for **104,** 20
State of arrest **79,** 426
double jeopardy **79,** 419 n. 7
drug-trafficking, jurisdiction, obligation to exercise **99,** 157
due process **61,** 194-8, **79,** 389, **84,** 102, 112, **86,** 100, **88,** 38, **90,** 652, 655-7
customary international law **104,** 92
deportation and **104,** 83
evidence of
official international bodies and **88,** 11, 21-2, 31
role of foreign armed forces **88,** 10-12
foreign naval deserters, arrest **42,** 232-8
foreign State's entitlement **107,** 341-2, **121,** 576, 597-9, 637-9

forum conveniens and **84,** 102-3
recognition of judgments not resulting from **79,** 411
duress
business compulsion **56,** 526-7, **63,** 157-8, 168
EEZ, establishment of **71,** 110, 121, 194
maritime boundary delimitation, effect on **71,** 194
effective remedy, need for **104,** 178
elections, non-intervention of military **82,** 339
embassy or consular bank account/funds, immunity, execution/attachment **89,** 362-6
mission to international organization **99,** 141-3
segregation, need for, whether **89,** 363
Vienna Convention on Diplomatic Relations (1961) **89,** 363
embassy of, territorial jurisdiction, whether within **81,** 548-9
eminent domain/*dominium eminens* **84,** 91, 197
employment contract, locally engaged staff, commercial/trade representation/mission
State immunity, jurisdiction **98,** 57-61
main terms as determining factor **98,** 59
nationality of employee, relevance **98,** 60 n. 7
employment contract, locally engaged staff, diplomatic mission, applicable law **116,** 674
enemy, definition **54,** 602-3
enemy property
confiscation, restrictions on **92,** 478
freezing/blocking, government's constitutional powers **42,** 198-205
sequestration of assets **42,** 198-205
environmental impact assessment (EIA), need for
activity on high seas **100,** 497, 501-3
activity within foreign jurisdiction **100,** 497-508
alternatives, need to consider **100,** 503–5
Antarctic Treaty, Protocol on Environmental Protection (1991), relevance **100,** 527-8
Antarctica, in relation to **100,** 523, 525-30
supplementary statement, need for **100,** 505
equitable discretion. *See* courts, municipal, equitable discretion *above*
equity **80,** 568, 578, 581
clean hands doctrine **66,** 84-5, **81,** 570, 576
failure to do **84,** 154-5
force majeure, in case of **107,** 212
escheatment **92,** 476-7
estoppel **79,** 382-3, 411-12, 598
agency, in case of reasonable belief in authorization **66,** 72-4, 131-2, 179
collateral, requirements **66,** 72-4, 131-2, 179, **72,** 660-2
international law and municipal law, effect in distinguished **91,** 423
statutory limitation **103,** 550
Eurocontrol, nexus **107,** 345-6
evidence **79,** 391-2, 395, 449-50, 453
admissibility **79,** 390, 434-5, 539-40
audiotape **107,** 439-40
hearsay **107,** 438
disclosure of documents. *See* disclosure of documents *above*
illegally acquired, effect **91,** 475
late presentation **107,** 437-8
persecution **79,** 613, 639-41

United States of America (USA) (*cont.*)
standard of proof **79,** 392, 419, 433, 527, 539
sufficiency **91,** 536-7, **107,** 436
translated documents **79,** 390, 434
evidence of
agency or instrumentality of a foreign State, control **103,** 511-12
marriage **107,** 438-9
excludability of alien
constitutionality of conditions **82,** 333-7
executive discretion **82,** 331
justiciability **82,** 333-5
Nicaraguan Interior Minister **82,** 334
PLO Permanent Observer to UN **82,** 331, 334-6
right of **104,** 66
security, relevance **82,** 331
waiver **82,** 331, 335
widow of former Chilean president **82,** 334
exclusion of alien. *See also* deportation *and* excludability of alien *above*; expulsion of alien *below*
arbitrary detention **87,** 451-60
burden of proof **95,** 538
criminal record, for **87,** 449, **95,** 573-4
deportation distinguished **95,** 580
detention, time-limit **87,** 452
executive, power of **87,** 450-1, 452
judicial review **87,** 451
executive **61,** 447, 452-4. *See also* separation of powers *below*
Congress and **61,** 11-15, 17-18, 21, 24-6
foreign relations, conduct of. *See* foreign relations *below*
powers of **61,** 9-15, 17-18, 20, 22-6
to wage war **60,** 15
executive agreements for release of hostages, taking without just compensation, whether **81,** 545, 550
executive certificate/statement **84,** 151
binding on courts, whether **72,** 659-60
conclusiveness, diplomatic protection, measures necessary to protect **121,** 511-12
'deferential respect' **82,** 312-13
effect **57,** 151
executive discretion, foreign relations **95,** 614
executive letter **88,** 96
conclusiveness **88,** 96-7
exhaustion of local remedies
exhaustion of State remedies **95,** 501-3
extraterritorial jurisdiction, anti-terrorist legislation **104,** 147 n. 14, 178
illusory, where **92,** 477
judicial system inoperable **107,** 459-60
expatriation, voluntary act of **82,** 318
expropriation/nationalization **61,** 49-51, 60-2, 75-7
as act of State **62,** 223-4, **63,** 98-9, **66,** 11-13, 56, 112-13, 147-51, 162, 315, 322-3, 342, 345, 366-8, **79,** 573-81, 584-9, **81,** 519, **94,** 151, 193, **103,** 462-3, 469, **107,** 211-12
debt, right to repayment **87,** 512, **92,** 411

enquiry into motives for **80,** 581 n. 28
right to repayment of debt **92,** 411
wartime measures **66,** 254-5
acta jure imperii, whether **101,** 549
applicable law
expropriating State **95,** 622-3
international law **95,** 623
arbitrability **62,** 221
caveat lodged as part of divorce proceedings **103,** 452-3
compensation
actual payment, need for, whether **92,** 397
generally accepted accounting principles **56,** 297-8, 299, 301-5
injury, need for **92,** 441
legality of expropriation and **92,** 397
prompt, adequate and effective **92,** 397
creditors' interests and, direct effect, need for **92,** 439-40
debt
act of State and **87,** 512, **92,** 411
assets relating to **92,** 410-11
right to collect **92,** 410-11
extinction of claim, whether **95,** 623
extraterritorial effect, enforcement of title **94,** 193 n. 17
Fifth Amendment taking **95,** 620-3
liabilities, assumption of **92,** 436
'measure tantamount to nationalization or expropriation', regulation as **121,** 178-9
own national, taking of property, whether **92,** 490
requirements
legislation **101,** 550
non-discrimination **103,** 467-8
public purpose **103,** 467-8
revocation **79,** 538
rights and obligations, express assumption, need for **107,** 207, 210-11
State responsibility
at prompting of forum State **95,** 616-23
direct and substantial involvement, need for **95,** 620-3
valuation
going concern **92,** 409
net asset value **92,** 409-11
property within forum **92,** 477
wartime exception **66,** 254-5, **92,** 478
expropriation/nationalization, compensation, act of State and **92,** 435-6
expropriation/nationalization, legality
non-discrimination **92,** 438, 439-40
prompt payment of just compensation **92,** 397
expulsion of alien **53,** 537-8. *See also* exclusion of alien *above*
expulsion of national **104,** 188
extraditable offence
conspiracy **104,** 5-6
drugs offence
customary international law **99,** 170
Single Convention on Narcotic Drugs (1961) **99,** 170-1
fraud involving political corruption **104,** 113-14

United States of America (USA) (*cont.*)
procuring an offence **104,** 6
treaty, defined by **104,** 6
extradition **51,** 270-88, 319-28, 340-60, 372-4, **61,** 446-69, **79,** 386-547
appeal **79,** 394, 416-22, 431-8, 441-58, 484-9, 493-533. *See also* habeas corpus *and* judicial review *below*
admissibility **104,** 106, 112
Declaratory Judgment Act, proceedings under **79,** 484-9
habeas corpus proceedings as **79,** 416, 417, 421, 431, 436, 442-3, 485-6, 493-533, 539-47, **104,** 45, 81, 106, 112, **122,** 671
refiling of request **79,** 485, 488
right of, whether **79,** 462-7, 488-9, 498 n. 3, 539
scope of review **79,** 420-2, 432, 443, 498 n. 3, 502-4, 539
armed conflict, laws of, applicability to **104,** 68-76
basis, reciprocity. *See* requirements, reciprocity *below*
comity **104,** 10, 115
conditions in requesting State **104,** 94-105
assurances regarding **104,** 102-3, 108
burden of proof **104,** 100-1
responsibility for determining **104,** 108
review **104,** 94-105, 107-8
Soering **104,** 98-100
constituent States, between **90,** 675
courts, role **90,** 685
customary international law
motivation of requesting State **104,** 115
narcotics offences as extraditable offence **99,** 170
danger, exposure to and **79,** 438, 493
delay **79,** 389-90, 529
deportation distinguished **104,** 47
discretion **90,** 688 n.20, **104,** 10, 47, 84
treaty provision **104,** 78 n. 21, 96
double criminality. *See* double criminality *above*
double jeopardy, multiple extradition requests **104,** 62 n. 2, 82
equity and **79,** 421
evidence
applicable law **104,** 49
assumption of validity **104,** 76-7
burden of proof **104,** 91
coerced **104,** 77-8, 85-6
law of requested State **104,** 21
right of challenge **104,** 85
sworn or affirmed statements, need for **104,** 48, 49
uncorroborated accomplice **104,** 85
executive power **87,** 188, **96,** 109
extraditable crimes **79,** 391, 420, 426, 441-2, 446, 494
fraud **79,** 424-9
trial for other offences **79,** 392
war crimes **79,** 391, 395
fair trial, need for
additional charges **104,** 115-16
bail, right to **104,** 116

right to be adequately informed of charges **104,** 50
right to cross-examine **104,** 49-50
right to discovery **104,** 50, 116
guilt, relevance **104,** 4
judicial review. *See* judicial review *below*
habeas corpus **79,** 416, 417, 418-19, 421, 431-8, **104,** 4, **122,** 661-80. *See also* judicial review *below*
as appeal **79,** 386-95, 416, 418 n. 5, 421, 431, 436, 442-3, 463-7, 517
scope **104,** 80-2, 105-6, 117
Hong Kong. *See* Hong Kong *and* Hong Kong Special Administrative Region (HKSAR) *below*
Hong Kong Special Administrative Region (HKSAR). *See* Hong Kong Special Administrative Region (HKSAR) *below*
judicial review **79,** 436, 487
jurisdiction **79,** 387, 420, 469-74, 485 n. 3, 493, 498-502, 531
double jeopardy. *See* double jeopardy *above*
'found' in the requested State **104,** 62-4, 82-3
illegal transfer from third country for sole purpose of extradition **104,** 62-4
requesting State **104,** 37, 78 n. 21, 83-4
motivation of requesting State **104,** 114-15
executive responsibility **104,** 115
nationals
aut dedere aut punire/judicare **95,** 364
of **57,** 322, **79,** 437-8, 494-5, 530, 533, 544
nexus, need for, conspiracy **104,** 5-6
objection to
extraditing State **90,** 658
individuals **90,** 658, 671, 689
offence 'within the jurisdiction of' **79,** 543
official of deposed government **81,** 623 n. 12
political offence **104,** 38-42, 64-76, 86-94, **106,** 64-76, 86-94, 173-7. *See also* political offence *below*
double jeopardy **104,** 62 n. 2
European Convention on the Suppression of Terrorism (1977) **104,** 87
First Additional Protocol to the Geneva Conventions (1977) **104,** 87
judicial review, power to review **104,** 81
UNGA Resolution 61 (1985) **104,** 87
prima facie case **79,** 380, 391-2, 395, 419, 420, 427-8, 433, 443-6, 461, 477, 497, 527-8, 539, **104,** 20-1, 22-37, 50-1, 76-8, 84-6, 117-18, **114,** 633-8
probable cause. *See* prima facie case *above*
procedure
appeal **79,** 394, 416-22, 431-8, 441-58, 460-75
criminal procedure rules, applicability **104,** 4
defects in **79,** 418 n. 5, 434
extraditing State, determination by **90,** 660, 687-8
hearing, judicial nature **104,** 78 n. 22
hearing, purpose **104,** 4
purpose
procedural **95,** 364
protection of sovereignty **95,** 364 n. 4
requesting State, motive **79,** 428-9, 452
requirements **104,** 22, 116

United States of America (USA) (*cont.*)
charges pending in requesting State **104,** 20
extraditable offence. *See* extraditable offence *above*
extradition agreement. *See* extradition agreement *above*
non-re-extradition **114,** 642-5
probable cause. *See* prima facie case *above*
proof of identity of person **104,** 20
waiver **90,** 664, 677-8
reciprocity **104,** 40
warranty of trial according to requesting State's laws **114,** 616, 630-1
res judicata **79,** 418-20
multiple extradition requests **104,** 82
responsibility, executive **79,** 436, 447-52, 458 n. 26, 487, 493, 547, **122,** 664
review. *See* appeal *above*
speciality **79,** 391, 451, **90,** 657-9, **104,** 4, 10-11
comity **104,** 10
extension of offences, by agreement **104,** 10
fairness to individual **90,** 678, **104,** 39-40
implied treaty provision **90,** 676, 682
individual's right to raise **90,** 583, 659, 684
purpose **90,** 677-80
sovereignty, protection of **90,** 674, 678
treaty, means of enforcement **104,** 11
violation **90,** 684
waiver by requested State **104,** 10-11
State and Federal offences **48,** 188-90
statutory limitation
analogous offence **104,** 21-2
treaty provision **104,** 22
sui generis nature of proceedings **88,** 46-7
treaties
need for **79,** 487
validity, requirement of **79,** 420
treaties. *See also* extradition agreement
extradition agreement
amendment, multilateral convention, by **99,** 170
breach **90,** 652, 657-8, 661, 671, 677-8, 679-85
exclusive, whether **95,** 364, 367, 369-73
forcible abduction as **95,** 358, 360-8
jurisdiction, effect on **95,** 363-8
official act **95,** 375-7
private act **95,** 375-7
as violation of international law **95,** 366 n. 14
conditions in signatory State, relevance **104,** 96
conflict with other obligations **104,** 95-6
discretionary right to surrender, effect on **104,** 10, 78 n. 21, 96
individual's rights under **114,** 599-600
interpretation. *See also* treaty interpretation *below*
liberal **104,** 115-16
military offence **104,** 37-8
need for **88,** 46-7, **96,** 107, **104,** 10, 46-7, **122,** 664
purpose **122,** 670-1, 677
self-executing **90,** 658, **95,** 366

special provision **104,** 115-16
State succession and **96,** 107-9, **104,** 46-7
extraterritorial effect of injunction **81,** 648-9
extraterritorial legislation **56,** 56, **69,** 4–6
alien exemption clause, effect **90,** 622, 626, 634-7
aliens on high seas **95,** 581-98
amendment of Statute, relevance **95,** 589-90, 591, 607
applicability to locally engaged staff on US military base abroad **94,** 268
bribery of foreign officials **92,** 500
choice of law and **100,** 526, 598-9
comity **96,** 133-4, **100,** 586-7, 599, 601
conduct primarily in legislating State **100,** 522, 524-6
conflict of interests **100,** 585, 600
conflict with law of third State, risk **95,** 589, **100,** 587, 601
Constitution **82,** 351, 353, 355 n. 24, **121,** 633
'direct effect' in forum State **92,** 445
effect in Antarctica **100,** 522-3, 526-7
employment by US companies of US citizens abroad **90,** 621-41
enforcement abroad, right to **90,** 621
extraterritorial adjudication distinguished **100,** 597
foreign relations, relevance **95,** 598, 609-10, **100,** 497-503, 523, 524-5, 527-8, 529
human rights legislation **90,** 622-41
implied by nature of offence **94,** 88, **99,** 157-8
national abroad, jurisdiction over and **87,** 102, **100,** 541-2
offences on high seas and against law of nations **82,** 351
political question doctrine **100,** 499
'possession' and **90,** 626, 636-7
prohibited effects in legislating country **87,** 101
protective principle and **87,** 101-2, **94,** 89-91, 95-6
reasonable exercise **100,** 600-1
requirements **82,** 351, 352, **90,** 624-5, 629, 630, 631-2, 633, 634, **95,** 598, **96,** 132, 133-4, **99,** 154, 157, 159-61, **100,** 498-501, 524, 536, 539
sovereignty, intrusion on **96,** 134
substantial effects **100,** 585
Trust Territory, applicability of laws to and **96,** 27, 30-1
extraterritoriality **61,** 203, 205
embassy premises **90,** 591, 592
inviolability distinguished **90,** 591 n. 9
Head of State **103,** 585
legislation. *See* extraterritorial legislation *above*; legislation, interpretation, presumption of territorial limitation *below*
military base **90,** 592
UN Headquarters **96,** 77
fair hearing **79,** 382, 389-96, 436
right to, legal counsel **107,** 449 n.
fair trial
extradition. *See* extradition, fair trial, need for *above*
failure to distinguish between different charges **107,** 442-3
identification procedures **107,** 440-1
joinder of cases **107,** 441-2
jury trial, right to **87,** 571-4. *See also* Foreign Sovereign Immunities Act (FSIA) 1976/82, jury trial, right to and *below*
prisoners of war, fair and impartial tribunal **99,** 167-8

United States of America (USA) (*cont.*)
FCN treaties **86,** 50-3. *See also* Freedom, Commerce and Navigation Treaty, Italy–USA (1948)
property protection clauses **86,** 52-3
Federal courts, external relations powers **72,** 273-4, 655-8
federal government
emergency powers **72,** 134, 274, 280
external relations powers **72,** 273-4, 655-8
treaty-making power **72,** 655-8
Federal Rules of Appellate Procedure **87,** 682-3
Federal Rules of Civil Procedure **87,** 551, 641-2, 681-2
4 **63,** 413-14
8(a) **99,** 60, 79 n. 5
8(e) **99,** 79 n. 5
9 **86,** 106-8
12 **88,** 57, 73, 96, **101,** 475, **107,** 386
12(b) **63,** 53, **66,** 200, 272, 289, 299, 314, **82,** 298-9, **99,** 60
13(b) **66,** 426, 431
17(a) **66,** 354
19 **66,** 80
24 **78,** 677-82
36 **66,** 312-13
37 **66,** 312-13
44.1 **66,** 465-6
54 **88,** 197
54(b) **66,** 289, 477
55 **84,** 60, 141, 142-3, 152, 154, 165 n. 3, 168-9
55(c) **107,** 267-8
55(e) **107,** 266
56 **66,** 272, 312, 476-7, **88,** 73, 96
60(b) **90,** 607-10, **98,** 85-8, **99,** 134, 143, **107,** 396
81(b) **80,** 591 n. 7
joinder of parties **57,** 23-4
Federal Rules of Criminal Procedure, extradition proceedings, applicability **104,** 4
Federal Rules of Evidence
803(8) **66,** 313
901(b)(7) **66,** 313
as federal State **68,** 220, 251
Federal Tort Claims Act (FTCA) 1938/1970/1982 **63,** 441, **72,** 142-3, **80,** 21
28 USC 1136 **63,** 104
28 USC 1346(b) **96,** 57, 59, **100,** 535-6, 537–8, 540
combatant activities exception **99,** 86-9
waiver of State immunity, whether **99,** 85–6
28 USC 2402 **63,** 248
28 USC 2671 **63,** 250
28 USC 2674 **88,** 90, **96,** 59
28 USC 2680 **63,** 388, 599, **88,** 59, 90
28 USC 2680(a) (discretionary function exception) **107,** 199-200, 401
28 USC 2680(d) **99,** 89, **100,** 538
28 USC 2680(j) **99,** 86
28 USC 2680(k) **100,** 537, 538
Antarctica, application to **100,** 532-44

cause of action, whether **96,** 59-60
'foreign country' **87,** 549, **100,** 526, 537-40, 553
government's immunity from suit, retention **80,** 22 n. 7
liability of foreign State, effect on **80,** 573 n. 11
Taiwan, application to **98,** 66-7
tort, discretionary functions, arising from **84,** 99, 100-2, **96,** 60-1
waiver of State immunity, whether **80,** 22
fishing zones **71,** 92, 105-6, 110-11
Florida
Laws 1989
c 20 **87,** 203
c 27 **87,** 202-3
nuisance law, maintenance of paramilitary training camps and **80,** 594
Survivor Statute, underlying tort, need for **99,** 64
Wrongful Death Act, underlying tort, need for **99,** 64
force majeure, State contract and **63,** 166, 276
force, use of **61,** 543-4, 569-70, 577-9, 580-1, 589
forced exile. *See* expulsion of national *above*
forcible abduction/unlawful arrest **91,** 474-5, 489 n. 1, 519-20, 531
breach of international law other than of treaty **91,** 519-20
breach of OAS Charter **90,** 661 n. 16, 665-6, 680
breach of treaty **90,** 647, 661, 662, 671, 673, 680-1, **91,** 475, 519-30, **95,** 358, 360-8, **99,** 174-7, **107,** 433, **121,** 597
evidence thus acquired **91,** 475
breach of UN Charter **90,** 661 n. 16, 665-6, 680
consent or acquiescence of extraditing State **90,** 662-5, 674, 691-2. *See also* protest *below*
ex post facto **90,** 680
consent of foreign government, effect **91,** 498
deportation and **104,** 64 n. 4
domestic and international distinguished **90,** 675
due process, violation **90,** 645, 655-7, 662
'shocking to the conscience' **104,** 63, 83
expulsion as **90,** 646, 663, **104,** 62-4
extradition and **104,** 62-4
extradition agreement, relevance **121,** 597
specific prohibition of forcible abduction, need for **107,** 433, **121,** 597
foreign relations, executive responsibility **104,** 63–4
general principle of international law **90,** 677, 679–80, **95,** 366
jurisdiction, effect on **90,** 645-8, 652-67, 673, 674, **104,** 62-4, **107,** 433-46
aut dedere aut punire/judicare **95,** 364
customary international law **95,** 365, 367 n. 15, 378 n. 34
due process violation **99,** 171-4
Harvard Research Draft Convention on Jurisdiction in Respect of Crime **95,** 365, 377
jurisdiction based on subsequent event **107,** 446
speciality doctrine **95,** 363
jurisprudence
Alvarez-Machain **107,** 434-5, 445-6, **112,** 596-7
Ker v. *Illinois* **107,** 433-5
Ker-Frisbie **90,** 645, 647, 655-7, 660, 661-2, 673-7, 692, **95,** 361-2, 363, **99,** 171-4, **103,** 213, **107,** 433-5, **121,** 611

United States of America (USA) (*cont.*)
Rauscher **95,** 361, 363, 371-3, 374-5
Toscanino **107,** 434-6
Verdugo **95,** 358, 360-1, 366
jus cogens/peremptory norm, whether **107,** 435 n. 5
motivation, relevance **107,** 444-5
protest **90,** 647. *See also* consent or acquiescence of extraditing State *above*
form **90,** 688-90, **95,** 361
relevance **90,** 663-71, 673, 680-1, 683-5, 687, 693-7, **95,** 358, 366, 367 n. 15
withdrawal **90,** 690
relevant factors, torture **107,** 435-6, 444-6
remedies
dependence on subsequent treatment **104,** 63
executive responsibility **95,** 367
foreign State **91,** 500
individuals **91,** 500
return of kidnapped person **90,** 665, 671, 687–8, 693-6, **95,** 358, 361, 367-8
State practice **95,** 367 n. 15
sovereignty, breach **90,** 680
State responsibility and **90,** 645-6
territorial integrity, breach **90,** 696-7, **95,** 368, 373-5, 378 n. 34
foreign affairs. *See* foreign relations *and* political question doctrine *below*
Foreign Claims Settlement Act 1982/86, s 1641 **84,** 163
Foreign Claims Settlement Commission **56,** 332, **66,** 123, 433, 456, **72,** 285, **84,** 163, 197
calculation of compensation **83,** 625 n. 31
decisions
corporate claims **46,** 392-3
review **56,** 332, 334
international law, application of **42,** 184-5, 191
foreign commerce
foreign relations distinguished **96,** 134
responsibility for, legislature **96,** 134
foreign enlistment **82,** 318
foreign judgment, recognition/enforcement **62,** 220-5, **81,** 570, 637
exceptions, property in USA **81,** 666
federal State, in **103,** 570-1
recognition of international organization, comity **107,** 424-6
requirements **81,** 561
due process **81,** 561
legality **60,** 37, 43
personal jurisdiction **81,** 561
foreign law
applicable law, as **104,** 183
choice of law, incorporation of foreign law distinguished **96,** 79
question of law, as **94,** 164
foreign law, recognition/enforcement **78,** 601-2, 680-2, **79,** 576-8, 579, 585-9, **80,** 35, **81,** 591
confiscatory legislation **63,** 2-4
public policy and **79,** 577, 579, 580, 589
retroactive legislation **92,** 477

foreign power, official representative, agent 'controlled' or 'dominated' distinguished **82,** 309-10
foreign relations
  Administrative Procedure Act 1946, executive and courts, relationship between **63,** 28
  authority of executive **57,** 26, **61,** 9-15, 17-18, 20, 22-6, **72,** 133-50, 275-92, 655-8
    attachment of foreign assets, nullification **72,** 274-82, **75,** 157-8, 196, 199-200, 215
  conduct of. *See* responsibility for *below*
  confiscation of enemy property **54,** 543
  Congress, power to legislate **43,** 17
  default judgment, effect on **84,** 144
  enforcement in municipal courts **72,** 133-40, 655
  executive agreements, conclusion of **72,** 133-40, 143-50, 275–7, 655-8
    constitutionality **72,** 143-50, 655-7
    enforcement in municipal courts **72,** 136-40, 655-8
    settlement of claims of foreign nationals **72,** 284-9
  executive and courts, relationship **57,** 26, 77, 151, **63,** 17, 27-9, 31, 36-7, 39-40, 55-6, 239-40, 247-8
  executive discretion **95,** 614
  executive responsibility **104,** 64, **107,** 288-9
  expulsion and **104,** 63-4
    executive responsibility **104,** 64
  foreign commerce distinguished **96,** 134
  inter-State relations distinguished **98,** 8
  legislative encroachment
    Department of State Authorization Act 1985 **82,** 311-12
    National Security Act 1947 **82,** 311
    War Powers Resolution 1982 **82,** 311
  President, powers of **56,** 22, **82,** 312
  private claims against foreign State
    recognition of foreign governments **72,** 655-6
    suspension **72,** 282-9
  responsibility for **53,** 20-2, 23, 532, 545-50, **56,** 525, **57,** 26, 77, 151, **60,** 15, 19, 20-1, **61,** 7, 11-13, 22-5, 447, 452-4, 657-8, **77,** 200, 212-15, 230-4, 253-6, **79,** 487, 499-502, 557, 572, 586, 588-9, **80,** 593, 595, **81,** 635, **82,** 289, 324, 333, **87,** 700-1, **90,** 685
    Congress **82,** 312
    federal government **56,** 7, 18-19, **98,** 7-8, **121,** 509-12
  right of suit to enforce laws and policies relating to **98,** 4-5, 11-12
  state of emergency, determination of **54,** 539
  State immunity, jurisdiction and **63,** 218-20, 332, 451-2, 640-1, **107,** 357
  States' powers **42,** 6
  under Constitution **56,** 7, **72,** 143-50, 277-92, 657-8, **77,** 212, 251
Foreign Sovereign Immunities Act (FSIA) 1976/82[xii] **63,** 198, 287-8, **64,** 224, **77,** 197, 201-2, 205, 218, 226, 228, 234, 518, **79,** 594-6, **80,** 22 n. 6, 572, 584-6, **81,** 540, 545-9, 549 n. 10, 553, 554, 556, 597, 601, 661, 662-9, **84,** 109-10, 135, 139, 140-1, 143, 146, 149, 164, 190, 197, **87,** 540, 614, **88,** 72, 192, 194, **90,** 588, 606, 610, **100,** 511, 512, **101,** 474, 512, 553, **103,** 449, 453, 546, 564, **107,** 263, 264, 265-7, 268, 365, **113,** 526, **121,** 606, 624

[xii] For the text of the Foreign Sovereign Immunities Act (FSIA) 1976/82, *see* 63 *ILR* 655.

United States of America (USA) (*cont.*)
28 USC 1330 (actions against foreign States) **63,** 207, 247, 293, 339-40, 393-8, 421, 443, 513, 533, 602, **66,** 415, **72,** 136, 288, **79,** 551, 558, **81,** 553, 554, **84,** 97, 109-10, 135, 140, 146, 157, 164, 190, 203 n. 1, **86,** 69, **87,** 598, 607, **90,** 588, **92,** 422, **121,** 483
action brought by alien **63,** 393-8
legislative history **63,** 444-5, **79,** 551, 555
28 USC 1330(a) (district court jurisdiction: non-jury civil action) **63,** 75, 103-4, 174, 185, 197-8, 206-7, 240, 265-6, 288-94, 330-1, 347, 361, 364-5, 366-7, 383-4, 478-9, 489, 541-6, 558, 572, 574-8, 634, **72,** 95-8, 112, 130, 158, 177-9, 661, **77,** 263, **79,** 551, 554-5, 557, **81,** 545-9, 556, **84,** 98, 112 n. 5, 137, 172-3, **86,** 89, **87,** 540-1, 600, 653, **90,** 599, **101,** 482, 532, **103,** 439, 518 n. 13, 567, **107,** 221-2, 348, 355-6, 396, **121,** 491
'any non-jury civil action' **63,** 397
legislative history **63,** 576-7
28 USC 1330(b) (personal jurisdiction over foreign State) **62,** 222, **63,** 75, 78-80, 151, 185, 187, 266, 334-7, 361-2, 376-7, 398-9, 492, 513, 520, 544-6, 559, 564, 572, 596, 612, 621, **72,** 112, 158, 164, 180, **73,** 151, **77,** 263, **81,** 549 n. 10, **84,** 98, 102-3, 112 n. 5, **86,** 64-5, 99-101, **87,** 525, 532-3, 543 n. 4, **88,** 82, **90,** 602-3, **98,** 90-1, **103,** 445, **107,** 340, **121,** 491, 495
legislative history **63,** 207, 213, 293-4, 377, 620
28 USC 1330(c) (appearance by foreign State) **63,** 240, **121,** 483 n. 1
28 USC 1330 ff **81,** 661, **86,** 58, 68
28 USC 1331 (federal jurisdiction) **56,** 22-4, **63,** 74-7, 443-4, 578, **79,** 399, 401-3, 485 n. 3, 558, **81,** 510, 511, 512, 514, 545, 546, 550, 589, 590, 661, 665, **95,** 488-9, **99,** 65, **104,** 147-8, 159, 176 n. 11, 193-4, **107,** 450 n. 2
28 USC 1331(a) (federal question: amount in controversy) **63,** 340
28 USC 1332 (diversity jurisdiction) **72,** 129-30, **77,** 228, **79,** 399, **81,** 499, 510, 511, 545, 546, 665 n. 5, **84,** 97, 109-10, 203, 205, **87,** 601, **103,** 612, **107,** 254, 339 n. 56, 357, **113,** 526-9, 545 n. 3
text of pre-FSIA legislation **63,** 541-2
28 USC 1332(a) **63,** 103, 140, 437, 438-9, 541-3, 643-4, **87,** 540, 586, **107,** 357-8
28 USC 1332(a)(2) (citizens of a State and citizens of a foreign State) **63,** 59, 102-3, 176, 246-9, 301, 331-2, 335, 364-5, 367, 438-9, 442-5, 543-5, 640, 642-4, **81,** 499, 545-7, **86,** 98-9, **87,** 542, 544-5, 600, 647-57, **90,** 607, **92,** 483, **108,** 496, **113,** 518
actions between aliens **63,** 102-3, 176, 574-83, **79,** 554-5, **88,** 81 n. 3, **94,** 150, **98,** 19 n. 6, **113,** 518
'citizen of a State' **63,** 443, **86,** 99
critical date **98,** 143
28 USC 1332(a)(3) (citizens of different States and of foreign States as additional parties) **99,** 79
28 USC 1332(a)(4) (foreign State as plaintiff) **63,** 112, 331, **107,** 413-15
28 USC 1332(c) ('corporation') **63,** 90, 177, 367, 368, 448
28 USC 1332(d) ('citizen of a state of the US') **63,** 367, 368
28 USC 1441(a) **63,** 639-40
28 USC 1441(d) (foreign State: removal of civil action to federal court) **63,** 74-6, 124, 177-8, 179, 332, 364, 368-9, 397-8, 444 n. 9, 468-73, 542-3, 544-6, 577, 639-40, 642, 644, **72,** 96-7, **79,** 554, **84,** 97, 111 n. 3, **87,** 540, 544-5, 598, 600, 607, 647, 653, **107,** 356
doing business as waiver of right **63,** 177-8

28 USC 1602 (findings and declaration of purpose) **63,** 75, 167, 171, 174, 179, 219, 257, 303, 367, 384, 437, 500, 501, 542, 561, **66,** 415, **72,** 112, 288, **77,** 262-3, **81,** 501, 554, 602, 603-4, 665, **87,** 609, **103,** 474, 614, **107,** 362, **119,** 58
28 USC 1603(a) ('foreign State') **62,** 222, **63,** 103, 124, 129-30, 174-6, 220, 234, 240, 247, 266, 314-15, 321, 331, 337, 352, 364-5, 367-8, 438, 542-3, 576, 616-17, 643-4, **72,** 96, 113, 158, 185, 187-8, **87,** 525 n. 7, 540, 647-8, 653, **98,** 52-3, **101,** 504, **103,** 449, 523, 539, **107,** 229, 230, 263, 324, 375, 376, 414
legislative history **63,** 103
28 USC 1603(b) ('agency or instrumentality') **63,** 90, 130, 174–6, 213, 234, 266, 278, 302, 309, 321, 331, 347, 364, 368, 438, 439, 454, 460, 514, 542-3, 576, 587, 606, 616, **72,** 96, 185-6, **87,** 525 n. 7, 540, **90,** 601, **101,** 546, **103,** 449, 468, 564, **104,** 175, **107,** 230, 247, 254, 263, 312, 316, 324-7, 375, 376, 414. *See also* agency or instrumentality of foreign State *above*
legislative history **63,** 175-6, 187, 651-2
28 USC 1603(b)(1) ('separate legal personality, corporate or otherwise') **63,** 103, 130, 167, 176, **107,** 312, 316-17
28 USC 1603(b)(2) ('organ of foreign State or political subdivision . . . or majority of shares or ownership interest owned by') **63,** 167, 174-6, 302, 334, 437, **81,** 540, **84,** 111, **88,** 82, **98,** 53, 120-2, 132, **103,** 509-10, **107,** 375, 376-8
28 USC 1603(b)(3) ('neither citizen of US nor created under laws of third country') **63,** 448, 651
28 USC 1603(c) ('United States') **63,** 602, **72,** 136, 141-2, **81,** 547, **87,** 548-9, **90,** 589, 590-3, **113,** 541
28 USC 1603(d) ('commercial activity' determined by nature of act) **63,** 90, 133-4, 154, 205, 229-31, 240-1, 266-7, 290, 343-4, 361, 422, 462, 473, 521, 530, 532, 558-9, 571, 588, 590, 609-10, 616-17, **64,** 234-5, **66,** 416, **72,** 107, 199, **79,** 568, **80,** 585, **81,** 555, **84,** 113 n. 6, 114 n. 7, 138, **86,** 71, 80, 91 n. 4, 93-4, **87,** 525 n. 10, 532, **88,** 83, 85, 195, 197, **89,** 364, **92,** 426, 427, 428, **98,** 122, **100,** 513, 515-16, 517, 558-9, **101,** 491-2, 503, 512-13, 515-16, **103,** 451-2, 464-5, 513, 514-15, 544, 607-8, **107,** 198, 265, 299-301, 329-30, 397, **121,** 492-4
diplomatic mission, expenses **63,** 526-7, **65,** 236
legislative history **63,** 154-5, 290, 526-7, 560-1, 588-9, 627
'regular course of commercial conduct' **63,** 133-4, 240-1, 292, 343-4, 398, 399-402, 449 n. 4, 521-2, 559, 610-12, **73,** 532, **98,** 18, 146
28 USC 1603(e) ('commercial activity carried on in the US by foreign State having substantial contact with US') **63,** 241, 267, 295, 360-2, 473, 521, 596, 617-18, **87,** 525 n. 10, 532, **88,** 195, **92,** 465-6, **98,** 18, 34-5, 115-17, **103,** 440
28 USC 1604 (immunity of foreign State from jurisdiction) **63,** 220, 309, 314, 352, 356, 384, 448, 473, 489, 490, 515, 533, 587, 603, **72,** 105, 112, 159, 177, 199, **77,** 263, **81,** 540, 547, 663, **84,** 90, **86,** 89, 91 n. 4, **87,** 525 n. 8, 609, 616, 683, **90,** 589, 611, **92,** 397-8, **101,** 551-2, **103,** 439, 445, 475-6, 524, 607, 611, **107,** 222, 235, 324, 374, 375, 387-9, **119,** 205, **121,** 483, 491
'existing international agreements' **63,** 606, 608, **77,** 266-7
28 USC 1605(a) (exceptions) **63,** 183, 205, 219, 336, **72,** 661-2, **79,** 5, **86,** 80, **107,** 374
waiver/nexus relationship **63,** 406-7, **79,** 555 n. 15
28 USC 1605(a)(1) (waiver) **62,** 222, **63,** 198, 303-4, 315, 321, 349, 352, 356, 421-2, 515, 537-8, 606-7, **72,** 127, 159-63, 178-9, **77,** 263, 267-8, **86,** 61-2, 69-70, 73-5, **87,** 540-1, 542, 543 n. 4, 609-10, 635, **89,** 358, **92,** 416, 488-90, **98,** 13, 17, 18-20, 32-4, 114, **101,** 474, 490, 543-5, 552, **103,** 451, 476-8, 496-500, 508, 539-41, 565-7, 607, 609-11, 615-21, **107,** 339 n. 57, 358, 380-1, 390-2, **113,** 537-40, 546-8. *See also* State immunity, jurisdiction, waiver *below*

United States of America (USA) (*cont.*)
legislative history **63,** 198, 321, 406-7, 422, 537-8
28 USC 1605(a)(2) (commercial activity exception) **63,** 132-4, 151-2, 180, 183-90, 205-6, 229-31, 234, 240-3, 266-7, 287, 289-90, 324-8, 352-3, 360, 422, 449-52, 489-92, 516, 522, 538-9, 559-64, 587-95, 608-12, 617-20, 626, 627-8, 629-32, **65,** 173, **72,** 96-7, 112-14, 163-71, 179, 199, 518 n . 2, **81,** 554-5, 667-8, **84,** 111-17, 157, 191-3, **86,** 59-61, 70-2, 78, 89-98, **87,** 525-30, 531-6, 542 n. 3, 549, **88,** 72, 82, 83, 194, 196, 197, **90,** 594-5, **92,** 378-80, 395-6, 427, 445-7, 451-4, 457-61, **98,** 35-6, 45-7, 75, 82-3, 88-9, 96-7, 100, 115, 132-3, 145-6, **100,** 513, 517, 547, 549, 550-2, 563-6, **101,** 491-2, 502-3, 512-18, 549-51, **103,** 439, 451-2, 464-7, 485, 488, 512-13, 515-18, 543, 607, **107,** 198, 227, 230-1, 235, 249-51, 265, 268, 299-302, 327-8, 334-8, 339 n. 57, 349, 368-70, 378, 389, 396-7, 403, **113,** 528, 548-9, **121,** 494 n. 6
'act performed in the United States in connection with a commercial activity of the foreign State elsewhere' **63,** 618-19, **92,** 378-80, **100,** 550-1, **103,** 441-2
Bahamian subsidiary of US firm, contractual rights **63,** 233-5, 242, 465
'carried on in the United States' **63,** 399-402, 609-10, 618
continuous and systematic/enduring relationship, need for **63,** 241, 322-3
legislative history **63,** 168, 206, 324-7, 402-3, 518, 520-1, 522, 588, 618-19
receipt of repudiation of letter of credit **63,** 402
'that causes a direct effect in the United States' **63,** 133, 168-9, 182-6, 212-14, 240-4, 295, 324, 356, 377, 402-8, 459, 462-6, 489-92, 496, 522-4, 538-9, 562-4, 598, 619-20, 637-8, **72,** 169-71, 179, **79,** 560, **86,** 59, 63-4, 72, **92,** 445-7, **107,** 229, 230-2, 234-7, 251 n. 26, 265, 334-8
28 USC 1605(a)(3) (taking of property exception) **63,** 603, **65,** 16, **72,** 127-8, **79,** 554, **81,** 663, **84,** 89-90, 193, **87,** 523, 530, 533, **88,** 81, 87, 92, **90,** 599-600, 602, **92,** 397, 490, **101,** 503, **103,** 452-3, 467, **107,** 229, 230, 232, 247-8, **113,** 549
in violation of international law **63,** 595, **79,** 16-17, **81,** 664, 666
28 USC 1605(a)(4) (immovable property exception) **63,** 179-80, 608, **79,** 554, **84,** 88, 89, 90-4, **101,** 494, **103,** 453, **107,** 198-9
breach of planning regulations **107,** 198-9
intangible property rights **84,** 90-1
legislative history **63,** 608
28 USC 1605(a)(5) (tortious activity exception) **63,** 133, 384-8, 422-3, 595-9, 602-3, 620, **65,** 173, **72,** 114-18, 136, 140-3, **79,** 4-7, 554, 563, 566, **81,** 547-8, 550 n. 10, 554, 666, **84,** 94-5, 98-102, **88,** 81, 87, 92, **90,** 587, 589, 593-5, **98,** 128, **101,** 482-3, 494-5, 503-6, 525-6, **103,** 453, 508, 517-18, **104,** 123, **107,** 198, 199-201, 222-4, 302, 307-8, 389-90, 397, **113,** 512, 541, 549-50, **121,** 483-7, **123,** 89
legislative history **63,** 385-7
as protection against acts of persons with diplomatic immunity **121,** 483
scope of employment **63,** 422-3, **101,** 493-4
28 USC 1605(a)(5)(A) (tortious acts: act or omission in case of discretionary function) **63,** 378-9, 384, 386-8, **72,** 141-3, **84,** 99, 100-2, **90,** 589-95, **98,** 108, 128-30, **99,** 162, **101,** 494-5, 504, 532, **107,** 199-201, 222-3, 401, **113,** 512-15
planning/operations distinguished **98,** 129
28 USC 1605(a)(5)(B) (tortious acts) **63,** 231, 384, 621,**107,** 398-404
interference with contract rights **63,** 169
libel **63,** 133
public act **63,** 386-7
28 USC 1605(a)(6) (enforcement of foreign arbitral award against foreign State) **103,** 563-4, 565, **113,** 550-1

28 USC 1605(b) (admiralty jurisdiction: enforcement of maritime lien) **63,** 77-80, 215-27, 252-8, 417-18, 529-34, 624-8, 632, 640, **79,** 554, **81,** 540-2, 664-6, **99,** 85 n. 4, **100,** 538-9
'based upon' **63,** 533-4
'based upon a commercial activity of foreign State' **63,** 532-4
legislative history **63,** 222-5, 418, 531-2, 533, 629
28 USC 1605(b)(1) (notice of suit) **63,** 226-7
28 USC 1605(b)(2) (date of notice) **63,** 226-7, 629
28 USC 1605-7 **86,** 58, **87,** 531
28 USC 1606 (State liability: private person liability: exclusion of punitive damages) **63,** 79, 205-6, 236, 418, 579, **79,** 554 n. 12, 558 n. 22, **86,** 79, **101,** 526, **103,** 550, **107,** 316
28 USC 1607 (counterclaims) **63,** 612, 626, 629, 630, **72,** 95, 127, 177-9, 661, **79,** 554
28 USC 1607(b) (counterclaims: arising out of transaction ... subject matter of claim) **63,** 303, 315-16, 607-8, **98,** 17, 20-1
28 USC 1607(c) (counterclaims: relief not exceeding amount sought by foreign State) **63,** 316, 317, **92,** 396
28 USC 1608 (service; time to answer; default) **62,** 222, **63,** 411-12, 612, **72,** 112, 158, **84,** 112 n. 5, **86,** 100, **88,** 82 n. 4, **103,** 546-7, **107,** 310-17
substitute form of service and **63,** 411-16
28 USC 1608(a) (service: foreign State or political subdivision) **63,** 124-6, 179, 198, **86,** 79, **106,** 280, **107,** 311-17
by mail to embassy **63,** 136-7
legislative history **63,** 136
notice of suit **63,** 125, 136, 212-13, 222, 413-15, 513, 520
28 USC 1608(a)(1) (service: in accordance with special arrangement) **63,** 125-7
28 USC 1608(a)(2) (service: in absence of special arrangement) **63,** 125-7, 287, 631
28 USC 1608(a)(3) (service: in case of failure of other prescribed methods) **63,** 149, 179-80, 263, 264, 551, **84,** 164, **121,** 624 n. 1
translation, need for **63,** 125-6, 136
28 USC 1608(a)(3)(B) (service: registered mail) **63,** 179-80, **121,** 624 n. 1
28 USC 1608(a)(3)(C) (service: as directed by the court), 'consistent with the law of the place where service is to be made' **63,** 412-13
28 USC 1608(a)(4) (service: mail with translation for transmission through diplomatic channels) **63,** 232, 381-2, **77,** 262, **84,** 143, 165, **106,** 280
28 USC 1608(b) (service: agency or instrumentality) **63,** 125, **86,** 79, **103,** 567-8, **107,** 311-17, 363-4
28 USC 1608(b)(2) (service: agency or instrumentality: in absence of special arrangement) **63,** 278, 627, 631, **72,** 180, **107,** 363-4
28 USC 1608(b)(3) (service: agency or instrumentality: in case of failure of other prescribed methods) **106,** 280-3, **107,** 363-5
28 USC 1608(b)(3)(B) (service: agency or instrumentality: registered mail) **63,** 263, 264, 266, **86,** 89 n. 3
28 USC 1608(b)(3)(C) (service: agency or instrumentality: as directed by court in accordance with place of service) **63,** 413, **72,** 180 n. 16, **106,** 280-1
28 USC 1608(c)(1) (date of service: transmission of diplomatic note) **63,** 413
28 USC 1608(c)(2) (date of service: date of certified or signed receipt or other proof) **63,** 413-16
28 USC 1608(d) (service: time to answer) **101,** 474-5, **107,** 264
28 USC 1608(e) (default judgment) **63,** 198, 287-8, 296-7, 382-3, 389-90, 421, **84,** 143, **107,** 264, 265-7, 268, 365, **121,** 606, 624

United States of America (USA) (*cont.*)
28 USC 1609 (immunity from attachment and execution of property of foreign State) **63,** 151, 180, 222, 256-7, 267-9, 270-2, 280-1, 305-10, 334, 336, 429-30, 625, **72,** 658-60, **89,** 358, 364, **98,** 8-11
legislative history **65,** 240-1
'subject to existing international agreements' **63,** 429-31
28 USC 1610 (exceptions to immunity from attachment or execution) **84,** 140, **89,** 358
28 USC 1610(a) (immunity from attachment or execution: exceptions) **63,** 125, 256-72, 280, 336, 502, 516, 518, 521, **65,** 174, **72,** 121-3, 184-5, 188, 658-60, **81,** 541, **86,** 79, 80, **89,** 359, 364, **98,** 31-2, **107,** 240, 241-2, 316
28 USC 1610(a)(1) (waiver of immunity from execution: withdrawal of waiver) **63,** 525-6, **65,** 190, 236
28 USC 1610(a)(2) (immunity from attachment or execution: property used for commercial activity on which claim based) **65,** 184, 242-3, **79,** 564, 566-9
28 USC 1610(a)(4) (execution of judgment relating to rights in property) **98,** 9-11, 13
28 USC 1610(a)(4)(b) (diplomatic/consular premises exception) **107,** 241
legislative history **72,** 141-3, 658-9
residential property **65,** 659-60
28 USC 1610(b) (immunity from attachment or execution: agency or instrumentality) **63,** 268-9, 280, **65,** 174, **86,** 79, **92,** 489, **98,** 52-4
legislative history **63,** 125, 431-2, **79,** 564-6
28 USC 1610(b)(1) (agency or instrumentality: waiver of immunity from attachment in aid of execution/execution) **63,** 309-10
28 USC 1610(d) (immunity from attachment or execution: agency or instrumentality: exceptions) **63,** 265 n. 9, 269-70, 280, 347, 431, 502, **65,** 239, **92,** 403-5
legislative history **63,** 269-70
28 USC 1610(d)(1) (pre-judgment attachment: explicit waiver requirement) **63,** 309-10, 431-3, **72,** 121, 184-6, 189
28 USC 1611 (certain types of property immune from jurisdiction) **63,** 265, 268, 272, 336, **89,** 364 n. 4
28 USC 1611(a) (property of international organizations: immunity from attachment or impediment to disbursement to foreign State) **63,** 341-2
28 USC 1611(b)(1) (property of central bank or monetary authority held for its own account) **63,** 599, **64,** 224-5, **92,** 401-3
28 USC 1611(b)(2)(A) (property of a military character) **63,** 430
28 USC 1611(b)(2)(B) (property for use in connection with military activity under control of military authority) **63,** 265 n. 9, 272, 280-3, 429-31, 433 n. 16
act of State doctrine and **66,** 418-19, **84,** 118 n. 12
Alien Tort Claims Statute, effect on **79,** 4-7
analysis of changes to previous legislation **63,** 541-2
antitrust actions and **63,** 201-3, 205-6, 294-7
applicability
acts against nationals abroad **121,** 629
criminal proceedings **119,** 58, 73-4
individual in official capacity **101,** 501, **104,** 175, **121,** 628-9, 643-5
natural persons **98,** 107, **104,** 175
Navy **82,** 340-1
personal holding company **121,** 586
Pope **81,** 608
applicable law
international law **80,** 574
lex fori **80,** 573 n. 11

State of incorporation **80,** 573
attachment, immunity and **63,** 147
claims settlement by executive agreement and **72,** 287-9
clear basis of jurisdiction/trial by jury balance **63,** 545-6
commercial activities **66,** 416-17, **72,** 112-14, 163-71, 179, 199, 654, 658-60, **81,** 554-5, 597, 666, **84,** 115, 137-8, 191-2, **86,** 59-61, 70-1, 89-98, 634-7, **88,** 82, 83-7, **121,** 492. *See also* State immunity, jurisdiction, classification of act, *below*
commercial emphasis **79,** 13
common law, effect on **92,** 486-8
confiscation of property and **63,** 595
Constitution and **63,** 366, 444, 472, 629 n. 12, **82,** 308-9, **103,** 528
control as test of independent status
evidence of **103,** 511-12
wholly owned and controlled **107,** 239-40
counterclaim, immunity from **80,** 572, 578-80
countermeasures and **63,** 503
critical date, change of status after cause of action or institution of legal proceedings **107,** 362
critical date for determining status, date of action **98,** 143
debts, liability for each other's **98,** 54
diplomatic privileges and immunities and **99,** 198, **103,** 589-90
domestic immunity **86,** 79-80
exceptions **87,** 616
violation of *jus cogens*/peremptory norm **103,** 474
expropriation/nationalization and **63,** 595
extent of liability under **79,** 558 n. 22
extraterritorial effect **82,** 340
foreign State agencies **72,** 95, 102, 105-9, 113, 115, 118, 122, 127-8
'foreign State or political subdivision'
distinction **103,** 239-41, **107,** 311-17, 365, 377
'organ thereof' **107,** 375-8
forum [non] conveniens and **86,** 65-7, 101-6, **87,** 542, **121,** 643
foreign policy considerations **86,** 105
public interest **86,** 105
government activity, impairment of and **84,** 102-3
government department **98,** 16, 23
Head of State immunity and **103,** 589-90, **121,** 572
high seas **81,** 664, 666-8
effects doctrine **81,** 666
imputability of acts to State **107,** 233
independent cause of action, whether **63,** 578-80
independent entity **80,** 570-2, 575-8
characteristics **80,** 575-6
individual acting in official capacity **113,** 527-8
intention of legislature **63,** 21, 75-6, 80, 90, 103, 108-13, 124, 175-6, 185, 206-7, 248-51, 256, 270, 281, 291, 309, 325, 336, 349, 396-7, 418, 422, 441-2, 450, 503, 518, 520, 534, 543-8, 576, 581, 587, 599, 610, 627, 631, 642, 651
international organizations and **63,** 94-5, 163, 338-43, **107,** 414-15, **113,** 501, 505 n. 1, 519-20
interpretation **79,** 550-60. *See also* legislative history *and* phrases *below*
ambiguity **86,** 60, 70, **103,** 438
vagueness **86,** 88-9
jurisdiction over foreign State or instrumentality, as basis for **63,** 444-5, **90,** 599-602

United States of America (USA) (*cont.*)
non-national **87,** 542
personal and subject-matter, merger **63,** 513-14, 558, 559, **81,** 549 n. 9, **121,** 491 n. 3
as sole basis **63,** 220, 444-5, 644, **79,** 4-5, 12, 14, 564, **81,** 663, 668-9, **84,** 90, 169, 171, **87,** 682-3, **98,** 30, 66-7, 73-4, 114, 152-3, **103,** 445, 450, 517-18, 537-8, 589, 605, **104,** 123, **107,** 197, 230, 246-7, 264-5, 339, 357-8, 374, 396, **113,** 545, **121,** 587, 629
subject-matter **63,** 75, 214, 266, 276, 288, 289, 335, 366-7, 383-8, 391-8, 421, 478-80, 545, 557-8, 561-4, 572, 609-12, 617-21, 627, 631, 634-5, **72,** 126-31, 137-43, 154-71, 177-80, 288, **84,** 98-9, 112 n. 5, 137-8, 166, **86,** 58-61, 63-4, 69-72, 88-9, **88,** 191, 195-8, **90,** 599-602, 607, 610-11
jury trial, right to and **63,** 245-51, 363-9, 438, 439-46, 546-9, 639-46, **72,** 95-100, 102-5, 109, **107,** 354-8
legislative history **63,** 219, 281 n. 14, 282, 296, 349, 365, 396-8, 438, 560-1, 588-9, 596, **79,** 5, 7, 12-13, **82,** 339, 340-1, **84,** 91, 99, 100, 116, 171, **86,** 59-60, 61, 71, 73, 79, 634-5, **87,** 530, 531, 533-4
burden of proof **98,** 41
'commercial activity' **98,** 58, **121,** 491-3
exemption from attachment of diplomatic/consular premises **107,** 241, 242
implied waiver for *jus cogens* violations **113,** 537-40
presumption of independence of State entities **98,** 54
'substantial and foreseeable' **98,** 97 n. 2, 165
waiver **98,** 114-15
liability for acts of Government **80,** 572, 576, 578
liability of foreign State and **80,** 572
liability for obligations of controlling body **107,** 248-9
maritime torts and **63,** 533
'minimum contacts'. *See* jurisdiction, nexus *below*
national airports authority **107,** 229, 230, 233
National Labour Relations Board and **63,** 595, 651-2
nationality, relevance **63,** 650. *See also* suit by alien *below*
official newspaper **98,** 84
personal injury **72,** 140-2
personal jurisdiction. *See* 28 USC 1330(b) (personal jurisdiction over foreign State)
phrases
agency or instrumentality of a foreign State. *See* agency or instrumentality of a foreign State *above*
'based upon' **63,** 450, 532-4, **88,** 197, **98,** 133-4, 155-8, **100,** 513, 550-1, **107,** 378
'based upon an act outside the US' **63,** 450, **100,** 513
'carried on in the USA' **72,** 163-7, 179, **86,** 96-9, **87,** 525-36, **98,** 34-5, **103,** 465
'commercial activity' **88,** 84, **98,** 58, **100,** 511, 513-17, **101,** 512-16, **103,** 485, 488-9
'connected with' **86,** 92
'doing business in' **63,** 322-3, 520-1, **96,** 76-8, **98,** 145
'foreign country', critical date **87,** 603
'political subdivision' **98,** 108 n. 13
'rights in property' **88,** 87
'substantial and foreseeable' **98,** 97 n. 2, 165
'USA' **87,** 548-9
piercing the corporate veil **80,** 574, 578
pre-judgment security and **63,** 417-18

presumption of immunity **84,** 167, 169, 192, **86,** 89
property of foreign State in US, immunity from attachment or execution **80,** 573 n. 8
public acts not benefiting from immunity **84,** 90
purpose **72,** 659-60, **79,** 12, 553-4, 559, **81,** 546, **84,** 95, **87,** 531, **88,** 82, 194, **92,** 445
codification of existing law **92,** 485, **103,** 537
codification of restrictive immunity doctrine **63,** 94, 151, 184-5, 219-20, 265, 326-7, 366, 385, 418-19, 461-2, 479, 488-9, 531, 586-7, 615, 641, **77,** 263, **84,** 90, 91, 99, **86,** 78-9, **87,** 534, **98,** 83, **100,** 514, **103,** 453, 474, 605, **104,** 125, **107,** 312-13, 355, 378
comity **84,** 117, **98,** 36
comprehensive procedure **63,** 360, 365-6, 396-7, 438
district court jurisdiction in civil cases **63,** 478-9
equalization of States and other defendants **63,** 80, 519
Explanatory Statement **63,** 418-19, 531, 641
harmonization of immunity from execution and immunity from jurisdiction **63,** 220, 419, 641
non-intervention in elections **82,** 339
partial provision of remedy **98,** 54
protection of litigation rights **84,** 100
provision of remedy in case of failure to comply with judgment **63,** 489, 531, 641
replacement of *in rem*/attachment jurisdiction with due process/sovereign immunity concepts **63,** 79-80, 151, 220, 222-4, 257-8, 289, 335-7, 349-50, 419, 461-2, 489, 531, 533-4, 627, 641, **86,** 64
transfer of competence to courts ensuring uniformity of decision-taking and reduction of foreign policy implications **63,** 74-6, 90, 124, 151, 171, 219, 239-40, 265, 289, 347-8, 366-7, 385-6, 451-2, 489, 501, 531, 545, 586-7, 615, 641, **77,** 263, 265, **84,** 112, 191, **87,** 524, **103,** 438, 537, **107,** 357, **121,** 491, 596
retroactive effect **63,** 75, 129 n. 1, 151-2, 155, 213, 256-7, 302-4, 478-9, 634-5, **84,** 142, 146-8, 172, 175, 183-5, **103,** 563-4, 565, 605-7, 614-15, **107,** 268
safeguarding/conservatory measures **65,** 239-40, 242-3
service of documents **79,** 594, **86,** 89
service of process **81,** 663, **84,** 138, 143
service of process out of the jurisdiction and **63,** 411-15
shipping line **103,** 575-6
sovereignty and **87,** 601
State agencies **66,** 511-12
State corporation, in process of privatisation **103,** 575-6
State department suggestions, effect on. *See* State Department suggestions *below*
State immunity, jurisdiction
absence as jurisdictional requirement **81,** 554
liability and immunity distinguished **103,** 510
State trading enterprise **103,** 563
statute of limitations and **84,** 172, 183, 184, **92,** 376-7, **121,** 641
structure **63,** 169
successor, liability **103,** 564, 567-8
Tate letter, codification **63,** 451-2, 599, **121,** 629
test for immunity **63,** 344, 462, 588-9, 618
Treasury Department regulations and **63,** 507-8
wholly owned State corporation **98,** 30
foreign State. *See also* Foreign Sovereign Immunities Act *above*; State immunity *below*
action against
acts within own territory **103,** 476 n. 17

United States of America (USA) (*cont.*)
common law, possibility under **107,** 354-8
due process, entitlement to **107,** 341-2, **121,** 576, 597-9, 637-9
proceedings involving, 'person', foreign State as **81,** 643
forum
determination by treaty, constitutionality **81,** 576
plaintiff's choice to be respected **98,** 147-8
forum [non] conveniens **66,** 287, 319-20, **81,** 559-80, 646, **86,** 57, 64, 65-7, **87,** 531, 536, 542, **98,** 147-8
absence of alternative forum **81,** 563-4, 568, 572-3, 577-80, **104,** 163-4, **113,** 532-3
burden of proof **113,** 532-3
clean hands doctrine **81,** 570, 576, 580
conditions for rejecting plea of **118,** 457
discretionary **81,** 574, 598
equitable basis **63,** 491, **81,** 563
Foreign Sovereign Immunities Act (FSIA) 1976/82 **86,** 65-7, 101-6, **87,** 542, **121,** 643
jurisdiction presupposed **81,** 565
public interest and **86,** 66
State immunity, jurisdiction distinguished **103,** 518-19
forum selection clause **87,** 543-4
freedom of expression
flag desecration and **122,** 575-6, 598
State immunity, jurisdiction and **82,** 309, 318
freedom from discrimination
bilateral commercial treaty, employees 'of their choice' **101,** 619-23
extraterritorial legislation effect **90,** 622-41
legislation **90,** 622
treaty trader legislation **101,** 621-2
freedom of the seas **57,** 84-5
freedom of speech **82,** 331-7
FRG
Offshore Procurement Treaty **45,** 74
Treaty of Friendship (1954) **45,** 74
recognition of government **72,** 655
GATT, countervailing duties
judicial review, timeliness **107,** 291-4
material injury, relevance **107,** 281-3, 290-1
retroactive application **107,** 290-1
GATT Panels, binding on Member States, whether **107,** 285-9
GDR, diplomatic property, agreement for reciprocal tax exemption **72,** 653-62
General Claims Commission **84,** 89
general principles of international law
source of obligation, whether **90,** 666 n. 25
State immunity, restrictive theory **103,** 474
Geneva Conventions (1949)
Additional Protocol relating to the Protection of Victims of International Armed Conflicts (1977), ratification **99,** 175 n. 32
individuals and **79,** 400, **99,** 176
municipal law, part of **123,** 172
self-executing, whether **79,** 399-401, **95,** 498, **99,** 67-8, 185, 188-90
genocide

forced expulsion **104,** 187 n. 35
individual responsibility
campaign coordinated with government **107,** 459
domestic legislation **104,** 155
Genocide Convention (1948) **104,** 154-5
Nuremberg Charter (1945) **104,** 154
UNGA Resolution 96(I) **104,** 154
war crimes. *See* war crimes, responsibility, individual *below*
German assets in, Settlement of War Claims Act 1928, release under **47,** 419, 426
Germany
relations with **81,** 511 n. 3
Treaty of Berlin 1955 **37,** 545, **42,** 203-4
Treaty of Commerce 1923 **43,** 197-8, 203
US Military Government in
Court of Restitution Appeals **81,** 512
Military Law 59 (1947) **81,** 511, 512-13
war with, termination **81,** 512
government
de facto, State immunity of de jure Head of State and **103,** 585-8
immunity from suit in own courts, discretionary acts by officials **80,** 22 n. 7
State distinguished **122,** 661-3
government, change
fundamental change of circumstances, whether **96,** 67
obligations of new government **96,** 67
State succession distinguished **96,** 65, 66-7
Gulf of Aqaba, statements on (1957) **41,** 124 n.
habeas corpus **57,** 319
death penalty **118,** 26-37
Antiterrorism and Effective Death Penalty Act 1996 and **118,** 27, 29
exhaustion of State remedies **95,** 502-3, **118,** 5, 28
extradition and. *See* extradition, habeas corpus *above*
failure to inform accused of rights under Vienna Convention on Consular Relations (1963) and **118,** 29-30, 33-7
official detention, need for **95,** 490-2
territorial limitation **95,** 492
Hague Conventions (1899/1907)
individuals, rights **103,** 611
State immunity, jurisdiction **103,** 611
Hawaii, boundaries, channels between islands **42,** 101
Head of State
'agency or instrumentality of foreign State', whether **103,** 589
definition
Convention on the Prevention and Punishment of Crimes against Internationally Protected Persons (1975) **99,** 162 n. 13
customary international law **99,** 162
diplomatic privileges and immunities, entitlement **99,** 165-7
evidence of, suggestion of immunity letter **103,** 584, 586, 587
extraterritoriality **103,** 585
recognition **81,** 512
anticipated **104,** 161
breach of international law, right to challenge and **99,** 176
immunity, jurisdiction and **99,** 161-3, **103,** 585-6
responsibility, executive **99,** 161, **103,** 587, **104,** 142-3, **113,** 512, 531

United States of America (USA) (*cont.*)
Head of State, former, immunity, execution/attachment, freezing of assets **81,** 613-57
Head of State, former, immunity, jurisdiction **81,** 597-8, 601-4, 632-3, **103,** 522-30, 555-8
criminal proceedings **121,** 572
judicial assistance, Procedures for Mutual Legal Assistance Agreement (MLAA) (1986) **121,** 570, 575-6
non-objection by present government **103,** 526
official acts, *Hatch* v. *Baez* **119,** 65, 81, 235
private acts **119,** 80, **121,** 572
Restatement of Foreign Relations Law (Third) **119,** 80
unauthorized acts while in power **81,** 601, 604, 605, 606, 607
Head of State, former, immunity, jurisdiction, waiver **81,** 601, 634, **121,** 571, 573
Head of State, immunity, jurisdiction **81,** 597, **101,** 504-5
absolute **103,** 584-5, 592, **121,** 573
absolute theory, legislation, affect on **103,** 588-92
'act of production' immunity **81,** 603-4
acts outside authority **104,** 125
common law **113,** 531
corporation owned by Head of State **101,** 506-8
criminal proceedings **103,** 590-2
customary international law **81,** 601, **99,** 161, 162, **103,** 585, **121,** 571-2
de facto Head of State **99,** 162, **103,** 585-6, **121,** 595-6
diplomatic immunity and **81,** 602, **99,** 165-7
discretionary **103,** 586
family members **81,** 605-6
brother **121,** 587
rationale **81,** 607
wife **121,** 571
Foreign Sovereign Immunities Act (FSIA) 1976/82 and **103,** 589-90, **121,** 572
functional basis **81,** 605 n. 1, 627
official acts while in power **81,** 601, 632, **99,** 161, **103,** 522-30, 556, 592
recognition, relevance **99,** 161-3, **103,** 585-6, **113,** 512, 531
responsibility for determining entitlement
courts **84,** 191, **87,** 524, **103,** 438, 537, **121,** 572, 596
executive **121,** 572
legislature **121,** 572
State immunity and **103,** 590, **119,** 57
Torture Victim Protection Act and **103,** 591-2
Head of State, immunity, jurisdiction, theory/doctrine, basis, comity **103,** 585, **119,** 62, 97, **121,** 572-3, 642
Head of State, immunity, jurisdiction, waiver
by de facto government **103,** 587-8
express **102,** 203-5, **121,** 571, 572-3
by government **103,** 586-7
right to waive State and diplomatic immunity compared **121,** 572-3
by successor government **103,** 555-6
Head of State, immunity, testimonial **101,** 506-7
waiver **101,** 507
headquarters agreement, UN
common law extension **104,** 161
service of process **104,** 160-1

Hickenlooper Amendment **42,** 46-8, **62,** 221, 224, **84,** 171 n. 5, 196-8, **87,** 513-14, **88,** 73 n. 1, 87
contract rights **66,** 16-18, 32-41, 182-5, 343-5, 363-5, 368-73
international law violations **66,** 41-7, 375-6, **87,** 514
property, claim of title or right **66,** 15-19, 33-4, 38-41, 77, 140, 184-5, 363, 365, 369-73, 410, 481
property, confiscation or taking **66,** 15-19, 32-42, 52-3, 55, 69, 95-6, 139-40, 150, 161, 182-5, 343-5, 363-73, 410, 428, 479-81
territoriality and **63,** 98-9, **87,** 514, 515
high seas
definition **63,** 353
sinking of ship, whether tort **79,** 15 n. 3
high seas, jurisdiction **81,** 664, 667
customs legislation **91,** 525-7
flag State **91,** 515, 518
customary international law **91,** 524
foreign ship **91,** 470-86
conspiracy **91,** 474
effects doctrine **91,** 474
High Seas Convention (1958) **91,** 475-6
High Seas Convention (1958), limitation of, whether **91,** 524-30
national ship **91,** 474
search and seizure **91,** 470-86, 488-92
Miranda warnings **91,** 533
reasonable suspicion or probable cause **91,** 478, 490, 497, 501-2, 516-18, 519, 535-6, 538
search warrant, need for **91,** 541
stateless ship **91,** 542
stateless ship **91,** 475 n. 15, 488-92
historic waters, claims in respect of **59,** 267-9
Hong Kong, extradition. *See also* Hong Kong Special Administrative Region (HKSAR) *below*
after reversion to China **104,** 46-7, **114,** 613-49, **122,** 603-19, 661-80
United States of America (Extradition) Order 1976 **87,** 321
Hong Kong Special Administrative Region (HKSAR)
extradition
HKSAR as foreign country for purposes of US legislation **122,** 661-80
Hong Kong Extradition Agreement (1996) **122,** 667-8, 670-80
UK–US Extradition Agreement (1972), applicability **114,** 611-49
treaties
capacity to conclude **122,** 678-9
continuity **114,** 619-20, **122,** 606-7, 667
hostages in Iran, rescue mission **71,** 601-2
human rights
American Convention on Human Rights (1969) **87,** 457
freedom from discrimination. *See* freedom from discrimination *above*
freedom of speech. *See* freedom of speech *above*
international treaties **87,** 455-60
summary execution, *jus cogens*/peremptory norm **104,** 185
Universal Declaration of Human Rights (1948) **87,** 456-7
Iceland, military cargo trade **86,** 22-32
treaty regulating **86,** 23, 24-31, 32
ICJ, provisional measures, compliance, refusal **118,** 54-5

United States of America (USA) (*cont.*)
immigration. *See also* excludability of alien *above*
Attorney-General's powers **95,** 586, 588-9, 605-8, 610
discretion **95,** 607
President's powers **95,** 586, 610
8 USC 1182(f) **95,** 588
immigration laws **53,** 528, 530
Immigration and Naturalization Service, limits of authority **42,** 235
immigration quotas **42,** 205-7
immunity, foreign State. *See* Foreign Sovereign Immunities Act (FSIA) 1976/82 *above*; State immunity *below*
independence, achievement of **39,** 65, 89-92, 110, 221, 254, 329
Indian tribes
fiduciary relationship **118,** 364
title to land **73,** 60, 69-70, 73-7, 100-1, 103-6, 109-11, 140, 152
compensation for loss of **73,** 73-7, 105-6
extinction **73,** 60, 69-70, 73-5
rights over the sea **125,** 463-6
individual in international law **81,** 514-15, **88,** 88, **99,** 66
breach **103,** 528-9, 530, **104,** 125 n. 8, 144-6, 147-8, 151-7, 158, 171-3, 174-5
human rights **95,** 632
justiciability **104,** 144-6
relations with foreign State **104,** 144
relations with own State **88,** 88-9, 92, **104,** 144
State as link **88,** 90
inhuman or degrading treatment
cause of action **104,** 187
customary international law. *See jus cogens*/peremptory norm *below*
definition **104,** 186-9
Torture Convention (1984), US reservation **104,** 186-7
forced exile **104,** 187-9
jus cogens/peremptory norm **104,** 185-9
clear criteria **104,** 185-6
requirements, discrimination **104,** 187-9
torture. *See* torture *below*
Torture Convention (1984), failure to prescribe penalty **104,** 186 n. 33
'well-founded fear of persecution' **104,** 189 n. 38
injunction
extraterritorial effect **81,** 648-9, 650
merits, relevance **81,** 503
Insular Cases **87,** 571-4
internal waters **91,** 413-15
bays as **91,** 431
claim **91,** 419, 421, 422
definition **91,** 413, 414, 431
Delaware Bay **91,** 418 n. 4
disclaimer **91,** 423-5
Mississippi Sound, whether **91,** 413-26
Nantucket Bay, whether **91,** 429-38
Territorial Sea and Contiguous Zone Convention (1958) **91,** 415-16
International Covenant on Civil and Political Rights (ICCPR) (1966), expulsion, national **104,** 188
international crimes, applicable law

international law **91,** 43, **99,** 66-7, **104,** 181-3
lex fori **104,** 101-4, 191-2
international law **87,** 455-60, **88,** 48, 50-4. *See also* comity *above*; treaties *below*
applicability between States of **59,** 218-27
applicable law, as **84,** 198, **95,** 566-8
absence of provision of municipal law, need for **95,** 636
adoption by federal courts and **96,** 16 n. 3
binding rule of international law, need for **95,** 567-8
coastline, determination of **91,** 431
State succession **94,** 180
binding, whether **84,** 215
defined rule, need for **95,** 631-2
jus cogens/peremptory norm **95,** 532
universal practice, need for **95,** 632
breach
applicable law **104,** 181-3
municipal law jurisdiction based on **103,** 530, **104,** 125-9
sovereign act, as **103,** 528-9
State action, need for **104,** 156-7
common law, part of **77,** 180, 187, 200, 240, **79,** 401
right of action, whether **79,** 401-3
compliance
choice of means **104,** 194
reciprocity and **99,** 197
conflict, avoidance of **82,** 292, 295
Constitution and **56,** 240, **77,** 174, **84,** 150, **121,** 515, 532-5
courts, role of **66,** 121, 225, 367, 420, 480
customary international law **88,** 48
difficulty of establishing **84,** 121-2
enforcement **79,** 401-3
evidence of **77,** 256, **79,** 411
treaty reservation **104,** 186-7
individual's right of relief **77,** 240
international commercial law, whether **96,** 134
jurisdiction, basis of **81,** 514-15
legislation
conformity with **81,** 547, 664
need for **81,** 515
multilateral trade agreements, whether **96,** 134
GATT **96,** 134
Uruguay Round Negotiations **96,** 134 n. 45
municipal courts
breach as cause of action **104,** 127-8, 176-84
creation by **104,** 189
development by **66,** 112
precedent **104,** 99
municipal law and **77,** 172, 179-82, 187, 207-11, **79,** 12, 13, 401, 545, **104,** 147, 159
incorporation, need for **103,** 610 n. 1
primacy **88,** 181
statutory limitation and **79,** 404
obligations
redress of violation **104,** 180 n. 21

United States of America (USA) (*cont.*)
respect for **90,** 648
unwritten **90,** 648
part of law of **80,** 574
Constitution, under **77,** 180
peremptory norm. *See jus cogens*/peremptory norm *above*
principles common to US law **80,** 574
private support for rebel forces, whether contrary to **80,** 590-2
remedies. *See* remedies *below*
sources **88,** 87 n. 13
executive or legislative acts **88,** 48
judicial and arbitral decisions **88,** 48
teachings of publicists **90,** 661 n. 14, **95,** 632, **104,** 151
usages and practices **104,** 151
statutory limitation and **79,** 404-11
subjects **88,** 87. *See also* individual in international law *above*
State acting against own nationals **104,** 144
teleological approach **77,** 175, 206, 218
rejected **77,** 241-5
violation
effect in municipal law **91,** 478-9
remedies **79,** 402-3
requirements **81,** 499
Statutory limitation and **79,** 404-11
international officials, asylum **83,** 288, 387-90
international officials, employment contract, as commercial act **63,** 343-6
international officials, immunity from jurisdiction
acts performed in official capacity **113,** 507, **121,** 402-4
illegal acts **113,** 507, 521
motivation, relevance **113,** 507
international officials, privileges and immunities
diplomatic agent, equivalence **113,** 506
former official **113,** 506-7
international organizations
applicable law, capacity to sue/be sued **107,** 423-4
capacity to sue/be sued **107,** 423-4
executive decision to deny **107,** 426-8
recognition of judgment of foreign court respecting **107,** 424-6
waiver **107,** 428
designation by President **63,** 93, 192-4, 340, 342
host State obligations, accordance of 'full facilities' for performance of Member State functions **99,** 142
recognition, need for **107,** 422
international organizations, immunity, jurisdiction, waiver
Articles of Agreement **99,** 96-103
seizure and detention of aircraft in settlement of bill **107,** 338-9
treaty undertaking not to permit racial discrimination **113,** 501
international organizations, privileges and immunities
absolute immunity **113,** 505
Privileges and Immunities Convention of the United Nations (1946) **113,** 501, 520
customary international law **105,** 21, **107,** 423-4
employment contract, multiple employment practices and **99,** 97-8
employment practices **113,** 501-2, 504-8

activity essential to fulfilment of purposes **113,** 501-2
functional **99,** 97-101
General Assembly, entitlement **113,** 501
racial discrimination **113,** 500-3
State immunity as measure **113,** 501
customary international law **107,** 319 n. 3, 324 n. 10
International Organizations Immunities Act (IOIA) **107,** 319 n. 3, 324 n. 10
international organizations, privileges and immunities, entitlement
presence in US for UN meeting **107,** 460
visitor to organization **104,** 159-61
international standards of procedural justice **91,** 479
International Tin Council (ITC), jurisdictional immunity **80,** 33
international tort/wrong
disappearances **95,** 634-5
inhuman and degrading treatment **95,** 635
jurisdiction **99,** 78-9
claim arising under municipal law, need for **99,** 65-7, **104,** 127-9, 178-84
murder by State authorities **95,** 634
official act **95,** 633
private act **95,** 633, **99,** 67
specific facts, need for **95,** 633
torture of wounded non-combatant civilian **99,** 78-9
Investment Guaranty Program **48,** 179
arbitration under **44,** 79-100
investment, definition **44,** 94-5, 98
investors, protection of **60,** 34-5
Iran. *See also* Iran–US Claims Settlement Declaration; Iran–US Claims Tribunal; Iran–US General Declaration
Claims Settlements Declaration. *See* Iran–US Claims Settlement Declaration
Claims Tribunal. *See* Iran–US Claims Tribunal
countermeasures **63,** 425-34, 455, 499, 504-9
hostages in
claims by **81,** 545-51
rescue mission **71,** 601-2
Iran–US Claims Tribunal. *See* Iran–US Claims Tribunal
pre-judgment attachment of Iranian assets
authorization **72,** 134, 275
nullification **72,** 134, 276-82
reprisals. *See* countermeasures *above*
status for purpose of FSIA **81,** 554
Ireland, Treaty of Friendship and Commerce (1950) **42,** 196
islands, Johnston Atoll, whether **100,** 507
Israel
extradition from **48,** 188-90
extradition to **79,** 538-47
Italy. *See also* Freedom, Commerce and Navigation (FCN) Treaty, Italy–USA (1948)
Peace Treaty, Memorandum on (1957) **40,** 250-2, 258
wartime claims, Memorandum concerning (1947) **40,** 449, 450
Japan
Pacific Islands, Treaty in respect of **37,** 545
Peace Treaty, confiscation of Japanese property under **44,** 490-1, 493
Jay Treaty (1794) **42,** 269-70
joinder of parties

United States of America (USA) (*cont.*)
joint tortfeasor **95,** 644
protection of absentee **95,** 643-4
judge, disqualification for lack of impartiality, 'reasonable man' test **121,** 335
judicial assistance
Head of State, in case of **121,** 574-6
Head of State, former, recovery of assets from, disclosure of information **121,** 569-77
judicial bias, extradition and **79,** 540
judicial discretion **78,** 679-80, **79,** 499
legislation, interpretation **83,** 128, 129
judicial notice **79,** 446 n. 9, 453, 509
diplomatic protest **90,** 696
Iran–Iraq conflict, facts relating to **99,** 83 n. 1
political turmoil **63,** 276
service of process **107,** 365
judicial restraint, act of State and **64,** 292-3
judicial review **88,** 14
act of State **82,** 323-4, 333-7
de novo **101,** 525
Chevron **96,** 130, 131
executive action in time of war **81,** 513
extradition. *See* extradition, judicial review *above*
extradition agreement, validity **104,** 45
failure to establish prima facie case and **88,** 9, 28, 30
Foreign Claims Act **80,** 22 n. 7
foreign relations **90,** 686
grounds
abuse of discretion **88,** 16, 17-19
unreasonableness **96,** 130, 131
new judge, need for **104,** 51, 62 n. 2, 78
political offence exception **104,** 62 n. 2
scope **104,** 4, 45, 48, 81-2, 93, 107-8
conditions in requesting State **104,** 81, 107-8
constitutionality of executive action **104,** 81
de novo examination of questions of law **104,** 82, 93
finding of fact not clearly erroneous **104,** 48, 82, 93
jurisdiction of original judge **104,** 4, 45, 81
new judge, need for **104,** 51, 62 n. 2, 78
offence within treaty **104,** 45, 81, 105
political offence exception **104,** 81
prima facie case **104,** 45, 81, 105, 107
procedural defects in extradition procedure **104,** 81
standard **88,** 19, 25-30, **90,** 672, **96,** 129-30
'facially legitimate and bona fide' **82,** 335-6
jurisdiction **60,** 16, 30, 32, 38-9, 45-6, 53, 57, 61-6, 72, **61,** 194-8, **79,** 387, 399, 401-3, 542-3, 547, **84,** 104. *See also* Alien Tort Claims Statute 1789 *and* Foreign Sovereign Immunities Act (FSIA) 1976/82 *above*; justiciability *and* State immunity, jurisdiction *below*
acquisition **66,** 9, 15, 149, 160, 170
attachment **63,** 11, 500 n. 4, **65,** 172, 239-40
act of State **66,** 147-51, 160-2, **84,** 104
admiralty. *See also* Foreign Sovereign Immunities Act (FSIA) 1976/82, 28 USC 1605(b) (admiralty jurisdiction: enforcement of maritime lien) *above*

alien, between **98,** 19 n. 6
Adra doctrine **77,** 215-17
advisory opinion, decision subject to suspension by executive **104,** 142-3
agent
attribution of acts of **92,** 378 n. 16
piercing the corporate veil **92,** 381
aircraft **107,** 390
Alien Tort Claims Act. *See* Alien Tort Claims Statute 1789 (28 USC 1350) *above*
aliens **54,** 224-9. *See also* Foreign Sovereign Immunities Act (FSIA) 1976/82, 28 USC 1332(a)(2) (citizens of a State and citizens of a foreign State)
abroad **72,** 129-31, **90,** 639, **104,** 125-7
foreign official acting under State authority **104,** 146-8
anti-terrorism conventions **86,** 37-40
antitrust claims **66,** 79-86, 293, 382-3, 490-1, 493-7, 500-2
arbitration, duty of and **82,** 288-91
'arising under Federal law' **79,** 555-60
'arising under treaties' **79,** 399-403, 485 n. 1
availability of evidence and **88,** 121, 123-4
awards of international commission, implementation **77,** 199
basis, international law, breach **104,** 125-9, 147-8
breach of treaty and, implied term **95,** 363, 366
burden of proof **63,** 102, 565, 588, 607, 608, 620, 623, 638, **107,** 346
claim arising under municipal law, need for **99,** 65-7
compétence de la compétence **84,** 154 n. 3, **90,** 610
concurrent **86,** 37, 42
connection, need for. *See* nexus *below*
conspiracy, to commit crime abroad **114,** 595-6
Constitution and **86,** 41
court's duty to determine *proprio motu* **81,** 589
criminal
acts committed abroad **54,** 231-2
irregular apprehension **45,** 103
stolen goods within jurisdiction **56,** 58-60
US embassy, in respect of **81,** 548
customs enforcement zone **91,** 473-4
district court **81,** 545-7
'claims arising under the Constitution, laws or treaties of the US' **81,** 512, 652
foreign State, over **81,** 554
supplemental jurisdiction **104,** 148-9
'violation of the law of nations or a treaty of the US' **81,** 512, 514-15, **104,** 143-6, 151-8
domicile **81,** 561
drug-trafficking, obligation to exercise **99,** 157
effectiveness of decision, need for **88,** 121, 124-5
effects doctrine **63,** 133, 150, 152, 185-6, 377, 402-5, **66,** 85-6, 279-86, 382-3, 490-1, 500, **81,** 500, 629, 643-4, 650, **84,** 99-100, 116-17, **91,** 531-3, **99,** 154-6
conspiracy **94,** 96-7, **99,** 155
'direct and foreseeable result', need for **81,** 555
FSIA and **81,** 550 n. 10, 555
national's possession of foreign shares **81,** 500-2
offences on high seas **81,** 667
overt act, need for **91,** 531-2
separable elements of crime distinguished **114,** 596, 599

United States of America (USA) (*cont.*)
embassy abroad **72,** 141-2, **81,** 548-9, **90,** 589-93
torts committed by foreign States in **90,** 590-3
enforcement of debt **87,** 514
exclusion
in favour of Iran–US Claims Tribunal **75,** 157-8, 160, 197
treaty, by **90,** 601-2
extradition **79,** 387, 420, 447-51, 469-74, 542-3, 547
extraterritorial **61,** 184-5, **66,** 79-86, 382-3, 490-1, 493-7, 500-2, **77,** 202, 250, **81,** 501, 549, 616-17, **82,** 340, **84,** 116 n. 9, **87,** 99-102, **90,** 622-41, **94,** 88-92, **99,** 154-61, **100,** 596-602, **103,** 524-30
aliens abroad. *See* aliens abroad *above*
anti-terrorism legislation **104,** 146-7
Constitution, under **82,** 351
death penalty, relevance **114,** 598-600
disuse of power **94,** 87
express legislative provision, need for **94,** 66-92
foreign territorial sea, national ship in **91,** 498-501
high seas. *See* high seas, jurisdiction *above*
internationally protected person, protection of **94,** 92-6
legislate, right to and **91,** 531, **94,** 86, **121,** 494 n. 6
legislation conferring, interpretation **114,** 596-7
limitations on **82,** 354-5
nexus **87,** 102
objection by foreign State, relevance **99,** 157
offence planned in forum State **114,** 590, 594-9, 605-6
reasonableness, need for **99,** 156-7
security, threat to **91,** 473
serious and universally condemned offences, limited to **99,** 156-7
subpoena, right of **90,** 638
terrorist offences **121,** 633-4
torture **104,** 180, 184 n. 25
Torture Convention (1984) **103,** 526-8
federal **63,** 74-7, 177-8, 234, 247-8, 301-2, 368-9, 395-6, 577-82, **77,** 181, 200, 212-15, 217, 219, 241, **81,** 510-13, 545-7, 589-91
federal common law **95,** 635-6, **104,** 193
foreign policy matters **81,** 589-91
foreign sovereign, over **92,** 483, **121,** 484
interpretation of international law **95,** 636, **104,** 193
treaty interpretation **104,** 193
waiver of **63,** 177-8
well-pleaded complaint rule **81,** 546, 651
foreign aircraft outside airspace **86,** 35-6, 37-43
place of landing **86,** 35-6, 38, 42
sexual offences **86,** 35-6, 37, 38
foreign law, violation of. *See* violation of foreign law *below*
foreign State, over **81,** 546-7
own territory, in **81,** 548
forum, implied choice, choice of law clause **107,** 350
forum [non] conveniens. See forum [non] conveniens above
Harvard Research Project (1935) **82,** 353
high seas. *See* high seas, jurisdiction *above*

in personam. See personal *below*
in rem **81,** 541
interests of foreign State **84,** 127
international crimes **91,** 43
international tort/wrong. *See* international tort/wrong *above*
justiciability distinguished **66,** 112, 293, 396-7, **99,** 46 n. 1
lex loci delicti commissi **77,** 174
lex locus delicti **79,** 5, 7
'long-arm' Statutes **72,** 116-17, 170
maritime **57,** 161
military courts **54,** 528-9
nationality **81,** 548, 561-2
  human rights cases, relevance **77,** 172
nationality in human rights cases, relevance **77,** 172, 178, 185
nationals **87,** 531
nationals abroad **81,** 500, **87,** 102, **90,** 621-41, **99,** 154 n. 4
  crime committed abroad **61,** 228-30
  crime committed against national in embassy **61,** 224-6
  injury to **63,** 212-14, 323-8, 447-52
  wrongful death **63,** 245-51, 612
nationals on high seas **51,** 230-2
nexus **63,** 168-9, 185, 266-7, 399-402, 491-2, 516-17, 520-1, 564-6, 571-2, 618-20, **72,** 169-71, 179-81, **79,** 554-5, 560, **81,** 563, 571-2, 574, **82,** 355, **84,** 90-5, 99-100, 112, 115-17, 192, **86,** 60-1, 64-5, 94-8, **87,** 526-36, 542, **88,** 83, 87 n. 12, 192, 195-8, **90,** 594, 595, 601, 602-3, **92,** 380-1, **98,** 17, **101,** 516-18
  advertising campaign **103,** 465, 466, 468
  agency or instrumentality of foreign State **98,** 90-2
  banking relationship **63,** 399-400
  between act and grievance **63,** 400-1, **92,** 457-8, **103,** 440
  causal connection **103,** 440, 478, 485, 488-9, 515-16, 609
  commercial activities in forum State **90,** 602, **103,** 439-43, 465-7, 488-9
  commercial/trade representation/mission **103,** 568
  constituent State, whether limited to **98,** 42, 92
  continuous and systematic/enduring relationship, need for **63,** 241, 322-3, 373-6, 496-7
  contract governed by foreign law **63,** 459, 463-5
  contract negotiated abroad **63,** 459, 463-5
  contractual payment **98,** 42, 89-90, 97, **100,** 517-19
  crash of foreign-owned plane abroad **98,** 23-5
  criminal investigations **121,** 640-1
  debt, *situs* **98,** 98-100, **103,** 545-6
  demand for payment in US **86,** 72
  destination of aircraft **98,** 74
  diplomatic mission in forum State, use of **86,** 60-1, 65
  diplomatic relations **121,** 640-1
  'direct effect in the United States'. *See* Foreign Sovereign Immunities Act (FSIA) 1976/82, 28 USC 1605(a)(2) (commercial activity exception: 'act . . . outside the United States ... that causes direct effect in the United States')
  'doing business in' **38,** 114, **63,** 212-14, 322-3, 324-5, 400-1, 496-7, **96,** 76-8, **98,** 145
  duty **98,** 134-5
  employment contract **98,** 135

United States of America (USA) (*cont.*)
expropriation/nationalization, 'commercial activity in the United States' **107,** 229-30, 232-3, 237, 247-51
expropriation/nationalization of national's property **63,** 457
extraterritorial legislation **92,** 445
failure to pay **121,** 494
failure to transfer funds **92,** 466-7
financial loss **98,** 89, **103,** 443, 466-7, **107,** 230-2, 236-7, 335-8
foreign State, in case of **107,** 340-6
foreseeable effect **92,** 460-1, **98,** 88, 97 n. 2, 146, **100,** 517, **101,** 550-1, **103,** 443-4, 489, 515-16
freezing-out of forum State directors **101,** 550-1
injury to nationals inflicted abroad **63,** 213-14, 611-12, **92,** 445-7, 451-4
issue of negotiable promissory notes **98,** 115-17
issue of ticket in forum State **92,** 458 n. 3, **98,** 46-7, 122-3
'legally significant acts' test **98,** 133, **107,** 335-6
letter of credit governed by foreign law **63,** 491
letter of credit payable in forum State **63,** 377, 403-8, 459-65, 491, 562-4
letter of credit payable in forum State, amendment abroad **63,** 186, 491, 563
letter of credit payable in forum State, repudiation abroad **63,** 403, 491, 563
local bank, use of **63,** 150-1, 187, **86,** 65, **101,** 516
loss of grain purchased through forum State's aid programme **63,** 611
loss and suffering of families of deceased **98,** 23-5, 75
'minimum contacts' **63,** 150, 168-9, 185, 204-5, 213-14, 234-5, 240-4, 266-7, 361-2, 372-7, 399-402, 461-6, 491-2, 496, 516-17, 520-1, 564-6, 571-2, 618-20, 626, 637-8
'minimum contacts', locus of injury test distinguished **63,** 491
mortgagee, loss of value of pledge **98,** 35-6
nationality of company suffering loss, relevance **98,** 97
non-UN activities **96,** 77-8
participation in aid programme **86,** 60-1
payment into bank account **98,** 98-100, **103,** 441
payment through bank account **63,** 152
payment on guarantee **103,** 443-4
payment of pensions using local infrastructure **103,** 608
payment of profits **103,** 467
payment for reservations **103,** 466
personal jurisdiction and **79,** 14, **121,** 588
personal jurisdiction and, in case of foreign State **63,** 57-8, **103,** 546-8, **107,** 340-6
place of business **107,** 350-1
place of incorporation **107,** 350
place of injury **63,** 491-2
previous visit by ship on which death occurred **98,** 164-6
'principal office' **90,** 648
representation by agent **98,** 146, 155
sale of air ticket **63,** 449-50
servicing of aircraft **98,** 75
settlement negotiations **103,** 441-2
signature of treaty **113,** 550
sovereign contacts **121,** 640-1
State-sponsored terrorism **121,** 639-41
subject-matter jurisdiction, need for **103,** 445, 453, 462, 528-30

substantial contact **81,** 509, **92,** 465-6, **100,** 563-4, **101,** 550-1
substantial effect **63,** 491, 522-4, **92,** 460-1, 466, **98,** 88, 97 n. 2, **100,** 517, **103,** 443
substantial sales **63,** 205-6
suffering following injury overseas **103,** 608-9
telex, overseas transaction by **63,** 241-3, 496, 620
tort and contract distinguished **63,** 323-4, **107,** 236
tortious injury in the State **63,** 323-8
transaction affecting control of bank **121,** 588
transaction as a whole **98,** 18-19
UN Permanent Observer's non-UN activities **96,** 77-8
US mail, use of **63,** 619-20, **86,** 65
US ship, collision with **63,** 610-12
wages claim by foreign seamen based on legislation of forum State **63,** 629-32
passive personality principle **82,** 348, 350-1, 353, **94,** 87
extradition based on **82,** 350-1, **104,** 83-4
terrorist acts **88,** 181, **121,** 612, 640
pendent **81,** 499, 644-5, 650, 651-3, 656
personal **60,** 62-6, **61,** 229, **66,** 133-5, 193-7, 251-3, 489-502, **72,** 115-18, 141-2, 158, 164, 167-71, **77,** 179, **79,** 14-15, **81,** 511, 560-2, **82,** 288, 298, 353, **86,** 41, **90,** 602-3, **92,** 380-1, **98,** 117
court's power to refuse **86,** 44
domicile **81,** 566
due process requirement **61,** 194-8, **63,** 612, **98,** 146-7, **121,** 495
foreign State/agency or instrumentality of foreign State (other than under the FSIA) **60,** 62-6, **61,** 229, **63,** 57, 62, 148-52, 207-8, 226, 322-3, 372-7, 398-405, 489, 495-7, 565-6, 627, 631, **90,** 603, **98,** 42-3, 91-2, **103,** 546-8, **107,** 642-58. *See also* Foreign Sovereign Immunities Act (FSIA) 1976/82, 28 USC 1330(b) (personal jurisdiction over foreign State) *and* nexus *above*
nexus. *See* nexus *above*
presence within jurisdiction **81,** 565, 577-8
presence within jurisdiction, enforced **86,** 41
presence within jurisdiction, voluntary **86,** 41
Securities Exchange Act 1934 **60,** 62-6
piracy **78,** 573-4
prisoners of war **99,** 166-70
proper law of contract **87,** 531
protective **79,** 556 n. 17
protective principle **81,** 548, 549, **84,** 214-15, **90,** 593 n. 11
drug-trafficking **84,** 214-15
protection of leading figures **94,** 89-92
security, threat to **82,** 351 n. 14, **94,** 87
terrorist offence **104,** 83, 181
public policy and **81,** 580
quasi in rem **63,** 145-8, 187, 252-60, 349, **103,** 444-5
reasonable exercise **84,** 103-4
reciprocity principle **81,** 549
responsibility for determining **114,** 591-4, 605-6
Restatement of Foreign Relations Law (Revised) **82,** 349
'special aircraft jurisdiction' **86,** 35-6, 38-9, 40-1
special maritime and territorial jurisdiction **91,** 474
standard of proof **114,** 591-4, 605-6

United States of America (USA) (*cont.*)
standards for decision and **88,** 121, 123
State, of the federation and national compared **56,** 58-61
subject-matter **60,** 53, 56-61, **66,** 147-51, 160-2, 170-2, 195-7, 200, 272, 284-6, 382-3, 490-1, 500-2, **72,** 126-31, 137-43, 154-71, 177-80, 288, **73,** 241, 250-1, **77,** 173, 271, **79,** 3, 554, **81,** 495, 499-502, 511, 512, 616-17, 628-9, 652, **82,** 288-91, 298, 352, **86,** 41, 88, **87,** 525, 531, 533-4, **90,** 599-602, 607, 610-11, **92,** 378-80, 395-9
consent, relevance **103,** 611
effects doctrine. *See* effects doctrine *above*
enforcement of foreign arbitral award **103,** 565
matter of law **107,** 349
nationality as basis **81,** 500
political question doctrine **81,** 566-7
presence of offender **82,** 354
Securities Exchange Act 1934 **60,** 56-62
substantial contact with forum, requirement **72,** 167-8, 178-81
territorial **63,** 610-12, 627-9, 630, **66,** 195-7, 200, 250-5, 279-86, 319-20, 382-8, **77,** 217, **81,** 548, **91,** 531
effects doctrine. *See* effects doctrine *above*
habeas corpus **95,** 492
special admiralty or maritime jurisdiction **63,** 353
State immunity and **90,** 590
territory subject to **72,** 141-2
tort **72,** 115-18, 130-1, 140-1, **95,** 489 n. 13
treaty
breach as bar **90,** 676
deprivation, need for express provision **99,** 170
treaty as limitation on **91,** 520-2
UN Headquarters **96,** 77
universal **77,** 217, 274, **79,** 14, **104,** 183 n. 25
attack on neutral ship in international waters **79,** 7, **81,** 662
civil cases excluded **79,** 7
crimes against humanity, International Criminal Tribunal for the Former Yugoslavia **103,** 619
extension of concept **94,** 93
jus cogens/peremptory norm **103,** 618-19, **104,** 193
presence of accused, need for **94,** 92, 94
terrorist offences **82,** 348-9, 351
unlawful arrest. *See* forcible abduction/unlawful arrest *above*
venue **90,** 603-4, 638
venue distinguished **114,** 592, 597-8
violation of foreign law **79,** 406-7
violations of international law **72,** 127, 130-1, 143, **77,** 172, 210-11, 215-17, **79,** 399-412
nexus with US law **77,** 217
waiver of objection by foreign State
ad hoc **84,** 211-12
bilateral agreement **84,** 211
withdrawal of immunity **72,** 127
jury trial, right to. *See* fair trial, right to *and* Foreign Sovereign Immunities Act (FSIA) 1976/82, jury trial, right to and *above*
jus cogens/peremptory norm

arbitrary detention **104,** 185
basis
consent, relevance **103,** 471, 617
customary international law **103,** 471, 616
criteria. *See* requirements *below*
definition
Committee of US Citizens in Nicaragua **103,** 609
Restatement of Foreign Relations Law (Third) **103,** 609, 616
Vienna Convention on the Law of Treaties (1961) **103,** 470, 615-16
disappearances **104,** 185
forcible abduction/unlawful arrest **107,** 435 n. 5
genocide **103,** 616-17
Holocaust **103,** 615-21
human rights **103,** 617
inhuman or degrading treatment **104,** 185-9
primacy
customary international law **103,** 471-2
treaty, over **103,** 471-2
requirements
clear criteria **104,** 184, 185
non-derogability **104,** 184
universality **104,** 184, 185-9
slavery **103,** 616-17
State immunity, jurisdiction and **103,** 473-5
implied waiver **103,** 609-10, **113,** 537-40, 547-8
summary execution **104,** 185
terrorist act **107,** 391-2
torture **103,** 472-5, **104,** 184-5, **119,** 206-7
universal jurisdiction **103,** 618, **104,** 193
justiciability **56,** 24, **77,** 218-20, **79,** 499-502, **81,** 517, **87,** 661-70. *See also* act of State *and* admissibility *above*; political question doctrine *below*
concession, grant **81,** 527
excludability of aliens **82,** 333-5
fact-finding, problems of and **87,** 662-5, 702
foreign relations questions **77,** 226, 231-2
individual in international law **104,** 144-6
international law
relations with foreign State **104,** 144
relations with own State **104,** 144
jurisdiction distinguished **66,** 112, 293, 396-7, **99,** 46 n. 1, **105,** 463, **107,** 256 n. 1
legality of actions, relevance **81,** 621
merits, prospect of succession, relevance **81,** 621
officials
acts purported to be official **81,** 596
official acts of, limited to **81,** 595
political question doctrine. *See* political question doctrine *below*
preliminary question **107,** 257
public interest, acts in **81,** 595, 623-4
purpose **81,** 646
rationale
foreign policy considerations **81,** 520-1, 525, 527-8, 536, 589, 590, 624-5, 626-7, 633, 636 n. 9
international comity **81,** 633

United States of America (USA) (*cont.*)
principles of international law **81,** 519
respect for foreign State **81,** 535, 594, 596, 619
separation of powers **81,** 519, 525, 528, 536, 595, 619-20, 624, 636 n. 9, 645, 654
sovereign authority, nature of **81,** 519
remedy, need for **104,** 159
ripeness of dispute **87,** 692-4, 703-5
separation of powers and **87,** 664, 675-9, 688, 700, 701
sovereign activity **81,** 525-6, 595, 622, 654-6
authorization, necessary, whether **81,** 525-6, 595, 622, 654-6
State Department suggestions **81,** 636 n. 8
State immunity distinguished **81,** 518-19
territorial restriction **81,** 535, 536, 594-5
torture claims **81,** 591
treaty exception **81,** 625 n. 12, 632 n. 4
treaty termination **77,** 226
laches **107,** 291-4
law of
Act of 3 March 1875 (Administration of Aliens) **87,** 451
Administrative Procedure Act 1946 **66,** 354, **80,** 591, 594
5 USC 555(1) **96,** 29
5 USC 701(a)(2) **95,** 486-7, 489
5 USC 702 **100,** 495-6
executive and judiciary, relations between **63,** 28
Age Discrimination in Employment Act (ADEA) 1967 **90,** 627, 628-9, 638
Agricultural Foreign Investment Disclosure Act 1978 **70,** 515
Agricultural Trade Development and Assistance Act 1954 (7 USC 1691) **42,** 173, **86,** 57
Aircraft Sabotage Act 1984 **86,** 41
Alien Tort Claims Statute 1789. *See* Alien Tort Claims Statute 1789 *above*
All Writs Act **95,** 492
Americans with Disabilities Act 1990 **90,** 623
Anti-Apartheid Act 1986
compatibility with treaty **82,** 291-2
s 306(a) **82,** 322, 324-8
Anti-Hijacking Act (49 USC App 1472) **88,** 181-2, 186
Anti-Smuggling Act 1935 **91,** 473, 527, 535
customs enforcement area **91,** 473-4
Anti-Terrorism Act 1987 **79,** 501 n. 7, **82,** 235, 236-44, 245-52, 254, 257, 261-7, 269-72, 275-7, 278, 279-80, 285, 286-8, 299
Bill of Attainder, whether **82,** 288 n. 16, 298, 314-18
constitutionality **82,** 304-18
enforcement **82,** 288
legislative history **82,** 287, 296-8
purpose **82,** 312
statutory finding of terrorist character, absence of appeal **82,** 315-16, 317
UN Headquarters Agreement, compatibility **82,** 295-8
Anti-Terrorism and Effective Death Penalty Act 1996 (28 USC 1605(a)(7)) **113,** 542, **121,** 611-13, 630-52
Chapter 153 **118,** 27
Chapter 154 **118,** 27
Flatow Amendment **121,** 630-1, 637, 642-52, **123,** 32, 42-3, 47-8
habeas corpus proceedings in states in case of death penalty **118,** 27

miscarriage of justice and **118,** 29
retroactive effect **121,** 611 n. 4, 631-2, 645
s 107(c) **118,** 27
Antidumping Act 1916 (15 USC 72) **63,** 201-2, 210
Antitrust Civil Process Act **92,** 384-9
Antitrust (Clayton) Act 1914 **63,** 106-20, 201-11, 294-7, **74,** 39, 44, 49-57, 59, 64, 68-9, 73, 80-2, **118,** 404
foreign State as 'person' **63,** 106-20, 207-8, 294-7
treble damages **63,** 107-20
antitrust legislation, *Noerr Pennington* doctrine **92,** 387-9
Antitrust (Sherman) Act 1890 **63,** 106-20, 201-11, 294-7, **64,** 261-2, **74,** 39, 44, 46, 49-57, 59, 64, 68-9, 73, 80-2, **81,** 518, 524
exported goods, applicability to **63,** 109
extraterritorial application **63,** 295, **100,** 585-7, 597, 599, **118,** 40-1, 396-8, 406
imported goods, applicability to **63,** 109
legislative history **63,** 108, 114-17, 294
'person', foreign State as **63,** 106-20, 207-8, 294-7
'person', foreign State as plaintiff **63,** 106-20, 294, 298
trade with 'foreign nations', applicability to **63,** 108
treble damages action **63,** 107-20, **118,** 397-8, 400-1, 406, 412-13
Arbitration Act 1966 **57,** 329-31, **63,** 536-7
Articles of Confederation **77,** 171
Aviation Act 1958 **74,** 44, 46, 74, **86,** 37, 40. *See also* Code, 49 USC app 1461(a) *above*
legislative history **82,** 324-7
s 306(a)(2) **82,** 324-8
s 801(a) **82,** 322
s 1006 **82,** 323
s 1102(a) **82,** 322-3, 325, 327
Banking Law **87,** 513
Bankruptcy Act **56,** 55-7
s 24 **81,** 504-5
Bankruptcy Code, State immunity, effect on **107,** 339
Bill of Rights 1791
Art. 6 **70,** 203
extraterritorial application **61,** 203, 205
Cargo Preference Act 1904 (10 USC 2631) **86,** 22-4, 28, 30, 32
Civil Aeronautics Board Sunset Act 1984 **82,** 356 n. 27
Civil Liability for Acts of State Sponsored Terrorism 1996 **121,** 612, 614
Civil Rights Act 1964
international organization, applicability **113,** 500
Title II **90,** 623
Title VII **90,** 621, 623, 626-7, 629, 634, 639-41
Title VII (employment discrimination) **113,** 500
Classified Information Procedures Act (CIPA) (18 USC App) **88,** 184
Coast Guard Act **90,** 628
Code. *See* Code (USC) *above and separate titles*
Code (Washington) **124,** 308, 315
Code of Federal Regulations (CFR) 1977 **79,** 380, **87,** 441, 443, 452, 465, 471, 481, 482, 503, 504
19 CFR s 148.2 **81,** 657
Compact of Free Association Act 1985 **84,** 204
Comprehensive Anti-Apartheid Act 1986 **90,** 628
Comprehensive Drug Abuse Prevention and Control Act 1970 **84,** 210, **91,** 473

United States of America (USA) (*cont.*)
Comprehensive Environmental Response, Compensation and Labor-Management Relations Act 1947 **90,** 632
Confederation Acts 1861/62 **88,** 44
Consumer Product Safety Act **90,** 623
Continuing Appropriations Act 1985 **76,** 390, 406
Copyright Act 1978, 17 USC 1041(b)(1) **96,** 84
Cuban Assets Control Regulations 1975 **42,** 138, **54,** 536-46, **66,** 20, 244-5
Cultural Property Implementation Act 1983 **108,** 507-9
Czechoslovakian Claims Settlement Act 1950 **84,** 534
International Development Act 1950 **84,** 534
Marshall Islands and **84,** 203-5
Czechoslovakian Claims Settlement Act 1981 **79,** 593, 597
amendment of US-Czechoslovakia Compensation Agreement by **79,** 593, 597-8
Death on the High Seas Act (DOHSA), waiver of sovereign immunity, whether **100,** 538-9
Declaration of the Rights of Man and the Citizen 1789, Art. 4 **79,** 332
Declaratory Judgment Act **79,** 485, 489, **88,** 46
Department of Defence Appropriations Act, congressional reporting requirement **100,** 505-7
Department of Transportation Final Order 86-11-29 **82,** 322
Destruction of Aircraft Act **82,** 346, 351-2, 353-7
Diplomatic Relations Act 1978 (Vienna Convention on Diplomatic Relations (1961)) **72,** 656, **98,** 6, **99,** 115, **121,** 601 n. 3
s 254(a) **99,** 116
s 254(d) **99,** 115-16, 117, 118
Displaced Persons Act 1948 **79,** 538
s 2(a) **95,** 518-19, 525 n. 7, 532
s 2(b) **95,** 517, 525 n. 5, 532
s 10 **95,** 508
Economic Opportunity Act 1964 **63,** 102
Economy Act 1932 **82,** 342
Edge Act(12 USC 632) **86,** 22-4, 28, 30, 32
Eight Hour Law **90,** 635
Emancipation Proclamation **88,** 44
Emergency Economic Powers Act 1977 **63,** 504-8
Congress, intentions of **63,** 506
Executive Orders
of 1 May 1985, declaring national emergency **76,** 404, 474, 876
7856 (passport area restrictions) **38,** 102-11
10422 (International Organizations Employees Loyalty Program) (1953) **83,** 515
12114 (application of NEPA to federal organs) **100,** 494, 502-3, 523, 529
12170 **72,** 241-2, 274
12205 **72,** 242
12211 **72,** 242
12283 **81,** 550, 554, 567
12283, constitutionality **72,** 137-40, 144-51
12283, extinction of claims of US hostages against Iran **72,** 133-40, 144-50, 276
12283, text **72,** 135
12293 **72,** 136
12294 **72,** 128-9, 136, 138, 144, 276, 282, 288
12333 **76,** 401
12571 **82,** 322

12807 (Interdiction of Illegal Immigrants)
12807, Immigration and Nationality Act, compatibility **95,** 584-98
12807, text **95,** 583 n. 13
12807, unreviewable discretion **95,** 606
Export Administrative Regulations, extraterritorial effect **87,** 99-102
Extension of Admiralty Jurisdiction Act **54,** 235-9
Extradition Act 1891 **79,** 464
Extradition Act 1981 **79,** 465-6, 488
Extradition Act (Proposed) 1984 **79,** 498 n. 3
Fair Labor Standards Act **90,** 626
Federal Arbitration Act 1976 **72,** 155-6
9 USC 201 **96,** 9
9 USC 202 **96,** 9
9 USC 203 **96,** 17
9 USC 207 **96,** 17, **103,** 568-9
compulsory arbitration under **72,** 156
New York Convention on the Recognition and Enforcement of Foreign Arbitral Awards (1958), implementation **96,** 9, **103,** 568-9, 578
Federal Communications Act 1934 **70,** 511
Federal Debt Collection Procedures Act (FDCPA) **120,** 421-2
Federal Employers Liability Act (FELA) **90,** 624, 632
Federal Food, Drug and Cosmetic Act (21 USC 32) **90,** 623
Federal Kidnapping Act **90,** 675
Federal Regulations (CFR), 32 CFR 213 **82,** 341-2
Federal Service Labor-Management Relations Act **94,** 268
Federal Tort Claims Act (FTCA). *See* Federal Tort Claims Act (FTCA) 1938/1970/1982 *above*
Fishery Conservation Act 1976 **91,** 526 n. 30
Fishery Conservation and Management Act 1976
Congress, intent of **63,** 353, 602
territorial jurisdiction and **63,** 353, 601-3, **71,** 110
Flag Protection Act 1989 **122,** 576
Foreign Assets Control Regulations **66,** 252-60, 426
blocking action, constitutionality **66,** 358-9
designated nationals **66,** 355-7
Foreign Assistance Act 1961 **44,** 80-1, 93-4, **59,** 373-5, 409-10, **63,** 96, **87,** 668-70. *See also* Hickenlooper Amendment *above*
22 USC 2304 **87,** 661, 662, 668
human rights and **87,** 668-9, **100,** 526
Sabbatino **42,** 40, 43, 46, 47-8, **43,** 13-18
Foreign Assistance Act 1964 **62,** 224, **63,** 98. *See also* Hickenlooper Amendment *above*
Foreign Banking Office Act 1973 **63,** 84-6
Foreign Claims Act (10 USC 2734)
10 USC 2734 **87,** 681
effective remedy, whether **123,** 136-8
waiver of State immunity, whether **80,** 22
Foreign Corrupt Practices Act (FCPA) 1977 **81,** 527-8
compliance as objective **92,** 499-500
private rights of action, whether **92,** 497-500
Foreign Intelligence Surveillance Act **82,** 313 n. 15
Foreign Sovereign Immunities Act (FSIA) 1976/82. *See* Foreign Sovereign Immunities Act (FSIA) 1976/82 *above*
Foreign Trade Antitrust Improvements Act 1982 **100,** 586 n. 23, 587

United States of America (USA) (*cont.*)
Freedom of Information Act **77,** 133, 134
arbitration rules of procedure and **125,** 108-9
Hong Kong Policy Act 1992 (22 USC 5701-32) **114,** 619-20, **122,** 606-77
Hostage Act 1868 **72,** 146, 283-4, 289
text **72,** 283
Hostage-taking Act (18 USC 1203) **82,** 346, 347, 352-3, **88,** 180, 186
legislative history **82,** 352-3
Human Rights Law **56,** 27
Immigration Act 1907, s 2 **53,** 525
Immigration Act 1917 **79,** 380-1, **87,** 467 n. 5
applicability **79,** 380-1
Immigration Act 1990, s 303 **95,** 573-4
Immigration and Nationality Act 1924, s 13(a) **95,** 520
Immigration and Nationality Act 1952 **42,** 205-7, 235, 237, **53,** 529, **56,** 558-60, 561, **60,** 239, **79,** 428 n. 11, 502 n. 8, 510, 606 n. 19, **87,** 452, 467, 472, 474, **88,** 28, 59, 90
acts of persecution **95,** 541 n. 5
amendment **87,** 466, **95,** 580 n. 2, 607
amendment (1978) **79,** 380-2
control of departure from US **43,** 126-30
s 203(a)(7) **79,** 618-20
s 203(e) **87,** 466, 471, 472
s 208 **95,** 538, 539, 559
s 208(a) **87,** 497
s 212(a)(20) **95,** 537, 538
s 215 **38,** 102-11
s 236 **95,** 538
s 243(a) **53,** 537-8
s 243(h) **53,** 533-6, **87,** 440, 441-2, 464-77, 482, 488, 496, **95,** 537, 538, 580-98, 605-10
s 316(a) **95,** 520, 528
s 318 **95,** 520
s 340(a) **95,** 506-7, 528
Immigration and Nationality Act 1952 (as amended 1978) **79,** 378-83
legislative history **79,** 380-1
Immigration and Nationality Act 1952 (as amended by the Refugee Act 1980)
8 USC 1101 **87,** 472, 482, 492, 494, 496, 503, 506
s 208(a) **79,** 612-41
s 243(h) **79,** 612-41
Immigration Reform and Control Act 1986 **79,** 614
Intelligence Authorization Act for Fiscal Year 1981 **80,** 593 n. 10
Intelligence Authorization Act for Fiscal Year 1984 **80,** 594
Internal Revenue Code
foreign investment, definition **56,** 327-8
foreign investment, treaty obligation and **56,** 551-2
s 911 **87,** 562
Internal Security Act 1950 **87,** 453
International Aviation Facilities Act, s 11 **102,** 283
International Claims Settlement Act 1949 **42,** 153-72, **56,** 538, **63,** 72, **72,** 285-6
22 USC 1621 **87,** 618
interest **42,** 191
'property' **42,** 178-9

International Emergency Economic Powers Act (IEEPA) **72,** 146, 274, 279-84, 286, 289, **94,** 216, 218-20
International Investment Survey Act 1976 **70,** 504
International Organizations Immunities Act (IOIA) 1945 **42,** 138, **63,** 92-5, 163, 288, 338-42, **72,** 199, **107,** 319 n. 3, 324, 415, 419-21
Congress, intentions of **63,** 92, 94
employment disputes **63,** 192-4, **113,** 501-2
Foreign Sovereign Immunities Act (FSIA), interrelationship **63,** 338-43, **113,** 501, 505 n. 1, 519-20
General Assembly, application to **113,** 501
'international organization' **80,** 34
legislative history **63,** 342-3
object and purpose **63,** 163, **107,** 420-1
official acts within functions **121,** 403
officials, applicability **113,** 502, 507
International Security and Development Act 1961 **87,** 668-70
human rights and **87,** 668
Iranian Assets Control Regulations (1979) **63,** 426-9, 455, 499, 504-9, **72,** 241-5
Jencks Act **91,** 505-6
Jones Act 1958 **54,** 224-9, **90,** 638
Judiciary Act 1789 **63,** 581, **77,** 172, 173, 179, 201, 204, 211, 213-15, 241, 243-5, **81,** 499. *See also* Alien Tort Claims Statute 1789 *above*
Labor Management Relations Act 1947 **81,** 591
Labor Management Reporting and Disclosure Act 1990 **90,** 623
Lanham Act **61,** 41, 59, **66,** 80-90, 130, 142-5, **90,** 624-5, 639
Law 85.861 **69,** 5
Law 87.693 **69,** 4-6
Limitation of Liability Act, 46 USC **87,** 181-9, 551
Longshoremen's and Harbor Workers' Compensation Act 1972 (33 USC 901-50) **63,** 440-2, **72,** 95
McCarran–Ferguson Act
15 USC 1011 ff **100,** 569
15 USC 1012(b) **100,** 574, 575-9, 600
15 USC 1013(b) **100,** 575, 578-84, 588-95, 600
Marine Mammal Protection Act 1972, waiver **95,** 613
Merchant Marine Acts 1920/1936 **70,** 515
Military Service Act 1961 **56,** 558-60
resident aliens **56,** 563
National Environmental Policy Act (NEPA)
alternatives to proposed action, need for **100,** 503-5
Antarctic Treaty, Protocol on Environmental Protection (1991) and **100,** 527-8
extraterritorial effect **100,** 497-501
high seas **100,** 501-3
s 102(2)(c) **100,** 523, 525, 526-30
s 102(2)(f) **100,** 528, 529
standing **100,** 495-7
supplementary EIS, need for **100,** 505
National Labor Relations Act (NLRA) **63,** 5-7, 18-21, 647-54, **90,** 624, 632-3
National Security Act 1947 **80,** 593
National Stolen Property Act 1934 **108,** 509
Nationality Act 1946 **72,** 465
Neutrality Act 1939 **87,** 486

United States of America (USA) (*cont.*)
Neutrality Act 1982 **80,** 593-4
non-recognition of government, effect **94,** 173
Nuclear Non-proliferation Act 1976 **100,** 526
Outer Continental Shelf Lands Act 1953 **43,** 113, **51,** 225-30, **54,** 235-9, **71,** 106
Passport Act 1918 **87,** 454
Passport Act 1926 **38,** 102-11
Posse Comitatus Act (18 USC 1385) **82,** 338-43, **88,** 183-4
legislative history **82,** 338-9
Poultry Product Inspection Act, s 17(d) **96,** 128-47
Presidential Proclamation 4865 (Interdiction of Illegal Immigrants) **95,** 581
Presidential Proclamation 5928 **81,** 667 n. 8
Presidential Proclamation in respect of sugar imports of 23 September 1983, **76,** 404
Prevention and Punishment of Crimes Against Internationally Protected Persons Act 1976 **77,** 274
Protection of Migratory Birds Act 1915 **83,** 157
Public Law 93-50 (prohibition of use of funds to support combat activity by US forces in South East Asia) **94,** 123, 126-7, 128-9, 132
Public Law 93-52 (prohibition of use of funds to support combat activity by US forces in South East Asia) **94,** 123, 126-7, 128-9, 132
Public Law 100-640 (Inter-American Convention on International Commercial Arbitration) **103,** 563
Public Vessels Act (PVA) 1925 **42,** 187
combatant activities exception **99,** 89
waiver of State immunity, whether **99,** 85-6, 91
Racketeer Influenced and Corrupt Organizations Act (RICO) **81,** 615, 616 n. 1, 642-5, 650-1, 656, **87,** 681, **88,** 96, **98,** 149-53, **99,** 152, 157
death of defendant, relevance **121,** 589-90
extraterritorial effect **81,** 616-17
mail/wire fraud **98,** 151-2
pattern of activity, need for **98,** 150-1, **121,** 497-8
service of process out of the jurisdiction **98,** 150
State immunity, jurisdiction and **98,** 152-3
Racketeering and Corrupt Influences Act **79,** 404 n. 3, **80,** 21
waiver of State immunity, whether **80,** 22
Reciprocal Trade Agreements Act 1945 **107,** 286
Reconstruction Act **79,** 404 n. 3
Refugee Act 1980 **79,** 505 n. 11, 605, 613, 615, 629, **87,** 480, 481, 503. *See also* Immigration and Nationality Act 1952 *above*
8 USC 1101 **95,** 485, 486, 487, 500
8 USC 1101(a)(42)(A) **88,** 6, 16, 20, 21, 24, 25-7, 28, 30, 33, **95,** 537, 538, 539-43, 549, 556, 564, 582 n. 11, 585
8 USC 1103 **88,** 16 n. 1
8 USC 1103(a) **95,** 568
8 USC 1105 **95,** 539 n. 3
8 USC 1105(a) **88,** 32-3
8 USC 1151 **95,** 486, 500
8 USC 1153 **88,** 13 n. 3, 28
8 USC 1158 **88,** 6, 16
8 USC 1158(a) **95,** 572, 582 n. 11
8 USC 1182(d)(5) **95,** 486, 500
8 USC 1253(h)(1) **95,** 549, 556, 558, 564, 605-8

purpose **79,** 621, 629, **87,** 466, 467, 474, 480, **88,** 7 n. 3, 12 n. 8, 16, 28, **95,** 549, 598, 599
retroactivity **79,** 605, 606
Refugee Escapee Act 1957 **79,** 621 n. 20
Refugee Relief Act 1953 **79,** 621 n. 20
Robinson–Patman Act (15 USC 13 ff) **81,** 524, **88,** 96
Rules of Decision Act (28 USC 1652) **104,** 190
Seamen's Wage Act, ss 596-7 **63,** 628-32
Secretarial Order 2918 (Trust Territories) **87,** 599
Secretarial Order 3039 (1979) (Recognition of Governmental Entities under Locally-ratified Constitutions in the Trust Territory of the Pacific Islands) **87,** 561
Secretarial Order 3119 **87,** 651
Securities Act 1933 **84,** 111 n. 4, 130 n. 33, **92,** 416
s 22(a) **81,** 499
Securities Exchange Act 1934 **60,** 30, 56-7, 61-2, 70-2, **63,** 67, 69-70, **81,** 501, **90,** 638-9, **92,** 417
amendments (1975) **63,** 70
corporations and **60,** 32, 33-5
extraterritorial effect **60,** 30, 32-4, **81,** 501-2
foreign government, application to **63,** 68-70
intention of legislature **60,** 32, 57, 59-60, 62, 63, **63,** 69-70
purpose **60,** 32-4
s 27 (jurisdiction) **60,** 56-66, **81,** 499
subject-matter jurisdiction **60,** 56-62
Selective Service Act 1967 **42,** 399
Settlement of War Claims Act 1928 **47,** 419, 426
Sherman Act 1890. *See* Antitrust (Sherman) Act 1890 *above*
Shipping Act 1916 **70,** 515, **92,** 385-6
Special Central American Assistance Act 1979 **76,** 403, 415
Presidential Determination (12 September 1980) **76,** 415
Speedy Trial Act 1982 (18 USC 3161) **84,** 209, **86,** 44
State immunity, jurisdiction, Bankruptcy Code **107,** 339
State involvement, need for **104,** 146-7
state of war, effect **94,** 173
Statute of Limitations. *See* Statute of Limitations *below*
Submerged Lands Act 1953 **42,** 86-102, **91,** 413-14, 415
boundaries, definition **57,** 94-6, 97-8, 107-8
coastline **57,** 106-17
inland waters **57,** 108
internal waters, failure to define **91,** 413, 415
international law, application **57,** 111
interpretation **59,** 219-27, 252-4
Subversive Activities Control Act 1950 **87,** 467 n. 5
Suits in Admiralty Act **88,** 56
waiver of State immunity, whether **99,** 85 n. 4, **100,** 538-9
Supplementary Rules for Certain Admiralty and Maritime Claims **87,** 558
Taiwan Relations Act 1982 **98,** 65, 665
Tariff Act 1897 **63,** 201-2, 210, **66,** 200-5, 289-95
Tariff Act 1930 **66,** 86-7, **107,** 294
Texas Securities Act **84,** 111 n. 4, 130 n. 33
Throughway (New York) Act **64,** 65-9
Torture Victim Protection Act 1991

United States of America (USA) (*cont.*)
cause of action **104,** 128, 176
exhaustion of local remedies requirement **107,** 459-60
'extrajudicial killing' **121,** 612, 634-6
Head of State immunity and **103,** 591-2
legislative history **104,** 172
responsibility of military commander **104,** 172
retroactivity **104,** 176-8
s 2(b) (exhaustion of remedies) **104,** 178, **107,** 460
Statute of Limitations **104,** 192
torture **104,** 156-7, **107,** 459
'under color of law' requirement **107,** 459
Trade Agreements Act 1979
s 104(b) **107,** 278, 279, 282-4
s 104(c) **107,** 283
s 303 **107,** 283-4
Trade and Tariff Act 1984 **107,** 295
Trading with the Enemy Acts (TWEA) 1917-42 **42,** 198-205, **54,** 532, 537-45, 548, **56,** 332, **60,** 19, 24, **61,** 41, 55, **63,** 72, **66,** 244, 255, 354, **72,** 280, **74,** 153-5
50 USC App 1-44 **107,** 257
50 USC App 9 **107,** 259-60
Alien Property Custodian **54,** 552, 572, 574
application **54,** 605-7
commercial transactions **54,** 548-9
constitutionality **54,** 548-9, **60,** 19-21, 24, **66,** 358-9
'enemy', burden of proof **54,** 573, 579, 581-2, 602-3, 606-7
'enemy' property, seizure **54,** 590
international relief organizations **54,** 548-9
jurisdiction **71,** 268
purpose **54,** 548-9, **60,** 20-3
recovery of seized property **54,** 584-7, 602
seizure of property **54,** 588
Transportation Safety Act 1974 **90,** 623
Travel Act **99,** 157
extraterritorial effect **99,** 159-61
treaties and **56,** 551-2
Trust Territories Code (TTC). *See* Trust Territories Code (TTC) *below*
Trusteeship Administration Act 1939 **87,** 560
Tucker Act **72,** 151, 291
28 USC 1491 **87,** 619
28 USC 1502 **87,** 619-20
UN staff, waiver of immunities **43,** 303
Uniform Commercial Code **78,** 674
Uniform Criminal Extradition and Rendition Act (11 ULA 3) **104,** 97
Uniform Foreign Money-Judgments Recognition Act (CPLR)
legislative history **81,** 577, 578
s 53 **81,** 561, 570
s 302 **81,** 578
s 327 **81,** 562, 563, 564 n. 4, 571, 574, 577-8
s 1015 **81,** 327, 562, 564 n. 4, 566
s 1021 **81,** 562, 571
s 5304 **81,** 561
s 5305 **81,** 561

Uniform Interstate and International Procedure Act (IIPA) **81,** 578
Uniform Military Justice Code **60,** 652-6
War Claims Act 1948 **56,** 538, 539, 544, 545
compensation for loss of property **56,** 332
War Crimes Act 1996 (18 USC 2441) **124,** 230
War Powers Resolution. *See* War Powers Resolution *below*
Water Pollution Control Act **63,** 357
Wilson Tariff Act. *See* Tariff Act 1897 *above*
law of nations. *See* international law *above*
League of Nations and **49,** 232
dissociation from, Mandates, effect on **37,** 61
legal assistance **79,** 389
legislation
common law, effect on **92,** 487-8
conformity with international law **81,** 547, 548
constitutionality
over-inclusiveness **121,** 523-5, 530-1, 538-41
under-inclusiveness **121,** 525-6, 541-4
ex post facto. *See* legislation, retroactive *below*
gaps, filled by analogy **104,** 189-92
repeal, implied **79,** 5-6, **81,** 665, **122,** 664
separation of powers and **91,** 107-9
legislation, interpretation **77,** 217-20, 240-5, 249-51, **79,** 464-7, **81,** 498 n. 26. *See also* treaties, primacy *below*
aids
absence of enforcement mechanisms **90,** 627
administrative interpretations **90,** 627-8, 629-30, 631, 632, 639-41
dictionary **96,** 131, 136-7, **100,** 534, 551
explanatory notes **92,** 459
external sources **83,** 128
international agreement **79,** 621-4
international law **91,** 500
legislative history **63,** 342-3, **77,** 211-15, 249-51, **79,** 5, 7, 12-13, 381, 463, 566, 567-8, 606, 618-25, 631, 636-8, **81,** 546, 547-8, 577, 663, 664, **82,** 296-7, 326, **84,** 91, 99, 100, 116, 155, 157, 171, 172, 173, **86,** 7, 36-40, **87,** 494, 552, **88,** 84, 186, **89,** 364, 365, **90,** 590-1, 595, 631, 632, 635-6, 639, 641, **91,** 498-9, **92,** 387, 395, 419, 451-2, 465, 466, 486, **94,** 91 n. 12, 92-3, **95,** 590-2, **96,** 131, **99,** 86, **101,** 423, 474-5, 512, 513, 543-4, 567, **104,** 147, 158, 176, 178, **107,** 312, 313, 316-17, 365, 402-3, 420-1, **122,** 676
location in text **95,** 586 n. 17, 588-90, 608
non-binding statements by UNHCR **79,** 638
other national legislation **79,** 569, **122,** 675-6
Restatement of Foreign Relations Law **92,** 451-2, 459-60
State practice **90,** 590, 591
treaty *travaux préparatoires* **95,** 587, 596-8
UNHCR *Handbook on Procedures and Criteria for Determining Refugee Status* **88,** 8-9, 30, 31, **95,** 551
writers **79,** 630
ambiguity **86,** 36
'boiler plate' language **90,** 623-4
contemporaneity **90,** 628
customary international law rules **104,** 181
guidelines

United States of America (USA) (*cont.*)
absurdity, avoidance of **96,** 132
ambiguities resolved in favour of alien **79,** 629
clear intention **79,** 630-1
clear language **84,** 148, 155, 172, 173, **95,** 605, **96,** 130, 131, 135, **99,** 160-1
common sense **99,** 86, 87
conflict with treaty **101,** 303-4, 567-9
conformity with international law **79,** 12
contemporary meaning **99,** 87, **100,** 514
expressio unius est exclusio alterius **107,** 400-1
foreign law, avoidance of conflict with **90,** 627, 637, 639
foreign relations, avoidance of embarrassment **90,** 592
'identical language' rule **96,** 137-9
intention of legislature **63,** 21, 69, 87-8, 107, 153, 194, 345, 506, 527, 564, 572, **90,** 592, 593, **94,** 95, **95,** 609, **96,** 39, 130-5, 144-7, **107,** 403. *See also* Foreign Sovereign Immunities Act (FSIA) 1976/82, intention of legislature *above*
intention of legislature, clearly expressed **79,** 630-1, **118,** 313, **121,** 633-4
language of Statute **87,** 494, **90,** 590-1, 639, 641, **101,** 564, **107,** 377
leges posteriores priores contrarias abrogant **82,** 296
lenity principle **86,** 36
liberal construction of tax law **87,** 553
logic and reason **79,** 568
narrow **82,** 314, 318
object and purpose **87,** 549, **96,** 141-2, **122,** 675-6
ordinary and natural meaning **79,** 617-18, **100,** 534, 551
plain language **82,** 353, **86,** 94-7, **90,** 595, 623, 628, **92,** 453, **95,** 529-30, 538 n. 3, 586, 587, **96,** 130-5, **103,** 526, **104,** 158, 182, **107,** 390, 400-1
plain meaning **79,** 629, **87,** 552, **122,** 672-3
purpose **83,** 128, **84,** 112, **92,** 387, 458, 487
reasonable **99,** 91
statute as a whole **100,** 533
statute as a whole, including amendment **121,** 631
motive, relevance **82,** 313
new circumstances and **91,** 499
phrases. *See also* Foreign Sovereign Immunities Act (FSIA) 1976/82, phrases *and under individual laws*
'agency' **90,** 612 n. 5, **96,** 29
'air carrier' **82,** 328
'air commerce' **86,** 37, 40
'alien' **95,** 585
'all territory and waters subject to the jurisdiction of the United States' **90,** 590-1
'any' **87,** 552
'arbitral award' **96,** 9
'arising under Federal law' **79,** 555-60, **81,** 546, **103,** 528-30, **104,** 176 n. 11, 178
'arising under the laws of the United States' **99,** 65-6
'arising under treaties' **79,** 399-403, 485 n. 1
'arising under a treaty' **81,** 513-14
'assisted the enemy in persecuting civilians' **95,** 508, 518-19
'between a [constituent] State and any place outside thereof' **90,** 623, 634
'boycott' **100,** 578-84, 588-95
'child' **95,** 486 n. 2
'clear probability of' **79,** 614, 617-20, 623-41

'coastline' **91,** 413-14
'color of law' **104,** 146, 158, 176, 178, **107,** 459
'combat activities' **94,** 126
'courts of justice or administrative agents' **90,** 602
'customs waters' **91,** 526 n. 28
'designated' **66,** 355-7
'discretionary function' **101,** 482-5
'displaced person' **95,** 508
'doing business in'. *See* jurisdiction, nexus *above*
'employee' **90,** 629
'employer' **90,** 623, 625, 634
'enemy' **94,** 172-3
'entity' **107,** 417
'extrajudicial killing' **121,** 612
'foreign country' **87,** 549, **100,** 526, 531, 537-40, 553, **122,** 673-7
'foreign State' **90,** 599, 611 n. 5
'found in the US' **88,** 180, 182
'henceforth' **103,** 614
'hostilities' **87,** 663-5, 672, 673, 675, 679
'immediate relative' **95,** 485
'immigrant' **45,** 334
'industry affecting commerce' **90,** 622, 623
'instrumentality of foreign State' **103,** 468
'laws of', common law **81,** 512, 590
'laws of', Executive Orders **81,** 513
'laws of', statutory **81,** 512
'national treatment' **101,** 578-80
'national of US' **90,** 628
'non-immigrant treaty trader' **54,** 259-63
offence 'within the jurisdiction of' **63,** 207-8, **79,** 543
'organ of a foreign State or political subdivision thereof' **101,** 482, 489
'overseas or foreign air commerce' **82,** 355-7
'particular social group'. *See* refugees, 'membership of a particular social group' *below*
'person', foreign State as **63,** 69-70, 106-20, 207-8, 294-6
'person within the jurisdiction' **118,** 35
'platforms or other man-made structures at sea' **100,** 507
'political incidence theory' **79,** 390
'possession' **90,** 626, 636
'proceedings' **89,** 573
'property' **42,** 178-9
'return' **95,** 607 n. 12
'rights in immovable property' **84,** 90-4
'special aircraft jurisdiction' **86,** 35-6, 37-8
'substantial and foreseeable' **103,** 515-16
'territory of the United States' **113,** 541
'the high seas and waters over which the US has jurisdiction' **91,** 498-500
'the same as' **96,** 128-47
'the special maritime and territorial jurisdiction of the US' **91,** 472, 474
'time of war' **99,** 86-9, 91
'transaction or occurrence' **63,** 316
'treaty' **101,** 564-9

United States of America (USA) (*cont.*)
'under actual or apparent authority' **104,** 147
'United States' **81,** 547, 548-9, 666-7, **87,** 548-9, **90,** 589, 590, **107,** 390
'United States forces' **94,** 126
'United States person' **107,** 413 n. 12
'violent political disturbance', 'well-founded fear of' **79,** 613, 616-20, 623-41
'voluntarily assisted enemy forces . . . in their operations' **95,** 508, 518-19
'war' **87,** 694
'waters' **81,** 667
policy coherence **90,** 594, 595
sovereignty, avoidance of conflict with **90,** 626-7
statute as whole **90,** 626, 635
presumption of conformity with international law **77,** 265, **81,** 664, **86,** 43, **88,** 180-1, **90,** 632-3, **95,** 610, **100,** 597-9, **101,** 566-7, **103,** 619, **122,** 676
presumption of conformity with treaty **94,** 93-4, **96,** 132, **101,** 303-4, 567-9, **107,** 281-9, **122,** 676
legislative intent, relevance **82,** 291-3, 295, 325, 326-7, **96,** 132-3
presumption of territorial limitation **63,** 87-8, **88,** 181, **90,** 622, 630, 632, 633, 634-5, **95,** 589, 609, **99,** 157, **100,** 498, 522, 523-5, 535-6, 597
foreign relations as basis for **121,** 634
presumption of validity **87,** 620
responsibility
courts **95,** 548 n. 6
implementing party **106,** 414-15
treaty, language of treaty, correspondence with **103,** 568-9
treaty as aid **87,** 474, 475, **94,** 92-5, **95,** 586, 592-6, 599
variety of meanings within Statute **96,** 130-2, 137-41
legislation, retroactive **79,** 381, 391, 411, 605, **82,** 315, **84,** 155-7, **87,** 617, **91,** 16, 20
anti-terrorist legislation **121,** 611 n. 4, 631-2, 645
bill of attainder **91,** 16, 83-6, 107-9
procedural legislation **104,** 177
State immunity legislation. *See* Foreign Sovereign Immunities Act (FSIA) 1976/82, retroactive effect *above*
torture **104,** 176-8
legislative encroachment **82,** 311-14
Lend-Lease, neutrality and **49,** 83
letter of credit, executory nature **106,** 415
limitation of liability
applicable law **87,** 558-9
venue **87,** 551-2, 559
Louisiana
boundary dispute, islands **59,** 211-17
Code of Civil Procedure, jurisdiction **63,** 347-50
Direct Action Statute **54,** 234-40
historic waters **59,** 264-73
territorial sea **59,** 275-305, 314-17
Texas, boundary with **59,** 200-17, 227-45
water boundaries **59,** 228-31
mail. *See* correspondence *above*
mandamus **63,** 24, 31-2, **79,** 467-8
Marshall Islands, Status of Forces Agreement (1982) **87,** 581
Massachusetts, Tort Claims Act, public employer's immunity for tortious acts **125,** 150-63

measure of damages/compensation including valuation of company/property/assets
lawfulness of taking, relevance **103,** 467-8
pain and suffering **107,** 460
unjust enrichment **92,** 436
Mexico
Claims Conventions (1923) **46,** 421, 465 n. 7, 468 n. 14, 472, 474, 506
Payne–Warren Agreement **66,** 188-9, 263-5
treaty status **66,** 263-5
military commission, basis **81,** 512-13
military courts, jurisdiction **54,** 528-9
military occupation
courts **81,** 512-13
legal basis **81,** 512-13
executive, responsibility of **81,** 513
military service, exception **56,** 563
resident aliens **56,** 563
most-favoured-nation status, UK **56,** 552
NAAEC (North American Agreement on Environment Cooperation) (1993), as precondition for conclusion of NAFTA **121,** 148
NAFTA Panels, binding on Member States, whether **107,** 288
Nantucket Bay
status **91,** 429-38
title **91,** 429-38
national emergency **60,** 19, **72,** 134, 274, 280
National Labor Relations Board
discretion **63,** 88-91
Foreign Sovereign Immunities Act (FSIA) 1976 and **63,** 595, 651-2
jurisdiction **63,** 7, 18-21, 81-92, 647-54
public policy and **63,** 81, 88-91, 653-4
nationality
citizenship distinguished **120,** 6
corporation, proof **70,** 500-18
renunciation of **60,** 240
nationality legislation, 'immigrant', meaning **45,** 334
nationals. *See also* jurisdiction, personal *above*
claims against foreign governments **56,** 333-4
'designated' **66,** 355-7
extradition of **79,** 437-8, 544
jurisdiction over **56,** 55-7
property, compensation for loss of **56,** 540
abroad **56,** 538-9, 541-2, 543, 544-5, 546-7
during war **56,** 332-4
protection of **87,** 582
standard of treatment **103,** 618
subrogation of rights **69,** 4-6
nationals abroad. *See also* jurisdiction, nationals abroad *above*
constitutional protection **56,** 241-2
postal service, in respect of **56,** 238
protection of **59,** 396
wrongful death **63,** 245-51
NATO Status of Forces Agreement and **60,** 37-8
naturalization
denaturalization

United States of America (USA) (*cont.*)
fraudulent procurement of citizenship **95,** 507, 513-15
wilful concealment of a material fact **95,** 507, 512-18, 530 n. 11, 534
requirements, good moral character **95,** 510 n. 11
necessity, American Law Institute Penal Code **122,** 638
New Jersey
Anti-Racketeering Act **88,** 96
political offence, offences within the jurisdiction **88,** 45-7
New York
Banking Law
jurisdiction, non-resident litigants **66,** 171
overseas deposits **66,** 471
s 138 **66,** 471
Business Corporation Law, s 1314 (non-resident corporations) **63,** 42
City Commission on Human Rights, scope of authority **66,** 306-10
Civil Practice Law and Rules **66,** 211
'doing business in New York' **38,** 114, **63,** 322-3, 400, **96,** 76-8
s 6213 (attachment) **63,** 410-11
s 6214 **63,** 146-8, 252-60
Civil Rights Law **56,** 22, 583
Decedent Estate Law **42,** 33
Judiciary Law
s 489 **66,** 408-9
s 495 **66,** 408-9
Statute of Limitations **66,** 211
New York City Commission on Human Rights, act of State **66,** 306-10
New York Convention on the Recognition and Enforcement of Foreign Arbitral Awards (1958)
date of award **103,** 568-70
State immunity and **103,** 563, 565-7, 577-80
nuclear weapons, deployment of cruise missiles in Europe, justiciability **99,** 45-53
Nuremberg Charter (1945), individual responsibility **104,** 154
obligation, *situs* **84,** 127-30
Office of Alien Property **71,** 267
overseas investment **59,** 373, 374, 375-6, 388, 423. *See also* Overseas Private Investment Corporation
Overseas Private Investment Corporation
functions **59,** 371
policy **59,** 394-5
private investment overseas, protection of **59,** 369-70, 389, 392-5, 413-18, 422, 431
expropriatory action, definition **59,** 375-6, 401-2
requirements **59,** 393-5, 397
purposes **59,** 390, 410
Panama, Isthmian Canal Convention (1902) **51,** 281
Panama Canal Zone, US territory, whether part of **56,** 50-2
parens patriae, limitation to proceedings abroad **118,** 475
passport
diplomatic
diplomatic status, whether conferring **99,** 165-6
discretionary power **99,** 166
retention by consul, right to recover **113,** 512-13
Pennsylvania, Uniform Commercial Code **66,** 195

permanent residence, international official **83,** 388
Philippines, Treaty concerning Independence (1964) **46,** 481
piracy, individual, responsibility for **104,** 152, 153
PLO, in. *See* Palestine Liberation Organization (PLO), USA, in
Poland, Claims Agreement (1960) **42,** 183-6
interest on awards **42,** 189-94
political offence **79,** 390, 395, 428, 435, 446-57, 461-2, 469-74, 493-4, 495, 497-533
burden of proof **104,** 93, 94
classification as
anarchism **79,** 455-6, 480 n. 4, 508, 514
applicable law **104,** 56, 67
bomb attack on civilians travelling by commercial bus **104,** 64-76
fraud involving political corruption **104,** 113-14
offence by official while suppressing rebellion **104,** 38-42
ordinary offence with political motivation **104,** 86
terrorism. *See* terrorism *below*
definition/requirements, 'pure'/'relative' **104,** 86
determination, executive or judicial role, whether **79,** 446-52, 469-74
extradition, double jeopardy **104,** 62 n. 2
incidence test
acts incidental to violent uprising **104,** 40-2, 65, 86-90, 93, 112-13
'political incidence' test **79,** 390
motivation of requesting party **79,** 428-9, 450-1, 452, 482
prescribed organization, membership **79,** 453, 454
reasons for exception
changed context **104,** 40, 88, 90
non-intervention in internal affairs of another country **104,** 39, 40
protection against authoritarian regime **104,** 39
protection against unfair trial and punishment **104,** 39
relevant factors
legality under international law **104,** 68-9, 90, 93
motivation **79,** 390, 435, 453
motive **104,** 65-8, 86, 89
nature of offence **79,** 390
place of offence **104,** 66 n. 8
prevailing circumstances at time of offence **79,** 390, 424, 435, 448
status of victim **104,** 89-90, 94
tactic previously used **104,** 66 n. 8
victim's status **79,** 390, 456-7
violent uprising at time of offence **104,** 40, 93, 94
responsibility for determining whether **104,** 38 n. 22, 87
executive certificate/statement, conclusiveness **104,** 87, 163
separation of powers **107,** 451
terrorist offence **104,** 79, 87-93
political by definition **104,** 92
'violent political disturbance'
definition **79,** 452, 453, 461
evidence of **79,** 453
political question doctrine **81,** 566-7, 637 n. 11, **82,** 289, **87,** 515, 662, 675, 676, 677-9, 687-9, 699-703, **88,** 57-9, 125-6. *See also* justiciability *above*
acts and omissions of State organ, warship **99,** 84
Constitution as basis **94,** 100, 109, 112-13, 117-21, **99,** 61
contras in Nicaragua **99,** 58-91

United States of America (USA) (*cont.*)
control of State's assets abroad **86,** 18
foreign relations question as **82,** 290, 333-5, **87,** 515, 664, **88,** 122
historical development **94,** 101-6
immunity of State vessel **94,** 105
implementation of law **94,** 126-7
internal affairs, relevance in **94,** 109-10
nationalization measures in course of war **94,** 109-10
jurisdictional bar **94,** 109
justiciability **42,** 393-401, 438, **63,** 72, **66,** 111-13, 119, 306, 333-8, 396-7, **77,** 225-7, 232, 252, 256, 270-1, **80,** 22, 590
maintenance of forces abroad **94,** 114-15
properly authorized, whether **94,** 114, 120
military operation **99,** 84-5
prisoner of war status **99,** 187
reasons for
absence of judicially discoverable and manageable standards **64,** 351, **94,** 110-11, 114, 126, **99,** 49-51, 53, 62-72, 77-8, 84-5, 181, **104,** 162, **107,** 257-8, 259, **114,** 628-9
confidentiality **94,** 110, 114, **95,** 619
difficulty in handling relevant information **94,** 110, 114, **95,** 618, **96,** 75
foreign policy considerations **104,** 162-3, **107,** 258
hierarchy, whether **99,** 49
international effects **94,** 110, 114, **99,** 52, 72-4, 79
policy decision, need for **104,** 162
prudence **95,** 618, 619
responsibility of another branch of government **95,** 618, 619, **96,** 75-6, **99,** 48-9, 53, **104,** 162, **107,** 258, 259
recognition, foreign State **86,** 3-4, 5-7, 12, 18, **96,** 48
recognition, government **94,** 102, 103-4
remedy, existence of alternative
complaint to executive agency **107,** 259-60
judicial review **107,** 260
remedy sought, relevance **99,** 49 n. 8, 51-3, 85
self-defence **94,** 114
separation of powers and **94,** 109, 115-16, 117-20, **95,** 620, **99,** 61, 177, 180, **123,** 147-8
State immunity, jurisdiction **63,** 71-3
State immunity, jurisdiction, classification of act, violation of international law **103,** 557-8
test **94,** 107-8, 124-5
treaty interpretation **82,** 290 n. 22, **90,** 685-6
US intervention in Panama (1989) **99,** 177-83
war, matters relating to **99,** 90-1
state of **94,** 113-14, **123,** 147
termination **94,** 106
post. *See* correspondence *above*
Potsdam Agreement 1945, violation of Constitution, whether **56,** 543
precedent in municipal courts, international tribunal decisions **104,** 99
preliminary injunction **86,** 4-8
balance of hardships **86,** 18-19, **96,** 51
irreparable harm **86,** 4-5, 18, **96,** 50-1

likelihood of success **86,** 5-8, 17-18, **96,** 48-50
public interest **86,** 19, **96,** 51
security **86,** 8
prescription **91,** 466. *See also* acquiescence *above*
requirements
absence of protest **91,** 450, 451
continuous and open exercise of authority **91,** 448-51
non-active nature of doctrine **91,** 448-9
passage of time **91,** 450
possession **91,** 448
President. *See also* law of, Executive Orders *above*
authority of **63,** 504-5
Commander in Chief, powers **42,** 394, 397, 399, 438
designation of international organizations **63,** 93, 192-4, 340, 342
emergency powers **63,** 504-5
foreign relations **56,** 22
immunity from suit, Commander-in-chief, acts committed as **80,** 22-3
liability for official acts of former **81,** 597-8
prerogative, disapproval of Order on foreign policy or national security grounds **82,** 322-4
President Wilson
annexation, opposition to **37,** 196, 528
Fourteen points **37,** 29, 401
'open door' clause **37,** 518
treaty-making capacity **44,** 279, **56,** 543
war, power to declare **56,** 22-4, 583, **60,** 16
prisoners of war
definition **99,** 167 n. 22, 185-6
fair trial
coerced confession **99,** 167-8
fair and impartial tribunal **99,** 167-8
internment, according to nationality **99,** 169
jurisdiction
equivalency principle **99,** 168
ex post facto legislation **99,** 168-9
offences committed before becoming prisoner of war **99,** 167, 168
repatriation after cessation of hostilities, criminal proceedings pending, where **99,** 169-70
transfer to third country **99,** 169
private international law, locus, aviation disaster **107,** 389-90
privileges and immunities, public officials **94,** 366
prize law, torture **81,** 591
prize proceedings **81,** 664-6. *See also* admiralty jurisdiction *above*
public interest, antitrust **81,** 520
procedural regulations, interpretation **79,** 382
property
compensation for loss of
abroad **56,** 538-9, 541-2, 543, 544-5, 546-7
during war **56,** 332-4
contract rights **62,** 224
expropriation by Government **56,** 541-2
just compensation **56,** 541-2

United States of America (USA) (*cont.*)
future or contingent interest **106,** 414-15
interest in, blocked account **63,** 427-9
letter of credit **106,** 414-15
'no property or interests in property', definition, responsibility **106,** 414
right to debt repayment as **92,** 439
taking. *See* expropriation/nationalization *above*
provisional measures **81,** 495
assets, prevention of dissipation **104,** 129-33
judicial review, time-limits **106,** 413
merits, likelihood of success and **81,** 638-40, **104,** 133
public interest **79,** 395, **81,** 520, **84,** 143
public order/public policy/*ordre public* **79,** 408, 412, 577, 579, 580
confiscation, compensation for **66,** 52, 56, 69-70, 77, 117, 132, 196, 215, 254-5, 375
expropriation, wartime validity **66,** 254-5
jurisdiction, assumption of and **81,** 580
racial discrimination, international organizations, privileges and immunities **113,** 500-3. *See also* government *above*
recognition, government **86,** 3-4, **87,** 587-8
access to municipal courts **96,** 52
act of State and **98,** 65
ambassador, appointment **86,** 6, 18, **107,** 258
China, People's Republic of, effect **96,** 85-7
conditional **98,** 5-6
diplomatic relations distinguished **94,** 214
foreign policy exception **86,** 9, 18
implied, access to courts **94,** 207-8
interference in internal affairs, whether **96,** 50
legal counsel, right to appoint and **96,** 51-2
Libya **94,** 201-8, **96,** 94-5
interim government's right of suit **96,** 92, 94
National Patriotic Reconstruction Assembly Government (NPRAG) **96,** 94-6
non-recognition, effect **86,** 8, 12
enforcement of arbitral award **94,** 201-2, 204-8
political question **86,** 3-4, 5-7, 12
Panama **96,** 46-54, **99,** 161-3
political weapon **94,** 214
property, right to and **96,** 48-9
applicable law **96,** 49
responsibility
Congress **94,** 102
courts **86,** 6, 12, 17-18
executive **86,** 4, 5, 12, 17, **87,** 586, 588-9, **94,** 207, 215, **96,** 48, 49-50, 94, **98,** 5-7, **99,** 161, **103,** 586, 587-8, **107,** 258-9, **122,** 672
right to sue and **94,** 201-2, 204-8, **96,** 94
treaties, effect on **96,** 86-9
withdrawal, continuation of diplomatic relations **96,** 86
recognition policy **61,** 49-51, 60-5, 75-7
recognition, State **88,** 40
constitutive theory **104,** 152 n. 2
non-recognition, effect
administrative act **108,** 503-5
legislation, expropriation of property **108,** 503-5

relevance, responsibility for violation of international law **104,** 158
responsibility, executive **63,** 30, **82,** 333, **108,** 504
Reconstruction Finance Corporation, immunity from suit **80,** 574 n. 1
refugees **79,** 612-41, **87,** 440-5
admission **70,** 347-53
qualification of applicants **70,** 348-53
definition **79,** 615, 618, 621-3, 635, 639, **87,** 482, 493, 496, **88,** 6, 16, **95,** 539 n. 4, 549, 572
deportation
appeals procedure **79,** 612, 616-18, 635
withhold **79,** 612-20, 623-9, 632-9
expulsion **70,** 361-2
'membership of a particular social group' **87,** 493-5, **95,** 573, **124,** 402, 483-5, 486, 495, 496, 506-7
'persecution' **79,** 381
well-founded fear **87,** 440-3, 466, 467, 472 n. 18, 473, 474, 482-3, 504-6
standard of proof **87,** 466, 470, 473, 481, 497-9
'persecution or well-founded fear of persecution' **88,** 6-7, 20-5, **95,** 548 n. 4
burden of proof **88,** 7, **95,** 564-5
categories specified in Geneva Convention on the Status of Refugees (1951), limited to **95,** 572
clear probability **79,** 614, 617-20, 623-41, **95,** 549-50, 554-6, 559, 564
conscientious objection **95,** 550-6, 558-60
evidence of **87,** 495-6
extended family **95,** 565-6
extortion **95,** 540-1
general conditions of political unrest **95,** 565
genuine fear **95,** 539, 553
group persecution **88,** 7, 20, 24, 31, 33-5
ideology as basis **88,** 13 n. 3, 28
military service evasion **88,** 7-13, 21, 24-5
motivation, relevance **95,** 553-4, 556
objective **95,** 540-2, 553, 565
past persecution **95,** 542-3
physical assault, relevance **95,** 541 n. 6
political opinion **87,** 486-8, **95,** 540-2
'reasonable person' **88,** 20, 32 n. 11, 36
reasonable possibility **95,** 539, 553, 565
refusal to join non-governmental group **95,** 560
relevant factors, punishment as key **88,** 9, **95,** 559
religious belief **95,** 554
requirements, discriminatory intent **95,** 550-1
requirements, government's knowledge or belief **95,** 559
responsibility for determining **88,** 23, 26-7
social group membership **87,** 491-6
standard of proof **95,** 548
State responsibility and **88,** 11, 23, 31
subjective **95,** 540, 572
substantial economic disadvantage **95,** 540-1
threat to life **79,** 616, 623, **87,** 485, **95,** 542
well-founded fear **79,** 613, 616-20, 623-41
well-founded fear, assumed belief **95,** 542, 555, 556
well-founded fear, balance of probabilities test **87,** 485-6

United States of America (USA) (*cont.*)
well-founded fear, more likely than not **95,** 549, 556
recognition as **88,** 6, 16
refoulement. *See* deportation withhold/bar *and* refugees, deportation *above*
standard of treatment, preferential immigrant status **87,** 472, 476
status
competence to accord **79,** 622, 635
determination **87,** 480, 482
UNHCR *Handbook on Procedures and Criteria for Determining Refugee Status* (1979) **87,** 493 n. 4, 494
remedies **80,** 591
breach of constitutional rights, for **80,** 592-3
corollary to right, whether **79,** 563, 569-70
courts' duty to adjust, violations of international law **79,** 402
diplomatic protection as **79,** 570 n. 4
illusory **79,** 580
need to exhaust **79,** 580
international law, breach, foreign State **104,** 153, 159, 180
non-monetary, discretionary **80,** 591-2
provision of, responsibility for **80,** 591-3
set-off **79,** 565
third party claim **104,** 189-92
res judicata **66,** 131-2, 178, **79,** 389, 395, 418-20, 498 n. 3
extradition, multiple extradition requests **104,** 82
responsibility, executive **79,** 626-8, 631-6
Restatement of Agency (Second) **99,** 131-2, 133, 136
Restatement of Conflict of Laws (1971) **77,** 188, **78,** 604, **79,** 407, 408 n. 5
Restatement of Conflict of Laws (Second) (1971) **84,** 119
31 **81,** 561, 573, 577
145 (tort: nexus) **107,** 389, **108,** 499
160 **87,** 638
161 **87,** 637
164 **87,** 637
175 (place of injury) **98,** 124, **121,** 632
177 **87,** 638
187 **87,** 635, 646
201 **87,** 636
222 (choice of law) **94,** 171
246 (choice of law) **94,** 171
351 **87,** 638
Restatement of Foreign Relations Law (Proposed Official Draft (1962)) **79,** 577
Restatement of Foreign Relations Law (1965) **77,** 179, 207, 217
18 (effects doctrine) **81,** 501
41 (act of State) **81,** 519, 595
65 (State immunity) **81,** 597
66 (State immunity) **81,** 597
Restatement of Foreign Relations Law (Revised) **84,** 91, 119 n. 13, 193, 195
428 **88,** 66, 125
469 **88,** 81
jurisdiction **82,** 349, 350
State immunity **86,** 73-4, 91 n. 3
Restatement of Foreign Relations Law (Revised) (Council Draft) **84,** 542
Restatement of Foreign Relations Law (Revised) (Tent. Draft 1)

304 (constitutional constraints on treaty-making) **81,** 576
329 ff (treaty interpretation) **81,** 575-6
Restatement of Foreign Relations Law (Revised) (Tent. Draft 2) (1981)
403 **87,** 525
jurisdiction **77,** 41, 217, 266
statehood **82,** 401
Restatement of Foreign Relations Law (Revised) (Tent. Draft 3) (1982), international crimes under **77,** 210
Restatement of Foreign Relations Law (Revised) (Tent. Draft 4) (1983) **77,** 273
428 (act of State) **81,** 595
464 (privileges and immunities of international organizations) **99,** 97, 98
Title B (diplomatic privileges and immunities) **99,** 109 n. 9
Restatement of Foreign Relations Law (Revised) (Tent. Draft 6) (1985) **79,** 10, 12, 14
702 (prolonged arbitrary detention) **95,** 634
effects doctrine **96,** 181-2, 183-4, 186
Restatement of Foreign Relations Law (Revised) (Tent. Draft 7) (1986) **79,** 601, 602,
469 (act of State) **81,** 595, 596
Restatement of Foreign Relations Law (Second) (1965) **84,** 91, 93, 116, 118, 125, 183, 199, 214, 669 n. 2
18 (effects doctrine) **66,** 281, **81,** 555, **92,** 445-6, 451-2, 459-60, **96,** 181-2
18 (extraterritorial legislation), jurisdiction distinguished **121,** 494 n. 6
30 (jurisdiction over national abroad) **66,** 285, **81,** 500, 548, **99,** 154 n. 4
33 **90,** 593 n. 11
40 (self-incrimination) **66,** 284-5, **104,** 608
41 (act of State) **66,** 251, 278, 286, 297, 402, 492, **88,** 117, 118, **101,** 534
43 **66,** 96, 310, 481-2
56 **66,** 432
65 (restrictive theory of State immunity) **92,** 484-5
66 (Head of State, definition) **103,** 586, **104,** 143 n. 7
68(b) (State immunity: immovable property exception) **107,** 199
69 **66,** 225
70(2)(b) **66,** 227
73 (consular functions) **101,** 482 n. 6
77 (territorial jurisdiction) **81,** 548
84 (privileges and immunities of international organization, waiver) **99,** 99, 100
154 (self-executing treaty) **95,** 614
159 **66,** 359-60
186 **66,** 375
187 **66,** 480
188 **66,** 375, 434, 480
189 **66,** 480
190 **66,** 480
192 **66,** 34, 42, 358
195 **66,** 34
198 **66,** 20
423 **88,** 181
443(1) **88,** 194
461 **88,** 40
extraterritorial jurisdiction **91,** 473, **100,** 523, 525
passive personality principle **94,** 87
internal waters **91,** 514 n. 9
international standards of procedural justice **91,** 479 n. 29
non-signatories to treaty, status **91,** 476

United States of America (USA) (*cont.*)
self-executing treaties **91,** 522, 523
ships' flags **91,** 475 n. 15
State immunity **86,** 72, 79
treaty ratification **86,** 24 n. 15
Restatement of Foreign Relations Law (Second) (Tent. Draft 2), jurisdiction **79,** 7
Restatement of Foreign Relations Law (Tent. Draft 2 (1981)) **79,** 7, 403
Restatement of Foreign Relations Law (Tent. Draft 5 (1984)) **79,** 542, 543, 545
Restatement of Foreign Relations Law (Tentative Final Draft) **84,** 513
Restatement of Foreign Relations Law (Third)
1 **82,** 312 n. 11
102 (sources of international law) **103,** 470, 472, 474, 609, 616, **107,** 285
102(2) (customary international law) **103,** 616
111(3) (self-executing treaties) **90,** 658, **99,** 188 n. 8
111(4) (self-executing treaties: presumption) **99,** 189
115 **82,** 292
115 (legislative interpretation in accordance with treaty) **107,** 285-6
201 (recognition) **87,** 653, **94,** 214, **104,** 157, **121,** 588
202 (recognition) **104,** 157
203 (recognition) **87,** 586
205(1) (non-recognized government: access to courts) **108,** 504
205(3) (non-recognized government: effect of acts) **108,** 503
207 (recognition) **104,** 158
207(c) **99,** 131
221 (international organization: definition) **107,** 421
223 (international organization: capacity) **107,** 421-2
235 (extraterritorial legislation) **100,** 597
301(1) (definition of treaty) **99,** 130
311 (authority to conclude treaties) **99,** 130, 131
321 (*pacta sunt servanda*) **107,** 285
331(2)(8) (invalidity of treaty) **99,** 136 n. 1
401-16 (extraterritorial jurisdiction) **100,** 598
402 (effects doctrine) **114,** 596
402(1) (effects doctrine) **99,** 154-6
403 (extraterritorial jurisdiction; reasonableness) **99,** 156-7, **100,** 523
403(1) (extraterritorial jurisdiction; reasonableness) **100,** 600
403(2) (extraterritorial jurisdiction; nexus) **100,** 600
403(3) (extraterritorial jurisdiction; conflict of interests) **100,** 600
404 (universal offences) **88,** 181, 182, **104,** 153, 183 n. 25, 193
415 (extraterritorial jurisdiction) **100,** 585-6, 587
432 (forcible abduction) **90,** 658, 689, 693-4, **95,** 369, 374
441 (foreign State compulsion) **104,** 541
443 (act of State; admissibility issue) **99,** 163, **119,** 107
451 (State immunity: sovereign acts) **107,** 403-4
452 (State instrumentality) **101,** 546
455 (diplomatic immunity) **103,** 585, **121,** 572
456 (waiver of immunity) **99,** 133
459 (default judgments against foreign State) **99,** 134
461(c) (State immunity: terrorist acts) **104,** 539
464 (diplomatic status) **99,** 166, **103,** 585
464 (immunities: former Head of State) **119,** 80, **121,** 572
465 (consular immunity) **99,** 123
467 (international organization: privileges and immunities) **107,** 422-3

469 (UN Headquarters: immunity of invitee) **104,** 161
476 (political offence) **104,** 86
477 (speciality) **104,** 102
481 (recognition of foreign judgment) **103,** 570
492 (expropriation) **100,** 525
702 (State violation of international law) **103,** 472, 473, **104,** 153, 187 n. 35, 193
703 (international law: remedies) **104,** 180, 194
712 (expropriation) **122,** 335
712(2) **99,** 131
888 (violation of international law) **104,** 180
901 **90,** 665
902 **90,** 658
908 **90,** 658
diplomatic protection, payment under claims agreement as property of State **108,** 612
jurisdiction, personal **86,** 41
Reporter's Note 14
Head of State immunity **103,** 592
UN convention on Special Missions **121,** 602
treaty interpretation **86,** 43
Restatement of Foreign Relations Law (Third) (Revised)
191 (intangible asset as property) **92,** 439
192 (intended deprivation of interests in property) **92,** 440
202 (recognition, States) **96,** 88
203 (recognition, States) **96,** 66
207 (State succession) **96,** 65
208 (State succession) **96,** 65
209 (State succession) **96,** 65
210 (State succession, treaties) **96,** 112
336 (fundamental change of circumstances) **96,** 67
451 (agency) **92,** 378 n. 16
451 (State immunity) **92,** 488, **100,** 553
453 (personal jurisdiction) **92,** 426 n. 11
453 (purpose of contract, relevance) **92,** 428, 429 n. 18
712 (non-discrimination in expropriation) **92,** 438, **122,** 335
Restatement of the Law of Judgments (Second) (1982) **79,** 382
65 (right to challenge default judgment) **92,** 425
Restatement of the Law of Restitution
160 **81,** 592
168 **81,** 592
Restatement of Torts (Second)
315 (duty to control conduct of third parties) **121,** 486
551 **87,** 637
901 (basis of liability) **99,** 88
retroactivity. *See* legislation, retroactive *above*
Rhodesia
Consular Office in **56,** 537
status **53,** 537-8
Romania, Release of Assets Agreement (1960) **43,** 210
Rules of Practice in Proceedings Relative to Mailability 1969 **56,** 236-7
Ryukyu Islands. *See* Ryukyu Islands
security, exclusion of alien and **82,** 331
Security Council Resolution
binding effect **95,** 612-14

United States of America (USA) (*cont.*)
individual's rights **95,** 613-14
self-executing, whether **95,** 613-14
as treaty **95,** 614
separation of powers **53,** 22, **56,** 22, **57,** 77-8, **63,** 29, **77,** 225, 228, 230-7, 242, 251, **79,** 6, 12, 487, **80,** 591 n. 5, 592-3, 595, **81,** 576, **82,** 312 n. 11, 316-17, **87,** 664, 670, 691, 700, 701, **88,** 58-9, **107,** 288-9. *See also* foreign relations *and* political question doctrine *above*
act of State and **63,** 567 n. 38, **79,** 6, 446-51, 586, 596-7, **81,** 519, **86,** 48, **88,** 66, 73, 97, 99, 119-20, 121-3, 125-6, **92,** 389, 496, **98,** 108-9, **99,** 162, 165
exceptions, speciality **104,** 11
political offence **107,** 451
political question doctrine and. *See* political question doctrine, separation of powers and *above*
relationship between courts, Congress and executive **94,** 125-7, 132
retroactive legislation and **91,** 107-9
State immunity, jurisdiction and **63,** 28-9, 35-6, **99,** 162
treaty interpretation and **90,** 685
service of process **81,** 663 n. 2, **84,** 138, 143, 164-6, 168
applicable law, *lex fori* **96,** 78, 79-80
requirements **42,** 175-7
return of document, effect **84,** 138
service of process at UN headquarters
UN Headquarters Agreement **104,** 159-61
designated representative of UN member **104,** 160
transit to and from airport **104,** 160
visitor to UN **104,** 160-1
service of process on foreign company or company based outside the jurisdiction
applicable law **96,** 78-80
dissolved company **103,** 567-8
service of process on foreign State or State agency **63,** 264-8, 288, 377, 388. *See also* Foreign Sovereign Immunities Act (FSIA) 1976/82, 28 USC 1608 (service, time to answer, default) *above*
appointment of agent for, waiver of immunity, whether **63,** 356-7
default judgment. *See* Foreign Sovereign Immunities Act (FSIA) 1976/82, 28 USC 1608(e) (default judgment) *above*
default judgment, foreign State, agency or instrumentality distinguished **107,** 365
foreign corporation distinguished **63,** 149
judicial notice **107,** 365
method
consular agent **63,** 97, 264, 266, 372, 377
delivery to mission to UN **63,** 60-2, 124-7, 136-7
diplomatic channels **84,** 138
lawyer **63,** 22
registered post **63,** 21-3, 46-8, 179-80, 232, 254 n. 1, 264, 381, **121,** 624 n. 1
service on ambassador/head of mission **92,** 395
service on diplomatic premises. *See* service on diplomatic premises *below*
service on Ministry of External Relations **63,** 21-3, 381
telex **63,** 415-16, 551
visiting government officials **63,** 70
mission to UN as State for purposes of **63,** 125
out of the jurisdiction **63,** 411-15

requirements
acknowledgement of receipt **63,** 198
actual notice **107,** 365
adequate notice **107,** 314-15
official language of foreign State **63,** 136, **79,** 389, **84,** 143
timeliness **63,** 410-11
service on diplomatic premises **63,** 21-3, 60-2, 198, 254 n. 1
diplomatic immunity and **63,** 21-3, 124-6, 254
service on ambassador distinguished **63,** 21-3
State immunity, jurisdiction and
mandatory nature of rules **90,** 602, **107,** 313-15
relevance **103,** 564
State-owned ship **63,** 626, 631
State/State agency distinguished **107,** 311-17
'substantial compliance' **107,** 364-6
service of process on international organization **63,** 61-2, 288
service of process out of the jurisdiction **98,** 150
foreign State or State agency **63,** 411-15
ships, jurisdiction
flag State **90,** 633
ship as territory of flag State **63,** 611 n. 8
foreign ship outside territorial sea **84,** 210-18
waiver of objection by foreign State **84,** 211-12
foreign ship in US port **63,** 628, 630-1
in foreign territorial sea **57,** 165, **63,** 603
ships, State-owned
attachment, immunity **81,** 541
waiver **81,** 541
classification as, fishing vessels **63,** 15
collision involving **63,** 14-15, 605-12
slave trade, individual, responsibility for **104,** 152, 153
Social Security Self-Employment Tax, income tax, whether **36,** 459, 460, 461-5
South West Africa, Mandate, consent to **37,** 131, 133 n.
sovereign act, concession **89,** 357
sovereign immunity. *See* State immunity *below*
sovereignty **61,** 107, 123-7, 133
respect for **90,** 660-1
extradition agreement and **90,** 660-1
speciality and **90,** 661
unlawful arrest as violation **90,** 648
Soviet Claims Fund **84,** 163
speciality. *See* extradition, speciality *above*
standard of proof, balance of probabilities **104,** 93, 101
standard of treatment of nationals **88,** 87-9, **103,** 618, **121,** 182-3
standing, citizen intervener **122,** 636-8
State, of United States, definition **101,** 483-4
State agency/State-owned corporation/State entity
as 'citizen of a State' **63,** 443
classification
municipal highways authority **64,** 64-9
Securities and Exchange Commission (SEC) **64,** 48-51
State contract

United States of America (USA) (*cont.*)
change of government, fundamental change of circumstance, whether **96,** 67
State succession
executed contract **96,** 65
executory contract **96,** 65
State department, statement on 'hot' Libyan oil **66,** 374
State Department suggestions (act of State doctrine) **66,** 50-8, 106, 108, 114-21, 140-1, 221, 226-9, 237, 428-30, 458-9
State Department suggestions (State immunity) **42,** 119-22, **63,** 49, 51, 60-5, **66,** 50-8, 60, 106, 108, 114-21, 140-1, 221, 226-9, 237, 336, 373-4, 428-31, 449, **79,** 4, 553, **81,** 601, 604, 605, 606, 607, **92,** 485, 487-8
conclusiveness **63,** 11, 17, 26-32, 34-7, 39-40, 51-2, 67, 69, 218-19, **81,** 606-7, **104,** 143 n. 7
earlier consideration by courts, effect **63,** 60
failure to make, effect **63,** 2, 11, 50-1, 63, 65
Foreign Sovereign Immunities Act (FSIA) 1976/82, effect **63,** 74-6, 171-2, 219, 239-40, 248, 265, 289, 366, 385-6, 451-2, 501, 531, 545, 586, 615, **121,** 586
importance of **63,** 49, 51, 52, 218-19
political questions **66,** 336
procedure **63,** 25
reasons, need for **63,** 29-31
refusal, effect **63,** 34-7, 53-5, 61-2
sovereign immunity **66,** 9, 60, 120, 223
State Department suggestions (State-owned ships, immunity from attachment) **63,** 24-31
State immunity, arbitral award, enforcement **62,** 220-5, **89,** 358, 362-6, **103,** 561-71
waiver, agreement for recognition and enforcement of arbitral awards **103,** 577-80
State immunity, execution, procedural aspects, freezing/blocking as attachment **63,** 427-9, 505, **81,** 646
State immunity, execution/attachment, applicability
default judgment, right to raise jurisdictional immunity **92,** 425-6
funds held by Tripartite Commission for the Restitution of Monetary Gold **63,** 71-3
funds of nationalized bank held by central/State-owned bank **63,** 1-4
State-owned ship **81,** 541
State immunity, execution/attachment, entitlement, agency or instrumentality of a foreign State **80,** 577, **86,** 79
State immunity, execution/attachment, procedural aspects
connection between property and claim, need for **65,** 174, 242-3, **79,** 566
pre- and post-judgment attachment distinguished **92,** 402-3
State immunity, execution/attachment, purpose of proceedings
debt repayment from blocked account **63,** 425-35
jurisdictional **63,** 349-50, 500 n. 4, **92,** 404
safeguarding/conservatory measures **65,** 172-5, 239-40
Iranian assets in USA **63,** 500-11
State immunity, execution/attachment, purpose/use of funds/assets
acquisition and use distinguished **98,** 9-12
blocked assets **63,** 427-9
burden of proof **98,** 12
consular premises **107,** 239-42
diplomatic premises, immovable property exception, whether **98,** 49
shipping fees **89,** 359-60
State immunity, execution/attachment, theory/doctrine
development of concept **42,** 40, **65,** 173-5, 239-40
execution and attachment distinguished **63,** 309-10

freezing/blocking of assets as negation of **63,** 504-9
State immunity, jurisdiction distinguished **63,** 60, 266 n. 13, 500 n. 4, **99,** 143
State immunity, execution/attachment, waiver
agency or instrumentality of a foreign State **107,** 240
'and its agencies' **98,** 52-4
arbitration agreement, express provision **63,** 526
post-judgment **92,** 402
requirements, explicit **92,** 403-5
treaty provision **63,** 267-8, 280-2, 347-9, 429-30, 433-4, 514-19, **72,** 178-9
express provision, need for **63,** 270-2, 430, 503
Iran–US Treaty of amity (1955). *See* Iran–US Treaty of Amity (1955), waiver of State immunity, whether
State immunity, jurisdiction **86,** 59 n. 3, 61-2, 73-5, 77-80, 90, 645-7, **98,** 34-5. *See also* diplomatic immunity, jurisdiction *and* Foreign Sovereign Immunities Act (FSIA) 1976/82 *above*
Foreign Sovereign Immunities Act (FSIA) 1976/82. *See* Foreign Sovereign Immunities Act (FSIA) 1976/82 *above*
State immunity, jurisdiction, acts of
agent, private person acting as **113,** 514-15
diplomatic agent, ambassador/head of mission **99,** 133-4, 138
official outside scope of authority **57,** 157-8, **104,** 123-5, 175-6
State immunity, jurisdiction, applicability
acts in own territory **63,** 389
counterclaim arising out of the same subject matter **63,** 311-17, **94,** 152 n. 2
cross-claim distinguished **98,** 17, 20-1
criminal proceedings **98,** 153
disclosure of documents **107,** 251-3, 254
immunity in own courts and **107,** 355, 356-7, **118,** 54, 55
in own courts
acts committed abroad **80,** 22 n. 7
combatant activities in time of war **80,** 22 n. 7
security, request for **103,** 550-1
State succession and, Holocaust **103,** 600-1
State immunity, jurisdiction, classification of act **64,** 43, **107,** 378
academic appointment, university **107,** 369-70
acquisition and use distinguished **98,** 12-13
act rather than actor **98,** 107
aid programme, participation in **86,** 60, 71, 635
air navigation charges **107,** 328-34
air ticket, sale of **63,** 449-50, 473
air transport **63,** 134, 195-6, 230, 292, 344, 449-50, 463, 588
aircraft overhaul **92,** 457
armed forces, foreign, training of **63,** 422
assassination **63,** 388-9, **81,** 554, **101,** 527-32
bullets, purchase of **63,** 388
caveat lodged as part of divorce proceedings **103,** 452
commercial activities **57,** 331, **81,** 518 n. 2, 663, **87,** 525-36, 542, 643, **88,** 193, **90,** 602, **103,** 439-44, 506, 513-15, 543-6, 607-9. *See also* Foreign Sovereign Immunities Act (FSIA) 1976/82, 28 USC 1605(a)(2) (commercial activity exception), 'that causes a direct effect in the United States' *and* jurisdiction, nexus *above*
act in private capacity **113,** 528
counterclaim anticipating main suit **92,** 396
definition **98,** 18, 58, 61

United States of America (USA) (*cont.*)
jurisdictional element, as **98,** 155
nexus, need for. *See* jurisdiction, nexus *above*
offset of loss from nationalization **92,** 396
substantial contact with non-forum State, need for. *See* jurisdiction, nexus *above*
concert performances, contract for **63,** 229-31
construction of government building **63,** 230, 344
consular activities **57,** 154-9, **98,** 128-31, **101,** 489-96
contract
for advice on aid to rural areas **92,** 426-30
breach **103,** 515
termination **107,** 368-70
contract to provide kidney transplants for nationals **101,** 514-18
conversion **63,** 597, 619-21
cruise ships, operation of **63,** 327
cultural exchange agreement, contract pursuant to **63,** 229-31
definition **86,** 59 n. 2, 60
demurrage, refusal to pay **63,** 153-4, 557-67
development programme, development **98,** 59
diplomatic activity **63,** 51, 57, 171-2, 218, 231
diplomatic activity, acts concerning, contract designed to embarrass government friendly to forum State **57,** 154-9
diplomatic agent, employment of **63,** 230, 344, 527
diplomatic premises
action relating to immovable property, whether **98,** 4, 9, 11-13
lease **63,** 179-80, 230
loan agreement for refurbishment **99,** 138
repair of **63,** 230, 588
effects doctrine **81,** 555
employment contract **101,** 514
employment of nationals **107,** 378-9
employment relationship **113,** 501
exchange control **84,** 112, 113
export promotion **98,** 59-61
export/import control **121,** 494
expropriation/nationalization **63,** 500, 599, **92,** 398, **101,** 549-50
presence of property in United States, need for **107,** 247 n. 10
taking in violation of international law **86,** 94 n. 7, **92,** 490, **103,** 452-3, 467-9, **113,** 549
expulsion of alien **101,** 503
fair value, relevance **100,** 516
foodstuffs, purchase of **63,** 495, 560, 569-71, 588
foreign assistance programme **63,** 230, 344
foreign exchange dealings **88,** 83-7
government policy, involvement in **98,** 60
grain, purchase of **63,** 495, 569-71
hospital operation **65,** 324, **100,** 556-8
hostage-taking for profit **107,** 299-302
hotel **63,** 327
humanitarian relief **113,** 520
implementation of currency controls **84,** 192-3
information centre, maintenance of **63,** 171-2, 231

insurance contract **63,** 454
internal administrative act **63,** 51, 57, 218, **96,** 220
investment promotion **98,** 68
investment in US corporation **63,** 205, 230, 588
judicial act **103,** 549-50
jus cogens/peremptory norm violation **103,** 472-5, 526
crimes against humanity **103,** 615-21
implied waiver **103,** 609-10, **113,** 537-40, 547-8
torture **103,** 472-5, **123,** 32, 42-3
kidnapping **101,** 503
labour, employment or engagement of **63,** 230, 588
lease of premises for consular purposes **101,** 491-2
legal suit **98,** 35
letter of credit **63,** 63-6, 140-5, 152, 182-90, 235-9, 347-50, 371-7, 391-407, 488-91, **121,** 492-4
libel in official newspaper **98,** 83-4
loan agreement **98,** 42
marketing agent, engagement of **63,** 230, 588
military procurement
cement for undefined purpose **63,** 63-6, 151-5, 182-90, 235-44, 480-93, 559-61
purchase of cement for military purposes **63,** 154-5
mineral extraction **63,** 134, 230, 292, 344, 449, 588, 617
mixed **98,** 68
motivation, relevance **113,** 527
nature or purpose of transaction as determining factor. *See* Foreign Sovereign Immunities Act (FSIA) 1976/82, 28 USC 1603(d) ('commercial activity' determined by nature of act) *above*
neutral ship in international waters, attack on **79,** 3-7, 9-17, **81,** 661-9
official article in government publication **63,** 133-4
oil, price-fixing **63,** 288-94, **66,** 416-17
oil, transportation of **63,** 257
operating naval chancery **107,** 198, 199-201
personal injury or death **99,** 143
personnel supervision **72,** 199
police power, abuse amounting to tort **100,** 552-4, 555-8, **124,** 435
policy in relation to **63,** 610
prisoners of war, hiring as slave labour **103,** 607-8
private acts, impossibility in certain cases **98,** 106-7, 108
private person test **63,** 290-1, 560, **98,** 42, 121, 145, **100,** 515, 516, 553-4, 555-6, 561-2, 565, **101,** 492, 513, 515, **103,** 452, 464-5, 488, 513, 544, 545, **107,** 332-4, 370, **121,** 492-3
profit, relevance **63,** 422, **101,** 493, 516, **103,** 464
provision for immunity from taxes, relevance **92,** 428-30
provision of kidney transplants for nationals **101,** 514-18
public loan **63,** 230, 588
public relations agents, engagement of **63,** 230, 588
purchase of goods or services **101,** 513
recruitment of engineer **88,** 195-7
recruitment of staff to work in third country **100,** 549, 551, 555, 559
refinancing of bonds **100,** 513-17, 518-19
reinsurance contract **63,** 454
reparations to Holocaust victims **113,** 548-9

United States of America (USA) (*cont.*)
repudiation of commercial debt **87,** 610
sale of bonds **84,** 142 n. 4, 155
sale of certificates of deposit **84,** 113
by State-owned bank **92,** 416
sale of golf carts **63,** 205-7
scientific research programme **63,** 39-40
seizure and detention of aircraft **107,** 331-4
service, sale of **63,** 230, 588
shipping services **63,** 267, 276
supply of military equipment for use of armed forces **63,** 43-5, 63-6, 152-5, 230, 344, 388, 560-1, 588
terrorist act **107,** 391-2, **113,** 539
State sponsor of terrorism, designation as and **113,** 542, **121,** 611-12, 630, 634
tort **79,** 563, **84,** 88, 89, 94-5, 98, 99-100, **88,** 82, 90-1, **101,** 493-6
abuse of police power **100,** 552-4, 555-8
commercial activity distinguished **90,** 589, **100,** 551-4, 556-60, **103,** 517-18, **107,** 396-404
committed in USA **81,** 666, 667
consul's retention of travel documents **113,** 512-13
criminal act **113,** 514
detention in hotel room **113,** 513-14
driving self for medical treatment during duty hours **107,** 307-8
effects doctrine and **84,** 95
failure to render compensation, effect on original taking **84,** 95
intentional **107,** 223-4
interference with private use and enjoyment of land **107,** 199
Letelier **121,** 486
locus, relevance **84,** 99-100, **90,** 587, 589-90, 593-5, **101,** 503-4, **103,** 453, **107,** 302, 389-90, **113,** 549-50
nature of conduct, relevance **107,** 200
nexus **84,** 94-5
'non-commercial tort' **72,** 140-2
ongoing **84,** 195
respondeat superior **107,** 307
scope of employment **63,** 422-3, **101,** 493-4, 526-32, **121,** 483-7
taking of property, whether **92,** 490
territorial jurisdiction **90,** 590, **103,** 470
torture **103,** 469-75, **104,** 123-5
traffic accident **107,** 199
transportation of people for public purpose **98,** 121-2
use of non-official agents, relevance **107,** 299-300
violation of human rights, Holocaust **103,** 600-2
violation of international law **72,** 127, 130-1, 143, **79,** 6-7, 8, 9-10, 11-13, 16-17, **84,** 193, **87,** 530, 682, **88,** 82, 83-7, **90,** 599-600, **103,** 452-3, 528-30, **118,** 34-5
general principles of international law **103,** 526
taking of property as **101,** 503
State immunity, jurisdiction, entitlement
agency or instrumentality of a foreign State
abuse of corporate form **79,** 565-6
authorization of act, need for **63,** 276 n. 5
burden of proof **79,** 565
individual as **92,** 484-90

liability and immunity distinguished **103,** 510
nationalized oil company **103,** 435-6, 483-90, 495-500
Presidential Commission on Good Government (PCGG) (Philippines) **103,** 508, 509-13
right of suit, waiver, whether **80,** 576
separate legal entity test **79,** 564-6, **90,** 611-16
courts' right/duty to raise *proprio motu* **80,** 432, 585, **104,** 143
denial of by executive **121,** 596
determination, responsibility **57,** 149-51, 156-7, 159, **79,** 4, 12, 14, **87,** 524, **119,** 74
discretion as to **98,** 144
executive, role **84,** 151, 170, 191
executive certificate/statement, conclusiveness **80,** 21, **98,** 10, **104,** 143 n. 7
executive letter **88,** 193
Head of State. *See* Head of State, immunity *above*
individual
official acts **92,** 484-8, **104,** 175-6
private acts **92,** 491-2
ultra vires acts **92,** 491-2, **104,** 175-6
officials **98,** 106-9
illegality of act **98,** 108, 129-31
in official capacity **101,** 501-2, 504
oral hearing, need for **107,** 307
personal holding company **121,** 587
PLO **96,** 73-5
UN Permanent Observer status and **96,** 74
Pope **81,** 601, 607-8
rationale, respect for foreign State **81,** 602
recognition of State/government, relevance **88,** 40
standard of proof **107,** 306-7
State agency/State-owned corporation/State entity, compliance with law and **63,** 474-5, **84,** 114-16
State immunity, jurisdiction, procedural aspects
appeal/judicial review, denial of evidentiary hearing **107,** 305-6
appearance required **84,** 168
reasonable misunderstanding **98,** 85-8
applicable law
classification of act **113,** 527
international law **84,** 170
sending State **103,** 538-9
burden of proof **63,** 220-1, 266, 280, 473, 579-80, 583, 588, **79,** 15, **87,** 525, **90,** 611, **92,** 395, 397-8, **98,** 41-2, 144-5, 156-7, 163-4, **101,** 489, 501, **103,** 403, 424, 425, 442-3, 451, 463-4, 468-9, 488, 512, 538-9, 555, 568, 576, 607, **107,** 230, 306, 378, 397-8, **113,** 545-6
default judgment
evidential requirement **107,** 265-6
impossibility of performance **107,** 267
defence, whether **63,** 43 n. 7, **92,** 422-3, **103,** 438
mistaken belief in entitlement **107,** 268
determination, legal question **84,** 165
enforceability of judgment, relevance **84,** 105
entitlement to raise **81,** 594
evidence, standard of proof **107,** 306-7
extent of liability **79,** 558 n. 22

United States of America (USA) (*cont.*)
forum [non] conveniens and **84,** 104-5, **103,** 518-19
interlocutory review, admissibility **98,** 73
jury trial and **63,** 245-51, 368-9, 438, 439-46, 546-9, 639-46, **72,** 95-100, 102-5, 109, **107,** 354-8
merits distinguished **90,** 589, **100,** 515-17
method of challenge **77,** 265
need to plead **77,** 264-5
nexus, need for. *See* jurisdiction, nexus *above*
non-appearance, effect **63,** 421-2
preliminary issue, whether **107,** 306, 378-9
presumption of **98,** 164, **103,** 445-6, **107,** 396, **113,** 468, 545
procedural problems **63,** 383-4, **79,** 12-13, 557 n. 20
right of suit in 'defendant' State's courts **103,** 601
State Department suggestions. *See* State Department suggestions (State immunity) *above*
subject-matter jurisdiction, need for, effect on immunity in related matters **103,** 518
substantial contact with non-forum State, need for. *See* jurisdiction, nexus *above*
'suggestions of immunity'. *See* State department suggestions (State immunity) *above*
State immunity, jurisdiction, theory/doctrine
absolute theory **84,** 142, 147, 169, 175-6, 183, 191, **87,** 524, **92,** 484
antecedent rights, whether **84,** 172-85
pre-Tate letter cases **84,** 183-5
act of State and. *See* act of State, State immunity, jurisdiction and *above*
acta jure imperii, limited to **107,** 403-4
basis
avoidance of burden of litigation **103,** 486
comity **63,** 506, **84,** 130, 150, 169-70, 172, 190, **88,** 193, **92,** 444, **103,** 617, 620, **107,** 381, **121,** 639
equality of States **107,** 381
foreign relations considerations **63,** 35, 218-20, 332, 451-2, 546-7, 640-1, **107,** 357
natural law **84,** 194
protection of prerogative **98,** 108
reciprocal standards **107,** 403
waiver of territorial jurisdiction, as **81,** 548 n. 7
development of concept **57,** 150, 156, **63,** 217-20, 248, 289, 385, 430-2, 437, 450-1, 464, 640-1, **64,** 7-10, 29-30, 36, 62, 104-6, 312-14, 317, 601-2, 640-2, 700, 712, **72,** 100-1, **79,** 4, 12, 552-4, **81,** 541-2, 663 n. 1, **88,** 193-4, **92,** 484-5, **98,** 8-9, 57, **103,** 437-8, 461-2
domestic immunity doctrine distinguished **80,** 591 n. 5
Draft Convention on the Competence of Courts in regard to Foreign States **88,** 194
freedom of speech, effect on **82,** 309, 318
international law, general principle **103,** 474
as privilege **63,** 506
restrictive **81,** 547 n. 6, 663, **87,** 524, **88,** 193-4, **92,** 484-5, **107,** 329-30
separation of powers and **63,** 28-9, 35-6, **99,** 162
territorial jurisdiction/sovereignty and **90,** 589-91
State immunity, jurisdiction, waiver
bankruptcy claim **107,** 339 n. 57
by State enterprise **72,** 127
Civil Aviation Board permit, provision **98,** 45-6, 74

contractual **87,** 541-2
contractual, interdependent contracts **92,** 448
counterclaim as **63,** 301, 304, 607-8, **66,** 109-10, 123-4, 411-12, 429
exception to immunity, whether **107,** 357-8
express **99,** 135, **103,** 555, 556
  Head of State immunity, effect on **103,** 556
failure to raise immunity promptly **101,** 543-4, **103,** 539-43, 547-8
Foreign Claims Act **80,** 22
Foreign Sovereign Immunities Act (FSIA) 1976/82, whether **81,** 546
guarantee of satisfaction in case of liability **107,** 390-1
human rights treaties **77,** 268-9
  Universal Declaration of Human Rights (1948) **103,** 475
implied **81,** 554, **87,** 541 n. 2
  acceptance of applicable law in respect of ships in port **63,** 40
  acknowledgement of receipt of complaint **92,** 424
  agreement to arbitrate in third country **63,** 405-7, 519-20, 537-8, 635, **72,** 159-63, **103,** 565-7, 570-1
  arbitral award, judgment confirming **98,** 33
  arbitration clause/agreement **62,** 222-3, 234-5, **63,** 197-8, **80,** 33, 36, 644-5, **92,** 426 n. 8, **103,** 576-80, **113,** 550-1
  charterparty **57,** 149, 151, **61,** 105-6
  choice of law clause **63,** 40, 198, 405-7, 520, 537, **107,** 349-52, **113,** 538
  contract as **63,** 422
  effect of waiver by one State agency on immunity of another **92,** 488-90
  extradition proceedings, participation in **42,** 245-6
  failure to raise immunity promptly **92,** 416
  forum selection clause **63,** 357-8, **92,** 447-8, **103,** 508
  guarantee of satisfaction in case of liability **113,** 540-1
  legal proceedings **98,** 114-15
  narrow interpretation **63,** 321-2
  service of process, appointment of agent for **63,** 356-7
  waiver of jurisdiction in third State **98,** 32
judgment in forum court, invocation as defence **98,** 33-4
knowledge and intent, need for **63,** 422, **101,** 491 n. 6, 544, **103,** 610, **113,** 538-9
letter to court **113,** 546
liability for suit provision **103,** 500-2
limitation to actions in own courts **63,** 48
nexus, relevance in case of **63,** 406-7, **79,** 555 n. 15
related action **103,** 570-1
relationship to legal proceedings, need for **113,** 538-40
requirements, knowledge and intent **103,** 620
restrictive interpretation **63,** 503-4, **103,** 577, **107,** 380, 390
statutory **96,** 40-1, 42, 58, **99,** 85-6, 91, **100,** 535, 539-40
submission to the jurisdiction as **66,** 56, **101,** 472-5
  conditional appearance **63,** 606-7, **101,** 472-5
  criminal proceedings **103,** 476-8
  submission to own courts distinguished **103,** 451
tortious act occurring within jurisdiction **81,** 547
treaty provision **81,** 554, 556, 668, **87,** 683, **98,** 31-2, **101,** 551-3, **103,** 475-6, **107,** 222
  conflict with legislation conferring immunity, need for **107,** 388
  critical date **107,** 388, **113,** 541

United States of America (USA) (*cont.*)
Hague Conventions (1899/1907) **103,** 611
Security Council Resolution **107,** 387-8
UN Charter **103,** 476, **113,** 541
Warsaw Convention (1955) **98,** 74
withdrawal **113,** 538
State immunity, taxation
real estate **65,** 547
social security contributions **63,** 195-6
State responsibility for
forcible abduction/unlawful arrest **90,** 645-6, 662, **95,** 359-60
authorization **95,** 361
international tort/wrong **104,** 158
intervention in Panama (1989), failure to restore and maintain public order **96,** 57-61
persecution **95,** 540-1
State responsibility for acts and omissions of
agency **90,** 660
agency or instrumentality of a foreign State **86,** 78-9, 80 n. 4
preliminary question, whether **98,** 42-3
agents of third State **90,** 656-7
armed forces
during armed conflict **99,** 87-9
off-duty soldier **63,** 423
consular agent **99,** 125
negligence, relevance **99,** 88-9
police officer, outside scope of authority **90,** 663
private persons or groups **95,** 540-1, **104,** 143-6
US officials in Antarctica **100,** 530-44
State responsibility for contract, breach of commercial contract **99,** 131
State responsibility, imputability **86,** 78
degree of control **101,** 545
State responsibility, requirements, breach of international law **99,** 131
State succession
contractual obligations
executed contract **96,** 65
executory contract **96,** 65
termination **96,** 65
definition
attainment of independence **96,** 65
closing of borders, relevance **96,** 66
declaration of state of emergency, relevance **96,** 66
military coup, relevance **96,** 66
partial takeover by another State **96,** 65
renaming of State, relevance **96,** 66
suspension of Constitution, relevance **96,** 66
total absorption by another State **96,** 65
extradition agreement, effect on. *See* extradition agreement, State succession and *above*
responsibility for determining, executive **107,** 256-9
State immunity, jurisdiction, Holocaust **103,** 600-1
treaties **78,** 110
State-sponsored terrorism
act of State and **121,** 642
applicable law **121,** 632-3

extraterritorial legislation **121,** 633-4
forum [non] conveniens **121,** 643
jurisdiction, extraterritorial **121,** 633-4
jurisdiction, requirements **113,** 542, **121,** 611-13
act within scope of office, agency or employment **121,** 634
designation as **113,** 542, **121,** 611-12, 630, 634
occurrence outside foreign State **121,** 612
offer of arbitration **121,** 634
terrorist act by or on behalf of foreign State **121,** 630, 634
victims as nationals of forum State **121,** 612, 634, **123,** 32, 47-8
shooting-down of plane 18 miles from coast **121,** 606-18
State responsibility for
act of agent or official consistent with State's policies **121,** 636
act of air force pilot **121,** 612
statehood, requirements/evidence of **104,** 146 n. 12
defined territory **104,** 158
government **104,** 158
non-recognition and **104,** 157-8
power to conclude treaties **104,** 158
recognition. *See* recognition, State, constitutive theory *above*
Restatement of Foreign Relations Law (Third) **104,** 157-8
Statute of Limitations **77,** 202, 271-3
absence of federal **81,** 533
affirmative defence **84,** 143 n. 7
applicable law
analogous federal law **95,** 639-40
lex loci delicti commissi **95,** 639-41
State law **95,** 641-3
counterclaim, right to raise **92,** 411-13
equitable tolling **95,** 641-3
flexibility **95,** 641
Foreign Sovereign Immunities Act (FSIA) 1976/82 and **84,** 172, 173, 183, 184, **92,** 376-7, **121,** 641
Torture Victim Protection Act 1991 **104,** 192
statutory limitation **66,** 211, **79,** 404-11, 494 n., 497, 526-7, 528-9, 530, 598
arbitral award, enforcement **103,** 564, 568-9
civil and criminal distinguished **79,** 405-6
Convention on the Non-applicability of Statutes of Limitation to War Crimes and Crimes against Humanity **79,** 405
date *a quo,* good faith requirement **108,** 506-7
due diligence, need for **108,** 501-2
estoppel **103,** 550
private international law rules **79,** 407-11
government interest test **79,** 409-11
procedural issue **79,** 407-9
tolling **79,** 406 n. 4, 408
torture **104,** 192
stay of judgment **87,** 645-6
Strategic Trust Territory agreement **37,** 536
strike, right to, public sector **94,** 250
Taiwan
State immunity, entitlement **98,** 66-7
status **98,** 65, 66

United States of America (USA) (*cont.*)
taking, compensation provision **81,** 550
Tate letter **42,** 121-2, **45,** 71, **63,** 11, 37-8, 42, 54, 61, 94, 168-9, 208, 218, 289, 326, 367, 385, 450-2, 464, 530-1, 534, 560, 586, 599, 627, 641, **64,** 2-3, 7, 29-30, 35-7, 104-6, 312, 314, 317, 576, 601, 640-1, 700, 712, **65,** 173, **66,** 222, 229-31, **72,** 101, 107, 112, 288, 659, **79,** 553, **84,** 147, 151, 171, 172, 183-5, **87,** 524, **88,** 193-4, **103,** 461
status **63,** 31 n. 8
taxation
Internal Revenue Code 1954, rates **56,** 551
State immunity, unemployment insurance **63,** 195-6
territorial sea **51,** 135-7, 157, 184, 185, **59,** 240-1
bays **57,** 62
breadth **81,** 667 n. 8
coastline **57,** 92
delimitation **57,** 61-2
measurement, straight baselines **59,** 280
rights over **57,** 60
sovereignty over **57,** 83, **125,** 400
States, rights over **57,** 91
seabed and subsoil **125,** 460-3
territory, whether seabed **91,** 413-15, 422 n. 12, 429 n. 1
territory
acquisition **91,** 424
cession **91,** 424
federal State and **91,** 413-15, 424
high seas, seabed **91,** 424
terrorism
definition/requirements
'international terrorism' **121,** 635-6
suicide bombing **121,** 634-6
jurisdiction **82,** 346-57
extraterritorial **104,** 146-7
passive personality principle **88,** 181, **121,** 612, 640
jus cogens/peremptory norm **107,** 391-2
measures against **82,** 313 n. 15, 346, 347, 351-2, 353-7
support for, Iran **96,** 7 n. 4
terrorist conventions
implementing legislation **86,** 37-40, 41
limited to offences under conventions, whether **86,** 37-40, 41
Texas
acts of rebel government, validity **70,** 23-6
boundaries, water **57,** 91-105, **59,** 231-8
Louisiana, boundary with **59,** 200-17, 227-45
purported secession of **39,** 123-4, 174, 175, 389
title, submerged lands below low-water mark **51,** 30
Tonkin Gulf Resolution 1964 **42,** 397, 400
tort, international. *See* international tort/wrong *above*
torture
customary international law **103,** 472-5, **104,** 153, 177
UN Declaration on the Protection of All Persons from Being Subjected to Torture **104,** 153
definition
psychological pressure **104,** 100

Restatement of Foreign Relations Law (Third) **103,** 470-1
Torture Convention (1984) **104,** 176 n. 12
US law **104,** 156-7, 176 n. 12, 178 n. 15
inhuman or degrading treatment **104,** 189
jurisdiction, extraterritorial **103,** 526-30
jus cogens/peremptory norm **103,** 472-5, **104,** 184-5, **119,** 206-7
prize law and **81,** 591
responsibility
individual **104,** 157
military commander **104,** 172
State **104,** 157
State immunity, jurisdiction **103,** 469-75, 555-7
statutory limitation **104,** 192
Torture Convention (1984)
private right of action **103,** 526-8
reservations **103,** 526-8
violation of international law **104,** 144, 153, 156-7
Trade Expansion Act 1962, **60,** 647, **61,** 7, 9, 10-13, 15, 17, 20-3
reprisals **60,** 647
trade union, political boycott, unprotected under First Amendment **82,** 309 n. 7
travaux préparatoires
interpretation, aid to **101,** 618-19, **107,** 455
plain meaning, where **101,** 603-7
travel restrictions **43,** 126-30
Treasury Department regulations, Foreign Sovereign Immunities Act (FSIA) 1976/82 and **63,** 507-8
treaties **53,** 18, **61,** 184-5, 199
acquired rights, effect on **101,** 561
amendment
change of name, whether **96,** 88-9
change of obligations, need for **96,** 89
multilateral convention, by **99,** 170
parties' agreement **101,** 614
practice, by **101,** 597-601
application by courts **86,** 51, 52
bar to jurisdiction, whether **90,** 676
forcible abduction, as **90,** 671
protest **90,** 659, 661, 693, 696
remedies **90,** 657, 671
breach **90,** 652, 657-8
executive's responsibility to determine response **79,** 438
inconsistent legislation as. *See* inconsistent laws and *below*
official act **95,** 375-7
private act **95,** 375-7
compliance
fairness, relevance **99,** 197
obligation **99,** 190
reciprocity and **99,** 197
Constitution and **56,** 543, **81,** 576, **121,** 533-5
contractual nature **95,** 371 n. 3, **96,** 87
definition **122,** 673
contract between sovereigns **107,** 454, **122,** 673
denunciation, power of Congress **82,** 327

United States of America (USA) (*cont.*)
direct effect **79,** 387, 485 n. 3
GATT **107,** 286
evidence of
embassy statement **96,** 108
executive intentions **96,** 107-8, 112
listing in *Treaties in Force* **96,** 108
State conduct **96,** 108
executive agreement, treaty status **101,** 563-9
executive responsibility
conclusion **96,** 88, **122,** 677
fulfilment of obligations **82,** 290
implementation **101,** 586, 592, 601
redress for violation **82,** 290
termination **82,** 290, **96,** 87
executory **77,** 198-200, 237-9
form
implementing regulation **101,** 585-7
press statement **99,** 111
fundamental change of circumstances, private person's right to assert against view of parties to treaty **101,** 596
implementation **79,** 613, 616, 621-4
applicable law **118,** 33
Congressional amendment of terms **79,** 593, 597-8
delay to be avoided **79,** 486
executive responsibility **101,** 586, 592, 601
judicial role **108,** 508
means **104,** 11
implementing legislation
need for **83,** 152, **90,** 657, **91,** 522, **99,** 189. *See also* self-executing *below*
presumption of conformity **63,** 270-2, 503
inconsistent laws and **82,** 235, 236-44, 245-52, 254, 257, 258-9, 262-7, 269-71, 275-9
Administration's attempts to resolve **82,** 236-8, 263-4, 265-8, 271-2, 275-6
interpretation as remedy **82,** 237-8, 292, 295-8, 304, 322, 326
State statutes and **43,** 201
incorporation into municipal law by ratification **99,** 187
individuals, rights **77,** 198-9, 202, 237-9, 241, **79,** 400, **81,** 513-14, **84,** 212-13, 315, **86,** 27, 28-32, **90,** 658-70, 674, 683-5, 686, **91,** 476, **95,** 498, **99,** 174-7, **104,** 84
enforcement **63,** 456, **86,** 52, **99,** 187-90, **100,** 507
extradition **107,** 433
Geneva Conventions (1949) **79,** 400, **99,** 176
Geneva Convention on the High Seas (1958) **81,** 668
Hague Conventions (1899/1907) **77,** 239, **79,** 400, **96,** 58-9, **99,** 175, **103,** 611
invocation of treaty **99,** 190
Iran–US Treaty of Amity (1955) **63,** 456
non-self-executing treaty **103,** 530
OAS Charter **99,** 175
Pan-American Maritime Neutrality Convention (1928) **81,** 668
UN Charter **77,** 238-9, **81,** 514, **99,** 175
unrecognized Head of State **99,** 176

inter-State, effect of boundary treaty on Congress' power to regulate commerce **91,** 445
jurisdiction, limitation on **91,** 520-2
municipal law and **56,** 551-2, **57,** 335, **66,** 497-8
conflict **101,** 618
constitutional requirements **104,** 95-6
evidence of intent **82,** 295-8, 325
implementing legislation. *See* implementing legislation *above*; primacy *below*
interpretation **101,** 621
leges posteriores priores contrarias abrogant **82,** 296
sovereign powers, need for, whether **96,** 88
subsequent treaty, effect **82,** 241-3, 246, 250, 258-9, 263-7, 275-6, 277, 278-9, 291, **83,** 152
Nuremberg Charter **99,** 176-7
obligations
reciprocity **90,** 690
waiver **90,** 680
operation and enforcement
courts, municipal **90,** 657-8
Federal Government **57,** 336
individual **63,** 456, **86,** 52, **99,** 187-90, **100,** 507
international plane **90,** 657
pre-existing legislation and **86,** 32
standing **90,** 658
State party, right limited to **90,** 658
as part of municipal law **81,** 513, **84,** 665, **90,** 672, **95,** 592, **98,** 8, **118,** 33-4
obligation to comply with **73,** 390
parties
change of name **96,** 89
diplomatic recognition, need for, whether **96,** 88
power to conclude **56,** 543
premature termination, statutory requirement **82,** 321-8
primacy
'equal in stature and force' **36,** 400-1, **99,** 141
subsequent legislation **36,** 400-1
ratification **86,** 24, 25
binding nature of executive certificate/statement, s **86,** 24-6, 28-9, 30
Constitution and **86,** 25
implicit authorization to State agencies to act in accordance with **91,** 500-1
relevance **56,** 240, **104,** 91-2
reciprocity **114,** 629
failure to accord as breach of treaty **79,** 438
reservations
as evidence of international law **104,** 186-7
Torture Convention (1984) **103,** 526-8
rights under **90,** 601-2
individual. *See* individual, rights *above*
waiver **90,** 693
self-executing **79,** 400, **84,** 213
Basle Convention on the Control of Transboundary Movements of Hazardous Wastes and Their Disposal (1989) **100,** 507
criteria **79,** 400

United States of America (USA) (*cont.*)
executory agreement distinguished **90,** 657
existing legislation, effect on **91,** 521, 530 n. 35, **122,** 679-80
express provision, need for **99,** 189
extradition agreement **90,** 658, **95,** 366
Geneva Convention on the High Seas (1958) **91,** 522-30
Geneva Convention on the Protection of Civilian Persons in Time of War (1949), First Additional Protocol (1977) **95,** 498, **99,** 67-8, **104,** 91
Geneva Convention (Protection of Prisoners of War) (1949) **79,** 399-401, **99,** 67-8, 185, 188-90
Hague Convention respecting the Laws and Customs of War on Land **79,** 399-401
implicit provisions, whether **90,** 686 n. 17
individuals' rights and **81,** 514, **95,** 613-14, **99,** 187-90
limitations on **91,** 523
multilateral treaties **91,** 528-9, **99,** 189
need for implementing legislation, effect **99,** 68
OAS Charter **90,** 665
partially **91,** 530 n. 35
power to determine whether **91,** 522, **95,** 614, **99,** 68
presumption **99,** 189
reciprocity, need for **91,** 524, 528-9
Refugees, Geneva Convention on the Status of (1951) **95,** 498
requirements **91,** 523, 524, **95,** 614
separability of provisions **99,** 188
subsequent legislation, effect **101,** 595-6
UN Charter **90,** 665, **99,** 175-6
Universal Declaration of Human Rights (1948) **95,** 498
US–HKSAR Extradition Agreement (1996) **122,** 679-80
Vienna Convention on Consular Relations (1963) **118,** 31
source of international law **88,** 48
source of judicially measurable and manageable standards **99,** 68
supreme law of the land, as **56,** 1-2
termination, subsequent legislation **101,** 595
treaty-making power
federal government **72,** 655-8
President **44,** 279, **56,** 543
Trusteeship Agreement **81,** 514
UN Resolutions **107,** 387-8
unincorporated treaty, enforceability **90,** 657-8
validity, presumption of official regularity **98,** 6-7
waiver of immunity and **63,** 267-8, 269-72, 280-2, 347-50, 433-4, 503-4, 514-19
treaties, State succession **78,** 110
agreement of all parties, need for **114,** 621-2
continuity of entity **96,** 108
evidence of treaty in force **96,** 107-9
exchange of notes prolonging **96,** 112
extradition agreement and. *See* extradition agreement, State succession and *above*
subsequent termination by predecessor State, effect **96,** 108, 112
tabula rasa **96,** 108
treaty interpretation **77,** 237, **79,** 543-5, 638-9, **84,** 124-5
agency's own **84,** 125
aids
applicable principles of international law **95,** 368-9

context **90,** 682, **91,** 522, 524, **95,** 371, **99,** 142, **107,** 454
customary international law **95,** 365
dictionary **95,** 594, 600
diplomatic correspondence **81,** 575
government guidelines **99,** 119
language of treaty **90,** 682, **91,** 522
legislation **107,** 455 n. 7
non-binding statements by UNHCR **79,** 638
other multilateral treaties **101,** 481
private law contract, principles of **81,** 575
ratification process **95,** 371 n. 15, **96,** 103, **99,** 108-9
State practice **95,** 366
subsequent practice **95,** 364, 371 n. 15, **101,** 242, 390, 391, 600-1
travaux préparatoires **81,** 575, **95,** 364, 371 n. 15, 587
applicable law
international law **101,** 602
municipal law **104,** 86
by executive **79,** 542, 635-6, 638, **90,** 681, 685, **99,** 102-3, 119
by municipal courts **82,** 290-1, 324, **90,** 685
executive certificate/statement, conclusiveness **86,** 24-6, 28-9, 30, **96,** 103, **101,** 618, 621
government interpretation, binding on court, whether **101,** 576, **104,** 87
guidelines
absence of provision **95,** 364
change of policy **95,** 378 n. 35
clear language **81,** 575, **95,** 587, 599, **101,** 574, 577, 579
constitution, compatibility **104,** 96
finality of boundaries **91,** 453
human rights, protection **104,** 95-6
implicit assumptions **90,** 682
liberal **107,** 454
literal **101,** 601-2
object and purpose **95,** 371, 586-7, **99,** 190, **107,** 420-1
of implementing legislation **103,** 578
ordinary meaning **79,** 469, **81,** 576, **95,** 600, **107,** 454
parties' construction **91,** 452-3, **95,** 582 n. 10, **96,** 103, **99,** 142, **101,** 577
purpose **90,** 682, **101,** 598
simplicity **91,** 453, 465-6
spirit **99,** 190
text **95,** 363, **96,** 102, 103, **99,** 142, 190
parties' intention **63,** 271-3, **79,** 435, **81,** 575, **91,** 465, 522, **101,** 577, 618, **107,** 454
practice and **82,** 292-4
separation of powers **90,** 685
travaux préparatoires **86,** 50, **99,** 142
UN interpretative statements **82,** 294
Truman Proclamation (1945). *See* Truman Proclamation (1945)
Trust Territories **61,** 106-7, 108, 109, 111-12, 123-7, 133, **64,** 547-8, 563, 565, **87,** 547-54, 556-64, 566-74, 577-83, 598-657. *See also* Trust Territories Code (TTC) *below*
applicability of US law **96,** 37-8
specific extension, need for **96,** 27, 30-1
government of, US agency, whether **96,** 27-9
State immunity, jurisdiction, entitlement **61,** 128-30
US government **96,** 40-1, 42

United States of America (USA) (*cont.*)
Trust Territories Code (TTC)
1 TTC 101 **87,** 561
1 TTC 103 **87,** 561, 564
5 TTC **87,** 53
5 TTC 501(1) **87,** 567
6 TTC 251(1)(a) **87,** 547, 548, 549-50, 552-3
6 TTC 355 **87,** 567, 570
63 TTC 292(3)(c) **87,** 567
77 TTC 53 **87,** 547, 552 n. 19
interpretation, drafter's intention **96,** 39
Part V **87,** 561
Trusteeship Agreements
draft, amendments to **37,** 536-9
judicially enforceable rights under **96,** 38-9
monetary damages, right to **96,** 38-9
Okinawa Islands **54,** 216, 218-21, 222-3
UN Headquarters Agreement
breach **82,** 235, 236-44, 245-52, 254, 257, 258-9, 262-7, 269-71, 275-9, 293-4
extraterritoriality **96,** 77
interpretation or application
obligation to arbitrate **82,** 230-82
practice, relevance **82,** 292-3
observers, obligation to admit **82,** 293, 331
UN Resolution, self-executing, whether **107,** 388-9
unilateral declaration/undertaking **101,** 585
Universal Declaration of Human Rights (1948), expulsion of national **104,** 188
US Code. *See* Code (USC) *and under separate titles*
USSR
Litvinov Assignment **42,** 32, 203, **84,** 162-4, 165, 175, 176, 177-8, 180 n. 11, 181
recognition **84,** 162-4
Vienna Convention on Consular Relations (1963)
consular access **118,** 4-21, 39-52
diplomatic protection, national other than diplomatic agent under death penalty **118,** 54
habeas corpus and **118,** 27-37
ratification **57,** 158-9
remedies **118,** 6-7, 10, 12-13, 15, 17, 19, 34-7
rights
individual **118,** 28-9, 31, 33-4, 35-6
States **118,** 34-6
self-executing **118,** 31
Vienna Convention on Diplomatic Relations (1961), implementation **88,** 40
visa, diplomatic, diplomatic status, whether conferring **99,** 166
war
congressional approval, need for **94,** 120, 132
constitutionality, remedy in case of unconstitutional war **94,** 120-1
declaration
constitutionality in absence of **99,** 87
power of **99,** 87
relevance **94,** 102, **99,** 86-7
duty of care to opponent, whether **99,** 89-90, 91
private contractors **99,** 89-90

effects, suspension of right to sue **94,** 172, 198
Iran–Iraq, US protection, whether **99,** 86-9
laws and customs
applicability to civil war **99,** 78-9
customary international law **99,** 78
individual liability **99,** 78-9
torture of wounded non-combatant civilian **99,** 78-9
legislature's approval, need for **99,** 87
nuclear weapons, deployment of cruise missiles in Europe, justiciability **99,** 45-53
political question doctrine. *See* political question doctrine, war, matters relating to *above*
power to declare **60,** 16, **87,** 665, 668, 686, 687-9, 699-703, **94,** 113
South East Asia, in
constitutionality **94,** 111-12, 114-15, 117-21
military assistance, lawfulness **94,** 123-7
war, whether **94,** 113-14
state of
effects **94,** 113
'hostilities' **87,** 663-5, 672, 673, 679
responsibility for determining **87,** 688-9, 699-703, **94,** 106
termination, political act **94,** 106
Vietnam
Gulf of Tonkin Resolution **54,** 529-30, **56,** 24
legality **42,** 393-401, 436-8, 439-41, **56,** 583
whether **60,** 15-16, 19-20, 654-5
war crimes
military commander's duty to control forces **104,** 155-6, 171-3
responsibility
Geneva Conventions (1949) **104,** 155-6
individual **104,** 155-6
insurgent military groups **104,** 156
War Powers Resolution **77,** 227, **80,** 593, **87,** 662-7, 668-70, 672-4
50 USC 1541 **87,** 672
50 USC 1541-8 **87,** 661, 698
50 USC 1542 **87,** 673
50 USC 1544 **87,** 666, 699
50 USC 1545 **87,** 666, 667, 699
50 USC 1547 **87,** 661
Byrd–Ward Amendment **87,** 675 n. 24
El Salvador and **87,** 663-70
judicial review **87,** 679
Persian Gulf and **87,** 672-9
purpose **87,** 665-6
reporting requirement **87,** 666-7, 675, 699
World Bank Group, privileges and immunities, statutory basis **63,** 88 n. 19
unity of the State principle 53, 415-16
Universal Declaration of Human Rights (1948) 37, 33, 50, 451, 454, 576, **45,** 151, 447, 451-2, **51,** 444, **60,** 137, **77,** 173, 247, 273, **88,** 556, 558
aliens, freedom of movement **60,** 268
arbitrary detention **87,** 456
Art. 1 **118,** 465-6, **124,** 482
Art. 2 **124,** 404, 482, 496
Art. 3 **77,** 273, **118,** 466, **122,** 84

Universal Declaration of Human Rights (*cont.*)
Art. 4 **53,** 552-3, **122,** 84
Art. 6 **118,** 466, **122,** 84
Art. 8 **118,** 466
Art. 9 **77,** 273, **122,** 84
Art. 10 **77,** 273
Art. 12 **77,** 273
criminal charges, penal offence not constituting **71,** 218-21
customary international law and **49,** 66, **87,** 456-7, **103,** 475
degrading treatment or punishment **71,** 307
detention of alien **92,** 551
effective remedy, need for **91,** 301, **118,** 483-4
equality before the law **41,** 345, **71,** 307
expulsion of national **104,** 188
fair and public hearing **70,** 203
fair trial **71,** 307
freedom from discrimination **124,** 482, 496, 505
racial **107,** 37
freedom of movement **83,** 458
within State **47,** 486
general principle of law **40,** 195
health, right to **110,** 83
international officials and **43,** 375, 376, **83,** 458
legal effect **47,** 196-7, 207, 208, 323, **87,** 456
legal rights, whether limited to **112,** 435
legislation, aid to interpretation **91,** 321
life, adequate and appropriate remedies, dependence on **118,** 466
marriage, right of **72,** 298
movement, freedom of **60,** 134-5, 268
national liberation struggles and **49,** 60
nationality
freedom to choose **60,** 207
loss or deprivation of **83,** 458
right to **79,** 294
presumption of innocence **44,** 104, 106, **71,** 307
property rights **91,** 321, **112,** 435, 445, 683
racial equality and **49,** 4, 36
retrospective criminal legislation **44,** 129-30
rights, direct enforceability **69,** 142-3
sexual discrimination **87,** 110
slavery **53,** 552-3
stateless person **40,** 195
summary execution **95,** 634
suppression or restriction of recognized rights, prohibition **116,** 364
torture **71,** 300
treaty, whether **103,** 475
UN Security Council and **60,** 642
violation as crime against humanity **122,** 84
universal jurisdiction. *See* jurisdiction, universal
Universal Postal Union (UPU)
language groups system **43,** 448, 452
Staff Regulations, applicability **43,** 449

Universal Postal Union (UPU) Convention (1957), treaty, whether **56,** 240
universality of law, double criminality rule **74,** 168-9, 482, **75,** 108-13
unjust enrichment 40, 112, 175, 183, **42,** 118, **48,** 215, **62,** 176, 213, **66,** 138, 144, **69,** 570, 583, **71,** 287, **75,** 128-9, 136, 147, 149, 159, 165, **83,** 564, 578, 587-8, 627, **89,** 572, 625-6
  act of State and **66,** 138, 448, **79,** 597
  damages/compensation
    as **88,** 702
    measure of **62,** 213, **83,** 564, 578, 627, **84,** 523, 638, **92,** 436
    offset **106,** 646-7
  equity, principle of **41,** 146 n. 4, **99,** 585
  general principle of law **41,** 142, 146, **44,** 449, 462, 471, **62,** 176
  State responsibility and **72,** 721-4
UNTAES. *See* Eastern Slavonia, United Nations Transitional Administration for Eastern Slavonia (UNTAES)
Upper Volta, State succession and **78,** 108
Uruguay
  appeal rights **71,** 349, 359
  arrests abroad **68,** 31, 35, 39, 45
  Constitution 1967
    Art. 8 **94,** 429
    Art. 55 **94,** 430
    habeas corpus **59,** 447
  consul, refusal of certification **70,** 239
  criminal procedure
    annulment and review of sentences, as local remedy **70,** 283-4, 292-4
    conditional release of detainees, as local remedy **70,** 283-4
    defence counsel, appointment of **78,** 78
    trial *in camera* **78,** 51, 52-3, 78
  detainees, rights **71,** 311-16, 347-53, 356-65
  detention
    conditions of **78,** 51-3, 78-80
    precautionary (*medidas eliminativas de seguridad*) **78,** 78
  freedom from discrimination, access to public service **94,** 428-32
  habeas corpus, 'prompt security measures' and **62,** 252-3, 255-6, 258-9, 261, 264, **68,** 45
  International Covenant on Civil and Political Rights (ICCPR) (1966)
    entry into force **62,** 241, 259
    Optional Protocol (1966) **59,** 437
    ratification **59,** 439
    violations of **62,** 241-70, **79,** 169-79, 181-6, 194-200, 202-10, 211-18, 220-5, 227-33, 235-41
  jurisdiction
    criminal, military courts **62,** 264, **71,** 311, 315, 347-53, 356-65
    International Covenant on Civil and Human Rights (1966) and **78,** 51
    nationals abroad **78,** 64, 67, 69
  law of
    Acta Institucional No 4, political rights, whether unreasonably restricting **70,** 257-8
    Constitution. *See* Constitution 1967 *above*
    Criminal Code **68,** 33, 43
      Art. 50 **79,** 183, 185

Uruguay (*cont.*)
Art. 237 **79,** 182-3, 185
Art. 340 **79,** 182, 185
Institution Act No 7 of June 1977 **94,** 428
Law 15,737 of 22 March 1985 **94,** 428, 431-2
Law 15,848 of 22 December 1986 (Limitations Act) **118,** 165-72
discriminatory, whether **94,** 428-31
Military Criminal Code **68,** 33, 43
Art. 60(V) **70,** 255, **79,** 182, 185
Military Criminal Procedure Code, Art. 489 **71,** 349
Organization of Military Courts Code
Art. 178 **71,** 361-2
Arts. 460 ff **71,** 362
State Security Act 1972 **62,** 264
military courts, criminal jurisdiction **62,** 264, **70,** 254, 283-4, **71,** 311, 315, 347-53, 356-65
nationals resident abroad, renewal of passports **70,** 236-40, **78,** 67-9
passport, refusal of **70,** 236-40, **78,** 69-71
political rights, derogation **62,** 269
prompt security measures **62,** 244-5, 248-9, 252-3, 256, 259, **70,** 250-8, 260-6, **73,** 312, 316, 347-8, 351-3, 357, **79,** 182, 185
International Covenant on Civil and Political Rights (ICCPR) (1966), whether violation of **71,** 316, 353
public hearings **62,** 264
subversive activities **62,** 245
torture **118,** 170-2
Uruguay Round. *See also* General Agreement on Tariffs and Trade (1947)
Agreement on Agriculture
'agreement negotiated under the GATT' **110,** 589-90
European Community competence **105,** 82-225
NAFTA and. *See* NAFTA (North American Free Trade Agreement) (1992), GATT/WTO and, WTO Agreement on Agriculture and
tariffication obligation **110,** 590-4
right distinguished **110,** 592
Agreement on the Application of Phytosanitary Measures, European Community competence **105,** 201
Agreement on Trade-Related Aspects of Intellectual Property Rights (TRIPS)
applicability, natural or legal persons **105,** 98
computer programmes, protection **105,** 100-1
copyright, defined **105,** 100
enforcement
criminal sanctions **105,** 105
damages **105,** 104-5
detention by customs authorities **105,** 105
disposal without compensation **105,** 105
inaudita altera parte **105,** 105
judicial order to desist **105,** 104
procedures to be fair and equitable **105,** 105-6
provisional measures **105,** 105
European Community competence **105,** 220-2
exhaustion of intellectual property rights **105,** 99-100
application within EU **105,** 100, 181
industrial property

geographical indications **105,** 101-2
industrial designs **105,** 102-3
integrated circuit topographies **105,** 103
patents **105,** 103
trademarks **105,** 101
undisclosed technical information **105,** 103
MFN treatment **105,** 98, 100
minimum level of treatment **105,** 98
national treatment **105,** 98-9, 100
purpose **105,** 97-8
recording and performance rights **105,** 100-1
scope **105,** 98-9
European Community (EC), common commercial policy **105,** 106-21, 202-24
General Agreement on Trade in Services (GATS)
Berne Convention (1948) and **105,** 99
exemptions **105,** 95
as framework **105,** 96-7
freedom of establishment **105,** 215-20
MFN treatment **105,** 95
monopoly supplier **105,** 95
national treatment **105,** 95-6
Paris Convention (1867) and **105,** 99
phrases
'commercial presence' **105,** 93-4, 204-5
'consumption abroad' **105,** 93, 204-5
'cross-border supply' **105,** 93, 204-5, 207, 215
'movement of persons' **105,** 94, 204-5
'services' **105,** 93-4, 204-5
publication of rules, need for **105,** 95
purpose **105,** 92
rules of GATT applied to services **105,** 92-3
transport provisions **105,** 213-15
Multilateral Agreements on Trade and Goods, European Community, competence **105,** 82-225
NAFTA and. *See* NAFTA (North American Free Trade Agreement) (1992), GATT/WTO and
Settlement of Disputes, Understanding on Rules and Procedures
Dispute Settlement Body, monitoring obligation **107,** 287
offending measures
cessation **107,** 287
compensation **107,** 287
recommendation to bring into conformity **107,** 287
suspension **107,** 287
subsidy, redefinition **107,** 121
World Trade Organization. *See* World Trade Organization (WTO)
usage 80, 135, 173, **90,** 211-12. *See also* comity; custom; customary international law; *jus cogens*/peremptory norm; State practice
as applicable law **86,** 456
custom distinguished **80,** 173
executive role **94,** 359
law distinguished **86,** 279
territorial sovereignty and **50,** 512
Ushant 81, 380

ut res magis valeat quam pereat **37,** 189, 192, 203, 282, **59,** 570, **88,** 272, 273, **91,** 363, **92,** 121, **97,** 645, **110,** 88, 695-6
uti possidetis **50,** 29, 407, 408, 470, **67,** 124-5, **77,** 657, **80,** 319, 469-72, 473, 531, 562-3, **83,** 56-85
acquiescence and **97,** 441
administering control as determining factor **97,** 311
administrative boundaries and **91,** 578-9, **97,** 303-5, 474-80
evidence of. *See* title, evidence of
maps, uncertainty **97,** 540
overlapping **97,** 310
titulos ejidales. See title, evidence of, *titulos ejidales*
transformation into international boundaries **97,** 481, 551, 556
Africa **80,** 470
Cairo Declaration (1964). *See* Cairo Declaration (1964) *below*
in **83,** 22, 35, 56-7, **100,** 84-90
as applicable law **83,** 57, **97,** 474, 547, 549-54, 582, 590
agreement between parties, absence of provision **97,** 302, 307-8
on basis of agreement between parties **83,** 57
land boundary **97,** 565, 566-7, 570-3
parties' wishes **97,** 554-6, 591
Argentina–Chile boundary **113,** 30
armed conflict and **100,** 82
automaticity **97,** 481
Cairo Declaration (1964) **77,** 657, **80,** 469, 470, 471, **83,** 22, 35, 38, 56, 60, **100,** 85-6
declaratory nature **80,** 471
retrospective effect **100,** 88-9
Cairo Resolution (1964) **67,** 59, 91, 124
Coast of Mosquitos Arbitral Award **83,** 71 n. 32
Colombia/Venezuela Arbitral Award (1922) **97,** 303
critical date **97,** 305, 474, 547-8, 551, 566, 572-3, **100,** 89
importance **97,** 553
separate legal entity test **100,** 89
subsequent events, relevance **97,** 547-9, 557-9, 566-7, 595-6, 620-1, 622-5
consent of all parties, need for **97,** 567
international law norms, priority **97,** 622-3
post-independence acts of sovereignty **97,** 313
post-independence changes **97,** 311, 312, 317, 324
uti possidetis de facto 479
decolonization and **80,** 471
effective control, need for **97,** 595-6, **100,** 82-4, 87-8, 90
El Salvador General Treaty of Peace (1980) **97,** 307-8
federal State, applicability **92,** 171
fisheries limits **83,** 37
Fonseca Bay Award **83,** 72-3
Fonseca Bay islands **97,** 474-81
freezing of title **80,** 473
Frontier Dispute **97,** 302-3
general principle of international law **80,** 469, 470, 531, **92,** 171-2, **97,** 551, 552, **100,** 86-7
general principles of law **83,** 58
Guatemala/Honduras (1933 Arbitral Award) **97,** 296

jus, administrative law of predecessor State **97,** 475
Latin America, in **97,** 551, **100,** 82-4, **113,** 30
administrative boundaries **83,** 35, 57, **97,** 303-5, 309
Brazilian rule distinguished **97,** 551, **100,** 84
general international law rule distinguished **97,** 552
territory granted to native community no longer extant **97,** 311
title, Spanish Crown **97,** 481
long-standing agreements, limited to, whether **83,** 38-9
maritime boundaries, applicability to **83,** 15, 35-9, 59-64, 68, 69, 71-3, 85
Middle East **114,** 32-4
Monroe Doctrine and **100,** 83
OAU Charter **80,** 470
overlapping jurisdictions **97,** 321, 330
prescriptive title and **97,** 480, 482, 485-6
consent, parties' conduct **97,** 549
contradiction of title, scope for **97,** 482
Treaty of Confederation (1847) **100,** 83
purpose, avoidance of instability **80,** 470
retrospective nature **97,** 304, 557-8
right to self-determination and **80,** 471, **92,** 168
Roman law origin **100,** 81-2
in Spanish America **80,** 470-1
State sovereignty, restriction on **83,** 67
terra nullius, denial of **97,** 303, **100,** 82-4
constructive occupation, *Colombia–Venezuela* Arbitral Award (1922) **100,** 82-3
territory retained by Spanish Crown **97,** 311, 321
title, source or recognition, whether **100,** 81-2
treaty arrangements distinguished **83,** 73, **100,** 37
uti possidetis de facto **80,** 324, **97,** 296
distinguished **80,** 324, **97,** 551
occupation followed by peaceful and continuous exercise of State functions **97,** 479, 623-5, 626-7
good faith, need for **97,** 623-4
vacuum of interest following independence **97,** 481-2
Yugoslavia **115,** 77

vagrancy, European Convention on Human Rights (1950) and **56,** 376-8, 401-3, 404-5, 411
valuation. *See* measure of damages/compensation including valuation of company/property/assets
Vancouver Island. *See* Canada, Vancouver Island; United Kingdom, Vancouver Island, colony of
vassal States 50, 414-15
Kutch area **50,** 2
Vatican City. *See* Holy See
Vattel 46, 490
expropriation/nationalization **41,** 12
punishment **36,** 28
treaty interpretation **49,** 173
Venezuela
Compania Anonima Venezolane de Navegación **63,** 416-19
Constitution 1961

Venezuela (*cont.*)
Art. 60(1) **94,** 403
Art. 68 **94,** 405
Art. 215(2) **94,** 404
Calvo Clause **66,** 319-20
Continental Shelf Convention, reservation **41,** 162, 205
Coordinating Commission for the Conservation of Commerce and Hydrocarbons **56,** 34-5
Corporacion de Mercadeo Agricola (CMA), status **64,** 677-82
Corporacion Venezolana de Fomento **63,** 301-4, 478-80
courts, municipal, exclusive jurisdiction **66,** 320
law of. *See also* Constitution 1961 *above*
Agricultural Marketing Law **64,** 680
Civil Procedure Code **66,** 320
Criminal Procedure Code, Art. 190 **94,** 404
Hydrocarbons Law 1943 **66,** 319
Military Justice Code
Art. 202 **94,** 403
Art. 203 **94,** 404
Nationalization Law **66,** 322-4
oil concessions, expropriation/nationalization **66,** 318-24
political question doctrine, state of exception **123,** 149-50
Versailles Peace Conference
Committee of the Supreme Council **37,** 11, 197, 198
Council of Principal Allied Powers **37,** 56-8, 65, 196
Dominions, representation **37,** 529
India, status at **37,** 529
Mandates (Milner) Mission **37,** 57-8, 170, 499-506
self-determination **37,** 29
Wilson
Fourteen Points **37,** 29
opposition to annexation **37,** 56-8, 65, 196
Versailles, Treaty of (1919). *See also* Dawes Plan (German reparations and liabilities); Young Plan (German reparations and liabilities)
German overseas possessions, renunciation **37,** 11, 29, 59, 64, 121, 197, 257, 545
Head of State, immunity **125,** 503
Kiel Canal provisions **37,** 72, 516, 600
seized German property, compensation for **40,** 176-7
State immunity, jurisdiction, as waiver **45,** 73
war crimes **82,** 436, **105,** 536, **108,** 14
as dictate **82,** 439
vested rights 46, 407, 484, **62,** 176, **77,** 314-16, **115,** 63
Vienna Convention[xiii] **on Consular Relations (1963) 68,** 176-80, **99,** 123-5. *See also* consular immunity, jurisdiction; consular premises; consular privileges and immunities; consular protection
applicability to non-signatories **57,** 158-90, **77,** 401
bilateral agreement, precedence **101,** 373, 480, **123,** 608
categories under **77,** 596-7
compliance with, importance **118,** 15
consular access **77,** 542, **107,** 81, **118,** 4-21, 40-52

[xiii] References to the Vienna Conventions are included in this index only when there is particular discussion of the Convention in question. Cursory references are to be found in the Table of Treaties.

consular functions **94,** 372, **98,** 128-9, 130, **101,** 372-3, 383, 469-70, 479 n. 3, **107,** 102-4
legality of actions, relevance **98,** 130-1
consular premises **55,** 586, **77,** 582-4
prevention of hostile acts **77,** 583
search, requisition or distraint **77,** 583
taxation, exemption **53,** 546
customary international law and **71,** 580-1, **77,** 401, 594, **101,** 481 n. 5
diplomatic protection, national other than diplomatic agent under death penalty **118,** 54
functional immunity under **71,** 581-2, **73,** 690
honorary consulate **77,** 582-4, 611-12
implementation under municipal law **75,** 97-9
interpretation
restrictive **89,** 66
travaux préparatoires **86,** 556
nationals of receiving State, fiscal liability **75,** 97-8
non-interference in internal affairs of another State **116,** 618
phrases
'consular employee' **77,** 401, 597
'consular office' **77,** 595
'member of service staff' **77,** 401
'official acts in the exercise of their functions' **86,** 556, **101,** 381, 481
remedies **118,** 6-7, 10, 12-13, 15, 17, 19, 34-7
restitutio in integrum **118,** 17
restoration of *status quo ante* **118,** 49
rights
individual **118,** 28-9, 31, 33-4, 35-6
States **118,** 34-6
self-executing **118,** 31
State immunity, jurisdiction, applicability, in own courts **118,** 54, 55
Vienna Convention on Diplomatic Relations (1961) 80, 423. *See also* customary international law, treaties and other international agreements reflecting; diplomatic privileges and immunities, Vienna Convention on Diplomatic Relations (1961)
administrative and technical staff **65,** 22, **74,** 518
amendment, possibility **99,** 203-4
applicability
acts committed abroad **119,** 60
acts committed in own country **119,** 60, 203
by analogy and special agreement **102,** 186
commercial/trade representation/mission **64,** 596
European Community (EC) **102,** 186-7
Head of State **102,** 202-3, **111,** 606, **119,** 42-8, 59-61, 89-90, 96-7, 102-3, 193
international officials **102,** 194
nationals of receiving State **75,** 88, **119,** 61
non-parties **65,** 254
signatory State **102,** 187
States/State entities **82,** 3
Art. 33, Art. 37 and **69,** 278
bilateral agreement, validity **102,** 187-8
breach as basis for award of damages **113,** 471-2
categories of officials distinguished **75,** 87-8

Vienna Convention on Diplomatic Relations (1961) (*cont.*)
customary international law and **65,** 186-7, **70,** 391, 395, 400, **71,** 549-51, 568-9, 571-2, **75,** 92, **78,** 4, 7-8, 103, 104, **82,** 98, **94,** 310, **101,** 309-10, 314-16
absence of express and unambiguous treaty provision **78,** 8
break from **116,** 628-9
residual matters **115,** 611
diplomatic agent **73,** 679-82, **74,** 521, **75,** 76, 92-4
special envoy **99,** 116
diplomat's right to sue and to protection from suit distinguished **78,** 8
'equivalent rank' **77,** 496
European Community (EC), applicability **102,** 186-7
evidence, requirement to give **82,** 16
family of diplomat **71,** 568, **73,** 680-2
fiscal exemption **75,** 87-9
ILC Draft Articles on Diplomatic Intercourse and Immunities compared **78,** 6 n. 1
immunity
arrest **119,** 61
civil jurisdiction **48,** 207, **82,** 16
personal **82,** 57
privileges distinguished **119,** 61
immunity, execution/attachment
Art. 22(3) provisions, limitation to **65,** 152, 161-2
embassy/consular bank accounts **65,** 152, **89,** 363
implementation **73,** 679, **74,** 518, 521, **75,** 92, **88,** 40, 326, **104,** 413, **111,** 606, 629-30, 634, **119,** 42
individual, rights under **111,** 158
institution of legal proceedings, sending State authorization, need for **82,** 16
international organizations, Member State missions and representatives **99,** 142
interpretation, strict **82,** 98
limitation of rights under **99,** 203-4
non-discrimination between States and **72,** 656
non-interference in internal affairs of another State **116,** 614, 618
permanent resident in receiving State **71,** 568, 571-2
persons, limitation to **82,** 3, 102
phrases
'a real action relating to private immovable property' **64,** 365-7, 392-3, **101,** 360, 378-9, **118,** 306-7
'private immovable property' **87,** 236
'ambassador' **104,** 413
'commercial activity exercised ... in the receiving State outside his official function' **118,** 305-6
'member of the staff of the mission' **104,** 636-43
'not permanently resident in the receiving State' **77,** 468-9
'part of his household' **77,** 456
child of spouse **77,** 457
minor living with separated partner **77,** 456-7
'premises of the mission' **64,** 391-3, **65,** 254
'professional or commercial activity' **111,** 635-6, **116,** 632
employment of domestic staff **107,** 453-6
joint control of funds for educational institution **104,** 413-17
personal profit, need for **107,** 454
translation **82,** 116-18

previous jurisprudence, relevance **82,** 117
private servants **71,** 549-51
property taxation, exemption **72,** 653-62
ratification, relevance **65,** 254, **70,** 391-6
receiving State's right to protect against abuse **106,** 291, 297
restricted immunity **87,** 235-6
sovereignty and **78,** 102
third State, inviolability in **88,** 326-7
travaux préparatoires **71,** 550, 558-9, **77,** 457
Art. 31(1)(c) **107,** 455
treaty codification **77,** 273
visa, need for **82,** 98
Vienna Convention on the Law of Treaties (1969). *See also* treaties; treaty interpretation
amendment of treaties **57,** 481
applicability
compulsory jurisdiction of ICJ, declarations accepting **123,** 214, 244
ratification, relevance **91,** 379, **116,** 71
resolutions of international organizations **110,** 142-3
third parties **82,** 611
as applicable law, NAFTA Tribunal **122,** 279
customary international law **56,** 111, **57,** 549, **59,** 579, **68,** 304, 419, **77,** 658, **82,** 98, 612, **83,** 32-3, **84,** 402, 403, **85,** 260, **88,** 627, **92,** 46, 125, 160, **97,** 633-4, 635, 645, **100,** 478, **101,** 211, 390, **105,** 25, 26, 30, 53, **106,** 207, 706, **110,** 576, **115,** 196, **116,** 71, **117,** 407, 409, **121,** 51, **122,** 279, **123,** 388, **125,** 499
duress **56,** 139, **83,** 534
effect on previous jurisprudence **82,** 117
entry into force **83,** 131, **100,** 478
force, prohibition on threat or use of **91,** 569
good faith **116,** 88, 121, 153, **120,** 573, **124,** 413-14
hostilities, effect **117,** 409
ILC **97,** 635, 645
international organizations, constituent instrument **48,** 415-16
international tribunals, practice of **77,** 658
interpretation **100,** 20-1, **101,** 211
intertemporal law **116,** 123
material breach **82,** 564, **116,** 70-1, 206, 230
measures before entry of treaty into force
in breach of **123,** 141 n. 1
defeating its object and purpose **113,** 323
multilateral treaties
breach **48,** 349-50, 353, 414-16, 434
modification **48,** 424
suspension **48,** 388, 414, 416, 432
necessity, absence of provision **116,** 197
pacta sunt servanda **53,** 332-3
reservations **107,** 20-1, 69, 69 n. 6
retroactive effect **100,** 486-7
separability **123,** 382-3
State responsibility **82,** 549-50, **117,** 409
State succession **117,** 409-10
termination
changed circumstances **55,** 198, **56,** 111-12

Vienna Convention on the Law of Treaties (1969) (*cont.*)
withdrawal **57,** 479
termination and suspension provisions **116,** 45-6, 47, 71, 73-6, 222-3, 224, **117,** 408-10, 430, 439, 445
threat or use of force, effect **55,** 194
treaties concluded before entry into force **68,** 303-4
treaty interpretation **46,** 477, **47,** 422, 450-1, **54,** 346, **57,** 213, 216, 217, 226, **62,** 605, **67,** 585, 602, 606, **68,** 262, 303-4, 416, 419-20, 535, 543, 554, 615, 634-5, 637, **70,** 465-6, **71,** 655, 695, 697, **72,** 483, 533, **73,** 540, **74,** 655, 660-2, 668, 673, **75,** 67, 187-8, 194, 202, 208-9, 219, 416, 423, 483-4, 522, 671, **79,** 291-2, 310, 329, 342, 357, **81,** 407, **83,** 131-2, 133, 188, **96,** 396-7
customary international law **82,** 612, **100,** 478, **121,** 51 n. 2, **124,** 439
good faith **87,** 153, **100,** 69-71, **101,** 379, **114,** 372, **124,** 15
multilingual text **82,** 647-8
principles **82,** 615
purposive requirement **122,** 538, 540-1
travaux préparatoires, restrictive use **82,** 634
UN Council for Namibia, signatory, whether **91,** 379
unilateral declaration/undertaking **106,** 371
Vienna Convention on the Succession of States in respect of Treaties (1978) 77, 657, **83,** 14, 54
applicability while not in force **95,** 30, **96,** 377
intangibility of boundaries **83,** 61
notification of succession **95,** 30
'treaties of a territorial character'. *See* treaties, State succession, treaties of a territorial character
Vietnam. *See also* Vietnam, Democratic Republic of; Vietnam, Socialist Republic of; Vietnam, South
banks
branch
foreign bank to operate through **107,** 205
funding responsibility **107,** 205
deposit, *situs* **107,** 207
expropriation/nationalization **107,** 206-19
law relating to **107,** 205, 207-10, 215-19
blocked assets, entitlement **107,** 256-60
force majeure **107,** 207-10, 216
France
concessions granted by, succession to **44,** 37-8
Judicial Assistance Protocol **47,** 266-7
Judicial Conventions (1949/54) **42,** 266-7, **44,** 297
nationals in **52,** 7
Geneva Accords (1954) **52,** 6, 312
law of
Commercial Code
Art. 701 **107,** 208 n. 3, 216 n. 6
Art. 1206 **107,** 208 n. 3, 210, 216 n. 6
Decree Law 18
Art. 12 **107,** 205
Art. 13 **107,** 205
Art. 26 **107,** 205
revolutionary change of government
rights and obligations

expropriation of property of departed institutions **107,** 211
undertaking by predecessor government immediately prior to take-over **107,** 210-11
separate legal entity test **39,** 405-11
Vietnam, Democratic Republic of. *See also* Vietnam; Vietnam, Socialist Republic of; Vietnam, South
adoption of children **95,** 499-500
commercial/trade representation/mission
immunity, execution/attachment **65,** 56
recognition **65,** 56
status **65,** 56
Geneva Agreement (1954) **48,** 148
hostilities (1952), acts of war **48,** 468
recognition **48,** 145, 148, **65,** 56
withdrawal **94,** 201-2
right to sue **94,** 201-2
State immunity, execution/attachment, entitlement **52,** 310-15
State immunity, jurisdiction, entitlement **52,** 310-15
Vietnam, Socialist Republic of. *See also* Vietnam; Vietnam, Democratic Republic of; Vietnam, South
Provisional Revolutionary Government, expropriation of bank assets **66,** 353-60, 462-70
South Vietnam as successor **66,** 359-60, **75,** 125
State succession **66,** 359-60
status **52,** 311-13
US military operation in, war, whether **60,** 16, 654-5
Vietnam, South. *See also* Vietnam; Vietnam, Democratic Republic of; Vietnam, Socialist Republic of
Banque Nationale du Vietnam **63,** 17
Credit Commercial du Vietnam **63,** 17
Virgin Islands. *See* British Virgin Islands
visa
application, misrepresentation of material fact, invalidity of visa **95,** 520-1, 522
diplomatic, diplomatic status and **99,** 166
exit visa
entitlement **73,** 391-2
refusal, public policy considerations **73,** 391-2
issue, responsibility for, Benelux Economic Union **99,** 41-2
visiting forces. *See* armed forces; belligerent occupation; jurisdiction, visiting forces; NATO Status of Forces Agreement (1951); State immunity, classification of act, military base; State responsibility for acts and omissions of, armed forces
Vitoria 46, 483, 490
conquered territory, treatment of inhabitants **37,** 434
tyrants, laws of **39,** 113-14, 172, 256-7
Voet, treason **39,** 291

Waitangi Treaty (1840). *See* New Zealand, Treaty of Waitangi (1840); New Zealand, Treaty of Waitangi Act 1975
Waitangi Tribunal. *See* New Zealand, Waitangi Tribunal
Walvis Bay
EEZ **91,** 375-8
fishing zone **91,** 375-8
Namibia, part of, whether **91,** 375-8
South Africa, law of, applicability **91,** 377-8
treatment as part of South Africa **82,** 470, 494-8

war. *See also* arms dealing; belligerent occupation; civil war; compensation for war-related events; enemy; enemy aliens; enemy property; espionage; Geneva Conventions (1949); Germany, capitulation; Germany, termination of hostilities with; Hague Conventions (1899/1907); Hague Regulations (1897/1907); martial law; neutrality; Nuremberg Charter (1945); Nuremberg Tribunal; peace, crime against; peace treaties; prisoners of war; rebellion; revolution; terrorism; war crimes; war damage
act of **90,** 402
confiscation of patents **48,** 468-9
definition **82,** 107
legitimacy **61,** 665-6
piracy distinguished **91,** 559
reprisals **61,** 665-7
'riot, social disorder and malicious damage' distinguished **82,** 107
terrorist act, whether **91,** 257-8
air warfare, bombing, Hungary-Western allies, secret agreement on **44,** 336
animus belligerendi **67,** 620-3
area of military conflict, whether confined to **87,** 265-7, 280
armed conflict. *See* armed conflict
assets, foreign
blocking of **61,** 658-61
confiscation **54,** 558-9
booty **40,** 463-7, **42,** 34-5, **44,** 486-7, **48,** 227-8
British Empire, declaration of war by Great Britain, effect **87,** 265, 266
ceasefire, declaration before UN Security Council **71,** 711
chemical weapons. *See* chemical weapons, deployment
Chicago Convention on International Civil Aviation (1944) and **48,** 417-18, 436, 437
civil commotion distinguished **74,** 33-4
civil war. *See* civil war
civilians, protection of **42,** 480, **83,** 142. *See also* Geneva Convention (Protection of Civilian Persons in Time of War) (1949)
co-belligerence, Italy and Germany (1943) **40,** 72
collective security system. *See* collective security system
combat action **106,** 448-51, 485-6
Adams v. *Naylor* **106,** 485-6
'combat activities' **94,** 126
guerrilla warfare **106,** 450, 485-6
Sri Lanka/Tamil Tigers **106,** 450, 485-6
'war or other armed conflict, revolution, a state of national emergency, revolt, insurrection or riot in the territory' **106,** 451
constitutionality, remedy in case of unconstitutional war **94,** 120-1
contraband, absolute, manganese ore in transit **44,** 495-8
contract
arbitration clause **67,** 628-9
effect on **52,** 475, 476-81, 483-5, 489-91, **53,** 609-12, **54,** 523-4, 525-7, **78,** 583-91
ipso facto, none **78,** 588-91
sale of arms **91,** 253-5
termination of, peace treaty, in **40,** 434-5, **42,** 421
Cuba–USA relations **42,** 202
cultural protection. *See* cultural property, protection, war, during
customary international law, non-discrimination between combatants and non-combatants **110,** 123, 152
de facto war **54,** 529-30

declaration **60,** 15, **67,** 616, 622, **71,** 709, 711
  date of commencement of war and **42,** 393-401
  as evidence of war **87,** 274, **105,** 533
  hostilities in absence of **53,** 623
  legislature's approval, need for **94,** 120, 132
  need for **52,** 508-9, **94,** 102
  power of **87,** 665, 668, 686, 687-9, 699-703
  prerogative right, as **80,** 594
  relevance **42,** 393-401, **87,** 269-70
  since 1945 **42,** 400-1
  State broadcast **67,** 616, 622
definition/characteristics **44,** 439-41, **54,** 523-4, 525-7, 529-30, **60,** 655, **67,** 620, **80,** 667-73, **87,** 270, 694, **91,** 10, 24, 32, 258. *See also* armed conflict
  hostile conflict distinguished **87,** 270
  intention to perpetrate acts of violence **80,** 668
  municipal and international distinguished **80,** 670
  non-hostile relations between belligerents **40,** 429-34
  severance of diplomatic relations **80,** 668
  States or recognized belligerents, need for **80,** 668-9
  suspension of general rules of international law of peace **80,** 668
  technical meaning **48,** 467-75
determination, Government prerogative **53,** 623
diplomatic relations and **80,** 668, 669
effects
  arbitration clause **67,** 628-9
  contract **53,** 609-12, **54,** 523-4, 525-7, **78,** 583-91
  enemy aliens, capacity to sue **71,** 710
  ipso facto, none **78,** 588-91
  right to sue **53,** 616-26
  suspension of right to sue **94,** 172, 198
enemy shareholder's rights. *See* enemy; enemy character; enemy corporation; enemy property; enemy taint
enforcement **87,** 93-5
'engine of war' **91,** 257-8
  actually used or intended for use in war **91,** 258
evidence of **87,** 278-9
  administrative regulations **67,** 617-18, 625
  ceasefire **67,** 617
  declaration of emergency **67,** 616-18
  declaration of war **87,** 274, **105,** 533
  diplomatic relations, breaking off **67,** 623-4
  expert **87,** 274
  martial law, declaration of **87,** 274
  self-defence rights, invocation of **67,** 622-3
  State broadcast **67,** 616-18
  State legislation **67,** 615, 616-18
  UN Secretary-General, statement of **67,** 619
existence. *See* state of *below*
General Treaty for Renunciation of (1928) **42,** 398
genocidal **42,** 439
Hague Regulations (1907). *See* Hague Regulations (1907)
hostilities **52,** 69, **53,** 614-15, 616, 622-3, **74,** 33, **87,** 663-5, 672, 673, 675, 679

war (*cont.*)
cessation **40,** 434-5, **56,** 543, **71,** 709-11, **72,** 468. *See also* termination *below*
declaration in Security Council **71,** 711
treaties, suspension during **48,** 337, 339, 348, 394, 413
illegal, conscription for **42,** 436-9
illegal transfers of property, UN Declaration (1943) **44,** 4-5, 470, 472-3, 474, 480-1, 482, 484
India and Pakistan (1965) **53,** 614-15, 622-3
insurance policy and **82,** 107-9, **107,** 507-16
insurrection **74,** 32
involvement of defence forces in **87,** 279-81
international law, as violation of **56,** 583
invasion **74,** 32
laws and customs **52,** 502
applicability
belligerent, recognition, relevance **105,** 446
civil war **99,** 78-9, **104,** 73-4, **105,** 444-50, 504-24, **112,** 178-82
customary international law **105,** 528-31
extradition proceedings **104,** 68-76
international conflict **105,** 528-31
Lieber Code (US Military Manual) **105,** 446
in occupied territories **83,** 165-6
Operational Code of Conduct for Nigerian Armed Forces (1967) **105,** 510
political offence exception **104,** 90-1
recognition of belligerency, relevance **105,** 446
until conclusion of peace **108,** 132
civilian population. *See also* means of waging, limitations on, non-discrimination between combatants and non-combatants *below*
attack on **110,** 256, 536-7
civil war or violent community conflict **104,** 73-6
collateral casualties **110,** 239, 536-7
commercial bus occasionally used as military vehicle **104,** 68-76
customary international law **110,** 537
protection of, emphasis on **104,** 90-1
combatants and non-combatants **42,** 480
customary international law **99,** 78, **104,** 91-2, **105,** 587-91
Hague Regulations 6.1907, **53,** 3
distinction, whether **105,** 587-9
equality of application **110,** 476-8
exceptions to **110,** 245, 251-2
gaps, Martens Clause **110,** 251, 261, 399
Geneva Conventions (1949), Second Protocol **108,** 43
Hague and Geneva Conventions, convergence **105,** 506, 517, 535-7
human rights and **105,** 500, 505-6, **123,** 135-6
individual liability **99,** 78-9
international humanitarian law. *See also* international humanitarian law
conflict **110,** 255-9, 261
replacement by **105,** 500-4, **110,** 206, 513
international and internal conflict distinguished **105,** 504-24, 528-31
jus ad bellum/jus in bello, interrelationship **83,** 142, **105,** 535-8, **110,** 240, 242, 386, 463, 469, 539
law of peace distinguished **110,** 445

'laws, customs and usages of war' **91,** 66-7, 68, 132
limitations on means of waging. *See* means of waging, limitations on *below*
private support for rebel forces, violation, whether **80,** 590-2
sources **42,** 479
sovereignty and **105,** 505-6
State responsibility for breach **76,** 722-3
subsequent treaties, effect **110,** 206
torture of wounded non-combatant civilian **99,** 78-9
US violations **76,** 723
usus in bello **52,** 502
'violation of the laws or customs of war' **105,** 442, 444-50, 489, 499-504, 528-31, 537-8, 587-91
weapons, prohibition, 'of a nature to cause superfluous injury' **108,** 47
legislation during, interpretation **42,** 421-2
length of, rebuttable presumption **78,** 588, 590
looted property, good faith of acquirer **44,** 473-5, 483-4
means of waging, limitations on **110,** 121-6, 206-9
acceptability to international community **110,** 331-7, 348-52, 353
Convention on the Modification of the Environment (1972) **110,** 155
Convention on the Prohibition of the Development, Production, Stockpiling and Use of Chemical Weapons (1993) **110,** 122
customary international law **110,** 122-3, 207, 347-52
UNGA Resolution 2444 (XXIII) **110,** 348
Declaration of Brussels (1874) **110,** 122
Declaration of St Petersburg (1868) **110,** 122, 150-1, 206-7, 534
environmental protection **110,** 124-6, 154-7, 191-3, 452-6
Geneva Conventions (1949) **110,** 124, 154
Geneva Conventions (1949) (Protocol I) **110,** 124-5, 154, 455
Hague Conventions (1897/1907) **110,** 124
proportionality **110,** 192-3
Rio Declaration on Environment and Development (1992) **110,** 126, 154, 192
Geneva Conventions (1949) (Protocol I) **110,** 536
Geneva Protocol (Prohibition of Asphyxiating, Poisonous or other Gases and Bacteriological Methods) (1925) **110,** 122, 151-2, 154
Hague Conventions (1899/1907) **110,** 122, 151-2
Hague Regulations (1907) **110,** 206-7, 534-5, 536
intent **110,** 441-2, 448-9, 537
Lucerne Conference of Governmental Experts on the Use of Certain Conventional Weapons (1974) **110,** 535
non-discrimination between combatants and non-combatants **42,** 469-70, **110,** 122-3, 156, 207, 261, 406, 466, 514
attack on civilians **110,** 256, 536-7
collateral damage **110,** 239, 536-7
customary international law **110,** 123, 152, 239
Geneva Conventions (1949) (Protocol I) **110,** 123, 152-3, 449-50
Hague Regulations (1907) **110,** 123
Hague Rules on Air Warfare (Draft) (1923) **110,** 123, 152
International Law Institute (Edinburgh 1969) **110,** 450
Martens Clause **110,** 124, 153-4, 207
nuclear weapons **110,** 123, 222-3
Toxin Weapons Convention (1972) **110,** 154

war (*cont.*)
UNGA Resolution 47/37 of 25 November 1992 (protection of environment in times of armed conflict) **110,** 192
unnecessary suffering **110,** 122, 154, 156, 206, 207, 239, 256, 261, 347, 351, 352-5, 376-7, 447-9, 464, 514, 524-5
civilians, applicability to **110,** 353-6, 534-7
customary international law **110,** 352, 435, 447-9
Lucerne Conference of Governmental Experts on the Use of Certain Conventional Weapons (1974) **110,** 535
proportionality **110,** 352-3, 534-7
mercenaries. *See* mercenaries
national emergency and **61,** 657
national liberation movements. *See* national liberation movements
naval warfare. *See* naval warfare; neutrality
necessity **91,** 52-3, 54, 68, 134
nuclear weapons. *See* nuclear disarmament; nuclear tests; nuclear weapons, deployment
ouster of jurisdiction, automatic, whether **87,** 274-5
peace conference. *See* Potsdam Conference 1945; Versailles Peace Conference; Yugoslavia, Socialist Federal Republic (SFRY), Conference on (1991)
peace treaties. *See* peace treaties
political offence and **79,** 509 n. 17, 520 n. 33
political question doctrine. *See* political question doctrine, war, matters relating to *above*
power to declare **94,** 113
power to wage **60,** 15, 16, 19-20
prisoners of war. *See* prisoners of war
prohibitory nature **91,** 40-1, 52, 160
property
instruments for protection of **46,** 544
private, respect for **53,** 4
purpose **110,** 473-4
recognition **80,** 669-70
collective prevention of **80,** 670
reparations. *See* compensation for war-related events
reprisals. *See* reprisals
resistance fighters **61,** 665-7
crimes against humanity and **122,** 81-3
status **47,** 463
rules of
customary **61,** 666
Laws and Customs of War on Land, Regulations **75,** 362-3
South East Asia, in
constitutionality **94,** 111-12, 114-15, 117-21
military assistance, lawfulness **94,** 123-7
war, whether **94,** 113-14
Spanish Civil War, whether **80,** 668-72
state of
'actually prevails' **87,** 262-75, 280-1
'actually raging' **87,** 262-3
between
Indonesia–Malaysia **52,** 498
UK–North Korea **52,** 69
declaration as to **71,** 709, 711
'defensive emergency' **106,** 348

determination
courts, by **87,** 273-5
difficulty of **87,** 662-5
responsibility for **87,** 688-9, 699-703, **94,** 106
effects **94,** 113
executive certificate/statement **87,** 183
existence of, executive or courts, whether a matter for **71,** 711-12
India/Pakistan. *See* India/Pakistan relations, state of war
termination of. *See* termination *below*
undeclared war outside State **87,** 269-70, 272
State responsibility. *See also* belligerent occupation, State responsibility for acts in occupied territory; State responsibility, liability of Iraq for 'any direct loss, damage . . . as a result of Iraq's unlawful invasion and occupation of Kuwait'
breach of the laws and customs of war **76,** 722-3
loss during war or civil disturbance not attributable to State **106,** 480, 487-94, 498-500
losses arising out of military operations **48,** 467-8
reparations **40,** 103-11, **41,** 480-2, **56,** 537-56, **94,** 61-2
State succession, war damage, offset **96,** 728-9
Suez operations, 1956, whether **48,** 467-8
termination **48,** 485, **67,** 628, **71,** 710-11, **72,** 468. *See also* hostilities, cessation *above*
armistice. *See* armistice; armistice agreement
ceasefire, declaration in Security Council **71,** 711
Japan, Instrument of Surrender **53,** 5-8
peace, declaration of **52,** 507-11
peace treaty, relevance **40,** 434-5. *See also* peace treaties
political act **94,** 106
threat of
Balkans **100,** 235-6, 237
evidence of, UN Secretary-General's report **100,** 237
'time of war' **87,** 275, **99,** 86-9, 91
treaties, effect on **37,** 71, **40,** 19, **44,** 318, **48,** 418, **59,** 492, **71,** 595-6, **74,** 118-19, 563-4
Institute of International Law (Helsinki Resolution (1985)) **96,** 305
multilateral treaties **74,** 564
reapplication, peace treaty **91,** 390
separability **37,** 71
suspension **91,** 390
unconditional surrender, effect on legal entity **44,** 302, 313
unprivileged **42,** 466-70, 480-3
Vietnam
aggressive **42,** 437
in **48,** 468, **60,** 15, 16
legality **56,** 583
US involvement in **42,** 393-401, 436-8, 439-41
weapons
'analogous materials or devices' **110,** 198
legality
authorization, need for **110,** 197
legitimacy of purpose, relevance **110,** 194
State practice **106,** 362-3, **110,** 197, 245-7, 261, 262-3
'poison or poisoned weapons', State practice **110,** 198

war crimes **42,** 436-8, 439-41, **61,** 665-8, **72,** 607-14, **77,** 220-1, **105,** 481-3. *See also* crimes against humanity; international crimes; international humanitarian law; Nuremberg Charter (1945); reprisals; Rwanda, International Criminal Tribunal for (ICTR); war; Yugoslavia, International Criminal Tribunal for the Former (ICTY), Statute
absolute liability **91,** 57
accused to be returned to country where acts carried out **78,** 129, 131
act of State and **36,** 23, 44-8, 254, 308-12
superior orders and **39,** 438
aiding and abetting. *See also* common purpose *below*; torture, aiding and abetting
acting with a common purpose distinguished **121,** 279-80, 320, **122,** 99 n. 310, 100, **124,** 155-6, 160
actus reus **121,** 273-86
ex post facto assistance **121,** 276-7, 284, 319-21
knowing presence **121,** 322-3
moral support **121,** 285, 295
presence as proof **122,** 99
substantial effect, need for **121,** 280-3, **122,** 160
case law relating to **121,** 274-83, 322-3
Almelo **121,** 276 n. 226
Auschwitz Concentration Camp **121,** 279-80
Dachau Concentration Camp **121,** 278-9
Einsatzgruppen **121,** 280-1, 286
Furundžija **122,** 99
Hechingen Deportation **121,** 282, 286-7, 289
Pig-cart parade case **121,** 277-8
Rohde **121,** 276-7, 289
Schonfeld **121,** 275-6
Stalag Luft III **121,** 276 n. 226
Synagogue case **121,** 277-8
Tadić Judgment **121,** 282-3, 287, 288
Zyklon B **121,** 281-2
customary international law **121,** 273-89, 322-3, **122,** 97-8
distinguished **122,** 99 n. 310
ILC Draft Code of Offences against the Peace and Security of Mankind (1996), aiding and abetting **121,** 283, 284, 287
mens rea **121,** 286-9. *See also* requirements, knowledge *below*
case law relating to **121,** 286-7, **122,** 99-100
Control Council Law No 10 **121,** 287 n. 262
customary international law **121,** 288
intent **121,** 288
international instruments **121,** 287-8
knowledge that action assists commission of offence **121,** 288-9, 295, **122,** 99-100
pre-existing conspiracy, relevance **121,** 319-21
Rome Statute (1998) **121,** 279-80, 288, 320
Schonfeld **121,** 286
Zyklon B **121** 286
applicable law
international law **91,** 43, 44-6, 47-8, **104,** 299-300
retroactivity and **91,** 43-4
military courts
international law **91,** 47-8
post-war Germany, correspondence of tribunal law with international law **91,** 48
municipal law **91,** 45, 47, 92-3, 94-6, **104,** 299-300, 306, 327

belligerent occupation, imprisonment of war criminal, costs **90,** 390-400
burden of proof **91,** 11, 68-9, 103-4, 134, **104,** 355-6
  knowledge that act constituted war crime or crime against humanity **98,** 542, 596-7, **104,** 395
classification as
  aerial bombardment **105,** 507-8
  attack on non-military buildings and civilians **42,** 458, 469-70
  attack on undefended towns or buildings **122,** 23, 72
  blocking of assets **66,** 352-60
  cruel treatment **112,** 93, 97, 102, 103, 250-2, 253, **122,** 72, 245
  destruction and appropriation of property **122,** 22, 66, 88, 139-40, 244
  destruction of sacred sites **108,** 91
  destruction or wilful damage to religious or other institutions **122,** 23, 73, 140, 244
  discriminatory attack **122,** 137, 166-8, 185, 196-9
  ethnic cleansing **95,** 150
  genocide **108,** 37, 133-6, **121,** 218
  hostage-taking **122,** 66, 73, 216-18, 224, 245
    intention to obtain advantage, need for **122,** 73
  human shields **122,** 73, 224-5
    UN hostages as **108,** 91, 132
  indiscriminate attack **108,** 47, 50-2, 91, 162-3, **122,** 136-7
  inhuman treatment **122,** 73, 210-16, 245
    human shields **122,** 73, 224-5
    trench digging **122,** 210-16, 223-4
  'murder of civilian population of or in occupied territory' **87,** 94-5
  'planned' attack on civilian population **122,** 127-43, 172-3, 184
  rape **121,** 267, 292
  sexual assault **108,** 37
  torture **121,** 262, 292, **122,** 65
  unlawful appropriation of property **108,** 91
  unlawful detention of civilians **108,** 91, **122,** 138
  violation of laws and customs of war **91,** 24-5, 40-1, **105,** 445, **111,** 381-2
  wanton destruction of cities or devastation unjustified by military necessity **108,** 162, **122,** 22, 23, 71, 133-7, 143-5, 178-82, 244
  wilful killing **108,** 62, **112,** 106, **122,** 22, 65, 72
  wilfully causing great suffering **108,** 62, **112,** 88, 93, 97, 102, 103, 107, **122,** 22, 65-6, 244
common purpose. *See also* aiding and abetting *above*
  actus reus
    common plan, design or purpose **124,** 159, 160-1
    crime provided for in the ICTY Statute **124,** 159-60
    participation in common purpose **124,** 160
    plurality of persons **124,** 159
  common design and common criminal intention (co-perpetration), requirements **124,** 139-43, 149-50, 154
    causation **124,** 144, 150-1, 153
    intention to achieve result **124,** 139, 159-60
    voluntary participation in part of common design **124,** 139
  common design leading to foreseeable act outside design **124,** 145-50, 152-4, 159-60
    psychological nexus, need for **124,** 151
    risk willingly taken **124,** 160
  common design and position of authority, requirements **124,** 143-5

war crimes (*cont.*)
intent to further common design **124,** 154, 160-1, 189
knowledge of nature of system **124,** 145, 154, 1104
Convention for the Suppression of Terrorist Bombing (1997) **124,** 154-5
customary international law **124,** 139-54
ICC (Rome) Statute (1998) **124,** 155-6
knowing participation with others in criminal activity **124,** 134
mens rea. See common purpose subheadings above
organization, relevance **124,** 159
post-WWII cases **124,** 139-54
complicity. *See* aiding and abetting *above*
customary international law **36,** 293, 294, **82,** 435, 439-41, **104,** 200-2, 299, 322, 335-6, 337-8, **108,** 162-3
common purpose **124,** 139-54
defence
act of State **36,** 44-8, 254, 308-12, **44,** 11
any defence available under international law at the time or at time of proceedings **104,** 331-4, 366
any defence available under *lex fori* at the time or at time of proceedings **104,** 297-8, 331-4, 366
autrefois convict **104,** 366
evidence of additional facts **91,** 69
judicial orders **91,** 26-7
lawful authority **98,** 597-602. *See also* superior orders
burden of proof **98,** 597
legality under laws of place where act committed **91,** 26-7, **104,** 296-7, 310, 334, 366, 377-80, 395-6
manifest illegality **104,** 379, 381, 395
mens rea, evidence of **104,** 380
peace officer defence distinguished **104,** 378-9
superior orders distinguished **104,** 378
legality under *lex fori* at time of act **104,** 203, 331
legitimate reprisals **72,** 609, 613-14
military necessity **104,** 331, **108,** 165-6
mistake of fact **104,** 367-8, 379
necessity **36,** 340
non-admissibility **91,** 25
peace officer defence. *See* peace officer defence *below*
permitted by laws, customs and usages of war **91,** 10, 25
proportionality **72,** 613-14, **108,** 46-7, 48, **122,** 177
reprisals **104,** 331, **108,** 46-7
superior orders. *See* superior orders
definition **36,** 275, 288, **42,** 482, **75,** 342, 359-60, 362-3, 365, **91,** 7, 8-10, 21-2, 23-8, 40-1, 47, 51-63, 66, 67, 68-9, 92, 121, 132-8. *See also* classification as *above*
breach of Geneva Conventions (1949) **105,** 521-2
Control Council Law No 10 **36,** 31, 39-41, **121,** 254-5, 266
as crimes against humanity **91,** 57-63. *See also* crimes against humanity, war crimes distinguished
international law, relevance **91,** 69, 132-8
International Military Tribunal for the Far East (Tokyo Tribunal) Charter **91,** 46
rape **121,** 266-7
jurists, writings of **105,** 445
municipal law **36,** 31, 288-9, **104,** 197, 335, 358

Nuremberg Charter (1945) **36,** 31, 288, **42,** 398, 437, **47,** 464, **78,** 143-4, **91,** 46, 122-3, **105,** 445
double criminality
notional transfer of act **104,** 198
offence under *lex fori* at the time **104,** 198, 202-4, 354
forced labour/kidnapping/forcible confinement, equivalence **104,** 202-3
enforcement of law
international military tribunals **91,** 46
military tribunal established by victorious power **91,** 46
municipal courts **91,** 47-8
obligation to seek out and prosecute. *See* obligation to seek out and prosecute *below*
State into whose hands alleged offender falls **91,** 46-7
evidence of **56,** 583-4, **75,** 341-3
admissibility **104,** 386-9
foreign **82,** 453-4
indiscriminate attack **108,** 49-52, **122,** 136-7
witnesses, judge's right to summon **104,** 389-93
exclusion of alien for **104,** 198
extradition for **75,** 339, 343, **79,** 386, 391, 395, 511, **88,** 279-301
fair trial
delay
introducing war crimes legislation **104,** 338
pre-trial **104,** 338
vagueness of legislation **104,** 337-8, 396-9
general principle of international law **82,** 438, **104,** 296, 322, 337-8
Hetherington Report **91,** 47, 50
individual responsibility. *See* responsibility *below*; superior orders
international character **36,** 293-4, 300, **104,** 356-7, **105,** 481-3
international law, existence in
absence of court/code, relevance **104,** 336
customary international law **91,** 123
Hague Conventions (1907), declaratory nature **104,** 200, 336
Nuremberg Charter (1945) **104,** 200-1
UNGA Resolution 95(1) (Nuremberg Charter) **91,** 123, **104,** 201-2, **112,** 204-6, **119,** 99
international military tribunals. *See* International Military Tribunal for the Far East (Tokyo Tribunal); Nuremberg Tribunal; Rwanda, International Criminal Tribunal for (ICTR); Yugoslavia, International Criminal Tribunal for the Former (ICTY), jurisdiction
jurisdiction **88,** 296-301. *See also* Yugoslavia, International Criminal Tribunal for the Former (ICTY), jurisdiction
accused within territory **82,** 445, **104,** 354
aut dedere aut punire/judicare **36,** 302-3, **88,** 296-7, **105,** 449, 497, 536. *See also* universal *below*
basis, breach of general principles of law recognized by the community of nations **104,** 299, 353
customary international law **104,** 353
extraterritorial **82,** 443-7, **91,** 10, 27-8, **104,** 298-9
Geneva Conventions (1949) **82,** 446-7, **104,** 298
non-national at time of offence **91,** 10, 27-8, **104,** 403-4
federal State, in **91,** 11
municipal courts **56,** 583, **105,** 521-2
national, over **57,** 170-3, **88,** 298-301

war crimes (*cont.*)
nexus, need for **91,** 27-8
non-national at time of offence **91,** 10, 27-8, **104,** 403-4
obligation **104,** 328, 330, **105,** 449
occupied territory, acts in **88,** 298-301
de facto jurisdiction, sufficiency **88,** 298-301
occupying forces after cessation of hostilities **91,** 44-6
occupying power **48,** 484, **57,** 170-3
over members of opposing forces **91,** 67
over members of own forces **91,** 67
par in parem non habet jurisdictionem **36,** 45
partisans, against **86,** 176
place where offender found **91,** 35
right **105,** 449
territorial **91,** 35, **119,** 226
universal **36,** 29, 40, 294, 298-304, **91,** 39-51, 119-21, **104,** 299-300, **105,** 485, **119,** 227-8, **120,** 367-71. *See also aut dedere aut punire/judicare above*
Land Warfare Regulations, breach of **87,** 94-5
lèse-humanité **105,** 482
limitation period. *See* statutory limitation *below*
mens rea. See also common purpose *above*
aiding and abetting **121,** 286-9, **122,** 99-100
of commander **122,** 98-9, 103-11, 113, 154-9, 182, 188-9
intent **121,** 288
reason to know **122,** 103-11, 221-3
Čelebići **122,** 104-5
post-WWII trials **122,** 105-9
Moscow Declaration (1943) **82,** 437-8
nullum crimen/poena sine lege **36,** 42-4, 279, 281-3, **91,** 43, 48, 50, **121,** 360
in case of customary international law **122,** 68
Nuremberg Charter (1945) **82,** 438
obligation to seek out and prosecute **91,** 34-51. *See also aut dedere aut punire/judicare*
customary international law **91,** 36-7, 116-17
Declaration of St James (1942) **91,** 34
ECOSOC Resolution 1074D(XXXIX) **91,** 35
Geneva Conventions (1949) **91,** 35-6, **105,** 449, 497
international obligation, whether **91,** 34-51
matter of international concern, whether **91,** 38-9, 116
Moscow Declaration (1943) **91,** 34
State practice **91,** 36-7
trial according to law, need for **91,** 34
UNGA Resolution 3(I) **91,** 35
UNGA Resolution 95(I) **91,** 35
UNGA Resolution 170(II) **91,** 35
UNGA Resolution 2712(XXV) **91,** 36
UNGA Resolution 3074(XXVIII) **91,** 35
occupied territory, in, partisans, against **86,** 179-81
origin of laws concerning **82,** 435
peace officer defence **104,** 331, 332, 366-7, 378-9
requirements **104,** 350-1
necessary force or violence **104,** 333, 367, 381

reasonable belief in lawful authority **104,** 333, 367, 380-1
reasonable to assume knowledge that act was war crime/crime against humanity **104,** 333
pillage. *See* pillage
planning, ordering or instigating **122,** 98-9
case law relating to, *Akayesu* **122,** 98-9
causal element, need for **122,** 98
mens rea of commander **122,** 98-9, 113, 154-9
political offence and **55,** 551, 553, 557, **86,** 179-81, **105,** 482
Preliminary Peace Conference of Paris 1919 **82,** 435-6
prisoners of war. *See* prisoners of war
prohibitory nature of law relating to **91,** 25-6, 40-1
Hague Conventions (1907) **91,** 41
punishment **74,** 710-13
requirements
armed conflict **36,** 289, **104,** 311, 312, **108,** 35, **111,** 382, **122,** 39-42. *See also* international conflict *below*
breach of international law at time of act **104,** 301, 335, 354
breach of laws of armed conflict **104,** 358
civilians in occupied territory **111,** 382, 383
combatants or prisoners of war **111,** 382
employment or service as State official **75,** 339, 346-8, 359, 361, 366, **124,** 119-21
fault **98,** 595
international conflict **105,** 444-50, 485-526, 528-31, 581-3, 592, 596, **108,** 35-6, 131-2, **122,** 20
customary international law **105,** 528-31
knowledge **122,** 103-4
proof, need for **122,** 104
knowledge that act a war crime or crime against humanity **98,** 536, 541, 542-6, 558-61, 594, 627-8, **104,** 312-23, 363-6
actus reus **104,** 312-14
burden of proof **98,** 542, 558-61, 596-7, **104,** 395
general principle of international law **104,** 321
natural law **104,** 321
rebuttable presumption **104,** 320
knowledge that action assists commission of offence **121,** 288-9, 295, **122,** 99-100
lack of clarity **104,** 328-9
mens rea **36,** 41, 42, 44, **104,** 363, 376-7, 380
non-nationals **79,** 401 n. 2, **111,** 382
'of or in occupied territory' **79,** 401 n. 2
treaty **104,** 337-8
responsibility **36,** 5-342
commander **122,** 98-9, 100-14, 142-62, 168-73, 182, 185-8
Alekovski **122,** 103
Čelibići **121,** 102-3
customary international law **122,** 100, 104-9
duty to control forces **104,** 155-6, 171-3
effective control test **122,** 102-3, 145-52, 186-7, 220-1
evidence of **122,** 152, 169-73, 186-8
Geneva Conventions, Additional Protocol I **122,** 109-10
High Command case **122,** 98 n. 308, 108
Hostage case **122,** 108

war crimes (*cont.*)
Israeli Commission of Enquiry into events at Shatilla and Sabra refugee camps **122,** 111
mens rea **122,** 98-9, 103-11, 113, 154-9, 182
multiple responsibility **122,** 103, 149-52
municipal law **122,** 109
obligation to prevent or punish **108,** 31-2, 120, 128-9, **122,** 94, 95, 100-14, 159-62, 187-8, 219-25, 226
Pohl **122,** 107
post-WWII trials **122,** 105-9
Roechling **122,** 107-8
superior-subordinate relationship, need for **122,** 101-3, 169-72
Toyoda **122,** 106-7
wanton disregard/risk **122,** 110-11, 223-5
widespread and systematic nature of attack **122,** 152, 204-6
Geneva Conventions (1949) **104,** 155-6, **122,** 70
individual **82,** 438, **91,** 69, 93, **104,** 155-6, **106,** 155-6, **122,** 70-1, **124,** 121 n. 175. *See also* aiding and abetting *and* common purpose *above*; superior orders
customary international law **105,** 520-4, **122,** 71
evidence of **108,** 165-6
Hague Conventions/Regulations (1907) **82,** 439, **122,** 70
internal conflict **105,** 520-4, 537-8
Nuremberg Charter (1945) **105,** 520
insurgent military groups **104,** 156
non-combatants **56,** 584
requirements
criminalization of offence **105,** 520-4
customary international law regulating **105,** 520-3
State responsibility. *See* State responsibility *below*
retroactivity **36,** 20-40, 43-4, **88,** 297, **98,** 564-5
breach of fundamental rights, whether **98,** 574-5, **104,** 335-7, 399-402
Canada **82,** 430-41, **98,** 564-5
Canadian Commission of Inquiry on War Criminals (Deschnes Commission) (1986) **91,** 49
Control Council Law No 10 **91,** 48
decisions of courts **82,** 434-5
Geneva Convention (Prisoners of War) (1949) **91,** 49-50
Hague Conventions (1899/1907) **104,** 400-1
incorporation into municipal law **105,** 450, 591
Hague Regulations (1907) **91,** 48
International Criminal Tribunal for Yugoslavia **105,** 449-50, 525-6, 591
international law as applicable law and **91,** 43-4
military tribunals in occupied Germany **91,** 48-9
nullum crimen sine lege **105,** 447, 449-50, **108,** 206
Nuremberg Charter (1945) **91,** 48, 49, **104,** 322, 400-2, **105,** 569-70
retrospectivity distinguished **98,** 574
State practice **82,** 434-5
treaties **82,** 434-5
retrospectivity. *See* retroactivity *above*
sabotage **44,** 440, **52,** 496-7
St James Declaration 1942 **82,** 436-7
State practice **82,** 440
State responsibility

applicability of rules relating to **108,** 155-6, **124,** 98
assimilation of civilians to State officials **124,** 119-21
statutory limitation **72,** 609, 611-12, **78,** 136, 139, **87,** 94-5, **91,** 35
arrest warrant interrupting **72,** 611
European Convention on the Non-applicability of Statutory Limitations to Crimes against Humanity and War Crimes (1974) **91,** 35
UN Convention on the Non-applicability of Statutory Limitations to War Crimes and Crimes against Humanity (1968) **91,** 35
superior orders. *See* defence, lawful authority *and* responsibility *above*; superior orders
Treaty of Versailles (1919) **82,** 436, **105,** 536, **108,** 14
as dictate **82,** 439
UN General Assembly (UNGA) **82,** 440-1
Resolutions, obligation to seek out and prosecute **91,** 35
Vietnam **42,** 436-8, 439-41
waging aggressive war, relative seriousness **121,** 355
war treason, whether **91,** 53-4
whether
question of fact for jury **98,** 528-9, 552-7
question of law for judge **98,** 536, 539-41, 570
war damage. *See* compensation for war-related events
war reparations. *See* compensation for war-related events
Warsaw Convention on International Carriage by Air (1929) and Hague Protocol (1955) 52, 428-35, 438, 442-6
air consignment note **41,** 426-36, **43,** 254-9
applicable law of contract and **87,** 372, 385
carrier's liability **61,** 626-7, 628-30, **74,** 633-83
contract of carriage **87,** 393
passengers, parties to, whether **87,** 293
relevance **87,** 293
Convention and Protocol distinguished **87,** 372, 387, 392
extraterritorial effect of implementing legislation **87,** 372-8, 381-9, 392-3
French text
primacy of **74,** 632, 641, 645, 650, 660, 663, 670-1, 673, 676, 679
recourse to **74,** 641, 650-4, 665-6, 669-71, 673, 676-81
gold clause
anachronistic nature, legitimacy of measures to compensate for **101,** 591-615
hijacking of aircraft and **60,** 445, 447-8, **89,** 27-8
phrases
'accident'
cause or event, whether **96,** 118, 122-4
French and English, coincidence of meaning **96,** 119
Guatemala City International Conference (1971) **96,** 121
Montreal Protocols (1975) **96,** 116-24
'occurrence', whether **96,** 116, 118
teachings of publicists **96,** 122
terrorist act **96,** 122
tortious act **96,** 122
unexpected or unusual event **96,** 119, 122
'agreed stopping place' **87,** 294, 374
'international carriage' **87,** 292-5, 367-9, 373-5, 383-4
'knowledge that damage would probably result' **101,** 324, 325-9, 330-2
'one undivided carriage' **87,** 292-5
'recklessly' **101,** 322-4, 330

Warsaw Convention on International Carriage by Air (1929) (*cont.*)
liability under
absolute **96,** 116, 123-4
consignment note **41,** 426-36
default equivalent to wilful misconduct **89,** 24-5, 29, 41-2
gold clause. *See* gold clause *above*
limitation **39,** 453-4, 458, **43,** 254-9, **45,** 386-9, **89,** 27-8, 41
waiver **89,** 28-9
nature of **77,** 409
presumption of **89,** 28
limitation period **39,** 406-9, **87,** 295
municipal law and, interpretation **41,** 426-36, **89,** 42, 43
nationality, relevance
aircraft **87,** 368, 392
carrier **87,** 374
purpose **87,** 372-3
elimination of conflict of laws problems **87,** 375, 384
unification of laws of contracting parties **77,** 407, **89,** 42
ratification provisions **42,** 259-63
rules **87,** 372, 396-8
State immunity, waiver **98,** 74
territory of operation **87,** 392
travaux préparatoires **74,** 634-6, 638, 642-5, 647, 650, 654-6, 660-2, 666-8, 674-5, 682
warship. *See also* High Seas Convention (1958), search and seizure by warship or other duly authorized ship or aircraft, prohibition; stateless ship
customs vessel as **91,** 475 n. 16, 500
immunity, arrest/attachment, Brussels Convention on Immunity of State-owned Ships (1926) **64,** 232-3
immunity, jurisdiction **55,** 419, **64,** 97, 232-3, **72,** 100, 104, 107
innocent passage **91,** 500
other ships distinguished from, whether **91,** 500
jurisdiction
ship's complement in foreign port **38,** 159, **42,** 232-8
vessel of neutral State driven into port in distress **64,** 97
obligation to notify passage **82,** 698
wartime emergency powers, State immunity, execution/attachment and **65,** 169, 428
waste disposal
Basel Convention on the Control of Transboundary Movements of Hazardous Wastes and Their Disposal (1989). *See also* hazardous activities
cross-border movement provisions, Canada–USA Transboundary Agreement (1986) compared **121,** 108-9
implementing measures **121,** 88-94
availability of alternative measures to achieve environmental objectives **121,** 105, 118, 133, 152, 175
compatibility with NAFTA (1992) **121,** 115-90
discriminatory, whether **121,** 115-17, 133, 174-5
protectionist nature **121,** 98-105, 118, 133, 159-67
NAFTA (1992) and. *See* NAFTA (North American Free Trade Agreement) (1992), Basel Convention on the Control of Transboundary Movements of Hazardous Waste and Their Disposal (1989) and
other treaties and, primacy **121,** 108-9, 150-1

Canada–USA, Agreement on the Transboundary Movement of Hazardous Wastes (1986) **121,** 107-8, 148-9
'applicable laws and regulations of the Parties' provision **121,** 149
weapons. *See* arms dealing; chemical weapons, deployment; nuclear weapons, deployment; war, weapons
West Africa, French
administration **80,** 473-550
boundaries, after independence **80,** 473-550
West Indian Associated States 90, 500, 501
common judicial system **90,** 501
Western European Union (WEU)
basis, UN Charter, Art. 51 **106,** 329
as collective security system **106,** 369
Petersberg Declaration (1992), treaty, whether **106,** 341-4
regional agreement or institution under UN Charter, Art. 52 **106,** 328
Western Sahara
colonization **59,** 154, 181
decolonization **59,** 51-4, 130-2, **88,** 700-2
compensation to Spanish national obliged to leave **88,** 700-2
continuity of law **88,** 705
Mauritania and **59,** 74-80, 82-4, 96-8, 120, 131-2, 136-9, 181, 188-9, 192-3
Morocco and. *See* Morocco, Western Sahara
Spain and **59,** 55, 126, 131-2, 154
special characteristics **59,** 80
status **59,** 52, 58, 93-4, 120, 136-9
Western Samoa, Trusteeship Agreement 37, 537-9
will, action to set aside, State immunity, jurisdiction and **64,** 673-4
Wilson Declaration (Fourteen Points) (1918) 37, 29, **46,** 485
winding-up proceedings 65, 84-5, **73,** 33-5. *See also* bankruptcy; international organizations, winding-up; jurisdiction, winding-up proceedings; State immunity, execution/attachment, applicability, bankruptcy/winding-up proceedings; United Kingdom, winding-up proceedings
foreign judgment, recognition/enforcement **77,** 30
international organizations **77,** 21-41
jurisdiction, in absence of establishment within the jurisdiction **65,** 84-5, **77,** 30
State immunity, jurisdiction **101,** 335-7
witnesses. *See* evidence, witnesses
women. *See also* married women
discrimination against women married to aliens **62,** 286-7, 290, 294-5
discrimination in the field of employment
Elimination of all Forms of Discrimination against Women, Convention on (1979) **125,** 524-6
public service appointments, Political Rights of Women Convention (1953) **47,** 196-7
domicile **118,** 302
international officials, residential status **48,** 249-53
nationality **41,** 380-3, **44,** 131-3, 141-3, **73,** 568, **79,** 297-9, 303-5
Elimination of all Forms of Discrimination against Women, Convention on (1979) **79,** 299
Nationality of Married Women, Montevideo Convention on (1933) **79,** 299, 303-4
as a 'particular social group' **104,** 263-4
Pakistan **124,** 477-511
public service appointments **47,** 196-7

women (*cont.*)
residential status, international officials **48,** 249-53
right to transmit citizenship through descent **103,** 133-7, 141-62, 170-2, 174-80, 183, 185-8, 192-7, 202
sexual harassment, measures to prevent **125,** 521-9
Guidelines and Norms (1997) (India) **125,** 526-9
UN Declaration on the Elimination of Discrimination against Women (1967) **103,** 178-9
World Bank Administrative Tribunal 83, 643-79, 681-716, 718-24. *See also* International Labour Organization Administrative Tribunal (ILOAT); United Nations Administrative Tribunal (UNAT); World Bank Group
admissibility. *See also* jurisdiction *below*
exhaustion of internal remedies **84,** 433-4
waiver of right to **84,** 447
timeliness **84,** 434-5, 437, 461, 463
appeals to **84,** 462
applicable law, internal law **83,** 649-50
function **83,** 669
judgment
finality **83,** 721, 724
reasoned, need for **83,** 723
review **83,** 723
revision **83,** 721-43
time-limits **83,** 722
jurisdiction **83,** 643, 646, 653. *See also* admissibility *above*
appeals against Appeals Committee **83,** 724
appropriate forum, whether **85,** 655-6
breach of contract **84,** 477, 482-3
determination of existence of contract **84,** 447-8
exceptional circumstances **84,** 434
procedure
amendment of plea **84,** 434-5
non-publication of applicant's name **84,** 456-7
third party intervention **85,** 656
time-limits **85,** 643-5, 653-6
discretion to waive **85,** 654
exceptional circumstances **85,** 654-5
Rules of Procedure
No 14 **83,** 681, 691
No 24 **84,** 456
No 25 **84,** 456
Statute
Art. II **83,** 643, 654, 710, 711, 723, 724, **85,** 653-5
Art. II(2) **84,** 434, 461, 463, 482-3
Art. XI **83,** 721, 723
Art. XIII **83,** 718, 721, 723, 724
Art. XVII **83,** 645, **85,** 653-5
superseded decision **84,** 437-8
World Bank Group. *See also* International Monetary Fund Agreement (IMF) (1944) (Bretton Woods Agreement); international officials; United Nations Economic and Social Council (ECOSOC); World Bank Administrative Tribunal
abuse of discretion **85,** 632, 666
Anniversary Evaluation
inconsistencies **85,** 634-5

procedure **85,** 668-9
arbitrariness **85,** 632, 666
discrimination **85,** 632, 666
improper motivation **85,** 632, 666-7
violation of fair and reasonable procedure **85,** 632, 666
discrimination, sexual **85,** 652-3
Principles of Staff Employment **85,** 652
employment contract, non-observance **85,** 631-2
fair and reasonable procedures **85,** 667-8
acquired rights **83,** 646, 651-2
Administrative Circular AC/23/79 of 25 May 1979 **83,** 644
Appeals Committee **83,** 704, 714, **84,** 462, 475
appeals against **83,** 724
appeals against World Bank Administrative Tribunal **83,** 724
function **84,** 482
jurisdiction **83,** 724
appointment, termination. *See* termination of appointment *below*
Articles of Agreement
Art. V **83,** 648, **85,** 632
Art. VII **83,** 648, 656, 666
waiver of immunity, whether **99,** 96-103
conditions of employment **83,** 647-56
Administrative Tribunal, right of recourse to **83,** 648-9
applicable law **83,** 652
Articles of Agreement **83,** 647
By-laws **83,** 647, 648
contractual relationship **83,** 647
fairness **83,** 698
Field Office Manual **83,** 649
fixed-term. *See* fixed-term appointment *below*
general principles of law **83,** 649
home-to-office transport **83,** 688
Memorandum of 14 February 1978 (treatment of tourism staff) **83,** 711-16
non-managerial staff **84,** 471
planned periodic reassignment **84,** 471, 475, 478-81
performance evaluation. *See* performance evaluation *below*
Personnel Manual Circular 1/80 of 21 January 1980 **83,** 664, 670
Personnel Manual Statement
No 1 **83,** 710
No 3 **83,** 661, 665-6
No 4 **83,** 698, 706, **85,** 633-4, 669
No 7 **83,** 707
physical injury, workman's compensation **83,** 688, 715
practice of organization **83,** 649, 673-7, **85,** 668-90
opinio juris **83,** 649
probation **83,** 691-9, **84,** 463-4
discretion and **83,** 699
unsatisfactory **83,** 697-8
reassignment
Administration's obligations **85,** 633, 667-8
employee's obligations **85,** 633
non-managerial staff, planned periodic **84,** 471, 475, 478-81
remedies

World Bank Group (*cont.*)
correction of personal record **84,** 454
damages, speculative **84,** 447
injury, need for **84,** 440
punitive damages **84,** 438
salary adjustment **83,** 670-9
discretion and **83,** 699
periodic review, obligation **83,** 678-9
Report R 68-140 of 30 June 1968 **83,** 671-2
tax reimbursement **83,** 648, 656-70
equitable requirement **83,** 663, 669-70
principle and method of implementation distinguished **83,** 667
training **85,** 634
unilateral amendment
discretionary **83,** 655, 669, 670
good faith **83,** 65
limitations **83,** 652, 655
non-discrimination **83,** 652
proportionality **83,** 652, 655
retroactivity **83,** 652, 655, 669
discrimination, age **84,** 435, 438-9, 453
employment contract
breach, compensation **84,** 453-4
customs and usages **84,** 452
estoppel, promissory **84,** 446
formation **84,** 445-6, 448-51
general principles of law **84,** 449
offer **84,** 448-9
parties' intention **84,** 449
procedures, applicant's knowledge of **84,** 450-1
fixed-term appointment **84,** 462. *See also* permanent appointment *below*
conversion into permanent **84,** 463-4
conduct, by **84,** 464
right to, whether **84,** 464
immunity, jurisdiction, waiver, Articles of Agreement **99,** 96-103
Joint Committee on Staff Compensation Issues. *See* Kafka Committee *below*
Kafka Committee **83,** 644, 662
Kafka Report **83,** 662-4, 669, 670, 677
officials. *See also* Personnel Manual Statement (PMS) *below*
F/I policy **84,** 462
interests of Bank, primacy **84,** 476, 478, 479
operations, audit **84,** 474
pensions, disability **84,** 436-7, 438
Pensions Benefits Administration Committee **84,** 434, 437, 438
performance evaluation
appeal against, grounds **84,** 464-6
arbitrariness **84,** 464-5, 478, 481, 483
discrimination **84,** 464-5, 478, 481, 482, 483
motivation **84,** 464, 465, 478, 481, 483
employee's right to know **84,** 482
finality **84,** 464
negative assessment, whether permitted **84,** 439
relevant factors **84,** 439

permanent appointment. *See also* fixed-term appointment *above*
'regular appointment' **84,** 463
Personnel Manual Circular 1/80 of 21 January 1980 **83,** 645
Personnel Manual Statement (PMS)
No 2.00 **84,** 449-50
No 4.01 **84,** 435
No 4.04 **84,** 440, 471, 476-7, 478, 479, 483
No 8.03 **84,** 476, 482
privileges and immunities
Convention on Privileges and Immunities of Specialized Agencies (1947) **83,** 657
statutory basis **63,** 88 n. 19
sexual harassment **85,** 652
Standards and Procedures for Operations Evaluation, status **84,** 479
termination of employment **83,** 681-9, **85,** 632, 666
authority **83,** 687, **85,** 632
change of basis for contract **84,** 440
discretion. *See* abuse of discretion *above*
disputed
finality of Administration's decision **85,** 632, 666
settlement **85,** 634, 644-5
due process **83,** 687
'for any cause' **83,** 686
grounds, unsatisfactory performance **85,** 632, 666
motivation **83,** 687
remedies **85,** 635, 670
compensation **83,** 687-8
equitable **83,** 699
publication of judgment **83,** 699
rescission of contested decision **83,** 687-8
retirement, disability **84,** 436, 438, 440
unsatisfactory performance **84,** 437
unsuitable appointment **84,** 453
World Health Assembly 62, 463, 496
competence **62,** 461, 483-5, 487-8, 491, 499, 537
functions **62,** 485, 487, 491
legality of acts, competence to determine **62,** 488, 496-7
World Health Organization (WHO). *See also* International Labour Organization Administrative Tribunal (ILOAT); International Sanitary Bureau; International Sanitary Regulations; World Health Organization Regional Office in Egypt
advisory opinion on legality of nuclear weapons, right to request **110,** 6-163
breach of obligations under WHO Constitution, limitation to **110,** 36-7
divided views of Member States **110,** 29-35, 44-51
Secretariat's views **110,** 29-35, 45
Alexandria Regional Office. *See* World Health Organization Regional Office in Egypt
amicus curiae **63,** 162
applicable law, international law **110,** 22
competence **110,** 15-19, 53-4, 68-71, 119-21, 134-5, 145
legality of underlying situation, relevance **110,** 15-19, 37
practice relating to legality of nuclear weapons **110,** 21-2, 145-6
practice relating to peace **110,** 91-2
transfer of seat of regional office **62,** 461, 483-5, 487-8, 491, 499, 511, 537
'within scope of activities' **110,** 14, 49-109
Constitution **62,** 460-3, 479, 483-5, 488, 491, 521, 547, 580

World Health Organization (WHO) (*cont.*)
interpretation. *See* constitution (international organization), interpretation
obligations **62,** 488
treaty, as **110,** 87
Eastern Mediterranean regional health organization. *See* World Health Organization Regional Office in Egypt
Effects of Nuclear War on Health and Health Services (WHO Management Group) **110,** 18
Egypt. *See also* World Health Organization Regional Office in Egypt
legal relationship **62,** 507-9
functions **62,** 485-7, 489, 537
headquarters agreement. *See* World Health Organization Regional Office in Egypt, host agreement
host agreement. *See* World Health Organization Regional Office in Egypt, host agreement
immunity, jurisdiction **72,** 197-200
interpretation. *See* constitution (international organization), interpretation
jurisdictional immunity **72,** 197-200
nuclear weapons, relevance **110,** 52-67, 72-7, 84, 86, 90-2
obligations, Member State **110,** 85
officials. *See also* international officials
employees not officials **38,** 420-7
immunity, jurisdiction **52,** 390-1, **72,** 199-200, **75,** 90-6
organs, role **62,** 487
Pan-American Health Organization and **43,** 459-62
Regional Board of Enquiry, procedure **48,** 278
regional office **62,** 461-3, 521-33. *See also* international organizations, regional office; World Health Organization Regional Office in Egypt
policy regarding **62,** 460-1, 527
Regional Office in Egypt. *See* World Health Organization Regional Office in Egypt
Resolutions
validity, form and substance distinguished **110,** 22-3, 29
WHA15.51, **110,** 21
WHA34.36 (Global Strategy for Health) **110,** 83-4
WHA34.38 **110,** 21
WHA36.28 **110,** 21
WHA42.26 **110,** 21
WHA45.31 **110,** 21
WHA46.40 (14 May 1993) (Request for Advisory Opinion on Legality of Use of Nuclear Weapons) **110,** 6-163
text **110,** 7-8
validity **110,** 35
Sanitary Regulations, municipal law and **48,** 231-2
staff
employment contract claims **72,** 197-200
summary dismissal, procedure **48,** 236-43
World Health Organization Regional Office in Egypt 62, 460-7
Agreement on privileges, immunities and facilities (1951) **62,** 466-9, 472-81, 490-1, 494, 507-8, 543-7, 558, 568, 573, 580
consultations **62,** 478-81, 493-6, 513, 538, 542, 546, 553, 558, 559-60, 568, 573
contractual nature **62,** 476-7, 509
cooperation, duty of **62,** 477-8, 538, 573
denunciation **62,** 475-6, 493-4, 507-8, 512, 514, 543, 547, 558, 569, 573
duration **62,** 536-7

establishment of regional office and **62,** 474-6, 492-3, 498-508, 511, 515, 532, 535-6, 543
good faith, duty to act in **62,** 479, 481, 508, 538, 573
host agreement, whether **62,** 466, 468, 478, 506, 515-33, 554-6, 569-70, 571
modifications **62,** 493-4, 512, 558, 568, 572
negotiations **62,** 476, 493-4, 542, 568
notice under **62,** 479-81, 494, 498, 515, 546, 553-4, 558-9, 568-9, 571
transitional period **62,** 480-1
obligations **62,** 477-81, 513, 546, 553, 573
purpose **62,** 474, 491, 498-9, 556
similar instruments **62,** 476, 492, 533-8
termination **62,** 475, 478-9, 491, 493-4, 496, 511-16, 534-7, 544, 570-1
transfer of regional office and. *See* seat, transfer, Agreement on privileges, immunities and facilities (1951), relevance
void, whether **62,** 572
agreements relating to
distinct, whether **62,** 490, 541, 553
objectives **62,** 490-1, 541
obligations **62,** 491, 508
Alexandria Regional Office **62,** 460-7, 485-7, 490-1
Alexandria Sanitary Bureau, integration of, **62,** 464-5, 468, 486-9, 499, 510-12, 528-9, 533, 557, 566-7. *See also* establishment *below*
constitutional framework **62,** 461-7
establishment **62,** 461-5, 474, 485-6, 492, 498-9, 505-7, 521-33, 557
existence assumed **62,** 505-6, 510, 533
history **62,** 461-8, 485-6, 492, 499-506, 515-31, 544, 553, 579
integration of Alexandria Sanitary Bureau distinguished **62,** 474, 505-6, 557
functions **62,** 485, 486-7, 489, 491
host agreement, drafting **62,** 463-8, 510-11
immunities. *See* Agreement on privileges, immunities and facilities (1951) *above*
legal status **62,** 464-9, 474-7, 484, 486, 490-1
privileges. *See* Agreement on privileges, immunities and facilities (1951) *above*
seat, transfer **62,** 460, 469-70, 477, 479-81, 483, 489-90, 494-5, 507-8, 536-7, 552, 558-9, 562, 568
Agreement on privileges, immunities and facilities (1951), relevance **62,** 472, 474, 476, 493, 498, 511, 515, 535-6, 542-4, 558-9, 570, 572-3, 576-7
revision/denunciation/termination and **62,** 469, 475-6, 478, 490, 493, 498, 507-8, 512, 521, 536, 544, 545-6, 560, 570, 572
competence to decide **62,** 461, 483-5, 487-8, 491, 499, 511, 537
conditions **62,** 494, 499, 508, 538, 552, 558-9, 573, 579-80
consultations **62,** 478-81, 493-6, 513, 538, 553, 559-60, 573
legal principles relating to **62,** 472-3, 476-7, 479-81, 495, 508, 513, 547, 550-1, 559-60, 573, 577-9
modalities **62,** 494-5, 508, 513, 538, 559, 573, 579-80
negotiations **62,** 478-81, 493-5, 498, 508, 513-15, 538, 553, 559-60, 573
obligations relating to **62,** 477, 479-81, 489
political question, whether **62,** 469-71, 483, 494, 547
reasonable period, within **62,** 477, 496, 508
World Trade Organization (WTO). *See also* General Agreement on Tariffs and Trade (GATT) (1947); Uruguay Round
Agreement on Agriculture. *See* Uruguay Round, Agreement on Agriculture
community competence **105,** 86, 149-52
European Communities

World Trade Organization (WTO) (*cont.*)
negotiation and signature **105,** 85
status **105,** 84
WTO Agreement **105,** 83-4
competence to conclude **105,** 84-225
dispute settlement
compensation in another sector **105,** 84
cross-retaliation **105,** 83-4
plurilateral agreements **105,** 84
dispute settlement **105,** 84
wrecks. *See also* collisions at sea
Australian territorial sea **70,** 54-101
Crown rights **70,** 80, 88, 97-8
definition **70,** 58, 70
derelict (*res derelicta*)
abandoned ship in international waters **56,** 45-6
distinguished **70,** 70, 77, 88
high seas, on
destruction **89,** 4-5
duty **74,** 199-200
removal costs **74,** 199-200
State responsibility and **89,** 5
diplomatic immunity and **89,** 363
historic wrecks, national heritage and **70,** 59-60, 67, 99-100
ownership **56,** 45-6, **87,** 523
expropriation/nationalization **87,** 523
possession of **70,** 80-3
removal
costs, liability
high seas **74,** 199-200
international rivers **74,** 124-7
duty **74,** 199-200
on rivers, removal costs, liability **74,** 124-7
seabed, whether distinguishable from **70,** 69-70

Yaoundé Conventions. *See* European Community treaties, Yaoundé I (1963); European Community treaties, Yaoundé Convention I (1963); European Community Treaties, Yaoundé II (1973)
Yemen, Arab Republic of
history **114,** 45
human rights **85,** 195, 196
Joint Yemeni–Eritrean Committee for Bilateral Cooperation, Treaty of 16 October 1998 **119,** 492-4
Memorandum of Understanding with Eritrea of 15 November 1994 **119,** 488-91
Red Sea Islands. *See* Red Sea Islands
right of residence **85,** 193-4, 198, 200-1
Yom Kippur War 63, 166
young people, protection of 92, 363-4. *See also* child care
Young Plan, German reparations and liabilities **47,** 419-20, 427, 429-30, 437-8, 443, 444, 456, 458
Yugoslavia, ethnicity, importance **122,** 58-60
Yugoslavia, Federal Republic (FRY) 95, 27-9, **96,** 722
International Tribunal for War Crimes **95,** 66

NATO bombing of Radio Television Serbia (RTS)
European Convention on Human Rights (1950), applicability **123,** 97-117
provisional measures, request to ICJ **123,** 99
recognition **92,** 207-8
succession to Socialist Federal Republic of Yugoslavia (SFRY)
date **96,** 722
treaties
Genocide Convention (1948) **115,** 169
statement of intention to be bound by **115,** 23, 166-9
Yugoslavia, whether **92,** 207-8, **96,** 722
Yugoslav State Commission for War Crimes and Genocide, Army of the Republic of Srpska and **95,** 80
Yugoslavia, International Criminal Tribunal for the Former (ICTY)
appeal
admissibility
audi alteram partem **110,** 682-4
right to challenge **110,** 683, 684-5
against acquittal **124,** 191-4
against sentencing judgment **124,** 236-59
deferment **124,** 79-80
alternative procedures **111,** 476
de novo review distinguished **121,** 308
expeditious procedure, need for **110,** 683
from final judgment of Trial Chamber **124,** 71
grounds. *See* grounds for appeal *and* judicial impartiality, disqualification for lack of *below*
interlocutory decision **105,** 542-3, **110,** 678-81
'directly affected' **110,** 679
'of general importance relating to the powers of the Tribunal' **110,** 679
rectification of appellant's errors in previous hearings **111,** 312
remedies
acquittal **111,** 313, 314
entry of non-guilty plea **111,** 429-30
opportunity to appellant to replead **111,** 313, 314, 374, 385, 396, 458
revision of sentence **111,** 313, 314, 385
right of **105,** 540-3, **124,** 247
Appeals Chamber
composition **124,** 215-16
decision, effect **105,** 595, 596
jurisdiction **105,** 540-3, **124,** 187
appeal against legality of Tribunal **105,** 455-6
proprio motu, **111,** 312-13
obiter dicta **124,** 163, 175-6, 187, 208
standard of review **121,** 304-8, 344-5
applicable law
any agreement binding on parties **105,** 526, **121,** 254-5
'any humanitarian law agreement in force in Former Yugoslavia' **105,** 493, 526, 591
armed conflict, relevance **112,** 178-9
customary international law **105,** 433-4, 442-3, 445-50, 587-91, **110,** 631, **111,** 336-44, **112,** 178, **121,** 360-2, **122,** 95, **124,** 139
at time of offence **112,** 220, **122,** 76, 104-5
avoidance of retroactivity **105,** 526, 569-70, 584-5
UN Secretary-General's Report **122,** 68-9, **124,** 180-1

Yugoslavia, ICTY (*cont.*)
'domestic law in so far as it incorporates customary international humanitarian law' **124,** 159
general principles of criminal law **122,** 95
international criminal law **108,** 207
international humanitarian law **111,** 395, 435
policy considerations **111,** 366-8, 395, 429
international law **111,** 395
law of accused **111,** 429
legal practice of the former Yugoslavia **108,** 194-6
lex loci delicti commissi **111,** 429
penalty
ICTY and ICTR case law **121,** 345
Statute and rules **121,** 345
Rules of Procedure and Evidence. *See* Yugoslavia, International Criminal Tribunal for the Former (ICTY), Rules of Procedure and Evidence
State practice
in conformity with nature and purposes of Tribunal **110,** 656, 658, 662, **111,** 388
limited relevance **110,** 696-7, 698, 709-10, 712, 713-14, **111,** 387-92, 395-6
Statute **111,** 395, **112,** 15
arrest
authority to issue order for. *See* orders, authority to issue *below*
definition **111,** 471-3
lawfulness, requirements
in accordance with procedures established by law **111,** 484-5
accused to be informed of charges **111,** 480-1
accused to be informed of rights **111,** 480-1
arrest warrant, entitlement to copy **111,** 483
forcible abduction/unlawful arrest. *See* forcible abduction/unlawful arrest *below*
non-disclosure of indictment, relevance **111,** 481-3
Office of the Prosecutor, role **111,** 480-1
power of
limited to States, whether **111,** 473-7
location, relevance **111,** 477
UNTAES **111,** 474-5, 477-80
procedures **111,** 474-7
burden of proof, grounds for appeal **121,** 306, 338
Chambers
constitution **110,** 732-5
Judge sitting alone, competence **110,** 732-5
characteristics
judicial body **105,** 553-4, **110,** 706
military tribunal **105,** 612
defence
alibi **112,** 155-69
nullum crimen/poena sine lege **121,** 360, **122,** 76
absence of precise penalty at time of offence **108,** 195-6, **121,** 271-2
detention. *See also* arrest *above*; enforcement of penalty *below*
compulsory residence (assignation … résidence) **108,** 76
conditions
amendment **108,** 71-85

European Prison Rules (1987) **108,** 209
UN Basic Principles for the Treatment of Prisoners (1990) **108,** 209
UN Body of Principles for the Protection of All Persons under Any Form of Detention or Imprisonment (1988) **108,** 209
UN Standard Minimum Rules for the Treatment of Prisoners (1957/1977) **108,** 209
house arrest (*arrêt domiciliaire*) **108,** 76-8
humane treatment, right to **108,** 84, 208-9
motions for release and modification of conditions distinguished **122,** 25
place
outside Detention Unit **108,** 79-81
outside territory of former Yugoslavia **108,** 206
release **108,** 81
Trial Chamber **108,** 76
Rules of. *See* Yugoslavia, International Criminal Tribunal for the Former (ICTY), Rules of Detention
diplomatic privileges and immunities, applicability **110,** 652
disclosure of documents, 'document' **122,** 27
due process **105,** 610-11. *See also* Yugoslavia, International Criminal Tribunal for the Former (ICTY), Statute, 21 (due process)
enforcement of penalty. *See also* detention *above*
absence of provision in Statute **110,** 697-8
applicable law, international criminal law **108,** 207
equality of treatment, need for **108,** 206-7
possibility **110,** 697-8
responsibility
provisional release **108,** 208
Registrar **108,** 206
remission of sentence **108,** 208
review **108,** 208
Tribunal **108,** 207
equality of arms **105,** 542-3, **124,** 80-90
applicability to conditions outside court's control **124,** 87-90
equal time to question witness **122,** 38
as essential element of fair trial **124,** 85-6
time to prepare defence and **124,** 86
establishment, legality. *See* legality *below*
evidence. *See also* Yugoslavia, International Criminal Tribunal for the Former (ICTY), Rules of Procedure and Evidence
additional **111,** 312
admissibility
authenticity considerations distinguished **122,** 30
deceased witness **122,** 31
evidence not available to confirming Judge **108,** 148, 171-2
evidence not submitted by witness **122,** 30
evidence relating to acts not under indictment **121,** 224, 310-11
hearsay. *See* hearsay *below*
affidavit **105,** 612
confidentiality
oral evidence **108,** 172-5
written evidence **108,** 172-5
corroboration, need for **111,** 374, **112,** 171-3, **124,** 92

Yugoslavia, ICTY (*cont.*)
customary international law **112,** 173
State practice **112,** 172-3
difficulty in obtaining. *See* protection of victims and witnesses *and* witnesses, attendance, lack of State cooperation *below*
disclosure, obligation **122,** 26-30, 31-5
of expert evidence **121,** 228
failure **121,** 26-30, 221
in indictment **121,** 326, 328
to expert witnesses **121,** 227-8
Trial Chamber's power to order **124,** 184-90, 194, 204-9
waiver of right to **121,** 222
effect of post-traumatic stress disorder **121,** 243-9, 321-2
evaluation
inconsistencies **121,** 249-51
judicial discretion **105,** 609
judicial obligation **124,** 189
exclusion, as irrelevant **121,** 314
hearsay **105,** 612, **112,** 177
best evidence rule **108,** 177
person taking victim's statements **108,** 148, 175-9
identity, of, photospread procedure **112,** 175-7
judge's *proprio motu* power to require new **105,** 609
national rules of evidence distinguished **108,** 12
notice of, right to **121,** 309-10, 324, 326, 328
obligation to provide **110,** 667-8
official nature, relevance **110,** 628
power to compel **110,** 627-8, 703-4. *See also* orders *below*
pre-trial media coverage **112,** 174
prima facie case **108,** 11-20
'sufficient evidence to provide reasonable grounds for believing' **108,** 12, 43, 68, 89, 139, 156, 158, 163-6
redaction in case of outstanding hearings against other indicted persons **121,** 223
standard of proof. *See* standard of proof *below*
technical rules, absence **105,** 609
witnesses. *See* protection of victims and witnesses *and* witnesses *below*
expert
disclosure of confidential evidence to **121,** 227
evidence
best evidence rule **108,** 177
disclosure of **121,** 228
fair trial **105,** 430, 485. *See also* prompt trial *below*
amendment of Rules of Procedure, retroactive effect **110,** 679
appeal, right of. *See* appeal *above*
balancing of interests of prosecution and defence **105,** 620-1, 636, 641-8
charges, right to be informed of **121,** 308-9
choice of counsel **110,** 722
delay **110,** 679, **111,** 385
not attributable to the defence **121,** 221
equality of arms. *See* equality of arms *above*
European Convention on Human Rights (1950) guarantees **110,** 723
hearsay evidence. *See* evidence, hearsay *above*
in absentia proceedings **110,** 722-3

legality of tribunal. *See* legality *below*
national security defence **110,** 668
overriding importance **112,** 172
power to compel evidence. *See* evidence, power to compel *above*
presumption of innocence **111,** 332, 393, 394, **121,** 245
Prosecution's decision not to pursue certain counts **121,** 220
Prosecution's negligent preparation of case, reopening of proceedings **121,** 223, 225-6, 243-4, 248, 342-3
protection of victims and witnesses. *See* protection of victims and witnesses *below*
public hearing **105,** 430
reasoned opinion, right to **121,** 312-13
specificity of charge, date and time of offence **112,** 170-1, **121,** 221
Statute **105,** 476
'tribunal established by law'. *See* status, 'tribunal established by law' *below*
witnesses, right to examine. *See* protection of victims and witnesses *and* witnesses *below*

forcible abduction/unlawful arrest
extradition agreement, relevance **111,** 487, 490
jurisdiction, effect on **111,** 485-92
luring into jurisdiction by trickery, whether **111,** 483-92
violation of territorial sovereignty **111,** 491-2

grounds for appeal
burden of proof **121,** 306
error in applying burden of proof test **124,** 133-6, 162
error in determining level of cooperation with Prosecutor **121,** 304-5
error in determining relative seriousness of crimes against humanity and war crimes **124,** 241, 255-6
error in determining starting point of sentence **124,** 241, 246-8
error in exercise of Tribunal's discretion **121,** 345-6
error of fact occasioning miscarriage of justice **121,** 305-7, 315
reasonableness test **121,** 315-17, 321-2, **124,** 92-3, 201-2
error of law invalidating decision **121,** 305-6, 315, 317-21
error in not giving credit for time spent in detention **124,** 241, 248-50, 258
error in respect of rank as a factor in determining sentence **124,** 241, 252-4
error in weight given to deterrence as sentencing factor **24,** 241, **124,** 250-2
error in weight given to sentencing practice of former Yugoslavia **124,** 256-7
lack of jurisdiction **105,** 453-596
legality of tribunal. *See* legality *below*
partiality of Judge **121,** 329-43. *See also* judicial impartiality *below*
primacy of jurisdiction. *See* primacy over national courts *below*
sentence unfair **124,** 240, 242-6

guilty plea **111,** 318-19
advantages **111,** 315, 392-3
common law basis **111,** 315, 317, 392
effect **111,** 318
mitigating circumstances distinguished **108,** 186-9
presumption of innocence, effect on **111,** 332, 393, 394
requirements
prima facie case **111,** 394, 431-2, 437
unambiguous **111,** 314, 319, 331-3, 335, 374, 379-81, 385, 394, 432-6, 438-9
understanding of nature of charge and consequences **108,** 185-6, **111,** 313, 319, 321-31, 374, 393-4, 432
voluntary **108,** 185-6, **111,** 313, 318-21, 393, 432

Yugoslavia, ICTY (*cont.*)
in absentia proceedings
admissibility **111,** 476
ancillary and primary jurisdiction distinguished **110,** 722
fair trial and **110,** 722-3
waiver of right to be present **110,** 722
independent and impartial tribunal **105,** 372, 437-8, 553, **121,** 212. *See also* judicial impartiality *and* legality *below*
individual, duty of compliance **110,** 651-5
communication with
customary international law **110,** 710-11
diplomatic channels **110,** 711
direct **110,** 642-3, 717-21
inherent power of Tribunal **110,** 720
notification to national authorities **110,** 723
State Agent before Tribunal **110,** 711
government officials **110,** 640-3, 652-5, 708-13, 730
duty to explain non-compliance to court **110,** 654-5, 712-13
former **110,** 653-4
onus on State **110,** 653-4
State prohibition **110,** 654-5, 712
State's residual responsibility **110,** 654-5, 713, 716
implementing legislation **110,** 651-2
orders. *See* orders, individual, application to *below*
in private capacity **110,** 713-16, 730
ancillary jurisdiction **110,** 714-15
government official refusing to carry out government policy **110,** 716
member of international peace force **110,** 715-16
object and purpose of Statute **110,** 714-15
witness to crime before taking office **110,** 715
witness to crime as result of exercising functions **110,** 715
witness to crime while exercising functions **110,** 715
Statute **110,** 651
inherent powers
direct communication with individual **110,** 720
judicial determination necessary for exercise of jurisdiction **110,** 704
penalties, power to impose **110,** 698
finding of contempt **110,** 722
procedure, determination of **105,** 430
subpoena duces tecum **110,** 624-31
judge
assignment of new **122,** 24-5
requirements, impartiality. *See* judicial impartiality *below*
sitting alone, status **110,** 644-5, 651
judicial assistance. *See also* Yugoslavia, International Criminal Tribunal for the Former (ICTY), Rules of Procedure and Evidence, 39 (Prosecutor's power to seek State assistance); Yugoslavia, International Criminal Tribunal for the Former (ICTY), Statute, 18(2) (Prosecutor's right to seek State assistance) *and* 29 (cooperation and judicial assistance)
designated authority **110,** 641-3, 717-18
implementing legislation
Australia **110,** 717 n. 70

Austria **110,** 717 n. 70, 719 nn. 73 *and* 75
Belgium **110,** 717 n. 70
Bosnia-Herzegovina **110,** 717 n. 70
Croatia **110,** 717 n. 70
Finland **110,** 717 n. 70, 719 nn. 73 *and* 75
FRG **110,** 719 n. 75
Hungary **110,** 717 n. 70
Netherlands **110,** 720 n. 75
New Zealand **110,** 717 n. 70
Norway **110,** 718 n. 70
Spain **110,** 717 n. 70
Sweden **110,** 717 n. 70
Switzerland **110,** 717 n. 70, 719 n. 75
UK **110,** 717 n. 70
judicial economy, Prosecution decision not to pursue certain counts **121,** 220
judicial impartiality
appearance of bias **121,** 333-42, 353-4
reasonable person test **121,** 336, 337-40
disqualification for lack of **121,** 329-43. *See also* appearance of bias *above*
burden of proof **121,** 338
contemporaneity of potential conflict, relevance **121,** 336-7
delay in raising **121,** 330-1
grounds for automatic **121,** 336
judge's obligation to withdraw distinguished **121,** 330
general principle of law recognized by civilized nations **121,** 350-4
participation in UN Commission on the Status of Women (UNCSW) and **121,** 329-30, 337-42
presumption of **121,** 333, 337-8
judicial review, Security Council **105,** 428-9, 433-5, 528
compliance with findings **105,** 555
jurisdiction. *See also* Yugoslavia, International Criminal Tribunal for the Former (ICTY), Statute, Arts. 2-5
accused brought unlawfully within the jurisdiction **111,** 492
advisory **105,** 586
ancillary **110,** 701
Appeals Chamber. *See* Appeals Chamber, jurisdiction *above*
Art. 3 offences **121,** 291-2
challenge, standing, individual **105,** 440-1
compétence de la compétence **105,** 460, 528, 553-5, 571, **110,** 626-7
power to determine own legality distinguished **105,** 430
compulsory **105,** 554
concurrent **105,** 574, **108,** 4-9, **110,** 702, **112,** 16
determination of own legality **105,** 428-33, 459-63, 528, 544-6, 596
'collateral examination' **105,** 552, 596
distinguished **105,** 428, 430
failure to punish **122,** 19
'grave breaches of the Geneva Conventions' **105,** 442-4, **108,** 44-5. *See also* Yugoslavia, International Criminal Tribunal for the Former (ICTY), Statute, 2 (grave breaches of the Geneva Conventions of 1949)
international conflict, need for **105,** 442-4, 494, 495-9, 596, **122,** 42-57
judicial review. *See* judicial review *above*
legality of Tribunal distinguished **105,** 455-6

Yugoslavia, ICTY (*cont.*)
limited **105,** 430, 585
natural persons **110,** 699, 701
political dimension, relevance **105,** 463
primacy over national courts. *See* primacy over national courts *below*
procedure. *See* procedure *below*
requirements
armed conflict **112,** 87, 207-10, **122,** 40-1. *See also* international conflict *below*
breach of customary international law **105,** 504, **108,** 61, **112,** 201-4, **121,** 292
breach of international humanitarian law **105,** 489-504, **108,** 61-3, **112,** 201, **121,** 292
breach of treaty **121,** 292
civilian population, action against **112,** 207-23
criminalization of humanitarian law **105,** 520-4
grave consequences for victim **108,** 61, **112,** 201-2
individual responsibility **105,** 504, 520-4, **108,** 48, 61-2, 163, **112,** 201, 202, **121,** 292
international conflict **105,** 444-50, 485-526, 528-31, 581-3, 592, 596, **108,** 131, **122,** 20
nexus between acts of accused and armed conflict **112,** 183-4, **121,** 236-7, 328, **122,** 41-2
serious violation **105,** 504, **108,** 48, 61, 163, **112,** 201-2, **121,** 292
undermining of important values **108,** 48, 163
serious violations of international humanitarian law in former Yugoslavia since 1991 **121,** 219, 222, **122,** 70
States, over **110,** 698-703
ancillary nature **110,** 701
territorial reach **101,** 4-5, **105,** 430
conflict with national law **101,** 8
universal **103,** 619, **105,** 485, 575
'violation of the laws or customs of war' **105,** 442, 444-50, 587-91
international conflict, need for **105,** 444-50, 528-31, 586-7, 592
legality **105,** 427-40, 560-71, 596
appealability **105,** 456-7
arbitrary, whether **105,** 432-3
establishment. *See* status, 'tribunal established by law' *below*
fair trial, expectation of **105,** 566
General Assembly role **105,** 339-40, 570, 571
individual, jurisdiction over **105,** 567-9
power to determine. *See* jurisdiction, determination of own legality *above*
retroactive jurisdiction **105,** 569-70
treaty, need for **105,** 570
waiver of national jurisdiction **105,** 576-7
individual's right to challenge **105,** 576-8
national security defence. *See also* national security defence
admissibility, responsibility for determining **110,** 668-76
State practice **110,** 670-3
burden of proof **110,** 673-4
Chapter VII obligations and **110,** 667-8
evidentiary privilege **110,** 661-2
fair trial **110,** 668
Rules of Procedure provisions **110,** 661-2

safeguards **110,** 666, 674, 728-30, 731-6
Statute **110,** 661-2
orders
authority to issue, Judge sitting alone **110,** 644, 651
binding nature
individuals **110,** 707-21
State **110,** 697-707
cancellation **110,** 730
challenge
automatic suspension **110,** 680
Trial Chamber as appropriate forum **110,** 658-9
channel of communication **110,** 641-3, 655
individual, application to **110,** 645, 652-5, 708-23
municipal law analogy, relevance **110,** 709-10
State's obligations in respect of **110,** 655, 730
suspension **110,** 686
inherent power **110,** 624-31
jurisdiction distinguished **110,** 641
limitations
national security **110,** 659-76. *See also* national security *above*
'required for conduct of trial' **110,** 655-9
non-compliance **122,** 32. *See also* penalty for non-compliance, relevance *and* remedies for non-compliance *below*
penalty for non-compliance, relevance **110,** 649 n. 135, 694-7, 698, 704-7. *See also* remedies for non-compliance *below*
remedies for non-compliance. *See also* penalty for non-compliance, relevance *above and* remedies *below*
finding of contempt **110,** 639, 722, 730
implementation by national courts **110,** 721-2
implementing legislation **110,** 721
in absentia proceedings **110,** 722
national equivalent **110,** 721
report to Security Council **110,** 730
request for assistance compared **110,** 645-7, 698
requirements, specificity **110,** 658, 703-4
review **110,** 677-81
State, application to **110,** 632-4, 698-703
sub-State immunity and **122,** 32-3
subpoena duces tecum
binding order distinguished **110,** 698
confidential **121,** 226-7
express provision **110,** 631-4
inherent powers **110,** 624-31
issue **110,** 616-17
State immunity and **122,** 32-5
suspension. *See subpoena duces tecum below*
suspension **110,** 617, 680, 681
balance of convenience **110,** 685
'execution while validity being challenged' **110,** 680, 685-6
individual, in case of **110,** 686
Parties' right of prior hearing **110,** 682-4
preservation of subject-matter of review **110,** 685

Yugoslavia, ICTY (*cont.*)
penalty **108,** 189-210
appeal against. *See* appeal, against sentencing judgment *above*
applicable law
ICTY and ICTR case law **121,** 345
Statute and Rules **121,** 345
Čelibići **122,** 228-9, **124,** 218
death **108,** 193, **112,** 288-91, **122,** 240, **124,** 220, 245, 326
developing practice **121,** 345
enforcement. *See* enforcement of penalty *above*
evidence relating to **122,** 39
factors determining
age **108,** 197, 223, 224, **121,** 298, **122,** 233-4
aggravating circumstances **108,** 196, **112,** 304-5, 308-9, **121,** 297, 298, **122,** 235-9, **124,** 223
appropriateness to the individual **108,** 196
changing balance **108,** 202
conditions in which sentence will be served **108,** 224
effect of crime on victims **122,** 236-7
form of participation **122,** 238-9
gravity of offence **108,** 196, 217, **121,** 348-9, 354-9, **122,** 235-6, 240-1
innocence, possibility of **121,** 349
intention **108,** 197
loss of life **121,** 347-9, 357
mitigating circumstances. *See* mitigating circumstances *below*
motive **108,** 197
personality **108,** 197
physical condition **108,** 197
premeditation **122,** 239
previous conduct **108,** 197
proportionality **108,** 196, 202, 205,**122,** 240
prospects for reform **108,** 223, **122,** 234-5
rank **108,** 217, 219, **122,** 237-8, **124,** 252-4
state of mind **108,** 197
Trial Chamber's discretion **108,** 197, **121,** 345, **124,** 245
war crimes/crimes against humanity, relative seriousness **121,** 346-7, 348, 354-9, **122,** 240-1, **124,** 225-6, 229-36, 255-6
guidelines, desirability **121,** 345
mitigating circumstances
behaviour towards victims **122,** 234
context of crimes **122,** 230-1
cooperation with the Prosecutor **108,** 196, 200, 220-2, 224, **112,** 309, **122,** 231-2, **124,** 224
duress **108,** 217, 218, **122,** 230
family circumstances **121,** 298, **122,** 234, **124,** 225
guilty plea **122,** 233
personal circumstances of accused **112,** 310-14, **121,** 300, **124,** 225
remorse **108,** 197, 219-20, 224, **122,** 232-3
superior orders **108,** 197-200, 218
voluntary surrender **122,** 233
multiple charges **124,** 235
benefit of doubt **124,** 226-7

single sentence **122,** 243
purpose
deterrence **105,** 608, **108,** 201-5, **121,** 299-300, **124,** 218, 250-2
object and purpose of Tribunal to determine **108,** 201
registration of public indignation **122,** 229
rehabilitation **122,** 228
retribution **108,** 201-5, **122,** 228, **124,** 218
State practice **108,** 202-4
review of sentence, standard **121,** 345-6
State practice **108,** 193-6
binding, whether **108,** 196, 204-5
underlying crime as measure **108,** 193-4, **122,** 242
plea-bargaining **105,** 609
precedent
absence **105,** 608-9
avoidance of errors **105,** 609
other tribunals **105,** 614
civil law jurisdictions **105,** 616-17
European Court of Human Rights **105,** 565, 611-12, 614-15, 621, 623-4
International Military Tribunal for the Far East (Tokyo Tribunal) **105,** 608-9
interpretation of Statute and Rules **105,** 607-12
municipal courts **105,** 480, 615-16, 620-1, 644-8
Nuremberg Tribunal **105,** 608-9
relevance **105,** 637
sentencing practice **121,** 345-9
primacy over national courts **101,** 4-9, **105,** 439, 440-1, 476-85, 571-9, 596, **112,** 16-17
appealability **105,** 456, 572-3
compliance, duty of and **110,** 628
deference, need for request **101,** 5, **105,** 574, **108,** 6
deference, requirements
investigations by Tribunal Prosecutor **108,** 6-7
national investigations or proceedings **108,** 6-7
significant factual or legal questions with implications for Tribunal investigations/proceedings **108,** 7
former Yugoslavia, limitation to **110,** 701-2
judicial and enforcement powers distinguished **110,** 714
political/military leadership, in cases concerning **108,** 8, 48-9, **110,** 667
powers of Tribunal, implications for **110,** 713-14, 718
State cooperation **105,** 481
Tribunal's discretion **105,** 574
procedure
adversarial nature **105,** 609, **124,** 189
amicus curiae brief. *See* Yugoslavia, International Criminal Tribunal for the Former (ICTY), Rules of Procedure and Evidence, 74 (*amicus curiae*)
confidentiality of proceedings **110,** 733-5
documentation, inadequacy **105,** 592-5, 596
evidence. *See* evidence *above*
full Trial Chamber, remission to **110,** 618
in absentia proceedings. *See in absentia* proceedings *above*
indictment, amendment **121,** 229-340
Prosecutor's prerogative **108,** 36
inherent power to determine **105,** 430

Yugoslavia, ICTY (*cont.*)
international arrest warrant
issue **108,** 39, 52, 66, 68, 90, 139, 168
transmission to IFOR **108,** 66, 168
joinder of cases **108,** 139
judge, exclusion **110,** 619
language **105,** 597-8
mixed common and civil law **100,** 646, **105,** 609, **110,** 631
municipal law proceedings distinguished **111,** 387-92
non-compliance with Rules, nullity dependent on non-compliance **111,** 481
pre-sentencing hearing, trial distinguished **111,** 430 n. 114
reopening of proceedings **121,** 225-6, 243-4, 248, 342-3
right to determine own **105,** 609-10
Rules of Procedure. *See* Yugoslavia, International Criminal Tribunal for the Former (ICTY), Rules of Procedure and Evidence
subpoena duces tecum. See orders, *subpoena duces tecum above*
time-limits, extension **105,** 456, **124,** 72-3, 74-5
value **121,** 248
proceedings, length, 'hearing day' **122,** 37
prompt trial, waiver of right to **121,** 222. *See also* fair trial *above*
Prosecutor
presumed good faith **122,** 28
separate legal entity test **112,** 16
protection of victims and witnesses **105,** 601-48, **121,** 221, **122,** 31-2
anonymity **105,** 620-48, **112,** 170, **122,** 36
ratione materiae/*ratione temporis*/*ratione loci* **122,** 36
right to examine witnesses and **105,** 624-6
temporary **105,** 624, **122,** 36
in case of rebuttal evidence **121,** 224-5
fair trial and **121,** 244-5, **124,** 88-90
Geneva Convention III (1949) (Prisoners of War) distinguished **105,** 612
limitation to protection requested **105,** 627
safe conduct **112,** 170
purpose **110,** 620-3
cessation of violations of humanitarian law **110,** 621, **111,** 366
court of record **105,** 553
development of international humanitarian law **111,** 366
justice **105,** 608
peace and reconciliation **108,** 202, **110,** 621
prosecution of all 'serious violations' of international humanitarian law **105,** 430, 503, 570
restoration and maintenance of peace **105,** 436-7, 560-1, 570, 608
rule of law **108,** 201, **111,** 373
remedies, judicial finding of failure to observe Statute or Rules, reported to Security Council **110,** 704-7, 730
review **110,** 677-81
Rule 61 proceedings **108,** 23-39, 42-52, 55-68, 89-141, 145-79
purpose
effectiveness of Tribunal in face of non-appearance of defendant **108,** 24, 55, 90, 147, 171
evidence, importance of safeguards **108,** 108, **111,** 492-4
public hearing of evidence **108,** 24, 56, 90, 147, 171, 177-9
trial *in absentia*, whether **108,** 24, 147, 177-8

accused's right to contest charges, effect on **108,** 24
ex parte nature **108,** 172, 177-8
verdict, absence **108,** 24, 147, 171
Trial Chamber's task
confirmation of finding of reasonable grounds **108,** 43, 55, 89, 139, 147, 171-2, 177-8
review of characterization of acts **108,** 89, 130-6
review of evidence **108,** 148
Security Council. *See also* United Nations Security Council, Chapter VII action
competence **105,** 427-40, 560-71
Resolution 827 (1993)
'approval of Secretary-General's Report' **124,** 180
innovatory nature **105,** 434-5
risk of interference **105,** 434, **110,** 706-7
subsidiary organ **105,** 459-60, 562-3, 568, **110,** 620-3, **112,** 15
implications **110,** 634, 666-7, 676
separate legal entity test **110,** 623, 634
special features **110,** 642, 646
sentencing practice. *See* penalty *above*
service of indictment
obligations of signatory State **108,** 23-4, 67
steps to secure, publication **108,** 38, 66, 166
standard of proof
beyond reasonable doubt **112,** 85-8, 92, 96, 102, 122-4, 131, 140-1, 144, 146, 149, 255-6, **121,** 248, 307-8, **122,** 206-10, **124,** 133-6
obligation to challenge inadequacy **112,** 87
production of body, need for **112,** 87
status. *See also* Security Council, subsidiary organ *above*
international tribunal **112,** 15
'tribunal established by law' **105,** 438, 470-6, 563-7
individual's right to challenge **105,** 439
pre-established **105,** 438
Statute. *See* Yugoslavia, International Criminal Tribunal for the Former (ICTY), Statute
superior orders, mitigating circumstance **100,** 218, **108,** 197-200
UN Human Rights Committee, role **105,** 444
waiver, right to trial **111,** 393
witnesses. *See also* protection of victims and witnesses *above*
attendance, lack of State cooperation **124,** 89-90
complaining party's obligation to raise **124,** 90
credibility **112,** 177
notification of identity **121,** 222, 227, **122,** 27-8
right to examine **121,** 313-14
anonymity and **105,** 624-6
victim as **112,** 173-4
Yugoslavia, International Criminal Tribunal for the Former (ICTY), Rules of Detention 108, 209
66 **108,** 82
Yugoslavia, International Criminal Tribunal for the Former (ICTY), Rules of Procedure and Evidence
2(A) (warrants of arrest: transmission) **108,** 38, 136
5 (non-compliance with Rules) **111,** 464-5
nullity dependent on miscarriage of justice **111,** 481
6(C) (amendment of rules: entry into force) **110,** 684-5

Yugoslavia, ICTY Rules of Procedure and Evidence (*cont.*)
6(D) (amendment of rules: entry into force) **124,** 80
7 (authentic languages) **105,** 597
7 *bis* (non-compliance) **110,** 704-7
text **110,** 705
8 **101,** 4
9 (deferral of proceedings) **101,** 3, 4, 5, **105,** 483, **108,** 2-9, **112,** 16-17
9(iii) (implications for investigations or prosecutions by Tribunal) **105,** 478, **108,** 2, 6-9
10 (diligent prosecution) **101,** 3, **105,** 477, 483, **108,** 2, 4-5, 8-9, **110,** 628, **112,** 16-17
11 **110,** 628
14 (judges: declaration on taking up office) **121,** 336 n. 259
15(A) (withdrawal of judge: partiality) **110,** 619, **121,** 336-41, 359-60, 362
15(B) (disqualification of judge) **121,** 332 n. 239, 363
15(E) **110,** 733
15(F) **122,** 24-5
21(4)(c) **122,** 37
34 (Victims and Witnesses Unit) **105,** 610
39 (Prosecutor's power to seek State assistance) **110,** 641 n. 105, 652-3, **122,** 33
42 **111,** 462
43 **111,** 462
47 ('reasonable grounds for believing') **108,** 11-20, 23, 170
intra vires, whether **108,** 11-12, 19-20
open hearing, absence of provision **108,** 171
47(A) ('sufficient reasons for believing') **108,** 18-20, 68, 170-1, 174-5
47(B) **122,** 20
47(C) (statement of facts and charge) **121,** 309, 324, 326, 328
47(D) (additional evidence) **108,** 18-20, 170-1
47(e) (additional evidence supporting new count) **108,** 171
50 (amendment of indictment) **108,** 36-7, **112,** 276-85, **121,** 328
51 (confirmation of indictment after open hearing) **108,** 171
52 (public character of indictment) **107,** 172-4
53 (non-disclosure of indictment) **108,** 172-5, **111,** 465, 481-3, **121,** 219
53(A) **108,** 20
54 (issue of orders) **110,** 627, 647 n. 125, 653, 676, 681, 687, 695-6, 733, **111,** 493, **122,** 28, 37-8, **124,** 204, 1136
general nature **110,** 632
revision **110,** 632, 639-40
text (English) **110,** 609
text (French) **110,** 610
55 (arrest warrants: transmission) **108,** 23, 38, **110,** 645 n. 115, **111,** 465, 473, 476-7, 482 n. 68, 483, 494
58 (primacy of Statute) **111,** 475-6
59 *bis* (arrest warrants: transmission) **108,** 52, 67, 138, **111,** 465-6, 473-85, 494, **124,** 88
adoption as supplement to Rule 55 **111,** 476
compatibility with Statute **111,** 476-7
59(A) (obligation of compliance) **108,** 67
60 (publication of indictment) **108,** 66
61 **108,** 52, 67, 139, 171, **110,** 733. *See also* Rule 61 proceedings *above*
61(A) (review in absentia) **108,** 23-4, 42, 148, 171
61(B) (presentation of indictment in open court) **108,** 148, 171, 174
61(C) (additional evidence) **108,** 148, 171-2

61(E) (notification to Security Council of State's failure to comply) **108,** 68, 139, 146, 169
62 (initial appearance) **108,** 185-6, **110,** 733, **111,** 317, 387, **112,** 17, **121,** 219
62(v) (pre-sentencing hearing) **108,** 184
64 (conditions of detention) **108,** 70 n. 1, 71, 76, 83-5, **122,** 25-6
65 (release of detainee) **108,** 70 n. 1, 71, 76, 80, 81-2, **122,** 26
65(B) (provisional release) **124,** 90
66(A) (disclosure of evidence) **110,** 661, **122,** 26-8, 31
66(A)(ii) (copies of witness statements) **121,** 221, 222, **124,** 206-7
66(B) (disclosure of evidence) **122,** 27, **124,** 206
66(C) (disclosure of evidence) **108,** 174-5, **110,** 661, 673-6, 728, 733-4
text **110,** 733-4, **122,** 27
67 (notice of alibi) **112,** 22
67(A) (identification of witnesses) **105,** 629-30
67(A)(ii)(a) (notification of defence of alibi) **112,** 155
67(C) (identification of witnesses) **105,** 630, **124,** 206
68 **121,** 225, **122,** 28, 31, **124,** 190
69 (protection of victims and witnesses) **105,** 606-7, 610, 614, 639
69(A) (identification of witnesses) **122,** 35-7
69(C) (identification of witnesses) **105,** 621
70 (disclosure) **105,** 639, **122,** 28-30, 32
70(A) (protection from disclosure) **122,** 27, 28-9, **124,** 185-6, 205-6
70(B) (protection from disclosure) **110,** 662, **122,** 29-30
70(F) (protection from disclosure) **122,** 29
71 (deposition) **105,** 610, **121,** 225
71(A) (deposition) **105,** 610, **121,** 225, **122,** 37
72 (general provisions) **105,** 453, 527, **111,** 494
72(B) (interlocutory appeal) **105,** 455, 539-43, **110,** 683
73 (preliminary motions by accused) **105,** 455
73(A)(i) (preliminary objections) **105,** 427, 430
73 *ter* (B) (pre-Defence Conference) **124,** 189-90, 207
74 (*amicus curiae*) **108,** 146, **110,** 618, 680, 681, **121,** 228, 330
value **121,** 248
75 (protection of victims and witnesses) **105,** 610, 617-20, 639
75(A) (consistency with rights of accused) **105,** 621, 639-40
75(B) (anonymity of witnesses) **107,** 174-5
75(B)(i) (anonymity of witnesses) **105,** 618
75(B)(iii) (anonymity of witnesses) **105,** 621, 640
77 (failure to answer relevant question) **110,** 651
77(B) **110,** 728
78 (public hearings) **105,** 613
79 (closed sessions) **105,** 607, 613, 614, **110,** 674
85 (presentation of evidence) **121,** 224, **124,** 217-18
87(C) (sentencing) **124,** 80
89 (rules of evidence) **105,** 607, **108,** 12, **112,** 177
89(A) (national rules of evidence) **110,** 638 n. 88
89(B) (rules of evidence: fair determination) **108,** 176, **110,** 703, 728, **124,** 185-6, 188, 204, 1239
89(C) (admissibility of evidence: Chamber's discretion) **108,** 176-7, 217, **112,** 172, **122,** 30-1, **124,** 190
89(D) (exclusion of evidence: fair trial) **108,** 176, **110,** 703, 728, **112,** 172, **124,** 190
89(E) (privileged communications) **124,** 190, 205

Yugoslavia, ICTY Rules of Procedure and Evidence (*cont.*)
90 *bis* (detention in Detention Unit) **108,** 183
90(A) (hearing of witnesses) **108,** 176-8
90(F) **124,** 185
91 (false testimony) **105,** 430
94 *bis* (A) **121,** 228
94 *bis* (B)(i) **121,** 228
94 *bis* (B)(ii) **121,** 228
95 (exclusion of evidence: integrity of proceedings) **108,** 176
96 (evidence in cases of sexual assault) **105,** 610
96(1) (corroboration) **112,** 172
97 (lawyer–client privilege) **124,** 185-6, 190, 205
98 (additional witnesses) **110,** 636, 640, **122,** 38
98 *bis* **122,** 38
100 (pre-sentencing procedure) **108,** 189-90, 210, 224, **112,** 287-8, **121,** 296
101 (penalties) **108,** 186, 190, 224, **112,** 288-91,**121,** 272, 296, 343, 344, **122,** 227-8, **124,** 218, 220, 246-8
101(A) (death penalty) **112,** 290, **122,** 240, **124,** 220, 236, 245
101(B) (factors affecting sentence) **108,** 196-7, **124,** 236
101(B)(i) (aggravating circumstances) **124,** 223
101(B)(ii) (mitigating circumstances) **108,** 197-201, **122,** 230, **124,** 239
cooperation with Prosecutor **108,** 200, **112,** 309, **124,** 224, 241, 254-5
101(B)(iii) (general practice in Yugoslav courts) **108,** 194-5, **121,** 298-9, **122,** 228, **124,** 219-21, 236, 256-7
101(C) (multiple conviction) **121,** 300-1
101(D) (credit for time detained in custody) **121,** 302, **122,** 239, **124,** 228, 241, 248-50
former rule 101(E) and **124,** 1311 n. 52
101(E) (credit for time detained in custody) **112,** 315-16
102 (detention in custody of Tribunal) **112,** 316, **121,** 302-3
103 (place of imprisonment) **108,** 191, 206, 224
104 (supervision of imprisonment) **108,** 191, 208-9
105 (attendance of third party in possession of property) **110,** 640
107 **110,** 687
107-8 (notice of appeal) **105,** 455
108 (notice of appeal) **110,** 82-7, 678-9, 682-7
text **110,** 678
108 *bis* (notice of appeal) **110,** 678-80, 684-6, **122,** 33-4
text **110,** 678-9
108 *bis* (B) (right to be heard by Appeals Chamber) **110,** 683-4
retroactivity **110,** 679, 684-5
108 *bis* (D) (suspension of order) **110,** 685-6
115 (additional evidence) **111,** 311-12, **124,** 74, 75
116 *bis* **105,** 527
117 **105,** 527, 595
119 (new fact: review of judgment) **124,** 74
amendment
retroactivity **110,** 679, 684-5
rights of accused and **110,** 684
compatibility with Statute, need for **111,** 476-7
human rights, protection of **105,** 610-11
interpretation
effectiveness **110,** 695-6
essence of term **110,** 639

multilingual nature **110,** 696
national concepts, relevance **110,** 638-9, **111,** 316, 317
object and purpose **111,** 316
plain and ordinary meaning **111,** 315, 316
reasonable **108,** 174
spirit of Statute **110,** 696
travaux préparatoires **111,** 315-16
Vienna Convention on the Law of Treaties (1969) **111,** 315-16
legislation, interpretation, phrases, 'enter a plea' **111,** 317
Rule 15 (judges) **121,** 364
Yugoslavia, International Criminal Tribunal for the Former (ICTY), Statute
1 (competence) **105,** 430, 442, 582, **108,** 48, **110,** 631, 632-3, 699, **112,** 178, **121,** 218, 360
'serious violations of international humanitarian law' **124,** 234
2 (grave breaches of the Geneva Conventions of 1949) **105,** 442-4, 489, 495-9, 528-31, 537-8, 586-7, 596, **108,** 31, 32, 35-6, 61-3, 149-58, **110,** 624 n. 21, 628, **112,** 178, 184-200, **121,** 218, **124,** 93-133, 234
customary international law **112,** 184
elements **122,** 64-6
Geneva Conventions (1949) and **105,** 586-7, **108,** 44-5, 149, **124,** 99-100
international armed conflict, need for **108,** 131, 149, **112,** 178-201, 261-76, **122,** 20, **124,** 96-8
protected persons or property, limitation to **108,** 132, 149, 159, **112,** 261-2, **124,** 94
responsibility, entity in de facto control **112,** 219-22, 262-76
2(a) (wilful killing) **108,** 62, **112,** 106, **122,** 22, 65, 72, 138-9, **124,** 162
'wilful' **122,** 65
2(b) (inhuman treatment) **122,** 210-16, 245
human shields **122,** 73, 218-19, 224-5
'inhuman treatment' **122,** 65
attack on human dignity **122,** 65
as question of fact **122,** 65
trench digging **122,** 210-16, 223-4
2(c) (wilfully causing great suffering) **108,** 62, **112,** 88, 93, 97, 102, 103, 107, **122,** 22, 65-6, 244
elements as alternative options **122,** 66
torture **122,** 65
2(d) (destruction and appropriation of property) **122,** 22, 66, 88, 244
'extensive' **122,** 66
2(h) (taking of civilians as hostages) **122,** 66, 73, 224, 245
intention to obtain advantage, need for **122,** 66, 216-18
2-5 (jurisdiction) **108,** 9, **110,** 701, 722, **121,** 218
3 (violation of the laws or customs of war) **105,** 444-50, 489, 499-504, 528-31, 537-8, 587-91, **108,** 31, 35-6, 43-52, 61-3, 162-3, **110,** 628, **111,** 381-2, **112,** 88, 93, 97, 106, 178, 201-3, 254, 255-6, 257, 258, 259, **121,** 218, 222, **122,** 22, 23, 245
armed conflict, need for **122,** 66-7
'civilian' **122,** 72
civilian population, planned attack against **122,** 127-42, 184
involvement of senior military figures **122,** 130-3, 142-3
'planned' **122,** 127-30, 142-3, 172-3
'civilian property' **122,** 71-2
devastation of property **122,** 72
discriminatory attack **122,** 137, 166-8, 185, 196-9
elements **122,** 71-3

Yugoslavia, ICTY Statute (*cont.*)
mens rea **122,** 71, 72
exhaustive, whether **105,** 444-5, 500-1, 589, 590-1, **108,** 44, 61, 162, **121,** 253-4, **122,** 67, 69
Geneva Conventions (1949) and **105,** 589-91, **108,** 31, 44-8, **122,** 72, 244
Additional Protocols I and II **122,** 69-70, 244
grave breaches **105,** 589, **108,** 44-8, 62
Hague Conventions (1899/1907) and **105,** 444, 446-50, 500-4, 583-4, 589-91
hostage-taking, intention to obtain advantage, need for **122,** 73, 216-18
indiscriminate attack **108,** 47, 50-2, 91, 162-3, **122,** 136-7
individual responsibility, need for **108,** 61-2, **121,** 253
infringement of international humanitarian law, need for **108,** 44, 61, **121,** 253
inhuman treatment **122,** 210-16
status of person, relevance **122,** 73
murder **122,** 72, 138-9
nature of armed conflict, relevance **121,** 253-4, 292-3, **122,** 40, 67
nexus between act or omission and armed conflict, need for **122,** 66-7
plunder of public or private property **122,** 72, 88, 244
rape **121,** 267, 292
relative severity **121,** 348
as serious breach of international humanitarian law **122,** 70
text **108,** 40 n. 2
torture **121,** 262, 292
as umbrella/residual provision **121,** 254, 262, **122,** 39
violation of agreements binding parties to conflict **122,** 69-70
violence to life and person **122,** 72
3(b) (wanton destruction of cities ... or devastation unjustified by military necessity) **108,** 162, **122,** 22, 23, 71, 133-7, 143-5, 173-82, 244
internal conflict, applicability **108,** 162
3(c) (attack on undefended towns or buildings) **122,** 23, 72
3(d) (destruction or wilful damage to religious or other institutions) **122,** 23, 73, 140, 244
3(1)(a) (cruel treatment) **112,** 93, 97, 102, 103, 250-2, 253, **122,** 72, 245
4 (genocide) **108,** 37, **121,** 218
4(2) (genocide) **108,** 133-6
5 (crimes against humanity) **105,** 450-2, 489, 494, 584, **108,** 30, 31, 32-3, 34-5, 63-8, 133-6, **110,** 628, **112,** 178, 204-23, **119,** 353, **124,** 162-73
act of a serious nature inflicted on human being **112,** 251-2
armed conflict, need for **112,** 87, 207-10, **122,** 40-2
intent to participate in, relevance **122,** 42
nexus between act or omission and armed conflict **112,** 208-10, 222-3, **122,** 40, 41-2, **124,** 164-73, 1248
as objective or jurisdictional element **124,** 165
as temporal condition **122,** 42
civilian population, action against **108,** 64, **112,** 207-23, 249
human shields **122,** 83-4
knowledge of widespread or systematic attack **122,** 90-4, **124,** 164, 167
knowledge that attack part of widespread or systematic attack **122,** 91, 92-3, **124,** 167, 172-3
nexus between act or omission and **124,** 165-6
presence of non-civilians, relevance **122,** 81-3
resistance movements and **122,** 81-3
status of victim, relevance **122,** 81-3

widespread or systematic policy **122,** 76, 77-81, 152, 164-6, 188-96, 225-6, **124,** 164, 183
customary international law distinguished **105,** 525, **124,** 166, 181
discrimination **112,** 218-19, 241-7, 249
as requirement **124,** 173-84
intent. *See* personal motives, relevance *below*
international conflict **105,** 596, **108,** 63
personal motives, relevance **112,** 222-3, **124,** 164-73, 193, 202-4
burden of proof **124,** 167, 172-3
customary international law **124,** 167-73
policy **112,** 207, 215-18, 219-22, 249
rape **121,** 267-8
retroactive, whether **105,** 525-6
5(a) (murder) **108,** 224, **112,** 106, 258, 259, **122,** 22, 138-9, 244
elements **122,** 83
'murder' **122,** 83
5(h) (persecution) **112,** 240-1, **122,** 21, 126, 206
deportation or forcible transfer of civilians **122,** 88, 179
discrimination **122,** 86-7, 88-9, **124,** 173-84, 191
evidence of **122,** 114-23
mens rea **122,** 88
as member of group **122,** 88-9
of which perpetrator is not a member **122,** 89
'persecution' **122,** 83-9
plunder of public or private property **122,** 88
on political, racial or religious grounds **122,** 88
serious bodily and mental harm **122,** 84-7
elements **122,** 90
mens rea **122,** 90-4
violation of human rights **122,** 84-7
wanton destruction and plunder of property not justified by necessity **122,** 88, 139-40, 179-82
5(i) (inhuman acts) **112,** 88, 93, 97, 102, 103, 107, 255, **122,** 22, 244
beating **112,** 253-4, 260
'calling-out' **112,** 258-9
in case of person already dead **112,** 255-6
'other inhumane acts' **122,** 89
sexual assault other than rape **121,** 268
wilful infliction of serious mental or physical injury and great suffering **122,** 89-90
6 (personal jurisdiction) **110,** 641
7 (individual responsibility) **108,** 4, **110,** 641, 667
text **108,** 40 n. 1
7(1) (individual responsibility: direct participation) **108,** 31-2, 119-20, 129-30, **112,** 87, 88, 97, 103, 106-7, 224-36, 253-60, **119,** 46, 66, **121,** 220, 272-3, **122,** 21, 94-100, 142-62, 168-73, 182, 185-8, 227
aiding and abetting **121,** 272-91, 294, 319-21, **122,** 95-100, 142-62
common purpose **124,** 134, 136-62
actus reus **124,** 159
mens rea **124,** 1104
customary international law **112,** 224-7, **122,** 71
planning, ordering or instigating **121,** 272-3
mens rea **122,** 98-9, 103-11, 113, 154-9
pre-existence, relevance **121,** 319-20

Yugoslavia, ICTY Statute (*cont.*)
7(2) (individual responsibility: action in official capacity) **108,** 48-9, **110,** 708-13, **119,** 87
Art. 7(3) distinguished **122,** 94, 113-14
customary international law **121,** 257
Head of State **119,** 71, 87, 162-3, 212, 243
7(3) (individual responsibility: failure to prevent) **108,** 31-2, 120, 128-9, **122,** 95, 100-14, 159-62, 187-8, 219-23, 226
effective control test **122,** 102-3, 145-52, 186-7, 220-1
7(4) (superior orders) **108,** 186-7, **110,** 708-13
mitigating circumstance **108,** 198-200, **122,** 230
8 (territorial and temporal jurisdiction) **101,** 4-5
9 (concurrent jurisdiction) **101,** 4, 9, **105,** 476-8, 483, **108,** 6-9, **110,** 702
9(2) (preliminary jurisdiction) **105,** 440, **108,** 2, 8, **110,** 628, 702
10 (*non bis in idem*) **124,** 191-3
10(2) (diligent prosecution) **105,** 478, 483
12 (composition of Chambers) **110,** 732-3
text **110,** 732-3
13(1) (judges: requirements) **121,** 332, 340-1, 350, 359, 362
15 (rules of procedure: Tribunal's power to adopt) **105,** 542, **108,** 12, **110,** 631, 733, **111,** 463-4, 474, **124,** 204
16(1) (Prosecutor's responsibility) **111,** 464
18 (collection of evidence) **110,** 632
18(2) (Prosecutor's right to seek State assistance) **110,** 641, 652, 653, 708-13, 714
18(4) (prima facie case) **108,** 11-20, 170-1, **110,** 733, **121,** 309, 326, 328, **122,** 20
19 (review of indictment) **110,** 632, 651, 655-9, **111,** 476, 480
19(1) (prima facie case: judicial confirmation) **108,** 11-20, 171, **110,** 733
absence of provision in Rules of Procedure **108,** 19-20
19(2) (issue of orders) **110,** 641, 647, 653, 714,**111,** 464, 474-5
20 (fair trial) **105,** 430, 613, 621, **108,** 176, **110,** 627, 734-5, **111,** 476, 480
20(1) (protection of victims) **105,** 613, 637, 641, **110,** 733, **111,** 318, 393, **124,** 85-90, 188-9, 1247
European Convention on Human Rights (1950) compared **124,** 188-9
International Covenant on Civil and Political Rights (Art. 14) compared **111,** 318, **124,** 188-9
20(2) (procedure on taking into custody) **111,** 464, 475, 485
20(3) (guilty plea) **108,** 185, **111,** 316-17, 387, 392-4
20(4) (public hearings) **105,** 613
21 (due process) **105,** 430, 476, 611, 614, 637, **111,** 462, **121,** 219, 308, 332, 362
21(2) (fair and public hearing) **105,** 613, 621, 637, 641, **111,** 393, **121,** 312, 332, 359
21(3) (presumption of innocence) **111,** 393, 394, **121,** 245, 337-8
21(4) (examination of witnesses) **105,** 623, **111,** 485, **121,** 308, **124,** 1247
21(4)(a) (right to be informed of charge) **111,** 464
21(4)(c) (undue delay) **110,** 679, **111,** 385
21(4)(d) (presence of accused at trial) **110,** 722
21(4)(d) (time for preparation of defence) **111,** 464, **124,** 85-90
21(4)(e) (accused's rights respecting witnesses) **110,** 627, **121,** 313-14
21(4)(g) (self-incrimination) **110,** 726, 727, **111,** 393, **124,** 185
22 (protection of victims and witnesses) **105,** 610, 614, 637, **124,** 188-9
exception to right of public hearing, whether **105,** 614, 637-9, 641
23 (judgment) **108,** 224, **121,** 296, 343-4, **122,** 227, 228
23(1) (judgment and sentencing) **108,** 189

23(2) (reasoned opinion) **121,** 312
24 (penalties) **108,** 190, 194, 224, **112,** 288-91, **121,** 272, 296, 344, **122,** 227, **124,** 217, 220
24(1) (penalty: general practice in courts of the former Yugoslavia) **121,** 301, **124,** 220, 235-6, 244, 256-7
24(2) (factors affecting sentence) **108,** 196-7, **122,** 239-40, **124,** 234
24(3) (return of property) **108,** 192
25 (appellate proceedings) **105,** 527, 540-3, **124,** 187, 191-4, 247
25(1)(a) (error of law invalidating decision) **121,** 305, 306, **124,** 164
25(1)(b) (error of fact occasioning miscarriage of justice) **121,** 305, 306-7, 315, **124,** 90-3, 175-6
27 (enforcement of sentences) **108,** 190-1, 205-10, 224,**112,** 316
28 (pardon/commutation) **108,** 191, 208
29 (cooperation and judicial assistance) **101,** 8, **105,** 477, **108,** 23-4, 136-8, 172, **110,** 617, 632, 633, 643-55, 660-1, 674, 680, 685, 687, 690, 698 n. 30, 699-707, 712-13, 715, 716, 722, 724-30, 731, **111,** 464, 473-4, 475, 476-7, **122,** 34, **124,** 88
  erga omnes application **110,** 699-700
  obligation of conduct **111,** 474 n. 38, 476
  sovereignty and **121,** 361
  text **110,** 609
29(1) (States' duty to cooperate) **110,** 644, 651
29(2) (duty to comply) **110,** 643, 696, 702, 703-4, **111,** 473-4
33(authentic languages) **105,** 597
applicability
  all signatory States **110,** 701
  members of the armed forces *hors de combat* **112,** 203
complicity, aiding and abetting (Art. 7) **121,** 273-91, 319-21. *See also* war crimes, aiding and abetting
customary international law, derogation **110,** 727
Head of State immunity **119,** 66, 71, 87, 155, 212, **125,** 462, 466
implementing legislation **110,** 665-6
  applicability, non-UN Member States **110,** 700
  Australia **110,** 650, 666
  Austria **110,** 640, 666
  Belgium **110,** 650, 665
  compatibility with Statute **110,** 718
  Denmark **110,** 650
  duty of compliance **110,** 650-1
  Finland **110,** 640-1, 721 n. 78
  FRG **110,** 721 n. 78
  individual, direct approach to **110,** 652-3
  Netherlands **110,** 640, 721 n. 78
  New Zealand **110,** 650, 666
  Security Council Resolution 827 **110,** 650
  Spain **110,** 721 n. 79
  Switzerland **110,** 640, 700
  UK **110,** 721 n. 78
incorporation of
  Geneva Conventions (1949) **105,** 442-4, 496
  International Covenant on Civil and Political Rights (ICCPR) (1966) **105,** 476
jus cogens and **124,** 181
obligations of signatory State

Yugoslavia, ICTY Statute (*cont.*)
breach
conflict with municipal law **110,** 650, **111,** 475-7
notification to Security Council **108,** 23-4, 39, 55-6, 67, 90, 139-41, 166-8
compliance with orders of Tribunal. *See also* Yugoslavia, International Criminal Tribunal for the Former (ICTY), individual, duty of compliance
collective responsibility **110,** 706-7
individual as addressee **110,** 655, 708-23
legal interest of all signatory States **110,** 699, 706
pre- and post-indictment, distinction **110,** 628, 633-4, 643-51
cooperation with Tribunal's requests for assistance **108,** 23-4, 136-8, **110,** 699, 703. *See also* Yugoslavia, International Criminal Tribunal for the Former (ICTY), Rules of Procedure and Evidence, 39 (Prosecutor's power to seek State assistance); Yugoslavia, International Criminal Tribunal for the Former (ICTY), Statute, 29 (cooperation and judicial assistance)
basis **110,** 699
in case of government official declining to carry out instructions **110,** 716
former Yugoslavia **110,** 717
giving effect to compared **110,** 645-7
judicial assistance procedures, expectation of **110,** 645, 718
mutual agreement, need for **110,** 643
obligation of conduct **108,** 74-5
exceptions, explicit provision, need for **110,** 726-7
judicial assistance. *See* cooperation with Tribunal's requests for assistance *above*; Yugoslavia, International Criminal Tribunal for the Former (ICTY), judicial assistance
municipal law, conflict, relevance **108,** 72-5
obligation of result **110,** 712
primacy of Tribunal **110,** 628
self-proclaimed entity, applicability to **108,** 24
service of indictment **108,** 23-4
sovereignty and **110,** 648-9, **121,** 361
relative seriousness of crimes against humanity/war crimes **111,** 327-31, 381-5, **121,** 346-7, 348, 354-9, **122,** 240-2, **124,** 225-6, 229-36, 255-6
remedies
collective action **110,** 706-7
Security Council responsibility **110,** 707
supplementary rules, admissibility **105,** 454-5
treaty distinguished **110,** 646
unlawful detention of civilians **122,** 88
Yugoslavia, International Criminal Tribunal for the Former (ICTY), Statute, interpretation
aids
Geneva Conventions (1949) **124,** 99-100
ILC Code of Crimes Against the Peace and Security of Mankind **122,** 83
International Criminal Court Statute **122,** 83
opinio juris **105,** 538
judicial and arbitral decisions **121,** 361-2
State practice **105,** 498-9
statements in Security Council **105,** 446, 493, 501-2,**112,** 209, **124,** 181-4
subsequent practice **105,** 538
UN Secretary-General's Report **105,** 442, 493, 498, 500-1, 581-7, 589-91, **124,** 138
conflict with Statute **124,** 180-1
status **124,** 180-1

guidelines
absence of provision **110,** 667-8
chapeau as umbrella **122,** 76
conformity with customary international law **112,** 247, **121,** 359-61, **124,** 178-80
context **105,** 490
effectiveness **105,** 494, 537
exceptions to State obligations, explicit **110,** 726
literal **105,** 489-90, 500
natural and ordinary meaning **124,** 176
object and purpose **105,** 490-5, 503, 537, 538, 608, **110,** 624 n. 21, 627, **121,** 361, **124,** 137-8, 176-7
in casc of language drawn from another treaty **105,** 611-12
plain language **110,** 711, 726
practice of other tribunals **105,** 607-12
Statute as a whole **105,** 502-3
teleological. *See* object and purpose *above*
text **105,** 498
treaty rules **105,** 608
phrases
'directed against any civilian population'
'civilian' **112,** 210-14
'population' **112,** 214-23
'protected persons or property' **105,** 497-8, **108,** 62, 132, 158-61, **112,** 184-200
'race, religion and politics' **112,** 246-7
'the general practice regarding prison sentences in the courts of the former Yugoslavia' **112,** 289-91, **124,** 219-21, 245
Yugoslavia, Socialist Federal Republic (SFRY). *See also* Bosnia-Herzegovina; Croatia; Macedonia, former Yugoslav Republic of (FYROM); Slovenia; Yugoslavia, Federal Republic of (FRY); Yugoslavia, International Criminal Tribunal for the Former
Badinter Commission. *See* Badinter Commission (Yugoslavia)
boundaries, *uti possidetis juris* **92,** 171
central/State-owned bank, State responsibility **96,** 735-6
Conference on (1991)
draft Convention **92,** 168-9
establishment **92,** 162-3
Constitution
Art. 5 **92,** 172
Art. 35 **63,** 103
Art. 181 **79,** 412
Art. 210 (incorporation of treaties) **105,** 522
boundary changes **92,** 172
community of peoples **115,** 128-30
history **115,** 123-9
secession, need for amendment **115,** 135-7
Constitution (1974), constituent republics, transfer of property to **96,** 732
Continental Shelf Convention 6.1958, **41,** 162, 205
reservation **41,** 162, 205
dissolution **92,** 164-6, **96,** 720-1
as fundamental change of circumstances **117,** 427-8, 432, 436-7, 442
France, Compensation Agreement (1951) **39,** 427-9, **44,** 100-1
German and Hungarian attack on **44,** 336
law of
Law of 26 December 1978 (Ratification of Geneva Convention Protocols) **105,** 522

Yugoslavia, Socialist Federal Republic (*cont.*)
nationality, collaborators with Germany **44,** 443
Penal Code 1965 **74,** 510-11
Art. 100 **79,** 406
Art. 125 **79,** 406, 407
Art. 134 **79,** 407, 408
Art. 135(2) **79,** 386
Art. 141 **79,** 406
Art. 142 **79,** 386, 391
Art. 145 **79,** 406
Art. 167 **79,** 390
Penal Code 1965/1990 **124,** 220
1990 amendment (application of Geneva Conventions (1949)) **105,** 522, 591, **112,** 289-90
Art. 33 **108,** 202-4
Art. 41(1) **112,** 291, **121,** 298-9, **122,** 228
Art. 42 **112,** 291
Art. 43 **112,** 291
Art. 125 (war crimes) **105,** 450
Art. 141 **108,** 3
Arts. 141-56 **108,** 194-5, **121,** 299, **122,** 228
Art. 142 **108,** 3, **112,** 289-91, **121,** 255, 266, 299
Art. 151 **108,** 3
Art. 179 (rape) **121,** 270 n. 207
Art. 180 **121,** 270 n. 213
State Monopolies Act 1964 **39,** 427-8
Statute of Limitations 1953, Art. 20 **79,** 406, 407-11
legislation, interpretation by ICTY **121,** 299
minorities
freedom from discrimination **92,** 186
human rights **92,** 168-9, 176
identity under international law **92,** 168
language, protection **92,** 186, 191
'national identity', protection **92,** 185-6, 191
nationality, right to choose **92,** 169
recognition of State and **92,** 174, 176, 180-1, 185-6, 210-11
self-determination **92,** 168-9, 211
special status areas **92,** 210-11
autonomy **92,** 211
demilitarization **92,** 211
State succession and **92,** 165, 166
National Bank of Yugoslavia
disintegration following dissolution of SFRY **96,** 735
entitlement to take decisions relating to distribution of property, rights and interests of SFRY **96,** 735
private banking functions, agreement relating to, jurisdiction **96,** 736, 737
State organ, whether **96,** 735-6
structure and responsibilities, applicable law **96,** 735
Nuklearna Elektrarna Krsko, agency or instrumentality of a foreign State **63,** 103-4
'process of dissolution' **115,** 116-17
property, archives and debts, ownership, transfer to constituent republics **96,** 732

referendum
legality **115,** 135-46
procedure **115,** 135-46
representation, federal organs **115,** 154-7
secession
amendment to Constitution, need for **115,** 135-7
State succession distinguished **115,** 116-17
Slovenijales, agency or instrumentality of a foreign State **63,** 647-54
social property, legal status of **63,** 103
State succession. *See also successor States*
dates **96,** 720-3
transfer of rights and obligations **96,** 723, 725-6
immovable property **96,** 731
movable property, archives and debts **96,** 731-3
National Bank of Yugoslavia
acts on behalf of State and private acts distinguished **96,** 736
agency of successor States, whether **96,** 735
disintegration and **96,** 735
distribution of assets following succession, applicable law **96,** 736
social ownership **96,** 732
public prerogative, exercise of as test **96,** 732
to Serbia **73,** 39-41, **79,** 387, 394, 395
war crimes
Hague Conventions (1899/1907), incorporation **105,** 450
individual responsibility **122,** 70-1, 113
proscription **79,** 386, 391
rape **121,** 266
retroactive **79,** 391
torture **121,** 255

Zaire. *See also* Belgian Congo; Congo, Democratic Republic of
amnesty **78,** 23-4, 26
arbitrary detention **78,** 26-7
criminal procedure, *in absentia* trial **78,** 24
death sentence, politically motivated, whether **78,** 25
expropriation measures **91,** 261-2
compensation **91,** 261-2
liability for **91,** 262
International Covenant on Civil and Political Rights (ICCPR) (1966), violation **79,** 188-92, 254-60
law of
Act No 78-012 of 28 June 1978 (amnesty) **78,** 23-4, 26
Act No 78-023 of 29 December 1978 (extension of amnesty) **78,** 26
Law No 78003 of 20 June 1978 (compensation for expropriation) **91,** 261
persecution **78,** 19-21
'Zairianization'. *See also* expropriation measures *above*
sovereign act **115,** 417
Zambia
burden of proof **79,** 39, 45
common law
definition **79,** 25

Zambia (*cont.*)
visiting forces under **79,** 25-6, 39
common purpose **124,** 1103 n. 291
Constitution **79,** 34
fundamental rights and freedoms
conscience **70,** 135-51
correspondence **70,** 154-83
expression **70,** 154-83
legal representation **70,** 185-91
permitted derogations **70,** 145-51, 154-83
property regarding **70,** 183
interpretation **70,** 143, 165-7
s 13 **70,** 144, 157, 169, 173-6
s 18 **70,** 155, 157-8, 165-6, 169
s 19 **70,** 155, 157-9, 165-6, 169, 176
s 20 **70,** 185-91
s 21 **70,** 143-7, 151
s 22 **70,** 155, 159, 165-6, 169, 182-3
s 27 **88,** 264
s 28 **70,** 135, 154
s 53 **88,** 268
deportation, contempt of court, as **79,** 49
detention, delegation of powers **88,** 268
evidence, newspaper report **79,** 39-40
exchange control regulations **70,** 159-64, 170-83
examination of correspondence **70,** 170-83
purposes **70,** 163-4
extradition
agreement
absence **88,** 266-7
ad hoc **88,** 266-7
Zambia, from **88,** 266
Zambia, to **88,** 264-7
forcible abduction/unlawful arrest, jurisdiction, effect on **88,** 265-8
habeas corpus proceedings **79,** 18-49
applicant outside jurisdiction **79,** 27-31, 41-4, 46-7, 48-9
enforcement **79,** 46
judicial notice **79,** 25, 45
jurisdiction
aliens **74,** 157-9
criminal **74,** 158-9
extraterritorial **74,** 158-9
visiting forces **79,** 22-6, 36-41, 45
death penalty, exception **79,** 40
justiciability **79,** 35-6, 48
law of. *See also* Constitution *above*
Criminal Procedure Code **74,** 159
Declaration of Rights, applicability to freedom fighters **79,** 34
Extradition Act **88,** 266
Extradition of Fugitive Offenders Act **88,** 266
Immigration and Deportation Act 1965 **79,** 20
employment permit, denial of **70,** 185-91
Penal Code

Art. 22 (common purpose) **124,** 158 n. 291
Art. 132 (rape) **121,** 270 n. 207
Penal Code Amendment Act 1970 **74,** 158-9
Preservation of Public Security Regulations **88,** 264, 268
liberation movement, status **79,** 25-6, 36-7
Rules of Court
Order 5 **84,** 26
Order 6 **84,** 20, 26
SWAPO
habeas corpus writ and **79,** 43-4
recognition
as Government in exile **79,** 37
liberation army as visiting force **79,** 37, 44-5
visiting forces
common law and **79,** 25-6, 40
liberation movement army, whether **79,** 25-6
Zanzibar. *See* Tanzania
Zarzis promontories 67, 291, 293, 307
Zimbabwe
abuse of power, misuse of discretionary power **88,** 250
aliens, residence permit, alien husband's right to **103,** 230-4
applicable law
human rights
European Convention on Human Rights (1950) **103,** 233-4
International Covenant on Civil and Political Rights (ICCPR) (1966) **103,** 232-3
burden of proof, human rights **100,** 630-1
conspiracy, liability for acts after withdrawal from conspiracy **103,** 218-24
Constitution 1961 **87,** 116
Amendment (No 2) Act 1981 **84,** 30
Declaration of Rights **90,** 581, 584
interpretation, guidelines, broad **103,** 228
s 11, preamble, whether **103,** 228-9
s 15(1) **100,** 625, 628-31, 653-4
s 16 **92,** 587, 593-4, 599, 601, 609
s 22(1) (freedom of movement) **103,** 229-34
s 24(1) **100,** 629
s 24(4) (power of Court to prevent contravention of human rights) **100,** 634
s 60(1) (inhuman or degrading punishment) **100,** 633-4
s 71(4) (power of court to prevent contravention of human rights) **100,** 634
s 89 **84,** 30, 31
courts, municipal, standing
condemned prisoners **100,** 628-31
wife in respect of refusal of residence permit to alien husband **103,** 231-2
customary law, modification by courts **87,** 116
death row as inhuman or degrading treatment **100,** 631-56
delay caused by appeal, relevance **100,** 648-51
personality of condemned person, relevance **100,** 653
time-limits **100,** 656
detention, pending expulsion **88,** 250-1, 257-9
diplomatic premises
extraterritorial, whether **84,** 9-10
recognition as **84,** 20
European Convention on Human Rights (1950) **90,** 581-3, **103,** 233-4

Zimbabwe (*cont.*)
family life, respect for, deportation and **103,** 233
European Court of Human Rights, precedent **90,** 581-3, 585, **103,** 234
exchange control **92,** 606-7
expropriation/nationalization
compensation
adequacy **92,** 587-8, 593, 596-600, 601-7, 609, 617
Bill of Rights and **92,** 599, 617-18
effect of expropriation and **92,** 591, 592, 602, 603, 613, 614
equitable nature **92,** 602
full monetary equivalent **92,** 597
market value **92,** 597, 598, 602-3, 610, 618
premium paid for purchase of foreign securities **92,** 587-618
prompt **92,** 599
public and private interests, balance **92,** 597, 602
deprivation and acquisition distinguished **92,** 607-8, 613, 614, 617
external securities, premium on purchase of, relevance to compensation **92,** 587-618
expulsion of alien, detention pending **88,** 250-1, 257-9
extradition
agreement, need for **88,** 251
disguised **88,** 248-59
family life, respect for, International Covenant on Civil and Political Rights (ICCPR) (1966) **103,** 232-3
forcible abduction/unlawful arrest
failure to observe extradition/deportation procedures **103,** 214-16
international law, breach **103,** 214
absence of force **103,** 214
jurisdiction, effect on **103,** 208-18
discretion to stay proceedings **103,** 209, 216-18
State responsibility and **103,** 214
freedom of movement, alien husband, refusal of residence permit **103,** 230-4
human rights
applicability, individuals who are not citizens of the country in which they live **103,** 229
burden of proof **100,** 630-1
derogation. *See* exceptions *below*
effective remedy, need for **100,** 654-6
exceptions, strict interpretation **103,** 228
inhuman or degrading punishment
changing standard **100,** 630
whipping **90,** 581-5
power of court to prevent abuse **100,** 634, 654-6
standing, condemned prisoners **100,** 628-31
inhuman or degrading treatment, death row. *See* death row as inhuman or degrading treatment *above*
international law
municipal law and **84,** 23
sources
State practice **90,** 584, 585
teachings of publicists **90,** 584
jurisdiction
criminal, territorial **88,** 251
nationality **84,** 3, 7-8

avoidance of injustice **84,** 7-8, 11
municipal law provision, necessity for **84,** 10-11
restrictive application **84,** 7
territorial principle, avoidance of conflict with **84,** 7, 11
passive personality principle **84,** 11
territorial **84,** 3
diplomatic service, membership of and **84,** 7, 17
effects doctrine **84,** 3-7, 8, 11-17
presence against will, relevance **103,** 209-16
law of. *See also* Constitution *above*
Criminal Laws Amendment Act 1992 **100,** 651
Criminal Procedure and Evidence Act **87,** 116
Chapter 59(Z) **84,** 2, 8
s 314(A) **100,** 650
Dangerous Drugs Act **88,** 282
Exchange Control (Amendment) Regulations 1984, s 12A **92,** 586-91, 597-600, 601-2, 609
Extradition Act 1963 **88,** 251
High Court of Zimbabwe Act 1981, s 44(2) **100,** 649
Immigration Act 1979
s 8(2)(b) **88,** 250, 257
s 14(1)(h) **88,** 250, 252, 257-9
s 21 **88,** 257
s 22 **88,** 257
Immigration Regulations 1979
s 17(1)(a) **103,** 230
s 38(1) **103,** 230
Land Acquisition Act 15/1979 **92,** 603
Reserve Bank of Zimbabwe Act **92,** 606
legislation, interpretation
aids
judicial and arbitral decisions **90,** 584, 585
ministerial statement **92,** 600, 604-5, 607
guidelines, ordinary meaning **92,** 598
phrases
'prohibited person' **88,** 250, 252
'remove or cause to be removed' **88,** 252
marriage, definition **103,** 231
precedent, European Court of Human Rights **90,** 581-3, 585, **103,** 234
proportionality, punishment and **90,** 584-5
South Africa law and **84,** 30
State immunity, jurisdiction, classification of act, breach of tenancy agreement **84,** 18-38
State immunity, jurisdiction, theory/doctrine, restrictive **84,** 32, 33
State responsibility for forcible abduction/unlawful arrest **103,** 214
theft, continuous offence **84,** 3
treaties, source of international law **90,** 585